W9-BZA-462

TEACHER WRAPAROUND EDITION

First-Year Course

GLENCOE

Accounting

Real-World Applications & Connections

Donald J. Guerrieri
Norwin High School
North Huntingdon,
Pennsylvania

F. Barry Haber
Fayetteville State University
Fayetteville,
North Carolina

William B. Hoyt
Wilton High School
Wilton,
Connecticut

Robert E. Turner
University of Louisiana at Monroe
Monroe,
Louisiana

Visit the *Glencoe Accounting* Web site at:
glencoeaccounting.glencoe.com

New York, New York Columbus, Ohio Chicago, Illinois Peoria, Illinois Woodland Hills, California

TEACHER WRAPAROUND EDITION

CONTENTS

Photo Credits: Cindy Charles/PhotoEdit T21; J. Clarke/Picture Perfect T4; Gary A. Conner/Photo Edit T35; Dorothy Littell Greco/Stock Boston T41; Jeffry W. Myers/Stock Boston T54; Elliott Smith Photography T43; Superstock T51, T52

The McGraw·Hill Companies

Printed in the United States of America.

Send all inquiries to:
Glencoe/McGraw-Hill
21600 Oxnard Street, Suite 500
Woodland Hills, CA 91367-4906

ISBN 0-07-845670-3 (Student Edition)
ISBN 0-07-846097-2 (Teacher Wraparound Edition)

1 2 3 4 5 6 7 8 9 071 08 07 06 05 04 03

MEET OUR AUTHORS

Donald J. Guerrieri

Donald J. Guerrieri is an accounting instructor at Norwin High School, North Huntingdon, Pennsylvania. He has taught accounting at both the secondary and college levels. He also has experience working for a firm of certified public accountants. Dr. Guerrieri has written numerous articles on the teaching of accounting for a variety of educational journals. He is also a program speaker at business education seminars and conferences.

F. Barry Haber

F. Barry Haber is Professor of Accounting at Fayetteville State University, Fayetteville, North Carolina. Dr. Haber has been teaching accounting principle courses for more than thirty-five years. He is a certified public accountant and has served on the American Institute of Certified Public Accountants (AICPA) Minority Doctoral Fellows Committee. In addition to teaching accounting principles, Dr. Haber has authored three other textbooks, as well as various articles and cases in accounting.

William B. Hoyt

William B. Hoyt is an accounting instructor at Wilton High School, Wilton, Connecticut. He has been involved in accounting curriculum development for many years. He was a member of the writing task force for the *National Standards for Business Education* and has published several articles in professional journals. In 1996, Mr. Hoyt was named Connecticut's *Outstanding Business Educator of the Year* and in 1997 was named *National Secondary Teacher of the Year* by the National Business Education Association.

Robert E. Turner

Robert E. Turner is the Vice President for Business Affairs at University of Louisiana at Monroe, Monroe, Louisiana. Mr. Turner has taught accounting and other business subjects at the high school and college levels. Mr. Turner has appeared on local, state, and national programs of a number of business education conferences. He is also a frequent speaker at educational seminars and workshops around the country.

Introducing *Glencoe's* Business Partners

Peachtree®

Peachtree® began in Atlanta over 25 years ago as a retail computer store selling hardware. In the early 1980s, Peachtree began developing a line of application software products for the home, education, and business markets, with emphasis on accounting products. Peachtree was the first company to provide off-the-shelf accounting software for personal computers. With more than a million packages of its software sold, Peachtree is recognized as a leader in the small business accounting market.

RHI Robert Half International Inc.

Robert Half International Inc. is the world's first and largest staffing service specializing in accounting, finance, banking, and technology systems. Founded in 1948, Robert Half provides services in both full-time and temporary professionals. They match ideal candidates to clients that have special staffing requirements. With over 300 offices in North America, Europe, Australia, and New Zealand, Robert Half is committed to quality, customer service, and professionalism.

The American Institute of Certified Public Accountants is a national professional organization for Certified Public Accountants in the United States. With more than 330,000 members, AICPA provides its members with resources and information, enabling them to provide valuable services to employers, clients, and the public.

EDUCATIONAL REVIEWERS

Jayne Abernathy
Accounting Teacher
Centerville High School
Centerville, OH

Barbara A. Berg
Vocational Business Teacher
Carey High School
Carey, ID

Sibyl Cole-Olfzewski
Computer Tech. Teacher
Medina High School
Medina, OH

Naomi Crane
Accounting Teacher
Southwest High School
Ft. Worth, TX

Johnsie Crawford
Accounting Teacher
Brandon High School
Brandon, FL

Carrie Davis
Business Teacher
Yoncalla High School
Yoncalla, OR

Melinda G. Dibenedetto
Business Department Chair
Shades Valley High School
Birmingham, AL

Christine Fink
Business Teacher
Cocalico High School
Denver, PA

Patricia Kay Fordham
Business Teacher
Central High School
Salt Lake City, UT

Patsy A. Frost
Business Department Chair
Scituate High School
North Scituate, RI

Ruby Garr
Business Department Head
I.H. Kempner High School
Sugar Land, TX

Karen King Gilliland
Business Department Chair
Winchester Community H.S.
Winchester, IN

Norma C. Isassi
Accounting Teacher
H. M. King High School
Kingsville, TX

Karen LaClair
Business Department Chair
Simsbury High School
Simsbury, CT

Chris Mendez
Accounting Teacher
Bel Air High School
El Paso, TX

Regena Morris
Business Education Teacher
Arlington Heights High School
Ft. Worth, TX

Jeff Noyes
Business Education Teacher
Minnetonka High School
Minnetonka, MN

Karen Poidomani
Business Teacher
William Floyd High School
Mastic Beach, NY

Martha Ramirez
Business Teacher
McCallum High School
Austin, TX

William Sinai
Computerized Accounting Dept. Chair
West Valley Occupational Center
Woodland Hills, CA

Violet Snell
Business Department Chair
MacArthur High School
San Antonio, TX

Alfonso Vargas
Accounting Teacher
Hueneme High School
Oxnard, CA

Karen Wood
Accounting Teacher
Centerville High School
Centerville, OH

Dianne L. Young
Dean of Students
Wilmington High School
Wilmington, DE

EDUCATIONAL CONSULTANTS

We wish to acknowledge the contributions of the following:

Jayne Abernathy, Xenia, OH
Jim Adams, New Albany, IN
G. Armstrong, Bath, NY
Ron Baldini, Pulaski, WI
Alan Balog, Ravenna, OH
B. A. Banks-Burke, Hudson, OH
Denise M. Barbaris, West Milford, NJ
E. Patricia Barnes, Evansville, IN
Lou Ellen Bass, Four Oaks, NC
Linda Becker, Cary, NC
Perry Beckerman, Brooklyn, NY
Kathleen Beetar, Houston, TX
Scott Behnke, Wales, WI
Len C. Bigler, Grand Rapids, MI
Jackie Billings, McAllen, TX
Lee Birnbaum, Farmingdale, NJ
Cheryl Birx, Canandaigua, NY
Linda J. Black, Mt. Airy, GA
Elbert F. Black, Hastings, MI
Cindi Blansfield, Auburn, WA
Josephine Bliss, Merced, CA
D. Bogataj, Flat Rock, MI
Kelly Brock, Columbus, GA
William A. Brogdon, German Town, TN
Rachelle Brown, Morocco, IN
Jessie Broxmeyer, Long Beach, NY
Margaret Broyles, Forest Park, OH
Gus Buchttolz, Wyoming, MI
Ronda K. Budd, Grove City, OH
Pete Bush, Leesburg, FL
Michelle Cardoza, Tulare, CA
Walter Carlson, Torrance, CA
Bill Christianson, Spokane, WA
Jodi S. Clark, Warner Robins, GA
Anthony Paul Corbisiero, West New York, NJ
Ron Craig, Anaheim, CA
Lynn Crawford, Cudahy, WI
Claudia Cullari, Fair Lawn, NJ
Jo Damron, Abilene, TX
Jan Davis, Port Neches, TX
Toni DeFuria, Old Tappan, NJ
Denise Deltondo, Girard, OH
Carolyn Deshler, Moorpark, CA
Diane DeWitt, Freeport, IL
Wanda Drake, Jackson, TN
Buzz Drake, Barrington, IL
Ray Dunavant, Denison, TX
Tearle Dwiggins, Pendleton, IN
Susan España, Rocklin, CA
Morris P. Fair, Sr., Jackson, TN
Glenn Fong, Sacramento, CA
Julie Fox, Wisconsin Rapids, WI
Carolyn Francis, Baytown, TX
Cherilynn Frost, Livonia, MI
Patricia T. Gardella, Vineland, NJ
Robert D. Garrison, Belleview, FL
Kimberly Morris Gehres, Adrian, MI
JoAnn Gipson, Garland, TX
Nancy Glavic, New Concord, OH
Joyce Greemon, Gastonin, NC
Sheree Green, Teaneck, NJ
Andrea Gross, Vidor, TX
Guzzeta, Plant City, FL
Ronald L. Hainds, Jacksonville, IL
Kellie Hair, Kennesaw, GA
Sheryl J. Hane, Norco, CA
Janice Hanes, Forth Worth, TX
Marion Hanneld, Omaha, NE
Farolyn Hanscom, Riverside, CA
Wanda Harris, Eden, NC
Tammy Hatfield, Tullahoma, TN
Felicia S. Hatten, Detroit, MI
Debra R. Hauser, Shrub Oak, NY
Richard Heim, Latham, NY
Audrey M. Hendry, Huntington Beach, CA
John Hodgins, Marysville, WA
Helen Hogan, Lithonia, GA
Betty L. Holloway, Maplewood, NJ
Carol Huprich, Dover, OH
Antoinette Hutchings, Slate Hill, NY
David Ifkovic, Wilton, CT
Steve Ingmire, Indianapolis, IN
Waydene C. Jackson, Stone Mountain, GA
M. Jackson, Houston, TX
Irma D. James, Dayton, OH
Carol Jekel, Flushing, MI
Lori Jepson, Montclair, CA
Kay Jernigan, Vanceboro, NC
Glenn Johnson, Mukwonago, WI
Mary K. Jones, Neenah, WI
Ted Juske, Mundelein, IL
Beverly Kaeser, Appleton, WI
Linda Keats, Stevens Point, WI
Sue Kelley, Hubbard, OH
Mary Kay King, Dickson, TN
Carol Kinney, Eau Claire, WI
Ann Klingelsmith, Greenville, MI
Tammy Koch, Minocqua, WI
Patrick Kubeny, Rhinelander, WI
Cheryl M. Lagan, Ossining, NY
Amelia Lard, Memphis, TN
Marianna Larkin, Waxahachie, TX
Becky Larsen, Irvine, CA
Sharon Larson, Crystal Lake, IL
Inez Lauerman, Shingle Springs, CA
Annette Laughlin, Oswego, IL
Steve Leighton, Brooklyn, NY
James Leonard, Palos Hills, IL
Sue Lewis, Littlerock, CA
Stan Lewis, Champaign, IL
Donna Lewis, Morehead City, NC
Theresa Lueras, Daly City, CA
Sherry Lund, Port Angeles, WA
Linda Lupi, W. Bloomfield, MI
A. Mallette, New York, NY
John Matera, Kenosha, WI
Alice Matthews, Artesia, CA
Sarah McBride, Hickory, NC
Rebecca McKnight, Gainesville, FL
Pam Meyer, The Woodlands, TX
J. Miller, Madison, OH
Gloria Morris, Fort Worth, TX
Ralph A. Muro, Binghamton, NY
Dianne Murphy, Rancho Cucamonga, CA
Jill N. Murphy-Totten, Middletown, OH
John Murray, Fraser, MI
Karen Neuman, Parma, OH
William Nitch, Niles, OH
Bonnie N. Nute, Munford, TN
Betty O'Dell, Escondido, CA
Deborah Ottmers, San Antonio, TX
RaeNell Parker, Menomonie, WI
Ronda Patrick, Kirkland, WA
Diane Personett, Rushville, IN
Hank Petite, Bloomfield, NJ
Glenn Philpott, Belleville, IL
Kip Pichel, Auburn Hills, MI
Patti Pletcher, Bristol, IN
Mark G. Pretz, Harlingen, TX
Diane A. Prom, Oak Creek, WI
Lydia Quinones, Dunwoody GA
Mary C. Rabb, Winchester, TN
Margaret Ralph, Portland, IN
Glenda Razor, Santa Ana, CA
Tom Reach, Aliso Viejo, CA
C. Redmond, Lakewood, CA
Suzanne Reisert, Floral Park, NY
Edlyn Reneau, Corpus Christi, TX
Ruth Riley, Poland, OH
Melanie Rodges, Keller, TX
Rosalinda Rodriguez, McAllen, TX
Mary R. Roth, Warner Robins, GA
Frank Rudnesky, Pine Hill, NJ
Joyce Sadd, Hastings, NE
Lawrence Sakalas, Southgate, MI
Gary L. Schepf, Irving, TX
Donna M. Scheuerer, Farmingdale, NY
Jerry Schlecher, Hartland, MI
Sue Smith, Whittier, CA
Pete Smith, Mishawaka, IN
James Smith, Greensboro, NC
Linda Songer, Orange Park, FL
Linda Spellich, Belleville, MI
Carolyn R. Spencer, E. St. Louis, IL
Camille Sroka, Toms River, NJ
Will Stauske, Cedarburg, WI
Beverly Stergeos, Fort Worth, TX
Anne Stewart, Clearwater, FL
Geoffrey Strauss, Endicott, NY
Amy C. Strickland, Columbus, GA
Debbie Stuebbe, Bakersfield, CA
Ken Swiergosz, Toledo, OH
Bonnie Toone, Evansville, IN
Robert Torres, Anaheim, CA
Jeff VanArsdel, W. Lafayette, IN
Jill Vicino, Darien, IL
Lina Volesky, West Bend, WI
Sandy Wainio, Durham, NC
David D. Weaver, Palmdale, CA
Irene Webb, Hackensack, NJ
Kathy Webb, Garland, TX
Gloria Wein, Aberdeen, NJ
Victoria Wenke, Burlington, WI
Donna Wheeler, Madison, IN
Patricia Williams, Tampa, FL
June Winkel, Plymouth, WI
Ann Wittmer, Waco, TX
Karen M. Wolf, West Carrollton, OH
William W. Wunrow, Green Bay, WI
Thomas F. YingLing, St. Marys, OH
Carol Young, Yorba Linda, CA
Cy Young, Garden Grove, CA
Cheri Zuccarelli, Phelan, CA

TABLE OF CONTENTS Student Edition

TABLE OF CONTENTS Student Edition

UNDERSTANDING THE LESSON

The textbook organization provides a structure that is easy for students to follow. New learning is based on previous knowledge, with each new concept building on a prior concept. Much like an accounting cycle where records are maintained through a sequence of procedures and activities, the text instruction follows an organized flow of concept development.

The **Chapter Opener** helps students organize their study of chapter concepts. Learning objectives help students preview what they will learn in the chapter. Students also get a chance to explore a real-world business.

CHAPTER 6

Recording Transactions in a General Journal

Learning Objectives

When you have completed this chapter, you will be able to:

- Explain the first three steps in the accounting cycle.
- Give and describe several examples of source documents.
- Explain the purpose of journalizing.
- Apply information from source documents.
- Describe the steps to make a general journal entry.
- Make accurate general journal entries.
- Correct errors in general journal entries.
- Define the accounting terms introduced in this chapter.

Exploring the Real World of Business

RECORDING FINANCIAL INFORMATION

Ben Cohen and Jerry Greenfield met in junior high school and graduated from Calhoun High School in Merrick, Long Island. After high school they decided that they wanted to start a business together. They researched products, market demand, and locations. A shared love for all-natural ice cream and a vision for a company that improves the quality of community life were the foundations for the beginnings of **Ben & Jerry's Ice Cream and Frozen Yogurt.** They purchased a used old-fashioned rock salt ice cream maker and took a correspondence course from Penn State about ice cream making.

Ben & Jerry's opened for business in May of 1978 in Burlington, Vermont, in a "roughly" renovated gas station. **Ben & Jerry's** products are now sold around the world. Recording financial information about the business keeps several full-time accountants busy.

What do you think?

If you were Ben and Jerry, what types of financial information would you record?

Ben & Jerry's Homemade, Inc.

Workplace Connections

Applying Your Accounting Knowledge

Have you ever kept a daily journal of the things that happen during your day? The general journal of a business is similar. The daily financial happenings are recorded there. Your local video store earns revenue by renting videos, buys advertising in the newspaper, pays its employees, and pays its bills. You'll learn how to record business transactions in a journal in this chapter.

Investigate:

1. In your workplace, why is it important to keep accurate records of daily transactions?
2. List five business transactions that happen in your workplace.

Glencoe Accounting Online

Visit the *Glencoe Accounting* Web site at **glencoeaccounting.glencoe.com** for additional activities and information.

120 Chapter 6 Recording Transactions in a General Journal

121

Special features like **Workplace Connections** provide an opportunity for students to apply their accounting knowledge.

Source Documents accompany each *Business Transaction Analysis Model* to help students visualize the forms used by real businesses.

Each section begins with **What You'll Learn, Why It's Important,** and **Key Terms** to help students connect what they learn to the real world of business.

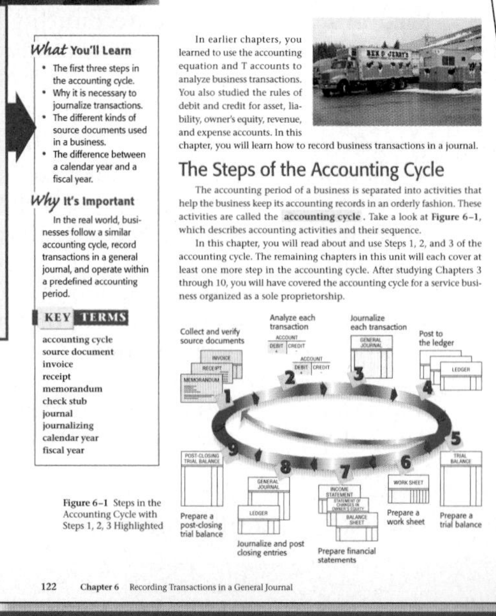

SECTION 1

The Accounting Cycle

***What* You'll Learn**

- The first three steps in the accounting cycle.
- Why it is necessary to journalize transactions.
- The different kinds of source documents used in a business.
- The difference between a calendar year and a fiscal year.

***Why* It's Important**

In the real world, businesses follow a similar accounting cycle, record transactions in a general journal, and operate within a predefined accounting period.

KEY TERMS

accounting cycle
source document
invoice
receipt
memorandum
check stub
journal
journalizing
calendar year
fiscal year

In earlier chapters, you learned to use the accounting equation and T accounts to analyze business transactions. You also studied the rules of debit and credit for asset, liability, owner's equity, revenue, and expense accounts. In this chapter, you will learn how to record business transactions in a journal.

The Steps of the Accounting Cycle

The accounting period of a business is separated into activities that help the business keep its accounting records in an orderly fashion. These activities are called the **accounting cycle**. Take a look at **Figure 6–1**, which describes accounting activities and their sequence.

In this chapter, you will read about and use Steps 1, 2, and 3 of the accounting cycle. The remaining chapters in this unit will each cover at least one more step in the accounting cycle. After studying Chapters 3 through 10, you will have covered the accounting cycle for a service business organized as a sole proprietorship.

Figure 6–1 Steps in the Accounting Cycle with Steps 1, 2, 3 Highlighted

122 Chapter 6 Recording Transactions in a General Journal

Business Transaction 8

On October 15 Roadrunner provided delivery services for the Sims Corporation. A check for $1,200 was received in full payment, Receipt 2.

RECEIPT No. 2 — Roadrunner Delivery Service — Oct. 15, 20-- — $1,200.00 — RECEIVED FROM Sims Corporation — One thousand two hundred and no/100 DOLLARS — FOR Delivery services — RECEIVED BY Maria Sanchez

ANALYSIS — *Identify* — 1. The accounts **Cash in Bank** and **Delivery Revenue** are affected.

Classify — 2. **Cash in Bank** is an asset account. **Delivery Revenue** is a revenue account.

+/− — 3. **Cash in Bank** is increased by $1,200. **Delivery Revenue** is increased by $1,200.

DEBIT-CREDIT RULE — 4. Increases in asset accounts are recorded as debits. Debit **Cash in Bank** for $1,200.
5. Increases in revenue accounts are recorded as credits. Credit **Delivery Revenue** for $1,200.

T ACCOUNTS — 6.

Cash in Bank		Delivery Revenue	
Debit + 1,200	Credit −	Debit −	Credit + 1,200

JOURNAL ENTRY — 7.

GENERAL JOURNAL PAGE 1

	DATE		DESCRIPTION	POST. REF.	DEBIT	CREDIT	
23	Oct.	15	Cash in Bank		1 200 00		23
24			Delivery Revenue			1 200 00	24
25			Receipt 2				25
26							26

Business Transaction 9

On October 16 Roadrunner mailed Check 103 for $700 to pay the month's rent.

No. 103 — $700.00 — Date October 16 — To Tooley & Co. Management — For rent

	Dollars	Cents
Balance brought forward	23,050	00
Add deposits		
Total	23,050	00
Less this check	700	00
Balance carried forward	22,350	00

ANALYSIS — *Identify* — 1. The accounts **Rent Expense** and **Cash in Bank** are affected.

Classify — 2. **Rent Expense** is an expense account. **Cash in Bank** is an asset account.

+/− — 3. **Rent Expense** is increased by $700. **Cash in Bank** is decreased by $700.

134 Chapter 6 Recording Transactions in a General Journal

Business Transaction Analysis Models help students not only learn how to record transactions, but also to think critically.

PRACTICE AND APPLY

The *Glencoe Accounting* program provides a variety of practice materials to help students transfer textbook learning to practical applications.

The **Check Your Understanding** activities and problems provide immediate reinforcement and help students apply accounting concepts and procedures. Answers to **Check Your Understanding** problems are provided in the back of the student textbook.

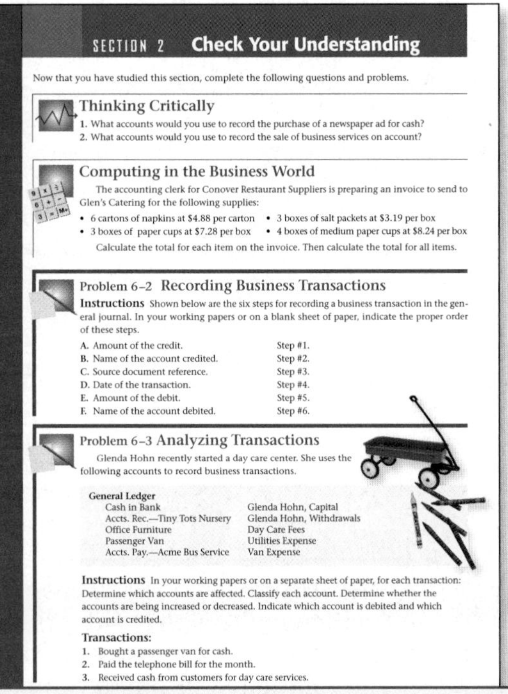

SECTION 2 Check Your Understanding

Now that you have studied this section, complete the following questions and problems.

Thinking Critically

1. What accounts would you use to record the purchase of a newspaper ad for cash?
2. What accounts would you use to record the sale of business services on account?

Computing in the Business World

The accounting clerk for Conover Restaurant Suppliers is preparing an invoice to send to Glen's Catering for the following supplies:

- 6 cartons of napkins at $4.88 per carton
- 3 boxes of salt packets at $3.19 per box
- 3 boxes of paper cups at $7.28 per box
- 4 boxes of medium paper cups at $8.24 per box

Calculate the total for each item on the invoice. Then calculate the total for all items.

Problem 6-2 Recording Business Transactions

Instructions Shown below are the six steps for recording a business transaction in the general journal. In your working papers or on a blank sheet of paper, indicate the proper order of these steps.

A. Amount of the credit.	Step #1.
B. Name of the account credited.	Step #2.
C. Source document reference.	Step #3.
D. Date of the transaction.	Step #4.
E. Amount of the debit.	Step #5.
F. Name of the account debited.	Step #6.

Problem 6-3 Analyzing Transactions

Glenda Hohn recently started a day care center. She uses the following accounts to record business transactions.

General Ledger

Cash in Bank	Glenda Hohn, Capital
Accts. Rec.—Tiny Tots Nursery	Glenda Hohn, Withdrawals
Office Furniture	Day Care Fees
Passenger Van	Utilities Expense
Accts. Pay.—Acme Bus Service	Van Expense

Instructions In your working papers or on a separate sheet of paper, for each transaction: Determine which accounts are affected. Classify each account. Determine whether the accounts are being increased or decreased. Indicate which account is debited and which account is credited.

Transactions:

1. Bought a passenger van for cash.
2. Paid the telephone bill for the month.
3. Received cash from customers for day care services.

The **Chapter Summary** visually lists key concepts in the chapter for quick review and reference.

CHAPTER 6 SUMMARY

KEY CONCEPTS

1. Accounting records are maintained in separate time periods called accounting periods.
2. The activities involved in maintaining the accounting records make up the accounting cycle.
3. The Accounting Cycle—Steps 1–3 is pictured to the right.
4. Journalizing a Business Transaction:
5. Correcting a Journal Entry with an Incorrect Amount (Manual System). Phillip Reyna invested $36,000 in his business on May 15, Memorandum 2. The amount of the transaction was recorded incorrectly. The original entry and the correction follows.
6. Correcting a Journal Entry with an Incorrect Account Name (Manual System).

Chapter 6 Summary 141

The **Chapter Review and Activities** helps students review important accounting terms, concepts, and procedures. Various activities offer students an opportunity to apply their critical thinking and decision-making skills.

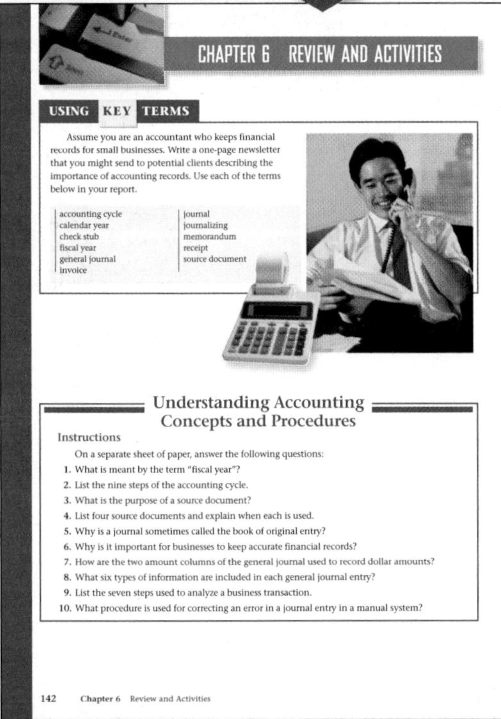

CHAPTER 6 REVIEW AND ACTIVITIES

USING KEY TERMS

Assume you are an accountant who keeps financial records for small businesses. Write a one-page newsletter that you might send to potential clients describing the importance of accounting records. Use each of the terms below in your report.

accounting cycle	journal
calendar year	journalizing
check stub	memorandum
fiscal year	receipt
general journal	source document
invoice	

Understanding Accounting Concepts and Procedures

Instructions

On a separate sheet of paper, answer the following questions:

1. What is meant by the term "fiscal year"?
2. List the nine steps of the accounting cycle.
3. What is the purpose of a source document?
4. List four source documents and explain when each is used.
5. Why is a journal sometimes called the book of original entry?
6. Why is it important for businesses to keep accurate financial records?
7. How are the two amount columns of the general journal used to record dollar amounts?
8. What six types of information are included in each general journal entry?
9. List the seven steps used to analyze a business transaction.
10. What procedure is used for correcting an error in a journal entry in a manual system?

142 Chapter 6 Review and Activities

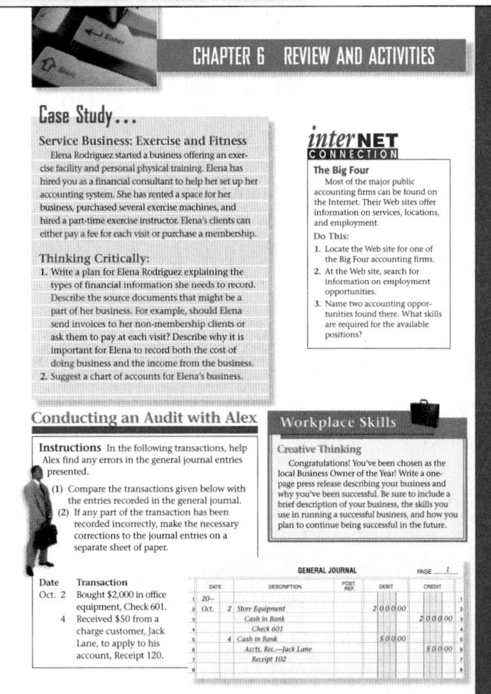

CHAPTER 6 REVIEW AND ACTIVITIES

Case Study...

Service Business: Exercise and Fitness

Elena Rodriguez started a business offering an exercise facility and personal physical training. Elena has hired you as a financial consultant to help her set up her accounting system. She has rented a space for her business, purchased several exercise machines, and hired a part-time exercise instructor. Elena's clients can either pay a fee for each visit or purchase a membership.

Thinking Critically:

1. Write a plan for Elena Rodriguez explaining the types of financial information she needs to record. Describe the source documents that might be a part of her business. For example, should Elena send invoices to her non-membership clients or ask them to pay at each visit? Describe why it is important for Elena to record both the cost of doing business and the income from the business.
2. Suggest a chart of accounts for Elena's business.

*inter*NET CONNECTION

The Big Four

Most of the major public accounting firms can be found on the Internet. Their Web sites offer information on services, locations, and employment.

Do This:

1. Locate the Web site for one of the Big Four accounting firms.
2. At the Web site, search for information on employment opportunities.
3. Name two accounting opportunities found there. What skills are required for the available positions?

Conducting an Audit with Alex

Instructions In the following transactions, help Alex find any errors in the general journal entries presented.

(1) Compare the transactions given below with the entries recorded in the general journal.
(2) If any part of the transaction has been recorded incorrectly, make the necessary corrections to the journal entries on a separate sheet of paper.

Date	Transaction
Oct. 2	Bought $2,000 in office equipment, Check 601.
4	Received $50 from a charge customer, Jack Lane, to apply to his account, Receipt 120.

GENERAL JOURNAL PAGE 1

	DATE		DESCRIPTION	POST. REF.	DEBIT	CREDIT	
1	20--						1
2	Oct.	2	Store Equipment		2 000 00		2
3			Cash in Bank			2 000 00	3
4			Check 601				4
5		4	Cash in Bank		500 00		5
6			Accts. Rec.—Jack Lane			500 00	6
7			Receipt 102				7

Workplace Skills

Creative Thinking

Congratulations! You've been chosen as the local Business Owner of the Year! Write a one-page press release describing your business and why you've been successful. Be sure to include a brief description of your business, the skills you use in running a successful business, and how you plan to continue being successful in the future.

Chapter 6 Review and Activities 143

Activities such as ***Case Studies, Internet Connection, Workplace Skills,*** and ***Conducting an Audit with Alex*** help students to apply their critical thinking and decision-making skills based on chapter concepts.

PRACTICE AND APPLY

Computerized Accounting activities help students make the transition from a manual system to a computerized system. Students also learn how to apply the chapter content in the Peachtree® system. For detailed instructions, refer to the *Peachtree User Guide* in the **Chapter Reviews and Working Papers**.

CHAPTER 6 COMPUTERIZED ACCOUNTING

General Journal Entries

Making the Transition from a Manual to a Computerized System

Task	Perform Accounting Procedures Using Manual Methods	Perform Accounting Procedures Using Automated Methods
Recording general journal entries	• Analyze the source document to determine which accounts are affected. • Using a general journal form, enter the details of the transaction. • Check for equality of debits and credits.	• Analyze the source document to determine which accounts are affected. • Enter the general journal using the account numbers for each ledger account. • The software will calculate the equality of debits and credits.

Peachtree®

Entering Transactions

Peachtree Question	Description
How do I enter general journal entries in Peachtree?	1. From the *Tasks* menu, select General Journal Entry. 2. Enter the date of the transaction in the Date box. 3. Enter the source document reference. TAB 4. Enter the account number to be debited. TAB. 5. Enter a brief description of the transaction. TAB. 6. Enter the debit amount. TAB. 7. Enter the account number to be credited. TAB 8. Enter the credit amount. TAB. 9. Click Save. (You will learn how to post to the general ledger in the next chapter.)
What does the software do "behind the scenes"?	The general journal screen automatically checks the equality of debits and credits in your journal entry. The software prompts you to correct the entry if it is out of balance.

For detailed instructions: See the **Peachtree User Guide** in your Glencoe Working Papers.

Chapter Problems reinforce students' accounting skills and enhance their accounting knowledge. They are arranged in ascending order of difficulty. The **Analysis** questions at the end of each problem encourage students to apply the concepts and skills they learned throughout the chapter. Additional reinforcement problems for each chapter are provided at the end of the textbook in Appendix G.

The last problem in each chapter is a **Challenge Problem**, and it is always accompanied by a source document. The **Challenge Problem** can be used as a class assignment or as an independent project. The challenge problem is identified with a challenge problem icon.

The **Peachtree Smart Guide** provides students with step-by-step instructions on how to solve specific problems. It also gives students practical tips to help them become more familiar with the Peachtree system.

CHAPTER 6 PROBLEMS

Peachtree® SMART GUIDE

Step-by-Step Instructions: Problem 6–7

1. Select the problem set for Outback Guide Service (Prob. 6–7).
2. Rename the company and set the system date.
3. Enter all of the general journal transactions.
4. Print a General Journal report.
5. Proof your work and make any needed corrections.
6. Answer the Analyze question.
7. End the session.

TIP: Press SHIFT+? in an *Account No.* field to display an account list.

Problem 6–7 Recording General Journal Transactions

Juanita Ortega is the owner of Outback Guide Service. The following accounts are used to record the transactions of her business.

General Ledger

101	Cash in Bank	205	Accts. Pay.—Peak Equipment Inc.
105	Accts. Rec.—M. Johnson	207	Accts. Pay.—Premier Processors
110	Accts. Rec.—Feldman, Jones, & Ritter	301	Juanita Ortega, Capital
115	Accts. Rec.—Podaski Systems Inc.	302	Juanita Ortega, Withdrawals
130	Office Equipment	310	Income Summary
135	Office Furniture	401	Guide Service Revenue
140	Computer Equipment	501	Advertising Expense
145	Hiking Equipment	505	Maintenance Expense
150	Rafting Equipment	515	Rent Expense
201	Accts. Pay.—A-1 Adventure Warehouse	520	Salaries Expense
		525	Utilities Expense

...the general ...r business: ...ipment, ...from A-1 ...g trip. The ...300. ...inting the ...e toward the amount owed, Check 517.

Date	Transactions
15	Received a check for $4,800 from Feldman, Jones, & Ritter in payment of their account, Receipt 252.
18	Juanita Ortega paid herself $600 by issuing Check 518.
22	Billed a client, Mary Johnson, $1,200 for completing guide services on a hiking expedition, Sales Invoice 301.
25	Paid the monthly telephone bill for $175 by issuing Check 519.
30	Purchased a $3,600 computer system from Premier Processors. Made a down payment for $1,800 and agreed to pay the balance within 30 days, Check 520 and Invoice 749.

Analyze: Did any of Outback's customers pay cash for services in January?

148 Chapter 6 Problems

...EMS

CHALLENGE PROBLEM Problem 6–8 SOURCE DOCUMENT PROBLEM Recording General Journal Transactions

Greg Failla operates Showbiz Video. The following accounts are used to record business transactions.

General Ledger

101	Cash in Bank	207	Accts. Pay.—New Media Suppliers
105	Accts. Rec.—G. Cohen	209	Accts. Pay.—Palace Films
110	Accts. Rec.—J. Coletti	301	Greg Failla, Capital
113	Accts. Rec.—S. Flannery	305	Greg Failla, Withdrawals
115	Accts. Rec.—Spring Branch School District	310	Income Summary
130	Office Equipment	401	Video Rental Revenue
135	Office Furniture	405	VCR Rental Revenue
140	Computer Equipment	501	Advertising Expense
145	Video Tapes	505	Equipment Repair Expense
150	Video Equipment	510	Maintenance Expense
201	Accts. Pay.—Broad Street Office Supply	520	Rent Expense
205	Accts. Pay.—Computer Horizons	525	Salaries Expense
		530	Utilities Expense

Instructions Record the following transactions on page 5 of the general journal in your working papers.

Date		Transactions
Jan.	1	Deposited $3,400 in receipts. Of that amount, $1,900 was VCR rentals and $1,500 was video tape rentals, Receipt 435.
	3	Wrote Check 1250 for $325 of equipment repairs.
	5	Purchased $400 in video tapes from Palace Films on account, Invoice PF32.
	7	Bought from New Media Suppliers $2,600 in video equipment. Made a down payment of $600 and agreed to pay the balance in two installments, Check 1251 and Invoice NM101.
	10	Rented videos to Spring Branch School District. The school district agreed to pay $1,800 at a later date, Sales Invoice 1650.
	12	Issued Check 1252 for $750 to Computer Horizons for the amount owed to them.
	15	Deposited $5,600 in receipts. VCR rentals amounted to $4,400 and video tape rentals were $1,200, Receipt 436.
	18	Paid Clear Vue Window Cleaners $100 for monthly window cleaning, Check 1253.
	25	Made a $1,000 installment payment toward the amount owed to New Media Suppliers by issuing Check 1254.

Analyze: What were the total expenses incurred in January?

Peachtree® SMART GUIDE

Step-by-Step Instructions: Problem 6–8

1. Select the problem set for Showbiz Video (Prob. 6–8).
2. Rename the company and set the system date.
3. Enter all of the general journal transactions.
4. Print a General Journal report.
5. Proof your work and make any needed corrections.
6. Answer the Analyze question.
7. End the session.

SOURCE DOCUMENT PROBLEM

Problem 6–8

Use the source documents in your working papers to record the transactions for this problem.

Chapter 6 Problems 149

FOCUS ON FEATURES

Each chapter includes special features designed to help students relate the study of accounting to certain aspects of the world around them.

Connect to... teaches students to apply their accounting concepts to various other disciplines.

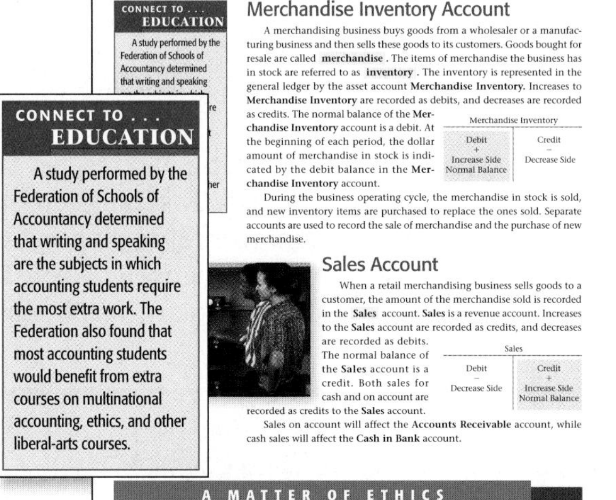

CONNECT TO . . .
EDUCATION

A study performed by the Federation of Schools of Accountancy determined that writing and speaking are the subjects in which accounting students require the most extra work. The Federation also found that most accounting students would benefit from extra courses on multinational accounting, ethics, and other liberal-arts courses.

Merchandise Inventory Account

A merchandising business buys goods from a wholesaler or a manufacturing business and then sells these goods to its customers. Goods bought for resale are called **merchandise**. The items of merchandise the business has in stock are referred to as **inventory**. The inventory is represented in the general ledger by the asset account **Merchandise Inventory**. Increases to **Merchandise Inventory** are recorded as debits, and decreases are recorded as credits. The normal balance of the **Merchandise Inventory** account is a debit. At the beginning of each period, the dollar amount of merchandise in stock is indicated by the debit balance in the **Merchandise Inventory** account.

Merchandise Inventory	
Debit + Increase Side Normal Balance	Credit − Decrease Side

During the business operating cycle, the merchandise in stock is sold, and new inventory items are purchased to replace the ones sold. Separate accounts are used to record the sale of merchandise and the purchase of new merchandise.

Sales Account

When a retail merchandising business sells goods to a customer, the amount of the merchandise sold is recorded in the **Sales** account. **Sales** is a revenue account. Increases to the **Sales** account are recorded as credits, and decreases are recorded as debits. The normal balance of the **Sales** account is a credit. Both sales for cash and on account are recorded as credits to the **Sales** account.

Sales	
Debit − Decrease Side	Credit + Increase Side Normal Balance

Sales on account will affect the **Accounts Receivable** account, while cash sales will affect the **Cash in Bank** account.

356

A Matter of Ethics describes common ethical issues in business. Students are encouraged to develop a decision model to help them evaluate alternative actions to reach an ethical decision.

A MATTER OF ETHICS

Confidentiality

Imagine that you work as an accounting clerk for a fast-food franchise like Taco Bell. You have access to all the accounting records for the business.

A friend of yours has promised to hire you as an accountant when he opens his own Mexican food restaurant. He has asked you to share information about Taco Bell's sales and expenses.

Ethical Decision Making:

- What are the ethical issues?
- What are the alternatives?
- Who are the affected parties?
- How do the alternatives affect the parties?
- What would you do?

ACCOUNTING CAREERS IN FOCUS

STERLING ELLSWORTH
Certified Public Accountant (CPA)

Q: Why did you choose accounting?
A: Because of its precision. I was a math major, but theoretical math, such as calculus, didn't interest me. I had taken an accounting class, and struggled with it, but enjoyed it at the same time. I took a second one and knew it was for me. It was challenging, but rewarding.

Q: What do you like about working for yourself?
A: I like the freedom to work when I want, take vacations when I want, to adjust my time around my workload. I work more intensely sometimes, but I have a lot of time off.

Q: How does your workload vary?
A: During tax season, I work 12 hours a day, or more, for about a 90-day period. It's very intense. Then it slows down. In late summer and early fall, I take a lot of four-day weekends. That's when I appreciate what I do.

Q: What skills are important to you?
A: Time management skills are the most critical. You have to be able to organize and work at maximum efficiency. You can't make mistakes that cost your client money, yet you have to work quickly. People skills are important too. Sometimes I have only 10 minutes to sell myself and convince clients they can trust me with their financial records.

Tips from . . .
Robert Half International Inc.
Learn to manage your time by planning ahead. Get organized with a "to do" list. Gather your supplies and resources for each task, then set priorities and schedule similar tasks together.

CAREER FACTS

Nature of the Work: Consult with clients, prepare tax forms, attend IRS audits, give financial advice.
Training or Education Needed: A bachelor's degree in accounting or business, the CPA exam, and continuing education.
Aptitudes, Abilities, and Skills: Time management skills, interpersonal skills, organizational skills, computer skills, and math.
Salary Range: Start at $40,000 to $400,000, depending on prior experience.
Career Path: Pass the CPA exam, work in an accounting field to gain work experience, build client base, then start your own business.

Thinking Critically: How would you convince clients that you can be trusted with their records?

36 Chapter 2 Accounting Careers in Focus

Accounting Careers in Focus introduces students to a wide range of interesting, attainable career choices in the field of accounting with tips from *Robert Half International*.

Analyzing Financial Reports gives students an opportunity to analyze financial statements of a business and to think critically.

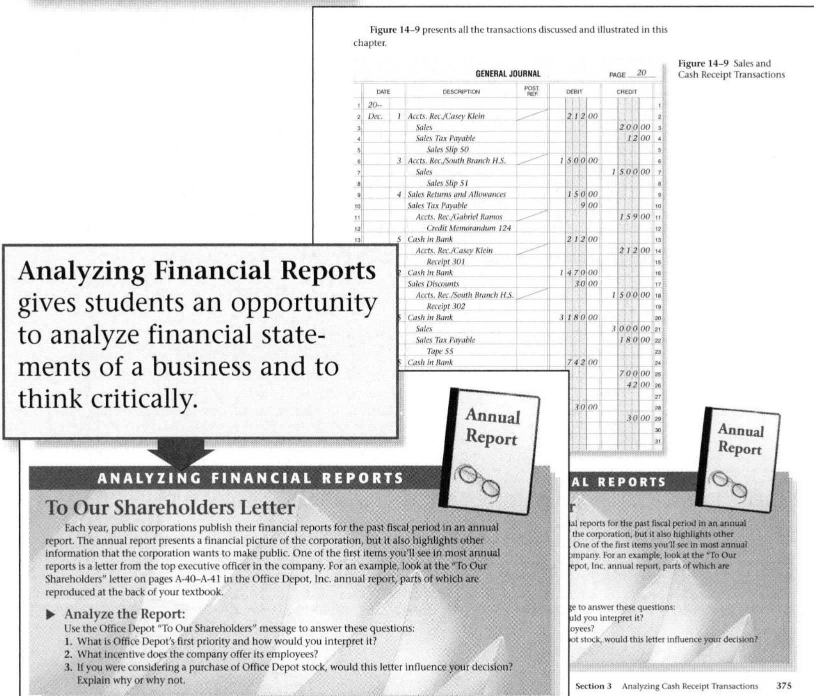

Figure 14–9 presents all the transactions discussed and illustrated in this chapter.

GENERAL JOURNAL PAGE 20

	DATE		DESCRIPTION	POST. REF.	DEBIT	CREDIT	
1	20--						1
2	Dec.	1	Accts. Rec./Casey Klein		212 00		2
3			Sales			200 00	3
4			Sales Tax Payable			12 00	4
5			Sales Slip 50				5
6		3	Accts. Rec./South Branch H.S.		1500 00		6
7			Sales			1500 00	7
8			Sales Slip 51				8
9		4	Sales Returns and Allowances		150 00		9
10			Sales Tax Payable		9 00		10
11			Accts. Rec./Gabriel Ramos			159 00	11
12			Credit Memorandum 124				12
13		5	Cash in Bank		212 00		13
14			Accts. Rec./Casey Klein			212 00	14
15			Receipt 301				15
16			Cash in Bank		1470 00		16
17			Sales Discounts		30 00		17
18			Accts. Rec./South Branch H.S.			1500 00	18
19			Receipt 302				19
20			Cash in Bank		3180 00		20
21			Sales			3000 00	21
22			Sales Tax Payable			180 00	22
23			Tape 55				23
24			Cash in Bank		742 00		24
25						700 00	25
26						42 00	26
27							27
28					30 00		28
29						30 00	29
30							30
31							31

Figure 14–9 Sales and Cash Receipt Transactions

ANALYZING FINANCIAL REPORTS

Annual Report

To Our Shareholders Letter

Each year, public corporations publish their financial reports for the past fiscal period in an annual report. The annual report presents a financial picture of the corporation, but it also highlights other information that the corporation wants to make public. One of the first items you'll see in most annual reports is a letter from the top executive officer in the company. For an example, look at the "To Our Shareholders" letter on pages A-40–A-41 in the Office Depot, Inc. annual report, parts of which are reproduced at the back of your textbook.

▶ Analyze the Report:
Use the Office Depot "To Our Shareholders" message to answer these questions:
1. What is Office Depot's first priority and how would you interpret it?
2. What incentive does the company offer its employees?
3. If you were considering a purchase of Office Depot stock, would this letter influence your decision? Explain why or why not.

Section 3 Analyzing Cash Receipt Transactions 375

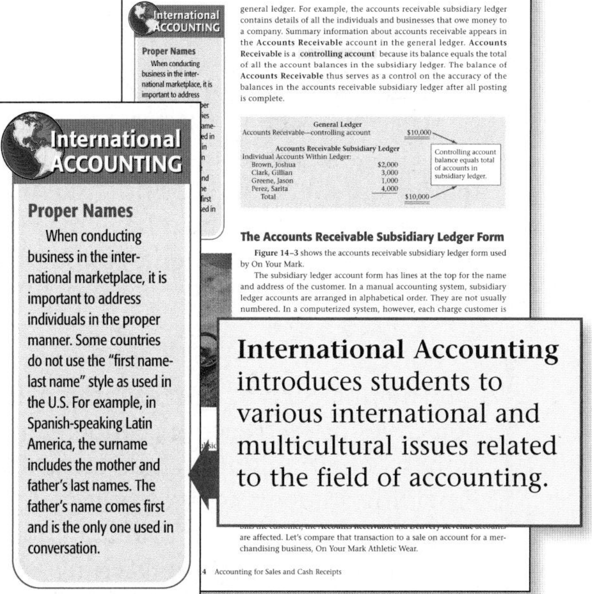

International ACCOUNTING

Proper Names

When conducting business in the international marketplace, it is important to address individuals in the proper manner. Some countries do not use the "first name-last name" style as used in the U.S. For example, in Spanish-speaking Latin America, the surname includes the mother and father's last names. The father's name comes first and is the only one used in conversation.

general ledger. For example, the accounts receivable subsidiary ledger contains details of all the individuals and businesses that owe money to a company. Summary information about accounts receivable appears in the **Accounts Receivable** account in the general ledger. **Accounts Receivable** is a **controlling account** because its balance equals the total of all the account balances in the subsidiary ledger. The balance of **Accounts Receivable** thus serves as a control on the accuracy of the balances in the accounts receivable subsidiary ledger after all posting is complete.

General Ledger
Accounts Receivable—controlling account $10,000
Accounts Receivable Subsidiary Ledger
Individual Accounts Within Ledger:
Brown, Joshua $2,000
Clark, Gillian 3,000
Greene, Jason 1,000
Perez, Sarita 4,000
Total $10,000
Controlling account balance equals total of accounts in subsidiary ledger.

The Accounts Receivable Subsidiary Ledger Form

Figure 14–3 shows the accounts receivable subsidiary ledger form used by On Your Mark.

The subsidiary ledger account form has lines at the top for the name and address of the customer. In a manual accounting system, subsidiary ledger accounts are arranged in alphabetical order. They are not usually numbered. In a computerized system, however, each charge customer is

are affected. Let's compare that transaction to a sale on account for a merchandising business, On Your Mark Athletic Wear.

Accounting for Sales and Cash Receipts

International Accounting introduces students to various international and multicultural issues related to the field of accounting.

INTRODUCTION

The *Teacher Wraparound Edition* highlights several contemporary issues facing accounting educators, such as the use of technology, global awareness, ethics, cooperative learning, assessment, and basic skills improvement. It also shows how Glencoe's comprehensive accounting program addresses these issues. The *Teacher Wraparound Edition* provides a description of the content and use of the numerous teacher and student components comprising the *Glencoe Accounting* program.

THE FOUR-STEP TEACHING PLAN

Each chapter in the *Teacher Wraparound Edition* is divided into instructional sections according to a four-step teaching plan designed to help you develop the chapter concepts and procedures. This widely accepted instructional method follows a mastery approach to developing student understanding of concepts and procedures. When utilized consistently, this four-step plan provides an instructional framework that makes it easy for you to teach and easy for your students to learn. The four steps in the instruction plan are Focus, Teach, Assess, and Close.

1 FOCUS

The first step in the teaching plan is to focus students' attention by piquing their interest with a Bell Ringer activity. This usually can be completed within the first several minutes of class and provides a motivational lead-in to the concepts that will be presented in the chapter.

2 TEACH

This section is the central part of the teaching plan. Teaching suggestions employing a variety of approaches, strategies, and activities appear in the side margins of the *Teacher Wraparound Edition*. These suggestions are provided to support your classroom instruction through supplementary accounting information, suggestions for the use of visuals, comments on the use of technology, and interesting facts that may be used to hold students' interest.

3 ASSESS

The third step in the teaching plan is used to evaluate students' understanding of accounting concepts and procedures. Each section ends with a *Check Your Understanding* that provides immediate reinforcement activities. Enrichment activities found here will allow you to enhance the learning experience for those who have mastered the section content and are ready for more in-depth learning. For further assessment, chapter quizzes, chapter tests, and unit tests are also available.

4 CLOSE

The final step in the teaching plan is used to determine whether students have mastered the objectives of each section. Students practice and apply what they have learned through a closing activity which might include a vocabulary review, review questions, short exercises, or problems. Providing students with a variety of ways to demonstrate what they have learned also gives you several opportunities to evaluate their learning and to identify students who need additional reinforcement through reteaching and practice activities.

UNIT RESOURCE MANAGER

To provide the best possible learning experience for your students, you need to know the variety of materials that are available to supplement your teaching. You cannot plan your lessons effectively unless you know what materials are available and the appropriate time needed to utilize each.

The **Unit Resource Manager** gives you a comprehensive reference to unit teaching resources such as videos, posters, business simulations, mini practice sets, Internet activities, assessment resources, accounting portfolio, and enrichment resources. Refer to these guides as you plan each unit so that you can make the best use of the numerous instructional materials that are included in the *Glencoe Accounting* program.

CHAPTER RESOURCE MANAGER

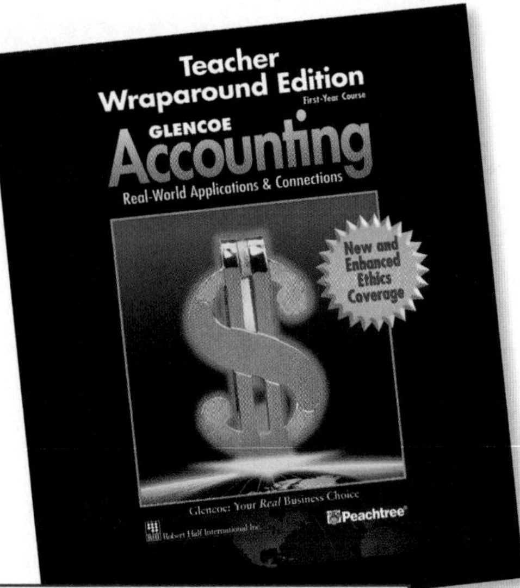

The *Glencoe Accounting* program offers a variety of teacher support materials for use in tailoring your course to best meet your course objectives and to maximize student learning.

The **Chapter Resource Manager** gives you a comprehensive reference to chapter teaching resources. It provides you a quick overview of all section objectives, the features covered, and a list of multimedia resources. Refer to these guides as you plan each chapter.

Section Resources provide a quick reference to the section objectives covered, including the National Standards for Business Education. You will find a list of all the activities, features, and reproducible masters that can be used to supplement your teaching.

The SCANS Correlation Chart shows you which foundation skills and workplace competencies are covered for the chapter.

CHAPTER 6 *Resource Manager*

Section Resources

	Objectives & Standards	Activities & Features	Reproducible Masters
Chapter Opener *Recording Transactions in a General Journal*	• Explain the first three steps in the accounting cycle. • Give and describe several examples of source documents. • Explain the purpose of journalizing. • Apply information from source documents. • Describe the steps to make a general journal entry. • Make accurate general journal entries. • Correct errors in general journal entries. • Define the accounting terms introduced in this chapter. **National Standards for Business Education**: IA1, IA4, IA6, IA7, IA8	Exploring the Real World of Business, p. 120 Workplace Connections, p. 121	School-to-Work Handbook
Section 1 *The Accounting Cycle*	• The first three steps in the accounting cycle. • Why it is necessary to journalize transactions. • The different kinds of source documents used in a business. • The difference between a calendar year and a fiscal year.	Spreadsheet Hints, p. 123 Connect To, p. 123 Accounting Flashbacks, p. 124 International Accounting, p. 124	Math Review for Accounting Strategies for Teaching International Accounting
Section 2 *Recording Transactions in the General Journal*	• The purpose of a general journal. • The parts and labeling of a general journal. • How information is entered in a general journal. • How to correct errors in a general journal.	Accounting Tips, p. 126 A Matter of Ethics, p. 139	Demonstration Problems Strategies for Teaching Ethics in Accounting Internet Resources and Activities Handbook

KEY

Posters | Blackline Masters | Transparency | CD-ROM | Software | Portfolio | Videocassette

SCANS Correlation Chart

FOUNDATION SKILLS

Basic Skills:	Reading	Writing	Math	Listening	Speaking	
Thinking Skills:	Creative Thinking	Decision Making	Problem Solving	Seeing Things in the Mind's Eye	Knowing How to Learn	Reasoning
Personal Qualities:	Responsibility	Self-Esteem	Sociability	Self-Management	Integrity/Honesty	

WORKPLACE COMPETENCIES

Resources:	Allocating Time	Allocating Money	Allocating Material and Facility Resources	Allocating Human Resources		
Information:	Acquiring and Evaluating Information	Organizing and Maintaining Information	Interpreting and Communicating Information	Using Computers to Process Information		
Interpersonal Skills:	Participating as a Member of a Team	Teaching Others	Serving Clients/Customers	Exercising Leadership	Negotiating to Arrive at a Decision	Working with Cultural Diversity
Systems:	Understanding Systems	Monitoring and Correcting Performance	Improving and Designing Systems			
Technology:	Selecting Technology	Applying Technology to Task	Maintaining and Troubleshooting Technology			

*Highlighted blocks indicate areas covered in the chapter. Additional SCANS skills are also covered throughout the *Teacher Wraparound Edition*.

MULTIMEDIA RESOURCE

Peachtree	QuickBooks	Spreadsheets	Videos	CD-ROMs
Problem 6–4 *Recording General Journal Transactions* Problem 6–5 *Recording General Journal Transactions* Problem 6–6 *Recording General Journal Transactions* Problem 6–7 *Recording General Journal Transactions* Problem 6–8 *Recording General Journal Transactions*	Problem 6–4 *Recording General Journal Transactions* Problem 6–5 *Recording General Journal Transactions*	None in this chapter.	***Video Segment: Business Ethics*** After viewing this video, students will be able to exercise judgment in evaluating ethical situations.	***Electronic Learning Center (ELC), Chapter 6*** This program is ideal for visual learners since it incorporates video images, animation, and graphics to enliven the content of each lesson. ***Interactive Lesson Planner (ILP), Chapter 6*** This CD-ROM combines the versatility of an electronic lesson planner with the convenience of teacher classroom resources.

Assessment

Student Edition
- Check Your Understanding, pp. 125, 140
- Chapter 6 Problems, pp. 145–149

Assessment and Evaluation Masters
- Chapter 6 Study Plan, *Glencoe Workbook*
- Chapter 6 Self-Test, *Glencoe Workbook*
- Chapter 6 Test, *Chapter Tests* Booklet
- Chapter 6 Activity, *School-to-Work Handbook*
- Chapter 6 Exam*View*

Teacher Wraparound Edition
- Critical Thinking Activity, p. 133
- Reteaching Section 1, p. 125
- Reteaching Section 2, p. 140
- Chapter 6 Quiz, p. 141

Transparencies

	Teaching Transparencies	Solution Transparencies
Section 1:	6–1, 6–2, 6–3	Problem 6–1
Section 2:	6–4, 6–5, 6–6, 6–7, 6–8, 6–9, 6–10, 6–11, 6–12, 6–13, 6–14, 6–15, 6–16, 6–17, 6–18, 6–19, 6–20	Problems 6–2, 6–3
End of Chapter:		Problems 6–4, 6–5, 6–6, 6–7, 6–8

Multimedia Resources provide an overview of resources such as CD-ROMs and videos. For your convenience, the chart identifies the chapter problems that can be completed using Peachtree Complete® Accounting software or QuickBooks® templates. It also identifies a spreadsheet problem, if available in the chapter.

Transparencies are listed by section. The chart includes both teaching transparencies and solution transparencies that are available in the chapter.

TEA ER CLASSROOM RESOURCES

One o)als of the *Teacher Wraparound Edition* is to coordinate for you the numerous teacher ar ent components that comprise the *Glencoe Accounting* program. Another goal is to provi and your students with the best possible learning opportunities and experiences. Th er Classroom Resources visually provides you with additional blackline masters av for your use with the chapter.

Teaching rovide a wide variety of alterna introduce, teach, or reinforce Transparencies provide visu ng for your students and enliv ontent of each lesson. Lesson Pl Block Scheduling help you ring for each chapter.

These resources help you in **Meeting Different Ability Levels** of your students, providing them with comprehensive reinforcement of chapter information and accounting skills. Use these activities to help students with various learning styles and abilities.

Use the **Multimedia CD-ROM** to introduce, reinforce, or summarize the concepts of each chapter.

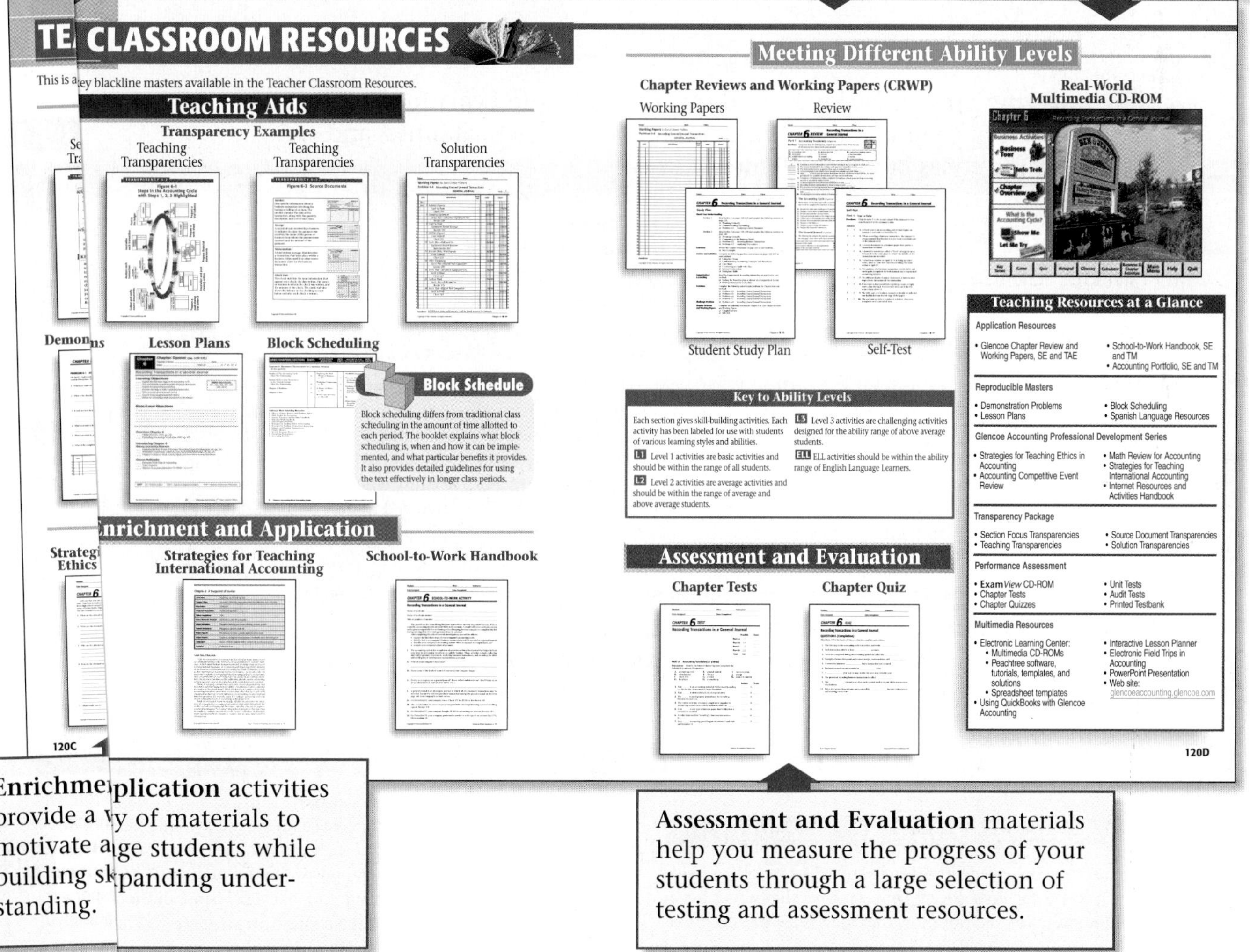

Enrichme plication activities provide a y of materials to motivate a ge students while building sk panding understanding.

Assessment and Evaluation materials help you measure the progress of your students through a large selection of testing and assessment resources.

ADDITIONAL FEATURES AND TEACHING STRATEGIES

The *Teacher Wraparound Edition* includes additional features and teaching strategies to support the concepts presented in the chapters. Use the following strategies to provide your students with the best possible learning opportunities.

MEETING SPECIAL NEEDS

English Language Learners Students who do not speak English as their native language face special challenges when dealing with large numbers. Generally, it is not the mathematical calculation that causes problems. Instead, native speakers tend to say the numbers very quickly and blur the soun[...] board along with the sign i[...]

ADDRESSING MULTIPLE LEARNING STYLES

Visual/Spatial Learner For some students, it may be difficult to visualize a real-life ledger when looking at images of miniature ledgers in the text or in the workbook. If possible, show students samples of actual ledgers from a real-life manual accounting system. If you do not have access to a business's ledger, create a notebook with sample, full-page ledger pages or cards. Be sure to use a four-column ledger account form so students can see the relationship between the real ledger and the forms illustrated in the text and workbook.

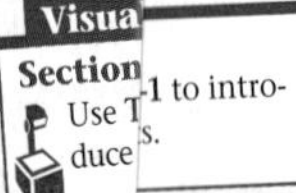

 **Meeting Special Needs** and **Addressing Multiple Learning Styles** provide appropriate guidelines for the special needs, abilities, and learning styles of your students.

MAKING CONNECTIONS TO DAILY LIFE

Using Checking Accounts Ask students who have checking accounts to explain what happens to their account when they withdraw money or deposit a check. (The transaction is posted to the account and the [...] explain why a bank must post [...] customer bank account balanc[...] ance is not up to date, an indiv[...] the account is not sufficient to[...]

HOME AND COMMUNITY CONNECTIONS ACTIVITY

Financial Planning What types of financial planning activities occur at home? Have students ask their parents or guardians about short-term and long-term financial planning. Does their family have a savings account? College fund? Investment portfolio? IRA? What are rules or limitations about the use or liquidity of those funds? How about wills or trusts? Does the student know where to locate that information in case of a family emergency? Have students report on the types of financial planning their family is involved in, not on the dollar amounts.

Making Connections to Daily Life and **Home and Community Connections Activity** enable you to bring the outside world into your accounting classroom.

COOPERATIVE LEARNING ACTIVITY

Make and Defend Divide students into groups of five or six and pro[...]ing scenario: "Monica Nan recently started a small business selling handmade [...] she posted journal entries at the end of each month. Business has increased and Monica wonders whether she should post more frequently. What recom[...]uld you make, and why?" Ask each group to make a decision and to appoint [...]n to present and defend the decision to the class. (All answers are correct if gro[...] defend their recommendations, which should refer to higher transaction vo[...]eed for timely information.)

CRITICAL THINKING ACTIVITY

Analyzing Information Give students this scenario: "Last month, Amelia [...] for $89.27 to pay the balance due for a doctor's bill. Amelia called about her a[...] today but her account information did not show that the $89.27 had been rece[...] Amelia has already received the canceled check from the bank." Give a reason([...] account still shows a balance due of $89.27. (The check was received and th[...] processed, but (a) the transaction was not posted to Amelia's account, (b) the t[...] have been posted to the wrong account, (c) the transaction was never journalized, or (d) the transaction was analyzed incorrectly and recorded incorrectly in the journal.)

 **Critical Thinking Activity** an[...]tive **Learning Activity** offer sugges[...]lp build students' critical thinking and skills.

SECTION 1

The General Ledger

In Chapter 6 you learned how to analyze business transactions and enter those transactions in a general journal.

In this chapter you will learn how to post journal entries to the general ledger and how to prepare a trial balance (Steps 4 and 5 in the accounting cycle illustrated in **Figure 7-1**). The Jeep dealership in your area records all business transactions in the journal and posts those transactions to the general ledger. An up-to-date ledger allows the accountant for the Jeep dealership to provide management with information such as:

- sales of vehicles
- service income
- salary and commission expense

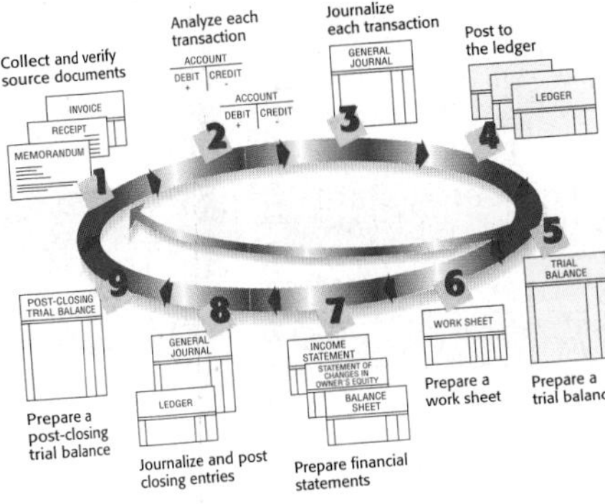

Setting Up the General Ledger

In a manual accounting system, the accounts used by a business are kept on separate pages or cards. These pages or cards are kept together in a book or file called a ledger. In a computerized accounting system, the electronic files containing the accounts are still referred to as the ledger, or the ledger accounts. In either system, the ledger is often called a **general ledger**.

Posting journal entries to the ledger accounts creates a record of the impact of business transactions on each account used by a business. After journal entries have been posted, a business owner or manager can look at a specific account and easily find its current balance. If, for example, Maria Sanchez wants to know how much money Roadrunner Delivery Service has in its bank account, she can simply look at the balance of the **Cash in Bank** account.

The Four-Column Ledger Account Form

In a manual accounting system, the accounting stationery used to record financial information about specific accounts is a **ledger account form**. There are several common ledger account forms. These forms—as well as other accounting stationery—are usually described by the number of amount columns they have. In other words, the number of columns refers only to those columns in which dollar amounts are recorded. For example, Roadrunner uses a four-column ledger account form.

The four-column account form has spaces to enter the account name, the account number, the date, a description of the entry, and the posting reference. It also has four columns in which to record dollar amounts. Look at the four-column account form shown in **Figure 7-2**.

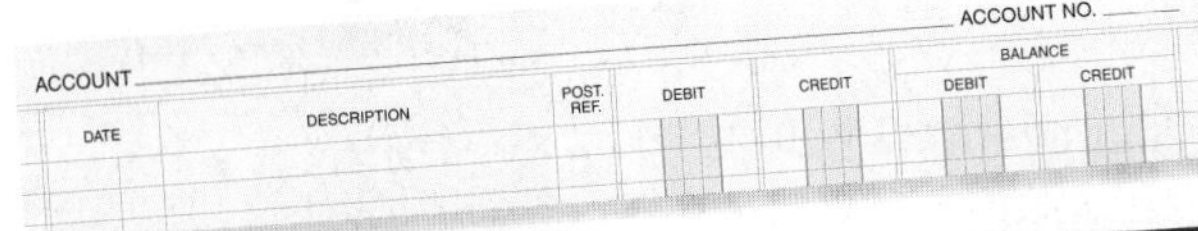

Figure 7-2 Four-Column Ledger Account Form

Notice the four amount columns: the debit column, the credit column, the debit balance column, and the credit balance column. The first two amount columns are used to enter debit and credit amounts posted from journal entries. The last two amount columns are used to enter the new account balance after a journal entry is posted. The balance columns show the current balance in the account. The type of account (expense, revenue, asset, etc.) determines which balance column to use. For example, accounts with a normal debit balance—such as asset or expense accounts—use the debit balance column. Accounts with a normal credit balance—such as liability or revenue accounts—use the credit balance column.

Did You Know?

Consumerism

U.S. cattle ranches produce 25 percent of the world's supply of beef. Consumers spend around $52 billion each year buying beef at their local supermarkets.

CHAPTER 7
SECTION 1, PAGES 152–156

2 TEACH
GUIDED PRACTICE

Reading Accounting

- Reinforce the accounting cycle by having students read the brief descriptions of Steps 1 to 3 in **Figure 7-1**. Then have them write descriptions of the actions accountants take at each step. L1
- If possible, obtain copies of accounting forms printed in your students' first language. Share copies with students and point out how they are similar to illustrations in the textbook. ELL

Concept Development: Setting Up the General Ledger

Discussion: Before learning how to post, students need to know what a ledger is. Point out that businesses have many different accounts and that, collectively, these accounts are referred to as a ledger. Although a business may have more than one ledger, the main ledger is the general ledger.

Explain to students that a ledger is similar to a card file but one that is not arranged alphabetically. Rather, the accounts in the ledger are arranged by classification: assets first, followed by liabilities, owner's equity, revenue, and expense accounts. Show students examples of actual ledgers to help them form an image of the general ledger. L1

Visual Learning

Figure 7-2 Four-Column Ledger Account Form
Using Transparency 7-3, demonstrate the information entered in the ledger during the posting process.

RESOURCE MANAGER

...e Masters
...s and Working Papers
...Problems
...cies
... Transparency
...sparencies

- Source Document Transparencies
- Solution Transparencies

Multimedia
- ExamView CD-ROM
- Electronic Learning Center CD-ROM
- Interactive Lesson Planner CD-ROM
- Electronic Field Trips in Accounting

Great Ideas *From the Classroom of...*

Posting to Ledger Accounts To help students better understand the posting process, I prepare transparencies to illustrate the relationship of the posting with the original transaction. First, I review the transaction and show a journal page with the recorded entry. Then I show a transparency with each of the ledger accounts. I write on the transparencies to complete the posting process so the class can see me perform each step in the posting process.

William Trouten
Platteville High School
Platteville, Wisconsin

EXTENDING THE CONTENT

Personal Finance Software Demonstrate a retail computer application for personal finance such as *Quicken* or *Microsoft Money*. Emphasize the ease with which you can enter transactions and how the computer automatically updates account balances, budgets, and reports. Discuss how the software automates daily tasks, provides reminders when bills are dues, and even prints checks. If possible, demonstrate how to use the online service features to pay bills and ...ing tasks.

ACCOUNTING ISSUES

Downsizing of CPA Firms In the last several years, many businesses have decreased their work forces at all levels. CPA firms are a part of this trend. Some of the downsizing is a result of new technology and its increased efficiency. Much downsizing, though, results from maximizing productivity and profitability by having the right staff at the right time. In other words, CPA firms must fit their work forces to their workloads. Many CPA firms use part-time employees and flexible work hours to cut labor costs and increase productivity. For example, part-time tax accountants work only during the tax season.

Accounting Issues and **Extending the Content** expand understanding of accounting concepts and procedures.

GLENCOE ACCOUNTING: ELECTRONIC LEARNING CENTER

The *Glencoe Accounting: Electronic Learning Center* is one of the most exciting parts of the *Glencoe Accounting* program. This dynamic and comprehensive package of learning and teaching materials includes a set of three *Real-World Multimedia CD-ROMs*, the *Peachtree Accounting Software and Applications CD-ROM*, and an integrated management system that allows you to monitor your students' progress, grade chapter problems, and navigate easily among tasks and activities.

New All-in-One Installation

- Teacher installation from one CD-ROM
- Easy-to-follow on-screen instructions
- User-friendly printed guide

Real-World Multimedia CD-ROMs

Many students today are visual learners who rely less on reading a textbook to gain knowledge and rely more on illustrations and visual images to acquire understanding of a subject. Glencoe's *Real-World Multimedia CD-ROMs* are ideal for visual learners, though all students will benefit from their use.

The Real-World Multimedia CD-ROMs contain lessons, chapter quizzes, vocabulary games, and real-world case studies for use throughout the textbook. Videos, animation, and graphics enliven the content of each lesson to capture and hold the attention of your students. Use these multimedia tools to introduce, reinforce, or summarize concepts of the course.

Real-World Case Studies are provided so that your students can understand how accounting plays a role in everyday life.

Business and Chapter Activities correlate to the textbook content, offering activities, lessons, and problems to enrich and extend learning.

Vocabulary Games challenge students to use newly learned accounting terms in a fun way.

Students may assess their own understanding of concepts and procedures at the close of each chapter using self-grading **Chapter Quizzes**.

- **Business Tour** video presentations grab the interest of your students and stimulate thinking on chapter concepts.
- **Real World Business** activities ask students to perform research on the featured business and practice their critical thinking skills.
- The **Chapter Overview** outlines primary learning goals and objectives for your students.
- **Show Me** lessons provide step-by-step instruction on chapter concepts and procedures.
- **Let Me Try** activities allow students to practice new skills and receive immediate feedback.
- **Audit with Alex** activities challenge students to review accounting transactions and entries for accuracy and completeness.

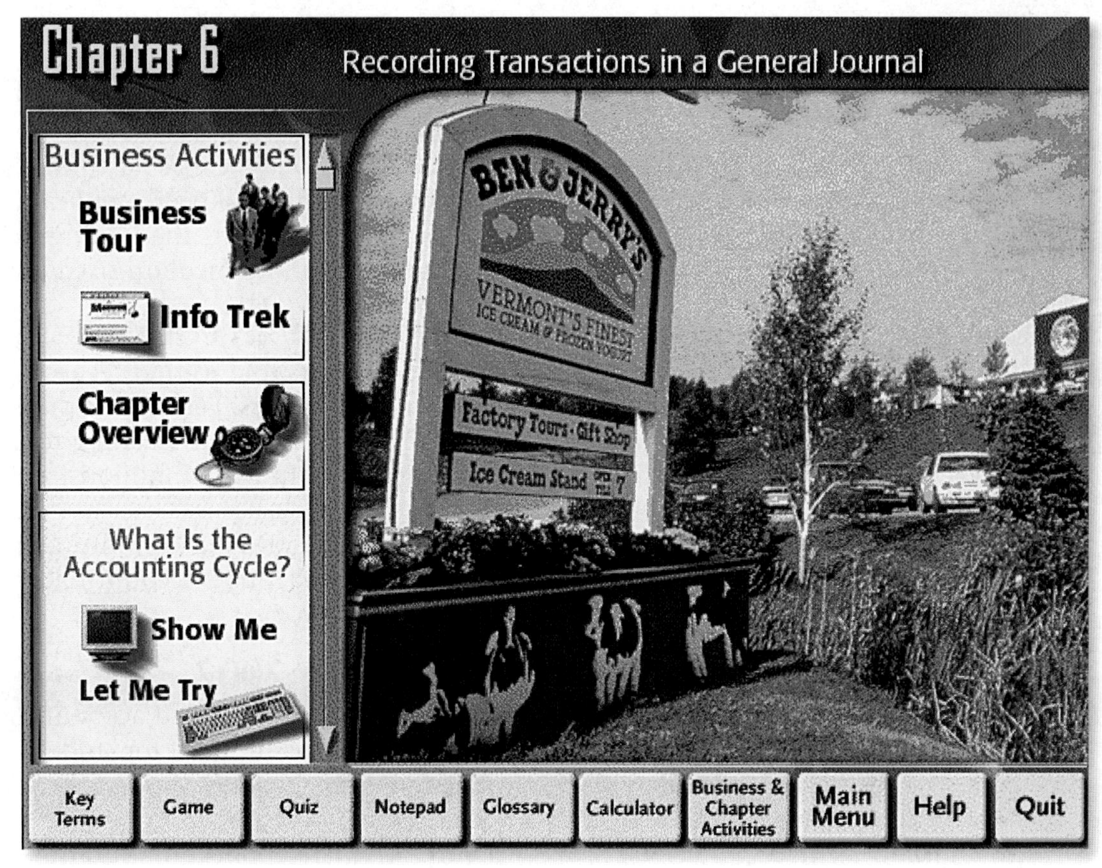

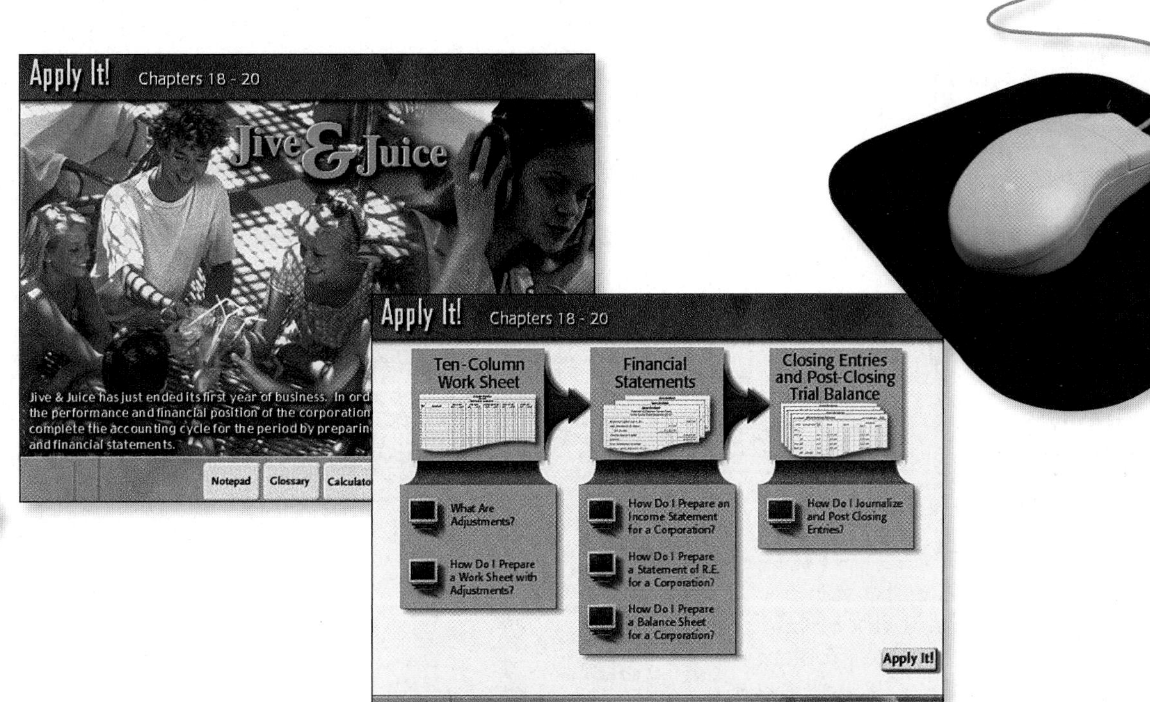

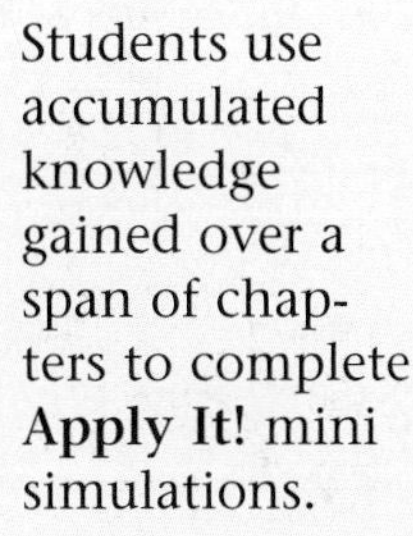

Students use accumulated knowledge gained over a span of chapters to complete **Apply It!** mini simulations.

PEACHTREE® ACCOUNTING SOFTWARE AND APPLICATIONS

Peachtree®

The *Peachtree Accounting Software and Applications CD-ROM* contains everything you'll need to train your students to use this leading small business accounting software application. Glencoe has formed an alliance with Peachtree Software, a subsidiary of Best Software, the leading supplier of business management software and related products and services to the small- to medium-sized business community worldwide.

The Perfect Real-World Partner for Accounting Classrooms

In our extensive work with focus groups, teachers told us that "real-world" software is needed to help students grasp accounting fundamentals relevant to business. Peachtree's products consistently received high ratings from teachers. By incorporating accounting software into your teaching tools, Glencoe gives students the advantage of being trained on accounting software currently in use by millions of businesses and taught in numerous colleges and postsecondary schools.

Glencoe's partnership with Peachtree Software demonstrates our commitment to giving students the best tools possible to prepare them for a future in business. By teaching Peachtree Accounting in the classroom, you can help students make a smooth transition from the classroom to the workforce.

Using Peachtree Complete® Accounting 2002

Peachtree Complete® Accounting 2002 is an easy-to-use, full-featured accounting solution designed for small business owners who want to manage their businesses more effectively. It's ideal for students who are learning accounting fundamentals. The software is user-friendly with features such as *Accounting Behind the Screens,* which displays the journal entries that happen when a student saves a transaction.

You'll find Peachtree problem sets, the Peachtree software application, multimedia tutorials, and solutions on the *Peachtree Accounting and Spreadsheet Templates CD-ROM*. All end-of-chapter problems, business simulations, and mini practice sets are correlated to the software and can be launched through an easy-to-use menu system. Glencoe supports Peachtree with these useful tools:

Peachtree User Guides. Easy-to-understand guides in student *Chapter Reviews and Working Papers (CRWP).*

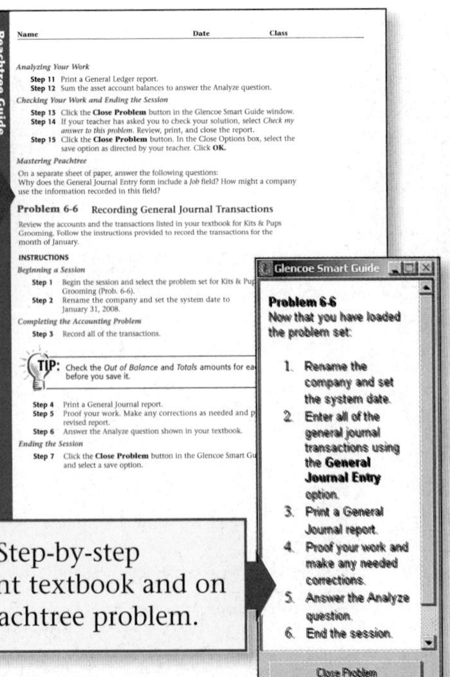

Glencoe Smart Guides. Step-by-step instructions in the student textbook and on the CD-ROM for each Peachtree problem.

Peachtree Solutions. Check your students' work electronically for each Peachtree problem.

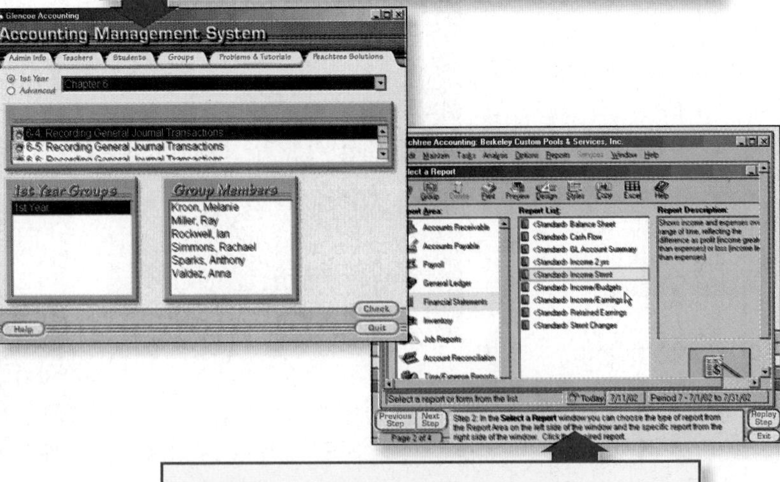

Peachtree Multimedia Tutorials. Animated tutorials to help students learn how to perform each accounting task.

SPREADSHEET TEMPLATES

From budgeting to analysis, basic calculations to advanced techniques, your students will benefit throughout their careers from the spreadsheet skills they will learn in this course. The spreadsheet problems provided with *Glencoe Accounting* will give your students realistic experience as they complete a variety of accounting tasks.

Spreadsheet problems are identified in the student text with a spreadsheet icon. The accompanying Excel spreadsheet templates are easily launched through the *Glencoe Accounting: Electronic Learning Center CD-ROM* menu system.

Spreadsheet activities range from working with the basic accounting equation to completing a ten-column work sheet. In order to meet the learning needs of your individual students, you may choose to provide spreadsheet templates that contain basic formulas or templates in which students will be required to set up their own formulas.

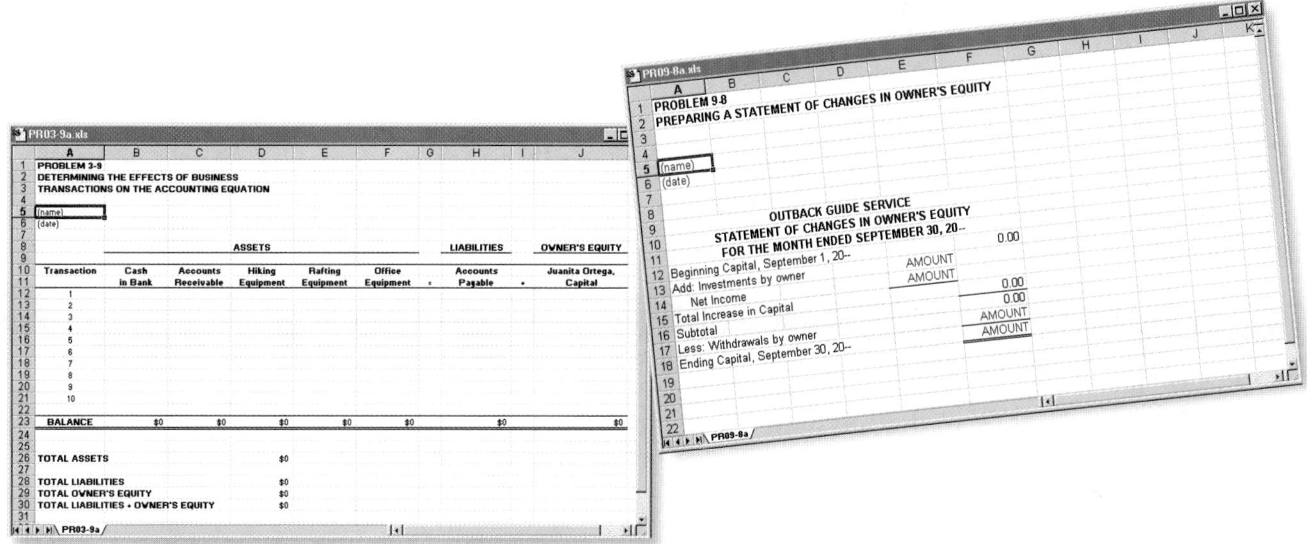

USING QUICKBOOKS® WITH *GLENCOE ACCOUNTING*

Once your students have mastered the principles and practices of a manual accounting system, they will be eager to transfer this knowledge to a computerized system. *Glencoe Accounting* provides you with introductory information on how your students can use QuickBooks software and template files. With these learning tools, they can learn how to set up a business and apply basic accounting principles and procedures.

Step-by-Step Instructions and Template Files

Glencoe Accounting offers *Using QuickBooks® with Glencoe Accounting* in which you'll find step-by-step instructions on how to work with QuickBooks. In addition, the CD-ROM in the back of the supplement contains QuickBooks template files for use in Chapters 6 through 28. As students use these files, they will learn to open accounts, establish account balances, set up charts of accounts and vendors, and process transactions. To get started, you'll need the QuickBooks® Pro 2001 accounting software.

CHARTING YOUR COURSE WITH THE *GLENCOE ACCOUNTING INTERACTIVE LESSON PLANNER CD-ROM (ILP)*

Planning and organizing an accounting program can be a challenging job. That's why we've gathered all the resources you'll need into one electronic "file cabinet" so that you can pick and choose the items needed for each day, week, or month of your accounting course.

The *Glencoe Accounting Interactive Lesson Planner CD-ROM (ILP)* is easily navigated through a central menu system. Using a calendar and a list of resources, you can arrange topics, add notes, and revise plans throughout the year. Point, click, and print selections from supplements like *Strategies for Teaching Ethics in Accounting, Lesson Plans*, or *Unit Tests*. View or print blackline masters. Print copies of your curriculum for your assistant, for home, or your administrator. You'll save time and energy. It's all within easy reach!

VIRTUAL BUSINESS® AND *GLENCOE ACCOUNTING*

Virtual Business® is a fully visual business and marketing simulation that introduces students to the principles of marketing by letting them start and run their own business. Designed and developed based on research conducted by Knowledge Matters, Inc. for the U.S. Department of Education, the CD-ROM contains the *Virtual Business* software, an interactive tutorial, 21 pre-saved modular activities with lesson plans, and the *Virtual Business Analyzer* companion software for post-activity classroom analysis and discussion.

Your students will be motivated to learn more about the world of business as they make merchandising, pricing, promotion, and market research decisions. Clearly relevant and fun to use, this multimedia tool adds an exciting dimension to your accounting program.

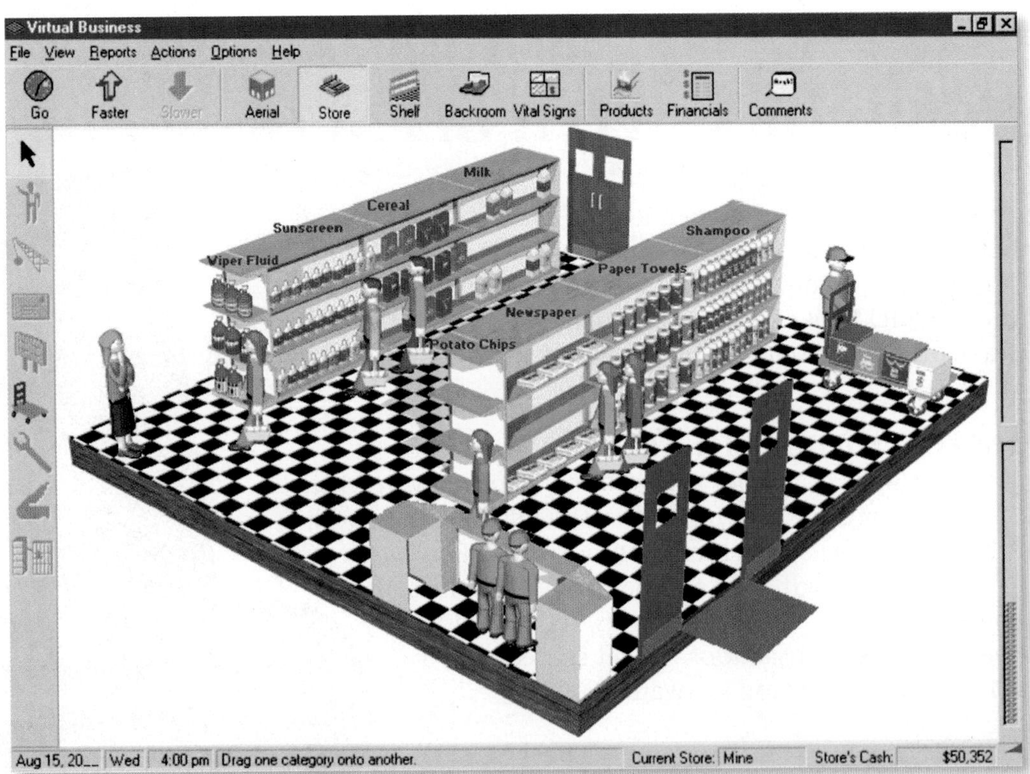

SCOPE AND SEQUENCE

Glencoe Chapters	Glencoe Accounting Real-World Multimedia	Peachtree Problems	QuickBooks Problems	Spreadsheet Problems	Internet Activities
1	✔				✔
2	✔				✔
3	✔			3-9	✔
4	✔			4-6	✔
5	✔	5-3, 5-4, 5-5, 5-6, 5-7		5-8	✔
6	✔	6-4, 6-5, 6-6, 6-7, 6-8	6-4, 6-5		✔
7	✔	7-5, 7-6, 7-7, 7-8, 7-9	7-5, 7-6		✔
Mini Practice Set 1: Canyon.com Web Sites		✔	✔		
8	✔	8-5, 8-6, 8-7	8-5, 8-6	8-4, 8-8	✔
9	✔	9-4, 9-5, 9-6, 9-7	9-6, 9-7	9-8	✔
10	✔	10-4, 10-5, 10-6, 10-7, 10-8	10-8, 10-9	10-9	✔
11	✔	11-4, 11-5, 11-7, 11-8	11-5, 11-7	11-6	✔
Mini Practice Set 2: Fast Track Tutoring Service		✔	✔		
Business Simulation: Adventure Travels		✔	✔		
12	✔	12-5, 12-7, 12-8, 12-9		12-6	✔
13	✔	13-7, 13-8, 13-9, 13-10	13-8, 13-9	13-6	✔
Mini Practice Set 3: Green Thumb Plant Service		✔			
14	✔	14-5, 14-6, 14-7, 14-8, 14-9	14-5, 14-7		✔
15	✔	15-6, 15-7, 15-8, 15-9, 15-10	15-7, 15-8	15-5	✔
16	✔	16-4, 16-5, 16-6	16-5, 16-6		✔
17	✔	17-4, 17-5, 17-6, 17-7, 17-8	17-5, 17-8		✔
18	✔	18-6, 18-7, 18-8	18-7, 18-8	18-5	✔
19	✔	19-6, 19-7, 19-8	19-5, 19-8	19-5	✔
Mini Practice Set 4: In-Touch Electronics		✔	✔		
20	✔	20-4, 20-5, 20-6, 20-8	20-5, 20-8	20-7	✔
Business Simulation: Outer Banks Marketplace, Inc.		✔	✔		
21	✔	21-6, 21-7, 21-9	21-6, 21-9	21-8	✔
22	✔	22-4, 22-5, 22-6, 22-7, 22-8	22-6, 22-7		
23	✔	23-7, 23-8, 23-9, 23-10	23-8, 23-10		✔
24	✔	24-4, 24-5, 24-6, 24-7, 25-8, 24-0	24-4, 24-6		✔
25	✔	25-4, 25-7, 25-8	25-4, 25-8	25-6	✔
26	✔	26-6, 26-7, 26-8, 26-9, 26-10	26-6, 26-10		✔
Mini Practice Set 5: Kite Loft, Inc.		✔	✔		
Business Simulation: Digital Express		✔	✔		
27	✔	27-6, 27-7, 27-8, 27-9	27-7, 27-8	27-5	✔
28	✔	28-6, 28-8	28-6, 28-8	28-4, 28-9	✔
Mini Practice Set 6: Fine Finishes		✔	✔		
29					✔
Appendix G				✔	

REINFORCEMENT

Chapter Reviews and Working Papers (CRWP)

The *Chapter Reviews and Working Papers (CRWP)* provides students with additional reinforcement problems and activities to review the content learned throughout the chapter. Solutions to all chapter review pages, chapter problems, and mini practice sets can be found in the *Teacher Annotated Edition* of the *Chapter Reviews and Working Papers*.

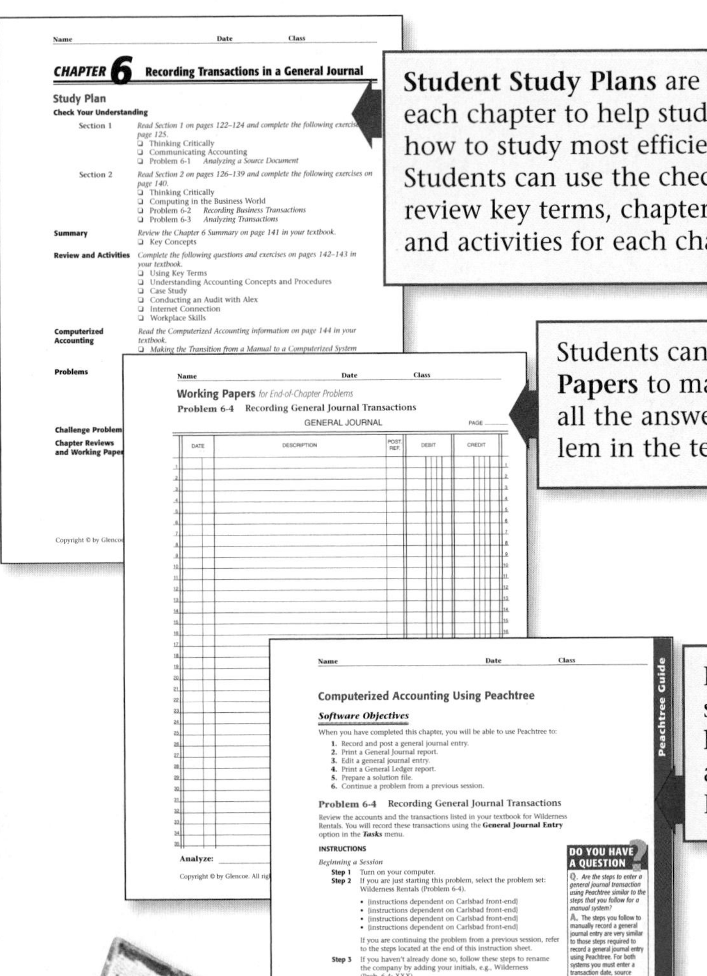

Name Date Class

CHAPTER 6 Recording Transactions in a General Journal

Study Plan

Check Your Understanding

Section 1 — *Read Section 1 on pages 122–124 and complete the following exercises on page 125.*
- ❑ Thinking Critically
- ❑ Communicating Accounting
- ❑ Problem 6-1 *Analyzing a Source Document*

Section 2 — *Read Section 2 on pages 126–139 and complete the following exercises on page 140.*
- ❑ Thinking Critically
- ❑ Computing in the Business World
- ❑ Problem 6-2 *Recording Business Transactions*
- ❑ Problem 6-3 *Analyzing Transactions*

Summary — *Review the Chapter 6 Summary on page 141 in your textbook.*
- ❑ Key Concepts

Review and Activities — *Complete the following questions and exercises on pages 142–143 in your textbook.*
- ❑ Using Key Terms
- ❑ Understanding Accounting Concepts and Procedures
- ❑ Case Study
- ❑ Conducting an Audit with Alex
- ❑ Internet Connection
- ❑ Workplace Skills

Computerized Accounting — *Read the Computerized Accounting information on page 144 in your textbook.*
- ❑ *Making the Transition from a Manual to a Computerized System*

Problems

Challenge Problem

Chapter Reviews and Working Paper

Copyright © by Glenco

Name Date Class

Working Papers *for End-of-Chapter Problems*

Problem 6-4 Recording General Journal Transactions

GENERAL JOURNAL PAGE

DATE	DESCRIPTION	POST. REF.	DEBIT	CREDIT

Analyze:

Copyright © by Glencoe. All rig

Name Date Class

Computerized Accounting Using Peachtree

Software Objectives

When you have completed this chapter, you will be able to use Peachtree to:

1. Record and post a general journal entry.
2. Print a General Journal report.
3. Edit a general journal entry.
4. Print a General Ledger report.
5. Prepare a solution file.
6. Continue a problem from a previous session.

Problem 6-4 Recording General Journal Transactions

Review the accounts and the transactions listed in your textbook for Wilderness Rentals. You will record these transactions using the **General Journal Entry** option in the ***Tasks*** menu.

INSTRUCTIONS

Beginning a Session

Step 1 Turn on your computer.

Step 2 If you are just starting this problem, select the problem set: Wilderness Rentals (Problem 6-4).

- [instructions dependent on Carlsbad front-end]
- [instructions dependent on Carlsbad front-end]
- [instructions dependent on Carlsbad front-end]
- [instructions dependent on Carlsbad front-end]

If you are continuing the problem from a previous session, refer to the steps located at the end of this instruction sheet.

Step 3 If you haven't already done so, follow these steps to rename the company by adding your initials, e.g., Wilderness (Prob. 6-4: XXX).

- Choose **Company Information** from the ***Maintain*** menu.
- Review the information in the Maintain Company Information window. (See Figure 6-4A.)
- Click in the *Company Name* field.
- Add your initials to the company name.
- Click to record the new company name.

DO YOU HAVE A QUESTION

Q. *Are the steps to enter a general journal transaction using Peachtree similar to the steps that you follow for a manual system?*

A. The steps you follow to manually record a general journal entry are very similar to those steps required to record a general journal entry using Peachtree. For both systems you must enter a transaction date, source document reference, account numbers, and debit/credit amounts. The Peachtree data entry form even looks like a manual journal.

Notes

Refer to the instructions in the Getting Started section (p. 000) if you need help selecting the problem set data.

Peachtree Guide

Copyright © by Glencoe. All rights reserved. Chapter 6 ■ 79

Student Study Plans are available for each chapter to help students learn how to study most efficiently. Students can use the checklist to help review key terms, chapter problems, and activities for each chapter.

Students can use the **Working Papers** to manually complete all the answers to each problem in the text.

Peachtree Guides provide step-by-step instructions on how to complete computerized accounting activities using Peachtree.

The **Self-Test** provides students an opportunity to take responsibility for assessing their own knowledge and skills.

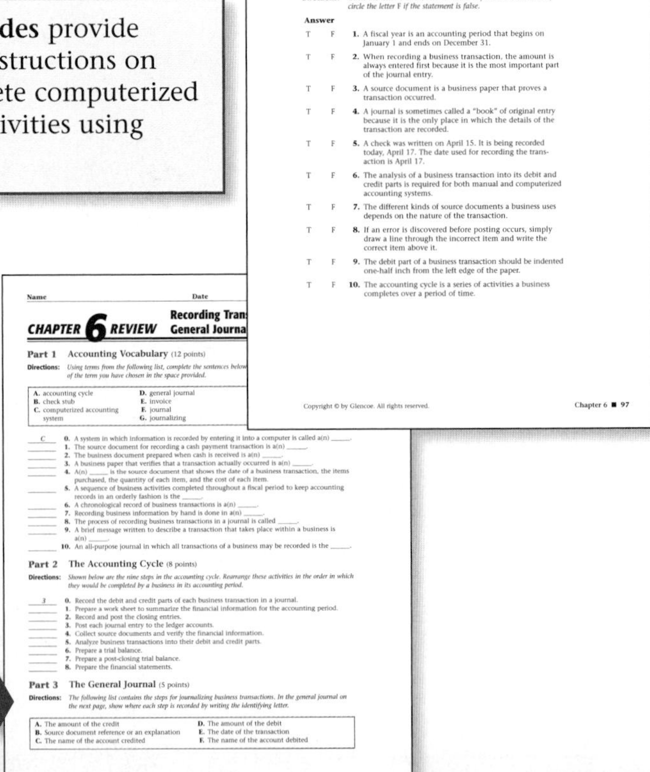

Name Date Class

CHAPTER 6 Recording Transactions in a General Journal

Self-Test

Part A True or False

Directions: *Circle the letter T in the Answer column if the statement is true; circle the letter F if the statement is false.*

Answer

T F **1.** A fiscal year is an accounting period that begins on January 1 and ends on December 31.

T F **2.** When recording a business transaction, the amount is always entered first because it is the most important part of the journal entry.

T F **3.** A source document is a business paper that proves a transaction occurred.

T F **4.** A journal is sometimes called a "book" of original entry because it is the only place in which the details of the transaction are recorded.

T F **5.** A check was written on April 15. It is being recorded today, April 17. The date used for recording the transaction is April 17.

T F **6.** The analysis of a business transaction into its debit and credit parts is required for both manual and computerized accounting systems.

T F **7.** The different kinds of source documents a business uses depends on the nature of the transaction.

T F **8.** If an error is discovered before posting occurs, simply draw a line through the incorrect item and write the correct item above it.

T F **9.** The debit part of a business transaction should be indented one-half inch from the left edge of the paper.

T F **10.** The accounting cycle is a series of activities a business completes over a period of time.

Copyright © by Glencoe. All rights reserved. Chapter 6 ■ 97

Name Date

CHAPTER 6 REVIEW Recording Tran General Journa

Part 1 Accounting Vocabulary (12 points)

Directions: *Using terms from the following list, complete the sentences below of the term you have chosen in the space provided.*

A. accounting cycle	**D.** general journal
B. check stub	**E.** invoice
C. computerized accounting system	**F.** journal
	G. journalizing

C **0.** A system in which information is recorded by entering it into a computer is called a(n) ______.
1. The source document for recording a cash payment transaction is a(n) ______.
2. The business document prepared when cash is received is a(n) ______.
3. A business paper that verifies that a transaction actually occurred is a(n) ______.
4. A(n) ______ is the source document that shows the date of a business transaction, the items purchased, the quantity of each item, and the cost of each item.
5. A sequence of business activities completed throughout a fiscal period to keep accounting records in an orderly fashion is the ______.
6. A chronological record of business transactions is a(n) ______.
7. Recording business information by hand is done in a(n) ______.
8. The process of recording business transactions in a journal is called ______.
9. A brief message written to describe a transaction that takes place within a business is a(n) ______.
10. An all-purpose journal in which all transactions of a business may be recorded is the ______.

Part 2 The Accounting Cycle (8 points)

Directions: *Shown below are the nine steps in the accounting cycle. Rearrange these activities in the order in which they would be completed by a business in its accounting period.*

3 **0.** Record the debit and credit parts of each business transaction in a journal.
1. Prepare a work sheet to summarize the financial information for the accounting period.
2. Record and post the closing entries.
3. Post each journal entry to the ledger accounts.
4. Collect source documents and verify the financial information.
5. Analyze business transactions into their debit and credit parts.
6. Prepare a trial balance.
7. Prepare a post-closing trial balance.
8. Prepare the financial statements.

Part 3 The General Journal (5 points)

Directions: *The following list contains the steps for journalizing business transactions. In the general journal on the next page, show where each step is recorded by writing the identifying letter.*

A. The amount of the credit	**D.** The amount of the debit
B. Source document reference or an explanation	**E.** The date of the transaction
C. The name of the account credited	**F.** The name of the account debited

76 ■ Chapter 6 Copyright © by Glencoe. All rights reserved.

The **Chapter Review** gives students an opportunity to review new accounting vocabulary and key accounting concepts and procedures presented in the chapter.

RETEACHING

Reteaching activities provide students with comprehensive reinforcement of chapter information and accounting skills.

Demonstration Problems can be used to make transparencies for introducing new concepts or procedures, for make-up work, as short quizzes, or as extra practice.

CHAPTER 6 Recording Transactions in a General Journal

PROBLEM 6–1 JOURNALIZING AN OWNER'S INVESTMENT

On April 2, Gail Gordan invested a calculator (Office Equipment) valued at $145 in her business, Gordan Enterprises, Memorandum 4.

1. Which accounts are affected?
2. What is the classification of each account? ______ is a(n) ______ account. ______ is a(n) ______ account.
3. Is each account increased or decreased? ______ is ______. ______ is ______.
4. Which account is debited, and for what amount? ______ is debited for $ ______.
5. Which account is credited, and for what amount? ______ is credited for $ ______.
6. What is the complete entry?

GENERAL JOURNAL PAGE 1

DATE	DESCRIPTION	POST. REF.	DEBIT	CREDIT

Demonstration Problems, Chapter

Copyright © by Glencoe/McGraw-Hill

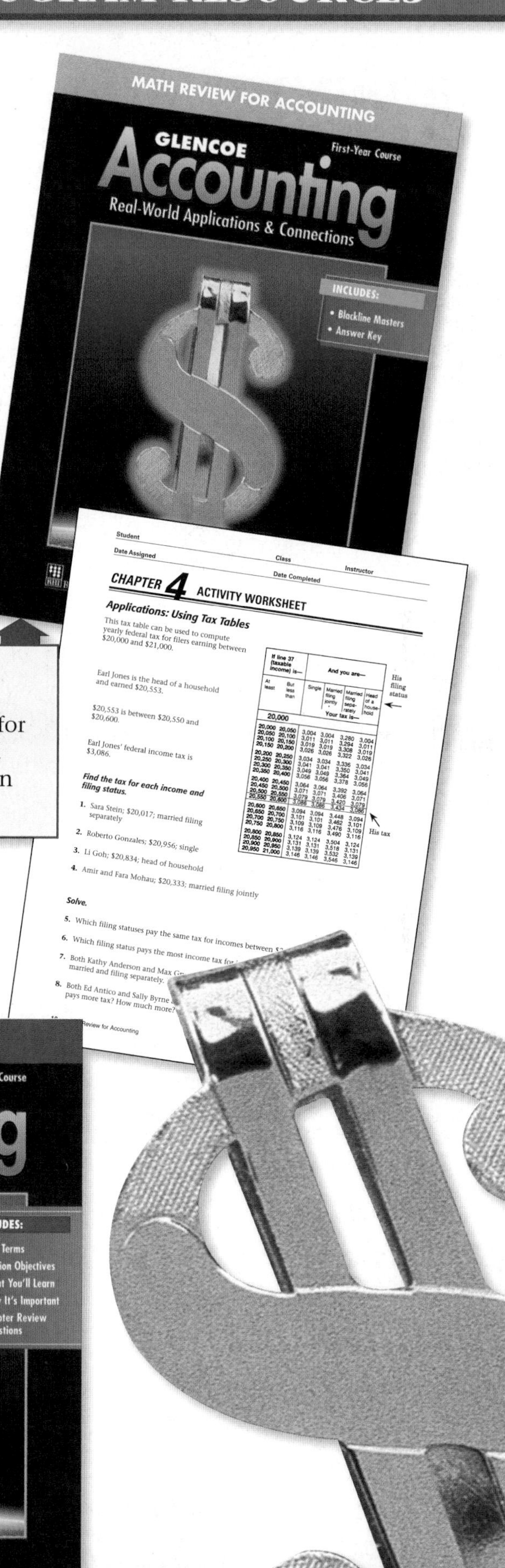

Student
Date Assigned Class Instructor
Date Completed

CHAPTER 4 ACTIVITY WORKSHEET

Applications: Using Tax Tables

This tax table can be used to compute yearly federal tax for filers earning between $20,000 and $21,000.

Earl Jones is the head of a household and earned $20,553.

$20,553 is between $20,550 and $20,600.

Earl Jones' federal income tax is $3,086.

If line 37 (taxable income) is— At least	But less than	And you are— Single	Married filing jointly	Married filing separately	Head of a household
		Your tax is—			
20,000					
20,000	20,050	3,004	3,004	3,280	3,004
20,050	20,100	3,011	3,011	3,294	3,011
20,100	20,150	3,019	3,019	3,308	3,019
20,150	20,200	3,026	3,026	3,322	3,026
20,200	20,250	3,034	3,034	3,336	3,034
20,250	20,300	3,041	3,041	3,350	3,041
20,300	20,350	3,049	3,049	3,364	3,049
20,350	20,400	3,056	3,056	3,378	3,056
20,400	20,450	3,064	3,064	3,392	3,064
20,450	20,500	3,071	3,071	3,406	3,071
20,500	20,550	3,079	3,079	3,420	3,079
20,550	20,600	3,086	3,086	3,434	3,086
20,600	20,650	3,094	3,094	3,448	3,094
20,650	20,700	3,101	3,101	3,462	3,101
20,700	20,750	3,109	3,109	3,476	3,109
20,750	20,800	3,116	3,116	3,490	3,116
20,800	20,850	3,124	3,124	3,504	3,124
20,850	20,900	3,131	3,131	3,518	3,131
20,900	20,950	3,139	3,139	3,532	3,139
20,950	21,000	3,146	3,146	3,546	3,146

His filing status

His tax

Find the tax for each income and filing status.

1. Sara Stein; $20,017; married filing separately
2. Roberto Gonzales; $20,956; single
3. Li Goh; $20,834; head of household
4. Amir and Fara Mohau; $20,333; married filing jointly

Solve.

5. Which filing statuses pay the same tax for incomes between
6. Which filing status pays the most income tax for
7. Both Kathy Anderson and Max G married and filing separately.
8. Both Ed Antico and Sally Byrne pays more tax? How much more?

Review for Accounting

Math Review for Accounting is an excellent resource for students who need additional review in basic math skills.

SPANISH LANGUAGE RESOURCES

First-Year Course

GLENCOE

Accounting

Real-World Applications & Connections

INCLUDES:
- Key Terms
- Section Objectives
- What You'll Learn
- Why It's Important
- Chapter Review Questions

Robert Half International Inc. Peachtree®

Spanish Language Resources provides translations of key terms, section objectives and review questions for each chapter to help you meet the needs of your Spanish-speaking students.

ENRICHMENT AND EXTENSION

Enrichment and Extension activities provide a wide variety of materials to motivate and challenge students while building skills and expanding understanding.

Strategies for Teaching International Accounting includes case studies from around the world. Individual worksheets are provided on such areas as business close-ups, doing business and financial reporting in other cultures, and developing global understandings.

Strategies for Teaching Ethics in Accounting provides strategies for teaching and integrating ethics into accounting. *Student Activity Sheets* are provided for each case study as well as a simulation for teacher implementation.

School-to-Work Handbook provides activities for every chapter and involves your students in work site analysis and working with mentors. The *Teacher Manual* includes scoring rubrics and an answer key.

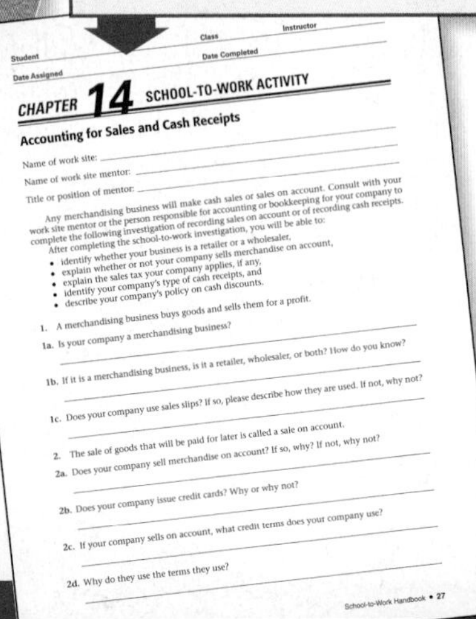
Student Class Instructor
Date Assigned Date Completed

CHAPTER 14 SCHOOL-TO-WORK ACTIVITY

Accounting for Sales and Cash Receipts

Name of work site:
Name of work site mentor:
Title or position of mentor:

Any merchandising business will make cash sales or sales on account. Consult with your work site mentor or the person responsible for accounting or bookkeeping for your company to complete the following investigation of recording sales on account or of recording cash receipts. After completing the school-to-work investigation, you will be able to:
- identify whether your business is a retailer or a wholesaler,
- explain whether or not your company sells merchandise on account,
- explain the sales tax your company applies, if any,
- identify your company's type of cash receipts, and
- describe your company's policy on cash discounts.

1. A merchandising business buys goods and sells them for a profit.
1a. Is your company a merchandising business?
1b. If it is a merchandising business, is it a retailer, wholesaler, or both? How do you know?
1c. Does your company use sales slips? If so, please describe how they are used. If not, why not?
2. The sale of goods that will be paid for later is called a sale on account.
2a. Does your company sell merchandise on account? If so, why? If not, why not?
2b. Does your company issue credit cards? Why or why not?
2c. If your company sells on account, what credit terms does your company use?
2d. Why do they use the terms they use?

Copyright © Glencoe/McGraw-Hill School-to-Work Handbook • 27

Accounting Portfolio includes real world assessment tools to help prepare your students for interviews in the business world. The *Teacher Manual* includes strategies for portfolio development and assessment, sample documents, and blackline masters.

ASSESSMENT

Glencoe's assessment and evaluation materials help you measure the progress of your students through a large selection of testing and assessment resources.

Chapter Quizzes can be used as pop quizzes to assess students' understanding of accounting concepts and procedures at the end of each chapter. Quizzes include true/false, completion, or short answer questions. All questions and answers to each chapter quiz are also located inside the *Teacher Wraparound Edition*.

Student ______ Class ______ Instructor ______

Date Assigned ______ Date Completed ______

CHAPTER 1 QUIZ

You and the World of Accounting

QUESTIONS (True-False)

Directions: In the space provided, indicate whether each statement is true or false.

___ 1. Everyone has skills, so only one's interests should be considered in choosing a career.

___ 2. One way to get to know yourself is to examine your values.

___ 3. Courage, compassion, and achievement are examples of values.

___ 4. How you want to live in the future is your lifestyle goal.

___ 5. Personal interest tests help you decide what your specific skills are.

___ 6. A personal career profile helps you compare your skills and interests with the requirements of a specific career.

___ 7. One step in setting a career goal is deciding what actions to take.

___ 8. Accountants who work for profit-making companies must have different training than those who work for non-profits.

___ 9. A public accountant provides accounting services to the general public or to businesses.

___ 10. The major public accounting firms are referred to as the Big Eight.

...r Quizzes • 3

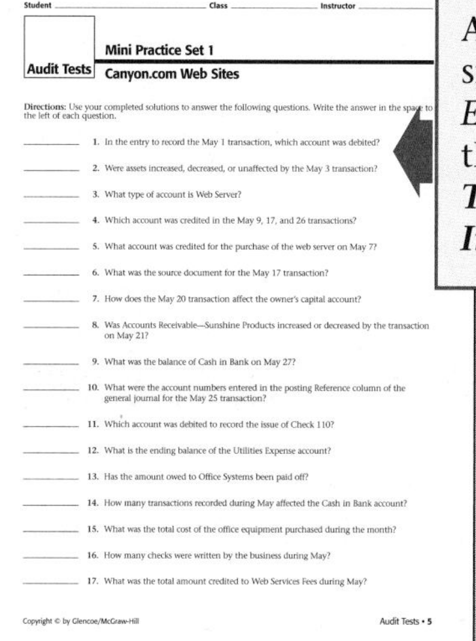

Student ______ Class ______ Instructor ______

Audit Tests

Mini Practice Set 1

Canyon.com Web Sites

Directions: Use your completed solutions to answer the following questions. Write the answer in the space to the left of each question.

______ 1. In the entry to record the May 1 transaction, which account was debited?

______ 2. Were assets increased, decreased, or unaffected by the May 3 transaction?

______ 3. What type of account is Web Server?

______ 4. Which account was credited in the May 9, 17, and 26 transactions?

______ 5. What account was credited for the purchase of the web server on May 7?

______ 6. What was the source document for the May 17 transaction?

______ 7. How does the May 20 transaction affect the owner's capital account?

______ 8. Was Accounts Receivable—Sunshine Products increased or decreased by the transaction on May 21?

______ 9. What was the balance of Cash in Bank on May 27?

______ 10. What were the account numbers entered in the posting Reference column of the general journal for the May 25 transaction?

______ 11. Which account was debited to record the issue of Check 110?

______ 12. What is the ending balance of the Utilities Expense account?

______ 13. Has the amount owed to Office Systems been paid off?

______ 14. How many transactions recorded during May affected the Cash in Bank account?

______ 15. What was the total cost of the office equipment purchased during the month?

______ 16. How many checks were written by the business during May?

______ 17. What was the total amount credited to Web Services Fees during May?

Copyright © by Glencoe/McGraw-Hill — Audit Tests • 5

Audit Tests include problems from the six Mini Practice Sets inside the *Student Edition*, as well as problems from the three business simulations: ***Adventure Travels, Outer Banks Marketplace, Inc.***, and ***Digital Express.***

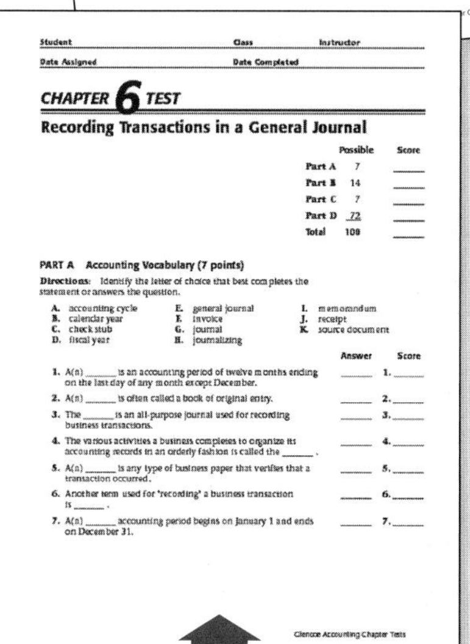

Student ______ Class ______ Instructor ______

Date Assigned ______ Date Completed ______

CHAPTER 6 TEST

Recording Transactions in a General Journal

	Possible	Score
Part A	7	____
Part B	14	____
Part C	7	____
Part D	72	____
Total	100	____

PART A Accounting Vocabulary (7 points)

Directions: Identify the letter of choice that best completes the statement or answers the question.

A. accounting cycle
B. calendar year
C. check stub
D. fiscal year
E. general journal
F. invoice
G. journal
H. journalizing
I. memorandum
J. receipt
K. source document

	Answer	Score
1. A(n) ______ is an accounting period of twelve months ending on the last day of any month except December.	____	1. ____
2. A(n) ______ is often called a book of original entry.	____	2. ____
3. The ______ is an all-purpose journal used for recording business transactions.	____	3. ____
4. The various activities a business completes to organize its accounting records in an orderly fashion is called the ______ .	____	4. ____
5. A(n) ______ is any type of business paper that verifies that a transaction occurred.	____	5. ____
6. Another term used for "recording" a business transaction is ______ .	____	6. ____
7. A(n) ______ accounting period begins on January 1 and ends on December 31.	____	7. ____

Glencoe Accounting Chapter Tests

Chapter Tests combine objective questions and problems that require students to apply the accounting procedures they learned in the chapter.

Exam*View*® allows you to develop tailor-made chapter, unit, or final tests using the Printed Test Bank, your own questions, and the software. *Test content is correlated to the National Standards for Business Education.*

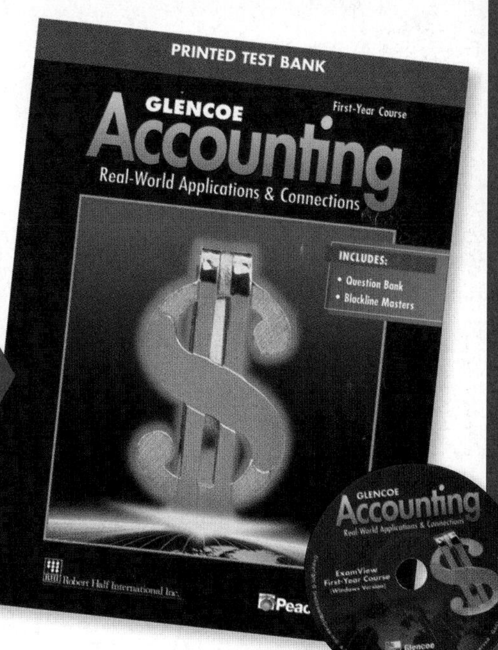

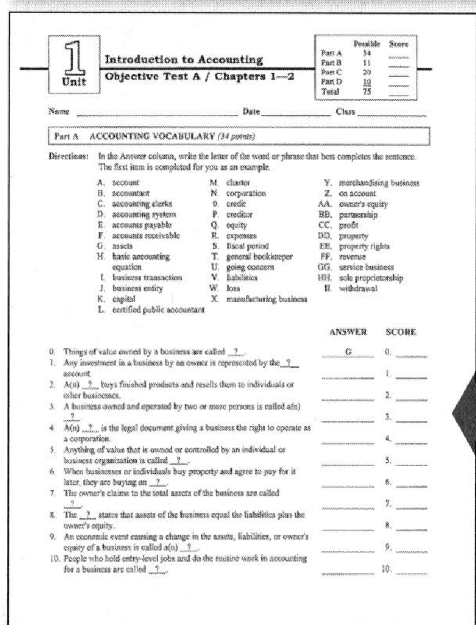

Unit 1

Introduction to Accounting

Objective Test A / Chapters 1—2

	Possible	Score
Part A	34	____
Part B	11	____
Part C	20	____
Part D	10	____
Total	75	____

Name ______ Date ______ Class ______

Part A ACCOUNTING VOCABULARY *(34 points)*

Directions: In the Answer column, write the letter of the word or phrase that best completes the sentence. The first item is completed for you as an example.

A. account
B. accountant
C. accounting clerks
D. accounting system
E. accounts payable
F. accounts receivable
G. assets
H. basic accounting equation
I. business transaction
J. business entity
K. capital
L. certified public accountant
M. charter
N. corporation
O. credit
P. creditor
Q. equity
R. expenses
S. fiscal period
T. general bookkeeper
U. going concern
V. liabilities
W. loss
X. manufacturing business
Y. merchandising business
Z. on account
AA. owner's equity
BB. partnership
CC. profit
DD. property
EE. property rights
FF. revenue
GG. service business
HH. sole proprietorship
II. withdrawal

	ANSWER	SCORE
0. Things of value owned by a business are called _?_.	G	0. ____
1. Any investment in a business by an owner is represented by the _?_ account.	____	1. ____
2. A(n) _?_ buys finished products and resells them to individuals or other businesses.	____	2. ____
3. A business owned and operated by two or more persons is called a(n) _?_.	____	3. ____
4. A(n) _?_ is the legal document giving a business the right to operate as a corporation.	____	4. ____
5. Anything of value that is owned or controlled by an individual or business organization is called _?_.	____	5. ____
6. When businesses or individuals buy property and agree to pay for it later, they are buying on _?_.	____	6. ____
7. The owner's claims to the total assets of the business are called _?_.	____	7. ____
8. The _?_ states that assets of the business equal the liabilities plus the owner's equity.	____	8. ____
9. An economic event causing a change in the assets, liabilities, or owner's equity of a business is called a(n) _?_.	____	9. ____
10. People who hold entry-level jobs and do the routine work in accounting for a business are called _?_.	____	10. ____

Copyright © by Glencoe/McGraw-Hill. All rights reserved. — Unit 1 Objective Test A • 1

Unit Tests are useful for evaluating students' understanding of accounting concepts and procedures over the study of several chapters.

BUSINESS SIMULATIONS

Three business simulations provide opportunities for students to keep accounting records for different types of businesses through an entire accounting cycle. Each simulation comes in a text-workbook format and includes all instructions for completing the simulation both manually and by computer. Source documents, all stationery, and an audit test are also provided for each simulation. A separate teacher manual provides teaching suggestions and complete solutions.

Adventure Travels

Adventure Travels is a service business that specializes in organizing and guiding tours in Seattle. In this simulation, students analyze source documents, journalize transactions, post transactions to the general ledger, write checks and maintain checking account records, and handle end-of-fiscal-period work. ***Adventure Travels*** is designed to be used after students have studied the first accounting cycle for a sole proprietorship.

Estimated completion time is 5 to 7 hours manually and 2 to 3 hours using the optional computer software.

The Beginning. . .

Tim Edwards was born and raised in Seattle. A competitive swimmer in high school, Tim went on to participate in local triathlons. As he trained for competitions, Tim explored the

hiking trails, national forests, and nearby lakes in the Seattle area. Tim graduated from college with a business degree. He volunteered time at the Seattle Chamber of Commerce and learned much about the city's historic beginnings.

While working at the information desk on Saturdays at the Chamber, Tim realized he wanted to open a travel-related business that would cater to the outdoor enthusiast. Visitors to the area often wanted to hike, camp, or kayak, but did not have the appropriate equipment. He wanted to offer tours, complete with equipment and maps. He also wanted to offer tours to help the visitor explore the city's "off-the-beaten-path" attractions.

Tim researched other travel services in the area. Only one other operation offered outdoor tours but did not include historic agendas, nor did they offer trips to Olympic National Forest. Tim had landed a great business idea that would combine his love of the outdoors, his business degree, and his knowledge of historic Seattle!

2 Adventure Travels Accounting Simulation

Services Offered by Adventure Travels

Organize and guide the following tours:
- walking and bus tours of historic Seattle
- harbor cruises of Puget Sound
- bus, cycling, day hiking, and backpacking tours in Olympic National Park
- customized regional tours
- mountain bike day trips
- kayak tours of Puget Sound

Equipment rentals:
- backpacks, tents, sleeping bags, daypacks
- kayaks
- bicycles

How Adventure Travels Will Attract Its Customers

Tim expects his busy season to run from June to September. During these months, Seattle experiences warmer, mild weather—perfect for travel adventures! Tim will distribute brochures to local hotels, cafes, and the Chamber of Commerce. He plans to advertise in the Seattle Spectator and offer a Web site with photos of the area, maps, and tour descriptions.

During the December holiday season, Tim will participate in the Chamber of Commerce event, Festival of Lights. Historical homes in downtown Seattle open their doors to allow visitors to view spectacular decorations provided by community florists and decorators. Tim hopes his tour will be a popular family activity for local residents and visitors alike.

Adventu

Outer Banks Marketplace, Inc.

Outer Banks Marketplace, Inc. is a closely held, merchandising corporation that sells products such as coffee mugs, candies, bumper stickers, and various other types of mementos from North Carolina. In this simulation, students analyze source documents, record transactions in special journals, post to general and subsidiary ledgers, and complete the end-of-period work for the business. ***Outer Banks Marketplace, Inc.*** is designed to be used at the end of the second accounting cycle, after students have studied special journals and the adjusting process.

Estimated completion time is 15 to 20 hours manually and 5 to 7 hours using the optional computer software.

Digital Express

Digital Express is a closely held, merchandising corporation that sells blank compact discs, VHS tapes, digital video disks (DVDs), and a variety of audio and video accessories. In this simulation, students analyze source documents, record transactions in special journals, and complete all work for a full accounting cycle. ***Digital Express*** is designed to be used after students have studied special journals and the procedures for petty cash, notes, depreciation, inventories, and uncollectible accounts.

Estimated completion time is 15 to 20 hours manually and 5 to 7 hours using the optional computer software.

Introduction

Do you remember your first cassette or CD player? How about the first time you recorded a favorite television show on a videotape? Let's face it—we love movies and music! And technology helps us record, playback, and record our favorites to enjoy again and again.

The evolving technology in audio and video reproduction has created a surge in the industry of CD, DVD, and VHS tape manufacturing and retailing. DVDs (Digital Versatile Discs), basically "super CDs," have enough storage space to handle video as well as sound. They combine sharp, high-resolution pictures with digital sound to create the ultimate home cinema experience, usually for a price very competitive with traditional VHS tapes. Most of the major movie studies like Warner Bros, Columbia Tri-Star, MCA Universal, Dreamworks, and New Line Cinema are creating DVDs. Foreign films, animation, and classics are getting new life from the digital format. Since DVD is an open format, even small studios can put out DVDs.

Whether you've watched a VHS tape of *Titanic* at home or know someone who is involved in DVD, audio tape, or compact disk production, you've probably observed the fascinating world of audio and video electronics change and evolve. *Digital Express*, a retail store that specializes in audio and video accessories and supplies, is reaping the rewards!

EXPLORING THE REAL WORLD OF BUSINESS

The Fifth Edition focuses on **a business perspective** by using examples from the business world to illustrate accounting concepts. Information on featured companies, organizations, their products and services is included for educational purposes only, and does not represent or imply endorsement of the *Glencoe Accounting* program. The following companies appear throughout the text:

Chapter 1
World Wildlife Fund
Home Office: Washington, D.C.
Web Address: www.worldwildlife.org

Chapter 2
Huey's Athletic Network
Home Office: Santa Monica, CA
Web Address: www.lahuey.com

Chapter 3
DreamWorks SKG
Home Office: Universal City, CA
Web Address: www.dreamworks.com

Chapter 4
American Airlines
Home Office: Fort Worth, TX
Web Address: www.aa.com

Chapter 5
Wendy's International
Home Office: Dublin, OH
Web Address: www.wendys.com

Chapter 6
Ben & Jerry's Homemade, Inc.
Home Office: South Burlington, VT
Web Address: www.benjerry.com

Chapter 7
King Ranch
Home Office: Kingsville, TX
Web Address: www.king-ranch.com

Chapter 8
Washington Metropolitan Area Transit Authority (WMATA)
Home Office: Washington, D.C.
Web Address: www.wmata.com

Chapter 9
New England Aquarium
Home Office: Boston, MA
Web Address: www.neaq.org

Chapter 10
ACTIONQuest
Home Office: Sarasota, FL
Web Address: www.actionquest.com

Chapter 11
The Timberland Company
Home Office: Stratham, NH
Web Address: www.timberland.com

Chapter 12
Robert Half International Inc.
Home Office: Menlo Park, CA
Web Address: www.rhii.com

Chapter 13
Rhino Records
Home Office: Westwood, CA
Web Address: www.rhino.com

Chapter 14
Rollerblade, Inc.
Home Office: Minneapolis, MN
Web Address: www.rollerblade.com

Chapter 15
Levi Strauss & Co.
Home Office: San Francisco, CA
Web Address: www.levistrauss.com

Chapter 16
Sony Corporation of America
Home Office: New York , NY
Web Address: www.sony.com

Chapter 17
PETCO Animal Supplies Inc.
Home Office: San Diego, CA
Web Address: www.petco.com

Chapter 18
Schwinn
Home Office: Boulder, CO
Web Address: www.schwinn.com

Chapter 19
Office Depot, Inc.
Home Office: Delray Beach, FL
Web Address: www.officedepot.com

Chapter 20
Bose Corporation
Home Office: Framingham, MA
Web Address: www.bose.com

Chapter 21
Microsoft Corporation
Home Office: Redmond, WA
Web Address: www.microsoft.com

Chapter 22
Outback Steakhouse
Home Office: La Jolla, CA
Web Address: www.outback.com

Chapter 23
Electronic Arts
Home Office: San Mateo, CA
Web Address: www.ea.com

Chapter 24
Bally Total Fitness
Home Office: Chicago, IL
Web Address: www.ballyfitness.com

Chapter 25
Gap
Home Office: New York, NY, San Francisco, CA
Web Address: www.gap.com

Chapter 26
Carnival Corporation
Home Office: Miami, FL
Web Address: www.carnival.com

Chapter 27
Intersal
Home Office: Boca Raton, FL
Web Address: www.ah.dcr.state.nc.us/qar (N.C. Depart. of Cultural Resources)

Chapter 28
Plum Creek Timber Company
Home Office: Seattle, WA
Web Address: www.plumcreek.com

Chapter 29

Institute of Internal Auditors
Home Office: Altamonte Springs, FL
Web Address: www.theiia.org

GREAT IDEAS . . .

Unit 1
Martha Eaton
Oxford High School
Oxford, Alabama

Chapter 3
Lynn Carmen Day
Northview High School
Covina, California

Chapter 7
William Trouten
Platteville High School
Platteville, Wisconsin

Chapter 11
Todd Karst
Plankinton High School
Plankinton, South Dakota

Unit 4
Susan Howe
Chariho Regional High School
Wood River Junction,
Rhode Island

Chapter 1
Claudia Cullari
Fair Lawn High School
Fair Lawn, New Jersey

Chapter 4
Mary Ann Constantini
Las Cruces High School
Las Cruces, New Mexico

Chapter 8
Dennis Conway
Grinnell High School
Grinnell, Iowa

Unit 3
Peggy Ross
Bozeman High School
Bozeman, Montana

Chapter 14
Chris Mendez
Bel Air High School
El Paso, Texas

Chapter 2
Beth Moody
Northview High School
Brazil, Indiana

Chapter 5
Don Black
Buhl High School
Buhl, Idaho

Chapter 9
Edward Schencks, Jr.
Sacopee Valley High School
Hiram, Maine

Chapter 12
Gwen H. Cruickshank
Laramie High School
Laramie, Wyoming

Chapter 15
Jackie Jacobellis
Winnacunnet High School
Hampton,
New Hampshire

Unit 2
James A. Wermes
Elk Grove High School
Elk Grove Village,
Illinois

Chapter 6
Barbara M. Young
Madison High School
Madison, Virginia

Chapter 10
Thelma H. Brooks
Southeast Career Center
Columbus, Ohio

Chapter 13
Bob Cox
Desert Vista High School
Phoenix, Arizona

Chapter 16
Missy Shea
Amherst Regional
High School
Amherst, Massachusetts

for the Accounting Classroom

Chapter 17
Laura Anderson
Adams City High School
Denver, Colorado

Chapter 21
Cynthia L.Greene
Centennial High School
Roswell, Georgia

Chapter 24
Robert E. Turner
University of Louisiana
at Monroe
Monroe, Louisiana

Chapter 27
F. Barry Haber
Fayetteville State University
Fayetteville, North Carolina

Chapter 18
Gale Woolsey
Texarkana Area
Vocational Center
Texarkana, Arkansas

Unit 5
Tammy Mathews
Hanna-Westside
Extension Campus
Anderson, South Carolina

Chapter 25
Scott A. Arcand
Columbus High School
Columbus, Nebraska

Chapter 28
William B. Hoyt
Wilton High School
Wilton, Connecticut

Chapter 19
Alfonso Vargas
Hueneme High School
Oxnard, California

Chapter 22
Louise P. Lochhead
Davis High School
Kaysville, Utah

Chapter 26
Donald J. Guerrieri
Norwin High School
Greensburg, Pennsylvania

Chapter 29
Martha Ramirez
McCallum High School
Austin, Texas

Chapter 20
Jacque Steinberger
Trimble Tech High School
Fort Worth, Texas

Chapter 23
Stephen Stengel
William Floyd High School
Mastic Beach, New York

Unit 6
Jerry Hawes
East Jordan High School
East Jordan, Michigan

INTEGRATING ETHICS

Introduction

In the business world today, newspaper and television broadcasts carry stories dealing with ethical issues in accounting with staggering frequency. The spotlight on ethics in accounting intensified with the well-publicized case of Enron, in which corporate officers allegedly hid debt by means of questionable accounting practices, and auditors were found guilty of obstruction of justice. With the emergence of similar cases of questionable corporate financial reporting, legislation was passed in 2002 limiting the ways in which auditors can work and holding corporate managers legally responsible for the accuracy of company financial statements.

As your students learn about the profession of accounting, they should understand the responsibilities that the accountant carries. The public demands integrity, professionalism, and reliable expertise from each accounting professional. To prepare your students for the ethical dilemmas they will face in their careers, it is important that you help equip them with ways to consider the ethical ramifications of their actions and decisions.

How Do You Teach Ethics in Accounting?

The purpose of introducing ethics into your accounting program is to help your students integrate ethical considerations and basic values into their decision-making process. Students are helped to develop this process of considering both the business and ethical ramifications of a decision *before* that decision is made. Even though basic values are set in childhood, people do make different decisions as they gain knowledge and insight into how their decisions affect society.

Ethics in the Student Text

To help you integrate ethics into your accounting instruction, the *Glencoe Accounting* program includes a chapter devoted entirely to the topic of ethics. **Chapter 29, Ethics in Accounting**, introduces your students to professional codes of ethics, ethical considerations in accounting, and how the industry governs itself in regard to professional conduct.

In addition, a special feature called **A Matter of Ethics** has been developed for every chapter of the student textbook. Students are given hypothetical business situations in which they need to make a decision about the most ethical course of action. These cases are excellent ways to stimulate class discussion and explore how your students approach decision making. The *Teacher Wraparound Edition* includes additional information related to the topic and includes strategies on how to teach the feature.

Ethics Cases in *Strategies for Teaching Ethics in Accounting*

As an added resource for your classroom, you can refer to the booklet titled *Strategies for Teaching Ethics in Accounting*. This booklet provides a brief overview of ethical theories and practical strategies for teaching ethics in accounting. It also provides guidelines to help you integrate cooperative learning activities into your classroom.

A MATTER OF ETHICS

Confidentiality

Imagine that you work as an accounting clerk for a fast-food franchise like Taco Bell. You have access to all the accounting records for the business.

A friend of yours has promised to hire you as an accountant when he opens his own Mexican food restaurant. He has asked you to share information about Taco Bell's sales and expenses.

Ethical Decision Making:

- What are the ethical issues?
- What are the alternatives?
- Who are the affected parties?
- How do the alternatives affect the parties?
- What would you do?

Strategies for Teaching Ethics in Accounting includes suggested answers and a reproducible *Student Activity Sheet* for every **A Matter of Ethics** feature. The activity sheets help students analyze the featured ethical dilemma using the decision model. This furthers their ability to analyze situations by considering the broad implications of possible decisions.

Ethics on the *Glencoe Accounting* Web Site

The *Glencoe Accounting* program provides online resources that can be used for independent study or extended learning in the field of ethics. The *Glencoe Accounting* Web site contains the following activities where students can research ethics and accounting in the news, practice their ethical decision-making skills, or extend the discussion of ethical issues by performing real-world explorations of ethics in their workplace or personal life.

Extend the discussion of **A Matter of Ethics** cases presented in the textbook. In these chapter-specific Internet assignments, students conduct online research to explore each topic and interpret the results. Answers are provided on the password-protected Teacher Web site.

Explore Ethics Online at glencoeaccounting.glencoe.com

ETHICS AND THE PROFESSION

- Ethics Links
- A Matter of Ethics
- Legislation

Use the **Ethics Links** as resources for teaching ethics in accounting. These links provide gateways to discussions on ethics in the business world and information about the ethical responsibilities of accountants.

Use the **Legislation** feature to learn about the landmark Sarbanes-Oxley Act of 2002. We present a brief background, a summary of the Act's provisions, and related links.

Links to current legislation on accounting reform and to the AICPA Code of Professional Conduct are provided for your use as you incorporate discussions of ethical actions into your accounting instruction.

The Ethical Decision-Making Model

Whether your students are discussing the ethical dilemma presented in **A Matter of Ethics** feature, or considering ethical issues in their own lives, the following ethical decision-making model can be used to evaluate options, analyze situations, consider ramifications, and choose among alternatives.

The Five-Step Decision-Making Model

1. What are the ethical issues?
2. What are the alternatives?
3. Who are the affected parties?
4. How do the alternatives affect the parties?
5. What would you do?

You may wish to use the first ethics feature in the student textbook (Chapter 1, page 12) as a sample and help students work through the decision model. Refer to *Strategies for Teaching Ethics in Accounting* for suggested answers to this feature. Students will also benefit from viewing the ethics segment on the **Electronic Field Trips** video that is part of the *Glencoe Accounting* multimedia program.

Encouraging Class Participation

Students need to understand that there is no right or wrong answer to the ethics cases. As they discuss each case, they are discussing possibilities. Students should feel that the classroom is a relatively "risk free" environment in which to make ethical decisions because no employee will be harmed and no business or stockholder will lose money as a result of a student's decision.

Strengthening Writing Skills

You can use these ethics cases to integrate writing activities into your accounting curriculum. Have students write their answers to the questions in the decision model using the *Student Activity Sheets* or utilizing a word processing program. You might also have them write descriptions of situations in which they have been required to make an ethical decision.

USING THE INTERNET

The Internet and the Accounting Classroom

Using the Internet in your accounting classroom can add an entirely new dimension to the learning experience of your students. From simple "surfing" on the Web to more sophisticated research skills, students can broaden their knowledge of accounting while they explore real-world news articles, professional organizations, and business resources.

Glencoe Accounting Web Site

An exciting way to enrich and extend learning for your accounting students is to utilize the many resources we have provided on the *Glencoe Accounting* Web site. Whether you need independent study activities for certain students, or seek cooperative learning experiences, the Student Site offers study plans, self-tests, case studies, career tips, and research activities.

Visit the *Glencoe Accounting* Web site at:

glencoeaccounting.glencoe.com

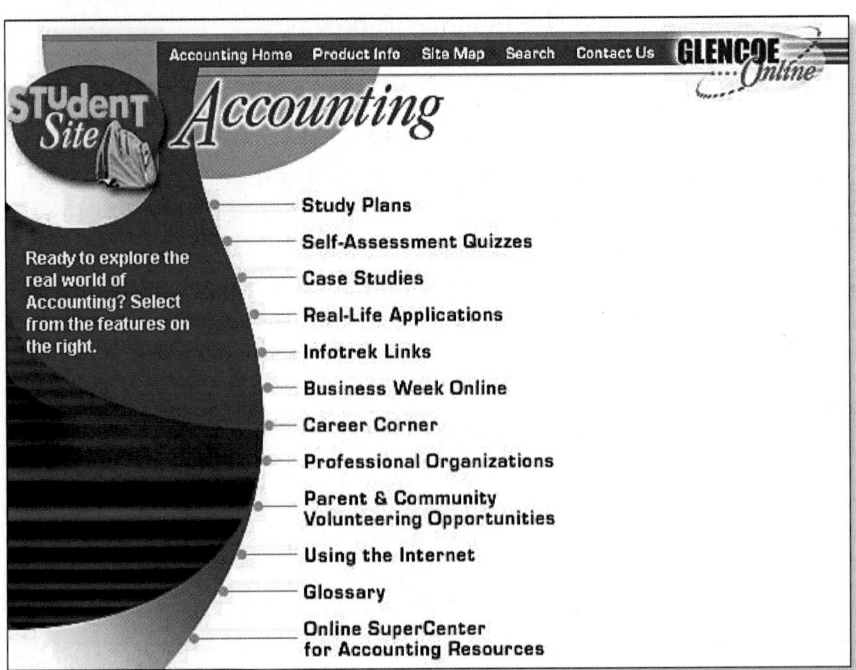

Internet Connection Activities

In the student text, you will find **Internet Connection** activities in each chapter. Using research skills, students will be challenged to find specific information on the Web that relates to the topic of the chapter. Use these assignments as homework activities, or assign them to groups for in-class practice.

interNET CONNECTION

Payroll and Tax Records

The federal government makes available a great deal of information related to wages and earnings.

Do This:

Use key words from the following questions to search the Internet for payroll-related statistics.

1. What is the current minimum hourly wage?
2. What are the annual earnings for a full-time employee who earns the minimum wage?
3. What is the average hourly wage in the United States?
4. What are the average annual earnings in the United States?
5. How many people are employed in the United States?

Internet Resources and Activities Handbook

Glencoe Accounting provides more Internet explorations in the *Internet Resources and Activities Handbook*. Photocopy the *Student Activity Sheets* to pass out to your class for independent practice or homework assignments.

ANALYZING FINANCIAL REPORTS

Analyzing Financial Reports for a Real Business

The *Glencoe Accounting* text is designed to link *real-world* experiences to classroom learning. Students have an opportunity to analyze financial reports from a real-world business—**Office Depot, Inc.** When students apply analytical techniques to actual business dealings, they increase their preparation and find relevance in their learning.

About Office Depot, Inc.

Office Depot, Inc., founded in 1986, is the world's largest seller of office products and an industry leader in every distribution channel, including stores, direct mail, contract delivery, the Internet, and business-to-business electronic commerce. Viking Office Products, a wholly owned subsidiary, operates one of the industry's leading direct mail marketers of office products worldwide. For more information about this corporation, refer students to the Office Depot Web site at www.officedepot.com.

Analyzing Financial Reports

Students are introduced to the feature *Analyzing Financial Reports* beginning with Chapter 9. This feature teaches students to learn how to analyze and evaluate information presented in a financial document. They also learn how to evaluate information and check their comprehension step-by-step. You may want to use the first feature appearing in Chapter 9 as a classroom activity in order to increase your students' familiarity with these exercises.

Analyzing Financial Reports incorporates a variety of critical thinking skills such as problem solving; analyzing, evaluating, and synthesizing information; decision making; and communication skills.

Your students' ability to apply accounting concepts to real-world problems is critical to their success in the financial profession.

ANALYZING FINANCIAL REPORTS AT A GLANCE

CHAPTER	FEATURE TITLE	ANALYSIS TOPIC
9	Return on Sales	Interpret an income statement.
10	Calculating Return on Owner's Equity	Analyze the income statement and the statement of changes in owner's equity.
11	Evaluating Working Capital	Analyze a balance sheet.
12	Analyzing Employee Productivity	Analyze an income statement.
13	Employee Costs	Analyze a payroll register and payroll tax information.
14	To Our Shareholders Letter	Analyze Office Depot's Letter to Our Shareholders from the company's annual report.
15	Identifying Corporate Goals	Analyze information from the Office Depot annual report.
16	Operating Results	Analyze information about sales.
17	Cost of Goods Sold	Analyze information about cost of goods sold.
18	The Income Statement: Return on Sales	Analyze Office Depot's income statement.
19	Evaluating Stockholders' Equity	Analyze the statement of stockholders' equity.
20	Classifying the Balance Sheet–Assets and Liabilities	Analyze the balance sheet to determine working capital.
21	Calculating Return on Stockholders' Equity	Analyze the statement of stockholders' equity to determine returns on investments.
22	Calculating Price-Earnings Ratios	Analyze the Consolidated Statements of Earnings.
23	The Income Statement: Vertical Analysis	Analyze the Consolidated Statements of Earnings to complete a vertical analysis.
24	The Balance Sheet	Analyze Office Depot's balance sheet and complete a horizontal analysis.
25	Inventories	Analyze Office Depot's balance sheet to determine inventory levels.
26	Evaluating Debt	Analyze the balance sheet for Office Depot's short-term and long-term debt.
27	Analyzing Partners' Equity	Analyze the T-account information.
28	Evaluating Partnership Operating Results	Analyze the income statement to determine the financial health of a company.

DEVELOPING THINKING SKILLS

Introduction

Teaching critical thinking skills is a goal of all educational disciplines. The use of critical thinking skills in an accounting profession is necessary in order to process, analyze, prepare, and communicate financial information. Achieving success in the workforce depends on an individual's ability to deal with the varied demands of the fast-paced world of business and finance. Employees are required to make insightful decisions, be creative problem solvers, interact with diverse groups—be it employees, management, investors, customers, or clients.

Critical thinking, which is the process of reasonably or logically deciding what to do or believe, involves the ability to:

- compare and contrast,
- solve problems,
- make decisions,
- analyze and evaluate,
- synthesize and transfer knowledge, and conduct metacognitive exercises.

Critical thinking skills are important for the following reasons:

- Helps students investigate their own ways of solving problems and finding creative resolutions.
- Leads students to investigations that compare and contrast what they know with unknowns.
- Allows students to make decisions about their own learning and makes them aware of the processes they use.

How to Teach Critical Thinking

All learning requires thinking. Benjamin Bloom's Taxonomy of the Cognitive Domain is probably the most widely recognized hierarchy for levels of thinking. Bloom's Taxonomy describes six levels of increasingly sophisticated thinking that educators can require of students. Each level is listed below, followed by action verbs describing learning objectives.

- *Knowledge:* define, recognize, recall, identify, label, understand, examine, show, collect
- *Comprehension:* translate, interpret, explain, describe, summarize, extrapolate
- *Application:* apply, solve, experiment, show, predict
- *Analysis:* connect, relate, differentiate, classify, arrange, check, group, distinguish, organize, categorize, detect, compare, infer
- *Synthesis:* produce, propose, design, plan, combine, formulate, compose, hypothesize, construct
- *Evaluation:* appraise, judge, criticize, decide

As educators, our goal is to move our students to the highest level they can achieve. In order to do this, *Glencoe Accounting* incorporates many critical thinking activities.

Critical Thinking in the *Glencoe Accounting* Program

Both the student text and this *Teacher Wraparound Edition* provide numerous activities and guidelines to help you incorporate and integrate critical thinking skills into your daily plans. The following are some guidelines for integrating and teaching critical thinking skills.

- *Let students know* they are engaging in aspects of critical thinking.
- *Use activities that focus* on open-ended problems to foster greater growth for creative problem solving.
- *Organize students* in cooperative learning groups so they can see how others solve problems, give each other feedback, and try out new ideas.
- *Use assessments* that measure students' growth and performance in their newly acquired skills.
- *Provide feedback* and encourage students to feel comfortable experimenting with new ideas and new ways to problem solve.

ASSESSMENT

Introduction

Evaluation of students' performance is fundamental to the teaching and learning process. In an accounting course, students' accounting skills typically are evaluated by using applications and written tests. Objective tests, however, cannot fully evaluate students' communication, critical-thinking, and interpersonal skills, or their problem-solving abilities. The evaluation of student performance should also relate to the personal skills that students will apply in the real world.

Performance Assessment

Glencoe recognizes the importance of providing several methods of assessing students' performance in accounting classrooms. *Glencoe Accounting* provides many activities, projects, and situations that create opportunities for performance assessment. The following are some tools to evaluate student performance:

- **Performance Assessment Package** includes **Exam***View*®, an easy-to-use computerized testing tool that allows you to create paper and online tests for your accounting students. Build your own customized tests or use the preloaded and correlated tests.
- **Chapter Quizzes**
- **Chapter Tests**
- **Audit Tests**
- **Unit Tests**

Additional assessment resources include:

- **Check Your Understanding** at the end of each section in the textbook.
- **Self Tests** in the *Chapter Reviews and Working Papers.*
- **Mini Practice Sets** in the textbook.
- **Business Simulations:** *Adventure Travels; Outer Banks Marketplace, Inc.;* and *Digital Express.*

For more information on **Assessment** resources, see page T29.

Assessing Student Work with Rubrics

A rubric is a set of descriptions of the quality of a process and/or a product. The set of descriptions includes a continuum of quality from excellent to poor. Rubrics are best used to help students periodically assess their quality of work. For example, use a rubric to assess their progress with a mini simulation or with a business simulation.

You or the student can assign a rubric score and explain why the score was chosen. If used as a self-assessment instrument, students will use a performance task assessment list in the rubric to examine the elements of each process and/or product. Students can easily justify their rubric scores. If you use the rubric for self-assessment, it is wise to review performance task assessment lists with the students before asking them to use the rubric for evaluation. For example, you can use Glencoe's rubric scoring suggestions when using the *School-to-Work Handbook.*

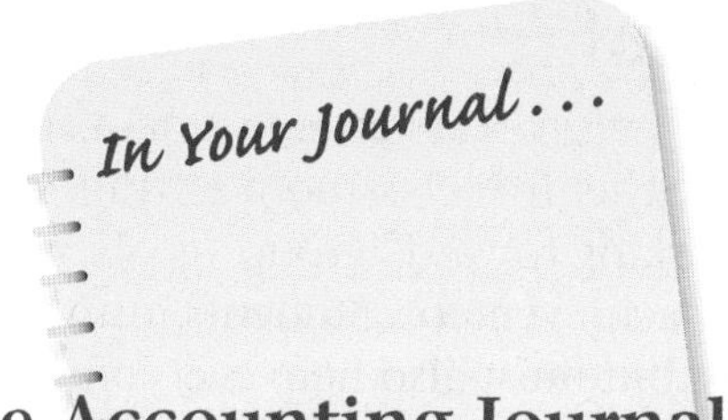

The Accounting Journal

The *In Your Journal* feature appears in every unit opener. The journal is a way to help students organize their thinking. It is for unstructured, creative responses. It is not designed to be used as a lecture or assignment notebook. It is a record that allows quick reference or reflection on various accounting concepts presented in the unit. This type of journal is another self-evaluation tool.

Portfolios: Putting It All Together

Portfolios help students visualize a body of work. In the accounting class, a portfolio may contain:

- examples of work—problems,
- written communications,
- cooperative learning projects,
- and/or documents related to extracurricular, community service, or work experience activities.

How students begin their portfolios and stay committed to the process is based on your introduction of this process. Introduce the portfolio assignment at the beginning of the course, offering specific objectives and examples in writing. Explain that developing a portfolio is a long-term project, a collection of evidence that allows prospective employers to evaluate a student's ability. A comprehensive portfolio should showcase a student's employability skills and demonstrate their readiness for an entry-level accounting position. For additional information on portfolios, refer to the *Accounting Portfolio* booklet.

COOPERATIVE LEARNING

Introduction

Studies show that students learn faster and retain more information when they are actively involved in the learning process. Studies also show that in a classroom setting, adolescents often learn more from each other about subject matter than from a traditional teacher-led lecture and discussion. Cooperative learning is one method that gets students actively involved in learning and at the same time allows for peer teaching.

The Basic Elements of Cooperative Learning

Cooperative learning involves assigning students to small groups to work together in a classroom setting. This structure emphasizes working toward "group" goals, as opposed to "individual" achievement. Students must learn the material themselves, but must also help everyone in the group learn the material. Emphasize to students that the success or failure of the group is shared by all of its members. Finally, remind group members that they must share equally in the responsibilities and goals of the group.

Preparation for Cooperative Learning

The following tips will help you set the stage for effective cooperative learning.

- **Classroom Arrangement**—Move the furniture in the room so that students can face each other as they work.
- **Group Size**—Decide on the size of the group. Groups of two to five students work best.
- **Group Assignments**—Assign students to groups. Each group should be mixed racially, socially, ethnically, and by gender and range of ability.
- **Rotation of Group Members**—Change groups periodically.
- **Student Preparation**—Prepare students for cooperation.
- **Initial Activities**—Start small. It is not necessary to incorporate all the characteristics of cooperative learning into the first activity.
- **Group Roles**—Explain group roles. Students need to learn the cooperative skills fundamental to each role before interacting in cooperative activities.

Teacher and Student Responsibilities

The success of the cooperative learning groups depends on the teacher's ability to coach each of the groups and the students' ability to accomplish a goal as a team.

The teacher:

- creates the environment and structures the process of learning, then guides the students' learning.
- motivates students to learn.
- states the goals of the instruction.
- teaches the fundamental concepts.
- interacts with and guides the work of many groups.
- acts as a resource to the groups as needed.
- monitors student behavior.
- evaluates the group process.

The students:

- work toward group goals, yet understand that individual responsibility is expected.
- contribute their own ideas.
- understand that they are responsible for one another's learning as well as their own.
- have tolerance for individual differences.
- draw upon their own creativity and on the strengths of their teammates.
- communicate effectively with one another.

Cooperative Learning in This Text

In this *Glencoe Accounting* text, students and teachers have a wealth of materials to assist with cooperative learning activities. The **Chapter Review and Activities** page includes several activities that can be completed in a cooperative learning environment: **Case Study**, **Internet Connection**, **Workplace Skills**, and **Conducting an Audit with Alex**.

Cooperative learning activities that are appropriate for the chapter topic are also included throughout the *Teacher Wraparound Edition.*

Additional cooperative learning resources appear in the *Strategies for Teaching Ethics in Accounting* booklet. See the sections in Part 3 titled "Cooperative Learning Strategies" and "Cooperative Learning Structures," as well as Part 6, "Collaborative Learning Through Role Playing."

PREPARING FOR COMPETITIVE EVENTS

Participating in Competitive Events

One way students can apply their accounting knowledge is by participating in organized competitive events. Both **Future Business Leaders of America** (**www.fbla.org**) and the **Business Professionals of America** (**www.bpa.org**) offer competitive examinations at the local, regional, state, and national levels. Students can test their skills, knowledge, and competency in many areas, but accounting continues to be one of the most in-demand contests.

If your state or school system allows professional organizations as a co-curricular activity, then use your *Accounting Competitive Event Review* booklet to help you implement a co-curricular teaching syllabus. If professional youth organizations are extra-curricular activities, you can encourage your clubs to use this booklet to gain a competitive edge!

Accounting Competitive Event Review

The *Accounting Competitive Event Review* booklet helps you prepare your students for accounting examinations and competitions. Use the strategies as guidelines or suggestions for enhancing your students' success in accounting.

The booklet includes study suggestions, a review of accounting terminology, and tips for test taking. It also provides a number of review questions and sample tests on basic accounting concepts.

MARKETING YOUR ACCOUNTING PROGRAM

Introduction

Education, like the business world, is competitive! In order for your students to gain that competitive edge in their education, you must take a proactive stand in marketing your accounting program. Accounting should be an interesting, challenging, enjoyable, and rewarding experience for all students. But how is that being communicated?

Your Marketing Plan

Accounting teachers must continually present their accounting course as dynamic and current. You may find it valuable to develop a marketing plan that maps out the specific marketing mix necessary for your marketing blitz. Research your target market—your students, your parents, and your business community.

- What do graduates say about the value of their secondary accounting program?
- What are local employers seeking in an entry-level accounting candidate?
- What do parents want their children to achieve from an accounting program?

Students, parents, community leaders, and education professionals will grow to appreciate the value of such a course. The *Glencoe Accounting* program offers you some tools to assist in your marketing efforts. However, your personal commitment to the success of the program makes you and your students the best salespersons for accounting.

Marketing Your Accounting Program with Back-to-School Night Activities

Many accounting teachers have asked us to develop creative ideas that can be used on Back-to-School night. This booklet contains 25 great activities, instructions on how to create a marketing plan, and a wealth of information on marketing your accounting program.

Accounting Posters

The *Glencoe Accounting* program includes posters for your use in classrooms, on bulletin boards, in display cases, or as promotional materials during career events. Each poster is designed to attract students' interest with an engaging photo and short quotes students can read quickly. Use these posters and their content to stimulate lively classroom discussions about career opportunities in accounting.

TEACHING ALL ASPECTS OF INDUSTRY

Introduction

As your students become employees in today's business world, it is imperative that they demonstrate the ability to make competent and independent decisions and understand how their decisions impact the business as a whole. They need the ability to see the "big picture" of an industry. During the 1990s, two pieces of legislation—the Carl D. Perkins Vocation and Applied Technology Education Act (1990) and the School-to-Work Opportunities Act (1994)—outlined the pertinent components of all aspects of industry:

- planning,
- management,
- finances,
- technical and production skills,
- underlying principles of technology,
- labor and community issues,
- health and safety issues, and
- environmental issues.

As students confront and examine accounting issues throughout this course, it is important to help them understand their role in the larger context of an applicable industry, as opposed to being an isolated and independent participant.

Benefits of Teaching All Aspects of Industry

Teaching students to understand all aspects of industry results in tangible benefits to both students and employers.

Benefits for Students

Students who enter the workforce equipped with a vision of all aspects of an industry are better prepared to contribute more positively to both their work environment and to their own career plans. In the workplace, these students:

- learn more quickly,
- adapt to anticipated and unexpected changes in the workplace,
- act as team players,
- see their role as part of a larger endeavor,
- move easily from one set of responsibilities to another, and
- transfer their skills to related tasks easily.

Because students understand how industries work as a whole, their career choices are more informed and generally lead to satisfying experiences. This awareness provides students with flexibility to try new opportunities and transfer their knowledge to new situations effectively.

Benefits for Employers

Employers benefit as well when workers are more fully trained in all aspects of an industry. For example, an employee's flexibility means that advances in technology or changes in workflow can be implemented more quickly and with less resistance. In addition, employers find that job cross-training and rotation of duties are more successful when workers value all aspects of an industry.

Implementing an All Aspects of Industry Approach

As you incorporate all aspects of industry into your teaching plan, it is essential to involve employers and mentors from the field. In this way, students can become actively engaged in the unique aspects of their chosen industry. Encourage your students to participate in job shadowing, workplace mentoring, and paid or unpaid internships. Invite industry specialists to present technical and academic programs to your classes.

Using Career Clusters

The U.S. Department of Education has identified the following 16 career clusters: Agriculture and Natural Resources; Architecture and Construction; Arts, A/V Technology, and Communications; Business and Administration; Education and Training; Finance; Government and Public Administration; Health Science; Hospitality and Tourism; Human Services; Information Technology; Law and Security; Manufacturing; Retail/Wholesale Sales and Service; Scientific Research/Engineering; and Transportation, Distribution, and Logistics. From these broad categories, students can begin to identify and develop skills needed to pursue their unique career goals.

More information on career clusters can be found at the U.S. Department of Education site:
www.ed.gov

INTEGRATING ACADEMIC STANDARDS OF LEARNING

Introduction

Integrating academics involves taking principles from other subjects and relating them to business education. Students who learn by a variety of examples and applied relations will greatly benefit from this approach. In this course, you will find a variety of exercises, problems, and readings that will help you connect the study of accounting to the disciplines of English Language Arts and Reading, Mathematics, Social Studies, Science, and Computers and Technology.

English Language Arts and Reading

Success in business requires effective communication and interaction. This textbook provides a framework for growth toward full language maturity. Encourage your students to pay special attention to instructions and questions. They will find that effective problem solving requires an understanding of the question posed. Use these activities and features to strengthen language arts skills:

Thinking Critically
Communicating Accounting
Using Key Terms
Connect to Literature
Connect to English
In Your Journal

Mathematics

In this course, mathematics inherently plays a role in the practices and procedures your students will learn. Issues like proper alignment in computations, legibility, and basic computational procedures are stressed. Use these activities and features to strengthen math skills:

Math Hints
Computing in the Business World
Analyzing Accounting
Calculator Hints
Connect to Mathematics

Social Studies

Social studies and social science furnish a wealth of material that can help students appreciate the cultural diversity in the global marketplace. As students better understand how accounting plays a role in the arena of arts, law, civics, and history, they can perform as more sensitive and well-informed business leaders. Use these features to stimulate thinking on the link between business education and history and the social sciences:

Connect to History
Connect to Civics
Connect to Foreign Language
Connect to Music
Connect to Law
Connect to Geography
Connect to Economics
Connect to Ethics
Connect to Education
Connect to Art

Science

The fundamental concepts of science may be applied to business education in a variety of ways. Use the following broad ideas to demonstrate the relationships between the scientific and business worlds:

- Physical energies propel technology changes in the business world.
- The study of a system can help in understanding its components.
- Business operates within constraints of scale and structure much like entities within the scientific world.
- The stability of business is defined by trends, cycles, or changes much like the equilibrium of organisms in the scientific world.

Use the following features to explore the intersections of science and business:

Connect to Environment
Connect to Ecology
Connect to Science
Connect to Health

Computer/Technology

Technology impacts the way we work, play, and live. Whether your students are researching ideas on the Web, practicing spreadsheet applications, or utilizing a computerized accounting program, their business careers will depend heavily on their familiarity and proficiencies with technology. Use these features and activities to connect your students' business education to computers and technology:

Connect to Technology
Computerized Accounting
Spreadsheet Hints
Peachtree Smart Guides

MEETING SPECIAL NEEDS

Introduction

Today's classrooms contain children of varying backgrounds—students who bring their own unique set of abilities, perceptions, and needs. In order to meet the special learning needs of your students, you may need to utilize more than one approach to teach accounting. When you provide a positive learning environment for *all* your students, you may be required to modify your teaching methods when you work with special needs students.

The *Teacher Wraparound Edition* provides a variety of teaching strategies to support the concepts presented in the chapter. The program also offers a variety of visual learning aids including full-color transparencies, demonstration problems, and blackline masters. You can select visuals, activities, and teaching strategies that are appropriate for the special needs, abilities, and learning styles of your students. Refer to the **Meeting Special Needs** chart on pages T46–T47 for tips on instructing students with special needs.

How Do You Prepare?

1. Identify the special needs of your students.
2. Identify areas in the curriculum that may present barriers to some students.
3. Define ways to remove any impediments to their learning.
4. Modify your teaching methods to meet your students' needs.

Ability Levels

In order to help you provide all your students with a positive learning experience, this text provides a variety of activities. This diversity will stimulate student interest, motivate learning, and facilitate understanding. The activities are broken down into three levels to accommodate all students. The *Glencoe Accounting, Teacher Wraparound Edition* designates the activities as follows:

L1 activities are basic activities designed to be within the ability range of all students. These activities reinforce the concepts presented.

L2 activities are application activities designed for students who have mastered the concepts presented. These activities give students an opportunity for practical application of the concepts presented.

L3 activities are challenging activities designed for students who are able to go beyond the basic concepts presented. These activities allow students to expand their perspectives on the basic concepts presented.

Physical Requirements

Your class may include students with various physical limitations that should be considered as you prepare your lectures, activities, and homework assignments.

For example, when an activity requires students to write on a whiteboard or chalkboard, students who use wheelchairs may require the board to be lowered or the use of an overhead projector. For students with visual impairments, you may consider activities in which oral responses can be substituted for written ones. Pay special attention to seating arrangements for students who need a clear view of the chalkboard or those who may need an environment free of sound distractions.

Individualized Projects

Assigning students individual projects allows them to progress at their own pace. Computers and computer software can enhance individual projects because of the practical applications and the consistent reinforcement of problem-solving skills. Using tutorial software can allow learners to progress at their own pace.

Refer to the chart called **Eight Ways of Learning** on pages T48–T49. The chart will help you identify your students' learning styles. It also gives a description of each type of learner; describes the likes of each type, what each type is good at, and how each learns best; and names some famous learners.

Web Site Resources

For more information and related links, visit "Mainstreaming in Your Classroom" on the Teacher Page of glencoeaccounting.glencoe.com.

ADDRESSING THE NEEDS OF ENGLISH LANGUAGE LEARNERS ELL

Your students come from a variety of cultural backgrounds. According to the National Assessment of Education Progress, the number of ELL students is growing at a rate of two-and-a-half times as fast as the general school population. For students who are English language learners, the focus needs to be on overcoming a language barrier. In the business world, these individuals will be expected to communicate effectively, both in oral and written forms.

Strategies for Teaching English Language Learners

As you help these students face the considerable challenges of mastering a new language, it is also important to honor the richness of diversity and cultural heritage they bring to your school. The ability to speak, write, and read English should not be confused with academic ability or intelligence. In general, the best method for dealing with ELL students is to provide them with a variety of ways to learn, apply, and be assessed on the concepts of the course.

- **Support the ELL Student's Culture**
  Display photographs, articles, and objects that are familiar to your ELL students. Ideally, these items might relate to the practice of accounting in their country. The goal is that all students develop an understanding of the differing backgrounds that learners possess.
- **Build Understanding Through Role Reversal**
  Invite a volunteer who speaks a language none of your students speak—or only one ELL student speaks—to present a financial issues lesson in that language. Give no explanation to the students and continue the lesson for about 10 minutes. English-speaking students are given an eye-opening experience into how difficult learning can be. This also gives the ELL student the opportunity to help others for a change.
- **Use Many Visuals and Handouts**
  While ELL students may have difficulty absorbing a rapid discussion of accounting issues, they may respond readily to a visual depicting the key concepts. Handouts and enrichment masters will give them resources to review as they prepare for exams at home.
- **Incorporate Cooperative Learning Activities**
  While it is important that each student become proficient in written and spoken English, it is also imperative for successful learning that the ELL student feels like a part of the classroom community. Constructing groups where ELL students are joined with especially helpful class members will facilitate this sense of belonging.
- **Simplify Your Language**
  As you deliver lessons and lectures to your class, simplify your language, not the content or questions. Speak directly to your students and emphasize important nouns and verbs. Repetition and speaking loudly does not help; rephrasing, accompanied by body language, does. Avoid slang and idiomatic expressions.
- **Outline the Objectives**
  Announce, list, and write the lesson's objectives and activities on the board. Review them orally before the class begins. It is also helpful to place the lesson in the context of its broader theme and preview the upcoming lesson.

ELL Activities in the Student Text

As you progress through the *Glencoe Accounting* course, use the following **Reading Accounting** activities, found in the side margin of the *Teacher Wraparound Edition*, to help you address the needs of your ELL students.

Chapter	TWE Page
1	15
2	27, 33
3	51
4	73
5	105
6	127
7	153
8	183
9	205
10	244
11	259
12	294
13	317
14	355, 359
15	389

Chapter	TWE Page
16	430
17	459
18	485
19	517
20	551
21	575
22	601, 602
23	627
24	653
25	681
26	703
27	735
28	758
29	777

Web Site Resources

For more information and related links, visit "English Language Learners" on the Teacher Page of glencoeaccounting.glencoe.com.

MEETING SPECIAL NEEDS

SUBJECT	DESCRIPTION	SOURCES OF INFORMATION
English Language Learners	Multicultural and/or bilingual children often speak English as a second language or not at all. The customs and behavior of people in the majority culture may be confusing for some of these students. Cultural values may inhibit some of these students from full participation in the classroom.	• *Teaching English as a Second Language* • *Mainstreaming and the Minority Child* • *Children with Limited English: Teaching Strategies for the Regular Classroom* • *Educational Services to Handicapped Students with Limited English Proficiency: A California Statewide Study/PBN B621*
Students with Behavior Disorders	Children with behavior disorders deviate from standards or expectations of behavior and impair the functioning of others and themselves. These children may also be gifted or have learning disabilities.	• *Exceptional Children* • *Journal of Special Education* • *Educating Students With Behavior Disorders* • *Characteristics of Emotional and Behavioral Disorders of Children and Youth*
Students with Orthopaedic Impairments	Children with physical impairments fall into two categories—those with orthopaedic impairments and those with other health impairments. Children with orthopaedic impairments have the use of one or more limbs severely restricted, so the use of wheelchairs, crutches, or braces may be necessary. Children with other health impairments may require the use of respirators or other medical equipment.	• *The Source Book for the Disabled* • *Teaching Exceptional Children* • *Children With Physical Disabilities* • *Vocational Preparation and Employment of Students with Physical and Multiple Disabilities*
Students with Visual Impairments	Students with visual impairments have partial or total loss of sight. Individuals with visual impairments are not significantly different from their sighted peers in ability range or personality. However, a visual impairment may affect cognitive, motor, and social development, especially if early intervention is lacking.	• *Journal of Visual Impairment and Blindness* • *Education of Visually Handicapped* • American Foundation for the Blind • Associated Services for the Blind (ASB) Information Center
Students with Hearing Impairments	Students with hearing impairments have partial or total loss of hearing. Individuals with hearing impairments are not significantly different from their hearing peers in ability range or personality. However, a chronic hearing impairment may affect cognitive, motor, social, and speech development if early intervention is lacking.	• *American Annals of the Deaf* • *Journal of Speech and Hearing Research* • *Sign Language Studies* • National Association of the Deaf • The National Captioning Institute
Students with Learning Disabilities	Students with learning disabilities have an academic problem in one or more areas, such as academic learning, language, perception, social-emotional adjustment, memory, or ability to pay attention.	• *Journal of Learning Disabilities* • *Learning Disability Quarterly* • *The ABCs of Learning Disabilities* • *Classroom Success for the LD and the ADHD Child*
Gifted Students	Although no formal definition exists, these students can be described as having above average ability, task commitment, and creativity. Gifted students rank in the top five percent of their class. They usually finish work more quickly than other students, and are capable of divergent thinking.	• *Journal for the Education of the Gifted* • *Gifted Child Quarterly* • *Gifted Creative/Talented* • The National Research Center on the Gifted and Talented

MEETING SPECIAL NEEDS

TIPS FOR INSTRUCTION	TWE CHAPTER*
With careful planning, all students' needs can be met in the accounting classroom. • Remember that students' ability to speak English does not reflect their academic ability. • Try to incorporate students' cultural experiences into your instruction. The help of a bilingual aide may be effective. • Include information about different cultures in your curriculum to help build students' self image. • Avoid cultural stereotypes. • Encourage students to share their cultures in the classroom.	4, 7, 13, 14, 22, 26, Appendix C, D
• Provide a clearly structured environment with regard to scheduling, rules, room arrangement and safety. • Clearly outline objectives and how you will help students obtain objectives. • Work for long-term improvement; do not expect immediate success. • Model appropriate behavior for students and reinforce proper behavior. • Adjust group requirements for individual needs.	15, 21, 29
• Discuss with the student when you should offer aid. • Help other students and adults understand students with orthopaedic impairments. • Allow students to participate in all activities including field trips, special events, and projects. • Learn about special devices or procedures and if any special safety precautions need to be taken.	5, 9, 23
• Help students become independent. Modify assignments as needed. • Provide tactile models whenever possible. • Team the students with sighted peers for laboratory work. • Teach classmates to serve as guides for students with visual impairments. • Tape lectures and reading assignments for students with visual impairments.	12, 20
• Seat students where they can see your lip movements easily; avoid visual directions. • Avoid standing with your back to the window or to a light source. • Using an overhead projector allows you to maintain eye contact while writing. • Seat students where they can see speakers. • Write all assignments on the board, or hand out written instructions.	3, 6, 16, 24
• Create a classroom environment that leads to success. • Provide assistance and direction; clearly define rules, assignments, and duties. • Allow for pair interaction during class time; utilize peer helpers. • Practice skills frequently. • Use games and drills to help maintain student interest. • Allow students to record answers on tape, and allow extra time to complete tests and assignments. • Provide outlines or tape lecture material.	8, 10, 11, 17, 19, 25, Appendix A
• Emphasize concepts, theories, relationships, ideas, and generalizations. • Let students express themselves in a variety of ways including drawing, creative writing, or acting. • Make arrangements for students to work on independent projects. • Make arrangements for students to take selected subjects early. • Utilize public services and resources, such as agencies providing free and inexpensive materials, community services and programs, and people in the community with specific expertise.	18, 27

*The student text has been carefully written to include in every chapter a variety of visuals, features, and activities to support students with special needs and individual learning styles. The *Teacher Wraparound Edition* integrates additional teaching strategies and activities to help you meet the needs of your classroom.

EIGHT WAYS OF LEARNING

TYPE	DESCRIPTION	LIKES TO...
Verbal/Linguistic Learner	Intelligence is related to words and language, written and spoken.	read, write, tell stories, play word games, and tell jokes and riddles.
Logical/Mathematical Learner	Intelligence deals with inductive and deductive thinking and reasoning, numbers, and abstractions.	perform experiments, solve puzzles, work with numbers, ask questions, and explore patterns and relationships.
Visual/Spatial Learner	Intelligence relies on the sense of sight and being able to visualize an object, including the ability to create mental images.	draw, build, design, and create things, daydream, do jigsaw puzzles and mazes, watch videos, look at photos, and draw maps and charts.
Musical/Rhythmic Learner	Intelligence is based on recognition of tonal patterns, including various environmental sounds, and on a sensitivity to rhythm and beats.	sing and hum, listen to music, play an instrument, move body when music is playing, and make up songs.
Bodily/Kinesthetic Learner	Intelligence is related to physical movement and the brain's motor cortex, which controls bodily motion.	learn by hands-on methods, demonstrate skill in crafts, tinker, perform, display physical endurance, and challenge self physically.
Interpersonal Learner	Intelligence operates primarily through person-to-person relationships and communication.	have lots of friends, talk to people, join groups, play cooperative games, solve problems as part of a group, and volunteer help when others need it.
Intrapersonal Learner	Intelligence is related to inner states of being, self-reflection, metacognition, and awareness of spiritual realities.	work alone, pursue own interests, daydream, keep a personal diary or journal, and think about starting own business.
Naturalistic Learner	Intelligence has to do with observing, understanding, and organizing patterns in the natural environment.	spend time outdoors and work with plants, animals, and other parts of the natural environment; good at identifying plants and animals and at hearing and seeing connections to nature.

EIGHT WAYS OF LEARNING

IS GOOD AT...	LEARNS BY...	FAMOUS LEARNERS	TWE CHAPTER*
memorizing names, dates, places, and trivia; spelling; using descriptive language; and creating imaginary worlds.	saying, hearing, and seeing words.	Maya Angelou—poet Abraham Lincoln—U.S. President and statesman Jerry Seinfeld—comedian Mary Hatwood Futrell—international teacher, leader, orator	8, 12, 13, 14, 22, 25, 26, 27
math, reasoning, logic, problem solving, computing numbers, moving from concrete to abstract, and thinking conceptually.	categorizing, classifying, and working with abstract patterns and relationships.	Stephen Hawking—physicist Albert Einstein—theoretical physicist Marilyn Burns—math educator Alexa Canady—neurosurgeon	4, 19
understanding the use of space and how to get around in it, thinking in three-dimensional terms, and imagining things in clear visual images.	visualizing, dreaming, using the mind's eye, and working with colors and pictures.	Pablo Picasso—artist Maria Martinez—Pueblo Indian famous for black pottery I. M. Pei—architect	1, 6, 7, 9, 15, 17, 18, 20, 21, 23, 24
remembering melodies; keeping time; mimicking beat and rhythm; noticing pitches, rhythms, and background and environmental sounds.	rhythm, melody, and music.	Henry Mancini—composer Marian Anderson—contralto Midori—violinist Paul McCartney—singer, song writer, musician	10
physical activities such as sports, dancing, acting, and crafts.	touching, moving, interacting with space, and processing knowledge through bodily sensations.	Marcel Marceau—mime Jackie Joyner-Kersey—Olympic gold medalist in track and field Katherine Dunham—modern dancer	3, 11
understanding people and their feelings, leading others, organizing, communicating, manipulating, mediating conflicts.	sharing, comparing, relating, cooperating, and interviewing.	Jimmy Carter—U.S. President and statesman Eleanor Roosevelt—Former First Lady Lee Iacocca—President of Chrysler Corporation Mother Teresa—winner of Nobel Peace Prize	16, Mini Practice Set 6
understanding self, focusing inward on feelings/dreams, following instincts, pursuing interests, and being original.	working alone, doing individualized projects, engaging in self-paced instruction.	Marva Collins—educator Maria Montessori—educator and physician Sigmund Freud—psychotherapist Anne Sexton—poet	5, Mini Practice Set 6
measuring, charting, mapping, observing plants and animals, keeping journals, collecting, classifying, and participating in outdoor activities.	visualizing, hands-on activities, bringing outdoors into the classroom, relating home/classroom to the natural world.	George Washington Carver—agricultural chemist Rachael Carson—scientific writer Charles Darwin—evolutionist John James Audubon—conservationist	28, 29

*The student text has been carefully written to include in every chapter a variety of visuals, features, and activities to support students with special needs and individual learning styles. The *Teacher Wraparound Edition* integrates additional teaching strategies and activities to help you meet the needs of your classroom.

NATIONAL STANDARDS FOR BUSINESS EDUCATION

Glencoe Correlated Standards

Chapter	Standard
1	IA1, IA2, IVA1, IVA3, IVD1
2	IA1, IA2, IIA10, IVA1, IVC1, IVD1
3	IA3, IA6, IIC1, IIC3
4	IA1, IA3, IA4, IA5, IA6, IA7
5	IA3, IA4, IA5
6	IA1, IA4, IA6, IA7, IA8
7	IA7, IA9, IA10, IA11
8	IA11
9	IA3-IA5, IA10, IA14, IA16, IIIA6, IIIB1
10	IA15, IA16
11	IA16, IIA2
12	IVB1, IVB2, IVB3
13	IVB4, IVB5, IVC1
14	IA6-10, IIA2, IIA3, IIA4, IVC1
15	IA7-IA10, IIA2, IIB2, IIB4
16	IA8-IA10, IA16, IIA2, IIA3, IIA4
17	IA6-IA10, IA16, IIA2, IIA3, IIA4, IIB2, IIB4, IVD1
18	IA11, IA12, IA16, IIIA1, IVC1
19	IA14, IA16, IIA1, IIB1, IIC4-5, IIIA1, IIIA3, IIIA5, IIIA9, IIIB1-2, IVA4
20	IA15, IA16
21	IA16, IIA1, IIC2–6, IIIA4, IIIA6, IVA4
22	IIA2, IIA9
23	IA13, IIA1, IIA7, IIA8, IIA9
24	IA13, IA16, IIA3, IIA4, IIA9, IIA10
25	IA13, IA16, IIA6
26	IIA5, IIB1, IIB3, IIB4
27	IA15, IA16, IIC1, IVA1, IVA2
28	IA14, IIC1, IVA1, IVA2
29	IIIA5
App. D	IA13

I. The Accounting Cycle

Achievement Standard: Complete and explain the purpose of the various steps in the accounting cycle.

Level 3-4 – Performance Expectations

I. A. 1. Define accounting and explain the purpose of the accounting system

I. A. 2. Define the concept of generally accepted accounting principles and ascertain the source of these standards

I. A. 3. Demonstrate an understanding of the fundamental accounting equation

I. A. 4. Classify items as assets, liabilities, or owner's equity

I. A. 5. Describe the purposes of the revenue, expense, and drawing accounts and illustrate their effects on owner's equity

I. A. 6. Analyze business transactions using source documents and describe the effect on the accounting equation

I. A. 7. Explain the double-entry system of accounting and apply debit and credit rules when analyzing business transactions

I. A. 8. Explain the purpose of the journal and the process of journalizing business transactions

I. A. 9. Analyze the relationship of the journal to the ledger

I. A. 10. Explain the purpose of a ledger account and post information from the journal to the ledger

I. A. 11. Prepare a trial balance and explain its uses and limitations

I. A. 12. Explain the purpose of adjusting entries

I. A. 13. Analyze the trial balance to determine the necessary adjustments (accruals and deferrals) to prepare financial statements

I. A. 14. Prepare and explain the purposes of each financial statement and describe the way they articulate with each other

I. A. 15. Explain the purposes of the closing process and journalize and post closing entries

I. A. 16. Use spreadsheet and accounting software to maintain accounting records and describe the differences between manual and computerized accounting systems

Level 3*-4 – Performance Expectations

(Advanced Course)

II. The Accounting Process

Achievement Standard: Apply generally accepted accounting principles to determine the value of assets, liabilities, and owner's equity.

A. Assets

Level 3-4 – Performance Expectations

II. A. 1. Define and identify current and long-term assets and explain their impact on financial statements

II. A. 2. Define cash; prepare bank reconciliations; establish, maintain and reconcile petty cash and change accounts; identify cash control techniques; explain the benefits of electronic fund transfers, automated teller machine transactions, electronic data interchange, automated bill paying, and uses of a debit card

II. A. 3. Create and maintain the accounts receivable subsidiary ledger and an account for credit card sales

II. A. 4. Apply appropriate accounting techniques for uncollectible accounts

II. A. 5. Establish and maintain accounts for receivables and related interest

II. A. 6. Compare and evaluate inventory concepts and costing procedures and apply these concepts and procedures to merchandising and manufacturing businesses

II. A. 7. Explain the purpose of depreciation

II. A. 8. Apply appropriate accounting concepts and techniques for acquisition, depreciation, and disposal of property, plant, and equipment

II. A. 9. Use spreadsheet or accounting software to maintain accounting records for short-term and long-term assets

Level 3*-4 – Performance Expectations

II. A. 10. Convert an amount of foreign currency into the equivalent U. S. dollar value

(Remaining performance expectations: Advanced Course)

B. Liabilities

Level 3-4 – Performance Expectations

II. B. 1. Define and identify current and long-term liabilities and explain their impact on financial statements

II. B. 2. Create and maintain the accounts payable subsidiary ledger

II. B. 3. Explain the purposes of notes payable; establish and maintain accounts for payables and related interest

II. B. 4. Use spreadsheet or accounting software to maintain accounting records for short-term and long-term liabilities

Level 3*-4 – Performance Expectations

(Advanced Course)

Level 4 – Performance Expectations

(Advanced Course)

C. Owner's Equity

Level 3-4 – Performance Expectations

II. C. 1. Explain the purpose of the capital and drawing accounts for a sole proprietorship and partnership

II. C. 2. Explain the purpose of the capital stock and retained earnings accounts for a corporation

Level 3*-4 – Performance Expectations

II. C. 3. Apply appropriate accounting techniques to account for investments and withdrawals by owners

II. C. 4. Explain the purpose of the following accounts, common stock, preferred stock, paid-in capital, retained earnings and dividends for a corporation

II. C. 5. Apply appropriate accounting concepts and techniques to analyze and record investments by stockholders and the declaration and payment of dividends

Level 4 – Performance Expectations

II. C. 6. Analyze the effect of cash dividends on financial statements

* Performance expectations appropriate for the second year of high school accounting are indicated by an asterisk.

III. Financial Statements

Achievement Standard: Prepare, interpret, and analyze financial statements using manual and computerized systems for service, merchandising, and manufacturing businesses.

A. Financial Statement Preparation and Analysis

Level 3-4 – Performance Expectations

III. A. 1. Analyze the income statement and balance sheet of a business by comparing a vertical analysis with industry standards

III. A. 2. Analyze the statement of cash flows by comparing it with previous statements

(Advanced Course)

III. A. 3. Use a spreadsheet or accounting software to evaluate the impact of changes in operating procedures, accounting methods, and estimates on the financial statements and ratios

III. A. 4. Use spreadsheet or accounting software to prepare charts and graphs useful in analyzing the financial condition of the business

III. A. 5. Explain the importance of high ethical standards in the preparation of financial statements

III. A. 6. Research and analyze financial statements of corporations using a variety of sources (e.g., the Internet and primary source documentation)

Level 3*-4 – Performance Expectations

III. A. 9. Perform horizontal and vertical analyses and compute appropriate ratios to evaluate solvency and earning power

III. A. 10. Analyze corporate financial data using a variety of sources (e.g., the Internet and primary source documentation)

(Remaining performance expectations: Advanced Course)

B. Income Statement for the Three Types of Business Operations

Level 3-4 – Performance Expectations

III. B. 1. Apply the revenue realization and matching principles in the preparation of an income statement or statement of operations for service and merchandising businesses

III. B. 2. Determine cost of goods sold and gross profit for a merchandising business

Level 3*-4 – Performance Expectations

(Advanced Course)

IV. Special Applications

Achievement Standard: Apply appropriate accounting principles to payroll, income taxation, managerial systems, and various forms of ownership.

A. Forms of Ownership

Level 3-4 – Performance Expectations

IV. A. 1. Explain the advantages and disadvantages of the three forms of business ownership—sole proprietorships, partnerships, and corporations

IV. A. 2. Apply appropriate accounting techniques for the formation and allocation of earnings of a partnership

Level 3*-4 – Performance Expectations

IV. A. 3. Apply appropriate accounting principles to government and not-for-profit entities

IV. A. 4. Apply appropriate accounting techniques for the formation and allocation of earnings of a corporation

B. Payroll

Level 3*-4 – Performance Expectations

IV. B. 1. Prepare and maintain payroll records using manual and computerized systems

IV. B. 2. Calculate earnings at an hourly and piece rate and on a salary, commission, and salary/commission basis

IV. B. 3. Calculate deductions including federal income tax, Social Security tax, Medicare tax, state income tax, and other deductions to determine net pay

IV. B. 4. Calculate employer's payroll taxes (e.g., Social Security, Medicare, federal unemployment, and state unemployment) and employee benefits paid by the employer

IV. B. 5. Prepare federal, state, and local payroll reports

C. Income Taxation

Level 3*-4 – Performance Expectations

IV. C. 1. Differentiate between taxation at the personal and business levels

D. Managerial Accounting Principles and Systems

Level 3*-4 – Performance Expectations

IV. D. 1. Describe the management process and the role of managerial accounting in this process

(Remaining performance expectations: Advanced Course)

V. Interpretation and Use of Data

Achievement Standard: Use planning and control principles to evaluate the performance of an organization and apply differential analysis and present-value concepts to make decisions

A. Planning and Control

Level 3*-4 – Performance Expectations

(Advanced Course)

PLANNING YOUR COURSE

A "typical" accounting course is a one-year, two-semester course. Your school may offer a second-year, advanced course, or you may be teaching in a different configuration—block schedule, staggered schedule, or quarter system. The materials in the *Glencoe Accounting* program were developed to give you flexibility and options to meet the needs of your students and the length and goals of your accounting course.

One-Year Course of Study

Glencoe Accounting is a two-year program that includes student textbooks, workbooks, and extensive supplemental materials for both manual and integrated computer applications. The *First-Year Course* includes a compre-hensive study of accounting, including chapters on accounting for depreciation of plant and equipment, uncollectible accounts receivable, inventories, notes payable and receivable, partnerships, and corporations. If your school does not offer a second-year course, you can be confident that your students will receive a strong foundation from the *First-Year Course.*

Computer Integration

The *First -Year Course* offers fully integrated computer activities with the accounting instruction. From performing Internet research to using a variety of computer applications, students will have ample opportunities to practice computer technology while learning accounting concepts. See the **Scope and Sequence** chart on page T25 for computer integrated activities.

Individualized Instruction

If you wish to individualize accounting instruction, the organization of the text provides clearly written steps that are easy for students to follow on their own. Review activities and student study plans are available in the *Chapter Reviews and Working Papers.*

Course Outlines

The chart on the next page will help you develop a course outline and lesson plans for the entire first-year course. The chart outlines a course of study for both six-week grading periods and nine-week grading periods. The chart identifies the estimated number of class periods required to complete each chapter and the mini practice sets. The suggested number of classes includes the approximate time required for students to complete end-of-chapter activities, computer activities, and chapter tests. Class periods are estimated at 50 minutes.

Simulations

Although three different business simulations are available for the first-year program, most teachers find that they do not have time to complete all three in a one-year course. If you choose to have students complete one or more business simulations, you will need to adjust the proposed outlines if you also wish to complete all the chapters in the textbook. See page T30 for detailed descriptions of all simulations and the estimated completion times of each.

Block Scheduling

Glencoe Accounting offers you an optional planning guide titled *Block Scheduling*. The guide is divided by unit, chapter, estimated days and additional days for each chapter, discussion activities, computer activities, and additional days to complete those activities. These guides include the use of TWE activities, end-of-unit activities, unit quizzes, transparencies, school-to-work activities, problems and simulations, and unit tests. The guide is designed to help you use the *Glencoe Accounting* program to meet your particular classroom needs and to accommodate your style of teaching.

Lesson Plans

Another guide that will help make your class planning flexible and save you time is the *Lesson Plans*. You can simply photocopy each chapter plan and customize it for your students' needs. The forms are prepared to allow you space to insert your local/state objectives. These completed lesson plans can also be submitted for supervisory evaluation.

SIX-WEEK AND NINE-WEEK GRADING PERIODS

Six-Week Grading Period		Chapter and Application Activity	Number of Classes	Nine-Week Grading Period
Grading Period 1	**Unit 1**	**Introduction to Accounting**		Grading Period 1
	Chapter 1	You and the World of Accounting	3	
	Chapter 2	The World of Business and Accounting	6	
	Unit 2	**The Basic Accounting Cycle**		
	Chapter 3	Business Transactions and the Accounting Equation	5	
	Chapter 4	Transactions that Affect Assets, Liabilities, and Owner's Equity	5	
	Chapter 5	Transactions that Affect Revenue, Expenses, and Withdrawals	5	
	Chapter 6	Recording Transactions in a General Journal	5	
Grading Period 2	Chapter 7	Posting Journal Entries to General Ledger Accounts	3	
	Mini Practice Set 1	***Canyon.com Web Sites***	6	
	Chapter 8	The Six-Column Work Sheet	6	
	Chapter 9	Financial Statements for a Sole Proprietorship	6	Grading Period 2
	Chapter 10	Completing the Accounting Cycle for a Sole Proprietorship	6	
Grading Period 3	Chapter 11	Cash Control and Banking Activities	6	
	Mini Practice Set 2	***Fast Track Tutoring Service***	3	
	Business Simulation	***Adventure Travels*** (Optional)		
	Unit 3	**Accounting for a Payroll System**		
	Chapter 12	Payroll Accounting	6	
	Chapter 13	Payroll Liabilities and Tax Records	6	
	Mini Practice Set 3	***Green Thumb Plant Service***	3	
	Unit 4	**The Accounting Cycle for a Merchandising Corporation**		
	Chapter 14	Accounting for Sales and Cash Receipts	6	
Grading Period 4	Chapter 15	Accounting for Purchases and Cash Payments	6	Grading Period 3
	Chapter 16	Special Journals: Sales and Cash Receipts	6	
	Chapter 17	Special Journals: Purchases and Cash Payments	6	
	Chapter 18	Adjustments and the Ten-column Work Sheet	5	
	Chapter 19	Financial Statements for a Corporation	6	
Grading Period 5	**Mini Practice Set 4**	***In-Touch Electronics***	3	
	Chapter 20	Completing the Accounting Cycle for a Merchandising Corporation	4	
	Business Simulation	***Outer Banks Marketplace, Inc.*** (Optional)		
	Chapter 21	Accounting for Publicly Held Corporations	6	
	Unit 5	**Accounting for Special Procedures**		Grading Period 4
	Chapter 22	Cash Funds	6	
	Chapter 23	Plant Assets and Depreciation	7	
	Chapter 24	Uncollectible Accounts Receivable	7	
Grading Period 6	Chapter 25	Inventories	6	
	Chapter 26	Notes Payable and Receivable	6	
	Mini Practice Set 5	***Kite Loft Inc.***	3	
	Business Simulation	***Digital Express*** (optional)		
	Unit 6	**Accounting for Partnerships**		
	Chapter 27	Introduction to Partnerships	5	
	Chapter 28	Financial Statements for a Partnership	6	
	Mini Practice Set 6	***Fine Finishes***		
	Chapter 29	Ethics in Accounting	2	
	TOTAL CLASS SESSIONS		176	

GLENCOE ACCOUNTING, ADVANCED COURSE

To be successful in the competitive business environment, today's students need not only to gain accounting knowledge but also to develop an understanding of the use of the computer in applying that knowledge. The *Glencoe Accounting, Advanced Course* provides a strong foundation in basic accounting theory and procedures and includes instruction on computerized accounting systems. Traditional methods for teaching accounting are combined with current applications of technology to ensure that students achieve mastery of basic accounting concepts and procedures while they gain computer literacy and a general understanding of how to use the computer to perform various accounting activities.

The *Glencoe Accounting, Advanced Course* is designed for both college-bound and vocational students. Much of the same material that students will study in a beginning college accounting course is included in the advanced text, but the material is written at a level suitable for high school students. Further, the coverage of practical accounting procedures helps prepare students for entry-level employment. Finally, the integration of computer applications throughout the text demonstrates the computer's use as a tool in accounting.

Glencoe Accounting, Advanced Course, is intended for use in the second-year accounting course. The advanced course materials include:

- 25-chapter student textbook
- Teacher Annotated Edition
- Chapter Reviews and Working Papers
- Teacher Annotated Edition of the Chapter Reviews and Working Papers
- Printed Chapter Tests
- Printed Unit Tests
- Test Bank with **Exam***View* software
- Blackline Masters
- Demonstration Problems
- Business Simulation *Import Expressions*

In addition, some items, such as the videos, *Math Review for Accounting, Strategies for Teaching International Accounting,* and *Internet Resources and Activities Handbook* may be used with either the first-year or the advanced course.

A complete listing of the components of the two-year program is included in a current Glencoe catalogue.

STUDENT TEXTBOOK AT A GLANCE

Glencoe Accounting, Advanced Course, is a textbook on financial accounting—the procedures and systems used to record transactions and to prepare reports such as the balance sheet and the income statement. The textbook is organized with learning in mind, allowing students to review the accounting cycle before moving on to more advanced procedures and applications.

The student textbook is organized into 6 units with 25 chapters.

Unit 1—The Accounting Cycle

The first unit of the textbook reviews the basic principles and procedures that students learned in their first-year study of accounting. Students begin by reviewing the basic accounting equation, the rules of debit and credit for the various types of accounts, and the steps in the accounting cycle.

Unit 2—Accounting for Assets, Liabilities, and Equity

The chapters in Unit 2 elaborate on many of the transactions and procedures first introduced in Units 5 and 6 of the first-year textbook. The content of the chapters in the unit is organized to follow the order accounts are presented on the balance sheet.

Unit 3—Understanding Business Information

In Unit 3, students learn how to use three different techniques to analyze the information contained on financial statements. These techniques include horizontal analysis, vertical analysis, and ratio analysis. Students also learn about the statement of cash flows.

Unit 4—The Accounting Cycle

This unit discusses two other forms of organization: the partnership and the not-for-profit organization. Students are introduced to the partnership form of business organization and to the transactions required to form, dissolve, and liquidate a partnership. They also learn about the budgeting process and the financial statements that are prepared by not-for-profit organizations.

Unit 5—Special Accounting Systems

The chapters in Unit 5 cover specialized accounting procedures. These specialized systems include procedures used by businesses to report departmental and branch operations, to control purchases and cash payments, and to record and report on manufacturing operations.

Unit 6—Accounting for Business Decisions

Unit 6 covers managerial and cost accounting. Students learn how costs behave in relation to business activities. Variable, fixed, and mixed costs are introduced, and students see how those costs change as production is increased or decreased. Graphs are used throughout the chapter.

TABLE OF CONTENTS

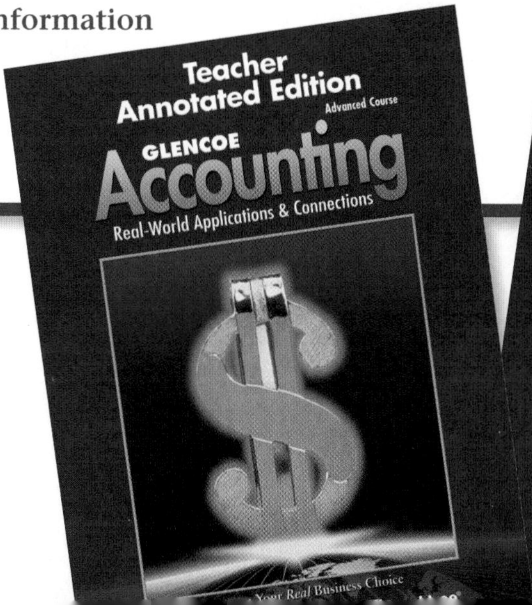

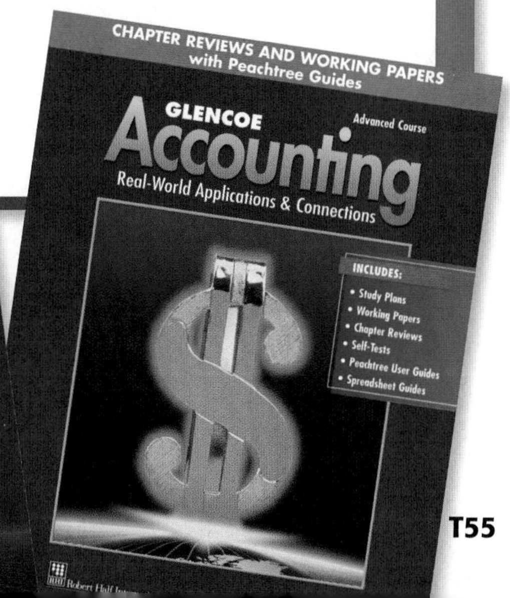

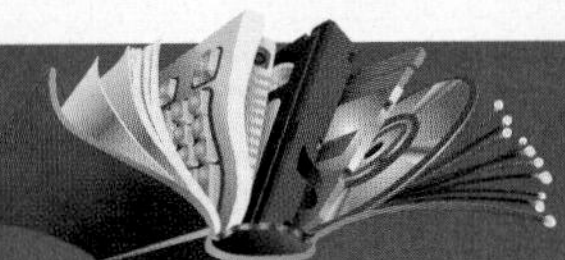

This is a representation of key resources available in the *Glencoe Accounting* program.

*inter*NET CONNECTION

Use the following Web resources to introduce, reinforce, or stimulate discussion on unit topics.

- Case Studies
- Study Plans
- Career Corner
- Real-Life Applications
- Self-Assessment Quizzes
- Games for the Classroom
- Ethics and the Profession

GLENCOE ACCOUNTING BULLETIN BOARD POSTER

Virtual Business® CD-ROM

Virtual Business **is a fully visual marketing and business simulation that lets students start and run their own business. For more information on the simulation, visit the teacher page on the *Glencoe Accounting* Web site.**

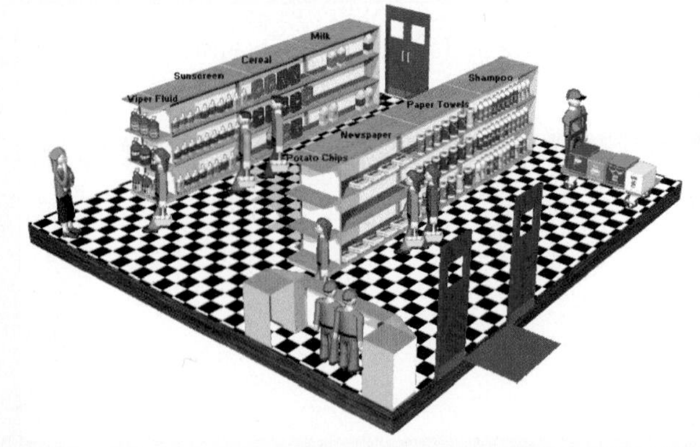

Unit Video Portfolio

Integrating *Electronic Field Trips* into Your Accounting Instruction

The *Electronic Field Trip* videos provide an excellent introduction to key accounting concepts taught in the textbook. You may want to use these video segments in **Unit 1**. The titles of the video segments are:

- *The Real World of Accounting*
- *Entrepreneurship*
- *Preparing for an Interview*
- *Entering the Workforce*
- *Knowing Your Legal Rights*

The Real World of Accounting

These Glencoe Resources may be used to teach, reteach, or enrich the concepts presented in this unit of study.

Knowing Your Legal Rights

Assessment and Evaluation

Unit 1 Test

1 Unit **Introduction to Accounting**
Objective Test A / Chapters 1—2

	Possible	Score
Part A	34	____
Part B	11	____
Part C	20	____
Part D	10	____
Total	75	____

Name ______________ Date ________ Class ________

Part A ACCOUNTING VOCABULARY *(34 points)*

Directions: In the Answer column, write the letter of the word or phrase that best completes the sentence. The first item is completed for you as an example.

A. account
B. accountant
C. accounting clerks
D. accounting system
E. accounts payable
F. accounts receivable
G. assets
H. basic accounting equation
I. business transaction
J. business entity
K. capital
L. certified public accountant
M. charter
N. corporation
0. credit
P. creditor
Q. equity
R. expenses
S. fiscal period
T. general bookkeeper
U. going concern
V. liabilities
W. loss
X. manufacturing business
Y. merchandising business
Z. on account
AA. owner's equity
BB. partnership
CC. profit
DD. property
EE. property rights
FF. revenue
GG. service business
HH. sole proprietorship
II. withdrawal

	ANSWER	SCORE
0. Things of value owned by a business are called _?_.	G	0. ____
1. Any investment in a business by an owner is represented by the _?_ account.	____	1. ____
2. A(n) _?_ buys finished products and resells them to individuals or other businesses.	____	2. ____
3. A business owned and operated by two or more persons is called a(n) _?_.	____	3. ____
4. A(n) _?_ is the legal document giving a business the right to operate as a corporation.	____	4. ____
5. Anything of value that is owned or controlled by an individual or business organization is called _?_.	____	5. ____
6. When businesses or individuals buy property and agree to pay for it later, they are buying on _?_.	____	6. ____
7. The owner's claims to the total assets of the business are called _?_.	____	7. ____
8. The _?_ states that assets of the business equal the liabilities plus the owner's equity.	____	8. ____
9. An economic event causing a change in the assets, liabilities, or owner's equity of a business is called a(n) _?_.	____	9. ____
10. People who hold entry-level jobs and do the routine work in accounting for a business are called _?_.	____	10. ____

Unit 1 Objective Test A • 1

Accounting Portfolio

Unit 1 Accounting Competencies

Student ______ **Class** ______ **Instructor** ______
Date Assigned ______ **Date Completed** ______

Unit ***1*** *Accounting Portfolio*

Accounting Competencies

The next three pages list the concepts and procedures typically covered in a first-year accounting course. The concepts and procedures learned in a second-year course are also listed.

Find out from your instructor if these competencies are covered in your accounting course. If so, remove these pages from the booklet and place them in the portfolio section or folder labeled "Accounting Competencies." If not, ask your teacher for a list of the competencies for your course. If you are studying only the first year of accounting, do not include the second-year competencies in your portfolio.

As you study each section of accounting concepts and procedures, you will complete textbook problems and take tests to gauge your knowledge for each competency. Enter your grade for each section in the space provided.

Accounting 1 Competencies	Demonstrated Proficiency (Grade)
A. Career and Principles of Accounting	
B. Introduction to Accounting Equation	
C. Accounting Cycle	
D. Computerization of Financial Data	
E. Accounting for Different Types of Ownership	
F. Special Accounting Transactions (for merchandising business)	
G. Journals and Subsidiary Ledgers	
H. Special Accounting Transactions (computerized accounts receivable and accounts payable)	
I. Partnership and Corporate Accounting	
J. Special Accounting Transactions for a Partnership and Corporations	
K. Skills for Business Employment	
L. Development of Leadership Skills	

Accounting Portfolio 3

Enrichment and Extension

Accounting Competitive Event Review

Student ______ **Class** ______ **Instructor** ______
Date Assigned ______ **Date Completed** ______

Reviewing for the Accounting Competitive Event

Basic Accounting Concepts

Accounting refers to the activities businesses and organizations carry out to record and report their financial transactions. All types of businesses need and use financial information—from the small, one-person repair shop to the huge multinational corporation, from the family doctor to the national not-for-profit charitable organization to governmental units at all levels.

Financial information is of interest to a wide variety of people: owners, investors, managers, creditors, employees, unions, government, and customers. Because accounting is used to gather and report this financial information, it is often called *the language of business*.

For further information: See Chapters 2 and 3, First Year; Chapters 1 and 2, Advanced.

For additional practice: Additional Reinforcement Problem 3A.

On a separate sheet of paper, answer the following questions.

True/False

1. A sole proprietorship is a business entity owned by two or more people.
2. The purpose of accounting is to provide financial information about a business entity.
3. The owners of a partnership business are known as stockholders.
4. The Financial Accounting Standards Board is responsible for the development of standards for business and not-for-profit organizations.
5. Each business follows accounting rules (or principles) that are specific to its particular needs.
6. Public accountants provide services to clients for a fee.
7. The three forms of business organization are the sole proprietorship, the partnership, and the not-for-profit organization.
8. Profit is one measure of business success.
9. The Internal Revenue Service has little effect on the accounting practices of businesses.
10. Passing a test on accounting theory and practices is required for one to become a certified public accountant.
11. Employees should have no particular interest in financial information about the business where they work.
12. Accounting information is reported in dollar amounts, regardless of inflation.
13. If a business spends more money to operate than it earns from the sale of goods and services, it is operating at a profit.

Multiple Choice

14. The financial affairs of a business and the financial affairs of the owner should be (A) kept totally separate, (B) combined in the firm's accounting records, (C) combined in the owner's accounting records, (D) reported in different parts of the firm's accounting records.
15. The type of business that buys finished products to resell to individuals or other businesses is called a (A) manufacturing business, (B) service business, (C) merchandising business, (D) partnership business.

Accounting Competitive Event Review • 11

OVERVIEW UNIT 1

Unit Objectives

1. Describe how personal interests and skills, values, and lifestyle goals affect one's career choices.
2. Explain how to conduct career research and set career goals.
3. Describe who entrepreneurs are and the types of businesses they form.
4. Explain the role of accounting in a private enterprise economy and the difference between financial and managerial accounting.

Unit 1 Contents

EXTENDING THE QUOTE

Henry Ford lived the idea of working with others to build success. With 11 other investors, he started Ford Motor Company in 1903 with $28,000 in cash. By the time the company made its first sale, its bank balance had declined to $223.65!

Ford's method of producing cars using an assembly line meant lower costs, making an automobile affordable for many people. For the assembly line, Ford needed people working together—each adding a part to the car—to create affordable automobiles. That spirit of working together helped turn Ford into a successful corporation that today sells its products all over the world.

UNIT 1

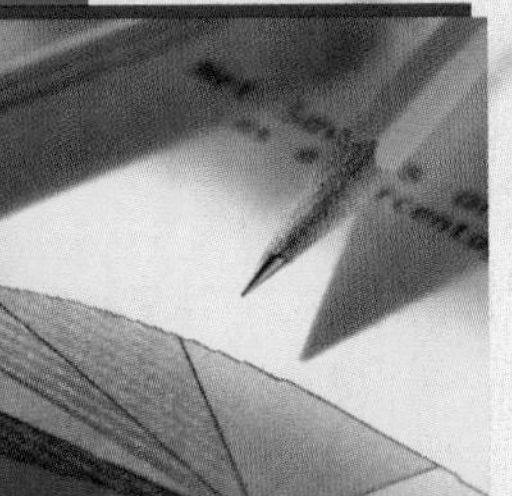

Introduction to Accounting

In this unit. . .

Accounting plays a vital role in the day-to-day activities of every business. In this first unit, you will learn about career planning, the variety of career opportunities available in accounting, and the importance of accounting in today's business environment. Accounting records and reports help businesses operate efficiently—and profitably—by keeping track of how much is earned and how much is spent.

Accounting is so much a part of the business world that much of its terminology has become a part of our everyday language. Throughout this book, you will learn why accounting has been called the "language of business."

Coming together is the beginning.
Keeping together is progress.
Working together is success.

—Henry Ford
American Automobile Manufacturer

2

Great Ideas *From the Classroom of...*

Martha Eaton
Oxford High School
Oxford, Alabama

Using Calculators Electronic calculators are among the many valuable technology tools used in accounting. During the first week of school, demonstrate proper techniques when using electronic calculators or pocket-sized computers. Ask each student to demonstrate how his or her calculator works, including using the percent keys and the memory keys. Then note the differences among the calculators within the group, and discuss the calculator features that are included with PDAs (personal digital assistants).

In Your Journal . . .

Think of all your daily activities, either at school or work. How do you keep track of all your goals? Your future plans? Do you have a daily planner to keep track? This exercise will help you develop time management skills by setting priorities for completing work as scheduled.

In your journal, record the following:

1. During the next two weeks, make a list of at least three goals you would like to accomplish.
2. Next to the goals, write the steps you will take to achieve these goals.
3. Keep track of your daily progress by recording your ideas and experiences in a journal.

After the two weeks, review your journal to see if you have accomplished the goals.

POWER READING STRATEGIES

To get the most out of your reading:

Predict what the section will be about.

Connect what you read with your own life.

Question as you read to make sure you understand the content.

Respond to what you've read.

In Your Journal. . .

Teacher Guidelines Have students add to their accounting portfolios by completing and including the *In Your Journal* writing activities. Remind students of how often they set informal, mental goals when they make plans to call a friend or talk to a school counselor about career information. Writing those and other goals will help them keep better track of what they need and want to do. It will also help them in accomplishing those goals. P

INTRODUCING UNIT 1

Previewing the Chapters

These first two chapters set the stage for the study of accounting by getting students to begin thinking about a future career. Students learn how to use their own interests and skills in searching for a career. They learn about the different types of businesses and the role of entrepreneurs in our economy. Finally, students learn how businesses use accounting information in making both financial and managerial decisions.

Tying to Previous Knowledge

Ask students who have part-time jobs to share their experiences in deciding where to look for a job and what personal skills they use in their work. Have students discuss how part-time employment or summer jobs can help them learn about different types of careers.

BULLETIN BOARD

Glencoe Poster Teaching Tip

Ask students what skills they think they'll need to be successful. Then point out the skills on the poster. Compare these skills with students' responses. Discuss each skill described on the poster and ask students to think about how they might acquire or enhance needed skills.

CHAPTER 1 Resource Manager

Section Resources

	Objectives & Standards	Activities & Features	Reproducible Masters
Chapter Opener *You and the World of Accounting*	• Describe how personal skills, values, and lifestyle goals affect career decisions. • Find information about a variety of careers. • Find specific information regarding careers in accounting. • Set career goals. • Describe the types of businesses and organizations that hire accountants. • Define the accounting terms introduced in this chapter. **National Standards for Business Education**: IA1, IA2, IVA1, IVD1	Exploring the Real World of Business, p. 4 Workplace Connections, p. 5	School-to-Work Handbook
Section 1 *Exploring Careers*	• How personal interests and skills, values, and lifestyle goals affect career decisions. • Where to find information on possible careers. • How to set career goals.	Did You Know?, p. 7 Connect To, p. 9 International Accounting, p. 10 Math Hints, p. 11 A Matter of Ethics, p. 12	Strategies for Teaching International Accounting Math Review for Accounting Strategies for Teaching Ethics in Accounting
Section 2 *Accounting Careers: The Possibilities Are Endless!*	• The variety of career opportunities available to accountants. • The types of businesses and organizations that hire accountants.	Accounting Flashbacks, p. 15 Accounting Careers in Focus, p. 18	Internet Resources and Activities Handbook

KEY

Posters
Blackline Masters
Transparency
CD-ROM
Software
Portfolio
Videocassette

MULTIMEDIA RESOURCE

Peachtree®	QuickBooks®	Spreadsheets	Videos	CD-ROMs
None in this chapter.	None in this chapter.	None in this chapter.	***Video Segments:*** ***The Real World of Accounting*** Discuss with students the career opportunities available to accountants. ***Preparing for an Interview*** Use this video to help students prepare for an interview. ***Entering the Workforce*** Discuss the importance of the first day on the job. ***Knowing Your Legal Rights*** Discuss with students the importance of knowing their legal rights.	***Electronic Learning Center (ELC), Chapter 1*** This program is ideal for visual learners since it incorporates video images, animation, and graphics to enliven the content of each lesson. ***Interactive Lesson Planner (ILP), Chapter 1*** This CD-ROM combines the versatility of an electronic lesson planner with the convenience of teacher classroom resources.

SCANS Correlation Chart

FOUNDATION SKILLS

Basic Skills:	Reading	Writing	Math	Listening	Speaking	
Thinking Skills:	Creative Thinking	Decision Making	Problem Solving	Seeing Things in the Mind's Eye	Knowing How to Learn	Reasoning
Personal Qualities:	Responsibility	Self-Esteem	Sociability	Self-Management	Integrity/Honesty	

WORKPLACE COMPETENCIES

Resources:	Allocating Time	Allocating Money	Allocating Material and Facility Resources	Allocating Human Resources		
Information:	Acquiring and Evaluating Information	Organizing and Maintaining Information	Interpreting and Communicating Information	Using Computers to Process Information		
Interpersonal Skills:	Participating as a Member of a Team	Teaching Others	Serving Clients/ Customers	Exercising Leadership	Negotiating to Arrive at a Decision	Working with Cultural Diversity
Systems:	Understanding Systems	Monitoring and Correcting Performance	Improving and Designing Systems			
Technology:	Selecting Technology	Applying Technology to Task	Maintaining and Troubleshooting Technology			

*Highlighted blocks indicate areas covered in the chapter. Additional SCANS skills are also covered throughout the *Teacher Wraparound Edition.*

Assessment

Student Edition
- Check Your Understanding, pp. 13, 17
- Chapter 1 Problems, pp. 22-23

Assessment and Evaluation Masters
- Chapter 1 Study Plan, *Glencoe Workbook*
- Chapter 1 Self-Test, *Glencoe Workbook*
- Chapter 1 Test, *Chapter Tests* Booklet
- Chapter 1 Activity, *School-to-Work Handbook*
- Chapter 1 **Exam***View*

Teacher Wraparound Edition
- Reteaching Section 1, p. 13
- Reteaching Section 2, p. 17
- Chapter 1 Quiz, p. 19

Transparencies

	Teaching Transparencies	Solution Transparencies
Section 1:	1–1, 1–2, 1–3, 1–4, 1–5, 1–6, 1–7, 1–8, 1–9	
Section 2:	1–10	
End of Chapter:		

TEACHER CLASSROOM RESOURCES

This is a representation of key blackline masters available in the Teacher Classroom Resources.

Teaching Aids

Transparency Examples

Section Focus Transparencies

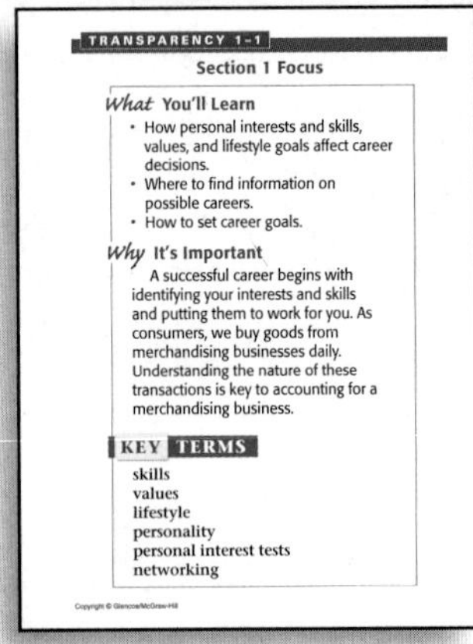

TRANSPARENCY 1-1

Section 1 Focus

What You'll Learn

- How personal interests and skills, values, and lifestyle goals affect career decisions.
- Where to find information on possible careers.
- How to set career goals.

Why It's Important

A successful career begins with identifying your interests and skills and putting them to work for you. As consumers, we buy goods from merchandising businesses daily. Understanding the nature of these transactions is key to accounting for a merchandising business.

KEY TERMS

skills
values
lifestyle
personality
personal interest tests
networking

Copyright © Glencoe/McGraw-Hill

Teaching Transparencies

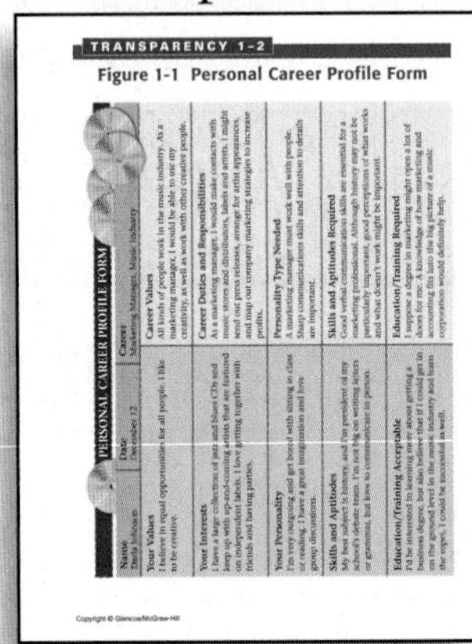

TRANSPARENCY 1-2

Figure 1-1 Personal Career Profile Form

PERSONAL CAREER PROFILE FORM

Copyright © Glencoe/McGraw-Hill

Teaching Transparencies

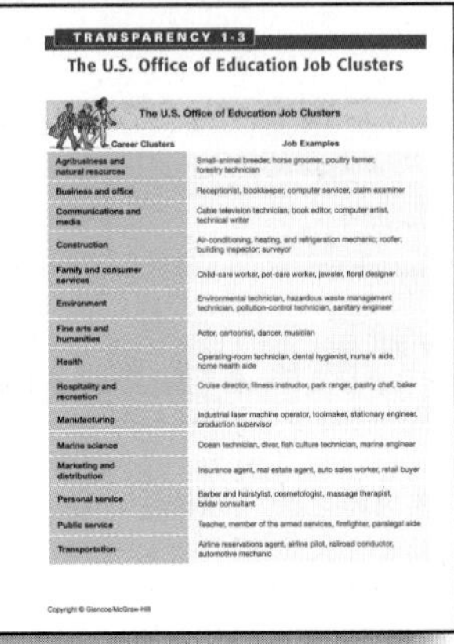

TRANSPARENCY 1-3

The U.S. Office of Education Job Clusters

The U.S. Office of Education Job Clusters

Career Clusters	Job Examples
Agribusiness and natural resources	Small animal breeder, horse groomer, poultry farmer, forestry technician
Business and office	Receptionist, bookkeeper, computer services, claim examiner
Communications and media	Cable television technician, book editor, computer artist, technical writer
Construction	Air-conditioning, heating, and refrigeration mechanic, roofer, building inspector, surveyor
Family and consumer services	Child-care worker, pet-care worker, jeweler, floral designer
Environment	Environmental technician, hazardous waste management technician, pollution-control technician, sanitary engineer
Fine arts and humanities	Actor, cartoonist, dancer, musician
Health	Operating room technician, dental hygienist, nurse's aide, home health aide
Hospitality and recreation	Cruise director, fitness instructor, park ranger, pastry chef, baker
Manufacturing	Industrial laser machine operator, toolmaker, stationary engineer, production supervisor
Marine science	Ocean technician, diver, fish culture technician, marine engineer
Marketing and distribution	Insurance agent, real estate agent, auto sales worker, retail buyer
Personal service	Barber and hairstylist, cosmetologist, massage therapist, bridal consultant
Public service	Teacher, member of the armed services, firefighter, paralegal aide
Transportation	Airline reservations agent, airline pilot, railroad conductor, automotive mechanic

Copyright © Glencoe/McGraw-Hill

Solution Transparencies

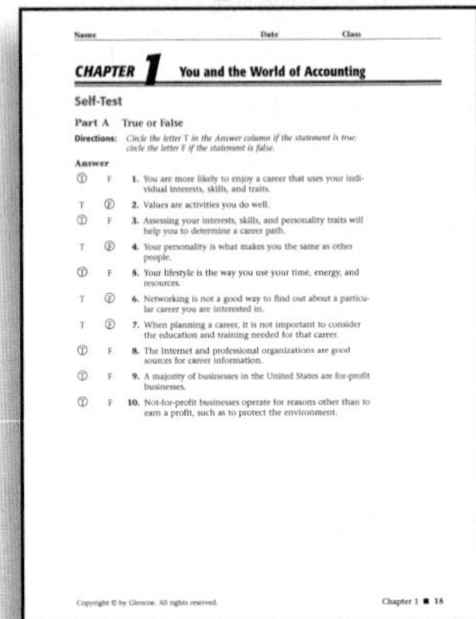

CHAPTER 1 You and the World of Accounting

Self-Test

Part A True or False

Copyright © by Glencoe. All rights reserved. Chapter 1 ■ 15

Lesson Plans

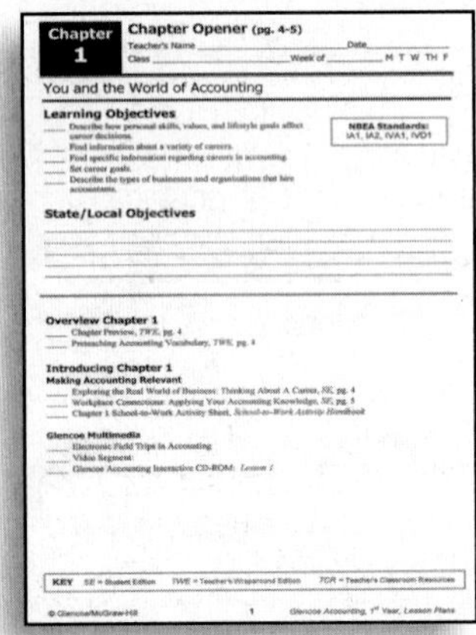

Chapter 1 Chapter Opener (pg. 4-5)

You and the World of Accounting

Learning Objectives

State/Local Objectives

Overview Chapter 1

Introducing Chapter 1

Glencoe Multimedia

© Glencoe/McGraw-Hill 1 Glencoe Accounting, 1st Year, Lesson Plans

Block Scheduling

Block scheduling differs from traditional class scheduling in the amount of time allotted to each period. The booklet explains what block scheduling is, when and how it can be implemented, and what particular benefits it provides. It also provides detailed guidelines for using the text effectively in longer class periods.

Enrichment and Application

Strategies for Teaching Ethics in Accounting

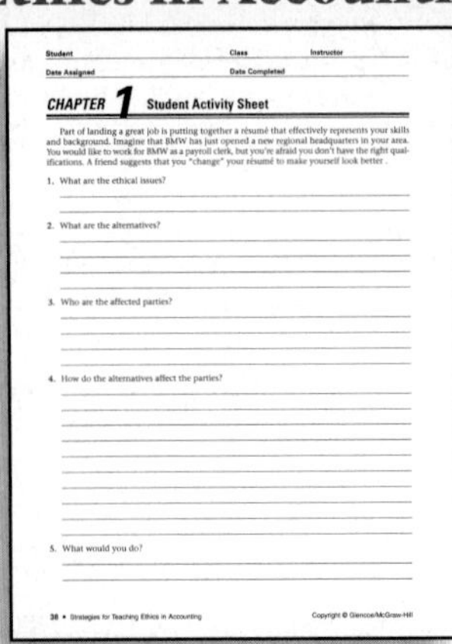

CHAPTER 1 Student Activity Sheet

1. What are the ethical issues?
2. What are the alternatives?
3. Who are the affected parties?
4. How do the alternatives affect the parties?
5. What would you do?

Strategies for Teaching International Accounting

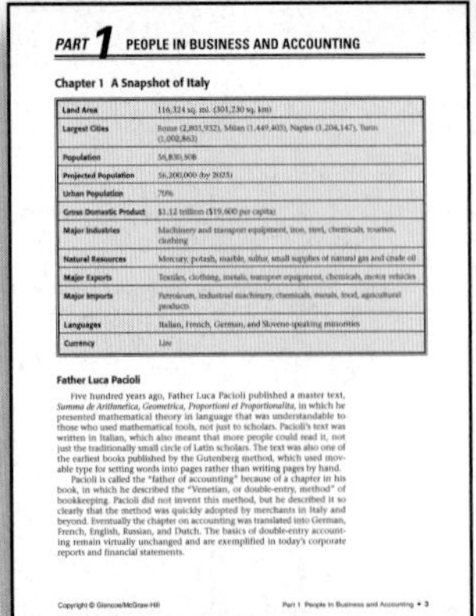

PART 1 PEOPLE IN BUSINESS AND ACCOUNTING

Chapter 1 A Snapshot of Italy

Father Luca Pacioli

School-to-Work Handbook

CHAPTER 1 SCHOOL-TO-WORK ACTIVITY

You and the World of Accounting

Meeting Different Ability Levels

Chapter Reviews and Working Papers (CRWP)

Working Papers

Review

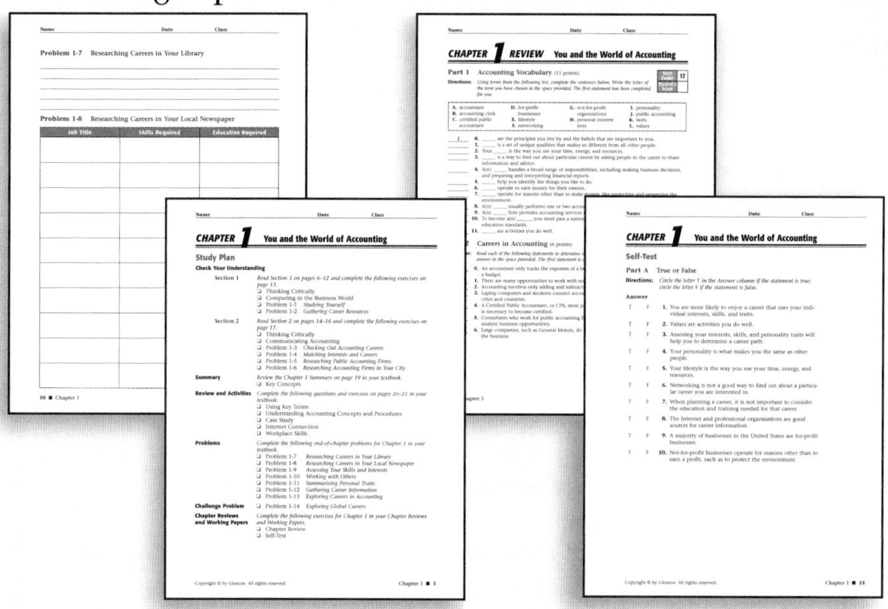

Student Study Plan

Self-Test

Real-World Multimedia CD-ROM

Key to Ability Levels

Each section gives skill-building activities. Each activity has been labeled for use with students of various learning styles and abilities.

L1 Level 1 activities are basic activities and should be within the range of all students.

L2 Level 2 activities are average activities and should be within the range of average and above average students.

L3 Level 3 activities are challenging activities designed for the ability range of above average students.

ELL ELL activities should be within the ability range of English Language Learners.

Teaching Resources at a Glance

Application Resources

- Glencoe Chapter Review and Working Papers, SE and TAE
- School-to-Work Handbook, SE and TM
- Accounting Portfolio, SE and TM

Reproducible Masters

- Demonstration Problems
- Lesson Plans
- Block Scheduling
- Spanish Language Resources

Glencoe Accounting Professional Development Series

- Strategies for Teaching Ethics in Accounting
- Accounting Competitive Event Review
- Math Review for Accounting
- Strategies for Teaching International Accounting
- Internet Resources and Activities Handbook

Transparency Package

- Section Focus Transparencies
- Teaching Transparencies
- Source Document Transparencies
- Solution Transparencies

Performance Assessment

- **Exam***View* CD-ROM
- Chapter Tests
- Chapter Quizzes
- Unit Tests
- Audit Tests
- Printed Testbank

Multimedia Resources

- Electronic Learning Center:
  - Multimedia CD-ROMs
  - Peachtree® software, tutorials, templates, and solutions
  - Spreadsheet templates
- Using QuickBooks® with Glencoe Accounting
- Interactive Lesson Planner
- Electronic Field Trips in Accounting
- PowerPoint® Presentation
- Web site: glencoeaccounting.glencoe.com

Assessment and Evaluation

Chapter Tests

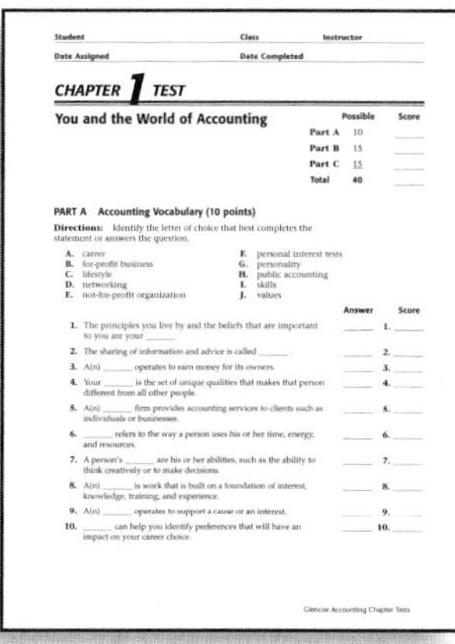

Chapter Quiz

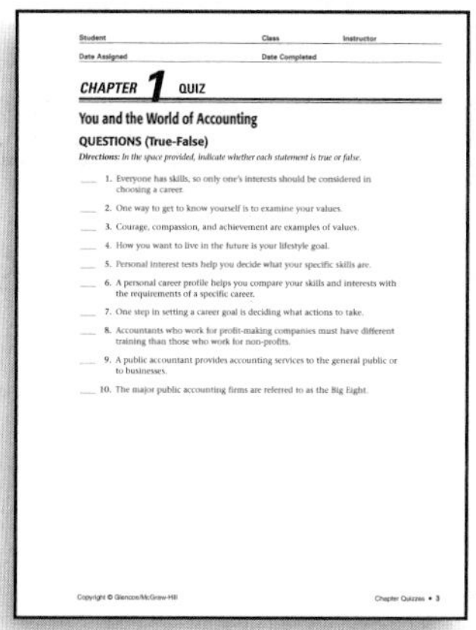

OVERVIEW CHAPTER 1

Correlations to National Standards for Business Education

(See pages T50–T51 for a detailed correlation chart.)

Standards: IA1, IA2, IVA1, IVD1

Chapter Preview

In this chapter students learn how to look at themselves for clues to future careers they might enjoy. Students are encouraged to do a personal inventory to identify personal skills and interests. They also learn how to research different careers and then match those careers to their personal values and lifestyle goals.

Students learn about the diversityof accounting career opportunities, as well as the types of businesses and organizations that hire accountants.

Section Overviews

- Section 1—*Exploring Careers*
- Section 2—*Accounting Careers: The Possibilities Are Endless!*

Chapter Vocabulary

skills
values
lifestyle
personality
personal interest tests
networking
accountant
for-profit business
not-for-profit organization
accounting clerk
certified public accountant
public accounting

Preteaching Accounting Vocabulary

Oral Exercise: Write each of the above vocabulary terms on the chalkboard. Ask for volunteers to explain each term and give an example. Ask students how they can use knowledge of these terms to help them start their career planning. L1

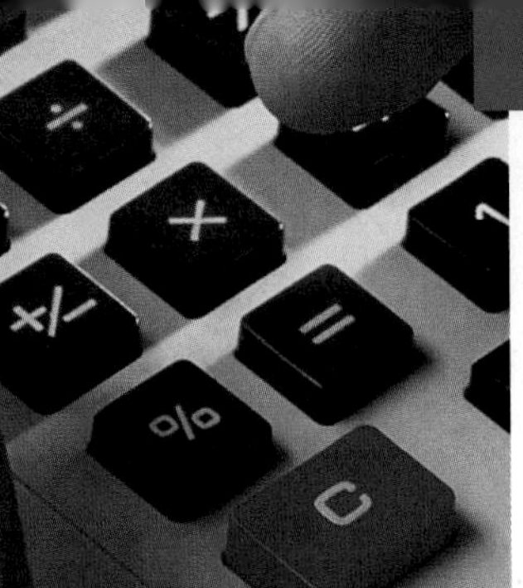

CHAPTER 1

You and the World of Accounting

Learning Objectives

When you have completed this chapter, you will be able to:

- Describe how personal skills, values, and lifestyle goals affect career decisions.
- Find information about a variety of careers.
- Identify career opportunities in the accounting field.
- Set career goals.
- Describe the types of businesses and organizations that hire accountants.
- Compare for-profit businesses and non-profit organizations.
- Define the accounting terms introduced in this chapter.

Exploring the Real World of Business

THINKING ABOUT A CAREER

Do you know what tigers, black rhinos, and giant pandas have in common? All three have uncertain futures because their numbers are dwindling. Poachers and land development threaten their survival.

The **World Wildlife Fund,** a nonprofit organization, works to save endangered species. Not so long ago, the bald eagle–the national symbol of the United States–was on the endangered species list. Today, thanks to the **WWF** and other conservationists, the bald eagle is once again thriving and has been removed from the endangered list. The **WWF** raises and spends millions of dollars each year on its efforts to protect animals and their habitats.

The **World Wildlife Fund** employs accountants, writers, fund-raisers, and many other professionals who care about wildlife and their habitats.

What do you think?

1. What job skills or interests do you think you would need to work for an organization like the **World Wildlife Fund?**
2. What kinds of interests do you think would attract someone to such an organization?

World Wildlife Fund

Exploring the Real World of Business

The World Wildlife Fund

The WWF is part of an international network of organizations with representatives in more than 50 countries. Their largest single source of operating funds is donations by individuals, followed by those from foundations and corporations.

What do you think? (Answers)

1. Interests might include taking care of animals or studying animal habitats. Skills might include math or an aptitude for plant and animal science.
2. Love of animals, desire to help prevent the loss of endangered species, a belief that the organization does valuable work.

Workplace Connections

Applying Your Accounting Knowledge

It's tough to figure out what you want to do with the rest of your life! Career counselors say that most people will have six to seven different careers throughout their lives. Some of us change careers entirely—from architect to teacher, or from freelance writer to photographer. Others stay within the same industry, but change specialties—from book designer to Web site designer, or from pediatrician to emergency care physician.

Investigate:

1. What type job do you have now or have you had in the past? Is it in a field you might continue to work in?
2. Imagine yourself in five years. What type of job do you have? Where are you living? What skills are you using?
3. Look at other people—your parents, other relatives, friends, coworkers, and people in the news. Do any of them have a career that you might enjoy? What skills would you need for this career?

5

Glencoe Accounting *Online*

Visit the *Glencoe Accounting* Web site at **glencoeaccounting.glencoe.com** for additional activities and information.

GLENCOE MULTIMEDIA

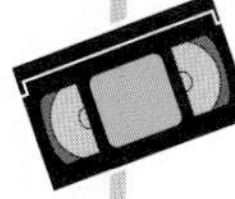

Electronic Field Trips in Accounting *Video Segment: The Real World of Accounting*
After viewing this video, students will be able to discuss a variety of businesses where people with accounting education may work.

Glencoe Accounting: Electronic Learning Center *Chapter 1*
The CD-ROM program is ideal for visual learners since it incorporates video images, animation, and graphics to enliven the content of each lesson.

INTRODUCING
CHAPTER 1

Making Accounting Relevant

Workplace Connections: Applying Your Accounting Knowledge

Discussion: Discuss the importance of planning when making career decisions. Point out that leaving a career to chance may mean a less enjoyable lifestyle and work satisfaction.

Investigate (Answers)

1. Answers will vary but might include a retail clerk, a fast-food cook, a tutor, or a cashier. Lead a classroom discussion based on students' answers and encourage students to share their career interests.
2. If students have difficulty, have students put themselves in the position of their older friends, siblings, or family members to help visualize what they might be doing in five years. Some skills might include technology, communications, human relations, reading, writing, and math.
3. Students' career choices will vary. Encourage them to explore a variety of career options.

School-to-Work Activity

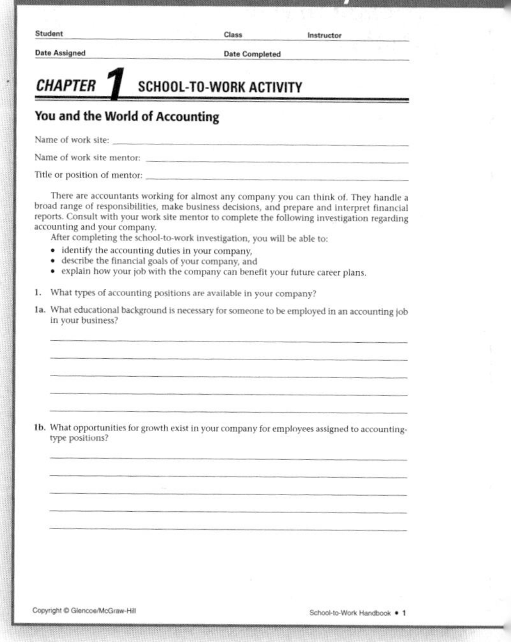

Student ______ Class ______ Instructor ______

Date Assigned ______ Date Completed ______

CHAPTER **1** SCHOOL-TO-WORK ACTIVITY

You and the World of Accounting

Name of work site: ______

Name of work site mentor: ______

Title or position of mentor: ______

There are accountants working for almost any company you can think of. They handle a broad range of responsibilities, make business decisions, and prepare and interpret financial reports. Consult with your work site mentor to complete the following investigation regarding accounting and your company.

After completing the school-to-work investigation, you will be able to:

- identify the accounting duties in your company,
- describe the financial goals of your company, and
- explain how your job with the company can benefit your future career plans.

1. What types of accounting positions are available in your company?

1a. What educational background is necessary for someone to be employed in an accounting job in your business?

1b. What opportunities for growth exist in your company for employees assigned to accounting-type positions?

 School-to-Work Handbook • 1

1 FOCUS

Introducing the Section

In this section students learn about the challenge of choosing a career even though they may not know what they really want to do. Examples of real-life work scenarios help students start thinking about careers they might enjoy. Students learn how to analyze their personal interests and skills and use those in researching potential careers. They also learn the importance of visualizing how and where they want to live and how to plan and set goals to achieve the careers they want.

Section Concepts

- How personal interests and skills, values, and lifestyle goals affect career decisions.
- Where to find information on possible careers.
- How to set career goals.

Visual Learning

Section 1 Focus

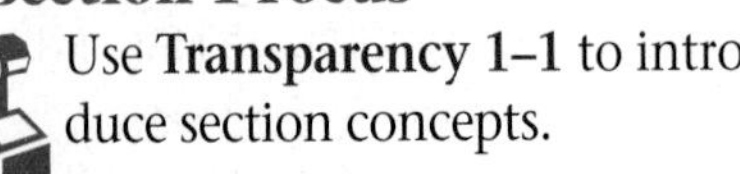

Use **Transparency 1–1** to introduce section concepts.

BELL RINGER

Writing: Have students write a list of five different careers they think they might want to pursue or learn more about. Tell students to choose any career of interest, not just those involving accounting. Have students save their lists for use in the Section Wrap-Up at the end of this section on page 13. L1

SECTION 1

Exploring Careers

***What* You'll Learn**

- How personal interests and skills, values, and lifestyle goals affect career decisions.
- Where to find information on possible careers.
- How to set career goals.

***Why* It's Important**

A successful career begins with identifying your interests and skills and putting them to work for you. As consumers, we buy goods from merchandising businesses daily. Understanding the nature of these transactions is key to accounting for a merchandising business.

KEY TERMS

skills
values
lifestyle
personality
personal interest tests
networking

Film producer? Animation engineer? Web site designer? History teacher? Pediatrician? Financial analyst? Environmental conservation consultant? Who me?

Choosing a Career

Let's face it: Not many of us know what we want to do with the rest of our lives, especially when we're still in high school. You may be thinking, "I'll just take some liberal arts courses in college and something will come up" or "I'll just work for a while to make some money and then fall into a career." You know what? Something may come up, and you may just fall into a career; but if you ask people who really love what they do, odds are that they took some time to really get to know themselves and what turned them on.

Danielle and Steve have been friends since their freshman year. Like most students, they've been too wrapped up with classes, homework, and activities to give thought to what their lives will be like after high school. This all changed at the start of their final year. Steve sees his senior year as the end of a long haul, but Danielle sees it as the beginning of a whole new life.

Closing his locker door with his elbow, Steve turns to see Danielle smiling at him.

"Hey Dani! How's it going?"

"Great," says Danielle, holding up her class schedule. "They say the last year in high school is always the best."

"What are you taking?"

"Let's see. I've got chemistry, literature, algebra, speech, and accounting."

"Ouch, tough schedule! Did you say accounting? I would've never guessed you to be a number cruncher."

"I don't think I want to just 'crunch numbers.' I've always aced math, so I figured if I take accounting now, I'll know if I really like it enough to study it as a career. Besides, there are tons of ads in the paper for accounting jobs. If you're good at it, you can write your own ticket. Think about it: Companies need

RESOURCE MANAGER

Reproducible Masters

- Lesson Plans
- Chapter Reviews and Working Papers (CRWP) TAE

Transparencies

- Section Focus Transparency
- Teaching Transparencies
- Solution Transparencies

Multimedia

- **Exam***View* CD-ROM
- Electronic Learning Center CD-ROM
- Interactive Lesson Planner CD-ROM
- Electronic Field Trips in Accounting

employees who know how to run their businesses. Plus it's not just sitting at a desk crunching numbers. My aunt is a financial advisor. She loves her job and travels all over the world."

"Slow down, Dani, it's only your senior year in high school. Don't you think it's a bit too soon to be playing career woman?"

"The sooner the better, Steve!"

"Maybe you're onto something here."

Unlike a job, which is simply work for pay, a career is built on a foundation of interest, knowledge, training, and experience. Have you given any thought to what you may want your career to be? If your answer is no, you're not alone.

Did You Know?

Donations
The World Wildlife Fund operates mostly on donations from people, charitable foundations, government, and corporations. The largest portion of the Fund's revenue, about 28 percent, comes from individuals.

Assess Your Career Vision

Before choosing a career, you'll want to do a little soul-searching. The more you know about yourself, the easier it will be to make career choices.

- What are your personal interests and skills?
- What are your values, and how will they affect your career?
- What lifestyle interests you?
- How will your personality affect a career choice?

Too many questions? You have all the answers; you just don't know it yet!

Your Interests, Skills, and Traits

You're more likely to enjoy a career that uses your individual interests, **skills**, and traits. Skills are activities that you do well. Take John King, for example. When John was a kid, he built an elaborate fort in his backyard. As a teenager John studied the architecture of major metropolitan cities. When he got out of high school, he was offered a job at a graphics company making calendars. The pay was good, but John lost interest and decided to go back to school to study his true passion, architecture. Today John is a partner in a successful architecture firm in Los Angeles, and he loves his job.

Are you good at math? Do you write well? Are you creative? Do you like to meet lots of new people, or like John, do you enjoy building things? Everyone has different skills and abilities—it's the combination that gives you a unique selling point. Here are some skills that employers have identified as being valuable. Although these skills are useful in a variety of situations, the chart on the next page provides examples of careers that require these skills and traits.

How many of these traits do you have? Make a list. It will come in handy when you begin to consider careers that interest you.

Values

One way to get to know yourself better is to examine your values. **Values** are the principles you live by and the beliefs that are important to you. It sounds good on paper, but values are really about actions, not words.

Great Ideas *From the Classroom of...*

Accounting Games Create bingo sheets with vocabulary terms and concepts and play "Accounting Bingo." Read the definitions and have students check off the correct terms. Award bonus points or treats for prizes. Accounting Jeopardy® or Accounting Password are also fun games to review various concepts and vocabulary.

Claudia Cullari
Fair Lawn High School
Fair Lawn, New Jersey

CHAPTER 1
SECTION 1, PAGES 6–13

2 TEACH

GUIDED PRACTICE

Reading Career Information

- Have students scan this section, looking at the headings and the illustrations. You may also have students outline the section to help them gain an overview of the content. L1
- Have students bring to class magazines and newspapers written in their first language. Have them search these resources for career ideas. ELL

Concept Development: Choosing a Career

Discussion: Take a poll and ask how many students have decided what they want their careers to be. Most will likely be undecided. Ask those who have made a career decision how they reached their decision. What factors influenced their choices? L1

Concept Development: Assess Your Career Vision

Discussion: Lead students in a discussion of how personal introspection can help them identify the following:
- personal interests, skills, and traits,
- values and how they affect career choices,
- lifestyle wants and needs, and
- the effect of personality on career choices.

Emphasize that employers hire people with the skills they need, so students will need to find employers—and careers—that value their skills. Discuss with students the types of skills they may have and those they may need to acquire to be employable. L1

CHAPTER 1
SECTION 1, PAGES 6–13

2 TEACH (Cont'd.)

Visual Learning

Skills & Traits

Use **Transparency 1–2** to discuss each of the skills and traits listed on the chart. Then have students identify their own skills and traits. Discuss the career examples given for each category of skills and traits. Have students think of other, similar careers for a person in each group of skills and traits.

Concept Development: Values

Discussion: Discuss each of the values listed here and on the next page; share examples from your own experiences. Ask students what other values people might have (for example, honesty and integrity, friendship, family, physical fitness, and so on). L1

Application: Have students make a list of their own values for use in evaluating potential careers. L1

Critical Thinking: Have students write a list of five interests or skills they would like to pursue in a future career. For each interest or skill, have them identify a possible career. L2

Teaching Tip

Bring to class several magazines that show people in a variety of lifestyles. Have students go through the magazines and identify lifestyles that appeal to them. Discuss how having a lifestyle goal can help guide the choice of a career.

Key Points

Determining a Career Path

Assessing your interests, skills, and personality traits will help you determine a career path.

SKILLS & TRAITS	CAREER EXAMPLE
Creative thinking	Fine arts and humanities careers, such as actor, artist, or musician
Knowing how to learn	Training or teaching careers, such as business consultant or training coordinator
Responsibility	Health-related careers, such as surgeon, dental hygienist, or home health aide
Friendliness	Hospitality and recreation careers, including cruise director, hotel manager, or park ranger
Honesty	Child care workers, veterinarians, and other family and consumer science workers
Decision making	Financial planners, accountants, and other business and office careers
Analytical	Construction careers, including surveyors, general contractors, or electricians
Adaptability	Any of the public service careers, such as teaching, fire fighting, or serving in the armed forces
Self-control	Entrepreneur or manager
Self-esteem	Communications and media occupations, such as computer artist or book editor

For example, if you like to spend your free time volunteering at a local hospital or community center, one of your values might be helping others.

What you value and believe may change as you get older. Most people, though, have a basic set of values that they follow throughout their life. As you read this section, think about your personal beliefs. Remember, values are actions, not aspirations. Which values are important to you? Can you think of careers that would benefit from these values?

Responsibility. Being responsible means being dependable and taking positive actions, such as showing up on time to take a friend to an appointment or honoring a commitment. If you value responsibility, you might think about a career as a supervisor or manager.

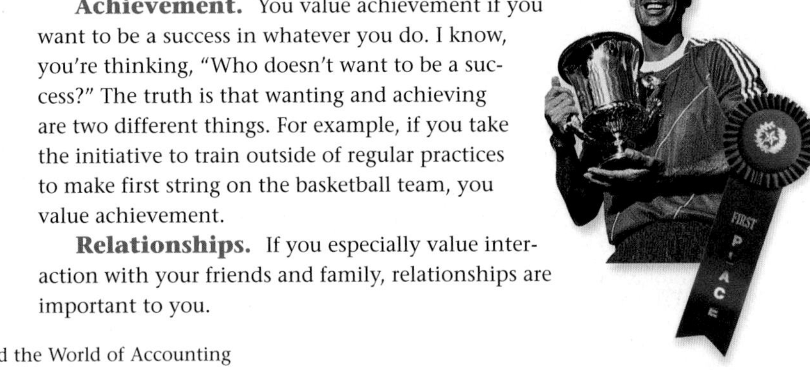

Achievement. You value achievement if you want to be a success in whatever you do. I know, you're thinking, "Who doesn't want to be a success?" The truth is that wanting and achieving are two different things. For example, if you take the initiative to train outside of regular practices to make first string on the basketball team, you value achievement.

Relationships. If you especially value interaction with your friends and family, relationships are important to you.

COOPERATIVE LEARNING ACTIVITY

Group Discussion In this activity, students are expected to follow oral instructions. Divide the class into groups of three to four students. Ask each group to create a list of ten jobs and to describe at least one personality trait that might be valuable in each job. (For example, an outgoing person would enjoy a sales job.) Also ask students to describe the skills and aptitudes that help a person be successful in that job. Have each group share its lists with the class, along with their reasons for matching personality traits, skills, and aptitudes to each job. Point out that choosing a career based on one's personal and unique characteristics is more likely to result in career success.

After all, sharing the joy of your accomplishments is half the fun. Those who value these types of connections might avoid occupations that require a lot of travel and might base their career decisions on the ability to live close to family and friends.

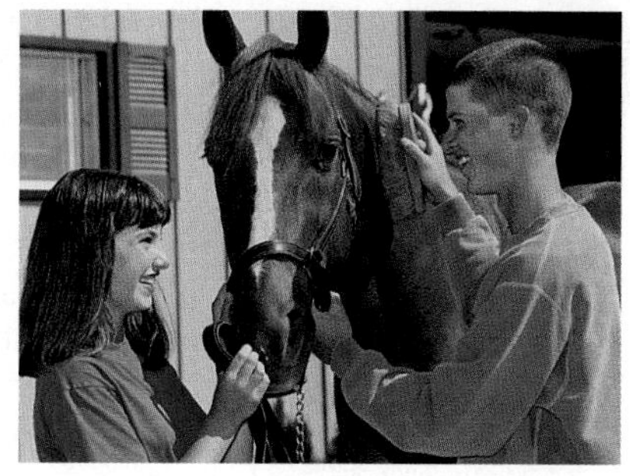

Compassion. Do you care deeply about people, animals, or special causes? For you, a compassionate career may outweigh all the money in the world. For example, if you love being around animals, you might enjoy a career in animal research or the marine sciences.

Courage. Courage is not just being brave in the face of physical danger. Courage is also the ability to overcome other fears. For example, it takes courage to make a speech to the whole school, even though you may be fearful or nervous. If you can put your beliefs on the line, you may be headed for a career in politics or law.

Recognition. If acknowledgement and appreciation of your work is important to you, then you value recognition. You might consider a career as a novelist or a television news reporter.

Many people share the same values, but how they apply them is unique to each person. To some, courage may be accepting the challenge of a job they know little about. To others, it may be turning down the big money to do something they really love. Think about your values. What can you learn from your values that will help you narrow your career choices?

CONNECT TO . . . GEOGRAPHY

Demographers study population density, distribution, and migration patterns. Using data from the census, records of vital statistics, and accounts of economic activity, demographers find out how different people react to certain events. For example, the rising cost of living has resulted in smaller families in America.

Lifestyle Goals

Your **lifestyle** is the way you use your time, energy, and resources. For example, many people devote themselves to work, earn lots of money, and put off the benefits of free time until they're older. Others accept smaller paychecks and work fewer hours in order to spend more time with family and friends now. If you want to work as a business manager or accountant for a professional sports team, you'll have to live in a city that has such a team, even if the weather's bad! Or, if you want to perform in a touring theater company, you'll have to get ready for life on the road.

- What's really important to you?
- Do you want to go for the big bucks?
- Do you want to live in a big city with endless activities or a small town where everyone knows your name?
- Do you want to collaborate with a group of people, or do you prefer working solo?

Make a list of how you'd like to spend your time, energy, and resources. These are your lifestyle goals. Try to focus on careers that closely match them.

Personality Traits

Try to imagine what it would be like if all your friends had the same personality. What if they were all shy or all serious? Even worse, what if they all had the same sense of humor? It's a good thing we each have our own **personality** —a set of unique qualities that makes us different from all other people.

What is your personality? Are you confident, dependable, funny, friendly, sympathetic? Be honest. Do you like being with people, or would you rather

INTERDISCIPLINARY CONNECTIONS ACTIVITY

Geography Tell students to imagine that they have an opportunity to open a business in a new community. Divide students into groups and have them study the geography, demographics, and economic conditions of a growing city of their choice. Ask each group to create a "city profile," including population numbers, economic trends, climate, and cost of living. Then have students select a business they think would be successful in this community. Does such a business currently exist? What would be the positive effects of opening a new business in this community? Are there any negative effects? Have each group present their city profile to the class.

2 TEACH (Cont'd.)

Concept Development: Lifestyle Goals and Personality Traits

Visualization: Have students think about a favorite television or movie character whose fictional lifestyle fits closely with their own lifestyle goals. Then discuss how they can set goals for career steps that will help them live the kind of life they envision. Also discuss the need to review goals periodically and to evaluate whether original goals are still applicable or need to be revised.

Discuss with students how personality affects career choices. For example, someone who is very competitive might choose to be a professional sports player such as a golfer. The same competitive spirit might also help another person become a successful salesperson. Ask students to think about their own personality traits and the types of careers in which those traits would help them be successful. L1

Teaching Tip

Bring real-world examples into your classroom by inviting local employers to talk about the jobs they offer and the skills they seek in their employees.

Try to form liaisons with Human Resources departments. Ask your contacts to be available when students need information. You might also set up a business advisory council that can serve as a resource for in-class presentations, interviews, and work-site observations.

Thinking Algebraically

Calculating: Have students learn about the formulas for calculating financial aid from an Internet site or from your school's guidance counselor. L2

CHAPTER 1
SECTION 1, PAGES 6–13

2 TEACH (Cont'd.)

Concept Development: Research the Possibilities

Researching: Have students use the Internet to research career information. If students do not have access to the Internet, provide students with books on careers to do their research. L2

Teaching Tip

Ask your school's guidance counselor to speak to your class on the types of career interest tests that are available.

Visual Learning

Figure1–1 Personal Career Profile Form

Use **Transparency 1–3** to discuss the personal career profile of Darla Johnson. Tell students that the more they know about themselves and how they might use their personal interests, skills, and traits in a career, the more likely they are to be successful in their chosen careers.

The U.S. Office of Education Job Clusters

Use **Transparency 1–4** to discuss the 15 job clusters based on similar job characteristics. Ask how many students are interested in each cluster. Tally responses and identify the most popular career cluster.

Application: Have students prepare a personal career profile. Have students evaluate whether they have a good match between themselves and the career they have chosen. L1

Strategies for Teaching International Accounting

To enrich study of International Accounting, refer to the additional critical thinking activities in the booklet.

International ACCOUNTING

Business Etiquette

In Japan, business cards are always offered with two hands. The receiver should accept the card with two hands, study it, and bow slightly before placing it into a shirt or jacket pocket. This shows respect for both the person and the company by placing the card near the heart.

spend your time with things, such as reading books or working with computers? You're probably wondering what in the world this has to do with accounting. Well, your personality affects your preferences for working with data, people, or things.

As you collect information about yourself, you'll want to complete a personal career profile such as the one shown in **Figure 1–1.** Use this profile to help you evaluate whether the careers you're considering match your skills, interests, values, and personality.

Research the Possibilities

Once you have a clear vision of yourself and how you want to live, the next step is to begin researching careers to find the one that's right for you. Here are some great places to start:

- Guidance counselors do a lot more than just show you the quickest way to get from your homeroom to the cafeteria. They can help you identify the things you like to do. One way they accomplish this is through testing, called **personal interest tests**, which help you identify your preferences.
- **Networking** is a way to find out about particular careers by asking people to share information and advice.

Figure 1–1 Personal Career Profile Form

PERSONAL CAREER PROFILE FORM

Name Darla Johnson	**Date** December 12	**Career** Marketing Manager, Music Industry

Your Values I believe in equal opportunities for all people. I like to be creative.	**Career Values** All kinds of people work in the music industry. As a marketing manager, I would be able to use my creativity, as well as work with other creative people.
Your Interests I have a large collection of jazz and blues CDs and keep up with up-and-coming artists that are featured on independent labels. I love getting together with friends and having parties.	**Career Duties and Responsibilities** As a marketing manager, I would make contacts with music stores and distributors, labels and artists. I might send out press releases, arrange for artist appearances, and map out company marketing strategies to increase profits.
Your Personality I'm very outgoing and get bored with sitting in class or reading. I have a great imagination and love group discussions.	**Personality Type Needed** A marketing manager must work well with people. Sharp communications skills and attention to details are important.
Skills and Aptitudes My best subject is history, and I'm president of my school's debate team. I'm not big on writing letters or grammar, but love to communicate in person.	**Skills and Aptitudes Required** Good verbal communication skills are essential for a marketing professional. Although history may not be particularly important, good perceptions of what works and what doesn't work might be important.
Education/Training Acceptable I'd be interested in learning more about getting a business degree, but also believe that if I could get in on the ground level in the music industry and learn the ropes, I could be successful as well.	**Education/Training Required** I suppose a degree in marketing might open a lot of doors for me. A knowledge of how marketing and accounting fits into the big picture of a music corporation would definitely help.

Teaching International ACCOUNTING

Role Playing Provide samples of business cards, and have students role-play exchanging the cards in a business interaction. First, have students exchange the business cards as they have seen it done in the United States. Then have students exchange the business cards as they would in Japan. Follow up the activity with a discussion about how the improper exchange of business cards could negatively affect a business relationship.

- Print materials on every career imaginable can be found in your public library. Try books on careers or magazines that focus on your interests like *House & Garden, Metropolitan Home,* or *Business Week.*
- The Internet is a great source of educational and career information. Check out ideas for putting together the perfect résumé or browse through job opportunities at Paramount Studios!
- Professional organizations are groups of people who have common career interests. In the accounting field, the American Institute of Certified Public Accountants (AICPA) and the Institute of Management Accountants might lead to interesting careers.

Set Career Goals

Once you have a clear vision of your interests and the types of careers you want to pursue, it's time to put a plan into action.

Map Out a Plan

For starters you'll need to make a list of the careers you've researched and compare possibilities. The easiest way to do this is by making a chart. List the careers you're interested in along the top and list your personal information along one side. Where they meet, X marks the spot.

After selecting the career choices that look the most promising, decide which one you'll pursue. Reaching your ultimate career goal is not going to happen overnight. There are many intermediate goals to achieve along the way. **Figure 1–2** provides some ideas on setting career goals.

Education

Most careers require some education or training beyond high school. Unfortunately, deciding to further your education and coming up with the cash to pay for it are two different things. For ideas on help in paying tuition, you can turn to many of the same places you turned to for career information: books, the Internet, and your friend, the guidance counselor.

On-the-Job Training

Imagine going to school, taking only your favorite subject, and getting paid for it! That's how on-the-job training works. Suppose you're thinking about eventually opening your own accounting firm. While in school, you might work as an office assistant at a local accounting firm to learn how accounting services are provided. It's a great way to find out if accounting is the career for you, and you'll be paid for your efforts.

Internships

Another way to obtain career experience is to work as an intern. Many companies offer summer internships to students. Others offer longer internships. Some offer modest pay. Successful interns are often offered positions in the company once their internships are completed. The key is to become so valuable that they miss you when you're gone!

Key Points

Career Resources
- Guidance counselors
- Friends and family
- Print materials
- The Internet
- Professional organizations

Math Hints

Financial Aid

To find out if you qualify for financial aid, check with organizations such as:
- The College Board, or
- The U.S. Department of Education.

You can check their Web sites for more information.

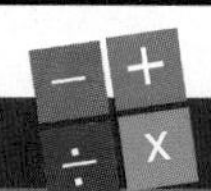

Math Skill Builder Activity

Calculating Financial Aid Help students conduct their own investigation for college financial aid by using the Internet. Have students do a keyword search on *college + financial aid.* Have students select a site that allows them to input financial information and helps them calculate the amount of aid for which they might qualify. Ask students to write a one-page summary on the Web sites they find most useful. Then have students share the list of Web sites with classmates.

2 TEACH (Cont'd.)

Concept Development: Set Career Goals

Discussion: Career advisors suggest that smart employees take charge of their own careers rather than relying on a company to guide their careers. Savvy employees decide the job they want and then identify the skills they need to get that job. To keep moving toward their career goals, they acquire new skills that employers want and need. With rapid changes in technology, most people will need to acquire new skills throughout their careers, either through formal education or on-the-job training.

Discuss with students how their careers may change over the next several years. For example, the first work they do after school (whether high school or college) is unlikely to be the work they stay with for an entire career. Also discuss the ways students can keep learning and gaining new skills that employers value. L1

Visual Learning

Ways That People Get Jobs

Use **Transparency 1–5** to discuss with students the ways people get jobs through various sources. Ask students to think of reasons why most people get jobs by networking and contacting employees directly.

Application: Have students make a list over a two- or three-day period of the people with whom they come in contact and their careers. Have students discuss how they can learn about careers from other people. L1

Math Review for Accounting

Photocopy appropriate *Activity Sheets* for students who need additional practice in basic math skills.

2 TEACH (Cont'd.)

Visual Learning

Figure 1–2 Setting Career Goals, p. 12

Use this illustration to help students learn how to set career goals and identify the steps they'll need to reach their goals.

Chronological Résumé and Skills Résumé

Use **Transparency 1–6** (Chronological Résumé) and **Transparency 1–7** (Skills Résumé) to discuss with students the advantages of both types of résumés.

Application: Have students choose a long-term career goal and write what they would do for each step in the process described in Figure 1–2. L1

Teaching Tip

Invite a career counselor to speak to your students about techniques they use to counsel people who are changing careers.

GO TO Strategies for Teaching Ethics in Accounting

Photocopy the Chapter 1 *Student Activity Sheet* for students. Answers are also provided in the booklet.

Visual Learning

The Effects of Unethical Behavior

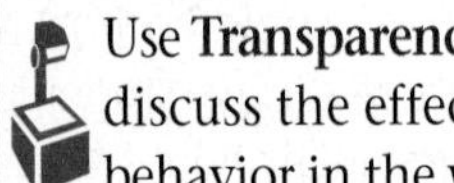

Use **Transparency 1–8** to further discuss the effects of unethical behavior in the workplace.

Observed Unethical Behavior

Use **Transparency 1–9** to show students the most common observations of unethical behavior in the workplace.

Setting Career Goals

STEP 1 Decide on a long-term goal. A couple of years ago, Donald Yang began a part-time job working for an entrepreneur who started a business providing temporary employees to local companies. Donald decided that he wanted to be an entrepreneur someday, too.

STEP 2 Decide on actions that will lead to the long-term goal. Knowing that he lacked business experience, Donald realized that he had several things to learn before he could start a business. Donald's first action was to choose a college that offers business degrees. He researched financial aid packages and grants.

STEP 3 Take action! Donald got financial aid, enrolled in college, and worked for his business degree. As he neared graduation, Donald decided he wanted to learn the sports management business. After graduation he took a job with the New York Yankees. His job helped him learn about the costs of running a sports team. He also developed negotiation skills as he helped negotiate licensing fees for baseball souvenirs.

STEP 4 Diversify your skills. After gaining experience with the Yankees, Donald moved to a new job working for the Chicago Bulls basketball team. Here he learned more about operational costs and added negotiation of player salaries to his skills.

STEP 5 Realize the long-term goal. Through his work Donald has made a lot of contacts in the sports field. He's now ready to put his long-term goal into action by starting his own sports management business, where he will be a financial consultant to sports teams.

Figure 1–2 Setting Career Goals

A MATTER OF ETHICS

Padding a Résumé

Part of landing a great job is putting together a résumé that effectively represents your skills and background. Imagine that BMW has just opened a new regional headquarters in your area. You would like to work for BMW as a payroll clerk, but you're afraid you don't have the right qualifications. A friend suggests that you "change" your résumé to make yourself look better.

Ethical Decision Making:

- What are the ethical issues?
- What are the alternatives?
- Who are the affected parties?
- How do the alternatives affect the parties?
- What would you do?

Teaching A MATTER OF ETHICS

Padding a Résumé After discussing this ethics case, point out that it is usually better to avoid stretching the truth about education or job qualifications. A résumé should present an accurate picture of a candidate, but it does not need to point out a person's weaknesses. Instead, it should highlight skills and knowledge that a potential employer would find valuable.

Check Your Understanding

Now that you have studied this section, complete the following questions and problems.

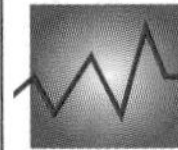

Thinking Critically

1. What consequences might result from choosing a career that conflicts with your values and lifestyle goals? Write one or two paragraphs describing these consequences.
2. Write three or four goals you can begin working toward now to help you choose a career. Include the steps you will need to take to reach each of your goals and the time within which you plan to accomplish each goal.

Computing in the Business World

Congratulations! The good news is that you've decided to attend a local community college after high school. The bad news is that tuition for an 18-week semester is $1,820. You estimate travel expenses of $20 per week and $300 for books and supplies. You plan to work 20 hours a week, earning $6.75 per hour. (I know it sounds weak, but hey, it's part-time!) Don't forget Uncle Sam. Social Security and income taxes will take about 15 percent of your earnings.

1. What is the total cost for a semester?
2. Assume that you've already saved $300 toward your first semester's costs. Approximately how long will it take to save enough to cover your tuition and books for one semester?

Problem 1–1 Studying Yourself

Instructions Think about the things you like to do and your particular skills. Make a list of at least five personal interests or skills, then use the career resource materials described in this section to identify one or more careers that match each interest or skill. Choose one career and write a one-page description of how your skills and interests fit this career.

Problem 1–2 Gathering Career Resources

Instructions Use the personal career profile form in **Figure 1–1** as a guide and compare three careers that you find interesting. Use the resources mentioned in this section to gather information: guidance counselors, networking, print materials, the Internet, and professional organizations. You may find other references in your school or local public library. After completing your comparison, write a brief summary; identify which of your choices you prefer and explain why.

RETEACHING SECTION 1

Networking To help students understand the concept of networking, ask students to list the names of all individuals they could contact to learn more about particular careers. Reinforce the idea that forming a good rapport with these individuals can help students form a network of contacts for now and the future. These contacts might be helpful in providing information, support, and advice as the student progresses in a career. (Students' responses may include family and personal friends, neighbors, family doctors, dentists, lawyers, or former employers.)

3 ASSESS

Productivity Skills
The student can practice productivity skills as they apply to accounting at the end of each section and chapter. In these activities the student is expected to follow written instructions.

Thinking Critically (Answers)

1. Answers might include a person who values spending time with the family but whose job requires frequent travel, or a person who loves the outdoors but works a desk job.
2. Answers might include improving grades, seeking an apprenticeship, applying to college, seeking financial aid, or writing a résumé.

Computing in the Business World (Answers)

1. $2,480.
2. 19 weeks, based on $2,180 ($2,480 – $300) / $114.75 (20 × $6.75 × .85).

Problem 1-1 (Answer)
Answers will vary. Students need to perform an honest analysis of their likes and dislikes. Refer students to the chart on page 8.

Problem 1-2 (Answer)
Answers will vary.

Chapter Reviews and Working Papers
Refer students to the Chapter 1 workbook pages to answer *Check Your Understanding* activities.

4 CLOSE

Section Wrap-Up
Writing: Have students use their lists from the Bell-Ringer activity. Tell students to use the information they learned in this section and write a plan for researching one of the careers. L1

1 FOCUS

Introducing the Section

In this section students learn about different types of accounting jobs and some of the businesses for which accountants work. Short profiles of people working in accounting help students identify the skills and interests that different people bring to accounting jobs. They also learn about the variety in work environments. The section shows the vital role that accountants play in all businesses, from private ones to public corporations to accounting firms.

Section Concepts

- The variety of career opportunities available to accountants.
- The types of businesses and organizations that hire accountants.

Visual Learning

Section 2 Focus

Use **Transparency 1–10** to introduce section concepts.

BELL RINGER

Comparison: Write the names of at least ten well-known local or regional businesses or organizations on the chalkboard. Use a variety of companies and organizations, from manufacturers to wholesalers to retail and service businesses to local not-for-profit groups. Ask students what all these organizations have in common. (They all employ accountants to record and analyze financial data.) L1

SECTION 2

Accounting Careers: The Possibilities Are Endless!

What You'll Learn

- The variety of career opportunities available to accountants.
- The types of businesses and organizations that hire accountants.

Why It's Important

Explore all the careers available in accounting! You wouldn't want to miss a great opportunity just because you didn't know it existed.

KEY TERMS

accountant
for-profit business
not-for-profit organization
accounting clerk
certified public accountant
public accounting

Some people believe accounting is boring. There, we said it. It's a pretty safe bet that you didn't enroll in an accounting course because you thought it would lead to a career in the spotlight. How often do you see Brad Pitt starring in an action thriller about a jet-setting accountant? Exactly. However, who do you think develops and approves the budget for his films to go into production? Who do you think advises Mr. Pitt how to invest the hefty salary he makes? You got it—someone just like you, who is good with accounting concepts and knows how to handle money.

The point is: Accounting can be a lot of things you would never have imagined. So, if an accounting career matches up with some of your interests and goals, hang in there. We promise there's a lot more to it than crunching numbers!

The Changing Horizon

Sure, some careers in accounting can be a little dry, but there are many more that are dynamic and exciting. Think of any business—Warner Music, Nike, the Hard Rock Cafe. They all look to accountants to help run their businesses. Think of your favorite celebrities—maybe Jim Carrey or Cameron Díaz. Most have financial advisors. Movie producers hire accountants to track production costs. Publishers of magazines, like *PC World* and *Sports Illustrated,* depend on accountants to work with national advertisers to keep things running smoothly. In this chapter, you will identify career opportunities in the accounting field.

Accounting is not just adding and subtracting. An **accountant** handles a broad range of responsibilities, makes business decisions, and prepares and interprets financial reports. These are skills that successful businesses can't do without. If you're good, the sky's the limit. So, if you still picture accountants huddled over pages of numbers in back offices, the following scenarios should set you straight.

On the Road

"Okay, everybody. Show time in five minutes." The announcement comes as the members of the band adjust guitar straps and prepare to go out on stage. A crowd of 30,000 fans, dropping thirty-five bucks a head, waits for their entrance. Drew Taylor jokes with the band just offstage and then watches as they head out to the fans' applause.

RESOURCE MANAGER

Reproducible Masters
- Lesson Plans
- Chapter Reviews and Working Papers (CRWP) TAE

Transparencies
- Section Focus Transparency
- Teaching Transparencies
- Solution Transparencies

Multimedia

- ExamView CD-ROM
- Electronic Learning Center CD-ROM
- Interactive Lesson Planner CD-ROM
- Electronic Field Trips in Accounting

Drew gets a rush being backstage amid all the excitement of a live show. As the financial assistant to the band's business manager, he often spends time at their performances. For Drew, working with numbers came as naturally as his love for music. He studied accounting throughout high school and college, and in his spare time he dabbled with the guitar and hung around recording studios with friends who were in the music business.

It wasn't long before they began to ask him for financial advice. His expertise landed him a position with one of the music industry's top business managers. Drew still dreams of recording his own music one day, but for now, he's quite content helping orchestrate the financial security of his music idols.

Accounting Professions in For-Profit Businesses. Entertainers perform to earn a profit. **For-profit businesses** operate to earn money for their owners. The majority of businesses in the United States are for-profit businesses.

Today, computers handle much of the basic accounting work, freeing accountants to do more planning for future operations. Computer technology means that accountants are no longer tied to a desk or an office. If you worked for artists like Moby, Radiohead, or Alicia Keys, you would probably spend part of your time traveling. Laptop computers and modems can connect you to your work as you travel to other cities and countries.

In order to explore accounting career opportunities, you need to compare the various forms of business organizations. Not all organizations are for-profit businesses.

For the Greater Good

"Listen up, folks! Here's the draft of the news release we're sending out tomorrow," shouts Darin Korman, waving a stack of papers in the air. "We need to get our position before the public while Congress is still considering the environmental legislation. Questions?"

"What else are we doing to alert voters to the potential value of this legislation?" a team member asks from the back of the room.

Darin, the team leader, opens a folder. "Here's our total plan. We begin filming a TV spot tomorrow. Next week, the art for our magazine ads will be finished, and they'll run in six different magazines. We'll also post a call-to-action on our Web site asking visitors for their support. We can all thank Maya for putting together a budget for the media campaign."

Accounting Professions in Not-For-Profit Organizations. Maya Cruz beams as her boss Darin describes a typical campaign put together for a group—like Sierra Club or Audubon Society—that works to protect and preserve the environment. Such groups operate as **not-for-profit organizations**, also known as *non-profit organizations*. When Maya was very young, her parents founded a similar group dedicated to cleaning up the waterways surrounding her hometown in New York. Maya helped her parents in the difficult task of soliciting donations within their community. As she grew older, Maya pursued the study of accounting with the sole purpose of continuing her involvement in environmental causes.

It is important to identify the various accounting functions involved with each form of business organization. Most not-for-profit organizations

ACCOUNTING *Flashbacks*

ARCHAIC RECORDKEEPING

The Inca Empire, which spanned the west coast of South America throughout the 11th–14th centuries, used knotted cords of different lengths and colors called *quipu* to keep accounting records.

EXTENDING THE CONTENT

Accounting Functions for a Non-Profit Organization Not-for-profit organizations use a fund accounting system. A fund is a set of accounts used to record the transactions for a particular activity or a particular part of the organization. In contrast to the account classifications used in this textbook, a not-for-profit organization might have several different funds. Ask students to name various types of funds that might be used in a not-for-profit organization. (Building fund, investment fund, scholarship fund, general fund.)

2 TEACH

GUIDED PRACTICE

Reading Accounting

- Have students analyze their reading skills. Are they good at reading and interpreting financial data? Do they have a good financial vocabulary? L1
- Suggest that students tape-record class discussions for later use in reviewing content and assignments. ELL

Concept Development: The Changing Horizon

Discussion: Ask students to describe what they think accountants do. List their responses on the chalkboard. Have students discuss whether their perceptions of accountants and what they do have changed as a result of reading the profiles in this section. L1

Concept Development: For-Profit Businesses and Not-for-Profit Organizations

Discussion: Ask students to name examples of several local businesses and organizations they think are either for-profit or not-for-profit. List the names of each group on the chalkboard. Then ask students to describe how the two groups might be alike and how they differ. (The major difference, of course, is the role of profit in the organization.) As prospective employees, have students list advantages and disadvantages of each form of business organization. L1

Chapter Reviews and Working Papers Refer students to the *Study Plan*, located at the beginning of Chapter 1 in the workbook.

2 TEACH (Cont'd.)

Concept Development: Accounting Professions in Public Accounting Firms

Discussion: Explore students' preconceptions about accountants by asking them to name several professions requiring accounting training. Some examples include careers in management, consulting, business ownership, or even teaching. L1

Application: If your school has an Internet connection, have students locate sites for the Big Four accounting firms. Have them find information about the types of services that each firm provides. Also, have them look at the employment opportunities described at each site. Ask students to make a list of the different types of jobs available. Then discuss the variety in class.

The Web site addresses are:

- Deloitte & Touche www.deloitte.com./us
- Ernst & Young www.ey.com
- KPMG www.kpmg.com
- PricewaterhouseCoopers www.pwcglobal.com

If your school is not connected to the Internet, bring in the employment ads from a local or regional newspaper. Have students look at the ads under the heading "Financial" or "Accounting." What are the different types of jobs employers are offering? L1

Teaching Tip

Invite one or more local accountants to to your class and have them describe the personal traits and skills they look for when interviewing potential employees. Have each student ask at least one question to investigate entry-level job requirements.

have the goal of balancing their income with expenses rather than earning a profit for owners or investors. Some not-for-profit organizations, like United Way or Boy Scouts of America, get their income from donations. Other organizations get income through tax dollars. Government agencies, such as your school or a federal agency, fall under this category.

There are thousands of opportunities in the not-for-profit arena. Like Maya, it may be just the place for you to combine your interest in accounting with a cause that you hold close to your heart.

In the Know

"Shelly, the manufacturer is on the line in Hong Kong, and the designers are standing by in Vermont. We're ready to start the videoconference."

"All right, I'm set. Good morning, everyone. Let's get right to the point. As The Gap's financial consultant, it is my responsibility to inform you that costs on the new fall line are coming in slightly over budget. The purpose of this meeting is to find a way to cut costs without sacrificing quality. As manufacturer, Mr. Chu, you must have some ideas why our costs are higher than budgeted and what we can do to get back in line."

Shelly Hale loves her job. In high school Shelly could be counted on for two things—a keen fashion sense and the ease with which she breezed through math and logic. However, like most students, she was lukewarm to the idea of a career in accounting. That is, until an internship became available in the accounting department of The Gap. Shelly took the internship as an **accounting clerk**, an entry level job usually performing one or two accounting tasks. She eventually landed a position that allowed her to combine her talents and interests. Shelly continued to work at The Gap while attending school at night to become a **certified public accountant**, or CPA. CPAs pass a national test and meet specified experience and education standards to become "certified" to practice accounting.

Accounting Professions in Public Accounting Firms. With experience like Shelly's, you too might work as a financial consultant for a large company like The Limited or Levi Strauss. Or, you might choose to work for a **public accounting** firm and provide accounting services to their clients. Public accounting firms can be small or large—from a local business specializing in personal tax returns to an international firm such as Ernst & Young, which provides a variety of services to businesses all around the globe.

> **Key Points**
>
> **Accountants in Demand**
>
> Every business must "account" for their financial activities.
>
> It's something successful businesses can't do without!

You might hear people refer to the "Big Four." These are the four major public accounting firms: PricewaterhouseCoopers, Deloitte & Touche, Ernst & Young, and KPMG. Accountants who work for these public accounting firms might work in tax planning or auditing. Auditing is the review of financial statements to confirm that they follow generally accepted accounting principles.

From entertainment to health care, conservation to entrepreneurship, the career possibilities in accounting are endless!

ADDRESSING MULTIPLE LEARNING STYLES

Visual/Spatial Learner Ask students to collect words, pictures from magazines, personal photos, and personal objects that illustrate the activities they enjoy doing. Encourage students to include a wide variety of things from as many activities as possible. Then have students create a collage, using the materials they've collected. Have them group items according to similar skills or interests. Then ask students to summarize each group in the collage. Does the activity involve primarily data, people, or things? The finished collage may reveal areas of interest students had not previously considered. Have the students write a paragraph regarding a possible career based on their interests.

Check Your Understanding

Now that you have studied this section, complete the following questions and problems.

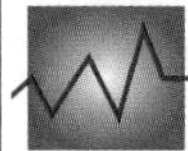

Thinking Critically

1. In business many decisions revolve around costs and potential earnings. For example, accountants might help create a picture, in numbers, of a proposed new product line; or they might be asked to suggest ways a company could cut its production costs. In addition to skill with numbers, what other skills do you think an accountant needs?
2. Make a list of five of your favorite products such as sports shoes, a favorite restaurant or food, or clothing. How do you think accountants who work for the companies that produce or sell these products might influence product decisions?

Communicating Accounting

Write a one-page article for a career newsletter. Describe the field of accounting and the types of businesses and organizations where accountants might work.

Problem 1–3 Checking Out Accounting Careers

Instructions Using the resources described in Section 1, research possible careers for people with accounting degrees. List at least five different careers and the formal training and work experience needed for each. Choose one career as your preference and write a paragraph describing why this career appeals to you.

Problem 1–4 Matching Interests and Careers

Instructions Using the three career examples described in this section, make a list of the personal interests and skills of the accountants described in each situation. Compare the list to your own interests and skills. Then think of three types of businesses (or actual companies) for which you might want to work. How would you learn about accounting career opportunities in those companies? Aside from pursuing needed training or education, what else would you do to prepare to work in that career? Share your ideas in class.

Problem 1–5 Researching Public Accounting Firms

Instructions Surf the World Wide Web or conduct research in your library to find information about the "Big Four" accounting firms. Create a table of information about each firm and the services the firm provides.

Problem 1–6 Interviewing Accountants

Instructions Interview members of the accounting field to investigate entry-level job requirements, career tracks for the profession, and projected trends for the future. Write a short report about your findings.

RETEACHING SECTION 2

Career Exploration Ask students to explore a variety of accounting positions. Have them identify each position and its work relationships by noting the data, people, and things involved with the position. For example, most jobs require working with other people. How much time does a person in that position spend working with other people? In contrast, some jobs require almost constant work with data or things. How much time is spent working with data or things? Have students examine each position closely and then list the aspects of each job that interest them.

3 ASSESS

Thinking Critically (Answers)

1. Answers might include computer, math, interpersonal, organization, and time management skills.
2. Answers will vary. Accountants compare costs with sales data to evaluate profitability and might suggest replacing unprofitable lines.

Communicating Accounting (Answer)

Answers will vary, but students should mention that both profit and non-profit businesses need accountants.

Problem 1–3 (Answer)

Answers will vary. Choices might be tax accountant, auditor, consultant, management accountant, or controller.

Problem 1–4 (Answer)

Answers will vary. Drew Taylor—interested in working with numbers and music; Maya Cruz—involved in environmental causes and studied accounting; Shelly Hale—interested in fashion, good with math and logic.

Problem 1–5 (Answer)

Answers will vary.

Problem 1–6 (Answer)

Answers will vary.

Chapter Reviews and Working Papers Refer students to the Chapter 1 workbook pages to answer *Check Your Understanding* activities.

4 CLOSE

Section Wrap-Up

Identify: Have students choose an area of accounting they might like. Ask them to describe the training they would need for this career. L1

CAREERS IN FOCUS
CHAPTER 1

SCANS in the Workforce

Foundation Skills Connection

Reading

Have students visit the local public library to investigate a career of interest. Have them research articles and create a list of information that will help them know more about the field. The list should include the education or training required, salary range, job skills needed, and availability of work in that career. Have students share their lists with the class. L1

Workplace Competencies Connection

Acquiring and Evaluating Information

Have students interview two people who work in career areas that interest them. Before the interview, have students compile a list of questions they would like to ask. After the interview, have them evaluate the information they've gathered and discuss their findings with the class. L2

Working with Cultural Diversity

Using the Internet, have students find articles on cultural diversity. Have them write a one-page summary of what they've learned. Then hold a classroom discussion on these questions: Did they learn anything new, and, if so, did it change their way of thinking? Is the local community experiencing a demographic change as a result of cultural diversity? How does that affect the workforce? L3

ACCOUNTING CAREERS IN FOCUS

JOYCE LUNDBOM
Senior Billing Manager
MCI

Q: What does your job entail?

A: I spend a lot of time answering revenue questions from other departments. I also answer my staff's questions and provide them with direction. I try to keep tabs on projects and keep them moving. I spend a lot of time problem-solving.

Q: What skills are most important to you?

A: Communication skills are critical. Analytical skills are also important. It's important to be able to see what has an impact on the profitability of a business. What appears to be small dollars could have a lot of significant numbers behind it. Knowing when to delve into something is a big part of the job.

Q: What do you like about your job?

A: I have a strong sense that my contribution to the company is relevant and that it is recognized. It is an exciting environment to work in. I like accounting because you take financial information and add meaning to it. You use your knowledge of the industry, the company, and the financial reports to understand trends. That's when you start contributing to the management of a company.

Tips from . . .
Robert Half International Inc.

Money is not all a company can offer. Some companies offer benefits such as advancement opportunities, stock options, tuition reimbursement, training, telecommuting, flex-time and child-care. Employees who feel valued work harder.

CAREER FACTS

Nature of the Work: Oversee billing of wholesale customers, answer management questions, oversee projects, and guide staff.
Training or Education Needed: A bachelor's degree in accounting or business, the CPA exam, auditing experience, and continuing education.
Aptitudes, Abilities, and Skills: Communication skills, analytical skills, problem-solving skills, organizational skills, and good judgment.
Salary Range: $40,000 to $60,000 depending on company size and industry.
Career Path: Start as a staff accountant and gradually take on more challenges, and then move into management.

Thinking Critically: What attributes can make a company exciting to work for?

ACCOUNTING CAREERS IN FOCUS

Thinking Critically (Answers)

Attributes that can make a company exciting to work for are innovative products, acquisition of other companies, participation in planning, different challenges, and opportunity for career growth.

ROBERT HALF CORNER

Benefits Many companies offer special benefits. Discuss with students these benefits: *flex-time* (flexible hours); *telecommuting* (working at home via computer); and *job sharing* (using two people to do the work for one position.)

KEY CONCEPTS

1. A successful career begins with insight into your own personal skills, interests, goals, and lifestyle preferences.
2. Personal skills and traits play major roles in how successful you may be in certain careers. Get to know yourself. What you value and believe plays a vital role in deciding what you want to pursue as a career.

3. As you decide on a career, consider lifestyle goals and personality traits.

4. Researching career possibilities can include sessions with a guidance counselor, networking with friends and family, magazines and books, the Internet, and seeking information from professional organizations. Do your homework. Research jobs, salaries, geographic locations, work environments, and growth potentials. You want to know what you are getting into, don't you?

5. To set and accomplish career goals, map out a plan, consider the education required, find a part-time job to get some on-the-job training, and check into internships available in your field of interest.
6. Accountants work for almost any company you can think of. Find a company you're interested in, and you can bet there's an accountant in the picture planning next year's budget, chasing down an expense report from the owner, or advising managers on financial issues.

Chapter 1 Quiz

Student ______ Class ______ Instructor ______
Date Assigned ______ Date Completed ______

CHAPTER 1 QUIZ

You and the World of Accounting

QUESTIONS (True-False)

Directions: In the space provided, indicate whether each statement is true or false.

___ 1. Everyone has skills, so only one's interests should be considered in choosing a career.
___ 2. One way to get to know yourself is to examine your values.
___ 3. Courage, compassion, and achievement are examples of values.
___ 4. How you want to live in the future is your lifestyle goal.
___ 5. Personal interest tests help you decide what your specific skills are.
___ 6. A personal career profile helps you compare your skills and interests with the requirements of a specific career.
___ 7. One step in setting a career goal is deciding what actions to take.
___ 8. Accountants who work for profit-making companies must have different training than those who work for non-profits.
___ 9. A public accountant provides accounting services to the general public or to businesses.
___ 10. The major public accounting firms are referred to as the Big Eight.

 Chapter Quizzes • 3

QUESTIONS (True-False)

1. Everyone has skills, so only one's interests should be considered in choosing a career.
2. One way to get to know yourself is to examine your values.
3. Courage, compassion, and achievement are examples of values.
4. How you want to live in the future is your lifestyle goal.
5. Personal interest tests help you decide what your specific skills are.
6. A personal career profile helps you compare your skills and interests with the requirements of a specific career.
7. One step in setting a career goal is deciding what actions to take.
8. Accountants who work for profit-making companies must have different training than those who work for non-profits.
9. A public accountant provides accounting services to the general public or to businesses.
10. The major public accounting firms are referred to as the Big Eight.

ANSWERS

1. False
2. True
3. True
4. True
5. False
6. True
7. True
8. False
9. True
10. False

REVIEW AND ACTIVITIES CHAPTER 1

USING KEY TERMS

See the *Glossary* for the definitions of these terms. Review students' questions in class. As students read their questions, verify that they've used the chapter terms appropriately.

Understanding Accounting Concepts and Procedures

(Answers)

1. Because you will be more likely to enjoy a career that appeals to your interests and utilizes your skills.
2. Careers may require travel, long hours, relocation, etc., that may or may not match lifestyle goals.
3. Responsibility, achievement, relationships, compassion, courage, and recognition.
4. You will be more content in your career if it matches your unique interests, skills, values, and personality traits.
5. Guidance counselors: Use tests to help identify preferences and find matching careers. Networking: Sharing information and advice with others. Print materials: Information about most any career, some with specific career advice. Internet: Information about potential careers and employers. Professional organizations: People with common career interests.
6. Networking gains information and contacts with people already working in a specific field.
7. Chart careers researched and personal interests, traits, values, and lifestyle goals. Where they meet, make a connection. When complete, chart will show a smaller group of potential careers.
8. The five steps are: Decide on a long-term goal, decide on actions that will lead to the long-term goal, take action, diversify your skills, and realize the long-term goal.

CHAPTER 1 REVIEW AND ACTIVITIES

USING KEY TERMS

Suppose you are preparing to interview a person who works in the accounting field. On a separate sheet of paper, write a list of questions you'll be asking in the interview. Incorporate each of the following terms in your questions:

accountant	lifestyle
accounting clerk	not-for-profit business
career	personal interest tests
certified public accountant	values
for-profit business	

Understanding Accounting Concepts and Procedures

Instructions

Answer the following questions on a separate sheet of paper:

1. Why should you consider your interests and skills when thinking about a career?
2. How does lifestyle affect career choices?
3. What are six common values that most people have?
4. Why should you consider your personality as you evaluate possible career choices?
5. List and describe at least three categories of career information resources.
6. Describe how networking is beneficial to career planning.
7. Describe how to create a personal career profile form.
8. Describe the five steps that are helpful when setting career goals.
9. List at least three types of organizations that offer accounting career opportunities.
10. What need would a not-for-profit organization have for an accounting professional?
11. Describe three ways that technology might be used by an accountant.
12. List three of the major public accounting firms.
13. List three possible functions that a Certified Public Accountant might provide for a business.

9. Examples are for-profits, not-for-profits, and public accounting firms.
10. Not-for-profit organizations have similar accounting needs to for-profit businesses. The only difference is that their goal is to match their income to their expenses, rather than to make a profit.
11. Examples are using the Internet for research, a spreadsheet to manipulate financial data, or a word processor to prepare a report.
12. Deloitte & Touche, Ernst & Young, KPMG, PricewaterhouseCoopers.
13. Public accounting firms provide services such as performing audits and preparing tax returns.

Case Study...

Career Advice

Sean Smith is a senior in high school. He's taking an accounting course this year because he wants to be an accountant. Sean likes working with numbers, but he also likes working with people. He plans to go to college but doesn't know which ones offer accounting programs and what costs are involved.

Thinking Critically:

Take the role of Sean's career counselor. Write a one-page report advising Sean. Include the following in your report:

- Information on how to find the resources he needs to choose a college.
- Details on how to set education and career goals.
- Define the steps Sean needs to take over the next several months.
- Prepare a list of resources Sean might use to learn more about accounting careers, colleges, and financial help.

*inter*NET CONNECTION

Finding Jobs on the Internet

Most large companies, and many smaller ones, can be found on the Internet. Along with product and service information, many companies post employment details and job openings.

Do This:

1. Find a company on the Internet that you might want to work for in the future. If you're not sure how to find a company on the Internet, ask your teacher for search engine sites like Yahoo, Excite, or Lycos.
2. What is the company's Web site address?
3. Does the company's site provide information about employment?
4. If employment information is provided, list the job opportunities you find.
5. Write a brief summary describing the company, its business purpose, and its products or services.

Workplace Skills

Acquiring and Evaluating Information

To make a decision, whether personal or business-related, you must be able to acquire and analyze data (information).

On the Job:

You've graduated and you're ready for that job that matches your skills and interests!

Thinking Critically:

1. Make a list of the businesses that advertise in one of your local or regional newspapers. You may want to use a Sunday issue since it's usually packed with ads.
2. Separate the businesses into for-profit and not-for-profit categories. For example, for-profit would include restaurants, retailers, entertainment providers (such as movie theaters or sports arenas), manufacturers, and so on. Not-for-profit may include schools, community organizations, and government agencies.
3. Write a summary of your findings, and describe the accounting career opportunities you think these businesses and organizations might offer.

Case Study...

Thinking Critically (Answers)

Answers will vary. Sean needs to consider many factors in choosing a college. First, he should develop a clear picture of what he is looking for. For a career in accounting, he will most likely need to start by obtaining a bachelor's degree. In selecting a college, he will require information concerning curriculum, accreditation, entrance requirements, tuition, and fees. He can start looking for financial aid immediately. Some possible resources for information include the Internet, phone book, professional organizations, and networking.

Workplace Skills

Thinking Critically (Answers)

Answers will vary. If your local newspaper has few employment ads, you may want to obtain issues of specialty papers such as the *National Employment Business Weekly* or *American Employment Weekly*.

Internet Resources and Activities Handbook

Refer students to the booklet for additional Internet activities.

*inter*NET CONNECTION www.glencoe.com

Do This (Answers)

Students should first identify a company they are interested in and would like to work for in the future. Using various search engines, demonstrate for students how to search for their specific companies on the Internet. Evaluate students' summaries for compiling a thorough summary of their selected companies, including information about the company, its business purpose, and its products or services.

PROBLEMS

CHAPTER 1

Problem 1-7 (Answer) Researching Careers in Your Library

Answers will vary. Students should use several different sources to research their career. Check to see that students' profiles include a description of the job, education or training requirements, potential earnings, and working conditions. Evaluate students' profiles for thorough research of available career information.

Problem 1-8 (Answer) Researching Careers in Your Local Newspaper

Answers will vary based on jobs listed in the local newspaper. Students should present summary information in a table format.

Problem 1-9 (Answer) Assessing Your Skills and Interests

Answers will vary. Refer students to the chart on page 8 for those having difficulty matching their skills and traits to careers examples.

Problem 1-10 (Answer) Working with Others

Answers will vary, but the list may include interpersonal, communication, analytical, and critical thinking skills. Students may have varying ideas on how to acquire these skills, and the steps they'll take to improve their skills.

CHAPTER 1 PROBLEMS

Problem 1–7 Researching Careers in Your Library

Instructions Using a reference book (such as the *Occupational Outlook Handbook*), choose a career area that interests you. Research the skills, education, and experience you would need to work in that area. Your research can utilize any number of resources including books, magazines, and the Internet. Write a brief profile of your chosen career, including a description of jobs in the field, education or training requirements, potential earnings, and working conditions. Present your profile to the class.

Problem 1–8 Researching Careers in Your Local Newspaper

Instructions Review the employment ads in a local or regional newspaper. Collect information on at least 10 job titles plus the skills and education required for each. Include at least two job titles related to the accounting field. Present your information in table format. If you have access to a word processing program, use it to create and print your table for your teacher.

Problem 1–9 Assessing Your Skills and Interests

Instructions Complete an assessment of your personal skills and interests by answering the questions in your working papers. Use the survey included in the working papers, or you can ask your guidance counselor to administer a personal interest test. Using the results of the test, find at least three careers that match your skills and interests.

Problem 1–10 Working with Others

Instructions As an accountant for a large business, you might be put in charge of training new hires in the accounting department. Or, you might be asked to discuss project cost overruns with a department manager or to present operating results to senior managers. In these situations, you need skills other than just your accounting knowledge. For each situation, make a list of the skills needed, then decide whether you have those skills and, if not, how you plan to acquire them.

ASSESSMENT RESOURCES

Choose assessment strategies from the following pages to evaluate your students' progress.

Student Edition

Check Your Understanding, pp. 13, 17

Chapter 1 Problems, pp. 22–23

Assessment and Evaluation Masters

Chapter 1 Study Plan, *Glencoe Workbook (CRWP)*

Chapter 1 Self-Test, *Glencoe Workbook (CRWP)*

Chapter 1 Test, *Chapter Tests* Booklet

Chapter 1 Activity, *School-to-Work Handbook*

Chapter 1 **Exam***View*

Teacher Wraparound Edition

Reteaching Sections 1–2, pp. 13, 17

Chapter 1 Quiz, p. 19

Problem 1–11 Summarizing Personal Traits

Instructions Sometimes you can learn about yourself by asking other people how they see you. Ask at least 10 people to name three words they think describe you. For example, someone might say you are dependable, fun, and quick-thinking. Do not just choose friends. Ask teachers, coworkers, relatives, and others who are willing to give you an honest opinion. Make a list of each person's descriptions; then summarize your findings by identifying the five characteristics or traits that were mentioned most often. Do these descriptions match your self-perception? Why or why not?

Problem 1–12 Gathering Career Information

Instructions Interview someone who currently works in a career area that interests you. Before the interview, prepare a list of the questions you want to ask. After the interview write two or three paragraphs describing your interview and the information you learned. Explain how this information will help you choose a career.

Problem 1–13 Exploring Careers in Accounting

Instructions Choose a local company that interests you, and find out who works as an accountant for the company. Call and ask whether you can observe the person at work for part of a day. Write a summary of your observations, and share the information with the class.

Problem 1–14 Exploring Global Careers

Instructions Many U.S. businesses operate in the global economy, which means they need accountants who understand international business. Find a local company that imports or exports products to or from one or more countries. Interview the accounting manager, and find out the skills, formal study, and personal traits they look for in an accountant who works in international accounting. Write a short report about your findings.

PROBLEMS
CHAPTER 1

Problem 1–11 (Answer) Summarizing Personal Traits
Answers will vary.

Problem 1–12 (Answer) Gathering Career Information
Answers will vary. Students should carefully prepare their list of questions beforehand. The report should first summarize the interview, then analyze how the information gained affects the student's attitude toward that career.

Problem 1–13 (Answer) Exploring Careers in Accounting
Answers will vary. Students should be able to get a clearer picture of the day-to-day activities involved in accounting. Evaluate students' summaries for correct usage of grammar and for including detailed observations.

Problem 1–14 (Answer) Exploring Global Careers
Answers will vary. Students should include a summary and an analysis of how the information affects them. Evaluate students' reports for clarity of ideas.

EXTENDING THE CONTENT

Interviewing Accounting Professionals Have students interview an individual who works in the field of accounting. To what extent does the individual work with people, data, and things? Did any of these factors affect the person's decision to accept the present job? Have students investigate career tracks for the profession in relation to people, data, and things. What steps does the interviewee suggest to investigate projected trends for the future? Ask students to present a brief summary of their findings to the class.

CHAPTER 2 Resource Manager

Section Resources

	Objectives & Standards	Activities & Features	Reproducible Masters
Chapter Opener *The World of Business and Accounting*	• Describe the role of profit, risk-taking, and the entrepreneur in the U.S. economy. • Describe the differences among service, merchandising, and manufacturing businesses. • Compare the sole proprietorship, partnership, and corporate forms of business. • List the advantages and disadvantages of each form of business organization. • Describe the purpose of accounting. • Explain the difference between financial and management accounting. • Describe the three basic assumptions that underlie accounting principles. • Define the accounting terms introduced in this chapter. **National Standards for Business Education**: IA1, IA2, IIA10, IVA1, IVC1, IVD1	Exploring the Real World of Business, p. 24 Workplace Connections, p. 25	School-to-Work Handbook
Section 1 *Exploring the World of Business*	• Profit and risk-taking. • The free enterprise system. • Starting and running your own business. • Three types of business operations. • Three forms of business organizations.	Accounting Flashbacks, p. 28 Did You Know?, p. 29 Math Hints, p. 30	Math Review for Accounting
Section 2 *Accounting: The Universal Language of Business*	• How the accounting system works. • Who uses financial accounting reports. • Who uses management accounting reports. • How accounting is used to help make business decisions. • What assumptions provide the foundation for accounting systems.	International Accounting, p. 33 Connect To, p. 33 A Matter of Ethics, p. 34 Accounting Careers in Focus, p. 36	Strategies for Teaching International Accounting Strategies for Teaching Ethics in Accounting Internet Resources and Activities Handbook

KEY

Posters — Transparency — Software — Videocassette

Blackline Masters — CD-ROM — Portfolio

MULTIMEDIA RESOURCE

Peachtree	QuickBooks	Spreadsheets	Videos	CD-ROMs
None in this chapter.	None in this chapter.	None in this chapter.	***Video Segment: Entrepreneurship*** After viewing this video, students will be able to recognize that entrepreneurs form the backbone of the private enterprise economy. Discuss with students some of the requirements for entrepreneurial success, such as a business plan.	***Electronic Learning Center (ELC), Chapter 2*** This program is ideal for visual learners since it incorporates video images, animation, and graphics to enliven the content of each lesson. ***Interactive Lesson Planner (ILP), Chapter 2*** This CD-ROM combines the versatility of an electronic lesson planner with the convenience of teacher classroom resources.

SCANS Correlation Chart

FOUNDATION SKILLS

Basic Skills:	Reading	Writing	Math	Listening	Speaking	
Thinking Skills:	Creative Thinking	Decision Making	Problem Solving	Seeing Things in the Mind's Eye	Knowing How to Learn	Reasoning
Personal Qualities:	Responsibility	Self-Esteem	Sociability	Self-Management	Integrity/Honesty	

WORKPLACE COMPETENCIES

Resources:	Allocating Time	Allocating Money	Allocating Material and Facility Resources	Allocating Human Resources		
Information:	Acquiring and Evaluating Information	Organizing and Maintaining Information	Interpreting and Communicating Information	Using Computers to Process Information		
Interpersonal Skills:	Participating as a Member of a Team	Teaching Others	Serving Clients/ Customers	Exercising Leadership	Negotiating to Arrive at a Decision	Working with Cultural Diversity
Systems:	Understanding Systems	Monitoring and Correcting Performance	Improving and Designing Systems			
Technology:	Selecting Technology	Applying Technology to Task	Maintaining and Troubleshooting Technology			

*Highlighted blocks indicate areas covered in the chapter. Additional SCANS skills are also covered throughout the *Teacher Wraparound Edition.*

Assessment

Student Edition
- Check Your Understanding, pp. 31, 35
- Chapter 2 Problems, pp. 40–41

Assessment and Evaluation Masters
- Chapter 2 Study Plan, *Glencoe Workbook*
- Chapter 2 Self-Test, *Glencoe Workbook*
- Chapter 2 Test, *Chapter Tests* Booklet
- Chapter 2 Activity, *School-to-Work Handbook*
- Chapter 2 **Exam***View*

Teacher Wraparound Edition
- Critical Thinking, p. 28
- Reteaching Section 1, p. 31
- Reteaching Section 2, p. 35
- Chapter 2 Quiz, p. 37

Transparencies

	Teaching Transparencies	Solution Transparencies
Section 1:	2–1, 2–2, 2–3, 2–4	Problem 2-1
Section 2:	2–5, 2–6	Problems 2-2, 2-3
End of Chapter:		Problems 2-4, 2-5, 2-6, 2-7, 2-8

TEACHER CLASSROOM RESOURCES

This is a representation of key blackline masters available in the Teacher Classroom Resources.

Teaching Aids

Transparency Examples

Section Focus Transparencies

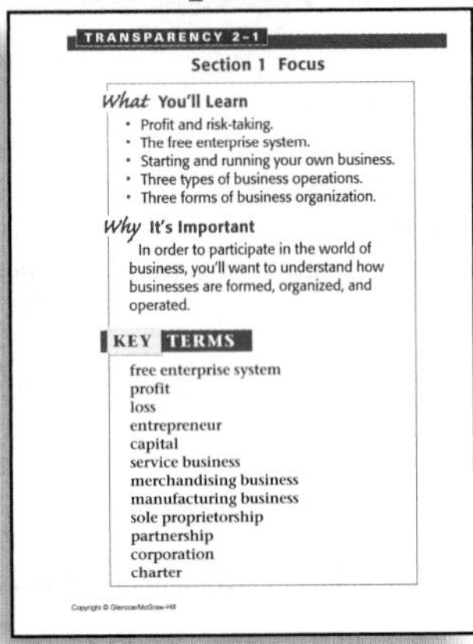

TRANSPARENCY 2-1

Section 1 Focus

What You'll Learn
- Profit and risk-taking.
- The free enterprise system.
- Starting and running your own business.
- Three types of business operations.
- Three forms of business organization.

Why It's Important

In order to participate in the world of business, you'll want to understand how businesses are formed, organized, and operated.

KEY TERMS

free enterprise system
profit
loss
entrepreneur
capital
service business
merchandising business
manufacturing business
sole proprietorship
partnership
corporation
charter

Copyright © Glencoe/McGraw-Hill

Teaching Transparencies

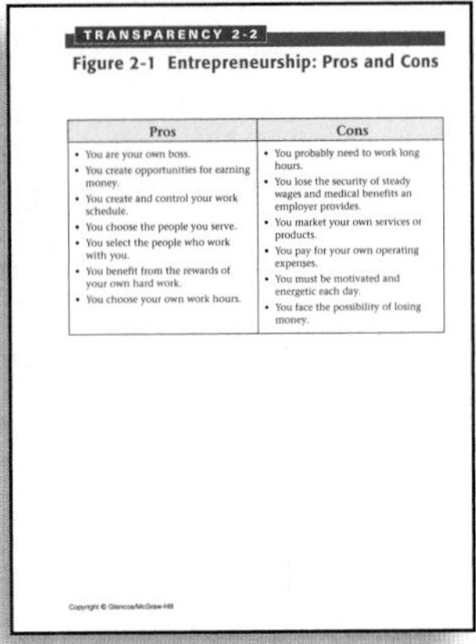

TRANSPARENCY 2-2

Figure 2-1 Entrepreneurship: Pros and Cons

Pros	Cons
• You are your own boss. • You create opportunities for earning money. • You create and control your work schedule. • You choose the people you serve. • You select the people who work with you. • You benefit from the rewards of your own hard work. • You choose your own work hours.	• You probably need to work long hours. • You lose the security of steady wages and medical benefits an employer provides. • You market your own services or products. • You pay for your own operating expenses. • You must be motivated and energetic each day. • You face the possibility of losing money.

Copyright © Glencoe/McGraw-Hill

Teaching Transparencies

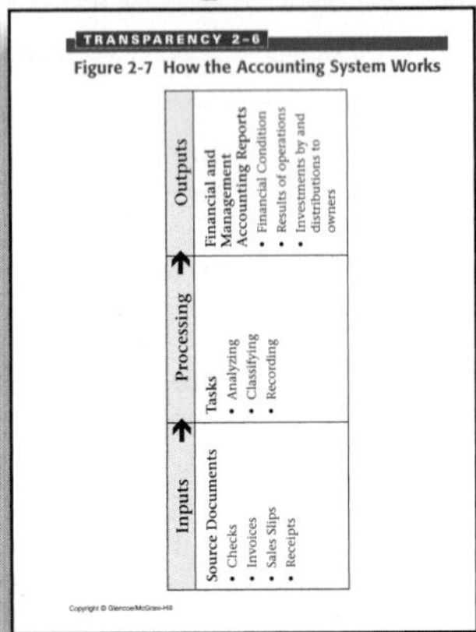

TRANSPARENCY 2-6

Figure 2-7 How the Accounting System Works

Inputs	→	Processing	→	Outputs
Source Documents • Checks • Invoices • Sales Slips • Receipts		Tasks • Analyzing • Classifying • Recording		Financial and Management Accounting Reports • Financial Condition • Results of operations • Investments by and distributions to owners

Copyright © Glencoe/McGraw-Hill

Solution Transparencies

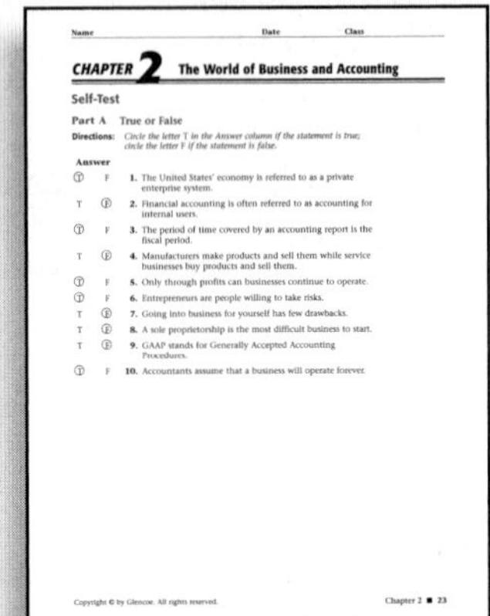

Name Date Class

CHAPTER 2 The World of Business and Accounting

Self-Test

Part A True or False

Directions: Circle the letter T in the Answer column if the statement is true; circle the letter F if the statement is false.

Answer
1. The United States' economy is referred to as a private enterprise system.
2. Financial accounting is often referred to as accounting for internal users.
3. The period of time covered by an accounting report is the fiscal period.
4. Manufacturers make products and sell them while service businesses buy products and sell them.
5. Only through profits can businesses continue to operate.
6. Entrepreneurs are people willing to take risks.
7. Going into business for yourself has few drawbacks.
8. A sole proprietorship is the most difficult business to start.
9. GAAP stands for Generally Accepted Accounting Procedures.
10. Accountants assume that a business will operate forever.

Copyright © by Glencoe. All rights reserved. Chapter 2 ■ 23

Lesson Plans

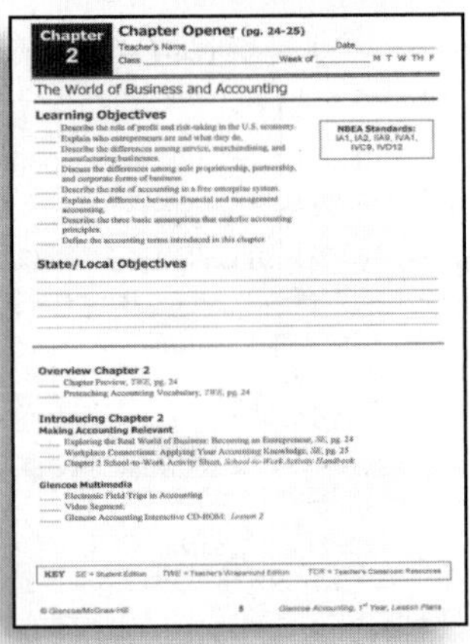

Chapter 2 Chapter Opener (pg. 24-25)

The World of Business and Accounting

Learning Objectives

State/Local Objectives

Overview Chapter 2

Introducing Chapter 2

Glencoe Multimedia

Block Scheduling

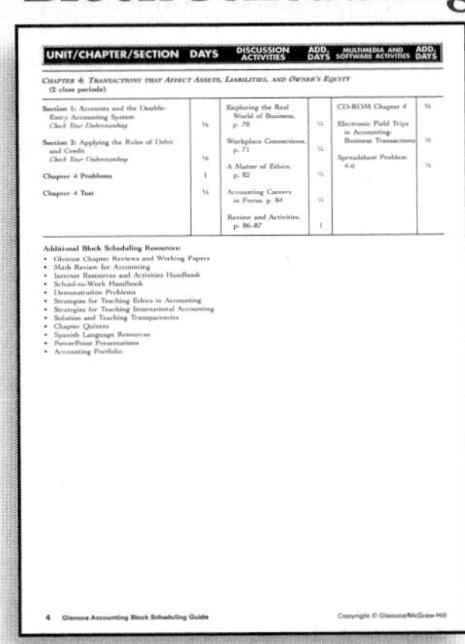

UNIT/CHAPTER/SECTION DAYS DISCUSSION ACTIVITIES ADD. DAYS MULTIMEDIA AND SOFTWARE ACTIVITIES ADD. DAYS

Additional Block Scheduling Resources

4 Glencoe Accounting Block Scheduling Guide Copyright © Glencoe/McGraw-Hill

Block Schedule

Block scheduling differs from traditional class scheduling in the amount of time allotted to each period. The booklet explains what block scheduling is, when and how it can be implemented, and what particular benefits it provides. It also provides detailed guidelines for using the text effectively in longer class periods.

Enrichment and Application

Strategies for Teaching Ethics in Accounting

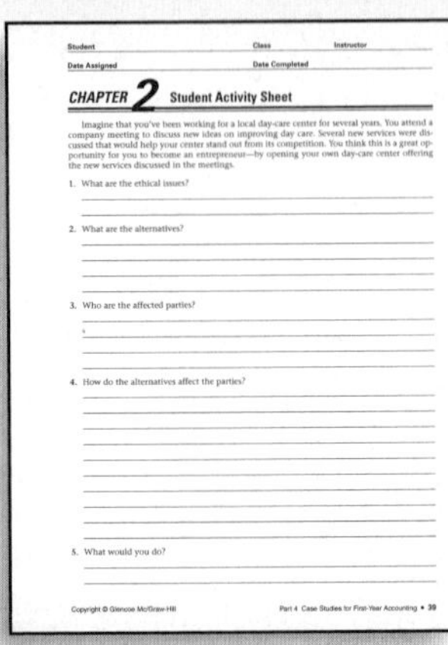

Student Class Instructor
Date Assigned Date Completed

CHAPTER 2 Student Activity Sheet

1. What are the ethical issues?
2. What are the alternatives?
3. Who are the affected parties?
4. How do the alternatives affect the parties?
5. What would you do?

Strategies for Teaching International Accounting

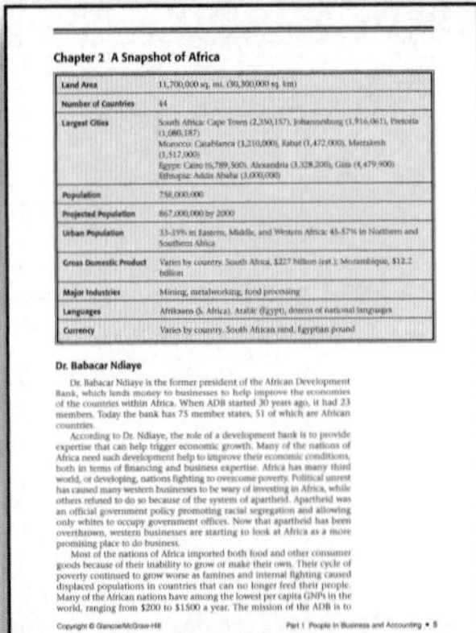

Chapter 2 A Snapshot of Africa

Dr. Babacar Ndiaye

School-to-Work Handbook

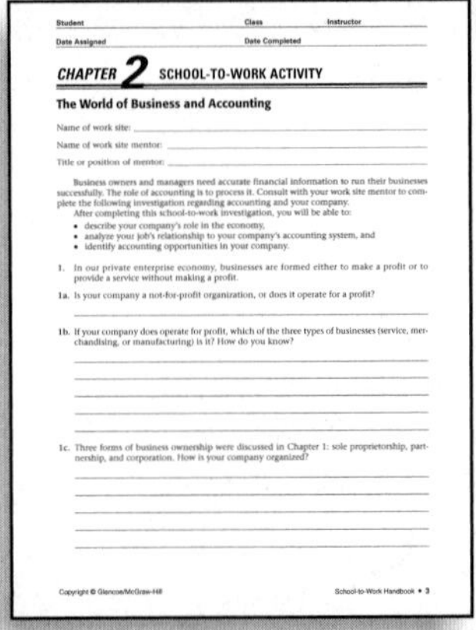

Student Class Instructor
Date Assigned Date Completed

CHAPTER 2 SCHOOL-TO-WORK ACTIVITY

The World of Business and Accounting

Name of work site:
Name of work site mentor:
Title or position of mentor:

Meeting Different Ability Levels

Chapter Reviews and Working Papers (CRWP)

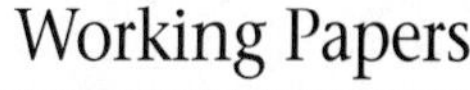

Working Papers

Review

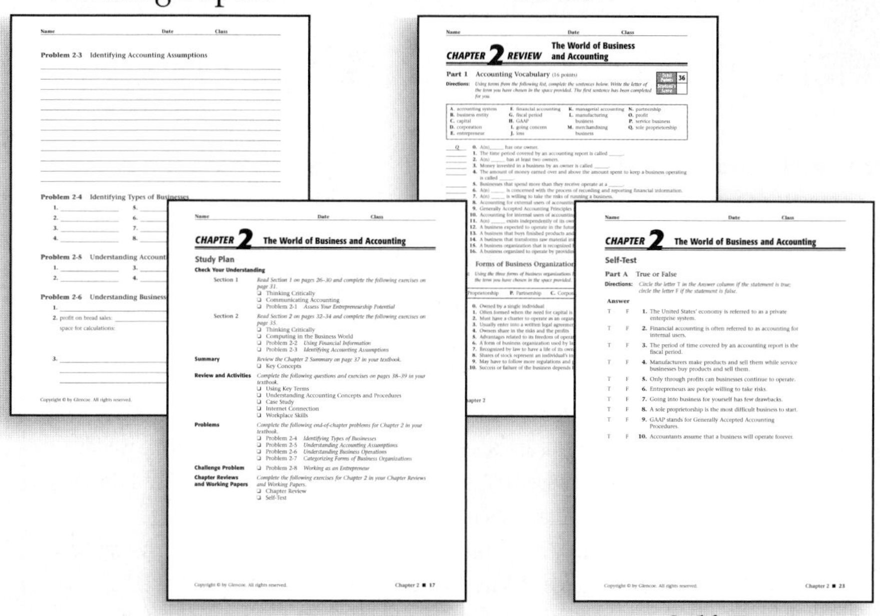

Student Study Plan

Self-Test

Real-World Multimedia CD-ROM

Key to Ability Levels

Each section gives skill-building activities. Each activity has been labeled for use with students of various learning styles and abilities.

L1 Level 1 activities are basic activities and should be within the range of all students.

L2 Level 2 activities are average activities and should be within the range of average and above average students.

L3 Level 3 activities are challenging activities designed for the ability range of above average students.

ELL ELL activities should be within the ability range of English Language Learners.

Assessment and Evaluation

Chapter Tests

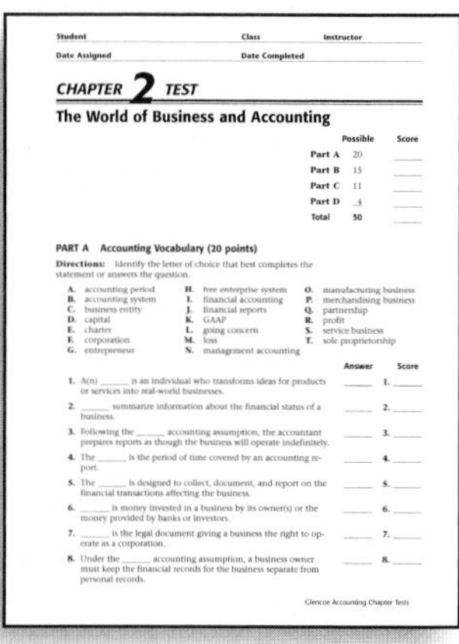

Chapter Quiz

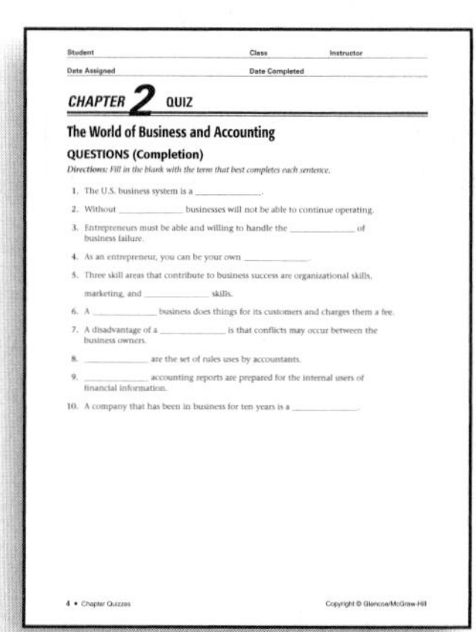

Teaching Resources at a Glance

Application Resources

- Glencoe Chapter Review and Working Papers, SE and TAE
- School-to-Work Handbook, SE and TM
- Accounting Portfolio, SE and TM

Reproducible Masters

- Demonstration Problems
- Lesson Plans
- Block Scheduling
- Spanish Language Resources

Glencoe Accounting Professional Development Series

- Strategies for Teaching Ethics in Accounting
- Accounting Competitive Event Review
- Math Review for Accounting
- Strategies for Teaching International Accounting
- Internet Resources and Activities Handbook

Transparency Package

- Section Focus Transparencies
- Teaching Transparencies
- Source Document Transparencies
- Solution Transparencies

Performance Assessment

- **Exam***View* CD-ROM
- Chapter Tests
- Chapter Quizzes
- Unit Tests
- Audit Tests
- Printed Testbank

Multimedia Resources

- Electronic Learning Center:
  - Multimedia CD-ROMs
  - Peachtree software, tutorials, templates, and solutions
  - Spreadsheet templates
- Using QuickBooks with Glencoe Accounting
- Interactive Lesson Planner
- Electronic Field Trips in Accounting
- PowerPoint Presentation
- Web site: glencoeaccounting.glencoe.com

OVERVIEW CHAPTER 2

Correlations to National Standards for Business Education

(See pages T50–T51 for a detailed correlation chart.)

Standards: IA1, IA2, IIA10, IVA1, IVC1, IVD1

Chapter Preview

In this chapter students learn about the need for financial recordkeeping and the role that profit and loss play in a free enterprise economy. Students also learn about different types of businesses and how they are organized. The accounting system is introduced, and students learn how information resulting from the accounting system is used in both financial and management decision making.

Section Overviews

- Section 1—*Exploring the World of Business*
- Section 2—*Accounting: The Universal Language of Business*

Chapter Vocabulary

free enterprise system	charter
profit	accounting system
loss	manual accounting system
entrepreneur	computerized accounting system
capital	GAAP
service business	financial reports
merchandising business	financial accounting
manufacturing business	management accounting
sole proprietorship	business entity
partnership	accounting period
corporation	going concern

Preteaching Accounting Vocabulary

Writing: Ask for volunteers to take turns writing each of the terms and its definition on the chalkboard. Discuss terms in related groups (such as service, merchandising, and manufacturing businesses). **L1**

CHAPTER 2

The World of Business and Accounting

Learning Objectives

When you have completed this chapter, you will be able to:

- Describe the role of profit, risk-taking, and the entrepreneur in the U.S. economy.
- Describe the differences among service, merchandising, and manufacturing businesses.
- Compare the sole proprietorship, partnership, and corporate forms of business.
- List the advantages and disadvantages of each form of business organization.
- Describe the purpose of accounting.
- Explain the difference between financial and management accounting.
- Describe the three basic assumptions that underlie accounting principles.
- Define the accounting terms introduced in this chapter.

Exploring the Real World of Business

BECOMING AN ENTREPRENEUR

Sports superstars like Venus Williams, Alex Rodriguez, and Kobe Bryant are among the best-conditioned athletes in the world; but even super athletes occasionally pull a muscle or suffer a stress fracture. That's when Lynda Huey comes to the rescue.

Huey's Athletic Network (HAN) uses aquatic therapy to help injured athletes rebuild body strength. As a track star at San Jose State University, Lynda Huey taught herself that water is beneficial because the body's buoyancy in water reduces the strain on injured muscles and bones. After college, she worked as a college coach and in 1986 started **Huey's Athletic Network.** The company's first job was aquatic training for Olympic athletes.

Today, **HAN** provides personal training and consulting not only to sports stars, but also to entertainers and weekend warriors who want to stay fit. Entertainment clients include Ben Stiller and Barbra Streisand. Lynda Huey regularly appears on television programs and has written books and magazine articles on water exercise.

What do you think?

1. What knowledge and special skills do you think Lynda Huey needed to start and manage her business?
2. What makes an entrepreneur successful?

Huey's Athletic Network

24 Chapter 2 The World of Business and Accounting

Exploring the Real World of Business

Huey's Athletic Network

Huey's Athletic Network is a service business. Many entrepreneurs start businesses by identifying a service they can provide to customers. Name several local businesses and have students determine which ones are service businesses.

What do you think? (Answers)

1. Huey needed to know which services to offer, how to market her services, what to charge, how to provide the services, and how to organize her business.
2. They work hard, provide good customer service, and pay close attention to the finances of the business.

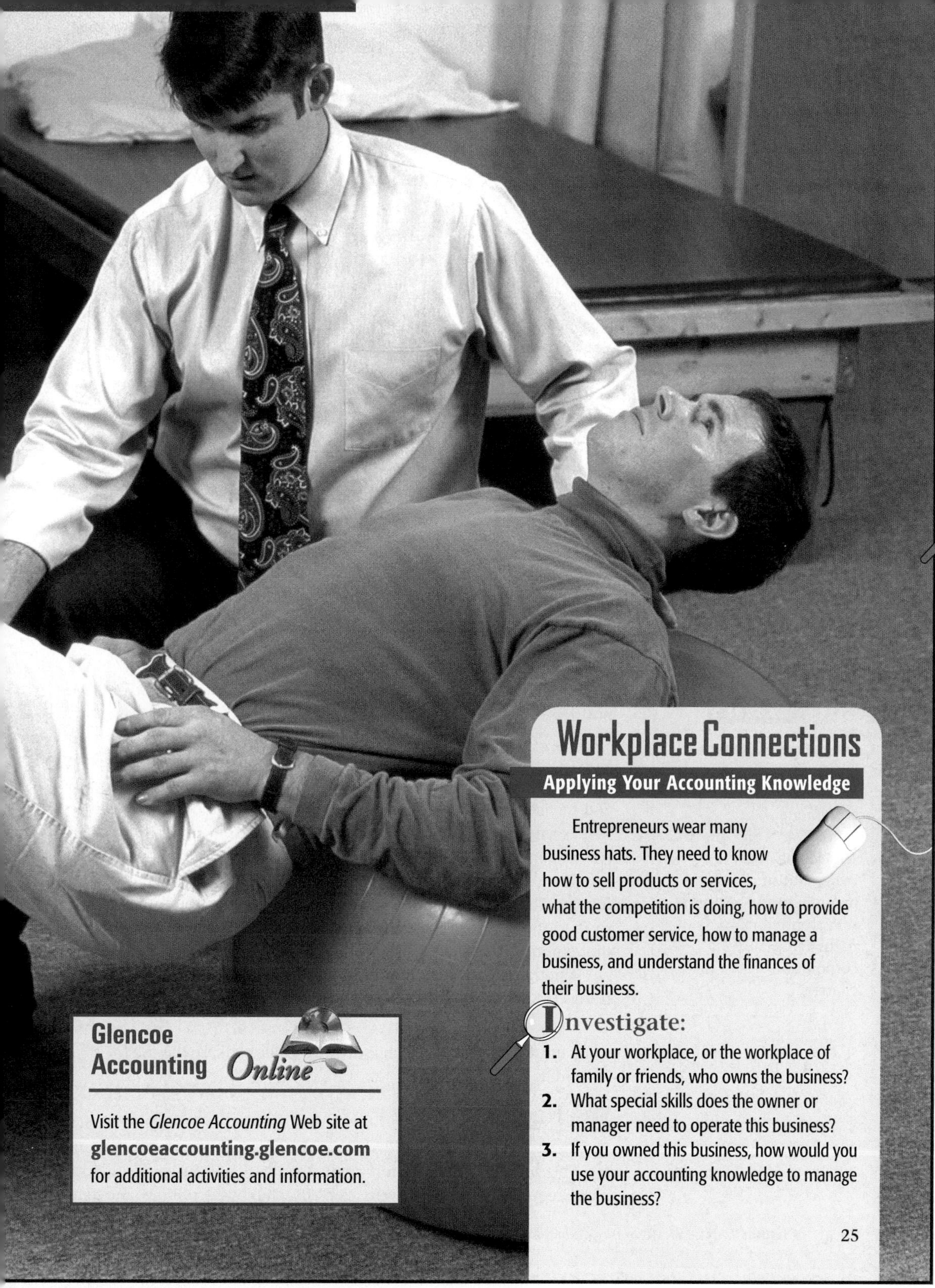

Workplace Connections

Applying Your Accounting Knowledge

Entrepreneurs wear many business hats. They need to know how to sell products or services, what the competition is doing, how to provide good customer service, how to manage a business, and understand the finances of their business.

Investigate:

1. At your workplace, or the workplace of family or friends, who owns the business?
2. What special skills does the owner or manager need to operate this business?
3. If you owned this business, how would you use your accounting knowledge to manage the business?

25

Glencoe Accounting Online

Visit the *Glencoe Accounting* Web site at **glencoeaccounting.glencoe.com** for additional activities and information.

INTRODUCING
CHAPTER 2

Making Accounting Relevant

Workplace Connections: Applying Your Accounting Knowledge

Discussion: Ask students how many of them have thought about owning their own business someday. What skills will they need to start and manage their business?

Investigate (Answers)

1. Answers will vary. Some will be local entrepreneurs while others may be branches or franchises of major public corporations.
2. Owners or managers need to know how to sell their products or services, hire good employees, promote the business, price products competitively, and make good financial decisions.
3. Students' responses will vary. Accounting knowledge is used to analyze sales and cost data, analyze costs and return of new products, and forecast business revenue and expenses.

School-to-Work Activity

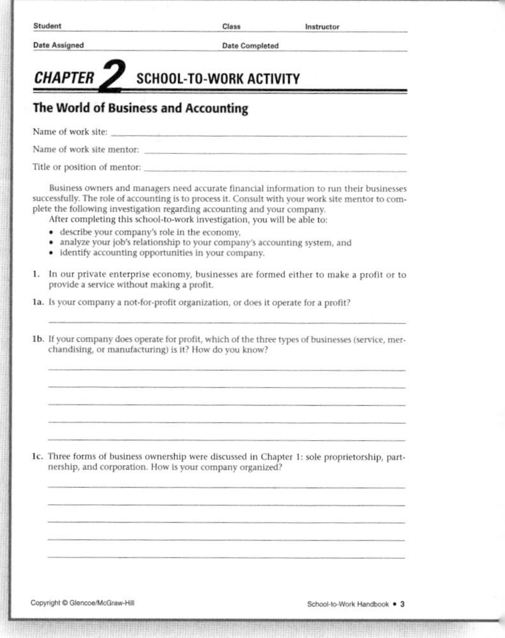

Student ____ Class ____ Instructor ____

Date Assigned ____ Date Completed ____

CHAPTER 2 SCHOOL-TO-WORK ACTIVITY

The World of Business and Accounting

Name of work site: ____

Name of work site mentor: ____

Title or position of mentor: ____

Business owners and managers need accurate financial information to run their businesses successfully. The role of accounting is to process it. Consult with your work site mentor to complete the following investigation regarding accounting and your company.

After completing this school-to-work investigation, you will be able to:

- describe your company's role in the economy,
- analyze your job's relationship to your company's accounting system, and
- identify accounting opportunities in your company.

1. In our private enterprise economy, businesses are formed either to make a profit or to provide a service without making a profit.

1a. Is your company a not-for-profit organization, or does it operate for a profit?

1b. If your company does operate for profit, which of the three types of businesses (service, merchandising, or manufacturing) is it? How do you know?

1c. Three forms of business ownership were discussed in Chapter 1: sole proprietorship, partnership, and corporation. How is your company organized?

School-to-Work Handbook • 3

GLENCOE MULTIMEDIA

Electronic Field Trips in Accounting *Video Segment: Entrepreneurship*

After viewing this video, students will be able to recognize that entrepreneurs form the backbone of the private enterprise economy. Discuss with students some of the requirements for entrepreneurial success, such as a business plan.

Glencoe Accounting: Electronic Learning Center *Chapter 2*

The CD-ROM program is ideal for visual learners since it incorporates video images, animation, and graphics to enliven the content of each lesson.

CHAPTER 2
SECTION 1, PAGES 26–31

1 FOCUS

Introducing the Section
In this section students will learn about the free enterprise system, in which businesses choose which products or services to offer their customers and how to price them. Students learn about the role of profit in this system. They also learn about entrepreneurs and the traits that help make entrepreneurs successful.

Several types of businesses operate within a free enterprise system. Students learn the types of businesses, along with the forms of business organization.

Section Concepts
- Profit and risk-taking
- The free enterprise system
- Starting and running your own business
- Three types of business operations
- Three forms of business organization

Visual Learning

Section 1 Focus

Use **Transparency 2–1** to introduce section concepts.

BELL RINGER

Compare and Contrast: Make a list of several local businesses and write their names on the chalkboard. Ask students to identify each as a service, merchandising, or manufacturing business. Then ask how the businesses differ. How are they alike? Do some businesses have operations that fall into more than one category (such as a manufacturer that also has a retail operation)? L1

SECTION 1

Exploring the World of Business

What **You'll Learn**
- Profit and risk-taking.
- The free enterprise system.
- Starting and running your own business.
- Three types of business operations.
- Three forms of business organization.

Why **It's Important**

In order to participate in the world of business, you'll want to understand how businesses are formed, organized, and operated.

KEY TERMS

free enterprise system
profit
loss
entrepreneur
capital
service business
merchandising business
manufacturing business
sole proprietorship
partnership
corporation
charter

In this chapter you will learn about different types of businesses and how they are organized. All businesses need information that is generated by accounting systems in the form of reports. You will learn about the different types of accounting and accounting reports.

In 1982 Howard Schultz joined Starbucks Coffee. When he purchased Starbucks, it consisted of six stores and fewer than 100 employees. Through his vision, energy, and imagination, he built the business to 4,000 stores with over 47,000 employees. By 2000 Starbucks was the top specialty coffee retailer in the nation, with coffee shops in 20 countries worldwide.

The Environment of Business

When you hear the word *business,* what do you think of? Nike, Microsoft, General Motors, IBM, Coca-Cola, or Tower Records? Large businesses like these are certainly players in the world of business today. Your neighborhood convenience store, clothing boutique, video rental store, and grocer are also important contributors in our free enterprise system. In a **free enterprise system** people are free to produce the goods and services they choose. Individuals are free to use their money as they wish: spend it, invest it, save it, or donate it. Business owners in this system must compete to attract the customers they need to continue operating.

One measure of success in a business operation is the amount of profit it earns. The amount of money earned over and above the amount spent to keep the business operating is called **profit**. Businesses that spend more money than they earn operate at a **loss**.

Whether small, medium, or large in size, a business must do two things to survive:

- It must operate at a profit.
- It must attract and keep an individual willing to take the risk to run it.

The Need for Profit

Continued operation and success of a business require profit. Your local pizza parlor must pay for raw materials (flour, sauce, cheese, toppings), equipment (mixers, ovens, freezers), employees, utilities, and rent.

RESOURCE MANAGER

Reproducible Masters
- Lesson Plans
- Chapter Reviews and Working Papers (CRWP) TAE

Transparencies
- Section Focus Transparency
- Teaching Transparencies
- Solution Transparencies

Multimedia
- Exam*View* CD-ROM
- Electronic Learning Center CD-ROM
- Interactive Lesson Planner CD-ROM
- Electronic Field Trips in Accounting

The selling price of the pizza must be high enough to cover all costs. Once the owner pays these costs, the money left over is profit.

The Need for a Risk-Taker

Within a business many people play different roles in daily operations, planning, and management. Inventors create ideas for producing new products or services. Investors provide money to help businesses get started. Employees supply the labor needed to operate the business. Managers handle supervision and planning. The role of the entrepreneur is special. **Entrepreneurs** transform ideas for products or services into real-world businesses. They are motivated self-starters willing to take the necessary risks to create profitable and useful businesses.

Key Points

Profit

A business must operate at a profit and have someone willing to take the risk to run it.

Entrepreneurship: Who Me?

Have you ever considered owning a business? Owning a business can offer flexible schedules, self-direction, and financial gain. Yet business ownership is not free from risk. Examine **Figure 2–1** for some pros and cons of entrepreneurship.

Pros	Cons
• You are your own boss. • You create opportunities for earning money. • You create and control your work schedule. • You choose the people you serve. • You select the people who work with you. • You benefit from the rewards of your own hard work. • You choose your own work hours.	• You probably need to work long hours. • You lose the security of steady wages and medical benefits an employer provides. • You market your own services or products. • You pay for your own operating expenses. • You must be motivated and energetic each day. • You face the possibility of losing money.

Figure 2–1
Entrepreneurship: Pros and Cons

Traits of Entrepreneurs

As you consider the path of entrepreneurship, take an inventory of your own skills and interests. Most entrepreneurs share certain behaviors and attitudes. Do you have good writing and speaking skills? Do you have a creative or mechanical mind? Are you a self-starter? Can you identify a community need and fill it? Do you have the capital to get started? Do you have accounting or marketing skills? Take a look at **Figure 2–2** to get an idea of the decisions that entrepreneurs face.

Owning your own business is not for everyone. An entrepreneur must possess the drive to overcome obstacles and be extremely resourceful. Strong organizational skills, marketing knowledge, and accounting skills are three areas of expertise that contribute to successful business ownership. If you are a visionary and have great energy and imagination, you may have the makings of an entrepreneur!

Key Points

Entrepreneurship

There are many benefits of starting and running your own business, but there are also drawbacks to consider.

Great Ideas *From the Classroom of...*

Student Challenge Divide students into groups of five or six. Set a time limit of two minutes and challenge each group to identify area businesses that do not keep financial records. Follow up with a discussion to help students understand that all businesses must keep financial records.

Beth Moody
Northview High School
Brazil, Indiana

2 TEACH

GUIDED PRACTICE

Reading Accounting

• Have students outline the chapter by writing the major heads and subheads, leaving space between the entries. As they read, have them jot notes about the content or the key terms defined in that section. L1

• If you have a substantial population of limited-English-speaking groups in your area, find local examples of businesses operated by entrepreneurs within that population group. Use these businesses in some of your discussion of entrepreneurs and also the different types of businesses. ELL

Concept Development: The Environment of Business

Discussion: Have students discuss the free enterprise system. Contrast this system to those in some other countries, such as China, where the government plays a much larger role in business decision making. L1

Concept Development: Entrepreneurship: Who Me?

Discussion: Take a poll of your students to find out how many of them plan to become entrepreneurs. Ask what type of business they plan to start. Discuss what they think it takes to be a successful entrepreneur. L1

Visual Learning

Figure 2–1 Entrepreneurship: Pros and Cons

Use **Transparency 2–2** to discuss the advantages and disadvantages of being an entrepreneur.

2 TEACH (Cont'd.)

Visual Learning

Figure 2–2 Traits of the Entrepreneur, p. 28
Use the illustration of the entrepreneurial process to discuss how entrepreneurs identify product or service ideas, plan their businesses, and then implement their plans.

Application: Have students choose a product or service and write a similar plan for their own business. L1

Concept Development: Types of Business Operations

Discussion: Discuss with students the different types of businesses—service, merchandising, and manufacturing—and why they operate. Point out that each type of business collects and records financial information about its operations. L1

Critical Thinking: Tell students to choose two types of businesses to start in your community: a service business and a merchandising business. Have them write a brief report comparing the businesses. In the report, the student is expected to contrast the characteristics of a service and a merchandising business. L3

Teaching Tip

Bring to class examples of products that represent each type of business. For example, a dry-cleaning receipt might represent your local dry-cleaner's service business, a sweatshirt from a local store might represent a merchandising business, and a car (toy) might represent an auto manufacturer.

Traits of the Entrepreneur

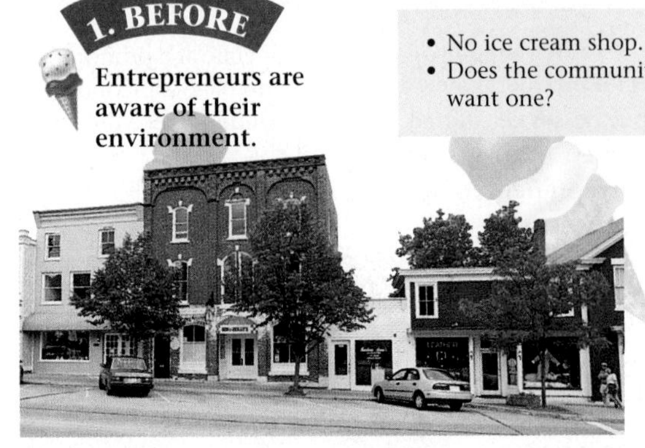

Figure 2–2

Types of Business Operations

In our free enterprise system there are three types of businesses that operate for profit: service, merchandising, and manufacturing.

Service, merchandising, and manufacturing businesses are alike in many ways. Each offers products or services, incurs expenses, and makes sales to customers. They differ from one another, however, in some basic ways. Each type of business needs money to begin and maintain operations. Money is needed to buy or to make products, and to cover operating costs like rent, utilities, and wages. Money supplied by investors, banks, or owners of a business is called **capital**.

ACCOUNTING Flashbacks

USING ELECTRONIC SPREADSHEETS
An electronic spreadsheet is software that can be used to create work sheets and trial balances and perform calculations. The first spreadsheet program, VisiCalc, was released in 1978.

Service Businesses

A **service business** provides a needed service for a fee. Service businesses include travel agencies, styling salons like Fantastic Sam's, movers, repair shops, real estate offices like Century 21, and medical centers.

Merchandising Businesses

A **merchandising business** buys finished products and resells them to individuals or other businesses. Department stores like JCPenney, new and used car dealers, supermarkets like Kroger, drugstores like Rite Aid, florists, and hobby shops are examples of merchandising businesses.

Key Points

Types of Businesses
There are three types of businesses:
- service
- merchandising
- manufacturing

Manufacturing Businesses

A **manufacturing business** buys raw materials, such as wood or iron ore, and transforms them into finished products through the use of labor and capital. It then sells the finished products to individuals or other businesses. Manufacturing businesses range from a shipbuilder, like Atlantic Marine Shipyard of Mobile, Alabama, to the Pioneer Bakery in Venice, California.

Forms of Business Organization

To start a business, a potential owner must have a sufficient amount of money (capital) and must choose an appropriate form of business

CRITICAL THINKING ACTIVITY

Analyzing Information The owner of a sole proprietorship, service business takes several risks in starting a new business. Among those risks are not earning enough revenue to stay in business or not being paid for services provided. In addition to the risks, the business owner is responsible for all aspects of operating the business. Ask students to name various tasks a business owner may have beyond providing a service or product. Write answers on the chalkboard. (Students' responses might include writing checks to pay bills, keeping accounting records, opening/closing the office/business each day, buying insurance, having the office cleaned, ordering supplies, writing letters to customers, and approving and placing advertising.)

Traits of the Entrepreneur

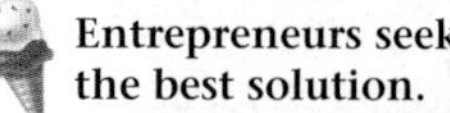

Entrepreneurs seek the best solution.

• Only used appliances are within budget guidelines.

3. AFTER

Entrepreneurs turn ideas into actions.

• Ben & Jerry's is a worldwide producer of ice cream and frozen yogurt.

organization. With a few exceptions, U.S. businesses are organized in one of three ways: sole proprietorship, partnership, or corporation, illustrated in **Figure 2–3.** Let's compare the various forms of business organization.

Type of Business	Form of Business		
	Sole Proprietorship	Partnership	Corporation
Service	X	X	X
Merchandising	X	X	X
Manufacturing	X	X	X

Figure 2–3 Forms of Business Organization

Key Points

Forms of Business Organization

There are three forms of business organization:

- sole proprietorship
- partnership
- corporation

Sole Proprietorship

Sole means "single" or "one." *Proprietor* means "owner." A **sole proprietorship**, therefore, is a business owned by one person. The term *proprietorship* is also used to describe this form of business organization. Being a sole proprietor does not mean working alone. Based on the size and scope of the operation, a sole proprietorship may have many managers and employees. The oldest and most common form of business organization, the sole proprietorship is the easiest form of business to start. Little or no legal paperwork (forms and documents) is required. The success or failure of the business depends heavily on the efforts and talent of the owner.

The advantages and disadvantages of organizing as a sole proprietorship are shown in **Figure 2–4**.

Did You Know?

Prices

Physical trainers and therapists charge from a low of about $30 an hour to more than $90 a session. Each session usually lasts from 30 to 60 minutes.

Advantages	Disadvantages
• Easy to set up • All profits go to owner • Owner has total control • Few regulations to follow	• Limited expertise • Hard to raise money • Owner has all the risks • Hard to attract talented employees

Figure 2–4 Advantages and Disadvantages of a Sole Proprietorship

INTERDISCIPLINARY CONNECTIONS ACTIVITY

(Refer to the *Connect To...Science* feature on page 33.)

Science Divide students into groups of four or five and discuss the importance of budget planning. Then tell students to imagine that they are a group of scientists assigned to a research project. In order to get a grant approved, they need to create a budget projecting their costs. Have each group create a budget totaling $75,000. Ask each group to prepare a report including a description of the project, the short and long-term goals, ideas for product development, and the cost of completing the project. Have each group present their report to the class.

2 TEACH (Cont'd.)

Concept Development: Forms of Business Organization

Discussion: Ask students whether they know any local sole proprietors. What type of business is it? If students cannot identify a local sole proprietor, be prepared with two or three business names. L1

Extending the Concept: Have students list advantages and disadvantages of operating a sole proprietorship. Ask how they would deal with the disadvantages. L2

Visual Learning

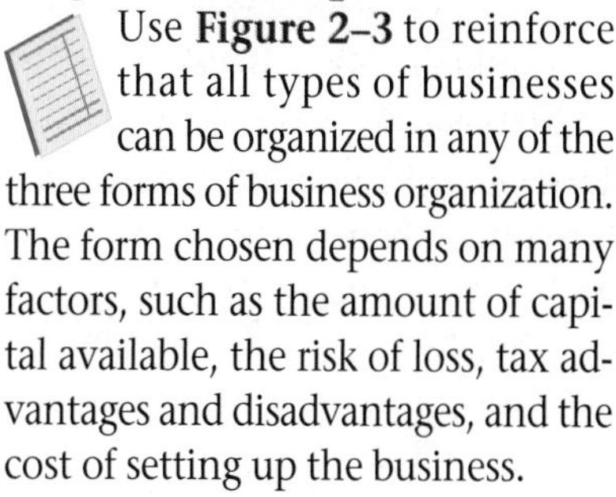

Figure 2-3 Forms of Business Organization, p. 29

Use **Figure 2–3** to reinforce that all types of businesses can be organized in any of the three forms of business organization. The form chosen depends on many factors, such as the amount of capital available, the risk of loss, tax advantages and disadvantages, and the cost of setting up the business.

Major Characteristics of Business Entities

Use **Transparency 2–3** to discuss with students the major characteristics of different types of businesses.

Figure 2–4 Advantages and Disadvantages of a Sole Proprietorship

Use **Transparency 2–4** to discuss the advantages and disadvantages of a sole proprietorship.

Teaching Tip

Invite a local sole proprietor to speak to your class. Ask the person to talk about his or her business idea, the steps in planning for and opening of the business, and the types of business tasks involved.

2 TEACH (Cont'd.)

Concept Development: Partnership

Discussion: Have students list advantages and disadvantages of a partnership. Ask students to think of local businesses that might be organized as partnerships. L1

Visual Learning

Figure 2–5 Advantages and Disadvantages of a Partnership

Use **Transparency 2–4** to reinforce the advantages and disadvantages of partnerships. Have students discuss how to deal with the disadvantages.

Concept Development: Corporation

Discussion: Have students list advantages and disadvantages of the corporate form of business organization. Then ask students to name some local corporations. L1

Visual Learning

Figure 2–6 Advantages and Disadvantages of a Corporation

Use **Transparency 2–4** to point out the advantages and disadvantages of organizing a business as a corporation. Discuss how to deal with the disadvantages. Refer back to **Figures 2–4** and **2–5** to compare the advantages and disadvantages from one form of organization to another.

Math Review for Accounting

Photocopy appropriate *Activity Sheets* for students who need additional practice in basic math skills.

Partnership

A **partnership** is a business owned by two or more persons, called partners, who agree to operate the business as co-owners. Business partners usually enter into a written, legal agreement. This agreement specifies the amount of money or property to be invested by each partner, the responsibilities of each partner, and how profits and losses are to be divided. Partnerships are often formed when the need for capital is greater than the amount of money one person can invest. Partnerships are not always small. For example, large accounting firms like Deloitte & Touche LLP are organized as partnerships and may have as many as 1,500 partners and over 20,000 employees. **Figure 2–5** provides advantages and disadvantages of the partnership.

Advantages	Disadvantages
• Easy to start • Skills and talents are pooled • More money available	• Conflicts between partners • Profits must be shared • Owners share all risks

Figure 2–5 Advantages and Disadvantages of a Partnership

Corporation

A **corporation** is a business organization that is recognized by law to have a life of its own. In contrast to a sole proprietorship and a partnership, a corporation must get permission from the state to operate. This legal permission, called a **charter**, gives a corporation certain rights and privileges. The charter spells out the rules under which the corporation is to operate.

Corporations often start out as sole proprietorships or partnerships. The owner(s) of a business may choose to "incorporate" to acquire additional money needed to expand. To raise this money, shares of stock are sold to hundreds or even thousands of people. These shares represent investments in and ownership of the corporation. *Shareholders,* who are also called stockholders, are the legal owners of a corporation. Starbucks is an example of a business organized as a corporation that has thousands of shareholders. **Figure 2–6** outlines a few advantages and disadvantages of organizing as a corporation.

Regardless of their form, sole proprietorship, partnership, or corporation, all businesses share common financial characteristics and methods for recording and reporting financial changes.

Math Hints

Setting Prices

When setting prices for products, most businesses:

- add all their costs of doing business,
- then calculate the prices to make an adequate profit.

Businesses might charge 20 or 25 percent over expenses.

Advantages	Disadvantages
• Easier to raise money • Easy to expand • Easy to transfer ownership • Losses limited to investment	• Costs more to start up • Complex to organize • More regulations • Higher taxes

Figure 2–6 Advantages and Disadvantages of a Corporation

Math Skill Builder Activity

Setting Prices Help students learn how businesses make profit. Tell students to imagine that they work as a sales clerk at The Gap. The fall merchandise has come in, and the store manager has asked you to price the crewneck sweaters at 25 percent over cost. A sweater costs $15 wholesale. What is the retail price? With a 6 percent sales tax, what is the cost of the sweater to the customer? If The Gap sold 100 sweaters at that price, what profit would the store make on the sale? ($18.75; $19.88; $375 [$3.75 markup per sweater × 100 units])

Check Your Understanding

Now that you have studied this section, complete the following questions and problem.

Thinking Critically

1. Would you say that the advantages of being an entrepreneur outweigh the disadvantages or vice versa? Why?
2. Explain how being influenced early in life by a role model might be critical to someone's success as an entrepreneur?

Communicating Accounting

Locate and read a current magazine article featuring a successful entrepreneur. Try periodicals like *Business Week, Forbes,* or *Working Woman.* Write a summary of the article, and explain why you think the person succeeded.

Problem 2–1 Assess Your Entrepreneurship Potential

Instructions The characteristics or traits needed to set up an owner-operated business and to run it successfully are listed below. Rank yourself, indicating if this trait is most like you or least like you. Use the form provided in your working papers.

	Most Like Me			Least Like Me	
Persistent	5	4	3	2	1
Creative	5	4	3	2	1
Responsible	5	4	3	2	1
Inquisitive	5	4	3	2	1
Goal-oriented	5	4	3	2	1
Independent	5	4	3	2	1
Demanding	5	4	3	2	1
Self-confident	5	4	3	2	1
Risk-taking	5	4	3	2	1
Restless	5	4	3	2	1

List the categories in which you ranked 3 or lower. Identify experiences, activities, and ways in which you could improve your entrepreneurial potential.

RETEACHING SECTION 1

Compare the Various Forms of Business Organizations Ask students to list four examples of area businesses for each type of business organization: sole proprietorship, partnership, and corporation. Students can speculate based on their knowledge of the business or simply by the name of the business. For example, Graybill and Jaehne, Attorneys at Law, is likely a partnership; and NetLink, Inc., is a corporation. Have students list the similarities and differences among the three groups.

Productivity Skills
The student can practice productivity skills as they apply to accounting at the end of each section and chapter. In these activities the student is expected to follow written instructions.

3 ASSESS

Thinking Critically (Answers)

1. Answers will vary. Have students discuss their analysis with the class.
2. Answers will vary. Evaluate students' answers for clear and logical progression of ideas.

Communicating Accounting (Answers)
Answers will vary. Students should include in the analysis the traits that made the entrepreneur successful. Evaluate students' summaries for correct grammar usage and reasoning.

Problem 2–1 (Answer)
Answers will vary.

Chapter Reviews and Working Papers Refer students to the Chapter 2 workbook pages to answer *Check Your Understanding* activities.

4 CLOSE

Section Wrap-Up
Demonstrate: Have students demonstrate their understanding of types of businesses and forms of organization by writing a paragraph about a local business, describing its purpose, form of organization, and the advantages and disadvantages of that business form. L1

CHAPTER 2
SECTION 2, PAGES 32–35

1 FOCUS

Introducing the Section

In this section students will learn about the role accounting plays in business operations. They'll learn about the foundation of an accounting system and how accounting information is used by people both inside and outside the business in making decisions.

Section Concepts

- How the accounting system works.
- Who uses financial accounting reports.
- Who uses management accounting reports.
- How accounting is used to help make business decisions.
- What assumptions provide the foundation for accounting systems.

Visual Learning

Section 2 Focus

Use **Transparency 2–5** to introduce section concepts.

BELL RINGER

Creative Thinking: Ask students what would happen if everyone used a different set of rules when driving. Then relate the rules of driving to the rules of accounting (GAAP). GAAP guides people through financial information that is presented in a consistent way from one company to another. L1

Visual Learning

Figure 2–7 How the Accounting System Works

Use **Transparency 2–6** to explain that financial data, resulting from a source document, are recorded in the accounting system and then used to create reports about operating costs and business earnings.

SECTION 2

Accounting: The Universal Language of Business

What You'll Learn

- How the accounting system works.
- Who uses financial accounting reports.
- Who uses management accounting reports.
- How accounting is used to help make business decisions.
- What assumptions provide the foundation for accounting systems.

Why It's Important

Understanding accounting systems is the key to understanding business.

KEY TERMS

- accounting system
- manual accounting system
- computerized accounting system
- GAAP
- financial reports
- financial accounting
- management accounting
- business entity
- accounting period
- going concern

Key Points

GAAP

GAAP stands for "generally accepted accounting principles."

Have you ever wondered how the band U2 determines which venues they will play, the cost of a tour, how profitable CD sales have been, or how much ticket prices should be? All these issues are probably tackled by the band's financial team: accountants, clerks, and financial advisors.

The Accounting System

Whether you are the accountant for a band or the financial manager for a chain of mountain bike stores, accounting methods are universal. The **accounting system** is designed to collect, document, and report on financial transactions affecting the business. In a **manual accounting system** the accounting information is processed by hand. In a **computerized accounting system** the financial information is recorded by entering it into a computer. Owners and investors who risk their money depend on accountants to report the results of operations and the financial condition of the businesses in which they invest. **Figure 2–7** outlines the inputs, processes, and outputs of an accounting system.

All accountants use the same set of rules, called **"generally accepted accounting principles"** or **GAAP** (pronounced "gap") to prepare their reports. Accounting principles provide a way to communicate financial information in a form understood by those interested in the operations and financial condition of a business. Because it is so fundamental to the communication of financial information, accounting is often called the "language of business." **Financial reports** are summarized information about the financial status of a business.

Inputs →	Processing →	Outputs
Source Documents • Checks • Invoices • Sales Slips • Receipts	**Tasks** • Analyzing • Classifying • Recording	**Financial and Management Accounting Reports** • Financial condition • Results of operations • Investments by and distributions to owners

Figure 2–7 How the Accounting System Works

RESOURCE MANAGER

Reproducible Masters
- Lesson Plans
- Chapter Reviews and Working Papers (CRWP) TAE

Transparencies
- Section Focus Transparency
- Teaching Transparencies
- Solution Transparencies

Multimedia
- Exam*View* CD-ROM
- Electronic Learning Center CD-ROM
- Interactive Lesson Planner CD-ROM
- Electronic Field Trips in Accounting

Using Accounting Reports for Making Business Decisions

The purpose of accounting is to provide financial information about a business or a not-for-profit organization. Individuals need financial information in order to make decisions.

The information found in accounting reports has a wide audience. In general, there are two groups that use accounting reports:

- individuals *outside* the business who have an interest in the business
- individuals *inside* the business

Financial Accounting

Financial accounting focuses on reporting information to external users. Financial accounting reports are prepared for individuals not directly involved in the day-to-day operations of the business. These reports are prepared using GAAP.

Who Uses Financial Accounting Reports?

- Suppose you wanted to invest in a business, such as Trek Mountain Bikes Inc. You would analyze financial accounting reports to estimate if an investment in the business would be profitable.
- Individuals or institutions, like banks that loan money to a business, use financial accounting reports to determine whether or not the business will be able to repay loans.
- Local, state, and federal governments review financial accounting reports. For example, the Internal Revenue Service may compare the tax return and financial reports of a business to determine whether the business is paying the proper amount of taxes.
- Workers, consumers, union leaders, and competitors are interested in the performance of businesses as presented in financial accounting reports.

Management Accounting

Management accounting, which focuses on reporting information to management, is often referred to as accounting for *internal* users of accounting information. Management accounting reports are prepared for managers involved in making the day-to-day operating decisions like purchasing, hiring, production, payments, sales, and collections.

Managers need accounting information so they can decide what to do, how to do it, when to do it, and whether or not the results match the plans for the future. **Figure 2–8** describes some of these decisions.

Accounting Assumptions

An assumption is something taken for granted as true. When you attend a movie, you assume the volume will be at a reasonable level, there will be a place to sit, and the film will be in focus. If these assumptions are wrong, the movie will be a disappointing experience.

International ACCOUNTING

Currency Conversion

When people need to convert U.S. dollars to a foreign currency, they can look up rates in newspapers, use the Internet, or use exchange counters in airports or banks. When converting currencies, a small fee is usually charged.

CONNECT TO . . . SCIENCE

Researchers who receive grant money from the government or private foundations are accountable for their expenditures. Before money is granted, scientists must project costs for their projects and delineate the immediate and long-term benefits of their work. While conducting research projects, they must tally their costs and report on their progress.

Teaching International ACCOUNTING

Researching Exchange Rates Have students research the current exchange rates for euros, Canadian dollars, Japanese yen, South African rand, Swiss francs, and so on. Ask students to calculate the conversion of 100 U.S. dollars to each of the foreign currencies. Have them share their information with the class and identify their sources of information. Ask students to name locations in your area where they could exchange U.S. dollars for foreign currencies. Have students inquire about the fee the bank or exchange agency would charge.

2 TEACH

GUIDED PRACTICE

Reading Accounting

- Have students skim the section and write questions that occur to them. Address their questions in your discussion of the section. L1
- Ask a language specialist to review exams and reading assignments to identify problems with wording, sentence structure, and vocabulary. ELL

Concept Development: The Accounting System

Discussion: Accounting records provide information about profits—and losses—by tracking the costs of operating a business and the income it produces. Because of its role in quantifying the results of business operations, an accounting system provides a common means of communicating financial information about the business. L1

Concept Development: Using Accounting Reports for Making Business Decisions

Discussion: Discuss with students that people can learn about a business from accounting reports. Some financial data are located in annual reports and are read by people outside the company. Other reports, such as those analyzing the costs or profits of a specific product line, are used by people inside the business to make decisions about how to operate the company. L1

Strategies for Teaching International Accounting

To enrich study of International Accounting, refer to the additional critical thinking activities in the booklet.

2 TEACH (Cont'd.)

Concept Development: Accounting Assumptions

Discussion: Have students apply basic accounting concepts and terminology by discussing the accounting assumptions in terms of a local business. For example, the costs and income for a local bowling alley (*business entity*) are recorded in an accounting system that excludes information about the personal finances of the bowling alley's owner. The bowling alley has an *accounting period* of a year. The business has been operating for several years and is assumed to be a *going concern.* L1

Teaching Tip

An exact business entity is sometimes hard to identify. Large corporations may report on separate divisions. Information from consolidated statements present information about the total entity.

Point out that businesses use a consistent time period for reporting their operating results so that results can be compared from one period to another. Such comparisons help company managers analyze whether their business is earning more or less profit than the previous financial period.

Visual Learning

Figure 2–8 Managerial Decisions, p. 34

Use this illustration when discussing the accounting assumptions underlying an accounting system.

Strategies for Teaching Ethics in Accounting

Photocopy the Chapter 2 *Student Activity Sheet* for students. Answers are also provided in the booklet.

Owners and managers use financial reports to make decisions.

- Which flowers are the best sellers?
- Can we purchase a new delivery van?
- Can we afford to attend floral conventions in Amsterdam?
- Should we hire more designers?

Figure 2–8 Managerial Decisions

Each business sets up an accounting system according to its specific needs, but all businesses follow GAAP. These generally accepted accounting principles are based on three very important assumptions summarized by the following terms:

- business entity
- accounting period
- going concern

For accounting purposes, a business is a separate entity. A **business entity** exists independently of its owner's personal holdings. The accounting records and reports are maintained separately and contain financial information related only to the business. The business owner's personal financial activities or other investments are not included in the reports of the business. For example, the personal residence of a pet store owner, valued at $100,000, is not reported in the accounting records of the pet store. Buildings owned by the business, however, are included in the financial records and reports of the pet store.

For reporting purposes, the life of a business is divided into specific periods of time. A period of time covered by an accounting report is referred to as an **accounting period** . The accounting period can cover one month or three months (quarterly), but the most common period is one year. This assumption is necessary when accountants assign the cost of buildings and equipment over the estimated period of time they will be used. Comparison of reports from one period to the next also makes the accounting period concept necessary.

Unless there is evidence to the contrary, accountants assume that a business has the ability to survive and operate indefinitely. In other words, a business is expected to continue as a **going concern** . Although many businesses fail within the first five years, the accountant assumes the business will continue to operate unless it is clear that it cannot survive.

Key Points

Accounting Assumptions
There are three important assumptions in accounting: business entity, accounting period, and going concern.

A MATTER OF ETHICS

Becoming an Entrepreneur

Imagine that you've been working for a local day-care center for several years. You attend a company meeting to discuss new ideas on improving day care. Several new services are discussed that would help your center stand out from its competition. You think that this is a great opportunity for you to become an entrepreneur—by opening your own day-care center offering the new services discussed in the meetings.

Ethical Decision Making:

- What are the ethical issues?
- What are the alternatives?
- Who are the affected parties?
- How do the alternatives affect the parties?
- What would you do?

Teaching A MATTER OF ETHICS

Becoming an Entrepreneur Since ideas are not tangible items of property, students may not immediately make a connection between using someone's ideas and stealing. Share this scenario with students: They have just thought up a clever new name for a new school sports team mascot and shared the name with a friend. Before they could enter the name in the contest to name the mascot, the friend submits the name and takes credit when it is chosen as the winning entry. How would students react? If the name had been a business idea that was taken by someone else, how would they react?

Check Your Understanding

Now that you have studied this section, complete the following questions and problems.

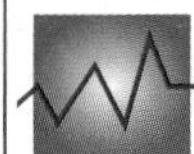

Thinking Critically

1. If a business owner failed to follow the assumption of "business entity," what complications might arise?
2. Consider creating an "accounting system" for your personal finances. How would you organize the system? What inputs would there be? How might you record your activities? How might you report on those activities?

Computing in the Business World

Suppose you are opening a 1,000 square foot baseball card store in a shopping center. You have signed a lease that requires you to pay a monthly rent of $1.75 per square foot, plus 5% of your gross annual sales. What is the total amount of rent you will pay in one year if you have sales of $85,000?

Problem 2–2 Using Financial Information

Instructions Imagine that you are the manager for Valley Skateboard Shop. The accountant for the business delivered the news that sales are down by 15% compared to last month. She also reports that the rent on the building will be increasing next month by $100. You believe the shop needs a more experienced salesperson and that the building needs new paint and awnings. How might the information delivered by the accountant affect your decisions and course of action?

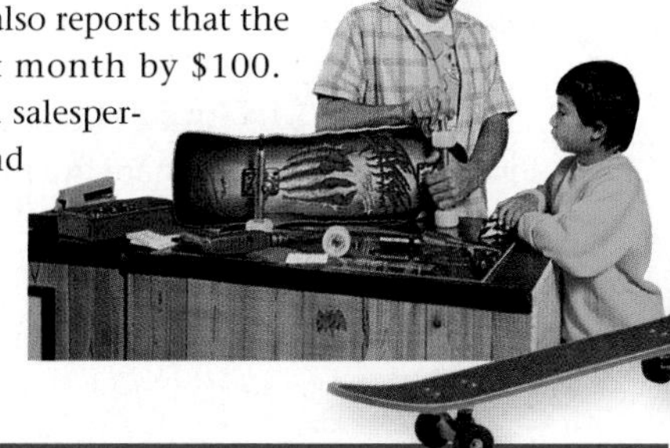

Problem 2–3 Identifying Accounting Assumptions

Suppose you work for a company called Greenwood Sky Divers as a sky-diving instructor. Since you have your pilot's license, you also give flying lessons on the side. You and the owner of Greenwood Sky Divers both belong to a local club, called the Greenwood Eagles, whose members get together for sky dives on weekends. Greenwood Sky Divers is a sole proprietorship that has been in business for six years. The owner of the company regularly reviews financial reports, and the company's accountant prepares end-of-the year reports to compare results from one year to the next.

Instructions Decide what information in this paragraph is relevant to accounting for Greenwood Sky Divers. Identify the accounting assumptions for Greenwood, and give an example of each assumption from the information given here.

RETEACHING SECTION 2

Understanding an Accounting System Students may have difficulty understanding what an accounting "system" is. At this point in their study of accounting, the important concept to communicate is that accounting information is recorded and reports are prepared to summarize information *following a specific set of steps*. The "system" consists of both the outline presented in **Figure 2–7** and the tools (types of accounting forms and/or software programs) used to prepare the accounting records.

Understanding accounting terminology is key to understanding an accounting system. Review the list of key terms, then call on students to use each of the terms in a sentence.

3 ASSESS

Thinking Critically (Answers)

1. Confusion could arise in separating business and personal income and in determining taxes. Some tax deductions allowed for a business are not allowed for individuals.
2. Students should consider creating accounts for their personal assets and liabilities (bank accounts, credit cards, investments, etc.), and recording their personal transactions.

Computing in the Business World (Answer)

$6,000.00

Problem 2–2 (Answer)

Answers may vary. The drop in sales could signal that a new salesperson is needed. Some owners, though, might be reluctant to invest more money in a business where sales are down. Reasons for the decrease in sales will be needed to make a final decision.

The manager might ask for new paint and awnings in return for the higher rent.

Problem 2–3 (Answer)

Greenwood Sky Divers is the name of the business entity. It has been in business for six years and is a going concern. The accounting period for Greenwood Sky Divers is one year.

Chapter Reviews and Working Papers Refer students to the Chapter 2 workbook pages to answer *Check Your Understanding* activities.

4 CLOSE

Section Wrap-Up

Writing: Have students write one or two paragraphs that describe the purpose of accounting in a free enterprise system. L1

CAREERS IN FOCUS
CHAPTER 2

SCANS in the Workforce

Foundation Skills Connection

Self-Management

To help students learn to be responsible, have them create a "to do" list. The list should include various tasks they need to complete in the next two weeks, including school assignments, home chores, and workplace duties. For each task, have students list who is responsible and when the task needs to be completed. Have students check off each task as they complete it. L1

Workplace Competencies Connection

Allocating Material and Facility Resources

Have students work in teams to design a model office using notebook paper, grid paper, or a software program. Have students list the type of materials, resources, and equipment they would need for this workplace. Have them select the type of business they will be operating. Point out that the office design should show how students would use materials and resources for a smooth workflow. L2

Serving Clients/Customers

Tell students to imagine that they are employees of Disney World. Then present the following scenario: "The Porter family is visiting Disney World for the first time. They have just finished the Small World ride, but their three young children refuse to leave the ride. The parents are exhausted and frustrated with their children." What can you do as the ride operator to assist the parents? Have students think of several solutions and practice with a partner what they would say to the family. L3

ACCOUNTING CAREERS IN FOCUS

STERLING ELLSWORTH
Certified Public Accountant (CPA)

Q: Why did you choose accounting?

A: Because of its precision. I was a math major, but theoretical math, such as calculus, didn't interest me. I had taken an accounting class, and struggled with it, but enjoyed it at the same time. I took a second one and knew it was for me. It was challenging, but rewarding.

Q: What do you like about working for yourself?

A: I like the freedom to work when I want, take vacations when I want, to adjust my time around my workload. I work more intensely sometimes, but I have a lot of time off.

Q: How does your workload vary?

A: During tax season, I work 12 hours a day, or more, for about a 90-day period. It's very intense. Then it slows down. In late summer and early fall, I take a lot of four-day weekends. That's when I appreciate what I do.

Q: What skills are important to you?

A: Time management skills are the most critical. You have to be able to organize and work at maximum efficiency. You can't make mistakes that cost your client money, yet you have to work quickly. People skills are important too. Sometimes I have only 10 minutes to sell myself and convince clients they can trust me with their financial records.

CAREER FACTS

Nature of the Work: Consult with clients, prepare tax forms, attend IRS audits, give financial advice.

Training or Education Needed: A bachelor's degree in accounting or business, the CPA exam, and continuing education.

Aptitudes, Abilities, and Skills: Time-management skills, interpersonal skills, organizational skills, computer skills, and math.

Salary Range: Start at $40,000 to $200,000, depending on prior experience.

Career Path: Pass the CPA exam, work in an accounting field to gain work experience, build client base, then start your own business.

Thinking Critically: How would you convince clients that you can be trusted with their records?

ACCOUNTING CAREERS IN FOCUS

Thinking Critically (Answers)

You will need to demonstrate knowledge about taxes, filing procedures, and the law. You also need good communication and organization skills. It's important that you keep information about other clients and accountants confidential.

ROBERT HALF CORNER

Entrepreneurial Traits In order to balance family and work demands, more accounting professionals are working at home. Have students brainstorm the advantages and disadvantages of becoming an entrepreneur.

CHAPTER 2 SUMMARY

KEY CONCEPTS

1. The free enterprise system is based on individual freedoms.
2. Competition among businesses to attract customers is a key element of the free enterprise system.
3. Businesses need to operate profitably in order to continue.

Money Earned from Sales > **Money Spent to Operate Business** = **Profit**

4. Entrepreneurs are willing to take risks and make things happen in business.
5. While everyone is different, people who become successful entrepreneurs tend to have similar traits, such as a strong desire to succeed, the ability to solve problems, and creative ideas for business services or products.
6. The three types of businesses are service, merchandising, and manufacturing.
7. Sole proprietorships, partnerships, and corporations are three forms of business.
8. Sole proprietorships are owned by one person, partnerships by two or more partners, and corporations by many shareholders who own stock in the corporation.
9. Accountants use "generally accepted accounting principles" or GAAP to prepare financial accounting reports.
10. Financial accounting reports are often used by individuals outside the business to make decisions, such as whether to buy stock in a company or to loan money to the company.
11. Management accounting reports are used by individuals inside the business to make decisions, such as whether to cut costs or to hire more workers.
12. Three important accounting assumptions are business entity, going concern, and accounting period.

SUMMARY CHAPTER 2

Chapter 2 Quiz

Student ____ Class ____ Instructor ____

Date Assigned ____ Date Completed ____

CHAPTER 2 QUIZ

The World of Business and Accounting

QUESTIONS (Completion)

Directions: *Fill in the blank with the term that best completes each sentence.*

1. The U.S. business system is a ______________.
2. Without ______________ businesses will not be able to continue operating.
3. Entrepreneurs must be able and willing to handle the ______________ of business failure.
4. As an entrepreneur, you can be your own ______________.
5. Three skill areas that contribute to business success are organizational skills, marketing, and ______________ skills.
6. A ______________ business does things for its customers and charges them a fee.
7. A disadvantage of a ______________ is that conflicts may occur between the business owners.
8. ______________ are the set of rules uses by accountants.
9. ______________ accounting reports are prepared for the internal users of financial information.
10. A company that has been in business for ten years is a ______________.

QUESTIONS (Completion)

1. The U.S. business system is a _____.
2. Without _____, businesses will not be able to continue operating.
3. Entrepreneurs must be able and willing to handle the _____ of business failure.
4. As an entrepreneur, you can be your own _____.
5. Three skill areas that contribute to business success are organizational skills, marketing, and _______ skills.
6. A _____ business does things for its customers and charges them a fee.
7. A disadvantage of a _____ is that conflicts may occur between the business owners.
8. _____ are the set of rules used by accountants.
9. _____ accounting reports are prepared for the internal users of financial information.
10. A company that has been in business for ten years is a _____.

ANSWERS

1. free enterprise system
2. profit
3. risk
4. boss
5. accounting
6. service
7. partnership
8. GAAP
9. Management
10. going concern

REVIEW AND ACTIVITIES CHAPTER 2

USING KEY TERMS

See the *Glossary* for the definitions of these terms. Spot check students' understanding of the vocabulary for this chapter by having volunteers read their definitions.

Understanding Accounting Concepts and Procedures

(Answers)

1. Businesses produce the goods and services they choose; individuals buy what they want.
2. Profit.
3. A merchandising business buys goods and then resells them to other businesses or individuals. A manufacturing business makes products and sells them to individuals or other businesses.
4. *Sole Proprietorship Advantages*: Easy to set up, all profits go to owner, owner has total control, few regulations to follow. *Sole Proprietorship Disadvantages*: Limited expertise, hard to raise money, owner has all the risks, hard to attract talented employees. *Partnership Advantages*: Easy to start, skills and talents are pooled, more money available than proprietorship. *Partnership Disadvantages*: Conflicts between partners, profits must be shared, owners share all risks. *Corporation Advantages*: Easier to raise money, easy to expand, easy to transfer ownership, losses limited to investment. *Corporation Disadvantages*: Costs more to start up, complex to organize, more regulations, higher taxes.
5. GAAP stands for generally accepted accounting principles.
6. The purpose of accounting is to provide financial information about a business or a not-for-profit organization. Individuals need financial information in order to make decisions.
7. Financial accounting focuses on information for external users. Management accounting focuses on information for internal users.
8. Business entity, a business independent of its owner's personal holdings; accounting period, the time covered by a financial report; going concern, a business assumed to have an ongoing life.
9. Answers may vary. Traits include being a self-starter, recognizing a need and filling it, having good writing and speaking skills.
10. The internal decision makers of a company.
11. Third parties such as current and potential investors and creditors.

CHAPTER 2 REVIEW AND ACTIVITIES

USING KEY TERMS

On a separate sheet of paper, write a brief definition for each of the following terms:

accounting period
accounting system
business entity
charter
computerized accounting system
corporation
entrepreneur
financial accounting
financial reports
free enterprise system
GAAP
going concern
management accounting
manual accounting system
manufacturing business
merchandising business
partnership
service business
sole proprietorship

Understanding Accounting Concepts and Procedures

Instructions

On a separate sheet of paper, answer the following questions:

1. The United States economy is referred to as a free enterprise system. What are the major characteristics of this system?
2. What is one measure of the success of a business?
3. What is the major difference between a merchandising business and a manufacturing business?
4. List advantages and disadvantages of each form of business organization: sole proprietorship, partnership, corporation.
5. What does GAAP mean?
6. Describe the pupose of accounting.
7. What are the major differences between financial and management accounting?
8. What are the three basic assumptions of accounting, and what do they mean?
9. What are some characteristics of the entrepreneur?
10. Who are the users of management accounting information?
11. Who are the users of financial accounting reports?

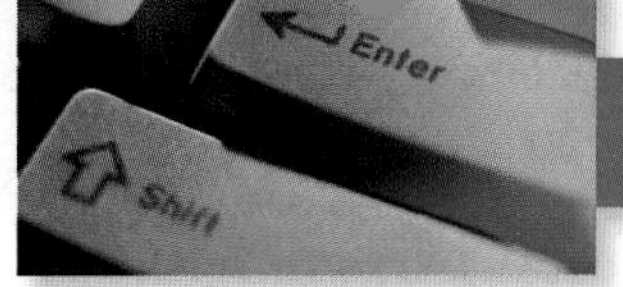

Case Study...

Entrepreneurship

Thousands of entrepreneurs start new businesses each year. Locate two or three entrepreneurs in your local area to interview. If you need help finding entrepreneurs, check with your local chamber of commerce or other business organizations. Telephone each entrepreneur and ask for an interview. Schedule the interview, then prepare questions such as these:

- How did you get the idea for your business?
- How did you finance the business?
- What skills have helped you start and run the business? How did you acquire these skills?
- What personal qualities have helped you be successful?
- What has been your biggest challenge in starting a business?
- What advice would you offer to other would-be entrepreneurs?

Thinking Critically:

1. Conduct the interviews, then write a general profile of the qualities and skills of a successful entrepreneur. Use information from all your interviews.
2. After writing your profile, decide whether you're entrepreneurial material. Explain why or why not.

interNET CONNECTION

The Small Business Administration

Some people dream of starting their own business because they want to be their own boss. Others desire financial independence or the opportunity to fully realize their creative freedom, skills, and knowledge. The Small Business Administration offers a wide variety of resources to the entrepreneur.

Do This:

1. Find the Small Business Administration Web site. What is the Web site address?
2. What features of the site do you think would be the most helpful to a person starting a business?
3. Based on information at the Web site, what goes into a business plan?

Workplace Skills

Individual Responsibility

High performance workers exhibit perseverance and excellence in their job duties. Working well and showing a high level of concentration on any task indicates you can assume individual responsibility for your work.

On the Job:

As an accounting clerk for Prints-in-a-Minute, a sole proprietorship, you prepare most of the financial statements for your employer, José Tirado. As you prepare for your year-end meeting with Mr. Tirado, you locate an error in the financial reports. How do you handle this situation?

Thinking Critically:

1. Mr. Tirado depends on you for accuracy. You write a memo to Mr. Tirado explaining what has occurred. Give Mr. Tirado a plan as to how you will correct the problem.
2. Mr. Tirado has read the memo and has called a conference with you. Pair up with another student and role-play the conference, one of you as the accounting clerk, the other as Mr. Tirado. Together discuss how you plan to fix the mistake.

Case Study...

Thinking Critically (Answers)

Answers will vary. Students should interview at least two entrepreneurs. Gathering information from the interviews, students should create an analysis of what makes a successful entrepreneur. Students should identify the skills and traits they have and explain why they are or are not entrepreneurial material.

Workplace Skills

Thinking Critically (Answers)

Answers will vary. Students should use a word processing program to create a brief memo explaining the error. You might suggest that students refer to the financial documents in Chapter 10 for examples of closing financial statements. Have students select at least one type of statement and choose a possible error (i.e., transposition of numbers, incorrect entry, or missing entry). As they create solutions to the problem, have them look not only for solutions to fix the error, but solutions that would show an investment of personal time beyond the workday to fix the problem.

Role-plays between students can be energizing. Circulate among students to help stimulate conversation, ideas, and interaction. Ask one pair of students to demonstrate their role-play for the entire class.

Internet Resources and Activities Handbook

Refer students to the booklet for additional Internet activities.

interNET CONNECTION www.glencoe.com

Do This (Answers)

1. www.sba.gov
2. Answers will vary.
3. The Web site specifies four major parts to a business plan, including: description of business, marketing plan, financial management plan, and the management plan.

PROBLEMS CHAPTER 2

Problem 2-4 (Answers) Identifying Types of Businesses

1. Manufacturing
2. Merchandising
3. Service
4. Service
5. Manufacturing
6. Service
7. Merchandising
8. Service
9. Merchandising
10. Merchandising
11. Service
12. Manufacturing

Problem 2-5 (Answers) Understanding Accounting Assumptions

1. Accounting Period
2. Going Concern
3. Business Entity
4. Going Concern
5. Business Entity
6. Accounting Period

Problem 2-6 (Answers) Understanding Business Operations

1. Manufacturing (bread) and merchandising (selling bread to public).
2. $225 before other expenses.
3. Answers may vary. Other expenses to consider when calculating profits are wages, utilities, rent, and supplies.

CHAPTER 2 PROBLEMS

Problem 2–4 Identifying Types of Businesses

Instructions In your working papers, indicate whether each of the following businesses is a service business, a merchandising business, or a manufacturing business.

1. International Business Machines (IBM)
2. The Gap
3. Glendale Medical Center
4. Avis Rent-a-Car
5. Ford Motor Company
6. The Chase Manhattan Bank
7. Ace Hardware Stores
8. Michigan City Animal Hospital
9. Office Depot
10. Wal-Mart Discount Department Store
11. Prudential Insurance Company of America
12. Bethlehem Steel Corporation

Problem 2–5 Understanding Accounting Assumptions

Instructions In your working papers, indicate the assumption from the list below that best matches each numbered statement.

Accounting Period | **Business Entity** | **Going Concern**

1. Accounting reports may cover a month, a quarter, or a year.
2. Accountants expect a business to last indefinitely.
3. The personal property of a business owner is not included in the accounting records of the business.
4. The business has been in operation for several years and is expected to continue.
5. An owner's personal activities or properties are not mixed with the business activities or properties.
6. The accountant's report shows how much profit the business earned for one month.

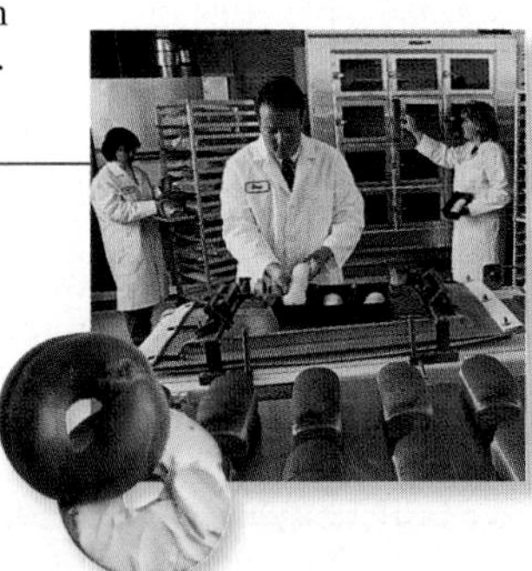

Problem 2–6 Understanding Business Operations

Mary Torres owns and operates a bakery. During the past week she sold 500 loaves of bread at $2.25 per loaf. The raw materials for each loaf cost Ms. Torres $1.80.

ASSESSMENT RESOURCES

Choose assessment strategies from the following pages to evaluate your students' progress.

Student Edition
Check Your Understanding, pp. 31, 35
Chapter 2 Problems, pp. 40–41

Assessment and Evaluation Masters
Chapter 2 Study Plan, *Glencoe Workbook (CRWP)*
Chapter 2 Self-Test, *Glencoe Workbook (CRWP)*
Chapter 2 Test, *Chapter Tests* Booklet
Chapter 2 Activity, *School-to-Work Handbook*
Chapter 2 **Exam***View*

Teacher Wraparound Edition
Critical Thinking, p. 28
Reteaching Sections 1–2, pp. 31, 35
Chapter 2 Quiz, p. 37

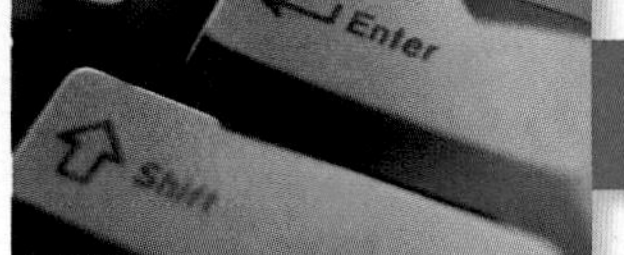

Instructions In your working papers, write the answers to the following questions:

1. What type of business does Ms. Torres operate?
2. What was the profit on bread sales for the week?
3. Aside from the costs for raw materials, what other costs will Ms. Torres use to calculate her profit for the week?

Problem 2–7 Categorizing Forms of Business Organizations

Instructions Match the letter next to each form of business with the appropriate items in the following list of advantages and disadvantages. You may use a letter more than once. Use the form provided in your working papers.

A. Sole Proprietorship B. Partnership C. Corporation

1. Easier to raise money
2. Limited expertise
3. Costs more to start up
4. Owner has total control
5. Must share the profits
6. Higher taxes
7. Fewer regulations to follow
8. Easy to transfer ownership
9. Conflict between owners
10. Easy to expand

Problem 2–8 Working as an Entrepreneur

Instructions Using the form in your working papers, identify each of the following as an advantage or disadvantage of being an entrepreneur. For each item you label a disadvantage, decide what actions you would take to overcome that disadvantage. Analyze and describe how your actions might affect the profit your business earns.

1. Risking the loss of your savings
2. Deciding what you and everyone else needs to do each day
3. Lacking steady wages and employee benefits
4. Choosing when and where to work
5. Keeping the financial benefits of your hard work
6. Choosing the people you want to work with
7. Paying all the expenses of a new business

Problem 2–7 (Answers) Categorizing Forms of Business Organization

1. C
2. A
3. C
4. A
5. B or C
6. C
7. A or B
8. C
9. B
10. C

Problem 2–8 (Answers) Working as an Entrepreneur

1. Disadvantage
2. Advantage
3. Disadvantage
4. Advantage
5. Advantage
6. Advantage
7. Disadvantage

Students should provide their own ideas in overcoming the disadvantages and explain how their actions might affect profits.

MAKING CONNECTIONS TO DAILY LIFE

Types of Credit Most students are familiar with the use of credit through credit-card purchases. Discuss with the class other types of credit, including loans and charge accounts. Then divide students into groups of four or five, and have each of them create a list of the advantages and disadvantages of using credit. Ask each group to name several local sources for borrowing money to purchase a car. (Group responses should include names of local banks, credit unions, savings and loans, auto dealerships, and finance companies.)

UNIT 2 *Resource Manager*

This is a representation of key resources available in the *Glencoe Accounting* program.

*inter*NET CONNECTION

Use the following Web resources to introduce, reinforce, or stimulate discussion on unit topics.

- Case Studies
- Study Plans
- Career Corner
- Real-Life Applications
- Self-Assessment Quizzes
- Games for the Classroom
- Ethics and the Profession

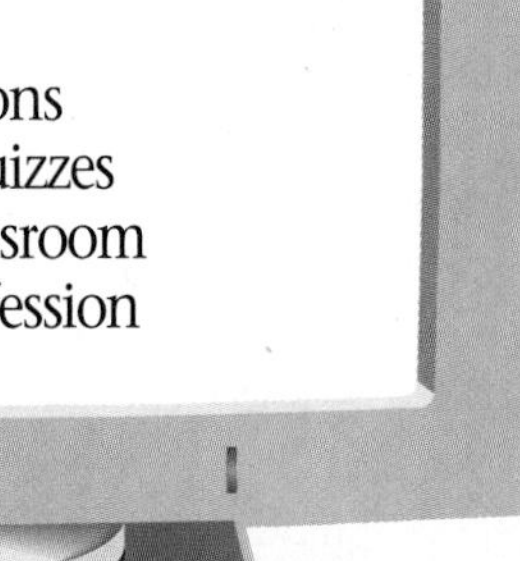

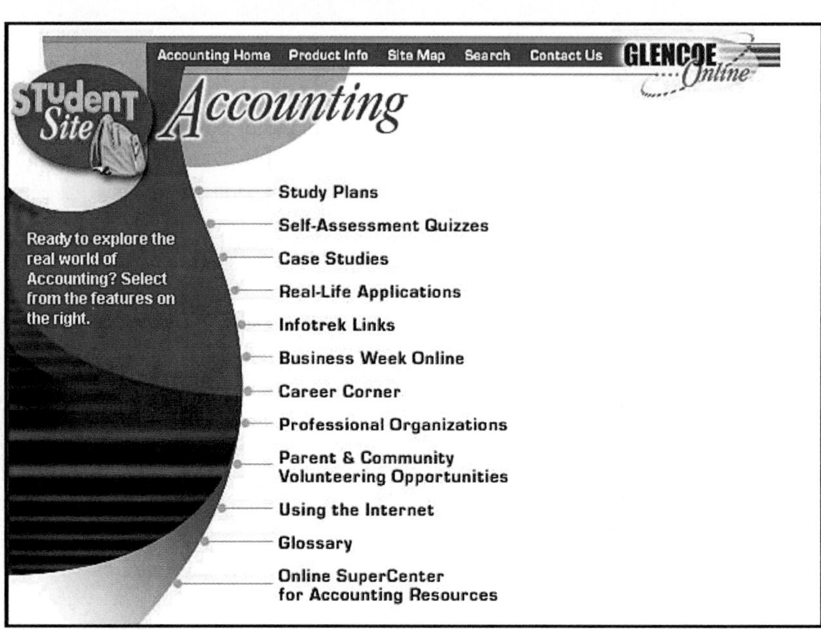

GLENCOE ACCOUNTING BULLETIN BOARD POSTER

Peachtree Complete® Accounting

Preparing you for the Real World

Virtual Business® CD-ROM

Virtual Business **is a fully visual marketing and business simulation that lets students start and run their own business. For more information on the simulation, visit the teacher page on the** ***Glencoe Accounting*** **Web site.**

Accounting in Action

Unit Video Portfolio

Integrating *Electronic Field Trips* into Your Accounting Instruction

The *Electronic Field Trip* videos provide an excellent introduction to key accounting concepts taught in the textbook. You may want to use these video segments in **Unit 2**. The titles of the video segments are:

- *Accounting All Around You*
- *Business Transactions*
- *Computerized Accounting*
- *Business Ethics*
- *Global Perspectives*
- *The Accounting Cycle*
- *Banking and Internal Control*

Business Simulation

Adventure Travels

(For use after Chapter 11)

Mini Practice Sets

Canyon.com Web Sites

Fast Track Tutoring Service

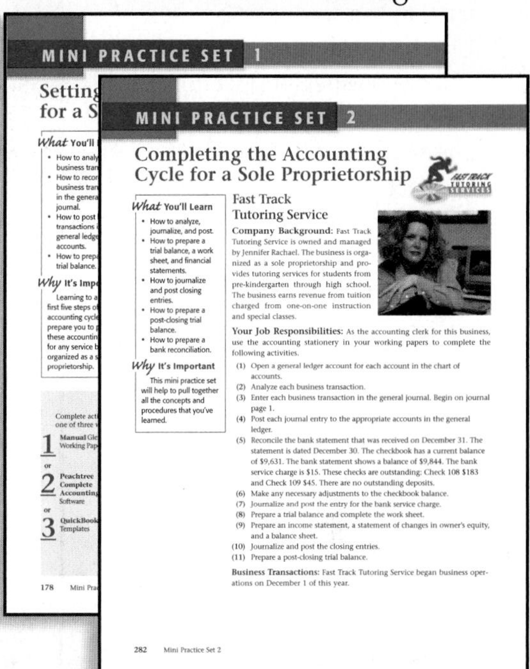

MINI PRACTICE SET 1

MINI PRACTICE SET 2

Completing the Accounting Cycle for a Sole Proprietorship

What **You'll Learn**

- How to analyze, journalize, and post.
- How to prepare a trial balance, a work sheet, and financial statements.
- How to journalize and post closing entries.
- How to prepare a post-closing trial balance.
- How to prepare a bank reconciliation.

Why **It's Important**

This mini practice set will help to pull together all the concepts and procedures that you've learned.

Fast Track Tutoring Service

Company Background: Fast Track Tutoring Service is owned and managed by Jennifer Rachael. The business is organized as a sole proprietorship and provides tutoring services for students from pre-kindergarten through high school. The business earns revenue from tuition charged from one-on-one instruction and special classes.

Your Job Responsibilities: As the accounting clerk for this business, use the accounting stationery in your working papers to complete the following activities.

(1) Open a general ledger account for each account in the chart of accounts.
(2) Analyze each business transaction.
(3) Enter each business transaction in the general journal. Begin on journal page 1.
(4) Post each journal entry to the appropriate accounts in the general ledger.
(5) Reconcile the bank statement that was received on December 31. The statement is dated December 30. The checkbook has a current balance of $9,631. The bank statement shows a balance of $9,844. The bank service charge is $15. These checks are outstanding: Check 108 $183 and Check 109 $45. There are no outstanding deposits.
(6) Make any necessary adjustments to the checkbook balance.
(7) Journalize and post the entry for the bank service charge.
(8) Prepare a trial balance and complete the work sheet.
(9) Prepare an income statement, a statement of changes in owner's equity, and a balance sheet.
(10) Journalize and post the closing entries.
(11) Prepare a post-closing trial balance.

Business Transactions: Fast Track Tutoring Service began business operations on December 1 of this year.

282 Mini Practice Set 2

Assessment and Evaluation

Unit 2 Test

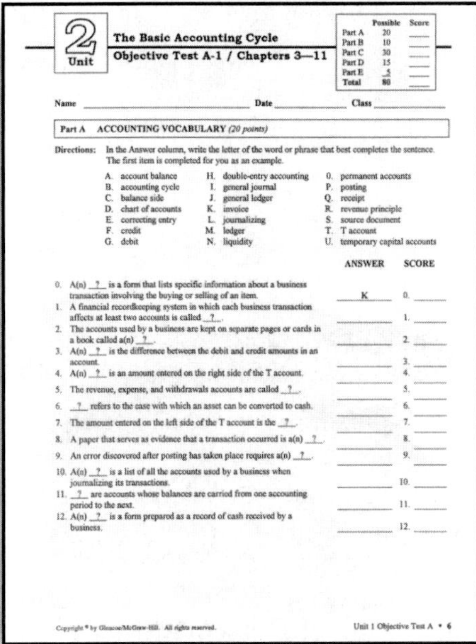

Unit 2 — The Basic Accounting Cycle

Objective Test A-1 / Chapters 3—11

	Possible	Score
Part A	20	
Part B	10	
Part C	30	
Part D	15	
Part E	5	
Total	80	

Name ______ Date ______ Class ______

Part A ACCOUNTING VOCABULARY *(20 points)*

Directions: In the Answer column, write the letter of the word or phrase that best completes the sentence. The first item is completed for you as an example.

A. account balance	H. double-entry accounting	O. permanent accounts
B. accounting cycle	I. general journal	P. posting
C. balance side	J. general ledger	Q. receipt
D. chart of accounts	K. invoice	R. revenue principle
E. correcting entry	L. journalizing	S. source document
F. credit	M. ledger	T. T account
G. debit	N. liquidity	U. temporary capital accounts

	ANSWER	SCORE
0. A(n) __?__ is a form that lists specific information about a business transaction involving the buying or selling of an item.	K	0.
1. A financial recordkeeping system in which each business transaction affects at least two accounts is called __?__.		1.
2. The accounts used by a business are kept on separate pages or cards in a book called a(n) __?__.		2.
3. A(n) __?__ is the difference between the debit and credit amounts in an account.		3.
4. A(n) __?__ is an amount entered on the right side of the T account.		4.
5. The revenue, expense, and withdrawals accounts are called __?__.		5.
6. __?__ refers to the ease with which an asset can be converted to cash.		6.
7. The amount entered on the left side of the T account is the __?__.		7.
8. A paper that serves as evidence that a transaction occurred is a(n) __?__.		8.
9. An error discovered after posting has taken place requires a(n) __?__.		9.
10. A(n) __?__ is a list of all the accounts used by a business when journalizing its transactions.		10.
11. __?__ are accounts whose balances are carried from one accounting period to the next.		11.
12. A(n) __?__ is a form prepared as a record of cash received by a business.		12.

Unit 1 Objective Test A • 6

Accounting Portfolio

Unit 2 Employability Skills

Student ______ Class ______ Instructor ______

Date Assigned ______ Date Completed ______

Unit 2 — *Accounting Portfolio*

Employability Skills

Employability skills are a combination of foundation skills (basic skills, thinking skills, and personal qualities) and knowledge of resources, information, interpersonal skills, systems, and technology that make up workplace competencies. A prospective employer will evaluate your employability skills. The better your skills, the better your chances for employment.

SELF-ASSESSMENT

Read the descriptions of the SCANS foundation skills and the workplace competencies on pages 11-14. Then consider your own skills and answer the following questions. The answers to these questions will not be evaluated by anyone else, so evaluate your strengths and weaknesses honestly.

1. Of the six basic skills (foundation skills), which do you consider your strongest skill? Why?
2. Which of the basic skills is your weakest? Why? How can you improve that skill?
3. Of the six thinking skills, which is your strongest? your weakest? How can you improve these skills?
4. How would you rate your personal qualities? For example, are you responsible? Do you do what you say you'll do? Which of your personal qualities do you want to improve?
5. If you were hired for a job tomorrow, would you know how to allocate each of the four resources under workplace competencies (time, money, material/facility, and human)? What do you need to improve?
6. Read the section on information under workplace competencies. Do you know how to acquire and use information to help you solve problems and make decisions on the job? What do you need to improve?

Accounting Portfolio 9

Enrichment and Extension

Accounting Competitive Event Review

Student ______ Class ______ Instructor ______

Date Assigned ______ Date Completed ______

Business Transactions and the Accounting Equation

The accounting process begins with the analysis of business transactions. The accountant analyzes each transaction to determine its effect on the basic accounting equation, which is:

Assets = Liabilities + Owner's Equity

Every transaction causes a change in the financial position of a business. These changes are recorded in the accounts of the business. Although each transaction affects the balances in two or more accounts, the basic accounting equation always remains in balance.

For further information: See Chapter 3, First Year; Chapters 1 and 2, Advanced.

For additional practice: Additional Reinforcement Problem 3A.

On a separate sheet of paper, answer the following questions.

True/False

1. When using the basic accounting equation, the accountant must make sure that the total assets always equal the total of the liabilities and the owner's equity.
2. Changes in owner's equity can result from revenue and expenses.
3. When cash is collected from accounts receivable, there is no change in the total amount of the assets.
4. When cash is paid to a creditor, the company's liabilities increase.
5. The property that a business owns is referred to as its liabilities.
6. Revenue decreases owner's equity.
7. Expenses decrease owner's equity.
8. Property rights are the financial claims to property.
9. The word *payable* indicates that an account is a liability.
10. Another way to express the basic accounting equation is Assets − Liabilities = Owner's Equity.
11. The companies or individuals to whom amounts are owed are called investors.
12. When the owner invests cash in a business, assets and revenue increase.
13. The money an owner withdraws from the business is considered to be an expense.

Multiple Choice

14. Examples of assets are (A) cash and accounts receivable, (B) cash and revenue, (C) withdrawals and accounts payable, (D) cash and rent expense.
15. If a business has assets of $45,670 and liabilities of $12,845, the owner's equity is (A) $12,845, (B) $32,825, (C) $91,340, (D) $58,515.
16. The word *equities* refers to claims against the assets of a business by (A) owners only, (B) customers only, (C) creditors only, (D) both owners and creditors.
17. A business transaction that involves a purchase on account is considered to be (A) an investment by the owner, (B) a credit transaction, (C) a cash transaction, (D) an expense transaction.

Accounting Competitive Event Review • 13

OVERVIEW
UNIT 2

Unit Objectives

1. Correctly use terminology related to the accounting cycle.
2. Use the accounting equation to analyze business transactions.
3. Describe accounting principles and practices for a sole proprietorship, service business.
4. Record and report operating results for a sole proprietorship, service business.

Unit 2 Contents

EXTENDING THE QUOTE

Martin Luther King, Jr., used his time campaigning tirelessly for voting rights and legislation ending discrimination in the schools, in business, and in public life.

UNIT 2

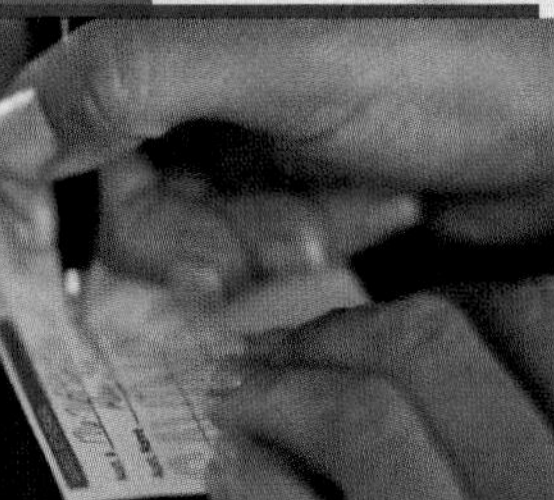

The Basic Accounting Cycle

In this unit. . .

All businesses keep financial records. In this unit, you will learn how business transactions affect the financial records of a business. Learning to analyze business transactions correctly is the first step toward learning accounting. The business used as an example in this unit is a sole proprietorship. The business, called **Roadrunner Delivery Service,** provides delivery services to its customers. After studying the chapters in this unit, you will have an understanding of the accounting cycle for a service business and will identify the accounting functions involved with a sole proprietorship.

We must use time creatively and forever realize that time is always hope to do great things.

—Martin Luther King, Jr.
American Civil
Rights Leader

42

Great Ideas *From the Classroom of...*

People Search Create a list of questions to review a topic, and establish a time limit for the game (answering the questions). Have each student **seek** another member of the class who can answer one of the questions correctly. That person should **share** the answer, **sign** below the question, **smile**, **shake** hands, and move on. Each student should seek other members of the class until all questions have been answered correctly. Each person may sign only once.

James A. Wermes
Elk Grove High School
Elk Grove Village, Illinois

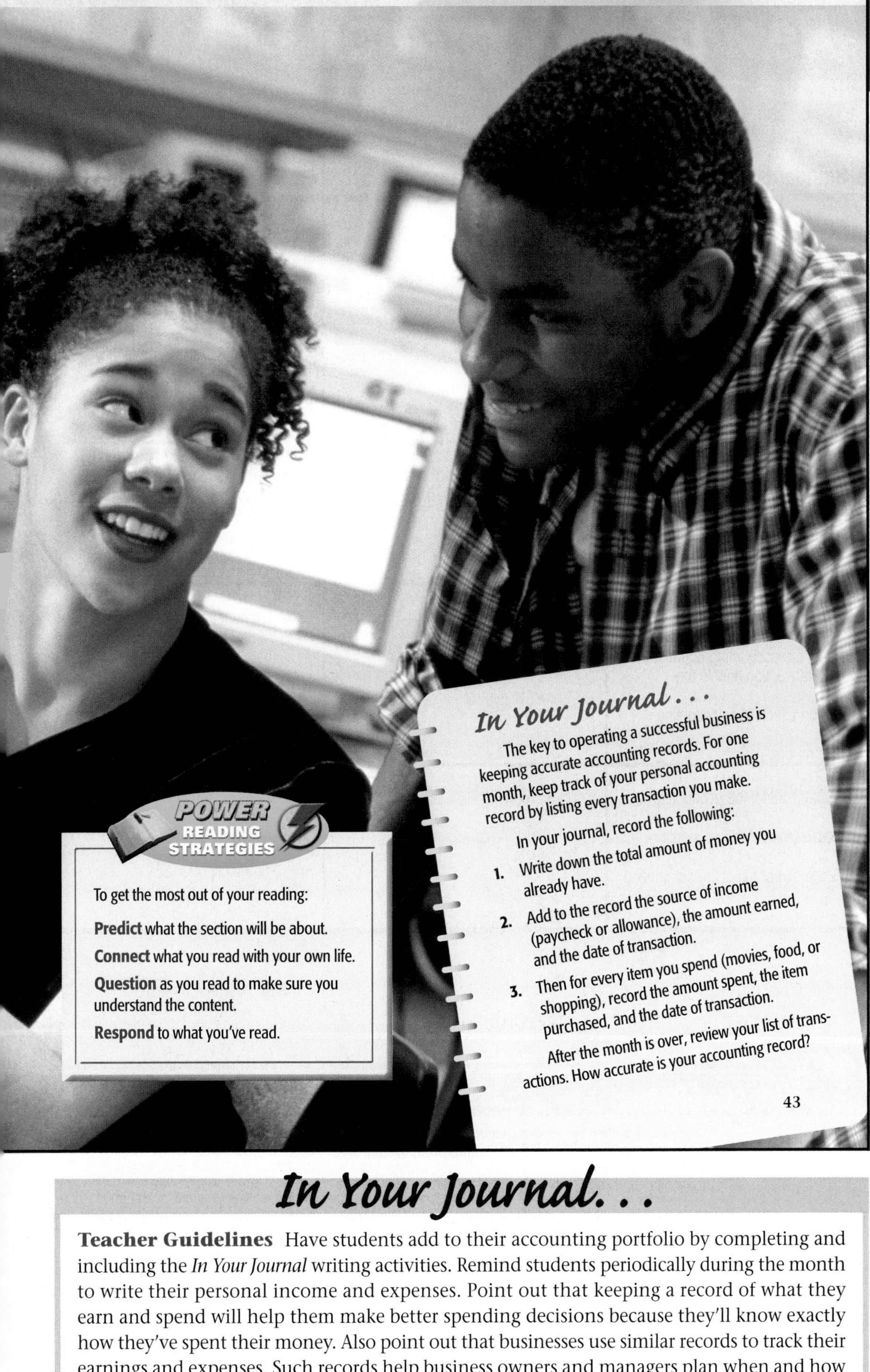

In Your Journal...

The key to operating a successful business is keeping accurate accounting records. For one month, keep track of your personal accounting record by listing every transaction you make.

In your journal, record the following:

1. Write down the total amount of money you already have.
2. Add to the record the source of income (paycheck or allowance), the amount earned, and the date of transaction.
3. Then for every item you spend (movies, food, or shopping), record the amount spent, the item purchased, and the date of transaction.

After the month is over, review your list of transactions. How accurate is your accounting record?

POWER READING STRATEGIES

To get the most out of your reading:

Predict what the section will be about.

Connect what you read with your own life.

Question as you read to make sure you understand the content.

Respond to what you've read.

INTRODUCING UNIT 2

Previewing the Chapters

In this unit students learn the basic accounting equation and how to use that equation to analyze business transactions. As they complete the unit, students analyze typical transactions for a sole proprietorship, service business and record those transactions in a double-entry accounting system. After completing an entire accounting cycle, students learn about banking and cash control.

Tying to Previous Knowledge

Unit 1 introduced students to career research and planning, along with the opportunities available for trained accountants. Students also learned about the forms of business organization, the role of profit and loss in a free enterprise economy, and the basic assumptions underlying an accounting system. In this unit, students will use their knowledge of business organization and accounting assumptions to learn how to analyze and prepare financial records for a business.

In Your Journal...

Teacher Guidelines Have students add to their accounting portfolio by completing and including the *In Your Journal* writing activities. Remind students periodically during the month to write their personal income and expenses. Point out that keeping a record of what they earn and spend will help them make better spending decisions because they'll know exactly how they've spent their money. Also point out that businesses use similar records to track their earnings and expenses. Such records help business owners and managers plan when and how to spend money to operate the business. P

BULLETIN BOARD

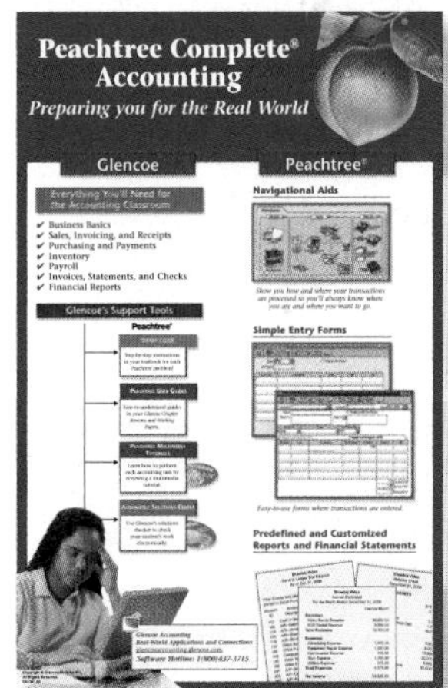

Glencoe Poster Teaching Tip

Ask students how using Peachtree Complete® Accounting software can benefit their study of accounting. Point out the Glencoe support tools listed on the poster as students start the Peachtree® problems beginning in Chapter 5 of this unit.

CHAPTER 3 Resource Manager

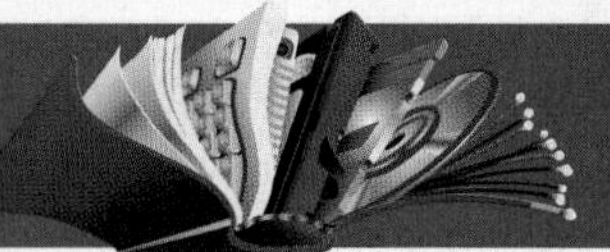

Section Resources

	Objectives & Standards	Activities & Features	Reproducible Masters
Chapter Opener *Business Transactions and the Accounting Equation*	• Describe the relationship between property and financial claims. • List and define each part of the accounting equation. • Show how various business transactions affect the accounting equation. • Check the balance of the accounting equation after a business transaction has been analyzed and recorded. • Define the accounting terms introduced in this chapter. **National Standards for Business Education**: IA3, IA6, IIC1, IIC3	Exploring the Real World of Business, p. 44 Workplace Connections, p. 45	School-to-Work Handbook
Section 1 *Property and Financial Claims*	• The relationship between property and financial claims. • The meaning of equity as it is used in accounting. • The parts of the accounting equation. • The definition of each part of the accounting equation.	International Accounting, p. 47 Accounting Flashbacks, p. 47 Math Hints, p. 48 A Matter of Ethics, p. 48	Demonstration Problems Strategies for Teaching International Accounting Strategies for Teaching Ethics in Accounting
Section 2 *Transactions That Affect Owner's Investment, Cash, and Credit*	• How accounts are used in business transactions. • The steps used to analyze business transactions. • How investments affect the accounting equation. • How a cash payment transaction affects the accounting equation. • How a credit transaction affects the accounting equation.	Accounting Tips, p. 51 Did You Know?, p. 51	Demonstration Problems Math Review for Accounting
Section 3 *Transactions That Affect Revenue, Expense, and Withdrawals by the Owner*	• How revenue transactions affect the accounting equation. • How expense transactions affect the accounting equation. • How withdrawals by the owner affect the accounting equation.	Connect To, p. 58	Demonstration Problems Internet Resources and Activities Handbook

KEY

Posters · Transparency · Software · Videocassette
Blackline Masters · CD-ROM · Portfolio

MULTIMEDIA RESOURCE

Peachtree	QuickBooks	Spreadsheets	Videos	CD-ROMs
None in this chapter.	None in this chapter.	Problem 3–9 *Determining the Effects of Business Transactions on the Accounting Equation*	***Video Segment: Accounting All Around You*** After viewing this video, students will be able to describe the role that accounting plays in providing decision-making information in a private enterprise economy.	***Electronic Learning Center (ELC), Chapter 3*** This program is ideal for visual learners since it incorporates video images, animation, and graphics to enliven the content of each lesson. ***Interactive Lesson Planner (ILP), Chapter 3*** This CD-ROM combines the versatility of an electronic lesson planner with the convenience of teacher classroom resources.

SCANS Correlation Chart

FOUNDATION SKILLS

Basic Skills:	Reading	Writing	Math	Listening	Speaking	
Thinking Skills:	Creative Thinking	Decision Making	Problem Solving	Seeing Things in the Mind's Eye	Knowing How to Learn	Reasoning
Personal Qualities:	Responsibility	Self-Esteem	Sociability	Self-Management	Integrity/Honesty	

WORKPLACE COMPETENCIES

Resources:	Allocating Time	Allocating Money	Allocating Material and Facility Resources	Allocating Human Resources		
Information:	Acquiring and Evaluating Information	Organizing and Maintaining Information	Interpreting and Communicating Information	Using Computers to Process Information		
Interpersonal Skills:	Participating as a Member of a Team	Teaching Others	Serving Clients/ Customers	Exercising Leadership	Negotiating to Arrive at a Decision	Working with Cultural Diversity
Systems:	Understanding Systems	Monitoring and Correcting Performance	Improving and Designing Systems			
Technology:	Selecting Technology	Applying Technology to Task	Maintaining and Troubleshooting Technology			

*Highlighted blocks indicate areas covered in the chapter. Additional SCANS skills are also covered throughout the *Teacher Wraparound Edition.*

Assessment

Student Edition
- Check Your Understanding, pp. 49, 56, 60
- Chapter 3 Problems, pp. 65–69

Assessment and Evaluation Masters
- Chapter 3 Study Plan, *Glencoe Workbook*
- Chapter 3 Self-Test, *Glencoe Workbook*
- Chapter 3 Test, *Chapter Tests* Booklet
- Chapter 3 Activity, *School-to-Work Handbook*
- Chapter 3 **Exam***View*

Teacher Wraparound Edition
- Critical Thinking Activity, p. 54
- Reteaching Section 1, p. 49
- Reteaching Section 2, p. 56
- Reteaching Section 3, p. 60
- Chapter 3 Quiz, p. 61

Transparencies

	Teaching Transparencies	Solution Transparencies
Section 1:	3–1	Problem 3–1
Section 2:	3–2, 3–3, 3–4, 3–5, 3–6, 3–7, 3–8, 3–9, 3–10	Problem 3–2
Section 3:	3–11, 3–12, 3–13, 3–14	Problem 3–3
End of Chapter:		Problems 3–4, 3–5, 3–6, 3–7, 3–8, 3–9, 3–10, 3–11

TEACHER CLASSROOM RESOURCES

This is a representation of key blackline masters available in the Teacher Classroom Resources.

Teaching Aids

Transparency Examples

Section Focus Transparencies

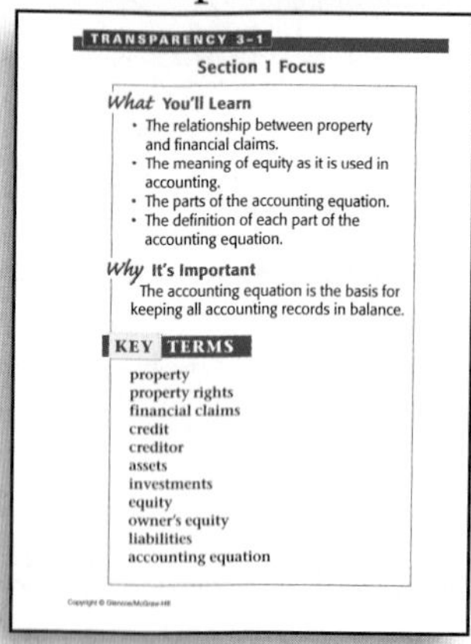

TRANSPARENCY 3-1

Section 1 Focus

What You'll Learn
- The relationship between property and financial claims.
- The meaning of equity as it is used in accounting.
- The parts of the accounting equation.
- The definition of each part of the accounting equation.

Why It's Important

The accounting equation is the basis for keeping all accounting records in balance.

KEY TERMS

property
property rights
financial claims
credit
creditor
assets
investments
equity
owner's equity
liabilities
accounting equation

Teaching Transparencies

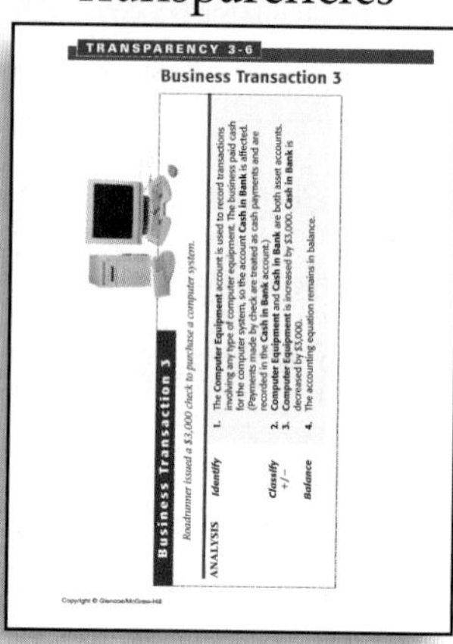

TRANSPARENCY 3-6

Business Transaction 3

Teaching Transparencies

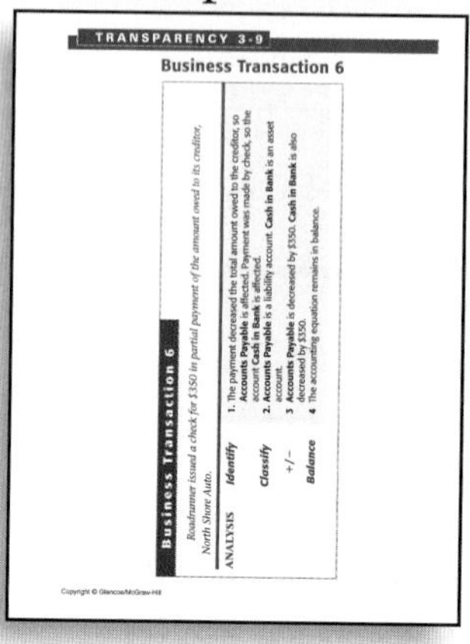

TRANSPARENCY 3-9

Business Transaction 6

Solution Transparencies

Working Papers for End-of-Chapter Problems

Problem 3-4 Classifying Accounts

Problem 3-5 Completing the Accounting Equation

Problem 3-6 Classifying Accounts within the Accounting Equation

Demonstration Problems

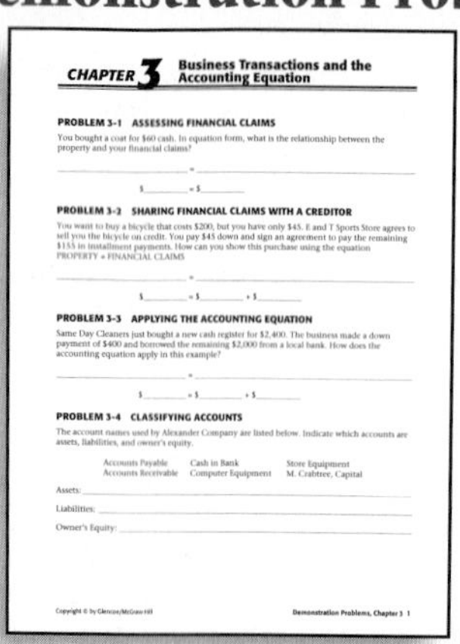

CHAPTER 3 Business Transactions and the Accounting Equation

PROBLEM 3-1 ASSESSING FINANCIAL CLAIMS

PROBLEM 3-2 SHARING FINANCIAL CLAIMS WITH A CREDITOR

PROBLEM 3-3 APPLYING THE ACCOUNTING EQUATION

PROBLEM 3-4 CLASSIFYING ACCOUNTS

Lesson Plans

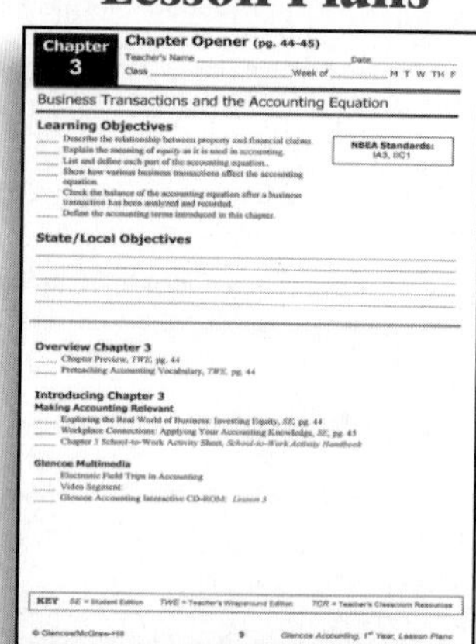

Chapter 3 Chapter Opener (pg. 44-45)

Business Transactions and the Accounting Equation

Learning Objectives

State/Local Objectives

Overview Chapter 3

Introducing Chapter 3

Glencoe Multimedia

Block Scheduling

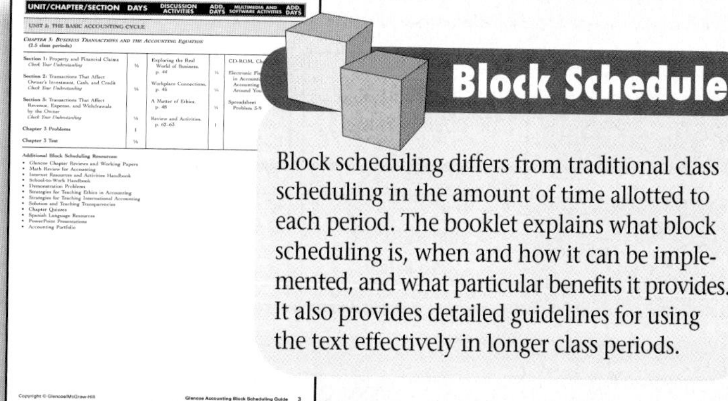

Block Schedule

Block scheduling differs from traditional class scheduling in the amount of time allotted to each period. The booklet explains what block scheduling is, when and how it can be implemented, and what particular benefits it provides. It also provides detailed guidelines for using the text effectively in longer class periods.

Enrichment and Application

Strategies for Teaching Ethics in Accounting

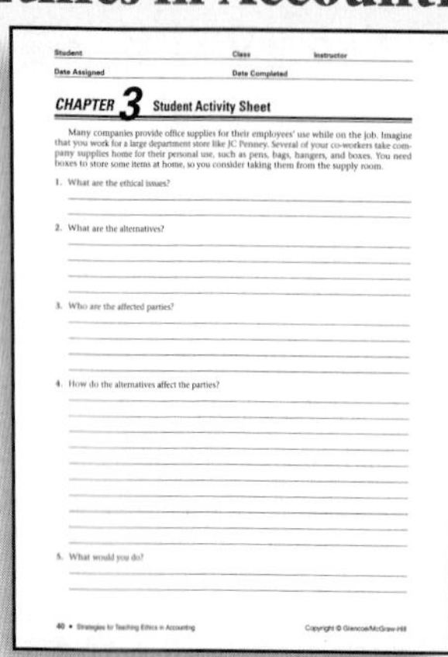

CHAPTER 3 Student Activity Sheet

1. What are the ethical issues?
2. What are the alternatives?
3. Who are the affected parties?
4. How do the alternatives affect the parties?
5. What would you do?

Strategies for Teaching International Accounting

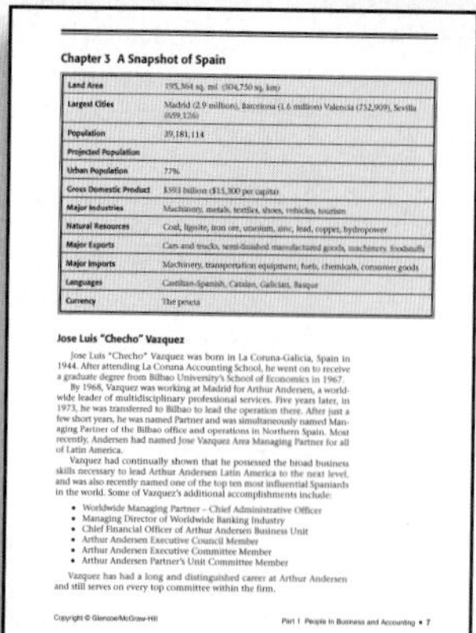

Chapter 3 A Snapshot of Spain

Jose Luis "Checho" Vasquez

School-to-Work Handbook

CHAPTER 3 SCHOOL-TO-WORK ACTIVITY

Business Transactions and the Accounting Equation

Meeting Different Ability Levels

Chapter Reviews and Working Papers (CRWP)

Working Papers

Review

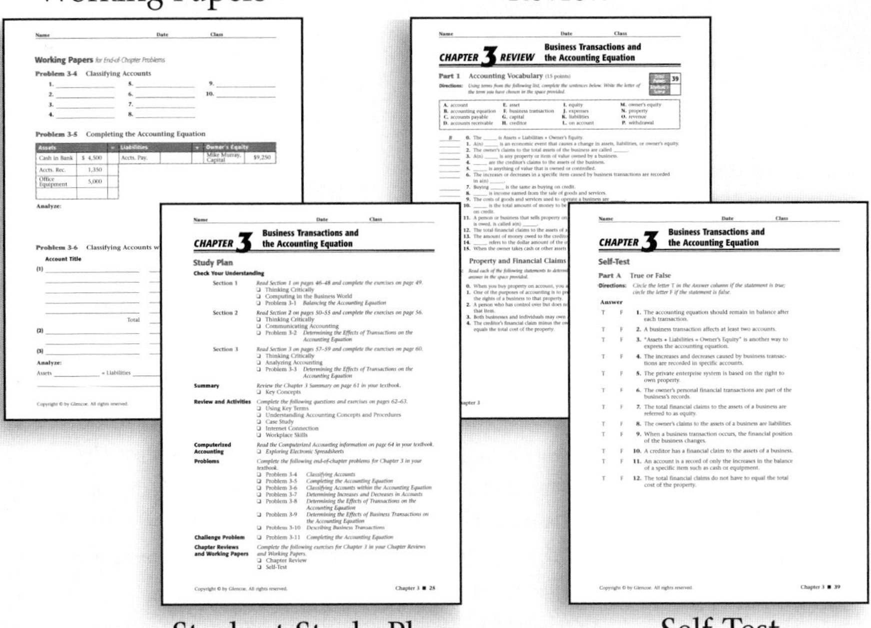

Student Study Plan

Self-Test

Real-World Multimedia CD-ROM

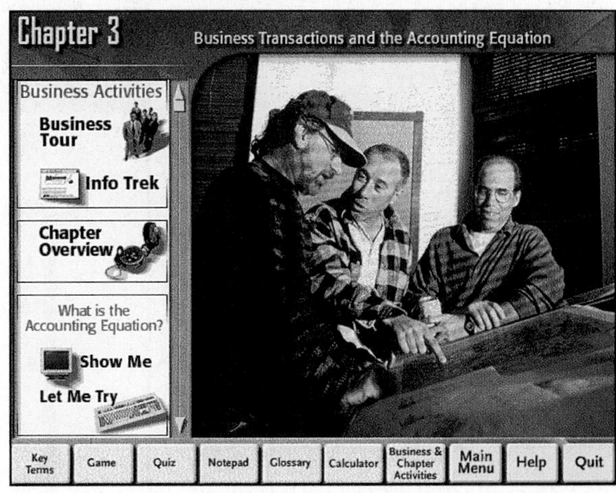

Key to Ability Levels

Each section gives skill-building activities. Each activity has been labeled for use with students of various learning styles and abilities.

L1 Level 1 activities are basic activities and should be within the range of all students.

L2 Level 2 activities are average activities and should be within the range of average and above average students.

L3 Level 3 activities are challenging activities designed for the ability range of above average students.

ELL ELL activities should be within the ability range of English Language Learners.

Assessment and Evaluation

Chapter Tests

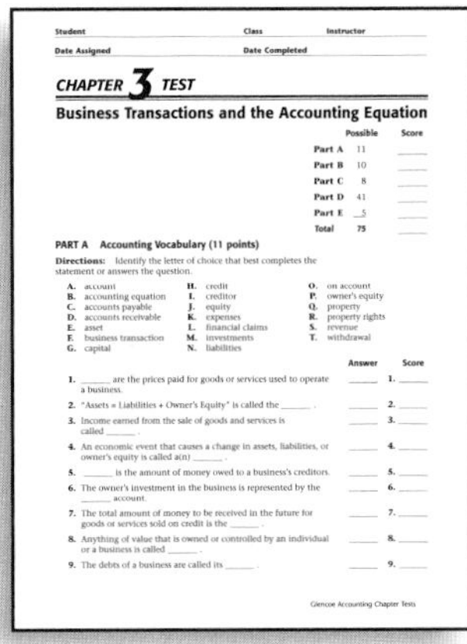

Chapter Quiz

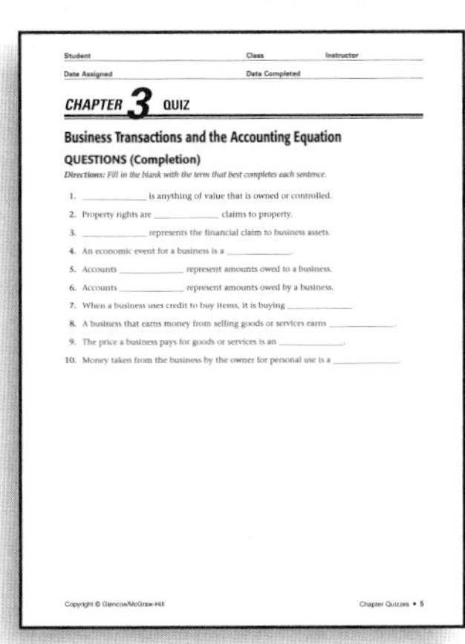

Teaching Resources at a Glance

Application Resources

- Glencoe Chapter Review and Working Papers, SE and TAE
- School-to-Work Handbook, SE and TM
- Accounting Portfolio, SE and TM

Reproducible Masters

- Demonstration Problems
- Lesson Plans
- Block Scheduling
- Spanish Language Resources

Glencoe Accounting Professional Development Series

- Strategies for Teaching Ethics in Accounting
- Accounting Competitive Event Review
- Math Review for Accounting
- Strategies for Teaching International Accounting
- Internet Resources and Activities Handbook

Transparency Package

- Section Focus Transparencies
- Teaching Transparencies
- Source Document Transparencies
- Solution Transparencies

Performance Assessment

- **Exam***View* CD-ROM
- Chapter Tests
- Chapter Quizzes
- Unit Tests
- Audit Tests
- Printed Testbank

Multimedia Resources

- Electronic Learning Center:
  - Multimedia CD-ROMs
  - Peachtree software, tutorials, templates, and solutions
  - Spreadsheet templates
- Using QuickBooks with Glencoe Accounting
- Interactive Lesson Planner
- Electronic Field Trips in Accounting
- PowerPoint Presentation
- Web site: glencoeaccounting.glencoe.com

OVERVIEW CHAPTER 3

Correlations to National Standards for Business Education

(See pages T50–T51 for a detailed correlation chart.)

Standards: IA3, IA6, IIC1, IIC3

Chapter Preview

In this chapter students will learn the basic accounting equation and the rules of debit and credit for accounts in each part of the equation. Using the equation and the rules of debit and credit, students will analyze the effects of typical business transactions for a sole proprietorship, service business.

Section Overviews

- Section 1—*Property and Financial Claims*
- Section 2—*Transactions That Affect Owner's Investment, Cash, and Credit*
- Section 3—*Transactions That Affect Revenue, Expense, and Withdrawals by the Owner*

Chapter Vocabulary

property
property rights
financial claims
credit
creditor
assets
investments
equity
owner's equity
liabilities
accounting equation
business transaction
account
accounts receivable
accounts payable
capital
on account
revenue
expense
withdrawal

Preteaching Accounting Vocabulary

Oral Contest: Set up a team competition to define new terms. Appoint teams to participate in a "Vocabulary Bee." Teams take turns defining terms, with team members consulting each other before giving a definition. If a team gives an incorrect definition, that team is eliminated. L1

CHAPTER 3

Business Transactions and the Accounting Equation

Learning Objectives

When you have completed this chapter, you will be able to:

- Appy basic accounting concepts.
- Apply basic accounting terminology.
- Describe the relationship between property and financial claims.
- Explain the meaning of *equity* as it is used in accounting.
- List and define each part of the accounting equation.
- Demonstrate the effects of transactions on the accounting equation.
- Check the balance of the accounting equation after a business transaction has been analyzed and recorded.
- Define the accounting terms introduced in this chapter.

Exploring the Real World of Business

INVESTING EQUITY

Born in Cincinnati, Ohio, Steven Spielberg shot his first movie in order to earn a Boy Scout merit badge. His homemade action film, called *Gunsmog,* featured a holdup, a sheriff, and a bad guy who plunged over a cliff. By the age of 46, Spielberg became a billionaire by producing movies like *ET, Back to the Future, Jurassic Park,* and several *Indiana Jones* movies.

DreamWorks SKG is a partnership he formed with Jeffrey Katzenberg and David Geffen. Each partner invested $33 million with plans to produce feature films and television series. **DreamWorks SKG** is located in Hollywood, California.

What do you think?

1. Making movies and television programs can cost millions of dollars. How do you think the money invested by the **DreamWorks'** partners helps the company operate?
2. What are the benefits of a partnership?

DreamWorks SKG

Exploring the Real World of Business

DreamWorks SKG

Steven Spielberg applied to the cinema school at the University of Southern California twice but was turned down both times because his grades had been too low. Fortunately for movie lovers, he persevered and became one of the most successful directors in the movie business.

What do you think? (Answers)

1. Money invested in the business is used to pay expenses such as making movies, which in turn brings in revenue for the company.
2. A partner can provide additional money needed to operate the business or expertise in managing the business.

Glencoe Accounting Online

Visit the *Glencoe Accounting* Web site at **glencoeaccounting.glencoe.com** for additional activities and information.

Workplace Connections

Applying Your Accounting Knowledge

Every business has assets, liabilities, and owner's equity—the elements in the basic accounting equation that you'll study in this chapter. The business uses an accounting system to record its assets, liabilities, and owner's equity. Your local bakery's assets (what it owns) probably include kitchen equipment and ovens. Its liabilities (debts) may include unpaid bills to food suppliers, and the owner's equity of the business (what the business is worth) may be money that the owner invested to get the bakery up and running.

Investigate:

1. In your workplace, what assets does the business have?
2. What types of debts or liabilities would you imagine the business to have?

45

INTRODUCING
CHAPTER 3

Making Accounting Relevant

Workplace Connections: Applying Your Accounting Knowledge

Discussion: Ask students to name several different types of businesses in your area. Have them think about the things that they see when they go into these businesses. What are possible assets, liabilities, and owner's equity?

Investigate (Answers)

1. Answers will vary. For example, if a student worked for a pizza restaurant, the assets might include kitchen equipment, furniture, and delivery trucks. For those working at a grocery store, the assets might include display cases and cash registers.
2. Answers will vary. For example, a restaurant might have liabilities for rent, equipment, or food purchases. Other businesses might owe for vehicles, advertising, or office furniture and computers.

School-to-Work Activity

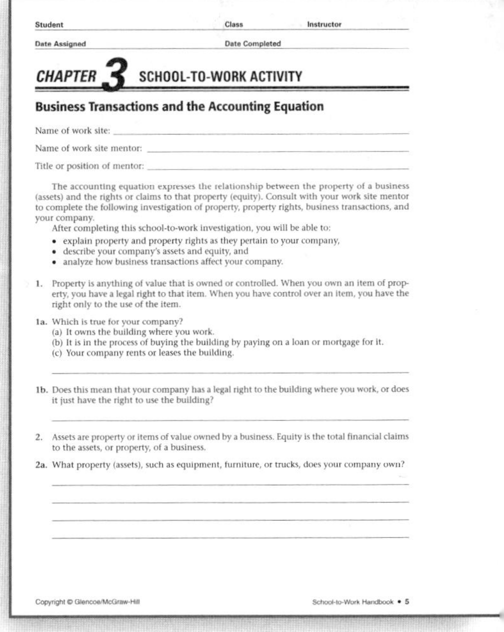

Student ____ Class ____ Instructor ____

Date Assigned ____ Date Completed ____

CHAPTER 3 SCHOOL-TO-WORK ACTIVITY

Business Transactions and the Accounting Equation

Name of work site: ____

Name of work site mentor: ____

Title or position of mentor: ____

The accounting equation expresses the relationship between the property of a business (assets) and the rights or claims to that property (equity). Consult with your work site mentor to complete the following investigation of property, property rights, business transactions, and your company.

After completing this school-to-work investigation, you will be able to:

- explain property and property rights as they pertain to your company,
- describe your company's assets and equity, and
- analyze how business transactions affect your company.

1. Property is anything of value that is owned or controlled. When you own an item of property, you have a legal right to that item. When you have control over an item, you have the right only to the use of the item.

1a. Which is true for your company?
(a) It owns the building where you work.
(b) It is in the process of buying the building by paying on a loan or mortgage for it.
(c) Your company rents or leases the building.

1b. Does this mean that your company has a legal right to the building where you work, or does it just have the right to use the building?

2. Assets are property or items of value owned by a business. Equity is the total financial claims to the assets, or property, of a business.

2a. What property (assets), such as equipment, furniture, or trucks, does your company own?

 School-to-Work Handbook • 5

GLENCOE MULTIMEDIA

Electronic Field Trips in Accounting *Video Segment: Accounting All Around You*
After viewing this video, students will be able to describe the role that accounting plays in providing decision-making information in a private enterprise economy.

Glencoe Accounting: Electronic Learning Center *Chapter 3*
The CD-ROM program is ideal for visual learners since it incorporates video images, animation, and graphics to enliven the content of each lesson.

CHAPTER 3
SECTION 1, PAGES 46–49

1 FOCUS

Introducing the Section

In this section, students will learn the balance between property and property rights—both their rights and those held by others to whom money is owed on the property. This presentation leads into a discussion of the accounting concepts of assets and equity. Students learn about an owner's claim to the assets of a business and creditors' claims to those same assets.

Section Concepts

- The relationship between property and financial claims.
- The meaning of *equity* as it is used in accounting.
- The parts of the accounting equation.
- The definition of each part of the accounting equation.

Visual Learning

Section 1 Focus

Use **Transparency 3–1** to introduce section concepts.

BELL RINGER

Observation: Ask students to consider their own property. What items of property are they wearing, such as watches or jewelry, sweatshirts, or shoes? Have students determine what rights they have in their property. Then have them name other items of property in which other people might have rights (e.g., cars or cycles, items of clothing, CD players or televisions). L1

SECTION 1

Property and Financial Claims

***What* You'll Learn**

- The relationship between property and financial claims.
- The meaning of *equity* as it is used in accounting.
- The parts of the accounting equation.
- The definition of each part of the accounting equation.

***Why* It's Important**

The accounting equation is the basis for keeping all accounting records in balance.

KEY TERMS

property
property rights
financial claims
credit
creditor
assets
investments
equity
owner's equity
liabilities
accounting equation

In Chapter 2, you learned that accounting is the language of business. In this chapter, you will learn how to apply basic accounting concepts and terminology. You will also learn how the accounting equation expresses the relationship between property and the rights, or claims, to the property.

United Parcel Service (UPS), a corporation that provides global delivery services, uses accounting reports to communicate to its managers, employees, and investors. The UPS financial reports identify the property used in the business, like airplanes, trucks, and computers. The reports also show how the company obtained the property, either from loans or from funds provided by investors.

Property: Ownership and Control

The right to own property is basic to a free enterprise system. **Property** is anything of value that is owned or controlled. When you own an item of property, you have a legal right or financial claim to that item. When you have control over an item, you have the right only to the use of the item. For example, suppose you paid $600 for a mountain bike. As a result of the payment, you own the bike. If you had rented the bike for the weekend instead of buying it, you would pay a much smaller amount of money, but you would have control of the bike for only a limited time. You would have the right to use the bike for the weekend, but you would not own it.

As you can see from this example, you can have certain rights, or claims, to the items that you either own or control. The following table illustrates the difference between ownership and control.

	Property Right	Financial Claim
Own	Yes	Yes
Control (like rent)	Yes	No

Businesses also own and control property. One of the purposes of accounting is to provide financial information about property and rights to

RESOURCE MANAGER

Reproducible Masters
- Lesson Plans
- Chapter Reviews and Working Papers (CRWP) TAE
- Demonstration Problems

Transparencies
- Section Focus Transparency
- Teaching Transparencies
- Solution Transparencies

Multimedia
- Exam*View* CD-ROM
- Electronic Learning Center CD-ROM
- Interactive Lesson Planner CD-ROM
- Electronic Field Trips in Accounting

that property. In accounting, property and financial claims are measured in dollar amounts. Dollar amounts measure both the cost of the property and the **property rights**, or **financial claims** to the property. In our mountain bike example, since you paid $600 cash to buy the bike, you have a property right *and* a financial claim of $600 to the bike. This relationship between property and financial claims is shown in the following equation.

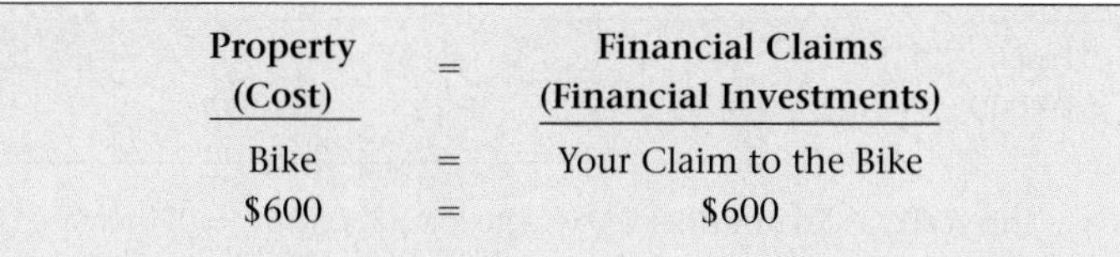

Property (Cost)	=	Financial Claims (Financial Investments)
Bike	=	Your Claim to the Bike
$600	=	$600

When you buy property with cash, you acquire all of the financial claims to that property at the time of purchase. What happens to the financial claim, however, when you don't pay for the property right away?

When you buy property and agree to pay for it later, you are buying on **credit**. The business or person selling you the property on credit is called a **creditor**. A creditor can be any person or business to which you owe money. When you buy property on credit, you do not have the only financial claim to the property. You share the financial claim to that property with your creditor. For example, suppose you want to buy a $100 lock for the mountain bike, but you have only $60. You pay the store $60 and sign an agreement to pay the remaining $40 over the next two months. Since you owe the store (the creditor) $40, you share the financial claim to the lock with the creditor. The creditor's financial claim to the lock is $40 and your claim is $60. The combined claims equal the cost of the property. Your purchase of the lock can be expressed in terms of the equation: PROPERTY = FINANCIAL CLAIMS.

Property	=	Financial Claims		
Bike Lock	=	Creditor's Financial Claim	+	Owner's Financial Claim
$100	=	$40	+	$60

As you can see, two (or more) people can have financial claims to the same property.

Financial Claims in Accounting

In accounting, property or items of value owned by a business are referred to as **assets**. Some examples of assets are cash, office equipment, manufacturing equipment, buildings, and land. The accounting term for the financial claims to these assets is **equity**. **Investments** are assets, generally long-term in nature, that are not intended to be converted to cash or to be used in the normal operations of the business in the next accounting period. If you have a financial claim to property, you are said to have equity in that property. Let's explore the meaning of the term equity by introducing Maria Sanchez and her new business, Roadrunner Delivery Service, organized as a sole proprietorship.

International ACCOUNTING

Overnight Guarantee

FedEx Corporation, the company that revolutionized the way people work, began when its founder Fred Smith was drawing a doodle of the distribution model—a hub and connecting spokes—used by major airlines to route flights. He proposed that if all mail were channeled through one major hub, it would reach its final destination more quickly. Smith's plan worked so well that FedEx was able to expand its overnight guarantee to include worldwide destinations.

ACCOUNTING *Flashbacks*

THE IRS WEB SITE

When the IRS put up its Web page in 1996, it received over a million hits during its first week. The site offers documents, guidelines, and help for taxpayers.

Teaching International ACCOUNTING

Researching Shipping Companies Have students research two or more U.S. shipping companies to answer the following questions: Where is their main hub? How many domestic locations do they serve? What mail services do they offer? Are there weight limits for international packages? Have students determine the costs for shipping a one-pound, letter-size package from your area to Frankfurt, Germany, for express mail service. How quickly can the package be delivered? Have students share their findings with the class.

CHAPTER 3
SECTION 1, PAGES 46–49

2 TEACH

GUIDED PRACTICE

Reading Accounting

- Have students turn each section head into a question. Mentally answering the questions will help students review the topic. L1

Concept Development: Property: Ownership and Control

Discussion: Emphasize that (1) the right to own property is fundamental to our free enterprise system, (2) the value of property in the United States is measured in dollars, and (3) accounting provides financial information about property and property rights. L1

Demonstration Problem Step-by-Step Practice

Use demonstration problem 3–1 to give students practice in assessing financial claims.

Visual Learning

Property = Financial Claims, p. 47

Use the illustrations on this page to guide the discussion of property and the claims that an owner and a creditor may have to the property. Point out the balance between the sides of the equation.

Strategies for Teaching International Accounting

To enrich study of International Accounting, refer to the additional critical thinking activities in the booklet.

CHAPTER 3
SECTION 1, PAGES 46–49

2 TEACH (Cont'd.)

Concept Development: Financial Claims in Accounting

Discussion: In accounting terms, property equals assets; claims to assets equal equity or property rights. Equity includes the claims of creditors (liabilities) and the owner (owner's equity).

Introduce the accounting equation and relate property to assets and financial claims to equity. Point out that creditors have first claim to assets, thus their claims are listed first on the equity side of the equation. L1

Demonstration Problem Step-by-Step Practice

Use demonstration problem 3–2 to give students practice in sharing financial claims with a creditor.

Visual Learning

Property = Creditor's Financial Claim + Owner's Financial Claim, p. 48

Use this illustration to help students make the transition from property and its financial claims to accounting terminology used in the accounting equation.

Strategies for Teaching Ethics in Accounting

Photocopy the Chapter 3 *Activity Sheet* for students. Answers are also provided in the booklet.

Using Algebra

You can calculate amounts in a financial equation using the rules of algebra.

The basic accounting equation is in the form of $a = b + c$.

- To find either b or c, re-write the equation as $b = a - c$, or $c = a - b$.

Suppose Roadrunner Delivery Service purchases a delivery truck for $10,000. Roadrunner makes a cash down payment of $3,000 to the seller. A local bank loans Roadrunner the remaining $7,000. Both Roadrunner and the bank now have financial claims to the truck.

Property	=	Creditor's Financial Claim	+	Owner's Financial Claim
Truck $10,000	=	$7,000	+	$3,000

Over the years, as Roadrunner repays the loan, its equity will increase. As less money is owed, the equity of the creditor (the bank) will decrease. When the loan is completely repaid, the creditor's financial claim will be canceled. In other words, the owner's equity will then equal the cost of the truck. Roadrunner will own the truck and will have full property rights to it.

As you can see from this example, equity is simply the claims—of both creditor(s) and owner(s)—to the assets of a business. In accounting, there are separate terms for owner's claims and creditor's claims. The owner's claims to the assets of the business are called **owner's equity**. Owner's equity is measured by the dollar amount of the owner's claims to the total assets of the business.

Property	=	Creditor's Financial Claim	+	Owner's Financial Claim
↓		↓		↓
Assets	=	Liabilities	+	Owner's Equity

Key Points

Equity

Equity includes both the creditor's claims (liabilities) and the owner's claims (owner's equity).

The creditor's claims to the assets of the business are called **liabilities**. Liabilities are the debts of a business. They are measured by the amount of money owed by a business to its creditors. The relationship between assets and both types of equity (liabilities and owner's equity) is shown in the **accounting equation**:

ASSETS = LIABILITIES + OWNER'S EQUITY

A MATTER OF ETHICS

Company Property

Many companies provide office supplies for their employees' use while on the job. Imagine that you work for a large department store like JC Penney. Several of your co-workers take company supplies home for their personal use, such as pens, bags, hangers, and boxes. You need boxes to store some items at home, so you consider taking them from the supply room.

Ethical Decision Making:

- What are the ethical issues?
- What are the alternatives?
- Who are the affected parties?
- How do the alternatives affect the parties?
- What would you do?

Teaching A MATTER OF ETHICS

Company Property Point out to students that many companies have written policies on the use or buying of company products by employees. Other companies may have informal guidelines about company property. For the boxes in this case, the company would probably discard them if they're not needed, in which case employees would likely be welcome to them. It's probably a good policy to ask a supervisor or manager, though, before assuming that a company is discarding items.

SECTION 1 Check Your Understanding

Now that you have studied this section, complete the following questions and problems.

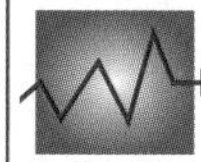

Thinking Critically

1. Explain the legal right of owning an item of property.
2. What is meant by having a financial claim to property?

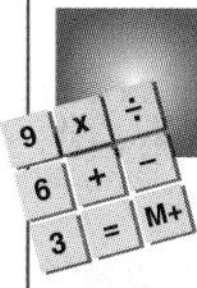

Computing in the Business World

Many types of work require you to convert fractions into decimals and vice versa. Convert the following fractions into decimals.

1. $\frac{1}{2}$
2. $\frac{1}{5}$
3. $\frac{1}{3}$
4. $\frac{4}{5}$
5. $\frac{7}{8}$
6. $\frac{7}{10}$

Convert the following decimals into fractions.

7. 0.889
8. 0.60
9. 0.375
10. 0.25
11. 0.667
12. 0.75

Problem 3–1 Balancing the Accounting Equation

Instructions Determine the missing dollar amount indicated by the question mark in each equation. Write each missing amount in your working papers.

	ASSETS	=	LIABILITIES	+	OWNER'S EQUITY
1.	$17,000	=	$ 7,000	+	?
2.	?	=	$ 6,000	+	$20,000
3.	$10,000	=	?	+	$ 7,000
4.	?	=	$ 9,000	+	$17,000
5.	$ 8,000	=	$ 2,000	+	?
6.	$20,000	=	$ 7,000	+	?
7.	?	=	$12,000	+	$ 4,000
8.	$30,000	=	?	+	$22,000
9.	$22,000	=	$ 1,000	+	?
10.	$25,000	=	$ 5,000	+	?
11.	?	=	$10,000	+	$25,000
12.	$ 7,500	=	?	+	$ 3,000

RETEACHING SECTION 1

Understanding the Concept of Equity In this reinforcement activity, the student is expected to follow oral instructions.

Have students check a dictionary for definitions of *equity*, *liability*, and *creditor*, then explain, in their own words, the role of the creditor and owner and their claims to business assets.

The concept of "equity" as a financial claim to assets may be confusing to students, especially as the term relates to liabilities. Students may reason that if the owner's claim is called "owner's equity," the creditors' claims should be called "creditors' equity" or "liabilities equity." Discuss these ideas with students.

3 ASSESS

Productivity Skills

The student can practice productivity skills as they apply to accounting at the end of each section and chapter. In these activities the student is expected to follow written instructions.

Thinking Critically (Answers)

1. You have a financial claim to that item and the right to use that item.
2. You have a claim to the property, either as an owner or a creditor.

Computing in the Business World (Answers)

1. .5
2. .2
3. .3333
4. .8
5. .875
6. .7
7. 889/1000
8. 6/10
9. 375/1000
10. 25/100
11. 667/1000
12. 75/100

Problem 3-1 (Answers)

1. $10,000
2. $26,000
3. $3,000
4. $26,000
5. $6,000
6. $13,000
7. $16,000
8. $8,000
9. $21,000
10. $20,000
11. $35,000
12. $4,500

Chapter Reviews and Working Papers
Refer students to the Chapter 3 workbook pages to answer *Check Your Understanding* activities.

4 CLOSE

Section Wrap-Up

Demonstrate: Have students write a short paragraph describing a business of their choice. Have them write an accounting equation for the business, giving amounts for each part of the equation. L1

1 FOCUS

Introducing the Section

In this section students will learn some typical business transactions for a service business. Using the accounting equation, students will analyze the effects of transactions involving an owner's investments, cash, and credit. Students will also learn how accounts are used in an accounting system for recording amounts affecting specific assets, liabilities, and owner's equity.

Section Concepts

- How accounts are used in business transactions.
- The steps used to analyze business transactions.
- How investments by the owner affect the accounting equation.
- How a cash payment transaction affects the accounting equation.
- How a credit transaction affects the accounting equation.

Visual Learning

Section 2 Focus

Use **Transparency 3–2** to introduce section concepts.

BELL RINGER

Critical Thinking: Ask students to describe some of their recent purchases. Write several of their examples on the chalkboard. Choose examples involving both cash and credit purchases. Then write the accounting equation on the chalkboard. Ask for volunteers to write their purchases in the appropriate spaces under the accounting equation. L1

SECTION 2

Transactions That Affect Owner's Investment, Cash, and Credit

***What* You'll Learn**

- How accounts are used in business transactions.
- The steps used to analyze business transactions.
- How investments by the owner affect the accounting equation.
- How a cash payment transaction affects the accounting equation.
- How a credit transaction affects the accounting equation.

***Why* It's Important**

You can analyze real-world business transactions by using the accounting equation.

KEY TERMS

business transaction
account
accounts receivable
accounts payable
on account

The last time you purchased a new sweater, bought popcorn at the movies, or deposited money into your savings account, you were participating in business transactions. Business transactions involve the purchase, sale, or exchange of goods and services. Some businesses have hundreds, or even thousands, of business transactions every day. When a business transaction occurs, the financial position of the business changes.

Business Transactions

A **business transaction** is an economic event that causes a change—either an increase or a decrease—in assets, liabilities, or owner's equity. The change is reflected in the accounting system of the business. Let's look at an example.

If a business buys a computer and pays cash for it, the amount of cash decreases. At the same time, the business increases its computer equipment. In an accounting system, the increases and decreases caused by business transactions are recorded in specific accounts. An **account** shows the balance for a specific item, such as cash or computer equipment. It also is a record of the increases or decreases for that specific item.

Accounts represent things in the real world, such as money invested in a business, office furniture, or money owed to a creditor. For example, an account for office furniture represents the dollar cost of all the office furniture owned by the business.

Every business sets up its accounts and its accounting system according to its needs. The number of accounts needed by a business will vary. Some businesses use only a few accounts, while others use hundreds. Regardless of the number of accounts a business has, all its accounts may be classified as either assets, liabilities, or owner's equity. Here are the accounts used by Roadrunner Delivery Service:

RESOURCE MANAGER

Reproducible Masters
- Lesson Plans
- Chapter Reviews and Working Papers (CRWP) TAE
- Demonstration Problems

Transparencies
- Section Focus Transparency
- Teaching Transparencies
- Solution Transparencies

Multimedia
- Exam*View* CD-ROM
- Electronic Learning Center CD-ROM
- Interactive Lesson Planner CD-ROM
- Electronic Field Trips in Accounting

Assets	=	Liabilities	+	Owner's Equity
Cash in Bank		Accounts Payable		Maria Sanchez, Capital
Accounts Receivable				
Computer Equipment				
Office Equipment				
Delivery Equipment				

The second asset account listed is **Accounts Receivable.** **Accounts receivable** is the total amount of money owed to a business. It represents money to be received later because of the sale of goods or services on credit. The **Accounts Receivable** account is an asset because it represents a claim to the assets of other people or businesses. It represents a future value that eventually will bring cash into the business. When the business receives payment, the claim will be canceled.

The liability account listed is **Accounts Payable.** **Accounts payable** is the amount of money owed, or payable, to the creditors of a business. It is a future obligation requiring the payment of cash or services to other people or businesses.

Finally, note that the owner's equity account in a business is identified by the owner's name followed by a comma and the word "Capital." Capital, as you learned in Chapter 2, refers to the dollar value of assets contributed to the business.

ACCOUNTING TIPS

Capital

The word *capital* has its roots in the Latin word *capitalis,* meaning "property." *Capital* first meant "main." Later the term came to stand for a person's wealth, which was the main source of a person's importance.

Did You Know?

Counting the Votes

When movies are nominated for an Academy Award, a professional accounting firm counts the votes and delivers the results on the night the prizes are awarded. PriceWaterhouse-Coopers is the firm, and it has been participating in the Academy Awards since 1935.

Effects of Transactions on the Accounting Equation

When a business transaction occurs, an accounting clerk analyzes the transaction to see how it affects each part of the accounting equation. Analyzing business transactions is simple. Use the following steps.

Business Transaction

ANALYSIS	***Identify***	**1.** Identify the accounts affected.
	Classify	**2.** Classify the accounts affected.
	+/−	**3.** Determine the amount of increase or decrease for each account affected.
	Balance	**4.** Make sure the accounting equation remains in balance.

The business transactions that follow are examples of transactions that occur in most businesses. To help you learn about various kinds of transactions, these examples are categorized as follows:

- investments by the owner,
- cash transactions,
- credit transactions,
- revenue and expense transactions, and
- withdrawals by the owner.

Great Ideas *From the Classroom of...*

Classifying Personal Inventories Have students brainstorm a list of assets and liabilities. Then have students create a list for their own personal inventory for each classification. When completed, have students represent the list and/or the accounting equation through a picture poster or mobile.

Lynn Carmen Day
Northview High School
Covina, California

2 TEACH

GUIDED PRACTICE

Reading Accounting

- As students read the account titles under the equation, ask what each account title describes. Point out that each account title gives a clue to its classification. L1
- Suggest that students form study teams. Pair bilingual students with students whose language skills are still developing. ELL

Concept Development: Business Transactions

Discussion: Businesses have hundreds of transactions each day in which they buy or sell products or services. Most transactions are repetitive and fall into specific types, such as buying an asset (e.g., supplies). Each business sets up accounts that are descriptive of its business operation. You may want to introduce the concept of a chart of accounts. L1

Concept Development: Effects of Transactions on the Accounting Equation

Discussion: Five types of business transactions are presented in this section to summarize the types of changes in assets, liabilities, and owner's equity resulting from business operations. Accounts are introduced as the means of analyzing the effects of each business transaction. L1

Visual Learning

Business Transaction Model

Use **Transparency 3–3** to demonstrate how to analyze the effect of a business transaction on business accounts.

2 TEACH (Cont'd.)

Demonstration Problem Step-by-Step Practice

Use demonstration problem 3–3 to give students practice in analyzing business transactions using the accounting equation.

Visual Learning

Business Transaction 1

Use **Transparency 3–4** to guide students through the analysis of the owner's investment of money in the business.

Business Transaction 2

Using **Transparency 3–5**, have students discuss the investment of equipment by the owner.

Teaching Tip

For Business Transaction 1, the owner's investment results in:

+ Asset (Cash in Bank)
+ Equity (Maria Sanchez, Capital)

For Business Transaction 2, the investment of equipment results in:

+ Asset (Office Equipment)
+ Equity (Maria Sanchez, Capital)

Remind students to refer to a list of account titles to be used in analyzing transactions. Classifying accounts correctly is key to understanding the effects of a transaction and how to determine whether an account increases or decreases.

Also remind students that the equation must balance after each transaction.

Math Review for Accounting

Photocopy appropriate *Activity Sheets* for students who need additional practice in basic math skills.

Key Points

Business Transactions
Every business transaction affects at least two accounts.

The first three categories are covered in this section. Transactions involving revenues, expenses, and withdrawals by the owner are covered in the next section.

Investments by the Owner

These transactions illustrate investments by the owner, Maria Sanchez, in her business, Roadrunner Delivery Service. The first involves a cash investment, while the second concerns a transfer of property.

Business Transaction 1

Maria Sanchez took $25,000 from personal savings and deposited that amount to open a business checking account in the name of Roadrunner Delivery Service.

ANALYSIS		
	Identify	1. Cash transactions are recorded in the account **Cash in Bank.** Maria Sanchez is investing personal funds in the business. Her investment in the business is recorded in the account called **Maria Sanchez, Capital.**
	Classify	2. **Cash in Bank** is an asset account. **Maria Sanchez, Capital** is an owner's equity account.
	+/−	3. **Cash in Bank** is increased by $25,000. **Maria Sanchez, Capital** is increased by $25,000.
	Balance	4. The accounting equation remains in balance.

	Assets	=	Liabilities	+	Owner's Equity
	Cash in Bank				Maria Sanchez, Capital
Trans. 1	+$25,000	=	0	+	+$25,000

Business Transaction 2

*The owner, Maria Sanchez, took two telephones valued at $200 each (total $400) from her home and transferred them to the business as **Office Equipment**.*

ANALYSIS		
	Identify	1. The business received two telephones. Since a telephone is office equipment, the account **Office Equipment** is affected. Maria Sanchez invested a personal asset in the business, so the account **Maria Sanchez, Capital** is affected.
	Classify	2. **Office Equipment** is an asset account. **Maria Sanchez, Capital** is an owner's equity account.
	+/−	3. **Office Equipment** is increased by $400. **Maria Sanchez, Capital** is increased by $400.
	Balance	4. The accounting equation remains in balance.

Math Skill Builder Activity

(Refer to the *Math Hints* feature on page 48.)

Using Algebra Write the basic algebraic formula: a = b + c and the basic accounting equation A = L + OE on the chalkboard and compare the two formulas. Have students solve the following equations:

1. If a = 5,000, c =3,000, then b = ? (2,000)
2. If a = 2,500, b = 1,200, then c = ? (1,300)
3. If b = 750, c = 1,985, then a = ? (2,735)
4. If a = 3,000, c = 475, then b = ? (2,525)
5. If b = 2,400, c = 200, then a = ? (2,600)
6. If a = 1,400, b = 220, then c = ? (1,180)

	Assets		= Liabilities	+ Owner's Equity
	Cash in Bank	Office Equipment		Maria Sanchez, Capital
Prev. Bal.	$25,000	0	0	$25,000
Trans. 2		+$400		+400
Balance	$25,000 +	$400 =	0 +	$25,400

Key Points

In Balance
After recording each transaction, the accounting equation must be in balance.

Cash Payment Transactions

Transaction 3 is an example of a transaction in which an asset is purchased for cash. Any asset that is purchased for cash will be recorded in the same manner, but the account name of the asset purchased may vary.

Business Transaction 3

Roadrunner issued a $3,000 check to purchase a computer system.

ANALYSIS

Identify
1. The **Computer Equipment** account is used to record transactions involving any type of computer equipment. The business paid cash for the computer system, so the account **Cash in Bank** is affected. (Payments made by check are treated as cash payments and are recorded in the **Cash in Bank** account.)

Classify
2. **Computer Equipment** and **Cash in Bank** are both asset accounts.

+/−
3. **Computer Equipment** is increased by $3,000. **Cash in Bank** is decreased by $3,000.

Balance
4. The accounting equation remains in balance.

	Assets			= Liabilities	+ Owner's Equity
	Cash in Bank	Computer Equipment	Office Equipment		Maria Sanchez, Capital
Prev. Bal.	$25,000	0	$400	0	$25,400
Trans. 3	−3,000	+$3,000			
Balance	$22,000 +	$3,000 +	$400 =	0 +	$25,400

Transaction 3 affects only the assets side of the equation. Roadrunner exchanged one asset (cash) for another asset (computer equipment).

Credit Transactions

Now that you have learned about cash transactions, let's look at how the use of credit affects the accounting equation. When a business buys an item on credit, it is buying **on account**. In the next four transactions, you will learn about a purchase on account, a sale on account, a payment made on account, and a payment received on account.

HOME AND COMMUNITY CONNECTIONS ACTIVITY

Being a Wise Consumer Buying on credit can be a way of purchasing needs or wants in advance of having the cash to pay for an item. However, becoming a wise credit consumer takes experience and self-discipline. Have students work with their family members to identify different types of credit purchases their families have made in the past year (e.g., buying groceries or gas for the family car or a loan for college tuition or to buy a car). Have students write at least three examples of how using credit wisely has affected their families.

2 TEACH (Cont'd.)

Concept Development: Cash Payment Transactions

Discussion: Have students discuss how they pay for the items they buy. The choices are either cash or on credit. Point out that business owners use the same means of buying the things they need to operate the business. L1

Visual Learning

Business Transaction 3
Use **Transparency 3–6** to guide students through the analysis of a cash payment made by the business. Point out the balance in the equation after the transaction has been analyzed. Also note that this transaction affects only one side of the accounting equation.

Teaching Tip

For Business Transaction 3, the purchase of equipment for cash results in:
− Asset (Cash in Bank)
+ Asset (Computer Equipment)

Concept Development: Credit Transactions

Discussion: Take a poll of students who have used a credit card—either theirs or one owned by their parents—to make purchases. When did they (or their parents) make payment for the purchase? Depending on the billing cycle, most people have from a few days to a couple of weeks before they make payment. Point out to students that when businesses use credit, they record the amount as a payable, which means it will be paid in the future. L1

2 TEACH (Cont'd.)

Visual Learning

Business Transaction 4

Using **Transparency 3–7**, have students analyze the purchase of delivery equipment on credit. Discuss the use of the word "Payable" in the account title to indicate that an amount is to be paid in the future.

Business Transaction 5

Use **Transparency 3–8** to help students analyze the sale of a business asset on credit. Point out that the business will receive payment for the asset at a later time. Discuss the word "Receivable" to indicate that an amount is to be received in the future.

Teaching Tip

For Business Transaction 4, the purchase of delivery equipment on account results in:

+ Asset (Delivery Equipment)
+ Liability (Accounts Payable)

Key words for students to look for in the transaction description include *bought, truck,* and *on account.*

For Business Transaction 5, the sale of a business asset on account results in:

+ Asset (Accounts Receivable)
− Asset (Office Equipment)

For an item sold on credit, the key words are *sold* and *on account.*

Thinking Algebraically

Solving an Equation: Ask students how they would find the balance for assets if they were given amounts for liabilities and owner's equity. L1

Business Transaction 4

Roadrunner bought a used truck on account from North Shore Auto for $12,000.

ANALYSIS

Identify 1. Roadrunner purchased a truck to be used as a delivery vehicle, so the account **Delivery Equipment** is affected. The business promised to pay for the truck at a later time. This promise to pay is a liability; therefore, the **Accounts Payable** account is affected.

Classify 2. **Delivery Equipment** is an asset account. **Accounts Payable** is a liability account.

+/− 3. **Delivery Equipment** is increased by $12,000. **Accounts Payable** is also increased by $12,000.

Balance 4. The accounting equation remains in balance.

	Assets				=	Liabilities +	Owner's Equity
	Cash in Bank	Computer Equipment	Office Equipment	Delivery Equipment		Accounts Payable	Maria Sanchez, Capital
Prev. Bal.	$22,000	$3,000	$400	0		0	$25,400
Trans. 4				+$12,000		+$12,000	
Balance	$22,000 +	$3,000 +	$400 +	$12,000	=	$12,000 +	$25,400

Business Transaction 5

Roadrunner sold one telephone to Green Company for $200 on account.

ANALYSIS

Identify 1. Since Roadrunner has agreed to receive payment for the telephone at a later time, the **Accounts Receivable** account is affected. The business sold the telephone, so the account **Office Equipment** is also affected.

Classify 2. Both **Accounts Receivable** and **Office Equipment** are asset accounts.

+/− 3. **Accounts Receivable** is increased by $200. **Office Equipment** is decreased by $200.

Balance 4. The accounting equation remains in balance.

	Assets					=	Liabilities +	Owner's Equity
	Cash in Bank	Accounts Receivable	Computer Equipment	Office Equipment	Delivery Equipment		Accounts Payable	Maria Sanchez, Capital
Prev. Bal.	$22,000	0	$3,000	$400	$12,000		$12,000	$25,400
Trans. 5		+$200		−200				
Balance	$22,000 +	$200 +	$3,000 +	$200 +	$12,000	=	$12,000 +	$25,400

CRITICAL THINKING ACTIVITY

Evaluating Information Ask students to list the assets and liabilities for the school's athletic department. Then ask each student to describe a transaction related to those assets or liabilities and to indicate whether the accounts affected are increased or decreased by the transaction. (Examples of assets might be uniforms, shoes, playing equipment, fixtures such as basketball hoops and boards, football field goals, soccer nets, lights, machines used to polish basketball courts or to maintain playing fields, and so on. Possible transactions include the purchase of items, sales of season tickets, concession sales, wages for referees, first aid, or security fees.)

Business Transaction 6

Roadrunner issued a check for $350 in partial payment of the amount owed to its creditor, North Shore Auto.

ANALYSIS		
	Identify	**1.** The payment decreased the total amount owed to the creditor, so **Accounts Payable** is affected. Payment was made by check, so the account **Cash in Bank** is affected.
	Classify	**2. Accounts Payable** is a liability account. **Cash in Bank** is an asset account.
	+/−	**3. Accounts Payable** is decreased by $350. **Cash in Bank** is also decreased by $350.
	Balance	**4.** The accounting equation remains in balance.

	Assets					= Liabilities	+ Owner's Equity
	Cash in Bank	Accounts Receivable	Computer Equipment	Office Equipment	Delivery Equipment	Accounts Payable	Maria Sanchez, Capital
Prev. Bal.	$22,000	$200	$3,000	$200	$12,000	$12,000	$25,400
Trans. 6	−350					−350	
Balance	$21,650 +	$200 +	$3,000 +	$200 +	$12,000 =	$11,650 +	$25,400

Business Transaction 7

Roadrunner received and deposited a check for $200 from Green Co. The check received is full payment for the telephone sold on account in Transaction 5.

ANALYSIS		
	Identify	**1.** The check decreases the amount owed to Roadrunner, so **Accounts Receivable** is affected. A check is given in payment, so **Cash in Bank** is affected.
	Classify	**2. Accounts Receivable** and **Cash in Bank** are asset accounts.
	+/−	**3. Accounts Receivable** is decreased by $200. **Cash in Bank** is increased by $200.
	Balance	**4.** The accounting equation remains in balance.

	Assets					= Liabilities	+ Owner's Equity
	Cash in Bank	Accounts Receivable	Computer Equipment	Office Equipment	Delivery Equipment	Accounts Payable	Maria Sanchez, Capital
Prev. Bal.	$21,650	$200	$3,000	$200	$12,000	$11,650	$25,400
Trans. 7	+200	−200					
Balance	$21,850 +	$0 +	$3,000 +	$200 +	$12,000 =	$11,650 +	$25,400

As you can see, each business transaction causes a change in assets, liabilities, or owner's equity. Analyzing each transaction to see how it affects the accounting equation keeps everything in balance.

REINFORCING STUDY SKILLS

Reading Technique Setting purposes for reading often helps students focus on the main points. Have students read the chapter introduction and then, in their own words, explain what they think this chapter will be about. As students read, have them refer back to the **Learning Objectives** and try to meet each one as they go along.

2 TEACH (Cont'd.)

Visual Learning

Business Transaction 6

Use **Transparency 3–9** to demonstrate the analysis of a payment for an item bought on account.

Business Transaction 7

Using **Transparency 3–10**, have students analyze the receipt of a cash payment for an item sold on credit.

Teaching Tip

For Business Transaction 6, the payment of an amount owed to a creditor results in:

− Liability (Accounts Payable)
− Asset (Cash in Bank)

For Business Transaction 7, the receipt of cash for an item sold on credit results in:

+ Asset (Cash in Bank)
− Asset (Accounts Receivable)

Remind students that the equation must remain in balance after each transaction.

Demonstration Problem Step-by-Step Practice

Use demonstration problem 3–4 to have students practice classifying accounts.

Chapter Reviews and Working Papers

Refer students to the *Study Plan* located at the beginning of Chapter 3 in the workbook.

CHAPTER 3
SECTION 2, PAGES 50–56

3 ASSESS

Thinking Critically (Answers)

1. Accounts Receivable is money to be received for goods or services sold on credit. It is an asset. Accounts Payable is money owed to creditors. It is a liability because it is a debt.
2. The accountant/accounting clerk analyzes the transaction to see the effects on the accounts of the business.

Communicating Accounting (Answers)

Answers may vary. Students' tips should be similar to the steps in the business transaction analysis model presented in the text.

Problem 3–2 (Answers)

1. Cash in Bank increased $30,000. Jan Swift, Cap. increased $30,000.
2. Office Furn. increased $700. Jan Swift, Cap. increased $700.
3. Cash in Bank decreased $4,000. Computer Equip. increased $4,000.
4. Office Furniture increased $5,000. Accts. Pay. increased $5,000.
5. Accts. Rec. increased $700. Office Furniture decreased $700.
6. Cash in Bank decreased $2,000. Accts. Pay. decreased $2,000.

Chapter Reviews and Working Papers Refer students to the Chapter 3 workbook pages to answer *Check Your Understanding* activities.

4 CLOSE

Section Wrap-Up

Writing: Have students write a paragraph describing how business transactions affect the accounting equation. L1

SECTION 2 Check Your Understanding

Now that you have studied this section, complete the following questions and problems.

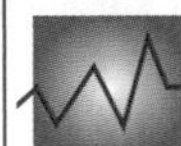

Thinking Critically

1. What is the difference between accounts receivable and accounts payable?
2. When a business transaction occurs, what is the role of the accountant or accounting clerk?

Communicating Accounting

In your business, Ace Tutoring Service, it is critical for your new accounting clerk to fully comprehend how a business transaction affects the accounts of your business. Using the four-step approach to transaction analysis, write a "tip sheet" to help your new employee remember the steps. Write a brief explanation and give an example of each step in the analysis. Create a business transaction to use in your explanation.

Problem 3–2 Determining the Effects of Transactions on the Accounting Equation

Instructions Use these accounts to analyze the business transactions of WordService.

Assets	=	Liabilities	+	Owner's Equity
Cash in Bank		Accounts Payable		Jan Swift, Capital
Accounts Receivable				
Computer Equipment				
Office Furniture				

On the form provided in your working papers, identify the accounts affected by each transaction and the amount of increase or decrease in each account. Make sure the accounting equation is in balance after each transaction. Your transaction analysis should be set up like Transactions 1 through 7 on pages 52–55.

1. Jan Swift, owner, deposited $30,000 in a checking account to start a business, WordService.
2. The owner transferred to the business a desk and chair valued at $700.
3. WordService issued a check for $4,000 for the purchase of a computer.
4. The business bought office furniture on account for $5,000 from Eastern Furniture Company.
5. The desk and chair previously transferred to the business by the owner were sold on account for $700.
6. WordService wrote a check for $2,000 in partial payment of the amount owed to Eastern Furniture Company.

RETEACHING SECTION 2

Analyzing Transactions Review the four-step process for analyzing transactions for any students who are having difficulty reading a transaction and deciding how it affects specific accounts. Explain each step, giving examples similar to those illustrated for Roadrunner Delivery Service in the text. Emphasize that every business transaction affects at least two accounts and that students should review the list of accounts used by the business when deciding which accounts are affected.

Transactions That Affect Revenue, Expense, and Withdrawals by the Owner

United Parcel Service (UPS) has thousands of shareholders who expect a return on their investment in the business. The most common way for a business to provide a return is by selling goods or providing services. UPS earns revenue by providing a global delivery service. To provide the delivery service, UPS incurs expenses like salaries, transportation, and insurance. In this section you will learn about revenue and expense transactions as well as owner's withdrawals.

What You'll Learn

- How revenue transactions affect the accounting equation.
- How expense transactions affect the accounting equation.
- How withdrawals by the owner affect the accounting equation.

Why It's Important

The experience you gain by analyzing revenue, expense, and withdrawal transactions will help you analyze transactions in real-world situations.

KEY TERMS

revenue
expense
withdrawal

Revenue and Expense Transactions

Income earned from the sale of goods or services is called **revenue**. Examples of revenue are fees earned for services performed and cash received from the sale of merchandise. Revenue increases owner's equity because it increases the assets of the business.

Both revenues and investments by the owner increase owner's equity, but these represent very different transactions. Revenue is income from the sale of goods and services. Investment by the owner is the dollar amount contributed to the business by the owner. To generate revenue by selling goods or services, most businesses must also incur expenses to buy goods, materials, and services. An **expense** is the price paid for goods or services used to operate a business. Examples of business expenses are rent, utilities, and advertising. Expenses decrease owner's equity because they decrease the assets of the business or increase liabilities.

Business Transaction 8

Roadrunner received a check for $1,200 from a customer, Sims Corporation, for delivery services.

ANALYSIS		
	Identify	**1.** Roadrunner received cash, so **Cash in Bank** is affected. The payment received is revenue. Revenue increases owner's equity, so **Maria Sanchez, Capital** is also affected.
	Classify	**2. Cash in Bank** is an asset account. **Maria Sanchez, Capital** is an owner's equity account.
	+/−	**3. Cash in Bank** is increased by $1,200. **Maria Sanchez, Capital** is also increased by $1,200.
	Balance	**4.** The accounting equation remains in balance.

1 FOCUS

Introducing the Section

In this section, students continue their analysis of business transactions by looking at transactions affecting revenue, expenses, and withdrawals. Students also learn how each transaction affects the accounting equation.

Section Concepts

- How revenue transactions affect the accounting equation.
- How expense transactions affect the accounting equation.
- How withdrawals by the owner affect the accounting equation.

Visual Learning

Section 3 Focus

Use **Transparency 3–11** to introduce section concepts.

BELL RINGER

Analyzing: Have students assume that they are business consultants. A business owner explains that the business had sales of $78,000 last year and it cost $42,000 to run the business. The owner took $54,000 out of the business for personal use. The owner started the business this year by depositing $20,000 of personal funds into the business bank account. The owner is having trouble paying business expenses. Ask students to apply basic accounting terminology to this scenario. Ask students to apply basic accounting concepts to analyze possible problems. What would they say to the business owner? L1

RESOURCE MANAGER

Reproducible Masters

- Lesson Plans
- Chapter Reviews and Working Papers (CRWP) TAE
- Demonstration Problems

Transparencies

- Section Focus Transparency
- Teaching Transparencies
- Solution Transparencies

Multimedia

- Exam*View* CD-ROM
- Electronic Learning Center CD-ROM
- Interactive Lesson Planner CD-ROM
- Electronic Field Trips in Accounting

2 TEACH

GUIDED PRACTICE

Reading Accounting

• Point out that students should look for key words such as "on account," "bought," "sold," or "paid" that indicate the type of transaction that has taken place. L1

Concept Development: Revenue and Expense Transactions

Discussion: Point out to students that every business must earn revenue if it is to continue operating. To earn revenue, businesses spend money on items such as equipment, advertising, or utilities. These expenditures are called expenses. The goal is to earn more revenue than the amount paid out for expenses. Discuss how revenue increases owner's equity while expenses decrease owner's equity. L1

Visual Learning

Business Transaction 8

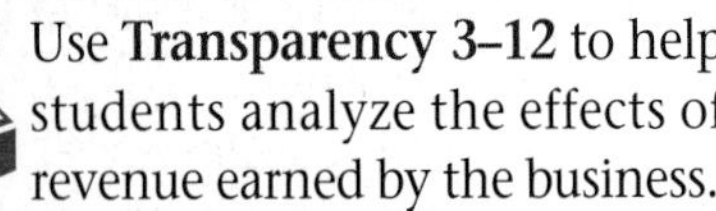

Use **Transparency 3–12** to help students analyze the effects of revenue earned by the business.

Business Transaction 9

Using **Transparency 3–13**, have students analyze the effect of using cash to pay an expense.

Teaching Tip

For Business Transaction 8:
+ Asset (Cash in Bank)
+ Owner's Equity (Maria Sanchez, Capital)

For Business Transaction 9:
– Owner's Equity (Maria Sanchez, Capital)
– Asset (Cash in Bank)

	Assets					= Liabilities	+ Owner's Equity
	Cash in Bank	Accounts Receivable	Computer Equipment	Office Equipment	Delivery Equipment	Accounts Payable	Maria Sanchez, Capital
Prev. Bal.	$21,850	$0	$3,000	$200	$12,000	$11,650	$25,400
Trans. 8	+1,200						+1,200
Balance	$23,050 +	$0 +	$3,000 +	$200 +	$12,000 =	$11,650 +	$26,600

Business Transaction 9

Roadrunner wrote a check for $700 to pay the rent for the month.

ANALYSIS

Identify 1. Roadrunner pays rent for use of building space. Rent is an expense. Expenses decrease owner's equity, so the account **Maria Sanchez, Capital** is affected. The business is paying cash for the use of the building, so **Cash in Bank** is affected.

Classify 2. **Maria Sanchez, Capital** is an owner's equity account. **Cash in Bank** is an asset account.

+/– 3. **Maria Sanchez, Capital** is decreased by $700. **Cash in Bank** is decreased by $700.

Balance 4. The accounting equation remains in balance.

	Assets					= Liabilities	+ Owner's Equity
	Cash in Bank	Accounts Receivable	Computer Equipment	Office Equipment	Delivery Equipment	Accounts Payable	Maria Sanchez, Capital
Prev. Bal.	$23,050	$0	$3,000	$200	$12,000	$11,650	$26,600
Trans. 9	−700						−700
Balance	$22,350 +	$0 +	$3,000 +	$200 +	$12,000 =	$11,650 +	$25,900

Withdrawals by the Owner

Generally, if a business earns revenue, the owner will take cash or other assets from the business for personal use. This transaction is called a **withdrawal**.

When the assets of a business are decreased because of a withdrawal by the owner, the owner's financial claim to the assets of the business is also decreased. A withdrawal, therefore, decreases both assets and owner's equity.

A withdrawal is not the same as an expense. Both expenses and owner's withdrawals decrease owner's equity, but these represent very different transactions. An expense is the price paid for goods and services used to operate a business. For example, a landscaping service might purchase fertilizer and lawncare supplies to conduct daily operations. Withdrawals by the owner are cash or other assets taken from the business for the owner's personal use. Transaction 10 illustrates the impact of a withdrawal on the accounting equation.

CONNECT TO . . . HEALTH

Actuaries in the insurance industry determine how much it costs to care for different clients and generate rates accordingly. For example, health insurance actuaries keep track of how much more it costs to cover smokers than non-smokers and adjust their rates to compensate for the difference.

INTERDISCIPLINARY CONNECTIONS ACTIVITY

Health Invite a guest speaker, an actuary if possible, from a local insurance group to speak on careers in the insurance industry. Have the speaker talk about his or her daily activities, including how he or she interacts with other people and the training required for the work. Ask the speaker to bring actuarial tables and show students how to read and interpret the data. Have the speaker give examples of people who apply for life insurance with different ages and genders. Then have students interpret the actuarial figures based on the different examples.

Business Transaction 10

Maria Sanchez withdrew $500 from the business for her personal use.

ANALYSIS

Identify 1. A withdrawal decreases the owner's claim to the assets of the business, so **Maria Sanchez, Capital** is affected. Cash is paid out, so the **Cash in Bank** account is affected.

Classify 2. **Maria Sanchez, Capital** is an owner's equity account. **Cash in Bank** is an asset account.

+/- 3. **Maria Sanchez, Capital** is decreased by $500. **Cash in Bank** is decreased by $500.

Balance 4. The accounting equation remains in balance.

	Assets					= Liabilities +	Owner's Equity
	Cash in Bank	Accounts Receivable	Computer Equipment	Office Equipment	Delivery Equipment	Accounts Payable	Maria Sanchez, Capital
Prev. Bal.	$22,350	$0	$3,000	$200	$12,000	$11,650	$25,900
Trans. 10	−500						−500
Balance	$21,850 +	$0 +	$3,000 +	$200 +	$12,000 =	$11,650 +	$25,400

The following summarizes the transactions of this chapter. Can you describe what is happening in each line?

	Cash in Bank	Accounts Receivable	Computer Equipment	Office Equipment	Delivery Equipment =	Accounts Payable +	Owner's Equity
Prev. Bal.	0	0	0	0	0	0	0
Trans. 1	+25,000						+25,000
Trans. 2				+400			+400
Trans. 3	−3,000		+3,000				
Trans. 4					+12,000	+12,000	
Trans. 5		+200		−200			
Trans. 6	−350					−350	
Trans. 7	+200	−200					
Trans. 8	+1,200						+1,200
Trans. 9	−700						−700
Trans. 10	−500						−500
Balance	$21,850 +	$0 +	$3,000 +	$200 +	$12,000 =	$11,650 +	$25,400

COOPERATIVE LEARNING ACTIVITY

Brainstorming Assign students to teams of four or five and ask each team to list all the assets that a video rental store would likely have. Set a time limit, and when the time limit has expired, ask each team to share its list with the class. Write the responses on the chalkboard and compile a comprehensive list. (Student responses could include videotapes, VCR rewinders, DVDs, video games, CD-ROM games, VCRs, concessions, and posters.)

2 TEACH (Cont'd.)

Concept Development: Withdrawals by the Owner

Discussion: Ask students why an owner might take money out of a business. Examples are for a salary or to reimburse business expenses paid out of personal money. Point out that most new businesses need several months of operation before they can pay their owners a salary. In a sole proprietorship, the owner can make withdrawals from the business as a salary or to pay other personal expenses. L1

Visual Learning

Business Transaction 10

Use **Transparency 3–14** to guide students through the analysis of an owner's withdrawal. Discuss the difference between an expense and a withdrawal. Both have the same effect on the accounting equation, but one is a cost of doing business while the other is a return of part of the owner's investment.

Teaching Tip

For Business Transaction 10, the results are:

- Owner's Equity (Maria Sanchez, Capital)
- Asset (Cash in Bank)

Point out that withdrawals decrease the owner's equity.

Demonstration Problem Step-by-Step Practice

Use demonstration problem 3–5 to review or reinforce the analysis of various types of business transactions.

CHAPTER 3
SECTION 3, PAGES 57–60

3 ASSESS

Thinking Critically (Answers)

1. Revenue increases owner's equity because it increases business assets.
2. A withdrawal decreases assets and owner's equity.

Analyzing Accounting (Answers)

1. Accounts affected are Paul Howard, Capital and Cash in Bank. Paul Howard, Capital: owner's equity; Cash in Bank: asset. Paul Howard, Capital – $500; Cash in Bank – $500. The equation remains in balance.
2. Accounts affected are Cash in Bank and Office Furniture. Both are assets. Cash in Bank – $250; Office Furniture + $250. The equation remains in balance.

Problem 3–3 (Answers)

1. Cash in Bank decreased by $50. Jan Swift, Cap. decreased by $50.
2. Cash in Bank increased by $1,000. Jan Swift, Cap. increased by $1,000.
3. Cash in Bank decreased by $600. Jan Swift, Cap. decreased by $600.
4. Cash in Bank decreased by $800. Jan Swift, Cap. decreased by $800.
5. Cash in Bank increased by $200. Accts. Rec. decreased by $200.

Chapter Reviews and Working Papers Refer students to the Chapter 3 workbook pages to answer *Check Your Understanding* activities.

4 CLOSE

Section Wrap-Up

Oral Exercise: Have students describe how revenue, expense, and withdrawals affect the accounting equation. L1

SECTION 3 Check Your Understanding

Now that you have studied this section, complete the following questions and problems.

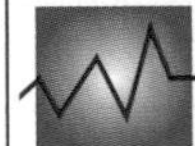

Thinking Critically

1. What effect does revenue have on a business?
2. What effect do withdrawals have on a business?

Analyzing Accounting

Analyze the following transactions using the format shown below.

Analysis	Identify:	?
	Classify:	?
	+/– :	?
	Balance:	?

1. Paul Howard withdrew $500 from his business, Kite Supply, for his personal use.
2. Kite Supply issued a check for $250 to purchase an office desk and chair.

Problem 3–3 Determining the Effect of Transactions on the Accounting Equation

Instructions Use the accounts of WordService, a secretarial service, to analyze these business transactions. The beginning balance for each account is shown following the account name.

Assets	=	Liabilities	+	Owner's Equity
Cash in Bank, $24,000		Accounts Payable		Jan Swift, Capital
Accounts Receivable, $700		$3,000		$30,700
Computer Equipment, $4,000				
Office Furniture, $5,000				

On the form provided in your working papers, identify the accounts affected by each transaction and the amount of the increase or decrease for each account. Make sure the accounting equation is in balance after each transaction.

1. Paid $50 for advertising in the local newspaper.
2. Received $1,000 as payment for preparing a report.
3. Wrote a $600 check for the month's rent.
4. Jan Swift withdrew $800 for her personal use.
5. Received $200 on account from the person who had purchased the old office furniture.

RETEACHING SECTION 3

Distinguishing Between Revenue and Expenses Review with students the distinction between (1) *revenue* and *investment* and (2) *expense* and *withdrawal*. Point out that *revenue* is money earned for services performed or goods sold by the business. An *investment* occurs when the owner contributes cash or transfers property to the business. An *expense* is the cost incurred for goods and services used to operate the business. A *withdrawal* occurs when the owner takes money from the business for personal use.

CHAPTER 3 SUMMARY

KEY CONCEPTS

1. For all property that is owned or controlled, there are corresponding financial claims equal to the cost of the property.
2. The accounting term for a financial claim to the assets of a business is *equity.*
3. Every business transaction changes one or more parts of the accounting equation.
4. When a business buys an item on account, the amount owed is called an account payable. When a business sells an item on account, the total amount to be received by the business is called an account receivable.
5. Revenues are earned by selling goods or services. Businesses must earn revenues to continue to operate and to provide a return on the owner's investment. Revenues increase the owner's equity in the business.
6. Expenses are the cost of items used in the operation of a business. Expenses decrease the owner's equity in the business.
7. Investments occur when an owner transfers cash or other assets to the business. Investments increase owner's equity.
8. Withdrawals occur when an owner takes cash or other assets from the business for personal use. Withdrawals decrease the owner's equity in the business.
9. The effects of typical business transactions on accounts are as follows:

Transaction	Effects On:		
	Assets	Liabilities	Owner's Equity
Investment of cash by owner	+		+
Investment of property	+		+
Cash payment, such as purchase of office equipment	+,−		
Purchase of an asset on account	+	+	
Sale of office equipment on account	−,+		
Make a payment on account	−	−	
Record revenue from a cash sale	+		+
Record a cash payment for an expense	−		−
Record a cash withdrawal by the owner	−		−

EXTENDING THE CONTENT

Analyzing Personal Business Transactions This activity will help students develop time management skills by setting priorities for completing work as scheduled.

Have students record all their personal business transactions for a week. Tell them to include every purchase, no matter how small. They should also include transactions in which they receive gifts or borrow money. Have students choose accounts they would use and analyze each transaction. At the end of the week, have students evaluate their financial activity for the week. Did their equity increase or decrease?

SUMMARY
CHAPTER 3

Chapter 3 Quiz

Student ______ Class ______ Instructor ______
Date Assigned ______ Date Completed ______

CHAPTER 3 QUIZ

Business Transactions and the Accounting Equation

QUESTIONS (Completion)

Directions: Fill in the blank with the term that best completes each sentence.

1. ______ is anything of value that is owned or controlled.
2. Property rights are ______ claims to property.
3. ______ represents the financial claim to business assets.
4. An economic event for a business is a ______.
5. Accounts ______ represent amounts owed to a business.
6. Accounts ______ represent amounts owed by a business.
7. When a business uses credit to buy items, it is buying ______.
8. A business that earns money from selling goods or services earns ______.
9. The price a business pays for goods or services is an ______.
10. Money taken from the business by the owner for personal use is a ______.

 Chapter Quizzes • 5

QUESTIONS (Completion)

1. _____ is anything of value that is owned or controlled.
2. Property rights are _____ claims to property.
3. _____ represents the financial claim to business assets.
4. An economic event for a business is a _____.
5. Accounts _____ represent amounts owed to a business.
6. Accounts _____ represent amounts owed by a business.
7. When a business uses credit to buy items, it is buying _____.
8. A business that earns money from selling goods or services earns _____.
9. The price a business pays for goods or services is an _____.
10. Money taken from the business by the owner for personal use is a _____.

ANSWERS

1. Property
2. financial
3. Owner's equity
4. business transaction
5. Receivable
6. Payable
7. on account
8. revenue
9. expense
10. withdrawal

REVIEW AND ACTIVITIES CHAPTER 3

USING KEY TERMS

See the *Glossary* for the definitions of these terms. Have students share their groupings of terms in class. For any terms that are grouped incorrectly, ask for volunteers to explain why the term belongs with a specific group.

Understanding Accounting Concepts and Procedures

(Answers)

1. Property is anything of value owned or controlled. Financial claims are financial rights to property held by creditors and owners.
2. Cash, office furniture, office equipment, manufacturing equipment, buildings; because they are used in business operations.
3. Creditors' claims for amounts owed (liabilities); owner's equity. Examples: Accounts Payable, Paul Howard, Capital.
4. Accounts show increases and decreases in balances for specific items such as cash, accounts receivable, and owner's equity.
5. Accounts receivable shows money owed to the business; accounts payable shows money owed by the business.
6. At least two accounts must change for the equation to balance.
7. (a) Identify accounts affected, (b) classify accounts, (c) determine increase or decrease for each account, (d) check that the equation remains in balance.
8. (a) Add all asset account balances, (b) add liability and owner's equity account balances, (c) Total assets = total liabilities + total equities.
9. Businesses need revenue to operate. Revenue also provides a return on the owner's investment.
10. Revenue is earned from the sale of goods or services. Revenue increases owner's equity. Expenses are costs for earning revenue; they decrease owner's equity.
11. Investment is money contributed by the owner. Revenue is money the business earns. Both increase owner's equity.
12. Expenses are costs incurred by the business. Withdrawals are money the owner takes out of the business. Both decrease owner's equity.
13. Cash withdrawals decrease owner's equity by decreasing assets and the owner's financial claim.

CHAPTER 3 REVIEW AND ACTIVITIES

USING KEY TERMS

Grouping, comparing, and contrasting terms often helps us understand definitions. Answer the following questions related to the terms in this chapter.

accounts payable	investments
accounts receivable	on account
credit	property
creditor	property rights
equity	revenue
expense	withdrawal
financial claims	

A. Which terms can be considered assets (or benefits) to the business? Why?
B. Which terms might be grouped under the heading "Owner's Equity"? Why?
C. Which terms relate to the liabilities of a business?

Understanding Accounting Concepts and Procedures

Instructions
Answer the following questions on a separate sheet of paper:

1. What is the relationship between property and financial claims?
2. List five examples of business assets. Explain why they are business assets rather than personal assets.
3. Name two types of equity in a business, and explain what each type represents. Give an example of each.
4. Why are accounts used in an accounting system?
5. Explain the difference between accounts receivable and accounts payable.
6. Why are at least two accounts affected by each business transaction?
7. What steps should be followed in analyzing a business transaction?
8. How does one determine if the accounting equation is in balance?
9. Why is it important for a business to earn revenue?
10. Explain the difference between revenue and expenses.
11. Explain the difference between revenue and owner's investment. How do transactions involving these items affect owner's equity?
12. Explain the difference between expense and owner's withdrawal. How do transactions involving these items affect owner's equity?
13. Why does withdrawal of cash by the owner for personal use decrease owner's equity?

Case Study...

Service Business: Health and Fitness

The Fitness Center, owned by Gail Chan, has been in business for two years. The business is successful with its expanded hours of operation and child care program. To meet the needs of its clients, the Fitness Center must buy additional exercise equipment.

You are a local business consultant and have worked with several other small businesses in the area. Ms. Chan has asked you about possible ways to obtain money for the new equipment. She has already borrowed money from family members and cannot use them as a source of more funds.

Thinking Critically:

1. As a consultant, your job is to evaluate possible sources of money for your client. Research alternatives with the Small Business Administration, the Chamber of Commerce, and local banks.
2. Make a list of alternatives. Include costs, interest rates, and advantages or disadvantages.
3. Make a recommendation to your client based on your list of alternatives.
4. Explain how the additional money will affect the accounting equation.

interNET CONNECTION

Careers: Salary Expectations

Part of choosing a career means assessing your financial expectations. How much money do you hope to make? If you're considering a career in accounting, you'll want to check out the possibilities.

Do This:

1. Locate Web sites that offer salary guides. Some guides are profession-specific, while others are general salary surveys. What sites did you locate?
2. Do you see a job title that sounds interesting to you? What is the entry level for that position?
3. List three accounting occupations and the entry-level salaries for those positions.

Workplace Skills

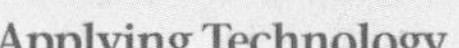

Applying Technology

Whether you work in a small or large business, technology is critical to efficiency in the workplace. Employees must be able to apply the technology appropriate to their work tasks.

On the Job:

After graduating from college and working for a year as a junior accountant in a CPA's office, you decide to open an accounting business from your home. You'll need a computer, software, and office furniture to get started. Answer the questions below to help you analyze and select the appropriate technology for your needs.

Thinking Critically:

1. List the kinds of financial services you would like to provide to your customers.
2. Research three accounting software packages that would help you deliver the services you listed. List the name, price, system requirements, and features of each software package.
3. Select the software package that best meets your anticipated needs. Write a paragraph explaining why you selected this product.

interNET CONNECTION www.glencoe.com

Do This (Answers)

1. Keyword: salary guide. Possible Web sites include:
   AICPA: www.aicpa.org
   JobSmart: jobsmart.org/tools/salary/
   Bureau of Labor Statistics: stats.bls.gov/oco/oco1001.htm
2. Answers will vary.
3. Answers will vary. Possibilities include: Junior Auditor, $36,000; Payroll Clerk, $24,000; Supervising Tax Accountant, $58,000; CPA/Partner, $135,000.

Case Study...

Thinking Critically (Answers)

1. Answers may vary. Possible sources are Small Business Administration, Chamber of Commerce, banks, and the Internet.
2. Answers may vary.
3. Answers may vary. Have students discuss recommendations in class.
4. Cash in Bank and owner's equity will increase, thus increasing both sides of the equation.

Workplace Skills

Thinking Critically (Answers)

1. Answers will vary. Some examples might include bookkeeping for small businesses, income tax preparation, personal budgeting, and debt repayment planning.
2. Answers will vary. Students may want to check out newspapers, magazines, or catalog advertisements for specifics on software packages. Example products are *Quicken, Turbo Tax, Peachtree Accounting,* and *Microsoft Money.* Suggest students to go online to find the most recent software packages on the market and download that information.
3. Answers will vary. Students should highlight how software features match their anticipated services.

Internet Resources and Activities Handbook

Refer students to the booklet for additional Internet activities.

Using Spreadsheets in Accounting

Spreadsheet applications are incorporated into the *Glencoe Accounting* program. Designated spreadsheet problems are identified in the student textbook with a spreadsheet icon. The spreadsheet activities range from working with the basic accounting equation to completing a 10-column work sheet to analyzing financial statements.

Completing the spreadsheet activities will help students gain realistic experience in using spreadsheet software for a variety of accounting tasks. Spreadsheet problem templates are provided for students working in a Windows environment using Microsoft Excel and can be launched through the CD-ROM menu system.

General instructions for completing each spreadsheet problem are provided in the student textbook beside the problem. Additional instructions for each spreadsheet activity are included in the student's *Chapter Reviews and Working Papers*.

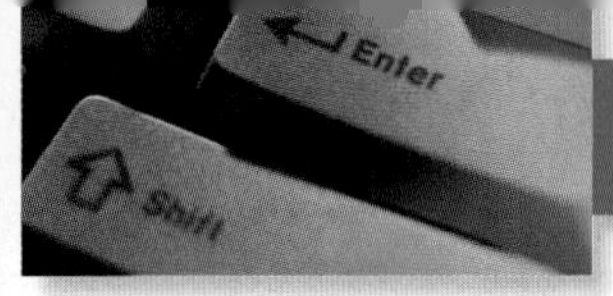

Exploring Electronic Spreadsheets

Computer spreadsheets are important tools for organizing and analyzing data. A spreadsheet is made up of rows and columns. The columns are identified by letters and the rows are identified by numbers. As you create a spreadsheet, you will enter numbers, labels, and formulas into cells. Spreadsheet applications that are commonly used in the business world include Lotus 1-2-3 and Microsoft Excel. The following is an example of a basic electronic spreadsheet:

	A	B	C	D	E	F	G	H
1		Jan	Feb	March	April	May	June	July
2	Sales	2,500	5,000	1,650	10,000	3,100	8,200	12,500
3	Expenses	700	1,200	225	3,550	1,800	2,300	5,600
4	Net income	1,800	3,800	1,425	6,450	1,300	5,900	6,900
5								
6								

Callouts: 1, 2, 3, 4, 5, 6, 7, 8

Before you create a computer spreadsheet, review the following spreadsheet terms.

	Spreadsheet Terms	Description
①	Row	Identified by numbers down the left side of the spreadsheet.
②	Column	Identified by letters along the top of the spreadsheet.
③	Cell address	Identified by a column letter and row number. For example, the cell address B4 indicates the cell where the number 1,800 is found.
④	Cell cursor	Indicated by a highlight of the cell.
⑤	Scroll arrows	Allows you to view other parts of the spreadsheet.
⑥	Labels	Text that identifies columns or rows of information; cannot be used for calculations.
⑦	Values	Numbers inserted in cells that can be used for calculations.
⑧	Formulas	Mathematical functions entered in a particular cell that tells the software to add, subtract, divide, or multiply values. For example, E2−E3 represents 10,000 − 3,550, or 6,450.

TEACHING NOTES

CHAPTER 3 PROBLEMS

APPLICATION OPTIONS

Complete chapter problems one of two ways:

1 **Manual** Glencoe Working Papers

or

2 **Spreadsheet** Templates (Problem 3–9)

Problem 3–4 Classifying Accounts

All accounts belong in one of the following classifications: Asset, Liability, Owner's Equity.

Instructions In your working papers indicate the classification for each of the following accounts.

1. John Jones, Capital
2. Cash in Bank
3. Accounts Receivable
4. Accounts Payable
5. Office Equipment
6. Delivery Equipment
7. Camping Equipment
8. Building
9. Land
10. Computer Equipment

Problem 3–5 Completing the Accounting Equation

The following accounts are used in a business owned and operated by Mike Murray.

Instructions Look at the following list of accounts and determine the missing amount for each of the question marks.

Assets		=	Liabilities	+	Owner's Equity
Cash in Bank	$4,500		Accounts Payable		Mike Murray,
Accounts Receivable	1,350		?		Capital $9,250
Office Equipment	5,000				
	?				

Analyze: Is the accounting equation in balance?

Problem 3–6 Classifying Accounts Within the Accounting Equation

Listed below are the account names and balances for Wilderness Rentals.

Accounts Payable	$ 7,000	Cash in Bank	$ 5,000
Accounts Receivable	2,000	Office Equipment	3,000
Camping Equipment	12,000	Ronald Hicks, Capital	15,000

Continued

PROBLEMS
CHAPTER 3

Problem 3–4 (Answers)
Classifying Accounts

1. Owner's Equity
2. Asset
3. Asset
4. Liability
5. Asset
6. Asset
7. Asset
8. Asset
9. Asset
10. Asset

Problem 3–5 (Answers)
Completing the Accounting Equation

Total Assets = $10,850
Liabilities (Accounts Payable) = $1,600

Analyze: The accounting equation is in balance.

Problem 3–6 (Answers)
Classifying Accounts Within the Accounting Equation

Total assets: $22,000
Liabilities: $7,000
Owner's Equity: $15,000

Analyze: The accounting equation is in balance ($22,000 = $7,000 + $15,000).

MEETING SPECIAL NEEDS

Students with Hearing Impairments When you talk to a student with a hearing impairment, be sure to look directly at the student and enunciate clearly. Remember to avoid talking when you are writing on the chalkboard, when your back is turned to the class, or when you are looking at the textbook. To further assist students, you may want to repeat questions that other students have asked. Also try to repeat answers you provide to the class.

Problem 3-7 (Answers) Determining Increases and Decreases in Accounts

1. Cash in Bank, asset, + $25,000; Regina Delgado, Capital, owner's equity, + $25,000
2. Car Wash Equipment, asset, + $12,000; Cash in Bank, asset, – $12,000
3. Office Equipment, asset, + $2,500; Accounts Payable, liability, + $2,500
4. Regina Delgado, Capital, owner's equity, – $800; Cash in Bank, asset, – $800
5. Cash in Bank, asset, + $1,000; Regina Delgado, Capital, owner's equity, + $1,000
6. Regina Delgado, Capital, owner's equity, – $600; Cash in Bank, asset, – $600
7. Office Furniture, asset, + $1,000; Cash in Bank, asset, – $200; Accounts Payable, liability, + $800
8. Accounts Receivable, asset, + $600; Regina Delgado, Capital, owner's equity, + $600

Analyze: Three accounts: Office Furniture, Cash in Bank, and Accounts Payable.

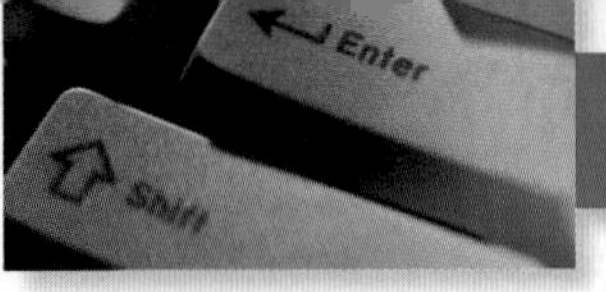

Instructions Using these account names and balances:
(1) List and total the assets of the business.
(2) Determine the amount owed by the business.
(3) Give the amount of the owner's equity in the business.

Analyze: Is the accounting equation in balance?

Problem 3–7 Determining Increases and Decreases in Accounts

Hot Suds Car Wash uses the following accounts:

Assets	=	Liabilities	+	Owner s Equity
Cash in Bank		Accounts Payable		Regina Delgado, Capital
Accounts Receivable				
Office Equipment				
Office Furniture				
Car Wash Equipment				

Instructions Use a form similar to the one that follows. For each transaction:
(1) Identify the accounts affected.
(2) Classify the accounts.
(3) Determine the amount of the increase (+) or decrease (−) for each account affected.

The first transaction is completed as an example.

Trans.	Accounts Affected	Classification	Amount of Increase (+) or Decrease (−)
1.	Cash in Bank	Asset	+$25,000
	Regina Delgado, Capital	Owner's Equity	+$25,000

Date		Transactions
Jan.	1	1. Regina Delgado, the owner, invested $25,000 cash in the business.
	4	2. Bought car wash equipment with cash for $12,000.
	5	3. Purchased, on account, $2,500 of office equipment.
	10	4. Wrote a check for the monthly rent, $800.
	12	5. Received cash for services performed, $1,000.
	15	6. The owner withdrew $600 cash from the business for personal use.
	20	7. Purchased a desk for $1,000, paying $200 cash and agreeing to pay the balance of $800 in 30 days.
	25	8. Provided services worth $600 on account.

Analyze: How many accounts are affected by Transaction 7?

ASSESSMENT RESOURCES

Choose assessment strategies from the following pages to evaluate your students' progress.

Student Edition
Check Your Understanding, pp. 49, 56, 60
Chapter 3 Problems, pp. 65–69

Assessment and Evaluation Masters
Chapter 3 Study Plan, *Glencoe Workbook (CRWP)*
Chapter 3 Self-Test, *Glencoe Workbook (CRWP)*
Chapter 3 Test, *Chapter Tests* Booklet
Chapter 3 Activity, *School-to-Work Handbook*
Chapter 3 **Exam***View*

Teacher Wraparound Edition
Critical Thinking Activity, p. 54
Reteaching Sections 1–3, pp. 49, 56, 60
Chapter 3 Quiz, p. 61

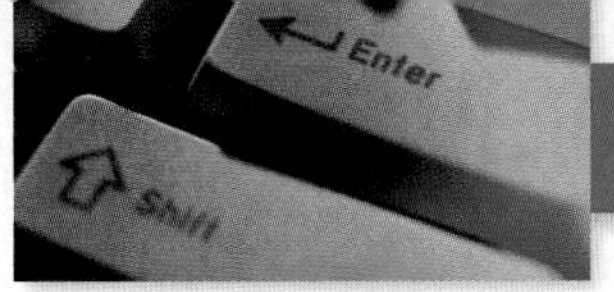

Problem 3–8 Determining the Effects of Transactions on the Accounting Equation

After graduating from college, Abe Shultz decided to start a pet grooming service called Kits & Pups Grooming.

Instructions Use a form similar to the one that follows. For each of the following transactions:

(1) Identify the accounts affected, using the account names on the form.
(2) Determine the amount of the increase or decrease for each account.
(3) Write the amount of the increase (+) or decrease (−) in the space under each account affected.
(4) On the following line, write the new balance for each account.
(5) Transaction 1 is completed as an example.

	Assets				=	Liabilities	+	Owner's Equity
Trans.	Cash in Bank	Accts. Rec.	Office Equip.	Grooming Equip.	=	Accounts Payable	+	Abe Shultz, Capital
1	+$10,000							+$10,000

Date	Transactions
Jan. 2	1. Abe Shultz began the business by depositing $10,000 in a checking account at the Shoreline National Bank in the name of the business, Kits & Pups Grooming.
3	2. Bought grooming equipment for cash, $1,000.
8	3. Issued a check for $900 for the monthly rent.
9	4. Bought $6,000 worth of new office equipment on account for use in the business.
15	5. Received $700 cash for services performed for customers during the first week of business.
21	6. Issued a $2,000 check to the creditor as partial payment for the office equipment purchased on account.
29	7. Performed grooming services and agreed to be paid for them later, $500.

Analyze: What is the amount of total liabilities and owner's equity?

Problem 3–8 (Answers) Determining the Effects of Transactions on the Accounting Equation

Ending account balances:
Cash in Bank $6,800
Accounts Receivable $500
Office Equipment $6,000
Grooming Equipment $1,000
Accounts Payable $4,000
Abe Schultz, Capital $10,300

Analyze: $14,300

ACCOUNTING ISSUES

The History of Public Accounting The profession of public accounting emerged in the late 19th century. The Institute of Accounts was founded in 1882 for public accountants, bookkeepers, and businesspeople interested in accounting. A rival organization, the American Association of Public Accountants, was founded in 1887. Both organizations issued members certificates of proficiency based on experience or the passing of an examination. The formation of contemporary accounting groups, including the American Institute of Certified Public Accountants, the Financial Accounting Standards Board, and the Financial Accounting Foundation, began in the 1970s.

Problem 3-9 (Answers) Determining the Effects of Business Transactions on the Accounting Equation

Ending account balances:
Cash in Bank $28,000
Accounts Receivable $1,200
Hiking Equipment $3,000
Rafting Equipment $24,000
Office Equipment $4,450
Accounts Payable $2,500
Juanita Ortega, Capital $58,150

Analyze: $2,500

Problem 3-10 (Answers) Describing Business Transactions

1. The owner invested $30,000 in the business.
2. Purchased office equipment with cash, $2,000.
3. Bought video equipment on account for $8,000.
4. Received payment for repair services, $700, or owner invested $700 in the business.
5. Performed repair services and customer agreed to pay later, $500. Or, rented video equipment or video tapes to customers who agreed to pay later.
6. Greg Failla invested office equipment, which was valued at $200, in the business.
7. Issued a $3,000 check to creditor.
8. Showbiz Video sold old office equipment for $200 on account.
9. Received payment on account for services previously performed, $500.
10. The owner withdrew $1,000 cash from the business for personal use.

Analyze: $30,400

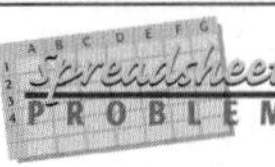

SPREADSHEET SMART GUIDE

Step-by-Step Instructions: Problem 3-9

1. Select the spreadsheet template for Problem 3-9.
2. Enter your name and the date in the spaces provided on the template.
3. Complete the spreadsheet using the instructions in your working papers.
4. Print the spreadsheet and proof your work.
5. Save your work and exit the spreadsheet program.

Spreadsheet PROBLEM Problem 3-9 Determining the Effects of Business Transactions on the Accounting Equation

Juanita Ortega is the owner of a professional guide service called Outback Guide Service.

Instructions Use a form similar to the one below. For each of the following transactions:

(1) Identify the accounts affected.
(2) Write the amount of the increase (+) or decrease (−) in the space provided on the form in your working papers.
(3) Determine the new balance for each account.

	Assets					=	Liabilities	+	Owner's Equity
Trans.	Cash in Bank	Accts. Rec.	Hiking Equip.	Rafting Equip.	Office Equip.	=	Accounts Payable	+	Juanita Ortega, Capital

Date	Transactions
Jan. 3	1. Ms. Ortega, the owner, opened a checking account for the business by depositing $60,000 of her personal funds.
6	2. Paid by check the monthly rent of $3,000.
8	3. Bought hiking equipment for the business by writing a check for $3,000.
9	4. Purchased $24,000 of rafting equipment by writing a check.
11	5. Purchased office equipment on account for $4,000.
15	6. Received payment for guide services, $2,500.
18	7. Ms. Ortega contributed a desk valued at $450 to the business.
21	8. Withdrew $3,000 cash from the business for personal use.
26	9. Wrote a check to a creditor as partial payment on account, $1,500.
30	10. Took a group on a tour and agreed to accept payment later, $1,200.

Analyze: How much is owed to creditors after Transaction 10?

Problem 3-10 Describing Business Transactions

Showbiz Video is a business owned by Greg Failla. The transactions that follow are shown as they would appear in the accounting equation.

Instructions In your working papers, describe what has happened in each transaction. Transaction 1 is completed as an example.

Example:
1. The owner invested $30,000 in the business.

ADDRESSING MULTIPLE LEARNING STYLES

Kinesthetic Learner Have students demonstrate physical skills they possess that will aid them in an accounting career. For example, students can demonstrate keyboarding and computer skills. Or, students can demonstrate how to use the various functions on an electronic calculator or PDA. Have each student explain the skill as he or she is demonstrating it, explain why it is important to his or her future in accounting, and tell the class how the skill was acquired. Involve as many students as possible.

	Assets				=	Liabilities	+	Owner's Equity
Trans.	Cash in Bank	Accts. Rec.	Office Equip.	Video Equip.	=	Accounts Payable	+	Greg Failla, Capital
1	+$30,000							+$30,000
2	−$ 2,000		+$2,000					
3				+$8,000		+$8,000		
4	+$ 700							+$ 700
5		+$500						+$ 500
6			+$ 200					+$ 200
7	−$ 3,000					−$3,000		
8		+$200	−$ 200					
9	+$ 500	−$500						
10	−$ 1,000							−$ 1,000

Analyze: What is the balance in the account, **Greg Failla, Capital?**

Problem 3–11 Completing the Accounting Equation

The account names and balances for Job Connect are listed below.

Instructions Determine the missing amount for each of the question marks. Use the form in your working papers and write in the missing amounts.

	Assets			=	Liabilities	+	Owner's Equity
Trans.	Cash in Bank	Accounts Receivable	Business Equipment	=	Accounts Payable	+	Richard Tang, Capital
1	?	$ 2,000	$ 1,000		$ 500		$ 7,500
2	$ 3,000	$ 9,000	?		$2,000		$16,000
3	$ 8,000	$ 1,000	$10,000		?		$15,000
4	$ 4,000	?	$ 4,000		$1,000		$17,000
5	$ 9,000	$ 7,000	$ 6,000		$5,000		?
6	$10,000	$14,000	?		$6,000		$32,000
7	$ 6,000	$ 4,000	$10,000		?		$15,000
8	?	$ 5,000	$ 9,000		$1,000		?

Hint: In line 8, total assets are $18,000.

Analyze: For line 8, if total liabilities and equity equals $20,000, what would the balance of **Cash in Bank** be?

Problem 3–11 (Answers) Completing the Accounting Equation

1. $5,000
2. $6,000
3. $4,000
4. $10,000
5. $17,000
6. $14,000
7. $5,000
8. $4,000, $17,000

Analyze: $6,000

MAKING CONNECTIONS TO DAILY LIFE

Personal Assets Ask students to list their personal assets on a sheet of paper; then ask them to consider how they acquired those assets. Did they purchase them? Were they gifts? Have students also list their liabilities, and then determine their equity. (Students' assets might include clothing, jewelry, savings/checking accounts, car, sports equipment, and stereo equipment. Liabilities might include money owed to parents or a friend, items in layaway or purchased on a credit card, or money due for car insurance or a car payment.)

CHAPTER 4 Resource Manager

Section Resources

	Objectives & Standards	Activities & Features	Reproducible Masters
Chapter Opener *Transactions That Affect Assets, Liabilities, and Owner's Equity*	• Prepare a chart of accounts. • Apply the rules of debit and credit to asset, liability, and owner's equity accounts. • Use T accounts to analyze a business transaction into its debit and credit parts. • Demonstrate the effects of transactions on the accounting equation using T accounts. • Identify the normal balance of accounts. • Calculate account balances after recording business transactions. • Analyze transactions that increase or decrease assets, liabilities, and owner's capital and record them in T accounts. • Define and use the accounting terms introduced in this chapter. **National Standards for Business Education**: IA1, IA3, IA4, IA5, IA6, IA7	Exploring the Real World of Business, p. 70 Workplace Connections, p. 71	School-to-Work Handbook
Section 1 *Accounts and the Double-Entry Accounting System*	• How to use T accounts. • Why you need a ledger. • The rules of debit and credit.	Did You Know?, p. 72 Accounting Flashbacks, p. 73 Math Hints, p. 74 International Accounting, p. 74 Connect To, p. 75 Accounting Tips, p. 76	Demonstration Problems Math Review for Accounting Strategies for Teaching International Accounting
Section 2 *Applying the Rules of Debit and Credit*	• How to analyze a transaction affecting assets, liabilities, and owner's equity.	A Matter of Ethics, p. 82 Accounting Careers in Focus, p. 84	Demonstration Problems Strategies for Teaching Ethics in Accounting Internet Resources and Activities Handbook

KEY

Posters · Transparency · Software · Videocassette · Blackline Masters · CD-ROM · Portfolio

MULTIMEDIA RESOURCE

Peachtree	QuickBooks	Spreadsheets	Videos	CD-ROMs
None in this chapter.	None in this chapter.	Problem 4–6 *Analyzing Transactions into Debit and Credit Parts*	***Video Segment: Business Transactions*** After viewing this video, students will be able to describe the great variety of business transactions that trigger an entry in the accounting records. Students will also learn to analyze a transaction from its source document to its effect on the accounting equation.	***Electronic Learning Center (ELC), Chapter 4*** This program is ideal for visual learners since it incorporates video images, animation, and graphics to enliven the content of each lesson. ***Interactive Lesson Planner (ILP), Chapter 4*** This CD-ROM combines the versatility of an electronic lesson planner with the convenience of teacher classroom resources.

SCANS Correlation Chart

FOUNDATION SKILLS

Basic Skills:	Reading	Writing	Math	Listening	Speaking	
Thinking Skills:	Creative Thinking	Decision Making	Problem Solving	Seeing Things in the Mind's Eye	Knowing How to Learn	Reasoning
Personal Qualities:	Responsibility	Self-Esteem	Sociability	Self-Management	Integrity/Honesty	

WORKPLACE COMPETENCIES

Resources:	Allocating Time	Allocating Money	Allocating Material and Facility Resources	Allocating Human Resources		
Information:	Acquiring and Evaluating Information	Organizing and Maintaining Information	Interpreting and Communicating Information	Using Computers to Process Information		
Interpersonal Skills:	Participating as a Member of a Team	Teaching Others	Serving Clients/ Customers	Exercising Leadership	Negotiating to Arrive at a Decision	Working with Cultural Diversity
Systems:	Understanding Systems	Monitoring and Correcting Performance	Improving and Designing Systems			
Technology:	Selecting Technology	Applying Technology to Task	Maintaining and Troubleshooting Technology			

*Highlighted blocks indicate areas covered in the chapter. Additional SCANS skills are also covered throughout the *Teacher Wraparound Edition.*

Assessment

Student Edition
- Check Your Understanding, pp. 77, 83
- Chapter 4 Problems, pp. 89–93

Assessment and Evaluation Masters
- Chapter 4 Study Plan, *Glencoe Workbook*
- Chapter 4 Self-Test, *Glencoe Workbook*
- Chapter 4 Test, *Chapter Tests* Booklet
- Chapter 4 Activity, *School-to-Work Handbook*
- Chapter 4 **Exam***View*

Teacher Wraparound Edition
- Critical Thinking Activity, p. 86
- Reteaching Section 1, p. 77
- Reteaching Section 2, p. 83
- Chapter 4 Quiz, p. 85

Transparencies

	Teaching Transparencies	Solution Transparencies
Section 1:	4–1, 4–2, 4–3	Problem 4–1
Section 2:	4–4, 4–5, 4–6, 4–7, 4–8, 4–9, 4–10, 4–11, 4–12	Problem 4–2
End of Chapter:		Problems 4–3, 4–4, 4–5, 4–6, 4–7

TEACHER CLASSROOM RESOURCES

This is a representation of key blackline masters available in the Teacher Classroom Resources.

Teaching Aids

Transparency Examples

Section Focus Transparencies

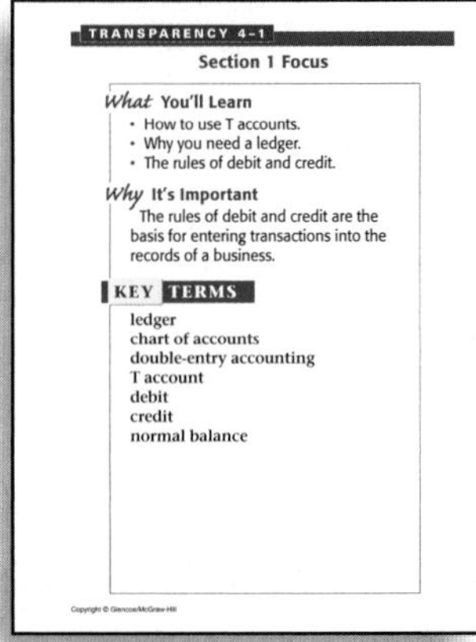

TRANSPARENCY 4-1

Section 1 Focus

What You'll Learn
- How to use T accounts.
- Why you need a ledger.
- The rules of debit and credit.

Why It's Important

The rules of debit and credit are the basis for entering transactions into the records of a business.

KEY TERMS

ledger
chart of accounts
double-entry accounting
T account
debit
credit
normal balance

Teaching Transparencies

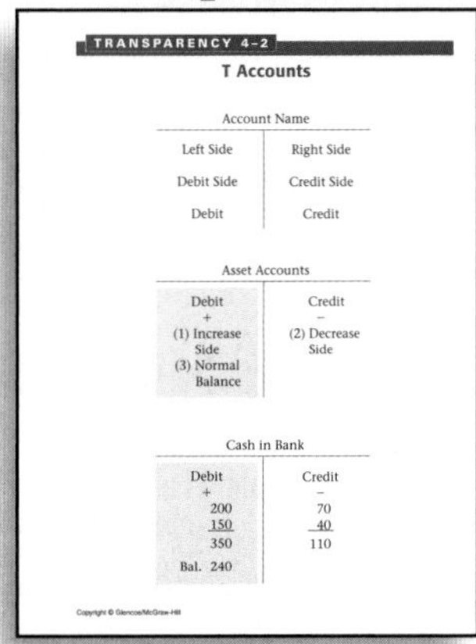

TRANSPARENCY 4-2

T Accounts

Teaching Transparencies

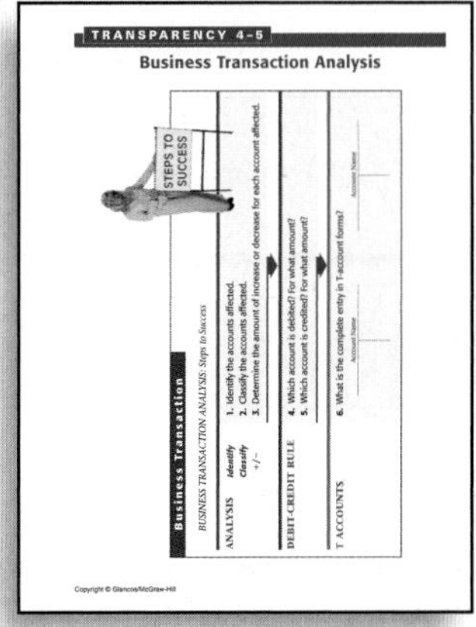

TRANSPARENCY 4-5

Business Transaction Analysis

Solution Transparencies

Demonstration Problems

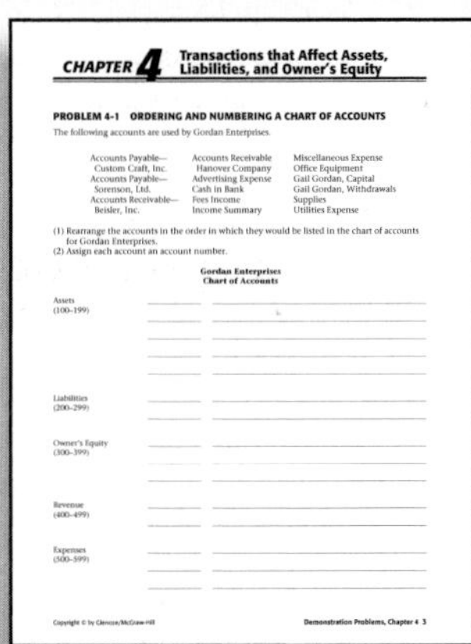

CHAPTER 4 Transactions that Affect Assets, Liabilities, and Owner's Equity

Lesson Plans

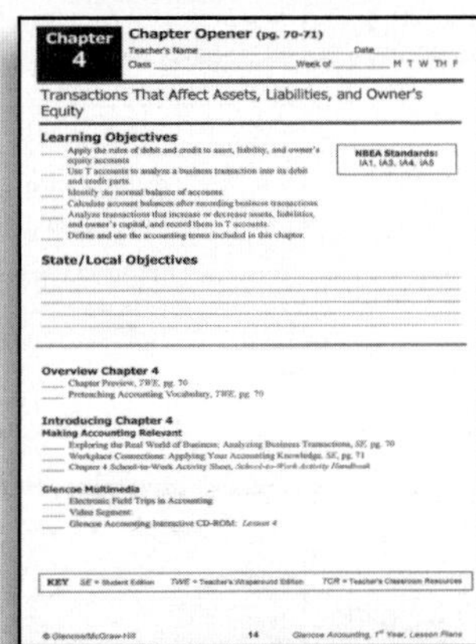

Chapter 4 Chapter Opener (pg. 70–71)

Transactions That Affect Assets, Liabilities, and Owner's Equity

Block Scheduling

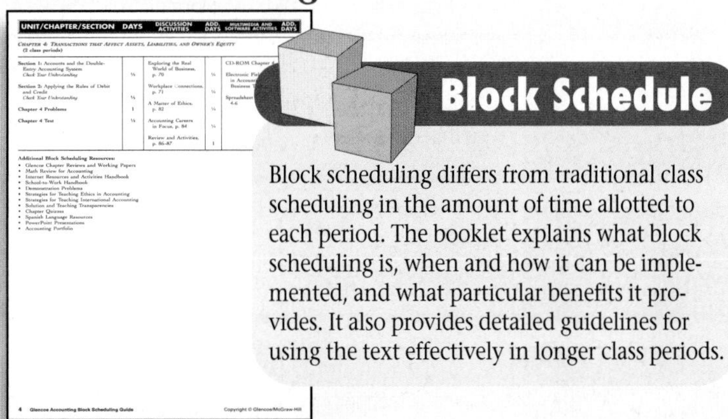

Block Schedule

Block scheduling differs from traditional class scheduling in the amount of time allotted to each period. The booklet explains what block scheduling is, when and how it can be implemented, and what particular benefits it provides. It also provides detailed guidelines for using the text effectively in longer class periods.

Enrichment and Application

Strategies for Teaching Ethics in Accounting

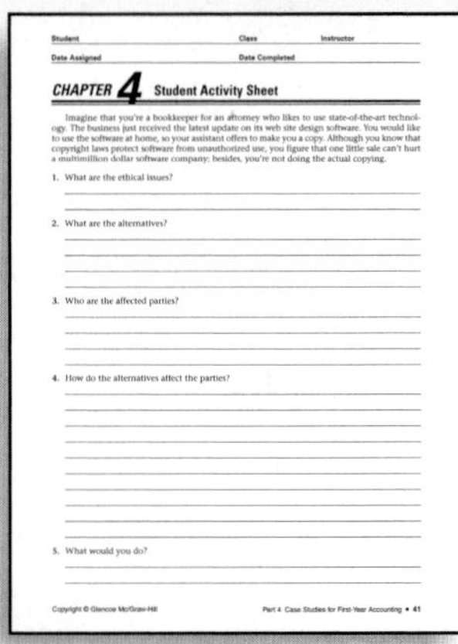

CHAPTER 4 Student Activity Sheet

Strategies for Teaching International Accounting

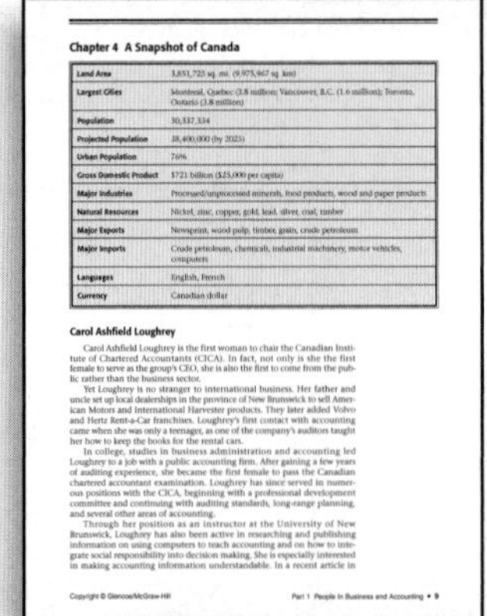

Chapter 4 A Snapshot of Canada

School-to-Work Handbook

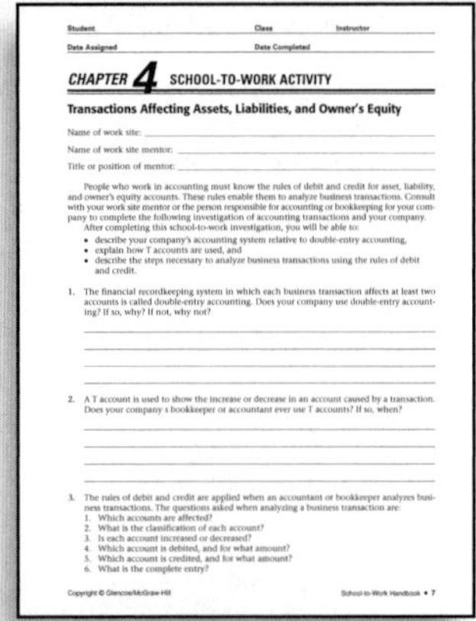

CHAPTER 4 SCHOOL-TO-WORK ACTIVITY

Transactions Affecting Assets, Liabilities, and Owner's Equity

Meeting Different Ability Levels

Chapter Reviews and Working Papers (CRWP)

Working Papers

Review

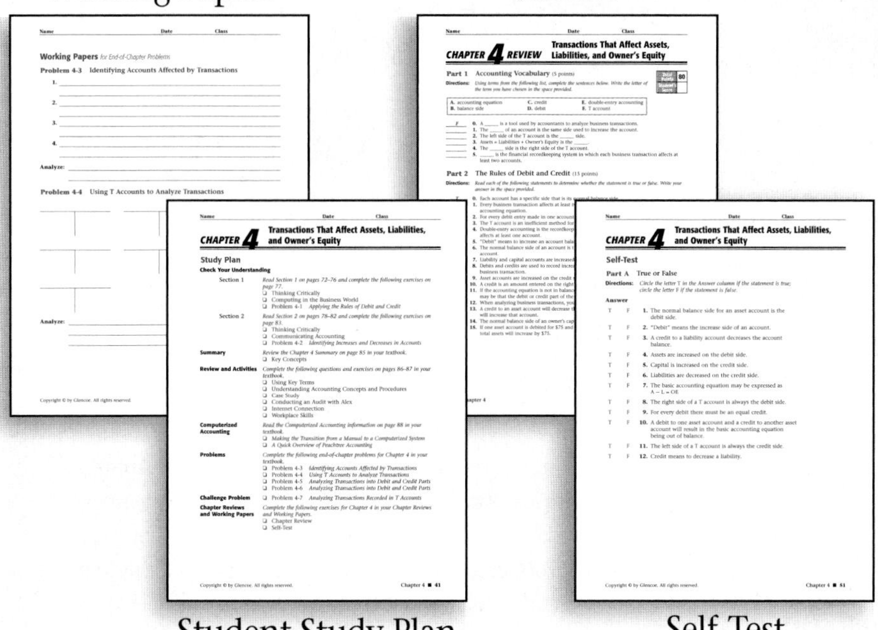

Student Study Plan

Self-Test

Real-World Multimedia CD-ROM

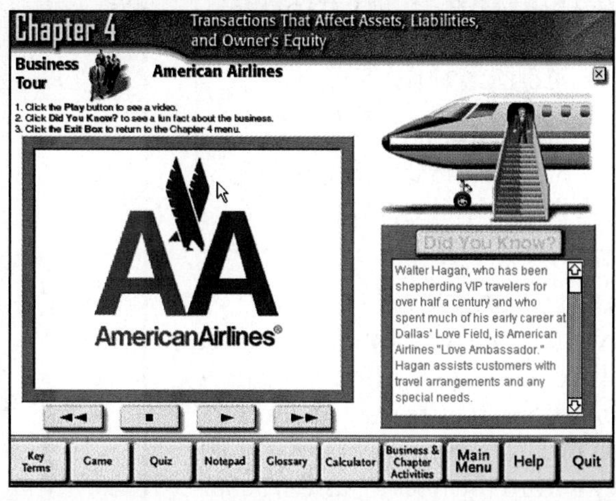

Key to Ability Levels

Each section gives skill-building activities. Each activity has been labeled for use with students of various learning styles and abilities.

L1 Level 1 activities are basic activities and should be within the range of all students.

L2 Level 2 activities are average activities and should be within the range of average and above average students.

L3 Level 3 activities are challenging activities designed for the ability range of above average students.

ELL ELL activities should be within the ability range of English Language Learners.

Teaching Resources at a Glance

Application Resources

- Glencoe Chapter Review and Working Papers, SE and TAE
- School-to-Work Handbook, SE and TM
- Accounting Portfolio, SE and TM

Reproducible Masters

- Demonstration Problems
- Lesson Plans
- Block Scheduling
- Spanish Language Resources

Glencoe Accounting Professional Development Series

- Strategies for Teaching Ethics in Accounting
- Accounting Competitive Event Review
- Math Review for Accounting
- Strategies for Teaching International Accounting
- Internet Resources and Activities Handbook

Transparency Package

- Section Focus Transparencies
- Teaching Transparencies
- Source Document Transparencies
- Solution Transparencies

Performance Assessment

- **Exam***View* CD-ROM
- Chapter Tests
- Chapter Quizzes
- Unit Tests
- Audit Tests
- Printed Testbank

Multimedia Resources

- Electronic Learning Center:
  - Multimedia CD-ROMs
  - Peachtree software, tutorials, templates, and solutions
  - Spreadsheet templates
- Using QuickBooks with Glencoe Accounting
- Interactive Lesson Planner
- Electronic Field Trips in Accounting
- PowerPoint Presentation
- Web site: glencoeaccounting.glencoe.com

Assessment and Evaluation

Chapter Tests

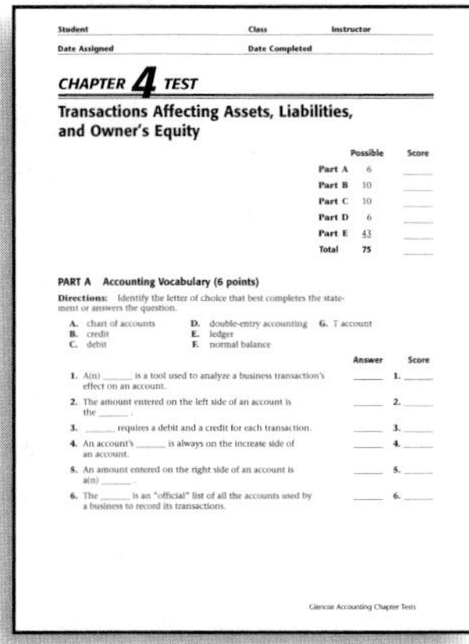

Chapter Quiz

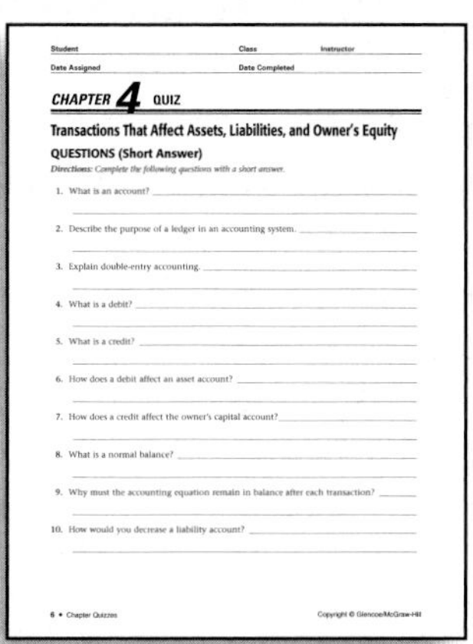

OVERVIEW CHAPTER 4

Correlations to National Standards for Business Education

(See pages T50–T51 for a detailed correlation chart.)

Standards: IA1, IA3, IA4, IA5, IA6, IA7

Chapter Preview

Now that students have learned to use the accounting equation to analyze transactions, they're ready to learn the rules of debit and credit. In this chapter, they'll learn the rules for assets, liabilities, and owner's equity accounts. Students will use those rules to analyze the debits and credits of the business transactions they studied in Chapter 2.

Section Overviews

- Section 1—*Accounts and the Double-Entry Accounting System*
- Section 2—*Applying the Rules of Debit and Credit*

Chapter Vocabulary

ledger
chart of accounts
double-entry accounting
T account
debit
credit
normal balance

Preteaching Accounting Vocabulary

Writing: Ask students to write a sentence using each of the new terms in context. Ask for volunteers to write their sentences on the chalkboard. Discuss any differences in the use of the terms. L1

Transactions That Affect Assets, Liabilities, and Owner's Equity

Learning Objectives

When you have completed this chapter, you will be able to:

- Prepare a chart of accounts.
- Apply the rules of debit and credit to asset, liability, and owner's equity accounts.
- Use T accounts to analyze a business transaction into its debit and credit parts.
- Demonstrate the effects of transactions on the accounting equation using T accounts.
- Identify the normal balance of accounts.
- Calculate account balances after recording business transactions.
- Analyze transactions that increase or decrease assets, liabilities, and owner's capital and record them in T accounts.
- Define and use the accounting terms introduced in this chapter.

Exploring the Real World of Business

ANALYZING BUSINESS TRANSACTIONS

Cruising at 30,000 feet is just part of a normal day at **American Airlines. American** is one of the largest passenger airlines in the world and flies to over 170 destinations. The company employs nearly 125,000 people. The airline earns its revenue primarily from passenger tickets and cargo shipments.

When you're as big as **American Airlines,** the things you buy to operate the business can also be very large expenditures. Have you ever wondered how much a Boeing 757 costs? Between $90 and $105 million each! In addition to large purchases, the airline also buys food, fuel, and even coloring books for young travelers. Each transaction affects the airline's assets, liabilities, and total equity.

What do you think?

Name at least three business transactions that would affect the assets and liabilities of **American Airlines.**

AmericanAirlines®

Exploring the Real World of Business

American Airlines

American Airlines is a public corporation whose stock is owned by over 15,000 stockholders. The stock symbol is AMR. Discuss with students the type of financial data that stockholders want to know about a corporation, such as its revenue, expenses, and increases or decreases to equity.

What do you think? (Answers)

Answers will vary. Students might mention the sale of a ticket, the purchase of snacks and meals, the purchase of jet fuel on account, payment to lease or buy an airplane, payment of airport landing fees, or purchases of parts for plane repairs.

Workplace Connections

Applying Your Accounting Knowledge

Business transactions occur around us everyday. A music store sells thousands of CDs in a day. You may stop by for a meal at a local sandwich shop. A cruise ship line may purchase new furniture for all its formal dining cabins. Successful businesses have hundreds, even thousands, of such transactions each day. Analyzing and recording these transactions are key duties of the accounting staff.

Investigate:

1. What types of business transactions occur in your workplace or the workplace of your family or friends?
2. Who records these transactions into the accounting records?

Glencoe Accounting *Online*

Visit the *Glencoe Accounting* Web site at **glencoeaccounting.glencoe.com** for additional activities and information.

71

INTRODUCING

CHAPTER 4

Making Accounting Relevant

Workplace Connections: Applying Your Accounting Knowledge

Discussion: Point out that accounting and finance staff are key employees in any business. Without financial records, the business owner would not know the amounts earned or spent. Ask students to discuss how the work of the accounting staff affects the day-to-day decisions made by a business owner or manager.

Investigate (Answers)

1. Answers will vary but could include examples such as the sale of a cruise by a travel agency or the sale of luggage by a department store.
2. Accountants and accounting staff record business transactions, then summarize the financial results. With computerized systems, basic transaction information may be recorded automatically into financial records. The accounting staff then checks that the records are correct and handles the process of summarizing and analyzing data.

School-to-Work Activity

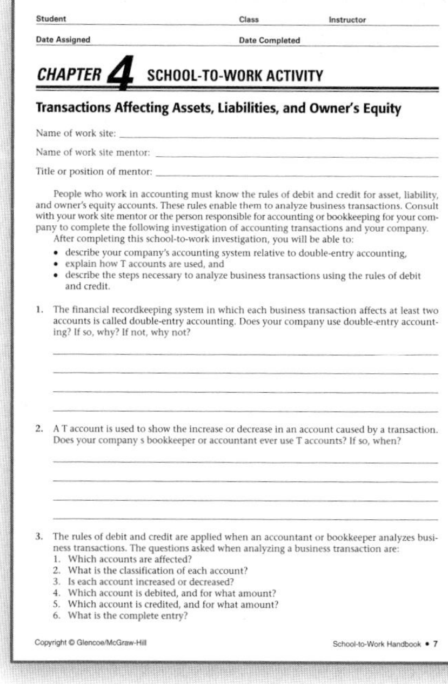

Student ______ Class ______ Instructor ______

Date Assigned ______ Date Completed ______

CHAPTER 4 SCHOOL-TO-WORK ACTIVITY

Transactions Affecting Assets, Liabilities, and Owner's Equity

Name of work site: ______

Name of work site mentor: ______

Title or position of mentor: ______

People who work in accounting must know the rules of debit and credit for asset, liability, and owner's equity accounts. These rules enable them to analyze business transactions. Consult with your work site mentor or the person responsible for accounting or bookkeeping for your company to complete the following investigation of accounting transactions and your company.

After completing this school-to-work investigation, you will be able to:

- describe your company's accounting system relative to double-entry accounting,
- explain how T accounts are used, and
- describe the steps necessary to analyze business transactions using the rules of debit and credit.

1. The financial recordkeeping system in which each business transaction affects at least two accounts is called double-entry accounting. Does your company use double-entry accounting? If so, why? If not, why not?

2. A T account is used to show the increase or decrease in an account caused by a transaction. Does your company s bookkeeper or accountant ever use T accounts? If so, when?

3. The rules of debit and credit are applied when an accountant or bookkeeper analyzes business transactions. The questions asked when analyzing a business transaction are:
   1. Which accounts are affected?
   2. What is the classification of each account?
   3. Is each account increased or decreased?
   4. Which account is debited, and for what amount?
   5. Which account is credited, and for what amount?
   6. What is the complete entry?

 School-to-Work Handbook • 7

GLENCOE MULTIMEDIA

Electronic Field Trips in Accounting *Video Segment: Business Transactions*
After viewing this video, students will be able to describe the great variety of business transactions that trigger an entry in the accounting records.

Glencoe Accounting: Electronic Learning Center *Chapter 4*
The CD-ROM program is ideal for visual learners since it incorporates video images, animation, and graphics to enliven the content of each lesson.

CHAPTER 4
SECTION 1, PAGES 72–77

1 FOCUS

Introducing the Section

In this section, students build on their knowledge of accounts by learning to place information about an account in T-account form. Using T accounts, students learn the rules of debit and credit for assets, liabilities, and owner's equity. Students learn these rules within the overall context of the accounting equation.

Section Concepts

- How to use T accounts.
- Why you need a ledger.
- The rules of debit and credit.

Visual Learning

Section 1 Focus

Use **Transparency 4–1** to introduce section concepts.

BELL RINGER

Conceptualize: Students learned about several different types of accounts and business transactions in Chapter 3. Point out that accounts can increase or decrease depending on the effects of a business transaction. For this activity, have students design an account form. How would they show the name of the account, the increases and decreases, and the balance? Have students share their ideas in class. As you present T accounts and the debit and credit sides of accounts, draw parallels to the forms students design. L2

SECTION 1

Accounts and the Double-Entry Accounting System

What You'll Learn

- How to use T accounts.
- Why you need a ledger.
- The rules of debit and credit.

Why It's Important

The rules of debit and credit are the basis for entering transactions into the records of a business.

KEY TERMS

ledger
chart of accounts
double-entry accounting
T account
debit
credit
normal balance

In Chapter 3 you learned about the accounting equation. In this chapter you will learn the double-entry accounting system that allows businesses to keep the accounting equation in balance. When The Coca-Cola Company records the dollar amount of a transaction in one account, it records an equal amount in another account. The same is true of the small computer repair shop or the McDonald's franchise in your community. In this chapter and following chapters, we will identify the various accounting functions involved in a sole proprietorship.

The Account

An account is a location within an accounting system in which the increases and decreases in a specific asset, liability, or owner's equity are recorded and stored. Accounts may have different physical forms, depending on the system. In a manual system, each account may be a separate page in a book or a separate card in a tray. In an electronic system, accounts are stored on disks or hard drives. Whether a system is manual or electronic, accounts are grouped together in a **ledger**. When people refer to "keeping the books," they are referring to maintaining accounts in the ledger. Grouping accounts in a ledger makes information easy to find. When financial statements are needed, the appropriate information is taken from the ledger and organized into reports.

The Chart of Accounts

To keep track of its accounts, a business develops a **chart of accounts**, or a list of all the accounts and their assigned account numbers. The number of accounts needed depends on the size of the business. A small business may require only 20 or 30 accounts. A large business may have several thousand accounts.

Did You Know?

Consumer Preferences

Southwest Airlines started the trend of offering only snacks and beverages on its flights. What is the flying public's favorite snack? About 49 percent prefer peanuts, 14 percent prefer pretzels, and the rest prefer other options.

RESOURCE MANAGER

Reproducible Masters
- Lesson Plans
- Chapter Reviews and Working Papers (CRWP) TAE
- Demonstration Problems

Transparencies
- Section Focus Transparency
- Teaching Transparencies
- Solution Transparencies

Multimedia
- ExamView CD-ROM
- Electronic Learning Center CD-ROM
- Interactive Lesson Planner CD-ROM
- Electronic Field Trips in Accounting

Numbering the Accounts

A system for numbering accounts makes it easy to locate individual accounts in the ledger. Account numbers have two or more digits. While a small company may use a three-digit system, a very large corporation may have 35 or more digits in its account numbers. The digits are used for sorting information based on the kinds of reports the business needs. A typical numbering system used to prepare a chart of accounts is as follows:

- Asset accounts begin with 1.
- Liability accounts begin with 2.
- Owner's equity accounts begin with 3.
- Revenue accounts begin with 4.
- Expense accounts begin with 5.

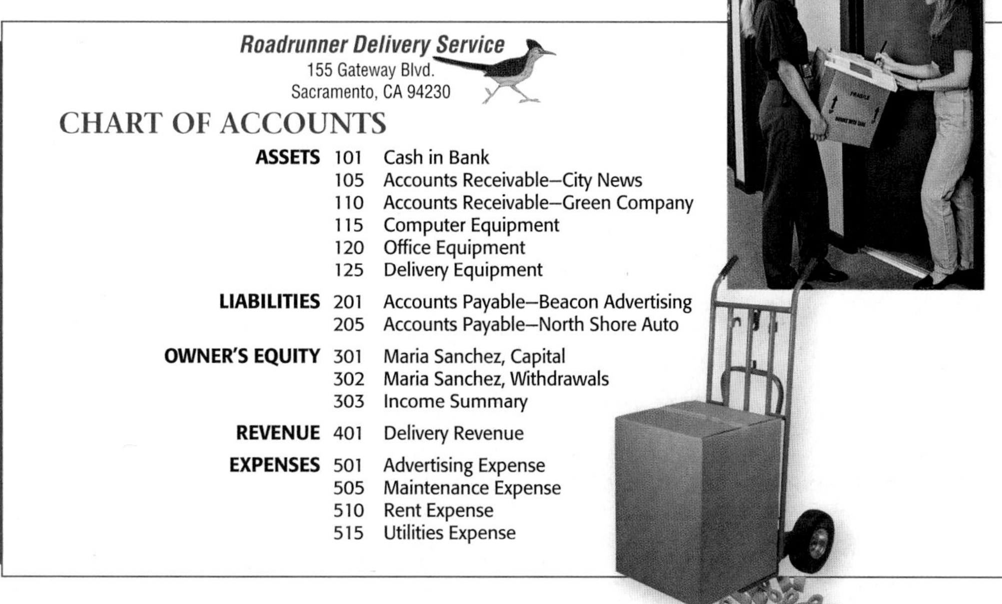

Roadrunner Delivery Service
155 Gateway Blvd.
Sacramento, CA 94230

CHART OF ACCOUNTS

ASSETS	101	Cash in Bank
	105	Accounts Receivable—City News
	110	Accounts Receivable—Green Company
	115	Computer Equipment
	120	Office Equipment
	125	Delivery Equipment
LIABILITIES	201	Accounts Payable—Beacon Advertising
	205	Accounts Payable—North Shore Auto
OWNER'S EQUITY	301	Maria Sanchez, Capital
	302	Maria Sanchez, Withdrawals
	303	Income Summary
REVENUE	401	Delivery Revenue
EXPENSES	501	Advertising Expense
	505	Maintenance Expense
	510	Rent Expense
	515	Utilities Expense

Double-Entry Accounting

The approach you used in Chapter 3 for analyzing and recording changes in account balances would work well if a business had only a few accounts. It becomes awkward, however, if a business has many accounts and many transactions to analyze. When accountants analyze and record a transaction, they use a system called **double-entry accounting**. Double-entry accounting is a system of recordkeeping in which each business transaction affects at least two accounts.

ACCOUNTING *Flashbacks*

ACCOUNTING TEXTBOOKS
Benjamin Workman published *The American Accountant,* the earliest-known American accounting textbook, in 1769. The State of New York passed its first CPA law 127 years later, in 1896.

T Accounts

An efficient way to apply double-entry accounting is to use what accountants call a T account. The **T account**, so called because of its T shape, shows the dollar increase or decrease in an account that is caused

CHAPTER 4
SECTION 1, PAGES 72-77

2 TEACH
GUIDED PRACTICE

Reading Accounting

- Learning to read a form is key to understanding accounting. Have students study T accounts to determine how the use of a graphic (the T) helps to clarify information. L1
- Help students learn basic rules, such as the rules of debit and credit, by arranging for a tutor to translate key information for them. ELL

Concept Development: The Account

Discussion: Point out that accounting records begin with the entry of a business transaction. Recording information in accounts makes it easy to identify and analyze each aspect of business operations. For example, the account for Office Equipment will show the amount of equipment purchased to date. A business owner might use this information in preparing an equipment budget for the next year. L1

Concept Development: The Chart of Accounts

Discussion: Emphasize that the chart of accounts is simply a list of the accounts used by a business. Small businesses may use few accounts while larger ones may use hundreds. L1

Visual Learning

Chart of Accounts, p. 73
Using the chart of accounts, point out the classification of accounts. Also, introduce the temporary equity accounts for revenue and expenses.

Great Ideas *From the Classroom of...*

Remembering Accounting Rules Point out to students that we were given two hands so we could learn keyboarding. Our left hand alone was given to us to remember the rules of plus/minus in the accounting equation. Assets and expenses, the two outside fingers are + –. Liabilities, owner's equity, and revenue, the three middle fingers, are – +.

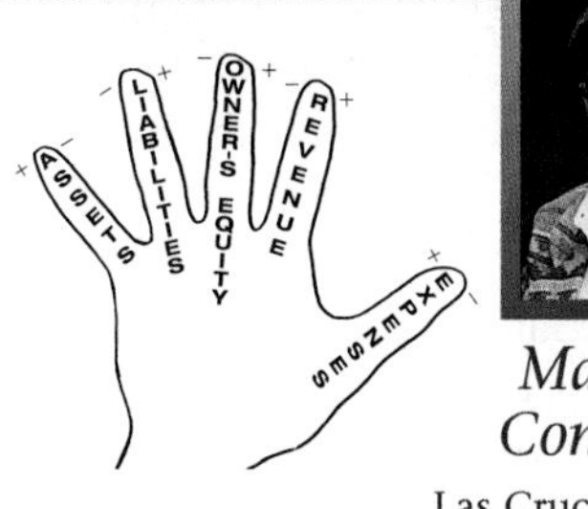

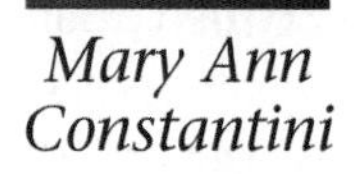

Mary Ann Constantini
Las Cruces High School
Las Cruces, New Mexico

CHAPTER 4
SECTION 1, PAGES 72–77

2 TEACH (Cont'd.)

Demonstration Problem Step-by-Step Practice

Use demonstration problem 4–1 to give students practice in setting up a chart of accounts.

Concept Development: Double-Entry Accounting

Discussion: Point out to students that the double-entry system requires each transaction to be entered into at least two accounts. This double entry of amounts forms the basis for the "balance" that is maintained within the accounting equation after each transaction. L1

Concept Development: T Accounts

Discussion: Emphasize that the T account is not a formal accounting record. Rather, it is a helpful tool for analyzing how a transaction affects accounts used by the business. T accounts can be likened to research notes students make to assist them in writing reports. L1

Visual Learning

T Accounts

Use **Transparency 4–2** of the rules of debit and credit to help students learn the rules for each account classification.

Math Review for Accounting

Photocopy appropriate *Activity Sheets* for students who need additional practice in basic math skills.

Teaching Tip

Have students prepare a chart of accounts for a sole proprietorship furniture repair business.

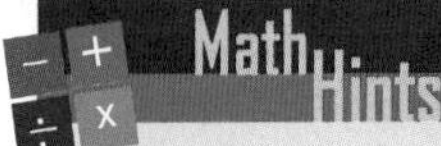

Math Hints

Decimals

When adding and subtracting whole dollar amounts:

- You do *not* need to enter a decimal point.

To add amounts that include dollars and cents:

- You *do* need to enter the decimal.

by a transaction. T accounts help the accountant analyze the parts of a business transaction.

As you can see from the illustration below, a T account has a place for an account name, a left side, and a right side. The top of the T is used for the account name. The left side of T accounts is *always* used for debit amounts. A **debit**, then, is an amount entered on the *left* side of the T account. The right side of T accounts is *always* used for credit amounts. A **credit** is an amount entered on the *right* side of the T account. The words *debit* and *credit* are simply the accountant's terms for *left* and *right*. Accountants sometimes use **DR** for debit and **CR** for credit.

Account Name	
Left Side	Right Side
Debit Side	Credit Side
Debit	Credit

Key Points

T Accounts

For all accounts:

Debit = Left Side
Credit = Right Side

The Rules of Debit and Credit

Debits and credits are used to record the increase or decrease in each account affected by a business transaction. Under double-entry accounting, for each debit entry made in one account, a credit of an equal amount must be made in another account. The rules of debit and credit vary according to whether an account is classified as an asset, a liability, or an owner's capital account. Regardless of the type of account, however, the left side of an account is always the debit side and the right side is always the credit side.

Each classification of account has a specific side that is its normal balance side. An account's **normal balance** is always on the side used to record increases to the account. The word *normal* used here means *usual*. Throughout this book, note that the normal balance side of each account will be shaded.

International ACCOUNTING

International Etiquette

When you make international phone calls or visits for business purposes, remember to consider the time differences and work schedules for that country.

Rules for Asset Accounts

There are three rules of debit and credit for asset accounts:

1. An asset account is *increased* (+) on the *debit* side (left side).
2. An asset account is *decreased* (−) on the *credit* side (right side).
3. The *normal balance* for an asset account is the *increase side,* or the *debit side.* The normal balance side is shaded in the T account on the next page. Assets normally have debit balances.

Math Skill Builder Activity

Efficient Keystroke Techniques Accountants often enter figures into a spreadsheet using a computer's numeric keypad. Have students practice these keystrokes.

- Place middle three fingers on the 4, 5, and 6 keys.
- Operate the 1, 4, and 7 keys with the index finger.
- Use the middle finger to operate the 2, 5, and 8 keys.
- Operate the 3, 6, and 9 keys with the ring finger.
- Use the little finger to strike the enter key.
- Use the thumb or index finger to strike the 0 key.

We can illustrate these rules using an asset T account and the basic accounting equation. Look at the left side of the equation below.

ASSETS = LIABILITIES + OWNER'S EQUITY

Asset Accounts

Debit	Credit
+	–
(1) Increase Side	(2) Decrease Side
(3) Normal Balance	

For asset accounts the *increase* side is the debit (left) side of the T account. The *decrease* side is the credit (right) side of the T account. Notice the (+) and (–) signs. These signs are used to indicate the increase and decrease sides of the account. They do not mean the same thing as *debit* and *credit.*

Since the increase side of an asset account is always the debit side, asset accounts have a normal debit balance. For example, in the normal course of business, total increases to assets are larger than total decreases. You would expect an asset account, then, to have a normal debit balance.

Let's apply these rules to an actual asset account. Look at the entries in the T account for **Cash in Bank** below. The increases in the account are recorded on the left, or debit, side. The decreases in the account are recorded on the right, or credit, side. Total debits equal $350 ($200 + $150). Total credits equal $110 ($70 + $40). To find the balance, subtract total credits from total debits ($350 – $110). The debit balance is $240.

Cash in Bank

Debit	Credit
+	–
200	70
150	40
350	110
Bal. 240	

CONNECT TO . . .
ECONOMICS

The first entrepreneurs surfaced during the Commercial Revolution of the 1500's. As the amount of trade and circulation of money increased, the size of businesses grew larger. Instead of creating goods or services to barter for other goods and services, individuals and groups began to work for profits.

Rules for Liability and Owner's Capital Accounts

The rules of debit and credit for liability and owner's capital accounts are:

1. Liability and owner's capital accounts are *increased* on the *credit* side (right side).
2. Liability and owner's capital accounts are *decreased* on the *debit* side (left side).
3. The *normal balance* for liability and owner's capital accounts is the *increase side*, or the *credit side*. Liability and owner's capital accounts normally have credit balances.

2 TEACH (Cont'd.)

Concept Development: The Rules of Debit and Credit

Discussion: Point out that debits and credits are the basis of double-entry accounting. Emphasize to students that they need to know the rules of debit and credit so well that they can analyze transactions without referring to the written rules. Also remind students that the + and – signs refer only to the terms "increase" and "decrease." Do not allow students to equate these signs with debit and credit. L1

Teaching Tips

Reinforce the rules of debit and credit for asset accounts by emphasizing that assets are on the left side of the accounting equation, assets are increased on the left side of the T account, and the normal balance for assets is on the left (increase) side of the T account. Use the same approach for other account classifications.

Emphasize that the normal balance of a T account is the same side (debit or credit) as its increase side.

When introducing the rules of debit and credit for liability and owner's equity accounts, write the accounting equation on the chalkboard. Draw T accounts for liabilities and owner's capital to emphasize that these accounts are on the right side of the equation. Point out that the right sides of the T accounts for liabilities and owner's capital are the increase sides, and the right sides are the normal balance sides.

INTERDISCIPLINARY CONNECTIONS ACTIVITY

Economics What type of entrepreneurial activities can your students do to make a profit? Divide your class into teams of three to four students. Have each team brainstorm a student-run enterprise that would offer a product or service of value. Ask each team to write a short business proposal describing the type of business, name of the product or service, charge for the product or service, targeted customers, etc. Have each team present its business proposal to the entire class. Encourage students to be professional and to use poster boards or transparencies to enhance their presentations.

2 TEACH (Cont'd.)

Visual Learning

T Account

Use **Transparency 4–3** to drill students on the increase, decrease, and normal balance sides for each classification of account.

Oral Checkup: Divide the class in half. As you name an account, have students in each half take turns quickly calling out the account's classification. L1

Teaching Tips

Emphasize that liabilities and capital are on the right side of the accounting equation, they are increased on the right (credit) side of the T account, and the normal balance is on the right (credit) side of the T account.

Use frequent, one- to two-minute drills to help students master the rules of debit and credit. After students learn those rules, also drill them on the normal balance side of each account classification.

Strategies for Teaching International Accounting

To enrich study of International Accounting, refer to the additional critical thinking activities in the booklet.

To illustrate these rules, let's look again at the accounting equation and the T accounts. Remember, the normal balance side is shaded.

Assets		=	Liabilities		+	Owner's Equity	
Debit + Increase Side Normal Balance	Credit – Decrease Side		Debit – (2) Decrease Side	Credit + (1) Increase Side (3) Normal Balance		Debit – (2) Decrease Side	Credit + (1) Increase Side (3) Normal Balance

ACCOUNTING TIPS

Rules of Debit and Credit

- Assets appear on the left side of the basic accounting equation. The left (debit) side of an asset account is the side used to increase that account and is its normal balance side.
- Liabilities and the owner's capital account appear on the right side of the basic accounting equation. The right (credit) side of liability and capital accounts is the side used to increase those accounts. It is also the normal balance side.

For all three types of accounts, the debit side is always the left side of the T account, and the credit side is always the right side. Notice, however, that the increase (+) and decrease (−) sides of the liability and owner's capital accounts are the opposite of those for assets. This difference exists because accounts classified as liabilities and owner's capital are on the opposite side of the accounting equation from accounts classified as assets. As a result, debit and credit rules on one side of the accounting equation—and the T accounts within it—are mirror images of those on the other side.

Let's apply these rules to actual accounts. First, look at the entries in the T account below for the liability account **Accounts Payable.** The increases in the account are recorded on the right, or credit, side. The decreases in the account are recorded on the left, or debit, side. Total credits equal $375 ($200 + $175); total debits equal $175 ($100 + $75). To find the balance, subtract the total debits from the total credits ($375 − $175). The credit balance is $200.

Accounts Payable	
Debit –	Credit +
100	200
75	175
175	375
	Bal. 200

Now look at the entries in the T account for the owner's equity account **Maria Sanchez, Capital.** Remember that the rules of debit and credit for the capital account are the same as for a liability account.

Increases to owner's capital are recorded on the right, or credit, side of the account. Decreases are recorded on the left, or debit, side. The capital account has a normal credit balance. If you subtract the total debits from the total credits ($4,000 − $550), you have a credit balance of $3,450.

Maria Sanchez, Capital	
Debit –	Credit +
350	1,500
200	2,500
550	4,000
	Bal. 3,450

Teaching International ACCOUNTING

(Refer to the *International Accounting* feature on page 74.)

Converting Time for International Time Zones Show students a time zone map illustrating the 24 time zones around the world. Have students identify other sources for time zone information (such as world atlases/almanacs, encyclopedias, and the Internet). Then provide several scenarios for international phone calls, and have students convert current U.S. time to the international location.

SECTION 1 Check Your Understanding

Now that you have studied this section, complete the following questions and problems.

Thinking Critically

1. In a chart of accounts, why are the accounts numbered?
2. Explain why the normal balance of an asset account is on the debit side of the account.

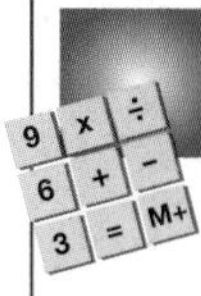

Computing in the Business World

During the month of December, Krusty's Pizza purchased computer equipment. According to your records, Krusty's Pizza took approximately $5,000 from the **Cash in Bank** account to purchase the computer equipment. Prior to that purchase, the owner's capital account had a credit balance of $10,000.

1. What is the balance in the owner's capital account after the purchase?
2. Is the owner's capital account balance a debit or a credit?

Problem 4–1 Applying the Rules of Debit and Credit

Speedy Appliance Repair, owned by R. Lewis, uses the following accounts:

General Ledger
- Cash in Bank
- Office Equipment
- Accounts Payable
- Accounts Receivable
- R. Lewis, Capital

Instructions In the form provided in your working papers:

(1) Classify each account as an asset, liability, or owner's capital account.

(2) Indicate whether the increase side is a debit or a credit.

(3) Indicate whether the decrease side is a debit or credit.

(4) Indicate whether the normal balance for the account is a debit or credit balance.

The **Cash in Bank** account is completed as an example.

Account Name	Account Classification	Increase Side	Decrease Side	Normal Balance
Cash in Bank	Asset	Debit	Credit	Debit

RETEACHING SECTION 1

Demonstrating the Effects of Transactions on the Accounting Equation Have students demonstrate the effects of transactions on the accounting equation, for example, T accounts. On the blackboard, draw several "blank" T accounts. Describe three simple transactions and have students write the transactions in the blank T-account forms. After each transaction, have the student write the accounting equation based on T-account totals.

3 ASSESS

Thinking Critically (Answers)

1. Businesses number their accounts to ease the location of individual accounts in a ledger. Most account numbers will have two or more digits.
2. The normal balance of an account is on the side that increases the account. Asset accounts are increased by debits, so they normally carry a debit balance.

Computing in the Business World (Answers)

1. $10,000
2. Credit

Problem 4–1 (Answers)

Office Equipment—asset, debit, credit, debit
Accounts Payable—liability, credit, debit, credit
Accounts Receivable—asset, debit, credit, debit
R. Lewis, Capital—owner's equity, credit, debit, credit

Chapter Reviews and Working Papers Refer students to the Chapter 4 workbook pages to answer *Check Your Understanding* activities.

4 CLOSE

Section Wrap-Up

Demonstrate: Have students demonstrate their mastery of the rules of debit and credit by having them write the accounting equation and the rules for each account classification within the equation. L1

1 FOCUS

Introducing the Section
In this section, students will learn to apply the rules of debit and credit as they analyze business transactions and determine debits and credits. Students will apply the rules of debit and credit to transactions involving assets, liabilities, and the owner's capital account.

Section Concepts
- How to analyze a transaction affecting assets, liabilities, and owner's equity.

Visual Learning

Section 2 Focus

Use **Transparency 4–4** to introduce section concepts.

BELL RINGER

Identification: Draw three T accounts on the chalkboard (without the accounting equation). Write Debit and Credit on the sides, but do not write an account title at the top. Add "Normal Balance" on the appropriate sides for asset, liability, and owner's capital. Then have students place the correct title on each T account. L1

Visual Learning

Business Transaction Analysis
Use **Transparency 4–5** to encourage students to use a step-by-step method for analyzing transactions into their debit and credit parts.

SECTION 2

Applying the Rules of Debit and Credit

What You'll Learn
- How to analyze a transaction affecting assets, liabilities, and owner's equity.

Why It's Important
You need to analyze transactions properly so that you record them correctly.

Now that you are familiar with the rules of debit and credit for asset, liability, and owner's capital accounts, the next step is to apply those rules to the analysis of business transactions.

Business Transaction Analysis

Whether a business is buying a new computer system, paying its utility bills, or receiving money for sales, the accountant must analyze how the transaction should be recorded. When analyzing business transactions, you should use the following step-by-step method:

Business Transaction

BUSINESS TRANSACTION ANALYSIS: Steps to Success

ANALYSIS	*Identify*	1. Identify the accounts affected.
	Classify	2. Classify the accounts affected.
	+/−	3. Determine the amount of increase or decrease for each account affected.
DEBIT-CREDIT RULE		4. Which account is debited? For what amount?
		5. Which account is credited? For what amount?
T ACCOUNTS		6. What is the complete entry in T-account form?

Account Name	Account Name

Key Points

Debits and Credits
For every transaction, total debits must equal total credits.

The business transactions that follow are for Roadrunner Delivery Service. Throughout the next several pages, you will learn how to analyze each Roadrunner transaction, apply the rules of debit and credit, and complete the entry in T-account form. The T accounts demonstrate the effects of transactions on the accounting equation. A debit in one account is offset by a credit in another account. Refer to the Roadrunner chart of accounts on page 73. These accounts will be used to analyze several business transactions.

RESOURCE MANAGER

Reproducible Masters
- Lesson Plans
- Chapter Reviews and Working Papers (CRWP) TAE
- Demonstration Problems

Transparencies
- Section Focus Transparency
- Teaching Transparencies
- Solution Transparencies

Multimedia
- ExamView CD-ROM
- Electronic Learning Center CD-ROM
- Interactive Lesson Planner CD-ROM
- Electronic Field Trips in Accounting

Business Transaction 1

On October 1 Maria Sanchez took $25,000 from personal savings and deposited that amount to open a business checking account in the name of Roadrunner Delivery Service.

ANALYSIS *Identify* **1.** The accounts **Cash in Bank** and **Maria Sanchez, Capital** are affected.

Classify **2. Cash in Bank** is an asset account. **Maria Sanchez, Capital** is an owner's capital account.

+/− **3. Cash in Bank** is increased by $25,000. **Maria Sanchez, Capital** is increased by $25,000.

DEBIT-CREDIT RULE **4.** Increases in asset accounts are recorded as debits. Debit **Cash in Bank** for $25,000.

5. Increases in the owner's capital account are recorded as credits. Credit **Maria Sanchez, Capital** for $25,000.

T ACCOUNTS **6.**

Cash in Bank			Maria Sanchez, Capital	
Debit + 25,000				Credit + 25,000

Business Transaction 2

On October 2 Maria Sanchez took two telephones valued at $200 each from her home and transferred them to the business as office equipment.

ANALYSIS *Identify* **1.** The accounts **Office Equipment** and **Maria Sanchez, Capital** are affected.

Classify **2. Office Equipment** is an asset account. **Maria Sanchez, Capital** is an owner's capital account.

+/− **3. Office Equipment** is increased by $400. **Maria Sanchez, Capital** is increased by $400.

DEBIT-CREDIT RULE **4.** Increases in asset accounts are recorded as debits. Debit **Office Equipment** for $400.

5. Increases in owner's capital accounts are recorded as credits. Credit **Maria Sanchez, Capital** for $400.

T ACCOUNTS **6.**

Office Equipment			Maria Sanchez, Capital	
Debit + 400				Credit + 400

REINFORCING STUDY SKILLS

Flash Card Practice Have students write new accounting vocabulary, examples of T accounts, debit balance, credit balance, accounting equation, and other basic accounting principles they have learned in this chapter on 3 × 5 cards. Have students write the terms or examples on the front of the card and the answers on the back. Then tell students to review each card and verbalize the answers. If they cannot think of the answer, have them flip the card over to check the correct response. Students should continue to flip through the stack until they can give correct responses for all cards.

2 TEACH

GUIDED PRACTICE

Reading Accounting

- As students read each transaction, have them draw their own T accounts and record amounts on the appropriate side. L1

Concept Development: Business Transaction Analysis

Discussion: The six-step approach for analyzing transactions takes students through the cognitive process needed to analyze typical business transactions. Urge students to learn the logic of the analysis rather than trying to memorize each type of transaction. L1

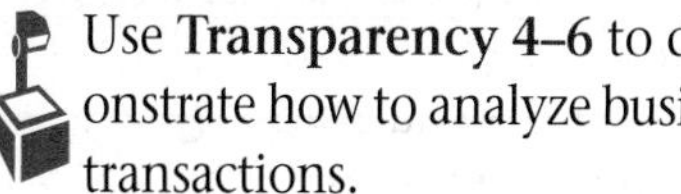

Visual Learning

Business Transaction 1

Use **Transparency 4–6** to demonstrate how to analyze business transactions.

Business Transaction 2

Using **Transparency 4–7**, have students give you the entry for each account.

Teaching Tips

For Business Transaction 1:

+ Asset (Debit Cash in Bank)
+ Owner's Equity (Credit Maria Sanchez, Capital)

For Business Transaction 2:

+ Asset (Office Equipment)
− Owner's Equity (Maria Sanchez, Capital)

Chapter Reviews and Working Papers

Refer students to the *Study Plan*, located at the beginning of Chapter 4 in the workbook.

2 TEACH (Cont'd.)

Teaching Tip

Keep the accounting equation on the chalkboard as students analyze transactions.

Visual Learning

Business Transaction 3

Use **Transparency 4–8** to discuss the effects of the transaction on the two accounts, Computer Equipment and Cash in Bank. Refer to the accounting equation on the chalkboard and ask students how the overall balance in the equation has changed as a result of this transaction.

Business Transaction 4

Use **Transparency 4–9** to discuss the effects of the transaction. Ask students to explain why a credit increases the balance in a liability account.

Teaching Tips

For Business Transaction 3:
+ Asset (Debit Computer Equipment
− Asset (Credit Cash in Bank)

For Business Transaction 4:
+ Asset (Debit Delivery Equipment)
+ Liability (Credit Accounts Payable—North Shore Auto)

Demonstration Problem Step-by-Step Practice

Use demonstration problem 4–2 to give students practice analyzing a cash purchase transaction.

Business Transaction 3

On October 4 Roadrunner issued Check 101 for $3,000 to buy a computer system.

ANALYSIS

Identify 1. The accounts **Computer Equipment** and **Cash in Bank** are affected.

Classify 2. **Computer Equipment** and **Cash in Bank** are asset accounts.

+/− 3. **Computer Equipment** is increased by $3,000. **Cash in Bank** is decreased by $3,000.

DEBIT-CREDIT RULE

4. Increases in asset accounts are recorded as debits. Debit **Computer Equipment** for $3,000.
5. Decreases in asset accounts are recorded as credits. Credit **Cash in Bank** for $3,000.

T ACCOUNTS

6.

Computer Equipment		Cash in Bank	
Debit + 3,000			Credit − 3,000

Business Transaction 4

On October 9 Roadrunner bought a used truck on account from North Shore Auto for $12,000.

ANALYSIS

Identify 1. The accounts **Delivery Equipment** and **Accounts Payable—North Shore Auto** are affected.

Classify 2. **Delivery Equipment** is an asset account. **Accounts Payable—North Shore Auto** is a liability account.

+/− 3. **Delivery Equipment** is increased by $12,000. **Accounts Payable—North Shore Auto** is increased by $12,000.

DEBIT-CREDIT RULE

4. Increases in asset accounts are recorded as debits. Debit **Delivery Equipment** for $12,000.
5. Increases in liability accounts are recorded as credits. Credit **Accounts Payable—North Shore Auto** for $12,000.

T ACCOUNTS

6.

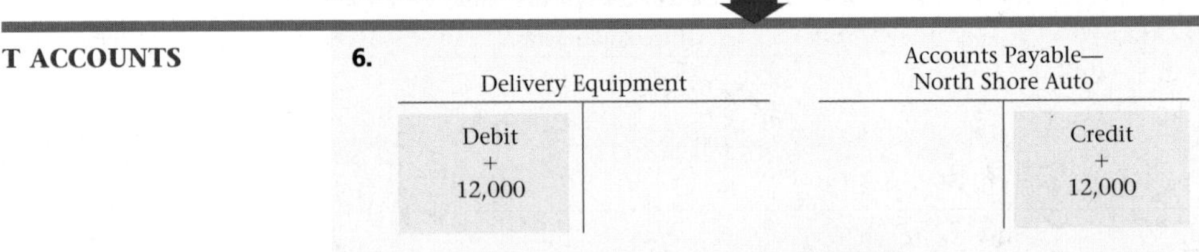

COOPERATIVE LEARNING ACTIVITY

Send-a-Question Divide students into teams of five or six. Give each student a 3 × 5 card. Ask each team member to write two typical business transactions for a video rental business on the front of the card. Then, as a team, have them analyze each transaction. Have one member write on the back of the card the accounts affected and whether they increase or decrease. Afterward, have each team pass the cards on to another team. Have the second team answer the questions, comparing their answers with those on the back of the cards. If there is disagreement among the teams regarding answers, have the teams work together to decide the correct answer.

Business Transaction 5

On October 11 Roadrunner sold one phone on account to Green Company for $200.

ANALYSIS

Identify 1. The accounts **Accounts Receivable—Green Company** and **Office Equipment** are affected.

Classify 2. **Accounts Receivable—Green Company** is an asset account. **Office Equipment** is also an asset account.

+/− 3. **Accounts Receivable—Green Company** is increased by $200. **Office Equipment** is decreased by $200.

DEBIT-CREDIT RULE

4. Increases in asset accounts are recorded as debits. Debit **Accounts Receivable—Green Company** for $200.
5. Decreases in asset accounts are recorded as credits. Credit **Office Equipment** for $200.

T ACCOUNTS

6.

Accounts Receivable—Green Company	
Debit + 200	

Office Equipment	
	Credit − 200

Business Transaction 6

On October 12 Roadrunner mailed Check 102 for $350 as the first installment payment on the truck purchased from North Shore Auto on October 9.

ANALYSIS

Identify 1. The accounts **Accounts Payable—North Shore Auto** and **Cash in Bank** are affected.

Classify 2. **Accounts Payable—North Shore Auto** is a liability account. **Cash in Bank** is an asset account.

+/− 3. **Accounts Payable—North Shore Auto** is decreased by $350. **Cash in Bank** is decreased by $350.

DEBIT-CREDIT RULE

4. Decreases in liability accounts are recorded as debits. Debit **Accounts Payable—North Shore Auto** for $350.
5. Decreases in asset accounts are recorded as credits. Credit **Cash in Bank** for $350.

T ACCOUNTS

6.

Accounts Payable—North Shore Auto	
Debit − 350	

Cash in Bank	
	Credit − 350

ADDRESSING MULTIPLE LEARNING STYLES

Logical/Mathematical Learner Drawing parallels between various businesses can help students understand that businesses of all sizes maintain accounts and keep the accounting equation in balance. Have students work in pairs. Have one student choose a local small business and the other student choose a large business. Ask each student to list several items that might be considered assets and liabilities for their business. Once they've completed the list, have students compare their lists with their partners. What are the similarities? What are the differences?

2 TEACH (Cont'd.)

Visual Learning

Business Transaction 5

Using **Transparency 4–10**, have students discuss the analysis. Have students explain why Accounts Receivable is an asset account. Also ask them to give you its normal balance side.

Business Transaction 6

Use **Transparency 4–11** to guide students through the effects of a payment made on account. Have students explain the normal balance side for both accounts affected.

Teaching Tips

For Business Transaction 5:
+ Asset (Debit Accounts Receivable—Green Company)
− Asset (Credit Office Equipment)

For Business Transaction 6:
− Liability (Debit Accounts Payable—North Shore Auto)
− Asset (Credit Cash in Bank)

GO TO **Demonstration Problem Step-by-Step Practice**

Use demonstration problem 4–3 to give students practice analyzing a credit purchase transaction.

Thinking Algebraically

Write "Debits = Credits" on the chalkboard. Point out that when total debits equal total credits in a transaction, the accounting equation remains in balance. L1

2 TEACH (Cont'd.)

Visual Learning

Business Transaction 7

Cover the right side (the shaded area) of **Transparency 4–12** and have students conduct the analysis and apply the rules of debit and credit.

Teaching Tip

For Business Transaction 7:

+ Asset (Debit Cash in Bank)
– Asset (Credit Accounts Receivable—Green Company)

Critical Thinking

Ask students to look at Business Transaction 7 again. If Green Company had issued a check for the telephone at the time of the purchase, what would have been different about the transaction? (Office Equipment would have been affected instead of Accounts Receivable.) How would the balances in the accounts have changed? (Cash in Bank still would have increased, and Office Equipment would have decreased.) Would the overall balance in the accounting equation be different? Why or why not? (No. Both transactions affected asset accounts only.) L2

Strategies for Teaching Ethics in Accounting

Photocopy the Chapter 4 *Student Activity Sheet* for students. Answers are also provided in the booklet.

Business Transaction 7

On October 14, Roadrunner received and deposited a check for $200 from Green Company. The check is full payment for the telephone sold on account to Green Company on October 11.

ANALYSIS

Identify 1. The accounts **Cash in Bank** and **Accounts Receivable—Green Company** are affected.

Classify 2. **Cash in Bank** is an asset account. **Accounts Receivable—Green Company** is an asset account.

+/– 3. **Cash in Bank** is increased by $200. **Accounts Receivable—Green Company** is decreased by $200.

DEBIT-CREDIT RULE

4. Increases in asset accounts are recorded as debits. Debit **Cash in Bank** for $200.
5. Decreases in asset accounts are recorded as credits. Credit **Accounts Receivable—Green Company** for $200.

T ACCOUNTS

6.

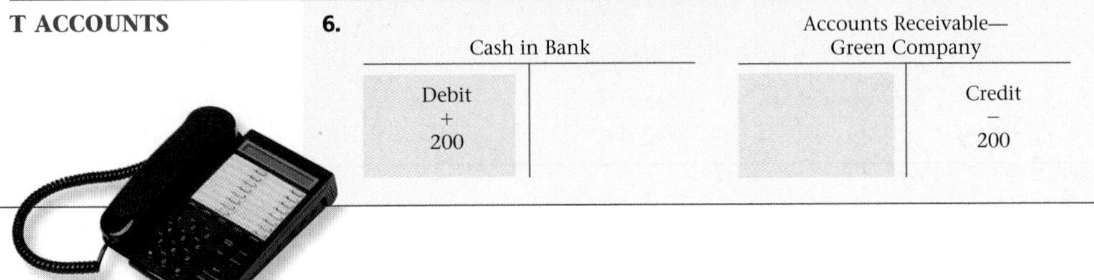

Cash in Bank	
Debit + 200	

Accounts Receivable—Green Company	
	Credit – 200

A MATTER OF ETHICS

Software Piracy

Imagine that you're a bookkeeper for an attorney who likes to use state-of-the-art technology. The business just received the latest update on its Web site design software. You would like to use the software at home, so your assistant offers to make you a copy. Although you know that copyright laws protect software from unauthorized use, you figure that one little sale can't hurt a multimillion dollar software company; and besides, you're not doing the actual copying.

Ethical Decision Making:

- What are the ethical issues?
- What are the alternatives?
- Who are the affected parties?
- How do the alternatives affect the parties?
- What would you do?

Teaching A MATTER OF ETHICS

Software Piracy It's estimated that software companies lose millions of dollars a year because people copy software rather than buying their own programs. Have students discuss this issue from the point of view of the software developer. Tell students to assume that they've written a unique software program, and they're selling it from their Internet site. How would they stay in business if people copied their software instead of buying the program?

Check Your Understanding

Now that you have studied this section, complete the following questions and problem.

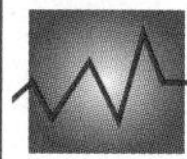

Thinking Critically

1. What is the debit-credit rule used in business transaction analysis?
2. In double-entry accounting, for each transaction there must be at least two entries. If you are increasing the **Cash in Bank** account, what other accounts might be affected?

Communicating Accounting

Philip Sanders, the owner of Bookworm Book Shops, believes his employees will be more responsible if they realize how their actions affect the records of the business. So Philip asks you to teach some basic accounting to the other managers in the company. You begin by explaining the double-entry accounting system. Explain how the purchase of delivery trucks used in the business affects different accounts.

1. Form a team. Divide the team into two groups.
2. Have one group explain the double-entry accounting system while the other group plays the role of the managers.

Problem 4–2 Identifying Increases and Decreases in Accounts

Alice Roberts uses the following accounts in her business:

General Ledger	
Cash in Bank	Office Equipment
Accounts Receivable	Accounts Payable
Office Furniture	Alice Roberts, Capital

Instructions Analyze each of the following transactions. In your working papers, explain the debit and the credit. Use the format shown in the example.

Example:

On June 2 Alice Roberts invested $5,000 of her own money in a business called Roberts Employment Agency.

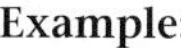

a. The asset account **Cash in Bank** is increased. Increases in asset accounts are recorded as debits.

b. The owner's capital account **Alice Roberts, Capital** is increased. Increases in the owner's capital account are recorded as credits.

Date	Transactions
June 3	1. Purchased a computer on account from Computer Inc. for $2,500.
9	2. Transferred a desk (Office Furniture) to the business. The desk is worth $750.
15	3. Made a partial payment on account of $1,000 to Computer Inc.

RETEACHING SECTION 2

Remembering Rules for Debit and Credit Provide students with a handout of the rules of debit and credit for use as a quick reference as they analyze transactions. If some students have difficulty remembering that debit is the left side of a T account and credit is the right, help them develop a mnemonic device to aid their memories. For example, the word "credit" has an "r" and so does "right." Debit and left do not have an "r."

3 ASSESS

Thinking Critically (Answers)

1. Decide which account is debited and for what amount, which account is credited and for what amount.
2. Your owner's equity or capital account will probably increase.

Communicating Accounting (Answers)

Answers may vary. Students should discuss the use of T accounts, the transaction analysis process, and debit-credit rules. You may want students to write out their thoughts before they explain to their groups. Circulate to make sure students are focused on the appropriate examples in their explanations.

Problem 4-2 (Answers)

1a. Office Equipment (asset) is increased (debit).
b. Accounts Payable (liability) is increased (credit).
2a. Office Furniture (asset) is increased (debit).
b. Alice Roberts, Capital (owner's equity) is increased (credit).
3a. Accounts Payable (liability) is decreased (debit).
b. Cash in Bank (asset) is decreased (credit).

Chapter Reviews and Working Papers Refer students to the Chapter 4 workbook pages to answer *Check Your Understanding* activities.

4 CLOSE

Section Wrap-Up

Oral Exercise: Have students explain to a new trainee how accountants use accounts to record the effects of business transactions. L1

SCANS in the Workforce

Foundation Skills Connection

Knowing How to Learn

Have students choose a career of interest in the accounting field. Some examples may include a CPA, a managerial accountant, or a government accountant. Then have students research the career and create a career profile. Require that the research involve interviews with accountants in the chosen field. Interview topics include entry level job requirements, career tracks for the profession, and projected trends for the future. The career profile should include education required, special skills, prior job experience, and personal traits that would help a person succeed. Have students share their profiles in class. L2

Workplace Competencies Connection

Selecting Technology

Have students visit a local computer store and locate at least three computer systems that will handle industry-standard financial software (e.g., *QuickBooks®*, *Peachtree Accounting®*, *MS Excel*). Have them identify the computer specifications, cost, and warranty information. Which computer system offers the most power? Which is the best buy? Have students evaluate the systems and present their conclusions to the class. L2

Maintaining and Troubleshooting Technology

Divide students into groups of four or five. Create a computer hardware problem (e.g., a jammed printer, an inactive cursor) or a software problem (e.g., can't save file to disk). Have each group write the steps they might take to troubleshoot the problem. Gather several computer, printer, and software manuals for students to refer to if necessary. L3

ACCOUNTING CAREERS IN FOCUS

ANNA ALVAREZ
Business Consultant, MCI

Q: Why did you choose accounting?

A: Initially, I chose accounting because my older brother was taking it. He went on to another career, but I stuck with it. I like making sure things are in the right place where money is concerned. I enjoy it when everything balances.

Q: What kind of training did you have?

A: I worked for an accounting firm at 17 and went to school at night. I got a business administration degree with an emphasis in accounting. I learned the software side on the job by working with a variety of databases. I also learned through training classes offered by software companies. I go to one-week training classes about every four months. It's not required, but I'd fall behind if I didn't, everything changes so quickly.

Q: How did you get into consulting?

A: I was a project accountant at another firm when we updated our old accounting system. I worked closely with the consultants and they told me I would make a good consultant. When a co-worker went to MCI, he recommended me.

Q: Are computer classes necessary for accounting students?

A: Computer experience is necessary for anyone in accounting. Any computer science course helps. You should understand relational databases. You still have to know accounting–to understand that purchasing affects accounts payable, which affects inventory–so that when problems occur, you know the most likely place to look for causes.

Tips from . . .

Robert Half International Inc.

When looking for a job, identify your ideal work environment. Do you want to work for a large or small company? Is pay or learning potential more important? Research companies at libraries, career centers, or through the Internet.

CAREER FACTS

Nature of the Work: Meet with and make presentations to business clients, install and debug financial systems, integrate new systems with the old, train new staff.
Training or Education Needed: A bachelor's or master's degree in accounting or business; experience in a variety of accounting areas.
Aptitudes, Abilities, and Skills: Computer skills, communication skills, analytical skills, business, and accounting.
Salary Range: Beginning consultant, $50,000 to $70,000; senior consultant, $85,000 to $100,000; managing consultant, $100,000 and up.
Career Path: Work in accounting in a variety of capacities, then move into a consulting firm.

Thinking Critically: What types of experience would you emphasize when applying for a job as a business consultant?

ACCOUNTING CAREERS IN FOCUS

Thinking Critically (Answer)

The types of experience you would emphasize are presentation skills and writing skills. Your familiarity with computer systems is also important, as well as your willingness to learn.

ROBERT HALF CORNER

Computer Literacy Computer literacy is critical for financial jobs. Create a three-column chart labeled *Current Skills*, *Employee Skills*, and *Education*. List skills students currently have, skills used by employees, and training needed to acquire skills.

CHAPTER 4 SUMMARY

KEY CONCEPTS

1. Double-entry accounting is a system of record-keeping in which each business transaction affects at least two accounts.

Accounting Equation: ASSETS = LIABILITIES + OWNER'S EQUITY

2. The T account is a tool for analyzing the debit and credit parts of a business transaction.
3. The top of a T account is used for the account name. Debits are entered on the left side and credits on the right side of the T account.

T Accounts:

Account Name	
Debit	Credit

4. Every account has an increase and a decrease side (a debit and a credit side).
5. For asset accounts:
   - The increase side is the debit side (left).
   - The decrease side is the credit side (right).
   - The normal balance is a debit.

Asset Rule:

Asset Accounts	
Debit Increase Side + Normal Balance	Credit Decrease Side −

6. For liability and owner's capital accounts:
   - The increase side is the credit side (right).
   - The decrease side is the debit side (left).
   - The normal balance is a credit.

Liability and Owner's Equity Rule:

Liability and Owner's Capital Accounts	
Debit Decrease Side −	Credit Increase Side + Normal Balance

SUMMARY CHAPTER 4

Chapter 4 Quiz

Student ______ Class ______ Instructor ______
Date Assigned ______ Date Completed ______

CHAPTER 4 QUIZ

Transactions That Affect Assets, Liabilities, and Owner's Equity

QUESTIONS (Short Answer)

Directions: Complete the following questions with a short answer.

1. What is an account? ______
2. Describe the purpose of a ledger in an accounting system. ______
3. Explain double-entry accounting. ______
4. What is a debit? ______
5. What is a credit? ______
6. How does a debit affect an asset account? ______
7. How does a credit affect the owner's capital account? ______
8. What is a normal balance? ______
9. Why must the accounting equation remain in balance after each transaction? ______
10. How would you decrease a liability account? ______

6 • Chapter Quizzes

QUESTIONS (Short Answer)

1. What is an account?
2. Describe the purpose of a ledger in an accounting system.
3. Explain double-entry accounting.
4. What is a debit?
5. What is a credit?
6. How does a debit affect an asset account?
7. How does a credit affect the owner's capital account?
8. What is a normal balance?
9. Why must the accounting equation remain in balance after each transaction?
10. How would you decrease a liability account?

ANSWERS

1. A specific asset, liability, or owner's equity used to record the financial transactions of the business.
2. A ledger organizes all the accounts used by a business, with all assets in one section, liabilities in another, and equity in another.
3. A system of recording business transactions in which each transaction affects at least two accounts.
4. A debit represents the left side of a T account.
5. A credit represents the right side of a T account.
6. A debit increases an asset account.
7. A credit increases the owner's capital account.
8. The normal balance is the side of the T account on which the account is increased.
9. Since each transaction affects at least two accounts, the accounting equation must balance or an error has occurred.
10. A liability account is decreased with a debit.

USING KEY TERMS

See the *Glossary* for the definitions of these terms. Have students share their definitions and explanations of the terms in class. Ask students to discuss how understanding business terminology might help them in their future careers.

Understanding Accounting Concepts and Procedures

(Answers)

1. To keep the accounting equation in balance.
2. Yes, because technology does not change accounting theory.
3. T accounts are used to analyze effects of transactions before recording them.
4. T accounts have a top (title), left side (debit), and right side (credit).
5. The left side is the debit side; the right is the credit side.
6. (a) Assets are increased by debits, decreased by credits. (b) Liabilities are increased by credits, decreased by debits. (c) Capital is increased by credits, decreased by debits.
7. The normal balance side for assets is the debit side; for liabilities and capital, the credit side.
8. (a) Asset, (b) Asset, (c) Asset, (d) Asset, (e) Asset, (f) Owner's Equity, (g) Asset, (h) Liability.
9. (a) Cash in Bank increased by $100. (b) Balance on the right side of a T account. (c) Accounts Payable increased by $500. (d) Balance on left side of a T account.
10. (1) Identify accounts affected. (2) Classify accounts affected. (3) Determine amount of increase or decrease for each account. (4) Which account is debited? For what amount? (5) Which account is credited? For what amount? (6) What is the complete entry in T-account form?

USING KEY TERMS

Your boss at Hillside Nurseries needs help understanding the concept of T accounts and the double-entry accounting system. Using the key terms listed below, draft a list of definitions and illustrations that would help in your explanation.

credit	ledger
chart of accounts	normal balance
debit	T account
double-entry accounting	

Understanding Accounting Concepts and Procedures

Instructions Answer the following questions on a separate sheet of paper:

1. Why is a business transaction entered in at least two accounts?
2. Would double-entry accounting be used in an electronic accounting system? Explain.
3. Why do accountants use T accounts?
4. Name the three basic parts of a T account.
5. What is the left side of a T account called? The right side?
6. State briefly the rules of debit and credit for increasing and decreasing (a) asset accounts, (b) liability accounts, (c) the owner's capital account.
7. What is the normal balance side for asset accounts? Liability accounts? The owner's capital account?
8. Classify the following accounts.
   a. Office Equipment
   b. Delivery Truck
   c. Accounts Receivable
   d. Store Supplies
   e. Cash in Bank
   f. Lee Jones, Capital
   g. Office Supplies
   h. Accounts Payable
9. Explain briefly what is meant by each of the following phrases.
   a. A debit of $100 to **Cash in Bank.**
   b. A credit balance.
   c. A credit of $500 to **Accounts Payable.**
   d. A debit balance.
10. What are the six steps involved in analyzing a business transaction?

ASSESSMENT RESOURCES

Choose assessment strategies from the following pages to evaluate your students' progress.

Student Edition
Check Your Understanding, pp. 77, 78
Chapter 4 Problems, pp. 89–93

Assessment and Evaluation Masters
Chapter 4 Study Plan, *Glencoe Workbook (CRWP)*
Chapter 4 Self-Test, *Glencoe Workbook (CRWP)*
Chapter 4 Test, *Chapter Tests* Booklet
Chapter 4 Activity, *School-to-Work Handbook*
Chapter 4 **Exam***View*

Teacher Wraparound Edition
Critical Thinking Activity, p. 90
Reteaching Sections 1–2, pp. 77, 83
Chapter 4 Quiz, p. 85

Case Study...

Service Business: Landscaping

While in school Martin Hamilton worked for a large landscaping company and gained work experience. Martin is planning to start a business called Landscapes and Beyond. Martin has made a list of everything he owns, with the estimated value for each.

Lawn mowers	$1,500
Shovels, and lawn-care tools	180
Truck	8,700
Stereo equipment	1,000
50 books on landscaping	400
Desk, chair, and file cabinet	700

Martin has also borrowed $5,000 from his family. He plans to repay the debt in one year.

Thinking Critically:

Write the accounting equation for Martin's new business, listing each item in the appropriate part of the equation.

*inter*NET CONNECTION

Currency Conversion

Traveling with family on a vacation to Brazil? Participating in an educational field trip to France? You'll want to know how much your U.S. dollar is worth in these locations. The Internet has the information you need.

Do This:

1. Locate a currency conversion site on the Internet. Use search terms: currency conversion or currency rates.
2. What is the name of the currency in Austria?
3. What is the current exchange rate for the Saudi Arabian riyal?
4. How much is the U.S. dollar worth in British pounds? In Japanese yen?

Conducting an Audit with Alex

In this and later chapters, you will be Conducting Audits with Alex. To audit *means to examine and verify financial records and reports.*

Instructions Review the T accounts below for errors. On a separate sheet of paper, make any corrections necessary.

1. Purchased a delivery truck for $27,000 on account from A-1 Trucks Inc.
2. Wrote a check for $1,500 to A-1 Trucks for payment on account.

Cash in Bank		Accounts Payable A-1 Trucks, Inc.	
	(2) 1,500	(1) 27,000	(2) 1,500

Delivery Equipment	
(1) 27,000	

Workplace Skills

Teaching Others

Keeping up with technology and learning new skills are important in today's workplace. Often, learning from co-workers and supervisors is the best way to increase your skills.

On the Job:

Assume that you work as the accountant for Westside Aquatics, a swim club in Florida. The club has 250 members. While some individuals pay cash on each visit, others are billed monthly for club use. A concession area featuring health foods and juices is a popular gathering place for members after swim lessons.

Thinking Critically:

List account names that would be used in a business like this. Describe to a classmate what kinds of transactions might affect each account. What is the normal balance side for each account?

REVIEW AND ACTIVITIES CHAPTER 4

Case Study...

Thinking Critically (Answers)

Assets: Cash in Bank $5,000, Lawn Mowers $1,500, Lawn Tools $180, Landscaping Books $400, Truck $8,700, Office Furniture $700. Liabilities $5000. Owner's Equity: Martin Hamilton, Capital $11,480.

Workplace Skills

Thinking Critically (Answers)

Answers will vary. Some account titles students may use are: Accounts Payable (credit balance), Utilities Expense (debit balance); Accounts Receivable (debit balance); Daily Membership Revenue (credit balance); Monthly Membership Revenue (credit balance); Cash in Bank (debit balance); Petty Cash (debit balance); Westside Aquatics, Capital (credit balance); Office Equipment (debit balance); and Office Furniture (debit balance).

Conducting an Audit with Alex

(Answers)

1. Mary debited the liability, Accounts Payable—A-1 Trucks Inc. She should have credited the account for an increase in liability.
2. Mary credited the liability, Accounts Payable—A-1 Trucks Inc. She should have debited the account for a decrease in liability.

Internet Resources and Activities Handbook

Refer students to the booklet for additional Internet activities.

*inter*NET CONNECTION www.glencoe.com

Do This (Answers)

1. The Universal Currency Converter Site: www.xe.net/ucc/
   TravelFinder.com: Currency Conversion: www.travelfinder.com/currency.html
2. Euros.
3. Answers will vary due to date.
4. Answers will vary due to date.

PEACHTREE CORNER

About Peachtree Complete® Accounting

Peachtree Complete Accounting is easy-to-use, full-featured accounting software that is designed for small business owners who want to use their accounting system to manage their businesses better, so it's ideal for students just learning accounting fundamentals. Students will be able to learn accounting on a system suited for virtually any type of small business and will be able to apply that knowledge elsewhere, both in education and in work environments.

Glencoe has formed a long-term alliance with Peachtree Software®, a subsidiary of the Best Software, U.S. Operations, a corporation with more than two decades of developing and marketing high-quality accounting software and electronic services specifically to meet the needs of small businesses. Glencoe's partnership with Peachtree Software demonstrates our commitment to giving students the best tools possible to prepare them for the future.

By incorporating Peachtree's accounting software into Glencoe's teaching tools, *Glencoe Accounting* gives students the advantage of being trained on accounting software that is currently in use by millions of businesses and is taught in numerous colleges and other post-secondary schools.

Introduction to Computerized Accounting Systems

Making the Transition from a Manual to a Computerized System

Perform Accounting Procedures Using Manual Methods	Perform Accounting Procedures Using Automated Methods
• Transactions are recorded into journals by hand. • The details of each transaction are then posted in the general ledger. • Account balances are calculated and a trial balance is prepared. The accountant prepares a trial balance to verify that the accounting equation is still in balance. • Account names and balances are then transferred to the proper financial report (income statement, balance sheet, or statement of owner's equity) and the report is summarized (totaled).	• Transactions are keyed to the appropriate screen in the accounting system. • Posting to the general ledger accounts occurs automatically. • The trial balance is generated by the accounting system. • Financial reports are predefined to pull the appropriate accounts and their current balances from the general ledger computer files. The reports automatically summarize and can be printed when the user chooses.

A Quick Overview

Peachtree Question	Description
What types of transactions can be entered in Peachtree Complete® Accounting?	You name it! You can enter: • General journal entries • Sales and cash receipts • Purchases and cash payments • Inventory adjustments • Payroll entries
What else will Peachtree do for the accountant?	• Reconciles bank statements • Prepares financial reports automatically • Prints checks • Prints invoices • Closes the accounting period • Creates cash, collections, and payment management charts and graphs.

For detailed instructions: See the **Peachtree User Guide** in your Glencoe Working Papers.

Peachtree® Accounting Software and Applications

Peachtree Accounting software and applications trains students in the leading accounting software for small businesses. All end-of-chapter problems, business simulations, and mini practice sets are launched through the CD-ROM menu system. Glencoe's Peachtree support includes:

- Peachtree User Guides in the workbook, *Chapter Reviews and Working Papers (CRWP)*
- Peachtree Smart Guides: Textbook instructions for each Peachtree problem
- Multimedia Peachtree Tutorials
- Automated Solutions Checker

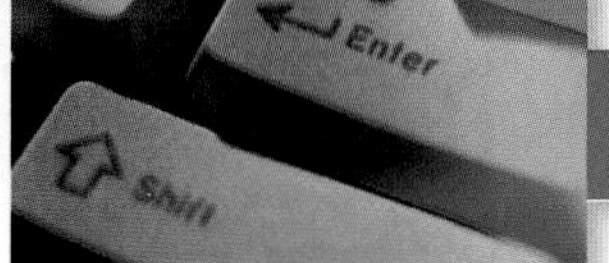

APPLICATION OPTIONS

Problem 4–3 Identifying Accounts Affected by Transactions

Ronald Hicks owns Wilderness Rentals and uses the following accounts in his business:

General Ledger

101	Cash in Bank		
105	Accounts Receivable—Helen Katz	201	Accounts Payable—Adventure Equipment Inc.
120	Office Equipment	301	Ronald Hicks, Capital
125	Camping Equipment		

Instructions For each of the following transactions:

(1) Indicate the two accounts affected.

(2) Indicate whether each account is debited or credited.

Date	Transactions
May 11	1. Sold on account to Helen Katz an unneeded office typewriter.
19	2. Purchased camping equipment on credit from Adventure Equipment Inc. Payment is due within 30 days.
22	3. Ronald Hicks brought a filing cabinet from home and transferred it to the business **(Office Equipment).**
23	4. Purchased tents and sleeping bags for cash.

Analyze: Which transactions affect the **Cash in Bank** account?

Complete chapter problems one of two ways:

1 **Manual** Glencoe Working Papers

or

2 **Spreadsheet** Templates (Problem 4–6)

Problem 4–4 Using T Accounts to Analyze Transactions

Regina Delgado owns a business called Hot Suds Car Wash. She uses the following accounts:

General Ledger

101	Cash in Bank	201	Accounts Payable—Allen Vacuum Systems
110	Accounts Receivable—Valley Auto	301	Regina Delgado, Capital
125	Office Equipment		
130	Office Furniture		
135	Car Wash Equipment		

Continued

PROBLEMS CHAPTER 4

Problem 4-3 (Answers) Identifying Accounts Affected by Transactions

1. Dr. Accts. Rec.—Helen Katz; Cr. Office Equipment
2. Dr. Camping Equipment; Cr. Accts. Pay.—Adventure Equipment Inc.
3. Dr. Office Furniture; Cr. Ronald Hicks, Capital
4. Dr. Camping Equipment; Cr. Cash in Bank

Analyze: Transaction number four

EXTENDING THE CONTENT

Interviewing Accountants and Bookkeepers Contact the Human Resources Departments of local business firms to find employees who are willing to speak with students about careers. Have students interview accountants or bookkeepers and ask these questions: Do they use a double-entry accounting system? How may accounts are used? What is the numbering system for accounts? Is a computer or manual system used? What technology skills must employees have to process accounting data? Have students collect samples of ledger accounts from the businesses they visit. Ask students to share with the class the information they've gathered from their interviews, including sample ledger accounts and any other forms.

PROBLEMS CHAPTER 4

Problem 4-4 (Answers)
Using T Accounts to Analyze Transactions

1. Dr. Cash in Bank $40,000;
   Cr. Regina Delgado, Capital $40,000
2. Dr. Car Wash Equipment $27,000;
   Cr. Accts. Pay.—Allen Vacuum Systems $27,000
3. Dr. Office Furniture $3,750;
   Cr. Regina Delgado, Capital $3,750
4. Dr. Office Equipment $7,500;
   Cr. Cash in Bank $7,500
5. Dr. Accts. Rec.—Valley Auto $1,200;
   Cr. Car Wash Equipment $1,200

Analyze: $27,000

Instructions For each transaction:

(1) Determine which accounts are affected.
(2) Prepare T accounts for the accounts affected.
(3) Enter the debit and credit amounts in the T accounts.

Date	Transactions
May 5	1. Regina Delgado invested an additional $40,000 cash in her business.
12	2. Bought another car wash system on account for $27,000 from Allen Vacuum Systems.
17	3. Regina Delgado transferred some of her personal office furniture, valued at $3,750, to her business.
24	4. Hot Suds Car Wash purchased additional office equipment for $7,500. Payment was made by check.
29	5. Hot Suds Car Wash sold some surplus car washing equipment on account to Valley Auto for $1,200.

Analyze: What is the ending balance for the liability account **Accounts Payable—Allen Vacuum Systems?**

Problem 4–5 Analyzing Transactions into Debit and Credit Parts

Abe Shultz uses the following accounts for his business, Kits & Pups Grooming:

General Ledger

101 Cash in Bank	205 Accounts Payable—Dogs & Cats Inc.
115 Accounts Receivable—Martha Giles	301 Abe Shultz, Capital
125 Office Equipment	
130 Office Furniture	
140 Grooming Equipment	

Instructions For each transaction:

(1) In your working papers prepare a T account for each account listed.
(2) Using the appropriate T accounts, analyze and record each of the following business transactions. Identify each transaction by number.
(3) After recording all transactions, write the word "Balance" on the normal balance side of each T account. Then compute and record the balance for each account.

CRITICAL THINKING ACTIVITY

Analyzing Information Tom Dunn started an automotive parts business two years ago. Except for a monthly salary, Tom has never taken money out of the business. He is considering withdrawing $5,000 to pay off the mortgage on his family home. What factors should Tom consider before making the withdrawal? (Students should ask questions such as, Is the cash currently available? Will the cash be needed to pay liabilities? Will there be enough cash left in the business to pay monthly expenses? Is future income anticipated to offset the withdrawal? After the withdrawal, will the business still realize a profit?)

Date	Transactions
May 1	1. Abe Shultz invested an additional $45,000 cash in his business.
5	2. Bought grooming equipment on account from Dogs & Cats Inc. for $8,500.
10	3. Purchased an office lamp for $85, Check 150.
14	4. Abe Shultz transferred his personal typewriter, worth $200, to the business.
19	5. Made a $3,000 payment on the grooming equipment bought on account, Check 151.
22	6. Sold the typewriter on account to Martha Giles for $200.
29	7. Bought a photocopier for $1,500, Check 152.
31	8. Received a $100 payment for the typewriter sold on account.

Analyze: How much cash did the business spend in all the above transactions?

Problem 4–6 Analyzing Transactions into Debit and Credit Parts

Juanita Ortega runs Outback Guide Service. The accounts she uses to record and report business transactions are listed below.

General Ledger

101 Cash in Bank	205 Accounts Payable—Peak Equipment Inc.
105 Accounts Receivable—Mary Johnson	207 Accounts Payable—Premier Processors
130 Office Equipment	301 Juanita Ortega, Capital
140 Computer Equipment	
145 Hiking Equipment	
150 Rafting Equipment	

Instructions For each transaction:

(1) In your working papers, prepare a T account for each account.

(2) Analyze and record each of the following business transactions in the appropriate T accounts. Identify each transaction by number.

(3) After recording all transactions, compute and record the account balance on the normal balance side of each T account.

(4) Add the balances of those accounts with normal debit balances.

(5) Add the balances of those accounts with normal credit balances.

(6) Compare the two totals. Are they the same?

Continued

SPREADSHEET SMART GUIDE

Step-by-Step Instructions: Problem 4–6

1. Select the spreadsheet template for Problem 4–6.
2. Enter your name and the date in the spaces provided on the template.
3. Complete the spreadsheet using the instructions in your working papers.
4. Print the spreadsheet and proof your work.
5. Save your work and exit the spreadsheet program.

Problem 4–5 (Answers) Analyzing Transactions into Debit and Credit Parts

Ending debit balances:
Cash in Bank $40,515
Accts. Rec.—Martha Giles $100
Office Equipment $1,500
Office Furniture $85
Grooming Equipment $8,500

Ending credit balances:
Accts. Pay.—Dogs & Cats Inc. $5,500
Abe Schultz, Capital $45,200

Analyze: $4,585

MAKING CONNECTIONS TO DAILY LIFE

Calculating Earnings and Expenses Tell students to imagine the following: You've been wanting to buy a new stereo that retails for $500. To earn extra cash, you plan to start mowing your neighbors' lawns. You decide to charge $20/yard for simple mowing and $30/yard for mowing, trimming, and cleanup. How will you plan to earn enough money for the stereo? What type of expenses might you have? What problems could arise? (Mowing 25 yards at $20 = $500 or 17 yards at $30 = $510. Expenses might include gasoline, oil, and mower repairs. Problems might include weather delays or competition from others who charge less.)

Problem 4-6 (Answers)
Analyzing Transactions into Debit and Credit Parts

Ending debit balances:
Cash in Bank $50,125
Accts. Rec.—Mary Johnson $850
Office Equipment $1,900
Computer Equipment $0
Hiking Equipment $550
Rafting Equipment $2,850

Ending credit balances:
Accts. Pay.—Peak Equipment $2,175
Accts. Pay.—Premier Processors $0
Juanita Ortega, Capital $54,100

Analyze: $0

Date	Transactions
May 2	1. Juanita Ortega transferred an additional $53,250 from her personal savings account into the business checking account.
6	2. Bought hiking equipment for $550, Check 367.
7	3. Bought rafting equipment on account from Peak Equipment Inc. for $2,675.
11	4. Juanita Ortega transferred her own computer, valued at $850, to the business.
16	5. Bought a cash register for the office on account from Premier Processors for $1,250.
19	6. Sold the computer on credit for $850 to Mary Johnson.
22	7. Paid $500 on account to Peak Equipment Inc., Check 368.
24	8. Purchased shelves for the office for $650, Check 369.
28	9. Paid $1,250 on account to Premier Processors, Check 370.
31	10. Bought rafting oars for $175, Check 371.

Analyze: What is the ending balance in the **Computer Equipment** account?

Problem 4–7 Analyzing Transactions Recorded in T Accounts

Richard Tang owns and operates a job placement service, Job Connect. The T accounts on the next page summarize several business transactions for May.

Instructions Use a form similar to the one presented on the next page. For each of the 10 transactions:

(1) Identify the account debited, and record the account name in the appropriate column.

(2) Indicate whether the account debited is being increased or decreased.

(3) Identify the account credited, and write the account name in the appropriate column.

(4) Indicate whether the account credited is being increased or decreased.

(5) Write a short description of the transaction.

MEETING SPECIAL NEEDS

English Language Learners Students who are English language learners will benefit from a preview of the vocabulary used in the chapter. Focus not only on the new terms introduced in the chapter but also on the other complex words that may be unfamiliar to these students, such as analysis, transaction, and concept. Define concepts and terms in more than one way. Also, have students define the concepts and terms in their own words. Help them correct or revise their definitions if necessary.

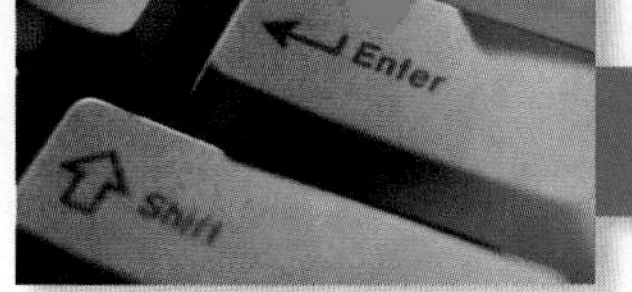

	(1)	(2)	(3)	(4)	(5)
Trans No.	Account Debited	Increase (I) or Decrease (D)	Account Credited	Increase (I) or Decrease (D)	Description
1	Cash in Bank	I	Richard Tang, Capital	I	Richard Tang invested $15,000 in the business.

Cash in Bank

Debit +	Credit –
(1) 15,000	(4) 1,225
(9) 225	(6) 900
	(7) 995
	(8) 2,000

Accounts Receivable

Debit +	Credit –
(5) 225	(9) 225

Office Equipment

Debit +	Credit –
(2) 225	(5) 225
(3) 8,000	
(4) 1,225	

Office Furniture

Debit +	Credit –
(6) 900	
(10) 145	

Computer Equipment

Debit +	Credit –
(7) 995	

Accounts Payable

Debit –	Credit +
(8) 2,000	(3) 8,000
	(10) 145

Richard Tang, Capital

Debit –	Credit +
	(1) 15,000
	(2) 225

Analyze: What is the ending balance for liabilities? For assets? For owner's equity?

Problem 4–7 (Answers) Analyzing Transactions Recorded in T Accounts

(2) Office Equipment Dr. (I)
Richard Tang, Capital Cr. (I)
Invested office equipment of $225 in the business

(3) Office Equipment Dr. (I)
Accounts Payable Cr. (I)
Bought office equipment of $8,000 on account

(4) Office Equipment Dr. (I)
Cash in Bank Cr. (D)
Paid cash for office equipment of $1,225

(5) Accounts Receivable Dr. (I)
Office Equipment Cr. (D)
Sold office equipment for $225 on account

(6) Office Furniture Dr. (I)
Cash in Bank Cr. (D)
Paid cash for office furniture of $900

(7) Computer Equipment Dr. (I)
Cash in Bank Cr. (D)
Paid cash for computer equipment of $995

(8) Accounts Payable Dr. (D)
Cash in Bank Cr. (D)
Paid $2,000 on account

(9) Cash in Bank Dr. (I)
Accounts Receivable Cr. (D)
Received cash of $225 on account

(10) Office Furniture Dr. (I)
Accounts Payable Cr. (I)
Bought office furniture on account for $145

Analyze: Assets $21,370, Liabilities $6,145, Owner's Equity $15,225

HOME AND COMMUNITY CONNECTIONS ACTIVITY

Cost of Preservation If your community has a historic preservation society, discuss with students the value of local historical sites. Are these sites assets or liabilities to the community? What criteria must a structure meet to be awarded the historic designation? Have students work in teams to contact local preservation agencies to get information about preservation. How much does it cost annually? Do the taxpayers support the preservation group? Who manages the funds? If your community does not have a local preservation group, ask students to research a well-known historic community in your state (e.g., Williamsburg or Mount Vernon; St. Augustine, Florida).

CHAPTER 5 Resource Manager

Section Resources

	Objectives & Standards	Activities & Features	Reproducible Masters
Chapter Opener *Transactions That Affect Revenue, Expenses, and Withdrawals*	• Explain the difference between permanent accounts and temporary capital accounts. • List and apply the rules of debit and credit for revenue, expense, and withdrawals accounts. • Use the six-step method to analyze transactions affecting revenue, expense, and withdrawals accounts. • Test a series of transactions for equality of debits and credits. • Define the new accounting terms introduced in this chapter. **National Standards for Business Education**: IA3, IA4, IA5	Exploring the Real World of Business, p. 94 Workplace Connections, p. 95	School-to-Work Handbook
Section 1 *The Relationship of Revenue, Expenses, and Withdrawals to Owner's Equity*	• The reason for having temporary and permanent accounts. • The rules of debit and credit for the revenue, expense, and withdrawals accounts.	International Accounting, p. 98 Did You Know?, p. 100 Math Hints, p. 100 Accounting Flashbacks, p. 101 A Matter of Ethics, p. 102	Strategies for Teaching International Accounting Math Review for Accounting Demonstration Problems Strategies for Teaching Ethics in Accounting
Section 2 *Applying the Rules of Debit and Credit to Revenue, Expense, and Owner's Equity Transactions*	• How to analyze transactions that affect revenue, expense, and withdrawals accounts.	Accounting Tips, p. 108 Connect To, p. 108 Accounting Careers in Focus, p. 110	Demonstration Problems Internet Resources and Activities Handbook

KEY

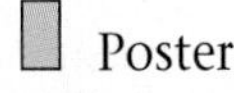

Posters

Transparency

Software

Videocassette

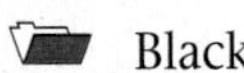

Blackline Masters

CD-ROM

Portfolio

MULTIMEDIA RESOURCE

Peachtree	QuickBooks	Spreadsheets	Videos	CD-ROMs
Problem 5–3 *Identifying Increases and Decreases in Accounts* Problem 5–4 *Using T Accounts to Analyze Transactions* Problem 5–5 *Analyzing Transactions into Debit and Credit Parts* Problem 5–6 *Analyzing Transactions into Debit and Credit Parts* Problem 5–7 *Analyzing Transactions*	Problem 5–7 *Analyzing Transactions*	Problem 5–8 *Completing the Accounting Equation*	***Video Segment: Computerized Accounting*** After viewing this video, students will be able to communicate how computers are used for accounting and accounting-related records in all types of businesses.	***Electronic Learning Center (ELC), Chapter 5*** This program is ideal for visual learners since it incorporates video images, animation, and graphics to enliven the content of each lesson. ***Interactive Lesson Planner (ILP), Chapter 5*** This CD-ROM combines the versatility of an electronic lesson planner with the convenience of teacher classroom resources.

SCANS Correlation Chart

FOUNDATION SKILLS

Basic Skills:	Reading	Writing	Math	Listening	Speaking	
Thinking Skills:	Creative Thinking	Decision Making	Problem Solving	Seeing Things in the Mind's Eye	Knowing How to Learn	Reasoning
Personal Qualities:	Responsibility	Self-Esteem	Sociability	Self-Management	Integrity/Honesty	

WORKPLACE COMPETENCIES

Resources:	Allocating Time	Allocating Money	Allocating Material and Facility Resources	Allocating Human Resources		
Information:	Acquiring and Evaluating Information	Organizing and Maintaining Information	Interpreting and Communicating Information	Using Computers to Process Information		
Interpersonal Skills:	Participating as a Member of a Team	Teaching Others	Serving Clients/ Customers	Exercising Leadership	Negotiating to Arrive at a Decision	Working with Cultural Diversity
Systems:	Understanding Systems	Monitoring and Correcting Performance	Improving and Designing Systems			
Technology:	Selecting Technology	Applying Technology to Task	Maintaining and Troubleshooting Technology			

*Highlighted blocks indicate areas covered in the chapter. Additional SCANS skills are also covered throughout the *Teacher Wraparound Edition*.

Assessment

Student Edition
- Check Your Understanding, pp. 103, 109
- Chapter 5 Problems, pp. 115–119

Assessment and Evaluation Masters
- Chapter 5 Study Plan, *Glencoe Workbook*
- Chapter 5 Self-Test, *Glencoe Workbook*
- Chapter 5 Test, *Chapter Tests* Booklet
- Chapter 5 Activity, *School-to-Work Handbook*
- Chapter 5 **Exam***View*

Teacher Wraparound Edition
- Critical Thinking Activity, p. 112
- Reteaching Section 1, p. 103
- Reteaching Section 2, p. 109
- Chapter 5 Quiz, p. 111

Transparencies

	Teaching Transparencies	Solution Transparencies
Section 1:	5–1, 5–2, 5–3, 5–4, 5–5	Problem 5–1
Section 2:	5–6, 5–7, 5–8, 5–9, 5–10, 5–11, 5–12, 5–13	Problem 5–2
End of Chapter:		Problems 5–3, 5–4, 5–5, 5–6, 5–7, 5–8

TEACHER CLASSROOM RESOURCES

This is a representation of key blackline masters available in the Teacher Classroom Resources.

Teaching Aids

Transparency Examples

Section Focus Transparencies

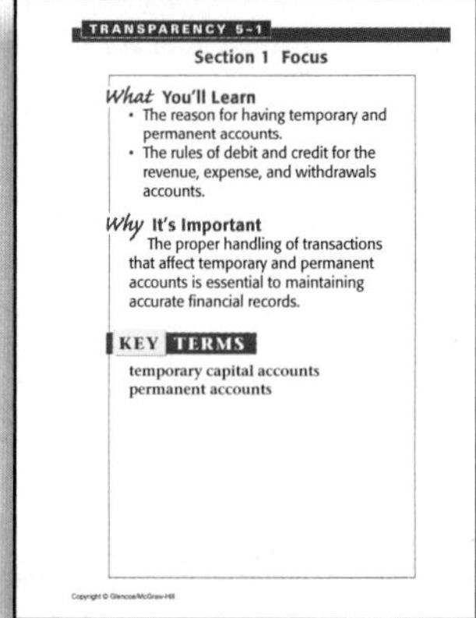

TRANSPARENCY 5-1

Section 1 Focus

What You'll Learn

- The reason for having temporary and permanent accounts.
- The rules of debit and credit for the revenue, expense, and withdrawals accounts.

Why It's Important

The proper handling of transactions that affect temporary and permanent accounts is essential to maintaining accurate financial records.

KEY TERMS

temporary capital accounts
permanent accounts

Teaching Transparencies

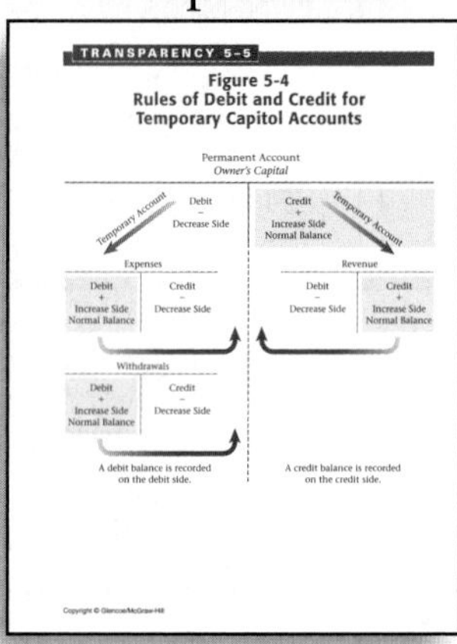

TRANSPARENCY 5-5

Figure 5-4
Rules of Debit and Credit for Temporary Capitol Accounts

Teaching Transparencies

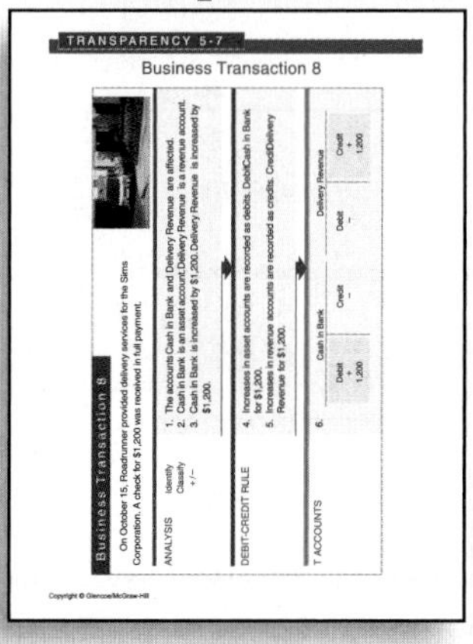

TRANSPARENCY 5-7

Business Transaction 8

Solution Transparencies

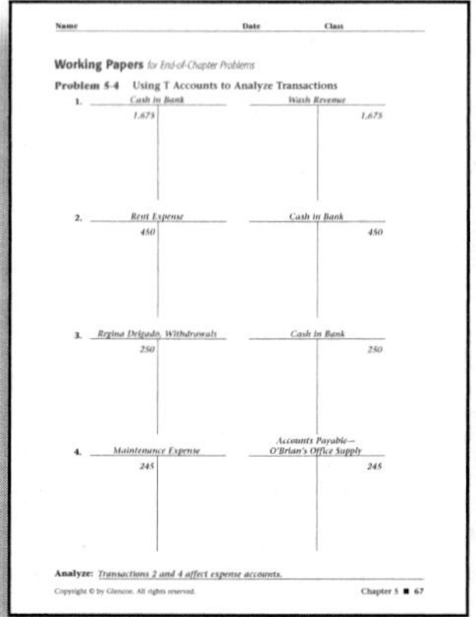

Working Papers

Problem 5-4 Using T Accounts to Analyze Transactions

Demonstration Problems

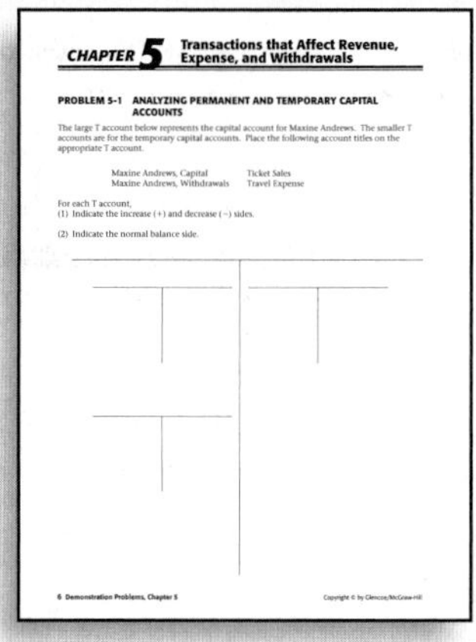

CHAPTER 5 Transactions that Affect Revenue, Expense, and Withdrawals

PROBLEM 5-1 ANALYZING PERMANENT AND TEMPORARY CAPITAL ACCOUNTS

Lesson Plans

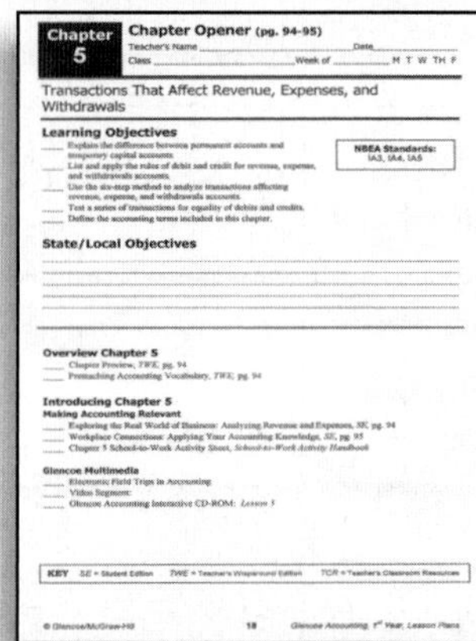

Chapter 5 Chapter Opener (pg. 94-95)

Transactions That Affect Revenue, Expenses, and Withdrawals

Learning Objectives

State/Local Objectives

Overview Chapter 5

Introducing Chapter 5

Glencoe Multimedia

Block Scheduling

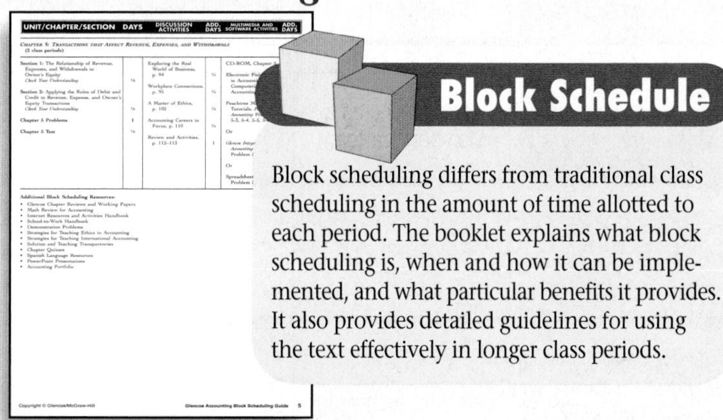

Block Schedule

Block scheduling differs from traditional class scheduling in the amount of time allotted to each period. The booklet explains what block scheduling is, when and how it can be implemented, and what particular benefits it provides. It also provides detailed guidelines for using the text effectively in longer class periods.

Enrichment and Application

Strategies for Teaching Ethics in Accounting

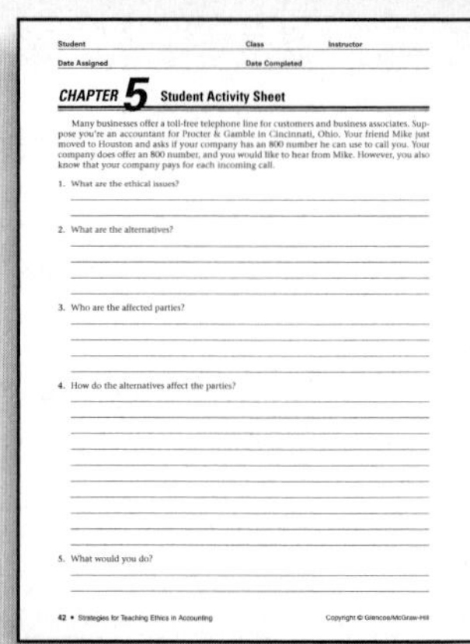

CHAPTER 5 Student Activity Sheet

Strategies for Teaching International Accounting

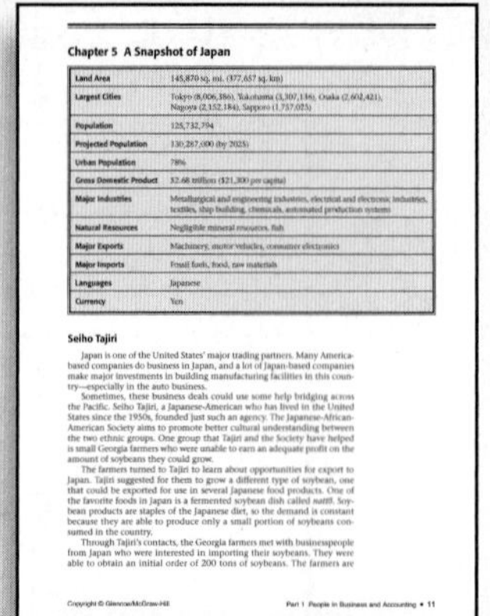

Chapter 5 A Snapshot of Japan

Seiho Tajiri

School-to-Work Handbook

CHAPTER 5 SCHOOL-TO-WORK ACTIVITY

Transactions Affecting Revenue, Expenses, and Withdrawals

Meeting Different Ability Levels

Chapter Reviews and Working Papers (CRWP)

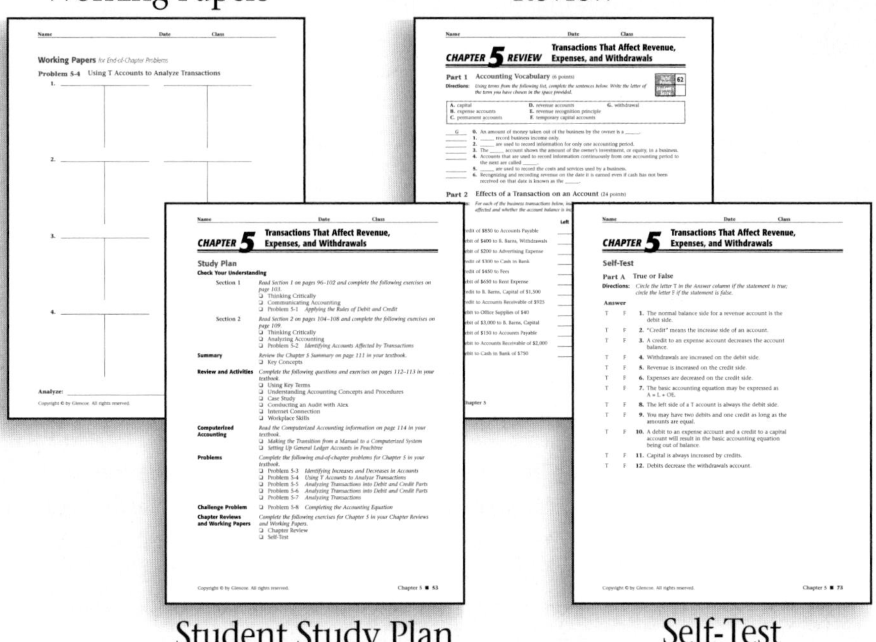

Real-World Multimedia CD-ROM

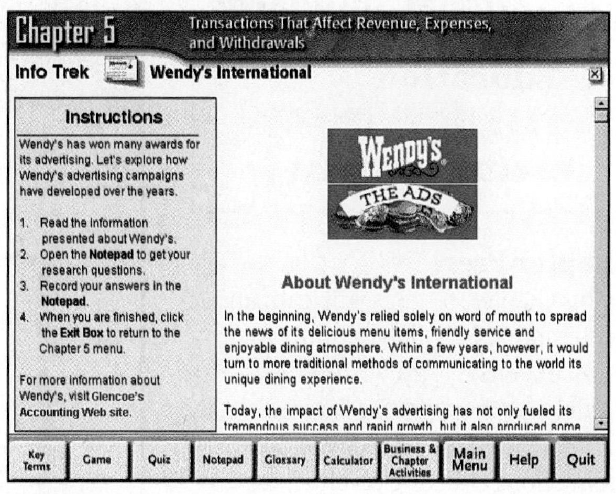

Key to Ability Levels

Each section gives skill-building activities. Each activity has been labeled for use with students of various learning styles and abilities.

L1 Level 1 activities are basic activities and should be within the range of all students.

L2 Level 2 activities are average activities and should be within the range of average and above average students.

L3 Level 3 activities are challenging activities designed for the ability range of above average students.

ELL ELL activities should be within the ability range of English Language Learners.

Teaching Resources at a Glance

Application Resources

- Glencoe Chapter Review and Working Papers, SE and TAE
- School-to-Work Handbook, SE and TM
- Accounting Portfolio, SE and TM

Reproducible Masters

- Demonstration Problems
- Lesson Plans
- Block Scheduling
- Spanish Language Resources

Glencoe Accounting Professional Development Series

- Strategies for Teaching Ethics in Accounting
- Accounting Competitive Event Review
- Math Review for Accounting
- Strategies for Teaching International Accounting
- Internet Resources and Activities Handbook

Transparency Package

- Section Focus Transparencies
- Teaching Transparencies
- Source Document Transparencies
- Solution Transparencies

Performance Assessment

- **Exam***View* CD-ROM
- Chapter Tests
- Chapter Quizzes
- Unit Tests
- Audit Tests
- Printed Testbank

Multimedia Resources

- Electronic Learning Center:
  - Multimedia CD-ROMs
  - Peachtree software, tutorials, templates, and solutions
  - Spreadsheet templates
- Using QuickBooks with Glencoe Accounting
- Interactive Lesson Planner
- Electronic Field Trips in Accounting
- PowerPoint Presentation
- Web site: glencoeaccounting.glencoe.com

Assessment and Evaluation

Chapter Tests

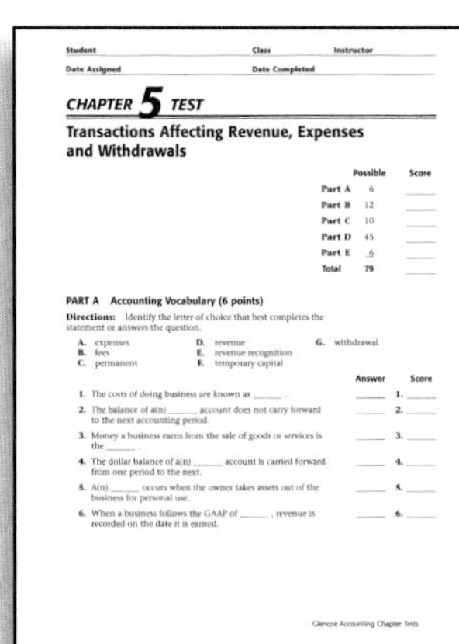

Chapter Quiz

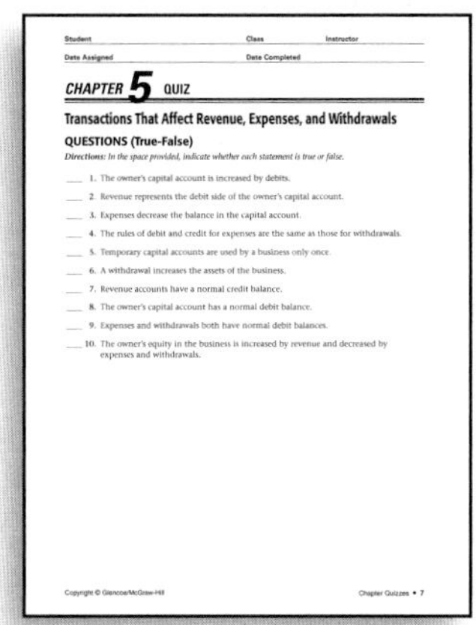

OVERVIEW CHAPTER 5

Correlations to National Standards for Business Education

(See pages T50–T51 for a detailed correlation chart.)

Standards: IA3, IA4, IA5

Chapter Preview

In this chapter students will learn about the temporary capital accounts for revenue, expenses, and withdrawals. Expanding on the rules of debit and credit, they'll learn how to analyze business transactions affecting revenue, expenses, and withdrawals into their debit and credit parts.

Section Overviews

- Section 1—*Relationship of Revenue, Expenses, and Withdrawals to Owner's Equity*
- Section 2—*Applying the Rules of Debit and Credit to Revenue, Expense, and Owner's Equity Transactions*

Chapter Vocabulary

temporary capital accounts
permanent accounts
revenue recognition

Preteaching Accounting Vocabulary

Oral Exercise: Write each of the new terms on the chalkboard. Review the meaning of each for students. Then have students discuss how these terms fit into an accounting system. L1

CHAPTER 5

Transactions That Affect Revenue, Expenses, and Withdrawals

Learning Objectives

When you have completed this chapter, you will be able to:

- Explain the difference between permanent accounts and temporary capital accounts.
- List and apply the rules of debit and credit for revenue, expense, and withdrawals accounts.
- Use the six-step method to analyze transactions affecting revenue, expense, and withdrawals accounts.
- Test a series of transactions for equality of debits and credits.
- Define the new accounting terms introduced in this chapter.

Exploring the Real World of Business

ANALYZING REVENUE AND EXPENSES

Dave Thomas was the man behind **Wendy's International.** The original restaurant in Columbus, Ohio, opened in 1969 and is called **Wendy's Old Fashioned Hamburgers.** Now more than 6,000 restaurants offer salads, sandwiches, hamburgers, fries, and drinks.

When you buy a meal at **Wendy's,** you are helping the business earn revenue. That revenue is used to pay expenses and to build new restaurants. **Wendy's** grew to its size today by selling meals to people just like you. Dave Thomas' motto for the restaurants is "Quality, Service, Cleanliness, and Value." Have you ever wondered where **Wendy's** name came from? Dave named his restaurant after one of his daughters, Melinda Lou, whose nickname is Wendy.

What do you think?

Wendy's earns revenue by selling meals. Can you think of at least six examples of expenses that a **Wendy's** restaurant might have?

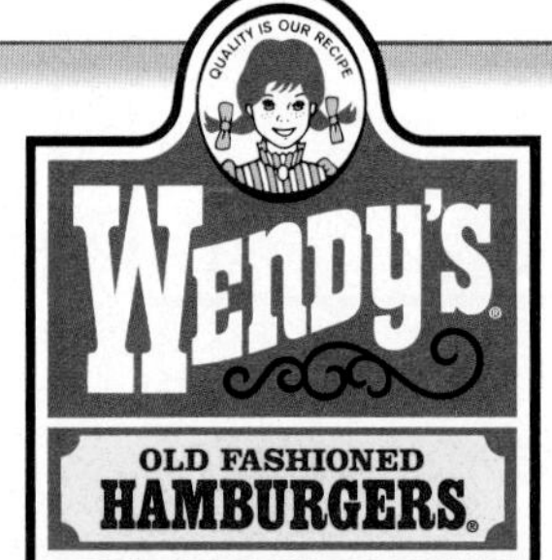

Exploring the Real World of Business

Wendy's Old Fashioned Hamburgers

Wendy's can be found in locations from Main Street USA to more exotic places such as Europe or Asia. Without revenue from selling its products, such growth would not have been possible. Discuss the impact on the revenue when buying another Wendy's franchise versus just starting a new restaurant.

What do you think? (Answers)

Answers will vary. Among expenses students might mention are advertising, franchise fees, costs of paper products, grounds maintenance, costs of flowers and shrubs, inside cleaning expense, and wages for full-time and part-time workers.

Workplace Connections

Applying Your Accounting Knowledge

When you receive a paycheck, you probably think about the amount of money you have and the things you'd like to buy. Businesses also earn money and spend it on items used to operate the business. In this chapter, you'll learn to analyze transactions involving revenue and expenses of a business.

Investigate:

1. How does your workplace (or the workplace of family or friends) earn revenue?
2. What does the business buy with that revenue?
3. How do these revenue and expense transactions affect the profits of a business?

Glencoe Accounting *Online*

Visit the *Glencoe Accounting* Web site at **glencoeaccounting.glencoe.com** for additional activities and information.

95

INTRODUCING CHAPTER 5

Making Accounting Relevant

Workplace Connections: Applying Your Accounting Knowledge

Discussion: Discuss with students how businesses earn revenue. Give examples of local companies. Include a variety of businesses, such as retailers, manufacturers, service businesses, and professionals.

Investigate (Answers)

1. Answers will vary. Examples might include a theater that sells goods (popcorn, soft drinks) and services (movies) to earn revenue or a dentist who earns revenue from services.
2. Businesses use revenue to pay operating expenses, for future growth, and to provide a return to the owner or others who invested money in the business.
3. Revenue increases business profits, expenses decrease it. Businesses must earn more revenue than they pay out in expenses if they are to continue operating in the future.

School-to-Work Activity

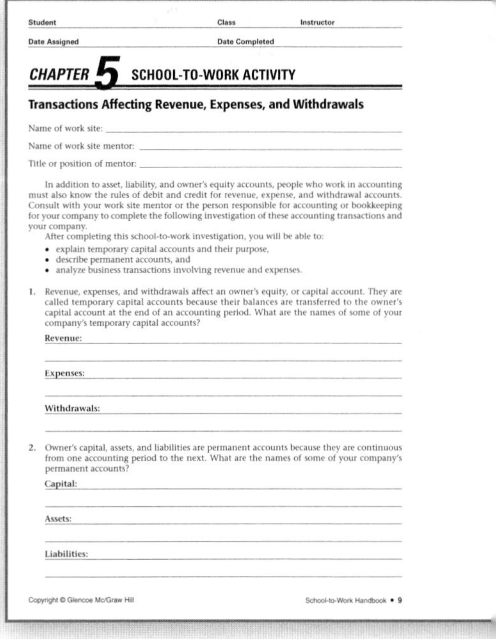

Student ______ Class ______ Instructor ______

Date Assigned ______ Date Completed ______

CHAPTER 5 SCHOOL-TO-WORK ACTIVITY

Transactions Affecting Revenue, Expenses, and Withdrawals

Name of work site: ______

Name of work site mentor: ______

Title or position of mentor: ______

In addition to asset, liability, and owner's equity accounts, people who work in accounting must also know the rules of debit and credit for revenue, expense, and withdrawal accounts. Consult with your work site mentor or the person responsible for accounting or bookkeeping for your company to complete the following investigation of these accounting transactions and your company.

After completing this school-to-work investigation, you will be able to:

- explain temporary capital accounts and their purpose,
- describe permanent accounts, and
- analyze business transactions involving revenue and expenses.

1. Revenue, expenses, and withdrawals affect an owner's equity, or capital account. They are called temporary capital accounts because their balances are transferred to the owner's capital account at the end of an accounting period. What are the names of some of your company's temporary capital accounts?

   Revenue: ______

   Expenses: ______

   Withdrawals: ______

2. Owner's capital, assets, and liabilities are permanent accounts because they are continuous from one accounting period to the next. What are the names of some of your company's permanent accounts?

   Capital: ______

   Assets: ______

   Liabilities: ______

 School-to-Work Handbook • 9

GLENCOE MULTIMEDIA

Electronic Field Trips in Accounting *Video Segment: Computerized Accounting*
After viewing this video, students will be able to communicate how computers are used for accounting and accounting-related records in all types of businesses.

Glencoe Accounting: Electronic Learning Center *Chapter 5*
The CD-ROM program is ideal for visual learners since it incorporates video images, animation, and graphics to enliven the content of each lesson.

1 FOCUS

Introducing the Section
Building on their knowledge of the rules of debit and credit for assets, liabilities, and owner's equity accounts, students will next learn to analyze accounts that are subsets of the owner's capital account. In this section, students will learn the rules of debit and credit for revenue, expense, and withdrawals accounts.

Section 1 Concepts
- The reason for having temporary and permanent accounts.
- The rules of debit and credit for the revenue, expense, and withdrawals accounts.

Visual Learning

Section 1 Focus

Use **Transparency 5–1** to introduce section concepts.

BELL RINGER

Compare and Contrast: Draw T accounts for revenue, expenses, and withdrawals on the chalkboard, with revenue on the right side and expenses and withdrawals on the left. Add the rules of debit and credit to each T account. Ask students to explain how the accounts relate to other accounts they have studied. How do they differ? Now draw a larger T account for the owner's capital, with the vertical part of the T separating the left side (expenses and withdrawals) and the right side (revenue). Given the rules of debit and credit for owner's capital, ask students how they think each account affects the capital account. L1

SECTION 1

Relationship of Revenue, Expenses, and Withdrawals to Owner's Equity

What You'll Learn
- The reason for having temporary and permanent accounts.
- The rules of debit and credit for the revenue, expense, and withdrawals accounts.

Why It's Important
The proper handling of transactions that affect temporary and permanent accounts is essential to maintaining accurate financial records.

KEY TERMS
temporary capital accounts
permanent accounts

In Chapter 4 you learned how to record transactions in asset, liability, and owner's capital accounts. In this chapter you will learn how to record transactions in revenue, expense, and owner's withdrawals accounts. These accounts provide information about how well the business is doing. A pilot for American Airlines or Delta would never take off in a 747 equipped with only a speedometer and a gas gauge. These two instruments, although necessary, do not give a pilot all of the information needed to keep such a complex aircraft on course and operating smoothly. Operating a business is a bit like operating a 747. Information about revenues and expenses is needed by the owner to keep the business on course.

Revenue, Expenses, and Withdrawals Account Transactions

You learned earlier that the owner's capital account shows the amount of the owner's investment, or equity, in a business. Owner's equity is increased or decreased by transactions other than owner's investments. For example, the revenue, or income, earned by the business increases owner's equity. Both expenses and owner's withdrawals decrease owner's equity. (Remember that revenue is not the same as an owner's investment, and expense is not the same as an owner's withdrawal.)

Revenue, expenses, and withdrawals could be recorded as increases or decreases directly in the capital account. This method, however, makes classifying information about these transactions difficult. A more informative way to record transactions affecting revenue and expenses is to set up separate accounts for each type of revenue or expense. Such information helps the owner decide, for example, whether some expenses need to be reduced to save money.

Temporary Capital Accounts

As you learned in Chapter 2, accounting is an activity that is divided into periods of time or accounting periods. This means that once all of the activities are completed for a given accounting period, that period is closed. Then a new period starts, and

RESOURCE MANAGER

Reproducible Masters
- Lesson Plans
- Chapter Reviews and Working Papers (CRWP) TAE
- Demonstration Problems

Transparencies
- Section Focus Transparency
- Teaching Transparencies
- Solution Transparencies

Multimedia
- ExamView CD-ROM
- Electronic Learning Center CD-ROM
- Interactive Lesson Planner CD-ROM
- Electronic Field Trips in Accounting

transactions for the new period are entered into the accounting system. The process continues for as long as the business exists.

Revenue, expense, and withdrawals accounts are used to collect information for a single accounting period. These accounts are called **temporary capital accounts**. Temporary capital accounts start each new accounting period with zero balances. That is, the amounts in these accounts are not carried forward from one accounting period to the next. Temporary capital accounts are not temporary in the sense that they are used for a short time and then discarded. They continue to be used in the accounting system, but the amounts recorded in them accumulate for only one accounting period. At the end of that period, the balances in the temporary capital accounts are transferred to the owner's capital account. (The procedure for transferring these balances to owner's capital is explained in Chapter 10.)

Illustrating Temporary Capital Accounts. Let's use **Utilities Expense**, a temporary capital account, as an example. During an accounting period, business transactions related to utilities such as electricity and telephones are recorded in **Utilities Expense.** By using this separate account, the owner can see at a glance how much money is being spent on this expense. The individual transaction amounts accumulate in the account as the accounting period progresses. At the end of the period, the total spent is transferred to the owner's capital account and subtracted from the capital account balance. Remember, expenses decrease owner's capital. In **Figure 5–1**, the account, **Utilities Expense**, starts the next accounting period with a zero balance—ready for the transactions in the new period.

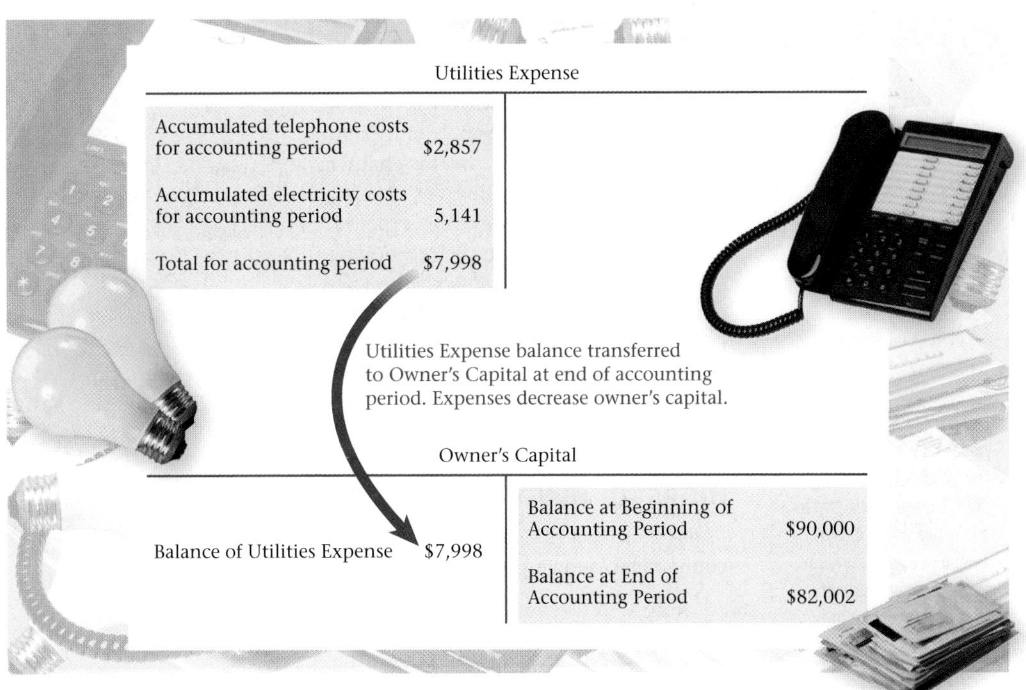

Figure 5–1 The Relationship of Temporary Capital Accounts to the Owner's Capital Account

Great Ideas *From the Classroom of...*

Computerized Accounting Computerized accounting systems provide an excellent opportunity for students to experience a real-life accounting system. Demonstrate a computer system and point out the ease and speed in accessing the chart of accounts or checking the equality of debits and credits in the ledger.

Don Black
Buhl High School
Buhl, Idaho

2 TEACH

GUIDED PRACTICE

Reading Accounting

- Have students make a table of key information gained from their reading. For example, you might suggest that students organize information in a tabular format. Under a heading such as "Topics," they might write a key concept or term. To the right, they might describe the concept under a heading such as "What I Need to Know." L1

Concept Development: Revenue, Expenses, and Withdrawals Account Transactions

Discussion: Discuss with students the relationship between the permanent and temporary capital accounts. Learning this relationship now will help students when they study the closing process in Chapter 10.

Emphasize that during an accounting period, the increases and decreases in owner's capital are recorded in temporary accounts to maintain a separate record of specific increases and decreases. Show the revenue and expense accounts within the capital account to demonstrate the relationship between permanent and temporary accounts. L1

Visual Learning

Figure 5–1 The Relationship of Temporary Capital Accounts to the Owner's Capital Account

Use **Transparency 5–2** to help students understand how expenses decrease the owner's capital account.

2 TEACH (Cont'd.)

Concept Development: The Rules of Debit and Credit for Temporary Capital Accounts

Discussion: To introduce the rules of debit and credit for revenue, expenses, and withdrawals, draw a T account for each classification on the chalkboard. Write the rules for revenue in that account. Discuss their effect on capital. Next, write the rules for expenses. Discuss the effect of expenses on capital. Continue with the rules for withdrawals and their effect on capital. L1

Thinking Algebraically

Point out that temporary capital accounts represent increases and decreases in capital. Since revenue increases capital, its rules of debit and credit are the same as for capital. Expenses and withdrawals decrease capital, so their rules are opposite those of revenue accounts. L1

Teaching Tips

Review the rules for increasing and decreasing owner's capital. Point out that revenue, expense, and withdrawals accounts are *classified* as temporary. They are not temporary in their use by the business. They collect account information until it is time to report it on a financial statement, after which their balances return to zero for use in data for another accounting period.

Strategies for Teaching International Accounting
To enrich study of International Accounting, refer to the additional critical thinking activities in the booklet.

Permanent Accounts

In contrast to the temporary accounts, the owner's capital account is a permanent account. Asset and liability accounts are also permanent accounts. **Permanent accounts** are continuous from one accounting period to the next. In permanent accounts, the dollar balances at the end of one accounting period become the dollar balances for the beginning of the next accounting period.

Illustrating Permanent Accounts. For example, if a business has supplies totaling $875 at the end of one accounting period, the business will start with $875 in supplies at the beginning of the next accounting period. That is, at the end of an accounting period, the ending balances in permanent accounts are carried forward to the next accounting period as the beginning balances.

End of Accounting Period

Supplies	
Debit	Credit
End Bal. 875	

Beginning of Next Accounting Period

Supplies	
Debit	Credit
Beg. Bal. 875	

The permanent accounts show balances on hand or amounts owed at any time. They also show the day-to-day changes in assets, liabilities, and owner's capital.

The Rules of Debit and Credit for Temporary Capital Accounts

In Chapter 4 you learned the rules of debit and credit for the asset, liability, and owner's capital accounts. In this chapter we will continue with the rules of debit and credit, this time for revenue, expense, and withdrawals accounts. Before looking at these rules, let's review quickly the T account showing the rules of debit and credit for the owner's capital account.

Owner's Capital Account	
Debit − Decrease Side	Credit + Increase Side Normal Balance

As you will see, the rules of debit and credit for accounts classified as revenue, expense, and withdrawals accounts are related to the rules for the owner's equity account.

International ACCOUNTING

Business Etiquette

In the United States, business people shake hands with a firm grip to show confidence. That is not always the case. In the Middle East, business people use a gentle grip to avoid suggesting aggression. If you meet someone from an unfamiliar culture, it's safest to let him or her set the precedent.

Rules for Revenue Accounts

Accounts set up to record business income are classified as revenue accounts. The following rules of debit and credit apply to revenue accounts:

Rule 1: A revenue account is *increased* (+) on the *credit* side.
Rule 2: A revenue account is *decreased* (−) on the *debit* side.
Rule 3: The *normal balance* for a revenue account is the *increase side,* or the *credit side.* Revenue accounts normally have credit balances.

Teaching International ACCOUNTING

Research Greeting Customs Assign students different countries (or let them choose a country) and ask them to research the greeting customs for that country. Students can find resources at the library or on the Internet. Have students present their findings to the class. They should discuss the importance of the greeting custom for their assigned country and contrast that country's greeting customs with greeting customs in the United States. If applicable, have them demonstrate the greeting.

Revenue earned from selling goods or services increases owner's capital. The relationship of revenue accounts to the owner's capital account is shown by the T accounts in **Figure 5–2.** Can you explain why the T account for revenue is used to represent the credit (right) side of the capital account?

Permanent Account
Owner's Capital

Debit – Decrease Side	Credit + Increase Side Normal Balance

Temporary Account

Revenue

Debit – Decrease Side	Credit + Increase Side Normal Balance

A credit balance is recorded on the credit side.

Figure 5–2 Rules of Debit and Credit for Revenue Accounts

Key Points

Normal Balances
The normal balance side of an account is the side used to increase the account.

Increases in owner's capital are shown on the credit side of that account. Since revenue increases owner's capital, the revenue account is used to represent the credit side of the owner's capital account.

We can summarize the rules of debit and credit for revenue accounts with a T account illustration.

Revenue Accounts

Debit – (2) Decrease Side	Credit + (1) Increase Side (3) Normal Balance

Let's apply the rules of debit and credit to an actual revenue account. Look at the entries in the following T account for the revenue account called **Fees.** The increases to the revenue account are recorded on the right, or credit, side of the T account. The decreases are recorded on the left, or debit, side. To find the balance, subtract total debits ($200) from total credits ($500 + $1,000 + $2,000 = $3,500). You get a balance of $3,300 on the credit side, the normal balance side for a revenue account.

Fees

Debit –	Credit +
200	500
	1,000
	2,000
	Bal. 3,300

2 TEACH (Cont'd.)

Visual Learning

Figure 5–2 Rules of Debit and Credit for Revenue Accounts

Use **Transparency 5–3** to emphasize the visual relationship between capital and revenue; i.e., revenue increases capital and is thus recorded as a credit. Likewise, the revenue account is increased by a credit and has a normal credit balance.

Teaching Tip

Emphasize that revenue represents an inflow of assets and an increase in equity.

Critical Thinking: Point out to students that businesses sometimes earn revenue from many different services. Have students choose a service business and analyze how the business earns revenue. Tell them to be specific (e.g., if they choose an advertising firm, they should mention different media, such as television, radio, magazines, etc.). Have students write one or two paragraphs describing the business and how it earns revenue. Also ask them to prepare a chart of accounts for the business. L2

Chapter Reviews and Working Papers
Refer students to the *Study Plan* located at the beginning of Chapter 5 in the workbook.

REINFORCING STUDY SKILLS

Time Management In this activity the student is expected to develop time management skills by setting priorities for completing work as scheduled. Set aside part of a class period to teach students how to organize their study activities and to set aside study time. A weekly schedule might be used to list assignments and their due dates. Fill out the schedules in class and periodically ask students whether they are on schedule. Ask students what problems they are having with their schedules and offer ideas for improvement.

2 TEACH (Cont'd.)

Concept Development: Rules for Expense Accounts

Discussion: Point out that during normal business operations the business spends money on many different things such as rent or mortgage payments, supplies used by the business, advertising, insurance, and utilities. During the fiscal period, the total of the expenses increases as the business continues to spend money. The money paid for expenses decreases the amount of capital. Thus, the rules of debit and credit for expense accounts are opposite those for revenue, which increases owner's capital. L1

Visual Learning

Figure 5–3 Rules of Debit and Credit for Expense Accounts

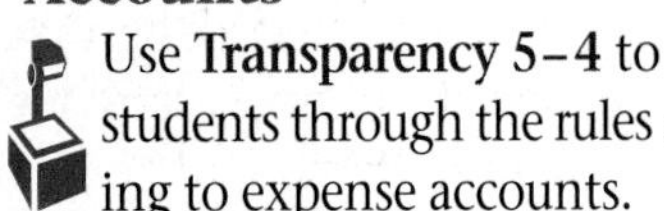

Use **Transparency 5–4** to guide students through the rules applying to expense accounts.

Teaching Tip

Emphasize that expenses represent an outflow of assets and a decrease in equity.

Math Review for Accounting

Photocopy appropriate *Activity Sheets* for students who need additional practice in basic math skills.

Did You Know?

Restaurant Industry

The restaurant industry is a key part of the U.S. economy, employing more than 11 million people. Restaurants take in revenue of about $400 billion a year.

Rules for Expense Accounts

Accounts set up to record the costs of goods and services a business uses are expense accounts. The following rules of debit and credit apply to expense accounts:

Rule 1: An expense account is *increased* on the *debit* side.
Rule 2: An expense account is *decreased* on the *credit* side.
Rule 3: The *normal balance* for an expense account is the *increase side,* or the *debit side.* Expense accounts normally have debit balances.

Expenses are the costs of doing business. Expenses decrease owner's capital. Note that revenues have the exact opposite impact; revenues increase owner's capital. Look at the T accounts in **Figure 5–3.** Can you explain why the T account for expenses is used to represent the debit (left) side of the capital account?

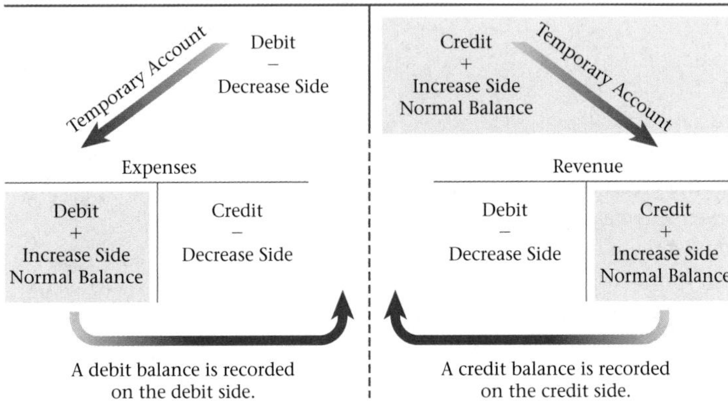

Figure 5–3 Rules of Debit and Credit for Expense Accounts

Math Hints

Computing the Balance in a T Account

To make it easier to find an account balance:

1. Add amounts and write a subtotal on each side of the account.
2. Subtract the lesser subtotal from the other subtotal to find the account balance.

Decreases in owner's capital are shown on the debit side of that account. Since expenses decrease owner's capital, expense accounts are used to represent the debit side of the owner's capital account.

Let's use a T account to summarize the rules of debit and credit for expense accounts.

Expense Accounts	
Debit + (1) Increase Side (3) Normal Balance	Credit – (2) Decrease Side

Now look at the entries recorded in the T account called **Advertising Expense.** The increases to the expense account are recorded on the left, or

Math Skill Builder Activity

T Account Balances Have students find T-account balances for these transactions: Eva's Style Shop paid rent of $700, bought a newspaper ad for $125, and paid $65 for plumbing repairs. Analyze the transactions and balance the accounts. The beginning debit balance of Cash in Bank is $25,000. (Dr. Rent Expense $700; Dr. Advertising Expense $125; Dr. Maintenance Expense $65; Cr. Cash in Bank $700, $125, $65. Expense accounts will have debit balances; Cash in Bank, $24,110 debit balance.)

debit, side of the T account. The decreases to the account are recorded on the right, or credit, side of the T account. When total credits ($125) are subtracted from total debits ($600), there is a balance of $475 on the debit side, which is the normal balance side for expense accounts.

Advertising Expense	
Debit +	Credit –
400	125
200	
Bal. 475	

Rules for the Withdrawals Account

A withdrawal is an amount of money or an asset the owner takes out of the business. Since withdrawals do not occur as frequently as expenses, no separate classification is used for the withdrawals account. Rather, it is classified as a temporary owner's equity account. Withdrawals, like expenses, decrease capital, so the rules of debit and credit are the same as for expense accounts.

Rule 1: The withdrawals account is *increased* on the *debit* side.
Rule 2: The withdrawals account is *decreased* on the *credit* side.
Rule 3: The *normal balance* for the withdrawals account is the *increase side* or the *debit side.* The withdrawals account normally has a debit balance.

Withdrawals Account	
Debit +	Credit –
(1) Increase Side	(2) Decrease Side
(3) Normal Balance	

Review the entries in the T account called **W. Smith, Withdrawals.** The increases are recorded on the left, or debit side, of the T account. The decreases are recorded on the right, or credit, side of the T account. When total credits ($200) are subtracted from total debits ($2,000), there is a balance of $1,800 on the debit side, which is the normal balance side for the withdrawals account.

W. Smith, Withdrawals	
Debit +	Credit –
500	200
1,500	
Bal. 1,800	

Key Points

Normal Balances
- The normal balance for a revenue account is a credit.
- The normal balance for an expense account is a debit.

ACCOUNTING *Flashbacks*

CURRENCIES

Following the Revolutionary War in the United States, Americans rejected everything British; so they embraced a money system from Bohemia–the Thaler. Americans mispronounced this unit as a "dollar."

COOPERATIVE LEARNING ACTIVITY

Co-op Co-op Assign students to small groups of four or five. Ask each group to develop an idea for a service business and to identify several revenue and expense accounts for the business. Instruct students to describe 10 typical transactions for their "business." Have students write the transactions and analyze each one using T accounts. Each T account should show the account balance on its normal balance side after all transactions are analyzed. Have each team select a spokesperson to present their "business" to the rest of the class. You may want to provide transparency markers and blank transparencies for students to use in preparing their presentations.

2 TEACH (Cont'd.)

Concept Development: Rules for the Withdrawals Account

Discussion: Have students discuss what happens when the owner takes money out of the business. The business now has fewer assets, so the owner's equity (or claim to those assets) is decreased. The owner's capital account represents equity in the business. Capital is decreased by debits, so withdrawals are shown on the debit side of the capital account. L1

Teaching Tip

Withdrawals by the owner are made in anticipation of income earned by the business.

Critical Thinking: Ask students what happens when the business does not earn enough income or the owner withdraws too much money. (The business will not have enough capital to operate. With too little capital, the owner may have to borrow money to operate, which adds to expenses because interest will have to be paid on the loan. If the additional capital does not result in greater revenue, the business could eventually be forced to stop operating.) L2

GO TO Demonstration Problem Step-by-Step Practice

Use demonstration problem 5–1 to give students practice indentifying the increase, decrease, and normal balance sides of capital and temporary capital accounts.

CHAPTER 5
SECTION 1, PAGES 96–103

2 TEACH (Cont'd.)

Visual Learning

Figure 5-4 Rules of Debit and Credit for Temporary Capital Accounts

Use **Transparency 5-5** of this illustration to summarize the rules of debit and credit for the temporary capital accounts.

Concept Development: Summary of the Rules of Debit and Credit for Temporary Capital Accounts

Application: Drill students on the rules of debit and credit by drawing T accounts on the chalkboard and omitting rules and titles. For example, draw a T account for revenue but omit the title, the words "Increase side," and "Normal balance." Have students determine the type of account and fill in the missing parts. Do the same for expenses and withdrawals, omitting different parts for each account. L1

Teaching Tip

Point out that the terms "capital" and "owner's equity" are often used interchangeably. Temporary owner's equity and temporary capital accounts are the same.

Strategies for Teaching Ethics in Accounting

Photocopy the Chapter 5 *Student Activity Sheet* for students. Answers are also provided in the booklet.

Key Points

Debits and Credits

Debits are used to:

1. Decrease (−) revenue.
2. Increase (+) expenses.
3. Increase (+) withdrawals.

Credits are used to:

1. Increase (+) revenue.
2. Decrease (−) expenses.
3. Decrease (−) withdrawals.

Summary of the Rules of Debit and Credit for Temporary Capital Accounts

Figure 5–4 summarizes the rules of debit and credit for the temporary capital accounts and the basic accounting relationships of these accounts to the owner's capital account.

Figure 5–4 Rules of Debit and Credit for Temporary Capital Accounts

A MATTER OF ETHICS

Using a Toll-Free Number

Many businesses offer a toll-free telephone line for customers and business associates. Suppose you're an accountant for Procter & Gamble in Cincinnati, Ohio. Your friend Mike just moved to Houston and asks if your company has an 800 number he can use to call you. Your company does offer an 800 number, and you would like to hear from Mike. However, you also know that your company pays for each incoming call.

Ethical Decision Making:

- What are the ethical issues?
- What are the alternatives?
- Who are the affected parties?
- How do the alternatives affect the parties?
- What would you do?

Teaching A MATTER OF ETHICS

Using a Toll-Free Number Ask students what issues other than the cost of the call to the company might affect a decision. Some possibilities are the loss of employee time spent talking to friends (another cost to the business) or giving the appearance of spending too much time on the telephone. Both supervisors and co-workers notice employees who abuse telephone privileges, and such practices could affect career success.

SECTION 1 Check Your Understanding

Now that you have studied this section, complete the following questions and problems.

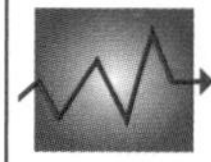

Thinking Critically

1. Changes to revenue accounts eventually affect another account. What other account is affected? Explain.
2. What type of transaction affects the debit side of the owner's capital account? Explain.

Communicating Accounting

As the financial director for the Southside Ballet Company, you determined it would be a good idea for Southside to open a ballet supply and dancewear shop. Write a memo to the ballet director and owner, Jonathan Booth, asking him to consider opening this shop. Explain how you view the impact of additional revenue on his capital account. Use the rules for revenue accounts in your explanation.

Problem 5–1 Applying the Rules of Debit and Credit

Caroline Palmer uses the following accounts in her San Francisco–Los Angeles commuter shuttle service.

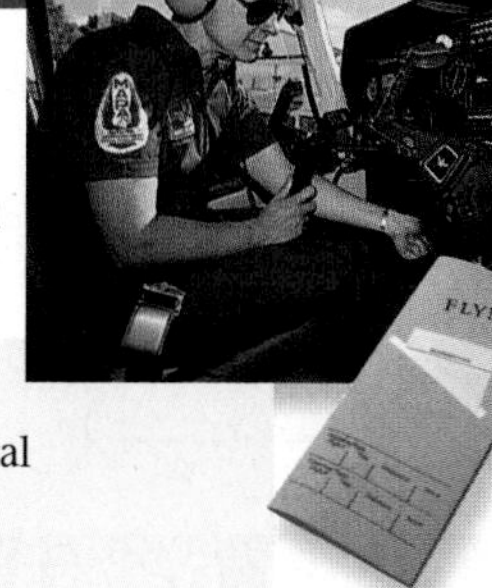

General Ledger

Cash in Bank	Caroline Palmer, Capital
Advertising Expense	Accounts Receivable
Caroline Palmer, Withdrawals	Food Expense
Airplanes	Flying Fees
Fuel and Oil Expense	Accounts Payable
Repairs Expense	

Instructions In the form provided in your working papers, provide the following information for each account.

(1) Classify the account as an asset, liability, owner's equity, revenue, or expense account.
(2) Indicate whether the increase side is a debit or a credit.
(3) Indicate whether the decrease side is a debit or a credit.
(4) Indicate whether the account has a normal debit balance or a normal credit balance. The first account is completed as an example.

Account Name	Account Classification	Increase Side	Decrease Side	Normal Balance
Cash in Bank	Asset	Debit	Credit	Debit

3 ASSESS

Thinking Critically (Answers)

1. Capital. Revenue represents increases to capital from selling goods or services.
2. Expenses and withdrawals decrease capital and represent the left, or debit, side of the capital account.

Communicating Accounting (Answers)

Answers will vary. Students should mention that additional revenue for the business means more operating capital and greater equity in the business.

Problem 5–1 (Answers)

Cash in Bank—asset, dr., cr., dr.
Accts. Rec.—asset, dr., cr., dr.
Airplanes—asset, dr., cr., dr.
Accts. Pay.—liability, cr., dr., cr.
Caroline Palmer, Capital—owner's equity, cr., dr., cr.
Caroline Palmer, Withdrawals—owner's equity, dr., cr., dr.
Flying Fees—revenue, cr., dr., cr.
Adv. Exp.—expense, dr., cr., dr.
Food Exp.—expense, dr., cr., dr.
Fuel & Oil Exp.—expense, dr., cr., dr.
Repairs Exp.—expense, dr., cr., dr.

Chapter Reviews and Working Papers Refer students to the Chapter 5 workbook pages to answer *Check Your Understanding* activities.

4 CLOSE

Section Wrap-Up

Demonstrate: Have students demonstrate their understanding of rules of debit and credit by drawing T accounts for capital, revenue, expenses, and withdrawals and identifying how each is increased and decreased and its normal balance. L1

RETEACHING SECTION 1

Understanding Temporary Accounts Use an analogy to help students understand the difference between permanent and temporary accounts. For example, relate temporary accounts to students' lockers, which are used only for a period of time to store books and other items. Likewise, temporary accounts are used only for an accounting period to "store" transactions involving revenue, expenses, and withdrawals. At the end of the period (semester), temporary account balances (books) are moved to capital (home) so that the temporary accounts (lockers) can be used during the next period (semester) for new transactions (by new students).

CHAPTER 5
SECTION 2, PAGES 104–109

1 FOCUS

Introducing the Section

In this section, students will use the rules of debit and credit they've just learned to analyze transactions involving temporary capital accounts. Students will again use the business transaction model for their analyses.

Section Concept

- How to analyze transactions that affect revenue, expense, and withdrawals accounts.

Visual Learning

Section 2 Focus

Use **Transparency 5-6** to introduce section concepts.

BELL RINGER

Conceptualize: Have students describe a student-run business, such as a weekend car wash or a lawn-care business. As a group, have them decide the purpose of the business and account titles they would use. L1

Visual Learning

Business Transaction 8

Use **Transparency 5-7** of this business transaction analysis to guide students through applying the rules of debit and credit to analyzing and recording revenue earned by the business.

Business Transactions 8, 9, and 10

Use **Transparencies 5-7, 5-8,** and **5-9** and have students analyze the effects using first the capital account only and then the temporary capital accounts.

SECTION 2

Applying the Rules of Debit and Credit to Revenue, Expense, and Owner's Equity Transactions

***What* You'll Learn**

- How to analyze transactions that affect revenue, expense, and withdrawals accounts.

***Why* It's Important**

You need to analyze revenue, expense, and owner's withdrawal transactions to record them correctly.

KEY TERMS

revenue recognition

In Section 1 you learned the rules of debit and credit for revenue, expense, and withdrawals accounts. Learning to apply these rules to typical business transactions is our next task. In the course of a week, a business might receive money, pay rent, or pay utility bills. Let's look at more transactions for Roadrunner Delivery Service.

Analyzing Transactions

In Chapter 4, Roadrunner's transactions dealt with asset and liability accounts and with the owner's equity account, **Maria Sanchez, Capital.** Using the rules of debit and credit, let's analyze several business transactions that affect revenue, expense, and owner's withdrawals accounts. Use the same six-step method you learned in Chapter 4. Refer to Roadrunner's chart of accounts on page 73 to analyze the following transactions.

Business Transaction 8

On October 15, Roadrunner provided delivery services for the Sims Corporation. A check for $1,200 was received in full payment.

ANALYSIS *Identify* *Classify* +/−

1. The accounts **Cash in Bank** and **Delivery Revenue** are affected.
2. **Cash in Bank** is an asset account. **Delivery Revenue** is a revenue account.
3. **Cash in Bank** is increased by $1,200. **Delivery Revenue** is increased by $1,200.

DEBIT-CREDIT RULE

4. Increases in asset accounts are recorded as debits. Debit **Cash in Bank** for $1,200.
5. Increases in revenue accounts are recorded as credits. Credit **Delivery Revenue** for $1,200.

T ACCOUNTS

6.

Cash in Bank		Delivery Revenue	
Debit + 1,200	Credit −	Debit −	Credit + 1,200

RESOURCE MANAGER

Reproducible Masters
- Lesson Plans
- Chapter Reviews and Working Papers (CRWP) TAE
- Demonstration Problems

Transparencies
- Section Focus Transparency
- Teaching Transparencies
- Solution Transparencies

Multimedia
- ExamView CD-ROM
- Electronic Learning Center CD-ROM
- Interactive Lesson Planner CD-ROM
- Electronic Field Trips in Accounting

Business Transaction 9

On October 16, Roadrunner mailed Check 103 for $700 to pay the month's rent.

ANALYSIS	*Identify*	1. The accounts **Rent Expense** and **Cash in Bank** are affected.
	Classify	2. **Rent Expense** is an expense account. **Cash in Bank** is an asset account.
	+/−	3. **Rent Expense** is increased by $700. **Cash in Bank** is decreased by $700.
DEBIT-CREDIT RULE		4. Increases in expense accounts are recorded as debits. Debit **Rent Expense** for $700. 5. Decreases in asset accounts are recorded as credits. Credit **Cash in Bank** for $700.
T ACCOUNTS		6.

Rent Expense		Cash in Bank	
Debit	Credit	Debit	Credit
+	−	+	−
700			700

Business Transaction 10

On October 18, Beacon Advertising prepared an advertisement for Roadrunner. Roadrunner will pay Beacon's $75 fee later.

ANALYSIS	*Identify*	1. The accounts **Advertising Expense** and **Accounts Payable—Beacon Advertising** are affected.
	Classify	2. **Advertising Expense** is an expense account. **Accounts Payable—Beacon Advertising** is a liability account.
	+/−	3. **Advertising Expense** is increased by $75. **Accounts Payable—Beacon Advertising** is increased by $75.
DEBIT-CREDIT RULE		4. Increases in expense accounts are recorded as debits. Debit **Advertising Expense** for $75. 5. Increases in liability accounts are recorded as credits. Credit **Accounts Payable—Beacon Advertising** for $75.
T ACCOUNTS		6.

Advertising Expense		Accounts Payable—Beacon Advertising	
Debit	Credit	Debit	Credit
+	−	−	+
75			75

MEETING SPECIAL NEEDS

Students with Orthopaedic Impairments Never assume that students with orthopaedic impairments can't do something, and make sure that they have the opportunity to participate fully in class. They must have access to the classroom. A barrier can be a stair, a curb, a narrow walkway, a heavy door, or an elevator door that does not allow time for a wheelchair to exit. Classroom tables need at least 27 ½ inches of clearance for a wheelchair to pull up under them.

2 TEACH

GUIDED PRACTICE

Reading Accounting

- Have students draw and complete their own T accounts as they analyze business transactions. Doing the actual analysis will help them learn the rules of debit and credit. L1
- Invite a local businessperson who is fluent in a language native to your students to speak about conducting business in other languages. ELL

Concept Development: Analyzing Transactions

Discussion: Relate the new learning in this chapter to the owner's equity transactions in Chapter 3. In that chapter students used the capital account to summarize transactions for revenue, expenses, and withdrawals.

Analyze transactions 8, 9, and 10 from Chapter 3. First draw a T account on the chalkboard only for the capital account and have students give you the amounts to enter for each transaction (place a balance of $25,400 in the capital account). Then draw T accounts for revenue, expenses, and withdrawals and have students tell you what to record in each account. Show students that if you add the balance in the revenue account to the original balance for capital and subtract the balances for expenses and withdrawals, the ending capital balance is the same as when the three transactions were recorded in the capital account. L1

Critical Thinking: Have students review transactions 9–14 in this chapter to identify the various accounting functions involved with a proprietorship. What important transaction is not shown here? (investment by owner) L2

CHAPTER 5
SECTION 2, PAGES 104–109

2 TEACH (Cont'd.)

Visual Learning

Business Transaction 11

Use the **Transparency 5-10** of this transaction analysis to help students determine how to record revenue amounts earned by the business. Discuss revenue's effect on business assets and on the owner's equity in the business.

Business Transaction 12

Use **Transparency 5-11** to demonstrate how to record an expense using a temporary capital account. Discuss the effects of an expense on the business and how tracking totals for different types of expenses (using a temporary capital account for each type) helps the business owner monitor total operating costs and make better spending decisions.

Demonstration Problem Step-by-Step Practice

Use demonstration problem 5-2 to have students analyze the entry for a revenue transaction.

Business Transaction 11

On October 20, Roadrunner billed City News $1,450 for delivery services.

ANALYSIS

Identify 1. The accounts **Accounts Receivable—City News** and **Delivery Revenue** are affected.

Classify 2. **Accounts Receivable—City News** is an asset account. **Delivery Revenue** is a revenue account.

+/− 3. **Accounts Receivable—City News** is increased by $1,450. **Delivery Revenue** is increased by $1,450.

DEBIT-CREDIT RULE

4. Increases in asset accounts are recorded as debits. Debit **Accounts Receivable—City News** for $1,450.
5. Increases in revenue accounts are recorded as credits. Credit **Delivery Revenue** for $1,450.

T ACCOUNTS

6.

Accounts Receivable—City News	
Debit + 1,450	Credit −

Delivery Revenue	
Debit −	Credit + 1,450

In Transaction 11 Roadrunner recorded revenue for services provided, even though the money had not been collected. Following the GAAP principle of **revenue recognition**, revenue should be recognized on the date earned, even if cash has not been received.

Business Transaction 12

On October 28, Roadrunner paid a $125 telephone bill with Check 104.

ANALYSIS

Identify 1. The accounts **Utilities Expense** and **Cash in Bank** are affected.

Classify 2. **Utilities Expense** is an expense account. **Cash in Bank** is an asset account.

+/− 3. **Utilities Expense** is increased by $125. **Cash in Bank** is decreased by $125.

DEBIT-CREDIT RULE

4. Increases in expense accounts are recorded as debits. Debit **Utilities Expense** for $125.
5. Decreases in asset accounts are recorded as credits. Credit **Cash in Bank** for $125.

T ACCOUNTS

6.

Utilities Expense	
Debit + 125	Credit −

Cash in Bank	
Debit +	Credit − 125

ADDRESSING MULTIPLE LEARNING STYLES

Intrapersonal Learner Have students research the background of a business they want to learn more about—a fast-food restaurant chain, a manufacturer of sports equipment or clothing, or a local business. Students should focus on the history of the business—when it was first established, the original owners, and the established form of business (proprietorship, partnership, or corporation). They can gather information through books, magazines, videos, the Internet, or personal interviews. Ask students to prepare a written report.

Business Transaction 13

On October 29, Roadrunner wrote Check 105 for $600 to have the office repainted.

ANALYSIS

Identify 1. The accounts **Maintenance Expense** and **Cash in Bank** are affected.

Classify 2. **Maintenance Expense** is an expense account. **Cash in Bank** is an asset account.

+/− 3. **Maintenance Expense** is increased by $600. **Cash in Bank** is decreased by $600.

DEBIT-CREDIT RULE

4. Increases in expense accounts are recorded as debits. Debit **Maintenance Expense** for $600.
5. Decreases in asset accounts are recorded as credits. Credit **Cash in Bank** for $600.

T ACCOUNTS

6.

Maintenance Expense		Cash in Bank	
Debit +	Credit −	Debit +	Credit −
600			600

Business Transaction 14

On October 31, Maria Sanchez wrote Check 106 to withdraw $500 cash for personal use.

ANALYSIS

Identify 1. The accounts **Maria Sanchez, Withdrawals** and **Cash in Bank** are affected.

Classify 2. **Maria Sanchez, Withdrawals** is an owner's equity account. **Cash in Bank** is an asset account.

+/− 3. **Maria Sanchez, Withdrawals** is increased by $500. **Cash in Bank** is decreased by $500.

DEBIT-CREDIT RULE

4. Increases in the owner's withdrawals account are recorded as debits. Debit **Maria Sanchez, Withdrawals** for $500.
5. Decreases in assets are recorded as credits. Credit **Cash in Bank** for $500.

T ACCOUNTS

6.

Maria Sanchez, Withdrawals		Cash in Bank	
Debit +	Credit −	Debit +	Credit −
500			500

2 TEACH (Cont'd.)

Visual Learning

Business Transaction 13

Cover the right (shaded) side of **Transparency 5–12** and have students give you the answers to each step in the analysis process.

Business Transaction 14

Again, cover the right side of **Transparency 5–13** and have students analyze the transaction. After the analysis, ask students how the transaction affects the owner's capital account and the accounting equation.

Teaching Tip

To reinforce students' analysis skills, write transactions 13 and 14 on the chalkboard and have students tell you which are the key words that tell what has happened in each transaction. Underline the key words students mention, then ask the class whether they all agree. Discuss any differences of opinion.

Demonstration Problem Step-by-Step Practice

Use demonstration problem 5–3 to give students practice in analyzing an expense transaction.

HOME AND COMMUNITY CONNECTIONS ACTIVITY

Accounting Skills On the Job Ask students to interview an accounting clerk, office manager, or bookkeeper about "real world" accounting. For example, have them talk with a financial professional who is responsible for analyzing financial transactions. What is the most difficult part of their job? What skills did they learn in school that are applicable to their current job duties? What skills did they learn on the job? What advice would they give to someone starting out in this business? Ask students to share their findings with the class and then compare similarities and differences between the different job responsibilities.

2 TEACH (Cont'd.)

Concept Development: Testing for the Equality of Debits and Credits

Discussion: Emphasize that total debits must equal total credits after all transactions have been recorded. Testing for the equality of debits and credits is one way to find out whether errors were made in recording the transactions.

Testing for the equality of debits and credits sets the stage for introducing the trial balance in Chapter 7. You may want to go ahead and introduce the trial balance here. L1

Critical Thinking: Tell students that total debits equal total credits, but an error has been made in recording the transactions. What type of error might have occurred that would not affect the total debit or credit amount? (Possible errors are an expense recorded in the wrong expense account or an owner's investment recorded as revenue.) L3

Teaching Tip

Point out the advantages of the double-entry system of accounting as a check on accuracy. Compare this system to keeping a balance in a checkbook where amounts are entered only once and errors are harder to find.

ACCOUNTING TIPS

Debits and Credits

Revenue represents the *right* side of the capital account. The *right* (credit) side of the revenue account is, therefore, the side used to increase that account. Expenses and withdrawals represent the *left* side of the capital account. The *left* (debit) side of these accounts is then the side used to increase the accounts.

Key Points

Owner's Withdrawals Account

Increases in the owner's withdrawals account are recorded as debits.

CONNECT TO . . . TECHNOLOGY

Popular Web sites, such as the IRS site, often indicate which Web browsers provide the best display. If your computer uses a different browser, or an earlier edition of a recommended browser, the Web site may not load correctly. You will need to upgrade your browser to the current edition.

Testing for the Equality of Debits and Credits

In a double-entry accounting system, correct analysis and recording of business transactions should result in total debits being equal to total credits. Testing for the equality of debits and credits is one way of finding out whether you have made any errors in recording transaction amounts. To test for the equality of debits and credits, follow these steps:

Step 1. Make a list of the account titles used by the business.
Step 2. To the right of each account title, list the balance of the account. Use two columns, one for debit balances and the other for credit balances.
Step 3. Add the amounts in each column.

If you have recorded all the amounts correctly, the total of the debit column will equal the total of the credit column. The test for equality of debits and credits for the transactions in Chapters 4 and 5 shows that total debits are equal to total credits, so the ledger is in balance.

ACCOUNT NAME		DEBIT BALANCES	CREDIT BALANCES
101	Cash in Bank	$ 21,125	
105	Accounts Receivable—City News	1,450	
110	Accounts Receivable—Green Company		
115	Computer Equipment	3,000	
120	Office Equipment	200	
125	Delivery Equipment	12,000	
201	Accounts Payable—Beacon Advertising		$ 75
205	Accounts Payable—North Shore Auto		11,650
301	Maria Sanchez, Capital		25,400
302	Maria Sanchez, Withdrawals	500	
303	Income Summary		
401	Delivery Revenue		2,650
501	Advertising Expense	75	
505	Maintenance Expense	600	
510	Rent Expense	700	
515	Utilities Expense	125	
		$ 39,775	$ 39,775

INTERDISCIPLINARY CONNECTIONS ACTIVITY

Technology Have students experiment with designing their own Web site. They can use a word processing or desktop publishing software program to draft their ideas. If a computer is not available, have them sketch out their ideas on paper. Also, have them visit at least three different Web sites to see how these pages are displayed and to identify the type of information illustrated.

Check Your Understanding

Now that you have studied this section, complete the following questions and problem.

Thinking Critically

1. What is the normal balance of a withdrawals account?
2. What other temporary account carries a normal balance on the same side as the normal balance for a withdrawals account?
3. The two accounts referred to above temporarily represent a permanent account. What is the name of the permanent account?

Analyzing Accounting

Your accounting clerk has just handed you the bar chart shown at right reflecting the revenue and expense for the first quarter. What month was the most revenue? What month had the highest expense? Overall, did the business have a profit or loss?

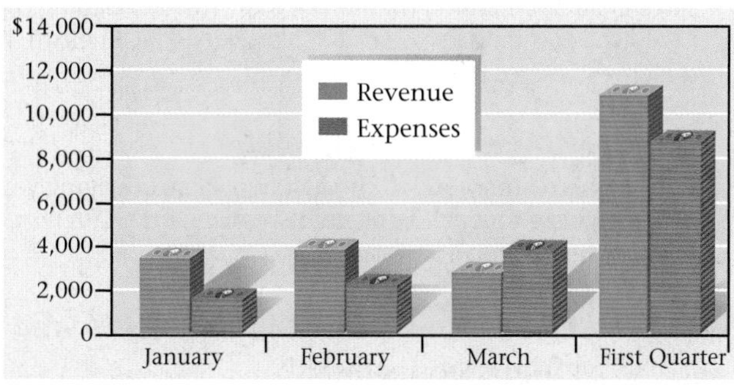

Problem 5-2 Identifying Accounts Affected by Transactions

John Albers uses the following accounts in his business.

General Ledger

Cash in Bank	John Albers, Capital	Advertising Expense
Accounts Receivable	John Albers, Withdrawals	Rent Expense
Office Equipment	Service Fees	Utilities Expense
Accounts Payable		

Instructions In your working papers:

(1) Identify the two accounts affected by each of the following transactions.

(2) Indicate whether each account is debited or credited.

Date	Transactions
July 1	1. Issued Check 543 to pay the electric bill for the month.
3	2. Billed a customer for services provided on account.
10	3. John Albers took cash from the business for his personal use.
17	4. Issued Check 544 to pay for an advertisement.

3 ASSESS

Thinking Critically (Answers)

1. Debit balance.
2. Expense accounts carry a debit balance.
3. Both withdrawals accounts and expense accounts act as temporary substitutes for the debit side of the account for owner's equity/capital.

Analyzing Accounting (Answer)

The month with the most revenue was February. The highest expense was incurred in March. The business is making a profit.

Problem 5-2 (Answers)

1. Dr. Utilities Expense;
   Cr. Cash in Bank
2. Dr. Accounts Receivable;
   Cr. Service Fees
3. Dr. John Albers, Withdrawals;
   Cr. Cash in Bank
4. Dr. Advertising Expense;
   Cr. Cash in Bank

Chapter Reviews and Working Papers Refer students to the Chapter 5 workbook pages to answer *Check Your Understanding* activities.

4 CLOSE

Section Wrap-Up

Demonstrate: Give students an accounting equation (for example, $50,500 = $10,150 + $40,350, where assets = $50,500, liabilities = $10,150, and owner's equity = $40,350). Provide one or more transactions that involve one permanent account and one temporary account (for example, "Write a check for $200 to pay the utility bill."). Have students write the transactions in T-account form and rewrite the accounting equation after each transaction. L2

RETEACHING SECTION 2

Testing the Equality of Debits and Credits Testing for the equality of debits and credits can be completed at any time. When the ledger is in balance, you can be sure that there was a corresponding credit for each debit. Unequal totals indicate an error. Point out that errors still could have occurred even with equal totals. Ask students to cite examples of possible errors that could exist. (The wrong amount could be recorded for a transaction; an entire transaction may have been omitted; a transaction could have been recorded twice.)

CHAPTER 5
SECTION 2, PAGES 104–109

SCANS in the Workforce

Foundation Skills Connection

Speaking

In this activity the student is expected to follow oral instructions. Have students work with a partner to practice speaking skills. Have them rehearse introducing themselves during a job interview. They should mention their goals, education, skills, and career interests. Then have each student present introductions to the entire class. L1

Workplace Competencies Connection

Teaching Others

Divide students into five teams. Have each team member share with others how he or she manages time. For example, who uses a daily planner? A check list? A "to-do" list? How does each person keep track of all the homework assignments, projects at work, chores at home, and after-school activities? Have each team share the best technique in managing time, and have a team member teach the rest of the class. Compare at least three different techniques with the entire class. L2

Interpreting and Communicating Information

Using books, periodicals, software, or Internet searches, have students research different résumé styles. Tell them to find a résumé style that fits their education, skills, and background. Have them study several approaches to résumé writing, then create their own. If time allows, hold mock interviews where the students are asked to talk to an interviewer about their résumés. L3

ACCOUNTING CAREERS IN FOCUS

BILL ALBRETS
Chief Accountant, Lockheed Martin Technical Operations

Q: How did you get into accounting?

A: I was a bookkeeper and liked it, but bookkeeping has a limited career growth and pay. There were two paths to business management: the MBA (Masters of Business Administration) and the CPA. The MBA takes two years, and since I had a family and no money, that was out. Getting my CPA involved sitting for the exam. It's a very difficult exam. It took me two tries to pass it.

Q: Is getting a CPA worthwhile?

A: I highly recommend it. The first two years of getting your experience are tough. I didn't enjoy working for a CPA firm, but it has only helped me in my career.

Q: What do you recommend to students who want to go into management?

A: Accounting is a very good path into management. As an internal auditor, you see all the operations of your employer. That's how I got my job here. I came in to do an audit, they liked what they saw, and they gave me a tremendous job offer.

Q: What skills are most important?

A: Excellent communication skills. You don't move ahead with just technical skills. You need to show your ideas to management in a way they'll understand and remember. I teach public speaking classes in community college because I believe so strongly in it.

Tips from . . .

RHI Robert Half International Inc.

Be enthusiastic and be ready to perform first-rate work no matter what you're asked to do. Enthusiasm can help you get a job done faster. You'll have time to take on exciting new challenges.

CAREER FACTS

Nature of the Work: Working with management on planning, guiding and directing staff, and doing accounting functions when necessary.

Training or Education Needed: A bachelor's degree in accounting, and the CPA exam.

Aptitudes, Abilities, and Skills: Accounting, time-management skills, problem-solving skills, communication skills and interpersonal skills.

Salary Range: $70,000 to $150,000 depending on company size and industry.

Career Path: Start as an internal auditor for a variety of firms to learn business, gain experience in lower management (such as project manager), and then move to chief accountant or controller.

Thinking Critically: In what ways would you use public speaking in your career?

ACCOUNTING CAREERS IN FOCUS

Thinking Critically (Answers)

In your career, there will be many public speaking opportunities. For example, you may need to make presentations during staff meetings, or you may need to give a report to upper management. You might even have an opportunity to represent your company and speak to the local community.

ROBERT HALF CORNER

The Job Interview Ask students to list qualities they think employers look for other than ability and willingness to do the job. Compare students' lists with qualities identified by business executives: honesty/integrity (32%); enthusiasm (29%); verbal skills (28%); appearance (3%); sense of humor (3%).

CHAPTER 5 SUMMARY

KEY CONCEPTS

1. The accounts used by a business can be separated into permanent accounts and temporary capital accounts.
2. Asset and liability accounts and the owner's capital account are permanent accounts.
3. Revenue, expense, and withdrawals accounts are temporary capital accounts.
4. Temporary capital accounts start each new accounting period with zero balances.
5. Revenue accounts temporarily represent the credit side of owner's capital.
6. Expense and withdrawals accounts temporarily represent the debit side of owner's capital.
7. Revenue accounts are increased by credits and have normal credit balances.
8. Expense and withdrawals accounts are increased by debits and have normal debit balances.
9. The rules of debit and credit for the permanent accounts—assets, liabilities, and the owner's capital account—are summarized below using T accounts and the basic accounting equation.

ASSETS = LIABILITIES + OWNER'S EQUITY

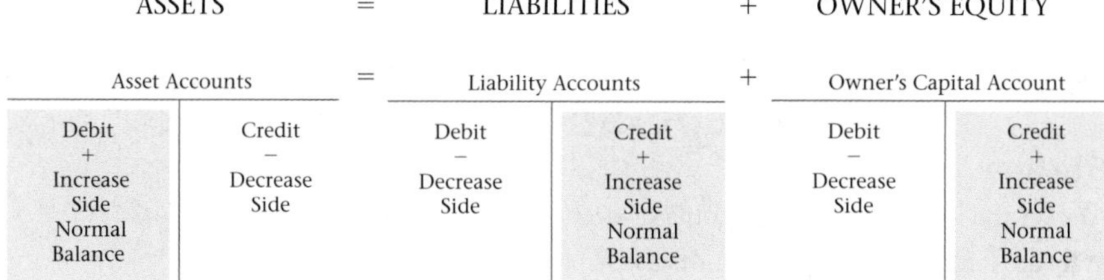

10. The rules of debit and credit for the temporary capital accounts—revenue, expenses, and the owner's withdrawals account—may also be summarized using T accounts.

Temporary Capital Accounts

Withdrawals		Expenses		Revenue	
Debit + Increase Side Normal Balance	Credit – Decrease Side	Debit + Increase Side Normal Balance	Credit – Decrease Side	Debit – Decrease Side	Credit + Increase Side Normal Balance

EXTENDING THE CONTENT

Visiting a Local Business Arrange to have students visit a local business that uses computers to process accounting data. Preferably, find a business that uses computers in several different departments. Have students observe the processing of accounting data in each department. Then have students summarize their observations in a short report. Follow up with a group discussion on what they saw and learned during the visit.

SUMMARY CHAPTER 5

Chapter 5 Quiz

Student ____ Class ____ Instructor ____
Date Assigned ____ Date Completed ____

CHAPTER 5 QUIZ

Transactions That Affect Revenue, Expenses, and Withdrawals

QUESTIONS (True-False)

Directions: In the space provided, indicate whether each statement is true or false.

____ 1. The owner's capital account is increased by debits.
____ 2. Revenue represents the debit side of the owner's capital account.
____ 3. Expenses decrease the balance in the capital account.
____ 4. The rules of debit and credit for expenses are the same as those for withdrawals.
____ 5. Temporary capital accounts are used by a business only once.
____ 6. A withdrawal increases the assets of the business.
____ 7. Revenue accounts have a normal credit balance.
____ 8. The owner's capital account has a normal debit balance.
____ 9. Expenses and withdrawals both have normal debit balances.
____ 10. The owner's equity in the business is increased by revenue and decreased by expenses and withdrawals.

 Chapter Quizzes • 7

QUESTIONS (True-False)

1. The owner's capital account is increased by debits.
2. Revenue represents the debit side of the owner's capital account.
3. Expenses decrease the balance in the capital account.
4. The rules of debit and credit for expenses are the same as those for withdrawals.
5. Temporary capital accounts are used by a business only once.
6. A withdrawal increases the assets of the business.
7. Revenue accounts have a normal credit balance.
8. The owner's capital account has a normal debit balance.
9. Expenses and withdrawals both have normal debit balances.
10. The owner's equity in the business is increased by revenue and decreased by expenses and withdrawals.

ANSWERS

1. False	6. False
2. False	7. True
3. True	8. False
4. True	9. True
5. False	10. True

REVIEW AND ACTIVITIES CHAPTER 5

USING KEY TERMS

See the *Glossary* for the definitions of these terms. Ask for volunteers to give their presentations. Compare examples and help students clarify differences.

Understanding Accounting Concepts and Procedures

(Answers)

1. To record specific revenue and expense information that would be mixed together if all such amounts were recorded in capital.
2. A temporary account is used for one accounting period (withdrawals, fees, advertising). Permanent accounts carry balances from one period to another (Cash in Bank, Capital Revenue).
3. Revenue: increased by credits, decreased by debits. Expense and withdrawals: increased by debits, decreased by credits.
4. (a) credit, (b) debit, (c) debit, (d) debit, (e) credit, (f) credit.
5. Revenue increases owner's capital, which is increased by credits, so revenue represents the credit side.
6. Revenues increase capital.
7. Expenses decrease capital, which is decreased by debits, so expenses represent the debit side.
8. Expenses decrease capital.
9. Expenses are costs of doing business. Withdrawals are owner reductions of cash or other assets. Both reduce owner's equity, are increased by debits, and have normal debit balances.
10. Revenue is earned from business operations; investments are placed in the business by the owner. Both increase owner's equity, are increased by credits, and have normal credit balances.
11. Add all balances using separate columns for debit and credit balances. The totals should be equal.

CHAPTER 5 REVIEW AND ACTIVITIES

USING KEY TERMS

You have been asked to make a presentation to your company's owners. For the owners to understand the difference in the accounts you manage, you must be able to explain the following key terms:

permanent accounts	temporary capital accounts
revenue recognition	

Create three examples that could be used as overhead transparencies. Each example (master) should show a term, a brief definition, and an illustration or example.

Understanding Accounting Concepts and Procedures

Instructions

Answer the following questions on a separate sheet of paper:

1. Why are temporary capital accounts used?
2. What is the difference between a temporary capital account and a permanent account? Give three examples of each type of account.
3. State briefly the rules of debit and credit for increasing and decreasing (a) revenue accounts, (b) expense accounts, (c) withdrawals accounts.
4. List the normal balance side of (a) revenue accounts, (b) expense accounts, (c) withdrawals accounts, (d) asset accounts, (e) liability accounts, (f) the owner's capital account.
5. Why does a revenue account temporarily represent the credit side of the owner's capital account?
6. What effect does a revenue transaction have on owner's capital?
7. Explain why the expense accounts temporarily represent the debit side of the owner's capital account.
8. What effect does an expense transaction have on owner's capital?
9. How is a withdrawal different from an expense? How are they the same?
10. How is an investment different from revenue? How are they the same?
11. How would you test for the equality of debits and credits?

CRITICAL THINKING ACTIVITY

Analyzing Information Jonathan Edwards was concerned that his electric bill for his dry-cleaning company was increasing monthly. To get an overview of the history of his electricity expenses, he decided to review the temporary account Utility Expense. What types of information would Jonathan gather from these temporary accounts? (Jonathan will be able to view a month-by-month total for all utility expenses and be able to compare electricity costs. If the amounts have continually increased, he may have the electric company check his meter for accuracy. Or, he may want to scale back the amount of electricity the business uses.)

Case Study...

Service Business: Web Site Design

Colleen Chapelli owns Web Design Source, a service that creates Web sites for local businesses. While Colleen is an expert with computers and software programming, her business finance expertise is limited. She has hired you as her accountant to organize her business information and suggest business accounts. Here are some of the items Colleen uses in the business:

- Computer
- Printer
- Software
- Desk and chair
- Bookcases
- Computer supplies

Colleen has been advertising in the local newspaper to find new clients. She manages the business from her home and has a separate telephone line for the business.

Thinking Critically:

1. Prepare a chart of accounts for Web Design Source.
2. Explain to Colleen why it is important to collect and organize the financial information resulting from business transactions.

Conducting an Audit with Alex

Instructions Review the T accounts below to verify that the following transactions are reflected properly. On a separate sheet of paper, make any necessary corrections.

1. Received $425 from Marty Prichard for printing services.
2. Provided printing services to Marty Prichard on account, $325.
3. Paid for repairs to the copier, $127.

Cash in Bank		Printing Revenue	
(1) 425 (2) 325	(3)127	(3) 127	(2) 325 (1) 425

interNET CONNECTION

Certified Public Accounting

The American Institute of Certified Public Accountants (AICPA) Web site offers an area for students that presents information on becoming a CPA.

Do This:

1. Locate the Web site for the AICPA. What is the Web site address?
2. Describe the features that exist on the AICPA site.
3. What other organizations might an accounting professional want to join?
4. List three scholarships available for accounting majors.

Workplace Skills

Acquiring and Analyzing Data

To make a decision, whether business or personal, you must be able to acquire and analyze data (information).

On the Job:

You are about to enter your senior year at Highland College, a small liberal arts college of 2,000 students in North Carolina. Eighty percent of the students live in dorms on campus or in apartments within one mile of the college. The student activities center closes at 9:00 P.M. during the school week, and students complain about the lack of a food and beverage service available for late night study sessions. You decide to analyze the market potential of starting a limited food and beverage delivery service.

Thinking Critically:

1. Develop a market survey of 5–10 questions related to the opening of an off-campus food and beverage delivery service.
2. Decide what type of food and beverage you can provide in a delivery service. How much investment would you need to begin? What do you anticipate your customer base to be?

interNET CONNECTION www.glencoe.com

Do This (Answers)

1. www.aicpa.org
2. News for CPAs, AICPA Student Affiliate Program, and other features
3. American Accounting Association, Association of Certified Fraud Examiners, Association of Government Accountants, Institute of Management Accountants, National Society of Public Accountants, and Accountants for the Public Interest.
4. Answers could include a fellowship offered by AAA; awards up to $5,000 offered by AICPA; and scholarships offered by American Society of Women Accountants.

Case Study...

Thinking Critically (Answers)

1. Possible accounts include: Computer Equipment, Utilities Expense, Supplies Expense, Office Furniture, Advertising Expense, and Design Fee Revenue.
2. Students should mention that it is necessary to collect and analyze financial data in order to determine how the business is performing.

Workplace Skills

Thinking Critically (Answers)

1. Students can use word processing or a spreadsheet to develop the survey. Survey questions should be related to students' eating and drinking preferences.
2. Have students write a one-paragraph synopsis of the food and beverage products they will offer in their delivery service. In evaluating the investment, have students look at a week's anticipated sales. Take that amount and multiply by the number of weeks they want to run their business. The customer base will vary, but students might assume 25 percent of the student population trying their service.

Conducting an Audit with Alex

(Answers)

1. The entry is correct.
2. Debit Accounts Receivable—Marty Pritchard, not Cash in Bank.
3. Debit Repairs Expense, not Printing Revenue.

Internet Resources and Activities Handbook

Refer students to the booklet for additional Internet activities.

PEACHTREE CORNER

Chart of Accounts Report
To print a Chart of Accounts report, choose **General Ledger** from the *Reports* menu. Then select the desired report from the Select a Report window.

Reports | Services | Window
Accounts Receivable...
Accounts Payable...
Payroll...
General Ledger...
Financial Statements...
Inventory...

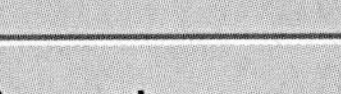

Maintain a Chart of Accounts
Choose the **Chart of Accounts** option in the ***Maintain*** menu to add or edit a general ledger account. Or, click the **General Ledger** navigation aid at the bottom of the screen and choose **Chart of Accounts**. The Navigation Aid provides an easy (visual) alternative for your students to select options.

Maintain | Tasks | Analysis
Customers/Prospects...
Vendors...
Employees/Sales Reps...
Chart of Accounts...
Inventory Items...
Item Prices...
Job Costs
Company Information...

The Chart of Accounts

Making the Transition from a Manual to a Computerized System

Task	Perform Accounting Procedures Using Manual Methods	Perform Accounting Procedures Using Automated Methods
Setting up the accounts in the general ledger	• Accounts are set up in the general ledger using general ledger account forms. • Accounts can be set up with or without beginning balances.	• Accounts are set up using defined account numbers and account types. • Accounts can be set up with or without beginning balances. • Peachtree offers hundreds of sample companies from which you can copy the chart of accounts instead of creating each account individually.

Chart of Accounts

Assets	Owner's Equity
Cash in Bank	Maria Sanchez, Capital
Accounts Receivable	Maria Sanchez, Withdrawals
Computer Equipment	
Office Equipment	**Revenue**
Delivery Equipment	Delivery Revenue
Liabilities	**Expenses**
Accounts Payable	Advertising Expense
	Maintenance Expense
	Rent Expense

Setting Up General Ledger Accounts

Peachtree Question	Description
How do I create general ledger accounts in Peachtree?	1. From the ***Maintain*** menu, select **Chart of Accounts.** 2. Enter the account number in the Account ID box. 3. Enter the account name in the Description box. 4. From the Account Type drop-down list, select the account type from options like accounts payable, accounts receivable, equity, expenses, income, and others.
What does the software do "behind the scenes"?	• General ledger accounts are opened for each account and stored in the chart of accounts. • These accounts will be accessible from a drop-down list for any transaction you wish to enter in the future. • Assigning each account an account type defines for the software where each account will be reported when you begin to print financial statements.

For detailed instructions: See the **Peachtree User Guide** in your Glencoe Working Papers.

Peachtree® Answers to Frequently Asked Questions

Q: How do you edit a general ledger account name or account type?
A: Go to **Chart of Accounts** in ***Maintain*** menu. Enter the general ledger account number, press *Enter*. Use *Description* and *Account Type* to change the account title and type.
For additional information, refer to your *Glencoe Peachtree Accounting User Guide.*

APPLICATION OPTIONS

Problem 5-3 Identifying Increases and Decreases in Accounts

Ronald Hicks uses the following accounts in his business, Wilderness Rentals.

General Ledger

101	Cash in Bank	301	Ronald Hicks, Capital
105	Accounts Receivable—Helen Katz	305	Ronald Hicks, Withdrawals
120	Office Equipment	401	Equipment Rental Revenue
125	Camping Equipment	505	Maintenance Expense
		525	Utilities Expense

Instructions Analyze each of the following transactions using the format shown in the example below. Record your answers in your working papers.

a. Explain the debit.
b. Explain the credit.

Example:
On Jan. 2, Ronald Hicks paid the bill for office cleaning, $100.

a. The expense account **505 Maintenance Expense** is increased. Increases in expenses are recorded as debits.
b. The asset account **101 Cash in Bank** is decreased. Decreases in assets are recorded as credits.

Date		Transactions
Jan.	3	1. Ronald Hicks withdrew $500 from his business for his own use, Check 225.
	8	2. The business received $1,200 cash in rental fees from various customers.
	12	3. The business paid a telephone bill of $85, Check 226.

Analyze: By what amount did the **Cash in Bank** balance change?

Complete chapter problems one of three ways:

1 **Manual** Glencoe Working Papers

or

2 **Peachtree Complete Accounting** Software

or

3 **Spreadsheet** Templates (Problem 5-8)

Peachtree®

SMART GUIDE

Step-by-Step Instructions: Problem 5-3

1. Select the problem set for Wilderness Rentals (Prob. 5-3).
2. Rename the company and set the system date.
3. Print a Chart of Accounts using the **General Ledger** option in the ***Reports*** menu.
4. Review the Chart of Accounts.
5. End the session.

Problem 5-4 Using T Accounts to Analyze Transactions

Regina Delgado, the owner of Hot Suds Car Wash, uses the following accounts:

Continued

Problem 5-3 (Answers) Identifying Increases and Decreases in Accounts

1a. The owner's equity account Ronald Hicks, Withdrawals is increased. Increases in withdrawals are recorded as debits.
b. The asset account Cash in Bank is decreased. Decreases in assets are recorded as credits.

2a. The asset account Cash in Bank is increased. Increases in assets are recorded as debits.
b. The revenue account Equipment Rental Revenue is increased. Increases in revenue are recorded as credits.

3a. The expense account Utilities Expense is increased. Increases in expenses are recorded as debits.
b. The asset account Cash in Bank is decreased. Decreases in assets are recorded as credits.

Analyze: Cash in Bank increased overall by $615.

SOFTWARE NOTES

Teachers can find detailed instructions for:

- **Peachtree Software**, in the *Glencoe Workbook* (CRWP)
- **Spreadsheets Templates**, in the *Glencoe Workbook* (CRWP)

Problem 5-4 (Answers)
Using T Accounts to Analyze Transactions

1. Dr. Cash in Bank: $1,675;
   Cr. Wash Revenue: $1,675
2. Dr. Rent Expense: $450;
   Cr. Cash in Bank: $450
3. Dr. Regina Delgado, Withdrawals: $250;
   Cr. Cash in Bank: $250
4. Dr. Maintenance Expense: $245;
   Cr. Accts. Pay.—O'Brian's Office Supply: $245

Analyze: transactions two and four

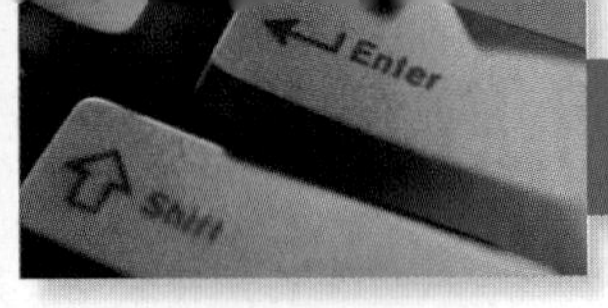

Peachtree®

SMART GUIDE

Step-by-Step Instructions: Problem 5-4

1. Select the problem set for Hot Suds Car Wash (Prob. 5-4).
2. Rename the company and set the system date.
3. Print a Chart of Accounts using the **General Ledger** option in the ***Reports*** menu.
4. Review the Chart of Accounts.
5. End the session.

TIP: You will learn how to enter transactions into the accounts in the next chapter.

General Ledger

101 Cash in Bank	401 Wash Revenue
125 Office Equipment	510 Maintenance Expense
205 Accounts Payable—O'Brian's Office Supply	520 Rent Expense
301 Regina Delgado, Capital	
305 Regina Delgado, Withdrawals	

Instructions In your working papers:
(1) Determine which accounts are affected for each transaction.
(2) Prepare T accounts for the accounts affected.
(3) Enter the amount of the debit and the amount of the credit in the T accounts.

Date	Transactions
Jan. 7	**1.** Received a check for $1,675 for car wash services.
12	**2.** Paid the monthly rent of $450 by writing Check 212.
15	**3.** Regina Delgado withdrew $250 for her personal use, Check 213.
29	**4.** Had the computer repaired at O'Brian's Office Supply for $245 and was given until next month to pay.

Analyze: Which transactions affect expense accounts?

Peachtree®

SMART GUIDE

Step-by-Step Instructions: Problem 5-5

1. Select the problem set for Kits & Pups Grooming (Prob. 5-5).
2. Rename the company and set the system date.
3. Add new general ledger accounts using the **Chart of Accounts** option in the ***Maintain*** menu.
4. Enter beginning balances using the **Chart of Accounts** option in the ***Maintain*** menu.
5. Print a Chart of Accounts using the **General Ledger** option in the ***Reports*** menu.
6. Proof your work.
7. End the session.

TIP: When a report list appears, double-click a report title to go directly to that report.

Problem 5-5 Analyzing Transactions into Debit and Credit Parts

Abe Shultz, owner of Kits & Pups Grooming, uses the following accounts to record transactions for the month.

General Ledger

101 Cash in Bank	401 Boarding Revenue
105 Accounts Receivable—Juan Alvarez	405 Grooming Revenue
140 Grooming Equipment	501 Advertising Expense
205 Accounts Payable—Dogs & Cats Inc.	505 Equipment Repair Expense
301 Abe Shultz, Capital	510 Maintenance Expense
305 Abe Shultz, Withdrawals	520 Rent Expense
	530 Utilities Expense

Instructions For each transaction:
(1) Prepare a T account for each account listed.
(2) Enter a balance of $15,000 in the **Cash in Bank** account; also enter a balance of $15,000 in the **Abe Shultz, Capital** account.
(3) Analyze and record each of the following business transactions, using the appropriate T accounts. Identify each transaction by number.

ASSESSMENT RESOURCES

Choose assessment strategies from the following pages to evaluate your students' progress.

Student Edition
Check Your Understanding, pp. 103, 109
Chapter 5 Problems, pp. 89–93

Assessment and Evaluation Masters
Chapter 5 Study Plan, *Glencoe Workbook* (CRWP)
Chapter 5 Self-Test, *Glencoe Workbook* (CRWP)
Chapter 5 Test, *Chapter Tests* Booklet
Chapter 5 Activity, *School-to-Work Handbook*
Chapter 5 **Exam***View*

Teacher Wraparound Edition
Reteaching Sections 1–2, pp. 103, 109
Chapter 5 Quiz, p. 111

(4) After all the business transactions have been recorded, write the word "Balance" on the normal balance side of each account.
(5) Compute and record the balance for each account.

Date	Transactions
Jan. 1	1. Purchased grooming equipment for $12,700, Check 283.
10	2. Wrote Check 284 for advertising, $125.
12	3. Received $1,850 cash for dog boarding services.
15	4. Paid $150 for equipment repair, Check 285.
17	5. Purchased a dog cage on account from Dogs & Cats Inc. for $75.
20	6. Abe Shultz withdrew $150 for personal use, Check 286.
22	7. Billed Juan Alvarez for $775 covering grooming services for all of the dogs boarded at the kennels he owns. Payment will be received later.
23	8. Paid the first two weeks' rent by writing Check 287 for $325.
25	9. Paid the electric bill at a cost of $115, Check 288.

Analyze: If you were asked to prepare a check on January 30 for another expense, what check number would you use?

Problem 5-6 Analyzing Transactions into Debit and Credit Parts

Juanita Ortega operates Outback Guide Service. She uses the following accounts to record and summarize her business transactions.

General Ledger

101	Cash in Bank	301	Juanita Ortega, Capital
105	Accounts Receivable—Mary Johnson	302	Juanita Ortega, Withdrawals
150	Rafting Equipment	401	Guide Service Revenue
205	Accounts Payable—Peak Equipment Inc.	505	Maintenance Expense
		515	Rent Expense
		520	Utilities Expense

Instructions For each transaction:
(1) Prepare a T account for each account the business uses.
(2) Analyze and record each of the following transactions using the appropriate T accounts. Identify each transaction by number.

Continued 

Peachtree®

SMART GUIDE

Step-by-Step Instructions: Problem 5-6

1. Select the problem set for Outback Guide Service (Prob. 5–6).
2. Rename the company and set the system date.
3. Add new general ledger accounts using the **Chart of Accounts** option in the ***Maintain*** menu.
4. Print a Chart of Accounts using the **General Ledger** option in the ***Reports*** menu.
5. Proof your work using the Chart of Accounts report.
6. End the session.

TIP: You can use General Ledger Navigation Aid to access the Maintain Chart of Accounts window.

Problem 5-5 (Answers) Analyzing Transactions into Debit and Credit Parts

Ending debit balances:
Cash in Bank $3,285
Accts. Rec.—Juan Alvarez $775
Grooming Equipment $12,775
Abe Schultz, Withdrawals $150
Advertising Expense $125
Equipment Repair Expense $150
Rent Expense $325
Maintenance Expense $0
Utilities Expense $115

Ending credit balances:
Accts. Pay.—Dogs & Cats Inc. $75
Abe Schultz, Capital $15,000
Boarding Revenue $1,850
Grooming Revenue $775

Analyze: Check number 289

MAKING CONNECTIONS TO DAILY LIFE

Freelance Business Options Tell students this scenario: "Marissa Lopez needed extra money for college so she decided to turn her computer skills into a small profit. She decided to offer a campus service for manuscript preparation (reports, essays, and theses). She plans to use savings (capital) to buy a computer, software, desk, stationery, printing supplies, and a telephone." How much money would Marissa need to start this business? What are the benefits of this type of business? the disadvantages? (Answers will vary. Marissa might need a minimum of $3,000; on-campus availability would be an incentive for students; Maria may have to work odd hours to meet deadlines.)

Problem 5-6 (Answers) Analyzing Transactions into Debit and Credit Parts

Ending debit balances:
Cash in Bank $10,032
Accts. Rec.—Mary Johnson $750
Rafting Equipment $3,750
Juanita Ortega, Withdrawals $250
Maintenance Expense $123
Rent Expense $225
Utilities Expense $95
Total $15,225

Ending credit balances:
Accts. Pay.—Peak Equipment Inc. $2,000
Juanita Ortega, Capital $12,000
Guide Service Revenue $1,225
Total $15,225

Analyze: $1,225

(3) After recording all transactions, compute and record the account balance on the normal balance side of each T account.
(4) Test for the equality of debits and credits.

Date	Transactions
Jan. 2	1. Juanita Ortega invested $12,000 cash in her business.
7	2. Purchased two new whitewater rafts on account for $3,750 from Peak Equipment Inc.
10	3. Billed, but did not collect, $750 for guide services provided to Mary Johnson.
12	4. Repaired a raft at a cost of $123, Check 411.
14	5. Wrote Check 412 to pay the electric bill of $95.
17	6. Received $225 for guide service fees.
21	7. Paid the $225 rent for the month, Check 413.
24	8. Paid $1,750 toward the rafts bought on account, Check 414.
27	9. Juanita Ortega withdrew $250 cash for personal use, Check 415.
29	10. Received guide service fees of $250.

Analyze: How much revenue was earned?

Peachtree®
SMART GUIDE

Step-by-Step Instructions: Problem 5-7
1. Select the problem set for Showbiz Video (Prob. 5-7).
2. Rename the company and set the system date.
3. Add a new record for each of the general ledger accounts.
4. Print a Chart of Accounts.
5. Proof your work.
6. End the session.

TIP: Peachtree requires that you group accounts by type: asset, liability, equity, income, and expense.

Problem 5-7 Analyzing Transactions

Greg Failla owns Showbiz Video. He uses the following accounts to record business transactions.

General Ledger

101	Cash in Bank	205	Accounts Payable—Computer Horizons
105	Accounts Receivable—Gabriel Cohen	207	Accounts Payable—New Media Suppliers
110	Accounts Receivable—James Coletti	301	Greg Failla, Capital
140	Computer Equipment	305	Greg Failla, Withdrawals
145	Video Tapes	401	Video Rental Revenue
		405	VCR Rental Revenue
		505	Equipment Repair Expense
		520	Rent Expense
		530	Utilities Expense

Instructions For each transaction:
(1) Prepare a T account for each account listed above.
(2) Analyze and record each of the following transactions using the appropriate T accounts. Identify each transaction by number.
(3) After recording all transactions, compute a balance for each account.
(4) Test for the equality of debits and credits.

ACCOUNTING ISSUES

Going Global Requirements for listing securities on a foreign stock exchange often vary from country to country. Companies that want to sell their securities on a foreign exchange must comply with several rules and regulations. For example, financial statements must contain information equivalent to that required in the foreign accounting standards. The International Organization of Securities (IOSCO) and the International Accounting Standards Board (IASB) are working together to create a comprehensive set of international standards for cross-border listings.

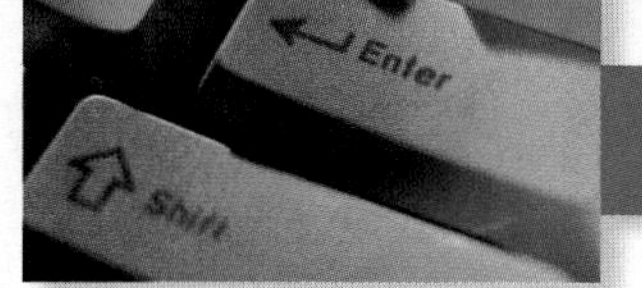

Date		Transactions
Jan.	1	1. Greg Failla invested $17,500 cash in Showbiz Video.
	3	2. Purchased computer equipment on account from Computer Horizons for $2,400.
	8	3. Purchased on account videos from New Media Suppliers for $375.
	10	4. Paid monthly rent of $750, Check 1183.
	13	5. Wrote Check 1184 to pay for new videos, $265.
	14	6. Sent a bill for $67 to Gabriel Cohen for a VCR rental.
	16	7. Deposited the receipts from video rentals, $233.
	19	8. Paid the gas and electric bill of $125, Check 1185.
	21	9. Sent Check 1186 for $375 to New Media Suppliers as payment on account.
	22	10. Greg Failla withdrew $150 for his personal use, Check 1187.
	25	11. Paid $45 for VCR repair, Check 1188.
	30	12. Deposited VCR rental receipts of $264 in the bank.

Analyze: What liabilities does Showbiz have after these transactions?

Problem 5–8 Completing the Accounting Equation

With the addition of temporary capital accounts, the basic accounting equation can be expanded as follows:

Assets = Liabilities + Owner's Equity − Withdrawals + Revenue − Expenses

Instructions Using the expanded equation, determine the missing amounts for the accounting equations shown below. Use the form in your working papers. The first equation is completed as an example.

	Assets	=	Liabilities	+	Owner's Equity	−	Withdrawals	+	Revenue	−	Expenses
1.	$64,400		$8,200		$56,300		$ 500		$10,000		$ 9,600
2.	$22,150		525		18,800		1,200		12,100		?
3.	17,500		75		21,650		?		4,115		3,250
4.	49,450		?		47,840		1,500		20,300		17,610
5.	21,900		1,150		20,005		950		?		16,570
6.	72,640		2,790		?		10,750		67,908		39,749
7.	?		1,988		41,194		6,196		52,210		42,597
8.	?		3,840		61,774		?		40,163		21,637
	(Expenses plus withdrawals equal $27,749.)										
9.	64,070		?		49,102		4,875		53,166		?
	(Total owner's equity after adding revenue and subtracting expenses and withdrawals is $50,643.)										

Analyze: Increases in temporary capital accounts result in an increase or a decrease in owner's equity?

SPREADSHEET SMART GUIDE

Step-by-Step Instructions: Problem 5–8

1. Select the spreadsheet template for Problem 5–8.
2. Enter your name and the date in the spaces provided on the template.
3. Complete the spreadsheet using the instructions in your working papers.
4. Print the spreadsheet and proof your work.
5. Save your work and exit the spreadsheet program.

TEACHING NOTES

Problem 5–7 (Answers) Analyzing Transactions

Ending debit balances:
Cash in Bank $16,287
Accts. Rec.—Gabriel Cohen $67
Accts. Rec.—James Colleti $0
Computer Equipment $2,400
Video Tapes $640
Greg Failla, Withdrawals $150
Equipment Repair Expense $45
Rent Expense $750
Utilities Expense $125
Total $20,464

Ending credit balances:
Accts. Pay.—Computer Horizons $2,400
Accts. Pay.—New Media Suppliers $0
Greg Failla, Capital $17,500
Video Rental Revenue $233
VCR Rental Revenue $331
Total $20,464

Analyze: $2,400

CHALLENGE PROBLEM

Problem 5-8 (Answer) Completing the Accounting Equation

2. $8,075
3. $5,090
4. $420
5. $18,265
6. $52,441
7. $46,599
8. $78,028; $6,112
9. $13,427; $46,750

Analyze: Increases in revenue result in increases in owner's equity. Increases in expenses and withdrawals result in decreases in owner's equity.

CHAPTER 6 Resource Manager

Section Resources

	Objectives & Standards	Activities & Features	Reproducible Masters
Chapter Opener *Recording Transactions in a General Journal*	• Explain the first three steps in the accounting cycle. • Give and describe several examples of source documents. • Explain the purpose of journalizing. • Apply information from source documents. • Describe the steps to make a general journal entry. • Make accurate general journal entries. • Correct errors in general journal entries. • Define the accounting terms introduced in this chapter. **National Standards for Business Education**: IA1, IA4, IA6, IA7, IA8	Exploring the Real World of Business, p. 120 Workplace Connections, p. 121	School-to-Work Handbook
Section 1 *The Accounting Cycle*	• The first three steps in the accounting cycle. • Why it is necessary to journalize transactions. • The different kinds of source documents used in a business. • The difference between a calendar year and a fiscal year.	Spreadsheet Hints, p. 123 Connect To, p. 123 Accounting Flashbacks, p. 124 International Accounting, p. 124	Math Review for Accounting Strategies for Teaching International Accounting
Section 2 *Recording Transactions in the General Journal*	• The purpose of a general journal. • The parts and labeling of a general journal. • How information is entered in a general journal. • How to correct errors in a general journal.	Accounting Tips, p. 126 A Matter of Ethics, p. 139	Demonstration Problems Strategies for Teaching Ethics in Accounting Internet Resources and Activities Handbook

KEY

Posters
Blackline Masters
Transparency
CD-ROM
Software
Portfolio
Videocassette

MULTIMEDIA RESOURCE

Peachtree	QuickBooks	Spreadsheets	Videos	CD-ROMs
Problem 6–4 *Recording General Journal Transactions* Problem 6–5 *Recording General Journal Transactions* Problem 6–6 *Recording General Journal Transactions* Problem 6–7 *Recording General Journal Transactions* Problem 6–8 *Recording General Journal Transactions*	Problem 6–4 *Recording General Journal Transactions* Problem 6–5 *Recording General Journal Transactions*	None in this chapter.	***Video Segment: Business Ethics*** After viewing this video, students will be able to exercise judgment in evaluating ethical situations.	***Electronic Learning Center (ELC), Chapter 6*** This program is ideal for visual learners since it incorporates video images, animation, and graphics to enliven the content of each lesson. ***Interactive Lesson Planner (ILP), Chapter 6*** This CD-ROM combines the versatility of an electronic lesson planner with the convenience of teacher classroom resources.

SCANS Correlation Chart

FOUNDATION SKILLS

Basic Skills:	Reading	Writing	Math	Listening	Speaking	
Thinking Skills:	Creative Thinking	Decision Making	Problem Solving	Seeing Things in the Mind's Eye	Knowing How to Learn	Reasoning
Personal Qualities:	Responsibility	Self-Esteem	Sociability	Self-Management	Integrity/Honesty	

WORKPLACE COMPETENCIES

Resources:	Allocating Time	Allocating Money	Allocating Material and Facility Resources	Allocating Human Resources		
Information:	Acquiring and Evaluating Information	Organizing and Maintaining Information	Interpreting and Communicating Information	Using Computers to Process Information		
Interpersonal Skills:	Participating as a Member of a Team	Teaching Others	Serving Clients/ Customers	Exercising Leadership	Negotiating to Arrive at a Decision	Working with Cultural Diversity
Systems:	Understanding Systems	Monitoring and Correcting Performance	Improving and Designing Systems			
Technology:	Selecting Technology	Applying Technology to Task	Maintaining and Troubleshooting Technology			

*Highlighted blocks indicate areas covered in the chapter. Additional SCANS skills are also covered throughout the *Teacher Wraparound Edition.*

Assessment

Student Edition
- Check Your Understanding, pp. 125, 140
- Chapter 6 Problems, pp. 145–149

Assessment and Evaluation Masters
- Chapter 6 Study Plan, *Glencoe Workbook*
- Chapter 6 Self-Test, *Glencoe Workbook*
- Chapter 6 Test, *Chapter Tests* Booklet
- Chapter 6 Activity, *School-to-Work Handbook*
- Chapter 6 **Exam***View*

Teacher Wraparound Edition
- Critical Thinking Activity, p. 133
- Reteaching Section 1, p. 125
- Reteaching Section 2, p. 140
- Chapter 6 Quiz, p. 141

Transparencies

	Teaching Transparencies	Solution Transparencies
Section 1:	6–1, 6–2, 6–3	Problem 6–1
Section 2:	6–4, 6–5, 6–6, 6–7, 6–8, 6–9, 6–10, 6–11, 6–12, 6–13, 6–14, 6–15, 6–16, 6–17, 6–18, 6–19, 6–20	Problems 6–2, 6–3
End of Chapter:		Problems 6–4, 6–5, 6–6, 6–7, 6–8

TEACHER CLASSROOM RESOURCES

This is a representation of key blackline masters available in the Teacher Classroom Resources.

Teaching Aids

Transparency Examples

Section Focus Transparencies

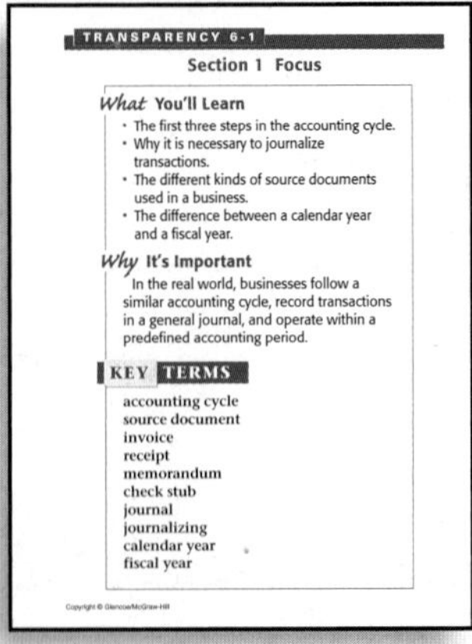

TRANSPARENCY 6-1

Section 1 Focus

What You'll Learn

- The first three steps in the accounting cycle.
- Why it is necessary to journalize transactions.
- The different kinds of source documents used in a business.
- The difference between a calendar year and a fiscal year.

Why It's Important

In the real world, businesses follow a similar accounting cycle, record transactions in a general journal, and operate within a predefined accounting period.

KEY TERMS

accounting cycle
source document
invoice
receipt
memorandum
check stub
journal
journalizing
calendar year
fiscal year

Teaching Transparencies

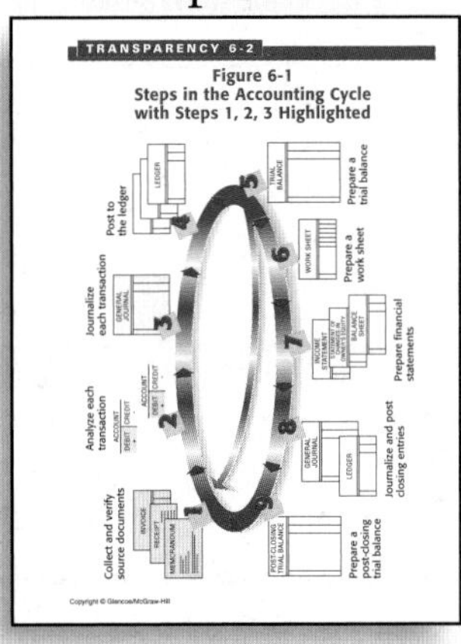

TRANSPARENCY 6-2

Figure 6-1
Steps in the Accounting Cycle with Steps 1, 2, 3 Highlighted

Teaching Transparencies

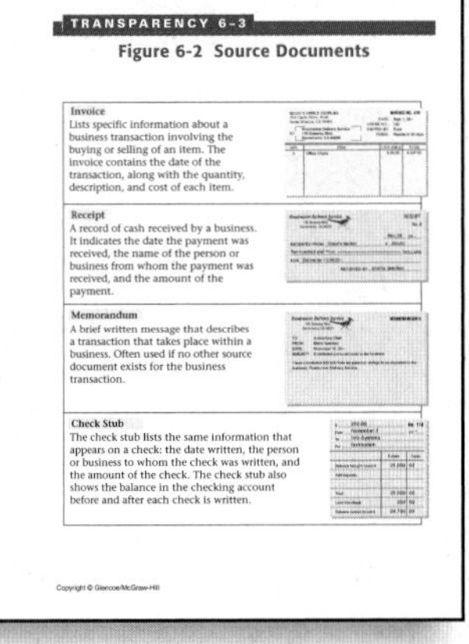

TRANSPARENCY 6-3

Figure 6-2 Source Documents

Invoice
Lists specific information about a business transaction involving the buying or selling of an item. The invoice contains the date of the transaction, along with the quantity, description, and cost of each item.

Receipt
A record of cash received by a business. It indicates the date the payment was received, the name of the person or business from whom the payment was received, and the amount of the payment.

Memorandum
A brief written message that describes a transaction that takes place within a business. Often used if no other source document exists for the business transaction.

Check Stub
The check stub lists the same information that appears on a check: the date written, the person or business to whom the check was written, and the amount of the check. The check stub also shows the balance in the checking account before and after each check is written.

Solution Transparencies

Working Papers for End-of-Chapter Problems
Problem 6-4 Recording General Journal Transactions

GENERAL JOURNAL

Analyze: $2,480 was deducted from the Cash in Bank account in January.

Demonstration Problems

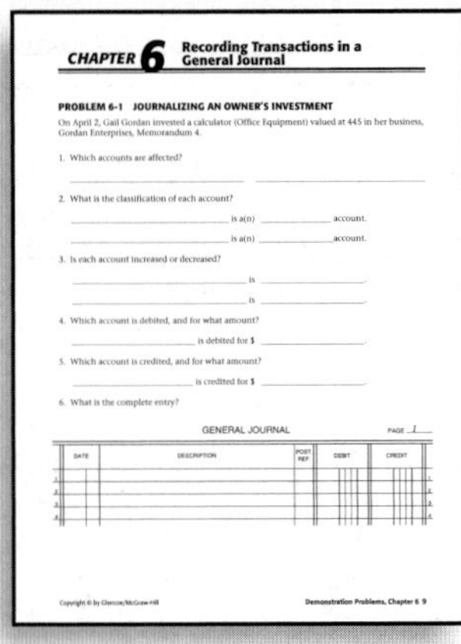

CHAPTER 6 Recording Transactions in a General Journal

PROBLEM 6-1 JOURNALIZING AN OWNER'S INVESTMENT

Lesson Plans

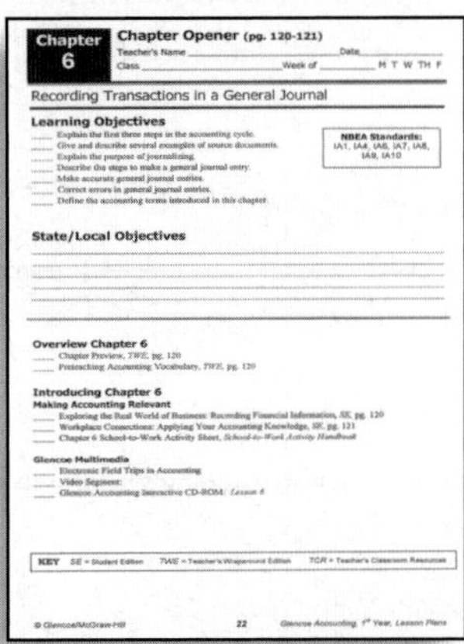

Chapter 6 Chapter Opener (pg. 120-121)

Recording Transactions in a General Journal

Learning Objectives

State/Local Objectives

Block Scheduling

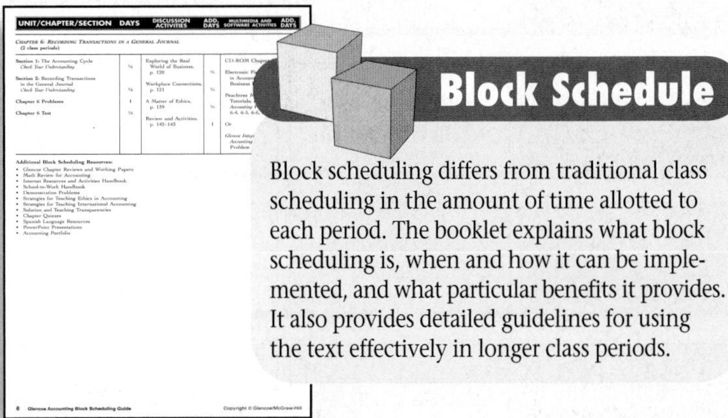

UNIT/CHAPTER/SECTION DAYS

Block Schedule

Block scheduling differs from traditional class scheduling in the amount of time allotted to each period. The booklet explains what block scheduling is, when and how it can be implemented, and what particular benefits it provides. It also provides detailed guidelines for using the text effectively in longer class periods.

Enrichment and Application

Strategies for Teaching Ethics in Accounting

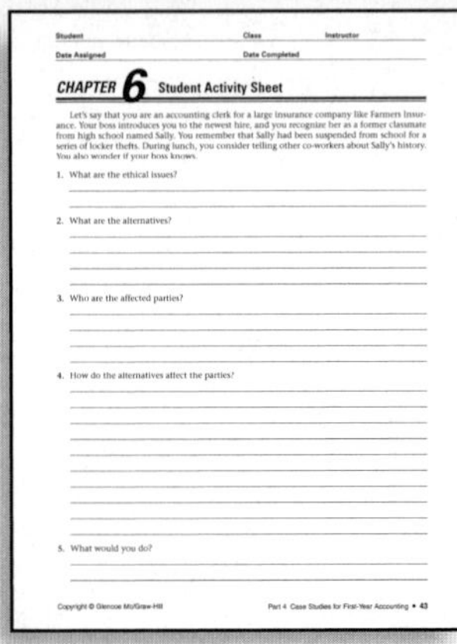

CHAPTER 6 Student Activity Sheet

1. What are the ethical issues?
2. What are the alternatives?
3. Who are the affected parties?
4. How do the alternatives affect the parties?
5. What would you do?

Strategies for Teaching International Accounting

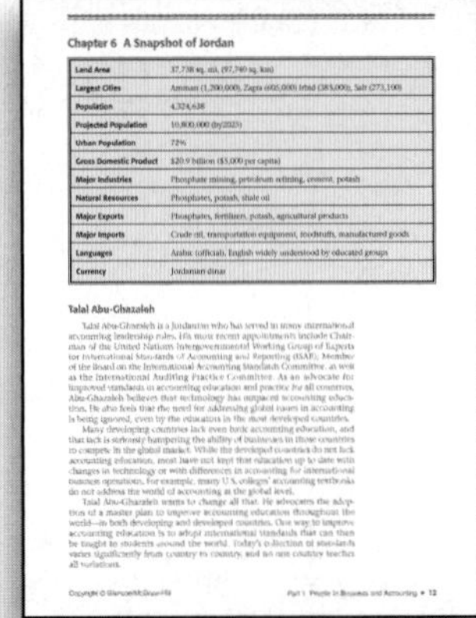

Chapter 6 A Snapshot of Jordan

Talal Abu-Ghazaleh

School-to-Work Handbook

CHAPTER 6 SCHOOL-TO-WORK ACTIVITY

Recording Transactions in a General Journal

Meeting Different Ability Levels

Chapter Reviews and Working Papers (CRWP)

Working Papers

Review

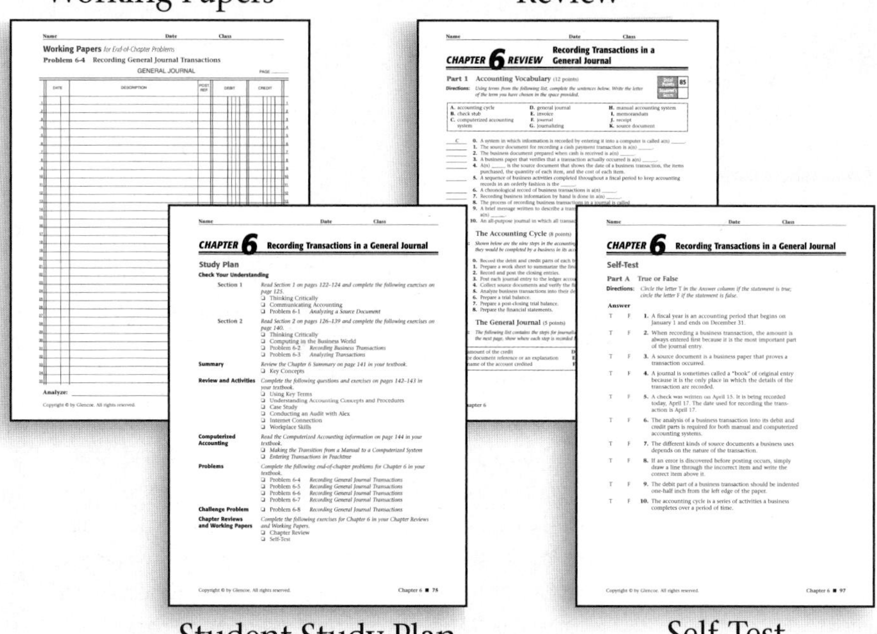

Student Study Plan

Self-Test

Real-World Multimedia CD-ROM

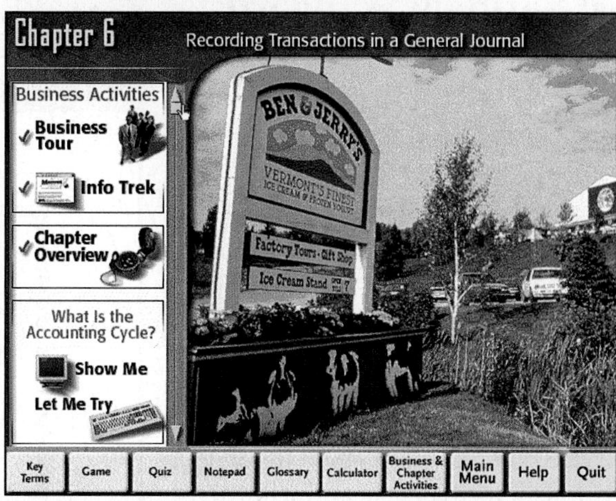

Key to Ability Levels

Each section gives skill-building activities. Each activity has been labeled for use with students of various learning styles and abilities.

L1 Level 1 activities are basic activities and should be within the range of all students.

L2 Level 2 activities are average activities and should be within the range of average and above average students.

L3 Level 3 activities are challenging activities designed for the ability range of above average students.

ELL ELL activities should be within the ability range of English Language Learners.

Teaching Resources at a Glance

Application Resources

- Glencoe Chapter Review and Working Papers, SE and TAE
- School-to-Work Handbook, SE and TM
- Accounting Portfolio, SE and TM

Reproducible Masters

- Demonstration Problems
- Lesson Plans
- Block Scheduling
- Spanish Language Resources

Glencoe Accounting Professional Development Series

- Strategies for Teaching Ethics in Accounting
- Accounting Competitive Event Review
- Math Review for Accounting
- Strategies for Teaching International Accounting
- Internet Resources and Activities Handbook

Transparency Package

- Section Focus Transparencies
- Teaching Transparencies
- Source Document Transparencies
- Solution Transparencies

Performance Assessment

- **Exam***View* CD-ROM
- Chapter Tests
- Chapter Quizzes
- Unit Tests
- Audit Tests
- Printed Testbank

Multimedia Resources

- Electronic Learning Center:
  - Multimedia CD-ROMs
  - Peachtree software, tutorials, templates, and solutions
  - Spreadsheet templates
- Using QuickBooks with Glencoe Accounting
- Interactive Lesson Planner
- Electronic Field Trips in Accounting
- PowerPoint Presentation
- Web site: glencoeaccounting.glencoe.com

Assessment and Evaluation

Chapter Tests

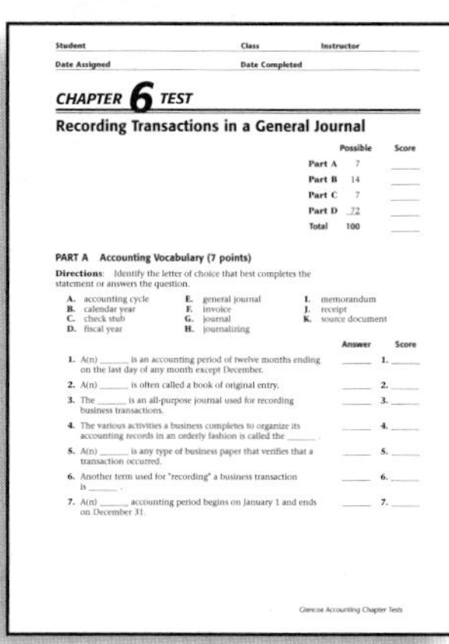

Chapter Quiz

OVERVIEW CHAPTER 6

Correlations to National Standards for Business Education

(See pages T50–T51 for a detailed correlation chart.)

Standards: IA1, IA4, IA6, IA7, IA8

Chapter Preview

In this chapter, students learn how to journalize the business transactions they have analyzed in the previous chapters. Students will first learn about the steps in the accounting cycle and will then use a general journal to record several typical business transactions.

Section Overviews

- Section 1—*The Accounting Cycle*
- Section 2—*Recording Transactions in the General Journal*

Chapter Vocabulary

accounting cycle
source document
invoice
receipt
memorandum
check stub
journal
journalizing
calendar year
fiscal year
general journal

Preteaching Accounting Vocabulary

Oral Exercise: Have students take turns using each of the vocabulary words in a sentence. Ask students to discuss their sentences and revise any whose meaning does not match the definition of the term. L1

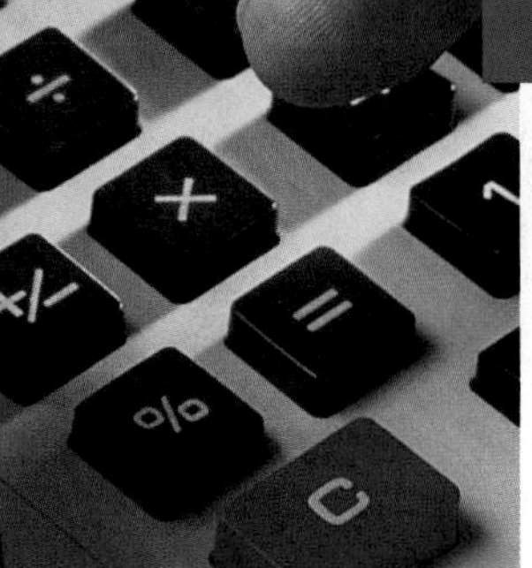

CHAPTER 6

Recording Transactions in a General Journal

Learning Objectives

When you have completed this chapter, you will be able to:

- Explain the first three steps in the accounting cycle.
- Give and describe several examples of source documents.
- Explain the purpose of journalizing.
- Apply information from source documents.
- Describe the steps to make a general journal entry.
- Make accurate general journal entries.
- Correct errors in general journal entries.
- Define the accounting terms introduced in this chapter.

Exploring the Real World of Business

RECORDING FINANCIAL INFORMATION

Ben Cohen and Jerry Greenfield met in junior high school and graduated from Calhoun High School in Merrick, Long Island. After high school they decided that they wanted to start a business together. They researched products, market demand, and locations. A shared love for all-natural ice cream and a vision for a company that improves the quality of community life were the foundations for the beginnings of **Ben & Jerry's Ice Cream and Frozen Yogurt.** They purchased a used old-fashioned rock salt ice cream maker and took a correspondence course from Penn State about ice cream making.

Ben & Jerry's opened for business in May of 1978 in Burlington, Vermont, in a "roughly" renovated gas station. **Ben & Jerry's** products are now sold around the world. Recording financial information about the business keeps several full-time accountants busy.

What do you think?

If you were Ben and Jerry, what types of financial information would you record?

Ben & Jerry's Homemade, Inc.

Exploring the Real World of Business

Ben & Jerry's

Like many corporations, Ben & Jerry's created a formal mission statement. Part of the mission statement is "to operate the Company on a sound financial basis of profitable growth. . . ." The accounting system provides the means of measuring the profitable growth of the company.

What do you think? (Answers)

Answers may vary. Among possible answers are purchases of ice cream ingredients, such as cream, chocolate, and cookies; sales for each ice cream, yogurt, or sorbet flavor; operating expenses such as electricity or gas; purchases of manufacturing equipment; advertising and promotion expenses.

Workplace Connections

Applying Your Accounting Knowledge

Have you ever kept a daily journal of the things that happen during your day? The general journal of a business is similar. The daily financial happenings are recorded there. Your local video store earns revenue by renting videos, buys advertising in the newspaper, pays its employees, and pays its bills. You'll learn how to record business transactions in a journal in this chapter.

Investigate:

1. In your workplace, why is it important to keep accurate records of daily transactions?
2. List five business transactions that happen in your workplace.

Glencoe Accounting *Online*

Visit the *Glencoe Accounting* Web site at **glencoeaccounting.glencoe.com** for additional activities and information.

INTRODUCING
CHAPTER 6

Making Accounting Relevant

Workplace Connections: Applying Your Accounting Knowledge

Discussion: Ask students what examples come to mind when they think of a journal. Some people keep a daily journal of their activities or their travel and expenses. A business journal is a record of financial activities. This journal tells what the business buys and sells each day.

Investigate (Answers)

1. Answers will vary. Students should note that without complete accurate financial records businesses will not know how much they have earned and spent.
2. Answers will vary depending on the business. For example, a movie theater would have sales of food items, sales of movie tickets, food purchases, payment of fees to show movies, payment of mortgage or rent, and advertising costs.

School-to-Work Activity

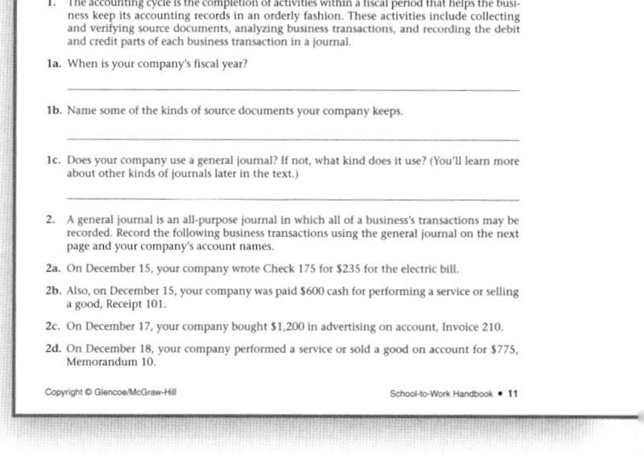

Student ____ Class ____ Instructor ____

Date Assigned ____ Date Completed ____

CHAPTER 6 SCHOOL-TO-WORK ACTIVITY

Recording Transactions in a General Journal

Name of work site: ____

Name of work site mentor: ____

Title or position of mentor: ____

The procedures for journalizing business transactions are very important because, if done correctly, accounting records are more likely to be accurate. Consult with your work site mentor or the person responsible for accounting or bookkeeping for your company to complete the following investigation of recording transactions in a journal.

After completing the school-to-work investigation, you will be able to:

- explain the first three steps of your company's accounting cycle,
- describe how your company's business transactions would be recorded in a general journal,
- describe your company's accounting system either as manual or computerized, and
- analyze your company's chart of accounts.

1. The accounting cycle is the completion of activities within a fiscal period that helps the business keep its accounting records in an orderly fashion. These activities include collecting and verifying source documents, analyzing business transactions, and recording the debit and credit parts of each business transaction in a journal.

1a. When is your company's fiscal year?

____

1b. Name some of the kinds of source documents your company keeps.

____

1c. Does your company use a general journal? If not, what kind does it use? (You'll learn more about other kinds of journals later in the text.)

____

2. A general journal is an all-purpose journal in which all of a business's transactions may be recorded. Record the following business transactions using the general journal on the next page and your company's account names.

2a. On December 15, your company wrote Check 175 for $235 for the electric bill.

2b. Also, on December 15, your company was paid $600 cash for performing a service or selling a good, Receipt 101.

2c. On December 17, your company bought $1,200 in advertising on account, Invoice 210.

2d. On December 18, your company performed a service or sold a good on account for $775, Memorandum 10.

 School-to-Work Handbook • 11

GLENCOE MULTIMEDIA

Electronic Field Trips in Accounting *Video Segment: Business Ethics*
After viewing this video, students will be able to exercise judgment in evaluating ethical situations.

Glencoe Accounting: Electronic Learning Center *Chapter 6*
The CD-ROM program is ideal for visual learners since it incorporates video images, animation, and graphics to enliven the content of each lesson.

1 FOCUS

Introducing the Section

In this section students learn all the steps in the accounting cycle and study the first three steps more closely. Students also learn about the accounting period and the various times businesses may choose for their fiscal periods.

Section Concepts

- The first three steps in the accounting cycle.
- Why it is necessary to journalize transactions.
- The different kinds of source documents used in a business.
- The difference between a calendar year and a fiscal year.

Visual Learning

Section 1 Focus

Use **Transparency 6–1** to introduce section concepts.

BELL RINGER

Creating Analogies: Have students choose an activity they do every day, such as opening their lockers to store or remove items. Ask students to write, in order, the steps they follow. Have volunteers share their steps. Introduce the accounting cycle, and make the point that accountants follow a set of steps to make the accounting system work. L1

Visual Learning

Figure 6–1 Steps in the Accounting Cycle with Steps 1, 2, 3 Highlighted

Use **Transparency 6–2** to discuss each step in the accounting cycle. Students will learn more about steps 4 through 9 in later chapters.

SECTION 1

The Accounting Cycle

What You'll Learn

- The first three steps in the accounting cycle.
- Why it is necessary to journalize transactions.
- The different kinds of source documents used in a business.
- The difference between a calendar year and a fiscal year.

Why It's Important

In the real world, businesses follow a similar accounting cycle, record transactions in a general journal, and operate within a predefined accounting period.

KEY TERMS

accounting cycle
source document
invoice
receipt
memorandum
check stub
journal
journalizing
calendar year
fiscal year

In earlier chapters, you learned to use the accounting equation and T accounts to analyze business transactions. You also studied the rules of debit and credit for asset, liability, owner's equity, revenue, and expense accounts. In this chapter, you will learn how to record business transactions in a journal.

The Steps of the Accounting Cycle

The accounting period of a business is separated into activities that help the business keep its accounting records in an orderly fashion. These activities are called the **accounting cycle**. Take a look at **Figure 6–1**, which describes accounting activities and their sequence.

In this chapter, you will read about and use Steps 1, 2, and 3 of the accounting cycle. The remaining chapters in this unit will each cover at least one more step in the accounting cycle. After studying Chapters 3 through 10, you will have covered the accounting cycle for a service business organized as a sole proprietorship.

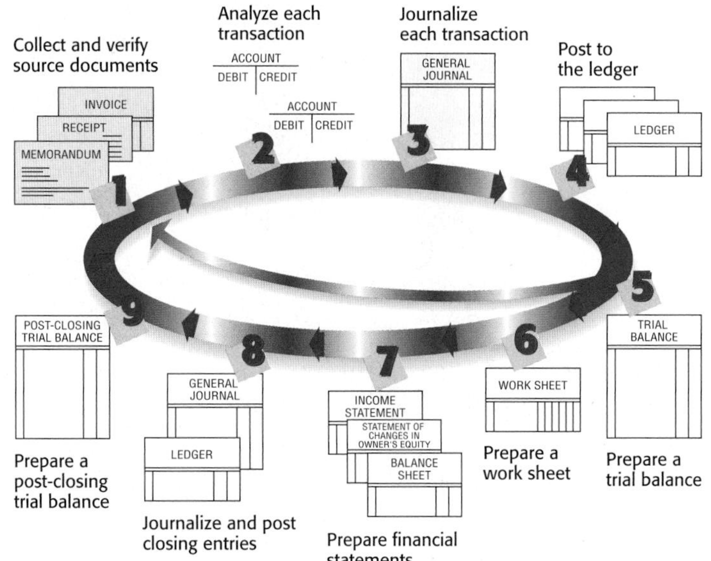

Figure 6–1 Steps in the Accounting Cycle with Steps 1, 2, 3 Highlighted

RESOURCE MANAGER

Reproducible Masters
- Lesson Plans
- Chapter Reviews and Working Papers (CRWP) TAE

Transparencies
- Section Focus Transparency
- Teaching Transparencies
- Source Document Transparencies
- Solution Transparencies

Multimedia
- Exam*View* CD-ROM
- Electronic Learning Center CD-ROM
- Interactive Lesson Planner CD-ROM
- Electronic Field Trips in Accounting

The First Step in the Accounting Cycle: Collecting and Verifying Source Documents

Most business transactions take place during the daily operations of a business. In the course of one day, a business may pay its rent, place an ad in a local newspaper, contract to have a Web site created, pay its employees, sell products, and purchase new equipment. When a business transaction occurs, a paper is prepared as evidence of that transaction. This paper is a **source document**. The business owner, accountant, or accounting clerk (depending on the size of the business) uses source documents generated by business transactions to keep the records of the business. The accounting cycle starts by collecting and verifying the accuracy of source documents. One important activity is to check the arithmetic on each source document.

There are several types of source documents that can be prepared by hand, by computer, or by a machine. The type of source document prepared depends on the nature of the transaction. **Figure 6–2** describes and illustrates commonly used source documents.

Invoice
Lists specific information about a business transaction involving the buying or selling of an item. The invoice contains the date of the transaction, along with the quantity, description, and cost of each item.

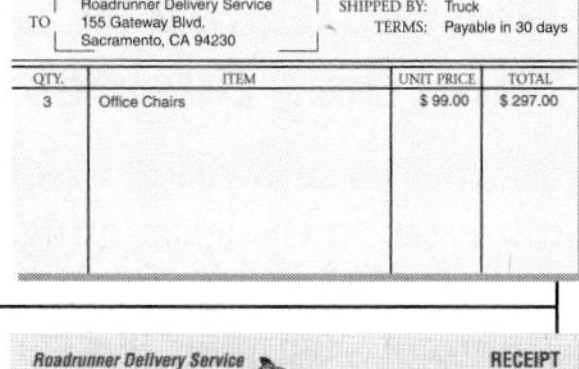
KELLY'S OFFICE SUPPLIES
354 Circle Drive, #150
Santa Monica, CA 90405

INVOICE NO. 479
DATE: Dec. 1, 20--
ORDER NO.: 150
SHIPPED BY: Truck
TERMS: Payable in 30 days

TO Roadrunner Delivery Service
155 Gateway Blvd.
Sacramento, CA 94230

QTY.	ITEM	UNIT PRICE	TOTAL
3	Office Chairs	$ 99.00	$ 297.00

Receipt
A record of cash received by a business. It indicates the date the payment was received, the name of the person or business from whom the payment was received, and the amount of the payment.

Roadrunner Delivery Service
155 Gateway Blvd.
Sacramento, CA 94230
RECEIPT
No. 2
Nov. 26 20 --
RECEIVED FROM Greer's Market $ 200.00
Two hundred and 00/100 DOLLARS
FOR Deliveries 11/26/20--
RECEIVED BY Maria Sanchez

Memorandum
A brief written message that describes a transaction that takes place within a business. Often used if no other source document exists for the business transaction.

Roadrunner Delivery Service
155 Gateway Blvd.
Sacramento, CA 94230
MEMORANDUM 6
TO: Accounting Clerk
FROM: Maria Sanchez
DATE: October 1, 20--
SUBJECT: Contributed personal funds to the business
I have contributed $25,000 from my personal savings to be deposited to the business, Roadrunner Delivery Service.

Check Stub
The check stub lists the same information that appears on a check: the date written, the person or business to whom the check was written, and the amount of the check. The check stub also shows the balance in the checking account before and after each check is written.

$ 250.00 No. 110
Date November 2 20 --
To Info-Systems
For fax/modem

	Dollars	Cents
Balance brought forward	25,000	00
Add deposits		
Total	25,000	00
Less this check	250	00
Balance carried forward	24,750	00

Figure 6–2 Source Documents

Spreadsheet Hints

Cell Addresses

Spreadsheets are divided into:

- Columns labeled A, B, C, and so on.
- Rows labeled 1, 2, 3, and so on.

The point where a column and a row meet is called a cell. Each cell has its own "address," identified by a letter and a number, such as A1.

Key Points

Source Documents

Source documents are evidence of business transactions. They are the basis for the information recorded in the accounting system.

CONNECT TO . . . ENVIRONMENT

Because businesses sometimes find it cheaper to pollute and pay fines than to take measures that protect the environment, the government is often forced to offer economic incentives. When accountants compare these benefits to the costs of environmental safeguarding, they must also factor in civic responsibility and public relations.

Math Skill Builder Activity

Identifying Spreadsheet Cell Addresses Ask students to locate a spreadsheet where the columns and rows are identified. Then have students read and interpret the data by locating the "cell addresses." To make this activity more exciting, play Spreadsheet Bingo. Use similar spreadsheet formats with different data and simply call out the cell address. Reward students who get Bingo with a small prize.

2 TEACH

GUIDED PRACTICE

Reading Accounting

• The ability to translate graphic information into text is an important skill for students to develop. Have students write a description of the steps in the accounting cycle, presenting the information in a form that is easy to read and understand. L1

Concept Development: The Steps of the Accounting Cycle

Discussion: Point out that all businesses operate in cycles referred to as accounting periods or fiscal periods (the terms are used interchangeably). Discuss source documents as evidence of business transactions. Without a source document, no evidence exists that a business transaction has occurred. Also mention that accountants verify information on source documents to avoid errors in the accounting records. L1

Visual Learning

Figure 6–2 Source Documents

Using **Transparency 6–3**, review source documents with students and point out that most businesses design forms to meet their particular needs. Collect samples of source documents from local businesses and have students identify the information used in accounting records.

GO TO **Math Review for Accounting**
Photocopy appropriate *Activity Sheets* for students who need additional practice in basic math skills.

2 TEACH (Cont'd.)

Teaching Tips

Remind students that a business transaction needs physical evidence of its occurrence. A telephone call to order an item does not prove that the transaction occurred. The source document (invoice) prepared as a result of the call does.

Emphasize that correctly analyzing business transactions is a key responsibility for an accountant. A transaction that is analyzed incorrectly will also be recorded incorrectly.

Concept Development: The Accounting Period

Discussion: Give students examples of several different kinds of businesses and identify the fiscal period used by each. Ask students why a business may use that particular fiscal period. For example, your local school system's accounting period may run from July 1 to June 30 because state legislation requires that time period. Point out that the accounting period of a business normally ends at a time when business activity is at its lowest level. L1

Strategies for Teaching International Accounting

To enrich study of International Accounting, refer to the additional critical thinking activities in the booklet.

ACCOUNTING Flashbacks

ARCHAIC RECORDKEEPING

The Sumerians in Mesopotamia kept records on clay tablets called cuneiforms. The shapes pressed into the clay eventually evolved into the Greek and Roman alphabets that we use today.

The Second Step in the Accounting Cycle: Analyzing Business Transactions

After collecting and verifying source documents, the second step in the accounting cycle can begin—analyzing information on the source documents to determine the debit and credit parts of each transaction.

You have already learned how to analyze business transactions using the rules of debit and credit. When you learned to analyze transactions, you were given a description of each transaction, such as: Roadrunner Delivery Service bought a computer system from Info-Systems Inc. for $3,000 and issued Check 101 in payment. On the job, you won't get a description of the transaction. Instead, you must examine a source document to determine what occurred during a business transaction.

The Third Step in the Accounting Cycle: Recording Business Transactions in a Journal

You are now ready to apply information from source documents. The third step in the accounting cycle is to record the debit and credit parts of each business transaction in a journal. A **journal** is a record of all of the transactions of a business. Journals are kept in chronological order, that is, in the order that the transactions occur. The process of recording business transactions in a journal is called **journalizing**. Keeping a journal can be compared to keeping a diary in which all important events are written. A journal contains the most important information relating to a business transaction. It is the only place where complete details of a transaction, including both the debit and credit parts, are recorded. For this reason, the journal is often called a *record* or *"book" of original entry.*

International ACCOUNTING

Lunch Meetings

Conducting business over a meal is a standard practice in the United States. However, when scheduling such meetings in other countries, consider that culture's dining habits.

The Accounting Period

As discussed in Chapter 2, accounting records are summarized for a certain period of time, called an accounting period. An accounting period may be for any designated length of time, such as a month, a quarter, or a year. Most businesses use a year as their accounting period. If the accounting period for a business begins on January 1 and ends on December 31, it is called a **calendar year** accounting period. A **fiscal year** is an accounting period of twelve months. Many businesses start their accounting periods in months other than January. For example, department stores often have fiscal years that begin on February 1 and end January 31 of the following year. School districts usually have fiscal years that begin on July 1 and end on June 30.

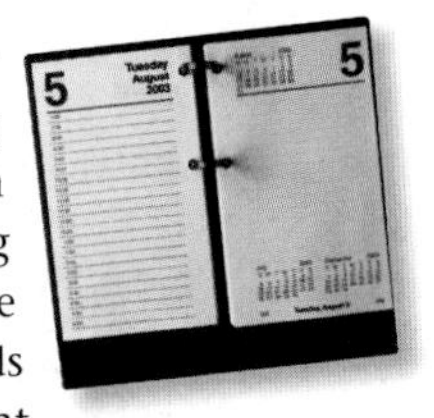

Teaching International ACCOUNTING

Researching Dining Habits Divide students into groups of three or four. Tell each group that they will be entertaining a business client from a foreign country. Then assign each group a different country and have them research the country's dining habits. Ask each group to respond to the following questions: Should you discuss business over a meal? If no, where and when should you discuss business? If yes, at which restaurant would you entertain the client, and what menu items would you recommend to the client? Have each group present its findings and share answers with the class.

Now that you have studied this section, complete the following questions and problems.

Thinking Critically

1. Businesses separate their accounting records into accounting periods. Why is this procedure important for keeping meaningful accounting records?
2. How are source documents used?

Communicating Accounting

Write a paragraph describing the content of invoices, check stubs, memorandums, and receipts. Explain how to verify and analyze these source documents before an entry in the journal is made.

Problem 6-1 Analyzing a Source Document

Instructions Analyze the invoice shown below and answer the following questions.

JAYMAX OFFICE SUPPLY
554 Town Square
Fort Myers, FL 33902

INVOICE NO. 479
DATE: Apr. 9, 20--
ORDER NO.:
SHIPPED BY: Truck
TERMS: Payable in 30 days

TO Dario's Accounting Services
5821 Gulf Blvd.
Naples, FL 33940

QTY.	ITEM	UNIT PRICE	TOTAL
1	Fax Machine	$ 299.00	$ 299.00

1. What is the name of the company providing the service?
2. What is the name of the business receiving the service?
3. What is the date of the invoice?
4. What is the invoice number?
5. What item was sold?
6. What is the price for this item?
7. What are the payment terms?

RETEACHING SECTION 1

Illustrating a Business Transaction with a Flow Chart To help students comprehend how source documents provide records of business transactions, develop a flow chart that shows the steps for completing a simple transaction, such as a sale, and recording the transaction in a journal. For example, when a customer purchases a CD, the customer receives a sales slip showing the date, the type of purchase, and the amount. The business keeps a copy of that same sales slip. The sales slip is the source document from which a journal entry is made in the accounting records.

3 ASSESS

Thinking Critically (Answers)

1. Comparing financial data is made possible by a standardized accounting period. Such comparisons of business performance would be impossible if fiscal periods varied in length.
2. Source documents capture the relevant details of a transaction. Accountants check the documents for accuracy, approve them, and enter their information into accounting records.

Communicating Accounting (Answers)

Answers may vary. Refer students to page 123 for descriptions of source documents.

Problem 6-1 (Answers)

1. JayMax Office Supply
2. Dario's Accounting Services
3. April 9, 20--
4. 479
5. Fax Machine
6. $299
7. Payable in 30 days

Chapter Reviews and Working Papers Refer students to the Chapter 6 workbook pages to answer *Check Your Understanding* activities.

4 CLOSE

Section Wrap-Up

Demonstrate: Have students write the first three steps in the accounting cycle and describe the actions accountants take at each step. L1

1 FOCUS

Introducing the Section

In this section students learn how to record business transactions in a general journal. Students will add a seventh step to the six-step transaction analysis by recording transactions in the journal.

Section Concepts

- The purpose of a general journal.
- The parts and labeling of a general journal.
- How information is entered in a general journal.
- How to correct errors in a general journal.

Visual Learning

Section 2 Focus

Use **Transparency 6–4** to introduce section concepts.

BELL RINGER

Summarizing: Tell students to think about the business transactions they analyzed in earlier chapters. Ask students what information they gained from analyzing each transaction. As students respond, list their responses on the chalkboard. (Students should include the account to be debited, debit amount, account to be credited, credit amount, account balances.) Refer to this list as you introduce the general journal. Show students where the information they gave you goes in the journal. L1

Visual Learning

Figure 6–3 General Journal for Roadrunner Delivery Service

Use **Transparency 6–5** to introduce students to the parts of the general journal.

SECTION 2

Recording Transactions in the General Journal

***What* You'll Learn**

- The purpose of a general journal.
- The parts and labeling of a general journal.
- How information is entered in a general journal.
- How to correct errors in a general journal.

***Why* It's Important**

The general journal is a permanent record of the financial transactions of a business.

KEY TERMS

general journal

In Section 1, you learned about the first three steps in the accounting cycle. Let's apply these steps to business transactions for Roadrunner Delivery Service.

Recording a General Journal Entry

Many kinds of accounting journals are used in business. One of the most common is the general journal. As its name suggests, the **general journal** is an all purpose journal in which all the transactions of a business may be recorded. **Figure 6–3** shows the general journal you will be using throughout the accounting cycle for Roadrunner Delivery Service. The general journal has two amount columns. The first amount column, the amount column on the left, is used to record debit amounts. (Remember that debit means left.) The second amount column, the amount column on the right, is used to record credit amounts. (Remember that credit means right.) Look at **Figure 6–3** to find where each component of a general journal entry appears.

1 Date of the transaction
2 Name of the account debited
3 Amount of the debit

GENERAL JOURNAL PAGE ______

	DATE		DESCRIPTION	POST. REF.	DEBIT	CREDIT	
1	*Year*						1
2	*Month*	*Day*	*Debited Account Name*		*1 000 00*		2
3			*Credited Account Name*			*1 000 00*	3
4			*Explanation*				4
5							5

6 Source document reference or an explanation
4 Name of the account credited
5 Amount of the credit

Figure 6–3 General Journal for Roadrunner Delivery Service

ACCOUNTING TIPS

Using Accounting Journals and Stationery

When using journals or other accounting stationery:

- Do not use dollar signs. A sloppy dollar sign might be mistaken for a number, causing an error in your records.
- The vertical lines in the amount columns take the place of commas and decimals.

In Chapters 4 and 5, you learned a step-by-step method for analyzing business transactions. In this chapter, you will learn to complete the journal entry for a business transaction in the same manner. Review the following steps before you continue.

RESOURCE MANAGER

Reproducible Masters
- Lesson Plans
- Strategies for Teaching Ethics in Accounting
- Chapter Reviews and Working Papers (CRWP) TAE
- Demonstration Problems

Transparencies
- Section Focus Transparency
- Teaching Transparencies
- Source Document Transparencies
- Solution Transparencies

Multimedia
- *ExamView* CD-ROM
- Electronic Learning Center CD-ROM
- Interactive Lesson Planner CD-ROM
- Electronic Field Trips in Accounting

Business Transaction

BUSINESS TRANSACTION ANALYSIS: Steps to Success

ANALYSIS	*Identify*	**1.** Identify the accounts affected.
	Classify	**2.** Classify the accounts affected.
	+/−	**3.** Determine the amount of increase or decrease for each account affected.
DEBIT-CREDIT RULE		**4.** Which account is debited? For what amount?
		5. Which account is credited? For what amount?
T ACCOUNTS		**6.** What is the complete entry in T-account form?
JOURNAL ENTRY		**7.** What is the complete entry in general journal form?

Use these steps to determine the debit and credit parts of each journal entry. Remember, it is always helpful to use T accounts to analyze transactions. After analyzing many transactions, you will find that you need these tools less and less to determine the debit and credit parts of a journal entry.

Now, let's examine business transactions and their analysis for Roadrunner Delivery Service.

Business Transaction 1

On October 1 Maria Sanchez took $25,000 from personal savings and deposited that amount to open a business checking account in the name of Roadrunner Delivery Service, Memorandum 1.

Roadrunner Delivery Service
155 Gateway Blvd.
Sacramento, CA 94230

MEMORANDUM 1

TO: Accounting Clerk
FROM: Maria Sanchez
DATE: October 1, 20--
SUBJECT: Contributed personal funds to the business

I have contributed $25,000 from my personal savings for a deposit to the business, Roadrunner Delivery Service.

ANALYSIS	*Identify*	**1.** The accounts **Cash in Bank** and **Maria Sanchez, Capital** are affected.
	Classify	**2.** **Cash in Bank** is an asset account. **Maria Sanchez, Capital** is an owner's capital account.
	+/−	**3.** **Cash in Bank** is increased by $25,000. **Maria Sanchez, Capital** is increased by $25,000.
DEBIT-CREDIT RULE		**4.** Increases in asset accounts are recorded as debits. Debit **Cash in Bank** for $25,000.
		5. Increases in the owner's capital account are recorded as credits. Credit **Maria Sanchez, Capital** for $25,000.

INTERDISCIPLINARY CONNECTIONS ACTIVITY

(Refer to the *Connect To...Environment* feature on page 123.)
Environment What safeguards does the EPA (Environmental Protection Agency) require for area parks, lakes, creeks, or common areas? Have students contact a local EPA office and ask for guidelines that businesses should adhere to when planning new development. Then divide students into small groups and discuss the potential cost of "doing business" and staying within environmental guidelines. What impact does the cost of compliance have on the amount of money needed to operate the business and on potential profit?

2 TEACH

GUIDED PRACTICE

Reading Accounting

- Point out that accountants must identify the pertinent information in a source document. Have students practice "reading" a source document by having them tell you the most pertinent information in Memorandum 1. L1
- Obtain copies of source documents printed in other languages. Point out the similarities between those documents and the ones illustrated in students' textbooks. ELL

Concept Development: Recording a General Journal Entry

Discussion: Point out to students that recording transactions in a journal provides a chronological record of all transactions. This record begins the process of recording and analyzing the financial data used by managers to make operating decisions and to determine whether the business is making an adequate profit. Ask students to discuss why they think it is important for a business to record its business transactions accurately. L1

Visual Learning

Business Transaction Model

Use **Transparency 6–6** to review the steps in analyzing a business transaction.

Teaching Tip

Have students apply information from a source document by journalizing the transaction shown in Problem 6–1 on page 125.

2 TEACH (Cont'd.)

Visual Learning

Business Transaction 1

Using **Transparency 6–7**, have students compare the information in the transaction description with the source document. Then have students look at the information recorded in the general journal entry. Point out where each type of information is found on the source document and in the T-account analysis.

Demonstration Problem Step-by-Step Practice

Use demonstration problem 6–1 to show students how to record an owner's additional investment in the business.

Teaching Tip

Remind students that the six steps in the analysis model are not written as formal accounting records. They are simply a tool for analyzing the effects of a business transaction on the accounts of the business.

Visual Learning

Business Transaction 2

Using **Transparency 6–8**, compare information in the transaction description and on the source document. Cover the general journal portion of the business transaction transparency and have students tell you what information they would record in the journal entry.

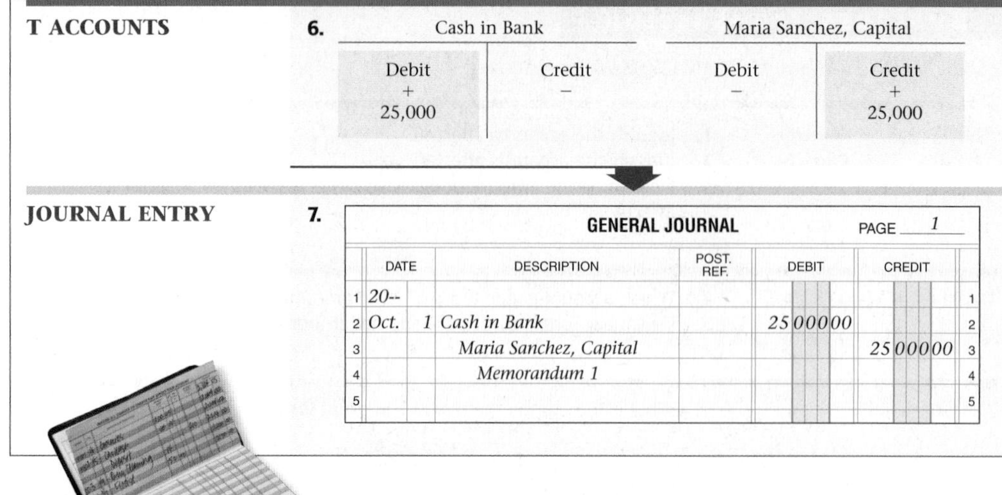

T ACCOUNTS

6.

Cash in Bank		Maria Sanchez, Capital	
Debit +	Credit −	Debit −	Credit +
25,000			25,000

JOURNAL ENTRY

7.

GENERAL JOURNAL PAGE 1

	DATE		DESCRIPTION	POST. REF.	DEBIT	CREDIT	
1	20--						1
2	Oct.	1	Cash in Bank		25 000 00		2
3			Maria Sanchez, Capital			25 000 00	3
4			Memorandum 1				4
5							5

Look again at the general journal entry shown above. Notice that in the upper right-hand corner there is a line for the page number. Journal pages are numbered in consecutive order; that is, 1, 2, 3, and so on. When you fill one page with journal entries, go on to the next page. Be sure to properly number each new page.

Business Transaction 2

On October 2 Maria Sanchez took two telephones valued at $200 each from her home and transferred them to the business as office equipment, Memorandum 2.

Roadrunner Delivery Service
155 Gateway Blvd.
Sacramento, CA 94230

MEMORANDUM 2

TO: Accounting Clerk
FROM: Maria Sanchez
DATE: October 2, 20--
SUBJECT: Contributed personal phones

I have contributed two telephones from my home to the business. The phones are valued at $200 each. Total contribution = $400.

ANALYSIS

Identify 1. The accounts **Office Equipment** and **Maria Sanchez, Capital** are affected.

Classify 2. **Office Equipment** is an asset account. **Maria Sanchez, Capital** is an owner's capital account.

+/− 3. **Office Equipment** is increased by $400. **Maria Sanchez, Capital** is increased by $400.

DEBIT-CREDIT RULE

4. Increases in asset accounts are recorded as debits. Debit **Office Equipment** for $400.
5. Increases in owner's capital accounts are recorded as credits. Credit **Maria Sanchez, Capital** for $400.

Great Ideas *From the Classroom of...*

Using TV Monitors A 36-inch computer/TV monitor helps to enhance automated accounting presentations. Use the monitor to display the lesson objectives when you introduce the lesson. Or use the monitor to guide students through beginning exercises, study guides, and problems and include class participation. Coordinate the learning exercises with the electronic field trips, and create custom presentations to introduce or reinforce lessons.

Barbara Young
Madison High School
Madison, Virginia

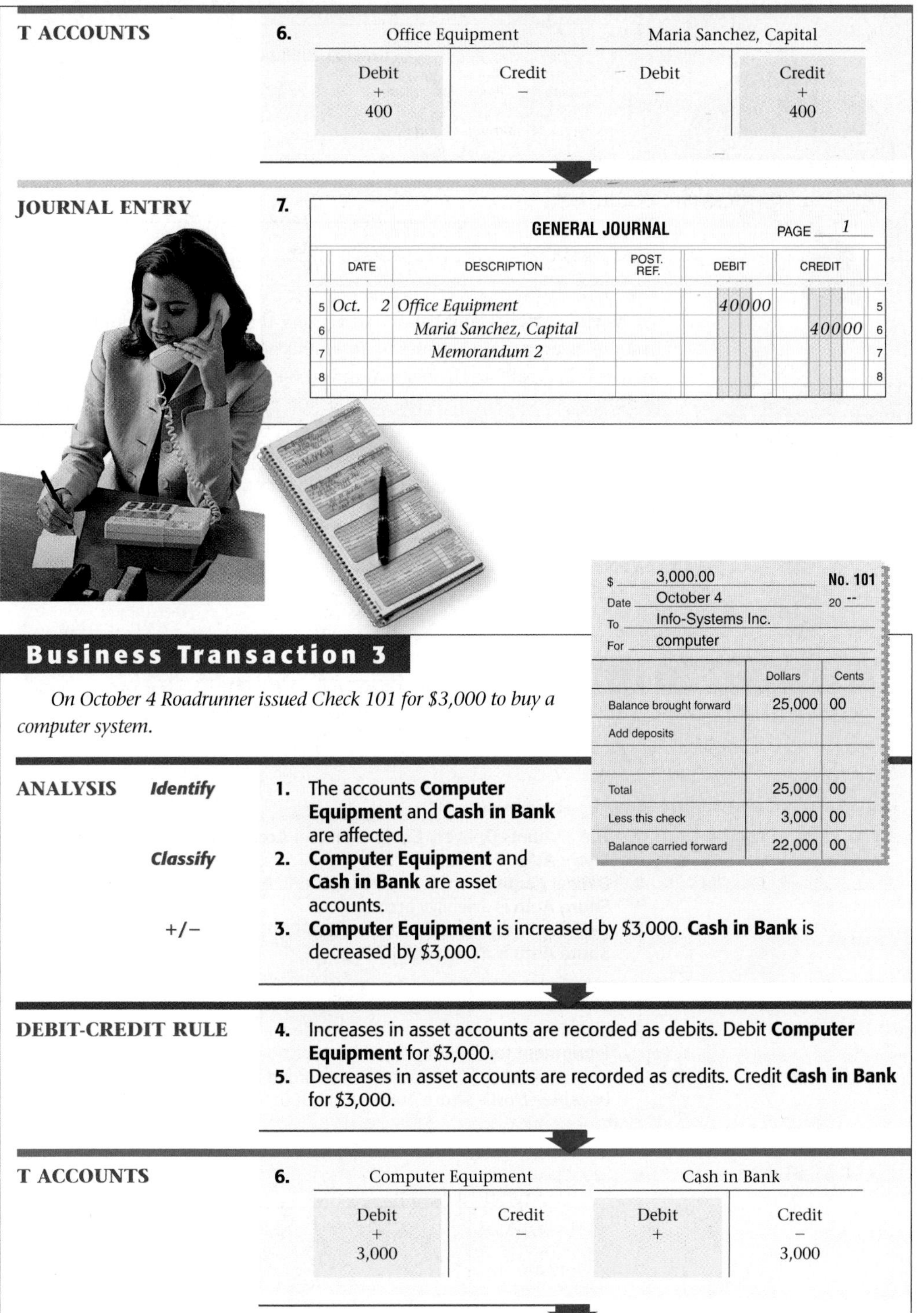

T ACCOUNTS

6.

Office Equipment		Maria Sanchez, Capital	
Debit + 400	Credit –	Debit –	Credit + 400

JOURNAL ENTRY

7.

GENERAL JOURNAL — PAGE 1

	DATE		DESCRIPTION	POST. REF.	DEBIT	CREDIT	
5	Oct.	2	*Office Equipment*		*400 00*		5
6			*Maria Sanchez, Capital*			*400 00*	6
7			*Memorandum 2*				7
8							8

Business Transaction 3

On October 4 Roadrunner issued Check 101 for $3,000 to buy a computer system.

$ 3,000.00	No. 101
Date October 4	20 --
To Info-Systems Inc.	
For computer	

	Dollars	Cents
Balance brought forward	25,000	00
Add deposits		
Total	25,000	00
Less this check	3,000	00
Balance carried forward	22,000	00

ANALYSIS

Identify 1. The accounts **Computer Equipment** and **Cash in Bank** are affected.

Classify 2. **Computer Equipment** and **Cash in Bank** are asset accounts.

+/– 3. **Computer Equipment** is increased by $3,000. **Cash in Bank** is decreased by $3,000.

DEBIT-CREDIT RULE

4. Increases in asset accounts are recorded as debits. Debit **Computer Equipment** for $3,000.
5. Decreases in asset accounts are recorded as credits. Credit **Cash in Bank** for $3,000.

T ACCOUNTS

6.

Computer Equipment		Cash in Bank	
Debit + 3,000	Credit –	Debit +	Credit – 3,000

2 TEACH (Cont'd.)

Teaching Tip

Have students analyze the check stub for Business Transaction 3 before looking at the transaction analysis. As students identify the pertinent information, write each part of their analysis on the chalkboard.

Visual Learning

Business Transaction 3

Use **Transparency 6–9** to guide students through recording a transaction involving a cash purchase of an asset.

Teaching Tip

Stress the importance of working neatly when recording accounting information. Sloppily prepared entries whose numbers are not clear can result in errors that are picked up and carried throughout the accounting process. Emphasize that the journal is the first record of entry, and errors made here will show up later when the accounts on each side of the equation do not balance.

MAKING CONNECTIONS TO DAILY LIFE

Apply Information from Source Documents Ask students to collect source documents for business transactions in their daily lives for a period of one week. (Samples of the source documents that students might collect include cash register receipts, handwritten receipts, order forms from catalogs, canceled checks, employee time cards, paycheck stubs, invoices, ATM bank receipts, credit card receipts, and telephone bills.) Have students prepare journal entries from the documents they collect.

2 TEACH (Cont'd.)

Visual Learning

Business Transaction 4

Using **Transparency 6–10**, have students analyze the transaction and explain how it is recorded in the general journal. Have students review the source document. What information on the invoice tells them that this purchase was made on account? Discuss installment credit and why it represents a purchase on account.

Critical Thinking: Ask students what other forms of credit might represent a purchase on account. (Answers could include credit-card purchases, an open line of credit with a business, or fixed credit terms such as payment within 15 days.) L1

Demonstration Problem Step-by-Step Practice

Use demonstration problem 6–2 to show students how to analyze and record a purchase made on account.

Chapter Reviews and Working Papers

Refer students to the *Study Plan* located at the beginning of Chapter 6 in the workbook.

JOURNAL ENTRY 7.

GENERAL JOURNAL PAGE 1

	DATE		DESCRIPTION	POST. REF.	DEBIT	CREDIT	
8	Oct.	4	*Computer Equipment*		3 000 00		8
9			*Cash in Bank*			3 000 00	9
10			*Check 101*				10
11							11

As you analyze a number of transactions, the rules of debit and credit will become clearer to you. Remember when you first learned to play a sport such as basketball? In the beginning you had to concentrate as you learned to dribble, shoot, and pass the ball. As you practiced, your skills improved. Learning to analyze business transactions is the same as learning anything else: The more you do it, the easier it gets.

Let's look at the remaining transactions for Roadrunner for the month of October.

Business Transaction 4

On October 9 Roadrunner bought a used truck on account from North Shore Auto for $12,000, Invoice 200.

North Shore Auto
440 Lake Drive
Sacramento, CA 94230

INVOICE NO. 200
DATE: Oct. 9, 20--
ORDER NO.: 99674
SHIPPED BY: n/a
TERMS: Installment

TO Roadrunner Delivery Service
155 Gateway Blvd.
Sacramento, CA 94230

QTY.	ITEM	UNIT PRICE	TOTAL
1	Dodge Truck Used	$ 12,000.00	$ 12,000.00

ANALYSIS

Identify 1. The accounts **Delivery Equipment** and **Accounts Payable—North Shore Auto** are affected.

Classify 2. **Delivery Equipment** is an asset account. **Accounts Payable—North Shore Auto** is a liability account.

+/− 3. **Delivery Equipment** is increased by $12,000. **Accounts Payable—North Shore Auto** is increased by $12,000.

DEBIT-CREDIT RULE

4. Increases in asset accounts are recorded as debits. Debit **Delivery Equipment** for $12,000.
5. Increases in liability accounts are recorded as credits. Credit **Accounts Payable—North Shore Auto** for $12,000.

T ACCOUNTS 6.

Delivery Equipment		Accounts Payable—North Shore Auto	
Debit +	Credit −	Debit −	Credit +
12,000			12,000

REINFORCING STUDY SKILLS

Taking Notes Some students find that an outline format is the best way to take notes, particularly notes from a textbook section or journal article. Making an outline for lecture notes may be more difficult, and students may have to use a combination of outline, narrative, and paragraph formats. Spend time with your students helping them to develop an outline format that is useful for accounting notes.

JOURNAL ENTRY

7.

GENERAL JOURNAL — PAGE 1

	DATE		DESCRIPTION	POST. REF.	DEBIT	CREDIT	
11	Oct.	9	Delivery Equipment		12 000 00		11
12			Accts. Pay.—North Shore Auto			12 000 00	12
13			Invoice 200				13
14							14

To separate the amounts to be paid to individual creditors, Roadrunner uses a different account name for each creditor. The account name consists of **Accounts Payable** followed by the name of the creditor. You may have to abbreviate the name to fit it on one line of the journal. An acceptable abbreviation in the preceding journal entry is **Accts. Pay.—North Shore Auto.**

Did You Know?

Teen Spending

Teens shop at malls an average of twice a month and spend just over $60 each trip.

Business Transaction 5

On October 11 Roadrunner sold one telephone on account to Green Company for $200, Memorandum 3.

Roadrunner Delivery Service
155 Gateway Blvd.
Sacramento, CA 94230

MEMORANDUM 3

TO: Accounting Clerk
FROM: Maria Sanchez
DATE: October 11, 20--
SUBJECT: Sold telephone

Sold one telephone on account to Green Company for $200.

ANALYSIS

Identify 1. The accounts **Accounts Receivable—Green Company** and **Office Equipment** are affected.

Classify 2. **Accounts Receivable—Green Company** is an asset account. **Office Equipment** is also an asset account.

+/− 3. **Accounts Receivable—Green Company** is increased by $200. **Office Equipment** is decreased by $200.

DEBIT-CREDIT RULE

4. Increases in asset accounts are recorded as debits. Debit **Accounts Receivable—Green Company** for $200.
5. Decreases in asset accounts are recorded as credits. Credit **Office Equipment** for $200.

T ACCOUNTS

6.

Accounts Receivable—Green Company	
Debit +	Credit −
200	

Office Equipment	
Debit +	Credit −
	200

CHAPTER 6
SECTION 2, PAGES 126–140

2 TEACH (Cont'd.)

Visual Learning

Business Transaction 5

Using **Transparency 6–11**, have students analyze the source document for this transaction amd then explain what information is recorded in the journal entry.

Teaching Tip

Remind students to look at each general journal entry as they analyze the business transaction given.

Critical Thinking: Ask students why the money from the sale of the telephone is not considered revenue for the business. (Since the business sells delivery services, revenue is earned from making deliveries. The sale of the telephone represents a reduction in the assets owned by the business rather than an increase in revenue earned by the business.) L1

COOPERATIVE LEARNING ACTIVITY

Round Table Divide students into groups of three or four and assign each group an example of a service business (such as carpet cleaners, hair salon, and heating/air conditioner repairs). Ask each group to list and describe the various source documents that their service business receives and generates for normal business activities. Ask students to interview local businesses and, if possible, collect samples of source documents from the business. Have each group appoint a spokesperson and share the lists and source documents with the class. Source documents should include the following: checks, cash receipts, credit card receipts, order forms, fax messages, letters, shipping forms, packing slips, and invoices.

CHAPTER 6
SECTION 2, PAGES 126–140

2 TEACH (Cont'd.)

Teaching Tip
To help students learn to analyze the information on a source document without relying on the transaction description in their textbooks, fill out several source documents and have students write descriptions of the transactions represented.

Demonstration Problem Step-by-Step Practice
Use demonstration problem 6–3 to show students how to record a partial payment to a creditor.

Visual Learning

Business Transaction 6
Using **Transparency 6–12**, have students describe the transaction represented by the check stub before they look at the transaction description in their textbooks. Then have students tell you what information to record in the general journal entry.

Critical Thinking: Ask students why it's a good idea when using T accounts to analyze a transaction to write the T account for the account debited first. (The debit part of the transaction is always entered first in the general journal, so writing the T account debited first makes it less likely to enter the wrong account first.) L1

Thinking Algebraically

Using Logic: Have students calculate the number of payments to pay off the $12,000 purchase price of the truck. (34 payments of $350 and a last payment of $100 = $12,000) L1

JOURNAL ENTRY 7.

GENERAL JOURNAL PAGE 1

	DATE		DESCRIPTION	POST. REF.	DEBIT	CREDIT	
14	Oct.	11	*Accts. Rec.—Green Company*		200 00		14
15			*Office Equipment*			200 00	15
16			*Memorandum 3*				16
17							17

To separate the amounts to be received from individual customers, Roadrunner uses a different account name for each customer. The account name consists of **Accounts Receivable** followed by the customer's name. You may have to abbreviate the name to fit it on one line of the journal. An acceptable abbreviation in the preceding journal entry is **Accts. Rec.—Green Co.**

$ 350.00 No. 102
Date October 12 20 --
To North Shore Auto
For installment on truck

	Dollars	Cents
Balance brought forward	22,000	00
Add deposits		
Total	22,000	00
Less this check	350	00
Balance carried forward	21,650	00

Business Transaction 6

On October 12 Roadrunner mailed Check 102 for $350 as the first installment payment on the truck purchased from North Shore Auto on October 9.

ANALYSIS

Identify 1. The accounts **Accounts Payable—North Shore Auto** and **Cash in Bank** are affected.

Classify 2. **Accounts Payable—North Shore Auto** is a liability account. **Cash in Bank** is an asset account.

+/− 3. **Accounts Payable—North Shore Auto** is decreased by $350. **Cash in Bank** is decreased by $350.

DEBIT-CREDIT RULE

4. Decreases in liability accounts are recorded as debits. Debit **Accounts Payable—North Shore Auto** for $350.
5. Decreases in asset accounts are recorded as credits. Credit **Cash in Bank** for $350.

T ACCOUNTS

6.

Accounts Payable—North Shore Auto		Cash in Bank	
Debit −	Credit +	Debit +	Credit −
350			350

MEETING SPECIAL NEEDS

Students with Hearing Impairments Students with hearing impairments may need to concentrate on lip reading your presentation or following an interpreter. Thus, taking notes may be difficult for these students. Try to help these students identify a reliable classmate who takes good notes. Contract with that student to share the notes and possibly provide a duplicate set of notes for the student with a hearing impairment.

JOURNAL ENTRY 7.

GENERAL JOURNAL — PAGE 1

	DATE		DESCRIPTION	POST. REF.	DEBIT	CREDIT	
17	Oct.	12	*Accts. Pay.—North Shore Auto*		350 00		17
18			*Cash in Bank*			350 00	18
19			*Check 102*				19
20							20

Business Transaction 7

On October 14 Roadrunner received and deposited a check for $200 from Green Company. The check is full payment for the telephone sold on account to Green on October 11, Receipt 1.

Roadrunner Delivery Service
155 Gateway Blvd.
Sacramento, CA 94230

RECEIPT
No. 1

Oct. 14 20 --

RECEIVED FROM Green Company $ 200.00

Two hundred and no/100 DOLLARS

FOR Telephone

RECEIVED BY *Maria Sanchez*

ANALYSIS

Identify 1. The accounts **Cash in Bank** and **Accounts Receivable—Green Company** are affected.

Classify 2. **Cash in Bank** is an asset account. **Accounts Receivable—Green Company** is an asset account.

+/− 3. Cash in Bank is increased by $200. **Accounts Receivable—Green Company** is decreased by $200.

DEBIT-CREDIT RULE

4. Increases in asset accounts are recorded as debits. Debit **Cash in Bank** for $200.
5. Decreases in asset accounts are recorded as credits. Credit **Accounts Receivable—Green Company** for $200.

T ACCOUNTS 6.

Cash in Bank	
Debit +	Credit −
200	

Accounts Receivable—Green Company	
Debit +	Credit −
	200

JOURNAL ENTRY 7.

GENERAL JOURNAL — PAGE 1

	DATE		DESCRIPTION	POST. REF.	DEBIT	CREDIT	
20	Oct.	14	*Cash in Bank*		200 00		20
21			*Accts. Rec.—Green Company*			200 00	21
22			*Receipt 1*				22
23							23

2 TEACH (Cont'd.)

Visual Learning

Business Transaction 7

Use **Transparency 6–13** to guide students through the analysis and recording of a receipt of cash for the sale of an asset on account. Remind students that this type of sale does not represent revenue for the business. Point out that the sale of assets is generally not a major source of cash for a business because the business uses its assets to generate revenue.

GO TO **Demonstration Probem Step-by-Step Practice**

Use demonstration problem 6–4 to show students how to record the receipt of a payment on account.

Teaching Tip

Emphasize the spelling of "receipt." Students frequently transpose the "e" and the "i."

CRITICAL THINKING ACTIVITY

Account Balances Last month, Amelia mailed a check for $89.27 to pay the balance due for a doctor's bill. Today, when Amelia called to schedule an appointment, she asked about her account balance. Amelia's account information did not show that the $89.27 had been received. However, Amelia has already received the canceled check from the bank. Give a reason(s) why Amelia's account still shows a balance due of $89.27. (The check was received and the payment was processed, but (a) the transaction was not posted to Amelia's account, (b) the transaction may have been posted to the wrong account, (c) the transaction was never journalized, or (d) the transaction was analyzed incorrectly and recorded incorrectly in the journal.)

2 TEACH (Cont'd.)

Visual Learning

Business Transaction 8

Use **Transparency 6–14** to discuss revenue transactions and the accounts affected. Have students explain how revenue affects owner's equity and the revenue account's relationship to the owner's capital account.

Critical Thinking: Ask students to explain how revenue affects both the current and future operations of the business. (Revenue is used to pay current operating expenses. It is also used to buy additional assets needed to operate or expand the business—thus generating additional revenue—and to pay future operating expenses.) L1

Visual Learning

Business Transaction 9

Use **Transparency 6–15** to analyze and record an expense transaction.

Critical Thinking: Have students contrast this transaction (check stub 103) with transaction 6 (check stub 102). Why does the same type of source document represent an expense transaction and a payment for an asset? (Businesses issue checks for all payments, whether for expenses or for purchase of assets such as equipment or supplies, for cash control and to provide an audit trail. Thus, a check stub can represent different types of business transactions.) L2

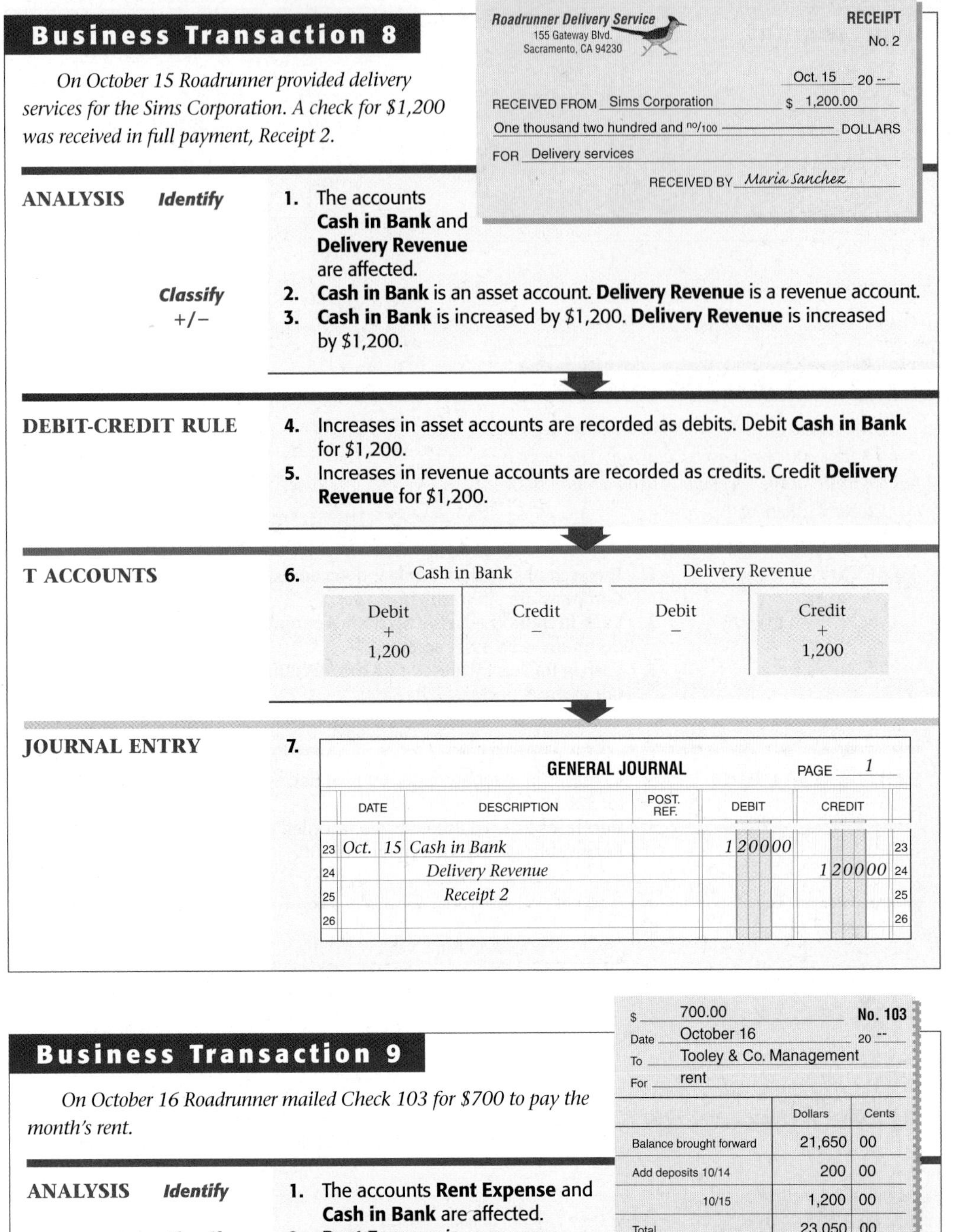

Business Transaction 8

On October 15 Roadrunner provided delivery services for the Sims Corporation. A check for $1,200 was received in full payment, Receipt 2.

Roadrunner Delivery Service
155 Gateway Blvd.
Sacramento, CA 94230

RECEIPT No. 2

Oct. 15 20 --

RECEIVED FROM Sims Corporation $ 1,200.00

One thousand two hundred and no/100 DOLLARS

FOR Delivery services

RECEIVED BY *Maria Sanchez*

ANALYSIS *Identify*
1. The accounts **Cash in Bank** and **Delivery Revenue** are affected.

Classify
2. **Cash in Bank** is an asset account. **Delivery Revenue** is a revenue account.

+/−
3. **Cash in Bank** is increased by $1,200. **Delivery Revenue** is increased by $1,200.

DEBIT-CREDIT RULE
4. Increases in asset accounts are recorded as debits. Debit **Cash in Bank** for $1,200.
5. Increases in revenue accounts are recorded as credits. Credit **Delivery Revenue** for $1,200.

T ACCOUNTS
6.

Cash in Bank		Delivery Revenue	
Debit +	Credit −	Debit −	Credit +
1,200			1,200

JOURNAL ENTRY
7.

GENERAL JOURNAL PAGE 1

	DATE		DESCRIPTION	POST. REF.	DEBIT	CREDIT	
23	Oct.	15	Cash in Bank		1 200 00		23
24			Delivery Revenue			1 200 00	24
25			Receipt 2				25
26							26

Business Transaction 9

On October 16 Roadrunner mailed Check 103 for $700 to pay the month's rent.

$ 700.00 No. 103
Date October 16 20 --
To Tooley & Co. Management
For rent

	Dollars	Cents
Balance brought forward	21,650	00
Add deposits 10/14	200	00
10/15	1,200	00
Total	23,050	00
Less this check	700	00
Balance carried forward	22,350	00

ANALYSIS *Identify*
1. The accounts **Rent Expense** and **Cash in Bank** are affected.

Classify
2. **Rent Expense** is an expense account. **Cash in Bank** is an asset account.

+/−
3. **Rent Expense** is increased by $700. **Cash in Bank** is decreased by $700.

134 Chapter 6 Recording Transactions in a General Journal

ACCOUNTING ISSUES

Using Neural Network Programs Typically, computers are used to perform repetitive tasks such as sorting, searching, and calculating. With innovative technology known as neural network programs, computers are also making decisions. Neural networks make the work of accountants easier and more productive by providing decision support software and services. The software simulates human intelligence. Neural networks are designed to learn from experience and to recognize patterns of data. By utilizing data analysis and prediction techniques, neural networks help accountants assess credit risk, detect fraud, forecast economic trends, establish credit ratings, and create financial models.

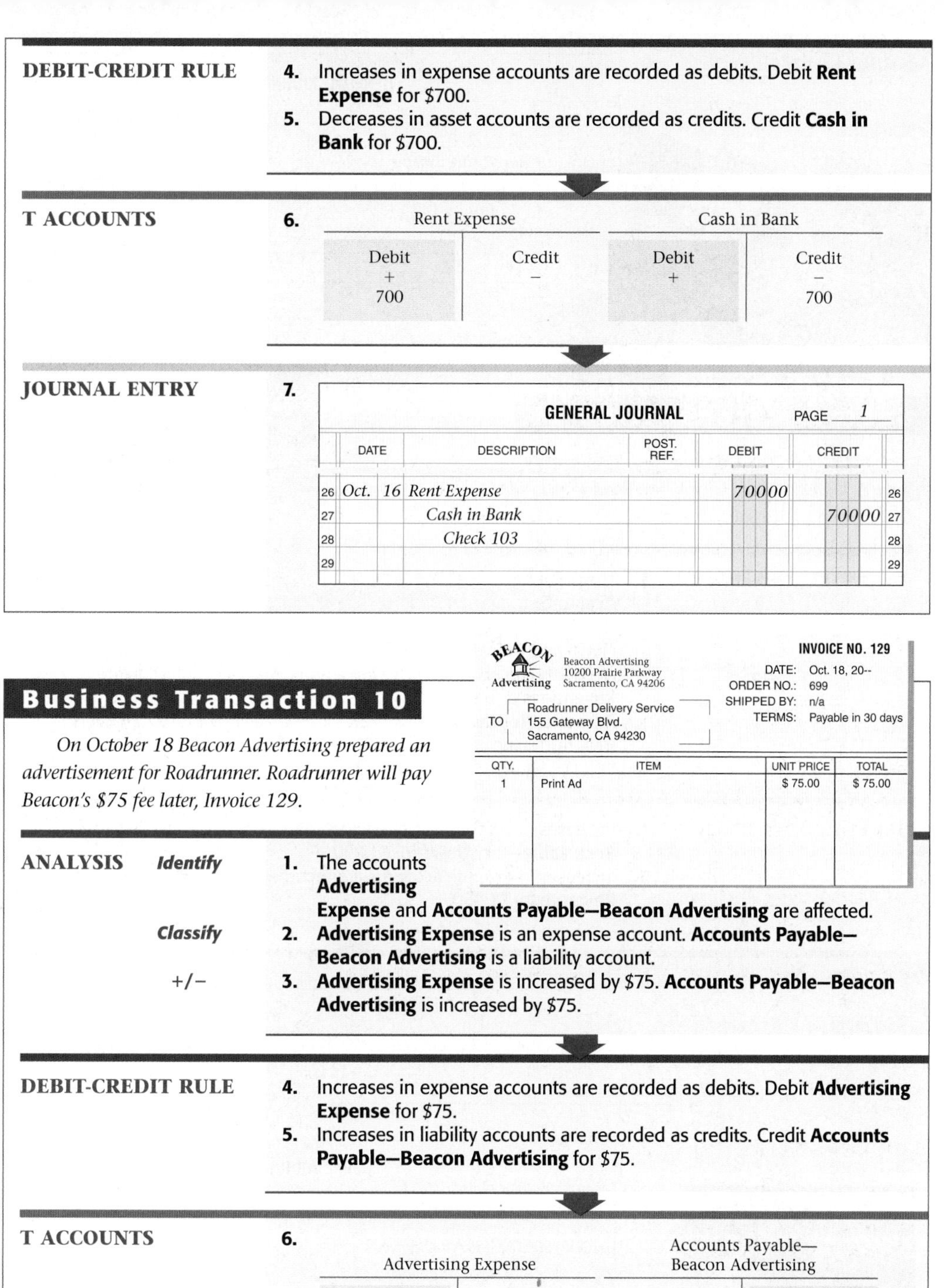

DEBIT-CREDIT RULE

4. Increases in expense accounts are recorded as debits. Debit **Rent Expense** for $700.
5. Decreases in asset accounts are recorded as credits. Credit **Cash in Bank** for $700.

T ACCOUNTS

6.

Rent Expense		Cash in Bank	
Debit +	Credit −	Debit +	Credit −
700			700

JOURNAL ENTRY

7.

GENERAL JOURNAL PAGE 1

	DATE		DESCRIPTION	POST. REF.	DEBIT	CREDIT	
26	Oct.	16	Rent Expense		700 00		26
27			Cash in Bank			700 00	27
28			Check 103				28
29							29

Business Transaction 10

On October 18 Beacon Advertising prepared an advertisement for Roadrunner. Roadrunner will pay Beacon's $75 fee later, Invoice 129.

BEACON Advertising
Beacon Advertising
10200 Prairie Parkway
Sacramento, CA 94206

INVOICE NO. 129

DATE: Oct. 18, 20--
ORDER NO.: 699
SHIPPED BY: n/a
TERMS: Payable in 30 days

TO Roadrunner Delivery Service
155 Gateway Blvd.
Sacramento, CA 94230

QTY.	ITEM	UNIT PRICE	TOTAL
1	Print Ad	$ 75.00	$ 75.00

ANALYSIS

Identify 1. The accounts **Advertising Expense** and **Accounts Payable—Beacon Advertising** are affected.

Classify 2. **Advertising Expense** is an expense account. **Accounts Payable—Beacon Advertising** is a liability account.

+/− 3. **Advertising Expense** is increased by $75. **Accounts Payable—Beacon Advertising** is increased by $75.

DEBIT-CREDIT RULE

4. Increases in expense accounts are recorded as debits. Debit **Advertising Expense** for $75.
5. Increases in liability accounts are recorded as credits. Credit **Accounts Payable—Beacon Advertising** for $75.

T ACCOUNTS

6.

Advertising Expense		Accounts Payable—Beacon Advertising	
Debit +	Credit −	Debit −	Credit +
75			75

CHAPTER 6
SECTION 2, PAGES 126–140

2 TEACH (Cont'd.)

Teaching Tip

Have students look at the source document for Business Transaction 10. How do they know this document represents a purchase on account? (The terms of the invoice show that the amount is payable in 30 days.)

Visual Learning

Business Transaction 10

Use **Transparency 6–16** to analyze the purchase of a service (an expense) on account. How does this transaction differ from a cash purchase?

Critical Thinking: Have students discuss why this transaction is represented by an invoice rather than a check stub. (The purchase was on account rather than for cash.) L1

HOME AND COMMUNITY CONNECTIONS ACTIVITY

Budgeting Ask students to visualize keeping their home budget by computer. What source documents would they need to gather from family members in order to key in accurate budget information? Have students talk with family members about different source documents critical to a budget. If possible, have them bring in at least two examples of such source documents. Collect the various examples and talk about their use for documenting information on the computer. (Examples of home source documents might be grocery receipts, sales slips, bills and invoices, check stubs.)

CHAPTER 6
SECTION 2, PAGES 126–140

2 TEACH (Cont'd.)

Visual Learning

Business Transaction 11

Use **Transparency 6–17** to analyze the accounts affected by a sale made on account.

GO TO Demonstration Problem Step-by-Step Practice

Use demonstration problem 6–5 to show students how to record a sale on account.

Observation: Have students contrast the invoice in business transaction 12 with the one in transaction 10 (a purchase invoice). Ask students to describe the differences. How will they know which type of invoice is a sales invoice and which is a purchase invoice? (A sales invoice is addressed to the buyer, while a purchase invoice is addressed to the business.) L1

Teaching Tip

Under the accrual basis of accounting, income is reported as being earned at the time the job is completed or the service provided, which is not necessarily the same time as the money is received.

JOURNAL ENTRY 7.

GENERAL JOURNAL — PAGE 1

	DATE		DESCRIPTION	POST. REF.	DEBIT	CREDIT	
29	Oct.	18	Advertising Expense		75 00		29
30			Accts. Pay.—Beacon Adv.			75 00	30
31			Invoice 129				31
32							32

Business Transaction 11

On October 20 Roadrunner provided delivery services for a customer, City News. Roadrunner billed City News $1,450, Sales Invoice 1.

Roadrunner Delivery Service
155 Gateway Blvd.
Sacramento, CA 94230

SALES INVOICE NO. 1
DATE: Oct. 20, 20--
ORDER NO.: 300
SHIPPED BY: n/a
TERMS: Payable in 30 days

TO City News
10900 Main St.
Sacramento, CA 94230

QTY.	ITEM	UNIT PRICE	TOTAL
1	Delivery Services	$ 1,450.00	$ 1,450.00

ANALYSIS

Identify 1. The accounts **Accounts Receivable—City News** and **Delivery Revenue** are affected.

Classify 2. **Accounts Receivable—City News** is an asset account. **Delivery Revenue** is a revenue account.

+/− 3. **Accounts Receivable—City News** is increased by $1,450. **Delivery Revenue** is increased by $1,450.

DEBIT-CREDIT RULE

4. Increases in asset accounts are recorded as debits. Debit **Accounts Receivable—City News** for $1,450.
5. Increases in revenue accounts are recorded as credits. Credit **Delivery Revenue** for $1,450.

T ACCOUNTS

6.

Accounts Receivable—City News		Delivery Revenue	
Debit +	Credit −	Debit −	Credit +
1,450			1,450

JOURNAL ENTRY 7.

GENERAL JOURNAL — PAGE 1

	DATE		DESCRIPTION	POST. REF.	DEBIT	CREDIT	
32	Oct.	20	Accts. Rec.—City News		1 450 00		32
33			Delivery Revenue			1 450 00	33
34			Sales Invoice 1				34
35							35

ADDRESSING MULTIPLE LEARNING STYLES

Visual/Spatial Learners Have students contact a local business and gather samples of source documents the business uses in its daily operations. Then have students display the various types of source documents on a bulletin board. Ask students to highlight the portions of each source document that provide the data for journal entries.

Business Transaction 12

On October 28 Roadrunner paid a $125 telephone bill with Check 104.

$ 125.00		No. 104
Date October 28		20 --
To Pacific Bell Telephone		
For telephone bill		
	Dollars	Cents
Balance brought forward	22,350	00
Add deposits		
Total	22,350	00
Less this check	125	00
Balance carried forward	22,225	00

ANALYSIS ***Identify*** 1. The accounts **Utilities Expense** and **Cash in Bank** are affected.

Classify 2. **Utilities Expense** is an expense account. **Cash in Bank** is an asset account.

+/− 3. **Utilities Expense** is increased by $125. **Cash in Bank** is decreased by $125.

DEBIT-CREDIT RULE

4. Increases in expense accounts are recorded as debits. Debit **Utilities Expense** for $125.
5. Decreases in asset accounts are recorded as credits. Credit **Cash in Bank** for $125.

T ACCOUNTS

6.

Utilities Expense		Cash in Bank	
Debit +	Credit −	Debit +	Credit −
125			125

JOURNAL ENTRY

7.

GENERAL JOURNAL — PAGE *1*

	DATE		DESCRIPTION	POST. REF.	DEBIT	CREDIT	
35	*Oct.*	*28*	*Utilities Expense*		*125 00*		35
36			*Cash in Bank*			*125 00*	36
37			*Check 104*				37
38							38

Business Transaction 13

On October 29 Roadrunner wrote Check 105 for $600 to have the office repainted.

$ 600.00		No. 105
Date October 29		20 --
To Rainbow Painting		
For office painted		
	Dollars	Cents
Balance brought forward	22,225	00
Add deposits		
Total	22,225	00
Less this check	600	00
Balance carried forward	21,625	00

ANALYSIS ***Identify*** 1. The accounts, **Maintenance Expense** and **Cash in Bank,** are affected.

Classify 2. **Maintenance Expense** is an expense account. **Cash in Bank** is an asset account.

+/− 3. **Maintenance Expense** is increased by $600. **Cash in Bank** is decreased by $600.

2 TEACH (Cont'd.)

Visual Learning

Business Transaction 12

Use **Transparency 6–18** to analyze the recording of a business expense. Ask students why expenses are paid with checks (to control cash and leave an audit trail).

Teaching Tips

Have students discuss how expenses affect the owner's capital account.

Also review the role of temporary capital accounts. Remind students that expense accounts begin each fiscal period with a zero balance and increase as expenses are incurred to operate the business during the fiscal period. Point out that each different type of expense is recorded in its own account. This practice helps owners and managers identify exactly what they are spending money on and whether these expenses are increasing or decreasing over a period of time.

TEACHING NOTES

CHAPTER 6
SECTION 2, PAGES 126–140

2 TEACH (Cont'd.)

Visual Learning

Business Transaction 13

Using **Transparency 6–19**, have students analyze the accounts affected and determine what information to record in the journal entry.

Business Transaction 14

Use **Transparency 6–20** to discuss the differences between a business expense and the withdrawal of cash or some other asset by the owner for personal use. Ask students to discuss the effect of a withdrawal on the owner's capital account.

Teaching Tip

Write "Expenses" and "Withdrawals" on the chalkboard. Have students tell you how the two are different and how they are alike. Write the similarities and differences on the board as students discuss the two types of accounts.

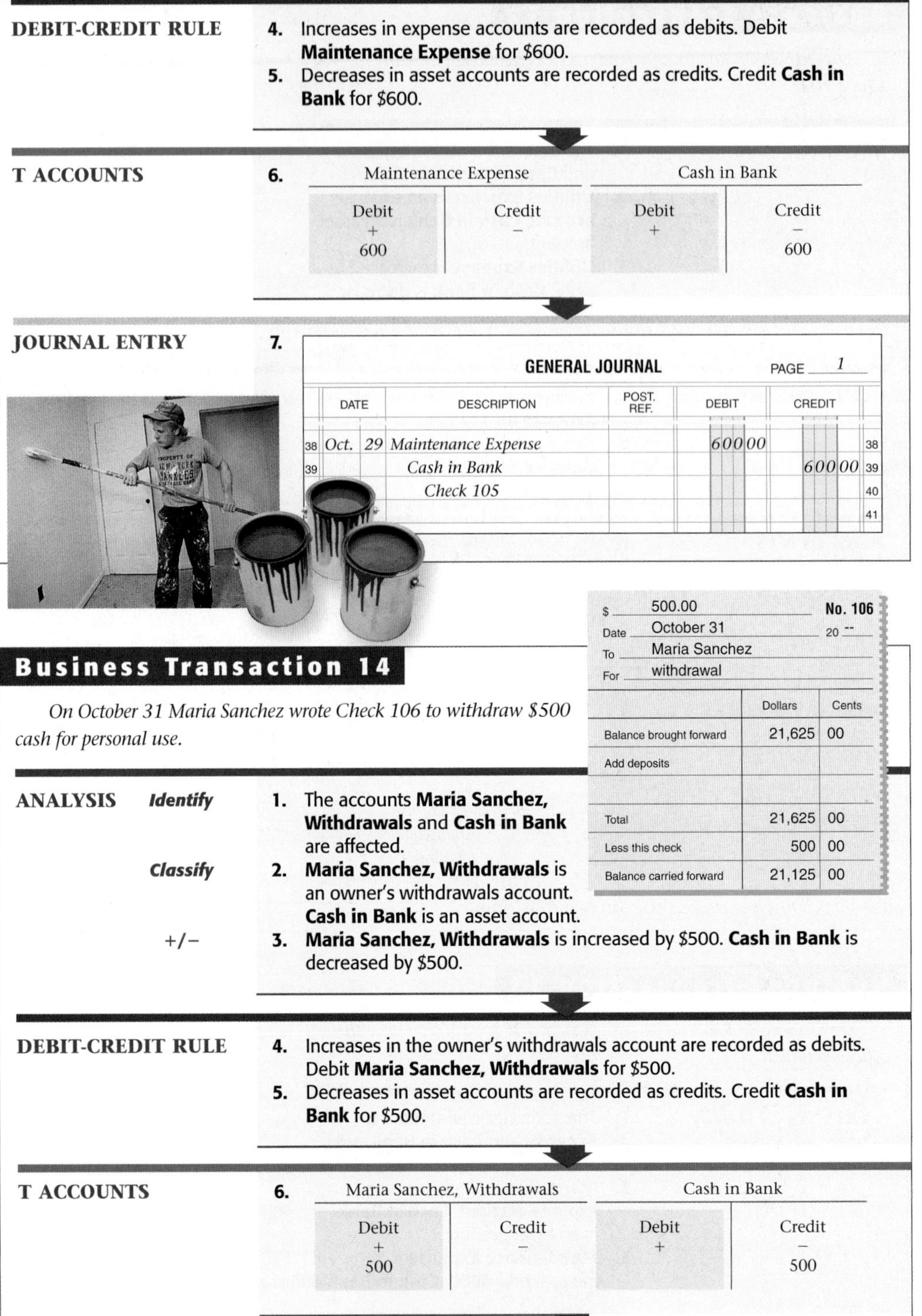

DEBIT-CREDIT RULE

4. Increases in expense accounts are recorded as debits. Debit **Maintenance Expense** for $600.
5. Decreases in asset accounts are recorded as credits. Credit **Cash in Bank** for $600.

T ACCOUNTS

6.

Maintenance Expense	
Debit +	Credit –
600	

Cash in Bank	
Debit +	Credit –
	600

JOURNAL ENTRY

7.

GENERAL JOURNAL — PAGE 1

	DATE		DESCRIPTION	POST. REF.	DEBIT	CREDIT	
38	Oct.	29	Maintenance Expense		600 00		38
39			Cash in Bank			600 00	39
			Check 105				40
							41

Business Transaction 14

On October 31 Maria Sanchez wrote Check 106 to withdraw $500 cash for personal use.

$ 500.00	No. 106
Date October 31	20 --
To Maria Sanchez	
For withdrawal	

	Dollars	Cents
Balance brought forward	21,625	00
Add deposits		
Total	21,625	00
Less this check	500	00
Balance carried forward	21,125	00

ANALYSIS

Identify 1. The accounts **Maria Sanchez, Withdrawals** and **Cash in Bank** are affected.

Classify 2. **Maria Sanchez, Withdrawals** is an owner's withdrawals account. **Cash in Bank** is an asset account.

+/– 3. **Maria Sanchez, Withdrawals** is increased by $500. **Cash in Bank** is decreased by $500.

DEBIT-CREDIT RULE

4. Increases in the owner's withdrawals account are recorded as debits. Debit **Maria Sanchez, Withdrawals** for $500.
5. Decreases in asset accounts are recorded as credits. Credit **Cash in Bank** for $500.

T ACCOUNTS

6.

Maria Sanchez, Withdrawals	
Debit +	Credit –
500	

Cash in Bank	
Debit +	Credit –
	500

EXTENDING THE CONTENT

Interviewing Employers Encourage students who have part-time jobs to interview their employers regarding how many different accounting computer applications are in use in their workplace. Ask students to obtain samples of input forms and computer-generated reports, if possible. Have students share their findings with the class. Students should be able to list the names of the various computer applications and describe their use.

JOURNAL ENTRY 7.

GENERAL JOURNAL — PAGE 1

	DATE		DESCRIPTION	POST. REF.	DEBIT	CREDIT	
41	Oct.	31	Maria Sanchez, Withdrawals		500 00		41
42			Cash in Bank			500 00	42
43			Check 106				43
44							44

Correcting Errors in General Journal Entries

Occasionally, errors occur when journalizing transactions. When an error is discovered, it must be corrected.

In a manual system, *an error should never be erased.* An erasure looks suspicious. It might be seen as an attempt to cover up a mistake or, worse, to change the accounting records illegally. To correct errors, use a pen and a ruler to draw a horizontal line through the entire incorrect item and write the correct information above the crossed-out error. A correction for an erroneous amount is shown in the general journal as follows:

GENERAL JOURNAL — PAGE 1

	DATE		DESCRIPTION	POST. REF.	DEBIT	CREDIT	
1	20--						1
2	Oct.	1	Cash in Bank		25 000 00 ~~52 000 00~~		2
3			Maria Sanchez, Capital			25 000 00 ~~52 000 00~~	3
4			Memorandum 1				4
5							5

To correct an error for an erroneous account name, cross out the incorrect information and write the correct names above.

Key Points

General Journal Entries

- Every transaction requires a debit and a credit entry.
- Debits are recorded before credits.
- Source document references are entered on a separate line.

A MATTER OF ETHICS

Gossip in the Workplace

Let's say that you are an accounting clerk for a large insurance company like Farmers Insurance. Your boss introduces you to the newest hire, and you recognize her as a former classmate from high school named Sally. You remember that Sally had been suspended from school for a series of locker thefts. During lunch, you consider telling other co-workers about Sally's history. You also wonder if your boss knows.

Ethical Decision Making:

- What are the ethical issues?
- What are the alternatives?
- Who are the affected parties?
- How do the alternatives affect the parties?
- What would you do?

2 TEACH (Cont'd.)

Concept Development: Correcting Errors in General Journal Entries

Discussion: Since errors are bound to occur, procedures have been developed for fixing them in the accounting records. Emphasize that errors should never be erased. Discuss with students the method of correcting an error by crossing out an incorrect account or amount in the journal entry.

Point out to students that following procedures for correcting errors maintains the audit trail. Explain that outside reviewers of accounting records are called auditors and the steps they follow in tracing financial data from its source (the journal entry) to its inclusion in financial reports is the audit trail. L1

Teaching Tip

Point out to students that while they're allowed to use pencil as they learn how to record financial data, in the business world financial records are kept either in ink or in a computerized system where entries cannot be erased.

Strategies for Teaching Ethics in Accounting

Photocopy the Chapter 6 *Student Activity Sheet* for students. Answers are also provided in the booklet.

Teaching A MATTER OF ETHICS

Gossip in the Workplace Ask students to think about times when they've been the victim of gossip. How did they feel? Did the gossip affect friendships or their work? Point out that gossip is rarely positive. People who gossip on the job are often viewed negatively by supervisors and co-workers. The temptation to gossip is strong, however, since it frequently makes people feel that they fit in. Students will need to decide how they will deal with workplace gossip.

CHAPTER 6
SECTION 2, PAGES 126–140

3 ASSESS

Thinking Critically (Answers)

1. Debit Advertising Expense; credit Cash in Bank.
2. Debit Accounts Receivable; credit Service Revenue.

Computing in the Business World (Answer)

Napkins $29.28; salt $9.57; paper cups $21.84; paper cups, medium $32.96; total $93.65 (amount to be used in the journal entry)

Problem 6–2 (Answers)

Step 1 D
Step 2 F
Step 3 E
Step 4 B
Step 5 A
Step 6 C

Problem 6–3 (Answers)

1. Passenger Van, asset, inc., dr.; Cash in Bank, asset, dec., cr.
2. Utilities Expense, expense, inc., dr.; Cash in Bank, asset, dec., cr.
3. Cash in Bank, asset, inc., dr.; Day Care Fees, revenue, inc., cr.

Chapter Reviews and Working Papers Refer students to the Chapter 6 workbook pages to answer *Check Your Understanding* activities.

4 CLOSE

Section Wrap-Up

Demonstration: Write this transaction on the chalkboard: "On October 31 Roadrunner Delivery Services bought gasoline and oil for $32.40 on account, Receipt 4." Have students record the transaction in a general journal. L1

SECTION 2 Check Your Understanding

Now that you have studied this section, complete the following questions and problems.

Thinking Critically

1. What accounts would you use to record the purchase of a newspaper ad for cash?
2. What accounts would you use to record the sale of business services on account?

Computing in the Business World

The accounting clerk for Conover Restaurant Suppliers is preparing an invoice to send to Glen's Catering for the following supplies:

- 6 cartons of napkins at $4.88 per carton
- 3 boxes of paper cups at $7.28 per box
- 3 boxes of salt packets at $3.19 per box
- 4 boxes of medium paper cups at $8.24 per box

Calculate the total for each item on the invoice. Then calculate the total for all items.

Problem 6–2 Recording Business Transactions

Instructions Shown below are the six steps for recording a business transaction in the general journal. In your working papers or on a blank sheet of paper, indicate the proper order of these steps.

A. Amount of the credit.	Step #1.
B. Name of the account credited.	Step #2.
C. Source document reference.	Step #3.
D. Date of the transaction.	Step #4.
E. Amount of the debit.	Step #5.
F. Name of the account debited.	Step #6.

Problem 6–3 Analyzing Transactions

Glenda Hohn recently started a day care center. She uses the following accounts to record business transactions.

General Ledger

Cash in Bank	Glenda Hohn, Capital
Accts. Rec.—Tiny Tots Nursery	Glenda Hohn, Withdrawals
Office Furniture	Day Care Fees
Passenger Van	Utilities Expense
Accts. Pay.—Acme Bus Service	Van Expense

Instructions In your working papers or on a separate sheet of paper, for each transaction: Determine which accounts are affected. Classify each account. Determine whether the accounts are being increased or decreased. Indicate which account is debited and which account is credited.

Transactions:

1. Bought a passenger van for cash.
2. Paid the telephone bill for the month.
3. Received cash from customers for day care services.

RETEACHING SECTION 2

The Purpose of the Journal Regardless of whether transactions are journalized manually or in a computerized system, the journal contains complete information about each of the daily transactions of the business in the order they occur. If instead transactions were recorded directly in the ledger accounts, there would be no chronological listing of all transactions. It would also be difficult to locate complete information about a specific transaction. To do so, you would need to search through each ledger account to find the debit and credit entries related to that transaction.

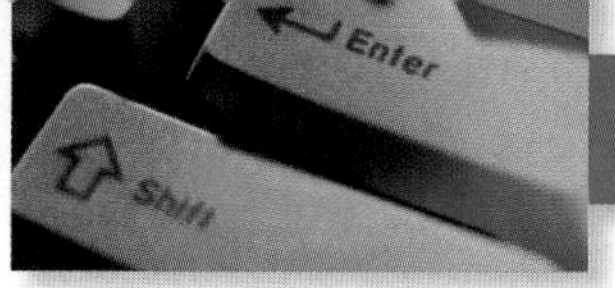

CHAPTER 6 SUMMARY

KEY CONCEPTS

1. Accounting records are maintained in separate time periods called accounting periods.
2. The activities involved in maintaining the accounting records make up the accounting cycle.
3. The Accounting Cycle—Steps 1–3 is pictured to the right.

4. Journalizing a Business Transaction:

GENERAL JOURNAL — PAGE ____

	DATE		DESCRIPTION	POST. REF.	DEBIT	CREDIT	
1	(1) Date		(2) Account to Debit		(3) Debit Amt.		1
2			(4) Account to Credit			(5) Credit Amt.	2
3			(6) Source Document Ref.				3
4							4

5. Correcting a Journal Entry with an Incorrect Amount (Manual System). Phillip Reyna invested $36,000 in his business on May 15, Memorandum 2. The amount of the transaction was recorded incorrectly. The original entry and the correction follows.

GENERAL JOURNAL — PAGE 1

	DATE		DESCRIPTION	POST. REF.	DEBIT	CREDIT	
1	20--						1
2	May	15	Cash in Bank		36 000 00 ~~63 000 00~~		2
3			Phillip Reyna, Capital			36 000 00 ~~63 000 00~~	3
4			Memorandum 2				4
5							5

6. Correcting a Journal Entry with an Incorrect Account Name (Manual System).

GENERAL JOURNAL — PAGE 1

	DATE		DESCRIPTION	POST. REF.	DEBIT	CREDIT	
1	20--						1
2	May	15	Cash in Bank ~~Office Supplies~~		36 000 00		2
3			Phillip Reyna, Capital			36 000 00	3
4			Memorandum 2				4
5							5

SUMMARY CHAPTER 6

Chapter 6 Quiz

Student ____ Class ____ Instructor ____
Date Assigned ____ Date Completed ____

CHAPTER 6 QUIZ

Recording Transactions in a General Journal

QUESTIONS (Completion)

Directions: Fill in the blank with the term that best completes each sentence.

1. The first step in the accounting cycle is to collect and verify ____.
2. Each transaction affects at least ____ accounts.
3. Activities completed during an accounting period are called the ____.
4. Examples of source documents are invoices, receipts, memorandums, and ____.
5. A source document is ____ that a transaction has occurred.
6. Business transactions are recorded in ____ order.
7. A ____ year may or may not be the same as a calendar year.
8. The process of recording business transactions is called ____.
9. The ____ journal is an all-purpose journal used to record all the transactions of a business.
10. Errors in a general journal entry are corrected by ____ incorrect information and entering correct data.

8 • Chapter Quizzes

QUESTIONS (Completion)

1. The first step in the accounting cycle is to collect and verify ____.
2. Each transaction affects at least ____ accounts.
3. Activities completed during an accounting period are called the ____.
4. Examples of source documents are invoices, receipts, memorandums, and ____.
5. A source document is ____ that a transaction has occurred.
6. Business transactions are recorded in ____ order.
7. A ____ year may or may not be the same as a calendar year.
8. The process of recording business transactions is called ____.
9. The ____ journal is an all-purpose journal used to record all the transactions of a business.
10. Errors in a general journal entry are corrected by ____ incorrect information and entering correct data.

ANSWERS

1. source documents
2. two
3. accounting cycle
4. check stubs
5. evidence
6. chronological
7. fiscal
8. journalizing
9. general
10. crossing out

USING KEY TERMS

See the *Glossary* for the definitions of these terms. Post students' newsletters on the bulletin board and give students time to read the newsletters. Have students note the terms they used incorrectly in their own newsletters.

Understanding Accounting Concepts and Procedures

(Answers)

1. An accounting period of twelve months ending on the last day of any month except December.
2. Collect/verify source documents, analyze transactions, journalize transactions, post to the ledger, prepare trial balance, prepare work sheet, prepare financial statements, journalize/post closing entries, prepare post-closing trial balance.
3. Evidence that a business transaction has occurred.
4. Invoices: buying or selling items; receipts: cash received; memorandums: transactions within business; check stubs: cash payments.
5. It is the only record of complete transaction details.
6. Businesses need to keep accurate financial records so that they know how well they are doing.
7. The first column records debits; the second, credits.
8. Date of the transaction, account debited, debit amount, account credited, credit amount, and reference to the source document or description of the entry.
9. Identify, classify, determine +/−, determine account to debit and amount, determine account to credit and amount, write the entry in T-account form, make a journal entry.
10. Draw a horizontal line through the incorrect item; write correct data above the crossed-out error.

USING KEY TERMS

Assume you are an accountant who keeps financial records for small businesses. Write a one-page newsletter that you might send to potential clients describing the importance of accounting records. Use each of the terms below in your report.

accounting cycle	journal
calendar year	journalizing
check stub	memorandum
fiscal year	receipt
general journal	source document
invoice	

Understanding Accounting Concepts and Procedures

Instructions

On a separate sheet of paper, answer the following questions:

1. What is meant by the term "fiscal year"?
2. List the nine steps of the accounting cycle.
3. What is the purpose of a source document?
4. List four source documents and explain when each is used.
5. Why is a journal sometimes called the book of original entry?
6. Why is it important for businesses to keep accurate financial records?
7. How are the two amount columns of the general journal used to record dollar amounts?
8. What six types of information are included in each general journal entry?
9. List the seven steps used to analyze a business transaction.
10. What procedure is used for correcting an error in a journal entry in a manual system?

ASSESSMENT RESOURCES

Choose assessment strategies from the following pages to evaluate your students' progress.

Student Edition
Check Your Understanding, pp. 125, 140
Chapter 6 Problems, pp. 145–149

Assessment and Evaluation Masters
Chapter 6 Study Plan, *Glencoe Workbook* (CRWP)
Chapter 6 Self-Test, *Glencoe Workbook* (CRWP)
Chapter 6 Test, *Chapter Tests* Booklet
Chapter 6 Activity, *School-to-Work Handbook*
Chapter 6 **Exam***View*

Teacher Wraparound Edition
Critical Thinking Activity, p. 133
Reteaching Section 1–2, pp. 125, 140
Chapter 6 Quiz, p. 141

Case Study...

Service Business: Exercise and Fitness

Elena Rodriguez started a business offering an exercise facility and personal physical training. Elena has hired you as a financial consultant to help her set up her accounting system. She has rented a space for her business, purchased several exercise machines, and hired a part-time exercise instructor. Elena's clients can either pay a fee for each visit or purchase a membership.

Thinking Critically:

1. Write a plan for Elena Rodriguez explaining the types of financial information she needs to record. Describe the source documents that might be a part of her business. For example, should Elena send invoices to her non-membership clients or ask them to pay at each visit? Describe why it is important for Elena to record both the cost of doing business and the income from the business.
2. Suggest a chart of accounts for Elena's business.

interNET CONNECTION

The Big Four

Most of the major public accounting firms can be found on the Internet. Their Web sites offer information on services, locations, and employment.

Do This:

1. Locate the Web site for one of the Big Four accounting firms.
2. At the Web site, search for information on employment opportunities.
3. Name two accounting opportunities found there. What skills are required for the available positions?

Conducting an Audit with Alex

Instructions In the following transactions, help Alex find any errors in the general journal entries presented.

(1) Compare the transactions given below with the entries recorded in the general journal.

(2) If any part of the transaction has been recorded incorrectly, make the necessary corrections to the journal entries on a separate sheet of paper.

Date	Transaction
Oct. 2	Bought $2,000 in office equipment, Check 601.
4	Received $50 from a charge customer, Jack Lane, to apply to his account, Receipt 120.

GENERAL JOURNAL PAGE 1

	DATE		DESCRIPTION	POST. REF.	DEBIT	CREDIT	
1	20--						1
2	Oct.	2	Store Equipment		2 000 00		2
3			Cash in Bank			2 000 00	3
4			Check 601				4
5		4	Cash in Bank		500 00		5
6			Accts. Rec.—Jack Lane			500 00	6
7			Receipt 102				7
8							8

Workplace Skills

Creative Thinking

Congratulations! You've been chosen as the local Business Owner of the Year! Write a one-page press release describing your business and why you've been successful. Be sure to include a brief description of your business, the skills you use in running a successful business, and how you plan to continue being successful in the future.

REVIEW AND ACTIVITIES CHAPTER 6

Case Study...

Thinking Critically (Answers)

Answers will vary. Students should mention that recording of financial information is necessary to evaluate the performance of the business.

Workplace Skills

Creative Thinking (Answers)

Answers will vary. Evaluate students' papers for use of correct grammar and the logical progression of ideas.

Conducting an Audit with Alex

(Answers)

Transaction 1:

Cross out "Store" and write "Office" above it.

Transaction 2:

Cross out the amount and write $50 above it. Cross out the receipt number and write "120" beside it.

GO TO Internet Resources and Activities Handbook

Refer students to the booklet for additional Internet activities.

interNET CONNECTION www.glencoe.com

Do This (Answers)

1. Answers may vary. Possibilities include:
   www.deloitte.com
   www.ey.com
   www.kpmg.com
   www.pwcglobal.com

2 and 3. Answers will vary.

PEACHTREE CORNER

General Journal Entry

Use the **General Journal Entry** task option to enter a transaction, or click the **General Ledger** navigation aid at the bottom of the screen and choose **General Journal Entry**. The Navigation Aid provides a (visual) alternative for students to select options.

Tasks Analysis Options Reports
- Quotes/Sales Orders ▶
- Sales/Invoicing...
- Receipts...
- Finance Charge...
- Select for Deposit...
- Purchase Orders...
- Purchases/Receive Inventory...
- Select for Payment...
- Payments...
- Write Checks...
- Time/Expense ▶
- Select for Payroll Entry...
- Payroll Entry...
- General Journal Entry...
- Inventory Adjustments...
- Assemblies...

Removing Data Files

After students completely finish a problem, you should remove their data files from your computer's hard drive or the network server. With Peachtree Complete Accounting 2002 (or higher), you must exit Peachtree and delete the company data folder using Windows Explorer. Identify the location of the company data files. Peachtree stores all files for a company in its own unique folder (directory). Delete the company folder and its content to remove the data files from the Peachtree system.

General Journal Entries

Making the Transition from a Manual to a Computerized System

Task	Perform Accounting Procedures Using Manual Methods	Perform Accounting Procedures Using Automated Methods
Recording general journal entries	• Analyze the source document to determine which accounts are affected. • Using a general journal form, enter the details of the transaction. • Check for equality of debits and credits.	• Analyze the source document to determine which accounts are affected. • Enter the general journal using the account numbers for each ledger account. • The software will calculate the equality of debits and credits.

Entering Transactions

Peachtree Question	Description
How do I enter general journal entries in Peachtree?	1. From the ***Tasks*** menu, select **General Journal Entry.** 2. Enter the date of the transaction in the Date box. 3. Enter the source document reference. TAB 4. Enter the account number to be debited. TAB. 5. Enter a brief description of the transaction. TAB. 6. Enter the debit amount. TAB. 7. Enter the account number to be credited. TAB 8. Enter the credit amount. TAB. 9. Click Save. (You will learn how to post to the general ledger in the next chapter.)
What does the software do "behind the scenes"?	The general journal screen automatically checks the equality of debits and credits in your journal entry. The software prompts you to correct the entry if it is out of balance.

For detailed instructions: See the **Peachtree User Guide** in your Glencoe Working Papers.

Peachtree® Answers to Frequently Asked Questions

Q: How do you correct a journal entry?

A: You can edit/delete a general journal entry at any time unless you have closed the current period. To make a change, choose **General Journal Entry**. Click the *Open* button and select an entry to update. Make the changes and click *Save* to post the corrected transaction. Peachtree automatically applies the corrections. To delete an entry, click the *Erase* button when the transaction is displayed in the **General Journal Entry** window.

For additional information, refer to your *Glencoe Peachtree Accounting User Guide.*

APPLICATION OPTIONS

Problem 6–4 Recording General Journal Transactions

Ronald Hicks owns and operates Wilderness Rentals. The following accounts are needed to journalize the month's transactions.

General Ledger

101	Cash in Bank	301	Ronald Hicks, Capital
105	Accts. Rec.—Helen Katz	305	Ronald Hicks, Withdrawals
110	Accts. Rec.—Polk and Co.	310	Income Summary
120	Office Equipment	401	Equipment Rental Revenue
125	Camping Equipment	501	Advertising Expense
201	Accts. Pay.—Adventure Equipment Inc.	505	Maintenance Expense
		515	Rent Expense
203	Accts. Pay.—Digital Tech Computers	520	Salaries Expense
		525	Utilities Expense
205	Accts. Pay.—Greg Mollaro		

Instructions Record the following transactions on page 1 of the general journal in your working papers. For each transaction:

(1) Enter the date. Use the current year.
(2) Enter the name of the account debited.
(3) Enter the amount of the debit.
(4) Enter the name of the account credited.
(5) Enter the amount of the credit.
(6) Enter a source document reference.

Date		Transactions
Jan.	1	Wrote Check 310 for the part-time secretary's salary, $270.
	3	Bought $2,000 of camping equipment on account from Adventure Equipment Inc., Invoice 320.
	5	Received $500 from a client for equipment rental, Receipt 150.
	7	Wrote Check 311 to pay the electricity bill of $110.
	11	Billed a client, Polk and Co., $1,700 for rental equipment, Sales Invoice 262.
	12	Ronald Hicks withdrew $800 for personal use, Check 312.
	14	Bought a $300 scanner for the office computer from Digital Tech Computers, on account, Invoice 270.
	16	Wrote Check 313 for $1,000 as an installment payment toward the amount owed to Adventure Equipment Inc.
	25	Received $1,700 from Polk and Co. in payment on their account, Receipt 151.
	30	Paid Digital Tech Computers $300 for the amount owed, Check 314.

Analyze: How much cash was deducted from the **Cash in Bank** account in January?

Complete chapter problems one of three ways:

1 **Manual** Glencoe Working Papers

or

2 **Peachtree Complete Accounting** Software

or

3 **QuickBooks®** Templates (Problems 6–4, 6–5)

Peachtree®

SMART GUIDE

Step-by-Step Instructions: Problem 6–4

1. Select the problem set for Wilderness Rentals (Prob. 6–4).
2. Rename the company and set the system date.
3. Enter all of the general journal transactions using the **General Journal Entry** option in the ***Tasks*** menu.
4. Print a General Journal report.
5. Proof your work and make any needed corrections.
6. Answer the Analyze question.
7. End the session.

Problem 6-4 (Answers) Recording General Journal Transactions

Jan. 1: Dr. Salaries Exp. $270; Cr. Cash in Bank $270; Check 310
Jan. 3: Dr. Camping Equip. $2,000; Cr. Accts. Pay.—Adventure Equip. Inc. $2,000; Invoice 320
Jan. 5: Dr. Cash in Bank $500; Cr. Equip. Rental Revenue $500; Receipt 150
Jan. 7: Dr. Utilities Exp. $110; Cr. Cash in Bank $110; Check 311
Jan. 11: Dr. Accts. Rec.—Polk and Co. $1,700; Cr. Equip. Rental Revenue $1,700; Invoice 262
Jan. 12: Dr. Ronald Hicks, Withdrawals $800; Cr. Cash in Bank $800; Check 312
Jan. 14: Dr. Office Equip. $300; Cr. Accts. Pay.—Digital Tech Computers $300; Invoice 270
Jan. 16: Dr. Accts. Pay.—Adventure Equip. Inc. $1,000; Cr. Cash in Bank $1,000; Check 313
Jan. 25: Dr. Cash in Bank $1,700; Cr. Accts. Rec.—Polk and Co. $1,700; Receipt 151
Jan. 30: Dr. Accts. Pay.—Digital Tech Computers $300; Cr. Cash in Bank $300; Check 314

Analyze: $2,480

SOFTWARE NOTES

Teachers can find detailed instructions for:

- **Peachtree Complete Accounting**, in the *Glencoe Workbook* (CRWP)
- **QuickBooks® Templates**, in *Using QuickBooks with Glencoe Accounting*
- **Spreadsheets Templates**, in the *Glencoe Workbook* (CRWP)

PROBLEMS CHAPTER 6

Problem 6-5 (Answers) Recording General Journal Transactions

Jan. 1: Dr. Cash in Bank $12,000; Cr. Regina Delgado, Capital $12,000; Memo. 41

Jan. 5: Dr. Office Furn. $5,000; Cr. Accts. Pay.—O'Brian's Office Supply $5,000; Invoice 1632

Jan. 8: Dr. Cash in Bank $1,600; Cr. Wash Revenue $1,600; Receipt 101

Jan. 10: Dr. Advertising Exp. $75; Cr. Cash in Bank $75; Check 301

Jan. 13: Dr. Regina Delgado, Withdrawals $900; Cr. Cash in Bank $900; Check 302

Jan. 17: Dr. Accts. Rec.—Valley Auto $400; Cr. Interior Detailing Revenue $400; Invoice 102

Jan. 18: Dr. Accts. Pay.—O'Brian's Office Supply $2,500; Cr. Cash in Bank $2,500; Check 303

Jan. 20: Dr. Office Equip. $350; Cr. Regina Delgado, Capital $350; Memo. 42

Jan. 22: Dr. Rent Exp. $600; Cr. Cash in Bank $600; Check 304

Jan. 24: Dr. Car Wash Equip. $1,500; Cr. Accts. Pay.—Allen Vacuum Systems $1,500; Invoice 312

Jan. 26: Dr. Cash in Bank $400; Cr. Accts. Rec.—Valley Auto $400; Receipt 102

Jan. 30: Dr. Accts. Pay.—O'Brian's Office Supply $2,500; Cr. Cash in Bank $2,500; Check 305

Analyze: $14,275

Peachtree®

SMART GUIDE

Step-by-Step Instructions: Problem 6-5

1. Select the problem set for Hot Suds Car Wash (Prob. 6-5).
2. Rename the company and set the system date.
3. Enter all of the general journal transactions using the **General Journal Entry** option in the ***Tasks*** menu.
4. Print a General Journal report.
5. Proof your work and make any needed corrections.
6. Answer the Analyze question.
7. End the session.

TIP: You can use General Ledger Navigation Aid as an alternative way to access the General Journal Entry window.

Problem 6-5 Recording General Journal Transactions

Regina Delgado owns a business called Hot Suds Car Wash. She uses the following chart of accounts.

General Ledger

101	Cash in Bank	401	Wash Revenue
105	Accts. Rec.—Linda Brown	405	Wax Revenue
110	Accts. Rec.—Valley Auto	410	Interior Detailing Revenue
125	Office Equipment	501	Advertising Expense
130	Office Furniture	505	Equipment Rental Expense
135	Car Wash Equipment	510	Maintenance Expense
201	Accts. Pay.—Allen Vacuum Systems	520	Rent Expense
		525	Salaries Expense
205	Accts. Pay.—O'Brian's Office Supply	530	Utilities Expense
301	Regina Delgado, Capital		
305	Regina Delgado, Withdrawals		
310	Income Summary		

Instructions Record the following transactions on page 1 of the general journal in your working papers.

Date	Transactions
Jan. 1	Regina Delgado invested $12,000 in the business, Memorandum 41.
5	Purchased $5,000 in desks, chairs, and cabinets from O'Brian's Office Supply on account, Invoice 1632.
8	Deposited $1,600 for income received from car washes for the week, Receipt 101.
10	Paid the *Village Bulletin* $75 for running an ad, Check 301.
13	Regina Delgado withdrew $900 for personal use, Check 302.
17	Billed Valley Auto $400 for interior detailing, Sales Invoice 102.
18	Paid O'Brian's Office Supply $2,500 as an installment payment on account, Check 303.
20	Regina Delgado transferred to the business an electronic calculator valued at $350, Memorandum 42.
22	Wrote Check 304 for $600 to Shadyside Realty for the office rent.
24	Purchased $1,500 in car wash equipment from Allen Vacuum Systems on account, Invoice 312.
26	Received a $400 check from Valley Auto in full payment of its account, Receipt 102.
30	Issued Check 305 for $2,500 to O'Brian's Office Supply for the balance due on account.

Analyze: What is the amount of total assets for Hot Suds Car Wash at January 31?

SOLUTION NOTES

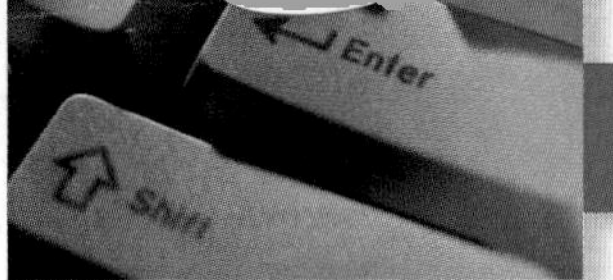

CHAPTER 6 PROBLEMS

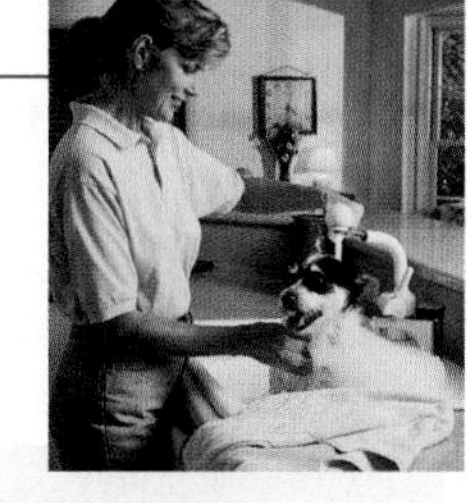

Problem 6-6 Recording General Journal Transactions

Abe Shultz owns and operates a pet grooming business called Kits & Pups Grooming. The following accounts are used to journalize transactions.

General Ledger

101	Cash in Bank	207	Accts. Pay.—Pet Gourmet
105	Accts. Rec.—Juan Alvarez	301	Abe Shultz, Capital
110	Accts. Rec.—N. Carlsbad	305	Abe Shultz, Withdrawals
115	Accts. Rec.—Martha Giles	310	Income Summary
125	Office Equipment	401	Boarding Revenue
130	Office Furniture	405	Grooming Revenue
135	Computer Equipment	501	Advertising Expense
140	Grooming Equipment	505	Equipment Repair Expense
145	Kennel Equipment	510	Maintenance Expense
201	Accts. Pay.—Able Store Equipment	520	Rent Expense
		525	Salaries Expense
205	Accts. Pay.—Dogs & Cats Inc.	530	Utilities Expense

Instructions Record the following transactions on page 7 of the general journal in your working papers.

Date		Transactions
Jan.	1	Received $125 for boarding a client's dog for one week, Receipt 300.
	3	Abe Shultz contributed to the business a computer valued at $2,500, Memorandum 33.
	5	Billed a client, Juan Alvarez, $80 for grooming his pets, Sales Invoice 212.
	9	Wrote Check 411 to Allegheny Power Co. for $150 in payment for the month's electricity bill.
	11	Abe Shultz withdrew $700 for personal use, Check 412.
	14	Purchased kennel equipment for $2,600 from Dogs & Cats Inc., on account, Invoice DC92.
	16	Paid the part-time receptionist's salary of $400 by issuing Check 413.
	18	Abe Shultz took from the business for his personal use a ten-key adding machine valued at $65, Memorandum 34.
	23	Juan Alvarez sent a check for $80 in full payment of his account, Receipt 301.
	28	Purchased on credit $250 in grooming equipment from the Pet Gourmet, Invoice PG333.
	31	Issued Check 414 for $1,300 as an installment payment for the amount owed to Dogs & Cats Inc.

Analyze: What is the total of the Accounts Receivable accounts at January 31?

Peachtree®

SMART GUIDE

Step-by-Step Instructions: Problem 6-6

1. Select the problem set for Kits & Pups Grooming (Prob. 6-6).
2. Rename the company and set the system date.
3. Enter all of the general journal transactions.
4. Print a General Journal report.
5. Proof your work and make any needed corrections.
6. Answer the Analyze question.
7. End the session.

TIP: As a shortcut, you can enter just the day of the month for a transaction date.

PROBLEMS
CHAPTER 6

Problem 6-6 (Answers) Recording General Journal Transactions

Jan. 1: Dr. Cash in Bank $125; Cr. Boarding Revenue $125; Receipt 300

Jan. 3: Dr. Computer Equip. $2,500; Cr. Abe Shultz, Capital $2,500; Memo. 33

Jan. 5: Dr. Accts. Rec.—Juan Alvarez $80; Cr. Grooming Revenue $80; Invoice 212

Jan. 9: Dr. Utilities Exp. $150; Cr. Cash in Bank $150; Check 411

Jan. 11: Dr. Abe Schultz, Withdrawals $700; Cr. Cash in Bank $700; Check 412

Jan. 14: Dr. Kennel Equip. $2,600; Cr. Accts. Pay.—Dogs & Cats Inc. $2,600; Invoice DC92

Jan. 16: Dr. Salaries Exp. $400; Cr. Cash in Bank $400; Check 413

Jan. 18: Dr. Abe Schultz, Withdrawals $65; Office Equip. $65; Memo. 34

Jan. 23: Dr. Cash in Bank $80; Cr. Accts. Rec.—Juan Alvarez $80; Receipt 301

Jan. 28: Dr. Grooming Equip. $250; Cr. Accts. Pay.—Pet Gourmet $250; Invoice PG333

Jan. 31: Dr. Accts. Pay.—Dogs & Cats Inc. $1,300; Cr. Cash in Bank $1,300; Check 414

Analyze: 0

SOLUTION NOTES

Problem 6-7 (Answers) Recording General Journal Transactions

Jan. 1: Dr. Cash in Bank $1,500, Hiking Equip. $2,000, Rafting Equip. $2,500, Office Furniture $500; Cr. Juanita Ortega, Capital $6,500; Memo. 21

Jan. 2: Dr. Advertising Exp. $75; Cr. Cash in Bank $75; Check 515

Jan. 4: Dr. Rafting Equip. $3,000; Cr. Accts. Pay.—A-1 Adventure Warehouse $3,000; Invoice AW45

Jan. 6: Dr. Dr. Accts. Rec.—Feldman, Jones, & Ritter $4,800; Cr. Guide Service Revenue $4,800; Invoice 300

Jan. 10: Dr. Maintenance Exp. $300; Cr. Cash in Bank $300; Check 516

Jan. 13: Dr. Accts. Pay.—A-1 Adventure Warehouse $1,000; Cr. Cash in Bank $1,000; Check 517

Jan. 15: Dr. Cash in Bank $4,800; Cr. Accts. Rec.—Feldman, Jones, & Ritter $4,800; Receipt 252

Jan. 18: Dr. Juanita Ortega, Withdrawals $600; Cash in Bank $600; Check 518

Jan. 22: Dr. Accts. Rec.—M. Johnson $1,200; Cr. Guide Service Revenue $1,200; Invoice 301

Jan. 25: Dr. Utilities Exp. $175; Cr. Cash in Bank $175; Check 519

Jan. 30: Dr. Computer Equip. $3,600; Cr. Cash in Bank $1,800, Accts. Pay.—Premier Processors $1,800; Invoice 749/Check 520

Analyze: No

Peachtree®

SMART GUIDE

Step-by-Step Instructions: Problem 6-7

1. Select the problem set for Outback Guide Service (Prob. 6-7).
2. Rename the company and set the system date.
3. Enter all of the general journal transactions.
4. Print a General Journal report.
5. Proof your work and make any needed corrections.
6. Answer the Analyze question.
7. End the session.

TIP: Press **SHIFT+?** in an ***Account No.*** field to display an account list.

Problem 6-7 Recording General Journal Transactions

Juanita Ortega is the owner of Outback Guide Service. The following accounts are used to record the transactions of her business.

General Ledger

101	Cash in Bank	205	Accts. Pay.—Peak Equipment Inc.
105	Accts. Rec.—M. Johnson	207	Accts. Pay.—Premier Processors
110	Accts. Rec.—Feldman, Jones, & Ritter	301	Juanita Ortega, Capital
		302	Juanita Ortega, Withdrawals
115	Accts. Rec.—Podaski Systems Inc.	310	Income Summary
		401	Guide Service Revenue
130	Office Equipment	501	Advertising Expense
135	Office Furniture	505	Maintenance Expense
140	Computer Equipment	515	Rent Expense
145	Hiking Equipment	520	Salaries Expense
150	Rafting Equipment	525	Utilities Expense
201	Accts. Pay.—A-1 Adventure Warehouse		

Instructions Record the following transactions on page 1 of the general journal in your working papers.

Date		Transactions
Jan.	1	Juanita Ortega contributed the following assets to her business: cash, $1,500; hiking equipment, $2,000; rafting equipment, $2,500; and office furniture, $500; Memorandum 21.
	2	Issued Check 515 to *Town News* for a $75 ad.
	4	Purchased $3,000 in rafting equipment on account from A-1 Adventure Warehouse, Invoice AW45.
	6	A group from Feldman, Jones, & Ritter went on a hiking trip. The group was billed $4,800 for guide services, Sales Invoice 300.
	10	Paid $300 to Dunn's Painting and Interior Co. for painting the office, Check 516.
	13	Made a $1,000 payment to A-1 Adventure Warehouse toward the amount owed, Check 517.
	15	Received a check for $4,800 from Feldman, Jones, & Ritter in payment of their account, Receipt 252.
	18	Juanita Ortega paid herself $600 by issuing Check 518.
	22	Billed a client, Mary Johnson, $1,200 for completing guide services on a hiking expedition, Sales Invoice 301.
	25	Paid the monthly telephone bill for $175 by issuing Check 519.
	30	Purchased a $3,600 computer system from Premier Processors. Made a down payment for $1,800 and agreed to pay the balance within 30 days, Check 520 and Invoice 749.

Analyze: Did any of Outback's customers pay cash for services in January?

SOLUTION NOTES

Problem 6–8 Recording General Journal Transactions

SOURCE DOCUMENT PROBLEM

Greg Failla operates Showbiz Video. The following accounts are used to record business transactions.

General Ledger

101 Cash in Bank	207 Accts. Pay.—New Media Suppliers
105 Accts. Rec.—G. Cohen	209 Accts. Pay.—Palace Films
110 Accts. Rec.—J. Coletti	301 Greg Failla, Capital
113 Accts. Rec.—S. Flannery	305 Greg Failla, Withdrawals
115 Accts. Rec.—Spring Branch School District	310 Income Summary
130 Office Equipment	401 Video Rental Revenue
135 Office Furniture	405 VCR Rental Revenue
140 Computer Equipment	501 Advertising Expense
145 Video Tapes	505 Equipment Repair Expense
150 Video Equipment	510 Maintenance Expense
201 Accts. Pay.—Broad Street Office Supply	520 Rent Expense
205 Accts. Pay.—Computer Horizons	525 Salaries Expense
	530 Utilities Expense

Instructions Record the following transactions on page 5 of the general journal in your working papers.

Date		Transactions
Jan.	1	Deposited $3,400 in receipts. Of that amount, $1,900 was VCR rentals and $1,500 was video tape rentals, Receipt 435.
	3	Wrote Check 1250 for $325 of equipment repairs.
	5	Purchased $400 in video tapes from Palace Films on account, Invoice PF32.
	7	Bought from New Media Suppliers $2,600 in video equipment. Made a down payment of $600 and agreed to pay the balance in two installments, Check 1251 and Invoice NM101.
	10	Rented videos to Spring Branch School District. The school district agreed to pay $1,800 at a later date, Sales Invoice 1650.
	12	Issued Check 1252 for $750 to Computer Horizons for the amount owed to them.
	15	Deposited $5,600 in receipts. VCR rentals amounted to $4,400 and video tape rentals were $1,200, Receipt 436.
	18	Paid Clear Vue Window Cleaners $100 for monthly window cleaning, Check 1253.
	25	Made a $1,000 installment payment toward the amount owed to New Media Suppliers by issuing Check 1254.

Analyze: What were the total expenses incurred in January?

Peachtree® SMART GUIDE

Step-by-Step Instructions: Problem 6–8

1. Select the problem set for Showbiz Video (Prob. 6–8).
2. Rename the company and set the system date.
3. Enter all of the general journal transactions.
4. Print a General Journal report.
5. Proof your work and make any needed corrections.
6. Answer the Analyze question.
7. End the session.

SOURCE DOCUMENT PROBLEM

Problem 6–8

Use the source documents in your working papers to record the transactions for this problem.

SOLUTION NOTES

SOURCE DOCUMENT PROBLEM

Problem 6–8 (Answers) Recording General Journal Transactions

Jan. 1: Dr. Cash in Bank $3,400; Cr. Video Rental Revenue $1,500; VCR Rental Revenue $1,900; Receipt 435

Jan. 3: Dr. Equip. Repair Exp. $325; Cr. Cash in Bank $325; Check 1250

Jan. 5: Dr. Video Tapes $400; Cr. Accts. Pay.—Palace Films $400; Invoice PF32

Jan. 7: Dr. Video Equip. $2,600; Cr. Cash in Bank $600, Accts. Pay.—New Media Suppliers $2,000; Invoice NM101/Check 1251

Jan. 10: Dr. Accts. Rec.—Spring Branch School District $1,800; Cr. Video Rental Revenue $1,800; Invoice 1650

Jan. 12: Dr. Accts. Pay.—Computer Horizons $750; Cr. Cash in Bank $750; Check 1252

Jan. 15: Dr. Cash in Bank $5,600; Cr. Video Rental Revenue $1,200; VCR Rental Revenue $4,400; Receipt 436

Jan. 18: Dr. Maintenance Exp. $100; Cr. Cash in Bank $100; Check 1253

Jan. 25: Dr. Accts. Pay.—New Media Supply $1,000; Cr. Cash in Bank $1,000; Check 1254

Analyze: $425

CHAPTER 7 Resource Manager

Section Resources

	Objectives & Standards	Activities & Features	Reproducible Masters
Chapter Opener *Posting Journal Entries to General Ledger Accounts*	• Describe the steps in the posting process. • Post general journal entries. • Prepare a trial balance. • Locate and correct trial balance errors. • Record correcting entries in the general journal. • Define the accounting terms introduced in this chapter. **National Standards for Business Education**: IA7, IA10, IA11	Exploring the Real World of Business, p. 150 Workplace Connections, p. 151	School-to-Work Handbook
Section 1 *The General Ledger*	• The purpose of the general ledger. • How to open accounts in the general ledger.	Did You Know?, p. 153 Connect To, p. 154 A Matter of Ethics, p. 155	Demonstration Problems Strategies for Teaching Ethics in Accounting
Section 2 *The Posting Process*	• The purpose and importance of posting. • How often a business posts transactions. • The six steps in the posting process. • How to compute an account balance. • How to show an account with a zero balance.	International Accounting, p. 158 Math Hints, p. 159 Accounting Careers in Focus, p. 165	Strategies for Teaching International Accounting Math Review for Accounting Demonstration Problems
Section 3 *Preparing a Trial Balance*	• The purpose of a trial balance. • How to prepare a trial balance. • How to identify and locate trial balance errors.	Accounting Tips, p. 166 Accounting Flashbacks, p. 168	Demonstration Problems Internet Resources and Activities Handbook

KEY

Posters — Transparency — Software — Videocassette

Blackline Masters — CD-ROM — Portfolio

MULTIMEDIA RESOURCE

Peachtree	QuickBooks	Spreadsheets	Videos	CD-ROMs
Problem 7–5 *Posting General Journal Transactions* Problem 7–6 *Preparing a Trial Balance* Problem 7–7 *Journalizing and Posting Business Transactions* Problem 7–8 *Journalizing and Posting Business Transactions* Problem 7–9 *Recording and Posting Correcting Entries*	Problem 7–5 *Posting General Journal Transactions* Problem 7–6 *Preparing a Trial Balance* Problem 7–7 *Journalizing and Posting Business Transactions*	None in this chapter.	***Video Segment: Global Perspectives*** After viewing this video, students will be able to describe how the United States is part of a global marketplace. They will also be able to describe differences for businesses that operate in the international market.	***Electronic Learning Center (ELC), Chapter 7*** This program is ideal for visual learners since it incorporates video images, animation, and graphics to enliven the content of each lesson. ***Interactive Lesson Planner (ILP), Chapter 7*** This CD-ROM combines the versatility of an electronic lesson planner with the convenience of teacher classroom resources.

SCANS Correlation Chart

FOUNDATION SKILLS

Basic Skills:	Reading	Writing	Math	Listening	Speaking	
Thinking Skills:	Creative Thinking	Decision Making	Problem Solving	Seeing Things in the Mind's Eye	Knowing How to Learn	Reasoning
Personal Qualities:	Responsibility	Self-Esteem	Sociability	Self-Management	Integrity/Honesty	

WORKPLACE COMPETENCIES

Resources:	Allocating Time	Allocating Money	Allocating Material and Facility Resources	Allocating Human Resources		
Information:	Acquiring and Evaluating Information	Organizing and Maintaining Information	Interpreting and Communicating Information	Using Computers to Process Information		
Interpersonal Skills:	Participating as a Member of a Team	Teaching Others	Serving Clients/ Customers	Exercising Leadership	Negotiating to Arrive at a Decision	Working with Cultural Diversity
Systems:	Understanding Systems	Monitoring and Correcting Performance	Improving and Designing Systems			
Technology:	Selecting Technology	Applying Technology to Task	Maintaining and Troubleshooting Technology			

*Highlighted blocks indicate areas covered in the chapter. Additional SCANS skills are also covered throughout the *Teacher Wraparound Edition.*

Assessment

Student Edition
- Check Your Understanding, pp. 156, 164, 170
- Chapter 7 Problems, pp. 175–177

Assessment and Evaluation Masters
- Chapter 7 Study Plan, *Glencoe Workbook*
- Chapter 7 Self-Test, *Glencoe Workbook*
- Chapter 7 Test, *Chapter Tests* Booklet
- Chapter 7 Activity, *School-to-Work Handbook*
- Chapter 7 **Exam***View*

Teacher Wraparound Edition
- Critical Thinking Activity, p. 168
- Reteaching Section 1, p. 156
- Reteaching Section 2, p. 164
- Reteaching Section 3, p. 170
- Chapter 7 Quiz, p. 171

Transparencies

	Teaching Transparencies	Solution Transparencies
Section 1:	7–1, 7–2, 7–3, 7–4, 7–5	Problems 7–1
Section 2:	7–6, 7–7, 7–8, 7–9a, 7–9b, 7–10, 7–11	Problem 7–2
Section 3:	7–12, 7–13, 7–14, 7–15	Problems 7–3, 7–4
End of Chapter:		Problems 7–5, 7–6, 7–7, 7–8, 7–9

TEACHER CLASSROOM RESOURCES

This is a representation of key blackline masters available in the Teacher Classroom Resources.

Teaching Aids

Transparency Examples

Section Focus Transparencies

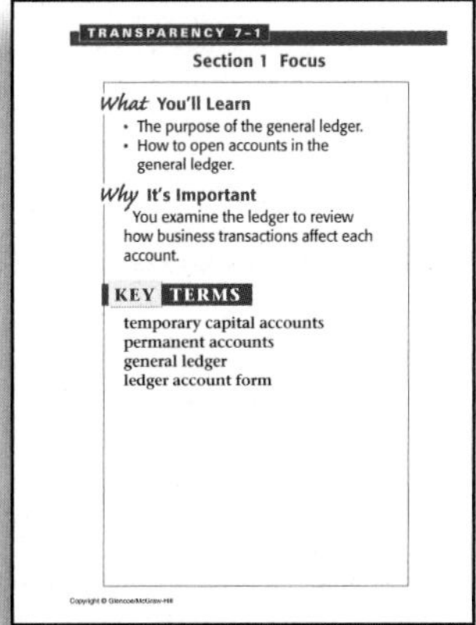

TRANSPARENCY 7-1

Section 1 Focus

What You'll Learn

- The purpose of the general ledger.
- How to open accounts in the general ledger.

Why It's Important

You examine the ledger to review how business transactions affect each account.

KEY TERMS

temporary capital accounts
permanent accounts
general ledger
ledger account form

Copyright © Glencoe/McGraw-Hill

Teaching Transparencies

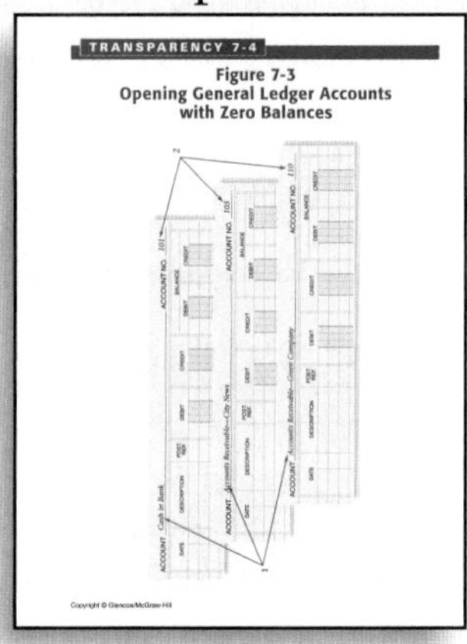

TRANSPARENCY 7-4

Figure 7-3
Opening General Ledger Accounts with Zero Balances

Copyright © Glencoe/McGraw-Hill

Teaching Transparencies

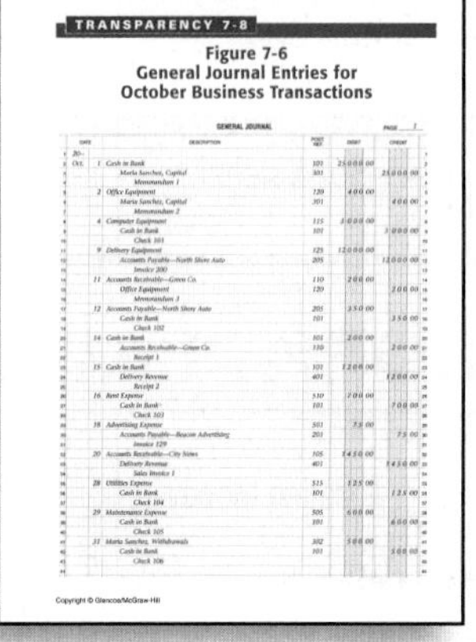

TRANSPARENCY 7-8

Figure 7-6
General Journal Entries for October Business Transactions

Copyright © Glencoe/McGraw-Hill

Solution Transparencies

Working Papers for End-of-Chapter Problems
Problem 7-5 Posting General Journal Transactions

Demonstration Problems

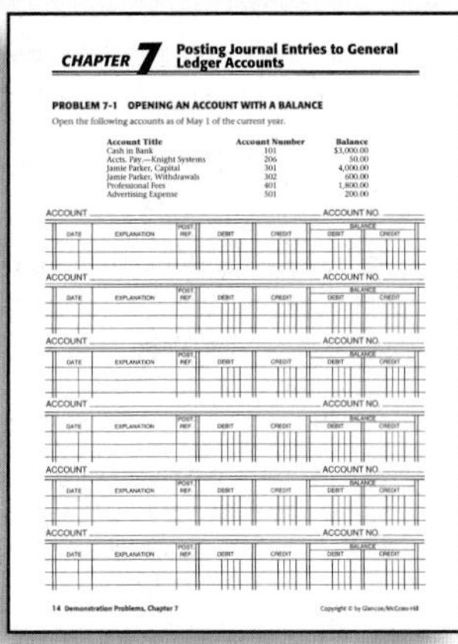

CHAPTER 7 Posting Journal Entries to General Ledger Accounts

PROBLEM 7-1 OPENING AN ACCOUNT WITH A BALANCE

Open the following accounts as of May 1 of the current year.

14 Demonstration Problems, Chapter 7

Copyright © Glencoe/McGraw-Hill

Lesson Plans

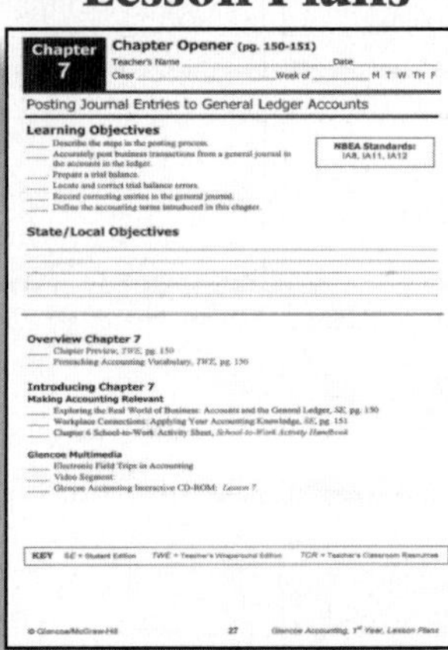

Chapter 7 Chapter Opener (pg. 150-151)

Posting Journal Entries to General Ledger Accounts

Learning Objectives

State/Local Objectives

Overview Chapter 7

Introducing Chapter 7

Glencoe Multimedia

Block Scheduling

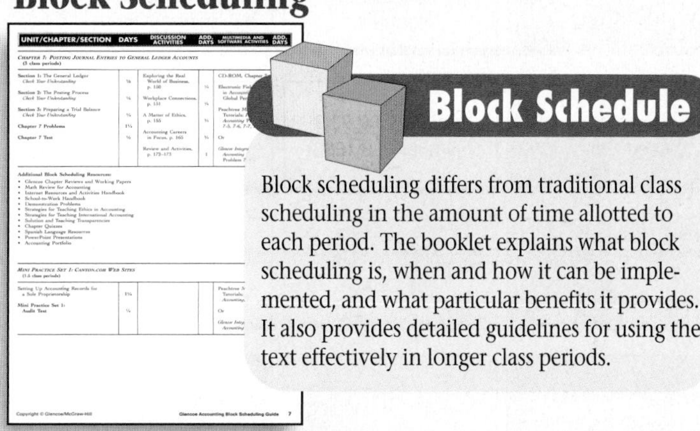

UNIT/CHAPTER/SECTION DAYS DISCUSSION ACTIVITIES ADD. DAYS MULTIMEDIA AND SOFTWARE ACTIVITIES ADD. DAYS

Block Schedule

Block scheduling differs from traditional class scheduling in the amount of time allotted to each period. The booklet explains what block scheduling is, when and how it can be implemented, and what particular benefits it provides. It also provides detailed guidelines for using the text effectively in longer class periods.

Enrichment and Application

Strategies for Teaching Ethics in Accounting

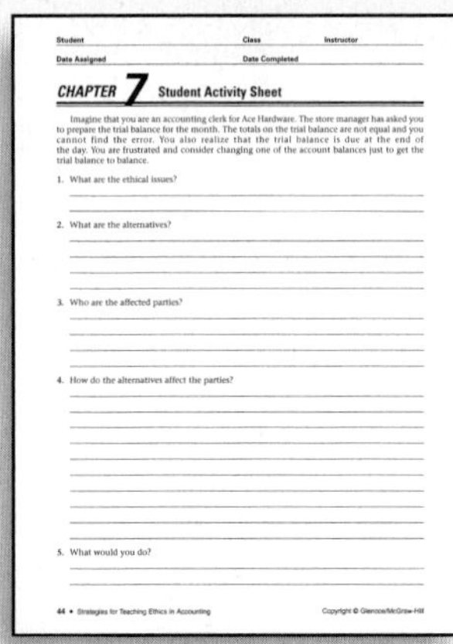

CHAPTER 7 Student Activity Sheet

1. What are the ethical issues?
2. What are the alternatives?
3. Who are the affected parties?
4. How do the alternatives affect the parties?
5. What would you do?

44 • Strategies for Teaching Ethics in Accounting

Copyright © Glencoe/McGraw-Hill

Strategies for Teaching International Accounting

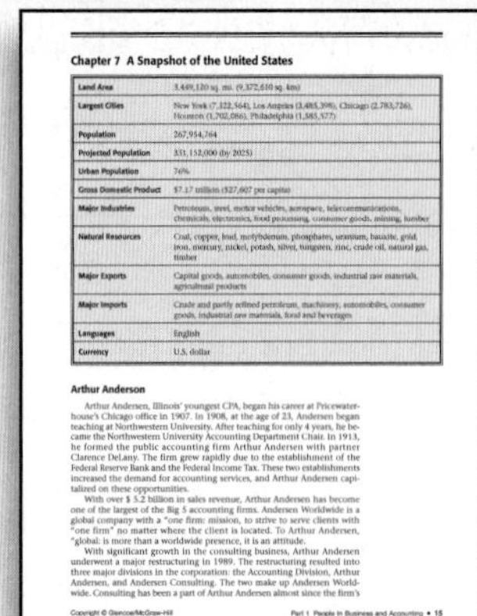

Chapter 7 A Snapshot of the United States

Arthur Andersen

School-to-Work Handbook

CHAPTER 7 SCHOOL-TO-WORK ACTIVITY

Posting Journal Entries to General Ledger Accounts

Meeting Different Ability Levels

Chapter Reviews and Working Papers (CRWP)

Working Papers

Review

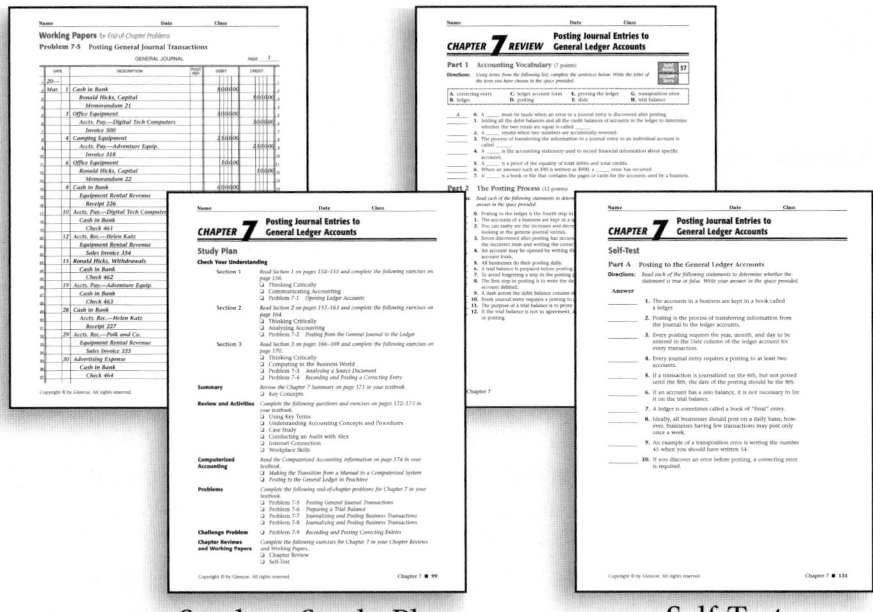

Student Study Plan

Self-Test

Real-World Multimedia CD-ROM

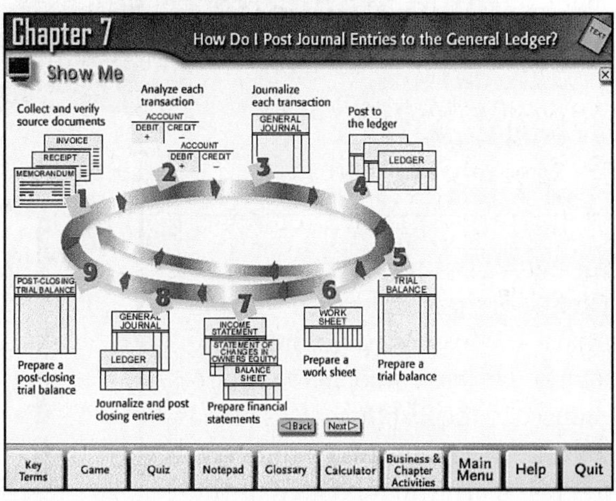

Key to Ability Levels

Each section gives skill-building activities. Each activity has been labeled for use with students of various learning styles and abilities.

L1 Level 1 activities are basic activities and should be within the range of all students.

L2 Level 2 activities are average activities and should be within the range of average and above average students.

L3 Level 3 activities are challenging activities designed for the ability range of above average students.

ELL ELL activities should be within the ability range of English Language Learners.

Teaching Resources at a Glance

Application Resources

- Glencoe Chapter Review and Working Papers, SE and TAE
- School-to-Work Handbook, SE and TM
- Accounting Portfolio, SE and TM

Reproducible Masters

- Demonstration Problems
- Lesson Plans
- Block Scheduling
- Spanish Language Resources

Glencoe Accounting Professional Development Series

- Strategies for Teaching Ethics in Accounting
- Accounting Competitive Event Review
- Math Review for Accounting
- Strategies for Teaching International Accounting
- Internet Resources and Activities Handbook

Transparency Package

- Section Focus Transparencies
- Teaching Transparencies
- Source Document Transparencies
- Solution Transparencies

Performance Assessment

- **Exam***View* CD-ROM
- Chapter Tests
- Chapter Quizzes
- Unit Tests
- Audit Tests
- Printed Testbank

Multimedia Resources

- Electronic Learning Center:
  - Multimedia CD-ROMs
  - Peachtree software, tutorials, templates, and solutions
  - Spreadsheet templates
- Using QuickBooks with Glencoe Accounting
- Interactive Lesson Planner
- Electronic Field Trips in Accounting
- PowerPoint Presentation
- Web site: glencoeaccounting.glencoe.com

Assessment and Evaluation

Chapter Tests

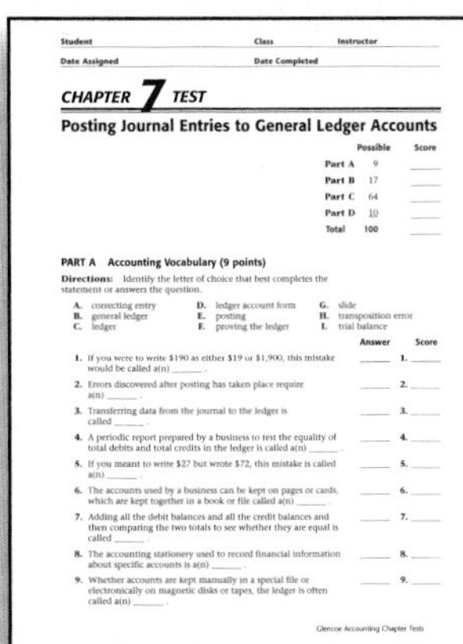

Chapter Quiz

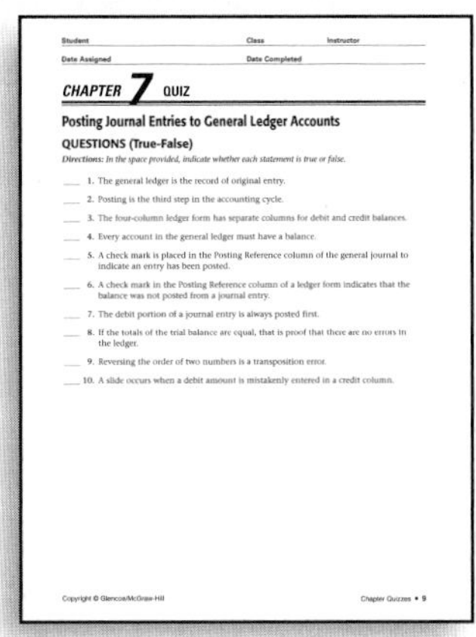

Correlations to National Standards for Business Education
(See pages T50–T51 for a detailed correlation chart.)
Standards: IA7, IA10, IA11

Chapter Preview

In Chapter 6 students learned that the journal is the first formal record in the accounting system. Students were also introduced to the first three steps in the accounting cycle. In this chapter students will learn the next step in the cycle: posting their journal entries to a general ledger.

Section Overviews

- Section 1—*The General Ledger*
- Section 2—*The Posting Process*
- Section 3—*Preparing a Trial Balance*

Chapter Vocabulary

general ledger
ledger account form
posting
proving the ledger
trial balance
transposition error
slide error
correcting entry

Preteaching Accounting Vocabulary

Oral Discussion: Discuss the definitions of the new terms in class. Ask students to give their definition of each term and to explain how each is used in accounting. L1

CHAPTER 7

Posting Journal Entries to General Ledger Accounts

Learning Objectives

When you have completed this chapter, you will be able to:

- Describe the steps in the posting process.
- Post general journal entries.
- Prepare a trial balance.
- Locate and correct trial balance errors.
- Record correcting entries in the general journal.
- Define the accounting terms introduced in this chapter.

Exploring the Real World of Business

ACCOUNTS AND THE GENERAL LEDGER

Can you imagine living on a ranch and riding a horse to work? One world-famous ranch on which you might work is the **King Ranch** in Texas. The ranch covers 825,000 acres, which is larger than the entire state of Rhode Island! It employs around 350 people full-time and another 350 as part-timers.

King Ranch is noted as the producer of the first registered American Quarter Horse and as the original breeder of Santa Gertrudis cattle. It is one of the oldest working ranches in the U.S. and also makes money from cotton crops, gas, and oil wells.

Accounting for an operation like **King Ranch** means keeping track of the number of calves born each year or the pounds of cotton produced. Computers handle much of the routine work of recording ranch information, leaving the ranch managers free to make decisions about how many horses to sell or how much feed to buy.

What do you think?

What are some general ledger accounts that might be used by **King Ranch?** List at least two accounts in each category (assets, liabilities, revenue, and expenses).

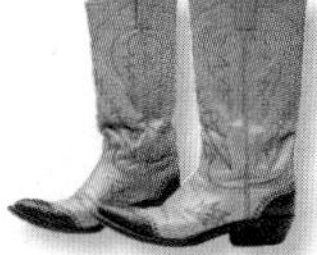

Exploring the Real World of Business

King Ranch
The King Ranch is part of an industry that has become big business in recent years. U.S. cattle ranches produce around 25 percent of the beef supplied to world markets while having only 10 percent of the cattle population. Since the early 1980s, beef exports have grown by over 400 percent.

What do you think? (Answers)
Answers will vary. Some examples are:
Assets: Cattle, Ranch Buildings, Horses
Liabilities: Accounts Payable for buying ranch equipment or digging oil wells
Revenue: Cattle Sales, Oil Revenue
Expenses: Oil Exploration Expense, Cotton Harvesting Expense, Cattle Feed

Workplace Connections

Applying Your Accounting Knowledge

In the last chapter, you learned how to record financial transactions in a journal. These journal entries show individual daily activities, but do not show the total of all transactions. You'll learn in this chapter that posting the journal entries is a means of organizing all the transactions affecting the accounts of a business. For example, all the transactions that might affect an account called "Revenue" are summarized and totaled. All the transactions that might affect an account called "Utilities Expense" are summarized and totaled.

Investigate:

What types of accounts would you imagine are used for accounting in your workplace?

Glencoe Accounting *Online*

Visit the *Glencoe Accounting* Web site at **glencoeaccounting.glencoe.com** for additional activities and information.

151

INTRODUCING
CHAPTER 7

Making Accounting Relevant

Workplace Connections: Applying Your Accounting Knowledge

Discussion: Take a poll of students who have part-time jobs. What types of businesses employ them? Make a list on the chalkboard, then discuss typical transactions for these businesses. Encourage students to think about various areas of a business, such as the different departments in a department store or in a home supply store. Choose one business and have students help you develop a chart of accounts for that business.

Investigate (Answers)

Students' responses will vary. For example, students working part-time at a grocery store might mention asset accounts such as shelving and store equipment; liability accounts for food vendors; owner's equity accounts; revenue from food and nonfood sales; and expenses such as advertising, utilities, food spoilage, maintenance, and cleaning.

School-to-Work Activity

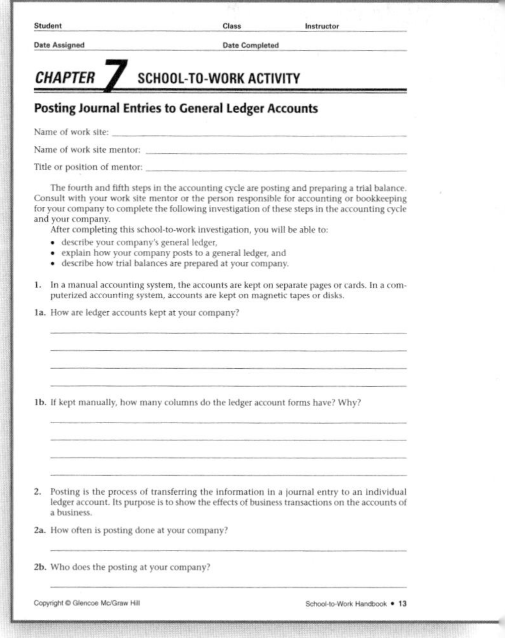

Student ____ Class ____ Instructor ____

Date Assigned ____ Date Completed ____

CHAPTER 7 SCHOOL-TO-WORK ACTIVITY

Posting Journal Entries to General Ledger Accounts

Name of work site: ____

Name of work site mentor: ____

Title or position of mentor: ____

The fourth and fifth steps in the accounting cycle are posting and preparing a trial balance. Consult with your work site mentor or the person responsible for accounting or bookkeeping for your company to complete the following investigation of these steps in the accounting cycle and your company.

After completing this school-to-work investigation, you will be able to:

- describe your company's general ledger,
- explain how your company posts to a general ledger, and
- describe how trial balances are prepared at your company.

1. In a manual accounting system, the accounts are kept on separate pages or cards. In a computerized accounting system, accounts are kept on magnetic tapes or disks.

1a. How are ledger accounts kept at your company?

1b. If kept manually, how many columns do the ledger account forms have? Why?

2. Posting is the process of transferring the information in a journal entry to an individual ledger account. Its purpose is to show the effects of business transactions on the accounts of a business.

2a. How often is posting done at your company?

2b. Who does the posting at your company?

School-to-Work Handbook • 13

GLENCOE MULTIMEDIA

Electronic Field Trips in Accounting *Video Segment: Global Perspectives*
After viewing this video, students will be able to describe how the United States is part of a global marketplace. Have students describe differences for businesses that operate in the international market.

Glencoe Accounting: Electronic Learning Center *Chapter 7*
The CD-ROM program is ideal for visual learners since it incorporates video images, animation, and graphics to enliven the content of each lesson.

1 FOCUS

Introducing the Section
In this section students learn the fourth step in the accounting cycle: posting to the general ledger. Students learn how to use a four-column account form and how to open accounts with and without existing balances.

Section Concepts
- The purpose of the general ledger.
- How to open accounts in the general ledger.

Visual Learning

Section 1 Focus
Use **Transparency 7–1** to introduce section concepts.

BELL RINGER

Creating Analogies: Have students write a paragraph or two describing the process they use when taking notes for a paper they have to write. How do they organize their notes, then prepare information for writing their papers? After students complete their paragraphs, discuss a few of their examples. Point out that taking notes is a way of organizing ideas. Posting is a means of organizing financial information. L1

Visual Learning

Figure 7–1 The Accounting Cycle with Steps 4 and 5 Highlighted
Use **Transparency 7–2** to review the first three steps in the cycle and to introduce Step 4.

SECTION 1

The General Ledger

***What* You'll Learn**
- The purpose of the general ledger.
- How to open accounts in the general ledger.

***Why* It's Important**
You examine the ledger to review how business transactions affect each account.

KEY TERMS
general ledger
ledger account form

In Chapter 6 you learned how to analyze business transactions and enter those transactions in a general journal.

In this chapter you will learn how to post journal entries to the general ledger and how to prepare a trial balance (Steps 4 and 5 in the accounting cycle illustrated in **Figure 7–1**). The Jeep dealership in your area records all business transactions in the journal and posts those transactions to the general ledger. An up-to-date ledger allows the accountant for the Jeep dealership to provide management with information such as:

- sales of vehicles
- service income
- salary and commission expense

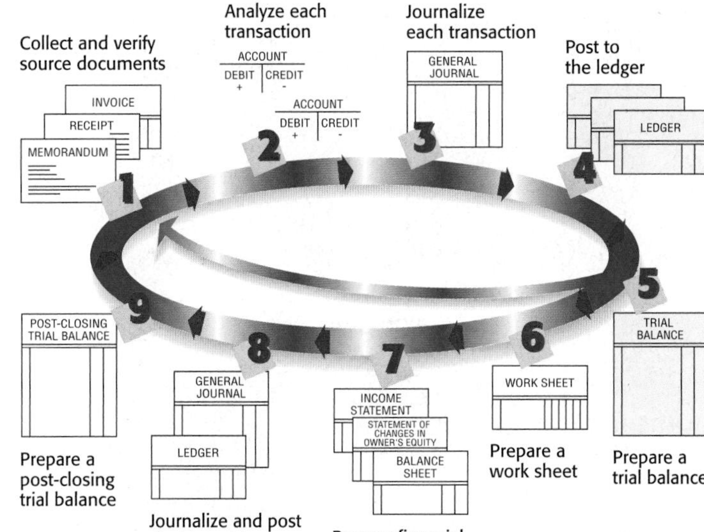

Figure 7–1 The Accounting Cycle with Steps 4 and 5 Highlighted

RESOURCE MANAGER

Reproducible Masters
- Lesson Plans
- Chapter Reviews and Working Papers (CRWP) TAE
- Demonstration Problems

Transparencies
- Section Focus Transparency
- Teaching Transparencies
- Source Document Transparencies
- Solution Transparencies

Multimedia
- Exam*View* CD-ROM
- Electronic Learning Center CD-ROM
- Interactive Lesson Planner CD-ROM
- Electronic Field Trips in Accounting

Setting Up the General Ledger

In a manual accounting system, the accounts used by a business are kept on separate pages or cards. These pages or cards are kept together in a book or file called a ledger. In a computerized accounting system, the electronic files containing the accounts are still referred to as the ledger, or the ledger accounts. In either system, the ledger is often called a **general ledger**.

Posting journal entries to the ledger accounts creates a record of the impact of business transactions on each account used by a business. After journal entries have been posted, a business owner or manager can look at a specific account and easily find its current balance. If, for example, Maria Sanchez wants to know how much money Roadrunner Delivery Service has in its bank account, she can simply look at the balance of the **Cash in Bank** account.

The Four-Column Ledger Account Form

In a manual accounting system, the accounting stationery used to record financial information about specific accounts is a **ledger account form**. There are several common ledger account forms. These forms—as well as other accounting stationery—are usually described by the number of amount columns they have. In other words, the number of columns refers only to those columns in which dollar amounts are recorded. For example, Roadrunner uses a four-column ledger account form.

The four-column account form has spaces to enter the account name, the account number, the date, a description of the entry, and the posting reference. It also has four columns in which to record dollar amounts. Look at the four-column account form shown in **Figure 7–2**.

ACCOUNT ______ ACCOUNT NO. ______

DATE	DESCRIPTION	POST. REF.	DEBIT	CREDIT	BALANCE DEBIT	BALANCE CREDIT

Figure 7–2 Four-Column Ledger Account Form

Notice the four amount columns: the debit column, the credit column, the debit balance column, and the credit balance column. The first two amount columns are used to enter debit and credit amounts posted from journal entries. The last two amount columns are used to enter the new account balance after a journal entry is posted. The balance columns show the current balance in the account. The type of account (expense, revenue, asset, etc.) determines which balance column to use. For example, accounts with a normal debit balance—such as asset or expense accounts—use the debit balance column. Accounts with a normal credit balance—such as liability or revenue accounts—use the credit balance column.

Did You Know?

Consumerism
U.S. cattle ranches produce 25 percent of the world's supply of beef. Consumers spend around $52 billion each year buying beef at their local supermarkets.

Great Ideas *From the Classroom of...*

Posting to Ledger Accounts To help students better understand the posting process, I prepare transparencies to illustrate the relationship of the posting with the original transaction. First, I review the transaction and show a journal page with the recorded entry. Then I show a transparency with each of the ledger accounts. I write on the transparencies to complete the posting process so the class can see me perform each step in the posting process.

William Trouten
Platteville High School
Platteville, Wisconsin

2 TEACH

GUIDED PRACTICE

Reading Accounting

- Reinforce the accounting cycle by having students read the brief descriptions of Steps 1 to 3 in **Figure 7–1**. Then have them write descriptions of the actions accountants take at each step. **L1**
- If possible, obtain copies of accounting forms printed in your students' first language. Share copies with students and point out how they are similar to illustrations in the textbook. **ELL**

Concept Development: Setting Up the General Ledger

Discussion: Before learning how to post, students need to know what a ledger is. Point out that businesses have many different accounts and that, collectively, these accounts are referred to as a ledger. Although a business may have more than one ledger, the main ledger is the general ledger.

Explain to students that a ledger is similar to a card file but one that is not arranged alphabetically. Rather, the accounts in the ledger are arranged by classification: assets first, followed by liabilities, owner's equity, revenue, and expense accounts. Show students examples of actual ledgers to help them form an image of the general ledger. **L1**

Visual Learning

Figure 7–2 Four-Column Ledger Account Form
Using **Transparency 7–3**, demonstrate the information entered in the ledger during the posting process.

CHAPTER 7
SECTION 1, PAGES 152–156

2 TEACH (Cont'd.)

Concept Development: Opening Accounts in the Ledger

Discussion and Demonstration: Create your own ledger by using 3 × 5 (or larger) note cards. Write the title of a different account on each note card. Use the list of accounts on page 108 as the source of information. After demonstrating with a few cards, have students participate in making the "ledger."

When introducing the ledger, point out how easy it is to find information about a particular account when everything related to that account is on one card. Demonstrate by naming an account such as Delivery Equipment and then locating it in the ledger you created. L1

Visual Learning

Figure 7–3 Opening General Ledger Accounts with Zero Balances

Use **Transparency 7–4** to guide students through the steps of opening a ledger account that has no balance. Also use the transparency of the Roadrunners chart of accounts to show students the source of the account titles and numbers.

Teaching Tip

Point out to students that a ledger is often called a book of "final" entry. Remind them that the journal is the book of "original," or first, entry.

Demonstration Problem Step-by-Step Practice

Use demonstration problem 7–1 to show students how to open an account with a balance.

CONNECT TO . . . GEOGRAPHY

Geographers study economics and accounting to understand how the location of resources affects the way people make, transport, and use goods. By comparing economic data with the physical features of an area, researchers can see relationships between the two properties.

Opening Accounts in the Ledger

Before journal entries can be posted, a general ledger account is opened for each account that appears on the chart of accounts. The number of steps required to open an account depends on whether or not the account has a zero balance.

Opening an Account with a Zero Balance

There are two steps required to open an account with a zero balance:

(1) Write the account name at the top of the ledger account form.
(2) Write the account number on the ledger account form.

These two steps are performed each time a new ledger account page is needed. The accounts that are opened for the first three asset accounts on Roadrunner's chart of accounts (page 73) are shown in **Figure 7–3.**

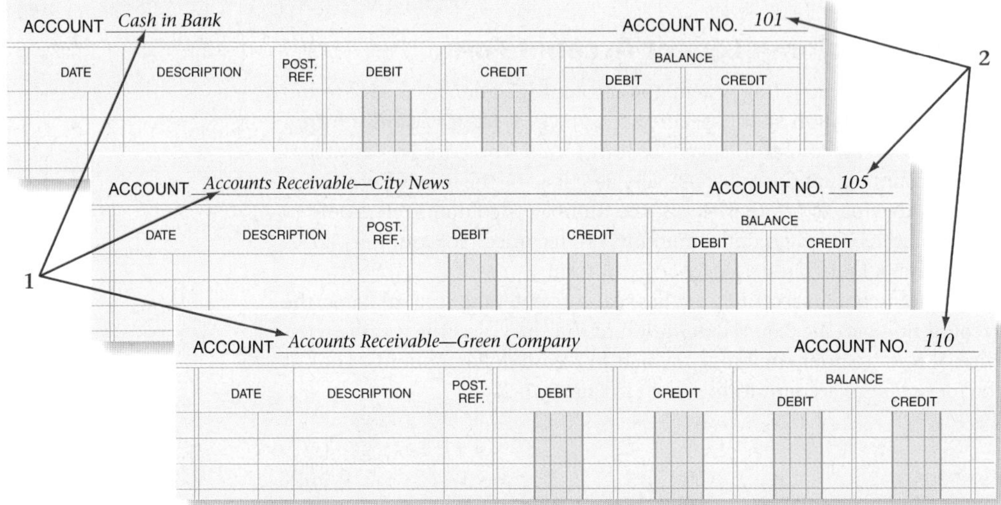

Figure 7–3 Opening General Ledger Accounts with Zero Balances

In a computerized accounting system, the procedure is similar. An account is opened by entering the account name and number on the chart of accounts. Computerized accounting systems vary, but all of them require that information such as the account numbers and names be entered into the computer files.

INTERDISCIPLINARY CONNECTIONS ACTIVITY

Geography By understanding the geography of a community, accountants can be more than just number crunchers—they can also be financial advisors. Assign students to teams and have them research your local community to find the land space in square miles, the proportion zoned for business and the types of zoning, transportation patterns, and business resources available to new and current business owners. Have each team present its findings to the class.

Opening an Account with a Balance

To open an account with a balance, six steps are required:

(1) Write the account name at the top of the ledger account form.
(2) Write the account number on the ledger account form.
(3) Enter the complete date (year, month, and day) in the date column.
(4) Write the word "Balance" in the Description column.
(5) Place a check mark (✓) in the Posting Reference column to show the amount entered on this line is not being posted from a journal.
(6) Enter the balance in the appropriate balance column of the ledger account form. Usually asset, expense, and owner's withdrawals accounts have debit balances. Liability, owner's capital, and revenue accounts have credit balances.

Figure 7–4 shows an example of an entry made to open an account with a balance.

ACCOUNT *Cash in Bank* 1 — ACCOUNT NO. *101* 2

DATE		DESCRIPTION	POST. REF.	DEBIT	CREDIT	BALANCE DEBIT	BALANCE CREDIT
3 *20--*							
Oct.	*1*	*Balance* 4	5 ✓			6 *25 000 00*	

Figure 7–4 Opening General Ledger Accounts with a Balance

The Usefulness of Journals and Ledgers to Managers

Managers continually make use of the information contained in the accounting records. To obtain information about a specific business transaction, a manager might refer to the journal entry. To learn the current balance of important accounts like **Cash in Bank**, **Accounts Receivable**, and **Accounts Payable**, managers will look to the ledger accounts. The organization of accounting data in ledgers makes it possible for managers to obtain summarized information before the financial statements are prepared.

A MATTER OF ETHICS

Meeting a Deadline

Imagine that you are an accounting clerk for Ace Hardware. The store manager has asked you to prepare the trial balance for the month. The totals on the trial balance are not equal and you cannot find the error. You also realize that the trial balance is due at the end of the day. You are frustrated and consider changing one of the account balances just to get the trial balance to balance.

Ethical Decision Making:

- What are the ethical issues?
- What are the alternatives?
- Who are the affected parties?
- How do the alternatives affect the parties?
- What would you do?

2 TEACH (Cont'd.)

Visual Learning

Figure 7–4 Opening General Ledger Accounts with a Balance

Use **Transparency 7–5** to explain how to open a general ledger account that has a balance.

Concept Development: The Usefulness of Journals and Ledgers to Managers

Discussion: Discuss with students the importance of financial data in making day-to-day business decisions. Ask students who have operated summer businesses to describe how they knew they were making a profit. They may not have written all their expenses and earnings in a formal record, but they probably knew how much they had spent and earned.

Since businesses have hundreds of transactions, managers need a way to analyze the details of the transactions. Accounts help them do this by providing total amounts earned and spent by type. For example, managers can track advertising expense to see if revenue increases. If it does not, a manager might decide to cut back on advertising and try some other form of promotion to increase revenue. L1

Strategies for Teaching Ethics in Accounting

Photocopy the Chapter 7 *Student Activity Sheet* for students. Answers are also provided in the booklet.

Teaching A MATTER OF ETHICS

Meeting a Deadline Discuss with students the pressure they feel when they know they're facing a deadline, such as a paper they've barely started that's due the next day or a job interview for which they haven't prepared. Point out that many people find it harder to think clearly when they're under pressure. As a result, they make decisions that may not be the best ones for the situation. Discuss the need to think through a problem before making a decision. For example, the accounting clerk could share the problem with the manager or ask a co-worker for help without changing balances that will only cause problems later.

CHAPTER 7
SECTION 1, PAGES 152–156

3 ASSESS

Thinking Critically (Answers)

1. (a) Write the account name, (b) write the account number.
2. (a) Write account name. (b) Enter ledger account number. (c) Enter complete date in date column. (d) Write "Balance" in Description column. (e) Place check mark in PR column. (f) Enter balance in appropriate column.

Communicating Accounting (Answers)

Answers will vary. Have students hold a class discussion on how to deal with these situations.

Problem 7–1 (Answers)

Cash in Bank $10,000 Dr.
Accts. Rec.—Mark Cohen $2,000 Dr.
Accts. Pay.—Jenco Industries $1,000 Cr.
Tom Torrie, Capital $35,000 Cr.
Admissions Revenue $0

Chapter Reviews and Working Papers Refer students to the Chapter 7 workbook pages to answer *Check Your Understanding* activities.

4 CLOSE

Section Wrap-Up

Writing Exercise: Have students choose a type of business, then write a paragraph or two explaining what information they would record in an accounting system and how they would use that information to make business decisions. L2

SECTION 1 Check Your Understanding

Now that you have studied this section, complete the following questions and problem.

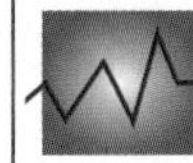

Thinking Critically

1. List the steps involved in opening an account with a zero balance.
2. List the steps involved in opening an account with a balance.

Communicating Accounting

Often the way we say things has a big impact on how our listeners respond to us. Angry words can bring an equally angry response, and no real communication will have taken place. Communication occurs when one person is able to express an idea in words and tone that are heard and understood in the way the speaker intended. See if you can identify why communication did not take place in the following examples. How would you have said things differently?

1. Supervisor: (Angrily) "You are late again, Wiley. If you're not here on time every day from now on, you're out of a job."
   Employee: "Aw, man. Get off my back. I'm trying as hard as I can."
2. First Employee: "I'm tired of always making the decisions and teaching you how to do your job. You should know how to open ledger accounts by yourself by now."
   Second Employee: "Well, you don't have to work with me anymore then. I'll find someone else to help me."

Problem 7–1 Opening Ledger Accounts

Instructions Use the step-by-step processes presented in this chapter to open the following ledger accounts. Use the accounting stationery provided in your working papers. January 1 of the current year is the date.

Account Name	Account Number	Balance
Cash in Bank	101	$10,000
Accounts Receivable—Mark Cohen	104	2,000
Accounts Payable—Jenco Industries	203	1,000
Tom Torrie, Capital	301	35,000
Admissions Revenue	401	- 0 -

RETEACHING SECTION 1

Making the Transition to the Four-Column Ledger Account Students are sometimes confused when they begin working with the four-column ledger account forms. Help them make the transition from the T account to the ledger form by showing the T-account relationship in the ledger account form. There are two Ts in the ledger form. The first T is in the Debit and Credit columns. The second T is in the Balance Debit and Credit columns.

The Posting Process

In the last section you learned how to open accounts in the general ledger. In this section you will learn how to post general journal entries to the ledger. **Posting** is the process of transferring information from the general journal to individual general ledger accounts, the fourth step in the accounting cycle. To provide current information to management, the accountant for the Jeep dealership in your area probably posts journal entries to the general ledger every day.

What **You'll Learn**

- The purpose and importance of posting.
- How often a business posts transactions.
- The six steps in the posting process.
- How to compute an account balance.
- How to show an account with a zero balance.

Why **It's Important**

Posting brings the records of the business up-to-date. If a business did not post its transactions, the balances in ledger accounts would not be current.

KEY TERMS

posting

The Fourth Step in the Accounting Cycle: Posting

The general journal is a sort of business diary containing all the transactions of a business. It is not easy to see the increases and decreases taking place in the account by looking at journal entries. To provide a clear picture of how each account is affected by a business transaction, the information in a journal entry is posted to the general ledger accounts. The purpose of posting, therefore, is to show the impact of business transactions on the individual accounts.

The size of the business, the number of transactions, and whether the accounting system is manual or computerized all affect how often posting occurs. Ideally, businesses post daily to keep their accounts up-to-date. Regardless of how often posting is performed, the process remains the same.

As in journalizing a transaction, posting to a ledger account is completed from left to right. Let's look at a journal entry for Roadrunner that is ready to be posted to the ledger.

Posting to the Roadrunner General Ledger

Roadrunner's first transaction affects two accounts: **Cash in Bank** and **Maria Sanchez, Capital.** The information in the journal entry is transferred item by item from the journal to each of the accounts affected. As you read about each step in the posting process, refer to **Figure 7–5.**

Locate the account to be debited in the ledger; in this example, **Cash in Bank** is to be debited.

RESOURCE MANAGER

Reproducible Masters
- Lesson Plans
- Chapter Reviews and Working Papers (CRWP) TAE
- Demonstration Problems

Transparencies
- Section Focus Transparency
- Teaching Transparencies
- Source Document Transparencies
- Solution Transparencies

Multimedia
- Exam*View* CD-ROM
- Electronic Learning Center CD-ROM
- Interactive Lesson Planner CD-ROM
- Electronic Field Trips in Accounting

1 FOCUS

Introducing the Section

In this section students apply their previous learning by posting general journal entries to the general ledger. Students will learn a step-by-step method for posting journal entries.

Section Concepts

- The purpose and importance of posting.
- How often a business posts transactions.
- The six steps in the posting process.
- How to compute an account balance.
- How to show an account with a zero balance.

Visual Learning

Section 2 Focus

Use **Transparency 7–6** to introduce section concepts.

BELL RINGER

Following Directions: Write this exercise on the chalkboard and ask students to complete the exercise. Be prepared for some noise and fun!

1. Don't do anything until I say the word "Go."
2. Write your name on a sheet of paper.
3. Fold the paper in half.
4. Stand up and clap your hands.
5. Recite the accounting equation.

How many students followed the first direction given and did nothing? Point out that following directions in accounting means completing all the steps in a process in the order required. L1

2 TEACH

GUIDED PRACTICE

Reading Accounting

- Have students convert data from the illustration into study notes by writing a list of the steps in the posting process. L1

Concept Development: The Fourth Step in the Accounting Cycle: Posting

Discussion: Use the transparency of the accounting cycle or the illustration in the textbook to point out the fourth step in the accounting cycle. Remind students that the accounting cycle is a series of steps taken in order to complete the activities of recording and reporting financial information. L1

Visual Learning

Figure 7–5 Posting from the General Journal to Ledger Accounts

Use **Transparency 7–7** to guide students through the steps in the posting process.

Teaching Tip

Point out that the posting process moves from left to right, the way we read, across the ledger form and then back to the journal with the account number. If students fill in all the information in this order, they are less likely to omit a part of the journal entry.

GO TO Strategies for Teaching International Accounting

To enrich study of International Accounting, refer to the additional critical thinking activities in the booklet.

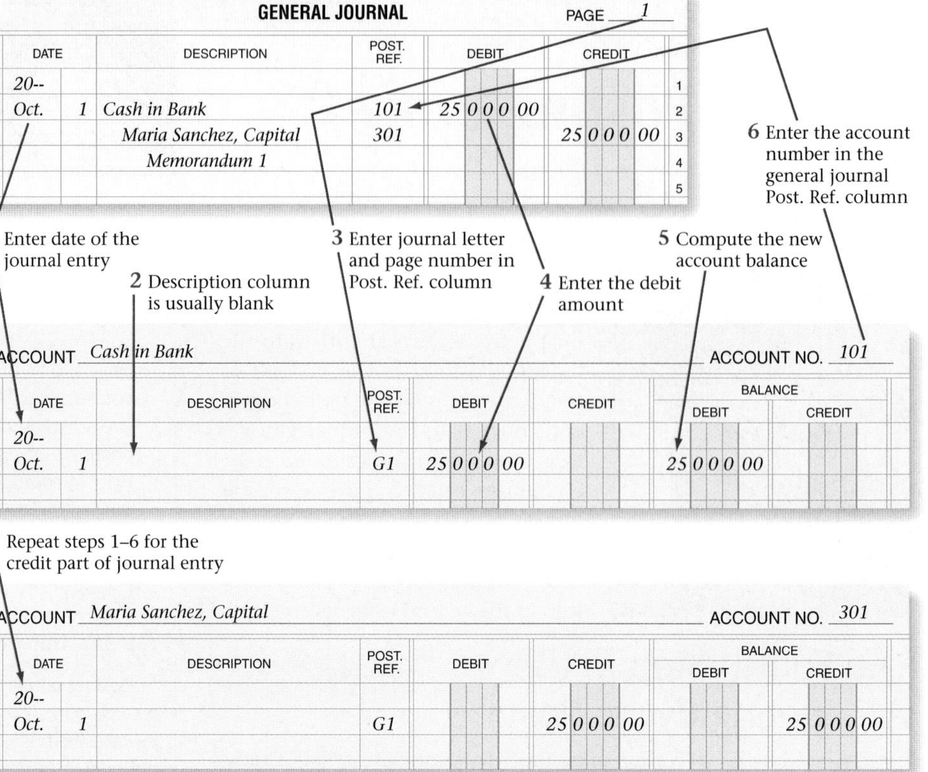

GENERAL JOURNAL — PAGE 1

	DATE		DESCRIPTION	POST. REF.	DEBIT	CREDIT	
1	20--						1
2	Oct.	1	Cash in Bank	101	25 000 00		2
3			Maria Sanchez, Capital	301		25 000 00	3
4			Memorandum 1				4
5							5

ACCOUNT Cash in Bank — ACCOUNT NO. 101

DATE		DESCRIPTION	POST. REF.	DEBIT	CREDIT	BALANCE DEBIT	BALANCE CREDIT
20--							
Oct.	1		G1	25 000 00		25 000 00	

ACCOUNT Maria Sanchez, Capital — ACCOUNT NO. 301

DATE		DESCRIPTION	POST. REF.	DEBIT	CREDIT	BALANCE DEBIT	BALANCE CREDIT
20--							
Oct.	1		G1		25 000 00		25 000 00

Figure 7–5 Posting from the General Journal to Ledger Accounts

International ACCOUNTING

Business Practices

Giving gifts to foreign business acquaintances can be tricky. Recognize that certain cultures attribute meaning to certain gifts and colors. For example, in Japan, white chrysanthemums are symbols of death.

1. Enter the date of the journal entry in the Date column of the account debited. Use the date of the journal entry, not the date on which the posting is done. Write the year and month in the left side of the Date column. It is not necessary to write the year and month for other postings to the same account on the same page unless the month or year changes. The day, however, is always entered.
2. The Description column on the ledger account is usually left blank. Some businesses use this space to write in the source document number.
3. In the ledger account Posting Reference (Post. Ref.) column, identify where the journal entry is recorded. Enter a letter for the journal and the journal page number. In this example, the letter "G" represents the general journal and the "1" indicates page one of the general journal.
4. Enter the debit amount in the Debit column of the ledger account.

Teaching International ACCOUNTING

Researching Appropriate Gifts Rules for gift giving in other countries can be quite complicated. Assign students to research cultural differences in business to learn about gift giving in a country of their choice. Students can find books on multiculturalism at their local library or find articles on the Internet. Have students write a short report on appropriate gifts for several different circumstances and share their findings in class.

5. Compute and record the new account balance in the appropriate balance column. Every amount posted will either increase or decrease the balance of that account.
6. Return to the journal and, in the Posting Reference column, enter the ledger account number of the account to which you just posted the debit part of the journal entry. Be sure it is entered on the same line as the debit entry. In this example, enter 101 in the Posting Reference column on the line for **Cash in Bank.**

   This step in the posting process is very important. The notation in the Posting Reference column of the journal indicates that the journal entry has been posted. The posting reference also shows the account to which the entry was posted. If the posting process is interrupted, perhaps by a telephone call, the posting reference signals the point at which posting stopped. *Never* write an account number in the posting reference column until *after* you have posted.
7. Repeat steps 1–6 for the credit part of the journal entry.
   - Locate the account to be credited. In this example, **Maria Sanchez, Capital,** is to be credited.
   - Enter the date.
   - Enter the posting reference on the ledger account form. In this example, G1 represents the first page of the general journal.
   - Enter the credit amount.
   - Compute the new account balance.
   - Enter the account number in the Posting Reference column of the general journal. In the example, enter 301 to show that the credit was posted to **Maria Sanchez, Capital.**

The journal entries made in Chapter 6 for Roadrunner's transactions are shown in **Figure 7–6.**

The Importance of Posting

Posting organizes business transaction details into the proper accounts. As discussed earlier, transactions that are itemized in the general journal are helpful, but do not summarize similar transactions into the same location. Posting summarizes all business transactions so managers can see the cumulative effects on accounts like **Utilities Expense** or **Salaries Expense.**

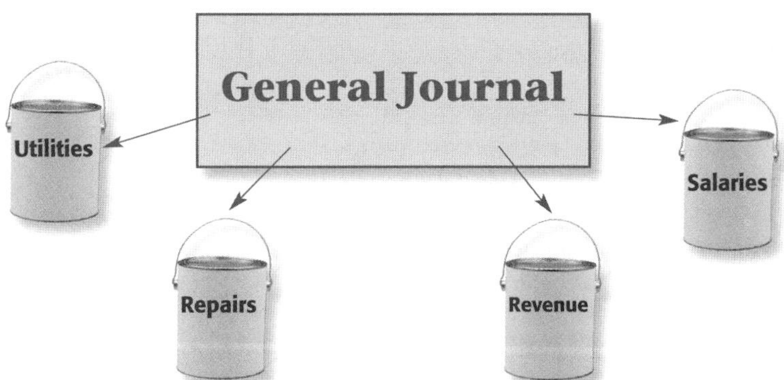

Key Points

Posting to General Ledger Accounts

For every journal entry, you will post to at least two ledger accounts. You will post the debit part of the entry to one ledger account and the credit part of the entry to another ledger account.

Math Hints

Balancing Transactions

When transactions affect both sides of the accounting equation:

- amounts *added* to one side must also be *added* to the other side, and
- amounts *subtracted* from one side must also be *subtracted* from the other side.

CHAPTER 7
SECTION 2, PAGES 157–164

2 TEACH (Cont'd.)

Teaching Tip

To help students understand the importance of posting, make copies (or a transparency) of a complete page of general journal entries. Ask students to look at the page and tell you the current balance in the Cash in Bank account or some other account that appears on the page. Point out that the journal simply records the information about transactions. Posting to the ledger provides the means of sorting the information into meaningful categories (account data).

Critical Thinking: Tell students that in a computerized accounting system, posting is handled automatically by the computer program. Have students write a paragraph or two explaining the benefits and disadvantages of having the posting process handled automatically. L3

Visual Learning

General Journal, p. 159

Use the graphic of the general journal and sample accounts on this page to remind students that posting sorts financial data according to accounts. The graphic shows some of those accounts in which information about a specific type of expense or revenue is collected.

Math Review for Accounting Photocopy appropriate *Activity Sheets* for students who need additional practice in basic math.

Math Skill Builder Activity

Balancing Transactions Ask students to practice balancing transactions by taking this information and posting to the appropriate accounts:

1. Check from Madelyn Warlick for $125 to pay on her account balance of $500.
   (Cr. AR—Madelyn Warlick for $125, Cr. balance $375; Dr. Cash in Bank, $125.)
2. Wrote Check 51 to City Utilities for water and sewer fees of $75.
   (Dr. Utilities Expense, $75.00; Cr. Cash in Bank, $75.00.)
3. Purchased a computer for the office for $2,000.
   (Dr. Office Equipment, $2,000; Cr. Cash in Bank, $2,000.)

2 TEACH (Cont'd.)

Visual Learning

Figure 7-6 General Journal Entries for October Business Transactions

Use **Transparency 7-8** to review the journal entries students learned in Chapter 6. Point out the account numbers in the Posting Reference column of the journal, and have students find the corresponding account in **Figure 7-7.**

Demonstration Problem Step-by-Step Practice

Use demonstration problem 7-2 to demonstrate the steps in the posting process.

Teaching Tip

Reinforce the classifying of accounts by having students look at the account name and the account numbers in the Posting Reference column and give each account's classification.

GENERAL JOURNAL PAGE 1

DATE		DESCRIPTION	POST. REF.	DEBIT	CREDIT
20--					
Oct.	1	Cash in Bank	101	25 000 00	
		Maria Sanchez, Capital	301		25 000 00
		Memorandum 1			
	2	Office Equipment	120	400 00	
		Maria Sanchez, Capital	301		400 00
		Memorandum 2			
	4	Computer Equipment	115	3 000 00	
		Cash in Bank	101		3 000 00
		Check 101			
	9	Delivery Equipment	125	12 000 00	
		Accounts Payable—North Shore Auto	205		12 000 00
		Invoice 200			
	11	Accounts Receivable—Green Co.	110	200 00	
		Office Equipment	120		200 00
		Memorandum 3			
	12	Accounts Payable—North Shore Auto	205	350 00	
		Cash in Bank	101		350 00
		Check 102			
	14	Cash in Bank	101	200 00	
		Accounts Receivable—Green Co.	110		200 00
		Receipt 1			
	15	Cash in Bank	101	1 200 00	
		Delivery Revenue	401		1 200 00
		Receipt 2			
	16	Rent Expense	510	700 00	
		Cash in Bank	101		700 00
		Check 103			
	18	Advertising Expense	501	75 00	
		Accounts Payable—Beacon Advertising	201		75 00
		Invoice 129			
	20	Accounts Receivable—City News	105	1 450 00	
		Delivery Revenue	401		1 450 00
		Sales Invoice 1			
	28	Utilities Expense	515	125 00	
		Cash in Bank	101		125 00
		Check 104			
	29	Maintenance Expense	505	600 00	
		Cash in Bank	101		600 00
		Check 105			
	31	Maria Sanchez, Withdrawals	302	500 00	
		Cash in Bank	101		500 00
		Check 106			

Figure 7–6 General Journal Entries for October Business Transactions

The postings made to the general ledger accounts from these entries are shown in **Figure 7–7.** Study these illustrations to check your understanding of the posting process.

MAKING CONNECTIONS TO DAILY LIFE

Using Checking Accounts Ask students who have checking accounts to explain what happens to their account when they withdraw money or deposit a check. (The transaction is posted to the account and the balance either increases or decreases.) Then ask students to explain why a bank must post transactions to checking and savings accounts daily. (To keep customer bank account balances up to date. If a customer's checking or savings account balance is not up to date, an individual may be permitted to withdraw cash when the balance in the account is not sufficient to cover the withdrawal.)

ACCOUNT *Cash in Bank* ACCOUNT NO. *101*

DATE		DESCRIPTION	POST. REF.	DEBIT	CREDIT	BALANCE DEBIT	BALANCE CREDIT
20--							
Oct.	*1*		*G1*	*25 000 00*		*25 000 00*	
	4		*G1*		*3 000 00*	*22 000 00*	
	12		*G1*		*3 5 0 00*	*21 6 5 0 00*	
	14		*G1*	*2 0 0 00*		*21 8 5 0 00*	
	15		*G1*	*1 2 0 0 00*		*23 0 5 0 00*	
	16		*G1*		*7 0 0 00*	*22 3 5 0 00*	
	28		*G1*		*1 2 5 00*	*22 2 2 5 00*	
	29		*G1*		*6 0 0 00*	*21 6 2 5 00*	
	31		*G1*		*5 0 0 00*	*21 1 2 5 00*	

ACCOUNT *Accounts Receivable—City News* ACCOUNT NO. *105*

DATE		DESCRIPTION	POST. REF.	DEBIT	CREDIT	BALANCE DEBIT	BALANCE CREDIT
20--							
Oct.	*20*		*G1*	*1 4 5 0 00*		*1 4 5 0 00*	

ACCOUNT *Accounts Receivable—Green Company* ACCOUNT NO. *110*

DATE		DESCRIPTION	POST. REF.	DEBIT	CREDIT	BALANCE DEBIT	BALANCE CREDIT
20--							
Oct.	*11*		*G1*	*2 0 0 00*		*2 0 0 00*	
	14		*G1*		*2 0 0 00*	—	

ACCOUNT *Computer Equipment* ACCOUNT NO. *115*

DATE		DESCRIPTION	POST. REF.	DEBIT	CREDIT	BALANCE DEBIT	BALANCE CREDIT
20--							
Oct.	*4*		*G1*	*3 0 0 0 00*		*3 0 0 0 00*	

ACCOUNT *Office Equipment* ACCOUNT NO. *120*

DATE		DESCRIPTION	POST. REF.	DEBIT	CREDIT	BALANCE DEBIT	BALANCE CREDIT
20--							
Oct.	*2*		*G1*	*4 0 0 00*		*4 0 0 00*	
	11		*G1*		*2 0 0 00*	*2 0 0 00*	

ACCOUNT *Delivery Equipment* ACCOUNT NO. *125*

DATE		DESCRIPTION	POST. REF.	DEBIT	CREDIT	BALANCE DEBIT	BALANCE CREDIT
20--							
Oct.	*9*		*G1*	*12 0 0 0 00*		*12 0 0 0 00*	

ACCOUNT *Accounts Payable—Beacon Advertising* ACCOUNT NO. *201*

DATE		DESCRIPTION	POST. REF.	DEBIT	CREDIT	BALANCE DEBIT	BALANCE CREDIT
20--							
Oct.	*18*		*G1*		*7 5 00*		*7 5 00*

Figure 7–7 Postings to General Ledger Accounts for the Month of October

2 TEACH (Cont'd.)

Visual Learning

Figure 7–7 Postings to General Ledger Accounts for the Month of October

Use **Transparency 7–9a** to help students trace posted items back to the original journal entry. Remind students that the last step in the posting process is to write the account number in the journal. This step tells an auditor the account to which the journal entry was posted.

Teaching Tip

Point out that the year is written at the top of the ledger form and is not repeated unless it changes. The month also is written only once until it changes.

Thinking Algebraically

Algebraic equations are written horizontally, just as the balance and debit/credit amounts are in a ledger form. Ask students how they would use algebra to find a new account balance. (The new account balance is the unknown, and they can solve just as they would with an unknown in an algebraic equation.) L1

Chapter Reviews and Working Papers Refer students to the *Study Plan* located at the beginning of Chapter 7 in the workbook.

REINFORCING STUDY SKILLS

Graphs and Charts Graphs and charts can convey certain kinds of information more quickly and succinctly than words. Some students may need help in reading and interpreting graphs or charts. For practice, ask students to explain in words the processes shown in one or more of the charts in this chapter. Ask students to explain what the arrows represent. If students have difficulty interpreting the data in the graphs or charts, explain in words the step-by-step processes shown in the illustrations.

2 TEACH (Cont'd.)

Visual Learning

Figure 7–7 Postings to General Ledger Accounts for the Month of October (Cont'd.)

Use **Transparency 7–9b** to continue tracing posted items to the general journal entries.

Critical Thinking: Point out to students that accounts are located in the general ledger in order of their account numbers. Ask students the advantage of this method over placing accounts in alphabetical order. (With this method, all accounts of the same classification are placed together so you know which section to go to if you are posting to an asset account, for example. In addition, since all accounts within a classification have the same rules of debit and credit, it is easier to remember which is the normal balance when posting to an account organized by its classification.) L2

ACCOUNT *Accounts Payable—North Shore Auto* ACCOUNT NO. *205*

DATE		DESCRIPTION	POST. REF.	DEBIT	CREDIT	BALANCE DEBIT	BALANCE CREDIT
20--							
Oct.	9		G1		12 000 00		12 000 00
	12		G1	350 00			11 650 00

ACCOUNT *Maria Sanchez, Capital* ACCOUNT NO. *301*

DATE		DESCRIPTION	POST. REF.	DEBIT	CREDIT	BALANCE DEBIT	BALANCE CREDIT
20--							
Oct.	1		G1		25 000 00		25 000 00
	2		G1		400 00		25 400 00

ACCOUNT *Maria Sanchez, Withdrawals* ACCOUNT NO. *302*

DATE		DESCRIPTION	POST. REF.	DEBIT	CREDIT	BALANCE DEBIT	BALANCE CREDIT
20--							
Oct.	31		G1	500 00		500 00	

ACCOUNT *Income Summary* ACCOUNT NO. *303*

DATE		DESCRIPTION	POST. REF.	DEBIT	CREDIT	BALANCE DEBIT	BALANCE CREDIT

ACCOUNT *Delivery Revenue* ACCOUNT NO. *401*

DATE		DESCRIPTION	POST. REF.	DEBIT	CREDIT	BALANCE DEBIT	BALANCE CREDIT
20--							
Oct.	15		G1		1 200 00		1 200 00
	20		G1		1 450 00		2 650 00

ACCOUNT *Advertising Expense* ACCOUNT NO. *501*

DATE		DESCRIPTION	POST. REF.	DEBIT	CREDIT	BALANCE DEBIT	BALANCE CREDIT
20--							
Oct.	18		G1	75 00		75 00	

ACCOUNT *Maintenance Expense* ACCOUNT NO. *505*

DATE		DESCRIPTION	POST. REF.	DEBIT	CREDIT	BALANCE DEBIT	BALANCE CREDIT
20--							
Oct.	29		G1	600 00		600 00	

ACCOUNT *Rent Expense* ACCOUNT NO. *510*

DATE		DESCRIPTION	POST. REF.	DEBIT	CREDIT	BALANCE DEBIT	BALANCE CREDIT
20--							
Oct.	16		G1	700 00		700 00	

ACCOUNT *Utilities Expense* ACCOUNT NO. *515*

DATE		DESCRIPTION	POST. REF.	DEBIT	CREDIT	BALANCE DEBIT	BALANCE CREDIT
20--							
Oct.	28		G1	125 00		125 00	

Figure 7–7 Postings to General Ledger Accounts for the Month of October (Continued)

COOPERATIVE LEARNING ACTIVITY

Make and Defend Divide students into groups of five or six and provide the following scenario: "Monica Nan recently started a small business selling handmade crafts. Initially she posted journal entries at the end of each month. Business has increased significantly, and Monica wonders whether she should post more frequently. What recommendations would you make, and why?" Ask each group to make a decision and to appoint a spokesperson to present and defend the decision to the class. (All answers are correct if groups adequately defend their recommendations, which should refer to higher transaction volume and the need for timely information.)

Computing a New Account Balance

On a four-column ledger account form, each time you post to an account, you also compute a new account balance. An easy rule of thumb for determining a new balance is that debits are added to debits, credits are added to credits, but debits and credits are subtracted. In other words, after you post to an account, you compute the new account balance as follows:

When the existing account balance is a debit, and

- the amount posted is a debit, ADD the amounts
- the amount posted is a credit, SUBTRACT the amounts.

When the existing account balance is a credit, and

- the amount posted is a debit, SUBTRACT the amounts
- the amount posted is a credit, ADD the amounts.

A ledger account usually has space for several postings. Often, blank lines remain after the journal entries for the month are posted. To save space, the journal entries for more than one month are entered on the same ledger page. Both the new month and day are entered in the Date column, as shown below in **Figure 7–8.**

Key Points

Calculating Balances

- Debit amounts are added together.
- Credit amounts are added together.
- Debit and credit amounts are subtracted.

ACCOUNT *Cash in Bank* ACCOUNT NO. *101*

DATE		DESCRIPTION	POST. REF.	DEBIT	CREDIT	BALANCE DEBIT	BALANCE CREDIT
20--							
Oct.	1		G1	25 000 00		25 000 00	
	31		G2		500 00	24 500 00	
Nov.	1		G2		125 00	24 375 00	

Figure 7–8 A Ledger Account with Several Postings

Showing a Zero Balance in a Ledger Account

Sometimes a ledger account will have a zero balance. To show a zero balance, a line should be drawn across the center of the column—where the normal balance would appear. For example, on October 11, Roadrunner sold a phone for $200 on account to Green Company. On October 14, Green Company paid for the phone in full with a $200 check. When the October 14 journal entry is posted, **Accounts Receivable—Green Company** has a zero balance. Look at the ledger account in **Figure 7–9.** The line across the debit balance column means that the account has a zero balance. The line is drawn in the debit column because the normal balance for this account is a debit.

ACCOUNT *Accounts Receivable—Green Company* ACCOUNT NO. *110*

DATE		DESCRIPTION	POST. REF.	DEBIT	CREDIT	BALANCE DEBIT	BALANCE CREDIT
20--							
Oct.	11		G1	200 00		200 00	
	14		G1		200 00	——	

Figure 7–9 Showing a Ledger Account with a Zero Balance

MEETING SPECIAL NEEDS

English Language Learners Students who do not speak English as their native language face special challenges when dealing with large numbers. Generally, it is not the mathematical calculation that causes problems. Instead, native speakers tend to say the numbers very quickly and blur the sounds. To help students understand, write the numbers on the chalkboard along with the sign indicating the operation being performed.

2 TEACH (Cont'd.)

Teaching Tips

This is the point at which students need to know the rules of debit and credit and normal balance sides very well. You may want to review the normal balance side of each account classification before discussing how to compute a new account balance.

Reinforce the classifying of accounts by having students look at the account numbers shown in **Figure 7–7** and give each account's classification.

Visual Learning

Figure 7–8 A Ledger Account with Several Postings

Use **Transparency 7–10** to point out that each time an entry is posted to the ledger, a new account balance is calculated. Suggest that students who have difficulty adding or subtracting horizontally write amounts on scrap paper to calculate new balances.

Figure 7–9 Showing a Ledger Account with a Zero Balance

Using **Transparency 7–11**, demonstrate how to show a zero balance in a ledger account.

Demonstration Problem
Step-by-Step Practice

Use demonstration problem 7–3 to show students how to indicate a zero balance in a ledger account.

CHAPTER 7

SECTION 2, PAGES 157–164

3 ASSESS

Thinking Critically (Answers)

1. The purpose of posting is to show the effects of business transactions on the accounts of the business.
2. The process involves transferring information in a journal entry to an individual account. Posting frequency depends on the size of a business, the number of transactions, and whether posting is done manually or by computer.

Analyzing Accounting (Answers)

Answers may vary. Students should analyze the graph, noting which months have the highest and lowest sales, and state the effects on overall profit.

Problem 7–2 (Answers)

Account balances:

Cash in Bank $10,000 (Dr.)

David Serlo, Capital $10,000 (Cr.)

Chapter Reviews and Working Papers

Refer students to the Chapter 7 workbook pages to answer *Check Your Understanding* activities.

4 CLOSE

Section Wrap-Up

Group Oral Presentation: Divide students into groups of four or five. Have each group prepare a short (2 minutes or so) presentation explaining the general ledger, how it is organized, and its purpose in an accounting system. Have groups give their presentations, then discuss any differences or questions. L1

Post General Journal Entries: As a reinforcement activity, have students draw general ledger account forms for the two accounts shown in the journal entry in Problem 7–2. Have students post the entry to their account forms. L2

SECTION 2 Check Your Understanding

Now that you have studied this section, complete the following questions and problem.

Thinking Critically

1. Explain the purpose for posting.
2. Explain the process of posting from a journal to the ledger.

Analyzing Accounting

As an employee of Always Fresh Bakery, you have been asked to analyze the impact that different sales levels have on the ultimate profit or loss of the business. After posting is completed, you prepare the following line graph to illustrate the sales figures for Always Fresh Bakery. Review the line graph and write a one-paragraph analysis of the impact of sales on the bakery's profit.

ANNUAL SALES AND REVENUE

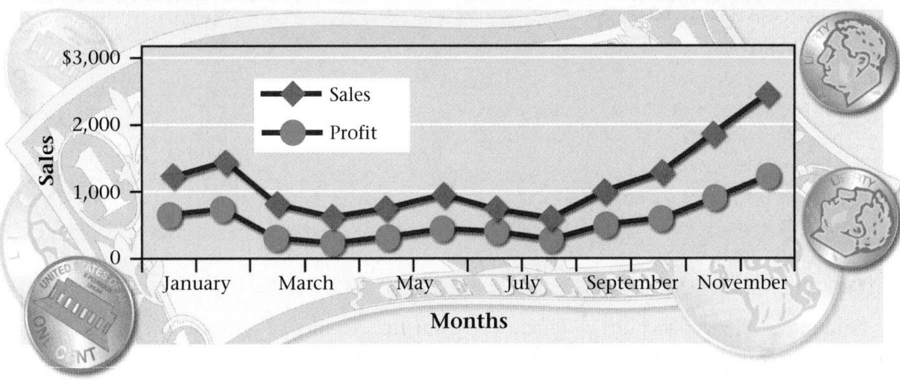

Problem 7–2 Posting from the General Journal to the Ledger

Instructions David Serlo made the following cash investment in his business. Use the six-step process to post the entry to the ledger accounts in your working papers.

GENERAL JOURNAL PAGE 1

	DATE		DESCRIPTION	POST. REF.	DEBIT	CREDIT	
1	20--						1
2	May	1	Cash in Bank		10 000 00		2
3			David Serlo, Capital			10 000 00	3
4			Memorandum 101				4
5							5

RETEACHING SECTION 2

Calculating Account Balances When calculating account balances after posting, some students may have difficulty remembering which accounts have a normal debit balance and which accounts have a normal credit balance. Encourage students to think of the rules of debit and credit to help them remember the normal balance side of an account.

Some account balances will be reduced to zero when all transactions are posted. Remind students that a dash is drawn across the normal balance column when a zero balance occurs. Otherwise, one might think that the balance amount was omitted in error.

ACCOUNTING CAREERS IN FOCUS

LORA HURRELBRINK
Accounts Payable Manager, National Veterinary Associates

Q: How did you get into accounting?

A: I started in a retail clothing warehouse tagging merchandise. Soon my responsibilities included checking receipts sent in by all the stores. That got boring, and I needed something more challenging and people-interactive. So, I became an accounts payable clerk. After a while, I wanted more responsibilities. So, I became an accounts payable bookkeeper and gained experience for five years. Then I applied for a supervisory position. I loved it! I have been a manager ever since.

Q: Why do you like managing?

A: I like being the boss, and I like teaching.

Q: What kind of degree do you need?

A: If someone wants to be an accounts payable manager, they don't necessarily need an accounting degree, although some companies like to see it. I've never been asked why I don't have one. If you want to move up to staff accountant, or controller, though, you need an accounting degree and a CPA. Business training is important. The best thing is to get experience while you're in school. Work anywhere you deal with money and math.

Tips from . . .

RHI Robert Half International Inc.

In business, success is usually a team effort. Help out whenever your help is necessary, even if it is "not your job." Show initiative, and give credit to the group when someone compliments a job well done.

CAREER FACTS

Nature of the Work: Oversee accounts payable staff, make decisions, and report to management.
Training or Education Needed: A bachelor's degree in accounting, or five to ten years experience.
Aptitudes, Abilities, and Skills: Analytical skills, problem-solving skills, computer skills, interpersonal skills, and communication skills.
Salary Range: $27,000 to $60,000 depending on company size and industry.
Career Path: First start as a clerk, then you can move to a lead clerk, and eventually move into management.

Thinking Critically: What qualities do you think employers look for when hiring?

CAREERS IN FOCUS CHAPTER 7

SCANS in the Workforce

Foundation Skills Connection

Sociability

Ask students to create a list of pros and cons related to their "sociability quotient." Are they extroverts or introverts? Do they possess empathy? How do they handle group situations? Do they prefer to have many acquaintances or just a few friends? Once they have identified their traits, discuss their ability to adapt to unfamiliar social situations. L1

Workplace Competencies Connection

Participating as a Member of a Team

Divide your class into small teams of four to five students. Ask each team to brainstorm a project that would be directed at community service and could be completed by the class. Then have them define the various duties, timeline, and end result of the project. Have the team develop a slogan or catchphrase for the project. Finally, ask the team to appoint a spokesperson to present their ideas. L2

Negotiating to Arrive at a Decision

Hold a classroom debate on a controversial issue. Pick a current event, social issue, school concern, or community problem. Divide the class into two teams to research the facts on the selected topic. Select two students per team to present the information. Select one student to act as the arbitrator to bring the class to a decision based on a majority vote. Discuss conflict resolution in the workplace and the role of arbitrators. L3

ACCOUNTING CAREERS IN FOCUS

Thinking Critically (Answers)

Employers look for people who are willing to work hard. They also look for employees who take on responsibilities and challenges for themselves.

ROBERT HALF CORNER

Networking Have students think about all the connections they have made so far, including personal/family references, professional associations, and volunteer organizations. Encourage students to continue to develop connections that can assist them in their future job searches.

1 FOCUS

Introducing the Section

Accounting is a system of checks and balances. In this section students learn how to check the accuracy of posting by preparing a trial balance. They'll also learn how to find and correct errors revealed by the trial balance.

Section Concepts

- The purpose of a trial balance.
- How to prepare a trial balance.
- How to identify and locate trial balance errors.

Visual Learning

Section 3 Focus

Use **Transparency 7–12** to introduce section concepts.

BELL RINGER

Exploring Meanings: Write the word "Trial" on the chalkboard. Have students tell you the different meanings of the word. Write each meaning on the chalkboard. You should get responses such as "a legal proceeding," "a test of endurance or patience," "an annoyance," and "to try something out." Focus on this last meaning: to try something out. Point out that the trial balance is a means of "trying out" the accuracy of the ledger. L1

SECTION 3

Preparing a Trial Balance

What You'll Learn

- The purpose of a trial balance.
- How to prepare a trial balance.
- How to identify and locate trial balance errors.

Why It's Important

To present accurate financial statements, the accounts must be in balance. The purpose of a trial balance is to prove that the general ledger is in balance.

KEY TERMS

proving the ledger
trial balance
transposition error
slide error
correcting entry

In the last section you learned how to post to the ledger. In this section you will learn how to prepare a trial balance. A trial balance is how accountants prove that the accounting system is in balance. Preparing a trial balance is the fifth step in the accounting cycle. Every time the accountant for the Jeep dealership in your area posts to the ledger, he or she prepares a trial balance. The trial balance provides assurance that the journal entries are posted properly.

The Fifth Step in the Accounting Cycle: The Trial Balance

After the journal entries are posted to the accounts in the general ledger, the total of all the debit balances should equal the total of all the credit balances. Adding all the debit balances, then adding all the credit balances, and finally comparing the two totals to see whether they are equal is called **proving the ledger**.

A formal way to prove that debits equal credits is to prepare a **trial balance**. A trial balance is a list of all the account names and their current balances. All of the debit balances are added. All of the credit balances are added. The totals are compared. If the totals are the same, the trial balance is in balance. If the totals are not equal, an error was made in journalizing, posting, or preparing the trial balance. You must find the error and correct it before continuing with the next step in the accounting cycle.

The trial balance for Roadrunner Delivery Service for the month of October is shown in **Figure 7–10.** The trial balance was prepared on two-column accounting stationery. The account numbers are listed in the far left column. The account names are listed in the next column. All of the debit balances are entered in the first amount column, and all of the credit balances are entered in the second amount column. Trial balances do not have to be prepared on accounting stationery. They can be handwritten on plain paper, typed, or prepared on a computer.

ACCOUNTING TIPS

Trial Balance

When preparing a trial balance, be sure to list all the general ledger accounts, in the order in which they appear in the ledger and on the chart of accounts. List even those accounts with a zero balance. Every account is listed to avoid omitting an account (and its balance) from the trial balance.

RESOURCE MANAGER

Reproducible Masters
- Lesson Plans
- Chapter Reviews and Working Papers (CRWP) TAE
- Demonstration Problems

Transparencies
- Section Focus Transparency
- Teaching Transparencies
- Source Document Transparencies
- Solution Transparencies

Multimedia
- ExamView CD-ROM
- Electronic Learning Center CD-ROM
- Interactive Lesson Planner CD-ROM
- Electronic Field Trips in Accounting

		Roadrunner Delivery Service Trial Balance October 31, 20--		
101	Cash in Bank		21 125 00	
105	Accounts Receivable—City News		1 450 00	
110	Accounts Receivable—Green Company		—	
115	Computer Equipment		3 000 00	
120	Office Equipment		200 00	
125	Delivery Equipment		12 000 00	
201	Accounts Payable—Beacon Advertising			75 00
205	Accounts Payable—North Shore Auto			11 650 00
301	Maria Sanchez, Capital			25 400 00
302	Maria Sanchez, Withdrawals		500 00	
303	Income Summary		—	—
401	Delivery Revenue			2 650 00
501	Advertising Expense		75 00	
505	Maintenance Expense		600 00	
510	Rent Expense		700 00	
515	Utilities Expense		125 00	
	Totals		39 775 00	39 775 00

Figure 7–10 Trial Balance

Finding Errors

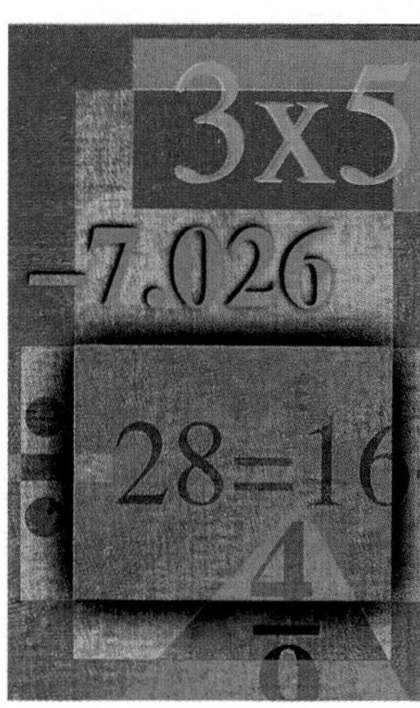

Most trial balance errors can be located easily and quickly. When total debits do not equal total credits, follow these steps:

1. Add the debit and credit columns again. You may have added one or both of the columns incorrectly.
2. Find the difference between the debit and credit columns. This is the amount that you are out of balance. If this amount is 10, 100, 1,000, and so on, you probably made an addition error. Suppose, for example, you have total debits of $35,245 and total credits of $35,345. The difference between the debits and credits is $100, which indicates an addition error is likely. Add the columns again to find the error.
3. Check if the amount you are out of balance is evenly divisible by 9. For example, suppose the difference between the debits and credits is $27. That amount is evenly divisible by 9 (27 ÷ 9 = 3). If the difference between the columns is evenly divisible by 9, you may have a transposition error or a slide error. A **transposition error** occurs when two digits within an amount are accidentally reversed, or transposed. For example, the amount $325 may have been written as $352.

   A **slide error** occurs when a decimal point is moved by mistake. For example, if you write $1,800 as either $180 or $18,000, you made a slide error.

   To find a transposition error or a slide error, check the trial balance amounts against the general ledger account balances to make sure you copied the balances correctly.
4. Make sure that you have included all of the general ledger accounts in the trial balance. Look in the general ledger for an account balance equal

ACCOUNTING ISSUES

Downsizing of CPA Firms In the last several years, many businesses have decreased their work forces at all levels. CPA firms are a part of this trend. Some of the downsizing is a result of new technology and its increased efficiency. Much downsizing, though, results from maximizing productivity and profitability by having the right staff at the right time. In other words, CPA firms must fit their work forces to their workloads. Many CPA firms use part-time employees and flexible work hours to cut labor costs and increase productivity. For example, part-time tax accountants work only during the tax season.

2 TEACH

GUIDED PRACTICE

Reading Accounting

• When preparing accounting records, it's important to read and transfer numbers correctly. Have students take turns practicing reading numbers in teams. Ask team members to point out any reading errors their teammate makes. L1

Concept Development: The Fifth Step in the Accounting Cycle: The Trial Balance

Discussion: Discuss the purpose of the trial balance as a "proof" that the ledger account balances are equal: total debits = total credits. Emphasize to students that the trial balance is a part of the system of balances that are characteristic of a double-entry system of accounting. If errors appear at this stage, they must be found and corrected before other work may proceed.

Remind students that all accounts are included in a trial balance, even those with zero balances. This practice follows computerized accounting systems, which print out all accounts. L1

Visual Learning

Figure 7–10 Trial Balance

Use **Transparency 7–13** to point out the information that is included on a trial balance.

2 TEACH (Cont'd.)

Demonstration Problem Step-by-Step Practice

Use demonstration problem 7–4 to show students how to prepare a trial balance.

Teaching Tips

Students are usually frustrated when errors appear. Help them use the information in the text to approach finding errors in a logical manner. Most general ledger errors result from either computation errors or incorrect postings. Math errors can be found simply by re-adding or subtracting amounts. Errors in postings may take longer to find. They are often caused by transposition or slides. Occasionally a debit amount is recorded as a credit or vice versa.

Demonstrate an example of a transposition error and a slide error.

Concept Development: Correcting Entries

Discussion: Explain to students that errors do occur even when one is careful. Remind students that they should not erase an error unless it is on the work sheet (covered in Chapter 8). Explain that errors discovered after a journal entry has been posted must be corrected with another journal entry whose purpose is to undo the incorrect entry and record the correct entry. L1

ACCOUNTING *Flashbacks*

ACCOUNTING HISTORY

The advent of the Industrial Revolution resulted in the growth of company size and ownership. As a result, the accounting profession grew to keep track of increasing business transactions.

to the amount you are out of balance. For example, if the difference between total debits and credits is $725, look in the general ledger for an account with a balance of $725.

5. If all the general ledger accounts and their balances are included in the trial balance, one of the account balances could be recorded in the wrong column. That is, a debit is entered in the credit column or a credit is entered in the debit column. To find out if this happened, divide the out-of-balance amount by 2 and check if the result matches the balance of an account. For example, suppose that the difference between the two columns is $300; $300 divided by 2 is $150. Look in the debit and credit columns for an account balance of $150. Then check to see if the $150 is entered in the wrong column.
6. If you still have not found the error, recompute the balance in each ledger account. You may have an addition or subtraction error on a ledger account form.
7. Finally, check the general ledger accounts to verify that the correct amounts are posted from the journal entries. Also, check to make sure that debit amounts are posted to the debit column and credit amounts are posted to the credit column.

Correcting Entries

Anyone who works in accounting understands the saying, "To err is human..." When mistakes are made in accounting, one rule applies: *Never erase an error.*

"Never erase an error"

The method for correcting an error depends on when and where the error is found. There are three types of errors:

- Error in a journal entry that is not posted.
- Error in posting to the ledger when the journal entry is correct.
- Error in a journal entry that is posted.

In Chapter 6 you learned that when an error in a journal entry is discovered before posting, you draw a single line through the incorrect item in the journal and write the correction directly above. If the journal entry is correct but is posted incorrectly to the ledger, you draw a single line through the incorrect item in the ledger and write the correction directly above.

When an error in a journal entry is discovered *after* posting, make a **correcting entry** to fix the error.

On November 15, the accountant for Roadrunner found an error in a journal entry made on November 2. A $100 check to pay the electricity bill was journalized and posted to the **Maintenance Expense** account by mistake. The original journal entry is shown in the following T accounts.

Maintenance Expense	
Debit + 100	Credit –

Cash in Bank	
Debit +	Credit – 100

TEACHING NOTES

The following T accounts show how the transaction *should* have been recorded.

Utilities Expense	
Debit	Credit
+	−
100	

Cash in Bank	
Debit	Credit
+	−
	100

As you can see, the $100 credit to **Cash in Bank** is correct. The error is in the debit part of the November 2 transaction. **Maintenance Expense** is incorrectly debited for $100. To correct the error, **Maintenance Expense** is credited for $100 and **Utilities Expense** is debited for $100.

The accountant wrote Memorandum 70 to notify the accounting clerk of the mistake. The correcting entry, recorded in the general journal, is shown in **Figure 7–11.**

GENERAL JOURNAL — PAGE 3

	DATE		DESCRIPTION	POST. REF.	DEBIT	CREDIT	
1	20--						1
2	Nov.	15	Utilities Expense		100 00		2
3			Maintenance Expense			100 00	3
4			Memorandum 70				4
5							5

Figure 7–11 Correcting Entry

Posting a correcting entry is similar to any other posting. In the Description column of the ledger accounts, however, the words "Correcting Entry" are written. **Figure 7–12** shows how the correcting entry is posted to the **Maintenance Expense** and **Utilities Expense** accounts.

ACCOUNT *Maintenance Expense* — ACCOUNT NO. 505

DATE		DESCRIPTION	POST. REF.	DEBIT	CREDIT	BALANCE DEBIT	BALANCE CREDIT
20--							
Oct.	29		G1			600 00	
Nov.	2		G2	100 00		700 00	
	15	Correcting Entry	G3		100 00	600 00	

ACCOUNT *Utilities Expense* — ACCOUNT NO. 515

DATE		DESCRIPTION	POST. REF.	DEBIT	CREDIT	BALANCE DEBIT	BALANCE CREDIT
20--							
Oct.	28		G1	125 00		125 00	
Nov.	15	Correcting Entry	G3	100 00		225 00	

Figure 7–12 Posting of Correcting Entry

HOME AND COMMUNITY CONNECTIONS ACTIVITY

Financial Planning What types of financial planning activities occur at home? Have students ask their parents or guardians about short-term and long-term financial planning. Does their family have a savings account? College fund? Investment portfolio? IRA? What are rules or limitations about the use or liquidity of those funds? How about wills or trusts? Does the student know where to locate that information in case of a family emergency? Have students report on the types of financial planning their family is involved in, not on the dollar amounts.

2 TEACH (Cont'd.)

Demonstration Problem Step-by-Step Practice

Use demonstration problem 7–5 to give students practice in identifying different types of errors.

Visual Learning

Figure 7–11 Correcting Entry

Using **Transparency 7–14**, demonstrate how to record a correcting entry. Remind students that the purpose is to undo the incorrect part of an entry and to make the correct entry.

Figure 7–12 Posting of Correcting Entry

Use **Transparency 7–15** to guide students through the posting of a correcting entry. Point out that once this entry is posted, the accounts in the ledger will be correct.

Demonstration Problem Step-by-Step Practice

Use demonstration problem 7–6 to give students practice in recording and posting a correcting entry.

Teaching Tip

Remind students that accounting records must be prepared in such a way that an independent person—the auditor—can follow the accountant's work through an audit trail. Correcting incorrect journal entries through correcting entries helps provide the audit trail.

CHAPTER 7

SECTION 3, PAGES 166–170

3 ASSESS

Thinking Critically (Answers)

1. Addition/subtraction errors, transpositions (reversing two numbers), slides (moving decimal point), omissions (dropping a number), incorrect debits or credits (posting to wrong column).
2. Line out the incorrect item and write the correction directly above it, or make a correcting entry if the error is discovered after posting.

Computing in the Business World (Answers)

1. Slide, omission, transposition, transposition, no error, omission
2. After all corrections have been made, the columns should be equal.

Problem 7–3 (Answers)

May 20: Dr. Office Equip. $1,500; Cr. Computer Equip. $1,500; Memo. 47

Problem 7–4 (Answers)

July 7: Dr. Advertising Expense $300; Cr. Rent Expense $300; Memo. 13

Chapter Reviews and Working Papers Refer students to the Chapter 7 workbook pages to answer *Check Your Understanding* activities.

4 CLOSE

Section Wrap-Up

Prepare a Trial Balance: Write the following account balances on the blackboard: Consulting Fee Revenue—$1,500; Cash in Bank—$3,500; Accounts Payable, Ace Inc.—$477; Mirren Paul, Capital—$1,523. Ask students to prepare a trial balance based on these accounts. [Correct order of accounts is: Cash in Bank (Dr.); Accounts Payable, Ace Inc. (Cr.); Mirren Paul, Capital (Cr.); Consulting Fee Revenue (Cr.).] L2

SECTION 3 Check Your Understanding

Now that you have studied this section, complete the following questions and problems.

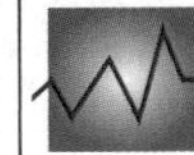

Thinking Critically

1. List some common errors made when posting. Give a brief description of each.
2. What is the best way to correct an error?

Computing in the Business World

1. Compare the numbers in Column 1 to those in Column 2. Find any transposition, slide, or omission errors. Identify the type of error for each line.

Column 1	Column 2
$18.00	$180.00
$15,000	$1,500
$222.52	$222.25
$187,235,499.05	$187,235,499.50
$47,988	$47,988
$578,334.99	$5,778,334.99

2. Using a calculator or adding machine, total Column 1. Correct any errors in Column 2, and then total Column 2. Do the totals of Columns 1 and 2 match?

Problem 7–3 Analyzing a Source Document

Instructions Analyze the transaction described in Memorandum 47, then record and post the required correcting entry in your working papers.

FUNTIME AMUSEMENT ARCADE — MEMORANDUM 47

TO: Accounting Clerk
FROM: Dan Vonderhaar
DATE: May 20, 20--
SUBJECT: Correction of error

On May 10, we purchased an office copier for $1,500. I noticed in the general journal that the entry was recorded and posted to the Computer Equipment account. Please record the necessary entry to correct this error.

Problem 7–4 Recording and Posting a Correcting Entry

Instructions On July 7, Video Connection's accounting supervisor discovered a July 3 transaction was recorded incorrectly. The transaction, involving the purchase of advertising in the local newspaper with a $300 check, was incorrectly journalized and posted to the **Rent Expense** account. In your working papers, record and post the correcting entry using Memorandum 13 as the source document.

VIDEO Connection — MEMORANDUM 13

TO: Accounting Clerk
FROM: Accounting Manager
DATE: July 7, 20--
SUBJECT: Correction of error

On July 3, we paid $300 for advertising in the *Daily News Record* that was incorrectly journalized and posted to the Rent Expense account. Please record the necessary entry to correct this error.

RETEACHING SECTION 3

Recording Correcting Entries Correcting entries are needed to correct an error detected after a journal entry has been posted. The correcting entry must undo the error. Therefore, if an account was debited in error, it must be credited for the same amount to "cancel out" and, in effect, undo the error. The second part of the correcting entry debits or credits the correct account. If the amount in the journal is incorrect, the correcting entry needs only to correct the amount. For example, if $100 was recorded instead of $1,000, the same accounts would be debited and credited for the difference—$900.

CHAPTER 7 SUMMARY

KEY CONCEPTS

1. Posting is the fourth step in the accounting cycle. It is the process of transferring information from a journal entry to specific accounts in the ledger.
2. The accounts used by a business are kept in the ledger. In a manual accounting system, each ledger account appears on its own page or card.
3. Ledger accounts are opened before posting can begin. An account is opened by writing the account name and its number at the top of the ledger account form.
4. A four-column ledger account form has four amount columns: one for a debit entry, one for a credit entry, one for a debit balance, and one for a credit balance.
5. Posting from the general journal to ledger accounts is illustrated below.

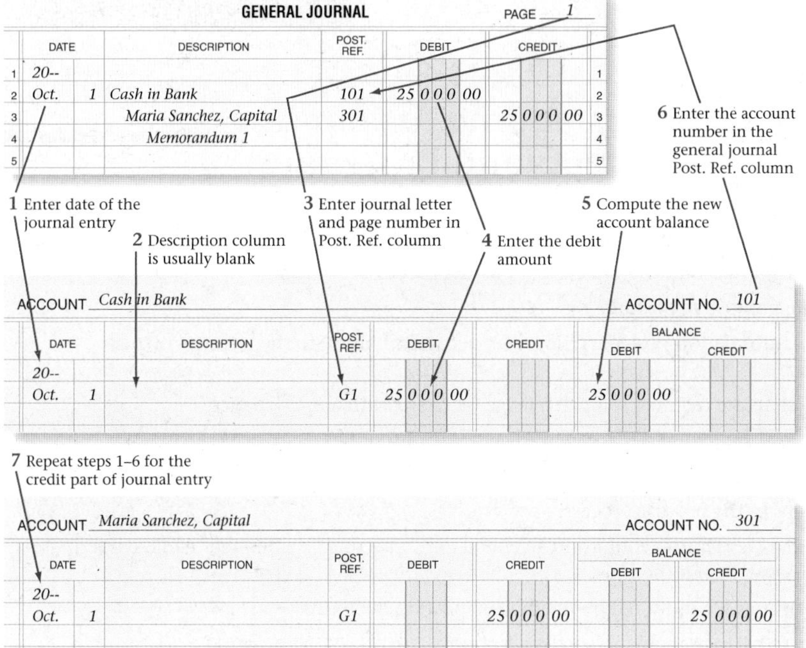

GENERAL JOURNAL — PAGE 1

	DATE		DESCRIPTION	POST. REF.	DEBIT	CREDIT	
1	20--						1
2	Oct.	1	Cash in Bank	101	25 000 00		2
3			Maria Sanchez, Capital	301		25 000 00	3
4			Memorandum 1				4
5							5

ACCOUNT Cash in Bank — ACCOUNT NO. 101

DATE		DESCRIPTION	POST. REF.	DEBIT	CREDIT	BALANCE DEBIT	BALANCE CREDIT
20--							
Oct.	1		G1	25 000 00		25 000 00	

ACCOUNT Maria Sanchez, Capital — ACCOUNT NO. 301

DATE		DESCRIPTION	POST. REF.	DEBIT	CREDIT	BALANCE DEBIT	BALANCE CREDIT
20--							
Oct.	1		G1		25 000 00		25 000 00

6. After posting is complete, the equality of the ledger is proved. A trial balance is prepared to prove that total debits equal total credits. Preparing a trial balance is the fifth step in the accounting cycle.
7. The most common errors made in accounting records are addition and subtraction errors, transpositions, slides, omissions, and incorrect debiting or crediting.
8. Errors discovered after posting require a correcting entry in both the general journal and the ledger.

ANSWERS

1. False
2. False
3. True
4. False
5. False
6. True
7. True
8. False
9. True
10. False

SUMMARY CHAPTER 7

Chapter 7 Quiz

Student Class Instructor
Date Assigned Date Completed
CHAPTER 7 QUIZ
Posting Journal Entries to General Ledger Accounts
QUESTIONS (True-False)
Directions: In the space provided, indicate whether each statement is true or false.
___ 1. The general ledger is the record of original entry.
___ 2. Posting is the third step in the accounting cycle.
___ 3. The four-column ledger form has separate columns for debit and credit balances.
___ 4. Every account in the general ledger must have a balance.
___ 5. A check mark is placed in the Posting Reference column of the general journal to indicate an entry has been posted.
___ 6. A check mark in the Posting Reference column of a ledger form indicates that the balance was not posted from a journal entry.
___ 7. The debit portion of a journal entry is always posted first.
___ 8. If the totals of the trial balance are equal, that is proof that there are no errors in the ledger.
___ 9. Reversing the order of two numbers is a transposition error.
___ 10. A slide occurs when a debit amount is mistakenly entered in a credit column.
 Chapter Quizzes • 9

QUESTIONS (True-False)

1. The general ledger is the record of original entry.
2. Posting is the third step in the accounting cycle.
3. The four-column ledger form has separate columns for debit and credit balances.
4. Every account in the general ledger must have a balance.
5. A check mark is placed in the Posting Reference column of the general journal to indicate an entry has been posted.
6. A check mark in the Posting Reference column of a ledger form indicates that the balance was not posted from a journal entry.
7. The debit portion of a journal entry is always posted first.
8. If the totals of the trial balance are equal, that is proof that there are no errors in the ledger.
9. Reversing the order of two numbers is a transposition error.
10. A slide occurs when a debit amount is mistakenly entered in a credit column.

USING KEY TERMS

See the *Glossary* for the definitions of these terms. Have students share their sentences in class. Discuss any misuse of terms.

Understanding Accounting Concepts and Procedures

(Answers)

1. Four
2. To show effects of business transactions on business accounts.
3. Accounts give a clear picture of what is happening in the business, aiding in decision making.
4. (a) Write the account name, (b) write the account number.
5. (a) Write the account name and (b) account number; (c) enter the date; (d) write "balance" in the description column; (e) place a check mark in the PR column; (f) enter the balance in the debit or credit balance column.
6. The size of the business, number of transactions, and whether posting is done manually or by computer.
7. (a) Enter date; (b) leave description column blank; (c) enter journal page reference; (d) enter debit amount; (e) compute account balance; (f) write debited account number in journal PR column; (g) repeat steps a–f for credit entry.
8. The source document number.
9. The entry has been posted and the accounts to which it was posted.
10. A dash across the balance column.
11. (a) Re-add columns; (b) look for transpositions, slides, amounts entered in wrong column; (c) check accuracy of account balances; (e) re-compute account balances; (f) verify postings.
12. Drawing a line through an incorrect entry; write the correction above it.
13. By making a correcting entry.

USING KEY TERMS

As a junior accounting clerk for Action Sports Outfitters, you are being evaluated for a raise. Your boss wants to see how well you understand basic accounting terminology. He asks you to write a sentence for each term below, showing how you would use each term in connection with Action Sports Outfitters.

correcting entry	proving the ledger
general ledger	slide error
ledger account form	transposition error
posting	trial balance

Understanding Accounting Concepts and Procedures

Instructions

On a separate sheet of paper, answer the following questions:

1. What step in the accounting cycle is the posting process?
2. What is the purpose of posting?
3. How is the information posted in the ledger accounts helpful to the business owner or manager?
4. What two steps are required to open a ledger account with a zero balance?
5. What six steps are required to open a ledger account that has a balance?
6. What determines the frequency of posting?
7. List the steps in the posting process.
8. Although the Description column in a general ledger account is often left blank, what do some businesses record there?
9. What two things are indicated by the journal posting reference?
10. How is a zero balance shown in a ledger account?
11. What steps should be followed to locate trial balance errors?
12. How does an accounting clerk correct a journal entry that has not been posted?
13. How does an accounting clerk correct an error in a journal entry that was posted?

ASSESSMENT RESOURCES

Choose assessment strategies from the following pages to evaluate your students' progress.

Student Edition
Check Your Understanding, pp. 156, 164, 170
Chapter 7 Problems, pp. 175–177

Assessment and Evaluation Masters
Chapter 7 Study Plan, *Glencoe Workbook* (CRWP)
Chapter 7 Self-Test, *Glencoe Workbook* (CRWP)
Chapter 7 Test, *Chapter Tests* Booklet
Chapter 7 Activity, *School-to-Work Handbook*
Chapter 7 **Exam***View*

Teacher Wraparound Edition
Critical Thinking Activity, p. 168
Reteaching Sections 1–3, pp. 156, 164, 170
Chapter 7 Quiz, p. 171

CHAPTER 7 REVIEW AND ACTIVITIES

Case Study...

Service Business: Accounting Services

Joel Rivlin studied accounting in college, then worked as an accountant for a local real estate company. After becoming a CPA, Joel decided to start his own company, Joel Rivlin, CPA.

Robert's Excavating Services came to Joel with a problem. The company's trial balance shows total debits of $76,240 and total credits of $75,090. The owner knows that clients paid for services worth at least $2,500 during the month, but the **Service Revenue** account balance is only $800. The owner also wrote a check for $550 for advertising, but the **Advertising Expense** account shows a zero balance.

Thinking Critically:

1. Describe what Joel should do to find the problems.
2. Suggest probable causes for the trial balance being out of balance.

Conducting an Audit with Alex

Instructions The owner of Frank Palmer's Flying School has given you the final general ledger balances and has provided the trial balance in your working papers. He has told you the Accounts Payable balance is wrong. Prepare a corrected trial balance on a separate sheet of paper.

Cash in Bank	$ 4,700
Accounts Receivable	1,600
Airplanes	90,000
Accounts Payable	2,680
Frank Palmer, Capital	68,650
Frank Palmer, Withdrawals	3,000
Flying Fees	40,000
Advertising Expense	150
Fuel and Oil Expense	5,600
Repairs Expense	6,200

*inter*NET CONNECTION

Peachtree Accounting Software

Assume that you are working part time and your employer is planning to change from a manual accounting system to a computerized system. She is not familiar with Peachtree software. She asks you to provide her with information about Peachtree software and how Peachtree can help her manage her business.

Do This:

1. Locate the Peachtree software Web site.
2. What Peachtree software is available for small businesses?
3. What is the cost?
4. Identify three advantages that Peachtree describes about its products.

Workplace Skills

Interpreting and Communicating Information

Every worker must learn how to interpret information and communicate effectively with co-workers, customers, and superiors.

On the Job:

As an accounting clerk for New Wave Inc., a surfboard manufacturer, one of your duties is to audit the accounting records and make the necessary corrections. Former employees did not always maintain the records accurately. The owner, Ron Lee, has asked you to provide written explanations for each error discovered in your audit.

Thinking Critically:

1. During an audit you discover a transposition error. An invoice for $510.00 payable to Marketing Pros was recorded and posted as $150.00. How do you correct this error?
2. Using word processing software, write a memo to Mr. Lee explaining how you corrected the error.

*inter*NET CONNECTION www.glencoe.com

Do This (Answers)

1. www.peachtree.com
2. Peachtree® Accounting, Peachtree First Accounting®, Peachtree Complete® Accounting
3. $169, $99, and $269, respectively
4. Some advantages are: it allows several people to enter data at the same time, it handles all math and "double entry" accounting behind the screens, it has navigation aids that serve as a roadmap to increase ease of use, the general ledger can be viewed or hidden, and it has tracking of sales orders for improved customer service.

Case Study...

Thinking Critically (Answers)

1. Answers will vary. Some possible steps include re-adding trial balance columns, checking ledger accounts for accuracy and omissions, recomputing ledger account balances, and verifying journal postings.
2. Answers will vary. Some possible causes are transposition errors, slides, and omissions.

Workplace Skills

Thinking Critically (Answers)

1. Students should communicate how to make a correcting entry and have the accounting clerk complete a memo noting the mistake. The correcting entry would need to be recorded in the general journal and posted.
2. Evaluate students' papers for use of correct grammar and for the logical progression of ideas.

Conducting an Audit with Alex

(Answers)

Ending debit balances:
Cash in Bank $4,700
Accounts Receivable $1,600
Airplanes $90,000
Frank Palmer, Withdrawals $3,000
Advertising Expense $150
Fuel and Oil Expense $5,600
Repairs Expense $6,200

Ending credit balances:
Accounts Payable $2,600
Frank Palmer, Capital $68,650
Flying Fees $40,000

Internet Resources and Activities Handbook

Refer students to the booklet for additional Internet activities.

PEACHTREE CORNER

General Ledger Report

The general ledger report produced by Peachtree is very similar to a manual general ledger report. A few of the differences include: (1) the Peachtree report does not show a running account balance after each transaction, (2) current period change debit, credit, and total amounts are provided, (3) Peachtree automatically updates the general ledger report every time you post an entry.

General Ledger Trial Balance

The general ledger trial balance is very similar to a manually prepared trial balance. By default, Peachtree does not print accounts with a zero (0.00) balance. You can, however, use ***Options*** to change the report settings to include all accounts.

General Ledger Report

To print a general ledger report, choose **General Ledger** from the ***Reports*** menu. Then select the desired report from the Select a Report window.

Reports Services Window
Accounts Receivable...
Accounts Payable...
Payroll...
General Ledger...

Financial Statements...
Inventory...
Jobs...
Account Reconciliation...
Time/Expense...
Company...
Report Groups...

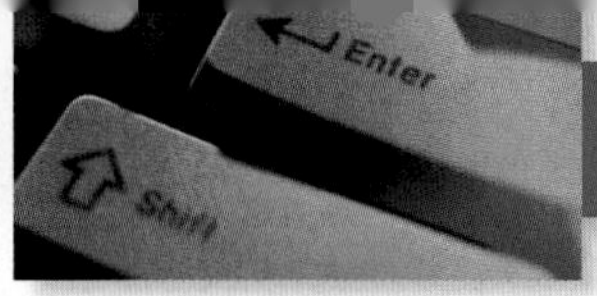

Posting to the General Ledger

Making the Transition from a Manual to a Computerized System

Task	Perform Accounting Procedures Using Manual Methods	Perform Accounting Procedures Using Automated Methods
Posting to the General Ledger	1. Transfer the details of each journal entry to individual ledger accounts. 2. Calculate the new account balance for each ledger account.	1. After each journal entry is entered, amounts are posted automatically into the general ledger. 2. New account balances are calculated for you.

Posting to the General Ledger

Peachtree Question	Description
How do I post general journal transactions?	• After entering a journal entry, click Save.
What does the software do "behind the scenes?"	• The software automatically posts the debit and credit amounts to the accounts you have indicated in the journal entry. New account balances are calculated for each account affected. • The software will not allow an out-of-balance journal entry to be posted. Therefore, the software always keeps the accounting records in balance (debits always equal credits).
What if I find an error in my journal entry after it has been posted?	Changes to journal entries can be made before or after the entry has been posted. 1. From the General Journal Entry window, drop down the Edit menu. Select *Edit Record.* 2. Select the entry you want to change. 3. Make the correction. 4. Click OK, then click the Save button.
What does the software do "behind the scenes"?	• When journal entries are edited, only the correct entry appears in the ledger account. Account balances are updated after each posting.

For detailed instructions: See the **Peachtree User Guide** in your Glencoe Working Papers.

Peachtree® Answers to Frequently Asked Questions

Q: Can you customize a report to allow for additional space for selected columns?
A: Yes. After you choose to display a report, click the **Design** button to display the report layout screen. Click on and drag the blue column markers to change the size of a column. Click the **Preview** button to return to the report screen.
Q: Does Peachtree produce an audit trail if you edit a general journal entry?
A: Yes, if you first select this option using ***Maintain*** > **Company Information**.
For additional information, refer to your *Glencoe Peachtree Accounting User Guide.*

APPLICATION OPTIONS

Problem 7–5 Posting General Journal Transactions

The accounts used by Wilderness Rentals have been opened and are included in the working papers accompanying this textbook. The general journal transactions for March of the current year are also included.

Instructions Post the transactions recorded on page 1 of the general journal to the accounts in the general ledger.

Analyze: After posting, what is the balance in the **Cash in Bank** account?

Problem 7–6 Preparing a Trial Balance

The ledger accounts for Hot Suds Car Wash are shown in your working papers.

Instructions Prepare a trial balance for the month of March of the current year.

Analyze: What is the amount of total debits?

Problem 7–7 Journalizing and Posting Business Transactions

A partial chart of accounts for Kits & Pups Grooming is provided below.

General Ledger

101	Cash in Bank	301	Abe Shultz, Capital
105	Accts. Rec.—J. Alvarez	305	Abe Shultz, Withdrawals
120	Grooming Supplies	401	Boarding Revenue
130	Office Furniture	405	Grooming Revenue
140	Grooming Equipment	525	Salaries Expense
205	Accts. Pay.—Dogs & Cats Inc.		

Instructions

(1) In your working papers, open an account in the general ledger for each account above.
(2) Record the March transactions on page 1 of the general journal.
(3) Post each journal entry to the appropriate ledger account.
(4) Prove the ledger by preparing a trial balance.

Date		Transactions
Mar.	1	Abe Shultz invested $5,000 in the business, Memorandum 51.
	3	Abe Shultz transferred a desk and chairs valued at $1,200 to the business, Memorandum 52.

Continued

Complete chapter problems one of three ways:

1 **Manual** Glencoe Working Papers

or

2 **Peachtree Complete Accounting** Software

or

3 **QuickBooks** Templates (Problems 7–5, 7–6, 7–7)

Peachtree® SMART GUIDE

Step-by-Step Instructions: Problem 7–5

1. Select the problem set for Wilderness Rentals (Prob. 7–5).
2. Rename the company and set the system date.
3. Print a General Ledger report.
4. Answer the Analyze question.
5. End the session.

Peachtree® SMART GUIDE

Step-by-Step Instructions: Problem 7–6

1. Select the problem set for Hot Suds Car Wash (Prob. 7–6).
2. Rename the company and set the system date.
3. Print a General Ledger Trial Balance report.
4. Answer the Analyze question.
5. End the session.

Problem 7–5 (Answers) Posting General Journal Transactions

Ending debit balances:
Cash in Bank $7,000
Accts. Rec.—Helen Katz $0
Accts. Rec.—Polk and Co. $2,400
Office Equipment $3,100
Camping Equipment $2,500
Ronald Hicks, Withdrawals $2,000
Advertising Expense $300

Ending credit balances:
Accts. Pay.—Adventure Equip. Inc. $1,300
Accts. Pay.—Digital Tech Computers $1,500
Ronald Hicks, Capital $5,100
Equipment Rental Revenue $9,400

Analyze: $7,000

Problem 7–6 (Answers) Preparing a Trial Balance

Ending debit balances:
Cash in Bank $17,000
Accts. Rec.—Valley Auto $1,000
Detergent Supplies $2,000
Car Wash Equipment $20,000
Regina Delgado, Withdrawals $4,000
Utilities Expense $6,500

Ending credit balances:
Accts. Pay.—Allen Vacuum Systems $500
Regina Delgado, Capital $40,000
Wash Revenue $7,500
Wax Revenue $1,300
Interior Detailing Revenue $1,200

Totals $50,500

Analyze: $50,500

ADDRESSING MULTIPLE LEARNING STYLES

Visual/Spatial Learner For some students, it may be difficult to visualize a real-life ledger when looking at images of miniature ledgers in the text or in the workbook. If possible, show students samples of actual ledgers from a real-life manual accounting system. If you do not have access to a business's ledger, create a notebook with sample, full-page ledger pages or cards. Be sure to use a four-column ledger account form so students can see the relationship between the real ledger and the forms illustrated in the text and workbook.

Problem 7-7 (Answers) Journalizing and Posting Business Transactions

Ending debit balances:
Cash in Bank $3,200
Accts. Rec.—J. Alvarez $0
Grooming Supplies $300
Office Furniture $1,200
Grooming Equipment $1,800
Abe Schultz, Withdrawals $1,000
Salaries Expense $500

Ending credit balances:
Accts. Pay.—Dogs & Cats Inc. $0
Abe Schultz, Capital $6,200
Boarding Revenue $1,400
Grooming Revenue $400

Totals $8,000

Analyze: $8,000

SOURCE DOCUMENT PROBLEM

Problem 7-8 (Answers) Journalizing and Posting Business Transactions

Ending debit balances:
Cash in Bank $17,900
Accts. Rec.—Podaski Systems Inc. $0
Computer Equipment $2,800
Hiking Equipment $600
Rafting Equipment $5,000
Juanita Ortega, Withdrawals $800
Advertising Expense $900

Ending credit balances:
Accts. Pay.—Peak Equipment Inc. $0
Accts. Pay.—Premier Processors $1,400
Juanita Ortega, Capital $25,000
Guide Service Revenue $1,600

Totals $28,000

Analyze: $17,900

Peachtree®

SMART GUIDE

Step-by-Step Instructions: Problem 7-7

1. Select the problem set for Kits & Pups Grooming (Prob. 7-7).
2. Rename the company and set the system date.
3. Enter all of the general journal transactions.
4. Print a General Journal report.
5. Proof your work.
6. Print a General Ledger report and a General Ledger Trial Balance report.
7. Answer the Analyze question.
8. End the session.

TIP: As a shortcut, you can enter just the day of the month for a transaction date.

Date	Problem 7-7 (cont.) Transactions
Mar. 5	Issued Check 551 for $300 for grooming supplies.
7	Bought grooming equipment on account for $1,800 from Dogs & Cats Inc., Invoice DC201.
9	Groomed Juan Alvarez's show dogs on account, $400, Sales Invoice 350.
12	Paid Dogs & Cats Inc. $900 on account, Check 552.
15	Issued Check 553 for $500 to pay the office secretary's salary.
18	Abe Shultz withdrew $1,000 cash from the business, Check 554.
20	Deposited $1,400 received from clients for boarding their pets, Receipts 477-480.
24	Wrote Check 555 for $900 to Dogs & Cats Inc. to apply on account.
26	Received a check for $400 from Juan Alvarez on account, Receipt 481.

Analyze: What are the total debits on the trial balance on March 31?

SOURCE DOCUMENT PROBLEM

Problem 7-8 Journalizing and Posting Business Transactions

The chart of accounts for Outback Guide Service is listed below.

General Ledger

101	Cash in Bank	301	Juanita Ortega, Capital
115	Accts. Rec.—Podaski Systems Inc.	302	Juanita Ortega, Withdrawals
140	Computer Equipment	401	Guide Service Revenue
145	Hiking Equipment	501	Advertising Expense
150	Rafting Equipment		
205	Accts. Pay.—Peak Equipment Inc.		
207	Accts. Pay.—Premier Processors		

Instructions

(1) In your working papers, open an account in the general ledger for each account in the chart of accounts.
(2) Record the following transactions on page 1 of the general journal.
(3) Post each journal entry to the appropriate accounts in the ledger.
(4) Prove the ledger by preparing a trial balance.

Date	Transactions
Mar. 1	Invested $20,000 in cash and transferred rafting equipment valued at $5,000 to the business, Memorandum 35.
3	Purchased $600 in hiking equipment on account from Peak Equipment Inc., Invoice 101.

Continued

Peachtree®

SMART GUIDE

Step-by-Step Instructions: Problem 7-8

1. Select the problem set for Outback Guide Service (Prob. 7-8).
2. Rename the company and set the system date.
3. Enter all of the general journal transactions.
4. Print a General Journal report.
5. Proof your work.
6. Print a General Ledger report and a General Ledger Trial Balance report.
7. Answer the Analyze question.
8. End the session.

TIP: Always double-check the account numbers and amounts in a general journal entry before you post it.

EXTENDING THE CONTENT

Personal Finance Software Demonstrate a retail computer application for personal finance such as *Quicken* or *Microsoft Money*. Emphasize the ease with which you can enter transactions and how the computer automatically updates account balances, budgets, and reports. Discuss how the software automates daily tasks, provides reminders when bills are dues, and even prints checks. If possible, demonstrate how to use the online service features to pay bills and do common banking tasks.

Date	Problem 7–8 (cont.) Transactions
Mar. 5	Bought a $2,800 computer from Premier Processors and agreed to pay for it within 60 days, Invoice 616.
7	Deposited $700 cash received from clients, Receipts 310–315.
9	Paid $400 to the *Daily Courier* for an ad, Check 652.
12	Sent a bill for $900 to Podaski Systems Inc. for conducting a group rafting trip for them, Sales Invoice 352.
15	Juanita Ortega wrote a check for $800 for personal use, Check 653.
18	Paid Premier Processors $1,400 to apply on account, Check 654.
22	Received $900 from Podaski Systems Inc. in full payment for the amount owed, Receipt 316.
27	Bought a $500 television ad with LIVE TV, Check 655.
28	Paid Peak Equipment Inc. $600 by writing Check 656.

Analyze: What is the balance of **Cash in Bank** at March 28?

SOURCE DOCUMENT PROBLEM

Problem 7–8

Use the source documents in your working papers to record the transactions for this problem.

Problem 7–9 Recording and Posting Correcting Entries

An auditor reviewed the accounting records of Showbiz Video. The auditor wrote a memo, outlined below, regarding the number of errors discovered in the March records. The general journal for March and a portion of the general ledger are included in your working papers.

Instructions

(1) Record correcting entries on general journal page 22.

(2) Use Memorandum 50 as the source document for all correcting entries and March 31 as the date. Some errors will not require correcting entries, but will require a general ledger correction. Make the appropriate general ledger corrections.

(3) Post all correcting entries to the general ledger accounts.

Date	Transactions
Mar. 3	The $125 purchase was for office supplies.
7	A $200 payment to a creditor, Broad Street Office Supply, was not posted to the account.
13	Greg Failla withdrew $1,200 from the business for personal use.
17	Cash totaling $2,000 was received for video rentals.
19	A $75 receipt from Shannon Flannery was posted as $57.
27	Greg Failla invested an additional $3,000 in the business.
29	The revenue of $1,000 was for video rentals.

Analyze: Once correcting entries have been posted, what are the balances of the owner's equity accounts?

Peachtree®

SMART GUIDE

Step-by-Step Instructions: Problem 7–9

1. Select the problem set for Showbiz Video (Prob. 7–9).
2. Rename the company and set the system date.
3. Correct the general journal entries based on the auditor's report.
4. Print a General Journal report and a General Ledger report.
5. Proof your work.
6. Answer the Analyze question.
7. End the session.

TIP: Use the **General Journal Entry** task option to edit the general journal entries.

Problem 7-9 (Answers) Recording and Posting Correcting Entries

Ending debit balances:

Cash in Bank $14,330
Accts. Rec.—Shannon Flannery $225
Office Supplies $245
Office Furniture $2,000
Greg Failla, Withdrawals $1,200

Ending credit balances:

Accts. Pay.—Broad Street Office Supply $2,000
Greg Failla, Capital $16,000
Video Rental Revenue $3,000
VCR Rental Revenue $0

Analyze: Greg Failla, Capital $16,000; Greg Failla, Withdrawals $1,200

SOLUTION NOTES

INTRODUCING
MINI PRACTICE SET 1

Mini Practice Set Overview
This mini practice set covers the material that students have studied through Chapter 7. In this activity students will open general ledger accounts and use those accounts to analyze and journalize business transactions in a general journal. The practice set ends with preparation of a trial balance.

Most students should be able to complete this practice set manually within two class periods.

Source documents and accounting stationery for completing this practice set are included in the *Chapter Reviews and Working Papers*.

Mini Practice Set Concepts
- How to analyze business transactions.
- How to record transactions in the general journal.
- How to post business transactions to the general ledger accounts.
- How to prepare a trial balance.

Visual Learning

Mini Practice Set Focus, p. 178

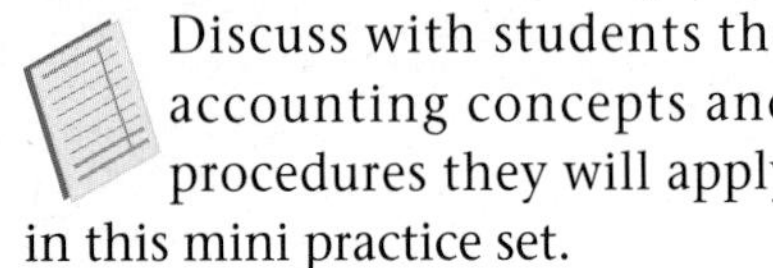

Discuss with students the accounting concepts and procedures they will apply in this mini practice set.

Chart of Accounts, p. 178

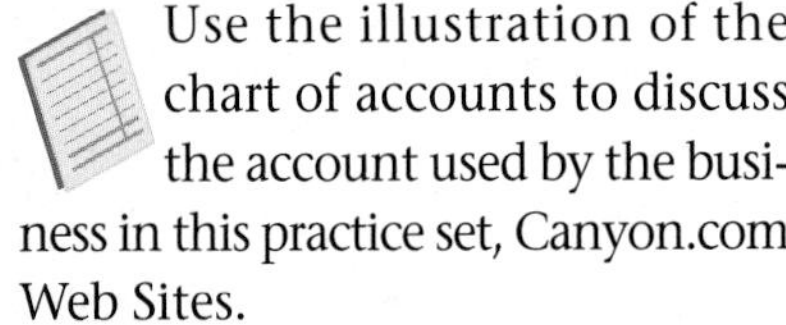

Use the illustration of the chart of accounts to discuss the account used by the business in this practice set, Canyon.com Web Sites.

Teaching Tips
The Income Summary account has been omitted from this practice set since students have not yet learned how it is used.

Quiz students on the chart of accounts by asking them to name the normal balance for each account.

Setting Up Accounting Records for a Sole Proprietorship

***What* You'll Learn**
- How to analyze business transactions.
- How to record business transactions in the general journal.
- How to post business transactions in the general ledger accounts.
- How to prepare a trial balance.

***Why* It's Important**
Learning to apply the first five steps of the accounting cycle will prepare you to perform these accounting tasks for any service business organized as a sole proprietorship.

Canyon.com Web Sites

Company Background: Whether you're interested in a Web site for your new hair salon or a corporate intranet site, Canyon.com provides design, hosting, and maintenance services for the small mom-and-pop business and the multi-national corporation alike. Jack Hines, owner of Canyon.com Web Sites is known for his unique and dynamic presentations on the Web. His creativity and knowledge of Web culture makes him a success in electronic content delivery.

Organization: Canyon.com is organized as a sole proprietorship. The business is fully owned and operated by Jack Hines.

Your Job Responsibilities: As the accounting clerk for the business, use the accounting stationery in your workbook to complete the following:

(1) Open a general ledger account for each account in the chart of accounts.
(2) Analyze each business transaction.
(3) Enter each business transaction in the general journal, page 1.
(4) Post each journal entry to the appropriate accounts in the general ledger.
(5) Prove the general ledger by preparing a trial balance.

APPLICATION OPTIONS

Complete activities one of three ways:

1 **Manual** Glencoe Working Papers

or

2 **Peachtree Complete Accounting** Software

or

3 **QuickBooks** Templates

CHART OF ACCOUNTS
Canyon.com Web Sites

ASSETS
101 Cash in Bank
105 Accts. Rec.–Andrew Hospital
110 Accts. Rec.–Indiana Trucking
115 Accts Rec.–Sunshine Products
130 Office Supplies
135 Office Equipment
140 Office Furniture
145 Web Server

LIABILITIES
205 Accts. Pay.–Computer Specialists Inc.
210 Accts. Pay.–Office Systems
215 Accts. Pay.–Service Plus Software Inc.

OWNER'S EQUITY
301 Jack Hines, Capital
305 Jack Hines, Withdrawals

REVENUE
401 Web Service Fees

EXPENSES
505 Membership Expense
506 Telecommunications Expense
507 Rent Expense
508 Utilities Expense

COOPERATIVE LEARNING ACTIVITY

Co-op Co-op Divide students into five groups and assign the topic "The Needs of a New Business." Instruct each group to gather information from one of the following sources: the local Chamber of Commerce, a bank, the library, an accountant, or the Small Business Administration. Have each group organize the information gained and present its findings to the class. Following the presentations, ask all students to summarize the findings of all the groups in a short report.

Canyon.com Web Sites

Business Transactions: Jack Hines, owner of Canyon.com Web Sites, began business operations on May 1 of this year. During the month of May, the business completed the transactions that follow.

Date	Transactions
May 1	Jack Hines invested $50,000 in the business, Memorandum 1.
2	The owner, Jack Hines, invested a desktop computer and printer (Office Equipment) $3,500, Memorandum 2.
2	Issued Check 101 for $125 for the purchase of office supplies.
3	Bought office furniture for $2,700 on account from Office Systems, Invoice 457.
7	Bought a Web server from Computer Specialists Inc. on account for $35,000, Invoice WS4658421.
9	Received $1,000 from James Market for Web site services, Receipt 101.
11	Completed Web site design services for Andrew Hospital to be paid later, Invoice 101, $3,000.
12	Bought software for the Web server (Web Server) on account from Service Plus Software Inc., Invoice 876, $10,000.
14	Wrote Check 102 for $118 to pay the electric bill.
15	Jack Hines withdrew $2,500 for personal expenses, Check 103.
17	Completed Web site design on account for Sunshine Products, Invoice 102, $5,000.
18	Bought a filing cabinet (Office Furniture) for $275, Check 104.
19	Received a check for $4,000 as payment for Web site maintenance for one year to a client, Receipt 102.
20	Provided design services on account to Indiana Trucking, Invoice 103 for $2,000.
21	Prepared Receipt 103, $2,500, received on account, Sunshine Products.
22	Paid $4,900 for telecommunication services for the period May 1–May 31, Check 105.
22	Wrote check 106 for $3,333 to Service Plus Software Inc. as payment on account.
25	Sent Check 107 for $2,000 to Office Systems as payment on account.
26	Received $1,000 for two months of Web services, Receipt 104.
27	Paid the dues for membership in the All Inclusive Group for $7,000, Check 108.
30	Wrote Check 109 for the monthly rent $750.
30	Withdrew $2,500 for personal expenses, Check 110.
30	Sent Check 111 for $25,000 to Computer Specialists Inc., as payment on account.

Analyze: How many checks were written by the business during May? What was the total of all checks written?

Peachtree®

SMART GUIDE

Step-by-Step Instructions:

1. Select the problem set for Canyon.Com Web Sites (MP-1).
2. Rename the company and set the system date.
3. Record all of the business transactions using the **General Journal Entry** option.
4. Print a General Journal report.
5. Proof your work.
6. Print a General Ledger report.
7. Print a Trial Balance.
8. Answer the Analyze questions and complete the Audit Test.
9. End the session.

MINI PRACTICE SET 1
PAGES 178–179

SOURCE DOCUMENT PROBLEM

ANSWERS

Ending ledger account balances:

Cash in Bank $9,999
Accts. Rec./Andrew Hospital $3,000
Accts. Rec./Indiana Trucking $2,000
Accts. Rec./Sunshine Products $2,500
Office Supplies $125
Office Equipment $3,500
Office Furniture $2,975
Web Server $45,000
Accts. Pay./Computer Specialists Inc. $10,000
Accts. Pay./Office Systems $700
Accts. Pay./Service Plus Software Inc. $6,667
Jack Hines, Capital $53,500
Jack Hines, Withdrawals $5,000
Web Services Fees $16,000
Membership Expense $7,000
Telecommunications Expense $4,900
Rent Expense $750
Utilities Expense $118

Trial balance totals $86,867

Analyze: Eleven checks were written during May. The total for all checks written is $48,501.

HOME AND COMMUNITY CONNECTIONS ACTIVITY

Entrepreneurial Experiences Ask students to interview a family member, relative, friend, or neighbor who owns a business. Have students compile a biographical report of the person they interview. The report should include the type of business he or she owns, how the person got started in the field, the skills needed to open the business, the positive and negative points of owning a business, and how a person can prepare to open that type of business. Have students get advice from the person and present a creative biographical sketch of the entrepreneur.

CHAPTER 8 Resource Manager

Section Resources

	Objectives & Standards	Activities & Features	Reproducible Masters
Chapter Opener *The Six-Column Work Sheet*	• Explain the purpose of the work sheet. • Describe the parts of a six-column work sheet. • Prepare a six-column work sheet. • Calculate net income and net loss. • Define the accounting terms introduced in this chapter. **National Standards for Business Education**: IA11	Exploring the Real World of Business, p. 180 Workplace Connections, p. 181	School-to-Work Handbook
Section 1 *Preparing the Work Sheet*	• The purpose of the work sheet. • The kinds of information contained in the heading. • How to prepare a trial balance on a work sheet. • How to rule a section of the work sheet.	Connect To, p. 183 Accounting Tips, p. 184 Did You Know?, p. 185	Demonstration Problems
Section 2 *Extending Amounts Across the Work Sheet*	• How to extend amounts to the Balance Sheet and Income Statement sections. • The importance of the matching principle. • How to calculate and show the net income or net loss on the work sheet.	Spreadsheet Hints, p. 191 International Accounting, p. 192 Accounting Flashbacks, p. 193 A Matter of Ethics, p. 193	Demonstration Problems Math Review for Accounting Strategies for Teaching International Accounting Strategies for Teaching Ethics in Accounting Internet Resources and Activities Handbook

KEY

Posters — Transparency — Software — Videocassette
Blackline Masters — CD-ROM — Portfolio

MULTIMEDIA RESOURCE

Peachtree	QuickBooks	Spreadsheets	Videos	CD-ROMs
Problem 8–5 *Preparing a Six-Column Work Sheet* Problem 8–6 *Preparing a Six-Column Work Sheet* Problem 8–7 *Preparing a Six-Column Work Sheet*	Problem 8–5 *Preparing a Six-Column Work Sheet* Problem 8–6 *Preparing a Six-Column Work Sheet*	Problem 8-4 *Preparing a Six-Column Work Sheet* Problem 8–8 *Completing the Work Sheet*	***Video Segment: Knowing Your Legal Rights*** Discuss with students the importance of knowing their legal rights.	***Electronic Learning Center (ELC), Chapter 8*** This program is ideal for visual learners since it incorporates video images, animation, and graphics to enliven the content of each lesson. ***Interactive Lesson Planner (ILP), Chapter 8*** This CD-ROM combines the versatility of an electronic lesson planner with the convenience of teacher classroom resources.

SCANS Correlation Chart

FOUNDATION SKILLS

Basic Skills:	Reading	Writing	Math	Listening	Speaking	
Thinking Skills:	Creative Thinking	Decision Making	Problem Solving	Seeing Things in the Mind's Eye	Knowing How to Learn	Reasoning
Personal Qualities:	Responsibility	Self-Esteem	Sociability	Self-Management	Integrity/Honesty	

WORKPLACE COMPETENCIES

Resources:	Allocating Time	Allocating Money	Allocating Material and Facility Resources	Allocating Human Resources		
Information:	Acquiring and Evaluating Information	Organizing and Maintaining Information	Interpreting and Communicating Information	Using Computers to Process Information		
Interpersonal Skills:	Participating as a Member of a Team	Teaching Others	Serving Clients/ Customers	Exercising Leadership	Negotiating to Arrive at a Decision	Working with Cultural Diversity
Systems:	Understanding Systems	Monitoring and Correcting Performance	Improving and Designing Systems			
Technology:	Selecting Technology	Applying Technology to Task	Maintaining and Troubleshooting Technology			

*Highlighted blocks indicate areas covered in the chapter. Additional SCANS skills are also covered throughout the *Teacher Wraparound Edition.*

Assessment

Student Edition
- Check Your Understanding, pp. 186, 194
- Chapter 8 Problems, pp. 199–201

Assessment and Evaluation Masters
- Chapter 8 Study Plan, *Glencoe Workbook*
- Chapter 8 Self-Test, *Glencoe Workbook*
- Chapter 8 Test, *Chapter Tests* Booklet
- Chapter 8 Activity *School-to-Work Handbook*
- Chapter 8 **Exam***View*

Teacher Wraparound Edition
- Critical Thinking Activity, p. 185
- Reteaching Section 1, p. 186
- Reteaching Section 2, p. 194
- Chapter 8 Quiz, p. 195

Transparencies

	Teaching Transparencies	Solution Transparencies
Section 1:	8–1, 8–2, 8–3, 8–4, 8–5	Problems 8–1, 8–2
Section 2:	8–6, 8–7, 8–8, 8–9, 8–10, 8–11, 8–12, 8–13	Problem 8–3
End of Chapter:		Problems 8–4, 8–5, 8–6, 8–7, 8–8

TEACHER CLASSROOM RESOURCES

This is a representation of key blackline masters available in the Teacher Classroom Resources.

Teaching Aids

Transparency Examples

Section Focus Transparencies

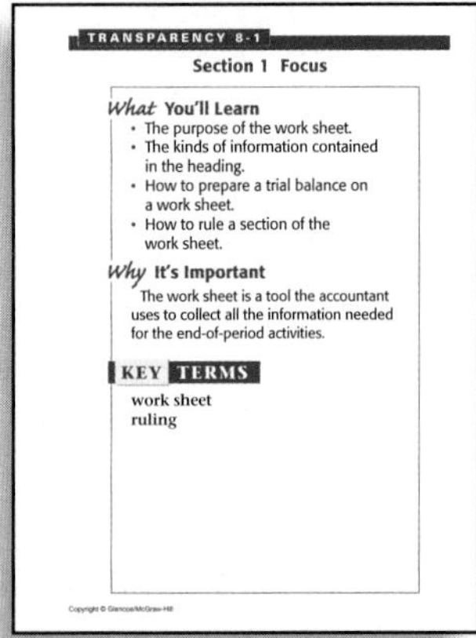

Teaching Transparencies

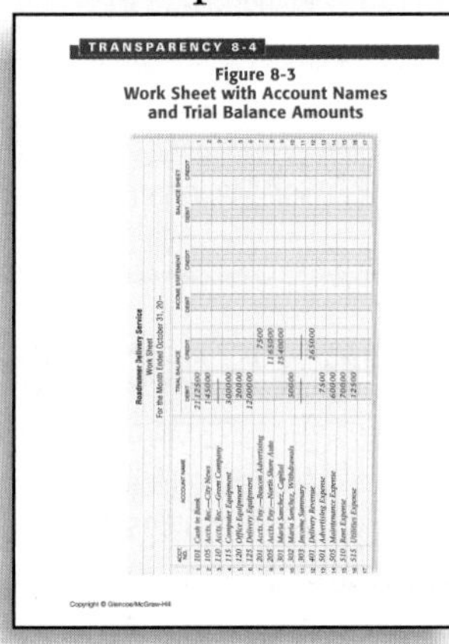

Teaching Transparencies

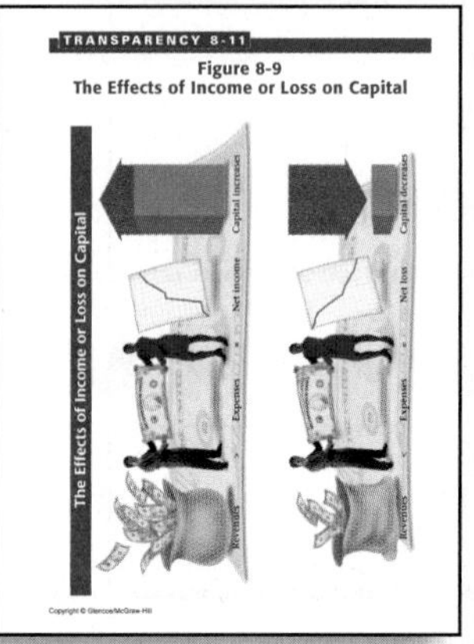

Solution Transparencies

Demonstration Problems

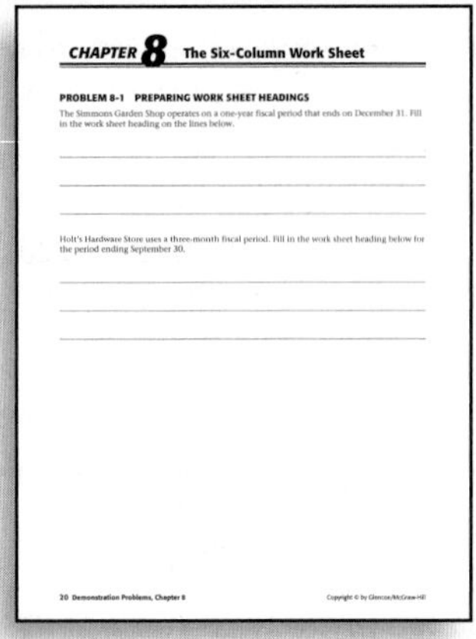

Lesson Plans

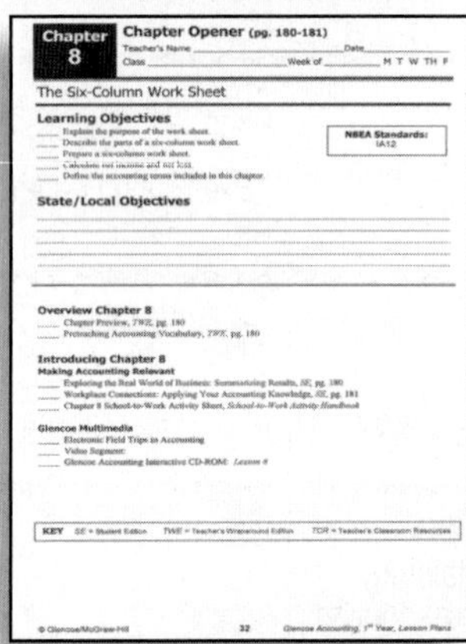

Block Scheduling

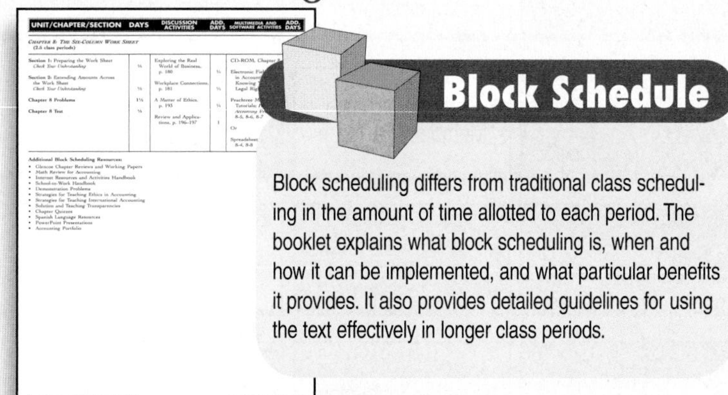

Block scheduling differs from traditional class scheduling in the amount of time allotted to each period. The booklet explains what block scheduling is, when and how it can be implemented, and what particular benefits it provides. It also provides detailed guidelines for using the text effectively in longer class periods.

Enrichment and Application

Strategies for Teaching Ethics in Accounting

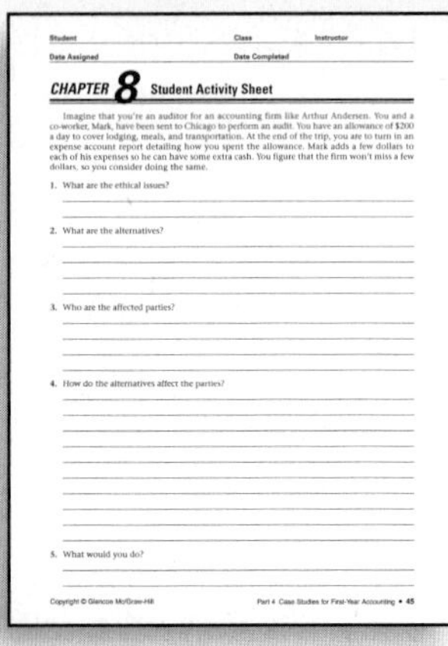

Strategies for Teaching International Accounting

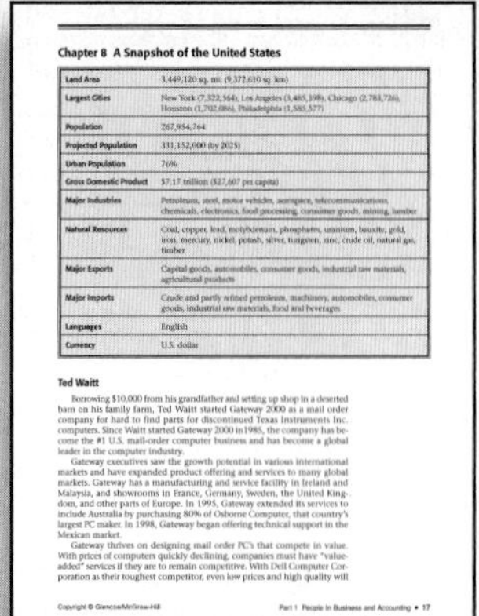

School-to-Work Handbook

Meeting Different Ability Levels

Chapter Reviews and Working Papers (CRWP)

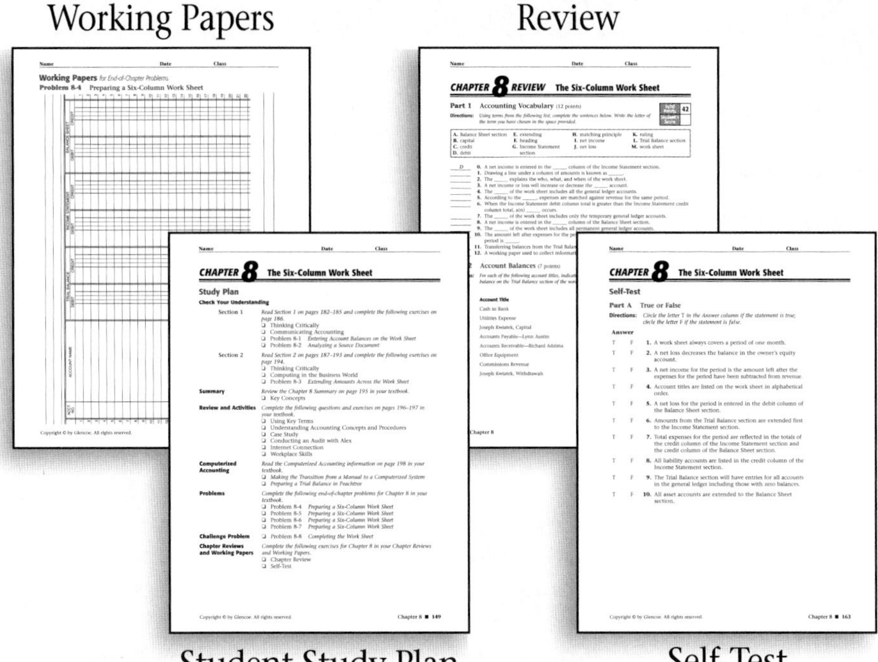

Real-World Multimedia CD-ROM

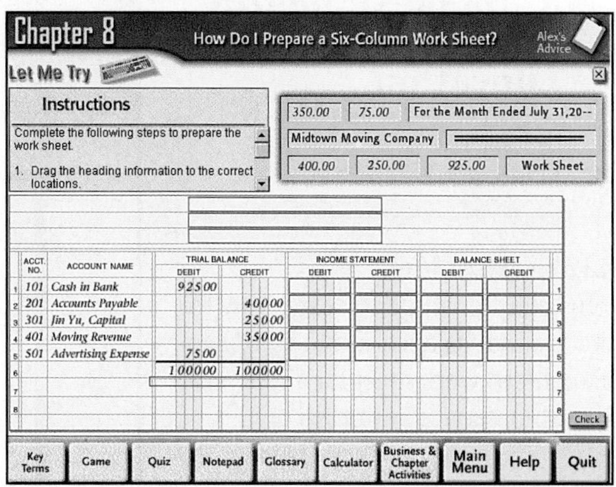

Key to Ability Levels

Each section gives skill-building activities. Each activity has been labeled for use with students of various learning styles and abilities.

L1 Level 1 activities are basic activities and should be within the range of all students.

L2 Level 2 activities are average activities and should be within the range of average and above average students.

L3 Level 3 activities are challenging activities designed for the ability range of above average students.

ELL ELL activities should be within the ability range of English Language Learners.

Teaching Resources at a Glance

Application Resources

- Glencoe Chapter Review and Working Papers, SE and TAE
- School-to-Work Handbook, SE and TM
- Accounting Portfolio, SE and TM

Reproducible Masters

- Demonstration Problems
- Lesson Plans
- Block Scheduling
- Spanish Language Resources

Glencoe Accounting Professional Development Series

- Strategies for Teaching Ethics in Accounting
- Accounting Competitive Event Review
- Math Review for Accounting
- Strategies for Teaching International Accounting
- Internet Resources and Activities Handbook

Transparency Package

- Section Focus Transparencies
- Teaching Transparencies
- Source Document Transparencies
- Solution Transparencies

Performance Assessment

- **Exam***View* CD-ROM
- Chapter Tests
- Chapter Quizzes
- Unit Tests
- Audit Tests
- Printed Testbank

Multimedia Resources

- Electronic Learning Center:
  - Multimedia CD-ROMs
  - Peachtree software, tutorials, templates, and solutions
  - Spreadsheet templates
- Using QuickBooks with Glencoe Accounting
- Interactive Lesson Planner
- Electronic Field Trips in Accounting
- PowerPoint Presentation
- Web site: glencoeaccounting.glencoe.com

Assessment and Evaluation

Chapter Tests

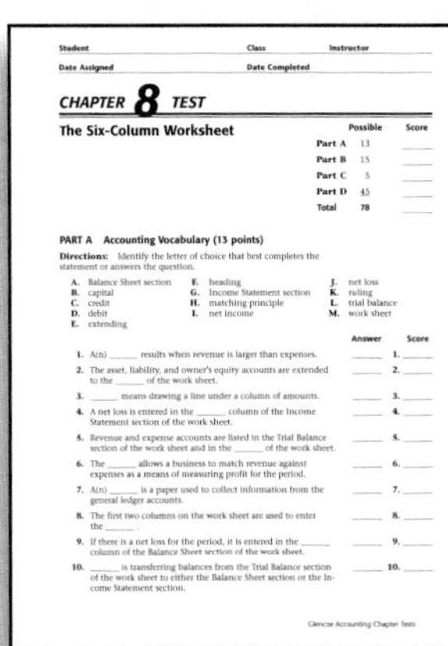

Chapter Quiz

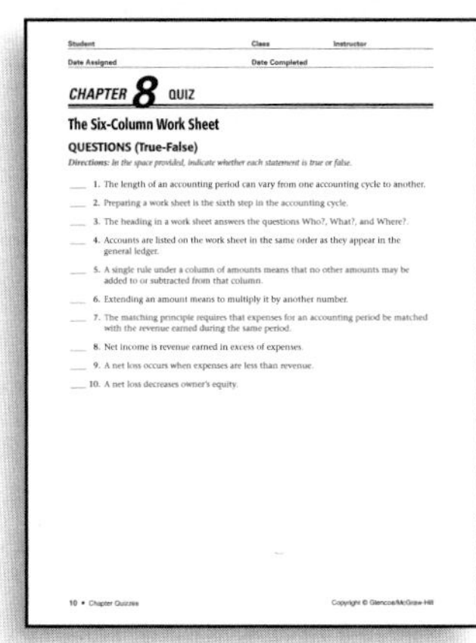

OVERVIEW CHAPTER 8

Correlations to National Standards for Business Education

(See pages T50–T51 for a detailed correlation chart.)

Standards: IA11

Chapter Preview

In this chapter students learn how to prepare a trial balance and to complete a six-column work sheet for a sole proprietorship, service business.

Section Overviews

- Section 1—*Preparing the Work Sheet*
- Section 2—*Extending Amounts Across the Work Sheet*

Appendix A Adjustments for a Service Business Using a Ten-Column Work Sheet

As students study the accounting cycle for a service business, you may wish to introduce the subject of adjusting entries. Use this appendix after your students study Chapter 8 to illustrate how to calculate and record end-of-period adjustments. If you prefer to cover the topic of adjusting entries later in the course, you may use Chapter 18 where end-of-period adjustments for a merchandising business are covered.

Chapter Vocabulary

work sheet
ruling
matching principle
net income
net loss

Preteaching Accounting Vocabulary

Apply Basic Accounting Terminology: Introduce each of the new terms in class. After discussing their meaning, ask for volunteers to write a sentence on the chalkboard using each of the terms. Then ask other students to explain why each of the sentences is correct. L1

CHAPTER 8

The Six-Column Work Sheet

Learning Objectives

When you have completed this chapter, you will be able to:

- Explain the purpose of the work sheet.
- Describe the parts of a six-column work sheet.
- Prepare a six-column work sheet.
- Calculate net income and net loss.
- Define the accounting terms introduced in this chapter.

Exploring the Real World of Business

SUMMARIZING RESULTS

Public transportation began as early as 1630. Today, most cities have public buses, and larger cities also have subway or rail lines.

The Washington D.C. metro system is the fourth largest transit system in the United States. The subway trains travel 103 miles of track each day and stop at 83 different stations in Washington and nearby communities in Maryland and Virginia.

The Metro system is operated by the **Washington Metropolitan Area Transit Authority (WMATA),** a not-for-profit organization. Revenues and expenses are monitored carefully by the **WMATA** managers since revenues must pay the full operating costs of the system. If they do not, fares must be increased. Work sheets that summarize the total revenue from fares and the expenses of operating the system help managers keep track of whether the system's income is in balance with its expenses.

What do you think?

If you worked for the **Washington Metro,** what information would you look for in monthly work sheets to alert you to revenue or expense problems?

Washington Metropolitan Area Transit Authority (WMATA)

Exploring the Real World of Business

Washington Metropolitan Area Transit Authority

It took over four decades to plan and build the Washington Metro. The Metro operates seven days a week, with bus service 24 hours a day and rail service until midnight. Convenience in getting around the city makes the Metro attractive to residents and visitors alike.

What do you think? (Answers)

Answers may vary. Managers would look at revenue to evaluate increases and decreases and try to find the reasons for each. For expenses, managers would monitor decreases to see if cost-cutting measures are effective and increases to verify that they were needed.

Workplace Connections

Applying Your Accounting Knowledge

When you prepare to write a research paper, you probably use note cards or a database program to collect and organize information. You may also write a rough draft of your paper, further organizing the information. In accounting, a work sheet serves to organize financial information. You'll learn how to create a work sheet in this chapter.

Investigate:

1. How might your ability to organize information be valuable to your employer?
2. Why is it important for financial and other information to be organized in a certain way?

Glencoe Accounting *Online*

Visit the *Glencoe Accounting* Web site at **glencoeaccounting.glencoe.com** for additional activities and information.

INTRODUCING CHAPTER 8

Making Accounting Relevant

Workplace Connections: Applying Your Accounting Knowledge

Discussion: The ability to organize information is an important skill for students to gain. They'll be called on in their work lives to present both ideas and data. Knowing how to organize both starts with an understanding of information and how to present it in ways others can grasp and use it.

Investigate (Answers)

1. To communicate well, you need to present information in an organized format that others can understand and use in their own work.
2. Financial information is read by many different people, both inside and outside the company. For all those people to understand the data and interpret it in the same way, the data must be organized according to accepted methods.

School-to-Work Activity

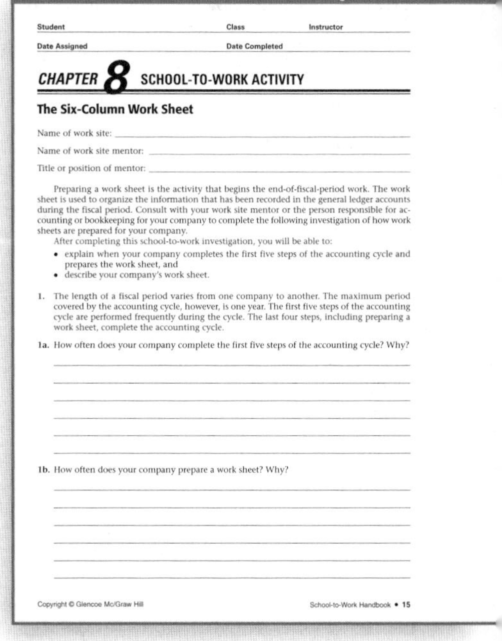

Student ______ Class ______ Instructor ______

Date Assigned ______ Date Completed ______

CHAPTER 8 SCHOOL-TO-WORK ACTIVITY

The Six-Column Work Sheet

Name of work site: ______

Name of work site mentor: ______

Title or position of mentor: ______

Preparing a work sheet is the activity that begins the end-of-fiscal-period work. The work sheet is used to organize the information that has been recorded in the general ledger accounts during the fiscal period. Consult with your work site mentor or the person responsible for accounting or bookkeeping for your company to complete the following investigation of how work sheets are prepared for your company.

After completing this school-to-work investigation, you will be able to:

- explain when your company completes the first five steps of the accounting cycle and prepares the work sheet, and
- describe your company's work sheet.

1. The length of a fiscal period varies from one company to another. The maximum period covered by the accounting cycle, however, is one year. The first five steps of the accounting cycle are performed frequently during the cycle. The last four steps, including preparing a work sheet, complete the accounting cycle.

1a. How often does your company complete the first five steps of the accounting cycle? Why?

1b. How often does your company prepare a work sheet? Why?

GLENCOE MULTIMEDIA

Electronic Field Trips in Accounting *Video Segment: Knowing Your Legal Rights*
Discuss with students the importance of knowing their legal rights.

Glencoe Accounting: Electronic Learning Center *Chapter 8*
The CD-ROM program is ideal for visual learners since it incorporates video images, animation, and graphics to enliven the content of each lesson.

1 FOCUS

Introducing the Section

In this section students learn the sixth step in the accounting cycle: the work sheet. Students learn what information goes in the work sheet heading and how to complete the trial balance section.

Section Concepts

- The purpose of the work sheet.
- The kinds of information contained in the heading.
- How to prepare a trial balance on a work sheet.
- How to rule a section of the work sheet.

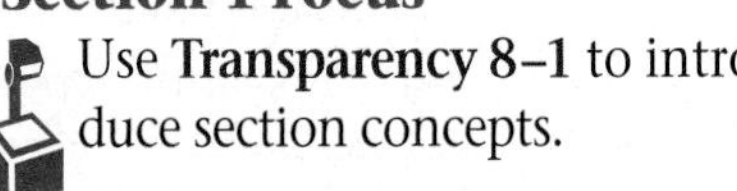

Visual Learning

Section 1 Focus

Use **Transparency 8–1** to introduce section concepts.

BELL RINGER

Compare and Contrast: Have students make a list of their personal sources of income (revenue) and expenses. Then ask for a few volunteers to share their lists. Did any of the students organize their information by listing all the income first followed by all the expenses? Have students compare their lists to a trial balance. How are the two similar? How are they different? L1

Visual Learning

Figure 8–1 Steps in the Accounting Cycle with Step 6 Highlighted

Use **Transparency 8–2** to reinforce the concept of the accounting cycle and the order in which each step is completed.

SECTION 1

Preparing the Work Sheet

What You'll Learn

- The purpose of the work sheet.
- The kinds of information contained in the heading.
- How to prepare a trial balance on a work sheet.
- How to rule a section of the work sheet.

Why It's Important

The work sheet is a tool the accountant uses to collect all the information needed for the end-of-period activities.

KEY TERMS

work sheet
ruling

As you learned in Chapter 6, the length of an accounting period can vary. The maximum period covered by the accounting cycle is one year. The first five steps of the accounting cycle are performed frequently during the cycle. The last four steps—preparing a work sheet, preparing financial statements, journalizing and posting closing entries, and preparing a post-closing trial balance—are performed at the end of the accounting period. Look at **Figure 8–1.** In this chapter you will learn how to prepare a work sheet, the sixth step of the accounting cycle. With this step, businesses like your local Midas Muffler shop or a Nike Outlet collect information from their ledger accounts and record this information on a single form.

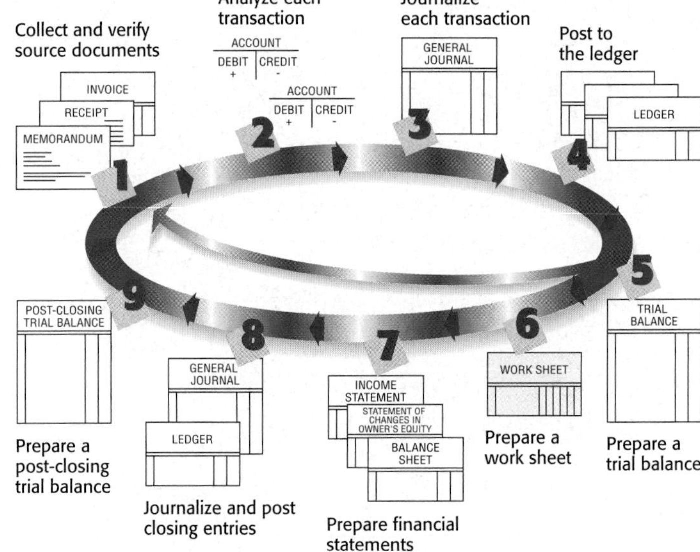

Figure 8–1 Steps in the Accounting Cycle with Step 6 Highlighted

RESOURCE MANAGER

Reproducible Masters

- Lesson Plans
- Chapter Reviews and Working Papers (CRWP) TAE
- Demonstration Problems

Transparencies

- Section Focus Transparency
- Teaching Transparencies
- Source Document Transparencies
- Solution Transparencies

Multimedia

- **Exam***View* CD-ROM
- Electronic Learning Center CD-ROM
- Interactive Lesson Planner CD-ROM

The Sixth Step of the Accounting Cycle: The Work Sheet

A **work sheet** is just what its name implies—a working paper used to collect information from the ledger accounts in one place. Like the T account, the work sheet is a tool that the accountant uses. With the work sheet, an accountant gathers all the information needed to prepare the financial statements and to complete the other end-of-period activities.

A work sheet may be prepared in pencil on standard multi-column accounting paper. The paper comes in several sizes and is usually printed without column headings. Blank spaces for column headings allow the accountant to enter the headings needed by a particular business. The work sheet can also be prepared using computer spreadsheet software.

The Roadrunner Delivery Service work sheet, shown in **Figure 8–2**, has five sections:

(1) the Heading
(2) the Account Name section
(3) the Trial Balance section
(4) the Income Statement section
(5) the Balance Sheet section.

CONNECT TO . . . ECOLOGY

Even in the age of computers, accountants have to handle a mountain of forms, paperwork, and records. They can lessen their impact on the environment by using recycled paper. One ton of recycled paper saves more than 4,000-kilowatt hours of energy, 7,000 gallons of water, and 17 trees.

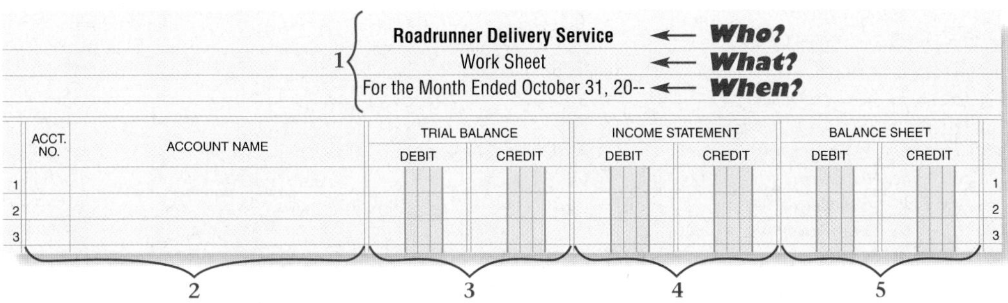

Figure 8–2 Six-Column Work Sheet

The Account Name section includes a column for the account number and a column for the account name. The Trial Balance, Income Statement, and Balance Sheet sections have debit and credit amount columns. The six amount columns give this work sheet its name: the six-column work sheet.

The Work Sheet Heading

The work sheet heading contains three kinds of information:

(1) The name of the business ***(Who?)***
(2) The name of the accounting form ***(What?)***
(3) The period covered by the work sheet ***(When?)***

Notice how these elements are positioned on the work sheet in **Figure 8–2.** Follow this format when preparing the heading of any work sheet.

INTERDISCIPLINARY CONNECTIONS ACTIVITY

Ecology Ask students to list several areas of conservation for a sole proprietorship. What are some things that might help businesses cut their expenses? Suggest that students research why some companies are labeled "green" or "clean" workplaces. What does a company do in order to be considered a green environment? (Businesses can recycle paper, magazines, computer disks, toner cartridges, water, food, plastic, or aluminum products. To be considered a "green" or "clean" environment, companies have strict requirements about clothing, sanitation, shoe wear, and air quality.)

2 TEACH

GUIDED PRACTICE

Reading Accounting

• Reading for meaning involves the reader's existing knowledge. Have students identify their underlying assumptions about material they are reading. For example, they might assume that all data in the trial balance is correct because the totals are equal, but that assumption may or may not be true. L2

• Give a blank work sheet to a language teacher, and ask the teacher to translate the list of accounts in the trial balance. Then copy for your students. ELL

Concept Development: The Sixth Step of the Accounting Cycle: The Work Sheet

Discussion: Point out that the work sheet is a "working paper" and thus is not part of the end-of-period financial statements. Since it is a working document, the work sheet may be prepared in pencil. Emphasize that its purpose is to gather all necessary information on one piece of paper to assist in the preparation of the financial statements for the period. L1

Visual Learning

Figure 8–2 Six-Column Work Sheet

Using **Transparency** 8–3, guide students through the information in the work sheet heading. Emphasize the mnemonic device of "Who? What? When?" to help students remember what information goes on each line.

2 TEACH (Cont'd.)

Demonstration Problem Step-by-Step Practice

Use demonstration problem 8–1 to show students how to write a work sheet heading.

Visual Learning

Figure 8–3 Work Sheet with Account Names and Trial Balance Amounts

Using **Transparency 8–4**, point out that the trial balance can be prepared at any time during the fiscal period after posting has been completed. When it is prepared as part of the end-of-period work, it is placed on a work sheet.

Teaching Tips

Point out to students that account numbers are listed on the work sheet to help in classifying accounts. Account numbers are also useful when entering data directly into a computer program, particularly for closing entries.

Remind students that erasing an error is permitted on a work sheet because it is a working document.

Review the meaning of "fiscal period," and stress the importance of consistency in time periods.

Demonstration Problem Step-by-Step Practice

Use demonstration problem 8–2 to show students how to enter accounts and their balances in the Trial Balance section of the work sheet.

ACCOUNTING TIPS

Rules

A *single rule* means that the column of figures is to be added or subtracted. *Double rules* mean that the last figure is a total and that no more entries are to be made below.

The Account Name and Trial Balance Sections

Information for the Account Name and Trial Balance sections comes from the general ledger accounts. In Chapter 7, you prepared a trial balance by listing the account names and their final balances. A trial balance can be prepared at any time during the fiscal period to prove the general ledger. When a trial balance is prepared at the end of an accounting period, though, it is prepared as a part of the work sheet.

Account Name Section. Look at the work sheet in **Figure 8–3.** The account numbers and names are from Roadrunner's general ledger and are listed on the work sheet in the same order that they appear in the general ledger. The order is:

- Assets
- Liabilities
- Owner's equity
- Revenues
- Expenses

Roadrunner Delivery Service
Work Sheet
For the Month Ended October 31, 20--

	ACCT. NO.	ACCOUNT NAME	TRIAL BALANCE		INCOME STATEMENT		BALANCE SHEET		
			DEBIT	CREDIT	DEBIT	CREDIT	DEBIT	CREDIT	
1	*101*	*Cash in Bank*	*21 125 00*						1
2	*105*	*Accts. Rec.—City News*	*1 450 00*						2
3	*110*	*Accts. Rec.—Green Company*	—						3
4	*115*	*Computer Equipment*	*3 000 00*						4
5	*120*	*Office Equipment*	*200 00*						5
6	*125*	*Delivery Equipment*	*12 000 00*						6
7	*201*	*Accts. Pay.—Beacon Advertising*		*75 00*					7
8	*205*	*Accts. Pay.—North Shore Auto*		*11 650 00*					8
9	*301*	*Maria Sanchez, Capital*		*25 400 00*					9
10	*302*	*Maria Sanchez, Withdrawals*	*500 00*						10
11	*303*	*Income Summary*	—	—					11
12	*401*	*Delivery Revenue*		*2 650 00*					12
13	*501*	*Advertising Expense*	*75 00*						13
14	*505*	*Maintenance Expense*	*600 00*						14
15	*510*	*Rent Expense*	*700 00*						15
16	*515*	*Utilities Expense*	*125 00*						16
17									17

Figure 8–3 Work Sheet with Account Names and Trial Balance Amounts

Key Points

The Work Sheet

On the work sheet, enter the number, name, and end-of-period balance of *every* account in the general ledger.

All the general ledger accounts are listed on the work sheet, even those that have a zero balance. Listing all the accounts avoids accidentally omitting an account and ensures that the work sheet contains all the accounts needed to prepare the financial reports.

Trial Balance Section. The end-of-period balance in the general ledger for each account is entered in the appropriate amount column of the Trial Balance section. Accounts with debit balances are entered in the Trial

Great Ideas *From the Classroom of...*

Solving the Six-Column Work Sheet If you like puzzles, you will like work sheets. Remember, "six column" means six money columns. I like my students to think of six areas in the six-column work sheet: (1) heading, (2) account titles and numbers, (3) trial balance amounts, (4) balance sheet amounts, (5) income statement amounts, and (6) net income or net loss. I see three purposes for the six columns: (a) prove the ledger (Do debits = credits?), (b) help set up for the financial statements, and (c) determine net income or net loss.

Dennis Conway
Grinnell High School
Grinnell, Iowa

Balance debit column. Accounts with credit balances are entered in the Trial Balance credit column. If an account has a zero balance at the end of the period, a line is drawn in the normal balance column. Notice in **Figure 8–3** that a line was drawn in the Trial Balance debit column for Accounts Receivable—Green Company. Lines were also recorded in the Trial Balance debit and credit columns for Income Summary since this account does not have a normal balance side. You'll learn more about the Income Summary account in Chapter 10.

Ruling and Totaling the Trial Balance Section

Ruling means "drawing a line." In accounting, a single rule drawn under a column of amounts means that the entries above the rule are to be added or subtracted. After all account names and balances are entered on the work sheet, a single line is drawn under the last entry and across both amount columns of the Trial Balance section as shown in **Figure 8–4.** The debit and credit columns are now ready for totaling. If the ledger balances, the total debits will equal the total credits. Look again at **Figure 8–4.** The totals match, with each column totaling $39,775. Since total debits equal total credits, a double rule is drawn across both amount columns just beneath the totals. This double rule means that the amounts just above are totals and that no other entries will be made in the Trial Balance columns.

If the total debits do not equal the total credits, there is an error. Find and correct the error before completing the work sheet. Procedures for locating errors are discussed in Chapter 7.

Did You Know?

Public Transit

U.S. public transit agencies spend a total of nearly $22 billion a year in operating expenses. Buses consume about 58 percent of that amount. Heavy rail and commuter rail lines are the next two largest forms of public transit.

Roadrunner Delivery Service
Work Sheet
For the Month Ended October 31, 20--

	ACCT. NO.	ACCOUNT NAME	TRIAL BALANCE DEBIT	TRIAL BALANCE CREDIT	INCOME STATEMENT DEBIT	INCOME STATEMENT CREDIT	BALANCE SHEET DEBIT	BALANCE SHEET CREDIT	
1	101	*Cash in Bank*	21125 00						1
2	105	*Accts. Rec.—City News*	1450 00						2
3	110	*Accts. Rec.—Green Company*	—						3
4	115	*Computer Equipment*	3000 00						4
5	120	*Office Equipment*	200 00						5
6	125	*Delivery Equipment*	12000 00						6
7	201	*Accts. Pay.—Beacon Advertising*		75 00					7
8	205	*Accts. Pay.—North Shore Auto*		11650 00					8
9	301	*Maria Sanchez, Capital*		25400 00					9
10	302	*Maria Sanchez, Withdrawals*	500 00						10
11	303	*Income Summary*	—	—					11
12	401	*Delivery Revenue*		2650 00					12
13	501	*Advertising Expense*	75 00						13
14	505	*Maintenance Expense*	600 00						14
15	510	*Rent Expense*	700 00						15
16	515	*Utilities Expense*	125 00						16
17			39775 00	39775 00					17
18									18

Figure 8–4 Work Sheet with Trial Balance Section Completed

2 TEACH (Cont'd.)

Visual Learning

Figure 8–4 Work Sheet with Trial Balance Section Completed

Use **Transparency 8–5** to demonstrate totaling and ruling the Trial Balance section of the work sheet.

Demonstration Problem Step-by-Step Practice

Use demonstration problem 8–3 to show students how to total and rule the Trial Balance section of the work sheet.

Teaching Tips

Point out to students that a work sheet is prepared in sections. The first section must balance before the next one can be completed.

Emphasize that the information for preparing the work sheet comes from the ledger accounts. Thus, students should find and correct any errors in the journalizing or posting steps before they prepare the work sheet. Otherwise, those errors will make it more difficult to prepare the work sheet, which must balance before it can be completed.

Critical Thinking: Tell students they have completed the trial balance section of the work sheet, and the totals do not balance. Have students write a list of the steps they would take to find and correct the errors. Tell students to be specific in their descriptions; for example, identifying the type of error and how to correct it. L2

CRITICAL THINKING ACTIVITY

Analyzing Information Ask students whether or not the following errors would be revealed by a trial balance.

a. A credit entry was never posted. (yes)
b. An entire entry was never posted. (no)
c. A transaction was not journalized. (no)
d. A transaction was posted to the wrong account. (no)
e. An amount was transposed during the posting process. (yes)

CHAPTER 8
SECTION 1, PAGES 182–186

3 ASSESS

Thinking Critically (Answers)

1. To organize ledger account balances for preparing financial statements.
2. To indicate stage of completion. A single rule means entries above are to be added or subtracted. A double rule means no other entries may be made.

Communicating Accounting (Answers)

Students should include specific instructions on the use of single and double rules and how to find and correct trial balance errors.

Problem 8–1 (Answers)

Rent Expense, Exp., Dr.
Service Fees Revenue, Rev., Cr.
Accts. Pay.—Rubino Supp., Liab., Cr.
Scott Lee, Capital, OE, Cr.
Advertising Expense, Exp., Dr.
Accts. Rec.—John Langer, Asset, Dr.
Scott Lee, Withdrawals, OE, Dr.
Maintenance Expense, Exp., Dr.
Office Supplies, Asset, Dr.

Problem 8–2 (Answers)

1. Hailey Office Supply
2. Garnet Electrical Co.
3. June 15
4. $6.23
5. Two
6. 220

Chapter Reviews and Working Papers Refer students to the Chapter 8 workbook pages to answer *Check Your Understanding* activities.

4 CLOSE

Section Wrap-Up

Oral Exercise: Have students explain how to set up a work sheet and complete the Trial Balance section. L1

SECTION 1 Check Your Understanding

Now that you have studied this section, complete the following questions and problems.

Thinking Critically

1. What is the purpose of the work sheet?
2. What is the purpose of ruling in accounting?

Communicating Accounting

Your accounting firm, AccountFast, volunteered to provide mentors to area schools for accounting and math programs. As a mentor, you are assigned to work with three accounting students. Your topic for this week is "Ruling and Totaling the Trial Balance." Create a handout to explain and illustrate this topic. Use any company, accounts, and account balances you wish. Remember, it is helpful to provide step-by-step instructions.

Problem 8–1 Entering Account Balances on the Work Sheet

The following accounts appear on the work sheet for Lee's Bike Shop.

Store Equipment
Rent Expense
Service Fees Revenue
Accts. Pay.—Rubino Supply
Scott Lee, Capital
Advertising Expense
Accts. Rec.—John Langer
Scott Lee, Withdrawals
Maintenance Expense
Office Supplies

Instructions Use a form similar to the one below in your working papers. Classify each account and use an "x" to indicate whether the account balance is entered in the debit or the credit column of the Trial Balance section. The first account is completed as an example.

Account Name	Classification	Trial Balance	
		Debit	Credit
Store Equipment	Asset	X	

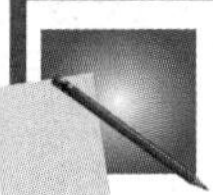

Problem 8–2 Analyzing a Source Document

Instructions Based on the invoice presented here, answer the following questions in your working papers.

1. Which company shipped the supplies?
2. Which company ordered the supplies?
3. On what date were the supplies received?
4. What does one box of file folders cost?
5. How many ring binders were ordered?
6. What is the invoice number?

Hailey Office Supply
2763 East Meadow Ave.
Richardson, TX 75080

INVOICE NO. 220

DATE: June 3, 20--
ORDER NO.: PO304
SHIPPED BY: Truck
TERMS: Net 30

TO Garmot Electrical Co.
15638 Lone Star Highway
Plano, TX 75074

QTY.	ITEM	UNIT PRICE	TOTAL
2	Ring Binders, 37546	$ 2.94	$ 5.88
1	Bond Paper, 27361	5.83	5.83
2	Rotary Cards, 62744	1.75	3.50
4	Fine-Tip Markers, 28733	.84	3.36
4	File Folders, Box 36206	6.23	24.92
			$43.49
	Sales Tax		2.17
	REC'D 6/15/20-- Total		$45.66

RETEACHING SECTION 1

Reviewing the Trial Balance Review the need for the Trial Balance section of the work sheet to be totaled, proved, and ruled before the account balances are extended to the other work sheet columns. The double rules at the bottom of the Trial Balance section indicate that the section is completed. The double rules are added only when total debits equal total credits.

To help students remember the source of information for preparing the work sheet, have them turn to pages 161 and 162 and compare the general ledger account balances from there to the Trial Balance section of **Figure 8–3**.

Extending Amounts Across the Work Sheet

In the previous section you learned how to prepare and prove the Trial Balance section of the work sheet. In this section, you will learn how to extend account balances across the work sheet to the Balance Sheet section and the Income Statement section.

What You'll Learn

- How to extend amounts to the Balance Sheet and Income Statement sections.
- The importance of the matching principle.
- How to calculate and show the net income or net loss on the work sheet.

Why It's Important

Preparing the work sheet helps you understand the relationship of all ledger accounts and where they are reported.

KEY TERMS

matching principle
net income
net loss

The Balance Sheet Section

The Balance Sheet section of the work sheet contains the "balance sheet accounts"—asset, liability, and owner's equity accounts. After the Trial Balance section is proved, the next step is to *extend,* or transfer, the appropriate amounts to the Balance Sheet section. To do this, copy the Trial Balance section amounts for the asset, liability, and owner's equity accounts to the appropriate Balance Sheet amount columns. Start with the first account and extend each account balance. Extend debit amounts to the Balance Sheet debit column. Extend credit amounts to the Balance Sheet credit column. The work sheet in **Figure 8–5** shows the balances extended to the Balance Sheet section.

The Income Statement Section

The next step in completing the work sheet is to extend the appropriate account balances to the Income Statement section. The Income Statement section of the work sheet contains the revenue and expense accounts. After the asset, liability, and owner's equity account balances are extended to the Balance Sheet section, the revenue and expense account balances are transferred to the Income Statement section. Because revenue accounts have a normal credit balance, revenue account balances are extended to the credit column of the Income Statement section. Since expense accounts have a normal debit balance, expense account balances are transferred to the debit column of the Income Statement section. Notice the amounts in the debit and credit columns of the Income Statement section in **Figure 8–6.**

RESOURCE MANAGER

Reproducible Masters
- Lesson Plans
- Chapter Reviews and Working Papers (CRWP) TAE
- Demonstration Problems

Transparencies
- Section Focus Transparency
- Teaching Transparencies
- Source Document Transparencies
- Solution Transparencies

Multimedia
- Exam*View* CD-ROM
- Electronic Learning Center CD-ROM
- Interactive Lesson Planner CD-ROM

1 FOCUS

Introducing the Section

In this section students learn how to complete the balance sheet and income statement sections of the work sheet. They also match expenses to revenue and calculate net income or loss.

Section Concepts

- How to extend amounts to the Balance Sheet and Income Statement sections.
- The importance of the matching principle.
- How to calculate and show the net income or net loss on the work sheet.

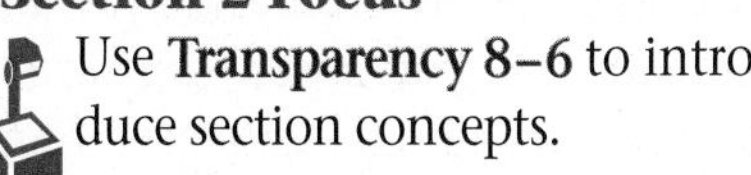

Section 2 Focus

Use **Transparency 8–6** to introduce section concepts.

BELL RINGER

Demonstration: Before class, write each account in the trial balance on a separate note card. Holding up each card, have students tell you the account's classification. Create a stack of balance sheet accounts and a stack of income statement accounts. Point out that the work sheet separates accounts into these two categories. L1

Concept Development: The Balance Sheet Section

Discussion: Discuss the role of the Balance Sheet columns for organizing the accounts that will be reported on the balance sheet. Point out that permanent accounts are included in this section. Each account balance is extended to the Debit or Credit column based on whether it was a debit or credit in the Trial Balance section. L1

2 TEACH

GUIDED PRACTICE

Reading Accounting

• When reading across an accounting form, it's very easy to drop up or down a line. Help students develop the habit of using a ruler or other straight edge to help them follow each line across. L1

Concept Development: The Income Statement Section

Discussion: Point out to students that the Income Statement section of the work sheet will be used to prepare the income statement. Accounts are organized on the work sheet as they will be on the income statement. This section includes the temporary capital accounts of revenue and expenses. L1

Visual Learning

Figure 8–5 Work Sheet with Trial Balance Amounts Extended to Balance Sheet Section

Use **Transparency 8–7** to demonstrate how to extend amounts to the Balance Sheet section. Tell students to extend amounts from the top of the work sheet down. They are less likely to miss an account balance.

Figure 8–6 Work Sheet with Trial Balance Amounts Extended to Income Statement Section

Using **Transparency 8–8**, have students describe how to extend amounts to the Income Statement section. Also point out the rule drawn across the Income Summary line to indicate the zero balance.

Roadrunner Delivery Service
Work Sheet
For the Month Ended October 31, 20--

ACCT. NO.	ACCOUNT NAME	TRIAL BALANCE		INCOME STATEMENT		BALANCE SHEET	
		DEBIT	CREDIT	DEBIT	CREDIT	DEBIT	CREDIT
101	Cash in Bank	21,125 00				21,125 00	
105	Accts. Rec.—City News	1,450 00				1,450 00	
110	Accts. Rec.—Green Company	—				—	
115	Computer Equipment	3,000 00				3,000 00	
120	Office Equipment	200 00				200 00	
125	Delivery Equipment	12,000 00				12,000 00	
201	Accts. Pay.—Beacon Advertising		75 00				75 00
205	Accts. Pay.—North Shore Auto		11,650 00				11,650 00
301	Maria Sanchez, Capital		25,400 00				25,400 00
302	Maria Sanchez, Withdrawals	500 00				500 00	
303	Income Summary	—	—				
401	Delivery Revenue		2,650 00				
501	Advertising Expense	75 00					
505	Maintenance Expense	600 00					
510	Rent Expense	700 00					
515	Utilities Expense	125 00					
		39,775 00	39,775 00				

Figure 8–5 Work Sheet with Trial Balance Amounts Extended to Balance Sheet Section

Roadrunner Delivery Service
Work Sheet
For the Month Ended October 31, 20--

ACCT. NO.	ACCOUNT NAME	TRIAL BALANCE		INCOME STATEMENT		BALANCE SHEET	
		DEBIT	CREDIT	DEBIT	CREDIT	DEBIT	CREDIT
101	Cash in Bank	21,125 00				21,125 00	
105	Accts. Rec.—City News	1,450 00				1,450 00	
110	Accts. Rec.—Green Company	—				—	
115	Computer Equipment	3,000 00				3,000 00	
120	Office Equipment	200 00				200 00	
125	Delivery Equipment	12,000 00				12,000 00	
201	Accts. Pay.—Beacon Advertising		75 00				75 00
205	Accts. Pay.—North Shore Auto		11,650 00				11,650 00
301	Maria Sanchez, Capital		25,400 00				25,400 00
302	Maria Sanchez, Withdrawals	500 00				500 00	
303	Income Summary	—	—	—	—		
401	Delivery Revenue		2,650 00		2,650 00		
501	Advertising Expense	75 00		75 00			
505	Maintenance Expense	600 00		600 00			
510	Rent Expense	700 00		700 00			
515	Utilities Expense	125 00		125 00			
		39,775 00	39,775 00				

Figure 8–6 Work Sheet with Trial Balance Amounts Extended to Income Statement Section

MEETING SPECIAL NEEDS

Students with Learning Disabilities Some students with learning disabilities have trouble with sequential tasks involving numbers and following step-by-step instructions. They may, for example, have trouble preparing a complete work sheet. Allow these students extra time to complete the assignment. For some students, it may be helpful to assign a peer helper who can guide the student through the series of steps needed to complete the work sheet.

Totaling the Income Statement and Balance Sheet Sections

After all the amounts in the Trial Balance section are extended to the Balance Sheet and Income Statement sections, each section is totaled. A single rule is drawn across the four debit and credit columns to indicate that the columns are ready to be added. Look now at **Figure 8–7.** After the four columns are totaled, notice that the debit and credit columns in each section are not equal. Unlike the Trial Balance section debit and credit totals, the column totals in these two sections will not be equal until the net income or net loss for the period is added.

Roadrunner Delivery Service
Work Sheet
For the Month Ended October 31, 20--

	ACCT. NO.	ACCOUNT NAME	TRIAL BALANCE		INCOME STATEMENT		BALANCE SHEET		
			DEBIT	CREDIT	DEBIT	CREDIT	DEBIT	CREDIT	
1	*101*	*Cash in Bank*	*21125 00*				*21125 00*		1
2	*105*	*Accts. Rec.—City News*	*1450 00*				*1450 00*		2
3	*110*	*Accts. Rec.—Green Company*	—				—		3
4	*115*	*Computer Equipment*	*3000 00*				*3000 00*		4
5	*120*	*Office Equipment*	*200 00*				*200 00*		5
6	*125*	*Delivery Equipment*	*12000 00*				*12000 00*		6
7	*201*	*Accts. Pay.—Beacon Advertising*		*75 00*				*75 00*	7
8	*205*	*Accts. Pay.—North Shore Auto*		*11650 00*				*11650 00*	8
9	*301*	*Maria Sanchez, Capital*		*25400 00*				*25400 00*	9
10	*302*	*Maria Sanchez, Withdrawals*	*500 00*				*500 00*		10
11	*303*	*Income Summary*	—	—	—	—			11
12	*401*	*Delivery Revenue*		*2650 00*		*2650 00*			12
13	*501*	*Advertising Expense*	*75 00*		*75 00*				13
14	*505*	*Maintenance Expense*	*600 00*		*600 00*				14
15	*510*	*Rent Expense*	*700 00*		*700 00*				15
16	*515*	*Utilities Expense*	*125 00*		*125 00*				16
17			*39775 00*	*39775 00*	*1500 00*	*2650 00*	*38275 00*	*37125 00*	17
18									18

Figure 8–7 Work Sheet with Income Statement and Balance Sheet Sections Totaled

Showing Net Income on the Work Sheet

The Income Statement section of the work sheet includes both the revenue and the expenses for the period. In accounting, expenses incurred in an accounting period are matched with the revenue earned during the same period. This comparison is referred to as the **matching principle**. Matching expenses of a period with revenue of the same period provides a reliable measure of profit, because it shows the cost (expense) of producing the revenue. This information helps the business owner or manager analyze results and then make decisions.

COOPERATIVE LEARNING ACTIVITY

Group Discussion Divide students into groups of three or four and give each group a list of several account names. Ask students to classify each account as a temporary or permanent account and then to determine whether each account balance is extended to the Income Statement or the Balance Sheet section of the work sheet.

2 TEACH (Cont'd.)

Demonstration Problem Step-by-Step Practice

Use demonstration problems 8–4 and 8–5 to show students how to extend amounts to the Balance Sheet and Income Statement columns and to complete the work sheet.

Concept Development: Totaling the Income Statement and Balance Sheet Sections

Discussion: Point out to students that they should make sure they've extended all amounts correctly before adding the columns. Review the process for finding and correcting errors. L1

Visual Learning

Figure 8–7 Work Sheet with Income Statement and Balance Sheet Sections Totaled

Using **Transparency** 8–9, call students' attention to the Balance Sheet and Income Statement column totals. Point out that the totals do not balance at this stage because net income or net loss has yet to be calculated.

Concept Development: Showing Net Income on the Work Sheet

Discussion: Discuss the matching principle by writing the heading "Revenue" on one side of the chalkboard and "Expenses" on the other. Draw an arrow connecting the two. Point out that businesses spend money to earn revenue. Matching expenses with revenue helps business owners and managers determine whether their expenses actually are producing more revenue. L1

2 TEACH (Cont'd.)

Visual Learning

Figure 8–8 Partial Work Sheet with Net Income

Using **Transparency 8–10**, explain why the net income amount is shown in the Income Statement Debit column and the Balance Sheet Credit column.

Teaching Tip

To help students understand how net income affects each of the financial statements, write these T accounts on the chalkboard.

Income Statement	
Dr.	Cr.
Expenses	Revenue
–	+

Balance Sheet	
Dr.	Cr.
	Capital
	+

Point out that if a business has a net income, the Credit column of the Income Statement section will be greater than the Debit column because revenue greater than expenses produces a net income. Since revenue increases capital and capital is increased by a credit, the net income amount is also placed in the Balance Sheet Credit column.

Chapter Reviews and Working Papers
Refer students to the *Study Plan* located at the beginning of Chapter 8 in the workbook.

After the Income Statement section columns are totaled, total expenses (the debit column total) are subtracted from total revenue (the credit column total) to find the net income. **Net income** is the amount of revenue that remains after expenses for the period are subtracted. Net income is entered as a debit at the bottom of the Income Statement section of the work sheet. Look at **Figure 8–8.** Roadrunner's net income is $1,150.

1. Skip a line after the last account and write the words "Net Income" in the Account Name column. A
2. On the same line, enter the net income amount in the Income statement debit column. B
3. On the same line, enter the net income amount in the Balance sheet credit column. C

Roadrunner Delivery Service
Work Sheet
For the Month Ended October 31, 20--

	ACCT. NO.	ACCOUNT NAME	TRIAL BALANCE		INCOME STATEMENT		BALANCE SHEET		
			DEBIT	CREDIT	DEBIT	CREDIT	DEBIT	CREDIT	
1	101	*Cash in Bank*	21125 00				21125 00		1
2	105	*Accts. Rec.—City News*	1450 00				1450 00		2
3	110	*Accts. Rec.—Green Company*	—				—		3
4	115	*Computer Equipment*	3000 00				3000 00		4
5	120	*Office Equipment*	200 00				200 00		5
6	125	*Delivery Equipment*	12000 00				12000 00		6
7	201	*Accts. Pay.—Beacon Advertising*		75 00				75 00	7
8	205	*Accts. Pay.—North Shore Auto*		11650 00				11650 00	8
9	301	*Maria Sanchez, Capital*		25400 00				25400 00	9
10	302	*Maria Sanchez, Withdrawals*	500 00				500 00		10
11	303	*Income Summary*	—	—	—	—			11
12	401	*Delivery Revenue*		2650 00		2650 00			12
13	501	*Advertising Expense*	75 00		75 00				13
14	505	*Maintenance Expense*	600 00		600 00				14
15	510	*Rent Expense*	700 00		700 00				15
16	515	*Utilities Expense*	125 00		125 00				16
17			39775 00	39775 00	1500 00	2650 00	38275 00	37125 00	17
18		*Net Income*			1150 00			1150 00	18
19									19

A B C

Figure 8–8 Partial Work Sheet with Net Income

The amount of net income is also reflected in the Balance Sheet section of the work sheet. Remember, revenue and expense accounts are temporary capital accounts. As you can see in **Figure 8–9**, revenues increase capital, while expenses decrease capital. Net income, therefore, increases capital since revenues exceed expenses. During the accounting period, revenue and expense amounts are recorded in the temporary capital accounts (like **Delivery Revenue** and **Utilities Expense**). At the end of the period, net income is transferred to the owner's capital account. Since the capital account is increased by credits, the amount of the net income is entered in the credit column of the Balance Sheet section of the work sheet.

REINFORCING STUDY SKILLS

Active Listening When information is given in a lecture rather than in a written text, students need to know how to listen actively and efficiently. Have students practice their listening skills as you lecture. Point out that to get the most out of a lecture, students should first focus their attention on the speaker, identify his or her main points, then listen carefully for supporting ideas and take clear notes.

The Effects of Income or Loss on Capital

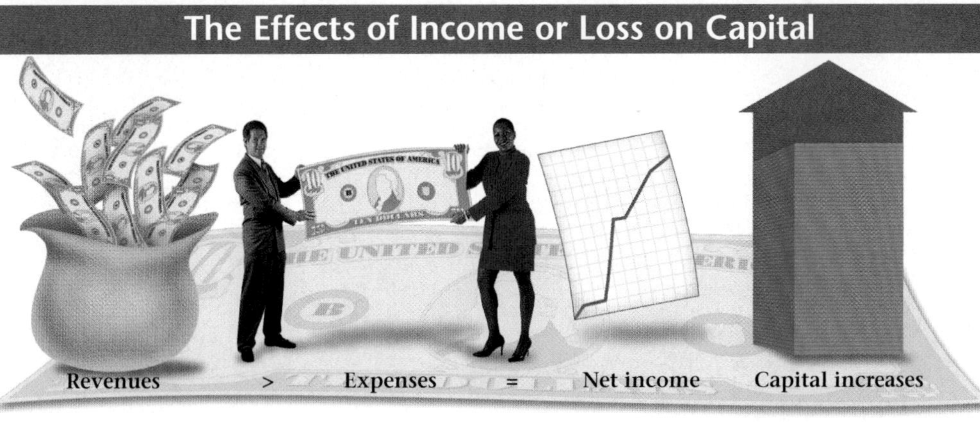

Figure 8–9 The Effects of Income or Loss on Capital

To check the accuracy of the net income amount in the Balance Sheet section, subtract the total of the credit column from the total of the debit column. If the result equals the net income computed in the Income Statement section, enter the net income in the credit column of the Balance Sheet section. If the result does not equal net income, there is an error. Before continuing, you must find and correct the error. To find the error, check that the amounts from the Trial Balance section are extended correctly and that the totals of all columns are added correctly.

Spreadsheet Hints

Writing Formulas

Spreadsheet programs use formulas to make calculations.

- Formulas must be identified to distinguish them from data entered in the spreadsheet.
- Most programs require formulas to be preceded by = or +.

Completing the Work Sheet

The completed work sheet for Roadrunner is shown in **Figure 8–10.** To complete the Income Statement and Balance Sheet sections, follow these steps:

1. On the line under the net income amount, draw a single rule across the four columns. D
2. In the Income Statement section debit column, add the net income amount to the previous total and enter the new total. Bring down the total of the Income Statement section credit column. Total debits should equal total credits. E

2 TEACH (Cont'd.)

Visual Learning

Figure 8-9 The Effects of Income or Loss on Capital

Using **Transparency 8-11**, point out that net income increases both capital and assets. Increases in assets are already reflected in the asset accounts through entries for cash received by the business from revenue or accounts receivable.

Discuss how a net loss decreases both assets and capital.

Thinking Algebraically

Conceptualize: Have students think about net income and loss in a formula format. (Example: "revenue > expenses = net income" or "expenses > revenue = net loss.") L1

Concept Development: Completing the Work Sheet

Discussion: Remind students that after calculating the net income or net loss, they must finish the work sheet by calculating totals for the Balance Sheet and Income Statement sections. Adding the amount of the net income or loss to both sections serves as a double check on the accuracy of the calculations. L1

Math Review for Accounting

Photocopy appropriate *Activity Sheets* for students who need additional practice in basic math.

Math Skill Builder Activity

Writing Formulas Have students practice writing spreadsheet formulas. Provide students with a spreadsheet that includes a variety of numbers. Call out the cell addresses and have students write the formulas on a separate piece of paper. Make sure that students get a chance to practice writing formulas for addition, subtraction, multiplication, and division.

2 TEACH (Cont'd.)

Visual Learning

Figure 8–10 Completed Work Sheet

Use **Transparency 8–12** to guide students through the completion of a work sheet. Remind students that the column totals in each section must balance after the net income is added. If they do not, an error has been made and must be corrected before they can continue.

Concept Development: Showing a Net Loss on the Work Sheet

Discussion: Emphasize the logic of why the entry on the work sheet for a net loss is opposite that for a net income. Refer to the T-account illustration given in the Teaching Tip for net income on page 190. L1

Strategies for Teaching International Accounting

To enrich study of International Accounting, refer to the additional critical thinking activities in the booklet.

Roadrunner Delivery Service
Work Sheet
For the Month Ended October 31, 20--

	ACCT. NO.	ACCOUNT NAME	TRIAL BALANCE DEBIT	TRIAL BALANCE CREDIT	INCOME STATEMENT DEBIT	INCOME STATEMENT CREDIT	BALANCE SHEET DEBIT	BALANCE SHEET CREDIT	
1	101	*Cash in Bank*	21 125 00				21 125 00		1
2	105	*Accts. Receivable—City News*	1 450 00				1 450 00		2
3	110	*Accts. Receivable—Green Company*	—				—		3
4	115	*Computer Equipment*	3 000 00				3 000 00		4
5	120	*Office Equipment*	200 00				200 00		5
6	125	*Delivery Equipment*	12 000 00				12 000 00		6
7	201	*Accts. Payable—Beacon Advertising*		75 00				75 00	7
8	205	*Accounts Pay.—North Shore Auto*		11 650 00				11 650 00	8
9	301	*Maria Sanchez, Capital*		25 400 00				25 400 00	9
10	302	*Maria Sanchez, Withdrawals*	500 00				500 00		10
11	303	*Income Summary*	—	—	—	—			11
12	401	*Delivery Revenue*		2 650 00		2 650 00			12
13	501	*Advertising Expense*	75 00		75 00				13
14	505	*Maintenance Expense*	600 00		600 00				14
15	510	*Rent Expense*	700 00		700 00				15
16	515	*Utilities Expense*	125 00		125 00				16
17			39 775 00	39 775 00	1 500 00	2 650 00	38 275 00	37 125 00	17
18		*Net Income*			1 150 00			1 150 00	18
19					2 650 00	2 650 00	38 275 00	38 275 00	19
20									20

A B D E F G C

Figure 8–10 Completed Work Sheet

3. In the Balance Sheet section credit column, add net income to the previous total and enter the new total. Bring down the total of the Balance Sheet section debit column. The total debit amount should equal the total credit amount. F
4. In the Balance Sheet and Income Statement sections, draw a double rule under the four column totals. The double rule indicates that the debit and credit columns are equal and that no more amounts are to be entered in these columns. G

Misinterpreting Gestures

When conducting business in another country, remember that gestures which are common in the U.S. are sometimes offensive to other cultures. For example, the good luck symbol (crossing one's fingers) and the okay symbol (the thumb and forefinger making a circle) are considered rude in Brazil.

Showing a Net Loss on the Work Sheet

When total expenses are greater than total revenue, a **net loss** occurs. A net loss decreases owner's equity. This decrease is shown as a debit to the capital account. On the work sheet when a net loss occurs, the Income Statement section debit column total (total expenses) is greater than the Income Statement section credit column total (total revenue). The steps

Teaching International ACCOUNTING

Comparing Gestures Divide students into groups of three or four and ask them to brainstorm common gestures used in America. Have each group share its list and describe the meaning of each gesture. Then have students research common gestures for another country. Ask students to compare the two lists. Are any of the gestures similar? If so, do those gestures have a different meaning in the foreign country? Have students explain the consequences of using the gesture in the foreign culture.

to complete the work sheet are the same as described for Net Income except that the words "Net Loss" are written in the Account Name column and the net loss amount is entered in the credit column of the Income Statement section and the debit column of the Balance Sheet section. The partial work sheet in **Figure 8–11** shows a net loss. Expenses exceed revenue by $746.

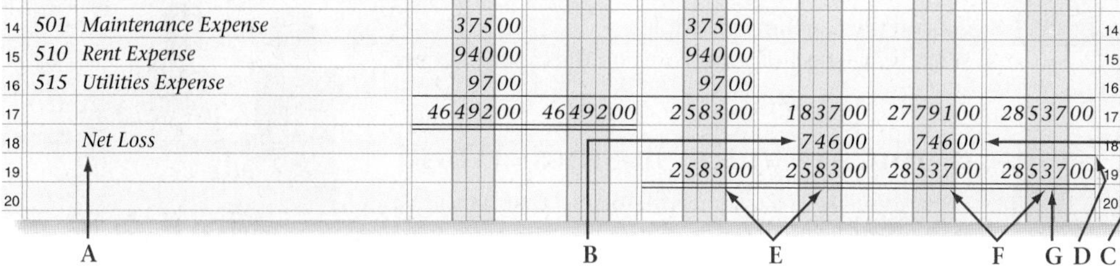

14	501	*Maintenance Expense*	375 00		375 00				14
15	510	*Rent Expense*	940 00		940 00				15
16	515	*Utilities Expense*	97 00		97 00				16
17			46,492 00	46,492 00	2,583 00	1,837 00	27,791 00	28,537 00	17
18		*Net Loss*				746 00	746 00		18
19					2,583 00	2,583 00	28,537 00	28,537 00	19
20									20

Figure 8–11 Partial Work Sheet Showing a Net Loss

A Review of the Steps in Preparing a Six-Column Work Sheet

Follow these steps when preparing a six-column work sheet:

1. Write the heading on the work sheet.
2. In the Account Name and Trial Balance sections, enter the account numbers, names, and balances for all accounts in the general ledger.
3. Prove the equality of total debits and total credits in the Trial Balance section.
4. Extend the amounts of the Trial Balance section to the appropriate columns in the Balance Sheet and Income Statement sections.
5. Total the columns in the Income Statement and Balance Sheet sections.
6. Determine the amount of the net income or the net loss for the period.
7. Enter the amount of the net income or the net loss in the appropriate columns in the Income Statement and Balance Sheet sections.
8. Total and rule the Income Statement and Balance Sheet sections.

ACCOUNTING *Flashbacks*

ACCOUNTING HALL OF FAME

The Accounting Hall of Fame was established at Ohio State University in 1950. It honors accountants who have contributed to the advancement of accounting.

A MATTER OF ETHICS

Padding Expense Accounts

Imagine that you're an auditor for an accounting firm like PricewaterhouseCoopers. You and a co-worker, Mark, have been sent to Chicago to perform an audit. You have an allowance of $200 a day to cover lodging, meals, and transportation. At the end of the trip, you are to turn in an expense account report detailing how you spent the allowance. Mark adds a few dollars to each of his expenses so he can have some extra cash. You figure that the firm won't miss a few dollars, so you consider doing the same.

Ethical Decision Making:

- What are the ethical issues?
- What are the alternatives?
- Who are the affected parties?
- How do the alternatives affect the parties?
- What would you do?

Teaching A MATTER OF ETHICS

Padding Expense Accounts Discuss reasons why employees might feel entitled to pad an expense account. For example, employees often travel for a company on their own time, for which they may not be reimbursed. Since most companies do not require receipts for expenses under $25, it's also easy to claim small expenses. Employees might reason that they can't keep track of every dollar spent, so claiming a few extra will ensure that they don't lose money. Contrast these reasons with a company's need to control expenses.

2 TEACH (Cont'd.)

Visual Learning

Figure 8–11 Partial Work Sheet Showing a Net Loss

Use **Transparency 8–13** to explain the differences between calculating a net loss and a net income. Remind students that a loss is opposite net income.

Demonstration Problem Step-by-Step Practice

Use demonstration problem 8–6 to show students how to calculate and enter a net loss on the work sheet.

Teaching Tip

Have students explain why a net income or loss occurs to test whether they understand the concept or are just memorizing rules.

Concept Development: A Review of the Steps in Preparing a Six-Column Work Sheet

Application: Make a transparency of a blank work sheet (also without column headings) and have students tell you what column headings should be used and where the information in Steps 1–8 should be placed on the work sheet. **L1**

Strategies for Teaching Ethics in Accounting

Photocopy the Chapter 8 *Student Activity Sheet* for students. Answers are also provided in the booklet.

CHAPTER 8
SECTION 2, PAGES 187–194

3 ASSESS

Thinking Critically (Answers)

1. Matching expenses from one accounting period to revenue earned during that same period.
2. Net income increases capital.

Computing in the Business World (Answers)

The third quarter net income is $2,225. The company seems to be recovering from earlier losses, but if the losses continue, it could be in trouble.

Problem 8-3 (Answers)

Store Equipment, Bal. Sheet, Dr.
Rent Expense, Inc. State., Dr.
Service Fees Revenue, Inc. State., Cr.
Accts. Pay.—Rubino Supply, Bal. Sheet, Cr.
Scott Lee, Capital, Bal. Sheet, Cr.
Advertising Expense, Inc. State., Dr.
Accts. Rec.—John Langer, Bal. Sheet, Dr.
Scott Lee, Withdrawals, Bal. Sheet, Dr.
Maintenance Exp., Inc. State., Dr.
Office Supplies, Bal. Sheet, Dr.

Chapter Reviews and Working Papers Refer students to the Chapter 8 workbook pages to answer *Check Your Understanding* activities.

4 CLOSE

Section Wrap-Up

Writing: Have students write a paragraph or two explaining the difference between the effect of a net income and a net loss on assets and the owner's capital account. L2

SECTION 2 Check Your Understanding

Now that you have studied this section, complete the following questions and problem.

Thinking Critically

1. Explain the matching principle.
2. What is the effect of net income on the capital account?

Computing in the Business World

For Art's Sake is a sole proprietorship that sells artwork. Even though the operating costs are low, the business relies on steady sales to make a profit. The first two quarterly financial statements for this year have been grim. Using the revenue and expense information for the third quarter, calculate the net profit or loss. (Balances of the Accounts Receivable accounts represent third-quarter revenue.) Compare the third quarter figure with the figures from the first and second quarters. What do you predict the future of For Art's Sake will be?

Third Quarter	
Rent Expense	$2,000
Utilities Expense	800
Advertising Expense	3,000
Maintenance Expense	1,200
Accounts Receivable—Sammy Wong	500
Accounts Receivable—The Artist Collection	5,525
Accounts Receivable—Vera Samuels	3,200
Second Quarter	Net Loss = $2,000
First Quarter	Net Loss = $1,200

Problem 8-3 Extending Amounts Across the Work Sheet

The following account balances appear in the Account Name section of the work sheet for Lee's Bike Shop.

Store Equipment	Advertising Expense
Rent Expense	Accounts Receivable—John Langer
Service Fees Revenue	Scott Lee, Withdrawals
Accounts Payable—Rubino Supply	Maintenance Expense
Scott Lee, Capital	Office Supplies

Instructions Use a form similar to the one below in your working papers or on a separate sheet of paper. For the above accounts, enter an "X" in the column where the account balance is transferred. The first account has been completed as an example.

Account Name	Income Statement		Balance Sheet	
	Debit	Credit	Debit	Credit
Store Equipment			X	

RETEACHING SECTION 2

Understanding Changes in Owner's Equity Students generally grasp the concepts of net income and net loss, but they sometimes have difficulty understanding the effects on owner's equity. Provide the following scenario to help explain: "Janet has $1,500 in savings. She earns $100 a week at her part-time job. Each week she sets aside $50 for car insurance and gasoline. This week she goes shopping and spends $80 on clothing. How will she pay for the car insurance and gasoline?" (She will have to take money from savings, which will reduce her equity.) What if she does not go shopping and spends less on gasoline than anticipated? (She will have more money to put in savings, which will increase her equity.)

KEY CONCEPTS

1. Preparing a work sheet is the sixth step in the accounting cycle.
2. A work sheet gathers all the information needed to complete the end-of-period work.
3. The work sheet heading contains three kinds of information:

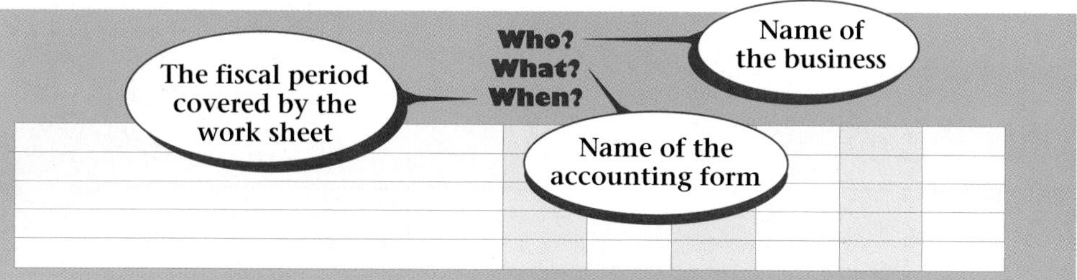

4. The Account Name section of the work sheet lists all general ledger account names, along with the account numbers.
5. Complete the Trial Balance section of the work sheet first. Total debits and total credits in the Trial Balance section must be equal.
6. Extend amounts from the Trial Balance section to the Balance Sheet section and then to the Income Statement section.
7. Use the work sheet to calculate the net income or net loss for the period. A net income results when revenue is greater than expenses. A net loss results when expenses are greater than revenue.
8. Show a net income as a debit on the Income Statement section and as a credit on the Balance Sheet section.

Account Name	Income Statement		Balance Sheet	
	Debit	Credit	Debit	Credit
Net Income	X			X

9. Show a net loss as a credit on the Income Statement section and as a debit on the Balance Sheet section.

Account Name	Income Statement		Balance Sheet	
	Debit	Credit	Debit	Credit
Net Loss		X	X	

10. A double rule means that the amount immediately above is a total and that no additional amounts will be entered in the amount column.

ANSWERS

1. False
2. True
3. False
4. True
5. False
6. False
7. True
8. True
9. False
10. True

SUMMARY CHAPTER 8

Chapter 8 Quiz

Student Class Instructor
Date Assigned Date Completed

CHAPTER 8 QUIZ

The Six-Column Work Sheet

QUESTIONS (True-False)

Directions: In the space provided, indicate whether each statement is true or false.

___ 1. The length of an accounting period can vary from one accounting cycle to another.
___ 2. Preparing a work sheet is the sixth step in the accounting cycle.
___ 3. The heading in a work sheet answers the questions Who?, What?, and Where?.
___ 4. Accounts are listed on the work sheet in the same order as they appear in the general ledger.
___ 5. A single rule under a column of amounts means that no other amounts may be added to or subtracted from that column.
___ 6. Extending an amount means to multiply it by another number.
___ 7. The matching principle requires that expenses for an accounting period be matched with the revenue earned during the same period.
___ 8. Net income is revenue earned in excess of expenses.
___ 9. A net loss occurs when expenses are less than revenue.
___ 10. A net loss decreases owner's equity.

10 • Chapter Quizzes Copyright © Glencoe/McGraw-Hill

QUESTIONS (True-False)

1. The length of an accounting period can vary from one accounting cycle to another.
2. Preparing a work sheet is the sixth step in the accounting cycle.
3. The heading in a work sheet answers the questions who, what, and where.
4. Accounts are listed on the work sheet in the same order as they appear in the general ledger.
5. A single rule under a column of amounts means that no other amounts may be added to or subtracted from that column.
6. Extending an amount means to multiply it by another number.
7. The matching principle requires that expenses for an accounting period be matched with the revenue earned during the same period.
8. Net income is revenue earned in excess of expenses.
9. A net loss occurs when expenses are less than revenue.
10. A net loss decreases owner's equity.

REVIEW AND ACTIVITIES CHAPTER 8

USING KEY TERMS

See the *Glossary* for the definitions of these terms. Ask for volunteers to share their memos. Discuss how each term is used and correct any misunderstanding.

Understanding Accounting Concepts and Procedures

(Answers)

1. The sixth.
2. To collect and organize information for end-of-period work.
3. Name of business, name of accounting form, and period covered.
4. Heading: name of business, title of form, period covered; Account Name: account numbers and names in general ledger order; Trial Balance: account balances; Income Statement: revenue and expense account balances; Balance Sheet: asset, liability, and owner's equity account balances.
5. Same order as the general ledger.
6. To avoid omitting an account and to have all accounts needed to prepare financial reports.
7. Total debits equal total credits.
8. Asset, liability, and OE accounts.
9. Revenue and expense accounts.
10. It provides data on the cost of producing revenue and a basis for making business decisions.
11. Write "Net Income" on the second line after the last account name. Enter amount in the Dr. column of the Inc. State. section and the Cr. column of the Bal. Sh. section.
12. Write "Net Loss" on the second line after the last account name. Enter loss in the Cr. column of the Inc. State. section and the Dr. column of the Bal. Sh. section.
13. It increases owner's equity.
14. Net Loss decreases owner's equity.
15. No other entries will be made in the columns.

CHAPTER 8 REVIEW AND ACTIVITIES

USING KEY TERMS

You just finished the work sheet for the third quarter and it looks like your company will make considerable profits. In the second quarter the company had experienced a net loss. On a separate sheet of paper, write a memo to your boss, Tonya Newman, asking her to review your trial balance and work sheet. Use the terms listed below in your memo.

matching principle	ruling
net income	work sheet
net loss	

Understanding Accounting Concepts and Procedures

Instructions

On a separate sheet of paper, answer the following questions:

1. Preparing the work sheet is which step of the accounting cycle?
2. Explain why a work sheet is prepared.
3. List the items that should be included in the work sheet heading.
4. Name and briefly describe the five parts of a six-column work sheet.
5. In what order are the account names listed on the work sheet?
6. Why are all accounts, including those with zero balances, listed on the work sheet?
7. What does the Trial Balance section of the work sheet prove when it has been totaled and ruled?
8. Which types of accounts are extended to the Balance Sheet section of the work sheet?
9. Which types of accounts are extended to the Income Statement section of the work sheet?
10. Why is the matching principle important?
11. Explain how to record net income on the work sheet.
12. Explain how to record a net loss on the work sheet.
13. What effect does net income have on owner's equity?
14. What effect does a net loss have on owner's equity?
15. What does a double rule on the work sheet indicate?

ASSESSMENT RESOURCES

Choose assessment strategies from the following pages to evaluate your students' progress.

Student Edition
Check Your Understanding, pp. 186, 194
Chapter 8 Problems, pp. 199–201

Assessment and Evaluation Masters
Chapter 8 Study Plan, *Glencoe Workbook (CRWP)*
Chapter 8 Self-Test, *Glencoe Workbook (CRWP)*
Chapter 8 Test, *Chapter Tests* Booklet
Chapter 8 Activity, *School-to-Work Handbook*
Chapter 8 Exam*View*

Teacher Wraparound Edition
Critical Thinking Activity, p. 185
Reteaching Sections 1–2, pp. 186, 194
Chapter 8 Quiz, p. 195

Case Study...

Service Business: Advertising Agency

You work for Creative Advertising as an assistant to the company's accountant. You're preparing a work sheet for the month of July. The trial balance totals are $127,750 and you've extended the account balances to the amount columns in the Balance Sheet and Income Statement sections. After adding the Balance Sheet and Income Statement columns and calculating net income, you find that the totals do not balance.

Thinking Critically:

1. What steps would you take to find the problem?
2. Provide a likely reason why the net income amounts do not match.

interNET CONNECTION

The Big Four

The largest public accounting firms are often referred to as the "Big Four." These firms practice internationally and provide accounting and business services to clients of all sizes.

Do This:

1. Consult the AICPA Web site, or other accounting-related Web sites to find the names of the "Big Four" firms.
2. List the Web site for each firm.
3. Do any of these firms have offices near you? If so, where are these offices located?

Conducting an Audit with Alex

Instructions The trial balance below is out of balance. Find and correct the errors, re-total the debit and credit columns, and prove the correctness of the account balances.

ACCT. NO.	ACCOUNT NAME	DEBIT	CREDIT
101	*Cash in Bank*	7,341.00	
105	*Accts. Rec.—Jon Vasi*	219.00	
110	*Accts. Rec.—Sheila Henry*	346.00	
115	*Accts. Rec.—Frank Gawle*	80.00	
120	*Supplies*		319.00
125	*Office Furniture*	3,683.00	
130	*Store Equipment*	2,047.00	
135	*Computer Equipment*	6,420.00	
205	*Accts. Pay.—Westport Supply*		231.00
210	*Accts. Pay.—Bradley Co.*		1,829.00
215	*Accts. Pay.—Jackson Brothers*	2,163.00	
301	*James Haily, Capital*		14,198.00
302	*James Haily, Withdrawals*		1,800.00
303	*Income Summary*		
405	*Delivery Revenue*	1,814.00	
410	*Repair Revenue*		7,203.00
501	*Advertising Expense*		600.00
505	*Maintenance Expense*	1,384.00	
510	*Miscellaneous Expense*	76.00	
515	*Rent Expense*	2,300.00	
520	*Repair Expense*	305.00	
525	*Utilities Expense*		518.00
		28,178.00	26,698.00

Workplace Skills

Understanding Social and Organizational Systems

- Can you read and interpret a company's organizational chart?
- Can you identify who reports to whom?

If you can answer "yes" to these questions, then you can probably work and operate effectively within an organizational system.

On the Job:

Your employer, The Teen Scene, was just bought out by a large, national clothing chain—Natural Fibers. The buyout has created a massive reorganization.

Thinking Critically:

1. The change from a small clothing store to a national chain store has affected employee morale. What do you think would help build loyalty to Natural Fibers?
2. How would an organizational chart that depicts who reports to whom help with the transition?

interNET CONNECTION www.glencoe.com

Do This (Answers)

1. Deloitte & Touche, Ernst and Young, KPMG, and PricewaterhouseCoopers
2. www.deloitte.com www.kpmg.com
   www.ey.com www.pwcglobal.com
3. Answers will vary.

Case Study...

Thinking Critically (Answer)

Students should check to see that the balances from the Trial Balance section have been extended properly and that totals of all columns have been added correctly.

Workplace Skills

Thinking Critically (Answers)

Answers will vary. Students may say that building loyalty and creating team spirit are most critical. Some methods for increasing loyalty and a sense of belonging might be through special employee incentives—clothing with company logos, employee social events, company newsletters, or employee input via surveys or interviews.

Conducting an Audit with Alex

(Answers)

Corrections:

Supplies: $319 Debit
Accts. Pay.—Jackson Brothers: $2,163 Credit
James Haily, Withdrawals: $1,800 Debit
Delivery Revenue: $1,814 Credit
Advertising Expense: $600 Debit
Utilities Expense: $518 Debit

Total: $27,438

Internet Resources and Activities Handbook

Refer students to the booklet for additional Internet activities.

PEACHTREE CORNER

General Ledger Trial Balance

To print a General Ledger Trial Balance, choose **General Ledger** from the ***Reports*** menu. Then select the General Ledger Trial Balance report from the Select a Report window.

Reports Services Window
Accounts Receivable...
Accounts Payable...
Payroll...
General Ledger...
Financial Statements...
Inventory...
Jobs...
Account Reconciliation...

The Navigation Aid provides an easy (visual) alternative for you to access the General Ledger reports.

The Trial Balance

Making the Transition from a Manual to a Computerized System

Task	Perform Accounting Procedures Using Manual Methods	Perform Accounting Procedures Using Automated Methods
Preparing the trial balance	1. After all journal entries have been posted and all general ledger balances have been updated, list account names and balances on two column accounting stationery. 2. List debit balances in one column and credit balances in the other. 3. Add all debit balances. 4. Add all credit balances. 5. Compare the totals. If totals are not in balance, locate and correct any journalizing or posting errors. 6. The trial balance is correct when total debits equal total credits.	1. Although the Trial Balance is not necessary to check the equality of debits and credits since out-of-balance entries cannot be posted, it is one of the most commonly used accounting statements. It provides a clear list format for reviewing accounts.

Preparing a Trial Balance

Peachtree Question	Description
How do I generate a trial balance in Peachtree?	1. Select **General Ledger** from the ***Reports*** menu. 2. Select General Ledger Trial Balance from the reports list. 3. Click Print.
What does the software do "behind the scenes?"	• The software automatically pulls up all account names and their current balances and lists them on a preformatted report. • The software will not allow an out-of-balance journal entry to be posted. Therefore, the accounting records stay in balance.

For detailed instructions: See the **Peachtree User Guide** in your Glencoe Working Papers.

Peachtree® Answers to Frequently Asked Questions

Q: Does Peachtree include an option to print a six-column work sheet?

A: No. Peachtree does not provide an option to print a work sheet. The program allows you to print an income statement and a balance sheet. To print an income statement or a balance sheet, choose the **Financial Statements** option from the ***Reports*** menu.

For additional information, see your *Glencoe Peachtree Accounting User Guide.*

APPLICATION OPTIONS

Problem 8–4 Preparing a Six-Column Work Sheet

The ending balances in the general ledger accounts of Wilderness Rentals for the period ended May 31 follow.

		Debit Balances	Credit Balances
101	Cash in Bank	$5,814	
105	Accts. Rec.—Helen Katz	717	
110	Accts. Rec.—Polk and Co.	590	
115	Office Supplies	847	
120	Office Equipment	4,360	
125	Camping Equipment	6,130	
201	Accts. Pay.—Adventure Equipment Inc.		$ 1,680
203	Accts. Pay.—Digital Tech Computers		3,554
205	Accts. Pay.—Greg Mollaro		635
301	Ronald Hicks, Capital		12,760
305	Ronald Hicks, Withdrawals	1,200	
310	Income Summary	—	—
401	Equipment Rental Revenue		9,716
501	Advertising Expense	1,940	
505	Maintenance Expense	1,083	
515	Rent Expense	3,500	
525	Utilities Expense	2,164	

Instructions Prepare a work sheet for the period ended May 31.

1. Write the heading on the work sheet.
2. List all of the accounts in the Account Name and Trial Balance sections. For each account, include the account number, name, and balance.

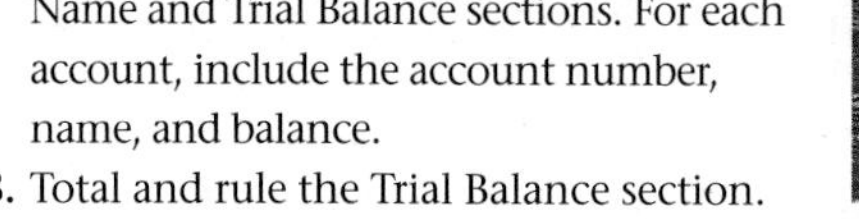

3. Total and rule the Trial Balance section. Do total debits equal total credits? If not, find and correct the problem before continuing.

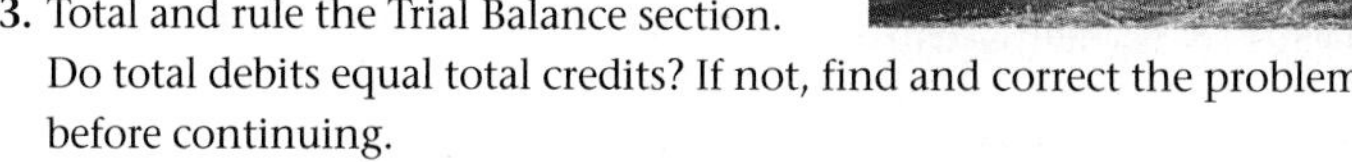

4. Extend the appropriate amounts to the Balance Sheet section.
5. Extend the appropriate amounts to the Income Statement section.
6. Total the amount columns in the Income Statement and Balance Sheet sections.
7. Enter the amount of net income or net loss in the appropriate columns in the Income Statement and Balance Sheet sections.
8. Total and rule the Income Statement and Balance Sheet sections.

Analyze: What is the net income or net loss for the period?

Complete chapter problems one of four ways:

1. **Manual** Glencoe Working Papers

or

2. **Peachtree Complete Accounting** Software

or

3. **QuickBooks** Templates (Problems 8–5, 8–6)

or

4. **Spreadsheet** Templates (Problems 8–4, 8–8)

SPREADSHEET SMART GUIDE

Step-by-Step Instructions: Problem 8–4

1. Select the spreadsheet template for Problem 8–4.
2. Enter your name and the date in the spaces provided on the template.
3. Complete the spreadsheet using the instructions in your working papers.
4. Print the spreadsheet and proof your work.
5. Save your work and exit the spreadsheet program.

PROBLEMS CHAPTER 8

Problem 8–4 (Answers) Preparing a Six-Column Work Sheet

Trial Balance totals: $28,345

Income Statement subtotals: $8,687 Debit, $9,716 Credit

Balance Sheet subtotals: $19,658 Debit, $18,629 Credit

Net Income: $1,029

Income Statement totals: $9,716

Balance Sheet totals: $19,658

Analyze: $1,029

MAKING CONNECTIONS TO DAILY LIFE

Work Sheet Preparation Tips When completing class assignments, such as writing a report, students often create a rough draft first. They may also prepare an outline to organize the information they plan to include in the report. As they write a first draft, students may choose to use a pencil rather than a pen so that they can erase mistakes and make revisions. Like the first draft of a report, the work sheet is a rough draft for the accountant. It is used to organize financial information prior to preparing the end-of-period financial statements. The columns of the work sheet help the accountant sort and classify information.

PROBLEMS CHAPTER 8

Problem 8–5 (Answers) Preparing a Six-Column Work Sheet

Trial Balance totals: $49,862
Income Statement subtotals: $11,339 Debit, $16,256 Credit
Balance Sheet subtotals: $38,523 Debit, $33,606 Credit
Net Income: $4,917

Analyze: The company's revenue is derived from different services (washing, waxing, and interior detailing). By using separate revenue accounts, they can better determine which service provides the most revenue.

Problem 8–6 (Answers) Preparing a Six-Column Work Sheet

Trial Balance totals: $51,136
Income Statement subtotals: $17,711 Debit, $16,092 Credit
Balance Sheet subtotals: $33,425 Debit, $35,044 Credit
Net Loss: $1,619

Analyze: Income Statement section

CHAPTER 8 PROBLEMS

Peachtree®

SMART GUIDE

Step-by-Step Instructions: Problem 8–5

1. Select the problem set for Hot Suds Car Wash (Prob. 8–5).
2. Rename the company and set the system date.
3. Print a General Ledger Trial Balance.
4. End the session.

TIP: As a shortcut, you can choose to print the trial balance from the **General Ledger** Navigation Aid.

Problem 8–5 Preparing a Six-Column Work Sheet

The general ledger for Hot Suds Car Wash shows the following account balances on May 31, the end of the period.

101	Cash in Bank	$9,400
105	Accts. Rec.—Linda Brown	429
110	Accts. Rec.—Valley Auto	372
115	Detailing Supplies	694
120	Detergent Supplies	418
125	Office Equipment	15,195
130	Office Furniture	2,029
135	Car Wash Equipment	7,486
201	Accts. Pay.—Allen Vacuum Systems	4,346
205	Accts. Pay.—O'Brian's Office Supply	2,730
301	Regina Delgado, Capital	26,530
305	Regina Delgado, Withdrawals	2,500
310	Income Summary	
401	Wash Revenue	7,957
405	Wax Revenue	5,329
410	Interior Detailing Revenue	2,970
501	Advertising Expense	1,940
505	Equipment Rental Expense	3,836
510	Maintenance Expense	1,424
520	Rent Expense	3,500
530	Utilities Expense	639

Instructions Prepare a work sheet for Hot Suds Car Wash in your working papers.

Analyze: Why are there three revenue accounts?

Peachtree®

SMART GUIDE

Step-by-Step Instructions: Problem 8–6

1. Select the problem set for Kits & Pups Grooming (Prob. 8–6).
2. Rename the company and set the system date.
3. Print a General Ledger Trial Balance.
4. End the session.

Problem 8–6 Preparing a Six-Column Work Sheet

The account balances in the general ledger of Kits & Pups Grooming at the end of May are:

101	Cash in Bank	$11,194
105	Accts. Rec.—Juan Alvarez	357
110	Accts. Rec.—Nathan Carlsbad	547
115	Accts. Rec.—Martha Giles	1,450
120	Grooming Supplies	842
125	Office Equipment	4,147
130	Office Furniture	935
135	Computer Equipment	2,200
140	Grooming Equipment	1,948
145	Kennel Equipment	7,305
201	Accts. Pay.—Able Store Equipment	7,945
205	Accts. Pay.—Dogs & Cats Inc.	1,205
207	Accts. Pay.—Pet Gourmet	2,846
301	Abe Shultz, Capital	23,048

EXTENDING THE CONTENT

Comparing Work Sheets from Various Businesses Contact local businesses to solicit multiple samples of both manual and computerized work sheets. Display these samples for students to review. Discuss the similarities and the differences among the work sheets. Explain to students that while the format and the number of columns may vary, the purpose of the work sheets is the same. Also note any edits, changes, or corrections on the manual work sheets. Emphasize that the work sheet is a tool to organize accounting data. Ask students to describe the advantages of working with electronic work sheets.

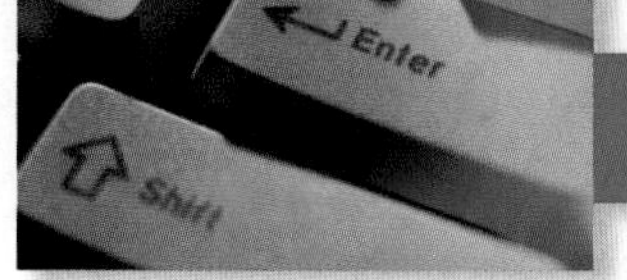

305	Abe Shultz, Withdrawals	2,500
310	Income Summary	—
401	Boarding Revenue	11,596
405	Grooming Revenue	4,496
501	Advertising Expense	3,675
505	Equipment Repair Expense	932
510	Maintenance Expense	2,658
520	Rent Expense	7,500
530	Utilities Expense	2,946

Instructions Prepare a work sheet for the month ended May 31 for Kits & Pups Grooming in your working papers.

Analyze: The balances of revenue and expense accounts are extended to which work sheet section?

Problem 8–7 Preparing a Six-Column Work Sheet

The general ledger account balances on May 31 for Outback Guide Service are:

101	Cash in Bank	$ 2,834
105	Accts. Rec.—Mary Johnson	384
125	Office Supplies	307
130	Office Equipment	5,902
135	Office Furniture	2,804
140	Computer Equipment	3,295
145	Hiking Equipment	922
150	Rafting Equipment	8,351
205	Accts. Pay.—Peak Equipment Inc.	1,204
301	Juanita Ortega, Capital	20,419
302	Juanita Ortega, Withdrawals	1,800
310	Income Summary	—
401	Guide Service Revenue	9,179
501	Advertising Expense	795
505	Maintenance Expense	125
515	Rent Expense	2,000
525	Utilities Expense	1,283

Instructions Prepare a work sheet for Outback Guide Service for the period ended May 31 in your working papers.

Analyze: What is the total of all of Outback's assets?

Problem 8–8 Completing the Work Sheet

The work sheet for Job Connect appears in your working papers. The amounts that have been entered are correct. Several amounts, however, are missing from various columns.

Instructions Calculate all missing amounts and complete the work sheet.

Analyze: What is the net income or net loss for Job Connect?

Peachtree®

SMART GUIDE

Step-by-Step Instructions: Problem 8–7

1. Select the problem set for Outback Guide Service (Prob. 8–7).
2. Rename the company and set the system date.
3. Print a General Ledger Trial Balance.
4. End the session.

SPREADSHEET SMART GUIDE

Step-by-Step Instructions: Problem 8–8

1. Select the spreadsheet template for Problem 8–8.
2. Enter your name and the date in the spaces provided on the template.
3. Complete the spreadsheet using the instructions in your working papers.
4. Print the spreadsheet and proof your work.
5. Save your work and exit the spreadsheet program.

PROBLEMS
CHAPTER 8

Problem 8–7 (Answer) Preparing a Six-Column Work Sheet

Trial Balance totals: $30,802
Income Statement subtotals: $4,203 Debit, $9,179 Credit
Balance Sheet subtotals: $26,599 Debit, $21,623 Credit
Net Income: $4,976

Analyze: $24,799

Problem 8–8 (Answers) Completing the Work Sheet

Trial Balance totals: $69,185
Income Statement subtotals: $8,151 Debit, $10,985 Credit
Balance Sheet subtotals: $61,034 Debit, $58,200 Credit
Net Income: $2,834

Analyze: $2,834

ADDRESSING MULTIPLE LEARNING STYLES

Linguistic Learner Display a transparency illustrating a blank work sheet form or provide students with a copy of a blank work sheet form. With the textbook closed, have students recall all the procedures in preparing a six-column work sheet. Ask students to write a description of each procedure with a brief explanation. Then have students refer to page 193 to check their descriptions with the steps presented in this chapter. Have students make any necessary corrections to their descriptions.

CHAPTER 9 Resource Manager

Section Resources

	Objectives & Standards	Activities & Features	Reproducible Masters
Chapter Opener *Financial Statements for a Sole Proprietorship*	• Explain the purpose of the income statement. • Prepare an income statement. • Explain the purpose of a statement of changes in owner's equity. • Prepare a statement of changes in owner's equity. • Explain the purpose of the balance sheet. • Explain and compute the return on sales percentage. • Calculate liquidity ratios and explain their function. • Prepare a balance sheet. • Define the accounting terms introduced in this chapter. **National Standards for Business Education**: IA3-5, IA10, IA14, IA16, IIIB1	Exploring the Real World of Business, p. 202 Workplace Connections, p. 203	School-to-Work Handbook
Section 1 *The Income Statement*	• Why financial statements are important for business decisions. • The purpose of the income statement. • How to prepare an income statement.	Did You Know?, p. 205 Connect To, p. 208	Demonstration Problems
Section 2 *The Statement of Changes in Owner's Equity*	• The purpose of the statement of changes in owner's equity. • How to prepare the statement of changes in owner's equity.	International Accounting, p. 211 A Matter of Ethics, p. 213 Accounting Careers in Focus, p. 215	Strategies for Teaching International Accounting Demonstration Problems Strategies for Teaching Ethics in Accounting
Section 3 *The Balance Sheet*	• The purpose of a balance sheet. • How to prepare a balance sheet. • How to analyze information on financial reports.	Math Hints, p. 217 Accounting Flashbacks, p. 220 Analyzing Financial Reports, p. 221	Math Review for Accounting Demonstration Problems Internet Resources and Activities Handbook

KEY

Posters — Transparency — Software — Videocassette
Blackline Masters — CD-ROM — Portfolio

MULTIMEDIA RESOURCE

Peachtree	QuickBooks	Spreadsheets	Videos	CD-ROMs
Problem 9–4 *Preparing an Income Statement* Problem 9–5 *Preparing a Statement of Changes in Owner's Equity* Problem 9–6 *Preparing Financial Statements* Problem 9–7 *Preparing Financial Statements*	Problem 9–6 *Preparing Financial Statements*	Problem 9–8 *Preparing a Statement of Changes in Owner's Equity*	***Video Segment: Business Transactions*** After viewing this video, students will be able to describe the great variety of business transactions that trigger an entry in the accounting records. Students will also learn to analyze a transaction from its source document to its effect on the accounting equation.	***Electronic Learning Center (ELC), Chapter 9*** This program is ideal for visual learners since it incorporates video images, animation, and graphics to enliven the content of each lesson. ***Interactive Lesson Planner (ILP), Chapter 9*** This CD-ROM combines the versatility of an electronic lesson planner with the convenience of teacher classroom resources.

SCANS Correlation Chart

FOUNDATION SKILLS

Basic Skills:	Reading	Writing	Math	Listening	Speaking	
Thinking Skills:	Creative Thinking	Decision Making	Problem Solving	Seeing Things in the Mind's Eye	Knowing How to Learn	Reasoning
Personal Qualities:	Responsibility	Self-Esteem	Sociability	Self-Management	Integrity/Honesty	

WORKPLACE COMPETENCIES

Resources:	Allocating Time	Allocating Money	Allocating Material and Facility Resources	Allocating Human Resources		
Information:	Acquiring and Evaluating Information	Organizing and Maintaining Information	Interpreting and Communicating Information	Using Computers to Process Information		
Interpersonal Skills:	Participating as a Member of a Team	Teaching Others	Serving Clients/ Customers	Exercising Leadership	Negotiating to Arrive at a Decision	Working with Cultural Diversity
Systems:	Understanding Systems	Monitoring and Correcting Performance	Improving and Designing Systems			
Technology:	Selecting Technology	Applying Technology to Task	Maintaining and Troubleshooting Technology			

*Highlighted blocks indicate areas covered in the chapter. Additional SCANS skills are also covered throughout the *Teacher Wraparound Edition.*

Assessment

Student Edition
- Check Your Understanding, pp. 209, 214, 222
- Chapter 9 Problems, pp. 227–229

Assessment and Evaluation Masters
- Chapter 9 Study Plan, *Glencoe Workbook*
- Chapter 9 Self-Test, *Glencoe Workbook*
- Chapter 9 Test, *Chapter Tests* Booklet
- Chapter 9 Activity, *School-to-Work Handbook*
- Chapter 9 **Exam***View*

Teacher Wraparound Edition
- Critical Thinking Activity, p. 206
- Reteaching Section 1, p. 209
- Reteaching Section 2, p. 214
- Reteaching Section 3, p. 222
- Chapter 9 Quiz, p. 223

Transparencies

	Teaching Transparencies	Solution Transparencies
Section 1:	9–1, 9–2, 9–3, 9–4, 9–5, 9–6	Problem 9–1
Section 2:	9–7, 9–8, 9–9, 9–10	Problem 9–2
Section 3:	9–11, 9–12, 9–13	Problem 9–3
End of Chapter:		Problems 9–4, 9–5, 9–6, 9–7, 9–8

TEACHER CLASSROOM RESOURCES

This is a representation of key blackline masters available in the Teacher Classroom Resources.

Teaching Aids

Transparency Examples

Section Focus Transparencies

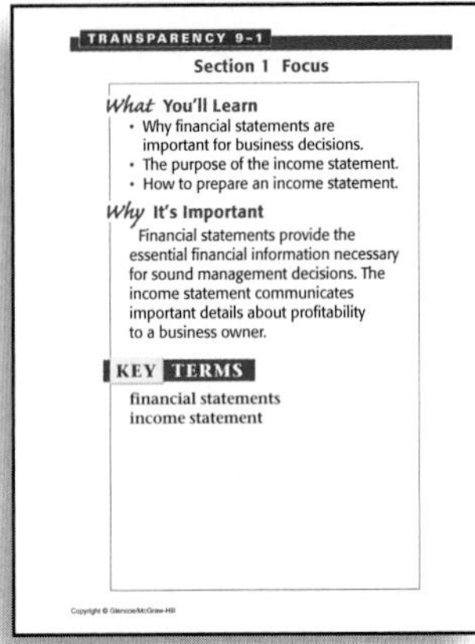

TRANSPARENCY 9-1

Section 1 Focus

What You'll Learn
- Why financial statements are important for business decisions.
- The purpose of the income statement.
- How to prepare an income statement.

Why It's Important

Financial statements provide the essential financial information necessary for sound management decisions. The income statement communicates important details about profitability to a business owner.

KEY TERMS

financial statements
income statement

Teaching Transparencies

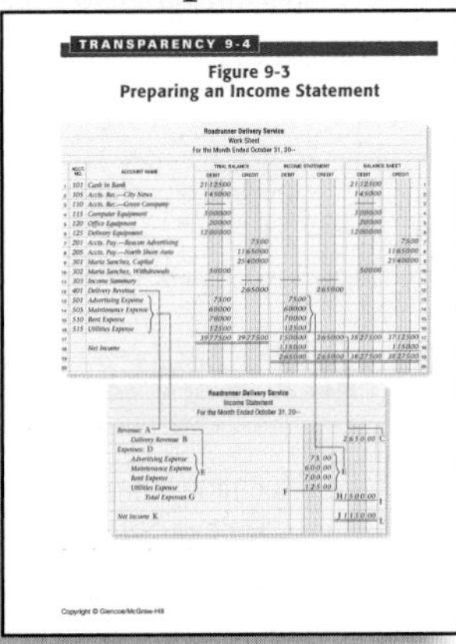

TRANSPARENCY 9-4

Figure 9-3
Preparing an Income Statement

Teaching Transparencies

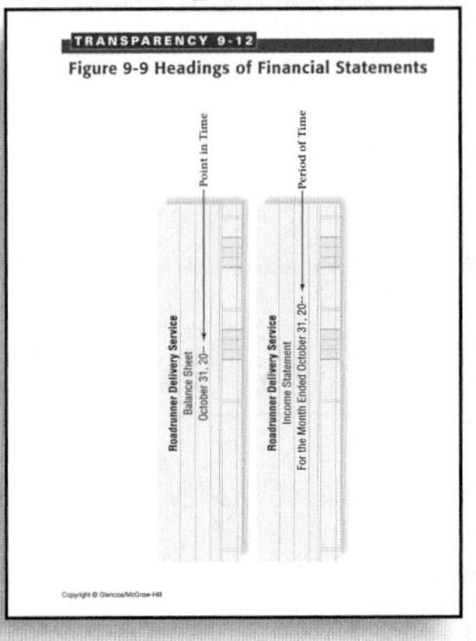

TRANSPARENCY 9-12

Figure 9-9 Headings of Financial Statements

Solution Transparencies

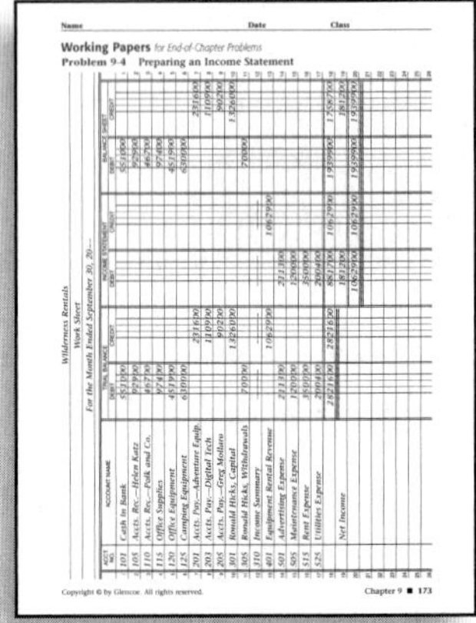

Working Papers for End-of-Chapter Problems
Problem 9-4 Preparing an Income Statement

Demonstration Problems

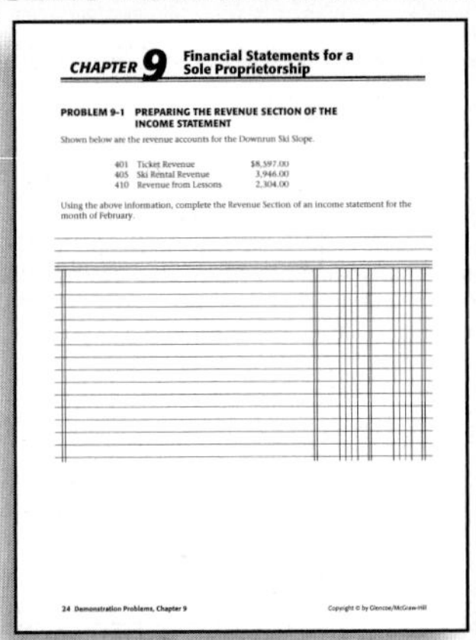

CHAPTER 9 Financial Statements for a Sole Proprietorship

PROBLEM 9-1 PREPARING THE REVENUE SECTION OF THE INCOME STATEMENT

Lesson Plans

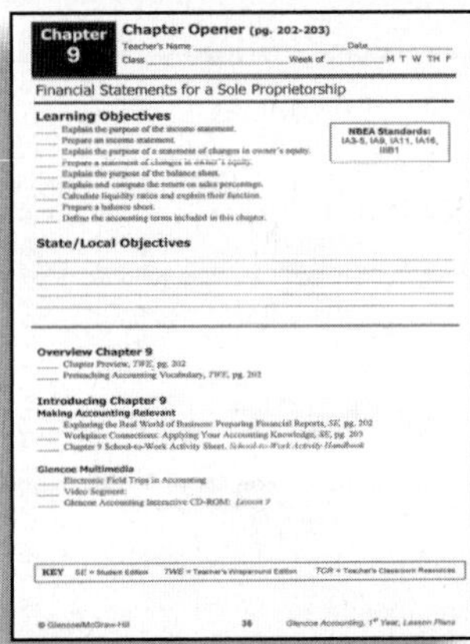

Chapter 9 Chapter Opener (pg. 202-203)

Financial Statements for a Sole Proprietorship

Learning Objectives

State/Local Objectives

Block Scheduling

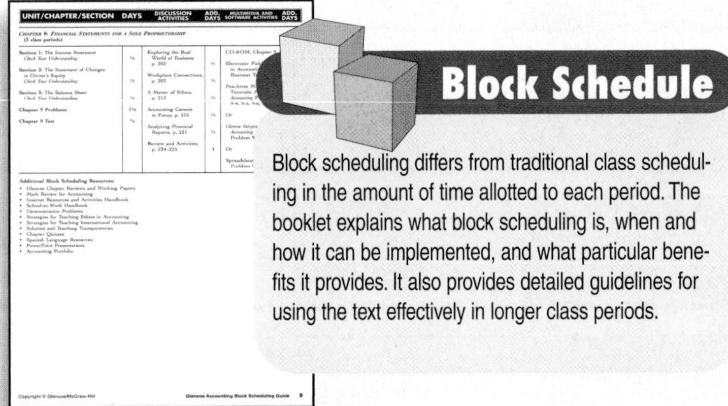

Block Schedule

Block scheduling differs from traditional class scheduling in the amount of time allotted to each period. The booklet explains what block scheduling is, when and how it can be implemented, and what particular benefits it provides. It also provides detailed guidelines for using the text effectively in longer class periods.

Enrichment and Application

Strategies for Teaching Ethics in Accounting

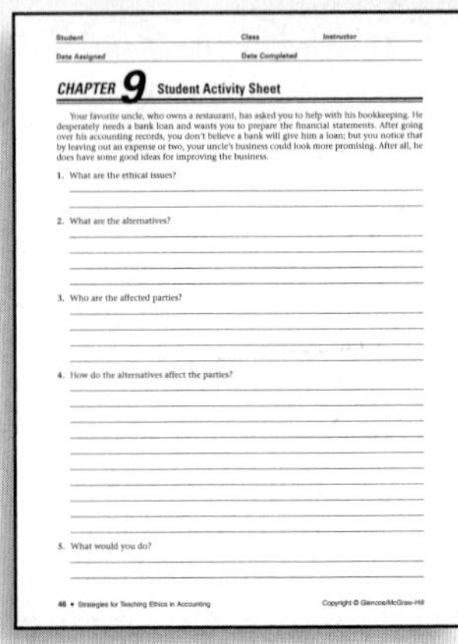

CHAPTER 9 Student Activity Sheet

Strategies for Teaching International Accounting

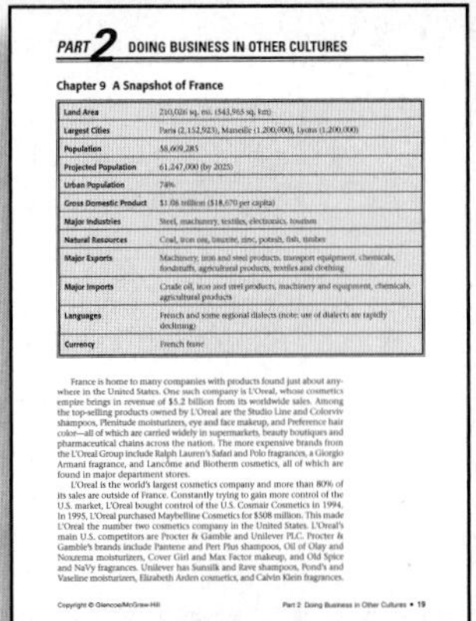

PART 2 DOING BUSINESS IN OTHER CULTURES

Chapter 9 A Snapshot of France

School-to-Work Handbook

CHAPTER 9 SCHOOL-TO-WORK ACTIVITY

Financial Statements for a Sole Proprietorship

Meeting Different Ability Levels

Chapter Reviews and Working Papers (CRWP)

Working Papers

Review

Student Study Plan

Self-Test

Real-World Multimedia CD-ROM

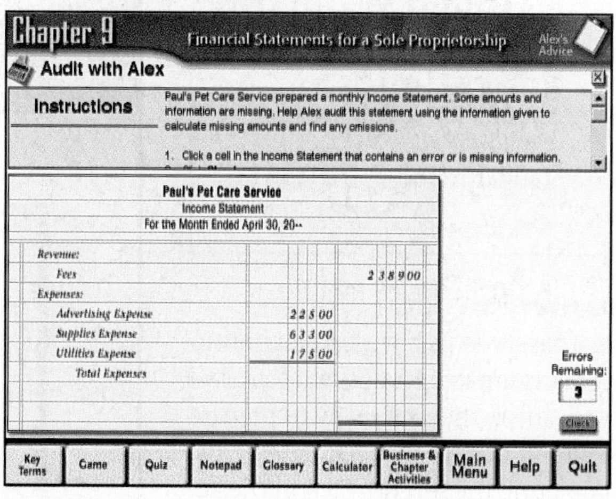

Key to Ability Levels

Each section gives skill-building activities. Each activity has been labeled for use with students of various learning styles and abilities.

L1 Level 1 activities are basic activities and should be within the range of all students.

L2 Level 2 activities are average activities and should be within the range of average and above average students.

L3 Level 3 activities are challenging activities designed for the ability range of above average students.

ELL ELL activities should be within the ability range of English Language Learners.

Assessment and Evaluation

Chapter Tests

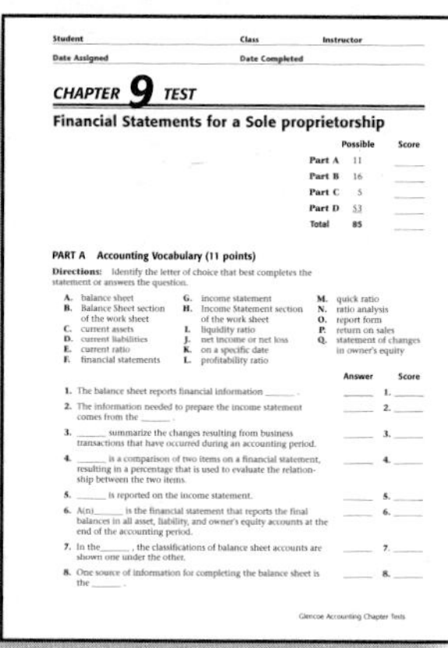
CHAPTER 9 TEST

Financial Statements for a Sole proprietorship

Chapter Quiz

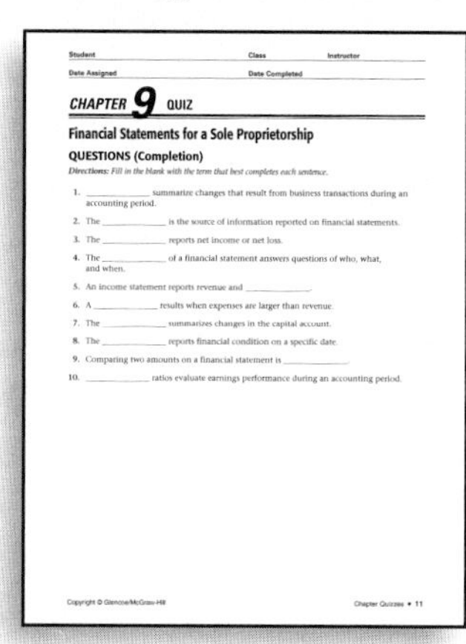
CHAPTER 9 QUIZ

Financial Statements for a Sole Proprietorship

Teaching Resources at a Glance

Application Resources

- Glencoe Chapter Review and Working Papers, SE and TAE
- School-to-Work Handbook, SE and TM
- Accounting Portfolio, SE and TM

Reproducible Masters

- Demonstration Problems
- Lesson Plans
- Block Scheduling
- Spanish Language Resources

Glencoe Accounting Professional Development Series

- Strategies for Teaching Ethics in Accounting
- Accounting Competitive Event Review
- Math Review for Accounting
- Strategies for Teaching International Accounting
- Internet Resources and Activities Handbook

Transparency Package

- Section Focus Transparencies
- Teaching Transparencies
- Source Document Transparencies
- Solution Transparencies

Performance Assessment

- **Exam***View* CD-ROM
- Chapter Tests
- Chapter Quizzes
- Unit Tests
- Audit Tests
- Printed Testbank

Multimedia Resources

- Electronic Learning Center:
  - Multimedia CD-ROMs
  - Peachtree software, tutorials, templates, and solutions
  - Spreadsheet templates
- Using QuickBooks with Glencoe Accounting
- Interactive Lesson Planner
- Electronic Field Trips in Accounting
- PowerPoint Presentation
- Web site: glencoeaccounting.glencoe.com

OVERVIEW CHAPTER 9

Correlations to National Standards for Business Education

(See pages T50–T51 for a detailed correlation chart.)

Standards: IA3–5, IA10, IA14, IA16, IIIB1

Chapter Preview

Now that students have learned how to collect account information and complete a work sheet, they are ready to prepare the end-of-period financial statements. Completing the seventh step in the accounting cycle, students will learn to prepare an income statement, a statement of changes in owner's equity, and a balance sheet in this chapter.

Section Overviews

- Section 1—*The Income Statement*
- Section 2—*The Statement of Changes in Owner's Equity*
- Section 3—*The Balance Sheet*

Chapter Vocabulary

financial statements
income statement
statement of changes in owner's equity
balance sheet
report form
ratio analysis
profitability ratio
return on sales
liquidity ratio
current ratio
current assets
current liabilities
quick ratio

Preteaching Accounting Vocabulary

Group Discussions: Discuss the definitions of the new terms in class. Then divide students into groups of four or five. Assign each group a list of terms. Have each group write sentences applying its terms. Ask a spokesperson for each group to share the group's sentences with the class. L1

CHAPTER 9

Financial Statements for a Sole Proprietorship

Learning Objectives

When you have completed this chapter, you will be able to:

- Explain the purpose of the income statement.
- Prepare an income statement.
- Explain the purpose of a statement of changes in owner's equity.
- Prepare a statement of changes in owner's equity.
- Explain the purpose of the balance sheet.
- Explain and compute the return on sales percentage.
- Calculate liquidity ratios and explain their function.
- Prepare a balance sheet.
- Define the accounting terms introduced in this chapter.

Exploring the Real World of Business

PREPARING FINANCIAL REPORTS

Imagine yourself just inches from the jaws of a shark–of course, from behind a thick glass wall.

The **New England Aquarium** in Boston allows you to do just that. Public aquariums date from the mid-1800s when it was discovered that marine life could live in glass containers. Modern aquariums do much more than just exhibit various forms of marine life, though. The **New England Aquarium** also supports projects that protect endangered whales and conserve coral reefs in the Indian Ocean. Staff members rescue hundreds of stranded seals, dolphins, whales, and turtles from local beaches each year.

As a public organization, the **New England Aquarium** funds its operations in several different ways. Sources of funds include memberships sold to the general public, admission fees, sales of **Aquarium**-sponsored books and films, and grants from corporate sponsors like Fleet Bank or Pepsi. The **Aquarium's** financial statements show the amounts of revenue from each source as well as how that revenue was spent during the year.

What do you think?

Why is it important for the **New England Aquarium** to prepare financial statements even though their purpose is not to earn a profit?

New England Aquarium

Exploring the Real World of Business

New England Aquarium

The New England Aquarium draws thousands of visitors each year, but admission fees alone do not support the cost of operating the Aquarium and its environmental programs. Like managers of for-profit businesses, Aquarium managers focus much of their attention on gaining revenue for the organization.

What do you think? (Answers)

Like any other organization, the Aquarium spends money on its operations. Its managers need financial records to tell them how much money is brought in from each revenue source. In turn, they use this information to monitor expenses and to determine which conservation programs to fund.

Workplace Connections

Applying Your Accounting Knowledge

A sole proprietorship can be a small business with a few employees or a large business with thousands of employees. In a small business, one person may handle the accounting duties. A larger business might have several employees working in an accounting department. Whether large or small, the preparation of financial statements is an important task.

Investigate:

1. Do you work for a sole proprietorship, a corporation, or a partnership?
2. In your work location, approximately how many people are employed?
3. If you were an accountant, do you think you would prefer to work for a large organization or a small one? Why?

Glencoe Accounting Online

Visit the *Glencoe Accounting* Web site at **glencoeaccounting.glencoe.com** for additional activities and information.

INTRODUCING CHAPTER 9

Making Accounting Relevant

Workplace Connections: Applying Your Accounting Knowledge

Discussion: Financial statements can be thought of as the map to what is happening in a business. Financial statements tell owners and managers how the business is changing as a result of operations. Those changes will help owners and managers decide how to operate the business in the future.

Investigate (Answers)

1. Students' responses will vary. Try to learn how several local businesses are organized so you can share that information with students.
2. Answers will vary.
3. Preferences will vary. Those who work in large organizations often have more opportunities to advance in their careers and may earn higher pay. Those who work in a small organization may learn more diverse skills because work is less specialized.

School-to-Work Activity

Student ______ Class ______ Instructor ______

Date Assigned ______ Date Completed ______

CHAPTER 9 SCHOOL-TO-WORK ACTIVITY

Financial Statements for a Sole Proprietorship

Name of work site: ______

Name of work site mentor: ______

Title or position of mentor: ______

At the end of a fiscal period, financial reports are prepared to show the effects of business transactions for the period. Consult with your work site mentor or the person responsible for accounting or bookkeeping for your company to complete the following investigation of the preparation of end-of-period financial statements at your company.

After completing this school-to-work investigation, you will be able to:

- identify who prepares and analyzes end-of-period financial statements at your company, and
- describe your company's income statements, changes in owner's equity statements, and balance sheets.

1. Financial statements are reports prepared to summarize the changes resulting from business transactions that have occurred during a fiscal period.

1a. Who prepares financial statements at your company?

1b. When are financial statements prepared at your company?

2. Comparing information shown on the financial statements for different fiscal periods helps owners spot trends that indicate the "health" of a business.

2a. Who analyzes financial statements at your company?

2b. What steps does he or she take to analyze financial statements? (You will learn about specific types of analyses in Chapter 28.)

School-to-Work Handbook • 17

GLENCOE MULTIMEDIA

Electronic Field Trips in Accounting *Video Segment: Business Transactions*
After viewing this video, students will be able to describe the great variety of business transactions that trigger an entry in the accounting records.

Glencoe Accounting: Electronic Learning Center *Chapter 9*
The CD-ROM program is ideal for visual learners since it incorporates video images, animation, and graphics to enliven the content of each lesson.

1 FOCUS

Introducing the Section

In this section students learn the purpose of financial statements. They also learn how to prepare an income statement and how to describe the fiscal period covered by the statement.

Section Concepts

- Why financial statements are important for business decisions.
- The purpose of the income statement.
- How to prepare an income statement.

Visual Learning

Section 1 Focus

Use **Transparency 9–1** to introduce section concepts.

BELL RINGER

Compare and Contrast: Write the questions Who?, What?, and When? on the chalkboard. Point out that students answered those questions when writing the heading of a work sheet. Have students tell you what information answers each question. Show the heading for an income statement, and have students compare the similarities and differences. L1

Visual Learning

Figure 9–1 The Accounting Cycle with the Seventh Step Highlighted

Use **Transparency 9–2** to review the first six steps in the accounting cycle and to introduce students to the next step in the end-of-period work.

SECTION 1

The Income Statement

***What* You'll Learn**

- Why financial statements are important for business decisions.
- The purpose of the income statement.
- How to prepare an income statement.

***Why* It's Important**

Financial statements provide the essential financial information necessary for sound management decisions. The income statement communicates important details about profitability to a business owner.

KEY TERMS

financial statements
income statement

To operate a business profitably, a business owner needs to have current financial information. Businesses ranging from Mobil Corporation to a rural dairy farm must organize financial information to evaluate profits or losses. **Financial statements** are prepared to summarize the changes resulting from business transactions that occur during an accounting period. As you can see from **Figure 9–1**, the preparation of financial statements is the seventh step in the accounting cycle.

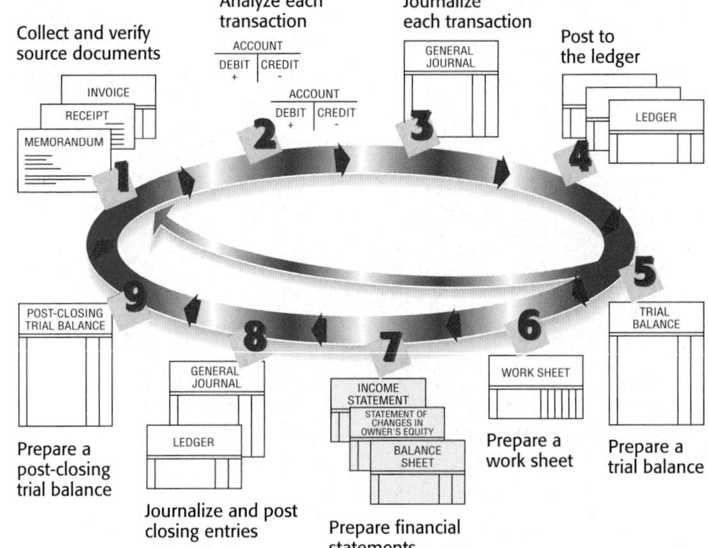

Figure 9–1 The Accounting Cycle with the Seventh Step Highlighted

Financial Statements

The primary financial statements prepared for a sole proprietorship are the income statement and the balance sheet. A third statement, the statement of changes in owner's equity, is also often prepared. The financial statements may be handwritten or typed but most often are prepared on a computer. When using a computerized accounting system, the information for preparing the financial statements is stored in the

RESOURCE MANAGER

Reproducible Masters
- Lesson Plans
- Chapter Reviews and Working Papers (CRWP) TAE
- Demonstration Problems

Transparencies
- Section Focus Transparency
- Teaching Transparencies
- Source Document Transparencies
- Solution Transparencies

Multimedia
- Exam*View* CD-ROM
- Electronic Learning Center CD-ROM
- Interactive Lesson Planner CD-ROM

computer. When a business owner needs financial statements, he or she can use the computer to generate them without first preparing a work sheet. Let's learn how to prepare financial statements for a service business such as Roadrunner.

The Income Statement

The **income statement** reports the net income or net loss for the period. As you recall from Chapter 8, net income or net loss is the difference between total revenue and total expenses. The main purpose of the income statement is to provide a report of the revenue earned and the expenses incurred over a specific period of time. For this reason, it is sometimes called a "profit-and-loss statement" or an "earnings statement."

The income statement contains the following sections:

- the heading
- the revenue for the period
- the expenses for the period
- the net income or net loss for the period

> **Did You Know?**
>
> **Earnings**
> Not-for-profit organizations earn about 5 percent, or about $430 billion, of total U.S. national income. For-profit organizations earn around 83 percent, with government accounting for the rest.

The Heading

Like the work sheet heading, the heading of an income statement has three parts:

1. The name of the business ***(Who?)***
2. The name of the report ***(What?)***
3. The period covered ***(When?)***

The heading for the Roadrunner Delivery Service income statement is shown in **Figure 9–2.** Each line of the heading is centered on the width of the statement.

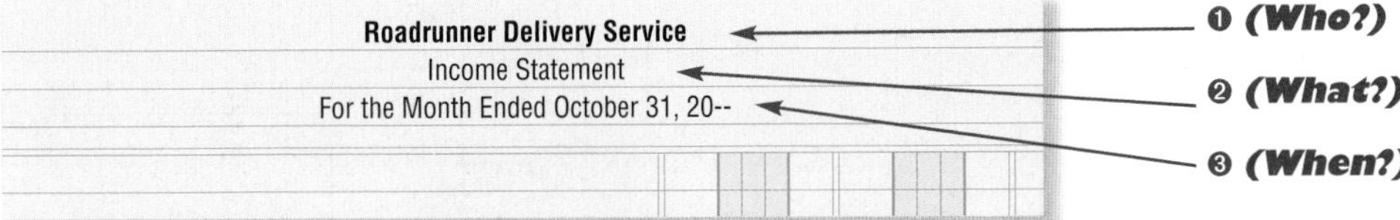

Figure 9–2 The Heading for an Income Statement

When preparing an income statement heading, be sure to follow the wording and capitalization shown in **Figure 9–2.** The wording of the date line is especially important. The reporting period will vary from business to business and must be clearly identified.

When preparing financial statements, a business owner uses the same fiscal periods year after year. This consistency allows the owner to compare and analyze the data on financial statements from one period to the next. This comparison is difficult if one statement covers a period of one month while another statement covers a period of six months.

Great Ideas *From the Classroom of...*

Checking Students' Computer Activities Using accounting software is easier when students save their work both before and after closing. Check your students' work before they perform the closing entries, and have them correct errors. Use the teacher check disk to identify errors after they perform the closing option.

Edward Schencks, Jr.
Sacopee Valley High School
Hiram, Maine

2 TEACH

GUIDED PRACTICE

Reading Accounting

- Have students read the section on preparing an income statement and then write their own guidelines for how to do the statement. For example, they might create an annotated outline where item 1 is the heading, 1(a) is who, 1(b) is what, and 1(c) is when. Items 2 and 3 would be revenue and expenses. Students could use their outlines for problems and other applications. L1
- Try to obtain an annual report or financial statements printed in your students' first language. Share the statements in class. ELL

Concept Development: Financial Statements

Discussion: After briefly reviewing the first six steps in the accounting cycle, introduce the topic of financial statements. Bring an annual report for a well-known business to class and share the financial statement section with students. Remind students that accountants prepare financial statements for a constant fiscal period so that data may be compared and analyzed from one period to the next. L1

Visual Learning

Figure 9–2 The Heading for an Income Statement
Use **Transparency** 9–3 to discuss the heading information for an income statement. Point out that the heading varies for each type of financial statement. The date line for an income statement indicates a period of time rather than a specific date.

2 TEACH (Cont'd.)

Concept Development: The Income Statement

Discussion: Have students look at the columns on the income-statement form. Explain that the two amount columns do not represent debit and credit columns. Discuss why expense account balances are entered in the first column, and the total is entered in the second column. Make sure students know that these amounts are taken from the Income Statement section of the work sheet. L1

Visual Learning

Figure 9–3 Preparing an Income Statement

Use **Transparency 9–4** to show students the work sheet data that is used to prepare the income statement. Guide students through preparing the revenue section. Explain that since there's only one revenue account, the total is entered in the right column. Then contrast the expenses section, which has several accounts. Those balances are listed in the first column, with the total going in the right column.

Demonstration Problem Step-by-Step Practice

Use demonstration problem 9–1 to show students how to complete the heading and the revenue section of the income statement.

Reporting Period	Wording of Date Line
One month	For the Month Ended October 31, 20--
One quarter	For the Quarter Ended March 30, 20--
One year	For the Year Ended June 30, 20--

The Revenue Section

After the heading is complete, enter the revenue earned for the period. Look at **Figure 9–3.** The Income Statement section of the work sheet is the information source used in preparing the income statement.

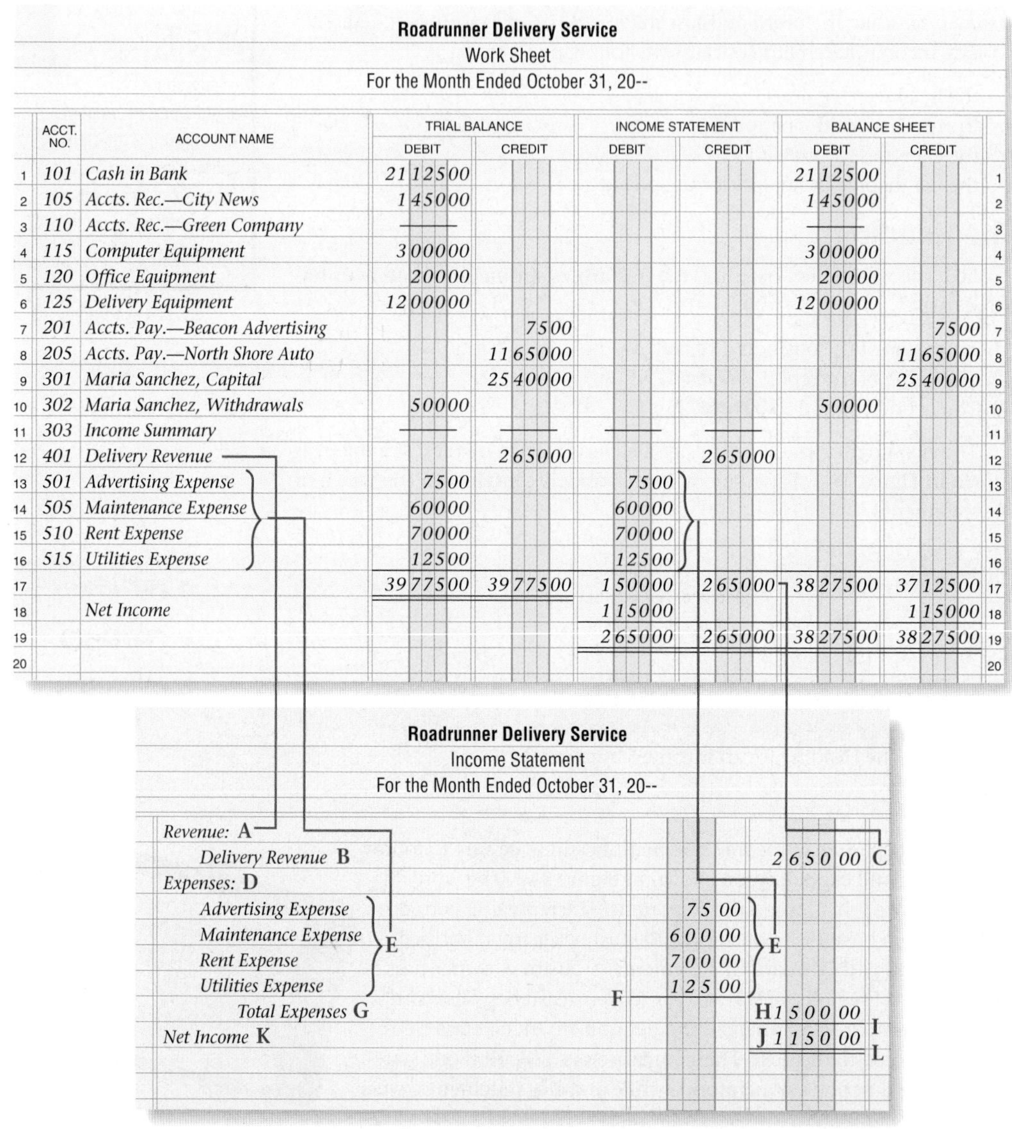

Roadrunner Delivery Service
Work Sheet
For the Month Ended October 31, 20--

	ACCT. NO.	ACCOUNT NAME	TRIAL BALANCE DEBIT	TRIAL BALANCE CREDIT	INCOME STATEMENT DEBIT	INCOME STATEMENT CREDIT	BALANCE SHEET DEBIT	BALANCE SHEET CREDIT	
1	101	Cash in Bank	21 125 00				21 125 00		1
2	105	Accts. Rec.—City News	1 450 00				1 450 00		2
3	110	Accts. Rec.—Green Company	—				—		3
4	115	Computer Equipment	3 000 00				3 000 00		4
5	120	Office Equipment	200 00				200 00		5
6	125	Delivery Equipment	12 000 00				12 000 00		6
7	201	Accts. Pay.—Beacon Advertising		75 00				75 00	7
8	205	Accts. Pay.—North Shore Auto		11 650 00				11 650 00	8
9	301	Maria Sanchez, Capital		25 400 00				25 400 00	9
10	302	Maria Sanchez, Withdrawals	500 00				500 00		10
11	303	Income Summary	—	—	—	—			11
12	401	Delivery Revenue		2 650 00		2 650 00			12
13	501	Advertising Expense	75 00		75 00				13
14	505	Maintenance Expense	600 00		600 00				14
15	510	Rent Expense	700 00		700 00				15
16	515	Utilities Expense	125 00		125 00				16
17			39 775 00	39 775 00	1 500 00	2 650 00	38 275 00	37 125 00	17
18		Net Income			1 150 00			1 150 00	18
19					2 650 00	2 650 00	38 275 00	38 275 00	19
20									20

Roadrunner Delivery Service
Income Statement
For the Month Ended October 31, 20--

Revenue: A		
Delivery Revenue B		2 650 00 C
Expenses: D		
Advertising Expense E	75 00 E	
Maintenance Expense	600 00	
Rent Expense	700 00	
Utilities Expense	125 00 F	
Total Expenses G		H 1 500 00 I
Net Income K		J 1 150 00 L

Figure 9–3 Preparing an Income Statement

CRITICAL THINKING ACTIVITY

Synthesizing Information Jane and Paul Schmidt own a pizza restaurant. All revenue comes from food sales in the restaurant. The Schmidts will begin offering carry-out service and free delivery next month. Explain why the Schmidts should maintain separate accounts for revenues generated from deliveries and carry-out services. (By recording revenues in separate accounts, the Schmidts will be able to assess the income from each new service. For example, if deliveries produce substantial revenue, the Schmidts might consider expanding the delivery area. If the free delivery does not generate sufficient revenue to justify the expense of the drivers, the Schmidts may want to discontinue the service.)

The income statement for Roadrunner is prepared on standard accounting stationery, which has a column for account names and two amount columns. The two amount columns are used to separate individual account balances from totals. The first amount column is used to enter the balances of the individual revenue and expense accounts. The second amount column is used to enter totals: total revenue, total expenses, and net income (or net loss).

Refer to **Figure 9–3** as you read the procedures for preparing an income statement:

1. Write "Revenue:" on the first line at the left side of the form. A
2. Enter the revenue account names beginning on the second line, indented about a half inch from the left edge of the form. B
3. Enter the balance of the revenue account(s). Since Roadrunner has only one revenue account, **Delivery Revenue**, total revenue is the same as the balance of the one revenue account. The balance is thus written in the second, or totals, column. C

Roadrunner uses one revenue account, which represents its only source of revenue. Many businesses have more than one source of revenue and thus have a separate revenue account for each source. For example, a swim club might have revenue accounts such as **Membership Fees**, **Pool Rental**, and **Instruction Revenue.**

If a business has more than one revenue account, the individual account balances are entered in the first amount column. Total revenue is then written on a separate line in the second amount column. **Figure 9–4** illustrates the revenue section of the income statement for a business with more than one revenue account. Notice that the words "Total Revenue" are indented about one inch from the left edge of the form.

Revenue:		
Rental Revenue	11 2 3 0 00	
Repair Revenue	4 8 5 0 00	
Total Revenue		16 0 8 0 00

Figure 9–4 Income Statement with More Than One Revenue Account

The Expenses Section

After total revenue is entered, the expenses incurred during the period are reported. The expense account names and the balances in the Income Statement section of the work sheet are used to prepare the expenses section of the income statement. Refer to **Figure 9–3** as you read the following instructions:

1. On the line following the revenue section, write "Expenses:" at the left side of the form. D
2. On the following lines, write the names of the expense accounts, indented half an inch, in the order that they appear on the work sheet. Since there are several expense accounts, enter the individual balances in the first amount column. E

COOPERATIVE LEARNING ACTIVITY

Co-Op Co-Op Divide the class into small groups of four or five students each. Give each group a list of account names and balances for a service business. Ask each group to complete a work sheet and prepare financial statements (income statement, statement of changes in owner's equity, and balance sheet). When the groups are finished, have them compare their statements. If differences in the statements are found, have the groups locate and correct the errors.

2 TEACH (Cont'd.)

Teaching Tips

Point out the accounting principle of matching revenue earned during an accounting period to the expenses of earning that revenue.

Also mention that totals are placed in the second amount column to make them stand out and be more easily read.

Suggest that students use a calculator or adding machine with a tape to help them find errors in their calculations.

Visual Learning

Figure 9–4 Income Statement with More Than One Revenue Account

Using **Transparency 9–5**, show students how to report revenue from more than one source. Point out that businesses track revenue from different sources just as they keep track of different kinds of expenses.

Demonstration Problem
Step-by-Step Practice

Use demonstration problem 9–2 to give students practice in preparing an income statement.

2 TEACH (Cont'd.)

Critical Thinking: Tell students that they are preparing an income statement. When they subtract total expenses from total revenue, they get a different amount of net income than they calculated on the work sheet. Ask students how they would go about finding and correcting the error. (Re-add columns to verify totals, check that amounts were transferred correctly from the work sheet and that all are included, check that amounts are in the correct columns.) L1

Visual Learning

Figure 9–5 Income Statement Showing a Net Loss

Use **Transparency 9–6** to show students how to report a net loss on the income statement.

Demonstration Problem
Step-by-Step Practice

Use demonstration problem 9-3 to give students practice preparing an income statement reporting a net loss.

Teaching Tip

Remind students that the income or loss is first calculated on the work sheet.

CONNECT TO . . . HISTORY

The issue of taxes toppled governments during the 1700s. Rallying under the cry of "No taxation without representation!" American colonists fought for their independence from England. Likewise, the lopsided tax structure that supported the lavish lifestyles of the aristocracy was a major cause of the French Revolution.

3. Draw a single rule under the last expense account balance. F
4. Write the words "Total Expenses" on the line following the last expense account name, indented about one inch. G
5. Add the balances for all the expense accounts. Write the total expenses amount in the second amount column, one line below the last expense account balance. H

The Net Income Section

The next step is to enter net income. Net income, remember, occurs when total revenue is greater than total expenses. Refer to **Figure 9–3** as you read the following instructions for the preparation of the net income section.

1. Draw a single rule under the total expenses amount. I
2. Subtract the total expenses from the total revenue to find net income. Enter the net income in the second amount column under the total expenses amount. J
3. On the same line, write the words "Net Income" at the left side of the form. K
4. If the amount of net income matches the amount shown on the work sheet, draw a double rule under the net income amount. L

The income statement is complete.

If the amount of net income shown on the work sheet does not equal the amount shown on the income statement, there is an error. Since the work sheet is balanced and ruled, the error probably occurred while the income statement was being prepared. An account balance may be omitted or entered incorrectly, or there may be an error in addition or subtraction. Find and correct the error.

Key Points

Net Income or Net Loss
The net income or net loss reported on the income statement must match the amount calculated on the work sheet.

Showing a Net Loss

If total expenses are greater than total revenue, there is a net loss. To determine the amount of net loss, subtract total revenue from total expenses. Enter the net loss in the second amount column under total expenses amount. Write the words "Net Loss" on the same line at the left side of the form. **Figure 9–5** illustrates how to report a net loss.

Revenue:		
Delivery Revenue		3 170 00
Expenses:		
Advertising Expense	275 00	
Maintenance Expense	750 00	
Miscellaneous Expense	270 00	
Rent Expense	1 900 00	
Utilities Expense	325 00	
Total Expenses		3 520 00
Net Loss	–	350 00

Figure 9–5 Income Statement Showing a Net Loss

INTERDISCIPLINARY CONNECTIONS ACTIVITY

History Before the twentieth century, taxation was a way to meet the financial obligations of the government. Today, taxes have three main functions: (1) to provide money for government functions; (2) for economic significance—it stabilizes the money supply through raising or lowering tax rates; and (3) to provide for the redistribution of wealth—to help level the financial inequalities in our society. Discuss with students the purpose of taxation. Encourage students who work to share their ideas.

SECTION 1 Check Your Understanding

Now that you have studied this section, complete the following questions and problems.

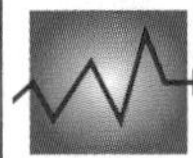

Thinking Critically

1. What three financial statements are prepared for a sole proprietorship?
2. Why is it important to divide the income statement into sections?

Communicating Accounting

Anna is the accounting clerk for the New Country Deli. For several months, Anna has tried to convince the owner to purchase a computer. Anna believes that a computer would save time, especially when financial statements are being prepared. She has explained that the information for preparing financial statements can be stored in the computer files. Then, when the financial statements are needed, it is not necessary to prepare a work sheet. The owner believes that a computer will cost too much money. What would you say to convince the owner that a computer should be purchased for use in the business?

Problem 9–1 Analyzing a Source Document

Instructions Based on the receipt shown below, answer the following questions in your working papers.

1. What is the name of the business that received the money?
2. How much money was received?
3. Who paid the money?
4. Why was the money paid?
5. When was the payment made?
6. Who received the money and made out the receipt?
7. Where is the business that received the money located?

Stratford Learning Center
243 Eastern Road
Roxbury, NY 14752

RECEIPT
No. 1834

Aug. 21 20 --

RECEIVED FROM Sandra Miller $ 832.00

Eight hundred thirty-two and no/100 DOLLARS

FOR On account

RECEIVED BY Rose Hughes

CHAPTER 9
SECTION 1, PAGES 204–209

3 ASSESS

Thinking Critically (Answers)

1. Income statement, balance sheet, and statement of changes in owner's equity.
2. To present information clearly so that revenue may be compared with the expenses incurred to produce that revenue.

Communicating Accounting (Answers)

Answers will vary. Students should mention that for most businesses the use of a computer will save time in data processing, which, in time, will cover the cost of the computer.

Problem 9–1 (Answers)

1. Stratford Learning Center
2. $832
3. Sandra Miller
4. Payment on account
5. August 21
6. Rose Hughes
7. Roxbury, New York

GO TO Chapter Reviews and Working Papers Refer students to the Chapter 9 workbook pages to answer *Check Your Understanding* activities.

4 CLOSE

Section Wrap-Up

Writing Exercise: Have students write a paragraph or two describing how the income statement follows the matching principle. L1

RETEACHING SECTION 1

Identifying the Fiscal Period on an Income Statement The date line in the heading of an income statement is critical because it identifies the fiscal period. Without the date line, you would not know whether the reported net income was earned in a month, a quarter, or a year. Call a local stockbroker and ask for copies of quarterly and annual reports to share with your class. Have students look at the report dates and discuss the fiscal periods indicated by those dates.

1 FOCUS

Introducing the Section
In this section students learn why and how a business prepares a statement of changes in owner's equity. They also learn how to report either net income or net loss on the statement.

Section Concepts
- The purpose of the statement of changes in owner's equity.
- How to prepare the statement of changes in owner's equity.

Visual Learning
Section 2 Focus
Use **Transparency 9–7** to introduce section concepts.

BELL RINGER
Observation and Analysis: Have students list the businesses in your local area that are sole proprietorships. Write the names on the chalkboard. Then ask students to discuss the answer to this question: How do the owners know how their capital accounts have changed each fiscal period as a result of business operations? L2

Concept Development: The Statement of Changes in Owner's Equity
Discussion: Emphasize to students that the purpose of this statement is to report all changes in owner's equity over an entire fiscal period. It is helpful to go through the statement and explain why each item is added or subtracted. Point out that information on this statement will be used to prepare a section of the balance sheet. Note that this financial statement is used for the proprietorship form of business organization, as indicated by its name. L1

SECTION 2

The Statement of Changes in Owner's Equity

***What* You'll Learn**
- The purpose of the statement of changes in owner's equity.
- How to prepare the statement of changes in owner's equity.

***Why* It's Important**
One way to evaluate how a business is performing is by tracking the increase or decrease in owner's equity.

KEY TERMS
statement of changes in owner's equity

One of the most important concerns of a business owner is whether the owner's equity in the business has increased or decreased during the period. An increase in owner's equity means the owner's claims to the assets of the business have grown. A decrease means the owner's claims to the assets of the business have been reduced.

The Statement of Changes in Owner's Equity

The **statement of changes in owner's equity** summarizes changes in the owner's capital account as a result of business transactions during the period. This statement is prepared at the end of the period and, as you will see in the next section, is a supporting document of the balance sheet.

The heading of the statement of changes in financial position is set up in the same manner as the heading for the income statement.

1. The first line consists of the name of the business ***(Who?)***
2. The second line indicates the name of the statement ***(What?)***
3. The third line indicates the period covered ***(When?)***

Because the statement of changes in financial position and the income statement cover the same period, the third line of the heading of both statements will include the same wording and date.

The information to prepare this statement is found in three places:

- the work sheet
- the income statement
- the owner's capital account in the general ledger

Completing the Statement of Changes in Owner's Equity

Look at **Figure 9–6** to see the statement of changes in owner's equity for Roadrunner Delivery Service for the month ended October 31.

In order to complete the statement of changes in owner's equity, follow these steps:

1. On the first line, write the words "Beginning Capital" followed by a comma and then by the first day of the period. For Roadrunner, that date is October 1, 20--. A

RESOURCE MANAGER

Reproducible Masters
- Lesson Plans
- Chapter Reviews and Working Papers (CRWP) TAE
- Demonstration Problems

Transparencies
- Section Focus Transparency
- Teaching Transparencies
- Source Document Transparencies
- Solution Transparencies

Multimedia
- ExamView CD-ROM
- Electronic Learning Center CD-ROM
- Interactive Lesson Planner CD-ROM

Roadrunner Delivery Service
Statement of Changes in Owner's Equity
For the Month Ended October 31, 20--

	Beginning Capital, October 1, 20-- A		—	B
C	*Add: Investments by Owner*	D 25 400 00		
	Net Income	E 1 150 00		
	Total Increase in Capital		26 550 00	F
	Subtotal		26 550 00	G
	Less: Withdrawals by Owner		500 00	H
	Ending Capital, October 31, 20-- I		26 050 00	J

Figure 9–6 Statement of Changes in Owner's Equity

2. In the second amount column, enter the balance of the capital account at the beginning of the period. The source of this information is the capital account. Since Roadrunner was formed after the beginning of the period, there is no beginning capital balance. Place a line in the second amount column. B
3. Next, enter the *increases* to the capital account: investments by the owner and net income. Investments made by the owner during the period are recorded in the capital account. Maria Sanchez, the owner of Roadrunner, invested a total of $25,400 during October. This includes $25,000 cash and two phones valued at $400. Write "Add: Investments by Owner." C Enter the total investment in the first amount column. D

   On the next line, write the words "Net Income." Indent so that "Net Income" aligns on the left with "Investments by Owner" above. In the first amount column, enter the net income amount from the income statement. Draw a single rule under the net income amount. E

4. Write the words "Total Increase in Capital" on the next line at the left side of the form. Add the investments by owner and net income amounts and enter the total in the second amount column. Draw a single rule under the amount. F
5. Write "Subtotal" on the next line, at the left side of the form. Add the amounts for beginning capital and total increase in capital. Enter the result in the second amount column. G
6. The next section of the statement lists the *decreases* to the capital account: withdrawals and net loss. Since Roadrunner did not have a net loss for the period, write the words "Less: Withdrawals by Owner" at the left side of the form. Find the withdrawals amount on the work sheet. Enter the withdrawals amount in the second amount column. Draw a single rule under the withdrawals amount. H
7. On the next line, at the left side of the form, write the words "Ending Capital" followed by a comma and the last day of the period. I
8. Subtract the withdrawals amount from the subtotal to determine the ending balance of the capital account. Finally, draw a double rule below the ending capital amount. J

International ACCOUNTING

Immunizations

If you are doing business in an industrialized country, immunizations are probably not necessary. However, it's important to take precautions in less industrialized areas. If you are unsure about the status of a country, seek medical advice at least six weeks prior to travel.

Teaching International ACCOUNTING

Get Professional Advice Invite a health-care professional to talk with the class about the importance of getting immunizations before traveling to foreign countries. Ask the guest speaker to explain the health risks involved and what precautionary measures individuals should take in addition to immunizations. Also ask the speaker to name resources where individuals can obtain information about immunizations for specific travel destinations.

2 TEACH

GUIDED PRACTICE

Reading Accounting

• Have students "interpret" the statement of changes in owner's equity by reading the words on the report. For example, what does "beginning capital" suggest to them? Why are investments and net income added? Why are withdrawals subtracted? Have students analyze why the report information is organized in this way rather than memorizing its format. L1

Visual Learning

Figure 9–6 Statement of Changes in Owner's Equity

Using **Transparency 9–8**, explain to students that the capital account balance at the beginning of the fiscal period reflects the account as of the end of the last fiscal period. The statement of changes in owner's equity summarizes changes affecting capital during the period and reports the new balance in capital at the end of the current fiscal period.

Teaching Tip

Point out to students that the letters A through J in the narrative match items shown in Figure 9–6.

Strategies for Teaching International Accounting

To enrich study of International Accounting, refer to the additional critical thinking activities in the booklet.

CHAPTER 9
SECTION 2, PAGES 210–214

2 TEACH (Cont'd.)

Teaching Tip

Review the accounting assumption of "ongoing business" for students. If needed, refer students to Chapter 5 for a review of the concepts relating to owner's equity.

Visual Learning

Figure 9–7 Statement of Changes in Owner's Equity for an Ongoing Business

Using **Transparency 9–9**, point out the balance in the account James Garo, Capital. This balance reflects the owner's previous investments and the results of business operations since Garo's Tree Service is an ongoing business that has been operating for some time. Also point out that the beginning balance used on the statement of changes in owner's equity is the balance at the beginning of the fiscal period for which the report is being prepared. Have students note that the current balance in the account ($24,800) is not used as the beginning balance because all changes affecting capital are reported on the statement of changes in owner's equity, which includes any additional investments (the April 15 entry for $1,000) made by the owner during the period.

Thinking Algebraically

Writing Formulas: Have students express the information on the statement of changes in owner's equity as a formula. (Example: beginning capital + investments + net income − withdrawals = ending capital.) L1

Figure 9–7 Statement of Changes in Owner's Equity for an Ongoing Business

Statement of Changes in Owner's Equity for an Ongoing Business

To prepare the statement of changes in owner's equity, you need to know the beginning balance of the owner's capital account. For an ongoing business, the balance entered on the work sheet for the capital account *may not* be the balance at the beginning of the period. If the owner made additional investments during the period, the investments would be recorded in the general journal, posted to the general ledger, and included in the amount shown on the work sheet.

For example, suppose the owner of Garo's Tree Service, James Garo, invested an additional $1,000 during the period. Look at **Figure 9–7.** The ledger account reflects the additional capital investment. The amount entered on the work sheet for **James Garo, Capital** includes the balance at the beginning of the period ($23,800) and the investment made during the period ($1,000).

ACCOUNT *James Garo, Capital* ACCOUNT NO. *301*

DATE		DESCRIPTION	POST. REF.	DEBIT	CREDIT	BALANCE DEBIT	BALANCE CREDIT
20--							
Apr.	*1*	*Balance*	✓				*23 800 00*
	15		*G1*		*1 000 00*		*24 800 00*

Garo's Tree Service
Work Sheet
For the Month Ended April 30, 20--

	ACCT. NO.	ACCOUNT NAME	TRIAL BALANCE DEBIT	TRIAL BALANCE CREDIT	INCOME STATEMENT DEBIT	INCOME STATEMENT CREDIT	BALANCE SHEET DEBIT	BALANCE SHEET CREDIT	
12	*301*	*James Garo, Capital*		*24 800 00*				*24 800 00*	12
13	*302*	*James Garo, Withdrawals*	*700 00*				*700 00*		13
20	*525*	*Utilities Expense*	*620 00*		*620 00*				20
21			*21 924 00*	*21 924 00*	*6 033 00*	*9 309 00*	*29 877 00*	*26 601 00*	21
22		*Net Income*			*3 276 00*			*3 276 00*	22
23					*9 309 00*	*9 309 00*	*29 877 00*	*29 877 00*	23
24									24

Garo's Tree Service
Statement of Changes in Owner's Equity
For the Month Ended April 30, 20--

Beginning Capital, April 1, 20--		*23 800 00*
Add: Investments by Owner	*1 000 00*	
Net Income	*3 276 00*	
Total Increase in Capital		*4 276 00*
Subtotal		*28 076 00*
Less: Withdrawals by Owner		*700 00*
Ending Capital, April 30, 20--		*27 376 00*

MEETING SPECIAL NEEDS

Students with Orthopaedic Impairments Students with orthopaedic impairments are often slow and/or awkward writers. For these students, do not place a great deal of emphasis on preparing accounting records and reports that are "neatly" handwritten. If computers are available, consider having students prepare their accounting assignments electronically.

There are two ways to determine the owner's capital account balance at the beginning of the period. One way is to look at the ledger. The other way is to subtract the additional investments from the account balance shown on the work sheet. For **James Garo, Capital**, the $1,000 additional investment is subtracted from the $24,800 account balance shown on the work sheet to arrive at the beginning account balance of $23,800.

Figure 9–7 shows the statement of changes in owner's equity for an ongoing business.

> **Key Points**
>
> **Owner Investments and Withdrawals**
>
> Investments by the owner and net income increase capital. Withdrawals by the owner and net loss decrease capital.

Statement of Changes in Owner's Equity Showing a Net Loss

Figure 9–8 shows a statement of changes in owner's equity for an ongoing business with a net loss. Notice that since there is only one item that increases capital, investments by owner, the amount of the individual item is entered in the second amount column. Since there are two items that decrease capital, withdrawals by owner and net loss, the amounts of the individual items are entered in the first amount column. The total decrease in capital is entered in the second amount column.

Island Burgers
Statement of Changes in Owner's Equity
For the Month Ended April 30, 20--

Beginning Capital, April 1, 20--		13 848 00
Add: Investments by Owner		1 500 00
Subtotal		15 348 00
Less: Withdrawals by Owner	900 00	
Net Loss	835 00	
Total Decrease in Capital		1 735 00
Ending Capital, April 30, 20--		13 613 00

Figure 9–8 Statement of Changes in Owner's Equity Showing a Net Loss

A MATTER OF ETHICS

Financial Report or Repair?

Your favorite uncle, who owns a restaurant, has asked you to help with his bookkeeping. He desperately needs a bank loan and wants you to prepare the financial statements. After going over his accounting records, you don't believe a bank will give him a loan; but you notice that by leaving out an expense or two, your uncle's business could look more promising. After all, he does have some good ideas for improving the business.

Ethical Decision Making:

- What are the ethical issues?
- What are the alternatives?
- Who are the affected parties?
- How do the alternatives affect the parties?
- What would you do?

2 TEACH (Cont'd.)

Demonstration Problem Step-by-Step Practice

Use demonstration problem 9–4 to give students practice in preparing a statement of changes in owner's equity.

Visual Learning

Figure 9–8 Statement of Changes in Owner's Equity Showing a Net Loss

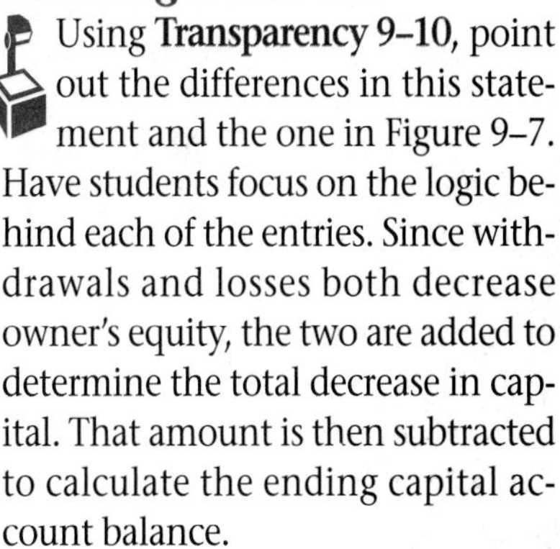

Using **Transparency 9–10,** point out the differences in this statement and the one in Figure 9–7. Have students focus on the logic behind each of the entries. Since withdrawals and losses both decrease owner's equity, the two are added to determine the total decrease in capital. That amount is then subtracted to calculate the ending capital account balance.

Teaching Tip

Review for students, or ask them to review, why investments by the owner and net income increase owner's equity, while withdrawals and net losses decrease owner's equity.

Strategies for Teaching Ethics in Accounting

Photocopy the Chapter 9 *Student Activity Sheet* for students. Answers are also provided in the booklet.

Teaching A MATTER OF ETHICS

Financial Report or Repair? Discuss with students why they might feel compelled to do something they know is wrong or unethical. For example, have they ever given in to peer pressure and stayed out too late? Ask students how they resist peer or family pressure. Under what circumstances do they resist? Ask students to explain the concept of integrity as related to the accounting profession. (*Integrity* is the principle that requires accountants to choose right over wrong. People make important decisions based on the information provided by accountants.)

3 ASSESS

Thinking Critically (Answers)

1. The work sheet, income statement, and the capital account in the general ledger.
2. It can highlight trends in earnings or losses over several periods. Losses or too small an increase in capital may signal a need for changes.

Analyzing Accounting (Answers)

Tracy shows a net profit, before taxes, of $24,400. In order to realize a higher profit margin, Tracy should consider working with her existing capital and bringing in more clients.

Problem 9–2 (Answers)

1. $62,500
2. $29,915
3. $29,470
4. $10,630
5. $7,060
6. $25,010

Chapter Reviews and Working Papers Refer students to the Chapter 9 workbook pages to answer *Check Your Understanding* activities.

4 CLOSE

Section Wrap-Up

Critical Thinking: Have students explain why it is better to show changes in the capital account on a statement of changes in owner's equity than keeping the capital account up to date by recording all transactions affecting capital in that account as they occur. (Students' responses should note that the capital account would be cluttered, and it would be much more difficult to calculate net income or loss.) L2

SECTION 2 Check Your Understanding

Now that you have studied this section, complete the following questions and problems.

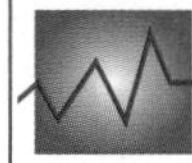

Thinking Critically

1. Where do you find the data needed to prepare a statement of changes in owner's equity?
2. How can the statement of changes in owner's equity help to determine the short- and long-term success of a business?

Analyzing Accounting

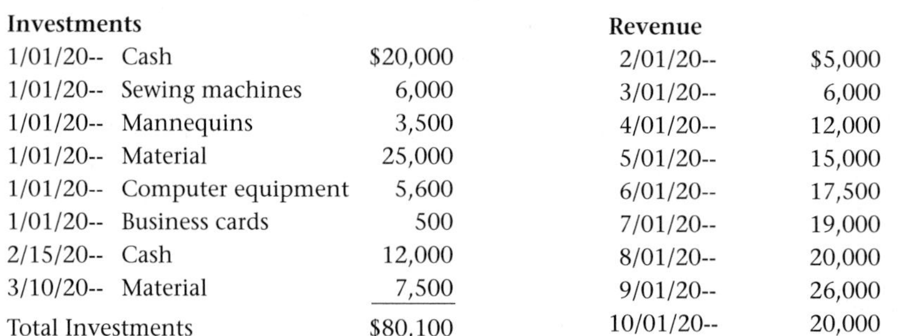

Tracy Murphy is a fashion designer who works from her home. She contributed her own funds and equipment to the business. She also continues to add new clients and increase her revenue. Tracy's investments in her business and the revenue she has earned over the past ten months are shown below. Create a line graph, by date, comparing Tracy's investments to her revenue. What can you determine from this chart?

Investments			Revenue	
1/01/20--	Cash	$20,000	2/01/20--	$5,000
1/01/20--	Sewing machines	6,000	3/01/20--	6,000
1/01/20--	Mannequins	3,500	4/01/20--	12,000
1/01/20--	Material	25,000	5/01/20--	15,000
1/01/20--	Computer equipment	5,600	6/01/20--	17,500
1/01/20--	Business cards	500	7/01/20--	19,000
2/15/20--	Cash	12,000	8/01/20--	20,000
3/10/20--	Material	7,500	9/01/20--	26,000
Total Investments		$80,100	10/01/20--	20,000

Problem 9–2 Determining Ending Capital Balances

The financial transactions affecting the capital accounts of several different businesses are summarized below.

Instructions Use the form in your working papers. Determine the ending capital balance for each business.

	Beginning Capital	Investments	Revenue	Expenses	Withdrawals
1.	$60,000	$ 500	$ 5,100	$2,400	$ 700
2.	24,075	0	13,880	7,240	800
3.	28,800	1,000	6,450	6,780	0
4.	0	10,500	5,320	4,990	200
5.	6,415	0	4,520	3,175	700
6.	20,870	1,300	13,980	9,440	1,700

RETEACHING SECTION 2

Calculating Changes in Owner's Equity The statement of changes in owner's equity not only shows the change in the balance of the capital account but also shows how that change occurred. For example, the statement shows whether an increase resulted from revenue or from further investment by the owner. Decreases are indicated as expenses or withdrawals. A quick way to calculate how much the owner's equity has increased or decreased is to compare the current balance of the capital account with the balance of the capital account at the beginning of the last fiscal period. Like other accounting records, this statement is analyzed for help in making future business decisions.

ACCOUNTING CAREERS IN FOCUS

ALFRED A. PEGUERO
Partner
PricewaterhouseCoopers LLP

Q: How did you become interested in accounting?

A: I was an economics major in college, but in my senior year I took two accounting classes that I really enjoyed. I realized that this is where the opportunities are. Accounting as a general profession is very broad. The basic principles are the same but you can focus on areas and industries that really interest you—anything from technology to farming. As an accountant, you have the opportunity to choose your industry.

Q: Which skills are most important?

A: Analytical and reasoning skills are critical. Mathematical ability can be helpful. Communication skills are essential.

Q: What do you enjoy most about your job?

A: I enjoy being able to offer solutions to my clients. Helping real people solve their problems and achieve peace of mind over their financial matters is very rewarding.

Q: What advice do you have for accountants just beginning their careers?

A: Find a good mentor—this is really important. Always follow through with what you say you're going to do and don't be afraid to ask questions.

Tips from . . .
Robert Half International Inc.
Many companies look for leadership potential in new employees. Look beyond your immediate area of responsibility. Help your colleagues, learn what motivates and inspires people, and take on new challenges.

CAREER FACTS

Nature of the Work: Specialize in personal financial and business consulting. Advise clients on complex accounting issues.
Training or Education Needed: Bachelor's degree in business administration, accounting, or economics (minor in communications and technology particularly useful); and the CPA exam.
Aptitudes, Abilities, and Skills: Communication skills, analytical skills, reasoning skills, and math.
Salary Range: $150,000 to $400,000 as a new partner, and up to $2,000,000 with more experience, based on the firm's performance.
Career Path: Gather hands-on experience with either a major accounting firm or a reputable local firm. Once you have a taste for the areas that most interest you, consider getting a master's degree. It usually takes about 10 to 15 years to make partner at most firms.

Thinking Critically: What kind of advice would you ask of a mentor?

CAREERS IN FOCUS
CHAPTER 9

SCANS in the Workforce

Foundation Skills Connection

Listening
Ask two students to role play situations in which each is applying for a job as an accounting clerk. One student is shy and retiring; the other is extroverted and bold. Have the students give brief descriptions of themselves to the class. Then ask the rest of the class what they've heard about each candidate. Have students describe their skills, job preparedness, and personality. Did some students hear and see things that others did not? L1

Workplace Competencies Connection

Allocating Human Resources
Tell students that they work for a local sports equipment store. The manager has asked them to clear the merchandise from the front of the store and set up a display of new seasonal products. Have students create a plan for accomplishing the work. Tell them to include the number of people they'll need and the tasks each person will complete. Encourage students to be creative with their plans. L2

Exercising Leadership
Assign students to review several case studies of CEOs or company presidents. Have them identify what made each person an effective business leader. Have students also investigate articles about new and creative approaches to business management by using the Internet. Have students write a short research paper about their findings. Make sure students cite their research references. L3

ACCOUNTING CAREERS IN FOCUS

Thinking Critically (Answer)
You can ask a mentor for help in planning your career path. You might also get some insight from the mentor's past career experiences. You can ask for help in dealing with interpersonal conflicts at work or suggestions for additional skills and training to acquire.

ROBERT HALF CORNER

Mentoring One strategy used to pass on wisdom and insight to junior-level employees is mentoring. Mentors provide knowledge and practical skills not learned in school. Mentors may teach the subtleties of business protocol or how to work with a challenging situation.

1 FOCUS

Introducing the Section

In this section students complete the financial statements by learning how to prepare a balance sheet. Students also learn how ratio analysis can be used to analyze the information reported on financial statements. Students learn to calculate the return on sales and the liquidity ratios such as the current and quick ratios.

Section Concepts

- The purpose of a balance sheet.
- How to prepare a balance sheet.
- How to analyze information on financial reports.

Visual Learning

Section 3 Focus

Use **Transparency 9–11** to introduce section concepts.

BELL RINGER

Critical Thinking: Tell students that they've just won the grand prize of $1,000 in a local contest, and they've decided to invest the money in the stock market. Would they invest all the money in one stock or buy several different ones? How would they decide which stocks to buy? What financial information would they want to know? How would they analyze this information? L2

SECTION 3

The Balance Sheet

***What* You'll Learn**

- The purpose of a balance sheet.
- How to prepare a balance sheet.
- How to analyze information on financial reports.

***Why* It's Important**

The balance sheet reports the financial position of a business at a specific point in time.

KEY TERMS

balance sheet
report form
ratio analysis
profitability ratio
return on sales
liquidity ratio
current ratio
current assets
current liabilities
quick ratio

The third financial report that is prepared at the end of a period is the balance sheet. The balance sheet provides a record of assets, and claims against those assets, for a business.

Your local bakery might prepare this statement to include amounts for items such as kitchen equipment, cash, and accounts receivable, as well as amounts for bills outstanding and owner's equity.

The Balance Sheet

The **balance sheet** is a report of the balances in all asset, liability, and owner's equity accounts at the end of the period. These accounts, you'll remember, are called permanent accounts. The main purpose of the balance sheet is to provide a record of the assets of the business and a summary of the claims (of both creditors and owners) against those *assets on a specific date.* In other words, the balance sheet states the financial position of a business at a specific point in time. It pinpoints what a business owns, owes, and is worth. For this reason, the balance sheet is sometimes called a *financial position statement.*

The balance sheet is prepared from the information in the Balance Sheet section of the work sheet and from the statement of changes in owner's equity. The balance sheet may be handwritten, typed, or, as in most cases, prepared by computer. Let's look at the sections of the balance sheet:

- the heading
- the assets section
- the liabilities and owner's equity sections

The Heading

Like the heading of the income statement, the heading of the balance sheet answers the questions *who? what? when?* The balance sheet heading includes:

1. The name of the business ***(Who?)***
2. The name of the financial statement ***(What?)***
3. The date of the balance sheet ***(When?)***

As you recall, the income statement reports the amount of net income (or net loss) for the period. Unlike the income statement, which covers

RESOURCE MANAGER

Reproducible Masters

- Lesson Plans
- Chapter Reviews and Working Papers (CRWP) TAE
- Demonstration Problems

Transparencies

- Section Focus Transparency
- Teaching Transparencies
- Source Document Transparencies
- Solution Transparencies

Multimedia

- **Exam***View* CD-ROM
- Electronic Learning Center CD-ROM
- Interactive Lesson Planner CD-ROM

the entire period, the balance sheet covers only one day in the period, the last day. The amounts shown on the balance sheet are the general ledger balances in the accounts on the last day of the period. Look at **Figure 9–9**. Notice the difference between the date lines on the income statement and on the balance sheet.

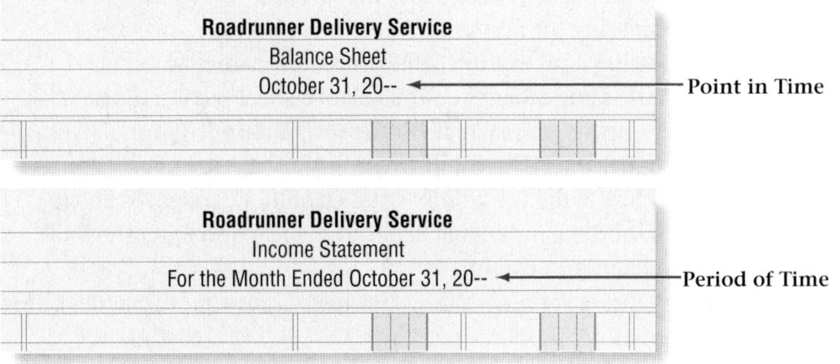

Figure 9–9 Headings of Financial Statements

The Assets Section

Refer to Roadrunner's balance sheet in **Figure 9–10** as you read how to prepare the balance sheet. Roadrunner's work sheet and statement of changes in owner's equity are also included to show the information sources used to prepare the balance sheet. Note that Roadrunner's balance sheet is prepared in report form. In **report form**, the balance sheet accounts are shown one under the other.

The asset section of the balance sheet is prepared as follows:

1. Write the word "Assets" on the first line in the center of the column containing the account names. A
2. On the following lines, enter the asset account names and their balances. List them in the same order as they appear in the Balance Sheet section of the work sheet. Enter the account balances in the first amount column. Draw a single rule under the last account balance. B
3. On the next line, write the words "Total Assets," indented about half an inch. Add the individual asset balances and enter the total in the second amount column. C

Do *not* draw a double rule under the total at this time. The double rule is entered when the liabilities and owner's equity sections are complete and equal to total assets.

Math Hints

Calculating Ratios

When calculating ratios, be sure to use the correct figures for the *divisor* and the *dividend.*

For example, to calculate the ratio of total expenses to total revenue:

- the revenue amount is the *dividend,*
- and the expense amount is the *divisor.*

Math Skill Builder Activity

Calculating Ratios Provide students with the following scenario and ask them to solve the problem by calculating the ratio of revenue to expenses: "At the City Bike Shop, the owner, Denise Buzby, has asked you to give her the revenue to expense ratios for the past two years. Her reported revenue for last year was $45,000 and expenses were $20,000; this year, her revenue is $125,000; expenses, $52,000." What are the ratios for both years? (45,000 ÷ 20,000 = 2.025; 125,000 ÷ 52,000 = 2.4)

2 TEACH

GUIDED PRACTICE

Reading Accounting

- Have students practice their classifying skills by reading the account names on the balance sheet. Which accounts are reported on this statement, and why? L1

Concept Development: The Balance Sheet

Discussion: Point out the heading on the balance sheet. Ask students why the date is different from the date line on the other two financial statements. Discuss the sources of information for preparing a balance sheet:

- The **work sheet** provides accounts and balances for the assets and liabilities sections.
- The **statement of changes in owner's equity** provides the new balance for the owner's capital account. L1

Teaching Tip

Ask students to explain the accounting assumption relating to time periods and why this assumption is important.

Visual Learning

Figure 9–9 Headings of Financial Statements

Use **Transparency 9–12** to help students contrast the dates on the balance sheet and the income statement.

Math Review for Accounting

Photocopy appropriate *Activity Sheets* for students who need additional practice in basic math.

2 TEACH (Cont'd.)

Teaching Tips

Compare the balance sheet to a photograph. The balance sheet shows the worth of a business at a single time—the date of the report.

Use annual reports to show students examples of balance sheets from both large and small companies. It is important for students to understand that the balance sheet is the same in principle no matter how large or small the company.

Remind students that the letters A through K refer to information on the balance sheet in Figure 9–10. Have students read each step and then identify the related information on the illustration.

Critical Thinking: Have students explain why the balance sheet proves the accuracy of the accounting equation. (The balance sheet reports total assets, total liabilities, and owner's equity—the three parts of the accounting equation.) L1

The Liabilities and Owner's Equity Sections

The information for the liabilities and owner's equity sections is taken from the work sheet and from the statement of changes in owner's equity. Use the following steps to complete the liabilities and owner's equity sections.

1. On the line after "Total Assets" enter the heading "Liabilities" in the column containing the account names. D
2. On the following lines, list the liability account names and their balances in the same order as on the Balance Sheet section of the work sheet. Enter the account balances in the first amount column. Draw a single rule under the last account balance. E
3. On the next line, write the words "Total Liabilities," indented about half an inch. Add the individual liability balances and enter the total in the second amount column. F
4. On the next line enter the heading "Owner's Equity" in the center of the column containing the account names. G
5. On the next line, write the name of the capital account. In the second amount column, enter the ending balance of the capital account as shown on the statement of changes in owner's equity. H

Proving the Equality of the Balance Sheet

Key Points

Source of Ending Capital Balance

Transfer the ending capital balance from the statement of changes in owner's equity to the owner's equity section of the balance sheet.

You learned in earlier chapters that the basic accounting equation must always be in balance. The balance sheet represents the basic accounting equation; thus, the assets section total must equal the total of the liabilities and owner's equity sections.

Assets = Liabilities + Owner's Equity

To prove the equality of the balance sheet, follow these steps:

1. Draw a single rule under the balance of the capital account. On the next line, write the words "Total Liabilities and Owner's Equity," indented about half an inch. I
2. Add the total liabilities amount and the ending capital balance. Enter the total in the second amount column. J This total must equal the total assets amount. If the totals are not equal, there is an error. Most errors occur when transferring amounts from the work sheet or from the statement of changes in owner's equity. Verify that each account balance has been transferred properly. Find and correct the error and then complete the balance sheet.
3. When total assets equal total liabilities and owner's equity, draw a double rule under the total assets amount *and* under the total liabilities and owner's equity amount. K The balance sheet is now complete.

Review the amounts and their placement in **Figure 9–10** again. As you can see, completion of the work sheet is the basis of all financial statement preparation.

MAKING CONNECTIONS TO DAILY LIFE

Applying for a Loan When an individual decides to purchase a car and applies for a loan, the lending institution inquires about financial position before it grants the loan. Ask students to brainstorm a list of questions the lending institution might ask about an individual's financial position and explain why. (Some typical questions may include: What is your weekly, monthly, or annual income? Do you have other current debts? What assets do you own? The lending institution needs to know whether the borrower can make the necessary loan payments. If the borrower's income is insufficient to repay the loan and current living expenses, the lender can assume that the loan is a bad risk.)

Roadrunner Delivery Service
Work Sheet
For the Month Ended October 31, 20--

	ACCT. NO.	ACCOUNT NAME	TRIAL BALANCE DEBIT	TRIAL BALANCE CREDIT	INCOME STATEMENT DEBIT	INCOME STATEMENT CREDIT	BALANCE SHEET DEBIT	BALANCE SHEET CREDIT	
	101	Cash in Bank	21 125 00				21 125 00		1
	105	Accts. Rec.—City News	1 450 00				1 450 00		2
	110	Accts. Rec.—Green Company	—				—		3
	115	Computer Equipment	3 000 00				3 000 00		4
	120	Office Equipment	200 00				200 00		5
	125	Delivery Equipment	12 000 00				12 000 00		6
	201	Accts. Pay.—Beacon Advertising		75 00				75 00	7
	205	Accts. Pay.—North Shore Auto		11 650 00				11 650 00	8
9	301	Maria Sanchez, Capital		25 400 00				25 400 00	9
10	302	Maria Sanchez, Withdrawals	500 00				500 00		10
11	303	Income Summary	—	—	—	—			11
12	401	Delivery Revenue		2 650 00		2 650 00			12
13	501	Advertising Expense	75 00		75 00				13
14	505	Mai	600 00		600 00				14
15	510	Ren							15
16	515	Util							16
17								37 125 00	17
18		Net						1 150 00	18
19								38 275 00	19
20									20

Roadrunner Delivery Service
Statement of Changes in Owner's Equity
For the Month Ended October 31, 20--

Beginning Capital, October 1, 20--		—
Add: Investments by Owner	25 400 00	
Net Income	1 150 00	
Total Increase in Capital		26 550 00
Subtotal		26 550 00
Less: Withdrawals by Owner		500 00
Ending Capital, October 31, 20--		26 050 00

Roadrunner Delivery Service
Balance Sheet
October 31, 20--

	A Assets			
B	Cash in Bank	21 125 00		
B	Accounts Receivable—City News	1 450 00		
B	Accounts Receivable—Green Company	—		
B	Computer Equipment	3 000 00		
B	Office Equipment	200 00		
B	Delivery Equipment	12 000 00		
	C Total Assets		37 775 00	K
	D Liabilities			
E	Accounts Payable—Beacon Advertising	75 00		
E	Accounts Payable—North Shore Auto	11 650 00		
	F Total Liabilities		11 725 00	
	G Owner's Equity			
H	Maria Sanchez, Capital		26 050 00	
	I Total Liabilities and Owner's Equity	J	37 775 00	K

H

Figure 9–10 Preparing a Balance Sheet

CHAPTER 9
SECTION 3, PAGES 216–222

2 TEACH (Cont'd.)

Visual Learning

Figure 9–10 Preparing a Balance Sheet

Use **Transparency 9–13** to point out the source of the accounts and balances reported on the balance sheet. Help students trace the transfer of information from the work sheet and the statement of changes in owner's equity to the balance sheet. Also discuss how to organize the information presented in the balance sheet.

Demonstration Problem
Step-by-Step Practice
Use demonstration problem 9–5 to guide students through the process of preparing a balance sheet or to give them independent practice in preparing the balance sheet.

Teaching Tip

Remind students that the double rule is not drawn under total assets until the total for liabilities and owner's equity has been calculated and is proven to equal total assets.

Chapter Reviews and Working Papers
Refer students to the *Study Plan* located at the beginning of Chapter 9 in the workbook.

REINFORCING STUDY SKILLS

Reading Technique Setting purposes for reading often helps students focus on the main points. Have students read the chapter introduction and then, in their own words, explain what they think this chapter will be about. As students read, have them refer back to the Learning Objectives and try to meet each one as they go along.

2 TEACH (Cont'd.)

Concept Development: Ratio Analysis

Discussion: Point out to students that one use of financial statements is to evaluate business performance. For example, if they were buying stock in a company, they would want to know that the company is financially healthy. Ratio analysis can help them evaluate companies and compare different companies within an industry.

Accountants and other analysts use ratio analysis to learn more about the business than would be possible simply by reading the financial statements. The process of comparing a set of figures and establishing their relationships enables one to gain a better understanding of a business. Ratios highlight unusual, unexpected, or otherwise unexplained changes in the operating results of a business. L2

Teaching Tips

Explain to students that return on sales is a measure of a company's profitability (its profit margin). The higher the return, the better the profit.

Point out that when using return on sales to evaluate the financial performance of a business, students should compare returns among several companies in the same industry.

Demonstration Problem Step-by-Step Practice

Use demonstration problem 9–6 to give students practice in calculating the return on sales.

Ratio Analysis

Ratio analysis involves the comparison of two amounts on a financial statement and the evaluation of the relationship between these amounts. A manager uses ratio analysis to determine the financial strength, activity, or debt-paying ability of a business.

Profitability ratios are used to evaluate the earnings performance of the business during the accounting period. The earning power of a business is an important measure of its ability to grow and continue to earn revenue. One commonly used profitability ratio is return on sales.

ACCOUNTING *Flashbacks*

THE FIRST CREDIT CARD
Frank McNamara launched Diner's Club, the first credit card, after he found himself short of cash in a Manhattan restaurant in 1950.

Return on Sales

Sales is a revenue account representing the sale of merchandise. Business owners use the **return on sales** ratio to examine the portion of each sales dollar that represents profit. To calculate this ratio, divide net income by sales. For example, the return on sales for Roadrunner Delivery Service is calculated as follows:

$$\frac{\$1{,}150 \text{ net income}}{\$2{,}650 \text{ sales}} = .434 \text{ or } 43.4\%$$

This percentage indicates that each dollar of sales produced 43.4 cents of profit for Roadrunner. It can be compared to other accounting periods to determine whether it is increasing or decreasing.

For example, if net income next year is $2,750 and net sales are $5,000, the return on sales would be computed as follows:

$$\frac{\$2{,}750 \text{ net income}}{\$5{,}000 \text{ sales}} = .550 \text{ or } 55.0\%$$

As you can see, profit per sales dollar would increase by 11.6 cents.

Liquidity Ratios

As you will recall from Chapter 6, liquidity refers to the ease with which an asset can be converted to cash. A **liquidity ratio** is a measure of the ability of a business to pay its current debts as they become due and to provide for unexpected needs of cash. Two common ratios used to determine liquidity follow.

Current Ratio. The **current ratio** is the relationship between current assets and current liabilities. The current ratio is calculated by dividing the dollar amount of current assets by the dollar amount of current liabilities. **Current assets** are those used up or converted to cash during the normal operating cycle of the business. These might include **Accounts Receivable**, **Cash in Bank**, and **Supplies.** **Current liabilities** are debts of the business that must be paid within the next accounting period. **Accounts Payable** is an example of current liabilities. The current ratio for Roadrunner based on the balance sheet in **Figure 9–10** is:

$$\frac{\text{Current Assets}}{\text{Current Liabilities}} = \text{Current Ratio} \quad \frac{\$\ 22{,}575}{\$\ 11{,}725} = 1.92 \text{ or } 1.9{:}1$$

The current liabilities of a business must be paid within a year. These liabilities are paid from current assets.

ACCOUNTING ISSUES

Using Charts in Financial Reports The purpose of financial reports is to provide the "big picture" of the financial condition of the business. Charts (or graphs) in financial reports help speed a reader's comprehension of complex data. Accountants use charts to simplify and summarize complicated and extensive numerical data. The charts also enhance the information by emphasizing trends and changes. Today's software applications easily and quickly convert numerical data into four color, 3-D charts. Choosing the correct type of chart can turn a dull report of numbers into an effective presentation with impact.

A ratio of 2:1 or higher is considered favorable by creditors. It indicates that a business is able to pay its debts, that a business has current assets which are two times its current liabilities. A low ratio may indicate that a company could have trouble paying its debts.

Quick Ratio. A **quick ratio** is a measure of the relationship between short-term assets and current liabilities. Short-term liquid assets—those that can be quickly converted to cash—are cash and net receivables. The quick ratio is computed by dividing the total cash and receivables by total current liabilities.

The quick ratio for Roadrunner based on the Balance Sheet in **Figure 9–10** is:

$$\frac{\text{Cash and Receivables}}{\text{Current Liabilities}} = \text{Quick Ratio} \qquad \frac{\$22{,}575}{\$\ 11{,}725} = 1.92{:}1$$

In some instances, the current ratio and the quick ratio can be the same, as in the case in this example.

A quick ratio of 1:1 is considered adequate. This indicates that a business can pay its current debts with cash in incoming receivables. If a business has a quick ratio of 1:1 or higher, the business has $1 in liquid assets for each $1 of its current liabilities.

Quick ratios may also be compared from one year to the next. For example, if cash and receivables for the previous year were $48,653 and current liabilities were $53,245, then that year's quick ratio would be computed as:

$$\frac{\$48{,}653}{\$53{,}245} = 0.91{:}1$$

As you can see, Roadrunner would have improved its liquidity position in the current year. $1.92 in liquid assets per $1 in current liabilities (current year) is stronger than $.91 in liquid assets per $1 in current liabilities (previous year).

ANALYZING FINANCIAL REPORTS

Return on Sales

In this chapter, you've learned about three basic financial reports that present different types of information about a business. One of these is the income statement. Owners and managers use the income statement to analyze the profit earned by the business and are especially interested in the return on sales.

To review, **return on sales** is calculated by dividing the net income by revenue, or sales. Take a look at the following example:

$$\frac{\text{Net Income}}{\text{Revenue}} = \frac{\$\ 3{,}600}{\$42{,}500} = 8.5 \text{ percent}$$

The resulting percentage shows the proportion of each revenue dollar that is profit to the business.

▶ Interpret the Report:

Use the income statement for Roadrunner Delivery Service on page 206 to complete these activities. Record your answers on a separate sheet of paper.

1. Calculate the return on sales for Roadrunner Delivery Service for the month of October.
2. Assume that total sales for Roadrunner are roughly equal from month to month. If return on sales decreases each month, what conclusions might you draw about the business? What suggestions would you offer to improve the return on sales?

2 TEACH (Cont'd.)

Teaching Tips

The ratios introduced in this section are but a few of the ratios analysts use when evaluating financial performance. The primary aim here is to show students how financial data may be used beyond reporting it on financial statements. Bring annual reports to class and have students use those to calculate the ratios introduced in this section.

Point out that the current ratio is a test for solvency. It provides clues to the financial margin of safety for businesses that grant credit. The quick ratio is a more stringent test of solvency since it includes only the most liquid assets.

Explain that the colon in a ratio is read as "to," which shows the relationship to the number "1."

Demonstration Problem Step-by-Step Practice

Use demonstration problem 9–7 to give students practice in calculating current and quick ratios.

ANALYZING FINANCIAL REPORTS

Roadrunner Delivery Service
155 Gateway Blvd.
Sacramento, CA 94230

Interpret the Report (Answers)

1. Net income of $1,150 ÷ revenue of $2,650 = 43.39%
2. Return on sales for Roadrunner is very high, perhaps reflecting lower-than-normal operating costs. A decrease in the return could signal greater competition or a loss of customers because of poor service or prices that are too high. The owner should find out the cause of the decreases and make changes to be more competitive—such as offering more or faster services—or to provide better customer service.

CHAPTER 9
SECTION 3, PAGES 216–222

3 ASSESS

Thinking Critically (Answers)

1. Probably in transferring an amount from the work sheet or statement of changes in owner's equity.
2. The income statement covers an entire reporting period; the balance sheet, the financial position on a specific date.

Communicating Accounting (Answers)

Answers may vary. The purpose of the balance sheet is to report assets and summarize the claims (of creditors and owners) to those assets, thus showing what the business owns, owes, and is worth at a specific time. The student is expected to apply basic accounting concepts, including the concept of equity.

Problem 9-3 (Answer)

Return on Sales = 20.53%

Chapter Reviews and Working Papers Refer students to the Chapter 9 workbook pages to answer *Check Your Understanding* activities.

4 CLOSE

Section Wrap-Up

Group Discussions: Divide the class into small groups. Assign each group either the income statement or the balance sheet. After discussing their statement, have each group present to the class an explanation of the purpose of the statement, the source of information for preparing the statement, and how the statement might be analyzed (with specific ratios). L2

SECTION 3 Check Your Understanding

Now that you have studied this section, complete the following questions and problems.

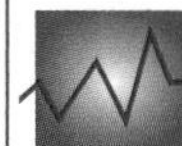

Thinking Critically

1. On the balance sheet, if the total of liabilities and owner's equity does not equal the total assets, where did the error most likely occur?
2. What is the difference between the heading sections of the income statement and the balance sheet?

Communicating Accounting

Interactive Communication is a company that specializes in voice and data communications. They have just experienced a fantastic year in sales and service. Team up with a classmate and, using the balance sheet provided below, give a brief presentation about the purpose and use of the balance sheet.

Interactive Communication
Balance Sheet
December 31, 20--

Assets		
Cash in Bank	944 000 00	
Accounts Receivable—Chamber of Commerce	200 000 00	
Office Equipment	850 000 00	
Computer Equipment	1,000 000 00	
Total Assets		2,994 000 00
Liabilities		
Accounts Payable—Tip Top Advertising	275 500 00	
Interest Payable	1 300 00	
Salaries Payable	2 100 00	
Total Liabilities		278 900 00
Owner's Equity		
Chuck Thompson, Capital		2,715 100 00
Total Liabilities and Owner's Equity		2,994 000 00

Problem 9-3 Calculating Return on Sales

The Gawle Company is a family-owned and operated appliance rental and repair business. The income statement for the month ended August 31 includes the following:

Rental Revenue	$3,256	Rent Expense	$2,100
Repair Revenue	2,140	Utilities Expense	483
Advertising Expense	575	Net Income	1,108
Maintenance Expense	1,130		

Instructions Calculate the return on sales for the month for the Gawle Company.

RETEACHING SECTION 3

Taking a Closer Look at a Balance Sheet Heading Obtain copies of balance sheets from quarterly or annual reports and have the class compare balance sheet headings. Remind students that the date line in the heading of a balance sheet specifies a specific day rather than a period of time. The balances of the accounts listed on the balance sheet can change daily. Thus, the balance sheet is up to date only on the date it is prepared.

CHAPTER 9 SUMMARY

KEY CONCEPTS

1. Preparing financial reports is the seventh step in the accounting cycle. The primary reports are the income statement and the balance sheet. Also, the statement of changes in owner's equity is often prepared.
2. The income statement reports the net income or net loss for the period.
3. The statement of changes in owner's equity summarizes the impact the period's business transactions had on the capital account.
4. The balance sheet reports the balances of asset, liability, and owner's equity accounts at the end of the period.
5. Financial reports may be handwritten, typewritten, or prepared using a computer.
6. The following chart lists the source of information and a description for each financial report.

Financial Report	Description	Source of Information
Income Statement	This statement reports revenue earned and the expenses incurred for a specific period of time. It also reports the net income or net loss for the period.	Work Sheet
Statement of Changes in Owner's Equity	This statement is a supporting document for the balance sheet. It reports the increases and decreases in the owner's capital account for the period.	Work Sheet General Ledger (Capital Account) Income Statement
Balance Sheet	This statement reports the financial position of the business on a specific date.	Work Sheet Statement of Changes in Owner's Equity

7. Ratio analysis is used to determine the financial strength, activity, or debt-paying ability of a business.
8. Liquidity ratios measure the ability of a business to pay its current debts as they become due.

SUMMARY CHAPTER 9

Chapter 9 Quiz

Student Class Instructor
Date Assigned Date Completed

CHAPTER 9 QUIZ

Financial Statements for a Sole Proprietorship

QUESTIONS (Completion)

Directions: Fill in the blank with the term that best completes each sentence.

1. ____________ summarize changes that result from business transactions during an accounting period.
2. The ____________ is the source of information reported on financial statements.
3. The ____________ reports net income or net loss.
4. The ____________ of a financial statement answers questions of who, what, and when.
5. An income statement reports revenue and ____________.
6. A ____________ results when expenses are larger than revenue.
7. The ____________ summarizes changes in the capital account.
8. The ____________ reports financial condition on a specific date.
9. Comparing two amounts on a financial statement is ____________.
10. ____________ ratios evaluate earnings performance during an accounting period.

QUESTIONS (Completion)

1. _____ summarize changes that result from business transactions during an accounting period.
2. The _____ is the source of information reported on financial statements.
3. The _____ reports net income or net loss.
4. The _____ of a financial statement answers questions of who, what, and when.
5. An income statement reports revenue and _____.
6. A _____ results when expenses are larger than revenue.
7. The _____ summarizes changes in the capital account.
8. The _____ reports financial condition on a specific date.
9. Comparing two amounts on a financial statement is _____.
10. _____ ratios evaluate earnings performance during an accounting period.

ANSWERS

1. Financial statements
2. work sheet
3. income statement
4. heading
5. expenses
6. net loss
7. statement of changes in owner's equity
8. balance sheet
9. ratio analysis
10. Profitability

REVIEW AND ACTIVITIES
CHAPTER 9

USING KEY TERMS

See the *Glossary* for the definitions of these terms. Make sure students note the importance of financial statement analysis.

Understanding Accounting Concepts and Procedures

(Answers)

1. To show effects of transactions for the period.
2. To report revenue earned and expenses incurred during the period.
3. To allow comparison of statement from two or more periods.
4. The Income Statement section of the work sheet.
5. To show changes in the owner's capital account resulting from business transactions.
6. The work sheet, the income statement, and the capital account in the general ledger.
7. To report the assets of the business and summarize claims to those assets on a specific date.
8. The Balance Sheet section of the work sheet and the statement of changes in owner's equity.
9. Balance sheet date line refers to a specific date; the others refer to the entire fiscal period.
10. The balance sheet.
11. To analyze profitability, debt-paying ability, and efficiency in use of resources.
12. Liquidity ratios show a company's ability to pay its short-term debts, which is important to creditors who need to know that they will be paid.
13. Both show the company's ability to pay its short-term debts. The difference is that the quick ratio does not consider inventory as a liquid asset.
14. A company's managers and its outside investors.

CHAPTER 9 REVIEW AND ACTIVITIES

USING KEY TERMS

Imagine that you are the owner of a video arcade. Develop an information sheet for your manager and explain the importance of financial statement preparation. Use each of the following key terms in your report.

balance sheet	profitability ratio
current assets	quick ratio
current liabilities	ratio analysis
current ratio	report form
financial statements	return on sales
income statement	statement of changes in owner's equity
liquidity ratio	

Understanding Accounting Concepts and Procedures

Instructions

On a separate sheet of paper, answer the following questions:

1. Why are financial statements prepared?
2. What is the purpose of the income statement?
3. Why does a business need to be consistent in the fiscal period it uses for its financial reports?
4. What is the source of information used to prepare the income statement?
5. What is the purpose of the statement of changes in owner's equity?
6. What sources of information are used to prepare the statement of changes in owner's equity?
7. What is the purpose of the balance sheet?
8. What sources of information are needed to prepare the balance sheet?
9. How does the date in the heading of a balance sheet differ from the date in the heading of an income statement and a statement of changes in owner's equity?
10. Which financial statement represents the basic accounting equation?
11. What is the purpose of computing ratios from amounts on financial statements?
12. Why might a creditor be interested in the liquidity ratios of a business?
13. How are the current ratio and the quick ratio similar? different?
14. Who might be interested in the profitability ratios of a business?

ASSESSMENT RESOURCES

Choose assessment strategies from the following pages to evaluate your students' progress.

Student Edition
Check Your Understanding, pp. 209, 214, 222
Chapter 9 Problems, pp. 227–229
Analyzing Financial Reports, p. 221

Assessment and Evaluation Masters
Chapter 9 Study Plan, *Glencoe Workbook (CRWP)*
Chapter 9 Self-Test, *Glencoe Workbook (CRWP)*
Chapter 9 Test, *Chapter Tests* Booklet
Chapter 9 Activity, *School-to-Work Handbook*
Chapter 9 **Exam***View*

Teacher Wraparound Edition
Critical Thinking Activity, p. 206
Reteaching Sections 1–2, pp. 209, 214
Chapter 9 Quiz, p. 223

Case Study...

Service Business: Video Arcade

Taki Yamamoto owns a video arcade business called Arcadia.

Taki hired your accounting firm to record Arcadia's financial information. Taki hands you a folder containing these documents:

- Canceled checks with June dates: $800 for rent, $120 for electricity, $70 for telephone service, $180 for insurance, $250 for newspaper advertising, and $200 for a cleaning service.
- Invoice dated June 16 for a used video game that was sold on account for $2,000.
- Cash register tapes for June showing total cash sales of $5,890.

Thinking Critically:

1. Using the preceding information, make a list of accounts needed to record the transactions indicated by the financial documents Taki gave you.
2. Prepare an income statement for Arcadia for the month of June.

*inter*NET CONNECTION

Preparing Financial Statements

Many national companies began as proprietorships or partnerships. Whether a company is a sole proprietorship or a corporation, financial statements provide information for making financial and operating decisions. Hoover's Online contains information about more than 18,000 public and private companies.

Do This:

1. Find the Hoover's Online Web site.
2. Within the site, locate financial information about The Gap and The Limited, Inc.
3. What was the amount of each company's sales last year?
4. What was the net income for each company?

Conducting an Audit with Alex

Instructions Using the amounts that are given below, calculate the missing amounts. Write the missing amounts on a separate sheet of paper.

SweepIt Carpet Cleaning Company
Statement of Changes in Owner's Equity
For the Month Ended July 31, 20--

Beginning Capital, July 1, 20--		?
Add: Investments by Owner		1 500 00
Subtotal:		?
Less: Withdrawals by Owner	1 600 00	
Net Loss	?	
Total Decrease in Capital		2 751 00
Ending Capital, July 31, 20--		19 729 00

Workplace Skills

Using Computers

Businesses of all sizes are becoming automated. Computers are integral to most business operations. The ability to use computers and software is essential to complete most business tasks.

On the Job:

As the accounting clerk for Jewels, Gems, and Treasures, a costume jewelry and gift shop, you are to prepare the quarterly income statement using a spreadsheet program. In the past you have prepared this statement using accounting stationery and a pencil.

Thinking Critically:

Prepare a list of reasons why using a spreadsheet program is an improvement over manually preparing financial reports.

REVIEW AND ACTIVITIES CHAPTER 9

Case Study...

Thinking Critically (Answers)

1. Answers may vary, but the list of accounts may include Rent Expense, Utilities Expense, Insurance Expense, Advertising Expense, and Maintenance Expense.
2. Net Income: $6,270

Workplace Skills

Thinking Critically (Answers)

Answers will vary. Some possible benefits are easier preparation and editing, automatic calculations, and the ability to conduct "what if" analyses.

Conducting an Audit with Alex

(Answer)

Beginning Capital: $20,980
Subtotal: $22,480
Net Loss: $1,151

Internet Resources and Activities Handbook

Refer students to the booklet for additional Internet activities.

*inter*NET CONNECTION www.glencoe.com

Do This (Answers)

1. www.hoovers.com
2. Answers will vary, depending on the year.
3. Answers will vary, depending on the year.

PEACHTREE CORNER

Income Statement/Balance Sheet

To print an Income Statement or a Balance Sheet, choose **Financial Statements** from the ***Reports*** menu. Then select the report you want to print from the Select a Report window.

Reports Services Window
Accounts Receivable...
Accounts Payable...
Payroll...
General Ledger...
Financial Statements...
Inventory...
Jobs...
Account Reconciliation...

Financial Statements

The Navigation Aid provides an easy (visual) alternative for you to print the financial statements.

Statement of Changes in Owner's Equity

Peachtree does not provide the capability to print the statement of changes in owner's equity. Instruct students to use the <Standard> Retained Earnings report and change the report title to "Statement of Changes in Owner's Equity."

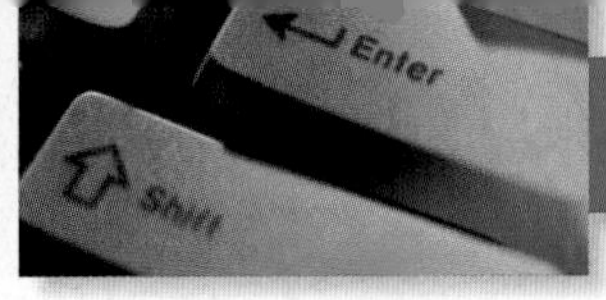

Preparing Financial Statements

Making the Transition from a Manual to a Computerized System

Task	Perform Accounting Procedures Using Manual Methods	Perform Accounting Procedures Using Automated Methods
Preparing an income statement	1. Transfer all revenue and expense accounts and their balances from the work sheet. 2. Subtract expenses from revenue to determine net income or net loss.	1. Select **Income Statement** from the ***Reports*** menu. 2. Click Print.
Preparing a statement of changes in owner's equity	1. Transfer the beginning balance of the capital account from the work sheet. 2. Add additional investments and net income or loss. 3. Subract withdrawals. 4. Calculate the ending balance for the capital account.	1. Since the software automatically computes the ending balance of the capital account for you, it is not necessary to prepare this statement.
Preparing a balance sheet	1. Transfer permanent accounts and their balances from the work sheet. 2. Transfer the ending capital account balance from the statement of changes in owner's equity. 3. Total all asset account balances. 4. Total all liabilities and owner's equity account balances. 5. Verify that assets equal liabilities and owner's equity.	1. Select **Balance Sheet** from the ***Reports*** menu. 2. Click Print.

Preparing Financial Statements

Peachtree Question	Description
How do I prepare financial statements in Peachtree?	1. Select **Financial Statements** from the ***Reports*** menu. 2. Choose the statement you wish to print from the reports list. 3. Click print when the statement appears on the screen.
What does the software do "behind the scenes"?	• The software automatically reads through the general ledger accounts, pulling account balances and names into the appropriate pre-formatted statements.

For detailed instructions: See the **Peachtree User Guide** in your Glencoe Working Papers.

Peachtree® Answers to Frequently Asked Questions

Q: Why do some problems include a customized income statement but no customized balance sheet?

A: The predefined <Standard> income statement includes two sets of income figures—current period and year to date. The customized report includes only the current period. For the balance sheet, the predefined <Standard> report includes only the current period so a customzied report is not necessary.

For additional information, see your *Glencoe Peachtree Accounting User Guide.*

APPLICATION OPTIONS

Problem 9–4 Preparing an Income Statement

The work sheet for Wilderness Rentals for the month ended September 30, 20-- is in your working papers.

Instructions Using the work sheet, prepare an income statement for Wilderness Rentals.

Analyze: What is the return on sales for the period?

Problem 9–5 Preparing a Statement of Changes in Owner's Equity

Instructions Using the work sheet for Wilderness Rentals in your working papers and the income statement prepared in Problem 9–4, prepare a statement of changes in owner's equity and a balance sheet. Ronald Hicks made an additional investment in the business of $500 during the period.

Analyze: What is the current ratio for Wilderness Rentals for this statement period?

Problem 9–6 Preparing Financial Statements

The trial balance for the Hot Suds Car Wash is listed below and in your working papers.

Instructions

1. Complete the work sheet in your working papers.
2. Prepare an income statement for the quarter ended September 30, 20--.
3. Prepare a statement of changes in owner's equity. Regina Delgado made no additional investments during the period.
4. Prepare a balance sheet in report form.

Analyze: What is the return on sales for the period?

Hot Suds Car Wash
Trial Balance
For the Quarter Ended September 30, 20--

		Debit	Credit
101	Cash in Bank	8,457.00	
105	Accts. Rec.—Linda Brown	584.00	
110	Accts. Rec.—Valley Auto	619.00	
115	Detailing Supplies	810.00	
120	Detergent Supplies	460.00	
125	Office Equipment	15,240.00	
130	Office Furniture	2,160.00	
135	Car Wash Equipment	7,522.00	
201	Accts. Pay.—Allen Vacuum Systems		3,528.00
205	Accts. Pay.—O'Brian's Office Supply		1,215.00
301	Regina Delgado, Capital		23,845.00
305	Regina Delgado, Withdrawals	1,500.00	
310	Income Summary	—	—
401	Wash Revenue		9,623.00
405	Wax Revenue		8,019.00
410	Interior Detailing Revenue		2,628.00
501	Advertising Expense	1,963.00	
505	Equipment Rental Expense	4,137.00	
510	Maintenance Expense	1,186.00	
520	Rent Expense	3,500.00	
530	Utilities Expense	720.00	
		48,858.00	48,858.00

Complete chapter problems one of four ways:

1. **Manual** Glencoe Working Papers

or

2. **Peachtree Complete Accounting** Software

or

3. **QuickBooks** Templates (Problem 9–6)

or

4. **Spreadsheet** Templates (Problem 9–8)

Peachtree®

SMART GUIDE

Step-by-Step Instructions: Problem 9–4, 9–5

1. Select the problem set for Wilderness Rentals (Prob. 9–4, 5).
2. Rename the company and set the system date.
3. Print a General Ledger Trial Balance.
4. Print an Income Statement.
5. Print a Statement of Changes in Owner's Equity.
6. Print a Balance Sheet.
7. Answer the Analyze question.
8. End the session.

Problem 9–4 (Answers) Preparing an Income Statement
Net Income: $1,812

Analyze: 17.04%

Problem 9–5 (Answers) Preparing a Statement of Changes in Owner's Equity
Ending Capital: $14,372
Total Assets: $18,699
Total Liabilities: $4,327

Analyze: 1.8:1

Problem 9–6 (Answers) Preparing Financial Statements
Net Income: $8,764
Ending Capital: $31,109
Total Assets: $35,852
Total Liabilities: $4,743

Analyze: 43.24%

HOME AND COMMUNITY CONNECTIONS ACTIVITY

Small-Business Loans To help students understand the time, effort, and information needed to secure a small-business loan, have them check out some local sources for loans. Have students call banks or credit unions, or use a business administration center in the community, if it exists. Have students ask the bank or the center what information is necessary to be considered for a small-business loan. Then have students write a one-page summary of the information they found.

Problem 9-7 (Answers) Preparing Financial Statements

Trial Balance totals: $55,240
Net Loss: $3,637
Ending Capital: $25,391
Total Assets: $33,294
Total Liabilities: $7,903

Analyze: 1:1

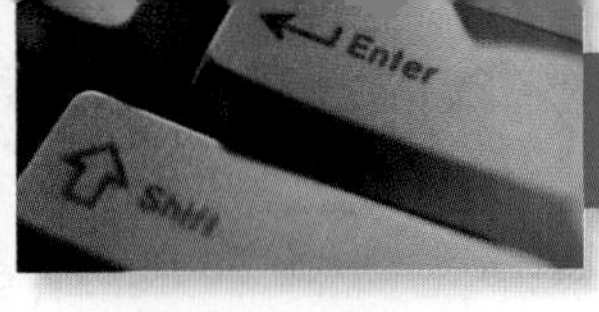

Peachtree®

SMART GUIDE

Step-by-Step Instructions: Problem 9-6

1. Select the problem set for Hot Suds Car Wash (Prob. 9-6).
2. Rename the company and set the system date.
3. Print a General Ledger Trial Balance.
4. Print an Income Statement.
5. Print a Statement of Changes in Owner's Equity.
6. Print a Balance Sheet.
7. Answer the Analyze question.
8. End the session.

Peachtree®

SMART GUIDE

Step-by-Step Instructions: Problem 9-7

1. Select the problem set for Kits & Pups Grooming (Prob. 9-7).
2. Rename the company and set the system date.
3. Print a General Ledger Trial Balance.
4. Print an Income Statement.
5. Print a Statement of Changes in Owner's Equity.
6. Print a Balance Sheet.
7. Answer the Analyze question.
8. End the session.

Problem 9-7 Preparing Financial Statements

The general ledger accounts and balances for Kits & Pups Grooming follow.

General Ledger

No.	Account	Balance
101	Cash in Bank	$ 4,296
105	Accts. Rec.—Juan Alvarez	1,528
110	Accts. Rec.—Nathan Carlsbad	904
115	Accts. Rec.—Martha Giles	1,219
120	Grooming Supplies	1,368
125	Office Equipment	8,467
130	Office Furniture	3,396
135	Computer Equipment	2,730
140	Grooming Equipment	1,974
145	Kennel Equipment	7,412
201	Accts. Pay.—Able Store Equipment	3,876
205	Accts. Pay.—Dogs & Cats Inc.	2,746
207	Accts. Pay.—Pet Gourmet	1,281
301	Abe Shultz, Capital	30,928
305	Abe Shultz, Withdrawals	1,900
310	Income Summary	—
401	Boarding Revenue	11,989
405	Grooming Revenue	4,420
501	Advertising Expense	3,934
505	Equipment Repair Expense	943
510	Maintenance Expense	2,483
520	Rent Expense	8,850
530	Utilities Expense	3,836

Instructions

1. Prepare a work sheet for the month ended September 30, 20--.
2. Prepare an income statement for the period.
3. Prepare a statement of changes in owner's equity. Abe Shultz made an additional investment of $2,500 during the period.
4. Prepare a balance sheet in report form.

Analyze: What is the quick ratio for Kits & Pups Grooming?

Problem 9-8 Preparing a Statement of Changes in Owner's Equity

Instructions Use the balance sheet and income statement shown to prepare a statement of changes in owner's equity. (The owner made an additional investment of $4,000 and withdrew $1,500 during the period.)

ADDRESSING MULTIPLE LEARNING STYLES

Visual Learner/Spatial Learner Have visual learners prepare a bulletin-board display with illustrations of financial statements for a sole proprietorship. If students cannot obtain real-life statements, they can create statements from examples in the text. Ask students to identify the key elements for each statement (the heading, the income section, the assets section, and so forth). Also have them include the purpose of each statement in their displays.

Outback Guide Service Income Statement For the Month Ended September 30, 20--		
Revenue:		
Guide Service Revenue		8 9 1 3 00
Expenses:		
Advertising Expense	3 7 5 00	
Maintenance Expense	1 3 8 00	
Rent Expense	1 2 5 0 00	
Salaries Expense	1 5 0 0 00	
Utilities Expense	1 1 6 1 00	
Total Expenses		4 4 2 4 00
Net Income		4 4 8 9 00

SPREADSHEET SMART GUIDE

Step-by-Step Instructions: Problem 9-8

1. Select the spreadsheet template for Problem 9-8.
2. Enter your name and the date in the spaces provided on the template.
3. Complete the spreadsheet using the instructions in your working papers.
4. Print the spreadsheet and proof your work.
5. Save your work and exit the spreadsheet program.

Outback Guide Service Balance Sheet September 30, 20--		
Assets		
Cash in Bank	3 1 1 7 00	
Accounts Receivable—Mary Johnson	4 2 3 00	
Accounts Receivable—Feldman, Jones, & Ritter	4 4 3 00	
Accounts Receivable—Podaski Systems Inc.	1 0 0 8 00	
Hiking Supplies	1 5 3 00	
Office Supplies	3 3 8 00	
Office Equipment	6 4 9 2 00	
Office Furniture	3 0 8 4 00	
Computer Equipment	3 6 2 4 00	
Hiking Equipment	1 0 1 5 00	
Rafting Equipment	9 1 8 6 00	
Total Assets		28 8 8 3 00
Liabilities		
Accounts Payable—A-1 Adventure Warehouse	6 5 4 5 00	
Accounts Payable—Peak Equipment Inc.	1 3 2 5 00	
Accounts Payable—Premier Processors	6 4 2 00	
Total Liabilities		8 5 1 2 00
Owner's Equity		
Juanita Ortega, Capital		20 3 7 1 00
Total Liabilities and Owner's Equity		28 8 8 3 00

Analyze: What was the largest expense for this business during the period?

PROBLEMS
CHAPTER 9

CHALLENGE PROBLEM

Problem 9-8 (Answers) Preparing a Statement of Changes in Owner's Equity
Ending Capital: $20,371

Analyze: Salaries Expense

EXTENDING THE CONTENT

Using Financial Statements on the Job Ask students who work to ask their supervisor or manager about the financial statements that have proven to be most helpful in running the business. How often are these statements prepared? How are they useful? Have students collect samples, if possible, and share their findings with the class. They should identify the financial statements, describe when they are prepared, and explain the reasons the supervisor or manager has found them to be helpful in the operations of the business.

CHAPTER 10 Resource Manager

Section Resources

	Objectives & Standards	Activities & Features	Reproducible Masters
Chapter Opener *Completing the Accounting Cycle for a Sole Proprietorship*	• Explain why it is necessary to update accounts through closing entries. • Explain the purpose of the Income Summary account. • Explain the relationship between the Income Summary account and the capital account. • Analyze and journalize closing entries. • Post the closing entries to the general ledger. • Prepare a post-closing trial balance. • Define the accounting terms introduced in this chapter. **National Standards for Business Education**: IA15, IA16	Exploring the Real World of Business, p. 230 Workplace Connections, p. 231	School-to-Work Handbook
Section 1 *Preparing Closing Entries*	• Why temporary capital accounts are closed at the end of the fiscal year. • The purpose of the Income Summary account. • The relationship between the Income Summary account and the capital account. • How to analyze and journalize closing entries.	International Accounting, p. 235 Did You Know?, p. 235 Math Hints, p. 236 Accounting Tips, p. 240 Connect To, p. 241 A Matter of Ethics, p. 241	Strategies for Teaching International Accounting Math Review for Accounting Demonstration Problem Strategies for Teaching Ethics in Accounting
Section 2 *Posting Closing Entries and Preparing a Post-Closing Trial Balance*	• How to record closing entries in the general ledger. • The purpose of a post-closing trial balance. • How to prepare a post-closing trial balance.	Accounting Flashbacks, p. 245 Analyzing Financial Reports, p. 245	Internet Resources and Activities Handbook

KEY

Posters · Transparency · Software · Videocassette
Blackline Masters · CD-ROM · Portfolio

MULTIMEDIA RESOURCE

Peachtree	QuickBooks	Spreadsheets	Videos	CD-ROMs
Problem 10–4 *Preparing Closing Entries* Problem 10–5 *Preparing a Post-Closing Trial Balance* Problem 10–6 *Journalizing Closing Entries* Problem 10–7 *Posting Closing Entries and Preparing a Post-Closing Trial Balance* Problem 10–8 *Completing End-of-Period Activities*	Problem 10–8 *Completing End-of-Period Activities* Problem 10–9 *Completing End-of-Period Activities*	Problem 10–9 *Completing End-of-Period Activities*	***Video Segment: The Accounting Cycle*** After viewing this video, students will be able to describe the concept of the cycle that businesses follow to complete the accounting records for a fiscal period. They will be able to describe each step in the accounting cycle and the activities that initiate that step or connect it to another part of the accounting cycle.	***Electronic Learning Center (ELC), Chapter 10*** This program is ideal for visual learners since it incorporates video images, animation, and graphics to enliven the content of each lesson. ***Interactive Lesson Planner (ILP), Chapter 10*** This CD-ROM combines the versatility of an electronic lesson planner with the convenience of teacher classroom resources.

SCANS Correlation Chart

FOUNDATION SKILLS

Basic Skills:	Reading	Writing	Math	Listening	Speaking	
Thinking Skills:	Creative Thinking	Decision Making	Problem Solving	Seeing Things in the Mind's Eye	Knowing How to Learn	Reasoning
Personal Qualities:	Responsibility	Self-Esteem	Sociability	Self-Management	Integrity/Honesty	

WORKPLACE COMPETENCIES

Resources:	Allocating Time	Allocating Money	Allocating Material and Facility Resources	Allocating Human Resources		
Information:	Acquiring and Evaluating Information	Organizing and Maintaining Information	Interpreting and Communicating Information	Using Computers to Process Information		
Interpersonal Skills:	Participating as a Member of a Team	Teaching Others	Serving Clients/ Customers	Exercising Leadership	Negotiating to Arrive at a Decision	Working with Cultural Diversity
Systems:	Understanding Systems	Monitoring and Correcting Performance	Improving and Designing Systems			
Technology:	Selecting Technology	Applying Technology to Task	Maintaining and Troubleshooting Technology			

*Highlighted blocks indicate areas covered in the chapter. Additional SCANS skills are also covered throughout the *Teacher Wraparound Edition.*

Assessment

Student Edition
- Check Your Understanding, pp. 242, 246
- Chapter 10 Problems, pp. 251–255

Assessment and Evaluation Masters
- Chapter 10 Study Plan, *Glencoe Workbook*
- Chapter 10 Self-Test, *Glencoe Workbook*
- Chapter 10 Test, *Chapter Tests* Booklet
- Chapter 10 Activity, *School-to-Work Handbook*
- Chapter 10 **Exam***View*

Teacher Wraparound Edition
- Critical Thinking Activity, p. 252
- Reteaching Section 1, p. 242
- Reteaching Section 2, p. 246
- Chapter 10 Quiz, p. 247

Transparencies

	Teaching Transparencies	Solution Transparencies
Section 1:	10–1, 10–2, 10–3, 10–4, 10–5, 10–6, 10–7, 10–8, 10–9	Problems 10–1, 10–2
Section 2:	10–10, 10–11a, 10–11b, 10–12	Problem 10–3
End of Chapter:		Problems 10–4, 10–5, 10–6, 10–7, 10–8, 10–9

TEACHER CLASSROOM RESOURCES

This is a representation of key blackline masters available in the Teacher Classroom Resources.

Teaching Aids

Transparency Examples

Section Focus Transparencies

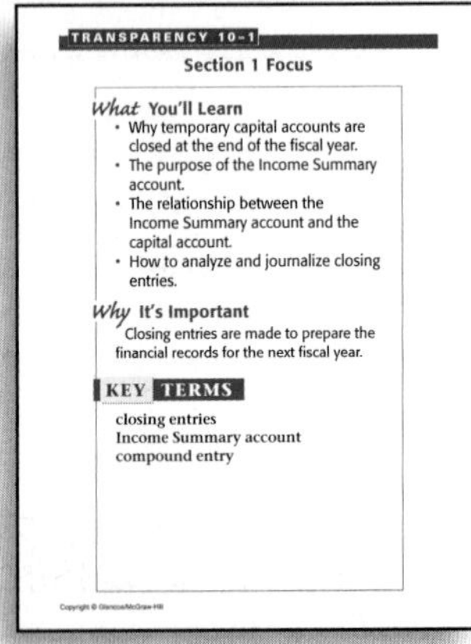

TRANSPARENCY 10-1

Section 1 Focus

What You'll Learn

- Why temporary capital accounts are closed at the end of the fiscal year.
- The purpose of the Income Summary account.
- The relationship between the Income Summary account and the capital account.
- How to analyze and journalize closing entries.

Why It's Important

Closing entries are made to prepare the financial records for the next fiscal year.

KEY TERMS

closing entries
Income Summary account
compound entry

Teaching Transparencies

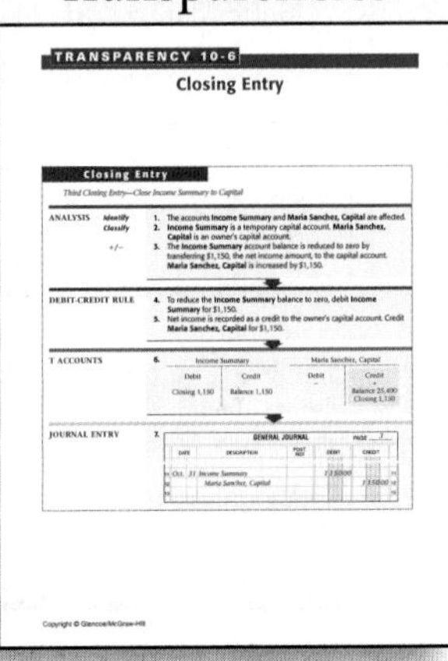

TRANSPARENCY 10-6

Closing Entry

Teaching Transparencies

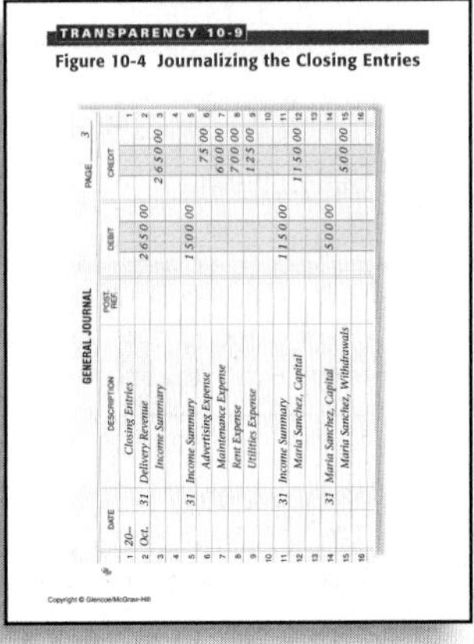

TRANSPARENCY 10-9

Figure 10-4 Journalizing the Closing Entries

Solution Transparencies

Working Papers for End-of-Chapter Problems

Problem 10-4 Preparing Closing Entries

Problem 10-5 Preparing a Post-Closing Trial Balance

Demonstration Problems

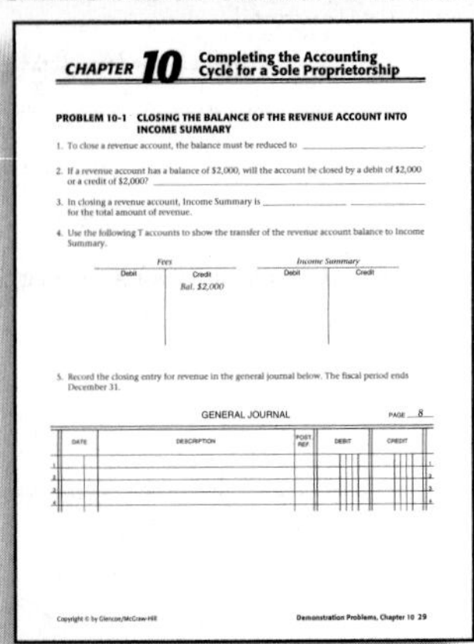

CHAPTER 10 Completing the Accounting Cycle for a Sole Proprietorship

PROBLEM 10-1 CLOSING THE BALANCE OF THE REVENUE ACCOUNT INTO INCOME SUMMARY

Lesson Plans

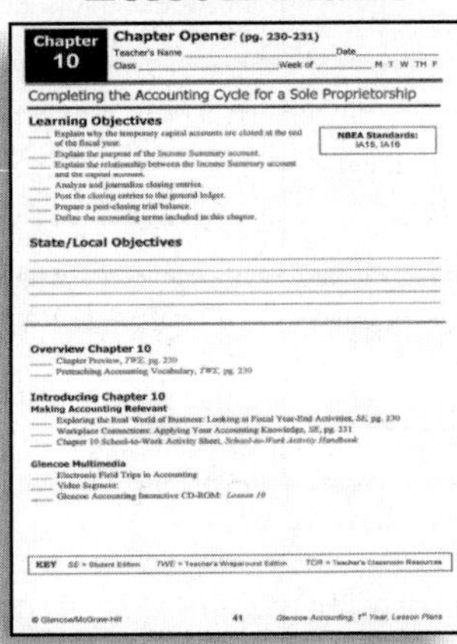

Chapter 10 Chapter Opener (pg. 230–231)

Completing the Accounting Cycle for a Sole Proprietorship

Learning Objectives

State/Local Objectives

Block Scheduling

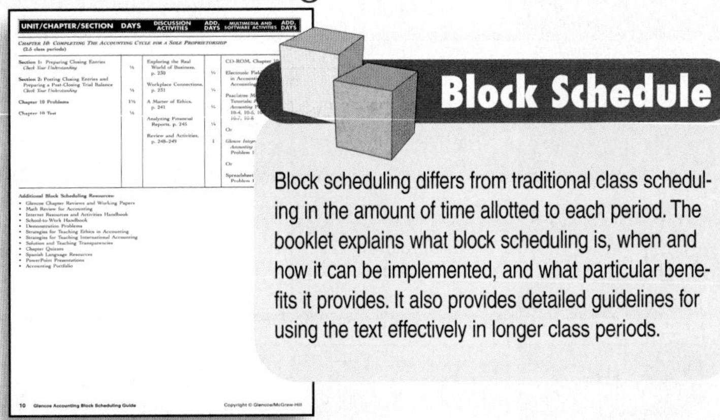

UNIT/CHAPTER/SECTION DAYS DISCUSSION ACTIVITIES ADD. DAYS MULTIMEDIA AND SOFTWARE ACTIVITIES ADD. DAYS

Block Schedule

Block scheduling differs from traditional class scheduling in the amount of time allotted to each period. The booklet explains what block scheduling is, when and how it can be implemented, and what particular benefits it provides. It also provides detailed guidelines for using the text effectively in longer class periods.

Enrichment and Application

Strategies for Teaching Ethics in Accounting

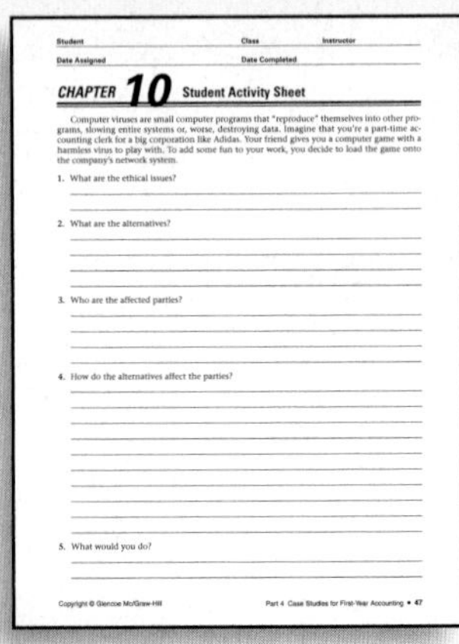

CHAPTER 10 Student Activity Sheet

Strategies for Teaching International Accounting

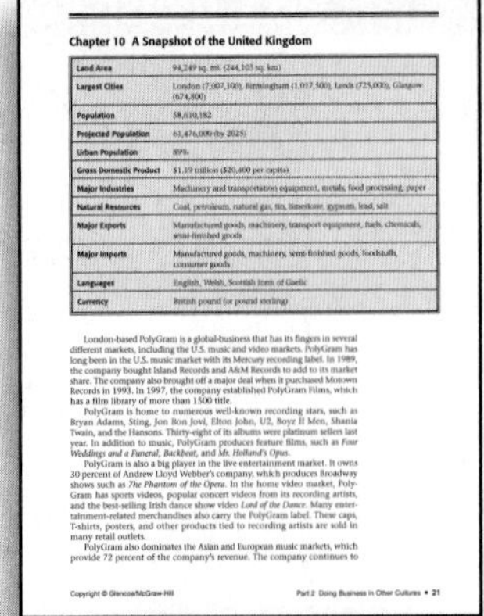

Chapter 10 A Snapshot of the United Kingdom

School-to-Work Handbook

CHAPTER 10 SCHOOL-TO-WORK ACTIVITY

Completing the Accounting Cycle for a Sole Proprietorship

Meeting Different Ability Levels

Chapter Reviews and Working Papers (CRWP)

Working Papers Review

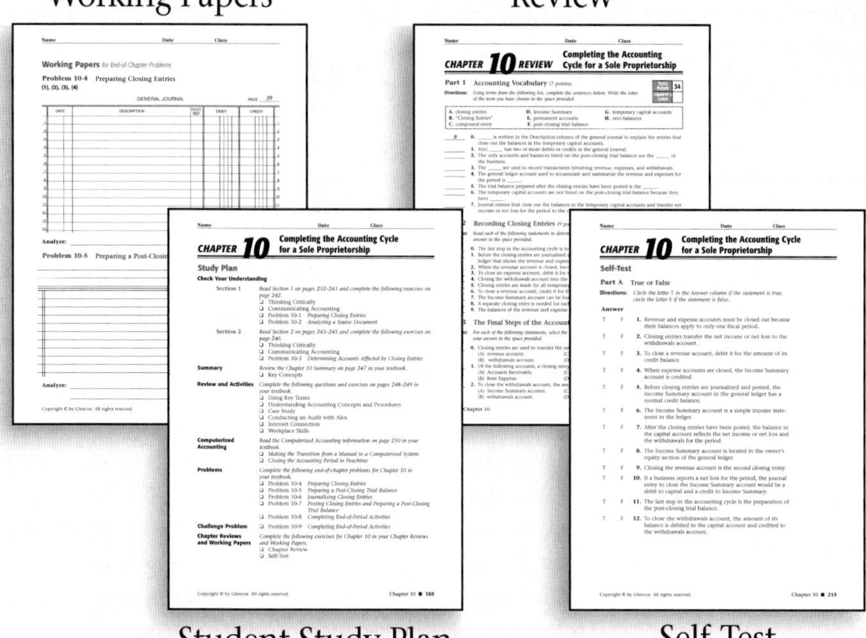

Student Study Plan Self-Test

Real-World Multimedia CD-ROM

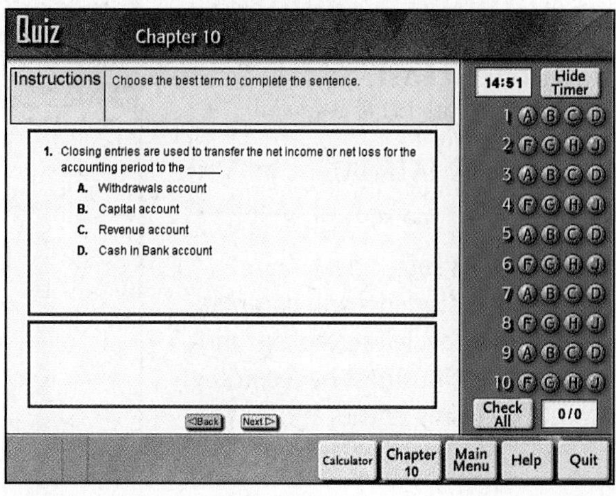

Key to Ability Levels

Each section gives skill-building activities. Each activity has been labeled for use with students of various learning styles and abilities.

L1 Level 1 activities are basic activities and should be within the range of all students.

L2 Level 2 activities are average activities and should be within the range of average and above average students.

L3 Level 3 activities are challenging activities designed for the ability range of above average students.

ELL ELL activities should be within the ability range of English Language Learners.

Assessment and Evaluation

Chapter Tests

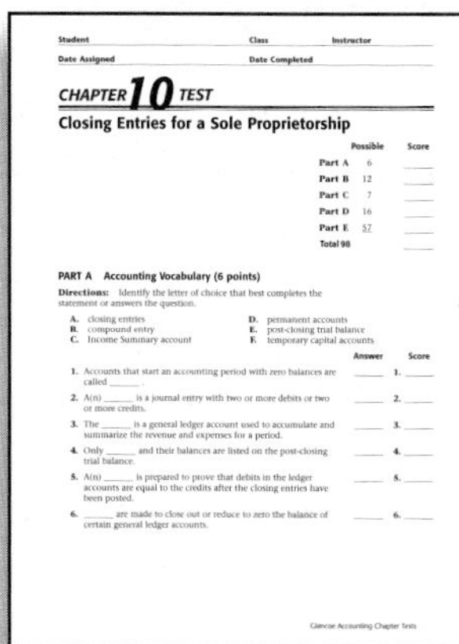

Chapter Quiz

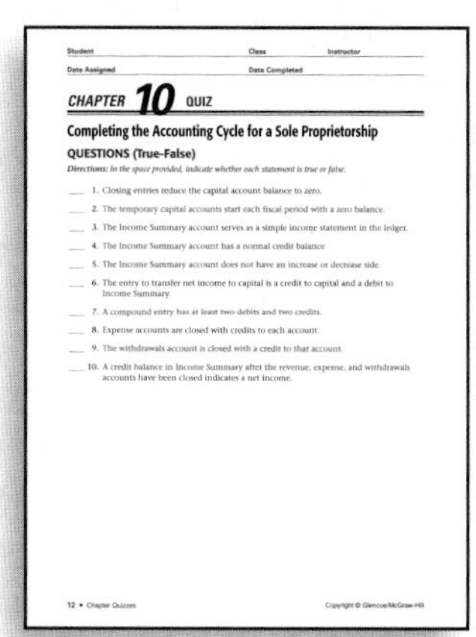

Teaching Resources at a Glance

Application Resources

- Glencoe Chapter Review and Working Papers, SE and TAE
- School-to-Work Handbook, SE and TM
- Accounting Portfolio, SE and TM

Reproducible Masters

- Demonstration Problems
- Lesson Plans
- Block Scheduling
- Spanish Language Resources

Glencoe Accounting Professional Development Series

- Strategies for Teaching Ethics in Accounting
- Accounting Competitive Event Review
- Math Review for Accounting
- Strategies for Teaching International Accounting
- Internet Resources and Activities Handbook

Transparency Package

- Section Focus Transparencies
- Teaching Transparencies
- Source Document Transparencies
- Solution Transparencies

Performance Assessment

- **Exam***View* CD-ROM
- Chapter Tests
- Chapter Quizzes
- Unit Tests
- Audit Tests
- Printed Testbank

Multimedia Resources

- Electronic Learning Center:
  - Multimedia CD-ROMs
  - Peachtree software, tutorials, templates, and solutions
  - Spreadsheet templates
- Using QuickBooks with Glencoe Accounting
- Interactive Lesson Planner
- Electronic Field Trips in Accounting
- PowerPoint Presentation
- Web site: glencoeaccounting.glencoe.com

OVERVIEW CHAPTER 10

Correlations to National Standards for Business Education
(See pages T50–T51 for a detailed correlation chart.)
Standards: IA15, IA16

Chapter Preview

In this chapter students will complete the accounting cycle for a sole proprietorship, service business by recording and posting closing entries and preparing a post-closing trial balance.

Section Overviews

- Section 1—*Preparing Closing Entries*
- Section 2—*Posting Closing Entries and Preparing a Post-Closing Trial Balance*

Chapter Vocabulary

closing entries
Income Summary account
compound entry
post-closing trial balance

Preteaching Accounting Vocabulary

Team Competition: Reinforce vocabulary through a team competition to define new terms. Include terms from earlier chapters as well. Appoint teams to participate in the "Vocabulary Bee." Have teams take turns defining a term you name, giving teams the opportunity to consult with each other before giving a definition (set a time limit of a minute or so). A team that gives an incorrect definition is eliminated until one team remains and is the winner. L1

CHAPTER 10

Completing the Accounting Cycle for a Sole Proprietorship

Learning Objectives

When you have completed this chapter, you will be able to:

- Explain why it is necessary to update accounts through closing entries.
- Explain the purpose of the Income Summary account.
- Explain the relationship between the Income Summary account and the capital account.
- Analyze and journalize closing entries.
- Post the closing entries to the general ledger.
- Prepare a post-closing trial balance.
- Define the accounting terms introduced in this chapter.

Exploring the Real World of Business

LOOKING AT FISCAL YEAR-END ACTIVITIES

Grind the winch? Trim the sail? Inflate your BCD? If any of these terms sound intriguing, you might be interested in sailing or scuba diving. **ActionQuest** is a company that offers certification in both. The company specializes in programs for teens, and you can even earn high school or college credits as you live aboard a sailing yacht and study marine sciences, oceanography, and tropical marine biology.

Located in Sarasota, Florida, **ActionQuest** trains teens from all over the United States, the Far East, South America, and Europe. Each voyage, which takes place in the waters of the Caribbean Islands, Mediterranean and Fiji, lasts from two and a half to three weeks. Instruction is provided by professional diving instructors and U.S. Coast Guard licensed skippers.

ActionQuest's revenue comes from fees teens pay for diving and sailing instruction. At the end of each fiscal period, the company closes its accounts and analyzes the revenue and costs of its diving and sailing programs. Part of the analysis might be looking at expenses or deciding whether fees are at an appropriate level to cover operating costs.

What do you think?

If you worked for **ActionQuest,** why would you want to be able to compare operating expenses from one fiscal period to another?

ACTIONQuest

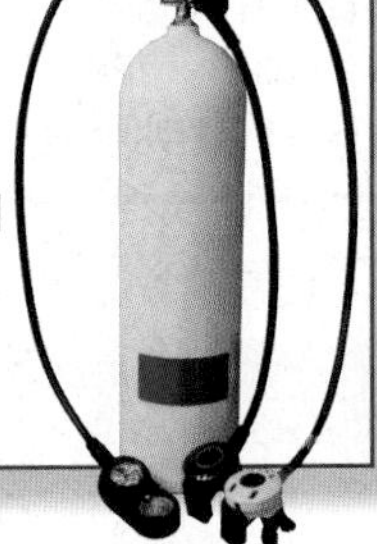

Exploring the Real World of Business

ActionQuest

ActionQuest is a private company, like thousands of other companies that employ accountants. Encourage students to consider such companies when planning their careers. Though less well known than major corporations, small companies may offer opportunities to learn a variety of job skills.

What do you think? (Answers)

Students' answers may vary. Comparing operating expenses from one period to another helps managers analyze whether expenses are as expected or higher or lower than expected. For a company such as ActionQuest, higher expenses may indicate a need to raise fees or to find ways to lower costs.

Workplace Connections

Applying Your Accounting Knowledge

Preparing financial statements can be a hectic time for an accounting staff. Professional accountants learn to manage stressful times using good organizational skills. Once the financial statements have been prepared, other tasks must be completed to close one accounting cycle and begin another. You will learn about these tasks in this chapter.

Investigate:

1. In your workplace, are there especially hectic times of the day or year?
2. How do you and your co-workers handle these busy times?

Glencoe Accounting Online

Visit the *Glencoe Accounting* Web site at **glencoeaccounting.glencoe.com** for additional activities and information.

INTRODUCING
CHAPTER 10

Making Accounting Relevant

Workplace Connections: Applying Your Accounting Knowledge

Discussion: Ask students who have part-time jobs to discuss how they manage stress during especially busy times. What personal skills help them manage busy times? How do they organize their work to be more efficient?

Investigate (Answers)

1. Students who work in retail stores might mention holidays as an especially busy time, while those who work in food service might mention weekend nights.
2. Answers will vary. Employees can handle especially busy times by being organized, having knowledge of their own and others' responsibilities, knowing products or services well, and pitching in to help—even if it's not their responsibility.

School-to-Work Activity

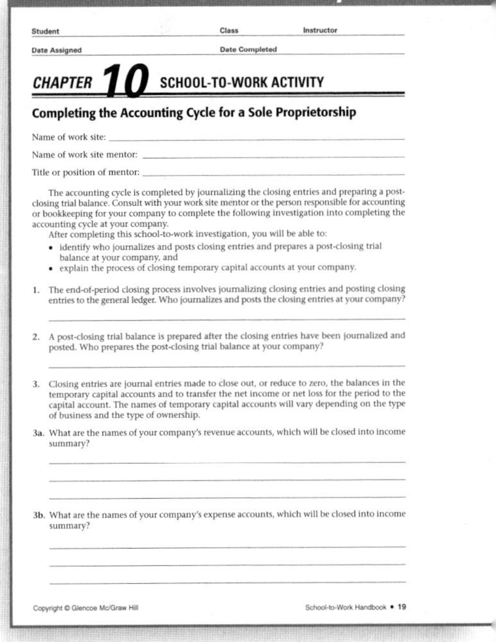

Student ____ Class ____ Instructor ____

Date Assigned ____ Date Completed ____

CHAPTER 10 SCHOOL-TO-WORK ACTIVITY

Completing the Accounting Cycle for a Sole Proprietorship

Name of work site: ____

Name of work site mentor: ____

Title or position of mentor: ____

The accounting cycle is completed by journalizing the closing entries and preparing a post-closing trial balance. Consult with your work site mentor or the person responsible for accounting or bookkeeping for your company to complete the following investigation into completing the accounting cycle at your company.

After completing this school-to-work investigation, you will be able to:

- identify who journalizes and posts closing entries and prepares a post-closing trial balance at your company, and
- explain the process of closing temporary capital accounts at your company.

1. The end-of-period closing process involves journalizing closing entries and posting closing entries to the general ledger. Who journalizes and posts the closing entries at your company?

2. A post-closing trial balance is prepared after the closing entries have been journalized and posted. Who prepares the post-closing trial balance at your company?

3. Closing entries are journal entries made to close out, or reduce to zero, the balances in the temporary capital accounts and to transfer the net income or net loss for the period to the capital account. The names of temporary capital accounts will vary depending on the type of business and the type of ownership.

3a. What are the names of your company's revenue accounts, which will be closed into income summary?

3b. What are the names of your company's expense accounts, which will be closed into income summary?

 School-to-Work Handbook • 19

GLENCOE MULTIMEDIA

Electronic Field Trips in Accounting *Video Segment: The Accounting Cycle*

After viewing this video, students will be able to describe the concept of the cycle that businesses follow to complete the accounting records for a fiscal period; describe each step in the accounting cycle and the activities that initiate that step or connect it to another part of the accounting cycle.

Glencoe Accounting: Electronic Learning Center *Chapter 10*

The CD-ROM program is ideal for visual learners since it incorporates video images, animation, and graphics to enliven the content of each lesson.

CHAPTER 10
SECTION 1, PAGES 232–242

1 FOCUS

Introducing the Section

In this section students learn which accounts are closed and how to record and post closing entries.

Section Concepts

- Why temporary capital accounts are closed at the end of the fiscal year.
- The purpose of the Income Summary account.
- The relationship between the Income Summary and the capital accounts.
- Analyze and journalize closing entries.

Appendix A Adjustments for a Service Business Using a Ten-Column Work Sheet

If your students learned about adjusting entries in Appendix A, point out that the accounting cycle has 10 steps:

Step 8: Journalize and post adjusting entries

Step 9: Journalize and post closing entries

Step 10: Prepare a post-closing trial balance

Visual Learning

Section 1 Focus

Use **Transparency 10–1** to introduce section concepts.

BELL RINGER

Creating Analogies: Ask students what they do at the end of a school year. Write responses on the chalkboard. If students do not mention it, point out that they clean out their lockers, leaving them ready for the next students to use. Tell students that closing entries are the accountant's way of cleaning out the temporary capital accounts for the next fiscal period. L1

SECTION 1

Preparing Closing Entries

What **You'll Learn**

- Why temporary capital accounts are closed at the end of the fiscal year.
- The purpose of the Income Summary account.
- The relationship between the Income Summary account and the capital account.
- How to analyze and journalize closing entries.

Why **It's Important**

Closing entries are made to prepare the financial records for the next fiscal year.

KEY TERMS

closing entries
Income Summary account
compound entry

In Chapter 9 you learned how to prepare the following financial statements:

- The income statement reports revenue, expenses, and net income or net loss for the period.
- The statement of changes in owner's equity summarizes the impact of the business transactions on the owner's capital account.
- The balance sheet reports the financial position of the business at the end of the period.

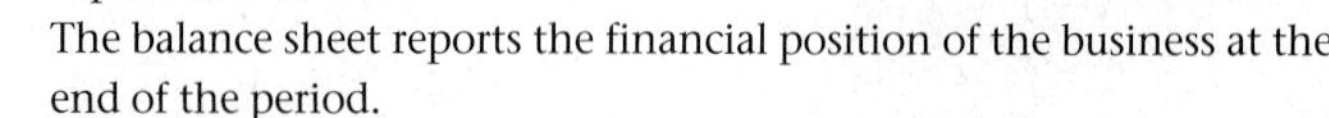

In a company like Mattel Toys, accountants prepare financial statements and then journalize and post closing entries. A post-closing trial balance is prepared to verify that the accounting records are still in balance.

Completing the Accounting Cycle

During the accounting period, the accountant records transactions involving revenue, expenses, and withdrawals in temporary capital accounts. At the end of the period, the accountant transfers the balances in the temporary capital accounts to the owner's capital account to bring it up to date and to prepare the accounting records for the next period.

Closing entries are journal entries made to close, or reduce to zero, the balances in the temporary capital accounts and to transfer the net income or net loss for the period to the capital account.

After the closing entries are journalized and posted, a trial balance is prepared to prove the equality of the general ledger after the closing process. The trial balance prepared after closing is called a post-closing trial balance. As you can see in **Figure 10–1**, the closing process and the post-closing trial balance complete the accounting cycle.

Starting the Eighth Step in the Accounting Cycle: Journalizing the Closing Entries

Preparing financial records for the start of a new period is a little like keeping stats for a basketball team. In keeping basketball stats, individual and team scores are recorded for every game, but each new game starts with a score of zero. Similarly, in keeping the stats or accounting for a

RESOURCE MANAGER

Reproducible Masters
- Lesson Plans
- Chapter Reviews and Working Papers (CRWP) TAE
- Demonstration Problems

Transparencies
- Section Focus Transparency
- Teaching Transparencies
- Source Document Transparencies
- Solution Transparencies

Multimedia
- ExamView CD-ROM
- Electronic Learning Center CD-ROM
- Interactive Lesson Planner CD-ROM
- Electronic Field Trips in Accounting

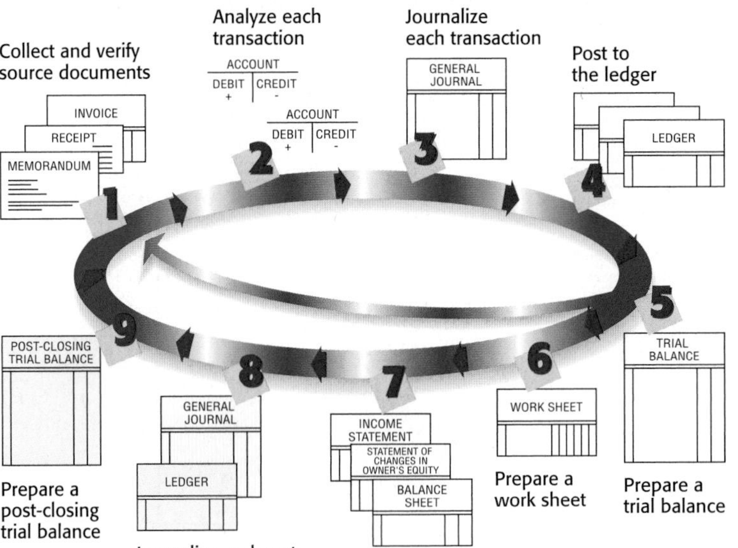

Figure 10–1 The Accounting Cycle with Steps 8 and 9 Highlighted

business, entries are recorded in the accounts during the year (game), but the temporary accounts (**Rent Expense**, **Maintenance Expense**, **Revenue**, etc.) start each new year (game) with zero balances.

The income statement, you'll remember, reports the net income or net loss for *one accounting period.* The statement is prepared from information recorded and accumulated in the revenue and expense accounts. At the end of the period, entries are recorded to close, or reduce to zero, the revenue and expense accounts because their balances also apply to only one accounting period. These closing entries also transfer the net income or net loss for the period to the capital account.

The need to complete the closing process can be seen in **Figure 10–2.**

- Prior to the closing process, you know that net income or net loss is calculated on the work sheet. A
- The net income or net loss amount then appears on the income statement. B
- On the statement of changes in owner's equity, the ending balance of the capital account includes net income or net loss. C
- The ending balance of the capital account then appears on the balance sheet. D
- At this point, however, the balance of the capital account in the general ledger does not equal the amount on the balance sheet because the closing entries need to be journalized and posted. E

CHAPTER 10
SECTION 1, PAGES 232–242

2 TEACH

GUIDED PRACTICE

Reading Accounting

- Accounting auditors need to trace financial data to its source. Have students read the financial reports in Figure 10–2 and choose one to "audit." Ask students to prepare a flowchart showing the stages from the report backwards to the original entry of data in the accounting system. L2

Concept Development: Completing the Accounting Cycle

Discussion: This section presents the final steps in the accounting cycle for a sole proprietorship, service business. Review the first seven steps in the cycle, then have students describe how the temporary accounts differ from the permanent accounts. L1

Concept Development: Starting the Eighth Step in the Accounting Cycle: Journalizing the Closing Entries

Discussion: Point out to students that, like any other information entered into the accounting system, the starting point is a journal entry. As with other journal entries, students will use T accounts to analyze the effects of an entry before journalizing. L1

Visual Learning

Figure 10–1 The Accounting Cycle with Steps 8 and 9 Highlighted

Using **Transparency 10–2**, introduce the last two steps in the accounting cycle.

Great Ideas *From the Classroom of...*

Ice Melts Ice is temporary and it melts. Temporary accounts melt away, too, because you close them out to a zero balance at the end of the fiscal period. Temporary accounts include:

I = Income (sales, sales returns and allowances, and sales discounts)
C = Cost (purchases, purchases returns and allowances, and purchases discounts)
E = Expenses

Thelma Brooks
Southeast Career Center
Columbus, Ohio

2 TEACH (Cont'd.)

Visual Learning

Figure 10–2 The Closing Process

Using **Transparency 10–3**, help students review the work leading up to the closing process.

Teaching Tips

Use a T account to demonstrate to students that the balance in the capital account ($25,400) does not match the balance reported on the balance sheet ($26,050). Remind students that during the fiscal period, transactions affecting capital (revenue, expenses, and withdrawals) were recorded in the temporary capital accounts rather than the owner's capital account. Now, at the end of the period, the totals need to be transferred to capital to bring that account up to date.

Point out that temporary capital accounts are temporary only in that their balances are maintained for an accounting period and then the accounts are cleared to prepare them for the next cycle. Emphasize that no entries are erased to clear them. Rather, closing journal entries are made to clear the temporary capital accounts by reducing their balances to zero. This process is similar to making a correcting entry to clear an amount that was posted to an incorrect account.

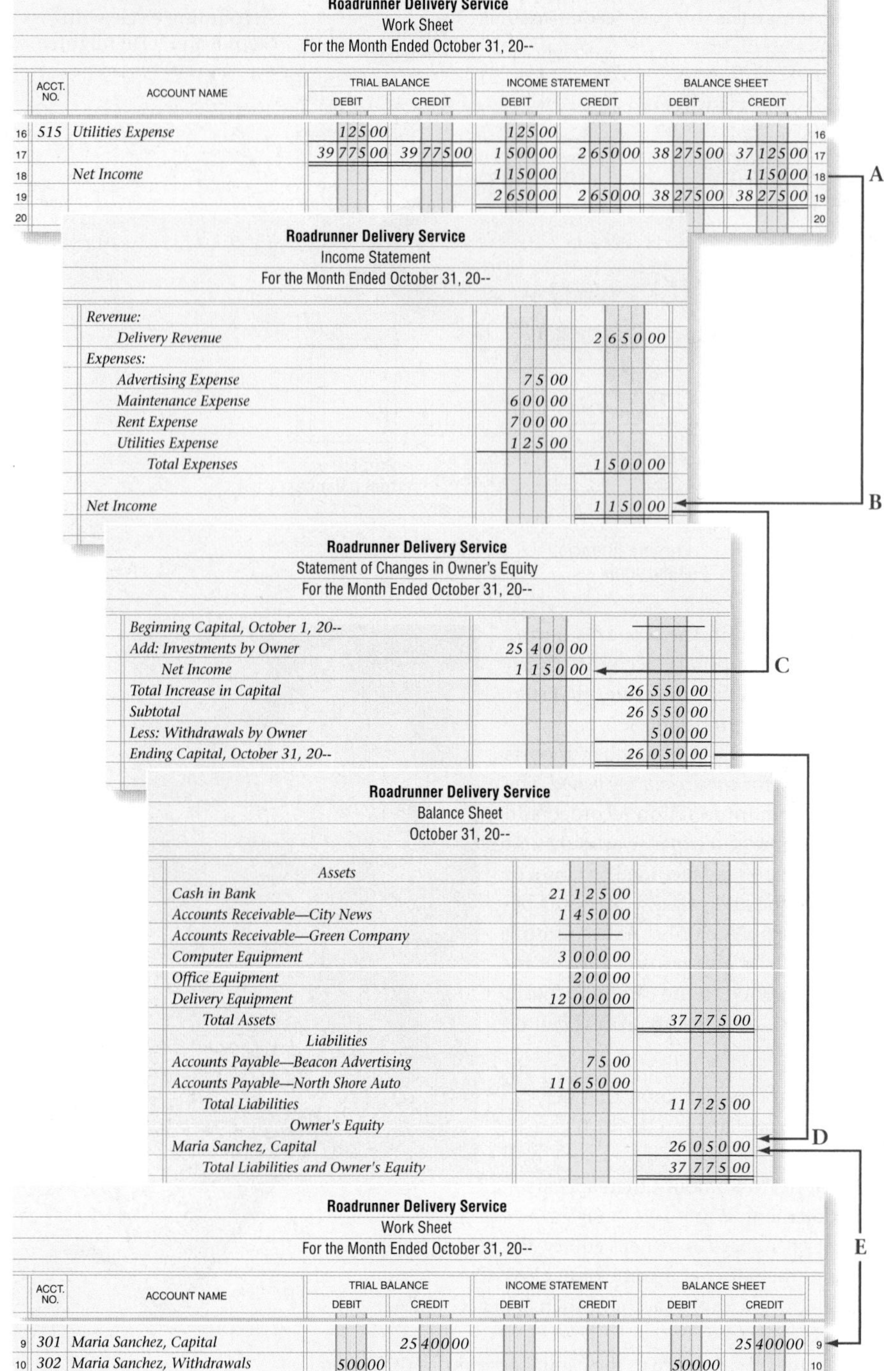

Roadrunner Delivery Service
Work Sheet
For the Month Ended October 31, 20--

	ACCT. NO.	ACCOUNT NAME	TRIAL BALANCE DEBIT	TRIAL BALANCE CREDIT	INCOME STATEMENT DEBIT	INCOME STATEMENT CREDIT	BALANCE SHEET DEBIT	BALANCE SHEET CREDIT	
16	515	Utilities Expense	125 00		125 00				16
17			39 775 00	39 775 00	1 500 00	2 650 00	38 275 00	37 125 00	17
18		Net Income			1 150 00			1 150 00	18
19					2 650 00	2 650 00	38 275 00	38 275 00	19
20									20

Roadrunner Delivery Service
Income Statement
For the Month Ended October 31, 20--

Revenue:		
Delivery Revenue		2 650 00
Expenses:		
Advertising Expense	75 00	
Maintenance Expense	600 00	
Rent Expense	700 00	
Utilities Expense	125 00	
Total Expenses		1 500 00
Net Income		1 150 00

Roadrunner Delivery Service
Statement of Changes in Owner's Equity
For the Month Ended October 31, 20--

Beginning Capital, October 1, 20--		—
Add: Investments by Owner	25 400 00	
Net Income	1 150 00	
Total Increase in Capital		26 550 00
Subtotal		26 550 00
Less: Withdrawals by Owner		500 00
Ending Capital, October 31, 20--		26 050 00

Roadrunner Delivery Service
Balance Sheet
October 31, 20--

Assets		
Cash in Bank	21 125 00	
Accounts Receivable—City News	1 450 00	
Accounts Receivable—Green Company	—	
Computer Equipment	3 000 00	
Office Equipment	200 00	
Delivery Equipment	12 000 00	
Total Assets		37 775 00
Liabilities		
Accounts Payable—Beacon Advertising	75 00	
Accounts Payable—North Shore Auto	11 650 00	
Total Liabilities		11 725 00
Owner's Equity		
Maria Sanchez, Capital		26 050 00
Total Liabilities and Owner's Equity		37 775 00

Roadrunner Delivery Service
Work Sheet
For the Month Ended October 31, 20--

	ACCT. NO.	ACCOUNT NAME	TRIAL BALANCE DEBIT	TRIAL BALANCE CREDIT	INCOME STATEMENT DEBIT	INCOME STATEMENT CREDIT	BALANCE SHEET DEBIT	BALANCE SHEET CREDIT	
9	301	Maria Sanchez, Capital		25 400 00				25 400 00	9
10	302	Maria Sanchez, Withdrawals	500 00				500 00		10

Figure 10–2 The Closing Process

HOME AND COMMUNITY CONNECTIONS ACTIVITY

Filing Income Taxes April 15th is the last day each year for taxpayers in the United States to file their tax returns. Have students interview family members to discover how and when they pay income taxes. Some questions students can ask are: (1) How do you file, jointly or separately? (2) Do you file before or on the deadline, or do you request an extension? (3) Who prepares the family's tax return? (4) How is the tax return filed, by mail or electronically? When students return with responses, discuss trends in income tax preparation and filing procedures (such as electronic filing). What procedures do students follow, or what procedures do they think they will follow when they are taxpayers?

For example, the balance for **Maria Sanchez, Capital** on the work sheet is $25,400 but the balance on the balance sheet is $26,050. These two amounts differ because the withdrawals and the net income are not yet recorded in the capital account in the general ledger. The closing process is used to update accounts through closing entries. The balance of the general ledger capital account is brought up-to-date.

The Income Summary Account

Before the closing entries are journalized and posted, there is no single account in the general ledger that shows all of the revenue and expenses for the period. This information is scattered among the individual revenue and expense accounts. There is, however, one general ledger account that, up to this point, has not been used. That is the **Income Summary** account.

The **Income Summary account** is used to accumulate and summarize the revenue and expenses for the period. This account serves as a simple income statement in the ledger. Expenses, which have debit balances, are transferred as debits to **Income Summary.** Revenues, which have credit balances, are transferred as credits to **Income Summary.** The balance of the account equals the net income or net loss for the fiscal period.

Look on page 73 at the chart of accounts for Roadrunner Delivery Service. Notice that **Income Summary** is located in the owner's equity section of the general ledger. It is located there because of its relationship to the owner's capital account. Remember, the revenue and expenses transferred to **Income Summary** actually represent increases and decreases to owner's equity. The balance of **Income Summary** (the net income or net loss for the period) is transferred to the capital account at the end of the closing process.

Like the withdrawals account, **Income Summary** is a temporary capital account. **Income Summary** is quite different, however, from the other temporary capital accounts.

- **Income Summary** is used only at the end of the fiscal year to summarize the balances from the revenue and expense accounts.
- **Income Summary** does not have a normal balance, which means that it does not have an increase or a decrease side. As shown in the T account below, the debit and credit sides of the account are simply used to summarize the period's revenue and expenses.

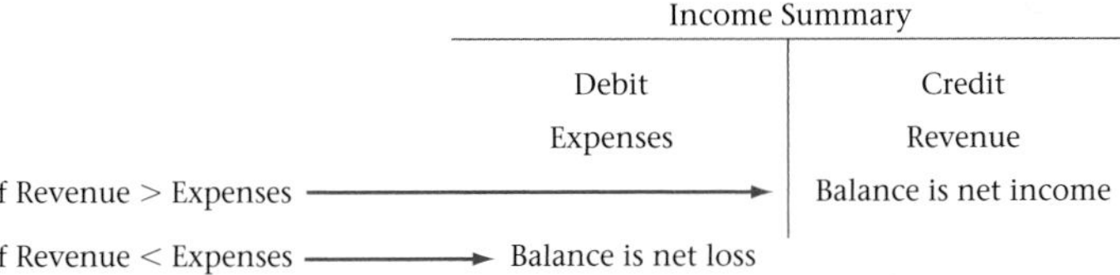

International ACCOUNTING

Bankcard Usage

Away from home on business? Using a bankcard is one of the best ways to acquire money when conducting business in another country because you get the bank's exchange rate.

Did You Know?

Sports

The America's Cup is the oldest trophy in international sporting events. Racing syndicates spend millions of dollars designing racing yachts and training crews with the goal of winning the America's Cup. The winner receives no prize money.

Teaching International ACCOUNTING

Remembering PINs at ATM Machines Discuss PINs and how they are used at ATM machines. Ask students to create their own PINs using all alphabetic characters. Provide a diagram of a ten-key pad displaying only numbers. Have students convert their PINs to numbers. Then have students check a keypad that displays letters and numbers to confirm their conversions.

2 TEACH (Cont'd.)

Concept Development: The Income Summary Account

Discussion: Point out to students that there is no account in the general ledger entitled net income or net loss. Thus, an account is needed to serve as a temporary repository for the net income or loss before it is transferred to the capital account. The Income Summary account:

- serves as a clearing account to reduce the temporary accounts to zero, and
- summarizes net income or net loss for the accounting period.

The Income Summary account is, in effect, a simple income statement in the ledger. L1

Visual Learning

Income Summary T Account, p. 235

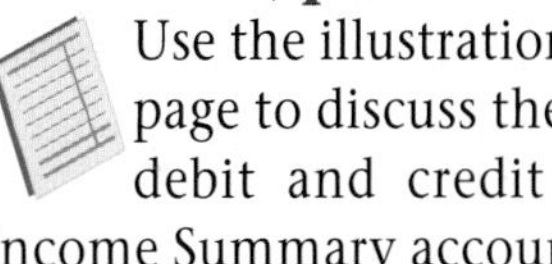

Use the illustration on this page to discuss the rules of debit and credit for the Income Summary account. Point out that, unlike other accounts, Income Summary does not have a normal balance side.

Teaching Tip

Point out that net income increases capital. Since capital is increased by credits, a balance on the credit side of Income Summary represents net income. Conversely, a balance on the debit side reduces capital, so a debit balance in Income Summary represents a net loss.

Strategies for Teaching International Accounting

To enrich study of International Accounting, refer to the additional critical thinking activities in the booklet.

2 TEACH (Cont'd.)

Concept Development: Preparing Closing Entries

Discussion: Explain to students that closing entries are recorded and posted only at the end of the accounting period. Revenue is the first of the temporary capital accounts to be closed. Draw T accounts on the chalkboard to analyze the process of closing revenue. For each of the four closing entries, discuss the steps in the closing entry analysis model in the student textbook. These steps are:

1. Identify the accounts affected.
2. Classify each account.
3. Determine whether each account is increasing or decreasing.
4. Determine which account is debited.
5. Determine which account is credited.
6. Use T accounts to show the entry.
7. Make the journal entry.

You may want to illustrate each of these steps on the chalkboard as you discuss the process. L1

Math Review for Accounting Photocopy appropriate *Activity Sheets* for students who need additional practice in basic math.

Adding Columns

To avoid errors in adding a column of figures, as for a post-closing trial balance, be sure to vertically align:

- the tens,
- the hundreds, and
- the thousands.

- The balance of the **Income Summary** account before and after the closing process is zero.
- The **Income Summary** account does not appear on any financial statement.

Preparing Closing Entries

Four journal entries are prepared to close the temporary capital accounts for Roadrunner.

1. The balance of the revenue account is transferred to the credit side of the **Income Summary** account.
2. The expense account balances are transferred to the debit side of the **Income Summary** account.
3. The balance of the **Income Summary** account is transferred to the capital account (net income to the credit side; net loss to the debit side).
4. The balance of the withdrawals account is transferred to the debit side of the capital account.

Closing the Balance of the Revenue Account to Income Summary

The first step in the closing procedure is to transfer the balance of the revenue account to **Income Summary.** The balance for the revenue account is found in the Income Statement section of the work sheet. (Refer to the work sheet in **Figure 9–3** on page 206 when reading about closing entries.)

Closing Entry

First Closing Entry—Close Revenue to Income Summary

ANALYSIS

Identify 1. Roadrunner has only one revenue account, **Delivery Revenue.** The accounts affected are **Delivery Revenue** and **Income Summary.**

Classify 2. **Delivery Revenue** is a revenue account. **Income Summary** is a temporary capital account.

+/− 3. The **Delivery Revenue** account balance is decreased by $2,650 to zero. That amount, $2,650 is transferred to the **Income Summary** account.

DEBIT-CREDIT RULE

4. Decreases in revenue accounts are recorded as debits. Debit **Delivery Revenue** for $2,650.
5. To transfer the revenue to the **Income Summary** account, credit **Income Summary** for $2,650.

T ACCOUNTS

6.

Delivery Revenue	
Debit − Closing 2,650	Credit + Balance 2,650

Income Summary	
Debit	Credit Closing 2,650

Math Skill Builder Activity

Adding Columns Ask students to write the following figures on a sheet of paper, putting them in the proper place columns: $5,000; $125.50; $44.75; $2,788; $35; $499. After students have completed their lists, write $5,000.00 on the chalkboard. Then ask for a volunteer to come to the chalkboard to write the next number. Continue this process until all numbers are written on the chalkboard.

JOURNAL ENTRY

GENERAL JOURNAL PAGE 3

	DATE		DESCRIPTION	POST. REF.	DEBIT	CREDIT	
1	20--		Closing Entries				1
2	Oct.	31	Delivery Revenue		2 650 00		2
3			Income Summary			2 650 00	3
4							4

To record closing entries in the general journal, follow these steps:

1. Enter "Closing Entries" in the center of the description column.
2. Enter the date (the last day of the fiscal period).
3. Enter the name(s) of the account(s) to be debited and the amount(s) to be debited.
4. Enter the name of the account, **Income Summary**, to be credited and the amount to be credited.

Closing the Balances of the Expense Accounts to Income Summary

The second closing entry transfers the balances of the expense accounts to **Income Summary.** The balances of the expense accounts are found in the Income Statement section of the work sheet.

Closing Entry

Second Closing Entry—Close Expenses to Income Summary

ANALYSIS

Identify
1. The accounts affected by the second closing entry are **Advertising Expense, Maintenance Expense, Rent Expense, Utilities Expense**, and **Income Summary.**

Classify
2. **Advertising Expense, Maintenance Expense, Rent Expense,** and **Utilities Expense** are expense accounts. **Income Summary** is a temporary capital account.

+/−
3. The balances of the four expense accounts are decreased to zero; the total decrease is $1,500. The total amount, $1,500, is transferred to the **Income Summary** account.

DEBIT-CREDIT RULE

4. To transfer the expenses to the **Income Summary** account, debit **Income Summary** for $1,500.
5. Decreases in expense accounts are recorded as credits. Credit **Advertising Expense,** $75; **Maintenance Expense,** $600; **Rent Expense,** $700; **Utilities Expense,** $125.

2 TEACH (Cont'd.)

Visual Learning

Closing the Revenue Accounts Analysis

Use **Transparency 10–4** to demonstrate the effect of the journal entry closing the revenue account into Income Summary. Have students explain the analysis of the closing entry and how each account is affected.

Demonstration Problem Step-by-Step Practice

Use demonstration problem 10–1 to show students how to record the entry to close the revenue account.

Teaching Tips

After explaining, illustrating, and using a demonstration problem on a closing entry, allow students to analyze and record the closing entry. After completing all four closing entries, use demonstration problem 10–5, which involves all four entries. Emphasize that the work sheet is the source of information for the account balances used in the closing entries.

MEETING SPECIAL NEEDS

Students with Learning Disabilities Many teachers grade students on their participation in class. However, class participation is hard for students who have oral expression difficulties. These students will need encouragement and, perhaps, special circumstances to contribute to class discussions. Create an environment and establish conditions that help students become successful. For example, you might ask factual questions such as "Why is the closing process necessary?" or "What is the purpose of a post-closing trial balance?" Allow students time to find the answers in the chapter before responding.

2 TEACH (Cont'd.)

Visual Learning

Closing Expense Accounts Analysis

Use **Transparency 10–5** to guide students through the analysis and recording of the entry to close the expense accounts.

Demonstration Problem Step-by-Step Practice

Use demonstration problem 10–2 to give students practice in recording the journal entry to close expense accounts.

Teaching Tips

Use T accounts to explain the closing of the expense accounts. Point out that one total is recorded in the Income Summary account because one total is recorded in the general journal entry that closes the expense accounts.

Explain to students that a compound entry saves space and posting time.

Thinking Algebraically

Showing Relationships: Have students describe the entry to close Income Summary using "if, then" statements. (If credit > debit, then debit Income Summary. If debit > credit, then credit Income Summary.) L1

T ACCOUNTS

6.

Income Summary

Debit	Credit
Closing 1,500	

Advertising Expense

Debit +	Credit −
Balance 75	Closing 75

Maintenance Expense

Debit +	Credit −
Balance 600	Closing 600

Rent Expense

Debit +	Credit −
Balance 700	Closing 700

Utilities Expense

Debit +	Credit −
Balance 125	Closing 125

JOURNAL ENTRY

7.

GENERAL JOURNAL — PAGE 3

	DATE		DESCRIPTION	POST. REF.	DEBIT	CREDIT	
5	Oct.	31	*Income Summary*		1 500 00		5
6			*Advertising Expense*			75 00	6
7			*Maintenance Expense*			600 00	7
8			*Rent Expense*			700 00	8
9			*Utilities Expense*			125 00	9
10							10

It is not necessary to use a separate closing entry for each expense account. As you can see, the above entry has one debit and four credits. A journal entry with two or more debits or two or more credits is called a **compound entry**. A compound entry saves both space and posting time. For example, each of Roadrunner's expense accounts could be closed to **Income Summary** separately. That, however, requires four entries and postings to the **Income Summary** account instead of one entry and posting.

Key Points

Closing Entries

To Close Revenue Accounts:
- Debit revenue account(s)
- Credit **Income Summary** account

To Close Expense Accounts:
- Debit **Income Summary** account
- Credit expense account(s)

Closing the Balance of the Income Summary Account to Capital

The third closing entry transfers the balance of the **Income Summary** account to the capital account. As shown in the T account, after closing Roadrunner's revenue and expense accounts, **Income Summary** has a credit balance of $1,150.

Income Summary

2 Closing entry for expenses	1,500	1 Closing entry for revenue	2,650
		Balance	1,150

ADDRESSING MULTIPLE LEARNING STYLES

Musical/Rhythmic Learner Ask students to choose a favorite song or advertising jingle. Have them write the words to the song or jingle. Then have them write new words to the song or jingle that would remind them of the nine steps in the accounting cycle. You may want to allow students to work in teams of two or three for this activity. If students are willing, have them perform their songs or jingles for the class.

A credit balance indicates net income for the period. It is the same amount that appears on the work sheet.

Closing Entry

Third Closing Entry—Close Income Summary to Capital

ANALYSIS *Identify* *Classify* +/−

1. The accounts **Income Summary** and **Maria Sanchez, Capital** are affected.
2. **Income Summary** is a temporary capital account. **Maria Sanchez, Capital** is an owner's capital account.
3. The **Income Summary** account balance is reduced to zero by transferring $1,150, the net income amount, to the capital account. **Maria Sanchez, Capital** is increased by $1,150.

DEBIT-CREDIT RULE

4. To reduce the **Income Summary** balance to zero, debit **Income Summary** for $1,150.
5. Net income is recorded as a credit to the owner's capital account. Credit **Maria Sanchez, Capital** for $1,150.

T ACCOUNTS

6.

Income Summary	
Debit	Credit
Closing 1,150	Balance 1,150

Maria Sanchez, Capital	
Debit −	Credit +
	Balance 25,400 Closing 1,150

JOURNAL ENTRY

7. GENERAL JOURNAL — PAGE 3

	DATE		DESCRIPTION	POST. REF.	DEBIT	CREDIT	
11	Oct.	31	Income Summary		1 150 00		11
12			Maria Sanchez, Capital			1 150 00	12
13							13

After the third closing entry is posted, the **Income Summary** account appears as follows:

Income Summary			
2 Closing entry for expenses	1,500	1 Closing entry for revenue	2,650
3 Closing balance to owner's capital account	1,150		

If a business reports a net loss for the period, **Income Summary** has a debit balance. In that situation, the third closing entry is a debit to the

2 TEACH (Cont'd.)

Visual Learning

Closing Entry Analysis

Use **Transparency 10–6** to analyze the closing entry for closing the Income Summary balance into the capital account.

GO TO Demonstration Problem Step-by-Step Practice

Use demonstration problem 10–3 to give students practice in recording the journal entry to close the Income Summary account balance into the owner's capital account.

Teaching Tips

Draw T accounts on the chalkboard to show students how to calculate the balance of the Income Summary account after the revenue and expense account balances have been recorded.

Remind students that the balance of the Income Summary account must be the same as the amount of net income or net loss calculated on the work sheet and reported on the income statement.

MAKING CONNECTIONS TO DAILY LIFE

Personal Budgeting Share this scenario with students: Assume you have set a budget for October, and throughout the month you record all your expenditures. At the end of October, you compare amounts you actually spent with amounts you budgeted and find that your total expenditures exceeded the budget. Is this a net loss or a net income? Explain why you would begin with zero balances to record expenses for November. (Net loss. By beginning with zero balances, you record only the expenses for November and do not add on to expenses for other months. Most people budget by the month so they can compare expenses by month—just as businesses compare revenue and expenses from one month to another.)

2 TEACH (Cont'd.)

Visual Learning

Figure 10–3 Closing Income Summary for the Amount of Net Loss

Using **Transparency 10–7,** explain to students the difference in journal entries for a net loss. Quiz students on why the Income Summary account would have a debit balance when the business has a net loss.

Closing Entry for Withdrawals

Use **Transparency 10–8** to explain the closing of the withdrawals balance into the capital account.

Demonstration Problem Step-by-Step Practice

Use demonstration problem 10–4 to give students practice in recording a journal entry to close the balance of the withdrawals account into capital.

ACCOUNTING TIPS

Closing Entries

Closing entries are sometimes called clearing entries because one of their functions is to *clear* the revenue and expense accounts and leave them with zero balances.

capital account and a credit to **Income Summary** for the amount of the net loss. **Figure 10–3** shows this entry as it appears in the general journal.

GENERAL JOURNAL — PAGE 3

	DATE		DESCRIPTION	POST. REF.	DEBIT	CREDIT	
1	20--		*Closing Entries*				1
2	Oct.	31	*Maria Sanchez, Capital*		700 00		2
3			*Income Summary*			700 00	3
4							4

Figure 10–3 Closing Income Summary for the Amount of Net Loss

Closing the Balance of the Withdrawals Account to Capital

The fourth and last closing entry transfers the balance of the withdrawals account to the capital account. As you recall, withdrawals decrease owner's equity. The balance of the withdrawals account is transferred to the capital account to reflect the decrease in owner's equity. The balance of the withdrawals account is found in the Balance Sheet section of the work sheet.

Closing Entry

Fourth Closing Entry—Close Withdrawals to Capital

ANALYSIS

Identify 1. The accounts affected by the fourth closing entry are **Maria Sanchez, Withdrawals** and **Maria Sanchez, Capital.**

Classify 2. **Maria Sanchez, Withdrawals** is a temporary capital account. **Maria Sanchez, Capital** is an owner's capital account.

+/− 3. **Maria Sanchez, Withdrawals** is decreased by $500. **Maria Sanchez, Capital** is decreased by $500.

DEBIT-CREDIT RULE

4. Decreases in owner's capital accounts are recorded as debits. Debit **Maria Sanchez, Capital** for $500.
5. Decreases in owner's withdrawal accounts are recorded as credits. Credit **Maria Sanchez, Withdrawals** for $500.

T ACCOUNTS

6.

Maria Sanchez, Capital	
Debit −	Credit +
Closing 500	Balance 26,550

Maria Sanchez, Withdrawals	
Debit +	Credit −
Balance 500	Closing 500

INTERDISCIPLINARY CONNECTIONS ACTIVITY

Literature Using ERIC or other Web sites, ask students to do a literature search on topics related to accounting, money, finances, or banking. Students should compose a list of possible articles, novels, or periodicals they discover in their search. Ask students to write a one-paragraph synopsis on an article or story they read that is related to their selected topic.

JOURNAL ENTRY

7.

GENERAL JOURNAL PAGE 3

	DATE		DESCRIPTION	POST. REF.	DEBIT	CREDIT	
14	Oct.	31	Maria Sanchez, Capital		500 00		14
15			Maria Sanchez, Withdrawals			500 00	15
16							16

The journal entries made to close the temporary capital accounts for Roadrunner are shown in **Figure 10–4**.

GENERAL JOURNAL PAGE 3

	DATE		DESCRIPTION	POST. REF.	DEBIT	CREDIT	
1	20--		Closing Entries				1
2	Oct.	31	Delivery Revenue		2 650 00		2
3			Income Summary			2 650 00	3
4							4
5		31	Income Summary		1 500 00		5
6			Advertising Expense			75 00	6
7			Maintenance Expense			600 00	7
8			Rent Expense			700 00	8
9			Utilities Expense			125 00	9
10							10
11		31	Income Summary		1 150 00		11
12			Maria Sanchez, Capital			1 150 00	12
13							13
14		31	Maria Sanchez, Capital		500 00		14
15			Maria Sanchez, Withdrawals			500 00	15
16							16

Figure 10–4 Journalizing the Closing Entries

CONNECT TO . . . LITERATURE

People often stereotype accounting as mechanical and plain. Johann von Goethe didn't. The Romantic author most famous for *Faust* described Luca Pacioli's system of accounting as possessing timeless beauty and simplicity—one of the greatest achievements of the human intellect.

A MATTER OF ETHICS

Computer Viruses

Computer viruses are small computer programs that "reproduce" themselves into other programs, slowing entire systems or, worse, destroying data. Imagine that you're a part-time accounting clerk for a big corporation like Adidas. Your friend gives you a computer game with a harmless virus to play with. To add some fun to your work, you decide to load the game onto the company's network system.

Ethical Decision Making:

- What are the ethical issues?
- What are the alternatives?
- Who are the affected parties?
- How do the alternatives affect the parties?
- What would you do?

CHAPTER 10
SECTION 1, PAGES 232–242

2 TEACH (Cont'd.)

Visual Learning

Figure 10–4 Journalizing the Closing Entries

Use **Transparency 10–9** to integrate the four entries needed to close the temporary capital accounts for a sole proprietorship, service business. Review the compound entry for closing the expense accounts.

Demonstration Problem Step-by-Step Practice

Use demonstration problem 10–5 to give students practice in recording all four closing entries.

Strategies for Teaching Ethics in Accounting

Photocopy the Chapter 10 *Student Activity Sheet* for students. Answers are also provided in the booklet.

Teaching Tips

Point out to students that it is not necessary to skip a line between closing entries if they need that space to fit their work onto the work paper.

Teaching A MATTER OF ETHICS

Computer Viruses Ask students to put themselves in the place of an employee who is trying to finish a spreadsheet for a meeting in one hour. Opening their computer file, they find that it's been ruined by a virus, and they'll have to redo all their previous work. They won't have time to finish the spreadsheet before the meeting. Have students discuss how they would feel about the person who introduced the virus to their computer system.

CHAPTER 10
SECTION 1, PAGES 232–242

3 ASSESS

Thinking Critically (Answers)

1. To reduce balances to zero and ready accounts for the next period.
2. To summarize the revenue and expenses for an accounting period.

Communicating Accounting (Answers)

Students' answers will vary. Discussion points: the balance of withdrawals is transferred into capital at end of fiscal period; withdrawals decrease capital (owner's equity); to close withdrawals, credit the account and debit capital.

Problem 10–1 (Answers)

1. Dr. Ticket Revenue $6,000; Cr. Income Summary $6,000
2. Dr. Income Summary $3,100; Cr. Gas and Oil Exp. $700, Misc. Exp. $600, Utilities Exp. $1,800

Problem 10–2 (Answers)

1. Dr. Utilities Expense $129; Cr. Cash in Bank $129
2. Dr. Income Summary $129; Cr. Utilities Expense $129

Chapter Reviews and Working Papers Refer students to the Chapter 10 workbook pages to answer *Check Your Understanding* activities.

4 CLOSE

Section Wrap-Up

Writing/Charting: Have students create a chart with T accounts to illustrate the four closing entries. Tell them to write brief descriptions of the steps for closing each account. L2

SECTION 1 Check Your Understanding

Now that you have studied this section, complete the following questions and problems.

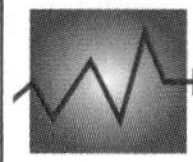

Thinking Critically

1. Why are closing entries for revenue and expense accounts recorded?
2. What is the purpose of the **Income Summary** account?

Communicating Accounting

It is 8:00 A.M. and your boss, Gregory Levi, posted a note on your phone asking you to come see him. He does not understand why his owner's equity account shows a decrease. You determine that the reason for the decrease in owner's equity is the amount of withdrawals made this quarter. Before you see your boss, you make a few notes. Write out some discussion points to help you explain the situation. Then pick a colleague to listen to your explanation, which should include proof that you understand the closing of the balance of a withdrawals account to a capital account.

Please see me... Gregory

Problem 10–1 Preparing Closing Entries

Instructions Prepare closing entries for the following in your working papers.

1. A closing entry must be made for the account **Ticket Revenue**, which has a balance of $6,000.
2. A business has three expense accounts: **Gas and Oil Expense** (balance, $700), **Miscellaneous Expense** (balance, $600), and **Utilities Expense** (balance, $1,800). The end of the fiscal year is June 30.

Problem 10–2 Analyzing a Source Document

Instructions Using the source document:

1. Journalize the transaction in a general journal in your working papers.
2. Post the entry to the appropriate T accounts.
3. Assume it is the end of the accounting period. Record the closing entry for this account in the general journal.
4. Post the closing entry to the appropriate T accounts.

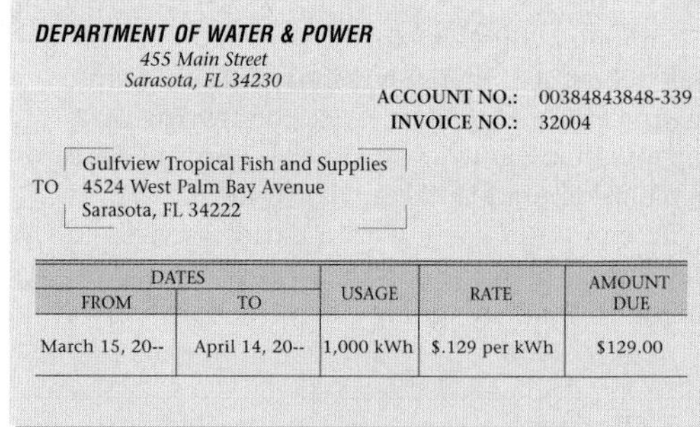

DEPARTMENT OF WATER & POWER
455 Main Street
Sarasota, FL 34230

ACCOUNT NO.: 00384843848-339
INVOICE NO.: 32004

TO Gulfview Tropical Fish and Supplies
4524 West Palm Bay Avenue
Sarasota, FL 34222

DATES FROM	DATES TO	USAGE	RATE	AMOUNT DUE
March 15, 20--	April 14, 20--	1,000 kWh	$.129 per kWh	$129.00

RETEACHING SECTION 1

Using a Clearing House Account Closing each revenue and expense account directly into capital would quickly fill up this ledger account. Only one amount, the net income or the net loss, needs to be transferred to the capital account. The Income Summary account is used as a "clearing house" to summarize all revenues and expenses for the period. After all revenue and expense account balances have been transferred to Income Summary (through closing entries), the balance of the account represents the net income or net loss for the period. The Income Summary account, which is also a temporary capital account, is then closed, and the balance (the net income or net loss) is transferred to the capital account.

SECTION 2

Posting Closing Entries and Preparing a Post-Closing Trial Balance

Completing the Eighth Step in the Accounting Cycle: Posting Closing Entries to the General Ledger

In the last section you learned how to prepare four closing entries. The next step in the closing process is to post the closing entries to the general ledger accounts. The posting procedure is the same as for any other general journal entry, with one exception. The word "Closing" is written in the Description column of the general ledger account. The posting of the closing entries for Roadrunner is shown in **Figure 10–5.**

What You'll Learn

- How to record closing entries in the general ledger.
- The purpose of a post-closing trial balance.
- How to prepare a post-closing trial balance.

Why It's Important

A post-closing trial balance verifies that the closing entries are properly recorded in the general ledger and that you are ready to start the next accounting period.

KEY TERMS

post-closing trial balance

GENERAL JOURNAL — PAGE 3

	DATE		DESCRIPTION	POST. REF.	DEBIT	CREDIT	
1	20--		Closing Entries				1
2	Oct.	31	Delivery Revenue	401	2 650 00		2
3			Income Summary	303		2 650 00	3
4							4
5		31	Income Summary	303	1 500 00		5
6			Advertising Expense	501		75 00	6
7			Maintenance Expense	505		600 00	7
8			Rent Expense	510		700 00	8
9			Utilities Expense	515		125 00	9
10							10
11		31	Income Summary	303	1 150 00		11
12			Maria Sanchez, Capital	301		1 150 00	12
13							13
14		31	Maria Sanchez, Capital	301	500 00		14
15			Maria Sanchez, Withdrawals	302		500 00	15

ACCOUNT Maria Sanchez, Capital — ACCOUNT NO. 301

DATE		DESCRIPTION	POST. REF.	DEBIT	CREDIT	BALANCE DEBIT	BALANCE CREDIT
20--							
Oct.	1		G1		25 000 00		25 000 00
	2		G1		400 00		25 400 00
	31	Closing	G3		1 150 00		26 550 00
	31	Closing	G3	500 00			26 050 00

Figure 10–5 Closing Entries Posted to the General Ledger

RESOURCE MANAGER

Reproducible Masters
- Lesson Plans
- Chapter Reviews and Working Papers (CRWP) TAE
- Demonstration Problems

Transparencies
- Section Focus Transparency
- Teaching Transparencies
- Source Document Transparencies
- Solution Transparencies

Multimedia
- ExamView CD-ROM
- Electronic Learning Center CD-ROM
- Interactive Lesson Planner CD-ROM
- Electronic Field Trips in Accounting

1 FOCUS

Introducing the Section

In this section students will learn to post the closing entries they journalized in the previous section. They'll also learn the importance of a post-closing trial balance and how to prepare this test of the equality of accounts in the ledger.

Section Concepts

- How to record closing entries in the general ledger.
- The purpose of a post-closing trial balance.
- How to prepare a post-closing trial balance.

Visual Learning

Section 2 Focus

Use **Transparency 10–10** to introduce section concepts.

BELL RINGER

Oral Exercise: Write the words "Trial Balance" on the chalkboard. Ask students to tell you the purpose of a trial balance and when it is prepared. Write their answers on the chalkboard. Then point out that a trial balance prepared at the end of the accounting period is called a post-closing trial balance. Its purpose is also to make sure that accounts in the ledger are in balance. L1

Visual Learning

Figure 10–5 Closing Entries Posted to the General Ledger

Use **Transparency 10–11a** to review the journalized closing entries for students.

2 TEACH

GUIDED PRACTICE

Reading Accounting

- Have students test their reading about the closing process by having them write a description of all the activities completed to close the records at the end of the accounting period. L1
- Prepare a bulletin-board display of the closing process. Include the work sheet, ledger accounts, T-account analyses, closing entries, and the post-closing trial balance, all translated into your students' first language. ELL

Concept Development: Completing the Eighth Step in the Accounting Cycle: Posting Closing Entries to the General Ledger

Discussion: Remind students that the only way to bring ledger accounts up to date is to record and post journal entries. Review the steps in the posting process, and remind students to enter information in the ledger form from left to right. L1

Visual Learning

Figure 10–5 Closing Entries Posted to the General Ledger (continued)

Use **Transparency 10–11b** to help students trace each part of the journal entries to the accounts in the ledger. Point out that accounts shown are the temporary capital accounts.

ACCOUNT *Maria Sanchez, Withdrawals* ACCOUNT NO. *302*

DATE		DESCRIPTION	POST. REF.	DEBIT	CREDIT	BALANCE DEBIT	BALANCE CREDIT
20--							
Oct.	*31*		*G1*	*500 00*		*500 00*	
	31	*Closing*	*G3*		*500 00*	—	—

ACCOUNT *Income Summary* ACCOUNT NO. *303*

DATE		DESCRIPTION	POST. REF.	DEBIT	CREDIT	BALANCE DEBIT	BALANCE CREDIT
20--							
Oct.	*31*	*Closing*	*G3*		*2 650 00*		*2 650 00*
	31	*Closing*	*G3*	*1 500 00*			*1 150 00*
	31	*Closing*	*G3*	*1 150 00*			—

ACCOUNT *Delivery Revenue* ACCOUNT NO. *401*

DATE		DESCRIPTION	POST. REF.	DEBIT	CREDIT	BALANCE DEBIT	BALANCE CREDIT
20--							
Oct.	*15*		*G1*		*1 200 00*		*1 200 00*
	20		*G1*		*1 450 00*		*2 650 00*
	31	*Closing*	*G3*	*2 650 00*			—

ACCOUNT *Advertising Expense* ACCOUNT NO. *501*

DATE		DESCRIPTION	POST. REF.	DEBIT	CREDIT	BALANCE DEBIT	BALANCE CREDIT
20--							
Oct.	*18*		*G1*	*75 00*		*75 00*	
	31	*Closing*	*G3*		*75 00*	—	

ACCOUNT *Maintenance Expense* ACCOUNT NO. *505*

DATE		DESCRIPTION	POST. REF.	DEBIT	CREDIT	BALANCE DEBIT	BALANCE CREDIT
20--							
Oct.	*29*		*G1*	*600 00*		*600 00*	
	31	*Closing*	*G3*		*600 00*	—	

ACCOUNT *Rent Expense* ACCOUNT NO. *510*

DATE		DESCRIPTION	POST. REF.	DEBIT	CREDIT	BALANCE DEBIT	BALANCE CREDIT
20--							
Oct.	*16*		*G1*	*700 00*		*700 00*	
	31	*Closing*	*G3*		*700 00*	—	

ACCOUNT *Utilities Expense* ACCOUNT NO. *515*

DATE		DESCRIPTION	POST. REF.	DEBIT	CREDIT	BALANCE DEBIT	BALANCE CREDIT
20--							
Oct.	*28*		*G1*	*125 00*		*125 00*	
	31	*Closing*	*G3*		*125 00*	—	

Figure 10–5 Closing Entries Posted to the General Ledger (continued)

COOPERATIVE LEARNING ACTIVITY

Think-Pair-Share Allow students to think about answers for the following questions and to discuss them with a partner. Ask students to then share their answers with the class.

1. What is the normal balance for the Income Summary account? (Income Summary has no normal balance.)
2. Which ledger accounts do not appear on the post-closing trial balance? (Temporary capital accounts.)
3. Is the post-closing trial balance dated for a point in time or for a period of time? Why? (A point in time because it represents ledger balances at a particular time.)

Key Points

Permanent Accounts
After closing, the only accounts with balances are permanent accounts.

The Ninth Step in the Accounting Cycle: Preparing a Post-Closing Trial Balance

The last step in the accounting cycle is to prepare a post-closing trial balance. The **post-closing trial balance** is prepared to make sure total debits equal total credits after the closing entries are posted. The post-closing trial balance for Roadrunner is shown in **Figure 10–6**.

Notice that only accounts with balances are listed on the post-closing trial balance. After the closing process, only permanent accounts have balances. Temporary accounts have zero balances, so there is no need to list those accounts on the post-closing trial balance.

Roadrunner Delivery Service
Post-Closing Trial Balance
October 31, 20--

Account	Debit	Credit
Cash in Bank	21 125 00	
Accounts Receivable—City News	1 450 00	
Computer Equipment	3 000 00	
Office Equipment	200 00	
Delivery Equipment	12 000 00	
Accounts Payable—Beacon Advertising		75 00
Accounts Payable—North Shore Auto		11 650 00
Maria Sanchez, Capital		26 050 00
Total	37 775 00	37 775 00

Figure 10–6 Post-Closing Trial Balance

ACCOUNTING *Flashbacks*

ACCOUNTING TEXTBOOKS
Friar Luca Pacioli published the first complete accounting textbook, *Summa de Arithmetica, Geometria: Proportioni et Proportionalita* in 1494. The double-entry system he described is still used today.

ANALYZING FINANCIAL REPORTS

Calculating Return on Owner's Equity

The statement of changes in owner's equity reports the amount of the owner's interest in the business. If the business is successful and growing, owner's equity should increase each fiscal period. One measure of business success is the **return on owner's equity.** Look at the following example.

$$\frac{\text{Net Income}}{\text{Beginning Owner's Equity} - \text{Withdrawals}} = \frac{\$3{,}600}{\$34{,}500 - \$2{,}500} = 11.25\%$$

The resulting percentage shows the amount earned during the period on each dollar invested by the owner.

▶ Analyze the Report:

Use the income statement on page 206 and the statement of changes in owner's equity for Roadrunner Delivery Service on page 211 to answer these questions.

1. Calculate the return on owner's equity for the month of October.
2. If you were the owner of Roadrunner Delivery Service, how would you evaluate the return on equity? For example, if current rates on savings paid by banks is 5 percent, how does your return on equity compare?

2 TEACH (Cont'd.)

Concept Development: The Ninth Step in the Accounting Cycle: Preparing a Post-Closing Trial Balance

Discussion: Emphasize that accounts listed on the post-closing trial balance should agree with the account balances found on the balance sheet. Note that temporary accounts are not listed on the post-closing trial balance because they all should have zero balances at this point.

Stress the purpose of the post-closing trial balance: to make sure the general ledger balances after closing entries have been posted. L1

Visual Learning

Figure 10–6 Post-Closing Trial Balance

Use **Transparency 10–12** to review the accounts included on the post-closing trial balance.

Teaching Tip

Remind students that "post" means "after."

Critical Thinking: Tell students that in preparing a post-closing trial balance they went through the ledger and listed all the accounts with balances. When added, the totals on the post-closing trial balances did not match. What are some possible errors? (A closing entry may not have been posted correctly or at all, or a posted amount may not have been subtracted correctly.) L1

Demonstration Problem Step-by-Step Practice

Use demonstration problem 10–6 to give students practice in preparing a post-closing trial balance.

ANALYZING FINANCIAL REPORTS

Roadrunner Delivery Service
155 Gateway Blvd.
Sacramento, CA 94230

Analyze the Report (Answers)

1. \$1,150 ÷ (\$25,400 − \$500) = \$1,150 ÷ \$24,900 = 4.6%
2. The current return on owner's equity is fairly low. However, since the business is new, the return can be expected to improve in the future. If it does not, the owner should consider ways to increase revenue and net income—such as increasing the delivery area, perhaps raising prices, or advertising more. The return offered for the savings account is greater, but it is less likely than the return on owner's equity to increase in the future.

CHAPTER 10
SECTION 2, PAGES 243–246

3 ASSESS

Thinking Critically (Answers)

1. Permanent accounts have balances; temporary accounts do not.
2. To record and post closing entries; to prepare a post-closing trial balance.

Communicating Accounting (Answers)

Answers will vary. Students can refer to a textbook example, but encourage them to write their own draft.

Problem 10-3 (Answers)

Accts. Rec.—L. Brown, Bal. Sh. No, Yes
Adv. Exp., Inc. St., Yes, No
Cash in Bank, Bal. Sh., No, Yes
Exer. Class Rev., Inc. St., Yes, No
Exercise Equip., Bal. Sh., No, Yes
Income Summary, N/A, Yes, No
Laundry Equip., Bal. Sh., No, Yes
Maintenance Exp., Inc. St., Yes, No
Membership Fees, Inc. St., Yes, No
Miscellaneous Exp., Inc. St., Yes, No
Office Furniture, Bal. Sh., No, Yes
Rent Exp., Inc. St., Yes, No
Repair Tools, Bal. Sh., No, Yes
T. Chapman, Cap., Bal. Sh., Yes, Yes
T. Chapman, With., Bal. Sh., Yes, No
Utilities Exp., Inc. St., Yes, No

Chapter Reviews and Working Papers Refer students to the Chapter 10 workbook pages to answer *Check Your Understanding* activities.

4 CLOSE

Section Wrap-Up

Writing: Have students write a paragraph explaining why the temporary accounts need zero balances to start a new fiscal period. L1

SECTION 2 Check Your Understanding

Now that you have studied this section, complete the following questions and problems.

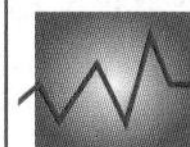

Thinking Critically

1. After the closing process, what types of accounts have balances other than zero, and what types of accounts have zero balances?
2. What is the purpose of the eighth and ninth steps in the accounting cycle?

Communicating Accounting

The Electric Light Company has a large accounting department, and every accounting clerk has specific duties. Your co-worker, Denise Doster, is ill today, and she usually completes the post-closing trial balance. You are too busy with your own work to complete this task, and Denise cannot be reached by phone, so you have to show another accounting clerk how to prepare the post-closing trial balance. Explain where the balances are pulled from and how to set up the post-closing trial balance. Using your computer or lined paper, draft an example for the accounting clerk to follow.

Problem 10-3 Determining Accounts Affected by Closing Entries

The following list contains some of the accounts used by the Living Well Health Spa.

General Ledger

Accts. Pay.—The Fitness Shop	Membership Fees
Accts. Rec.—Linda Brown	Miscellaneous Expense
Advertising Expense	Office Furniture
Cash in Bank	Rent Expense
Exercise Class Revenue	Repair Tools
Exercise Equipment	Ted Chapman, Capital
Income Summary	Ted Chapman, Withdrawals
Laundry Equipment	Utilities Expense
Maintenance Expense	

Instructions Using the form in your working papers:

1. In the first column, indicate the financial statement where each account appears: balance sheet or income statement.
2. In the next column, indicate whether or not the account is affected by a closing entry.
3. In the last column, indicate whether or not the account appears on the post-closing trial balance.

The first account is shown as an example.

Account Name	Financial Statement	Is the account affected by a closing entry?	Does the account appear on the post-closing trial balance?
Accts. Pay.—The Fitness Shop	Balance Sheet	No	Yes

RETEACHING SECTION 2

Post-Closing Trial Balance Students may question the need for creating the post-closing trial balance. Explain that errors could have been made after the trial balance was prepared. For example, a closing entry could have been posted to the wrong ledger account, or an entire closing entry may not have been posted. In preparing the post-closing trial balance, all the balances in the ledger accounts are checked. All temporary accounts should have zero balances. The second, or post-closing, trial balance provides proof that the ledger is in balance after all the temporary accounts have been closed. Give students a set of permanent account balances and have them prepare a post-closing trial balance.

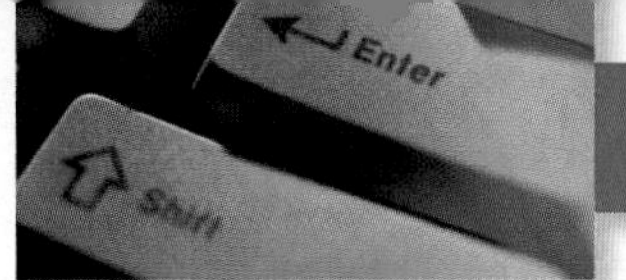

CHAPTER 10 SUMMARY

KEY CONCEPTS

1. The eighth step in the accounting cycle is to journalize and post the closing entries.
2. The ninth step in the accounting cycle is to prepare a post-closing trial balance.
3. Closing is the process of transferring the balances in the temporary capital accounts to the owner's capital account. The work sheet shows the balances of the temporary capital accounts.
4. Only temporary capital accounts are closed. The asset, liability, and owner's capital accounts are never closed.
5. The first closing entry transfers the balance of the revenue account(s) to **Income Summary.**
6. The second closing entry transfers the balances of the expense accounts to **Income Summary.**
7. The third closing entry transfers the balance of the **Income Summary** account (the net income or net loss for the period) to the owner's capital account.
8. The fourth closing entry transfers the balance of the withdrawals account to the owner's capital account.
9. After the closing entries are journalized, they are posted to the general ledger. A post-closing trial balance is prepared to verify the equality of total debits and total credits in the general ledger after the closing entries are posted.

	Date		Description	Debit	Credit	
1	20--					1
2	Dec.	31	*Revenue Account*	XXX XX		2
3			*Income Summary*		XXX XX	3
4		31	*Income Summary*	XXX XX		4
5			*Expense Account*		XXX XX	5
6			*Expense Account*		XXX XX	6
7			*Expense Account*		XXX XX	7
8		31	*Income Summary*	XXX XX		8
9			*Owner's Capital Account*		XXX XX	9
12		31	*Owner's Capital Account*	XXX XX		12
13			*Withdrawals Account*		XXX XX	13

Roadrunner Delivery Service
Post-Closing Trial Balance
December 31, 20--

Account	Debit	Credit
Cash in Bank	21 125 00	
Accts. Rec.—City News	1 450 00	
Computer Equipment	3 000 00	
Office Equipment	200 00	
Delivery Equipment	12 000 00	
Accts. Pay.—Beacon Advertising		75 00
Accts. Pay.—North Shore Auto		11 650 00
Maria Sanchez, Capital		26 050 00
Totals	37 775 00	37 775 00

SUMMARY CHAPTER 10

Chapter 10 Quiz

Student Class Instructor
Date Assigned Date Completed

CHAPTER 10 QUIZ

Completing the Accounting Cycle for a Sole Proprietorship

QUESTIONS (True-False)

Directions: In the space provided, indicate whether each statement is true or false.

___ 1. Closing entries reduce the capital account balance to zero.
___ 2. The temporary capital accounts start each fiscal period with a zero balance.
___ 3. The Income Summary account serves as a simple income statement in the ledger.
___ 4. The Income Summary account has a normal credit balance
___ 5. The Income Summary account does not have an increase or decrease side.
___ 6. The entry to transfer net income to capital is a credit to capital and a debit to Income Summary.
___ 7. A compound entry has at least two debits and two credits.
___ 8. Expense accounts are closed with credits to each account.
___ 9. The withdrawals account is closed with a credit to that account.
___ 10. A credit balance in Income Summary after the revenue, expense, and withdrawals accounts have been closed indicates a net income.

12 • Chapter Quizzes

QUESTIONS (True-False)

1. Closing entries reduce the capital account balance to zero.
2. The temporary capital accounts start each fiscal period with a zero balance.
3. The Income Summary account serves as a simple income statement in the ledger.
4. The Income Summary account has a normal credit balance.
5. The Income Summary account does not have an increase or decrease side.
6. The entry to transfer net income to capital is a credit to capital and a debit to Income Summary.
7. A compound entry has at least two debits and two credits.
8. Expense accounts are closed with credits to each account.
9. The withdrawals account is closed with a credit to that account.
10. A credit balance in Income Summary after the revenue, expense, and withdrawals accounts have been closed indicates a net income.

ANSWERS

1. False
2. True
3. True
4. False
5. False
6. True
7. False
8. True
9. True
10. True

USING KEY TERMS

See the *Glossary* for the definitions of these terms. Have students share their definitions in class. Correct definitions as needed.

Understanding Accounting Concepts and Procedures

(Answers)

1. To reduce their balances to zero for use in the new fiscal period.
2. Revenues, Expenses, and Withdrawals.
3. To summarize the revenue and expenses for a fiscal period.
4. Income Summary is a temporary capital account used to record net income or net loss; its debit balance (loss) decreases capital while a credit balance (income) increases capital.
5. It is used only at the end of the fiscal period and does not have a normal balance side.
6. Its balance is either a net loss or a net income.
7. (a) Transfer revenue to credit side of Income Summary. (b) Transfer expenses to debit side. (c) Transfer Income Summary balance to capital. (d) Transfer withdrawals to debit side of Capital.
8. The work sheet.
9. It saves space in the journal and posting time.
10. Balance of Income Summary is transferred to debit side of capital.
11. Withdrawals is a temporary account that does not affect net income or loss and so is closed separately.
12. They are the same except for writing "Closing Entry" in accounts.
13. To test that total debits in the ledger are equal to total credits after closing entries are posted.
14. Only permanent accounts have balances.

USING KEY TERMS

On a separate sheet of paper, write a brief definition for each term below.

closing entries	**Income Summary** account
compound entry	post-closing trial balance

Understanding Accounting Concepts and Procedures

Instructions

On a separate sheet of paper, answer the following questions:

1. Why are the temporary capital accounts closed at the end of the fiscal year?
2. Which accounts are considered temporary capital accounts?
3. What is the purpose of the **Income Summary** account?
4. Explain the relationship between the **Income Summary** account and the capital account.
5. How is the **Income Summary** account different from the other temporary capital accounts?
6. Why doesn't the **Income Summary** account have a normal balance?
7. List the steps for closing the temporary capital accounts.
8. What is the source of information for the closing entries?
9. Why is a compound entry useful when closing the expense accounts?
10. How does the closing procedure for net loss differ from the closing procedure for net income?
11. Why is the balance of the withdrawals account closed to the capital account?
12. How are the posting procedures for closing entries and for other general journal entries different?
13. Why is the post-closing trial balance prepared?
14. Why do only the balances of permanent accounts appear on the post-closing trial balance?

ASSESSMENT RESOURCES

Choose assessment strategies from the following pages to evaluate your students' progress.

Student Edition
Check Your Understanding, pp. 242, 246
Chapter 10 Problems, pp. 251–255
Analyzing Financial Reports, p. 245

Assessment and Evaluation Masters
Chapter 10 Study Plan, *Glencoe Workbook (CRWP)*
Chapter 10 Self-Test, *Glencoe Workbook (CRWP)*
Chapter 10 Test, *Chapter Tests* Booklet
Chapter 10 Activity, *School-to-Work Handbook*
Chapter 10 **Exam***View*

Teacher Wraparound Edition
Critical Thinking Activity, p. 252
Reteaching Sections 1–2, pp. 242, 246
Chapter 10 Quiz, p. 247

Case Study...

Service Business: Computer Consulting

You are the accountant for Computer Works, a computer consulting business. After preparing financial statements and completing the closing entries below, you notice that the owner's capital account balance in the general ledger of $34,400 differs from the ending capital balance of $43,400 on the statement of changes in owner's equity. The capital account balance was $38,900 at the beginning of the month.

Date	Description	Debit	Credit
Aug. 31	Consulting Fee Revenue	9,240	
	Income Summary		9,240
Aug. 31	Income Summary	870	
	Advertising Expense		300
	Internet Access Expense		20
	Rent Expense		550
Aug. 31	Rex Moran, Capital	8,100	
	Income Summary		8,100

Thinking Critically:
1. Identify the mistakes in the closing entries.
2. What is the correct capital account balance?

Conducting an Audit with Alex

The work sheet and financial statements for Bennett Company for November are complete. The balances of revenue, expense and equity accounts are:

Service Revenue	$ 6,200
Advertising Expense	900
Miscellaneous Expense	300
Rent Expense	1,400
Utilities Expense	600
Dale Bennett, Capital	30,000
Dale Bennett, Withdrawals	2,000

Instructions Answer the following questions about the closing entries that will be prepared:
1. What is the amount of the debit to the **Income Summary** to close out the expense accounts?
2. What is the amount of the credit to the **Income Summary** to close out the revenue account?

*inter*NET CONNECTION

Accounting Publications

When using the Internet, the accountant has many resources at his or her fingertips. Whether you're interested in the latest tax laws, accounting software, or professional conduct tips, you'll find publications that cover these topics and others.

Do This:
1. Locate and list five accounting publications on the Internet.
2. Describe the information each publication contains.
3. Imagine you have landed your first accounting job in a CPA office. Which publication do you think would be most helpful?

Workplace Skills

Working in a Team

Completion of projects at work often requires a variety of talents and skills. You may be asked to work as part of a team to complete a budget for your department or create a presentation on your group's latest achievement.

On the Job:

Imagine that you work in the accounting department for the multimedia division of MTV. The CD-ROM project manager wants to produce a new CD-ROM that will contain clips from the latest music videos to sell in stores. You and your co-workers in accounting have questions:
- What are the engineering costs for the CD-ROM?
- When will the CD-ROM be on the shelves at music stores?
- What will be the price of the product?

Thinking Critically:
1. Form a team of five students. Outline other questions you may have for the project manager.
2. Compile your questions and opinions about the product (from a financial perspective) into a one-page report.
3. Present your report to the class.

*inter*NET CONNECTION www.glencoe.com

Do This (Answers)
1. Answers will vary.
2. Answers will vary, depending on the publication.
3. Answers will vary.

REVIEW AND ACTIVITIES
CHAPTER 10

Case Study...

Thinking Critically (Answers)

1. The entry closing the Income Summary account to the Capital account should be: Dr. Income Summary $8,370; Cr. Rex Moran, Capital $8,370.
2. $47,270

Workplace Skills

Thinking Critically (Answers)

Answers will vary. Some possible areas to question include distribution costs, forecasts of sales volume, and marketing costs/strategy.

Conducting an Audit with Alex

(Answers)
1. $3,200
2. $6,200

Internet Resources and Activities Handbook

Refer students to the booklet for additional Internet activities.

Teaching Tip: Prepare a Post-Closing Trial Balance

Extend the Case Study activity by having students prepare a post-closing trial balance. Give students the following balances: Cash in Bank, $5,320; Accounts Payable, Riverside Electronics, $450; Rex Moran, Withdrawals, $0; Computer Equipment, $3,500. (Cash in Bank Dr., $5,320; Computer Equipment Dr., $3,500; Accounts Payable, Riverside Electronics Cr. $450; Rex Moran, Capital Cr. $8,370. Note that Rex Moran, Withdrawals, does not appear on the post-closing trial balance because it is a temporary account.)

PEACHTREE CORNER

Close Fiscal Year

To close the fiscal year, choose **System** from the *Tasks* menu and then choose **Year-End Wizard**. Closing the fiscal year automatically closes all temporary accounts, updates the general ledger, and selects the next accounting period. **Note:** This process cannot be reversed.

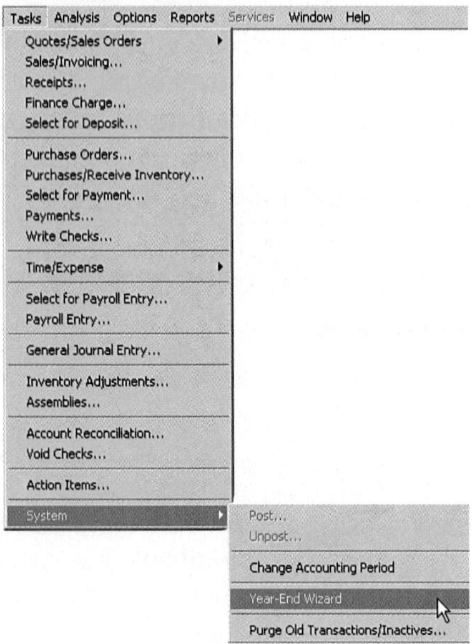

Backup/Restore

Making a backup of a company's accounting data files is an important task that should be performed on a regular basis. Peachtree provides an easy way to backup/restore data files.

File Edit Maintain Tasks Analysis
Open Company... Ctrl+O
New Company... Ctrl+N
Print... Ctrl+P
Print Preview Ctrl+W
Page Setup...
Back Up... Ctrl+B
Restore... Ctrl+R
Select Import/Export...

CHAPTER 10 COMPUTERIZED ACCOUNTING

Closing the Accounting Period

Making the Transition from a Manual to a Computerized System

Task	Perform Accounting Procedures Using Manual Methods	Perform Accounting Procedures Using Automated Methods
Closing Entries	• Using a general journal form, prepare closing entries for revenue, expense, income summary, and withdrawals accounts. Post the closing entries in the general ledger accounts.	• It is not necessary to journalize closing entries. Closing entries are performed by the computerized system.

Closing the Accounting Period

Peachtree Question	Description
What is the difference between changing the accounting period and closing the fiscal year in Peachtree?	• At the end of an accounting period (usually at month-end), you should change to the next accounting period. For example, at March 30, 20— you would select the next accounting period, April 1, 20— through April 30, 20—. • The fiscal year should be closed only when you are sure that all entries have been recorded and all reports have been printed for the year.
How do I change the accounting period?	When you finish entering all transactions for the month and are ready to move to the next month, you must change the accounting period. **1.** Select Systems from the Tasks menu. **2.** Select Change Accounting Period. **3.** Select the next accounting period from the pull-down menu. **4.** Peachtree asks if you would like to print monthly reports before continuing. Do so if necessary. Click OK.
What does the software do "behind the scenes"?	• The software will change the accounting period and it will appear in the status bar at the bottom of the screen. • Now you may enter transactions for the new month.
How do I close the fiscal year?	**1.** Post and print all journal entries before closing the fiscal year. Closing the fiscal year cannot be reversed. **2.** From the Tasks menu, select Systems. **3.** Select Year-End Wizard. **4.** You will be prompted to complete Year-End closing procedures.
What does the software do "behind the scenes"?	• Closing the fiscal year will zero all income and expense accounts and post them to the Retained Earnings account, essentially preparing and posting all closing entries.

For detailed instructions: See the **Peachtree User Guide** in your Glencoe Working Papers.

250 **Chapter 10** Computerized Accounting

Peachtree® Answers to Frequently Asked Questions

Q: What if you notice a mistake after you close the fiscal year?
A: You have two options. If you made a backup before the closing, you can restore the company data, correct the error, and then close the fiscal year again. If you did not make a backup, make a correcting entry in the new period.
Q: How do you print a post-closing trial balance since Peachtree does not include this report?
A: Use the General Ledger Trial Balance and change the title using the report options.
For additional information, see your *Glencoe Peachtree Accounting User Guide.*

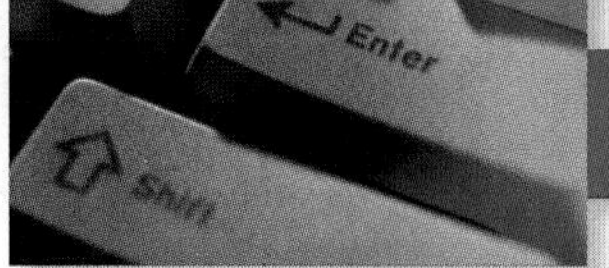

APPLICATION OPTIONS

Problem 10–4 Preparing Closing Entries

A portion of the work sheet for Wilderness Rentals for the period ended December 31 appears below.

Instructions Using the information from the work sheet, prepare the journal entries to close the temporary capital accounts.

1. Record the closing entry for the revenue account.
2. Record the closing entry for the expense accounts.
3. Record the closing entry for the **Income Summary** account.
4. Record the closing entry for the withdrawals account.

Wilderness Rentals
Work Sheet
For the Period Ended December 31, 20--

ACCT. NO.	ACCOUNT NAME	INCOME STATEMENT DEBIT	INCOME STATEMENT CREDIT	BALANCE SHEET DEBIT	BALANCE SHEET CREDIT
101	*Cash in Bank*			7 000 00	
105	*Accts. Rec.—Helen Katz*			2 000 00	
110	*Accts. Rec.—Polk and Co.*			1 000 00	
115	*Office Supplies*			900 00	
120	*Office Equipment*			12 000 00	
125	*Camping Equipment*			6 000 00	
201	*Accts. Pay.—Adventure Equip. Inc.*				900 00
203	*Accts. Pay.—Digital Tech Computers*				400 00
205	*Accts. Pay.—Greg Mollaro*				500 00
301	*Ronald Hicks, Capital*				19 775 00
305	*Ronald Hicks, Withdrawals*			2 350 00	
310	*Income Summary*	—	—		
401	*Equipment Rental Revenue*		14 965 00		
501	*Advertising Expense*	1 500 00			
505	*Maintenance Expense*	1 560 00			
515	*Rent Expense*	1 000 00			
525	*Utilities Expense*	1 230 00			
		5 290 00	14 965 00	31 250 00	21 575 00
	Net Income	9 675 00			9 675 00
		14 965 00	14 965 00	31 250 00	31 250 00

Analyze: What is the capital account balance after posting the closing entries?

Complete chapter problems one of four ways:

1. **Manual** Glencoe Working Papers

or

2. **Peachtree Complete Accounting** Software

or

3. **QuickBooks** Templates (Problems 10–8, 10–9)

or

4. **Spreadsheet** Templates (Problem 10–9)

Peachtree®

SMART GUIDE

Step-by-Step Instructions: Problem 10–4

1. Select the problem set for Wilderness Rentals (Prob. 10–4).
2. Rename the company and set the system date.
3. Select **System** from the ***Tasks*** menu and then choose **Year-End Wizard.**
4. Answer the Analyze question.
5. End the session.

TIP: Print the General Ledger or General Ledger Trial Balance report to find an account balance.

Problem 10–5 Preparing a Post-Closing Trial Balance

Instructions Use the accounts shown on the next two pages to prepare a Dec. 31 post-closing trial balance for Hot Suds Car Wash.

Continued

Problem 10–4 (Answers) Preparing Closing Entries

1. Dr. Equipment Rental Revenue $14,965; Cr. Income Summary $14,965
2. Dr. Income Summary $5,290; Cr. Advertising Expense $1,500, Maintenance Expense $1,560, Rent Expense $1,000, Utilities Expense $1,230
3. Dr. Income Summary $9,675; Cr. Ronald Hicks, Capital $9,675
4. Dr. Ronald Hicks, Capital $2,350; Cr. Ronald Hicks, Withdrawals $2,350

Analyze: $27,100

Chapter Reviews and Working Papers Refer students to the *Study Plan* located at the beginning of Chapter 10 in the workbook.

REINFORCING STUDY SKILLS

Note Taking The skill of taking good notes is important in enabling students to recall and study what they have heard in lectures. Help students develop good note-taking habits by explaining that notes should be brief but complete enough to provide clear information when they're read hours or days after a lecture. Have pairs of students compare their notes and note-taking techniques.

Problem 10-5 (Answers) Preparing a Post-Closing Trial Balance

Post-closing trial balance totals: $93,925

Analyze: Zero

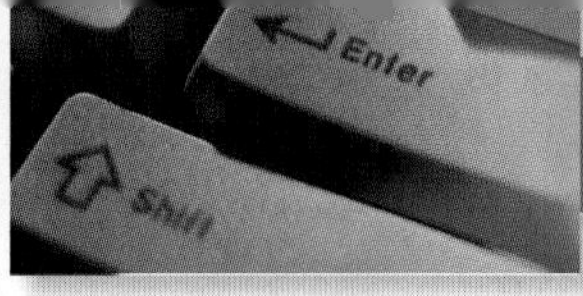

Peachtree®

SMART GUIDE

Step-by-Step Instructions: Problem 10-5

1. Select the problem set for Hot Suds Car Wash (Prob. 10-5).
2. Rename the company and set the system date.
3. Print a General Ledger Trial Balance.
4. Answer the Analyze question.
5. End the session.

TIP: Print the General Ledger Trial Balance after you complete the closing process to generate a post-closing trial balance.

Cash in Bank

Debit +	Credit −
Balance 8,000	

Accounts Receivable—Linda Brown

Debit +	Credit −
Balance 875	

Accounts Receivable—Valley Auto

Debit +	Credit −
Balance 5,050	

Office Equipment

Debit +	Credit −
Balance 6,000	

Office Furniture

Debit +	Credit −
Balance 9,000	

Car Wash Equipment

Debit +	Credit −
Balance 65,000	

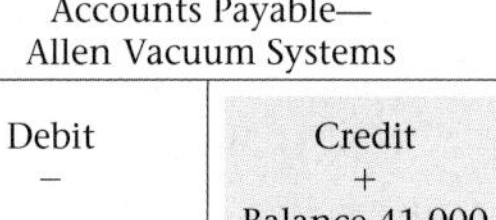

Accounts Payable—Allen Vacuum Systems

Debit −	Credit +
	Balance 41,000

Accounts Payable—O'Brian's Office Supply

Debit −	Credit +
	Balance 2,500

Regina Delgado, Capital

Debit −	Credit +
Closing 1,500	35,925
	Closing 16,000

Regina Delgado, Withdrawals

Debit +	Credit −
Balance 1,500	Closing 1,500

Income Summary

Debit	Credit
Closing 19,000	Closing 35,000
Closing 16,000	

Wash Revenue

Debit −	Credit +
Closing 15,000	Balance 15,000

Wax Revenue

Debit −	Credit +
Closing 8,000	Balance 8,000

Interior Detailing Revenue

Debit −	Credit +
Closing 12,000	Balance 12,000

Advertising Expense

Debit +	Credit −
Balance 2,500	Closing 2,500

Equipment Rental Expense

Debit +	Credit −
Balance 3,000	Closing 3,000

Continued

CRITICAL THINKING ACTIVITY

Making Comparisons Have students assume that they have been asked to review financial statements and the post-closing trial balance. They notice that the Capital balance on the post-closing trial balance does not match the balance sheet amount. In checking the ledger account balances, they also notice that the revenue and expense accounts still have end-of-period balances. Is there a reason to explain this situation, or does this imply an error in the accounting records? (The closing entries have not been posted to the ledger, which results in an incorrect capital balance being reported on the post-closing trial balance. After posting, the capital account balance should equal the amount shown on the balance sheet.)

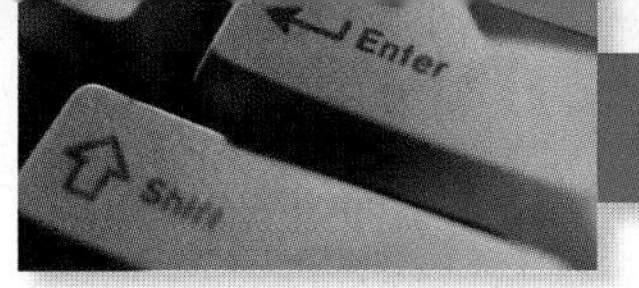

Maintenance Expense	
Debit +	Credit –
Balance 5,000	Closing 5,000

Rent Expense	
Debit +	Credit –
Balance 5,000	Closing 5,000

Utilities Expense	
Debit +	Credit –
Balance 3,500	Closing 3,500

Analyze: What is the balance of the temporary accounts after the closing entries are posted?

Peachtree®

SMART GUIDE

Step-by-Step Instructions: Problem 10–6

1. Select the problem set for Kits & Pups Grooming (Prob. 10–6).
2. Rename the company and set the system date.
3. Close the current fiscal year.
4. Answer the Analyze question.
5. End the session.

Problem 10–6 Journalizing Closing Entries

The following account names and balances appear on the work sheet for Kits & Pups Grooming for the month ended December 31.

Kits & Pups Grooming
Work Sheet
For the Month Ended December 31, 20--

	ACCT. NO.	ACCOUNT NAME	INCOME STATEMENT DEBIT	INCOME STATEMENT CREDIT	BALANCE SHEET DEBIT	BALANCE SHEET CREDIT	
1		*Cash in Bank*			9 300 00		1
2		*Accts. Rec.—Juan Alvarez*			3 000 00		2
3		*Accts. Rec.—Nathan Carlsbad*			10 000 00		3
4		*Accts. Rec.—Martha Giles*			5 000 00		4
5		*Office Equipment*			8 000 00		5
6		*Office Furniture*			10 000 00		6
7		*Computer Equipment*			9 000 00		7
8		*Grooming Equipment*			15 000 00		8
9		*Kennel Equipment*			21 000 00		9
10		*Accts. Pay.—Able Store Equip.*				5 000 00	10
11		*Accts. Pay.—Dogs & Cats Inc.*				1 500 00	11
12		*Accts. Pay.—Pet Gourmet*				15 000 00	12
13		*Abe Shultz, Capital*				52 700 00	13
14		*Abe Shultz, Withdrawals*			7 000 00		14
15		*Income Summary*					15
16		*Boarding Revenue*		20 000 00			16
17		*Grooming Revenue*		8 000 00			17
18		*Advertising Expense*	700 00				18
19		*Equipment Repair Expense*	1 200 00				19
20		*Maintenance Expense*	500 00				20
21		*Rent Expense*	1 700 00				
22		*Utilities Expense*	800 00				

Instructions Using the above information, record the closing entries for Kits & Pups Grooming. Use general journal page 11.

Analyze: What was the change in the capital account for the period?

PROBLEMS
CHAPTER 10

Problem 10–6 (Answer)
Journalizing Closing Entries

1. Dr. Boarding Revenue $20,000, Grooming Revenue $8,000; Cr. Income Summary $28,000
2. Dr. Income Summary $4,900; Cr. Advertising Expense $700, Equipment Repair Expense $1,200, Maintenance Expense $500, Rent Expense $1,700, Utilities Expense $800
3. Dr. Income Summary $23,100; Cr. Abe Schultz, Capital $23,100
4. Dr. Abe Schultz, Capital $7,000; Cr. Abe Schultz, Withdrawals $7,000

Analyze: $16,100 increase

ACCOUNTING ISSUES

Guides for Doing Business in Foreign Countries The AICPA publishes guides for CPAs whose clients are interested in doing business in foreign countries. These guides provide an in-depth look at business conditions in various countries. Among the topics addressed are:

- history, geography, climate, population, and religion
- political environment
- currency, customs regulations, transportation, communications, business hours, public holidays
- banking and finance, foreign exchange, and acounting and auditing considerations

Problem 10–7 (Answers) Posting Closing Entries and Preparing a Post-Closing Trial Balance

Post-closing trial balance totals: $79,500

Analyze: $52,500

Problem 10–8 (Answers) Completing End-of-Period Activities

Work sheet trial balance totals: $79,775
Net Income: $8,525
Ending Capital: $38,300
Total Assets: $71,200

Closing entries:

1. Dr. Video Rental Revenue $9,600, VCR Rental Revenue $3,500; Cr. Income Summary $13,100
2. Dr. Income Summary $4,575; Cr. Advertising Expense $1,600, Equipment Repair Expense $1,200, Maintenance Expense $400, Rent Expense $1,000, Utilities Expense $375
3. Dr. Income Summary $8,525; Cr. Greg Failla, Capital $8,525
4. Dr. Greg Failla, Capital $4,000; Cr. Greg Failla, Withdrawals $4,000

Post-closing trial balance totals: $71,200

Analyze: $7,200

Peachtree®

SMART GUIDE

Step-by-Step Instructions: Problem 10–7

1. Select the problem set for Outback Guide Service (Prob. 10–7).
2. Rename the company and set the system date.
3. Close the fiscal year.
4. Print a General Ledger Trial Balance.
5. Answer the Analyze question.
6. End the session.

Problem 10–7 Posting Closing Entries and Preparing a Post-Closing Trial Balance

The closing entries for Outback Guide Service for the period ended December 31 appear below.

GENERAL JOURNAL — PAGE 1

	DATE		DESCRIPTION	POST. REF.	DEBIT	CREDIT	
1	20--		*Closing Entries*				1
2	Dec.	31	*Guide Service Revenue*		16 300 00		2
3			*Income Summary*			16 300 00	3
4		31	*Income Summary*		10 000 00		4
5			*Advertising Expense*			3 000 00	5
6			*Maintenance Expense*			1 100 00	6
7			*Rent Expense*			4 000 00	7
8			*Utilities Expense*			1 900 00	8
9		31	*Income Summary*		6 300 00		9
10			*Juanita Ortega, Capital*			6 300 00	10
11		31	*Juanita Ortega, Capital*		4 000 00		11
12			*Juanita Ortega, Withdrawals*			4 000 00	12

Instructions In your working papers:

1. Post the closing entries to the appropriate general ledger accounts.
2. Using the general ledger in your working papers, prepare a post-closing trial balance.

Analyze: What is the balance of the capital account after closing?

Peachtree®

SMART GUIDE

Step-by-Step Instructions: Problem 10–8

1. Select the problem set for Showbiz Video (Prob. 10–8).
2. Rename the company and set the system date.
3. Print a General Ledger Trial Balance.
4. Print an Income Statement and a Balance Sheet.
5. Close the fiscal year.
6. Print a General Ledger Trial Balance.
7. Answer the Analyze question.
8. End the session.

TIP: You can use the General Ledger navigation aid to access the financial statements.

Problem 10–8 Completing End-of-Period Activities

The general ledger for Showbiz Video shows the following at December 31:

General Ledger

No.	Account	Balance
101	Cash in Bank	12,000
105	Accts. Rec.—G. Cohen	3,000
110	Accts. Rec.—J. Coletti	900
113	Accts. Rec.—S. Flannery	1,800
115	Accts. Rec.—Spring Branch School District	1,500
130	Office Equipment	5,000
135	Office Furniture	8,000
140	Computer Equipment	10,000
145	Video Tapes	20,000
150	Video Equipment	9,000
201	Accts. Pay.—Broad Street Office Supply	400
205	Accts. Pay.—Computer Horizons	15,500
207	Accts. Pay.—New Media Suppliers	3,000
209	Accts. Pay.—Palace Films	14,000
301	Greg Failla, Capital	33,775
305	Greg Failla, Withdrawals	4,000
310	Income Summary	—
401	Video Rental Revenue	9,600
405	VCR Rental Revenue	3,500
501	Advertising Expense	1,600
505	Equipment Repair Expense	1,200
510	Maintenance Expense	400
520	Rent Expense	1,000
530	Utilities Expense	375

EXTENDING THE CONTENT

Identifying and Classifying Revenue and Expense Accounts Write two headings on the chalkboard: *Revenue* and *Expense*. Have students brainstorm the temporary accounts for a pizza delivery service business. As students name an account, ask them to classify the account as a revenue or an expense. Then list the account on the chalkboard under the appropriate heading. Accept all responses, and do not stop to evaluate whether they are correct. After all responses have been offered, ask students to review the lists. Edit the lists as needed so only temporary accounts are included.

Instructions Using the preceding account names and balances:

1. Prepare the six-column work sheet. The period covered is one month.
2. Prepare the financial statements. Greg Failla invested $10,000 during the month.
3. Record the closing entries on page 12 of the general journal.
4. Post the closing entries.
5. Prepare a post-closing trial balance.

Analyze: What is the total amount of all the accounts receivable accounts on December 31?

Problem 10–9 Completing End-of-Period Activities

At the end of December, the general ledger for Job Connect showed the following account balances:

General Ledger

101	Cash in Bank	6,000	207	Accts. Pay.—Wildwood Furniture Sales	2,000
105	Accts. Rec.—CompuRite Systems	1,000	301	Richard Tang, Capital	23,600
110	Accts. Rec.—Marquez Manufact.	500	302	Richard Tang, Withdrawals	3,000
113	Accts. Rec.—Roaring Rivers Water Park	600	303	Income Summary	—
115	Accts. Rec.—M. Spencer	200	401	Placement Fees Revenue	6,900
130	Office Equipment	7,000	405	Technology Classes Revenue	2,400
135	Office Furniture	5,000	501	Advertising Expense	3,000
140	Computer Equipment	8,500	505	Maintenance Expense	800
201	Accts. Pay.—Micro Solutions Inc.	2,800	510	Miscellaneous Expense	800
205	Accts. Pay.—Vega Internet Services	1,600	520	Rent Expense	2,000
			530	Utilities Expense	900

SPREADSHEET SMART GUIDE

Step-by-Step Instructions: Problem 10–9

1. Select the spreadsheet template for Problem 10–9.
2. Enter your name and the date in the spaces provided on the template.
3. Complete the spreadsheet using the instructions in your working papers.
4. Print the spreadsheet and proof your work.
5. Save your work and exit the spreadsheet program.

Instructions Using the preceding account names and balances:

1. Prepare the six-column work sheet. The period covered is one month.
2. Prepare the financial statements.
3. Record the closing entries on page 28 of the general journal.
4. Post the closing entries.
5. Prepare a post-closing trial balance.

Analyze: What was the greatest expenditure for the period?

PROBLEMS CHAPTER 10

Problem 10–9 (Answers) Completing End-of-Period Activities

Work sheet trial balance totals: $39,300
Net Income: $1,800
Ending Capital: $22,400
Total Assets: $28,800

Closing entries:

1. Dr. Placement Fees Revenue $6,900, Technology Classes Revenue $2,400; Cr. Income Summary $9,300
2. Dr. Income Summary $7,500; Cr. Advertising Expense $3,000, Maintenance Expense $800, Miscellaneous Expense $800, Rent Expense $2,000, Utilities Expense $900
3. Dr. Income Summary $1,800; Cr. Richard Tang, Capital $1,800
4. Dr. Richard Tang, Capital $3,000; Cr. Richard Tang, Withdrawals $3,000

Post-closing trial balance totals: $28,800

Analyze: Advertising Expense $3,000

SOLUTION NOTES

Section Resources

	Objectives & Standards	Activities & Features	Reproducible Masters
Chapter Opener *Cash Control and Banking Activities*	• Describe the internal controls used to protect cash. • Describe the forms needed to open and use a checking account. • Accurately record information on check stubs. • Prepare a check correctly. • Prepare bank deposits. • Reconcile a bank statement. • Journalize and post entries relating to bank service charges. • Define the terms introduced in this chapter. **National Standards for Business Education**: IA16, IIA2	Exploring Real World of Business, p. 256 Workplace Connections, p. 257	School-to-Work Handbook
Section 1 *Banking Procedures*	• What controls a business uses to protect cash and why these controls are needed. • To complete forms used to open a checking account. • To record information on check stubs. • To prepare a check correctly.	International Accounting, p. 260 A Matter of Ethics, p. 263	Strategies for Teaching International Accounting Demonstration Problems Strategies for Teaching Ethics in Accounting
Section 2 *Reconciling the Bank Account*	• Why a business reconciles a bank statement. • How to journalize and post entries relating to bank service charges. • The accounting procedure for stopping payment on a check. • How to record an NSF check. • How electronic funds transfer systems enable banks to transfer funds quickly and accurately.	Accounting Flashbacks, p.266 Connect To, p. 267 Did You Know?, p. 268 Calculator Hints, p. 270 Analyzing Financial Reports, p. 272 Accounting Careers in Focus, p. 274	Demonstration Problems Math Review for Accounting Internet Resources and Activities Handbook

KEY

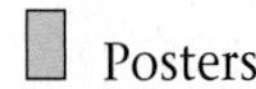

Posters · Transparency · Software · Videocassette

Blackline Masters · CD-ROM · Portfolio

MULTIMEDIA RESOURCE

Peachtree

- Problem 11-4 *Maintaining the Checkbook*
- Problem 11-5 *Reconciling the Bank Statement*
- Problem 11-7 *Reconciling the Bank Statement*
- Problem 11-8 *Reconciling the Bank Statement Using the Account Form*

QuickBooks

- Problem 11-5 *Reconciling the Bank Statement*
- Problem 11-7 *Reconciling the Bank Statement*

Spreadsheets

- Problem 11-6 *Reconciling the Bank Statement*

Videos

Video Segment: Banking and Internal Controls
After viewing this video, students will be able to describe the need for protecting cash and various means of doing so. Discuss with students how a checking account is used as one means of internal control.

CD-ROMs

Electronic Learning Center (ELC), Chapter 11
This program is ideal for visual learners since it incorporates video images, animation, and graphics to enliven the content of each lesson.

Interactive Lesson Planner (ILP), Chapter 11
This CD-ROM combines the versatility of an electronic lesson planner with the convenience of teacher classroom resources.

SCANS Correlation Chart

FOUNDATION SKILLS

Basic Skills:	Reading	Writing	Math	Listening	Speaking	
Thinking Skills:	Creative Thinking	Decision Making	Problem Solving	Seeing Things in the Mind's Eye	Knowing How to Learn	Reasoning
Personal Qualities:	Responsibility	Self-Esteem	Sociability	Self-Management	Integrity/Honesty	

WORKPLACE COMPETENCIES

Resources:	Allocating Time	Allocating Money	Allocating Material and Facility Resources	Allocating Human Resources		
Information:	Acquiring and Evaluating Information	Organizing and Maintaining Information	Interpreting and Communicating Information	Using Computers to Process Information		
Interpersonal Skills:	Participating as a Member of a Team	Teaching Others	Serving Clients/ Customers	Exercising Leadership	Negotiating to Arrive at a Decision	Working with Cultural Diversity
Systems:	Understanding Systems	Monitoring and Correcting Performance	Improving and Designing Systems			
Technology:	Selecting Technology	Applying Technology to Task	Maintaining and Troubleshooting Technology			

*Highlighted blocks indicate areas covered in the chapter. Additional SCANS skills are also covered throughout the *Teacher Wraparound Edition.*

Assessment

Student Edition
- Check Your Understanding, pp. 264, 273
- Chapter 11 Problems, pp. 279–281

Assessment and Evaluation Masters
- Chapter 11 Study Plan, *Glencoe Workbook*
- Chapter 11 Self-Test, *Glencoe Workbook*
- Chapter 11 Test, *Chapter Tests* Booklet
- Chapter 11 Activity, *School-to-Work Handbook*
- Chapter 11 **Exam***View*

Teacher Wraparound Edition
- Critical Thinking Activity, p. 269
- Reteaching Section 1, p. 264
- Reteaching Section 2, p. 273
- Chapter 11 Quiz, p. 275

Transparencies

	Teaching Transparencies	Solution Transparencies
Section 1:	11–1, 11–2, 11–3, 11–4, 11–5, 11–6, 11–7, 11–8, 11–9	Problem 11–1
Section 2:	11–10, 11–11, 11–12, 11–13, 11–14, 11–15, 11–16, 11–17, 11–18, 11–19	Problem 11–2
End of Chapter:		Problems 11–3, 11–4, 11–5, 11–6, 11–7, 11–8

TEACHER CLASSROOM RESOURCES

This is a representation of key blackline masters available in the Teacher Classroom Resources.

Teaching Aids

Transparency Examples

Section Focus Transparencies

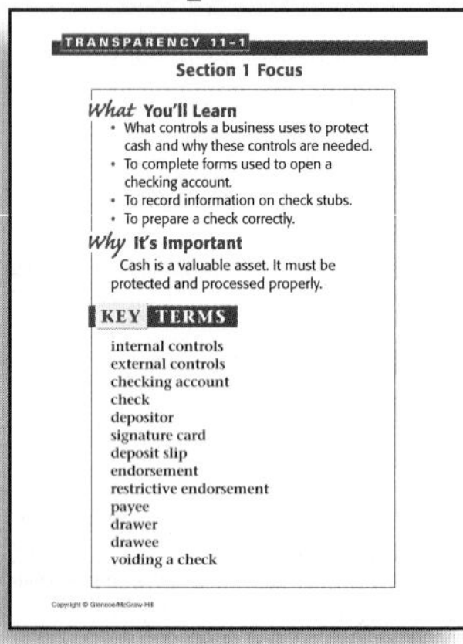

TRANSPARENCY 11-1

Section 1 Focus

What You'll Learn
- What controls a business uses to protect cash and why these controls are needed.
- To complete forms used to open a checking account.
- To record information on check stubs.
- To prepare a check correctly.

Why It's Important

Cash is a valuable asset. It must be protected and processed properly.

KEY TERMS

internal controls
external controls
checking account
check
depositor
signature card
deposit slip
endorsement
restrictive endorsement
payee
drawer
drawee
voiding a check

Teaching Transparencies

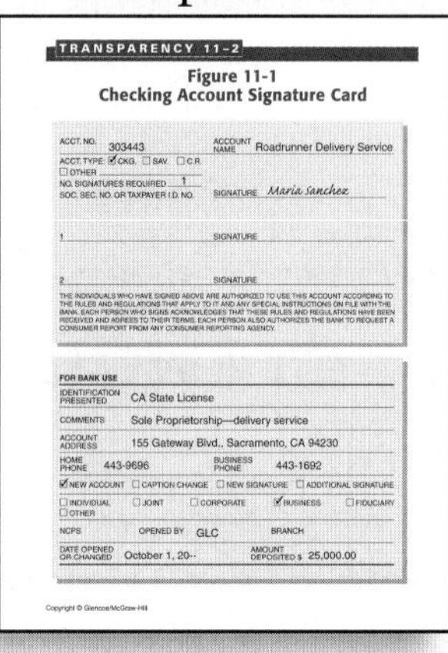

TRANSPARENCY 11-2

Figure 11-1
Checking Account Signature Card

Teaching Transparencies

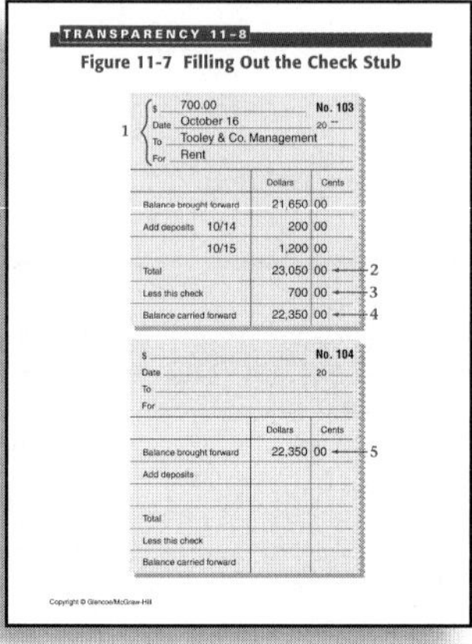

TRANSPARENCY 11-8

Figure 11-7 Filling Out the Check Stub

Solution Transparencies

Working Papers for End-of-Chapter Problems
Problem 11-3 Handling Deposits

Demonstration Problems

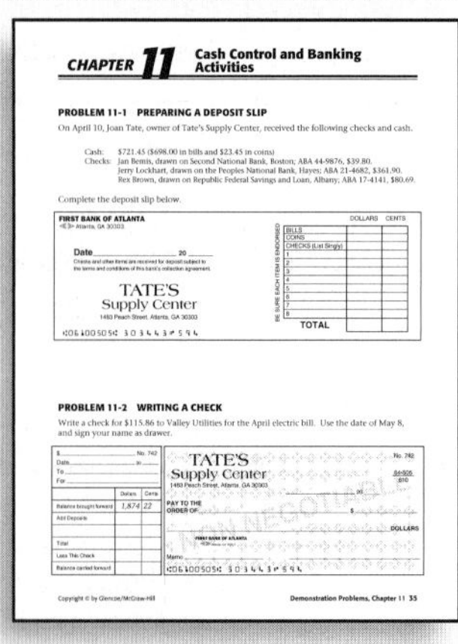

CHAPTER 11 Cash Control and Banking Activities

PROBLEM 11-1 PREPARING A DEPOSIT SLIP

PROBLEM 11-2 WRITING A CHECK

Lesson Plans

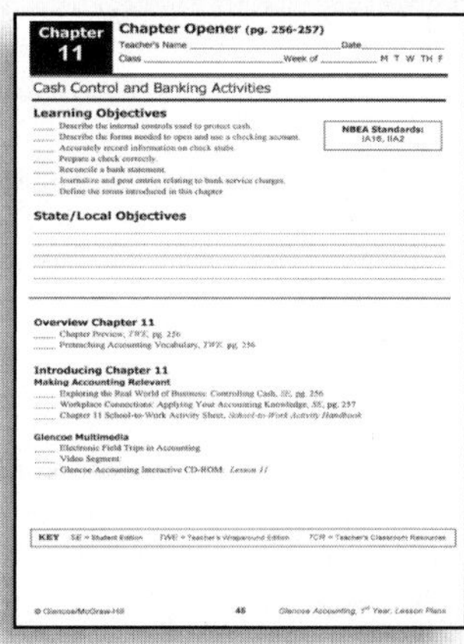

Chapter 11 Chapter Opener (pg. 256-257)

Cash Control and Banking Activities

Learning Objectives

State/Local Objectives

Block Scheduling

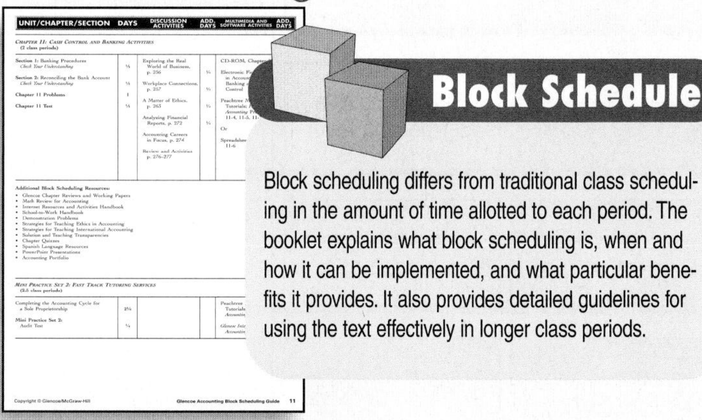

Block Schedule

Block scheduling differs from traditional class scheduling in the amount of time allotted to each period. The booklet explains what block scheduling is, when and how it can be implemented, and what particular benefits it provides. It also provides detailed guidelines for using the text effectively in longer class periods.

Enrichment and Application

Strategies for Teaching Ethics in Accounting

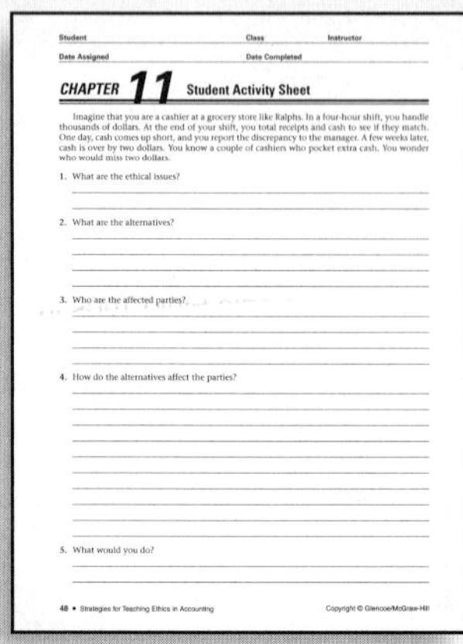

CHAPTER 11 Student Activity Sheet

Strategies for Teaching International Accounting

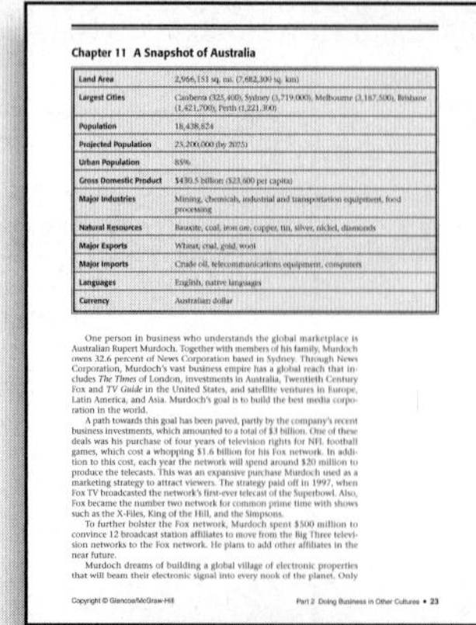

Chapter 11 A Snapshot of Australia

School-to-Work Handbook

CHAPTER 11 SCHOOL-TO-WORK ACTIVITY

Cash Control and Banking Activities

Meeting Different Ability Levels

Chapter Reviews and Working Papers (CRWP)

Working Papers

Review

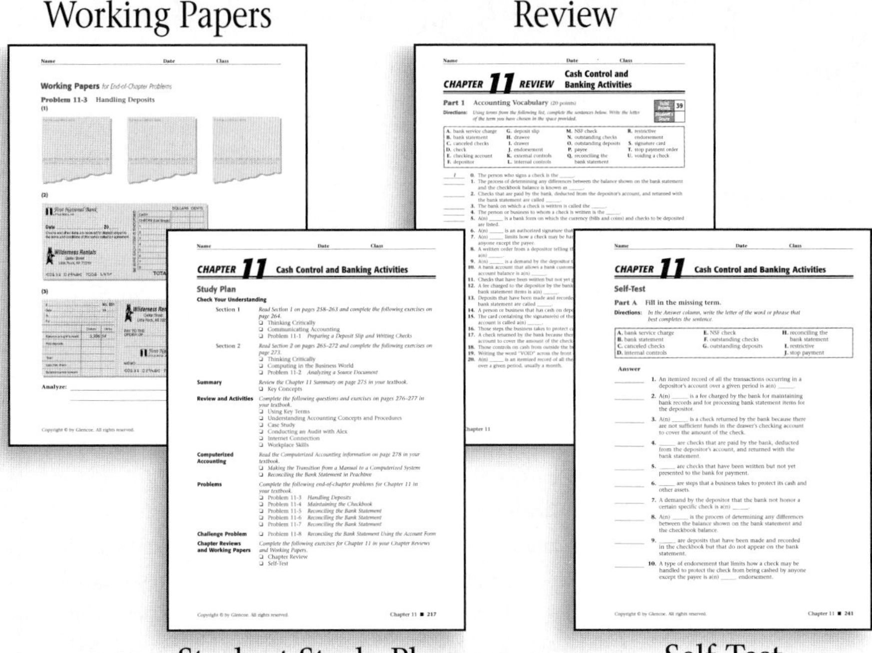

Student Study Plan

Self-Test

Real-World Multimedia CD-ROM

Key to Ability Levels

Each section gives skill-building activities. Each activity has been labeled for use with students of various learning styles and abilities.

L1 Level 1 activities are basic activities and should be within the range of all students.

L2 Level 2 activities are average activities and should be within the range of average and above average students.

L3 Level 3 activities are challenging activities designed for the ability range of above average students.

ELL ELL activities should be within the ability range of English Language Learners.

Teaching Resources at a Glance

Application Resources

- Glencoe Chapter Review and Working Papers, SE and TAE
- School-to-Work Handbook, SE and TM
- Accounting Portfolio, SE and TM

Reproducible Masters

- Demonstration Problems
- Lesson Plans
- Block Scheduling
- Spanish Language Resources

Glencoe Accounting Professional Development Series

- Strategies for Teaching Ethics in Accounting
- Accounting Competitive Event Review
- Math Review for Accounting
- Strategies for Teaching International Accounting
- Internet Resources and Activities Handbook

Transparency Package

- Section Focus Transparencies
- Teaching Transparencies
- Source Document Transparencies
- Solution Transparencies

Performance Assessment

- **Exam***View* CD-ROM
- Chapter Tests
- Chapter Quizzes
- Unit Tests
- Audit Tests
- Printed Testbank

Multimedia Resources

- Electronic Learning Center:
  - Multimedia CD-ROMs
  - Peachtree software, tutorials, templates, and solutions
  - Spreadsheet templates
- Using QuickBooks with Glencoe Accounting
- Interactive Lesson Planner
- Electronic Field Trips in Accounting
- PowerPoint Presentation
- Web site: glencoeaccounting.glencoe.com

Assessment and Evaluation

Chapter Tests

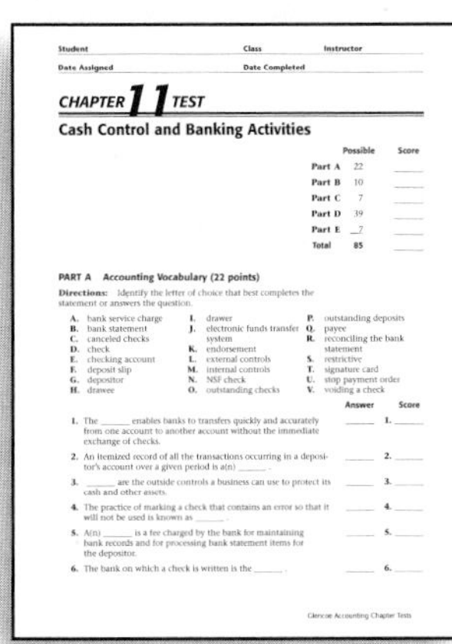

Chapter Quiz

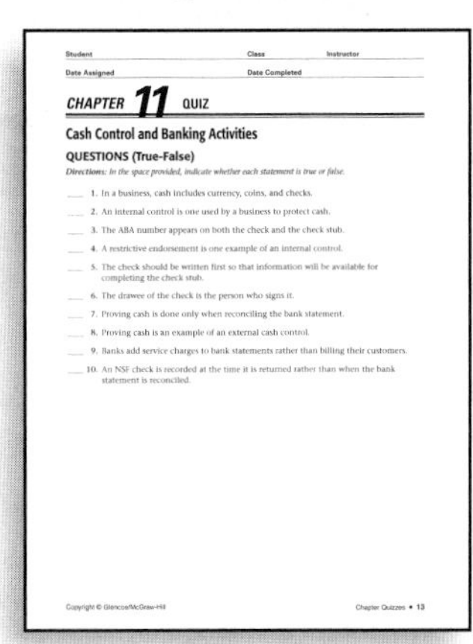

Correlations to National Standards for Business Education

(See pages T50–T51 for a detailed correlation chart.)

Standards: IA16, IIA2

Chapter Preview

To this point, students have learned to record receipts and payments of cash in ledger accounts. Another part of accounting relates to cash control and banking activities. In this chapter students will learn to use a checking account and to record bank service charges in the accounting records for a business.

Section Overviews

- Section 1—*Banking Procedures*
- Section 2—*Reconciling the Bank Account*

Chapter Vocabulary

internal controls
external controls
checking account
check
depositor
signature card
deposit slip
endorsement
restrictive endorsement
payee
drawer
drawee
voiding a check
bank statement
canceled checks
reconciling the bank statement
outstanding checks
outstanding deposits
bank service charge
stop payment order
NSF check
electronic funds transfer system (EFTS)

Preteaching Accounting Vocabulary

Oral Exercise: Write the new terms on the chalkboard. Ask students for ideas for each term's meaning. Review the meanings of terms that are not familiar to students. L1

Cash Control and Banking Activities

Learning Objectives

When you have completed this chapter, you will be able to:

- Describe the internal controls used to protect cash.
- Describe the forms needed to open and use a checking account.
- Accurately record information on check stubs.
- Prepare a check correctly.
- Prepare bank deposits.
- Reconcile a bank statement.
- Journalize and post entries relating to bank service charges.
- Define the terms introduced in this chapter.

Exploring the Real World of Business

CONTROLLING CASH

If you're shopping for waterproof boots or a new waistpack, you could be looking at **Timberland**® products.

The **Timberland Company** designs and sells footwear, clothing, and accessories. **Timberland**® products are sold in more than 90 countries through specialty and department stores, in addition to its own retail locations. The company's flagship store is on Madison Avenue in New York. When you shop at a **Timberland**® store, you might pay for your purchase in cash or use a credit card.

What do you think?

If you worked at a **Timberland**® store, what are at least three cash controls you would use to help protect money received by the company?

Exploring the Real World of Business

Timberland

Timberland was started as a family business 30 years ago by the Schwartz family. The company started out selling just its trademark yellow boot. Timberland now sells to retailers and operates over 70 of its own retail stores. In those stores, cash controls are an important part of protecting cash taken in from product sales.

What do you think? (Answers)

Students' answers may vary. Cash controls may include making all payments by check, bonding employees who frequently handle cash, using restrictive endorsements on all checks to be deposited, using a safe, depositing cash received daily, or separating cash handling and cash accounting responsibilities.

Workplace Connections

Applying Your Accounting Knowledge

You cash your paycheck, stuff the cash in your wallet, and before you know it, it's gone! It's easy to lose track of how you spend your money. Businesses also have to watch their money carefully. One way of safeguarding cash is to keep it in the bank and write checks to make payments. You'll learn about a business checking account in this chapter.

Investigate:

1. Do you handle cash, checks, or credit cards in your job?
2. What procedures are in place to help protect cash?

Glencoe Accounting Online

Visit the *Glencoe Accounting* Web site at **glencoeaccounting.glencoe.com** for additional activities and information.

257

INTRODUCING CHAPTER 11

Making Accounting Relevant

Workplace Connections: Applying Your Accounting Knowledge

Discussion: Businesses deposit all cash in a bank account and make all payments using checks. This policy helps to protect cash from loss or theft, and it also leaves an audit trail for accountants to follow.

Investigate (Answers)

1. Answers will vary. Ask students who have part-time jobs in retail businesses to describe how they handle cash on the job.
2. List students' responses to question 2 on the chalkboard, then discuss which activities help protect cash. Activities students may mention are filling out forms recording the amount of cash in a cash drawer, signing in to obtain a change fund, and making deposits in a bank.

School-to-Work Activity

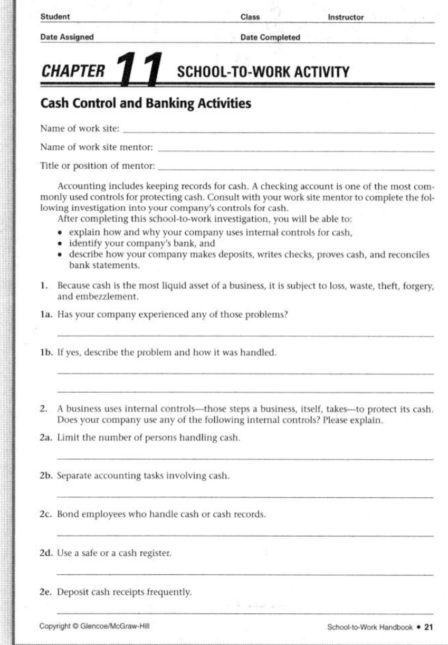

Student ______ Class ______ Instructor ______

Date Assigned ______ Date Completed ______

CHAPTER 11 SCHOOL-TO-WORK ACTIVITY

Cash Control and Banking Activities

Name of work site: ______

Name of work site mentor: ______

Title or position of mentor: ______

Accounting includes keeping records for cash. A checking account is one of the most commonly used controls for protecting cash. Consult with your work site mentor to complete the following investigation into your company's controls for cash.

After completing this school-to-work investigation, you will be able to:

- explain how and why your company uses internal controls for cash,
- identify your company's bank, and
- describe how your company makes deposits, writes checks, proves cash, and reconciles bank statements.

1. Because cash is the most liquid asset of a business, it is subject to loss, waste, theft, forgery, and embezzlement.

1a. Has your company experienced any of those problems?

1b. If yes, describe the problem and how it was handled.

2. A business uses internal controls—those steps a business, itself, takes—to protect its cash. Does your company use any of the following internal controls? Please explain.

2a. Limit the number of persons handling cash.

2b. Separate accounting tasks involving cash.

2c. Bond employees who handle cash or cash records.

2d. Use a safe or a cash register.

2e. Deposit cash receipts frequently.

 School-to-Work Handbook • 21

GLENCOE MULTIMEDIA

Electronic Field Trips in Accounting *Video Segment: Banking and Internal Controls*
After viewing this video, students will be able to describe the need for protecting cash and various means of doing so and discuss how a checking account is used as one means of internal control.

Glencoe Accounting: Electronic Learning Center *Chapter 11*
The CD-ROM program is ideal for visual learners since it incorporates video images, animation, and graphics to enliven the content of each lesson.

1 FOCUS

Introducing the Section

In this section students will learn about the internal and external controls that businesses use to protect cash. Students will also learn how to open a checking account and to record information accurately on checks and check stubs.

Section Concepts

- What controls a business uses to protect cash and why these controls are needed.
- To complete forms used to open a checking account.
- To record information on check stubs.
- To prepare a check correctly.

Visual Learning

Section 1 Focus

Use **Transparency 11–1** to introduce section concepts.

BELL RINGER

Creative Thinking: Using play money or photocopies of hand-drawn hundred dollar bills, distribute several hundred dollars to each student. Then ask students how they would protect their "cash." How would they keep track of how they spend the money? Write their responses on the chalkboard. L1

Concept Development: Protecting Cash

Discussion: Refer to the list of examples given in items 1–6 and have students respond with how each example helps to protect cash. Mention that when business records are audited, internal controls of cash are reviewed in detail. Also discuss how external controls are not under the direct control of the business but may also protect cash. L1

SECTION 1

Banking Procedures

What You'll Learn

- What controls a business uses to protect cash and why these controls are needed.
- To complete forms used to open a checking account.
- To record information on check stubs.
- To prepare a check correctly.

Why It's Important

Cash is a valuable asset. It must be protected and processed properly.

KEY TERMS

internal controls
external controls
checking account
check
depositor
signature card
deposit slip
endorsement
restrictive endorsement
payee
drawer
drawee
voiding a check

In any business, cash (currency, coins, and checks) is used in daily transactions. A business receives cash in return for the goods or services it sells. It pays out cash to purchase goods and services and to pay its expenses. An important part of accounting for a business, therefore, involves tracking the cash received and paid out. For example, McDonald's has established procedures for processing the cash received from the sale of food and drinks. McDonald's also has a system of monitoring and controlling cash paid out for wages, utilities, supplies, and the numerous other expenses involved in operating a restaurant.

Cash needs protection to prevent loss or waste. One of the most commonly used controls is a checking account. The use of a checking account not only helps protect cash but also provides a separate record of cash transactions.

Protecting Cash

It is important to protect cash from loss, waste, theft, forgery, and embezzlement. Cash is protected through internal controls and external controls. **Internal controls** refer to those steps the business itself takes to protect cash and other assets. Internal controls for cash include:

1. Limiting the number of persons handling cash.
2. Separating accounting tasks involving cash. For example, one person handles cash receipts and payments, and a different person keeps the accounting records showing the amounts received or paid.
3. Bonding (insuring) employees who handle cash or cash records.
4. Using a cash register and a safe.
5. Depositing cash receipts in the bank daily.
6. Using checks to make all cash payments.

External controls are the measures and procedures provided outside the business to protect cash and other assets. For

RESOURCE MANAGER

Reproducible Masters
- Lesson Plans
- Chapter Reviews and Working Papers (CRWP) TAE
- Demonstration Problems

Transparencies
- Section Focus Transparency
- Teaching Transparencies
- Source Document Transparencies
- Solution Transparencies

Multimedia
- *ExamView* CD-ROM
- Electronic Learning Center CD-ROM
- Interactive Lesson Planner CD-ROM
- Electronic Field Trips in Accounting

example, banks maintain controls to protect the funds their customers deposit. These controls include verifying the accuracy of signatures on checks and maintaining records of monetary transactions.

Opening a Checking Account

A **checking account** allows a person or business to deposit cash in a bank and to write checks against the account balance. A **check** is a written order from a depositor telling the bank to pay a stated amount of cash to the person or business named on the check. A **depositor** is a person or business that has cash on deposit in a bank.

Signature Card

To open a checking account, a business owner fills out a **signature card** and deposits cash in the bank. A signature card contains the signature(s) of the person(s) authorized to write checks on the account. The signature card is kept on file so that it can be matched against signed checks presented for payment. The use of a signature card protects both the account holder and the bank against checks with forged signatures. **Figure 11–1** shows the signature card used to open the checking account for Roadrunner Delivery Service.

ACCT. NO. 303443 ACCOUNT NAME Roadrunner Delivery Service
ACCT. TYPE: ☑ CKG. ☐ SAV. ☐ C.R.
☐ OTHER
NO. SIGNATURES REQUIRED 1
SOC. SEC. NO. OR TAXPAYER I.D. NO. SIGNATURE *Maria Sanchez*
1 SIGNATURE
2 SIGNATURE
THE INDIVIDUALS WHO HAVE SIGNED ABOVE ARE AUTHORIZED TO USE THIS ACCOUNT ACCORDING TO THE RULES AND REGULATIONS THAT APPLY TO IT AND ANY SPECIAL INSTRUCTIONS ON FILE WITH THE BANK. EACH PERSON WHO SIGNS ACKNOWLEDGES THAT THESE RULES AND REGULATIONS HAVE BEEN RECEIVED AND AGREES TO THEIR TERMS. EACH PERSON ALSO AUTHORIZES THE BANK TO REQUEST A CONSUMER REPORT FROM ANY CONSUMER REPORTING AGENCY.

FOR BANK USE
IDENTIFICATION PRESENTED CA State License
COMMENTS Sole Proprietorship—delivery service
ACCOUNT ADDRESS 155 Gateway Blvd., Sacramento, CA 94230
HOME PHONE 443-9696 BUSINESS PHONE 443-1692
☑ NEW ACCOUNT ☐ CAPTION CHANGE ☐ NEW SIGNATURE ☐ ADDITIONAL SIGNATURE
☐ INDIVIDUAL ☐ JOINT ☐ CORPORATE ☑ BUSINESS ☐ FIDUCIARY
☐ OTHER
NCPS OPENED BY GLC BRANCH
DATE OPENED OR CHANGED October 1, 20-- AMOUNT DEPOSITED $ 25,000.00

Figure 11–1 Checking Account Signature Card

Checkbook

When a depositor opens a checking account, checks are printed for the depositor's use. Printed checks are packaged together in *checkbooks* shown in **Figure 11–2,** which looks like a spiral-bound notebook. Each page has several detachable checks attached to check stubs, both numbered in sequence. Using checks with preprinted numbers helps a business keep track of every check that is written, an important internal control.

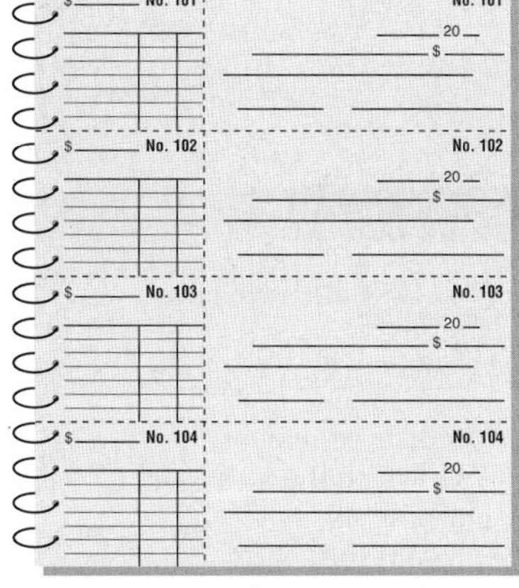

Figure 11–2 Checkbook

ABA Number

In addition to the check number, each check is printed with the account number and an American Bankers Association (ABA) number. The ABA number is the fractional number printed in the upper right corner of a check, just below the check number. The ABA number is a code that identifies the bank. For example, look at the ABA number on the check in **Figure 11–3.** The number above the line and to the left of the hyphen represents the city or state where the bank is located. The number to the right of the hyphen indicates the specific bank. The number below the line is the code for the Federal Reserve district where the bank is located.

Great Ideas *From the Classroom of...*

Finding the "Best Bank" To teach students about checking accounts, divide the class into groups and assign each group a local bank. Have each group research the different types of checking accounts offered at their bank and present their findings to the class. After all groups have shared, all class members vote to decide on the "best bank." Then arrange for the class to visit the "best bank."

Todd Karst
Plankinton High School
Plankinton, South Dakota

2 TEACH

GUIDED PRACTICE

Reading Accounting

- Make a list of the new terms as a handout for students. As students read the chapter, have them write a sentence about each term. **L1**
- For students who have difficulty connecting text information to illustrations, use transparencies of the textbook illustrations when presenting new concepts. Point out related text, and have students follow along as you discuss each concept. **ELL**

Concept Development: Opening a Checking Account

Discussion: Point out to students that checking accounts are a major feature of our economic system. Seventy-five to eighty percent of the money supply can be found in checking accounts. Some banks may require a financial statement and references before opening an account for a business. **L1**

Visual Learning

Figure 11–1 Checking Account Signature Card
Use **Transparency 11–2** to discuss the information that banks require on a signature card.

Figure 11–2 Checkbook
Use **Transparency 11–3** to point out the features of a typical checkbook used by a business. If possible, obtain an actual sample from a local bank to share with students.

2 TEACH (Cont'd.)

Visual Learning

Figure 11–3 Printed Check
Use **Transparency 11–4** to discuss the features of a typical check. Students will learn how to fill out a check later in this section.

Concept Development: Making Deposits to a Checking Account

Discussion: The deposit slip is a summary of the cash receipts for a specific period of time, usually daily. The daily deposit should match the journal entries made for cash received. Emphasize the importance of using a restrictive endorsement. Call students' attention to the importance of controlling checks received from customers. Make sure students understand why businesses do not accept checks from every customer. (Some customers may have a history of writing checks without sufficient funds to cover them.)

Point out that each daily deposit is recorded in the checkbook to maintain a daily record of the balance in the Cash in Bank account. L1

Teaching Tip

There are 12 Federal Reserve districts in the United States. Ask students whether they know the district to which your area belongs. Discuss the Federal Reserve system in class, or have students write short (1–2 pages) research papers on the topic.

Strategies for Teaching International Accounting

To enrich study of international accounting, refer to the additional critical thinking activities in the booklet.

Figure 11–3 Printed Check

Roadrunner Delivery Service
155 Gateway Blvd.
Sacramento, CA 94230

No. 101
71-627
3222

DATE ______________ 20____

PAY TO THE ORDER OF ______________________________ $ __________

____ DOLLARS

American National Bank
SACRAMENTO, CALIFORNIA

MEMO ______________ ______________

⑆322271627⑆ 303443⑈ 101

International ACCOUNTING

Netiquette

When sending e-mail to any business-related accounts, keep your message brief and relevant. Treat it as a formal letter, using proper capitalization, grammar and spelling. Avoid smiley faces and other e-mail tricks that create an unprofessional image.

The ABA number was developed to speed the sorting of checks by hand. An updated version of the ABA number is also printed on the bottom of each check for electronic sorting. The ABA number, the depositor's account number, and sometimes the check number are printed at the bottom of the check in a special ink and typeface. These specially printed numbers are called MICR (magnetic ink character recognition) numbers. Can you identify the MICR numbers on the check in **Figure 11–3?**

Making Deposits to a Checking Account

Businesses make regular deposits to protect the currency, coins, and checks received. Most businesses make daily deposits. These deposits are accompanied by a **deposit slip**, a bank form listing the cash and checks to be deposited. The deposit slip, also called a deposit ticket, gives both the depositor and the bank a detailed record of the deposit. Most banks provide deposit slips with the depositor's name, address, and account number printed on the form. A deposit slip for Roadrunner Delivery Service is shown in **Figure 11–4.**

Let's learn how to prepare commercial bank deposits. To complete a deposit slip, follow these steps:

1. Write the date on the Date line.
2. On the Cash line, indicate the total amount of currency and coins to be deposited.
3. List checks separately by their ABA numbers. Write on the deposit slip only the two numbers that appear above the line in the ABA number. If there are many checks, list the checks by amount on a calculator tape and attach the tape to the deposit slip. On the first Checks line, write "See tape listing," followed by the total amount of the checks.
4. Add the cash and checks amounts, and write the total amount to be deposited on the Total line.

When the deposit slip is completed, the checks are arranged in the order listed on the deposit slip. The deposit slip and the cash and checks are handed to a bank teller. The teller verifies the deposit and gives the depositor a receipt. The deposit receipt may be a copy of the deposit slip stamped and initialed by the teller or it may be a machine-printed form.

Key Points

Verify the Deposit Slip Information

- Be sure that the cash to be deposited equals the amount shown on the deposit slip.
- Be sure each check to be deposited is listed on the deposit slip by ABA number.

Teaching International ACCOUNTING

Writing an E-Mail Provide the following scenario and ask students to compose an e-mail response. "You will travel to Singapore the last week of next month to your firm's international office. Your colleague, Lu-yin Shen, offered to make hotel reservations for you when you last spoke. You wish to confirm your hotel accommodations and request a non-smoking room with a king-size bed. You also wish to meet with your client's co-workers while you are there to discuss a new marketing strategy." Have several students share their e-mails with the class. Make sure students' messages are professional and evaluate them for correct usage of grammar and spelling.

American National Bank
SACRAMENTO, CALIFORNIA

Date November 6 20 --

Checks and other items are received for deposit subject to the terms and conditions of this bank's collection agreement.

Roadrunner Delivery Service
155 Gateway Blvd.
Sacramento, CA 94230

⑆322271627⑆ 303443⑈

BE SURE EACH ITEM IS ENDORSED

	DOLLARS	CENTS	
CASH	48	69	2
CHECKS (List Singly)			
1 5-2	300	00	3
2 53-116	250	00	
3			
4			
5			
6			
7			
8			
TOTAL	598	69	4

1 (Date)

Figure 11–4 Deposit Slip

Endorsing Checks

A check is a form of property. When a business receives a check in payment for a product or service, it acquires the right to that check. To deposit the check in a checking account, the depositor endorses the check to transfer ownership to the bank. An **endorsement** is an authorized signature written or stamped on the back of a check representing a promise to pay.

Burton Company wrote a check to Roadrunner to pay for delivery services. After Roadrunner endorses the check on the back, the check is deposited in Roadrunner's account at American National Bank. The endorsement by Roadrunner authorizes American National Bank to add the amount of the check to Roadrunner's account. Suppose American National Bank cannot collect the amount of the check from Burton Company—that is, Burton's account does not have sufficient funds to cover the check. Roadrunner must go back to Burton Company to collect payment.

There are several types of endorsements, but most businesses use restrictive endorsements. A **restrictive endorsement** limits, or restricts, how a check may be handled. To protect checks from being cashed by anyone else, Roadrunner stamps a restrictive endorsement, "For Deposit Only," on the back of each check as soon as it is received. By doing so, Roadrunner ensures that the check will be deposited in its checking account. See **Figure 11–5** for a typical restrictive endorsement.

PLEASE ENDORSE HERE

FOR DEPOSIT ONLY
Roadrunner Delivery Service
ACCT. 303443

DO NOT WRITE, STAMP OR SIGN BELOW THIS LINE
RESERVED FOR FINANCIAL INSTITUTION USE ★ (0)

Figure 11–5 Restrictive Endorsement

Recording Deposits in the Checkbook

The check stubs in the checkbook are a record of the **Cash in Bank** account. That is, the completed stubs reflect all checking account transactions: payments, deposits, and bank service charges.

To see how to record a deposit in the checkbook, refer to **Figure 11–6** and follow these procedures:

1. Enter the date of the deposit on the Add Deposits line of the check stub for the next unused check.
2. Enter the total amount of the deposit on the same line in the Dollars and Cents (amount) columns.
3. Add the deposit amounts to the amount on the Balance Brought Forward line. Enter the result on the Total line. This total is the new checkbook balance.

$ ______ No. 103
Date ______ 20 --
To ______
For ______

	Dollars	Cents	
Balance brought forward	21,650	00	
Add deposits 1 10/14	200	00	2
10/15	1,200	00	
Total	23,050	00	3
Less this check			
Balance carried forward			

Figure 11–6 Recording a Deposit in the Checkbook

REINFORCING STUDY SKILLS

Time Management Skills Remind students that time management skills are important in helping them complete homework assignments and projects. One effective time management tool is a priority chart. If prepared on a weekly basis, the chart will help students identify their most important tasks. For example, due dates for assignments and test dates should be on their list of priorities. Weeks in which short-term assignments are not due or in which major tests are not given are the best time to schedule work on a long-term assignment.

2 TEACH (Cont'd.)

Visual Learning

Figure 11–4 Deposit Slip

Use **Transparency 11–5** to point out the different entries for cash and checks. Explain the ABA number shown on the deposit slip.

GO TO Demonstration Problem Step-by-Step Practice

Use demonstration problem 10–11 to show students how to fill out a deposit slip.

Concept Development: Endorsing Checks

Discussion: Explain to students why banks require endorsements. Then discuss with the class the difference between a blank endorsement and a restrictive endorsement. L1

Visual Learning

Figure 11–5 Restrictive Endorsement

Use **Transparency 11–6** to explain what makes an endorsement restrictive.

Concept Development: Recording Deposits in the Checkbook

Discussion: Students with checking accounts may be more familiar with the check register, but many businesses use checks having check stubs. If possible, obtain a sample of a business checkbook from a local bank to share with students. L1

Visual Learning

Figure 11–6 Recording a Deposit in the Checkbook

Use **Transparency 11–7** to show students how to record a deposit on the check stub.

CHAPTER 11
SECTION 1, PAGES 258–264

2 TEACH (Cont'd.)

Concept Development: Writing Checks

Discussion: Emphasize the importance of completing the check stub *before* writing the check. Many people have shared the frustrating experience of having written a check without recording it and then being unable to determine their account balance. For businesses, the stub is even more important because it serves as a source document for journalizing entries involving cash payments. L1

Visual Learning

Figure 11–7 Filling Out the Check Stub

Use **Transparency 11–8** to explain how to complete a check stub.

Demonstration Problem
Step-by-Step Practice
Use demonstration 11–2 to show students how to fill out a check stub and a check, or photocopy it for students to practice completing a check stub and a check.

Teaching Tip

Invite a local bank representative to explain banking procedures and requirements for opening a business checking account.

Chapter Reviews and Working Papers
Refer students to the *Study Plan* located at the beginning of Chapter 11 in the workbook.

Writing Checks

Writing a check involves a simple procedure. You need to follow a few important rules, however, to ensure correct recordkeeping and proper handling of the money represented by the check.

- Write checks in ink, or prepare typewritten or computer-generated checks. It is difficult to alter checks written in ink, prepared on a typewriter, or generated on a computer. Checks written in pencil are not acceptable because they can be easily altered.
- Complete the check stub *before* writing the check. This reduces the chance of forgetting to complete the stub. Because the stub serves as a permanent record of the check, it is important that the stub be complete and accurate.

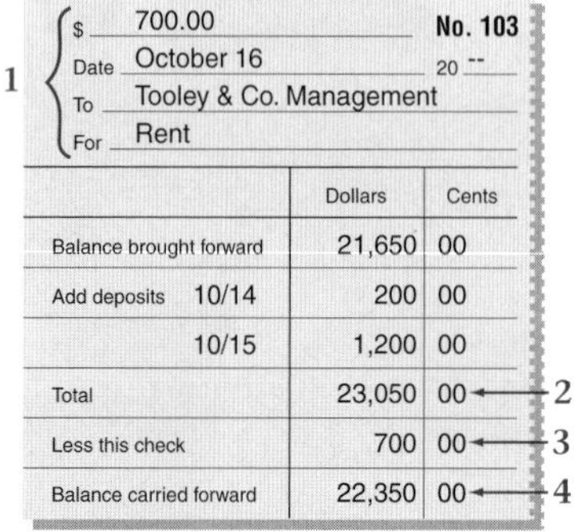

1 $ 700.00 No. 103
Date October 16 20 --
To Tooley & Co. Management
For Rent

	Dollars	Cents	
Balance brought forward	21,650	00	
Add deposits 10/14	200	00	
10/15	1,200	00	
Total	23,050	00	2
Less this check	700	00	3
Balance carried forward	22,350	00	4

$ No. 104
Date 20
To
For

	Dollars	Cents	
Balance brought forward	22,350	00	5
Add deposits			
Total			
Less this check			
Balance carried forward			

Figure 11–7 Filling Out the Check Stub

Completing the Check Stub

A check stub is divided into two parts. The upper part summarizes the details of the cash payment transaction. The lower part is a record of how the transaction affects the checking account. It contains the balance before the transaction, any current deposits, the transaction amount, and the balance after the transaction. To see how to complete the check stub, refer to **Figure 11–7** and follow these steps:

1. In the upper part of the stub, enter the amount of the check, the date, the name of the payee (on the To line), and the purpose of the check (on the For line). A **payee** is the person or business to whom a check is written.
2. If it is not already done, enter the balance on the Total line on the lower part of the stub.
3. Enter the amount of the check on the Less This Check line. This amount is the same as the amount shown on the first line in the upper part of the stub.
4. Subtract the check amount from the total. Enter the new balance on the Balance Carried Forward line.
5. Enter the new balance on the first line of the bottom part of the *next* check stub, the Balance Brought Forward line.

Key Points

The Check Stub
Always complete the check stub *before* you write a check.

Filling Out the Check

When the check stub is complete, the next step is to write the check. Remember to write the check in ink so that it cannot easily be changed. To see how to write a check, refer to **Figure 11–8** and follow these steps:

1. Write the date on which the check is being issued.
2. Write the payee's name on the Pay To The Order Of line. Start the payee's name as far left as possible.
3. Enter the amount of the check in numbers. Write clearly, and begin the first number as close to the printed dollar sign as possible.
4. On the next line, write the dollar amount of the check *in words*. Start at the left edge of the line. Write any cents as a fraction. For example, write 22 cents as 22/100. Draw a line from the cents fraction to the word "Dollars."

MAKING CONNECTIONS TO DAILY LIFE

Writing Checks Review the information recorded on a check by photocopying or making a transparency of a sample blank check. If you photocopy an actual check, be sure to cover the account number and the bank name. Have students practice writing a check, then have them describe the information they have written and explain how that information is used in an accounting system. If you are using a transparency, have students give you information as you fill in the check.

$ 700.00	No. 103
Date October 16	20 --
To Tooley & Co. Management	
For Rent	

	Dollars	Cents
Balance brought forward	21,650	00
Add deposits 10/14	200	00
10/15	1,200	00
Total	23,050	00
Less this check	700	00
Balance carried forward	22,350	00

Roadrunner Delivery Service
155 Gateway Blvd.
Sacramento, CA 94230

103
71-627
3222

DATE Oct. 16 20 --

PAY TO THE ORDER OF Tooley & Co. Management $ 700.00

Seven hundred and no/100 DOLLARS

American National Bank
SACRAMENTO, CALIFORNIA

MEMO

Maria Sanchez

⑆322271627⑆ 3034431⑈ 103

1 2 3 4 5

Figure 11–8 Completed Check and Stub

5. Sign the check. Only an authorized person—one who has signed the signature card for the account—may sign the check. The person who signs a check is the **drawer**. The bank on which the check is written is the **drawee**.

The checkbook is now ready for the next transaction.

Some businesses prepare checks using a check-writing machine, which perforates the amount of the check in words on the Dollars line. These perforations protect a check from alteration, since the holes in the check are almost impossible to alter.

Voiding a Check

If an error is made while writing a check, that check is not used. Corrected checks look suspicious to banks. Instead, the incorrect check is marked "Void" and a new check is prepared. Writing the word "Void" in large letters across the front of a check (in ink) is known as **voiding a check**. When a check is voided, the stub is also voided.

Since a business needs to account for each check used, a voided check is never destroyed. Instead it is filed with the business records. A voided check may be placed in a special file, or it may simply be folded and stapled to the check stub.

A MATTER OF ETHICS

Pocketing Differences

Imagine that you are a cashier at a grocery store like Ralphs. In a four-hour shift, you handle thousands of dollars. At the end of your shift, you total receipts and cash to see if they match. One day, cash comes up short, and you report the discrepancy to the manager. A few weeks later, cash is over by two dollars. You know a couple of cashiers who pocket extra cash. You wonder who would miss two dollars.

Ethical Decision Making:

- What are the ethical issues?
- What are the alternatives?
- Who are the affected parties?
- How do the alternatives affect the parties?
- What would you do?

2 TEACH (Cont'd.)

Visual Learning

Figure 11-8 Completed Check and Stub

Use **Transparency 11-9** to guide students through writing a check. Point out the numbers in the textbook narrative (1 through 5) that correspond to numbers in the illustration.

Teaching Tips

Explain the advantages of using a check-writing machine for businesses that write many checks. If possible, obtain a sample to show students how these checks differ in appearance.

When explaining voided checks, draw the outline of a check on the chalkboard and demonstrate where to write the word "VOID."

Point out reasons why a check may be voided. Mention that the signature portion of a voided check is usually torn from the check and destroyed. Emphasize that for internal control purposes, all voided checks must be accounted for.

Strategies for Teaching Ethics in Accounting

Photocopy the Chapter 11 *Student Activity Sheet* for students. Answers are also provided in the booklet.

Teaching A MATTER OF ETHICS

Pocketing Differences Ask students who have part-time jobs in which they handle cash to describe the cash control procedures used by their employers. Also ask what their experiences have been when they or their co-workers have cash shortages or overages. Ask students to put themselves in the place of the store owner. How would they want their employees to handle these situations?

3 ASSESS

Thinking Critically (Answers)

1. Internal controls refer to steps a business takes to protect cash and other assets. External controls are provided outside the business.
2. ABA stands for the American Bankers Association. The number is printed on each check and appears as a fraction in the upper right corner of a check just below the check number. The ABA number is a code that identifies the bank. It was developed to speed the sorting of checks.

Communicating Accounting (Answers)

Answers may vary. Students should comment on how this is a poor example of internal control and increases the risk of theft.

Problem 11-1 (Answers)

1. Total deposit $967.08
2. Subtotal $2,609.04
3. Balance $2,394.24
4. Check $214.80
5. Balance $2,119.24

Chapter Reviews and Working Papers Refer students to the Chapter 11 workbook pages to answer *Check Your Understanding* activities.

4 CLOSE

Section Wrap-Up

Creating Posters: Have students create posters presenting information on internal and external cash controls. Encourage students to illustrate their posters. L1

SECTION 1 Check Your Understanding

Now that you have studied this section, complete the following questions and problems.

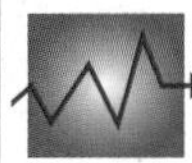

Thinking Critically

1. Cash is protected through internal controls and external controls. Describe controls over cash.
2. Define and describe the purpose of an ABA number.

Communicating Accounting

Assume you work for a sporting goods store that is open six days a week from 9:00 A.M. to 9:00 P.M. Due to a major promotion, the store is making record sales and the manager has been too busy to make daily cash deposits. Discuss with your classmates and teacher why it is important to take time each day to deposit cash receipts.

Problem 11-1 Preparing a Deposit Slip and Writing Checks

On August 14, Loretta Harper, owner of Peabody Cards and Gifts, deposited the following items in the checking account of the business.

Cash: $784.29

Checks: Charles Ling, drawn on American Bank of Commerce, ABA No. 32-7091; $39.44
Keith Lopez, drawn on People's Bank, ABA No. 84-268; $22.95
Marjorie Luke, drawn on Horizon Federal Savings and Loan, ABA No. 84-6249; $52.95
Mable Parker, drawn on Security National Bank, ABA No. 84-2242; $67.45

On August 15, Peabody Cards and Gifts received a bill from Northeast Telephone for $214.80 for July telephone services.

On August 17, Peabody received a bill from the Bayside News for $275.00.

Instructions Using the forms provided in your working papers:

1. Complete a deposit slip.
2. Record the deposit on the check stub for Check 41.
3. Check 41 is issued to pay the telephone bill on August 16. Record the information for Check 41 on the check stub and complete the check stub.
4. Prepare Check 41 to pay the telephone bill. Use August 16 as the date and sign your name as drawer.
5. Prepare Check 42 to pay the bill for advertising. Use August 17 as the date and sign your name as drawer.

RETEACHING SECTION 1

Prepare Commercial Bank Deposits As a reinforcement activity, have students draw a deposit slip for an imaginary business. The deposit slip should include all the elements shown in Figure 11-4 on page 261 (bank name, company name, etc.). Have students deposit the following items in the business bank account:

Cash: $1,952.06
Checks: Hank Sheldon, Dundee Bank, ABA No. 51-212, $60.69
Ayesha Wadood, Western Bank, ABA No. 26-1956, $98.50

Have students "endorse" the checks on a blank piece of paper.

SECTION 2

Reconciling the Bank Account

Have you ever forgotten to record a cash withdrawal from your bank account and then been surprised to find that you have less money than you thought? If so, you understand the importance of reconciling (bringing into agreement) your checkbook with your bank statement. Business owners and their accountants also need to keep their records up-to-date when it comes to cash. An important part of accounting for cash for both large multinational companies, like General Motors, and small local companies, like the video game arcade at the mall, is the comparison and reconciliation of the bank statement with company records.

Proving Cash

The balance in the **Cash in Bank** account in the general ledger is regularly compared with the balance in the checkbook. If all cash receipts are deposited, all cash payments are made by check, and all transactions are journalized and posted, the **Cash in Bank** account balance should agree with the checkbook balance. Comparing these two cash balances regularly is part of the internal control of cash. Some businesses prove cash daily or weekly, while others prove cash on a monthly basis.

If the **Cash in Bank** balance does not agree with the checkbook balance, and the trial balance is proved, the error is probably in the checkbook. A checkbook error is usually the result of (1) faulty addition or subtraction, (2) failure to record a deposit or a check, or (3) a mistake in copying the balance forward amount to the Balance Brought Forward line of the next check stub.

If an error is made in the checkbook, the proper place to enter the correction is on the next unused check stub. For example, suppose Check 22 for $84.60 was recorded on the check stub as $48.60. The error is found when cash is proved. By this time, several other checks have been written, so the next unused check stub is 31. In this case, the amount of the error ($84.60 − $48.60 = $36.00) is subtracted from the balance brought forward on Check Stub 31 (see **Figure 11–9**). A note is made on Check Stub 22 to indicate that the error is corrected on Check Stub 31.

What You'll Learn

- Why a business reconciles a bank statement.
- How to journalize and post entries relating to bank service charges.
- The accounting procedure for stopping payment on a check.
- How to record an NSF check.
- How electronic funds transfer systems enable banks to transfer funds quickly and accurately.

Why It's Important

Reconciling the bank account ensures that a business owner is aware of all transactions that affect cash.

KEY TERMS

bank statement
canceled checks
reconciling the bank statement
outstanding checks
outstanding deposits
bank service charge
stop payment order
NSF check
electronic funds transfer system (EFTS)

CHAPTER 11
SECTION 2, PAGES 265–273

1 FOCUS

Introducing the Section

In this section students will learn to prove cash and to reconcile a bank statement. They'll also learn how to record and post journal entries for bank service charges. The section closes with information on special banking procedures, such as a stop-payment order, NSF checks, and electronic funds transfers.

Section Concepts

- Why a business reconciles a bank statement.
- How to journalize and post entries relating to bank service charges.
- The accounting procedure for stopping payment on a check.
- How to record an NSF check.
- How electronic funds transfer systems enable banks to transfer funds quickly and accurately.

Visual Learning

Section 2 Focus

Use **Transparency 11–10** to introduce section concepts.

BELL RINGER

Identifying: Have students describe the types of banking services they know about, along with charges for those services. Write responses on the chalkboard. Discuss how banks "bill" for their services. L1

Concept Development: Proving Cash

Discussion: Discuss the reasons for comparing the checkbook balance with the Cash in Bank balance. Point out that cash should be proved *before* the Cash in Bank balance is reconciled with the bank statement balance. L1

RESOURCE MANAGER

Reproducible Masters
- Lesson Plans
- Chapter Reviews and Working Papers (CRWP) TAE
- Demonstration Problems

Transparencies
- Section Focus Transparency
- Teaching Transparencies
- Source Document Transparencies
- Solution Transparencies

Multimedia
- Exam*View* CD-ROM
- Electronic Learning Center CD-ROM
- Interactive Lesson Planner CD-ROM
- Electronic Field Trips in Accounting

CHAPTER 11
SECTION 2, PAGES 265–273

2 TEACH
GUIDED PRACTICE

Reading Accounting

• Have students take notes about concepts in this section. Then pair students and have them "teach" each other the concepts using their notes. L2

Visual Learning

Figure 11–9 Entering an Error Correction on the Check Stub

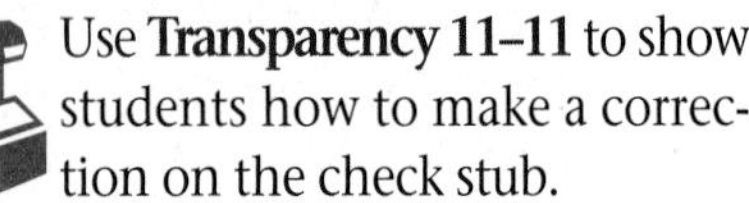
Use **Transparency 11–11** to show students how to make a correction on the check stub.

Figure 11–10 Bank Statement

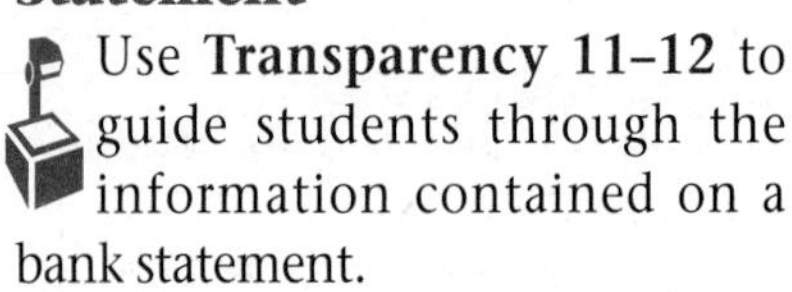
Use **Transparency 11–12** to guide students through the information contained on a bank statement.

Concept Development: The Bank Statement

Discussion: Have students locate five items of information on the bank statement shown in Figure 11–10:

- the checking account balance,
- deposits made,
- checks paid,
- other deductions, and
- ending account balance.

Give a short explanation of each item. When introducing the bank statement, you may want to bring an actual bank statement and canceled checks to class to share with students. L1

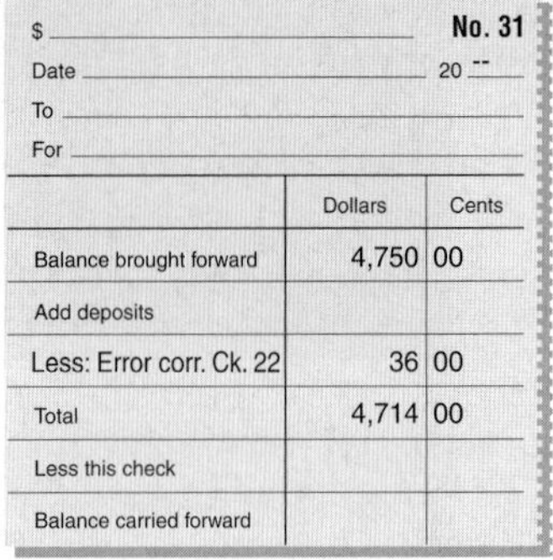

$ ______ No. 31
Date ______ 20 --
To ______
For ______

	Dollars	Cents
Balance brought forward	4,750	00
Add deposits		
Less: Error corr. Ck. 22	36	00
Total	4,714	00
Less this check		
Balance carried forward		

Figure 11–9 Entering an Error Correction on the Check Stub

The Bank Statement

A **bank statement** is an itemized record of all the transactions in a depositor's account over a given period, usually a month. Typical bank statements include the following information:

(1) the checking account balance at the beginning of the period
(2) a list of all deposits made by the business during the period
(3) a list of all checks paid by the bank
(4) a list of any other deductions from the depositor's account
(5) the checking account balance at the end of the period

Find each of these items on the bank statement for Roadrunner Delivery Service in **Figure 11–10.**

When a bank sends a statement to a depositor, it may return the checks paid by the bank and deducted from the depositor's account. These returned checks are called **canceled checks**. Canceled checks are stamped or marked with the word "Paid" and the date of payment. They can be used to verify the information on the bank statement. These checks should be kept in a file or storage box in case they are needed later as proof of payment.

ACCOUNTING *Flashbacks*

MODERN BANKING

The oldest bank in the world is reported to be the Monte dei Paschi di Siena. This Italian bank, established in 1472, is still in operation and has a network of over 1,800 branches.

American National Bank
SACRAMENTO, CALIFORNIA

Roadrunner Delivery Service
155 Gateway Boulevard
Sacramento, CA 94230

FDIC

Account Number: 303443
Statement Date: 10/31/20--

Balance Last Statement	Deposits & Other Credits No.	Deposits & Other Credits Amount	Checks & Other Debits No.	Checks & Other Debits Amount	Balance This Statement
1 00.00	3	26,400.00	5	4,183.00	5 22,217.00

Description	Checks & Other Debits	Deposits & Other Credits	Date	Balance
Balance Forward				00.00
Deposit		2 25,000.00	10/01	25,000.00
Check 101	3 3,000.00		10/04	22,000.00
Deposit		200.00	10/14	22,200.00
Check 102	350.00		10/15	21,850.00
Deposit		1,200.00	10/16	23,050.00
Check 103	700.00		10/20	22,350.00
Check 104	125.00		10/31	22,225.00
Service Charge	4 8.00		10/31	22,217.00

PLEASE EXAMINE YOUR STATEMENT AT ONCE. IF NO ERROR IS REPORTED IN 10 DAYS THE ACCOUNT WILL BE CONSIDERED CORRECT AND VOUCHERS GENUINE. ALL ITEMS ARE CREDITED SUBJECT TO FINAL PAYMENT.

The Bank for All Your Business Needs

Figure 11–10 Bank Statement

Key Points

Bank Service Charges

Before reconciling the bank statement, record in the checkbook those bank service charges and other deductions listed on the bank statement, but not previously entered in the checkbook.

HOME AND COMMUNITY CONNECTIONS ACTIVITY

Banking Options Many students do not know the various options they have for banking in their community. Divide students into small groups and have them identify at least three banking services available to them in your community (e.g., branch banking, ATMs, electronic funds transfer). Have students prepare a bulletin-board or tri-board display illustrating the banking services available to their peers. Encourage groups to visit local banks, speak to professionals, and gather banking-related materials for their displays.

Upon receipt, the bank statement is compared to the checkbook. The process of determining any differences between the bank statement and the checkbook is called **reconciling the bank statement**. The ending balance on the bank statement seldom agrees with the balance in the checkbook. There are three common reasons why the bank statement balance and the checkbook balance disagree:

- outstanding checks
- outstanding deposits
- bank charges

CONNECT TO . . . HEALTH

When businesses need to evaluate the performance of their health care providers, they turn to CPAs. A trained accountant can assess and report on the quality of care and comparisons of cost and delivery of services, and ensure that employees get the best possible service for their money.

Outstanding Checks and Deposits

In banking terms, the word "outstanding" simply means "not yet received." **Outstanding checks**, therefore, are checks that have been written but have not yet been presented to the bank for payment. It is not unusual for checks written in one statement period to reach the bank in a later period. **Outstanding deposits** are deposits that have been made and recorded in the checkbook but do not appear on the bank statement. Deposits made the same day the bank statement is prepared may not appear on the statement.

Bank Service Charges

The bank statement balance also reflects any service charges made by the bank during the statement period. A **bank service charge** is a fee the bank charges for maintaining bank records and processing bank statement items for the depositor. This charge varies from bank to bank, but is frequently based on either the number of checks and deposits handled during the statement period or the balance in the depositor's account. The bank subtracts the service charge from the depositor's account. The depositor usually does not know about the service charge, or other bank charges handled in the same manner, until the statement is received.

Before the bank statement is reconciled, the checkbook balance is adjusted by the amount of the bank service charge. As shown in **Figure 11–11**, the words "Less: Service Charge" are written on the next unused check stub on the line above the Total line. The amount of the service charge is entered in the amount column, preceded by a minus sign. The balance is recalculated and entered on the Total line.

$ ______ **No. 107**
Date ______ 20 __
To ______
For ______

	Dollars	Cents
Balance brought forward	21,125	00
Add deposits		
Less: Svc. Charge	–8	00
Total	21,117	00
Less this check		
Balance carried forward		

Figure 11–11 Entering a Bank Service Charge on the Check Stub

Reconciling a Bank Statement

Promptly reconciling the bank statement is a good way to ensure orderly cash records and guard against cash losses. The bank expects to be notified immediately of any errors on the statement. Failure to do so may release the bank from responsibility for the errors.

On the back of the bank statement is a form for reconciling the bank statement. This form documents the differences between the bank balance and the checkbook balance. Refer to **Figure 11–12** and follow these steps to reconcile a bank statement:

2 TEACH (Cont'd.)

Teaching Tips

Remind students that bank service charges and NSF checks should be entered in the checkbook *before* reconciling the bank statement.

Point out that the bank statement reconciliation process updates both the checkbook balance and the bank statement balance. After both are updated, the balances should be the same.

Ask students who have checking accounts to explain how their bank statements differ from the illustration in Figure 11–10.

Visual Learning

Figure 11–11 Entering a Bank Service Charge on the Check Stub

Using **Transparency 11–13**, point out the recording of the bank service charge on the check stub.

Demonstration Problem
Step-by-Step Practice

Use demonstration problem 11–3 to give students practice in journalizing a bank service charge.

INTERDISCIPLINARY CONNECTIONS ACTIVITY

Health The health-care industry may offer students a wide range of financial career opportunities. Ask students to talk with financial professionals, visit a health-care site, or look in the newspaper for financial jobs in the health-care industry. Ask students to identify the education and skill preparation needed to secure one of these jobs. Have students discuss their findings with the class.

2 TEACH (Cont'd.)

Visual Learning

Figure 11–12 Bank Reconciliation Using a Bank Statement Form

Use **Transparency 11–14** to point out information recorded on a bank reconciliation form.

Demonstration Problem Step-by-Step Practice

Use demonstration problem 11–4 to show students how to complete a bank reconciliation, or photocopy for students to give them practice in completing a bank reconciliation.

Teaching Tip

Most bank statements have reconciliation forms printed on their backs. Reconciliation forms vary from bank to bank. If possible, collect several samples to share with the class.

Visual Learning

Figure 11–13 Bank Account Reconciliation Using a Two Column Account Form

Use **Transparency 11–15** to demonstrate how to reconcile the bank statement using accounting stationery.

Compare and Contrast: Have students look at each type of information in Figures 11–12 and 11–13. Ask them to write a paragraph or two explaining how the two procedures are alike and how they are different. L2

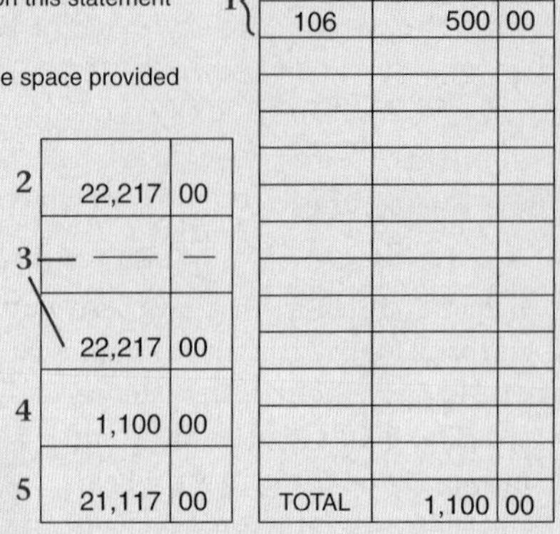

BANK RECONCILIATION FORM

PLEASE EXAMINE YOUR STATEMENT AT ONCE. ANY DISCREPANCY SHOULD BE REPORTED TO THE BANK IMMEDIATELY.

1. Record any transactions appearing on this statement but not listed in your checkbook.
2. List any checks still outstanding in the space provided to the right.
3. Enter the balance shown on this statement here. — 22,217 00
4. Enter deposits recorded in your checkbook but not shown on this statement. — —
5. Total lines 3 and 4 and enter here. — 22,217 00
6. Enter total checks outstanding here. — 1,100 00
7. Subtract line 6 from line 5. This adjusted bank balance should agree with your checkbook balance. — 21,117 00

CHECKS OUTSTANDING	
Number	Amount
105	600 00
106	500 00
TOTAL	1,100 00

Figure 11–12 Bank Reconciliation Using a Bank Statement Form

1. Arrange the canceled checks in numerical order. Compare the canceled checks with those listed on the statement and with the stubs. When you match a check and a stub, place a check mark beside the check amount on the bank statement and on the check stub. After all the checks and stubs are matched, list on the reconciliation form, by number and amount, all the stubs without check marks. These stubs indicate the outstanding checks.
2. Enter the ending balance shown on the bank statement.
3. Compare deposits listed on the bank statement to deposits listed in the checkbook. Enter the total of any outstanding deposits on the reconciliation form. Add this total to the bank statement balance and enter the result on the form.
4. Subtract the total of the outstanding checks from the amount calculated in Step 3. The result is the adjusted bank balance.
5. Compare the adjusted bank balance to the checkbook balance. When the balances match, the bank statement is reconciled.

Figure 11–13 illustrates the same bank reconciliation using a two-column account form.

If the adjusted bank balance does not match the checkbook balance, find and correct the error. Notify the bank immediately if it is a bank error. It is more likely, however, that the error is in the checkbook. Check the addition

Did You Know?

Ticket Sales

Ticketmaster is the world's largest computerized ticketing service. The company sells more than 86 million tickets a year and earns annual revenue of $600 million to $675 million on ticket sales.

Roadrunner Delivery Service
Bank Reconciliation Statement
October 31, 20--

Balance on bank statement		22 217 00
Additions:		
Deposits in transit	—	
		22 217 00
Deductions for outstanding checks:		
Check 105	600 00	
Check 106	500 00	
Total outstanding checks		1 100 00
Adjusted bank balance		21 117 00

Figure 11–13 Bank Account Reconciliation Using a Two Column Account Form

MEETING SPECIAL NEEDS

Students with Learning Disabilities Students with learning disabilities are often distracted by noise and movement in the classroom. Help identify and eliminate distractions by examining students' classroom behavior. While students are silently reading a section of the chapter, periodically call out the word "check." Students should keep a record of whether they were paying attention ("on task") or whether their minds were wandering ("off task"). If they were off task, ask them if they know what distracted them. Try to create an atmosphere that eliminates those distractions.

and subtraction on the check stubs and on the bank reconciliation form. Also look for any outstanding checks or deposits that are not included in your calculations.

Recording Bank Service Charges

Like any other business, banks charge fees for their services. A bank service charge is an expense that is recorded in the accounting records.

The bank deducted the service charge from Roadrunner's account, so it is not necessary to write a check for this expense. The bank statement is the source document for recording the bank service charge.

Business Transaction

On November 1 Roadrunner received the bank statement. A bank service charge of $8 appeared on the statement.

ANALYSIS

Identify 1. Bank service charges are often recorded in the **Miscellaneous Expense** account. Therefore, **Miscellaneous Expense** and **Cash in Bank** are affected.

Classify 2. **Miscellaneous Expense** is an expense account. **Cash in Bank** is an asset account.

+/− 3. **Miscellaneous Expense** is increased by $8. **Cash in Bank** is decreased by $8.

DEBIT-CREDIT RULE

4. Increases in expense accounts are recorded as debits. Debit **Miscellaneous Expense** for $8.
5. Decreases in asset accounts are recorded as credits. Credit **Cash in Bank** for $8.

T ACCOUNTS

6.

Miscellaneous Expense	
Debit +	Credit −
8	

Cash in Bank	
Debit +	Credit −
	8

JOURNAL ENTRY

7.

GENERAL JOURNAL PAGE 42

	DATE		DESCRIPTION	POST. REF.	DEBIT	CREDIT	
1	20--						1
2	Nov.	1	Miscellaneous Expense		8 00		2
3			Cash in Bank			8 00	3
4							4

CRITICAL THINKING ACTIVITY

Understanding Cause and Effect Carlos owns a miniature golf business. When he needs to purchase supplies, he often takes money out of the cash register drawer to pay for the items. Also, Carlos occasionally takes $5 or $10 out to buy his lunch. Explain why these are poor business practices. (Carlos should pay for all supplies by check so that he has a record of all payments made. He should also deposit all cash receipts in the bank to have a record of cash received. When Carlos takes money from the cash drawer for personal use, that amount will never be accounted for in the records of the business, thus presenting an inaccurate picture of the revenue and expenses of the business.)

2 TEACH (Cont'd.)

Concept Development: Recording Bank Service Charges

Discussion: Banks do not send bills to businesses for the various fees they charge for their services. Rather, they add the charges to the monthly bank statement sent to a business. Accountants check bank statements carefully to verify that service charges are appropriate and correct.

Analyze the transaction for the bank service charge using T accounts drawn on the chalkboard or pointing to the illustration on page 269. Emphasize that any bank charge that increases or decreases the checkbook balance requires a journal entry. L1

Visual Learning

Business Transaction Analysis

Use **Transparency 11–16** to guide students through the analysis and recording of a bank service charge.

Thinking Algebraically

Analyzing: Tell students that they neglected to write the amount of a recent check on the stub and that the check does not appear on the bank statement. How could they find the likely amount of the check? (By completing the reconciliation and then solving for the unknown by subtracting the checkbook balance from the bank statement balance. Point out that the check could not be recorded until its amount has been verified.) L1

CHAPTER 11
SECTION 2, PAGES 265–273

2 TEACH (Cont'd.)

Concept Development: Special Banking Procedures

Discussion: Have students suggest reasons for stopping payment on a check; for example, a check gets lost in the mail or a disagreement occurs on a transaction.

Explain the effect of an NSF check on the accounting records of the business. Analyze the transaction using T accounts. First, show how the receipt of the check was recorded. Next, establish the need to reverse the cash receipt entry. Finally, show the entry in T-account form. Then illustrate the recording of an NSF check in the journal.

Point out that NSF check notices may arrive throughout the month and that a journal entry is made each time the bank sends a notice. L1

Visual Learning

Figure 11–14 Recording a Stopped Check on the Check Stub

Use **Transparency 11–17** to point out the notation entered in the checkbook records to note a stopped payment.

Math Review for Accounting

Photocopy appropriate *Activity Sheets* for students who need additional practice in basic math.

Check Stub for Stopped Check

$ 500.00	No. 633	
Date January 12	20 --	
To Smith Engineering		
For Electrical Work		
	Dollars	Cents
Balance brought forward	12,723	00
Add deposits		
Total		
Less this check	500	00
Balance carried forward	12,223	00

STOPPED PAYMENT

Next Unused Check Stub

$	No. 652	
Date	20	
To		
For		
	Dollars	Cents
Balance brought forward	10,452	00
Add deposits Stopped		
Payment on Ck 633	500	00
Total	10,952	00
Less this check		
Balance carried forward		

Figure 11–14 Recording a Stopped Check on the Check Stub

Special Banking Procedures

Checks are usually written or received and deposited without any problems. However, two problems that may happen are:

- A business does not want the bank to pay a check that was issued.
- A business receives and deposits a check from a customer whose account does not have enough money to cover the check.

Stopping Payment on a Check

Occasionally, a drawer (Roadrunner) will order the drawee (bank) not to honor, or pay, a check. A **stop payment order** is a demand by the drawer that the bank not honor a certain check. A stop payment order is often used when a check is lost. The drawer must issue a stop payment order *before* the check is presented to the bank for payment. Usually, a stop payment order is made in writing.

To record a stop payment order, the accountant writes the words "Stopped Payment" on the check stub for the stopped check. The accountant then adds the amount of the stopped check on the next unused check stub, illustrated in **Figure 11–14.** If appropriate, the accountant then issues a replacement check.

Most banks charge a fee for a stop payment order. The fee appears on the bank statement and is subtracted from the checkbook balance. A journal entry, similar to that made for the bank service charge, is prepared. Most businesses record the fee in **Miscellaneous Expense.** The source document for this entry is the bank statement.

Calculator Hints

Subtracting the Same Number

If you're subtracting one number several times, such as $20 three times in a row:

- enter the number once,
- then press the = key for each additional time you want to subtract the number.

Recording NSF Checks

An **NSF check** is a check returned to the depositor by the bank because there are not sufficient funds in the drawer's checking account to cover the check. For example, suppose Roadrunner deposits a check from a customer. If the customer does not have enough money in the bank to cover the check, Roadrunner's bank deducts the amount of the check from Roadrunner's account and returns the check to Roadrunner. Roadrunner notifies the customer that the bank returned the check. The customer then deposits enough money in the bank to cover the check or finds another means of payment.

When the bank returns an NSF check, the amount of the check is subtracted from the checkbook balance, and a journal entry is made to record the returned check.

Math Skill Builder Activity

Subtracting the Same Number Tell students that they are practicing for an employment test at their local grocery store. The total on the cash register tape reads $200, and the customer complains that there is obviously an error in the total. In reviewing the charges, the employee finds an overcharge caused by inputting the cost for fish fillets at $10 ten times instead of one time. The employee must subtract nine entries from the $200 total. What is the new total? ($200 – $90 = $110)

Business Transaction

On November 15 a check for $450, written by Burton Company for payment on account and deposited by Roadrunner, was returned by the bank due to insufficient funds in Burton's account.

ANALYSIS *Identify* *Classify* +/−

1. **Accounts Receivable—Burton Company** and **Cash in Bank** are affected.
2. **Accounts Receivable—Burton Company** and **Cash in Bank** are both asset accounts.
3. **Accounts Receivable—Burton Company** is increased by the amount of the check returned by the bank, $450. **Cash in Bank** is decreased by $450.

DEBIT-CREDIT RULE

4. Increases in asset accounts are recorded as debits. Debit **Accounts Receivable—Burton Company** for $450.
5. Decreases in asset accounts are recorded as credits. Credit **Cash in Bank** for $450.

T ACCOUNTS

6.

Accounts Receivable—Burton Company	
Debit +	Credit −
450	

Cash in Bank	
Debit +	Credit −
	450

JOURNAL ENTRY

7.

GENERAL JOURNAL PAGE 43

	DATE		DESCRIPTION	POST. REF.	DEBIT	CREDIT	
1	20--						1
2	Nov.	15	Accts. Rec.—Burton Company		450 00		2
3			Cash in Bank			450 00	3
4							4

Electronic Funds Transfer System

Look at **Figure 11–15.** It illustrates the route a check follows from the time it is written until the time it is returned with the bank statement.

Since millions of checks are written each day, the transfer of checks and funds is routine. This transfer of funds among banks is a huge job, however. To handle such a large volume of transfers, banks use the **electronic funds transfer system (EFTS)**. The EFTS allows banks to transfer funds among accounts quickly and accurately without the exchange of checks.

An example of EFTS is the direct deposit of payroll. Many employees do not receive paychecks. Their pay is electronically transferred from the employer's account to the employees' accounts using the EFTS.

In the United States, the EFTS is not fully implemented because the general public does not yet want a completely check-less system.

2 TEACH (Cont'd.)

Visual Learning

Business Transaction Analysis

Use **Transparency 11–18** to guide students through the analysis and recording of an NSF check.

GO TO **Demonstration Problem** **Step-by-Step Practice**

Use demonstration problem 11–5 to give students practice in recording the journal entry for an NSF check.

Concept Development: Electronic Funds Transfer System

Discussion: Discuss the route a check follows from the time it is written until it is returned with the bank statement (refer to Figure 11–15 on page 272). Make students aware of what takes place at each point in the flow. Emphasize that the ABA number on the bottom of each check is used in an electronic system. Bring checks to class to show students this number. Also call students' attention to how the amount is entered at the bottom of the check for electronic sorting. L1

COOPERATIVE LEARNING ACTIVITY

Corners Provide the following report topics and allow students to choose the topic they want to learn about. Group students based on the topic they select, and instruct each group to research the topic and prepare a report. Ask each group to present its report to the class.

- ATM Fraud
- Innovations in ATM Technology
- Mandatory Direct Payroll Deposit
- Automated Clearinghouse Security Risks and Fraud Prevention Systems
- Online/Home Banking Services

2 TEACH (Cont'd.)

Visual Learning

Figure 11–15 Routing of Checks

Use **Transparency 11–19** to guide students through the steps a check takes on its journey from origination by the business to its return to the business.

Critical Thinking: Explain to students that many banks do not return canceled checks for personal checking accounts. Ask students whether they think this practice would be an advantage or disadvantage for their own checking accounts. Then ask them how the practice might be a disadvantage for a business checking account. (For a personal checking account, the advantage is mostly for the bank through less work to collect checks and lower postage costs to send them to customers. The disadvantage for the customer is not having a returned check as proof of a payment. For a business, the disadvantage is not having canceled checks as proof of payment and as a part of the audit trail.) L2

Routing of Checks

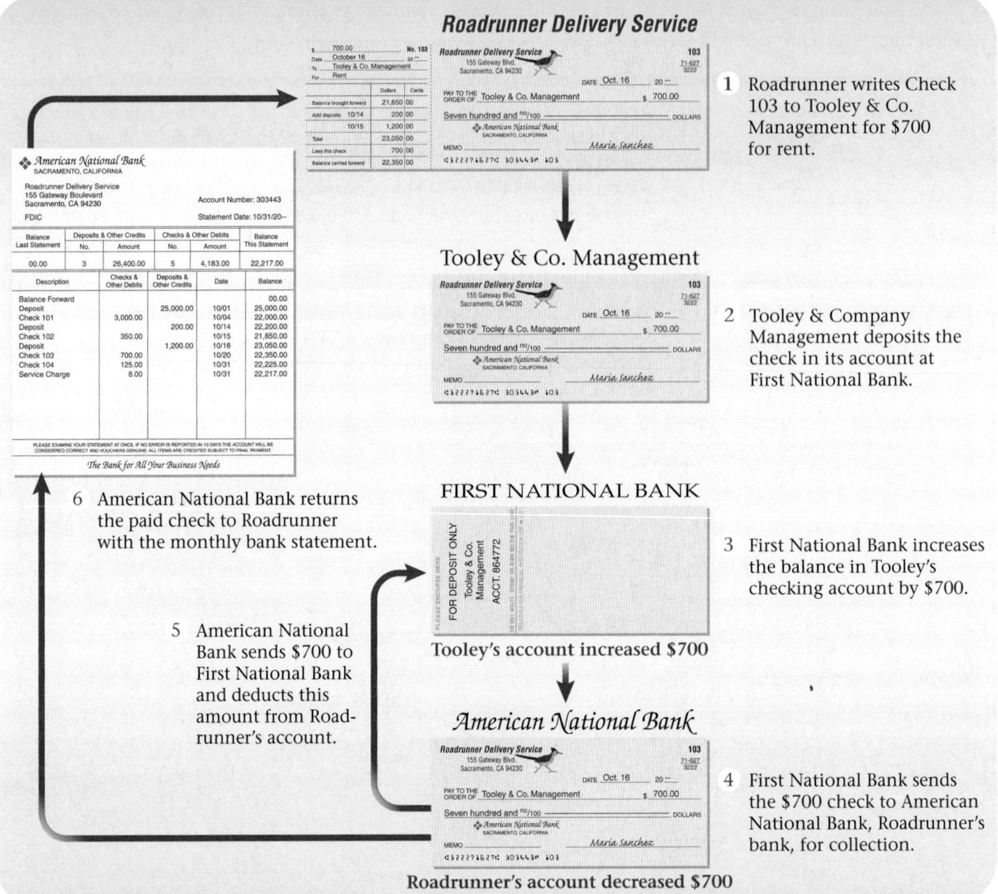

Figure 11–15 Routing of Checks

ANALYZING FINANCIAL REPORTS

Evaluating Working Capital

When analyzing the balance sheet, one thing owners and managers want to know is whether the business has enough assets to pay its debts. One measure of a company's ability to pay debts is its working capital.

Working Capital = Current Assets − Current Liabilities

Current assets are cash and assets that will be converted to cash within the next accounting period. *Current liabilities* are debts that must be paid within the next accounting period.

▶ Analyze the Report:

Use the balance sheet for Roadrunner Delivery Service on page 219 to answer these questions.

1. What is the total amount of current assets?
2. What is the total amount of current liabilities?
3. Calculate the working capital for Roadrunner Delivery Service.

ANALYZING FINANCIAL REPORTS

Roadrunner Delivery Service
155 Gateway Blvd.
Sacramento, CA 94230

Analyze the Report (Answers)

1. Current assets = $22,575
2. Current liabilities = $11,725
3. Working capital = $22,575 − $11,725 = $10,850
4. The owner would look at working capital to determine whether the business would have enough money on hand to pay the new debit when it became due.

SECTION 2 Check Your Understanding

Now that you have studied this section, complete the following questions and problems.

Thinking Critically

1. List the standard information that appears on a bank statement.
2. If you have problems reconciling a bank statement, what steps may uncover the errors?

Computing in the Business World

The balance in the checkbook of Valleyview Tennis Center on April 30 is $2,944.20. The balance shown on the April bank statement is $3,085.95. A deposit of $345.00 was made on April 29, and another deposit of $290.00 was made on April 30. Neither of these deposits appears on the bank statement. The service charge for the month was $5.25. Valleyview has four outstanding checks:

Check 344	$202.00	Check 350	$ 25.00
Check 346	55.00	Check 351	500.00

Instructions

1. Record the bank service charge in the checkbook.
2. Reconcile the bank statement.

Problem 11–2

Analyzing a Source Document

Instructions Review the Global Travel Agency bank statement and answer the following questions in your working papers.

1. What is the amount of the returned check?
2. What is the bank charging Global Travel Agency for the returned check?
3. What account will be debited for the $12 bank service charge?

Security National Bank
155 Flower Street, Cambridge, MA 02138

STATEMENT

Global Travel Agency
200 Brattle Street
Cambridge, MA 02138

Account Number: 2649-84
Statement Date: 2/28/20--

FDIC

Balance Last Statement	Deposits & Other Credits No.	Deposits & Other Credits Amount	Checks & Other Debits No.	Checks & Other Debits Amount	Balance This Statement
2,714.00	3	2,395.00	7	4,036.00	1,073.00

Checks & Other Debits	Deposits & Other Credits	Date	Balance
	1,250.00	2/05	3,964.00
700.00		2/10	3,264.00
900.00		2/10	2,364.00
	845.00	2/15	3,209.00
600.00		2/15	2,609.00
(R) 100.00		2/20	2,509.00
(S) 25.00		2/20	2,484.00
725.00		2/25	1,759.00
600.00		2/25	1,159.00
(S) 12.00		2/26	1,147.00
214.00		2/26	933.00
	300.00	2/27	1,233.00
160.00		2/27	1,073.00

PLEASE EXAMINE YOUR STATEMENT AT ONCE. IF NO ERROR IS REPORTED IN 10 DAYS THE ACCOUNT WILL BE CONSIDERED CORRECT AND VOUCHERS GENUINE. ALL ITEMS ARE CREDITED SUBJECT TO FINAL PAYMENT.

C=CERTIFIED CHECK T=DEBIT OR CREDIT S=SERVICE CHARGE L=LIST CR=OVERDRAFT R=RETURNED CHECK

CHAPTER 11

SECTION 2, PAGES 265–273

3 ASSESS

Thinking Critically (Answers)

1. The checking account balance at the beginning of the period, a list of all deposits made during the period, a list of all checks paid by the bank, a list of other deductions from the account, and the balance at the end of the period.
2. Double-check for any outstanding checks or deposits; check the mathematics; check the bank listing of checks, deposits, and withdrawals. If an error still occurs, contact the bank for assistance.

Computing in the Business World (Answer)

Reconciled balance: $2,938.95

Problem 11–2 (Answers)

1. $100
2. $25
3. Miscellaneous Expense

Chapter Reviews and Working Papers Refer students to the Chapter 11 workbook pages to answer *Check Your Understanding* activities.

4 CLOSE

Section Wrap-Up

Writing: Have students write a paragraph by completing this sentence: "The bank statement balance and the checkbook balance are reconciled by . . . ." L1

RETEACHING SECTION 2

Reconcile a Bank Statement Give students the following information about Problem 11-2 and have them reconcile the bank statement.

- Global Travel Agency made a $2,000.00 deposit on February 28.
- The following checks are still outstanding: Check 401 for $100.00 and Check 402 for $53.00.
- The balance in the checkbook as of February 28 is $3,057.00.
(Reconciled balance is $2,920.00.)

CAREERS IN FOCUS
CHAPTER 11

SCANS in the Workforce

Foundation Skills Connection

Writing
Have students write in their journals, reflecting on an experience when they were part of a team. How did they feel to be part of a group? Was the team a competitive team? If so, what was their individual contribution to the team? Do they prefer to work in a group or alone? Allow about five minutes for this writing exercise, then hold an informal discussion about the benefits of journal writing. L1

Workplace Competencies Connection

Interpreting and Communicating Information
Locate an accounts receivable ledger or a spreadsheet that lists a number of accounts. Have students read the document, then interpret the financial information in a written memorandum. Tell students to address the memo to the CFO of the company and to explain the status of each account in the ledger or spreadsheet. L2

Participating as a Member of a Team
Divide students into groups of at least five members. Ask each group to select a professional sports team they can research together. Ask a spokesperson from the group to provide you with a list of each member's research responsibilities. Have each group present findings about the team they chose. L3

ACCOUNTING CAREERS IN FOCUS

KEVIN HART
Controller
Pittsburgh Penguins

Q: What are some of the special concerns of a controller for a hockey team?

A: You have to handle personnel with more care than you would in another organization. You have young fellows making a lot of money and their superstar status creates some problems. You have to have superb people skills.

Q: What kinds of reporting do you do?

A: We have the regular reporting requirements everyone has: state, local, federal, and the reports to our lending institution. We also make reports to the National Hockey League. We let them know what's happened after each game and after each payroll.

Q: Do you enjoy your work?

A: It's a lot of fun. I enjoy talking to the league or to players or to their agents. I can walk into the locker room when I want and talk to players and coaches about questions I have for them or questions they have for me.

Q: How did you get this job?

A: I joined a large public accounting firm out of college. I worked on the acquisition of the Penguin franchise from its previous owners. It took about four months. During that time I got familiar with the organization and they got familiar with me. They offered me the position.

Tips from . . .
Robert Half International Inc.
Communication is very important in a team-oriented work environment. Learn to communicate your ideas to others through written memos or verbal updates. Always keep your supervisor updated on the status of your projects.

CAREER FACTS

Nature of the Work: Supervise accounting and finance, motivate and oversee staff, oversee accounts receivable, accounts payable and payroll, and meet reporting deadlines.
Training or Education Needed: A bachelor's degree in accounting.
Aptitudes, Abilities, and Skills: Accounting, time-management skills, problem-solving skills, communication skills, and interpersonal skills.
Salary Range: \$50,000 to \$100,000 depending on the team's city.
Career Path: Work for an accounting firm and become familiar with a variety of organizations, and then move to the right job when it becomes available.

Thinking Critically: In what ways could a sports team player's "superstar status" create problems for a controller?

ACCOUNTING CAREERS IN FOCUS

Thinking Critically (Answers)
Superstars usually have superstar salaries, and the controller must juggle the budget to pay that salary along with those of the other team members. The controller may look at ways to raise revenue to pay the salaries, such as increasing ticket prices.

ROBERT HALF CORNER

Communication Skills Communication is very important in a team-oriented work environment. Learn to communicate your ideas to others through written memos or verbal updates. Always keep your supervisor updated on the status of your projects.

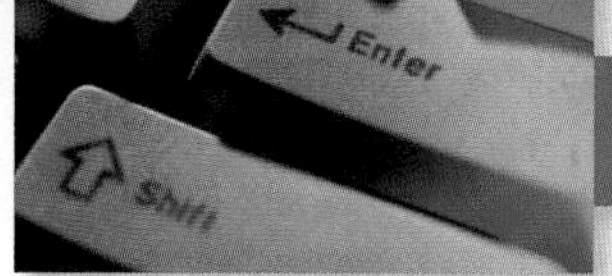

CHAPTER 11 SUMMARY

KEY CONCEPTS

1. The use of a checking account by a business provides an important control of cash. The checking account protects cash and also serves as a record of all cash transactions.
2. Deposit slips are prepared when cash and checks are deposited in a bank account. Copies of deposit slips are the proof of deposits.
3. Checks are endorsed before they are deposited. Most businesses stamp a restrictive endorsement on checks as soon as the checks are received. A restrictive endorsement limits how checks are handled and helps protect the checks from misuse.
4. Correctly written checks and accurate check stubs help prevent cash loss through carelessness or fraud.
5. As a part of their control of cash, businesses regularly prove cash by comparing the **Cash in Bank** balance to the checkbook balance. The reasons for any differences between the two balances are determined, and appropriate corrections are made.
6. A bank statement is sent to each depositor, usually once a month. A bank statement is reconciled promptly upon receipt. Any errors found on the bank statement are reported to the bank immediately.
7. Before reconciling the bank statement, record bank service charges and NSF checks in the checkbook.
8. Follow these steps when reconciling a bank statement:
   a. Arrange the canceled checks in numerical order.
   b. On the bank reconciliation form, enter the ending balance shown on the bank statement.
   c. Identify outstanding deposits and add them to the bank statement balance.
   d. Identify outstanding checks and subtract them from the bank statement balance.
   e. Compare the adjusted bank statement balance with the checkbook balance. When the amounts are equal, the bank statement is reconciled.
9. After the bank statement is reconciled, journalize and post the bank service charges, stop payment order charges, and NSF checks.

GENERAL JOURNAL PAGE *1*

	DATE		DESCRIPTION	POST. REF.	DEBIT	CREDIT	
1	*20--*						1
2	*Date*		*Miscellaneous Expense*		*xx xx*		2
3			*Cash in Bank*			*xx xx*	3
4			*10/31/20—Bank Statement*				4
5							5

EXTENDING THE CONTENT

Exploring Cash-Handling Procedures Ask students who work in restaurants and retail stores to explain the cash-handling procedures in their workplaces. Are only selected employees permitted to handle cash? Is money locked in a safe? How often are cash receipts deposited in the bank? Are employees bonded? What precautions do the cashiers at the workplace take to avoid short-change artists? Has a customer ever attempted to short them or a fellow employee? If so, have students explain what happened.

SUMMARY
CHAPTER 11

Chapter 11 Quiz

Student ______ Class ______ Instructor ______
Date Assigned ______ Date Completed ______

CHAPTER 11 QUIZ

Cash Control and Banking Activities

QUESTIONS (True-False)

Directions: In the space provided, indicate whether each statement is true or false.

___ 1. In a business, cash includes currency, coins, and checks.
___ 2. An internal control is one used by a business to protect cash.
___ 3. The ABA number appears on both the check and the check stub.
___ 4. A restrictive endorsement is one example of an internal control.
___ 5. The check should be written first so that information will be available for completing the check stub.
___ 6. The drawee of the check is the person who signs it.
___ 7. Proving cash is done only when reconciling the bank statement.
___ 8. Proving cash is an example of an external cash control.
___ 9. Banks add service charges to bank statements rather than billing their customers.
___ 10. An NSF check is recorded at the time it is returned rather than when the bank statement is reconciled.

 Chapter Quizzes • 13

QUESTIONS (True-False)

1. In a business, cash includes currency, coins, and checks.
2. An internal control is one used by a business to protect cash.
3. The ABA number appears on both the check and the check stub.
4. A restrictive endorsement is one example of an internal control.
5. The check should be written first so that information is available for completing the check stub.
6. The drawee of the check is the person who signs it.
7. Proving cash is done only when reconciling the bank statement.
8. Proving cash is an example of an external cash control.
9. Banks add service charges to bank statements rather than billing their customers.
10. An NSF check is recorded at the time it is returned rather than when the bank statement is reconciled.

ANSWERS

1. True	5. False	8. False
2. True	6. False	9. True
3. False	7. False	10. True
4. True		

REVIEWS AND ACTIVITIES CHAPTER 11

USING KEY TERMS

See the *Glossary* for the definitions of these terms. Ask for volunteers to share paragraphs in class, or have students meet in groups to exchange papers and discuss use of terms.

Understanding Accounting Concepts and Procedures

(Answers)

1. Cash is the most liquid asset and thus easily stolen.
2. Limit people handling cash, separate accounting tasks involving cash, bond employees, use a safe, deposit cash daily, pay by check.
3. Verify signatures, keep checking account records.
4. (a) Signature card, (b) deposit slips to record deposits, (c) checks/stubs to make/record payments.
5. Transfer ownership of check to another person, business, or bank.
6. To avoid leaving the stub blank.
7. (a) Beginning account balance, (b) deposits, (c) checks paid, (d) other deductions, (e) ending account balance.
8. (a) Subtract service charge in checkbook, (b) order canceled checks, (c) compare canceled checks with statement/check stubs, (d) enter bank balance on reconciliation form, (e) verify deposits, (f) add outstanding deposits to bank balance, (g) subtract total outstanding checks from revised bank balance, (h) compare adjusted bank and checkbook balances.
9. Stub: Write "Service Charge" and amount on line above total; subtract from balance. Dr. Misc. Exp., Cr. Cash in Bank.
10. The amount of the check is subtracted from the checkbook balance and a journal entry is made to record the returned check.

CHAPTER 11 REVIEW AND ACTIVITIES

USING KEY TERMS

The manager of Valley View Bowling Center is concerned about cash control and banking procedures for his business. On a separate sheet of paper, write a paragraph explaining how the list of terms relates to each of the four group headings.

External Controls
check
checking account
depositor
signature card

Internal Controls
deposit slip
drawee
drawer
endorsement
payee
restrictive endorsement

Personal Banking Controls
bank statement
canceled checks
reconciling the bank statement
voiding a check

Financial Record Controls
bank service charge
electronic funds transfer system (EFTS)
NSF check
outstanding checks
outstanding deposits
stop payment order

Understanding Accounting Concepts and Procedures

Instructions

On a separate sheet of paper, answer the following questions:

1. Why is it important for businesses to protect cash?
2. What internal controls can businesses use to protect cash?
3. What external controls help businesses protect cash?
4. Describe the forms that are needed to open and use a checking account.
5. What is the purpose of a check endorsement?
6. Why should you always complete the check stub *before* writing the check?
7. What information does a bank statement contain?
8. List the steps to reconcile a bank statement.
9. Explain how bank service charges are recorded in the checkbook and in the accounting records of a business.
10. Explain how NSF checks and related charges are recorded in the checkbook and in the accounting records of a business.

ASSESSMENT RESOURCES

Choose assessment strategies from the following pages to evaluate your students' progress.

Student Edition
Check Your Understanding, pp. 264, 273
Chapter 11 Problems, pp. 279–281
Analyzing Financial Reports, p. 272

Assessment and Evaluation Masters
Chapter 11 Study Plan, *Glencoe Workbook (CRWP)*
Chapter 11 Self-Test, *Glencoe Workbook (CRWP)*
Chapter 11 Test, *Chapter Tests* Booklet
Chapter 11 Activity, *School-to-Work Handbook*
Chapter 11 Exam*View*

Teacher Wraparound Edition
Critical Thinking Activity, p. 269
Reteaching Sections 1–2, pp. 264, 273
Chapter 11 Quiz, p. 275

Case Study...

Service Business: Entertainment

Dexter Shuman owns a bowling alley called Ten Pin Alley. Each night, Dexter counts the cash in the two cash registers and makes a night deposit at the local bank. For the month of May, Dexter made deposits totaling $6,400.

During May, Dexter wrote checks totaling $2,900. The last three checks he wrote were Check 1408 for $180; Check 1409 for $560; and Check 1410 for $212. The beginning cash balance for the month was $13,840, which is the amount shown as the beginning balance on the May bank statement. The May bank statement also includes a $12 service charge and an $18 charge for printing new checks.

Thinking Critically:

1. What is the ending bank statement balance if all checks written have cleared?
2. If Checks 1408, 1409, and 1410 are outstanding, what is the ending bank statement balance?
3. After reconciling the bank statement, what is the ending balance in the cash account?

interNET CONNECTION

Cash Control and Banking Activities

The Federal Reserve System is the central bank of the United States. Locate the Web site for the Board of Governors of the Federal Reserve System and complete the following activities.

Do This:

1. From the Board of Governors' site, access the related Web site for the National Information Center of Banking. Name the three largest banks and the headquarters of each bank.
2. From the Board of Governors' site, access the site for Federal Reserve Banks. The United States is divided into 12 federal reserve districts. In which district is your city located?

Workplace Skills

Serving Customers

Working with others and satisfying expectations are essential skills in any work environment. Listening, communicating, and solving problems shows your employer you have strong interpersonal skills.

On the Job:

You are a personal banker for Citizens First National Bank. Your job duties include opening personal bank accounts, taking loan applications, and serving bank customers. Today, Ms. Kelly Myer wants to open a bank account. How will you assist her?

Thinking Critically:

1. Before you can assist Ms. Myer, you put together a packet of information and forms needed to open her account. List the items that are in her packet.
2. Review with Ms. Myer how to write a check and complete a deposit ticket. Use examples from your textbook to explain how to complete each document. Pair up with a student and role-play this situation.

Conducting an Audit with Alex

The accountant for Jack's Produce received the March bank statement. While proving cash and reviewing the bank statement, the accountant discovered the following:

1. A stop payment bank charge for $20, dated March 12, found on the March bank statement, was not recorded in the accounting records.
2. A monthly bank service charge for $15, dated March 31, was not recorded in the accounting records, but appeared on the March bank statement.

Instructions Record these bank charges in the general journal on a separate sheet of paper.

REVIEWS AND ACTIVITIES CHAPTER 11

Case Study...

Thinking Critically (Answers)

1. $17,310
2. $18,262
3. $17,310

Workplace Skills

Thinking Critically (Answers)

1. Students may not know all of the forms necessary, but at a minimum they should include signature card(s), temporary checks and deposit slips, and bank account information brochures in their list.
2. Circulate around the room to help students with this role-play. Choose one pair of students to role-play the check-writing and deposit instructions for the rest of the class.

Conducting an Audit with Alex

(Answers)

1. Dr. Miscellaneous Expense $20; Cr. Cash in Bank $20
2. Dr. Miscellaneous Expense $15; Cr. Cash in Bank $15

GO TO **Internet Resources and Activities Handbook**

Refer students to the booklet for additional Internet activities.

interNET CONNECTION www.glencoe.com

Do This (Answers)

1. The Board of Governor's web site: www.federalreserve.gov; Citigroup Inc., New York City; J.P. Morgan Chase & Co., New York City; Bank of America Corporation, Charlotte, North Carolina.
2. Answers will vary.

PEACHTREE CORNER

Account Reconciliation

Choose **Account Reconciliation** from the ***Tasks*** menu to access the Peachtree feature that allows you to reconcile a bank statement. Or, you can click the **General Ledger** navigation aid to choose this option.

Tasks | Analysis | Options | Reports

- Quotes/Sales Orders ▸
- Sales/Invoicing...
- Receipts...
- Finance Charge...
- Select for Deposit...
- Purchase Orders...
- Purchases/Receive Inventory...
- Select for Payment...
- Payments...
- Write Checks...
- Time/Expense ▸
- Select for Payroll Entry...
- Payroll Entry...
- General Journal Entry...
- Inventory Adjustments...
- Assemblies...
- Account Reconciliation...
- Void Checks...
- Action Items...
- System ▸

Account Reconciliation Reports

Once you complete the account reconciliation, choose **Account Reconciliation** from the ***Reports*** menu to print the following reports: Account Register, Account Reconciliation, Deposits in Transit, and Outstanding Checks.

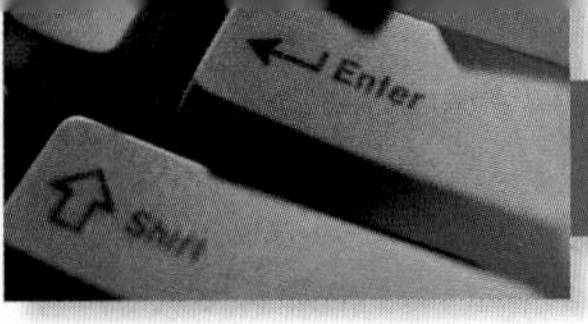

Reconciling the Bank Statement

Making the Transition from a Manual to a Computerized System

Task	Perform Accounting Procedures Using Manual Methods	Perform Accounting Procedures Using Automated Methods
Reconciling the bank statement	1. Using the form on the back of the bank statement or accounting stationery, follow the steps on page 268 to reconcile the bank statement.	1. Before attempting to reconcile the bank statement, make sure all transactions of the month have been posted. 2. A computerized system will list all cash transactions and allow you to check off the appropriate cleared items. 3. You may enter adjustments such as bank fees. These will be posted to the general ledger.

Reconciling the Bank Statement

Peachtree Question	Description
How do I reconcile the cash account in Peachtree?	1. Select **Account Reconciliation** from the ***Tasks*** menu. 2. Select the cash account to be reconciled. 3. Enter the bank statement date. 4. Enter the ending bank statement balance. 5. Click the *Clear* box for all items that appear on the bank statement. 6. When the unreconciled difference is $0.00, the account has been reconciled. 7. Click OK to save the reconciliation.
How do I enter an adjustment to the cash account?	1. When reconciling the bank statement, you may find bank charges that have not yet been entered into the accounting records. 2. After you have cleared all items listed on the bank statement, click the Adjust button at the top of the screen. 3. Enter the account number that the adjustment should be posted to and enter the amount. 4. Click OK.
What does the software do "behind the scenes"?	1. Peachtree automatically pulls up a list of cash transactions to help you verify bank statement activity. 2. Any adjustments that must be entered at the time of the reconciliation are posted to the general ledger accounts, updating the balances of each account.

For detailed instructions: See the **Peachtree User Guide** in your Glencoe Working Papers.

Peachtree® Answers to Frequently Asked Questions

Q: How do you edit/delete a transaction entered using the Account Reconciliation feature?

A: Close the Account Reconciliation window and choose **General Journal Entry**. Click **Open** and select the entry you want to change.

Q: When you record an adjustment (e.g., bank service charge) using Account Reconciliation, do you have to make a separate entry to update the general ledger?

A: No. A general journal entry is created when you use the **Account Reconciliation** option.

For additional information, see your *Glencoe Peachtree Accounting User Guide.*

CHAPTER 11 PROBLEMS

APPLICATION OPTIONS

Problem 11–3 Handling Deposits

On October 4, the owner of Wilderness Rentals deposited the following in the checking account at First National Bank. The beginning balance in the account is $3,306.54 before these transactions.

Cash: Currency, $374.00; Coins, $7.42

Checks: Bob Warner, drawn on Consumers Bank, ABA No. 63-706; $64.98
Joan Walkman, drawn on Mountain Bank, ABA No. 63-699; $349.81
Ernesto Garcia, drawn on Progressive Savings and Loan, ABA No. 63-710; $29.44

Instructions In your working papers:

1. Place a restrictive endorsement on each check. Use "Wilderness Rentals."
2. Fill out a deposit slip. Use the ABA number to identify each check.
3. Record the deposit in the checkbook on Check Stub 651.

Analyze: What is the checkbook balance after recording the deposit on the check stub?

Problem 11–4 Maintaining the Checkbook

As the accounting clerk for Hot Suds Car Wash, you write checks and make deposits. The current checkbook balance is $3,486.29.

Instructions For each transaction:

1. Record the necessary information on the check stub. Determine the new balance and carry the balance forward.
2. Prepare the necessary checks and sign your name as drawer.

Date	Transactions
Oct. 3	Issued Check 504 for $868.45 to Custom Construction for construction supplies.
3	Deposited $601.35 in the checking account.
6	Issued Check 505 for $299.60 to CP Lumber for paint.
7	Issued Check 506 to Laverne Brothers for $1,000.00 for completing a painting job.
10	Deposited $342.80 in the checking account.
10	Issued Check 507 to Union Utilities for the September electricity bill of $175.50.

Analyze: What is the balance brought forward amount on Check Stub 508?

Complete chapter problems one of four ways:

1. **Manual** Glencoe Working Papers

or

2. **Peachtree Complete Accounting** Software

or

3. **QuickBooks** Templates (Problems 11–5, 11–7)

or

4. **Spreadsheet** Templates (Problem 11–6)

Peachtree®

SMART GUIDE

Step-by-Step Instructions: Problem 11–4

1. Select the problem set for Hot Suds Car Wash (Prob. 11–4).
2. Rename the company and set the system date.
3. Use the **Payments** option in the ***Tasks*** menu to record the checks issued.
4. Record the deposits using the **General Journal Entry** option.
5. Print an Account Register report using the **Account Reconciliation** option from the ***Reports*** menu.
6. Answer the Analyze question.
7. End the session.

PROBLEMS CHAPTER 11

Problem 11–3 (Answer) Handling Deposits
Total deposit $825.65

Analyze: $4,132.19

Problem 11–4 (Answers) Maintaining the Checkbook
Check stub balances:

504	$2,617.84
505	$2,919.59
506	$1,919.59
507	$2,086.89

Analyze: Ending balance $2,086.89

ADDRESSING MULTIPLE LEARNING STYLES

Kinesthetic Learner Have students work in groups of three or four to create and present skits on how to protect cash in a retail business. Ask groups to demonstrate ineffective ways of safekeeping money; for example, leaving an unlocked cash register unattended, or frequently changing cashiers without changing the money drawer. After each presentation, have the class discuss the situation and offer suggestions for a solution.

PROBLEMS CHAPTER 11

Problem 11-5 (Answers) Reconciling the Bank Statement

Adjusted balances $950

Bank service charge:

Oct 31: Dr. Miscellaneous Expense, $10; Cr. Cash in Bank, $10; October Bank Statement

Analyze: Two, $835

Problem 11-6 (Answers) Reconciling the Bank Statement

Adjusted balances $2,468.90

Bank service charge:

Oct 31: Dr. Miscellaneous Expense, $20; Cr. Cash in Bank, $20; Bank Service Charge October

NSF Check:

Oct 31: Dr. Accounts Receivable—Podaski Systems Inc., $62.44; Cr. Cash in Bank, $62.44; NSF Check

Analyze: $70

Peachtree®

SMART GUIDE

Step-by-Step Instructions: Problem 11-5

1. Select the problem set for Kits & Pups Grooming (Prob. 11-5).
2. Rename the company and set the system date.
3. Reconcile the bank statement using the **Account Reconciliation** option in the ***Tasks*** menu.
4. Print the following Account Reconciliation reports: Account Register, Account Reconciliation, Deposits in Transit, and Outstanding Checks.
5. Answer the Analyze question.
6. End the session.

TIP: Peachtree automatically updates the general ledger when you record an adjustment such as a bank service charge.

Problem 11-5 Reconciling the Bank Statement

On October 31, George Flaum, the accountant for Kits & Pups Grooming, received the bank statement dated October 30. After comparing the company's checkbook with the bank statement, George found the following:

1. The checkbook balance on October 31 is $960.
2. The ending bank statement balance is $1,380.
3. The bank statement shows a service charge of $10.
4. A deposit of $405 was made on October 30, but does not appear on the bank statement.
5. Check 768 for $529 and Check 772 for $306 are outstanding.

Instructions In your working papers:

1. Record the bank service charge in the checkbook.
2. Reconcile the bank statement.
3. Journalize the bank service charge in the general journal, page 4.
4. Post the bank service charge journal entry to the appropriate general ledger accounts.

Analyze: How many checks are outstanding? What is the total amount outstanding?

SPREADSHEET SMART GUIDE

Step-by-Step Instructions: Problem 11-6

1. Select the spreadsheet template for Problem 11-6.
2. Enter your name and the date in the spaces provided on the template.
3. Complete the spreadsheet using the instructions in your working papers.
4. Print the spreadsheet and proof your work.
5. Save your work and exit the spreadsheet program.

Problem 11-6 Reconciling the Bank Statement

On October 31, Juanita Ortega, owner of Outback Guide Service, received a bank statement dated October 30. Juanita found the following:

1. The checkbook has a balance of $2,551.34.
2. The bank statement shows a balance of $2,272.36.
3. The statement shows a bank service charge of $20.00.
4. A check from Podaski Systems for $62.44, deposited on October 18, was returned by the bank. There is no fee for handling the NSF check.
5. A deposit of $672.48 made on October 30 does not appear on the bank statement.
6. These checks are outstanding:

Check 872 for	$126.84	Check 883 for	$192.80
Check 881 for	87.66	Check 887 for	68.64

Instructions Using the preceding information:

1. Record the service charge and the NSF check in the checkbook.
2. Reconcile the bank statement.
3. Record the service charge and NSF check on page 7 of the general journal.
4. Post the journal entries to the appropriate general ledger accounts.

Analyze: Review the **Miscellaneous Expense** account found in your working papers. What is the balance of the **Miscellaneous Expense** account after posting the October 31 entry?

ACCOUNTING ISSUES

Preparing for the Future A survey of commercial banks and savings institutions from across the United States reveals that the industry feels it must change to prepare for the future. To ensure continued success, the owners and managers believe they must take several steps, including the following:

- Employ technology
- Offer a greater diversity of financial products
- Use the Internet to deliver services

Problem 11–7 Reconciling the Bank Statement

On October 31, Showbiz Video received the bank statement dated October 30. After comparing the company's checkbook with the bank statement, the accountant found the following:

1. The checkbook balance on October 31 is $13,462.96.
2. The ending bank statement balance is $13,883.80.
3. The bank statement shows a service charge of $17.50.
4. Deposits of $675.00 on October 28 and $925.00 on October 29 do not appear on the bank statement.
5. The following checks are outstanding:

Check 1766	$125.00	Check 1770	$1,462.19
Check 1768	69.42	Check 1771	381.73

Instructions In your working papers:

1. Record the bank service charge in the checkbook in your working papers.
2. Reconcile the bank statement.
3. Record the entry for the bank service charge on general journal page 13.
4. Post the bank service charge journal entry to the appropriate ledger accounts.

Analyze: What is the balance of the **Cash in Bank** account after posting the October 31 entry? Does it agree with the adjusted checkbook balance?

Peachtree®

SMART GUIDE

Step-by-Step Instructions: Problem 11–7

1. Select the problem set for Showbiz Video (Prob. 11–7).
2. Rename the company and set the system date.
3. Reconcile the bank statement using the **Account Reconciliation** option in the ***Tasks*** menu.
4. Print the Account Reconciliation reports.
5. Answer the Analyze question.
6. End the session.

TIP: Make sure that you mark any adjustments as "cleared."

Problem 11–8 Reconciling the Bank Statement Using the Account Form

SOURCE DOCUMENT PROBLEM

On Oct. 20, Job Connect received its bank statement dated Oct. 18.

1. The checkbook balance on Oct. 20 is $880.84.
2. The ending bank statement balance is $344.58.
3. A $14.00 service charge appears on the bank statement.
4. The following checks are outstanding:

Check 864	$ 88.41	Check 871	$129.88
Check 869	69.34	Check 873	14.25

5. A $68.42 check from Tom McCrary deposited on Oct. 13 was returned by the bank for insufficient funds. The bank charged Job Connect's account $7.00 for the NSF check. No journal entry was made for the NSF check.
6. A deposit of $938.72 made on Oct. 19 does not appear on the bank statement.
7. A check for $200.00 to Fontenot Inc. was lost in the mail and has not been deposited. A stop payment order, which cost $10.00, was issued on Oct. 15. No new check was issued.

Instructions Reconcile the bank statement using the account form in your working papers.

Analyze: What accounts will be debited for the NSF check and the bank handling charge on the check?

Peachtree®

SMART GUIDE

Step-by-Step Instructions: Problem 11–8

1. Select the problem set for Job Connect (Prob. 11–8).
2. Rename the company and set the system date.
3. Reconcile the bank statement.
4. Print the Account Reconciliation reports.
5. Answer the Analyze question.
6. End the session.

SOURCE DOCUMENT PROBLEM

Problem 11–8

Use the source documents in your working papers to record the transactions for this problem.

PROBLEMS CHAPTER 11

Problem 11–7 (Answer) Reconciling the Bank Statement

Adjusted balances $13,445.46

Bank service charge:

Oct 30: Dr. Miscellaneous Expense, $17.50; Cr. Cash in Bank, $17.50; Bank Service Charge October

Analyze: $13,445.46. This amount agrees with the checkbook.

SOURCE DOCUMENT PROBLEM

Problem 11–8 (Answer) Reconciling the Bank Statement Using the Account Form

Adjusted balances $981.42

Analyze: Accounts Receivable—Tom McCrary will be debited for both charges.

EXTENDING THE CONTENT

Prepare Commercial Bank Deposits As a reinforcement activity, have students draw a deposit slip for an imaginary business. The deposit slip should include all the elements shown in Figure 11-4 on page 261 (bank name, company name, etc.). Have students deposit the following items in the business bank account:

Cash: $1,944.66

Checks: Jasmine Yaralian, First Street Bank, ABA No. 61-313, $197.20
Leonard Mott, Western Bank, ABA No. 26-1956, $625.30

Have students "endorse" the checks on a blank piece of paper.

INTRODUCING
MINI PRACTICE SET 2

Mini Practice Set Overview

This practice set is a culminating activity that helps students integrate the steps in the accounting cycle. In this activity students record business transactions for a sole proprietorship, service business called Fast Track Tutoring Service. Students will go through each step in the accounting cycle and will also reconcile the business's bank statement and record bank service charges.

Most students should be able to complete this activity manually within an assigned time frame (three to four class periods).

Source documents and the accounting stationery needed to complete this mini practice set are included in the student workbook, *Chapter Reviews and Working Papers*.

Mini Practice Set Concepts

- How to analyze, journalize, and post.
- How to prepare a trial balance, a work sheet, and financial statements.
- How to journalize and post closing entries.
- How to prepare a post-closing trial balance.
- How to prepare a bank reconciliation.

Visual Learning

Mini Practice Set Focus, p. 282

Discuss with students the accounting concepts and procedures they will apply in this mini practice set.

MINI PRACTICE SET 2

Completing the Accounting Cycle for a Sole Proprietorship

FAST TRACK TUTORING SERVICES

***What* You'll Learn**

- How to analyze, journalize, and post.
- How to prepare a trial balance, a work sheet, and financial statements.
- How to journalize and post closing entries.
- How to prepare a post-closing trial balance.
- How to prepare a bank reconciliation.

***Why* It's Important**

This mini practice set will help to pull together all the concepts and procedures that you've learned.

Fast Track Tutoring Service

Company Background: Fast Track Tutoring Service is owned and managed by Jennifer Rachael. The business is organized as a sole proprietorship and provides tutoring services for students from pre-kindergarten through high school. The business earns revenue from tuition charged from one-on-one instruction and special classes.

Your Job Responsibilities: As the accounting clerk for this business, use the accounting stationery in your working papers to complete the following activities.

(1) Open a general ledger account for each account in the chart of accounts.
(2) Analyze each business transaction.
(3) Enter each business transaction in the general journal. Begin on journal page 1.
(4) Post each journal entry to the appropriate accounts in the general ledger.
(5) Reconcile the bank statement that was received on December 31. The statement is dated December 30. The checkbook has a current balance of $9,631. The bank statement shows a balance of $9,844. The bank service charge is $15. These checks are outstanding: Check 108 $183 and Check 109 $45. There are no outstanding deposits.
(6) Make any necessary adjustments to the checkbook balance.
(7) Journalize and post the entry for the bank service charge.
(8) Prepare a trial balance and complete the work sheet.
(9) Prepare an income statement, a statement of changes in owner's equity, and a balance sheet.
(10) Journalize and post the closing entries.
(11) Prepare a post-closing trial balance.

Business Transactions: Fast Track Tutoring Service began business operations on December 1 of this year.

CRITICAL THINKING ACTIVITY

Formulating Questions Tell students to imagine that they have an opportunity to interview with an accounting firm for an entry-level position. What type of questions should they anticipate during the interview? What information should they ask? Have students brainstorm a list of questions and discuss with the class. (The interviewer may ask questions about the student's previous work experience, education, and desire to work for them. The student should ask questions about job duties, company benefits, pay rate, and start date.)

Fast Track Tutoring Service

APPLICATION OPTIONS

CHART OF ACCOUNTS
Fast Track Tutoring Service

ASSETS
101 Cash in Bank
110 Accts. Rec.–Carla DiSario
120 Accts. Rec.–George McGarty
140 Office Supplies
150 Office Equipment
155 Instructional Equipment

LIABILITIES
210 Accts. Pay.–Educational Software
215 Accts. Pay.–T & N School Equip.

OWNER'S EQUITY
301 Jennifer Rachael, Capital
305 Jennifer Rachael, Withdrawals
310 Income Summary

REVENUE
401 Group Lessons Fees
405 Private Lessons Fees

EXPENSES
505 Maintenance Expense
510 Miscellaneous Expense
515 Rent Expense
525 Utilities Expense

Complete activities one of three ways:

1 **Manual** Glencoe Working Papers

or

2 **Peachtree Complete Accounting** Software

or

3 **QuickBooks** Templates

Date	Transactions
Dec. 1	Jennifer Rachael invested $25,000 in Fast Track Tutoring Service, Memorandum 1.
2	Bought a cash register (**Office Equipment**) for $525, Check 101.
2	Purchased $73 in office supplies, Check 102.
5	Purchased educational instructional computers for $13,924, Check 103.
5	Received $950 for private instruction, Receipt 1.
6	Bought $8,494 of instructional material, Invoice 395, from Educational Software on account.
8	Carla DiSario billed for two group classes, $36, Invoice 101.
9	Wrote Check 104 for $850 for the December rent.
10	Billed George McGarty $275 for special group classes, Invoice 102.
10	Received Invoice 5495 for a $2,375 microcomputer system, for office use, bought on account from T & N School Equipment.
11	Prepared Receipt 2 for $695 for 20 private lessons given between December 1 and December 10.
13	Received $36 from Carla DiSario on account, Receipt 3.
14	Sent Check 105 for $200 to Educational Software on account.
15	Wrote Check 106 for $750 to repaint two classrooms.
18	Jennifer Rachael withdrew $500 for personal use, Check 107.
20	Sent Check 108 for the electric bill of $183.
24	Issued Check 109 for $45 for stamps (**Miscellaneous Expense**).

Analyze: To which creditors did Fast Track Tutoring Service owe the most money on December 31?

Peachtree®

SMART GUIDE

Step-by-Step Instructions:

1. Select the problem set for Fast Track Tutoring Service (MP-2).
2. Rename the company and set the system date.
3. Record all of the transactions.
4. Reconcile the bank statement.
5. Print the Account Reconciliation reports.
6. Print a General Journal report and proof your work.
7. Print a General Ledger report and a Trial Balance.
8. Print the financial statements.
9. Close the fiscal year.
10. Print a Post-Closing Trial Balance.
11. Answer the Analyze questions and complete the Audit Test.
12. End the session.

MINI PRACTICE SET 2
PAGES 282–283

Visual Learning

Chart of Accounts, p. 283
Use the illustration of the chart of accounts to discuss the accounts used by the business in this practice set, Fast Track Tutoring Service.

SOURCE DOCUMENT PROBLEM

ANSWERS

Ending ledger account balances:
Cash in Bank $9,616
Accts. Rec./Carla DiSario $0
Accts. Rec./George McGarty $275
Office Supplies $73
Office Equipment $2,900
Instructional Equipment $22,418
Accts. Pay./Educational Software $8,294
Accts. Pay./T&N School Equipment $2,375
Jennifer Rachael, Capital $24,613

Reconciled bank balance $9,616

Work sheet totals:
Trial balance $37,625
Income statement $1,956
Balance sheet $35,782

Net Income $113
Ending Owner's Equity $24,613
Total Assets $35,282
Total Liabilities $10,669

Post-Closing Trial Balance $35,282

Analyze: Educational Software

MAKING CONNECTIONS TO DAILY LIFE

Comparing Local Businesses Ask students to name several local businesses that are profit-making organizations. Then ask them to name some local nonprofit organizations. Ask students to cite similarities and differences between the two types of organizations. For example, a similarity is that a nonprofit art museum sells products in its gift shop. A for-profit business also sells items or services. A major difference is the purpose of each type of organization. The for-profit organization is operated to earn revenue and return a profit to its owners. The nonprofit organization is operated to provide a service to the community and may be supported by taxes, donations, and revenue earned from selling products.

UNIT 3 Resource Manager

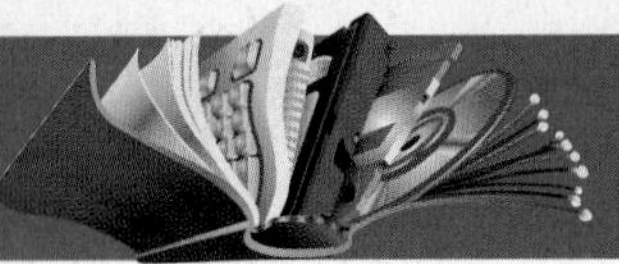

This is a representation of key resources available in the *Glencoe Accounting* program.

interNET CONNECTION

Use the following Web resources to introduce, reinforce, or stimulate discussion on unit topics.

- Case Studies
- Study Plans
- Career Corner
- Real-Life Applications
- Self-Assessment Quizzes
- Games for the Classroom
- Ethics and the Profession

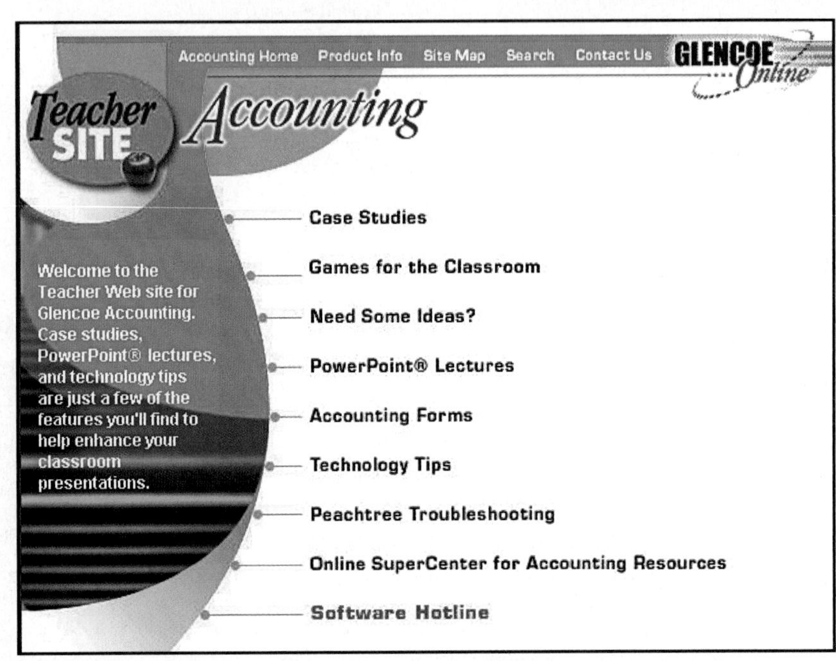

GLENCOE ACCOUNTING BULLETIN BOARD POSTER

Virtual Business® CD-ROM

Virtual Business is a fully visual marketing and business simulation that lets students start and run their own business. For more information on the simulation, visit the teacher page on the *Glencoe Accounting* Web site.

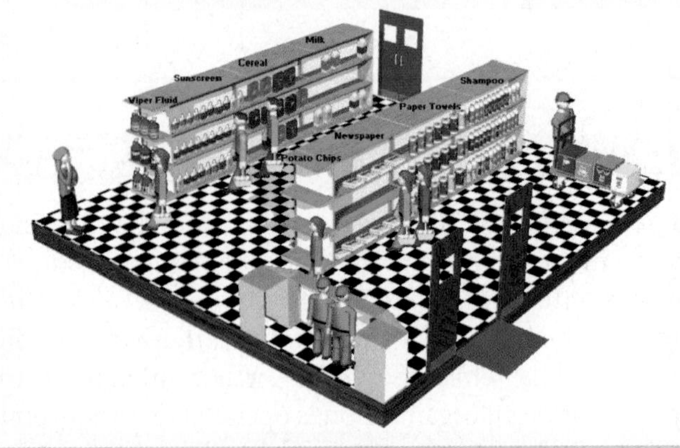

Accounting in Action

Unit Video Portfolio

Integrating *Electronic Field Trips* into Your Accounting Instruction

The *Electronic Field Trip* videos provide an excellent introduction to key accounting concepts taught in the textbook. You may want to use this video segment in **Unit 3**. The title of the video segment is:

- *Payroll Accounting*

Accounting Mini Practice Set

Green Thumb Plant Service

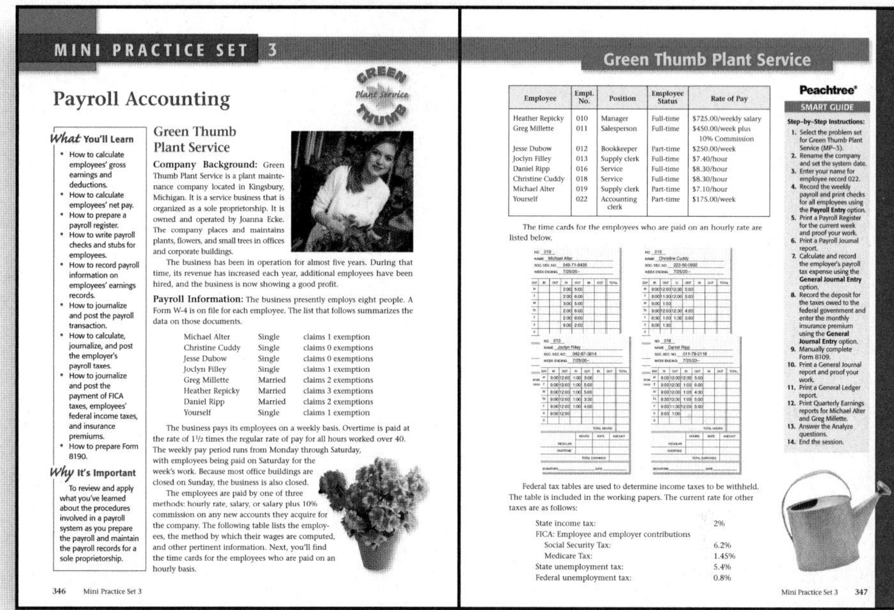

MINI PRACTICE SET 3

Payroll Accounting

What You'll Learn

- How to calculate employees' gross earnings and deductions.
- How to calculate employees' net pay.
- How to prepare a payroll register.
- How to write payroll checks and stubs for employees.
- How to record payroll information on employees' earnings records.
- How to journalize and post the payroll transaction.
- How to calculate, journalize, and post the employer's payroll taxes.
- How to journalize and post the payment of FICA taxes, employees' federal income taxes, and insurance premiums.
- How to prepare Form 8190.

Why It's Important

To review and apply what you've learned about the procedures involved in a payroll system as you prepare the payroll and maintain the payroll records for a sole proprietorship.

Green Thumb Plant Service

Company Background: Green Thumb Plant Service is a plant maintenance company located in Kingsbury, Michigan. It is a service business that is organized as a sole proprietorship. It is owned and operated by Joanna Ecke. The company places and maintains plants, flowers, and small trees in offices and corporate buildings.

The business has been in operation for almost five years. During that time, its revenue has increased each year, additional employees have been hired, and the business is now showing a good profit.

Payroll Information: The business presently employs eight people. A Form W-4 is on file for each employee. The list that follows summarizes the data on those documents.

Michael Alter	Single	claims 1 exemption
Christine Cuddy	Single	claims 0 exemptions
Jesse Dubow	Single	claims 0 exemptions
Joclyn Filley	Single	claims 1 exemption
Greg Millette	Married	claims 2 exemptions
Heather Repicky	Married	claims 3 exemptions
Daniel Ripp	Married	claims 2 exemptions
Yourself	Single	claims 1 exemption

The business pays its employees on a weekly basis. Overtime is paid at the rate of $1\frac{1}{2}$ times the regular rate of pay for all hours worked over 40. The weekly pay period runs from Monday through Saturday, with employees being paid on Saturday for the week's work. Because most office buildings are closed on Sunday, the business is also closed.

The employees are paid by one of three methods: hourly rate, salary, or salary plus 10% commission on any new accounts they acquire for the company. The following table lists the employees, the method by which their wages are computed, and other pertinent information. Next, you'll find the time cards for the employees who are paid on an hourly basis.

346 Mini Practice Set 3

Green Thumb Plant Service

Employee	Empl. No.	Position	Employee Status	Rate of Pay
Heather Repicky	010	Manager	Full-time	$725.00/weekly salary
Greg Millette	011	Salesperson	Full-time	$450.00/week plus 10% Commission
Jesse Dubow	012	Bookkeeper	Part-time	$250.00/week
Joclyn Filley	013	Supply clerk	Full-time	$7.40/hour
Daniel Ripp	016	Service	Full-time	$8.30/hour
Christine Cuddy	018	Service	Full-time	$8.30/hour
Michael Alter	019	Supply clerk	Part-time	$7.10/hour
Yourself	022	Accounting clerk	Part-time	$175.00/week

The time cards for the employees who are paid on an hourly rate are listed below.

Federal tax tables are used to determine income taxes to be withheld. The table is included in the working papers. The current rate for other taxes are as follows:

State income tax:	2%
FICA: Employee and employer contributions	
Social Security Tax:	6.2%
Medicare Tax:	1.45%
State unemployment tax:	5.4%
Federal unemployment tax:	0.8%

Peachtree® SMART GUIDE

Step-by-Step Instructions:

1. Select the problem set for Green Thumb Plant Service (MP-3).
2. Rename the company and set the system date.
3. Enter your name for employee record 022.
4. Record the weekly payroll and print checks for all employees using the **Payroll Entry** option.
5. Print a Payroll Register for the current week and proof your work.
6. Print a Payroll Journal report.
7. Calculate and record the employer's payroll tax expense using the **General Journal Entry** option.
8. Record the deposit for the taxes owed to the federal government and enter the monthly insurance premium using the **General Journal Entry** option.
9. Manually complete Form 8109.
10. Print a General Journal report and proof your work.
11. Print a General Ledger report.
12. Print Quarterly Earnings reports for Michael Alter and Greg Millette.
13. Answer the Analyze questions.
14. End the session.

Mini Practice Set 3 347

*Can be found after Chapter 13

Assessment and Evaluation

Unit 3 Test

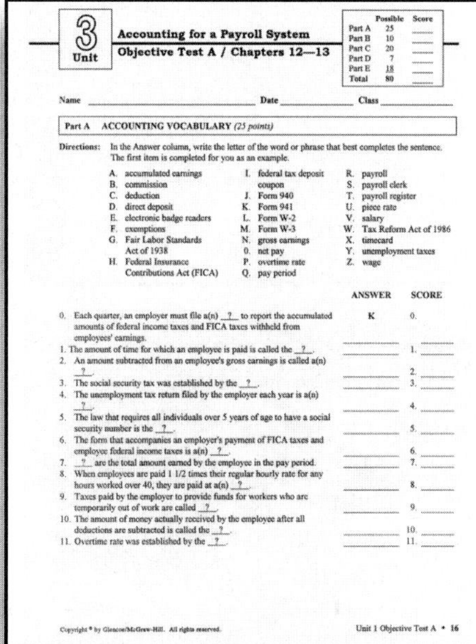

3 Unit

Accounting for a Payroll System

Objective Test A / Chapters 12—13

	Possible	Score
Part A	25	
Part B	10	
Part C	20	
Part D	7	
Part E	18	
Total	80	

Name ______ Date ______ Class ______

Part A ACCOUNTING VOCABULARY *(25 points)*

Directions: In the Answer column, write the letter of the word or phrase that best completes the sentence. The first item is completed for you as an example.

A. accumulated earnings	I. federal tax deposit coupon	R. payroll
B. commission	J. Form 940	S. payroll clerk
C. deduction	K. Form 941	T. payroll register
D. direct deposit	L. Form W-2	U. piece rate
E. electronic badge readers	M. Form W-3	V. salary
F. exemptions	N. gross earnings	W. Tax Reform Act of 1986
G. Fair Labor Standards Act of 1938	O. net pay	X. timecard
H. Federal Insurance Contributions Act (FICA)	P. overtime rate	Y. unemployment taxes
	Q. pay period	Z. wage

	ANSWER	SCORE
0. Each quarter, an employer must file a(n) _?_ to report the accumulated amounts of federal income taxes and FICA taxes withheld from employees' earnings.	K	0.
1. The amount of time for which an employee is paid is called the _?_.		1.
2. An amount subtracted from an employee's gross earnings is called a(n) _?_.		2.
3. The social security tax was established by the _?_.		3.
4. The unemployment tax return filed by the employer each year is a(n) _?_.		4.
5. The law that requires all individuals over 5 years of age to have a social security number is the _?_.		5.
6. The form that accompanies an employer's payment of FICA taxes and employee federal income taxes is a(n) _?_.		6.
7. _?_ are the total amount earned by the employee in the pay period.		7.
8. When employees are paid 1 1/2 times their regular hourly rate for any hours worked over 40, they are paid at a(n) _?_.		8.
9. Taxes paid by the employer to provide funds for workers who are temporarily out of work are called _?_.		9.
10. The amount of money actually received by the employee after all deductions are subtracted is called the _?_.		10.
11. Overtime rate was established by the _?_.		11.

Unit 1 Objective Test A • 16

Accounting Portfolio

Unit 3 Career Goals

Student ______ Class ______ Instructor ______

Date Assigned ______ Date Completed ______

Unit 3 *Accounting Portfolio*

Career Goals

Do you have career goals, or are you still searching for a career interest? There are many ways to find out about possible careers. The first step is to evaluate yourself and your personal interests. Complete the self-valuation that follows. Then complete the activities.

1. Self-Evaluation

1. What are the things you love to do (music, sports, gardening, computers, working with animals, and so on)?
2. What are your values, the things that are most important to you (such as family, knowledge, independence)?
3. What are your particular skills and aptitudes (for example, playing a musical instrument, fluency in a foreign language, working with people, working with your hands, working with data)?
4. What is your personality (shy or outgoing, thoughtful or boisterous, deliberate or spontaneous)? Write ten words that describe your personality.

Accounting Portfolio 19

Enrichment and Extension

Accounting Competitive Event Review

Student ______ Class ______ Instructor ______

Date Assigned ______ Date Completed ______

Payroll Accounting

Payroll is one of the most important accounting systems in any business. A business must not only account for the salaries and wages of its employees, but must also account for various deductions and withholdings from those earnings. Some deductions are required by law. These "involuntary" deductions include federal, state, and local income taxes and social security taxes. Voluntary deductions include union dues, health insurance, life insurance, and U.S. Savings Bonds. The business itself is also liable for payroll taxes.

You should also be familiar with the different payroll records and forms. In addition to the payroll register, a business maintains or prepares an Employee Withholding Allowance Certificate (Form W4); the Wage and Tax Statement (Form W2); the employee's earnings record; the Employer's Quarterly Federal Tax Return (Form 941); the employer's annual unemployment tax return (Form 940); and the Transmittal of Income and Tax Statements (Form W3).

For further information: See Chapters 12 and 13, First Year.

For additional practice: Additional Reinforcement Problems 12A and 13A.

On a separate sheet of paper, answer the following questions.

True/False

1. When a business records its payroll, the amount of federal income tax withheld from employees is entered as a liability.
2. The net pay of employees is the amount of salaries or wages expense for the period.
3. The amounts for FICA taxes withheld depends on an employee's gross earnings, marital status, and number of withholding allowances.
4. FICA taxes are levied in an equal amount on both employers and employees.
5. The gross pay of an hourly employee is determined by subtracting overtime earnings from the regular earnings.
6. Once an employee's year-to-date earnings reach a certain amount set by law, Social Security taxes are no longer withheld.
7. FICA taxes include social security and Medicare tax.
8. FUTA tax, like FICA tax, is levied on both the employer and the employee and so is withheld from each employee's pay.
9. The entry to record the employer's payroll taxes would include a debit to an expense account and a credit to one or more liability accounts.
10. Gross wages are wages before deductions.
11. Many hourly employees keep track of the number of hours they work on time cards.

Multiple Choice

12. Information about the cumulative (year-to-date) earnings of employees would be found in (A) the payroll register, (B) the withholding allowance certificate, (C) employees' earnings records, (D) Form 941.
13. Lisa Ramos has a regular hourly rate of $8.75. In a week when she worked 40 hours and had deductions of $45 for federal income tax, $5.32 for Medicare, and $22.68 for social security, her net pay was (A) $350, (B) $305, (C) $322, (D) $277.

Accounting Competitive Event Review • 41

OVERVIEW UNIT 3

Unit Objectives

1. Correctly use terminology related to accounting for a payroll system.
2. Describe the principles and practices of accounting for a payroll system.
3. Demonstrate the accounting procedures used in a payroll system.

Unit 3 Contents

EXTENDING THE QUOTE

Margaret Thatcher is an example of where hard work, talent, and education can take a person. She is the first and only woman to serve as prime minister of Great Britain, serving three consecutive terms from 1979 to 1990. The daughter of a grocer and a dressmaker, she set an early goal of being in the English Parliament. She surpassed that goal when she became prime minister.

UNIT 3

Accounting for a Payroll System

In this unit. . .

You have now learned how to record business transactions for a service business. Service businesses and merchandising businesses, like the ones you'll learn about in Unit 4, employ people and must keep records on the money paid to their employees and on the taxes paid to local, state, and federal governments. In this unit, you will learn how to perform payroll procedures. You will learn how to keep records on employee earnings and how to record the payment of wages in the accounting records of the business.

Success is having a flair for the thing that you are doing; knowing that is not enough, you have got to have hard work and a sense of purpose.

—Margaret Thatcher
Former Prime Minister of England

284

Great Ideas *From the Classroom of...*

Developing a Pay Plan Divide the students into groups of four or five and present the following scenario: A local beauty salon is having difficulty making a profit. Of the six employees, three have worked at the salon for three years or less. Ask students to study the five pay plans and develop an efficient pay plan for the salon. Then have each group share their plan with the class. Students must provide sufficient rationale for their plans.

Peggy Ross
Bozeman High School
Bozeman, Montana

POWER READING STRATEGIES

To get the most out of your reading:

Predict what the section will be about.

Connect what you read with your own life.

Question as you read to make sure you understand the content.

Respond to what you've read.

In Your Journal . . .

The next time you get paid, take a good look at your pay stub. If you're not employed, ask your parents if you can take a look at their paycheck. Record your responses to the following questions in a journal entry.

1. What do you think of when you hear the word *taxes*?
2. Now take a close look at the pay stub. What percentage of your income was withheld from your paycheck?
3. What are the different types of taxes?
4. Where do you think your tax dollars go?

In Your Journal. . .

Teacher Guidelines Have students add to their accounting portfolios by completing and including the *In Your Journal* writing activities. Ask students to discuss their answers to each of the four questions. Ask for volunteers to share the percentage of their earnings they pay in taxes. Discuss how government would operate if people paid no taxes. Query students about how they think tax dollars are used in your community (examples might be building roads, expanding water and sewer services, or funding schools). To have students add to their accounting portfolios, have them write how they think tax dollars should be used and who should pay taxes. P

INTRODUCING UNIT 3

Previewing the Chapters

The payroll unit's two chapters provide full and realistic coverage of general payroll records and related accounting procedures. While manual payroll and accounting procedures are emphasized, students also learn about computerized payroll systems.

Tying to Previous Knowledge

In the previous unit, students learned to analyze transactions and keep the accounting records for external business transactions. Records must also be kept for internal activities such as payroll. In this unit students learn about payroll records and accounting entries made to record payroll information. They will also learn about typical payroll taxes and how to record the accrual and payment of taxes.

BULLETIN BOARD

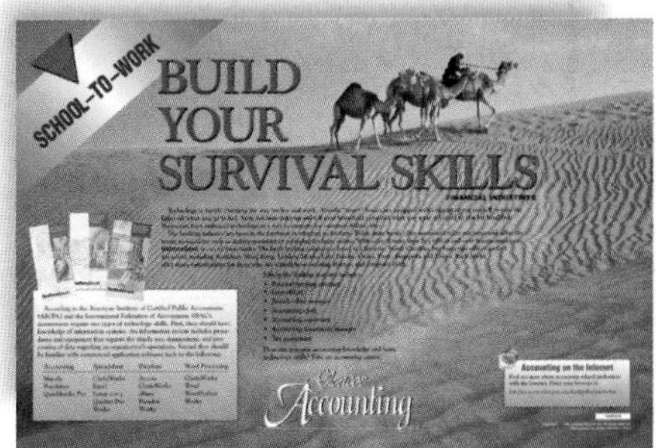

Glencoe Poster Teaching Tip

Discuss the need for technology skills for future careers. Then poll students and ask which software packages they know or have used. Compare students' responses with the software programs listed on the poster. How many of these programs have students used? Ask students how they plan to acquire or improve their technology skills.

CHAPTER 12 Resource Manager

Section Resources

	Objectives & Standards	Activities & Features	Reproducible Masters
Chapter Opener *Payroll Accounting*	• Explain the importance of accurate payroll records. • Compute gross pay using different methods. • Explain and compute employee-paid withholdings. • Compute net pay. • Prepare payroll registers. • Explain and determine methods of dissemination of payroll funds. • Prepare an employee's earnings record. • Define the accounting terms introduced in this chapter. **National Standards for Business Education**: IVB1, IVB2, IVB3	Exploring Real World of Business, p. 286 Workplace Connections, p. 287	School-to-Work Handbook
Section 1 *Calculating Gross Earnings*	• The importance of accurate payroll records. • How to calculate gross earnings.	Did You Know?, p. 289	Demonstration Problems
Section 2 *Payroll Deductions*	• Why deductions are calculated and reported. • How to calculate deductions required by the federal government. • How to determine voluntary deductions.	Calculator Hints, p. 295 Accounting Flashbacks, p. 296 Connect To, p. 297 Analyzing Financial Reports, p. 297	Math Review for Accounting Demonstration Problems
Section 3 *Payroll Records*	• The purpose of a payroll register. • How to prepare a payroll register. • How to prepare a payroll check. • The purpose of an employee's earnings record. • How to prepare an employee's earnings record.	Accounting Tips, p. 300 International Accounting, p. 301 Accounting Tips, p. 302 A Matter of Ethics, p. 303	Demonstration Problems Strategies for Teaching International Accounting Strategies for Teaching Ethics in Accounting Internet Resources and Activities Handbook

KEY

Posters — Transparency — Software — Videocassette
Blackline Masters — CD-ROM — Portfolio

MULTIMEDIA RESOURCE

Peachtree	QuickBooks	Spreadsheets	Videos	CD-ROMs
Problem 12-5 *Calculating Gross Pay* Problem 12-7 *Preparing Payroll Checks and Employee's Earnings Records* Problem 12-8 *Preparing the Payroll* Problem 12-9 *Preparing the Payroll Register* Problem 12-10 *Calculating Gross Earnings*	None in this chapter	Problem 12-6 *Preparing a Payroll Register*	***Video Segment: Payroll Accounting*** After viewing this video, students will be able to explain a payroll system and that deductions can be both voluntary and mandated by law; illustrate both the employee's deductions and the employer's taxes that are based on payroll.	***Electronic Learning Center (ELC), Chapter 12*** This program is ideal for visual learners since it incorporates video images, animation, and graphics to enliven the content of each lesson. ***Interactive Lesson Planner (ILP), Chapter 12*** This CD-ROM combines the versatility of an electronic lesson planner with the convenience of teacher classroom resources.

SCANS Correlation Chart

FOUNDATION SKILLS

Basic Skills:	Reading	Writing	Math	Listening	Speaking	
Thinking Skills:	Creative Thinking	Decision Making	Problem Solving	Seeing Things in the Mind's Eye	Knowing How to Learn	Reasoning
Personal Qualities:	Responsibility	Self-Esteem	Sociability	Self-Management	Integrity/Honesty	

WORKPLACE COMPETENCIES

Resources:	Allocating Time	Allocating Money	Allocating Material and Facility Resources	Allocating Human Resources		
Information:	Acquiring and Evaluating Information	Organizing and Maintaining Information	Interpreting and Communicating Information	Using Computers to Process Information		
Interpersonal Skills:	Participating as a Member of a Team	Teaching Others	Serving Clients/ Customers	Exercising Leadership	Negotiating to Arrive at a Decision	Working with Cultural Diversity
Systems:	Understanding Systems	Monitoring and Correcting Performance	Improving and Designing Systems			
Technology:	Selecting Technology	Applying Technology to Task	Maintaining and Troubleshooting Technology			

*Highlighted blocks indicate areas covered in the chapter. Additional SCANS skills are also covered throughout the *Teacher Wraparound Edition.*

Assessment

Student Edition
- Check Your Understanding, pp. 292, 298, 304
- Chapter 12 Problems, pp. 309–313

Assessment and Evaluation Masters
- Chapter 12 Study Plan, *Glencoe Workbook*
- Chapter 12 Self-Test, *Glencoe Workbook*
- Chapter 12 Test, *Chapter Tests* Booklet
- Chapter 12 Activity, *School-to-Work Handbook*
- Chapter 12 **Exam***View*

Teacher Wraparound Edition
- Critical Thinking Activity, p. 300
- Reteaching Section 1, p. 292
- Reteaching Section 2, p. 298
- Reteaching Section 3, p. 304
- Chapter 12 Quiz, p. 305

Transparencies

	Teaching Transparencies	Solution Transparencies
Section 1:	12–1, 12–2, 12–3	Problem 12–1
Section 2:	12–4, 12–5, 12–6	Problems 12–2, 12–3
Section 3:	12–7, 12–8, 12–9, 12–10	Problem 12–4
End of Chapter:		12–5, 12–6, 12–7, 12–8, 12–9, 12–10

TEACHER CLASSROOM RESOURCES

This is a representation of key blackline masters available in the Teacher Classroom Resources.

Teaching Aids

Transparency Examples

Section Focus Transparencies

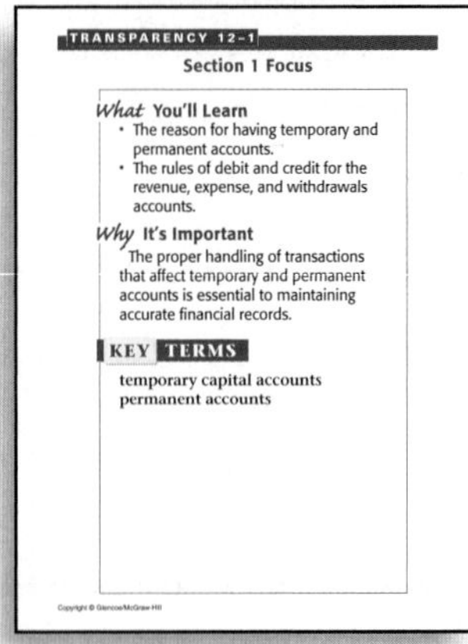
TRANSPARENCY 12-1
Section 1 Focus

What You'll Learn
- The reason for having temporary and permanent accounts.
- The rules of debit and credit for the revenue, expense, and withdrawals accounts.

Why It's Important
The proper handling of transactions that affect temporary and permanent accounts is essential to maintaining accurate financial records.

KEY TERMS
temporary capital accounts
permanent accounts

Teaching Transparencies

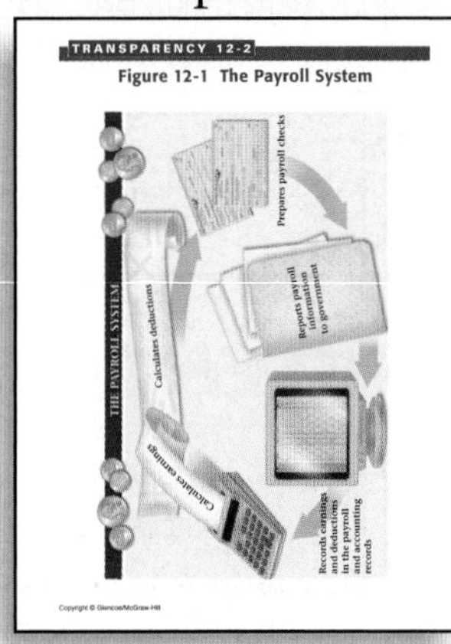
TRANSPARENCY 12-2
Figure 12-1 The Payroll System

Teaching Transparencies

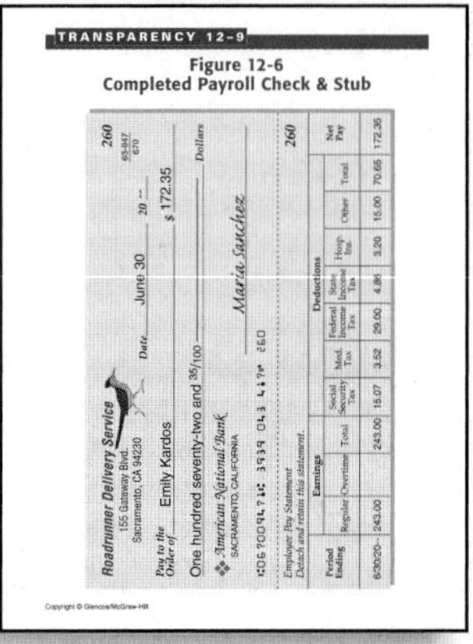
TRANSPARENCY 12-9
Figure 12-6
Completed Payroll Check & Stub

Solution Transparencies

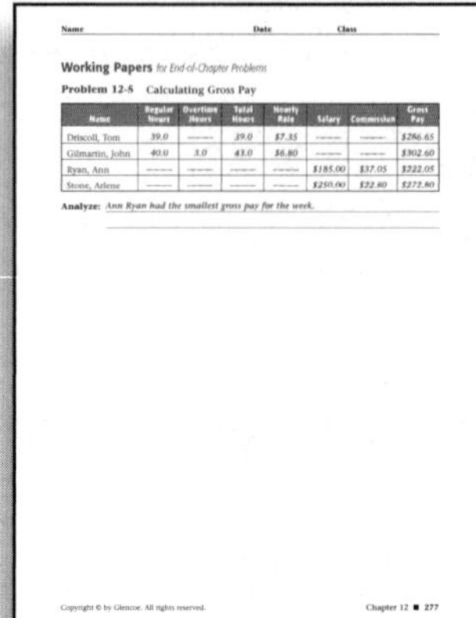
Working Papers for End-of-Chapter Problems
Problem 12-5 Calculating Gross Pay

Analyze: Ann Ryan had the smallest gross pay for the week.

Demonstration Problems

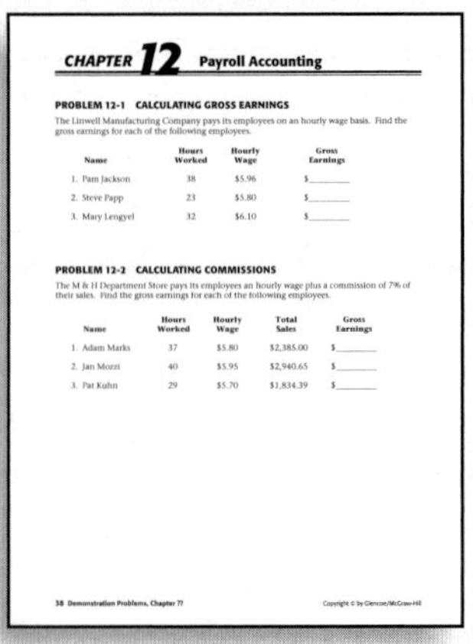
CHAPTER 12 Payroll Accounting

PROBLEM 12-1 CALCULATING GROSS EARNINGS

PROBLEM 12-2 CALCULATING COMMISSIONS

Lesson Plans

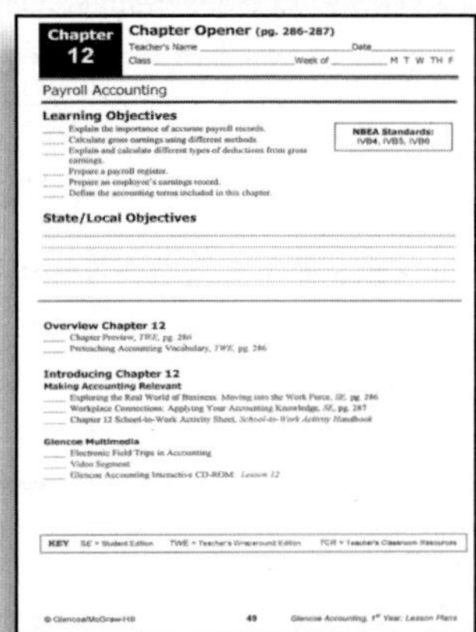
Chapter 12 Chapter Opener (pg. 286-287)

Payroll Accounting

Learning Objectives

State/Local Objectives

Overview Chapter 12

Introducing Chapter 12

Glencoe Multimedia

Block Scheduling

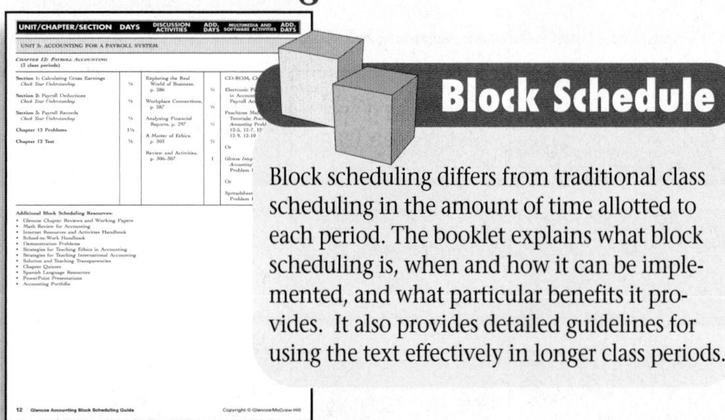
UNIT/CHAPTER/SECTION DAYS

UNIT 3: ACCOUNTING FOR A PAYROLL SYSTEM

Block Schedule

Block scheduling differs from traditional class scheduling in the amount of time allotted to each period. The booklet explains what block scheduling is, when and how it can be implemented, and what particular benefits it provides. It also provides detailed guidelines for using the text effectively in longer class periods.

Enrichment and Application

Strategies for Teaching Ethics in Accounting

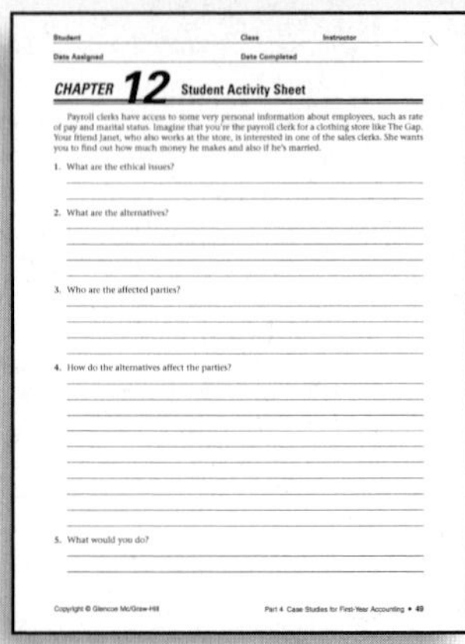
CHAPTER 12 Student Activity Sheet

1. What are the ethical issues?
2. What are the alternatives?
3. Who are the affected parties?
4. How do the alternatives affect the parties?
5. What would you do?

Strategies for Teaching International Accounting

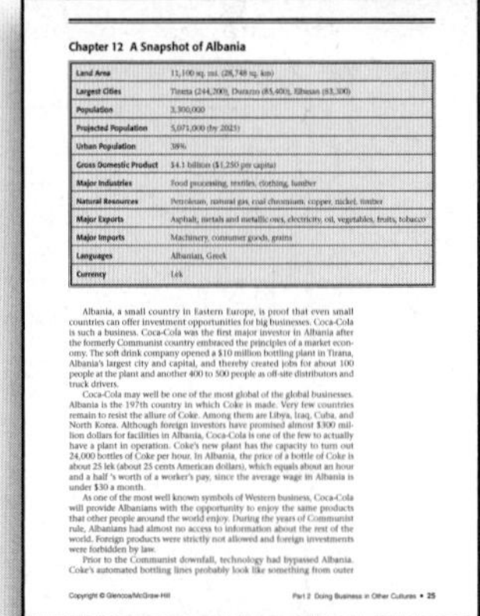
Chapter 12 A Snapshot of Albania

School-to-Work Handbook

CHAPTER 12 SCHOOL-TO-WORK ACTIVITY
Payroll Accounting

Meeting Different Ability Levels

Chapter Reviews and Working Papers (CRWP)

Working Papers

Review

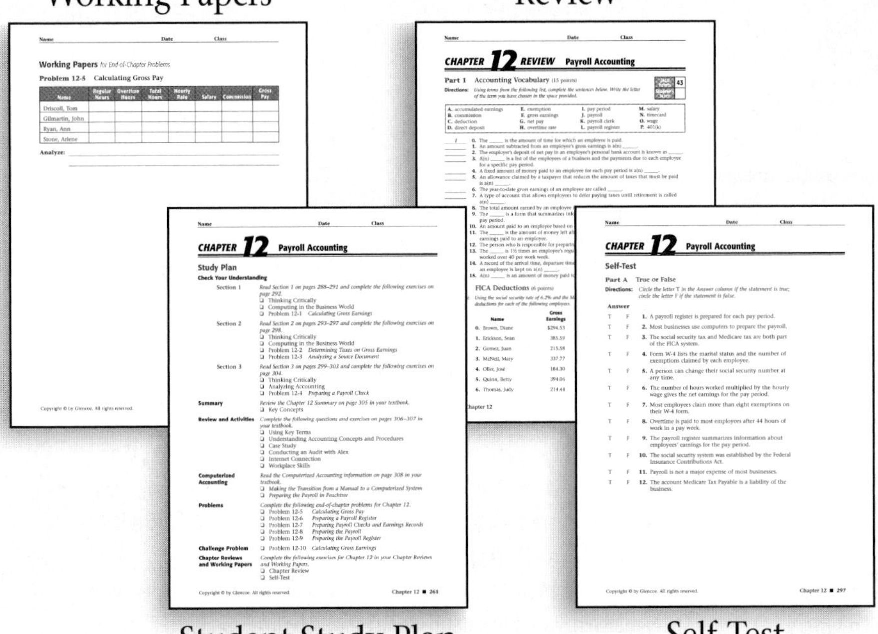

Student Study Plan

Self-Test

Real-World Multimedia CD-ROM

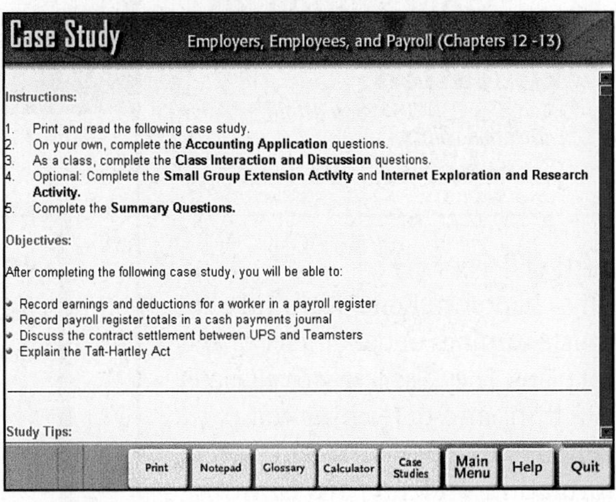

Key to Ability Levels

Each section gives skill-building activities. Each activity has been labeled for use with students of various learning styles and abilities.

L1 Level 1 activities are basic activities and should be within the range of all students.

L2 Level 2 activities are average activities and should be within the range of average and above average students.

L3 Level 3 activities are challenging activities designed for the ability range of above average students.

ELL ELL activities should be within the ability range of English Language Learners.

Assessment and Evaluation

Chapter Tests

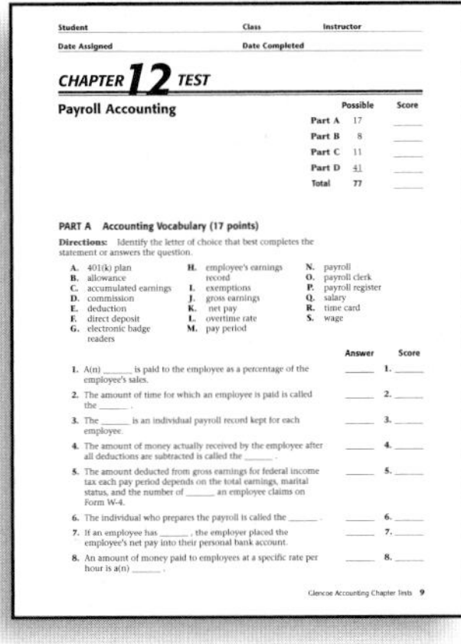

Chapter Quiz

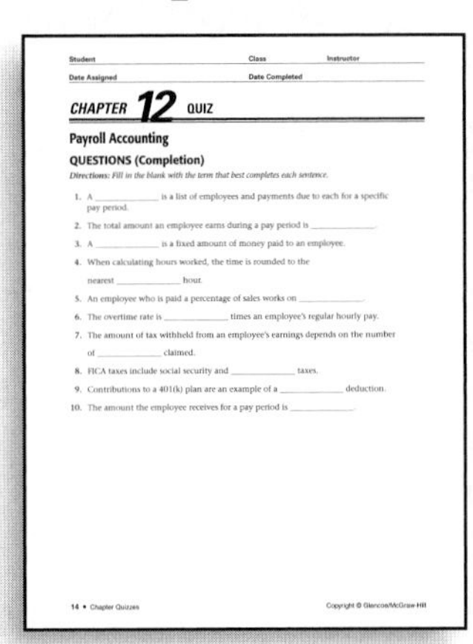

Teaching Resources at a Glance

Application Resources

- Glencoe Chapter Review and Working Papers, SE and TAE
- School-to-Work Handbook, SE and TM
- Accounting Portfolio, SE and TM

Reproducible Masters

- Demonstration Problems
- Lesson Plans
- Block Scheduling
- Spanish Language Resources

Glencoe Accounting Professional Development Series

- Strategies for Teaching Ethics in Accounting
- Accounting Competitive Event Review
- Math Review for Accounting
- Strategies for Teaching International Accounting
- Internet Resources and Activities Handbook

Transparency Package

- Section Focus Transparencies
- Teaching Transparencies
- Source Document Transparencies
- Solution Transparencies

Performance Assessment

- **Exam***View* CD-ROM
- Chapter Tests
- Chapter Quizzes
- Unit Tests
- Audit Tests
- Printed Testbank

Multimedia Resources

- Electronic Learning Center:
  - Multimedia CD-ROMs
  - Peachtree software, tutorials, templates, and solutions
  - Spreadsheet templates
- Using QuickBooks with Glencoe Accounting
- Interactive Lesson Planner
- Electronic Field Trips in Accounting
- PowerPoint Presentation
- Web site: glencoeaccounting.glencoe.com

Correlations to National Standards for Business Education

(See pages T50–T51 for a detailed correlation chart.)

Standards: IVB1, IVB2, IVB3

Chapter Preview

In this chapter students learn how to calculate earnings under different payment plans. They also learn to calculate deductions and determine net pay. Finally, they learn how to record payroll information and prepare earnings reports.

Section Overviews

- Section 1—*Calculating Gross Earnings*
- Section 2—*Payroll Deductions*
- Section 3—*Payroll Records*

Chapter Vocabulary

payroll
pay period
payroll clerk
gross earnings
salary
wage
time card
electronic badge readers
commission
overtime rate
deduction
allowance
401(k) plan
payroll register
net pay
direct deposit
employee's earnings record
accumulated earnings

Preteaching Accounting Vocabulary

Writing Exercise: Have students look up definitions of terms in the *Glossary* and write a sentence using each term. Ask for volunteers to share their sentences in class. L1

CHAPTER 12

Payroll Accounting

Learning Objectives

When you have completed this chapter, you will be able to:

- Explain the importance of accurate payroll records.
- Compute gross pay using different methods.
- Explain and compute employee-paid withholdings.
- Compute net pay.
- Prepare payroll registers.
- Explain and determine methods of dissemination of payroll funds.
- Prepare an employee's earnings record.
- Define the accounting terms introduced in this chapter.

Exploring the Real World of Business

MOVING INTO THE WORKFORCE

It's graduation day! You've studied hard, and now you're ready for the next big step–looking for your first job. Where do you start looking? How will you know whether you'll like the company? How do you prepare for a job interview? What will you earn? **Robert Half International** can help!

Robert Half is an international staffing service that specializes in matching employers and workers for jobs in accounting, finance, and information systems. The company offers job placement for both full-time and temporary jobs. Job seekers can find a database of job listings for openings around the world. If you choose temporary work, you might find assignments lasting from a few weeks to several months. Such assignments give you an opportunity to work at a variety of jobs.

What do you think?

Why do you think it is beneficial for some companies to hire temporary employees rather than full-time staff? Give at least two specific examples.

Robert Half International Inc.

Exploring the Real World of Business

Robert Half International Inc.

Robert Half has over 300 offices worldwide. The company charges employers a fee for its services. It does not charge job applicants. Robert Half has seven operating divisions: Accountemps®, Robert Half®, OfficeTeam®, RHI Consulting®, RHI Management Resources®, The Affiliates®, and The Creative Group®.

What do you think? (Answers)

Answers may vary. Employers hire temporary employees when they have jobs they know will last only a few months. They also hire temps to fill in during peak work hours or especially busy times. Other employers may hire temps to save on overhead and personnel administration costs.

Glencoe Accounting Online

Visit the *Glencoe Accounting* Web site at **glencoeaccounting.glencoe.com** for additional activities and information.

Workplace Connections

Applying Your Accounting Knowledge

When you get your paycheck, do you look at it carefully to see how much you've earned and what amounts have been deducted from the total? Employers are required to make certain deductions from your pay. You'll learn about those deductions in this chapter.

Investigate:

1. Look at your last pay stub. Was money deducted from your earnings?
2. What do you think those deductions were taken for?

INTRODUCING CHAPTER 12

Making Accounting Relevant

Workplace Connections: Applying Your Accounting Knowledge

Discussion: Ask students who have part-time jobs whether they verify the amount of their gross earnings and deductions. Have they ever found an error? How would they get the error corrected? Discuss ways to approach the problem.

Investigate (Answers)

1. Most students will have deductions from their gross earnings.
2. The largest deductions are usually for local, state, and federal taxes. Some students may also have deductions for health-care plans or savings.

School-to-Work Activity

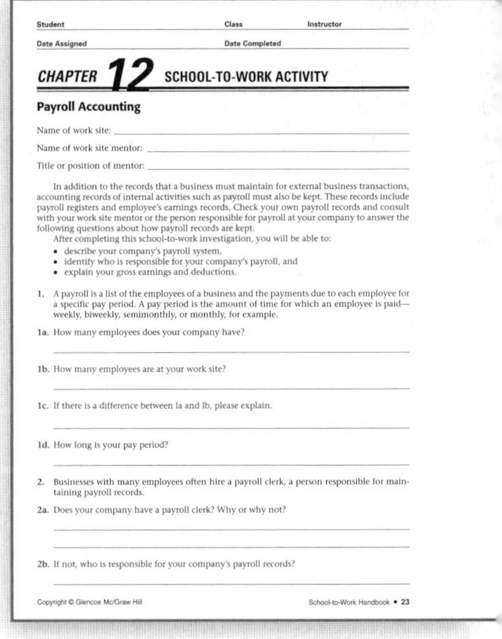

Student ________ Class ________ Instructor ________

Date Assigned ________ Date Completed ________

CHAPTER 12 SCHOOL-TO-WORK ACTIVITY

Payroll Accounting

Name of work site: ________

Name of work site mentor: ________

Title or position of mentor: ________

In addition to the records that a business must maintain for external business transactions, accounting records of internal activities such as payroll must also be kept. These records include payroll registers and employee's earnings records. Check your own payroll records and consult with your work site mentor or the person responsible for payroll at your company to answer the following questions about how payroll records are kept.

After completing this school-to-work investigation, you will be able to:

- describe your company's payroll system,
- identify who is responsible for your company's payroll, and
- explain your gross earnings and deductions.

1. A payroll is a list of the employees of a business and the payments due to each employee for a specific pay period. A pay period is the amount of time for which an employee is paid—weekly, biweekly, semimonthly, or monthly, for example.

1a. How many employees does your company have?

1b. How many employees are at your work site?

1c. If there is a difference between la and lb, please explain.

1d. How long is your pay period?

2. Businesses with many employees often hire a payroll clerk, a person responsible for maintaining payroll records.

2a. Does your company have a payroll clerk? Why or why not?

2b. If not, who is responsible for your company's payroll records?

GLENCOE MULTIMEDIA

Electronic Field Trips in Accounting *Video Segment: Payroll Accounting*

After viewing this video, students will be able to explain a payroll system and that deductions can be both voluntary and mandated by law.

Glencoe Accounting: Electronic Learning Center *Chapter 12*

The CD-ROM program is ideal for visual learners since it incorporates video images, animation, and graphics to enliven the content of each lesson.

CHAPTER 12
SECTION 1, PAGES 288–292

1 FOCUS

Introducing the Section

In this section students learn that payroll records provide information for calculating employee pay and for recording payroll costs in the accounting system. Students also learn how to calculate gross earnings based on salary, hourly wage, commission, salary plus commission or bonus, and overtime pay.

Section Concepts

- The importance of accurate payroll records.
- How to calculate gross earnings.

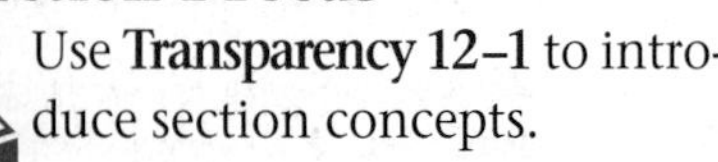

Visual Learning

Section 1 Focus

Use **Transparency 12–1** to introduce section concepts.

BELL RINGER

Comparing Experiences: Take a poll of students in the class who have part-time jobs. How many of them are paid a salary? How many are paid by the hour? Are any of them paid a commission? How many earn overtime? Have students discuss how they calculate their earnings. L1

SECTION 1

Calculating Gross Earnings

What You'll Learn

- The importance of accurate payroll records.
- How to calculate gross earnings.

Why It's Important

For many businesses payroll is the largest expense. It is essential that the payroll system accurately determine the gross pay for each employee for every pay period.

KEY TERMS

payroll
pay period
payroll clerk
gross earnings
salary
wage
time card
electronic badge readers
commission
overtime rate

In a private enterprise economy, people are free to work for any business they choose—as long as they meet the requirements for employment. Employers such as Ford Motor Company, Pier 1, and Borders Books & Music rely on their employees to operate the business and pay their employees for the services they perform. In paying their employees, businesses follow certain guidelines. For example, both federal and state laws require businesses to keep accurate payroll records and to report on employees' earnings.

Most companies set up a payroll system to ensure that their employees are paid on time and that payroll checks are accurate. In this chapter, you will learn about the payroll system.

The Importance of Payroll Records

A **payroll** is a list of the employees and the payments due to each employee for a specific pay period. A **pay period** is the amount of time over which an employee is paid. Most businesses use weekly, biweekly (every two weeks), semimonthly (twice a month), or monthly pay periods.

The payroll expense is a major expense for most companies. To compute salary expenses, most businesses set up a payroll system for recording and reporting employee earnings information. A well-designed payroll system achieves two goals:

(1) The collection and processing of all the information needed to prepare and issue payroll checks.
(2) The generation of payroll records needed for accounting purposes and for reporting to government agencies, management, and others.

Businesses with many employees often hire a **payroll clerk** who is responsible for preparing the payroll. The payroll clerk:

- Makes sure employees are paid on time.
- Makes sure each employee is paid the correct amount.
- Completes payroll records.
- Submits payroll reports.
- Pays payroll taxes.

All payroll systems have certain tasks in common, as shown in **Figure 12–1.**

RESOURCE MANAGER

Reproducible Masters
- Lesson Plans
- Chapter Reviews and Working Papers (CRWP) TAE
- Demonstration Problems

Transparencies
- Section Focus Transparency
- Teaching Transparencies
- Source Document Transparencies
- Solution Transparencies

Multimedia
- *ExamView* CD-ROM
- Electronic Learning Center CD-ROM
- Interactive Lesson Planner CD-ROM
- Electronic Field Trips in Accounting

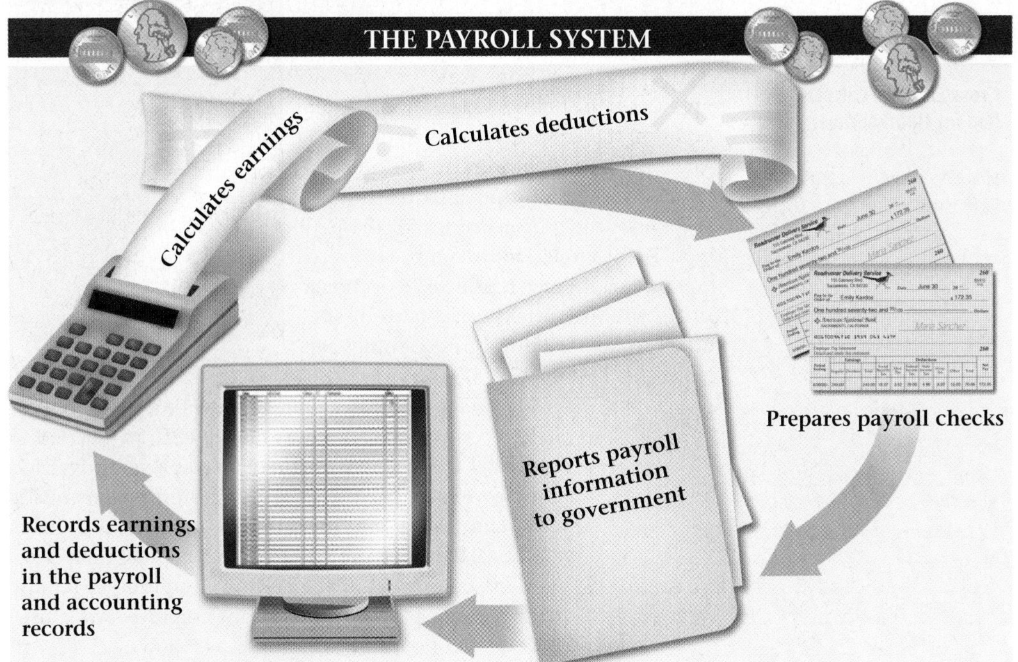

Figure 12–1 The Payroll System

Computing Gross Pay

Most employees are paid for the specific amount of time they work during a pay period. The total amount of money an employee earns in a pay period is the employee's **gross earnings**, or *gross pay*. The gross earnings expense is sometimes called salary expense. The method used to compute gross pay depends on the basis on which an employee is paid. An employee's pay can be based on:

- salary
- hourly wage
- commission
- salary plus commission or bonus
- overtime pay

Let's look at each method of paying employees.

Salary

One common method of paying employees, especially those who are managers or supervisors, is by salary. A **salary** is a fixed amount of money paid to an employee for each pay period. In other words, an employee who is paid a salary earns the same amount regardless of the number of hours worked during the pay period. For example, Paula Ferguson, an administrative assistant, is paid a salary of $2,000 a month. Her gross earnings are $2,000 for each monthly pay period. Paula may work 160 hours in one month and 170 hours in the next, but her gross earnings for each of the two months are the same—$2,000.

Did You Know?

Teen Income

Teens get a large portion of the money they spend from parents, who provide 55 percent of teen income. Other sources of income are part-time jobs, allowances, and even full-time jobs.

Great Ideas *From the Classroom of...*

Bring the Chapter to Life! Bring the payroll chapter to life with a field trip to a McDonald's restaurant. Ask the manager to begin the tour with a discussion about the history of the corporation. Then have the manager discuss employment policies including hiring, employee evaluations, sexual harassment, labor costs, and payroll procedures. At the end of the tour, ask questions reviewing what students have learned; and when students provide correct answers, reward students with coupons for "free food."

Gwen H. Cruickshank
Laramie High School
Laramie, Wyoming

2 TEACH

GUIDED PRACTICE

Reading Accounting

- Reading time cards can be confusing for some students. Obtain samples of time cards used by local employers, and have students practice reading the cards and calculating the hours worked. L1

Concept Development: The Importance of Payroll Records

Discussion: Point out to students that payroll is often one of the largest expenses for a business. Inaccuracies in payroll calculations could cost a business thousands of dollars, both in payroll amounts and in taxes paid on the payroll. Discuss the importance of controlling payroll expenses and the cost to businesses of wasted employee time. L1

Visual Learning

Figure 12–1 The Payroll System

Use **Transparency 12–2** to discuss the steps in calculating earnings and recording payroll in the accounting records.

Concept Development: Computing Gross Pay

Discussion: Five methods of determining gross earnings are presented in this section. These methods include salary, hourly wage, commission, salary plus commission, and overtime. Emphasize why employers choose different ways of compensating employees. L1

2 TEACH (Cont'd.)

Teaching Tip

Students sometimes confuse terms such as *biweekly* or *semimonthly*. Point out that "bi" means two, so biweekly is every two weeks. "Semi" means half, so semimonthly means half a month or being paid twice a month.

Visual Learning

Figure 12–2 An Employee Time Card

Use **Transparency 12–3** to guide students through the calculations to determine total hours worked and total earnings.

Demonstration Problem

Step-by-Step Practice

Use demonstration problem 12–1 to give students practice in calculating hourly wages.

Chapter Reviews and Working Papers

Refer students to the *Study Plan* located at the beginning of Chapter 12 in the workbook.

Key Points

Gross Earnings Calculation for Hourly Wage

Hours Worked × Hourly Wage = Gross Earnings

Hourly Wage

Another common way of paying employees is the hourly wage. A **wage** is an amount of money paid to an employee at a specified rate per hour worked. The number of hours worked multiplied by the hourly wage equals the gross earnings for the pay period. For example, Emily Kardos, a delivery driver for Roadrunner, is paid $6.75 per hour. During the last weekly pay period, she worked 36 hours. Emily's gross earnings are $243.00 (36 hours × $6.75).

NO. 11
NAME Emily Kardos
SOC. SEC. NO. 201-46-8319
WEEK ENDING 6/30/20--

DAY	IN	OUT	IN	OUT	IN	OUT	TOTAL
M	7:58	12:25	1:32	4:18			7 1/4
T	8:00	12:00	12:45	4:00			7 1/4
W	7:56	12:01	1:10	4:15			7
Th	8:01	11:55	1:02	4:16			7 1/4
F	7:45	12:02	1:05	3:58			7 1/4
S							
S							
					TOTAL HOURS		36

	HOURS	RATE	AMOUNT
REGULAR	36	$6.75	$243.00
OVERTIME	0		
	TOTAL EARNINGS		$243.00

SIGNATURE *Emily Kardos* DATE *6/30/20--*

Figure 12–2 An Employee Time Card

Many employees are required to use time cards to accurately record their work hours during each pay period. A **time card** is a record of the times an employee arrives and leaves work each day. The times may be recorded manually or by a time clock. The time card also shows the total hours worked each day. **Figure 12–2** shows a manual time card.

Many companies divide an hour into four 15-minute quarters for the purpose of measuring employee work time. These quarter hours are determined as follows:

Quarter Hour	Example
On the hour	2:00 P.M.
15 minutes after the hour	2:15 P.M.
30 minutes after the hour	2:30 P.M.
45 minutes after the hour	2:45 P.M.

Employees seldom arrive and leave exactly on the quarter hour. As a result, some companies round arrival and departure times to the nearest quarter hour. Employees, therefore, are paid for working to the nearest quarter hour. Look at **Figure 12–2.** The times appearing on the time card for Emily Kardos for Monday will be rounded to the nearest quarter hour as follows:

Actual Time Recorded	Nearest Quarter Hour
7:58 A.M.	8:00 A.M.
12:25 P.M.	12:30 P.M.
1:32 P.M.	1:30 P.M.
4:18 P.M.	4:15 P.M.

Key Points

Determining Hours Worked

For hourly workers, the actual arrival and departure times may not be used to calculate the hours worked.

Emily will be paid for working on Monday from 8:00 A.M. to 12:30 P.M. (4½ hours) and from 1:30 P.M. to 4:15 P.M. (2¾ hours) for a total of 7¼ hours.

Some businesses use computer technology to track employee arrival and departure times. One method uses **electronic badge readers**. With this method the employee is issued an identification badge with a magnetic strip that contains employee information. When the employee inserts the identification badge into a badge reader, the magnetic strip is scanned and the following information is transferred directly to the computer: the employee's name,

REINFORCING STUDY SKILLS

Applying Questioning Skills Review the SQ3R strategy with students: *Survey, Question, Read, Recite, Review*. Ask students to skim (survey) the main heads in the chapter and apply the second step by turning the heads into questions that students can answer in their reading. For example, "How are hourly wages calculated?" "How are commissions paid on sales calculated?"

the department or area where the employee works, and the arrival or departure times.

This electronic equipment makes it fast and easy to prepare a daily print-out on employee work hours.

Regardless of how employee work hours are recorded (manually, time clock, or electronic reader), business owners and supervisors check the accuracy of the hours reported and analyze the labor costs for every pay period.

Commission

A **commission** is an amount paid to an employee based on a percentage of the employee's sales. Sales employees are often paid a commission to encourage them to increase their sales. For example, Joyce Torrez is paid a 5% commission on all her sales. Last week Joyce's total sales were $8,254. Joyce's gross earnings for the week are $412.70 ($8,254 × .05).

Salary Plus Commission or Bonus

Some salespeople earn a base salary plus a commission or a bonus on the amount of their sales. For example, Juan Espito, who works at a car stereo shop, is paid a salary of $200 per week plus a commission of 3% of his sales. Juan's sales were $4,810 last week. His gross earnings are $344.30 [$200 + ($4,810 × .03)].

Overtime Pay

State and federal laws regulate the number of hours some employees may work in a week. Generally, employers are required to pay overtime when employees covered by these laws work more than 40 hours per week. The **overtime rate**, set by the Fair Labor Standards Act of 1938, is 1½ (1.5) times the employee's regular hourly pay rate. For example, Jesse Dubow, a photo-lab clerk at Fast Photo, worked 43 hours last week. Jesse's hourly rate of pay is $6.60. His hourly overtime rate is $9.90 ($6.60 × 1.5). His gross earnings for the week are $293.70 determined as follows:

	Hours		Rate		
Regular	40	×	$6.60	=	$264.00
Overtime	3	×	$9.90	=	29.70
Total					$293.70

Some employees who are paid a salary are also entitled to overtime pay. If a salaried employee is paid overtime, the salary is converted to an hourly rate using a standard number of hours for the period covered by the salary. Then the hourly overtime rate is calculated. For example, Jim Halley's salary is $600 per week. His hourly rate is $15 assuming a standard 40-hour work week. His hourly overtime rate is $22.50 ($15 × 1.5). Jim's gross earnings for a 44-hour week are $690, determined as follows:

	Hours		Rate		
Regular				=	$600.00
Overtime	4	×	$22.50	=	90.00
Total					$690.00

Key Points

Overtime Pay
Some employees who work more than 40 hours per week are paid overtime. The usual overtime rate is 1½ times the employee's hourly rate of pay.

2 TEACH (Cont'd.)

Teaching Tip

Ask students whether any of them have worked in companies using electronic identification devices. If not, have students describe the identification methods their employers use.

Demonstration Problem Step-by-Step Practice

Use demonstration problem 12–2 to give students practice in calculating commission wages.

Demonstration Problem Step-by-Step Practice

Use demonstration problem 12–3 to give students practice in calculating overtime pay.

HOME AND COMMUNITY CONNECTIONS ACTIVITY

Payroll Survey Have students conduct a payroll survey of their friends and family to learn about methods of pay. Encourage students to develop a written questionnaire, allowing spaces for them to write respondents' answers. Questions might include:

- How are you paid?
- How often are you paid?
- How is your total pay determined?

Lead a class discussion to determine methods of dissemination of payroll funds, for example, direct deposit and mail.

CHAPTER 12
SECTION 1, PAGES 288–292

3 ASSESS

Thinking Critically (Answers)

1. Collect and process information to prepare and issue payroll checks; produce payroll records for accounting and reports to government, management, and others.
2. Each badge has a magnetic strip with employee information embedded. The badge reader scans the strip and feeds information to a computer.

Computing in the Business World (Answers)

Potentially, the Charleston Group has the better offer. You would have to bring in at least eight new clients to equal Bryson's offer. With Bryson, you would start higher but could add only $900 to your income, and you would need to gain 10 new clients.

Problem 12-1 (Answers)

Lang: $296.40, $0, $296.40
Longas: $290, $32.64, $322.62
Quinn: $332.00, $52.19, $384.91
Sullivan: $327.85, $0, $327.85
Talbert: $300, $0, $300
Trimbell: $390, $36.58, $426.58
Varney: $299.69, $0, $299.69
Wallace: $370, $83.28, $453.22

Chapter Reviews and Working Papers Refer students to the Chapter 12 workbook pages to answer *Check Your Understanding* activities.

4 CLOSE

Section Wrap-Up

Writing Exercise: Have students write a paragraph describing how to calculate wages using at least four different methods. L1

SECTION 1 Check Your Understanding

Now that you have studied this section, complete the following questions and problems.

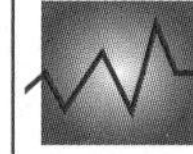

Thinking Critically

1. List the two goals a payroll system should achieve.
2. How does an electronic badge reader record the correct arrival and departure times?

Computing in the Business World

You have been interviewing with several financial consulting firms for entry-level management positions, and you received two job offers. One company, Bryson Consulting, offers you a starting salary of $30,000 with a 2% bonus (on salary) if you can bring 10 new clients into the firm. The other company, The Charleston Group, offers a salary of $25,000 plus a 3% commission on all new client billings. Which job offers the highest earnings potential? Explain.

Problem 12–1 Calculating Gross Earnings

Cleary's Music Center has nine employees. The employees are paid weekly with overtime after 40 hours per week. The overtime rate is 1½ times the regular rate of pay. Payroll information for the week ending June 12 follows:

Employee	Pay Rate	Hours
David Clune	$6.95	33½
Richard Lang	$7.80	38
Jane Longas	$7.25	43
Betty Quinn	$8.30	44¼
John Sullivan	$8.30	39½
Kelly Talbert	$7.50	40
Gene Trimbell	$9.75	42½
Heidi Varney	$8.75	34¼
Kevin Wallace	$9.25	46

Instructions Prepare a form similar to the one that follows. Calculate regular earnings, overtime earnings, and gross earnings for each employee.

Employee	Total Hours	Pay Rate	Regular Earnings	Overtime Earnings	Gross Earnings
Clune, David	33½	$6.95	$232.83	– 0 –	$232.83

RETEACHING SECTION 1

Calculating Gross Earnings Accurate payroll records must be maintained for several reasons:

- To ensure that the employee salaries and wages are computed accurately.
- To ensure that the wages and salaries are paid to employees promptly.
- Because the business must comply with tax law provisions.

Give students extra practice in calculating gross earnings by making up several payroll examples and writing them on the chalkboard. Ask students who have learned the calculations to help those who have not yet mastered the various means of calculating gross earnings.

Payroll Deductions

Whether you work at Target, McDonald's, or CompUSA, your earnings and deductions are prepared in the same manner. In this section, you will learn how to compute employee-paid withholdings.

***What* You'll Learn**

- Why deductions are calculated and reported.
- How to calculate deductions required by the federal government.
- How to determine voluntary deductions.

***Why* It's Important**

To prepare the payroll accurately and to comply with the law, both mandatory and voluntary deductions must be calculated correctly.

KEY TERMS

deduction
allowance
401(k) plan

Computing Employee-Paid Withholdings

The first time you received a payroll check, you were probably surprised to see that the amount of the check was less than your gross earnings. Various amounts are taken out of gross earnings. An amount that is subtracted from gross earnings is called a **deduction**. Deductions include those required by law and those an employee wishes to have withheld from earnings.

Deductions Required by Law

An employer is required by law to withhold payroll taxes. These taxes include the federal income tax and the social security tax. In addition, most cities and states require employers to withhold city and state income tax.

Federal Income Tax. Most people pay the federal government a tax based on their annual income. To ensure that employees have the funds to pay their income taxes, employers are required to withhold a certain amount of money from each payroll check. The employer sends the money withheld to the federal government. The employer, thus, acts as a collection agent for the federal government.

The amount of income tax withheld is based on an estimate of the amount of income tax the employee will actually owe. The exact amount of income tax is determined when the employee prepares an income tax return. If too much money is withheld, the Internal Revenue Service (IRS) will refund the overpayment. If too little money is withheld, the employee pays the amount due when the income tax return is filed. To avoid penalties, an employee should have at least 90% of the actual tax liability deducted from his or her pay.

Form W-4. The amount withheld for federal income taxes depends on three factors:

(1) the employee's marital status
(2) the number of allowances claimed by the employee
(3) the employee's gross earnings

RESOURCE MANAGER

Reproducible Masters
- Lesson Plans
- Chapter Reviews and Working Papers (CRWP) TAE
- Demonstration Problems

Transparencies
- Section Focus Transparency
- Teaching Transparencies
- Source Document Transparencies
- Solution Transparencies

Multimedia
- ExamView CD-ROM
- Electronic Learning Center CD-ROM
- Interactive Lesson Planner CD-ROM
- Electronic Field Trips in Accounting

1 FOCUS

Introducing the Section

Now that students have learned how to calculate gross earnings, in this section they'll learn about deductions from earnings. They will calculate mandatory deductions for taxes, as well as voluntary deductions for items such as health plans and savings.

Section Concepts

- Why deductions are calculated and reported.
- How to calculate deductions required by the federal government.
- How to determine voluntary deductions.

Visual Learning

Section 2 Focus

Use **Transparency 12–4** to introduce section concepts.

BELL RINGER

Oral Exercise: Ask students to name part-time jobs they would like to do to earn money. What skills do they need to get the jobs? How much do the jobs pay? How is the pay determined (salary, hourly, commission)? How much take-home pay would they earn? L1

Concept Development: Computing Employee-Paid Withholdings

Discussion: Point out to students that some payroll deductions are required by law, while others are voluntary. Before explaining each deduction, describe the employer's role as a "collection agent" for federal, state, and local governments. Remind students that deductions are part of the total earnings of the employees. L1

2 TEACH

GUIDED PRACTICE

Reading Accounting

- Have students learn how to read tax tables by giving them several examples and having them give you the tax amount to withhold. L1

- Tax tables may be especially confusing to students whose first language is not English. If possible, obtain copies of tax information printed in your students' first language. ELL

Teaching Tips

To help students understand the concept of withholding, you may want to obtain the publication *Understanding Taxes*, available from the IRS, to share with your students.

Explain to students that the payroll tax money withheld from employees' earnings is deposited with the appropriate taxing agency either weekly or monthly depending on the amount of the payroll.

Try to obtain blank copies of Form W-4 and have students complete them in class. Discuss qualifications for dependents. Point out that each dependent claimed results in a specific decrease in the amount of taxes paid.

Visual Learning

Figure 12–3 Employee's Withholding Allowance Certificate—Form W-4

Use **Transparency 12–5** to discuss how to complete a Form W-4 to claim withholding allowances.

The first two items of information are found on Form W-4, the Employee's Withholding Allowance Certificate. Form W-4 is filled out by each employee when starting a job. A revised Form W-4 is filed if the employee's marital status or number of allowances changes. Employers keep a current Form W-4 on file for each employee.

Figure 12–3 shows the completed Form W-4 for Emily Kardos. As you can see, Form W-4 includes the employee's name, address, social security number, and marital status. In addition, the employee lists the number of allowances claimed (see line 4). An **allowance** reduces the amount of income tax to be withheld. The greater the number of allowances claimed by a taxpayer, the lower the amount of income tax withheld from earnings. Usually, a taxpayer is allowed one personal allowance and one allowance for each person the taxpayer supports, such as a child or an elderly parent.

Figure 12–3 Employee's Withholding Allowance Certificate—Form W-4

Cut here and give the certificate to your employer. Keep the top portion for your records.

Form **W-4** Department of the Treasury Internal Revenue Service | **Employee's Withholding Allowance Certificate** ► **For Privacy Act and Paperwork Reduction Act Notice, see reverse.** | OMB No. 1545-0010 20--

1 Type or print your first name and middle initial: Emily M. | Last Name: Kardos | **2** Your social security number: 201-46-8319

Home address (number and street or rural route): 809 East Main Street

City or town, state, and ZIP code: Sacramento, CA 94230

3 Marital Status: ☑ Single ☐ Married ☐ Married, but withhold at higher Single rate
Note: *If married, but legally separated, or spouse is a nonresident alien, check the Single box.*

4 Total number of allowances you are claiming (from line G above or from the Worksheets on back if they apply) . . . **4** 0

5 Additional amount, if any, you want deducted from each pay . . . **5** $

6 I claim exemption from withholding and I certify that I meet **ALL** of the following conditions for exemption:
- Last year I had a right to a refund of **ALL** federal income tax withheld because I had **NO** tax liability: **AND**
- This year I expect a refund of **ALL** Federal income tax withheld because I expect to have **NO** tax liability; **AND**
- This year if my income exceeds $500 and includes nonwage income, another person cannot claim me as a dependent.

If you meet all of the above conditions, enter the year effective and "EXEMPT" here . . . ► **6**

7 Are you a full-time student? (**Note:** Full-time students are not automatically exempt.) . . . **7** ☐ Yes ☑ No

Under penalty of perjury, I certify that I am entitled to the number of withholding allowances claimed on this certificate or entitled to claim exempt status.

Employee's signature ► *Emily M. Kardos* **Date** ► *January 3* 20 --

8 Employer's name and address (**Employer:** Complete 8 and 10 **only if sending to IRS**): Roadrunner Delivery Service, 155 Gateway Blvd., Sacramento, CA 94230 | **9** Office code (optional) | **10** Employee identification number: 31-8042398

In certain circumstances as defined in the tax laws, some employees do not pay federal income tax. An employee who does not pay federal income tax can be "exempt" from withholding if he or she:

- Did not have a federal income tax liability in the previous year.
- Expects no tax liability this year.
- Has income of $700 or less including nonwage income such as interest on a savings account.
- Cannot be claimed as a dependent on someone else's tax return.

If an employee writes "EXEMPT" on Form W-4, the employer will not withhold federal income taxes.

Tax Tables. An employee's gross earnings also affect the amount withheld for federal income taxes. Once gross earnings are calculated, most employers use tables supplied by the IRS to determine the amount of federal tax to withhold. **Figure 12–4** shows tables for single and married persons who are paid weekly. Other tax tables are available.

Let's use the tables to determine the tax withheld for Emily Kardos. Emily is single and claims no allowances. For the week ending June 30, she earned

COOPERATIVE LEARNING ACTIVITY

Jigsaw Divide students into groups of five persons each. Each member of the group learns one of the following methods of calculating earnings: salary, hourly wage, commission, salary plus commission or bonus, and overtime pay. Each person returns to the group and teaches the other members of the group what she or he has learned.

Assign Problem 12–10 on page 313. Have each student work independently to complete the exercise, but grade the students as a group.

SINGLE Persons—**WEEKLY** Payroll Period

If the wages are –		And the number of withholding allowances claimed is –										
At least	But less than	0	1	2	3	4	5	6	7	8	9	10
		The amount of income tax to be withheld is –										
$0	$55	0	0	0	0	0	0	0	0	0	0	0
55	60	1	0	0	0	0	0	0	0	0	0	0
60	65	2	0	0	0	0	0	0	0	0	0	0
65	70	2	0	0	0	0	0	0	0	0	0	0
70	75	3	0	0	0	0	0	0	0	0	0	0
75	80	4	0	0	0	0	0	0	0	0	0	0
80	85	5	0	0	0	0	0	0	0	0	0	0
85	90	5	0	0	0	0	0	0	0	0	0	0
90	95	6	0	0	0	0	0	0	0	0	0	0
95	100	7	0	0	0	0	0	0	0	0	0	0
100	105	8	0	0	0	0	0	0	0	0	0	0
105	110	8	1	0	0	0	0	0	0	0	0	0
110	115	9	2	0	0	0	0	0	0	0	0	0
115	120	10	2	0	0	0	0	0	0	0	0	0
120	125	11	3	0	0	0	0	0	0	0	0	0
125	130	11	4	0	0	0	0	0	0	0	0	0
130	135	12	5	0	0	0	0	0	0	0	0	0
135	140	13	5	0	0	0	0	0	0	0	0	0
140	145	14	6	0	0	0	0	0	0	0	0	0
145	150	14	7	0	0	0	0	0	0	0	0	0
150	155	15	8	0	0	0	0	0	0	0	0	0
155	160	16	8	1	0	0	0	0	0	0	0	0
160	165	17	9	1	0	0	0	0	0	0	0	0
165	170	17	10	2	0	0	0	0	0	0	0	0
170	175	18	11	3	0	0	0	0	0	0	0	0
175	180	19	11	4	0	0	0	0	0	0	0	0
180	185	20	12	4	0	0	0	0	0	0	0	0
185	190	20	13	5	0	0	0	0	0	0	0	0
190	195	21	14	6	0	0	0	0	0	0	0	0
195	200	22	14	7	0	0	0	0	0	0	0	0
200	210	23	15	8	0	0	0	0	0	0	0	0
210	220	25	17	9	2	0	0	0	0	0	0	0
220	230	26	18	11	3	0	0	0	0	0	0	0
230	240	28	20	12	5	0	0	0	0	0	0	0
240	250	29	21	14	6	0	0	0	0	0	0	0
250	260	31	23	15	8	0	0	0	0	0	0	0
260	270	32	24	17	9	2	0	0	0	0	0	0
270	280	34	26	18	11	3	0	0	0	0	0	0
280	290	35	27	20	12	5	0	0	0	0	0	0
290	300	37	29	21	14	6	0	0	0	0	0	0
300	310	38	30	23	15	8	0	0	0	0	0	0
310	320	40	32	24	17	9	1	0	0	0	0	0
320	330	41	33	26	18	11	3	0	0	0	0	0
330	340	43	35	27	20	12	4	0	0	0	0	0
340	350	44	36	29	21	14	6	0	0	0	0	0

MARRIED Persons—**WEEKLY** Payroll Period

If the wages are –		And the number of withholding allowances claimed is –										
At least	But less than	0	1	2	3	4	5	6	7	8	9	10
		The amount of income tax to be withheld is –										
$0	$125	0	0	0	0	0	0	0	0	0	0	0
125	130	1	0	0	0	0	0	0	0	0	0	0
130	135	1	0	0	0	0	0	0	0	0	0	0
135	140	2	0	0	0	0	0	0	0	0	0	0
140	145	3	0	0	0	0	0	0	0	0	0	0
145	150	4	0	0	0	0	0	0	0	0	0	0
150	155	4	0	0	0	0	0	0	0	0	0	0
155	160	5	0	0	0	0	0	0	0	0	0	0
160	165	6	0	0	0	0	0	0	0	0	0	0
165	170	7	0	0	0	0	0	0	0	0	0	0
170	175	7	0	0	0	0	0	0	0	0	0	0
175	180	8	0	0	0	0	0	0	0	0	0	0
180	185	9	1	0	0	0	0	0	0	0	0	0
185	190	10	2	0	0	0	0	0	0	0	0	0
190	195	10	3	0	0	0	0	0	0	0	0	0
195	200	11	3	0	0	0	0	0	0	0	0	0
200	210	12	5	0	0	0	0	0	0	0	0	0
210	220	14	6	0	0	0	0	0	0	0	0	0
220	230	15	8	0	0	0	0	0	0	0	0	0
230	240	17	9	1	0	0	0	0	0	0	0	0
240	250	18	11	3	0	0	0	0	0	0	0	0
250	260	20	12	4	0	0	0	0	0	0	0	0
260	270	21	14	6	0	0	0	0	0	0	0	0
270	280	23	15	7	0	0	0	0	0	0	0	0
280	290	24	17	9	1	0	0	0	0	0	0	0
290	300	26	18	10	3	0	0	0	0	0	0	0
300	310	27	20	12	4	0	0	0	0	0	0	0
310	320	29	21	13	6	0	0	0	0	0	0	0
320	330	30	23	15	7	0	0	0	0	0	0	0
330	340	32	24	16	9	1	0	0	0	0	0	0

Figure 12–4 Internal Revenue Service Tax Tables

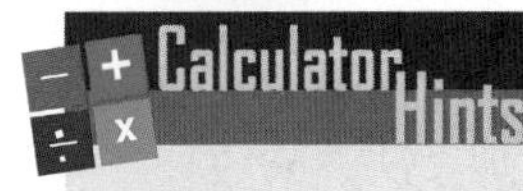

Calculating Gross Earnings

To calculate gross earnings:

- multiply the pay rate by the hours worked,
- place that amount in memory by pressing M+,
- then multiply the regular rate by 1.5 and the number of overtime hours,
- press MR,
- then + to find the total.

2 TEACH (Cont'd.)

Visual Learning

Figure 12–4 Internal Revenue Service Tax Tables

Using **Transparency 12–6**, show students how to use the tax tables. Have students determine withholding for several different situations.

Teaching Tip

Explain to students that employees can adjust their withholding at any time by filing a new W-4 form with their employer's payroll department.

Thinking Algebraically

Calculating Gross Earnings: Have students write a formula for calculating gross earnings for an hourly worker earning $6 an hour plus overtime at 1.5 times the regular rate. (For example, gross earnings = $6x + [(1.5 \times 6) \times y]$ where x equals regular hours worked and y equals overtime hours.) L1

Math Review for Accounting Photocopy appropriate *Activity Sheets* for students who need additional practice in basic math.

Math Skill Builder Activity

Calculating Gross Earnings Have students calculate the gross earnings for Joyce Hogan, who worked 48 hours at $6.50/hr. using these steps:

1. Multiply the pay rate by the hours worked. ($6.50 × 40 hrs. = $260.00)
2. Place that amount in memory by pressing M+.
3. Multiply the regular rate by 1.5 and the number of overtime hours. ($6.50 × 1.5 = $9.75 × 8 = $78)
4. Press MR.
5. Then press + to find the total. ($338.00)

2 TEACH (Cont'd.)

Teaching Tips

Discuss procedures for paying personal income, social security, and Medicare taxes.

Mention the procedure for securing a social security number by filling out a Form SS-5.

When discussing social security and Medicare taxes, emphasize that these taxes are not options for either the employee or the employer. You may also want to discuss the role the U.S. Congress plays in setting social security and Medicare tax rates and the maximum earnings on which taxes are to be withheld.

All employees begin paying social security and Medicare taxes at the beginning of each tax year.

Discuss any payroll taxes imposed by your local and state governments.

Demonstration Problem Step-by-Step Practice

Use demonstration problem 12–4 to give students practice in calculating social security and Medicare taxes.

$243. This amount falls between $240 and $250 on the tax table for single persons. Reading across this line to the column for zero withholding allowances, you find that $29 is withheld from Emily's gross earnings for federal income taxes.

Social Security Tax. In addition to federal income tax, employers also collect social security taxes for the federal government. The present social security system was established by the Federal Insurance Contributions Act (FICA) in 1935. Social security taxes are therefore often referred to as FICA taxes. The FICA taxes finance programs that provide income to certain individuals:

1. The old-age and disability insurance programs provide income to retired and disabled persons and their dependent children.
2. The survivors' benefits program provides income to the spouse and dependent children of a deceased worker.
3. The Medicare program provides health insurance benefits for the elderly.

ACCOUNTING *Flashbacks*

FINANCIAL RECORDS

The ancient Egyptians wrote on an early form of paper known as papyrus. The Zenon Papyri are the oldest complete set of financial records, dated to 250 BC.

The FICA taxes are exact taxes in that, unlike the federal income tax, they do not involve estimation and are not affected by allowances or marital status. The FICA tax rates are set by Congress, and can be changed at any time. Most employees are subject to FICA taxes, even those who are exempt from federal income taxes.

There are two FICA taxes: social security and Medicare. Each tax is separately recorded on payroll documents. The tax rates are as follows:

Social security tax	6.20%
Medicare tax	1.45%
Total FICA taxes	7.65%

The social security tax is deducted from each employee's earnings until the maximum taxable earnings amount for the year is reached. This amount increases each year. For 2002, the maximum taxable earnings amount is $84,900. Therefore the maximum amount of social security tax that can be withheld from an employee in one year is $5,263.80 ($84,900 × .062). There is no maximum taxable earnings amount for the Medicare tax. For example, Lisa Gustavson earns $87,000 per year as a manager at a CPA firm. The $6,525.30 in FICA taxes withheld from her earnings is calculated as follows:

	Earnings Subject to Tax		Tax Rate		Tax
Social security tax	$84,900	×	.062	=	$5,263.80
Medicare tax	87,000	×	.0145	=	1,261.50
Total withheld					$6,525.30

Key Points

Calculation of FICA Taxes

Social security tax 6.2% (.062) of annual gross earnings up to $84,900.

Medicare tax 1.45% (.0145) of gross annual earnings.

State and Local Income Taxes. Most states and cities tax the earnings of the people who live or work within their boundaries. In some states and cities, the tax rates are set as a percentage of gross earnings, like social security taxes. In others, the amounts to be deducted are indicated on tables similar to the ones used for federal income tax.

INTERDISCIPLINARY CONNECTIONS ACTIVITY

Civics Using the Internet or the classified section of a major newspaper (e.g., *The Wall Street Journal, Business Journal*), have students look for job opportunities with the Internal Revenue Service. What type of jobs are currently available? What are the education requirements? What are the expected duties? Is the benefit or salary package mentioned? As a class, discuss the findings and talk about the advantages and disadvantages of working for the IRS.

Voluntary Deductions

Most employers agree to deduct other amounts from their employees' payroll check to accommodate the wishes of the employees. Once an employee requests that deductions be made, they are withheld from each payroll check until the employee notifies the employer to stop. Common voluntary deductions include:

- union dues
- health insurance payments
- life insurance payments
- pension and other retirement contributions
- credit union deposits and payments
- U.S. savings bonds
- charitable contributions.

A popular payroll deduction is a contribution to a **401(k) plan**. An employee contributes a portion of gross earnings to an account in the 401(k) plan. The employee does not pay income tax on the contributed earnings. In other words, taxable income is reduced by the amount of the contribution. The 401(k) contribution and earnings on the contribution are not taxed until the money is withdrawn from the plan, usually after age 59½. In some 401(k) plans, employers make matching and profit-sharing contributions to their employees' accounts.

Angelo Cappelli, a graphic artist, earns $644 each week and contributes $75 to his 401(k) account. Angelo will pay income tax on $569 ($644 – $75). He will not pay income tax on his $75 contribution until it is withdrawn from his 401(k) account.

CONNECT TO . . . CIVICS

The Internal Revenue Service is the number-one employer of accountants in the world. Sixty-three district offices across the United States hire Revenue Agents, Revenue Officers, Special Agents, Tax Auditors, and Computer Specialists. Together, they use their accounting backgrounds in reviewing tax returns and investigating tax fraud.

ANALYZING FINANCIAL REPORTS

Analyzing Employee Productivity

The cost of wages and benefits is often one of a company's largest expenses. Before hiring additional employees, managers and owners carefully calculate whether another person will contribute to the overall profitability of the company.

One measure of profitability is the average sales dollars generated by each employee. This measure is calculated by dividing the total revenue by the number of all employees.

$$\frac{\textbf{Total Revenue}}{\textbf{Number of Employees}} = \textbf{Sales per Employee}$$

For example, in a company with total revenue of $1,480,000 and 20 employees, sales per employee are $74,000. Calculating this measure of profitability from period to period or from one part of a company to another allows an owner to see changes in employee productivity. If sales per employee increase or decrease greatly, the owner would want to learn why.

▶ Analyze the Report:

Use the income statement for Roadrunner Delivery Service on page 206 to answer these questions.

1. Assume that Roadrunner Delivery Service has two employees, including the owner. What is the monthly revenue per employee?
2. Suppose Maria Sanchez hires two more delivery people. The revenue for the next month increases to $5,400.00. How has the productivity per employee changed?

2 TEACH (Cont'd.)

Teaching Tips

When introducing voluntary deductions, emphasize that the employer decides which deductions will be included in the payroll system. Common voluntary deductions are for credit union savings or payments, savings bonds, health or life insurance premiums, charitable contributions, union dues, and so on.

You may want to obtain a kit of teaching materials about the financing of social security and how benefits are paid. The Social Security Teachers Kit is available for download at no charge from the Social Security Administration Web site at www.ssa.gov/teacher/teacher.html.

Research: Have students who work part-time check out the voluntary deductions their employer offers. Have students who do not work choose a local company and research the voluntary deductions it offers. Ask students to share their findings with the class. L1

ANALYZING FINANCIAL REPORTS

Roadrunner Delivery Service
155 Gateway Blvd.
Sacramento, CA 94230

Analyze the Report (Answers)

1. Monthly revenue per employee = $2,650 ÷ 2 = $1,325
2. The new monthly revenue per employee is $1,350 ($5,400 ÷ 4). The increase in revenue per employee indicates an increase in employee productivity because the employees are generating more revenue per person.

CHAPTER 12
SECTION 2, PAGES 293–298

3 ASSESS

Thinking Critically (Answers)

1. Federal income and FICA taxes, possibly city and state income taxes.
2. Employee's marital status, number of exemptions claimed, gross earnings.

Computing in the Business World (Answer)

$21,240.50

Problem 12–2 (Answers)

Cleary, Kevin: S, 0, $155.60, $9.65, $2.26, $16, $3.11, $31.02, $124.58
Halley, James: S, 1, $184.10, $11.41, $2.67, $12, $3.68, $29.76, $154.34
Hong, Kim: S, 0, $204.65, $12.69, $2.97, $23, $4.09, $42.75, $161.90
Jackson, Marvin: M, 1, $216.40, $13.42, $3.14, $6, $4.33, $26.89, $189.51
Sell, Richard: M, 2, $196.81, $12.20, $2.85, $0, $3.94, $18.99, $177.82
Totals: $957.56, $59.37, $13.89, $57, $19.15, $149.41, $808.15

Problem 12–3 (Answers)

1. Medicare $4.57
2. Social Security $19.53
3. Federal Income Tax $32.00

Chapter Reviews and Working Papers Refer students to the Chapter 12 workbook pages to answer *Check Your Understanding* activities.

4 CLOSE

Section Wrap-Up

Compute Salary Expenses: Have students compute the total annual salary expense incurred for the five new sales consultants in the "Computing in the Business World" activity. ($115,000)

SECTION 2 Check Your Understanding

Now that you have studied this section, complete the following questions and problems.

Thinking Critically

1. Which taxes are required to be withheld from employees' pay?
2. What three factors determine the amount of federal income tax withheld each pay period?

Computing in the Business World

As the president of Creative Craft Memory Books, you have decided to add five new sales consultants to your sales force. You offer these sales consultants a gross salary of $23,000 each, but the consultants will not take home $23,000. Calculate the FICA taxes to be withheld from each consultant's gross pay. What remains of their gross pay after you deduct FICA taxes?

Problem 12–2 Determining Taxes on Gross Earnings

Information related to the just-completed pay period of MegaCom Computer Upgrades is provided in the chart below. Determine the amounts to be withheld from each employee's gross earnings for FICA and income taxes. It is a weekly pay period, so use the tables on page 295 to determine the amount of federal income tax to be withheld. The state income tax is 2% of gross earnings. The social security tax rate is 6.2%, and the Medicare tax rate is 1.45%. Use the format shown in your working papers.

Employee	Marital Status	Allowances	Gross Earnings
Cleary, Kevin	S	0	$155.60
Halley, James	S	1	184.10
Hong, Kim	S	0	204.65
Jackson, Marvin	M	1	216.40
Sell, Richard	M	2	196.81
Total			$957.56

Problem 12–3 Analyzing a Source Document

Examine the following partially completed payroll check stub. The employee, Melanie Galvin, is single and claims one allowance.

What amount should be deducted for:

1. Medicare tax?
2. Social Security tax?
3. Federal Income tax?

Employee Pay Statement
Detach and retain this statement. **260**

Period Ending	Earnings			Deductions							Net Pay
	Regular	Overtime	Total	Social Security Tax	Med. Tax	Federal Income Tax	State Income Tax	Hosp. Ins.	Other	Total	
1/15/20--	315.00		315.00								

RETEACHING SECTION 2

Explaining Exemptions Students sometimes need reinforcement to understand the concept of exemptions. Explain that an exemption is an allowance that reduces your tax liability. In addition to having an allowance for yourself, you are entitled to additional allowances for each person to whom you provide more than one-half of their support during the year. The more exemptions (allowances) you have, the lower your taxes.

Payroll Records

In the previous sections you learned how to calculate gross earnings and deductions. Now you will learn how to compute net pay, prepare the payroll records for each period, and prepare payroll checks. Whether a business has many employees, like the Boeing Corporation, or a small staff, like a veterinarian's office, it is essential that the payroll be prepared on time and accurately.

What You'll Learn

- The purpose of a payroll register.
- How to prepare a payroll register.
- How to prepare a payroll check.
- The purpose of an employee's earnings record.
- How to prepare an employee's earnings record.

Why It's Important

To comply with federal and state laws, payroll records must be kept accurately.

KEY TERMS

payroll register
net pay
direct deposit
employee's earnings record
accumulated earnings

Preparing the Payroll Register

Federal and state laws require businesses to keep accurate payroll records. To help meet these requirements, businesses use a payroll register. The **payroll register** is a form that summarizes information about employees' earnings for each pay period. Let's learn how to prepare payroll registers.

Figure 12–5 shows the payroll register for Roadrunner. As you can see, the payroll register lists each employee's I.D. number, name, marital status, and the number of allowances claimed. Refer to **Figure 12–5** as you read the descriptions of the payroll register.

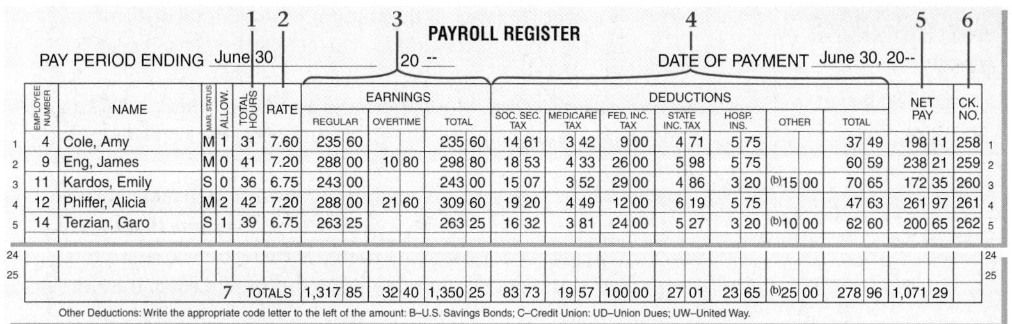

PAYROLL REGISTER

PAY PERIOD ENDING June 30 20 -- DATE OF PAYMENT June 30, 20--

EMPLOYEE NUMBER	NAME	MAR. STATUS	ALLOW.	TOTAL HOURS	RATE	EARNINGS REGULAR	EARNINGS OVERTIME	EARNINGS TOTAL	SOC. SEC. TAX	MEDICARE TAX	FED. INC. TAX	STATE INC. TAX	HOSP. INS.	OTHER	DEDUCTIONS TOTAL	NET PAY	CK. NO.
4	Cole, Amy	M	1	31	7.60	235 60		235 60	14 61	3 42	9 00	4 71	5 75		37 49	198 11	258
9	Eng, James	M	0	41	7.20	288 00	10 80	298 80	18 53	4 33	26 00	5 98	5 75		60 59	238 21	259
11	Kardos, Emily	S	0	36	6.75	243 00		243 00	15 07	3 52	29 00	4 86	3 20	(b)15 00	70 65	172 35	260
12	Phiffer, Alicia	M	2	42	7.20	288 00	21 60	309 60	19 20	4 49	12 00	6 19	5 75		47 63	261 97	261
14	Terzian, Garo	S	1	39	6.75	263 25		263 25	16 32	3 81	24 00	5 27	3 20	(b)10 00	62 60	200 65	262
			7		TOTALS	1,317 85	32 40	1,350 25	83 73	19 57	100 00	27 01	23 65	(b)25 00	278 96	1,071 29	

Other Deductions: Write the appropriate code letter to the left of the amount: B–U.S. Savings Bonds; C–Credit Union: UD–Union Dues; UW–United Way.

Figure 12–5 Completed Payroll Register

RESOURCE MANAGER

Reproducible Masters
- Lesson Plans
- Chapter Reviews and Working Papers (CRWP) TAE
- Demonstration Problems

Transparencies
- Section Focus Transparency
- Teaching Transparencies
- Source Document Transparencies
- Solution Transparencies

Multimedia
- Exam*View* CD-ROM
- Electronic Learning Center CD-ROM
- Interactive Lesson Planner CD-ROM
- Electronic Field Trips in Accounting

1 FOCUS

Introducing the Section

In this section students learn how to prepare a payroll register, write payroll checks, and complete earnings records.

Section Concepts

- The purpose of a payroll register.
- How to prepare a payroll register.
- How to prepare a payroll check.
- The purpose of an employee's earnings record.
- How to prepare an employee's earnings record.

Visual Learning

Section 3 Focus

Use **Transparency** 12–7 to introduce section concepts.

BELL RINGER

Critical Thinking: Ask students how temporary employees affect payroll records. (Temps may not be allowed payroll deductions for savings, health insurance, or other voluntary deductions.) L1

Concept Development: Preparing the Payroll Register

Discussion: Explain that a payroll register is completed for each pay period. All payroll information for a pay period is included in the payroll register, which is the source document for journalizing payroll entries. L1

Visual Learning

Figure 12–5 Completed Payroll Register

Use **Transparency 12–8** to explain the information that is recorded in a payroll register.

CHAPTER 12
SECTION 3, PAGES 299–304

2 TEACH
GUIDED PRACTICE

Reading Accounting

• Knowing how to set up a form to make financial information easier to read is an excellent skill for students to acquire. Have students study the earnings record in Figure 12–7 and identify how the form makes data easier to read. (Columns are clearly separated, amounts are vertically aligned to avoid confusion of dollars and cents, commas are used to indicate thousands, horizontal rules separate information by date.) L1

Teaching Tips

Remind students that information recorded in a payroll register is not posted and, thus, does not appear in the accounting records. Only journal entries are posted and create an accounting record.

Have students compute net pay based on the source document in Problem 12–3 on page 298.

Demonstration Problem Step-by-Step Practice

Use demonstration problem 12–5 to give students practice in filling out a payroll register.

ACCOUNTING TIPS

Social Security Numbers

Under the Tax Reform Act of 1986, most individuals over the age of five should have a social security number. A person has the same social security number for life. This number is used when reporting an employee's earnings to state and federal governments.

1. *Total Hours Column.* Regular and overtime hours from the employee's time card are added together, and the total is entered in this column.
2. *Rate Column.* This column shows the employee's current rate of pay, found on the employee's earnings record.
3. *Earnings Section.* The earnings section is divided into three columns: regular, overtime, and total earnings. To complete these columns, the payroll clerk multiplies the hours worked by the employee's regular hourly rate or, when applicable, overtime hourly rate.

Employee 4, Amy Cole, worked 31 hours. Her regular hourly rate is $7.60. Amy earned $235.60 (31 × $7.60) for the week. Since there are no overtime hours, regular and total earnings are the same.

Alicia Phiffer, Employee 12, worked 2 overtime hours in addition to 40 regular hours. Her regular hourly rate is $7.20. Her overtime hourly rate is $10.80 ($7.20 × 1.5). Her regular earnings are $288.00 (40 × $7.20) and her overtime earnings are $21.60 (2 × $10.80). Her total earnings are $309.60 ($288.00 + $21.60).

4. *Deductions Section.* The illustrated payroll register has seven deduction columns. The number of deduction columns, however, varies among businesses depending on the specific needs of each business. In the illustration, columns are provided for the deductions required by law—FICA taxes (social security and Medicare), federal income tax, and state income tax. Columns are also provided for voluntary deductions. Certain voluntary deductions taken by many employees on a regular basis will usually have their own columns, such as the column shown in the illustration for hospital insurance. Deductions taken less frequently are often placed in a column titled "Other." In the illustration these deductions include credit union, union dues, savings bonds, and charitable contributions. Finally, a column is provided for the total deductions of each employee.

Look at the deductions for Garo Terzian, Employee 14. Garo's deductions include the taxes required by law. He also has two voluntary deductions, $3.20 for hospital insurance and $10.00, shown in the Other column, for U.S. Savings Bonds. The total deductions for Garo are $62.60 as shown in the "Total" column.

Key Points

Net Pay

Gross (total) earnings minus total deductions equal net pay.

5. *Net Pay Column.* **Net pay** is the amount left after total deductions are subtracted from gross earnings. The net pay for Garo Terzian is $200.65.
6. *Check Number Column.* Most employees are paid by check. After the payroll checks are prepared, the check numbers are recorded in this column.
7. *Column Totals.* Each amount column is totaled, and the totals are entered on the last line of the payroll register. To ensure that there are no mathematical errors, subtract the Total Deductions column total from Total Earnings column total. The result should equal the Net Pay column total.

CRITICAL THINKING ACTIVITY

Income Tax Systems Explain to students that the U.S. federal income system is a progressive tax system, which means that as taxable income increases so does the tax rate and the total amount of taxes paid. Have students research the current U.S. system and a different tax method, such as a flat tax. Ask students to evaluate the two systems and write a short paper (one to two pages) outlining the advantages and disadvantages of each system. Have students make a recommendation about which tax system they prefer and give reasons for their recommendations.

Preparing Payroll Checks

Once the accuracy of the payroll register is verified, a payroll check is prepared for each employee. Most businesses pay their employees by check as a means of cash control. When a company has only a few employees, payroll checks are written from the company's regular checking account. Companies with many employees have a separate checking account for payroll.

When a separate payroll checking account is used, funds are transferred to this account each pay period. A check for the total net pay amount is written from the company's regular checking account and deposited in the payroll checking account. Then, individual payroll checks are issued to employees from the payroll account.

The payroll register is the source of information for preparing the payroll checks. Along with a payroll check, each employee is given a written or printed explanation showing how the employee's net pay is calculated. This explanation is provided on a stub attached to the payroll check. **Figure 12–6** shows a typical payroll check and stub. Notice that for Emily Kardos, the amounts on the stub are the same as the amounts in the payroll register. After each payroll check is written, the check number is recorded in the payroll register.

Employees are not always paid by check. The accountant reviews the records to determine methods of dissemination of payroll funds, for example, direct deposit, and mail. With **direct deposit**, the net pay is deposited in the employee's personal bank account by the employer. No payroll check is prepared. The employee does, however, receive a printed record of the payroll calculation. Direct deposits are made through electronic funds transfer. With this system, the employer informs the employee's bank of the amount to be deposited.

Roadrunner Delivery Service 260
155 Gateway Blvd.
Sacramento, CA 94230 63-947/670

Date June 30 *20* --

Pay to the Order of Emily Kardos $ 172.35

One hundred seventy-two and 35/100 *Dollars*

American National Bank
SACRAMENTO, CALIFORNIA

Maria Sanchez

⑆067009471⑆ 3939 043 417⑈ 260

Employee Pay Statement
Detach and retain this statement. 260

Period Ending	Earnings			Deductions							Net Pay
	Regular	Overtime	Total	Social Security Tax	Med. Tax	Federal Income Tax	State Income Tax	Hosp. Ins.	Other	Total	
6/30/20--	243.00		243.00	15.07	3.52	29.00	4.86	3.20	15.00	70.65	172.35

Figure 12–6 Completed Payroll Check and Stub

International ACCOUNTING

Voltage Power

Accountants who travel frequently and carry laptop computers should be aware of the voltage used in the countries of their destination. Power in the United States is 110V, but in most other countries it is 220V.

2 TEACH (Cont'd.)

Concept Development: Preparing Payroll Checks

Discussion: Explain why employers often use separate checking accounts for issuing payroll checks. Discuss the advantages of this procedure (include the control of cash).

Ask students who work whether they have the option of having their paychecks deposited directly to their checking accounts. Ask students to think of advantages of direct deposit for the employer, the employee, and the bank.

Visual Learning

Figure 12–6 Completed Payroll Check and Stub

Use **Transparency 12–9** to explain how a paycheck is prepared and the information included on the paycheck and stub.

Teaching Tip

Have students compare the column headings on the pay stub with the column headings in the payroll register on page 299.

Strategies for Teaching International Accounting

To enrich study of international accounting, refer to the additional critical thinking activities in the booklet.

Teaching International ACCOUNTING

What Does a Voltage Adaptor Look Like? Bring in a voltage adaptor to demonstrate what one looks like and how it works with laptop computers or even portable hair dryers. Ask students what other uses travelers to foreign countries might have for voltage adaptors. Have students research where you can purchase adaptors and how much they cost.

2 TEACH (Cont'd.)

Concept Development: The Employee's Earnings Record

Discussion: Explain to students that the employees' earnings records are prepared primarily to assist in the preparation of reports required for employees, government taxing authorities, and stockholders. L1

Visual Learning

Figure 12–7 Employee's Earnings Record

Use **Transparency 12–10** to guide students through the information included on an employee's earnings record.

Teaching Tips

Emphasize the need for accurate, up-to-date information for preparing payroll records.

Have students compare the amounts in the earnings record with the payroll register (page 299) and the payroll check and stub (page 301).

ACCOUNTING TIPS

Work Experience

Research shows that employers would rather hire people who can do things rather than people who know about things. If you can get experience doing anything in the accounting field, you'd have a better chance of getting a job than an applicant who has taken the same classes as you have but doesn't have your work experience.

The Employee's Earnings Record

In addition to the payroll register, an employer must also keep an **employee's earnings record** for each employee. This record contains all of the payroll information related to an employee. **Figure 12–7** shows an example of an employee's earnings record. The earnings record has the same amount columns that appear on the payroll register. An additional column for the employee's accumulated earnings is also provided. **Accumulated earnings** are the employee's year-to-date gross earnings, or the employee's gross earnings from the beginning of the year through the end of each pay period. The accumulated earnings for Emily Kardos as of June 30 are computed by adding her gross earnings for the pay period just completed to her accumulated earnings for the previous pay period as follows:

Gross Earnings for Pay Period Just Completed	+	Accumulated Earnings for Previous Pay Period	=	Accumulated Earnings for Pay Period Just Completed
$243.00	+	$4,178.60	=	$4,421.60

Businesses keep employee's earnings records on a quarterly basis. This makes it easier to complete government reports that are required each

This amount was carried forward from the previous quarter's record.

EMPLOYEE'S EARNINGS RECORD FOR QUARTER ENDING June 30, 20--

Kardos (Last Name) Emily (First) M (Initial)   EMPLOYEE NO. 11   MARITAL STATUS S   ALLOWANCES 0
809 East Main Street (Address)   POSITION Delivery Driver
Sacramento, CA 94230   RATE OF PAY 6.75   SOC. SEC. NO. 201-46-8319

PAY PERIOD		EARNINGS			DEDUCTIONS							NET PAY	ACCUMULATED EARNINGS
NO.	ENDED	REGULAR	OVERTIME	TOTAL	SOC. SEC. TAX	MEDICARE TAX	FED. INC. TAX	STATE INC. TAX	HOSP. INS.	OTHER	TOTAL		1,490 39
1	4/07/--	199 13		199 13	12 35	2 89	22 00	3 98	3 20	(B) 15 00	59 42	139 71	1,689 52
2	4/14/--	205 88		205 88	12 76	2 99	23 00	4 12	3 20		46 07	159 81	1,895 40
3	4/21/--	270 00	30 38	300 38	18 62	4 36	38 00	6 01	3 20		70 19	230 19	2,195 78
4	4/28/--	222 75		222 75	13 81	3 23	26 00	4 46	3 20		50 70	172 05	2,418 53
5	5/05/--	229 50		229 50	14 23	3 33	26 00	4 59	3 20	(B) 15 00	66 35	163 15	2,648 03
6	5/12/--	162 00		162 00	10 04	2 35	17 00	3 24	3 20		35 83	126 17	2,810 03
7	5/19/--	256 50		256 50	15 90	3 72	31 00	5 13	3 20		58 95	197 55	3,066 53
8	5/26/--	270 00	20 25	290 25	18 00	4 21	37 00	5 81	3 20		68 22	222 03	3,356 78
9	6/02/--	204 19		204 19	12 66	2 96	23 00	4 08	3 20	(B) 15 00	60 90	143 29	3,560 97
10	6/09/--	212 63		212 63	13 18	3 08	25 00	4 25	3 20		48 71	163 92	3,773 60
11	6/16/--	189 00		189 00	11 72	2 74	20 00	3 78	3 20		41 44	147 56	3,962 60
12	6/23/--	216 00		216 00	13 39	3 13	25 00	4 32	3 20		49 04	166 96	4,178 60
13	6/30/--	243 00		243 00	15 07	3 52	29 00	4 86	3 20	(B) 15 00	70 65	172 35	4,421 60
QUARTERLY TOTALS		2,880 58	50 63	2,931 21	181 73	42 51	342 00	58 63	41 60	60 00	726 47	2,204 74	

Other Deductions: B—U.S. Savings Bonds; C—Credit Union; UD—Union Dues; UW—United Way.

Figure 12–7 Employee's Earnings Record

This amount will be carried forward to the next quarter's record.

MEETING SPECIAL NEEDS

Students with Visual Impairments Students with visual impairments may have difficulty interpreting and using accounting records such as the payroll register. Discuss the column headings with students to ensure they understand where the information comes from and how the amounts are calculated. Be sure students see the relationship between the payroll register (Figure 12–5), the payroll check and stub (Figure 12–6), and an employee's earnings record (Figure 12–7).

quarter. At the end of a quarter, the amount columns on each employee's earnings record are totaled. The final amount in the Accumulated Earnings column is carried forward to the top of the employee's earnings record for the next quarter, (refer to **Figure 12–7**).

As you can see from this chapter, preparing payroll is time consuming and detail oriented. A mistake that is not promptly detected and corrected can mean hours of rework. To reduce simple mathematical errors and to improve productivity, many businesses use computers and special software to prepare payroll. In a computerized system, the computer:

- performs all the payroll calculations
- prepares and prints the payroll register
- prints the payroll checks and stubs
- maintains the employee's earnings records

Managerial Implications for Payroll Accounting

Payroll procedures and records must comply with state, federal, and local laws. Withholding amounts must be accurately computed and care should be taken that necessary reports are prepared on time.

Wages and salaries form a large part of the expenses of a business. Thus, an adequate set of payroll records is essential as an aid to management in controlling expenses. These records help pinpoint the labor cost for each area of the business by showing management exactly what amounts have been spent. These records also indicate how much of the amount spent was for overtime. Although overtime is fully justified in many cases, it may also be a sign of inefficiency. Large or frequent expenditures for overtime should therefore be investigated by management. To prevent errors or fraud, management should make sure that the payroll records are audited carefully and that payroll procedures are evaluated periodically.

A MATTER OF ETHICS

Payroll Information

Payroll clerks have access to some very personal information about employees, such as rate of pay and marital status. Imagine that you're the payroll clerk for a clothing store like The Gap. Your friend Janet, who also works at the store, is interested in one of the sales clerks. She wants you to find out how much money he makes and also if he's married.

Ethical Decision Making:

- What are the ethical issues?
- What are the alternatives?
- Who are the affected parties?
- How do the alternatives affect the parties?
- What would you do?

2 TEACH (Cont'd.)

Concept Development: Managerial Implications for Payroll Accounting

Discussion: Point out to students that payroll costs are regularly reviewed by a company's managers. Some managers use a percentage of sales as a means of evaluating payroll costs. For example, the manager may have determined that, in the past, payroll costs were generally about 6 percent of revenue. If payroll begins to exceed that amount, the manager may determine ways to cut payroll costs, such as downsizing or not hiring additional staff when an employee leaves. L1

Critical Thinking: Have students discuss how current unemployment rates and the condition of the economy affect an employer's payroll costs. (With low unemployment, employees may have to pay higher wages, which also increases their taxes. With high unemployment, wages tend to remain the same or decrease. If the economy is booming, employers tend to be more optimistic and hire people, thus adding to payroll costs. If the economy is slow, employers tend to be reluctant to hire.) L3

Strategies for Teaching Ethics in Accounting

Photocopy the Chapter 12 *Student Activity Sheet* for students. Answers are also provided in the booklet.

Teaching A MATTER OF ETHICS

Payroll Information Point out that companies have a responsibility to employees to keep some information confidential. Give students the definition of *confidentiality*: "The requirement that information acquired in the course of work be protected and not be disclosed without the legal or professional responsibility to do so." Have students explain the concept of confidentiality as related to the accounting profession.

3 ASSESS

Thinking Critically (Answers)

1. Net pay is deposited directly into an employee's personal bank account. No paycheck is prepared, but the employee receives a record of earnings and amounts withheld for taxes and other deductions.
2. A payroll register summarizes payroll information for all employees. An earnings record is kept for each employee.

Analyzing Accounting (Answers)

Answers will vary. The graph shows that over the last year payroll has steadily increased with little change in revenue. During the first year, revenue increased dramatically with very little change in payroll. This seems to indicate that revenue is not dependent upon payroll being at its highest level, so it can probably be reduced. Further analysis would be necessary to find the actual causes of the variation in revenue.

Problem 12-4 (Answer)

Check number 79, net pay $263.94

Chapter Reviews and Working Papers Refer students to the Chapter 12 workbook pages to answer *Check Your Understanding* activities.

4 CLOSE

Section Wrap-Up

Oral Discussion: Ask students to describe the information recorded in the payroll register and the source of that information. L1

SECTION 3 Check Your Understanding

Now that you have studied this section, complete the following questions and problems.

Thinking Critically

1. Describe the direct deposit process.
2. What is the difference between a payroll register and an employee's earnings record?

Analyzing Accounting

While reviewing payroll records from the past three years for Sports Junction, an athletic supply store, you notice that the increasing payroll cost could be holding down overall company profits. Review the graph comparing the cost of payroll with the revenue realized. Make a recommendation to the management of Sports Junction about the salary levels. Do you recommend downsizing to increase profit?

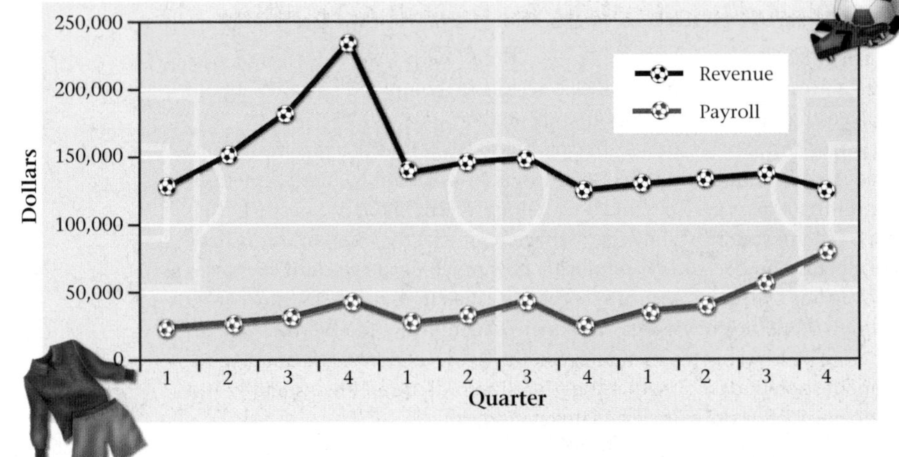

Problem 12–4 Preparing a Payroll Check

Use the information on the payroll register for Heather's Dance School and the form in the working papers to prepare a payroll check for Janice Burns for the week ending March 23, 20—.

PAYROLL REGISTER

PAY PERIOD ENDING March 23 20 -- DATE OF PAYMENT March 23, 20--

	EMPLOYEE NUMBER	NAME	MAR. STATUS	ALLOW.	TOTAL HOURS	RATE	EARNINGS REGULAR	EARNINGS OVERTIME	EARNINGS TOTAL	DEDUCTIONS SOC. SEC. TAX	MEDICARE TAX	FED. INC. TAX	STATE INC. TAX	HOSP. INS.	OTHER	DEDUCTIONS TOTAL	NET PAY	CK. NO.	
1	18	Burns, Janice	S	1	42	7.80	312 00	23 40	335 40	20 79	4 86	35 00	6 71	4 10	—	71 46	263 94	79	1
2																			2

RETEACHING SECTION 3

Prepare Payroll Registers Review the process with students. (The first step is to make sure the payroll register is complete with each employee's I.D. number, name, marital status, and number of allowances.)

- Enter the hours worked and the pay rate.
- Compute and enter earnings.
- Compute and enter deductions and net pay.
- Enter the check number.
- After all entries are made, total the columns.

CHAPTER 12 SUMMARY

KEY CONCEPTS

1. Federal and state laws require employers to keep accurate records of all payroll information. Most employers have a payroll system to ensure that employees are paid on time and that their payroll checks and payroll records are accurate.
2. Gross earnings may be calculated by various methods including:
   - salary,
   - hourly wage,
   - commission,
   - overtime pay, or
   - a combination of these methods.
3. Some employees who work more than 40 hours in a week are paid overtime. Usually the overtime rate is 1½ times the regular rate of pay.

Regular Hourly Rate				Overtime Hourly Rate
$8.20	×	1.5	=	$12.30

4. Some deductions from gross earnings are required by law. Other deductions are voluntary.

Deductions Required By Law	Voluntary Deductions
federal income tax	union dues
social security tax	insurance payments
medicare tax	401(k) plans
city and state tax	charitable contributions
	other retirement-related contributions

5. Form W-4 is used to determine federal income tax withholding.
6. Payroll Deductions
   - Federal income tax withholding is determined by tables.
   - Social security tax rate is 6.2% (.062) of gross earnings.
   - Medicare tax rate is 1.45% (.0145) of gross earnings.
   - State income tax is determined by each state.
   - Voluntary deductions are agreed to by employer and employees.
7. A payroll register, prepared for each pay period, summarizes the payroll information for all employees.
8. The employee's earnings record contains all of the payroll information, including earnings and deductions, for an employee for each period.
9. Gross pay is the amount that an employee earns before deductions.
10. Net pay is the amount of money actually received by an employee.
    Gross Pay − Total Payroll Deductions = Net Pay
11. Many businesses use computers to process payroll. In a computerized payroll system, the computer is used to perform all the calculations and to prepare and print the payroll register, the employee payroll checks and stubs, and the employee's earnings records.

EXTENDING THE CONTENT

Investigating Employee Benefits Have students investigate the employee benefits provided to full-time employees in the business where they work. Does the employer bear all the cost, or does the employer share the costs with the employees? Ask students to share their information with the class. Compile a list of employee benefits and have students explain each of the benefits.

SUMMARY CHAPTER 12

Chapter 12 Quiz

Student ______ Class ______ Instructor ______
Date Assigned ______ Date Completed ______

CHAPTER 12 QUIZ

Payroll Accounting

QUESTIONS (Completion)

Directions: Fill in the blank with the term that best completes each sentence.

1. A ______ is a list of employees and payments due to each for a specific pay period.
2. The total amount an employee earns during a pay period is ______.
3. A ______ is a fixed amount of money paid to an employee.
4. When calculating hours worked, the time is rounded to the nearest ______ hour.
5. An employee who is paid a percentage of sales works on ______.
6. The overtime rate is ______ times an employee's regular hourly pay.
7. The amount of tax withheld from an employee's earnings depends on the number of ______ claimed.
8. FICA taxes include social security and ______ taxes.
9. Contributions to a 401(k) plan are an example of a ______ deduction.
10. The amount the employee receives for a pay period is ______.

14 • Chapter Quizzes Copyright © Glencoe/McGraw-Hill

QUESTIONS (Completion)

1. A _____ is a list of employees and payments due to each for a specific pay period.
2. The total amount an employee earns during a pay period is _____.
3. A _____ is a fixed amount of money paid to an employee.
4. When calculating hours worked, the time is rounded to the nearest _____ hour.
5. An employee who is paid a percentage of sales works on _____.
6. The overtime rate is _____ times an employee's regular hourly pay.
7. The amount of tax withheld from an employee's earnings depends on the number of _____ claimed.
8. FICA taxes include social security and _____ taxes.
9. Contributions to a 401(k) plan are an example of a _____ deduction.
10. The amount the employee receives for a pay period is _____.

ANSWERS

1. payroll
2. gross earnings
3. salary
4. quarter
5. commission
6. 1.5
7. exemptions
8. Medicare
9. voluntary
10. net pay

REVIEW AND ACTIVITIES CHAPTER 12

USING KEY TERMS

See the *Glossary* for the definitions of these terms. Ask for volunteers to read their papers in class. Discuss any misuses of terms.

Understanding Accounting Concepts and Procedures

(Answers)

1. Collecting and processing information to prepare payroll checks, and producing payroll records for accounting purposes and reports.
2. Calculating earnings, calculating deductions, recording amounts in accounting and payroll records, preparing paychecks, and reporting information to federal and state governments.
3. A salary is a fixed amount of money paid to an employee for a pay period; a wage is a specific rate per hour worked.
4. To encourage them to increase their sales.
5. Federal income taxes, social security taxes, and Medicare taxes.
6. The employee's marital status, number of exemptions claimed, and gross earnings.
7. To indicate marital status and number of exemptions claimed.
8. The FICA system provides income to retired and disabled persons and to the spouses and dependent children of deceased workers. It also finances health insurance through Medicare.
9. An exact tax means that the amount deducted is the exact tax owed, not an estimated amount.
10. Union dues, insurance premiums, pension fund contributions, credit union deposits and payments, and charitable contributions.

CHAPTER 12 REVIEW AND ACTIVITIES

USING KEY TERMS

You are the payroll clerk for Wild West Amusement Park. The new sales manager for the Western region, Will Klein, called and asked you to explain the items on his payroll check, dated January 31, 20--. He also asked you to explain any relevant company payroll procedures. Use the following key terms in your written explanation of his payroll check and the payroll process. Use your imagination!

401(k) plan	net pay
accumulated earnings	overtime rate
allowance	pay period
commission	payroll
deduction	payroll clerk
direct deposit	payroll register
electronic badge readers	salary
employee's earnings record	time card
gross earnings	wage

Understanding Accounting Concepts and Procedures

Instructions

On a separate sheet of paper, answer the following questions:

1. What are the two goals of a payroll system?
2. What five tasks does an effective payroll system perform?
3. What is the difference between a salary and a wage?
4. Why do some businesses pay their employees on a commission basis?
5. List the three federal taxes that businesses are required to withhold from employees' wages.
6. List three factors that determine the amount of federal income tax withheld from employee earnings each pay period.
7. Why do all employees complete Form W-4?
8. Describe the three programs that are financed by the Federal Insurance Contributions Act (FICA).
9. Explain the statement, "The social security tax is an exact tax."
10. What are some common voluntary deductions that are withheld from employee payroll checks?

ASSESSMENT RESOURCES

Choose assessment strategies from the following pages to evaluate your students' progress.

Student Edition
Check Your Understanding, pp. 292, 298, 304
Chapter 12 Problems, pp. 309–313
Analyzing Financial Reports, p. 297

Assessment and Evaluation Masters
Chapter 12 Study Plan, *Glencoe Workbook (CRWP)*
Chapter 12 Self-Test, *Glencoe Workbook (CRWP)*
Chapter 12 Test, *Chapter Tests* Booklet
Chapter 12 Activity, *School-to-Work Handbook*
Chapter 12 **Exam***View*

Teacher Wraparound Edition
Critical Thinking Activity, p. 300
Reteaching Sections 1–3, pp. 292, 298, 304
Chapter 12 Quiz, p. 305

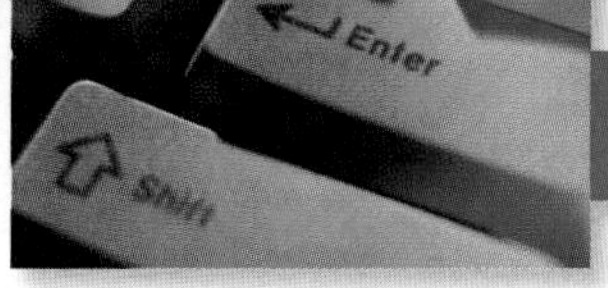

CHAPTER 12 REVIEW AND ACTIVITIES

Case Study...

Payroll: Financial Planning

You are employed by Tallman Financial Advisors, owned by Marcy Tallman. Parker's Framing hired Tallman to design its payroll system. Parker's Framing will offer group health insurance to its employees and a retirement plan that will require contributions from both the employer and employees. Marcy has assigned the Parker's Framing payroll project to you.

Thinking Critically:

Write a one-page report describing the payroll system you would design for Parker's Framing. Include information on:

- payroll forms
- how hours worked will be collected
- payroll deductions

interNET CONNECTION

Payroll and Tax Records

The federal government makes available a great deal of information related to wages and earnings.

Do This:

Use key words from the following questions to search the Internet for payroll-related statistics.

1. What is the current minimum hourly wage?
2. What are the annual earnings for a full-time employee who earns the minimum wage?
3. What is the average hourly wage in the United States?
4. What are the average annual earnings in the United States?
5. How many people are employed in the United States?

Conducting an Audit with Alex

Philip Wagner is paid an hourly rate of $8.20. Last week Philip worked 41 hours. He is paid overtime for all work over 40 hours. The social security tax is 6.2%, the Medicare tax is 1.45%, and the state income tax is 2½% of gross earnings. Philip is single and claims one allowance.

Instructions Examine the following check. Check all calculations, and create a replacement check using a separate sheet of paper.

Horizons Garden Supply
5295 Southwest Parkway
Cape Coral, Florida 33990

58

63-947/670

Date August 19 20 --

Pay to the Order of Philip Wagner $ 291.14

Two hundred ninety-one and 14/100 Dollars

State Street Bank
CAPE CORAL, FLORIDA

Angela Armstrong

⑆06700947⑆ 3939 043 417⑈ 58

Employee Pay Statement
Detach and retain this statement.

58

Period Ending	Earnings			Deductions							Net Pay
	Regular	Overtime	Total	Social Security Tax	Med. Tax	Federal Income Tax	State Income Tax	Hosp. Ins.	Other	Total	
8/19/20--	328.00	36.90	364.09	22.57	5.28	36.00	9.10	6.25	—	72.95	291.14

Workplace Skills

Integrity

Employees who demonstrate integrity are persons who can make ethical decisions. Employers expect you to have integrity on the job. Your ability to make decisions that uphold your company's codes, operating standards, and practices will indicate that you have integrity.

On the Job:

As a payroll clerk for the Fun 'n Games Amusement Park, you have access to confidential payroll information about all park employees. Your friend and co-worker, Mark Arnold, asked you to divulge payroll information about his associate, Melissa Porter. Melissa and Mark have the same job title. Melissa just received a pay raise. Mark did not.

Thinking Critically:

How do you respond to Mark's request? Write a few sentences explaining your response.

REVIEW AND ACTIVITIES CHAPTER 12

Case Study...

Thinking Critically (Answers)

Answers may vary. Evaluate students' papers for correct grammar and the logical progression of ideas.

Workplace Skills

Thinking Critically (Answers)

Answers will vary. Students should say that sharing payroll information with other workers is unethical and illegal. If you are caught, you may lose your job.

Conducting an Audit with Alex

Overtime earnings $12.30
Social security tax $21.10
Medicare tax $4.93
State income tax $8.51
Net pay $263.51

GO TO Internet Resources and Activities Handbook

Refer students to the booklet for additional Internet activities.

interNET CONNECTION www.glencoe.com

Do This (Answers)

Find U.S. Dept. of Labor at www.dol.gov to find these answers:

1. $5.15 as of September 1, 1997
2. $10,300
3. $14.63 as of April 2002
4. $33,089 as of April 2002
5. 133,894,000 people are employed in the United States as of April 2002

PEACHTREE CORNER

Payroll Entry

Use the **Payroll Entry** task option to calculate employee gross earnings, enter payroll taxes and deductions, and print payroll checks. Select **Payroll Entry** from the ***Tasks*** menu.

Tasks Analysis Options Reports
Quotes/Sales Orders
Sales/Invoicing...
Receipts...
Finance Charge...
Select for Deposit...
Purchase Orders...
Purchases/Receive Inventory...
Select for Payment...
Payments...
Write Checks...
Time/Expense
Select for Payroll Entry...
Payroll Entry...
General Journal Entry...

Payroll Entry Window

You can also click the **Payroll** navigation aid at the bottom of the screen and choose **Payroll Entry**. The Payroll Entry window allows you to record earnings and payroll deductions. The software automatically posts the required entries to the general ledger accounts.

Reports

To print a Payroll Register or a Current Earnings report, choose **Payroll** from the ***Reports*** menu. Select the desired report from the Select a Report window.

Preparing the Payroll

Making the Transition from a Manual to a Computerized System

Task	Perform Accounting Procedures Using Manual Methods	Perform Accounting Procedures Using Automated Methods
Enter and maintain employee information; process payroll.	1. Calculate employee gross earnings based on time cards or salary information. 2. Calculate required and voluntary deductions for each employee. 3. Complete the payroll register. 4. Prepare payroll checks. 5. Update employee earnings records. 6. Prepare journal entries. 7. Post journal entries to the general ledger.	1. Set up information related to employee earnings and deductions in employees' records. 2. Based on rate, deduction, and withholding information for each employee, the software automatically calculates gross earnings and deductions. 3. The payroll checks, journal entries, and ledger postings are generated automatically.

Preparing the Payroll

Peachtree Question	Description
How do I set up payroll information for employees in Peachtree?	1. Standard or default information for each employee can be entered and maintained by using the ***Maintain*** menu. 2. Click on **Employees/Sales Reps.** 3. Enter employee names, addresses, deductions, tax rates, rates of pay, and filing status.
How do I process a payroll?	1. Select **Payroll Entry** from the ***Tasks*** menu. 2. Select the employee(s) to be paid. 3. Verify the pay amounts that are automatically entered for you. (These amounts are pulled from employee records stored in the system.) 4. Click *Save*. 5. To print payroll checks, click on *Open* then *OK* to select checks to print. 6. Click *Print*.
What does the software do "behind the scenes?"	• Gross pay, taxes, and other deductions are calculated automatically. • Journal entries are prepared and posted automatically. • Earnings and deductions are posted to employee earnings records.

For detailed instructions: See the **Peachtree User Guide** in your Glencoe Working Papers.

Peachtree® Answers to Frequently Asked Questions

Q: How can you correct a payroll entry with the wrong employee ID, earnings, or deductions?
A: Choose **Payroll Entry** and click *Open*. Select and correct the entry, print a new payroll check if needed, and save the updated entry.
Q: Can you change the default data entry format for amount fields?
A: Yes. To change, choose **Global** from the ***Options*** menu and change the Decimal Entry setting to manual.
For additional information, see your *Glencoe Peachtree Accounting User Guide*.

CHAPTER 12 PROBLEMS

APPLICATION OPTIONS

Problem 12–5
Calculating Gross Pay

Wilderness Rentals pays employees either an hourly wage or a salary plus commission based on rental revenue. Hourly wage employees can earn overtime. The overtime rate is 1½ times the regular hourly rate of pay for hours worked over 40 in a week.

Instructions For each of the following employees, determine the total gross pay for the pay period.

John Gilmartin
- Earns an hourly wage of $6.80.
- Worked 43 hours this week.

Arlene Stone
- Receives a salary of $250 per week plus a 3% commission on rental revenue.
- Had rental revenue of $760 this week.

Tom Driscoll
- Earns an hourly wage of $7.35.
- Worked 39 hours this week.

Ann Ryan
- Receives a salary of $185 per week plus 3% commission.
- Had rental revenue of $1,235 this week.

Analyze: Which employee had the smallest gross pay for the week?

Problem 12–6
Preparing a Payroll Register

Hot Suds Car Wash has four employees. They are paid on a weekly basis with overtime paid for all hours worked over 40 in a week. The overtime rate is 1½ times the regular rate of pay. The payroll information follows.

Employee	Employee Number	Rate per Hour	Marital Status	Allowances	Union Member
James Dumser	108	$6.40	Single	0	No
Gail Job	112	$7.22	Married	1	Yes
James Liptak	102	$6.70	Married	2	Yes
Bruce Stern	109	$7.80	Single	1	Yes

During the week ending October 9, Dumser worked 39 hours, Job worked 41 hours, and Liptak and Stern each worked 36 hours.

Continued 

Complete chapter problems one of three ways:

1 **Manual** Glencoe Working Papers

or

2 **Peachtree Complete Accounting** Software

or

3 **Spreadsheet Templates** (Problem 12–6)

Peachtree®

SMART GUIDE

Step-by-Step Instructions: Problem 12–5

1. Select the problem set for Wilderness Rentals (Prob. 12-5).
2. Rename the company and set the system date.
3. Enter John Gilmartin's regular and overtime pay rates using the **Employees/Sales Reps** option.
4. Calculate the employees' gross pay using the **Payroll Entry** option.
5. Print a Payroll Register report.
6. Proof your work and make any needed corrections.
7. Answer the Analyze question.
8. End the session.

PROBLEMS CHAPTER 12

Problem 12–5 (Answers)
Calculating Gross Pay

Driscoll, Tom $286.65
Gilmartin, John $302.60
Ryan, Ann $222.05
Stone, Arlene $272.80

Analyze: Ann Ryan

Problem 12–6 (Answers)
Preparing a Payroll Register

Net pay:
Dumser, James $196.51
Job, Gail $241.47
Liptak, James $210.43
Stern, Bruce $215.45

Payroll register totals:
Reg. earnings $1,060.40
Overtime $10.83
Total earnings $1,071.23
Social security tax $66.42
Medicare tax $15.53
FIT $77.00
State income tax $21.42
Hospital insurance $13.50
Other $13.50
Total deductions $207.37
Net pay $863.86

Analyze: James Dumser

MAKING CONNECTIONS TO DAILY LIFE

How Workers Are Paid Many different jobs exist in our economy. Students will be familiar with jobs that pay an hourly rate. Pay for other jobs may be calculated in different ways. For example, sales is a type of job that usually pays a commission on total sales for the month. Ask students to describe jobs they are familiar with and to explain how earnings are calculated. Also ask students to determine methods of dissemination of payroll funds.

Problem 12-7 (Answers)
Preparing Payroll Checks and Employee's Earnings Records

Net pay:
Hurd, Mildred $219.48
Montego, José $241.73
Pilly, Amanda $239.40
Stearns, Margaret $243.39

Record the check numbers in the box on the far right of the payroll register (labeled CK NO.).

Total accumulated earnings:
Montego, José $10,283.32
Pilly, Amanda $10,538.20

Analyze: $241.73

SPREADSHEET SMART GUIDE

Step-by-Step Instructions: Problem 12-6

1. Select the spreadsheet template for Problem 12-6.
2. Enter your name and the date in the spaces provided on the template.
3. Complete the spreadsheet using the instructions in your working papers.
4. Print the spreadsheet and proof your work.
5. Save your work and exit the spreadsheet program.

Instructions On the forms provided in your working papers:

1. Prepare a payroll register for the week ending October 9. The date of payment is also October 9. List employees in alphabetical order by *last* name. Use the tables on page 295 to determine the federal income tax withholding. The rate for the state income tax is 2%. Compute social security tax at 6.2% and Medicare tax at 1.45%. Union members pay weekly dues of $4.50. Both Gail Job and Bruce Stern had $6.75 deducted for health and hospital insurance.
2. Total the amount columns. Subtract total deductions from total earnings. Does the result equal the sum of the Net Pay column? If not, find and correct any error(s) on the payroll register.

Analyze: Which employee had the greatest amount withheld for federal income tax for the week?

Problem 12-7 Preparing Payroll Checks and Employee's Earnings Records

The payroll register for Kits & Pups Grooming is presented below and also appears in your working papers.

PAYROLL REGISTER

PAY PERIOD ENDING October 17 20 --   DATE OF PAYMENT October 17, 20--

EMPLOYEE NUMBER	NAME	MAR. STATUS	ALLOW.	TOTAL HOURS	RATE	EARNINGS REGULAR	EARNINGS OVERTIME	EARNINGS TOTAL	SOC. SEC. TAX	MEDICARE TAX	FED. INC. TAX	STATE INC. TAX	HOSP. INS.	OTHER	DEDUCTIONS TOTAL	NET PAY	CK. NO.
162	Hurd, Mildred	S	0	38	7.60	288 80		288 80	17 91	4 19	35 00	7 22		(B) 5 00	69 32	219 48	
157	Montego, José	S	1	39	7.90	308 10		308 10	19 10	4 47	30 00	7 70	5 10		66 37	241 73	
151	Pilly, Amanda	M	2	36	8.10	291 60		291 60	18 08	4 23	10 00	7 29	7 60	(B) 5 00	52 20	239 40	
163	Steams, Margaret	S	0	41	7.60	304 00	11 40	315 40	19 55	4 57	40 00	7 89			72 01	243 39	
					TOTALS	1,192 50	11 40	1,203 90	74 64	17 46	115 00	30 10	12 70	(B)10 00	259 90	944 00	

Other Deductions: Write the appropriate code letter to the left of the amount: B–U.S. Savings Bonds; C–Credit Union: UD–Union Dues; UW–United Way.

Peachtree® SMART GUIDE

Step-by-Step Instructions: Problem 12-7

1. Select the problem set for Kits & Pups Grooming (Prob. 12-7).
2. Rename the company and set the system date.
3. Print payroll checks using the **Payroll Entry** option.
4. Print a Payroll Register report and a Current Earnings report.
5. End the session.

Instructions On the forms in your working papers:

1. Prepare a payroll check and stub for each employee. Where would you record the check numbers in the payroll register?
2. Record the payroll information in the employee's earnings records for José Montego and Amanda Pilly.

Analyze: What was the net pay for José Montego for this week?

Problem 12-8 Preparing the Payroll

Outback Guide Service has six employees and pays each week. Hourly employees are paid overtime for all hours worked over 40 in a week. The overtime rate is 1½ times the regular rate of pay. Outback pays its employees by hourly rate, salary, or salary plus a 5% commission on total sales.

ACCOUNTING ISSUES

Getting Information about Your Social Security Benefits Social security provides retirement benefits to workers who retire. The retirement age for reduced benefits is currently 62, and the retirement age for full benefits is currently 65. By 2027 the retirement age for full benefits will rise to 67. Up to a certain amount, the higher your average yearly earnings, the higher your retirement benefits. Employees can contact the Social Security Administration to request a form that will enable them to obtain a copy of their personal earnings and benefit statements. Included in the information are the employee's earnings for every year worked and an estimate of the benefits the employee can expect to receive at different retirement ages.

Method of Computing Earnings

Employee	Hourly Wage	Salary	Salary Plus Commission
Cummings, Carol		$270.00	
Dame, Ted	$6.95		
Lengyel, Tom			$160.00 plus 5%
Robinson, Jean			$140.00 plus 5%
Usdavin, James	$6.65		
Wong, Kim			$140.00 plus 5%

Employee deductions include federal income taxes (use the tables on page 295), FICA taxes at 6.2% for social security and 1.45% for Medicare, state income taxes of 1.5%, and hospital insurance premiums of $5.43 for single employees and $9.37 for married employees. Also, Kim Wong and Tom Lengyel have $10.00 withheld each week to purchase U.S. savings bonds.

During the pay period ending October 17, the sales were: Tom Lengyel $1,204.76, Jean Robinson $1,925.80, and Kim Wong $2,135.65.

The hourly employees filled in the following time cards.

NO. 73
NAME Ted Dame
SOC. SEC. NO. 093-48-7423
WEEK ENDING 10/17/20--

DAY	IN	OUT	IN	OUT	IN	OUT
M	8:58	12:03	12:55	5:09		
T	8:55	11:55	1:00	4:00		
W	9:30	12:10	1:04	3:30		
Th	8:57	12:03	12:59	6:00		
F	8:58	12:00	1:00	6:05		
S	9:00	12:00				
S						

TOTAL HOURS

	HOURS	RATE
REGULAR		
OVERTIME		
TOTAL EARNINGS		

SIGNATURE ________ DATE ________

NO. 92
NAME James Usdavin
SOC. SEC. NO. 087-46-3875
WEEK ENDING 10/17/20--

DAY	IN	OUT	IN	OUT	IN	OUT	TOTAL
M	8:55	12:06	1:01	5:35			
T	7:58	11:01	12:03	6:38			
W	9:03	1:10	2:00	6:00			
Th	7:59	11:55	1:10	4:51			
F	9:01	12:06	1:05	3:47			
S	9:00	12:03					
S							

TOTAL HOURS

	HOURS	RATE	AMOUNT
REGULAR			
OVERTIME			
TOTAL EARNINGS			

SIGNATURE ________ DATE ________

Continued

Peachtree®

SMART GUIDE

Step-by-Step Instructions: Problem 12–8

1. Select the problem set for Outback Guide Service (Prob. 12–8).
2. Rename the company and set the system date.
3. Record the payroll and print a check for each employee using the **Payroll Entry** option.
4. Print a Payroll Register report and a Current Earnings report.
5. Proof your work and make any needed corrections.
6. Answer the Analyze question.
7. End the session.

TIP: Use the Windows calculator accessory if you need to make a calculation (e.g., commission)

PROBLEMS
CHAPTER 12

Problem 12–8 (Answers)
Preparing the Payroll

Total hours:
Ted Dame 37.5
James Usdavin 41.75

Payroll register totals:
Regular earnings $1,499.94
Overtime earnings $17.47
Total earnings $1,517.41
Social Security tax $94.08
Medicare tax $22.01
Federal income tax $139.00
State income tax $22.75
Hospital insurance $40.46
Other deductions $20.00
Total deductions $338.30
Net pay $1,179.11

Net pay:
Cummings, Carol $220.92
Dame, Ted $199.35
Lengyel, Tom $172.73
Robinson, Jean $189.24
Usdavin, James $217.10
Wong, Kim $179.77

Total accumulated earnings:
Cummings, Carol $12,690.00
Dame, Ted $4,540.95
Lengyel, Tom $5,257.64
Robinson, Jean $3,231.94
Usdavin, James $3,661.77
Wong, Kim $4,130.43

Analyze: $116.09

ADDRESSING MULTIPLE LEARNING STYLES

Verbal/Linguistic Learner After discussing the various types of pay periods (weekly, biweekly, monthly, and so forth), ask students to consider the advantages for each pay plan from the employer's viewpoint and from the employee's viewpoint. Ask students to write a short essay that summarizes these advantages and disadvantages. Their essay should include the pay period they would prefer and why.

Problem 12–9 (Answers)
Preparing the Payroll Register

Payroll register totals:
Regular earnings $1,593.49
Overtime earnings $10.88
Total earnings $1,604.37
Social security tax $99.48
Medicare tax $23.27
Federal income tax $84.00
State income tax $28.88
Hospital insurance $25.00
Total deductions $260.63
Net pay $1,343.74

Analyze: $1,343.74

Instructions On the forms in your working papers:

1. Complete the time cards to the nearest quarter hour.
2. Prepare a payroll register for the week ending October 17. The date of payment is also October 17. Each employee's number, marital status, and number of allowances claimed are listed on her or his employee's earnings record.
3. Prepare a payroll check and stub for each employee.
4. Record the payroll information for each employee on her or his employee's earnings record.

Analyze: What is the total amount deducted from employees' gross pay for FICA taxes (social security and Medicare)?

Peachtree®

SMART GUIDE

Step-by-Step Instructions: Problem 12–9

1. Select the problem set for Showbiz Video (Prob. 12-9).
2. Rename the company and set the system date.
3. Record the payroll for each employee.
4. Print a Payroll Register report.
5. Proof your work and make any needed corrections.
6. Answer the Analyze question.
7. End the session.

Problem 12–9 Preparing the Payroll Register

Showbiz Video has six employees who are paid weekly. The hourly employees are paid overtime for hours worked over 40 in a week, at a rate 1½ times their regular rate of pay. Employee information follows:

Employee	Employee Number	Marital Status	Allowances
Mary Arcompora	105	Married	2
Barbara Fox	137	Married	1
John French	135	Single	1
Chris German	141	Married	4
David Ifkovic	139	Single	0
Susan Tilbert	129	Married	1

Mary Arcompora, the store manager, is paid a salary of $300.00 per week plus 1% of all rental sales. Barbara Fox and John French, salespeople, are paid a salary of $200.00 per week plus a 6% commission on all rentals from the "Oldies but Goodies" section. Chris German and David Ifkovic, office workers, are paid an hourly wage of $7.25. Susan Tilbert, a stock person, is paid $6.40 per hour.

The payroll deductions include federal income tax, social security tax of 6.2%, Medicare tax of 1.45%, and state income tax of 1.8%. Chris German and Susan Tilbert have $12.50 deducted each week for hospital insurance.

NO. 141
NAME Chris German
SOC. SEC. NO. 449-42-6721
WEEK ENDING October 24, 20--

DAY	IN	OUT	IN	OUT	IN	OUT	TOTAL
M	8:05	12:03	1:00	5:05			
T	8:00	12:05	1:10	5:00			
W	9:05	12:05	1:15	6:05			
Th	8:30	11:55	1:15	6:00			
F	8:00	12:00	1:00	6:15			
S							
S							
						TOTAL HOURS	

	HOURS	RATE	AMOUNT
REGULAR			
OVERTIME			
		TOTAL EARNINGS	

During the week ending October 24, "Oldies but Goodies" rentals were $484.90 for Barbara Fox and $641.70 for John French. Total rental revenue for the week was $3,917.30.

SOFTWARE NOTES

Teachers can find detailed instructions for:

- **Peachtree Complete Accounting Software**, in the *Glencoe Workbook (CRWP)*
- **Spreadsheet Templates**, in the *Glencoe Workbook (CRWP)*

CHAPTER 12 PROBLEMS

Instructions Prepare a payroll register in your working papers for the week ending October 24. Use the federal income tax tables provided in the chapter.

Analyze: What is the total net pay of all employees for the pay period?

NO. 139
NAME David Ifkovic
SOC. SEC. NO. 461-24-4422
WEEK ENDING October 24, 20--

DAY	IN	OUT	IN	OUT	IN	OUT	TOTAL
M	8:00	12:05	1:00	5:00			
T	8:10	12:00	1:00	5:05			
W	8:05	12:30	1:30	5:00			
Th	8:00	12:00	1:00	5:10			
F	8:05	12:05	1:05	3:30			
S							
S							

TOTAL HOURS

	HOURS	RATE	AMOUNT
REGULAR			
OVERTIME			
TOTAL EARNINGS			

SIGNATURE ________ DATE ________

NO. 129
NAME Susan Tilbert
SOC. SEC. NO. 401-32-0977
WEEK ENDING October 24, 20--

DAY	IN	OUT	IN	OUT	IN	OUT	TOTAL
M	8:05	12:00	1:00	5:00			
T	8:10	12:00	1:15	5:00			
W	8:30	12:00	1:00	6:00			
Th	9:00	12:00	12:45	5:00			
F	9:00	11:50					
S							
S							

TOTAL HOURS

	HOURS	RATE	AMOUNT
REGULAR			
OVERTIME			
TOTAL EARNINGS			

SIGNATURE ________ DATE ________

Problem 12–10 Calculating Gross Earnings

SOURCE DOCUMENT PROBLEM

Job Connect has 7 employees, all of whom are paid weekly. For hourly wage employees, overtime is paid at 1½ times the regular rate of pay for hours worked over 40 in a week.

Barbara Miller, the office manager, is paid a salary of $375.00 per week plus a bonus of 3% of all revenue *over* $6,000 per week. Lynn Austin, an office assistant, is paid a salary of $250.00 per week plus 5% of all telephone sales made in the office. Charlene Womack, the office secretary, is paid a salary of $230.00 per week. Susan Dilloway and Doris Franco, placement workers, are paid an hourly wage of $8.95. Pam Darrah is also a placement worker but is paid a commission of $35.00 for every job placement that she completes. David Facini, a part-time maintenance worker, is paid $6.75 per hour.

For the week ending October 24, the office recorded the following payroll information.

- Total office sales for the week were $8,420.00.
- Susan Dilloway worked a total of 38½ hours.
- Doris Franco worked a total of 41¼ hours.
- Phone sales for the week were $1,375.00.
- Pam Darrah made seven job placements.
- David Facini worked a total of 23 hours.

Instructions Using the form provided in your working papers, calculate the gross earnings for the workers at Job Connect for the week ending October 24.

Analyze: Who had the largest gross earnings?

Peachtree®

SMART GUIDE

Step-by-Step Instructions: Problem 12–10

1. Select the problem set for Job Connect (Prob. 12–10).
2. Rename the company and set the system date.
3. Calculate the employees' gross pay using the **Payroll Entry** option.
4. Print a Payroll Register report.
5. Proof your work.
6. Answer the Analyze question.
7. End the session.

SOURCE DOCUMENT PROBLEM

Problem 12–10

Use the source documents in your working papers to record the transactions for this problem.

SOLUTION NOTES

PROBLEMS CHAPTER 12

SOURCE DOCUMENT PROBLEM

Problem 12–10 (Answers) Calculating Gross Earnings

Gross earnings:
Austin, Lynn $318.75
Darrah, Pam $245.00
Dilloway, Susan $344.58
Facini, David $155.25
Franco, Doris $374.78
Miller, Barbara $447.60
Womack, Charlene $230.00

Total $2,115.96

Analyze: Barbara Miller

CHAPTER 13 Resource Manager

Section Resources

	Objectives & Standards	Activities & Features	Reproducible Masters
Chapter Opener *Payroll Liabilities and Tax Records*	• Record payroll information in the general journal. • Describe and calculate the employer's payroll taxes. • Record payroll transactions in the general journal. • Record the payment of tax liabilities in the general journal. • Complete payroll tax forms. • Compute and complete payroll tax expense forms. • Define the accounting terms introduced in this chapter. **National Standards for Business Education**: IVB4, IVB5	Exploring Real World of Business, p. 314 Workplace Connections, p. 315	School-to-Work Handbook
Section 1 *Journalizing and Posting the Payroll*	• How to compute the business payroll deductions. • How to record the payroll entry in the general journal.	Did You Know?, p. 317 A Matter of Ethics, p. 320	Demonstration Problems Strategies for Teaching Ethics in Accounting
Section 2 *Employer's Payroll Taxes*	• How to calculate the employer's FICA taxes. • How to calculate federal and state unemployment taxes. • How to journalize and post employer's payroll taxes.	Accounting Tips, p. 323	Demonstration Problems
Section 3 *Tax Liability Payments and Tax Reports*	• How to pay payroll tax liabilities. • Which tax reports are prepared and filed.	International Accounting, p. 327 Calculator Hints, p. 334 Accounting Flashbacks, p. 334 Connect To, p. 336 Analyzing Financial Reports, p. 336 Accounting Careers in Focus, p. 338	Strategies for Teaching International Accounting Demonstration Problems Math Review for Accounting Internet Resources and Activities Handbook

KEY

Posters — Transparency — Software — Videocassette
Blackline Masters — CD-ROM — Portfolio

MULTIMEDIA RESOURCE

Peachtree	QuickBooks	Spreadsheets	Videos	CD-ROMs
Problem 13–7 *Recording the Payment of the Payroll* Problem 13–8 *Journalizing Payroll Transactions* Problem 13–9 *Recording and Posting Payroll Transactions* Problem 13–10 *Recording and Posting Payroll Transactions*	Problem 13–8 *Journalizing Payroll Transactions* Problem 13–9 *Recording and Posting Payroll Transactions*	Problem 13–6 *Calculating Employer's Payroll Taxes*	***Video Segment: Payroll Accounting*** After viewing this video, students will be able to explain a payroll system and that deductions can be both voluntary and mandated by law; illustrate both the employee's deductions and the employer's taxes that are based on payroll.	***Electronic Learning Center (ELC), Chapter 13*** This program is ideal for visual learners since it incorporates video images, animation, and graphics to enliven the content of each lesson. ***Interactive Lesson Planner (ILP), Chapter 13*** This CD-ROM combines the versatility of an electronic lesson planner with the convenience of teacher classroom resources.

SCANS Correlation Chart

FOUNDATION SKILLS

Basic Skills:	Reading	Writing	Math	Listening	Speaking	
Thinking Skills:	Creative Thinking	Decision Making	Problem Solving	Seeing Things in the Mind's Eye	Knowing How to Learn	Reasoning
Personal Qualities:	Responsibility	Self-Esteem	Sociability	Self-Management	Integrity/Honesty	

WORKPLACE COMPETENCIES

Resources:	Allocating Time	Allocating Money	Allocating Material and Facility Resources	Allocating Human Resources		
Information:	Acquiring and Evaluating Information	Organizing and Maintaining Information	Interpreting and Communicating Information	Using Computers to Process Information		
Interpersonal Skills:	Participating as a Member of a Team	Teaching Others	Serving Clients/ Customers	Exercising Leadership	Negotiating to Arrive at a Decision	Working with Cultural Diversity
Systems:	Understanding Systems	Monitoring and Correcting Performance	Improving and Designing Systems			
Technology:	Selecting Technology	Applying Technology to Task	Maintaining and Troubleshooting Technology			

*Highlighted blocks indicate areas covered in the chapter. Additional SCANS skills are also covered throughout the *Teacher Wraparound Edition.*

Assessment

Student Edition
- Check Your Understanding, pp. 321, 326, 337
- Chapter 13 Problems, pp. 343-345

Assessment and Evaluation Masters
- Chapter 13 Study Plan, *Glencoe Workbook*
- Chapter 13 Self-Test, *Glencoe Workbook*
- Chapter 13 Test, *Chapter Tests* Booklet
- Chapter 13 Activity *School-to-Work Handbook*
- Chapter 13 **Exam***View*

Teacher Wraparound Edition
- Critical Thinking Activity, p. 323
- Reteaching Section 1, p. 321
- Reteaching Section 2, p. 326
- Reteaching Section 3, p. 337
- Chapter 13 Quiz, p. 339

Transparencies

	Teaching Transparencies	Solution Transparencies
Section 1:	13–1, 13–2, 13–3a, 13–3b	Problem 13–1
Section 2:	13–4, 13–5, 13–6	Problems 13–2, 13–3
Section 3:	13–7, 13–8a, 13-8b, 13–9, 13–10, 13–11, 13–12, 13–13, 13–14, 13–15, 13–16, 13–17	Problems 13–4, 13–5
End of Chapter:		13–6, 13–7, 13–8, 13–9, 13–10

TEACHER CLASSROOM RESOURCES

This is a representation of key blackline masters available in the Teacher Classroom Resources.

Teaching Aids

Transparency Examples

Section Focus Transparencies

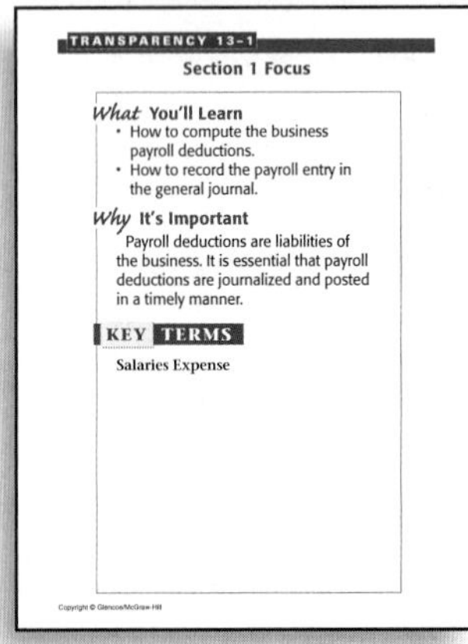

TRANSPARENCY 13-1

Section 1 Focus

What You'll Learn
- How to compute the business payroll deductions.
- How to record the payroll entry in the general journal.

Why It's Important

Payroll deductions are liabilities of the business. It is essential that payroll deductions are journalized and posted in a timely manner.

KEY TERMS

Salaries Expense

Teaching Transparencies

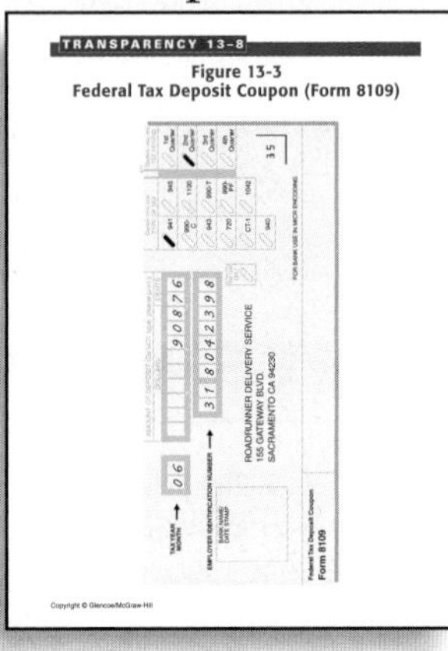

TRANSPARENCY 13-8

Figure 13-3
Federal Tax Deposit Coupon (Form 8109)

Teaching Transparencies

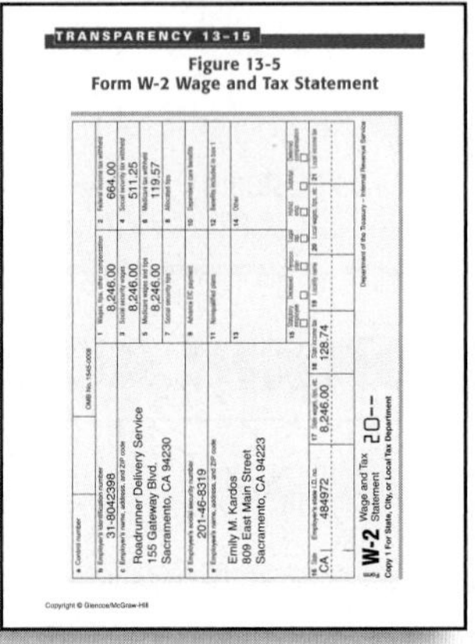

TRANSPARENCY 13-15

Figure 13-5
Form W-2 Wage and Tax Statement

Solution Transparencies

Working Papers for End-of-Chapter Problems

Problem 13-6 Calculating Employer's Payroll Taxes

Problem 13-7 Recording the Payment of the Payroll

Demonstration Problems

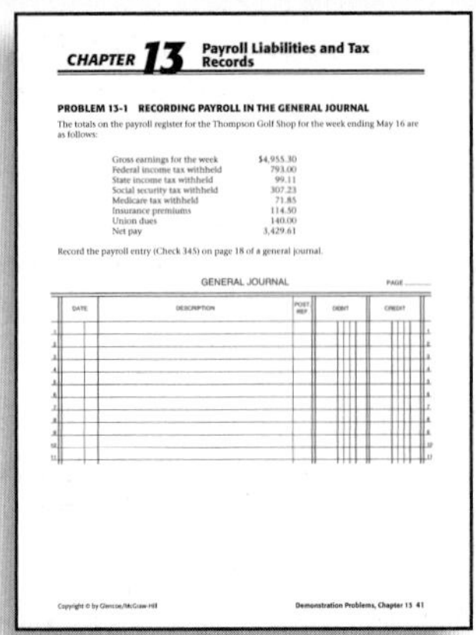

CHAPTER 13 Payroll Liabilities and Tax Records

PROBLEM 13-1 RECORDING PAYROLL IN THE GENERAL JOURNAL

GENERAL JOURNAL

Lesson Plans

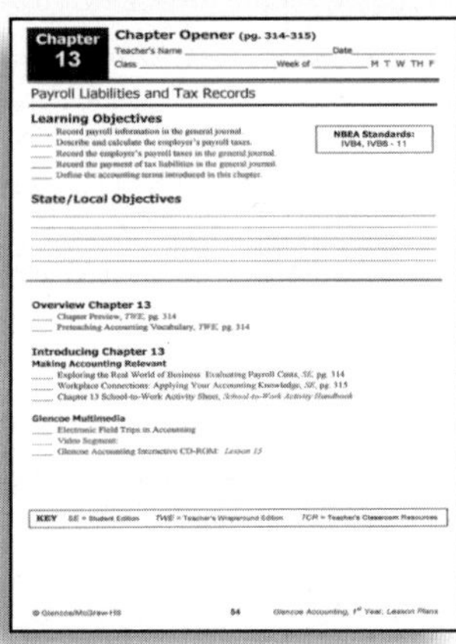

Chapter 13 Chapter Opener (pg. 314-315)

Payroll Liabilities and Tax Records

Learning Objectives

State/Local Objectives

Overview Chapter 13

Introducing Chapter 13

Glencoe Multimedia

Block Scheduling

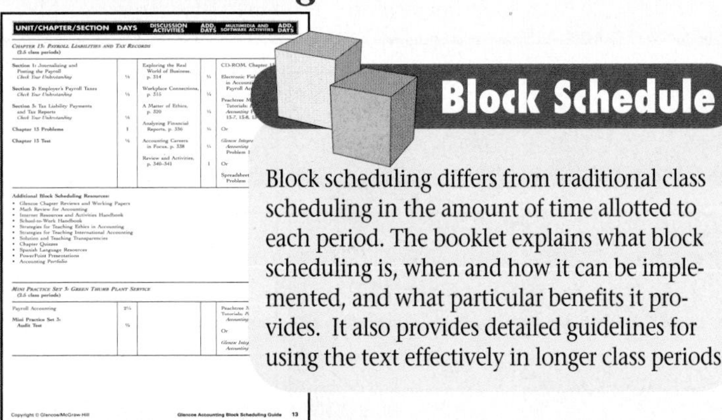

Block Schedule

Block scheduling differs from traditional class scheduling in the amount of time allotted to each period. The booklet explains what block scheduling is, when and how it can be implemented, and what particular benefits it provides. It also provides detailed guidelines for using the text effectively in longer class periods.

Enrichment and Application

Strategies for Teaching Ethics in Accounting

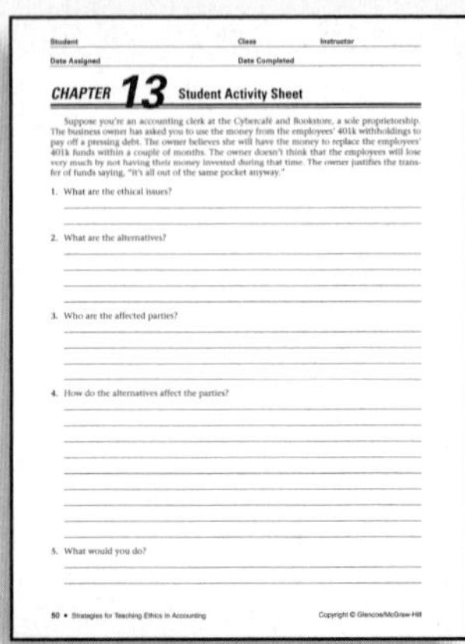

CHAPTER 13 Student Activity Sheet

1. What are the ethical issues?
2. What are the alternatives?
3. Who are the affected parties?
4. How do the alternatives affect the parties?
5. What would you do?

Strategies for Teaching International Accounting

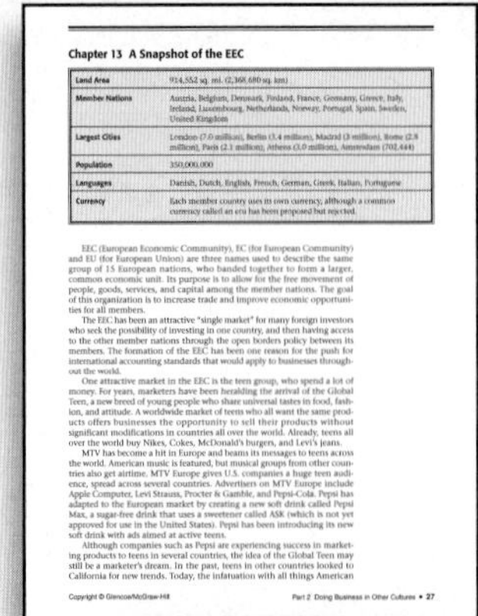

Chapter 13 A Snapshot of the EEC

School-to-Work Handbook

CHAPTER 13 SCHOOL-TO-WORK ACTIVITY

Payroll Liabilities and Tax Records

Meeting Different Ability Levels

Chapter Reviews and Working Papers (CRWP)

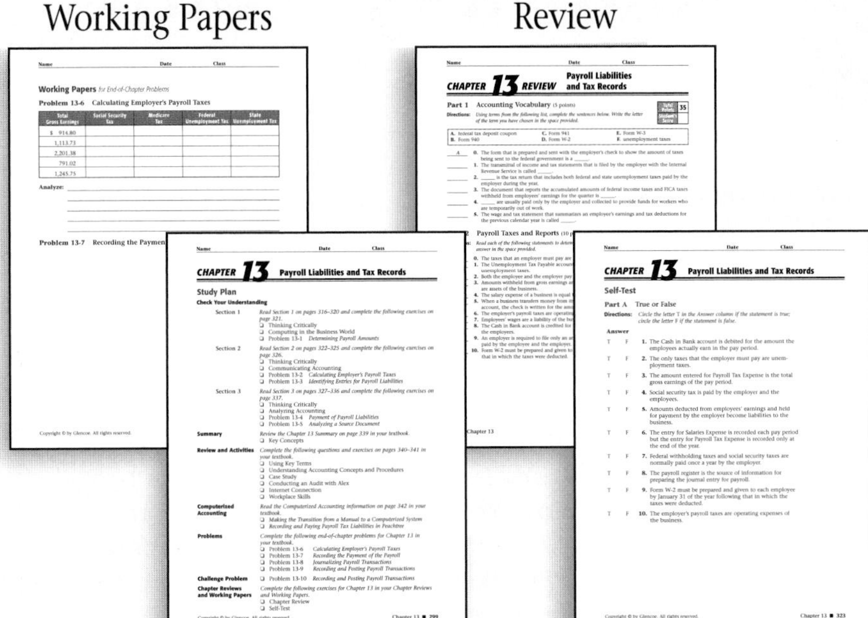

Real-World Multimedia CD-ROM

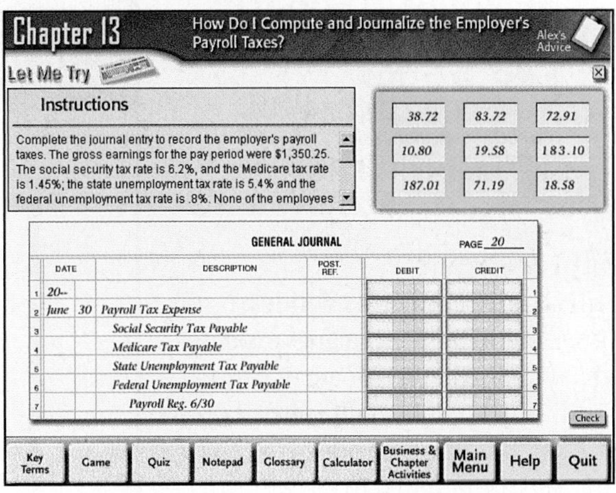

Key to Ability Levels

Each section gives skill-building activities. Each activity has been labeled for use with students of various learning styles and abilities.

L1 Level 1 activities are basic activities and should be within the range of all students.

L2 Level 2 activities are average activities and should be within the range of average and above average students.

L3 Level 3 activities are challenging activities designed for the ability range of above average students.

ELL ELL activities should be within the ability range of English Language Learners.

Assessment and Evaluation

Chapter Tests

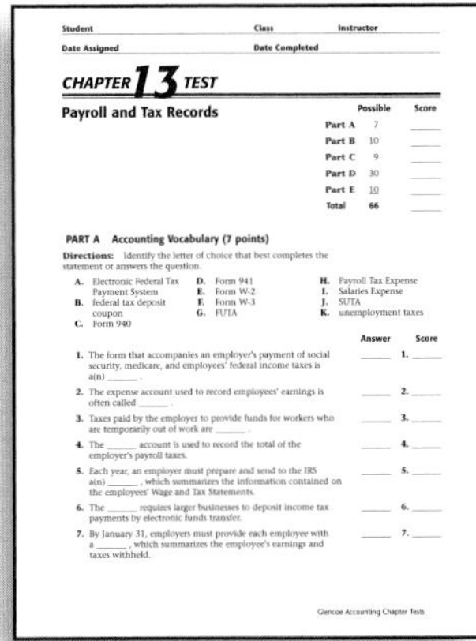

Chapter Quiz

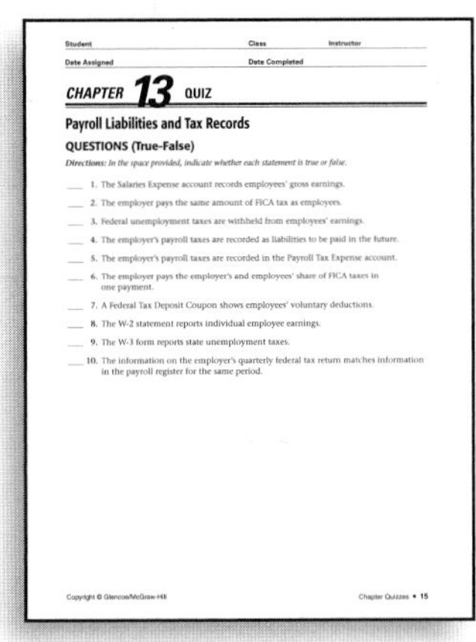

Teaching Resources at a Glance

Application Resources

- Glencoe Chapter Review and Working Papers, SE and TAE
- School-to-Work Handbook, SE and TM
- Accounting Portfolio, SE and TM

Reproducible Masters

- Demonstration Problems
- Lesson Plans
- Block Scheduling
- Spanish Language Resources

Glencoe Accounting Professional Development Series

- Strategies for Teaching Ethics in Accounting
- Accounting Competitive Event Review
- Math Review for Accounting
- Strategies for Teaching International Accounting
- Internet Resources and Activities Handbook

Transparency Package

- Section Focus Transparencies
- Teaching Transparencies
- Source Document Transparencies
- Solution Transparencies

Performance Assessment

- **Exam***View* CD-ROM
- Chapter Tests
- Chapter Quizzes
- Unit Tests
- Audit Tests
- Printed Testbank

Multimedia Resources

- Electronic Learning Center:
  - Multimedia CD-ROMs
  - Peachtree software, tutorials, templates, and solutions
  - Spreadsheet templates
- Using QuickBooks with Glencoe Accounting
- Interactive Lesson Planner
- Electronic Field Trips in Accounting
- PowerPoint Presentation
- Web site: glencoeaccounting.glencoe.com

OVERVIEW
CHAPTER 13

Correlations to National Standards for Business Education

(See pages T50–T51 for a detailed correlation chart.)

Standards: IVB4, IVB5

Chapter Preview

In this chapter students will learn to journalize and post the salaries expense and payroll expenses for a pay period. In addition, students will learn about some of the reports and forms that employers are required to file with government agencies.

Section Overviews

- Section 1—*Journalizing and Posting the Payroll*
- Section 2—*Employer's Payroll Taxes*
- Section 3—*Tax Liability Payments and Tax Reports*

Chapter Vocabulary

salaries expense
Federal Unemployment Tax Act (FUTA)
State Unemployment Tax Act (SUTA)
unemployment taxes
payroll tax expense
Federal Tax Deposit Coupon
Electronic Federal Tax Payment System (EFTPS)
Form 940
Form 941
Form W-2
Form W-3

Preteaching Accounting Vocabulary

Oral Exercise: Explain all terms, then ask students to use each term in a sentence that relates to accounting for payroll. Encourage students to be grammatically and factually correct in their sentences. L1

CHAPTER 13

Payroll Liabilities and Tax Records

Learning Objectives

When you have completed this chapter, you will be able to:

- Record payroll transactions in the general journal.
- Describe the employer's payroll taxes.
- Compute and complete payroll tax expense forms.
- Record the payment of tax liabilities in the general journal.
- Complete payroll tax reports.
- Define the accounting terms introduced in this chapter.

Exploring the Real World of Business

EVALUATING PAYROLL COSTS

Back in the early '70s, Richard Foos sold used records from the trunk of his car. Eventually, Richard sold so many records that he opened up a store. He hired a store manager, and together they turned the business into one of the hippest record stores in Los Angeles. Thus, **Rhino Records** was born. Soon after, the owner created his own record label.

Rhino Records' issues of *Billboard Top Hits* include '50s and '60s rhythm and blues and pop-rock, '70s and '80s disco, hip-hop, show tunes, and television theme songs. The company does more than just earn money. Its mission is to "put out great stuff, have some fun, make some money, learn from each other, and make a difference where we can." The company donates money to charitable causes and encourages employees to volunteer for community programs by allowing them time off during work hours to do so.

What do you think?

How do you think **Rhino Records'** commitment to social responsibility affects its payroll costs?

Exploring the Real World of Business

Rhino Records

Rhino Records is one of many companies that are committed to social responsibility. Have students discuss corporate responsibility from the viewpoint of shareholders, employees, and the community. If possible, have students survey local businesses to learn how they are involved in the community.

What do you think? (Answers)

When employees are given time off to work on community programs, the company pays for the hours they would have worked. Payroll costs may not increase directly, but productivity costs increase because the employees work fewer hours.

Workplace Connections

Applying Your Accounting Knowledge

Almost everyone must pay taxes. You learned about the taxes you pay on your earnings in the last chapter. Your employer also pays taxes on what you and other employees earn. That money must then be paid to the appropriate government agency within a certain amount of time. You'll learn about the employer's payroll taxes in this chapter.

Investigate:

1. Do you receive your paycheck in person, in the mail, or by direct deposit?
2. What do you imagine would happen if the accounting department failed to pay the taxes collected to the appropriate government agencies?

Glencoe Accounting *Online*

Visit the *Glencoe Accounting* Web site at **glencoeaccounting.glencoe.com** for additional activities and information.

INTRODUCING CHAPTER 13

Making Accounting Relevant

Workplace Connections: Applying Your Accounting Knowledge

Discussion: Discuss with students how and why tax laws are passed. For example, local government may need additional money to provide adequate fire and police protection; the state, highway construction; or the federal government, education loan programs, armed forces, and bridge and road construction.

Investigate (Answers)

1. Answers may vary. Most students who work probably receive their checks in person.
2. Companies that collect taxes but fail to pay them to the government are subject to fines. Employees might also have to prove to the IRS that their personal income taxes had been withheld by the company.

School-to-Work Activity

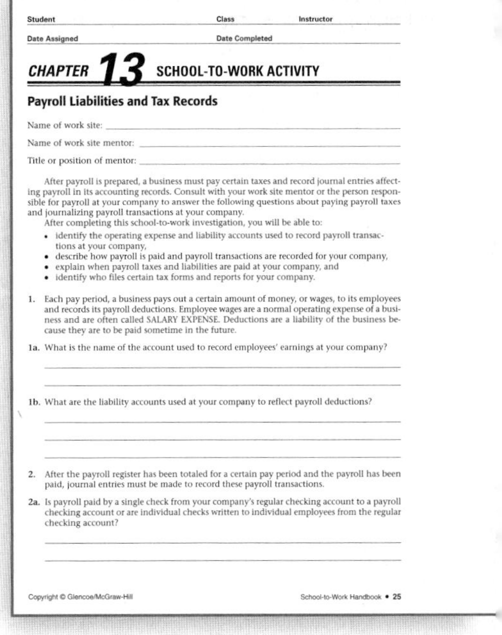

Student ____ Class ____ Instructor ____

Date Assigned ____ Date Completed ____

CHAPTER 13 SCHOOL-TO-WORK ACTIVITY

Payroll Liabilities and Tax Records

Name of work site: ____

Name of work site mentor: ____

Title or position of mentor: ____

After payroll is prepared, a business must pay certain taxes and record journal entries affecting payroll in its accounting records. Consult with your work site mentor or the person responsible for payroll at your company to answer the following questions about paying payroll taxes and journalizing payroll transactions at your company.

After completing this school-to-work investigation, you will be able to:

- identify the operating expense and liability accounts used to record payroll transactions at your company,
- describe how payroll is paid and payroll transactions are recorded for your company,
- explain when payroll taxes and liabilities are paid at your company, and
- identify who files certain tax forms and reports for your company.

1. Each pay period, a business pays out a certain amount of money, or wages, to its employees and records its payroll deductions. Employee wages are a normal operating expense of a business and are often called SALARY EXPENSE. Deductions are a liability of the business because they are to be paid sometime in the future.

1a. What is the name of the account used to record employees' earnings at your company?

1b. What are the liability accounts used at your company to reflect payroll deductions?

2. After the payroll register has been totaled for a certain pay period and the payroll has been paid, journal entries must be made to record these payroll transactions.

2a. Is payroll paid by a single check from your company's regular checking account to a payroll checking account or are individual checks written to individual employees from the regular checking account?

GLENCOE MULTIMEDIA

Electronic Field Trips in Accounting *Video Segment: Payroll Accounting*
After viewing this video, students will be able to explain a payroll system and that deductions can be both voluntary and mandated by law.

Glencoe Accounting: Electronic Learning Center *Chapter 13*
The CD-ROM program is ideal for visual learners since it incorporates video images, animation, and graphics to enliven the content of each lesson.

1 FOCUS

Introducing the Section

In this section students learn how to analyze and record journal entries needed to incorporate payroll expenses into the accounting records. Students will learn about liability accounts used to record amounts owed for required tax deductions, as well as accounts used to record voluntary employee deductions.

Section Concepts

- How to compute the business payroll deductions.
- How to record the payroll entry in the general journal.

Visual Learning

Section 1 Focus

Use **Transparency 13–1** to introduce section concepts.

BELL RINGER

Analyzing: Write this phrase on the chalkboard: "Hourly earnings, $6.50." Tell students they've just taken a new job, and they need to determine how much take-home pay they'll have. Have students decide how much they would earn in a week (without overtime) and then discuss how they would determine take-home pay. What amounts do they think would be deducted from their pay? L1

Journalizing and Posting the Payroll

What **You'll Learn**

- How to compute the business payroll deductions.
- How to record the payroll entry in the general journal.

Why **It's Important**

Payroll deductions are liabilities of the business. It is essential that payroll deductions are journalized and posted in a timely manner.

KEY TERMS

Salaries Expense

Employees, ranging from design engineers at Ford Motor Company to the waitresses at a neighborhood coffee shop, expect their payroll checks to arrive on time and to be accurate. You have learned that various amounts are withheld from employees' earnings for taxes and other voluntary deductions. Once the payroll register is complete, the payroll entry is journalized and the amounts are posted to the general ledger.

Journalizing and Posting the Payroll

After the payroll is prepared, a check is written to transfer the *total net pay* amount from the regular checking account of a business to the payroll checking account. The check is deposited in the payroll account, and all payroll checks for the period are written on the payroll account. The next step is to record the payroll in the accounting records.

Analyzing the Payroll Transaction

Let's analyze the effect of payroll on the employer's accounting system. Each pay period, the business pays out a certain amount of money to its employees in the form of wages and salaries. Employee earnings are a normal operating expense of a business. The expense account often used to record employees' earnings is called **Salaries Expense**. To increase the amount in **Salaries Expense**, the account is debited for the gross earnings for the pay period.

Various deductions, such as income and FICA taxes, are withheld from gross earnings each pay period. The employer retains the amounts withheld until it is time to pay the appropriate government agencies and businesses. The amounts withheld but not yet paid are liabilities of the business. Remember, a liability is an amount *owed* by a business.

Each type of payroll liability is recorded in a separate account.

Type of Deduction	Ledger Account
Federal income tax	**Employees' Federal Income Tax Payable**
Medicare tax	**Medicare Tax Payable**
Hospital insurance premiums	**Hospital Insurance Premiums Payable**

RESOURCE MANAGER

Reproducible Masters
- Lesson Plans
- Chapter Reviews and Working Papers (CRWP) TAE
- Demonstration Problems

Transparencies
- Section Focus Transparency
- Teaching Transparencies
- Source Document Transparencies
- Solution Transparencies

Multimedia
- Exam*View* CD-ROM
- Electronic Learning Center CD-ROM
- Interactive Lesson Planner CD-ROM

Depending on the business, it is possible that several different types of deductions are recorded in the Other Deductions column of the payroll register. If so, the total for each type of deduction is credited to the appropriate liability account. Refer to the Roadrunner Delivery Service payroll register shown in **Figure 12–5** on page 299. To accommodate the deductions that may appear in the Other Deductions column, Roadrunner's ledger includes:

- **U.S. Savings Bonds Payable,**
- **Credit Union Payable,**
- **Union Dues Payable,** and
- **United Way Payable.**

The credit part of the payroll journal entry is made up of several items. The largest item is for net pay. Net pay is the amount actually paid out in cash by the employer to the employees. **Cash in Bank** is credited for total net pay.

The difference between gross earnings and net pay equals the employer's payroll liabilities. Each payroll liability account is separately credited for the total amount shown on the payroll register.

Did You Know?

Teen Spending

Teens number over 25 million today and spend an average of $3,000 a year. With the additional money their parents spend on them, teens influence over $250 billion in spending each year.

Business Transaction

Roadrunner's payroll register in Figure 12–5 on page 299 is the source document for the payroll journal entry.

ANALYSIS

Identify

1. The accounts **Salaries Expense, Employees' Federal Income Tax Payable, Employees' State Income Tax Payable, Social Security Tax Payable, Medicare Tax Payable, Hospital Insurance Premiums Payable, U.S. Savings Bonds Payable,** and **Cash in Bank** are affected.

Classify

2. **Salaries Expense** is an expense account. **Employees' Federal Income Tax Payable, Employees' State Income Tax Payable, Social Security Tax Payable, Medicare Tax Payable, Hospital Insurance Premiums Payable,** and **U.S. Savings Bonds Payable** are liability accounts. **Cash in Bank** is an asset account.

+/−

3. **Salaries Expense** is increased by $1,350.25; **Employees' Federal Income Tax Payable** is increased by $100.00; **Employees' State Income Tax Payable** is increased by $27.01; **Social Security Tax Payable** is increased by $83.73; **Medicare Tax Payable** is increased by $19.57; **Hospital Insurance Premiums Payable** is increased by $23.65; **U.S. Savings Bonds Payable** is increased by $25.00; **Cash in Bank** is decreased by $1,071.29

DEBIT-CREDIT RULE

4. Increases in expense accounts are recorded as debits. Debit **Salaries Expense** for $1,350.25.
5. Decreases in asset accounts are recorded as credits. Credit **Cash in Bank** for $1,071.29. Increases in liability accounts are recorded as credits. Credit **Employees' Federal Income Tax Payable** for $100; **Employees' State Income Tax Payable** for $27.01; **Social Security Tax Payable** for $83.73; **Medicare Tax Payable** for $19.57; **Hospital Insurance Premiums Payable** for $23.65; **U.S. Savings Bonds Payable** for $25.00.

Great Ideas *From the Classroom of...*

Tax Accounting Service At Desert Vista High School, one of our core values is service to others. With this in mind, I established an annual project to enhance the understanding of taxes in my accounting classes. The students provide a tax accounting service for the entire student body. We provide the stamps, envelopes, forms, and expertise.

Bob Cox
Desert Vista High School
Phoenix, Arizona

2 TEACH

GUIDED PRACTICE

Reading Accounting

- Calculating payroll costs requires accountants to apply several different percentages. Have students go through the chapter and make a list of percentages (e.g., social security, 6.2%) and then write the decimal equivalent beside each percentage. L1
- Arrange for a translator who speaks your students' first language to interpret your comments as you present major concepts. Point out to all students that many businesspeople work through interpreters to do business in other countries. ELL

Concept Development: Journalizing and Posting the Payroll

Discussion: Point out to students that businesses use the account Salaries Expense to record the total payroll. Like other expenses, this account has a debit balance. The credit portion of the entry is then divided according to amounts owed for the individual deductions—such as income taxes, social security and Medicare taxes, and voluntary deductions—and the amount actually paid to employees (net pay), which is recorded as a credit to Cash in Bank. L1

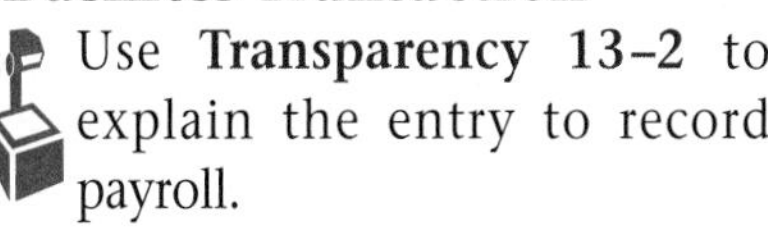

Visual Learning

Business Transaction

Use **Transparency 13–2** to explain the entry to record payroll.

2 TEACH (Cont'd.)

Teaching Tips

Remind students that the payroll register is the source document for the journal entry.

Point out that Salaries Expense is equal to gross earnings. The amount of gross earnings for the pay period is debited to Salaries Expense.

The amount of net pay is equal to the entry to record the total payment to employees, which is a credit to Cash in Bank. The net pay is the only amount actually paid at the time the payroll is recorded, since the business will hold amounts withheld and pay them later.

Demonstration Problem Step-by-Step Practice

Use demonstration problem 13–1 to show students how to record the payroll entry in the general journal.

T ACCOUNTS

6.

Salaries Expense	
Debit +	Credit −
1,350.25	

Employees' Federal Income Tax Payable	
Debit −	Credit +
	100.00

Employees' State Income Tax Payable	
Debit −	Credit +
	27.01

Social Security Tax Payable	
Debit −	Credit +
	83.73

Medicare Tax Payable	
Debit −	Credit +
	19.57

Hospital Insurance Premiums Payable	
Debit −	Credit +
	23.65

U.S. Savings Bonds Payable	
Debit −	Credit +
	25.00

Cash in Bank	
Debit +	Credit −
	1,071.29

JOURNAL ENTRY

7.

GENERAL JOURNAL — PAGE 29

	DATE		DESCRIPTION	POST. REF.	DEBIT	CREDIT	
1	20--						1
2	June	30	Salaries Expense		1 350 25		2
3			Emplys' Fed. Inc. Tax Pay.			100 00	3
4			Emplys' State Inc. Tax Pay.			27 01	4
5			Social Sec. Tax Pay.			83 73	5
6			Medicare Tax Pay.			19 57	6
7			Hosp. Ins. Premiums Pay.			23 65	7
8			U.S. Savings Bonds Pay.			25 00	8
9			Cash in Bank			1 071 29	9
10			Pay. Reg. 6/30—Ck 186				10
11							11

The payroll expense is $1,350.25. The employees receive $1,071.29 in cash (net pay). Later the business will pay the federal government $203.30 ($100.00 federal income tax, $83.73 social security tax, and $19.57 Medicare tax). The business will also pay the state $27.01 for state income tax. A check for $23.65 will be written to the insurance company for hospital insurance premiums. Finally, a check for $25 will be sent to the federal government to purchase savings bonds.

In the next section, you will learn about the payroll tax liabilities of the employer and how those liabilities are calculated and recorded.

COOPERATIVE LEARNING ACTIVITY

Corners Have students choose one of the following topics: social security and Medicare taxes, federal unemployment tax, state unemployment tax, federal income tax, or state income tax. Then have students work in groups to learn as much as they can about the topic. For each topic, students should answer these questions: Who pays the tax—employee or employer? What is the current tax rate? What forms is the employer required to submit? When must the employer pay the taxes?

Ask a spokesperson from each group to present the group findings to the class.

Posting the Payroll Entry to the General Ledger

Figure 13–1 shows the general journal entry and the individual ledger accounts after posting.

GENERAL JOURNAL PAGE *29*

DATE		DESCRIPTION	POST. REF.	DEBIT	CREDIT
20--					
June	*30*	*Salaries Expense*	*514*	*1,350.25*	
		Employees' Fed. Inc. Tax Pay.	*210*		*100.00*
		Employees' State Inc. Tax Pay.	*215*		*27.01*
		Social Security Tax Pay.	*220*		*83.73*
		Medicare Tax Pay.	*225*		*19.57*
		Hosp. Ins. Premiums Pay.	*230*		*23.65*
		U.S. Savings Bonds Pay.	*235*		*25.00*
		Cash in Bank	*101*		*1,071.29*
		Payroll Reg. 6/30—Ck. 186			

ACCOUNT *Salaries Expense* ACCOUNT NO. *514*

DATE		DESCRIPTION	POST. REF.	DEBIT	CREDIT	BALANCE DEBIT	BALANCE CREDIT
20--							
June	*23*	*Balance*	✓			*34,683.10*	
	30		*G29*	*1,350.25*		*36,033.35*	

ACCOUNT *Employees' Federal Income Tax Payable* ACCOUNT NO. *210*

DATE		DESCRIPTION	POST. REF.	DEBIT	CREDIT	BALANCE DEBIT	BALANCE CREDIT
20--							
June	*23*	*Balance*	✓				*293.18*
	30		*G29*		*100.00*		*393.18*

ACCOUNT *Employees' State Income Tax Payable* ACCOUNT NO. *215*

DATE		DESCRIPTION	POST. REF.	DEBIT	CREDIT	BALANCE DEBIT	BALANCE CREDIT
20--							
June	*23*	*Balance*	✓				*321.12*
	30		*G29*		*27.01*		*348.13*

ACCOUNT *Social Security Tax Payable* ACCOUNT NO. *220*

DATE		DESCRIPTION	POST. REF.	DEBIT	CREDIT	BALANCE DEBIT	BALANCE CREDIT
20--							
June	*23*	*Balance*	✓				*250.35*
	30		*G29*		*83.73*		*334.08*

Figure 13–1 Posting the Payroll Entry to the General Ledger

Continued

Key Points

The Payroll Entry

Gross pay
Amount debited to **Salaries Expense**

Net pay
Amount credited to **Cash in Bank**

Payroll deductions
Amounts credited to various liability accounts

ADDRESSING MULTIPLE LEARNING STYLES

Linguistic Learner After discussing the different types of taxes, ask students to consider a world without taxes. Ask them to write a short essay that shows how tax-based services such as education, law enforcement, and mail service would be paid for. They should reflect on the advantages and disadvantages of such a system for individuals and for society.

2 TEACH (Cont'd.)

Visual Learning

Figure 13–1 Posting the Payroll Entry to the General Ledger

Use **Transparency 13–3a** to guide students through the process of posting the general journal entry to the payroll accounts.

Teaching Tips

Direct students' attention to Figure 12–5 on page 299. Have students compare the column headings in the payroll register with the corresponding account names in the general journal entry.

Invite a local business owner or manager who hires teenagers to speak to the class about the criteria she or he uses to decide when to hire additional employees. Ask the speaker to discuss how payroll costs are factored into the decision.

2 TEACH (Cont'd.)

Visual Learning

Figure 13–1 Posting the Payroll Entry to the General Ledger (continued)

Use **Transparency 13–3b** to continue tracing the posting of the general journal payroll entry.

Teaching Tips

Remind students that the word "payable" indicates an amount owed. The employer "owes" the tax money and other deductions withheld on behalf of the employees. The employer will pay amounts owed on a schedule determined by the dollar amount owed. Failure to pay amounts owed to government agencies on the due date can result in fines.

Debating: Divide students into debate teams. Have teams debate the services and benefits they think should be paid for through payroll taxes and who should pay these taxes. Allow teams to choose whether they want to take the employer's or the employees' position on benefits and taxes. Reserve the right to assign positions to ensure enough teams to debate. L2

Strategies for Teaching Ethics in Accounting

Photocopy the Chapter 13 *Student Activity Sheet* for students. Answers are also provided in the booklet.

ACCOUNT *Medicare Tax Payable* — ACCOUNT NO. *225*

DATE		DESCRIPTION	POST. REF.	DEBIT	CREDIT	BALANCE DEBIT	BALANCE CREDIT
20--							
June	*23*	*Balance*	✓				*58 63*
	30		*G29*		*19 57*		*78 20*

ACCOUNT *Hospital Insurance Premiums Payable* — ACCOUNT NO. *230*

DATE		DESCRIPTION	POST. REF.	DEBIT	CREDIT	BALANCE DEBIT	BALANCE CREDIT
20--							
June	*23*	*Balance*	✓				*4 73*
	30		*G29*		*23 65*		*28 38*

ACCOUNT *U.S. Savings Bonds Payable* — ACCOUNT NO. *235*

DATE		DESCRIPTION	POST. REF.	DEBIT	CREDIT	BALANCE DEBIT	BALANCE CREDIT
20--							
June	*23*	*Balance*	✓				*75 00*
	30		*G29*		*25 00*		*100 00*

ACCOUNT *Cash in Bank* — ACCOUNT NO. *101*

DATE		DESCRIPTION	POST. REF.	DEBIT	CREDIT	BALANCE DEBIT	BALANCE CREDIT
20--							
June	*23*	*Balance*	✓			*19610 30*	
	30		*G29*		*1071 29*	*18539 01*	

Figure 13–1 Posting the Payroll Entry to the General Ledger (continued)

A MATTER OF ETHICS

Money Shuffling

Suppose you're an accounting clerk at the Cybercafé and Bookstore, a sole proprietorship. The business owner has asked you to use the money from the employees' 401(k) withholdings to pay off a pressing debt. The owner believes she will have the money to replace the employees' 401(k) funds within a couple of months. The owner doesn't think that the employees will lose very much by not having their money invested during that time. The owner justifies the transfer of funds saying, "It's all out of the same pocket anyway."

Ethical Decision Making:

- What are the ethical issues?
- What are the alternatives?
- Who are the affected parties?
- How do the alternatives affect the parties?
- What would you do?

Teaching A MATTER OF ETHICS

Money Shuffling In this case the business owner wants to use employees' money without their knowledge. Ask students whether her plans to repay the money make a difference in their attitudes. Would students' opinions change if the owner explained the situation to employees and asked to borrow the funds for two months? Would they feel differently if some employees had to be laid off so the business could pay its debts?

Check Your Understanding

Now that you have studied this section, complete the following questions and problems.

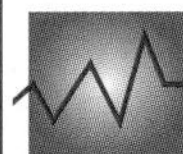

Thinking Critically

1. Why are income and FICA taxes that are withheld from employees' gross earnings considered liabilities to the employer?
2. What is the source of information for recording the payroll transaction in the general journal? What accounts are debited and what accounts are credited?

Computing in the Business World

You are the payroll clerk for Queen City Motors. As you review the payroll records, you notice that two employees are nearing the $84,900 limit for social security tax. As commission-only sales employees, Marcie Laliberte and Kevin Hogan have earned $74,500 and $78,500 respectively.

1. How much more must Marcie and Kevin earn in commission to reach the social security tax limit?
2. If Marcie and Kevin are paid 7% commission on each sale, how much more in sales must each make to reach the social security tax limit?

Problem 13–1 Determining Payroll Amounts

The SweepIt Cleaning Service reported the following amounts for the week ending November 4. The total amount earned by all employees is $2,193.40. The amount withheld for federal income tax is $263.00. Social security tax is $136.00, and Medicare tax is $31.80. Three employees each have $11.25 deducted for hospital insurance. The amount withheld for state income tax is $38.70.

Instructions Answer the following questions concerning the November 4 payroll for the SweepIt Cleaning Service.

1. What amount is recorded in the **Salaries Expense** account?
2. What amount is recorded in the **Medicare Tax Payable** account?
3. What is the total amount of liabilities for the weekly payroll?
4. What amount is entered in the **Hospital Insurance Premiums Payable** account?
5. What amount is recorded as a credit for the **Cash in Bank** account?

3 ASSESS

Thinking Critically (Answers)

1. The employer holds amounts deducted until the specified time to pay them. The amounts are liabilities since they are to be paid in the future.
2. Totals line of the payroll register. Salaries Expense is debited for total gross earnings; payroll liability accounts are credited for individual column total.

Computing in the Business World (Answers)

1. Marcie: an additional $10,400; Kevin: an additional $6,400.
2. Marcie: an additional $148,571.42; Kevin: an additional $91,428.57.

Problem 13–1 (Answers)

1. $2,193.40
2. $31.80
3. $503.25
4. $33.75
5. $1,690.15

Chapter Reviews and Working Papers Refer students to the Chapter 13 workbook pages to answer *Check Your Understanding* activities.

4 CLOSE

Section Wrap-Up

Writing: Have students write a paragraph describing how employee deductions are recorded in the accounting system. L1

RETEACHING SECTION 1

Recording the Payment of Payroll The journal entry to record the payment of payroll is easy when you get the information from the payroll register. Refer students to Figure 12–5 on page 299. The total earnings is the amount debited to payroll expense. Each total under Deductions represents a liability for the employer. The employer owes this money to the federal and state governments for taxes, the Social Security Administration for social security and Medicare taxes, the insurance company for hospital insurance, and the federal government for savings bonds. The Net Pay in the payroll register is the total amount the employer actually pays the employees, so the Cash in Bank account is credited for that amount.

CHAPTER 13
SECTION 2, PAGES 322–326

1 FOCUS

Introducing the Section
In this section students will learn how to calculate several taxes that employers are required to pay on their payrolls. These taxes include social security and Medicare taxes and state and federal unemployment taxes.

Section Concepts
- How to calculate the employer's FICA taxes.
- How to calculate federal and state unemployment taxes.
- How to journalize and post employer's payroll taxes.

Visual Learning

Section 2 Focus
Use **Transparency 13–4** to introduce section concepts.

BELL RINGER

Collecting Information: Have students list the kinds of taxes they or their parents pay. Write responses on the chalkboard. (Responses might include gasoline taxes, sales tax, property tax, income taxes, FICA taxes.) Then ask students what taxes employers pay, and write those on the chalkboard. Help students by asking questions such as "Who pays benefits for workers who are unemployed?" L1

SECTION 2

Employer's Payroll Taxes

What You'll Learn
- How to calculate the employer's FICA taxes.
- How to calculate federal and state unemployment taxes.
- How to journalize and post employer's payroll taxes.

Why It's Important
In addition to the amounts withheld from employees' payroll checks, the employer owes taxes based on the weekly payroll. These taxes are liabilities of the business.

KEY TERMS
- Federal Unemployment Tax Act (FUTA)
- State Unemployment Tax Act (SUTA)
- unemployment taxes
- Payroll Tax Expense

Key Points
FICA Taxes
Both employees and employers pay FICA taxes using the same tax rates.

In Section 1, you learned how to journalize and post the payroll entry. This entry, in part, records taxes employees are required to pay on their earnings. Your local florist, employing designers, delivery workers, and sales clerks, must also pay taxes on their worker's earnings. These amounts need to be calculated, journalized, and posted.

Computing Payroll Tax Expenses

In addition to withholding taxes from employees' wages, the employer *pays* taxes on these wages. The employer's taxes, considered operating expenses of the business, consist of the employer's FICA taxes, the federal unemployment tax, and the state unemployment tax.

The Employer's FICA Taxes

Under the Federal Insurance Contributions Act, both the employee and the employer pay FICA taxes. As you recall, the employer withholds a percentage of gross earnings for social security and Medicare taxes. In addition, the employer pays FICA taxes using the same percentage of gross earnings. Recall that the current rates are 6.2% for social security tax and 1.45% for Medicare tax.

The employer and the employee pay social security tax on gross earnings up to the maximum taxable limit per employee ($84,900 in 2002). The employer and the employee pay Medicare tax on all gross earnings; there is no maximum taxable limit. The payroll clerk checks the accumulated earnings on each employee's earnings record to determine if that employee has reached the maximum taxable amount. When an employee reaches the limit, the social security tax is no longer computed.

In determining social security tax and Medicare tax for both employee and employer, it makes no difference if the employees are full-time, part-time, temporary, or permanent. A full-time adult employee and a student employed part-time only for the summer are subject to the same taxes.

At Roadrunner Delivery Service for the week ending June 30, the employees' total social security taxes are $83.73 and total Medicare taxes are $19.57. The employer's taxes on the total gross earnings are $83.72

RESOURCE MANAGER

Reproducible Masters
- Lesson Plans
- Chapter Reviews and Working Papers (CRWP) TAE
- Demonstration Problems

Transparencies
- Section Focus Transparency
- Teaching Transparencies
- Source Document Transparencies
- Solution Transparencies

Multimedia
- ExamView CD-ROM
- Electronic Learning Center CD-ROM
- Interactive Lesson Planner CD-ROM

(6.2% of $1,350.25) and $19.58 (1.45% of $1,350.25) respectively. Notice that the social security tax for the employees ($83.73) and the employer ($83.72) do not match. The same situation exists for the Medicare tax. This is because the employer's tax is calculated on the total gross earnings ($1,350.25). The employees' taxes are calculated on each employee's gross earnings and the individual tax amounts are totaled. This may result in small differences between the employees' and employer's taxes.

ACCOUNTING TIPS

Check Your Work

If you're a payroll clerk, always double-check the obvious. The IRS says that problems on tax filings most often result from obvious mistakes like incorrect employer identification numbers and social security numbers, misspelled employee names, and incorrect addresses.

Federal and State Unemployment Taxes

The **Federal Unemployment Tax Act (FUTA)** and the **State Unemployment Tax Act (SUTA)** require employers to pay unemployment taxes. Unemployment taxes are based on a percentage of the employees' gross earnings. **Unemployment taxes** are collected to provide funds for workers who are temporarily unemployed.

The employer pays both federal and state unemployment taxes. The maximum federal unemployment tax is 6.2% on the first $7,000 of an employee's annual wages. State unemployment tax rates and maximum taxable amounts vary among states. Employers may deduct up to 5.4% of the state unemployment taxes from federal unemployment taxes. Most employers, therefore, pay a federal tax of .8% (6.2%–5.4%) of taxable gross earnings.

In a few states, employees are also required to pay unemployment taxes. The percentage amounts vary among these states.

For Roadrunner, since none of the employees has reached the maximum taxable amount, the federal unemployment tax for the week ended June 30 is $10.80 ($1,350.25 × .8%). The state unemployment tax is $72.91 ($1,350.25 × 5.4%).

HELP WANTED

Journalizing the Employer Payroll Taxes

The employer's payroll taxes are business expenses recorded in the **Payroll Tax Expense** account. Until paid, the employer's payroll taxes are liabilities of the business.

Use the **Social Security Tax Payable** and the **Medicare Tax Payable** accounts to record both the employees' and the employer's FICA taxes. Record the employer's unemployment taxes in the **Federal Unemployment Tax Payable** and **State Unemployment Tax Payable** accounts.

In the next business transaction we will analyze the accounts affected when an employer pays its payroll taxes. This entry takes place in each payroll period.

CRITICAL THINKING ACTIVITY

Analyzing Employee Costs Explain to students that paying employees to work overtime is often less expensive for employers than hiring additional staff. Have students discuss why it may be less expensive to pay overtime wages than to hire new employees. (The employer must pay taxes on each employee, including the employer's share of social security and Medicare, federal unemployment taxes, and state unemployment taxes. Overtime wages for an existing employee may be less than the taxes paid for a new employee.)

2 TEACH

GUIDED PRACTICE

Reading Accounting

- Comparing numbers and proofreading numbers accurately are skills accountants need. Give students practice comparing numbers by photocopying the solution to an end-of-chapter problem and having students proofread and check each other's solutions. L1

Concept Development: Computing Payroll Tax Expenses

Discussion: Show students how to calculate the two parts of FICA taxes: social security and Medicare. Point out that the employer is obligated to calculate the correct amount.

Employers also are required to calculate federal and state unemployment taxes on their total payroll. Employers also pay these taxes at times specified by the taxing agency. L1

Concept Development: Journalizing the Employer Payroll Taxes

Discussion: Point out that the employer pays both the employees' and the employer's share of social security and Medicare taxes at the same time. The employer also pays additional taxes for federal and state unemployment programs. Employers consider taxes a part of the cost of hiring an employee. L1

2 TEACH (Cont'd.)

Visual Learning

Business Transaction

Use **Transparency 13–5** to guide students through the analysis and recording of the journal entry to record the employer's payroll tax liabilities.

Demonstration Problem
Step-by-Step Practice

Use demonstration problem 13–2 to give students practice in calculating the employer's payroll taxes.

Teaching Tip

Ask students to explain the source of information in each line of the journal entry.

Thinking Algebraically

Conceptualize: Tell students that they have been asked to estimate future payroll expenses if FICA tax rates and limits are increased to pay for social security and Medicare benefits. Have students write a formula for estimating the employer's FICA taxes if the result of the tax increase will cause the total amount of tax paid to increase by 20 percent over current amounts paid. (Estimated taxes = 1.2 × current total FICA taxes) **L1**

Chapter Reviews and Working Papers
Refer students to the *Study Plan* located at the beginning of Chapter 13 in the workbook.

Business Transaction

Roadrunner's payroll register in ***Figure 12–5*** *on page 299 is the source document for the payroll tax journal entry.*

ANALYSIS

Identify

1. The accounts **Payroll Tax Expense**, **Social Security Tax Payable**, **Medicare Tax Payable**, **State Unemployment Tax Payable**, and **Federal Unemployment Tax Payable** are affected.

Classify

2. **Payroll Tax Expense** is an expense account. **Social Security Tax Payable**, **Medicare Tax Payable**, **State Unemployment Tax Payable**, and **Federal Unemployment Tax Payable** are liability accounts.

+/−

3. **Payroll Tax Expense** is increased by $187.01; **Social Security Tax Payable** is increased by $83.72; **Medicare Tax Payable** is increased by $19.58; **State Unemployment Tax Payable** is increased by $72.91; **Federal Unemployment Tax Payable** is increased by $10.80.

DEBIT-CREDIT RULE

4. Increases in expense accounts are recorded as debits. Debit **Payroll Tax Expense** for $187.01.
5. Increases in liability accounts are recorded as credits. Credit **Social Security Tax Payable** for $83.72; **Medicare Tax Payable** for $19.58; **State Unemployment Tax Payable** for $72.91; **Federal Unemployment Tax Payable** for $10.80.

T ACCOUNTS

6.

Payroll Tax Expense	
Debit + 187.01	Credit −

Social Security Tax Payable	
Debit −	Credit + 83.72

Medicare Tax Payable	
Debit −	Credit + 19.58

State Unemployment Tax Payable	
Debit −	Credit + 72.91

Federal Unemployment Tax Payable	
Debit −	Credit + 10.80

JOURNAL ENTRY

7.

GENERAL JOURNAL — PAGE 30

	DATE		DESCRIPTION	POST. REF.	DEBIT	CREDIT	
1	20--						1
2	June	30	Payroll Tax Expense		187 01		2
3			Social Security Tax Pay.			83 72	3
4			Medicare Tax Pay.			19 58	4
5			State Unemplymnt. Tax Pay.			72 91	5
6			Fed. Unemplymnt. Tax Pay.			10 80	6
7			Payroll Reg. 6/30				7

REINFORCING STUDY SKILLS

Reading Skills Remind students that the learning objectives listed at the begining of each chapter provide a good "road map" for their approach to the chapter. As they read the chapter, students should try to reach each of the stated goals before going on to the next main objective. Reading for a specific objective should help students retain information more easily.

Posting Payroll Taxes to the General Ledger

Figure 13–2 shows the individual ledger accounts after posting the payroll taxes entry.

Notice that the **Social Security Tax Payable** and the **Medicare Tax Payable** accounts have two entries for the June 30 payroll. The first entry is the amount of taxes withheld from the *employees'* earnings. The second entry is the amount of taxes paid by the *employer.*

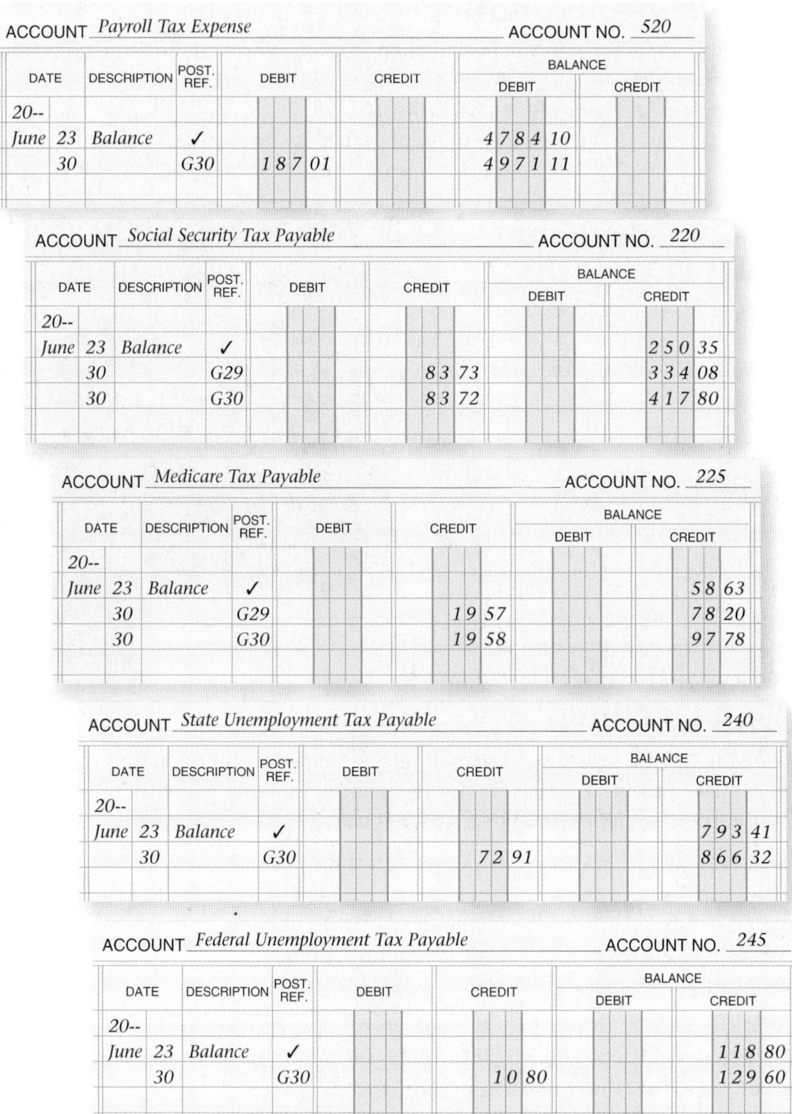

ACCOUNT *Payroll Tax Expense* ACCOUNT NO. *520*

DATE		DESCRIPTION	POST. REF.	DEBIT	CREDIT	BALANCE DEBIT	BALANCE CREDIT
20--							
June	23	Balance	✓			4,784.10	
	30		G30	187.01		4,971.11	

ACCOUNT *Social Security Tax Payable* ACCOUNT NO. *220*

DATE		DESCRIPTION	POST. REF.	DEBIT	CREDIT	BALANCE DEBIT	BALANCE CREDIT
20--							
June	23	Balance	✓				250.35
	30		G29		83.73		334.08
	30		G30		83.72		417.80

ACCOUNT *Medicare Tax Payable* ACCOUNT NO. *225*

DATE		DESCRIPTION	POST. REF.	DEBIT	CREDIT	BALANCE DEBIT	BALANCE CREDIT
20--							
June	23	Balance	✓				58.63
	30		G29		19.57		78.20
	30		G30		19.58		97.78

ACCOUNT *State Unemployment Tax Payable* ACCOUNT NO. *240*

DATE		DESCRIPTION	POST. REF.	DEBIT	CREDIT	BALANCE DEBIT	BALANCE CREDIT
20--							
June	23	Balance	✓				793.41
	30		G30		72.91		866.32

ACCOUNT *Federal Unemployment Tax Payable* ACCOUNT NO. *245*

DATE		DESCRIPTION	POST. REF.	DEBIT	CREDIT	BALANCE DEBIT	BALANCE CREDIT
20--							
June	23	Balance	✓				118.80
	30		G30		10.80		129.60

Figure 13–2 General Ledger Accounts after Posting the Payroll Taxes Entry

HOME AND COMMUNITY CONNECTIONS ACTIVITY

Filing System for Bill Payments Have students find out what type of system their families use to keep track of monthly expenses, payment due dates, and receipt retention. Who is responsible for the monthly/semi-monthly payment of invoices and bills in their home? Do they agree with their family's filing system? Can they recommend a more efficient system? Have several students share their ideas and then discuss with the entire class the need for financial organization in the home.

2 TEACH (Cont'd.)

Concept Development: Posting Payroll Taxes to the General Ledger

Discussion: Have students describe the posting process and explain why each amount is posted to the ledger column shown. Ask students how they know whether the normal balance of each account is a debit or a credit. L1

Visual Learning

Figure 13–2 General Ledger Accounts After Posting the Payroll Taxes Entry

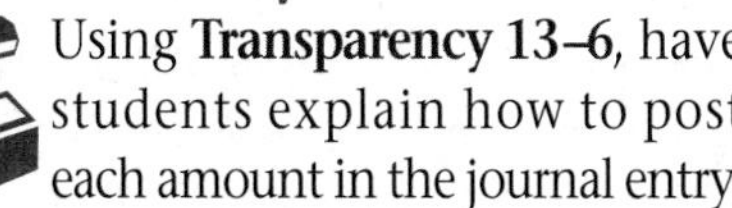

Using **Transparency 13–6**, have students explain how to post each amount in the journal entry.

Teaching Tip

Have students look at the ledger accounts for Social Security Tax Payable and Medicare Tax Payable. Point out the two amounts posted for the June 30 entries. The first June 30 amount in each account represents the employees' share of the taxes; the second amount is the employer's share. Since the employer's share is calculated on the total payroll, there is often a difference of a penny or so between the two amounts.

Demonstration Problem Step-by-Step Practice

Use demonstration problem 13–3 to give students practice in journalizing the employer's payroll taxes.

CHAPTER 13
SECTION 2, PAGES 322–326

3 ASSESS

Thinking Critically (Answers)
1. Both pay the same percentage of FICA taxes on employees' earnings.
2. They are paid by the business at a future date and are thus a liability.

Communicating Accounting (Answers)
Answers may vary. Students should list the deductions and explain each.

Problem 13–2 (Answers)
Social Security Tax Pay.: $299.87
Medicare Tax Pay.: $70.13
Federal Unemploy. Tax Pay.: $38.69
State Unemploy. Tax Pay.: $261.18

Problem 13–3 (Answers)
Employees' fed. income tax, payroll
Employer's soc. sec. tax, payroll tax
U.S. savings bonds, payroll
Employer's Medicare tax, payroll tax
Federal unemployment tax, payroll tax
Employees' state income tax, payroll
Union dues, payroll
Employees' social security tax, payroll
State unemployment tax, payroll tax
Employee's Medicare tax, payroll

Chapter Reviews and Working Papers Refer students to the Chapter 13 workbook pages to answer *Check Your Understanding* activities.

4 CLOSE

Section Wrap-Up
Presenting Information in a Table: Have students create a table showing the employer's payroll taxes and percentages paid. Tell students to write a table title and use an appropriate table format. L1

SECTION 2 Check Your Understanding

Now that you have studied this section, complete the following questions and problems.

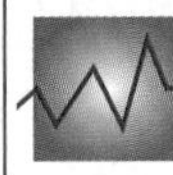

Thinking Critically

1. What does the Federal Insurance Contributions Act require of employers and employees?
2. Explain why the employer's payroll taxes are a liability of the business.

Communicating Accounting

As the payroll clerk for Fashion Square Gift Shop, you are to explain the deductions from employees' payroll checks.
1. Prepare an outline of the items you'll need to discuss.
2. Team up with a classmate and present your list of deductions. Explain each deduction.

Problem 13–2 Calculating Employer's Payroll Taxes

For the week ending June 30, EZ Copy Center's payroll has total gross earnings of $4,836.60. Calculate the employer's payroll taxes. Use the following percentages:

Social security tax	6.2%
Medicare tax	1.45%
Federal unemployment tax	.8%
State unemployment tax	5.4%

Problem 13–3 Identifying Entries for Payroll Liabilities

The following list includes several payroll-related items used in preparing the weekly payroll for Outdoor Adventures. These items are included in either the entry to record the payroll or the entry to record the employer's payroll taxes.

Employees' federal income tax	Employees' state income tax
Employer's social security tax	Union dues
U.S. savings bonds	Employees' social security tax
Employer's Medicare tax	State unemployment tax
Federal unemployment tax	Employees' Medicare tax

Instructions Use the form provided in your working papers. Place a check mark in the column that describes the entry in which the item is recorded: the entry to record the payroll, or the entry to record the employer's payroll taxes.

RETEACHING SECTION 2

Explaining FICA Taxes Employees pay FICA taxes so that they can receive retirement benefits. Like income taxes, FICA taxes are calculated as a percentage of the money the employee earns. The maximum wage for FICA taxes can change each year based on inflation and the cost of living. The employer must contribute an amount equal to the amount that each employee pays. The federal government uses FICA taxes to provide disability benefits, survivor's benefits, retirement income, and hospitalization insurance to those employees who have contributed through their employment.

Tax Liability Payments and Tax Reports

After the payroll entries are journalized and posted, the amounts owed to government agencies and other institutions (credit unions, charitable organizations, etc.) must be paid in a timely manner. Depending on the balance, the payroll liabilities are paid biweekly, monthly, or quarterly. Payroll reports and payroll tax returns are also prepared and filed. In this section you will learn how to complete payroll tax forms.

What **You'll Learn**

- How to pay payroll tax liabilities.
- Which tax reports are prepared and filed.

Why **It's Important**

Business owners must pay their payroll liabilities and file payroll tax reports promptly and accurately.

KEY TERMS

Federal Tax Deposit Coupon
Electronic Federal Tax Payment System (EFTPS)
Form 940
Form 941
Form W-2
Form W-3

Paying the Payroll Tax Liabilities

At regular intervals, the payroll taxes and the amounts withheld from employees are paid by the employer. These items include **(1)** FICA and employees' federal income taxes, **(2)** employees' state income taxes, **(3)** federal and state unemployment taxes, and **(4)** amounts voluntarily withheld from employees' earnings.

FICA and Federal Income Taxes

One payment is made for:

- social security and Medicare taxes (both the employees' and the employer's shares), and
- employees' federal income taxes withheld.

The payment is made at an authorized financial institution or a Federal Reserve Bank. For most small businesses, like Roadrunner, this payment is made monthly. The payment is due by the 15th day of the month following the payroll month. For example, for the month ending June 30, the payment is due by July 15. Larger businesses make the payment every two weeks, or even within days of the payroll date.

For many small businesses, the **Federal Tax Deposit Coupon** (Form 8109) is prepared and sent with the check. The form identifies the type of tax and the tax period. **Figure 13–3** shows Form 8109 for Roadrunner. Notice the ovals on the right side of the form. One oval, 941, is filled in to indicate FICA and federal income taxes. Another oval, 2nd Quarter, is filled in to indicate the period ending June 30.

International ACCOUNTING

Netiquette

Make considerations for foreign users who browse your Web site. Using simple text with few colloquialisms will help accommodate foreign users.

CHAPTER 13
SECTION 3, PAGES 327–337

1 FOCUS

Introducing the Section

Now that students have learned to calculate and record the employer's payroll tax liabilities, they'll next learn how to record the payment of those liabilities. They'll also learn about several tax forms that accompany payments.

Section Concepts

- How to pay payroll tax liabilities.
- Which tax reports are prepared and filed.

Visual Learning

Section 3 Focus

Use **Transparency 13–7** to introduce section concepts.

BELL RINGER

Consulting: Tell students that they've been asked to advise a small-business client about the information they would need to give an outside firm if they wanted to contract out their payroll work. Have students decide what information the business would need to provide to the contractor. Ask students what information the employer should expect from the contractor in return. L2

Concept Development: Paying the Payroll Tax Liabilities

Discussion: Explain the employer's obligation to pay the correct amount of each tax at the appropriate time. Depending upon total amounts being held, employers are required to pay taxes weekly, monthly, or quarterly. L1

RESOURCE MANAGER

Reproducible Masters
- Lesson Plans
- Chapter Reviews and Working Papers (CRWP) TAE
- Demonstration Problems

Transparencies
- Section Focus Transparency
- Teaching Transparencies
- Source Document Transparencies
- Solution Transparencies

Multimedia
- Exam*View* CD-ROM
- Electronic Learning Center CD-ROM
- Interactive Lesson Planner CD-ROM

2 TEACH

GUIDED PRACTICE

Reading Accounting

• Tax forms require careful preparation. Have students look at the form in Figure 13–3. What information would they verify for accuracy on this form? (The tax month, amount being paid, employer ID number, type of form—941, and quarter.) L1

Visual Learning

Figure 13–3 Federal Tax Deposit Coupon (Form 8109)

Use **Transparencies 13–8a and 13–8b** to point out the information that is recorded on a tax coupon to accompany payment of federal income taxes withheld from employees' pay.

Business Transaction

Using **Transparency 13–9**, guide students through the analysis and recording of the entry for payment of federal income taxes.

Teaching Tip

Explain to students that the check accompanying the federal tax deposit coupon is made out to a local bank that is a member of the Federal Reserve System. This bank then forwards the funds to the IRS.

Strategies for Teaching International Accounting

To enrich study of International Accounting, refer to the additional critical thinking activities in the booklet.

Figure 13–3 Federal Tax Deposit Coupon (Form 8109) for FICA and Federal Income Taxes

AMOUNT OF DEPOSIT (Do NOT type, please print.)
DOLLARS | CENTS

TAX YEAR MONTH → 0 6

9 0 8 7 6

EMPLOYER IDENTIFICATION NUMBER → 3 1 8 0 4 2 3 9 8

BANK NAME/ DATE STAMP

ROADRUNNER DELIVERY SERVICE
155 GATEWAY BLVD.
SACRAMENTO CA 94230

IRS USE ONLY

Darken only one TYPE OF TAX: 941 (marked), 945, 990-C, 1120, 943, 990-T, 720, 990-PF, CT-1, 1042, 940

Darken only one TAX PERIOD: 1st Quarter, 2nd Quarter (marked), 3rd Quarter, 4th Quarter

35

FOR BANK USE IN MICR ENCODING

Federal Tax Deposit Coupon
Form 8109

Larger businesses deposit income tax payments by electronic funds transfer through the **Electronic Federal Tax Payment System (EFTPS)**. Eventually even small businesses will make payments using EFTPS.

Business Transaction

After recording the June 30 payroll and the employer's payroll taxes, Roadrunner pays its payroll tax liabilities of $908.76, which include employees' federal income taxes of $393.18 (refer to ledger account in ***Figure 13–1****), social security taxes of $417.80, and Medicare taxes of $97.78 on July 15 (refer to ledger accounts in* ***Figure 13–2****).*

ANALYSIS

Identify 1. The accounts **Employees' Federal Income Tax Payable, Social Security Tax Payable, Medicare Tax Payable,** and **Cash in Bank** are affected.

Classify 2. **Employees' Federal Income Tax Payable, Social Security Tax Payable,** and **Medicare Tax Payable** are liability accounts. **Cash in Bank** is an asset account.

+/− 3. **Employees' Federal Income Tax Payable** is decreased by $393.18; **Social Security Tax Payable** is decreased by $417.80; **Medicare Tax Payable** is decreased by $97.78; **Cash in Bank** is decreased by $908.76.

DEBIT-CREDIT RULE

4. Decreases in liability accounts are recorded as debits. Debit **Employees' Federal Income Tax Payable** for $393.18; **Social Security Tax Payable** for $417.80; **Medicare Tax Payable** for $97.78.
5. Decreases in asset accounts are recorded as credits. Credit **Cash in Bank** for $908.76.

T ACCOUNTS

6.

Employees' Federal Income Tax Payable

Debit −	Credit +
393.18	

Social Security Tax Payable

Debit −	Credit +
417.80	

Medicare Tax Payable

Debit −	Credit +
97.78	

Cash in Bank

Debit +	Credit −
	908.76

Teaching International ACCOUNTING

(Refer to the *International Accounting* feature on page 327.)

Identifying Colloquialisms A colloquialism is an informal expression that is not recognized as standard dialect. Foreign browsers may misinterpret or simply not understand colloquialisms posted on a Web site. Provide examples of colloquialisms for students. (For example, "plastic" means a credit card or a debit card; "bounced check" means a check returned for nonsufficient funds.) Have students expand the list with examples of their own. Then have students visit various Web sites and search for colloquialisms that should be avoided. Ask them to share their findings with the class.

JOURNAL ENTRY

7.

	DATE		DESCRIPTION	POST. REF.	DEBIT	CREDIT	
			GENERAL JOURNAL		PAGE 31		
1	20--						1
2	July	15	Emplys' Fed. Inc. Tax Pay.		393 18		2
3			Social Security Tax Pay.		417 80		3
4			Medicare Tax Pay.		97 78		4
5			Cash in Bank			908 76	5
6			Check 208				6
7							7

State Income Taxes

At regular intervals, businesses pay the amounts withheld for state income taxes. Each state determines how and when the payments are made and what reports are filed.

Business Transaction

Roadrunner pays $348.13 to the state. This is the amount of state income tax withheld from employees earnings, as indicated in the ***Employees' State Income Tax Payable*** *account shown in* ***Figure 13–1.***

ANALYSIS

Identify 1. The accounts **Employees' State Income Tax Payable** and **Cash in Bank** are affected.

Classify 2. **Employees' State Income Tax Payable** is a liability account. **Cash in Bank** is an asset account.

+/− 3. **Employees' State Income Tax Payable** is decreased by $348.13. **Cash in Bank** is decreased by $348.13.

DEBIT-CREDIT RULE

4. Decreases in liability accounts are recorded as debits. Debit **Employees' State Income Tax Payable** for $348.13.
5. Decreases in asset accounts are recorded as credits. Credit **Cash in Bank** for $348.13.

T ACCOUNTS

6.

Employees' State Income Tax Payable		Cash in Bank	
Debit −	Credit +	Debit +	Credit −
348.13			348.13

JOURNAL ENTRY

7.

	DATE		DESCRIPTION	POST. REF.	DEBIT	CREDIT	
			GENERAL JOURNAL		PAGE 32		
1	20--						1
2	July	15	Emplys' State Inc. Tax Pay.		348 13		2
3			Cash in Bank			348 13	3
4			Check 209				4
5							5

2 TEACH (Cont'd.)

Visual Learning

Business Transaction

Using **Transparency 13–10**, have students analyze the entry to pay the state income taxes. Discuss how this payment differs from the payment of federal taxes. If your area has a local income tax, also discuss that tax and its payment.

Writing: Have students write letters to your state representative and to your federal members of Congress. In the letters, have students query legislators about how tax laws are proposed and how the legislators decide whether to raise or lower taxes. If you have access to E-mail services, you may want students to use that means of communication. Have students share responses in class. L1

Research: Have students research recent tax proposals made by your state's congressional representatives. Ask students to discuss the impact of the proposals on employers and employees, and whether they agree or disagree with the proposals. L2

MEETING SPECIAL NEEDS

English Language Learners To make studying easier for any students who are English language learners, ask other students to help tape this chapter for home study. Have several students divide up the chapter, with each student recording one section. Ask students who use the tapes to summarize orally the main ideas in each section. These students could also develop questions for quizzes.

2 TEACH (Cont'd.)

Visual Learning

Business Transaction
Use **Transparency 13–11** to guide students through the analysis and recording of the entry for payment of federal unemployment taxes.

Teaching Tip

The IRS has information and forms you may want to download from their Internet site. The Teachers' Toolkit is intended for use in secondary schools and contains tax forms, a lesson plan, student handouts, and sample cases, all of which can be downloaded. Available tax forms include the following:

- Form W-2
- Form W-4
- Form 1099-INT
- Form 1040EZ
- Form 1040A
- Form 1040A Schedule 1
- Tax Tables
- Form 1040A Instructions
- Form 1040EZ Instructions

You can access the Toolkit from the IRS Web site at www.irs.gov. Enter a search, using "Teacher's Toolkit" for the keywords.

Federal Unemployment Taxes

Most businesses pay the federal unemployment or FUTA tax quarterly. If a business has accumulated federal unemployment taxes of less than $100 for the year, only one annual payment is necessary.

Business Transaction

*Roadrunner pays $129.60 for FUTA taxes. This is the balance of the **Federal Unemployment Tax Payable** account shown in **Figure 13–2**.*

ANALYSIS

Identify
1. The accounts **Federal Unemployment Tax Payable** and **Cash in Bank** are affected.

Classify
2. **Federal Unemployment Tax Payable** is a liability account. **Cash in Bank** is an asset account.

+/−
3. **Federal Unemployment Tax Payable** is decreased by $129.60. **Cash in Bank** is decreased by $129.60.

DEBIT-CREDIT RULE

4. Decreases in liability accounts are recorded as debits. Debit **Federal Unemployment Tax Payable** for $129.60.
5. Decreases in asset accounts are recorded as credits. Credit **Cash in Bank** for $129.60.

T ACCOUNTS

6.

Federal Unemployment Tax Payable	
Debit −	Credit +
129.60	

Cash in Bank	
Debit +	Credit −
	129.60

JOURNAL ENTRY

7. GENERAL JOURNAL — PAGE 33

	DATE		DESCRIPTION	POST. REF.	DEBIT	CREDIT	
1	20--						1
2	July	15	Fed. Unemployment Tax Pay.		129 60		2
3			Cash in Bank			129 60	3
4			Check 210				4
5							5

When a business pays the FUTA tax, a Federal Tax Deposit Coupon (Form 8109) is prepared and sent with the check. When FUTA taxes are paid, the "940" oval is filled in instead of the "941" oval. **Figure 13–4** shows the Form 8109 that Roadrunner sends with the federal unemployment tax payment.

MAKING CONNECTIONS TO DAILY LIFE

Observing Taxes at Work Have students keep a "tax log" for a week. Ask them to observe the things around them that are provided through tax dollars. At the end of the week, ask students to share their logs in class and discuss whether they agree or disagree that taxes should fund all the items in their logs. (Students' logs might list education, highways, fire and police protection, aid for the poor and homeless, sewer and water, business development grants or tax relief, public libraries, programs for abused children, medical care through a public hospital, or training for displaced workers.)

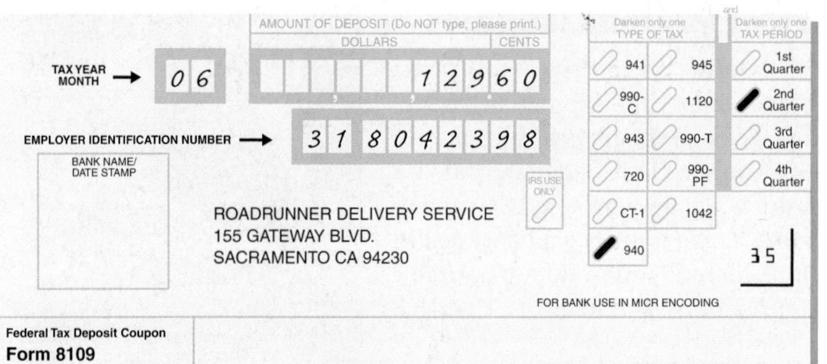
AMOUNT OF DEPOSIT (Do NOT type, please print.)
DOLLARS | CENTS
TAX YEAR MONTH → 06
12960
EMPLOYER IDENTIFICATION NUMBER → 31 8042398
BANK NAME/ DATE STAMP
ROADRUNNER DELIVERY SERVICE
155 GATEWAY BLVD.
SACRAMENTO CA 94230
Darken only one TYPE OF TAX: 941, 945, 990-C, 1120, 943, 990-T, 720, 990-PF, CT-1, 1042, 940 (marked)
Darken only one TAX PERIOD: 1st Quarter, 2nd Quarter (marked), 3rd Quarter, 4th Quarter
IRS USE ONLY
35
FOR BANK USE IN MICR ENCODING
Federal Tax Deposit Coupon
Form 8109

Figure 13–4 Federal Tax Deposit Coupon (Form 8109) for Federal Unemployment Taxes

State Unemployment Taxes

State unemployment taxes are usually paid on a quarterly basis.

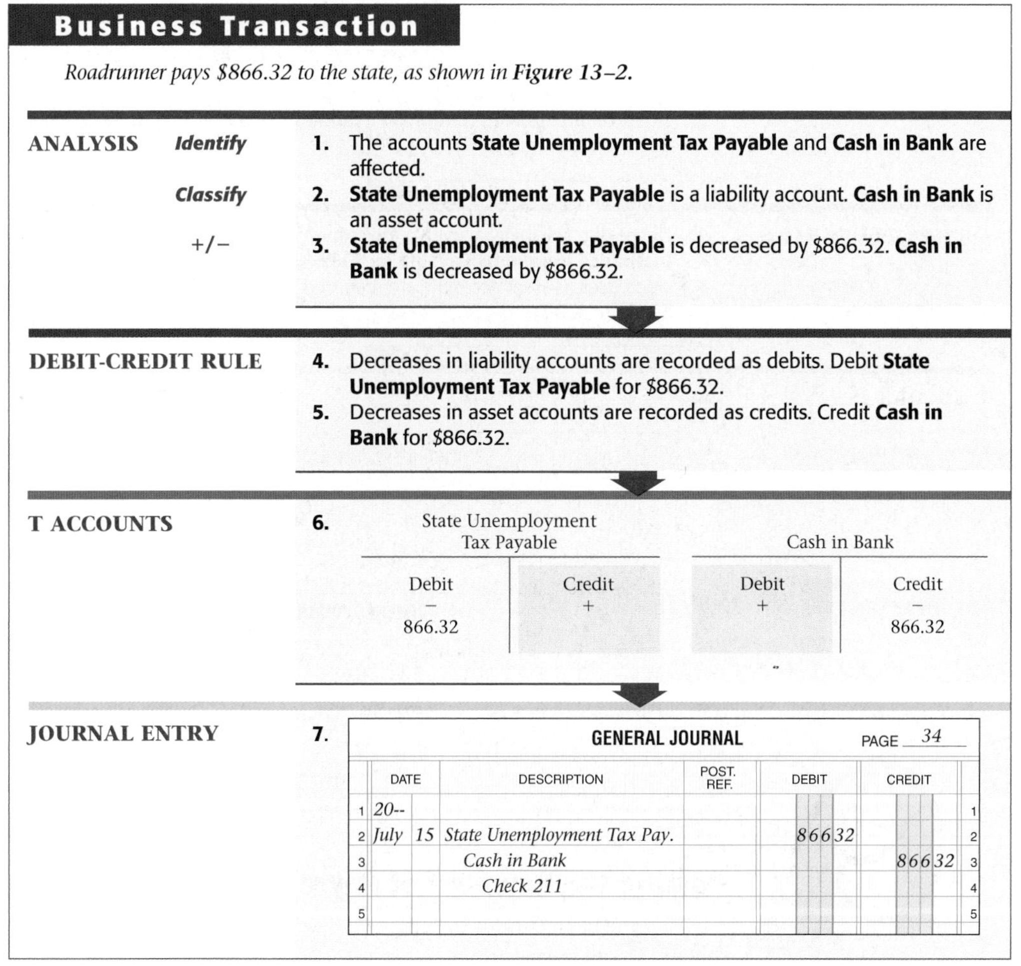

Business Transaction

Roadrunner pays $866.32 to the state, as shown in ***Figure 13–2.***

ANALYSIS

Identify 1. The accounts **State Unemployment Tax Payable** and **Cash in Bank** are affected.

Classify 2. **State Unemployment Tax Payable** is a liability account. **Cash in Bank** is an asset account.

+/− 3. **State Unemployment Tax Payable** is decreased by $866.32. **Cash in Bank** is decreased by $866.32.

DEBIT-CREDIT RULE

4. Decreases in liability accounts are recorded as debits. Debit **State Unemployment Tax Payable** for $866.32.
5. Decreases in asset accounts are recorded as credits. Credit **Cash in Bank** for $866.32.

T ACCOUNTS

6.

State Unemployment Tax Payable	
Debit −	Credit +
866.32	

Cash in Bank	
Debit +	Credit −
	866.32

JOURNAL ENTRY

7. GENERAL JOURNAL PAGE 34

	DATE		DESCRIPTION	POST. REF.	DEBIT	CREDIT	
1	20--						1
2	July	15	State Unemployment Tax Pay.		866 32		2
3			Cash in Bank			866 32	3
4			Check 211				4
5							5

ACCOUNTING ISSUES

Balancing Work and Family Responsibilities A recent survey of more than 1,000 U.S. employers indicates that an increasing number of employers are providing programs and policies that help their employees balance work and family responsibilities. Among the popular programs are child-care assistance, employee assistance, flexible scheduling, and home offices. The increase in the number of programs shows the changing attitude of employers. Among the advantages of such programs are that workers are very productive and satisfied employees.

2 TEACH (Cont'd.)

Visual Learning

Business Transaction
Use **Transparency 13–12** to have students analyze the entry to record payment of the state unemployment taxes.

Demonstration Problem Step-by-Step Practice
Use demonstration problem 13–4 to give students practice in journalizing the entries to record payment of the employer's payroll tax liabilities, including federal and state income taxes and federal and state unemployment taxes.

Teaching Tip
Invite a local CPA who works with small-business clients to discuss how small businesses handle payroll and tax reporting tasks.

CHAPTER 13
SECTION 3, PAGES 327–337

2 TEACH (Cont'd.)

Visual Learning

Business Transaction

Using **Transparency 13–13**, have students analyze the entry to record payment of liabilities for voluntary deductions withheld from employees' pay.

GO TO Demonstration Problem Step-by-Step Practice

Use demonstration problem 13–5 to give students practice in journalizing entries to pay liabilities for employees' voluntary withholdings.

Critical Thinking: Point out to students that employers are required to make all payments for employees' voluntary deductions within a timely manner. Ask students what are some possible problems that could result if an employer fails to make timely payments. (Some possibilities are: health insurance could be canceled; employees would lose interest on savings accounts; investments in 401(k) funds would be delayed, thus lowering the return on cash funds or forgoing dividends or investment gains. If the employer uses the cash for business payments, which is both unethical and illegal, it could signal that the business is in financial trouble.) L3

Other Payroll Liabilities

In addition to the payroll taxes, employers pay the appropriate organizations for all voluntary deductions. For Roadrunner, these deductions are for insurance premiums and U.S. savings bonds. Other types of voluntary deductions include union dues, charitable contributions, and so on.

Business Transaction

On July 15, Roadrunner pays $28.38 for hospital insurance premiums. This is the balance of the ***Hospital Insurance Premiums Payable*** *account shown in* ***Figure 13–1,*** *page 320.*

ANALYSIS

Identify 1. The accounts **Hospital Insurance Premiums Payable** and **Cash in Bank** are affected.

Classify 2. **Hospital Insurance Premiums Payable** is a liability account. **Cash in Bank** is an asset account.

+/− 3. **Hospital Insurance Premiums Payable** is decreased by $28.38. **Cash in Bank** is decreased by $28.38.

DEBIT-CREDIT RULE

4. Decreases in liability accounts are recorded as debits. Debit **Hospital Insurance Premiums Payable** for $28.38.
5. Decreases in asset accounts are recorded as credits. Credit **Cash in Bank** for $28.38.

T ACCOUNTS

6.

Hospital Insurance Premiums Payable	
Debit −	Credit +
28.38	

Cash in Bank	
Debit +	Credit −
	28.38

JOURNAL ENTRY

7.

GENERAL JOURNAL — PAGE 35

	DATE		DESCRIPTION	POST. REF.	DEBIT	CREDIT	
1	20--						1
2	July	15	Hospital Ins. Premiums Pay.		28 38		2
3			Cash in Bank			28 38	3
4			Check 212				4
5							5

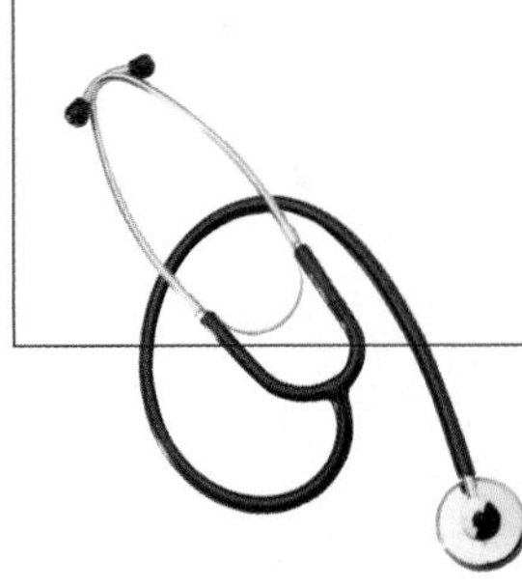

Posting the Payment of Payroll Liabilities

After the payments for the employer's payroll liabilities are journalized, the entries are posted to the appropriate general ledger accounts. **Figure 13–5** shows Roadrunner's general ledger accounts after posting.

EXTENDING THE CONTENT

Exploring Taxes for Government Services Explain to students that there is always a conflict between increased government services and lower taxes—the more services offered, the higher the taxes. Divide students into small groups and have each group research a service organization in your area that receives tax money. Students should interview the organization's personnel to learn how the organization spends its tax money. Ask a spokesperson from each group to present the group's findings to the class.

Figure 13–5 General Ledger Accounts after Posting of Payroll Liabilities Payments

ACCOUNT *Employee's Federal Income Tax Payable* ACCOUNT NO. *210*

DATE		DESCRIPTION	POST. REF.	DEBIT	CREDIT	BALANCE DEBIT	BALANCE CREDIT
20--							
June	23	Balance	✓				293 18
	30		G29		100 00		393 18
July	15		G31	393 18			—

ACCOUNT *Employee's State Income Tax Payable* ACCOUNT NO. *215*

DATE		DESCRIPTION	POST. REF.	DEBIT	CREDIT	BALANCE DEBIT	BALANCE CREDIT
20--							
June	23	Balance	✓				321 12
	30		G29		27 01		348 13
July	15		G32	348 13			—

ACCOUNT *Social Security Tax Payable* ACCOUNT NO. *220*

DATE		DESCRIPTION	POST. REF.	DEBIT	CREDIT	BALANCE DEBIT	BALANCE CREDIT
20--							
June	23	Balance	✓				250 35
	30		G29		83 73		334 08
	30		G30		83 72		417 80
July	15		G31	417 80			—

ACCOUNT *Medicare Tax Payable* ACCOUNT NO. *225*

DATE		DESCRIPTION	POST. REF.	DEBIT	CREDIT	BALANCE DEBIT	BALANCE CREDIT
20--							
June	23	Balance	✓				58 63
	30		G29		19 57		78 20
	30		G30		19 58		97 78
July	15		G31	97 78			—

ACCOUNT *Hospital Insurance Premium Payable* ACCOUNT NO. *230*

DATE		DESCRIPTION	POST. REF.	DEBIT	CREDIT	BALANCE DEBIT	BALANCE CREDIT
20--							
June	23	Balance	✓				4 73
	30		G29		23 65		28 38
July	15		G35	28 38			—

ACCOUNT *State Unemployment Tax Payable* ACCOUNT NO. *240*

DATE		DESCRIPTION	POST. REF.	DEBIT	CREDIT	BALANCE DEBIT	BALANCE CREDIT
20--							
June	23	Balance	✓				793 41
	30		G30		72 91		866 32
July	15		G34	866 32			—

ACCOUNT *Federal Unemployment Tax Payable* ACCOUNT NO. *245*

DATE		DESCRIPTION	POST. REF.	DEBIT	CREDIT	BALANCE DEBIT	BALANCE CREDIT
20--							
June	23	Balance	✓				118 80
	30		G30		10 80		129 60
July	15		G33	129 60			—

2 TEACH (Cont'd.)

Visual Learning

Figure 13–5 General Ledger Accounts After Posting of Payroll Liabilities Payments

Using **Transparency 13–14**, have students trace the posting of each of the journal entries for payment of the payroll liabilities.

Interviewing: Have students interview a payroll accounting supervisor for a local company to find out how the company handles the preparation and reporting of payroll information. Ask students to make a flow chart summarizing the steps in the process and present their flow charts to the class. L2

TEACHING NOTES

2 TEACH (Cont'd.)

Concept Development: Preparing Payroll Tax Reports

Discussion: This is a good time to mention to students that employees are given copies of Form W-2 to file with their personal tax returns. The employer makes out the form each year to report each employee's earnings and total taxes paid. L1

Visual Learning

Figure 13–6 Form W-2 Wage and Tax Statement

Use **Transparency 13–15** to explain the information contained on a W-2 statement.

Teaching Tip

Have students who work at part-time jobs share their experiences in filing personal tax returns.

Application: Obtain copies of the simple 1040 forms, and have students complete a personal tax return. L3

Math Review for Accounting Photocopy appropriate *Activity Sheets* for students who need additional practice in basic math.

Finding Tax Amounts

To find the amount of taxes on earnings using a calculator:

- simply enter the amount of earnings,
- press X,
- then enter the tax percentage followed by the % key.

Preparing Payroll Tax Reports

Employers must complete a variety of payroll-related tax forms.

Form	Name of Form	Filed
W-2	Wage and Tax Statement	Annually
940	Employer's Annual Federal Unemployment (FUTA) Tax Return	Annually
941	Employer's Quarterly Federal Tax Return	Quarterly
W-3	Transmittal of Wage and Tax Statements	Annually

Wage and Tax Statement

The Wage and Tax statement, **Form W-2**, summarizes an employee's earnings and withholdings for the calendar year. Form W-2 reports:

(1) gross earnings
(2) federal income tax withheld
(3) FICA taxes withheld
(4) state and local income taxes withheld

Each employee receives a Form W-2 by January 31 of the following year. The information reported on Form W-2 assists employees in preparing their individual income tax returns. **Figure 13–6** shows Emily Kardos' Form W-2.

Employers prepare many copies of Form W-2. The employer sends Copy A to the IRS and gives Copies B and C to the employee. The employer keeps Copy D. Additional copies are sent to city or state government if necessary.

Figure 13–6 Form W-2 Wage and Tax Statement

a Control number	OMB No. 1545-0008	
b Employer's identification number 31-8042398	1 Wages, tips, other compensation 8,246.00	2 Federal income tax withheld 664.00
c Employer's name, address, and ZIP code Roadrunner Delivery Service 155 Gateway Blvd. Sacramento, CA 94230	3 Social security wages 8,246.00	4 Social security tax withheld 511.25
	5 Medicare wages and tips 8,246.00	6 Medicare tax withheld 119.57
	7 Social security tips	8 Allocated tips
d Employee's social security number 201-46-8319	9 Advance EIC payment	10 Dependent care benefits
e Employee's name, address, and ZIP code Emily M. Kardos 809 East Main Street Sacramento, CA 94230	11 Nonqualified plans	12 Benefits included in box 1
	13	14 Other
	15 Statutory employee ☐ Deceased ☐ Pension plan ☐ Legal rep. ☐ Hshld. emp. ☐ Subtotal ☐ Deferred compensation ☐	

16 State	Employer's state I.D. no.	17 State wages, tips, etc.	18 State income tax	19 Locality name	20 Local wages, tips, etc.	21 Local income tax
CA	484972	8,246.00	128.74			

Form **W-2** Wage and Tax Statement 20-- Department of the Treasury – Internal Revenue Service
Copy 1 For State, City, or Local Tax Department

ACCOUNTING Flashbacks

ELECTRIC CALCULATORS

Electric calculators were developed in the early 1960s and miniature types were marketed to consumers in the early 70s. The first pocket calculator was sold in 1971 for $100.

Forms 940 and 941

Use **Form 940** to report the employer's unemployment (state and federal) taxes. **Form 941** illustrated in **Figure 13–7**, is the employer's quarterly federal tax return on which accumulated amounts of FICA and federal income tax withheld from employees' earnings, as well as FICA tax owed by the employer, are reported.

Math Skill Builder Activity

Finding Tax Amounts Diane Porter is an independent contractor. Last year she earned $40,000, and she owes the government about 33% in taxes. Have students use a calculator to find the amount of taxes on her earnings. ($40,000 × 33% = $13,200)

Form **941** — **Employer's Quarterly Federal Tax Return**

Department of the Treasury
Internal Revenue Service

► See separate instructions for information on completing this return.
Please type or print.

Enter state code for state in which deposits were made ONLY if different from state in address to the right ► (see page 3 of instructions).

		OMB No. 1545-0029
Name (as distinguished from trade name): Roadrunner Delivery Service	Date quarter ended: June 30, 20--	T
Trade name, if any	Employer identification number: 31-8042398	FF
Address (number and street): 155 Gateway Blvd.	City, state, and ZIP code: Sacramento, CA 94230	FD
		FP
		I
		T

If address is different from prior return, check here ► ☐ — IRS Use

If you do not have to file returns in the future, check here ► ☐ and enter date final wages paid ►
If you are a seasonal employer, see **Seasonal employers** on page 1 of the instructions and check here ► ☐

Line	Description		Amount
1	Number of employees in the pay period that includes March 12th . ► 1		
2	Total wages and tips, plus other compensation	2	9,252 96
3	Total income tax withheld from wages, tips, and sick pay	3	747 64
4	Adjustment of withheld income tax for preceding quarters of calendar year	4	0 00
5	Adjusted total of income tax withheld (line 3 as adjusted by line 4—see instructions)	5	773 55
6	Taxable social security wages . . . 6a 9,252 96 × 12.4% (.124) =	6b	1,147 37
	Taxable social security tips . . . 6c × 12.4% (.124) =	6d	0 00
7	Taxable Medicare wages and tips . . . 7a 9,252 96 × 2.9% (.029) =	7b	268 33
8	Total social security and Medicare taxes (add lines 6b, 6d, and 7b). Check here if wages are not subject to social security and/or Medicare tax ► ☐	8	1,415 70
9	Adjustment of social security and Medicare taxes (see instructions for required explanation) Sick Pay $ ____ ± Fractions of Cents $ ____ ± Other $ ____ =	9	0 00
10	Adjusted total of social security and Medicare taxes (line 8 as adjusted by line 9—see instructions)	10	1,415 70
11	**Total taxes** (add lines 5 and 10)	11	2,163 34
12	Advance earned income credit (EIC) payments made to employees	12	0 00
13	Net taxes (subtract line 12 from line 11). **This should equal line 17, column (d) below (or line D of Schedule B (Form 941))**	13	2,163 34
14	Total deposits for quarter, including overpayment applied from a prior quarter	14	2,163 34
15	**Balance due** (subtract line 14 from line 13). See instructions	15	0 00
16	**Overpayment,** if line 14 is more than line 13, enter excess here ► $ ____ and check if to be: ☐ Applied to next return **OR** ☐ Refunded.		

- **All filers:** If line 13 is less than $500, you need not complete line 17 or Schedule B (Form 941).
- **Semiweekly schedule depositors:** Complete Schedule B (Form 941) and check here ► ☐
- **Monthly schedule depositors:** Complete line 17, columns (a) through (d), and check here ► ☐

17 Monthly Summary of Federal Tax Liability. Do not complete if you were a semiweekly schedule depositor.

(a) First month liability	(b) Second month liability	(c) Third month liability	(d) Total liability for quarter
627.29	627.29	908.76	2,163.34

Sign Here Under penalties of perjury, I declare that I have examined this return, including accompanying schedules and statements, and to the best of my knowledge and belief, it is true, correct, and complete.
Signature ► *Maria Sanchez* Print Your Name and Title ► Maria Sanchez, Owner Date ► *6/30/20--*

Figure 13–7—Form 941

2 TEACH (Cont'd.)

Visual Learning

Figure 13–7 Form 941
Using **Transparency 13–16,** explain the information reported on this form. Point out that this is a quarterly form, so the employer prepares and files the form four times a year to report the wages paid to employees and the taxes withheld from employees' earnings.

Teaching Tips

When discussing this section, try to obtain actual forms to share with students. Point out that the employer has an obligation to file this and other reports with the correct information and to file them on time.

Show students how the payroll register and the employees' earnings records are used to prepare the payroll reports and forms. For example, point out the taxable social security wages.

INTERDISCIPLINARY CONNECTIONS ACTIVITY

(Refer to the *Connect To...Ethics* feature on page 336.)
Ethics The most commonly quoted ethics theory is the Golden Rule, "Do unto others as you would have them do unto you." Ask students to discuss the application of this theory to their daily lives. Do they agree that the interpreted meaning is to treat people with respect? Have they ever been in a situation when they have been mistreated or disrespected? How important is ethical behavior in their lives?

CHAPTER 13
SECTION 3, PAGES 327–337

2 TEACH (Cont'd.)

Visual Learning

Figure 13–8 Transmittal of Wage and Tax Statements

Using **Transparency 13–17**, explain to students that the employer files a summary of the employee wage and tax information by filing Form W-3. This form summarizes the information on the employees' W-2 forms and is sent along with those forms to the Internal Revenue Service.

Research: Have students collect information from their local newspaper employment ads offering jobs working in payroll. Ask students to make a chart listing each job, the skills required, and the wages (if given). Have students discuss their findings in class. L1

CONNECT TO . . . ETHICS

According to a study by Ernst & Young LLP, one in five American workers is personally aware of fraud in the workplace. While infractions range from stealing office supplies to taking kickbacks from suppliers, the problem appears to be on the rise. Asset misappropriation accounts for approximately 80 percent of all reported business fraud cases. Because accountants are often the discoverers of fraud, accounting educators and firms offer ethics training.

Transmittal of Wage and Tax Statements

The employer files **Form W-3**, Transmittal of Wage and Tax Statements, with the federal government. Form W-3 summarizes the information contained on the employees' Forms W-2. Form W-3 is due by February 28. Along with Form W-3, the employer includes Copy A of each employee's Form W-2. The federal government uses the Form W-2 information to check individual income tax returns. **Figure 13–8** shows Roadrunner's Form W-3.

DO NOT STAPLE

a Control number	33333	For Official Use Only ▶ OMB No. 1545-0008	
b Kind of Payer	941 ☑ Military ☐ 943 ☐ CT-1 ☐ Hshld. emp. ☐ Medicare govt. emp. ☐	1 Wages, tips, other compensation	67,210.35
		2 Federal income tax withheld	5,396.00
		3 Social security wages	67,210.35
		4 Social security tax withheld	4,167.04
c Total number of Forms W-2	5	5 Medicare wages and tips	67,210.35
d Establishment number	7210	6 Medicare tax withheld	974.55
e Employer identification number	31-8042398	7 Social security tips	
		8 Allocated tips	
f Employer's name	Roadrunner Delivery Service	9 Advance EIC payments	
		10 Dependent care benefits	
g Employer's address and ZIP code	155 Gateway Blvd. Sacramento, CA 94230	11 Nonqualified plans	
		12 Deferred compensation	
		13	
		14	
h Other EIN used this year		15 Income tax withheld by third-party payer	
i Employer's state I.D. No.			
Contact person		Telephone number	( )
Fax number	( )	E-mail address	

Under penalties of perjury, I declare that I have examined this return and accompanying documents, and, to the best of my knowledge and belief, they are true, correct, and complete.

Signature ▸ *Maria Sanchez* Title ▸ *Owner* Date ▸ *1/29/20--*

Form **W-3 Transmittal of Wage and Tax Statements** Department of the Treasury Internal Revenue Service

Figure 13–8 Transmittal of Wage and Tax Statements

ANALYZING FINANCIAL REPORTS

Employee Costs

Business owners and managers monitor employee costs by tracking the number of employees, total salary costs, and the cost of providing employee benefits. Employee benefits might include paid vacations, employer contributions to employee retirement plans, and health insurance. Many employers calculate the cost of benefits as a percentage of total salaries. For example, if a company's total costs for salaries are $58,600 and the cost of benefits paid by the company is $12,900, benefits as a percentage of salaries are 22%. Owners and managers use this percentage when calculating the total cost of hiring a new employee.

▶ Analyze the Report:

Use the payroll register on page 299 and payroll tax information in this chapter to answer these questions.

1. If the company's employee benefits cost 24% of employee earnings, what would be the benefits cost for this salary period?
2. If a new employee is to be hired for a 40-hour work week at wages of $7 an hour, what would be the total cost for the new employee? The company estimates its employee benefits cost at 22%.

ANALYZING FINANCIAL REPORTS

Roadrunner Delivery Service
155 Gateway Blvd.
Sacramento, CA 94230

Analyze the Report (Answers)

1. 24% × $1,317.85 = $316.28
2. Costs for the new employee are:
   Earnings: $7 × 40 = $280
   Employer's FICA taxes = 7.65% × $280 = $21.42
   Federal and state unemployment taxes = 6.2% × $280 = $17.36
   Benefits = 22% × $280 = $61.60
   Total weekly cost = $280.00 + $21.42 + $17.36 + $61.60 = $380.38

SECTION 3 Check Your Understanding

Now that you have studied this section, complete the following questions and problems.

Thinking Critically

1. What accounts are affected when a business pays the federal unemployment tax?
2. What information is included on a Form W-2?

Analyzing Accounting

Small businesses (those with revenues less than $200,000 per year) pay their federal taxes by the 15th day of the month following the payroll month. Large businesses pay their taxes every two weeks. Review the graph, and answer the following questions.

1. Which businesses pay their taxes every two weeks?
2. What percent of businesses represented in the circle graph are large businesses?

Problem 13–4 Payment of Payroll Liabilities

The following account balances appear in the general ledger for Soap Box Laundry on April 30.

General Ledger	
Social Security Tax Payable	$318.55
State Income Tax Payable	205.60
Medicare Tax Payable	113.28
Employees' Federal Income Tax Payable	286.00

Instructions Record the payment of the four liability accounts on page 34 of the general journal. (Hint: Two checks are written.)

Problem 13–5 Analyzing a Source Document

PAYROLL REGISTER

PAY PERIOD ENDING May 19 20 --   DATE OF PAYMENT May 19, 20--

	EMPLOYEE NUMBER	NAME	MAR. STATUS	ALLOW.	TOTAL HOURS	RATE	EARNINGS REGULAR	EARNINGS OVERTIME	EARNINGS TOTAL	DEDUCTIONS SOC. SEC. TAX	DEDUCTIONS MEDICARE TAX	DEDUCTIONS FED. INC. TAX	DEDUCTIONS STATE INC. TAX	DEDUCTIONS HOSP. INS.	DEDUCTIONS OTHER	DEDUCTIONS TOTAL	NET PAY	CK. NO.	
25																			25
		TOTALS					1,218 93	109 14	1,328 07	82 34	19 26	184 00	26 56	20 00	—	332 16	995 91		

Other Deductions: Write the appropriate code letter to the left of the amount: B–U.S. Savings Bonds; C–Credit Union: UD–Union Dues; UW–United Way.

Instructions Based on the payroll register above, record the appropriate journal entry in your working papers. Use page 14 in the general journal.

RETEACHING SECTION 3

Categorizing Taxes Some students may have difficulty remembering the various taxes that businesses must pay on their payrolls. Having students categorize the taxes may help them remember. For example, in the illustration given in the textbook, four federal taxes are paid: employees' federal income taxes, social security taxes, Medicare taxes, and the federal unemployment tax. Two state taxes are paid: employee state income tax and the state unemployment tax. The optional withholdings will vary by company.

3 ASSESS

Thinking Critically (Answers)

1. Federal Unemployment Tax Payable is decreased (debit); Cash in Bank is decreased (credit).
2. Gross earnings for the year, federal income tax withheld, FICA taxes withheld, state and local tax withheld.

Analyzing Accounting (Answers)

1. Morgan Manufacturing, Stanford Tools, Lights & More
2. 50% are large businesses

Problem 13–4 (Answers)

April 30: Dr. Employees' Fed. Inc. Tax Pay. $286, Soc. Sec. Tax Pay. $318.55, Med. Tax Pay. $113.28; Cr. Cash in Bank $717.83

April 30: Dr. State Income Tax Pay. $205.60; Cr. Cash in Bank $205.60

Problem 13–5 (Answers)

May 19: Dr. Salaries Expense $1,328.07, Cr. Soc. Sec. Tax Pay. $82.34, Med. Tax Pay. $19.26, Employee's Fed. Inc. Tax Pay. $184, Employee's St. Inc. Tax Pay. $26.56, Hosp. Ins. Prem. Pay. $20, Cash in Bank $995.91.

Chapter Reviews and Working Papers Refer students to the Chapter 13 workbook pages to answer *Check Your Understanding* activities.

4 CLOSE

Section Wrap-Up

Oral Discussion: Have students describe the purpose of each of the tax forms presented in this section (W-2, 940, 941, W-3). L1

SCANS in the Workforce

Foundation Skills Connection

Creative Thinking

If students were employed by a Big 4 accounting firm that had to deliver a presentation to a new client group from France, how would they present information? Ask students to brainstorm the best way to communicate to foreign clients. L1

Workplace Competencies Connection

Acquiring and Evaluating Information

Ask students to assume the role of consultant for a land developer. The land developer wants to expand by building multi-family housing, retail businesses, and theme parks. The students have been hired to advise the land developer if this business expansion will be profitable. What questions should the students ask in their consultant role? What information do they need to obtain from the developer? L2

Serving Clients/Customers

Ask a few students to role-play this scenario: A group seated at a well-known restaurant has been waiting over an hour for their dinner. The waiter/waitress must keep them happy while the meal is prepared. How would your students handle this situation? Ask students who are observing to critique the customer-service skills of the waiter/waitress. L3

ACCOUNTING CAREERS IN FOCUS

GRACE KIM
Tax Specialist
KPMG LLP

Q: How did you get into accounting?

A: I was an economics major as an undergraduate, and I wanted to do something practical in which I could be licensed. I like numbers because they're so concrete. You have to be creative when you work with words, but numbers are given to you as a fact. I see a lot of different issues and deal with a lot of different companies.

Q: What's the most difficult part of your job?

A: I have a hard time asking for help when I run into a wall. When I was in school, I didn't take any group study classes. I worked on my own, but anyone going into public accounting has to develop interpersonal skills and be willing to ask for help.

Q: Is tax season difficult?

A: Tax season gets the juices flowing. I find it exciting, and it's never so long that a person can't handle it. You can always see the light at the end of the tunnel.

Q: How should students present themselves at an on-campus interview?

A: Be mature and confident and talk about yourself articulately. Also, having an idea of what you want to be doing in the next five years will be helpful.

Q: What is the future like for tax specialists?

A: It's definitely good. The field is moving toward tax consultants who can advise companies about changing tax laws.

Tips from . . .

Numbers are important to accountants, but 96 percent of financial executives say communication skills are essential. Learn what it takes to clearly put your ideas into writing, and practice speaking to large groups of people.

CAREER FACTS

Nature of the Work: Prepare tax returns and research tax questions.
Training or Education Needed: A bachelor's or master's degree in accounting or tax, and the CPA exam.
Aptitudes, Abilities, and Skills: Accounting, time-management skills, problem-solving skills, analytical skills, computer skills, communication skills, interpersonal skills, and willingness to learn.
Salary Range: $60,000 to $100,000 with a master's degree.
Career Path: Do an on-campus interview to find a job with a public accounting firm.

Thinking Critically: Why is it important to be willing to ask for help?

ACCOUNTING CAREERS IN FOCUS

Thinking Critically (Answers)

It's important to be willing to ask for help because you can get information from more experienced co-workers, learn their methods to become more efficient, reduce research time, and reduce errors. Asking for help shows your willingness to learn new information.

ROBERT HALF CORNER

Importance of Verbal Skills Strong verbal skills for accountants are required in the workplace. The ability to deliver an effective financial presentation to management and clients is highly desirable. Students should strive to practice their public-speaking skills whenever possible.

CHAPTER 13 SUMMARY

KEY CONCEPTS

1. Employees' earnings are an operating expense of the business. The total gross earnings is debited to the **Salaries Expense** account.
2. Amounts withheld from employees' earnings are liabilities of the business. The employer makes regular payments of the amounts withheld to the appropriate government agencies, businesses, and organizations.
3. Employers pay taxes on their employees' gross earnings. These taxes are operating expenses of the business. The amounts are debited to the **Payroll Tax Expense** account. Employer's payroll taxes include FICA taxes (Social security & Medicare) and Unemployment taxes (Federal & State).
4. Both employees and employers are liable for payroll taxes. Payroll tax rates can change and vary by state. To calculate the tax, multiply gross earnings by the tax rate.
5. To journalize various payroll items, the related journal entries include the following:

Payroll Item	Required in Journal Entry
Total gross earnings →	Debit to **Salaries Expense**
Total net pay →	Credit to **Cash in Bank**
Federal income tax withholding →	Credit to **Employees' Federal Income Tax Payable**
Social security tax withholding →	Credit to **Social Security Tax Payable**
Medicare tax withholding →	Credit to **Medicare Tax Payable**
State income tax withholding →	Credit to **State Income Tax Payable**

6. The payroll register is the source of information for preparing the entry to record the payment of the payroll.
7. When payroll liabilities accounts are paid, the related liability accounts are debited and **Cash in Bank** is credited.

GENERAL JOURNAL PAGE *12*

	DATE	DESCRIPTION	POST. REF.	DEBIT	CREDIT	
1	*20--*					1
2	*Date*	*Medicare Tax Payable*		*xxx xx*		2
3		*State Income Tax Payable*		*xxx xx*		3
4		*Cash in Bank*			*xxx xx*	4
5						5

8. Employers file quarterly and annual tax reports on employee earnings and on taxes paid by the employee and the employer.
9. Employers report earnings and tax information to employees once a year on Form W-2.

ANSWERS

1. False
2. True
3. False
4. True
5. True
6. True
7. False
8. True
9. False
10. True

SUMMARY CHAPTER 13

Chapter 13 Quiz

Student ____ Class ____ Instructor ____
Date Assigned ____ Date Completed ____

CHAPTER 13 QUIZ

Payroll Liabilities and Tax Records

QUESTIONS (True-False)

Directions: In the space provided, indicate whether each statement is true or false.

___ 1. The Salaries Expense account records employees' gross earnings.
___ 2. The employer pays the same amount of FICA tax as employees.
___ 3. Federal unemployment taxes are withheld from employees' earnings.
___ 4. The employer's payroll taxes are recorded as liabilities to be paid in the future.
___ 5. The employer's payroll taxes are recorded in the Payroll Tax Expense account.
___ 6. The employer pays the employer's and employees' share of FICA taxes in one payment.
___ 7. A Federal Tax Deposit Coupon shows employees' voluntary deductions.
___ 8. The W-2 statement reports individual employee earnings.
___ 9. The W-3 form reports state unemployment taxes.
___ 10. The information on the employer's quarterly federal tax return matches information in the payroll register for the same period.

 Chapter Quizzes • 15

QUESTIONS (True-False)

1. The Salaries Expense account records employees' gross earnings.
2. The employer pays the same amount of FICA tax as employees.
3. Federal unemployment taxes are withheld from employees' earnings.
4. The employer's payroll taxes are recorded as liabilities to be paid in the future.
5. The employer's payroll taxes are recorded in the Payroll Tax Expense account.
6. The employer pays the employer's and employees' share of FICA taxes in one payment.
7. A Federal Tax Deposit Coupon shows employees' voluntary deductions.
8. The W-2 statement reports individual employee earnings.
9. The W-3 form reports state unemployment taxes.
10. The information on the employer's quarterly federal tax return matches information in the payroll register for the same period.

REVIEW AND ACTIVITIES CHAPTER 13

USING KEY TERMS

See the *Glossary* for the definitions of these terms. Ask for volunteers to make their presentations in class. Discuss any misuses of terms.

Understanding Accounting Concepts and Procedures

(Answers)

1. Because gross earnings represent total wages paid to employees by the employer, which is a cost of operating the business.
2. The employer holds the money until it is to be paid in the future.
3. Cash in Bank.
4. Multiply total gross earnings by tax rates (currently 6.2% and 1.45%).
5. Multiply individual gross earnings by tax rates (6.2% and 1.45%).
6. Employee's gross earnings.
7. Social security and Medicare taxes, state and federal unemployment taxes.
8. Social security and Medicare taxes (both shares), employees' federal income taxes withheld.
9. January 31 of the following year.
10. Copies B and C go to employees. Two additional copies are provided for attachment to state or local tax returns. The employer keeps Copy D.
11. Gross earnings for the year, federal income tax withheld, FICA tax withheld, state and local tax withheld.
12. Form 940: reports employer's state and federal unemployment taxes; Form 941: employer's quarterly federal tax return reporting total wages paid, accumulated FICA and federal income tax withheld from employees' earnings, and FICA tax owed by the employer.
13. A summary of information contained on employees' W-2 forms.

CHAPTER 13 REVIEW AND ACTIVITIES

USING KEY TERMS

You are the owner of Accurate Financial Services. You have just been hired by Brad Justice, the owner of a new company called Snack Shack, to help establish a payroll system. As a new business owner, Brad understands the importance of complying with government requirements, but he is concerned that he may not be aware of all of the requirements related to payroll. Using the following key terms, prepare a presentation for Brad describing the government requirements for payroll.

- Electronic Federal Tax Payment System (EFTPS)
- Federal Tax Deposit Coupon (Form 8109)
- Federal Unemployment Tax Act (FUTA)
- Form 940
- Form 941
- Form W-2
- Form W-3
- **Payroll Tax Expense**
- **Salaries Expense**
- State Unemployment Tax Act (SUTA)
- unemployment taxes

Understanding Accounting Concepts and Procedures

Instructions

On a separate sheet of paper, answer the following questions:

1. Explain why gross earnings, not net pay, is debited to the **Salaries Expense** account.
2. Explain why the amounts withheld from employees' payroll checks are liabilities of the employer.
3. What account is credited for net pay?
4. How is the employer's share of FICA tax calculated?
5. How is the employee's share of FICA tax calculated?
6. State and federal unemployment taxes are percentages of what amount?
7. The debit to **Payroll Tax Expense** is the total of what amounts?
8. What payroll taxes are deposited monthly in a Federal Reserve Bank or other authorized financial institution?
9. When does an employee receive a Form W-2?
10. Explain how different copies of Form W-2 are distributed.
11. What information is reported on Form W-2?
12. What is the difference between a Form 940 and Form 941?
13. What information is contained on Form W-3?

ASSESSMENT RESOURCES

Choose assessment strategies from the following pages to evaluate your students' progress.

Student Edition
Check Your Understanding, pp. 321,326, 337
Chapter 13 Problems, pp. 343–345
Analyzing Financial Reports, p. 336

Assessment and Evaluation Masters
Chapter 13 Study Plan, *Glencoe Workbook (CRWP)*
Chapter 13 Self-Test, *Glencoe Workbook (CRWP)*
Chapter 13 Test, *Chapter Tests* Booklet
Chapter 13 Activity, *School-to-Work Handbook*
Chapter 13 **Exam***View*

Teacher Wraparound Edition
Critical Thinking Activity, p. 323
Reteaching Sections 1–3, pp. 321, 326, 337
Chapter 13 Quiz, p. 339

CHAPTER 13 REVIEW AND ACTIVITIES

Case Study...

Payroll: Warehousing Center

Morrison Distribution Center offers warehousing services to local businesses. Morrison has 40 full-time employees and operates two shifts. The company is considering adding a third shift, which would require 12 additional employees.

The accountant estimates that a third shift could bring in additional revenue of $390,000. Prepare an estimate of the third shift payroll costs. Assume: **(1)** The average warehouse employee earns $21,000 per year. **(2)** The state unemployment tax is 5.4%, and the federal unemployment tax is 0.8%. (Both applied to the first $7,000 of earnings.) **(3)** The employer's cost of health insurance averages 22% of an employee's earnings.

Thinking Critically:

1. What is the salary expense related to adding the new employees?
2. How much in additional payroll taxes will Morrison pay?
3. What is the total cost to add the third shift?

Conducting an Audit with Alex

The journal entry for the March 12 payroll was recorded in the general journal of Milan's Painting. Later some water spilled on the journal making two amounts illegible.

Instructions

Based on the remaining amounts shown below, determine what the illegible amounts should be.

GENERAL JOURNAL — PAGE 14

	DATE		DESCRIPTION	POST. REF.	DEBIT	CREDIT	
1	20--						1
2	Mar.	12	Salaries Expense		3 840 00		2
3			Empl. Fed. Inc. Tax Pay.			274 00	3
4			Social Security Tax Pay.			?	4
5			Medicare Tax Pay.			55 68	5
6			State Income Tax Payable			63 00	6
7			Hosp. Ins. Premiums Pay.			?	7
8			Cash in Bank			3 144 24	8
9							9

*inter*NET CONNECTION

The Internal Revenue Service

The Internal Revenue Service (IRS), the largest agency in the Department of the Treasury, employs 100,000 people. The IRS processes approximately 226 million tax returns in a year while assisting more than 100 million taxpayers by telephone and at more than 400 walk-in offices throughout the country.

Do This:

1. Locate the IRS Web site online. What is the Web site address?
2. Name 6 services or kinds of information that the Web site offers.
3. Who is the Commissioner of the IRS?
4. What is e-file?

Workplace Skills

Self-Management

Are you a "self-starter"? If the answer is yes, then you have strong self-management skills. People who possess these skills can assess their own abilities and skills, set attainable goals, and motivate themselves to accomplish those goals. Employers are always eager to hire and promote employees with self-management skills.

On the Job:

As an accounting clerk in the payroll department of Trendy Threads, you are responsible for processing all payroll and tax reports. It is December, and your tax reports are due soon. What steps do you need to take now to make sure you process your reports on time?

Thinking Critically:

Describe the reports you'll need to file and what payroll ledgers and registers you'll need to complete each one.

REVIEW AND ACTIVITIES CHAPTER 13

Case Study...

Thinking Critically (Answers)

1. $252,000
2. $24,486
3. $331,926

Workplace Skills

Thinking Critically (Answers)

Answers may vary. Some of the forms required include the reporting of wages, Federal income tax withheld, social security tax withheld, Medicare tax withheld, the employer's ID number, the employee's social security number, the employer's address, the employee's address, and state income tax (if the state has a state income tax).

Conducting an Audit with Alex

(Answer)

Social Security Tax Payable $238.08

Hospital Insurance Premium Payable $65.00

Internet Resources and Activities Handbook

Refer students to the booklet for additional Internet activities.

*inter*NET CONNECTION

www.glencoe.com

Do This (Answers)

1. www.irs.gov
2. Services and information available include electronic filing of tax returns, direct deposit of tax return checks, order a CD-ROM of various tax forms, order tax forms and publications, tax filing locations, and notes on important changes to the tax code.
3. Charles O. Rossotti
4. E-file allows you to file your federal tax return online. It uses automation to replace most of the manual processing of paper returns and is thus faster and more accurate.

PEACHTREE CORNER

General Journal Entry
To record the payroll entries, choose the **General Journal Entry** from the ***Tasks*** menu.

Tasks | Analysis | Options | Reports

- Quotes/Sales Orders ▸
- Sales/Invoicing...
- Receipts...
- Finance Charge...
- Select for Deposit...
- Purchase Orders...
- Purchases/Receive Inventory...
- Select for Payment...
- Payments...
- Write Checks...
- Time/Expense ▸
- Select for Payroll Entry...
- Payroll Entry...
- General Journal Entry...
- Inventory Adjustments...
- Assemblies...
- Account Reconciliation...
- Void Checks...
- Action Items...
- System ▸

You can also access the General Journal Entry option by clicking on the **General Ledger** navigation aid at the bottom of the screen and choosing **General Journal Entry**. The Navigation Aid provides an easy (visual) alternative for your students to select options.

Recording and Paying Payroll Tax Liabilities

Making the Transition from a Manual to a Computerized System

Task	Perform Accounting Procedures Using Manual Methods	Perform Accounting Procedures Using Automated Methods
Record and post payroll entries; pay payroll tax liabilities	1. Prepare the journal entry based on the payroll register totals for the employee and employer's tax liabilities. 2. Post the payroll entries to the general ledger. 3. Prepare tax liability checks to pay federal, state, and local taxing authorities. 4. Prepare journal entries to record the payment of the liabilities.	1. When the payroll checks are generated, the payroll tax journal entries are automatically prepared and posted.

Recording and Paying Payroll Taxes

Peachtree Question	Description
How do I journalize the employer's tax liabilities?	• When payroll checks were issued, the software automatically journalized the tax liabilities.
How do I pay the payroll tax liabilities?	• Select **Payments** from the ***Tasks*** menu. • Select the taxing authority ID to be paid. • Enter the amount and cash account number. • Enter description and general ledger account (tax liability account). • Click *Print*.
What does the software do "behind the scenes?"	• When payroll checks are issued, the software automatically journalizes and posts both the tax liabilities of the employee and the employer. • When a check is prepared to pay a tax liability, the software automatically journalizes and posts the payment. • Employee earnings records are updated for you.

For detailed instructions: See the **Peachtree User Guide** in your Glencoe Working Papers.

Peachtree® Answers to Frequently Asked Questions

Q: Can you print a Form 8109 using the Peachtree software?
A: No, Peachtree does not include a Form 8109 report. You must prepare this form manually when you submit a payroll tax deposit.
For additional information, see your *Glencoe Peachtree Accounting User Guide.*

CHAPTER 13 PROBLEMS

APPLICATION OPTIONS

Problem 13-6 Calculating Employer's Payroll Taxes

Instructions For each of the following total gross earnings amounts recorded in the past five pay weeks for Hot Suds Car Wash, determine the employer's FICA taxes (social security 6.2%, Medicare 1.45%), the federal unemployment tax (.8%), and the state unemployment tax (5.4%). Use the form provided in the working papers. None of the employees has reached the taxable earnings limit.

Total gross earnings:

1. $914.80
2. $1,113.73
3. $2,201.38
4. $791.02
5. $1,245.75

Analyze: Explain the relationship between federal and state unemployment tax rates.

Complete chapter problems one of four ways:

1 **Manual** Glencoe Working Papers

or

2 **Peachtree Complete Accounting** Software

or

3 **QuickBooks** Templates (Problems 13–8, 13–9)

or

4 **Spreadsheet** Templates (Problem 13–6)

Problem 13-7 Recording the Payment of the Payroll

The totals of the payroll register for Kits & Pups Grooming are shown in your working papers. On December 31, the owner, Abe Shultz, wrote Check 1400 to pay the payroll.

Instructions In your working papers:

1. Record the payroll entry in the general journal.
2. Post the entry to the general ledger accounts.

Analyze: Which payroll liability account has the largest credit entry?

SPREADSHEET SMART GUIDE

Step-by-Step Instructions: Problem 13-6

1. Select the spreadsheet template for Problem 13–6.
2. Enter your name and the date in the spaces provided on the template.
3. Complete the spreadsheet using the instructions in your working papers.
4. Print the spreadsheet and proof your work.
5. Save your work and exit the spreadsheet program.

Problem 13-8 Journalizing Payroll Transactions

The Outback Guide Service payroll register for the week ending Dec. 31 appears on the next page.

PROBLEMS CHAPTER 13

Problem 13-6 (Answers) Calculating Employer's Payroll Taxes

1. Soc. sec. tax $56.72, Med. tax $13.27, FUT $7.32, SUT $49.40
2. Soc. sec. tax $69.05, Med. tax $16.15, FUT $8.91, SUT $60.14
3. Soc. sec. tax $136.49, Med. tax $31.92, FUT $17.61, SUT $118.87
4. Soc. sec. tax $49.04, Med. tax $11.47, FUT $6.33, SUT $42.72
5. Soc. sec. tax $77.24, Med. tax $18.06, FUT $9.97, SUT $67.27

Analyze: Maximum federal rate is 6.2%. Employers may deduct up to 5.4% of state unemployment taxes. Thus, most employers pay .8% (6.2% − 5.4%) of taxable gross earnings.

Problem 13-7 (Answers) Recording the Payment of the Payroll

1. Dec. 31: Dr. Salaries Exp. $1,069.34; Cr. Social Security Tax Pay. $66.30, Medicare Tax Pay. $15.51, Employees' Federal Income Tax Pay. $78.00, Employees' State Income Tax Pay. $21.39, Hospital Insurance Prem. Pay. $11.65, Cash in Bank $876.49; Check 1400
2. *Ending debit balances:*
   Cash in Bank $16,475.61
   Salaries Expense $49,487.20

   Ending credit balances:
   Social Security Tax Pay. $257.55
   Medicare Tax Payable $60.82
   Employees' Fed. Inc. Tax Pay. $318.00
   Employees' St. Inc. Tax Pay. $202.18
   Hospital Ins. Premium Pay. $63.91

Analyze: Employees' Federal Income Tax Payable

SOFTWARE NOTES

Teachers can find detailed instructions for:

- **Peachtree Complete Accounting Software**, in the *Glencoe Workbook (CRWP)*
- **QuickBooks Templates**, in *Using QuickBooks with Glencoe Accounting*
- **Spreadsheet Templates**, in the *Glencoe Workbook (CRWP)*

Problem 13–8 (Answers) Journalizing Payroll Transactions

1. Dec. 31: Dr. Sal. Exp. $1,091.90; Cr. Soc. Sec. Tax Pay. $67.69, Med. Tax Pay. $15.82, Empl. Fed. Inc. Tax Pay. $74.00, Empl. St. Inc. Tax Pay. $21.84, Union Dues Pay. $10.80, Cash in Bank $901.75; Check 1201, Payroll Reg. 12/31
2. Dec. 31: Dr. Pay. Tax Exp. $151.21; Cr. Soc. Sec. Tax Pay. $67.69, Med. Tax Pay. $15.82, Fed. Unempl. Tax Pay. $8.74, St. Unempl. Tax Pay. $58.96; Payroll Reg. 12/31

Analyze: Employees' Federal Income Tax Payable.

SOURCE DOCUMENT PROBLEM

Problem 13–9 (Answers) Recording and Posting Payroll Transactions

Journal Entries

Dec. 13: Dr. Sal. Exp. $3,840.58; Cr. Soc. Sec. Tax Pay. $238.12, Med. Tax Pay. $55.69, Empl. Fed. Inc. Tax Pay. $639.00, Empl. St. Inc. Tax Pay. $96.02, Insur. Prem. Pay. $21.00, U.S. Sav. Bonds Pay. $20.00, Cash in Bank $2,770.75; Check 2206, Payroll Reg. 12/13

Dec. 13: Dr. Pay. Tax Exp. $531.92; Cr. Soc. Sec. Tax Pay. $238.12, Med. Tax Pay. $55.69, Fed. Unempl. Tax Pay. $30.72, St. Unempl. Tax Pay. $207.39; Payroll Reg. 12/13

Dec. 16: Dr. Empl. Fed. Inc. Tax Pay. $639.00, Soc. Sec. Tax Pay. $476.24, Med. Tax Pay. $111.38; Cr. Cash in Bank $1,226.62; Check 2215

Dec. 16: Dr. U.S. Savings Bonds Payable $100.00; Cr. Cash in Bank $100.00; Check 2216

Dec. 16: Dr. Hospital Insurance Premiums Payable $148.00; Cr. Cash in Bank $148.00; Check 2217

Ending debit balances:

Cash in Bank $17,686.77
Payroll Tax Expense $5,146.05
Salaries Expense $37,495.80

Ending credit balances:

Employees' Fed. Inc. Tax Pay. $0
Employees' St. Inc. Tax Pay. $382.10
Social Security Tax Payable $0
Medicare Tax Payable $0
Hospital Insurance Premiums Payable $0
U.S. Savings Bonds Payable $0
Federal Unempl. Tax Pay. $30.72
State Unempl. Tax Pay. $207.39

Analyze: Employees' State Inc. Tax Pay., Fed. Unempl. Tax Pay., State Unempl. Tax Pay., Payroll Tax Expense, Salaries Expense

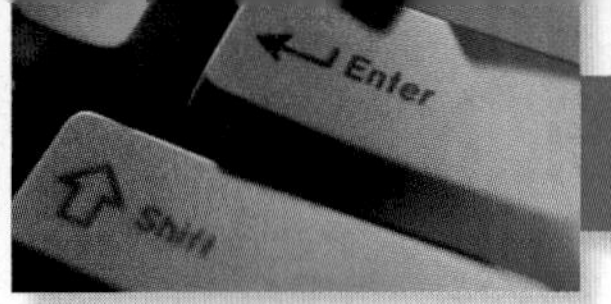

Peachtree®

SMART GUIDE

Step-by-Step Instructions: Problem 13–7

1. Select the problem set for Kits & Pups Grooming (Prob. 13–7).
2. Rename the company and set the system date.
3. Record the payroll entry using the **General Journal Entry** option.
4. Print a General Journal report and a General Ledger report.
5. Proof your work.
6. Answer the Analyze question.
7. End the session.

TIP: As a shortcut, you can type just the day in most date fields.

PAYROLL REGISTER

PAY PERIOD ENDING Dec. 31 20 -- DATE OF PAYMENT Dec. 31, 20--

	EMPLOYEE NUMBER	NAME	MAR. STATUS	ALLOW.	TOTAL HOURS	RATE	EARNINGS REGULAR	EARNINGS OVERTIME	EARNINGS TOTAL	DEDUCTIONS SOC. SEC. TAX	DEDUCTIONS MEDICARE TAX	DEDUCTIONS FED. INC. TAX	DEDUCTIONS STATE INC. TAX	DEDUCTIONS HOSP. INS.	DEDUCTIONS OTHER	DEDUCTIONS TOTAL	NET PAY	CK. NO.	
1	31	Coleman, Clarence	M	1	41	7.60	304 00	11 40	315 40	19 55	4 57	21 00	6 31			51 43	263 97		1
2	28	Lorman, Victoria	S	1	30	8.00	240 00		240 00	14 88	3 48	21 00	4 80		(UD)5 40	49 56	190 44		2
3	33	Peterson, Peg	S	1	38	7.25	275 50		275 50	17 08	3 99	26 00	5 51			52 58	222 92		3
4	35	Torrez, Joyce	M	2	36	7.25	261 00		261 00	16 18	3 78	6 00	5 22		(UD)5 40	36 58	224 42		4
24																			24
25																			25
						TOTALS	1,080 50	11 40	1,091 90	67 69	15 82	74 00	21 84	—	10 80	190 15	901 75		

Other Deductions: Write the appropriate code letter to the left of the amount: B–U.S. Savings Bonds; C–Credit Union; UD–Union Dues; UW–United Way.

Instructions In your working papers:

1. Record the entry for the payment of the payroll on page 15 of the general journal. (Check 1201, dated Dec. 31).
2. Use the information in the payroll register to compute the employer's payroll taxes. These include FICA taxes (6.2% for social security, 1.45% for Medicare) and federal (.8%) and state (5.4%) unemployment taxes. None of the employees has reached the taxable earnings limit.
3. Record the entry for the employer's payroll taxes on page 15 of the general journal.

Analyze: In the entry recording the payment of payroll, which account, **Social Security Tax Payable** or **Employees' Federal Income Tax Payable**, had the largest credit?

Peachtree®

SMART GUIDE

Step-by-Step Instructions: Problem 13–8

1. Select the problem set for Outback Guide Service (Prob. 13–8).
2. Rename the company and set the system date.
3. Record the payment of the payroll and the employer's payroll taxes.
4. Print a General Journal report.
5. Proof your work.
6. Answer the Analyze question.
7. End the session.

TIP: You can press ALT+S to post a General Journal entry.

SOURCE DOCUMENT PROBLEM

Problem 13–9

Use the source documents in your working papers to record the transactions for this problem.

SOURCE DOCUMENT PROBLEM

Problem 13–9 Recording and Posting Payroll Transactions

Showbiz Video completed the following payroll transactions during the first two weeks of December. Showbiz Video pays its employees on a biweekly (every two weeks) basis.

Instructions In your working papers:

1. Record the December 13 transactions on page 38 in the general journal.
2. Post both payroll entries to the appropriate general ledger accounts.
3. Journalize and post the December 16 transactions.

Date	Transactions
Dec. 13	Wrote Check 2206 to pay the payroll of $3,840.58 (gross earnings) for the pay period ending December 13. The following amounts were withheld: FICA taxes, $238.12 for social security and $55.69 for Medicare; employees' federal income taxes, $639.00; employees' state income taxes, $96.02; insurance premium, $21.00; U.S. savings bonds, $20.00.
13	Recorded the employer's payroll taxes (FICA tax rates, 6.2% for social security and 1.45% for Medicare; federal unemployment tax rate, 0.8%; state unemployment tax rate, 5.4%). No employee has reached the maximum taxable amount.

Continued

Date	Transactions (cont.)
16	Paid the amounts owed to the federal government for employees' federal income taxes and FICA taxes, Check 2215.
16	Purchased U.S. savings bonds for employees for $100.00, Check 2216.
16	Paid $148.00 to American Insurance Company for employees' insurance, Check 2217.

Analyze: Which payroll accounts have a balance after entries are posted?

Problem 13-10 Recording and Posting Payroll Transactions

Job Connect pays its employees twice a month. Employee earnings and tax amounts for the pay period ending December 31 are:

Gross Earnings	$12,543.40
Social Security Tax	777.69
Medicare Tax	181.88
Employees' Federal Income Tax	662.00
Employees' State Income Tax	250.87

Instructions In your working papers:

1. Prepare Check 1602 (payable to "Job Connect Payroll Account") to transfer the net pay amount to the payroll checking account.
2. On page 19 of the general journal, record the payment of the payroll.
3. Post the payroll transaction to the general ledger.
4. Compute payroll tax expense forms and journalize the entry to record employer's payroll taxes. (Social security rate = 6.2%; Medicare rate = 1.45%; state unemployment rate = 5.4%; federal unemployment rate = .8%.) No employee has reached the taxable earnings limit.
5. Post the entry to the general journal.
6. Prepare checks dated December 31 to pay the following payroll liabilities:
   (a) Federal unemployment taxes, payable to First City Bank (Check 1603).
   (b) State unemployment taxes, payable to the State of North Carolina (Check 1604).
   (c) Employees' federal income taxes and FICA taxes, payable to First City Bank (Check 1605).
7. Journalize and post the entries for the payment of the payroll liabilities.
8. Complete payroll tax expense forms. Prepare a Form 8109 for each of the two federal tax deposits paid in Instruction 6, parts (a) and (c). The oval for FICA and federal income tax is 941. The oval for the federal unemployment tax is 940.

Analyze: What is the balance in the **Salaries Expense** account on December 31 after the payroll entries have been posted?

Peachtree®

SMART GUIDE

Step-by-Step Instructions: Problem 13-9

1. Select the problem set for Showbiz Video (Prob. 13-9).
2. Rename the company and set the system date.
3. Record the December transactions.
4. Print a General Journal report and a General Ledger report.
5. Proof your work.
6. Answer the Analyze question.
7. End the session.

Peachtree®

SMART GUIDE

Step-by-Step Instructions: Problem 13-10

1. Select the problem set for Job Connect (Prob. 13-10).
2. Rename the company and set the system date.
3. Record all of the entries using the **General Journal Entry** option.
4. Print a General Journal report and a General Ledger report.
5. Proof your work.
6. Manually prepare Form 8109 for the federal tax deposits.
7. Answer the Analyze question.
8. End the session.

Problem 13-10 (Answers) Recording and Posting Payroll Transactions

Journal Entries

Dec. 31: Dr. Sal. Exp. $12,543.40; Cr. Soc. Sec. Tax Pay. $777.69, Med. Tax Pay. $181.88, Empl. Fed. Inc. Tax Pay. $662.00, Empl. St. Inc. Tax Pay. $250.87, Cash in Bank $10,670.96; Payroll Reg. 12/31, Check 1602

Dec. 31: Dr. Pay. Tax Exp. $1,737.26; Cr. Soc. Sec. Tax Pay. $777.69, Med. Tax Pay. $181.88, Fed. Unempl. Tax Pay. $100.35, St. Unempl. Tax Pay. $677.34; Payroll Reg. 12/31

Dec. 31: Dr. Fed. Unempl. Tax Pay. $564.46; Cr. Cash in Bank $564.46; Ck. 1603

Dec. 31: Dr. St. Unempl. Tax Pay. $3,810.07; Cr. Cash in Bank $3,810.07; Ck. 1604

Dec. 31: Dr. Empl. Fed. Inc. Tax Pay. $662.00, Soc. Sec. Tax Pay. $1,555.38, Med. Tax Pay. $363.76; Cr. Cash in Bank $2,581.14; Check 1605

Ledger Balances

Ending debit balances:

Cash in Bank $11,814.98
Salaries Expense $70,556.85

Ending credit balances:

Employees' Fed. Inc. Tax Pay. $0
Employees' St. Inc. Tax Pay. $250.87
Social Security Tax Payable $0
Medicare Tax Payable $0
Federal Unemployment Tax Payable $0
State Unemployment Tax Payable $0

Analyze: $70,556.85

INTRODUCING
MINI PRACTICE SET 3

Mini Practice Set Overview

This practice set reinforces students' learning of how to keep payroll records and how to record the cost of the payroll in the accounting records for Green Thumb Plant Service. In this activity students complete all the payroll functions they learned in Chapters 12 and 13. Those activities include calculating earnings and deductions, preparing earnings records and a payroll register, writing checks, and recording journal entries for payroll amounts.

Most students should be able to complete this activity manually within three class periods.

Source documents and the accounting stationery needed to complete the practice set are included in the student workbook, *Chapter Reviews and Working Papers*.

Mini Practice Set Concepts

- How to calculate employees' gross earnings and deductions.
- How to calculate employees' net pay.
- How to prepare a payroll register.
- How to write payroll checks and stubs for employees.
- How to record payroll information on employees' earnings records.
- How to journalize and post the payroll transactions.
- How to calculate, journalize, and post the employer's payroll taxes.
- How to journalize and post the payment of FICA taxes, employees' federal income taxes, and insurance premiums.
- How to prepare Form 8190.

Visual Learning

Mini Practice Set Focus, p. 346

Discuss with students the payroll and accounting concepts they will apply in this mini practice set.

GREEN THUMB Plant Service

Payroll Accounting

***What* You'll Learn**

- How to calculate employees' gross earnings and deductions.
- How to calculate employees' net pay.
- How to prepare a payroll register.
- How to write payroll checks and stubs for employees.
- How to record payroll information on employees' earnings records.
- How to journalize and post the payroll transaction.
- How to calculate, journalize, and post the employer's payroll taxes.
- How to journalize and post the payment of FICA taxes, employees' federal income taxes, and insurance premiums.
- How to prepare Form 8190.

***Why* It's Important**

To review and apply what you've learned about the procedures involved in a payroll system as you prepare the payroll and maintain the payroll records for a sole proprietorship.

Green Thumb Plant Service

Company Background: Green Thumb Plant Service is a plant maintenance company located in Kingsbury, Michigan. It is a service business that is organized as a sole proprietorship. It is owned and operated by Joanna Ecke. The company places and maintains plants, flowers, and small trees in offices and corporate buildings.

The business has been in operation for almost five years. During that time, its revenue has increased each year, additional employees have been hired, and the business is now showing a good profit.

Payroll Information: The business presently employs eight people. A Form W-4 is on file for each employee. The list that follows summarizes the data on those documents.

Michael Alter	Single	claims 1 exemption
Christine Cuddy	Single	claims 0 exemptions
Jesse Dubow	Single	claims 0 exemptions
Joclyn Filley	Single	claims 1 exemption
Greg Millette	Married	claims 2 exemptions
Heather Repicky	Married	claims 3 exemptions
Daniel Ripp	Married	claims 2 exemptions
Yourself	Single	claims 1 exemption

The business pays its employees on a weekly basis. Overtime is paid at the rate of $1\frac{1}{2}$ times the regular rate of pay for all hours worked over 40. The weekly pay period runs from Monday through Saturday, with employees being paid on Saturday for the week's work. Because most office buildings are closed on Sunday, the business is also closed.

The employees are paid by one of three methods: hourly rate, salary, or salary plus 10% commission on any new accounts they acquire for the company. The following table lists the employees, the method by which their wages are computed, and other pertinent information. Next, you'll find the time cards for the employees who are paid on an hourly basis.

TEACHING NOTES

Green Thumb Plant Service

Employee	Empl. No.	Position	Employee Status	Rate of Pay
Heather Repicky	010	Manager	Full-time	$725.00/weekly salary
Greg Millette	011	Salesperson	Full-time	$450.00/week plus 10% Commission
Jesse Dubow	012	Bookkeeper	Part-time	$250.00/week
Joclyn Filley	013	Supply clerk	Full-time	$7.40/hour
Daniel Ripp	016	Service	Full-time	$8.30/hour
Christine Cuddy	018	Service	Full-time	$8.30/hour
Michael Alter	019	Supply clerk	Part-time	$7.10/hour
Yourself	022	Accounting clerk	Part-time	$175.00/week

The time cards for the employees who are paid on an hourly rate are listed below.

NO. 019
NAME Michael Alter
SOC. SEC. NO. 049-71-8436
WEEK ENDING 7/25/20--

DAY	IN	OUT	IN	OUT	IN	OUT	TOTAL
M			2:00	5:00			
T			2:00	6:00			
W			3:00	5:00			
Th			2:00	6:00			
F			2:00	6:00			
S			9:00	2:00			
S							

NO. 018
NAME Christine Cuddy
SOC. SEC. NO. 223-56-0992
WEEK ENDING 7/25/20--

DAY	IN	OUT	IN	OUT	IN	OUT	TOTAL
M	9:00	12:00	12;30	5:00			
T	9:00	11:30	12:00	5:00			
W	9:00	1:00					
Th	9:00	12:00	12:30	4:00			
F	8:30	1:00	1:30	3:00			
S	9:00	1:30					
S							

NO. 013
NAME Joclyn Filley
SOC. SEC. NO. 042-97-3814
WEEK ENDING 7/25/20--

DAY	IN	OUT	IN	OUT	IN	OUT	TOTAL
M	9:00	12:00	1:00	3:00			
T	9:00	12:00	1:00	5:00			
W	8:00	12:00	1:00	5:00			
Th	9:00	12:00	1:00	3:30			
F	9:00	12:00	1:00	4:00			
S	9:00	12:00					
S							
						TOTAL HOURS	

	HOURS	RATE	AMOUNT
REGULAR			
OVERTIME			
TOTAL EARNINGS			

SIGN.
SIGNATURE ______ DATE ______

NO. 016
NAME Daniel Ripp
SOC. SEC. NO. 011-79-2118
WEEK ENDING 7/25/20--

DAY	IN	OUT	IN	OUT	IN	OUT	TOTAL
M	9:00	12:00	12:30	5:00			
T	9:00	12:30	1:00	6:00			
W	9:00	12:00	1:00	4:30			
Th	8:30	12:30	1:00	5:00			
F	9:00	11:30	12:00	5:00			
S	9:00	1:00					
S							
						TOTAL HOURS	

	HOURS	RATE	AMOUNT
REGULAR			
OVERTIME			
TOTAL EARNINGS			

SIGN.
SIGNATURE ______ DATE ______

Federal tax tables are used to determine income taxes to be withheld. The table is included in the working papers. The current rate for other taxes are as follows:

State income tax:	2%
FICA: Employee and employer contributions	
Social Security Tax:	6.2%
Medicare Tax:	1.45%
State unemployment tax:	5.4%
Federal unemployment tax:	0.8%

Peachtree®

SMART GUIDE

Step-by-Step Instructions:

1. Select the problem set for Green Thumb Plant Service (MP–3).
2. Rename the company and set the system date.
3. Enter your name for employee record 022.
4. Record the weekly payroll and print checks for all employees using the **Payroll Entry** option.
5. Print a Payroll Register for the current week and proof your work.
6. Print a Payroll Journal report.
7. Calculate and record the employer's payroll tax expense using the **General Journal Entry** option.
8. Record the deposit for the taxes owed to the federal government and enter the monthly insurance premium using the **General Journal Entry** option.
9. Manually complete Form 8109.
10. Print a General Journal report and proof your work.
11. Print a General Ledger report.
12. Print Quarterly Earnings reports for Michael Alter and Greg Millette.
13. Answer the Analyze questions.
14. End the session.

Visual Learning

Time Cards, p. 347

Use the illustration of the time cards in the textbook to review the calculation of hours worked with the class.

SOLUTION NOTES

Teaching Tips
Review the "job responsibilities" with students to be sure they know what they are to do to complete the mini practice set.

Remind students to check employees' accumulated earnings for FUTA and FICA limits.

APPLICATION OPTIONS

Complete activities one of two ways:

1 **Manual** Glencoe Working Papers

or

2 **Peachtree Complete Accounting** Software

YOUR JOB RESPONSIBILITIES
Green Thumb Plant Service

The business entered the third quarter of its fiscal year at the beginning of July. It is presently the last week of July. Jesse Dubow, the bookkeeper, is leaving on vacation. In his absence, you are to prepare this week's payroll.

(1) Complete the timecards for the four hourly employees. Enter the total hours worked at the bottom of each card.

(2) Greg Millette recorded additional clients that brought in $925.00 in new business. Calculate his commission and add it to his salary to determine his gross earnings.

(3) Enter the payroll information for all employees in the payroll register. Each employee was recently assigned an employee number because the business is soon converting to an automated payroll preparation system. Since this payroll is being prepared manually, list the employees in the payroll register in alphabetical order by last name.

(4) Use the following information to complete the payroll register.

- **(a)** Use the federal tax chart to determine income tax amounts to be withheld.
- **(b)** Michael Alter, Christine Cuddy, Joclyn Filley, and Greg Millette each have $5.00 deducted for the purchase of U.S. savings bonds.
- **(c)** Jesse Dubow, Heather Repicky, and Daniel Ripp each have $4.00 deducted for donations to the United Way.
- **(d)** All employees pay an insurance premium each week. Married employees pay $9.00 and single employees pay $6.00.
- **(e)** None of Green Thumb's employees has reached the maximum taxable amount for the social security tax.

(5) Calculate the net pay for each employee.

(6) Total all amount columns in the payroll register. Prove the accuracy of the totals.

MEETING SPECIAL NEEDS

Students with Orthopaedic Impairments A wheelchair is part of a student's "space." Do not automatically hang over or lean on the chair. Do not automatically assume that students need help. Most students who use wheelchairs will ask for help if they need it.

(7) Write Check 972 on the business's regular checking account for the amount of the total net pay. Make the check payable to the Green Thumb Plant Service—Payroll Account. In Jesse's absence, Joanna Ecke will sign the check for you. Complete the deposit slip for the payroll account.

(8) Record the payroll transaction in the general journal, page 21. Use the information contained in the payroll register and Check 972 as the source documents. Post the transaction to the general ledger accounts.

(9) Write the paychecks for the employees. Use the information in the payroll register to complete the check stubs. After a check has been written for an employee, enter the check number in the payroll register.

(10) Enter this week's payroll information on the employee's earnings records for Michael Alter and Greg Millette only. Be sure to add the current gross earnings amount to the accumulated total.

(11) Calculate and record the employer's taxes for this pay period in the general journal. The source of information is the payroll register. Post the journal entry to the general ledger.

(12) Make a deposit for the taxes owed to the federal government. The total includes the amounts withheld for employees' federal income tax, social security tax, and medicare tax. Complete Form 8109 by entering the amount owed. Write Check 973, payable to the First Federal Bank for the taxes.

(13) Enter the transaction in the general journal and post the entry to the general ledger.

(14) Pay the monthly insurance premium by writing Check 974 to the American Insurance Company for $228.00. Record the payment in the general journal and post the entry to the general ledger.

Analyze:

1. What is the total net pay for this pay period?
2. For what amount is the deposit to the federal government for taxes owed?

SOLUTION NOTES

MINI PRACTICE SET 3
PAGES 346–349

SOURCE DOCUMENT PROBLEM

ANSWERS

Hours worked:
Alter 22
Cuddy 36
Filley 34.5
Ripp 42

Millette's commission $92.50

Payroll register column totals:
Regular $2,734.80
Overtime $24.90
Total $2,759.70
Social Security $171.11
Medicare $40.02
FIT $244.00
SIT $55.20
Hospital Insurance $57.00
Other $32.00
Total $599.33
Net pay $2,160.37

Employees' net pay:
Alter $122.14
Cuddy $221.96
Dubow $184.87
Filley $196.66
Millette $428.14
Repicky $575.04
Ripp $290.45
Student $141.11

Employer's taxes:
Social Security $171.10
Medicare $40.02
FUT $22.08
SUT $149.02

Federal tax deposit $1,121.65

Analyze:
1. $2,160.37
2. $1,121.65

UNIT 4 *Resource Manager*

This is a representation of key resources available in the *Glencoe Accounting* program.

*inter*NET CONNECTION

Use the following Web resources to introduce, reinforce, or stimulate discussion on unit topics.

- Case Studies
- Study Plans
- Career Corner
- Real-Life Applications
- Self-Assessment Quizzes
- Games for the Classroom
- Ethics and the Profession

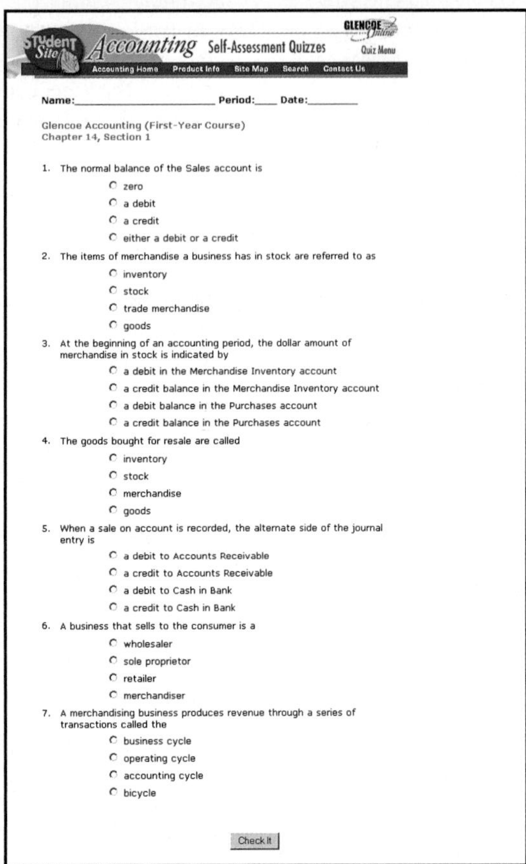

Student Site Accounting Self-Assessment Quizzes — Glencoe Online — Quiz Menu

Accounting Home | Product Info | Site Map | Search | Contact Us

Name:______________ Period:___ Date:________

Glencoe Accounting (First-Year Course)
Chapter 14, Section 1

1. The normal balance of the Sales account is
   - zero
   - a debit
   - a credit
   - either a debit or a credit
2. The items of merchandise a business has in stock are referred to as
   - inventory
   - stock
   - trade merchandise
   - goods
3. At the beginning of an accounting period, the dollar amount of merchandise in stock is indicated by
   - a debit in the Merchandise Inventory account
   - a credit balance in the Merchandise Inventory account
   - a debit balance in the Purchases account
   - a credit balance in the Purchases account
4. The goods bought for resale are called
   - inventory
   - stock
   - merchandise
   - goods
5. When a sale on account is recorded, the alternate side of the journal entry is
   - a debit to Accounts Receivable
   - a credit to Accounts Receivable
   - a debit to Cash in Bank
   - a credit to Cash in Bank
6. A business that sells to the consumer is a
   - wholesaler
   - sole proprietor
   - retailer
   - merchandiser
7. A merchandising business produces revenue through a series of transactions called the
   - business cycle
   - operating cycle
   - accounting cycle
   - bicycle

Check It

GLENCOE ACCOUNTING BULLETIN BOARD POSTER

Virtual Business® CD-ROM

Virtual Business is a fully visual marketing and business simulation that lets students start and run their own business. For more information on the simulation, visit the teacher page on the *Glencoe Accounting* Web site.

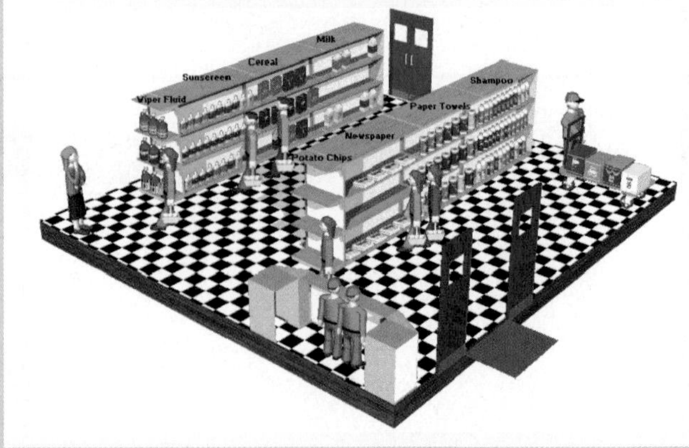

Accounting in Action

Unit Video Portfolio

Integrating *Electronic Field Trips* into Your Accounting Instruction

The *Electronic Field Trip* videos provide an excellent introduction to key accounting concepts taught in the textbook. You may want to use these video segments in **Unit 4.** The titles of the video segments are:

- *Sales and Cash Receipts*
- *Purchases and Cash Payments*
- *Adjusting Entries*
- *Financial Statements and Analysis*
- *Closing Entries*
- *Partnerships and Corporations*

Business Simulation
Outer Banks Marketplace, Inc.

*For use after Chapter 20

Mini Practice Set
In-Touch Electronics

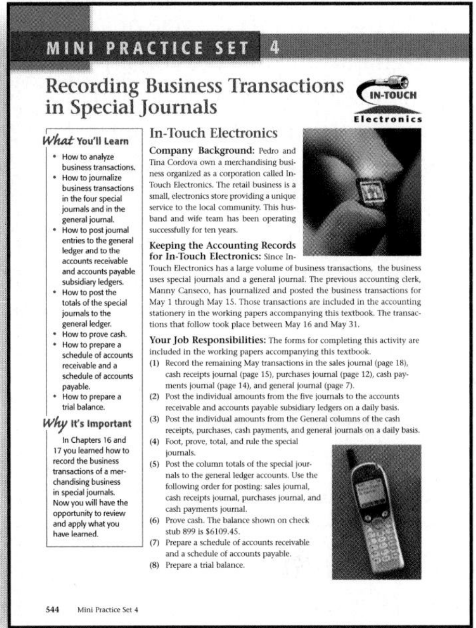

MINI PRACTICE SET 4

Recording Business Transactions in Special Journals

IN-TOUCH Electronics

What **You'll Learn**

- How to analyze business transactions.
- How to journalize business transactions in the four special journals and in the general journal.
- How to post journal entries to the general ledger and to the accounts receivable and accounts payable subsidiary ledgers.
- How to post the totals of the special journals to the general ledger.
- How to prove cash.
- How to prepare a schedule of accounts receivable and a schedule of accounts payable.
- How to prepare a trial balance.

Why **It's Important**

In Chapters 16 and 17 you learned how to record the business transactions of a merchandising business in special journals. Now you will have the opportunity to review and apply what you have learned.

In-Touch Electronics

Company Background: Pedro and Tina Cordova own a merchandising business organized as a corporation called In-Touch Electronics. The retail business is a small, electronics store providing a unique service to the local community. This husband and wife team has been operating successfully for ten years.

Keeping the Accounting Records for In-Touch Electronics: Since In-Touch Electronics has a large volume of business transactions, the business uses special journals and a general journal. The previous accounting clerk, Manny Canseco, has journalized and posted the business transactions for May 1 through May 15. Those transactions are included in the accounting stationery in the working papers accompanying this textbook. The transactions that follow took place between May 16 and May 31.

Your Job Responsibilities: The forms for completing this activity are included in the working papers accompanying this textbook.

(1) Record the remaining May transactions in the sales journal (page 18), cash receipts journal (page 15), purchases journal (page 12), cash payments journal (page 14), and general journal (page 7).
(2) Post the individual amounts from the five journals to the accounts receivable and accounts payable subsidiary ledgers on a daily basis.
(3) Post the individual amounts from the General columns of the cash receipts, purchases, cash payments, and general journals on a daily basis.
(4) Foot, prove, total, and rule the special journals.
(5) Post the column totals of the special journals to the general ledger accounts. Use the following order for posting: sales journal, cash receipts journal, purchases journal, and cash payments journal.
(6) Prove cash. The balance shown on check stub 899 is $6109.45.
(7) Prepare a schedule of accounts receivable and a schedule of accounts payable.
(8) Prepare a trial balance.

544 Mini Practice Set 4

*Can be found after Chapter 19

Assessment and Evaluation

Unit 4 Test

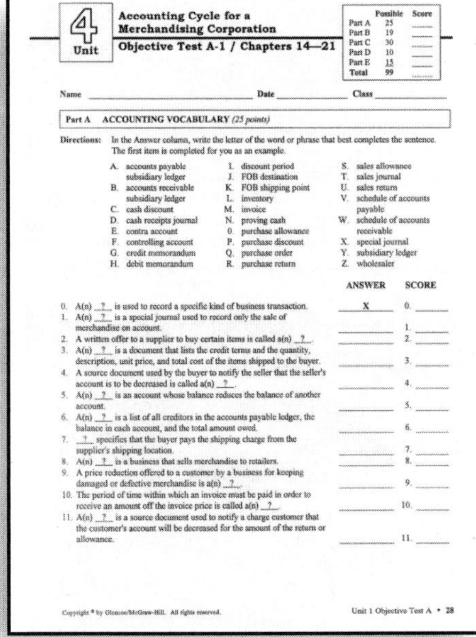

4 Unit — **Accounting Cycle for a Merchandising Corporation**

Objective Test A-1 / Chapters 14—21

	Possible	Score
Part A	25	____
Part B	19	____
Part C	30	____
Part D	10	____
Part E	15	____
Total	99	____

Name ____________ Date ________ Class ________

Part A ACCOUNTING VOCABULARY *(25 points)*

Directions: In the Answer column, write the letter of the word or phrase that best completes the sentence. The first item is completed for you as an example.

A. accounts payable subsidiary ledger
B. accounts receivable subsidiary ledger
C. cash discount
D. cash receipts journal
E. contra account
F. controlling account
G. credit memorandum
H. debit memorandum
I. discount period
J. FOB destination
K. FOB shipping point
L. inventory
M. invoice
N. proving cash
0. purchase allowance
P. purchase discount
Q. purchase order
R. purchase return
S. sales allowance
T. sales journal
U. sales return
V. schedule of accounts payable
W. schedule of accounts receivable
X. special journal
Y. subsidiary ledger
Z. wholesaler

	ANSWER	SCORE
0. A(n) __?__ is used to record a specific kind of business transaction.	X	0. ____
1. A(n) __?__ is a special journal used to record only the sale of merchandise on account.	____	1. ____
2. A written offer to a supplier to buy certain items is called a(n) __?__.	____	2. ____
3. A(n) __?__ is a document that lists the credit terms and the quantity, description, unit price, and total cost of the items shipped to the buyer.	____	3. ____
4. A source document used by the buyer to notify the seller that the seller's account is to be decreased is called a(n) __?__.	____	4. ____
5. A(n) __?__ is an account whose balance reduces the balance of another account.	____	5. ____
6. A(n) __?__ is a list of all creditors in the accounts payable ledger, the balance in each account, and the total amount owed.	____	6. ____
7. __?__ specifies that the buyer pays the shipping charge from the supplier's shipping location.	____	7. ____
8. A(n) __?__ is a business that sells merchandise to retailers.	____	8. ____
9. A price reduction offered to a customer by a business for keeping damaged or defective merchandise is a(n) __?__.	____	9. ____
10. The period of time within which an invoice must be paid in order to receive an amount off the invoice price is called a(n) __?__.	____	10. ____
11. A(n) __?__ is a source document used to notify a charge customer that the customer's account will be decreased for the amount of the return or allowance.	____	11. ____

Unit 1 Objective Test A • 28

Accounting Portfolio

Unit 4 Service and Leadership

Student ________ Class ________ Instructor ________

Date Assigned ________ Date Completed ________

Unit ***4*** — *Accounting Portfolio*

Service and Leadership

Extracurricular activities are important because they show employers your ability to work within a team, get along with others, and demonstrate your leader, ship skills. Being a member of a school club, participating in community projects, and competing in academic contests shows that you actively develop your skills and knowledge.

For this section of your portfolio, collect documents that represent your service and leadership activities. Some ideas follow.

LOCAL SERVICE PROJECTS

Look around your community and decide how you might help others in the community. For example, if you run for exercise, you may want to participate in a local fund-raising effort such as a 10K race. Ask for a letter or certificate of participation from the race sponsors and place the letter/certificate in your portfolio. An example is shown on page 34.

SCHOOL CLUBS OR CONTESTS

Organizations such as Business Professionals of America or Future Business Leaders of America orlyanize statewide and national accounting competitions for students.

Business Professionals of America is a national group of vocational students preparing for careers in the business world. The competitive events in accounting sponsored by Business Professionals of America include:

- Financial Assistant
- Financial Specialist
- Financial Analyst Team
- Computerized Accounting
- Payroll Accounting
- Cost Accounting

Certificates of merit can be earned at the local or state level. Students who win at the state level are allowed to compete at Business Professionals of America's national leadership conference. Include documents evidencing such competition in your portfolio (see page 32 for a sample). To participate in one or more of these categories requires many of the SCANS foundation skills and workplace competencies.

The Future Business Leaders of America also sponsors similar competitive events. A sample certificate from the FBLA leadership event is shown on page 33.

YOUR SERVICE AND LEADERSHIP GOALS

Volunteering your services to the community is an excellent way to demonstrate good citizenship and an effort to get to know others in your community. Ask teachers, parents, or friends to suggest community projects that might interest you.

Go to your local library and research charitable organizations and events in your area. Look for activities that you might like to participate in, then complete the lists on the next page. For each activity, include information such as the date and time of an event.

Accounting Portfolio 30

Enrichment and Extension

Accounting Competitive Event Review

Student ________ Class ________ Instructor ________

Date Assigned ________ Date Completed ________

Accounting for Corporations

A publicly held corporation is one whose stock is traded on a stock exchange such as the New York Stock Exchange. There are two kinds of stock commonly issued by a corporation: (1) common stock and (2) preferred stock. If only one class of stock is issued, it is called common stock. Preferred stock has a preference over common stock, usually in the form of dividends.

If stock is issued at a price more than its par value, the amount of cash received above par value is credited to the account Paid-in Capital in Excess of Par.

Stockholders receive a return on their investment in the form of dividends. A record of the corporation's dividends is recorded in the temporary contra stockholders' equity account Dividends.

For further information: See Chapters 19 and 21, First Year; Chapters 9 and 10, Advanced.

For additional practice: Additional Reinforcement Problems 19A and 21A.

On a separate sheet of paper, answer the following questions.

True/False

1. A corporation's profits are first taxed at the corporate tax rate and then taxed again at personal income tax rates when the profits are paid to the stockholders in the form of dividends.
2. All stockholders are guaranteed the right to receive annual dividends.
3. When common stock is issued, the par or stated value of the shares is recorded in the Common Stock account.
4. Stockholders have no personal liability for a corporation's debts.
5. A separate Common Stock account is kept in the general ledger for each common stockholder of a corporation.
6. Dividends are a distribution of a corporation's net income.
7. At the end of the period, any balance in the Dividends (Paid) account is debited to Retained Earnings.
8. No journal entry is necessary on the date a dividend is declared.
9. The stock of closely held corporations is traded on stock exchanges.
10. Par value is the dollar amount printed on a stock certificate.
11. A corporation may not own property.
12. A company's stock that has never been issued is called authorized capital stock.
13. The death, disability, or withdrawal of a major stockholder does not end the existence of a corporation.

Multiple Choice

14. Common stockholders will receive a dividend (A) in every year that the corporation is profitable, (B) in every year that the board of directors declares a dividend, (C) in every year, whether the corporation is profitable or not, (D) in those years when preferred stockholders do not receive dividends.
15. The right to vote in the election of directors and on other matters involving a corporation normally belongs to (A) corporate creditors, (B) corporate officers, (C) preferred stockholders, (D) common stockholders.

Accounting Competitive Event Review • 53

Unit Objectives

1. Correctly use terminology related to the accounting cycle of a merchandising business organized as a closely held corporation.
2. Describe accounting procedures for a merchandising business organized as a corporation.
3. Demonstrate accounting procedures for recording transactions in special journals and general and subsidiary ledgers.
4. Describe how managers and investors use financial information to analyze the operating performance of a business.

Unit 4 Contents

EXTENDING THE QUOTE

All businesses want to make a profit, but some do not succeed. Others may not make enough profit to operate the business successfully or to keep it growing. Managers use accounting data to help them identify reasons for losses and ways to improve profits.

UNIT 4

The Accounting Cycle for a Merchandising Corporation

In this unit. . .

You will learn how to keep the accounting records for a business that sells merchandise. The business we will use in our examples is organized as a corporation. You will study the complete accounting cycle for the merchandise business called **On Your Mark Athletic Wear.** We'll examine cash sales, sales on account, cash receipts, cash payments, and purchases. In addition, you'll learn how to record adjusting entries, prepare financial statements for a corporation, and prepare closing entries. The chart of accounts for **On Your Mark Athletic Wear** is shown on page 355.

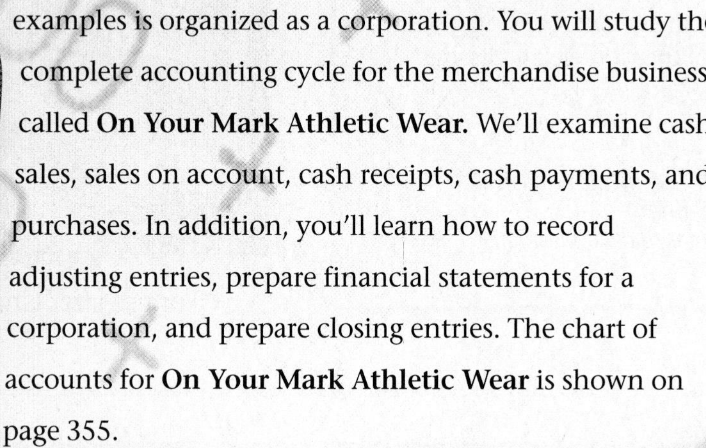

Where profit is, loss is hidden nearby.

Japanese Proverb

350

Great Ideas *From the Classroom of...*

Computers in Accounting Have students return to the beginning of the text and complete all the computer problems, chapter by chapter, on their own. This provides a great reinforcement of the materials while creating a work-like atmosphere in which the teacher is the "supervisor" answering questions related to the computer program.

Susan Howe
Chariho Regional High School
Wood River Junction, Rhode Island

In Your Journal . . .

The next time you visit your local CD store, examine the inventory—the various types of products that are available to purchase. The managers of merchandising businesses are responsible for the quality and popularity of their stores.

In your journal, record the following:

1. Make a list of all the product groups for sale (CDs, tapes, magazines, t-shirts, etc).
2. What items are the least expensive for sale? Most expensive?
3. Make a list of items that the store does not currently carry that you feel would be a beneficial addition.

POWER READING STRATEGIES

To get the most out of your reading:

Predict what the section will be about.

Connect what you read with your own life.

Question as you read to make sure you understand the content.

Respond to what you've read.

In Your Journal. . .

Teacher Guidelines Have students add to their accounting portfolios by completing and including the *In Your Journal* writing activities. Tell students to write a paragraph explaining how a store's inventory influences their shopping habits and buying decisions. Ask them also to explain how inventory can influence customer loyalty and a store's profits. P

OVERVIEW UNIT 4

Previewing the Chapters

In this unit students complete an accounting cycle for a merchandising business organized as a closely held corporation. Students learn about general purchasing and sales procedures, as well as accounts payable and receivable. Using special journals, students analyze and record merchandising transactions. They also learn how to use the general journal in a special journal system.

Adjusting entries are introduced in this unit. After learning adjustments, students complete the accounting cycle, then learn to analyze financial reports for business evaluation and decision making.

Tying to Previous Knowledge

In previous units students learned the basic accounting cycle, using the general journal and general ledger. This unit will build on prior learning by expanding the cycle to include special journals, subsidiary ledgers, and adjustments.

BULLETIN BOARD

Glencoe Poster Teaching Tip

Before discussing the poster, ask students what skills and knowledge they think will help them find and keep a job. Make a list of their responses on the chalkboard. Then introduce the poster and have students compare their answers to those of employers.

CHAPTER 14 Resource Manager

Section Resources

	Objectives & Standards	Activities & Features	Reproducible Masters
Chapter Opener *Accounting for Sales and Cash Receipts*	• Explain the difference between a service business and a merchandising business. • Analyze transactions relating to the sale of merchandise. • Explain the difference between a retailer and a wholesaler. • Record a variety of sales and cash receipt transactions in a general journal. • Define the accounting terms introduced in this chapter. **National Standards for Business Education**: IA6–10, IIA2–4	Exploring the Real World of Business, p. 352 Workplace Connections, p. 353	School-to-Work Handbook
Section 1 *Accounting for a Merchandising Business*	• The purpose of a merchandising business. • The difference between a retailer and a wholesaler. • Uses of the **Merchandise Inventory** account, and its rules of debit and credit. • Uses of the **Sales** account, and its rules of debit and credit.	Connect To, p. 356 A Matter of Ethics, p. 356	Demonstration Problems Strategies for Teaching Ethics in Accounting
Section 2 *Analyzing Sales Transactions*	• How to record the sale of merchandise on account. • How to use the accounts receivable subsidiary ledger. • How to post to the accounts receivable subsidiary ledger. • The use of the **Sales Tax Payable** account, and its rules of debit and credit. • The use of the **Sales Returns and Allowances** account, and its rules of debit and credit.	Did You Know?, p. 359 International Accounting, p. 360 Accounting Tips, p. 362 Spreadsheet Hints, p. 365	Demonstration Problems Strategies for Teaching International Accounting Math Review for Accounting
Section 3 *Analyzing Cash Receipt Transactions*	• How to record cash receipt transactions. • The use of the **Sales Discounts** account, and its rules of debit and credit.	Accounting Flashbacks, p. 369 Analyzing Financial Reports, p. 375	Demonstration Problems Internet Resources and Activities Handbook

KEY

Posters — Transparency — Software — Videocassette

Blackline Masters — CD-ROM — Portfolio

MULTIMEDIA RESOURCE

Peachtree

- Problem 14–5 *Recording Sales and Cash Receipts*
- Problem 14–6 *Posting Sales and Cash Receipts*
- Problem 14–7 *Recording Sales and Cash Receipts*
- Problem 14–8 *Recording Sales and Cash Receipt Transactions*
-  Problem 14–9 *Recording and Posting Sales and Cash Receipts*

QuickBooks

- Problem 14–5 *Recording Sales and Cash Receipts*
- Problem 14–7 *Recording Sales and Cash Receipts*
- Problem 14–9 *Recording and Posting Sales and Cash Receipts*

Spreadsheets

None in this chapter.

Videos

Video Segment: Sales and Cash Receipts

After viewing this video, students will be able to describe the need for special journals using examples of both credit and cash sales. Students will be able to explain the difference between cash and credit sales and why they are recorded in cash receipts and sales journals, respectively.

CD-ROMs

Electronic Learning Center (ELC), Chapter 14

This program is ideal for visual learners since it incorporates video images, animation, and graphics to enliven the content of each lesson.

Interactive Lesson Planner (ILP), Chapter 14

This CD-ROM combines the versatility of an electronic lesson planner with the convenience of teacher classroom resources.

SCANS Correlation Chart

FOUNDATION SKILLS

Basic Skills:	Reading	Writing	Math	Listening	Speaking	
Thinking Skills:	Creative Thinking	Decision Making	Problem Solving	Seeing Things in the Mind's Eye	Knowing How to Learn	Reasoning
Personal Qualities:	Responsibility	Self-Esteem	Sociability	Self-Management	Integrity/Honesty	

WORKPLACE COMPETENCIES

Resources:	Allocating Time	Allocating Money	Allocating Material and Facility Resources	Allocating Human Resources		
Information:	Acquiring and Evaluating Information	Organizing and Maintaining Information	Interpreting and Communicating Information	Using Computers to Process Information		
Interpersonal Skills:	Participating as a Member of a Team	Teaching Others	Serving Clients/ Customers	Exercising Leadership	Negotiating to Arrive at a Decision	Working with Cultural Diversity
Systems:	Understanding Systems	Monitoring and Correcting Performance	Improving and Designing Systems			
Technology:	Selecting Technology	Applying Technology to Task	Maintaining and Troubleshooting Technology			

*Highlighted blocks indicate areas covered in the chapter. Additional SCANS skills are also covered throughout the *Teacher Wraparound Edition.*

Assessment

Student Edition
- Check Your Understanding, pp. 357, 366, 376
- Chapter 14 Problems, pp. 381–385

Assessment and Evaluation Masters
- Chapter 14 Study Plan, *Glencoe Workbook*
- Chapter 14 Self-Test, *Glencoe Workbook*
- Chapter 14 Test, *Chapter Tests* Booklet
- Chapter 14 Activity, *School-to-Work Handbook*
- Chapter 14 **Exam***View*

Teacher Wraparound Edition
- Critical Thinking Activity, p. 369
- Reteaching Section 1, p. 357
- Reteaching Section 2, p. 366
- Reteaching Section 3, p. 376
- Chapter 14 Quiz, p. 377

Transparencies

	Teaching Transparencies	Solution Transparencies
Section 1:	14–1, 14–2	Problem 14–1
Section 2:	14–3, 14–4, 14–5, 14–6, 14–7, 14–8, 14–9, 14–10	Problem 14–2
Section 3:	14–11, 14–12, 14–13, 14–14, 14–15, 14–16, 14–17, 14–18, 14–19, 14–20	Problems 14–3, 14–4
End of Chapter:		Problems 14–5, 14–6, 14–7, 14–8, 14–9

TEACHER CLASSROOM RESOURCES

This is a representation of key blackline masters available in the Teacher Classroom Resources.

Teaching Aids

Transparency Examples

Section Focus Transparencies

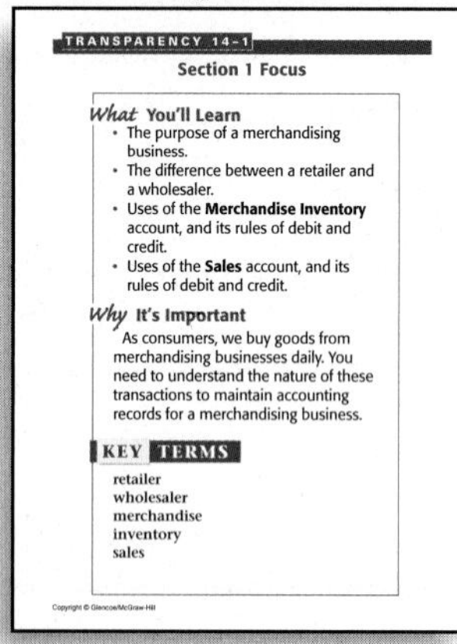
TRANSPARENCY 14–1

Section 1 Focus

What You'll Learn
- The purpose of a merchandising business.
- The difference between a retailer and a wholesaler.
- Uses of the **Merchandise Inventory** account, and its rules of debit and credit.
- Uses of the **Sales** account, and its rules of debit and credit.

Why It's Important

As consumers, we buy goods from merchandising businesses daily. You need to understand the nature of these transactions to maintain accounting records for a merchandising business.

KEY TERMS

retailer
wholesaler
merchandise
inventory
sales

Teaching Transparencies

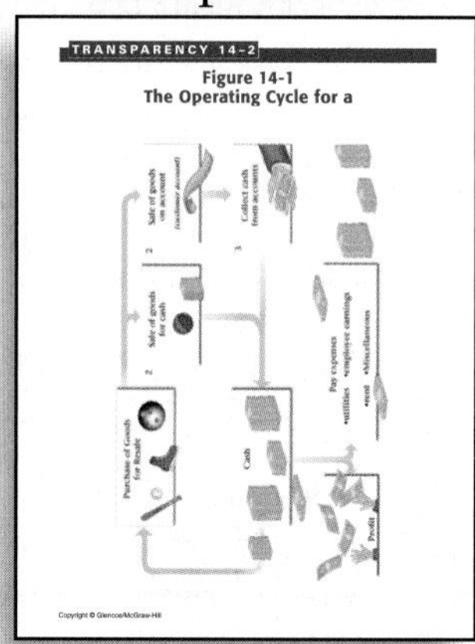
TRANSPARENCY 14–2

Figure 14-1
The Operating Cycle for a

Source Document Transparencies

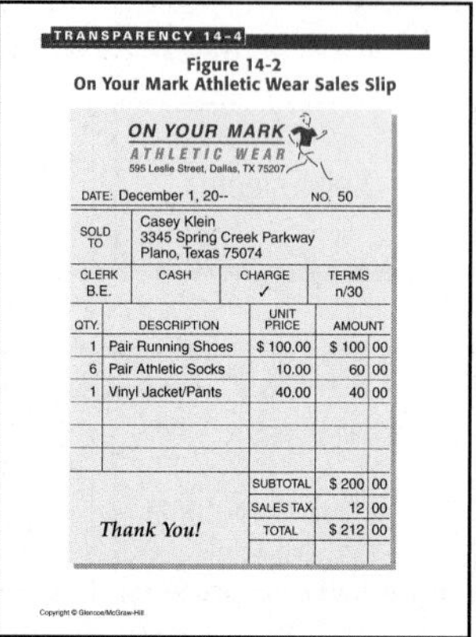
TRANSPARENCY 14–4

Figure 14-2
On Your Mark Athletic Wear Sales Slip

ON YOUR MARK ATHLETIC WEAR
595 Leslie Street, Dallas, TX 75207

DATE: December 1, 20-- NO. 50

SOLD TO: Casey Klein, 3345 Spring Creek Parkway, Plano, Texas 75074

CLERK	CASH	CHARGE	TERMS
B.E.		✓	n/30

QTY.	DESCRIPTION	UNIT PRICE	AMOUNT
1	Pair Running Shoes	$ 100.00	$ 100 00
6	Pair Athletic Socks	10.00	60 00
1	Vinyl Jacket/Pants	40.00	40 00
		SUBTOTAL	$ 200 00
		SALES TAX	12 00
	Thank You!	TOTAL	$ 212 00

Solution Transparencies

Working Papers for End-of-Chapter Problems

Problem 14-5 Recording Sales and Cash Receipts

GENERAL JOURNAL

Demonstration Problems

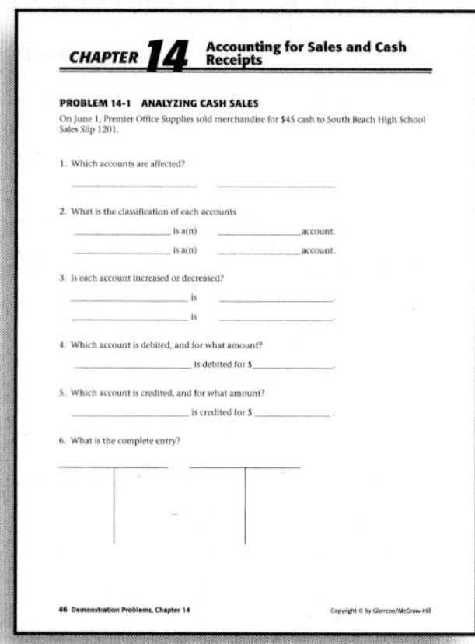
CHAPTER 14 Accounting for Sales and Cash Receipts

PROBLEM 14-1 ANALYZING CASH SALES

Lesson Plans

Chapter 14 — Chapter Opener (pg. 352-353)

Accounting for Sales and Cash Receipts

Learning Objectives

State/Local Objectives

Block Scheduling

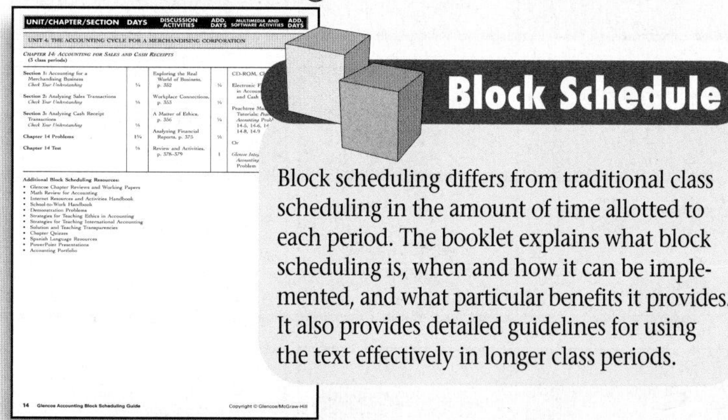
Block Schedule

Block scheduling differs from traditional class scheduling in the amount of time allotted to each period. The booklet explains what block scheduling is, when and how it can be implemented, and what particular benefits it provides. It also provides detailed guidelines for using the text effectively in longer class periods.

Enrichment and Application

Strategies for Teaching Ethics in Accounting

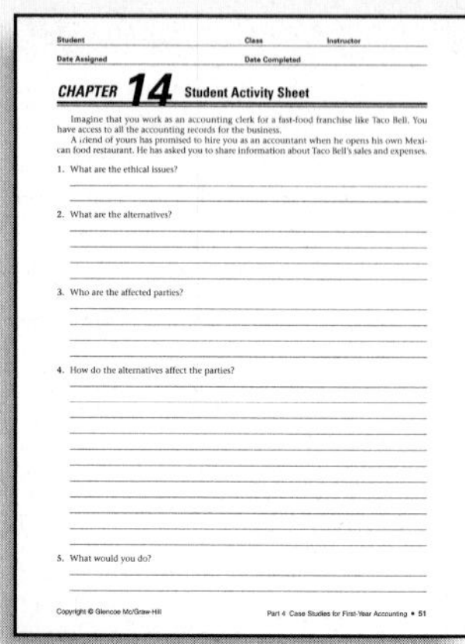
CHAPTER 14 Student Activity Sheet

1. What are the ethical issues?
2. What are the alternatives?
3. Who are the affected parties?
4. How do the alternatives affect the parties?
5. What would you do?

Strategies for Teaching International Accounting

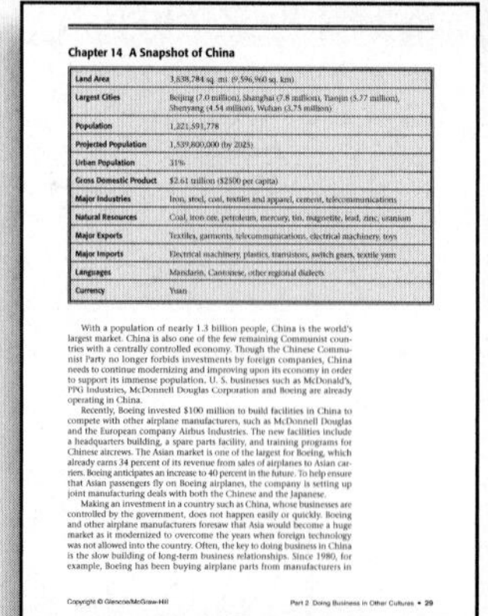
Chapter 14 A Snapshot of China

School-to-Work Handbook

CHAPTER 14 SCHOOL-TO-WORK ACTIVITY

Accounting for Sales and Cash Receipts

Meeting Different Ability Levels

Chapter Reviews and Working Papers (CRWP)

Working Papers

Review

Student Study Plan

Self-Test

Real-World Multimedia CD-ROM

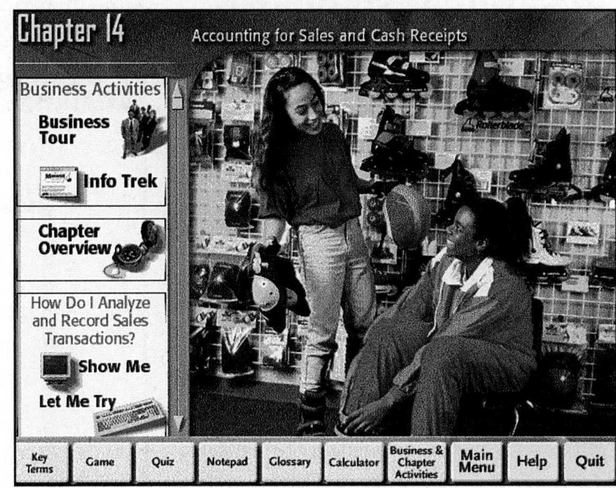

Key to Ability Levels

Each section gives skill-building activities. Each activity has been labeled for use with students of various learning styles and abilities.

L1 Level 1 activities are basic activities and should be within the range of all students.

L2 Level 2 activities are average activities and should be within the range of average and above average students.

L3 Level 3 activities are challenging activities designed for the ability range of above average students.

ELL ELL activities should be within the ability range of English Language Learners.

Assessment and Evaluation

Chapter Tests

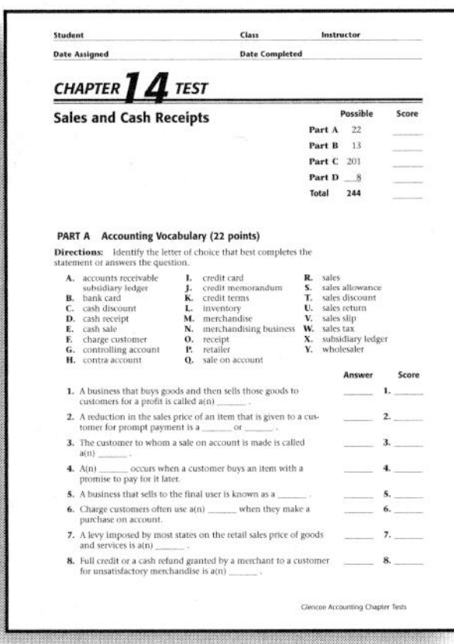

CHAPTER 14 TEST

Sales and Cash Receipts

	Possible	Score
Part A	22	
Part B	13	
Part C	201	
Part D	8	
Total	244	

PART A Accounting Vocabulary (22 points)

Chapter Quiz

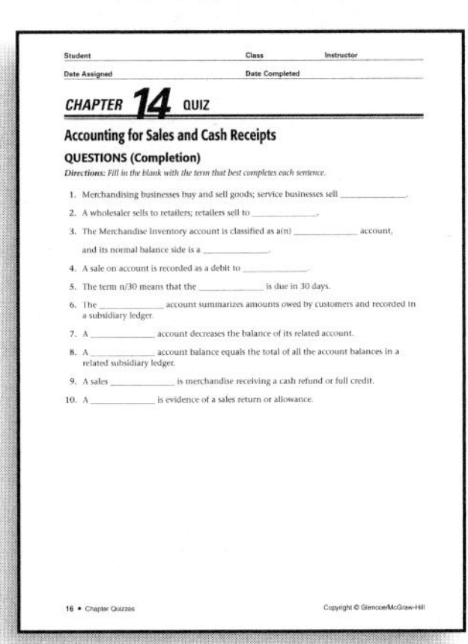

CHAPTER 14 QUIZ

Accounting for Sales and Cash Receipts

QUESTIONS (Completion)

Teaching Resources at a Glance

Application Resources

- Glencoe Chapter Review and Working Papers, SE and TAE
- School-to-Work Handbook, SE and TM
- Accounting Portfolio, SE and TM

Reproducible Masters

- Demonstration Problems
- Lesson Plans
- Block Scheduling
- Spanish Language Resources

Glencoe Accounting Professional Development Series

- Strategies for Teaching Ethics in Accounting
- Accounting Competitive Event Review
- Math Review for Accounting
- Strategies for Teaching International Accounting
- Internet Resources and Activities Handbook

Transparency Package

- Section Focus Transparencies
- Teaching Transparencies
- Source Document Transparencies
- Solution Transparencies

Performance Assessment

- **Exam***View* CD-ROM
- Chapter Tests
- Chapter Quizzes
- Unit Tests
- Audit Tests
- Printed Testbank

Multimedia Resources

- Electronic Learning Center:
  - Multimedia CD-ROMs
  - Peachtree software, tutorials, templates, and solutions
  - Spreadsheet templates
- Using QuickBooks with Glencoe Accounting
- Interactive Lesson Planner
- Electronic Field Trips in Accounting
- PowerPoint Presentation
- Web site: glencoeaccounting.glencoe.com

OVERVIEW CHAPTER 14

Correlations to National Standards for Business Education

(See pages T50–T51 for a detailed correlation chart.)

Standards: IA6–10, IIA2–4

Chapter Preview

In this chapter students learn to analyze and record sales and cash receipt transactions. They post to the general ledger and the accounts receivable subsidiary ledger. Students will also analyze source documents for sales and cash receipts.

Section Overviews

- Section 1—*Accounting for a Merchandising Business*
- Section 2—*Analyzing Sales Transactions*
- Section 3—*Analyzing Cash Receipt Transactions*

Chapter Vocabulary

retailer
wholesaler
merchandise
inventory
sales
sale on account
charge customer
credit cards
sales slip
sales tax
credit terms
accounts receivable subsidiary ledger
subsidiary ledger
controlling account
sales return
sales allowance
credit memorandum
contra account
cash receipt
cash sale
bankcard
cash discount
sales discount

Preteaching Accounting Vocabulary

Oral Exercise: Write each of the new terms on the chalkboard, then ask students for ideas for each term's meaning. Write correct responses on the chalkboard. See the chapter and the *Glossary* for definitions. L1

CHAPTER 14 Accounting for Sales and Cash Receipts

Learning Objectives

When you have completed this chapter, you will be able to:

- Explain the difference between a service business and a merchandising business.
- Analyze transactions relating to the sale of merchandise.
- Explain the difference between a retailer and a wholesaler.
- Record a variety of sales and cash receipt transactions in a general journal.
- Define the accounting terms introduced in this chapter.

Exploring the Real World of Business

ANALYZING SALES

Twenty years ago, the now-popular sport of in-line skating didn't exist. Today, in-line skating attracts nearly 29 million participants and is one of the fastest growing sports in the U.S.

Rollerblade, a leading producer of in-line skates based in Minnesota, was created when two brothers found a used pair of in-line skates while rummaging through a sporting goods store. In the basement of their parents' home, they modified the skates for their off-season hockey training. Other hockey players and skiers in training soon adapted the in-line skates into their training routines. Professional marketing efforts helped the sport gain public attention, and soon in-line skaters were a common sight along city streets, beaches, and college campuses.

Although the company does not release its accounting records because it is privately owned, it has become a multi-million dollar business, maintaining a 33 percent market share.

What do you think?

1. What products and accessories do you think a company like **Rollerblade** sells?
2. When **Rollerblade** sells its products to sporting goods stores and skate shops, what general ledger accounts do you imagine would be affected?

Exploring the Real World of Business

Rollerblade

In-line skates may date back to the early 1700s, but only conventional roller skates were used in this country until Rollerblade began promoting a new sport of in-line skating to help sell its products. Businesses often become successful through creative adaptations or marketing of existing products.

What do you think? (Answers)

1. Students' responses might include in-line skates and protective gear such as helmets, gloves, and knee pads.
2. Sales and Accounts Receivable. Students may mention Sales Tax Payable. Point out that sales taxes are paid only by retail customers. Rollerblade is a wholesaler.

Workplace Connections

Applying Your Accounting Knowledge

Making sales is key to the financial success of a business. Sales dollars come from selling products or services to customers. In Chapters 3 through 11, you learned about accounting for a business that sells services to its customers. In this Unit, you'll learn about selling merchandise to customers and how to record these sales into the accounting records.

Investigate:

1. Does your work or the work of friends or family involve selling merchandise to customers?
2. What products are sold?
3. What information from these sales do you think should be recorded into the accounting records?

Glencoe Accounting Online

Visit the *Glencoe Accounting* Web site at **glencoeaccounting.glencoe.com** for additional activities and information.

INTRODUCING
CHAPTER 14

Making Accounting Relevant

Workplace Connections: Applying Your Accounting Knowledge

Discussion: Ask students how many of them have made sales of products or services in their work. How did they learn to make a sale? What did their sale mean to the business? Have students discuss the actions involved in a sale and the effect of the sale on the financial records of the business.

Investigate (Answers)

1. Answers will vary. Have students discuss any jobs where friends or family are in sales.
2. Answers will vary. Have students discuss the differences between selling a service and a product.
3. The product or service sold, amount of the sale, terms, amount of any tax, and name/account of the buyer.

School-to-Work Activity

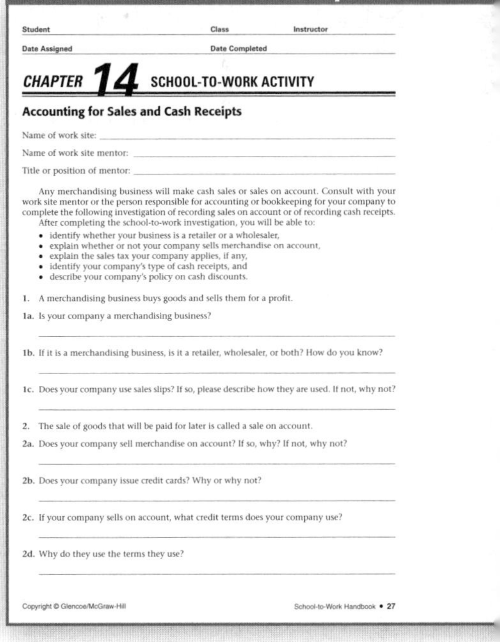

Student ______ Class ______ Instructor ______

Date Assigned ______ Date Completed ______

CHAPTER 14 SCHOOL-TO-WORK ACTIVITY

Accounting for Sales and Cash Receipts

Name of work site: ______

Name of work site mentor: ______

Title or position of mentor: ______

Any merchandising business will make cash sales or sales on account. Consult with your work site mentor or the person responsible for accounting or bookkeeping for your company to complete the following investigation of recording sales on account or of recording cash receipts.

After completing the school-to-work investigation, you will be able to:

- identify whether your business is a retailer or a wholesaler,
- explain whether or not your company sells merchandise on account,
- explain the sales tax your company applies, if any,
- identify your company's type of cash receipts, and
- describe your company's policy on cash discounts.

1. A merchandising business buys goods and sells them for a profit.

1a. Is your company a merchandising business?

1b. If it is a merchandising business, is it a retailer, wholesaler, or both? How do you know?

1c. Does your company use sales slips? If so, please describe how they are used. If not, why not?

2. The sale of goods that will be paid for later is called a sale on account.

2a. Does your company sell merchandise on account? If so, why? If not, why not?

2b. Does your company issue credit cards? Why or why not?

2c. If your company sells on account, what credit terms does your company use?

2d. Why do they use the terms they use?

 School-to-Work Handbook • 27

GLENCOE MULTIMEDIA

Electronic Field Trips in Accounting *Video Segment: Sales and Cash Receipts*

After viewing this video, students will be able to describe the need for special journals using examples of both credit and cash sales; explain the difference between cash and credit sales and why they are recorded in cash receipts and sales journals, respectively.

Glencoe Accounting: Electronic Learning Center *Chapter 14*

The CD-ROM program is ideal for visual learners since it incorporates video images, animation, and graphics to enliven the content of each lesson.

1 FOCUS

Introducing the Section

In this section students learn about merchandising businesses and how they differ from a service business. They also learn the difference between retailers and wholesalers. Two key accounts, Merchandise Inventory and Sales, are introduced, along with a chart of accounts for a merchandising business.

Section Concepts

- The purpose of a merchandising business.
- The difference between a retailer and a wholesaler.
- Uses of the Merchandise Inventory account and its rules of debit and credit.
- Uses of the Sale account and its rules of debit and credit.

Visual Learning

Section 1 Focus

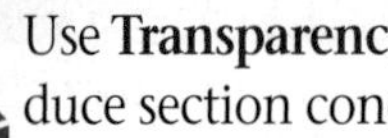
Use **Transparency 14–1** to introduce section concepts.

BELL RINGER

Compare and Contrast: Write this list on the chalkboard:

theater tickets
gasoline
soft drinks
car wash
CDs
music concert
jeans
haircut and style
ticket to a sports event
car

Have students decide which item is provided by a service business and which by a merchandising business. Ask students to explain what makes each a service or merchandise. L1

SECTION 1

Accounting for a Merchandising Business

What You'll Learn

- The purpose of a merchandising business.
- The difference between a retailer and a wholesaler.
- Uses of the **Merchandise Inventory** account, and its rules of debit and credit.
- Uses of the **Sales** account, and its rules of debit and credit.

Why It's Important

As consumers, we buy goods from merchandising businesses daily. You need to understand the nature of these transactions to maintain accounting records for a merchandising business.

KEY TERMS

retailer
wholesaler
merchandise
inventory
sales

As you remember, a service business is one that provides a service to the public for a fee. In contrast, a merchandising business buys goods (such as computers, clothing, or furniture) and then sells those goods to customers for a profit. You're probably familiar with merchandising businesses like Tower Records or Wal-Mart. Most merchandising businesses operate either as retailers or as wholesalers. Some merchandising businesses are both retailers and wholesalers. A **retailer** is a business that sells to the final user, that is, to you—the consumer. A **wholesaler** is a business that sells to retailers. In this chapter, we will analyze transactions relating to the sale of merchandise for On Your Mark Athletic Wear, a retailer. Refer to the chart of accounts for On Your Mark Athletic Wear.

The Operating Cycle of a Merchandising Business

A merchandising business produces revenue through a series of transactions called the operating cycle, as illustrated in **Figure 14–1** below.

The collection of cash from sales enables the business to purchase more items to sell, pay expenses, and make a profit. As long as the company is in business, this is a continuous, repeating sequence.

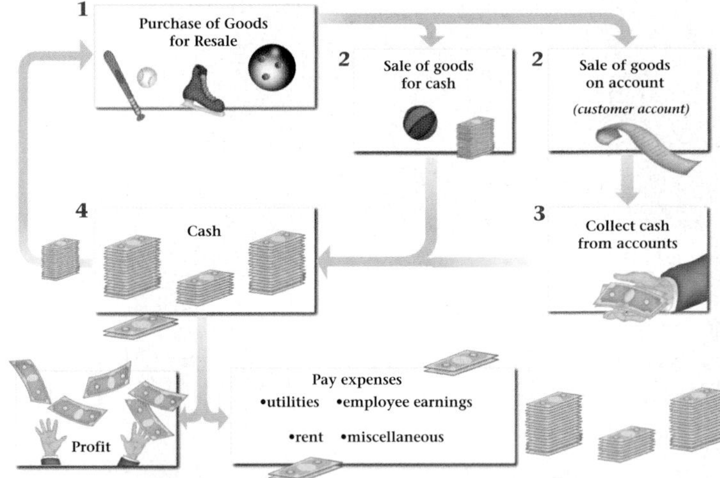

Figure 14–1 The Operating Cycle for a Merchandising Business

RESOURCE MANAGER

Reproducible Masters
- Lesson Plans
- Chapter Reviews and Working Papers (CRWP) TAE
- Demonstration Problems

Transparencies
- Section Focus Transparency
- Teaching Transparencies
- Source Document Transparencies
- Solution Transparencies

Multimedia
- Exam*View* CD-ROM
- Electronic Learning Center CD-ROM
- Interactive Lesson Planner CD-ROM

CHART OF ACCOUNTS

ASSETS

101	Cash in Bank	130	Supplies
105	Change Fund	135	Prepaid Insurance
110	Petty Cash Fund	140	Delivery Equipment
115	Accounts Receivable	142	Accumulated Depreciation—Delivery Equipment
117	Allowance for Uncollectible Accounts	145	Office Equipment
118	Notes Receivable	147	Accumulated Depreciation—Office Equipment
120	Interest Receivable	150	Store Equipment
125	Merchandise Inventory	152	Accumulated Depreciation—Store Equipment

LIABILITIES

201	Accounts Payable	212	Social Security Tax Payable
202	Notes Payable	213	Medicare Tax Payable
203	Discount on Notes Payable	214	Federal Unemployment Tax Payable
204	Federal Corporate Income Tax Payable	215	State Unemployment Tax Payable
205	Employees' Federal Income Tax Payable	220	Sales Tax Payable
211	Employees' State Income Tax Payable		

STOCKHOLDERS' EQUITY

301	Capital Stock	310	Income Summary
305	Retained Earnings		

REVENUE

401	Sales	410	Sales Returns and Allowances
405	Sales Discounts	415	Interest Income

COST OF MERCHANDISE

501	Purchases	510	Purchases Discounts
505	Transportation In	515	Purchases Returns and Allowances

EXPENSES

601	Advertising Expense	645	Loss/Gain on Disposal of Plant Assets
605	Bankcard Fees Expense	650	Maintenance Expense
610	Cash Short and Over	655	Miscellaneous Expense
612	Delivery Expense	657	Payroll Tax Expense
615	Depreciation Expense—Delivery Equipment	660	Rent Expense
620	Depreciation Expense—Office Equipment	665	Salaries Expense
625	Depreciation Expense—Store Equipment	670	Supplies Expense
630	Federal Corporate Income Tax Expense	675	Uncollectible Accounts Expense
635	Insurance Expense	680	Utilities Expense
640	Interest Expense		

▶ Accounts Receivable Subsidiary Ledger		▶ Accounts Payable Subsidiary Ledger	
BRE	Break Point Sports Club	CHA	Champion Store Supply
DIM	Dimaio, Joe	COM	Computer Solutions
GAL	Galvin, Robert	DAR	Dara's Delivery Service
KLE	Klein, Casey	FAS	FastLane Athletics
MON	Montero, Anita	GEA	Geary Office Supply
RAH	Rahim, Shashi	PRO	Pro Runner Warehouse
RAM	Ramos, Gabriel	SLF	Sports Link Footwear
SOU	South Branch High School Athletics	SNS	Sports Nutrition Supply
SUL	Sullivan, Megan		
TAM	Tammy's Fitness Club		
WON	Wong, Kim		
YOU	Young, Lara		

Great Ideas *From the Classroom of...*

Researching Jobs in Accounting Beginning with the first day of school, students look in newspapers every day for a week and find jobs available for accounting clerks, bookkeepers, payroll clerks, CPAs, and accountants. The students cut out classified ads and highlight job requirements and the starting salaries. They make a collage of the ads and compare salaries to other available jobs.

Chris Mendez
Bel Air High School
El Paso, TX

2 TEACH

GUIDED PRACTICE

Reading Accounting

- Have students look at the headings in this section. Ask them to make a list of the topics being presented and connect each topic to an accounting concept. L1
- Have students look at the illustrations. Discuss how they connect to the major concepts in the section. For example, look at the chart of accounts to find Merchandise Inventory and Sales. Then connect those accounts to the T-account analysis on the next page. ELL

Concept Development: The Operating Cycle of a Merchandising Business

Discussion: Discuss the differences between service and merchandising businesses. Have students give examples of each. Discuss how retailers and wholesalers differ. Explain the new accounts in this section (Sales and Merchandise Inventory). L1

Visual Learning

Figure 14–1 The Operating Cycle for a Merchandising Business

Using **Transparency 14–2**, discuss the steps in how a business buys and sells goods. Relate each step to an account such as Sales or Merchandise Inventory.

Chart of Accounts, p. 355

Point out the new accounts students will study in this accounting cycle, but at this point discuss only the Sales and Merchandise Inventory accounts.

2 TEACH (Cont'd.)

Concept Development: Merchandise Inventory and Sales Accounts

Discussion: Discuss why the account is called Merchandise Inventory (it represents the inventory a merchandiser has for sale). As the business sells merchandise, the money it receives is recorded in the Sales account. Ask students to name an item they just bought, such as a CD or tape. In which account is the sale recorded by the merchant selling the CD or tape? L1

Critical Thinking: Using the preceding example, tell students to assume this is a cash sale. In keeping with the double-entry system, which account other than Sales would the merchant use to record the sale? (Cash in Bank) L2

Demonstration Problem Step-by-Step Practice

Use demonstration problem 14–1 to guide students through the analysis and recording of a cash sale.

Thinking Algebraically

Conceptualize: Ask students to think about the double-entry system of accounting. Have them discuss why the rules of debit and credit are opposite for the Sales and Merchandise Inventory accounts. L2

Strategies for Teaching Ethics in Accounting

Photocopy the Chapter 14 *Student Activity Sheet* for students. Answers are also provided in the booklet.

CONNECT TO . . . EDUCATION

A study performed by the Federation of Schools of Accountancy determined that writing and speaking are the subjects in which accounting students require the most extra work. The Federation also found that most accounting students would benefit from extra courses on multinational accounting, ethics, and other liberal-arts courses.

Merchandise Inventory Account

A merchandising business buys goods from a wholesaler or a manufacturing business and then sells these goods to its customers. Goods bought for resale are called **merchandise**. The items of merchandise the business has in stock are referred to as **inventory**. The inventory is represented in the general ledger by the asset account **Merchandise Inventory.** Increases to **Merchandise Inventory** are recorded as debits, and decreases are recorded as credits. The normal balance of the **Merchandise Inventory** account is a debit. At the beginning of each period, the dollar amount of merchandise in stock is indicated by the debit balance in the **Merchandise Inventory** account.

Merchandise Inventory	
Debit + Increase Side Normal Balance	Credit – Decrease Side

During the business operating cycle, the merchandise in stock is sold, and new inventory items are purchased to replace the ones sold. Separate accounts are used to record the sale of merchandise and the purchase of new merchandise.

Sales Account

When a retail merchandising business sells goods to a customer, the amount of the merchandise sold is recorded in the **Sales** account. **Sales** is a revenue account. Increases to the **Sales** account are recorded as credits, and decreases are recorded as debits. The normal balance of the **Sales** account is a credit. Both sales for cash and on account are recorded as credits to the **Sales** account.

Sales	
Debit – Decrease Side	Credit + Increase Side Normal Balance

Sales on account will affect the **Accounts Receivable** account, while cash sales will affect the **Cash in Bank** account.

A MATTER OF ETHICS

Confidentiality

Imagine that you work as an accounting clerk for a fast-food franchise like Taco Bell. You have access to all the accounting records for the business.

A friend of yours has promised to hire you as an accountant when he opens his own Mexican food restaurant. He has asked you to share information about Taco Bell's sales and expenses.

Ethical Decision Making:

- What are the ethical issues?
- What are the alternatives?
- Who are the affected parties?
- How do the alternatives affect the parties?
- What would you do?

Teaching A MATTER OF ETHICS

Confidentiality Businesses expect that employees will learn confidential information just by doing their jobs. They also expect them to keep that information confidential. Discuss what is confidential (e.g., salaries, specific costs) versus public information (e.g., information printed in an annual report).

SECTION 1 Check Your Understanding

Now that you have studied this section, complete the following questions and problems.

Thinking Critically

1. Explain the two types of merchandising businesses.
2. What type of account is **Merchandise Inventory?**

Communicating Accounting

You and your best friend, Inga Swenson, graduated from a prestigious art school. You have a degree in art history and business management; Inga has a degree in fine art. Inga is an award-winning weaver and creates wall hangings that are extremely popular in your community. Together you decide to form a business partnership. You want to open a retail store. Inga wants to sell directly to the customers at fairs and art shows. Draft a report to Inga that explains why selling art through a retail store is more profitable than seasonal shows and fairs.

Problem 14–1 Recording Merchandising Transactions

Instructions Record the following transactions in T-account form in your working papers for Sharp Shot Camera Shop. A partial chart of accounts follows:

General Ledger
Cash in Bank
Accounts Receivable
Merchandise Inventory
Accounts Payable
Sales

Date	Transactions
Apr. 4	Sold 10 Canon cameras on account for $3,000, Sales Slip 224.
10	Sold 2 dozen photo albums for $150, cash, Sales Slip 225.
20	Sold 4 rolls of 35mm film for $24 cash, Sales Slip 226.
25	Sold a Canon camera to a customer for $380 cash, Sales Slip 227.

CHAPTER 14
SECTION 1, PAGES 354–357

3 ASSESS

Thinking Critically (Answers)

1. A retailer buys goods and sells to the consumer. A wholesaler sells those products to the retailers.
2. Merchandise Inventory is an asset account.

Communicating Accounting (Answers)

Students' proposals will vary. Evaluate student papers for correct grammar and a logical progression of ideas.

Problem 14–1 (Answers)

Ending account balances:
Cash in Bank $554
Accounts Receivable $3,000
Sales $3,554

Chapter Reviews and Working Papers Refer students to the Chapter 14 workbook pages to answer *Check Your Understanding* activities.

4 CLOSE

Section Wrap-Up

Demonstrate: Draw two T accounts on the chalkboard and write the titles Merchandise Inventory and Sales on them. Ask for volunteers to come up and add the increase/decrease and normal balance sides for the two accounts. L1

RETEACHING SECTION 1

Rules of Debit and Credit Reinforce the rules of debit and credit by drawing blank T accounts on the chalkboard for the new accounts in this section: Merchandise Inventory, Sales, and Sales Tax Payable. Have students analyze each account and tell you the rules of debit and credit and the normal balance side for each. Then ask for volunteers to describe a transaction involving these accounts. Remind students of the information they should learn about each new account: (1) its classification; (2) its increase, decrease, and balance sides; and (3) how the account is used.

1 FOCUS

Introducing the Section

In this section students learn about the information recorded on a sales slip, including sales tax and credit terms. Students learn how to analyze and record sales transactions using a general journal model. They also learn how to analyze and record sales returns and allowances using a general journal. After recording transactions, students will post to the accounts receivable ledger.

Section Concepts

- How to record the sale of merchandise on account.
- How to use the accounts receivable subsidiary ledger.
- How to post to the accounts receivable subsidiary ledger.
- The use of the Sales Tax Payable account and its rules of debit and credit.
- The use of the Sales Returns and Allowances account and its rules of debit and credit.

Visual Learning

Section 2 Focus

Use **Transparency 14–3** to introduce section concepts.

BELL RINGER

Role-Play: Bring an item students might buy, such as candy bars or soda, to class and role-play its purchase from a merchant. Have a student take the role of the buyer while you play the merchant. Using a transparency of a blank sales slip, fill out the source document for the purchase. Then ask students to describe the transaction and how it affects the merchant's accounts. L1

SECTION 2

Analyzing Sales Transactions

What You'll Learn

- How to record the sale of merchandise on account.
- How to use the accounts receivable subsidiary ledger.
- How to post to the accounts receivable subsidiary ledger.
- The use of the **Sales Tax Payable** account, and its rules of debit and credit.
- The use of the **Sales Returns and Allowances** account, and its rules of debit and credit.

Why It's Important

It is essential to record sales transactions correctly as they reflect the revenue of the business.

KEY TERMS

sale on account
charge customer
credit cards
sales slip
sales tax
credit terms
accounts receivable subsidiary ledger
subsidiary ledger
controlling account
sales return
sales allowance
credit memorandum
contra account

In a merchandising business, the most frequent transaction is the sale of merchandise. Some businesses sell on a cash only basis. Others sell only on credit. Most businesses handle both cash and credit sales. Think about how many sales transactions a single Sears store records on a December day. Some customers pay with cash, some use a Sears credit card, and others use a bankcard such as VISA, MasterCard, or Discover. Each transaction is recorded so that at the end of the day, the store can report sales by each category (cash, credit card, and bankcard) and total sales. In this section, you will learn how to analyze transactions relating to sale of merchandise on account.

The sale of merchandise that will be paid for at a later date is called a **sale on account**, a charge sale, or a credit sale. The sale on account is made to a **charge customer**. Charge customers use **credit cards** issued by the business to make their purchases. A credit card, imprinted with the customer's name and account number, facilitates the sale on account.

The Sales Slip

A **sales slip** is a form that lists the details of a sale:

- The date of the sale.
- The name of the customer.
- The description, quantity, and price of the item(s) sold.

The description may include the physical details (such as "white athletic socks"), a stock number, or both. A sales slip is usually prepared in multiple copies. The customer receives the original as a receipt and as proof of purchase. The number of copies kept by the business varies with its needs. A copy is always used for accounting purposes as the source document for recording the journal entry.

Pre-numbered sales slips help businesses keep track of all sales made on account. On Your Mark uses pre-numbered sales slips printed with its name and address. On Your Mark's sales slip is shown in **Figure 14–2**.

Notice that the total amount on the sales slip includes cost of the items sold and sales tax.

RESOURCE MANAGER

Reproducible Masters
- Lesson Plans
- Chapter Reviews and Working Papers (CRWP) TAE
- Demonstration Problems

Transparencies
- Section Focus Transparency
- Teaching Transparencies
- Source Document Transparencies
- Solution Transparencies

Multimedia
- Exam*View* CD-ROM
- Electronic Learning Center CD-ROM
- Interactive Lesson Planner CD-ROM

Sales Tax

Most states and some cities tax the retail sale of goods and services. This tax is called a **sales tax**. Items subject to sales tax and sales tax rates vary from state to state. The sales tax rate is usually stated as a percentage of the sale, such as 5%. Sales tax rates are determined by each state's taxing authority.

The sales tax is paid by the customer and collected by the business. The business acts as the collection agent for the state or city government. (In the future, we will refer only to the state government.) At the time of the sale, the business adds the sales tax to the total selling price of the goods. Periodically, the business sends the collected sales tax to the state. Until the state is paid, however, the sales tax collected from customers represents a liability of the business. The business keeps a record of the sales tax owed to the state in a liability account called **Sales Tax Payable.** For **Sales Tax Payable,** the increase and balance side is a credit and the decrease side is a debit.

Sales Tax Payable	
Debit – Decrease Side	Credit + Increase Side Normal Balance

ON YOUR MARK
ATHLETIC WEAR
595 Leslie Street, Dallas, TX 75207

DATE: December 1, 20-- NO. 50

SOLD TO: Casey Klein, 3345 Spring Creek Parkway, Plano, Texas 75074

CLERK	CASH	CHARGE	TERMS
B.E.		✓	n/30

QTY.	DESCRIPTION	UNIT PRICE	AMOUNT
1	Pair Running Shoes	$ 100.00	$ 100 00
6	Pair Athletic Socks	10.00	60 00
1	Vinyl Jacket/Pants	40.00	40 00
		SUBTOTAL	$ 200 00
		SALES TAX	12 00
	Thank You!	TOTAL	$ 212 00

Figure 14–2 On Your Mark Athletic Wear Sales Slip

Calculating Sales Tax

To calculate the sales tax, multiply the total selling price of the merchandise by the sales tax rate. Refer to **Figure 14–2.** Casey Klein bought $200 worth of merchandise. The sales tax rate is 6%. The sales clerk multiplied $200 by 6% (.06) to compute the $12 sales tax. The total transaction amount is $212.

Not all sales of retail merchandise are taxed. In most states, sales made to tax-exempt organizations, such as schools, are not taxed. For example, South Branch High School purchased $1,500 worth of merchandise on account. Since schools are tax exempt, no sales tax is added to the amount of the sale.

Credit Terms

On the sales slip in **Figure 14–2,** space is provided to indicate the credit terms of the sale. **Credit terms** state the time allowed for payment. The credit terms for the sale to Casey Klein are n/30. The "n" stands for the *net,* or total, amount of the sale. The "30" stands for the number of days the customer has to pay for the merchandise. Casey Klein owes On Your Mark $212 (the net amount) by December 31 (30 days after December 1).

Did You Know?

Teen Spending
Teens are major consumers in the U.S. economy, spending over $103 billion each year. Transactions per teen average $67 per week on clothing, health and beauty aids, and entertainment.

The Accounts Receivable Ledger

Businesses with few charge customers usually include an Accounts Receivable account for each customer in the general ledger. A large business, however, with many charge customers, sets up a separate ledger that contains an account for each charge customer. This ledger is the **accounts receivable subsidiary ledger**. A **subsidiary ledger** is a ledger, or book, that contains detailed data summarized to a controlling account in the

INTERDISCIPLINARY CONNECTIONS ACTIVITY

(Refer to the *Connect to...Education* feature on page 356.)
Education Accountants are required to have many skills in addition to their expertise with numbers. Being able to communicate clearly, in writing and orally, is a skill that many employers value. Have students discuss how they can improve their communication skills; for example, by participating in clubs or student government, joining a debate team, or taking extra English courses.

2 TEACH

GUIDED PRACTICE

Reading Accounting

- Have students write each of the major heads in this section on a sheet of paper. As they read the section, have them write a brief description of the content under each heading. L1
- Summarize the sales procedure by drawing a diagram on the chalkboard. Connect a sales slip with arrows to a T-account analysis, a journal entry, and an account in the accounts receivable subsidiary ledger. ELL

Concept Development: The Sales Slip

Discussion: Bring a credit card and a sales slip to class. Ask students whether they have bought items using a credit card. Relate their purchases to buying on account. Then discuss the information on a sales slip, including (a) the purpose, (b) why there are multiple copies, (c) the information on the sales slip, (d) how sales tax is determined, (e) what happens to sales tax collected by the business, and (f) credit terms such as n/30 or 2/10, n/30. L1

Visual Learning

Figure 14–2 On Your Mark Athletic Wear Sales Slip
Use **Transparency 14–4** to review sales slip information. Bring in examples of other sales slips, and have students compare the information recorded on each.

Concept Development: Sales Tax and Credit Terms

Discussion: Ask students the local sales tax rate. What are the credit terms on items they buy on account? L1

2 TEACH (Cont'd.)

Demonstration Problem Step-by-Step Practice

Use demonstration problem 14–2 to give students practice in calculating sales tax and determining the total sale.

Teaching Tip

Ask students if they know the sales tax rate in your state and community. Give them a few sales amounts and have them calculate the sales tax on each amount.

Concept Development: The Accounts Receivable Ledger

Discussion: Explain the Accounts Receivable controlling account and how the accounts in the subsidiary ledger equal the total of the controlling account. Point out that the rules of debit and credit for the subsidiary ledger accounts are the same as their controlling account. Compare the subsidiary ledger account form and the general ledger account form, pointing out the differences. L1

Visual Learning

Figure 14–3 Subsidiary Ledger Account Form

Use **Transparency 14–5** to demonstrate the differences between a subsidiary ledger form and a general ledger form.

Strategies for Teaching International Accounting

To enrich study of International Accounting, refer to the additional critical thinking activities in the booklet.

Proper Names

When conducting business in the international marketplace, it is important to address individuals in the proper manner. Some countries do not use the "first name-last name" style as used in the U.S. For example, in Spanish-speaking Latin America, the surname includes the mother and father's last names. The father's name comes first and is the only one used in conversation.

general ledger. For example, the accounts receivable subsidiary ledger contains details of all the individuals and businesses that owe money to a company. Summary information about accounts receivable appears in the **Accounts Receivable** account in the general ledger. **Accounts Receivable** is a **controlling account** because its balance equals the total of all the account balances in the subsidiary ledger. The balance of **Accounts Receivable** thus serves as a control on the accuracy of the balances in the accounts receivable subsidiary ledger after all posting is complete.

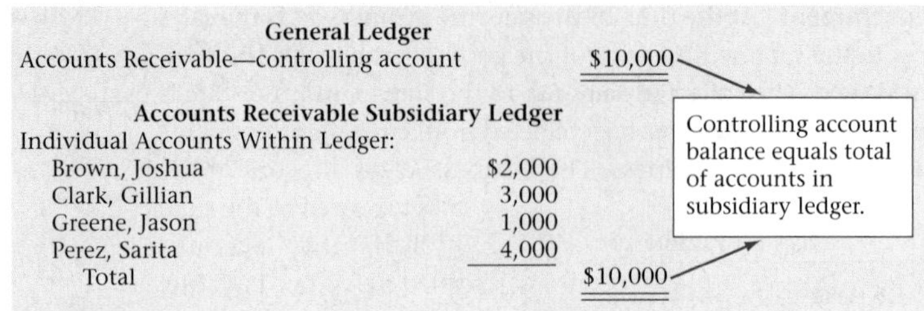

General Ledger

Accounts Receivable—controlling account		$10,000

Accounts Receivable Subsidiary Ledger

Individual Accounts Within Ledger:		
Brown, Joshua	$2,000	
Clark, Gillian	3,000	
Greene, Jason	1,000	
Perez, Sarita	4,000	
Total		$10,000

The Accounts Receivable Subsidiary Ledger Form

Figure 14–3 shows the accounts receivable subsidiary ledger form used by On Your Mark.

The subsidiary ledger account form has lines at the top for the name and address of the customer. In a manual accounting system, subsidiary ledger accounts are arranged in alphabetical order. They are not usually numbered. In a computerized system, however, each charge customer is assigned a specific account number.

Notice that the subsidiary ledger account form has only three amount columns. The Debit and Credit columns are used to record increases and decreases to the customer's account. There is only one Balance column. Since **Accounts Receivable** is an asset account, the normal balance is a debit, so one balance amount is sufficient.

NAME ______

ADDRESS ______

DATE	DESCRIPTION	POST. REF.	DEBIT	CREDIT	BALANCE

Figure 14–3 Subsidiary Ledger Account Form

Recording Sales on Account

Recall that Roadrunner Delivery Service is a service business organized as a sole proprietorship. When Roadrunner provides delivery services and bills the customer, the **Accounts Receivable** and **Delivery Revenue** accounts are affected. Let's compare that transaction to a sale on account for a merchandising business, On Your Mark Athletic Wear.

Teaching International ACCOUNTING

U.S. Businesses Overseas Obtain business magazines such as *BusinessWeek*, *Forbes*, and *Fortune* that have articles about U.S. companies doing business in other countries. Share with students and have them choose a country to research. Have students write a short one-page report about the country and its major industries. Ask students to share reports and discuss what knowledge accountants would need to work in that country.

Business Transaction

On December 1 On Your Mark sold merchandise on account to Casey Klein for $200 plus sales tax of $12, Sales Slip 50.

ON YOUR MARK
ATHLETIC WEAR
595 Leslie Street, Dallas, TX 75207

DATE: December 1, 20-- NO. 50

SOLD TO: Casey Klein, 3345 Spring Creek Parkway, Plano, Texas 75074

CLERK	CASH	CHARGE	TERMS
B.E.		✓	n/30

QTY.	DESCRIPTION	UNIT PRICE	AMOUNT
1	Pair Running Shoes	$ 100.00	$ 100 00
6	Pair Athletic Socks	10.00	60 00
1	Vinyl Jacket/Pants	40.00	40 00
		SUBTOTAL	$ 200 00
		SALES TAX	12 00
	Thank You!	TOTAL	$ 212 00

ANALYSIS

Identify 1. The accounts affected are **Accounts Receivable** (controlling), **Accounts Receivable–Casey Klein** (subsidiary), **Sales,** and **Sales Tax Payable.**

Classify 2. **Accounts Receivable** (controlling) and **Accounts Receivable–Casey Klein** (subsidiary) are asset accounts. **Sales** is a revenue account. **Sales Tax Payable** is a liability account.

+/− 3. **Accounts Receivable** (controlling) and **Accounts Receivable–Casey Klein** (subsidiary) are increased by the total amount, $212 (dollar amount of merchandise sold plus sales tax). **Sales** is increased by the dollar amount of merchandise sold, $200. **Sales Tax Payable** is increased by the amount of sales tax charged, $12.

DEBIT-CREDIT RULE

4. Increases to asset accounts are recorded as debits. Debit **Accounts Receivable** (controlling) for $212. Also debit **Accounts Receivable–Casey Klein** (subsidiary) for $212.
5. Increases to revenue and liability accounts are recorded as credits. Credit **Sales** for $200 and **Sales Tax Payable** for $12.

T ACCOUNTS

6.

Accounts Receivable	
Debit + 212	Credit −

Sales	
Debit −	Credit + 200

Accounts Receivable Subsidiary Ledger Casey Klein	
Debit + 212	Credit −

Sales Tax Payable	
Debit −	Credit + 12

JOURNAL ENTRY

7. **GENERAL JOURNAL** PAGE 20

	DATE		DESCRIPTION	POST. REF.	DEBIT	CREDIT	
1	20--						1
2	Dec.	1	Accts. Rec./Casey Klein		212 00		2
3			Sales			200 00	3
4			Sales Tax Payable			12 00	4
5			Sales Slip 50				5
6							6

MAKING CONNECTIONS TO DAILY LIFE

The Sales Process Ask students how they participate in the sales process. For example, what do they buy on a given day? Perhaps lunch at school or a candy bar after school. Have students make a list of at least ten things they and other family members buy each week. For each item on the list, tell whether the business is selling a service (dry-cleaning) or a product (groceries).

2 TEACH (Cont'd.)

Visual Learning

Business Transaction
Use **Transparency 14–6** to walk students through each of the steps in analyzing a sales transaction and recording it in a general journal. As you go through each step in the analysis, ask students to explain why the transaction affects each account and why each is increasing or decreasing.

Concept Development: Recording Sales on Account

Discussion: Explain the accounts affected by a sale on account. Read the business transaction and point out the sales slip as the source of information for the transaction. You may want to show the transparency of the sales slip again and have students relate the information in the written description to the data recorded on the sales slip.

For the business transaction analysis, have students do the following:

1. Identify the accounts affected.
2. Classify each account.
3. Determine whether each account increases or decreases.
4. Decide which account is debited.
5. Decide which account is credited.
6. Complete T accounts for the transaction.
7. Describe the general journal entry.

Demonstration Problem Step-by-Step Practice
Use demonstration problem 14–3 to show students how to record a sale on account.

CHAPTER 14
SECTION 2, PAGES 358–366

2 TEACH (Cont'd.)

Visual Learning

Business Transaction

Use **Transparency 14–7** to give students practice in analyzing the information in a source document and deciding how the transaction is to be recorded. Have students go through each step in the analysis model.

Concept Development: Sales Returns and Allowances

Discussion: Customers are not always satisfied with merchandise they purchase. The merchandise may have been the wrong size or color, or it may have damage the customer did not notice in the store. When customers return merchandise, the seller must issue a credit or return cash paid. A full return of the purchase price is a sales return. If the customer wants to keep the merchandise but receive a partial credit, a sales allowance is granted.

A sales return or allowance decreases the Sales account, but businesses record these amounts in a separate account to better track its lost sales. The Sales account shows the gross sales or revenue for the accounting period. L1

Teaching Tips

Ask students who work in retail environments to share some of their experiences with returned merchandise. Point out that merchandise returned to a business must be in the same condition as when purchased, or full credit may not be granted for a return.

Chapter Reviews and Working Papers Refer students to the *Study Plan* located at the beginning of Chapter 14 in the workbook.

ACCOUNTING TIPS

Errors

To lessen the risk of error, use a calculator—preferably one that prints out a tape—to check your work.

Notice that the debit in the general journal entry is to "Accounts Receivable/Casey Klein." The slash indicates that two accounts are debited: **Accounts Receivable** (controlling) and **Accounts Receivable—Casey Klein** (subsidiary).

As mentioned earlier, when merchandise is sold to tax-exempt organizations, such as school districts, sales tax is not charged. An example of such a transaction follows.

This transaction is analyzed and recorded in the same manner as the December 1 entry for Casey Klein *except* there is no sales tax. On Your Mark's accountant debits **Accounts Receivable/South Branch High School Athletics** for $1,500 and credits the **Sales** account for $1,500.

Business Transaction

On December 3 On Your Mark sold merchandise on account to South Branch High School Athletics for $1,500, Sales Slip 51.

JOURNAL ENTRY

ON YOUR MARK ATHLETIC WEAR
595 Leslie Street, Dallas, TX 75207

DATE: December 3, 20-- NO. 51

SOLD TO: South Branch High School, 1750 Rutgers Dr., Dallas, TX 75207

CLERK	CASH	CHARGE	TERMS
B.E.		✓	2/10, n/30

QTY.	DESCRIPTION	UNIT PRICE	AMOUNT
15	Baseball Uniforms	$ 40.00	$ 600 00
15	Baseball Caps	20.00	300 00
15	Baseball Mitts	35.00	525 00
2	Baseballs	15.00	30 00
3	Baseball Bats	15.00	45 00
		SUBTOTAL	$ 1,500 00
		SALES TAX	0 00
	Thank You!	TOTAL	$ 1,500 00

GENERAL JOURNAL PAGE 20

	DATE	DESCRIPTION	POST. REF.	DEBIT	CREDIT	
6	3	Accts. Rec./So. Branch H.S.		1 500 00		6
7		Sales			1 500 00	7
8		Sales Slip 51				8
9						9

Sales Returns and Allowances

All merchandising businesses expect that some customers will be dissatisfied with their purchases. The reasons for dissatisfaction vary. An item may be damaged or defective. The color or size may be incorrect. Whatever the reason, merchants usually allow dissatisfied customers to return merchandise. Any merchandise returned for credit or a cash refund is called a **sales return**.

Sometimes a customer discovers that merchandise is damaged or defective but still usable. When this happens, the merchant may reduce the sales price for the damaged merchandise. A price reduction granted for damaged goods kept by the customer is called a **sales allowance**.

The Credit Memorandum. If the sales return or allowance occurs on a charge sale, the business usually prepares a credit memorandum. A **credit memorandum** lists the details of a sales return or allowance. The charge customer's account is credited (decreased) for the amount of the return or allowance.

Figure 14–4 shows a credit memorandum, or credit memo, used by On Your Mark. The credit memo was prepared when Gabriel Ramos returned merchandise that he bought on account on November 29. Note that the credit memo includes a description of the returned item, the reasons for the return, and the amount to be credited to Gabriel Ramos' account.

Key Points

Posting a Sale on Account

For sales on account, the accounts receivable portion of the journal entry is posted to both the controlling account in the general ledger and the customer's account in the subsidiary ledger.

REINFORCING STUDY SKILLS

Vocabulary Technique Understanding terminology is essential to retaining information gained from reading. To help students understand the new terms in this chapter related to sales transactions, use real-world examples of merchandise, sales taxes, sales slips, credit cards, credit terms, and so on. Then ask students to give you other examples of these same terms.

On Your Mark's credit memo also includes spaces for the date and sales slip number of the original sale. Notice too that the total on the credit memo includes the sales tax charged on the original sale.

The same form is used if Gabriel Ramos is instead given a sales allowance. Of course, the amount credited to his account would be less. The credit granted for an allowance is the difference between the original sales price and the reduced price.

ON YOUR MARK ATHLETIC WEAR
595 Leslie Street, Dallas, TX 75207

CREDIT MEMORANDUM NO. 124

DATE: December 4, 20--
NAME: Gabriel Ramos
ADDRESS: 278 Summit Avenue
Dallas, TX 75206

Gabriel Ramos
CUSTOMER SIGNATURE

ORIGINAL SALES DATE	ORIGINAL SALES SLIP	APPROVAL	
Nov. 29, 20--	No. 35	J.R.	X MDSE RET

QTY	DESCRIPTION	AMOUNT
1	Athletic Suit	$ 150 00
REASON FOR RETURN: wrong color	SUB TOTAL	$ 150 00
THE TOTAL SHOWN AT THE RIGHT WILL BE CREDITED TO YOUR ACCOUNT.	SALES TAX	9 00
	TOTAL	$ 159 00

Figure 14–4 Credit Memorandum

On Your Mark's credit memos are pre-numbered and prepared in duplicate. The original is given to the customer. The copy is kept by the business and is the source document used for the journal entry to record the transaction.

The Sales Returns and Allowances Account. Sales returns and allowances decrease the total revenue earned by a business. This decrease, however, is not recorded in the **Sales** account. Instead, a separate account called **Sales Returns and Allowances** is used. **Sales Returns and Allowances** summarizes the total returns and allowances for damaged, defective, or otherwise unsatisfactory merchandise. If the **Sales Returns and Allowances** account balance is large in proportion to the **Sales** account balance, there may be merchandising problems. The **Sales Returns and Allowances** account is carefully analyzed to detect any trouble.

The **Sales Returns and Allowances** account is a contra account. As a **contra account**, its balance decreases the balance of its related account. **Sales Returns and Allowances** is more specifically classified as a *contra revenue* account because it is related to a revenue account, **Sales.** Since the normal balance side of **Sales** is a credit, the normal balance side of **Sales Returns and Allowances** is a debit. This relationship is shown below:

Sales		Sales Returns and Allowances	
Debit – Decrease Side	Credit + Increase Side Normal Balance	Debit + Increase Side Normal Balance	Credit – Decrease Side

Key Points

Contra Accounts

A contra account balance decreases the balance of its related account. The normal balance side of any contra account is always the opposite of the normal balance side of its related account.

Cash Refunds

Sometimes a merchant will give a customer a cash refund instead of a credit. On Your Mark's store policy is to give a cash refund only if the original sale was a cash sale. For cash refunds, the **Cash in Bank** account is credited instead of **Accounts Receivable.**

COOPERATIVE LEARNING ACTIVITY

Group Discussion Many cities and states levy taxes on retail sales. Assign students to groups of four or five and ask them to investigate and report on the tax percentage imposed by our city and state. Group reports should include information on the goods and services that are tax exempt. You may also want students to include information about which government agencies are allowed to impose taxes and how they go about doing so.

2 TEACH (Cont'd.)

Visual Learning

Figure 14–4 Credit Memorandum

Use **Transparency 14–8** to show students the information recorded on a credit memorandum. Relate the information on the form to accounts used by On Your Mark Athletic Wear.

Teaching Tips

Ask students why a separate account is used for sales returns and allowances. Such an account is especially useful to business managers because it gives the manager an indication of customer dissatisfaction with the seller's merchandise. Large increases or decreases in the account from one period to the next can also indicate whether customers are more or less happy with the merchandise.

Emphasize the association between "credit" memorandum and "credit" being granted to a customer by decreasing the customer's account balance through a "credit" entry.

Critical Thinking: Draw a T account on the chalkboard and label it Sales Returns and Allowances. Ask students to supply the increase, decrease, and normal balance sides and to explain why they are opposite those of the Sales account. L1

Writing: Have students write 1–2 paragraphs describing a business's sales returns policies (for example, what can be returned and for what reasons). Ask for a few volunteers to read their policies, then discuss how the policies might affect business profits. L2

2 TEACH (Cont'd.)

Visual Learning

Business Transaction

Using **Transparency 14–9**, have students read the transaction description. Review the information on the credit memorandum. Have students go through each step in the transaction analysis model.

Demonstration Problem
Step-by-Step Practice

Use demonstration problem 14–4 to give students practice in recording sales returns and allowances transactions in a general journal and posting to the general and subsidiary ledgers.

Teaching Tip

Point out that the controlling account is always entered before the subsidiary ledger account when journalizing a credit for a sales return.

Concept Development: Posting to the Accounts Receivable Ledger

Discussion: Remind students that they learned to post from the general journal in Unit 2. Most students will remember the process after a quick demonstration. L1

Oral Demonstration: Ask for a volunteer to explain the process of posting from a general journal to the general ledger. L2

Business Transaction

On December 4 On Your Mark issued Credit Memorandum 124 to Gabriel Ramos for the return of merchandise purchased on account, $150 plus $9 sales tax.

ON YOUR MARK ATHLETIC WEAR
595 Leslie Street, Dallas, TX 75207

CREDIT MEMORANDUM — NO. 124

DATE: December 4, 20--
NAME: Gabriel Ramos
ADDRESS: 278 Summit Avenue
Dallas, TX 75206

ORIGINAL SALES DATE	ORIGINAL SALES SLIP	APPROVAL	MDSE RET
Nov. 29, 20--	No. 35	J.R.	X

QTY	DESCRIPTION	AMOUNT
1	Athletic Suit	$ 150 00

REASON FOR RETURN: wrong color — SUB TOTAL $ 150 00
THE TOTAL SHOWN AT THE RIGHT WILL BE CREDITED TO YOUR ACCOUNT. — SALES TAX 9 00
TOTAL $ 159 00

Gabriel Ramos
CUSTOMER SIGNATURE

ANALYSIS

Identify 1. The accounts affected are **Accounts Receivable** (controlling), **Accounts Receivable–Gabriel Ramos** (subsidiary), **Sales Returns and Allowances,** and **Sales Tax Payable.**

Classify 2. **Accounts Receivable** (controlling) and **Accounts Receivable–Gabriel Ramos** (subsidiary) are asset accounts. **Sales Returns and Allowances** is a contra revenue account. **Sales Tax Payable** is a liability account.

+/– 3. **Sales Returns and Allowances** is increased by $150. **Sales Tax Payable** is decreased by $9. **Accounts Receivable** (controlling) and **Accounts Receivable–Gabriel Ramos** (subsidiary) are decreased by $159.

DEBIT-CREDIT RULE

4. Increases to a contra revenue account are recorded as debits. Debit **Sales Returns and Allowances** for $150. Decreases to liability accounts are recorded as debits. Debit **Sales Tax Payable** for $9.
5. Decreases to asset accounts are recorded as credits. Credit **Accounts Receivable** (controlling) for $159. Also credit **Accounts Receivable–Gabriel Ramos** (subsidiary) for $159.

T ACCOUNTS

6.

Accounts Receivable	
Debit +	Credit –
	159

Sales Returns and Allowances	
Debit +	Credit –
150	

Accounts Receivable Subsidiary Ledger Gabriel Ramos	
Debit +	Credit –
	159

Sales Tax Payable	
Debit –	Credit +
9	

JOURNAL ENTRY

7.

GENERAL JOURNAL — PAGE 20

	DATE	DESCRIPTION	POST. REF.	DEBIT	CREDIT	
9	4	*Sales Returns and Allowances*		150 00		9
10		*Sales Tax Payable*		9 00		10
11		*Accts. Rec./Gabriel Ramos*	/		159 00	11
12		*Credit Memorandum 124*				12
13						13

MEETING SPECIAL NEEDS

English Language Learners Encourage all students to participate in class. Fluency and accuracy in English will increase with use. Students who are not native to the United States may not be familiar with a participatory learning environment and may need your encouragement to share comments in class. Active participation will also enable you to judge ELL students' understanding of accounting concepts and procedures.

Posting to the Accounts Receivable Subsidiary Ledger

Refer to **Figure 14–5.** Look at the general journal entry. The credit is to **Accts Rec./Gabriel Ramos.** The slash indicates that both **Accounts Receivable** (controlling) and **Accounts Receivable—Gabriel Ramos** (subsidiary) are credited. Notice that a diagonal line is entered in the Post. Ref. column. This diagonal line indicates that the amount, $159, is posted in *two* places: *first* to the **Account Receivable** controlling account in the general ledger and *then* to the **Gabriel Ramos** account in the accounts receivable subsidiary ledger.

After the amount is posted to the Accounts Receivable controlling account, the account number (115) is entered to the *left* of the diagonal line in the Posting Reference column. After the amount is posted to the subsidiary ledger account, Gabriel Ramos, a check mark (✓) is entered to the *right* of the diagonal line.

Spreadsheet Hints

Using Symbols

Spreadsheet software uses symbols to indicate mathematical operations. Here are the common symbols:

- + means addition,
- − means subtraction (or a negative number),
- × means multiplication, and
- / means division.

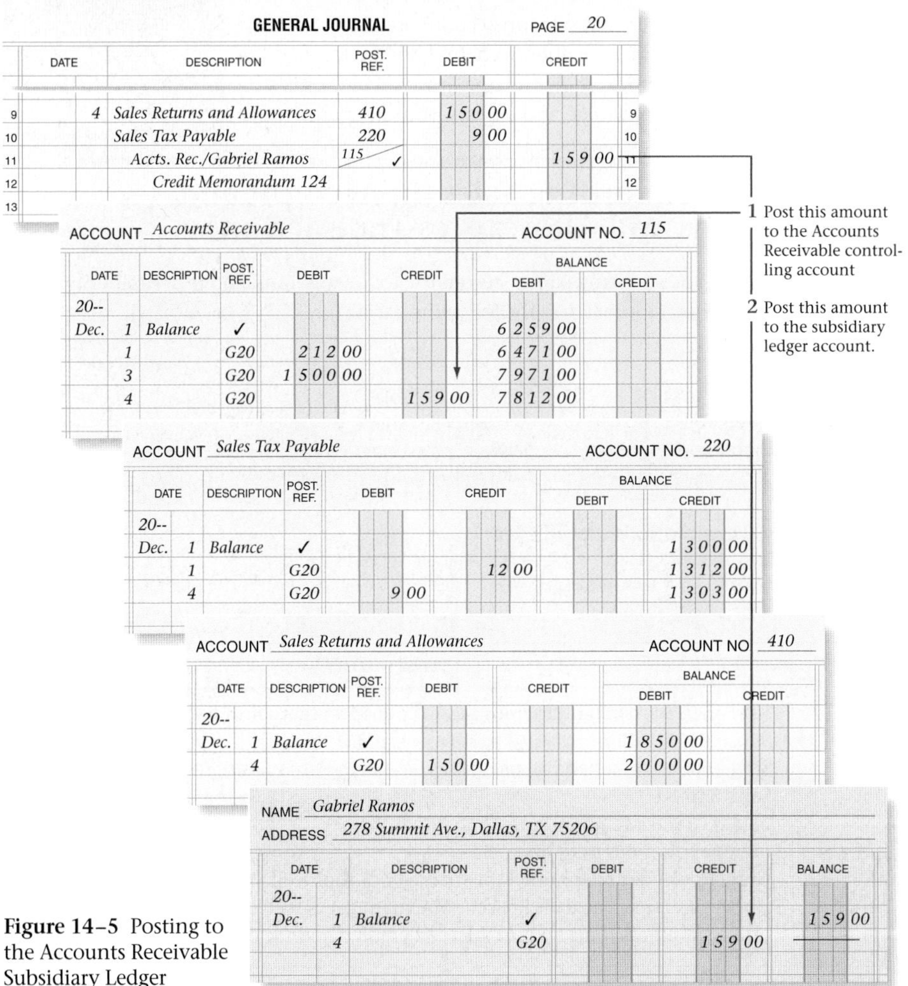

GENERAL JOURNAL — PAGE 20

	DATE		DESCRIPTION	POST. REF.	DEBIT	CREDIT	
9		4	Sales Returns and Allowances	410	150 00		9
10			Sales Tax Payable	220	9 00		10
11			Accts. Rec./Gabriel Ramos	115/✓		159 00	11
12			Credit Memorandum 124				12
13							

ACCOUNT Accounts Receivable — ACCOUNT NO. 115

DATE		DESCRIPTION	POST. REF.	DEBIT	CREDIT	BALANCE DEBIT	BALANCE CREDIT
20--							
Dec.	1	Balance	✓			6259 00	
	1		G20	212 00		6471 00	
	3		G20	1500 00		7971 00	
	4		G20		159 00	7812 00	

ACCOUNT Sales Tax Payable — ACCOUNT NO. 220

DATE		DESCRIPTION	POST. REF.	DEBIT	CREDIT	BALANCE DEBIT	BALANCE CREDIT
20--							
Dec.	1	Balance	✓				1300 00
	1		G20		12 00		1312 00
	4		G20	9 00			1303 00

ACCOUNT Sales Returns and Allowances — ACCOUNT NO 410

DATE		DESCRIPTION	POST. REF.	DEBIT	CREDIT	BALANCE DEBIT	BALANCE CREDIT
20--							
Dec.	1	Balance	✓			1850 00	
	4		G20	150 00		2000 00	

NAME Gabriel Ramos
ADDRESS 278 Summit Ave., Dallas, TX 75206

DATE		DESCRIPTION	POST. REF.	DEBIT	CREDIT	BALANCE
20--						
Dec.	1	Balance	✓			159 00
	4		G20		159 00	—

Figure 14–5 Posting to the Accounts Receivable Subsidiary Ledger

2 TEACH (Cont'd.)

Visual Learning

Figure 14–5 Posting to the Accounts Receivable Subsidiary Ledger

Use **Transparency 14–10** to review the posting process. Point out the Posting Reference column and explain the use of the general ledger account number and the check mark for the subsidiary ledger account.

Teaching Tips

Make transparencies of a general journal with entries, general ledger accounts, and subsidiary ledger accounts. Demonstrate the posting of journal transactions to the ledger accounts. Point out the differences between the general ledger and the subsidiary ledger. Demonstrate calculating new account balances for each.

Ask students how knowing the account's classification helps them determine the column in which to write the new balance after an amount has been posted.

Math Review for Accounting Photocopy appropriate *Activity Sheet* for students who need additional practice in basic math.

Math Skill Builder Activity

Using Symbols Review spreadsheet software symbols with your students. Write several math formulas on the board or on an overhead transparency, then quiz students about the meaning of each symbol. Have students explain whether the formula indicates an addition, subtraction, multiplication, or division problem.

CHAPTER 14
SECTION 2, PAGES 358–366

3 ASSESS

Thinking Critically (Answers)

1. Sales Tax Payable
2. The net amount is due in 30 days.
3. If the customer has paid more money than is owed.

Analyzing Accounting (Answers)

Answers will vary. Make sure students incorporate these steps: merchandise is sold on credit; sales slip (with credit terms) is prepared; sale is recorded as debit to Accts. Rec. and credit to Sales and Sales Tax Pay. (if applicable); uncollected payments become a cost to the business.

Problem 14–2 (Answers)

Jan. 1: Dr. Accts. Rec./James Palmer $318; Cr. Sales $300 and Sales Tax Pay. $18; Sales Slip 101

Jan. 4: Dr. Accts. Rec./Anna Rodriguez $636; Cr. Sales $600 and Sales Tax Payable $36; Sales Slip 102

Jan. 7: Dr. Sales Ret. and Allow. $300 and Sales Tax Pay. $18; Cr. Accts. Rec./James Palmer $318; Credit Memo 15

Jan. 19: Dr. Sales Ret. and Allow. $40 and Sales Tax Pay. $2.40; Cr. Accts. Rec./Anna Rodriguez $42.40; Credit Memo 16

Chapter Reviews and Working Papers Refer students to the Chapter 14 workbook pages to answer *Check Your Understanding* activities.

4 CLOSE

Section Wrap-Up

Analyzing: Have students draw T accounts on plain paper for Sales, Sales Ret. and Allow., and Accts. Rec. Have them add rules of debit and credit for each account. L1

SECTION 2 Check Your Understanding

Now that you have studied this section, complete the following questions and problems.

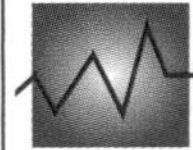

Thinking Critically

1. Businesses collect sales tax from customers. In what account is the sales tax recorded?
2. Explain this term: n/30.
3. The normal balance for an Accounts Receivable subsidiary account is a debit. Under what circumstances would a customer's account have a credit balance?

Analyzing Accounting

From Rags to Riches is a local consignment clothing store. You are the office manager for the store. The owner, Patty Potter, has extended quite a bit of "in store credit" to her customers. As you analyze the books, you can see that sales on account are significant and many accounts may be uncollectible. To help Patty understand her problem, design a diagram to show the operating cycle for sales on account. Pair up with a classmate and explain your diagram.

Problem 14–2 Recording Sales on Account and Sales Returns and Allowances Transactions

Instructions In your working papers, record the following transactions of Alpine Ski Shop on page 2 of the general journal. Use the following accounts:

General Ledger

Cash in Bank	Sales Tax Payable
Accounts Receivable	Accounts Payable
Merchandise Inventory	Sales
	Sales Returns and Allowances

Accounts Receivable Subsidiary Ledger
Palmer, James
Rodriguez, Anna

Date	Transactions
Sept. 1	Sold $300 in merchandise plus sales tax of $18 on account to James Palmer, Sales Slip 101.
4	Sold $600 in merchandise plus $36 sales tax to Anna Rodriguez on account, Sales Slip 102.
7	Issued Credit Memorandum 15 to James Palmer for the return of $300 in merchandise plus sales tax of $18.
19	Anna Rodriguez telephoned the manager of Alpine Ski Shop and said that the zipper on her ski jacket is broken. The manager agreed to give her a $40 credit on her purchase, plus a $2.40 sales tax credit, Credit Memorandum 16.

RETEACHING SECTION 2

Understanding Returns and Allowances Use the following scenario to help students understand returns and allowances. Ask students to name the accounts affected in both situations: "Sachi bought a new bike, took it home, and checked the parts before assembling it. Sachi found that the kickstand and the handle grips were both missing. Sachi packed all the parts in the box and took it back. The retailer had no more of this model in stock and offered to take the bike back and return the purchase price or to give a $10 discount if Sachi keeps the bike."

SECTION 3

Analyzing Cash Receipt Transactions

Whether it's the Los Angeles Metropolitan Transit Authority collecting fares from its bus passengers or Baskin-Robbins ringing up sales for ice cream, each business must account for cash receipts. In this section, you'll explore cash sales, charge sales, bankcard sales, and cash discounts.

What You'll Learn

- How to record cash receipt transactions.
- The use of the **Sales Discounts** account, and its rules of debit and credit.

Why It's Important

It is essential to understand the various ways that businesses receive cash and how to record the receipt of cash.

KEY TERMS

cash receipt
cash sale
bankcard
cash discount
sales discount

Kinds of Cash Receipts

A transaction in which money comes in to a business is referred to as a **cash receipt**. The three most common sources of cash for a merchandising business are payments from charge customers, cash sales, and bankcard sales. Cash is also received, though much less frequently, from such transactions as the sale of an asset other than merchandise inventory. Let's learn how to handle these four kinds of cash receipts.

Cash Sales

In a **cash sale** transaction, the business receives full payment for the merchandise sold *at the time of the sale.* The proof of sale and the source document generated by a cash sale transaction differ from those for a sale on account.

Most retailers use a cash register to record cash sales. Instead of using preprinted sales slips, cash sales are recorded on two rolls of paper tape inside the cash register. When a cash sale occurs, the details of the sale are printed on the two tapes at the same time. The portion of one tape that contains a record of the sale is torn off and handed to the customer as a receipt. The other tape remains in the register.

Totaling Cash Sales

At the end of the day, the cash register is totaled and cleared. The total cash sales and the total sales taxes collected on those sales are listed on the cash register tape. The tape also shows the total charge sales for the day. A proof is usually prepared to show that the amount of cash in the cash register equals the amount of cash sales and sales tax recorded on the cash register tape. The proof and the tape are sent to the accounting clerk, who uses the tape, **Figure 14–6**, as the source document for the journal entry to record the day's cash sales.

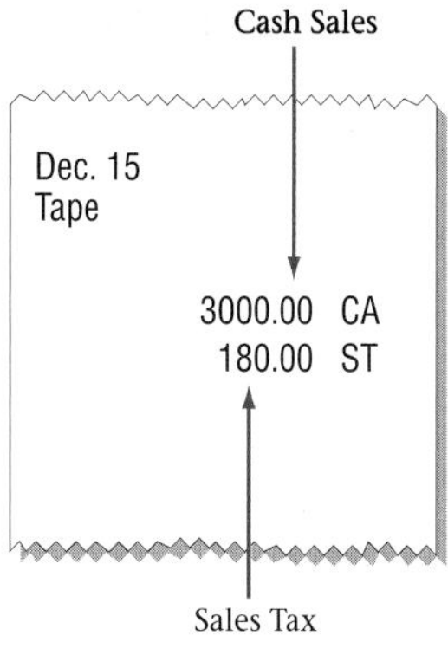

Figure 14–6 Cash Register Tape

CHAPTER 14
SECTION 3, PAGES 367–376

1 FOCUS

Introducing the Section

In this section students learn how to analyze and record transactions involving the receipt of cash. Students learn how to record sales discounts and payments received from charge customers. Continuing the pattern in the first two sections, students will use a general journal to record cash receipt transactions and post to the ledgers.

Section Concepts

- How to record cash receipt transactions.
- The use of the Sales Discounts account, and its rules of debit and credit.

Visual Learning

Section 3 Focus

Use **Transparency 14–11** to introduce section concepts.

BELL RINGER

Teaching: Tell students that they've been hired to give accounting advice to a business owner who does not think it's necessary to record sales on account in both Accounts Receivable and individual customer accounts. Have students explain why recording sales and cash receipts this way benefits the business owner. L1

Visual Learning

Figure 14–6 Cash Register Tape

Using **Transparency 14–12**, discuss the use of a cash register tape as a source document. Bring in some examples from your own purchases, or ask students to bring in their cash receipts. Discuss the total sale and the tax amount.

RESOURCE MANAGER

Reproducible Masters
- Lesson Plans
- Chapter Reviews and Working Papers (CRWP) TAE
- Demonstration Problems

Transparencies
- Section Focus Transparency
- Teaching Transparencies
- Source Document Transparencies
- Solution Transparencies

Multimedia
- ExamView CD-ROM
- Electronic Learning Center CD-ROM
- Interactive Lesson Planner CD-ROM

2 TEACH

GUIDED PRACTICE

Reading Accounting

- Have students spend five minutes skimming the content of this section. Ask them to jot down ideas that occur to them as they skim. Point out that skimming headings and key terms can give a general idea about the content. L1

Concept Development: Kinds of Cash Receipts

Discussion: Try to borrow a used cash register from a local dealer. Have students create some cash sales transactions and enter them into the cash register. Point out that the cash register has two rolls of tape—one for the customer and one for the business—and that every transaction is recorded on both tapes. After the cash register is totaled and cleared for the day, the tape becomes the source document for recording total cash sales and sales taxes collected for the day. L1

Teaching Tips

Remind students that a business receives cash for things other than cash sales; for example, from charge customers paying on account, from banks for bankcard sales, from selling assets owned by the business, or from borrowing money.

Bring to class some bankcard sales slips. Have students create a few bankcard sales transactions and enter them into a cash register. The cash register tape becomes the source document for recording total bankcard sales and sales taxes for the day.

Cash from Charge Customers

Businesses record cash received on account from charge customers by preparing receipts. A receipt, shown in **Figure 14–7**, is a form that serves as a record of cash received. Receipts are pre-numbered and may be prepared in multiple copies. The receipt is a source document for the journal entry. As you can see, the receipt lists the date the cash was received, the customer's name, the amount received, and an explanation of the transaction.

Figure 14–7 Receipt for Cash Received from a Charge Customer

ON YOUR MARK
ATHLETIC WEAR
595 Leslie Street, Dallas, TX 75207

RECEIPT
No. 301

Dec. 5 20 --

RECEIVED FROM Casey Klein $ 212.00

Two hundred twelve and no/100 DOLLARS

FOR On account

RECEIVED BY *Michael Smith*

Bankcard Sales

Many businesses accept bankcards. Unlike a credit card, which is issued by a business and is used for purchases only at that business, a **bankcard** is issued by a bank and honored by many businesses. The most widely used bankcards in North America are VISA, MasterCard, and Discover.

Bankcard sales are processed differently from a store's credit card sales. Since the bankcard holder has an account with the bank that issued the card, and not with the businesses where the card is used, a store receives cash from the bank soon after it deposits its bankcard sales slips. The store does not have to wait until the bank collects from the card holder. Therefore, bankcard sales are recorded as though they are cash sales.

Processing Bankcard Sales. When a bankcard sale occurs, the sales clerk completes a multi-copy bankcard sales slip. The sales slip is inserted into the cash register, which records the details of the sale on both the sales slip and the cash register tape. When the cash register is totaled at the end of the day, the total bankcard sales and the sales taxes for those sales are listed on the cash register tape. Since the cash register tape includes the bankcard sales, those sales are included on the daily cash proof. Bankcard sales are journalized from the same tape as the cash sales for the day. **Figure 14–8** shows a cash register tape indicating the day's bankcard sales and related sales tax.

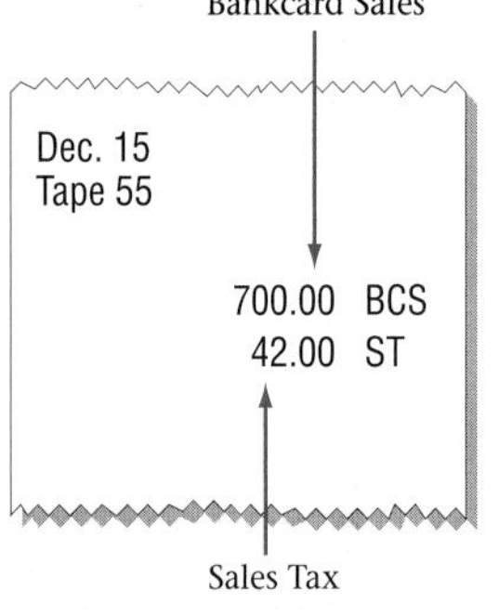

Figure 14–8 Bankcard Sales Tape

ACCOUNTING ISSUES

Female Accountants Approximately half of all graduating accounting students are female. One concern of many businesses is how to retain female accountants, who often must choose between advancing in their careers and spending time caring for children. Many companies have instituted programs that provide for flexible work schedules, child-care options, and alternative career paths. Such programs can result in higher employee morale and lower turnover among both females and males, many of whom are taking on more child-care responsibilities.

A business deposits all bankcard sales slips in its checking account, using a special deposit slip. Deposits of bankcard sales slips are treated the same as cash deposits. There is often a three or four-day delay before the amount of the deposit is credited to the business's checking account. This is due to the time it takes the bank to collect the funds from the various banks that issued the customers' bankcards.

Key Points

Bankcard Accounts The bankcard holder has an account with the bank that issued the card, not with the businesses where the card is used.

Other Cash Receipts

Most of the cash receipts of a merchandising business result from the sale of merchandise. Cash may also be received from infrequently occurring transactions, such as the sale of assets other than merchandise or a loan from a bank.

When such transactions do occur, a receipt is prepared to indicate the source of the cash received. This receipt is similar to that prepared for cash received from a charge customer. All the information needed for the journal entry is listed on the explanation line.

Cash Discounts

To encourage charge customers to pay promptly, some merchandising businesses offer a cash discount. A **cash discount**, or **sales discount**, is the amount a customer can deduct from the amount owed for purchased merchandise if payment is made within a certain time. A cash discount is an advantage to both the buyer and seller. Therefore, the buyer gets merchandise at a reduced cost, and the seller receives cash quickly.

Businesses do not automatically offer cash discounts to all customers. Some businesses may offer cash discounts only to business customers. On Your Mark offers a cash discount to charge customers who buy merchandise in large quantities. Its credit terms are *2/10, n/30*. These terms mean that the customer can deduct 2% of the cost of the merchandise if payment is made within 10 days of the sale date. Otherwise, the full (net) amount is due within 30 days. A cash discount, then, decreases the amount the business actually receives from the sale. Let's look at an example.

Cash Discount Transactions

On December 3 On Your Mark sold $1,500 worth of merchandise on account to South Branch High School Athletics. This transaction was recorded as a credit to **Sales** and a debit to **Accounts Receivable** for $1,500. If South Branch pays within 10 days (by December 13), On Your Mark will receive $1,470, or the original price less the cash discount of $30. These amounts are determined as follows:

	Merchandise Sold	×	Discount Rate	=	Discount
1.	$1,500	×	.02	=	$30

	Sales Slip Amount	−	Discount Amount	=	Amount Paid Within Discount Period
2.	$1,500	−	$30	=	$1,470

ACCOUNTING *Flashbacks*

THE FIRST COMPUTER Remington Rand introduced the UNIVAC, the first commercially successful computer, in 1951. It contained 5,500 vacuum tubes, was large enough to consume the space in several rooms, and was sold to businesses and scientists.

CRITICAL THINKING ACTIVITY

Analyzing Information Have students decide which errors would be detected when comparing the Accounts Receivable balance with the total of the subsidiary ledger balances.

1. The transaction was never journalized. (not detected)
2. The transaction was posted to the wrong account in the subsidiary ledger. (not detected)
3. The amount was transposed during posting. (detected)
4. The journal entry was never posted. (detected)
5. The amount was recorded incorrectly in the journal. (not detected)

2 TEACH (Cont'd.)

Visual Learning

Figure 14–7 Receipt for Cash Received from a Charge Customer

Use **Transparency 14–13** to review the information on a cash receipt. Point out that cash receipts are numbered to track all cash receipt transactions. If someone filling out a pre-numbered cash receipt makes an error, the word "VOID" is written across the receipt. The ruined receipt and the correct one are thus available to auditors.

Figure 14–8 Bankcard Sales Tape

Use **Transparency 14–14** to discuss the tape as the source document for recording bankcard sales. Point out that the bank pays the business and the customer actually pays the bank the amount of the sale. The business pays a percentage of all sales to the bank for collecting payments from customers.

Concept Development: Cash Discounts

Discussion: Explain that a cash discount is a reduction in the selling price of an item. To the seller, a cash discount is called a sales discount, and this amount is recorded in an account called Sales Discounts. This account is classified as a contra revenue account because its balance decreases the revenue account Sales. Use a T account on the chalkboard to review the increase, decrease, and normal balance sides of the Sales Discounts account.

Write "2/10,n/30" on the chalkboard, then explain each part of the term. Emphasize that the discount period begins on the date of the sales slip or invoice. L1

2 TEACH (Cont'd.)

Teaching Tip

Emphasize these points about a contra account: (1) A contra account decreases the balance of its related account. (2) The increase and balance side is always opposite the increase and balance side of the account it decreases.

Demonstration Problem Step-by-Step Practice

Use demonstration problem 14–5 to give students practice analyzing sales terms and calculating cash discounts.

For students who need a review of percentages, refer to the *Math Review for Accounting* booklet accompanying the *Glencoe Accounting* program.

Concept Development: Recording Cash Received from Charge Customers

Discussion: Point out to students that since the charge sale has already been recorded in the Sales account, when cash is received in payment, the Sales account is not affected—only Accounts Receivable, the subsidiary ledger, and Cash in Bank accounts. L1

Visual Learning

Business Transaction

Use **Transparency 14–15** to analyze the receipt of cash from a charge customer. At each step in the analysis model, ask students to explain why particular accounts are affected and why the transaction increases or decreases an account.

Key Points

Sales Discounts Account
Sales Discounts, a contra revenue account, reduces the balance of its related account, **Sales.**

Which accounts are involved in this cash receipt transaction? **Cash in Bank** is debited for $1,470, the amount of cash actually received. **Accounts Receivable** is credited for the full $1,500 because the customer paid for the merchandise and doesn't owe any more on the purchase. The difference between $1,500 and $1,470, $30, is the discount amount.

A separate account is used to record cash discounts taken by customers. The $30 discount is entered in a contra revenue account called **Sales Discounts**, which reduces the revenue earned from sales. The normal balance of the **Sales** account is a credit. The normal balance of the **Sales Discounts** account is a debit.

Sales	
Debit – Decrease Side	Credit + Increase Side Normal Balance

Sales Discounts	
Debit + Increase Side Normal Balance	Credit – Decrease Side

A cash discount is recorded only when the customer pays for the merchandise within the time stated. The discount is on the price of the merchandise *before* taxes.

Recording Cash Received from Charge Customers

Let's look at a business transaction involving receipt of cash from a charge customer.

Business Transaction

On December 5 On Your Mark received $212 from Casey Klein to apply to her account, Receipt 301.

ON YOUR MARK
ATHLETIC WEAR
595 Leslie Street, Dallas, TX 75207

RECEIPT
No. 301

Dec. 5 20 --

RECEIVED FROM Casey Klein $ 212.00
Two hundred twelve and no/100 DOLLARS
FOR On account
RECEIVED BY *Michael Smith*

ANALYSIS

Identify
1. The accounts affected are **Cash in Bank**, **Accounts Receivable** (controlling), **Accounts Receivable—Casey Klein** (subsidiary).

Classify
2. **Cash in Bank, Accounts Receivable** (controlling), and **Accounts Receivable—Casey Klein** (subsidiary) are asset accounts.

+/–
3. **Cash in Bank** is increased by $212. **Accounts Receivable** (controlling) and **Accounts Receivable—Casey Klein** (subsidiary) are decreased by $212.

DEBIT-CREDIT RULE

4. Increases to asset accounts are recorded as debits. Debit **Cash in Bank** for $212.
5. Decreases to asset accounts are recorded as credits. Credit **Accounts Receivable** (controlling) for $212. Also credit **Accounts Receivable—Casey Klein** (subsidiary) for $212.

ADDRESSING MULTIPLE LEARNING STYLES

Linguistic Learner Have students imagine that they've been asked to help train a new accounting clerk who will be in charge of recording sales transactions. Tell students to think of the different types of sales transactions, then write descriptions of how to record each of the transactions. Students should include a cash sale, sale on account, bankcard sale, and sale on account with cash discount. Tell students to write titles of specific accounts for each transaction, debits and credits, and directions for calculating discounts.

T ACCOUNTS

6.

Cash in Bank	
Debit +	Credit −
212	

Accounts Receivable	
Debit +	Credit −
	212

Accounts Receivable Subsidiary Ledger
Casey Klein

Debit +	Credit −
	212

JOURNAL ENTRY

7.

GENERAL JOURNAL — PAGE 20

	DATE	DESCRIPTION	POST. REF.	DEBIT	CREDIT	
13	5	*Cash in Bank*		*212 00*		13
14		*Accts. Rec./Casey Klein*			*212 00*	14
15		*Receipt 301*				15
16						16

Recording Cash Received on Account with a Cash Discount

When a customer pays for a purchase on account within the discount period, the amount paid equals the amount of the invoice less the cash discount. Let's record a cash discount transaction.

Business Transaction

On December 12 On Your Mark received $1,470 from South Branch High School Athletics in payment of Sales Slip 51 for $1,500 less the discount of $30, Receipt 302.

ON YOUR MARK ATHLETIC WEAR
595 Leslie Street, Dallas, TX 75207
RECEIPT No. 302
Dec. 12 20 --
RECEIVED FROM South Branch H.S. Athletics $ 1,470.00
One thousand four hundred seventy and no/100 DOLLARS
FOR On account
RECEIVED BY *Michael Smith*

ANALYSIS

Identify 1. The accounts affected are **Cash in Bank, Sales Discounts, Accounts Receivable** (controlling), and **Accounts Receivable—South Branch High School Athletics** (subsidiary).

Classify 2. **Cash in Bank, Accounts Receivable** (controlling), and **Accounts Receivable—South Branch High School Athletics** (subsidiary) are asset accounts. **Sales Discounts** is a contra revenue account.

+/− 3. **Cash in Bank** is increased by $1,470. **Sales Discounts** is increased by $30. **Accounts Receivable** (controlling), and **Accounts Receivable—South Branch High School Athletics** (subsidiary) are decreased by $1,500.

TEACHING NOTES

2 TEACH (Cont'd.)

Concept Development: Recording Cash Received on Account with a Cash Discount

Discussion: Explain that a cash discount results in a reduction in the selling price of an item. To the seller, a cash discount is called a sales discount, and the amount is recorded in an account called Sales Discounts. Write "2/10, n/30" on the chalkboard, then ask students to tell you the meaning. Emphasize that when determining the discount period, the calculation is always based on the date of the sales slip or invoice. Write several sales amounts on the chalkboard, and give students practice in calculating sales discounts. L1

Visual Learning

Business Transaction

Use **Transparency 14–16** to analyze a cash payment from a customer that involves a cash discount taken by the customer. As you go through each step in the analysis model, check students' understanding of the analysis by asking them why certain accounts are affected and why those accounts are either increased or decreased by the transaction.

Demonstration Problem Step-by-Step Practice

Use demonstration problem 14–6 to guide students through the analysis and recording of cash received from a charge customer.

2 TEACH (Cont'd.)

Concept Development: Recording Cash Sales

Discussion: For retail businesses, cash sales make up a large part of the daily business transactions. Have students recount their own experiences in buying an item for cash.

Explain to students that the examples in their textbook show cash sales being recorded every two weeks to save space in journal illustrations. In reality, cash sales are recorded daily. L1

Visual Learning

Business Transaction

Use **Transparency 14–17** to analyze the receipt of cash in a cash sale. When discussing this transaction, you may want to cover the "Analysis" part of the transparency and ask students to give you the information in items 1 through 3. Then uncover those items and have students verify their own analyses. Do the same for the remaining steps in the model.

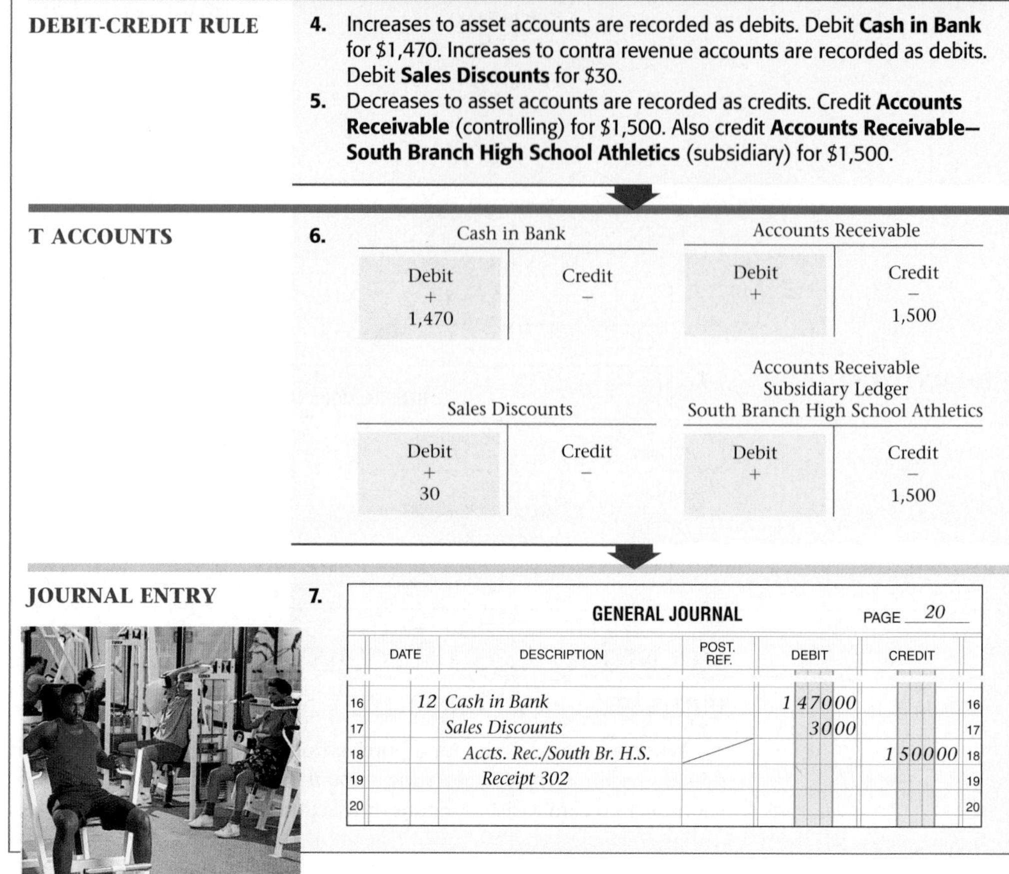

DEBIT-CREDIT RULE

4. Increases to asset accounts are recorded as debits. Debit **Cash in Bank** for $1,470. Increases to contra revenue accounts are recorded as debits. Debit **Sales Discounts** for $30.
5. Decreases to asset accounts are recorded as credits. Credit **Accounts Receivable** (controlling) for $1,500. Also credit **Accounts Receivable—South Branch High School Athletics** (subsidiary) for $1,500.

T ACCOUNTS

6.

Cash in Bank	
Debit + 1,470	Credit −

Accounts Receivable	
Debit +	Credit − 1,500

Sales Discounts	
Debit + 30	Credit −

Accounts Receivable Subsidiary Ledger South Branch High School Athletics	
Debit +	Credit − 1,500

JOURNAL ENTRY

7.

GENERAL JOURNAL PAGE 20

	DATE	DESCRIPTION	POST. REF.	DEBIT	CREDIT	
16	12	Cash in Bank		1 470 00		16
17		Sales Discounts		30 00		17
18		Accts. Rec./South Br. H.S.			1 500 00	18
19		Receipt 302				19
20						20

Recording Cash Sales

As a rule, businesses journalize cash sales and make cash deposits daily. Let's analyze transactions relating to sale of merchandise for cash on December 15.

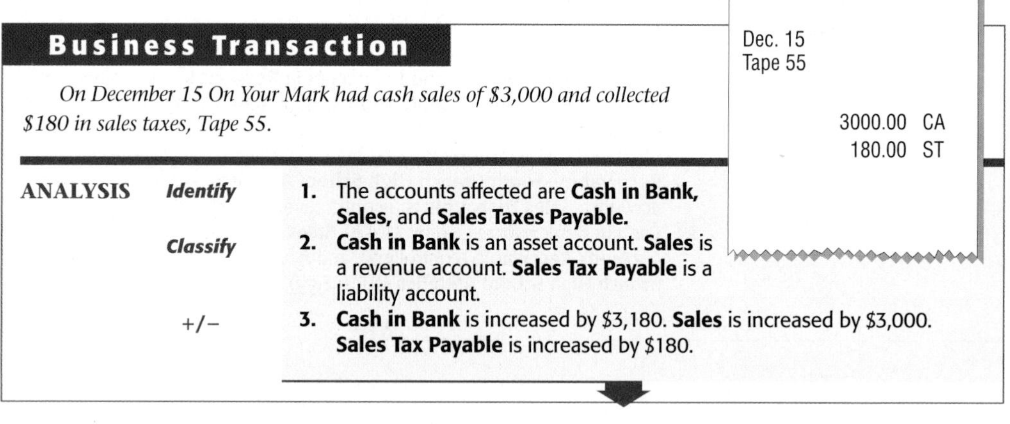

Business Transaction

On December 15 On Your Mark had cash sales of $3,000 and collected $180 in sales taxes, Tape 55.

ANALYSIS

Identify 1. The accounts affected are **Cash in Bank, Sales,** and **Sales Taxes Payable.**

Classify 2. **Cash in Bank** is an asset account. **Sales** is a revenue account. **Sales Tax Payable** is a liability account.

+/− 3. **Cash in Bank** is increased by $3,180. **Sales** is increased by $3,000. **Sales Tax Payable** is increased by $180.

HOME AND COMMUNITY CONNECTIONS ACTIVITY

Fund-Raising Activities Have students choose a local organization for which they would like to raise money. Have them plan a fund-raising day. In planning the activity, tell students to answer these questions: What services would they provide, and what would they charge? What products would they sell, and at what prices? Will they be required to charge sales tax? You may want to have students work in groups on this activity. Have each group write a plan for its fund-raising activities. Have students decide whether to implement their plans.

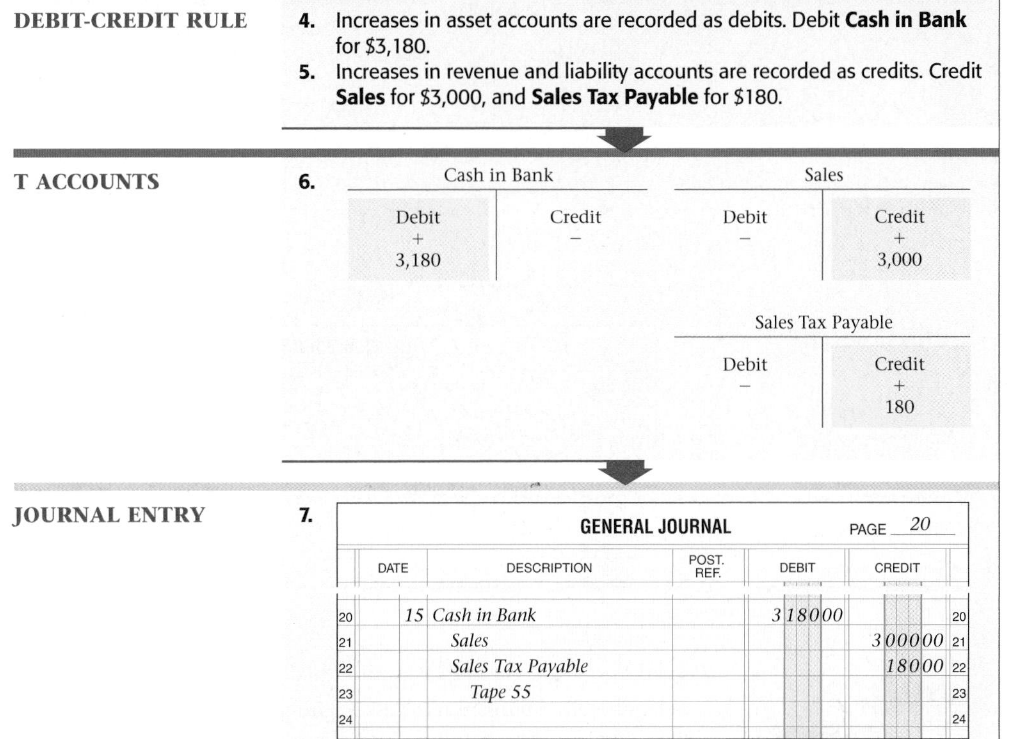

DEBIT-CREDIT RULE	**4.** Increases in asset accounts are recorded as debits. Debit **Cash in Bank** for $3,180. **5.** Increases in revenue and liability accounts are recorded as credits. Credit **Sales** for $3,000, and **Sales Tax Payable** for $180.

T ACCOUNTS

6.

Cash in Bank	
Debit + 3,180	Credit –

Sales	
Debit –	Credit + 3,000

Sales Tax Payable	
Debit –	Credit + 180

JOURNAL ENTRY

7.

GENERAL JOURNAL PAGE 20

	DATE		DESCRIPTION	POST. REF.	DEBIT	CREDIT	
20		15	Cash in Bank		3 180 00		20
21			Sales			3 000 00	21
22			Sales Tax Payable			180 00	22
23			Tape 55				23
24							24

Recording Bankcard Sales

Now let's record sales paid by bankcard. Notice how this is similar to recording cash sales.

Business Transaction

On Your Mark had bankcard sales of $700 and collected $42 in related sales taxes on December 15, Tape 55.

Dec. 15
Tape 55

700.00 BCS
42.00 ST

ANALYSIS	***Identify***	**1.** The accounts affected are **Cash in Bank, Sales,** and **Sales Tax Payable.**
	Classify	**2.** **Cash in Bank** is an asset account. **Sales** is a revenue account. **Sales Tax Payable** is a liability account.
	+/–	**3.** **Cash in Bank** is increased by $742. **Sales** is increased by $700. **Sales Tax Payable** is increased by $42.
DEBIT-CREDIT RULE		**4.** Increases in asset accounts are recorded as debits. Debit **Cash in Bank** for $742. **5.** Increases in revenue and liability accounts are recorded as credits. Credit **Sales** for $700 and **Sales Tax Payable** for $42.

2 TEACH (Cont'd.)

Concept Development: Recording Bankcard Sales

Discussion: Point out to students that the same accounts are affected by a bankcard sale as for a cash sale. Remind students that the banks issuing cards used for bankcard sales pay the business directly, which means that the business receives its money soon after it deposits the bankcard sales slips. L1

Visual Learning

Business Transaction

Use **Transparency 14–18** to analyze the receipt of cash from bankcard sales. Point out that bankcard sales are handled the same way as cash sales.

Teaching Tip

When discussing bankcard sales, ask students to think about why transactions involving bankcards (such as VISA or MasterCard) are handled differently than transactions involving credit cards (such as a Bloomingdale's or Gap charge card). Discuss when the merchant receives the cash from the sale and who is making payment to the merchant.

EXTENDING THE CONTENT

Business Plan Have students choose a retail business they would like to operate and write a two-page short business plan. Students should include a short paragraph describing the business, a simple chart of accounts, hours of operation, competitive advantages (such as lower prices), and policies relating to sales returns, allowances, and cash discounts. Tell students also to decide whether they will accept bankcards and make sales on account. Ask for volunteers to share their plans in class. Have students discuss why they chose specific accounts for their businesses.

2 TEACH (Cont'd.)

Concept Development: Recording Other Cash Receipts

Discussion: Explain to students that not all cash received by a business is from the sale of merchandise. Ask students if they can think of examples. They might mention the sale of assets or cash received from a loan. L1

Visual Learning

Business Transaction

Use **Transparency 14–19** to analyze the receipt of cash from selling an asset owned by the business. Have students go through each step in the analysis model explaining why the accounts given are affected and why each is increasing or decreasing.

Teaching Tip

Ask students how many of them work for a retail business in which scanners are used to scan barcodes and enter sales amounts in the cash register. These electronic systems provide a lot of information that managers use in deciding how much of a product to order and when. They may also record sales on account, cash sales, and bankcard sales directly on a business's accounting system.

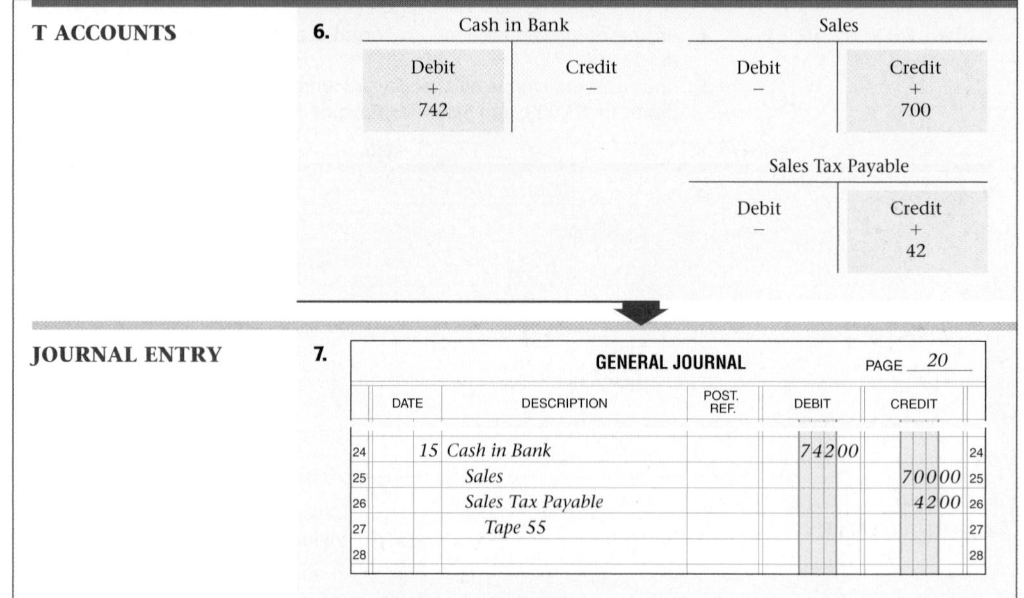

T ACCOUNTS

6.

Cash in Bank	
Debit	Credit
+	–
742	

Sales	
Debit	Credit
–	+
	700

Sales Tax Payable	
Debit	Credit
–	+
	42

JOURNAL ENTRY

7.

GENERAL JOURNAL PAGE 20

	DATE	DESCRIPTION	POST. REF.	DEBIT	CREDIT	
24	15	Cash in Bank		742 00		24
25		Sales			700 00	25
26		Sales Tax Payable			42 00	26
27		Tape 55				27
28						28

Recording Other Cash Receipts

Occasionally a business receives cash from a transaction that does not involve the sale of merchandise. The **Sales** account is not used because the item is not a *merchandise* item.

Business Transaction

On December 16 On Your Mark received $30 from Mandy Harris, an office employee. She purchased a calculator that the business was no longer using, Receipt 303.

ON YOUR MARK
ATHLETIC WEAR
595 Leslie Street, Dallas, TX 75207

RECEIPT
No. 303

Dec. 16 20 --

RECEIVED FROM Mandy Harris $ 30.00

Thirty and no/100 DOLLARS

FOR calculator

RECEIVED BY *Michael Smith*

JOURNAL ENTRY

GENERAL JOURNAL PAGE 20

	DATE	DESCRIPTION	POST. REF.	DEBIT	CREDIT	
28	16	Cash in Bank		30 00		28
29		Office Equipment			30 00	29
30		Receipt 303				30
31						31

TEACHING NOTES

Figure 14–9 presents all the transactions discussed and illustrated in this chapter.

Figure 14–9 Sales and Cash Receipt Transactions

GENERAL JOURNAL PAGE 20

DATE		DESCRIPTION	POST. REF.	DEBIT	CREDIT
20--					
Dec.	1	Accts. Rec./Casey Klein		212 00	
		Sales			200 00
		Sales Tax Payable			12 00
		Sales Slip 50			
	3	Accts. Rec./South Branch H.S.		1 500 00	
		Sales			1 500 00
		Sales Slip 51			
	4	Sales Returns and Allowances		150 00	
		Sales Tax Payable		9 00	
		Accts. Rec./Gabriel Ramos			159 00
		Credit Memorandum 124			
	5	Cash in Bank		212 00	
		Accts. Rec./Casey Klein			212 00
		Receipt 301			
	12	Cash in Bank		1 470 00	
		Sales Discounts		30 00	
		Accts. Rec./South Branch H.S.			1 500 00
		Receipt 302			
	15	Cash in Bank		3 180 00	
		Sales			3 000 00
		Sales Tax Payable			180 00
		Tape 55			
	15	Cash in Bank		742 00	
		Sales			700 00
		Sales Tax Payable			42 00
		Tape 55			
	16	Cash in Bank		30 00	
		Office Equipment			30 00
		Receipt 303			

ANALYZING FINANCIAL REPORTS

To Our Shareholders Letter

Each year, public corporations publish their financial reports for the past fiscal period in an annual report. The annual report presents a financial picture of the corporation, but it also highlights other information that the corporation wants to make public. One of the first items you'll see in most annual reports is a letter from the top executive officer in the company. For an example, look at the "To Our Shareholders" letter on pages A-40–A-41 in the Office Depot, Inc. annual report, parts of which are reproduced at the back of your textbook.

▶ **Analyze the Report:**

Use the Office Depot "To Our Shareholders" message to answer these questions:

1. What is Office Depot's first priority and how would you interpret it?
2. What incentive does the company offer its employees?
3. If you were considering a purchase of Office Depot stock, would this letter influence your decision? Explain why or why not.

2 TEACH (Cont'd.)

Visual Learning

Figure 14–9 Sales and Cash Receipt Transactions

Use **Transparency 14–20** to summarize the transactions involving the receipt of cash for different types of sales. For each transaction, ask students whether it was a cash sale, a sale on account, or a sales return or allowance.

Teaching Tip

To evaluate students' understanding of the transactions behind the journal entries, you may want to ask students to look at a journal entry and describe the transaction.

Writing and Analyzing: Choose four or five of the journal entries and have students write transaction descriptions for each of the entries. L2

The Office Depot 2001 Annual Report

Refer students to pages A-39–A-48 in the back of the book.

ANALYZING FINANCIAL REPORTS

Analyze the Report (Answers)

1. The delivery of "fanatical" customer service; the company is determined to provide the best possible service to meet the needs and demands of all customers.
2. Office Depot has improved opportunities for employees and tied recognition and reward directly to employee performance.
3. Answers will vary. Students might answer "Yes" because the company leadership has a clear vision for the future; its new management team has experience, skills, and financial acumen; and it is concerned about its customers, employees, and shareholders.

CHAPTER 14
SECTION 3, PAGES 367–376

3 ASSESS

Thinking Critically (Answers)

1. Business sends bankcard slips to bank, receives cash; customer pays bank.
2. Buyer has lower costs; seller gets quicker payment.
3. Incorrect ledger account balance or amount not posted; to find the error, recalculate account balances, re-add totals, check posting.

Analyzing Accounting (Answers)

1. February and May
2. Iris
3. Purchases can be aligned with anticipated sales.

Problem 14–3 (Answer)

May 15: Dr. Cash in Bank $1,060; Cr. Sales $1,000, Sales Tax Pay. $60; Tape 40

May 15: Dr. Cash in Bank $848; Cr. Sales $800, Sales Tax Pay. $48; Tape 40

Problem 14–4 (Answers)

Mar. 1: Dr. Cash in Bank $140.40; Cr. Sales $130, Sales Tax Pay. $10.40; Sales Slip 49

Mar. 5: Dr. Accts. Rec./Kelly Wilson $324; Cr. Sales $300, Sales Tax Pay. $24; Sales Slip 55

Mar. 17: Dr. Cash in Bank $810; Cr. Sales $750, Sales Tax Pay. $60; Tape 65

Chapter Reviews and Working Papers Refer students to the Chapter 14 workbook pages to answer *Check Your Understanding* activities.

4 CLOSE

Section Wrap-Up

Analyzing: Have students analyze this transaction. "On January 31, On Your Mark Athletic Wear had bankcard sales of $2,800 plus sales tax of $168." L1

SECTION 3 Check Your Understanding

Now that you have studied this section, complete the following questions and problems.

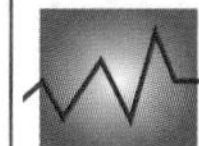

Thinking Critically

1. Explain the process behind a bankcard transaction.
2. Explain the benefits of a cash discount.
3. The balance of the controlling account should equal the sum of the related subsidiary ledger accounts. What error might cause the sum of the subsidiary ledger accounts to be less than the controlling account balance? How would you find the error?

Analyzing Accounting

The following graph illustrates the sales of flowers throughout the year for Randy's Florist.

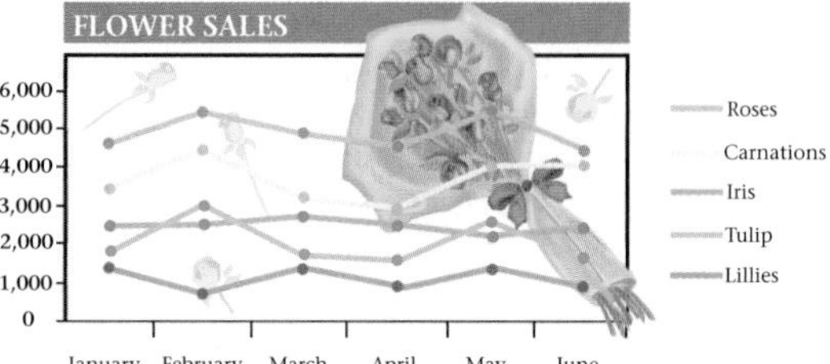

1. The sale of tulips was highest in which month?
2. Which type of flower sells at a steady rate, regardless of the month?
3. How would this graph be helpful in planning purchases for the year? Explain.

Problem 14–3 Analyzing a Source Document

As the accounting clerk for Super Cycle Shop, you record the business transactions. The store's manager hands you the source document shown here.

Instructions Analyze the source document and record the necessary entries on page 17 of the general journal.

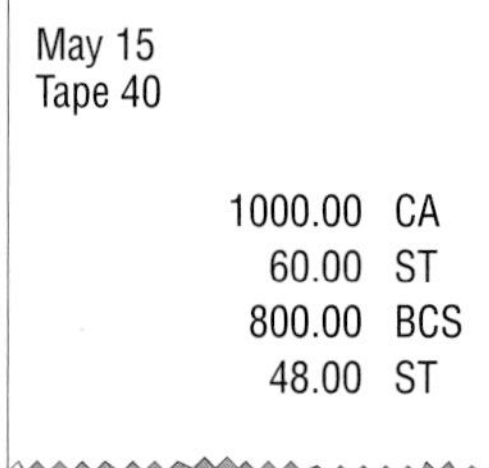

May 15
Tape 40

1000.00 CA
60.00 ST
800.00 BCS
48.00 ST

Problem 14–4 Recording Cash Receipts

Commerce Technology, a computer equipment retailer, had the following selected transactions in March.

Instructions Record each transaction on page 4 of the general journal in your working papers.

Date	Transactions
Mar. 1	Sold one modem for $130 plus $10.40 sales tax, Sales Slip 49.
5	Sold one computer monitor to Kelly Wilson on account for $300 plus $24 sales tax, Sales Slip 55.
17	Bankcard sales totaled $750 plus $60 sales tax, Tape 65.

RETEACHING SECTION 3

Analyzing Cash Receipt Transactions When a customer uses a bankcard to buy goods from a merchandising business, the customer is buying on credit. However, the business will get cash for the sale from the customer's bank, and the customer will pay the bank the amount of the sale. The customer is receiving credit from the bank issuing the bankcard rather than the business selling the goods. As a result, the business records the transaction in the same way as it would a cash sale.

CHAPTER 14 SUMMARY

KEY CONCEPTS

1. Retail firms buy merchandise to resell to consumers. Two of the accounts used by merchandising businesses are **Merchandise Inventory** and **Sales.**

2. The **Merchandise Inventory** account is an asset account used to record the value of the merchandise in stock.

Merchandise Inventory	
Debit + Increase Side Normal Balance	Credit – Decrease Side

3. The **Sales** account is a revenue account used to record business income.

4. A sales slip, prepared in multiple copies, lists the details of a sale on account. It is the source document for the journal entry.

Sales	
Debit – Decrease Side	Credit + Increase Side Normal Balance

5. Most states and some cities tax the retail sale of goods. Businesses collect sales tax and record it as a liability in the **Sales Tax Payable** account. Later the business sends a check to the state for the sales tax collected.

Sales Tax Payable	
Debit – Decrease Side	Credit + Increase Side Normal Balance

6. The **Sales Returns and Allowances** account is used to record the credit granted to charge customers for returned or damaged merchandise.

Sales Returns and Allowances	
Debit + Increase Side Normal Balance	Credit – Decrease Side

7. The cash received by a business is recorded on receipts and cash register tapes. These receipts and tapes are the source documents for the journal entries.

8. Bankcard sales are recorded as cash sales.

9. Some merchandising businesses grant cash discounts to customers who pay for their credit purchases within a certain time period. The time period and amount of the discount are indicated in the credit terms of the purchases.

10. The **Sales Discounts** account is used to record the amount of any cash discount taken by charge customers.

11. **Accounts Receivable** is a controlling account. Its balance must equal the sum of the customer account balances in the accounts receivable subsidiary ledger.

Sales Discounts	
Debit + Increase Side Normal Balance	Credit – Decrease Side

SUMMARY CHAPTER 14

Chapter 14 Quiz

Student ______ Class ______ Instructor ______
Date Assigned ______ Date Completed ______

CHAPTER 14 QUIZ

Accounting for Sales and Cash Receipts

QUESTIONS (Completion)

Directions: Fill in the blank with the term that best completes each sentence.

1. Merchandising businesses buy and sell goods; service businesses sell ______.
2. A wholesaler sells to retailers; retailers sell to ______.
3. The Merchandise Inventory account is classified as a(n) ______ account, and its normal balance side is a ______.
4. A sale on account is recorded as a debit to ______.
5. The term n/30 means that the ______ is due in 30 days.
6. The ______ account summarizes amounts owed by customers and recorded in a subsidiary ledger.
7. A ______ account decreases the balance of its related account.
8. A ______ account balance equals the total of all the account balances in a related subsidiary ledger.
9. A sales ______ is merchandise receiving a cash refund or full credit.
10. A ______ is evidence of a sales return or allowance.

16 • Chapter Quizzes

QUESTIONS (Completion)

1. Merchandising businesses buy and sell goods; service businesses sell ______.
2. A wholesaler sells to retailers; retailers sell to ______.
3. The Merchandise Inventory account is classified as a(n) ______ account, and its normal balance side is a ______.
4. A sale on account is recorded as a debit to ______.
5. The term *n/30* means that the ______ is due in 30 days.
6. The ______ account summarizes amounts owed by customers and recorded in a subsidiary ledger.
7. A ______ account decreases the balance of its related account.
8. A ______ account balance equals the total of all the account balances in a related subsidiary ledger.
9. A sales ______ is merchandise receiving a cash refund or full credit.
10. A ______ is evidence of a sales return or allowance.

ANSWERS

1. services
2. the consumer or final user
3. asset, debit
4. Accounts Receivable
5. net amount
6. controlling account
7. contra
8. controlling
9. return
10. credit memorandum

USING KEY TERMS

See the *Glossary* for the definitions of these terms. After students prepare their note cards for the activity, you may want to collect some of them and use them as flash cards to help students review the meanings of terms.

Understanding Accounting Concepts and Procedures

(Answers)

1. A merchandising business buys items and resells them to customers for a profit. A service business provides a service to the general public for a fee.
2. A wholesaler sells to retailers; a retailer sells to the consumer.
3. Merchandise Inventory—Asset; Sales—Revenue; Sales Returns and Allowances—Contra Revenue; Sales Discounts—Contra Revenue; and Sales Tax Payable—Liability.
4. The business adds the amount of the sales tax to the selling price of the goods and periodically sends the taxes collected to the state government.
5. Sales, Sales Tax Payable, Accounts Receivable, and the name of the charge customer.
6. To indicate that two postings are required, one to the Accounts Receivable account in the general ledger and the other to the charge customer's account in the accounts receivable subsidiary ledger.
7. Cash Sales and Bankcard Sales—cash register tape; Cash received from a charge customer—receipt.
8. Because the business receives cash from the bank soon after depositing its bankcard sales slips. The bank collects from the bankcard holder.
9. To encourage prompt payment.
10. Cash in Bank, Sales Discounts, and Accounts Receivable.

CHAPTER 14 REVIEW AND ACTIVITIES

USING KEY TERMS

You have just hired Geoffrey Hillman to be the accounting clerk for the Hats Off Corporation, a merchandiser of hats, caps, and scarves. Geoffrey worked as a payroll clerk, but not in sales or cash receipts jobs. To help him, you've offered to write on note cards the definitions of the following terms. Provide an example of each term when possible.

accounts receivable subsidiary ledger	inventory
bankcard	merchandise
cash discount	retailer
cash receipt	sale on account
cash sale	**Sales**
charge customer	sales allowance
contra account	sales discount
controlling account	sales return
credit cards	sales slip
credit memorandum	sales tax
credit terms	subsidiary ledger
	wholesaler

Understanding Accounting Concepts and Procedures

Instructions:

On a separate sheet of paper, answer the following questions:

1. Contrast the characteristics of a service and a merchandising business.
2. What is the difference between a wholesaler and a retailer?
3. Classify the following accounts: Merchandise Inventory, Sales, Sales Returns and Allowances, Sales Discounts, and Sales Tax Payable.
4. How does a merchandising business act as a collection agency for the state government?
5. What four accounts are affected by a sale of merchandise on account?
6. Why is a diagonal line drawn in the posting reference column when journalizing a sale of merchandise on account?
7. What are the source documents for recording cash sales, bankcard sales, and cash received from a charge customer?
8. Why are bankcard sales considered a form of cash sales?
9. Why would a business offer a cash discount to its customers?
10. Which accounts are affected when a business receives a payment from a charge customer who has taken a cash discount?

ASSESSMENT RESOURCES

Choose assessment strategies from the following pages to evaluate your students' progress.

Student Edition
Check Your Understanding, pp. 357, 366, 376
Chapter 14 Problems, pp. 381–385
Analyzing Financial Reports, p. 375

Assessment and Evaluation Masters
Chapter 14 Study Plan, *Glencoe Workbook (CRWP)*
Chapter 14 Self-Test, *Glencoe Workbook (CRWP)*
Chapter 14 Test, *Chapter Tests* Booklet
Chapter 14 Activity, *School-to-Work Handbook*
Chapter 14 ExamView

Teacher Wraparound Edition
Critical Thinking Activity, p. 369
Reteaching Sections 1–3, pp. 357, 366, 376
Chapter 14 Quiz, p. 377

Case Study...

Merchandising Business: Videotapes

Felix Andersen is a film buff. His business, Video Source, specializes in foreign titles and classic film collections. Video Source uses a manual accounting system. Sales are recorded from cash register tapes at the end of the day. Felix is thinking of updating to an electronic cash register that records sales information directly into a computerized accounting system.

Thinking Critically:

1. What are the benefits of converting to an electronic system?
2. Explain how an analysis of sales would help when making decisions about what types of videos to stock.

interNET CONNECTION

Becoming Part of an Organization

Becoming part of an organization helps us feel vibrant and involved. The same holds true in the world of work. Accounting organizations provide a place for professionals to exchange ideas, discuss issues, and gather information about current trends.

Do This:

1. Find out which accounting organizations have Web sites. Make a list of three accounting organizations you find on the Internet.
2. For each organization, where would you write or call for membership information?
3. How would membership in this organization help accounting students?

Conducting an Audit with Alex

You are an accounting intern for Computer Solutions Incorporated. Your supervisor, Lisa Lane, would like you to review the accounts receivable subsidiary ledger. You decide to prepare a schedule of accounts receivable.

Instructions

Use the information below to prepare the schedule on a separate sheet of paper. Does the controlling account balance equal the sum of the subsidiary accounts?

Accounts Receivable Subsidiary Ledger

Amanda Shively	$ 47.90
Kate Right	98.50
St. Andrews Community Center	359.60
West Heights School District	885.45
Randy Sabin	145.50

Accounts Receivable

Controlling Account Balance	$1,536.95

Workplace Skills

Allocating Time, Money, Materials, Space, and Staff

When you operate a business, you are constantly evaluating the effective use of your company's resources. These resources include time, money, materials, space, and staff.

On the Job:

You are the owner of the Retro Café, a late-night spot for young professionals and college students. The café is open from 11:00 A.M. until midnight. You review the month's financial reports and find that the café is showing a net loss for the third month in a row.

Thinking Critically:

1. To help you gather information from your employees, design a staff evaluation form regarding menu, staffing, and hours of operation.
2. In reviewing sales figures, you discover that most of your sales happen after 3:00 P.M. What are the possible staffing implications?

Case Study...

Thinking Critically (Answers)

1. An electronic cash register system would automatically compute sales for the day. It would account for overages and shortages in the cash received and could track peak sales times. The system might generate journal entries, therefore saving staff time.
2. The owner could avoid making purchases of unpopular videos and focus on those that seem to be hot.

Workplace Skills

Thinking Critically (Answers)

1. Some possible questions:

Menu: What items are most popular on the menu? What items do you receive the most complaints about? What requests do you receive most often for items to add to the menu?

Staffing: Which shift do you find the most hectic? Why? How many tables can you effectively serve?

Hours: Which hours are the busiest? For employees who close, are customers rushed to leave at the end of the night? At what times do you have few customers?

2. The café may need less staff before 3 P.M. and more staff after.

Conducting an Audit with Alex

(Answer)

The total of the subsidiary ledger accounts ($1,536.95) equals the controlling account ($1,536.95).

Internet Resources and Activities Handbook

Refer students to the booklet for additional Internet activities.

interNET CONNECTION www.glencoe.com

Do This (Answers)

Use search terms such as *accounting* or *accounting organizations*.

1. AICPA: www.aicpa.org/
   Institute of Management Accountants: www.imanet.org/
   American Society of Women Accountants: www.aswa.org/
2. Answers may vary.
3. Gain knowledge about the accounting profession, working environment, networking opportunities, upcoming events or seminars, scholarships, and grants.

PEACHTREE CORNER

Sales on Account

Use the **Sales/Invoicing** task option to enter sales on account. Unlike a manual system, you cannot enter sales on account in the general journal using the Peachtree software. To enter invoices (sales slips), select **Sales/Invoicing** from the ***Tasks*** menu. Or click the **Sales** navigation aid at the bottom of the screen and choose **Sales/Invoicing**.

Tasks Analysis Options Reports
Quotes/Sales Orders
Sales/Invoicing...
Receipts...
Finance Charge...

Credit Memos

To enter a credit memo, you must first use the **Sales/Invoicing** option to enter a "negative" invoice (sales slip). Then, apply the credit memo to a specific invoice using the **Receipts** option. Mark the credit memo and the invoice to which it applies as paid. The net result is a $0.00 cash receipt.

Cash Receipts

To enter cash sales, bankcard sales, or cash receipts on account, select **Receipts** from the ***Tasks*** menu. Or click the **Sales** navigation aid at the bottom of the screen and choose **Receipts**.

Tasks Analysis Options Reports
Quotes/Sales Orders
Sales/Invoicing...
Receipts...
Finance Charge...

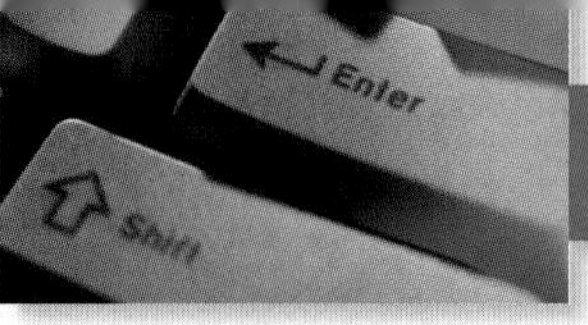

Sales and Cash Receipts

Making the Transition from a Manual to a Computerized System

Task	Perform Accounting Procedures Using Manual Methods	Perform Accounting Procedures Using Automated Methods
Recording Sales Transactions	1. General journal entries are prepared based on a sales slip or an invoice. 2. Journal entries are prepared and posted to the appropriate general ledger accounts. 3. New account balances must be calculated.	1. Invoices can be created with the software and posted to the general ledger accounts at the same time. 2. New account balances are calculated for you.
Recording Cash Receipts Transactions	1. Journal entries are prepared based on deposit slips, receipts, or cash register tapes. 2. Journal entries are prepared and posted to the appropriate general ledger accounts. 3. New account balances must be calculated.	1. Deposits are recorded and posted to the general ledger using the cash receipts task item. 2. General ledger accounts are updated automatically.

Entering Sales and Cash Receipts

Peachtree Question	Description
How do I record a cash sale or a miscellaneous receipt?	1. From the ***Tasks*** menu, select **Receipts.** 2. Enter a reference number (generally the customer's check number). 3. In the *Cash Account* list, enter the bank account in which the receipt is deposited. 4. Select the *Apply to Revenues* tab. Then, enter the line items on the receipt. (For a miscellaneous receipt, select the appropriate general ledger account. The Sales account is the default account.) 5. Click *Save.*
How do I record a sale on account?	1. From the ***Tasks*** menu, select **Sales/Invoicing.** 2. Enter customer ID and invoice number. 3. Click on the *Apply to Sales* tab. 4. Enter details of the invoice and amount. 5. Click *Save.*
How do I record a cash receipt from a customer on account?	1. From the ***Tasks*** menu, select **Receipts.** 2. Enter a reference number (generally the customer's check number). 3. In the *Cash Account* list, enter the bank account in which the receipt is to be deposited. 4. Select the *Apply to Invoices* tab. Then, select the invoices being paid. 5. Click *Save.*

For detailed instructions: See the **Peachtree User Guide** in your Glencoe Working Papers.

Peachtree® Answers to Frequently Asked Questions

Q: How do you correct a sales entry with the wrong customer ID code or sale amount?

A: If you enter the wrong information for a sales invoice, you can correct it even if you have already posted the transaction. Choose the **Sales/Invoicing** option and click *Open*. Select the invoice (sales slip) you want to change. When the invoice appears in the Sales/Invoicing data entry window, make the necessary corrections and then post the updated transaction.

For additional information, see your *Glencoe Accounting Peachtree User Guide.*

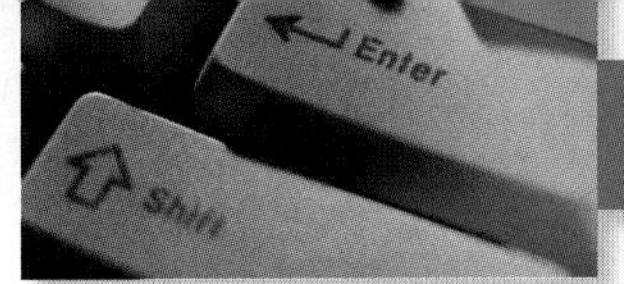

APPLICATION OPTIONS

Problem 14–5 Recording Sales and Cash Receipts

Sunset Surfwear, a California-based merchandising store, had the following sales and cash receipt transactions for January. The partial chart of accounts for Sunset Surfwear follows.

General Ledger

101 Cash in Bank	401 Sales
115 Accounts Receivable	405 Sales Discounts
215 Sales Tax Payable	410 Sales Returns and Allowances

Accounts Receivable Subsidiary Ledger

ADA Adams, Martha	**MOU** Moulder, Nate
HAM Hamilton, Alex	**WES** Westwood High School Athletics
JUN1 Jun, Helen	

Instructions Record the following transactions on page 20 of the general journal.

Date	Transactions
Jan. 1	Sold $300 in merchandise plus a sales tax of $18 on account to Martha Adams, Sales Slip 777.
5	Sold $1,500 in merchandise on account to Westwood High School Athletics, Sales Slip 778.
7	Received $400 from Alex Hamilton on account, Receipt 345.
10	Issued Credit Memorandum 102 to Martha Adams for $318 covering $300 in returned merchandise plus $18 sales tax.
15	Recorded cash sales of $800 plus $48 in sales tax, Tape 39.
15	Recorded bankcard sales of $900 plus $54 in sales tax, Tape 39.
20	Received $1,500 from Westwood High School Athletics in payment of Sales Slip 778, Receipt 346.
25	Sold $1,200 in merchandise plus sales tax of $72 on account to Helen Jun, Sales Slip 779.
28	Granted a $106 sales allowance to Helen Jun, which includes $100 for damaged merchandise she kept and sales tax of $6, Credit Memorandum 103.
30	Received $500 from a charge customer, Nate Moulder, in payment of his $500 account, Receipt 347.

Analyze: What is the sum of all the debits to the **Sales Returns and Allowances** account during January?

Complete chapter problems one of three ways:

1 **Manual** Glencoe Working Papers

or

2 **Peachtree Complete Accounting** Software

or

3 **QuickBooks** Templates (Problems 14–5, 14–7)

Peachtree®

SMART GUIDE

Step-by-Step Instructions: Problem 14–5

1. Start Peachtree and open Sunset Surfwear (Prob. 14-5).
2. Rename the problem set by using your initials.
3. Enter all sales on account transactions using the **Sales/Invoicing** option in the *Tasks* menu.
4. Process all credit memorandums using the **Sales/Invoicing** and **Receipts** options.
5. Record all cash receipts transactions using the Receipts option.
6. Print a Sales Journal report and a Cash Receipts Journal report.
7. Proof your work and make any needed corrections.
8. Print a GL report to answer the Analyze question.
9. End the session.

Problem 14–5 (Answers) Recording Sales and Cash Receipts

Jan. 1: Dr. Accts. Rec./Martha Adams $318; Cr. Sales $300 and Sales Tax Payable $18; Sales Slip 777

Jan. 5: Dr. Accts. Rec./Westwood H.S. Athletics $1,500; Cr. Sales $1,500; Sales Slip 778

Jan. 7: Dr. Cash in Bank $400; Cr. Accts. Rec./Alex Hamilton $400; Receipt 345

Jan. 10: Dr. Sales Returns & Allowances $300 and Sales Tax Payable $18; Cr. Accts. Rec./Martha Adams $318; Credit Memo 102

Jan. 15: Dr. Cash in Bank $848; Cr. Sales $800 and Sales Tax Payable $48; Tape 39

Jan. 15: Dr. Cash in Bank $954; Cr. Sales $900 and Sales Tax Payable $54.

Jan. 20: Dr. Cash in Bank $1,500; Cr. Accts. Rec./Westwood H.S. Athletics $1,500; Receipt 346

Jan. 25: Dr. Accts. Rec./Helen Jun $1,272; Cr. Sales $1,200 and Sales Tax Payable $72; Sales Slip 779

Jan. 28: Dr. Sales Ret. and Allow. $100 and Sales Tax Payable $6; Cr. Accts. Rec./Helen Jun $106; Credit Memo 103

Jan. 30: Dr. Cash in Bank $500; Cr. Accts. Rec./Nate Mouler $500; Receipt 347

Analyze: $400

SOFTWARE NOTES

Teachers can find detailed instructions for:

- **Peachtree Complete Accounting Software**, in the *Glencoe Workbook (CRWP)*
- **QuickBooks Templates**, in *Using QuickBooks with Glencoe Accounting*
- **Spreadsheet Templates**, in the *Glencoe Workbook (CRWP)*

Problem 14-6 (Answers) Posting Sales and Cash Receipts

Ending GL account balances:
Cash in Bank $13,061
Accounts Receivable $1,130
Sales Tax Payable $470
Sales $14,985
Sales Discounts $204
Sales Rets. & Allow. $1,060

Ending SL account balances:
Alvarez $420
Greenburg $500
Montoya $0
Wright $210

Analyze: $204

CHAPTER 14 PROBLEMS

Peachtree®

SMART GUIDE

Step-by-Step Instructions: Problem 14-6

1. Start Peachtree and open InBeat CD Shop (Prob. 14-6).
2. Rename the problem set by using your initials.
3. Choose General Ledger from the Reports menu.
4. Print a General Ledger report.
5. Select the Accounts Receivable report area.
6. From the list on the right, select and print the Customer Ledgers report.
7. Compare each GL entry in your working papers to the GL report and Customer Ledgers report.
8. Use the GL report to answer the Analyze question.
9. End the session.

Problem 14-6 Posting Sales and Cash Receipts

The January transactions for InBeat CD Shop are recorded on page 15 of the general journal.

Instructions Post the transactions to the general ledger and subsidiary ledger in your working papers.

GENERAL JOURNAL PAGE *15*

DATE		DESCRIPTION	POST. REF.	DEBIT	CREDIT
20--					
Jan.	*1*	*Cash in Bank*		388 00	
		Sales Discounts		12 00	
		Accts. Rec./Alicia Alvarez	/		400 00
		Receipt 92			
	4	*Accts. Rec./Dena Greenburg*	/	735 00	
		Sales			700 00
		Sales Tax Payable			35 00
		Sales Slip 60			
	6	*Cash in Bank*		2 100 00	
		Sales			2 000 00
		Sales Tax Payable			100 00
		Tape 32			
	6	*Cash in Bank*		3 150 00	
		Sales			3 000 00
		Sales Tax Payable			150 00
		Tape 32			
	8	*Sales Returns and Allowances*		700 00	
		Sales Tax Payable		35 00	
		Accts. Rec./ Dena Greenburg	/		735 00
		Credit Memorandum 15			
	10	*Cash in Bank*		1 358 00	
		Sales Discounts		42 00	
		Accts. Rec./Joe Montoya	/		1 400 00
		Receipt 93			
	15	*Accts. Rec./Alicia Alvarez*	/	420 00	
		Sales			400 00
		Sales Tax Payable			20 00
		Sales Slip 61			
	27	*Cash in Bank*		1 365 00	
		Accts. Rec./Chelsea Wright	/		1 365 00
		Receipt 94			

Analyze: What is the ending balance in the **Sales Discounts** account for January?

SOLUTION NOTES

Problem 14–7 Recording Sales and Cash Receipts

Shutterbug Cameras had the following transactions during January. The partial chart of accounts for Shutterbug is shown below.

General Ledger

101 Cash in Bank	401 Sales
115 Accounts Receivable	405 Sales Discounts
130 Supplies	410 Sales Returns and Allowances
215 Sales Tax Payable	

Accounts Receivable Subsidiary Ledger

DIA Diaz, Arturo	**NAK** Nakata, Yoko
FAS FastForward Productions	**SUL** Sullivan, Heather

Instructions Record the transactions on page 5 of the general journal in your working papers.

Date	Transactions
Jan. 1	Sold merchandise on account to Yoko Nakata for $250 plus a 4% sales tax of $10, Sales Slip 90.
3	Received $50 in cash from the sale of supplies to Betty's Boutique, Receipt 201.
7	Sold $300 in merchandise plus a sales tax of $12 to Arturo Diaz on account, Sales Slip 91.
12	Sold on account $1,500 in merchandise plus a sales tax of $60 to FastForward Productions, credit terms 2/10, n/30, Sales Slip 92.
13	Issued Credit Memorandum 20 for $312 to Arturo Diaz, which includes $300 in merchandise returned by him plus sales tax of $12.
14	Received a check for $260 from Yoko Nakata in full payment of his account, Receipt 202.
15	Cash sales amounted to $2,500 plus $100 in sales tax, Tape 75.
15	Bankcard sales were $3,000 plus $120 in sales tax, Tape 75.
21	Received a check for $1,530 from FastForward Productions in payment of their $1,560 account balance less a cash discount of $30, Receipt 203.
28	Granted Heather Sullivan a $104 allowance for damaged merchandise of $100 plus a 4% sales tax of $4, Credit Memorandum 21.

Analyze: What is the net amount of sales tax for the month based on these transactions?

Peachtree®

SMART GUIDE

Step-by-Step Instructions: Problem 14–7

1. Start Peachtree and open Shutterbug Cameras (Prob. 14–7).
2. Rename the problem set by using your initials.
3. Enter all sales on account transactions using the **Sales/Invoicing** option.
4. Process all credit memorandums using the **Sales/Invoicing** and **Receipts** options.
5. Record all cash receipts using the **Receipts** option.
6. Print a Sales Journal and a Cash Receipts Journal report.
7. Proof your work. Make any needed corrections.
8. Print a GL report to answer the Analyze question.
9. End the session.

Problem 14–7 (Answers) Recording Sales and Cash Receipts

Jan. 1: Dr. Accts. Rec./ Yoko Nakata $260; Cr. Sales $250, Sales Tax Pay. $10; Sales Slip 90

Jan. 3: Dr. Cash in Bank $50; Cr. Supplies $50; Receipt 201

Jan. 7: Dr. Accts. Rec./Arturo Diaz $312; Cr. Sales $300, Sales Tax Pay. $12; Sales Slip 91

Jan. 12: Dr. Accts. Rec./FastForward Productions $1,560; Cr. Sales $1,500, Sales Tax Pay. $60; Sales Slip 92

Jan. 13: Dr. Sales Ret. and Allow. $300, Sales Tax Pay. $12; Cr. Accts. Rec./Arturo Diaz $312; Credit Memo 20

Jan. 14: Dr. Cash in Bank $260; Cr. Accts. Rec./Yoko Nakata $260; Receipt 202

Jan. 15: Dr. Cash in Bank $2,600; Cr. Sales $2,500, Sales Tax Pay. $100; Tape 75

Jan. 15: Dr. Cash in Bank $3,120; Cr. Sales $3,000, Sales Tax Pay. $120; Tape 75

Jan. 21: Dr. Cash in Bank $1,530, Sales Discounts $30; Cr. Accts. Rec./ FastForward Productions $1,560; Receipt 203

Jan. 28: Dr. Sales Ret. and Allow. $100, Sales Tax Pay. $4; Cr. Accts. Rec./ Heather Sullivan $104; Credit Memo 21

Analyze: $286

SOLUTION NOTES

PROBLEMS
CHAPTER 14

Problem 14–8 (Answers) Recording Sales and Cash Receipt Transactions

Jan. 1: Dr. Accts. Rec./Wildwood Resorts $2,000; Cr. Sales $2,000; Sales Slip 103

Jan. 5: Dr. Sales Ret. and Allow. $150; Cr. Accts. Rec./Wildwood Resorts $150; Credit Memo 33

Jan. 8: Dr. Cash in Bank $485 and Sales Discounts $15; Cr. Accts. Rec./Adventure River Tours $500; Receipt 96

Jan. 10: Dr. Accts. Rec./Paul Drake $525; Cr. Sales $500 and Sales Tax Payable $25; Sales Slip 104

Jan. 12: Dr. Cash in Bank $1,794.50 and Sales Discounts $55.50; Cr. Accts. Rec./Wildwood Resorts $1,850; Receipt 97

Jan. 15: Dr. Cash in Bank $3,675; Cr. Sales $3,500 and Sales Tax Payable $175; Tape 22

Jan. 15: Dr. Cash in Bank $4,200; Cr. Sales $4,000 and Sales Tax Payable $200; Tape 22

Jan. 20: Dr. Cash in Bank $75; Cr. Supplies $75; Receipt 98

Jan. 22: Dr. Sales Ret. and Allow. $60 and Sales Tax Payable $3; Cr. Accts. Rec./Kim Wu $63; Credit Memo 34

Jan. 25: Dr. Cash in Bank $510 and Sales Discounts $15; Cr. Accts. Rec./Paul Drake $525; Receipt 99

Analyze: $85.50

Peachtree®

SMART GUIDE

Step-by-Step Instructions: Problem 14–8

1. Start Peachtree and open River's Edge (Prob. 14–8).
2. Rename the problem set by using your initials.
3. Enter all sales on account transactions using the **Sales/Invoicing** option.
4. Process all credit memorandums using the **Sales/Invoicing** and **Receipts** options.
5. Record all cash receipts using the Receipts option.
6. Print a Sales Journal and Cash Receipts journal report.
7. Proof your work. Make any needed corrections.
8. Print a GL report to answer the Analyze question.
9. End the session.

Problem 14–8 Recording Sales and Cash Receipt Transactions

River's Edge Canoe & Kayak is a merchandising business in Wyoming. The partial chart of accounts follows:

General Ledger

101 Cash in Bank	401 Sales
115 Accounts Receivable	405 Sales Discounts
135 Supplies	410 Sales Returns and Allowances
215 Sales Tax Payable	

Accounts Receivable Subsidiary Ledger

ADV Adventure River Tours	WILD Wildwood Resorts
DRA Drake, Paul	WU Wu, Kim

Instructions Record January transactions on page 10 of the general journal.

Date	Transactions
Jan. 1	Sold $2,000 in merchandise on account to Wildwood Resorts, a tax-exempt agency, credit terms 3/15, n/30, Sales Slip 103.
5	Granted Wildwood Resorts a $150 credit allowance for defective merchandise, Credit Memorandum 33.
8	Received $485 from Adventure River Tours for $500 in merchandise sold to them on Dec. 27 less a 3% cash discount of $15, Receipt 96.
10	Sold $500 in merchandise plus a 5% sales tax of $25 to Paul Drake on account, credit terms 3/15, n/30, Sales Slip 104.
12	Received a check for $1,794.50 from Wildwood Resorts on account ($1,850 less a 3% cash discount of $55.50), Receipt 97.
15	Cash sales were $3,500 plus sales tax of $175, Tape 22.
15	Bankcard sales amounted to $4,000 plus sales tax of $200, Tape 22.
20	Sold to Adventure River Tours $75 in supplies. Cash received recorded on Receipt 98.
22	Granted Kim Wu $63 credit for $60 in damaged merchandise sold to her last month and 5% sales tax of $3 on the merchandise, Credit Memorandum 34.
25	Paul Drake sent a check for $510 in payment of his account. The account balance was $525 ($500 in merchandise and $25 sales tax). He took a 3% cash discount of $15 on the merchandise, Receipt 99.

Analyze: If customers had not taken any cash discounts, how much more cash would have been collected in the month of January?

SOLUTION NOTES

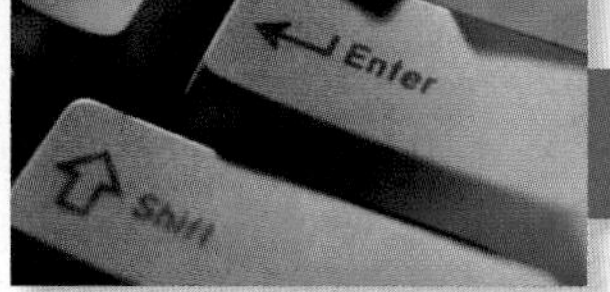

Problem 14–9 Recording and Posting Sales and Cash Receipts

SOURCE DOCUMENT PROBLEM

Buzz Newsstand had the following transactions for the month of January.

General Ledger

101 Cash in Bank	401 Sales
115 Accounts Receivable	405 Sales Discounts
135 Supplies	410 Sales Returns and Allowances
215 Sales Tax Payable	

Accounts Receivable Subsidiary Ledger

ADK Adkins, Lee	NAD Nadal, Saba
JAV Java Shops Inc.	ROL Rolling Hills Pharmacies

Instructions

1. Record the transactions on page 9 of the general journal.
2. Post each transaction to the appropriate general ledger and accounts receivable subsidiary ledger accounts. A partial general ledger and accounts receivable subsidiary ledger are included in the working papers. The current account balances are recorded in the accounts.

Date	Transactions
Jan. 1	Lee Adkins returned $200 in damaged merchandise purchased on account last month, issued Credit Memorandum 10 for $212 ($200 in merchandise plus 6% sales tax of $12).
3	Received a check from Rolling Hills Pharmacies for $2,256.62 in payment of their account of $2,300 less a 2% cash discount of $43.38, Receipt 75.
7	Gave credit to Saba Nadal for the return of $300 in merchandise sold to him on account, plus sales tax of $18. Issued Credit Memorandum 11 for $318.
10	Java Shops Inc. sent a check for $1471.70 in payment of their account of $1,500 less a 2% cash discount of $28.30, Receipt 76.
15	Cash sales were $2,500 plus $150 in sales tax, Tape 25.
15	Bankcard sales were $2,000 plus $120 in sales tax, Tape 25.
20	Janson Lee, a neighboring store, needed supplies urgently. Sold them $40 in supplies and received cash from the sale, Receipt 77.
25	Received a check for $636 from Lee Adkins on account, Receipt 78.
31	Sold $3,000 in merchandise plus sales tax of $180 on account to Rolling Hills Pharmacies, Sales Slip 114.

Analyze: What is the balance of the Sales account at January 31?

Peachtree®

SMART GUIDE

Step-by-Step Instructions: Problem 14–9

1. Start Peachtree and open Buzz Newsstand (Prob. 14–9).
2. Rename the problem set by using your initials.
3. Enter all sales on account transactions.
4. Process all credit memorandums.
5. Record all cash receipts.
6. Print the following reports: Sales Journal, Cash Receipts Journal, Customer Ledgers, and General Ledger.
7. Proof your work. Make any needed corrections.
8. Use the GL report to answer the Analyze question.
9. End the session.

SOURCE DOCUMENT PROBLEM

Problem 14–9

Use the source documents in your working papers to record the transactions in this problem.

CHALLENGE PROBLEM

SOURCE DOCUMENT PROBLEM

Problem 14–9 (Answers) Recording and Posting Sales and Cash Receipts

Jan. 1: Dr. Sales Ret. & Allow. $200, Sales Tax Pay. $12; Cr. Accts. Rec./Lee Adkins $212; Credit Memo 10

Jan. 3: Dr. Cash in Bank $2,256.62, Sales Discounts $43.38; Cr. Accts. Rec./Rolling Hills Pharmacies $2,300; Receipt 75

Jan. 7: Dr. Sales Ret. & Allow. $300, Sales Tax Pay. $18; Cr. Accts. Rec./Saba Nadal, $318; Credit Memo 11

Jan. 10: Dr. Cash in Bank $1,471.70, Sales Discounts $28.30; Cr. Accts. Rec./Java Shops Inc. $1,500; Receipt 76

Jan. 15: Dr. Cash in Bank $2,650; Cr. Sales $2,500, Sales Tax Pay. $150; Tape 25

Jan. 15: Dr. Cash in Bank $2,120; Cr. Sales $2,000, Sales Tax Pay. $120; Tape 25

Jan. 20: Dr. Cash in Bank $40; Cr. Supplies $40; Receipt 77

Jan. 25: Dr. Cash in Bank $636; Cr. Accts. Rec./Lee Adkins $636; Receipt 78

Jan. 31: Dr. Accts. Rec./Rolling Hills Pharmacies $3,180; Cr. Sales $3,000, Sales Tax Pay. $180; Sales Slip 114

Analyze: $18,300

SOLUTION NOTES

CHAPTER 15 Resource Manager

Section Resources

	Objectives & Standards	Activities & Features	Reproducible Masters
Chapter Opener *Accounting for Purchases and Cash Payments*	• Explain the procedures for processing a purchase on account. • Describe the accounts used in the purchasing process. • Analyze transactions relating to the purchase of mechandise. • Record a variety of purchases and cash payment transactions. • Post to the accounts payable subsidiary ledger. • Define the accounting terms introduced in this chapter. **National Standards for Business Education**: IA7–IA10, IIA2, IIB2, IIB4	Exploring the Real World of Business, p. 386 Workplace Connections, p. 387	School-to-Work Handbook
Section 1 *Purchasing Items Needed by a Business*	• Paperwork involved in the purchasing process. • The purpose of the **Purchases Discounts** account. • The purpose of the **Purchases** account and its rules of debit and credit.	Connect To, p. 389	
Section 2 *Analyzing and Recording Purchases on Account*	• How the accounts payable subsidiary ledger is used. • How to record the purchase of merchandise on account. • How to record the purchase of other assets on account. • How to record purchases returns and allowances transactions. • How to post to creditor accounts in the accounts payable subsidiary ledger.	Accounting Flashbacks, p. 394 Did You Know?, p. 397 Calculator Hints, p. 397 Analyzing Financial Reports, p. 399 Accounting Careers in Focus, p. 401	Demonstration Problems Math Review for Accounting
Section 3 *Analyzing and Recording Cash Payments*	• The different kinds of cash payments made by a business. • The rules of debit and credit for the **Purchases Discounts** account. • How shipping charges are recorded and whether the buyer or the seller pays for them.	International Accounting, p. 402 A Matter of Ethics, p. 407	Strategies for Teaching International Accounting Demonstration Problems Strategies for Teaching Ethics in Accounting Internet Resources and Activities Handbook

KEY

Posters — Transparency — Software — Videocassette — Blackline Masters — CD-ROM — Portfolio

MULTIMEDIA RESOURCE

Peachtree	QuickBooks	Spreadsheets	Videos	CD-ROMs
Problem 15–6 *Analyzing Purchases and Cash Payments* Problem 15–7 *Recording Purchases Transactions* Problem 15–8 *Recording Cash Payment Transactions* Problem 15–9 *Recording Purchases and Cash Payment Transactions* Problem 15–10 *Recording and Posting Purchases and Cash Payment Transactions*	Problem 15–7 *Recording Purchases Transactions* Problem 15–9 *Recording Purchases and Cash Payment Transactions*	Problem 15–5 *Determining Due Dates and Discount Amounts*	***Video Segment: Purchases and Cash Payments*** After viewing this video, students will be able to explain the difference between purchases of assets for use in the business and purchases of merchandise for resale. Students will be able to describe the purchasing process and how purchases and payments are recorded.	***Electronic Learning Center (ELC), Chapter 15*** This program is ideal for visual learners since it incorporates video images, animation, and graphics to enliven the content of each lesson. ***Interactive Lesson Planner (ILP), Chapter 15*** This CD-ROM combines the versatility of an electronic lesson planner with the convenience of teacher classroom resources.

SCANS Correlation Chart

FOUNDATION SKILLS

Basic Skills:	Reading	Writing	Math	Listening	Speaking	
Thinking Skills:	Creative Thinking	Decision Making	Problem Solving	Seeing Things in the Mind's Eye	Knowing How to Learn	Reasoning
Personal Qualities:	Responsibility	Self-Esteem	Sociability	Self-Management	Integrity/Honesty	

WORKPLACE COMPETENCIES

Resources:	Allocating Time	Allocating Money	Allocating Material and Facility Resources	Allocating Human Resources		
Information:	Acquiring and Evaluating Information	Organizing and Maintaining Information	Interpreting and Communicating Information	Using Computers to Process Information		
Interpersonal Skills:	Participating as a Member of a Team	Teaching Others	Serving Clients/ Customers	Exercising Leadership	Negotiating to Arrive at a Decision	Working with Cultural Diversity
Systems:	Understanding Systems	Monitoring and Correcting Performance	Improving and Designing Systems			
Technology:	Selecting Technology	Applying Technology to Task	Maintaining and Troubleshooting Technology			

*Highlighted blocks indicate areas covered in the chapter. Additional SCANS skills are also covered throughout the *Teacher Wraparound Edition.*

Assessment

Student Edition
- Check Your Understanding, pp. 392, 400, 408
- Chapter 15 Problems, pp. 413–417

Assessment and Evaluation Masters
- Chapter 15 Study Plan, *Glencoe Workbook*
- Chapter 15 Self-Test, *Glencoe Workbook*
- Chapter 15 Test, *Chapter Tests* Booklet
- Chapter 15 Activity, *School-to-Work Handbook*
- Chapter 15 **Exam***View*

Teacher Wraparound Edition
- Critical Thinking Activity, p. 404
- Reteaching Section 1, p. 392
- Reteaching Section 2, p. 400
- Reteaching Section 3, p. 408
- Chapter 15 Quiz, p. 409

Transparencies

	Teaching Transparencies	Solution Transparencies
Section 1:	15–1, 15–2, 15–3, 15–4	Problem 15–1
Section 2:	15–5, 15–6, 15–7, 15–8, 15–9, 15–10, 15–11	Problems 15–2, 15–3
Section 3:	15-12, 15-13, 15–14, 15–15, 15–16, 15–17	Problem 15–4
End of Chapter:		Problems 15–5, 15–6, 15–7, 15–8, 15–9, 15–10

TEACHER CLASSROOM RESOURCES

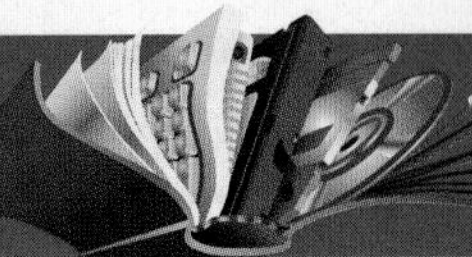

This is a representation of key blackline masters available in the Teacher Classroom Resources.

Teaching Aids

Transparency Examples

Section Focus Transparencies

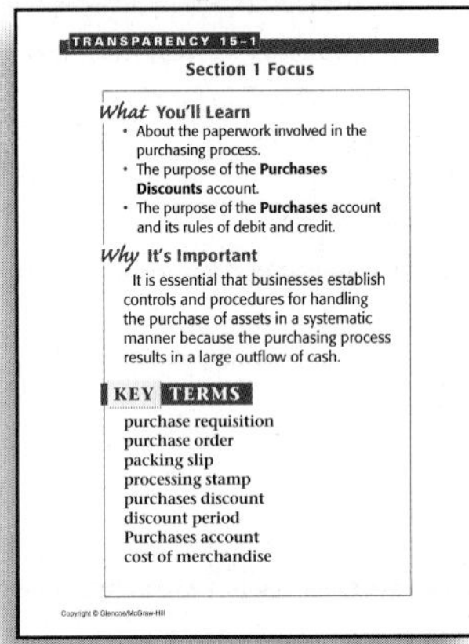

TRANSPARENCY 15-1

Section 1 Focus

What You'll Learn
- About the paperwork involved in the purchasing process.
- The purpose of the **Purchases Discounts** account.
- The purpose of the **Purchases** account and its rules of debit and credit.

Why It's Important

It is essential that businesses establish controls and procedures for handling the purchase of assets in a systematic manner because the purchasing process results in a large outflow of cash.

KEY TERMS

purchase requisition
purchase order
packing slip
processing stamp
purchases discount
discount period
Purchases account
cost of merchandise

Copyright © Glencoe/McGraw-Hill

Teaching Transparencies

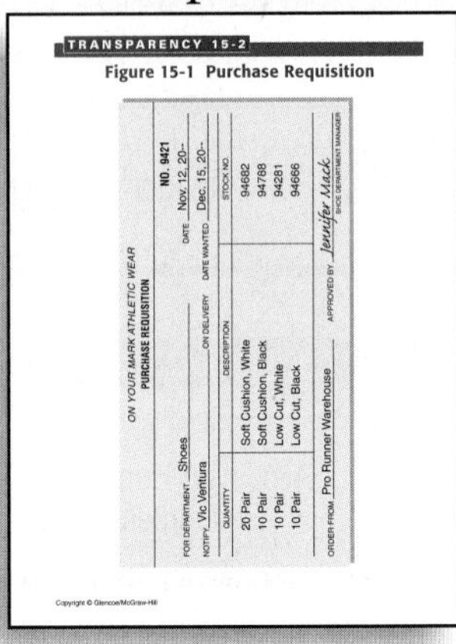

TRANSPARENCY 15-2

Figure 15-1 Purchase Requisition

ON YOUR MARK ATHLETIC WEAR — PURCHASE REQUISITION — NO. 9421

FOR DEPARTMENT: Shoes — DATE: Nov. 12, 20-- — NOTIFY: Vic Ventura — DATE WANTED: Dec. 15, 20--

QUANTITY	DESCRIPTION	STOCK NO.
20 Pair	Soft Cushion, White	94682
10 Pair	Soft Cushion, Black	94788
10 Pair	Low Cut, White	94281
10 Pair	Low Cut, Black	94666

ORDER FROM: Pro Runner Warehouse — APPROVED BY: Jennifer Mack

Copyright © Glencoe/McGraw-Hill

Source Document Transparencies

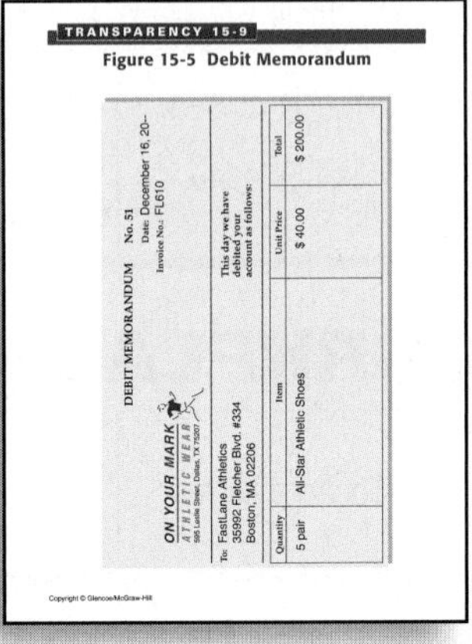

TRANSPARENCY 15-9

Figure 15-5 Debit Memorandum

ON YOUR MARK ATHLETIC WEAR — DEBIT MEMORANDUM — No. 51 — Date: December 16, 20-- — Invoice No. FL610

To: FastLane Athletics, 3099 Fletcher Blvd. #334, Boston, MA 02206

This day we have debited your account as follows:

Quantity	Item	Unit Price	Total
5 pair	All-Star Athletic Shoes	$ 40.00	$ 200.00

Copyright © Glencoe/McGraw-Hill

Solution Transparencies

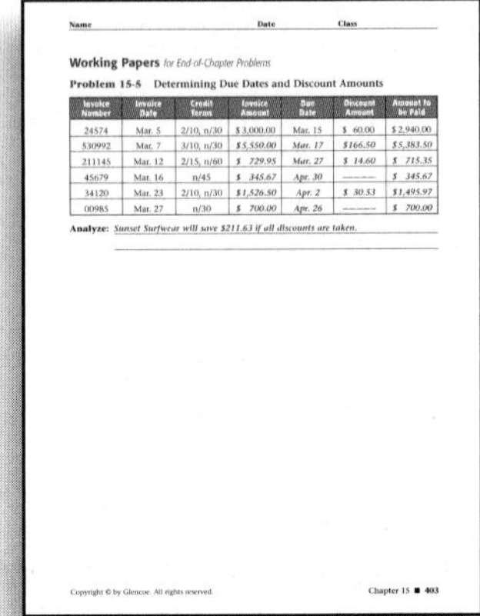

Working Papers for End-of-Chapter Problems

Problem 15-5 Determining Due Dates and Discount Amounts

Analyze: Sunset Surfwear will save $211.63 if all discounts are taken.

Copyright © by Glencoe. All rights reserved. — Chapter 15 ■ 403

Demonstration Problems

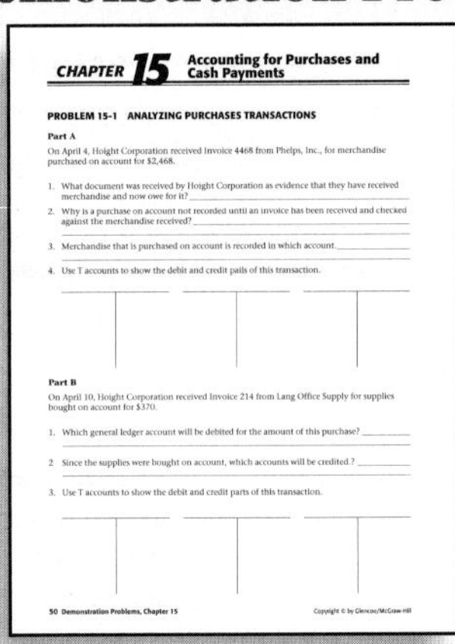

CHAPTER 15 Accounting for Purchases and Cash Payments

PROBLEM 15-1 ANALYZING PURCHASES TRANSACTIONS

Lesson Plans

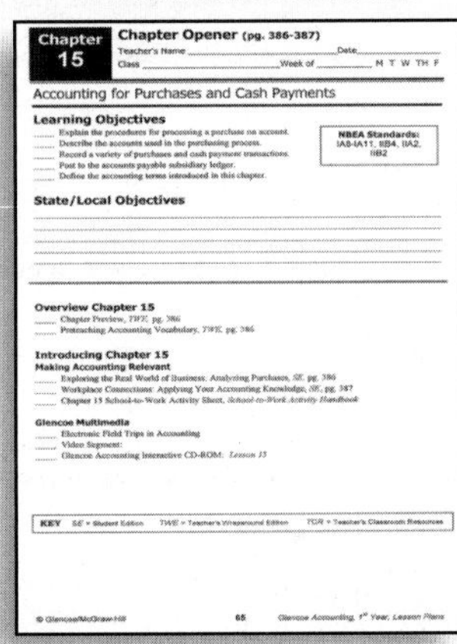

Chapter 15 — Chapter Opener (pg. 386-387)

Accounting for Purchases and Cash Payments

Learning Objectives

State/Local Objectives

Overview Chapter 15

Introducing Chapter 15

Glencoe Multimedia

Block Scheduling

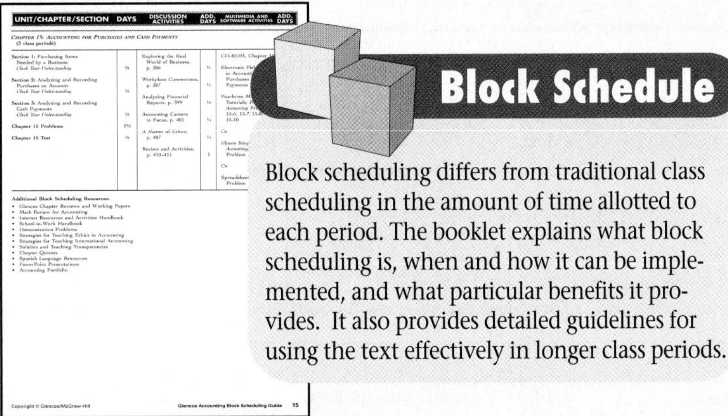

UNIT/CHAPTER/SECTION — DAYS — DISCUSSION ACTIVITIES — ADD. DAYS — MULTIMEDIA AND SOFTWARE ACTIVITIES — ADD. DAYS

Block Schedule

Block scheduling differs from traditional class scheduling in the amount of time allotted to each period. The booklet explains what block scheduling is, when and how it can be implemented, and what particular benefits it provides. It also provides detailed guidelines for using the text effectively in longer class periods.

Enrichment and Application

Strategies for Teaching Ethics in Accounting

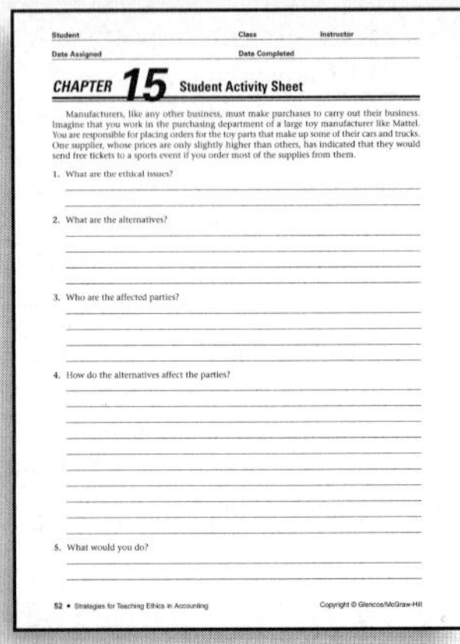

CHAPTER 15 Student Activity Sheet

Strategies for Teaching International Accounting

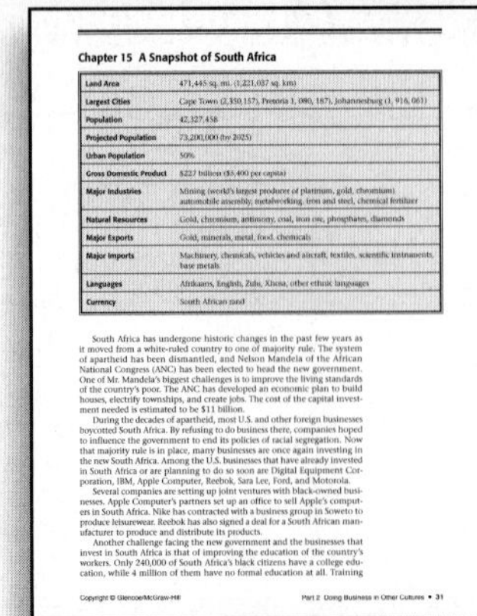

Chapter 15 A Snapshot of South Africa

School-to-Work Handbook

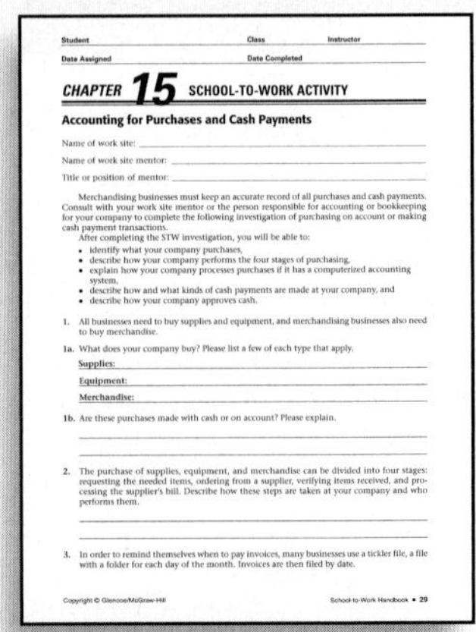

CHAPTER 15 SCHOOL-TO-WORK ACTIVITY

Accounting for Purchases and Cash Payments

Meeting Different Ability Levels

Chapter Reviews and Working Papers (CRWP)

Working Papers

Review

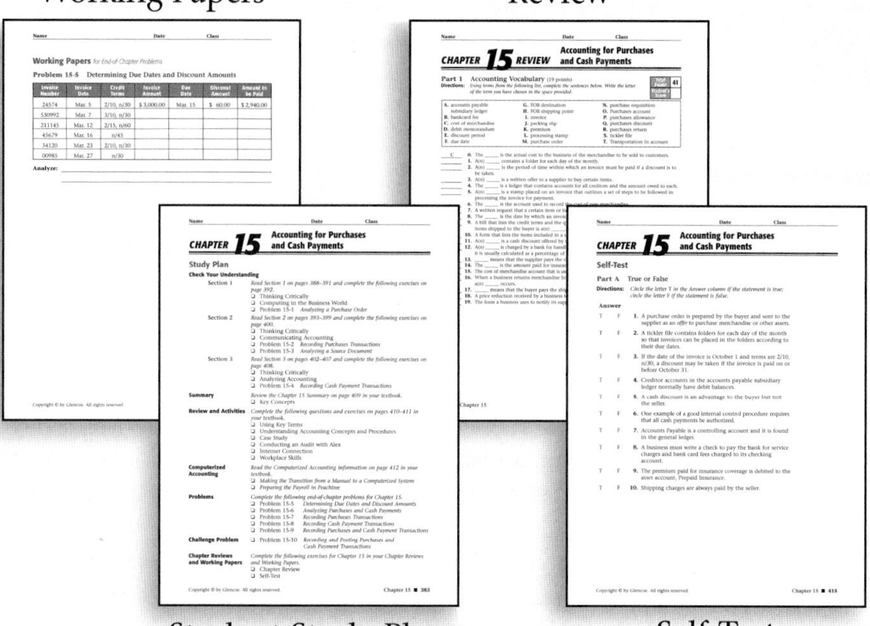

Student Study Plan

Self-Test

Real-World Multimedia CD-ROM

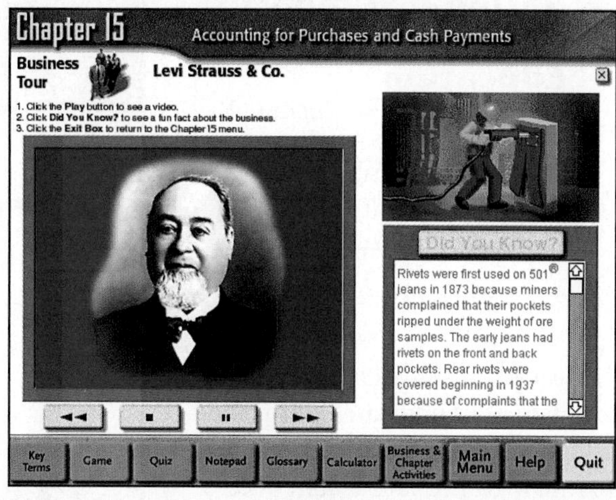

Key to Ability Levels

Each section gives skill-building activities. Each activity has been labeled for use with students of various learning styles and abilities.

L1 Level 1 activities are basic activities and should be within the range of all students.

L2 Level 2 activities are average activities and should be within the range of average and above average students.

L3 Level 3 activities are challenging activities designed for the ability range of above average students.

ELL ELL activities should be within the ability range of English Language Learners.

Assessment and Evaluation

Chapter Tests

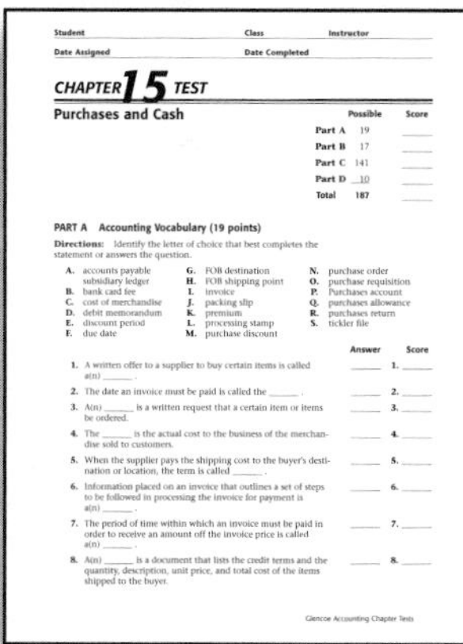

Chapter Quiz

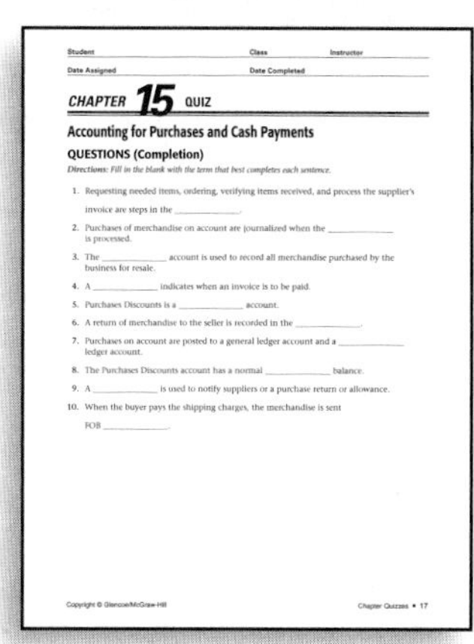

Teaching Resources at a Glance

Application Resources

- Glencoe Chapter Review and Working Papers, SE and TAE
- School-to-Work Handbook, SE and TM
- Accounting Portfolio, SE and TM

Reproducible Masters

- Demonstration Problems
- Lesson Plans
- Block Scheduling
- Spanish Language Resources

Glencoe Accounting Professional Development Series

- Strategies for Teaching Ethics in Accounting
- Accounting Competitive Event Review
- Math Review for Accounting
- Strategies for Teaching International Accounting
- Internet Resources and Activities Handbook

Transparency Package

- Section Focus Transparencies
- Teaching Transparencies
- Source Document Transparencies
- Solution Transparencies

Performance Assessment

- **Exam***View* CD-ROM
- Chapter Tests
- Chapter Quizzes
- Unit Tests
- Audit Tests
- Printed Testbank

Multimedia Resources

- Electronic Learning Center:
  - Multimedia CD-ROMs
  - Peachtree software, tutorials, templates, and solutions
  - Spreadsheet templates
- Using QuickBooks with Glencoe Accounting
- Interactive Lesson Planner
- Electronic Field Trips in Accounting
- PowerPoint Presentation
- Web site: glencoeaccounting.glencoe.com

OVERVIEW CHAPTER 15

Correlations to National Standards for Business Education

(See pages T50–T51 for a detailed correlation chart.)

Standards: IA8–IA11, IIA2, IIB2, IIB4

Chapter Preview

In this chapter students will continue their study of the special journals by learning to use a purchases journal and a cash payments journal. They'll also learn how to prepare a schedule of accounts payable.

Section Overviews

- Section 1—*Purchasing Items Needed by a Business*
- Section 2—*Analyzing and Recording Purchases on Account*
- Section 3—*Analyzing and Recording Cash Payments*

Chapter Vocabulary

purchase requisition	**tickler file**
purchase order	**due dates**
packing slip	**purchases returns**
processing stamp	**purchases allowances**
purchases discount	**debit memorandum**
discount period	**premium**
Purchases account	**FOB destination**
cost of merchandise	**FOB shipping point**
accounts payable subsidiary ledger	**bankcard fee**

Preteaching Accounting Vocabulary

Discussion: Ask students to name items they have purchased recently, such as jeans or a sweater. Using the item as an example, discuss each term in the chapter. For example, the store selling the jeans would have issued a purchase requisition before buying the merchandise. L1

CHAPTER 15

Accounting for Purchases and Cash Payments

Learning Objectives

When you have completed this chapter, you will be able to:

- Explain the procedures for processing a purchase on account.
- Describe the accounts used in the purchasing process.
- Analyze transactions relating to the purchase of merchandise.
- Record a variety of purchases and cash payment transactions.
- Post to the accounts payable subsidiary ledger.
- Define the accounting terms introduced in this chapter.

Exploring the Real World of Business

ANALYZING PURCHASES

Levi's® jeans are one of the oldest and most successful products ever made. **Levi Strauss** is the largest manufacturer of branded clothing in the world, with recent sales of over $4 billion. That's a lot of jeans!

Born in Bavaria, Levi Strauss emigrated to New York in 1847. Several years later, he moved to San Francisco and started a small dry-goods store. In 1873, Strauss and a tailor, Jacob Davis, received a patent for riveted men's pants. Originally called waist overalls, the pants were made of denim purchased from the Amoskeag Mill in New Hampshire and were fastened with copper rivets. Around 1890, the company started numbering their styles and the 501® style came into existence. These original pants were made only for men. It was not until 1981 that 501® jeans for women were introduced.

Today, **Levi Strauss** operates not only as a wholesaler, but also as a retailer of its products from its own retail stores.

What do you think?

Levi Strauss buys denim for making its jeans from a fabric manufacturer. What are at least three other items the company might purchase for use in making its jeans?

Exploring the Real World of Business

Levi's

Levi's is well known for its jeans products, but the company has also followed the trend toward more casual wear in the office and created a line of casual business wear. These products include slacks, jackets, sweaters, and shirts (all made from non-denim fabrics) that employees wear in the office on "casual day."

What do you think? (Answers)

Answers may vary. Among other items Levi's would buy for use in manufacturing its jeans products are cotton fabrics for pockets, thread, metal snaps, buttons, and zippers. The company also would buy equipment used in the manufacturing process.

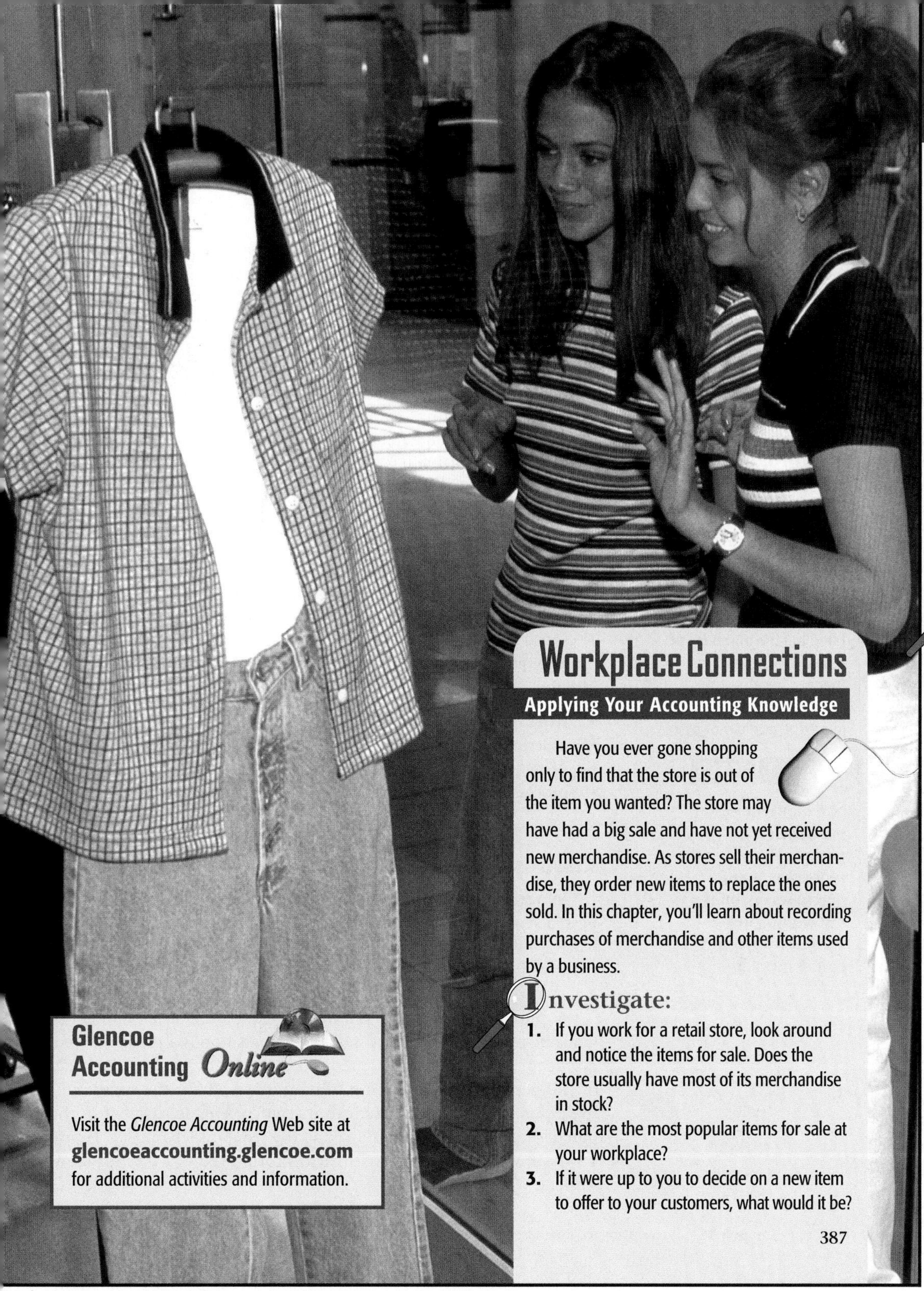

Workplace Connections

Applying Your Accounting Knowledge

Have you ever gone shopping only to find that the store is out of the item you wanted? The store may have had a big sale and have not yet received new merchandise. As stores sell their merchandise, they order new items to replace the ones sold. In this chapter, you'll learn about recording purchases of merchandise and other items used by a business.

Investigate:

1. If you work for a retail store, look around and notice the items for sale. Does the store usually have most of its merchandise in stock?
2. What are the most popular items for sale at your workplace?
3. If it were up to you to decide on a new item to offer to your customers, what would it be?

Glencoe Accounting Online

Visit the *Glencoe Accounting* Web site at **glencoeaccounting.glencoe.com** for additional activities and information.

INTRODUCING CHAPTER 15

Making Accounting Relevant

Workplace Connections: Applying Your Accounting Knowledge

Discussion: Most students will have had the experience of not being able to buy something they wanted because it was out of stock or the store did not have their size. Discuss the effect of out-of-stock situations on business revenue, emphasizing that businesses use a purchasing process to help avoid such situations.

Investigate (Answers)

1. Answers will vary. Ask students whether local stores offer rain checks for special sale items when they are out of stock on that item. How does the rain check help promote customer goodwill?
2. Answers will vary.
3. Answers will vary. Ask students to name the type of store in which the items they mention would be sold. Look for answers that include products that are related to the purpose of the business.

School-to-Work Activity

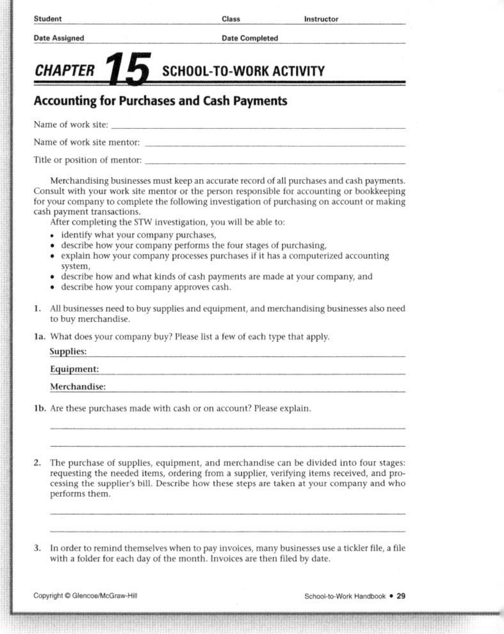

Student ______ Class ______ Instructor ______

Date Assigned ______ Date Completed ______

CHAPTER 15 SCHOOL-TO-WORK ACTIVITY

Accounting for Purchases and Cash Payments

Name of work site: ______

Name of work site mentor: ______

Title or position of mentor: ______

Merchandising businesses must keep an accurate record of all purchases and cash payments. Consult with your work site mentor or the person responsible for accounting or bookkeeping for your company to complete the following investigation of purchasing on account or making cash payment transactions.

After completing the STW investigation, you will be able to:

- identify what your company purchases,
- describe how your company performs the four stages of purchasing,
- explain how your company processes purchases if it has a computerized accounting system,
- describe how and what kinds of cash payments are made at your company, and
- describe how your company approves cash.

1. All businesses need to buy supplies and equipment, and merchandising businesses also need to buy merchandise.

1a. What does your company buy? Please list a few of each type that apply.

Supplies: ______

Equipment: ______

Merchandise: ______

1b. Are these purchases made with cash or on account? Please explain.

2. The purchase of supplies, equipment, and merchandise can be divided into four stages: requesting the needed items, ordering from a supplier, verifying items received, and processing the supplier's bill. Describe how these steps are taken at your company and who performs them.

3. In order to remind themselves when to pay invoices, many businesses use a tickler file, a file with a folder for each day of the month. Invoices are then filed by date.

 School-to-Work Handbook • 29

GLENCOE MULTIMEDIA

Electronic Field Trips in Accounting *Video Segment: Purchases and Cash Payments*
After viewing this video, students will be able to describe the purchasing process and how purchases and payments are recorded.

Glencoe Accounting: Electronic Learning Center *Chapter 15*
The CD-ROM program is ideal for visual learners since it incorporates video images, animation, and graphics to enliven the content of each lesson.

CHAPTER 15
SECTION 1, PAGES 388–392

1 FOCUS

Introducing the Section

In this section students will learn the steps for ordering new merchandise. They'll also learn how to calculate due dates and purchases discounts. Students will learn how to use the Purchases account for recording purchases of merchandise and its rules of debit and credit.

Section Concepts

- About the paperwork involved in the purchasing process.
- The purpose of the Purchases Discounts account.
- The purpose of the Purchases account and its rules of debit and credit.

Visual Learning

Section 1 Focus

Use **Transparency 15–1** to introduce section concepts.

BELL RINGER

Observation: A day or two before you plan to present this section, have students visit local stores to shop for something they want. In class, ask students to share their experiences. How many of them found exactly the item they wanted? Did any of them find similar items they would have bought instead? How many of them found their items out of stock? L1

SECTION 1

Purchasing Items Needed by a Business

What You'll Learn

- About the paperwork involved in the purchasing process.
- The purpose of the **Purchases Discounts** account.
- The purpose of the **Purchases** account and its rules of debit and credit.

Why It's Important

It is essential that businesses establish controls and procedures for handling the purchase of assets in a systematic manner because the purchasing process results in a large outflow of cash.

KEY TERMS

purchase requisition
purchase order
packing slip
processing stamp
purchases discount
discount period
Purchases account
cost of merchandise

In Chapter 14 you learned that the primary source of income for a merchandising business is from the sale of its merchandise. However, to sell merchandise, a business must first buy the items. The items you find for sale at Wal-Mart—housewares, clothing, sporting goods, jewelry—are all purchased from wholesalers and suppliers. In this chapter you will learn how to analyze transactions relating to the purchase of merchandise.

The Purchasing Process

All businesses, from the corner grocery store to a giant international corporation, are involved in the purchasing process. Retail businesses need shopping bags for customers, sales slips, and cash register tapes. They also need to purchase supplies, equipment, and merchandise.

The purchase of supplies, equipment, and merchandise is divided into four stages:

- requesting needed items
- ordering from a supplier
- verifying items received
- processing the supplier's invoice

Let's take a look at each of these stages.

Requesting Needed Items

In a small business, the owner does all the buying. In a large business, a separate purchasing department buys items for the entire company. When the company needs to buy equipment or supplies, or when the inventory of merchandise on hand is low, a purchase requisition is prepared.

A **purchase requisition** is a written request that a certain item or items be purchased. Usually a purchase requisition is a pre-numbered, multicopy form. The purchase requisition is approved by the manager of the department requesting the purchase. Then, the original of the purchase requisition is sent to the purchasing department or the purchasing agent. The person making the request keeps a copy. **Figure 15–1** shows the purchase requisition form used by On Your Mark Athletic Wear.

RESOURCE MANAGER

Reproducible Masters
- Lesson Plans
- Chapter Reviews and Working Papers (CRWP) TAE

Transparencies
- Section Focus Transparency
- Teaching Transparencies
- Source Document Transparencies
- Solution Transparencies

Multimedia
- Exam*View* CD-ROM
- Electronic Learning Center CD-ROM
- Interactive Lesson Planner CD-ROM

ON YOUR MARK ATHLETIC WEAR
PURCHASE REQUISITION

NO. 9421

FOR DEPARTMENT Shoes DATE Nov. 12, 20--

NOTIFY Vic Ventura ON DELIVERY DATE WANTED Dec. 15, 20--

QUANTITY	DESCRIPTION	STOCK NO.
20 Pair	Soft Cushion, White	94682
10 Pair	Soft Cushion, Black	94788
10 Pair	Low Cut, White	94281
10 Pair	Low Cut, Black	94666

ORDER FROM Pro Runner Warehouse APPROVED BY *Jennifer Mack*
SHOE DEPARTMENT MANAGER

Figure 15–1
Purchase Requisition

Ordering from a Supplier

A **purchase order** is a written *offer* to a supplier to buy certain items. Much of the information on the purchase order comes directly from the purchase requisition. Other information may be obtained from the supplier's catalog.

Look at the purchase order prepared by On Your Mark in **Figure 15–2.** The purchase order contains:

1. quantity
2. description
3. unit price
4. total cost
5. supplier's name and address
6. date needed
7. shipping method (optional)

The purchase order is a pre-numbered multi-copy form. The original of the purchase order is sent to the supplier. One copy of the purchase order is sent to the department requesting the items. Another copy is kept in the purchasing department.

Key Points

Forms Used in Purchasing

The purchase requisition stays inside the company (from the department making the request to the purchasing department). The purchase order is sent outside (from the purchasing department to the supplier).

ON YOUR MARK
ATHLETIC WEAR
595 Leslie Street, Dallas, TX 75207

PURCHASE ORDER
No. 9784

To
Pro Runner Warehouse 5
22009 Ben White Blvd.
Austin, TX 78705

Date: November 15, 20-- 6
Date Needed: December 15, 20--

Quantity 1	Item 2	Unit Price 3	Total 4
20 pair	Soft Cushion: White, #94682	$ 50.00	$ 1,000.00
10 pair	Soft Cushion: Black #94788	50.00	500.00
10 pair	Low Cut: White, #94281	40.00	400.00
10 pair	Low Cut: Black, #94666	40.00	400.00
	Total		$ 2,300.00

Figure 15–2
Purchase Order

CONNECT TO . . . ART

At television and motion picture awards ceremonies, accounting firms are called on to tally and verify vote results. The accounting firms' involvement with such programs adds authenticity to the vote counting and lends exposure to the accounting industry.

INTERDISCIPLINARY CONNECTIONS ACTIVITY

Art Can your students identify accounting or other financial occupations in the performing or fine arts career fields? Ask students to research organizations such as local symphony orchestras, dance companies, art galleries, television or radio stations, opera guilds, or community theaters. What financial jobs are needed to keep these arts organizations alive and thriving? Have students make a list of possible job opportunities in these fields.

2 TEACH

GUIDED PRACTICE

Reading Accounting

- As students read about the steps in the purchasing process, have them diagram or flowchart the steps and make notes about the forms prepared at each step. L1
- Ask a local businessperson who speaks both English and your students' first language to explain the purchasing process used in his or her business. ELL

Concept Development: The Purchasing Process

Discussion: When introducing the purchasing process, show students real-life examples of the forms. Try to obtain samples from local businesses of a purchase requisition, purchase order, verification form, and supplier's invoice. Or, invite a local businessperson who works with purchasing forms to explain the procedures used in her or his business. Ask the speaker to bring samples of the purchasing forms used by the business. L1

Visual Learning

Figure 15–1 Purchase Requisition

Using **Transparency 15–2,** discuss the purchase requisition. Ask students why the purchase requisition is not a source document. (It is not evidence of a transaction; no dollar amounts are included.)

Figure 15–2 Purchase Order

Using **Transparency 15–3,** discuss the purchase order. Point out the number of the purchase order (No. 9784), and explain how prenumbered forms are a part of internal control.

2 TEACH (Cont'd.)

Teaching Tips

Ask your principal for an office supply catalog your students could look at for sample forms and equipment.

Ask a local office supply store if they have samples of purchasing forms you might borrow.

Point out that purchasing procedures vary from one business to another, but the basic elements of a purchase are the same.

If you have a business simulation that includes source documents, remove examples of the purchasing forms to show to students.

Explain that an invoice is prepared by the supplier's accounting department and mailed to the buyer's accounting department. To the seller, this document is a sales invoice; to the buyer, it is a purchase invoice. Tell students they are keeping the accounting records for On Your Mark Athletic Wear. Is the invoice in Figure 15–3 a sales invoice or a purchase invoice? (Purchase invoice)

Explain why a business uses a date stamp.

Research: Have students interview local business owners about the purchasing procedures they use in their businesses. Ask the students to share their findings in class. L1

Verifying Items Received

Note that a purchase order is only an *offer* to buy items. Until the items are actually received, the buyer does not know whether or not the supplier has accepted the offer. A supplier may not be able to fill the purchase order because an item is out of stock or has been discontinued. The mailing of a purchase order, therefore, does not require a journal entry. A supplier accepts a purchase order by shipping the items requested and billing the buyer for these items.

When an order is shipped to a buyer, a packing slip is included with the order. A **packing slip** is a form that lists the items included in the shipment. When a shipment is received, it is immediately unpacked and checked against the quantities and items listed on the packing slip. If the contents of the shipment do not agree with those listed on the packing slip, a note about the differences is made on the packing slip. The packing slip is then sent to the accounting department to be checked against both the purchase order and the supplier's bill. A buyer does not have to pay for items that were not received or for damaged or unordered items that were returned to the supplier.

Processing the Supplier's Invoice

When items are shipped to a buyer, the supplier prepares a bill called an invoice. An invoice lists the credit terms; the quantity, description, unit price, and total cost of the items shipped; the buyer's purchase order number; and the method of shipment.

Key Points

Purchase Order

A purchase order is only an *offer* to buy and does not require a journal entry.

The invoice is sent directly to the buyer's accounting department, where it is date stamped to indicate when the invoice was received. The accounting clerk checks each detail (item, quantity, and price) on the invoice against the packing slip and the purchase order. This procedure verifies that the buyer is billed for the quantities and items actually ordered and received and that the prices are correct.

Once verified, the invoice is the source document for a journal entry. Before the invoice is recorded, a **processing stamp** is placed on the invoice to enter the following information: the date the invoice is to be paid, the discount amount, if any, the amount to be paid, and the check number.

The first three lines on the processing stamp are completed at the time the invoice is received. The check number is entered later, when the check is issued.

Look at the invoice in **Figure 15–3.** Notice the date stamp, which indicates when the invoice was received. The processing stamp information is complete except for the check number, which means that the invoice has been verified but not yet paid.

Key Points

Recording an Invoice

After a supplier's invoice is verified, a journal entry is made to record the amount owed.

Purchases Discounts

Suppliers frequently offer charge customers a cash discount for early payment. For the buyer, this discount is called a **purchases discount**. A purchases discount and cash discount are calculated in the same way.

Great Ideas *From the Classroom of...*

Collaboration and Creativity After initial presentation of the new chapter material, assign students to teams. Ask each team to create purchases and cash payments transactions for a business of their choice (a favorite sports team, Santa, Tom Turkey, Bill Gates, and so forth). Have teams trade transactions, then journalize and compare answers.

Jackie Jacobellis
Winnacunnet High School
Hampton, New Hampshire

PRO RUNNER WAREHOUSE
22009 Ben White Blvd.
Austin, TX 78705

REC'D DEC. 14, 20--

TO On Your Mark Athletic Wear
595 Leslie Street
Dallas, TX 75207

INVOICE NO. 7894

DATE: Dec. 14, 20--
ORDER NO.: 9784
SHIPPED BY: Federal Trucking
TERMS: 2/10, n/30

QTY.	ITEM	UNIT PRICE	TOTAL
20 pair	Soft Cushion: White, #94682	$ 50.00	$ 1,000.00
10 pair	Soft Cushion: Black, #94788	50.00	500.00
10 pair	Low Cut: White, #94281	40.00	400.00
10 pair	Low Cut: Black, #94666	40.00	400.00
	Total		$ 2,300.00

Due Date: 12/24
Discount: $ 46.00
Net Amount: $ 2,254.00
Check No.:

Figure 15–3 Invoice

For example, On Your Mark purchased $2,300 of merchandise on account from Pro Runner Warehouse. **Figure 15–3** shows the invoice dated December 14. The credit terms are 2/10, n/30. If On Your Mark pays for the merchandise on or before December 24, it may deduct 2% of the value of the merchandise. The 10 days, called the **discount period**, is the time within which an invoice must be paid if the discount is taken. If On Your Mark does not pay for the merchandise within the discount period, it pays the net, or total, amount within 30 days of the invoice date.

On Your Mark can save $46 if the invoice is paid within the 10-day discount period ending December 24. The end of the discount period can be determined by adding 10 days to the date of the invoice (December 14 + 10 days = December 24). The amount to be paid within the discount period is calculated as follows:

	Merchandise Purchased	×	Discount Rate	=	Discount
1.	$2,300	×	.02	=	$46

	Invoice Amount	−	Discount Amount	=	Amount Paid Within Discount Period
2.	$2,300	−	$46	=	$2,254

The Purchases Account

When a business buys merchandise to sell to customers, the cost of the merchandise is recorded in the **Purchases account**. The **Purchases** account is a temporary account, classified as a **cost of merchandise** account. Cost of merchandise accounts contain the actual cost to the business of the merchandise sold to customers.

Merchandise that is purchased for resale is a cost of doing business. Therefore, the **Purchases** account follows the rules of debit and credit for expense accounts. The **Purchases** account is increased by debits and decreased by credits. The normal balance of the **Purchases** account is a debit.

Key Points

Discount Period
The discount period is calculated from the date of the invoice, not the date the invoice is received.

Key Points

The Purchases Account
The **Purchases** account is classified as a cost of merchandise account. The cost of merchandise bought during the period is recorded in the **Purchases** account.

Purchases	
Debit + Increase Side Normal Balance	Credit − Decrease Side

Visual Learning

Figure 15–3 Invoice
Use **Transparency 15–4** to explain the different types of information on an invoice.

Concept Development: Purchases Discounts

Discussion: Review credit terms, how to calculate discounts, how to determine the amount to be paid, and how to determine the last day in the discount period. Point out that well-managed businesses usually pay within the discount period to avoid paying what are, in effect, very high interest charges for having the use of the invoice amount for the full term of the invoice (such as 30 days). L1

Thinking Algebraically

Evaluate: Give students this scenario: On the Mark Athletic Wear has purchased merchandise for $1,000, with terms of 2/10, n/30. Should the business save $20 by paying the invoice within 10 days, or should it conserve cash and treat the $20 as a reasonable charge for having use of $980 for an additional 20 days? Have students use the simple interest formula to calculate the interest rate represented by the charge of $20 for 20 days. (I = PRT; $20 = $980 × ? × 20/365. Restated to solve for the missing amount, $20 ÷ ($980 × 20/365) = .372 or 37.2%. The interest rate is very high, and the business should pay within the 10 days.) L2

Chapter Reviews and Working Papers
Refer students to the *Study Plan* located at the beginning of Chapter 15 in the workbook.

REINFORCING STUDY SKILLS

Using Active Listening Skills Learning through active listening may be difficult for many students who are skillful readers. Encourage students to participate actively in listening to lectures or oral reports. As they listen, they should focus on both the information presented and the actual task of listening attentively. Active listeners do the following: read assignments beforehand, keep their minds on the presentation, anticipate what the speaker will say next, relate information to personal life experiences, and formulate questions.

3 ASSESS

Thinking Critically (Answers)

1. A purchase requisition requests items to be ordered; the requisition is approved and a purchase order issued to a supplier; when received, the shipment is verified with the packing slip and approved for payment; the packing slip is checked against the invoice and payment is made.
2. The Purchases account and cash (or accounts payable if a credit sale).

Computing in the Business World (Answers)

Copy paper $34.00, art paper $60.00, globes $110.00, pencils $12.00, markers $26.00

Problem 15-1 (Answers)

1. Case Construction Company
2. Westmoreland Paint & Supply Co.
3. 7894
4. November 15, 20—
5. December 1, 20—
6. 25 gallons
7. 5 colors
8. White, gray, brown, beige, peach
9. $20.00
10. $500.00

Chapter Reviews and Working Papers Refer students to the Chapter 15 workbook pages to answer *Check Your Understanding* activities.

4 CLOSE

Section Wrap-Up

Writing: Have students write a paragraph describing the process of getting a music CD from the manufacturer to a local music store where they might buy it. L1

SECTION 1 Check Your Understanding

Now that you have studied this section, complete the following questions and problems.

Thinking Critically

1. Explain the steps in the purchasing process from the request for merchandise to the payment of the invoice.
2. When a business purchases merchandise for resale, what accounts are affected?

Computing in the Business World

As a new accountant for the South City School District, one of your primary duties involves preparing purchase requisitions. For each item ordered, you compute the extensions (quantity ordered multiplied by the cost per unit). On a separate sheet of paper, calculate the extensions for each of the following items ordered.

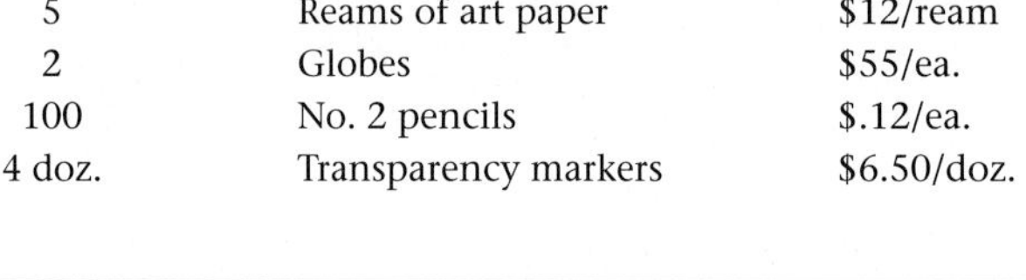

Quantity	Item Description	Unit Price
1	Box of copy paper	$34.00/box
5	Reams of art paper	$12/ream
2	Globes	$55/ea.
100	No. 2 pencils	$.12/ea.
4 doz.	Transparency markers	$6.50/doz.

Problem 15-1 Analyzing a Purchase Order

Instructions Analyze the purchase order shown below and answer the following questions in your working papers.

CASE CONSTRUCTION COMPANY
601 Mt. Lebanon Road, Shaker Heights, OH 44120

PURCHASE ORDER
No. 7894

To: Westmoreland Paint and Supply Co.
1714 Peak Road
Cleveland, OH 44109

Date: November 15, 20--
Date Needed: December 1, 20--

Quantity	Item	Unit Price	Total
4 gal.	Exterior paint, white, #682	$ 20.00	$ 80.00
4 gal.	Exterior paint, gray, #788	20.00	80.00
6 gal.	Exterior paint, brown, #281	20.00	120.00
6 gal.	Exterior paint, beige, #66	20.00	120.00
5 gal.	Exterior paint, peach, #711	20.00	100.00
	Total		$ 500.00

1. What company ordered the merchandise?
2. What company was asked to supply the merchandise?
3. What is the purchase order number?
4. When was the purchase order prepared?
5. When is the merchandise needed?
6. How many gallons of paint were ordered?
7. How many different colors of paint were ordered?
8. What colors were ordered?
9. How much does each gallon of paint cost?
10. What is the total cost of the order?

RETEACHING SECTION 1

Role-Playing the Purchasing Process Write the four stages of the purchasing process on the chalkboard. Ask five students to stand before the class, each one representing one of the following: the person requesting a purchase, the purchasing department, the supplier, the receiving department, and the accounting department. Write these form names on large pieces of cardboard: purchase requisition, purchase order, packing slip, invoice. Have the five students role-play the flow of the forms through the steps in the purchasing process. This activity will help students understand the purpose of each form and its relationship to the other purchasing forms.

SECTION 2

Analyzing and Recording Purchases on Account

In the previous section, you learned about the purchasing process. In this section you will learn how to record transactions involving the purchases of merchandise and other assets on account. You will also learn how to record purchases returns and purchases allowances.

A small retailer may rely on a bookkeeper or part-time accountant to record purchase transactions. A large company, like Kohl's Department Store, can have thousands of suppliers and therefore needs an entire accounts payable department to verify invoices and handle any discrepancies before recording purchases in the accounting records.

Analyzing Purchases of Assets on Account

Regardless of its type, size, or purpose, a retail business needs to buy supplies, equipment, and other assets. Most importantly, it needs to buy merchandise to resell to customers. These items may be bought on a cash basis or on account. Purchases on account are recorded in the accounts payable subsidiary ledger.

The Accounts Payable Subsidiary Ledger

In Chapter 14 you learned that when a business sells to many customers on credit, it is efficient to set up an accounts receivable subsidiary ledger. Likewise, when a business purchases from many suppliers on account, it is efficient to set up an **accounts payable subsidiary ledger** that contains an account for each supplier or creditor. The individual accounts in the accounts payable subsidiary ledger are summarized in the general ledger controlling account, **Accounts Payable.** The balance of the **Accounts Payable** controlling account and the total of all the account balances in the accounts payable subsidiary ledger must agree after posting.

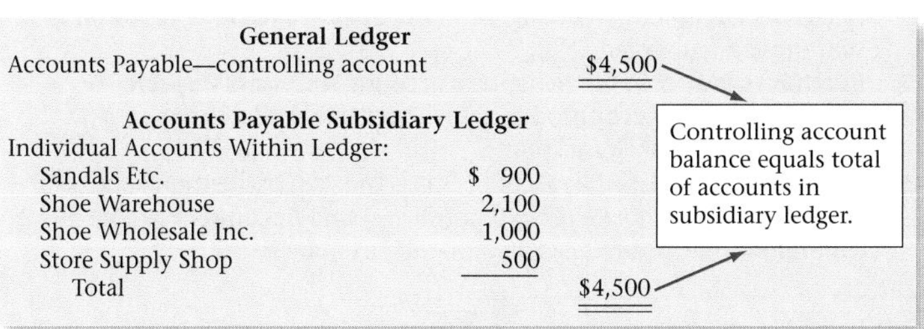

General Ledger

Accounts Payable—controlling account		$4,500

Accounts Payable Subsidiary Ledger

Individual Accounts Within Ledger:

Sandals Etc.	$ 900	
Shoe Warehouse	2,100	
Shoe Wholesale Inc.	1,000	
Store Supply Shop	500	
Total		$4,500

Controlling account balance equals total of accounts in subsidiary ledger.

***What* You'll Learn**

- How the accounts payable subsidiary ledger is used.
- How to record the purchase of merchandise on account.
- How to record the purchase of other assets on account.
- How to record purchases returns and allowances transactions.
- How to post to creditor accounts in the accounts payable subsidiary ledger.

***Why* It's Important**

Purchasing is a critical, ongoing process in a merchandising business; therefore, it is essential that you learn how to record the different kinds of purchases transactions.

KEY TERMS

accounts payable subsidiary ledger
tickler file
due dates
purchases returns
purchases allowances
debit memorandum

1 FOCUS

Introducing the Section

In this section students learn how to record several transactions relating to the purchase of merchandise on account. Students will learn how to use a purchases journal and an accounts payable subsidiary ledger.

Section Concepts

- How the accounts payable subsidiary ledger is used.
- How to record the purchase of merchandise on account.
- How to record the purchase of other assets on account.
- How to record purchases returns and allowances transactions.
- How to post to creditor accounts in the accounts payable subsidiary ledger.

Visual Learning

Section 2 Focus

Use **Transparency 15–5** to introduce section concepts.

BELL RINGER

Take a Poll: Ask your students how many of them (or their parents) have bought something on credit within the last month. Have students discuss the similarities between their purchases on credits and a business buying merchandise on account. Ask them how buying on account affects a business's accounting records. L1

Visual Learning

Accounts Payable Subsidiary Ledger, p. 393

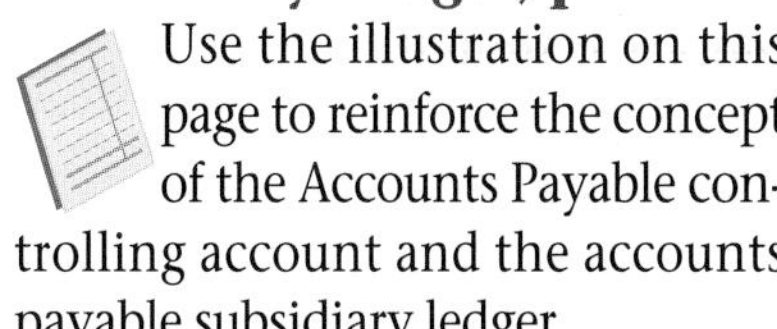
Use the illustration on this page to reinforce the concept of the Accounts Payable controlling account and the accounts payable subsidiary ledger.

RESOURCE MANAGER

Reproducible Masters
- Lesson Plans
- Chapter Reviews and Working Papers (CRWP) TAE
- Demonstration Problems

Transparencies
- Section Focus Transparency
- Teaching Transparencies
- Source Document Transparencies
- Solution Transparencies

Multimedia
- Exam*View* CD-ROM
- Electronic Learning Center CD-ROM
- Interactive Lesson Planner CD-ROM

CHAPTER 15
SECTION 2, PAGES 393–400

2 TEACH
GUIDED PRACTICE

Reading Accounting

• Learning to read source documents (such as invoices or purchase orders) accurately is a valuable skill for accountants. Try to obtain several examples of actual source documents from local businesses and have students practice reading and analyzing the documents. L1

Concept Development: Analyzing Purchases of Assets on Account

Discussion: Remind students that items purchased on account are liabilities for the business and are recorded as accounts payable. Organizing all accounts payable in a separate ledger helps the business owner or manager quickly analyze total amounts owed as well as amounts owed to each creditor. Point out that the accounts payable subsidiary ledger is similar to the accounts receivable ledger. The difference is that one records amounts owed to the business by customers and the other records amounts owed by the business.

Emphasize that the normal balance of an accounts payable account in the subsidiary ledger is a credit balance—just like its controlling account in the general ledger. Also point out that the forms for the two subsidiary ledgers are identical. The Balance column represents either a debit or a credit balance depending on whether the account is an account receivable or an account payable. L1

The Accounts Payable Subsidiary Ledger Form

The ledger account form used for the accounts payable subsidiary ledger, shown in **Figure 15–4**, is the same form that is used for the accounts receivable subsidiary ledger.

Figure 15–4 Subsidiary Ledger Account Form

NAME
ADDRESS

DATE		DESCRIPTION	POST. REF.	DEBIT	CREDIT	BALANCE

As you can see, the ledger account form has lines at the top for the creditor's name and address. In a manual accounting system, the accounts payable subsidiary ledger is arranged in alphabetical order. There are no account numbers. In a computerized accounting system, each creditor is assigned an account number.

The ledger account form has three amount columns. The Debit column records decreases to the account. Therefore, payments to creditors on account are recorded in the Debit column. The Credit column records increases to the account. Therefore, purchases on account are recorded in the Credit column. The Balance column shows the amount that is owed to the creditor. The normal balance of an Accounts Payable subsidiary account is a credit.

ACCOUNTING *Flashbacks*

ACCOUNTING ORGANIZATIONS

In 1973, an independent, seven-member, full-time Financial Accounting Standards Board was established. The private sector organization is responsible for the development of new financial accounting standards.

Recording the Purchase of Merchandise on Account

On Your Mark's first purchase transaction in December involves a purchase of merchandise on account.

Business Transaction

On December 14 On Your Mark purchased $2,300 in merchandise on account from Pro Runner Warehouse, Invoice 7894.

PRO RUNNER WAREHOUSE
22009 Ben White Blvd.
Austin, TX 78705

INVOICE NO. 7894
REC'D DEC. 14, 20--
DATE: Dec. 14, 20--
ORDER NO.: 9784
SHIPPED BY: Federal Trucking
TERMS: 2/10, n/30

TO On Your Mark Athletic Wear
595 Leslie Street
Dallas, TX 75207

QTY.	ITEM	UNIT PRICE	TOTAL
20 pair	Soft Cushion: White, #94682	$ 50.00	$ 1,000.00
10 pair	Soft Cushion: Black, #94788	50.00	500.00
10 pair	Low Cut: White, #94281	40.00	400.00
10 pair	Low Cut: Black, #94666	40.00	400.00
	Total		$ 2,300.00

Due Date: 12/24
Discount: $ 46.00
Net Amount: $ 2,254.00
Check No.:

ANALYSIS

Identify 1. The accounts affected are **Purchases**, **Accounts Payable** (controlling), and **Accounts Payable—Pro Runner Warehouse** (subsidiary).

Classify 2. **Purchases** is a cost of merchandise account. **Accounts Payable** (controlling) and **Accounts Payable—Pro Runner Warehouse** (subsidiary) are liability accounts.

+/− 3. **Purchases** is increased by $2,300. This is the cost of the merchandise purchased. **Accounts Payable** (controlling) and **Accounts Payable—Pro Runner Warehouse** (subsidiary) are increased by $2,300.

ACCOUNTING ISSUES

Document Management Systems It can take hours, or days, to track down filed or stored documents. The costs of time and productivity in maintaining paper document storage can be staggering. For example, studies show that professionals spend up to two hours a day retrieving files. Electronic document management systems that scan, store, retrieve, and manage information can save money and make business operations more efficient. Documents can be located quickly by searching for key words in the document. By adding a password to designated files, users can keep certain information confidential.

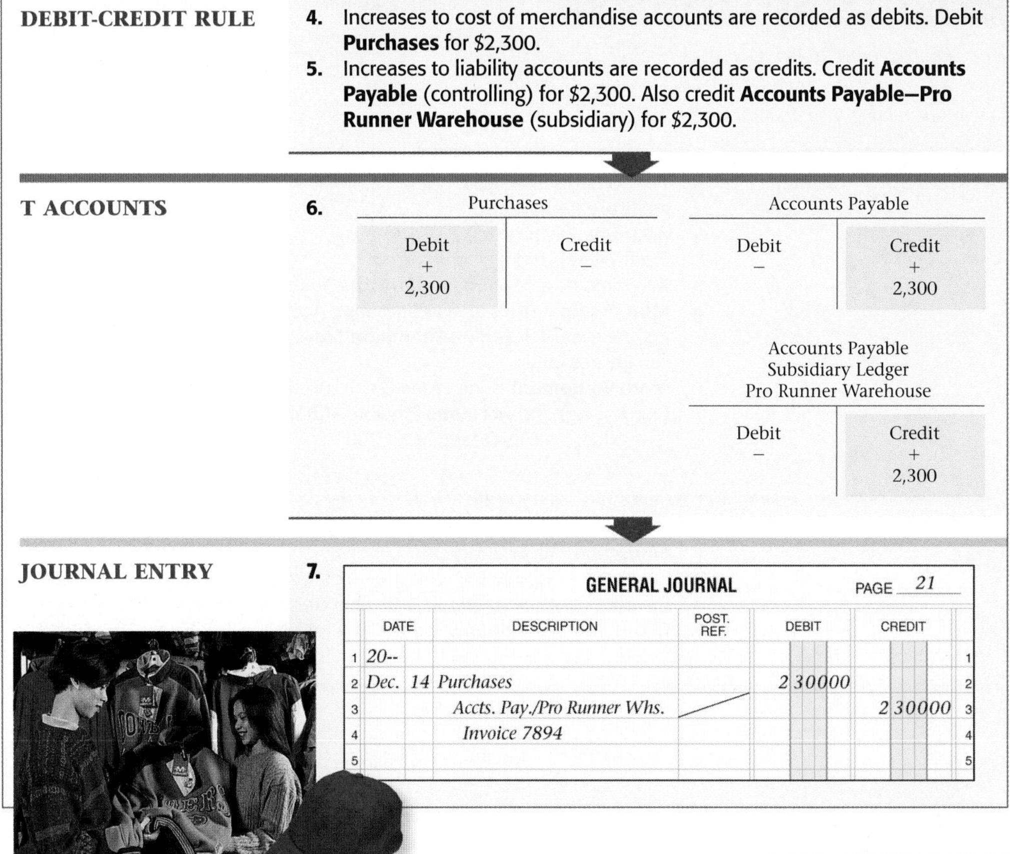

DEBIT-CREDIT RULE

4. Increases to cost of merchandise accounts are recorded as debits. Debit **Purchases** for $2,300.
5. Increases to liability accounts are recorded as credits. Credit **Accounts Payable** (controlling) for $2,300. Also credit **Accounts Payable–Pro Runner Warehouse** (subsidiary) for $2,300.

T ACCOUNTS

6.

Purchases	
Debit + 2,300	Credit –

Accounts Payable	
Debit –	Credit + 2,300

Accounts Payable Subsidiary Ledger Pro Runner Warehouse	
Debit –	Credit + 2,300

JOURNAL ENTRY

7. GENERAL JOURNAL PAGE 21

	DATE		DESCRIPTION	POST. REF.	DEBIT	CREDIT	
1	20--						1
2	Dec.	14	Purchases		2 300 00		2
3			Accts. Pay./Pro Runner Whs.	/		2 300 00	3
4			Invoice 7894				4
5							5

When this entry is recorded in the journal, a diagonal line is entered in the Posting Reference column to indicate that the credit amount is posted in *two* places.

- *First* post to the **Accounts Payable** controlling account in the general ledger.
- *Then* post to the **Pro Runner Warehouse** account in the accounts payable subsidiary ledger.

After the invoice from Pro Runner Warehouse is journalized, it is placed in a tickler file. A **tickler file** has a folder for each day of the month. Invoices are placed in the folders according to their **due dates**, that is, the dates that they are to be paid. For example, an invoice due on December 24 is placed in the folder marked "24."

Key Points

Recording and Posting a Purchase on Account

The purchase of merchandise on account is recorded in the journal as a debit to **Purchases** and a credit to **Accounts Payable.** The credit is posted to **Accounts Payable** (controlling) and to the accounts payable subsidiary ledger.

Recording Other Purchases on Account

On Your Mark purchases assets other than merchandise, such as supplies, computer equipment, and store equipment. The following example illustrates the purchase of store equipment on account.

2 TEACH (Cont'd.)

Visual Learning

Figure 15–4 Subsidiary Ledger Account Form

Use **Transparency 15–6** and have students explain the columns on a subsidiary ledger form.

Business Transaction

Use **Transparency 15–7** to guide students through the analysis and recording of a purchase of merchandise on account.

Teaching Tip

Remind students that the diagonal in the Posting Reference column means that the amount is posted to two different accounts: the Accounts Payable account in the general ledger and the subsidiary ledger account; in the example in the business transaction, Pro Runner Warehouse.

Demonstration Problem Step-by-Step Practice

Use demonstration problem 15–1 to give students practice in using T accounts to analyze purchases transactions.

MAKING CONNECTIONS TO DAILY LIFE

Purchasing Car Insurance Many students are responsible for purchasing their own car insurance. Ask students whether they must pay the premium for the insurance at the beginning or at the end of the insurance period. The response will be that they prepay. Ask students if they consider the cost of the premium to be an asset or an expense. Most students will consider it an expense. To illustrate how prepaid insurance is an asset, ask students to describe the benefit of purchasing insurance. The major benefit is protection, which is an asset until the insurance coverage expires.

2 TEACH (Cont'd.)

Visual Learning

Business Transaction

Use **Transparency 15–8** to guide students through the analysis and recording of purchase of equipment on account.

Teaching Tip

Explain to students why purchases on account of items other than merchandise are not recorded in the Purchases account. Point out that the Purchases account is used only for merchandise bought by the business so business owners and managers have a summary of the cost of all merchandise purchased during a fiscal period.

Demonstration Problem Step-by-Step Practice

Use demonstration problem 15–2 to give students practice in recording purchases transactions in the general journal.

Business Transaction

On December 15 On Your Mark received Invoice 3417, dated December 13, from Champion Store Supply for store equipment bought on account for $1,200, terms n/30.

CHAMPION STORE SUPPLY
47249 Randall Parkway
Dallas, TX 75207

INVOICE NO. 3417

REC'D DEC. 15, 20--

TO: On Your Mark Athletic Wear, 595 Leslie Street, Dallas, TX 75207

DATE: Dec. 13, 20--
ORDER NO.: 9795
SHIPPED BY: Federal Trucking
TERMS: n/30

QTY.	ITEM	UNIT PRICE	TOTAL
3	Corner Shelf Units	$ 300.00	$ 900.00
1	Shirt Rack	300.00	300.00
	Total		$ 1,200.00

Due Date: 1/12
Discount: $0.00
Net Amount: $1,200.00
Check No.:

ANALYSIS

Identify 1. The accounts affected are **Store Equipment, Accounts Payable** (controlling), and **Accounts Payable—Champion Store Supply** (subsidiary).

Classify 2. **Store Equipment** is an asset account. **Accounts Payable** (controlling) and **Accounts Payable—Champion Store Supply** (subsidiary) are liability accounts.

+/− 3. **Store Equipment** is increased by $1,200. **Accounts Payable** (controlling) and **Accounts Payable—Champion Store Supply** (subsidiary) are increased by $1,200.

DEBIT-CREDIT RULE

4. Increases to asset accounts are recorded as debits. Debit **Store Equipment** for $1,200.
5. Increases to liability accounts are recorded as credits. Credit **Accounts Payable** (controlling) for $1,200. Also credit **Accounts Payable—Champion Store Supply** (subsidiary) for $1,200.

T ACCOUNTS

6.

Store Equipment	
Debit +	Credit −
1,200	

Accounts Payable	
Debit −	Credit +
	1,200

Accounts Payable Subsidiary Ledger — Champion Store Supply

Debit −	Credit +
	1,200

JOURNAL ENTRY

7.

GENERAL JOURNAL — PAGE 21

	DATE		DESCRIPTION	POST. REF.	DEBIT	CREDIT	
5	Dec.	15	Store Equipment		1 200 00		5
6			Accts. Pay./Champion Store			1 200 00	6
7			Invoice 3417				7
8							8

Purchases Returns and Allowances

Occasionally, a business buys merchandise that, upon inspection, is unacceptable. A **purchases return** occurs when a business returns merchandise to the supplier for full credit. A **purchases allowance** occurs when a business keeps less than satisfactory merchandise and pays a reduced price.

MEETING SPECIAL NEEDS

Students with Behavior Disorders Students who have attention difficulties may find it easier to stay on target if they are actively involved in learning. Have students select one section of this chapter, such as "Purchases Returns and Allowances" on page 396, to teach to another student. Afterward, discuss with the students whether they learn better when they are the teacher or the student.

A **debit memorandum**, or debit memo, is used to notify suppliers (creditors) of a return or to request an allowance. The "debit" in debit memorandum indicates that the creditor's account will be debited, or decreased.

Figure 15–5 shows a debit memorandum prepared by On Your Mark. As you can see, the debit memorandum is prenumbered and has spaces for the creditor's name and address, and the invoice number. The original is sent to the creditor. The copy is the source document for the journal entry.

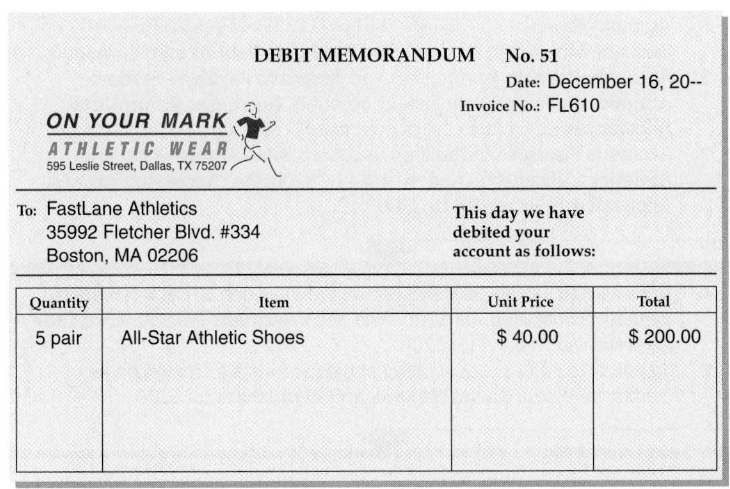
DEBIT MEMORANDUM No. 51

Date: December 16, 20--

Invoice No.: FL610

ON YOUR MARK ATHLETIC WEAR

595 Leslie Street, Dallas, TX 75207

To: FastLane Athletics
35992 Fletcher Blvd. #334
Boston, MA 02206

This day we have debited your account as follows:

Quantity	Item	Unit Price	Total
5 pair	All-Star Athletic Shoes	$ 40.00	$ 200.00

Figure 15–5 Debit Memorandum

Did You Know?

Vintage Clothing

In May 2001, Levi Strauss paid $46,532 at auction for what is thought to be the oldest pair of jeans in the world: a pair of men's denim work pants probably made in the 1880s. Found in Nevada in relatively good condition, the jeans were replicated in a new design by Levi's Vintage Clothing line.

A debit memorandum always results in a debit (decrease) to the **Accounts Payable** controlling account in the general ledger and to the creditor's account in the subsidiary ledger. The account credited depends upon whether the debit memorandum is for merchandise or for some other asset.

The **Purchases Returns and Allowances** account is used to record the return of merchandise to a supplier or to record an allowance. **Purchases Returns and Allowances** is classified as a *contra cost of merchandise* account. As a contra account, its balance reduces the balance of the related account, **Purchases.** The normal balance of **Purchases** is a debit, so the normal balance of **Purchases Returns and Allowances** is a credit. This relationship is shown in the T accounts below.

Purchases	
Debit + Increase Side Normal Balance	Credit – Decrease Side

Purchases Returns and Allowances	
Debit – Decrease Side	Credit + Increase Side Normal Balance

Calculator Hints

Clearing Amounts

If you have entered an incorrect amount while adding a long column of numbers:

- press the CE button *once* to clear that amount;
- previously entered numbers will not be deleted,
- and you can continue entering amounts to find the total.

Recording a Purchases Returns and Allowances Transaction

Now let's record a purchases return. On Your Mark prepared and sent the debit memorandum shown in **Figure 15–5.**

2 TEACH (Cont'd.)

Concept Development: Purchases Returns and Allowances

Discussion: Students learned in Chapter 14 how the seller of merchandise grants credit to dissatisfied customers. Businesses are also customers, and they buy items such as merchandise, supplies, and equipment that may need to be returned to the supplier. Such returns for credit are purchases returns or allowances.

Emphasize the difference between a return and an allowance. Point out that the buyer prepares a debit memorandum to inform the seller that items purchased were unsatisfactory. Use a T account to emphasize the association between "debit" memorandum and a "debit" to the creditor's account.

A purchases return or allowance decreases Purchases, but a separate account is used to record such amounts so they can more easily be traced in the accounting system. The Purchases account should always show the total amount of merchandise purchased for the accounting period and should not be "cluttered" with purchases returns and allowances. L1

Visual Learning

Figure 15–5 Debit Memorandum

Using **Transparency 15–9,** ask students to explain the information in a debit memorandum.

Math Review for Accounting

Photocopy appropriate *Activity Sheets* for students who need additional practice in basic math.

Math Skill Builder Activity

Clearing Amounts Have students use calculators to review the steps involved in clearing an incorrect amount. Ask students to enter two or three numbers and then purposely enter an incorrect number. To clear the incorrect entry, have them follow these steps: (1) press the CE button once to clear the incorrect entry; (2) enter the correct number—the first numbers entered should not have been erased; (3) complete the calculation.

CHAPTER 15
SECTION 2, PAGES 393–400

2 TEACH (Cont'd.)

Visual Learning

Business Transaction

Use **Transparency 15–10** to guide students through the analysis and recording of a purchases return.

Teaching Tips

Point out that Purchases Returns and Allowances is a contra cost of merchandise account; therefore, its balance decreases the balance of the Purchases account. Use T accounts to explain this relationship.

Remind students that Purchases Returns and Allowances is used only for returns or allowances for merchandise. Use T accounts to show students how the return of other items, such as office equipment, would be recorded.

Emphasize that the controlling account is always listed before the subsidiary ledger account name when recording a debit to the creditor's account for a purchases return or allowance.

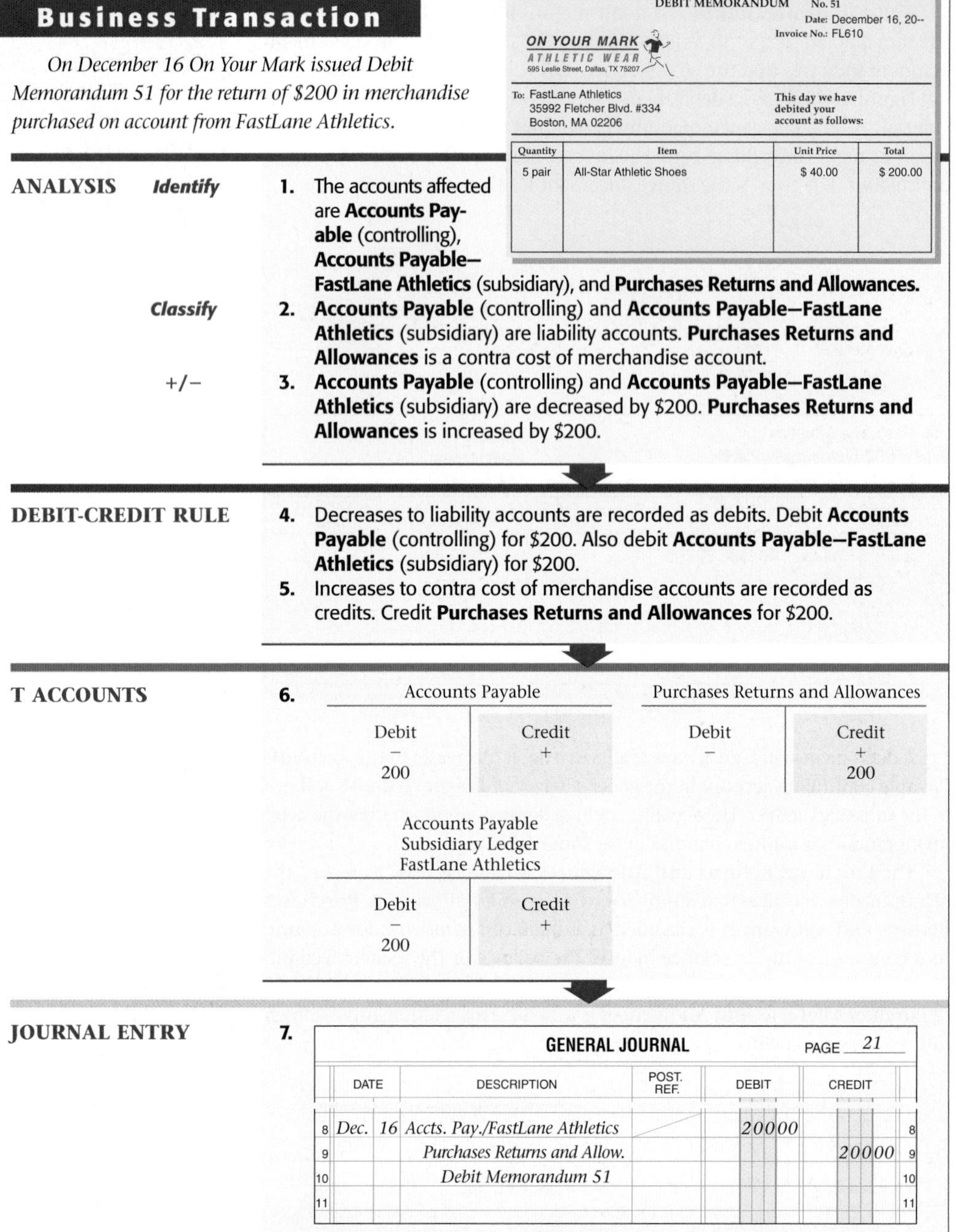

Business Transaction

On December 16 On Your Mark issued Debit Memorandum 51 for the return of $200 in merchandise purchased on account from FastLane Athletics.

DEBIT MEMORANDUM No. 51
Date: December 16, 20--
Invoice No.: FL610

ON YOUR MARK ATHLETIC WEAR
595 Leslie Street, Dallas, TX 75207

To: FastLane Athletics
35992 Fletcher Blvd. #334
Boston, MA 02206

This day we have debited your account as follows:

Quantity	Item	Unit Price	Total
5 pair	All-Star Athletic Shoes	$ 40.00	$ 200.00

ANALYSIS

Identify 1. The accounts affected are **Accounts Payable** (controlling), **Accounts Payable—FastLane Athletics** (subsidiary), and **Purchases Returns and Allowances.**

Classify 2. **Accounts Payable** (controlling) and **Accounts Payable—FastLane Athletics** (subsidiary) are liability accounts. **Purchases Returns and Allowances** is a contra cost of merchandise account.

+/− 3. **Accounts Payable** (controlling) and **Accounts Payable—FastLane Athletics** (subsidiary) are decreased by $200. **Purchases Returns and Allowances** is increased by $200.

DEBIT-CREDIT RULE

4. Decreases to liability accounts are recorded as debits. Debit **Accounts Payable** (controlling) for $200. Also debit **Accounts Payable—FastLane Athletics** (subsidiary) for $200.
5. Increases to contra cost of merchandise accounts are recorded as credits. Credit **Purchases Returns and Allowances** for $200.

T ACCOUNTS

6.

Accounts Payable

Debit −	Credit +
200	

Purchases Returns and Allowances

Debit −	Credit +
	200

Accounts Payable Subsidiary Ledger
FastLane Athletics

Debit −	Credit +
200	

JOURNAL ENTRY

7.

GENERAL JOURNAL PAGE 21

	DATE		DESCRIPTION	POST. REF.	DEBIT	CREDIT	
8	Dec.	16	Accts. Pay./FastLane Athletics		200 00		8
9			Purchases Returns and Allow.			200 00	9
10			Debit Memorandum 51				10
11							11

Posting to the Accounts Payable Subsidiary Ledger

In **Figure 15–6** notice how the transaction is posted. The $200 debit amount is posted to two accounts—the **Accounts Payable** controlling account

COOPERATIVE LEARNING ACTIVITY

Co-Op Co-Op Divide students into groups of two or three persons. Ask each group to research and prepare a report about a real-life case where employees embezzled money or stole merchandise from their employer. The report should include a discussion of internal controls that could have prevented the loss. Students must outline the necessary steps to complete the project and plan and negotiate their activities. When each group member has shared individual findings with other group members, the students combine the information, write a report, and choose a spokesperson to present findings to the class.

and the accounts payable subsidiary ledger account, **FastLane Athletics.** After the amount is posted to **Accounts Payable**, the account number *201* is entered to the *left* of the diagonal in the Posting Reference column. After the amount is posted to **FastLane Athletics**, a check mark (✓) is entered to the *right* of the diagonal line.

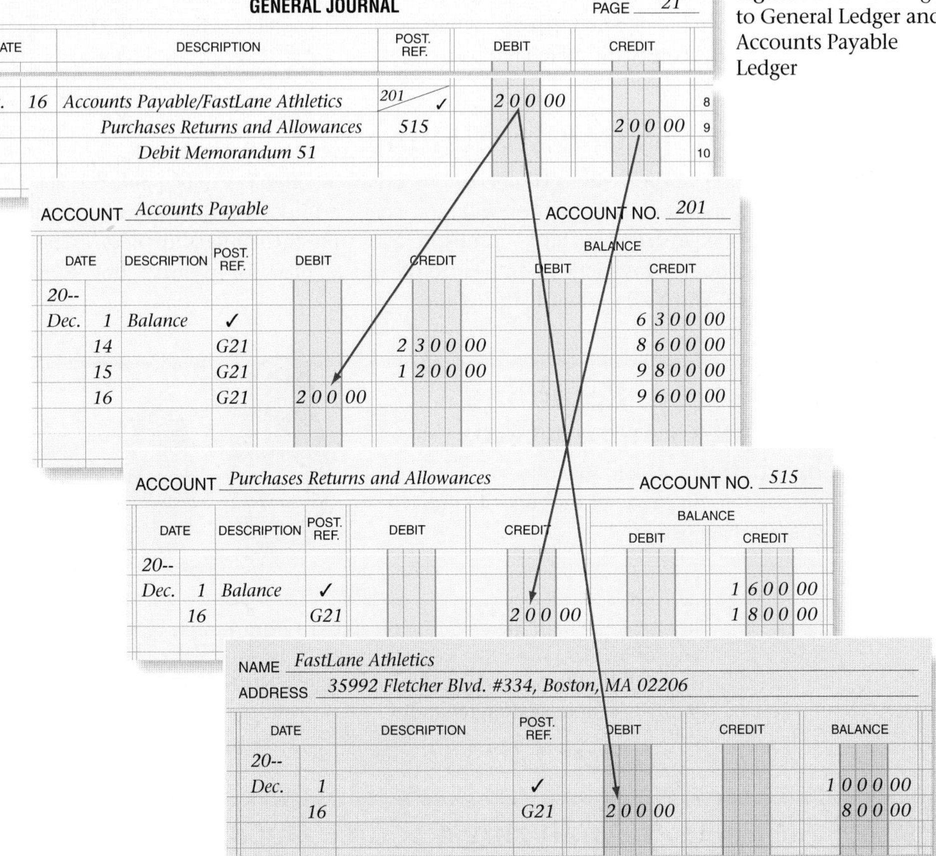

GENERAL JOURNAL — PAGE 21

	DATE		DESCRIPTION	POST. REF.	DEBIT	CREDIT	
8	Dec.	16	Accounts Payable/FastLane Athletics	201/✓	200 00		8
9			Purchases Returns and Allowances	515		200 00	9
10			Debit Memorandum 51				10
11							

ACCOUNT Accounts Payable — ACCOUNT NO. 201

DATE		DESCRIPTION	POST. REF.	DEBIT	CREDIT	BALANCE DEBIT	BALANCE CREDIT
20--							
Dec.	1	Balance	✓				6 300 00
	14		G21		2 300 00		8 600 00
	15		G21		1 200 00		9 800 00
	16		G21	200 00			9 600 00

ACCOUNT Purchases Returns and Allowances — ACCOUNT NO. 515

DATE		DESCRIPTION	POST. REF.	DEBIT	CREDIT	BALANCE DEBIT	BALANCE CREDIT
20--							
Dec.	1	Balance	✓				1 600 00
	16		G21		200 00		1 800 00

NAME FastLane Athletics
ADDRESS 35992 Fletcher Blvd. #334, Boston, MA 02206

DATE		DESCRIPTION	POST. REF.	DEBIT	CREDIT	BALANCE
20--						
Dec.	1		✓			1 000 00
	16		G21	200 00		800 00

Figure 15–6 Posting to General Ledger and Accounts Payable Ledger

ANALYZING FINANCIAL REPORTS

Identifying Corporate Goals

The information in an annual report is directed to a number of different audiences: potential buyers of company stock; existing shareholders; financial analysts and advisors; government regulators, such as the Securities and Exchange Commission (SEC); employees; and creditors.

▶ **Analyze the Report:**

Use the pages labeled "To Our Shareholders" at the back of your textbook. Answer these questions using the section titled "Forging Ahead."

1. List three goals for Office Depot.
2. How does Office Depot plan to communicate the differences between the company and its competitors?

2 TEACH (Cont'd.)

Visual Learning

Figure 15–6 Posting to General Ledger and Accounts Payable Ledger

Using **Transparency 15–11**, have students describe the process of posting to each type of ledger account. Have students explain why the debit amount is posted twice.

Critical Thinking: Have students explain why the debit amount in Figure 15–6 is posted twice, while the credit amount is posted only once. Why does this double posting not cause the accounting records of total debits and credits to balance incorrectly? (The debit amount is posted twice to keep the total amount the business owes up to date and to record the amount owed to the individual creditor. The credit amount is posted only once because only the general ledger account is affected since the effect of the transaction on the creditor's account was taken care of in the debit part of the entry. The records remain in balance because the posting to the general ledger is the only one that affects total debits and credits.) L1

The Office Depot 2001 Annual Report
Refer students to pages A-39–A-48 in the back of the book.

ANALYZING FINANCIAL REPORTS

Analyze the Report (Answers)

1. Answers may vary, but could include finding new ways to drive sales, manage costs, and increase shareholder value.
2. Office Depot is undertaking new branding and advertising initiatives that will define the differences between the company and its competitors.

CHAPTER 15
SECTION 2, PAGES 393–400

3 ASSESS

Thinking Critically (Answers)

1. A business with many creditors can track financial data more easily with an account for each creditor.
2. The business can send a debit memo to notify the creditor of the unacceptable merchandise.

Communicating Accounting (Answers)

Answers will vary but should include these points: A tickler file contains a folder for each day of the month. Invoices are placed in the file in due date order. Pull invoices due on the 15th and pay those first.

Problem 15–2 (Answers)

Sept. 2: Dr. Purchases $900; Cr. Accts. Pay./Sunrise Novelty Supply $900; Invoice SN110

Sept. 7: Dr. Accts. Pay./Sunrise Novelty Supply $50; Cr. Purchases Ret. & Allow. $50; Debit Memo 18

Problem 15–3 (Answers)

Nov. 12: Dr. Accts. Pay./Kaleidoscope Comics $16; Cr. Purchases Ret. & Allow. $16; Debit Memo 559

Chapter Reviews and Working Papers Refer students to the Chapter 15 workbook pages to answer *Check Your Understanding* activities.

4 CLOSE

Section Wrap-Up

Oral Exercise: Write T accounts on the chalkboard for Purchases, Purchases Discounts, and Purchases Returns and Allowances. Have students give you the rules of debit and credit and the normal balance for each account. L1

SECTION 2 Check Your Understanding

Now that you have studied this section, complete the following questions and problems.

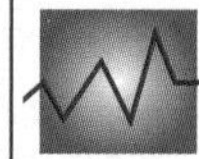

Thinking Critically

1. When and why would a business use an accounts payable subsidiary ledger?
2. When merchandise purchased by a business is unacceptable, what can the business do to recover the cost of the merchandise?

Communicating Accounting

Your job at The Writer's Desk is to process all the invoices to be paid. You keep a tickler file of invoices due. This year you will be on vacation from March 13 through April 2, so you leave detailed instructions for your substitute about how to process invoices. Prepare a memo with step-by-step instructions on how to prepare invoices for payment, how to record journal entries, and how to use the tickler file.

Problem 15–2 Recording Purchases Transactions

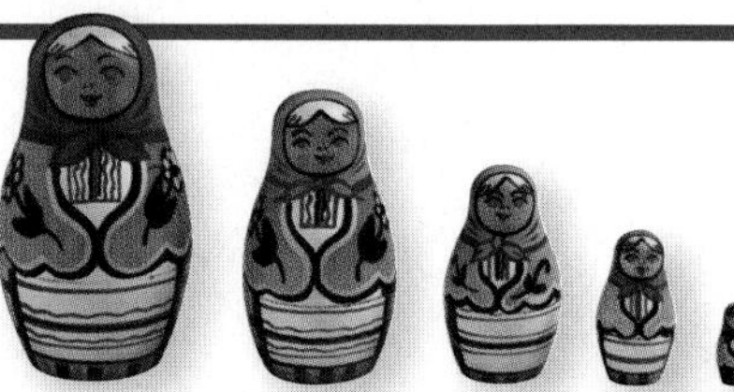

Instructions Record the following purchases transactions on page 7 of the general journal in your working papers.

Date	Transactions
Sept. 2	Purchased $900 in merchandise on account from Sunrise Novelty Supply, Invoice SN110.
7	Issued Debit Memorandum 18 to Sunrise Novelty Supply for a $50 allowance granted on damaged merchandise.

Problem 15–3 Analyzing a Source Document

As an accounting intern for Kaleidoscope Comics, you are expected to perform a variety of accounting tasks. Kaleidoscope's accountant gives you the debit memorandum shown at right.

Instructions

1. Analyze the source document. Determine which accounts are to be debited or credited.
2. Record the entry on page 15 of the general journal in your working papers.

DEBIT MEMORANDUM No. 559
Date: November 12, 20--
Invoice No.: 2260

Kaleidoscope Comics
2110 Brady Lane, Austin, TX 78748

To: Randall's Cafe and Bookstore

This day we have debited your account as follows:

Quantity	Item	Unit Price	Total
1 dz	Best of Dilbert	$ 7.50	$ 7.50
1 dz	Banzai Anime	8.50	8.50
			$ 16.00

RETEACHING SECTION 2

Using the Purchases Account Remind students that they have already learned about subsidiary ledgers and controlling accounts. Ask them to compare the accounts payable subsidiary ledger to the accounts receivable subsidiary ledger. How are they similar? How are they different? Both ledger forms have three amount columns. The two ledgers are different in their purpose: the accounts payable subsidiary ledger records amounts owed by the business and the accounts have a normal credit balance; the accounts receivable ledger records amounts owed to the business and the accounts have a normal debit balance.

ACCOUNTING CAREERS IN FOCUS

MICHELE MOLYNEUX
Credit Analyst
3Com Corporation

Q: How do you evaluate a company's credit?
A: I get reports from agencies such as Dun & Bradstreet and the SEC. I analyze financial statements. I look at the type of business, the number of years in business, and how the company is run.

For international businesses, I may get an opinion on the country from the state department, or read about it in a periodical such as the *Economist* or *The Wall Street Journal.* I also check with people who specialize in research. Then I make a judgment.

Tips from . . .

Robert Half International Inc.

When focusing on an accounting career, consider learning a second language. Among executives surveyed, 63 percent said Spanish is the most important language to know as business becomes more global.

Q: What do you like about your work?
A: I like the variety, the challenges, and the diversity. I work with people all over the world.

Q: What kind of attitude do you need?
A: Curiosity. You need to want to know the big picture. Because most companies do a lot of work overseas, you need an international perspective or you'll lose ground very quickly in this profession.

Q: Do you suggest learning another language?
A: I highly recommend proficiency in an Asian language. A Latin-American language and one of the European languages would also be helpful.

Q: Is a degree necessary?
A: I'm just finishing my bachelor's degree. Without it, I have been handicapped in terms of promotions and getting other jobs. Get your education early. You just can't compete without it.

CAREER FACTS

Nature of the Work: Analyze credit worthiness of corporate customers, evaluate credit risk and set credit line, and decide whether to extend credit.
Training or Education Needed: A bachelor's degree in accounting or finance, and a good working knowledge of one or two other languages.
Aptitudes, Abilities, and Skills: Time management skills, accounting, good judgement, investigative skills, analytical skills, communication skills, and interpersonal skills.
Salary Range: $30,000 to $65,000
Career Path: Get experience in different areas of accounting, purchasing, or customer service, then move into credit analysis.

Thinking Critically: In determining credit worthiness, why would it be important to get information about the country in which the company is located?

SCANS in the Workforce

Foundation Skills Connection

Reasoning
Have students practice their reasoning skills by reviewing this problem: An Asian firm has approached your students, who are bank loan representatives, to secure a loan for the purchase of a small U.S. computer manufacturer. What items should the students consider before agreeing to make the loan to the firm? L1

Workplace Competencies Connection

Allocating Money
Create a projected budget for a school-based T-shirt printing business. The school is allowed to charge enough money to recoup the cost of supplies and processing. Since the school has nonprofit tax status, the revenue gain must be kept low. L2

Cultural Diversity
If your students wanted to learn a foreign language through an "immersion experience" (that is, living in a foreign country), what information would they need to know before going to another country? Have students check with colleges, foreign exchange programs, or *au pair* services to learn about existing cultural exchange opportunities. Ask students to present their findings in a short report. L3

ACCOUNTING CAREERS IN FOCUS

Thinking Critically (Answer)
Cultural attitudes may affect payment and invoicing policies as well as how business is conducted. Also, monetary systems and government stability can affect businesses and their ability to pay for products and services.

ROBERT HALF CORNER

Learning a Second Language If your students intend to be active participants in the global workplace, they'll need to be fluent in a second language. Preferred languages are Spanish or French.

CHAPTER 15
SECTION 3, PAGES 402–408

1 FOCUS

Introducing the Section
In this section students will learn about cash payments businesses make and how to record such payments. They'll also learn how to calculate purchases discounts and to record shipping charges.

Section Concepts
- The different kinds of cash payments made by a business.
- The rules of debit and credit for the Purchases Discounts account.
- How shipping charges are recorded and whether the buyer or seller pays for them.

Visual Learning
Section 3 Focus
Use **Transparency 15–12** to introduce section concepts.

BELL RINGER
Analyzing: Share examples of business statements that require payment by check or money order. Have students read the notes on the statements advising the payer not to send cash. How does this policy benefit the business? How does it benefit the customer? (The business's employees will not be handling actual cash, which could be lost or stolen. The customer has a record of payment—the check or money order. Also, if the payment is lost in the mail, no cash is lost.) L1

Visual Learning
Business Transaction
Use **Transparency 15–13** to guide students through the analysis and recording of a cash payment for an insurance premium.

SECTION 3

Analyzing and Recording Cash Payments

What You'll Learn
- The different kinds of cash payments made by a business.
- The rules of debit and credit for the **Purchases Discounts** account.
- How shipping charges are recorded and whether the buyer or the seller pays for them.

Why It's Important
About half of all business transactions result in the outflow of cash; therefore, it is essential that you understand how businesses record various cash payment transactions.

KEY TERMS
premium
FOB destination
FOB shipping point
bankcard fee

International ACCOUNTING
International Cuisine
When inviting international clients to a meal, consider the customary diets of different religions and cultures.

If cash is the lifeblood of a business, the accounting department is its heart. All cash entering or leaving a business is "pumped" through the accounting department at some time. If it is not, cash losses may occur.

Controls over Cash

Earlier chapters explained ways to guard against losses of cash receipts. For example, businesses should deposit all cash receipts in a bank account. Cash payments must also be properly managed so that losses don't occur. The following are procedures to manage cash payments:

- Authorize all cash payments. Each payment is supported by an approved source document, such as an invoice.
- Write checks for all payments. Only authorized persons can sign checks.
- Use prenumbered checks.
- Retain and account for spoiled checks. Mark these checks "Void," and file them in sequence.

Analyzing Cash Payment Transactions

Businesses buy merchandise and other assets on account or by paying cash. At On Your Mark, all cash payments are made by check. When a cash payment is made, the details are recorded on the check stub. The check stub is the source document for the journal entry. Then, a check is prepared and signed by an authorized person. Let's look at two cash payment transactions that occur frequently.

Recording Cash Purchase of Insurance

Businesses buy insurance to protect against losses from hazards such as theft, fire, and flood. Insurance policies cover varying time periods, such as six months or one year. The cost of insurance protection is called the **premium**. A premium is paid in advance at the beginning of the covered period. Insurance paid in advance is an asset because until the insurance protection expires, it represents a benefit to the company. The insurance premium is recorded in the asset account, **Prepaid Insurance.**

RESOURCE MANAGER

Reproducible Masters
- Lesson Plans
- Chapter Reviews and Working Papers (CRWP) TAE
- Demonstration Problems

Transparencies
- Section Focus Transparency
- Teaching Transparencies
- Source Document Transparencies
- Solution Transparencies

Multimedia
- *ExamView* CD-ROM
- Electronic Learning Center CD-ROM
- Interactive Lesson Planner CD-ROM

Business Transaction

On December 17 On Your Mark paid $1,500 to Keystone Insurance Company for the premium on a six-month insurance policy, Check 1001.

ON YOUR MARK ATHLETIC WEAR
595 Leslie Street, Dallas, TX 75207
1001
22-523
4210
DATE Dec. 17 20--
PAY TO THE ORDER OF Keystone Insurance Company $ 1,500.00
One thousand five hundred and no/100 DOLLARS
Security National Bank
DALLAS, TEXAS
MEMO
Michael Brown
⑆4210225231⑆ 727596⑈ 1001

ANALYSIS ***Identify***
1. The accounts affected are **Prepaid Insurance** and **Cash in Bank.**

Classify
2. Both **Prepaid Insurance** and **Cash in Bank** are asset accounts.

+/−
3. **Prepaid Insurance** is increased by $1,500. **Cash in Bank** is decreased by $1,500.

DEBIT-CREDIT RULE
4. Increases to asset accounts are recorded as debits. Debit **Prepaid Insurance** for $1,500.
5. Decreases to asset accounts are recorded as credits. Credit **Cash in Bank** for $1,500.

T ACCOUNTS
6.

Prepaid Insurance	
Debit + 1,500	Credit −

Cash in Bank	
Debit +	Credit − 1,500

JOURNAL ENTRY
7.

GENERAL JOURNAL PAGE 21

	DATE		DESCRIPTION	POST. REF.	DEBIT	CREDIT	
11	Dec.	17	Prepaid Insurance		1 500 00		11
12			Cash in Bank			1 500 00	12
13			Check 1001				13
14							14

Recording Cash Purchases of Merchandise

Usually businesses purchase merchandise on account. Sometimes a business buys merchandise for cash. Let's look at an example of a cash purchase of merchandise.

Business Transaction

On December 19 On Your Mark purchased merchandise from FastLane Athletics for $1,300, Check 1002.

ON YOUR MARK ATHLETIC WEAR
595 Leslie Street, Dallas, TX 75207
1002
22-523
4210
DATE Dec. 19 20--
PAY TO THE ORDER OF FastLane Athletics $ 1,300.00
One thousand three hundred and no/100 DOLLARS
Security National Bank
DALLAS, TEXAS
MEMO
Michael Brown
⑆4210225231⑆ 727596⑈ 1002

ANALYSIS ***Identify***
1. The accounts affected are **Purchases** and **Cash in Bank.**

Classify
2. **Purchases** is a cost of merchandise account. **Cash in Bank** is an asset account.

+/−
3. **Purchases** is increased by $1,300. **Cash in Bank** is decreased by $1,300.

Teaching International ACCOUNTING

International Cuisine Divide the class into small groups and assign each group a country. Tell students that they are to choose a menu for entertaining a business client from their assigned country. They are to research the culture and plan an appropriate menu. Each group is to determine the appropriate time of the day to entertain the client and describe the appropriate attire for the occasion. Ask groups to share their plans in class.

2 TEACH

GUIDED PRACTICE

Reading Accounting

- Have students make a list of T accounts for the accounts used in purchases and cash payments transactions. Tell students to add the rules of debit and credit and the normal balance for each account. Students can then use their lists as a study aid. L1

Concept Development: Controls over Cash

Discussion: Emphasize that cash is a key asset and should be protected in these ways: (1) All cash payments must be authorized and supported by a source document, which demonstrates the importance of source documents and systems for routing them; (2) all checks should be prenumbered and should be signed only after the amount and the payee have been entered on the check; and (3) all voided checks must be accounted for. L1

Concept Development: Analyzing Cash Payment Transactions

Discussion: Point out to students that cash payments are made with checks, not with actual cash. The source document for most cash payment transactions is the check stub. Emphasize that making payments by check is a good internal control practice. L1

Strategies for Teaching International Accounting

To enrich study of International Accounting, refer to the additional critical thinking activities in the booklet.

2 TEACH (Cont'd.)

Visual Learning

Business Transaction

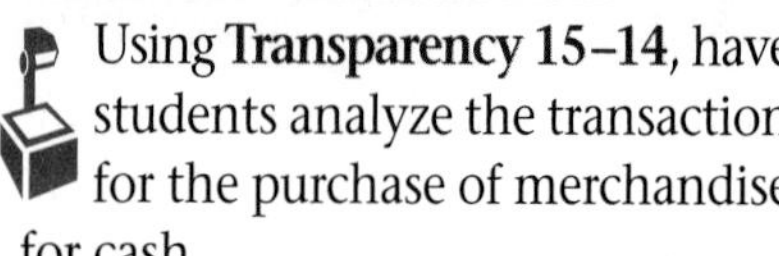

Using **Transparency 15–14**, have students analyze the transaction for the purchase of merchandise for cash.

Teaching Tips

Good internal control of cash requires that employees who keep the accounting records should not also write checks. Another safeguard is to require checks for large dollar amounts to be signed by two people.

Point out that many businesses pay invoices two to three days before the due date to allow for mail delivery.

When discussing the Purchases Discounts account, review the concept of contra accounts.

Team Thinking: Explain that department stores and other retail establishments that sell merchandise on credit do not typically offer cash discounts to customers. Divide students into teams and have each team come up with reasons for this practice. (Stores that issue their own credit cards have no incentive to collect payments early because they can collect interest on unpaid balances and on late payments. Banks issuing credit cards have no incentive because they earn money from customers who carry balances from month to month and pay interest on those balances.) L2

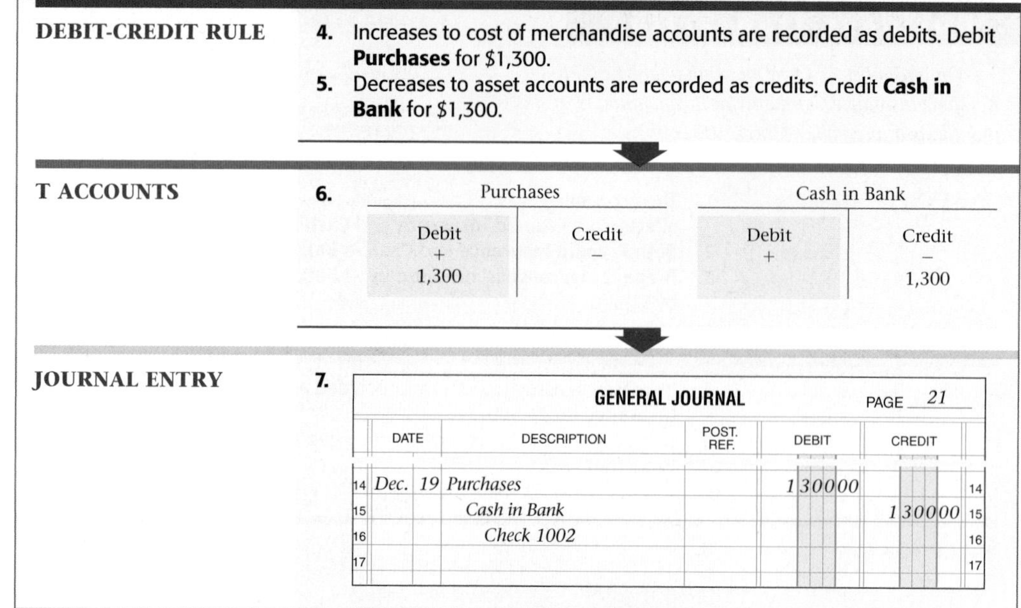

DEBIT-CREDIT RULE

4. Increases to cost of merchandise accounts are recorded as debits. Debit **Purchases** for $1,300.
5. Decreases to asset accounts are recorded as credits. Credit **Cash in Bank** for $1,300.

T ACCOUNTS

6.

Purchases	
Debit + 1,300	Credit –

Cash in Bank	
Debit +	Credit – 1,300

JOURNAL ENTRY

7.

GENERAL JOURNAL PAGE 21

	DATE		DESCRIPTION	POST. REF.	DEBIT	CREDIT	
14	Dec.	19	Purchases		1 300 00		14
15			Cash in Bank			1 300 00	15
16			Check 1002				16
17							17

Key Points

Recording Purchases

Regardless of when payment is made, now (cash) or later (on account), the **Purchases** account is debited when merchandise for resale is purchased.

Recording Cash Payments for Items Purchased on Account

An invoice received by a business is verified for items, quantities, and prices, recorded in the journal, and filed by due date in a tickler file.

Each day, the invoices due for payment are removed from the tickler file. Checks are prepared, signed by an authorized person, and mailed to creditors.

The amount of the check in payment of an invoice depends on the credit terms and the payment date. For example, On Your Mark purchased $2,300 of merchandise on account from Pro Runner Warehouse. The invoice, dated December 14, listed credit terms of 2/10, n/30. If On Your Mark pays for the merchandise on or before December 24, it can take a discount of $46.

When the invoice is paid on December 24, On Your Mark debits **Accounts Payable** (controlling) and **Accounts Payable—Pro Runner Warehouse** for the full amount of the invoice, $2,300. On Your Mark is paying for all of the merchandise and doesn't owe any more money on this purchase. **Cash in Bank** is credited for $2,254, the actual amount of the check. The difference between $2,300 and $2,254 is the cash discount, which is debited to the **Purchases Discounts** account.

The **Purchases Discounts** account tracks the cash discounts a business takes. **Purchases Discounts** is a contra cost of merchandise account. Its balance reduces the balance of the **Purchases** account. Its normal balance is therefore a credit.

Purchases	
Debit + Increase Side Normal Balance	Credit – Decrease Side

Purchases Discounts	
Debit – Decrease Side	Credit + Increase Side Normal Balance

Key Points

Purchases discounts

Taking all purchases discounts is a good business practice. Over a period of time, these discounts can add up to sizable cost savings.

CRITICAL THINKING ACTIVITY

Paying by Check Have students assume that they are accounting clerks for a local business and they misplace an invoice from a supplier. They telephone the supplier to get the current account balance. Why should they not write a check for payment without the invoice? (Any payment must be supported by a source document. In addition, invoices need to be verified and shipments checked before payment is made. The audit trail also is incomplete without an invoice.)

Business Transaction

On December 24 On Your Mark paid $2,254 to Pro Runner Warehouse for merchandise purchased on account, $2,300 less a discount of $46, Check 1003.

ON YOUR MARK ATHLETIC WEAR
595 Leslie Street, Dallas, TX 75207
1003
22-523
4210
DATE Dec. 24 20 --
PAY TO THE ORDER OF Pro Runner Warehouse $ 2,254.00
Two thousand two hundred fifty-four and no/100 DOLLARS
Security National Bank
DALLAS, TEXAS
MEMO
Michael Brown
⑆4210225 23⑆ 727596⑈ 1003

ANALYSIS

Identify
1. The accounts affected are **Accounts Payable** (controlling), **Accounts Payable–Pro Runner Warehouse** (subsidiary), **Cash in Bank**, and **Purchases Discounts.**

Classify
2. **Accounts Payable** (controlling) and **Accounts Payable–Pro Runner Warehouse** (subsidiary) are liability accounts. **Cash in Bank** is an asset account. **Purchases Discounts** is a contra cost of merchandise account.

+/−
3. **Accounts Payable** (controlling) and **Accounts Payable–Pro Runner Warehouse** (subsidiary) are decreased by $2,300. **Cash in Bank** is decreased by $2,254. **Purchases Discounts** is increased by $46.

DEBIT-CREDIT RULE

4. Decreases to liability accounts are recorded as debits. Debit **Accounts Payable** (controlling) for $2,300. Also debit **Accounts Payable–Pro Runner Warehouse** (subsidiary) for $2,300.
5. Decreases to asset accounts are recorded as credits. Credit **Cash in Bank** for $2,254. Increases to contra cost of merchandise accounts are recorded as credits. Credit **Purchases Discounts** for $46.

T ACCOUNTS

6.

Accounts Payable	
Debit −	Credit +
2,300	

Cash in Bank	
Debit +	Credit −
	2,254

Accounts Payable Subsidiary Ledger Pro Runner Warehouse	
Debit −	Credit +
2,300	

Purchases Discounts	
Debit −	Credit +
	46

JOURNAL ENTRY

7.

GENERAL JOURNAL PAGE *21*

	DATE		DESCRIPTION	POST. REF.	DEBIT	CREDIT	
17	*Dec.*	*24*	*Accts. Pay./Pro Runner Ware.*		*2 300 00*		17
18			*Cash in Bank*			*2 254 00*	18
19			*Purchases Discounts*			*46 00*	19
20			*Check 1003*				20
21							21

Other Cash Payments

When a company buys merchandise from a supplier, there is often a charge for shipping the goods. The shipping terms determine who will pay the shipping charges, either the buyer or the supplier.

Shipping terms are stated as either FOB destination or FOB shipping point. "FOB" stands for "free on board." **FOB destination** means that the

2 TEACH (Cont'd.)

Visual Learning

Business Transaction

Use **Transparency 15–15** to guide students through the analysis and recording of a cash payment involving a purchases discount.

Demonstration Problem Step-by-Step Practice

Use demonstration problem 15–3 to give students practice in analyzing cash payments transactions.

Critical Thinking: Have students discuss the advantages and disadvantages of taking cash discounts. (Advantages: Items purchased cost less in the long term; the business has more money to buy other items. Disadvantages: By making quick payment, the business pays out cash that could be used for other things; the business could have a negative cash flow if it pays out more money than it takes in.) L2

ADDRESSING MULTIPLE LEARNING STYLES

Visual/Spatial Learner Have visual learners prepare a flow chart describing the purchasing process. Have students include in the flow chart either a text reference or a visual image of the following source documents: (1) a purchase requisition, (2) a purchase order, (3) a packing slip, and (4) a debit memorandum.

2 TEACH (Cont'd.)

Teaching Tips

Another term for "transportation in" is "freight in."

Transportation In is classified as a cost of merchandise account because it increases the cost of merchandise purchased for resale.

To help students remember who pays for the shipping costs, point out that FOB destination means that the buyer takes ownership of a shipment at its destination; thus, the shipping costs are paid by the seller. FOB shipping point means that the buyer takes ownership of the shipment at the shipping point; thus, the buyer pays to get the merchandise to its location.

Visual Learning

Business Transaction

Use **Transparency 15–16** to discuss how to record shipping charges paid for by the buyer.

supplier pays the shipping cost to the buyer's destination or location. **FOB shipping point** means that the *buyer* pays the shipping charge from the supplier's shipping point.

Terms	Shipping Cost Paid By
FOB destination	Supplier
FOB shipping point	Buyer

Transportation In	
Debit + Increase Side Normal Balance	Credit – Decrease Side

A shipping charge is an additional cost of the merchandise. The account set up to handle shipping charges is **Transportation In**, which is a cost of merchandise account. **Transportation In** follows the rules of debit and credit for expense accounts. **Transportation In** is increased by debits and decreased by credits. The normal balance of **Transportation In** is a debit.

Here is an example of the payment of shipping charges.

Business Transaction

On December 24 On Your Mark issued Check 1004 for $275 to Dara's Delivery Service for shipping charges on merchandise purchased from Sports Link Footwear.

ON YOUR MARK ATHLETIC WEAR
595 Leslie Street, Dallas, TX 75207
1004
22-523
4210
DATE Dec. 24 20 --
PAY TO THE ORDER OF Dara's Delivery Service $ 275.00
Two hundred seventy-five and no/100 DOLLARS
Security National Bank
DALLAS, TEXAS
MEMO
Michael Brown
⑆4210225231⑆ 727596⑈ 1004

JOURNAL ENTRY

GENERAL JOURNAL PAGE 21

	DATE		DESCRIPTION	POST. REF.	DEBIT	CREDIT	
21	Dec.	24	Transportation In		275 00		21
22			Cash in Bank			275 00	22
23			Check 1004				23
24							24

Recording Bankcard Fees

The following transaction is made to record the bankcard fee deducted from the business checking account. Banks charge a fee for handling bankcard sales slips. This **bankcard fee** is usually a percentage of the total of the amounts recorded on the bankcard sales slips processed.

Business Transaction

On December 31 On Your Mark records the bankcard fee of $75, December bank statement.

JOURNAL ENTRY

GENERAL JOURNAL PAGE 21

	DATE		DESCRIPTION	POST. REF.	DEBIT	CREDIT	
24	Dec.	31	Bankcard Fees Expense		75 00		24
25			Cash in Bank			75 00	25
26			December Bank Statement				26
27							27

HOME AND COMMUNITY CONNECTIONS ACTIVITY

Bank Loans Have students work with family members or community members who can provide them information about applying for loans from a bank. Ask students to prepare a one-page paper on the various bank loan options for cars, college, or to start a business.

The journal entries for all the transactions discussed and illustrated in this chapter are shown in **Figure 15–7.**

GENERAL JOURNAL PAGE 21

DATE		DESCRIPTION	POST. REF.	DEBIT	CREDIT
20--					
Dec.	14	Purchases		2 300 00	
		Accounts Payable/Pro Runner Warehouse			2 300 00
		Invoice 7894			
	15	Store Equipment		1 200 00	
		Accounts Payable/Champion Store Supply			1 200 00
		Invoice 3417			
	16	Accounts Payable/FastLane Athletics		200 00	
		Purchases Returns & Allowances			200 00
		Debit Memorandum 51			
	17	Prepaid Insurance		1 500 00	
		Cash in Bank			1 500 00
		Check 1001			
	19	Purchases		1 300 00	
		Cash in Bank			1 300 00
		Check 1002			
	24	Accounts Payable/Pro Runner Warehouse		2 300 00	
		Cash in Bank			2 254 00
		Purchases Discounts			46 00
		Check 1003			
	24	Transportation In		275 00	
		Cash in Bank			275 00
		Check 1004			
	31	Bankcard Fees Expense		75 00	
		Cash in Bank			75 00
		December Bank Statement			

Figure 15–7 Journal Entries for December Business Transactions

A MATTER OF ETHICS

Showing Favoritism

Manufacturers, like any other business, must make purchases to carry out their business. Imagine that you work in the purchasing department of a large toy manufacturer like Mattel. You are responsible for placing orders for the toy parts that make up some of their cars and trucks. One supplier, whose prices are only slightly higher than others, has indicated that they would send free tickets to a sports event if you order most of the supplies from them.

Ethical Decision Making:

- What are the ethical issues?
- What are the alternatives?
- Who are the affected parties?
- How do the alternatives affect the parties?
- What would you do?

Teaching A MATTER OF ETHICS

Showing Favoritism Have students think about items they purchase and where they buy them. Do they have favorite stores or favorite salespeople, such as friends who work for retail stores? Discuss why students may prefer to buy from people they know and like. Then have students think about buying from the viewpoint of the business owner. As owners, would they rather have their employees buy from people they like or from companies that give the best product at the best price?

2 TEACH (Cont'd.)

Visual Learning

Figure 15–7 Journal Entries for December Business Transactions

Use **Transparency 15–17** to review the purchases and cash payments transactions students learned in this chapter.

Demonstration Problem Step-by-Step Practice

Use demonstration problem 15–4 to give students practice in analyzing and recording cash payment transactions in the general journal.

Teaching Tip

Point out that bankcard fees are a percentage of total bankcard sales. For example, banks handling the collection of VISA® or MasterCard® sales might charge a business 2 to 2.5 percent of the total sales charged on those cards.

Strategies for Teaching Ethics in Accounting

Photocopy the Chapter 15 *Student Activity Sheet* for students. Answers are also provided in the booklet.

CHAPTER 15
SECTION 3, PAGES 402–408

3 ASSESS

Thinking Critically (Answers)

1. An accounting clerk removes the invoices due for payment from a tickler file. Checks are prepared, signed by the authorized person, and mailed to creditors.
2. Premiums paid for insurance coverage are debited to an asset account, Prepaid Insurance.

Analyzing Accounting (Answer)

The shipping charges are 10 percent of the cost of the item.

Problem 15–4 (Answers)

May 1: Dr. Purchases $10,500; Cr. Cash in Bank $10,500; Check 1150
May 5: Dr. Transportation In $325; Cr. Cash in Bank $325; Check 1151
May 7: Dr. Prepaid Insurance $2,500; Cr. Cash in Bank $2,500; Check 1152

Chapter Reviews and Working Papers Refer students to the Chapter 15 workbook pages to answer *Check Your Understanding* activities.

4 CLOSE

Section Wrap-Up

Writing Exercise: Have students write a paragraph describing at least three types of cash payments a business might make and how those payments would be entered in the accounting records. L1

SECTION 3 Check Your Understanding

Now that you have studied this section, complete the following questions and problems.

Thinking Critically

1. What steps are involved in the payment of an invoice?
2. How do businesses record premium payments for insurance coverage?

Analyzing Accounting

Clara's Designs is a crafts store with a large inventory of seasonal crafts items. As the inventory clerk, you are to create a chart or graph to compare the cost of the items purchased and the related shipping charges. Using the data given below, design a chart or graph that depicts both sets of data. What conclusions can you draw from your chart or graph?

	Cost of Item	Shipping Charges
Holiday decorator ribbon	$2,000	$200
Door wreaths and hangers	3,200	320
Potpourri	1,200	120
Styrofoam trees	4,350	435

Problem 15–4 Recording Cash Payment Transactions

Meadow Link Golf Club had the following cash payment transactions.

Instructions Record the following transactions on page 6 of the general journal in your working papers.

Date	Transactions
May 1	Purchased $10,500 in golf equipment (merchandise) from TopMax Golf Manufacturers, Check 1150.
5	Issued Check 1151 for $325 to Franco's Trucking for delivery charges on merchandise bought from TopMax Golf Manufacturers.
7	Paid Lone Star Insurance Company $2,500 for the annual premium on an insurance policy, Check 1152.

RETEACHING SECTION 3

Mastering the Posting Process Review the reason for posting to both the accounts payable controlling account and the accounts payable subsidiary ledger. Point out in Figure 15–7 on page 407 that a diagonal is used in the posting reference column in the general journal to show amounts that are to be posted to the general ledger and to a subsidiary ledger. If any students are having difficulty with the posting process, ask for volunteers among students who have mastered posting to help those who are having difficulties. Allow them several minutes of class time, while others are working on problems, to work together on posting.

CHAPTER 15 SUMMARY

KEY CONCEPTS

1. There are four documents used in the purchasing process:
   - The purchase requisition is a request to order goods.
   - The purchase order is an offer to buy goods.
   - The packing slip is a list of the goods shipped.
   - The invoice lists the quantity, description, unit price, and total cost of the items shipped to the buyer.
2. When an invoice is received by the accounting department, it is checked against the purchase order and the packing slip for items, quantities, and prices.
3. After the invoices are recorded in the journal, they are filed according to their due dates in a tickler file. A tickler file contains a folder for each day of the month.
4. The **Purchases** account is used to record the cost of merchandise purchased during the period. **Purchases** is a cost of merchandise account. The rules of debit and credit for **Purchases** are the same as those for expense accounts.
5. Suppliers may offer cash discounts to their credit customers to encourage prompt payment. Buyers who take a cash discount record it in the **Purchases Discounts** account. **Purchases Discounts** is a contra cost of merchandise account.
6. When the buyer receives credit for returned or damaged merchandise, the amount is recorded in the **Purchases Returns and Allowances** account. **Purchases Returns and Allowances** is a contra cost of merchandise account.
7. The shipping charges for merchandise purchased from suppliers are considered an additional cost of merchandise. Shipping charges are debited to the **Transportation In** account, which is a cost of merchandise account.
8. The accounts payable subsidiary ledger contains an account for each creditor. The total of the account balances in the accounts payable subsidiary ledger must match the balance of the **Accounts Payable** controlling account in the general ledger.
9. The premium paid for insurance coverage is debited to **Prepaid Insurance. Prepaid Insurance** is an asset account.
10. Good internal controls include proper management of cash payments. All cash payments should be authorized, all cash payments should be made by check, and all checks should be signed by an authorized person.

Purchases	
Debit + Increase Side Normal Balance	Credit – Decrease Side

Purchases Discounts	
Debit – Decrease Side	Credit + Increase Side Normal Balance

Purchases Returns and Allowances	
Debit – Decrease Side	Credit + Increase Side Normal Balance

Transportation In	
Debit + Increase Side Normal Balance	Credit – Decrease Side

Prepaid Insurance	
Debit + Increase Side Normal Balance	Credit – Decrease Side

ANSWERS

1. purchasing process
2. supplier's invoice
3. Purchases
4. processing stamp
5. contra
6. Purchases Returns and Allowances
7. subsidiary
8. credit
9. debit memorandum
10. shipping point

Chapter 15 Quiz

Student ____ Class ____ Instructor ____
Date Assigned ____ Date Completed ____

CHAPTER 15 QUIZ

Accounting for Purchases and Cash Payments

QUESTIONS (Completion)

Directions: Fill in the blank with the term that best completes each sentence.

1. Requesting needed items, ordering, verifying items received, and process the supplier's invoice are steps in the ______.
2. Purchases of merchandise on account are journalized when the ______ is processed.
3. The ______ account is used to record all merchandise purchased by the business for resale.
4. A ______ indicates when an invoice is to be paid.
5. Purchases Discounts is a ______ account.
6. A return of merchandise to the seller is recorded in the ______.
7. Purchases on account are posted to a general ledger account and a ______ ledger account.
8. The Purchases Discounts account has a normal ______ balance.
9. A ______ is used to notify suppliers or a purchase return or allowance.
10. When the buyer pays the shipping charges, the merchandise is sent FOB ______.

 Chapter Quizzes • 17

QUESTIONS (Completion)

1. Requesting needed items, ordering, verifying items received, and processing the supplier's invoice are steps in the ______.
2. Purchases of merchandise on account are journalized when the ______ is processed.
3. The ______ account is used to record all merchandise purchased by the business for resale.
4. A ______ indicates when an invoice is to be paid.
5. Purchases Discounts is a ______ account.
6. A return of merchandise to the seller is recorded in the ______ account.
7. Purchases on account are posted to a general ledger account and a ______ ledger account.
8. The Purchases Discounts account has a normal ______ balance.
9. A ______ is used to notify suppliers or a purchase return or allowance.
10. When the buyer pays the shipping charges, the merchandise is sent FOB ______.

USING KEY TERMS

See the *Glossary* for the definitions of these terms. Have students share their lists of paired terms in class. Discuss any differences in the way students pair the terms.

Understanding Accounting Concepts and Procedures

(Answers)

1. To verify that the company is being billed only for the quantities and items actually ordered and received.
2. (a) The date the invoice is to be paid; (b) the discount amount, if any; (c) the amount to be paid, or the net amount of the invoice less the discount; and (d) the check number.
3. To encourage the customer to pay promptly.
4. A tickler file is a file that contains a folder for each day of the month. Invoices are placed in the tickler file according to their due dates.
5. A purchases return occurs when a business returns merchandise bought on account to the supplier for full credit. A purchases allowance occurs when a business keeps unsatisfactory merchandise but pays less than its original purchase price.
6. (a) All cash payments should be authorized; (b) each authorization should be supported by an approved source document; (c) all payments should be made by check; (d) all checks should be signed only by an authorized person or persons.
7. Shipping charges are a cost of doing business and add to the cost of merchandise.
8. The monthly bank statement.
9. On the dollar volume of the bankcard sales processed.
10. Bankcard Fees Expense.

USING KEY TERMS

Work with a partner to pair these terms. Discuss the relationship between the terms. Is one the result of another? Are they opposite? Once you agree, write out your explanation for each pair.

accounts payable subsidiary ledger
bankcard fee
cost of merchandise
debit memorandum
discount period
due dates
FOB destination
FOB shipping point
packing slip
premium
processing stamp
purchase order
purchase requisition
Purchases account
purchases allowances
purchases discount
purchases returns
tickler file

Understanding Accounting Concepts and Procedures

Instructions

On a separate sheet of paper, answer the following questions:

1. Why is an invoice checked against both the purchase order and the packing slip?
2. What information is included on a processing stamp?
3. Why do suppliers give cash discounts to credit customers?
4. What is a tickler file? How are invoices filed in a tickler file?
5. What is a purchases return? What is a purchases allowance?
6. List four procedures that a business should use to control its cash payments.
7. Why are shipping charges an additional cost of merchandise purchased for resale?
8. What is the source document for recording the bank card fees?
9. On what amount is the bank card fee based?
10. To which account are bank card fees debited?

ASSESSMENT RESOURCES

Choose assessment strategies from the following pages to evaluate your students' progress.

Student Edition
Check Your Understanding, pp. 392, 400, 408
Chapter 15 Problems, pp. 413–417
Analyzing Financial Reports, p. 399

Assessment and Evaluation Masters
Chapter 15 Study Plan, *Glencoe Workbook (CRWP)*
Chapter 15 Self-Test, *Glencoe Workbook (CRWP)*
Chapter 15 Test, *Chapter Tests* Booklet
Chapter 15 Activity, *School-to-Work Handbook*
Chapter 15 **Exam***View*

Teacher Wraparound Edition
Critical Thinking Activity, p. 404
Reteaching Sections 1–3, pp. 392, 400, 408
Chapter 15 Quiz, p. 409

Case Study...

Merchandising Business: Sportswear Store

The Sports Loft is a retail store that sells sports clothing, accessories, and equipment. Janet wants you to design a more automated system for ordering merchandise that will free her for other management duties.

Thinking Critically:

1. Identify issues involved in creating a new purchasing process. For example, how is low stock to be identified? If you think an electronic system is needed, specify the information it should collect and how new orders would be triggered.
2. Write a one-page report suggesting a purchasing system for The Sports Loft. Include a description of any forms needed. Draw a diagram if necessary.

*inter*NET CONNECTION

Fraud Detection

The Association of Certified Fraud Examiners considers occupational fraud and abuse to be a serious problem in the U.S. Most accountants believe that fraud cannot be eliminated, but that it can be reduced.

Do This:

Locate sites on the Internet related to occupational fraud and abuse and answer the following questions.

1. What organizations are most vulnerable to occupational fraud and abuse? Why?
2. Are regular audits designed to detect fraud and abuse?
3. How is most fraud discovered?

Conducting an Audit with Alex

The following entries were made in the general journal for Nova Shoe Shop.

Instructions

Review each transaction and record any errors on a separate sheet of paper.

On June 1 Nova issued Check 557 for $105 to Don's Deliveries for shipping charges on merchandise purchased from E-Z Shoe Supply.

GENERAL JOURNAL — PAGE 3

	DATE		DESCRIPTION	POST. REF.	DEBIT	CREDIT	
1	20--						1
2	June	6	Purchases		105 00		2
3			Cash in Bank			105 00	3
4			Check 557				4
5							5

On June 6 Nova purchased $200 in supplies from Bayside Office Supply, Check 558.

GENERAL JOURNAL — PAGE 3

	DATE		DESCRIPTION	POST. REF.	DEBIT	CREDIT	
1	20--						1
2	June	9	Purchases		200 00		2
3			Cash in Bank			200 00	3
4			Check 585				4
5							5

Workplace Skills

Monitoring and Correcting Performance of Systems

Identifying trends, predicting changes, finding problems, and applying solutions are skills of a "systems thinker."

On the Job:

After working for Action Athletics for one year, you recognize your customers' growing interest in cycling. Your community is hosting a large mountain bike competition. You see an opportunity for Action Athletics to increase sales of cycling gear. You recommend to management that they adjust and upgrade their cycling merchandise line to appeal to this growing market.

Thinking Critically:

1. Pair up with a student and role play your "sales pitch" to persuade your employer to add to their current merchandise line.
2. Using a spreadsheet program, make a list of 10 biking accessories to add to the inventory. For each item, provide reasonable estimates for price and one month's sales. Assume that approximately 200 cyclists will visit the store in one month.

*inter*NET CONNECTION www.glencoe.com

Do This (Answers)

Search the Association of Certified Fraud Examiners' Web site www.cfenet.com, or on terms such as "occupational fraud."

1. Companies with fewer than 100 employees; because sophisticated internal controls are less common in smaller organizations.
2. Few cases of fraud are discovered through routine audits.
3. As a result of tips and complaints from other employees.

Case Study...

Thinking Critically (Answers)

1. Answers may vary. This could be anything from a simple system where you would periodically enters sales data to see the new inventory level, to a fully functional perpetual inventory system that would scan merchandise when sold and automatically update the inventory.
2. Answers may vary. Evaluate students' papers for correct grammar and the logical progression of ideas.

Workplace Skills

Thinking Critically (Answers)

1. Answers will vary. Circulate around the room and help students with the art of sales and persuasion. Ask a pair of students to role-play their conversation for the class.
2. Answers will vary. Spreadsheets should show names of merchandise, unit costs, projected sales, and projected revenues.

Conducting an Audit with Alex

(Answers)

Corrected entries:

June 1: Dr. Transportation In $105; Cr. Cash in Bank $105; Check 557

June 6: Dr. Supplies $200; Cr. Cash in Bank $200; Check 558

Internet Resources and Activities Handbook

Refer students to the booklet for additional Internet activities.

PEACHTREE CORNER

Purchases on Account

You cannot enter purchases on account in the general journal using Peachtree software. To enter invoices, select **Purchases/Receive Inventory** from the ***Tasks*** menu. Or click the **Purchases** navigation aid at the bottom of the screen and choose **Purchases/Receive Inventory**.

Tasks Analysis Options Reports
Quotes/Sales Orders
Sales/Invoicing...
Receipts...
Finance Charge...
Select for Deposit...
Purchase Orders...
Purchases/Receive Inventory...
Select for Payment...
Payments...

Cash Payments

To enter cash payments, select **Payments** from the ***Tasks*** menu. Or click the **Purchases** navigation aid at the bottom of the screen and choose **Payments**.

Tasks Analysis Options Reports
Quotes/Sales Orders
Sales/Invoicing...
Receipts...
Finance Charge...
Select for Deposit...
Purchase Orders...
Purchases/Receive Inventory...
Select for Payment...
Payments...
Write Checks...

Recording Purchases and Cash Payments

Making the Transition from a Manual to a Computerized System

Task	Perform Accounting Procedures Using Manual Methods	Perform Accounting Procedures Using Automated Methods
Recording purchases transactions	1. General journal entries are prepared and then posted based on an invoice for merchandise purchased on account or for cash.	1. The purchase can be recorded when the merchandise is received, when the invoice is received, or when the cash purchase is made. Journal entries are automatically generated from the invoice information and posted to the general ledger.
Recording cash payment transactions	1. Checks are prepared in payment of an invoice or memorandum. 2. Journal entries are prepared to record the check. 3. Journal entries are posted to the general ledger. 4. New account balances are calculated.	1. Journal entries are automatically generated as the check for payment is prepared. 2. Journal entries are posted and account balances updated.

Recording Purchases and Cash Payments

Peachtree Question	Description
How do I record the purchase of merchandise on account?	1. Select **Purchases/Receive Merchandise** from the ***Tasks*** menu. 2. Enter Vendor ID, Invoice No., and Date. 3. Select the *Apply to Purchases* tab. 4. Enter quantity, description, GL account, and unit price for each item. 5. Click *Save*.
How do I record cash (check) purchases for merchandise or miscellaneous expenses?	1. Select **Payments** from the ***Tasks*** menu. 2. Enter the Vendor ID, Check No., Date, and Cash GL account number. 3. Click the *Apply to Expenses* tab. 4. Enter quantity, description, GL account, and unit price for each item. 5. Click *Save*.
How do I record payments on account?	1. Select **Payments** from the ***Tasks*** menu. 2. Enter the Vendor ID, Check No., Date, and Cash GL account number. 3. Click the *Apply to Invoices* tab. 4. Select the invoice to be paid. 5. Verify or enter the amount being paid. Click *Save*.
What does the software do "behind the scenes"?	• For purchases and cash payments, the software automatically updates the vendor's or creditor's account and the general ledger accounts.

For detailed instructions: See the **Peachtree User Guide** in your Glencoe Working Papers.

Peachtree® Answers to Frequently Asked Questions

Q: Which general ledger account should you use to record a debit memorandum transaction for damaged supplies?

A: Use the **Supplies** account, not the **Purchases Returns and Allowances** account. Only use **Purchases Returns and Allowances** when you record a debit memo for damaged merchandise.

For additional information, refer to your *Glencoe Peachtree Accounting User Guide*.

APPLICATION OPTIONS

Problem 15–5 Determining Due Dates and Discount Amounts

Sunset Surfwear frequently purchases merchandise on account. When invoices are received, a processing stamp is placed on the invoice indicating the due date, the amount of any discount, and the amount to be paid. The following invoices were received during March.

	Invoice Number	Invoice Date	Credit Terms	Invoice Amount
1.	24574	March 5	2/10, n/30	$3,000.00
2.	530992	March 7	3/10, n/30	5,550.00
3.	211145	March 12	2/15, n/60	729.95
4.	45679	March 16	n/45	345.67
5.	34120	March 23	2/10, n/30	1,526.50
6.	00985	March 27	n/30	700.00

Instructions Prepare a form similar to the one shown below. The first invoice has been completed as an example. For each invoice:

1. Determine the due date. Assume that Sunset Surfwear always pays invoices within the discount period.
2. Compute the discount amount, if any.
3. Compute the amount to be paid.

Invoice Number	Invoice Date	Credit Terms	Invoice Amount	Due Date	Discount Amount	Amount To Be Paid
24574	Mar. 5	2/10, n/30	$3,000.00	Mar. 15	$60.00	$2,940.00

Analyze: If all discounts are taken, how much money will Sunset Surfwear save?

Complete chapter problems one of four ways:

1 **Manual** Glencoe Working Papers

or

2 **Peachtree Complete Accounting** Software

or

3 **QuickBooks** Templates (Problems 15–7, 15–9)

or

4 **Spreadsheet** Templates (Problem 15–5)

SPREADSHEET SMART GUIDE

Step-by-Step Instructions: Problem 15–5

1. Select the spreadsheet template for Problem 15–5.
2. Enter your name and the date in the spaces provided on the template.
3. Complete the spreadsheet using the instructions in your working papers.
4. Print the spreadsheet and proof your work.
5. Save your work and exit the spreadsheet program.

Problem 15–5 (Answers) Determining Due Dates and Discount Amounts

2. Invoice 530992: Due date Mar. 17, discount amount $166.50, amount to be paid $5,383.50
3. Invoice 211145: Due date Mar. 27, discount amount $14.60, amount to be paid $715.35
4. Invoice 45679: Due date Apr. 30, discount amount $0, amount to be paid $345.67
5. Invoice 34120: Due date Apr. 2, discount amount $30.53, amount to be paid $1,495.97
6. Invoice 00985: Due date Apr. 26, discount amount $0, amount to be paid $700.00

Analyze: $271.63

SOFTWARE NOTES

Teachers can find detailed instructions for:

- **Peachtree Complete Accounting Software**, in the *Glencoe Workbook (CRWP)*
- **QuickBooks Templates**, in *Using QuickBooks with Glencoe Accounting*
- **Spreadsheet Templates**, in the *Glencoe Workbook (CRWP)*

PROBLEMS CHAPTER 15

Problem 15–6 (Answers) Analyzing Purchases and Cash Payments

Refer to the *Teacher Annotated Edition* of *Chapter Reviews and Working Papers* for answers.

Analyze: $5,900

Problem 15–7 (Answers) Recording Purchases Transactions

Mar. 3: Dr. Purchases $4,500; Cr. Accts. Pay/Photo Emporium $4,500; Invoice 1221

Mar. 5: Dr. Supplies $750; Cr. Accts. Pay/State Street Office Supply $750; Invoice 873

Mar. 9: Dr. Accts. Pay./Photo Emporium $225; Cr. Purchases Returns and Allowances $225; Debit Memo 72

Mar. 10: Dr. Purchases $3,600; Cr. Accts. Pay./Video Optics Inc. $3,600; Invoice V094

Mar. 15: Dr. Accts. Pay./State Street Office Supply $60; Cr. Supplies $60; Debit Memo 73

Mar. 20: Dr. Store Equipment $4,800; Cr. Accts. Pay./Digital Precision Equipment $4,800; Invoice 1288

Mar. 25: Dr. Accts. Pay./Video Optics Inc. $120; Cr. Purchases Returns and Allowances $120; Debit Memo 74

Mar. 28: Dr. Purchases $1,800; Cr. Accts. Pay./U-Tech Products $1,800; Invoice UT66

Mar. 29: Dr. Supplies $270; Cr. Accts. Pay./Prostudio Supply $270; Invoice 4574

Mar. 30: Dr. Accts. Pay./U-Tech Products $150; Cr. Purchases Returns and Allowances $150; Debit Memo 75

Mar. 31: Dr. Accts. Pay./ProStudio Supply $35; Cr. Supplies $35; Debit Memo 76

Analyze: $495

Peachtree®

SMART GUIDE

Step-by-Step Instructions: Problem 15–6

1. Select the problem set for InBeat CD Shop (Prob. 15–6).
2. Rename the company and set the system date.
3. Enter all of the purchases on account transactions using the **Purchases/ Receive Inventory** option in the ***Tasks*** menu.
4. Process all debit memorandums using the **Purchases/Receive Inventory** and the **Payments** options.
5. Record all cash payments using the **Payments** option.
6. Print a Purchases Journal report and a Cash Disbursements Journal report.
7. Proof your work and make any needed corrections.
8. Print a General Ledger report to answer the Analyze question.
9. End the session.

TIP: To save time entering transactions, group them by type and then enter the transactions in batches.

Problem 15–6 Analyzing Purchases and Cash Payments

InBeat CD Shop had the following transactions in March.

Instructions Use the T accounts in your working papers. For each transaction:

1. Determine which accounts are affected.
2. Enter the debit and credit amounts in the T accounts.

Date	Transactions
Mar. 2	Purchased merchandise on account from NightVision and Company, $2,000, Invoice NV-20, terms 2/10, n/30.
6	Issued Check 250 for $85 to Penn Trucking Company for delivering merchandise from NightVision and Company.
7	Purchased $300 in supplies on account from Temple Store Supply, Invoice 6011, terms n/30.
12	Issued Check 251 for $1,960 to NightVision and Company in payment of Invoice NV-20 for $2,000 less a cash discount of $40.
15	Paid Keystone Insurance Company $2,500 for the annual premium on business insurance, Check 252.
16	Purchased $3,000 in merchandise on account from NightVision and Company, Invoice NV-45, terms 2/10, n/30.
18	Issued Debit Memorandum 25 for $100 to NightVision and Company for the return of merchandise.
20	Purchased $900 in merchandise from Dandelion Records, Check 253.
22	Issued Check 254 to Temple Store Supplies for $300 for Invoice 6011.

Analyze: What is the Purchases account balance at the end of March?

Problem 15–7 Recording Purchases Transactions

Shutterbug Cameras, a retail merchandising store, had the following purchases transactions in March.

Instructions In your working papers, record the transactions on page 31 of the general journal.

Date	Transactions
Mar. 3	Purchased $4,500 in merchandise on account from Photo Emporium, Invoice 1221, terms 2/10, n/30.
5	Bought $750 in supplies on account from State Street Office Supply, Invoice 873, terms n/30.

Continued

EXTENDING THE CONTENT

Comparing Purchase Order and Invoice Forms Ask several local businesses for blank copies of their invoice and purchase order forms. Have students compare the formats and analyze the forms for ease of use. You can also provide samples of computer template forms for invoices and purchase orders. Then, provide a sampling of mail-order catalogs and ask students to compare and contrast the methods for determining shipping and handling charges. For example, do companies base their charges on weight and distance, or do they assess a charge based on the amount of the order?

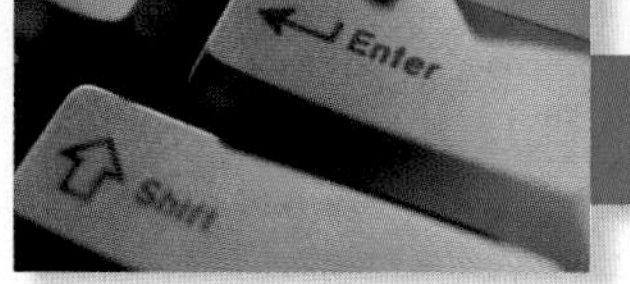

Date	Prob. 15–7 (cont.) Transactions
Mar. 9	Returned $225 in merchandise to Photo Emporium, issued Debit Memorandum 72.
10	Purchased $3,600 in merchandise on account from Video Optics Inc., Invoice VO94, terms 3/15, n/45.
15	State Street Office Supply granted a $60 credit for damaged supplies purchased on August 5, Debit Memorandum 73.
20	Bought $4,800 in store equipment from Digital Precision Equipment on account, Invoice 1288, terms n/30.
25	Issued Debit Memorandum 74 to Video Optics Inc. for the return of $120 in merchandise.
28	Purchased $1,800 in merchandise on account from U-Tech Products, Invoice UT66, terms n/30.
29	Bought $270 in supplies on account from ProStudio Supply, Invoice 4574, terms n/30.
30	Returned $150 in merchandise to U-Tech Products, Debit Memorandum 75.
31	Issued Debit Memorandum 76 to ProStudio Supply for the return of $35 in supplies bought on March 29.

Analyze: What are the total credits made to the **Purchases Returns and Allowances** account for the month?

Problem 15–8 Recording Cash Payment Transactions

Cycle Tech Bicycles had the following cash payment transactions in March.

Instructions In your working papers, record the transactions on page 19 of the general journal.

Date	Transactions
Mar. 1	Purchased $1,800 in merchandise from Summit Bicycles, Check 2111.
3	Issued Check 2112 for $2,450 to Spaulding Inc. in payment of the $2,500 account balance less a 2% cash discount of $50.
7	Issued Check 2113 for $3,100 to Desert Palms Insurance Company for the annual business insurance premium.
12	Paid $175 to Viking Express for delivery of merchandise purchased from Schwinn Inc., FOB shipping point, Check 2114.
17	Issued Check 2115 to Suspension Specialists for $3,880 in payment of Invoice 1492 for $4,000 less a 3% cash discount of $120.

Continued

Peachtree®

SMART GUIDE

Step-by-Step Instructions: Problem 15–7

1. Select the problem set for Shutterbug Cameras (Prob. 15–7).
2. Rename the company and set the system date.
3. Enter all of the purchases on account transactions using the **Purchases/Receive Inventory** option in the ***Tasks*** menu.
4. Process all debit memorandums using the **Purchases/Receive Inventory** and the **Payments** options.
5. Print a Purchases Journal report and a Cash Disbursements Journal report.
6. Proof your work. Make any needed corrections.
7. Print a GL report to answer the Analyze question.
8. End the session.

TIP: Using the **Vendors** option, Peachtree lets you set the terms offered by each vendor.

Problem 15–8 (Answers) Recording Cash Payment Transactions

Mar. 1: Dr. Purchases $1,800; Cr. Cash in Bank $1,800; Check 2111
Mar. 3: Dr. Accts. Pay./Spaulding Inc. $2,500; Cr. Cash in Bank $2,450, Purchases Discount $50; Check 2112
Mar. 7: Dr. Prepaid Insurance $3,100; Cr. Cash in Bank $3,100; Check 2113
Mar. 12: Dr. Transportation In $175; Cr. Cash in Bank $175; Check 2114
Mar. 17: Dr. Accts. Pay./Suspension Specialists $4,000; Cr. Cash in Bank $3,880, Purchases Discounts $120; Check 2115
Mar. 20: Bankcard Fees Expense $275; Cr. Cash in Bank $275; March Bank Statement
Mar. 24: Dr. Advertising Expense $130; Cr. Cash in Bank $130; Check 2116
Mar. 28: Dr. Supplies $100, Store Equipment $700; Cr. Cash in Bank $800; Check 2117
Mar. 31: Dr. Salaries Expense $3,000; Cr. Employees' Federal Income Tax Pay. $480, Employees' State Income Tax Pay. $105, Social Security Tax Pay. $186, Medicare Tax Pay. $43.50, Cash in Bank $2,185.50; Check 2118

Analyze: $14,795.50

SOLUTION NOTES

Problem 15-9 (Answers) Recording Purchases and Cash Payment Transactions

Mar. 1: Dr. Purchases $8,200; Cr. Accts. Pay./Trailhead Canoes $8,200; Invoice TC202

Mar. 5: Dr. Transportation In $98; Cr. Cash in Bank $98; Check 887

Mar. 7: Dr. Supplies $230; Cr. Accts. Pay./StoreMart Supply $230; Invoice SM101

Mar. 9: Dr. Prepaid Insurance $2,500; Cr. Cash in Bank $2,500; Check 888

Mar. 11: Dr. Accts. Pay./Trailhead Canoes $8,200; Cr. Cash in Bank $8,036, Purchases Discounts $164; Check 889

Mar. 15: Dr. Purchases $6,200; Cr. Accts. Pay./Mohican Falls Kayak $6,200; Invoice 45332

Mar. 18: Dr. Accts. Pay./StoreMart Supply $25; Cr. Supplies $25; Debit Memo 67

Mar. 21: Dr. Accts. Pay./StoreMart Supply $205; Cr. Cash in Bank $205; Check 890

Mar. 25: Dr. Accts. Pay./Mohican Falls Kayak $200; Cr. Purchases Returns and Allowances $200; Debit Memo 68

Mar. 28: Dr. Maintenance Expense $120; Cr. Accts. Pay./Rollins Plumbing Service $120; Invoice RP432

Analyze: $14,400

Peachtree®

SMART GUIDE

Step-by-Step Instructions: Problem 15-8

1. Select the problem set for Cycle Tech (Prob. 15-8).
2. Rename the company and set the system date.
3. Record all cash payments using the **Payments** option.
4. Print a Cash Disbursements Journal report.
5. Proof your work. Make any needed corrections.
6. Answer the Analyze question.
7. End the session.

TIP: Remember that you may need to change the G/L Account in the Payments window to enter a cash payment for the purchase of an asset (e.g., supplies, office equipment).

Date	Prob. 15-8 (cont.) Transactions
Mar. 20	Received the March bank statement and recorded bankcard fees of $275.
24	Paid All-Star News $130 to run an advertisement promoting the store, Check 2116.
28	Bought $100 in supplies and $700 in store equipment from Superior Store Equipment Inc., Check 2117 for $800.
31	Issued Check 2118 for $2,185.50 in payment of monthly wages of $3,000 less deductions for the following taxes: Employees' Federal Income Tax Payable, $480; Employees' State Income Tax Payable, $105; Social Security Tax Payable, $186; and Medicare Tax Payable, $43.50.

Analyze: What is the total decrease to the checking account for the month?

Problem 15-9 Recording Purchases and Cash Payment Transactions

River's Edge Canoe & Kayak had the following purchases and cash payment transactions for the month of March.

Instructions In your working papers, record the following transactions on page 16 of the general journal.

Date	Transactions
Mar. 1	Purchased $8,200 in merchandise on account from Trailhead Canoes, Invoice TC202, terms 2/10, n/30.
5	Issued Check 887 for $98 to Santini Trucking Company for delivery of merchandise purchased from Trailhead Canoes.
7	Bought $230 in supplies on account from StoreMart Supply, Invoice SM101, terms n/30.
9	Issued Check 888 to World-Wide Insurance Company for $2,500 in payment of business insurance premium.
11	Issued Check 889 to Trailhead Canoes for $8,036 in payment of Invoice TC202 for $8,200 less a 2% cash discount of $164.
15	Purchased $6,200 in merchandise on account from Mohican Falls Kayak Wholesalers, Invoice 45332, terms 3/15, n/45.
18	Issued Debit Memorandum 67 for $25 to StoreMart Supply for damaged supplies purchased on March 7.
21	Paid StoreMart Supply the balance due on their account, $205 ($230 less $25 credit), Check 890.
25	Returned $200 in merchandise to Mohican Falls Kayak Wholesalers, Debit Memorandum 68.
28	Rollins Plumbing Service completed $120 in repair work **(Maintenance Expense)** on account, Invoice RP432.

Analyze: What are the total debits to the **Purchases** account for the month?

Peachtree®

SMART GUIDE

Step-by-Step Instructions: Problem 15-9

1. Select the problem set for River's Edge (Prob. 15-9).
2. Rename the company and set the system date.
3. Enter all of the purchases on account.
4. Process all debit memorandums.
5. Record all cash payments.
6. Print the following reports: Purchases Journal, Cash Disbursements Journal, and General Ledger.
7. Proof your work.
8. Answer the Analyze question.
9. End the session.

TIP: Peachtree automatically calculates a purchases discount if the terms are included in a vendor's account.

SOLUTION NOTES

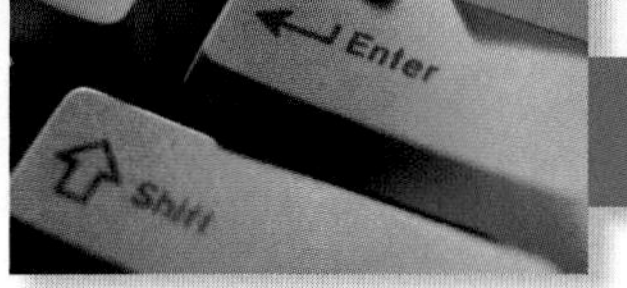

CHALLENGE PROBLEM

Problem 15–10 Recording and Posting Purchases and Cash Payment Transactions

SOURCE DOCUMENT PROBLEM

Buzz Newsstand's purchases and cash payment transactions for the month of March are described below.

Instructions In your working papers:

1. Record the transactions in the general journal, page 7.
2. Post the transactions to the ledger accounts.

Date		Transactions
Mar.	1	Purchased $5,600 in merchandise on account from ADC Publishing, Invoice 785, terms 3/15, n/45.
	3	Issued Check 1400 for $735 to Pine Forest Publications in payment of Invoice PFP98 for $750 less a 2% cash discount of $15.
	5	Issued Check 1401 for $275 to Rizzo's Trucking Company for transportation charges.
	7	Issued Check 1402 for $588 to Delta Press in payment of Invoice DP166 for $600 less a 2% cash discount of $12.
	9	American Trend Publishers granted a $100 allowance for damaged merchandise, Debit Memorandum 33.
	11	Issued Check 1403 for $3,200 to Keystone Insurance Company for the annual premium for business insurance.
	15	Issued Check 1404 for $5,432 to ADC Publishing in payment of Invoice 785 for $5,600 less a 3% cash discount of $168.
	18	Bought $2,800 in merchandise on account from Delta Press, Invoice DP204, terms 2/10, n/30.
	22	Issued Debit Memorandum 34 to Delta Press for the return of $300 in merchandise.
	28	Paid American Trend Publishers the balance due on their account, $800, no discount, Check 1405.
	30	Bought $120 in merchandise for cash from ADC Publishing, Check 1406.

Analyze: How much did Buzz Newsstand save in March by taking cash discounts available?

Peachtree® SMART GUIDE

Step-by-Step Instructions: Problem 15–10

1. Select the problem set for Buzz Newsstand (Prob. 15–10).
2. Rename the company and set the system date.
3. Enter all of the purchases on account.
4. Process all debit memorandums.
5. Record all cash payments.
6. Print the following reports: Purchases Journal, Cash Disbursements Journal, Vendor Ledgers, and General Ledger.
7. Proof your work.
8. Answer the Analyze question.
9. End the session.

SOURCE DOCUMENT PROBLEM

Problem 15–10

Use the source documents in your working papers to record the transactions for this problem.

SOLUTION NOTES

CHALLENGE PROBLEM

SOURCE DOCUMENT PROBLEM

Problem 15–10 (Answers) Recording and Posting Purchases and Cash Payment Transactions

Mar. 1: Dr. Purchases $5,600; Cr. Accts. Pay./ADC Publish. $5,600; Inv. 785

Mar. 3: Dr. Accts. Pay./Pine Forest Pub. $750; Cr. Cash in Bank $735, Purchases Disc. $15; Check 1400

Mar. 5: Dr. Transportation In $275; Cr. Cash in Bank $275; Check 1401

Mar. 7: Dr. Accts. Pay./Delta Press $600; Cr. Cash in Bank $588, Purchases Disc. $12; Check 1402

Mar. 9: Dr. Accts. Pay./American Trend Publishers $100; Cr. Purchases Ret. & Allow. $100; Debit Memo 33

Mar. 11: Dr. Prepaid Insurance $3,200; Cr. Cash in Bank $3,200; Check 1403

Mar. 15: Dr. Accts. Pay./ADC Publishing $5,600; Cr. Cash in Bank $5,432, Pur. Disc. $168; Check 1404

Mar. 18: Dr. Purchases $2,800; Cr. Accts. Pay./Delta Press $2,800; Invoice DP204

Mar. 22: Dr. Accts. Pay./Delta Press $300; Cr. Purchases Ret. & Allow. $300; Debit Memo 34

Mar. 28: Dr. Accts. Pay./American Trend Publishers $800; Cr. Cash in Bank $800; Check 1405

Mar. 30: Dr. Purchases $120; Cr. Cash in Bank $120; Check 1406

Ending debit balances:

Cash in Bank $850
Prepaid Insurance $3,200
Purchases $16,520
Transportation In $1,775

Ending credit balances:

Accounts Payable $2,500
Purchases Discounts $195
Purchases Ret. & Allow. $400
Accts. Pay./ADC Publishing $0
Accts. Pay./American Trend Pubs. $0
Accts. Pay./Delta Press $2,500
Accts. Pay./Pine Forest Publications $0

Analyze: $195

CHAPTER 16 Resource Manager

Section Resources

	Objectives & Standards	Activities & Features	Reproducible Masters
Chapter Opener *Special Journals: Sales and Cash Receipts*	• Identify the special journals and explain how they are used in a merchandising business. • Record transactions in sales and cash receipts journals. • Post from the sales and cash receipts journals to customer accounts in the accounts receivable subsidiary ledger. • Foot, prove, total, and rule the sales and cash receipts journals. • Post column totals from the sales and cash receipts journals to general ledger accounts. • Prepare a schedule for the accounts receivable subsidiary ledger. • Define the accounting terms introduced in this chapter. **National Standards for Business Education**: IA8–IA10, IA16, IIA2, IIA3, IIA4	Exploring the Real World of Business, p. 418 Workplace Connections, p. 419	School-to-Work Handbook
Section 1 *The Sales Journal*	• Identify the special journals and how they are used. • How to record sales of merchandise on account in a sales journal. • How to post from the sales journal to the accounts receivable subsidiary ledger accounts. • How to foot, prove, total, and rule the sales journal. • How to post column totals from the sales journal to the general ledger.	International Accounting, p. 427 A Matter of Ethics, p. 427	Demonstration Problems Strategies for Teaching International Accounting Strategies for Teaching Ethics in Accounting
Section 2 *The Cash Receipts Journal*	• How to record transactions in the cash receipts journal. • How to post from the cash receipts journal to accounts receivable subsidiary ledger accounts. • How to post amounts in the General Credit column of the cash receipts journal to general ledger accounts. • How to post column totals from the cash receipts journal to the general ledger. • How to prepare a schedule of accounts receivable.	Math Hints, p. 435 Connect To, p. 436 Did You Know?, p. 438 Accounting Flashbacks, p. 438 Analyzing Financial Reports, p. 439	Demonstration Problems Math Review for Accounting Internet Resources and Activities Handbook

KEY

Posters   Transparency   Software   Videocassette

 Blackline Masters   CD-ROM   Portfolio

MULTIMEDIA RESOURCE

Peachtree	QuickBooks	Spreadsheets	Videos	CD-ROMs
Problem 16–4 *Recording and Posting Sales and Cash Receipts* Problem 16–5 *Recording and Posting Cash Receipts* Problem 16–6 *Recording and Posting Sales and Cash Receipts*	Problem 16–5 *Recording and Posting Cash Receipts* Problem 16–6 *Recording and Posting Sales and Cash Receipts*	None in this chapter.	***Video Segment: Sales and Cash Receipts*** After viewing this video, students will be able to describe the need for special journals using examples of both credit and cash sales. Students will be able to explain the difference between cash and credit sales and why they are recorded in cash receipts and sales journals, respectively.	***Electronic Learning Center (ELC), Chapter 16*** This program is ideal for visual learners since it incorporates video images, animation, and graphics to enliven the content of each lesson. ***Interactive Lesson Planner (ILP), Chapter 16*** This CD-ROM combines the versatility of an electronic lesson planner with the convenience of teacher classroom resources.

SCANS Correlation Chart

FOUNDATION SKILLS

Basic Skills:	Reading	Writing	Math	Listening	Speaking	
Thinking Skills:	Creative Thinking	Decision Making	Problem Solving	Seeing Things in the Mind's Eye	Knowing How to Learn	Reasoning
Personal Qualities:	Responsibility	Self-Esteem	Sociability	Self-Management	Integrity/Honesty	

WORKPLACE COMPETENCIES

Resources:	Allocating Time	Allocating Money	Allocating Material and Facility Resources	Allocating Human Resources		
Information:	Acquiring and Evaluating Information	Organizing and Maintaining Information	Interpreting and Communicating Information	Using Computers to Process Information		
Interpersonal Skills:	Participating as a Member of a Team	Teaching Others	Serving Clients/ Customers	Exercising Leadership	Negotiating to Arrive at a Decision	Working with Cultural Diversity
Systems:	Understanding Systems	Monitoring and Correcting Performance	Improving and Designing Systems			
Technology:	Selecting Technology	Applying Technology to Task	Maintaining and Troubleshooting Technology			

*Highlighted blocks indicate areas covered in the chapter. Additional SCANS skills are also covered throughout the *Teacher Wraparound Edition.*

Assessment

Student Edition
- Check Your Understanding, pp. 428, 440
- Chapter 16 Problems, pp. 445–447

Assessment and Evaluation Masters
- Chapter 16 Study Plan, *Glencoe Workbook*
- Chapter 16 Self-Test, *Glencoe Workbook*
- Chapter 16 Test, *Chapter Tests* Booklet
- Chapter 16 Activity, *School-to-Work Handbook*
- Chapter 16 **Exam***View*

Teacher Wraparound Edition
- Critical Thinking Activity, p. 423
- Reteaching Section 1, p. 428
- Reteaching Section 2, p. 440
- Chapter 16 Quiz, p. 441

Transparencies

	Teaching Transparencies	Solution Transparencies
Section 1:	16–1, 16–2, 16–3, 16–4, 16–5, 16–6, 16–7, 16–8, 16–9, 16–10	Problems 16–1, 16–2
Section 2:	16–11, 16-12, 16–13, 16–14, 16–15, 16–16, 16–17, 16-18, 16–19, 16–20, 16–21, 16–22	Problem 16–3
End of Chapter:		Problems 16–4, 16–5, 16–6

TEACHER CLASSROOM RESOURCES

This is a representation of key blackline masters available in the Teacher Classroom Resources.

Teaching Aids

Transparency Examples

Section Focus Transparencies

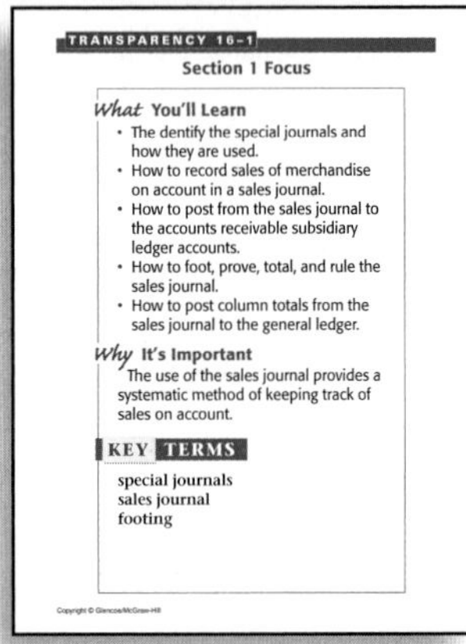

TRANSPARENCY 16-1

Section 1 Focus

What You'll Learn

- The dentify the special journals and how they are used.
- How to record sales of merchandise on account in a sales journal.
- How to post from the sales journal to the accounts receivable subsidiary ledger accounts.
- How to foot, prove, total, and rule the sales journal.
- How to post column totals from the sales journal to the general ledger.

Why It's Important

The use of the sales journal provides a systematic method of keeping track of sales on account.

KEY TERMS

special journals
sales journal
footing

Teaching Transparencies

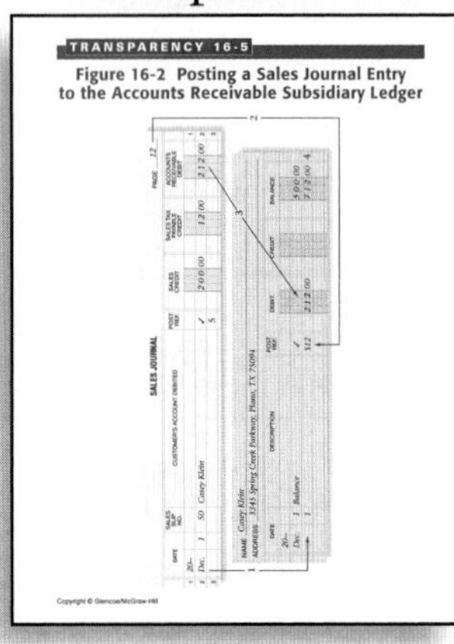

TRANSPARENCY 16-5

Figure 16-2 Posting a Sales Journal Entry to the Accounts Receivable Subsidiary Ledger

Teaching Transparencies

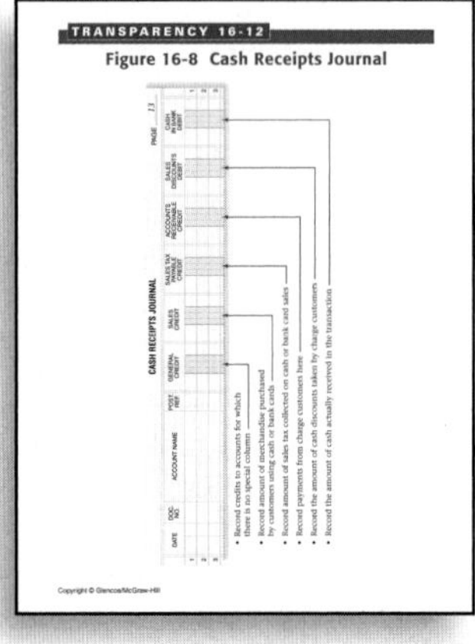

TRANSPARENCY 16-12

Figure 16-8 Cash Receipts Journal

Solution Transparencies

Working Papers for End-of-Chapter Problems

Problem 16-4 Recording and Posting Sales and Cash Receipts

Demonstration Problems

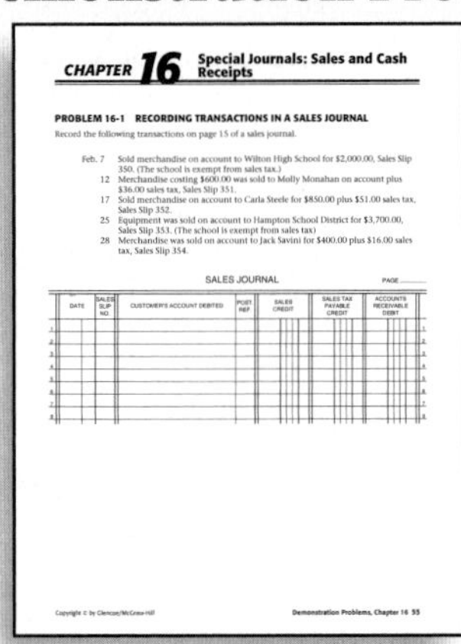

CHAPTER 16 Special Journals: Sales and Cash Receipts

PROBLEM 16-1 RECORDING TRANSACTIONS IN A SALES JOURNAL

SALES JOURNAL

Lesson Plans

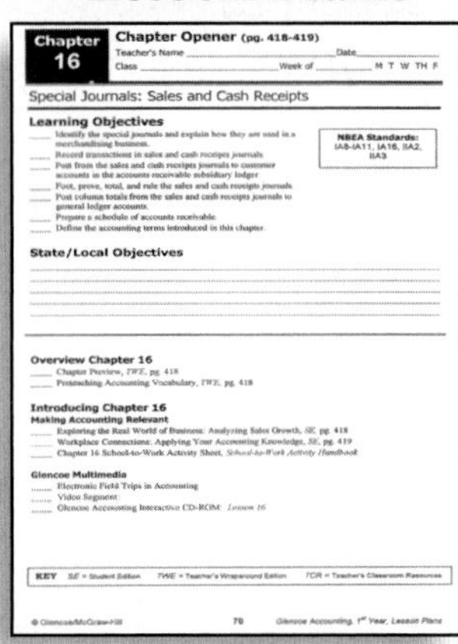

Chapter 16 Chapter Opener (pg. 418-419)

Special Journals: Sales and Cash Receipts

Learning Objectives

State/Local Objectives

Overview Chapter 16

Introducing Chapter 16

Glencoe Multimedia

Block Scheduling

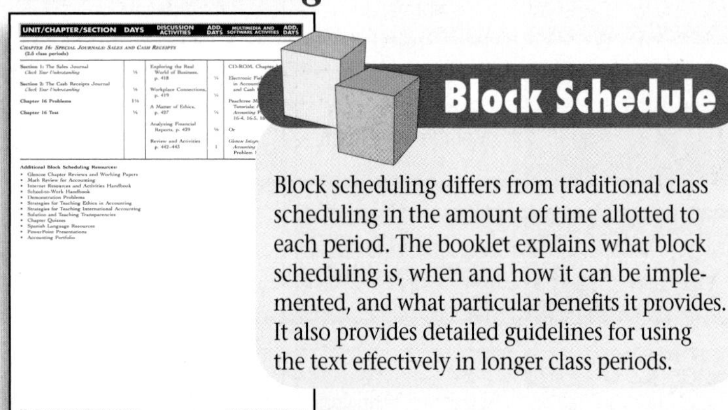

UNIT/CHAPTER/SECTION DAYS DISCUSSION ACTIVITIES

Block Schedule

Block scheduling differs from traditional class scheduling in the amount of time allotted to each period. The booklet explains what block scheduling is, when and how it can be implemented, and what particular benefits it provides. It also provides detailed guidelines for using the text effectively in longer class periods.

Enrichment and Application

Strategies for Teaching Ethics in Accounting

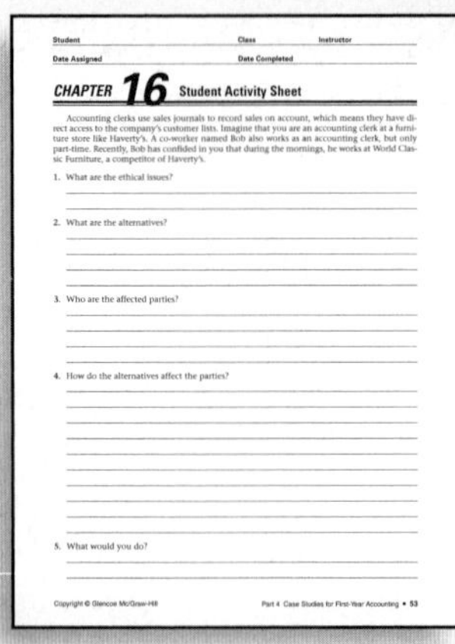

CHAPTER 16 Student Activity Sheet

1. What are the ethical issues?
2. What are the alternatives?
3. Who are the affected parties?
4. How do the alternatives affect the parties?
5. What would you do?

Strategies for Teaching International Accounting

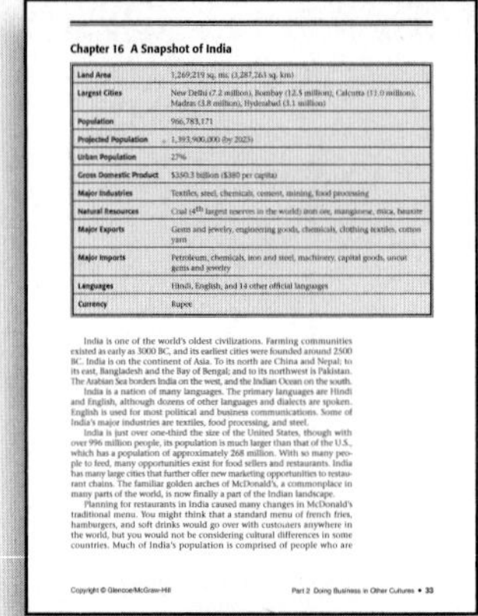

Chapter 16 A Snapshot of India

School-to-Work Handbook

CHAPTER 16 SCHOOL-TO-WORK ACTIVITY

Special Journals: Sales and Cash Receipts

Meeting Different Ability Levels

Chapter Reviews and Working Papers (CRWP)

Working Papers

Review

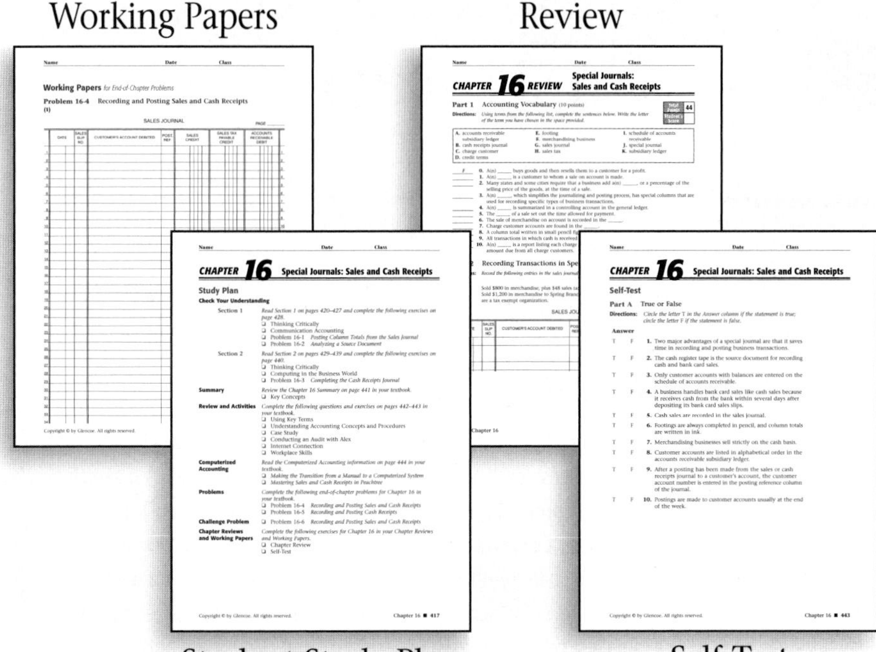

Student Study Plan

Self-Test

Real-World Multimedia CD-ROM

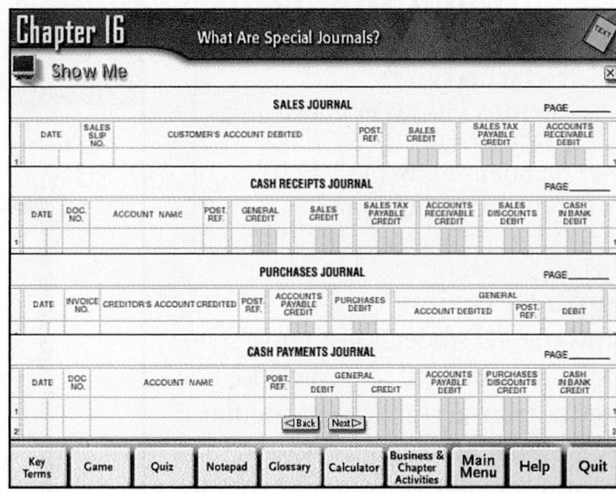

Key to Ability Levels

Each section gives skill-building activities. Each activity has been labeled for use with students of various learning styles and abilities.

L1 Level 1 activities are basic activities and should be within the range of all students.

L2 Level 2 activities are average activities and should be within the range of average and above average students.

L3 Level 3 activities are challenging activities designed for the ability range of above average students.

ELL ELL activities should be within the ability range of English Language Learners.

Assessment and Evaluation

Chapter Tests

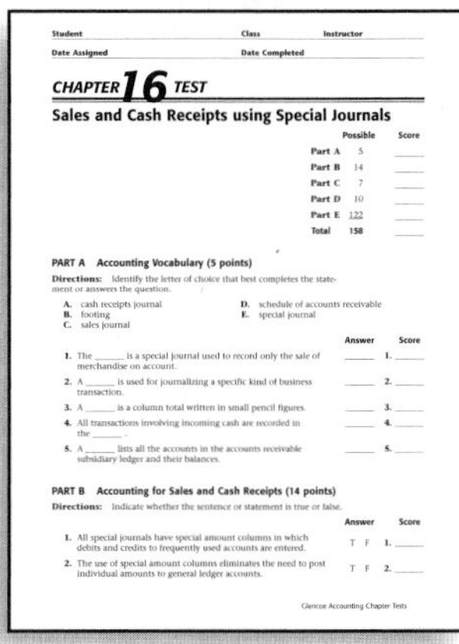

Chapter Quiz

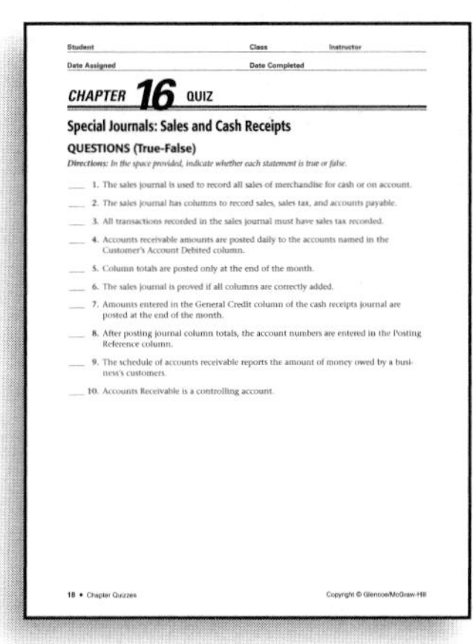

Teaching Resources at a Glance

Application Resources

- Glencoe Chapter Review and Working Papers, SE and TAE
- School-to-Work Handbook, SE and TM
- Accounting Portfolio, SE and TM

Reproducible Masters

- Demonstration Problems
- Lesson Plans
- Block Scheduling
- Spanish Language Resources

Glencoe Accounting Professional Development Series

- Strategies for Teaching Ethics in Accounting
- Accounting Competitive Event Review
- Math Review for Accounting
- Strategies for Teaching International Accounting
- Internet Resources and Activities Handbook

Transparency Package

- Section Focus Transparencies
- Teaching Transparencies
- Source Document Transparencies
- Solution Transparencies

Performance Assessment

- **Exam***View* CD-ROM
- Chapter Tests
- Chapter Quizzes
- Unit Tests
- Audit Tests
- Printed Testbank

Multimedia Resources

- Electronic Learning Center:
  - Multimedia CD-ROMs
  - Peachtree software, tutorials, templates, and solutions
  - Spreadsheet templates
- Using QuickBooks with Glencoe Accounting
- Interactive Lesson Planner
- Electronic Field Trips in Accounting
- PowerPoint Presentation
- Web site: glencoeaccounting.glencoe.com

Correlations to National Standards for Business Education

(See pages T50–T51 for a detailed correlation chart.)

Standards: IA8–IA10, IA16, IIA2–IIA4

Chapter Preview

In this chapter students learn how special journals are used to record specific types of transactions. In particular, they'll learn how to record entries in the sales and cash receipts journals. They'll also learn how to post from those journals and to total, prove, and rule each one.

Section Overviews

- Section 1—*The Sales Journal*
- Section 2—*The Cash Receipts Journal*

Chapter Vocabulary

special journals
sales journal
footing
cash receipts journal
schedule of accounts receivable

Preteaching Accounting Vocabulary

Writing Exercise: Have students write a sentence using each of the new terms in context. Ask for volunteers to write their sentences on the chalkboard. Discuss any differences in the use of the terms. L1

CHAPTER 16

Special Journals: Sales and Cash Receipts

Learning Objectives

When you have completed this chapter, you will be able to:

- Identify the special journals and explain how they are used in a merchandising business.
- Record transactions in sales and cash receipts journals.
- Post from the sales and cash receipts journals to customer accounts in the accounts receivable subsidiary ledger.
- Foot, prove, total, and rule the sales and cash receipts journals.
- Post column totals from the sales and cash receipts journals to general ledger accounts.
- Prepare a schedule for the accounts receivable subsidiary ledger.
- Define the accounting terms introduced in this chapter.

Exploring the Real World of Business

ANALYZING SALES GROWTH

Imagine yourself with your headphones on, jamming to the latest release of REM. Perhaps you're using a Sony Walkman cassette player, a product that started a revolution in personal music listening.

Sony Corporation was the first to see the potential for a portable, battery-operated cassette player. **Sony** has a lot of other firsts, a few of which are the home videotape recorder, the world's smallest color TV, the water-resistant Sports Walkman, and the digital video disc. The company has dozens of electronic products that have become market leaders.

If you've listened to music, been to the movies, watched music videos, or watched television recently, chances are you've come into contact with something made by **Sony.** The **Sony** brands include Columbia Pictures, Epic Records, and PlayStation game consoles. **Sony Corporation of America** has annual sales of more than $18 billion. The company has grown to this size because sales of its early products helped to pay for the research needed to develop even better electronics products that consumers want to buy.

What do you think?

If you were making a presentation to a group of potential investors, what would you say about **Sony's** sales?

Sony Corporation

Exploring the Real World of Business

Sony Corporation

Sony has used its profits from sales to expand into many entertainment areas. Through Columbia and Sony Records, the company publishes many of today's most popular recording artists. The company produces movies, television programs, and home videos. Without sales, none of this would be possible.

What do you think? (Answers)

Students might say that Sony's sales reflect its reputation for quality products. Its position as a market leader also means that it can compete on product features and reputation rather than the lowest price. Mention could also be made of the effect of high sales on appreciation in stock prices.

Workplace Connections

Applying Your Accounting Knowledge

In this chapter, you will learn more about the cycle of buying and selling merchandise. Dollars from sales are used to buy merchandise, which is in turn sold to customers. Some sales dollars come from customers who pay cash, while others come from sales on credit. Both types are recorded in the accounting records.

Investigate:

1. In your job, do you handle cash and personal checks?
2. Do you handle credit card sales?
3. If a business did not accept credit cards, how do you think it would affect overall sales?

Glencoe Accounting Online

Visit the *Glencoe Accounting* Web site at **glencoeaccounting.glencoe.com** for additional activities and information.

419

OVERVIEW CHAPTER 16

Making Accounting Relevant

Workplace Connections: Applying Your Accounting Knowledge

Discussion: In a merchandising business, revenue from sales fuels business operations. Business managers pay close attention to sales and may even monitor sales totals on a daily basis. Have students discuss tactics local businesses use to increase sales (such as holiday or 2-for-1 special sales, appearances by local celebrities, coupons, or advertising in local newspapers).

Investigate (Answers)

1. Answers may vary.
2. Answers may vary.
3. Sales would likely be lower because people who could not use credit might delay purchases or not buy at all. Or, they might go to other stores where they could use credit cards.

School-to-Work Activity

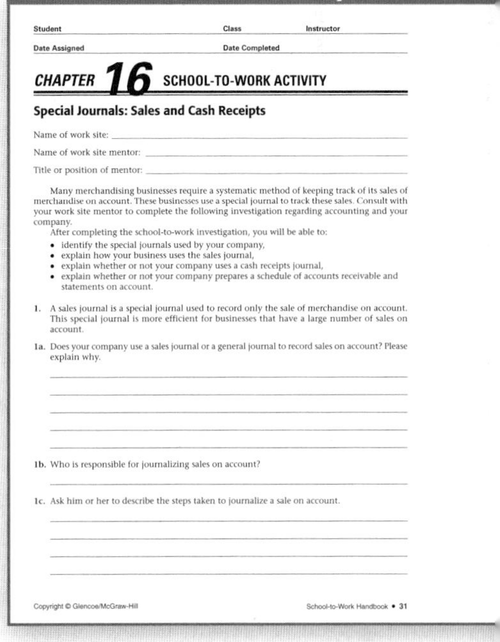

Student ______ Class ______ Instructor ______

Date Assigned ______ Date Completed ______

CHAPTER 16 SCHOOL-TO-WORK ACTIVITY

Special Journals: Sales and Cash Receipts

Name of work site: ______

Name of work site mentor: ______

Title or position of mentor: ______

Many merchandising businesses require a systematic method of keeping track of its sales of merchandise on account. These businesses use a special journal to track these sales. Consult with your work site mentor to complete the following investigation regarding accounting and your company.

After completing the school-to-work investigation, you will be able to:

- identify the special journals used by your company,
- explain how your business uses the sales journal,
- explain whether or not your company uses a cash receipts journal,
- explain whether or not your company prepares a schedule of accounts receivable and statements on account.

1. A sales journal is a special journal used to record only the sale of merchandise on account. This special journal is more efficient for businesses that have a large number of sales on account.

1a. Does your company use a sales journal or a general journal to record sales on account? Please explain why.

______

1b. Who is responsible for journalizing sales on account?

______

1c. Ask him or her to describe the steps taken to journalize a sale on account.

______

 School-to-Work Handbook • 31

GLENCOE MULTIMEDIA

Electronic Field Trips in Accounting *Video Segment: Sales and Cash Receipts*

After viewing this video, students will be able to describe the need for special journals using examples of both credit and cash sales; explain the difference between cash and credit sales and why they are recorded in cash receipts and sales journals, respectively.

Glencoe Accounting: Electronic Learning Center *Chapter 16*

The CD-ROM program is ideal for visual learners since it incorporates video images, animation, and graphics to enliven the content of each lesson.

1 FOCUS

Introducing the Section

In this section students will learn how to record transactions in the sales journal. They will also learn how to post individual amounts to the accounts receivable subsidiary ledger and column totals to the general ledger.

Section Concepts

- To identify the special journals and how they are used.
- How to record sales of merchandise on account in a sales journal.
- How to post from the sales journal to the accounts receivable subsidiary ledger.
- How to foot, prove, total, and rule the sales journal.
- How to post column totals from the sales journal to the general ledger.

Visual Learning

Section 1 Focus

Use **Transparency 16–1** to introduce section concepts.

BELL RINGER

Analyzing: Have students tell you the accounts affected by sales transactions. Then tell students that they are to design a special journal used only to record sales on account. What column headings would they use? L2

Concept Development: Special Journals

Discussion: Explain why special journals are needed in businesses that have large numbers of repetitive transactions. Emphasize that all special journals have three significant characteristics: (1) Each special journal records a specific type of transaction. (2) Special journals simplify the journalizing process. (3) Special journals save time in posting. L1

SECTION 1

The Sales Journal

What You'll Learn

- To identify the special journals and how they are used.
- How to record sales of merchandise on account in a sales journal.
- How to post from the sales journal to the accounts receivable subsidiary ledger accounts.
- How to foot, prove, total, and rule the sales journal.
- How to post column totals from the sales journal to the general ledger.

Why It's Important

The use of the sales journal provides a systematic method of keeping track of sales on account.

KEY TERMS

special journals
sales journal
footing

You have learned how to record a variety of business transactions in a general journal. A merchandising business can record all of its transactions in a general journal. However, each transaction requires at least three journal lines—one line for the debit, one line for the credit, and one line for the explanation. Each debit and credit is posted separately to the general ledger. For merchandising businesses with many sales transactions, such as Crate & Barrel, this would be very time consuming. To improve efficiency many merchandising businesses use special journals. In this chapter and the next chapter, you will learn how to record transactions in special journals.

Special Journals

Special journals have amount columns used to record debits and credits to specific general ledger accounts. Most transactions are recorded on one line. Special journals thus simplify the journalizing and posting process. The four most commonly used special journals and the type of transaction recorded in each journal are:

Journal	Transaction
Sales journal	sale of merchandise on account
Cash receipts journal	receipt of cash
Purchases journal	purchase of any asset on account
Cash payments journal	payment of cash, including payment by check

Businesses that use special journals still need the general journal to record transactions that cannot be entered in the special journals. Let's now look at the sales journal.

The Sales Journal

The **sales journal** is a special journal used to record sales of merchandise on account. **Figure 16–1** shows the sales journal used by On Your Mark Athletic Wear.

Like the general journal, the sales journal has a space for the page number and columns for the date and the posting reference. There is a separate column in which to record the sales slip number and a column

RESOURCE MANAGER

Reproducible Masters
- Lesson Plans
- Chapter Reviews and Working Papers (CRWP) TAE
- Demonstration Problems

Transparencies
- Section Focus Transparency
- Teaching Transparencies
- Source Document Transparencies
- Solution Transparencies

Multimedia
- Exam*View* CD-ROM
- Electronic Learning Center CD-ROM
- Interactive Lesson Planner CD-ROM

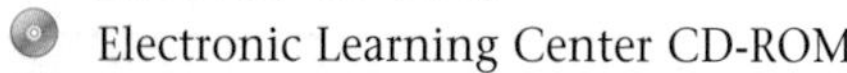
Electronic Field Trips in Accounting

in which to record the name of the charge customer. There are also three special amount columns. **Figure 16–1** illustrates what is to be recorded in each column.

Figure 16–1 Sales Journal

SALES JOURNAL — PAGE ____

	DATE		SALES SLIP NO.	CUSTOMER'S ACCOUNT DEBITED	POST. REF.	SALES CREDIT	SALES TAX PAYABLE CREDIT	ACCOUNTS RECEIVABLE DEBIT	
1									1
2									2
3									3

Record the amount of the merchandise sold on account (Sales Credit)
Record the amount of sales tax on the sale (Sales Tax Payable Credit)
Record the total amount to be received from the customer on account (Accounts Receivable Debit)

Recording Sales of Merchandise on Account

Are you ready to record a sale on account in the sales journal? It's simple. Let's look at the same transactions you analyzed in Chapter 14 for On Your Mark Athletic Wear. This time we'll record transactions using the sales journal.

ON YOUR MARK ATHLETIC WEAR
595 Leslie Street, Dallas, TX 75207

DATE: December 1, 20-- NO. 50

SOLD TO: Casey Klein, 3345 Spring Creek Parkway, Plano, Texas 75094

CLERK	CASH	CHARGE	TERMS
B.E.		✓	n/30

QTY.	DESCRIPTION	UNIT PRICE	AMOUNT
1	Pair Running Shoes	$ 100.00	$ 100 00
6	Pair Athletic Socks	10.00	60 00
1	Vinyl Jacket/Pants	40.00	40 00
		SUBTOTAL	$ 200 00
		SALES TAX	12 00
		TOTAL	$ 212 00

Thank You!

Business Transaction

On December 1 On Your Mark sold merchandise on account to Casey Klein for $200 plus $12 sales tax, Sales Slip 50.

JOURNAL ENTRY

SALES JOURNAL — PAGE 12

	DATE		SALES SLIP NO.	CUSTOMER'S ACCOUNT DEBITED	POST. REF.	SALES CREDIT	SALES TAX PAYABLE CREDIT	ACCOUNTS RECEIVABLE DEBIT	
1	20--								1
2	Dec.	1	50	Casey Klein		200 00	12 00	212 00	2
3	1		2	3		4	5	6	3

To record the transaction in the sales journal, journalize from left to right by following these steps.

1. Enter the date of the sales slip in the Date column.
2. Enter the sales slip number in the Sales Slip No. column.
3. Enter the name of the customer in the Customer's Account Debited column.
4. Enter the total of the merchandise sold in the Sales Credit column. (This is the amount shown in the subtotal box of the sales slip.)
5. Enter the amount of the sales tax in the Sales Tax Payable Credit column.

Great Ideas *From the Classroom of...*

Designing Your Own Business Have students design their own business by planning and producing a business portfolio that includes the business logo, a chart of accounts, and a variety of business transactions that reflect an active, profitable business. Students prepare a final report that analyzes the financial status of the business from all data generated from the financial statements. Students utilize critical thinking, reasoning, logic, communication, and interpersonal skills.

Missy Shea
Amherst Regional High School
Amherst, Massachusetts

2 TEACH

GUIDED PRACTICE

Reading Accounting

- Give students a handout of a blank sales journal. As they read the section, have them annotate the handout explaining the information that goes in each column of the journal. L1

Concept Development: The Sales Journal

Discussion: Refer students back to the business transaction analyses in Chapter 14 and Figure 14–5 on page 365. Point out the repetition both in journalizing and in posting the transactions in the general journal. Then introduce the need for a special journal to record only sales on account. Using a sales slip, develop the special columns needed for a sales journal: (1) date; (2) source document and number; (3) name of customer; (4) posting reference; (5) amount columns—Sales Credit, Sales Tax Payable Credit, and Accounts Receivable Debit. L1

Visual Learning

Figure 16–1 Sales Journal
Using **Transparency 16–2**, discuss the columns in a sales journal. Point out that only sales on account are recorded in this journal.

Business Transaction
Use **Transparency 16–3** to analyze how information is taken from a sales slip and recorded in the sales journal.

CHAPTER 16
SECTION 1, PAGES 420–428

2 TEACH (Cont'd.)

Visual Learning

Business Transaction
Use **Transparency 16–4** to demonstrate how to record a transaction in which sales tax is not collected.

Demonstration Problem
Step-by-Step Practice
Use demonstration problem 16–1 to give students practice in analyzing and recording transactions in a sales journal.

Teaching Tip
Point out to students that the number of amount columns in a special journal will vary with the needs of the business. For example, a manufacturing business would not collect sales taxes on its products and thus would have no need for a sales tax column.

Concept Development: Posting a Sales Journal Entry to the Accounts Receivable Subsidiary Ledger
Discussion: Point out the accounts receivable subsidiary ledger form and review the purpose of each column. Demonstrate how an amount entered in the Debit column increases the account balance while an amount entered in the Credit column decreases the account balance. You might have students place a "+" above the Debit column and a "−" above the Credit column. L1

6. Enter the total amount to be received from the customer in the Accounts Receivable Debit column. (This is the amount shown in the total box of the sales slip.)

You learned in Chapter 14 that sales tax is not imposed on sales of merchandise to tax-exempt organizations. The next transaction involves a tax-exempt sale.

ON YOUR MARK
ATHLETIC WEAR
595 Leslie Street, Dallas, TX 75207

DATE: December 3, 20-- NO. 51

SOLD TO: South Branch High School, 1750 Rutgers Dr., Dallas, TX 75207

CLERK	CASH	CHARGE	TERMS
B.E.		✓	2/10, n/30

QTY.	DESCRIPTION	UNIT PRICE	AMOUNT
15	Baseball Uniforms	$ 40.00	$ 600 00
15	Baseball Caps	20.00	300 00
15	Baseball Mitts	35.00	525 00
2	Baseballs	15.00	30 00
3	Baseball Bats	15.00	45 00
		SUBTOTAL	$ 1,500 00
		SALES TAX	0 00
	Thank You!	TOTAL	$ 1,500 00

Business Transaction

On December 3 On Your Mark sold merchandise on account to South Branch High School Athletics for $1,500, Sales Slip 51.

JOURNAL ENTRY

SALES JOURNAL — PAGE 12

	DATE	SALES SLIP NO.	CUSTOMER'S ACCOUNT DEBITED	POST. REF.	SALES CREDIT	SALES TAX PAYABLE CREDIT	ACCOUNTS RECEIVABLE DEBIT	
3	3	51	South Branch H.S. Ath.		1 500 00		1 500 00	3
4	1	2	3		4		5	4

This transaction is analyzed in the same manner as the previous transaction—except there is no sales tax. There are only five steps involved in journalizing this transaction. The first four steps are the same. The fifth step is to skip the Sales Tax Payable Credit column. Enter the total amount to be received from the customer in the Accounts Receivable Debit column.

For sales that do not include a sales tax, amounts entered in the Sales Credit column and in the Accounts Receivable Debit column are the same.

Key Points

Sales Journal Entry
For each line of the sales journal, make sure that the credits (**Sales** and **Sales Tax Payable**) equal the debit (**Accounts Receivable**).

Posting a Sales Journal Entry to the Accounts Receivable Subsidiary Ledger

In Chapter 14 you learned about posting to the accounts receivable subsidiary ledger. To keep the balances of the customer accounts current, sales journal transactions are posted daily to the accounts receivable subsidiary ledger. Whether you use the general journal or the sales journal when posting to the accounts receivable subsidiary ledger, the process is similar. Refer to **Figure 16–2** and follow these steps.

1. Enter the date of the transaction in the Date column of the subsidiary ledger account. Use the same date as the journal entry.
2. In the Posting Reference column of the subsidiary ledger account, enter the journal letter and the journal page number. "S" is the letter used for the sales journal.
3. In the Debit column of the subsidiary ledger account, enter the total amount to be received from the customer.
4. Compute the new balance and enter it in the Balance column. To find the new balance, add the amount in the Debit column to the previous balance amount.

COOPERATIVE LEARNING ACTIVITY

Send-a-Question Divide students into teams of five or six. Ask each student to describe, on a 3 × 5 card, a typical sales transaction for a retail store, including the total amount of the sale, the sales tax rate, and the terms of payment if on account. Have team members analyze each transaction and, on the back side of the card, write the special journal in which the transaction would be recorded, the accounts affected, and the amount each account increases or decreases. Then have each team pass its card to another team and repeat the process, comparing their answers with those of the first team. If there is disagreement regarding an answer, have teams work together to decide the correct answer.

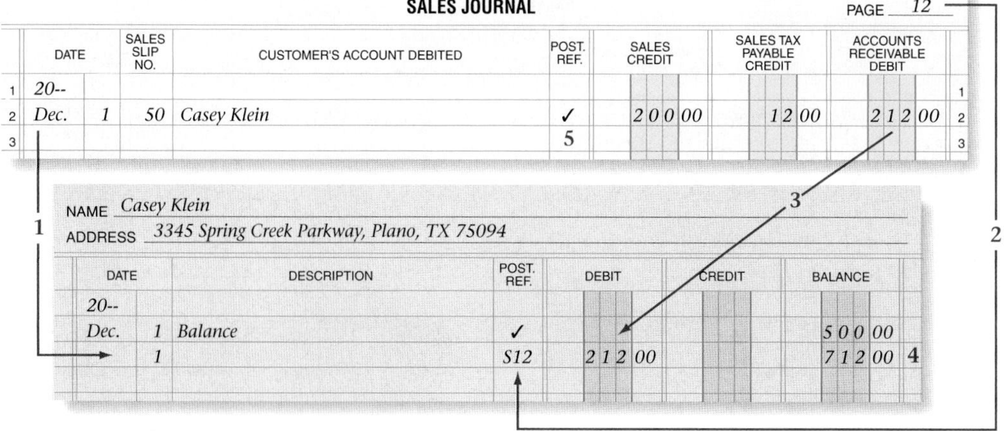

Figure 16–2 Posting a Sales Journal Entry to the Accounts Receivable Subsidiary Ledger

5. Return to the sales journal and enter a check mark (✓) in the Posting Reference column. The check mark indicates that the transaction has been posted to the accounts receivable subsidiary ledger. In manual accounting systems, customer accounts are not numbered, so a check mark is used in the Posting Reference column.

Completing the Sales Journal

All special journals have amount columns used to record debits and credits to specific general ledger accounts. These amount columns simplify posting. Instead of posting each transaction separately to the general ledger, only the amount column totals are posted. For the sales journal, the column totals posted are the Sales Credit, the Sales Tax Payable Credit, and the Accounts Receivable Debit. Therefore, only three postings are made to the general ledger from the sales journal.

Footing, Totaling, Proving, and Ruling the Sales Journal

Before amounts are posted to the general ledger, the accountant calculates and verifies the column totals. Refer to **Figure 16–3** as you follow each step.

1. Draw a single rule across the three amount columns, just below the last transaction.
2. Foot the amount columns. A **footing** is a column total written in small penciled figures. A footing must be verified. It is written in pencil so that it can be erased if a mistake is discovered.
3. On a separate sheet of paper, test for the equality of debits and credits. The total of the debit column should equal the total of the two credit columns.

Debit Column		Credit Columns	
Accounts Receivable	$11,305	Sales Tax Payable	$ 555
		Sales	10,750
Total	$11,305	Total	$11,305

Key Points

Posting from a Special Journal

When posting from a special journal, post information from left to right across the ledger form. By following this procedure, you will remember to enter all the information from the journal entry.

CRITICAL THINKING ACTIVITY

Sales Returns An electronic parts manufacturer offers a rebate on sales to wholesalers if their returns are less than 20 percent. Ask students why a business would offer this rebate. (Returns are expensive for the business to process. When a sale is made, the business incurs expenses in processing the order and shipping it to the customer. When the customer returns the merchandise, not only does the business lose the revenue, it also incurs additional expenses to handle the return. By providing incentives to keep returns low, the business avoids the cost of processing those returns.)

2 TEACH (Cont'd.)

Visual Learning

Figure 16–2 Posting a Sales Journal Entry to the Accounts Receivable Subsidiary Ledger

Review the posting process using **Transparency 16–5**. Point out that the sales journal entry is posted from left to right, the same as posting from the general journal.

Demonstration Problem Step-by-Step Practice

Use demonstration problem 16–2 to give students practice in posting from the sales journal to the accounts receivable subsidiary ledger.

Concept Development: Completing the Sales Journal

Discussion: Explain the need to total, prove, and rule the sales journal. Remind students that the use of special amount columns saves posting time since the column totals—rather than individual transactions—are posted to the account named in the column heading. L1

Thinking Algebraically

Conceptualize: Have students write an equation for proving the equality of the debits and credits in the sales journal. (For example, they might write AR = STP + S, which stands for Accounts Receivable = Sales Tax Payable + Sales.) L2

CHAPTER 16
SECTION 1, PAGES 420–428

2 TEACH (Cont'd.)

Demonstration Problem Step-by-Step Practice

Use demonstration problem 16–3 to show students how to foot, total, prove, and rule the sales journal.

Visual Learning

Figure 16–3 Totaled and Ruled Sales Journal

Use **Transparency 16–6** to guide students through the process of totaling, ruling, and proving the sales journal. Reinforce the meanings of single and double rulings by asking students to explain what they mean in this illustration.

Teaching Tips

To emphasize the time saved in posting from a special journal, ask students to look at Figure 16–3 and count the number of postings saved by posting only the column totals.

Chapter Reviews and Working Papers

Refer students to the *Study Plan* located at the beginning of Chapter 16 in the workbook.

SALES JOURNAL — PAGE 12

	DATE		SALES SLIP NO.	CUSTOMER'S ACCOUNT DEBITED	POST. REF.	SALES CREDIT	SALES TAX PAYABLE CREDIT	ACCOUNTS RECEIVABLE DEBIT	
1	20--								1
2	Dec.	1	50	Casey Klein	✓	200 00	12 00	212 00	2
3		3	51	South Branch High School Athletics	✓	1 500 00		1 500 00	3
4		5	52	Break Point Sports Club	✓	3 500 00	210 00	3 710 00	4
5		9	53	Gabriel Ramos	✓	300 00	18 00	318 00	5
6		10	54	Kim Wong	✓	100 00	6 00	106 00	6
7		12	55	Robert Galvin	✓	250 00	15 00	265 00	7
8		18	56	Joe Dimaio	✓	400 00	24 00	424 00	8
9		20	57	Megan Sullivan	✓	500 00	30 00	530 00	9
10		24	58	Tammy's Fitness Club	✓	1 000 00	60 00	1 060 00	10
11		26	59	Anita Montero	✓	350 00	21 00	371 00	11
12		28	60	Shashi Rahim	✓	200 00	12 00	212 00	12
13		30	61	Lara Young	✓	2 450 00	147 00	2 597 00	13
14		31		Totals		10 750 00 10 750 00	555 00 555 00	11 305 00 11 305 00	14
15									15

Figure 16–3 Totaled and Ruled Sales Journal

4. In the Date column, on the line below the single rule, enter the date the journal is being totaled.
5. On the same line, in the Customer's Account Debited column, enter the word "Totals."
6. Enter the column totals, in ink, just below the footings.
7. Double-rule the three amount columns. A double rule, as you know, indicates that the totals have been verified.

After the sales journal is footed, proved, totaled, and ruled, the column totals are posted to the general ledger.

Key Points

Footing the Amount Columns

Use a pencil when first totaling the columns. If an error is made, column totals entered in pencil are much easier to correct.

Posting the Total of the Sales Credit Column

Refer to **Figure 16–4** as you read the procedure for posting the total of the Sales Credit column to the **Sales** account in the general ledger.

1. In the Date column of the **Sales** account in the general ledger, enter the date from the "Totals" line of the sales journal.
2. Enter the sales journal letter and page number in the Posting Reference column. Remember, "S" is the letter for the sales journal.
3. In the Credit column, enter the total from the Sales Credit column of the sales journal.
4. Compute the new balance and enter it in the Credit Balance column. To determine the new balance, add the amount entered in the Credit column to the previous balance.
5. Return to the sales journal and enter the **Sales** account number, in parentheses, below the double rule in the Sales Credit column. The number written in parentheses indicates that the column total has been posted to the general ledger account.

REINFORCING STUDY SKILLS

Using Skimming Skills Skimming is a reading skill that helps in surveying or previewing new material, looking for specific information, and reviewing for a test. In skimming a chapter, students should quickly read the title, skim the introduction and the first and last paragraphs, find the relationships between section and subsection heads, and look for key terms.

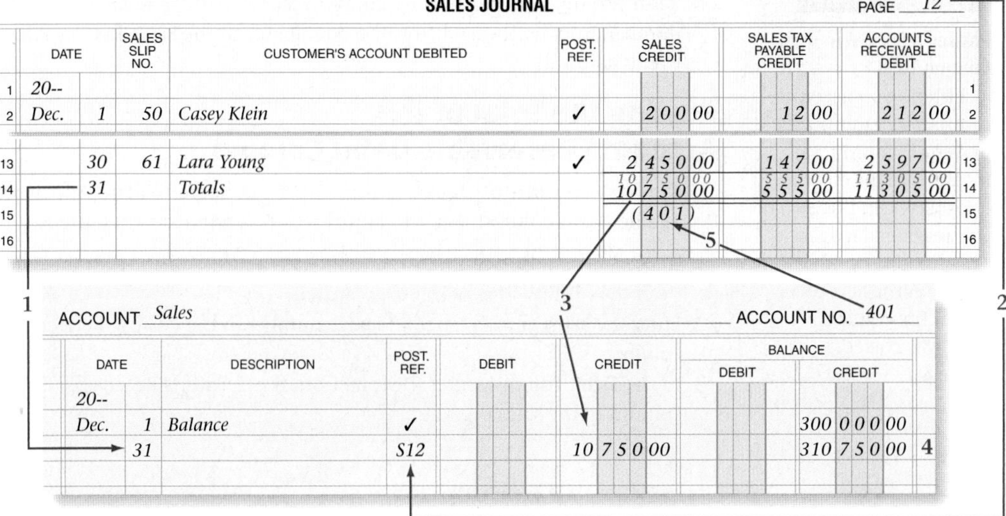

SALES JOURNAL — PAGE 12

	DATE		SALES SLIP NO.	CUSTOMER'S ACCOUNT DEBITED	POST. REF.	SALES CREDIT	SALES TAX PAYABLE CREDIT	ACCOUNTS RECEIVABLE DEBIT	
1	20--								1
2	Dec.	1	50	Casey Klein	✓	200 00	12 00	212 00	2
13		30	61	Lara Young	✓	2 450 00	147 00	2 597 00	13
14		31		Totals		10 750 00	555 00	11 305 00	14
15						(401)			15
16									16

ACCOUNT Sales — ACCOUNT NO. 401

DATE		DESCRIPTION	POST. REF.	DEBIT	CREDIT	BALANCE DEBIT	BALANCE CREDIT
20--							
Dec.	1	Balance	✓				300 000 00
	31		S12		10 750 00		310 750 00

Figure 16–4 Posting the Sales Credit Total to the General Ledger Account

Posting the Total of the Sales Tax Payable Credit Column

The next amount to be posted is the Sales Tax Payable Credit column total. Refer to **Figure 16–5** as you read the following procedure.

1. In the Date column of the **Sales Tax Payable** account, enter the date from the "Totals" line of the sales journal.
2. Enter the sales journal letter and page number in the Posting Reference column.
3. In the Credit column, enter the total from the Sales Tax Payable Credit column of the sales journal.

SALES JOURNAL — PAGE 12

	DATE		SALES SLIP NO.	CUSTOMER'S ACCOUNT DEBITED	POST. REF.	SALES CREDIT	SALES TAX PAYABLE CREDIT	ACCOUNTS RECEIVABLE DEBIT	
1	20--								1
2	Dec.	1	50	Casey Klein	✓	200 00	12 00	212 00	2
13		31	61	Lara Young	✓	2 450 00	147 00	2 597 00	13
14		31		Totals		10 750 00	555 00	11 305 00	14
15						(401)	(220)		15
16									16

ACCOUNT Sales Tax Payable — ACCOUNT NO. 220

DATE		DESCRIPTION	POST. REF.	DEBIT	CREDIT	BALANCE DEBIT	BALANCE CREDIT
20--							
Dec.	1	Balance	✓				1 300 00
	4		G20	9 00			1 291 00
	31		S12		555 00		1 846 00

Figure 16–5 Posting the Sales Tax Payable Credit Total to the General Ledger

CHAPTER 16
SECTION 1, PAGES 420–428

2 TEACH (Cont'd.)

Visual Learning

Figure 16–4 Posting the Sales Credit Total to the General Ledger Account

Use **Transparency 16–7** to guide students through the posting of a column total. Point out that the Posting Reference column is not used to record the account number when column totals are posted. Rather, the number is written directly under the column total.

Figure 16–5 Posting the Sales Tax Payable Credit Total to the General Ledger

Using **Transparency 16–8**, have students explain how to post this column total. Point out the difference between the general ledger account form and a subsidiary ledger account form.

GO TO **Demonstration Problem Step-by-Step Practice**

Use demonstration problem 16–4 to give students practice in posting sales journal column totals.

MEETING SPECIAL NEEDS

Students with Hearing Impairments When speaking with students who wear hearing aids, be sure to stand close to them. Hearing aids have a limited range. The hearing aids also amplify all sound, so try to restrict background noise as much as possible by keeping the classroom quiet or speaking to the student in a quiet office. Speak in a normal tone of voice. Shouting is not necessary, but speaking clearly is. Try not to let your voice trail off at the ends of sentences. In class, repeat the questions of other students.

CHAPTER 16
SECTION 1, PAGES 420–428

2 TEACH (Cont'd.)

Visual Learning

Figure 16–6 Posting Accounts Receivable Debit Total to the General Ledger

Using **Transparency 16–9**, ask students to describe what is taking place when the Accounts Receivable column total is posted to the general ledger.

Teaching Tip

Remind students that Accounts Receivable is a controlling account whose total must match the total of all the accounts in the accounts receivable subsidiary ledger. The details of the accounts receivable transactions are recorded in the accounts receivable subsidiary ledger through daily postings to the accounts named in the Customer's Account Debited column of the sales journal.

Critical Thinking: Ask students how accounting records would be affected if amounts in the Accounts Receivable Debit column were posted only as a column total. (The customers' accounts would not have up-to-date balances, and the total of the accounts receivable subsidiary ledger would not match the balance of the Accounts Receivable controlling account.) L1

Demonstration Problem Step-by-Step Practice

Use demonstration problem 16–5 to give students practice in proving the sales journal.

Strategies for Teaching International Accounting

To enrich study of International Accounting, refer to the additional critical thinking activities in the booklet.

Key Points

Posting a Special Journal Column Total

Entering an account number in parentheses under a column total means that the column total has been posted to the general ledger. The account number indicates the account where the column total was posted.

4. Compute the new balance and enter it in the Credit Balance column.
5. Return to the sales journal and enter the Sales Tax Payable account number, in parentheses, below the double rule in the Sales Tax Payable Credit column.

Posting the Total of the Accounts Receivable Debit Column

The last column of the sales journal to be posted is the Accounts Receivable Debit column. Refer to **Figure 16–6** as you read these steps.

1. In the Date column of the **Accounts Receivable** account, enter the date from the "Totals" line of the sales journal.
2. Enter the sales journal letter and page number in the Posting Reference column.
3. In the Debit column, enter the total from the Accounts Receivable Debit column of the sales journal.

SALES JOURNAL PAGE 12

	DATE		SALES SLIP NO.	CUSTOMER'S ACCOUNT DEBITED	POST. REF.	SALES CREDIT	SALES TAX PAYABLE CREDIT	ACCOUNTS RECEIVABLE DEBIT	
1	20--								1
2	Dec.	1	50	Casey Klein	✓	200 00	12 00	212 00	2
13		30	61	Lara Young	✓	2 450 00	147 00	2 597 00	13
14		31		Totals		10 750 00	555 00	11 305 00	14
15						(401)	(220)	(115)	15
16									16

ACCOUNT *Accounts Receivable* ACCOUNT NO. 115

DATE		DESCRIPTION	POST. REF.	DEBIT	CREDIT	BALANCE DEBIT	BALANCE CREDIT
20--							
Dec.	1	Balance	✓			6 259 00	
	4		G20		159 00	6 100 00	
	31		S12	11 305 00		17 405 00	

Figure 16–6 Posting Accounts Receivable Debit Total to the General Ledger

4. Compute the new balance and enter it in the Debit Balance column.
5. Return to the sales journal and enter the **Accounts Receivable** account number, in parentheses, below the double rule in the Accounts Receivable Debit column.

Proving the Sales Journal at the End of a Page

All special journals are totaled and proved at the end of every month. Sometimes, however, a business has so many transactions in one month that it is impossible to fit them all on one journal page. When this occurs, the journal page is totaled and ruled before a new page is started.

Refer to **Figure 16–7** and follow these steps to record the totals and carry them forward to the next page.

Teaching International ACCOUNTING

Using Laptop Computers in Foreign Countries Contact a local computer store or office supply store and obtain catalogs of computer products. Mail-order companies are another source of catalogs. Have students search catalogs and identify the types of products that are intended for use in adapting to a foreign country's power supply or creating cordless connections to the Internet.

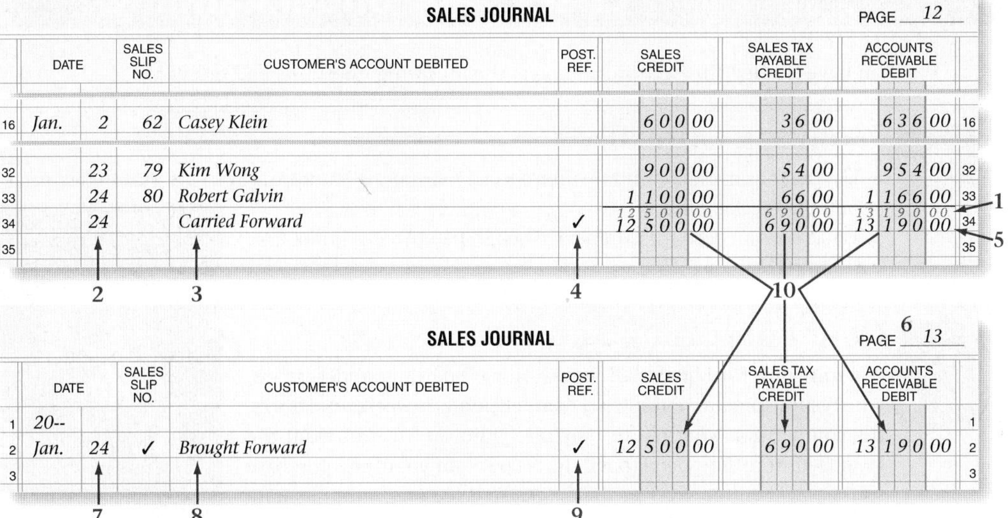

SALES JOURNAL — PAGE 12

	DATE		SALES SLIP NO.	CUSTOMER'S ACCOUNT DEBITED	POST. REF.	SALES CREDIT	SALES TAX PAYABLE CREDIT	ACCOUNTS RECEIVABLE DEBIT	
16	Jan.	2	62	Casey Klein		600 00	36 00	636 00	16
32		23	79	Kim Wong		900 00	54 00	954 00	32
33		24	80	Robert Galvin		1 100 00	66 00	1 166 00	33
						12 500 00	690 00	13 190 00	
34		24		Carried Forward	✓	12 500 00	690 00	13 190 00	34
35									35

SALES JOURNAL — PAGE 13

	DATE		SALES SLIP NO.	CUSTOMER'S ACCOUNT DEBITED	POST. REF.	SALES CREDIT	SALES TAX PAYABLE CREDIT	ACCOUNTS RECEIVABLE DEBIT	
1	20--								1
2	Jan.	24	✓	Brought Forward	✓	12 500 00	690 00	13 190 00	2
3									3

Figure 16–7 Starting a New Journal Page

1. Draw a single rule across the three amount columns below the last transaction. Foot the columns and prove the equality of debits and credits.
2. On the line following the last transaction, enter the date of the last transaction in the Date column.
3. In the Customer's Account Debited column, write "Carried Forward."
4. Place a check mark (✓) in the Posting Reference column. This check mark indicates that these totals are not to be posted.
5. Enter the column totals in ink. *Do not* double-rule the columns.
6. On the next journal page, enter the new page number.
7. On line 1 and 2 enter the complete date (year, month, and day) in the Date column. Use the same date as on the last line of the previous page.
8. Write "Brought Forward" in the Customer's Account Debited column.
9. Place a check mark (✓) in the Posting Reference column.
10. Enter the column totals from the previous page on line 2.

The journal page is now ready for the recording of the next transaction.

Laptop Safety

Business travelers who carry a laptop should test the phone lines to make sure that power surges don't ruin their computers.

A MATTER OF ETHICS

Working for a Competitor

Accounting clerks use sales journals to record sales on account, which means they have direct access to the company's customer lists. Imagine that you are an accounting clerk at a furniture store like Haverty's. A co-worker named Bob also works as an accounting clerk, but only part-time. Recently, Bob has confided in you that during the mornings, he works at World Classic Furniture, a competitor of Haverty's.

Ethical Decision Making:

- What are the ethical issues?
- What are the alternatives?
- Who are the affected parties?
- How do the alternatives affect the parties?
- What would you do?

Teaching A MATTER OF ETHICS

Working for a Competitor Ask students who in their class they consider competitors, whether on sports teams, club officer positions, or just getting top grades. Tell students to imagine that they are running for a student government office. Would they want a person assisting in their campaign also to work for a competitor running for the same office? Discuss business competition and the loyalty businesses expect of employees.

2 TEACH (Cont'd.)

Visual Learning

Figure 16–7 Starting a New Journal Page

Use **Transparency 16–10** to show students how to carry forward a balance when one journal page is filled and a new one must be started.

Teaching Tips

Explain that a special journal page may become filled before the end of the month for businesses having a lot of sales transactions. When that happens, the columns are totaled, and the totals are carried forward to a new journal page. New entries continue to be made. At the end of the month, the column totals are posted as one amount to the general ledger accounts.

Point out that balances carried forward must be identified clearly on the new page so that an auditing trail can be maintained.

Strategies for Teaching Ethics in Accounting

Photocopy the Chapter 16 *Student Activity Sheet* for students. Answers are also provided in the booklet.

CHAPTER 16
SECTION 1, PAGES 420–428

3 ASSESS

Thinking Critically (Answers)

1. SJ: record sales of merchandise on account; CRJ: record all cash received by business; PJ: record purchase of assets on account; CPJ: record all payments of cash.
2. The column total has been posted to the general ledger account.

Communicating Accounting (Answers)

Answers will vary. Memos should mention the accounts affected (Feed and Accounts Payable), the name of the store, the total purchase price, with the amount of sales tax calculated. (Tax \$5.10, total purchase \$90.10)

Problem 16–1 (Answers)

Ending debit balance:
Accounts Receivable \$27,720
Ending credit balances:
Sales Tax Payable \$2,020
Sales \$37,000

Problem 16–2 (Answers)

Sales Cr. \$820, Sales Tax Payable Cr. \$41, Accounts Receivable Dr. \$861
Ending balance \$1,161

Chapter Reviews and Working Papers Refer students to the Chapter 16 workbook pages to answer *Check Your Understanding* activities.

4 CLOSE

Section Wrap-Up

Oral Exercise: Have students discuss the difference between posting to a general ledger account and a subsidiary ledger account. Ask them to describe which transactions are posted to each type of account. L1

SECTION 1 Check Your Understanding

Now that you have studied this section, complete the following questions and problems.

Thinking Critically

1. List the four most commonly used special journals. What transactions are recorded in each of these special journals?
2. What does an account number written in parentheses under a column total mean?

Communicating Accounting

You work for Equestrian Steps—Horse Boarding and Lessons, which sponsored an equestrian competition last weekend. During the competition you had to purchase grain on account from the local feed store. You need to tell the accountant about the purchase so that she can record it in the accounting records. On a separate sheet of paper, write a brief memo explaining the transaction. The grain cost \$85. The feed store charged a 6% sales tax.

Problem 16–1 Posting Column Totals from the Sales Journal

Instructions Here are the column totals of the sales journal for the month of April. In your working papers, post these totals to the appropriate general ledger accounts.

SALES JOURNAL — PAGE 4

	DATE		SALES SLIP NO.	CUSTOMER'S ACCOUNT DEBITED	POST. REF.	SALES CREDIT	SALES TAX PAYABLE CREDIT	ACCOUNTS RECEIVABLE DEBIT	
1	20--								1
2	Apr.	1	47	Amy Anderson	✓	800 00	48 00	848 00	2
32		30		Totals		12 000 00	720 00	12 720 00	32
33									33

Problem 16–2 Analyzing a Source Document

Metro Sports Distributors had the following transaction on June 15.

Instructions

1. Analyze the sales slip shown. In your working papers, record the required entry on page 3 of the sales journal.
2. Post to the customer's account in the accounts receivable subsidiary ledger.

METRO
SPORTS DISTRIBUTORS
Kingston Mall, Williamsburg, Virginia 23185

DATE: June 15, 20-- NO. 113

SOLD TO: M&M Consultants, 2816 Mt. Odin Drive, Williamsburg, VA 23185

CLERK	CASH	CHARGE	TERMS
RDP		✓	3/15, n/45

QTY.	DESCRIPTION	UNIT PRICE	AMOUNT
10	Golf Bags	\$ 50.00	\$ 500 00
2 doz.	Ladies Golf Shirts	100.00/doz	200 00
20	Golf Caps	6.00	120 00
		SUBTOTAL	\$ 820 00
		SALES TAX	41 00
	Thank You!	TOTAL	\$ 861 00

RETEACHING SECTION 1

Using the Sales Journal Identify a retail business in your community, and ask students to describe several sales on account transactions generated at that store. Record the examples on the chalkboard or an overhead transparency, and have students name the three accounts affected in each transaction (Accounts Receivable, Sales, and Sales Tax Payable). Refer to Figure 16–1 on page 421 and note the differences between the sales journal and the general journal. Demonstrate how the sales journal simplifies the journalizing and posting process. Remind students that for each entry the total credits equal the debit amount.

The Cash Receipts Journal

In Chapter 14 you learned about cash receipts. The three most common sources of cash for a merchandising business are payments from charge customers, cash sales, and bank card sales. Cash is also received, though less frequently, from the sale of other business assets.

Think about cable television, electric, and telephone companies in your area. Can you imagine how many checks these companies receive every day? You can be sure they have streamlined the cash receipts process so that checks are recorded as efficiently as possible and deposited in the bank promptly. In this section, you will learn a more efficient way to record cash receipts by using a special journal called the six-column cash receipts journal.

What You'll Learn

- How to record transactions in the cash receipts journal.
- How to post from the cash receipts journal to accounts receivable subsidiary ledger accounts.
- How to post amounts in the General Credit column of the cash receipts journal to general ledger accounts.
- How to post column totals from the cash receipts journal to the general ledger.
- How to prepare a schedule of accounts receivable.

Why It's Important

Use of the cash receipts journal will save time and reduce errors.

KEY TERMS

cash receipts journal
schedule of accounts receivable

The Cash Receipts Journal

The **cash receipts journal** is a special journal used to record all cash receipt transactions. Every transaction recorded in the cash receipts journal requires a debit to the **Cash in Bank** account, so there is always a Cash in Bank Debit column. The number of credit columns varies, depending on the needs of the business.

The cash receipts journal used by On Your Mark Athletic Wear is shown in **Figure 16–8**. In addition to the date, source document, account name and posting reference columns, it contains six amount columns.

To keep the customer account balances current, the entries in the Accounts Receivable Credit column are posted daily to the accounts receivable subsidiary ledger. The entries in the General Credit column are posted daily to the individual general ledger accounts. At the end of the month, the totals of all the special amount columns are posted to the general ledger accounts named in the column headings.

RESOURCE MANAGER

Reproducible Masters
- Lesson Plans
- Chapter Reviews and Working Papers (CRWP) TAE
- Demonstration Problems

Transparencies
- Section Focus Transparency
- Teaching Transparencies
- Source Document Transparencies
- Solution Transparencies

Multimedia
- ExamView CD-ROM
- Electronic Learning Center CD-ROM
- Interactive Lesson Planner CD-ROM
- Electronic Field Trips in Accounting

1 FOCUS

Introducing the Section

In this section students will learn which transactions are recorded in the cash receipts journal; how to post individual amounts and column totals; and how to total, prove, and rule the journal.

Section Concepts

- How to record transactions in the cash receipts journal.
- How to post from the cash receipts journal to accounts receivable subsidiary ledger accounts.
- How to post amounts in the General Credit column of the cash receipts journal to general ledger accounts.
- How to post column totals from the cash receipts journal to the general ledger.
- How to prepare a schedule of accounts receivable.

Visual Learning

Section 2 Focus

Use **Transparency 16–11** to introduce section concepts.

BELL RINGER

Role-Play: Ask for volunteers to role-play a cash sale. Have students observe the role-play and write notes about the transaction. Ask them to identify accounts affected by the sales transaction. Then record the entry in a cash receipts journal. L2

Concept Development: The Cash Receipts Journal

Discussion: Point out that the cash receipts journal has two major advantages over a general journal: (1) all cash receipts are entered together on a journal page, and (2) the cash receipts journal saves time in posting. Point out the six amount columns in the journal, and explain how each is used. L1

2 TEACH

GUIDED PRACTICE

Reading Accounting

- Reinforce terminology and accounting concepts by having students read each column heading in the cash receipts journal, explain its meaning, and describe how it fits in the accounting system. L1
- Create a bulletin-board display of special journals, the types of transactions recorded in each, and the ledger accounts related to each journal. Include information in English and in your students' first language. ELL

Visual Learning

Figure 16–8 Cash Receipts Journal

Display **Transparency 16–12** and explain the information that is recorded in each column of the cash receipts journal.

Business Transaction

Use **Transparency 16–13** to guide students through the analysis and recording of cash received from a charge customer.

Teaching Tip

Emphasize that the word "General" in the first amount column heading in the cash receipts journal refers to the general ledger; thus, the amounts recorded as credits in this column are to be posted to the accounts entered in the "Account Name" column.

CASH RECEIPTS JOURNAL PAGE 13

	DATE	DOC. NO.	ACCOUNT NAME	POST. REF.	GENERAL CREDIT	SALES CREDIT	SALES TAX PAYABLE CREDIT	ACCOUNTS RECEIVABLE CREDIT	SALES DISCOUNTS DEBIT	CASH IN BANK DEBIT	
1											1
2											2
3											3

- Record credits to accounts for which there is no special column
- Record amount of merchandise purchased by customers using cash or bank cards
- Record amount of sales tax collected on cash or bank card sales
- Record payments from charge customers here
- Record the amount of cash discounts taken by charge customers
- Record the amount of cash actually received in the transaction

Figure 16–8 Cash Receipts Journal

Recording Cash from Charge Customers

Let's record a transaction for cash received from a charge customer. The source document for this transaction is the receipt.

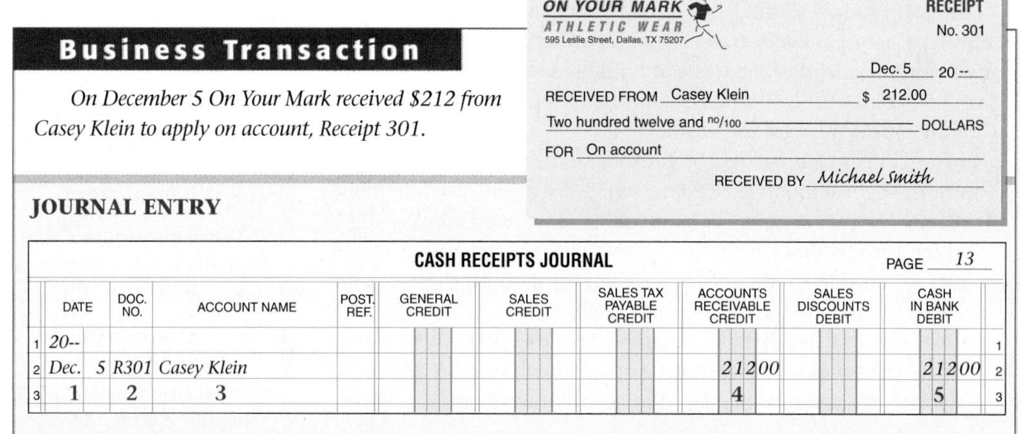

Business Transaction

On December 5 On Your Mark received $212 from Casey Klein to apply on account, Receipt 301.

ON YOUR MARK ATHLETIC WEAR
595 Leslie Street, Dallas, TX 75207

RECEIPT
No. 301

Dec. 5 20 --

RECEIVED FROM Casey Klein $ 212.00

Two hundred twelve and no/100 DOLLARS

FOR On account

RECEIVED BY *Michael Smith*

JOURNAL ENTRY

CASH RECEIPTS JOURNAL PAGE 13

	DATE	DOC. NO.	ACCOUNT NAME	POST. REF.	GENERAL CREDIT	SALES CREDIT	SALES TAX PAYABLE CREDIT	ACCOUNTS RECEIVABLE CREDIT	SALES DISCOUNTS DEBIT	CASH IN BANK DEBIT	
1	20--										1
2	Dec. 5	R301	Casey Klein					212 00		212 00	2
3	1	2	3					4		5	3

Follow these steps when journalizing cash receipts from charge customers:

1. Enter the date of the transaction in the Date column.
2. Enter the receipt number in the Document Number column. Write the letter "R" (for receipt) before the receipt number.
3. Enter the name of the customer in the Account Name column.
4. Enter the decrease in the amount owed by the customer in the Accounts Receivable Credit column.
5. Enter the amount of cash received in the Cash in Bank Debit column.

Key Points

Cash Receipts Journal Entry

Be sure that for each line of the cash receipts journal, the debit and credit entries are equal.

When this entry is posted to the customer's account in the accounts receivable subsidiary ledger, a check mark (✓) is entered in the Posting Reference column of the cash receipts journal.

HOME AND COMMUNITY CONNECTIONS ACTIVITY

Consumer Trends How do businesses stay on top of consumer buying trends? Have students choose a merchandising business in the community and interview someone at the management level about buying trends. Suggest that students ask questions such as: What drives a consumer's interest in a particular product? How do they track buying trends? What product is currently in high demand, and which product is in low demand? What was the store's highest selling product in its history? Have students share their interviews with the class.

Recording Cash Received on Account, Less a Cash Discount

Now let's record a cash receipt transaction with a cash discount.

Business Transaction

On December 12 On Your Mark received $1,470 from South Branch High School Athletics in payment of Sales Slip 51 for $1,500 less the discount of $30, Receipt 302.

ON YOUR MARK ATHLETIC WEAR
595 Leslie Street, Dallas, TX 75207

RECEIPT
No. 302

Dec. 12 20 --

RECEIVED FROM South Branch H.S. Athletics $ 1,470.00

One thousand four hundred seventy and no/100 DOLLARS

FOR On account

RECEIVED BY *Michael Smith*

JOURNAL ENTRY

CASH RECEIPTS JOURNAL PAGE 13

	DATE	DOC. NO.	ACCOUNT NAME	POST. REF.	GENERAL CREDIT	SALES CREDIT	SALES TAX PAYABLE CREDIT	ACCOUNTS RECEIVABLE CREDIT	SALES DISCOUNTS DEBIT	CASH IN BANK DEBIT	
3	12	R302	South Branch H.S. Ath.					1 500 00	30 00	1 470 00	3
4	1	2	3					4	5	6	4

Follow these steps to journalize this transaction:

1. Enter the date of the receipt in the Date column.
2. Enter the receipt number in the Document Number column. Remember to write the letter "R" before the receipt number.
3. Enter the name of the customer in the Account Name column.
4. In the Accounts Receivable Credit column, enter the amount of the original sales transaction (the amount that was debited in the sales journal) less any related sales returns or allowances.
5. Enter the cash discount amount in the Sales Discounts Debit column.
6. Enter the amount of cash received in the Cash in Bank Debit column.

Recording Cash Sales

Many businesses journalize cash sales and make cash deposits daily. In this chapter, however, we assume that On Your Mark records cash sales every two weeks.

Business Transaction

On December 15 On Your Mark records the cash sales for the first two weeks of December, $3,000, and $180 in related sales taxes, Tape 55.

Dec. 15
Tape 55

3000.00 CA
180.00 ST

JOURNAL ENTRY

CASH RECEIPTS JOURNAL PAGE 13

	DATE	DOC. NO.	ACCOUNT NAME	POST. REF.	GENERAL CREDIT	SALES CREDIT	SALES TAX PAYABLE CREDIT	ACCOUNTS RECEIVABLE CREDIT	SALES DISCOUNTS DEBIT	CASH IN BANK DEBIT	
4	15	T55	Cash Sales	—		3 000 00	180 00			3 180 00	4
5	1	2	3	4		5	6			7	5

CHAPTER 16
SECTION 2, PAGES 429–440

2 TEACH (Cont'd.)

Visual Learning

Business Transaction

Using **Transparency 16–14**, have students analyze the transaction and tell you how to record it in the cash receipts journal.

Business Transaction

Using **Transparency 16–15**, have students explain how to record the cash sales for the period in the cash receipts journal.

Critical Thinking: Have students write a short paragraph explaining why cash sales are not recorded in the sales journal. (The sales journal records sales made on account, so the business has clear records of how much cash they have taken in from sales versus cash that is to be received in the future from sales made on account.) L2

ACCOUNTING ISSUES

Using Barcode Technology Barcodes provide a fast and efficient way to keep track of data in the front office, the back office, the factory, and the warehouse. A portable barcode scanner can capture information for almost anything from manufactured goods to tax records and load it into a computer quickly and accurately. Tracking inventory is one of the most popular applications for barcoding. CPA firms use barcode technology to track work papers and tax records.

2 TEACH (Cont'd.)

Visual Learning

Business Transaction

Using **Transparency 16–16**, guide students through the analysis and recording of bankcard sales.

Teaching Tips

Remind students that bankcard sales are similar to cash sales in that the business receives its money when it deposits the bankcard receipts in the bank. The bank then collects the amount owed from the customer.

Have students prove the equality of each journal entry by adding all the debit amounts entered and all the credit amounts to see whether the totals match.

Explain that cash and bankcard sales are recorded every two weeks in the examples used here merely to save space in the journal illustrations. In reality, most businesses make daily deposits of cash and bankcard sales as a part of their internal control of cash.

Key Points

Journalizing Cash Receipts

When journalizing a cash receipt transaction involving a sales discount, be sure to credit **Accounts Receivable** for the amount of the original sales transaction less any related sales returns or allowances.

Follow these steps when entering cash sales in the cash receipts journal. The source document for this transaction is the cash register tape.

1. Enter the date written on the cash register tape in the Date column.
2. Enter the number of the tape in the Document Number column. Write the letter "T" (for tape) before the tape number.
3. Enter the words "Cash Sales" in the Account Name column.
4. Enter a dash in the Posting Reference column. The amounts recorded in the cash sales entry are posted to the general ledger as part of the column totals at the end of the month. The dash indicates that the entry is not posted individually to the general ledger accounts.
5. Enter the amount of merchandise sold in the Sales Credit column.
6. Enter the amount of the sales taxes collected in the Sales Tax Payable Credit column.
7. Enter the total cash received in the Cash in Bank Debit column.

Recording Bankcard Sales

A business can record and deposit bankcard sales slips at any interval. For illustration purposes, we assume that On Your Mark processes bankcard sales every two weeks. Let's record a bankcard sales transaction. Notice how this is similar to recording a cash sale.

Business Transaction

On December 15 On Your Mark recorded bankcard sales of $700 for the first two weeks of December and related sales taxes of $42, Tape 55.

Dec. 15
Tape 55

700.00 BCS
42.00 ST

JOURNAL ENTRY

CASH RECEIPTS JOURNAL PAGE *13*

	DATE	DOC. NO.	ACCOUNT NAME	POST. REF.	GENERAL CREDIT	SALES CREDIT	SALES TAX PAYABLE CREDIT	ACCOUNTS RECEIVABLE CREDIT	SALES DISCOUNTS DEBIT	CASH IN BANK DEBIT	
5	*15*	*T55*	*Bankcard Sales*	—		*700 00*	*42 00*			*742 00*	5
6	1	2	3	4		5	6			7	6

Follow these steps when entering bankcard sales in the cash receipts journal. The source document for this entry is the cash register tape.

1. Enter the date of the cash register tape in the Date column.
2. Enter the number of the tape in the Document Number column. Remember to write the letter "T" before the tape number.
3. Enter the words "Bankcard Sales" in the Account Name column.
4. Enter a dash in the Posting Reference column. The amounts recorded in the bankcard sales entry are posted to the general ledger as part of the column totals at the end of the month.
5. Enter the amount of merchandise sold in the Sales Credit column.

MAKING CONNECTIONS TO DAILY LIFE

Merchandise Returns Almost everyone has probably returned merchandise to a retailer. Perhaps they did not like the fit of clothing, or maybe their name was misspelled on the return address labels they ordered through a catalog. Ask students to describe occasions when they have returned merchandise. Have them discuss how the store's accountants would have handled their return.

6. Enter the amount of sales taxes collected in the Sales Tax Payable Credit column.
7. Enter the total cash received in the Cash in Bank Debit column.

Recording Other Cash Receipts

Occasionally, a retail business will receive cash from a transaction that does not involve the sale of merchandise. Since the business is receiving cash, the transaction is entered in the cash receipts journal.

Business Transaction

On December 16 On Your Mark received $30 from Mandy Harris, an office employee. She purchased a calculator that the business was no longer using, Receipt 303.

ON YOUR MARK
ATHLETIC WEAR
595 Leslie Street, Dallas, TX 75207

RECEIPT
No. 303

Dec. 16 20 --

RECEIVED FROM Mandy Harris $ 30.00

Thirty and no/100 DOLLARS

FOR calculator

RECEIVED BY *Michael Smith*

JOURNAL ENTRY

CASH RECEIPTS JOURNAL — PAGE *13*

	DATE	DOC. NO.	ACCOUNT NAME	POST. REF.	GENERAL CREDIT	SALES CREDIT	SALES TAX PAYABLE CREDIT	ACCOUNTS RECEIVABLE CREDIT	SALES DISCOUNTS DEBIT	CASH IN BANK DEBIT	
6	*16*	*R303*	*Office Equipment*		*30 00*					*30 00*	6
7	1	2	3		4					5	7

Follow these steps to enter this transaction into the cash receipts journal:

1. Enter the date of the receipt in the Date column.
2. Enter the letter "R" and the receipt number in the Document Number column.
3. Enter "Office Equipment" in the Account Name column.
4. Enter the amount of the credit in the General Credit column. Use the General Credit column whenever the credit part of the entry is to an account that does not have a special amount column.
5. Enter the amount of cash received in the Cash in Bank Debit column.

Posting to the Accounts Receivable Subsidiary Ledger

Daily postings are made from the Accounts Receivable Credit column to the accounts receivable subsidiary ledger. This ensures that customer accounts are always current. To post a cash receipt transaction to an account in the accounts receivable subsidiary ledger, refer to **Figure 16–9** and follow these steps.

1. Enter the date of the transaction in the Date column of the subsidiary ledger account.
2. In the Posting Reference column of the subsidiary ledger, enter the journal letters and the page number. Use the letters "CR" for the cash receipts journal.

2 TEACH (Cont'd.)

Visual Learning

Business Transaction

Display **Transparency 16–17** and explain how to record an entry in the General Credit column of the cash receipts journal. Remind students that this amount is posted to the account entered in the Account Name column; in this example, Office Equipment.

Demonstration Problem Step-by-Step Practice

Use demonstration problem 16–6 to give students practice in recording transactions in the cash receipts journal.

Concept Development: Posting to the Accounts Receivable Subsidiary Ledger

Discussion: Explain to students that posting from the cash receipts journal requires posting to the accounts receivable subsidiary ledger and to the general ledger. Amounts entered in the Accounts Receivable Credit column are posted daily to the customer accounts in the accounts receivable ledger. During the month, amounts in the General Credit column are posted to the general ledger accounts named in the Account Name column. At the end of the month, column totals are posted to the general ledger. L1

TEACHING NOTES

2 TEACH (Cont'd.)

Visual Learning

Figure 16–9 Posting from the Cash Receipts Journal to the Accounts Receivable Subsidiary Ledger

Using **Transparency 16–18**, have students explain the steps in posting from the cash receipts journal to the accounts receivable ledger.

Teaching Tip

Check students' understanding of accounts receivable by asking them whether the account in Figure 16–9 has a normal debit or credit balance.

Critical Thinking: Ask students to list types of errors that might occur during the posting process. How would they find and correct errors? (Slides, transpositions, posting to the wrong account, posting to the wrong column, math errors. To find errors, check addition and subtraction, retrace postings, and check account names against journal entries.) L1

3. In the Credit column of the subsidiary ledger account, enter the amount shown in the Accounts Receivable Credit column of the cash receipts journal.
4. Compute the new balance and enter it in the Balance column. If the account has a zero balance, draw a line through the Balance column.
5. Return to the cash receipts journal and enter a check mark (✓) in the Posting Reference column.

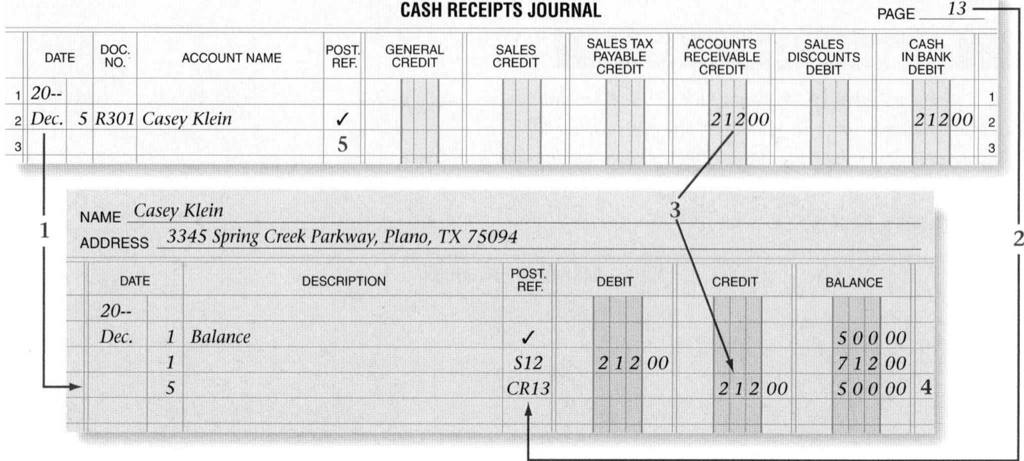

Figure 16–9 Posting from the Cash Receipts Journal to the Accounts Receivable Subsidiary Ledger

Posting the General Credit Column

Daily postings are made from the General Credit column of the cash receipts journal to the appropriate accounts in the general ledger. Refer to **Figure 16–10** as you read the steps for posting amounts from this column.

> **Key Points**
>
> **Posting from the Cash Receipts Journal**
> When posting a cash receipts journal entry to the accounts receivable subsidiary ledger, be sure to post the amount recorded in the Accounts Receivable Credit column.

1. Enter the date of the transaction in the Date column of the general ledger account.
2. Enter the journal letters and page number in the Posting Reference column of the ledger account. Be sure to use the letters "CR" for cash receipts journal.
3. In the Credit column of the ledger account, enter the amount from the General Credit column of the cash receipts journal.
4. Compute and enter the new account balance in the proper Balance column. For the **Office Equipment** account shown in **Figure 16–10**, the Debit Balance column is used. If the account has a zero balance, draw a line through the appropriate Balance column.
5. Return to the cash receipts journal and enter the general ledger account number in the Posting Reference column.

The cash receipts journal entry for the December 16 transaction is now posted. All transactions recorded in the General Credit column are posted in the same manner.

ADDRESSING MULTIPLE LEARNING STYLES

Interpersonal Learner Changes in technology often require new workplace skills. Have students interview someone whose daily work involves computerized accounting. Among the questions students should ask are: What computer skills do you use? How did you acquire those skills? How often do you need to upgrade your skills? How do you upgrade your skills? What new computer and communications hardware makes your work easier? Ask students to share the information they obtain with the class.

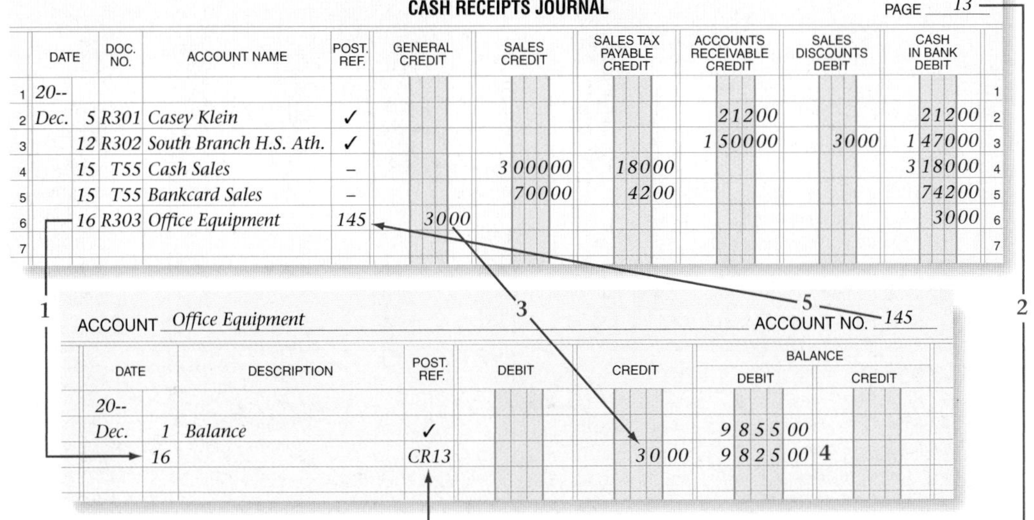

CASH RECEIPTS JOURNAL PAGE 13

	DATE	DOC. NO.	ACCOUNT NAME	POST. REF.	GENERAL CREDIT	SALES CREDIT	SALES TAX PAYABLE CREDIT	ACCOUNTS RECEIVABLE CREDIT	SALES DISCOUNTS DEBIT	CASH IN BANK DEBIT	
1	20--										1
2	Dec. 5	R301	Casey Klein	✓				212 00		212 00	2
3	12	R302	South Branch H.S. Ath.	✓				1 500 00	30 00	1 470 00	3
4	15	T55	Cash Sales	–		3 000 00	180 00			3 180 00	4
5	15	T55	Bankcard Sales	–		700 00	42 00			742 00	5
6	16	R303	Office Equipment	145	30 00					30 00	6
7											7

ACCOUNT Office Equipment ACCOUNT NO. 145

DATE		DESCRIPTION	POST. REF.	DEBIT	CREDIT	BALANCE DEBIT	BALANCE CREDIT
20--							
Dec.	1	Balance	✓			9 855 00	
	16		CR13		30 00	9 825 00	

Figure 16–10 Posting from the General Credit Column of the Cash Receipts Journal

Footing, Totaling, Proving, and Ruling the Cash Receipts Journal

To complete the cash receipts journal, refer to **Figure 16–11** and follow these steps:

1. Draw a single rule across the six amount columns, just below the last transaction.
2. Foot the columns.
3. Test for the equality of debits and credits.

Debit Columns		**Credit Columns**	
Sales Discounts	$ 30	General	$ 30
Cash in Bank	17,283	Sales	9,700
		Sales Tax Payable	582
		Accounts Receivable	7,001
Total	$ 17,313	Total	$ 17,313

4. In the Date column, on the line below the single rule, enter the date the journal is being totaled.
5. On the same line in the Account Name column, enter the word "Totals."
6. Enter the column totals, in ink, just below the footings.
7. Double-rule the amount columns.

Take a look at the completed Cash Receipts Journal. As you can see, a business saves time by using this special journal to record its cash receipts in one location instead of using many general journal pages.

After the cash receipts journal is footed, proved, totaled, and ruled, the column totals are posted to the general ledger.

Calculating Sales Discount

To calculate the amount of a sales discount, multiply the percentage times the sale amount *before* sales taxes are added to the total.

Math Skill Builder Activity

Calculating Sales Discount Have students calculate the following sales discount: Marsha wants to purchase two pairs of shoes that are on the 50% off sales rack. One pair of shoes is priced at $45 and the other is priced at $22. What is the discount and the total cost? ($45 × .50 = $22.50; $22 × .50 = $11.00; $22.50 + $11.00 = $33.50; $45 + $22 = $67.00 – $33.50 = $33.50; $33.50 + ($33.50 × 6%), or other amount of sales tax = $35.51.)

2 TEACH (Cont'd.)

Visual Learning

Figure 16–10 Posting from the General Credit Column of the Cash Receipts Journal

Using **Transparency 16–19**, have students describe how to post an amount entered in the General Credit column.

Critical Thinking: Ask students to explain why the Posting Reference column of the cash receipts journal in Figure 16–10 shows a check mark for amounts posted from the Accounts Receivable Credit column but an account number for amounts posted from the General Credit column. How might this differ in a computerized system? (Accounts with a check mark are subsidiary ledger accounts, which have not been numbered. Amounts in the General Credit column are posted to general ledger accounts, so the account number is entered in the Posting Reference column. In a computerized system, customer accounts would likely have numbers and those numbers would be entered in the Posting Reference column.) L2

Teaching Tips

Point out that totaling, proving, and ruling takes place before the column totals are posted. Footings are written in pencil because they are a test of total debits and credits and can be changed to correct errors.

Have students explain why a check mark rather than an account number is written below the double rule in the General Credit column.

Math Review for Accounting

Photocopy appropriate *Activity Sheets* for students who need additional practice in basic math.

CHAPTER 16
SECTION 2, PAGES 429–440

2 TEACH (Cont'd.)

Visual Learning

Figure 16–11 Totaled and Ruled Cash Receipts Journal

Display **Transparency 16–20** to review each step in footing, totaling, proving, and ruling the cash receipts journal.

Teaching Tip

Have students test the equality of debits and credits using the journal entry in Figure 16–11. Have students explain why they should check the equality of their journal entries.

Demonstration Problem Step-by-Step Practice

Use demonstration problem 16–7 to give students practice in posting column totals from the cash receipts journal to general ledger accounts.

CASH RECEIPTS JOURNAL — PAGE 13

	DATE		DOC. NO.	ACCOUNT NAME	POST. REF.	GENERAL CREDIT	SALES CREDIT	SALES TAX PAYABLE CREDIT	ACCOUNTS RECEIVABLE CREDIT	SALES DISCOUNTS DEBIT	CASH IN BANK DEBIT	
1	20--											1
2	Dec.	5	R301	Casey Klein	✓				212 00		212 00	2
3		12	R302	South Branch H.S. Ath.	✓				1 500 00	30 00	1 470 00	3
4		15	T55	Cash Sales	–		3 000 00	180 00			3 180 00	4
5		15	T55	Bankcard Sales	–		700 00	42 00			742 00	5
6		16	R303	Office Equipment	145	30 00					30 00	6
7		18	R304	Break Point Sports Club	✓				1 000 00		1 000 00	7
8		20	R305	Anita Montero	✓				100 00		100 00	8
9		22	R306	Gabriel Ramos	✓				500 00		500 00	9
10		23	R307	South Branch H.S. Ath.	✓				1 000 00		1 000 00	10
11		24	R308	Tammy's Fitness Club	✓				1 300 00		1 300 00	11
12		26	R309	Kim Wong	✓				300 00		300 00	12
13		27	R310	Lara Young	✓				200 00		200 00	13
14		27	R311	Robert Galvin	✓				465 00		465 00	14
15		28	R312	Joe Dimaio	✓				424 00		424 00	15
16		31	T56	Cash Sales	–		5 000 00	300 00			5 300 00	16
17		31	T56	Bankcard Sales	–		1 000 00	60 00			1 060 00	17
18		31		Totals		30 00 30 00	9 700 00 9 700 00	582 00 582 00	7 001 00 7 001 00	30 00 30 00	17 283 00 17 283 00	18
19						(✓)						19

Figure 16–11 Totaled and Ruled Cash Receipts Journal

Posting Column Totals to the General Ledger

There are six amount columns in the cash receipts journal used by On Your Mark. Only five of the column totals, however, are posted to the general ledger. The total of the General Credit column is *not* posted. The entries in this column have already been posted, individually, to the general ledger accounts. (See **Figure 16–10.**)

As shown in **Figure 16–12**, the total in each of the other five amount columns is posted to the general ledger account named in the column heading. The column heading indicates whether the amount is to be posted to the Debit or Credit column of the ledger account.

Refer to **Figure 16–12** and follow these steps:

1. Place a check mark in parenthesis under the General column total to indicate that this total is not posted.
2. Post the **Sales** total to the **Sales** account Credit column.
3. Post the **Sales Tax Payable** total to the **Sales Tax Payable** account Credit column.
4. Post the **Accounts Receivable** total to the **Accounts Receivable** controlling account Credit column.
5. Post the **Sales Discount** total to the **Sales Discounts** account Debit column.
6. Post the **Cash in Bank** total to the **Cash in Bank** account Debit column.
7. Compute new balances for each general ledger account.
8. Write the number of each account below the double rule in the cash receipts journal.

CONNECT TO . . . FOREIGN LANGUAGE

If an American buys a Japanese product and promises to pay in yen 90 days after receiving it, does he or she pay the dollar/yen exchange rate at date of purchase or the settlement date? Accountants must make such decisions when translating foreign currency for international business.

INTERDISCIPLINARY CONNECTIONS ACTIVITY

Foreign Currency Have students create a chart of foreign currency with exchange rates into U.S. dollars. Students can locate the information on the Internet, at local banks, or at airports. If students are particularly interested in one foreign country, ask them to find out the products that are most often purchased from that country (for example, watches from Switzerland, diamonds from Africa, or consumer electronics from Japan).

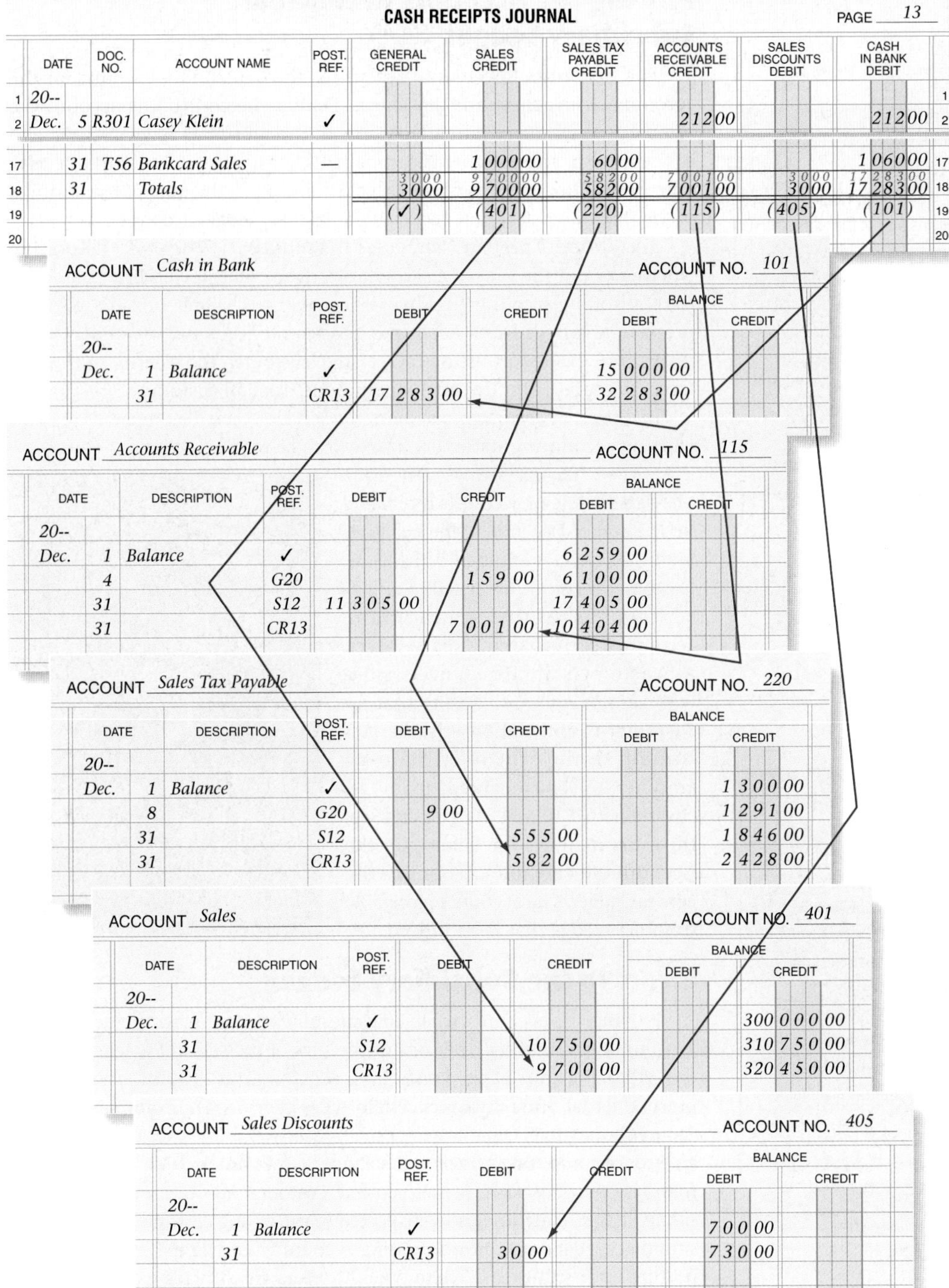

CASH RECEIPTS JOURNAL PAGE 13

	DATE		DOC. NO.	ACCOUNT NAME	POST. REF.	GENERAL CREDIT	SALES CREDIT	SALES TAX PAYABLE CREDIT	ACCOUNTS RECEIVABLE CREDIT	SALES DISCOUNTS DEBIT	CASH IN BANK DEBIT	
1	20--											1
2	Dec.	5	R301	Casey Klein	✓				212 00		212 00	2
17		31	T56	Bankcard Sales	—		1 000 00	60 00			1 060 00	17
18		31		Totals		30 00	9 700 00	582 00	7 001 00	30 00	17 283 00	18
19						(✓)	(401)	(220)	(115)	(405)	(101)	19
20												20

ACCOUNT *Cash in Bank* ACCOUNT NO. *101*

DATE		DESCRIPTION	POST. REF.	DEBIT	CREDIT	BALANCE DEBIT	BALANCE CREDIT
20--							
Dec.	1	Balance	✓			15 000 00	
	31		CR13	17 283 00		32 283 00	

ACCOUNT *Accounts Receivable* ACCOUNT NO. *115*

DATE		DESCRIPTION	POST. REF.	DEBIT	CREDIT	BALANCE DEBIT	BALANCE CREDIT
20--							
Dec.	1	Balance	✓			6 259 00	
	4		G20		159 00	6 100 00	
	31		S12	11 305 00		17 405 00	
	31		CR13		7 001 00	10 404 00	

ACCOUNT *Sales Tax Payable* ACCOUNT NO. *220*

DATE		DESCRIPTION	POST. REF.	DEBIT	CREDIT	BALANCE DEBIT	BALANCE CREDIT
20--							
Dec.	1	Balance	✓				1 300 00
	8		G20	9 00			1 291 00
	31		S12		555 00		1 846 00
	31		CR13		582 00		2 428 00

ACCOUNT *Sales* ACCOUNT NO. *401*

DATE		DESCRIPTION	POST. REF.	DEBIT	CREDIT	BALANCE DEBIT	BALANCE CREDIT
20--							
Dec.	1	Balance	✓				300 000 00
	31		S12		10 750 00		310 750 00
	31		CR13		9 700 00		320 450 00

ACCOUNT *Sales Discounts* ACCOUNT NO. *405*

DATE		DESCRIPTION	POST. REF.	DEBIT	CREDIT	BALANCE DEBIT	BALANCE CREDIT
20--							
Dec.	1	Balance	✓			700 00	
	31		CR13	30 00		730 00	

Figure 16–12 Posting Column Totals from the Cash Receipts Journal

2 TEACH (Cont'd.)

Visual Learning

Figure 16–12 Posting Column Totals from the Cash Receipts Journal

Using **Transparency 16–21**, have students review the process for posting column totals. Ask students to explain the effect of posting each column total to the general ledger.

Teaching Tips

Remind students that the date of the posting is always the same as the date of the journal entry. When column totals are posted, the last day of the month is used.

Tell students to write account numbers neatly and in the correct column. These numbers form a part of the audit trail that allows an auditor to trace transactions to their source documents.

TEACHING NOTES

2 TEACH (Cont'd.)

Concept Development: Proving the Accounts Receivable Subsidiary Ledger

Discussion: Explain that a schedule of accounts receivable is simply a list of each charge customer, the balance in each customer's account, and the total amount due from all customers. Tell students to list all customers on the schedule, even those with zero balances. By listing all customers, they will be less likely to omit an account accidentally. This practice also corresponds to computerized accounting programs, which print out the complete customer list.

Emphasize that the total of the schedule of accounts receivable must match the total of the Accounts Receivable controlling account in the general ledger. L1

Teaching Tip

Point out that business managers review the schedule of accounts receivable to determine which customers are not paying on time or those who may have stopped buying from the company for some reason. Following up with those customers can help the managers improve their collections of amounts owed or improve products or services to regain customers.

Did You Know?

Theaters

Sony Corporation owns part of the largest theater company in the world. Loews Cineplex Entertainment is the result of a merger between Sony's Loews Theatres and Cineplex Odeon. The combined company has over 2,500 movie screens in 290 locations in North America.

ACCOUNTING *Flashbacks*

EGYPTIAN ACCOUNTANTS

In ancient Egypt, accountants were highly respected members of society. They were the pharaohs' right hands, summarizing detailed daily records into monthly and yearly financial statements.

Proving the Accounts Receivable Subsidiary Ledger

The **Accounts Receivable** account is the controlling account for the accounts receivable subsidiary ledger. That is, the controlling account is a summary of all the customer accounts in the subsidiary ledger. At the end of the month, after posting is completed, the balance of **Accounts Receivable** (controlling) in the general ledger should equal the total of the balances of the individual accounts receivable subsidiary ledger accounts.

Accountants prepare schedules for subsidiary ledgers to determine whether or not the sum of a subsidiary ledger equals the ending balance of the controlling account. To prove the accounts receivable subsidiary ledger, prepare a schedule of accounts receivable. A **schedule of accounts receivable** is a report listing each charge customer, the balance in the customer's account, and the total amount due from all customers.

In a manual accounting system, the schedule may be prepared on plain paper or accounting stationery. It may also be prepared on a computer.

Figure 16–13 shows On Your Mark's schedule of accounts receivable for the end of December. The heading identifies the schedule and the date. Customer accounts are listed in alphabetical order, as they appear in the accounts receivable subsidiary ledger. All customers are listed, even those with zero balances, to ensure that no customer is omitted by mistake. According to the schedule, the total amount to be received from all customers is $10,404. As you can see, this total matches the balance of the **Accounts Receivable** account in the general ledger. The accounts receivable subsidiary ledger has been proved.

Errors in the Subsidiary Ledger

Proving the accounts receivable subsidiary ledger with the controlling account determines whether or not the sum of the subsidiary ledger equals the ending balance of the controlling account. This is an internal control procedure that often uncovers certain types of errors. For example, this procedure should detect a failure to post a transaction to the subsidiary ledger or an error in computing an account balance. It does **not** provide assurance that transactions were posted to the correct customer account within the subsidiary ledger. If an amount were posted to the wrong customer account, the subsidiary ledger and the controlling account would be in balance, but the posting error still exists. These types of errors are difficult to detect. These errors are often detected by a customer who finds the error on a monthly billing.

EXTENDING THE CONTENT

Customer Preferences for Payment of Goods and Services Ask students to interview managers of local businesses to learn about the payment method customers prefer. Have students gather information regarding the percentage of customers who use cash, debit cards, personal checks, and credit cards to pay for their goods and services. Have students compare their findings and then discuss the differences between the businesses they contacted.

ACCOUNT *Accounts Receivable* ACCOUNT NO. *115*

DATE		DESCRIPTION	POST. REF.	DEBIT	CREDIT	BALANCE DEBIT	BALANCE CREDIT
20--							
Dec.	*1*	*Balance*	✓			*6 259 00*	
	4		*G20*		*159 00*	*6 100 00*	
	31		*S12*	*11 305 00*		*17 405 00*	
	31		*CR13*		*7 001 00*	*10 404 00*	

On Your Mark Athletic Wear
Schedule of Accounts Receivable
December 31, 20--

Break Point Sports Club	*3 710 00*	
Joe Dimaio	—	
Robert Galvin	—	
Casey Klein	*500 00*	
Anita Montero	*371 00*	
Shashi Rahim	*212 00*	
Gabriel Ramos	*318 00*	
South Branch High School Athletics	*1 000 00*	
Megan Sullivan	*530 00*	
Tammy's Fitness Club	*1 060 00*	
Kim Wong	*106 00*	
Lara Young	*2 597 00*	
		10 404 00

The balance of the **Accounts Receivable** account should equal the total of the schedule of accounts receivable.

Figure 16–13 Schedule of Accounts Receivable

ANALYZING FINANCIAL REPORTS

Operating Results

As you learned earlier, public corporations publish the financial results of their business operations each year in an annual report. The annual report contains much more than just financial data about the business. The company usually includes a description of the business activities of the past fiscal period, new products in development, and the business actions taken by the company's management to help make the business successful in the future.

The description of business activities includes management's analysis and interpretation of the financial data. For example, if revenue has decreased, the description might provide reasons for the decrease and projections for the next fiscal period.

▶ Analyze the Report:

Refer to the "Results of Operations" section on pages A-43–A-44 for Office Depot to answer these questions.

1. Did sales increase or decrease over the prior year?
2. What reasons are given for the change in sales from the prior fiscal period?
3. Why do you think an analysis of sales would be important to people reading an annual report?

ANALYZING FINANCIAL REPORTS

Analyze the Report (Answers)

1. Sales decreased in 2001 from the prior year.
2. The decrease in sales was due to the slowing U.S. economy and the closing of 73 stores, following a comprehensive business review.
3. Investors want to know if the company will grow in profitability, while creditors need to know that the company can pay its debts. Since the company's revenue comes primarily from sales, the sales data is important to just about all readers.

2 TEACH (Cont'd.)

Visual Learning

Figure 16–13 Schedule of Accounts Receivable

Use **Transparency 16–22** to show students how to prepare a schedule of accounts receivable.

Teaching Tip

Review types of errors that might occur when preparing a schedule of accounts receivable; for example, slide, transposition, omitted account, incorrect math. Have students explain how they would find and correct each type of error.

Analysis: Point out that accounts receivable represents money due to the company. How might a manager use the schedule of accounts receivable and the accounts receivable subsidiary ledger to manage the amount of credit allowed to customers? (The schedule gives the manager an overall picture of the total owed to the company. If this amount increases significantly each month, the company may be granting too much credit and could have trouble collecting some of the money owed to it. If the amount goes down each month, the company may be granting too little credit or customers may be going elsewhere for some other reason. Using accounts in the subsidiary ledger, the manager could identify which customers are not buying as much and try to find out whether the company has a problem with products or services.) L3

The Office Depot 2001 Annual Report
Refer students to pages A-39–A-48 in the back of the book.

CHAPTER 16
SECTION 2, PAGES 429–440

3 ASSESS

Thinking Critically (Answers)

1. Cash in Bank is debited because bankcard sales increase cash. Sales is credited since revenue is increased. Sales Tax Payable is credited because liabilities are increased.
2. All charge customers, ending account balances, and total amount due from all customers. The schedule is proved if the total matches the balance of the Accounts Receivable account.

Computing in the Business World (Answers)

1. 6% × $550 = $33; $33 + $550 = $583
2. 1% × $49.32 = $0.49; $49.32 – $0.49 = $48.83

Problem 16–3 (Answers)

General Credit $105
Sales Credit $6,200
Sales Tax Payable Credit $372
Accounts Receivable Credit $5,580
Sales Discounts Debit $110
Cash in Bank Debit $12,147
Total debits/credits $12,257

Chapter Reviews and Working Papers Refer students to the Chapter 16 workbook pages to answer *Check Your Understanding* activities.

4 CLOSE

Section Wrap-Up

Writing: Have students write a paragraph or two describing why they would use special journals. Ask them also to explain the types of information that special journals provide and how they could use this information in making business decisions. L2

SECTION 2 Check Your Understanding

Now that you have studied this section, complete the following questions and problems.

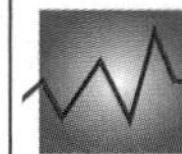

Thinking Critically

1. Explain the rules of debit and credit for recording bank card sales.
2. What is included in a schedule of accounts receivable? Explain how to prove the accounts receivable subsidiary ledger.

Computing in the Business World

You are hired to audit the books for a computer software retailer, Software Biz. As you review the books, you realize that the sales tax was not calculated on a sales slip. You also want to estimate cash receipts from a sale. On a separate sheet of paper, make the following calculations:

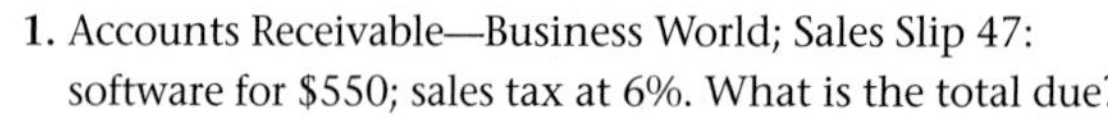

1. Accounts Receivable—Business World; Sales Slip 47: software for $550; sales tax at 6%. What is the total due?
2. Accounts Receivable—Cindy Caskey; Sales Slip 48:

Software	$46.53
Sales tax	2.79
Total	$49.32

Terms: 1/10, n/30.
How much will be received if paid within the discount period?

Problem 16–3 Completing the Cash Receipts Journal

The cash receipts journal for the month of January is provided in your working papers and illustrated below.

Instructions In your working papers, foot, prove, total, and rule the cash receipts journal.

CASH RECEIPTS JOURNAL PAGE *10*

DATE		DOC. NO.	ACCOUNT NAME	POST. REF.	GENERAL CREDIT	SALES CREDIT	SALES TAX PAYABLE CREDIT	ACCOUNTS RECEIVABLE CREDIT	SALES DISCOUNTS DEBIT	CASH IN BANK DEBIT
20--										
Jan.	*3*	*R502*	*Jennifer Smith*	✓				*80 00*		*80 00*
	5	*R503*	*Wilton High School*	✓				*3 100 00*	*62 00*	*3 038 00*
	8	*R504*	*Store Equipment*	*155*	*75 00*					*75 00*
	15	*T42*	*Cash Sales*	—		*5 000 00*	*300 00*			*5 300 00*
	15	*T42*	*Bankcard Sales*	—		*1 200 00*	*72 00*			*1 272 00*
	20	*R505*	*Norwin High School*	✓				*2 400 00*	*48 00*	*2 352 00*
	30	*R506*	*Supplies*	*115*	*30 00*					*30 00*

RETEACHING SECTION 2

Recording Cash Discounts When a business sells goods on account, it records the full amount of the sale without taking account of any discount offered for quick payment. The reason for this is that the business does not know whether the customer will pay for the goods in time to take advantage of the discount offer. If payment is received within the specified time, the amount of the cash discount is recorded along with the cash payment. By recording cash discounts at the time payment is received, businesses can keep a record of the total cash discounts allowed.

CHAPTER 16 SUMMARY

KEY CONCEPTS

1. Special journals are used by businesses that have many transactions. The most commonly used special journals are: the sales journal, the cash receipts journal, the purchases journal, and the cash payments journal.
2. A sales journal is used to record all sales of merchandise on account. The entry to record the sale of merchandise on account in the sales journal is illustrated below.

SALES JOURNAL PAGE *1*

	DATE	SALES SLIP NO.	CUSTOMER'S ACCOUNT DEBITED	POST. REF.	SALES CREDIT	SALES TAX PAYABLE CREDIT	ACCOUNTS RECEIVABLE DEBIT	
1	*Date*	*Sales*	*Customer's Account Name*		*x x x xx*	*x x xx*	*x x x xx*	1
2		*Slip*						2
3		*No.*						3

3. Daily postings are made from the Accounts Receivable Debit column to customer accounts in the accounts receivable subsidiary ledger. At the end of the month, the totals of the amount columns in the sales journal are posted to the accounts named in the column headings.
4. The cash receipts journal is used to record all cash received by a business.
5. The following illustrates the use of the cash receipts journal:
   (a) the receipt of cash from a charge customer
   (b) the receipt of cash from a charge customer less a cash discount
   (c) the receipt of cash from cash sales
   (d) the receipt of cash from bankcard sales
   (e) the receipt of cash from the sale of other assets

CASH RECEIPTS JOURNAL PAGE *1*

		DATE	DOC. NO.	ACCOUNT NAME	POST. REF.	GENERAL CREDIT	SALES CREDIT	SALES TAX PAYABLE CREDIT	ACCOUNTS RECEIVABLE CREDIT	SALES DISCOUNTS DEBIT	CASH IN BANK DEBIT	
(a)	1	*Date of Receipt*	*Receipt No.*	*Customer's Name*					*x x x xx*		*x x x xx*	1
(b)	2	*Date of Receipt*	*Receipt No.*	*Customer's Name*					*x x x xx*	*x x xx*	*x x x xx*	2
(c)	3	*Date of Deposit*	*Tape No.*	*Cash Sale*			*x x x xx*	*x x xx*			*x x x xx*	3
(d)	4	*Date of Deposit*	*Tape No.*	*Bankcard Sales*			*x x x xx*	*x x xx*			*x x x xx*	4
(e)	5	*Date of Receipt*	*Receipt No.*	*Account Affected*		*x x x xx*					*x x x xx*	5

6. The schedule of accounts receivable lists all charge customers and the amount each customer owes.

ANSWERS

1. False
2. False
3. False
4. True
5. True
6. False
7. False
8. False
9. True
10. True

SUMMARY CHAPTER 16

Chapter 16 Quiz

Student Class Instructor
Date Assigned Date Completed

CHAPTER 16 QUIZ

Special Journals: Sales and Cash Receipts

QUESTIONS (True-False)

Directions: In the space provided, indicate whether each statement is true or false.

___ 1. The sales journal is used to record all sales of merchandise for cash or on account.
___ 2. The sales journal has columns to record sales, sales tax, and accounts payable.
___ 3. All transactions recorded in the sales journal must have sales tax recorded.
___ 4. Accounts receivable amounts are posted daily to the accounts named in the Customer's Account Debited column.
___ 5. Column totals are posted only at the end of the month.
___ 6. The sales journal is proved if all columns are correctly added.
___ 7. Amounts entered in the General Credit column of the cash receipts journal are posted at the end of the month.
___ 8. After posting journal column totals, the account numbers are entered in the Posting Reference column.
___ 9. The schedule of accounts receivable reports the amount of money owed by a business's customers.
___ 10. Accounts Receivable is a controlling account.

18 • Chapter Quizzes Copyright © Glencoe/McGraw-Hill

QUESTIONS (True-False)

1. The sales journal is used to record all sales of merchandise for cash or on account.
2. The sales journal has columns for sales, sales tax, and accounts payable.
3. All transactions recorded in the sales journal must have sales tax recorded.
4. Accounts receivable amounts are posted daily to the accounts named in the Customer's Account Debited column.
5. Column totals are posted only at the end of the month.
6. The sales journal is proved if all columns are correctly added.
7. Amounts entered in the General Credit column of the cash receipts journal are posted at the end of the month.
8. After posting journal column totals, the account numbers are entered in the Posting Reference column.
9. The schedule of accounts receivable reports the amount of money owed by a business's customers.
10. Accounts Receivable is a controlling account.

USING KEY TERMS

See the *Glossary* for the definitions of these terms. Have several students share their memos in class. Discuss ways to communicate effectively in writing, such as stating the purpose and giving supporting information.

Understanding Accounting Concepts and Procedures

(Answers)

1. When the volume of transactions requires a more efficient system for recording transactions that are similar in nature.
2. (a) Sales journal, used to record all sales of merchandise on account; (b) cash receipts journal, used to record all cash received; (c) purchases journal, used to record any purchase on account; (d) cash payments journal, used to record all payments of cash.
3. Sales, Sales Tax Payable, and Accounts Receivable.
4. Daily; to be certain that the balances in customers' accounts are always current.
5. Receipts and cash register tapes.
6. Every transaction recorded in the cash receipts journal requires a debit to Cash in Bank.
7. Cash receipts from charge customers are posted to the customer accounts in the accounts receivable subsidiary ledger. Cash receipts for the transactions recorded in the General Credit column are posted to the appropriate general ledger accounts.
8. Daily; to ensure that customer accounts are always up to date.
9. To indicate that the column total is not posted.
10. To prove the subsidiary ledger.

USING KEY TERMS

Imagine that you are the accounting manager for EarthWear Clothing. Recently you noticed that several sales associates are not keeping good records of sales transactions. Write an informational memorandum to the sales staff about the need for accurate, complete sales records. Use the terms listed below, and describe a systematic method to track sales.

cash receipts journal	schedule of accounts receivable
footing	special journals
sales journal	

Understanding Accounting Concepts and Procedures

Instructions

Answer the following questions on a separate sheet of paper.

1. When are special journals used in an accounting system?
2. Name and describe four commonly used special journals.
3. What three accounts are affected by a sale on account?
4. When are sales transactions posted to the accounts receivable subsidiary ledger? Why?
5. What are the source documents for transactions recorded in the cash receipts journal?
6. Why does a cash receipts journal always have a Cash in Bank Debit column.
7. What are the two kinds of postings made from the cash receipts journal?
8. When are amounts in the Accounts Receivable Credit column of the cash receipts journal posted to the accounts receivable subsidiary ledger?
9. Why is a check mark in parentheses placed below the double rule in the General Credit column of the cash receipts journal?
10. What is the purpose of preparing a schedule of accounts receivable?

ASSESSMENT RESOURCES

Choose assessment strategies from the following pages to evaluate your students' progress.

Student Edition
Check Your Understanding, pp. 428, 440
Chapter 16 Problems, pp. 445–447
Analyzing Financial Reports, p. 439

Assessment and Evaluation Masters
Chapter 16 Study Plan, *Glencoe Workbook (CRWP)*
Chapter 16 Self-Test, *Glencoe Workbook (CRWP)*
Chapter 16 Test, *Chapter Tests* Booklet
Chapter 16 Activity, *School-to-Work Handbook*
Chapter 16 Exam*View*

Teacher Wraparound Edition
Critical Thinking Activity, p. 423
Reteaching Sections 1–2, pp. 428, 440
Chapter 16 Quiz, p. 441

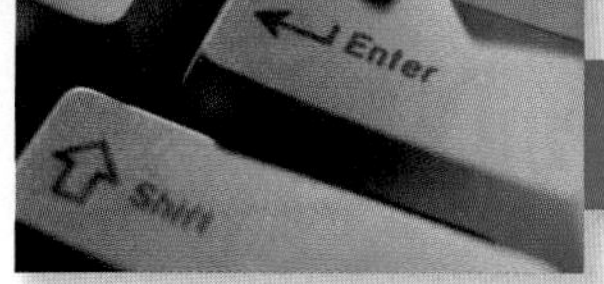

CHAPTER 16 REVIEW AND ACTIVITIES

Case Study...

Merchandising Business: Movie Theater

You work in the accounting department for Springdale Movie Theaters and have been asked to analyze ticket and concession food sales. The owners are considering enlarging the concession area to offer a greater variety of foods. No theater seats would be lost. The cost of enlarging the concession area to one and one-half times its current size is estimated at $200,000. Review the following sales figures for the past three years.

Year	Ticket Sales	Concession Sales
Year 1	$4,800,000	$1,800,000
Year 2	5,100,000	1,600,000
Year 3	5,400,000	1,480,000

Thinking Critically:

1. What percentage of sales are ticket sales and concession sales for each year?
2. What percentage increase in concession revenue would be needed to pay for the renovation costs in the first year?

Conducting an Audit with Alex

Alex is the chief auditor for the Mega Byte Corporation. You are working as an accounting intern under Alex's supervision. In April a number of errors are discovered in the sales journal. Alex asked you to identify and correct the errors. All sales were made on account and are taxable at a rate of 6%.

Instructions

1. What possible error has been made in the Sales Slip No. column?
2. What errors have been made in the three amount columns?

SALES JOURNAL PAGE 1

	DATE		SALES SLIP NO.	CUSTOMER'S ACCOUNT DEBITED	POST. REF.	SALES CREDIT	SALES TAX PAYABLE CREDIT	ACCOUNTS RECEIVABLE DEBIT	
1	20--								1
2	Apr.	25	3110	Suzette Simons		330 00		330 00	2
3		25	3101	John Joyce		450 00	27 00	477 00	3
4		26	3102	Fred Woodburn		170 00		190 00	4
5									5

*inter*NET CONNECTION

Bankcards

As you learned in Chapter 14, VISA and MasterCard are the two most widely used bankcards. Locate the Internet site for each company and answer the following questions.

Do This:

1. Which card, VISA or MasterCard, has greater acceptance or use by shoppers?
2. How many merchants accept VISA and MasterCard? What volume of sales is charged to each card?
3. List at least three additional services offered by the two major bankcard companies.
4. What is the cost to a merchant for accepting these bankcards?

Workplace Skills

Designing and Improving Systems

The ultimate in "systems thinking" is predicting trends, making adjustments, and improving the current system to benefit the organization.

On the Job:

At Ice Cream Express, you keep the financial records and maintain inventory. You noticed that some ice cream flavors are only popular during certain seasons of the year. For example, peppermint-flavored ice cream is very popular during the winter season, but sales decrease dramatically in the summer. You decide to get feedback from regular customers.

Thinking Critically:

1. Design a survey that will help determine the likes and dislikes of your customers. Include questions that will gather information about the gender, age, and income levels of respondents.
2. What incentives might prompt customers to participate?

REVIEW AND ACTIVITIES
CHAPTER 16

Case Study...

Thinking Critically (Answers)

1. Year One: ticket sales 72.7%, concession sales 27.3%; Year Two: ticket sales 76.1%, concession sales 23.9%; Year Three: ticket sales 78.5%, concession sales 21.5%
2. 13.5%

Workplace Skills

Thinking Critically (Answers)

1. Answers will vary.
2. Answers will vary. Students may use computer software or they can create a one-page flyer by hand. The flyer should announce the customer online survey and give some reasons for the company's interest in their customer's opinions.

Conducting an Audit with Alex

(Answers)

1. The sales slips are not in order. They should be checked to ensure that all are accounted for.
2. Sales tax has not been accrued for Simons and Woodburn.

Internet Resources and Activities Handbook

Refer students to the booklet for additional Internet activities.

*inter*NET CONNECTION www.glencoe.com

Do This (Answers)

1. www.visa.com and www.mastercard.com; Visa is first in dollar volume, MasterCard second.
2. Visa is accepted at 24 million locations; MasterCard has 24 million acceptance locations (including merchants and ATMs). Visa has sales volume of $2.1 trillion worldwide; MasterCard, $986 billion worldwide (2001 data).
3. Debit cards, Internet payment systems, smart cards, and travelers' checks.
4. 2.5%

PEACHTREE CORNER

Sales on Account

Use the **Sales/Invoicing** task option or click the **Sales** navigation aid to enter a sale on account.

Tasks | Analysis | Options | Reports
- Quotes/Sales Orders
- Sales/Invoicing...
- Receipts...
- Finance Charge...
- Select for Deposit...
- Purchase Orders...

Sales/Invoicing

Your students learned how to use the Sales/Invoicing data entry form in Chapter 14, but you may want to review the steps to record a sale on account.

Cash Receipts

Remind your students to select **Receipts** from the ***Tasks*** menu to enter any kind of cash receipt: cash sales, bankcard sales, and sale of an asset (e.g., supplies, store equipment).

Tasks | Analysis | Options | Reports
- Quotes/Sales Orders
- Sales/Invoicing...
- Receipts...
- Finance Charge...
- Select for Deposit...

Receipts

To record a customer payment, enter a deposit ticket ID (transaction date), customer ID, reference (receipt number), and transaction date. In the Apply to Invoices tab, mark the invoice (sales slip) to which you want to apply the cash received from the customer. Peachtree uses the term invoice instead of sales slip.

Mastering Sales and Cash Receipts

Making the Transition from a Manual to a Computerized System

Task	Perform Accounting Procedures Using Manual Methods	Perform Accounting Procedures Using Automated Methods
Setting up customer records	1. Ledger sheets or cards are prepared with customer account details such as customer name, address, and contact information. 2. Account activities are posted to the customer's subsidiary ledger account.	1. Assign each customer an ID code. 2. Record details of customer accounts into customer records. 3. The software will access this information automatically each time the ID code is used. 4. The customer's sales and payment history is maintained automatically.
Issuing and Recording a Credit Memorandum	1. A credit memorandum is prepared. 2. A journal entry is prepared to record the credit memorandum. 3. The journal entry is posted to the customer's account and to the general ledger.	1. A credit memorandum is prepared. 2. Record the credit memorandum as a negative amount using the Sales/Invoice option. 3. The software applies the credit memorandum to the appropriate outstanding invoice and posts the amount to the customer's account and to the general ledger.

Mastering Sales and Cash Receipts

Peachtree Question	Description
How do I set up a new customer account?	1. Select **Customers/Prospects** from the ***Maintain*** menu. 2. Assign a Customer ID to the customer account. 3. Enter customer name and contact information. 4. Click on the *Sales Defaults* tab. 5. Verify or enter the appropriate sales default GL account number. 6. Click *Save*.
How do I issue and record a credit memorandum?	1. Select **Sales/Invoicing** from the ***Tasks*** menu. 2. Enter a reference number, usually the Credit Memorandum number. 3. Enter the return or allowance as a negative amount for the appropriate invoice listed. 4. Click *Save*.
What does the software do "behind the scenes"?	• Using Customer ID codes, the software can update customer sales and payment history records when you enter invoices or cash receipts. • Credit memorandums are applied directly to the appropriate outstanding invoice and posted to the general ledger and subsidiary ledger automatically.

For detailed instructions: See the **Peachtree User Guide** in your Glencoe Working Papers.

Peachtree® Answers to Frequently Asked Questions

Q: What steps are required to correct a cash receipt entry?

A: You can change any information on a cash receipt unless you have closed the current period. To make a change, choose the **Receipts** option. Click the *Open* button and select the receipt you want to update. Make the changes and post the corrected transaction. Peachtree automatically applies the corrections.

For additional information, refer to your *Glencoe Peachtree Accounting User Guide*.

APPLICATION OPTIONS

Problem 16–4 Recording and Posting Sales Transactions

Shutterbug Cameras uses special journals for recording its transactions. The accounts receivable subsidiary ledger and certain general ledger accounts are included in your working papers.

Instructions In your working papers:

1. Record each transaction on page 12 of the sales journal or on page 13 of the cash receipts journal.
2. Post to the customer accounts in the accounts receivable subsidiary ledger on a daily basis.
3. Foot, prove, total, and rule the sales journal.
4. Post the column totals from the sales journal and the cash receipts journal to the general ledger accounts named in the column headings.
5. Prepare a schedule of accounts receivable.

Date	Transactions
May 1	Sold merchandise on account to Yoko Nakata, $500 plus 4% sales tax of $20, Sales Slip 220.
3	Sold to Click Studios $1,500 in camera equipment plus sales tax of $60, Sales Slip 221.
7	Sold telescopic lens to Jimmy Thompson for $200 plus sales tax of $8, Sales Slip 222.
9	Sold merchandise on account to Heather Sullivan for $100 plus sales tax of $4, Sales Slip 223.
12	Sold camera tripod to Arturo Diaz for $400 plus sales tax of $16, Sales Slip 224.
15	Sold $3,000 in merchandise on account to FastForward Productions plus sales tax of $120, Sales Slip 225.
18	Sold merchandise on account to Yoko Nakata, $200 plus sales tax of $8, Sales Slip 226.

Analyze: Based on the transactions above, how much cash was collected for the month?

Problem 16–5 Recording and Posting Cash Receipts

River's Edge Canoe & Kayak uses special journals and an accounts receivable subsidiary ledger for recording business transactions. The accounts receivable subsidiary ledger accounts and certain general ledger accounts are included in your working papers. The current account balances are recorded in the accounts.

Continued

Complete chapter problems one of three ways:

1 **Manual** Glencoe Working Papers

or

2 **Peachtree Complete Accounting** Software

or

3 **QuickBooks** Templates (Problems 16–5, 16–6)

Peachtree®

SMART GUIDE

Step-by-Step Instructions: Problem 16–4

1. Select the problem set for Shutterbug Cameras (Prob. 16–4).
2. Rename the company and set the system date.
3. Enter all sales on account transactions using the **Sales/Invoicing** option.
4. Record all cash sales using the **Receipts** option.
5. Print a Sales Journal report and a Cash Receipts Journal report.
6. Proof your work. Make any needed corrections.
7. Print a General Ledger report and Customer Ledgers report.
8. Answer the Analyze question.
9. End the session.

TIP: When you print a report, such as the General Ledger, you can use the filter options to customize the information that appears on the report.

PROBLEMS CHAPTER 16

Problem 16-4 (Answers) Recording and Posting Sales and Cash Receipts

Sales Journal totals:
Sales Cr. $3,800
Sales Tax Pay. Cr. $152
Accts. Rec. Dr. $3,952

Cash Receipts Journal totals:
Sales Cr. $2,100
Sales Tax Pay. Cr. $84
Cash in Bank Dr. $2,184

Ending debit balances:
Cash in Bank $7,184
Accts. Rec. $4,602
Accts. Rec./Fast Forward $3,120
Accts. Rec./Yoko Nakata $1,328
Accts. Rec./Heather Sullivan $154

Ending credit balances:
Sales Tax Pay. $1,436
Sales $35,900

Analyze: $2,184

SOFTWARE NOTES

Teachers can find detailed instructions for:

- **Peachtree Complete Accounting Software**, in the *Glencoe Workbook (CRWP)*
- **QuickBooks Templates**, in *Using QuickBooks with Glencoe Accounting*
- **Spreadsheet Templates**, in the *Glencoe Workbook (CRWP)*

Problem 16–5 (Answers) Recording and Posting Cash Receipts

Cash Receipts Journal totals:
General Cr. $50
Sales Cr. $13,300
Sales Tax. Pay. Cr. $665
Accts. Rec. Cr. $6,150
Sales Discounts Dr. $135
Cash in Bank Dr. $20,030

Total Debits/Credits $20,165

Ending debit balances:
Cash in Bank $27,530
Accts. Rec. $750
Store Equipment $2,950
Sales Discounts $1,335
Accts. Rec./Adventure River Tours $0
Accts. Rec./Paul Drake $400
Accts. Rec./Celeste Everett $250
Accts. Rec./Isabel Rodriguez $100
Accts. Rec./Wildwood Resorts $0

Ending credit balances:
Sales Tax Pay. $915
Sales $53,300

Schedule of Accounts Receivable $750

Analyze: A tape from the cash register

Peachtree®

SMART GUIDE

Step-by-Step Instructions: Problem 16–5

1. Select the problem set for River's Edge Canoe & Kayak (Prob. 16–5).
2. Rename the company and set the system date.
3. Record all cash receipts using the **Receipts** option.
4. Print the following reports: Cash Receipts Journal, General Ledger, and Customer Ledgers.
5. Proof your work. Make any needed corrections.
6. Answer the Analyze question.
7. End the session.

TIP: You can apply a partial payment from a customer.

Instructions In your working papers:

1. Record the transactions on page 7 in the cash receipts journal.
2. Post the amounts from the Accounts Receivable Credit column to the customers' accounts in the accounts receivable subsidiary ledger. Post the individual amounts in the General Credit column to the general ledger accounts.
3. Foot, prove, total, and rule the cash receipts journal.
4. Post the column totals to the general ledger accounts named in the column headings.
5. Prepare a schedule of accounts receivable.

Date	Transactions
May 2	Received $400 from Paul Drake to apply on his account, Receipt 505.
5	Received $2,940 from Adventure River Tours in payment of their $3,000 account less a 2% cash discount of $60, Receipt 506.
7	Sold old shelving **(Store Equipment)** for $50, Receipt 507.
10	Wildwood Resorts sent us a check for $2,425 in payment of their account, $2,500 less a 3% cash discount of $75, Receipt 508.
15	Cash sales totaled $2,000 plus $100 in sales tax, Tape 20.
15	Bankcard sales were $3,000 plus $150 in sales tax, Tape 20.
18	Celeste Everett sent us a check for $150 to apply on her account, Receipt 509.
20	Isabel Rodriquez sent us $100 to apply on her account, Receipt 510.
30	Cash sales were $4,500 plus $225 sales tax, Tape 21. Bankcard sales totaled $3,800 plus sales tax of $190, Tape 21.

Analyze: What source document would be used to record bankcard sales and cash sales?

SOURCE DOCUMENT PROBLEM

Problem 16–6

Use the source documents in your working papers to record the transactions for this problem.

CHALLENGE PROBLEM Problem 16–6 Recording and Posting Sales and Cash Receipts

SOURCE DOCUMENT PROBLEM

Buzz Newsstand had the following sales and cash receipt transactions for May. In your working papers, the accounts receivable subsidiary ledger and general ledger accounts have been opened with current balances.

Instructions

1. Record the sales and cash receipts for May on page 11 of the sales journal and page 11 of the cash receipts journal.
2. Post to the customer accounts in the accounts receivable subsidiary ledger on a daily basis.
3. Post from the General Credit column of the cash receipts journal on a daily basis.

SOLUTION NOTES

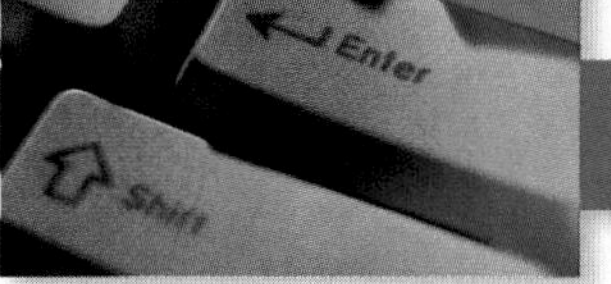

4. Foot, prove, total, and rule both journals.
5. Post the column totals of the sales journal to the general ledger accounts named in the column headings.
6. Post the column totals from the cash receipts journal to the general ledger accounts named in the column headings.
7. Prepare a schedule of accounts receivable.

Date	Transactions
May 1	Sold $300 in merchandise plus 6% sales tax of $18 on account to Ilya Bodonski, Sales Slip 170.
3	Received $490.00 from Katz Properties in payment of their $500 account balance less a 2% discount of $10.00, Receipt 145.
5	As a favor, sold $60 in supplies to Straka Stores, received cash, Receipt 146.
7	Rothwell Management Inc. sent us a check for $294.00 in payment of their $300 account balance less a $6.00 cash discount, Receipt 147.
9	Sold $100 in merchandise plus $6 sales tax on account to Saba Nadal, Sales Slip 171.
10	Sold $600 in merchandise plus $36 sales tax on account to Java Shops Inc., terms 2/10, n/30, Sales Slip 172.
12	Sold $50 in merchandise plus $3 sales tax on account to Lee Adkins, Sales Slip 173.
15	Received a check for $196.00 from Rolling Hills Pharmacies in payment of their $200 account less a 2% cash discount of $4.00, Receipt 148.
15	Cash sales were $2,400 plus $144 sales tax, Tape 33.
15	Bankcard sales totaled $2,000 plus sales tax of $120, Tape 33.
18	Sold $1,000 in merchandise plus sales tax of $60 on account to Katz Properties, terms 2/10, n/30, Sales Slip 174.
20	Received $100 from Ilya Bodonski to apply on her account, Receipt 149.
22	Sold $800 in merchandise plus $48 sales tax on account to Rothwell Management Inc., terms 2/10, n/30, Sales Slip 175.
23	Lee Adkins sent us a check for $53 in payment of his account, Receipt 150.
24	Received a $106 check from Saba Nadal to apply on account, Receipt 151.
26	Java Shops Inc. sent us a check for $200 to apply on account, Receipt 152.
27	Sold $200 in merchandise plus sales tax of $12 on account to Lee Adkins, Sales Slip 176.
28	Received $75 from the sale of excess store equipment, Receipt 153.
30	Cash sales totaled $2,600 plus $156 sales tax, Tape 34.
30	Bankcard sales were $2,200 plus sales tax of $132, Tape 34.

Analyze: If all Buzz Newsstand's customers pay their accounts within the cash discount period, what total amount will be forfeited by Buzz?

Peachtree®

SMART GUIDE

Step-by-Step Instructions: Problem 16–6

1. Select the problem set for Buzz Newsstand (Prob. 16–6).
2. Rename the company and set the system date.
3. Enter all sales on account transactions.
4. Record all cash receipts.
5. Print a Sales Journal report and a Cash Receipts Journal report.
6. Proof your work.
7. Print a General Ledger report and Customer Ledgers report.
8. Answer the Analyze question.
9. End the session.

SOLUTION NOTES

CHALLENGE PROBLEM

Problem 16–6 (Answers) Recording and Posting Sales and Cash Receipts

Sales Journal totals:
Sales Cr. $3,050
Sales Tax Pay. Cr. $183
Accts. Rec. Dr. $3,233
Total Debits/Credits $3,233

Cash Receipts Journal totals:
General Cr. $135
Sales Cr. $9,200
Sales Tax Pay. Cr. $552
Accts. Rec. Cr. $1,459
Sales Discounts Dr. $20.00
Cash in Bank Dr. $11,326.00
Total Debits/Credits $11,346

Ending debit balances:
Cash in Bank $16,326
Accts. Rec. $2,774
Supplies $240
Store Equipment $3,925
Sales Discounts $520

Ending credit balances:
Sales Tax Pay. $1,135
Sales $32,250

Accounts receivable ledger balances:
Lee Adkins $212
Ilya Bodonski $218
Java Shops Inc. $436
Katz Properties $1,060
Saba Nadal $0
Rolling Hills Pharmacies $0
Rothwell Management Inc. $848

Schedule of Accounts Receivable $2,774

Analyze: $55.48

CHAPTER 17 Resource Manager

Section Resources

	Objectives & Standards	Activities & Features	Reproducible Masters
Chapter Opener *Special Journals: Purchases and Cash Payments*	• Explain the purpose of the purchases and cash payments journals. • Record transactions in the purchases and cash payments journals. • Record payroll transactions in the cash payments journal. • Post from the purchases and cash payments journals to the general and accounts payable subsidiary ledgers. • Total, prove, and rule the purchases and cash payments journals. • Prepare a schedule of accounts payable. • Prove cash. • Define the accounting terms introduced in this chapter. **National Standards for Business Education**: IA–IA10, IA16, IIA2, IIA3, IIA4, IIB2, IIB4	Exploring the Real World of Business, p. 448 Workplace Connections, p. 449	School-to-Work Handbook
Section 1 *The Purchases Journal*	• The purpose of the purchases journal. • How to record purchases on account in the purchases journal. • How to post from the purchases journal to the general and accounts payable subsidiary ledger accounts. • How to total, prove, and rule the purchases journal.	Math Hints, p. 452 Did You Know?, p. 453 Accounting Flashbacks, p. 454 International Accounting, p. 455 A Matter of Ethics, p. 456	Demonstration Problems Math Review for Accounting Strategies for Teaching International Accounting Strategies for Teaching Ethics in Accounting
Section 2 *The Cash Payments Journal*	• The purpose of the cash payments journal. • How to record transactions in the cash payments journal. • How to post from the cash payments journal. • How to prepare a schedule of accounts payable. • How to prove cash.	Connect To, p. 460 Analyzing Financial Reports, p. 470 Accounting Careers in Focus, p. 472	Demonstration Problems Internet Resources and Activities Handbook

KEY

Posters · Transparency · Software · Videocassette
Blackline Masters · CD-ROM · Portfolio

MULTIMEDIA RESOURCE

Peachtree	QuickBooks	Spreadsheets	Videos	CD-ROMs
Problem 17–4 *Recording Payment of the Payroll* Problem 17–5 *Recording Transactions in the Purchases Journal* Problem 17–6 *Recording and Posting Purchases* Problem 17–7 *Recording and Posting Cash Payments* Problem 17–8 *Recording and Posting Purchases and Cash Payments*	Problem 17–5 *Recording Transactions in the Purchases Journal* Problem 17–8 *Recording and Posting Purchases and Cash Payments*	None in this chapter.	***Video Segment: Purchases and Cash Payments*** After viewing this video, students will be able to explain the difference between purchases of assets for use in the business and purchases of merchandise for resale. Students will be able to describe the purchasing process and how purchases and payments are recorded.	***Electronic Learning Center (ELC), Chapter 17*** This program is ideal for visual learners since it incorporates video images, animation, and graphics to enliven the content of each lesson. ***Interactive Lesson Planner (ILP), Chapter 17*** This CD-ROM combines the versatility of an electronic lesson planner with the convenience of teacher classroom resources.

SCANS Correlation Chart

FOUNDATION SKILLS

Basic Skills:	Reading	Writing	Math	Listening	Speaking	
Thinking Skills:	Creative Thinking	Decision Making	Problem Solving	Seeing Things in the Mind's Eye	Knowing How to Learn	Reasoning
Personal Qualities:	Responsibility	Self-Esteem	Sociability	Self-Management	Integrity/Honesty	

WORKPLACE COMPETENCIES

Resources:	Allocating Time	Allocating Money	Allocating Material and Facility Resources	Allocating Human Resources		
Information:	Acquiring and Evaluating Information	Organizing and Maintaining Information	Interpreting and Communicating Information	Using Computers to Process Information		
Interpersonal Skills:	Participating as a Member of a Team	Teaching Others	Serving Clients/ Customers	Exercising Leadership	Negotiating to Arrive at a Decision	Working with Cultural Diversity
Systems:	Understanding Systems	Monitoring and Correcting Performance	Improving and Designing Systems			
Technology:	Selecting Technology	Applying Technology to Task	Maintaining and Troubleshooting Technology			

*Highlighted blocks indicate areas covered in the chapter. Additional SCANS skills are also covered throughout the *Teacher Wraparound Edition.*

Assessment

Student Edition
- Check Your Understanding, pp. 457, 471
- Chapter 17 Problems, pp. 477–481

Assessment and Evaluation Masters
- Chapter 17 Study Plan, *Glencoe Workbook*
- Chapter 17 Self-Test, *Glencoe Workbook*
- Chapter 17 Test, *Chapter Tests* Booklet
- Chapter 17 Activity, *School-to-Work Handbook*
- Chapter 17 **Exam***View*

Teacher Wraparound Edition
- Critical Thinking Activity, p. 463
- Reteaching Section 1, p. 457
- Reteaching Section 2, p. 471
- Chapter 17 Quiz, p. 473

Transparencies

	Teaching Transparencies	Solution Transparencies
Section 1:	17–1, 17–2, 17–3, 17–4, 17–5, 17–6, 17–7, 17–8,	Problem 17–1
Section 2:	17–9, 17–10, 17–11, 17–12, 17–13, 17–14, 17–15, 17–16, 17–17, 17–18, 17–19, 17–20a, 17–20b, 17–21, 17–22, 17–23, 17–24, 17–25	Problems 17–2, 17–3
End of Chapter:		Problems 17–4, 17–5, 17–6, 17–7, 17–8

TEACHER CLASSROOM RESOURCES

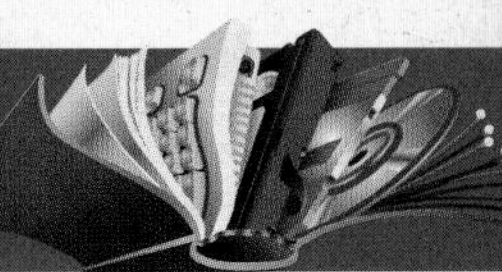

This is a representation of key blackline masters available in the Teacher Classroom Resources.

Teaching Aids

Transparency Examples

Section Focus Transparencies

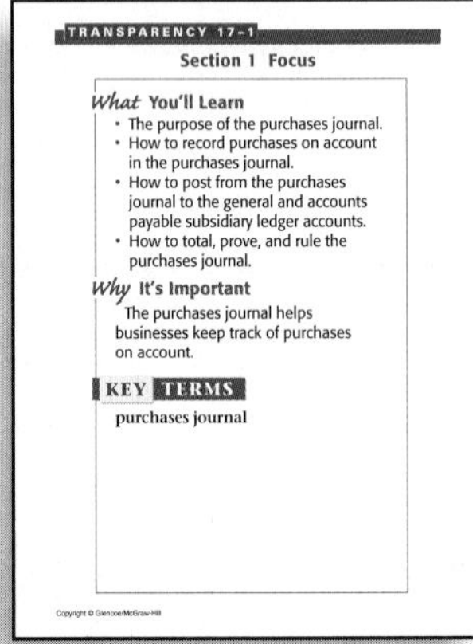

TRANSPARENCY 17-1

Section 1 Focus

What You'll Learn
- The purpose of the purchases journal.
- How to record purchases on account in the purchases journal.
- How to post from the purchases journal to the general and accounts payable subsidiary ledger accounts.
- How to total, prove, and rule the purchases journal.

Why It's Important

The purchases journal helps businesses keep track of purchases on account.

KEY TERMS

purchases journal

Teaching Transparencies

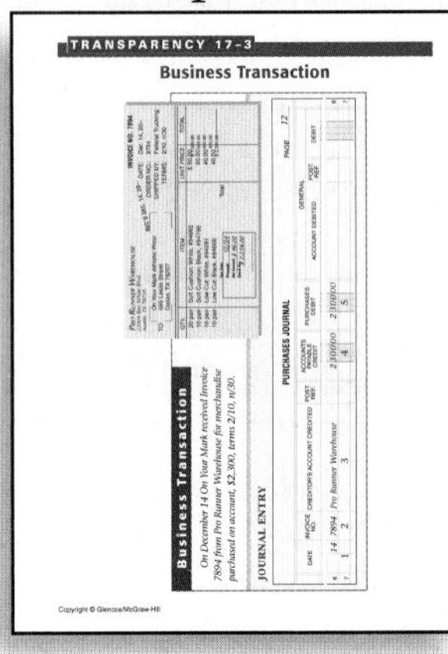

TRANSPARENCY 17-3

Business Transaction

Teaching Transparencies

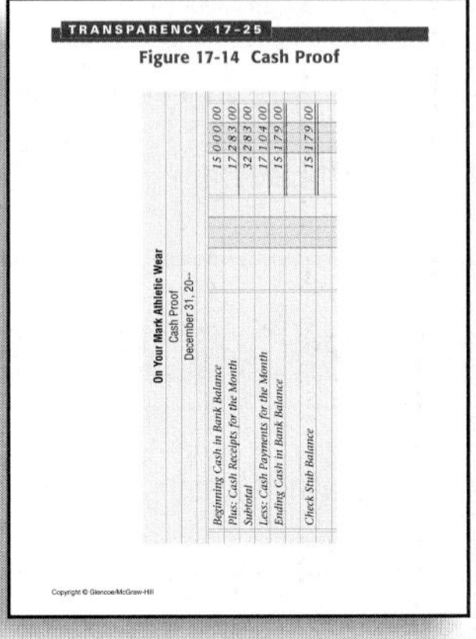

TRANSPARENCY 17-25

Figure 17-14 Cash Proof

On Your Mark Athletic Wear
Cash Proof
December 31, 20--

Beginning Cash in Bank Balance	15 0 0 0 00
Plus: Cash Receipts for the Month	12 2 8 1 00
Subtotal	27 2 8 1 00
Less: Cash Payments for the Month	12 1 0 2 00
Ending Cash in Bank Balance	15 1 7 9 00
Check Stub Balance	15 1 7 9 00

Solution Transparencies

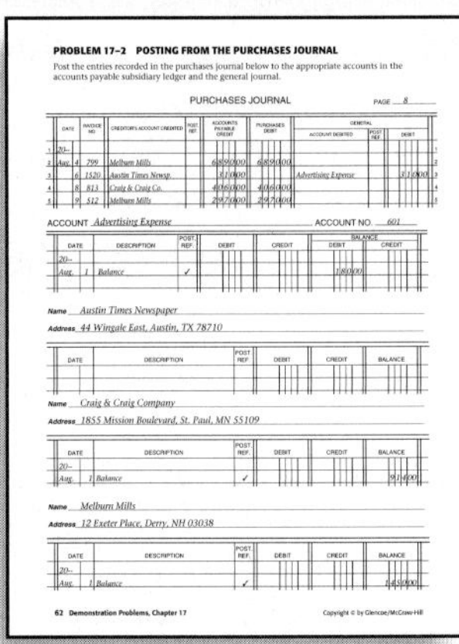

Demonstration Problems

PROBLEM 17-2 POSTING FROM THE PURCHASES JOURNAL

Lesson Plans

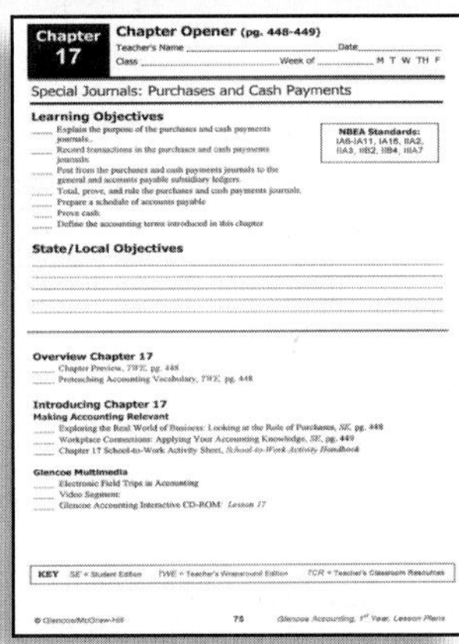

Chapter 17 Chapter Opener (pg. 448-449)

Special Journals: Purchases and Cash Payments

Block Scheduling

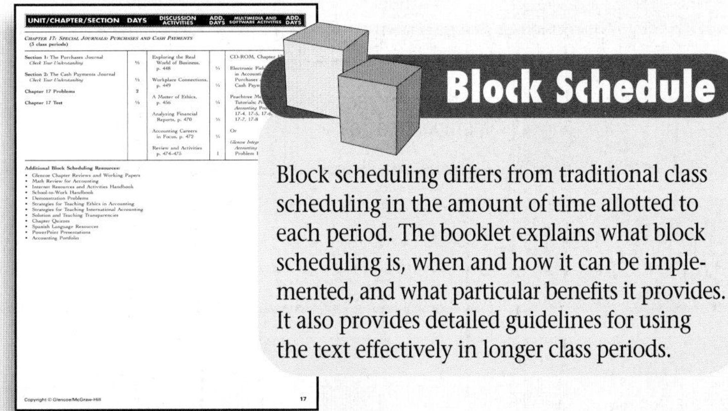

UNIT/CHAPTER/SECTION DAYS DISCUSSION ACTIVITIES ADD. DAYS MULTIMEDIA AND SOFTWARE ACTIVITIES ADD. DAYS

Block Schedule

Block scheduling differs from traditional class scheduling in the amount of time allotted to each period. The booklet explains what block scheduling is, when and how it can be implemented, and what particular benefits it provides. It also provides detailed guidelines for using the text effectively in longer class periods.

Enrichment and Application

Strategies for Teaching Ethics in Accounting

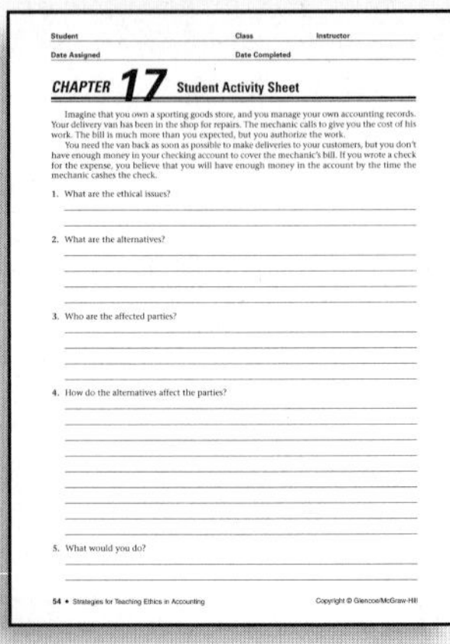

CHAPTER 17 Student Activity Sheet

1. What are the ethical issues?
2. What are the alternatives?
3. Who are the affected parties?
4. How do the alternatives affect the parties?
5. What would you do?

Strategies for Teaching International Accounting

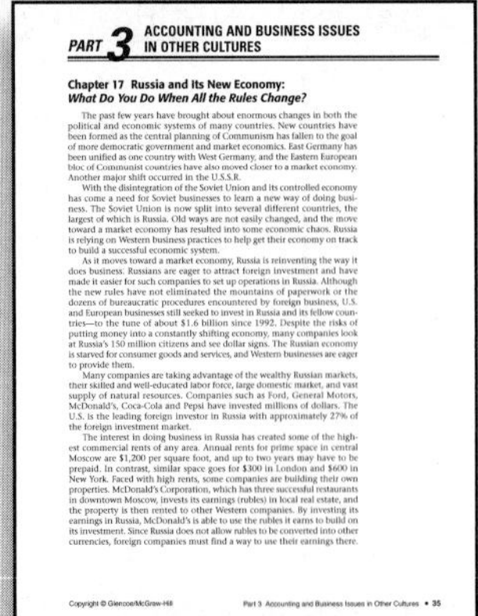

PART 3 ACCOUNTING AND BUSINESS ISSUES IN OTHER CULTURES

Chapter 17 Russia and Its New Economy: *What Do You Do When All the Rules Change?*

School-to-Work Handbook

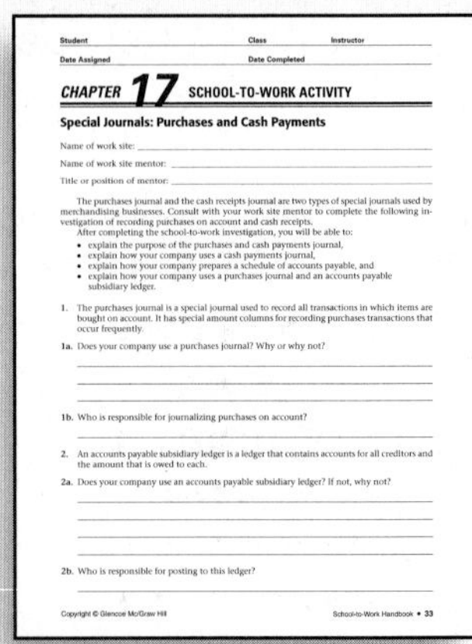

CHAPTER 17 SCHOOL-TO-WORK ACTIVITY

Special Journals: Purchases and Cash Payments

Meeting Different Ability Levels

Chapter Reviews and Working Papers (CRWP)

Working Papers   Review

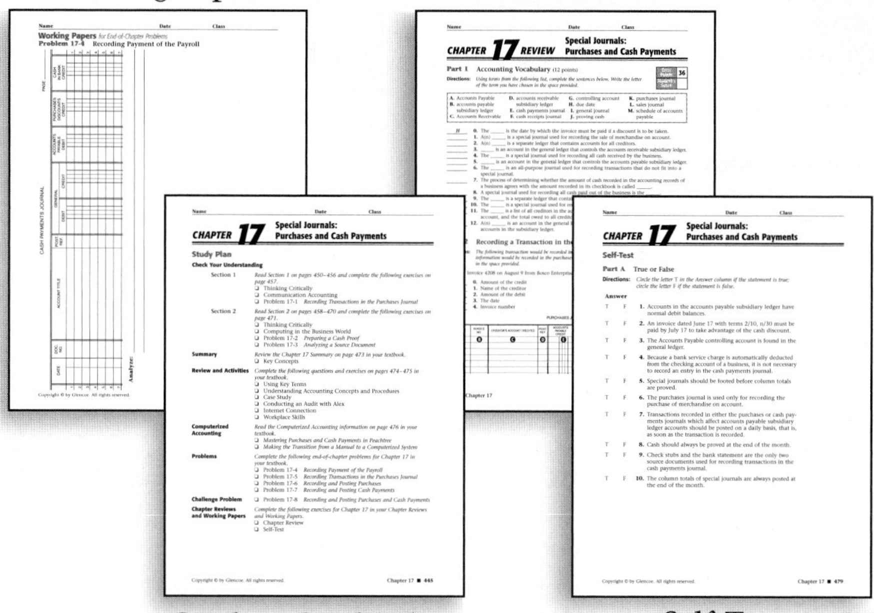
Working Papers for End-of-Chapter Problems
Problem 17-4 Recording Payment of the Payroll

CHAPTER 17 REVIEW Special Journals: Purchases and Cash Payments
Part 1 Accounting Vocabulary

CHAPTER 17 Special Journals: Purchases and Cash Payments
Study Plan
Check Your Understanding

CHAPTER 17 Special Journals: Purchases and Cash Payments
Self-Test
Part A True or False

Student Study Plan   Self-Test

Real-World Multimedia CD-ROM

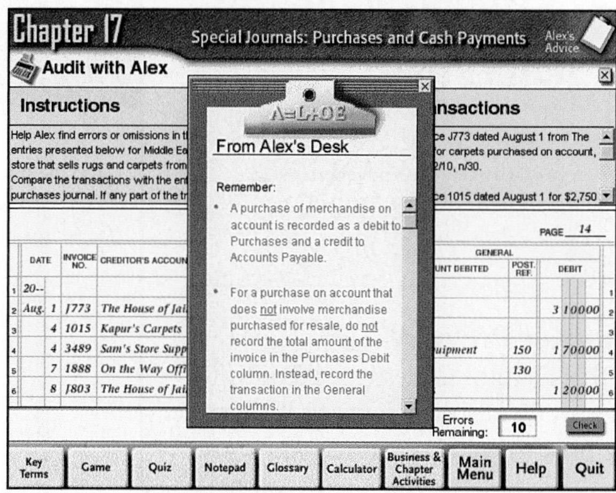

Key to Ability Levels

Each section gives skill-building activities. Each activity has been labeled for use with students of various learning styles and abilities.

L1 Level 1 activities are basic activities and should be within the range of all students.

L2 Level 2 activities are average activities and should be within the range of average and above average students.

L3 Level 3 activities are challenging activities designed for the ability range of above average students.

ELL ELL activities should be within the ability range of English Language Learners.

Assessment and Evaluation

Chapter Tests

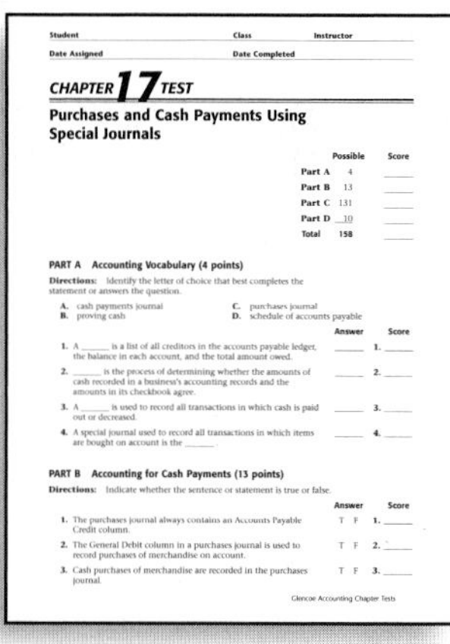
CHAPTER 17 TEST
Purchases and Cash Payments Using Special Journals

Chapter Quiz

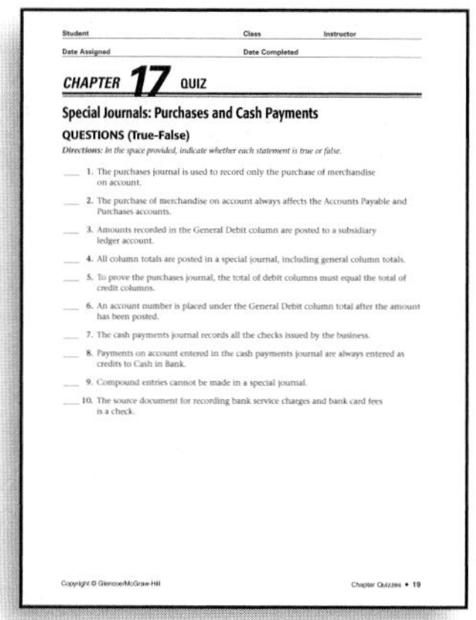
CHAPTER 17 QUIZ
Special Journals: Purchases and Cash Payments
QUESTIONS (True-False)

Teaching Resources at a Glance

Application Resources

- Glencoe Chapter Review and Working Papers, SE and TAE
- School-to-Work Handbook, SE and TM
- Accounting Portfolio, SE and TM

Reproducible Masters

- Demonstration Problems
- Lesson Plans
- Block Scheduling
- Spanish Language Resources

Glencoe Accounting Professional Development Series

- Strategies for Teaching Ethics in Accounting
- Accounting Competitive Event Review
- Math Review for Accounting
- Strategies for Teaching International Accounting
- Internet Resources and Activities Handbook

Transparency Package

- Section Focus Transparencies
- Teaching Transparencies
- Source Document Transparencies
- Solution Transparencies

Performance Assessment

- **Exam***View* CD-ROM
- Chapter Tests
- Chapter Quizzes
- Unit Tests
- Audit Tests
- Printed Testbank

Multimedia Resources

- Electronic Learning Center:
  - Multimedia CD-ROMs
  - Peachtree software, tutorials, templates, and solutions
  - Spreadsheet templates
- Using QuickBooks with Glencoe Accounting
- Interactive Lesson Planner
- Electronic Field Trips in Accounting
- PowerPoint Presentation
- Web site: glencoeaccounting.glencoe.com

OVERVIEW
CHAPTER 17

Correlations to National Standards for Business Education

(See pages T50–T51 for a detailed correlation chart.)

Standards: IA6–IA10, IA16, IIA2, IIA3, IIA4, IIB2, IIB4

Chapter Preview

In this chapter students will continue their study of special journals by learning how to record transactions in the purchases and cash payments journals. They'll also learn how to post from both journals to the general and subsidiary ledgers.

Section Overviews

- Section 1—*The Purchases Journal*
- Section 2—*The Cash Payments Journal*

Chapter Vocabulary

purchases journal
cash payments journal
schedule of accounts payable
proving cash

Preteaching Accounting Vocabulary

Demonstration: Write each of the new vocabulary terms on the chalkboard. Ask for volunteers to come to the board and write a sentence using one of the terms in context. Discuss any misuses of terms. L1

CHAPTER 17

Special Journals: Purchases and Cash Payments

Learning Objectives

When you have completed this chapter, you will be able to:

- Explain the purpose of the purchases and cash payments journals.
- Record transactions in the purchases and cash payments journals.
- Record payroll transactions in the cash payments journal.
- Post from the purchases and cash payments journals to the general and accounts payable subsidiary ledgers.
- Total, prove, and rule the purchases and cash payments journals.
- Prepare a schedule of accounts payable.
- Prove cash.
- Define the accounting terms introduced in this chapter.

Exploring the Real World of Business

LOOKING AT THE ROLE OF PURCHASES

The U.S. population loves pets, spending $23 billion a year on pet-care products and services.

PETCO is one of the country's largest providers of these products and services. In addition to large selections of pet foods, toys, grooming supplies, books, and pet care accessories, the company also sells fish, birds, snakes, cats, dogs, and other companion animals.

Operating in 42 states, plus the District of Columbia, **PETCO** has 575 pet food, supply and services stores. An expanded product line offers more products to customers and provides more supplies used in their grooming service operations. Using its accounting records to analyze which products and services pet owners buy helps the company anticipate future demand. Offering the right products and services is the key to continued growth.

What do you think?

Name at least three different products that **PETCO** might purchase for resale to its customers. Name three products the company might buy for use in operating the business.

Exploring the Real World of Business

PETCO

Through aggressive growth, PETCO has become the largest U.S. retailer of pet food and supplies. PETCO stores stock over 10,000 different pet-related products. The company expanded sales with competitive prices and superior customer service.

What do you think? (Answers)

Answers may vary. Products for resale include pet food, collars or leashes, or pets such as fish or rabbits. Items bought to operate the business might include display shelving, electronic cash registers, and plastic or paper bags for customer purchases.

Workplace Connections

Applying Your Accounting Knowledge

Do you, or anyone you know, make regular payments to anyone—perhaps for car insurance or for a purchase you made on an installment plan? Businesses make a lot of similar payments. Retail businesses buy the merchandise they sell to customers. They also buy many items used to operate the business, such as china and silverware for a restaurant. Businesses buy most items on credit and must keep track of when payments are due. You'll learn how that's done through the accounting records as you study this chapter.

Investigate:

1. What items might your employer buy on credit?
2. Do you have any ideas on how you might keep track of purchases and when payments are due on those items?

449

Glencoe Accounting Online

Visit the *Glencoe Accounting* Web site at **glencoeaccounting.glencoe.com** for additional activities and information.

GLENCOE MULTIMEDIA

Electronic Field Trips in Accounting *Video Segment: Purchases and Cash Payments*
After viewing this video, students will be able to describe the purchasing process and how purchases and payments are recorded.

Glencoe Accounting: Electronic Learning Center *Chapter 17*
The CD-ROM program is ideal for visual learners since it incorporates video images, animation, and graphics to enliven the content of each lesson.

INTRODUCING CHAPTER 17

Making Accounting Relevant

Workplace Connections: Applying Your Accounting Knowledge

Discussion: Merchandising businesses operate on a cycle of buying and selling goods. Choose a local merchandising business and have students describe its operations, including the items the business buys for resale, how often they see new merchandise being stocked, and how the business pays for its merchandise.

Investigate (Answers)

1. Answers may vary. Most businesses use credit to buy merchandise for resale, office supplies, computer hardware, office or warehouse equipment, or to build offices, warehouses, or manufacturing facilities.
2. Answers may vary. Students might keep all their credit card receipts in one place and review them at the end of the month to see how much they owe and when they will be billed.

School-to-Work Activity

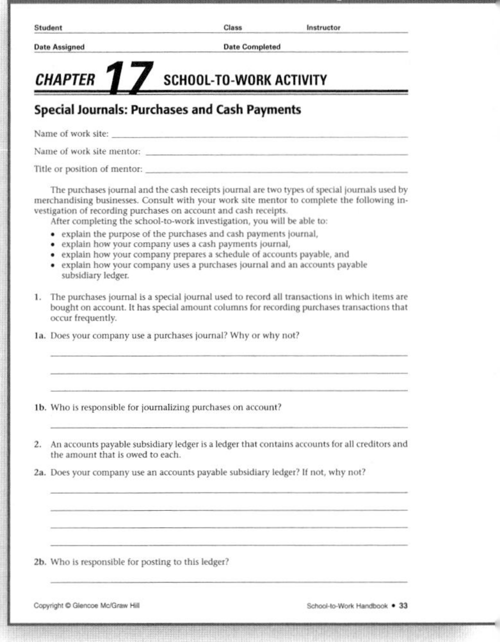

Student ______ Class ______ Instructor ______

Date Assigned ______ Date Completed ______

CHAPTER 17 SCHOOL-TO-WORK ACTIVITY

Special Journals: Purchases and Cash Payments

Name of work site: ______

Name of work site mentor: ______

Title or position of mentor: ______

The purchases journal and the cash receipts journal are two types of special journals used by merchandising businesses. Consult with your work site mentor to complete the following investigation of recording purchases on account and cash receipts.

After completing the school-to-work investigation, you will be able to:

- explain the purpose of the purchases and cash payments journal,
- explain how your company uses a cash payments journal,
- explain how your company prepares a schedule of accounts payable, and
- explain how your company uses a purchases journal and an accounts payable subsidiary ledger.

1. The purchases journal is a special journal used to record all transactions in which items are bought on account. It has special amount columns for recording purchases transactions that occur frequently.

1a. Does your company use a purchases journal? Why or why not?

1b. Who is responsible for journalizing purchases on account?

2. An accounts payable subsidiary ledger is a ledger that contains accounts for all creditors and the amount that is owed to each.

2a. Does your company use an accounts payable subsidiary ledger? If not, why not?

2b. Who is responsible for posting to this ledger?

 School-to-Work Handbook • 33

1 FOCUS

Introducing the Section

Students have learned about the purchasing process and the accounts used to record purchases transactions. In this section students will build on their prior knowledge by learning how to record transactions in the purchases journal and post from that journal.

Section Concepts

- The purpose of the purchases journal.
- How to record purchases on account in the purchases journal.
- How to post from the purchases journal to the general and accounts payable subsidiary ledger accounts.
- How to total, prove, and rule the purchases journal.

Visual Learning

Section 1 Focus

Use **Transparency 17–1** to introduce section concepts.

BELL RINGER

Compare and Contrast: Display a general journal with an entry for the purchase of merchandise on account. Have students compare the column headings in the purchases journal with the general journal entry. Then ask them to explain how the general journal entry and the purchases journal column headings are alike. How are the two journals different? L1

Visual Learning

Figure 17–1 Purchases Journal

Using **Transparency 17–2**, guide students through the information recorded in a purchases journal.

SECTION 1

The Purchases Journal

***What* You'll Learn**

- The purpose of the purchases journal.
- How to record purchases on account in the purchases journal.
- How to post from the purchases journal to the general and accounts payable subsidiary ledger accounts.
- How to total, prove, and rule the purchases journal.

***Why* It's Important**

The purchases journal helps businesses keep track of purchases on account.

KEY TERMS

purchases journal

In the last chapter, you learned that businesses use special journals to record transactions that are similar and occur frequently. If the accounting system is like a transit system, then special journals help accountants avoid accounting traffic jams. Special journals channel incoming data into appropriate "lanes" and provide a shortcut for much of the data headed for the general ledger.

In the last chapter, you learned that the sales and cash receipts journals record the sale of merchandise and other assets. In this chapter you'll learn about purchases and cash payments journals and how these journals are used to record the purchase of merchandise and other assets. You will also learn about the accounts payable subsidiary ledger.

Kmart purchases merchandise for resale from hundreds of suppliers. Businesses like Kmart use purchases and cash payments journals to simplify the purchase and payment processes.

The Purchases Journal

The **purchases journal** is a special journal used to record all purchases on account. **Figure 17–1** shows the purchases journal used by On Your Mark Athletic Wear.

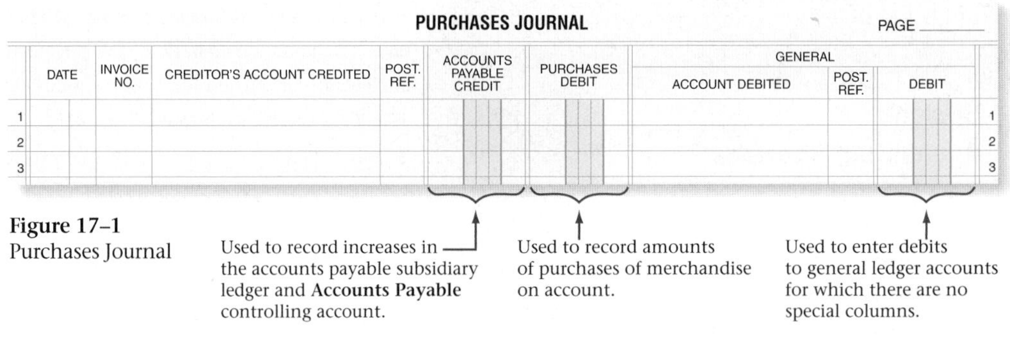

PURCHASES JOURNAL — PAGE ______

	DATE	INVOICE NO.	CREDITOR'S ACCOUNT CREDITED	POST. REF.	ACCOUNTS PAYABLE CREDIT	PURCHASES DEBIT	GENERAL: ACCOUNT DEBITED	GENERAL: POST. REF.	GENERAL: DEBIT	
1										1
2										2
3										3

Figure 17–1
Purchases Journal

RESOURCE MANAGER

Reproducible Masters
- Lesson Plans
- Chapter Reviews and Working Papers (CRWP) TAE
- Demonstration Problems

Transparencies
- Section Focus Transparency
- Teaching Transparencies
- Source Document Transparencies
- Solution Transparencies

Multimedia
- Exam*View* CD-ROM
- Electronic Learning Center CD-ROM
- Interactive Lesson Planner CD-ROM
- Electronic Field Trips in Accounting

The purchases journal includes: space for the page number, a column for the date, a column for the invoice number, a column for the name of the creditor, and a column for the posting reference. There are also three amount columns. Refer to **Figure 17–1** for a description of what amounts should be recorded in each column.

Recording the Purchase of Merchandise on Account

After an invoice is verified by the accounting clerk, the purchase is recorded in the purchases journal.

Business Transaction

On December 14 On Your Mark received Invoice 7894 from Pro Runner Warehouse for merchandise purchased on account, $2,300, terms 2/10, n/30.

PRO RUNNER WAREHOUSE
22009 Ben White Blvd.
Austin, TX 78705

INVOICE NO. 7894

REC'D DEC. 14, 20--

DATE: Dec. 14, 20--
ORDER NO.: 9784
SHIPPED BY: Federal Trucking
TERMS: 2/10, n/30

TO On Your Mark Athletic Wear
595 Leslie Street
Dallas, TX 75207

QTY.	ITEM	UNIT PRICE	TOTAL
20 pair	Soft Cushion: White, #94682	$ 50.00	$ 1,000.00
10 pair	Soft Cushion: Black, #94788	50.00	500.00
10 pair	Low Cut: White, #94281	40.00	400.00
10 pair	Low Cut: Black, #94666	40.00	400.00
	Total		$ 2,300.00

Due Date: *12/24*
Discount: *$ 46.00*
Net Amount: *$ 2,254.00*
Check No.:

JOURNAL ENTRY

PURCHASES JOURNAL PAGE *12*

	DATE	INVOICE NO.	CREDITOR'S ACCOUNT CREDITED	POST. REF.	ACCOUNTS PAYABLE CREDIT	PURCHASES DEBIT	GENERAL ACCOUNT DEBITED	GENERAL POST. REF.	GENERAL DEBIT	
6	*14*	*7894*	*Pro Runner Warehouse*		*2 300 00*	*2 300 00*				6
7	1	2	3		4	5				7

Refer to the purchases journal and follow these steps:

1. Enter the date in the Date column. Use the date the invoice was *received,* not the date the invoice was prepared.
2. Enter the invoice number in the Invoice Number column.
3. Enter the creditor's name in the Creditor's Account Credited column.
4. Enter the *total* of the invoice in the Accounts Payable Credit column.
5. For purchases of merchandise on account, enter the total amount of the invoice in the Purchases Debit column.

After the invoice from Pro Runner Warehouse is journalized, it is placed in a tickler file by due date. In this case, it is filed in the December 24 folder. On Your Mark plans to take the discount, and December 24 is ten days after the invoice date.

Key Points

Recording a Purchase on Account

A purchase of merchandise on account is recorded as a debit to **Purchases** and a credit to **Accounts Payable.**

Journalizing Other Purchases on Account

On Your Mark also purchases supplies and other assets on account. These purchases do not occur often enough to set up special columns in the purchases journal. When these purchases do occur, they are recorded in the General Debit column of the purchases journal.

CHAPTER 17
SECTION 1, PAGES 450–457

2 TEACH

GUIDED PRACTICE

Reading Accounting

- Reading numbers correctly helps accountants avoid errors. Have students practice reading numbers by giving them a list of business transactions and asking them to write the key numbers beside each transaction. Have students check each other's lists. L1

Concept Development: The Purchases Journal

Discussion: Using actual invoices, have students identify information to be recorded in the purchases journal. Explain column headings and emphasize that: (1) All purchases on account require an entry in the Accounts Payable Credit column. (2) Only merchandise purchased on account is recorded in the Purchases Debit column. (3) All purchases on account other than merchandise are recorded in the General Debit column. L1

Visual Learning

Business Transaction

Using **Transparency 17–3**, have students analyze the transaction for merchandise purchased on account.

Critical Thinking: Ask students to explain why the purchases discount of $46 is not recorded in the purchases journal or at the same time as the purchase. (The discount is not recorded until payment is made. At that time, the discount is recorded in the cash payments journal since it represents a decrease in the amount of cash the company pays out.) L2

Great Ideas *From the Classroom of...*

Career Exploration I use a three-step approach to career exploration:

1. **Investigate!** Guest speakers talk to students about the variety of accounting careers.
2. **Explore!** Visit international CPA firms and large corporations to see textbook accounting theory in action.
3. **Shadow!** Pick a specific area of interest and go to work for a day.

Laura Anderson
Adams City High School
Denver, Colorado

CHAPTER 17
SECTION 1, PAGES 450–457

2 TEACH (Cont'd.)

Visual Learning

Business Transaction
Using **Transparency 17–4**, have students analyze the entry to record the purchase of equipment on account. Ask for volunteers to draw T accounts on the chalkboard for their analysis.

Teaching Tips

Remind students that all purchases on account are recorded in the purchases journal. Emphasize that students should not confuse the Purchases account with the purchases journal.

Point out that the journal entry is made when the invoice (bill) is received, not when the purchase order is mailed. The invoice is the source document for the entry, not the purchase order.

Examples of purchases on account other than for merchandise may include store or factory supplies and various types of equipment.

Emphasize that all items bought on account are recorded in the purchases journal.

Demonstration Problem Step-by-Step Practice
Use demonstration problem 17–1 to give students practice in recording transactions in the purchases journal.

Math Review for Accounting
Photocopy appropriate *Activity Sheets* for students who need additional practice in basic math skills.

Business Transaction

On December 15 On Your Mark received Invoice 3417, dated December 13, from Champion Store Supply for store equipment bought on account, $1,200, terms n/30.

CHAMPION STORE SUPPLY
47249 Randall Parkway
Dallas, TX 75207

REC'D DEC. 15, 20--

INVOICE NO. 3417
DATE: Dec. 13, 20--
ORDER NO.: 9795
SHIPPED BY: Federal Trucking
TERMS: n/30

TO On Your Mark Athletic Wear
595 Leslie Street
Dallas, TX 75207

QTY.	ITEM	UNIT PRICE	TOTAL
3	Corner Shelf Units	$ 300.00	$ 900.00
1	Shirt Rack	300.00	300.00
	Total		$ 1,200.00

Due Date: *1/12*
Discount: *$0.00*
Net Amount: *$1,200.00*
Check No.:

JOURNAL ENTRY

PURCHASES JOURNAL — PAGE *12*

	DATE	INVOICE NO.	CREDITOR'S ACCOUNT CREDITED	POST. REF.	ACCOUNTS PAYABLE CREDIT	PURCHASES DEBIT	GENERAL ACCOUNT DEBITED	GENERAL POST. REF.	GENERAL DEBIT	
7	*15*	*3417*	*Champion Store Supply*		*1 200 00*		*Store Equipment*		*1 200 00*	7
8	1	2	3		4		5		6	8

Refer to the purchases journal above and follow these steps:

1. Enter the date the invoice was *received* in the Date column.
2. Enter the invoice number in the Invoice Number column.
3. Enter the creditor's name in the Creditor's Account Credited column.
4. Enter the *total* of the invoice in the Accounts Payable Credit column.
5. Store equipment is not merchandise purchased for resale, so this transaction is not recorded in the Purchases Debit column. Instead, it is recorded in the General columns. Write the name of the general ledger account being debited in the General Account Debited column.
6. Enter the total amount of the invoice in the General Debit column.

Proving Cash
Proving cash is easy when you remember a simple formula:
- Beginning balance
  \+ Cash in
  − Cash out
  Ending balance
- The ending balance is then compared with the ending checkbook balance.

After journalizing the invoice, the accounting clerk places it in the tickler file. Because Champion Store Supply does not offer its credit customers a cash discount, the due date is January 12, 30 days after the date of the invoice. The invoice is filed in folder "12" to indicate the bill is to be paid on January 12.

Posting to the Accounts Payable Subsidiary Ledger

Each transaction in the purchases journal is a purchase on account. Therefore, each transaction is separately posted to the accounts payable subsidiary ledger. Transactions are posted *daily* to the accounts payable subsidiary ledger to keep creditor accounts current.

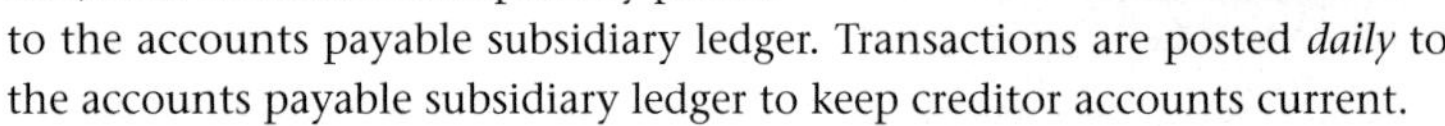

Refer to **Figure 17–2** as you read about posting to the accounts payable subsidiary ledger.

1. In the Date column of the subsidiary ledger account, enter the date of the transaction.

Math Skill Builder Activity

Proving Cash Teach students that proving cash is easy when you remember a simple formula: Beginning balance + cash in − cash out = ending balance. The ending balance is then compared with the ending checkbook balance. Give students this example: Cash at the beginning of the month is $6,880; the business has cash sales of $21,600 and has issued checks that total $17,200. Bank fees for the month were $18. The checkbook balance *before* bank service charges is $11,280. Have students prove cash. (Ending balance/checkbook balance: $11,262.)

2. In the Posting Reference column of the subsidiary ledger account, record the journal letter and the page number. "P" is the letter used for the purchases journal.
3. In the Credit column of the subsidiary ledger account, enter the amount owed to the creditor.
4. Compute the new account balance by adding the amount in the Credit column to the previous balance amount. Since there was no previous balance in Pro Runner's account, enter $2,300 in the Balance column.
5. Return to the purchases journal and place a check mark (✓) in the *first* Posting Reference column (the column following the Creditor's Account Credited column).

> **Did You Know?**
>
> **Pets**
>
> Owning and caring for a pet can be expensive. People spend an average of $530 a year taking care of their pets.

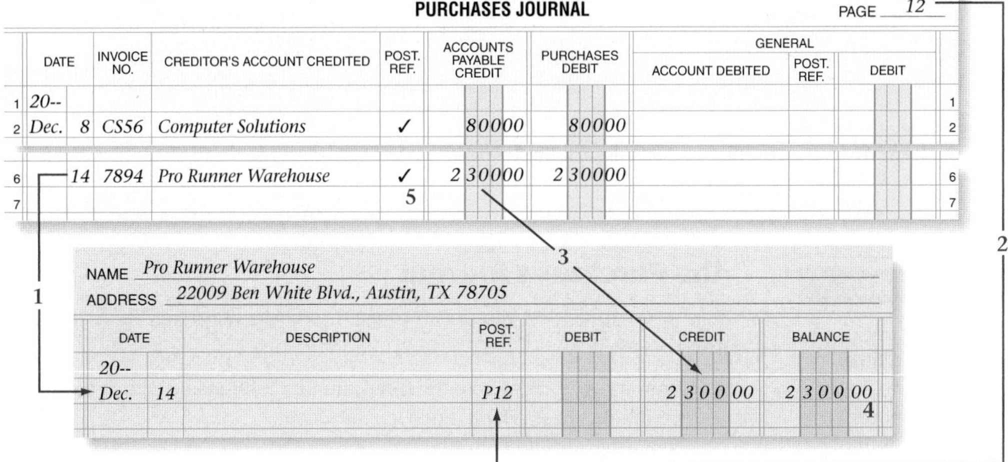

PURCHASES JOURNAL — PAGE 12

	DATE		INVOICE NO.	CREDITOR'S ACCOUNT CREDITED	POST. REF.	ACCOUNTS PAYABLE CREDIT	PURCHASES DEBIT	GENERAL ACCOUNT DEBITED	GENERAL POST. REF.	GENERAL DEBIT	
1	20--										1
2	Dec.	8	CS56	Computer Solutions	✓	800 00	800 00				2
6		14	7894	Pro Runner Warehouse	✓	2,300 00	2,300 00				6
7											7

NAME Pro Runner Warehouse
ADDRESS 22009 Ben White Blvd., Austin, TX 78705

DATE		DESCRIPTION	POST. REF.	DEBIT	CREDIT	BALANCE
20--						
Dec.	14		P12		2,300 00	2,300 00

Figure 17–2 Posting from the Purchases Journal to the Accounts Payable Subsidiary Ledger

Posting from the General Debit Column

Daily postings are made from the General Debit column of the purchases journal to the appropriate accounts in the general ledger.

Refer to **Figure 17–3** as you read the following steps:

1. Enter the date of the transaction in the Date column of the general ledger account.
2. In the Posting Reference column of the general ledger account, record the journal letter and page number. Be sure to use the letter "P" for purchases journal.
3. In the Debit column of the general ledger account, enter the amount recorded in the General Debit column of the purchases journal.
4. Compute and record the new balance in the Debit Balance column.
5. Return to the purchases journal and place the general ledger account number in the General Posting Reference column (the column following the General Account Debited column).

> **Key Points**
>
> **Accounts Payable Subsidiary Ledger**
>
> Normally, accounts in the accounts payable subsidiary ledger have credit balances.

MAKING CONNECTIONS TO DAILY LIFE

Making Purchases and Payments Many students are responsible for buying items for their personal use, such as gasoline for cars or some of their clothing. Have students discuss the benefits and disadvantages of paying cash for all their purchases or buying some items on credit and making payments later. If students use credit, how would they plan ahead to make sure they have the money to pay for their purchases in the future?

2 TEACH (Cont'd.)

Visual Learning

Figure 17–2 Posting from the Purchases Journal to the Accounts Payable Subsidiary Ledger

Use **Transparency 17–5** to review the steps in the posting process with students.

Teaching Tips

Remind students that the accounts listed in the Creditor's Account Credited column are accounts in the accounts payable subsidiary ledger. Point out that the column headings *Accounts Payable Credit* and *Purchases Debit* stand for those accounts in the general ledger. The account names given in the General Account Debited column are also general ledger accounts.

Emphasize that errors are easily made when posting to the subsidiary ledger by placing amounts in the wrong column.

Demonstration Problem Step-by-Step Practice

Use demonstration problem 17–2 to give students practice in posting entries in the purchases journal.

Thinking Algebraically

Conceptualize: Have students write an equation for proving cash. (Example: $a + b - c$ = cash proof, where a = beginning cash, b = cash in, c = cash out) L2

CHAPTER 17
SECTION 1, PAGES 450–457

2 TEACH (Cont'd.)

Visual Learning

Figure 17-3 Posting from the Purchases Journal to the General Ledger

Display **Transparency 17-6** to review posting to the general ledger.

Teaching Tips

Explain the purpose of the General Debit column. Point out that it is similar to the General Credit column in the cash receipts journal. Remind students that accounts listed in this column are names of general ledger accounts.

Remind students that posting from the purchases journal is similar to posting from the other special journals. As with other special journals, students will post to two ledgers: the accounts payable subsidiary ledger and the general ledger.

Chapter Reviews and Working Papers Refer students to the *Study Plan* located at the beginning of Chapter 17 in the workbook.

PURCHASES JOURNAL PAGE *12*

	DATE		INVOICE NO.	CREDITOR'S ACCOUNT CREDITED	POST. REF.	ACCOUNTS PAYABLE CREDIT	PURCHASES DEBIT	GENERAL ACCOUNT DEBITED	GENERAL POST. REF.	GENERAL DEBIT	
1	*20--*										1
2	*Dec.*	*8*	*CS56*	*Computer Solutions*	✓	*800 00*	*800 00*				2
7		*15*	*3417*	*Champion Store Supply*	✓	*1 200 00*		*Store Equipment*	*150*	*1 200 00*	7
8									5		8

ACCOUNT *Store Equipment* ACCOUNT NO. *150*

DATE		DESCRIPTION	POST. REF.	DEBIT	CREDIT	BALANCE DEBIT	BALANCE CREDIT
20--							
Dec.	*1*	*Balance*	✓			*4 000 00*	
	15		*P12*	*1 200 00*		*5 200 00* 4	

1 2 3

Figure 17–3 Posting from the Purchases Journal to the General Ledger

Key Points

Ruling the Purchases Journal

When ruling the purchases journal, the ruling is drawn across the amount columns only.

ACCOUNTING *Flashbacks*

ACCOUNTING HISTORY

In the Roman Empire, Julius Caesar strengthened the state economy by improving auditing and accounting. Augustus Caesar used one year's state tax receipts to plan the next year's expenditures.

Totaling, Proving, and Ruling the Purchases Journal

To complete the purchases journal, refer to **Figure 17–4** and follow these steps:

1. Draw a single rule across the three amount columns: Accounts Payable Credit, Purchases Debit, and General Debit.
2. Foot each amount column.
3. Test for the equality of debits and credits.

Debit Columns		Credit Column	
Purchases	$15,400	Accounts Payable	$16,850
General	1,450		
	$16,850		$16,850

4. In the Date column, on the line below the single rule, enter the date the journal is being totaled.
5. On the same line, write the word "Totals" in the Creditor's Account Credited column.
6. Enter the three column totals, in ink, just below the footings.
7. Draw a double rule across the three amount columns.

The completed purchases journal is a quick reference tool for the accountant to review current transactions that affect the **Purchases** account and the **Accounts Payable** account. Miscellaneous purchases are also reflected here. If a general journal had been used, these transactions would have been mingled with other transactions (cash receipts, payments, and more) of the period.

REINFORCING STUDY SKILLS

Creating Outlines Some students learn best by writing down their thoughts, study points, or notes. Show students how building a simple outline of the chapters they study can assist them with triggering these key thoughts when they study. Use section titles as the main headings of the outline, then fill in the headings within each section. Show students how to list important points under each subsection. Point out that students should include as much detail as they feel they need to review the content.

			PURCHASES JOURNAL							PAGE 12	
	DATE		INVOICE NO.	CREDITOR'S ACCOUNT CREDITED	POST. REF.	ACCOUNTS PAYABLE CREDIT	PURCHASES DEBIT	GENERAL			
								ACCOUNT DEBITED	POST. REF.	DEBIT	
1	20--										1
2	Dec.	8	CS56	Computer Solutions	✓	800 00	800 00				2
3		10	4692	Sports Link Footwear	✓	4 000 00	4 000 00				3
4		12	SN63	Sports Nutrition Supply	✓	600 00	600 00				4
5		14	2560	FastLane Athletics	✓	3 000 00	3 000 00				5
6		14	7894	Pro Runner Warehouse	✓	2 300 00	2 300 00				6
7		15	3417	Champion Store Supply	✓	1 200 00		Store Equipment	150	1 200 00	7
8		15	9881	Geary Office Supply	✓	250 00		Supplies	130	250 00	8
9		18	8560	FastLane Athletics	✓	2 000 00	2 000 00				9
10		20	6593	Computer Solutions	✓	1 200 00	1 200 00				10
11		27	5200	Sports Link Footwear	✓	1 500 00	1 500 00				11
12		31		Totals		16 850 00 16 850 00	15 400 00 15 400 00			1 450 00 1 450 00	12
13		4		5							13

Figure 17–4 The Completed Purchases Journal

What else can the accountant verify from the completed purchases journal? A quick review of the Post. Ref. column tells the accountant that amounts have been posted to the accounts payable subsidiary ledger.

Posting the Special Column Totals of the Purchases Journal

After the purchases journal is totaled and ruled, post the totals of the Accounts Payable Credit column and the Purchases Debit column to the general ledger accounts. Calculate the new balance for each account, and enter the new balance in the appropriate Balance column. **Figure 17–5** shows the posting of these column totals.

After posting each column total, write the general ledger account number, in parentheses, in the column below the double rule as shown in **Figure 17–5**. The total of the General Debit column is not posted because the individual amounts were posted during the month. Place a check mark (✓) in parentheses below the double rule in the General Debit column to indicate that the total is not posted.

International ACCOUNTING

Local Dialogue

Although English is the official language of business in numerous non-English speaking countries, it is generally appreciated if you make an attempt to learn the local tongue. Learning polite phrases such as "hello" and "thank you" show that you respect their culture.

CHAPTER 17
SECTION 1, PAGES 450–457

2 TEACH (Cont'd.)

Visual Learning

Figure 17–4 The Completed Purchases Journal

Using **Transparency 17–7**, have students explain the process of totaling, proving, and ruling the purchases journal.

Demonstration Problem Step-by-Step Practice

Use demonstration problem 17–3 to give students practice in completing the purchases journal and posting the column totals.

Teaching Tips

Emphasize that posting should be done systematically to reduce errors. Posting from left to right helps students avoid omissions. Point out that students should not skip or combine steps to try to save time.

Strategies for Teaching International Accounting

To enrich study of International Accounting, refer to the additional critical thinking activities in the booklet.

Teaching International ACCOUNTING

Local Dialogue Divide students into six groups and ask each group to learn how to say "hello," "please," "thank you," "good-bye," "yes," and "no" in the following languages: French, Spanish, German, Japanese, Russian, and Chinese. Have each group share what they have learned with the class. If any of your students can speak other languages, develop scenarios such as asking for directions, ordering entrées from a menu, or reserving a hotel room. Then have those students role-play the scenarios, speaking in another language.

2 TEACH (Cont'd.)

Visual Learning

Figure 17–5 Posting Column Totals from the Purchases Journal to the General Ledger

Using **Transparency 17–8**, ask students to describe the steps in posting column totals to the general ledger accounts. Review the meaning of a check mark under a column total.

Teaching Tip

Point out that the normal balance of an accounts payable account is a credit balance. Also mention that the account forms for the two subsidiary ledgers are identical. The Balance column represents either a debit or a credit balance depending on whether the account is an account receivable or an account payable. When posting, students should think about whether they are posting to a customer's account or to a creditor's account as a reminder of the account's normal balance.

Critical Thinking: Tell students that total debits and credits in the purchases journal column totals do not match. They have re-added the columns and found no math errors. What would they do next? (Check individual debit and credit entries to be sure amounts are correct. If each entry's debits and credits match, the column totals should also match.) L2

Strategies for Teaching Ethics in Accounting

Photocopy the Chapter 17 *Student Activity Sheet* for students. Answers are also provided in the booklet.

PURCHASES JOURNAL — PAGE 12

	DATE		INVOICE NO.	CREDITOR'S ACCOUNT CREDITED	POST. REF.	ACCOUNTS PAYABLE CREDIT	PURCHASES DEBIT	GENERAL ACCOUNT DEBITED	GENERAL POST. REF.	GENERAL DEBIT	
1	20--										1
2	Dec.	8	CS56	Computer Solutions	✓	800 00	800 00				2
11		27	5200	Sports Link Footwear	✓	1 500 00	1 500 00				11
12		31		Totals		16 850 00	15 400 00			1 450 00	12
13						(201)	(501)			(✓)	13
14											14

ACCOUNT *Accounts Payable* — ACCOUNT NO. *201*

DATE		DESCRIPTION	POST. REF.	DEBIT	CREDIT	BALANCE DEBIT	BALANCE CREDIT
20--							
Dec.	1	Balance	✓				6 300 00
	16		G21	200 00			6 100 00
	31		P12		16 850 00		22 950 00

ACCOUNT *Purchases* — ACCOUNT NO. *501*

DATE		DESCRIPTION	POST. REF.	DEBIT	CREDIT	BALANCE DEBIT	BALANCE CREDIT
20--							
Dec.	1	Balance	✓			190 000 00	
	19		CP14	1 300 00		191 300 00	
	31		P12	15 400 00		206 700 00	

Figure 17–5 Posting Column Totals from the Purchases Journal to the General Ledger

A MATTER OF ETHICS

Insufficient Funds

Imagine that you own a sporting goods store, and you manage your own accounting records. Your delivery van has been in the shop for repairs. The mechanic calls to give you the cost of his work. The bill is much more than you expected, but you authorize the work.

You need the van back as soon as possible to make deliveries to your customers, but you don't have enough money in your checking account to cover the mechanic's bill. If you write a check for the expense, you believe that you will have enough money in the account by the time the mechanic cashes the check.

Ethical Decision Making:

- What are the ethical issues?
- What are the alternatives?
- Who are the affected parties?
- How do the alternatives affect the parties?
- What would you do?

Teaching A MATTER OF ETHICS

Insufficient Funds Ask students how many of them have a checking account. Have they ever had a check returned for insufficient funds? Sometimes people don't keep track of their balances, and they think they have enough money in the account to cover a check. Point out that banks charge a fee for returning NSF checks, so writing a check when you know your balance is inadequate may not be the best move. Have students think about alternatives, such as using a credit card or negotiating to pay part now and part later.

Check Your Understanding

Now that you have studied this section, complete the following questions and problems.

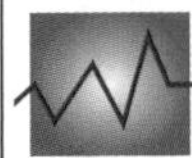

Thinking Critically

1. Describe the two types of purchases on account that are recorded in the purchases journal.
2. In the purchases journal, the General Debit column *total* is not posted. Explain why.

Communicating Accounting

Thomas Sampson is a purchasing agent for Complete Offices, a small office supply company. He recently returned from a 10-day business trip to California and gave you an envelope full of receipts. He did not provide any explanations about the purchases represented by the receipts. Write a memo to Thomas asking him to identify which receipts represent purchases for cash and which receipts represent purchases on account. Explain the information you need to analyze the transactions. Refer specifically to payment terms.

Problem 17–1 Recording Transactions in the Purchases Journal

The Design Den, a retail merchandising business, uses special journals. On page 3 of the purchases journal in the working papers, record the following purchases:

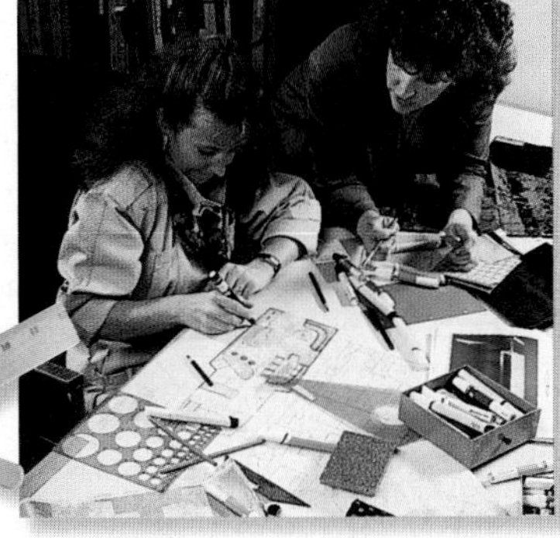

Date	Transactions
Feb. 1	Purchased $1,400 in merchandise on account from Woodstock Furnishings, terms 3/15, n/30, Invoice WF39.
2	Bought $900 in store equipment on account from Holmes Equipment Company, terms n/30, Invoice 98.
4	Purchased $700 in merchandise from Fuller Fabrics, terms 3/10, n/30, Invoice 72.
7	Purchased computer speakers on account for $50 from Digital Solutions, terms 2/10, n/30, Invoice AB220.
10	Purchased fabric from Valley Upholstery for $1,500, terms 2/10, n/30, Invoice 947.

3 ASSESS

Thinking Critically (Answers)

1. Most purchases on account are for merchandise to be resold to customers. The other type of purchases on account is for the purchase of any asset for use in the business.
2. The total from the General Debit column is not posted because the individual amounts were posted during the month.

Communicating Accounting (Answers)

Answers will vary. Students should ask for confirmation of total due, any payment terms, and the date of purchase.

Problem 17–1 (Answers)

See *Chapter Reviews and Working Papers TAE* for journal entries.

Chapter Reviews and Working Papers Refer students to the Chapter 17 workbook pages to answer *Check Your Understanding* activities.

4 CLOSE

Section Wrap-Up

Oral Exercise: Have students describe typical transactions recorded in the purchases journal. Then ask for an explanation of totaling, proving, and ruling the journal. L1

RETEACHING SECTION 1

Calculating the Due Date of an Invoice Students may be confused about which date to use when calculating the due date of an invoice. Review with students that the date used to record an invoice in the purchases journal is the date the invoice is received. However, when determining the discount period and the due date of an invoice, students are to use the date of the invoice, not the date the invoice was received. For example, a company receives an invoice on September 5. The date of the invoice is September 1, and the terms of the invoice are net 30. The date for the journal entry is September 5. The invoice is to be paid on October 1 (counting from the date of September 1).

1 FOCUS

Introducing the Section

In this section students will learn how to record cash payments in a cash payments journal. They will also post individual amounts and column totals to the subsidiary and general ledgers, prepare a schedule of accounts payable, and prove cash.

Section Concepts

- The purpose of the cash payments journal.
- How to record transactions in the cash payments journal.
- How to post from the cash payments journal.
- How to prepare a schedule of accounts payable.
- How to prove cash.

Visual Learning

Section 2 Focus

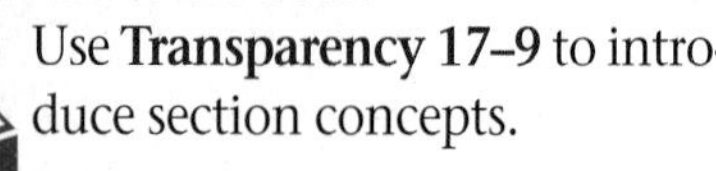
Use **Transparency 17–9** to introduce section concepts.

BELL RINGER

Compare and Contrast: Have students make a list of their recent cash payments. Ask volunteers to read their lists. Choose two or three examples and analyze them (e.g., the amount paid for a product or service and the sales tax). Then ask students how a business's cash payments might be different from theirs. (Businesses generally do not pay sales taxes and may receive discounts.) L1

Visual Learning

Figure 17-6 Cash Payments Journal

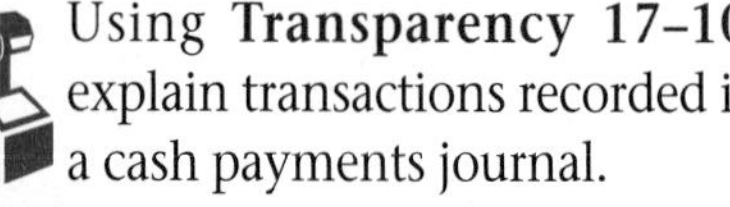
Using **Transparency 17–10**, explain transactions recorded in a cash payments journal.

SECTION 2

The Cash Payments Journal

***What* You'll Learn**

- The purpose of the cash payments journal.
- How to record transactions in the cash payments journal.
- How to post from the cash payments journal.
- How to prepare a schedule of accounts payable.
- How to prove cash.

***Why* It's Important**

Cash is a major asset of a business; therefore, it is essential that a business keep accurate records of both the inflow and the outflow of cash.

KEY TERMS

cash payments journal
schedule of accounts payable
proving cash

You have learned about three special journals: the sales journal, the cash receipts journal, and the purchases journal. Now you will study the cash payments journal. For many businesses, like grocers who must pay for the purchases of a wide variety of merchandise and florists who constantly pay to keep fresh flowers in stock, frequent payments make the use of the cash payments journal necessary.

The Cash Payments Journal

The **cash payments journal** is used to record all transactions in which cash is paid out or decreased. These transactions include: payments to creditors for items bought on account, cash purchases of merchandise and other assets, payments for various expenses, payments for wages and salaries, and cash decreases for bank service charges and bank card fees. The source documents for the journal entries are check stubs and the bank statement.

Figure 17–6 shows the cash payments journal used by On Your Mark. Notice that there are five amount columns.

The seven transactions that follow are typical of those recorded in the cash payments journal. Note that each transaction in the cash payments journal results in a credit to the **Cash in Bank** account.

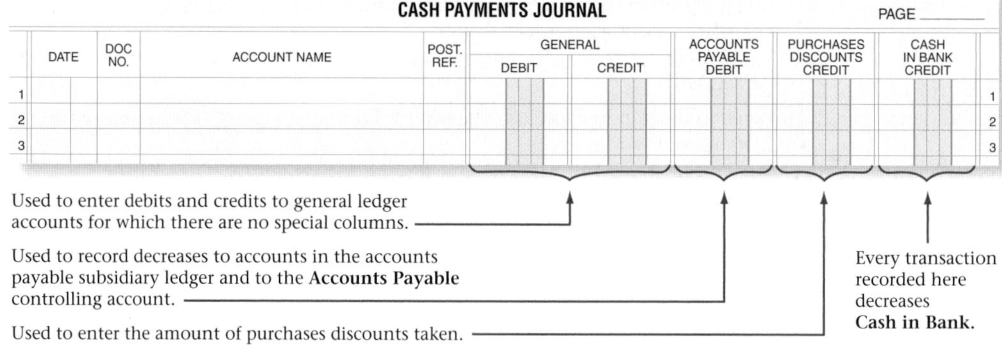

Figure 17–6 Cash Payments Journal

RESOURCE MANAGER

Reproducible Masters
- Lesson Plans
- Chapter Reviews and Working Papers (CRWP) TAE
- Demonstration Problems

Transparencies
- Section Focus Transparency
- Teaching Transparencies
- Source Document Transparencies
- Solution Transparencies

Multimedia
- Exam*View* CD-ROM
- Electronic Learning Center CD-ROM
- Interactive Lesson Planner CD-ROM
- Electronic Field Trips in Accounting

Recording the Cash Purchase of an Asset

Cash purchases of various assets are recorded in the cash payments journal. One asset commonly purchased for cash is insurance. Let's record a transaction involving a cash purchase of insurance.

Business Transaction

On December 17 On Your Mark paid $1,500 to Keystone Insurance Company for the premium on a six-month insurance policy, Check 1001.

ON YOUR MARK ATHLETIC WEAR
595 Leslie Street, Dallas, TX 75207
1001
22-523 / 4210
DATE Dec. 17 20--
PAY TO THE ORDER OF Keystone Insurance Company $ 1,500.00
One thousand five hundred and no/100 DOLLARS
Security National Bank DALLAS, TEXAS
MEMO Michael Brown
⑆4210225231⑆ 727596⑈ 1001

JOURNAL ENTRY

CASH PAYMENTS JOURNAL PAGE 14

	DATE		DOC NO.	ACCOUNT NAME	POST. REF.	GENERAL DEBIT	GENERAL CREDIT	ACCOUNTS PAYABLE DEBIT	PURCHASES DISCOUNTS CREDIT	CASH IN BANK CREDIT	
1	20--										1
2	Dec.	17	1001	Prepaid Insurance		1 500 00				1 500 00	2
3		1	2	3		4				5	3

Refer to the cash payments journal above and follow these steps:

1. Enter the date of the transaction in the Date column.
2. Enter the check number in the Document Number column.
3. Enter the name of the account debited in the Account Name column.
4. Because there is no special column for **Prepaid Insurance**, enter the amount of the debit in the General Debit column.
5. Enter the amount of the credit in the Cash in Bank Credit column.

After payment, the invoice for the insurance is filed.

Recording a Cash Purchase of Merchandise

Retail businesses are constantly purchasing merchandise for resale. While most purchases are on account, many are for cash. Let's record a cash purchase of merchandise for resale.

Business Transaction

On December 19 On Your Mark purchased merchandise from FastLane Athletics for $1,300, Check 1002.

ON YOUR MARK ATHLETIC WEAR
595 Leslie Street, Dallas, TX 75207
1002
22-523 / 4210
DATE Dec. 19 20--
PAY TO THE ORDER OF FastLane Athletics $ 1,300.00
One thousand three hundred and no/100 DOLLARS
Security National Bank DALLAS, TEXAS
MEMO Michael Brown
⑆4210225231⑆ 727596⑈ 1002

JOURNAL ENTRY

CASH PAYMENTS JOURNAL PAGE 14

	DATE		DOC NO.	ACCOUNT NAME	POST. REF.	GENERAL DEBIT	GENERAL CREDIT	ACCOUNTS PAYABLE DEBIT	PURCHASES DISCOUNTS CREDIT	CASH IN BANK CREDIT	
3		19	1002	Purchases		1 300 00				1 300 00	3
4		1	2	3		4				5	4

ACCOUNTING ISSUES

The PFS Specialty Designation The AICPA has established a specialty designation for its members who have achieved a high level of financial planning expertise. The personal financial specialist (PFS) designation is awarded to those CPAs who successfully complete a comprehensive six-hour exam. The exam covers seven subject areas: PFP process, estate planning, retirement planning, personal income tax planning, risk management and insuranc planning, investment planning, and professional responsibilities (regulations and standards). To qualify for the exam, applicants must have 750 hours of personal financial planning experience over the three years immediately preceding the exam.

2 TEACH
GUIDED PRACTICE

Reading Accounting

- As students read each section, have them make a list of the types of transactions recorded in each special journal for use as a study aid. L1
- Divide students into teams, assigning LEP students to different teams. Have each team prepare a poster presenting purchases and cash payments. Tell teams to present their explanations of journals, ledgers, and accounts in English and in your students' first language. ELL

Concept Development: The Cash Payments Journal

Discussion: After studying the other special journals, students should be familiar with the use of a multicolumn journal. You may want to review the type of transactions recorded in each journ Remind students that column head relate to accounts in the general L1

Visual Learning

Business Transac

Use **Transparenc** students throu recording of

Business T
Using **Tra** stud fo

CHAPTER 17
SECTION 2, PAGES 458–471

2 TEACH (Cont'd.)

Teaching Tip

Point out that purchases of merchandise for actual cash rather than a check are infrequent and would be discouraged by an auditor for cash control reasons.

Visual Learning

Business Transaction

Use **Transparency 17–13** to go through the analysis and recording of a cash payment for merchandise purchased on account. When discussing this transaction, refer students to the invoice on page 451. Point out the terms and the amount of the discount. Also point out the space to enter the check number on the processing stamp placed on the invoice.

Critical Thinking: Ask students to review the payroll entry in the cash payments journal. Why is the entry recorded this way rather than recording the amount of each check issued to employees? (Recording the total cost of payroll as a payment to Salaries Expense saves having to make many more entries to record each employee's check. This entry gives the total while leaving the details in the payroll register and the separate payroll checking account that businesses maintain.) L3

Key Points

The General Column The General column of a special journal refers to the general ledger. The account named in the Account Name column is the general ledger account affected by the transaction.

Refer to the cash payments journal and follow these steps:

1. Enter the date of the transaction in the Date column.
2. Enter the check number in the Document Number column.
3. Enter the name of the account debited in the Account Name column.
4. Because there is no special column for **Purchases,** enter the amount of the debit in the General Debit column.
5. Enter the amount of the check in the **Cash in Bank** Credit column.

After recording the transaction, the receipt for the cash purchase is filed.

Recording a Payment on Account

Now let's learn how to make a payment on account and take a purchase discount.

Business Transaction

On December 24 On Your Mark paid $2,254 to Pro Runner Warehouse for merchandise purchased on account, $2,300 less a discount of $46, Check 1003.

ON YOUR MARK ATHLETIC WEAR
595 Leslie Street, Dallas, TX 75207
1003
22-523
4210
DATE Dec. 24 20 --
PAY TO THE ORDER OF Pro Runner Warehouse $ 2,254.00
Two thousand two hundred fifty-four and no/100 DOLLARS
Security National Bank
DALLAS, TEXAS
MEMO
Michael Brown
⑆4210225231⑆ 727596⑈ 1003

JOURNAL ENTRY

CASH PAYMENTS JOURNAL PAGE 14

	DATE	DOC NO.	ACCOUNT NAME	POST. REF.	GENERAL DEBIT	GENERAL CREDIT	ACCOUNTS PAYABLE DEBIT	PURCHASES DISCOUNTS CREDIT	CASH IN BANK CREDIT	
4	24	1003	Pro Runner Warehouse				2 300 00	46 00	2 254 00	4
5	1	2	3				4	5	6	5

Refer to the purchases journal above and follow these steps:

1. Enter the date of the transaction in the Date column.
2. Enter the check number in the Document Number column.
3. Enter the creditor's name in the Account Name column.
4. Enter the amount of the original purchase in the Accounts Payable Debit column.
5. Enter the amount of the purchase discount in the Purchases Discounts Credit column.
6. Enter the amount of the check in the **Cash in Bank** Credit column.

Remember that a processing stamp is placed on each invoice when it is verified. After the cash payment is journalized, the accounting clerk records the check number on the "Check No." line of the processing stamp. The paid invoice is then filed.

For some purchases a discount is not offered. For others a discount is offered, but the business cannot pay within the discount period. In these cases the check is written for the amount of the purchase.

CONNECT TO . . . LAW

The FBI and other law enforcement agencies recruit accountants to investigate criminal conduct and claimed damages. Perhaps the most famous use of accounting by law enforcers is the conviction of Al Capone for tax evasion after he could not be jailed for his ties to organized crime.

INTERDISCIPLINARY CONNECTIONS ACTIVITY

Law To encourage students to learn more about taxes, tax law, and tax crimes, have them research past tax-evasion cases. Students can use your school's media center, the public library, or the Internet to search for such cases. If you have a law school in your area, you might also make arrangements to borrow materials or to have students search their collection. Once students have located a case study, have them write an article (as if for a newspaper) on the who, what, where, when, and why of the case.

Recording Other Cash Payments

Let's record a check written to pay for shipping charges when merchandise is sent FOB shipping point.

Business Transaction

On December 24 On Your Mark issued Check 1004 for $275 to Dara's Delivery Service for shipping charges on merchandise purchased from Sports Link Footwear.

ON YOUR MARK ATHLETIC WEAR
595 Leslie Street, Dallas, TX 75207
1004
22-523
4210
DATE Dec. 24 20 --
PAY TO THE ORDER OF Dara's Delivery Service $ 275.00
Two hundred seventy-five and no/100 DOLLARS
Security National Bank
DALLAS, TEXAS
MEMO
Michael Brown
⑆4210225234⑆ 727596⑈ 1004

JOURNAL ENTRY

CASH PAYMENTS JOURNAL PAGE 14

	DATE	DOC NO.	ACCOUNT NAME	POST. REF.	GENERAL DEBIT	GENERAL CREDIT	ACCOUNTS PAYABLE DEBIT	PURCHASES DISCOUNTS CREDIT	CASH IN BANK CREDIT	
5	24	1004	*Transportation In*		275 00				275 00	5
6	1	2	3		4				5	6

Refer to the cash payments journal above and follow these steps:

1. Enter the date of the transaction in the Date column.
2. Enter the check number in the Document Number column.
3. Enter the name of the account debited in the Account Name column.
4. Because there is no special column for **Transportation In**, enter the amount of the expense in the General Debit column.
5. Enter the amount of the check in the Cash in Bank Credit column.

Recording Payment of Payroll

In an earlier chapter, you learned how to record the payroll entry in the general journal. When a business uses special journals, the entry for payment of the payroll is recorded in the cash payments journal. The information to record payroll transactions in journals is taken from the payroll register.

To record the payroll transaction, refer to the cash payments journal and follow these steps:

1. On the first line of the entry, enter the date of the transaction in the Date column.
2. Enter the check number in the Document Number column.
3. Enter the name of the account debited in the Account Name column.
4. Enter the amount of the payroll (gross pay) in the General Debit column.
5. Enter the net pay in the Cash in Bank Credit column.
6. On the next four lines, enter the names of the accounts credited in the Account Name column. Enter the amount of each liability in the General Credit column.

2 TEACH (Cont'd.)

Visual Learning

Business Transaction

Using **Transparency 17–14**, have students analyze and explain how to record the payment of shipping charges.

Teaching Tips

When discussing shipping charges, review the meaning of FOB destination and FOB shipping point.

Point out that the check for the salaries expense is made out to the payroll checking account. When discussing this entry, you may want to refer students back to the payroll register in Chapter 12 (see page 299).

MEETING SPECIAL NEEDS

Students with Learning Disabilities Students with learning disabilities may require additional guidelines or study aids to get the most out of text material. You may wish to make audiotapes for students who find written text difficult to use. Establish a relaxed reading pace, and use a bell or clicker to signal page turns. Elicit the help of classmates who have clear voices.

CHAPTER 17
SECTION 2, PAGES 458–471

2 TEACH (Cont'd.)

Visual Learning

Business Transaction
Use **Transparency 17–15** to guide students through the recording of the payroll entry. Point out that this entry is a compound entry in the cash payments journal.

Teaching Tip
Point out that the entry to pay the employer's payroll tax liabilities would be similar to that for issuing the check for the total payroll.

Visual Learning

Business Transaction
Use **Transparency 17–16** to guide students through the analysis and recording of the bank service charges.

Teaching Tips
Point out that some businesses prefer to record transactions for bank charges in the general journal since no checks are issued.

Some banks may send a separate memo notifying a business of the charge for processing bankcard sales for the month.

Business Transaction

On December 31 On Your Mark wrote Check 1012 for $2,974 to pay the payroll of $4,000 (gross earnings) for the pay period ended December 31. The following amounts were withheld: Employees' Federal Income Tax, $640; Employees' State Income Tax, $80; Social Security Tax, $248; and Medicare Tax, $58.

JOURNAL ENTRY

CASH PAYMENTS JOURNAL — PAGE 14

	DATE	DOC NO.	ACCOUNT NAME	POST. REF.	GENERAL DEBIT	GENERAL CREDIT	ACCOUNTS PAYABLE DEBIT	PURCHASES DISCOUNTS CREDIT	CASH IN BANK CREDIT	
13	31	1012	*Salaries Expense* 3		4 000 00				5 2 974 00	13
14	1	2	*Employees' Fed. Inc. Tax Pay.*		4	640 00				14
15			*Employees' State Inc. Tax Pay.*	6		80 00				15
16			*Social Security Tax Pay.*			248 00				16
17			*Medicare Tax Pay.*			58 00				17
18										18

Recording Bank Service Charges

Bank service charges are automatically deducted from the checking account. No check is written. Since the charges result in decreases to **Cash in Bank**, the transactions are recorded in the cash payments journal.

Business Transaction

On December 31 On Your Mark recorded a bank service charge for $20 indicated on the bank statement.

JOURNAL ENTRY

CASH PAYMENTS JOURNAL — PAGE 14

	DATE	DOC NO.	ACCOUNT NAME	POST. REF.	GENERAL DEBIT	GENERAL CREDIT	ACCOUNTS PAYABLE DEBIT	PURCHASES DISCOUNTS CREDIT	CASH IN BANK CREDIT	
18	31		*Miscellaneous Expense*		20 00				20 00	18
19										19

Recording Bankcard Fees

Most banks charge a fee for handling bankcard sales. This fee is automatically deducted from the business' checking account. On Your Mark's bank deducted a bankcard fee of $75. The fee appeared on the bank statement as a deduction from the checking account balance. This decrease in cash is recorded in the cash payments journal.

COOPERATIVE LEARNING ACTIVITY

Group Discussion Provide several samples of actual invoices for a specific type of business (for merchandise, supplies, equipment, and so forth). Divide students into groups of two or three persons, and ask each group to do the following:

1. Identify the accounts affected for each invoice and determine whether each account is increased or decreased.
2. Identify the kinds of information common to all the invoices.
3. Identify the special journal columns that should be included to record this information.
4. Design a purchases journal.

Business Transaction

On December 31 On Your Mark recorded the bankcard fee of $75 that appeared on the bank statement.

JOURNAL ENTRY

CASH PAYMENTS JOURNAL — PAGE 14

	DATE	DOC NO.	ACCOUNT NAME	POST. REF.	GENERAL DEBIT	GENERAL CREDIT	ACCOUNTS PAYABLE DEBIT	PURCHASES DISCOUNTS CREDIT	CASH IN BANK CREDIT	
19	31		Bankcard Fees Expense		75 00				75 00	19
20										20

The bank charges are also entered in the checkbook records. **Figure 17–7** illustrates one way to adjust the balance on the check stub. The deposit heading is crossed out, and the words "Bankcard Fees" are written in its place. A deduction of $75 is entered on the stub. On the next line, the words "Less Bank Service Charge" are written and an entry is made for the $20 deduction. Both amounts are subtracted from the balance brought forward.

$ ______ No. 1013
Date ______ 20 ___
To ______
For ______

	Dollars	Cents
Balance brought forward	15,274	00
~~Add deposits~~ Bankcard Fees	–75	00
Less Bank Svc. Chg.	–20	00
Total	15,179	00
Less this check		
Balance carried forward		

Figure 17–7 Recording Bankcard Fees and Service Charges in the Checkbook

Posting to the Accounts Payable Subsidiary Ledger

To keep creditors' accounts current, daily postings are made from the Accounts Payable Debit column to the accounts payable subsidiary ledger. Refer to **Figure 17–8** and follow these steps:

1. Enter the date of the transaction in the Date column of the subsidiary ledger account.
2. In the subsidiary ledger account's Posting Reference column, enter the journal letters and the page number. The letters "CP" represent the cash payments journal.
3. In the Debit column of the subsidiary ledger account, enter the amount recorded in the Accounts Payable Debit column of the journal.
4. Compute the new account balance and enter it in the Balance column. If the account has a zero balance, draw a line through the Balance column.

Key Points

Posting from the Cash Payments Journal
Every day individual amounts in the Accounts Payable Debit column are posted to the accounts payable subsidiary ledger.

2 TEACH (Cont'd.)

Visual Learning

Business Transaction
Using **Transparency 17–17**, have students analyze and describe how to record the bank's charge for processing bankcard sales.

Demonstration Problem
Step-by-Step Practice
Use demonstration problem 17–4 to give students practice in recording transactions in the cash payments journal.

Visual Learning

Figure 17–7 Recording Bankcard Fees and Service Charges in the Checkbook
Use **Transparency 17–18** to review how to record bankcard fees on the check stub. Remind students that the check stub is the source document for the cash payments journal entry.

Teaching Tip
Point out the minus signs in Figure 17–7. Explain to students that accountants generally use parentheses around a number rather than a minus to indicate an amount that is to be subtracted.

CRITICAL THINKING ACTIVITY

Verifying Invoices Tell students that they work as accounting clerks for The Computer Store. They paid an invoice in March and then realized in April that some of the items on the invoice had been back ordered and had never been received. Where would they find a record of the back-ordered items, and how could they have avoided this error? (The back-ordered items would have been noted on the packing slip. The error could have been avoided by verifying the invoice against the packing slip before paying the invoice.)

2 TEACH (Cont'd.)

Visual Learning

Figure 17–8 Posting from the Cash Payments Journal to the Accounts Payable Subsidiary Ledger

Using **Transparency 17–19**, have students describe how to post amounts to the subsidiary ledger. Review the normal balance for accounts payable accounts.

Demonstration Problem Step-by-Step Practice

Use demonstration problem 17–5 to give students practice in posting individual amounts from the cash payments journal.

Visual Learning

Figure 17–9 The Completed Accounts Payable Subsidiary Ledger

Using **Transparency 17–20a**, review the relationship between the accounts payable ledger and the *Accounts Payable* controlling account.

5. Return to the cash payments journal and enter a check mark (✓) in the Posting Reference column.

CASH PAYMENTS JOURNAL PAGE 14

	DATE		DOC NO.	ACCOUNT NAME	POST. REF.	GENERAL DEBIT	GENERAL CREDIT	ACCOUNTS PAYABLE DEBIT	PURCHASES DISCOUNTS CREDIT	CASH IN BANK CREDIT	
1	20--										1
2	Dec.	17	1001	Prepaid Insurance	135	1 500 00				1 500 00	2
3		19	1002	Purchases	501	1 300 00				1 300 00	3
4		24	1003	Pro Runner Warehouse	✓			2 300 00	46 00	2 254 00	4
5					5						5

NAME *Pro Runner Warehouse*
ADDRESS *22009 Ben White Blvd., Austin, TX 78705*

DATE		DESCRIPTION	POST. REF.	DEBIT	CREDIT	BALANCE
20--						
Dec.	14		P12		2 300 00	2 300 00
	24		CP14	2 300 00		—

Figure 17–8 Posting from the Cash Payments Journal to the Accounts Payable Subsidiary Ledger

Figure 17–9 shows On Your Mark's accounts payable subsidiary ledger after all postings are completed. Notice that the accounts contain entries from the purchases, cash payments, and general journals.

NAME *Champion Store Supply*
ADDRESS *99455 Williams Lane #334, Dallas, TX 75214*

DATE		DESCRIPTION	POST. REF.	DEBIT	CREDIT	BALANCE
20--						
Dec.	1	Balance	✓			1 000 00
	15		P12		1 200 00	2 200 00
	26		CP14	1 200 00		1 000 00

NAME *Computer Solutions*
ADDRESS *6990 Baker Circle, Dallas, TX 75219*

DATE		DESCRIPTION	POST. REF.	DEBIT	CREDIT	BALANCE
20--						
Dec.	1	Balance	✓			500 00
	8		P12		800 00	1 300 00
	20		P12		1 200 00	2 500 00
	31		CP14	1 200 00		1 300 00

Figure 17–9 The Completed Accounts Payable Subsidiary Ledger

TEACHING NOTES

NAME Dara's Delivery Service
ADDRESS 14500 Ellis Blvd., Plano, TX 75093

DATE		DESCRIPTION	POST. REF.	DEBIT	CREDIT	BALANCE
20--						
Dec.	1	Balance	✓			300 00
	30		CP14	300 00		—

NAME FastLane Athletics
ADDRESS 35992 Fletcher Blvd. #334, Boston, MA 02106

DATE		DESCRIPTION	POST. REF.	DEBIT	CREDIT	BALANCE
20--						
Dec.	1	Balance	✓			1 000 00
	14		P12		3 000 00	4 000 00
	16		G21	200 00		3 800 00
	18		P12		2 000 00	5 800 00
	28		CP14	2 000 00		3 800 00

NAME Geary Office Supply
ADDRESS 3300 Fulton Street, Dallas, TX 75219

DATE		DESCRIPTION	POST. REF.	DEBIT	CREDIT	BALANCE
20--						
Dec.	15		P12		250 00	250 00

NAME Pro Runner Warehouse
ADDRESS 22009 Ben White Blvd., Austin, TX 78705

DATE		DESCRIPTION	POST. REF.	DEBIT	CREDIT	BALANCE
20--						
Dec.	14		P12		2 300 00	2 300 00
	24		CP14	2 300 00		—

NAME Sports Link Footwear
ADDRESS 300 Page St. #910, San Francisco, CA 94107

DATE		DESCRIPTION	POST. REF.	DEBIT	CREDIT	BALANCE
20--						
Dec.	1	Balance	✓			2 000 00
	10		P12		4 000 00	6 000 00
	27		P12		1 500 00	7 500 00
	31		CP14	1 500 00		6 000 00

NAME Sports Nutrition Supply
ADDRESS 348 11th Street, Cleveland, OH 44112

DATE		DESCRIPTION	POST. REF.	DEBIT	CREDIT	BALANCE
20--						
Dec.	1	Balance	✓			1 500 00
	12		P12		600 00	2 100 00
	27		CP14	600 00		1 500 00

Figure 17–9 The Completed Accounts Payable Subsidiary Ledger (continued)

2 TEACH (Cont'd.)

Visual Learning

Figure 17–9 The Completed Accounts Payable Subsidiary Ledger (continued)

Using **Transparency 17–20b**, review the accounts in the accounts payable ledger.

Critical Thinking: Have students explain how they know whether the amount shown in the Balance column in Figure 17–9 is a debit balance or a credit balance. (The account is in the accounts payable ledger, which has the same rules as the controlling account, Accounts Payable. The normal balance is thus a credit balance.) L1

HOME AND COMMUNITY CONNECTIONS ACTIVITY

Categorizing Purchases Have students work with a family member to develop a list, by categories, of the different types of purchases made by their family (e.g., clothing, hair care, car maintenance, household supplies, groceries, etc.). Have students write a projected budgeted amount for each item. Then have students monitor purchases by all family members for one week. Did the original list agree with the types of purchases made? Will the projected budget work based on the results gathered in a week's time? What changes might be needed? Discuss general observations with the class.

2 TEACH (Cont'd.)

Visual Learning

Figure 17–10 Posting from the General Debit Column of the Cash Payments Journal

Using **Transparency 17–21**, have students describe the process of posting the amounts in the General Debit column.

Teaching Tips

Remind students that the word "General" in the column heading of the cash payments journal refers to the general ledger. Thus, amounts entered in this column are posted to a general ledger account that is entered in the Account Name column.

If any students are having difficulties with posting, form special tutoring teams and have students teach each other how to post accurately.

Key Points

Footing and Totaling a Special Journal

First, columns are footed with the total entered in pencil. Verified totals are then written in ink.

Posting from the General Debit Column

Daily postings are made from the General Debit column to the appropriate general ledger accounts.

Refer to **Figure 17–10** as you read the following steps.

1. Enter the date of the transaction in the Date column of the general ledger account.
2. Enter the journal letters and the page number in the Posting Reference column of the general ledger account. Be sure to use the letters "CP" for the cash payments journal.
3. In the Debit column, enter the amount from the General Debit column of the cash payments journal.
4. Compute the new balance and enter it in the appropriate Balance column. (In this example there is no previous balance, so the amount recorded in the Debit column is also entered in the Debit Balance column.)
5. Return to the cash payments journal and enter the account number in the Posting Reference column.

All transactions in the General Debit column are posted to the general ledger accounts in the same way.

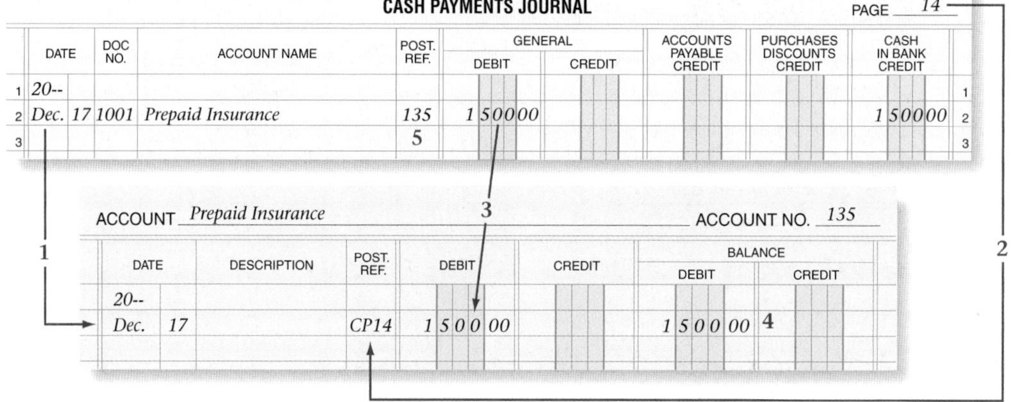

Figure 17–10 Posting from the General Debit Column of the Cash Payments Journal

Totaling, Proving, and Ruling the Cash Payments Journal

The cash payments journal is totaled in the same manner as the other special journals. Before the journal is ruled, prove the equality of debits and credits.

TEACHING NOTES

Debit Columns		Credit Columns	
General	$ 9,170	General	$ 1,026
Accounts Payable	9,100	Purchases Discounts	140
		Cash in Bank	17,104
	$18,270		$18,270

Since debits equal credits, the cash payments journal can be double-ruled, as shown in **Figure 17–11.**

CASH PAYMENTS JOURNAL PAGE *14*

DATE		DOC NO.	ACCOUNT NAME	POST. REF.	GENERAL DEBIT	GENERAL CREDIT	ACCOUNTS PAYABLE DEBIT	PURCHASES DISCOUNTS CREDIT	CASH IN BANK CREDIT
20--									
Dec.	*17*	*1001*	*Prepaid Insurance*	*135*	*1 500 00*				*1 500 00*
	19	*1002*	*Purchases*	*501*	*1 300 00*				*1 300 00*
	24	*1003*	*Pro Runner Warehouse*	✓			*2 300 00*	*46 00*	*2 254 00*
	24	*1004*	*Transportation In*	*505*	*275 00*				*275 00*
	26	*1005*	*Champion Store Supply*	✓			*1 200 00*		*1 200 00*
	27	*1006*	*Sports Nutrition Supply*	✓			*600 00*		*600 00*
	28	*1007*	*FastLane Athletics*	✓			*2 000 00*	*40 00*	*1 960 00*
	30	*1008*	*Dara's Delivery Service*	✓			*300 00*		*300 00*
	31	*1009*	*Rent Expense*	*660*	*2 000 00*				*2 000 00*
	31	*1010*	*Computer Solutions*	✓			*1 200 00*	*24 00*	*1 176 00*
	31	*1011*	*Sports Link Footwear*	✓			*1 500 00*	*30 00*	*1 470 00*
	31	*1012*	*Salaries Expense*	*665*	*4 000 00*				*2 974 00*
			Employee's Federal Inc. Tax Pay.	*205*		*640 00*			
			Employee's State Inc. Tax Pay.	*211*		*80 00*			
			Social Security Tax Payable	*212*		*248 00*			
			Medicare Tax Payable	*213*		*58 00*			
	31	—	*Miscellaneous Expense*	*655*	*20 00*				*20 00*
	31	—	*Bankcard Fees Expense*	*605*	*75 00*				*75 00*
	31		*Totals*		*9 170 00*	*1 026 00*	*9 100 00*	*140 00*	*17 104 00*

Figure 17–11 The Completed Cash Payments Journal

Posting Column Totals to the General Ledger

At the end of the month, the total of each special amount column is posted to the general ledger account named in the column heading. For the cash payments journal, column totals are posted to **Accounts Payable, Purchases Discounts,** and **Cash in Bank. Figure 17–12** shows the posting of the three special column totals to the general ledger accounts. Note that the account numbers for the three general ledger accounts are written in parentheses below the double rule in the appropriate columns of the cash payments journal.

The totals of the General Debit and Credit columns are not posted. Each entry in those columns was posted individually to the general ledger accounts. A check mark (✓) is entered below the double rule in the General Debit and Credit columns.

Key Points

General Columns in Special Journals

To show that General column totals are not posted, place a check mark in parentheses (✓) below the double rule.

2 TEACH (Cont'd.)

Visual Learning

Figure 17–11 The Completed Cash Payments Journal

Using **Transparency 17–22,** have students describe how to total, prove, and rule the cash payments journal.

Critical Thinking: Ask students to explain why the General column of the cash payments journal allows for both debit and credit entries. In the purchases journal, only general debits are made. In the cash receipts journal, only general credits are made. Why is the cash payments journal different? (Most entries affecting general ledger accounts are recorded as credits because cash payments result in credits to Cash in Bank and corresponding debits to the general ledger accounts affected. Even though all payments result in a credit to Cash in Bank, other credits may occasionally be recorded, as when payroll liabilities for which payment will be made later are recorded.) **L3**

ADDRESSING MULTIPLE LEARNING STYLES

Visual/Spatial Learners A visual/spatial learner relies on the sense of sight and the ability to visualize an object. Identify a local businessperson who has videoconferencing facilities and arrange for your students to visit the business and observe a videoconference in action. Ask students to watch for the exchange of images and voice. When you return to the classroom, discuss how businesses can use teleconferencing to save money and to communicate better with its customers and/or suppliers.

2 TEACH (Cont'd.)

Visual Learning

Figure 17–12 Posting Column Totals from the Cash Payments Journal

Using **Transparency 17–23**, ask students to describe the posting of column totals to the general ledger accounts.

Demonstration Problem Step-by-Step Practice

Use demonstration problem 17–6 to give students practice in posting column totals to the general ledger accounts.

Concept Development: Proving the Accounts Payable Subsidiary Ledger

Discussion: Point out that the schedule of accounts payable is a list of creditors and the amounts the business owes each creditor. The key point for students to remember is that the total on the schedule of accounts payable must match the balance of the Accounts Payable controlling account in the general ledger. L1

Teaching Tips

Point out that the schedule of accounts payable is prepared in the same format as the schedule of accounts receivable. One is a list of amounts owed to the business, the other is a list of amounts owed by the business.

Remind students that all accounts are listed on the schedule of accounts payable, even those with zero balances.

CASH PAYMENTS JOURNAL PAGE 14

	DATE		DOC. NO.	ACCOUNT NAME	POST. REF.	GENERAL DEBIT	GENERAL CREDIT	ACCOUNTS PAYABLE DEBIT	PURCHASES DISCOUNTS CREDIT	CASH IN BANK CREDIT	
1	20--										1
2	Dec.	17	1001	Prepaid Insurance	135	1 500 00				1 500 00	2
19		31	—	Bankcard Fees Expense	605	75 00				75 00	19
20		31		Totals		9 170 00	1 026 00	9 100 00	140 00	17 104 00	20
21						(✓)	(✓)	(201)	(510)	(101)	21
22											22

ACCOUNT Cash in Bank ACCOUNT NO. 101

DATE		DESCRIPTION	POST. REF.	DEBIT	CREDIT	BALANCE DEBIT	BALANCE CREDIT
20--							
Dec.	1	Balance	✓			15 000 00	
	31		CR13	17 283 00		32 283 00	
	31		CP14		17 104 00	15 179 00	

ACCOUNT Accounts Payable ACCOUNT NO. 201

DATE		DESCRIPTION	POST. REF.	DEBIT	CREDIT	BALANCE DEBIT	BALANCE CREDIT
20--							
Dec.	1	Balance	✓				6 300 00
	16		G21	200 00			6 100 00
	31		P12		16 850 00		22 950 00
	31		CP14	9 100 00			13 850 00

ACCOUNT Purchases Discounts ACCOUNT NO. 510

DATE		DESCRIPTION	POST. REF.	DEBIT	CREDIT	BALANCE DEBIT	BALANCE CREDIT
20--							
Dec.	1	Balance	✓				1 200 00
	31		CP14		140 00		1 340 00

Figure 17–12 Posting Column Totals from the Cash Payments Journal

Proving the Accounts Payable Subsidiary Ledger

After the column totals are posted, prepare a **schedule of accounts payable**. This schedule lists all creditors in the accounts payable ledger, the balance in each account, and the total amount owed to all creditors. The accounts payable subsidiary ledger is proved when the total of the schedule of accounts payable agrees with the balance of the **Accounts Payable** (controlling) account in the general ledger.

Figure 17–13 shows On Your Mark's schedule of accounts payable for December. The accounts are listed in alphabetical order. All creditors are listed, even those with zero balances. Notice that the total listed on the schedule ($13,850) agrees with the balance of the **Accounts Payable** account.

TEACHING NOTES

ACCOUNT *Accounts Payable* ACCOUNT NO. *201*

DATE		DESCRIPTION	POST. REF.	DEBIT	CREDIT	BALANCE DEBIT	BALANCE CREDIT
20--							
Dec.	1	Balance	✓				6 300 00
	16		G21	200 00			6 100 00
	31		P12		16 850 00		22 950 00
	31		CP14	9 100 00			13 850 00

On Your Mark Athletic Wear
Schedule of Accounts Payable
December 31, 20--

Champion Store Supply	1 000 00	
Computer Solutions	1 300 00	
Dara's Delivery Service	—	
FastLane Athletics	3 800 00	
Geary Office Supply	250 00	
Pro Runner Warehouse	—	
Sports Link Footwear	6 000 00	
Sports Nutrition Supply	1 500 00	
Total Accounts Payable		13 850 00

The balance of the Accounts Payable account should equal the total of the schedule of accounts payable.

Figure 17–13 Schedule of Accounts Payable

Proving Cash

Proving cash is the process of verifying that cash recorded in the accounting records agrees with the amount entered in the checkbook. Ideally businesses prove cash each day. When a business uses special journals, however, the **Cash in Bank** account in the general ledger is updated at the end of the month. For many businesses, then, proving cash is done at the end of the month.

Preparing a Cash Proof

The cash proof may be prepared on plain paper, on accounting stationery, on a special cash proof form, or on a computer. The cash proof for On Your Mark, shown in **Figure 17–14**, is prepared on two-column accounting stationery. To prove cash, follow these steps:

1. On the first line, record the beginning balance of **Cash in Bank** according to the general ledger account.
2. On the next line, enter the total cash received during the month. This is the total of the Cash in Bank Debit column from the cash receipts journal.
3. Add the first and second lines.
4. From the subtotal, subtract the cash payments for the month. This is the total of the Cash in Bank Credit column from the cash payments journal.
5. Compare this figure to the balance shown on the last check stub in the checkbook. If the ending balance of **Cash in Bank** and the balance on

2 TEACH (Cont'd.)

Visual Learning

Figure 17–13 Schedule of Accounts Payable

Using **Transparency 17–24**, discuss the preparation of the list of business creditors and the amount owed to each.

Concept Development: Proving Cash

Discussion: Proving cash regularly is a part of the internal controls used to protect cash. It is also done as a check on the records of cash receipts and cash payments. Most businesses prove cash when they receive their bank statements. Many businesses also prove cash at other times during a month, especially if they handle large amounts of cash. L1

Teaching Tip

Ask students who work in a job where they use a cash register to share how they prove the cash in their cash register drawers each day.

EXTENDING THE CONTENT

Internal Controls Cash proofs are a part of the internal controls for protecting cash. Although many businesses prove cash only when they receive their bank statements, it is recommended that businesses prove cash daily. Invite a local CPA or accountant to your classroom to discuss what auditors look for during an audit. Have the speaker emphasize the importance of internal controls. Ask the speaker to discuss how businesses guard against embezzlement and how auditors are able to detect fraud.

CHAPTER 17
SECTION 2, PAGES 458–471

2 TEACH (Cont'd.)

Visual Learning

Figure 17–14 Cash Proof

Using **Transparency 17–25**, have students describe how to prepare a cash proof.

Teaching Tip

Remind students that cash proofs are important for the control of cash. Cash proofs may also point to errors in the accounting records.

Error Analysis: Have students write a paragraph describing how they would analyze the cash records to find the error if the ending Cash in Bank balance and the check stub balance did not match. (Check all calculations, check that account balances and column totals are written correctly on the cash proof form, re-check addition and subtraction in the checkbook, make sure that all bank service charges are recorded in the checkbook and in the accounting records.) L1

The Office Depot 2001 Annual Report

Refer students to pages A-39–A-48 in the back of the book.

the check stub match, cash is proved. The ending balance of **Cash in Bank** is $15,179. The balance shown on the last check stub is also $15,179; therefore, cash is proved.

If the balances are not equal, the error should be located and corrected. Errors can occur if a bank service charge or a bankcard fee was recorded in the checkbook, but not recorded in the general ledger. Next, you should verify that all disbursements and deposits were recorded in the accounting records. If cash is being proved at month-end, the accountant can then continue with month-end entries.

On Your Mark Athletic Wear
Cash Proof
December 31, 20--

Beginning Cash in Bank Balance	15 000 00
Plus: Cash Receipts for the Month	17 283 00
Subtotal	32 283 00
Less: Cash Payments for the Month	17 104 00
Ending Cash in Bank Balance	15 179 00
Check Stub Balance	15 179 00

Figure 17–14 Cash Proof

ANALYZING FINANCIAL REPORTS

Cost of Goods Sold

For most corporations, increasing profits is a primary goal. To increase profits, either sales must increase or costs must decrease. Managers analyze both sales and costs carefully, and share information about both in the corporation's annual report. For example, in the Office Depot annual report at the back of your textbook, you'll see a section labeled "Management's Discussion & Analysis of Financial Condition and Results of Operations" on pages A-43–A-44. This section contains information about sales and the cost of goods sold.

Management's discussion refers to the company's gross profit, which is sometimes called gross margin. Here's how gross profit is calculated:

Sales
– Cost of goods sold
Gross Profit

In the Office Depot Financial reports, occupancy costs such as rent and common area maintenance are included in cost of goods sold based on the industry's general practices.

▶ Analyze the Report:

1. For Office Depot, what other items do you think would be included in cost of goods sold?
2. By what percentage did "cost of goods sold and occupancy costs" change from 2000 to 2001? Was this an increase or a decrease?

ANALYZING FINANCIAL REPORTS

Analyze the Report (Answers)

1. Answers will vary. Students should mention the cost of merchandise when discussing the cost of goods sold. Occupancy costs can include taxes and utilities. In the Office Depot financial reports, occupancy costs are included in cost of goods sold based on the industry's general practices.
2. Cost of goods sold and occupancy costs decreased 5.84% from 2000 to 2001. ($8,479,437 – $7,983,973 = $495,464; $495,464 ÷ $8,479,437 = 0.0584)

SECTION 2 Check Your Understanding

Now that you have studied this section, complete the following questions and problems.

Thinking Critically

1. How is the accounts payable subsidiary ledger proved?
2. How does an accountant prove cash? How often is cash proved?

Computing in the Business World

At Car Wash Palace, hourly-wage earners are paid weekly. These employees earned $8,000 in total gross earnings this week.

1. Calculate each withholding amount.
2. What is the total net pay for this week?

Tax	Rate
Social Security	6.2%
Medicare	1.45%
Federal Unemployment	0.8%
State Unemployment	5.4%
State Income	4%

Problem 17–2 Preparing a Cash Proof

The Apple Tree Boutique uses special journals. On September 30 the total of the Cash in Bank Debit column of the cash receipts journal is $18,750.12. The total of the Cash in Bank Credit column of the cash payments journal is $16,890.43. The checkbook balance on September 30 is $5,610.59.

Instructions Prepare a cash proof for September in your working papers. The balance of **Cash in Bank** on September 1 is $3,750.90.

Problem 17–3 Analyzing a Source Document

The Country Peddler, which is a retail merchandising store, had the following transaction on November 2.

Instructions Analyze Check Stub 104 shown here. In your working papers, record the necessary entry on page 11 of the cash payments journal.

$ 873.00 No. 104
Date November 2 20 --
To Colonial Products Inc.
For Inv. 323 $900 less 3% disc. $27.00

	Dollars	Cents
Balance brought forward	3,468	29
Add deposits		
Total	3,468	29
Less this check	873	00
Balance carried forward	2,595	29

3 ASSESS

Thinking Critically (Answers)

1. By verifying that the total of the schedule of accounts payable agrees with the balance of Accounts Payable.
2. By adding cash received during the month to the beginning balance and subtracting cash payments. The ending balance must match the check stub balance. Cash is usually proved at the end of the month.

Computing in the Business World (Answers)

Social Security $496, Medicare $116, Federal Unemployment $64, State Unemployment $432, State Income Tax $320, Total Net Pay $6,572

Problem 17–2 (Answer)

Ending Cash in Bank balance $5,610.59

Problem 17–3 (Answer)

Nov. 2: Dr. Accts. Pay./Colonial Products $900; Cr. Purchases Disc. $27, Cash in Bank $873; Check 104

Chapter Reviews and Working Papers Refer students to the Chapter 17 workbook pages to answer *Check Your Understanding* activities.

4 CLOSE

Section Wrap-Up

Teamwork: Divide students into teams. Assign half the teams the AP ledger and the other half, the AR ledger. Have each team make a short presentation explaining its ledger and how purchases and cash payments transactions affect the accounts in the ledger. L1

RETEACHING SECTION 2

Checking the Accuracy of the Accounts Payable Ledger The schedule of accounts payable is a check on the accuracy of the posting to the individual accounts in the accounts payable subsidiary ledger. Review typical posting errors that may have occurred if the balance on the schedule of accounts payable does not match the balance of the Accounts Payable account. Numbers could be transposed during the posting process; the column totals may not have been posted; journal entries may not have been posted; or journal entries may have been posted twice.

SCANS in the Workforce

Foundation Skills Connection

Seeing Things in the Mind's Eye

Ask students to design a flow chart or an organizational chart from a verbal description. Give students an example of a company's management structure and their work flow. From your description, have students use their creativity to design the chart that best depicts this description. Have students share their charts with the class. L1

Workplace Competencies Connection

Using Computers to Process Information

What type of computer skills do your students possess? Ask students to list the software and hardware skills they currently possess. Then have them make a separate list of the computer skills they feel they lack or want to improve. Ask students to project a learning time line for acquiring these skills well enough to perform them in a work environment. L2

Improving and Designing Systems

Have students select a business, a procedure, or a project they feel suffers from a poor operational design. Have students brainstorm in small groups. Then have students write a one-page proposal of the adjustments or changes they would make to improve the business, procedure, or project. L3

ACCOUNTING CAREERS IN FOCUS

SETH PRATT, CPA
Software Developer
Peachtree Software, Inc.

Q: What is your background?

A: After I got my Bachelor of Science in accounting, I worked for three and a half years as a junior accountant and an accountant. Then I passed the CPA exam and went to work for a local CPA firm. I had my own business for a while, but I got excited about computers in the late 1970s. So I went to work for a computer store, then worked as a programmer. After a year and a half, I started a software company and developed accounting software for Windows. Peachtree noticed me and bought my company.

Q: Now what do you do?

A: I lead a team that produces new releases of the product. We improve the product by finding out what our customers complain about and what the competition is doing. We try to see opportunities that no one has thought of.

Q: What skills are most important?

A: Simple math is really important, especially the ability to do word problems. The ability to write concisely is also important. Have the desire to learn new things.

Q: What advice do you have for students interested in developing accounting software?

A: Study accounting in school rather than programming. Programming technology changes rapidly, but accounting procedures don't. Then learn as much about accounting as you can in a small company where you get the opportunity to look at the big picture.

Tips from . . .
RHI Robert Half International Inc.
When hiring, many companies find applicants who do not have basic math, reading, writing or leadership skills. You can improve your chances of being hired by working on weaknesses in these areas before you go to a job interview.

CAREER FACTS

Nature of the Work: Talk to clients, evaluate products on the market, and design products to fit niches.
Training or Education Needed: A bachelor's degree in accounting, the CPA exam, and broad computer experience.
Aptitudes, Abilities, and Skills: Accounting, problem-solving skills, computer skills, communication skills, listening skills, and analytical skills.
Salary Range: $50,000 to $100,000
Career Path: Start by getting accounting experience in a small firm. Then gain some experience in computer sales, programming, and eventually move into development.

Thinking Critically: Why is it important for software designers to be able to see the big accounting picture?

ACCOUNTING CAREERS IN FOCUS

Thinking Critically (Answer)
It's important for software designers to be able to see the "big accounting picture" because familiarity with accounting procedures and its use in the business world helps the designer make efficient programs.

RHI ROBERT HALF CORNER

Basic Skills Students will be more competitive if they possess strong analytical, communications, and organizational skills. Motorola Corp. once turned away 90 percent of applicants for manufacturing positions because of insufficient math and communications abilities.

CHAPTER 17 SUMMARY

KEY CONCEPTS

1. The purchases journal is used to record all purchases on account. The source document for a purchases journal entry is an invoice.

PURCHASES JOURNAL PAGE 12

	DATE	INVOICE NO.	CREDITOR'S ACCOUNT CREDITED	POST. REF.	ACCOUNTS PAYABLE CREDIT	PURCHASES DEBIT	GENERAL: ACCOUNT DEBITED	GENERAL: POST. REF.	GENERAL: DEBIT
1	*Date*	*Invoice No.*	*Creditor's Name*		*xx xx*	*xx xx*			
2									
3									

2. The accounts payable subsidiary ledger contains an account for each creditor. The total of the account balances in the accounts payable subsidiary ledger must match the balance of the **Accounts Payable** controlling account in the general ledger.
3. Transactions are posted from the purchases journal to the accounts payable subsidiary ledger daily. Transactions entered in the General Debit column of the purchases journal are posted daily to the general ledger accounts.
4. At the end of the month, the totals of the special amount columns of special journals are posted to the general ledger.
5. Good internal controls require that all cash payments are authorized, all payments are made by check, and all checks are signed by an authorized person.
6. The cash payments journal, illustrated below, is used to record all transactions in which cash is paid out. The source documents for the journal entry are check stubs and the bank statement.

CASH PAYMENTS JOURNAL PAGE 14

	DATE	DOC NO.	ACCOUNT NAME	POST. REF.	GENERAL DEBIT	GENERAL CREDIT	ACCOUNTS PAYABLE DEBIT	PURCHASES DISCOUNTS CREDIT	CASH IN BANK CREDIT
1	*Date*	*Ck #*	*Purchases*		*xx xx*				*xx xx*
2	*Date*	*Ck #*	*Creditor's Account Name*				*xx xx*		*xx xx*
3	*Date*	*Ck #*	*Creditor's Account Name*				*xx xx*	*xx xx*	*xx xx*
4	*Date*	---	*Account Name to be Debited*		*xx xx*				*xx xx*
5									

7. Transactions are posted from the cash payments journal to the accounts payable subsidiary ledger daily. Transactions entered in the General Debit column of the cash payments journal are posted daily to the general ledger accounts.
8. A schedule of accounts payable is a list of all creditors, the amount owed to each, and the total amount owed to all creditors. The total of the schedule of accounts payable must agree with the balance of the **Accounts Payable** controlling account in the general ledger.
9. At the end of the month, cash is proved by verifying that the cash recorded in the accounting records agrees with the amount shown in the checkbook.

ANSWERS

1. False
2. True
3. False
4. False
5. True
6. False
7. True
8. True
9. False
10. False

SUMMARY

CHAPTER 17

Chapter 17 Quiz

Student ____ Class ____ Instructor ____
Date Assigned ____ Date Completed ____

CHAPTER **17** QUIZ

Special Journals: Purchases and Cash Payments

QUESTIONS (True-False)

Directions: In the space provided, indicate whether each statement is true or false.

___ 1. The purchases journal is used to record only the purchase of merchandise on account.
___ 2. The purchase of merchandise on account always affects the Accounts Payable and Purchases accounts.
___ 3. Amounts recorded in the General Debit column are posted to a subsidiary ledger account.
___ 4. All column totals are posted in a special journal, including general column totals.
___ 5. To prove the purchases journal, the total of debit columns must equal the total of credit columns.
___ 6. An account number is placed under the General Debit column total after the amount has been posted.
___ 7. The cash payments journal records all the checks issued by the business.
___ 8. Payments on account entered in the cash payments journal are always entered as credits to Cash in Bank.
___ 9. Compound entries cannot be made in a special journal.
___ 10. The source document for recording bank service charges and bank card fees is a check.

 Chapter Quizzes • 19

QUESTIONS (True-False)

1. The purchases journal is used to record only the purchase of merchandise on account.
2. The purchase of merchandise on account always affects the Accounts Payable and Purchases accounts.
3. Amounts recorded in the General Debit column are posted to a subsidiary ledger account.
4. All column totals are posted in a special journal, including general column totals.
5. To prove the purchases journal, the total of debit columns must equal the total of credit columns.
6. An account number is placed under the General Debit column total after the amount has been posted.
7. The cash payments journal records all checks issued by a business.
8. Payments on account are entered in the cash payments journal as credits to Cash in Bank.
9. Compound entries cannot be made in a special journal.
10. The source document for recording bank service charges and bankcard fees is a check.

USING KEY TERMS

See the *Glossary* for the definitions of these terms. Ask for volunteers to share their definitions in class. Discuss the job skills students would need to obtain a job as an accounting clerk.

Understanding Accounting Concepts and Procedures

(Answers)

1. All assets bought on account.
2. Accounts Payable.
3. Daily. By posting daily, creditors' accounts in the accounts payable subsidiary ledger are kept current.
4. Credit. Subsidiary ledger accounts have the same balance as the controlling account; Accounts Payable has a normal credit balance.
5. The total of the General Debit column of the purchases journal is not posted because the transactions in the General Debit column were posted during the month.
6. All transactions in which cash is paid out by the business.
7. Specific information for each creditor, such as amount owed.
8. No. Daily posting of amounts to creditors' accounts means that their total will be higher because the column total is not posted to Accounts Payable until the end of the month.
9. To prove that Accounts Payable equals the total of all accounts in the accounts payable subsidiary ledger.
10. (a) Determine the beginning cash balance. (b) Add total cash received during the month. (c) Subtract total cash payments for the month. (d) Compare the result with balance on the last completed check stub. If the ending balances of Cash in Bank and the check stub match, cash is proved.

CHAPTER 17 REVIEW AND ACTIVITIES

USING KEY TERMS

Imagine that you are an applicant for an accounting clerk position with PETCO. You are asked to write definitions for the terms listed below. You really want to get the job, so make sure you connect your knowledge of these accounting terms to the financial activities you believe take place at PETCO.

cash payments journal	purchases journal
proving cash	schedule of accounts payable

Understanding Accounting Concepts and Procedures

Instructions

On a separate sheet of paper, answer the following questions:

1. What kinds of transactions are recorded in the purchases journal?
2. Which account is credited when merchandise is purchased on account?
3. How often are amounts in the Accounts Payable Credit column of the purchases journal posted? Explain.
4. What is the normal balance of an account in the accounts payable subsidiary ledger? Explain.
5. Explain why the total of the General Debit column in the purchases journal is not posted.
6. What kinds of transactions are recorded in the cash payments journal?
7. What information is available in the accounts payable subsidiary ledger that cannot be found in the **Accounts Payable** controlling account?
8. Should the balance of the **Accounts Payable** account in the general ledger always equal the total of the accounts payable subsidiary ledger? Explain.
9. Why is a schedule of accounts payable prepared?
10. List the steps to prove cash at the end of the month.

ASSESSMENT RESOURCES

Choose assessment strategies from the following pages to evaluate your students' progress.

Student Edition
Check Your Understanding, pp. 457, 471
Chapter 17 Problems, pp. 477–481
Analyzing Financial Reports, p. 470

Assessment and Evaluation Masters
Chapter 17 Study Plan, *Glencoe Workbook (CRWP)*
Chapter 17 Self-Test, *Glencoe Workbook (CRWP)*
Chapter 17 Test, *Chapter Tests* Booklet
Chapter 17 Activity, *School-to-Work Handbook*
Chapter 17 **Exam***View*

Teacher Wraparound Edition
Critical Thinking Activity, p. 463
Reteaching Sections 1–2, pp. 457, 471
Chapter 17 Quiz, p. 473

Case Study...

Merchandising Business: Books & More

Books & More is a retail store that sells hardcover and paperback books, plus a large selection of music tapes and CDs. Books & More keeps a large stock of merchandise on hand and places frequent orders for new merchandise. For fast-selling items, such as a popular new CD, the store may place an order each week.

You work in the accounting department for Books & More. Recently, you noticed two invoices for three dozen CDs ordered from the same music wholesaler. The CDs ordered and the amounts are identical on both invoices.

Thinking Critically:

1. How would you determine whether the invoices are for two different orders or are duplicate invoices for one order?
2. What steps would you take to ensure that payments are not made for duplicate invoices?

Conducting an Audit with Alex

Alpha Enterprises had the following business transactions in May:

- Alpha issued a check to Metro Ace Realty for rent, $800.
- Alpha issued a check to Cray Hardware for $1,940 in payment for a $2,000 invoice due, less cash discount of $60.
- Alpha paid $300 to Ron's Paint Shop for painting supplies.

The accounting clerk for Alpha Enterprises made the following postings:
$800 was posted as a credit to **Rent Expense;**
$1,940 was posted as a debit to **Accounts Payable;**
$300 was posted as a credit to **Paint Supplies.**

Instructions Determine whether the transactions were posted correctly. If not, what error(s) were made?

*inter*NET CONNECTION

Electronic Commerce

Electronic commerce on the Internet is becoming increasingly popular. You should be aware of the basics of e-commerce and its benefits.

Do This:

Explore e-commerce on the Internet and then answer the following questions:

1. Define electronic commerce.
2. A smart card is one method for making electronic payments. Locate an Internet site that discusses smart cards. What is a smart card?
3. List two advantages electronic commerce provides for consumers.

Workplace Skills

Selecting Equipment and Tools

For your business to be competitive, you must be able to look at your company's needs, assess the best technology to help solve problems, and find the best equipment to produce results.

On the Job:
Web Works is an online computer assistance service for people who use computers. The company specializes in applications accessible through the Internet. In a recent staff meeting, Shelly Lazarus, your manager, asked you to assess online banking and invoice payment.

Thinking Critically:

1. Investigate online banking on the Internet. Find out what type of computer equipment is required, and how much the service will cost. Prepare a table showing comparative data.
2. Next, review different options for paying invoices online. Look at software product reviews and prepare a table showing the comparative data for this type of service.
3. Write a memorandum with your recommendations to Ms. Lazarus for the types of equipment Web Works will need to facilitate both online banking and online invoice payment.

*inter*NET CONNECTION www.glencoe.com

Do This (Answers)

1. Searching for "electronic commerce" should bring students to the Electronic Commerce Page of the WWW Virtual Library Project (www.elib.org/econ.html). Electronic commerce generally covers business transactions executed electronically.
2. Examples: (www.slb.com/smartcards/) or (www.smart–card.com). Smart cards are wallet-sized plastic cards with microprocessors that interface with network terminal devices.
3. Answers may include the convenience (shopping anytime from home), increased product availability, or improved product quality at reduced cost.

Case Study...

Thinking Critically (Answers)

1. Check the invoice numbers and dates to determine if these are two separate orders or a duplicate.
2. Ensure that checks are not printed for an invoice without proper authorization and that they are supported by receiving reports and purchase orders. Attach a copy of the check to paid invoices and stamp them "Paid."

Workplace Skills

Thinking Critically (Answers)

1. Answers will vary. Ask students to work in teams to locate the information—either by phone or through the Internet.
2. Answers will vary. Use your school's media center to have students conduct a periodical review for information about online accounting programs and financial services. You may also do an Internet search.
3. Answers will vary. Recommendations will depend on current software trends, pricing structures, and services available in your area.

Conducting an Audit with Alex

(Answers)

The accounting clerk for Alpha Enterprises made the following postings:

- $800 was credited to **Rent Expense.**
- $1,940 was debited to **Accounts Payable.**
- $300 was credited to **Paint Supplies.**

Internet Resources and Activities Handbook

Refer students to the booklet for additional Internet activities.

PEACHTREE CORNER

Purchases on Account

Use the **Purchases/Receive Inventory** task option or click the **Purchases** navigation aid to enter purchases on account.

Tasks | Analysis | Options | Reports
- Quotes/Sales Orders
- Sales/Invoicing...
- Receipts...
- Finance Charge...
- Select for Deposit...
- Purchase Orders...
- Purchases/Receive Inventory...
- Select for Payment...
- Payments...

Cash Payments

Select **Payments** from the ***Tasks*** menu or click the **Purchases** navigation aid to enter a cash payment.

Tasks | Analysis | Options | Reports
- Quotes/Sales Orders
- Sales/Invoicing...
- Receipts...
- Finance Charge...
- Select for Deposit...
- Purchase Orders...
- Purchases/Receive Inventory...
- Select for Payment...
- Payments...
- Write Checks...

Payments

For a cash payment on account, enter the transaction details. In the Apply to Invoices tab, mark the invoice to apply the payment.

For a cash payment not on account, record transaction information then enter it in the Apply to Expenses tab.

Mastering Purchases and Cash Payments

Making the Transition from a Manual to a Computerized System

Task	Perform Accounting Procedures Using Manual Methods	Perform Accounting Procedures Using Automated Methods
Setting up vendor records	1. Ledger sheet or card is prepared with vendor details such as name, address, and contact information. 2. Account activities are posted to the vendor subsidiary ledger accounts.	1. Assign each vendor an ID code. 2. Record details of vendor accounts into vendor records. 3. The software will access this information automatically each time the ID code is used.
Recording a debit memorandum	1. A debit memorandum is prepared when merchandise is damaged or an allowance is due. 2. A journal entry is prepared to record the debit memorandum. 3. The journal entry is posted to the subsidiary account and to the general ledger.	1. Record the debit memorandum as a negative amount using the Purchases/Receive Inventory option. 2. The debit memorandum will appear on the outstanding invoices list. 3. The debit memorandum data is posted automatically to the vendor's account record and the general ledger.

Mastering Purchases and Cash Payments

Peachtree Question	Description
How do I set up a new vendor record?	1. Select **Vendors** from the ***Maintain*** menu. 2. Assign a **Vendor ID** to the new vendor. 3. Enter vendor name and contact information. 4. Click on the *Purchase Defaults* tab. 5. Verify or enter the appropriate Purchase default GL account number. 6. Click *Save*.
How do I record a debit memorandum?	1. Select **Purchases/Receive Merchandise** from the ***Tasks*** menu. 2. Select the appropriate **Vendor ID** from the pull-down list. 3. Enter the Debit Memorandum number in the Invoice field. 4. Select or verify the GL A/P account number. 5. Enter the line items of the return or allowance as a negative amount. 6. Click *Save*.
What does the software do "behind the scenes"?	• Using Vendor ID codes, the software can update vendor purchases and payments when purchase or cash payments are recorded. • Debit memorandums are applied directly to the appropriate vendor account and posted to the general ledger and subsidiary ledger automatically.

For detailed instructions: See the **Peachtree User Guide** in your Glencoe Working Papers.

Peachtree® Answers to Frequently Asked Questions

Q: What steps are required to correct a cash payment entry?

A: You can change any information on a cash payment unless you have closed the current period. To make a change, choose the **Payments** option. Click the *Open* button and select the payment you want to update. Make the changes and post the corrected transaction. Peachtree automatically applies the corrections.

For additional information, refer to your *Glencoe Peachtree Accounting User's Guide*.

CHAPTER 17 PROBLEMS

APPLICATION OPTIONS

Problem 17–4 Recording Payment of the Payroll

Denardo's Country Store pays its employees on a biweekly basis. This week the payroll is $2,000. You issued Check 949 for $1,487 in payment of the payroll less the following amounts: Employees' Federal Income Tax, $320; Employees' State Income Tax, $40; Social Security Tax, $124; and Medicare Tax, $29.

Instructions In your working papers, record the July 15 payroll on page 4 of the cash payments journal.

Analyze: Calculate the total deductions from employees wages for federal, state, social security, and Medicare taxes. What percentage of gross payroll is this amount?

Problem 17–5 Recording Transactions in the Purchases Journal

Sunset Surfwear had the following purchases transactions for July.

Instructions Use the purchases journal in your working papers.

1. Record the following transactions on page 4 of the purchases journal.
2. Foot, prove, total, and rule the purchases journal.

Date	Transactions
July 1	Purchased merchandise on account from Waverunner Designs for $1,200, Invoice WD121.
3	Received Invoice CA552 from Capital Accessories for the purchase of $1,600 in merchandise on account.
5	Purchased $2,000 in store equipment on account from Neilson Store Equipment, Invoice NS444.
9	Purchased $870 in merchandise on account from Kelley Apparel Inc., Invoice KA772.
12	Purchased $250 in supplies from Moore Paper & Office Supply Co., Invoice MPS266.
15	Purchased $1,800 in merchandise on account from AcaTan Products, Invoice ATP99.

Continued

Complete chapter problems one of three ways:

1. **Manual** Glencoe Working Papers

or

2. **Peachtree Complete Accounting** Software

or

3. **QuickBooks** Templates (Problems 17–5, 17–8)

Peachtree®

SMART GUIDE

Step-by-Step Instructions: Problem 17–4

1. Select the problem set for Denardo's Country Store (Prob. 17–4).
2. Rename the company and set the system date.
3. Record the payment of the payroll using the **Payments** option.
4. Print a Cash Disbursements Journal report.
5. Proof your work.
6. Answer the Analyze question.
7. End the session.

TIP: Remember to update the *G/L Account* field for each line of a multi-part cash payment transaction.

PROBLEMS CHAPTER 17

Problem 17-4 (Answers) Recording Payment of the Payroll

General Debit, Salaries Expense $2,000; General Credit, Employees' Fed. Income Tax Pay. $320, Employees' State Income Tax Pay. $40, Social Security Tax Pay. $124, Medicare Tax Pay. $29; Cash in Bank Credit $1,487

Analyze: $513, 25.65% of gross payroll

Problem 17-5 (Answers) Recording Transactions in the Purchases Journal

Column totals:

Accounts Payable $11,185
Purchases $7,235
General $3,950

Total Debits/Credits $11,185

Analyze: $11,185

SOFTWARE NOTES

Teachers can find detailed instructions for:

- **Peachtree Complete Accounting Software**, in the *Glencoe Workbook (CRWP)*
- **QuickBooks Templates**, in *Using QuickBooks with Glencoe Accounting*
- **Spreadsheet Templates**, in the *Glencoe Workbook (CRWP)*

Problem 17-6 (Answers) Recording and Posting Purchases

Purchases journal column totals:
Accounts Payable $7,500
Purchases $4,250
General $3,250

Total Debits/Credits $7,500

Accounts payable subsidiary ledger balances:
Allen's Repair $210
Digital Precision Equipment $3,500
Photo Emporium $750
Prostudio Supply $2,400
State Street Office Supply $140
U-Tech Products $4,000
Video Optics Inc. $1,000

General ledger debit balances:
Supplies $840
Store Equipment $5,000
Purchases $19,250
Maintenance Expense $410

General ledger credit balances:
Accounts Payable $12,000

Analyze: The accounts payable subsidiary ledger would be understated and out of balance with the Accounts Payable controlling account.

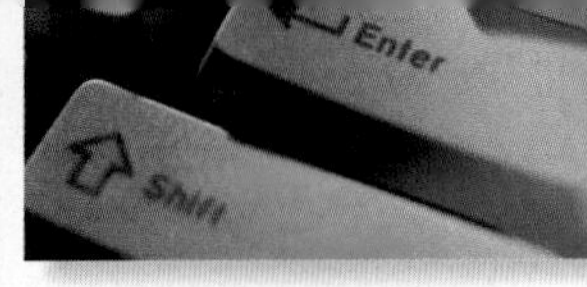

Peachtree®

SMART GUIDE

Step-by-Step Instructions: Problem 17-5

1. Select the problem set for Sunset Surfwear (Prob. 17-5).
2. Rename the company and set the system date.
3. Record all of the purchases on account using the **Purchases/Receive Inventory** option.
4. Print a Purchases Journal report.
5. Proof your work.
6. Answer the Analyze question.
7. End the session.

TIP: Remember to change the *G/L Account* field as needed for general purchases.

Date	Problem 17-5 (cont.) Transactions
July 18	Purchased $500 in office equipment on account from Moore Paper & Office Supply Co., Invoice MPS275.
22	Received Invoice WD156 from Waverunner Designs for the purchase of $900 in merchandise on account.
25	Purchased $475 in merchandise on account from Capital Accessories, Invoice CA560.
28	Purchased from Kelley Apparel Inc. $390 in merchandise on account, Invoice KA800.
30	Received Invoice NS460 from Neilson Store Equipment for the purchase of $1,200 in store equipment on account.

Analyze: What are the total purchases on account for the month?

Problem 17-6 Recording and Posting Purchases

Shutterbug Cameras, a retail merchandising business, had the following purchases on account for the month of July. In the working papers, the beginning balances in the accounts are opened for you.

Instructions In your working papers:

1. Record July's transactions on page 18 of the purchases journal.
2. Post to the accounts payable subsidiary ledger accounts daily.
3. Post amounts entered in the General Debit column daily.
4. Foot, prove, total, and rule the purchases journal at the end of the month.
5. Post the column totals at the end of the month to the account named in the column heading.
6. Prepare a schedule of accounts payable.

Peachtree®

SMART GUIDE

Step-by-Step Instructions: Problem 17-6

1. Select the problem set for Shutterbug Cameras (Prob. 17-6).
2. Rename the company and set the system date.
3. Record all of the purchases on account using the **Purchases/Receive Inventory** option.
4. Print a Purchases Journal report.
5. Proof your work.
6. Print a General Ledger report and a Vendor Ledgers report.
7. Answer the Analyze question.
8. End the session.

TIP: Remember to change the *G/L Account* field for purchases other than merchandise.

Date	Transactions
July 1	Purchased $1,200 in merchandise on account from U-Tech Products, Invoice UT220.
3	Purchased $140 in supplies on account from State Street Office Supply, Invoice 983, n/30.
6	Received Invoice 1338 from Photo Emporium for the purchase of $150 in merchandise on account, 2/10, n/30.
9	Invoice 445 for $90 was sent by Allen's Repair for plumbing repairs completed at the store **(Maintenance Expense).**
12	Purchased $800 in merchandise on account from Video Optics Inc., Invoice VO167, 3/15, n/45.
15	Received Invoice 1322 from Digital Precision Equipment for the purchase of $2,500 in store equipment on account, n/30.

Continued

SOLUTION NOTES

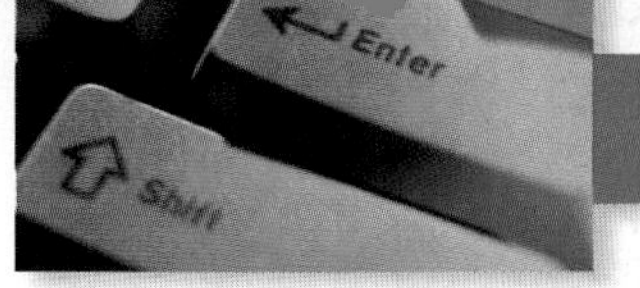

Date	Problem 17–6 (cont.) Transactions
July 18	Purchased $1,300 in merchandise on account from U-Tech Products, Invoice UT257.
20	Purchased $400 in supplies on account from ProStudio Supply, Invoice 4677.
23	Photo Emporium sent Invoice 1359 for the purchase of $600 of merchandise on account.
26	Received Invoice 478 for $120 from Allen's Repair for additional plumbing work completed at the store.
28	Purchased $200 in merchandise on account from Video Optics Inc., Invoice VO183.

Analyze: If the transaction of July 23 (Photo Emporium) was posted to the accounts payable subsidiary ledger as $60, what problems would occur?

Problem 17–7 Recording and Posting Cash Payments

River's Edge Canoe & Kayak is a retail merchandising business located in Jackson Hole, Wyoming. The beginning balances of the accounts needed to complete this problem are opened in your working papers.

Instructions In your working papers:

1. Record the transactions on page 19 of the cash payments journal.
2. Post the individual amounts in the Accounts Payable Credit column on a daily basis to the creditors' accounts.
3. Post the individual amounts in the General Debit and Credit columns on the date the transaction occurred.
4. Foot, prove, total, and rule the cash payments journal.
5. Post the column totals at the end of the month.
6. Prepare a schedule of accounts payable.
7. Prove cash at the end of the month. The beginning **Cash in Bank** balance was $8,000; cash receipts were $7,000; and the ending check stub balance is $8,404.

Date	Transactions
July 1	Issued Check 1405 for $1,372 to North American Waterways Suppliers in payment on account of $1,400 invoice less a 2% discount.
3	Received insurance premium statement from Rocky Mountain Insurance Company. Issued Check 1406 for $1,800.

Continued

Peachtree®

SMART GUIDE

Step-by-Step Instructions: Problem 17–7

1. Select the problem set for River's Edge Canoe & Kayak (Prob. 17–7).
2. Rename the company and set the system date.
3. Record all of the cash payments using the **Payments** option.
4. Print a Cash Disbursements Journal report.
5. Proof your work.
6. Print a General Ledger report and a Vendor Ledgers report.
7. Answer the Analyze question.
8. End the session.

TIP: Sometimes you may have to manually entry a cash discount when you record a cash payment.

INTRODUCING
CHAPTER 17

Problem 17–7 (Answers) Recording and Posting Cash Payments

Cash payments journal column totals:
General Dr. $3,090
Accounts Payable $3,550
Purchases Discounts $42
Cash in Bank $6,598

Total Debits/Credits $6,640

Accounts payable subsidiary ledger balances:
Mohican Falls Kayak Wholesalers $300
North American Waterways Suppliers $0
Office Max $0
Pacific Wholesalers $800
Rollins Plumbing Service $0
StoreMart Supply $500
Trailhead Canoes $0

General ledger debit balances:
Cash in Bank $8,402
Supplies $240
Prepaid Insurance $1,800
Store Equipment $3,700
Transportation In $775
Advertising Expense $2,100
Miscellaneous Expense $75

General ledger credit balances:
Accounts Payable $1,600
Purchases Discounts $1,542

Schedule of Accounts Payable $1,600

Cash proof $8,402

Analyze: $1,600

SOLUTION NOTES

CHALLENGE PROBLEM | SOURCE DOCUMENT PROBLEM

Problem 17-8 (Answers)
Recording and Posting Purchases and Cash Payments

Cash payments journal totals:
General Dr. $1,880
Accounts Payable $7,550
Purchases Discounts $108
Cash in Bank $9,322

Total Debits/Credits $9,430

Purchases journal column totals:
Accounts Payable $4,900
Purchases $2,600
General $2,300

Total Debits/Credits $4,900

Accounts payable subsidiary ledger balances:
ADC Publishing $600
American Trend Publishers $0
Candlelight Software $500
CorpTech Office Supply $300
Delta Press $750
Nomad Computer Sales $600
Pine Forest Publications $300

General ledger debit balances:
Cash in Bank $10,178
Supplies $450
Prepaid Insurance $1,600
Store Equipment $8,000
Purchases $27,600
Transportation In $925
Bankcard Fees Expense $1,230
Miscellaneous Expense $225

General ledger credit balances:
Accounts Payable $3,050
Purchases Discounts $1,708

Schedule of Accounts Payable $3,050

Cash Proof $10,178

Analyze: $2,600

Date		Problem 17–7 (cont.) Transactions
July	5	Issued Check 1407 to Pacific Wholesalers for $500 to apply on account.
	8	Received an invoice for $300 from Jackson News for advertising. Issued Check 1408.
	12	Issued Check 1409 for $686 to Trailhead Canoes in payment on account of $700 invoice less a 2% discount.
	15	Issued Check 1410 for $200 to Rollins Plumbing Service in full payment of the amount owed on account.
	18	Issued Check 1411 for $75 to Ben Jacobs for completing odd jobs in the store (Miscellaneous Expense).
	20	Purchased $90 in supplies from StoreMart Supply by issuing Check 1412.
	22	Paid StoreMart Supply $400 to apply on account, Check 1413.
	24	Issued Check 1414, $700 to Office Max, store equipment.
	25	Paid Mohican Falls Kayak Wholesalers $200 to apply on account, Check 1415.
	26	Issued Check 1416 to Office Max, $150 to apply on account.
	28	Paid transportation charges of $125 to Stein's Trucking, Check 1417.

Analyze: At month end, how much does River's Edge owe to its creditors?

Peachtree®

SMART GUIDE

Step-by-Step Instructions: Problem 17–8

1. Select the problem set for Buzz Newsstand (Prob. 17-8).
2. Rename the company and set the system date.
3. Enter the purchases on account.
4. Record all of the cash payments.
5. Print the following reports: Purchases Journal, Cash Disbursements Journal, and Vendor Ledgers.
6. Proof your work.
7. Print a General Ledger report.
8. Answer the Analyze question.
9. End the session.

SOURCE DOCUMENT PROBLEM

Problem 17–8

Use the source documents in your working papers to record the transactions for this problem.

CHALLENGE PROBLEM

Problem 17–8 Recording and Posting Purchases and Cash Payments

SOURCE DOCUMENT PROBLEM

Buzz Newsstand had the following purchases and cash payment transactions for July. The balance in the accounts payable subsidiary ledger and general ledger accounts are opened in the working papers.

Instructions In your working papers:

1. Record the purchases and cash payment transactions on page 12 of the purchases journal and page 12 of the cash payments journal.
2. Post to the creditors' accounts in the accounts payable subsidiary ledger daily.
3. Post from the General Debit and Credit columns of the journals on the date the transaction occurred.
4. Foot, prove, total, and rule both journals.
5. Post the column totals of the purchases journal to the general ledger accounts named in the column headings.
6. Post the column totals of the cash payments journal to the general ledger accounts named in the column headings.
7. Prepare a schedule of accounts payable.

SOLUTION NOTES

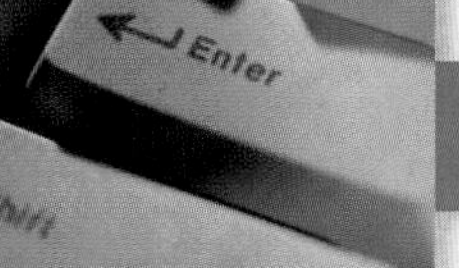

8. Prepare a cash proof at the end of the month. The beginning **Cash in Bank** balance was $9,000. Cash receipts were $10,500. The check stub balance on July 31 is $10,178.

Date		Transactions
July	1	Issued Check 2455 for $1,552 to ADC Publishing in payment on account of $1,600 invoice less a 3% discount.
	2	Purchased $400 in merchandise on account from Pine Forest Publications, Invoice PFP144, terms 2/10, n/30.
	2	Paid Candlelight Software $1,358 in payment of $1,400 account less a 3% discount, Check 2456.
	4	Issued Check 2457 to Nomad Computer Sales for $350 to apply on account.
	5	Purchased $2,000 in store equipment on account from CorpTech Office Supply, Invoice CT67.
	7	Issued Check 2458 for $125 to Wolfe Trucking for transportation charges.
	9	Purchased $900 in merchandise on account from American Trend Publishers, Invoice ATP98.
	12	Purchased $300 in supplies on account from CorpTech Office Supply, Invoice CT72.
	14	Issued Check 2459 to Delta Press for $750 to apply on account.
	15	Received insurance premium statement from SeaTac Insurance Co. for $1,600. Issued Check 2460.
	16	Check 2461 was issued for $882 to American Trend Publishers in payment of $900 account less a 2% discount.
	18	Purchased $500 in merchandise on account from Candlelight Software, Invoice CS101, terms n/30.
	20	Purchased $200 in merchandise on account from Nomad Computer Sales, Invoice NC56, terms 2/10, n/30.
	22	Paid Pine Forest Publications $100 to apply on account, Check 2462.
	23	Issued Check 2463 for $2,000 to CorpTech Office Supply to apply on account.
	25	Purchased $600 in merchandise on account from ADC Publishing, Invoice ADC70.
	28	Issued Check 2464 for $450 to Nomad Computer Sales to apply on account.
	30	Recorded the bank service charge of $25. Recorded the bankcard fees, $130. July bank statement.

Analyze: Of the purchases made during July, what dollar amount increased merchandise inventory?

SOLUTION NOTES

CHAPTER 18 Resource Manager

Section Resources

	Objectives & Standards	Activities & Features	Reproducible Masters
Chapter Opener *Adjustments and the Ten-Column Work Sheet*	• Describe the parts of a ten-column work sheet. • Generate trial-balances and end-of-period adjustments. • Determine which general ledger accounts are adjusted. • Calculate the adjustments. • Prepare a ten-column work sheet. • Journalize the adjustments. • Define the accounting terms introduced in this chapter. **National Standards for Business Education**: IA11, IA12, IA16	Exploring the Real World of Business, p. 482 Workplace Connections, p. 483	School-to-Work Handbook
Section 1 *Identifying Accounts To Be Adjusted and Adjusting Merchandise Inventory*	• How to complete the Trial Balance section of the work sheet. • Why certain general ledger accounts are adjusted. • Why **Merchandise Inventory** is adjusted. • How to calculate and record the adjustment for **Merchandise Inventory**.	Did You Know?, p. 485 Math Hints, p. 486 A Matter of Ethics, p. 489	Math Review for Accounting Demonstration Problems Strategies for Teaching Ethics in Accounting
Section 2 *Adjusting Supplies, Prepaid Insurance, and Federal Corporate Income Tax*	• Why the **Supplies**, **Prepaid Insurance**, and **Federal Corporate Income Tax Expense** accounts are adjusted. • How to calculate the adjustments for supplies, insurance, and federal corporate income tax. • How to enter the adjustments on the work sheet.	International Accounting, p. 494	Demonstration Problems Strategies for Teaching International Accounting
Section 3 *Completing the Work Sheet and Journalizing and Posting the Adjusting Entries*	• How to complete the Adjusted Trial Balance section. • How to extend amounts to the Income Statement and Balance Sheet sections. • How to report the net income or net loss for the period. • How to journalize the adjusting entries in the general journal. • How to post the adjusting entries to the general ledger.	Connect To, p. 499 Accounting Flashbacks, p. 500 Analyzing Financial Reports, p. 503	Demonstration Problems Internet Resources and Activities Handbook

KEY

Posters — Transparency — Software — Videocassette
Blackline Masters — CD-ROM — Portfolio

MULTIMEDIA RESOURCE

Peachtree
- Problem 18–6 *Completing a Ten-Column Work Sheet*
- Problem 18–7 *Completing a Ten-Column Work Sheet*
- Problem 18–8 *Completing a Ten-Column Work Sheet*

QuickBooks
- Problem 18–7 *Completing a Ten-Column Work Sheet*
- Problem 18–8 *Completing a Ten-Column Work Sheet*

Spreadsheets
- Problem 18–5 *Completing a Ten-Column Work Sheet*

Videos

Video Segment: Adjusting Entries
After viewing this video, students will be able to describe items that are paid for in advance and are used in the operation of the business. They will also be able to explain the need for adjustments and describe a typical adjustment.

CD-ROMs

Electronic Learning Center (ELC), Chapter 18
This program is ideal for visual learners since it incorporates video images, animation, and graphics to enliven the content of each lesson.

Interactive Lesson Planner (ILP), Chapter 18
This CD-ROM combines the versatility of an electronic lesson planner with the convenience of teacher classroom resources.

SCANS Correlation Chart

FOUNDATION SKILLS

Basic Skills:	Reading	Writing	Math	Listening	Speaking	
Thinking Skills:	Creative Thinking	Decision Making	Problem Solving	Seeing Things in the Mind's Eye	Knowing How to Learn	Reasoning
Personal Qualities:	Responsibility	Self-Esteem	Sociability	Self-Management	Integrity/Honesty	

WORKPLACE COMPETENCIES

Resources:	Allocating Time	Allocating Money	Allocating Material and Facility Resources	Allocating Human Resources		
Information:	Acquiring and Evaluating Information	Organizing and Maintaining Information	Interpreting and Communicating Information	Using Computers to Process Information		
Interpersonal Skills:	Participating as a Member of a Team	Teaching Others	Serving Clients/ Customers	Exercising Leadership	Negotiating to Arrive at a Decision	Working with Cultural Diversity
Systems:	Understanding Systems	Monitoring and Correcting Performance	Improving and Designing Systems			
Technology:	Selecting Technology	Applying Technology to Task	Maintaining and Troubleshooting Technology			

*Highlighted blocks indicate areas covered in the chapter. Additional SCANS skills are also covered throughout the *Teacher Wraparound Edition.*

Assessment

Student Edition
- Check Your Understanding, pp. 490, 495, 504
- Chapter 18 Problems, pp. 509–513

Assessment and Evaluation Masters
- Chapter 18 Study Plan, *Glencoe Workbook*
- Chapter 18 Self-Test, *Glencoe Workbook*
- Chapter 18 Test, *Chapter Tests* Booklet
- Chapter 18 Activity, *School-to-Work Handbook*
- Chapter 18 **Exam***View*

Teacher Wraparound Edition
- Critical Thinking Activity, p. 487
- Reteaching Section 1, p. 490
- Reteaching Section 2, p. 495
- Reteaching Section 3, p. 504
- Chapter 18 Quiz, p. 505

Transparencies

	Teaching Transparencies	Solution Transparencies
Section 1:	18–1, 18–2, 18–3, 18–4	Problem 18–1
Section 2:	18–5, 18–6, 18–7, 18–8	Problem 18–2
Section 3:	18–9, 18–10, 18–11a, 18–11b, 18–12, 18–13a, 18–13b	Problems 18–3, 18–4
End of Chapter:		Problems 18–5, 18–6, 18–7, 18–8, 18–9

TEACHER CLASSROOM RESOURCES

This is a representation of key blackline masters available in the Teacher Classroom Resources.

Teaching Aids

Transparency Examples

Section Focus Transparencies

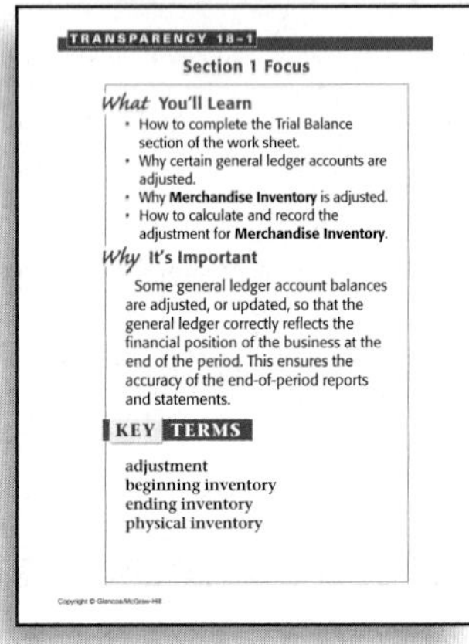

TRANSPARENCY 18-1

Section 1 Focus

What You'll Learn

- How to complete the Trial Balance section of the work sheet.
- Why certain general ledger accounts are adjusted.
- Why **Merchandise Inventory** is adjusted.
- How to calculate and record the adjustment for **Merchandise Inventory**.

Why It's Important

Some general ledger account balances are adjusted, or updated, so that the general ledger correctly reflects the financial position of the business at the end of the period. This ensures the accuracy of the end-of-period reports and statements.

KEY TERMS

adjustment
beginning inventory
ending inventory
physical inventory

Teaching Transparencies

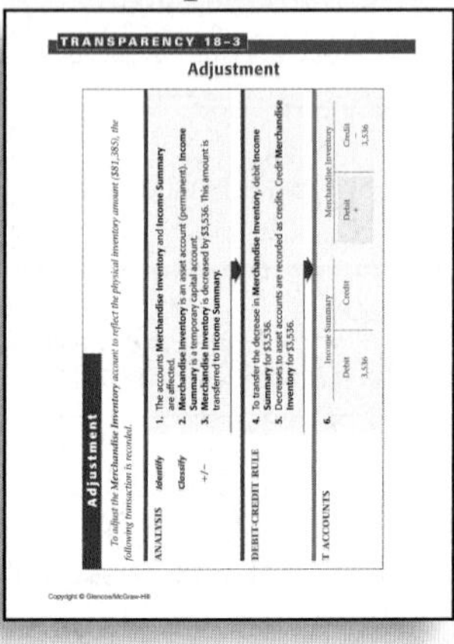

TRANSPARENCY 18-3

Adjustment

Teaching Transparencies

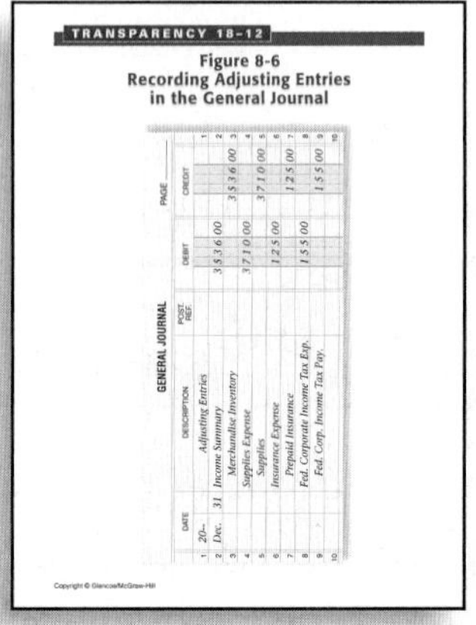

TRANSPARENCY 18-12

Figure 8-6
Recording Adjusting Entries
in the General Journal

Solution Transparencies

Working Papers for End-of-Chapter Problems
Problem 18-5 Completing a Ten-Column Work Sheet

Demonstration Problems

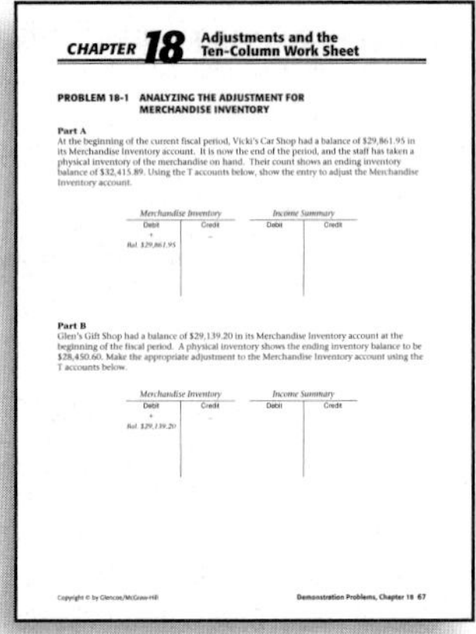

CHAPTER 18 Adjustments and the Ten-Column Work Sheet

PROBLEM 18-1 ANALYZING THE ADJUSTMENT FOR MERCHANDISE INVENTORY

Lesson Plans

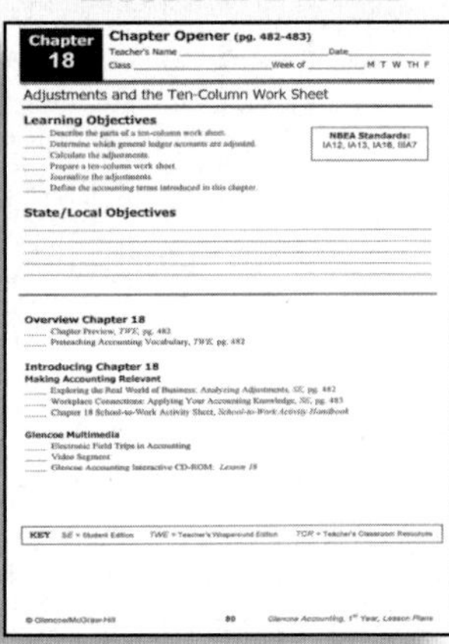

Chapter 18 Chapter Opener (pg. 482-483)

Adjustments and the Ten-Column Work Sheet

Learning Objectives

State/Local Objectives

Block Scheduling

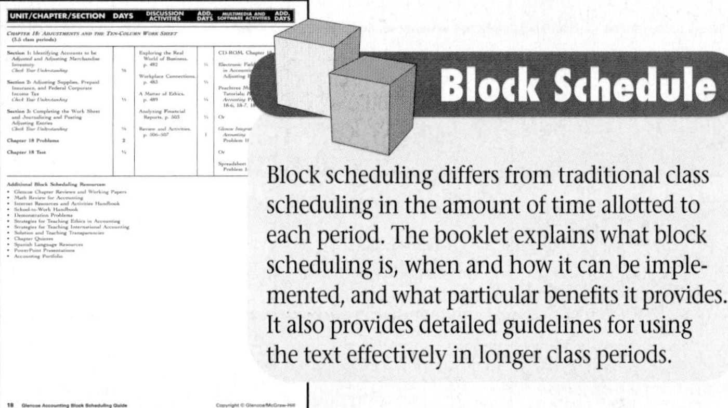

Block Schedule

Block scheduling differs from traditional class scheduling in the amount of time allotted to each period. The booklet explains what block scheduling is, when and how it can be implemented, and what particular benefits it provides. It also provides detailed guidelines for using the text effectively in longer class periods.

Enrichment and Application

Strategies for Teaching Ethics in Accounting

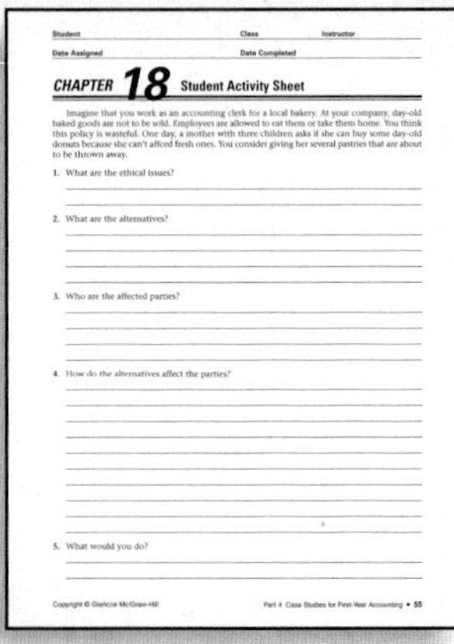

CHAPTER 18 Student Activity Sheet

Strategies for Teaching International Accounting

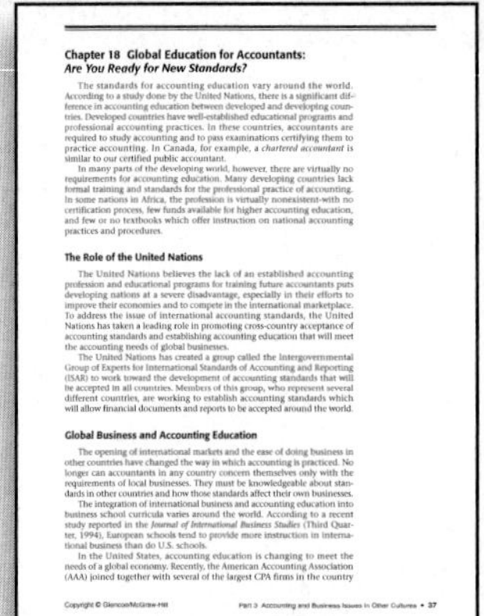

Chapter 18 Global Education for Accountants: Are You Ready for New Standards?

School-to-Work Handbook

CHAPTER 18 SCHOOL-TO-WORK ACTIVITY

Adjustments and a Ten-Column Work Sheet

Meeting Different Ability Levels

Chapter Reviews and Working Papers (CRWP)

Working Papers

Review

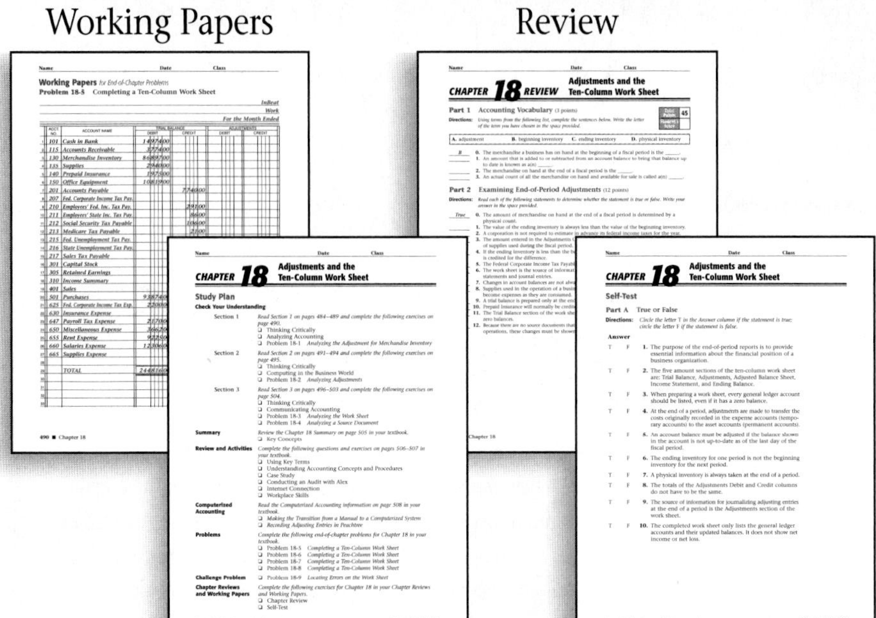

Student Study Plan

Self-Test

Real-World Multimedia CD-ROM

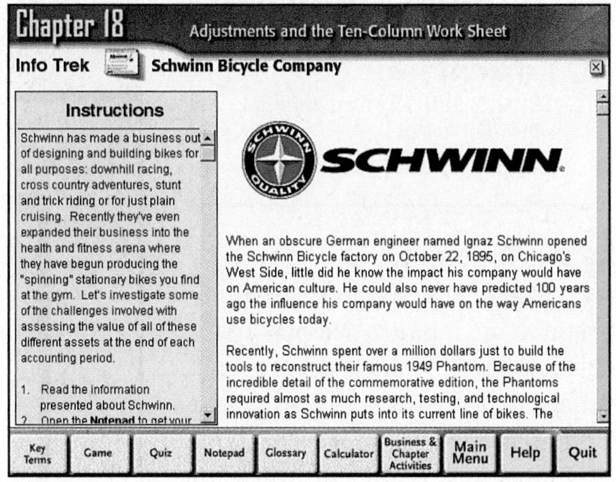

Key to Ability Levels

Each section gives skill-building activities. Each activity has been labeled for use with students of various learning styles and abilities.

L1 Level 1 activities are basic activities and should be within the range of all students.

L2 Level 2 activities are average activities and should be within the range of average and above average students.

L3 Level 3 activities are challenging activities designed for the ability range of above average students.

ELL ELL activities should be within the ability range of English Language Learners.

Teaching Resources at a Glance

Application Resources

- Glencoe Chapter Review and Working Papers, SE and TAE
- School-to-Work Handbook, SE and TM
- Accounting Portfolio, SE and TM

Reproducible Masters

- Demonstration Problems
- Lesson Plans
- Block Scheduling
- Spanish Language Resources

Glencoe Accounting Professional Development Series

- Strategies for Teaching Ethics in Accounting
- Accounting Competitive Event Review
- Math Review for Accounting
- Strategies for Teaching International Accounting
- Internet Resources and Activities Handbook

Transparency Package

- Section Focus Transparencies
- Teaching Transparencies
- Source Document Transparencies
- Solution Transparencies

Performance Assessment

- **Exam***View* CD-ROM
- Chapter Tests
- Chapter Quizzes
- Unit Tests
- Audit Tests
- Printed Testbank

Multimedia Resources

- Electronic Learning Center:
  - Multimedia CD-ROMs
  - Peachtree software, tutorials, templates, and solutions
  - Spreadsheet templates
- Using QuickBooks with Glencoe Accounting
- Interactive Lesson Planner
- Electronic Field Trips in Accounting
- PowerPoint Presentation
- Web site: glencoeaccounting.glencoe.com

Assessment and Evaluation

Chapter Tests

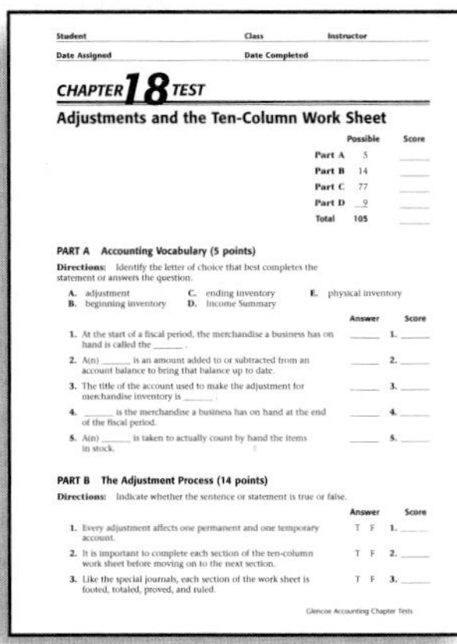

Chapter Quiz

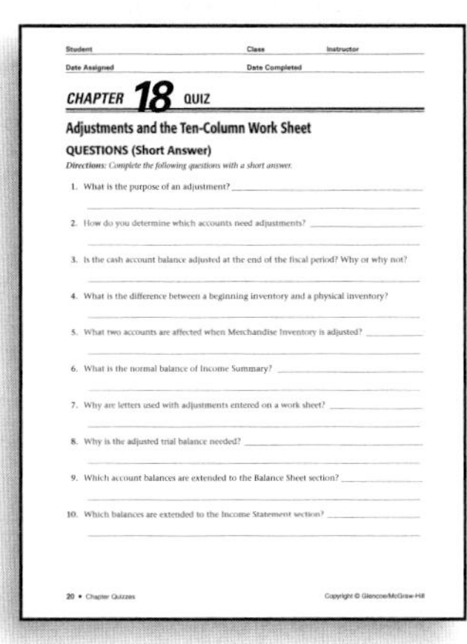

OVERVIEW
CHAPTER 18

Correlations to National Standards for Business Education

(See pages T50–T51 for a detailed correlation chart.)

Standards: IA11, IA12, IA16

Chapter Preview

Now that students have learned to analyze and record business transactions for a merchandising business using special journals, they are ready to learn about the end-of-period work for such a business. In this chapter students will learn to calculate adjustments and enter them on a ten-column work sheet.

Section Overviews

- Section 1—*Identifying Accounts to Be Adjusted and Adjusting Merchandise Inventory*
- Section 2—*Adjusting Supplies, Prepaid Insurance, and Federal Corporate Income Tax*
- Section 3—*Completing the Work Sheet and Journalizing and Posting the Adjusting Entries*

Chapter Vocabulary

adjustment
beginning inventory
ending inventory
physical inventory

Preteaching Accounting Vocabulary

Oral Exercise: Have students read the list of new terms. Ask for ideas for each term's meaning. Write correct responses on the chalkboard. Review the meanings of terms that are not familiar to students. **L1**

CHAPTER 18

Adjustments and the Ten-Column Work Sheet

Learning Objectives

When you have completed this chapter, you will be able to:

- Describe the parts of a ten-column work sheet.
- Generate trial balances and end-of-period adjustments.
- Determine which general ledger accounts are adjusted.
- Calculate the adjustments.
- Prepare a ten-column work sheet.
- Journalize the adjustments.
- Define the accounting terms introduced in this chapter.

Exploring the Real World of Business

ANALYZING ADJUSTMENTS

The Black Phantom rides again! Is it a superspy? Batman's sidekick? A new James Bond car? Actually, it's a bicycle. The original Black Phantom was made in 1949 and was recently re-introduced as a collector's item by the **Schwinn Bicycle Company.** Since 1895, German engineer Ignaz Schwinn has been making bicycles in his factory in Chicago.

Today, if you visit any local health club, you might find Schwinn stationary bicycles, treadmills, weight stacks, and steppers. Many health clubs use **Schwinn's** Johnny G SPINNER stationary bikes, which give users the same exercise as if they were cycling through hilly terrain. The SPINNER bike was developed by **Schwinn** with Johnny Goldberg, a world-class cyclist who used the bike to train for the Race Across America.

Schwinn counts these and its other products as part of its inventory. Each year, items in inventory are counted and adjustments are made to show changes in beginning and ending inventories. Analysis of inventory shortages or excesses often help companies make production decisions and develop marketing strategies.

What do you think?

What other adjustments do you think **Schwinn** would need to make at the end of their fiscal period?

Exploring the Real World of Business

Schwinn

Like many other manufacturers, Schwinn has created a cyberstore to sell its products via the Internet. Some of the products sold in the cyberstore are T-shirts and other casual wear; cycling posters, stickers, and videos; and BMX race clothing and accessories.

What do you think? (Answers)

Answers may vary. Among adjustments the company might make are those for expired insurance; office supplies; and federal, state, and local taxes the business pays.

Workplace Connections

Applying Your Accounting Knowledge

A merchandising business uses the work sheet for collecting and organizing financial information. In really big businesses, several people might work on different parts of the work sheet. For example, one person might be responsible for accounts payable information and others for accounts receivable and payroll. The staff works as a team to prepare the work sheet.

Investigate:

1. In your workplace, are you asked to participate in group or team assignments?
2. How do team members work with each other?
3. What skills are needed to work well in a team?

483

Glencoe Accounting Online

Visit the *Glencoe Accounting* Web site at **glencoeaccounting.glencoe.com** for additional activities and information.

Making Accounting Relevant

Workplace Connections: Applying Your Accounting Knowledge

Discussion: Financial data is like any other type of information: it must be communicated before it can be used effectively. Whether informing through financial reports or through oral or written messages, communication skills are important to success in the workplace.

Investigate (Answers)

1. Answers may vary. An example might be students who work in fast-food restaurants work as a team making hamburgers or preparing tacos and burritos.
2. Each team member knows his or her responsibility and works with other team members to identify what to do and when to make the work efficient.
3. Good communication skills, a sense of responsibility, and a willingness to work with others.

School-to-Work Activity

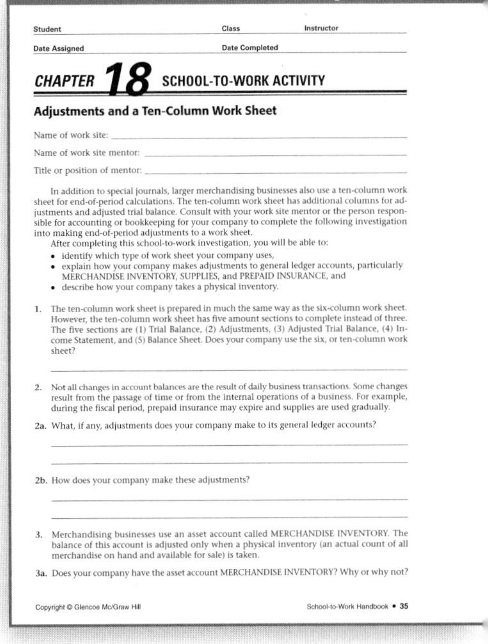

Student ______ Class ______ Instructor ______

Date Assigned ______ Date Completed ______

CHAPTER 18 SCHOOL-TO-WORK ACTIVITY

Adjustments and a Ten-Column Work Sheet

Name of work site: ______

Name of work site mentor: ______

Title or position of mentor: ______

In addition to special journals, larger merchandising businesses also use a ten-column work sheet for end-of-period calculations. The ten-column work sheet has additional columns for adjustments and adjusted trial balance. Consult with your work site mentor or the person responsible for accounting or bookkeeping for your company to complete the following investigation into making end-of-period adjustments to a work sheet.

After completing this school-to-work investigation, you will be able to:

- identify which type of work sheet your company uses,
- explain how your company makes adjustments to general ledger accounts, particularly MERCHANDISE INVENTORY, SUPPLIES, and PREPAID INSURANCE, and
- describe how your company takes a physical inventory.

1. The ten-column work sheet is prepared in much the same way as the six-column work sheet. However, the ten-column work sheet has five amount sections to complete instead of three. The five sections are (1) Trial Balance, (2) Adjustments, (3) Adjusted Trial Balance, (4) Income Statement, and (5) Balance Sheet. Does your company use the six, or ten-column work sheet?

______

2. Not all changes in account balances are the result of daily business transactions. Some changes result from the passage of time or from the internal operations of a business. For example, during the fiscal period, prepaid insurance may expire and supplies are used gradually.

2a. What, if any, adjustments does your company make to its general ledger accounts?

______

2b. How does your company make these adjustments?

______

3. Merchandising businesses use an asset account called MERCHANDISE INVENTORY. The balance of this account is adjusted only when a physical inventory (an actual count of all merchandise on hand and available for sale) is taken.

3a. Does your company have the asset account MERCHANDISE INVENTORY? Why or why not?

 School-to-Work Handbook • 35

GLENCOE MULTIMEDIA

Electronic Field Trips in Accounting *Video Segment: Adjusting Entries*

After viewing this video, students will be able to describe items that are paid for in advance and are used in the operation of the business.

Glencoe Accounting: Electronic Learning Center *Chapter 18*

The CD-ROM program is ideal for visual learners since it incorporates video images, animation, and graphics to enliven the content of each lesson.

CHAPTER 18
SECTION 1, PAGES 484–490

1 FOCUS

Introducing the Section

In this section students will learn how to prepare a ten-column work sheet. They will prepare a trial balance on the work sheet and then calculate the adjustment for merchandise inventory.

Section Concepts

- How to complete the Trial Balance section of the work sheet.
- Why certain general ledger accounts are adjusted.
- Why Merchandise Inventory is adjusted.
- How to calculate and record the adjustment for Merchandise Inventory.

Visual Learning

Section 1 Focus

Use **Transparency 18–1** to introduce section concepts.

BELL RINGER

Analysis: Ask students to name several local retailers and the type of merchandise each sells. Ask students whether these retailers have times when they have a low stock of merchandise (such as after holiday sales in late December/early January). Discuss how the retailers' stock at that time might differ from the level at the beginning of the year. L1

Concept Development: Completing End-of-Period Work

Discussion: Review the steps in the accounting cycle. Point out that preparing the work sheet is the beginning of the end-of-period work. Note that the accounting cycle from Chapters 3–11 showed nine steps. A tenth step—journalizing and posting adjusting entries—has been added. L1

SECTION 1

Identifying Accounts To Be Adjusted and Adjusting Merchandise Inventory

What You'll Learn

- How to complete the Trial Balance section of the work sheet.
- Why certain general ledger accounts are adjusted.
- Why **Merchandise Inventory** is adjusted.
- How to calculate and record the adjustment for **Merchandise Inventory**.

Why It's Important

Some general ledger account balances are adjusted, or updated, so that the general ledger correctly reflects the financial position of the business at the end of the period. This ensures the accuracy of the end-of-period reports and statements.

KEY TERMS

adjustment
beginning inventory
ending inventory
physical inventory

The work sheet in Chapter 8 had six amount columns. The work sheet in this chapter, however, has ten amount columns. The additional columns are for the Adjustments and Adjusted Trial Balance sections. Companies like Taco Bell make adjustments at the end of each accounting period. In this chapter you will learn how to generate trial balances and end-of-period adjustments.

Completing End-of-Period Work

The general ledger summarizes the effects of business transactions on individual accounts for an accounting period. However, managers, stockholders, and creditors need more than a list of account totals to evaluate performance. They need to know net income and the value of owners' equity. Sound business decisions cannot be made without this vital information.

The purpose of all end-of-period reports is to provide essential information about the financial position of a business organization. In Chapters 8 and 9, you learned about the work sheet prepared for a service business organized as a sole proprietorship. In this chapter you will prepare a work sheet for a merchandising business organized as a corporation. This work sheet is the basis for preparing end-of-period financial statements and journal entries.

The Ten-Column Work Sheet

The ten-column work sheet is prepared in the same way as the six-column work sheet. The ten-column work sheet, however, has five amount sections instead of three. The five sections are:

RESOURCE MANAGER

Reproducible Masters
- Lesson Plans
- Chapter Reviews and Working Papers (CRWP) TAE
- Demonstration Problems

Transparencies
- Section Focus Transparency
- Teaching Transparencies
- Source Document Transparencies
- Solution Transparencies

Multimedia
- **Exam***View* CD-ROM
- Electronic Learning Center CD-ROM
- Interactive Lesson Planner CD-ROM
- Electronic Field Trips in Accounting

- Trial Balance
- Adjustments
- Adjusted Trial Balance
- Income Statement
- Balance Sheet

Completing the Trial Balance Section

A trial balance is prepared to prove the equality of debits and credits in the general ledger. **Figure 18–1** shows the end-of-period trial balance for On Your Mark Athletic Wear.

To prepare the trial balance, the number and name of each account in the general ledger are entered on the work sheet in the Account Number

Key Points

The Trial Balance Section of the Work Sheet
The Debit and Credit columns of the Trial Balance section must be equal. If they are not, find and correct any errors before continuing.

	ACCT. NO.	ACCOUNT NAME	TRIAL BALANCE	
			DEBIT	CREDIT
1	101	Cash in Bank	15 179 00	
2	115	Accounts Receivable	10 404 00	
3	125	Merchandise Inventory	84 921 00	
4	130	Supplies	5 549 00	
5	135	Prepaid Insurance	1 500 00	
6	140	Delivery Equipment	19 831 00	
7	145	Office Equipment	9 825 00	
8	150	Store Equipment	5 200 00	
9	201	Accounts Payable		13 850 00
10	204	Fed. Corp. Inc. Tax Payable		
11	205	Employees' Fed. Inc. Tax Pay.		640 00
12	211	Employees' State Inc. Tax Pay.		80 00
13	212	Social Security Tax Payable		248 00
14	213	Medicare Tax Payable		58 00
15	214	Fed. Unemployment Tax Payable		18 36
16	215	State Unemployment Tax Payable		114 73
17	220	Sales Tax Payable		2 428 00
18	301	Capital Stock		75 000 00
19	305	Retained Earnings		19 771 19
20	310	Income Summary		
21	401	Sales		320 450 00
22	405	Sales Discounts	730 00	
23	410	Sales Returns & Allowances	2 000 00	
24	501	Purchases	206 700 00	
25	505	Transportation In	4 036 18	
26	510	Purchases Discounts		1 340 00
27	515	Purchases Returns & Allowances		1 800 00
28	601	Advertising Expense	2 450 00	
29	605	Bankcard Fees Expense	4 199 27	
30	630	Fed. Corp. Income Tax Expense	9 840 00	
31	635	Insurance Expense		
32	650	Maintenance Expense	3 519 25	
33	655	Miscellaneous Expense	348 28	
34	657	Payroll Tax Expense	3 826 83	
35	660	Rent Expense	14 000 00	
36	665	Salaries Expense	29 374 60	
37	670	Supplies Expense		
38	680	Utilities Expense	2 364 87	
39			435 798 28	435 798 28
40				

Figure 18–1 The Trial Balance Section of the Work Sheet

Did You Know?

Sports
Companies like Schwinn sponsor cycle teams that compete in biking events called BMX (which stands for bicycle motocross) competitions. Sponsoring events is a form of advertising for companies like Schwinn.

2 TEACH

GUIDED PRACTICE

Reading Accounting

- Have students read through the list of accounts in the trial balance. What do the account numbers tell them? L1
- Ask a local retailer who speaks your students' first language to speak to the class about end-of-period merchandise adjustments. ELL

Concept Development: The Ten-Column Work Sheet

Discussion: The ten-column work sheet is an expansion of the work sheet presented in earlier chapters. The four new columns are used to record adjustments and to calculate an adjusted trial balance. Point out that service businesses also have adjustments, but discussion was postponed to give students a basic foundation of accounting concepts before they encountered less frequent accounting activities. L1

Concept Development: Completing the Trial Balance Section

Discussion: Remind students that the trial balance is prepared to test the equality of the ledger. If total debits equal total credits, the work sheet can be completed. L1

Visual Learning

Figure 18–1 The Trial Balance Section of the Work Sheet
Display **Transparency 18–2** to review the preparation of a trial balance.

Great Ideas *From the Classroom of...*

Adjusting Entries Tip Sometimes we need to make "attitude" adjustments to change the way we think or feel to bring ourselves up to date. Adjusting entries are like attitude adjustments. Some account balances change every day, but there are no transactions to record the change. For example, although you don't record a transaction every time you open a new ream of paper, a box of pens, or a box of staples, your supplies decrease. An adjusting entry brings the supplies account up to date.

Gale Woolsey
Texarkana Area Vocational Center
Texarkana, Arkansas

2 TEACH (Cont'd.)

Concept Development: Calculating Adjustments

Discussion: Explain the adjustments that must be made for a merchandising corporation. Emphasize why these adjustments must be made before the financial statements are prepared. Also remind students that revenue and expenses must be matched in a fiscal period.

Briefly discuss the fact that consumed assets are an expense of doing business. Point out that items purchased are initially recorded as assets (for example, office supplies). The supplies are used during the year, but no entry is made to record the amount used. An adjustment is needed at the end of the period to bring the balance in the supplies account up to date. L1

Teaching Tips

Review the concept of permanent and temporary accounts. For each adjustment, have students identify which accounts are permanent and which are temporary.

Emphasize that the Adjustments section is used to collect the information for journalizing and posting the entries that will update the balances in the accounts needing adjustments.

Math Review for Accounting
Photocopy appropriate *Activity Sheets* for students who need additional practice in basic math skills.

Getting the Right Balance
When calculating the adjusted trial balance amounts, use these simple rules:

- When trial balance and adjustment amounts are both debits (or credits), add the amounts.
- When one amount is a debit and the other is a credit, subtract the amounts.

and Account Name columns. The accounts are listed in the order that they appear in the general ledger (Asset, Liability, Owner's Equity, Revenue, Cost of Merchandise, Expense). The balance of each account is entered in the appropriate column, either the Debit or the Credit column, of the Trial Balance section. Notice that every general ledger account is listed, even those with zero balances. After all balances are entered, the Trial Balance Debit and Credit columns are ruled, totaled, and proved. Then, a double rule is drawn across both columns.

Calculating Adjustments

Not all changes in account balances are the result of daily business transactions. Some changes result from the internal operations of the business or from the passage of time. For example, supplies such as paper, pens, shopping bags, and sales slips are bought for use by the business. They are recorded in an asset account called **Supplies.** These supplies are used gradually during the accounting period. Another example is insurance premiums, which cover a certain period of time. The premiums are recorded in an asset account called **Prepaid Insurance.** During the period, some of the insurance is used up, or expires. At the end of the period, the balances in accounts such as **Supplies** and **Prepaid Insurance** are brought up-to-date.

To illustrate, suppose that supplies costing $500 were purchased during an accounting period and recorded in the **Supplies** account. At the end of the period, the **Supplies** account balance is $500; however, only $200 of supplies are still on hand. The account balance for **Supplies** is adjusted downward to show that the business used $300 of supplies.

Up to this point, the general ledger account balances have been changed by journal entries made to record transactions that are supported by source documents. There are no source documents, however, for the changes in account balances caused by the internal operations of a business or the passage of time. Such changes are recorded through adjustments made at the end of the period to the account balance. An **adjustment** is an amount that is added to or subtracted from an account balance to bring that balance up-to-date. Every adjustment affects at least one permanent account and one temporary account.

At the end of the period, adjustments are made to transfer the costs of the assets consumed from the asset accounts (permanent accounts) to the appropriate expense accounts (temporary accounts). Accountants say that these assets are "expensed" because the costs of consumed assets are expenses of doing business. Thus, when an adjustment is recorded, the expenses for a given period are matched with the revenue for that period.

The Adjustments section of the work sheet is used to record the adjustments made at the end of the period to bring various account balances up-to-date.

Determining the Adjustments Needed

How do you generate end-of-period adjustments? Review each account balance in the Trial Balance columns of the work sheet. If the balance shown

Math Skill Builder Activity

Getting the Right Balance Ask students to calculate adjusted balances for two entries in the work sheet for Linens & China:
Merchandise Inventory: Debit Trial Balance = $125,000; Debit Adjustment = $30,000
Maintenance Expense: Debit Trial Balance = $850; Credit Adjustment = $75
(Merchandise Inventory, Debit Adjusted Trial Balance = $155,000;
Maintenance Expense, Debit Adjusted Trial Balance = $775)

for an account is not up-to-date *as of the last day of the fiscal period,* then that account balance must be adjusted.

Refer to **Figure 18–1.** The first account listed is **Cash in Bank.** All cash received or paid out during the period was journalized and posted to the **Cash in Bank** account. The balance in this account is up-to-date. The next account, **Accounts Receivable** (controlling), is also up-to-date since all amounts owed or paid by charge customers were journalized and posted.

The third account is **Merchandise Inventory,** used to report the cost of merchandise on hand. The balance reported in the Trial Balance section ($84,921) is the merchandise on hand at the *beginning* of the period.

The amount of merchandise on hand is constantly changing during the period. The changes are not recorded in the **Merchandise Inventory** account. During the period the cost of merchandise purchased is recorded in the **Purchases** account. As inventory is reduced by the sale of merchandise, the amount of each sale is recorded in the **Sales** account. No entries are posted to **Merchandise Inventory.** At the end of the period, the balance in the **Merchandise Inventory** account does not reflect the amount of merchandise on hand. So, the **Merchandise Inventory** account balance must be adjusted.

The other account balances on the work sheet are reviewed in the same manner. Additional adjustments are made as described later in this chapter.

Adjusting the Merchandise Inventory Account

Merchandise Inventory is an asset account used by merchandising businesses. **Beginning inventory** is the merchandise a business has on hand and available for sale at the *beginning* of a period. **Ending inventory** is the merchandise a business has on hand at the *end* of a period. The ending inventory for one period becomes the beginning inventory for the next period.

The account balance of **Merchandise Inventory** does not change during the period. It is changed *only* when a physical inventory is taken. A **physical inventory** is an actual count of all the merchandise on hand and available for sale. A physical inventory can be taken at any time. One is always taken at the end of a period.

Key Points

Adjustments

Adjustments help match expenses with related revenue.

For example, if inventory is counted in a toy store at the end of a period, the cost of inventory can be calculated. This is done by multiplying the quantity of each item by its unit cost.

At the end of each period, after the physical inventory is taken and the cost of ending inventory is calculated, the beginning inventory amount recorded in **Merchandise Inventory** is replaced by the ending inventory amount. This is accomplished by an adjustment to **Merchandise Inventory.**

Calculating the Adjustment for Merchandise Inventory

When calculating the adjustment for **Merchandise Inventory,** you need to know:

2 TEACH (Cont'd.)

Teaching Tips

Point out that adjustments are entered on the work sheet from the top down and that not every account needs an adjustment. An important aspect of the accountant's job is to identify all accounts needing adjustment.

Remind students that the Merchandise Inventory account is not used to record sales or purchases of merchandise during the period.

Briefly discuss taking an inventory. Have students relate job experiences with inventories, or have them take an inventory of the classroom.

You may want to point out that there are several ways to determine the cost of an inventory. These methods are presented in Chapter 25.

Critical Thinking: Ask students why it is better to record sales and purchases of merchandise in separate accounts rather than the Merchandise Inventory account. (Separating specific types of information, such as sales and purchases, into accounts helps analysts readily determine totals for merchandise bought and sold during a fiscal period. Separate sales and purchases amounts also are needed to calculate gross profit and net income.) L2

CRITICAL THINKING ACTIVITY

Inventory Discrepancies When an inventory of supplies was completed at the end of the fiscal period, it was found that the amount of the supplies on hand was greater than the balance in the Supplies account. Explain how this could happen. (When new supplies were purchased, the transaction was never journalized and posted to the Supplies account.)

2 TEACH (Cont'd.)

Visual Learning

Adjustment

Use **Transparency 18–3** to guide students through the analysis of the adjustment to the Merchandise Inventory account.

Teaching Tips

Remind students that Income Summary is a temporary capital account. Have students discuss why Income Summary does not have a +/– side or a normal balance side.

Thinking Algebraically

Stating Relationships: Have students express the Key Point, Adjustment to Merchandise Inventory, algebraically. (Example: If beginning inventory > ending inventory, – Merchandise Inventory; if beginning inventory < ending inventory, + Merchandise Inventory) L2

Demonstration Problem Step-by-Step Practice

Use demonstration problem 18–1 to give students practice in analyzing an adjustment for Merchandise Inventory.

- The **Merchandise Inventory** account balance
- The physical inventory amount

For On Your Mark:

Merchandise Inventory account balance	$84,921
Physical inventory	81,385

The effect of all the purchases and sales during the period is a decrease to **Merchandise Inventory** of $3,536 ($84,921 – $81,385). This reduction in inventory needs to be recorded as an adjustment in the accounting records. The two accounts affected by the inventory adjustment are **Merchandise Inventory** and **Income Summary.**

Adjustment

*To adjust the **Merchandise Inventory** account to reflect the physical inventory amount ($81,385), the following transaction is recorded.*

ANALYSIS

Identify 1. The accounts **Merchandise Inventory** and **Income Summary** are affected.

Classify 2. **Merchandise Inventory** is an asset account (permanent). **Income Summary** is a stockholder's equity account.

+/– 3. **Merchandise Inventory** is decreased by $3,536. This amount is transferred to **Income Summary.**

DEBIT-CREDIT RULE

4. To transfer the decrease in **Merchandise Inventory**, debit **Income Summary** for $3,536.
5. Decreases to asset accounts are recorded as credits. Credit **Merchandise Inventory** for $3,536.

T ACCOUNTS

6.

Income Summary		Merchandise Inventory	
Debit	Credit	Debit +	Credit –
3,536			3,536

Key Points

Adjustment to Merchandise Inventory

When beginning inventory is greater than ending inventory, credit **Merchandise Inventory.** When beginning inventory is less than ending inventory, debit **Merchandise Inventory.**

If ending inventory is greater than beginning inventory, **Merchandise Inventory** is debited and **Income Summary** is credited. For example, suppose that the beginning inventory was $84,921 and the ending inventory is $88,226. Inventory increased by $3,305 ($88,226 – $84,921). The **Merchandise Inventory** account is debited for $3,305, and **Income Summary** is credited for $3,305.

Merchandise Inventory		Income Summary	
Debit +	Credit –	Debit	Credit
3,305			3,305

MAKING CONNECTIONS TO DAILY LIFE

Taking Inventory Ask students if they have ever seen a sign on a business saying "Closed for Inventory." Companies sometimes close for a day or two to complete a physical inventory of the merchandise on hand. Many times they hire temporary help to complete the task much faster. Ask students to describe occasions when a business in their community closed for taking inventory. Have any students participated in taking a physical inventory as part of their job responsibilities?

Entering the Adjustment for Merchandise Inventory on the Work Sheet

Adjustments are entered in the Adjustments columns of the work sheet. The debit and credit parts of each adjustment are given a unique label. The label consists of a small letter in parentheses and is placed just above and to the left of the adjustment amounts. The adjustments are labeled as follows:

First adjustment	(a)
Second adjustment	(b)
Third adjustment	(c)

The number of adjustments vary depending on the business. Once the adjustments are entered, the work sheet provides the information needed to make the adjusting journal entries.

Use the T accounts in step 6 of the preceding example as a guide to entering the inventory adjustment on the work sheet. Refer to **Figure 18–2**. To record the adjustment for **Merchandise Inventory:**

1. In the Adjustments Debit column, enter the debit amount of the adjustment on the Income Summary line. Label this amount (a).
2. In the Adjustments Credit column, enter the credit amount of the adjustment on the Merchandise Inventory line. Label this amount (a) also.

Key Points

Adjustments on the Work Sheet
Label the debit and credit amounts of each adjustment.

	ACCT. NO.	ACCOUNT NAME	TRIAL BALANCE DEBIT	TRIAL BALANCE CREDIT	ADJUSTMENTS DEBIT	ADJUSTMENTS CREDIT
1	101	*Cash in Bank*	15 179 00			
2	115	*Accounts Receivable*	10 404 00			
3	125	*Merchandise Inventory*	84 921 00			(a) 3 536 00
20	310	*Income Summary*			(a) 3 536 00	
21						

Figure 18–2 Recording the Adjustment for Merchandise Inventory on the Work Sheet

A MATTER OF ETHICS

Out-of-Date Goods

Imagine that you work as an accounting clerk for a local bakery. At your company, day-old baked goods are not to be sold. Employees are allowed to eat them or take them home. You think this policy is wasteful. One day, a mother with three children asks if she can buy some day-old donuts because she can't afford fresh ones. You consider giving her several pastries that are about to be thrown away.

Ethical Decision Making:

- What are the ethical issues?
- What are the alternatives?
- Who are the affected parties?
- How do the alternatives affect the parties?
- What would you do?

Teaching A MATTER OF ETHICS

Out-of-Date Goods Have students discuss the waste versus the need for business profits. For example, if businesses give away products or reduce prices, will customers wait to buy? Ask students to think of alternatives to throwing away perishable food products that must be used quickly. Ask students to discuss the advantages and disadvantages to the business of giving away its products. Relate the concept of social conscience to the discussion. You may want to have a panel debate with some groups taking the side of a business having a social responsibility and the others taking the position that business is to create profit for its shareholders.

2 TEACH (Cont'd.)

Teaching Tip
You may want to mention that there are other methods of adjusting the Merchandise Inventory account. For example, some accountants adjust the Merchandise Inventory account by closing out the beginning inventory balance and entering the new balance.

Visual Learning

Figure 18–2 Recording the Adjustment for Merchandise Inventory on the Work Sheet
Display **Transparency 18–4** to explain how to enter the Merchandise Inventory adjustment on the work sheet. Point out the letter "a" in parentheses in both the Debit and Credit columns. Point out that this letter identifies the adjustment for Merchandise Inventory and the debit and credit parts of the entry.

Demonstration Problem Step-by-Step Practice
Use demonstration problem 18–2 to have students calculate and enter the adjustment for Merchandise Inventory on the work sheet.

Strategies for Teaching Ethics in Accounting
Photocopy the Chapter 18 *Student Activity Sheet* for students. Answers are also provided in the booklet.

CHAPTER 18

SECTION 1, PAGES 484–490

3 ASSESS

Thinking Critically (Answers)

1. Find the errors and correct them before continuing.
2. If ending inventory is less than beginning inventory, Merchandise Inventory is credited for the amount of the difference. If ending inventory is greater, Merchandise Inventory is debited for the difference.

Analyzing Accounting (Answer)

Students should create a bar graph by hand or computer. Analysis shows that merchandise sold increased $2,100 between 2001 and 2002, and $1,000 between 2002 and 2003.

Problem 18–1 (Answers)

1. Greater
2. $1,533
3. Merchandise Inventory
4. Income Summary

Chapter Reviews and Working Papers Refer students to the Chapter 18 workbook pages to answer *Check Your Understanding* activities.

4 CLOSE

Section Wrap-Up

Demonstrate: Give students the following amounts and have them write T accounts showing the adjustment for Merchandise Inventory: beginning inventory, $45,220; ending inventory, $48,670. (Dr. Merchandise Inventory $3,450; Cr. Income Summary $3,450) L1

SECTION 1 Check Your Understanding

Now that you have studied this section, complete the following questions and problems.

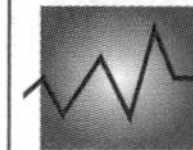

Thinking Critically

1. What would you do if the Debit and Credit columns of the Trial Balance section of the work sheet are not equal?
2. After the physical inventory is taken, what happens to the **Merchandise Inventory** account?

Analyzing Accounting

Jim Warren, accounting manager, asked you to analyze inventory for the past three years. Your company, Photo Shots, is looking to expand its merchandise, but Jim wants to analyze inventory data for the last three years before he recommends expansion. Using the data given, create a bar graph to depict the total amount of merchandise sold by year. Write a paragraph summarizing your analysis of inventory trends.

	Merchandise Inventory		
Year	**Beginning**	**Ending**	**Purchases**
2001	900	1,000	5,000
2002	1,000	2,000	8,000
2003	2,000	1,500	7,500

Problem 18–1 Analyzing the Adjustment for Merchandise Inventory

The Ely Corporation, a custom furniture manufacturer, has a general ledger account balance of $73,395 for **Merchandise Inventory** as of July 1. On the following June 30, the end of the fiscal period, Ely took a physical inventory and determined there was $74,928 in merchandise on hand. In your working papers, answer the following questions regarding the adjustment for **Merchandise Inventory:**

1. Is the value of the ending inventory greater than or less than the value of the beginning inventory?
2. What is the amount of the inventory adjustment?
3. Which account is debited?
4. Which account is credited?

RETEACHING SECTION 1

Adjusting Merchandise Inventory For the text example on adjusting Merchandise Inventory, use a mnemonic device such as the acronym BEA, which stands for Beginning Inventory – Ending Inventory = Adjustment Amount. Give students plenty of practice in analyzing the adjustment for Merchandise Inventory. The chapter example shows beginning inventory greater than ending inventory. After helping students analyze that situation, give them an example of ending inventory being higher than beginning inventory. Write the calculations on the chalkboard as you walk students through this analysis.

SECTION 2

Adjusting Supplies, Prepaid Insurance, and Federal Corporate Income Tax

In Section 1 you learned that the **Merchandise Inventory** account is updated at the end of the period. Other accounts in the general ledger are also adjusted. For example, high-risk businesses, like building construction and demolition, spend a lot of money on insurance. Therefore, it is important that the financial statements reflect the proper insurance expenses each period. Supplies and federal corporate income taxes also represent significant expenses that must be reported accurately.

What You'll Learn

- Why the **Supplies, Prepaid Insurance,** and **Federal Corporate Income Tax Expense** accounts are adjusted.
- How to calculate the adjustments for supplies, insurance, and federal corporate income tax.
- How to enter the adjustments on the work sheet.

Why It's Important

Account balances related to supplies, insurance, and federal corporate income tax require adjustment in order to prepare accurate financial reports.

Adjusting the Supplies Account

A merchandising business buys various supplies to be used by employees in the everyday operations of the business. Pencils, pens, computer paper, shopping bags, sales slips, price tags, and cash register tapes are purchased, and the cost is debited to the **Supplies** account.

Supplies are used every day. As they are consumed, they become expenses of the business. It is inefficient to keep daily records of each item as it is used, so the **Supplies** account is updated at the end of the period.

In the Trial Balance section of the work sheet in **Figure 18–1**, the balance of the **Supplies** account is $5,549. This amount is the cost of the supplies on hand on January 1 *plus* the cost of the additional supplies purchased during the period.

At the end of December, On Your Mark took a physical inventory and found that there were $1,839 of supplies on hand. This means that $3,710 of supplies were used during the period ($5,549 − $1,839 = $3,710). The amount of supplies on hand decreased by $3,710. Therefore, **Supplies** (a permanent asset account) is credited for $3,710. **Supplies Expense** (a temporary account) is debited (increased) to record the cost of supplies used during the period.

Adjustment

Record the adjustment for supplies.

ANALYSIS		
	Identify	1. The accounts affected are **Supplies** and **Supplies Expense.**
	Classify	2. **Supplies** is an asset account (permanent). **Supplies Expense** is an expense account (temporary).
	+/−	3. **Supplies** is decreased by $3,710. **Supplies Expense** is increased by $3,710.

1 FOCUS

Introducing the Section

In this section students will learn how to calculate adjustments for other accounts, such as Supplies, Prepaid Insurance, and Corporate Income Tax Expense.

Section Concepts

- Why the Supplies, Prepaid Insurance, and Federal Corporate Income Tax Expense accounts are adjusted.
- How to calculate the adjustments for supplies, insurance, and federal corporate income tax.
- How to enter the adjustments on the work sheet.

Visual Learning

Section 2 Focus

Use **Transparency 18–5** to introduce section concepts.

BELL RINGER

Demonstration: Bring to class a stack of notebooks and pens and pencils. Place them on the desk, and tell students these supplies cost $48. Then take away roughly half the supplies, and ask students how much is left (about $24 worth). Ask students how they would bring the accounting records up to date if they show $48 worth of supplies but you have only $24 left. L1

RESOURCE MANAGER

Reproducible Masters
- Lesson Plans
- Chapter Reviews and Working Papers (CRWP) TAE
- Demonstration Problems

Transparencies
- Section Focus Transparency
- Teaching Transparencies
- Source Document Transparencies
- Solution Transparencies

Multimedia
- ExamView CD-ROM
- Electronic Learning Center CD-ROM
- Interactive Lesson Planner CD-ROM
- Electronic Field Trips in Accounting

2 TEACH

GUIDED PRACTICE

Reading Accounting

• As students read about adjustments, have them make a list of each type of adjustment and the accounts affected for use as a study aid. L1

Concept Development: Adjusting the Supplies Account

Discussion: Point out that businesses buy supplies throughout the year and record the cost in the Supplies account, but no accounting entry is made each time an employee uses supplies. At the end of the period, an inventory is taken and the amount of supplies used is determined. The Supplies account is then adjusted to make its balance match the amount of supplies on hand. L1

Visual Learning

Adjustment

Use **Transparency 18–6** to guide students through the adjustment for supplies.

Demonstration Problem Step-by-Step Practice

Use demonstration problem 18–3 to have students calculate and enter the supplies adjustment on the work sheet.

Concept Development: Adjusting the Prepaid Insurance Account

Discussion: Businesses need insurance to protect their property from loss, just as individual property owners do. Ask students to suggest other types of insurance a business may have (for example, liability insurance to cover delivery vehicles). L1

DEBIT-CREDIT RULE

4. Increases to expense accounts are recorded as debits. Debit **Supplies Expense** for $3,710.
5. Decreases to asset accounts are recorded as credits. Credit **Supplies** for $3,710.

T ACCOUNTS

6.

Supplies Expense	
Debit +	Credit −
3,710	

Supplies	
Debit +	Credit −
	3,710

The adjustment for supplies is shown in **Figure 18–3.** To enter the adjustment on the work sheet, follow these steps:

1. In the Adjustments Debit column, enter the debit amount of the adjustment on the Supplies Expense line. Since this is the second adjustment, label it (b).
2. In the Adjustments Credit column, enter the credit amount of the adjustment on the Supplies line. Label it (b) also.

Adjusting the Prepaid Insurance Account

On December 17 On Your Mark purchased an insurance policy. The insurance coverage is for six months, mid-December through mid-May. The premium of $1,500 ($250 per month) was debited to the **Prepaid Insurance** account.

At the end of December, the balance of **Prepaid Insurance** is $1,500, as shown in the Trial Balance section of the work sheet in **Figure 18–1.** However, the coverage for half of a month, costing $125, has expired. Since the value of the unexpired portion of the coverage has decreased to $1,375 ($1,500 − $125), **Prepaid Insurance** is adjusted with a credit for $125 to bring its balance up-to-date. The adjustment records the expired portion of the coverage as a business expense.

Adjustment

Record the adjustment for the expiration of one-half month's insurance coverage.

ANALYSIS

Identify 1. The accounts affected are **Insurance Expense** and **Prepaid Insurance.**

Classify 2. **Insurance Expense** is an expense account (temporary). **Prepaid Insurance** is an asset account (permanent).

+/− 3. **Insurance Expense** is increased by $125. **Prepaid Insurance** is decreased by $125.

DEBIT-CREDIT RULE

4. Increases to expense accounts are recorded as debits. Debit **Insurance Expense** for $125.
5. Decreases to asset accounts are recorded as credits. Credit **Prepaid Insurance** for $125.

HOME AND COMMUNITY CONNECTIONS ACTIVITY

School Finance Business Invite your school's financial secretary, bookkeeper, or controller to speak about managing a school's finances. Ask them to discuss the types of accounts kept, their method for preparing end-of-the-month statements, and who receives this financial information. Have students create a list of questions to ask your guest speaker. Afterward, ask students to share their impressions of the "business" of keeping a school in good operation.

T ACCOUNTS

6.

Insurance Expense		Prepaid Insurance	
Debit +	Credit −	Debit +	Credit −
125			125

	ACCT. NO.	ACCOUNT NAME	TRIAL BALANCE DEBIT	TRIAL BALANCE CREDIT	ADJUSTMENTS DEBIT	ADJUSTMENTS CREDIT
1	101	Cash in Bank	15 179 00			
2	115	Accounts Receivable	10 404 00			
3	125	Merchandise Inventory	84 921 00			(a) 3 536 00
4	130	Supplies	5 549 00			(b) 3 710 00
5	135	Prepaid Insurance	1 500 00			(c) 125 00
6	140	Delivery Equipment	19 831 00			
7	145	Office Equipment	9 825 00			
8	150	Store Equipment	5 200 00			
9	201	Accounts Payable		13 850 00		
10	204	Fed. Corp. Inc. Tax Payable				(d) 155 00
11	205	Employees' Fed. Inc. Tax Pay.		640 00		
12	211	Employees' State Inc. Tax Pay.		80 00		
13	212	Social Security Tax Payable		248 00		
14	213	Medicare Tax Payable		58 00		
15	214	Fed. Unemployment Tax Payable		18 36		
16	215	State Unemployment Tax Payable		114 73		
17	220	Sales Tax Payable		2 428 00		
18	301	Capital Stock		75 000 00		
19	305	Retained Earnings		19 771 19		
20	310	Income Summary			(a) 3 536 00	
21	401	Sales		320 450 00		
22	405	Sales Discounts	730 00			
23	410	Sales Returns and Allowances	2 000 00			
24	501	Purchases	206 700 00			
25	505	Transportation In	4 036 18			
26	510	Purchases Discounts		1 340 00		
27	515	Purchases Returns and Allowances		1 800 00		
28	601	Advertising Expense	2 450 00			
29	605	Bankcard Fees Expense	4 199 27			
30	630	Fed. Corp. Income Tax Expense	9 840 00		(d) 155 00	
31	635	Insurance Expense			(c) 125 00	
32	650	Maintenance Expense	3 519 25			
33	655	Miscellaneous Expense	348 28			
34	657	Payroll Tax Expense	3 826 83			
35	660	Rent Expense	14 000 00			
36	665	Salaries Expense	29 374 60			
37	670	Supplies Expense			(b) 3 710 00	
38	680	Utilities Expense	2 364 87			
39			435 798 28	435 798 28	7 526 00	7 526 00
40						

Figure 18–3 Recording the Adjustments on the Work Sheet

The adjustment for **Prepaid Insurance** is shown in **Figure 18–3**. To enter the adjustment on the work sheet, follow these steps:

1. In the Adjustments Debit column, enter the debit amount of the adjustment on the Insurance Expense line. Since this is the third adjustment, label it (c).

2 TEACH (Cont'd.)

Teaching Tip
Explain that Prepaid Insurance represents a future value to the company, which is why it is classified as an asset account.

Visual Learning

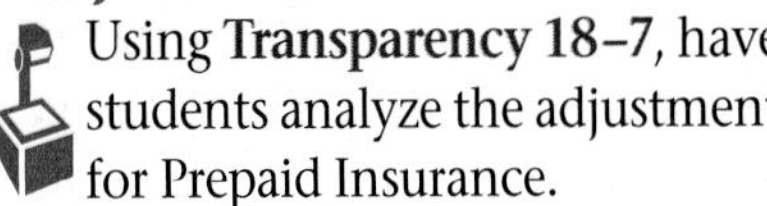

Adjustment
Using **Transparency 18–7**, have students analyze the adjustment for Prepaid Insurance.

Figure 18–3 Recording the Adjustments on the Work Sheet
Using **Transparency 18–8**, ask students to describe each of the adjustments and how to enter each in the work sheet. Review the use of the letters in parentheses to identify each adjustment and its debit and credit parts.

Demonstration Problem Step-by-Step Practice
Use demonstration problem 18–4 to give students practice in calculating the adjustment for Prepaid Insurance and entering it on the work sheet.

Chapter Reviews and Working Papers
Refer students to the *Study Plan* located at the beginning of Chapter 18 in the workbook.

REINFORCING STUDY SKILLS

Time Management Many students need help in organizing their time to allow for reading and studying as well as sports and social activities. Have students analyze their study habits with the idea of improving them. Can they concentrate long enough to read a chapter, or do they need to arrange shorter study sessions? Do they have a good study space? Can they avoid distractions at home such as TV?

CHAPTER 18
SECTION 2, PAGES 491–495

2 TEACH (Cont'd.)

Concept Development: Adjusting the Federal Corporate Income Tax Expense Account

Discussion: Point out that corporations pay income tax, but sole proprietorships and partnerships do not. Explain that corporations estimate their net income tax for the year and make regular tax payments during the year based on the estimate. If the estimate is too high or too low, the corporation will either receive a refund or pay an additional amount when it files its corporate tax return. The accounting records are adjusted to show the difference between the estimated amount paid and the amount actually due. L1

Demonstration Problem Step-by-Step Practice

Use demonstration problem 18–5 to have students calculate and enter the adjustment for corporate income tax expense on the work sheet.

Teaching Tip

Point out that accountants calculate the amount of corporate income tax for the year based on the company's earnings. Any additional taxes owed will not be paid until the company files its corporate tax return, so the taxes owed are recorded in the liability account, Federal Corporate Income Tax Payable.

Strategies for Teaching International Accounting

To enrich study of international accounting, refer to the additional critical thinking activities in the booklet.

International ACCOUNTING

World Congress of Accountants

In November 2002 thousands of accountants from over 100 countries attended the XVI World Congress of Accountants in Hong Kong. Scheduled Topics of discussion included the "one size fits all" approach to international accounting standards as well as corporate response to public demand for greater transparency.

Key Points

The Work Sheet

The Adjustments section of the work sheet, like the Trial Balance section, must be proved before continuing on to the Adjusted Trial Balance section.

2. In the Adjustments Credit column, enter the credit amount of the adjustment on the Prepaid Insurance line. Label it (c) also.

Adjusting the Federal Corporate Income Tax Expense Account

On Your Mark is organized as a corporation. A corporation is considered to be a legal entity separate from its owners. On Your Mark owns assets, pays its own debts, and enters into legal contracts.

A corporation pays federal corporate income taxes on its net income. Many states and cities also tax corporate income. For now, we will discuss only federal corporate income taxes. A corporation estimates its federal corporate income taxes for the coming year and pays that amount to the federal government in quarterly installments. At the end of the year, the exact net income and the tax on that income are determined. If the corporation owes additional taxes, they are paid when the corporate income tax return is filed.

At the beginning of the year, On Your Mark's accountant estimated that federal corporate income taxes would be $9,840. The business made quarterly payments of $2,460 in March, June, September, and December. These payments were journalized as debits to **Federal Corporate Income Tax Expense** and credits to **Cash in Bank.**

At the end of the year, On Your Mark's accountant determines that the federal corporate income tax for the year is $9,995. Since On Your Mark has already paid $9,840, the business owes an additional $155 ($9,995 – $9,840).

To bring the accounting records up-to-date, **Federal Corporate Income Tax Expense** and **Federal Corporate Income Tax Payable** must both be increased by $155. The T accounts below illustrate this adjustment.

Federal Corporate Income Tax Expense	
Debit +	Credit –
155	

Federal Corporate Income Tax Payable	
Debit –	Credit +
	155

The adjustment for **Federal Corporate Income Tax Expense** is shown in **Figure 18–3.** Since this is the fourth adjustment, it is labeled (d).

Totaling and Ruling the Adjustments Section

After all adjustments are entered, the Adjustments section of the work sheet is totaled and ruled. Each adjustment has an equal debit and credit, so the totals of the Adjustments Debit and Credit columns should be the same. When the Adjustments section is proved, a double rule is drawn under the totals and across both columns, as shown in **Figure 18–3.**

Teaching International ACCOUNTING

World Congress of Accountants Have students research the World Congress of Accountants to find answers to these questions:

1. Who attends the conference? (Accountants from around the world.)
2. What is the purpose of the World Congress? (To provide an opportunity for accountants to meet and learn about accounting practices in other countries.)
3. How often does the World Congress meet? (Once every five years.)
4. Where do they meet? (Each meeting is held in a different country.)

SECTION 2 Check Your Understanding

Now that you have studied this section, complete the following questions and problems.

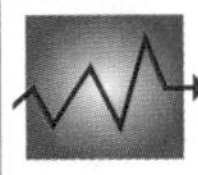

Thinking Critically

1. Explain how to record the cost of supplies purchased for use in a business.
2. Explain how to make an adjustment for prepaid insurance.

Computing in the Business World

You own a personal-training franchise called Your Body. You want to provide health insurance for your ten employees. As you review the alternative plans, you have to make a decision based not only on affordability, but also on total benefits. Determine the total annual premium of each plan and decide which plan best fits your needs.

Type of plan	Plan #1	Plan #2	Plan #3
Monthly cost per employee	$600	$500	$800
Co-pay for each employee	$10	$20	None

Problem 18–2 Analyzing Adjustments

Information related to accounts requiring adjustment on the work sheet for the year ended December 31 for Star City Resorts Corporation follows. Indicate in your working papers the amount of each adjustment, which account is debited, and which account is credited.

1. The Trial Balance section shows a balance of $3,347.45 for **Supplies.** The amount of supplies actually on hand is $892.75.
2. Star City paid an annual insurance premium of $4,440 on November 1.
3. Star City made quarterly federal corporate income tax payments of $945 each. Its actual tax, calculated at the end of the year, is $3,885.

RETEACHING SECTION 2

Analyzing Adjustments Help students learn to analyze each adjustment using the basic rules of debit and credit and increase and decrease. Remind students to think of each account's normal balance when they are analyzing an adjustment for that account. For example, if the amount of supplies on hand is less than the balance amount in the Supplies account, then the account balance must be decreased to bring it up to date. Supplies has a normal debit balance and, therefore, is decreased by a credit. Thus, the amount of the adjustment is a credit to the Supplies account.

3 ASSESS

Thinking Critically (Answers)

1. Their cost is debited to Supplies and credited to Cash in Bank (cash) or Accounts Payable (on account).
2. Enter the amount of a decrease in the Adjustments Credit column on the Prepaid Insurance line and in the Adjustments Debit column on the Insurance Expense line. Label both entries with a letter.

Computing in the World of Business (Answers)

#1 $6,000, #2 $5,000, #3 $8,000
Answers may vary. Plan #2 is the most affordable to Your Body. Plan #3 has no co-pay for employees. The company will have to weigh the two factors in making a final decision.

Problem 18–2 (Answers)

1. Amount $2,454.70; Dr. Supplies Expense; Cr. Supplies
2. Amount $740; Dr. Insurance Expense; Cr. Prepaid Insurance
3. Amount $105; Dr. Federal Corporate Income Tax Expense; Cr. Federal Corporate Income Tax Payable

Chapter Reviews and Working Papers Refer students to the Chapter 18 workbook pages to answer *Check Your Understanding* activities.

4 CLOSE

Section Wrap-Up

Writing: Have students write a paragraph explaining the adjustment process and why certain accounts need to be adjusted at the end of a fiscal period. L1

CHAPTER 18
SECTION 3, PAGES 496–504

1 FOCUS

Introducing the Section

In this section students will learn how to complete the work sheet and journalize and post the adjusting entries.

Section Concepts

- How to complete the Adjusted Trial Balance section.
- How to extend amounts to the Income Statement and Balance sheet sections.
- How to report the net income or net loss for the period.
- How to journalize the adjusting entries in the general journal.
- How to post the adjusting entries to the general ledger.

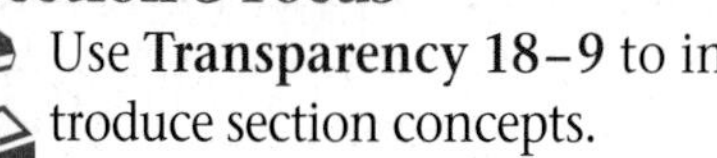

Visual Learning

Section 3 Focus

Use **Transparency 18–9** to introduce section concepts.

BELL RINGER

Consulting: Tell students that they've been hired by a local entrepreneur to give advice on a business plan. Have students describe the information the entrepreneur should collect for preparing the financial statements to include in the business plan. L1

SECTION 3

Completing the Work Sheet and Journalizing and Posting the Adjusting Entries

What You'll Learn

- How to complete the Adjusted Trial Balance section.
- How to extend amounts to the Income Statement and Balance Sheet sections.
- How to report the net income or net loss for the period.
- How to journalize the adjusting entries in the general journal.
- How to post the adjusting entries to the general ledger.

Why It's Important

The work sheet is the source of information for journalizing the adjusting entries and preparing the financial statements.

Once the adjustments are entered in the Adjustments section of the work sheet, it is important to prove that the accounts are still in balance. This is done by completing an adjusted trial balance. Once the Adjusted Trial Balance section is proved, the work sheet can be completed.

Completing the Adjusted Trial Balance Section

After all the adjustments are entered on the work sheet, the Adjusted Trial Balance section can be completed. This section of the work sheet shows the updated balances of all the general ledger accounts. To complete this section, the balance of each account in the Trial Balance section is combined with the adjustment, if any, in the Adjustments section. The new balance is then entered in the appropriate Adjusted Trial Balance column.

Refer to **Figure 18–4** and look at how new balances are computed. If there is no adjustment, the account balance shown in the Trial Balance section is simply extended to the same column (Debit or Credit) in the Adjusted Trial Balance section. There are no adjustments for the first two accounts, **Cash in Bank** and **Accounts Receivable**, so those balances are extended to the Adjusted Trial Balance Debit column.

If the account balance in the Trial Balance section has an adjustment, a new balance is calculated. The amount of the adjustment (from the Adjustments section) is added to or subtracted from the amount in the Trial Balance section. Add debits to debits; add credits to credits; subtract debits and credits.

The first account in the Trial Balance section to have an adjustment is **Merchandise Inventory. Merchandise Inventory** has an unadjusted debit balance of $84,921. Adjustment (a) is a credit of $3,536. To calculate the new balance, the credit adjustment is subtracted from the debit balance. The adjusted balance of $81,385 ($84,921 − $3,536) is extended to the Adjusted Trial Balance Debit column.

The adjusted balances for **Supplies**, **Prepaid Insurance**, and **Federal Corporate Income Tax Expense** are calculated in the same way.

If an account has a zero balance in the Trial Balance section, the amount listed in the Adjustments section is extended to the Adjusted Trial Balance section. **Federal Corporate Income Tax Payable**, for example, has a zero

RESOURCE MANAGER

Reproducible Masters
- Lesson Plans
- Chapter Reviews and Working Papers (CRWP) TAE
- Demonstration Problems

Transparencies
- Section Focus Transparency
- Teaching Transparencies
- Source Document Transparencies
- Solution Transparencies

Multimedia
- ExamView CD-ROM
- Electronic Learning Center CD-ROM
- Interactive Lesson Planner CD-ROM
- Electronic Field Trips in Accounting

	ACCT. NO.	ACCOUNT NAME	TRIAL BALANCE DEBIT	TRIAL BALANCE CREDIT	ADJUSTMENTS DEBIT	ADJUSTMENTS CREDIT	ADJUSTED TRIAL BALANCE DEBIT	ADJUSTED TRIAL BALANCE CREDIT
1	101	Cash in Bank	15 179 00				15 179 00	
2	115	Accounts Receivable	10 404 00				10 404 00	
3	125	Merchandise Inventory	84 921 00			(a) 3 536 00	81 385 00	
4	130	Supplies	5 549 00			(b) 3 710 00	1 839 00	
5	135	Prepaid Insurance	1 500 00			(c) 125 00	1 375 00	
6	140	Delivery Equipment	19 831 00				19 831 00	
7	145	Office Equipment	9 825 00				9 825 00	
8	150	Store Equipment	5 200 00				5 200 00	
9	201	Accounts Payable		13 850 00				13 850 00
10	204	Fed. Corp. Inc. Tax Payable				(d) 155 00		155 00
11	205	Employees' Fed. Inc. Tax Pay.		640 00				640 00
12	211	Employees' State Inc. Tax Pay.		80 00				80 00
13	212	Social Security Tax Payable		248 00				248 00
14	213	Medicare Tax Payable		58 00				58 00
15	214	Fed. Unemployment Tax Payable		18 36				18 36
16	215	State Unemployment Tax Payable		114 73				114 73
17	220	Sales Tax Payable		2 428 00				2 428 00
18	301	Capital Stock		75 000 00				75 000 00
19	305	Retained Earnings		19 771 19				19 771 19
20	310	Income Summary			(a) 3 536 00		3 536 00	
21	401	Sales		320 450 00				320 450 00
22	405	Sales Discounts	730 00				730 00	
23	410	Sales Returns and Allowances	2 000 00				2 000 00	
24	501	Purchases	206 700 00				206 700 00	
25	505	Transportation In	4 036 18				4 036 18	
26	510	Purchases Discounts		1 340 00				1 340 00
27	515	Purchases Returns and Allowances		1 800 00				1 800 00
28	601	Advertising Expense	2 450 00				2 450 00	
29	605	Bankcard Fees Expense	4 199 27				4 199 27	
30	630	Fed. Corp. Income Tax Expense	9 840 00		(d) 155 00		9 995 00	
31	635	Insurance Expense			(c) 125 00		125 00	
32	650	Maintenance Expense	3 519 25				3 519 25	
33	655	Miscellaneous Expense	348 28				348 28	
34	657	Payroll Tax Expense	3 826 83				3 826 83	
35	660	Rent Expense	14 000 00				14 000 00	
36	665	Salaries Expense	29 374 60				29 374 60	
37	670	Supplies Expense			(b) 3 710 00		3 710 00	
38	680	Utilities Expense	2 364 87				2 364 87	
39			435 798 28	435 798 28	7 526 00	7 526 00	435 953 28	435 953 28
40								

Figure 18–4 Extending Balances to the Adjusted Trial Balance Section of the Work Sheet

balance in the Trial Balance section. Adjustment (d) is a credit of $155. This amount is extended to the Adjusted Trial Balance Credit column.

After all account balances are extended to the Adjusted Trial Balance section, both columns are totaled. If total debits equal total credits, this section is proved. A double rule is drawn under the totals and across both columns. If total debits do not equal total credits, there is an error. To find the error, re-add each column. Also, make sure amounts in the Trial Balance and Adjustments sections are extended properly to the Adjusted Trial Balance section.

2 TEACH

GUIDED PRACTICE

Reading Accounting

- As students extend amounts to complete the work sheet, have them read carefully across columns to make sure they are extending the correct amount. L1

Concept Development: Completing the Adjusted Trial Balance Section

Discussion: Point out that amounts are extended from the Trial Balance section of the work sheet to the Adjusted Trial Balance section, beginning with line 1. New account balances are calculated for those accounts with adjustments. The resulting adjusted trial balance holds the ending balances for the accounts that will be reported on the financial statements. L1

Visual Learning

Figure 18–4 Extending Balances to the Adjusted Trial Balance Section of the Work Sheet

Use **Transparency 18–10** to guide students through the process of extending amounts and calculating new balances for the accounts with adjustments.

ACCOUNTING ISSUES

Going Online CPA firms can use the Web to describe the services they offer. It is estimated that 88 percent of online users go online to learn and explore new things. Thus, a Web site is an excellent way to attract prospective clients. Free information such as articles, tax tips, and checklists can attract visitors. Photos and illustrations are easy and inexpensive and help to create a visually appealing site. If the information is updated frequently, browsers will have a reason to come back.

2 TEACH (Cont'd.)

Concept Development: Extending Amounts to the Balance Sheet and Income Statement Sections

Discussion: Emphasize to students that all permanent accounts balances are extended to the Balance Sheet section, and all temporary account balances are extended to the Income Statement section of the work sheet. Although Income Summary represents neither revenue nor expense, it is a temporary account used only at the end of the fiscal period and is thus included in the Income Statement section of the work sheet. L1

Visual Learning

Figure 18–5 On Your Mark Athletic Wear Completed Work Sheet

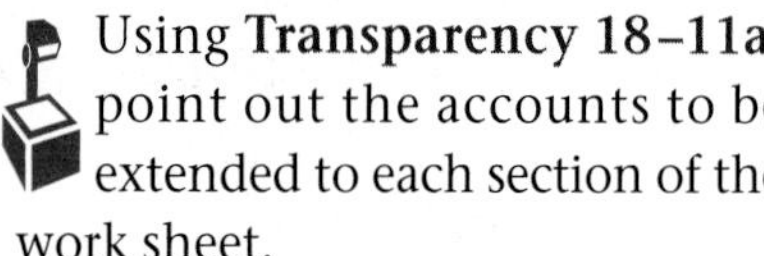

Using **Transparency 18–11a**, point out the accounts to be extended to each section of the work sheet.

Extending Amounts to the Balance Sheet and Income Statement Sections

Beginning with line 1, each account balance in the Adjusted Trial Balance section is extended to the appropriate column of either the Balance Sheet section or the Income Statement section. **Figure 18–5** shows these extensions.

Figure 18–5 On Your Mark Athletic Wear Completed Work Sheet

On Your Mark
Work
For Year Ended

	ACCT. NO.	ACCOUNT NAME	TRIAL BALANCE DEBIT	TRIAL BALANCE CREDIT	ADJUSTMENTS DEBIT	ADJUSTMENTS CREDIT
1	101	Cash in Bank	15 179 00			
2	115	Accounts Receivable	10 404 00			
3	125	Merchandise Inventory	84 921 00			(a) 3 536 00
4	130	Supplies	5 549 00			(b) 3 710 00
5	135	Prepaid Insurance	1 500 00			(c) 125 00
6	140	Delivery Equipment	19 831 00			
7	145	Office Equipment	9 825 00			
8	150	Store Equipment	5 200 00			
9	201	Accounts Payable		13 850 00		
10	204	Fed. Corp. Inc. Tax Payable				(d) 155 00
11	205	Employees' Fed. Inc. Tax Pay.		640 00		
12	211	Employees' State Inc. Tax Pay.		80 00		
13	212	Social Security Tax Payable		248 00		
14	213	Medicare Tax Payable		58 00		
15	214	Fed. Unemployment Tax Payable		18 36		
16	215	State Unemployment Tax Payable		114 73		
17	220	Sales Tax Payable		2 428 00		
18	301	Capital Stock		75 000 00		
19	305	Retained Earnings		19 771 19		
20	310	Income Summary			(a) 3 536 00	
21	401	Sales		320 450 00		
22	405	Sales Discounts	730 00			
23	410	Sales Returns and Allowances	2 000 00			
24	501	Purchases	206 700 00			
25	505	Transportation In	4 036 18			
26	510	Purchases Discounts		1 340 00		
27	515	Purchases Returns and Allowances		1 800 00		
28	601	Advertising Expense	2 450 00			
29	605	Bankcard Fees Expense	4 199 27			
30	630	Fed. Corp. Income Tax Expense	9 840 00		(d) 155 00	
31	635	Insurance Expense			(c) 125 00	
32	650	Maintenance Expense	3 519 25			
33	655	Miscellaneous Expense	348 28			
34	657	Payroll Tax Expense	3 826 83			
35	660	Rent Expense	14 000 00			
36	665	Salaries Expense	29 374 60			
37	670	Supplies Expense			(b) 3 710 00	
38	680	Utilities Expense	2 364 87			
39			435 798 28	435 798 28	7 526 00	7 526 00
40		Net Income				
41						

MEETING SPECIAL NEEDS

Gifted Gifted students may find that the material in the text gives them their first look into the real world of business and finance. Encourage students to take on a wide variety of enrichment and independent practice activities that put them in contact with people in the accounting profession and allow them to observe the daily practices that lead to success. Explore with them what they have observed, and ask them to summarize their findings in writing.

The Income Statement section contains the balances of all the temporary accounts. This section includes **Income Summary** and all revenue, cost of merchandise, and expense accounts.

The Balance Sheet section contains the balances of all the permanent accounts. Here you will find all asset, liability, and capital accounts (**Capital Stock** and **Retained Earnings**).

Athletic Wear
Sheet
December 31, 20--

Adjusted Trial Balance Debit	Adjusted Trial Balance Credit	Income Statement Debit	Income Statement Credit	Balance Sheet Debit	Balance Sheet Credit	
15 179 00				15 179 00		1
10 404 00				10 404 00		2
81 385 00				81 385 00		3
1 839 00				1 839 00		4
1 375 00				1 375 00		5
19 831 00				19 831 00		6
9 825 00				9 825 00		7
5 200 00				5 200 00		8
	13 850 00				13 850 00	9
	155 00				155 00	10
	640 00				640 00	11
	80 00				80 00	12
	248 00				248 00	13
	58 00				58 00	14
	18 36				18 36	15
	114 73				114 73	16
	2 428 00				2 428 00	17
	75 000 00				75 000 00	18
	19 771 19				19 771 19	19
3 536 00		3 536 00				20
	320 450 00		320 450 00			21
730 00		730 00				22
2 000 00		2 000 00				23
206 700 00		206 700 00				24
4 036 18		4 036 18				25
	1 340 00		1 340 00			26
	1 800 00		1 800 00			27
2 450 00		2 450 00				28
4 199 27		4 199 27				29
9 995 00		9 995 00				30
125 00		125 00				31
3 519 25		3 519 25				32
348 28		348 28				33
3 826 83		3 826 83				34
14 000 00		14 000 00				35
29 374 60		29 374 60				36
3 710 00		3 710 00				37
2 364 87		2 364 87				38
435 953 28	435 953 28	290 915 28	323 590 00	145 038 00	112 363 28	39
		32 674 72			32 674 72	40
		323 590 00	323 590 00	145 038 00	145 038 00	41
						42
						43

Figure 18–5 On Your Mark Athletic Wear Completed Work Sheet (continued)

CONNECT TO . . . MUSIC

When you buy a CD, your money doesn't just go to the performer. Music company accountants also have to consider writers, publishers, and administrative fees when checking royalty payments. Keeping track of who gets paid can get even more complicated when a song incorporates samples of other songs.

2 TEACH (Cont'd.)

Visual Learning

Figure 18–5 On Your Mark Athletic Wear Completed Work Sheet (continued)

Using **Transparency 18–11b**, point out the account balances extended to the Balance Sheet and Income Statement sections.

Teaching Tips

Remind students that if the adjusted trial balance does not balance, errors must be found and corrected before the work sheet can be completed.

Briefly discuss the Capital Stock and Retained Earnings accounts. Students will learn more about these accounts in Chapter 19.

Demonstration Problem
Step-by-Step Practice

Use demonstration problem 18–6 to give students practice in extending amounts and completing a ten-column work sheet.

INTERDISCIPLINARY CONNECTIONS ACTIVITY

Music What would it cost to get a song or a musical score copyrighted? Ask students to check into the process and the cost. What does the copyright protect, and for how long? What benefit is it to an artist to seek a copyright? After students have found some answers, talk about the impact of copyright protection on the entertainment industry and artist's profits. Students may have some interesting opinions!

2 TEACH (Cont'd.)

Concept Development: Completing the Work Sheet

Discussion: Review the steps in totaling and ruling an accounting form. Point out that the totals for the two financial statement sections do not match because the net income or loss earned during the fiscal period covered by the work sheet has yet to be calculated and added to the subtotals. L1

Concept Development: Journalizing Adjustments

Discussion: Review adjustments to Merchandise Inventory, Supplies, Prepaid Insurance, and Federal Corporate Income Tax Expense. Analyze each adjusting entry in T-account form. Review the adjustments on the work sheet, and remind students why the debit and credit parts are identified by a small letter in parentheses. Point out that entering adjustments on the work sheet is simply a way of collecting information. The adjustment amounts still need to be recorded in the accounts affected. Journal entries must be made and then posted to bring the ledger accounts up to date. L1

ACCOUNTING *Flashbacks*

MODERN ACCOUNTING

AC Littleton, a founder of modern accounting, determined that a civilization must have seven "Antecedents of Bookkeeping" before accounting develops: writing, arithmetic, private property, money, credit, commerce, and capital.

Completing the Work Sheet

After all amounts are extended to the Balance Sheet and Income Statement sections, a single rule is drawn across the columns in these sections. All four columns are then totaled as shown in **Figure 18–5.** As you learned in Chapter 8, the totals of the debit and credit columns within the Balance Sheet and Income Statement sections are not equal at this point. The difference between the two column totals in each section is the amount of net income (or net loss) for the period.

After the net income (or net loss) is recorded, the columns in the Balance Sheet and Income Statement sections are ruled and totaled as shown in **Figure 18–5.** Notice that the words "Net Income" are written in the Account Name column on the same line as the net income amount.

If the totals of the two Income Statement columns are equal, and the totals of the two Balance Sheet columns are equal, a double rule is drawn across all four columns. The double rule indicates that these sections of the work sheet are proved.

Journalizing Adjustments

The journal entries that update the general ledger accounts at the end of a period are called adjusting entries. The source of information for journalizing the adjusting entries is the Adjustments section of the work sheet. The accounts debited and credited in the Adjustments section are entered in the general journal.

Before recording the first adjusting entry, the words "Adjusting Entries" are written in the Description column of the general journal. This heading eliminates the need to write an explanation after each adjusting entry.

Refer to **Figure 18–6.** The following entries are recorded in the Adjustments columns of the work sheet:

(a) adjusting merchandise inventory
(b) adjusting supplies
(c) adjusting insurance
(d) adjusting income tax

The first adjustment, labeled **(a)** on the work sheet, is recorded in the general journal as a debit to **Income Summary** for $3,536 and a credit to **Merchandise Inventory** for $3,536. The label **(a)** is not recorded in the general journal.

Remaining adjustments are entered in the general journal in the same manner, with the debit part of the entry recorded first. The date for each adjusting entry is the last day of the period.

COOPERATIVE LEARNING ACTIVITY

Group Discussion Assign students to pairs and give each pair 20 beans. The beans represent inventory. Ask each pair to read the transactions recorded in the sales journal in Figure 16–3 on page 424 and from the purchases journal in Figure 17–4 on page 455. For each sales transaction, students are to remove one bean from inventory; for each purchases transaction, students are to add one bean. The partners count the ending inventory and report the changes. (There should be 18 beans in inventory.) Ask students to explain why the Merchandise Inventory balance is not up to date. (The account is not used in any of the transactions.)

	DATE		DESCRIPTION	POST. REF.	DEBIT	CREDIT	
1	20--		Adjusting Entries				1
2	Dec.	31	Income Summary		3 5 3 6 00		2
3			Merchandise Inventory			3 5 3 6 00	3
4		31	Supplies Expense		3 7 1 0 00		4
5			Supplies			3 7 1 0 00	5
6		31	Insurance Expense		1 2 5 00		6
7			Prepaid Insurance			1 2 5 00	7
8		31	Fed. Corporate Income Tax Exp.		1 5 5 00		8
9			Fed. Corp. Income Tax Pay.			1 5 5 00	9
10							10

GENERAL JOURNAL — PAGE 22

Figure 18–6 Recording Adjusting Entries in the General Journal

Posting Adjusting Entries to the General Ledger

After the adjusting entries are recorded in the general journal, they are posted to the general ledger accounts. Once the adjusting entries are posted, the general ledger accounts are up-to-date. The balances in the general ledger accounts all agree with the amounts entered on the Income Statement and Balance Sheet sections of the work sheet.

Once these entries are posted, the following has been accomplished:

- The **Supplies Expense** account has been "charged" with the value of the supplies used in the period.
- The **Supplies** account now reflects only the amount of items still remaining in inventory.
- The **Merchandise Inventory** account now reflects the correct inventory value.
- The **Income Summary** account has been "charged" with the cost of goods sold for the period.
- The **Insurance Expense** account now reflects the appropriate insurance expense for the period.
- The **Prepaid Insurance** account has been reduced by the amount of insurance expired.
- The **Federal Corporate Income Tax Expense** account now reflects the tax expense for the period.
- The **Federal Corporate Income Tax Payable** account has been increased to reflect the appropriate payable amount.

Figure 18–7 shows the general journal and the general ledger accounts after the posting of the adjusting entries is completed. Notice that the words "Adjusting Entry" are written in the Description column of the general ledger accounts.

2 TEACH (Cont'd.)

Visual Learning

Figure 18–6 Recording Adjusting Entries in the General Journal

Use **Transparency 18–12** to review the entire process of entering adjustments on the work sheet, calculating adjusted balances, extending amounts to the Balance Sheet and Income Statement columns, calculating net income (or loss), totaling and ruling the work sheet, and recording the adjustments in the general journal.

Concept Development: Posting Adjusting Entries to the General Ledger

Discussion: Students are already familiar with the posting procedure, but you may want to review the steps with them in Figure 18–7. Point out the words "Adjusting Entry" written in the general ledger account to identify the entry. L1

ADDRESSING MULTIPLE LEARNING STYLES

Visual/Spatial Learners Have students record adjusting entries in a journal on separate journal pages. Then have students assemble all the journal entries in a collage. Students should label each journal entry with a caption or callout to explain the need for the adjusting entry. If desired, students can also explain how the amount for the adjustment is determined. The finished collages will summarize the accounts that must be adjusted at the end of the fiscal period, and students will have a visual reminder of which accounts are debited and which accounts are credited.

2 TEACH (Cont'd.)

Visual Learning

Figure 18–7 Adjusting Entries Posted to the General Ledger

Use **Transparency 18–13a** to explain each of the journal entries to record the work sheet adjustments. Point out the heading "Adjusting Entries." Ask students why these entries need to be identified as adjusting entries (for the audit trail).

Teaching Tips

Remind students that each adjusting entry affects a permanent account and a temporary account.

Point out that the debit and credit parts of each adjusting entry are found by matching the letters of the entries on the work sheet.

GENERAL JOURNAL PAGE 22

DATE		DESCRIPTION	POST. REF.	DEBIT	CREDIT
20--		Adjusting Entries			
Dec.	31	Income Summary	310	3536 00	
		Merchandise Inventory	125		3536 00
		Supplies Expense	670	3710 00	
		Supplies	130		3710 00
		Insurance Expense	635	125 00	
		Prepaid Insurance	135		125 00
		Fed. Corporate Income Tax Exp.	630	155 00	
		Fed. Corp. Income Tax Pay.	204		155 00

ACCOUNT Merchandise Inventory ACCOUNT NO. 125

DATE		DESCRIPTION	POST. REF.	DEBIT	CREDIT	BALANCE DEBIT	BALANCE CREDIT
20--							
Jan.	1	Balance	—			84921 00	
Dec.	31	Adjusting Entry	G22		3536 00	81385 00	

ACCOUNT Supplies ACCOUNT NO. 130

DATE		DESCRIPTION	POST. REF.	DEBIT	CREDIT	BALANCE DEBIT	BALANCE CREDIT
20--							
Dec.	1	Balance	✓			5299 00	
	15		P12	250 00		5549 00	
	31	Adjusting Entry	G22		3710 00	1839 00	

ACCOUNT Prepaid Insurance ACCOUNT NO. 135

DATE		DESCRIPTION	POST. REF.	DEBIT	CREDIT	BALANCE DEBIT	BALANCE CREDIT
20--							
Dec.	17	Balance	CP14	1500 00		1500 00	
	31	Adjusting Entry	G22		125 00	1375 00	

ACCOUNT Federal Corporate Income Tax Payable ACCOUNT NO. 204

DATE		DESCRIPTION	POST. REF.	DEBIT	CREDIT	BALANCE DEBIT	BALANCE CREDIT
20--							
Dec.	31	Adjusting Entry	G22		155 00		155 00

Figure 18–7 Adjusting Entries Posted to the General Ledger

TEACHING NOTES

ACCOUNT *Income Summary* ACCOUNT NO. *310*

DATE		DESCRIPTION	POST. REF.	DEBIT	CREDIT	BALANCE DEBIT	BALANCE CREDIT
20--							
Dec.	31	Adjusting Entry	G22	3 536 00		3 536 00	

ACCOUNT *Federal Corporate Income Tax Expense* ACCOUNT NO. *630*

DATE		DESCRIPTION	POST. REF.	DEBIT	CREDIT	BALANCE DEBIT	BALANCE CREDIT
20--							
Dec.	1	Balance	—			9 840 00	
	31	Adjusting Entry	G22	155 00		9 995 00	

ACCOUNT *Insurance Expense* ACCOUNT NO. *635*

DATE		DESCRIPTION	POST. REF.	DEBIT	CREDIT	BALANCE DEBIT	BALANCE CREDIT
20--							
Dec.	31	Adjusting Entry	G22	125 00		125 00	

ACCOUNT *Supplies Expense* ACCOUNT NO. *670*

DATE		DESCRIPTION	POST. REF.	DEBIT	CREDIT	BALANCE DEBIT	BALANCE CREDIT
20--							
Dec.	31	Adjusting Entry	G22	3 710 00		3 710 00	

Figure 18–7 Adjusting Entries Posted to the General Ledger (continued)

ANALYZING FINANCIAL REPORTS

The Income Statement: Return on Sales

One use of the income statement is to analyze the return on sales. You first analyzed return on sales for a sole proprietorship in Chapter 9. Analyzing return on sales for a corporation is similar. Look at the following example:

$$\text{Return on Sales} = \frac{\text{Net Income}}{\text{Net Sales}} \quad \frac{\$59{,}000}{\$5{,}655{,}000} = 0.0104 = 1.04\%$$

▶ Analyze the Report:

Use the information found on the Office Depot income statement and "To Our Shareholders" letter to answer these questions. Note that Office Depot chooses to use the term "Consolidated Statements of Earnings" instead of "income statement." For our purposes, they are the same. Net income is called "net earnings" and net sales is called "sales."

1. Calculate the return on sales for each of the three years given.
2. What possible factors affected the return on sales over the last two years?

2 TEACH (Cont'd.)

Visual Learning

Figure 18–7 Adjusting Entries Posted to the General Ledger (continued)
Use **Transparency 18–13b** to review the posting process.

Critical Thinking: Have students discuss how the adjustment of account balances at the end of a fiscal period supports the matching principle. L1

The Office Depot 2001 Annual Report
Refer students to pages A-39–A-48 in the back of the book.

ANALYZING FINANCIAL REPORTS

Analyze the Report (Answers)

1. Return on Sales: 1999, 2.51%; 2000, 0.43%; 2001, 1.80%
2. Answers will vary, but might include the following factors. In 2000, the office supply superstore industry was beginning to mature and the environment was becoming more competitive. Office Depot's new leadership team plotted a strategic course to meet goals. Throughout 2001, the team continued the process. Strategies included increased emphasis on customer service, closure of underperforming stores, and growth in international markets.

CHAPTER 18
SECTION 3, PAGES 496–504

3 ASSESS

Thinking Critically (Answers)

1. The Balance Sheet section contains balances of all permanent general ledger accounts, which includes assets, liabilities, and stockholders' equity.
2. Insurance Expense and Prepaid Insurance.

Communicating Accounting (Answers)

Answers may vary. The Balance Sheet section contains balances of all permanent general ledger accounts. The Income Statement section contains balances of all temporary general ledger accounts.

Problem 18–3 (Answers)

1. $9,995
2. Balance Sheet
3. $3,710
4. $155

Problem 18–4 (Answers)

1. Rotary Supply Corporation
2. 6
3. $177.09
4. Accts. Pay.—K & L Electrical
5. Purchases Returns and Allowances

Chapter Reviews and Working Papers Refer students to the Chapter 18 workbook pages to answer *Check Your Understanding* activities.

4 CLOSE

Section Wrap-Up

Writing: Have students write a paragraph explaining the adjusting process and why it is needed. L1

SECTION 3 Check Your Understanding

Now that you have studied this section, complete the following questions and problems.

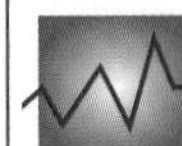

Thinking Critically

1. Which types of general ledger accounts appear in the Balance Sheet section of the work sheet?
2. What accounts are affected by the adjustment for prepaid insurance?

Communicating Accounting

You are making a presentation to the board of directors of your organization, Kids-n-Teens. As you review the financial statements for this quarter, you notice that the bookkeeper extended the account balances from the Adjusted Trial Balance section to the Balance Sheet section but not to the Income Statement section. What a mistake! You can fix it this time, but you need to explain to the bookkeeper how to extend to both sections of the work sheet. Select a classmate and practice your explanation.

Problem 18–3 Analyzing the Work Sheet

Refer to **Figure 18–5** and answer the following questions in your working papers:

1. What amount is extended to the Income Statement section for **Federal Corporate Income Tax Expense**?
2. To which section of the work sheet is the balance of **Prepaid Insurance** extended?
3. What is the total amount of supplies consumed during the period?
4. What is the total amount still owed to the federal government for corporate income tax?

Problem 18–4 Analyzing a Source Document

Based on the debit memorandum, answer the following questions.

1. Which company is returning the merchandise?
2. How many items are being returned?
3. What amount is entered in the journal entry?
4. Which account is debited?
5. Which account is credited?

DEBIT MEMORANDUM No. 284
Date: May 4, 20--
Invoice No.: 378456

ROTARY SUPPLY CORPORATION
634 West Washington Avenue, Lincoln, SC 30856

To: K & L Electrical
845 Morgan Street
Plantsville, SC 30455

This day we have debited your account as follows:

Quantity	Item	Unit Price	Total
4	Locking Fixture #27304-78	$ 36.95	$ 147.80
2	Mirror/Reflectors #8935-231	11.24	22.48
	Subtotal		$ 170.28
	Tax		6.81
	Total		$ 177.09

RETEACHING SECTION 3

Extending Account Balances Review with students that temporary account balances are extended to the Income Statement section of the work sheet, and permanent account balances are extended to the Balance Sheet section. Point out to students that they can use the account numbers as a guide for extending the account balances. The balances of the permanent accounts numbered 101 through 399 are extended to the Balance Sheet columns. The balances of the temporary accounts numbered 401 through 699 are extended to the Income Statement columns.

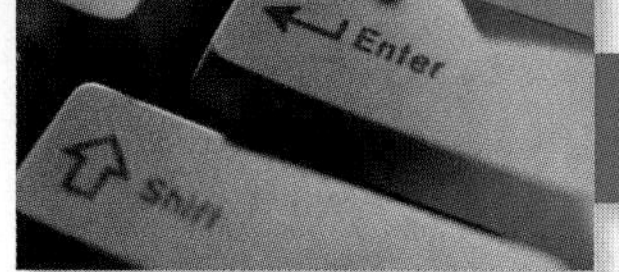

CHAPTER 18 SUMMARY

KEY CONCEPTS

1. The work sheet is prepared, either manually or on a spreadsheet, to organize all the data needed to update the accounts, to prepare the financial statements, and to record end-of-period adjusting journal entries.
2. The ten-column work sheet contains columns for the following:
   - trial balance
   - adjustments
   - adjusted trial balance
   - income statement
   - balance sheet
3. The Trial Balance section of the work sheet includes all accounts listed in the chart of accounts, even those with zero balances. The ending balances for all accounts are listed, and the equality of debits and credits is proved.
4. Some general ledger accounts must be updated at the end of a period by entering adjustments. Adjustments are often made to the following accounts:
   - inventory
   - supplies
   - insurance
   - tax liabilities
5. Every adjustment affects one permanent and one temporary general ledger account.
6. The beginning inventory is the amount of merchandise a business has on hand at the beginning of a period. The ending inventory is the amount of merchandise on hand at the end of a period. The balance of the **Merchandise Inventory** account changes after the physical inventory count, when it is adjusted to reflect the actual amount of merchandise on hand.
7. A corporation pays income taxes on its net income for the year.
8. All account balances are extended to the Adjusted Trial Balance section of the work sheet. Adjustments are reflected in the balances entered in the Adjusted Trial Balance section.
9. The Balance Sheet section of the work sheet contains the balances of all the permanent accounts, including assets, liabilities, and owners' equity.
10. The Income Statement section of the work sheet contains the balances of all the temporary accounts, including **Income Summary** and revenue, cost of merchandise, and expense accounts.
11. The completed work sheet lists all general ledger accounts and their updated balances and shows the net income (or net loss) for the period.

SUMMARY CHAPTER 18

Chapter 18 Quiz

Student ______ Class ______ Instructor ______
Date Assigned ______ Date Completed ______

CHAPTER 18 QUIZ

Adjustments and the Ten-Column Work Sheet

QUESTIONS (Short Answer)

Directions: Complete the following questions with a short answer.

1. What is the purpose of an adjustment? ______
2. How do you determine which accounts need adjustments? ______
3. Is the cash account balance adjusted at the end of the fiscal period? Why or why not? ______
4. What is the difference between a beginning inventory and a physical inventory? ______
5. What two accounts are affected when Merchandise Inventory is adjusted? ______
6. What is the normal balance of Income Summary? ______
7. Why are letters used with adjustments entered on a work sheet? ______
8. Why is the adjusted trial balance needed? ______
9. Which account balances are extended to the Balance Sheet section? ______
10. Which balances are extended to the Income Statement section? ______

20 • Chapter Quizzes

QUESTIONS (Short Answer)

1. What is the purpose of an adjustment?
2. How do you determine which accounts need adjustments?
3. Is the cash account balance adjusted at the end of the fiscal period? Why or why not?
4. What is the difference between a beginning inventory and a physical inventory?
5. What two accounts are affected when Merchandise Inventory is adjusted?
6. What is the normal balance of Income Summary?
7. Why are letters used with adjustments entered on a work sheet?
8. Why is the adjusted trial balance needed?
9. Which account balances are extended to the Balance Sheet section?
10. Which balances are extended to the Income Statement section?

ANSWERS

1. To bring account balances up to date at the end of a fiscal period.
2. If the trial balance amount is not up to date, the account must be adjusted.
3. No. Cash is continually updated through journal entries and posting.
4. A beginning inventory is the cost of inventory on hand at the beginning of a fiscal period. A physical inventory is the actual count made to determine the cost of the inventory on hand.
5. Merchandise Inventory, Income Summary.
6. It has no normal balance.
7. To identify the debit and credit parts of each adjustment.
8. To calculate final balances for all accounts prior to preparing the financial statements.
9. Permanent account.
10. Temporary accounts.

REVIEW AND ACTIVITIES CHAPTER 18

USING KEY TERMS

See the *Glossary* for the definitions of these terms. Ask for volunteers to share their memos in class. Discuss any misuses of the terms.

Understanding Accounting Concepts and Procedures

(Answers)

1. To enable the accountant to determine net income (or loss) for the fiscal period.
2. (a) Trial Balance, (b) Adjustments, (c) Adjusted Trial Balance, (d) Income Statement, (e) Balance Sheet
3. All accounts are listed in the Trial Balance section of the work sheet, even those with zero balances, to allow for their potential use for adjustments.
4. To show the changes caused by internal operations or passage of time.
5. Merchandise Inventory, Supplies, Prepaid Insurance, and Federal Income Tax Expense.
6. Transferring the costs of the assets consumed to an appropriate expense account.
7. Purchases of merchandise are recorded in the Purchases account. Sales of merchandise are recorded in the Sales account.
8. To update the balances of all the general ledger accounts.
9. The permanent general ledger accounts for assets, liabilities, and owner's equity.
10. The temporary accounts for revenue and expenses.

USING KEY TERMS

As the accounting manager for several Homemade Fresh Ice Cream stores in your region, it is your responsibility to oversee the preparation of end-of-period financial statements. Before you complete your end-of-period reports, you need your staff to verify their work sheets and trial balances. Write a memorandum to the staff to remind them to verify their data, make adjustments where needed, give beginning and ending inventory figures, and complete a physical inventory. In the body of your memorandum, provide a brief definition of each term.

adjustment	ending inventory
beginning inventory	physical inventory

Understanding Accounting Concepts and Procedures

Instructions

On a separate sheet of paper, answer the following questions:

1. Why is a work sheet completed before the financial statements are prepared?
2. What are the five sections of the ten-column work sheet?
3. Why are general ledger accounts with zero balances entered in the Trial Balance section of the work sheet?
4. Why are some general ledger accounts updated at the end of the period?
5. Name four accounts of a merchandising business that are typically adjusted at the end of the period.
6. What is meant by "expensing" an asset?
7. Why does the balance of the **Merchandise Inventory** account not change during the period?
8. What is the purpose of completing the Adjusted Trial Balance section of the work sheet?
9. Which accounts are included on the Balance Sheet section of the work sheet?
10. Which accounts are included on the Income Statement section of the work sheet?

ASSESSMENT RESOURCES

Choose assessment strategies from the following pages to evaluate your students' progress.

Student Edition
Check Your Understanding, pp. 490, 495, 503
Chapter 18 Problems, pp. 509–513
Analyzing Financial Reports, p. 503

Assessment and Evaluation Masters
Chapter 18 Study Plan, *Glencoe Workbook (CRWP)*
Chapter 18 Self-Test, *Glencoe Workbook (CRWP)*
Chapter 18 Test, *Chapter Tests* Booklet
Chapter 18 Activity, *School-to-Work Handbook*
Chapter 18 **Exam***View*

Teacher Wraparound Edition
Critical Thinking Activity, p. 487
Reteaching Sections 1–3, pp. 490, 495, 504
Chapter 18 Quiz, p. 505

Case Study...

Merchandising Business: Training Videos

You're an accountant for Millennium Training Systems, a company that creates and sells training videos. The company CEO asks you to prepare financial statements for the month without the appropriate adjusting entries.

Thinking Critically:

1. Look at the information for adjustments:

	Beginning	Ending
Supplies	$5,000	$1,200
Prepaid Insurance	6,400	800

Net income, before adjustments, is $22,400. What is net income after the adjustments are made?

2. Explain why the financial statements do not present an accurate picture of the company without considering the adjusting entries.

interNET CONNECTION

Purchase versus Lease

Whether you are ready to buy your first car or your business needs to replace a delivery vehicle, you can use the Internet to research the costs and convenience factors of purchasing or leasing a vehicle.

Do This:

1. Select an automobile that you wish to purchase or lease.
2. Find the lowest interest rate for new cars in your area.
3. Locate an online calculator that will calculate the cost:
   - if you take a loan on the car
   - if you lease the vehicle

   What is the cost of each option over a four-year term?
4. Will you lease or purchase the vehicle? Explain your decision.

Conducting an Audit with Alex

Florence Loch works part-time as a clerk at Tiger Corporation. She was asked to take a physical count of the lamp area and complete an inventory sheet. Her completed sheet is presented below. Check Florence's work.

Instructions Locate any errors on the inventory sheet. On a separate sheet of paper, make a list of the corrections.

INVENTORY SHEET

STOCK NO.	ITEM	UNIT	QUANTITY	UNIT COST		TOTAL VALUE	
27485	Lamp Shade	Each	23	$ 27	56	$ 633	88
27847	Lamp Socket	Each	162	3	85	579	96
23186	Electrical Wire	Feet	895		73	653	35
21965	Lamp Shade	Each	11	32	05	325	55
22625	Lamp Shade	Each	13	29	11	378	43
52335	Lamp Base	Each	9	27	30	245	00
55894	Lamp Base	Each	17	24	91	423	47
			TOTAL FOR THIS SHEET			$ 3,239	64

Workplace Skills

Leadership

Effective leaders are those who provide positive examples for others to follow. Leaders listen, encourage, motivate, persuade, and take initiative.

On the Job:

You have just been promoted to director of accounting for a national toy store chain. In reviewing the end-of-period financial reports, you notice that the net income was not as great as past reporting periods. In your weekly management meeting, you mention to the director of marketing that perhaps a new line of toys should be considered to boost the net income for the next financial reporting period.

Thinking Critically:

Prior to the management meeting, you meet with Leonard Rainwater, Director of Marketing. Leonard has been with the company for 25 years, and his decisions are rarely questioned. How would you approach Leonard to discuss a new line of toys being added to the inventory?

REVIEW AND ACTIVITIES CHAPTER 18

Case Study...

Thinking Critically (Answers)

1. $13,000
2. Answers may vary. The financial statements would not be accurate without adjusting entries because some changes occur over time or internally, without individual transactions being recorded.

Workplace Skills

Thinking Critically (Answers)

Answers will vary. Assist students with an approach that shows respect for job longevity, initiative, and decisiveness. You may want to hold a brief classroom discussion prior to this assignment.

Conducting an Audit with Alex

(Answer)

Lamp socket #27847 should be $623.70
Lamp base #52335 should be $245.70
Total $3,311.08

Internet Resources and Activities Handbook

Refer students to the booklet for additional Internet activities.

interNET CONNECTION www.glencoe.com

Do This (Answers)

1. Answers may vary.
2. This information can be found at a number of sites: www.financenter.com; www.peoplefirst.com; www.bankrate.com.
3. Calculator can be found at www.calculatorzone.com or at specific finance locations such as www.fordcredit.com.
4. Answers will vary.

PEACHTREE CORNER

Adjusting Entries

Use the **General Journal Entry** task to enter adjusting entries. You must use an account called **Inventory Adjustment**, not the **Income Summary** account, to make the adjustment to Merchandise Inventory. The procedures to record the other adjustments using Peachtree are the same as in a manual system.

Tasks Analysis Options Reports

- Quotes/Sales Orders ▸
- Sales/Invoicing...
- Receipts...
- Finance Charge...
- Select for Deposit...
- Purchase Orders...
- Purchases/Receive Inventory...
- Select for Payment...
- Payments...
- Write Checks...
- Time/Expense ▸
- Select for Payroll Entry...
- Payroll Entry...
- General Journal Entry...
- Inventory Adjustments...
- Assemblies...

Reports

The ten-column work sheet is a convenient way to manually prepare adjusted trial balances and financial statements. Computerized systems automatically prepare financial statements so a work sheet is not needed.

Peachtree does, however, include a Working Trial Balance report to aid in recording adjustments. To print this report, go to the ***Reports*** menu, choose **General Ledger**, *Select a Report*, then select Working Trial Balance.

Adjusting Entries

Making the Transition from a Manual to a Computerized System

Task	Perform Accounting Procedures Using Manual Methods	Perform Accounting Procedures Using Automated Methods
Recording adjusting entries	1. From the general ledger, prepare a trial balance in the first two columns of a work sheet. 2. Record adjustments on the work sheet. 3. Calculate adjusted account balances in the Adjusted Trial Balance columns. 4. Extend account balances to Income Statement or Balance Sheet columns of work sheet. 5. Calculate net income (loss) for the accounting period. 6. Record adjusting entries in the general journal. 7. Post adjusting entries to general ledger accounts.	1. Print a Trial Balance. 2. Record the adjusting entries in the general journal. 3. General ledger accounts are automatically updated.

Recording Adjusting Entries

Peachtree Question	Description
How do I generate a trial balance for use in preparing adjustments?	1. Choose **General Ledger** from the ***Reports*** menu. 2. From the *Report List*, select Working Trial Balance. 3. Click the *Print* button.
How do I journalize the adjusting entries?	1. List necessary adjustments on the Working Trial Balance form. 2. From the ***Tasks*** menu, select **General Journal Entry**. 3. Enter the adjusting entries. 4. Click *Save*.
What does the software do "behind the scenes?"	1. Peachtree automatically updates the general ledger accounts when the adjusting entries are posted. 2. A trial balance can be generated at any time.

For detailed instructions: See the **Peachtree User Guide** in your Glencoe Working Papers.

Peachtree® Answers to Frequently Asked Questions

Q: Why doesn't the chart of accounts include an Income Summary account to make an adjustment to **Merchandise Inventory**?

A: You should use the **Inventory Adjustment** account, not the **Income Summary** account to make an adjustment to **Merchandise Inventory**. Peachtree requires that you use the **Inventory Adjustment** account so that the program can correctly compute the Cost of Merchandise Sold section on an Income Statement.

For additional information, refer to your *Glencoe Peachtree Accounting User's Guide*.

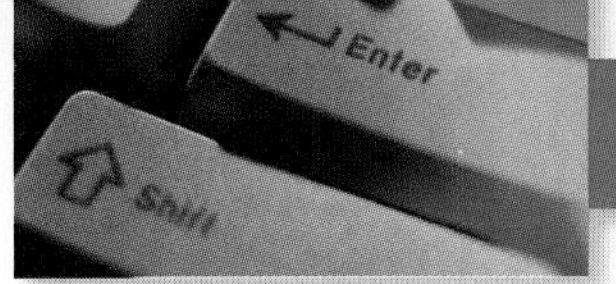

APPLICATION OPTIONS

Problem 18–5 Completing a Ten-Column Work Sheet

The August 31 trial balance for InBeat CD Shop is entered on the work sheet in your working papers. Listed below is the data needed to make the adjustments.

Instructions In your working papers, complete the ten-column work sheet for InBeat CD Shop for the month ended August 31.

Data for Adjustments	
Merchandise Inventory, August 31	$ 77,872
Supplies consumed during the period	2,171
Insurance premium expired during the period	489
Additional federal corporate income taxes owed	118

Analyze: After the adjustments are made on the work sheet, which expense account has the highest balance?

Complete chapter problems one of four ways:

1 **Manual** Glencoe Working Papers

or

2 **Peachtree Complete Accounting** Software

or

3 **QuickBooks** Templates (Problems 18–7, 18–8)

or

4 **Spreadsheet** Templates (Problem 18–5)

Problem 18–6 Completing a Ten-Column Work Sheet

The August 31 trial balance for Shutterbug Cameras is listed on the next page. Also listed is the data needed for the adjustments.

Instructions In your working papers, complete the ten-column work sheet for Shutterbug Cameras for the month ended August 31.

SPREADSHEET SMART GUIDE

Step-by-Step Instructions: Problem 18–5

1. Select the spreadsheet template for Problem 18–5.
2. Enter your name and the date in the spaces provided on the template.
3. Complete the spreadsheet using the instructions in your working papers.
4. Print the spreadsheet and proof your work.
5. Save your work and exit the spreadsheet program.

Continued 

Problem 18–5 (Answers) Completing a Ten-Column Work Sheet

Adjustments:

(a) $9,025
(b) $2,171
(c) $489
(d) $118

Adjusted Trial Balance totals $244,934
Net Income $13,896

Analyze: Salaries Expense

EXTENDING THE CONTENT

Interviewing a Bookkeeper Invite a local bookkeeper or businessperson who prepares and uses work sheets to speak to your class. Ask the speaker to discuss the procedures for preparing the documents and focus on how they determine the adjusting entries. The discussion should also include how the work sheets are used by others in the business. Ask the speaker to bring work sheet samples to share with your class. Have students prepare questions in advance and set aside time for a question-and-answer session. After the interview, ask students what one item of information was most surprising to them.

PROBLEMS CHAPTER 18

Problem 18–6 (Answers) Completing a Ten-Column Work Sheet

Adjustments:

(a) $4,309
(b) $2,008
(c) $490
(d) $252

Adjusted Trial Balance totals $214,541
Net Income $11,766

Analyze: Accounts Payable

Peachtree®

SMART GUIDE

Step-by-Step Instructions: Problem 18–6

1. Select the problem set for Shutterbug Cameras (Prob. 18–6).
2. Rename the company and set the system date.
3. Print a Working Trial Balance and use it to help you prepare the adjustments.
4. Record the adjustments using the **General Journal Entry** option.
5. Print a General Journal report and proof your work.
6. Print a General Ledger Trial Balance report.
7. Answer the Analyze question.
8. End the session.

TIP: Use the Inventory Adjustment account, not the Income Summary account to record the adjustment for Merchandise Inventory.

		Trial Balance	
		Debit	Credit
101	Cash in Bank	$13,873	
115	Accounts Receivable	5,382	
125	Merchandise Inventory	82,981	
130	Supplies	2,397	
135	Prepaid Insurance	1,350	
140	Store Equipment	30,769	
201	Accounts Payable		$ 8,481
207	Federal Corporate Income Tax Payable		—
210	Employees' Federal Income Tax Payable		194
211	Employees' State Income Tax Payable		48
212	Social Security Tax Payable		119
213	Medicare Tax Payable		25
215	Sales Tax Payable		381
216	Federal Unemployment Tax Payable		19
217	State Unemployment Tax Payable		92
301	Capital Stock		80,000
305	Retained Earnings		28,568
310	Income Summary	—	—
401	Sales		95,487
405	Sales Discounts	37	
410	Sales Returns and Allowances	945	
501	Purchases	39,491	
505	Transportation In	2,039	
510	Purchases Discounts		656
515	Purchases Returns and Allowances		219
601	Advertising Expense	128	
605	Bankcard Fees Expense	219	
620	Federal Corporate Income Tax Expense	1,580	
630	Insurance Expense	—	
640	Maintenance Expense	2,513	
645	Miscellaneous Expense	652	
647	Payroll Tax Expense	1,953	
650	Rent Expense	9,000	
655	Salaries Expense	18,631	
660	Supplies Expense	—	
670	Utilities Expense	349	

Data for Adjustments

Merchandise Inventory, August 31	$78,672
Supplies on hand, August 31	389
Insurance premium expired during the period	490
Additional federal income taxes owed	252

Analyze: On the Balance Sheet section, which account has the higher balance, **Accounts Payable** or **Accounts Receivable**?

SOFTWARE NOTES

Teachers can find detailed instructions for:

- **Peachtree Complete Accounting Software**, in the *Glencoe Workbook (CRWP)*
- **QuickBooks Templates**, in *Using QuickBooks with Glencoe Accounting*
- **Spreadsheet Templates**, in the *Glencoe Workbook (CRWP)*

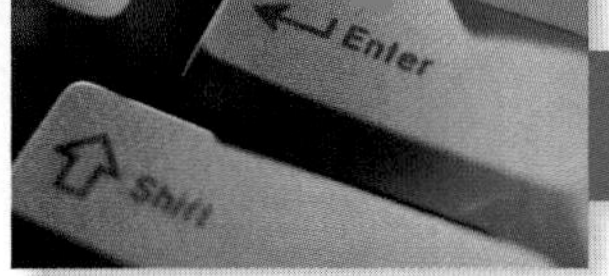

Problem 18-7 Completing a Ten-Column Work Sheet

The balances of the general ledger accounts of Cycle Tech Bicycles, as of August 31, are listed below. Also listed is the data needed for the adjustments.

Instructions In your working papers:

Prepare a ten-column work sheet for Cycle Tech Bicycles for the month ended August 31.

101	Cash in Bank	$ 22,323
115	Accounts Receivable	1,737
125	Merchandise Inventory	23,654
130	Supplies	3,971
135	Prepaid Insurance	1,800
140	Store Equipment	25,395
145	Office Equipment	15,239
201	Accounts Payable	11,051
210	Federal Corporate Income Tax Payable	—
211	Employees' Federal Income Tax Payable	519
212	Employees' State Income Tax Payable	142
213	Social Security Tax Payable	408
214	Medicare Tax Payable	137
215	Sales Tax Payable	1,871
216	Federal Unemployment Tax Payable	51
217	State Unemployment Tax Payable	263
301	Capital Stock	40,000
305	Retained Earnings	14,908
310	Income Summary	—
401	Sales	128,231
405	Sales Discounts	214
410	Sales Returns and Allowances	1,289
501	Purchases	67,118
505	Transportation In	1,172
510	Purchases Discounts	810
515	Purchases Returns and Allowances	322
601	Advertising Expense	2,938
605	Bankcard Fees Expense	185
625	Federal Corporate Income Tax Expense	3,650
630	Insurance Expense	—
645	Maintenance Expense	2,450
650	Miscellaneous Expense	3,929
655	Payroll Tax Expense	834
657	Rent Expense	10,750
660	Salaries Expense	4,670
665	Supplies Expense	—
675	Utilities Expense	5,395

Continued

Peachtree®

SMART GUIDE

Step-by-Step Instructions: Problem 18-7

1. Select the problem set for Cycle Tech Bicycles (Prob. 18-7).
2. Rename the company and set the system date.
3. Print a Working Trial Balance and use it to help you prepare the adjustments.
4. Record the adjustments using the **General Journal Entry** option.
5. Print a General Journal report and proof your work.
6. Print a General Ledger Trial Balance report.
7. Answer the Analyze question.
8. End the session.

Problem 18-7 (Answers) Completing a Ten-Column Work Sheet

Adjustments:

(a) $534
(b) $2,922
(c) $675
(d) $177

Adjusted Trial Balance totals $199,424
Net Income $21,529

Analyze: The Balance Sheet section

SOLUTION NOTES

Problem 18–8 (Answers)
Completing a Ten-Column Work Sheet

Adjustments:
(a) $3,536
(b) $2,408
(c) $700
(d) $155

Adjusted Trial Balance totals $240,534
Net Income $20,727

Adjusting entries:
Aug. 31: Dr. Income Summary $3,536; Cr. Merchandise Inventory $3,536
Aug. 31: Dr. Supplies Exp. $2,408; Cr. Supplies $2,408
Aug. 31: Dr. Insurance Exp. $700; Cr. Prepaid Insurance $700
Aug. 31: Dr. Federal Corporate Income Tax Exp. $155; Cr. Federal Corporate Income Tax Pay. $155

Ending debit balances:
Merchandise Inventory $45,669
Supplies $619
Prepaid Insurance $980
Income Summary $3,536
Federal Corporate Income Tax Exp. $2,635
Insurance Exp. $700
Supplies Exp. $2,408

Ending credit balances:
Federal Corporate Income Tax Pay. $155

Analyze: $1,292

Data for Adjustments	
Ending merchandise inventory	$ 24,188
Ending supplies inventory	1,049
Insurance premium expired	675
Federal income tax expense for the month	3,827

Analyze: Which section of the work sheet had the higher balance for **Merchandise Inventory**, the Trial Balance section or the Balance Sheet section?

Peachtree®

SMART GUIDE

Step-by-Step Instructions: Problem 18–8

1. Select the problem set for River's Edge Canoe & Kayak (Prob. 18–8).
2. Rename the company and set the system date.
3. Print a Working Trial Balance and use it to help you prepare the adjustments.
4. Record the adjustments using the **General Journal Entry** option.
5. Print a General Journal report and proof your work.
6. Print a General Ledger report.
7. Print a General Ledger Trial Balance report.
8. Answer the Analyze question.
9. End the session.

TIP: Enter the adjustments as one multi-part entry to save time.

Problem 18–8 Completing a Ten-Column Work Sheet

The balances of the general ledger accounts of River's Edge Canoe & Kayak, as of August 31, are listed below.

Instructions In your working papers:

(1) Prepare a ten-column work sheet for River's Edge Canoe & Kayak for the month ended August 31. The account names are entered on the work sheet. The data for the adjustments follows:
  (a) The cost of the ending merchandise inventory is $45,669.
  (b) The cost of the supplies on hand on August 31 is $619.
  (c) The one-year insurance premium of $1,680 was paid on April 1.
  (d) The total federal income taxes owed for the year are $2,635.
(2) Enter the journal entries for the adjustments on page 31 of the general journal.
(3) Post the journal entries to the general ledger accounts.

101	Cash in Bank	$ 15,387
115	Accounts Receivable	2,852
130	Merchandise Inventory	49,205
135	Supplies	3,027
140	Prepaid Insurance	1,680
145	Delivery Equipment	19,437
150	Store Equipment	29,504
201	Accounts Payable	13,339
204	Federal Corporate Income Tax Payable	—
210	Employees' Federal Income Tax Payable	632
211	Employees' State Income Tax Payable	117
212	Social Security Tax Payable	472
213	Medicare Tax Payable	108
215	Sales Tax Payable	2,931
216	Federal Unemployment Tax Payable	77
217	State Unemployment Tax Payable	315
219	U.S. Savings Bonds Payable	150
301	Capital Stock	50,000
305	Retained Earnings	25,425
310	Income Summary	—

SOLUTION NOTES

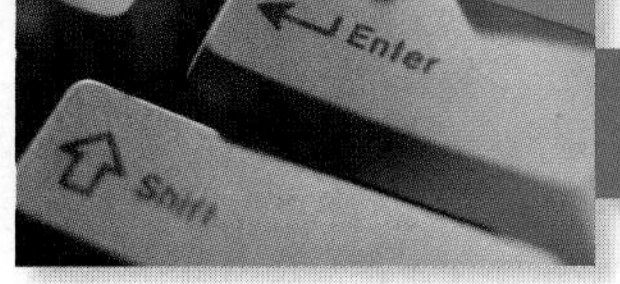

401	Sales	144,945
405	Sales Discounts	203
410	Sales Returns and Allowances	1,381
501	Purchases	79,310
505	Transportation In	1,192
510	Purchases Discounts	1,292
515	Purchases Returns and Allowances	576
601	Advertising Expense	3,151
605	Bankcard Fees Expense	288
625	Federal Corporate Income Tax Expense	2,480
635	Insurance Expense	—
650	Maintenance Expense	1,381
655	Miscellaneous Expense	3,772
658	Payroll Tax Expense	1,219
660	Rent Expense	10,350
665	Salaries Expense	11,965
670	Supplies Expense	—
680	Utilities Expense	2,595

Analyze: How much in discounts did River's Edge earn by paying the amounts owed to creditors within the discount period?

Problem 18–9 Locating Errors on the Work Sheet

The Trial Balance and adjustment sections for Buzz Newsstand have been prepared in your working papers. It is apparent from the totals on the work sheet that errors have been made in preparing these portions of the work sheet.

The accounting records show:

1. The merchandise on hand at the end of the month is valued at $12,950.
2. The supplies on hand on August 31 are valued at $529.
3. The insurance premium was paid on August 1. The premium was $980 and covers the period from August 1 to November 30.
4. The total federal income tax owed for the period is $249.

Instructions In your working papers:

(1) Find and correct the error(s) in the Trial Balance section.
(2) On the line provided on the work sheet, write in the corrected totals for the Trial Balance section.
(3) Find and correct the error(s) in the Adjustments section.
(4) Write in the corrected totals for the Adjustments columns.

Analyze: Explain your calculations for the Merchandise Inventory adjustment.

Problem 18-9 (Answers) Locating Errors on the Work Sheet

1. Employee's State Income Tax Payable should be a $26 credit. Sales Returns and Allowances should be a $126 debit.
2. Trial Balance totals $46,600.
3. Merchandise Inventory adjustment should be a $7,830 debit. Supplies adjustment should be a $445 credit. Income Summary should be a $7,830 credit. Supplies Expense should be a $445 debit.
4. Adjustment totals $8,769.

Analyze:

Merchandise on hand	$12,950
Less Beg. Inventory	5,120
Adjustment	$ 7,830

SOLUTION NOTES

CHAPTER 19 Resource Manager

Section Resources

	Objectives & Standards	Activities & Features	Reproducible Masters
Chapter Opener *Financial Statements for a Corporation*	• Explain how to record ownership of a corporation. • Explain the relationship between the work sheet and the financial statements for a merchandising corporation. • Explain how the financial statements for a corporation differ from those for a sole proprietorship. • Prepare an income statement, balance sheet, and statement of retained earnings for a merchandising corporation. • Analyze the financial data contained on the statements. • Define the accounting terms introduced in this chapter. **National Standards for Business Education**: IA14, IA16, IIA1, IIB1, IIC4–5, IIIA1, IIIA3, IIIA5, IIIA9, IIIB1–2	Exploring the Real World of Business, p. 514 Workplace Connections, p. 515	School-to-Work Handbook
Section 1 *The Ownership of a Corporation*	• Which equity accounts are used in corporation accounting. • How equity earned through business profits is reported. • Which end-of-period financial statements are prepared for a corporation.	Did You Know?, p. 518 Connect To, p. 520 A Matter of Ethics, p. 520	Strategies for Teaching Ethics in Accounting
Section 2 *The Income Statement*	• What is included in each of the five sections of the income statement. • How to prepare an income statement using four amount columns. • How to calculate the cost of merchandise sold. • How to calculate the gross profit on sales. • How to analyze the information on the income statement.	International Accounting, p. 526 Accounting Careers in Focus, p. 530	Demonstration Problems Strategies for Teaching International Accounting
Section 3 *The Statement of Retained Earnings and the Balance Sheet*	• How to prepare a statement of retained earnings for a merchandising corporation. • Prepare a balance sheet for a merchandising corporation. • How to analyze the balance sheet.	Accounting Flashbacks, p. 532 Math Hints, p. 535 Analyzing Financial Reports, p. 535	Demonstration Problems Math Review for Accounting Internet Resources and Activities Handbook

KEY

Posters — Transparency — Software — Videocassette

Blackline Masters — CD-ROM — Portfolio

MULTIMEDIA RESOURCE

Peachtree

- Problem 19–6 *Preparing a Statement of Retained Earnings and a Balance Sheet*
- Problem 19–7 *Preparing Financial Statements*
- Problem 19–8 *Completing a Work Sheet and Financial Statements*

QuickBooks

- Problem 19–5 *Preparing an Income Statement*
- Problem 19–8 *Completing a Work Sheet and Financial Statements*

Spreadsheets

- Problem 19–5 *Preparing an Income Statement*

Videos

Video Segment: Financial Statements and Analysis

After viewing this video, students will be able to explain how financial information is used by both public and private readers. Have students give an example of how financial information is analyzed and how the results are used in business decision making.

CD-ROMs

Electronic Learning Center (ELC), Chapter 19

This program is ideal for visual learners since it incorporates video images, animation, and graphics to enliven the content of each lesson.

Interactive Lesson Planner (ILP), Chapter 19

This CD-ROM combines the versatility of an electronic lesson planner with the convenience of teacher classroom resources.

SCANS Correlation Chart

FOUNDATION SKILLS

Basic Skills:	Reading	Writing	Math	Listening	Speaking	
Thinking Skills:	Creative Thinking	Decision Making	Problem Solving	Seeing Things in the Mind's Eye	Knowing How to Learn	Reasoning
Personal Qualities:	Responsibility	Self-Esteem	Sociability	Self-Management	Integrity/Honesty	

WORKPLACE COMPETENCIES

Resources:	Allocating Time	Allocating Money	Allocating Material and Facility Resources	Allocating Human Resources		
Information:	Acquiring and Evaluating Information	Organizing and Maintaining Information	Interpreting and Communicating Information	Using Computers to Process Information		
Interpersonal Skills:	Participating as a Member of a Team	Teaching Others	Serving Clients/ Customers	Exercising Leadership	Negotiating to Arrive at a Decision	Working with Cultural Diversity
Systems:	Understanding Systems	Monitoring and Correcting Performance	Improving and Designing Systems			
Technology:	Selecting Technology	Applying Technology to Task	Maintaining and Troubleshooting Technology			

*Highlighted blocks indicate areas covered in the chapter. Additional SCANS skills are also covered throughout the *Teacher Wraparound Edition.*

Assessment

Student Edition
- Check Your Understanding, pp. 521, 529, 536
- Chapter 19 Problems, pp. 541–543

Assessment and Evaluation Masters
- Chapter 19 Study Plan, *Glencoe Workbook*
- Chapter 19 Self-Test, *Glencoe Workbook*
- Chapter 19 Test, *Chapter Tests* Booklet
- Chapter 19 Activity, *School-to-Work Handbook*
- Chapter 19 **Exam***View*

Teacher Wraparound Edition
- Critical Thinking Activity, p. 528
- Reteaching Section 1, p. 521
- Reteaching Section 2, p. 529
- Reteaching Section 3, p. 536
- Chapter 19 Quiz, p. 537

Transparencies

	Teaching Transparencies	Solution Transparencies
Section 1:	19–1, 19–2	Problems 19–1, 19–2
Section 2:	19–3, 19–4, 19–5, 19–6, 19–7	Problem 19–3
Section 3:	19–8, 19–9, 19–10, 19–11	Problem 19–4
End of Chapter:		Problems 19–5, 19–6, 19–7, 19–8, Challenge Problem 19–9

TEACHER CLASSROOM RESOURCES

This is a representation of key blackline masters available in the Teacher Classroom Resources.

Teaching Aids

Transparency Examples

Section Focus Transparencies

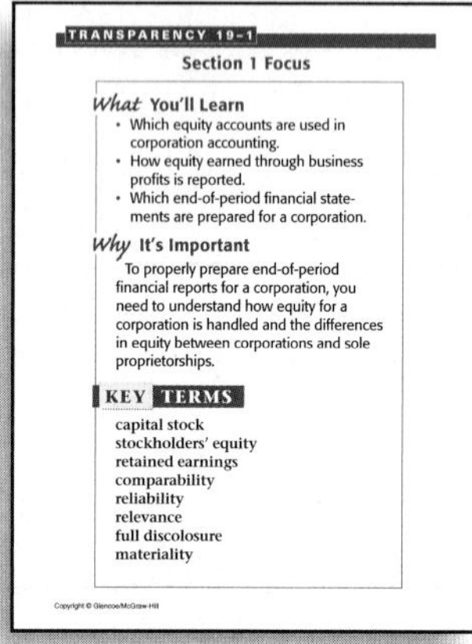

TRANSPARENCY 19-1

Section 1 Focus

What You'll Learn
- Which equity accounts are used in corporation accounting.
- How equity earned through business profits is reported.
- Which end-of-period financial statements are prepared for a corporation.

Why It's Important

To properly prepare end-of-period financial reports for a corporation, you need to understand how equity for a corporation is handled and the differences in equity between corporations and sole proprietorships.

KEY TERMS

capital stock
stockholders' equity
retained earnings
comparability
reliability
relevance
full discolosure
materiality

Teaching Transparencies

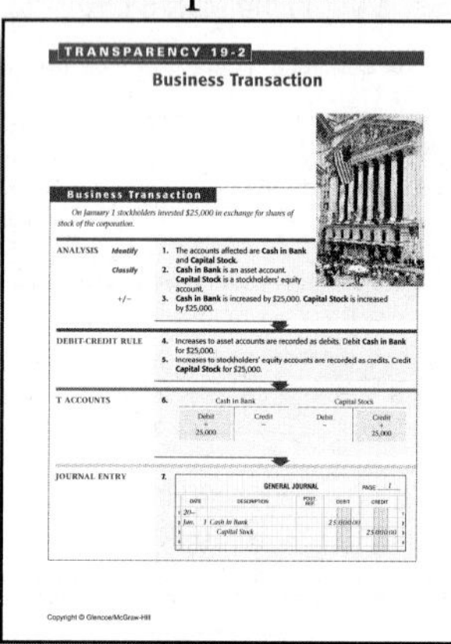

TRANSPARENCY 19-2

Business Transaction

Teaching Transparencies

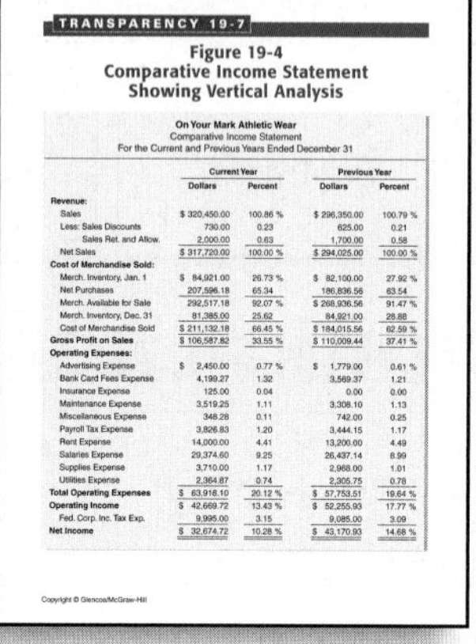

TRANSPARENCY 19-7

Figure 19-4
Comparative Income Statement
Showing Vertical Analysis

Solution Transparencies

Working Papers for End-of-Chapter Problems
Problem 19-5 Preparing an Income Statement

Demonstration Problems

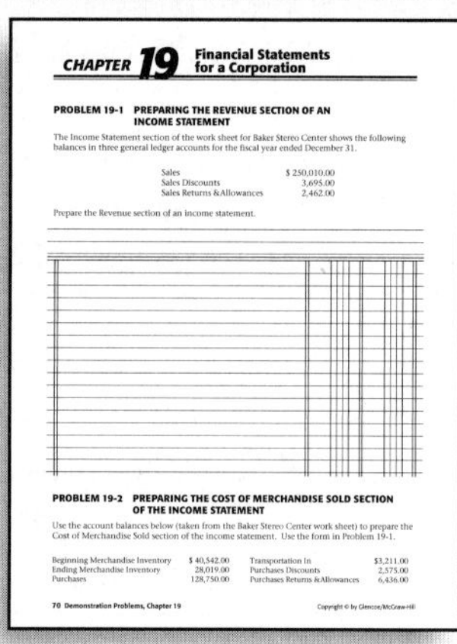

CHAPTER 19 Financial Statements for a Corporation

PROBLEM 19-1 PREPARING THE REVENUE SECTION OF AN INCOME STATEMENT

PROBLEM 19-2 PREPARING THE COST OF MERCHANDISE SOLD SECTION OF THE INCOME STATEMENT

Lesson Plans

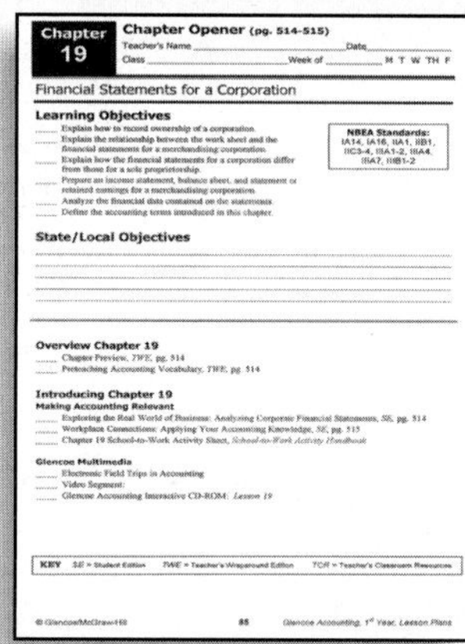

Chapter 19 Chapter Opener (pg. 514-515)

Financial Statements for a Corporation

Learning Objectives

State/Local Objectives

Overview Chapter 19

Introducing Chapter 19

Glencoe Multimedia

Block Scheduling

Block Schedule

Block scheduling differs from traditional class scheduling in the amount of time allotted to each period. The booklet explains what block scheduling is, when and how it can be implemented, and what particular benefits it provides. It also provides detailed guidelines for using the text effectively in longer class periods.

Enrichment and Application

Strategies for Teaching Ethics in Accounting

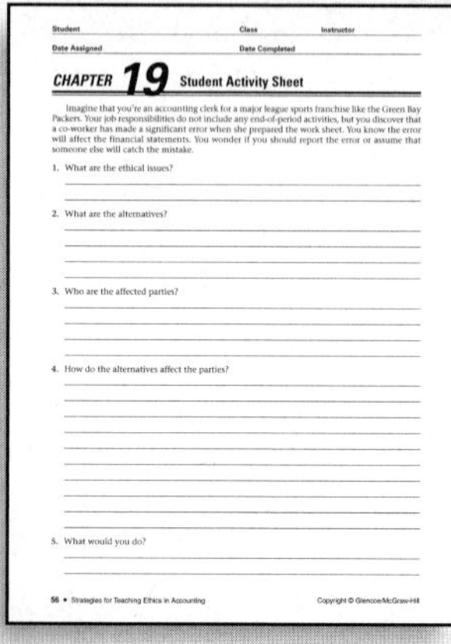

CHAPTER 19 Student Activity Sheet

1. What are the ethical issues?
2. What are the alternatives?
3. Who are the affected parties?
4. How do the alternatives affect the parties?
5. What would you do?

Strategies for Teaching International Accounting

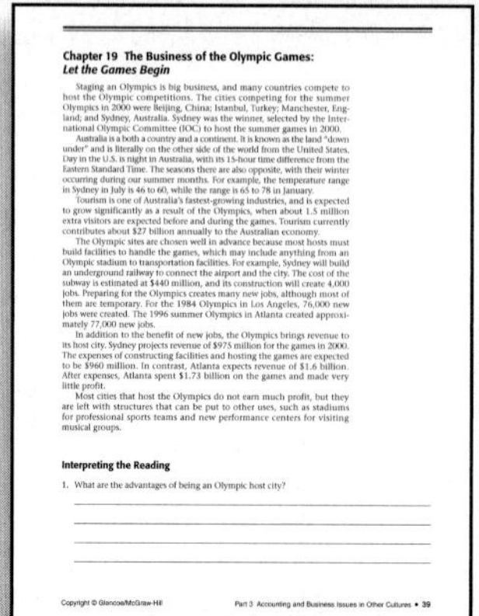

Chapter 19 The Business of the Olympic Games: *Let the Games Begin*

Interpreting the Reading

School-to-Work Handbook

CHAPTER 19 SCHOOL-TO-WORK ACTIVITY

Financial Statements for a Corporation

Meeting Different Ability Levels

Chapter Reviews and Working Papers (CRWP)

Working Papers

Review

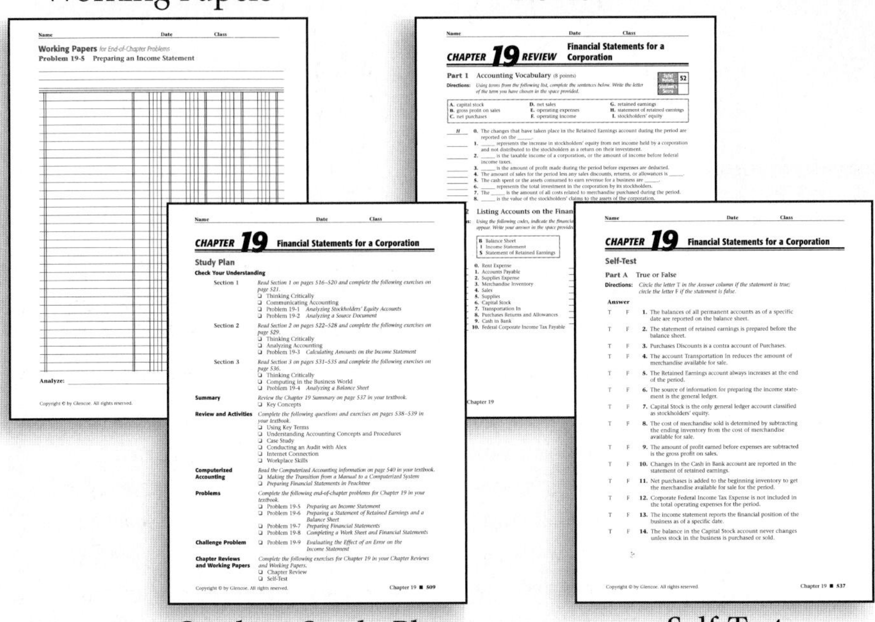

Student Study Plan

Self-Test

Real-World Multimedia CD-ROM

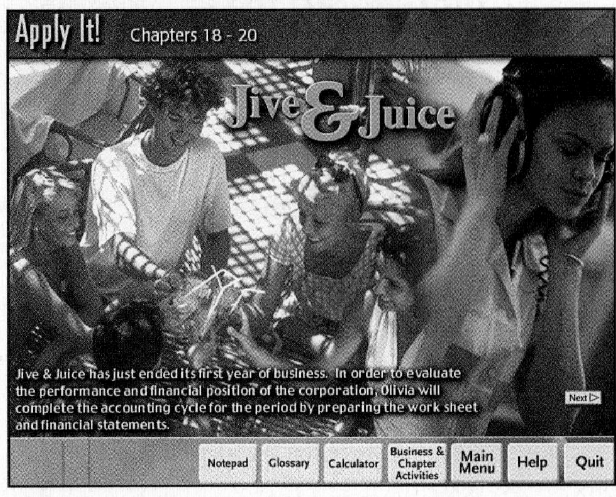

Key to Ability Levels

Each section gives skill-building activities. Each activity has been labeled for use with students of various learning styles and abilities.

L1 Level 1 activities are basic activities and should be within the range of all students.

L2 Level 2 activities are average activities and should be within the range of average and above average students.

L3 Level 3 activities are challenging activities designed for the ability range of above average students.

ELL ELL activities should be within the ability range of English Language Learners.

Teaching Resources at a Glance

Application Resources

- Glencoe Chapter Review and Working Papers, SE and TAE
- School-to-Work Handbook, SE and TM
- Accounting Portfolio, SE and TM

Reproducible Masters

- Demonstration Problems
- Lesson Plans
- Block Scheduling
- Spanish Language Resources

Glencoe Accounting Professional Development Series

- Strategies for Teaching Ethics in Accounting
- Accounting Competitive Event Review
- Math Review for Accounting
- Strategies for Teaching International Accounting
- Internet Resources and Activities Handbook

Transparency Package

- Section Focus Transparencies
- Teaching Transparencies
- Source Document Transparencies
- Solution Transparencies

Performance Assessment

- **Exam***View* CD-ROM
- Chapter Tests
- Chapter Quizzes
- Unit Tests
- Audit Tests
- Printed Testbank

Multimedia Resources

- Electronic Learning Center:
  - Multimedia CD-ROMs
  - Peachtree software, tutorials, templates, and solutions
  - Spreadsheet templates
- Using QuickBooks with Glencoe Accounting
- Interactive Lesson Planner
- Electronic Field Trips in Accounting
- PowerPoint Presentation
- Web site: glencoeaccounting.glencoe.com

Assessment and Evaluation

Chapter Tests

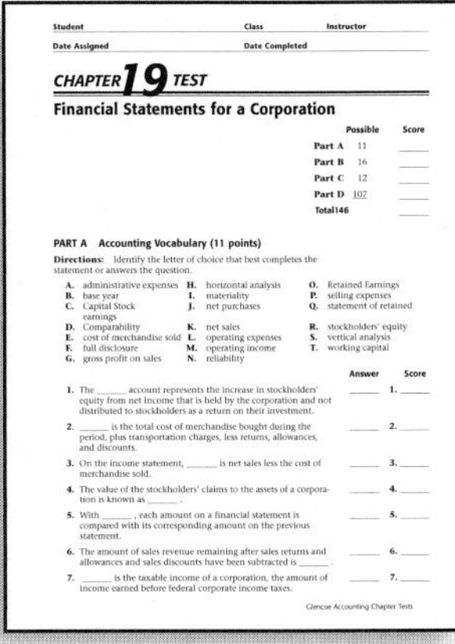

Chapter Quiz

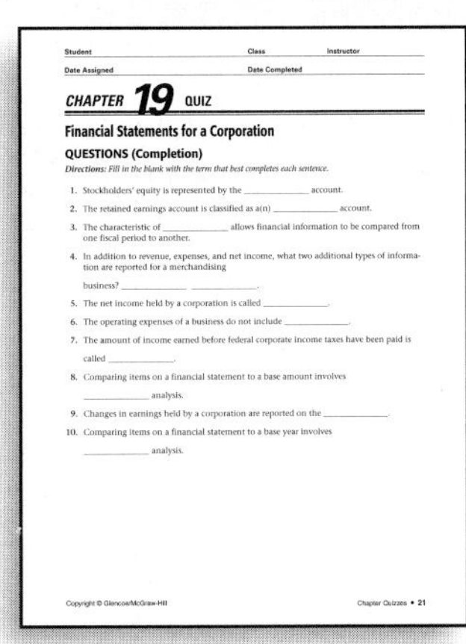

OVERVIEW
CHAPTER 19

Correlations to National Standards for Business Education
(See pages T50–T51 for a detailed correlation chart.)
Standards: IA14, IA16, IIA1, IIB1, IIC4–5, IIIA1, IIIA3, IIIA7, IIIA9, IIIB1–2

Chapter Preview
In this chapter students will learn to use work sheet information to prepare the financial statements for a merchandising business organized as a privately held corporation.

Section Overviews
- Section 1—*The Ownership of a Corporation*
- Section 2—*The Income Statement*
- Section 3—*The Statement of Retained Earnings and the Balance Sheet*

Chapter Vocabulary
capital stock
stockholders' equity
retained earnings
comparability
reliability
relevance
full disclosure
materiality
cost of merchandise sold
net sales
net purchases
gross profit on sales
operating expenses
selling expenses
administrative expenses
operating income
vertical analysis
statement of retained earnings
horizontal analysis
base year
working capital

Preteaching Accounting Vocabulary
Analysis: Bring to class several samples of published annual reports. Have students look at the reports and make a list of the types of financial information presented. Ask students how accounting records play a role in the information given. L1

CHAPTER 19

Financial Statements for a Corporation

Learning Objectives
When you have completed this chapter, you will be able to:

- Explain how to record ownership of a corporation.
- Explain the relationship between the work sheet and the financial statements for a merchandising corporation.
- Explain how the financial statements for a corporation differ from those for a sole proprietorship.
- Prepare an income statement, balance sheet, and statement of retained earnings for a merchandising corporation.
- Analyze the financial data contained on the statements.
- Define the accounting terms introduced in this chapter.

Office DEPOT

Exploring the Real World of Business
ANALYZING CORPORATE FINANCIAL STATEMENTS

Whether you need a backpack and a three-ring binder for school, or an assortment of office supplies, desks, chairs, and computers for your new business, **Office Depot** can serve you in 21 countries at over 1,000 company-owned and licensed stores and from its worldwide delivery channel through catalog sales, contract account sales, or one of its 20 unique Web sites. Founded in 1986, the company began with one modest store in Fort Lauderdale, Florida. In two short years, **Office Depot** went public and by the end of 1990, customers could shop at 173 stores in 27 states.

International joint ventures and licensing agreements placed **Office Depot** in countries like France, Japan, Mexico, Israel, Poland, and Hungary. In addition, an impressive Internet presence boosted sales by approximately $1.6 billion in 2001.

As **Office Depot** grows and strengthens, the owners of the corporation must be properly informed of the financial value and condition of the entity through the issuance of audited financial statements. Other parties like creditors, government agencies, employees, and internal managers must also be given relevant and reliable financial data upon which decisions can be based.

What do you think?
As a potential investor in **Office Depot** stock, what types of information would you be interested in?

Exploring the Real World of Business

Office Depot
Office Depot is the world's largest seller of office products and an industry leader in most distribution channels, including direct mail, contract delivery, the Internet, and business-to-business electronic commerce. Have students discuss these distribution channels.

What do you think? (Answers)
Answers will vary. Students should recognize the importance of growth in sales and net income, sufficient assets, reasonable debt levels, and liquidity. Potential investors would be interested in stock price trends and capital spending policies.

Workplace Connections

Applying Your Accounting Knowledge

Once the work sheet is completed, the accounting staff is ready to prepare financial statements. If you've listened to the evening news on television, you might remember an announcer reporting earnings increases or decreases for a large national corporation. This information is found in the financial statements or annual reports of the company.

Investigate:

1. Is your employer a public corporation?
2. Are the financial statements available for you to look at?
3. Can they be found on the Internet or in your local library?

Glencoe Accounting Online

Visit the *Glencoe Accounting* Web site at **glencoeaccounting.glencoe.com** for additional activities and information.

GLENCOE MULTIMEDIA

Electronic Field Trips in Accounting *Video Segment: Financial Statements and Analysis*
After viewing this video, students will be able to explain how financial information is used by both public and private readers; give an example of how financial information is analyzed and how the results are used in business decision making.

Glencoe Accounting: Electronic Learning Center *Chapter 19*
The CD-ROM program is ideal for visual learners since it incorporates video images, animation, and graphics to enliven the content of each lesson.

INTRODUCING
CHAPTER 19

Making Accounting Relevant

Workplace Connections: Applying Your Accounting Knowledge

Discussion: Spend some time with students discussing how to find financial information about public corporations. Many corporations have Web sites where they provide financial data. Corporations are also required to file financial data with the SEC, and much data is available through the federal government's EDGAR database, which is accessible online (www.sec.gov).

Investigate (Answers)

1. Answers will vary.
2. Answers will vary. If the corporation is public, financial statements will be available in annual reports. If the corporation is privately held, financial data may not be available to the public.
3. Many annual reports are available via the Internet. Public libraries often have annual reports, though they may have only those for the largest, best-known corporations.

School-to-Work Activity

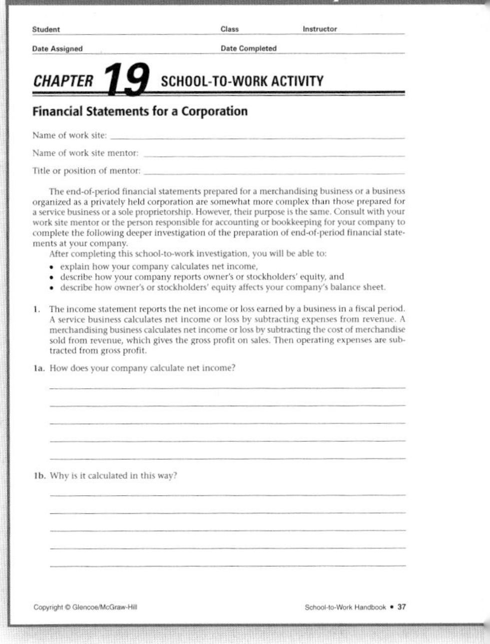

Student ______ Class ______ Instructor ______

Date Assigned ______ Date Completed ______

CHAPTER 19 SCHOOL-TO-WORK ACTIVITY

Financial Statements for a Corporation

Name of work site: ______

Name of work site mentor: ______

Title or position of mentor: ______

The end-of-period financial statements prepared for a merchandising business or a business organized as a privately held corporation are somewhat more complex than those prepared for a service business or a sole proprietorship. However, their purpose is the same. Consult with your work site mentor or the person responsible for accounting or bookkeeping for your company to complete the following deeper investigation of the preparation of end-of-period financial statements at your company.

After completing this school-to-work investigation, you will be able to:

- explain how your company calculates net income,
- describe how your company reports owner's or stockholders' equity, and
- describe how owner's or stockholders' equity affects your company's balance sheet.

1. The income statement reports the net income or loss earned by a business in a fiscal period. A service business calculates net income or loss by subtracting expenses from revenue. A merchandising business calculates net income or loss by subtracting the cost of merchandise sold from revenue, which gives the gross profit on sales. Then operating expenses are subtracted from gross profit.

1a. How does your company calculate net income?

______

1b. Why is it calculated in this way?

______

1 FOCUS

Introducing the Section
In this section students learn how the equity for a corporation differs from that for a sole proprietorship. Students learn about the Retained Earnings account and how it is used, along with the characteristics of financial statements that make the information they report useful to a broad variety of readers.

Section Concepts
- Which equity accounts are used in corporation accounting.
- How equity earned through business profits is reported.
- Which end-of-period financial statements are prepared for a corporation.

Visual Learning

Section 1 Focus

Use **Transparency 19–1** to introduce section concepts.

BELL RINGER

Compare and Contrast: Have students bring to class the business section of a local or regional newspaper, or provide a few copies for the class. Have students look up the stock listings for well-known companies such as IBM or Procter and Gamble (NYSE). Then have students search for companies such as SAS Institute or Kinko's, both of which are privately held corporations and thus will not be listed. Have students discuss the differences between privately held and public corporations. L1

SECTION 1

The Ownership of a Corporation

What You'll Learn
- Which equity accounts are used in corporation accounting.
- How equity earned through business profits is reported.
- Which end-of-period financial statements are prepared for a corporation.

Why It's Important
To properly prepare end-of-period financial reports for a corporation, you need to understand how equity for a corporation is handled and the differences in equity between corporations and sole proprietorships.

KEY TERMS
Capital Stock
stockholders' equity
retained earnings
comparability
reliability
relevance
full disclosure
materiality

In Chapter 18 you learned that some accounts in the general ledger are not up-to-date at the end of a period. You learned how to determine which accounts to adjust, how to calculate the amount of each adjustment, and how to enter each adjustment on a ten-column work sheet.

The work sheet is a working paper, organizing all the accounting data needed to prepare the financial statements and the end-of-period journal entries. In this chapter you will use the information on the work sheet to prepare the financial statements for a merchandising corporation. Businesses like John Deere & Co. focus a lot of time and attention on the preparation of financial statements.

Accounting for a Corporation

A sole proprietorship is owned by one person. A corporation may be owned by one person or by thousands of people. The ownership of a corporation is represented by shares of stock. After completing this chapter and following chapters, you will be able to identify the various accounting functions involved with a corporation.

Recording the Ownership of a Corporation

As you recall, investments made by the owner of a sole proprietorship are recorded in the owner's capital account. An owner's investment of $25,000 in a sole proprietorship is recorded as shown in the T accounts. **Cash in Bank** is debited for $25,000, and **Maria Sanchez, Capital** is credited for $25,000.

Cash in Bank		Maria Sanchez, Capital	
Debit + 25,000	Credit –	Debit –	Credit + 25,000

If a business is organized as a corporation, the owner's capital account used in a sole proprietorship is replaced by an account named **Capital Stock. Capital Stock** represents the investments in the corporation by its stockholders (owners).

RESOURCE MANAGER

Reproducible Masters
- Lesson Plans
- Chapter Reviews and Working Papers (CRWP) TAE

Transparencies
- Section Focus Transparency
- Teaching Transparencies
- Source Document Transparencies
- Solution Transparencies

Multimedia
- Exam*View* CD-ROM
- Electronic Learning Center CD-ROM
- Interactive Lesson Planner CD-ROM
- Electronic Field Trips in Accounting

Capital Stock is classified as a stockholders' equity account. **Stockholders' equity** is the value of the stockholders' claims to the corporation. Like the owner's capital account in a sole proprietorship, increases to the **Capital Stock** account are recorded as credits and decreases are recorded as debits.

Business Transaction

On January 1 stockholders invested $25,000 in exchange for shares of stock of the corporation, Receipt 997.

ANALYSIS

Identify 1. The accounts affected are **Cash in Bank** and **Capital Stock.**

Classify 2. **Cash in Bank** is an asset account. **Capital Stock** is a stockholders' equity account.

+/− 3. **Cash in Bank** is increased by $25,000. **Capital Stock** is increased by $25,000.

DEBIT-CREDIT RULE

4. Increases to asset accounts are recorded as debits. Debit **Cash in Bank** for $25,000.
5. Increases to stockholders' equity accounts are recorded as credits. Credit **Capital Stock** for $25,000.

T ACCOUNTS

6.

Cash in Bank	
Debit + 25,000	Credit −

Capital Stock	
Debit −	Credit + 25,000

JOURNAL ENTRY

7.

GENERAL JOURNAL PAGE 1

	DATE		DESCRIPTION	POST. REF.	DEBIT	CREDIT	
1	20--						1
2	Jan.	1	Cash in Bank		25 000 00		2
3			Capital Stock			25 000 00	3
4			Receipt 997				4

Reporting Stockholders' Equity in a Corporation

The form of business organization does not affect the amount of equity in the business. That is, one person may have an ownership interest in a sole proprietorship worth $80,000, or ten people may have shares of stock in a corporation worth a total of $80,000. The difference is in the way these two amounts are reported on the balance sheet.

2 TEACH

GUIDED PRACTICE

Reading Accounting

- Show students how to read the information provided in the stock listings in your local newspaper's financial section. L1
- Have students find information about the stock exchange in the country of their first language (for example, the Hong Kong Stock Exchange). If possible, have students discuss the differences between U.S. and foreign stock exchanges. ELL

Concept Development: Accounting for a Corporation

Discussion: Discuss the difference in equity accounts for the sole proprietorship versus the corporation. The corporation used as an example in this accounting cycle is organized as a privately held corporation, so its capital stock is not traded on a public stock exchange. Publicly held corporations may issue several different kinds of stock, as well as declaring dividends and issuing bonds. L1

Visual Learning

Business Transaction

Use **Transparency 19–2** to guide students through the analysis and recording of the issuance of capital stock.

Great Ideas *From the Classroom of...*

Mnemonics Have students remember the six steps in analyzing transactions by using mnemonics. For example:

1. **Identify** the accounts affected.
2. **Classify** the accounts affected.
3. **Determine** the amount of increase or decrease for each account affected.
4. Which account is **debited**?
5. Which account is **credited**?
6. What is the complete entry in **T-account** form?

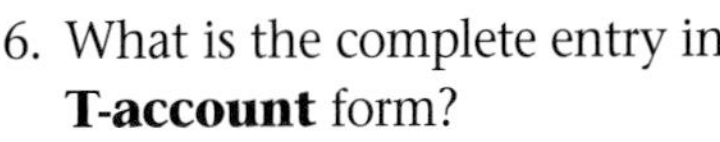

"**I** can **d**ream, **d**ance, **c**reate, and **t**hink."

Alfonso Vargas
Hueneme High School
Oxnard, CA

2 TEACH (Cont'd.)

Teaching Tips

Compare the different types of equity for a corporation (equity contributed by stockholders) versus equity earned by the business (retained earnings). Explain why both are needed for an organization to remain financially healthy.

Review the rules of debit and credit for the capital account for a sole proprietorship and then relate them to the Capital Stock account.

Remind students that an ownership interest is the same as a financial claim to the assets of the business.

Capital Stock is also the legal capital of a corporation, which means that it cannot be paid back to the stockholders and must remain with the corporation to protect the interests of creditors.

The Retained Earnings account represents the profits made and kept by the corporation (versus profits paid out as dividends to stockholders). Corporations retain profits to grow the business through investments in operating assets.

Did You Know?

Ticket Prices
Season tickets to NHL games cost from as little as $500 to over $3,000 for regular seats. Tickets for individual games average from $20 to $75.

A sole proprietorship reports the balance of the owner's capital account in the owner's equity section of the balance sheet. For a corporation the owner's equity section of the balance sheet is called stockholders' equity. The law requires that stockholders' equity be reported in two parts: (1) equity contributed by stockholders and (2) equity earned through business profits.

Equity Contributed by Stockholders

The first part of stockholders' equity is the amount of money invested by stockholders. This amount is comparable to the investments made by the owner in a sole proprietorship. In a corporation stockholders contribute to equity by buying shares of stock issued by the corporation. Stockholders' investments are recorded in the **Capital Stock** account.

Equity Earned Through Business Profits

The second part of stockholders' equity is the amount of accumulated net income earned and retained by the corporation. This amount is comparable to the amount of net income less any withdrawals by the owner in a sole proprietorship. In a corporation this amount, called **Retained Earnings**, represents the increase in stockholders' equity from the portion of net income not distributed to the stockholders.

Earnings retained by a corporation are recorded in the **Retained Earnings** account. **Retained Earnings** is classified as a stockholders' equity account. Like the **Capital Stock** account, it is increased by credits and decreased by debits. **Retained Earnings** has a normal credit balance.

Retained Earnings	
Debit – Decrease Side	Credit + Increase Side Normal Balance

In a sole proprietorship, net income increases owner's capital. This increase in owner's capital represents an increase in the assets of the business. In a corporation net income increases retained earnings, which represents the growth, or increase, in the assets of the corporation.

Balance Sheet Presentation

A comparison of the capital section of the balance sheet for a sole proprietorship and for a corporation follows:

Sole Proprietorship	Corporation
Owner's Equity:	Stockholders' Equity:
Owner's Capital	Capital Stock
	Retained Earnings

MAKING CONNECTIONS TO DAILY LIFE

Direct Sales Avon Products, Inc. now accepts orders through its online stores. Its traditional direct sales approach, however, continues to generate much of the company's revenue. Many people, including teenagers, have become successful entrepreneurs selling Avon products. To calculate their net income, Avon representatives must determine their cost of goods sold. The cost of goods sold includes the cost of purchasing Avon products from the Avon distribution centers and the shipping costs to have the products delivered to the sales representative's home.

Characteristics of Financial Information

At the end of a period, a business prepares various financial statements. These statements summarize the changes that have taken place during the period and report the financial condition of the business at the end of the period. Financial statements are used by many groups:

- Managers analyze the financial statements to help evaluate past performance and to make informed decisions and predictions that will affect future operations.
- Stockholders are interested in the performance, potential future growth, and success of the business.
- Creditors want to know the ability of the business to pay its debts in a timely manner and the amount of credit that should be extended to the business.
- Government agencies, employees, consumers, and the general public are also interested in the financial position of the business.

Key Points

The Accounting Equation

The basic accounting equation applies to the accounting system in any business regardless of the form of business organization:

Assets = Liabilities + Stockholders' (Owner's) Equity

Increases in owner's capital or in retained earnings also represent increases in assets.

Comparability

For accounting information to be useful, it must be understandable and comparable. Thus, for the financial reports to be useful, the data must be presented in a way that lets users recognize similarities, differences, and trends from one period to another. **Comparability** allows accounting information to be compared from one fiscal period to another. The same types of statements, therefore, are prepared at the end of each period. The length of time covered by the financial statements is the same from one period to another (for example, one month or one year). By comparing financial statements in different periods of equal length, financial patterns and relationships can be identified and analyzed and the information from the analysis can be used in making decisions regarding business operations. Comparability also allows the comparison of financial information between businesses.

Reliability

Users of accounting data assume that the data are reliable. **Reliability** relates to the confidence users have that the financial information is reasonably free from bias and error.

Relevance

Not all information about a business is relevant to financial decision making. In accounting, **relevance** means that the information "makes a difference" to a user in reaching a business decision.

Full Disclosure

To "disclose" means "to uncover or to make known." **Full disclosure** means that financial reports include enough information so that the report is complete.

2 TEACH (Cont'd.)

Concept Development: Characteristics of Financial Information

Discussion: Discuss the characteristics and guidelines accountants follow when preparing financial statements. Relate each of the characteristics to something students will understand. For example, ask students what information is relevant when reporting the outcome of a sporting event.

Point out that full disclosure requires reports to be complete enough not to mislead a reader.

Also review some of the other basic accounting concepts students have learned in previous chapters of the book: business entity, going concern, unit of measure, time period, revenue principle, matching principle, guideline of conservatism. **L1**

Teaching Tips

The assumption of time period means that the same time span is used from one fiscal period to another.

The accounting characteristic of comparability allows data to be compared over several fiscal periods. When discussing comparability, ask students whether they could tell which school has the best team if game scores were reported using different rules for each school.

Explain that materiality is not just a matter of size. It relates to whether the inclusion of specific information would have any impact on interpretations by readers of a report.

INTERDISCIPLINARY CONNECTIONS ACTIVITY

(Refer to the *Connect To...Health* feature on page 520.)

Health Have your students do some comparison shopping of financial software programs specifically for the medical and health-care industry. Students can check with computer hardware and software vendors, catalogs, magazine advertisements, or other media. Ask students to create a table with the comparison information. Once they have completed their lists, facilitate a classroom discussion about the various pros and cons of each software package.

2 TEACH (Cont'd.)

Teaching Tips
Discuss the characteristics that financial statements for U.S. businesses have in common. Point out that the characteristics result from accounting standards that all businesses are required to follow.

Corporations prepare the same types of financial statements at the end of each fiscal period. Remind students that the same time period is used so that financial statements may be compared from one period to the next. For example, if the fiscal period is a calendar year, the financial statements would cover January through December each year, not January through December one year and April through March the next year.

Remind students that the work sheet is the source of information for preparing the financial statements.

Critical Thinking: Ask students how they think the U.S. accounting system helps make financial statements reliable. (Accounting requirements are strict, especially as compared with those in other countries. Since all U.S. companies must follow the same rules, financial reports tend to be reliable unless a company deliberately breaks accounting rules and misreports financial data.) L3

Strategies for Teaching Ethics in Accounting
Photocopy the Chapter 19 *Student Activity Sheet* for students. Answers are also provided in the booklet.

CONNECT TO . . . HEALTH

Because each patient may have a different insurance plan or payment plan, professionals in the health field, such as doctors and dentists, have to handle accounting as well. As a result, programmers have developed specialized software that both prints out proper paperwork and keeps track of the bills.

Materiality

If something is "material," it is important. In accounting, **materiality** means that information deemed relative should be included in financial reports.

Computerized Accounting Systems

Today most businesses rely on automated equipment or computers to maintain the general and subsidiary ledgers and to prepare the end-of-period financial statements. Computers offer the advantages of speed and accuracy. Even small businesses can afford computers and accounting software designed for their needs. On the other hand, some businesses prefer to have an outside company maintain their accounting records and prepare their financial statements.

Financial Statements for a Merchandising Corporation

On Your Mark Athletic Wear, a merchandising corporation, prepares three financial statements: the income statement, the statement of retained earnings, and the balance sheet. The first two statements report the changes that have taken place over the period. The third statement, the balance sheet, shows the financial position of the business on a specific date—the last day of the period. The data needed to complete all three statements come from the work sheet.

A MATTER OF ETHICS

Reporting a Mistake

Imagine that you're an accounting clerk for a major league sports franchise like the Green Bay Packers. Your job responsibilities do not include any end-of-period activities, but you discover that a co-worker has made a significant error when she prepared the work sheet. You know the error will affect the financial statements. You wonder if you should report the error or assume that someone else will catch the mistake.

Ethical Decision Making:

- What are the ethical issues?
- What are the alternatives?
- Who are the affected parties?
- How do the alternatives affect the parties?
- What would you do?

Teaching A MATTER OF ETHICS

Reporting a Mistake Have students discuss the circumstances that might affect their decisions. For example, do they get along well with the person who has made the mistake? Will pointing out the mistake cause hard feelings? How does being a good team member affect the decision? Do they have a sense of pride and responsibility in seeing that the work of the group is accurate? Do students think it's better to mind your own business or to help others at work?

SECTION 1 Check Your Understanding

Now that you have studied this section, complete the following questions and problems.

Thinking Critically

1. What two parts of stockholders' equity are required by law to be reported on the balance sheet?
2. What is the purpose of preparing the same types of financial statements at the end of each period?

Communicating Accounting

As the CEO of First Rate Products, you are expected to present accurate financial statements at your next stockholders' meeting. It is imperative that your recently-hired accounting clerk, Vanessa Fuller, understand the importance of the end-of-period financial statements. Write a clear, concise memorandum to her outlining the end-of-period financial statements you are required to present at the meeting. Make sure Vanessa understands the importance of each financial statement and the relationships of those statements to the overall performance of First Rate Products.

Problem 19–1 Analyzing Stockholders' Equity Accounts

1. An investment of $60,000 by Kevin Cleary in his sole proprietorship is recorded as a credit to which account?
2. The sale of 100 shares of stock, for $8,500, by the Sims Corporation is recorded as a credit to which account?
3. Stockholders' equity consists of which two accounts?

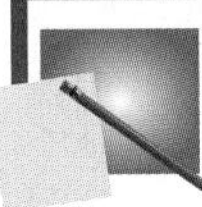

Problem 19–2 Analyzing a Source Document

A sales slip for Cindy's Curtains is presented at right. The accountant noticed errors in the calculations.

Instructions Check all calculations and recalculate the sales tax using a rate of 4 percent.

Cindy's Curtains
432 Meadowbrook Street
Wilcoxson, Georgia 30345-8417
404-555-2488

DATE: June 26, 20-- NO. 1441

SOLD TO: Rachel C. Washington
59 Priscilla Drive
Park Ridge, IL 60068

CLERK	CASH	CHARGE	TERMS
K.C.	✓		

QTY.	DESCRIPTION	UNIT PRICE	AMOUNT
2	Curtain Rods #21847	$ 14.95	$ 29 09
4	Anchor Pieces #23104	6.75	27 00
15	Feet of ribbon per ft.	0.89	13 00
		SUBTOTAL	$ 69 09
		SALES TAX	2 76
	Thank You!	TOTAL	$ 71 85

RETEACHING SECTION 1

Explaining Retained Earnings Some students may be confused by the Retained Earnings account. A sole proprietorship does not need a Retained Earnings account because the revenue is closed into the owner's capital account. The revenue of a corporation, however, cannot be closed into capital because that account represents the stockholders' equity. Stockholders cannot withdraw funds from a corporation (in contrast to the sole proprietor's ability to withdraw funds). Funds can only be paid out to stockholders through dividends if the corporate board decides to do so. If no dividends are declared for the stockholders, the corporation retains all the revenue (thus, the name Retained Earnings).

3 ASSESS

Thinking Critically (Answers)

1. Equity contributed by stockholders, equity earned through business profits.
2. To enable comparisons of financial data to identify financial patterns and relationships for use in making decisions about the business.

Communicating Accounting (Answers)

Answers will vary. Students should emphasize the importance of comparability, reliability, relevance, and full disclosure.

Problem 19–1 (Answers)

Kevin Cleary, Capital
Capital Stock
Capital Stock and Retained Earnings

Problem 19–2 (Answers)

Subtotal $70.25
Sales Tax $2.81
Total $73.06

Chapter Reviews and Working Papers Refer students to the Chapter 19 workbook pages to answer *Check Your Understanding* activities.

4 CLOSE

Section Wrap-Up

Demonstrate: Write the characteristics of financial statements on the chalkboard, leaving space for students to add descriptions. Ask for volunteers to write a description of each characteristic and give an example. L1

1 FOCUS

Introducing the Section
Now that students have learned some of the characteristics of financial statements, in this section they will learn how to prepare an income statement for a corporation.

Section Concepts
- What is included in each of the five sections of the income statement.
- How to prepare an income statement using four amount columns.
- How to calculate the cost of merchandise sold.
- How to calculate the gross profit on sales.
- How to analyze the information on the income statement.

Visual Learning

Section 2 Focus

Use **Transparency 19–3** to introduce section concepts.

BELL RINGER

Identifying: Bring several annual reports to class. Have students form groups, and give each group a report. Ask each group to look at the income statement (also called the statement of operations) and make a list of the different sections on the statement. Have groups share their lists. Relate information in the section to the published reports. L1

SECTION 2

The Income Statement

What **You'll Learn**
- What is included in each of the five sections of the income statement.
- How to prepare an income statement using four amount columns.
- How to calculate the cost of merchandise sold.
- How to calculate the gross profit on sales.
- How to analyze the information on the income statement.

Why **It's Important**

The income statement reports the net income or loss for the period and indicates whether or not the business is operating efficiently.

KEY TERMS

net sales
net purchases
gross profit on sales
operating expenses
selling expenses
administrative expenses
operating income
vertical analysis

In Section 1 you learned that there are three financial statements prepared by corporations at the end of each period. In this section you will learn how to prepare and analyze the income statement. Every year John Deere & Co. expects the March income statement to show a large profit as farmers get ready for the new growing season.

The Income Statement

As you know, the income statement reports the net income or loss earned by a business. In Chapter 9 you prepared an income statement for Roadrunner Delivery Service, a service business organized as a sole proprietorship. You subtracted total expenses from revenue to determine the net income or loss for the period.

Merchandising businesses have an additional cost—the cost of the merchandise that is purchased and then resold to customers. The income statement for a merchandising business is thus expanded to include the cost of merchandise sold.

An income statement for a merchandising business has five sections:

- Revenue
- Cost of Merchandise Sold
- Gross Profit on Sales
- Operating Expenses
- Net Income (or Loss)

A comparison of the income statements for a service business and for a merchandising business follows:

Service Business	Merchandising Business
Roadrunner Delivery Service	*On Your Mark Athletic Wear*
Revenue	Revenue
− Expenses	− Cost of Merchandise Sold
Net Income (Loss)	Gross Profit on Sales
	− Operating Expenses
	Net Income (Loss)

As you can see from **Figure 19–1**, On Your Mark's income statement has four amount columns. The far right column is used to enter totals. The other columns are used to enter balances that are added or subtracted. Note that the format of a computer-generated income statement may vary from the format of an income statement prepared manually on accounting stationery. Regardless of how an income statement is prepared, the formats are very similar.

RESOURCE MANAGER

Reproducible Masters
- Lesson Plans
- Chapter Reviews and Working Papers (CRWP) TAE
- Demonstration Problems

Transparencies
- Section Focus Transparency
- Teaching Transparencies
- Source Document Transparencies
- Solution Transparencies

Multimedia
- Exam*View* CD-ROM
- Electronic Learning Center CD-ROM
- Interactive Lesson Planner CD-ROM
- Electronic Field Trips in Accounting

On Your Mark Athletic Wear				
Income Statement				
For the Year Ended December 31, 20--				
Revenue:				
Sales			320 450 00	
Less: Sales Discounts		730 00		
Sales Returns and Allowances		2 000 00	2 730 00	
Net Sales				317 720 00

Figure 19–1 The Heading and Revenue Section of the Income Statement

All of the information needed to prepare the income statement comes from the work sheet, particularly the Income Statement section. As with all other financial statements, the income statement begins with a three-line heading. The income statement for On Your Mark is prepared for the year ended December 31.

The Revenue Section

The first section on the income statement is the revenue section. This section reports the net sales for the period. The balances of the **Sales** revenue account and the **Sales Discounts** and **Sales Returns and Allowances** contra revenue accounts are reported in this section. Remember, contra revenue accounts decrease the revenue account. Therefore, **net sales** is the amount of sales for the period less any sales discounts, returns, and allowances. Refer to **Figure 19–1** as you learn how to complete the revenue section.

1. On the first line, enter the classification "Revenue:" at the left edge of the stationery.
2. On the second line, enter the name of the revenue account "**Sales**," indented about half an inch. Enter the balance of the account in the *third* amount column.
3. On the next lines, enter the deductions from **Sales.** Write the word "Less:" followed by the names and balances of the two contra revenue accounts. (You may have to abbreviate the account names.) Enter the balances of the accounts in the *second* amount column.
4. Add the balances of the two contra revenue accounts. Write the total below the **Sales** balance on the fourth line, in the *third* amount column.
5. On the next line, enter the words "Net Sales," indented about an inch. Subtract the total of the two contra accounts from the balance of the **Sales** account. Enter the amount in the *fourth* amount column. On Your Mark's net sales for the year are $317,720.

The Cost of Merchandise Sold Section

The next section reports the cost of merchandise sold. As the words indicate, the "cost of merchandise sold" is the actual cost to the business of the merchandise that was sold to customers during the period.

ACCOUNTING ISSUES

The Power of Information Technology Information technology has changed the way financial statements are prepared, audited, and used. In the early 1900s, financial statements provided a large part of the information available about a business to its investors. Today, however, investors can get up-to-the-minute data about companies through public and proprietary databases without waiting for quarterly or annual reports. Using information technology, CPAs can provide financial statements in a more timely manner. With so much information available, auditors also use technology to help clients interpret information and determine what data is relevant.

2 TEACH

GUIDED PRACTICE

Reading Accounting

- Using published annual reports, have students read a section and make a list of the words they do not know. Have them look up the words, then discuss their use in class. L1

Concept Development: The Income Statement

Discussion: Refer back to the income statement students learned in Chapter 9, which had these parts: revenue, expenses, and net income (or loss). Two additional sections used by a merchandising business are added in this chapter: cost of merchandise sold and gross profit on sales. Discuss each section and how it relates to a merchandising business. L1

Visual Learning

Figure 19–1 The Heading and Revenue Section of the Income Statement

Using **Transparency 19–4,** review the information in the heading of the income statement. Discuss the four amount columns and the order of entering information in each column.

Teaching Tip

When introducing the revenue section, discuss the difference between net sales and total revenue.

Demonstration Problem Step-by-Step Practice

Use demonstration problem 19–1 here to give students practice in preparing the revenue section of an income statement.

2 TEACH (Cont'd.)

Teaching Tips

When presenting the cost of merchandise sold section, write each entry on the chalkboard and have students explain each item. Help students to think each step through logically rather than memorizing each label.

Point out that the inventory balance represents the amount the business paid for the merchandise sold by the business. Remind students that the beginning and ending inventory balances are taken from the Trial Balance and Balance Sheet sections of the work sheet.

Remind students that Purchases, Transportation In, Purchases Discounts, and Purchases Returns and Allowances are all classified as cost of merchandise accounts. All are temporary accounts, thus their balances are found in the Income Statement section of the work sheet.

Demonstration Problem Step-by-Step Practice

Use demonstration problem 19–2 to give students practice in completing the cost of merchandise sold section of the income statement.

The cost of merchandise sold is calculated as follows:

Beginning Merchandise Inventory
+ Net Purchases During the Period
Cost of Merchandise Available for Sale
– Ending Merchandise Inventory
Cost of Merchandise Sold

There are two steps involved in calculating the cost of merchandise sold. The first step is to determine the cost of all the merchandise available for sale. The second step is to calculate the cost of merchandise sold.

Net Purchases

To calculate the cost of merchandise available for sale, add net purchases to the beginning inventory amount. **Net purchases** is all the costs related to merchandise purchased during the period. To calculate net purchases, add the transportation charges for the period (**Transportation In**) to the **Purchases** balance and then subtract the balances of **Purchases Discounts** and **Purchases Returns and Allowances.**

Purchases
+ Transportation In
Cost of Delivered Merchandise
– Purchases Discounts
– Purchases Returns and Allowances
Net Purchases

> **Key Points**
>
> **Cost of Merchandise**
> **Transportation In** increases the cost of merchandise. **Purchases Discounts** and **Purchases Returns and Allowances** decrease the cost of the merchandise.

Cost of Merchandise Sold

To calculate the cost of merchandise sold, subtract the ending merchandise inventory amount from the cost of merchandise available for sale. Refer to **Figure 19–2** as you learn how to complete the cost of merchandise sold section.

1. On the line below net sales, enter the words "Cost of Merchandise Sold:" at the left edge.
2. Next, enter "Merchandise Inventory, January 1, 20—" indented about half an inch. Enter the amount of the beginning inventory in the *third* amount column. (The beginning inventory is found on the work sheet, in the Trial Balance section, on the Merchandise Inventory line.)
3. Next, enter "Purchases", indented about half an inch, and place the **Purchases** account balance in the *first* amount column.
4. On the next line, enter "Plus: Transportation In" indented about half an inch. Enter the balance of the **Transportation In** account in the *first* amount column, below the **Purchases** amount. Draw a line across the *first* amount column under the **Transportation In** amount.
5. On the next line, enter "Cost of Delivered Merchandise" indented about half an inch. Add the balances of the **Purchases** and **Transportation In** accounts. Enter the result in the *second* amount column.
6. On the next line, enter "Less: Purchases Discounts," indented about half an inch, and place the **Purchases Discounts** account balance in the *first* amount column.

MEETING SPECIAL NEEDS

Students with Learning Disabilities Students with learning disabilities may have trouble acquiring information from the written word. Show them how to get information focusing on the learning objectives, the list of key terms and highlighted vocabulary, the chapter headings, illustrations, and the chapter summaries. Emphasize the value in studying the Business Transaction Analysis boxes, and encourage students to read the notes for key points and accounting tips.

On Your Mark Athletic Wear
Income Statement
For the Year Ended December 31, 20--

Revenue:				
Sales			320,450.00	
Less: Sales Discounts		730.00		
Sales Returns and Allowances		2,000.00	2,730.00	
Net Sales				317,720.00
Cost of Merchandise Sold:				
Merchandise Inventory, January 1, 20--			84,921.00	
Purchases	206,700.00			
Plus: Transportation In	4,036.18			
Cost of Delivered Merchandise		210,736.18		
Less: Purchases Discounts	1,340.00			
Purchases Returns and Allowances	1,800.00	3,140.00		
Net Purchases			207,596.18	
Cost of Merchandise Available			292,517.18	
Merchandise Inventory, December 31, 20--			81,385.00	
Cost of Merchandise Sold				211,132.18
Gross Profit on Sales				106,587.82

Figure 19–2 Income Statement Through Gross Profit on Sales

7. On the next line, enter "Purchases Returns and Allowances" indented about half an inch, and place the **Purchases Returns and Allowances** account balance in the *first* amount column.
8. To find the total deduction from **Purchases,** add the balances of the **Purchases Discounts** and **Purchases Returns and Allowances** accounts. Enter the total, on the Purchases Returns and Allowances line, in the *second* amount column. Draw a line across the *first* and *second* amount columns under this total.

9. On the next line, enter "Net Purchases" indented about half an inch. Subtract the total of the **Purchases Discounts** and **Purchases Returns and Allowances** accounts from the cost of delivered merchandise. The difference is the net purchases for the period. Enter the amount in the *third* amount column. Draw a line across the *third* amount column under this amount.
10. On the next line, enter "Cost of Merchandise Available" indented about half an inch. Add the net purchases amount to the beginning inventory amount. The total is the cost of merchandise available for sale. Enter the total in the *third* amount column.
11. On the next line, write "Merchandise Inventory, December 31, 20—" indented about half an inch. Enter the amount of the ending inventory in the *third* amount column. (The ending inventory is found on the work sheet, in the Balance Sheet section, on the Merchandise Inventory line.) Draw a line across the *third* amount column under this amount.
12. On the next line, enter "Cost of Merchandise Sold" indented about one inch. Subtract the ending inventory amount from the cost of merchandise available for sale. The difference is the cost of merchandise sold during the period. Enter the amount in the *fourth* amount column. Draw a line across the *fourth* amount column under this amount.

2 TEACH (Cont'd.)

Visual Learning

Figure 19–2 Income Statement Through Gross Profit on Sales

Use **Transparency 19–5** to guide students through the recording of the information to calculate the cost of merchandise sold and gross profit on sales.

Teaching Tips

Explain the purpose behind each item of information reported in the cost of merchandise sold section.

Point out that cost of merchandise sold may also be called cost of goods sold.

Help students understand the logic of entering account balances in each column on the income statement. Point out that the net sales and gross profit on sales amounts are in the right column. Each set of subtotals needed to calculate each of those amounts moves to the left one column.

GO TO **Chapter Reviews and Working Papers** Refer students to *Study Plans* located at the beginning of Chapter 19 in the workbook.

REINFORCING STUDY SKILLS

Taking Notes Taking notes while listening for information can be challenging, but shortcuts can make it easier. Share these hints with students: Have pen and paper ready to take notes at the beginning of every class. Make up your own "shorthand" using symbols and abbreviations. Write faster, but keep your writing legible. Use an outline format and use phrases, not complete sentences.

CHAPTER 19
SECTION 2, PAGES 522–529

2 TEACH (Cont'd.)

Teaching Tips

Gross profit on sales is sometimes referred to as gross margin on sales.

Remind students that the costs of operating the business are recorded as expenses. Point out that since corporations are allowed to deduct operating expenses to reduce total federal corporate income taxes, the income tax expense is listed separately on the income statement after other expenses have been totaled.

Demonstration Problem Step-by-Step Practice

Use demonstration problem 19–3 to give students practice in calculating gross profit on sales and entering it on the income statement.

Strategies for Teaching International Accounting

To enrich study of international accounting, refer to the additional critical thinking activities in the booklet.

The Gross Profit on Sales Section

Once the cost of merchandise sold is calculated, the gross profit on sales can be determined. The **gross profit on sales** is the profit made during the period before operating expenses are deducted. Gross profit on sales is found by subtracting the cost of merchandise sold from net sales. "Gross Profit on Sales" is entered at the left edge, and the amount is placed in the *fourth* amount column. In **Figure 19–2** you can see that On Your Mark's gross profit on sales is $106,587.82.

The Operating Expenses Section

The next section of the income statement shows the operating expenses for the period. **Operating expenses** are the costs of the goods and services used in the process of earning revenue for the business. Some businesses choose to further classify operating expenses into **selling expenses** (incurred to sell or market the merchandise sold) and **administrative expenses** (costs related to the management of the business). Look at **Figure 19–3.** "Operating Expenses" is entered at the left edge on the line following the gross profit on sales. On the following lines, the names and balances of all expense accounts except **Federal Corporate Income Tax Expense** are listed in the same order as on the work sheet. While federal corporate income tax is a normal expense for a corporation, it is not considered to be an operating expense. Rather than a cost related to earning revenue, income tax represents a cost *resulting* from the revenue earned.

Notice that the balances of the expense accounts are entered in the *third* amount column. The balances are totaled. The total, $63,918.10, is entered in the *fourth* amount column.

> **International ACCOUNTING**
>
> **European Union**
>
> The European Economic Community was formed in 1958 to allow goods, services, workers, and money to move freely among its member countries. Now known as the European Union, the organization has developed a single currency, the *euro*. The euro is divided into one hundred cents.

The Net Income Section

The final section of the income statement reports the net income (or net loss) for the period, both before and after federal corporate income taxes. It is customary to present the federal corporate income tax amount separately on the income statement. This is done so that the income statement shows the amount of operating income. **Operating income** is the amount of income earned before federal corporate income taxes are deducted.

Look at **Figure 19–3** again. To calculate operating income, subtract the total operating expenses from the gross profit on sales. On Your Mark's operating income for the period is $42,669.72.

To calculate net income:

1. Enter "Less: Federal Corporate Income Tax Expense" on the next line, indented about half an inch.
2. Enter the amount of income taxes, $9,995, in the *fourth* amount column. Federal corporate income taxes appear in the Income Statement section of the work sheet. Draw a line across the *fourth* column under this amount.
3. Enter "Net Income" (or "Net Loss") on the next line at the left edge.
4. Subtract the amount of federal corporate income taxes from the operating income. The result is net income or net loss.
5. Enter the difference, $32,674.72, in the *fourth* amount column. Net income on the income statement must agree with the net income

Teaching International ACCOUNTING

European Union Have students research the status of the European Union (also referred to as the European Economic Community). Students should find out which European countries are members and which are not, the requirements for membership, and the political and other barriers a country's leaders face in deciding whether to become a part of the EU. Also have students research how common regulations affect marketing and accounting opportunities for U.S. businesses and accounting professionals.

On Your Mark Athletic Wear Income Statement For the Year Ended December 31, 20--				
Revenue:				
Sales			320 450 00	
Less: Sales Discounts		730 00		
Sales Returns and Allowances		2 000 00	2 730 00	
Net Sales				317 720 00
Cost of Merchandise Sold:				
Merchandise Inventory, January 1, 20--			84 921 00	
Purchases	206 700 00			
Plus: Transportation In	4 036 18			
Cost of Delivered Merchandise		210 736 18		
Less: Purchases Discounts	1 340 00			
Purchases Returns and Allowances	1 800 00	3 140 00		
Net Purchases			207 596 18	
Cost of Merchandise Available			292 517 18	
Merchandise Inventory, December 31, 20--			81 385 00	
Cost of Merchandise Sold				211 132 18
Gross Profit on Sales				106 587 82
Operating Expenses:				
Advertising Expense			2 450 00	
Bank Card Fees Expense			4 199 27	
Insurance Expense			125 00	
Maintenance Expense			3 519 25	
Miscellaneous Expense			348 28	
Payroll Tax Expense			3 826 83	
Rent Expense			14 000 00	
Salaries Expense			29 374 60	
Supplies Expense			3 710 00	
Utilities Expense			2 364 87	
Total Operating Expenses				63 918 10
Operating Income				42 669 72
Less: Federal Corporate Income Tax Expense				9 995 00
Net Income				32 674 72

Figure 19–3 On Your Mark's Completed Income Statement

shown on the work sheet. If it does, draw a double rule under the amount to show that the income statement is proved and complete. If it does not, check the addition and subtraction on the income statement. Also check that all the accounts and balances in the Income Statement section of the work sheet appear correctly on the income statement.

Analyzing Amounts on the Income Statement

The income statement is analyzed to evaluate the financial performance of the business. The information reported on the income statement and other financial statements is expressed in dollars. Although dollar amounts are useful, the analysis of financial statements can be expanded and made more meaningful by expressing the dollar amounts as percentages. These

COOPERATIVE LEARNING ACTIVITY

Think-Pair-Share Write the following account balances on the chalkboard: Beginning Inventory, 1/1 $65,112; Purchases $114,549; Transportation In $2,546; Purchases Discounts $4,897; Purchases Ret. & Allow. $4,311; Ending Inventory, 12/31 $68,335. Ask students to calculate the cost of merchandise sold. Allow students a specified amount of time to calculate answers and to discuss them with a partner. Then ask students to share their answers with the class. (Cost of delivered merchandise, $117,095; net purchases, $107,887; cost of merchandise available for sale, $172,999; cost of merchandise sold, $104,664.)

2 TEACH (Cont'd.)

Visual Learning

Figure 19–3 On Your Mark's Completed Income Statement

Using **Transparency 19–6**, have students explain each part of the income statement.

Thinking Algebraically

Expressing Relationships: Have students write an equation describing the calculations needed to determine net income (or loss), using only major categories. (Example: net sales − cost of merchandise sold = gross profit on sales − operating expenses = operating income − federal corporate income tax = net income) L1

Concept Development: Analyzing Amounts on the Income Statement

Discussion: Explain vertical analysis and how it is used to evaluate all items on the income statement in relation to net sales. Point out that the base amount used in vertical analysis of the income statement is net sales. All other items are stated as a percentage of that amount. A vertical analysis can be used to evaluate changes in key amounts, such as net income, over a span of years. For example, negative changes might indicate a need to reduce expenses or to expand sales. L1

Demonstration Problem
Step-by-Step Practice

Use demonstration problem 19–4 to give students practice in completing an income statement for a merchandising corporation.

2 TEACH (Cont'd.)

Visual Learning

Figure 19–4 Comparative Income Statement Showing Vertical Analysis
Use **Transparency 19–7** to explain to students how to interpret the relationship of items on the income statement to net sales.

Teaching Tip

Demonstrate the calculation of a few of the percentages in Figure 19–4. Then discuss how year-to-year changes are used to evaluate operating results. For example, the percentage of operating expenses increased over the past year. Management would want to learn the reason for this increase, which might signal a need to look at costs more closely.

Analyzing Data: Point out that in Figure 19–4 gross profit as a percentage of net sales changed from 37.41% in the previous year to 33.55% in the current year. Ask students whether this change is positive or negative. Have them explain their answer. (The change is negative since it represents less profit.) L2

percentages more clearly indicate the relationships among the items on the financial statements. They also enable users of the financial statements to compare the relationships within an accounting period and changes in these relationships between accounting periods.

Key Points

Vertical Analysis
Vertical analysis is useful for determining relationships among items in a financial statement and changes in these relationships from one period to the next.

One type of analysis is called **vertical analysis**. With vertical analysis, each dollar amount reported on a financial statement is also reported as a percentage of another amount, called a base amount, appearing on that same statement. For example, on the income statement, each amount is reported as a percentage of net sales. Current-period percentages can be compared with percentages from past periods or with percentages from other companies within the same industry.

Figure 19–4 illustrates a comparative income statement. As you can see, the net sales amount for each year is assigned a percentage of 100. Every other amount on the income statement is stated as a percentage of the net sales amount. Notice that net income was 14.68 percent of net sales in the previous year and only 10.28 percent of net sales for the current year. Analysis of this and other percentages will help management make informed decisions regarding the operation of the business.

Figure 19–4 Comparative Income Statement Showing Vertical Analysis

On Your Mark Athletic Wear
Comparative Income Statement
For the Current and Previous Years Ended December 31

	Current Year		Previous Year	
	Dollars	Percent	Dollars	Percent
Revenue:				
Sales	$ 320,450.00	100.86 %	$ 296,350.00	100.79 %
Less: Sales Discounts	730.00	0.23	625.00	0.21
Sales Ret. and Allow.	2,000.00	0.63	1,700.00	0.58
Net Sales	$ 317,720.00	100.00 %	$ 294,025.00	100.00 %
Cost of Merchandise Sold:				
Merch. Inventory, Jan. 1	$ 84,921.00	26.73 %	$ 82,100.00	27.92 %
Net Purchases	207,596.18	65.34	186,836.56	63.54
Merch. Available for Sale	292,517.18	92.07 %	$ 268,936.56	91.47 %
Merch. Inventory, Dec. 31	81,385.00	25.62	84,921.00	28.88
Cost of Merchandise Sold	$ 211,132.18	66.45 %	$ 184,015.56	62.59 %
Gross Profit on Sales	$ 106,587.82	33.55 %	$ 110,009.44	37.41 %
Operating Expenses:				
Advertising Expense	$ 2,450.00	0.77 %	$ 1,779.00	0.61 %
Bankcard Fees Expense	4,199.27	1.32	3,569.37	1.21
Insurance Expense	125.00	0.04	0.00	0.00
Maintenance Expense	3,519.25	1.11	3,308.10	1.13
Miscellaneous Expense	348.28	0.11	742.00	0.25
Payroll Tax Expense	3,826.83	1.20	3,444.15	1.17
Rent Expense	14,000.00	4.41	13,200.00	4.49
Salaries Expense	29,374.60	9.25	26,437.14	8.99
Supplies Expense	3,710.00	1.17	2,968.00	1.01
Utilities Expense	2,364.87	0.74	2,305.75	0.78
Total Operating Expenses	$ 63,918.10	20.12 %	$ 57,753.51	19.64 %
Operating Income	$ 42,669.72	13.43 %	$ 52,255.93	17.77 %
Fed. Corp. Inc. Tax Exp.	9,995.00	3.15	9,085.00	3.09
Net Income	$ 32,674.72	10.28 %	$ 43,170.93	14.68 %

CRITICAL THINKING ACTIVITY

Account Balances At the end of an accounting period, an accountant for a merchandising business was checking the accuracy of the financial statements. When comparing the statements with the general ledger account balances, the accountant found that some account balances did not match. Why would some of the balances in the ledger be different from those reported on the financial statements? (The balance sheet and income statement are prepared after the work sheet is completed. The ledger account balances are not up to date until the adjusting and closing entries are journalized and posted.)

SECTION 2 Check Your Understanding

Now that you have studied this section, complete the following questions and problems.

Thinking Critically

1. An income statement for a merchandising business has five sections. Name and briefly describe each section.
2. How do transportation charges affect the cost of merchandise?

Analyzing Accounting

Look at the comparative income statement at the right and answer the following questions about the vertical analysis of this financial statement.

1. What is the trend in sales?
2. How is that trend affecting the net income?
3. What expenses have decreased in the past year?
4. Are there any significant changes in inventory?
5. What is the largest expense?
6. Would you invest your money in this business? Why or why not?

Comparative Income Statement
For the Current and Previous Years Ended December 31

	Current Year		Previous Year	
	Dollars	Percent	Dollars	Percent
Revenue:				
Sales	$ 1,500,000	100.13 %	$ 850,000	100.26 %
Less: Sales Ret. and Allow.	2,000	0.13	2,200	0.26
Net Sales	$ 1,498,000	100.00 %	$ 847,800	100.00 %
Cost of Merchandise Sold:				
Merch. Inventory, Jan. 1	$ 250,000	16.69 %	$ 100,000	11.80 %
Net Purchases	800,000	53.40	650,000	76.67
Merch. Available for Sale	$ 1,050,000	70.09 %	$ 750,000	88.46 %
Merch. Inventory, Dec. 31	60,000	4.01	250,000	29.49
Cost of Merchandise Sold	$ 990,000	66.09 %	$ 500,000	58.98 %
Gross Profit on Sales	$ 508,000	33.91 %	$ 347,800	41.02 %
Operating Expenses:				
Advertising Expense	$ 50,000	3.34 %	$ 25,000	2.95 %
Bankcard Fees Expense	10,000	0.67	8,000	0.94
Insurance Expense	5,300	0.35	5,300	0.63
Maintenance Expense	9,000	0.60	7,500	0.88
Payroll Tax Expense	6,200	0.41	3,200	0.38
Rent Expense	20,000	1.34	20,000	2.36
Salaries Expense	58,000	3.87	48,000	5.66
Supplies Expense	3,000	0.20	2,200	0.26
Utilities Expense	2,400	0.16	1,850	0.22
Total Operating Expenses	$ 163,900	10.94 %	$ 121,050	14.28 %
Operating Income	$ 344,100	22.97 %	$ 226,750	26.75 %
Fed. Corp. Inc. Tax Exp.	44,940	3.00	25,434	3.00
Net Income	$ 299,160	19.97 %	$ 201,316	23.75 %

Problem 19–3 Calculating Amounts on the Income Statement

Instructions

For each group of figures that follows, determine the missing amount.

1.	Beginning merchandise inventory	$81,367
	Net purchases	15,139
	Cost of merchandise available for sale	?
2.	Net sales	$52,935
	Cost of merchandise sold	36,232
	Gross profit on sales	?
3.	Purchases	$26,472
	Transportation in	1,311
	Cost of delivered merchandise	?
4.	Cost of merchandise available for sale	$49,769
	Ending merchandise inventory	32,621
	Cost of merchandise sold	?

RETEACHING SECTION 2

Calculating a Vertical Analysis Businesses analyze their income statements to see how well they are doing. A vertical analysis compares amounts within the same year. Students may need help performing the calculations for percentages. Explain the use of net sales as the base amount. To find any given item's percentage of the net sales, divide the account balance by the net sales figure. Guide students step by step through the vertical analysis calculations illustrated in Figure 19–4 on page 528, and then provide several additional examples so that students can practice calculating the percentages for each.

3 ASSESS

Thinking Critically (Answers)

1. (1) Revenue: reports net sales for the period, (2) Cost of Merchandise Sold: actual cost of merchandise sold to customer, (3) Gross Profit on Sales: profit before expenses are deducted, (4) Operating Expenses: cash spent or assets consumed to earn revenue, (5) Net Income (or Loss): profit (or loss) after taxes are paid.
2. Transportation charges increase the cost of merchandise.

Analyzing Accounting (Answers)

1. A large increase
2. Net income decreasing.
3. Bankcard fees, Insurance, Rent, Salaries, Maintenance, Supplies, and Utilities
4. End. Inv. is down significantly.
5. Salaries

Problem 19–3 (Answers)

1. $96,506
2. $16,703
3. $27,783
4. $17,148

Chapter Reviews and Working Papers Refer students to the Chapter 19 workbook pages to answer *Check Your Understanding* activities.

4 CLOSE

Section Wrap-Up

Writing: Have students write a paragraph explaining the six major items listed on the income statement and how to calculate each. L1

SCANS in the Workforce

Foundation Skills Connection

Reasoning

Have students use the *Directory of Occupational Titles* to find a career area and read about the information provided. Then have them create a list of the top three priorities for skills, training, or experience needed to prepare for the career. Remind students to read, think logically, and look for the main points listed under their chosen field. L1

Workplace Competencies Connection

Allocating Human Resources

Have students act as employment directors for a company of their choice. Ask them to write a help-wanted ad for an entry-level accounting position. Have students bring in some examples of employment ads from the local newspaper to use as a guide. L2

Serving Clients/Customers

Ask students to put themselves into the role of an employment recruiter for a large accounting firm. Their job is to go to nearby colleges and recruit graduates to join their firm. Have students pair up, with one student assuming the role of the recruiter; the other, the college graduate. Ask the recruiter to develop a list of five interview questions that will be "thought provoking" to the interviewee. Circulate through the classroom and observe the interviewing sessions. L3

ACCOUNTING CAREERS IN FOCUS

RAJ KHANNA
Recruiting Manager
Robert Half

Q: How did you become a recruiter?

A: Like most people, I sort of fell into recruiting. I was a CPA for eight years, working in both public and private accounting, when my sister introduced me to a friend who owned a small recruiting firm. I had been there just a few months when the firm was acquired by Robert Half. That's when things really started to happen for me. I had the opportunity to travel and attend key training workshops, which really gave my career momentum.

Q: What are some factors that have been key to your success?

A: Intense daily activity is critical, and, in providing customer service, thinking outside the box is also important. These factors have enabled me to establish long-standing relationships with my clients and candidates.

Q: What advice do you have for people considering a degree in accounting?

A: It is still one of the most solid business foundations out there. Even in light of recent developments, accounting and finance is a discipline that transcends any industry and is relevant at any level throughout one's career.

Tips from . . .
Robert Half International Inc.

The way you present yourself is important throughout your career, not just during a job interview. Be confident and friendly. Always be prompt, and work hard. Put in the hours necessary to do first-rate work.

CAREER FACTS

Nature of the Work: Identify qualified candidates for available employment opportunities with client companies.
Training or Education Needed: For recruiting firm specializing in accounting and finance, a bachelor's degree in accounting or related experience.
Aptitudes, Abilities, and Skills: Interpersonal skills; communication skills; aptitude for sales. To work with a specialized recruiter in accounting and finance, familiarity with industry jobs.
Salary Range: $50,000 to $150,000, depending on personal performance, company size and performance.
Career Path: Work in a public accounting firm or corporate accounting department to gain experience and knowledge; transfer to a recruiting position with a specialized recruiting firm in accounting and finance.

Thinking Critically: What might a job applicant look for in deciding whether or not a company's culture is right?

ACCOUNTING CAREERS IN FOCUS

Thinking Critically (Answers)

There are many things to look for when deciding whether a company's culture is right for you. Issues to consider: training and promotion opportunities; flexible hours; retirement, health, and education benefits; dress code; child-care facilities; and community involvement.

ROBERT HALF CORNER

Workplace Skills When beginning a new job, remember to accept additional responsibilities and exhibit a cooperative, can-do attitude; ask for input about your performance and be open to guidance and constructive criticism; and ask questions about policy, procedures, and office etiquette.

The Statement of Retained Earnings and the Balance Sheet

In the previous section, you learned how to prepare and analyze the income statement, which reports the net income or loss for the period. In this section you will learn how to prepare and analyze the statement of retained earnings and the balance sheet. The stockholders of John Deere & Co. study the balance sheet to understand the financial position of the company.

What You'll Learn

- How to prepare a statement of retained earnings for a merchandising corporation.
- How to prepare a balance sheet for a merchandising corporation.
- How to analyze the balance sheet.

Why It's Important

The statement of retained earnings reports how the Retained Earnings stockholders' equity account changes from the beginning to the end of the period. The balance sheet reports the financial position of the business on the last day of the period.

KEY TERMS

- statement of retained earnings
- horizontal analysis
- base year
- working capital

The Statement of Retained Earnings

In a corporation there are two stockholders' equity accounts: **Capital Stock** and **Retained Earnings.** The **Capital Stock** account represents the stockholders' investment in the corporation. The balance of this account changes only when additional shares of stock are issued by the corporation. The **Retained Earnings** account summarizes the accumulated profits of a corporation less any amounts paid to stockholders as returns on their investments.

In Chapter 9 you learned how to prepare a statement of changes in owner's equity for a sole proprietorship to show the changes that occur in the owner's capital account during the period. A similar statement, the statement of retained earnings, is prepared for a corporation. A **statement of retained earnings** reports the changes that take place in the **Retained Earnings** account during the period. These changes result from business operations and the distribution of earnings to stockholders through dividends.

The changes to **Retained Earnings** are summarized as follows:

Retained Earnings

Debit – Decreased by: net loss dividends	Credit + Increased by: net income

RESOURCE MANAGER

Reproducible Masters
- Lesson Plans
- Chapter Reviews and Working Papers (CRWP) TAE
- Demonstration Problems

Transparencies
- Section Focus Transparency
- Teaching Transparencies
- Source Document Transparencies
- Solution Transparencies

Multimedia
- ExamView CD-ROM
- Electronic Learning Center CD-ROM
- Interactive Lesson Planner CD-ROM
- Electronic Field Trips in Accounting

1 FOCUS

Introducing the Section

In this section students will learn how to prepare a statement of retained earnings and a balance sheet for a privately held corporation. Students will also learn how to use horizontal analysis to analyze the balance sheet.

Section Concepts

- How to prepare a statement of retained earnings for a merchandising corporation.
- How to prepare a balance sheet for a merchandising corporation.
- How to analyze the balance sheet.

Visual Learning

Section 3 Focus

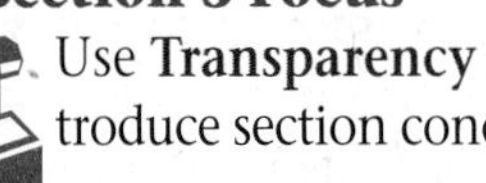

Use **Transparency 19–8** to introduce section concepts.

BELL RINGER

Evaluating: Tell students that they have $1,000 to invest in the stock market. What would they want to know about a company before buying its stock? Have students choose a stock to "purchase" and follow its price changes for a week. Discuss their results in class. L1

Concept Development: The Statement of Retained Earnings

Discussion: Discuss the function of the Retained Earnings account as a repository for net income. Point out that public corporations may pay dividends to shareholders. If so, the amount comes out of Retained Earnings. L1

Teaching Tip

Point out that the rules of debit and credit for the Retained Earnings account are the same as for a revenue account because it is increased by net income.

2 TEACH

GUIDED PRACTICE

Reading Accounting

- Have students explain how percentages can provide a clearer picture of financial data than the actual data. L1

Visual Learning

Figure 19–5 Statement of Retained Earnings

Use **Transparency 19–9** to guide students through the steps in preparing a statement of retained earnings.

Demonstration Problem
Step-by-Step Practice

Use demonstration problem 19–5 to give students practice in completing a statement of retained earnings.

Concept Development: The Balance Sheet

Discussion: When introducing the balance sheet, remind students of the format they learned in Chapter 9. Point out that the information for preparing the balance sheet is taken from the Balance Sheet section of the work sheet and from the statement of retained earnings.

Reinforce the need for adjustments on the work sheet by pointing out how the account balances reported on the balance sheet differ from the beginning trial balance amounts. The account balances for Merchandise Inventory, Prepaid Insurance, Supplies, and Federal Corporate Income Tax Payable were all changed as a result of adjustments. L1

The statement of retained earnings is prepared from information found on the work sheet. The statement of retained earnings is a supporting document for the balance sheet. The final balance of the **Retained Earnings** account, as calculated on the statement of retained earnings, is used when preparing the balance sheet.

Figure 19–5 shows the statement of retained earnings for On Your Mark. The first line shows the balance of the **Retained Earnings** account at the beginning of the period. This balance comes from the Balance Sheet section of the work sheet. The second line is the net income for the period. This is from the Income Statement columns of the work sheet. Add net income to the beginning balance of the **Retained Earnings** account. Since On Your Mark did not distribute any of its net income to stockholders during the period, there are no deductions from **Retained Earnings.** The new balance of the **Retained Earnings** account is $52,445.91.

On Your Mark Athletic Wear
Statement of Retained Earnings
For the Year Ended December 31, 20--

Retained Earnings, January 1, 20--		19 771 19
Net Income		32 674 72
Retained Earnings, December 31, 20--		52 445 91

Figure 19–5 Statement of Retained Earnings

The Balance Sheet

The balance sheet reports the balances of all asset, liability, and stockholders' equity accounts for a specific date. The balance sheet is prepared from the information in the Balance Sheet section of the work sheet and from the statement of retained earnings.

Figure 19–6 shows On Your Mark's balance sheet. This balance sheet is prepared in report form. In the report form, classifications (assets, liabilities, and stockholders' equity) are shown one under the other.

The assets are listed first. The classification "Assets" is centered on the first line. The account names are listed at the left edge in the same order as they appear on the work sheet. The individual balances are entered in the first amount column. "Total Assets" is entered on the line below the last account name, indented about half an inch. The total assets amount is entered in the second amount column. The double rule, however, is not entered until the Liabilities and Stockholders' Equity sections are complete, and the total of these two sections equals the total of the Assets section.

ACCOUNTING *Flashbacks*

ADDING MACHINES

In 1692, 19-year-old French mathematical prodigy Blaise Pascal invented an adding and subtracting machine to help his father compute taxes. Today, a computer language is named after him.

HOME AND COMMUNITY CONNECTIONS ACTIVITY

Income Tax Savings Have students check with local income tax experts, CPAs, or financial planners to find at least three methods for lowering their family's tax bill. For example, if their family can invest before-tax dollars in a 401k or an IRA, their taxable income will be lower. Once students have located the information, ask them to discuss it with their families. Does their family use tax-deferred savings plans? If not, will they consider another approach to reducing income tax?

On Your Mark Athletic Wear Balance Sheet December 31, 20--		
Assets		
Cash in Bank	15 179 00	
Accounts Receivable	10 404 00	
Merchandise Inventory	81 385 00	
Supplies	1 839 00	
Prepaid Insurance	1 375 00	
Delivery Equipment	19 831 00	
Office Equipment	9 825 00	
Store Equipment	5 200 00	
Total Assets		145 038 00
Liabilities		
Accounts Payable	13 850 00	
Federal Corporate Income Tax Payable	155 00	
Employees' Federal Income Tax Payable	640 00	
Employees' State Income Tax Payable	80 00	
Social Security Tax Payable	248 00	
Medicare Tax Payable	58 00	
Federal Unemployment Tax Payable	18 36	
State Unemployment Tax Payable	114 73	
Sales Tax Payable	2 428 00	
Total Liabilities		17 592 09
Stockholders' Equity		
Capital Stock	75 000 00	
Retained Earnings	52 445 91	
Total Stockholders' Equity		127 445 91
Total Liabilities and Stockholders' Equity		145 038 00

Figure 19–6 On Your Mark's Balance Sheet

The Liabilities section begins on the second line below the total assets. "Liabilities" is centered on this line. Again, the account names are listed at the left edge in the same order as they appear on the work sheet. The individual balances are entered in the first amount column. "Total Liabilities" is entered on the line below the last account name, indented about half an inch. The total liabilities amount is entered in the second amount column.

Next, the Stockholders' Equity section begins on the second line below total liabilities. "Stockholders' Equity" is centered on this line. Stockholders' equity consists of two accounts: **Capital Stock** and **Retained Earnings.** The balance of the **Capital Stock** account is from the Balance Sheet section of the work sheet. The balance of the **Retained Earnings** account is from the statement of retained earnings. Again, the account names are listed at the left edge and the individual balances are listed in the first amount column. "Total Stockholders' Equity" is entered on the line below the last account name, indented about half an inch. The stockholders' equity total is entered in the second amount column.

Key Points

The Balance Sheet

The balance sheet represents the basic accounting equation:

Assets = Liabilities + Stockholders' (Owners') Equity

2 TEACH (Cont'd.)

Visual Learning

Figure 19–6 On Your Mark's Balance Sheet

Using **Transparency 19–10,** review the format of a balance sheet. Remind students that the balance sheet mirrors the accounting equation: Assets = Liabilities + Stockholders' (or Owner's) Equity.

Teaching Tips

Have students explain why the date of the balance sheet does not span a fiscal period.

Emphasize that information reported on the balance sheet comes from two different sources: the Balance Sheet section of the work sheet and the statement of retained earnings.

Demonstration Problem Step-by-Step Practice

Use demonstration problem 19–6 to have students prepare a balance sheet for a merchandising corporation.

ADDRESSING MULTIPLE LEARNING STYLES

Logical/Mathematical Learner Have students read the help-wanted ads in your local newspaper to determine how many job listings specify knowledge of accounting procedures and/or knowledge of a specific accounting software application. Ask students to prepare a grid to illustrate the number of job openings in accounting and the percentage of those jobs that require technology skills. If you have access to spreadsheet software, have students create a spreadsheet and/or chart to display the results of their research.

CHAPTER 19
SECTION 3, PAGES 531–536

2 TEACH (Cont'd.)

Concept Development: Analyzing Amounts on the Balance Sheet

Discussion: Contrast horizontal analysis to vertical analysis. With horizontal analysis, a base year is chosen and all other amounts are stated as a percentage of the amounts in that year. Horizontal analysis is especially useful in detecting significant changes or trends from year to year. L1

Teaching Tip

Explain that working capital is really the excess net current assets of the business (those not needed to pay current debts). The term "net working capital" is actually more accurate, but convention dictates the use of the term "working capital."

Critical Thinking: Tell students they are small business owners selling products on account to several other businesses. Why should they be concerned about selling on account to a business with insufficient working capital? (Working capital is used to pay current debts. A business with insufficient working capital may not have enough cash to pay its creditors on time—or at all. Small businesses are especially vulnerable, since they need prompt payment to continue financing their own operations.) L2

Math Review for Accounting Photocopy appropriate *Activity Sheets* for students who need additional practice in basic math skills.

On the line following total stockholders' equity, "Total Liabilities and Stockholders' Equity" is entered at the left edge. The total of the Liabilities section and the total of the Stockholders' Equity section are added. The total is entered in the second amount column. This total must agree with the total assets amount. If it does, the balance sheet is double ruled. If it does not, check the addition on the balance sheet. Also check that the accounts and amounts are transferred from the work sheet accurately.

Analyzing Amounts on the Balance Sheet

When analyzing financial statements, you learned that while the dollar amounts provided on the statements are useful, the analysis can be expanded and made more meaningful by expressing the dollar amounts as percentages. In addition to using percentage amounts in vertical analysis as described earlier, they can also be used in horizontal analysis. **Horizontal analysis** is the comparison of the same items on financial statements for two or more accounting periods or dates and the determination of changes from one period or date to the next. With horizontal analysis, each amount on the current statement is compared with its corresponding amount on the previous statement. A **base year** is a year or period that is used for comparison.

Look at the example of a comparative balance sheet in **Figure 19–7.** By comparing the amounts for the two years, you can see that **Cash in Bank** increased by 25.3 percent and **Accounts Payable** decreased by 38.26 percent. The accountant might use this information to assess why cash has increased or why accounts payable have decreased. Perhaps the business is receiving more sales in cash instead of on account. The business may also be purchasing less inventory on account. These are trends that would be of interest to management.

Key Points

Analysis of Financial Statements
Vertical analysis involves the comparison of financial statement amounts within a single period or date. Horizontal analysis involves the comparison of financial statement amounts between periods or dates. Vertical and horizontal analysis can be applied to both the income statement and the balance sheet.

Working Capital

The amount by which current assets exceed current liabilities is known as **working capital**. Because current liabilities are usually paid for out of current assets, working capital represents the excess assets available to continue operations. The working capital for On Your Mark is calculated as follows:

Current Assets	–	Current Liabilities	=	Working Capital
$110,182.00	–	$17,592.09	=	$92,589.91

In this example, current assets include **Cash in Bank**, **Accounts Receivable**, **Merchandise Inventory**, **Supplies**, and **Prepaid Insurance**. Current liabilities are all those listed in the liability section of the balance sheet in **Figure 19–7**.

Math Skill Builder Activity

(Refer to the *Math Hints* feature on page 535.)

Percentage Change Ask students to solve this problem about the percentage of change over a period of time. At the end of its first year of operation, The Chocolate Shoppe reported $50,000 in total assets. Three years later, total assets had increased to $250,000. What is the percentage change over the three years? ($250,000 – $50,000 = $200,000 increase; $200,000 ÷ $250,000 = .80 or 80% percent increase.)

On Your Mark Athletic Wear Comparative Balance Sheet December 31, Current Year and Previous Year				
	Current Year	Previous Year	Increase (Decrease) Current over Previous: Dollars	Percent
Assets				
Cash in Bank	$ 15,179.00	$ 12,114.57	$ 3,064.43	25.30 %
Accounts Receivable	10,404.00	8,220.00	2,184.00	26.57
Merchandise Inventory	81,385.00	84,921.00	(3,536.00)	(4.16)
Supplies	1,839.00	1,587.00	252.00	15.88
Prepaid Insurance	1,375.00	0.00	1,375.00	—
Delivery Equipment	19,831.00	12,462.00	7,369.00	59.13
Office Equipment	9,825.00	5,854.00	3,971.00	67.83
Store Equipment	5,200.00	3,500.00	1,700.00	48.57
Total Assets	$ 145,038.00	$ 128,658.57	$ 16,379.43	12.73 %
Liabilities				
Accounts Payable	$ 13,850.00	$ 22,433.00	$ (8,583.00)	(38.26)%
Fed. Corp. Inc. Tax Payable	155.00	140.00	15.00	10.71
Employees' Fed. Inc. Tax Pay.	640.00	608.00	32.00	5.26
Employees' State Inc. Tax Pay.	80.00	72.00	8.00	11.11
Social Security Tax Payable	248.00	241.00	7.00	2.90
Medicare Tax Payable	58.00	56.35	1.65	2.93
Federal Unemployment Tax Pay.	18.36	16.50	1.86	11.27
State Unemployment Tax Pay.	114.73	103.17	11.56	11.20
Sales Tax Payable	2,428.00	3,158.00	(730.00)	(23.12)
Total Liabilities	$ 17,592.09	$ 26,828.02	$ (9,235.93)	(34.43)%
Stockholders' Equity				
Capital Stock	$ 75,000.00	$ 75,000.00	$ 0.00	0.00 %
Retained Earnings	52,445.91	26,830.55	25,615.36	95.47
Total Stockholders' Equity	$ 127,445.91	$ 101,830.55	$ 25,615.36	25.15 %
Total Liab. and Stockhldrs' Equity	$ 145,038.00	$ 128,658.57	$ 16,379.43	12.73 %

Figure 19–7 Comparative Balance Sheet Showing Horizontal Analysis

Percentage Change

To find the percent of increase, subtract the base year amount from the current year, then divide by the base year.

For example:

- if assets in the base year are $240,000 and $280,000 this year,
- the increase is $40,000.
- The percentage change is 17 percent ($40,000 ÷ $240,000).

Is company better financial position this year than last year?

ANALYZING FINANCIAL REPORTS

Evaluating Stockholders' Equity

Although the balance sheet provides information about stockholders' equity, corporations also prepare a report called the statement of stockholders' equity. This report might also be called a statement of retained earnings.

Look at the consolidated statements of stockholders' equity for Office Depot on pages A-47–A-48. This statement provides details about changes in capital through stock issuance and in retained earnings over a period of years. This information helps investors and analysts get a better picture of the company's capital. Successful companies earn money for future operations (reported as retained earnings) through sales, and rely less on raising new capital through the issuance of stock.

▶ Analyze the Report:

Use the consolidated statements of stockholders' equity on pages A-47–A-48 to answer these questions.

1. Explain how retained earnings changed from a balance of $1,516,691,000 in 2000 to a balance of $1,717,734,000 at the end of 2001.
2. How much did additional paid-in capital increase during this same time?

2 TEACH (Cont'd.)

Visual Learning

Figure 19–7 Comparative Balance Sheet Showing Horizontal Analysis

Use **Transparency 19–11** to guide students through the calculation of percentages for horizontal analysis. Point out that the previous year is the base year, and all amounts on the balance sheet are compared to this year.

Teaching Tips

Point out that a percentage change reveals more than an actual dollar change.

Remind students that calculating the percentages in horizontal and vertical analyses is simply an arithmetic function. You may want to review the calculation of a few percentages using the financial statements presented in the chapter. Refer students who need a review of percentages to the booklet *Math Review for Accounting*.

The Office Depot 2001 Annual Report

Refer students to pages A-39–A-48 in the back of the book.

ANALYZING FINANCIAL REPORTS

Analyze the Report (Answers)

1. Retained earnings increased by the amount of net income for 2001, $201,043,000.
2. Additional paid-in capital increased $67,874,000 (from $939,214,000 to $1,007,088,000).

CHAPTER 19
SECTION 3, PAGES 531–536

3 ASSESS

Thinking Critically (Answers)

1. Changes resulting from business operations (net income/net loss) and the distribution of earnings as dividends.
2. To compare changes over two or more accounting periods.

Computing in the Business World (Answers)

Year 1: Gross Profit, 60%; Total Oper. Exp., 3%; Net Income, 57%
Year 2: Gross Profit, 50%; Total Oper. Exp., 1%; Net Income, 49%
Year 3: Gross Profit, 49%; Total Oper. Exp., 1%; Net Income, 48%

Problem 19–4 (Answers)

1. Office Equip., Merch. Inventory
2. Fed. Unemployment Tax Payable
3. Increased $16,379.43, or 12.73%.
4. 95.47%
5. Increase in Accts. Rec. indicates the company is selling more product or is less efficient at collecting payments. Decrease in Accts. Pay. indicates that they are paying bills earlier.
6. Company prepaid new insurance contract.

Chapter Reviews and Working Papers Refer students to the Chapter 19 workbook pages to answer *Check Your Understanding* activities.

4 CLOSE

Section Wrap-Up

Calculation and Writing: Give students a completed balance sheet and have them calculate working capital. Have students write a paragraph explaining why working capital is important to a business. L1

SECTION 3 Check Your Understanding

Now that you have studied this section, complete the following questions and problems.

Thinking Critically

1. What is reported on a statement of retained earnings?
2. Explain the use of a horizontal analysis.

Computing in the Business World

Larry Campbell is the owner of Craftsman Furniture, a successful family-owned furniture store. As the accountant for Craftsman Furniture, it is your responsibility to run a vertical analysis on the income statement. Mr. Campbell asks you to prepare an Executive Summary of a three-year vertical analysis. Using the information provided, in your working papers calculate the percentages for each year and complete the columns of the draft report. Mr. Campbell will review the draft with you so he clearly understands the trends in sales for Craftsman Furniture.

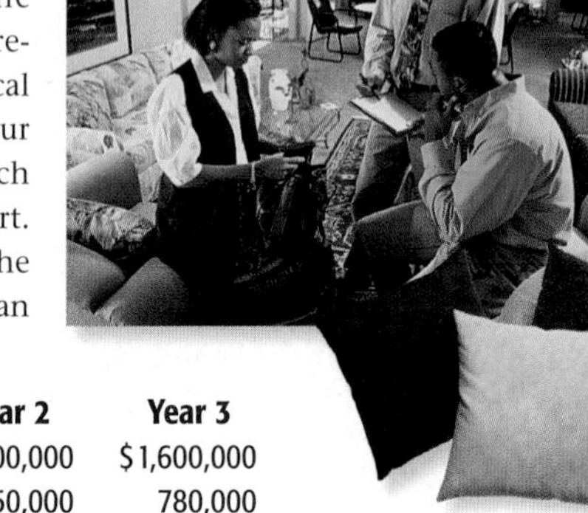

	Year 1	Year 2	Year 3
Net Sales	$1,000,000	$1,500,000	$1,600,000
Gross Profit on Sales	600,000	750,000	780,000
Total Operating Expenses	25,000	21,000	23,000
Net Income	$ 575,000	$ 729,000	$ 757,000

Problem 19–4 Analyzing a Balance Sheet

Use the comparative balance sheet for On Your Mark in **Figure 19–7** to answer the following questions.

1. Which asset account has the greatest percentage increase between the two years? Greatest decrease?
2. Which liability account has the greatest increase between the two years?
3. Did the overall value of the corporation increase or decrease between the two years? What is the dollar amount? What is the percentage?
4. What is the percentage increase in retained earnings between the two years?
5. What conclusions might you draw based on the change in Accounts Receivable? Accounts Payable?
6. Can you provide a possible explanation for the difference in the balance of the **Prepaid Insurance** account?

RETEACHING SECTION 3

Calculating a Horizontal Analysis A horizontal analysis is the comparison of financial data over two or more accounting periods. Managers and stockholders are interested in a horizontal analysis because it identifies change over a period of time. Dollar amounts are compared and expressed as a percentage increase or decrease. The percentage of change indicates whether or not the business is improving. Guide students step by step through the horizontal analysis calculations illustrated in Figure 19–7 on page 535, and then provide several additional examples so that students can practice calculating the percentages for each.

CHAPTER 19 SUMMARY

KEY CONCEPTS

1. Accounting for sole proprietorships and for corporations is very similar except for reporting owner's equity on the balance sheet. Corporations have two stockholders' equity accounts: **Capital Stock** and **Retained Earnings. Capital Stock** represents the stockholders' investments in the corporation. **Retained Earnings** summarizes the profits accumulated less distributions to stockholders.
2. Three financial statements prepared by merchandising corporations are the income statement, the statement of retained earnings, and the balance sheet.
3. Accounting information must be understandable and comparable. Comparability allows information to be compared from one fiscal period to another.
4. Accounting information must also be relevant, reliable, fully-disclosed, and material.
5. The income statement for a merchandising business contains the following elements:
   - (a) Net sales, which is total sales less deductions for sales discounts, returns, and allowances
   - (b) Net purchases, which is the total cost of merchandise bought plus transportation charges less deductions for purchases discounts, returns, and allowances
   - (c) The cost of merchandise sold
   - (d) Gross profit on sales, which is net sales minus the cost of merchandise sold.
   - (e) Operating expenses
   - (f) Operating income
   - (g) The federal income tax paid by a corporation, listed separately on the income statement
   - (h) Net income or net loss
6. The statement of retained earnings reports the changes in the **Retained Earnings** account due to net income or loss and distributions to stockholders.
7. The cost of merchandise sold is calculated as follows:

   Beginning Merchandise Inventory
   \+ Net Purchases During the Period
   Cost of Merchandise Available for Sale
   − Ending Merchandise Inventory
   Cost of Merchandise Sold

8. The balance sheet reports the financial position of the business on a specific date. The balance sheet includes all the permanent general ledger accounts: assets, liabilities, and stockholders' equity accounts.
9. Vertical analysis helps the accountant determine the relationships among items on a financial statement and the changes in these relationships from one period to the next.
10. Horizontal analysis compares items on a financial statement for two or more accounting periods. Each amount on a current statement is compared with its corresponding amount on the previous statement.

ANSWERS

1. Capital Stock
2. stockholders' equity
3. comparability
4. cost of merchandise sold and gross profit on sales
5. retained earnings
6. federal corporate income tax
7. operating income
8. vertical analysis
9. statement of retained earnings
10. horizontal analysis

SUMMARY CHAPTER 19

Chapter 19 Quiz

Student ______ Class ______ Instructor ______

Date Assigned ______ Date Completed ______

CHAPTER 19 QUIZ

Financial Statements for a Corporation

QUESTIONS (Completion)

Directions: Fill in the blank with the term that best completes each sentence.

1. Stockholders' equity is represented by the ______ account.
2. The retained earnings account is classified as a(n) ______ account.
3. The characteristic of ______ allows financial information to be compared from one fiscal period to another.
4. In addition to revenue, expenses, and net income, what two additional types of information are reported for a merchandising business? ______ ______.
5. The net income held by a corporation is called ______.
6. The operating expenses of a business do not include ______.
7. The amount of income earned before federal corporate income taxes have been paid is called ______.
8. Comparing items on a financial statement to a base amount involves ______ analysis.
9. Changes in earnings held by a corporation are reported on the ______.
10. Comparing items on a financial statement to a base year involves ______ analysis.

 Chapter Quizzes • 21

QUESTIONS (Completion)

1. Stockholders' equity is represented by the _____ account.
2. The retained earnings account is classified as a(n) _____ account.
3. The characteristic of _____ allows financial information to be compared from one fiscal period to another.

4. In addition to revenue, expenses, and net income, what two additional types of information are reported for a merchandising business?

5. The net income held by a corporation is called _____.
6. The operating expenses of a business do not include _____.

7. The amount of income earned before federal corporate income taxes have been paid is called _____.

8. Comparing items on a financial statement to a base amount involves _____ analysis.
9. Changes in earnings held by a corporation are reported on the _____.
10. Comparing items on a financial statement to a base year involves _____ analysis.

USING KEY TERMS

See the *Glossary* for the definitions of these terms. Have students share their definitions in class. Discuss how the terms relate to each of the financial statements.

Understanding Accounting Concepts and Procedures

(Answers)

1. Owner's equity: investments and earnings of a sole proprietorship; stockholders' equity: stockholders' investments (Capital Stock) and earnings (Retained Earnings).
2. Income statement, statement of retained earnings, balance sheet.
3. A merchandising business includes cost of merchandise sold and gross profit on sales; a service business does not include these categories.
4. Net sales: deduct sales returns, allowances, discounts from total sales. Net purchases: add transportation charges to Purchases, subtract returns, allowances, discounts.
5. Cost of merchandise available for sale = beginning inventory + net purchases. Subtracting ending inventory = cost of merchandise sold.
6. By subtracting the ending merchandise inventory from the cost of merchandise available for sale.
7. To identify the amount of taxable income on the income statement.
8. Operating income is gross margin less operating expenses; net income is the amount after expenses and federal corporate income taxes are deducted.
9. Because Retained Earnings summarizes profits accumulated and kept by a corporation, less any distributions made to stockholders.
10. Net income is needed to calculate the balance of Retained Earnings. The balance of Retained Earnings is reported on the balance sheet.

USING KEY TERMS

Your company, The Neighborhood Bookworm, was purchased several months ago by an international bookstore chain—The Best Seller. Your new boss, Gabriella Sitta, asks you to create the end-of-year financial statements. Gabriella is not native to the U.S. and does not understand all the English-language business terms. On a separate sheet of paper, write for each term its definition and its relationship to the preparation of financial statements.

administrative expenses	operating income
base year	relevance
Capital Stock	reliability
comparability	retained earnings
full disclosure	selling expenses
gross profit on sales	statement of retained earnings
horizontal analysis	stockholders' equity
materiality	vertical analysis
net purchases	working capital
net sales	
operating expenses	

Understanding Accounting Concepts and Procedures

Instructions

On a separate sheet of paper, answer the following questions:

1. How does stockholders' equity differ from owner's equity?
2. What three financial statements are prepared by a merchandising corporation?
3. How does an income statement for a merchandising business differ from that for a service business?
4. How is net sales calculated? Net purchases?
5. What is the difference between the cost of merchandise available for sale and the cost of merchandise sold?
6. How is the cost of merchandise sold calculated?
7. Why are the income taxes paid by a corporation listed separately on the income statement?
8. What is the difference between operating income and net income?
9. Why is the net income for the period added to **Retained Earnings** rather than to **Capital Stock?**
10. Why is the income statement prepared before the statement of retained earnings? Why is the statement of retained earnings prepared before the balance sheet?

ASSESSMENT RESOURCES

Choose assessment strategies from the following pages to evaluate your students' progress.

Student Edition
Check Your Understanding, pp. 521, 529, 536
Chapter 19 Problems, pp. 541–543
Analyzing Financial Reports, p. 535

Assessment and Evaluation Masters
Chapter 19 Study Plan, *Glencoe Workbook (CRWP)*
Chapter 19 Self-Test, *Glencoe Workbook (CRWP)*
Chapter 19 Test, *Chapter Tests* Booklet
Chapter 19 Activity, *School-to-Work Handbook*
Chapter 19 **Exam***View*

Teacher Wraparound Edition
Critical Thinking Activity, p. 528
Reteaching Sections 1–3, pp. 521, 529, 536
Chapter 19 Quiz, p. 537

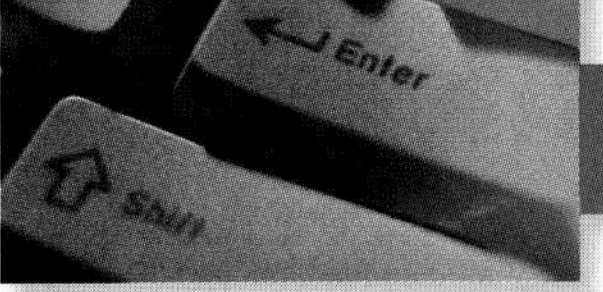

Case Study...

Merchandising Business: Gourmet Food Gifts

The Gourmet Express sells cookies, candies, food baskets, and other gourmet items. Valentine's Day and Mother's Day are the busiest days. The store sells directly to customers and also ships items through catalog orders. Recently, prices have increased for some food ingredients, such as sugar and chocolate. As a result, net income has decreased. The manager does not want to use lower-priced ingredients because they might change the quality of the finished products.

In preparation for the Valentine's Day rush, you've been asked to suggest some ideas for increasing net income.

Thinking Critically:

1. What items affect net income?
2. Think about the gourmet food gift business, both the retail and the catalog operations. What are some areas for possibly cutting costs?
3. Recommend at least three ideas for cutting costs.

interNET CONNECTION

Corporate Financial Statements

Many corporations publish financial statements online. By accessing a company's financial information, potential investors can locate annual earnings, stock prices, and growth trends for the company.

Do This:

1. Find a well-known company's corporate site on the Web. Try companies like Toys "R" Us, Coca-Cola, Intel, or AT&T. Which company did you choose? What is the Web site address?
2. Locate the company's annual report or earnings release for the current year or the most recent quarter. Did the company have a profit or loss for the period?
3. What is the value of the company's total assets?

Conducting an Audit with Alex

The following account balances are from the Income Statement section of the work sheet.

Account Name	Debit	Credit
Purchases	121,520	
Transportation In	1,306	
Purchases Discounts		4,840
Purchases Returns and Allowances		1,641

The beginning merchandise inventory is $36,813, and the ending merchandise inventory is $54,709.

Instructions

(1) Determine the amount of net purchases for the period.
(2) Determine the cost of merchandise sold.

Workplace Skills

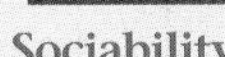

Sociability

Most jobs require you to be adaptable to any situation. Your social skills on the job are equally important. How well you can relate to others, demonstrate an understanding, and respond appropriately to any situation is an indicator of your interpersonal skills development.

On the Job:

Friday night you are attending the annual stockholders' meeting and reception for Big League Sports—a professional-sports merchandising company. Your boss, Lily Chang, asks you to make a presentation about trends in professional sports. She recommends that you keep it colorful, simple, humorous, and appropriate for the event.

Thinking Critically:

Together with several of your colleagues (classmates), develop an outline for your presentation. Decide on visuals to use and topics to cover. Prepare a question and answer segment.

REVIEW AND ACTIVITIES CHAPTER 19

Case Study...

Thinking Critically (Answers)

1. Net income is affected by all of the company's revenues and expenses.
2. Answers may vary. Some costs that could be lowered include advertising expense and payroll expense.
3. Answers may vary. Expenditures for advertising could be lowered. Schedules could be gone over to determine if there are times when there is less work and fewer employees could be used. Analysis of customer buying trends might allow production to occur so as to reduce waste.

Workplace Skills

Thinking Critically (Answers)

Answers may vary. The point of this exercise is to increase students' comfort level with prepared and impromptu speaking opportunities.

Conducting an Audit with Alex

(Answers)

1. $116,345
2. $98,449

Internet Resources and Activities Handbook

Refer students to the booklet for additional Internet activities.

interNET CONNECTION www.glencoe.com

Do This (Answers)

1. Coca-Cola http://www.cocacola.com
   Intel http://www.intel.com
   Corporate Financials Online http://www.cfonews.com/
   Answers may vary.
2. Answers may vary.
3. Answers may vary.

PEACHTREE CORNER

Financial Statements
Peachtree includes several standard financial statements. Choose **Financial Statements** from the ***Reports*** menu to access the standard Income Statement, Statement of Retained Earnings, and Balance Sheet reports.

You may want to discuss with your students the formatting differences between the Peachtree financial statements and the manual reports presented in this chapter. For example, the Peachtree Balance sheet is divided into more segments, including Current Assets, Property and Equipment, Other Assets, Current Liabilities, Long-Term Liabilities, and Capital. As another example, the Cost of Merchandise Sold section on the Peachtree Income Statement shows the **Inventory Adjustment** account balance instead of the beginning and ending inventory balances.

Reports Services Window
Accounts Receivable...
Accounts Payable...
Payroll...
General Ledger...
Financial Statements...
Inventory...
Jobs...
Account Reconciliation...

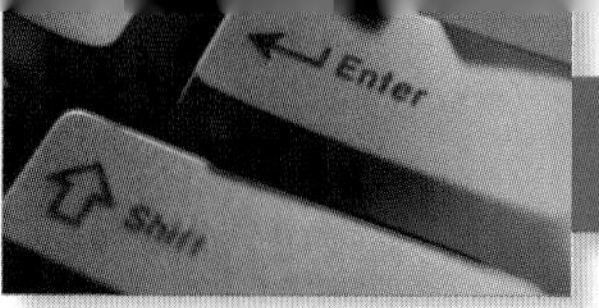

Preparing Financial Statements
Making the Transition from a Manual to a Computerized System

Task	Perform Accounting Procedures Using Manual Methods	Perform Accounting Procedures Using Automated Methods
Preparing financial statements	1. After all business transactions have been journalized and posted, prepare the trial balance. 2. Calculate, journalize, and post the adjusting entries. 3. Prepare the income statement, statement of retained earnings, and balance sheet.	1. After all business transactions have been journalized and posted, print a working trial balance. 2. Journalize the adjusting entries. 3. Print the income statement, statement of retained earnings, and balance sheet.

Preparing Financial Statements

Peachtree Question	Description
Why should I display a financial statement on the screen before printing it?	1. Displaying reports on the screen allows you to review the report before printing. 2. Viewing the report on the screen avoids printing a report that may contain no data or including data that you do not want included. 3. If a transaction in a report is outlined by a blue box, the "drill-down" feature allows you to double-click on the entry and go directly to the Tasks edit screen to make corrections. 4. Changes are reflected in the displayed report before it is printed.
How do I print the Income Statement, Statement of Retained Earnings, and Balance Sheet?	1. Select **Financial Statements** from the ***Reports*** menu. 2. Select *Income Statement, Retained Earnings Statement,* or *Balance Sheet* from the Reports list. 3. Click the Screen icon to display the Options window. 4. Select a time frame for the information to be included in the report. Current period is the default. 5. Review the statement on screen. 6. Click *Print.*
What does the software do "behind the scenes"?	• Financial statements are generated from information stored in the general ledger. Selections made at the Options window and the defaults established when the company was set up determine the appearance of the report and the amount of information included.

For detailed instructions: See the **Peachtree User Guide** in your Glencoe Working Papers.

Peachtree® Answers to Frequently Asked Questions

Q: Why does the Income Statement include current month and year-to-date totals?
A: The current month and year-to-date totals are included because they are part of the standard Income Statement report. You can change the design to remove the current month columns.

For additional information, refer to your *Glencoe Peachtree Accounting User Guide.*

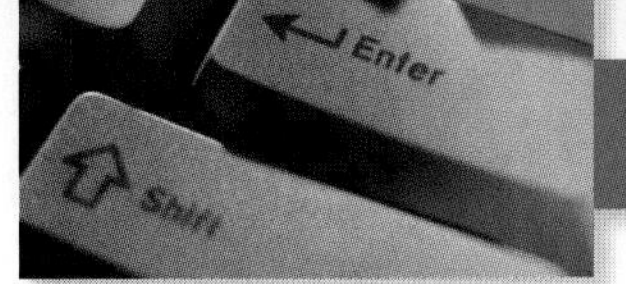

CHAPTER 19 PROBLEMS

APPLICATION OPTIONS

Problem 19–5 Preparing an Income Statement

The work sheet for Sunset Surfwear for the year ended December 31 is shown in your working papers.

Instructions Prepare an income statement for Sunset Surfwear in your working papers. Refer to **Figure 19–3** for guidance in setting up the income statement.

Analyze: Which is larger for this period, purchases discounts or purchases returns and allowances?

Problem 19–6 Preparing a Statement of Retained Earnings and a Balance Sheet

Instructions Use the work sheet and the income statement from **Problem 19–5** to prepare a statement of retained earnings and a balance sheet for Sunset Surfwear. Use the accounting stationery provided in your working papers.

Analyze: Calculate working capital for Sunset Surfwear.

Problem 19–7 Preparing Financial Statements

Instructions The partially completed work sheet for Shutterbug Cameras is included in your working papers.

(1) Complete the work sheet.
(2) Prepare an income statement.
(3) Prepare a statement of retained earnings.
(4) Prepare a balance sheet.

Analyze: Was the ending merchandise inventory greater or less than the beginning inventory?

Complete chapter problems one of four ways:

1 **Manual** Glencoe Working Papers

or

2 **Peachtree Complete Accounting** Software

or

3 **QuickBooks** Templates (Problems 19–5, 19–8)

or

4 **Spreadsheet** Templates (Problem 19–5)

SPREADSHEET SMART GUIDE

Step-by-Step Instructions: Problem 19–5

1. Select the spreadsheet template for Problem 19–5.
2. Enter your name and the date in the spaces provided on the template.
3. Complete the spreadsheet using the instructions in your working papers.
4. Print the spreadsheet and proof your work.
5. Save your work and exit the spreadsheet program.

PROBLEMS CHAPTER 19

Problem 19–5 (Answers) Preparing an Income Statement
Net Income $20,618

Analyze: Purchases Returns and Allowances

Problem 19–6 (Answers) Preparing a Statement of Retained Earnings and a Balance Sheet
Ending Retained Earnings $35,538
Total Assets $108,394
Total Liabilities $12,856
Total Stockholders' Equity $95,538

Analyze: $83,688

Problem 19–7 (Answers) Preparing Financial Statements
Adjusted Trial Balance Totals $209,089
Net Income $10,113
Ending Retained Earnings $29,305
Total Assets $125,460
Total Liabilities $16,155
Total Stockholders' Equity $109,305

Analyze: Less than beginning inventory

EXTENDING THE CONTENT

Telecommuting and Home-based Businesses Have each student find and read an article about telecommuting and/or home-based businesses that rely on the computer. Discuss how people who work in accounting careers can establish a home-based business or do much of their work through telecommuting. Ask students to identify friends and neighbors who have home-based businesses or telecommute. Invite one or more of these individuals to speak to your class about how they established their home-based business and/or how much time they spend telecommuting.

Problem 19–8 (Answers) Completing a Work Sheet and Financial Statements

Adjusted Trial Balance Totals $195,412
Net Income $26,208
Ending Retained Earnings $37,299
Total Assets $92,108
Total Liabilities $14,809
Total Stockholders' Equity $77,299

Analyze: Net income would be higher.

Peachtree®

SMART GUIDE

Step-by-Step Instructions: Problem 19–6

1. Select the problem set for Sunset Surfwear (Prob. 19–6).
2. Rename the company and set the system date.
3. Print a Statement of Retained Earnings and a Balance Sheet.
4. Answer the Analyze question.
5. End the session.

Peachtree®

SMART GUIDE

Step-by-Step Instructions: Problem 19–7

1. Select the problem set for Shutterbug Cameras (Prob. 19–7).
2. Rename the company and set the system date.
3. Print the following reports: Adjusted Trial Balance, Balance Sheet, Income Statement, and Statement of Retained Earnings.
4. Answer the Analyze question.
5. End the session.

Problem 19–8 Completing a Work Sheet and Financial Statements

The trial balance for Cycle Tech Bicycles, prepared on a ten-column work sheet, is included in your working papers.

Cycle Tech Bicycles
Work Sheet
For the Year Ended December 31, 20--

	ACCT. NO.	ACCOUNT NAME	TRIAL BALANCE DEBIT	TRIAL BALANCE CREDIT
1	101	*Cash in Bank*	21 931 00	
2	115	*Accounts Receivable*	1 782 00	
3	125	*Merchandise Inventory*	24 028 00	
4	130	*Supplies*	4 159 00	
5	135	*Prepaid Insurance*	1 800 00	
6	140	*Store Equipment*	24 895 00	
7	145	*Office Equipment*	16 113 00	
8	201	*Accounts Payable*		11 224 00
9	210	*Fed. Corp. Income Tax Payable*		
10	211	*Emplys' Fed. Inc. Tax Payable*		522 00
11	212	*Emplys' State Inc. Tax Payable*		144 00
12	213	*Social Security Tax Payable*		413 00
13	214	*Medicare Tax Payable*		134 00
14	215	*Sales Tax Payable*		1 915 00
15	216	*Fed. Unemployment Tax Payable*		54 00
16	217	*State Unemployment Tax Payable*		271 00
17	301	*Capital Stock*		40 000 00
18	305	*Retained Earnings*		11 091 00
19	310	*Income Summary*		
20	401	*Sales*		127 151 00
21	405	*Sales Discounts*	246 00	
22	410	*Sales Returns and Allowances*	1 328 00	
23	501	*Purchases*	66 107 00	
24	505	*Transportation In*	983 00	
25	510	*Purchases Discounts*		822 00
26	515	*Purchases Ret. and Allowances*		376 00
27	601	*Advertising Expense*	2 380 00	
28	605	*Bankcard Fees Expense*	181 00	
29	625	*Fed. Corp. Income Tax Expense*	3 340 00	
30	630	*Insurance Expense*		
31	645	*Maintenance Expense*	1 950 00	
32	650	*Miscellaneous Expense*	1 831 00	
33	655	*Payroll Tax Expense*	834 00	
34	657	*Rent Expense*	10 800 00	
35	660	*Salaries Expense*	4 734 00	
36	665	*Supplies Expense*		
37	675	*Utilities Expense*	4 695 00	
38				
39			194 117 00	194 117 00
40		*Net Income*		
41				
42				

Instructions

(1) Complete the work sheet for the year ended December 31. Use the following information to make the adjustments.

Ending merchandise inventory	$25,191
Ending supplies inventory	1,221
Expired insurance	825
Total federal corporate income taxes for the year	3,472

(2) Prepare an income statement.
(3) Prepare a statement of retained earnings.
(4) Prepare a balance sheet.

Analyze: If the ending value of **Merchandise Inventory** was actually $28,000, would net income be higher or lower?

SOFTWARE NOTES

Teachers can find detailed instructions for:

- **Peachtree Complete Accounting Software**, in the *Glencoe Workbook (CRWP)*
- **QuickBooks Templates**, in *Using QuickBooks with Glencoe Accounting*
- **Spreadsheet Templates**, in the *Glencoe Workbook (CRWP)*

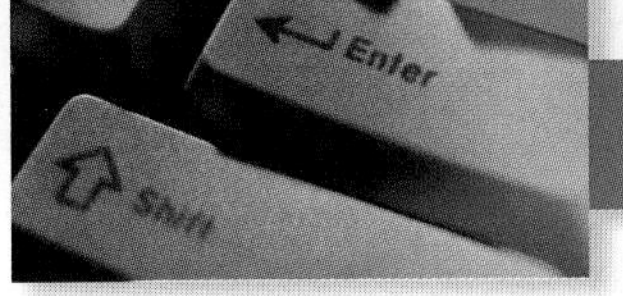

CHALLENGE PROBLEM

Problem 19–9 Evaluating the Effect of an Error on the Income Statement

The accounting clerk for River's Edge Canoe & Kayak prepared the income statement for the year ended December 31. The accounting supervisor at River's Edge noticed that the balance of the **Transportation In** account was erroneously omitted from this statement. **Transportation In** has a balance of $562.

Instructions Use the income statement shown in your working papers to answer the following questions.

1. In which section of the income statement is the account **Transportation In** entered?
2. How is net purchases affected by this omission (understated or overstated)? By what amount?
3. How does the omission of the **Transportation In** balance affect gross profit on sales? By what amount?
4. What is the correct amount for the cost of merchandise sold for the period?
5. What is the correct amount for net income?

Analyze: An overstatement of expenses has what effect on net income?

Peachtree®

SMART GUIDE

Step-by-Step Instructions: Problem 19–8

1. Select the problem set for Cycle Tech Bicycles (Prob. 19–8).
2. Rename the company and set the system date.
3. Print a Working Trial Balance to help you prepare the adjustments.
4. Record the adjustments using the **General Journal Entry** option.
5. Print a General Journal report and proof your work.
6. Print the following reports: Adjusted Trial Balance, Income Statement, Statement of Retained Earnings, and Balance Sheet.
7. Answer the Analyze question.
8. End the session.

CHALLENGE PROBLEM

Problem 19–9 (Answers) Evaluating the Effect of an Error on the Income Statement

1. Cost of Merchandise Sold
2. Understated, $562
3. Overstated, $562
4. $198,170
5. $46,914

Analyze: An overstatement of expenses causes net income to be understated.

SOLUTION NOTES

INTRODUCING
MINI PRACTICE SET 4

Mini Practice Set Overview

This reinforcement activity helps students integrate their learning of how to use the special journals and the general journal to record business transactions for a merchandising business called In-Touch Electronics. In the activity students journalize and post business transactions. They will use the four special journals, the general journal, the general ledger, and the accounts receivable and accounts payable subsidiary ledgers. Students will also prove cash and prepare schedules of accounts receivable and payable.

Most students should be able to complete this activity manually within two to three class periods.

Source documents and the accounting stationery needed for completing the practice set are included in the student workbook, *Chapter Reviews and Working Papers*.

Mini Practice Set Concepts

- How to analyze business transactions.
- How to journalize business transactions in the four special journals and in the general journal.
- How to post journal entries to the general ledger and to the accounts receivable and accounts payable subsidiary ledgers.
- How to post the totals of the special journals to the general ledger.
- How to prove cash.
- How to prepare a schedule of accounts receivable and a schedule of accounts payable.
- How to prepare a trial balance.

Visual Learning

Mini Practice Set Focus, p. 544
Discuss with students the accounting concepts and procedures they will apply in this mini practice set.

Recording Business Transactions in Special Journals

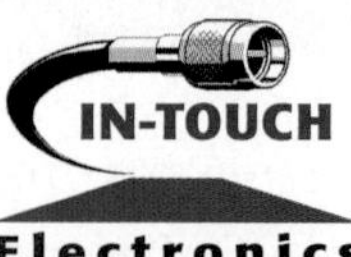

***What* You'll Learn**

- How to analyze business transactions.
- How to journalize business transactions in the four special journals and in the general journal.
- How to post journal entries to the general ledger and to the accounts receivable and accounts payable subsidiary ledgers.
- How to post the totals of the special journals to the general ledger.
- How to prove cash.
- How to prepare a schedule of accounts receivable and a schedule of accounts payable.
- How to prepare a trial balance.

***Why* It's Important**

In Chapters 16 and 17 you learned how to record the business transactions of a merchandising business in special journals. Now you will have the opportunity to review and apply what you have learned.

In-Touch Electronics

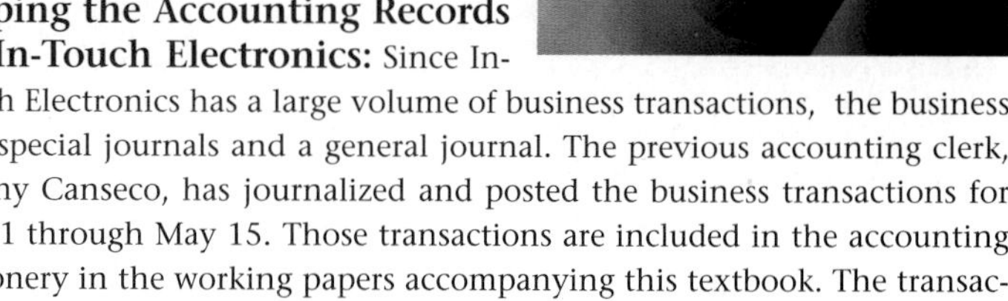

Company Background: Pedro and Tina Cordova own a merchandising business organized as a corporation called In-Touch Electronics. The retail business is a small, electronics store providing a unique service to the local community. This husband and wife team has been operating successfully for ten years.

Keeping the Accounting Records for In-Touch Electronics: Since In-Touch Electronics has a large volume of business transactions, the business uses special journals and a general journal. The previous accounting clerk, Manny Canseco, has journalized and posted the business transactions for May 1 through May 15. Those transactions are included in the accounting stationery in the working papers accompanying this textbook. The transactions that follow took place between May 16 and May 31.

Your Job Responsibilities: The forms for completing this activity are included in the working papers accompanying this textbook.

(1) Record the remaining May transactions in the sales journal (page 18), cash receipts journal (page 15), purchases journal (page 12), cash payments journal (page 14), and general journal (page 7).
(2) Post the individual amounts from the five journals to the accounts receivable and accounts payable subsidiary ledgers on a daily basis.
(3) Post the individual amounts from the General columns of the cash receipts, purchases, cash payments, and general journals on a daily basis.
(4) Foot, prove, total, and rule the special journals.
(5) Post the column totals of the special journals to the general ledger accounts. Use the following order for posting: sales journal, cash receipts journal, purchases journal, and cash payments journal.
(6) Prove cash. The balance shown on check stub 899 is $6109.45.
(7) Prepare a schedule of accounts receivable and a schedule of accounts payable.
(8) Prepare a trial balance.

TEACHING NOTES

In-Touch Electronics

APPLICATION OPTIONS

CHART OF ACCOUNTS
In-Touch Electronics

ASSETS

101 Cash in Bank
105 Accounts Receivable
110 Merchandise Inventory
115 Supplies
120 Prepaid Insurance
150 Store Equipment
155 Office Equipment

LIABILITIES

201 Accounts Payable
205 Sales Tax Payable
210 Employees' Federal Income Tax Payable
211 Employees' State Income Tax Payable
212 Social Security Tax Payable
213 Medicare Tax Payable
214 Federal Unemployment Tax Payable
215 State Unemployment Tax Payable

STOCKHOLDERS' EQUITY

301 Capital Stock
302 Retained Earnings
303 Income Summary

REVENUE

401 Sales
405 Sales Discounts
410 Sales Returns and Allowances

COST OF MERCHANDISE

501 Purchases
505 Transportation In
510 Purchases Discounts
515 Purchases Returns and Allowances

EXPENSES

605 Advertising Expense
610 Bankcard Fees Expense
615 Miscellaneous Expense
620 Payroll Tax Expense
625 Rent Expense
630 Salaries Expense
635 Utilities Expense

Accounts Receivable Subsidiary Ledger

LOR Sam Lorenzo
MAR Marianne Martino
MCC Mark McCormick
SCO Sue Ellen Scott
TRO Tom Trout

Accounts Payable Subsidiary Ledger

COM Computer Systems Inc.
DES Desktop Wholesalers
HIT Hi-Tech Electronics Outlet
LAS Laser & Ink-Jet Products
OFF Office Suppliers Inc.

Complete activities one of three ways:

1 **Manual** Glencoe Working Papers

or

2 **Peachtree Complete Accounting** Software

or

3 **QuickBooks** Templates

MINI PRACTICE SET 4
PAGES 544–547

Visual Learning

Chart of Accounts, p. 545

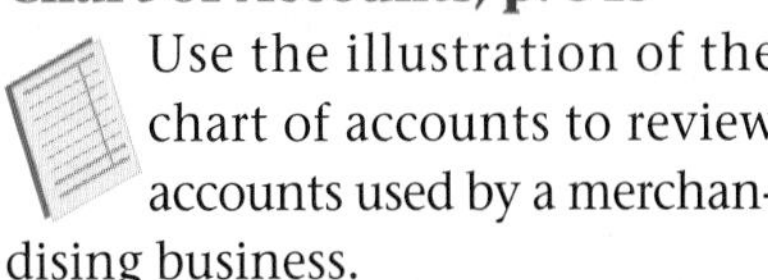

Use the illustration of the chart of accounts to review accounts used by a merchandising business.

ACCOUNTING ISSUES

The Impact of NAFTA The ratification of the North American Free Trade Agreement (NAFTA) has had a great impact on the accounting profession. CPA firms are now called upon to manage foreign currency transactions and solve international tax problems for firms that have established operations or alliances in Mexico, Canada, and the United States. To accommodate client demands for cross-border expertise, CPA firms employ personnel who are multilingual and multicultural. These individuals must understand international laws, rules, and general business protocol as they work with people in foreign offices.

MINI PRACTICE SET 4
PAGES 544–547

SOURCE DOCUMENT PROBLEM

ANSWERS

Sales Journal totals:
Sales $2,110.00
Sales Tax Payable $105.50
Accounts Receivable $2,215.50

Cash Receipts Journal totals:
General $90.00
Sales $9,660.00
Sales Tax Payable $483.00
Accounts Receivable $2,434.50
Sales Discounts $19.30
Cash in Bank $12,648.20

Purchases Journal totals:
Accounts Payable $7,770.00
Purchases $4,850.00
General $2,920.00

Cash Payments Journal totals:
General Debit $6,025.00
General Credit $641.25
Accounts Payable $8,670.00
Purchases Discounts $15.00
Cash in Bank $14,038.75

Cash proof $6,109.45

Schedule of Accounts Receivable $1,176.00
Schedule of Accounts Payable $4,575.00

Trial Balance totals $126,535.00

Peachtree®

SMART GUIDE

Step-by-Step Instructions:

1. Select the problem set for In-Touch Electronics (MP–4).
2. Rename the company and set the system date.
3. Enter all of the sales on account using the **Sales/Invoicing** option.
4. Record and apply any sales returns.
5. Process all of the cash receipts using the **Receipts** option.
6. Enter the purchases on account using the **Purchases/Receive Inventory** option.
7. Record and apply any purchases returns.
8. Process all of the cash payments with the **Payments** option.
9. Use the **General Journal Entry** option to record the error discovered on May 26.
10. Record the employer's payroll taxes using the **General Journal Entry** option.
11. Print the following reports: General Journal, Purchases Journal, Cash Disbursements Journal, Sales Journal, and Cash Receipts Journal.
12. Proof your work.
13. Print the following reports: General Ledger, Vendor Ledgers, and Customer Ledgers.
14. Print a General Ledger Trial Balance.
15. Answer the Analyze questions.
16. End the session.

Business Transactions: In-Touch Electronics had the following transactions in the month of May.

Date	Transactions
May 16	Sold $120.00 in merchandise plus 5% sales tax to Sam Lorenzo on account, Sales Slip 607.
17	Received $126.00 from Tom Trout to apply on his account, Receipt 356.
17	Issued Check 892 for $800.00 to Desktop Wholesalers in payment of our account balance.
18	Issued Debit Memo 38 to Laser & Ink Jet Products for our return of $75.00 in merchandise.
19	Wrote Check 893 for $1,200.00 to Computer Systems Inc. to apply on our account.
19	Paid Hi-Tech Electronics Outlet $1,750.00 in full payment of our account balance by issuing Check 894.
19	Issued Check 895 to Office Suppliers, Inc. for $770.00 in full payment of our account balance.
20	Sold $90.00 in office equipment for cash to an employee, Bob Bell, Receipt 357.
20	Purchased $1,200.00 in store equipment on account from Desktop Wholesalers, DW87, n/30.
20	Received $210.00 from Mark McCormick to apply on his account, Receipt 358.
20	Sue Ellen Scott sent us a check for $308.70 in payment of her $315.00 account less a 2% discount, Receipt 359.
21	Purchased $1,500.00 in merchandise on account from Hi-Tech Electronics Outlet, Invoice HT99, terms 2/10, n/30.
21	Marianne Martino sent us a $94.50 check to apply on her account, Receipt 360.
21	Sold $400.00 in merchandise plus 5% sales tax to Mark McCormick on account, Sales Slip 608, terms 2/10, n/30.
22	Issued Check 896 for $1,200.00 to Desktop Wholesalers, in payment of our account.
23	Sold $500.00 in merchandise to Sue Ellen Scott on account plus 5% sales tax, Sales Slip 609, terms 2/10, n/30.
24	Mark McCormick returned merchandise purchased on account, $100.00, plus 5% sales tax, Credit Memo 55.
25	Paid the annual insurance premium of $1,600.00 by issuing Check 897 to Surfside Insurance Co.
26	Discovered that **Transportation In** account should have been debited last month for $50.00 instead of the **Purchases** account. Recorded the correcting entry, Memorandum 26.
27	Bought $1,400.00 in merchandise on account from Computer Systems, Inc., CS75, terms 2/10, n/30.

Continued

MAKING CONNECTIONS TO DAILY LIFE

Doing Business with Corporations Most people deal with one or more corporations every day. If you make a telephone call, you are using the services of a corporation. If you purchase gasoline for your car, you are most likely using a product of a corporation. Ask your students to think of corporations they do business with frequently.

Date	Transactions (cont.)
28	Sold $200.00 in merchandise on account plus 5% sales tax to Marianne Martino, Sales Slip 610, terms 2/10, n/30.
29	Purchased $150.00 in supplies on account from Office Suppliers Inc., Invoice 9489.
30	Issued Check 898 for $1,500.00 in payment for the monthly rent.
31	Recorded cash sales of $1,200.00 plus 5% sales tax, Tape 22.
31	Recorded bankcard sales of $900.00 plus 5% sales tax, Tape 22.
31	Recorded bank service charge of $25.00 and bankcard fees of $100.00, May bank statement (record compound entry).
31	Wrote Check 899 to pay the payroll of $2,500.00 (gross earnings) for the pay period ended May 31. The following amounts were withheld: employees' federal income taxes, $400.00; employees' state income taxes, $50.00; FICA taxes, $155.00 for social security and $36.25 for Medicare.
31	Recorded the employer's payroll taxes for the May 31 payroll: FICA tax rate, 6.2% for social security and 1.45% for Medicare; federal unemployment tax rate, 0.8%; and state unemployment tax rate, 5.4%.

Peachtree®

SMART GUIDE

TIP: To save time entering transactions, group them by type and then enter the transactions in batches.

TIP: Remember that you need to change the G/L Account in the Receipts window to enter a cash receipt for the sale of an asset (e.g., supplies, office equipment.

TIP: Always verify the *G/L Account* field when you enter a purchases on account transaction.

Analyze:

1. How much has **Cash in Bank** increased by throughout the month?
2. What is the amount of the trial balance debit and credit columns on May 31?
3. What is the amount debited to the **Payroll Tax Expense** account on May 31?

MINI PRACTICE SET 4
PAGES 544–547

Analyze:
1. It has been reduced by $1,374.55.
2. $126,535.00
3. $346.25

SOLUTION NOTES

CHAPTER 20 *Resource Manager*

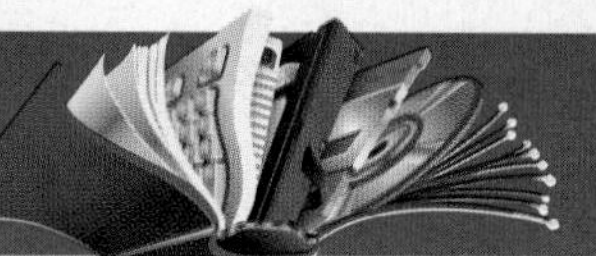

Section Resources

	Objectives & Standards	Activities & Features	Reproducible Masters
Chapter Opener *Completing the Accounting Cycle for a Merchandising Corporation*	• Journalize closing entries for a merchandising corporation. • Post closing entries to the general ledger accounts. • Prepare a post-closing trial balance. • Describe the steps in the accounting cycle. **National Standards for Business Education**: IA15, IA16	Exploring the Real World of Business, p. 548 Workplace Connections, p. 549	School-to-Work Handbook
Section 1 *Journalizing Closing Entries*	• What steps are followed to close the ledger. • What closing entries are required for a merchandising business organized as a corporation. • What closing entry is required when a corporation reports a loss.	Did You Know?, p. 550 International Accounting, p. 552 Accounting Flashbacks, p. 553 Accounting Tips, p. 554 A Matter of Ethics, p. 554	Strategies for Teaching International Accounting Demonstration Problems Strategies for Teaching Ethics in Accounting
Section 2 *Posting Closing Entries*	• How to post closing entries. • How to prepare a post-closing trial balance. • The accounting cycle for a merchandising business.	Spreadsheet Hints, p. 559 Connect To, p. 560 Analyzing Financial Reports, p. 561	Demonstration Problems Math Review for Accounting Internet Resources and Activities Handbook

KEY

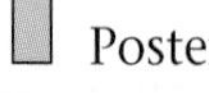

- Posters
- Blackline Masters
- Transparency
- CD-ROM
- Software
- Portfolio
- Videocassette

MULTIMEDIA RESOURCE

Peachtree	QuickBooks	Spreadsheets	Videos	CD-ROMs
Problem 20–4 *Journalizing Closing Entries* Problem 20–5 *Journalizing and Posting Closing Entries* Problem 20–6 *Identifying Accounts for Closing Entries* Problem 20–8 *Preparing Adjusting and Closing Entries*	Problem 20–5 *Journalizing and Posting Closing Entries* Problem 20–8 *Preparing Adjusting and Closing Entries*	Problem 20–7 *Completing End-of-Period Activities*	***Video Segment: Closing Entries*** After viewing this video, students will be able to describe the result of the closing process. They will also be able to explain the concept of closing entries and how the process is achieved.	***Electronic Learning Center (ELC), Chapter 20*** This program is ideal for visual learners since it incorporates video images, animation, and graphics to enliven the content of each lesson. ***Interactive Lesson Planner (ILP), Chapter 20*** This CD-ROM combines the versatility of an electronic lesson planner with the convenience of teacher classroom resources.

SCANS Correlation Chart

FOUNDATION SKILLS

Basic Skills:	Reading	Writing	Math	Listening	Speaking	
Thinking Skills:	Creative Thinking	Decision Making	Problem Solving	Seeing Things in the Mind's Eye	Knowing How to Learn	Reasoning
Personal Qualities:	Responsibility	Self-Esteem	Sociability	Self-Management	Integrity/Honesty	

WORKPLACE COMPETENCIES

Resources:	Allocating Time	Allocating Money	Allocating Material and Facility Resources	Allocating Human Resources		
Information:	Acquiring and Evaluating Information	Organizing and Maintaining Information	Interpreting and Communicating Information	Using Computers to Process Information		
Interpersonal Skills:	Participating as a Member of a Team	Teaching Others	Serving Clients/ Customers	Exercising Leadership	Negotiating to Arrive at a Decision	Working with Cultural Diversity
Systems:	Understanding Systems	Monitoring and Correcting Performance	Improving and Designing Systems			
Technology:	Selecting Technology	Applying Technology to Task	Maintaining and Troubleshooting Technology			

*Highlighted blocks indicate areas covered in the chapter. Additional SCANS skills are also covered throughout the *Teacher Wraparound Edition.*

Assessment

Student Edition
- Check Your Understanding, pp. 555, 562
- Chapter 20 Problems, pp. 567–571

Assessment and Evaluation Masters
- Chapter 20 Study Plan, *Glencoe Workbook*
- Chapter 20 Self-Test, *Glencoe Workbook*
- Chapter 20 Test, *Chapter Tests* Booklet
- Chapter 20 Activity *School-to-Work Handbook*
- Chapter 20 **Exam***View*

Teacher Wraparound Edition
- Critical Thinking Activity, p. 557
- Reteaching Section 1, p. 555
- Reteaching Section 2, p. 562
- Chapter 20 Quiz, p. 563

Transparencies

	Teaching Transparencies	Solution Transparencies
Section 1:	20–1, 20–2, 20–3, 20–4, 20–5, 20–6	Problem 20–1
Section 2:	20–7, 20–8a, 20–8b, 20–8c, 20–8d, 20–9, 20–10	Problems 20–2, 20–3
End of Chapter:		Problems 20–4, 20–5, 20–6, 20–7, 20–8

TEACHER CLASSROOM RESOURCES

This is a representation of key blackline masters available in the Teacher Classroom Resources.

Teaching Aids

Transparency Examples

Section Focus Transparencies

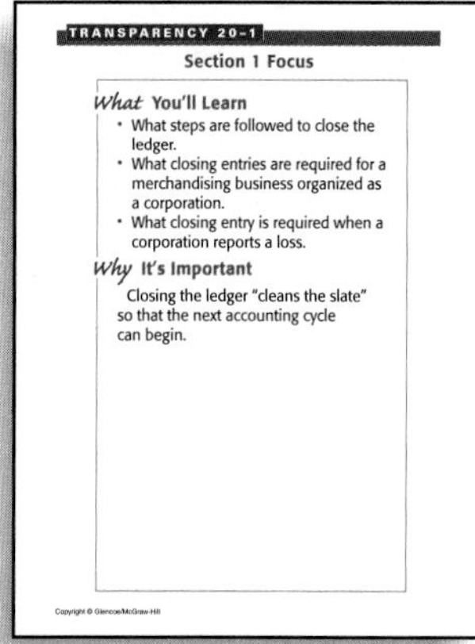

TRANSPARENCY 20-1

Section 1 Focus

What You'll Learn

- What steps are followed to close the ledger.
- What closing entries are required for a merchandising business organized as a corporation.
- What closing entry is required when a corporation reports a loss.

Why It's Important

Closing the ledger "cleans the slate" so that the next accounting cycle can begin.

Teaching Transparencies

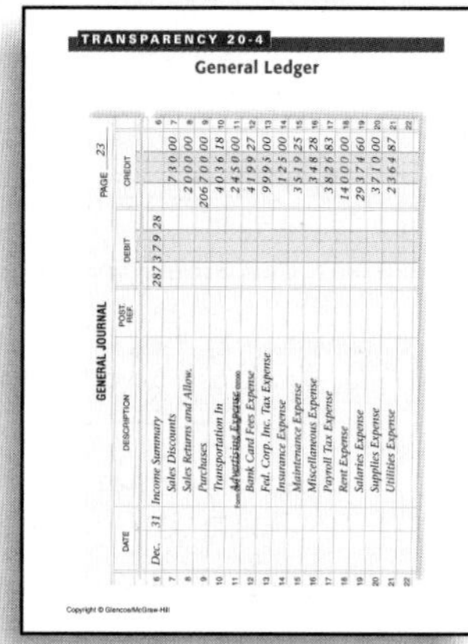

TRANSPARENCY 20-4

General Ledger

Teaching Transparencies

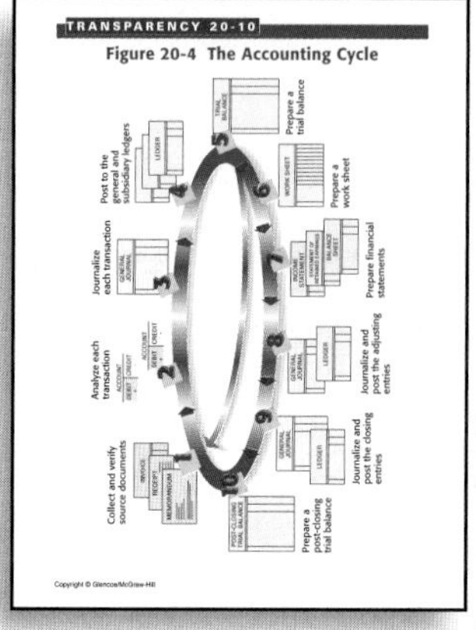

TRANSPARENCY 20-10

Figure 20-4 The Accounting Cycle

Solution Transparencies

Demonstration Problems

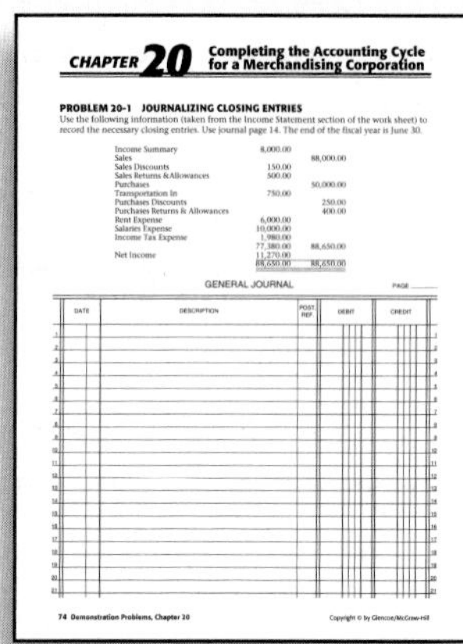

CHAPTER 20 Completing the Accounting Cycle for a Merchandising Corporation

PROBLEM 20-1 JOURNALIZING CLOSING ENTRIES

GENERAL JOURNAL

Lesson Plans

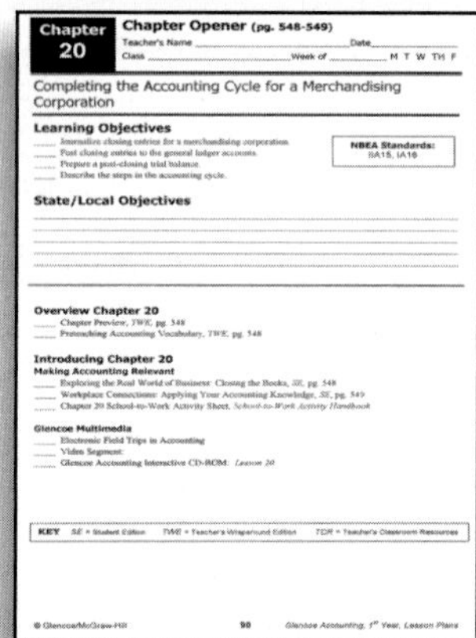

Chapter 20 Chapter Opener (pg. 548-549)

Completing the Accounting Cycle for a Merchandising Corporation

Learning Objectives

State/Local Objectives

Block Scheduling

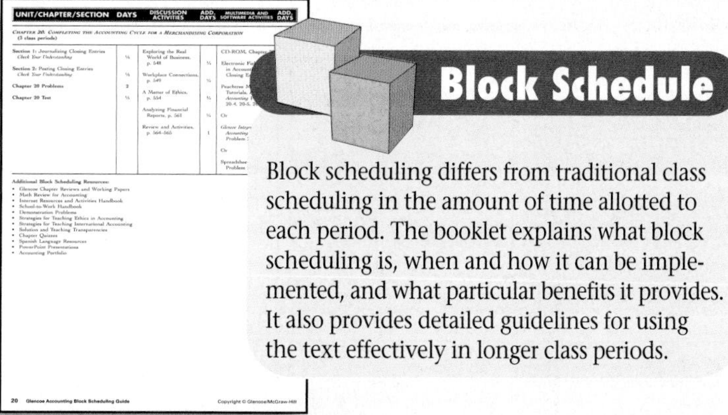

Block Schedule

Block scheduling differs from traditional class scheduling in the amount of time allotted to each period. The booklet explains what block scheduling is, when and how it can be implemented, and what particular benefits it provides. It also provides detailed guidelines for using the text effectively in longer class periods.

Enrichment and Application

Strategies for Teaching Ethics in Accounting

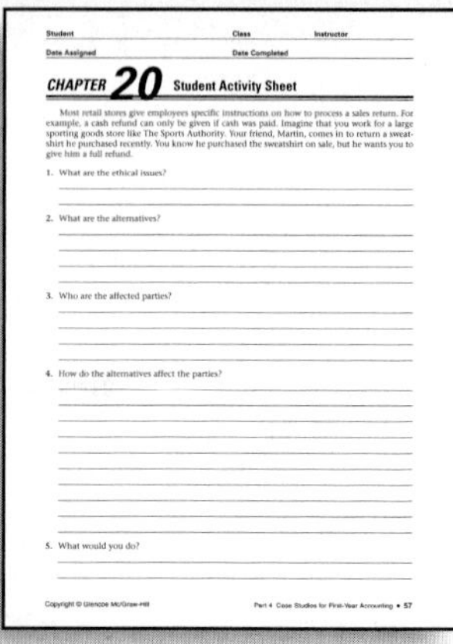

CHAPTER 20 Student Activity Sheet

Strategies for Teaching International Accounting

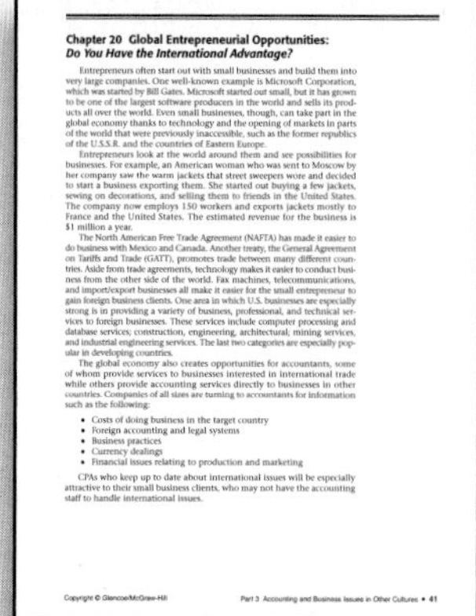

Chapter 20 Global Entrepreneurial Opportunities: Do You Have the International Advantage?

School-to-Work Handbook

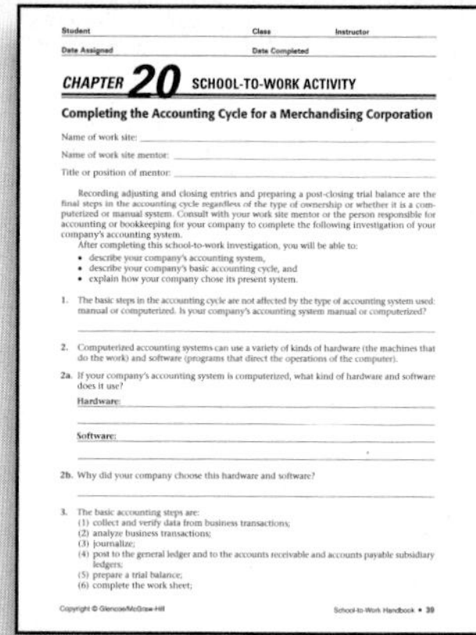

CHAPTER 20 SCHOOL-TO-WORK ACTIVITY

Completing the Accounting Cycle for a Merchandising Corporation

Meeting Different Ability Levels

Chapter Reviews and Working Papers (CRWP)

Working Papers

Review

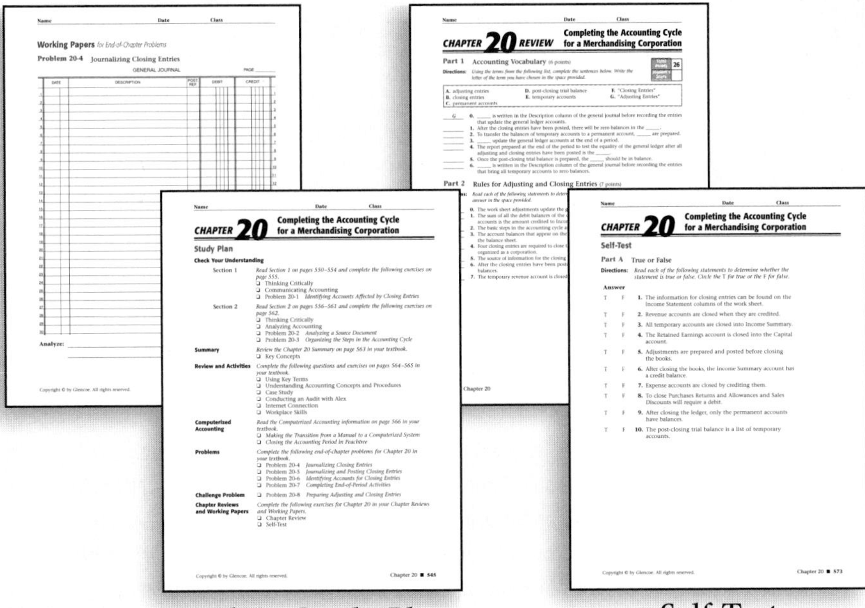

Student Study Plan

Self-Test

Real-World Multimedia CD-ROM

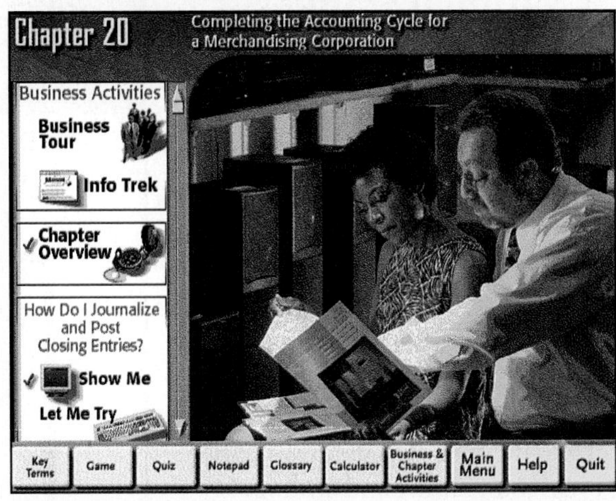

Key to Ability Levels

Each section gives skill-building activities. Each activity has been labeled for use with students of various learning styles and abilities.

L1 Level 1 activities are basic activities and should be within the range of all students.

L2 Level 2 activities are average activities and should be within the range of average and above average students.

L3 Level 3 activities are challenging activities designed for the ability range of above average students.

ELL ELL activities should be within the ability range of English Language Learners.

Teaching Resources at a Glance

Application Resources

- Glencoe Chapter Review and Working Papers, SE and TAE
- School-to-Work Handbook, SE and TM
- Accounting Portfolio, SE and TM

Reproducible Masters

- Demonstration Problems
- Lesson Plans
- Block Scheduling
- Spanish Language Resources

Glencoe Accounting Professional Development Series

- Strategies for Teaching Ethics in Accounting
- Accounting Competitive Event Review
- Math Review for Accounting
- Strategies for Teaching International Accounting
- Internet Resources and Activities Handbook

Transparency Package

- Section Focus Transparencies
- Teaching Transparencies
- Source Document Transparencies
- Solution Transparencies

Performance Assessment

- **Exam***View* CD-ROM
- Chapter Tests
- Chapter Quizzes
- Unit Tests
- Audit Tests
- Printed Testbank

Multimedia Resources

- Electronic Learning Center:
  - Multimedia CD-ROMs
  - Peachtree software, tutorials, templates, and solutions
  - Spreadsheet templates
- Using QuickBooks with Glencoe Accounting
- Interactive Lesson Planner
- Electronic Field Trips in Accounting
- PowerPoint Presentation
- Web site: glencoeaccounting.glencoe.com

Assessment and Evaluation

Chapter Tests

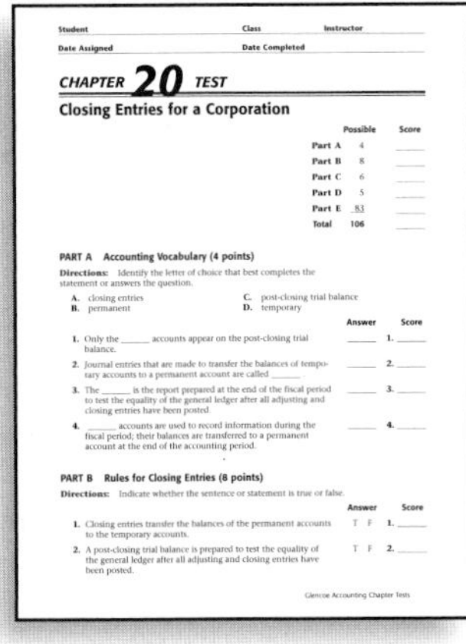

Chapter Quiz

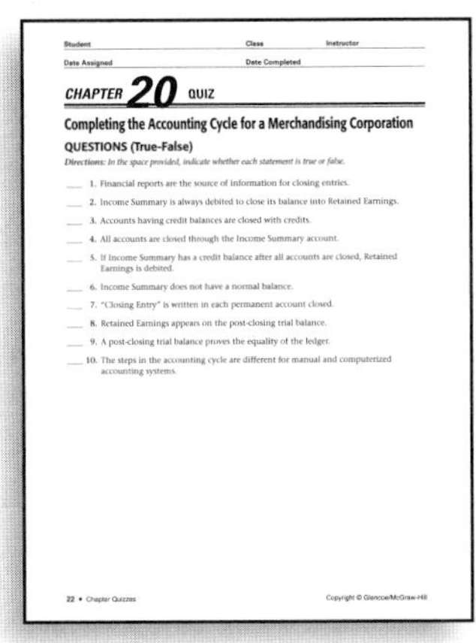

OVERVIEW
CHAPTER 20

Correlations to National Standards for Business Education
(See pages T50–T51 for a detailed correlation chart.)
Standards: IA15, IA16

Chapter Preview
Now that students have learned to record transactions for a merchandising business and prepare a work sheet and financial statements, they are ready to complete the final step in the accounting cycle: journalizing and posting closing entries and preparing a post-closing trial balance.

Section Overviews
- Section 1—*Journalizing Closing Entries*
- Section 2—*Posting Closing Entries*

Chapter Vocabulary
No new terms are introduced in this chapter. Review the meaning of **closing entries**.

Preteaching Accounting Vocabulary
Oral Exercise: Have students tell you each of the steps, in order, in the accounting cycle for a merchandising business. Write their responses on the chalkboard. Ask students to discuss why each step has its particular order in the cycle. Review definitions of terms in each step. L1

CHAPTER 20

Completing the Accounting Cycle for a Merchandising Corporation

Learning Objectives
When you have completed this chapter, you will be able to:
- Journalize closing entries for a merchandising corporation.
- Post closing entries to the general ledger accounts.
- Prepare a post-closing trial balance.
- Describe the steps in the accounting cycle.

Exploring the Real World of Business
CLOSING THE BOOKS

If you've ever purchased a set of speakers for your stereo system, you've probably heard of **Bose Corporation.** Noted for high-performance audio equipment, **Bose** products are sold in retail stores and found in many luxury automobiles. You'll find **Bose** products in homes as well as in stadiums, arenas, computers, restaurants, public spaces, and even on the space shuttle.

Bose Corporation was started in 1964 by Dr. Amar Bose, a professor at the Massachusetts Institute of Technology. Dr. Bose believes in using research and technology to create the best possible products. Research is expensive, and the company tracks costs through its accounting system.

Making closing entries at the end of each fiscal period helps the company match the specific expenses of developing new loudspeakers or other equipment to a fiscal period and to the products developed.

What do you think?
If you worked for **Bose Corporation,** what accounts would you use to track the costs for a new line of home audio loudspeakers?

Bose Corporation

Exploring the Real World of Business

Bose Corporation
To continue growing, Bose relies on introducing new merchandise, such as different types of speakers and sound systems. Selling its products into new markets, such as pilots who use Bose's Noise Cancelling® headsets to improve communications sound, adds to the company's success.

What do you think? (Answers)
Answers will vary. You might use a research account for research and development costs, an advertising and promotion account, a dealer rebates account if special incentives are offered, an account for packaging costs, and accounts for manufacturing costs.

Workplace Connections

Applying Your Accounting Knowledge

You've nearly completed another accounting cycle–this time for a merchandising company. After the financial statements are prepared, closing entries are made to get the accounting records ready for the next fiscal period. You might think of closing entries as "wiping the slate clean" to make it ready for more entries. Closing entries for a merchandising business are similar to those you learned about for a service business. There are just more of them.

Investigate:

1. In your job, are there duties that you perform at the end of a night or week that "wipe the slate clean" or "close out" the day's activities?
2. If you were preparing the closing entries for your workplace, what accounts do you imagine would be involved?

549

Glencoe Accounting Online

Visit the *Glencoe Accounting* Web site at **glencoeaccounting.glencoe.com** for additional activities and information.

INTRODUCING
CHAPTER 20

Making Accounting Relevant

Workplace Connections: Applying Your Accounting Knowledge

Discussion: Discuss with students the things they do at the end of a school year, such as cleaning out lockers, getting ready for graduation, or planning for a summer job. Businesses have a similar need to organize their operations for a new fiscal period.

Investigate (Answers)

1. Answers will vary. Students who work in retail environments might mention tallying their change funds and closing out their cash registers.
2. Answers will vary. Students should mention that the temporary accounts—such as Sales, Purchases, and expense accounts—are closed.

School-to-Work Activity

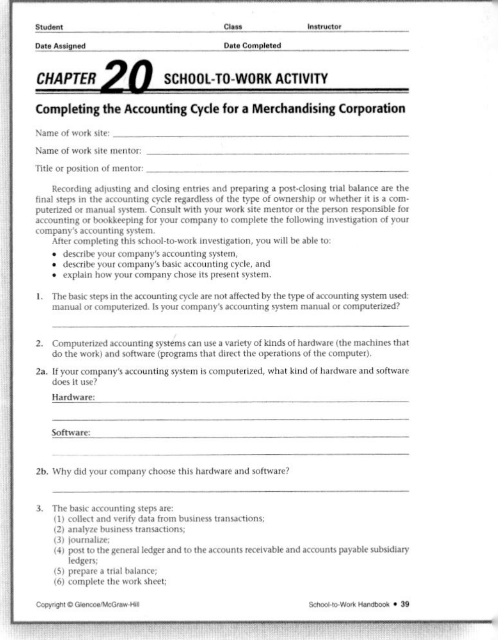

Student ________ Class ________ Instructor ________

Date Assigned ________ Date Completed ________

CHAPTER 20 SCHOOL-TO-WORK ACTIVITY

Completing the Accounting Cycle for a Merchandising Corporation

Name of work site: ________

Name of work site mentor: ________

Title or position of mentor: ________

Recording adjusting and closing entries and preparing a post-closing trial balance are the final steps in the accounting cycle regardless of the type of ownership or whether it is a computerized or manual system. Consult with your work site mentor or the person responsible for accounting or bookkeeping for your company to complete the following investigation of your company's accounting system.

After completing this school-to-work investigation, you will be able to:

- describe your company's accounting system,
- describe your company's basic accounting cycle, and
- explain how your company chose its present system.

1. The basic steps in the accounting cycle are not affected by the type of accounting system used: manual or computerized. Is your company's accounting system manual or computerized?

2. Computerized accounting systems can use a variety of kinds of hardware (the machines that do the work) and software (programs that direct the operations of the computer).

2a. If your company's accounting system is computerized, what kind of hardware and software does it use?

Hardware: ________

Software: ________

2b. Why did your company choose this hardware and software?

3. The basic accounting steps are:
(1) collect and verify data from business transactions;
(2) analyze business transactions;
(3) journalize;
(4) post to the general ledger and to the accounts receivable and accounts payable subsidiary ledgers;
(5) prepare a trial balance;
(6) complete the work sheet;

School-to-Work Handbook • 39

GLENCOE MULTIMEDIA

Electronic Field Trips in Accounting *Video Segment: Closing Entries*

After viewing this video, students will be able to describe the result of the closing process and explain the concept of closing entries and how the process is achieved.

Glencoe Accounting: Electronic Learning Center *Chapter 20*

The CD-ROM program is ideal for visual learners since it incorporates video images, animation, and graphics to enliven the content of each lesson.

CHAPTER 20
SECTION 1, PAGES 550–555

1 FOCUS

Introducing the Section

In this section students will learn which of a merchandising corporation's accounts are closed at the end of an accounting cycle. They'll learn how to journalize all the closing entries using information from the work sheet.

Section Concepts

- What steps are followed to close the ledger.
- What closing entries are required for a merchandising business organized as a corporation.
- What closing entry is required when a corporation reports a loss.

Visual Learning

Section 1 Focus

Use **Transparency 20–1** to introduce section concepts.

BELL RINGER

Compare and Contrast: Have students recall the closing entries they prepared in Chapter 10 for a sole proprietorship, service business (see page 243). Ask how they think the closing entries for a merchandising corporation might be different. (The process is the same; some of the accounts closed will be different because they are unique to a merchandising business.) L1

SECTION 1

Journalizing Closing Entries

What You'll Learn

- What steps are followed to close the ledger.
- What closing entries are required for a merchandising business organized as a corporation.
- What closing entry is required when a corporation reports a loss.

Why It's Important

Closing the ledger "cleans the slate" so that the next accounting cycle can begin.

In Chapter 10 you learned how to journalize and post the closing entries for a service business operated as a sole proprietorship. In this chapter you will learn how to journalize and post the closing entries for a merchandising business organized as a corporation. Whether a business is organized as a sole proprietorship or a corporation, and whether it is a service or merchandising business, the procedures for journalizing closing entries are the same. Because closing entries are important, the accountant for a business like Newman's Own reviews them for accuracy and completeness.

Closing entries transfer the balances of all the temporary accounts to a permanent account. After the closing entries are posted, all of the temporary accounts have zero balances. The general ledger is then ready for the next accounting period. Information needed to prepare the

Did You Know?

Financial Statements

Like other privately owned companies, Bose does not publish its financial statements each year after closing its books. Only public companies whose stock is traded on a stock exchange are required to publish their operating results each year.

On Your Mark
Work
For the Year Ended

	ACCT. NO.	ACCOUNT NAME	TRIAL BALANCE DEBIT	TRIAL BALANCE CREDIT	ADJUSTMENTS DEBIT	ADJUSTMENTS CREDIT
20	310	Income Summary			(a)3 536 00	
21	401	Sales		320 450 00		
22	405	Sales Discounts	730 00			
23	410	Sales Returns and Allowances	2 000 00			
24	501	Purchases	206 700 00			
25	505	Transportation In	4 036 18			
26	510	Purchases Discounts		1 340 00		
27	515	Purchases Returns and Allow.		1 800 00		
28	601	Advertising Expense	2 450 00			
29	605	Bankcard Fees Expense	4 199 27			
30	630	Fed. Corporate Income Tax Exp.	9 840 00		(d) 155 00	
31	635	Insurance Expense			(c) 125 00	
32	650	Maintenance Expense	3 519 25			
33	655	Miscellaneous Expense	348 28			
34	657	Payroll Tax Expense	3 826 83			
35	660	Rent Expense	14 000 00			
36	665	Salaries Expense	29 374 60			
37	670	Supplies Expense			(b)3 710 00	
38	680	Utilities Expense	2 364 87			
39			435 798 28	435 798 28	7 526 00	7 526 00
40		Net Income				
41						
42						

Figure 20–1
Closing Entries Needed for a Corporation

RESOURCE MANAGER

Reproducible Masters
- Lesson Plans
- Chapter Reviews and Working Papers (CRWP) TAE
- Demonstration Problems

Transparencies
- Section Focus Transparency
- Teaching Transparencies
- Source Document Transparencies
- Solution Transparencies

Multimedia
- **Exam***View* CD-ROM
- Electronic Learning Center CD-ROM
- Interactive Lesson Planner CD-ROM
- Electronic Field Trips in Accounting

closing entries is found in the Income Statement section of the work sheet, which contains the balances of all the temporary accounts.

Steps for Closing the Ledger

In Chapter 10 you made four entries to close the temporary general ledger accounts of a sole proprietorship:

1. close the temporary accounts with credit balances to **Income Summary**
2. close the temporary accounts with debit balances to **Income Summary**
3. close the balance of **Income Summary** to capital
4. close the withdrawals account to capital

Only the first three closing entries are made to close the temporary accounts for a merchandising business organized as a corporation. Since a corporation does not have a withdrawals account, the fourth closing entry is not needed.

The portion of On Your Mark's work sheet in **Figure 20–1** shows the account balances that are closed. Let's look closely at each closing entry.

1. Close the accounts with balances in the Credit column of the Income Statement section of the work sheet (revenue and contra cost of merchandise accounts) to **Income Summary.**

Sales	
Debit –	Credit +
Clos. 320,450.00	Bal. 320,450.00

Income Summary	
Debit	Credit
Adj. 3,536.00	Clos. 323,590.00

Purchases Discounts	
Debit –	Credit +
Clos. 1,340.00	Bal. 1,340.00

Purchases Returns and Allowances	
Debit –	Credit +
Clos. 1,800.00	Bal. 1,800.00

Athletic Wear
Sheet
December 31, 20--

ADJUSTED TRIAL BALANCE		INCOME STATEMENT		BALANCE SHEET		
DEBIT	CREDIT	DEBIT	CREDIT	DEBIT	CREDIT	
3 536 00		3 536 00				20
	320 450 00		320 450 00			21
730 00		730 00				22
2 000 00		2 000 00				23
206 700 00		206 700 00				24
4 036 18		4 036 18				25
	1 340 00		1 340 00			26
	1 800 00		1 800 00			27
2 450 00		2 450 00				28
4 199 27		4 199 27				29
9 995 00		9 995 00				30
125 00		125 00				31
3 519 25		3 519 25				32
348 28		348 28				33
3 826 83		3 826 83				34
14 000 00		14 000 00				35
29 374 60		29 374 60				36
3 710 00		3 710 00				37
2 364 87		2 364 87				38
435 953 28	435 953 28	290 915 28	323 590 00	145 038 00	112 363 28	39
		32 674 72			32 674 72	40
		323 590 00	323 590 00	145 038 00	145 038 00	41
						42

1 Close temporary accounts with balances in the Income Statement Credit column to Income Summary.

2 Close temporary accounts with balances in the Income Statement Debit column to Income Summary.

3 Close Income Summary to Retained Earnings by the amount of the net income or loss.

Figure 20–1
Closing Entries Needed for a Corporation

CHAPTER 20
SECTION 1, PAGES 550–555

2 TEACH

GUIDED PRACTICE

Reading Accounting

- Have students read this section with the specific goal of identifying the classifications of all accounts that are closed at the end of the fiscal period. **L1**
- Prepare a bulletin-board display of the closing process. Include descriptions in English and in your students' first language. **ELL**

Concept Development: Steps for Closing the Ledger

Discussion: Ask students to explain the difference between permanent and temporary accounts. Point out the Income Statement section of the work sheet. Remind students that temporary accounts are reported on the income statement and that these accounts are closed at the end of the fiscal period. **L1**

Visual Learning

Figure 20–1 Closing Entries Needed for a Corporation

Using **Transparency 20–2,** discuss each step in the closing process.

Teaching Tip

Point out the T accounts for Sales, Purchases Discounts, and Purchases Returns and Allowances. Review the normal balance and how to make an entry to bring each account's balance to zero.

Great Ideas *From the Classroom of...*

Teaching Closing Entries Choose a work sheet problem that contains as many accounts as you have students in the class. Create a poster with an envelope labeled for each account and assign each student one of the accounts. Display the completed work sheet and ask students to record their account balance on a 3 × 5 card and then place the card in the correct account envelope. Review the closing entries, post the entries by moving the cards to the correct envelopes, and prepare a post-closing trial balance.

Jacque Steinberger
Trimble Tech High School
Fort Worth, Texas

2 TEACH (Cont'd.)

Visual Learning

General Journal

Use **Transparency 20–3** to show students how to record closing entries for accounts with credit balances.

Teaching Tips

Remind students of the purpose of the Income Summary account: to serve as a mini income statement in the general ledger. Discuss why this account is used as a clearing account.

Have students compare T-account balances on pages 552–553 with the balances in the Income Statement section of the work sheet in Figure 20–1 (page 551). These are all the temporary accounts with debit balances.

Critical Thinking: Have students look at the T accounts on this page and then offer reasons why the accounts with debit balances are all added and the total closed to Income Summary rather than each account being closed individually. (To save space and time making separate journal entries.) L1

Strategies for Teaching International Accounting

To enrich study of international accounting, refer to the additional critical thinking activities in the booklet.

Key Points

Closing Temporary Accounts with Credit Balances

The sum of the balances in the Credit column of the Income Statement section of the work sheet, which includes revenue and contra cost of merchandise accounts, is the amount *credited* to **Income Summary.**

GENERAL JOURNAL PAGE 23

	DATE		DESCRIPTION	POST. REF.	DEBIT	CREDIT	
1	20--		*Closing Entries*				1
2	Dec.	31	*Sales*		320 450 00		2
3			*Purchases Discounts*		1 340 00		3
4			*Purchases Returns and Allow.*		1 800 00		4
5			*Income Summary*			323 590 00	5
6							6

After this closing entry is journalized and posted, the **Sales**, **Purchases Discounts**, and **Purchases Returns and Allowances** accounts have zero balances.

2. Close the accounts with balances in the Debit column of the Income Statement section of the work sheet (contra revenue, cost of merchandise, and expense accounts) to **Income Summary.**

Income Summary

Debit	Credit
Adj. 3,536.00 Clos. 287,379.28	Clos. 323,590.00

Insurance Expense

Debit +	Credit –
Bal. 125.00	Clos. 125.00

Sales Discounts

Debit +	Credit –
Bal. 730.00	Clos. 730.00

Maintenance Expense

Debit +	Credit –
Bal. 3,519.25	Clos. 3,519.25

Sales Returns and Allowances

Debit +	Credit –
Bal. 2,000.00	Clos. 2,000.00

Miscellaneous Expense

Debit +	Credit –
Bal. 348.28	Clos. 348.28

Purchases

Debit +	Credit –
Bal. 206,700.00	Clos. 206,700.00

Payroll Tax Expense

Debit +	Credit –
Bal. 3,826.83	Clos. 3,826.83

Transportation In

Debit +	Credit –
Bal. 4,036.18	Clos. 4,036.18

Rent Expense

Debit +	Credit –
Bal. 14,000.00	Clos. 14,000.00

Advertising Expense

Debit +	Credit –
Bal. 2,450.00	Clos. 2,450.00

Salaries Expense

Debit +	Credit –
Bal. 29,374.60	Clos. 29,374.60

International ACCOUNTING

Regional Preferences

When conducting business, the customer's tastes should be considered. Consumers around the world have different preferences in product packaging. For example, in France and Italy consumers expect stylish looks, while in Germany many consumers look for recyclable materials. Accountants who work with international clients should consider national preferences when designing letterhead, creating portfolios, or choosing paper quality.

Teaching International ACCOUNTING

Designing an Invoice Tell students that they work for an accounting firm in San Francisco. Although many clients are in the United States, they also have clients in Germany, France, and Italy. The office manager wants a new invoice form for billing clients. Have students design two or more invoice forms appropriate for billing the firm's clients. If available, use a document template form provided in a software application. Ask students to describe the kind and color of paper they would recommend for printing and the ink colors they would use.

Bankcard Fees Expense	
Debit +	Credit −
Bal. 4,199.27	Clos. 4,199.27

Supplies Expense	
Debit +	Credit −
Bal. 3,710.00	Clos. 3,710.00

Federal Corporate Income Tax Expense	
Debit +	Credit −
Bal. 9,995.00	Clos. 9,995.00

Utilities Expense	
Debit +	Credit −
Bal. 2,364.87	Clos. 2,364.87

ACCOUNTING *Flashbacks*

EARLY INVENTIONS
Paper was probably invented by artisans in China by 100 BC. Used first for wrapping and clothing, paper was soon recognized as an ideal writing and record-keeping material.

GENERAL JOURNAL PAGE 23

	DATE		DESCRIPTION	POST. REF.	DEBIT	CREDIT	
6	Dec.	31	Income Summary		287 379 28		6
7			Sales Discounts			730 00	7
8			Sales Returns and Allow.			2 000 00	8
9			Purchases			206 700 00	9
10			Transportation In			4 036 18	10
11			Advertising Expense			2 450 00	11
12			Bankcard Fees Expense			4 199 27	12
13			Fed. Corp. Inc. Tax Expense			9 995 00	13
14			Insurance Expense			125 00	14
15			Maintenance Expense			3 519 25	15
16			Miscellaneous Expense			348 28	16
17			Payroll Tax Expense			3 826 83	17
18			Rent Expense			14 000 00	18
19			Salaries Expense			29 374 60	19
20			Supplies Expense			3 710 00	20
21			Utilities Expense			2 364 87	21
22							22

After this closing entry is journalized and posted, contra revenue, cost of merchandise, and expense accounts have zero balances.

After the two preceding closing entries are journalized and posted, **Income Summary** has a credit balance of $32,674.72.

$ 323,590.00	closing credit
− 3,536.00	adjustment debit
−287,379.28	closing debit
$ 32,674.72	credit balance

3. Close **Income Summary** to **Retained Earnings.**

Income Summary	
Debit	Credit
Adj. 3,536.00 Clos. 287,379.28 Clos. 32,674.72	Clos. 323,590.00

Retained Earnings	
Debit −	Credit +
	Bal. 19,771.19 Clos. 32,674.72

After the entry to close **Income Summary** to **Retained Earnings** is journalized and posted, **Income Summary** has a zero balance. The balance of **Retained Earnings** is increased to $52,445.91.

Key Points

Closing Temporary Accounts with Debit Balances
The sum of the balances in the Debit column of the Income Statement section of the work sheet, which includes contra revenue, cost of merchandise, and expense accounts, is the amount *debited* to **Income Summary.**

MAKING CONNECTIONS TO DAILY LIFE

Communications Knowing about computers has become a necessary skill in most offices and businesses. Have students research and analyze some of the accounting software programs now available. They should look at these programs in terms of their being "user-friendly" and suitable for small businesses, large corporations, or individual users. Students should then prepare a business report summarizing their findings and listing their recommendations. This activity could also be used as a cooperative learning experience.

2 TEACH (Cont'd.)

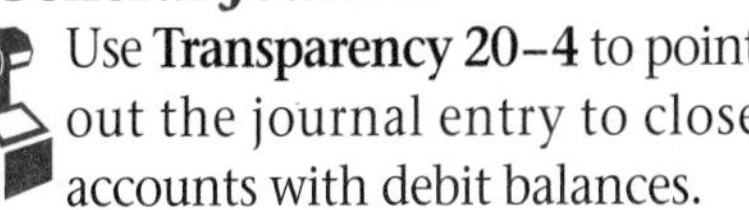

Visual Learning

General Journal
Use **Transparency 20–4** to point out the journal entry to close accounts with debit balances.

Teaching Tips
Point out that the adjustment debit of $3,536.00 is from the adjusting entries journalized in Chapter 18.

Remind students that Income Summary does not have a normal balance side.

Demonstration Problem Step-by-Step Practice
Use demonstration problem 20–1 to give students practice in journalizing the closing entries.

Critical Thinking: Have students look at the journal entries on this page. If they were asked to reconstruct an income statement from these entries, what additional information would they need? (Beginning and ending Merchandise Inventory balances.) L2

Thinking Algebraically

Theorizing: Have students explain why Income Summary is debited to close the accounts with debit balances. (Students should think of the simple equation, debits = credits. For an equation to balance, amounts added to or subtracted from one side must also be added to or subtracted from the other side. Since accounts with debit balances are credited to close them, the same amount must be debited to another account to keep the equation balanced.) L3

2 TEACH (Cont'd.)

Visual Learning

General Journal

Display **Transparency 20–5** and explain the entry to close the balance of Income Summary into the Retained Earnings account.

Concept Development: Closing Entry to Transfer a Net Loss

Discussion: Use T accounts for the Income Summary and Retained Earnings accounts to show how Income Summary is closed if a business incurs a net loss. After analyzing the net loss in T-account form, point out the general journal entry. Mention that the closing entry for a net loss is opposite the entry for a net income. L1

Visual Learning

General Journal

Use **Transparency 20–6** to demonstrate how to record the entry to close a net loss into the Retained Earnings account. Point out that a loss decreases the amount of money held by the business, thus Retained Earnings is debited.

Demonstration Problem Step-by-Step Practice

Use demonstration problem 20–2 to give students practice in journalizing the entry to close Income Summary with a net loss.

Strategies for Teaching Ethics in Accounting

Photocopy the Chapter 20 *Student Activity Sheet* for students. Answers are also provided in the booklet.

GENERAL JOURNAL PAGE 23

	DATE		DESCRIPTION	POST. REF.	DEBIT	CREDIT	
22	Dec.	31	*Income Summary*		32 674 72		22
23			*Retained Earnings*			32 674 72	23
24							24

Closing Entry to Transfer a Net Loss

Sometimes businesses incur net losses. For example, suppose the **Income Summary** account of a business after posting the first two entries closing the temporary accounts is as follows:

Income Summary	
Debit	**Credit**
Adj. 3,612.00	Clos. 63,790.00
Clos. 65,178.00	

Before it is closed, **Income Summary** has a debit balance of $5,000.00:

$ 3,612.00	adjustment debit
+ 65,178.00	closing debit
− 63,790.00	closing credit
$ 5,000.00	debit balance

To close **Income Summary**, it is credited for $5,000. **Retained Earnings** is debited for $5,000. The earnings retained by the business are *decreased* by the amount of the net loss. This closing entry is recorded in the general journal as follows:

ACCOUNTING TIPS

Entrepreneurs

Entrepreneurs often try more than once to become successful. The owner of Laugh-O-Gram Corporation in Kansas City did so poorly that he filed for bankruptcy after two years. Not discouraged, the owner decided to try again. Walt Disney left Kansas City in 1923 for Hollywood with all his belongings—one set of clothes and some drawings.

GENERAL JOURNAL PAGE ____

	DATE		DESCRIPTION	POST. REF.	DEBIT	CREDIT	
1			*Closing Entries*				1
22	Dec.	31	*Retained Earnings*		5 000 00		22
23			*Income Summary*			5 000 00	23
24							24

A MATTER OF ETHICS

Handling Sales Returns

Most retail stores give employees specific instructions on how to process a sales return. For example, a cash refund can only be given if cash was paid. Imagine that you work for a large sporting goods store like The Sports Authority. Your friend, Martin, comes in to return a sweatshirt he purchased recently. You know he purchased the sweatshirt on sale, but he wants you to give him a full refund.

Ethical Decision Making:

- What are the ethical issues?
- What are the alternatives?
- Who are the affected parties?
- How do the alternatives affect the parties?
- What would you do?

Teaching A MATTER OF ETHICS

Handling Sales Returns Have students who work in retail positions describe the returns policies for their employers. For example, are customers allowed to return items without a sales slip? What are the procedures employees use to process refunds? If students do not mention it, ask whether they are required to gain the approval of a supervisor for any part of a return transaction. Have students discuss their own experiences with returns and the decisions they've made in either accepting or rejecting returns.

SECTION 1 Check Your Understanding

Now that you have studied this section, complete the following questions and problems.

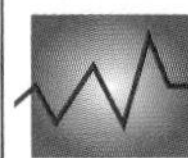

Thinking Critically

1. During the closing process, which account balances are credited to the **Income Summary** account? Which account balances are debited to the **Income Summary** account?
2. When a business has a net loss, the **Retained Earnings** account is debited for the loss during the closing process. Explain why.

Communicating Accounting

As you are completing the closing entries for the fourth quarter, you realize that your company, Dynamic Sound, has a net loss. You know that your boss is not aware that the fourth quarter financial statements are so bleak. Practice an explanation to your boss of how the **Income Summary** and **Retained Earnings** accounts are affected by the loss. Select a partner from your class and ask him or her to critique your style of delivery and the accuracy of your explanation.

Problem 20–1 Identifying Accounts Affected by Closing Entries

The following account names appear in the chart of accounts of Larkin's Department Store.

General Ledger

Accounts Receivable	Purchases
Bankcard Fees Expense	Purchases Discounts
Capital Stock	Purchases Returns and Allowances
Cash in Bank	Retained Earnings
Equipment	Sales
Fed. Corp. Income Tax Expense	Sales Discounts
Fed. Corp. Income Tax Payable	Sales Returns and Allowances
Income Summary	Sales Tax Payable
Insurance Expense	Supplies
Merchandise Inventory	Supplies Expense
Miscellaneous Expense	Transportation In
Prepaid Insurance	Utilities Expense

Instructions Use the form in your working papers to answer the following questions about each account. Assume that all accounts have normal balances.

(1) Is the account affected by a closing entry?
(2) During closing, is the account debited or credited?
(3) During closing, is **Income Summary** debited or credited?

RETEACHING SECTION 1

Closing Temporary Accounts Emphasize that the Income Summary account is used only at the end of the accounting period for the purpose of closing temporary accounts. The only time the Income Summary account has a balance is during the closing procedure. After the closing entries are posted, the balance in the Income Summary account is reduced to zero.

Remind students that the amount used in the third closing entry is the amount of the net income or loss, not the balance of the Retained Earnings account.

3 ASSESS

Thinking Critically (Answers)

1. The sum of all credit balances of revenue and contra cost of merchandise accounts is credited to Income Summary. The sum of all debit balances of contra revenue, cost of merchandise, and expense accounts is debited to Income Summary.
2. Because the earnings retained by the business have decreased by the amount of the net loss.

Communicating Accounting (Answers)

Answers will vary. Since the business has a net loss, the closing debit entry to Retained Earnings will decrease that account balance. The Retained Earnings account is an equity account, and its balance will roll forward to the next fiscal period. Income Summary is a temporary account that will show a zero balance after closing.

Problem 20–1 (Answer)

See solution in the *Teacher Annotated Edition of Chapter Reviews and Working Papers.*

Chapter Reviews and Working Papers Refer students to the Chapter 20 workbook pages to answer *Check Your Understanding* activities.

4 CLOSE

Section Wrap-Up

Summarizing: Have students write a short summary of the steps needed to close the accounts for a merchandising corporation. L1

CHAPTER 20
SECTION 2, PAGES 556–562

1 FOCUS

Introducing the Section

In this section students will learn to post the closing entries to the general ledger and to prepare a post-closing trial balance. Students will also review the complete accounting cycle for a merchandising business.

Section Concepts

- How to post closing entries.
- How to prepare a post-closing trial balance.
- The accounting cycle for a merchandising business.

Visual Learning

Section 2 Focus

Use **Transparency 20–7** to introduce section concepts.

BELL RINGER

Classifying: Use this activity to reinforce learning of the closing process. Make a handout listing each of the temporary account names in scrambled order at the top of a page. In the lower half of the page, draw four columns and add these labels: Normal Debit Balance, Normal Credit Balance, Closed with a Debit, Closed with a Credit. Have students write the account names in the appropriate columns. For example, Sales goes in the "Normal Credit Balance" and the "Closed with a Debit" columns. L1

SECTION 2

Posting Closing Entries

***What* You'll Learn**

- How to post closing entries.
- How to prepare a post-closing trial balance.
- The accounting cycle for a merchandising business.

***Why* It's Important**

To prepare the general ledger for the next period, you need to transfer the temporary account balances to the permanent **Retained Earnings** account.

Key Points

Posting to the General Ledger

Use a systematic procedure when posting. Begin with the date of the transaction. Continue posting by moving from the left of the account to the right. Remember to enter the account number in the Posting Reference column of the journal after you post a transaction to the ledger.

After closing entries are recorded in the general journal, they are posted to the general ledger.

Closing the General Ledger

Figure 20–2 shows the portion of On Your Mark's general ledger affected by the closing process after the closing entries have been posted. For each posting the term "Closing Entry" is written in the Description column of the general ledger account.

ACCOUNT *Retained Earnings* ACCOUNT NO. *305*

DATE		DESCRIPTION	POST. REF.	DEBIT	CREDIT	BALANCE DEBIT	BALANCE CREDIT
20--							
Dec.	1	Balance	✓				19 771 19
	31	Clos. Ent.	G23		32 674 72		52 445 91

ACCOUNT *Income Summary* ACCOUNT NO. *310*

DATE		DESCRIPTION	POST. REF.	DEBIT	CREDIT	BALANCE DEBIT	BALANCE CREDIT
20--							
Dec.	31	Adj. Ent	G22	3 536 00		3 536 00	
	31	Clos. Ent.	G23		323 590 00		320 054 00
	31	Clos. Ent.	G23	287 379 28			32 674 72
	31	Clos. Ent.	G23	32 674 72			—

ACCOUNT *Sales* ACCOUNT NO. *401*

DATE		DESCRIPTION	POST. REF.	DEBIT	CREDIT	BALANCE DEBIT	BALANCE CREDIT
20--							
Dec.	1	Balance	✓				300 000 00
	31		S12		10 750 00		310 750 00
	31		CR13		9 700 00		320 450 00
	31	Clos. Ent.	G23	320 450 00			—

Figure 20–2 Partial General Ledger at the End of the Period

RESOURCE MANAGER

Reproducible Masters
- Lesson Plans
- Chapter Reviews and Working Papers (CRWP) TAE
- Demonstration Problems

Transparencies
- Section Focus Transparency
- Teaching Transparencies
- Source Document Transparencies
- Solution Transparencies

Multimedia
- Exam*View* CD-ROM
- Electronic Learning Center CD-ROM
- Interactive Lesson Planner CD-ROM
- Electronic Field Trips in Accounting

ACCOUNT *Sales Discounts* ACCOUNT NO. *405*

DATE		DESCRIPTION	POST. REF.	DEBIT	CREDIT	BALANCE DEBIT	BALANCE CREDIT
20--							
Dec.	1	Balance	✓			700 00	
	31		CR13	30 00		730 00	
	31	Clos. Ent.	G23		730 00	—	

ACCOUNT *Sales Returns and Allowances* ACCOUNT NO. *410*

DATE		DESCRIPTION	POST. REF.	DEBIT	CREDIT	BALANCE DEBIT	BALANCE CREDIT
20--							
Dec.	1	Balance	✓			1 850 00	
	4		G20	150 00		2 000 00	
	31	Clos. Ent.	G23		2 000 00	—	

ACCOUNT *Purchases* ACCOUNT NO. *501*

DATE		DESCRIPTION	POST. REF.	DEBIT	CREDIT	BALANCE DEBIT	BALANCE CREDIT
20--							
Dec.	1	Balance	✓			190 000 00	
	19		CP14	1 300 00		191 300 00	
	31		P12	15 400 00		206 700 00	
	31	Clos. Ent.	G23		206 700 00	—	

ACCOUNT *Transportation In* ACCOUNT NO. *505*

DATE		DESCRIPTION	POST. REF.	DEBIT	CREDIT	BALANCE DEBIT	BALANCE CREDIT
20--							
Dec.	1	Balance	✓			3 761 18	
	24		CP14	275 00		4 036 18	
	31	Clos. Ent.	G23		4 036 18	—	

ACCOUNT *Purchases Discounts* ACCOUNT NO. *510*

DATE		DESCRIPTION	POST. REF.	DEBIT	CREDIT	BALANCE DEBIT	BALANCE CREDIT
20--							
Dec.	1	Balance	✓				1 200 00
	31		CP14		140 00		1 340 00
	31	Clos. Ent.	G23	1 340 00			—

ACCOUNT *Purchases Returns and Allowances* ACCOUNT NO. *515*

DATE		DESCRIPTION	POST. REF.	DEBIT	CREDIT	BALANCE DEBIT	BALANCE CREDIT
20--							
Dec.	1	Balance	✓				1 600 00
	16		G21		200 00		1 800 00
	31	Clos. Ent.	G23	1 800 00			—

Figure 20–2 Partial General Ledger at the End of the Period (continued)

2 TEACH (Cont'd.)

GUIDED PRACTICE

Reading Accounting

- Have students read the ledger accounts in this section. Ask how they know which entries are from business transactions and which are end-of-period entries. L1

Concept Development: Closing the General Ledger

Discussion: By now students should be thoroughly familiar with the posting process. The only thing new about posting the closing entries is writing the words "Closing Entry" in the Description column of the ledger account. Point out that all journal entries point back to a source document. Writing "Closing Entry" in the ledger account identifies the work sheet as the source document for that entry. L1

Visual Learning

Figure 20–2 Partial General Ledger at the End of the Fiscal Period

Use **Transparencies 20–8a** and **20–8b** to review the posting of the closing entries. Point out the words "Closing Entry" in the accounts.

CRITICAL THINKING ACTIVITY

Predicting Consequences Share this scenario with students: Joan is always looking for shortcuts. She decided she would journalize adjusting and closing entries at the same time. Do you think Joan has a good idea? Explain. (No, it is not a good idea. Every adjusting entry affects a temporary account. You do not want to journalize closing entries to close the temporary accounts until the ledger has been updated. Joan will need to journalize and post adjusting entries first. Only after all the necessary accounts—both permanent and temporary—have been updated can Joan journalize the entries to close the temporary accounts.)

CHAPTER 20
SECTION 2, PAGES 556–562

2 TEACH (Cont'd.)

Visual Learning

Figure 20–2 Partial General Ledger at the End of the Fiscal Period (continued)

Use **Transparencies 20–8c** and **20–8d** to continue reviewing the posted closing entries.

Demonstration Problem
Step-by-Step Practice

Use demonstration problem 20–3 to give students practice in posting closing entries to the general ledger.

Analyzing: Ask students why it is not necessary to write identifying remarks in the Description section of the general ledger accounts for entries other than adjusting or closing entries. (The posting reference column indicates the journal page on which the entry can be found, and the source document will be identified in that entry. The terms "Adjusting Entry" and "Closing Entry" identify the work sheet as the source document for these entries.) L1

Chapter Reviews and Working Papers

Refer students to the *Study Plan* located at the beginning of Chapter 20 in the workbook.

ACCOUNT *Advertising Expense* ACCOUNT NO. *601*

DATE		DESCRIPTION	POST. REF.	DEBIT	CREDIT	BALANCE	
						DEBIT	CREDIT
20--							
Dec.	1	Balance	✓			2450 00	
	31	Clos. Ent.	G23		2450 00	—	

ACCOUNT *Bankcard Fees Expense* ACCOUNT NO. *605*

DATE		DESCRIPTION	POST. REF.	DEBIT	CREDIT	BALANCE	
						DEBIT	CREDIT
20--							
Dec.	1	Balance	✓			4124 27	
	31		CP14	75 00		4199 27	
	31	Clos. Ent.	G23		4199 27	—	

ACCOUNT *Federal Corporate Income Tax Expense* ACCOUNT NO. *630*

DATE		DESCRIPTION	POST. REF.	DEBIT	CREDIT	BALANCE	
						DEBIT	CREDIT
20--							
Dec.	1	Balance	✓			9840 00	
	31	Adj. Ent.	G22	155 00		9995 00	
	31	Clos. Ent.	G23		9995 00	—	

ACCOUNT *Insurance Expense* ACCOUNT NO. *635*

DATE		DESCRIPTION	POST. REF.	DEBIT	CREDIT	BALANCE	
						DEBIT	CREDIT
20--							
Dec.	31	Adj. Ent.	G22	125 00		125 00	
	31	Clos. Ent.	G23		125 00	—	

ACCOUNT *Maintenance Expense* ACCOUNT NO. *650*

DATE		DESCRIPTION	POST. REF.	DEBIT	CREDIT	BALANCE	
						DEBIT	CREDIT
20--							
Dec.	1	Balance	✓			3519 25	
	31	Clos. Ent.	G23		3519 25	—	

ACCOUNT *Miscellaneous Expense* ACCOUNT NO. *655*

DATE		DESCRIPTION	POST. REF.	DEBIT	CREDIT	BALANCE	
						DEBIT	CREDIT
20--							
Dec.	1	Balance	✓			328 28	
	31		CP14	20 00		348 28	
	31	Clos. Ent.	G23		348 28	—	

Figure 20–2 Partial General Ledger at the End of the Fiscal Period (continued)

REINFORCING STUDY SKILLS

Study Buddies Some students will benefit from having a "study buddy" for special projects or for certain unit exams. How do students make an appropriate selection of a study buddy? Help students analyze what they need—it is not always a best friend. Tell students to evaluate their needs and prioritize them by doing the following: (1) Identify the subject/topic with which they need help. (2) Find someone who is well-versed in that subject/topic and ask for help. (3) If they do not know someone, ask the teacher for a recommendation. (4) Check the school's guidance office or the front office for a list of mentors or tutors.

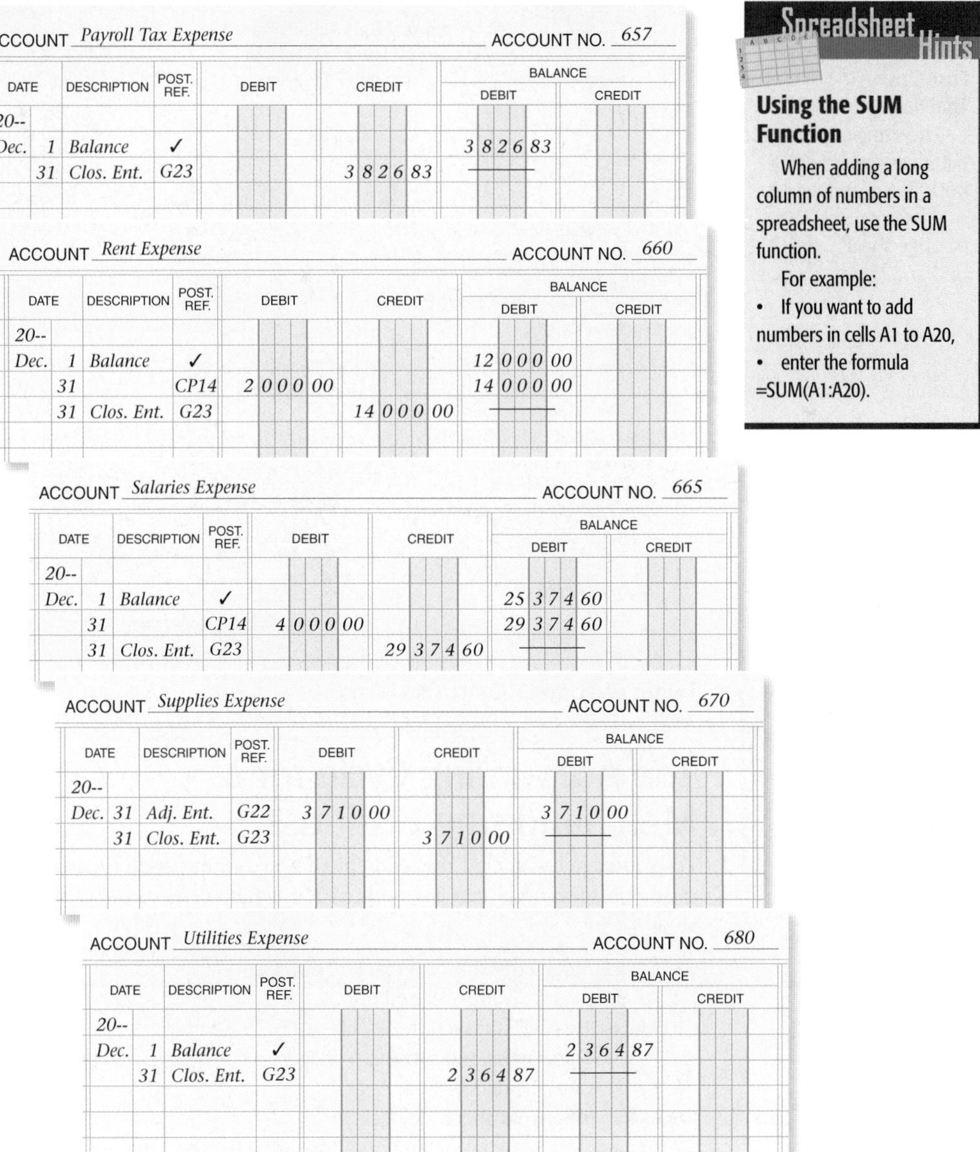

ACCOUNT *Payroll Tax Expense* ACCOUNT NO. *657*

DATE		DESCRIPTION	POST. REF.	DEBIT	CREDIT	BALANCE DEBIT	BALANCE CREDIT
20--							
Dec.	1	Balance	✓			3 826 83	
	31	Clos. Ent.	G23		3 826 83	—	

ACCOUNT *Rent Expense* ACCOUNT NO. *660*

DATE		DESCRIPTION	POST. REF.	DEBIT	CREDIT	BALANCE DEBIT	BALANCE CREDIT
20--							
Dec.	1	Balance	✓			12 000 00	
	31		CP14	2 000 00		14 000 00	
	31	Clos. Ent.	G23		14 000 00	—	

ACCOUNT *Salaries Expense* ACCOUNT NO. *665*

DATE		DESCRIPTION	POST. REF.	DEBIT	CREDIT	BALANCE DEBIT	BALANCE CREDIT
20--							
Dec.	1	Balance	✓			25 374 60	
	31		CP14	4 000 00		29 374 60	
	31	Clos. Ent.	G23		29 374 60	—	

ACCOUNT *Supplies Expense* ACCOUNT NO. *670*

DATE		DESCRIPTION	POST. REF.	DEBIT	CREDIT	BALANCE DEBIT	BALANCE CREDIT
20--							
Dec.	31	Adj. Ent.	G22	3 710 00		3 710 00	
	31	Clos. Ent.	G23		3 710 00	—	

ACCOUNT *Utilities Expense* ACCOUNT NO. *680*

DATE		DESCRIPTION	POST. REF.	DEBIT	CREDIT	BALANCE DEBIT	BALANCE CREDIT
20--							
Dec.	1	Balance	✓			2 364 87	
	31	Clos. Ent.	G23		2 364 87	—	

Figure 20–2 Partial General Ledger at the End of the Fiscal Period (continued)

Spreadsheet Hints

Using the SUM Function

When adding a long column of numbers in a spreadsheet, use the SUM function.

For example:

- If you want to add numbers in cells A1 to A20,
- enter the formula =SUM(A1:A20).

Preparing a Post-Closing Trial Balance

A post-closing trial balance is prepared at the end of the accounting period to prove that the general ledger accounts are in balance after all adjusting and closing entries are posted. **Figure 20–3** shows the post-closing trial balance for On Your Mark.

CHAPTER 20

SECTION 2, PAGES 556–562

2 TEACH (Cont'd.)

Concept Development: Preparing a Post-Closing Trial Balance

Discussion: Students have already learned how to prepare a post-closing trial balance (in Chapter 10). Remind students that the post-closing trial balance is prepared as a check on the accuracy of the ledger account balances. If total debits do not equal total credits, the reason must be found and corrected before the accounting records are ready for use during the next fiscal period. **L1**

Teaching Tip

The word "post" means after, and the post-closing trial balance is sometimes called the after-closing trial balance.

GO TO **Math Review for Accounting** Photocopy appropriate *Activity Sheets* for students who need additional practice in basic math skills.

Math Skill Builder Activity

Using the SUM Function To practice the SUM function, have students create a simple spreadsheet keying in these amounts in a column: \$22.50, \$750.00, \$15.33, \$75.74, \$1,683.00, \$32.99, \$200.00, \$7,500.00, \$138.66. Ask students the total of the numbers. Have students share the formulas they create to sum the column. (Total = \$10,418.22; = SUM(A1:A9) sample formula.)

2 TEACH (Cont'd.)

Visual Learning

Figure 20–3 Post-Closing Trial Balance

Display **Transparency 20–9** and review the process of preparing a post-closing trial balance. Have students explain why no temporary accounts appear on this form.

Teaching Tip

Discuss types of errors students might find on a post-closing trial balance. Review actions students should take to find and correct errors.

Concept Development: The Accounting Cycle for a Merchandising Business

Discussion: To review the accounting cycle, trace one business transaction from the first step in the cycle to the last. For each step, ask students to name the types of accounting stationery used and what is recorded on each. L1

Key Points

Post-Closing Trial Balance

The same account balances appear on both the post-closing trial balance and the balance sheet.

CONNECT TO . . . HISTORY

In response to the American stock market crash and the Great Depression, President Franklin Delano Roosevelt created the Securities and Exchange Commission in 1934. It regulates and supervises the sale of securities and the brokers, dealers, and bankers who sell them—to prevent stock market fraud.

On Your Mark Athletic Wear
Post-Closing Trial Balance
December 31, 20--

Account	Debit	Credit
Cash in Bank	15 179 00	
Accounts Receivable	10 404 00	
Merchandise Inventory	81 385 00	
Supplies	1 839 00	
Prepaid Insurance	1 375 00	
Delivery Equipment	19 831 00	
Office Equipment	9 825 00	
Store Equipment	5 200 00	
Accounts Payable		13 850 00
Fed. Corp. Income Tax Payable		155 00
Employees' Fed. Income Tax Payable		640 00
Employees' State Income Tax Payable		80 00
Social Security Tax Payable		248 00
Medicare Tax Payable		58 00
Fed. Unemployment Tax Payable		18 36
State Unemployment Tax Payable		114 73
Sales Tax Payable		2 428 00
Capital Stock		75 000 00
Retained Earnings		52 445 91
Totals	145 038 00	145 038 00

Figure 20–3 Post-Closing Trial Balance

The Accounting Cycle for a Merchandising Business

You have completed the study of the accounting cycle for a merchandising business organized as a corporation, which consists of the following steps:

1. Collect and verify source documents.
2. Analyze each business transaction.
3. Journalize each transaction.
4. Post to the general and subsidiary ledgers.
5. Prepare a trial balance.
6. Complete a work sheet.
7. Prepare the financial statements—income statement, statement of retained earnings, and balance sheet.
8. Journalize and post the adjusting entries.
9. Journalize and post the closing entries.
10. Prepare a post-closing trial balance.

The accounting cycle for other types of businesses, such as a service business, would follow the same steps. Also, regardless of how a business is organized—sole proprietorship, partnership, or corporation—the basic steps of the accounting cycle are the same. **Figure 20–4** illustrates the accounting cycle.

INTERDISCIPLINARY CONNECTIONS ACTIVITY

History The Securities and Exchange Commission is the governing body that would "blow the whistle" on insider trading—the illegal practice of using information known only by a few people to make profits from buying or selling stocks before the information is made public. Each year the SEC brings between 400 and 500 legal actions against individuals and companies who commit securities infractions, such as insider trading or accounting fraud.

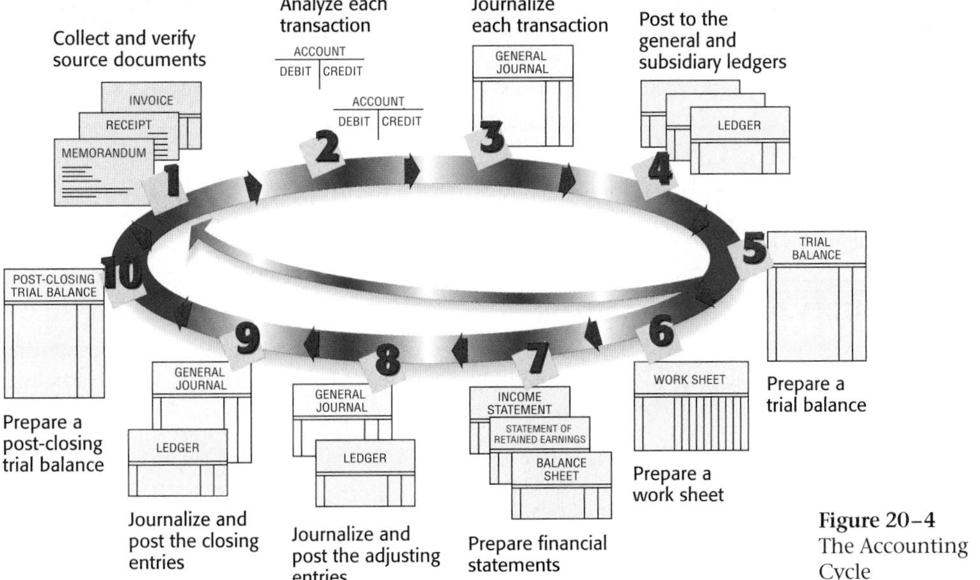

Figure 20–4
The Accounting Cycle

The accounting system used, whether manual or computerized, does not affect the steps in the accounting cycle. In a computerized accounting system, however, many of the routine procedures, such as posting, are performed by the computer.

ANALYZING FINANCIAL REPORTS

Classifying the Balance Sheet—Assets and Liabilities

To classify a balance sheet, accounts are grouped into related categories. For example, assets can generally be divided into these categories: *Current assets* (to be converted to cash or used within the next fiscal year); *investments* (assets not to be converted to cash in the next fiscal year and not used in business operations); *property, plant, and equipment* (physical assets used in business operations); and *other assets* (such as trademarks, copyrights, patents).

Liabilities are generally divided into *current liabilities* (to be paid within the next fiscal year) and *long-term liabilities* (debts that will not be paid fully within the next fiscal year), such as long-term notes payable or mortgages.

One use of the classified balance sheet is to compute the company's working capital, which is the excess of current assets over current liabilities. To review, here is the formula:

Working Capital

Current Assets	$123,220
Current Liabilities	−95,765
Working Capital	$ 27,455

▶ **Analyze the Report:**

Use the Office Depot balance sheet on page A-45 to answer these questions:

1. What categories of current assets are listed on the balance sheet?
2. What categories of current liabilities are listed?
3. What is the working capital?

2 TEACH (Cont'd.)

Visual Learning

Figure 20–4 The Accounting Cycle

Using **Transparency 20–10**, have students discuss what happens at each step in the cycle.

Teaching Tips

Explain that the accounting cycle for a merchandising business has 10 steps because adjustments have been added to the cycle students first learned about in Chapter 6 (page 122).

Bring in examples of annual reports to share with students. Explain how to classify a balance sheet, then show students examples from the annual reports. To give students additional practice analyzing financial data, have them calculate the current and quick ratios from a few of the annual reports.

The Office Depot 2001 Annual Report
Refer students to pages A-39–A-48 at the back of the book.

ANALYZING FINANCIAL REPORTS

Analyze the Report (Answers)

1. Current assets: cash and cash equivalents, receivables, merchandise inventories, deferred income taxes, prepaid expenses.
2. Current liabilities: accounts payable, accrued expenses and other liabilities, income taxes payable, current maturities of long-term debt.
3. $2,806,190,000 – $2,101,514,000 = $704,676,000.

CHAPTER 20
SECTION 2, PAGES 556–562

3 ASSESS

Thinking Critically (Answers)

1. Zero.
2. Post from left to right, beginning with the transaction date. End by entering the account number in the journal's Posting Reference column.

Analyzing Accounting (Answers)

Revenue: Sales, Sales Discounts
Expenses: Rent Exp., Purchases, Trans. In, Salaries Exp., Ins. Exp.
Owner's Equity: Retained Earnings

Problem 20–2 (Answers)

July 12: Dr. Rent Exp. $750; Cr. Cash in Bank $750

Problem 20–3 (Answers)

1. Collect/verify source documents
2. Analyze business transactions
3. Journalize business transactions
4. Post journal entries to ledgers
5. Prepare trial balance
6. Complete work sheet
7. Prepare financial statements
8. Journalize/post adjusting entries
9. Journalize/post closing entries
10. Prepare post-closing trial balance

Chapter Reviews and Working Papers Refer students to the Chapter 20 workbook pages to answer *Check Your Understanding* activities.

4 CLOSE

Section Wrap-Up

Preparing a Chart: Have students draw a chart illustrating the 10 steps in the accounting cycle. Have them label each step and write a brief description of the work done at that step. L1

SECTION 2 Check Your Understanding

Now that you have studied this section, complete the following questions and problems.

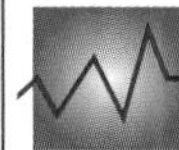

Thinking Critically

1. After all closing journal entries are posted, what is the balance of the temporary accounts?
2. Describe a systematic procedure for posting.

Analyzing Accounting

Can you identify which general ledger accounts are closed at the end of the accounting period? Examine the list of accounts below. On a separate sheet of paper, list the accounts that are closed. Group your lists by account classification.

Rent Expense	Insurance Expense
Delivery Equipment	Sales
Cash in Bank	Sales Discounts
Purchases	Notes Payable
Transportation In	Retained Earnings
Salaries Expense	

Problem 20–2 Analyzing a Source Document

Instructions Review the source document and prepare the journal entry to record this transaction in your working papers. Your Backpack Inc. uses a cash payments journal to record disbursements.

Your Backpack Inc.
29000 White Road
Cold Springs, TX 77282-4513

MEMORANDUM
No. 42

TO: Robert Chan, Chief Accountant
FROM: James Perkins, President
DATE: July 12, 20--
SUBJECT: New Storage Facility Rent

Would you please make a check out to Warehouse Inc. for $750. The check is for the new storage facility we are renting. Please mail the check to:

Mr. James Skiller, Controller
Warehouse Inc.
7576 County Line Highway
Crossplains, TX 77361-8411

Problem 20–3 Organizing the Steps in the Accounting Cycle

Instructions List the following steps of the accounting cycle in their proper order. Use the form provided in your working papers or a separate sheet of paper.

Analyzing business transactions	Journalizing and posting closing entries
Collecting and verifying source documents	Posting journal entries to ledgers
Completing the work sheet	Preparing financial statements
Journalizing business transactions	Preparing a post-closing trial balance
Journalizing and posting adjusting entries	Preparing a trial balance

RETEACHING SECTION 2

Preparing for the Post-Closing Trial Balance After closing entries are posted for a corporation, the totals for the columns on the post-closing trial balance should equal the totals in the Balance Sheet section on the work sheet. Only the permanent accounts appear on the balance sheet and on the post-closing trial balance. Have students discuss in class the types of errors that may occur on a trial balance and what causes those errors.

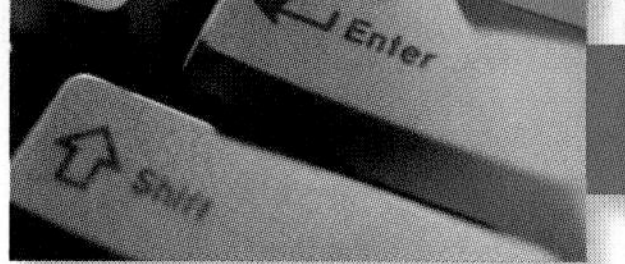

CHAPTER 20 SUMMARY

KEY CONCEPTS

1. Closing entries are made to transfer the balances of the temporary accounts to the permanent **Retained Earnings** account.
2. The information for journalizing closing entries is taken from the Income Statement section of the work sheet.
3. Four entries are made to close the temporary general ledger accounts of a sole proprietorship:
   - close the temporary accounts with credit balances to **Income Summary**
   - close the temporary accounts with debit balances to **Income Summary**
   - close the balance of **Income Summary** to capital
   - close the withdrawals account to capital
4. The first closing entry:

   Debit: All temporary accounts with credit balances
   Credit: **Income Summary**
5. The second closing entry:

   Debit: **Income Summary**
   Credit: All temporary accounts with debit balances
6. The third closing entry:
   Close the balance of **Income Summary** to the **Retained Earnings** account.

Net Income	Net Loss
Debit: **Income Summary**	Debit: **Retained Earnings**
Credit: **Retained Earnings**	Credit: **Income Summary**

7. After posting the closing entries, prepare a post-closing trial balance. The post-closing trial balance contains only Balance Sheet (permanent) accounts.
8. The temporary accounts are ready for the next accounting period after the closing entries are posted.
9. The Accounting Cycle

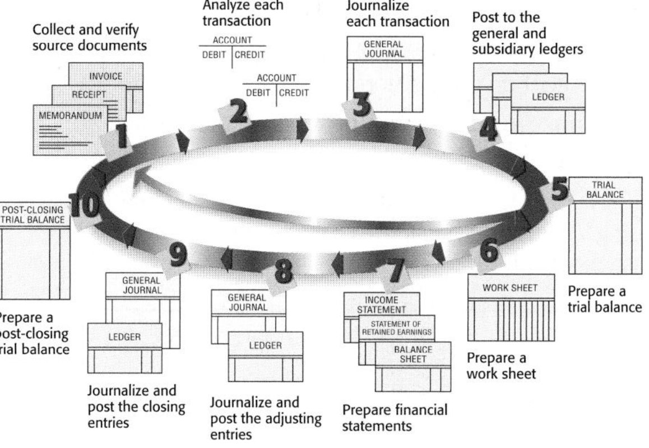

MEETING SPECIAL NEEDS

Students with Visual Impairments One of the ways students with visual impairments cope with classroom printed material is by listening to taped classroom lectures. To that end, think carefully about what you say in class. When writing on the chalkboard or while presenting information on a transparency, be clear and specific. "This (pointing) account increases and this (pointing) account is credited" will not mean anything to students listening to an audio tape of the presentation. "The Income Summary account increases, and the Retained Earnings account is credited" provides a clear explanation.

SUMMARY CHAPTER 20

Chapter 20 Quiz

Student ____ Class ____ Instructor ____
Date Assigned ____ Date Completed ____

CHAPTER 20 QUIZ

Completing the Accounting Cycle for a Merchandising Corporation

QUESTIONS (True-False)

Directions: In the space provided, indicate whether each statement is true or false.

___ 1. Financial reports are the source of information for closing entries.
___ 2. Income Summary is always debited to close its balance into Retained Earnings.
___ 3. Accounts having credit balances are closed with credits.
___ 4. All accounts are closed through the Income Summary account.
___ 5. If Income Summary has a credit balance after all accounts are closed, Retained Earnings is debited.
___ 6. Income Summary does not have a normal balance.
___ 7. "Closing Entry" is written in each permanent account closed.
___ 8. Retained Earnings appears on the post-closing trial balance.
___ 9. A post-closing trial balance proves the equality of the ledger.
___ 10. The steps in the accounting cycle are different for manual and computerized accounting systems.

22 • Chapter Quizzes

QUESTIONS (True–False)

1. Financial reports are the source of information for closing entries.
2. Income Summary is always debited to close its balance into Retained Earnings.
3. Accounts having credit balances are closed with credits.
4. All accounts are closed through the Income Summary account.
5. If Income Summary has a credit balance after all accounts are closed, Retained Earnings is debited.
6. Income Summary does not have a normal balance.
7. "Closing Entry" is written in each permanent account closed.
8. Retained Earnings appears on the post-closing trial balance.
9. A post-closing trial balance proves the equality of the ledger.
10. The steps in the accounting cycle are different for manual and computerized accounting systems.

ANSWERS

1. False	6. True
2. False	7. False
3. False	8. True
4. True	9. True
5. False	10. False

REVIEW AND ACTIVITIES CHAPTER 20

USING KEY TERMS

See the *Glossary* for the definitions of these terms. Have students share their explanations in class. Discuss any differences in use of terms.

Understanding Accounting Concepts and Procedures

(Answers)

1. To transfer balances of temporary accounts to a permanent account.
2. The Income Statement section of the work sheet.
3. (a) Close balances of revenue and contra cost of merchandise accounts into Income Summary. (b) Close balances of contra revenue, cost of merchandise, and expense accounts into Income Summary. (c) Close balance of Income Summary into Retained Earnings.
4. Because net income increases stockholders' equity.
5. Because a net loss decreases earnings retained by the business.
6. Permanent general ledger accounts; balance sheet.
7. No. Income Summary is a temporary account, and only permanent accounts appear on the post-closing trial balance.
8. (a) Collect/verify transaction data. (b) Analyze transactions. (c) Journalize transactions. (d) Post journal entries to general ledger and accounts receivable/payable ledgers. (e) Prepare trial balance. (f) Complete work sheet. (g) Prepare financial statements. (h) Journalize/post adjusting entries. (i) Journalize/post closing entries. (j) Prepare post-closing trial balance.
9. All steps are automatic except collecting, verifying, and inputting transaction data.

CHAPTER 20 REVIEW AND ACTIVITIES

USING KEY TERMS

The following key terms were introduced in Chapter 10. Let's review the terms as they relate to a merchandising corporation such as Bose Corporation. What differences exist between the closing entries for a sole proprietorship and the closing entries for a merchandising corporation? Use the following terms in your explanation.

closing entries	temporary accounts
permanent accounts	

Understanding Accounting Concepts and Procedures

Instructions

On a separate sheet of paper, answer the following questions:

1. What is the purpose of closing entries?
2. Where can you find the information needed to prepare the closing entries?
3. Explain the closing entries for a business organized as a corporation.
4. Why is **Retained Earnings** credited when the business earns a profit?
5. Why is **Retained Earnings** debited when the business has a net loss?
6. Which type of general ledger accounts appear on the post-closing trial balance? On which financial statement do these accounts appear?
7. Does the **Income Summary** account appear on the post-closing trial balance? Why or why not?
8. Name the ten steps in the accounting cycle.
9. When using a computerized accounting system, which tasks in the accounting cycle are performed automatically?

ASSESSMENT RESOURCES

Choose assessment strategies from the following pages to evaluate your students' progress.

Student Edition
Check Your Understanding, pp. 555, 562
Chapter 20 Problems, pp. 567–571
Analyzing Financial Reports, p. 561

Assessment and Evaluation Masters
Chapter 20 Study Plan, *Glencoe Workbook (CRWP)*
Chapter 20 Self-Test, *Glencoe Workbook (CRWP)*
Chapter 20 Test, *Chapter Tests* Booklet
Chapter 20 Activity, *School-to-Work Handbook*
Chapter 20 **Exam***View*

Teacher Wraparound Edition
Critical Thinking Activity, p. 557
Reteaching Sections 1–2, pp. 555, 562
Chapter 20 Quiz, p. 563

CHAPTER 20 REVIEW AND ACTIVITIES

Case Study...

Merchandising Business: Department Store

Pearl's is a department store chain located throughout the southeastern United States. It is known for trendy women's wear and elegant home furnishings.

You work in the accounting department in the Fort Lauderdale location. Your manager asks you to review the work completed by an accounting intern. The intern prepared financial statements and completed the closing process. When looking at the post-closing trial balance, the manager noticed that some of the temporary accounts still have balances.

Thinking Critically:

1. How would you determine which accounts should have zero balances after closing?
2. How would you determine which accounts are closed and which are not?
3. What would you say to the intern to explain why temporary accounts have zero balances after closing?
4. What human-relations skills might you use in your explanation to the intern?

interNET CONNECTION

Financial Accounting Standards Board

The Financial Accounting Standards Board (FASB) serves an important role in determining how financial information is reported to owners and managers and to stockholders.

Do This:

1. Locate the FASB Web site to learn more about the FASB's work.
2. What is the mission of the FASB?
3. When was the FASB established?
4. List at least three ways the FASB works to achieve its mission.
5. Can an accountant serve on the FASB and continue to work as a practicing accountant?

Conducting an Audit with Alex

Mr. Raheev Singh's accountant made the following closing entry.

GENERAL JOURNAL PAGE 45

	DATE		DESCRIPTION	POST. REF.	DEBIT	CREDIT	
1	20--						1
2	Dec.	31	Income Summary		17 000 00		2
3			Purchases Discounts			8 000 00	3
4			Purchases Ret. and Allow.			3 200 00	4
5			Sales Discounts			2 300 00	5
6			Sales Returns and Allow.			3 500 00	6
7							7

Instructions Review the closing entry. On a separate sheet of paper, prepare the closing entries that the accountant should have made.

Workplace Skills

Maintaining and Troubleshooting Technologies

Maintaining and troubleshooting technological equipment is the job of a computer technician. It is also the responsibility of every person who owns or operates computer equipment. To be competent with technology, you should be able to detect problems, generate solutions, and know when to get assistance.

On the Job:

In the accounting department of KidsWear Inc., you are responsible for processing the closing entries. This morning you are having problems with the printer—you are not getting printouts of the ledgers or journals.

Thinking Critically:

What steps do you need to take to troubleshoot this problem? Write down each step and prioritize your list. In one column indicate whom you should call if you can't resolve the problem after each step is completed.

interNET CONNECTION www.glencoe.com

Do This (Answers)

1. www.fasb.org
2. Their mission is to establish and improve financial accounting standards for the public.
3. 1973
4. Keep standards current to reflect changes in economic environment; promote the international convergence of accounting standards; and consider any significant areas of deficiency in financial reporting through the standard-setting process.
5. No. A board member can have no contact with her or his accounting firm while serving on the board.

REVIEW AND ACTIVITIES CHAPTER 20

Case Study...

Thinking Critically (Answers)

1. Only permanent accounts should have balances after closing.
2. Temporary (income statement) accounts are closed; permanent (balance sheet) accounts are not.
3. The accounts must begin each period with zero balances to separate data by fiscal period.
4. Answers may vary. A manager might praise work well done and explain areas that need improvement. Clear oral and written communications should be used to reinforce and document expected improvements.

Workplace Skills

Thinking Critically (Answers)

Answers will vary. Check to see that the printer has power and is turned on. If the printer displays an error message, check the owner's manual for troubleshooting suggestions. If none of this helps, consult an expert in your company, or call to get help from the manufacturer.

Conducting an Audit with Alex

(Answers)

Dec. 31: Dr. Purchases Disc. $8,000, Purchases Returns & Allowances $3,200; Cr. Sales Disc. $2,300, Sales Returns & Allowances $3,500, Income Summary $5,400

Internet Resources and Activities Handbook

Refer students to the booklet for additional Internet activities.

PEACHTREE CORNER

Close the Fiscal Year

To close the fiscal year, choose **System** from the ***Tasks*** menu and then **Year-End Wizard**. Closing the fiscal year automatically closes the temporary capital accounts, updates the general ledger, and selects the next accounting period. **Note:** This process cannot be reversed.

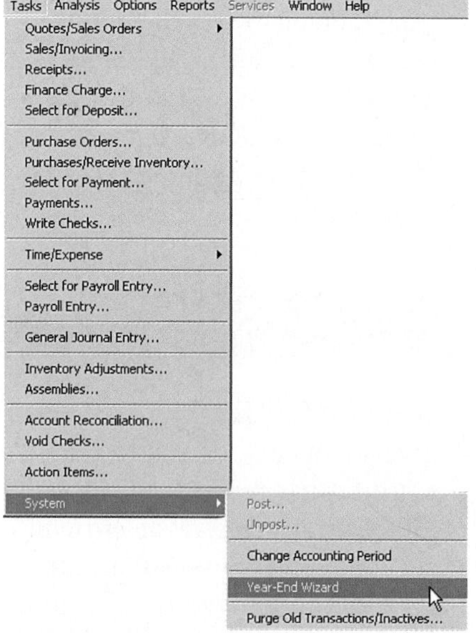

Backup/Restore

Making a backup of data files should be done regularly and before completing tasks that cannot be reversed, such as closing a fiscal year. Peachtree provides an easy way to backup/restore data files.

File Edit Maintain Tasks Analysis
Open Company... Ctrl+O
New Company... Ctrl+N
Print... Ctrl+P
Print Preview Ctrl+W
Page Setup...
Back Up... Ctrl+B
Restore... Ctrl+R
Select Import/Export...

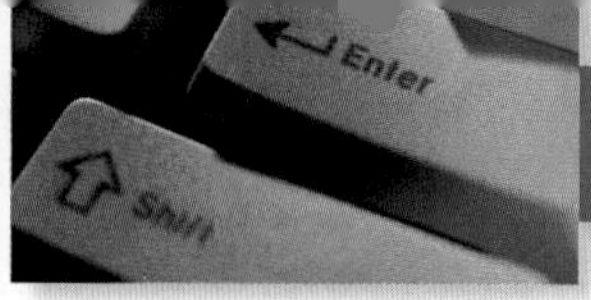

Closing the Fiscal Year

Making the Transition from a Manual to a Computerized System

Task	Perform Accounting Procedures Using Manual Methods	Perform Accounting Procedures Using Automated Methods
Closing a fiscal year	1. Journalize the entry to close the revenue, expense, Income Summary, and Withdrawals accounts. 2. Post the closing entries.	1. Closing the fiscal year is only performed if you want to clear income and expense accounts at the end of the fiscal year. 2. If you have selected the closing option, closing entries are journalized for you.
Post-closing trial balance	1. After the closing entries have been posted to the ledger, prepare a trial balance to verify the equality of debits and credits. 2. All expense and revenue accounts should have zero balances.	1. A post-closing trial balance can be printed to verify that all revenue and expense accounts have been closed.

Closing the Accounting Period

Peachtree Question	Description
What is the difference between changing an accounting period and closing a fiscal year?	1. Typically you will *change* an accounting period when moving from one month to another. 2. You will *close* a fiscal year at the end of a calendar or fiscal year.
What tasks should I perform before closing a fiscal year?	1. Post and print all journal entries before you close the fiscal year. 2. Back up all files before closing. Closing the fiscal year cannot be reversed.
How do I close the fiscal year?	1. From the ***Tasks*** menu, select **System**. 2. Choose Year-End Wizard. 3. You will be prompted if any procedures need to be completed before the system continues the closing process.
What does the software do "behind the scenes"?	1. Peachtree detects any unposted entries and reminds you to print reports. 2. Peachtree reminds you to back up your files before closing. 3. When you close the fiscal period, the software will create closing entries and post them. All income and expense account balances will be transferred to the **Retained Earnings** account.

For detailed instructions: See the **Peachtree User Guide** in your Glencoe Working Papers.

Peachtree® Answers to Frequently Asked Questions

Q: What if you notice a mistake after you close the fiscal year?
A: If you made a backup before the closing, restore the company data, correct the error, and close the fiscal year again. If you did not make a backup or do not want to restore company data, make a correcting entry in the new period.
Q: How do you print a post-closing trial balance?
A: Use the GL Trial Balance and change the report title using the report options.
For additional information, refer to your *Glencoe Peachtree Accounting User Guide.*

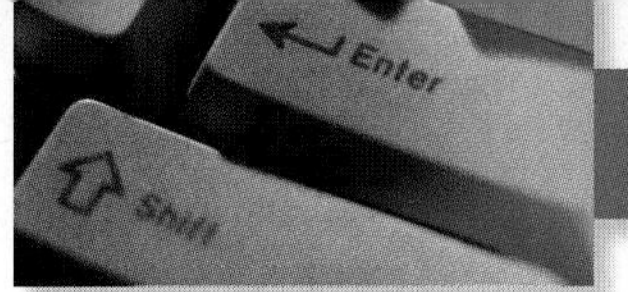

APPLICATION OPTIONS

Problem 20–4 Journalizing Closing Entries

The following amounts appeared in the Income Statement section of Sunset Surfwear's work sheet.

Instructions In your working papers, record the closing entries for the year ended December 31. Start with general journal page 13.

ACCT. NO.	ACCOUNT NAME	INCOME STATEMENT DEBIT	INCOME STATEMENT CREDIT
310	*Income Summary*		7 000 00
401	*Sales*		90 000 00
405	*Sales Discounts*	1 000 00	
410	*Sales Returns and Allowances*	2 400 00	
501	*Purchases*	25 000 00	
505	*Transportation In*	3 000 00	
510	*Purchases Discounts*		500 00
515	*Purchases Returns and Allowances*		1 500 00
625	*Federal Corporate Income Tax Exp.*	5 532 00	
635	*Insurance Expense*	300 00	
650	*Miscellaneous Expense*	6 000 00	
655	*Rent Expense*	12 000 00	
665	*Supplies Expense*	450 00	
675	*Utilities Expense*	14 000 00	
		69 682 00	99 000 00
	Net Income	29 318 00	
		99 000 00	99 000 00

Analyze: What is the effect of the closing entries on the **Retained Earnings** account?

Complete chapter problems one of four ways:

1. **Manual** Glencoe Working Papers

or

2. **Peachtree Complete Accounting** Software

or

3. **QuickBooks** Templates (Problems 20–5, 20–8)

or

4. **Spreadsheet** Templates (Problem 20–7)

Peachtree®

SMART GUIDE

Step-by-Step Instructions: Problem 20–4

1. Select the problem set for Sunset Surfwear (Prob. 20–4).
2. Rename the company and set the system date.
3. Choose **System** from the **Tasks** menu and then select **Year-End Wizard** to close the fiscal year.
4. Print a Post-Closing Trial Balance.
5. Answer the Analyze question.
6. End the session.

PROBLEMS CHAPTER 20

Problem 20–4 (Answers) Journalizing Closing Entries

Dec. 31: Dr. Sales $90,000, Purchases Discounts $500, Purchases Returns and Allowances $1,500; Cr. Income Summary $92,000

Dec. 31: Dr. Income Summary $69,682; Cr. Sales Discounts $1,000, Sales Returns and Allowances $2,400, Purchases $25,000, Transportation In $3,000, Federal Corporate Income Tax Exp. $5,532, Insurance Expense $300, Miscellaneous Exp. $6,000, Rent Exp. $12,000, Supplies Exp. $450, Utilities Exp. $14,000

Dec. 31: Dr. Income Summary $29,318; Cr. Retained Earnings $29,318

Analyze: It increases Retained Earnings by $29,318.

EXTENDING THE CONTENT

Keeping Up with New Developments It is a challenge for many people to keep up with new technology and how it changes both personal and professional lives. Have students keep portfolios where they can place newspaper clippings, notes, articles, and advertisements of the newest products and trends in the computer industry. As students gather information, have them identify how the new products and developments impact accounting-related jobs. Ask students to reflect on how people working with technology can keep up with the new developments.

Problem 20-5 (Answers) Journalizing and Posting Closing Entries

Closing entries:

Dec. 31: Dr. Sales $150,000, Purchases Disc. $1,000, Purchases Returns & Allowances $1,500; Cr. Income Summary $152,500

Dec. 31: Dr. Income Summary $115,630; Cr. Sales Returns & Allowances $5,000, Purchases $90,000, Trans. In $5,000, Misc. Exp. $300, Rent Exp. $6,000, Supplies Exp. $1,630, Utilities Exp. $3,000, Fed. Corp. Inc. Tax Exp. $4,700

Dec. 31: Dr. Inc. Summary $32,870; Cr. Retained Earnings $32,870

Analyze: The balance of the account would be carried over into the next accounting period, and Retained Earnings for the year would be overstated.

Problem 20-6 (Answers) Identifying Accounts for Closing Entries

Accounts debited:

401 Sales
515 Purchases Ret. & Allow.
310 (Income Summary for credits and profits)
305 (Retained Earnings for losses)

Accounts credited:

650 Miscellaneous Expense
665 Supplies Expense
505 Transportation In
405 Sales Discounts
501 Purchases
601 Advertising Expense
625 Fed. Corp. Income Tax Exp.
657 Rent Expense
310 (Income Summary for debits and losses)
305 (Retained Earnings for profits)

Analyze: No, because some of the accounts are not affected by closing entries.

CHAPTER 20 PROBLEMS

Peachtree®

SMART GUIDE

Step-by-Step Instructions: Problem 20-5

1. Select the problem set for Shutterbug Cameras (Prob. 20-5).
2. Rename the company and set the system date.
3. Close the fiscal year.
4. Print a Post-Closing Trial Balance.
5. Answer the Analyze question.
6. End the session.

TIP: Choose the General Ledger Trial Balance report whenever you are instructed to print a Post-Closing Trial Balance.

Problem 20-5 Journalizing and Posting Closing Entries

The following account balances appeared in the Income Statement section of the work sheet of Shutterbug Cameras.

Instructions

(1) Journalize the closing entries for the year ended December 31. Start with page 14 of a general journal (in your working papers).

(2) Post the closing entries to the general ledger accounts, which are included in your working papers.

	ACCT. NO.	ACCOUNT NAME	INCOME STATEMENT DEBIT	INCOME STATEMENT CREDIT
20	310	*Income Summary*	4 000 00	
21	401	*Sales*		150 000 00
22	410	*Sales Returns and Allowances*	5 000 00	
23	501	*Purchases*	90 000 00	
24	505	*Transportation In*	5 000 00	
25	510	*Purchases Discounts*		1 000 00
26	515	*Purchases Returns and Allowances*		1 500 00
27	620	*Federal Corporate Income Tax Exp.*	4 700 00	
28	645	*Miscellaneous Expense*	300 00	
29	650	*Rent Expense*	6 000 00	
30	660	*Supplies Expense*	1 630 00	
31	670	*Utilities Expense*	3 000 00	
32			119 630 00	152 500 00
33		*Net Income*	32 870 00	
34			152 500 00	152 500 00
35				

Analyze: What would happen if the accountant for Shutterbug Cameras made a mistake and did not close the **Transportation In** account?

Problem 20-6 Identifying Accounts for Closing Entries

The following is a partial list of the accounts used by Cycle Tech Bicycles. All of the accounts have nonzero balances.

COOPERATIVE LEARNING ACTIVITY

Co-Op Co-Op Assign students to groups of four or five persons. Ask each group to research the following topic: How does the income tax that U.S. citizens pay compare with the taxes of citizens in Japan and most European countries? Have each group present a report to the class. Groups are to divide responsibilities and apply a cooperative effort to accomplish their task. If you have access to a software presentation program, have students make their class presentation using the software.

General Ledger
101 Cash in Bank
650 Miscellaneous Expense
125 Merchandise Inventory
665 Supplies Expense
215 Sales Tax Payable
505 Transportation In
305 Retained Earnings
401 Sales
405 Sales Discounts
310 Income Summary
501 Purchases
515 Purchases Returns and Allowances
601 Advertising Expense
625 Federal Corporate Income Tax Expense
657 Rent Expense
135 Prepaid Insurance

Peachtree®

SMART GUIDE

Step-by-Step Instructions: Problem 20–6

1. Select the problem set for Cycle Tech Bicycles (Prob. 20–6).
2. Rename the company and set the system date.
3. Print a Chart of Accounts report.
4. List the accounts that will be debited and those that will be credited when closed.
5. Answer the Analyze question.
6. End the session.

Instructions In your working papers, list all the account numbers and names for accounts that will be debited when closed. Next, list all the account numbers and names for accounts that will be credited when closed.

Analyze: Did you list all of the accounts? If not, why?

Spreadsheet PROBLEM Problem 20–7 Completing End-of-Period Activities

The general ledger accounts for River's Edge Canoe & Kayak as of December 31, the end of the period, appear in the working papers.

Instructions In your working papers:

(1) Prepare a trial balance on a ten-column work sheet.

(2) Complete the work sheet. Use the following adjustment information.

Merchandise inventory, December 31	$20,000
Supplies inventory, December 31	900
Unexpired insurance, December 31	1,800
Total federal corporate income taxes for the year	2,965

(3) Prepare an income statement from the work sheet information.

(4) Prepare a statement of retained earnings.

(5) Prepare a balance sheet.

(6) Journalize and post the adjusting entries. Begin on general journal page 14.

(7) Journalize and post the closing entries.

(8) Prepare a post-closing trial balance.

Analyze: Did the company make a profit for the year?

SPREADSHEET SMART GUIDE

Step-by-Step Instructions: Problem 20–7

1. Select the spreadsheet template for Problem 20–7.
2. Enter your name and the date in the spaces provided on the template.
3. Complete the spreadsheet using the instructions in your working papers.
4. Print the spreadsheet and proof your work.
5. Save your work and exit the spreadsheet program.

HOME AND COMMUNITY CONNECTIONS ACTIVITY

Stock Market Investing Have students check with friends, family members, or work associates to see if anyone invests in the stock market. Ask students to make a list of stock market investment tips by asking these questions: (1)What stocks have been most successful for them? (2) How did they learn to invest? (3) What advice would they give a beginning investor? If students do not know anyone who has invested in stocks, have them contact a local stock broker to ask about building a stock market portfolio and how to begin. Ask students to submit a one-page summary of their findings.

Problem 20–7 (Answers) Completing End-of-Period Activities

Trial balance totals $261,826.57
Adj. trial balance totals $261,851.57
Net Income $41,285
Ending Retained Earnings $66,685
Total Assets $120,236.57

Adjusting entries:
Dec. 31: Dr. Income Summary $5,000; Cr. Merchandise Inv. $5,000
Dec. 31: Dr. Supplies Exp. $3,200; Cr. Supplies $3,200
Dec. 31: Dr. Insur. Exp. $1,200; Cr. Prepaid Insur. $1,200
Dec. 31: Dr. Fed. Inc. Tax Exp. $25; Cr. Fed. Inc. Tax Pay. $25

Closing entries:
Dec. 31: Dr. Sales $175,000, Purchases Disc. $2,300, Purchases Rets. & Allow. $5,600; Cr. Income Summary $182,900
Dec. 31: Dr. Income Summary $136,615; Cr. Sales Disc. $3,775, Sales Rets. & Allow. $2,500, Purchases $75,300, Trans. In $5,000, Bankcard Fees $3,515, Fed. Inc. Tax Exp. $2,965, Insur. Exp. $1,200, Misc. Exp. $5,960, Rent Exp. $9,000, Salaries Exp. $22,200, Supplies Exp. $3,200, Utilities Exp. $2,000
Dec. 31: Dr. Inc. Summary $41,285; Cr. Retained Earnings $41,285
Post-Closing TB totals $120,236.57

Ending debit balances:
Cash in Bank $22,236.57
Accounts Receivable $7,400
Merchandise Inventory $20,000
Supplies $900
Prepaid Insurance $1,800
Delivery Truck $67,900

Ending credit balances:
Accounts Payable $13,000
Federal Corp. Income Tax Payable $25
Sales Tax Payable $526.57
Capital Stock $40,000
Retained Earnings $66,685

Analyze: Yes

Problem 20-8 (Answers) Preparing Adjusting and Closing Entries

Adjusting entries:

Dec. 31: Dr. Income Summary $4,400; Cr. Merchandise Inventory $4,400

Dec. 31: Dr. Insurance Exp. $1,800; Cr. Prepaid Insurance $1,800

Dec. 31: Dr. Supplies Exp. $2,744; Cr. Supplies $2,744

Dec. 31: Dr. Federal Corporate Income Tax Exp. $2,413; Cr. Federal Corporate Income Tax Pay. $2,413

Closing entries:

Dec. 31: Dr. Sales $299,156, Purchases Discounts $2,950, Purchases Returns and Allowances $2,108; Cr. Income Summary $304,214

Dec. 31: Dr. Income Summary $242,517; Cr. Sales Returns and Allowances $9,500, Purchases $168,624, Transportation In $8,236, Advertising Exp. $4,000, Federal Corporate Income Tax Exp. $14,913, Insurance Exp. $1,800, Miscellaneous Exp. $1,600, Salaries Exp. $26,900, Supplies Exp. $2,744, Utilities Exp. $4,200, Dec. 31: Dr. Income Summary $57,297; Cr. Retained Earnings $57,297

Post-Closing Trial Balance totals $129,419

Analyze: They lowered net income.

Peachtree®

SMART GUIDE

Step-by-Step Instructions: Problem 20-8

1. Select the problem set for Buzz Newsstand (Prob. 20-8).
2. Rename the company and set the system date.
3. Print a Working Trial Balance to help you prepare the adjustments.
4. Record the adjustments using the **General Journal Entry** option.
5. Print a General Journal report and proof your work.
6. Answer the Analyze question.
7. Close the fiscal year.
8. Print a Post-Closing Trial Balance.
9. End the session.

TIP: Peachtree automatically updates the general ledger accounts when you close the fiscal year.

CHALLENGE PROBLEM Problem 20-8 Preparing Adjusting and Closing Entries

In the middle of the end-of-period activities, the accountant for Buzz Newsstand was called away because of an illness in the family. Before leaving, the accountant prepared the work sheet and the financial statements. However, the business manager can only locate a trial balance (before adjustments) and the income statement.

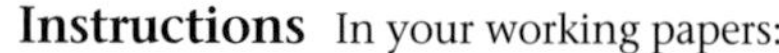

Instructions In your working papers:

(1) Journalize the adjusting and closing entries on page 16 of the general journal.

(2) Using the information provided, prepare a post-closing trial balance.

Buzz Newsstand
Trial Balance, Before Adjustments
December 31, 20--

		Debit	Credit
101	*Cash in Bank*	12 035 00	
115	*Accounts Receivable*	6 106 00	
130	*Merchandise Inventory*	64 800 00	
135	*Supplies*	3 916 00	
140	*Prepaid Insurance*	5 400 00	
145	*Delivery Truck*	46 106 00	
201	*Accounts Payable*		4 690 00
204	*Fed. Corp. Income Tax Pay.*		—
215	*Sales Tax Payable*		416 00
301	*Capital Stock*		40 000 00
305	*Retained Earnings*		24 603 00
310	*Income Summary*		
401	*Sales*		299 156 00
410	*Sales Returns and Allowances*	9 500 00	
501	*Purchases*	168 624 00	
505	*Transportation In*	8 236 00	
510	*Purchases Discounts*		2 950 00
515	*Purchases Returns and Allowances*		2 108 00
601	*Advertising Expense*	4 000 00	
625	*Fed. Corp. Income Tax Expense*	12 500 00	
635	*Insurance Expense*	—	
650	*Miscellaneous Expense*	1 600 00	
660	*Salaries Expense*	26 900 00	
665	*Supplies Expense*	—	
675	*Utilities Expense*	4 200 00	
	Totals	373 923 00	373 923 00

ADDRESSING MULTIPLE LEARNING STYLES

Visual/Spatial Learner Brainstorm the variety of daily activities accountants perform. Then ask students to use photos and graphics from magazines to create posters showing accountants in the workplace: working at computers; processing source documents; completing tax forms; meeting with clients; using fax machines, videoconferencing, and so on. After students complete the posters, review the activities they have displayed and discuss the changes they think will occur in the next few years because of technology.

Buzz Newsstand
Income Statement
For the Year Ended December 31, 20--

Revenue:				
Sales			299 156 00	
Less: Sales Ret. and Allow.			9 500 00	
Net Sales				289 656 00
Cost of Merch. Sold:				
Merch. Inv., Jan 1, 20--			64 800 00	
Purchases	168 624 00			
Plus: Transportation In	8 236 00			
Cost of Del. Merch.		176 860 00		
Less: Purch. Discounts	2 950 00			
Purch. Ret. and Allow.	2 108 00	5 058 00		
Net Purchases			171 802 00	
Cost of Merch. Avail.			236 602 00	
Merch. Inv., Dec. 31, 20--			60 400 00	
Cost of Merch. Sold				176 202 00
Gross Profit on Sales				113 454 00
Operating Expenses:				
Advertising Expense			4 000 00	
Insurance Expense			1 800 00	
Miscellaneous Expense			1 600 00	
Salaries Expense			26 900 00	
Supplies Expense			2 744 00	
Utilities Expense			4 200 00	
Total Oper. Expenses				41 244 00
Operating Income				72 210 00
Less: Fed. Inc. Tax Exp.				14 913 00
Net Income				57 297 00

Analyze: What was the impact of adjusting entries on net income?

ACCOUNTING ISSUES

Electronic Tax Deposits The old way of paying taxes was to deposit federal taxes and corporate income taxes in a government depository and accompany each deposit with a paper coupon. In 1994 the IRS offered Taxlink to allow businesses to pay employment, excise, and corporate income taxes electronically to replace the paper coupon system. The IRS replaced Taxlink in 1996 with a more advanced system called the Electronic Federal Tax Payment System (EFTPS). By 2001 over three million businesses enrolled in EFTPS, and over $1 trillion in federal tax deposits were made electronically each year.

CHAPTER 21 Resource Manager

Section Resources

	Objectives & Standards	Activities & Features	Reproducible Masters
Chapter Opener *Accounting for Publicly Held Corporations*	• Describe the characteristics of the corporate form of business organization. • Prepare journal entries to record the issue of stock to investors. • Prepare journal entries to record the distribution of earnings to owners. • Prepare financial statements for publicly held corporations. • Define the accounting terms introduced in this chapter. **National Standards for Business Education**: IA16, IIA1, IIC2, IIC3, IIC4, IIC5	Exploring the Real World of Business, p. 572 Workplace Connections, p. 573	School-to-Work Handbook
Section 1 *Publicly Held Corporations*	• The characteristics of a corporation. • How to record the issue of capital stock.	Did You Know?, p. 576	Demonstration Problems
Section 2 *Distributing the Earnings of a Corporation*	• Why and how corporations distribute their earnings. • How to record dividends on preferred stock. • How to record dividends on common stock.	Connect To, p. 579 Calculator Hints, p. 580 Accounting Tips, p. 582 Analyzing Financial Reports, p. 582 Accounting Careers in Focus, p. 584	Math Review for Accounting Demonstration Problems
Section 3 *Financial Reporting for a Publicly Held Corporation*	• How to prepare a statement of stockholders' equity for a publicly held corporation. • How to prepare a balance sheet for a publicly held corporation.	International Accounting, p. 585 Accounting Flashbacks, p. 586 A Matter of Ethics, p. 587	Demonstration Problems Strategies for Teaching International Accounting Strategies for Teaching Ethics in Accounting Internet Resources and Activities Handbook

KEY

Posters — Transparency — Software — Videocassette

Blackline Masters — CD-ROM — Portfolio

MULTIMEDIA RESOURCE

Peachtree

- Problem 21–6 *Journalizing the Issue of Stock*
- Problem 21–7 *Journalizing Common and Preferred Stock Dividend Transactions*
- Problem 21–9 *Recording Stockholders' Equity Transactions*

QuickBooks

- Problem 21–6 *Journalizing the Issue of Stock*
- Problem 21–9 *Recording Stockholders' Equity Transactions*

Spreadsheets

- Problem 21–8 *Preparing Corporate Financial Statements*

Videos

Video Segment: Partnerships and Corporations

After viewing this video, students will be able to describe the organizational differences between partnerships and corporations. Have students list the major advantages and disadvantages of a corporation.

CD-ROMs

Electronic Learning Center (ELC), Chapter 21

This program is ideal for visual learners since it incorporates video images, animation, and graphics to enliven the content of each lesson.

Interactive Lesson Planner (ILP), Chapter 21

This CD-ROM combines the versatility of an electronic lesson planner with the convenience of teacher classroom resources.

SCANS Correlation Chart

FOUNDATION SKILLS

Basic Skills:	Reading	Writing	Math	Listening	Speaking	
Thinking Skills:	Creative Thinking	Decision Making	Problem Solving	Seeing Things in the Mind's Eye	Knowing How to Learn	Reasoning
Personal Qualities:	Responsibility	Self-Esteem	Sociability	Self-Management	Integrity/Honesty	

WORKPLACE COMPETENCIES

Resources:	Allocating Time	Allocating Money	Allocating Material and Facility Resources	Allocating Human Resources		
Information:	Acquiring and Evaluating Information	Organizing and Maintaining Information	Interpreting and Communicating Information	Using Computers to Process Information		
Interpersonal Skills:	Participating as a Member of a Team	Teaching Others	Serving Clients/ Customers	Exercising Leadership	Negotiating to Arrive at a Decision	Working with Cultural Diversity
Systems:	Understanding Systems	Monitoring and Correcting Performance	Improving and Designing Systems			
Technology:	Selecting Technology	Applying Technology to Task	Maintaining and Troubleshooting Technology			

*Highlighted blocks indicate areas covered in the chapter. Additional SCANS skills are also covered throughout the *Teacher Wraparound Edition.*

Assessment

Student Edition
- Check Your Understanding, pp. 578, 583, 588
- Chapter 21 Problems, pp. 593–595

Assessment and Evaluation Masters
- Chapter 21 Study Plan, *Glencoe Workbook*
- Chapter 21 Self-Test, *Glencoe Workbook*
- Chapter 21 Test, *Chapter Tests* Booklet
- Chapter 21 Activity, *School-to-Work Handbook*
- Chapter 21 **Exam***View*

Teacher Wraparound Edition
- Critical Thinking Activity, p. 593
- Reteaching Section 1, p. 578
- Reteaching Section 2, p. 583
- Reteaching Section 3, p. 588
- Chapter 21 Quiz, p. 589

Transparencies

	Teaching Transparencies	Solution Transparencies
Section 1:	21–1, 21–2, 21–3, 21–4	Problem 21–1
Section 2:	21–5, 21–6, 21–7, 21–8	Problems 21–2, 21–3
Section 3:	21–9, 21–10, 21–11, 21–12	Problem 21–4
End of Chapter:		Problems 21–5, 21–6, 21–7, 21–8, 21–9

TEACHER CLASSROOM RESOURCES

This is a representation of key blackline masters available in the Teacher Classroom Resources.

Teaching Aids

Transparency Examples

Section Focus Transparencies

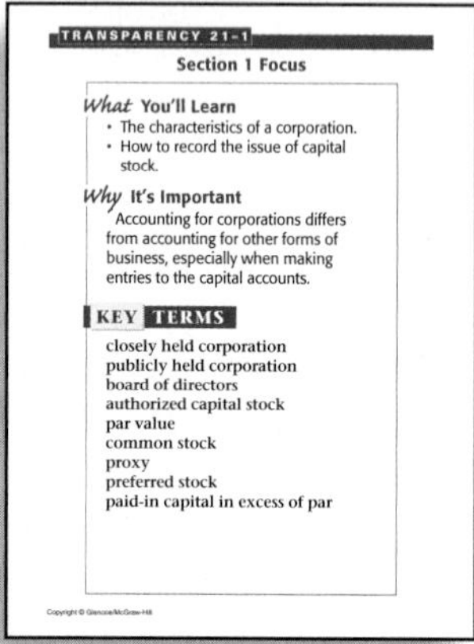

TRANSPARENCY 21-1

Section 1 Focus

What You'll Learn
- The characteristics of a corporation.
- How to record the issue of capital stock.

Why It's Important

Accounting for corporations differs from accounting for other forms of business, especially when making entries to the capital accounts.

KEY TERMS

closely held corporation
publicly held corporation
board of directors
authorized capital stock
par value
common stock
proxy
preferred stock
paid-in capital in excess of par

Teaching Transparencies

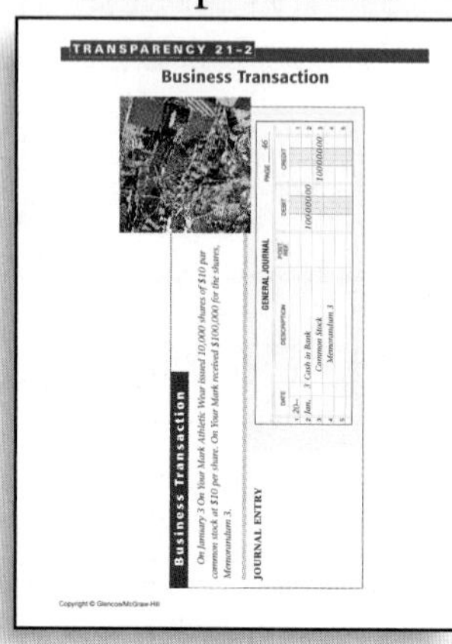

TRANSPARENCY 21-2

Business Transaction

Teaching Transparencies

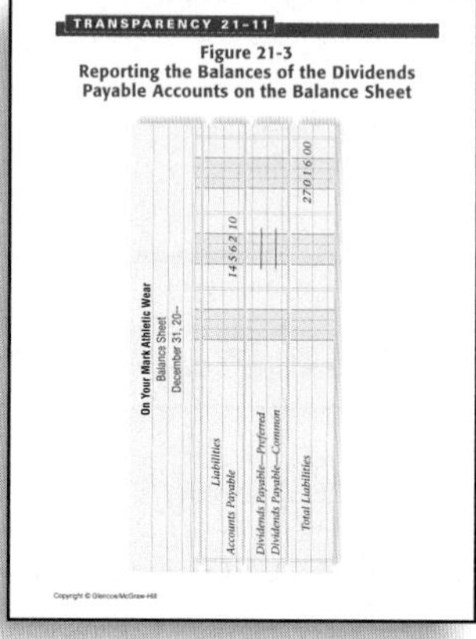

TRANSPARENCY 21-11

Figure 21-3
Reporting the Balances of the Dividends Payable Accounts on the Balance Sheet

Solution Transparencies

Working Papers for End-of-Chapter Problems

Problem 21-5 Distributing Corporate Earnings

Problem 21-6 Distributing Corporate Earnings

Demonstration Problems

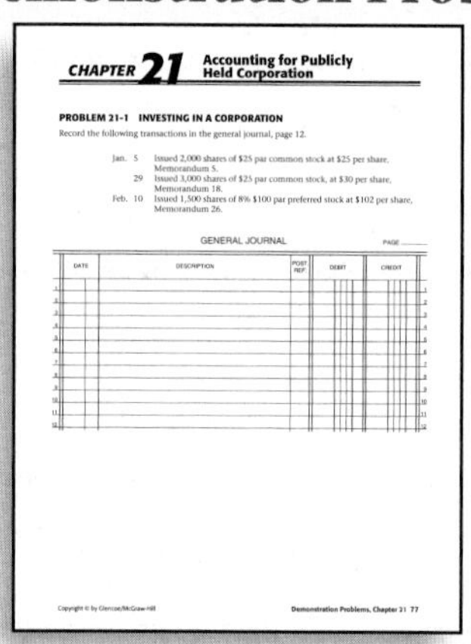

CHAPTER 21 Accounting for Publicly Held Corporation

PROBLEM 21-1 INVESTING IN A CORPORATION

Lesson Plans

Chapter 21 Chapter Opener (pg. 572-573)

Accounting for Publicly Held Corporations

Block Scheduling

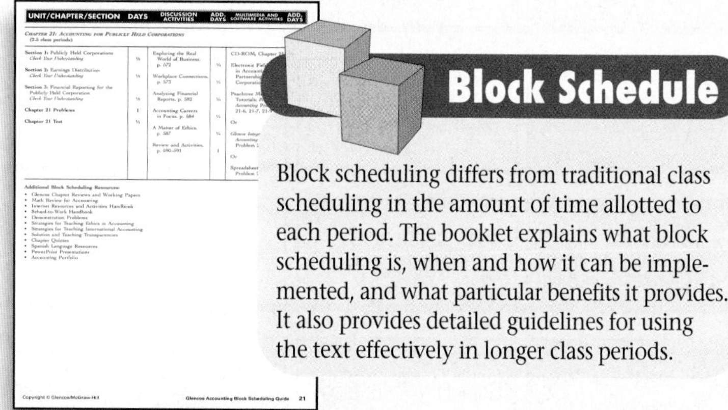

Block Schedule

Block scheduling differs from traditional class scheduling in the amount of time allotted to each period. The booklet explains what block scheduling is, when and how it can be implemented, and what particular benefits it provides. It also provides detailed guidelines for using the text effectively in longer class periods.

Enrichment and Application

Strategies for Teaching Ethics in Accounting

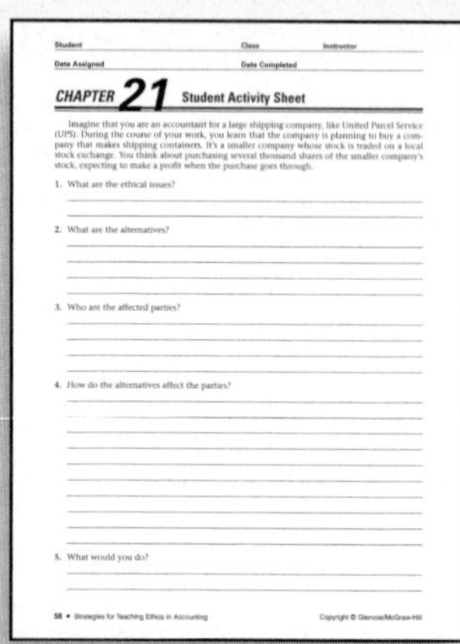

CHAPTER 21 Student Activity Sheet

Strategies for Teaching International Accounting

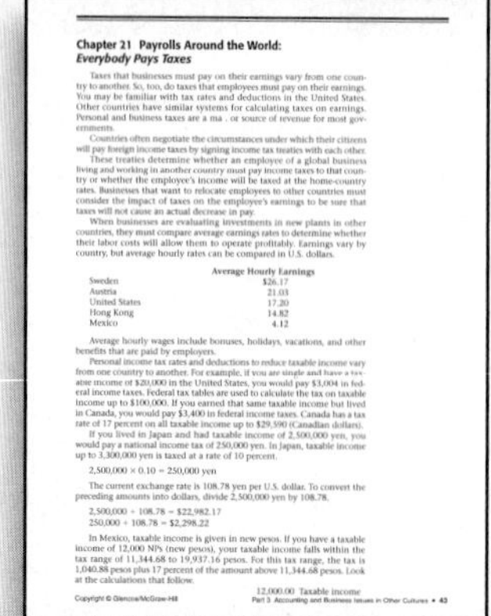

Chapter 21 Payrolls Around the World: *Everybody Pays Taxes*

School-to-Work Handbook

CHAPTER 21 SCHOOL-TO-WORK ACTIVITY

Accounting for Publicly Held Corporations

Meeting Different Ability Levels

Chapter Reviews and Working Papers (CRWP)

Working Papers

Review

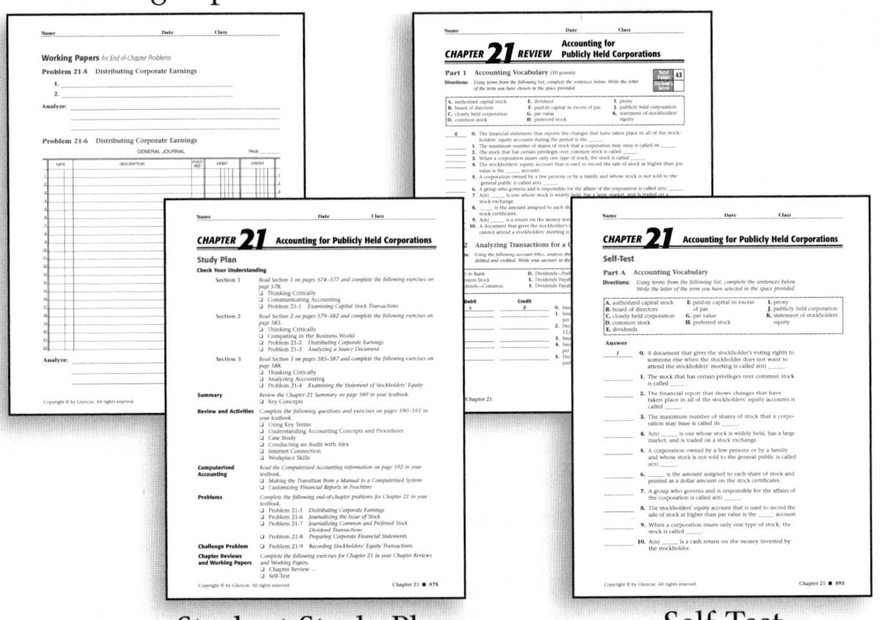

Student Study Plan

Self-Test

Real-World Multimedia CD-ROM

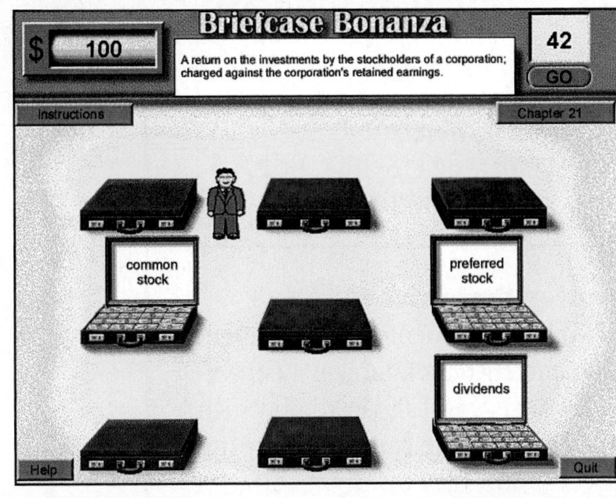

Key to Ability Levels

Each section gives skill-building activities. Each activity has been labeled for use with students of various learning styles and abilities.

L1 Level 1 activities are basic activities and should be within the range of all students.

L2 Level 2 activities are average activities and should be within the range of average and above average students.

L3 Level 3 activities are challenging activities designed for the ability range of above average students.

ELL ELL activities should be within the ability range of English Language Learners.

Teaching Resources at a Glance

Application Resources

- Glencoe Chapter Review and Working Papers, SE and TAE
- School-to-Work Handbook, SE and TM
- Accounting Portfolio, SE and TM

Reproducible Masters

- Demonstration Problems
- Lesson Plans
- Block Scheduling
- Spanish Language Resources

Glencoe Accounting Professional Development Series

- Strategies for Teaching Ethics in Accounting
- Accounting Competitive Event Review
- Math Review for Accounting
- Strategies for Teaching International Accounting
- Internet Resources and Activities Handbook

Transparency Package

- Section Focus Transparencies
- Teaching Transparencies
- Source Document Transparencies
- Solution Transparencies

Performance Assessment

- **Exam***View* CD-ROM
- Chapter Tests
- Chapter Quizzes
- Unit Tests
- Audit Tests
- Printed Testbank

Multimedia Resources

- Electronic Learning Center:
  - Multimedia CD-ROMs
  - Peachtree software, tutorials, templates, and solutions
  - Spreadsheet templates
- Using QuickBooks with Glencoe Accounting
- Interactive Lesson Planner
- Electronic Field Trips in Accounting
- PowerPoint Presentation
- Web site: glencoeaccounting.glencoe.com

Assessment and Evaluation

Chapter Tests

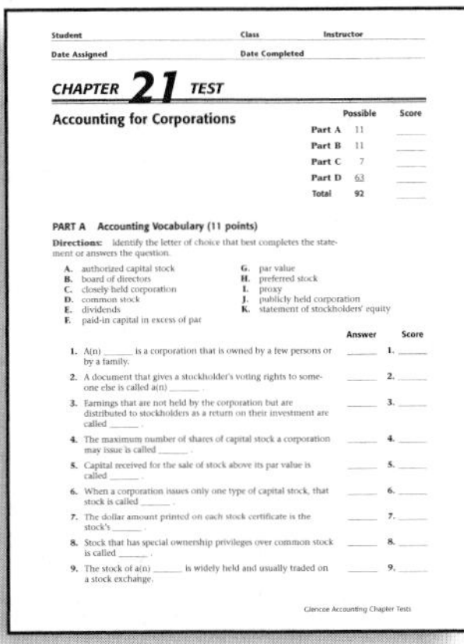

Chapter Quiz

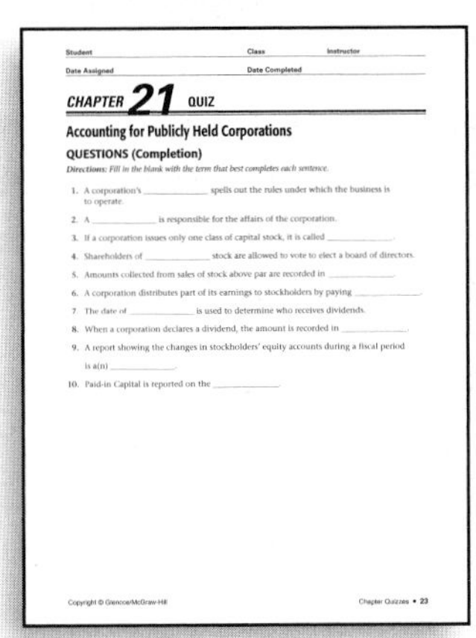

OVERVIEW CHAPTER 21

Correlations to National Standards for Business Education

(See pages T50–T51 for a detailed correlation chart.)

Standards: IA16, IIA1, IIC2, IIC3, IIC4, IIC5

Chapter Preview

In this chapter students will learn about the characteristics of publicly held corporations. They will also learn how such corporations raise capital by issuing stock and how they distribute earnings to shareholders.

Section Overviews

- Section 1—*Publicly Held Corporations*
- Section 2—*Distributing the Earnings of a Corporation*
- Section 3—*Financial Reporting for a Publicly Held Corporation*

Chapter Vocabulary

closely held corporation
publicly held corporation
board of directors
authorized capital stock
par value
common stock
proxy
preferred stock
paid-in capital in excess of par
dividend
statement of stockholders' equity

Preteaching Accounting Vocabulary

Oral Exercise: Write each term on the chalkboard, and then ask for volunteers to explain the meaning of each term. Discuss how each term relates to a publicly held corporation. L1

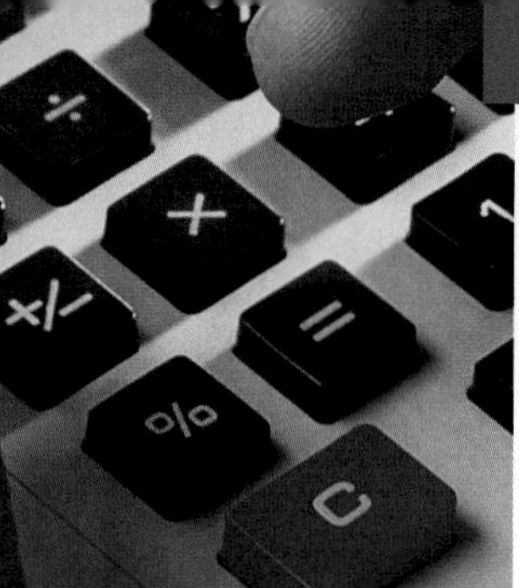

CHAPTER 21

Accounting for Publicly Held Corporations

Learning Objectives

When you have completed this chapter, you will be able to:

- Describe the characteristics of the corporate form of business organization.
- Prepare journal entries to record the issue of stock to investors.
- Prepare journal entries to record the distribution of earnings to owners.
- Prepare financial statements for publicly held corporations.
- Define the accounting terms introduced in this chapter.

Exploring the Real World of Business

EVALUATING CORPORATE STOCK

Computer technologies affect almost everything we do today—from banking to pumping gas at your local Shell station. Small business owners advertise on the Internet. Database technologies bring stock quotes, weather reports, and airline reservations to our fingertips. One of the biggest companies involved in this technology revolution is **Microsoft.**

Microsoft was started in 1975 by Bill Gates and Paul Allen, based on a belief that every business and home would one day have a personal computer. Rather than building the computer itself, they decided to focus on the software that would run the computer. **Microsoft's** Windows operating systems and computer applications are used in millions of personal computers today. **Microsoft** products are available in 40 languages and are sold in more than 60 countries.

As a public corporation, **Microsoft's** stock is traded on the National Association of Securities Dealers Automated Quotations (NASDAQ). Investors who are interested in buying stock can review the company's financial statements to analyze earnings and dividends paid to preferred stockholders over a period of years.

What do you think?

If you were considering buying stock in **Microsoft,** what financial information would you want to know about the company?

Microsoft

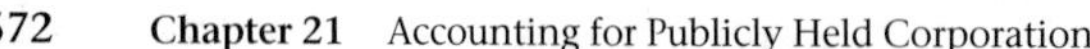

Exploring the Real World of Business

Microsoft

Microsoft has capitalized on the explosive growth in the use of personal computers by bundling its operating system software with new computers. Have students research Microsoft's stock price over a period of years and calculate how investors have benefited from this growth.

What do you think? (Answers)

Answers may vary. Investors would want to know information such as trends in earnings, return on equity, whether the stock pays dividends, the history of stock prices, the return on investment over a period of years, the profitability of the company, and anticipated future demand for the company's products.

Workplace Connections

Applying Your Accounting Knowledge

Many people look at a corporation's financial reports. Some analyze the reports to decide whether to buy stock in the company. Others analyze the reports to decide whether to loan money to the company. Still others analyze the reports to plan for the future including staffing, purchasing, and budget plans. In this chapter, you'll learn how to analyze financial statements using ratios and comparisons.

Investigate:

1. If your employer's financial statements are available, did the company earn a profit last year?
2. If your employer's statements are not available, locate the annual report of a public company on the Internet or in your library. Did this company earn a profit, or record a loss for last year?

573

Glencoe Accounting *Online*

Visit the *Glencoe Accounting* Web site at **glencoeaccounting.glencoe.com** for additional activities and information.

INTRODUCING CHAPTER 21

Making Accounting Relevant

Workplace Connections: Applying Your Accounting Knowledge

Discussion: All public corporations publish their operating results each year. In addition to printed and online annual reports, students can find corporate financial data in a variety of reference materials, such as *Hoover's Handbooks* or financial magazines and newspapers. Have students visit the local public library and make a list of sources where they can find corporate financial data.

Investigate (Answers)

1. Answers will vary. Have students who do not have part-time jobs research local public corporations (or the corporate owner of local companies) to find whether they earned a profit.
2. Answers will vary.

School-to-Work Activity

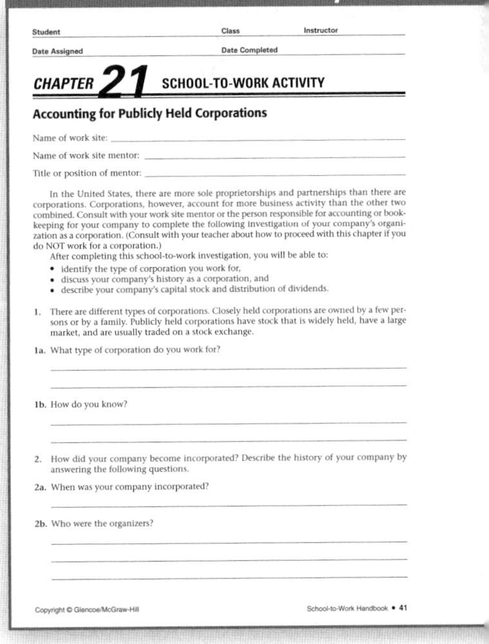

Student ____ Class ____ Instructor ____

Date Assigned ____ Date Completed ____

CHAPTER 21 SCHOOL-TO-WORK ACTIVITY

Accounting for Publicly Held Corporations

Name of work site: ____

Name of work site mentor: ____

Title or position of mentor: ____

In the United States, there are more sole proprietorships and partnerships than there are corporations. Corporations, however, account for more business activity than the other two combined. Consult with your work site mentor or the person responsible for accounting or bookkeeping for your company to complete the following investigation of your company's organization as a corporation. (Consult with your teacher about how to proceed with this chapter if you do NOT work for a corporation.)

After completing this school-to-work investigation, you will be able to:

- identify the type of corporation you work for,
- discuss your company's history as a corporation, and
- describe your company's capital stock and distribution of dividends.

1. There are different types of corporations. Closely held corporations are owned by a few persons or by a family. Publicly held corporations have stock that is widely held, have a large market, and are usually traded on a stock exchange.

1a. What type of corporation do you work for?

1b. How do you know?

2. How did your company become incorporated? Describe the history of your company by answering the following questions.

2a. When was your company incorporated?

2b. Who were the organizers?

GLENCOE MULTIMEDIA

Electronic Field Trips in Accounting *Video Segment: Partnerships and Corporations*
After viewing this video, students will be able to describe the organizational differences between partnerships and corporations.

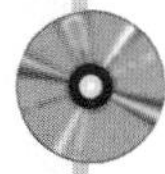

Glencoe Accounting: Electronic Learning Center *Chapter 21*
The CD-ROM program is ideal for visual learners since it incorporates video images, animation, and graphics to enliven the content of each lesson.

1 FOCUS

Introducing the Section

In this section students will learn how a corporation is different from other types of business organizations. They'll also learn the types of stocks public corporations may issue and how to record sales of capital stock in the accounting records.

Section Concepts

- The characteristics of a corporation.
- How to record the issuance of capital stock.

Visual Learning

Section 1 Focus

Use **Transparency 21–1** to introduce section concepts.

BELL RINGER

Identifying: Ask students to name companies located in your general area. Write the names on the chalkboard, and then help students decide which of the companies is a publicly held corporation. L1

Concept Development: Publicly Held Corporations

Discussion: Bring in the financial section of a daily newspaper or *The Wall Street Journal.* As students look at the stock reports, explain that all companies listed are publicly held corporations. Suggest that students interested in a specific company write to request a copy of its annual report. L1

Concept Development: Characteristics of a Corporation

Discussion: Explain the characteristics of a corporation. Contrast with the sole proprietorship and the partnership. Point out that legal permission to operate is generally granted by a state's secretary of state. L1

SECTION 1

Publicly Held Corporations

***What* You'll Learn**

- The characteristics of a corporation.
- How to record the issue of capital stock.

***Why* It's Important**

Accounting for corporations differs from accounting for other forms of business, especially when making entries to the capital accounts.

KEY TERMS

closely held corporation
publicly held corporation
board of directors
authorized capital stock
par value
common stock
proxy
preferred stock
paid-in capital in excess of par

In the United States, there are more sole proprietorships and partnerships than there are corporations. Corporations, however, account for more business activity than the other two forms of business combined. Many high profile companies like The Coca-Cola Company and General Motors are organized as corporations.

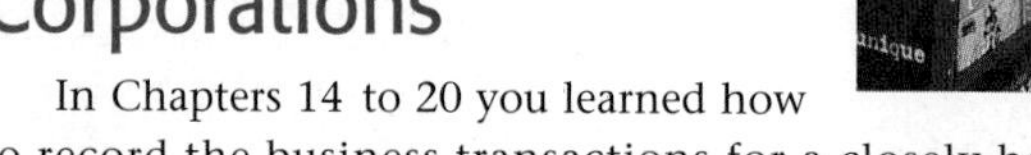

Publicly Held Corporations

In Chapters 14 to 20 you learned how to record the business transactions for a closely held corporation. **Closely held corporations** are corporations owned by a few persons or by a family. The stock of a closely held corporation is not sold to the general public.

In this chapter you will learn about another type of corporation—the publicly held corporation. A **publicly held corporation** is one whose stock is widely held, has a large market, and is usually traded on the New York Stock Exchange or the American Stock Exchange.

Characteristics of a Corporation

The corporation has several unique features:

- **Legal Permission to Operate**—To operate a business as a corporation, the incorporators (organizers) file an application with state officials for permission to operate. Once the application is approved, it becomes the corporation's charter. The charter indicates the purpose of the business and spells out the rules under which the business is to operate. The charter also states the type and amount of stock a corporation is authorized to issue.
- **Separate Legal Entity**—A corporation is a separate legal entity that is created and exists only by law. A corporation may enter into contracts, borrow money, and conduct business in the same manner as a person. It may acquire, own, and sell property in its name. It can also sue and be sued in the courts.
- **Stockholders**—The ownership of a corporation is divided into units called shares of stock. The owners of a corporation are called stockholders. Each stockholder receives a *stock certificate* as proof of ownership. The stock certificate lists the name of the stockholder, the number of shares issued, and the date the shares were issued.

RESOURCE MANAGER

Reproducible Masters
- Lesson Plans
- Chapter Reviews and Working Papers (CRWP) TAE
- Demonstration Problems

Transparencies
- Section Focus Transparency
- Teaching Transparencies
- Source Document Transparencies
- Solution Transparencies

Multimedia
- Exam*View* CD-ROM
- Electronic Learning Center CD-ROM

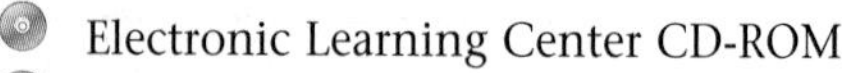

- Interactive Lesson Planner CD-ROM
- Electronic Field Trips in Accounting

- **Professional Management**—Stockholders own the corporation, but they do not manage it. The stockholders elect a **board of directors**, who govern and are responsible for the affairs of the corporation.

Stockholders' Equity

Stockholders' equity is the value of the stockholders' claims to the assets of the corporation. As you learned in Chapter 19, corporations report stockholders' equity in two parts:

- the equity that is paid into the corporation by stockholders
- the equity earned by the corporation and retained in the business

Let's look at how transactions affecting stockholders' equity are handled.

Capital Stock

The maximum number of shares a corporation may issue is called its **authorized capital stock**. The authorized number of shares is usually much greater than the number of shares the corporation plans to sell right away. This allows the corporation to sell additional shares at a later time.

State laws may require that an amount or value be assigned to each share of stock before it is sold to the public. The amount assigned to each share is referred to as **par value**, the per-share dollar amount printed on the stock certificates. The par value is used to determine the amount credited to the capital stock account. Par values of $1, $5, and $25 are common.

The corporate charter specifies the types of capital stock that a corporation may issue. The two main types of stock are common and preferred.

Common Stock

If the corporation issues only one class of capital stock, it is called **common stock**. The owners of common stock participate in the corporation as follows:

- Elect the board of directors and, through them, exercise control over the operations of the corporation. Stockholders are entitled to one vote for each share of stock they own. The election occurs at the stockholders' meeting, which is usually held once a year. If a stockholder cannot attend the meeting, he or she may send in a **proxy**, which gives the stockholder's voting rights to someone else.
- Share in the earnings of the corporation by receiving dividends declared by the board of directors.
- Entitled to share in the assets of the corporation if it goes out of business.

Preferred Stock

To appeal to as many investors as possible, a corporation may also issue preferred stock. **Preferred stock** has certain privileges (or preferences) over common stock. Preferred stockholders participate as follows:

2 TEACH

GUIDED PRACTICE

Reading Accounting

- Have students make a table with Preferred Stock and Common Stock as the headings. As they read, have them make notes about the rights of each type of stockholder and the accounts used to record transactions related to each type of stock. L1
- Have students search the Internet for financial reference materials and resources that are available in their first language. ELL

Concept Development: Stockholders' Equity

Discussion: Remind students that stockholders' equity is made up of two parts: the capital paid into the corporation by purchasers of shares of stock and prior earnings retained in the business. L1

Concept Development: Capital Stock

Discussion: Remind students that all corporations—closely or publicly held—are owned in the form of capital stock. The capital stock account changes only when a corporation issues additional stock or buys its own stock from the public. Shares of stock traded on a stock exchange by members of the public do not affect the corporation's accounting records because the corporation receives no income from such stock trades. L1

Great Ideas *From the Classroom of...*

Exploring Cyberbanking Surf the Net and visit Internet banking sites. Provide some URL addresses for your students and let them explore cyberbanking. Ask them to compare the methods used and services offered on the Web with the services available at your local banks. Discuss the issues related to Internet security and have students investigate the security features implemented at the various sites.

Cynthia L. Greene
Centennial High School
Roswell, Georgia

CHAPTER 21
SECTION 1, PAGES 574–578

2 TEACH (Cont'd.)

Teaching Tips

Common stock carries these rights: the right to vote, to share in profits, to share in assets at liquidation, and the first option to buy additional shares issued (pre-emptive right).

Preferred stock has no vote, is preferred in dividends and assets at liquidation, and may be callable at the option of the corporation.

Visual Learning

Business Transaction

Using **Transparency 21–2**, help students analyze the entry for the issuance of common stock.

Teaching Tips

Point out that corporations generally do not issue all their authorized shares at one time. Some shares may be held for future capital needs or for use as stock options to reward key employees.

Amounts recorded in the Paid-in Capital in Excess of Par account do not represent profits, but rather investments in the company. Profits result from the sale of goods and services, not from the sale of stock.

No-par stock is quite common. No-par stock requires that a "stated value" be used. Accounting for stated value and par value are the same except for the terminology.

Did You Know?

Shareholders

Shareholders of Microsoft Corporation own around 5.4 billion shares of stock in the company. Company employees own many shares, and several became millionaires as the value of a share grew from a few dollars to more than $150.

- Entitled to receive dividends before common stockholders. The preferred stock dividend is stated in specific dollars, such as $6, or as a percentage of the stock's par value, such as 6 percent. The stock itself is then referred to as "preferred $6 stock" or "preferred 6% stock."
- Given preference over common stockholders to the assets of the corporation should it go out of business.

In return for these special privileges, the preferred stockholders give up the right to vote and to participate in the control of the corporation. Usually, investors buy preferred stock to receive the stated dividend.

Issuing Common Stock

When common stock is issued, the **Common Stock** account is credited for the par value of the stock. Let's look at some examples.

Issuing Common Stock at Par Value. When On Your Mark was incorporated, it had the following transaction.

Business Transaction

On January 3 On Your Mark Athletic Wear issued 10,000 shares of $10 par common stock at $10 per share. On Your Mark received $100,000 for the shares, Memorandum 3.

JOURNAL ENTRY

GENERAL JOURNAL — PAGE 46

	DATE		DESCRIPTION	POST. REF.	DEBIT	CREDIT	
1	20--						1
2	Jan.	3	Cash in Bank		100 000 00		2
3			Common Stock			100 000 00	3
4			Memorandum 3				4
5							5

Key Points

Recording the Issuance of Common Stock

When common stock is issued by a corporation,

- **Common Stock** is credited for the par value of the stock.
- **Paid-in Capital in Excess of Par** is credited for any amount received in excess of par value.

Issuing Common Stock in Excess of Par Value. Investors are often willing to pay more than par value for the stock of a corporation. When a corporation sells its stock at a price that is above par, the excess over par is credited to a separate stockholders' equity account called **Paid-in Capital in Excess of Par**. **Paid-in Capital in Excess of Par** appears in the chart of accounts immediately following the **Common Stock** account. The amounts recorded in this account are not profits to the corporation. Rather, they represent part of the stockholders' investment in the corporation. This account follows the same rules of debit and credit as other stockholders' equity accounts.

Paid-in Capital in Excess Par	
Debit – Decrease Side	Credit + Increase Side Normal Balance

One year after On Your Mark was incorporated, it had the following transaction.

ADDRESSING MULTIPLE LEARNING STYLES

Visual/Spatial Learner Provide several examples of annual reports for students to review. Ask students to locate the statements of stockholders' equity in each report. Then ask them to compare the statements from each of the reports and choose two or three of the samples they feel are easiest to read and understand. Students should be able to identify the fiscal period, the net income for the period, the number of shares of stock issued, the total amount received for those shares, and any dividends declared during the period. Ask one of your students to create a poster illustrating the two or three statements that are easiest to read and understand.

Business Transaction

On January 5 On Your Mark issued 5,000 shares of $10 par common stock at $11.50 per share, Memorandum 147. On Your Mark received $57,500 for the shares.

Before recording the transaction, determine how much of the $57,500 is credited to **Common Stock** and how much is credited to **Paid-in Capital in Excess of Par.**

Credit to **Common Stock:**	
5,000 shares at $10 par value	$50,000
Credit to **Paid-in Capital in Excess of Par:**	
5,000 shares at $1.50	
($11.50 issue price − $10.00 par value) per share	+ 7,500
Total cash received	$57,500

Remember, the amount credited to the **Common Stock** account is the par value of the shares issued.

JOURNAL ENTRY

GENERAL JOURNAL — PAGE 99

	DATE		DESCRIPTION	POST. REF.	DEBIT	CREDIT	
1	20--						1
2	Jan.	5	Cash in Bank		57 500 00		2
3			Common Stock			50 000 00	3
4			Paid-in Cap. in Ex. of Par			7 500 00	4
5			Memorandum 147				5
6							6

Issuing Preferred Stock

When preferred stock is issued, the **Preferred Stock** account is credited for the par value of the stock. Preferred stock is almost always issued at its par value.

On Your Mark was incorporated on January 3, and was authorized to issue 1,000 shares of preferred stock with a par value of $100 and a stated dividend of $6. The next day the company had the following transaction.

Business Transaction

On January 4 On Your Mark issued 250 shares of preferred $6 stock, $100 par, at $100 per share. On Your Mark received $25,000 for the shares, Memorandum 5.

JOURNAL ENTRY

GENERAL JOURNAL — PAGE 47

	DATE		DESCRIPTION	POST. REF.	DEBIT	CREDIT	
1	20--						1
2	Jan.	4	Cash in Bank		25 000 00		2
3			Preferred Stock			25 000 00	3
4			Memorandum 5				4
5							5

MEETING SPECIAL NEEDS

Students with Behavioral Disorders If your students have attention difficulties, try setting a time limit for a particular activity. For example, have students read the "Characteristics of a Corporation" section, which contains just over 300 words. Give them about 5 to 6 minutes to read the section (enough time for average readers). Discuss with students whether the time limit helped them focus on the activity.

2 TEACH (Cont'd.)

Visual Learning

Business Transaction

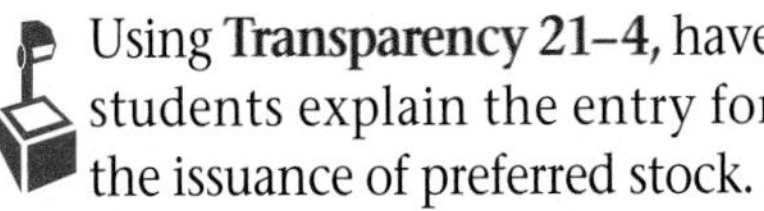

Use **Transparency 21–3** to guide students through the analysis and recording of the transaction to issue common stock at a price above par.

Business Transaction

Using **Transparency 21–4,** have students explain the entry for the issuance of preferred stock.

Demonstration Problem Step-by-Step Practice

Use demonstration problem 21–1 to give students practice in making journal entries to record the issuance of stock.

Critical Thinking: Ask students this question: As an investor, why would you want to know how much money the corporation has raised through sales of common and preferred stock? (Capital raised through stock issues represents a significant part of corporate equity, which in turn reflects the corporation's capacity for paying operating expenses and long-term debt and for growing the business. Corporations that are undercapitalized with too little stockholders' equity may be high-risk investments.) L3

CHAPTER 21
SECTION 1, PAGES 574–578

3 ASSESS

Thinking Critically (Answers)

1. Closely held: owned by few people, stock not sold to public. Publicly held: issues stock shares to public, shares traded on a stock exchange.
2. Preferred stockholders have first claim to dividends and company assets at liquidation. Only common stockholders may vote and participate in the control of the corporation.

Communicating Accounting (Answers)

Answers will vary. Students might include information about legal permission to operate, a corporation's charter, separate legal entity, stockholders, professional management, and organization costs.

Problem 21-1 (Answers)

1. Issued 30,000 shares common stock at par, $10 per share in cash.
2. Issued 2,000 shares of preferred stock at par, $100 per share in cash.
3. Issued 50,000 shares of common stock at $14 per share, par $10.

Chapter Reviews and Working Papers Refer students to the Chapter 21 workbook pages to answer *Check Your Understanding* activities.

4 CLOSE

Section Wrap-Up

Teamwork: Assign students to teams. Have each team create a poster describing the characteristics of a corporation and presenting information on common and preferred stock. L1

SECTION 1 Check Your Understanding

Now that you have studied this section, complete the following questions and problems.

Thinking Critically

1. What is the difference between a closely held corporation and a publicly held corporation?
2. Describe the difference between common and preferred stock.

Communicating Accounting

You work for a locally owned partnership that was just purchased by a corporation. You decide to share information about corporations with your coworkers. Write a one-page information sheet identifying the characteristics of a corporation. Provide an explanation paragraph for each characteristic.

Problem 21-1 Examining Capital Stock Transactions

The Dublin Corporation was organized and authorized to issue 10,000 shares of $100 par, preferred 8% stock and 500,000 shares of $10 par common stock. The three transactions recorded in the following T accounts took place during the first month of operations.

Instructions In your working papers, describe each of the three transactions.

Cash in Bank

Debit +	Credit −
(1) 300,000	
(2) 200,000	
(3) 700,000	

Preferred Stock

Debit −	Credit +
	(2) 200,000

Common Stock

Debit −	Credit +
	(1) 300,000
	(3) 500,000

Paid-in Capital in Excess of Par

Debit −	Credit +
	(3) 200,000

RETEACHING SECTION 1

Explaining Corporate Charter The corporate charter spells out the number of shares of common and preferred stock that a corporation may issue. The charter also indicates the par value assigned to each share of stock. Many investors prefer to buy common stock because it has voting privileges and offers greater potential for growth than does preferred stock. If possible, bring in a stockholders' proxy card to show your students, along with the proxy booklet that describes the issues on which shareholders are voting.

Distributing the Earnings of a Corporation

In Section 1 you learned to record stock issue transactions for a corporation. In this section you will learn how corporations distribute earnings to the stockholders. Corporations like General Motors have a long history of distributing a portion of earnings to their stockholders every year, making their stock an attractive investment.

Dividends

When an owner of a sole proprietorship or a partnership wishes to take money out of the business, a check is written on the checking account of the business. The amount of the check is recorded as a debit in the owner's withdrawals account, which reduces the owner's equity.

The owners (stockholders) of a publicly held corporation cannot withdraw cash whenever they want. Instead, a **dividend** is a distribution of cash to stockholders. Dividends reduce retained earnings.

The corporation's board of directors declares, or authorizes, dividends. Before a dividend is declared, the corporation should have a sufficient amount of cash available to pay the dividend. In addition, since dividends decrease retained earnings, there must be an adequate balance in the **Retained Earnings** account. **Figure 21–1** illustrates the important dates in the dividend process.

A separate account named **Dividends** is used to record dividends declared. The **Dividends** account is a contra-stockholders' equity account. At the end of the year, the **Dividends** account is closed to the **Retained Earnings** account. The rules of debit and credit for **Dividends** are shown in the T account. Notice that they are the opposite of the rules for the stockholders' equity accounts.

Dividends	
Debit + Increase Side Normal Balance	Credit – Decrease Side

Dividend amounts could be debited directly to the **Retained Earnings** account. Most corporations, however, prefer to use a separate account so that the dividend amounts can be easily determined.

A liability account, **Dividends Payable**, is used to record the amount of dividends that will be paid on the payment date. Like all liability accounts, **Dividends Payable** is increased by credits and decreased by debits. The normal balance of the **Dividends Payable** account is a credit balance.

What You'll Learn

- Why and how corporations distribute their earnings.
- How to record dividends on preferred stock.
- How to record dividends on common stock.

Why It's Important

When the board of directors of a corporation decides to distribute profits in the form of dividends, a general journal entry is recorded.

KEY TERMS

dividend

CONNECT TO . . . ENGLISH

In 1776, Adam Smith published *The Wealth of Nations.* In his book, the Scots professor argued that individual welfare was more important than national power, and that allowing people to struggle for their own wealth benefits everyone. This was the first written explanation of capitalism and laissez-faire economics.

RESOURCE MANAGER

Reproducible Masters
- Lesson Plans
- Chapter Reviews and Working Papers (CRWP) TAE
- Demonstration Problems

Transparencies
- Section Focus Transparency
- Teaching Transparencies
- Source Document Transparencies
- Solution Transparencies

Multimedia
- Exam*View* CD-ROM
- Electronic Learning Center CD-ROM
- Interactive Lesson Planner CD-ROM
- Electronic Field Trips in Accounting

1 FOCUS

Introducing the Section

In this section students will learn that corporations with earnings often pay dividends to their shareholders. Students will learn how to record dividends paid on both common and preferred stock.

Section Concepts

- Why and how corporations distribute their earnings.
- How to record dividends on preferred stock.
- How to record dividends on common stock.

Visual Learning

Section 2 Focus

Use **Transparency 21–5** to introduce section concepts.

BELL RINGER

Analyzing Financial Data: Bring in the financial section of a newspaper. Have students read the stock listings and identify several companies that have paid dividends this year. Ask students whether they would prefer to invest in a company that pays dividends versus one that does not. Have them explain their reasons. L1

Concept Development: Dividends

Discussion: Have students look at the stock listings on the financial pages of your local newspaper or a financial publication. Have students select three companies and then compare the stock price and dividends paid by each company. Ask students which stock is the best buy in terms of dividends paid. The price-earnings ratio is commonly used to evaluate a corporation's financial performance. L1

2 TEACH

GUIDED PRACTICE

Reading Accounting

• Have students make an outline of the major headings in the section. As they read the text related to each heading, have them make notes about the information under the heading. L1

Visual Learning

Figure 21–1 Important Dates in the Dividend Process

Use **Transparency 21–6** to help students determine which stockholders are entitled to receive dividend payments.

Critical Thinking: Ask students this question: Since dividends must be paid on preferred stock before common stockholders can be paid any dividends, why might investors prefer common stock? (The dividend rate on preferred stock is a set rate that does not change with the profits of the business. Dividends on common stock are voted by the board of directors, and these dividends are often higher than those paid on preferred shares. Thus investors earn a better return.) L3

Math Review for Accounting Photocopy appropriate *Activity Sheets* for students who need additional practice in basic math skills.

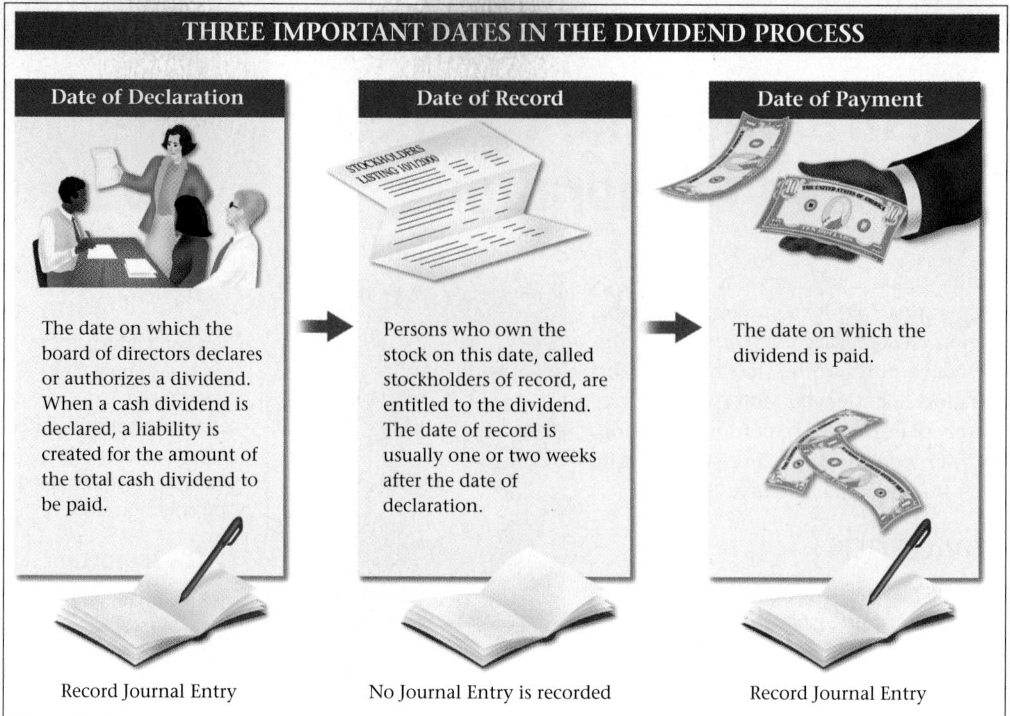

Figure 21–1 Important Dates in the Dividend Process

If a corporation is authorized to issue two types of stock, separate dividend and dividend payable accounts are used for each type of stock. On Your Mark uses the following accounts:

Dividends—Preferred	**Dividends Payable—Preferred**
Dividends—Common	**Dividends Payable—Common**

Let's look at the transactions involved when dividends are declared by the board of directors of On Your Mark during its second year of incorporation.

Calculator Hints

Starting New Calculations

If you want to start a new calculation:

- press C, or Clear twice to clear all numbers and mathematical functions.

If you're starting a new calculation and you ended the preceding one with the equal key:

- you do *not* need to press C.

Dividends on Preferred Stock

As mentioned earlier, preferred stockholders have certain preferences over common stockholders; one preference is the right to receive dividends before common stockholders. The amount of the dividend for preferred stock is predetermined or stated. The stated dividend indicates the amount that will be paid to preferred stockholders per year. On Your Mark issued 250 shares of preferred $6 stock. A $6 dividend will be paid for each share of preferred stock per year. The dividend amount can be paid annually, or in semiannual or quarterly installments.

	Dividend Payment	
Annually	$6.00	
Semiannually	$3.00	($6.00 ÷ 2)
Quarterly	$1.50	($6.00 ÷ 4)

Math Skill Builder Activity

Starting New Calculations Have students practice using the Clear key on their printing calculators. Have each student key in this series of numbers: Assets: $150,680, $639,298, $406,010, $750,000, $262,500, $45,000, $22,558; Liabilities: $62,412, $363,009, $20,000, $772,478, $316,315; Capital: $735,000, $500,000, $305,990. Tell students to find a subtotal after each set of numbers, clear that section, then continue adding the next. When finished, they are to add the subtotals to find the grand total and then check the calculator tape against the figures for proof. (Asset subtotal = $2,276,046; Liabilities subtotal = $1,534,214; Capital subtotal = $1,540,990; Grand total = $5,351,250)

Date of Declaration

A journal entry is made to record the dividend on preferred stock on the date of declaration.

Business Transaction

On November 15 the board of directors for On Your Mark declared an annual cash dividend on the 250 shares of preferred $6 stock issued. The dividend is payable to preferred stockholders of record on November 29. The dividend will be paid on December 15. The total amount of the preferred dividends is $1,500 (250 shares × $6), Memorandum 215.

JOURNAL ENTRY

GENERAL JOURNAL — PAGE 72

	DATE		DESCRIPTION	POST. REF.	DEBIT	CREDIT	
1	20--						1
2	Nov.	15	Dividends—Preferred		1 500 00		2
3			Dividends Payable—Preferred			1 500 00	3
4			Memorandum 215				4
5							5

Date of Record

On November 29 the corporation checks its records and prepares a list of preferred stockholders entitled to receive the dividend. No journal entry is required on this date.

Date of Payment

On December 15 a check for $1,500, the total amount of the dividend payable on preferred stock, is written and then deposited in a special dividends checking account. Separate checks are written on the dividends checking account and are made payable to each preferred stockholder entitled to receive the dividend.

Business Transaction

On December 15 On Your Mark issued Check 1373 for $1,500 in payment of the dividend on preferred stock declared November 15.

JOURNAL ENTRY

GENERAL JOURNAL — PAGE 81

	DATE		DESCRIPTION	POST. REF.	DEBIT	CREDIT	
1	20--						1
2	Dec.	15	Dividends Payable—Preferred		1 500 00		2
3			Cash in Bank			1 500 00	3
4			Check 1373				4
5							5

2 TEACH (Cont'd.)

Visual Learning

Business Transaction

Use **Transparency 21–7** to guide students through the analysis and recording of a declaration of a preferred stock dividend.

Teaching Tips

Even in years when a profit does not exist, some corporations will pay dividends if there is adequate cash.

Stockholders are the owners of a corporation and are entitled to a share of its profits, but dividends are not guaranteed. The size and frequency of dividends depend on the corporation's earnings, the amount of cash available, and the plans of the board of directors.

The board of directors is under no legal obligation to declare dividends. A corporation must retain some of its assets for emergencies, for future distribution to stockholders as dividends in those years when earnings are not sufficient to pay normal dividends, and—most important—for use in expanding operations.

Visual Learning

Business Transaction

Using **Transparency 21–8**, have students analyze the transaction and explain the journal entry to record payment of a preferred stock dividend.

INTERDISCIPLINARY CONNECTIONS ACTIVITY

(Refer to the *Connect to...English* feature on page 579.)

English Have students conduct an author search for literature, essays, or articles written on any of these topics: economics, capitalism, taxation, stock market, corporate accounting. Ask students to list the author, the title of the work, and the subject. When the searches are complete, compile the lists into a "Recommended Reading List" for your accounting classes. Ask students to choose one author or article, read the work, and write a synopsis of the material.

2 TEACH (Cont'd.)

Teaching Tips

Remind students that the process for paying dividends on common stock is the same as on preferred stock. Only the account names are different.

Point out that the declaration of a stock dividend creates a liability for the corporation. The actual payment of the dividend usually occurs weeks after a dividend is declared.

Discuss return on stockholders' equity and how investors use such calculations to aid their decision about buying stock in a corporation. The more a corporation earns as a percentage of equity, the higher the likelihood of long-term growth, which usually leads to increases in stock prices and higher dividends.

Demonstration Problem Step-by-Step Practice

Use demonstration problem 21–2 to give students practice in recording entries to declare and pay stock dividends.

Thinking Algebraically

Writing Formulas: Have students write a formula to calculate the dividend per share of common stock using the information described in item (2) on this page (582). (Example: common stock dividend = [a – (b × c)] ÷ d, which is solved as [$3,000 – (250 × $6)] ÷ 15,000 = $0.10, or 10 cents per share) L2

The Office Depot 2001 Annual Report

Refer students to pages A-39–A-48 at the back of the book.

ACCOUNTING TIPS

Stock Issues

Large issues of stock sold by a corporation to the public must have the approval of the Securities and Exchange Commission of the federal government. This indicates that the sellers of the stock have revealed all pertinent information about the business to potential stock buyers.

Dividends on Common Stock

Dividends on common stock may be declared in one of two ways.

(1) The board of directors may declare a dividend amount per common share. For example, the board of directors of On Your Mark declared a 50¢ per common share dividend. Thus, a 50¢ dividend will be paid for each share of common stock.

(2) The board of directors may decide to declare the total cash dividend for both preferred and common stock. In this case the preferred dividends are paid first and the remaining amount is divided equally among the common stockholders. For example, suppose the board of directors of On Your Mark declared a total cash dividend of $3,000. Preferred stockholders will receive $1,500 (250 shares × $6). The remaining amount, $1,500 ($3,000 – $1,500) will be split among the common stockholders. Each share of common stock will receive a 10¢ dividend ($1,500 ÷ 15,000 shares).

Like preferred stock, dividends on common stock can be paid annually, semiannually, or quarterly. Most publicly held corporations pay dividends on a quarterly basis.

ANALYZING FINANCIAL REPORTS

Calculating Return on Stockholders' Equity

Stockholders' equity is used to evaluate a company's profitability. One measure of profitability is the return on common stockholders' equity. You calculated this ratio for a sole proprietorship business in Chapter 10. The calculation for a corporation is similar.

$$\frac{\text{Net Earnings}}{\text{Average Common Stockholders' Equity}} \quad \frac{\$20{,}990}{\$200{,}832} = 0.1045 \text{ or } 10.45\%$$

To find the average common stockholders' equity, add the stockholders' equity at the beginning of the year to that at the end of the year and divide by 2. For example:

Beginning stockholders' equity	$186,178	
Ending stockholders' equity	215,486	
Total	$401,664 ÷ 2 =	$200,832

The return on common stockholders' equity shows how much the business earned for each dollar invested by the common stockholders.

▶ **Analyze the Report:**

1. Calculate the return on stockholders' equity for 2001 using Office Depot's balance sheet and income statement on pages A-45–A-46.
2. Why do you think the return on common stockholders' equity would be important to potential buyers of a company's common stock?

ANALYZING FINANCIAL REPORTS

Analyze the Report (Answers)

1. Return on stockholders' equity = 11.66%
   $201,043.00 ÷ $1,724,844.50 = 11.66%
2. The ratio shows how well the corporation's managers are using the equity invested in the company to produce revenue and profit. The higher the ratio, the better the return on the equity invested. Investors usually prefer companies that deliver high (or at least average) returns because other investors will continue to buy the stock, thus driving up the value of their own stock holdings.

SECTION 2 Check Your Understanding

Now that you have studied this section, complete the following questions and problems.

Thinking Critically

1. What two conditions should exist before a cash dividend is declared?
2. Explain how dividends are recorded when a corporation has issued two types of stock.

Computing in the Business World

On January 28 the board of directors for Jelly Bean Works declared an annual cash dividend on 200 shares of preferred $10 stock. What is the total amount of the dividend? How is this dividend accounted for in the company's books?

Problem 21–2 Distributing Corporate Earnings

During its first year of operation, Longhorn Corporation issued 17,500 shares of $10 par common stock. At the end of the year, the corporation had a net income of $350,000. The board of directors declared a cash dividend of $5 per share.

Instructions Answer the following questions in your working papers:

1. How much of the net income was distributed to the stockholders?
2. How much of the net income was retained by the corporation?

Problem 21–3 Analyzing a Source Document

Information related to the first quarter dividend on the common stock of Rob Williams Thrift Market Inc. is provided on the following memorandum.

Instructions Prepare the journal entries required to record the following in your working papers. Use page 18 in a general journal.

- declaration of the first quarter dividend
- payment of the first quarter dividend, Check 221

Rob Williams Thrift Market Inc.
2347 Eastern Parkway
Orange, IA 50322-6922

MEMORANDUM 37

TO: Chief Financial Officer
FROM: Albert MacFish, Chairman of the Board
DATE: April 8, 20--
SUBJECT: 1st quarter dividend

On April 1, 20--, the board of directors declared a $1 per share dividend on the 5,679 shares of common stock issued. The date of record is April 15, 20--. The date of payment is April 30, 20--.

RETEACHING SECTION 2

Payment of Cash Dividends Unlike owners of sole proprietorships, stockholders cannot withdraw cash from the business. The return on the money they invest in stock is paid in the form of dividends. However, companies do not have to pay dividends. If the company has a poor year, the board of directors for the company may decide not to pay a dividend. When cash dividends are paid, the effect is a decrease in the company's Retained Earnings account and a decrease in the Cash in Bank account.

3 ASSESS

Thinking Critically (Answers)

1. Authorization by board of directors, sufficient cash to pay the dividend.
2. Preferred dividends are paid first and recorded in Dividends—Preferred; common dividends are recorded in the Dividends—Common account.

Computing in the Business World (Answers)

Dividend is $2,000 (200 shares × $10); debited to Dividends—Preferred and credited to Dividends Payable—Preferred; memo number is recorded in description line below the entries.

Problem 21–2 (Answers)

1. $87,500
2. $262,500

Problem 21–3 (Answers)

Apr. 1: Dr. Dividends—Common $5,679; Cr. Dividends Payable—Common $5,679; Memorandum 37
Apr. 30: Dr. Dividends Payable—Common $5,679; Cr. Cash in Bank $5,679; Check 221

Chapter Reviews and Working Papers Refer students to the Chapter 21 workbook pages to answer *Check Your Understanding* activities.

4 CLOSE

Section Wrap-Up

Writing: Have students write a paragraph describing the important dates related to dividends and the accounts used to record dividend transactions. L1

SCANS in the Workforce

Foundation Skills Connection

Creative Thinking

Ask students to think creatively and create a learning strategy for one of their accounting principles (e.g., the accounting equation, double-entry accounting). They may want to create a bulletin-board display, a game, a simulated project, or an academic activity. Ask students to write their ideas and share with other students for constructive criticism. L1

Workplace Competencies Connection

Using Computers to Process Information

Ask students to choose a stock and follow its activity for one week. Have students write down the daily activity. At the end of the week, have students use computer software with charting or graphing tools to create a graph plotting the stock activity. L2

Teaching Others

Divide students into small groups of four to five members. Have each group choose a math or business skill they could teach to others. Have each group prepare a lesson plan, handouts, and tests for its topic. Then schedule the groups to teach their subjects to others (e.g., in your class, in an academic class, in another school). Ask the students who were taught to evaluate the lesson. L3

ACCOUNTING CAREERS IN FOCUS

JOHNSIE CRAWFORD
Accounting Teacher
Brandon High School

Q: What do you like about your job?
A: Writing the school's accounting curriculum and teaching it are the most exciting things I've done in the 35 years I've been teaching. I feel like I've been on the cutting edge of a revolution in education. I'm helping students step into the real world before they leave high school.

Once students see they can succeed in the accounting class, and get college credit, they realize they do have the skills to succeed in college. They have the motivation and self-esteem to move forward.

Q: Do your students go into the accounting field?
A: Some do. But I emphasize how many careers and fields require at least a year of accounting—doctors, construction workers, farmers, lawyers, mechanics, and so on. Accounting is a valuable course for all students.

Q: Do you need computer skills?
A: Yes. Students learn manual entry first, but then they have to apply those skills to the computer. In addition to training them for business, the computer makes the course come alive.

In 1993, I got 25 new classroom computers. I spent hours learning how to use them. But I learned where the bugs were. Wherever I got stuck, I knew my students might get stuck there too.

Tips from . . .
Robert Half International Inc.
Technology is part of the accounting profession. Spend some time on the Internet and see what's available about accounting. Discover the latest business trends, and learn to research new information about the industry.

CAREER FACTS

Nature of the Work: Create lesson plans and exams, advise students, teach classes, and motivate students and help them achieve mastery.
Training or Education Needed: A bachelor's degree in business education.
Aptitudes, Abilities, and Skills: Accounting, time-management skills, communication skills, and interpersonal skills.
Salary Range: \$25,000 to \$60,000 depending on your experience.
Career Path: Major in business education, intern in high school, and seek a business education teaching position.

Thinking Critically: What would be the most difficult part of teaching accounting?

ACCOUNTING CAREERS IN FOCUS

Thinking Critically (Answers)
Managing time; grading detailed, number-oriented papers; explaining accounting concepts; motivating students; and keeping up to date on accounting technology and software used in accounting practice.

ROBERT HALF CORNER

Accounting Trends Roles for accounting and finance professionals are growing. Beyond theory and practical knowledge, future employees will be expected to show expertise in strategic planning, revenue enhancement, technology, interpersonal skills, and communication skills.

Financial Reporting for a Publicly Held Corporation

Many corporations prepare a statement of stockholders' equity instead of a statement of retained earnings. In this section we'll examine the information that is reported on the statement of stockholders' equity and see how this statement is prepared. We'll also see how stockholders' equity is reported on a corporation's balance sheet.

The Income Statement

The income statement of a publicly held corporation is similar to that prepared by a closely held corporation. Remember, the federal corporate income taxes paid by a corporation are reported separately on the income statement.

Statement of Stockholders' Equity

In Chapter 19 you learned how to prepare a statement of retained earnings for a closely held corporation. That statement reports the changes in the **Retained Earnings** account during the period. It showed:

Retained Earnings, beginning balance
+ Net Income
Retained Earnings, ending balance

An increasing number of corporations prepare a statement of stockholders' equity rather than a statement of retained earnings. The **statement of stockholders' equity** reports the changes in all of the stockholders' equity accounts during the period. It also provides information about the transactions affecting stockholders' equity during the period. The information reported on a statement of stockholders' equity includes the number of shares of each type of stock issued and the total amount received for those shares, the net income for the period, and dividends declared during the period.

Figure 21–2 shows the statement of stockholders' equity for On Your Mark at the end of its second year of incorporation. The information needed for the statement comes from the work sheet and from the general ledger accounts. The statement is prepared as follows:

- The names of the four stockholders' equity accounts appear at the top of the amount columns. There is also a Totals column at the far right.

What You'll Learn

- How to prepare a statement of stockholders' equity for a publicly held corporation.
- How to prepare a balance sheet for a publicly held corporation.

Why It's Important

Stockholders and managers examine financial reports to determine the health of a corporation.

KEY TERMS

statement of stockholders' equity

International ACCOUNTING

Advertising

When promoting your accounting practice in the international marketplace, it's important to be aware of how businesses are promoted there. Studying the details of the marketplace will help you promote knowledgeably.

RESOURCE MANAGER

Reproducible Masters
- Lesson Plans
- Chapter Reviews and Working Papers (CRWP) TAE
- Demonstration Problems

Transparencies
- Section Focus Transparency
- Teaching Transparencies
- Source Document Transparencies
- Solution Transparencies

Multimedia
- ExamView CD-ROM
- Electronic Learning Center CD-ROM
- Interactive Lesson Planner CD-ROM
- Electronic Field Trips in Accounting

1 FOCUS

Introducing the Section

In this section students will learn how to prepare financial statements for a publicly held corporation, focusing on the statement of stockholders' equity and the balance sheet.

Section Concepts

- How to prepare a statement of stockholders' equity for a publicly held corporation.
- How to prepare a balance sheet for a publicly held corporation.

Visual Learning

Section 3 Focus

Use **Transparency 21–9** to introduce section concepts.

BELL RINGER

Making Comparisons: Collect several annual reports to share with students. Have them look at the different types of financial statements. Explore the meaning of "consolidated," which they'll find on many financial statements. L1

Concept Development: The Income Statement

Discussion: Point out that the income statement for a publicly held corporation is similar to that for a privately held corporation. Both report the earnings and expenses of doing business. L1

Concept Development: Statement of Stockholders' Equity

Discussion: Explain that the statement of stockholders' equity reports changes in the corporation's equity that occurred during the period. Its purpose is similar to the statement of changes in owner's equity. L1

2 TEACH

GUIDED PRACTICE

Reading Accounting

- Have students read the statement of stockholders' equity. Ask what it means when amounts are shown in parentheses. L1

Visual Learning

Figure 21–2 Statement of Stockholders' Equity

Using **Transparency 21–10,** point out information reported on a statement of stockholders' equity. Emphasize the equity account names in the column headings.

Demonstration Problem Step-by-Step Practice

Use demonstration problem 21–3 to give students practice in preparing a statement of stockholders' equity.

Concept Development: Balance Sheet

Discussion: Emphasize that the assets section of the balance sheet is the same for a publicly held corporation as for one that is privately held. The liabilities section may include a liability account for dividends payable if the corporation pays dividends. The other difference is in the equity section, which reports the issuance of common and preferred stock and the capital acquired from stock sold above par value. L1

Strategies for Teaching International Accounting

To enrich the study of international accounting, refer to the additional critical thinking activities in the booklet.

On Your Mark Athletic Wear
Statement of Stockholders' Equity
For the Year Ended December 31, 20--

		$100 Par Preferred $6 Stock	$10 Par Common Stock	Paid-in Capital in Excess of Par	Retained Earnings	Totals	
1	*Balance, January 1, 20--*	25 000 00	100 000 00		27 600 00	152 600 00	1
2	*Issuance of 5,000 shares of common stock*		50 000 00	7 500 00		57 500 00	2
3	*Net Income*				13 525 00	13 525 00	3
4	*Cash Dividends:*						4
5	*Preferred Stock*				(1 500 00)	(1 500 00)	5
6	*Common Stock*				(7 500 00)	(7 500 00)	6
7	*Balance, December 31, 20--*	25 000 00	150 000 00	7 500 00	32 125 00	214 625 00	7
8							8

Figure 21–2 Statement of Stockholders' Equity

- The first line shows the balance of each account at the beginning of the period.
- The next lines describe various transactions affecting the stockholders' equity accounts, such as issuance of stock, net income, and dividends declared. The transactions are described in the left column. The increase or decrease amounts are recorded in the individual account columns and in the Totals column. For example, the second line on the statement indicates that the company issued 5,000 shares of common stock during the period. The issuance of the 5,000 shares increased the balance of the **Common Stock** account by $50,000. Since the shares were issued at a price above par value, the **Paid-in Capital in Excess of Par** account increased by $7,500.
- The final line shows the balance of each account at the end of the period.

As you review **Figure 21–2**, notice that amounts which decrease account balances, like dividends declared, are enclosed in parentheses. The cash dividends declared on preferred and common stock are each listed separately. Also notice that the Retained Earnings column of the statement of stockholders' equity contains the same information that is reported on a statement of retained earnings. Remember that net income increases retained earnings, and dividends declared decrease retained earnings. The statement of stockholders' equity is used to prepare the corporation's balance sheet.

ACCOUNTING *Flashbacks*

ARABIC NUMERALS
Around 300 AD, Gupta mathematicians in India advanced algebra and introduced concepts of infinity and zero. Adopted by Middle Eastern travelers, their mathematical symbols became known as Arabic numerals.

Balance Sheet

The assets and liabilities sections of a balance sheet for a publicly held corporation are similar to those of a balance sheet for a closely held corporation. Notice in **Figure 21–3** that the **Dividends Payable** accounts are reported in the liabilities section. Since On Your Mark paid the dividends before the end of the year, zero balances are reported in these liability accounts.

The stockholders' equity section of a publicly held corporation's balance sheet is more detailed than that of a closely held corporation. As you can see in **Figure 21–4**, each type of stock issued by On Your Mark is listed separately under the heading "Paid-in Capital." Preferred stock is listed before common stock. Each listing describes:

Teaching International ACCOUNTING

(Refer to the *International Accounting* feature on page 585.)

Evaluating Commercials and Advertisements Ask students to identify a favorite commercial or advertisement. Then ask students to assume that they work for the company marketing the product in the United States. The firm has decided to begin exporting the product to Saudi Arabia, France, and Russia. Instruct students to research the cultures of the three countries to determine if the commercial or advertisement is appropriate for each of the three countries. If adjustments are necessary, students should describe the necessary changes and defend the changes by explaining the cultural differences or similarities.

- the par value,
- the number of shares authorized, and
- the number of shares issued.

The **Dividends** accounts are not listed in the stockholders' equity section because they are closed to **Retained Earnings** at the end of the year. Thus, the retained earnings amount shown on the balance sheet has been reduced by the dividends declared during the period.

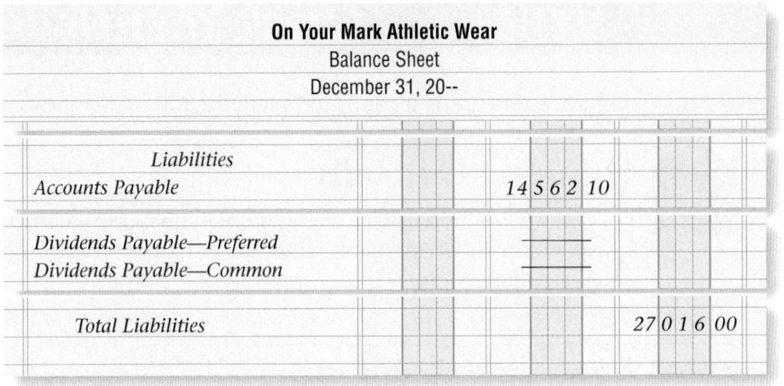

On Your Mark Athletic Wear Balance Sheet December 31, 20--			
Liabilities			
Accounts Payable		14 562 10	
Dividends Payable—Preferred			
Dividends Payable—Common			
Total Liabilities			27 016 00

Figure 21–3 Reporting the Balances of the Dividends Payable Accounts on the Balance Sheet

On Your Mark Athletic Wear Balance Sheet December 31, 20--			
Stockholders' Equity			
Paid-in Capital:			
$6 Preferred Stock, $100 par, 1,000 shares authorized,			
250 shares issued	25 000 00		
Common stock, $10 par, 20,000 shares authorized,			
15,000 shares issued	150 000 00		
Paid-in Capital in Excess of Par	7 500 00		
Total Paid-in Capital		182 500 00	
Retained Earnings		32 125 00	
Total Stockholders' Equity			214 625 00
Total Liabilities and Stockholders' Equity			241 641 00

Figure 21–4 The Stockholders' Equity Section of the Balance Sheet

A MATTER OF ETHICS

Using Insider Information

Imagine that you are an accountant for a large shipping company, like United Parcel Service (UPS). During the course of your work, you learn that the company is planning to buy a company that makes shipping containers. It's a smaller company whose stock is traded on a local stock exchange. You think about purchasing several thousand shares of the smaller company's stock, expecting to make a profit when the purchase goes through.

Ethical Decision Making:

- What are the ethical issues?
- What are the alternatives?
- Who are the affected parties?
- How do the alternatives affect the parties?
- What would you do?

Teaching A MATTER OF ETHICS

Using Insider Information Have students research business magazines and newspapers to find articles about insider trading. Tell students to make notes about their findings so they can share the information in class. Also ask students to find the penalties for being found guilty of insider trading. Hold a class discussion about the pros and cons of insider trading.

2 TEACH (Cont'd.)

Visual Learning

Figure 21–3 Reporting the Balances of the Dividends Payable Accounts on the Balance Sheet

Using **Transparency 21–11**, explain the reporting of the dividends payable accounts on the balance sheet. Remind students that Dividends Payable is a liability account and its balance will be included as a part of total liabilities.

Figure 21–4 The Stockholders' Equity Section of the Balance Sheet

Using **Transparency 21–12**, explain the stockholders' equity section of the balance sheet.

GO TO Demonstration Problem Step-by-Step Practice

Use demonstration problem 21–4 to give students practice in preparing the stockholders' equity section of the balance sheet.

Teaching Tip

Have students compare the information in the statement of stockholders' equity with that in the equity section of the balance sheet. Help them trace the source of each balance reported on the balance sheet.

Strategies for Teaching Ethics in Accounting

Photocopy the Chapter 21 *Student Activity Sheet* for students. Answers are also provided in the booklet.

CHAPTER 21
SECTION 3, PAGES 585–588

3 ASSESS

Thinking Critically (Answers)

1. The number of shares of stock issued and the total amount received for the shares, net income for the period, dividends declared.
2. The statement of stockholders' equity shows total equity (investments made in the company by its shareholders and net income). The statement of retained earnings shows only the changes in that account during the period.

Analyzing Accounting (Answers)

Answers will vary. Students might mention that stock growth and dividend activity have increased and yielded higher dividends over the past three years. For stock activity to be so high, profits and sales must be equally high. Potential buyers will be able to purchase a company with a strong customer base. The fact that stockholders have received several dividend checks should create goodwill and loyalty to the company.

Problem 21-4 (Answers)

Transactions that are reported on the statement of stockholders' equity are 2, 3, 6, and 8.

Chapter Reviews and Working Papers Refer students to the Chapter 21 workbook pages to answer *Check Your Understanding* activities.

4 CLOSE

Section Wrap-Up

Writing: Have students write a paragraph explaining why investors would be interested in the statement of stockholders' equity and the equity section of the balance sheet. L1

SECTION 3 Check Your Understanding

Now that you have studied this section, complete the following questions and problems.

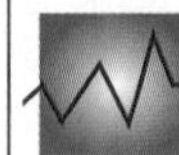

Thinking Critically

1. What information is reported on the statement of stockholders' equity?
2. Explain the difference between the statement of retained earnings and the statement of stockholders' equity.

Analyzing Accounting

As the accounting manager for Sunny Days, a Hawaiian-based sun care products manufacturer and retailer, you are asked to review the stock price and dividends declared over the past three years. The president, Ron Kanai, is looking for a buyer for Sunny Days and thinks an analysis of stock prices and dividends may appeal to potential corporate buyers. Review the following graph and write a one-paragraph report of what may attract potential buyers.

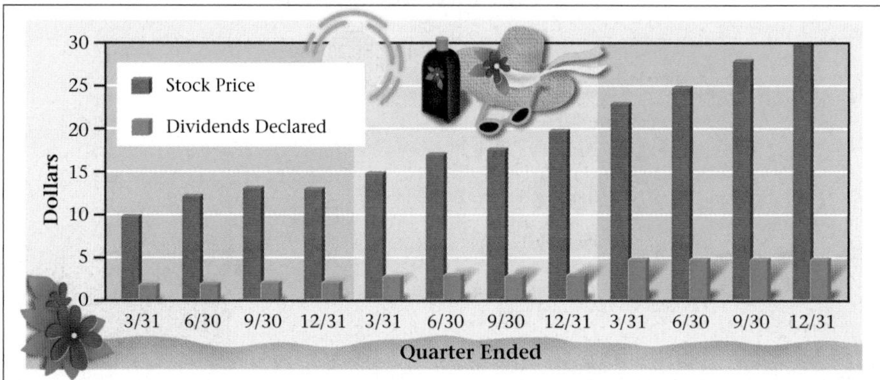

Problem 21–4 Examining the Statement of Stockholders' Equity

The following transactions of Victor Jewelry Corporation took place during the period.

Instructions Use the form in your working papers to indicate which of the transactions is reported on the statement of stockholders' equity.

Transactions:

1. Paid accounts payable of $50,000.
2. Issued 2,000 shares of $10 par common stock, receiving $15 per share.
3. The board of directors declared a cash dividend of $12,000 for all common stockholders.
4. Bought equipment on account at a total cost of $125,000.
5. Paid the cash dividend declared in Transaction 3.
6. Issued 500 shares of $100 par, $7 preferred stock.
7. Paid the federal income tax installment of $5,000.
8. Earned a net income of $150,000 for the period.

RETEACHING SECTION 3

Analyzing the Statement of Stockholders' Equity Point out that net income earned by a corporation increases the Retained Earnings account. Any dividends declared by a corporation decrease Retained Earnings. The statement of stockholders' equity reports the changes that have taken place in all of the stockholders' equity accounts during the accounting period. Any amounts that decrease account balances are enclosed in parentheses. The dividends for preferred stock and for common stock are reported separately on the statement.

CHAPTER 21 SUMMARY

KEY CONCEPTS

1. A closely held corporation is one that is owned by a few persons or by a family. A publicly held corporation is one whose stock is widely held, has a large market, and is usually traded on a stock exchange.
2. A corporation must have permission from the state to operate. It is considered to be a separate legal entity, is owned by its stockholders, and is usually run by professional managers.
3. Two types of stock a corporation may issue are common and preferred.
4. The par value of stock is the dollar amount printed on the stock certificate. Par value is used to determine the amount credited to the capital stock account when stock is issued.
5. Common stockholders have the right to vote and elect the board of directors of the corporation, to share in the earnings of the corporation, and to share in the assets of the corporation should it go out of business.
6. Preferred stockholders do not have the right to vote but are entitled to receive dividends before the common stockholders.
7. If stock is issued at a price higher than its par value, the amount received over par is credited to an account called **Paid-in Capital in Excess of Par.**
8. Corporations distribute part of their earnings to stockholders in the form of dividends.
9. Corporations may prepare a statement of stockholders' equity, which reports the changes that occurred in all of the stockholders' equity accounts during the period.
10. T account analysis of typical stock transactions:

(a) Issuing preferred stock at par value

Cash in Bank	
Debit + XXX	Credit –

Preferred Stock	
Debit –	Credit + XXX

(b) Issuing common stock at par value

Cash in Bank	
Debit + XXX	Credit –

Common Stock	
Debit –	Credit + XXX

(c) Declaration of cash dividend

Dividends—Preferred (or Common)	
Debit + XXX	Credit –

Dividends Payable—Preferred (or Common)	
Debit –	Credit + XXX

ANSWERS

1. charter
2. board of directors
3. common
4. common
5. Paid-in Capital in Excess of Par
6. dividends
7. record
8. Dividends Payable
9. statement of stockholders' equity
10. balance sheet

Chapter 21 Quiz

Student ____ Class ____ Instructor ____

Date Assigned ____ Date Completed ____

CHAPTER 21 QUIZ

Accounting for Publicly Held Corporations

QUESTIONS (Completion)

Directions: Fill in the blank with the term that best completes each sentence.

1. A corporation's ____ spells out the rules under which the business is to operate.
2. A ____ is responsible for the affairs of the corporation.
3. If a corporation issues only one class of capital stock, it is called ____.
4. Shareholders of ____ stock are allowed to vote to elect a board of directors.
5. Amounts collected from sales of stock above par are recorded in ____.
6. A corporation distributes part of its earnings to stockholders by paying ____.
7. The date of ____ is used to determine who receives dividends.
8. When a corporation declares a dividend, the amount is recorded in ____.
9. A report showing the changes in stockholders' equity accounts during a fiscal period is a(n) ____.
10. Paid-in Capital is reported on the ____.

 Chapter Quizzes • 23

QUESTIONS (Completion)

1. A corporation's ____ spells out the rules under which the business is to operate.
2. A ____ is responsible for the affairs of the corporation.
3. If a corporation issues only one class of capital stock, it is called ____.
4. Shareholders of ____ stock are allowed to vote to elect a board of directors.
5. Amounts collected from sales of stock above par are recorded in ____.
6. A corporation distributes part of its earnings to stockholders by paying ____.
7. The date of ____ is used to determine who receives dividends.
8. When a corporation declares a dividend, the amount is recorded in ____.
9. A report showing the changes in stockholders' equity accounts during a fiscal period is a(n) ____.
10. Paid-in Capital is reported on the ____.

USING KEY TERMS

See the *Glossary* for the definitions of these terms. Have students share examples in class. Discuss how their study of accounting helps them understand terms used in business magazine and newspaper articles.

Understanding Accounting Concepts and Procedures

(Answers)

1. Closely held corporation does not sell stock and is owned by small number of people; publicly held corporations sell stock that is traded on an exchange and owned by hundreds or thousands of investors.
2. Legal permission to operate, a separate legal entity, and owned by stockholders.
3. Right to vote and elect board of directors, to share in earnings, and to share in assets should the corporation be liquidated.
4. Common shareholders may attend stockholders' meetings and vote for the board of directors. Preferred stock owners do not vote but do receive dividends before common stockholders.
5. The total par value of shares sold.
6. Stockholders' equity account; it has a normal credit balance.
7. (a) Date of declaration, board of directors votes to pay dividend, (b) date of record, ownership of shares is set, (c) date of actual payment.
8. A temporary contra stockholders' equity account.
9. Dr. dividends account; Cr. Dividends Payable.
10. Date of declaration. Once a dividend is declared, the corporation is obligated to pay it.
11. Issuance of stock (at and above par), net income, and amount of any dividends declared.

USING KEY TERMS

For each key term, give or find an example of the term in a newspaper, periodical, annual report, or on an Internet site. Then use the example in a sentence.

authorized capital stock	par value
board of directors	preferred stock
closely held corporation	proxy
common stock	publicly held corporation
dividend	statement of stockholders' equity
Paid-in Capital in Excess of Par	

Understanding Accounting Concepts and Procedures

Instructions

On a separate sheet of paper, answer the following questions:

1. Explain the difference between a closely held corporation and a publicly held corporation.
2. Name three characteristics of a corporation.
3. What are some of the rights of common stockholders?
4. List the differences between common and preferred stock.
5. When stock is sold at a price above its par value, what amount is credited to the capital stock account?
6. What is the classification of the **Paid-in Capital in Excess of Par** account? What is its normal balance?
7. Name and explain the three dates important to the dividend process.
8. What type of account is **Dividends**?
9. When a dividend is declared, which accounts are debited and which accounts are credited?
10. At what date does a dividend become a liability to the corporation? Explain.
11. What type of information is reported on the statement of stockholders' equity?

ASSESSMENT RESOURCES

Choose assessment strategies from the following pages to evaluate your students' progress.

Student Edition
Check Your Understanding, pp. 578, 583, 588
Chapter 21 Problems, pp. 593–595
Analyzing Financial Reports, p. 582

Assessment and Evaluation Masters
Chapter 21 Study Plan, *Glencoe Workbook (CRWP)*
Chapter 21 Self-Test, *Glencoe Workbook (CRWP)*
Chapter 21 Test, *Chapter Tests* Booklet
Chapter 21 Activity, *School-to-Work Handbook*
Chapter 21 Exam*View*

Teacher Wraparound Edition
Critical Thinking Activity, p. 593
Reteaching Sections 1–3, pp. 578, 583, 588
Chapter 21 Quiz, p. 589

CHAPTER 21 REVIEW AND ACTIVITIES

Case Study...

Merchandising Business: Coffee Shop

Cyber Café is a retail store that sells a variety of coffees, along with gourmet pastries and other snacks. Besides food and beverages, the store offers computer stations where customers can surf the Web.

The owners of Cyber Café started the business three years ago. Early success helped them decide to incorporate and franchise the business. They now have franchises in 15 cities. The owners want to raise additional money to open cafés in Japan.

Thinking Critically:

1. Name at least three ways the business could raise money for the new franchises.
2. If you were considering investing in Cyber Café, what ratios and analyses would you calculate from their financial statements?
3. How would these calculations help you make an investment decision?

interNET CONNECTION

Stocks Online

The Web offers many sites that help investors track their stock holdings. Investors may trade (buy and sell) stocks, check the current prices, or watch trends.

Do This:

1. Locate a Web site that offers online trading capabilities. Use the search terms "stock quote" or "stock reports."
2. What is the current price for Microsoft and Coca Cola stocks? (If you don't know the stock symbol, use the search engine provided on the site.)

Workplace Skills

Working in Teams

Teamwork is essential in any job. Whether you work for a small company or a large corporation, you will seldom make decisions by yourself. If you can work cooperatively with others, contribute to a group, listen and respond accordingly, and take responsibility for accomplishing goals, then your ability to be a team player is definitely an employment strength.

On the Job:

Aussie Diners, owned by Annabelle Brandly, are located in Australia and North America. The corporation is about to go public and offer common stock on the New York Stock Exchange. Ms. Brandly calls you from the corporate office in Perth, Australia. She wants you to invite the North American executive management team to meet before she makes the final decision about going public.

Thinking Critically:

1. What would you do to get all the members of the executive management team together quickly?
2. Group with five students in your class and role play an executive management meeting. Ask each student to assume the role of one of these managers: Marketing, Accounting, Personnel, Facilities, and Purchasing. As a team, make a list of concerns from each department.

Conducting an Audit with Alex

The balance sheet of Automart Inc. includes the following amounts:

Preferred 6% Stock, $100 par value	$ 90,000
Common Stock, $10 par value	150,000
Paid-in Capital in Excess of Par—Common	40,000
Retained Earnings	55,000

Instructions Audit the balance sheet and report the number of shares of preferred and common stock issued as well as the selling price per share. Prepare a brief memorandum that contains your findings.

REVIEW AND ACTIVITIES CHAPTER 21

Case Study...

Thinking Critically (Answers)

1. Three possibilities include selling new stock, obtaining a loan from a bank, and saving the company's profits.
2. Answers may vary. Some ratios include the current ratio, quick ratio, debt ratio, return on equity, and price-earnings ratio.
3. Answers may vary. Evaluate student responses for the logical progression of ideas.

Workplace Skills

Thinking Critically (Answers)

1. Answers will vary. Students may not be familiar with teleconferencing, but you may want to suggest the various options available to today's business professional. Ask students to submit a copy of the memo to you.
2. Answers will vary.

Conducting an Audit with Alex

(Answers)

Number of preferred stock shares 900
Number of common stock shares 15,000
Price per share of common stock $12.67

Internet Resources and Activities Handbook

Refer students to the booklet for additional Internet activities.

interNET CONNECTION www.glencoe.com

Do This (Answers)

The Web offers many sites that help the investor track stock holdings. Investors may trade (buy and sell) stocks, check the current prices, or watch trends.

1. Big Charts: bigcharts.marketwatch.com
   Wall Street City: www.wallstreetcity.com/stocks/stocks_main.html
   Yahoo! Finance: Finance.yahoo.com/
2. Answers may vary.

PEACHTREE CORNER

Report Options

When entering transactions over multiple accounting periods, you must change the time frame for a report so that it will include all of the relevant transactions. For example, if a date range is set from October 1 to December 31, Peachtree will include only the transactions that occurred in this time frame in the report.

To change the date range, select **General Journal** from the ***Reports*** menu.

General Journal

Filter | Fields | Fonts

Report Order: Transaction Date
☑ Include Accounts with Zero Amounts
☑ Truncate Transaction Description
☐ Print Report in Summary Format

Date: Range From: Oct 1, 2008 To: Dec 31, 2008

Filter Range:

Filter	Type	From	To
Transaction Reference	All		

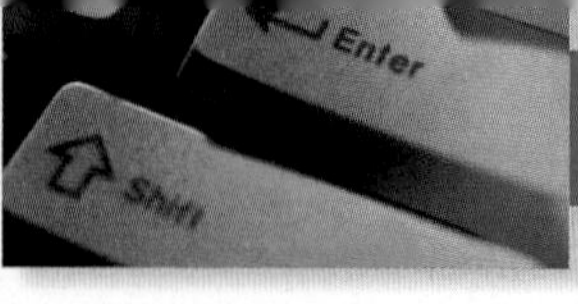

Customizing Financial Statements

Making the Transition from a Manual to a Computerized System

Task	Perform Accounting Procedures Using Manual Methods	Perform Accounting Procedures Using Automated Methods
Customizing financial statements	1. Using accounting stationery, you may wish to reorganize information or add details to financial statements.	1. Using the Report Designer option, you may select and sort data that appears on each financial statement. 2. You may also alter information on a report by using the Filter option.

Customizing Financial Reports

Peachtree Question	Description
How do I change the appearance or content of financial reports in Peachtree?	1. Select **Reports** from the ***Tasks*** menu. 2. Select the report you wish to customize from the Reports list. 3. Display it on the screen. 4. Select the Design icon above the report. 5. The following features can be adjusted: the size of the columns, the types of information displaying in the report, the font style and size of the print, and the location of information on the report. 6. If you wish to save the report in the new format, rename the file, leaving the original files in their original form.
How do I filter information on preformatted reports?	1. After you have selected a report from the Reports list, click the Preview icon to display it on your screen. 2. At the Filter option, you may accept the current settings, or make changes to the displayed fields. 3. The information that can be filtered varies according to the report.
What does the software do "behind the scenes"?	1. Peachtree retrieves general ledger account balances and names and includes them on various financial reports as defined by the parameters of the predefined reports. 2. Changes made to reports are immediately reflected on the screen, ensuring that the printed report will be in a desired format.

For detailed instructions: See the **Peachtree User Guide** in your Glencoe Working Papers.

Peachtree® Answers to Frequently Asked Questions

Q: Why doesn't Peachtree show all transactions when you choose **Open**?

A: Peachtree shows only the transactions entered in the current period. Suppose the current period is October and you enter a transaction dated November 15. If you choose **Open**, the November transaction will not be listed. Click the *Show* button in the Select General Journal Entry window and choose *All Transactions* or select the desired period to display the transactions you want to see.

For additional information, refer to your *Glencoe Peachtree Accounting User Guide*.

CHAPTER 21 PROBLEMS

APPLICATION OPTIONS

Problem 21–5 Distributing Corporate Earnings

During the first year of operations, Sunset Surfwear issued 18,500 shares of $10 par common stock. At the end of the year, the corporation had net income of $380,000. The board of directors declared a $5 cash dividend per share of common stock.

Instructions Answer the following questions in your working papers:

(1) How much of the net income earned for the year was paid to the common stockholders?

(2) How much of the net income was retained by the corporation?

Analyze: The journal entries for this cash dividend are required on which of the following dates: date of declaration, date of record, date of payment? Why are journal entries required on those dates?

Problem 21–6 Journalizing the Issue of Stock

On June 1 InBeat CD Shop was incorporated and authorized to issue 1,000 shares of $100 par, preferred 9% stock, and 10,000 shares of $25 par common stock.

Instructions In your working papers, record the following transactions on general journal page 1.

Date		Transactions
June	1	Issued 200 shares of preferred 9% stock at $100 per share, Memorandum 3.
	2	Issued 3,000 shares of common stock at $25 per share, Memorandum 7.
	6	Received $31 per share for 2,000 shares of common stock issued, Memorandum 10.
	7	Issued 50 shares of preferred 9% stock at par, Memorandum 11.

Analyze: Was any of the stock issued at a price above par? If yes, what amount was credited to the **Paid-in Capital in Excess of Par** account?

Complete chapter problems one of four ways:

1. **Manual** Glencoe Working Papers

or

2. **Peachtree Complete Accounting** Software

or

3. **QuickBooks** Templates (Problems 21–6, 21–9)

or

4. **Spreadsheet** Templates (Problem 21–8)

Peachtree®

SMART GUIDE

Step-by-Step Instructions: Problem 21–6

1. Select the problem set for InBeat CD Shop (Prob. 21–6).
2. Rename the company and set the system date.
3. Record all of the transactions using the **General Journal Entry** option.
4. Print a General Journal report and proof your work.
5. Answer the Analyze question.
6. End the session.

Problem 21–5 (Answers) Distributing Corporate Earnings

1. $92,500
2. $287,500

Analyze: Date of declaration, to record the liability; date of payment, to record the actual payment.

Problem 21–6 (Answers) Journalizing the Issue of Stock

June 1: Dr. Cash in Bank $20,000; Cr. 9% Preferred Stock $20,000; Memorandum 3

June 2: Dr. Cash in Bank $75,000; Cr. Common Stock $75,000; Memorandum 7

June 6: Dr. Cash in Bank $62,000; Cr. Common Stock $50,000, Paid-in Capital in Excess of Par $12,000; Memorandum 10

June 7: Dr. Cash in Bank $5,000; Cr. 9% Preferred Stock $5,000; Memorandum 11

Analyze: Yes, $12,000 (2,000 shares of common stock × $6).

CRITICAL THINKING ACTIVITY

Identifying Alternatives Fred and Edmond co-own a plastics manufacturing business that their father started several years ago. The business currently has some large debts, but sales have grown steadily during the last five years, with revenues of more than $50 million last year. One of the brothers is contemplating leaving the business. Recently, they have talked about incorporating the business. What would the advantages be to incorporating the business? (They could sell stock to raise capital for the business to help pay off the debts. If the business cannot pay its debts, there will be limited liability. Even if one brother does leave the business, the business will continue to operate.)

Problem 21-7 (Answers) Journalizing Common and Preferred Stock Dividend Transactions

Oct. 15: Dr. Dividends—Preferred $44,800; Cr. Dividends Payable—Preferred $44,800; Memorandum 407

Nov. 5: Dr. Dividends—Common $43,750; Cr. Dividends Payable—Common $43,750; Memorandum 415

Dec. 1: Dr. Dividends Payable—Preferred $44,800; Cr. Cash in Bank $44,800; Check 1163

Dec. 17: Dr. Dividends Payable—Common $43,750; Cr. Cash in Bank $43,750; Check 1201

General ledger balance at
Dec. 31: Cash $10,100,
Dividend Payable—Preferred 0
Dividend Payable—Common 0

Analyze: No dividends are payable on either stock at the end of December.

Problem 21-8 (Answers) Preparing Corporate Financial Statements

Ending stockholders' equity balances:
Preferred Stock $500,000
Common Stock $750,000
Paid-in Capital in Excess of Par $300,000
Retained Earnings $852,500
Total $2,402,500

Total assets $2,661,912
Total Liabilities $259,412
Total Stockholders' Equity $2,402,500

Analyze: $2,402,500

Peachtree®

SMART GUIDE

Step-by-Step Instructions: Problem 21-7

1. Select the problem set for Shutterbug Cameras (Prob. 21-7).
2. Rename the company and set the system date.
3. Record all of the transactions using the **General Journal Entry** option. Remember to enter each transaction in the proper accounting period (month).
4. Print a General Journal report for the entire quarter and proof your work.
5. Print a General Ledger report.
6. Answer the Analyze question.
7. End the session.

TIP: Set the date filter options to print a General Journal report that includes all of the entries for the quarter.

Problem 21-7 Journalizing Common and Preferred Stock Dividend Transactions

Shutterbug Cameras issued 8,000 shares of $80 par, preferred 7% stock and 35,000 shares of $25 par common stock.

Instructions In your working papers:
(1) Record the following transactions on general journal page 14.
(2) Post the transactions to the general ledger accounts provided in your working papers. Net income was $296,490.

Date	Transactions
Oct. 15	The board of directors declared an annual cash dividend on the preferred 7% stock, payable on December 1, Memorandum 407.
Nov. 5	Declared an annual cash dividend of $1.25 on 35,000 shares of common stock, payable on December 17, Memorandum 415.
Dec. 1	Paid the dividend declared on October 15, Check 1163.
17	Paid the dividend declared on November 5, Check 1201.

Analyze: What are the amounts of dividends payable on common stock and dividends payable on preferred stock at the end of December?

SPREADSHEET SMART GUIDE

Step-by-Step Instructions: Problem 21-8

1. Select the spreadsheet template for Problem 21-8.
2. Enter your name and the date in the spaces provided on the template.
3. Complete the spreadsheet using the instructions in your working papers.
4. Print the spreadsheet and proof your work.
5. Save your work and exit the spreadsheet program.

Problem 21-8 Preparing Corporate Financial Statements

River's Edge Canoe & Kayak is authorized to issue 10,000 shares of $100 par, preferred 9% stock and 500,000 shares of $5 par common stock. The following balances appeared in the Balance Sheet section of the company's work sheet for the year ended December 31.

Instructions
(1) Prepare the statement of stockholders' equity.
  (a) During the period the corporation issued 500 shares of 9% preferred stock at par and 25,000 shares of common stock at $9.
  (b) The net income for the year was $425,000.
(2) Prepare the balance sheet.

101	Cash in Bank	$506,010
115	Accounts Receivable	850,680
120	Notes Receivable	400,000
130	Merchandise Inventory	388,815
135	Prepaid Ins.	3,600
140	Supplies	10,500
145	Delivery Truck	139,298
150	Store Equipment	363,009
201	Accounts Payable	62,412
202	Dividends Payable—Preferred	22,500

EXTENDING THE CONTENT

Making Investments Assign students to work in small groups of three or four. Ask each group to "invest" a specified sum, say $1,000, in stock holdings. Allow students to choose the type of investment, then have them track the performance of their investment over a period of time (minimum one month). Students can visit several Web sites to gather information. Have each group create a graph to illustrate the stock dividend activity during the time period and then share their results with the rest of the class.

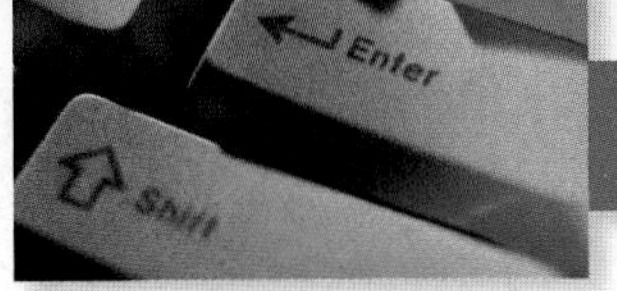

203 Dividends Payable—Common	$150,000
210 Fed. Corp. Income Tax Payable	20,000
215 Sales Tax Payable	4,500
301 Preferred Stock	500,000
303 Common Stock	750,000
304 Paid-in Capital in Excess of Par	300,000
305 Retained Earnings	735,000
307 Dividends—Common	262,500
308 Dividends—Preferred	45,000

Analyze: What is the total stockholders' equity on December 31?

SOURCE DOCUMENT PROBLEM

Problem 21–9

Use the source documents in your working papers to record the transactions for this problem.

CHALLENGE PROBLEM Problem 21–9 Recording Stockholders' Equity Transactions

SOURCE DOCUMENT PROBLEM

Buzz Newsstand is authorized to issue 100,000 shares of $5 par common stock and 5,000 shares of $100 par, preferred 8% stock. On January 1, the beginning of the period, the stockholders' equity accounts had the following balances:

301 Preferred Stock	$150,000
302 Paid-in Capital in Excess of Par—Preferred	11,250
303 Common Stock	225,000
304 Paid-in Capital in Excess of Par—Common	112,500
305 Retained Earnings	366,800
307 Dividends—Preferred	0
308 Dividends—Common	0

Instructions In your working papers:

(1) Record the following transactions on general journal page 42. Close the Dividends and Retained Earnings accounts.

(2) Prepare the stockholders' equity section of the balance sheet.

Date	Transactions
Mar. 15	The board of directors approved a semiannual cash dividend of $62,250 for both preferred and common stockholders. The dividend is payable to stockholders of record as of April 15 with payment on May 1, Memorandum 635.
Apr. 19	Issued 500 shares of preferred stock at $108, Memorandum 651.
May 1	Paid the dividends declared on March 15, Check 1256.
Sept. 1	The board of directors approved a semiannual cash dividend of $79,250 for both preferred and common stockholders. The dividend is payable to stockholders of record as of October 1 with payment on November 1, Memorandum 828.
Nov. 1	Paid the dividend declared on September 1, Check 2451.

Analyze: What is the December 31 balance of **Retained Earnings**? Why did the balance change from the beginning of the year?

Peachtree®

SMART GUIDE

Step-by-Step Instructions: Problem 21–9

1. Select the problem set for Buzz Newsstand (Prob. 21–9).
2. Rename the company and set the system date.
3. Record all of the transactions. Enter each transaction in the proper accounting period (month).
4. Print a General Journal report and proof your work.
5. Print a Balance Sheet.
6. Answer the Analyze questions.
7. End the session.

CHALLENGE PROBLEM

SOURCE DOCUMENT PROBLEM

Problem 21–9 (Answers) Recording Stockholders' Equity Transactions

Mar 15: Dr. Dividends—Preferred $6,000, Dividends—Common $56,250; Cr. Dividends Payable—Preferred $6,000, Dividends Payable—Common $56,250; Memorandum 635

Apr. 19: Dr. Cash in Bank $54,000; Cr. 8% Preferred Stock $50,000, Paid-in Capital in Excess of Par—Preferred $4,000; Memorandum 651

May 1: Dr. Dividends Payable—Preferred $6,000, Dividends Payable—Common $56,250; Cr. Cash in Bank $62,250; Check 2956

Sept. 1: Dr. Dividends—Preferred $8,000, Dividends—Common $71,250; Cr. Dividends Payable—Preferred $8,000, Dividends Payable—Common $71,250; Memorandum 828

Nov. 1: Dr. Dividends Payable—Preferred $8,000, Dividends Payable—Common $71,250; Cr. Cash in Bank $79,250; Check 4837

Closing entries:

Dec. 31: Dr. Income Summary $296,490; Cr. Ret. Earnings $296,490

Dec. 31: Dr. Ret. Earnings $141,500; Cr. Dividends—Preferred $14,000, Dividends—Common $127,500

Total Stockholders' Equity $1,074,540

Analyze: $521,790. The balance of Retained Earnings was increased by net income and decreased by dividends paid.

HOME AND COMMUNITY CONNECTIONS ACTIVITY

Reading an Annual Report Ask students to request a copy of an annual report for any business. Students might contact a local corporation or use the school media center, the public library, or the Internet to obtain a copy of an annual report. Have students review the report and note the type of stock available, type of corporation, profit and loss figures, and distribution of stock premiums or stock splits. Once students have reviewed those sections, ask them to write a paragraph on whether they would recommend the company's stock as a good investment.

This is a representation of key resources available in the *Glencoe Accounting* program.

*inter*NET CONNECTION

Use the following Web resources to introduce, reinforce, or stimulate discussion on unit topics.

- Case Studies
- Study Plans
- Career Corner
- Real-Life Applications
- Self-Assessment Quizzes
- Games for the Classroom
- Ethics and the Profession

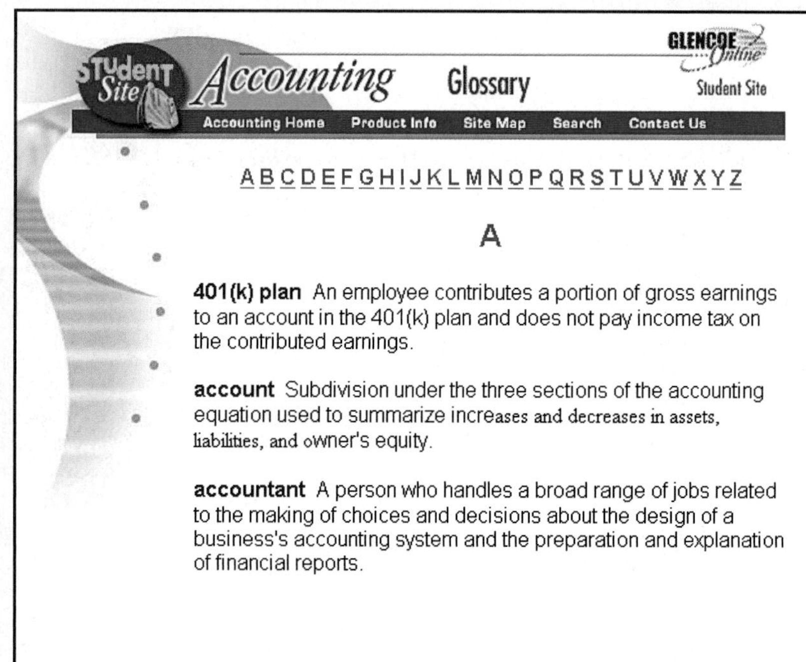

GLENCOE ACCOUNTING BULLETIN BOARD POSTER

Virtual Business® CD-ROM

Virtual Business is a fully visual marketing and business simulation that lets students start and run their own business. For more information on the simulation, visit the teacher page on the *Glencoe Accounting* Web site.

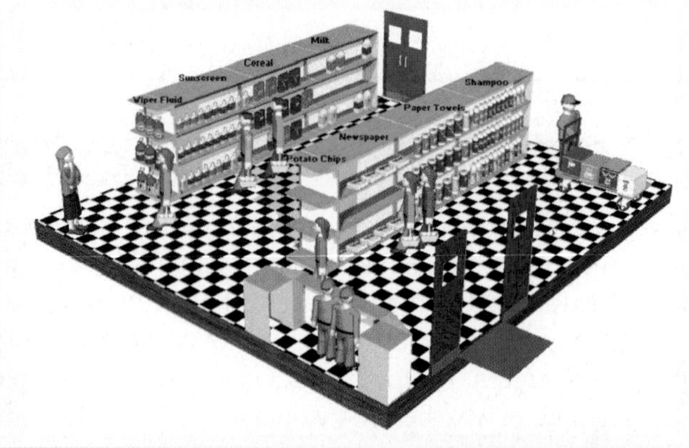

Accounting in Action

Unit Video Portfolio

Integrating *Electronic Field Trips* into Your Accounting Instruction

The *Electronic Field Trip* videos provide an excellent introduction to key accounting concepts taught in the textbook. You may want to use these video segments in **Unit 5.** The titles of the video segments are:

- *Depreciation*
- *Inventory*

Business Simulation
Digital Express

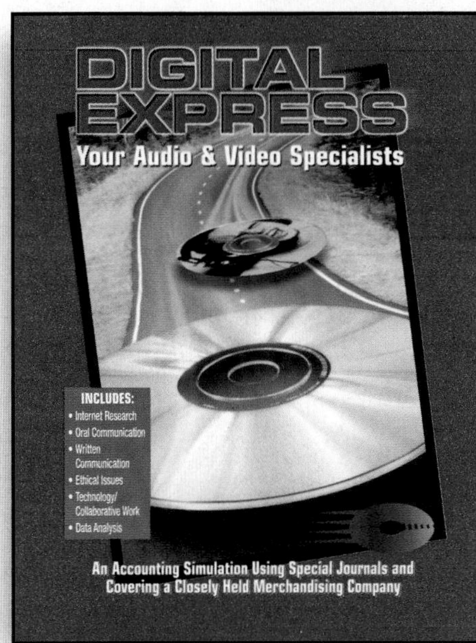

*For use after Chapter 26

Mini Practice Set
Kite Loft Inc.

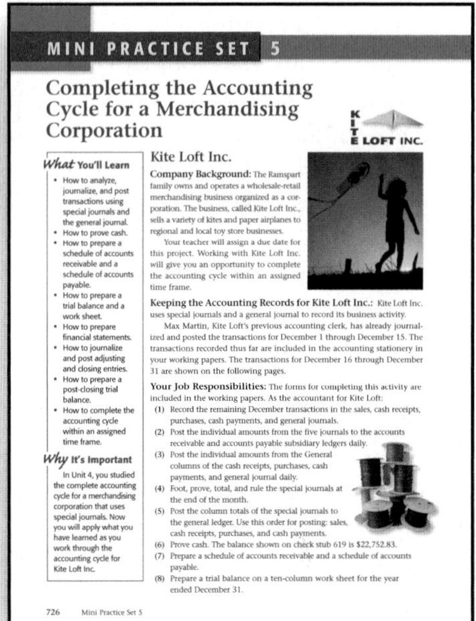

MINI PRACTICE SET 5

Completing the Accounting Cycle for a Merchandising Corporation

KITE LOFT INC.

What You'll Learn

- How to analyze, journalize, and post transactions using special journals and the general journal.
- How to prove cash.
- How to prepare a schedule of accounts receivable and a schedule of accounts payable.
- How to prepare a trial balance and a work sheet.
- How to prepare financial statements.
- How to journalize and post adjusting and closing entries.
- How to prepare a post-closing trial balance.
- How to complete the accounting cycle within an assigned time frame.

Why It's Important

In Unit 4, you studied the complete accounting cycle for a merchandising corporation that uses special journals. Now you will apply what you have learned as you work through the accounting cycle for Kite Loft Inc.

Kite Loft Inc.

Company Background: The Ramspart family owns and operates a wholesale-retail merchandising business organized as a corporation. The business, called Kite Loft Inc., sells a variety of kites and paper airplanes to regional and local toy store businesses.

Your teacher will assign a due date for this project. Working with Kite Loft Inc. will give you an opportunity to complete the accounting cycle within an assigned time frame.

Keeping the Accounting Records for Kite Loft Inc.: Kite Loft Inc. uses special journals and a general journal to record its business activity.

Max Martin, Kite Loft's previous accounting clerk, has already journalized and posted the transactions for December 1 through December 15. The transactions recorded thus far are included in the accounting stationery in your working papers. The transactions for December 16 through December 31 are shown on the following pages.

Your Job Responsibilities: The forms for completing this activity are included in the working papers. As the accountant for Kite Loft:

(1) Record the remaining December transactions in the sales, cash receipts, purchases, cash payments, and general journals.
(2) Post the individual amounts from the five journals to the accounts receivable and accounts payable subsidiary ledgers daily.
(3) Post the individual amounts from the General columns of the cash receipts, purchases, cash payments, and general journal daily.
(4) Foot, prove, total, and rule the special journals at the end of the month.
(5) Post the column totals of the special journals to the general ledger. Use this order for posting: sales, cash receipts, purchases, and cash payments.
(6) Prove cash. The balance shown on check stub 619 is $22,752.83.
(7) Prepare a schedule of accounts receivable and a schedule of accounts payable.
(8) Prepare a trial balance on a ten-column work sheet for the year ended December 31.

726 Mini Practice Set 5

*Can be found after Chapter 26

Assessment and Evaluation

Unit 5 Test

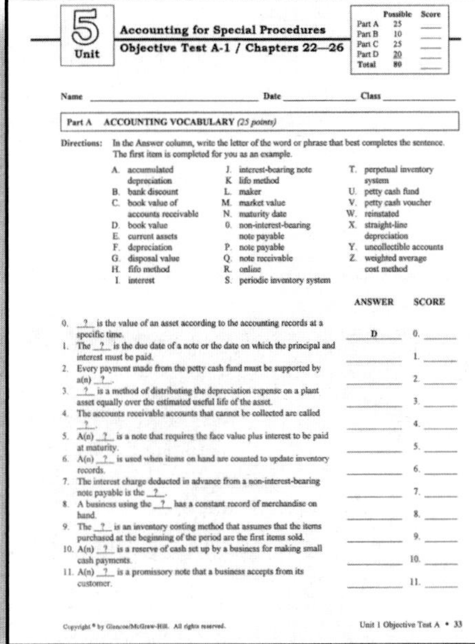

5 Unit

Accounting for Special Procedures
Objective Test A-1 / Chapters 22—26

	Possible	Score
Part A	25	___
Part B	10	___
Part C	25	___
Part D	20	___
Total	80	___

Name ______________ Date ________ Class ________

Part A ACCOUNTING VOCABULARY *(25 points)*

Directions: In the Answer column, write the letter of the word or phrase that best completes the sentence. The first item is completed for you as an example.

A. accumulated depreciation
B. bank discount
C. book value of accounts receivable
D. book value
E. current assets
F. depreciation
G. disposal value
H. fifo method
I. interest
J. interest-bearing note
K. lifo method
L. maker
M. market value
N. maturity date
0. non-interest-bearing note payable
P. note payable
Q. note receivable
R. online
S. periodic inventory system
T. perpetual inventory system
U. petty cash fund
V. petty cash voucher
W. reinstated
X. straight-line depreciation
Y. uncollectible accounts
Z. weighted average cost method

	ANSWER	SCORE
0. __?__ is the value of an asset according to the accounting records at a specific time.	D	0. ___
1. The __?__ is the due date of a note or the date on which the principal and interest must be paid.	___	1. ___
2. Every payment made from the petty cash fund must be supported by a(n) __?__.	___	2. ___
3. __?__ is a method of distributing the depreciation expense on a plant asset equally over the estimated useful life of the asset.	___	3. ___
4. The accounts receivable accounts that cannot be collected are called __?__.	___	4. ___
5. A(n) __?__ is a note that requires the face value plus interest to be paid at maturity.	___	5. ___
6. A(n) __?__ is used when items on hand are counted to update inventory records.	___	6. ___
7. The interest charge deducted in advance from a non-interest-bearing note payable is the __?__.	___	7. ___
8. A business using the __?__ has a constant record of merchandise on hand.	___	8. ___
9. The __?__ is an inventory costing method that assumes that the items purchased at the beginning of the period are the first items sold.	___	9. ___
10. A(n) __?__ is a reserve of cash set up by a business for making small cash payments.	___	10. ___
11. A(n) __?__ is a promissory note that a business accepts from its customer.	___	11. ___

Copyright © by Glencoe/McGraw-Hill. All rights reserved. Unit 1 Objective Test A • 33

Accounting Portfolio

Unit 5 Model Employment Letters

Student ______ Class ______ Instructor ______

Date Assigned ______ Date Completed ______

Unit 5 *Accounting Portfolio*

Model Employment Letters

When applying for a job or asking for an interview, you'll generally be writing one of three or four different types of letters.

- Letter asking for an informational interview
- Letter asking about job opportunities
- Letter responding to an advertised position
- Follow-up letter after an interview

No matter what their purpose is, all business letters have common elements. Each letter has a date line, an inside address, salutation, body (2-3 paragraphs), complimentary close, and the name of the sender. Your letters should be error-free and typed or printed on good quality bond paper. If you use a word processor, remember that spell-checking programs are not infallible. Errors of sense will not be caught.

Examples of the four types of employment letters described below are shown on pages 36-39.

LETTER ASKING FOR AN INFORMATIONAL INTERVIEW

Send this letter to a specific company when you want to know more about an industry or a career field. Your letter may be addressed to the Director of Human Resources, but if you can find out who heads the department that interests you, address the letter to him or her. In your letter, explain your specific interest in the company and your desire to set up an interview to gain information about particular jobs or departments within the company. Include a resume with your letter.

LETTER ASKING ABOUT JOB OPPORTUNITIES

If you know you want to work for a certain company, let the company know. Even if the company is not advertising new positions, your letter might arrive at a time when a new position is being created or a job has become open. If there are no immediate positions, many companies still keep applicants' letters on file for several months. When writing this type of letter, explain your background and describe why the company interests you. Explain how you think you can be valuable to the company and close the letter with a positive comment about the company, reaffirming your interest in working there. Include a resume with your letter.

LETTER RESPONDING TO AN ADVERTISEMENT

When responding to an advertisement for a job opening, mention the job you're applying for in the first sentence. Then present a brief overview of your background, emphasizing your education and experience as they relate to the advertised job. Connect your education and experience with the described job duties by explaining how you performed similar duties in other situations. You need not repeat information that is on your resume (to be included with the letter), but you may want to refer to a particular strength or work experience that relates strongly to the advertised job. In the final paragraph, affirm your interest in the company and ask for an interview.

FOLLOW- UP TO AN INTERVIEW

Letters sent as follow-up to an interview are an important way to make a positive impression. When writing this type of letter, reaffirm your interest in the company and thank the interviewer for discussing the position and its requirements with you. As soon as you leave an interview, jot down key points the interviewer made when describing the job, the responsibilities, or the company. Refer to at least one of these points in your follow-up letter, and indicate how your skills fit the job requirement. Express confidence in your ability to be an asset to the organization. The purpose of this letter is not only to show that you have good business manners, but also to remind the interviewer of your strong points.

If you were interviewed by several people, address your letter to the primary interviewer, but mention the other people by name in your letter.

Copyright © Glencoe/McGraw-Hill Accounting Portfolio 35

Enrichment and Extension

Accounting Competitive Event Review

Student ______ Class ______ Instructor ______

Date Assigned ______ Date Completed ______

Accounting for Cash Funds

It is usually not practical for a business to write checks for all of its cash payments. Some cash payments are for small amounts, such as paying the newscarrier and reimbursing an employee for a small business expense. To make these small cash payments, most businesses set up a petty cash fund. The size of the petty cash fund varies according to the size of the business. Many businesses also record their petty cash disbursements in a petty cash register.

Retail stores such as drugstores and supermarkets also have change funds. A change fund is an amount of money, of various denominations and coins, placed in a cash register and used to make change for customers in business transactions.

For further information: See Chapter 11, First Year.

For additional practice: Additional Reinforcement Problem 11A.

On a separate sheet of paper, answer the following questions.

True/False

1. The Petty Cash Fund account is debited when a check is written to replenish petty cash.
2. The Petty Cash Fund account has a debit balance.
3. If the amount of cash available for deposit is less than the amount listed on the cash register tape, the Cash Short and Over account is debited.
4. Businesses often have both a change fund and a petty cash fund.
5. The Petty Cash Fund account is credited each time a petty cash voucher is issued.
6. Because the amount of the change fund cannot be changed, a business must consider carefully the original amount.
7. The petty cash fund may be used to cash employees' personal checks.
8. Always credit Cash in Bank when replenishing the petty cash fund.
9. The petty cash register is a book of original entry.
10. The reconciled petty cash balance is the amount of money that should be in the petty cash box when it's time to replenish the fund.
11. On the cash proof, total cash sales and net cash received must agree.
12. The petty cashier should be the only one with access to the petty cash fund.

Multiple Choice

13. The entry to replenish a petty cash fund includes (A) debits to various expense and asset accounts and a credit to Cash in Bank, (B) debits to various expense accounts and a credit to Petty Cash Fund, (C) a debit to Petty Cash Fund and a credit to Cash in Bank, (D) debits to various asset and expense accounts and credits to Cash in Bank and Petty Cash Fund.
14. The Cash Short and Over account (A) usually has a normal debit balance, (B) usually has a normal credit balance, (C) does not have a normal balance, (D) usually has a zero balance.
15. A cash shortage is usually recorded in the (A) cash receipts journal, (B) cash payments journal, (C) purchases journal, (D) general journal.
16. The entry to establish a change fund requires (A) a debit to Petty Cash Fund and a credit to Change Fund, (B) a debit to Change Fund and a credit to Cash in Bank, (C) a debit to Change Fund and a credit to Petty Cash Fund, (D) a debit to Change Fund and a credit to Sales.

Copyright © Glencoe/McGraw-Hill Accounting Competitive Event Review • 39

OVERVIEW UNIT 5

Unit Objectives

1. Learn to account for cash funds.
2. Calculate depreciation and determine book value of plant assets and maintain accounting records for depreciation.
3. Estimate uncollectible amounts and record them in the accounting records.
4. Value inventories using different methods and record inventory amounts in the accounting records.
5. Explain how notes are used, calculate interest, and record notes in the accounting records.

Unit 5 Contents

EXTENDING THE QUOTE

Albert Einstein is considered one of the world's greatest scientists. In his early life, Einstein had planned to study electrical engineering, but he failed to pass the university entrance exams! Looking for other opportunities, Einstein trained to be a teacher of mathematics and physics. Einstein wrote that he lacked imagination and practical ability, but, if so, he turned his difficulties into tremendous achievements, including a Nobel Prize.

UNIT 5

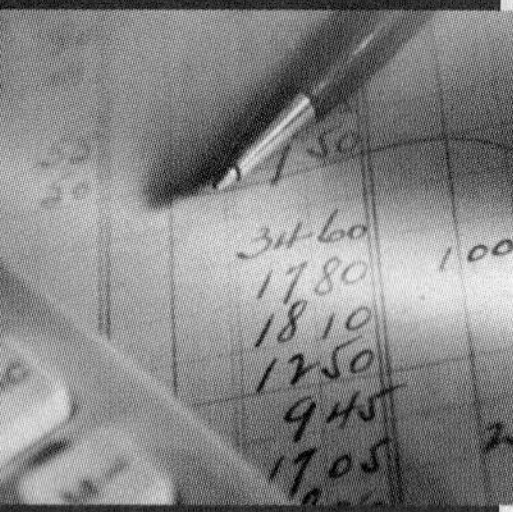

Accounting for Special Procedures

In this unit. . .

Now that you have learned about the tasks in the accounting cycle for both a service and merchandising business, you will learn how to perform specialized accounting procedures. You will continue to follow the operations of **On Your Mark Athletic Wear**, exploring transactions that include accounting for cash funds, recording the depreciation of assets, accounting for accounts receivable that cannot be collected, and accounting for the cost of inventories. Transactions that include money that is borrowed or loaned to a business will also be analyzed and recorded.

In the middle of difficulty lies opportunity.

—Albert Einstein
Physicist

596

Great Ideas *From the Classroom of...*

The Knuckle Rule I use the "knuckle rule" to teach students how many days are in a month. Begin with the index finger and count each finger and space between fingers. Months on knuckles have 31 days; months in spaces have 30 days. Of course, February only has 28 days most years, and 29 days in a leap year.

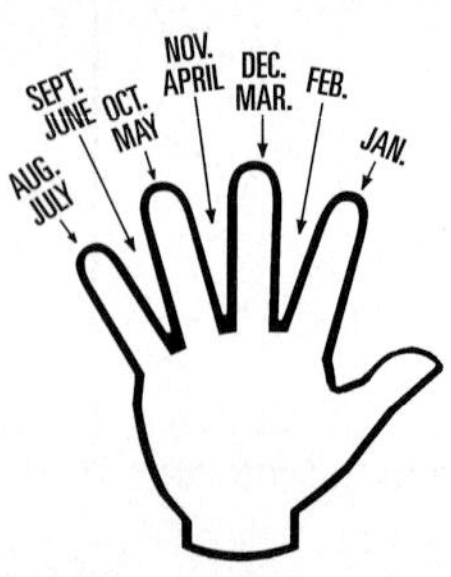

Tammy Mathews
Hanna-Westside
Extension Campus
Anderson, South Carolina

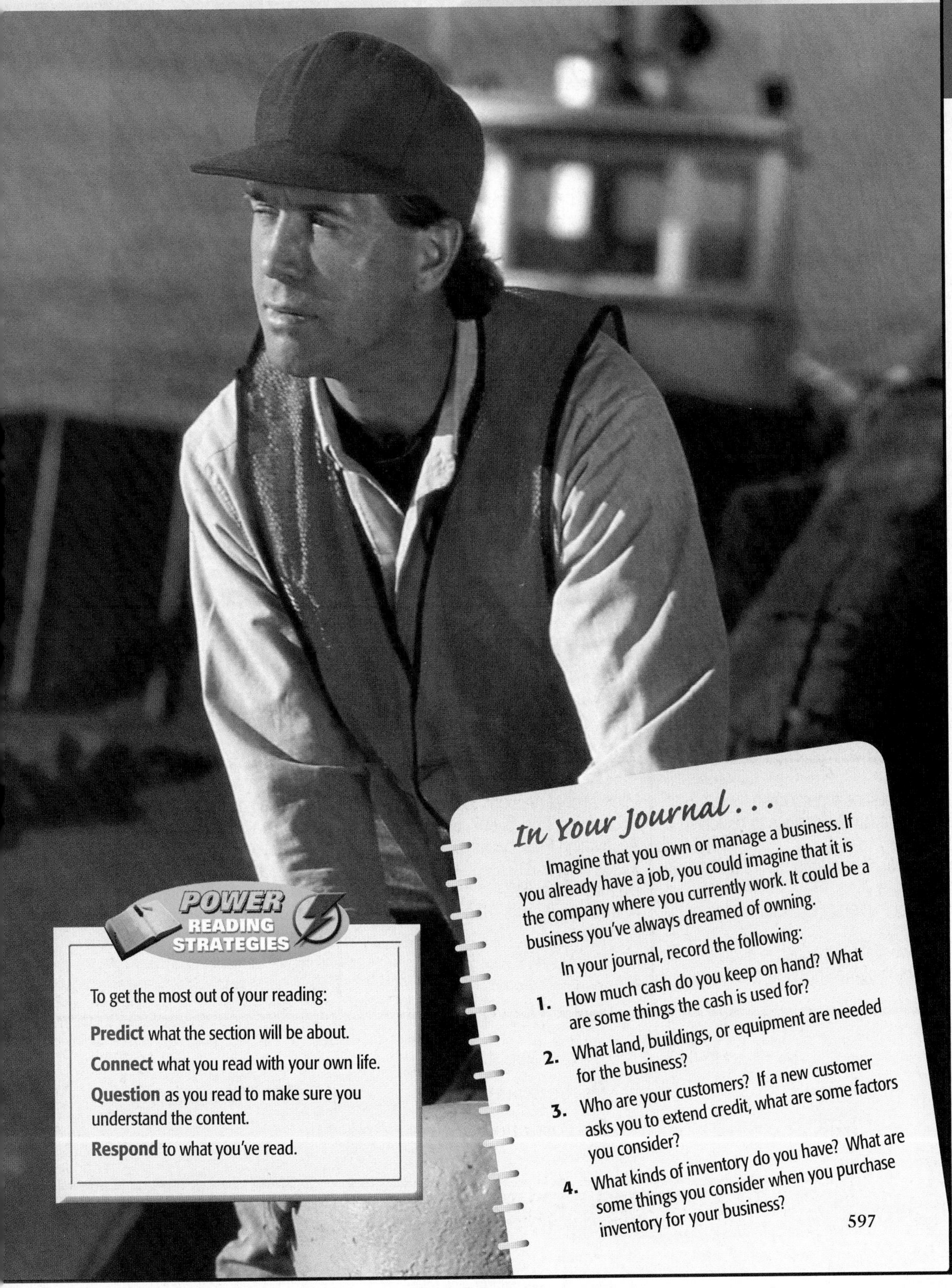

In Your Journal . . .

Imagine that you own or manage a business. If you already have a job, you could imagine that it is the company where you currently work. It could be a business you've always dreamed of owning.

In your journal, record the following:

1. How much cash do you keep on hand? What are some things the cash is used for?
2. What land, buildings, or equipment are needed for the business?
3. Who are your customers? If a new customer asks you to extend credit, what are some factors you consider?
4. What kinds of inventory do you have? What are some things you consider when you purchase inventory for your business?

POWER READING STRATEGIES

To get the most out of your reading:

Predict what the section will be about.

Connect what you read with your own life.

Question as you read to make sure you understand the content.

Respond to what you've read.

In Your Journal. . .

Teaching Guidelines Have students add to their accounting portfolios by completing and including the *In Your Journal* writing activities. To help students describe business activities, have them think of a local business that interests them and write answers to the questions based on that business. Ask for volunteers to share their answers. Discuss how being a business owner or manager requires one to know about several different types of business activities. Have students write how they would prepare to become a business owner or manager. Urge them to explore creative actions such as apprenticeships and internships, as well as formal and on-the-job training. P

INTRODUCING UNIT 5

Previewing the Chapters

In Unit 5 students will learn accounting procedures for cash funds, depreciation of plant assets, uncollectible accounts receivable, inventories, and notes payable and receivable.

Tying to Previous Knowledge

Students will build on their knowledge of journalizing and posting to create accounting records for the special procedures in this unit. Have students who have part-time jobs involving change funds describe how they reconcile their fund each day. Other students may be familiar with notes if they've signed a note to buy a car.

BULLETIN BOARD

Glencoe Poster Teaching Tip

Ask students how many of them plan to gain further accounting training in college. Have them discuss how they will obtain information about the various college programs offered. Point out the sources of college information on the poster. Also discuss the types of accounting positions and the training students would need for each position.

CHAPTER 22 Resource Manager

Section Resources

	Objectives & Standards	Activities & Features	Reproducible Masters
Chapter Opener *Cash Funds*	• Record the entry to establish a change fund. • Prove the cash in the cash register drawers at the end of each business day. • Open and replenish a petty cash fund. • Journalize opening a petty cash fund. • Prepare a petty cash requisition to replenish the petty cash fund. • Use a petty cash register to record petty cash disbursements. • Journalize replenishing a petty cash fund. • Determine whether cash is short or over, and record the amount of the shortage or overage. • Define the accounting terms introduced in this chapter. **National Standards for Business Education**: IIA2, IIA9	Exploring the Real World of Business, p. 598 Workplace Connections, p. 599	School-to-Work Handbook
Section 1 *The Change Fund*	• Why a business needs to have a small amount of cash on hand. • How to record the entry to establish a change fund. • How to prove the cash in the cash register drawer at the end of each business day.	Did You Know?, p. 602 A Matter of Ethics, p. 603	Demonstration Problems Strategies for Teaching Ethics in Accounting
Section 2 *The Petty Cash Fund*	• How a business establishes a petty cash fund. • How to prepare petty cash requisitions to replenish the petty cash fund. • How to use a petty cash register to record petty cash disbursements. • How to record the journal entry to replenish the petty cash fund. • How to determine whether petty cash is short or over and record the amount of the shortage of overage.	International Accounting, p. 606 Accounting Tips, p. 607, 609 Accounting Flashbacks, p. 607 Math Hints, p. 610 Connect To, p. 612 Analyzing Financial Reports, p. 613	Demonstration Problems Strategies for Teaching International Accounting Math Review for Accounting Internet Resources and Activities Handbook

KEY

Posters — Transparency — Software — Videocassette
Blackline Masters — CD-ROM — Portfolio

MULTIMEDIA RESOURCE

Peachtree	QuickBooks	Spreadsheets	Videos	CD-ROMs
Problem 22–4 *Establishing a Change Fund* Problem 22–5 *Establishing and Replenishing a Petty Cash Fund* Problem 22–6 *Establishing and Replenishing a Petty Cash Fund* Problem 22–7 *Using a Petty Cash Register* Problem 22–8 *Handling a Petty Cash Fund*	Problem 22–6 *Establishing and Replenishing a Petty Cash Fund* Problem 22–7 *Using a Petty Cash Register*	None in this chapter.	***Video Segment: Global Perspectives*** After viewing this video, students will be able to describe how the United States is part of a global marketplace. They will also be able to describe differences for businesses that operate in the international market.	***Electronic Learning Center (ELC), Chapter 22*** This program is ideal for visual learners since it incorporates video images, animation, and graphics to enliven the content of each lesson. ***Interactive Lesson Planner (ILP), Chapter 22*** This CD-ROM combines the versatility of an electronic lesson planner with the convenience of teacher classroom resources.

SCANS Correlation Chart

FOUNDATION SKILLS

Basic Skills:	Reading	Writing	Math	Listening	Speaking	
Thinking Skills:	Creative Thinking	Decision Making	Problem Solving	Seeing Things in the Mind's Eye	Knowing How to Learn	Reasoning
Personal Qualities:	Responsibility	Self-Esteem	Sociability	Self-Management	Integrity/Honesty	

WORKPLACE COMPETENCIES

Resources:	Allocating Time	Allocating Money	Allocating Material and Facility Resources	Allocating Human Resources		
Information:	Acquiring and Evaluating Information	Organizing and Maintaining Information	Interpreting and Communicating Information	Using Computers to Process Information		
Interpersonal Skills:	Participating as a Member of a Team	Teaching Others	Serving Clients/ Customers	Exercising Leadership	Negotiating to Arrive at a Decision	Working with Cultural Diversity
Systems:	Understanding Systems	Monitoring and Correcting Performance	Improving and Designing Systems			
Technology:	Selecting Technology	Applying Technology to Task	Maintaining and Troubleshooting Technology			

*Highlighted blocks indicate areas covered in the chapter. Additional SCANS skills are also covered throughout the *Teacher Wraparound Edition.*

Assessment

Student Edition
- Check Your Understanding, pp. 604, 614
- Chapter 22 Problems, pp. 619–623

Assessment and Evaluation Masters
- Chapter 22 Study Plan, *Glencoe Workbook*
- Chapter 22 Self-Test, *Glencoe Workbook*
- Chapter 22 Test, *Chapter Tests* Booklet
- Chapter 22 Activity, *School-to-Work Handbook*
- Chapter 22 **Exam***View*

Teacher Wraparound Edition
- Critical Thinking Activity, p. 609
- Reteaching Section 1, p. 604
- Reteaching Section 2, p. 614
- Chapter 22 Quiz, p. 615

Transparencies

	Teaching Transparencies	Solution Transparencies
Section 1:	22–1, 22–2, 22–3, 22–4	Problems 22–1, 22–2
Section 2:	22–5, 22–6, 22–7, 22–8, 22–9, 22–10, 22–11, 22–12	Problem 22–3
End of Chapter:		Problems 22–4, 22–5, 22–6, 22–7, 22–8, 22–9

TEACHER CLASSROOM RESOURCES

This is a representation of key blackline masters available in the Teacher Classroom Resources.

Teaching Aids

Transparency Examples

Section Focus Transparencies

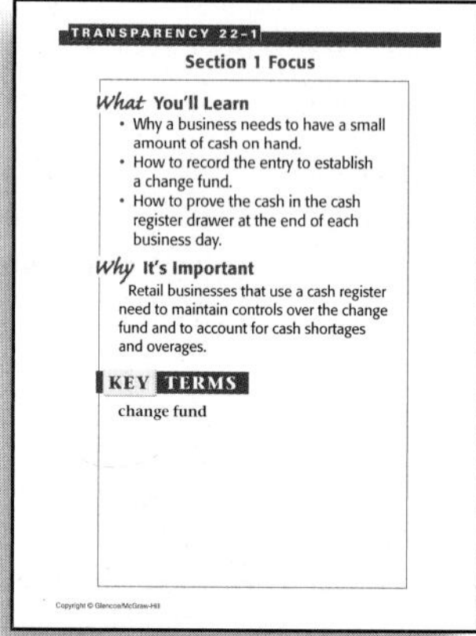

TRANSPARENCY 22-1

Section 1 Focus

What You'll Learn
- Why a business needs to have a small amount of cash on hand.
- How to record the entry to establish a change fund.
- How to prove the cash in the cash register drawer at the end of each business day.

Why It's Important

Retail businesses that use a cash register need to maintain controls over the change fund and to account for cash shortages and overages.

KEY TERMS

change fund

Teaching Transparencies

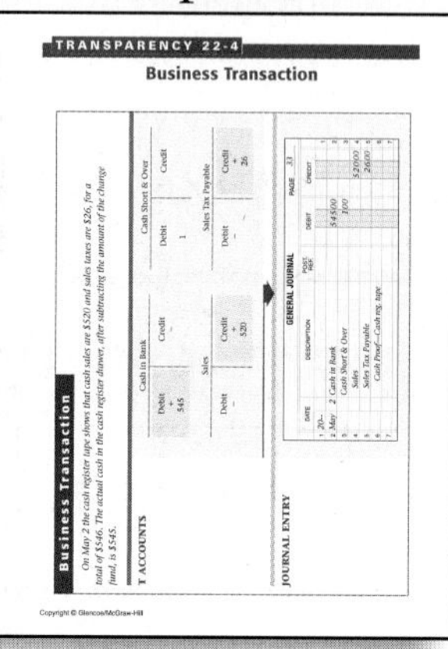

TRANSPARENCY 22-4

Business Transaction

Source Document Transparencies

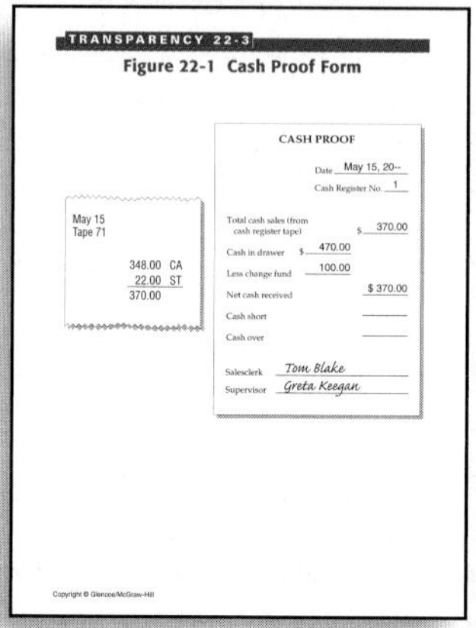

TRANSPARENCY 22-3

Figure 22-1 Cash Proof Form

CASH PROOF

Date May 15, 20--

Cash Register No. 1

May 15 Tape 71

348.00 CA
22.00 ST
370.00

Total cash sales (from cash register tape) $ 370.00

Cash in drawer $ 470.00

Less change fund 100.00

Net cash received $ 370.00

Cash short

Cash over

Salesclerk Tom Blake

Supervisor Greta Keegan

Solution Transparencies

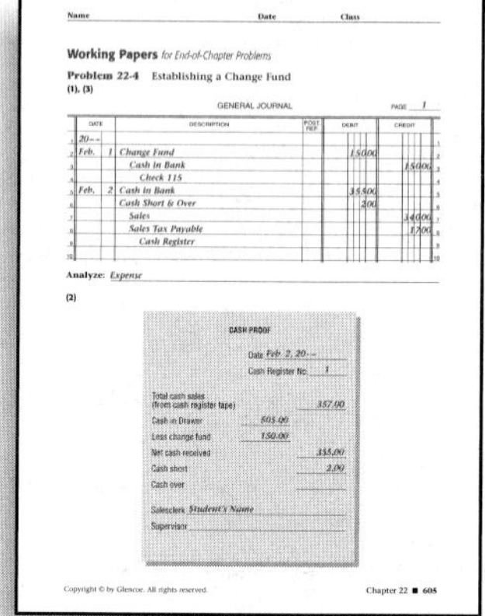

Working Papers for End-of-Chapter Problems

Problem 22-4 Establishing a Change Fund

Demonstration Problems

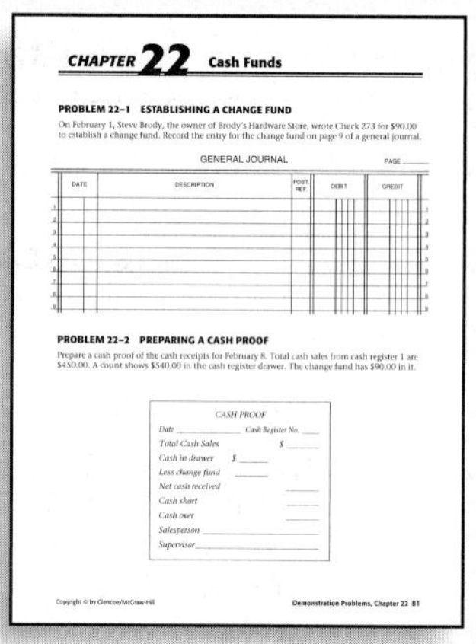

CHAPTER 22 Cash Funds

PROBLEM 22-1 ESTABLISHING A CHANGE FUND

PROBLEM 22-2 PREPARING A CASH PROOF

Lesson Plans

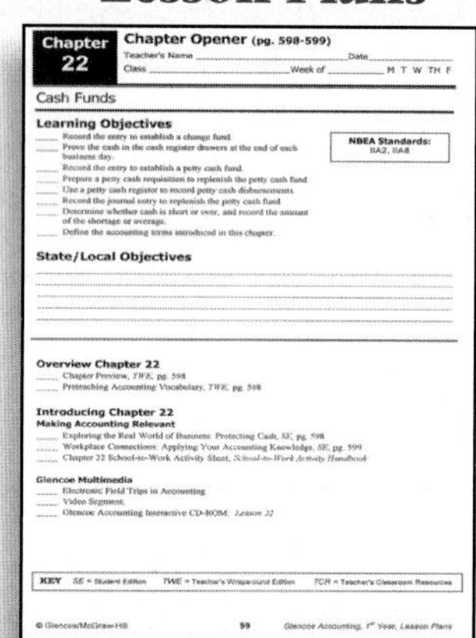

Chapter 22 Chapter Opener (pg. 598-599)

Cash Funds

Learning Objectives

State/Local Objectives

Overview Chapter 22

Introducing Chapter 22

Glencoe Multimedia

Block Scheduling

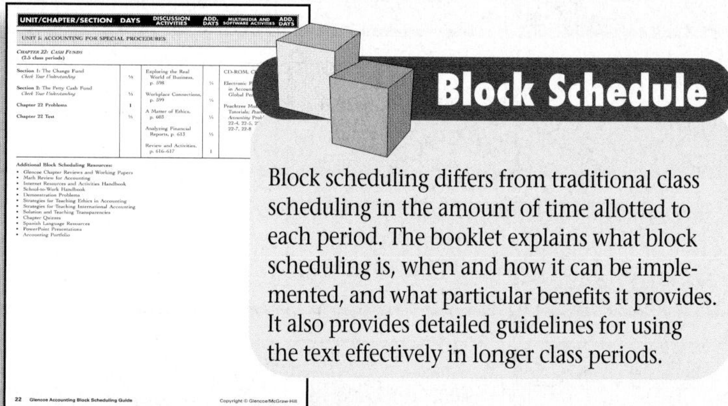

Block Schedule

Block scheduling differs from traditional class scheduling in the amount of time allotted to each period. The booklet explains what block scheduling is, when and how it can be implemented, and what particular benefits it provides. It also provides detailed guidelines for using the text effectively in longer class periods.

Enrichment and Application

Strategies for Teaching Ethics in Accounting

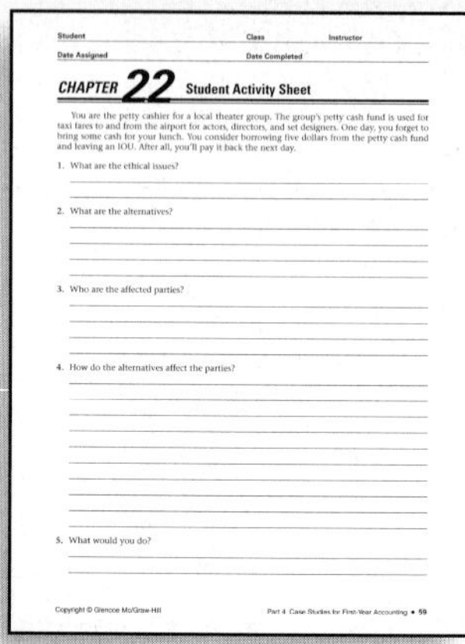

CHAPTER 22 Student Activity Sheet

1. What are the ethical issues?
2. What are the alternatives?
3. Who are the affected parties?
4. How do the alternatives affect the parties?
5. What would you do?

Strategies for Teaching International Accounting

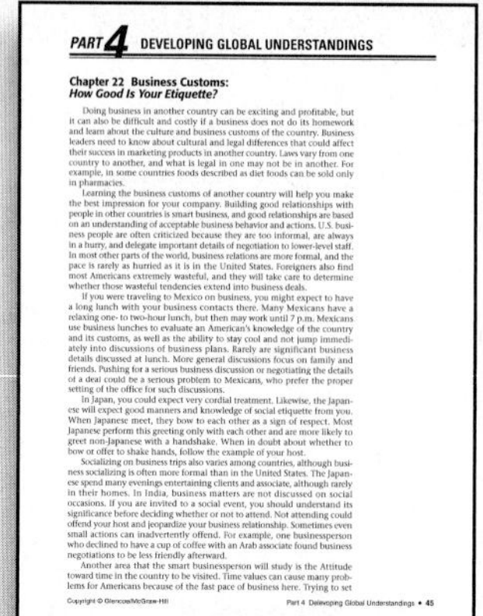

PART 4 DEVELOPING GLOBAL UNDERSTANDINGS

Chapter 22 Business Customs: How Good Is Your Etiquette?

School-to-Work Handbook

CHAPTER 22 SCHOOL-TO-WORK ACTIVITY

Cash Funds

Meeting Different Ability Levels

Chapter Reviews and Working Papers (CRWP)

Working Papers | Review

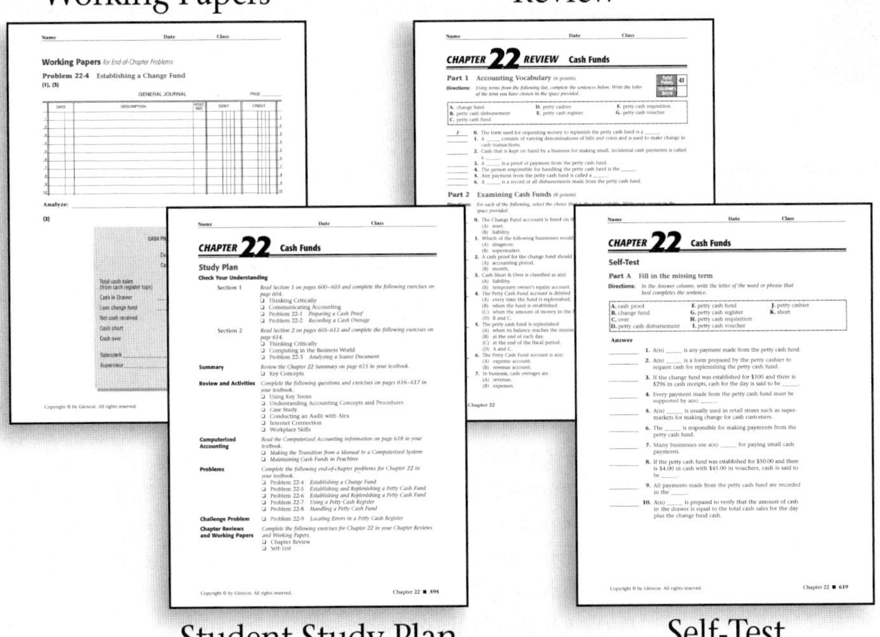

Student Study Plan | Self-Test

Real-World Multimedia CD-ROM

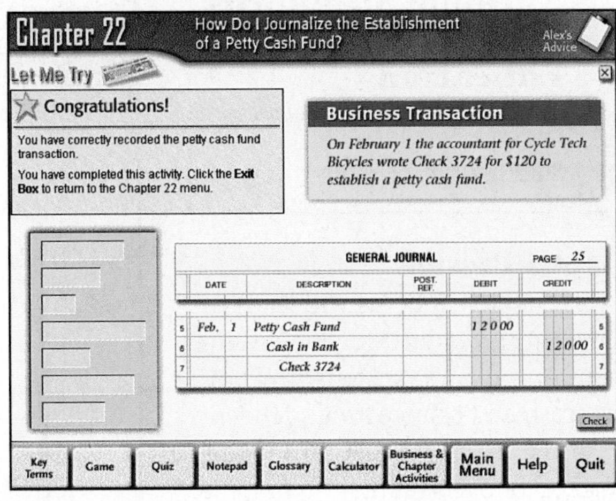

Key to Ability Levels

Each section gives skill-building activities. Each activity has been labeled for use with students of various learning styles and abilities.

L1 Level 1 activities are basic activities and should be within the range of all students.

L2 Level 2 activities are average activities and should be within the range of average and above average students.

L3 Level 3 activities are challenging activities designed for the ability range of above average students.

ELL ELL activities should be within the ability range of English Language Learners.

Teaching Resources at a Glance

Application Resources

- Glencoe Chapter Review and Working Papers, SE and TAE
- School-to-Work Handbook, SE and TM
- Accounting Portfolio, SE and TM

Reproducible Masters

- Demonstration Problems
- Lesson Plans
- Block Scheduling
- Spanish Language Resources

Glencoe Accounting Professional Development Series

- Strategies for Teaching Ethics in Accounting
- Accounting Competitive Event Review
- Math Review for Accounting
- Strategies for Teaching International Accounting
- Internet Resources and Activities Handbook

Transparency Package

- Section Focus Transparencies
- Teaching Transparencies
- Source Document Transparencies
- Solution Transparencies

Performance Assessment

- **Exam***View* CD-ROM
- Chapter Tests
- Chapter Quizzes
- Unit Tests
- Audit Tests
- Printed Testbank

Multimedia Resources

- Electronic Learning Center:
  - Multimedia CD-ROMs
  - Peachtree software, tutorials, templates, and solutions
  - Spreadsheet templates
- Using QuickBooks with Glencoe Accounting
- Interactive Lesson Planner
- Electronic Field Trips in Accounting
- PowerPoint Presentation
- Web site: glencoeaccounting.glencoe.com

Assessment and Evaluation

Chapter Tests

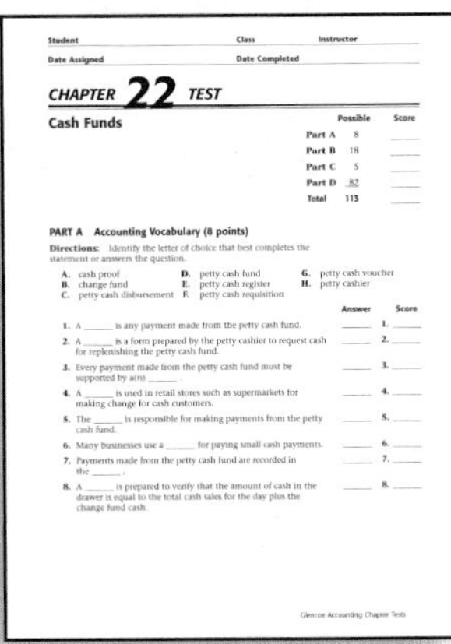

Chapter Quiz

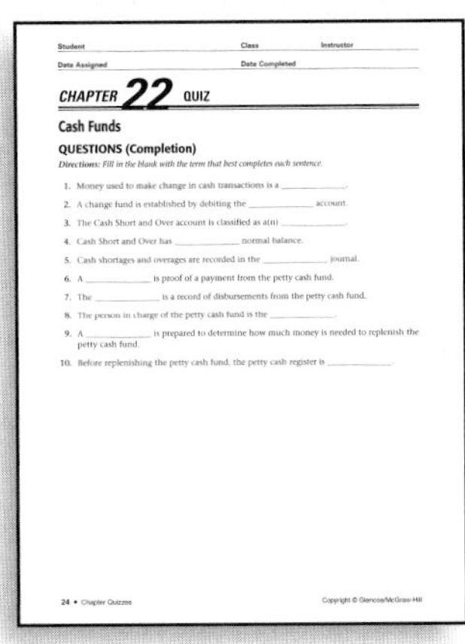

OVERVIEW CHAPTER 22

Correlations to National Standards for Business Education

(See pages T50–T51 for a detailed correlation chart.)

Standards: IIA2, IIA9

Chapter Preview

In this chapter students will learn the accounting procedures for establishing, maintaining, and replenishing both petty cash and change funds. Students will also learn how to account for any shortages or overages that occur in the use of the funds.

Section Overviews

- Section 1—*The Change Fund*
- Section 2—*The Petty Cash Fund*

Chapter Vocabulary

change fund
petty cash fund
petty cash disbursement
petty cashier
petty cash voucher
petty cash requisition
petty cash register

Preteaching Accounting Vocabulary

Writing Exercise: Ask students to write a sentence using each of the new terms in context. Have volunteers write their sentences on the chalkboard. Discuss any differences in the use of the terms. L1

CHAPTER 22

Cash Funds

Learning Objectives

When you have completed this chapter, you will be able to:

- Record the entry to establish a change fund.
- Prove the cash in the cash register drawers at the end of each business day.
- Open and replenish a petty cash fund.
- Journalize opening a petty cash fund.
- Prepare a petty cash requisition to replenish the petty cash fund.
- Use a petty cash register to record petty cash disbursements.
- Journalize replenishing a petty cash fund.
- Determine whether cash is short or over, and record the amount of the shortage or overage.
- Define the accounting terms introduced in this chapter.

Exploring the Real World of Business

PROTECTING CASH

"G'day, mate. Welcome to **Outback Steakhouse.**"

No, you're not really in Australia, but the **Outback Steakhouse** chain of restaurants uses Australia as the theme for decorations and menu items. One of the fastest-growing restaurant chains in the country, **Outback** has opened 750 restaurants around the country since 1988. On average, about 4,000 people eat at an **Outback Steakhouse** every week.

With so many customers and meals served, each restaurant takes in a lot of cash. In any cash business, employees must know how to handle money quickly and accurately, and also how to protect it from theft or loss. Job applicants who want to work for **Outback** must take an aptitude test on basic skills, including making correct change. Ethical questions regarding money handling and business transactions are covered as well. The company also says that a friendly and outgoing personality is an absolute requirement.

What do you think?

If you were applying for a job at an **Outback Steakhouse,** and you were asked to describe your money handling skills and how to protect cash taken in by the company, how would you respond?

Outback Steakhouse

Exploring the Real World of Business

Outback Steakhouse

On New Year's Day, college football teams from the SEC and the Big Ten meet in the Outback Bowl, which is sponsored by the Outback Steakhouse. Outback uses its sponsorship to advertise its restaurants and to make its name better known to potential customers.

What do you think? (Answers)

Answers will vary. Students might mention other experience working in a retail environment. They might also mention their accounting study and what they have learned about handling and protecting cash, such as doing cash proofs, paying bills by check, and having more than one employee verify cash.

Workplace Connections

Applying Your Accounting Knowledge

Waiters and waitresses are important employees in the restaurant industry. A portion of their earnings is likely to be cash tips from their customers. Businesses that take in a lot of cash need to protect their money from theft or loss. You'll learn about the records used to account for cash funds in this chapter.

Investigate:

1. What measures are taken in your workplace to protect cash?
2. If you were a store manager, how would you prevent employee theft?

Glencoe Accounting Online

Visit the *Glencoe Accounting* Web site at **glencoeaccounting.glencoe.com** for additional activities and information.

599

Making Accounting Relevant

Workplace Connections: Applying Your Accounting Knowledge

Discussion: Many people handle cash at work. Have students give you examples (such as grocery checkers, fast-food order takers, retail clerks, restaurant workers, and so on). Protecting cash from theft or loss is important to businesses that handle a lot of cash. Good cash controls can provide the protection that businesses need.

Investigate (Answers)

1. Answers may vary. Among controls used to protect cash are having two people handle cash (as when a waiter has to take a payment to the cashier for processing), making daily deposits of cash, and verifying actual cash against sales slips.
2. Answers will vary. Students might mention cash controls such as paying all bills by check, making daily deposits, or having two employees handle different parts of cash transactions.

School-to-Work Activity

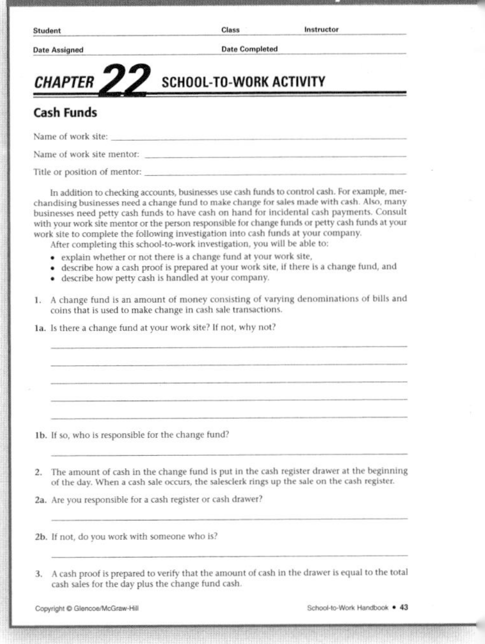

Student ______ Class ______ Instructor ______

Date Assigned ______ Date Completed ______

CHAPTER 22 SCHOOL-TO-WORK ACTIVITY

Cash Funds

Name of work site: ______

Name of work site mentor: ______

Title or position of mentor: ______

In addition to checking accounts, businesses use cash funds to control cash. For example, merchandising businesses need a change fund to make change for sales made with cash. Also, many businesses need petty cash funds to have cash on hand for incidental cash payments. Consult with your work site mentor or the person responsible for change funds or petty cash funds at your work site to complete the following investigation into cash funds at your company.

After completing this school-to-work investigation, you will be able to:

- explain whether or not there is a change fund at your work site,
- describe how a cash proof is prepared at your work site, if there is a change fund, and
- describe how petty cash is handled at your company.

1. A change fund is an amount of money consisting of varying denominations of bills and coins that is used to make change in cash sale transactions.

1a. Is there a change fund at your work site? If not, why not?

1b. If so, who is responsible for the change fund?

2. The amount of cash in the change fund is put in the cash register drawer at the beginning of the day. When a cash sale occurs, the salesclerk rings up the sale on the cash register.

2a. Are you responsible for a cash register or cash drawer?

2b. If not, do you work with someone who is?

3. A cash proof is prepared to verify that the amount of cash in the drawer is equal to the total cash sales for the day plus the change fund cash.

 School-to-Work Handbook • 43

GLENCOE MULTIMEDIA

Electronic Field Trips in Accounting *Video Segment: Global Perspectives*
After viewing this video, students will be able to describe how the United States is part of a global marketplace. Have students describe differences for businesses that operate in the international market.

Glencoe Accounting: Electronic Learning Center *Chapter 22*
The CD-ROM program is ideal for visual learners since it incorporates video images, animation, and graphics to enliven the content of each lesson.

CHAPTER 22
SECTION 1, PAGES 600–604

1 FOCUS

Introducing the Section

In this section students will learn the purpose of a change fund and how to account for it. They'll also learn how to prove cash in the cash register drawer.

Section Concepts

- Why a business needs to have a small amount of cash on hand.
- How to record the entry to establish a change fund.
- How to prove the cash in the cash register drawer at the end of each business day.

Visual Learning

Section 1 Focus

Use **Transparency 22–1** to introduce section concepts.

BELL RINGER

Comparing Information: Take a poll of students whose jobs require them to make change. Ask what their job duties are and how they use money on the job. Write responses on the chalkboard and have students compare ways in which change funds are used in different types of businesses. L1

Concept Development: Establishing a Change Fund

Discussion: When introducing the change fund, point out that any retail business using a cash register needs to keep a small amount of money in the cash drawer for making change. The change fund consists of varying denominations of bills and coins. L1

SECTION 1

The Change Fund

***What* You'll Learn**

- Why a business needs to have a small amount of cash on hand.
- How to record the entry to establish a change fund.
- How to prove the cash in the cash register drawer at the end of each business day.

***Why* It's Important**

Retail businesses that use a cash register need to maintain controls over the change fund and to account for cash shortages and overages.

KEY TERMS

change fund

In earlier chapters you learned that businesses use checking accounts for depositing cash receipts and making cash payments. Merchandising businesses, such as Sears or Blockbuster, keep some cash on hand to make change for customers who pay with cash.

Establishing a Change Fund

A **change fund** is an amount of money, consisting of varying denominations of bills and coins, that is used to make change in cash transactions. For example, a customer who pays for a $13.80 purchase with a $20 bill will receive $6.20 in change.

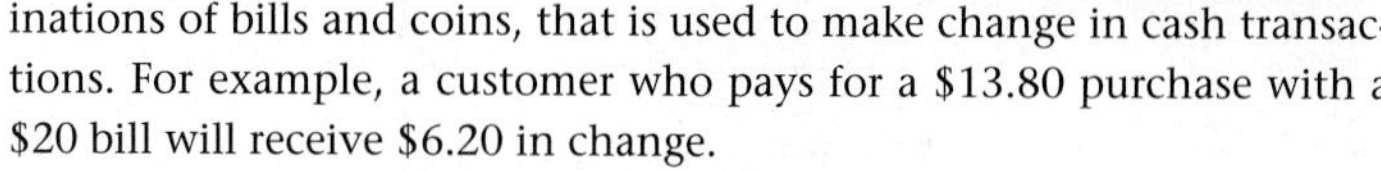

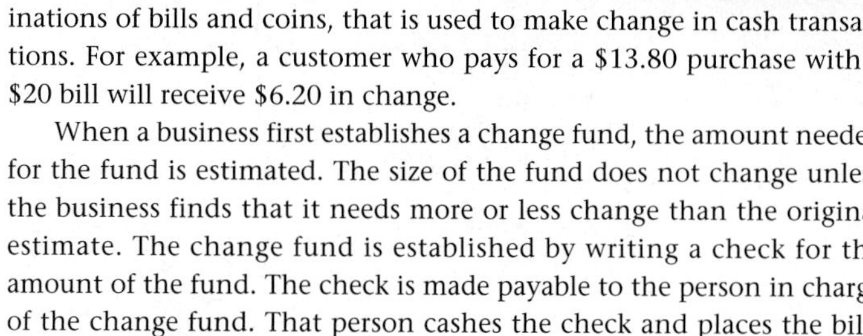

When a business first establishes a change fund, the amount needed for the fund is estimated. The size of the fund does not change unless the business finds that it needs more or less change than the original estimate. The change fund is established by writing a check for the amount of the fund. The check is made payable to the person in charge of the change fund. That person cashes the check and places the bills and coins in the cash register drawer. The transaction is recorded in an asset account called **Change Fund.** Let's look at an example.

Business Transaction

On May 1 the accountant for On Your Mark wrote Check 2150 for $100 to establish a change fund.

ANALYSIS	*Identify* / *Classify* / +/−	1. The accounts affected are **Change Fund** and **Cash in Bank.** 2. Both **Change Fund** and **Cash in Bank** are asset accounts. 3. **Change Fund** is increased by $100. **Cash in Bank** is decreased by $100.
DEBIT-CREDIT RULE		4. Increases to asset accounts are recorded as debits. Debit **Change Fund** for $100. 5. Decreases to asset accounts are recorded as credits. Credit **Cash in Bank** for $100.

RESOURCE MANAGER

Reproducible Masters
- Lesson Plans
- Chapter Reviews and Working Papers (CRWP) TAE
- Demonstration Problems

Transparencies
- Section Focus Transparency
- Teaching Transparencies
- Source Document Transparencies
- Solution Transparencies

Multimedia
- **Exam***View* CD-ROM
- Electronic Learning Center CD-ROM
- Interactive Lesson Planner CD-ROM

T ACCOUNTS	6.	Change Fund		Cash in Bank	
		Debit +	Credit −	Debit +	Credit −
		100			100

JOURNAL ENTRY 7.

GENERAL JOURNAL PAGE 32

	DATE		DESCRIPTION	POST. REF.	DEBIT	CREDIT	
1	20--						1
2	May	1	Change Fund		100 00		2
3			Cash in Bank			100 00	3
4			Check 2150				4
5							5

If the business needs to increase the size of the change fund, a check is written for the amount of the cash increase. For example, suppose that On Your Mark needs to increase the change fund from $100 to $125. A check is written for $25. In the journal entry, **Change Fund** is debited for $25 and **Cash in Bank** is credited for $25. This brings the **Change Fund** account balance to $125.

Using the Change Fund

The amount of cash in the change fund is put into the cash register drawer at the beginning of the day. When a cash sale occurs, the salesclerk rings the sale on the cash register. The sale is automatically recorded on the cash register tape. At the end of the day, the cash in the cash register drawer is counted. A cash proof is prepared to verify that the amount of cash in the drawer equals the total cash sales for the day plus the change fund. The amount of cash in the change fund is set aside for use as change for the next day. The balance of the cash from the drawer is deposited in the checking account.

Let's look at an example. Suppose On Your Mark has $470 in the cash register drawer at the end of the day on May 15. The cash register tape shows that cash sales, including sales tax, total $370. **Figure 22–1** shows the cash proof. As you can see, the amount of cash in the drawer at the end of the day minus the amount of cash in the change fund equals the total sales shown on the cash register tape.

Most businesses require that salesclerks sign the cash proof to indicate that they have counted the cash in the drawer and verified its accuracy. The supervisor also checks these amounts and signs the cash proof. The cash proof form is attached to the cash register tape, which is the source document for recording the cash sales for the day.

CHAPTER 22
SECTION 1, PAGES 600–604

2 TEACH
GUIDED PRACTICE

Reading Accounting

- Have students outline the section, then make notes about the content described under each heading. L1
- Ask a local retail businessperson who speaks your students' first language to address the class about change-handling procedures used in her or his business. ELL

Visual Learning
Business Transactions

Using **Transparency** 22–2, discuss how the business establishes a change fund by writing a check for the amount of the fund. Guide students through the analysis of the debit and credit parts of the transaction and its recording in the general journal.

Concept Development: Using the Change Fund

Discussion: Some of your students will already have a basic understanding of the process of using a change fund from their part-time jobs. Have these students share their experiences with the class. L1

Demonstration Problem Step-by-Step Practice

Use demonstration problem 22–1 to give students practice in recording an entry to establish a change fund.

Great Ideas *From the Classroom of...*

Teaching the Change Fund I prepare *different* problems with a cash proof form, monopoly money, cash receipts, and a cash payment journal. I place everything for a problem in an envelope and write "Change Fund" on the cash proof form. Students count the money, prepare the form, and journalize entries for establishing the change fund and recording the transactions. Check the solutions and repeat the process.

Louise P. Lochhead
Davis High School
Kaysville, Utah

2 TEACH (Cont'd.)

Visual Learning

Figure 22–1 Cash Proof Form

Use **Transparency 22–3** to guide students through the preparation of a cash proof for the change fund. Remind students that this cash proof is similar to proving cash when reconciling the bank statement.

Concept Development: Recording Cash Short and Over

Discussion: Occasionally errors are made in making change to customers, and the amount of cash in the register drawer does not agree with the amount recorded on the register tape. When this occurs, there may be too little or too much cash in the drawer. The difference is recorded in a temporary equity account called Cash Short and Over. Draw a T account on the chalkboard for Cash Short and Over. Emphasize that this account has no normal balance. Cash shortages are considered to be expenses of the business and are thus recorded as debits (since, like other expenses, debits decrease equity). Cash overages are considered to be revenue and are recorded as credits (since revenue increases equity). L1

Demonstration Problem Step-by-Step Practice

Use demonstration problem 22–2 to give students practice in preparing a cash proof of the change fund.

Did You Know?

Managers

To become a manager of an Outback Steakhouse restaurant, a manager must invest personal savings of $25,000 in the restaurant. The company believes that it gets better results when managers have a personal stake in the success of the restaurant.

Figure 22–1 Cash Proof Form

May 15
Tape 71

348.00	CA
22.00	ST
370.00	

CASH PROOF

Date May 15, 20--
Cash Register No. 1

Total cash sales (from cash register tape)		$ 370.00
Cash in drawer	$ 470.00	
Less change fund	100.00	
Net cash received		$ 370.00
Cash short		
Cash over		

Salesclerk *Tom Blake*
Supervisor *Greta Keegan*

Recording Cash Short and Over

Many cash transactions occur during each business day. Occasionally, a salesclerk makes an error and gives the incorrect amount of change to a customer. When this happens, the amount of cash in the cash register drawer, less the beginning change fund, does not agree with the cash sales amount recorded on the cash register tape. If the salesclerk gives a customer too much change, the amount of cash in the drawer at the end of the day is *short*. If the salesclerk gives a customer too little change, the cash amount is *over*.

The amount of cash either gained or lost because of errors is recorded in the **Cash Short & Over** account. **Cash Short & Over** is a temporary account. Cash shortages are expenses to the business; they are recorded as debits to **Cash Short & Over.** Cash overages are revenue for the business; they are recorded as credits to **Cash Short & Over.** The **Cash Short & Over** account does not have a normal balance.

Cash Short & Over	
Debit Cash Shortages	Credit Cash Overages

At the end of the fiscal period, the balance of the **Cash Short & Over** account is closed to Income Summary. Let's look at an example.

MEETING SPECIAL NEEDS

English Language Learners In classroom lectures or discussions, slow down your speech patterns but do not use choppy, syllable-by-syllable pronunciations. One way to speak more slowly is to increase the length of pauses between groups of words or between sentences. These longer pauses give students who are English language learners more time to process what they are hearing.

Business Transaction

On May 2 the cash register tape shows that cash sales are $520 and sales taxes are $26, for a total of $546. The actual cash in the cash register drawer, after subtracting the amount of the change fund, is $545.

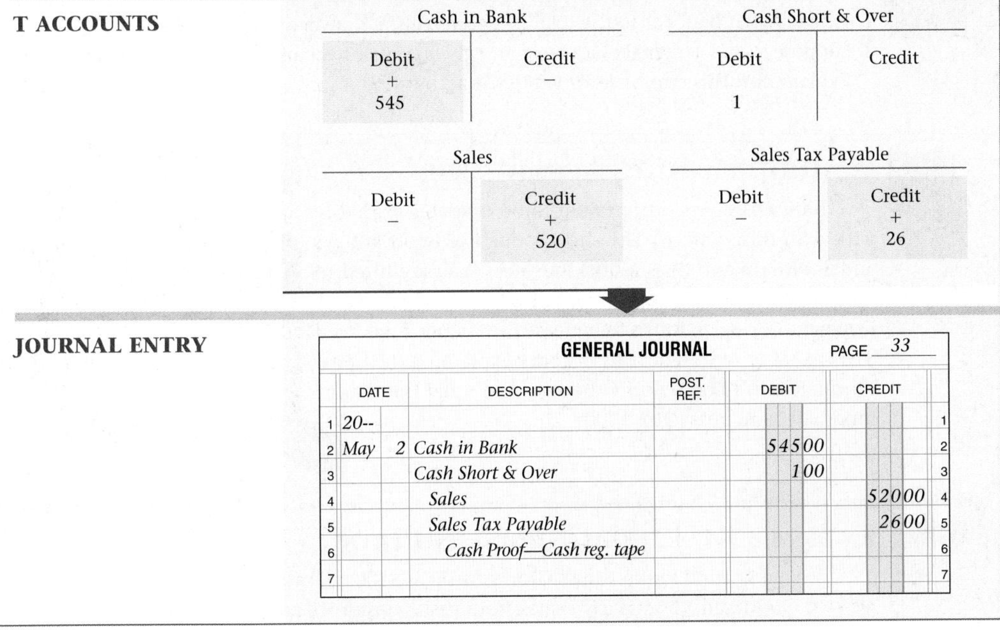

T ACCOUNTS

Cash in Bank	
Debit +	Credit −
545	

Cash Short & Over	
Debit	Credit
1	

Sales	
Debit −	Credit +
	520

Sales Tax Payable	
Debit −	Credit +
	26

JOURNAL ENTRY

GENERAL JOURNAL PAGE 33

	DATE		DESCRIPTION	POST. REF.	DEBIT	CREDIT	
1	20--						1
2	May	2	Cash in Bank		545 00		2
3			Cash Short & Over		1 00		3
4			Sales			520 00	4
5			Sales Tax Payable			26 00	5
6			Cash Proof—Cash reg. tape				6
7							7

The journal entry to record a cash overage is similar to that for a cash shortage, except that **Cash Short & Over** is *credited* for the amount of the overage. In the previous example, suppose that the amount of cash in the drawer is $547 after the amount of the change fund is subtracted. In the journal entry, **Cash in Bank** would be debited for $547 and **Cash Short & Over** would be credited for $1. The credits to **Sales** and **Sales Tax Payable** would remain the same.

A MATTER OF ETHICS

Petty Cash Funds

You are the petty cashier for a local theater group. The group's petty cash fund is used for taxi fares to and from the airport for actors, directors, and set designers. One day, you forget to bring some cash for your lunch. You consider borrowing five dollars from the petty cash fund and leaving an IOU. After all, you'll pay it back the next day.

Ethical Decision Making:

- What are the ethical issues?
- What are the alternatives?
- Who are the affected parties?
- How do the alternatives affect the parties?
- What would you do?

2 TEACH (Cont'd.)

Visual Learning

Business Transaction
Use **Transparency 22–4** to show students how to analyze and record a transaction involving a cash shortage.

Teaching Tip

Compare the Cash Short and Over account to Income Summary, which also has no normal balance. Its balance depends on the entries in the account.

Critical Thinking: Ask students what they would do as managers if they had an employee who had frequent cash shortages. Have students write a paragraph or two describing what they would do. L1

Demonstration Problem Step-by-Step Practice

Use demonstration problem 22–3 to give students practice in recording an entry with a cash shortage.

Demonstration Problem Step-by-Step Practice

Use demonstration problem 22–4 to give students practice in recording an entry with a cash overage.

Strategies for Teaching Ethics in Accounting

Photocopy the Chapter 22 *Student Activity Sheet* for students. Answers are also provided in the booklet.

Teaching A MATTER OF ETHICS

Petty Cash Funds Ask students if they've ever found themselves short of funds a few days before payday or if they've just forgotten to bring money to school for a special event. How did they handle their need for cash? Have students discuss the "borrowing" of money from petty cash or change funds from the position of the business owner and the position of the employee. You may want to form teams for each side and debate the issue of employee use of cash funds.

3 ASSESS

Thinking Critically (Answers)

1. Cash is counted; the amount of the change fund is set aside for use the next day; the balance of cash from the drawer is deposited in the bank.
2. Cash shortages are expenses to the business and are debited to Cash Short and Over. Cash overages are revenue for the business and are credited to Cash Short and Over.

Communicating Accounting (Answers)

Answers will vary. Have students share their notes in class.

Problem 22-1 (Answers)

1. Net cash $1,016.84; Cash short $5
2. Mar. 31: Dr. Cash in Bank $1,016.84, Cash Short and Over $5; Cr. Sales $964, Sales Tax Pay. $57.84

Problem 22-2 (Answers)

1. Net cash $1,595.77; Cash over $10
2. Apr. 14: Dr. Cash in Bank $1,595.77; Cr. Sales $1,496, Sales Tax Pay. $89.77, Cash Short & Over $10

Chapter Reviews and Working Papers
Refer students to the Chapter 22 workbook pages to answer *Check Your Understanding* activities.

4 CLOSE

Section Wrap-Up

Demonstrate: Prepare "change funds" for each student using fake money. Use slightly differing amounts for each fund. Tell students the amount of the change fund (such as $50), and have them prepare a cash proof. L1

SECTION 1 Check Your Understanding

Now that you have studied this section, complete the following questions and problems.

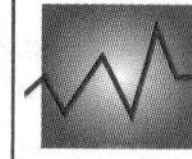

Thinking Critically

1. Explain what happens to the cash in a cash register drawer at the end of a business day.
2. Suppose a salesclerk makes an error and gives an incorrect amount of change to a customer. Explain how this error is recorded in the accounting records.

Communicating Accounting

The Children's Consignment Shop operates primarily with cash transactions. The shop is open only on Fridays and Saturdays and does a brisk business. You are hired to maintain the accounting records for the shop. Dorothy Douglas, the owner, wants to increase the change fund from $100 to $200. Write a note to Dorothy explaining the transaction. Remind her to notify the salesclerks that the change fund will be increased by $100.

Problem 22–1 Preparing a Cash Proof

The change fund for Messina's Grocery Store is $200 per cash register. On March 31 total cash sales from cash register six are $964 and sales taxes are $57.84. A count of cash shows $1,216.84 in the cash register drawer.

Mar 31
Tape 49

964.00 CA
57.84 ST

Instructions

(1) Use the form in your working papers to prepare a cash proof. Sign your name as the salesclerk.
(2) Record the March 31 cash sales on page 2 of a general journal.

Problem 22–2 Recording a Cash Overage

The change fund for Visions Hair Salon is $300 per register. On April 14, at the end of the business day, the manager counts the funds in the register. Cash sales total $1,496 and sales taxes amount to $89.77 in register two. The cash drawer contains $1,895.77.

Instructions

(1) Use the form in your working papers to prepare a cash proof. Sign your name as the salesclerk.
(2) Record the April 14 cash sales and overage on page 4 of the general journal.

RETEACHING SECTION 1

Proving Cash Provide a cash drawer with play money, and write the amount of the change fund on the chalkboard or an overhead transparency. Ask one student to act as the cashier, making change for each sale, as students role-play a few business transactions. As students exchange money, record the increases and decreases to the change fund on the chalkboard or transparency. When the role-play is over, ask the cashier to count the money in the cash drawer. Ask the rest of the students to calculate the balance that should be in the change fund. Have students complete a cash proof form, and, if necessary, indicate the amount of cash short or over.

The Petty Cash Fund

Businesses often make small cash payments for delivery fees, postage stamps, supplies, and other similar purchases. To handle these payments, businesses establish a special cash fund called petty cash. In this section you will learn how to open and replenish a petty cash fund.

Establishing the Petty Cash Fund

Small, incidental cash payments are made from the **petty cash fund**. The word "petty"

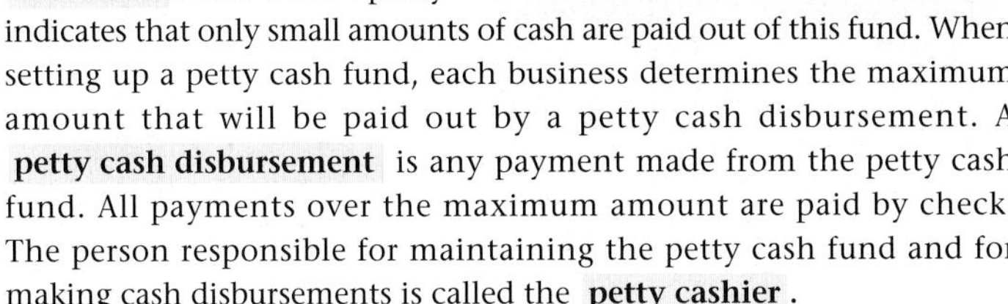

indicates that only small amounts of cash are paid out of this fund. When setting up a petty cash fund, each business determines the maximum amount that will be paid out by a petty cash disbursement. A **petty cash disbursement** is any payment made from the petty cash fund. All payments over the maximum amount are paid by check. The person responsible for maintaining the petty cash fund and for making cash disbursements is called the **petty cashier**.

To establish a petty cash fund, a business estimates the amount of cash needed in the fund for a certain period of time, usually a month. This estimate is based on the company's past experiences.

On Your Mark decides to establish a petty cash fund. Crystal Casteel, an office clerk, is appointed petty cashier. The petty cash fund will contain \$100. Any payments under \$10 will be paid from the petty cash fund. Any payments over \$10 will be paid by check. The company accountant, Greta Keegan, prepares a check for \$100, payable to "Petty Cashier Crystal Casteel," to establish the fund. The transaction is recorded in an asset account called **Petty Cash Fund.** Crystal cashes the check and places the money, consisting of small denominations of bills and coins, in a petty cash box. For better internal control, the petty cash box is kept in an office safe or a locked desk drawer. Crystal is responsible for the \$100 in the petty cash fund. When members of the staff need small amounts of cash for items like stamps or office supplies, Crystal will disburse the cash and store the receipts in the petty cash box. Let's learn how to journalize transactions to open a petty cash fund.

What You'll Learn

- How a business establishes a petty cash fund.
- How to prepare petty cash requisitions to replenish the petty cash fund.
- How to use a petty cash register to record petty cash disbursements.
- How to record the journal entry to replenish the petty cash fund.
- How to determine whether petty cash is short or over and record the amount of the shortage or overage.

Why It's Important

Businesses use petty cash funds because writing checks for small amounts is impractical, costly, and time consuming.

KEY TERMS

petty cash fund
petty cash disbursement
petty cashier
petty cash voucher
petty cash requisition
petty cash register

CHAPTER 22
SECTION 2, PAGES 605–614

1 FOCUS

Introducing the Section

In this section students will learn how to set up and use a petty cash fund. They'll learn how to write petty cash requisitions, record disbursements in a petty cash register, replenish the petty cash fund, and record journal entries related to petty cash.

Section Concepts

- How a business establishes a petty cash fund.
- How to prepare petty cash requisitions to replenish the petty cash fund.
- How to use a petty cash register to record petty cash disbursements.
- How to record the journal entry to replenish the petty cash fund.
- How to determine whether petty cash is short or over and record the amount of the shortage or overage.

Visual Learning

Section 2 Focus

Use **Transparency 22–5** to introduce section concepts.

BELL RINGER

Collecting Data: Assign students to teams. Have each team make a list of how they spend money each week for small items. Tell teams to omit large payments, such as car or insurance payments. Ask teams to share their lists and discuss how the types of payments might be similar to payments made from a petty cash fund. L1

RESOURCE MANAGER

Reproducible Masters
- Lesson Plans
- Chapter Reviews and Working Papers (CRWP) TAE
- Demonstration Problems

Transparencies
- Section Focus Transparency
- Teaching Transparencies
- Source Document Transparencies
- Solution Transparencies

Multimedia
- Exam*View* CD-ROM
- Electronic Learning Center CD-ROM
- Interactive Lesson Planner CD-ROM

CHAPTER 22
SECTION 2, PAGES 605–614

2 TEACH
GUIDED PRACTICE

Reading Accounting

- Have students skim the section and make a list of terms and concepts they need to study. Have them write definitions of the terms and summaries of the concepts. L1

Concept Development: Establishing the Petty Cash Fund

Discussion: Make the explanation of the petty cash fund as realistic as possible by bringing to class a petty cash box, fake money, and petty cash vouchers. Point out that the amount of the fund depends on payments the business plans to make from the fund. A petty cash fund may be as small as $25 or as large as several hundred dollars. Emphasize that the petty cashier is the only person who should have access to the cash fund and the authority to disburse cash. L1

Visual Learning

Business Transaction

Use **Transparency 22–6** to guide students through the analysis and recording of the entry to establish a petty cash fund.

Demonstration Problem Step-by-Step Practice

Use demonstration problem 22–5 to give students practice in recording the entry to establish a petty cash fund.

Strategies for Teaching International Accounting

To enrich study of international accounting, refer to the additional critical thinking activities in the booklet.

Business Transaction

On May 1 Check 2151 for $100 was issued to establish the petty cash fund.

ANALYSIS

Identify
1. The accounts affected are **Petty Cash Fund** and **Cash in Bank.**

Classify
2. Both **Petty Cash Fund** and **Cash in Bank** are asset accounts.

+/−
3. **Petty Cash Fund** is increased by $100. **Cash in Bank** is decreased by $100.

DEBIT-CREDIT RULE

4. Increases to asset accounts are recorded as debits. Debit **Petty Cash Fund** for $100.
5. Decreases to asset accounts are recorded as credits. Credit **Cash in Bank** for $100.

T ACCOUNTS

6.

Petty Cash Fund	
Debit +	Credit −
100	

Cash in Bank	
Debit +	Credit −
	100

JOURNAL ENTRY

7. GENERAL JOURNAL — PAGE *32*

	DATE		DESCRIPTION	POST. REF.	DEBIT	CREDIT	
5	*May*	*1*	*Petty Cash Fund*		*100 00*		5
6			*Cash in Bank*			*100 00*	6
7			*Check 2151*				7
8							8

International ACCOUNTING

Weather Forecasts

Before embarking on a business trip, find out the current weather of your destination. Selecting the proper clothes can make a big difference in how comfortable you feel during a presentation or meeting.

Sometimes petty cash disbursements occur more often than expected, and the petty cash fund is used up before the end of the specified time period. If this happens often, the company may decide to increase the amount of the fund. To increase the petty cash fund, debit the **Petty Cash Fund** account and credit the **Cash in Bank** account for the amount of the increase.

Making Petty Cash Payments

The petty cashier is responsible for making payments from the petty cash fund. Whenever a cash payment is made, a petty cash voucher is completed. A **petty cash voucher** is a proof of payment from the petty cash fund.

Figure 22–2 shows a petty cash voucher. Petty cash vouchers are usually prenumbered. If they are not, the petty cashier numbers them as they are issued.

Teaching International ACCOUNTING

Finding Weather Forecasts Ask students how they can find information about the current weather and weather forecasts for specific destinations. (Newspapers, local TV news stations, The Weather Channel, and Web sites.) Allow students to choose a destination and a date for travel within the next week. Have them research the current weather and weather forecast for that destination. Ask students to compare the forecast with local conditions and to explain how the weather forecast might affect the clothes they would pack for their trip.

The petty cash voucher includes the following information:

1. the date of the payment
2. the person or business to whom the payment is made
3. the amount of the payment
4. the reason for the payment
5. the account to be debited
6. the signature of the person approving the payment (usually the petty cashier)
7. the signature of the person receiving the payment

After the petty cash disbursement is made, the voucher is filed in the petty cash box until the fund is reimbursed.

ACCOUNTING TIPS

Petty Cash Vouchers

For internal control of petty cash, most businesses use prenumbered petty cash vouchers.

PETTY CASH VOUCHER

No. 001 — 1 Date May 2, 20--

2 Paid to Premier Office Supply Co. — 3 $ 7.10

4 For Printer paper

5 Account Supplies

Approved by 6 *Crystal Casteel* — Payment received by 7 *John Marks*

Figure 22–2
Petty Cash Voucher

Replenishing the Petty Cash Fund

To *replenish* a petty cash fund means to restore the fund to its original cash balance. As payments are made from the petty cash fund, the amount of cash in the petty cash box decreases. Some businesses set a minimum amount that must be kept in the petty cash box. When the amount of cash in the petty cash box reaches the minimum amount, the petty cash fund is replenished.

The petty cash fund is replenished once a month, when the balance reaches the minimum amount, or at the end of the fiscal period. When the petty cash fund is replenished, the general ledger accounts affected by petty cash disbursements (such as **Supplies** and **Delivery Fees**) are updated.

To replenish the petty cash fund, you reconcile the cash balance in the fund and then prepare a petty cash requisition form.

Reconciling the Petty Cash Fund

The petty cash fund is reconciled to determine whether or not the fund is in balance. To reconcile the petty cash fund, the petty cashier first adds all the paid petty cash vouchers. This total is then subtracted from the original cash balance of the petty cash fund. The difference is the *reconciled petty cash balance,* or the amount of money that *should be* in the petty cash box. If the count of the cash in the petty cash box agrees with the reconciled balance, the petty cash fund is in balance. If the two amounts do not agree, the petty cash fund is either short or over.

ACCOUNTING *Flashbacks*

THE BARTER SYSTEM

In Europe, the inconvenience of the barter system for the rising merchant class led to the development of currencies, banking, and the money economy system around 1000 AD.

2 TEACH (Cont'd.)

Concept Development: Making Petty Cash Payments

Discussion: An important point for students to understand is that the petty cash fund operates on an *imprest* basis, which means that the sum of all the paid vouchers, plus the amount of cash in the petty cash box, must be equal to the amount for which the fund was originally established. A petty cash voucher must be completed as a record of each cash disbursement. L1

Teaching Tip

On a piece of paper, have students journalize a transaction to open a petty cash fund.

Visual Learning

Figure 22–2 Petty Cash Voucher

Using **Transparency 22–7**, discuss the information on the petty cash voucher. Point out that a voucher is prepared every time cash is disbursed from the petty cash fund.

Chapter Reviews and Working Papers
Refer students to the *Study Plan* located at the beginning of Chapter 22 in the workbook.

REINFORCING STUDY SKILLS

Skimming Techniques The techniques used for reading a textbook can also be applied to reading articles in professional journals and other periodicals. To preview an article, read the title and the notes about the author. Then apply the techniques of skimming the first and last paragraphs, noticing the points in heads and subheads, and looking at graphics.

2 TEACH (Cont'd.)

Teaching Tip

Explain each step in reconciling the petty cash fund; then explain the journal entry that is made to replenish the fund.

Visual Learning

Figure 22–3 Petty Cash Requisition

Use **Transparency 22–8** to discuss the petty cash requisition form. Point out the accounts on the form showing how petty cash has been disbursed.

Concept Development: Using a Petty Cash Register

Discussion: Many businesses keep files of vouchers issued for petty cash disbursements and do not record them in a petty cash register. Businesses that have frequent petty cash disbursements may need to record them in a petty cash register. Remind students that this register is not a journal; it is not a record of original entry, and no amounts are transferred (posted) from the register to any accounts. When information from petty cash transactions is ready to be entered in the accounting records, journal entries must be made and posted. L1

On May 31 the total of all the petty cash vouchers for the month was $87.75. As you recall, the original petty cash balance was $100. The reconciled petty cash balance is:

Original balance	$100.00
Total of paid petty cash vouchers	− 87.75
Reconciled petty cash balance	$ 12.25

The amount of cash in the petty cash box that Crystal counted was $12.25. The petty cash fund, therefore, is in balance.

Preparing a Petty Cash Requisition Form

After the petty cash fund is reconciled, the petty cashier prepares a petty cash requisition. A **petty cash requisition** is a form requesting money to replenish the petty cash fund. **Figure 22–3** shows a typical petty cash requisition. This form serves as the source of information for the check written to replenish the petty cash fund. The check stub then serves as the source document for the entry recorded in the general journal.

PETTY CASH REQUISITION

Accounts for which payments were made:	Amount
Supplies	$24.45
Advertising Expense	14.80
Delivery Expense	19.00
Miscellaneous Expense	29.50
TOTAL CASH NEEDED TO REPLENISH FUND	$87.75

Requested by: *Crystal Casteel* Date *5/31/20--*

Approved by: *Greta Keegan* Date *5/31/20--*

Check No. *2341*

Figure 22–3 Petty Cash Requisition

To prepare the petty cash requisition, the petty cashier first sorts the paid petty cash vouchers by account. The vouchers for each account are totaled. The account title and the total amount to be debited to that account are recorded on the petty cash requisition. Look at **Figure 22–3** again. During May, On Your Mark made petty cash disbursements affecting the general ledger accounts **Supplies, Advertising Expense, Delivery Expense,** and **Miscellaneous Expense.**

The total of all the paid petty cash vouchers is the amount of cash needed to replenish the petty cash fund. When the accountant receives the petty cash requisition from the petty cashier, a check is written for the total of the paid vouchers. The check is made payable to the petty cashier, who cashes the check and places the money in the petty cash box.

Using a Petty Cash Register

Some businesses use a **petty cash register** to record all disbursements made from the petty cash fund. The petty cash register is a supplemental record that summarizes the types of petty cash disbursements. It is not an accounting journal because amounts from this register are not posted to general ledger accounts.

Recording Petty Cash Vouchers in a Petty Cash Register

Not all businesses that have a petty cash fund use a petty cash register. Those who do might use a form similar to that shown in **Figure 22–4.** This illustration shows how On Your Mark's petty cash vouchers are recorded. In the example, the establishment of the fund is followed by the month's disbursements.

COOPERATIVE LEARNING ACTIVITY

Group Discussion Assign students to groups of four or five and ask them to recommend internal controls for the management of petty cash. (Group suggestions will vary, but the following internal controls should be included: (1) Determine the maximum amount and/or types of expenses to be paid from the petty cash fund. (2) Keep the money in a safe or in a locked box. (3) Use prenumbered petty cash voucher forms. (4) Record all disbursements in a petty cash register or on a petty cash envelope. (5) Replenish the fund at the end of each accounting period.)

	DATE	VOU. NO.	DESCRIPTION	PAYMENTS	DISTRIBUTION OF PAYMENTS					
					SUPPLIES	DELIVERY EXPENSE	MISC. EXPENSE	GENERAL		
								ACCOUNT NAME	AMOUNT	
1	20--									1
2	May 1	—	Est. Petty Cash ($100)							2
3	2	1	Printer paper	7 10	7 10					3
4	3	2	Postage on incoming mail	2 50			2 50			4
5	4	3	Newspaper Ad.	9 80				Adv. Expense	9 80	5
6	5	4	Gas & Parking	9 50			9 50			6
7	7	5	Daily newspaper	3 50			3 50			7
8	8	6	Collect telegram	1 25			1 25			8
9	10	7	Pens and pencils	2 50	2 50					9
10	12	8	Dara's Delivery Service	9 50		9 50				10
11	16	9	Daily newspaper	3 50			3 50			11
12	18	10	Memo pads	8 45	8 45					12
13	20	11	Postage stamps	1 00			1 00			13
14	22	12	Ad in H.S. yearbook	5 00				Adv. Expense	5 00	14
15	26	13	File folders	6 40	6 40					15
16	29	14	Dara's Delivery Service	9 50		9 50				16
17	30	15	Gas & tolls	8 25			8 25			17
18	31		Totals	87 75 87 75	24 45 24 45	19 00 19 00	29 50 29 50		14 80 14 80	18
19										19
20			Reconciled bal. $ 12.25							20
21			Replen. check +87.75							21
22			Total $100.00							22
23										23

Figure 22–4 A Typical Petty Cash Register

Notice that the establishment of the petty cash fund on May 1 is noted on line 2 of the register. On each line that follows, each petty cash payment is identified by date, voucher number, and a brief explanation. The amount of each disbursement is entered in the Payments column *and* in the appropriate Distribution of Payments column. There are three special amount columns: Supplies, Delivery Expense, and Miscellaneous Expense. The General Amount column is used for petty cash payments that do not belong in one of the three special amount columns. The Account Name is written to the left of the amount.

Totaling and Proving the Petty Cash Register

When the petty cash fund is replenished, the petty cash register is totaled and proved. Refer to **Figure 22–4** as you read the following steps on totaling and proving a petty cash register:

ACCOUNTING TIPS

Internships

Internships at accounting firms and the IRS provide part-time jobs for students. In addition to earning a salary, students gain practical experience in the field of accounting. They can also investigate possible career paths in some specialized fields of accounting.

CRITICAL THINKING ACTIVITY

Evaluating Information Since cash overages result in revenue for the business, why not just include the overage with sales rather than using a separate account for cash short and over? (The sales account would be overstated. By maintaining a separate account, management can track shortages and overages. Excessive or frequent shortages or overages may indicate dishonesty or incompetence.)

2 TEACH (Cont'd.)

Visual Learning

Figure 22–4 A Typical Petty Cash Register

Use **Transparency 22–9** to discuss the petty cash register. Review each of the column headings and the information that is recorded in each column. Go through several entries with students to make sure they understand how to use the register.

Drawing Conclusions: Ask students how a business might design a petty cash register if it regularly makes payments from petty cash for office supplies, store supplies, deliveries, and advertising expenses. (The business might have a column for each type of payment rather than entering more of them in the General column.) L1

Teaching Tips

Errors in the petty cash register are likely to result from incorrect addition or from amounts recorded incorrectly in the distribution and payments columns.

Remind students that only amount columns are ruled.

2 TEACH (Cont'd.)

Teaching Tips

Emphasize that the total of the payments column must equal the sum of all other column totals.

Try to obtain a petty cash envelope from a local business or an office supply store to share with students.

Research: Have students contact a few local companies to determine how many of them use a petty cash fund and the types of payments they make from the fund. Ask students to share their findings in class. L1

Math Review for Accounting Photocopy appropriate *Activity Sheets* for students who need additional practice in basic math skills.

Avoiding Errors

To help you find errors:

- use a printing calculator to add column totals or figure account balances,
- then compare the amounts on the calculator tape to those in your accounting records.

1. Enter the date the fund is being replenished in the Date column. Also enter the word "Totals" in the Description column.
2. Single rule the amount columns.
3. Foot each amount column.
4. Verify that the total of the Payments column is equal to the total of the Distribution of Payments columns.

Payments		Distribution of Payments	
		$24.45	Supplies
		14.80	Advertising Expense
		19.00	Delivery Expense
		29.50	Miscellaneous Expense
$87.75	=	$ 87.75	

Once verified, the totals are recorded below the footings.

5. Draw a double rule under the amount columns to show that the totals are proved.
6. You will now enter the petty cash fund replenishment information. Skip one line, then enter the reconciled petty cash balance (the amount of cash that should be in the petty cash box before it is replenished). For On Your Mark, that amount is $12.25.
7. On the next line, write the amount of the check written to replenish the petty cash fund.
8. Add the balance that should be in the petty cash fund and the amount of the check. The sum should equal the original amount of the petty cash fund.

As you can see, the petty cash register helps the petty cashier keep track of the petty cash disbursements by account. When the petty cash fund is replenished, the totals of the special columns and the amounts recorded in the General column are listed on the petty cash requisition form.

Using a Petty Cash Envelope

Small businesses sometimes use petty cash envelopes for recording petty cash disbursements. A form very similar to the petty cash register is printed on the front of the petty cash envelope. Petty cash disbursements are recorded on the form on the envelope.

The paid petty cash vouchers are placed in the petty cash envelope. When the petty cash fund is replenished, the petty cash envelope, containing all the paid vouchers for the period, is sealed and filed. A new envelope is used to record the next period's petty cash disbursements.

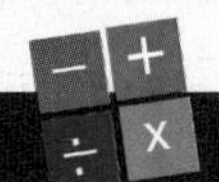

Key Points

Petty Cash Fund

The only time the **Petty Cash Fund** account is debited is when the petty cash fund is initially established or when the amount of money in the petty cash fund is increased.

Journalizing the Check to Replenish the Petty Cash Fund

When a check is written to replenish the petty cash fund, the check stub and the petty cash requisition are the source documents for recording the journal entry. Let's learn how to journalize transactions to replenish a petty cash fund.

Notice that the **Petty Cash Fund** account is not affected by this transaction. When replenishing petty cash, always credit **Cash in Bank** and debit the accounts for which petty cash payments were made.

Math Skill Builder Activity

Avoiding Errors Using the illustration of the petty cash register in this chapter, have students key the payments column of figures into a printing calculator. Ask students to prove their calculations by comparing their paper tape with the figures in the text. If students make errors, have them key the column of numbers until they can match the total in the register.

Business Transaction

On May 31 Check 2341 is written to replenish the petty cash fund.

ANALYSIS

Identify
1. The accounts affected are **Supplies, Advertising Expense, Delivery Expense, Miscellaneous Expense**, and **Cash in Bank.**

Classify
2. **Supplies** is an asset account. **Advertising Expense, Delivery Expense,** and **Miscellaneous Expense** are expense accounts. **Cash in Bank** is an asset account.

+/−
3. **Supplies** is increased by $24.45. **Advertising Expense** is increased by $14.80. **Delivery Expense** is increased by $19. **Miscellaneous Expense** is increased by $29.50. **Cash in Bank** is decreased by $87.75.

DEBIT-CREDIT RULE

4. Increases in asset accounts are recorded as debits. Debit **Supplies** for $24.45. Increases in expense accounts are recorded as debits. Debit **Advertising Expense** for $14.80. Debit **Delivery Expense** for $19; and **Miscellaneous Expense** for $29.50.
5. Decreases in asset accounts are recorded as credits. Credit **Cash in Bank** for $87.75.

T ACCOUNTS

6.

Supplies	
Debit + 24.45	Credit −

Advertising Expense	
Debit + 14.80	Credit −

Delivery Expense	
Debit + 19.00	Credit −

Cash in Bank	
Debit +	Credit − 87.75

Miscellaneous Expense	
Debit + 29.50	Credit −

JOURNAL ENTRY

7. GENERAL JOURNAL — PAGE 41

	DATE		DESCRIPTION	POST. REF.	DEBIT	CREDIT	
1	20--						1
2	May	31	Supplies		24 45		2
3			Advertising Expense		14 80		3
4			Delivery Expense		19 00		4
5			Miscellaneous Expense		29 50		5
6			Cash in Bank			87 75	6
7			Check 2341				7
8							8

2 TEACH (Cont'd.)

Visual Learning

Business Transaction

Use **Transparency 22–10** to guide students through the analysis and recording of the transactions to replenish petty cash.

GO TO Demonstration Problem Step-by-Step Practice

Use demonstration problem 22–6 to give students practice in recording the entry to replenish the petty cash fund.

HOME AND COMMUNITY CONNECTIONS ACTIVITY

Keeping Track of Allowances Almost all students have received an allowance at some age. In many ways, an allowance is similar to a petty cash fund. It is a liquid amount of money that can be used to purchase small items. Have students design a procedure for keeping track of allowance money for an elementary child, a middle school child, and a high school student. Have them check with their family to see if their allowance-tracking design seems reasonable. Ask for volunteers to share some of their responses in class.

2 TEACH (Cont'd.)

Concept Development: Handling Cash Short and Over in the Petty Cash Fund

Discussion: If the amount of money in the petty cash fund does not agree with the petty cash record, the difference must be recorded in the accounting records. Shortages and overages are recorded as part of the replenishment process. L1

Teaching Tip

Remind students that shortages are an expense to the business, while overages are revenue to the business.

Thinking Algebraically

Explaining Relationships: Have students describe the relationship of the Cash Short and Over balance to revenue or expense. (Example: debit balance > credit balance = expense; credit balance > debit balance = revenue.) L1

Visual Learning

Figure 22–5 Journal Entry to Replenish the Petty Cash Fund

Using **Transparency 22–11**, have students explain each part of the entry to replenish the petty cash fund and to record a cash shortage.

Handling Cash Short and Over in the Petty Cash Fund

CONNECT TO . . . LAW

Hammurabi's code, perhaps the first written laws, gave ancient Mesopotamia several economic guidelines. Inheritance rules, interest rates on loans, and damage assessments on cattle fields were all defined.

The petty cashier may occasionally make an error when paying out cash from the petty cash fund. When this happens, the amount of cash in the petty cash box will not agree with the reconciled petty cash balance. Any amounts of cash gained or lost through errors made by the petty cashier are recorded in the **Cash Short & Over** account.

Let's look at an example. At the end of June, Crystal Casteel, the petty cashier at On Your Mark, classified and totaled the petty cash vouchers. The accounts affected by the petty cash disbursements are:

Supplies	$15.75
Advertising Expense	25.00
Delivery Expense	20.45
Miscellaneous Expense	21.80

The total petty cash disbursements for June were $83. Crystal then reconciled the petty cash fund.

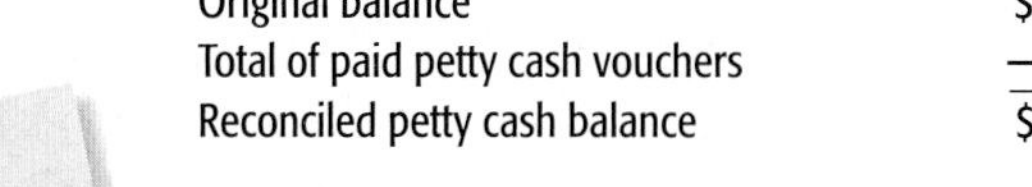

Original balance	$100
Total of paid petty cash vouchers	− 83
Reconciled petty cash balance	$ 17

Short $1.50

When Crystal counted the cash in the petty cash box, she found that there was only $15.50. The petty cash fund was short $1.50. To bring the petty cash fund up to the original $100, $84.50 is needed ($83 + $1.50). The $1.50 cash shortage is an expense and is debited to the **Cash Short & Over** account.

When Crystal prepared the petty cash requisition form, she listed the accounts to be debited for the petty cash disbursements. She also indicated that the **Cash Short & Over** account is to be debited for $1.50. **Figure 22–5** shows the journal entry to record the replenishment.

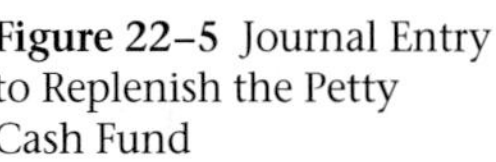

Figure 22–5 Journal Entry to Replenish the Petty Cash Fund

GENERAL JOURNAL — PAGE 43

	DATE		DESCRIPTION	POST. REF.	DEBIT	CREDIT	
1	20--						1
2	June	30	Supplies		15 75		2
3			Advertising Expense		25 00		3
4			Delivery Expense		20 45		4
5			Miscellaneous Expense		21 80		5
6			Cash Short & Over		1 50		6
7			Cash in Bank			84 50	7
8							8

INTERDISCIPLINARY CONNECTIONS ACTIVITY

Law Did you know that U.S. citizens have made several contributions to the development of economic laws? Here are just a few Nobel Prize winners in the area of economic sciences:

- Simon Kuznets developed the Gross National Product as a measure of economic output.
- Gerard Debreu researched how prices operate to balance supply with demand.
- Gary Becker applied economic theory to family relationships, welfare, racial discrimination, and crime.

A petty cash overage is recorded in a similar manner. If, for example, the cash in the petty cash box is $17.75, there is a cash overage of 75¢. **Cash Short & Over** is credited for that amount in the journal entry. Instead of needing $83 to replenish the fund, only $82.25 is required.

If a business uses a petty cash register, the cash shortage or overage is also reported in that record. **Figure 22–6** shows how the June cash shortage of $1.50 would be recorded in the petty cash register.

PETTY CASH REGISTER PAGE 2

	DATE		VOU. NO.	DESCRIPTION	PAYMENTS	DISTRIBUTION OF PAYMENTS					
						SUPPLIES	DELIVERY EXPENSE	MISC. EXPENSE	GENERAL ACCOUNT NAME	GENERAL AMOUNT	
1	20--										1
2	June	1	16	Postage stamps	5 00			5 00			2
14		30	29	Button	1 25				Adv. Expense	1 25	14
15		30		Totals	83 00	15 75	20 45	21 80		25 00	15
16											16
17				Reconciled bal. $ 17.00							17
18				Cash short (1.50)							18
19				Replen. check 84.50							19
20				Total $100.00							20
21											21

Figure 22–6 Recording a Cash Shortage in the Petty Cash Register

ANALYZING FINANCIAL REPORTS

Calculating Price-Earnings Ratios

When deciding whether to buy stock, analysts and investors look at stock price information, such as highs and lows over a period of time. They might also calculate the price-earnings (PE) ratio. The PE ratio compares the current market value of a stock with its earnings per share. Usually, the higher the ratio, the less attractive the stock to investors. Here's the formula to calculate the PE ratio:

$$\text{Price-earnings ratio} = \frac{\text{Current market value per share}}{\text{Earnings per share}}$$

You'll find earnings per share reported in the "Financial Highlights" for Office Depot.

▶ Analyze the Report:

Use the "Financial Highlights" on page A-42 to answer these questions. Use the "Basic" earnings per share figure and round your answer to the nearest whole number.

1. Calculate the price-earnings ratio for 2001, assuming Office Depot stock is selling at $17.50 per share.
2. Calculate the PE ratio for 2001, assuming Office Depot stock is selling at $20.00 per share.
3. Describe how stock price affects the PE ratio. How would you use this ratio in deciding which stocks to buy?

2 TEACH (Cont'd.)

Visual Learning

Figure 22–6 Recording a Cash Shortage in the Petty Cash Register

Use **Transparency 22–12** to show students how to record the replenishment and cash shortage in the petty cash register.

Teaching Tips

Remind students that recording the replenishment and cash shortages or overages in the petty cash register does not result in an accounting record. No amounts are posted from this register. A journal entry must be recorded and posted to enter information in the accounting system.

Discuss the price-earnings ratio. Invite a local stockbroker to speak to the class about the use of the PE ratio for analyzing stock prices and comparing potential investments.

The Office Depot 2001 Annual Report
Refer students to pages A-39–A-48 in the back of the book.

ANALYZING FINANCIAL REPORTS

Analyze the Report (Answers)

1. The price-earnings ratio is 26. ($17.50 ÷ $0.67)
2. The price-earnings ratio is 30. ($20.00 ÷ $0.67)
3. The price-earnings ratio is calculated by dividing the price of the stock by its earnings per share, so the higher the stock price, the higher the PE ratio. Generally, you would want a stock with a lower PE ratio because it means that the stock is earning more for your purchase price.

CHAPTER 22
SECTION 2, PAGES 605–614

3 ASSESS

Thinking Critically (Answers)

1. If the amounts of cash in the petty cash box do not agree with the balance, then the account is either short or over.
2. The accounts for which petty cash payments have been made are debited; the Cash in Bank account is credited.

Computing in the Business World (Answers)

Revenue $600
Expenses $63
Total deposit $563
Ending drawer balance $225
Ending petty cash $37

Problem 22–3 (Answers)

Check $39.51
New check stub balance $77,393.35

Chapter Reviews and Working Papers Refer students to the Chapter 22 workbook pages to answer *Check Your Understanding* activities.

4 CLOSE

Section Wrap-Up

Demonstrate: Have students use the information in Problem 22–3 and prepare the journal entry to replenish the petty cash fund. Have students use plain paper and write their entries in general journal form. L1

SECTION 2 Check Your Understanding

Now that you have studied this section, complete the following questions and problems.

Thinking Critically

1. How do you determine if a petty cash fund is short or over?
2. When replenishing the petty cash fund, which accounts are debited and which are credited?

Computing in the Business World

It is another busy day at Olde Time Swimming Hole, a private swimming facility for your neighborhood. You have a summer job running the concession stand, and you maintain the petty cash fund. To make your accounting easier, you record the cash sales and the petty cash transactions in one report at the end of the day. You always attach the cash register tape to prove the cash drawer. Using the following figures, determine the revenue and expenses for the day. How much money will remain in the cash drawer?

Opening cash drawer	$225
Petty cash fund	100
Cash sales	600
Pool supplies bought	55
Photocopy paper purchased	8

Problem 22–3 Analyzing a Source Document

The petty cash clerk for Riddle's Card Shop prepared the following petty cash requisition:

Instructions Review the document and prepare Check 973 to replenish the petty cash fund in your working papers.

PETTY CASH REQUISITION

Accounts for which payments were made:	Amount
Office Supplies	$12.40
Postage Expense	12.00
Misc. Expense	16.00
Cash Short and Over	(.89)
TOTAL CASH NEEDED TO REPLENISH FUND	$39.51

Requested by: *Brent Roy* Date *2/28/20--*
Approved by: *Hugh Morrison* Date ______
Check No. *941*

RETEACHING SECTION 2

Replenishing Petty Cash Use the cash drawer again to help explain how to establish and replenish the petty cash fund. Explain that a check is written to establish the fund. Have students record the journal entry. Assign one student the role of petty cashier and have the other students complete petty cash vouchers and role-play typical requests for petty cash. Then have students prepare a cash proof of the petty cash fund and record the journal entries. Discuss the need to write a check to replenish the petty cash fund, and record the journal entry.

CHAPTER 22 SUMMARY

KEY CONCEPTS

1. A change fund is the money used to make change for cash transactions.
2. The asset account **Change Fund** is usually debited only once—when the change fund is established.
3. To record the establishment of a change fund:

Debit: **Change Fund**	Credit: **Cash in Bank**

4. At the end of each business day, a cash proof is prepared to reconcile the cash in the register to the recorded cash sales.
5. The **Cash Short & Over** account is used to record errors in making change and in petty cash disbursements.
6. To record a cash shortage:

Debit: **Cash in Bank**	Credit: **Sales**
Debit: **Cash Short & Over**	Credit: **Sales Tax Payable**

7. To record a cash overage:

Debit: **Cash in Bank**	Credit: **Sales**
	Credit: **Sales Tax Payable**
	Credit: **Cash Short & Over**

8. A petty cash fund is the cash a business has on hand for making small, incidental cash payments.
9. The asset account **Petty Cash Fund** is usually debited only once—when the petty cash fund is established.
10. To record the establishment of a petty cash fund:

Debit: **Petty Cash Fund**	Credit: **Cash in Bank**

11. A petty cash voucher is prepared by the petty cashier when a disbursement is made from the petty cash fund.
12. The petty cashier prepares a petty cash requisition to request that the petty cash fund be replenished.
13. To record the replenishment of the petty cash fund with no shortages or overages:

Debit: **Various Assets and Expenses**	Credit: **Cash in Bank**

14. To record the replenishment of the petty cash fund with a shortage:

Debit: **Various Assets and Expenses**	Credit: **Cash in Bank**
Debit: **Cash Short & Over**	

15. To record the replenishment of the petty cash fund with an overage:

Debit: **Various Assets and Expenses**	Credit: **Cash in Bank**
	Credit: **Cash Short & Over**

16. A petty cash register or a petty cash envelope is used to keep a record of all petty cash disbursements on one form.

CHAPTER 22

SECTION 2, PAGES 605–614

Chapter 22 Quiz

Student ______ Class ______ Instructor ______
Date Assigned ______ Date Completed ______

CHAPTER 22 QUIZ

Cash Funds

QUESTIONS (Completion)

Directions: Fill in the blank with the term that best completes each sentence.

1. Money used to make change in cash transactions is a ______.
2. A change fund is established by debiting the ______ account.
3. The Cash Short and Over account is classified as a(n) ______.
4. Cash Short and Over has ______ normal balance.
5. Cash shortages and overages are recorded in the ______ journal.
6. A ______ is proof of a payment from the petty cash fund.
7. The ______ is a record of disbursements from the petty cash fund.
8. The person in charge of the petty cash fund is the ______.
9. A ______ is prepared to determine how much money is needed to replenish the petty cash fund.
10. Before replenishing the petty cash fund, the petty cash register is ______.

24 • Chapter Quizzes

QUESTIONS (Completion)

1. Money used to make change in cash transactions is a _____.
2. A change fund is established by debiting the _____ account.
3. The Cash Short and Over account is classified as a(n) _____.
4. Cash Short and Over has _____ normal balance.
5. Cash shortages and overages are recorded in the _____ journal.
6. A _____ is proof of a payment from the petty cash fund.
7. The _____ is a record of disbursements from the petty cash fund.
8. The person in charge of the petty cash fund is the _____.
9. A _____ is prepared to determine how much money is needed to replenish the petty cash fund.
10. Before replenishing the petty cash fund, the petty cash register is _____.

ANSWERS

1. change fund
2. Change Fund
3. temporary equity account
4. no
5. general
6. petty cash voucher
7. petty cash register
8. petty cashier
9. petty cash requisition
10. totaled and proved

REVIEW AND ACTIVITIES CHAPTER 22

USING KEY TERMS

See the *Glossary* for the definitions of these terms. Have students share their memos in class. Discuss the reasons they give for establishing the fund and any disagreements in use of accounting terms.

Understanding Accounting Concepts and Procedures

(Answers)

1. Dr. Change Fund; Cr. Cash in Bank.
2. When too much change is given to a customer or when theft or wrongful or negligent entering of amounts on the register tape occurs.
3. Because it is considered a cost of doing business.
4. To make small, incidental cash payments rather than writing checks.
5. Maintain the petty cash fund and make disbursements.
6. Postage stamps, small amounts of supplies, and newspaper delivery.
7. Dr. Petty Cash; Cr. Cash in Bank.
8. Date of payment, payee, amount, reason for payment, account to debit, approving signature, signature of person being paid.
9. When the fund is established or when the business increases the amount of the fund.
10. To update the balances of the accounts for which payments have been made.
11. Totaling paid vouchers and subtracting the total from the original fund balance. The difference is reconciled if it agrees with the amount in the petty cash box.
12. (a) Reconcile fund. (b) Prepare petty cash requisition. (c) Have accountant write replenishment check. (d) Record journal entry.
13. Because no amounts entered are posted to the ledger accounts.
14. Petty cash disbursements are written on the envelope, and the vouchers are stored inside.

CHAPTER 22 REVIEW AND ACTIVITIES

USING KEY TERMS

As the financial manager of The Tennis Center, you believe a petty cash fund should be established. Using the terms below, prepare a one-page memorandum to convince your boss, Megan Long, to open a petty cash fund.

change fund	petty cash requisition
petty cash disbursement	petty cash voucher
petty cash fund	petty cashier
petty cash register	

Understanding Accounting Concepts and Procedures

Instructions

On a separate sheet of paper, answer the following questions:

1. Which accounts are debited and credited when a change fund is established?
2. When does a cash shortage occur?
3. Explain why a cash shortage is treated like an expense.
4. Why would a business set up a petty cash fund?
5. What are the responsibilities of the petty cashier?
6. List three payments that might be made from a petty cash fund.
7. Which accounts are debited and credited to establish a petty cash fund?
8. What information is contained on a petty cash voucher?
9. How often is the **Petty Cash Fund** account debited?
10. Why should the petty cash fund be replenished at the end of the fiscal period?
11. What is meant by reconciling the petty cash fund?
12. Explain the procedure for replenishing the petty cash fund.
13. Why is the petty cash register not considered a journal?
14. How are petty cash envelopes used?

ASSESSMENT RESOURCES

Choose assessment strategies from the following pages to evaluate your students' progress.

Student Edition
Check Your Understanding, pp. 604, 614
Chapter 22 Problems, pp. 619–623
Analyzing Financial Reports, p. 613

Assessment and Evaluation Masters
Chapter 22 Study Plan, *Glencoe Workbook (CRWP)*
Chapter 22 Self-Test, *Glencoe Workbook (CRWP)*
Chapter 22 Test, *Chapter Tests* Booklet
Chapter 22 Activity, *School-to-Work Handbook*
Chapter 22 **Exam***View*

Teacher Wraparound Edition
Critical Thinking Activity, p. 609
Reteaching Sections 1–2, pp. 604, 614
Chapter 22 Quiz, p. 615

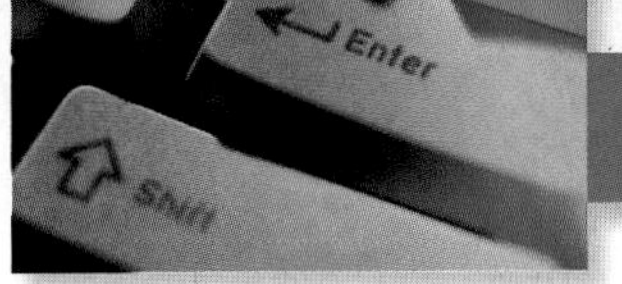

CHAPTER 22 REVIEW AND ACTIVITIES

Case Study...

Merchandising Business: Health Foods

The Healthy Alternative is an organic food store that sells vitamins and natural health-care products. The store has two electronic cash registers that track inventory and record sales directly to the computerized accounting system. The owner of the store is concerned because the actual cash on hand is usually short when compared to the sales records.

Thinking Critically:

1. You work for a local CPA firm that is auditing the accounting records for The Healthy Alternative. What advice would you give the owner about cash controls and protection?
2. Explain to the owner why it is important for the cash records to match the accounting records.

interNET CONNECTION

Online Banking

Need to check your bank balance? Apply for a loan? Transfer money from savings to checking? If you have a computer with Internet access, you can do all these things from your home.

Do This:

1. Do the banks in your community have Web sites?
2. List three banks and their Web site addresses.
3. Choose one site listed above. List the services that are provided to online customers.
4. Make a list of the advantages and disadvantages of online banking.

Conducting an Audit with Alex

Alex is auditing the petty cash transactions of Donnell's Decorating. He has asked you to review the journal entry and the list of petty cash vouchers from which the entry was prepared.

Date	Voucher No.	Account	Amount
July 1	1	Misc. Expense	$ 6.25
6	2	Delivery Expense	3.50
8	3	Voided	—
19	4	Samples Expense	8.10
19	5	Misc. Expense	2.10
30	6	Delivery Expense	7.35

GENERAL JOURNAL PAGE 12

	DATE		DESCRIPTION	POST. REF.	DEBIT	CREDIT	
1	20--						1
2	July	31	Misc. Expense		16 45		2
3			Delivery Expense		10 85		3
4			Petty Cash Fund			27 30	4
5			Check 327				5
6							6

Instructions Determine if the journal entry is correct. If not, why?

Workplace Skills

Integrity

In the workplace you may face situations where you are asked to make a decision that breaks with commonly held personal or societal values. Your ability to comprehend and choose the ethical course of action is a mark of integrity.

On the Job:

Fun Farm is a hands-on, educational working farm where elementary students learn about planting crops, harvesting, and raising animals. As you review the activity of Fun Farm's petty cash fund, you notice some unusual disbursements and cash shortages.

Thinking Critically:

In the course of your audit, you begin to suspect that someone in the company is taking funds out of petty cash and either not preparing a voucher or falsifying a voucher. Discuss with a partner how you should handle this situation.

REVIEW AND ACTIVITIES CHAPTER 22

Case Study...

Thinking Critically (Answers)

1. Answers may vary. One possibility would be to reconcile the cash drawer to the sales records for each shift. The earlier a mistake is discovered, the easier it is to track down. If an employee is consistently short, the person is either in need of training or is taking the money.
2. Answers may vary. If the actual cash does not match the accounting records, then there is a problem with internal control.

Workplace Skills

Thinking Critically (Answers)

Answers will vary. Students should be encouraged to brainstorm this case study and discuss the effects of "white collar" crime in the workplace.

Conducting an Audit with Alex

(Answers)

July 31: Dr. Misc. Expense $8.35, Delivery Expense $10.85, Samples Expense $8.10; Cr. Cash in Bank $27.30; Check 327

Internet Resources and Activities Handbook

Refer students to the booklet for additional Internet activities.

interNET CONNECTION www.glencoe.com

Do This (Answers)

1. Answers will vary.
2. Answers will vary. Possibilities include: Bank One, www.bankone.com; JPMorgan Chase Bank, www.chase.com; Citibank, www.citibank.com.
3. Services could include credit card applications, investment and retirement planning, stock quotes, banking transactions, bill paying, loan information and applications.
4. Possible advantages include 24-hour access, quick turnaround on requests to bank. Possible disadvantages include lack of Internet access, lack of "personalized" service.

PEACHTREE CORNER

Cash Funds

Use the **General Journal Entry** task to enter cash fund transactions unless you prefer to use the **Payments and Receipts** options. Students can use any of these options to record the transactions.

Instruct your students that they must manually complete the petty cash register and the petty cash requisition whenever requested since Peachtree does not support these functions.

Tasks Analysis Options Reports

- Quotes/Sales Orders ▸
- Sales/Invoicing...
- Receipts...
- Finance Charge...
- Select for Deposit...
- Purchase Orders...
- Purchases/Receive Inventory...
- Select for Payment...
- Payments...
- Write Checks...
- Time/Expense ▸
- Select for Payroll Entry...
- Payroll Entry...
- General Journal Entry...
- Inventory Adjustments...
- Assemblies...
- Account Reconciliation...
- Void Checks...
- Action Items...
- System ▸

Maintaining Cash Funds

Making the Transition from a Manual to a Computerized System

Task	Perform Accounting Procedures Using Manual Methods	Perform Accounting Procedures Using Automated Methods
Maintaining the check register	1. A check stub or deposit slip is the source document for journalizing cash payments. 2. A running balance must be calculated in the check register as deposits are made or checks are written.	1. Checks and deposits are automatically entered in the check register when transactions are journalized and posted. 2. The checking account balance is updated as each transaction is posted.
Reconciling the bank statement	1. Compare the check register with bank statement. 2. Add deposits in transit to the statement balance. 3. Deduct outstanding checks. 4. Deduct bank charges from check register. 5. Journalize and post bank charges.	1. Enter bank statement balance. 2. Verify outstanding checks and deposits not included on statement. 3. Record bank charges as a payment.

Maintaining Cash Funds

Peachtree Question	Description
How do I review the check register in Peachtree?	1. From the Reports menu, select Accounts Payable. 2. Select Check Register from the Reports list. 3. Select Options. 4. At the Filter window, set the range of checks to be displayed. 5. The register shows the check number, date, payee, cash account, and the amount of the check.
How do I reconcile the bank statement?	1. From the ***Tasks*** menu, choose **Account Reconciliation**. 2. Enter the Cash in Bank number you wish to reconcile. 3. Enter the ending balance from the bank statement. 4. Mark the clear box for each check listed on the statement. 5. Mark deposits that have cleared. 6. Click Adjust to record the journal entry for the service charge. 7. The reconciliation process is complete when the Unreconciled difference equals $0.00.
What does the software do "behind the scenes"?	1. During Account Reconciliation, Peachtree will prompt you until the difference between the cash account and the bank statement has been reconciled, thus assuring that the check register is accurate. 2. Each time the Account Reconciliation is accessed, it contains the previously reconciled information.

For detailed instructions: See the **Peachtree User Guide** in your Glencoe Working Papers.

Peachtree® Answers to Frequently Asked Questions

Q: Can you use the **General Journal Entry** option for cash fund transactions?

A: You have used the **Payments** and **Receipts** options to record cash payments and cash receipts, respectively. However, you can always use the **General Journal Entry** option to record transactions involving cash. The only disadvantage to using this option is that Peachtree will not print checks for any cash payment transactions you record. This is not an issue if you manually write checks.

For additional information, refer to your *Glencoe Peachtree Accounting User Guide*.

APPLICATION OPTIONS

Problem 22-4 Establishing a Change Fund

On February 1 Sunset Surfwear issued Check 115 to establish a change fund of $150. At the end of the business day on February 2, the shop's cash register tape showed cash sales of $340 plus sales taxes of $17. An actual cash count of the money indicated that $505 was in the cash register drawer.

Instructions

(1) Record the entry to establish the change fund on page 1 of the general journal.

(2) Prepare a cash proof for Feb. 2. Sign your name on the Salesclerk line.

(3) Record the cash sales for Feb. 2 on page 1 of the general journal.

Analyze: Does the shortage or overage represent revenue or expense to the business?

Problem 22-5 Establishing and Replenishing a Petty Cash Fund

InBeat CD Shop established a petty cash fund for $100.

Instructions

(1) In your working papers, record the entry to establish the petty cash fund on page 6 of a general journal.

(2) Record the entry for replenishing the petty cash fund on page 10 of the general journal. There was $5 cash in the petty cash fund box on February 28.

Date	Transactions
Feb. 1	Issued Check 112 for $100 to establish the petty cash fund.
28	Issued Check 146 to replenish the petty cash fund. Paid petty cash vouchers included Supplies, $40; Advertising Expense, $16; Maintenance Expense, $27; and Miscellaneous Expense, $12.

Analyze: Was cash short or over?

Complete chapter problems one of three ways:

1 **Manual** Glencoe Working Papers

or

2 **Peachtree Complete Accounting** Software

or

3 **QuickBooks** Templates (Problems 22–6, 22–7)

Peachtree®

SMART GUIDE

Step-by-Step Instructions: Problem 22-4

1. Select the problem set for Sunset Surfwear (Prob. 22-4).
2. Rename the company and set the system date.
3. Record the entry to establish the change fund using the **General Journal Entry** option.
4. Manually prepare a cash proof.
5. Record the cash sales using the **General Journal Entry** option.
6. Print a General Journal report and proof your work.
7. Answer the Analyze question.
8. End the session.

PROBLEMS CHAPTER 22

Problem 22-4 (Answers) Establishing a Change Fund

1. Feb. 1: Dr. Change Fund $150; Cr. Cash in Bank $150; Check 115
2. Net cash received $355, Cash short $2
3. Feb. 2: Dr. Cash in Bank $355, Cash Short and Over $2; Cr. Sales $340, Sales Tax Pay. $17; Cash Register Tape

Analyze: Expense

Problem 22-5 (Answers) Establishing and Replenishing a Petty Cash Fund

1. Feb. 1: Dr. Petty Cash Fund $100; Cr. Cash in Bank $100; Check 112
2. Feb. 28: Dr. Supplies $40, Advertising Expense $16, Maintenance Expense $27, Miscellaneous Expense $12; Cr. Cash in Bank $95; Check 146

Analyze: Cash was neither over nor short; it was in balance.

EXTENDING THE CONTENT

Safeguarding Cash on the Job Every employee who uses a cash register should be familiar with some safeguards against the theft of money. Ask students who work with cash registers at their jobs to describe the procedures and/or rules their employers enforce regarding the handling of the change fund. Also ask students to explain what happens when a salesclerk makes an error and gives the incorrect amount of change to a customer. Have students get permission to share forms such as cash proofs.

Problem 22-6 (Answers) Establishing and Replenishing a Petty Cash Fund

1. Feb. 1: Dr. Petty Cash Fund $70; Cr. Cash in Bank $70; Check 1018
2. Feb. 28: Dr. Supplies $14, Advertising Expense $25, Delivery Expense $16.90, Miscellaneous Expense $12.60; Cr. Cash in Bank $68.50; Check 1191

Analyze: $16.90

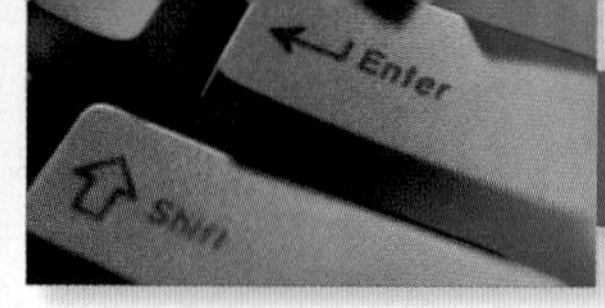

Peachtree®

SMART GUIDE

Step-by-Step Instructions: Problem 25-5

1. Select the problem set for InBeat CD Shop (Prob. 22-5).
2. Rename the company and set the system date.
3. Record the entry to establish the petty cash fund.
4. Record the entry to replenish the petty cash fund.
5. Print a General Journal report and proof your work.
6. Answer the Analyze question.
7. End the session.

TIP: Use the **General Journal Entry** option to record the cash fund transactions.

Peachtree®

SMART GUIDE

Step-by-Step Instructions: Problem 22-6

1. Select the problem set for Shutterbug Cameras (Prob. 22-6).
2. Rename the company and set the system date.
3. Record the entry to establish the petty cash fund.
4. Make a list of the petty cash vouchers and then manually prepare a petty cash requisition.
5. Record the entry to replenish the petty cash fund.
6. Print a General Journal report and proof your work.
7. Answer the Analyze question.
8. End the session.

TIP: Use the **General Journal Entry** option to record the cash fund transactions.

Problem 22-6 Establishing and Replenishing a Petty Cash Fund

Shutterbug Cameras, a camera store, decided to establish a petty cash fund. On February 1 the accountant, Al Rosen, issued Check 1018 for $70 to establish the fund. The following disbursements were made.

Instructions

(1) In your working papers, record the entry to establish the petty cash fund on page 9 of a general journal.
(2) Make a list of the paid petty cash vouchers.
(3) Classify the petty cash disbursements by account. Calculate the total amount paid out for each account.
(4) Prepare a petty cash requisition, signing your name as the petty cashier. On February 28 there was $1.50 in the petty cash box.
(5) Record the entry in the general journal (page 11) to replenish the petty cash fund on February 28. Use Check 1191.

Date		Transactions
Feb.	1	Purchased memo pads for the office, $2.75, Voucher 101 **(Supplies)**.
	3	Prepared Voucher 102 for a newspaper ad, $7.50 **(Advertising Expense)**.
	5	Prepared Voucher 103 for the postage on an outgoing package, $1.75 **(Miscellaneous Expense)**.
	8	Paid Dandy Delivery Service $5.65, Voucher 104 **(Delivery Expense)**.
	10	Prepared Voucher 105 for pens and pencils, $3.75 **(Supplies)**.
	12	Paid $2.20 for postage stamps, Voucher 106 **(Miscellaneous Expense)**.
	15	Paid Dandy Delivery Service $6.75, Voucher 107 **(Delivery Expense)**.
	20	Paid the news carrier $4.25 for delivery of the daily newspaper, Voucher 108 **(Miscellaneous Expense)**.
	22	Bought typing paper for $7.50, Voucher 109 **(Supplies)**.
	25	Paid $4.50 to Dandy Delivery Service, Voucher 110 **(Delivery Expense)**.
	27	Prepared Voucher 111 for an advertisement, $10 **(Advertising Expense)**.
	28	Paid $4.40 for postage stamps, Voucher 112 **(Miscellaneous Expense)**.
	28	Prepared Voucher 113 for an advertisement, $7.50 **(Advertising Expense)**.

Analyze: What were the total petty cash disbursements for **Delivery Expense** during February?

ACCOUNTING ISSUES

The FASB Since 1973, the Financial Accounting Standards Board (FASB) has been the designated organization to establish standards of financial accounting and reporting. Those standards govern the preparation of financial reports. The FASB also develops broad accounting concepts. These concepts are useful to the Board in establishing financial reporting standards and resolving accounting issues. You can locate the FASB on the Web at http://www.fasb.org to find general information, announcements of board actions and meetings, press releases, summaries of FASB statements, and to order FASB products and services. You can also e-mail board members and staff at this site.

SOURCE DOCUMENT PROBLEM

Problem 22–7 Using a Petty Cash Register

Cycle Tech Bicycles decided to establish a petty cash fund. On February 1 the accountant issued Check 3724 for $120 to establish the fund. The following disbursements were made.

Instructions

(1) In your working papers, record the entry to establish the petty cash fund in a general journal, page 5.

(2) Enter the information about the establishment of the petty cash fund on line 1 of a petty cash register, page 1.

(3) Record the petty cash disbursements in the petty cash register.

(4) Foot, total, and prove the petty cash register on February 28.

(5) Record the petty cash fund replenishment information in the explanation column below the totals. On February 28 there was $4.35 in the petty cash box.

(6) Prepare a petty cash requisition form. Use the form provided in your working papers and sign your name as petty cashier.

(7) Record the issuance of Check 3875 to replenish the petty cash fund in the general journal, page 8.

Date	Transactions
Feb. 2	Prepared Voucher 1 for a $9.25 newspaper advertisement **(Advertising Expense).**
5	Prepared Voucher 2 for pens and pencils, $5 **(Supplies).**
9	Paid $12.50 for flowers for an employee's birthday, Voucher 3 **(Miscellaneous Expense).**
12	Bought cash register tape for $3.95, Voucher 4 **(Supplies).**
19	Prepared Voucher 5 for $15 to pay National Express for parts delivered **(Delivery Expense).**
20	Paid $3.90 for postage stamps, Voucher 6 **(Miscellaneous Expense).**
22	Paid $16 to have the show window cleaned, Voucher 7 **(Miscellaneous Expense).**
24	Bought an $11 advertisement in the local newspaper, Voucher 8 **(Advertising Expense).**
25	Bought stationery for $10, Voucher 9 **(Supplies).**
26	Prepared Voucher 10 to National Express for packages delivered, $8.25 **(Delivery Expense).**
27	Prepared Voucher 11 incorrectly and voided it.
27	Purchased memo pads for the office for $3, Voucher 12 **(Supplies).**
28	Paid the news carrier a $4 tip for the daily newspaper delivery, Voucher 13 **(Miscellaneous Expense).**
	Continued

Peachtree®

SMART GUIDE

Step-by-Step Instructions: Problem 22–7

1. Select the problem set for Cycle Tech Bicycles (Prob. 22–7).
2. Rename the company and set the system date.
3. Record the entry to establish the petty cash fund.
4. Manually record the petty cash disbursements.
5. Prepare a petty cash requisition.
6. Record the entry to replenish the petty cash fund.
7. Print a General Journal report and proof your work.
8. Answer the Analyze question.
9. End the session.

SOURCE DOCUMENT PROBLEM

Problem 22–7

Use the source documents in your working papers to record the transactions in this problem.

SOURCE DOCUMENT PROBLEM

Problem 22–7 (Answers) Using a Petty Cash Register

1. Feb. 1: Dr. Petty Cash Fund $120; Cr. Cash in Bank $120; Check 3724
2. Reconciled balance $1.35, Cash over $3, Replenishment check $115.65
3. Feb. 28: Dr. Supplies $21.95, Delivery Expense $23.25, Miscellaneous Expense $43.20; Advertising Expense $30.25, Cr. Cash Short and Over $3, Cash in Bank $115.65; Check 3785

Analyze: 14

MAKING CONNECTIONS TO DAILY LIFE

Incorrect Change Ask students to share their experiences of receiving incorrect change from a cashier. As students mention their experiences, write a short phrase on the chalkboard describing the situation. For each situation, have students decide whether the change fund for the business would have been short or over as a result of the error.

Problem 22-8 (Answers) Handling a Petty Cash Fund

1. Feb. 1: Dr. Petty Cash Fund $100; Cr. Cash in Bank $100; Check 1763
2. Reconciled balance $2.25, Cash short $.75, Replenishment Check $98.50
3. Feb. 28: Dr. Supplies $20.30, Delivery Expense $22.50, Miscellaneous Expense $27.15, Advertising Expense $13.00, Gas Expense $14.80, Cash Short and Over $.75; Cr. Cash in Bank $98.50; Check 1798
4. Feb. 28: Dr. Petty Cash Fund $25; Cr. Cash in Bank $25; Check 1799

Analyze: Flowers, postage stamps, window washing, newspaper delivery

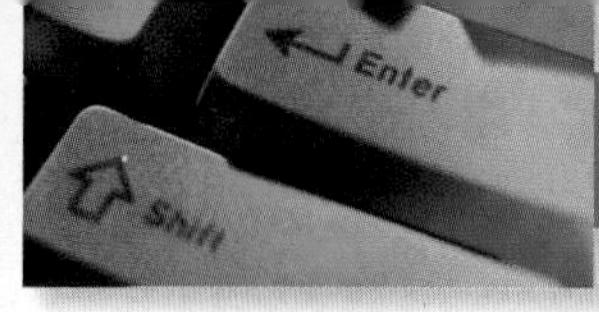

Peachtree®

SMART GUIDE

Step-by-Step Instructions: Problem 22-8

1. Select the problem set for River's Edge Canoe & Kayak (Prob. 22-8).
2. Rename the company and set the system date.
3. Record the entry to establish the petty cash fund.
4. Manually record the petty cash disbursements.
5. Reconcile the petty cash register and prepare a petty cash requisition.
6. Record the entry to replenish the petty cash fund.
7. Record the entry to increase the petty cash fund.
8. Print a General Journal report and proof your work.
9. Answer the Analyze question.
10. End the session.

Date	Problem 22-7 (cont.) Transactions
28	Paid $6.80 for postage stamps, Voucher 14 **(Miscellaneous Expense).**
28	Prepared Voucher 15 for a $10 newspaper advertisement **(Advertising Expense).**

Analyze: How many payments were made from the petty cash fund during the month of February?

Problem 22-8 Handling a Petty Cash Fund

River's Edge Canoe & Kayak petty cash fund was established on February 1 for $100, by writing check 1763. The accounts for which petty cash disbursements are likely to be made include **Supplies, Gas Expense, Advertising Expense, Delivery Expense,** and **Miscellaneous Expense.**

Instructions

(1) In your working papers, record the entry to establish the petty cash fund on page 12 of a general journal.
(2) Record the establishment of the fund on the first line of the petty cash register, page 1.
(3) Record each petty cash disbursement in the petty cash register.
(4) Foot, prove, total, and rule the petty cash register on February 28.
(5) Reconcile the petty cash fund. The amount in the petty cash box is $1.50.
(6) Prepare a petty cash requisition. Sign your name as petty cashier.
(7) Record the entry to replenish the petty cash fund by issuing Check 1798 in the general journal, page 15.
(8) Record the replenishment information in the petty cash register.
(9) The accountant believes the petty cash fund should be increased by $25. Record the issuance of Check 1799 on February 28.

Date	Transactions
Feb. 1	Bought an $8 advertisement in the local newspaper, Voucher 101.
2	Prepared Voucher 102 for $7.50 to pay Mercury Messenger for packages delivered.
3	Bought adding machine tape for 75¢, Voucher 103.
5	Paid $9.50 for flowers for an employee's birthday, Voucher 104.

Continued

ADDRESSING MULTIPLE LEARNING STYLES

Linguistic Learner Tell students that they own and operate a small coffee shop. The business employs seven servers who work flexible hours each week. Each server collects money from customers and operates the electronic cash register to record sales. One of the servers consistently has lower sales than the other servers when they work the same time period. That person may be failing to enter all sales and instead keeping the money. Ask students to create some policies and procedures they would implement for safeguarding cash. Students should write a report describing the policies and outlining the procedures.

Date	Problem 22–8 (cont.) Transactions
7	Prepared Voucher 105 for $5.25 for a typewriter ribbon.
9	Paid $4.40 for postage stamps, Voucher 106.
12	Bought $9 worth of gasoline, Voucher 107.
15	Paid $8.50 to have the shop's windows washed, Voucher 108.
18	Bought memo pads, pencils, and pens for office use, $6.30, Voucher 109.
20	Prepared Voucher 110 for $7.50 to pay Mercury Messenger for packages delivered.
23	Prepared Voucher 111 incorrectly and voided it.
23	Bought stationery for $8, Voucher 112.
27	Paid the news carrier $4.75 for the daily newspaper, Voucher 113.
28	Prepared Voucher 114 for $7.50 to pay Mercury Messenger for packages delivered.
28	Bought gasoline, $5.80, Voucher 115.
28	Prepared Voucher 116 for a newspaper advertisement, $5.

Analyze: List the petty cash disbursements that are charged to the **Miscellaneous Expense** account.

Problem 22–9 Locating Errors in a Petty Cash Register

On February 1 a petty cash fund of $150 was established for Buzz Newsstand, Check 1198. The petty cashier writes a voucher for each petty cash disbursement. The vouchers are entered in a petty cash register, which is included in your working papers. When the petty cash register was totaled on February 28, the accounting clerk discovered that the footings of the Distribution of Payments columns did not equal the total of the Payments column.

Instructions

(1) Compare the following petty cash disbursement information in your working papers with the entries in the petty cash register.

(2) Correct any errors you find in the petty cash register by drawing a line through the incorrect item and writing the correction above it.

(3) Total all columns after the corrections are made.

(4) Record the replenishment information on the register. The amount in the petty cash box on February 28 was $8.10.

Analyze: How did you determine the amount of the check to replenish the petty cash fund on February 28?

SOLUTION NOTES

PROBLEM CHAPTER 22

Problem 22–9 (Answers) Locating Errors in a Petty Cash Register

Errors:

Feb. 4: Delivery charges were recorded under Miscellaneous Expense; amount was $7.60, not $6.70.

Feb. 9: Writing tablets were recorded as $9.34; it should have been $9.43.

Feb. 10: Newspaper ad was recorded under Miscellaneous Expense; amount in Payments column should be $8.50, not $8.52.

Feb. 11: Stamps were recorded under Postage, which should have been Miscellaneous Expense.

Feb. 27: Delivery charge was recorded as $6.75; it should have been $8.75.

Feb. 28: Telephone directory of $4.30 was omitted from the Miscellaneous Expense column.

Reconciled balance $7.06
Cash Over $1.04
Replenishment check $141.90

Analyze: Petty cash fund of $150.00 less amount in cash box of $8.10 = $141.90.

CHAPTER 23 Resource Manager

Section Resources

	Objectives & Standards	Activities & Features	Reproducible Masters
Chapter Opener *Plant Assets and Depreciation*	• Identify plant assets. • Explain the need to depreciate plant assets. • Calculate annual depreciation of plant assets. • Calculate partial-year depreciation of plant assets. • Determine the book value of a plant asset. • Record depreciation of plant assets. • Prepare depreciation schedules. • Define the accounting terms introduced in this chapter. **National Standards for Business Education**: IA13, IIA7, IIA8, IIA9	Exploring the Real World of Business, p. 624 Workplace Connections, p. 625	School-to-Work Handbook
Section 1 *Plant Assets and Equipment*	• How to identify plant assets. • How to allocate the cost of a plant asset over its useful life.	Did You Know?, p. 627 Accounting Tips, p. 628 Analyzing Financial Reports, p. 628	
Section 2 *Calculating Depreciation*	• How to calculate the annual depreciation of a plant asset. • How to calculate depreciation for a partial year. • How to determine the book value of a plant asset.	Accounting Flashbacks, p. 630 Accounting Tips, p. 631	Demonstration Problems
Section 3 *Accounting for Depreciation Expense at the End of a Year*	• How to record adjusting entries in the general journal for depreciation. • How to record depreciation adjustments on a work sheet. • How to report **Depreciation Expense** and **Accumulated Depreciation** on financial statements.	Calculator Hints, p. 634 International Accounting, p. 636 Connect To, p. 637 A Matter of Ethics, p. 640 Accounting Careers in Focus, p. 642	Demonstration Problems Math Review for Accounting Strategies for Teaching International Accounting Strategies for Teaching Ethics in Accounting Internet Resources and Activities Handbook

KEY

Posters — Transparency — Software — Videocassette
Blackline Masters — CD-ROM — Portfolio

MULTIMEDIA RESOURCE

Peachtree	QuickBooks	Spreadsheets	Videos	CD-ROMs
Problem 23–7 *Recording Adjusting Entries for Depreciation* Problem 23–8 *Reporting Depreciation Expense on the Work Sheet and Financial Statements* Problem 23–9 *Calculating and Recording Depreciation Expense* Problem 23–10 *Calculating and Recording Adjustments*	Problem 23–8 *Reporting Depreciation Expense on the Work Sheet and Financial Statements* Problem 23–10 *Calculating and Recording Adjustments*	None in this chapter.	***Video Segment: Depreciation*** After viewing this video, students will be able to explain the difference between book value and market value of items that are depreciated. They will be able to calculate straight-line depreciation.	***Electronic Learning Center (ELC), Chapter 23*** This program is ideal for visual learners since it incorporates video images, animation, and graphics to enliven the content of each lesson. ***Interactive Lesson Planner (ILP), Chapter 23*** This CD-ROM combines the versatility of an electronic lesson planner with the convenience of teacher classroom resources.

SCANS Correlation Chart

FOUNDATION SKILLS

Basic Skills:	Reading	Writing	Math	Listening	Speaking	
Thinking Skills:	Creative Thinking	Decision Making	Problem Solving	Seeing Things in the Mind's Eye	Knowing How to Learn	Reasoning
Personal Qualities:	Responsibility	Self-Esteem	Sociability	Self-Management	Integrity/Honesty	

WORKPLACE COMPETENCIES

Resources:	Allocating Time	Allocating Money	Allocating Material and Facility Resources	Allocating Human Resources		
Information:	Acquiring and Evaluating Information	Organizing and Maintaining Information	Interpreting and Communicating Information	Using Computers to Process Information		
Interpersonal Skills:	Participating as a Member of a Team	Teaching Others	Serving Clients/ Customers	Exercising Leadership	Negotiating to Arrive at a Decision	Working with Cultural Diversity
Systems:	Understanding Systems	Monitoring and Correcting Performance	Improving and Designing Systems			
Technology:	Selecting Technology	Applying Technology to Task	Maintaining and Troubleshooting Technology			

*Highlighted blocks indicate areas covered in the chapter. Additional SCANS skills are also covered throughout the *Teacher Wraparound Edition.*

Assessment

Student Edition
- Check Your Understanding, pp. 629, 632, 641
- Chapter 23 Problems, pp. 647–649

Assessment and Evaluation Masters
- Chapter 23 Study Plan, *Glencoe Workbook*
- Chapter 23 Self-Test, *Glencoe Workbook*
- Chapter 23 Test, *Chapter Tests* Booklet
- Chapter 23 Activity, *School-to-Work Handbook*
- Chapter 23 **Exam***View*

Teacher Wraparound Edition
- Critical Thinking Activity, p. 639
- Reteaching Section 1, p. 629
- Reteaching Section 2, p. 632
- Reteaching Section 3, p. 641
- Chapter 23 Quiz, p. 643

Transparencies

	Teaching Transparencies	Solution Transparencies
Section 1:	23–1	Problem 23–1
Section 2:	23–2, 23–3	Problems 23–2, 23–3
Section 3:	23–4, 23–5, 23–6, 23–7, 23–8, 23–9, 23–10, 23–11	Problems 23–4, 23–5
End of Chapter:		Problems 23–6, 23–7, 23–8, 23–9, 23–10, CHALLENGE PROBLEM 23–11

TEACHER CLASSROOM RESOURCES

This is a representation of key blackline masters available in the Teacher Classroom Resources.

Teaching Aids

Transparency Examples

Section Focus Transparencies

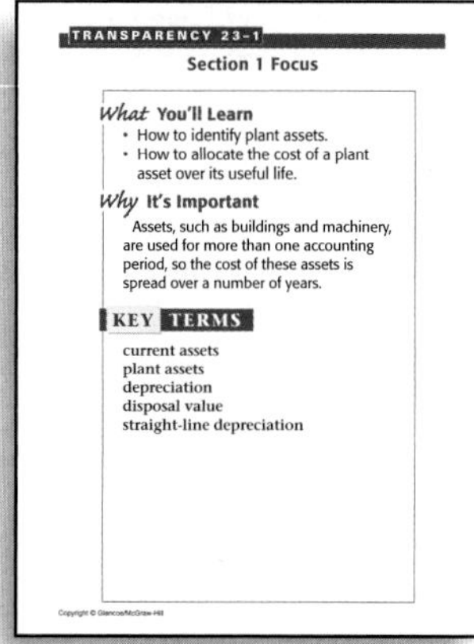

TRANSPARENCY 23-1

Section 1 Focus

What You'll Learn
- How to identify plant assets.
- How to allocate the cost of a plant asset over its useful life.

Why It's Important

Assets, such as buildings and machinery, are used for more than one accounting period, so the cost of these assets is spread over a number of years.

KEY TERMS

current assets
plant assets
depreciation
disposal value
straight-line depreciation

Teaching Transparencies

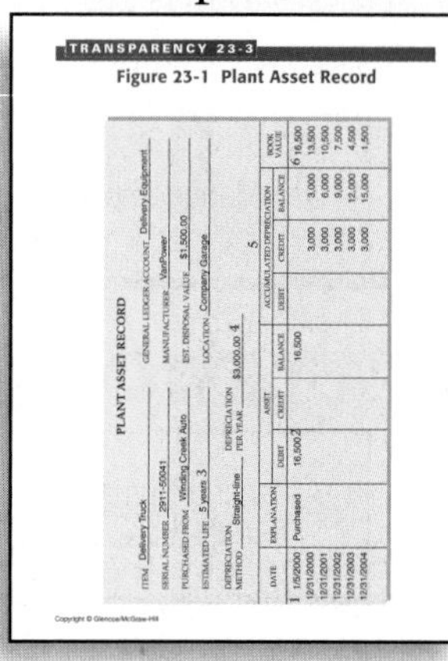

TRANSPARENCY 23-3

Figure 23-1 Plant Asset Record

Teaching Transparencies

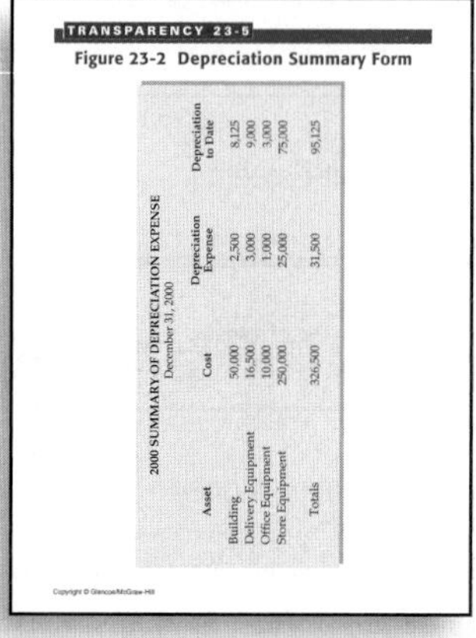

TRANSPARENCY 23-5

Figure 23-2 Depreciation Summary Form

Solution Transparencies

Working Papers

Problem 23-6 Opening a Plant Asset Record

Problem 23-7 Recording Adjusting Entries for Depreciation

Demonstration Problems

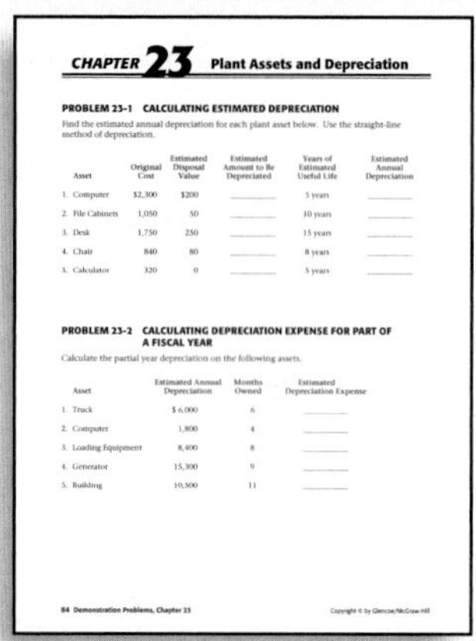

CHAPTER 23 Plant Assets and Depreciation

PROBLEM 23-1 CALCULATING ESTIMATED DEPRECIATION

PROBLEM 23-2 CALCULATING DEPRECIATION EXPENSE FOR PART OF A FISCAL YEAR

Lesson Plans

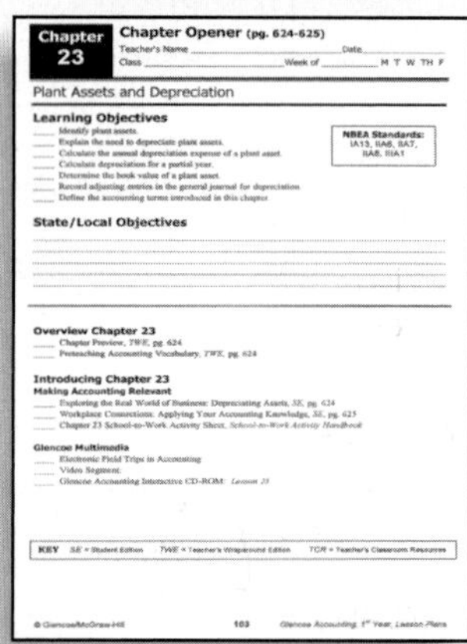

Chapter 23 Chapter Opener (pg. 624-625)

Plant Assets and Depreciation

Learning Objectives

State/Local Objectives

Overview Chapter 23

Introducing Chapter 23

Glencoe Multimedia

Block Scheduling

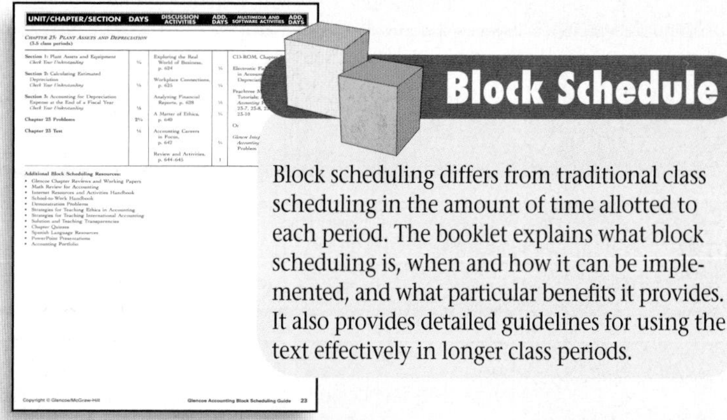

Block Schedule

Block scheduling differs from traditional class scheduling in the amount of time allotted to each period. The booklet explains what block scheduling is, when and how it can be implemented, and what particular benefits it provides. It also provides detailed guidelines for using the text effectively in longer class periods.

Enrichment and Application

Strategies for Teaching Ethics in Accounting

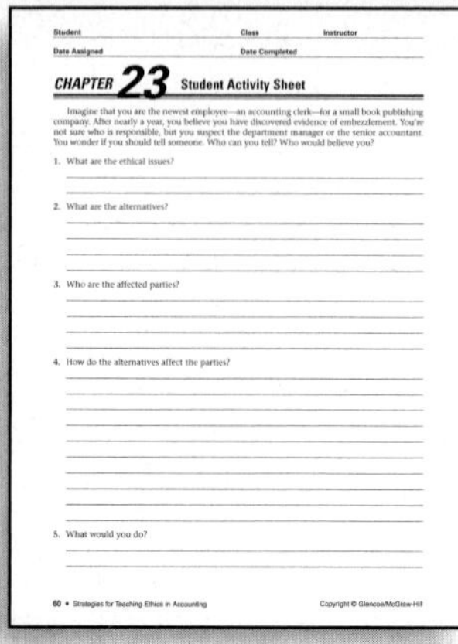

CHAPTER 23 Student Activity Sheet

1. What are the ethical issues?
2. What are the alternatives?
3. Who are the affected parties?
4. How do the alternatives affect the parties?
5. What would you do?

Strategies for Teaching International Accounting

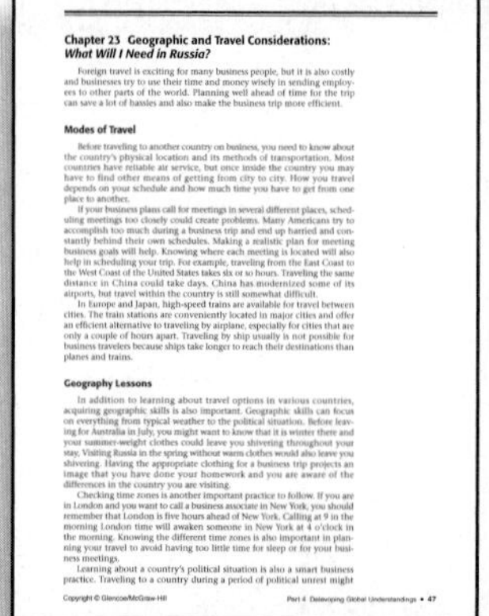

Chapter 23 Geographic and Travel Considerations: *What Will I Need in Russia?*

Modes of Travel

Geography Lessons

School-to-Work Handbook

CHAPTER 23 SCHOOL-TO-WORK ACTIVITY

Plant Assets and Depreciation

Meeting Different Ability Levels

Chapter Reviews and Working Papers (CRWP)

Working Papers

Review

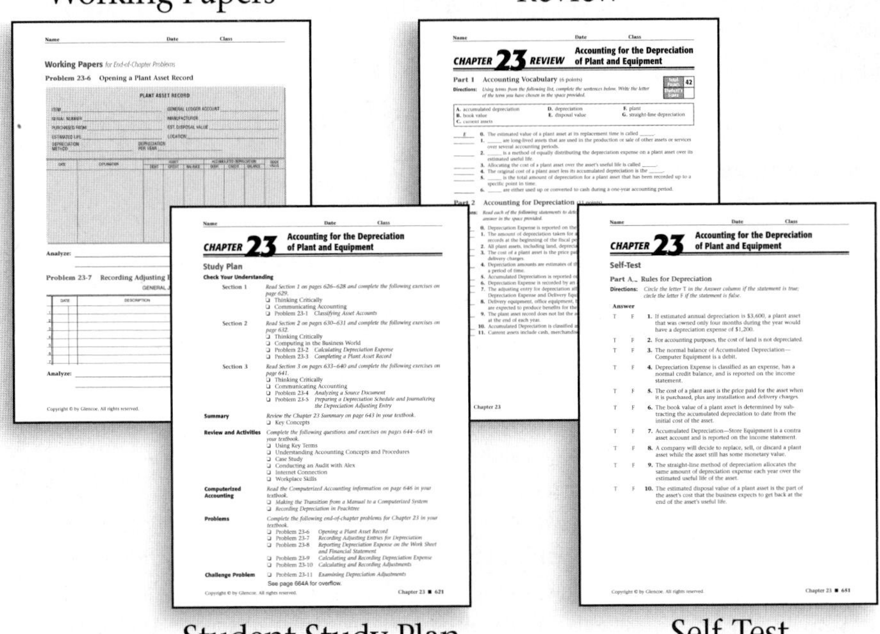
CHAPTER 23 REVIEW Accounting for the Depreciation of Plant and Equipment

CHAPTER 23 Accounting for the Depreciation of Plant and Equipment
Study Plan

CHAPTER 23 Accounting for the Depreciation of Plant and Equipment
Self-Test

Student Study Plan

Self-Test

Real-World Multimedia CD-ROM

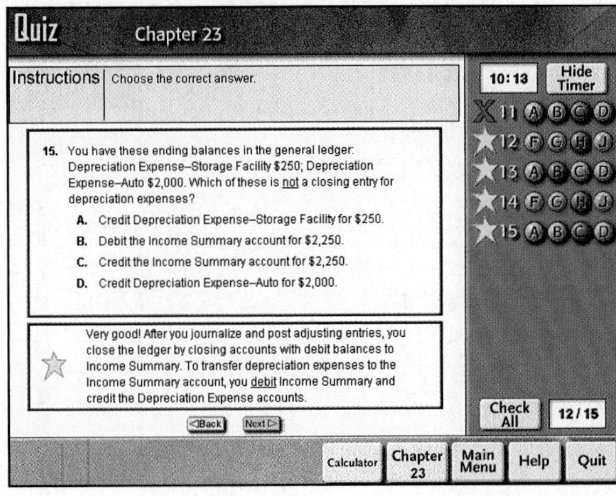

Key to Ability Levels

Each section gives skill-building activities. Each activity has been labeled for use with students of various learning styles and abilities.

L1 Level 1 activities are basic activities and should be within the range of all students.

L2 Level 2 activities are average activities and should be within the range of average and above average students.

L3 Level 3 activities are challenging activities designed for the ability range of above average students.

ELL ELL activities should be within the ability range of English Language Learners.

Teaching Resources at a Glance

Application Resources

- Glencoe Chapter Review and Working Papers, SE and TAE
- School-to-Work Handbook, SE and TM
- Accounting Portfolio, SE and TM

Reproducible Masters

- Demonstration Problems
- Lesson Plans
- Block Scheduling
- Spanish Language Resources

Glencoe Accounting Professional Development Series

- Strategies for Teaching Ethics in Accounting
- Accounting Competitive Event Review
- Math Review for Accounting
- Strategies for Teaching International Accounting
- Internet Resources and Activities Handbook

Transparency Package

- Section Focus Transparencies
- Teaching Transparencies
- Source Document Transparencies
- Solution Transparencies

Performance Assessment

- **Exam***View* CD-ROM
- Chapter Tests
- Chapter Quizzes
- Unit Tests
- Audit Tests
- Printed Testbank

Multimedia Resources

- Electronic Learning Center:
  - Multimedia CD-ROMs
  - Peachtree software, tutorials, templates, and solutions
  - Spreadsheet templates
- Using QuickBooks with Glencoe Accounting
- Interactive Lesson Planner
- Electronic Field Trips in Accounting
- PowerPoint Presentation
- Web site: glencoeaccounting.glencoe.com

Assessment and Evaluation

Chapter Tests

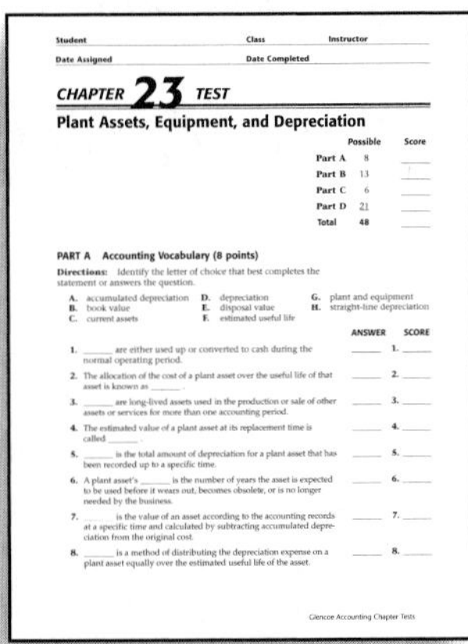
CHAPTER 23 TEST
Plant Assets, Equipment, and Depreciation

Chapter Quiz

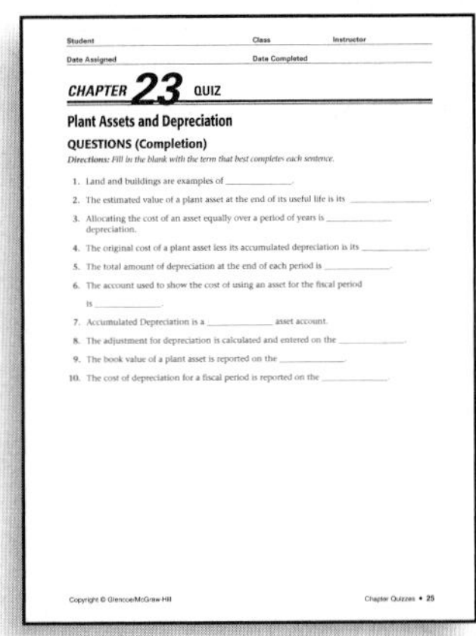
CHAPTER 23 QUIZ
Plant Assets and Depreciation

Correlations to National Standards for Business Education

(See pages T50–T51 for a detailed correlation chart.)

Standards: IA13, IIA7, IIA8, IIA9

Chapter Preview

In this chapter students will learn that certain assets provide long-term economic benefits to a business. They will learn that the cost of those assets is allocated over the life of each asset through depreciation. Students will also learn to classify assets as current or long-term assets and to calculate depreciation using the straight-line method.

Section Overviews

- Section 1—*Plant Assets and Equipment*
- Section 2—*Calculating Depreciation*
- Section 3—*Accounting for Depreciation Expense at the End of a Year*

Chapter Vocabulary

current assets
plant assets
depreciation
disposal value
straight-line depreciation
accumulated depreciation
book value

Preteaching Accounting Vocabulary

Oral Exercise: Write each new term on the chalkboard. Have students give you the meaning of each term and use it in the context of operating a business. Discuss any differences in understanding of term meanings. L1

Plant Assets and Depreciation

Learning Objectives

When you have completed this chapter, you will be able to:

- Identify plant assets.
- Explain the need to depreciate plant assets.
- Calculate annual depreciation of plant assets.
- Calculate partial-year depreciation of plant assets.
- Determine the book value of a plant asset.
- Record depreciation of plant assets.
- Prepare depreciation schedules.
- Define the accounting terms introduced in this chapter.

Exploring the Real World of Business

DEPRECIATING ASSETS

Have you ever tested your skill as a hot-shot pilot or a professional sports coach? Video games give you the chance to put yourself in many different virtual worlds.

The world's largest interactive entertainment software publisher is **Electronic Arts (EA),** located in Redwood City, California. **EA** or its wholly-owned subsidiaries have created such popular video games as Madden NFL,™ NBA Live,™ Medal of Honor,™ and Ultima Onlines.™ The games run on hardware such as the PlayStation,® Nintendo® GameCube™, and personal computers.

To create their products, **Electronic Arts** uses high-technology equipment, such as professional graphics software and computers. Video editing computers and special sound equipment are also needed. Professional level computer equipment costs thousands of dollars, and the company places each piece of equipment on a depreciation schedule. Because technology changes so quickly, the company frequently needs to upgrade its computers and software so it can remain the premier developer of software video games.

What do you think?

How do you think changes in computer technology affect the useful lives of depreciable assets such as computers?

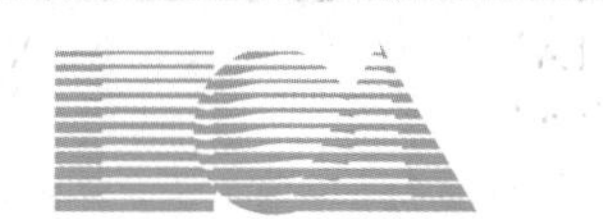

Exploring the Real World of Business

Electronic Arts

One use of Electronic Arts' high-technology equipment is to maintain its Web site (www.ea.com). Video gamers can find information about new products, software patches, help guides, "how to" documents, hardware links, and even hints for playing specific games created by the company.

What do you think? (Answers)

Answers may vary. Computers will last physically for quite a long time. They will become obsolete long before they wear out. Businesses that rely on the latest technology will depreciate their electronic equipment faster than businesses that use computers only for basic applications such as word processing and accounting.

Workplace Connections

Applying Your Accounting Knowledge

All businesses have assets. Some of those assets become less useful over time because they wear out or become out-of-date. Examples of these assets might be company trucks or computers. Other assets, such as cash or accounts receivable, are not depreciated because their value remains the same over time. You'll learn how to identify depreciable assets and how to set up depreciation schedules in this chapter.

Investigate:

1. In your workplace, are there assets that are wearing out or need to be replaced? What are they?

625

Glencoe Accounting Online

Visit the *Glencoe Accounting* Web site at **glencoeaccounting.glencoe.com** for additional activities and information.

INTRODUCING CHAPTER 23

Making Accounting Relevant

Workplace Connections: Applying Your Accounting Knowledge

Discussion: Have students discuss how assets are used to earn revenue for the business. For example, a delivery truck earns revenue for a parcel delivery service such as FedEx. Since revenue is to be matched against the expenses of producing it, part of the cost of an asset becomes an expense for each year it is used. Explain that depreciation is a way of calculating this expense.

Investigate (Answers)

1. Answers will vary depending on the types of employers. For example, a retail store might have display cases or cash register terminals that need to be upgraded. A restaurant might need new tables and chairs.

School-to-Work Activity

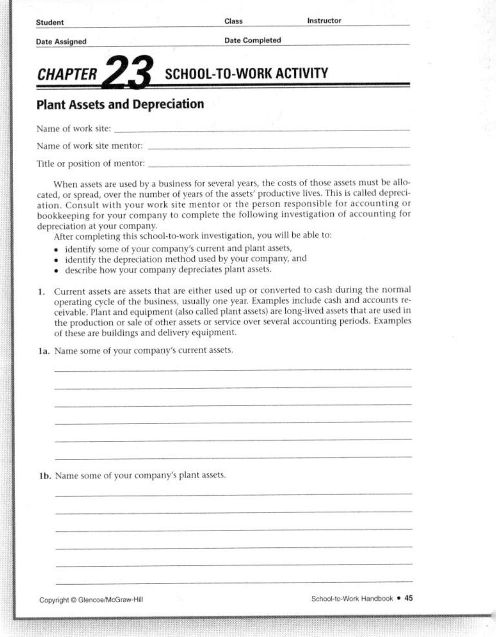

Student ______ Class ______ Instructor ______

Date Assigned ______ Date Completed ______

CHAPTER 23 SCHOOL-TO-WORK ACTIVITY

Plant Assets and Depreciation

Name of work site: ______

Name of work site mentor: ______

Title or position of mentor: ______

When assets are used by a business for several years, the costs of those assets must be allocated, or spread, over the number of years of the assets' productive lives. This is called depreciation. Consult with your work site mentor or the person responsible for accounting or bookkeeping for your company to complete the following investigation of accounting for depreciation at your company.

After completing this school-to-work investigation, you will be able to:

- identify some of your company's current and plant assets,
- identify the depreciation method used by your company, and
- describe how your company depreciates plant assets.

1. Current assets are assets that are either used up or converted to cash during the normal operating cycle of the business, usually one year. Examples include cash and accounts receivable. Plant and equipment (also called plant assets) are long-lived assets that are used in the production or sale of other assets or service over several accounting periods. Examples of these are buildings and delivery equipment.

1a. Name some of your company's current assets.

1b. Name some of your company's plant assets.

School-to-Work Handbook • 45

GLENCOE MULTIMEDIA

Electronic Field Trips in Accounting *Video Segment: Depreciation*
After viewing this video, students will be able to explain the difference between book value and market value of items that are depreciated and calculate straight-line depreciation.

Glencoe Accounting: Electronic Learning Center *Chapter 23*
The CD-ROM program is ideal for visual learners since it incorporates video images, animation, and graphics to enliven the content of each lesson.

CHAPTER 23
SECTION 1, PAGES 626–629

1 FOCUS

Introducing the Section

In this section students will learn how to identify assets as current or plant (long-term) assets. They'll also learn how to estimate useful life and allocate cost of an asset over its life.

Section Concepts

- How to identify plant assets.
- How to allocate the cost of a plant assets over its useful life.

Visual Learning

Section 1 Focus

Use **Transparency 23–1** to introduce section concepts.

BELL RINGER

Compare and Contrast: Bring in magazine or newspaper ads for a sale of new cars at the end of a model year. Ask students why a new truck or car sold at the end of a model year is worth less than at the beginning of the year. (Some students may know that the car has depreciated in value because it's considered a year old when the new models appear—even though it is just as good a car as it was a few months before.) L1

Concept Development: Current and Plant Assets

Discussion: Write a list of assets that students have learned to date on the chalkboard, asking students to tell you the names of assets. Define current and plant assets; then have students tell you which of the assets on the list fall into each category. Ask students for reasons for their choices. Stress that plant assets will be used over a number of fiscal periods to produce revenue. L1

SECTION 1

Plant Assets and Equipment

What You'll Learn

- How to identify plant assets.
- How to allocate the cost of a plant asset over its useful life.

Why It's Important

Assets, such as buildings and machinery, are used for more than one accounting period, so the cost of these assets is spread over a number of years.

KEY TERMS

current assets
plant assets
depreciation
disposal value
straight-line depreciation

Businesses own many different types of assets. One type of asset requires special treatment in the accounting records. These assets, such as office equipment and buildings, have two things in common:

- They are expected to produce benefits for the business for more than one year.
- They are purchased for use in operating the business, not for resale.

Electronic Arts owns many assets in this category, including computer, office, and delivery equipment. Let's explore how businesses account for these types of assets.

Current and Plant Assets

Throughout this textbook you have learned about various assets that are used in the operation of a business. These assets can be classified as current assets or plant assets.

Current Assets	Plant Assets
Assets that are either consumed or converted to cash during the normal operating cycle of the business, usually one year. Examples are: • cash • accounts receivable (collect cash from charge customers within a short period of time) • merchandise (sold within a short period of time)	Long-lived assets that are used in the production or sale of other assets or services over several accounting periods. Examples are: • land • buildings • delivery equipment • store equipment • office equipment

Key Points

Plant and Current Assets

Plant assets are used for more than one accounting period. Current assets are consumed or converted to cash in one accounting period.

In Chapter 18 you learned about assets such as supplies and prepaid insurance. As these assets are used, their costs are converted to expenses. This conforms to the matching principle of accounting, which states that during an accounting period expenses must be matched with the revenue earned. Since current assets are consumed during one accounting period, the costs of current assets are easily matched to the revenue for the period.

RESOURCE MANAGER

Reproducible Masters
- Lesson Plans
- Chapter Reviews and Working Papers (CRWP) TAE

Transparencies
- Section Focus Transparency
- Teaching Transparencies
- Source Document Transparencies
- Solution Transparencies

Multimedia
- ExamView CD-ROM
- Electronic Learning Center CD-ROM
- Interactive Lesson Planner CD-ROM
- Electronic Field Trips in Accounting

Plant assets, however, are used over a number of accounting periods. To follow the matching principle, the cost of a plant asset is spread, or allocated, over the periods that the asset will be used to produce revenue.

Allocating the Cost of Plant Assets

Allocating the cost of a plant asset over that asset's useful life is called **depreciation**. For accounting purposes, all plant assets are depreciated, except for land. The cost of land is not depreciated, since land is considered to have an unlimited useful life. In this chapter you will learn how to calculate and record depreciation of plant assets.

For example, suppose that a plant asset costs $40,000 and has a useful life of ten years. The cost of the asset is depreciated over ten years. A portion of the $40,000 is transferred to an expense account each year. At the end of ten years, the cost of the plant asset will have been expensed.

Estimating Depreciation of a Plant Asset

It is important to remember that depreciation is an *estimate*. No one can predict with certainty the useful life or the disposal value of an asset.

Four factors are used to calculate depreciation of plant assets:

- the cost of the plant asset
- the estimated useful life of the asset
- the estimated disposal value of the asset
- the depreciation method used

Plant Asset Cost

The cost of a plant asset is the price paid for the asset plus any sales taxes, delivery charges, and installation charges. The total cost is the amount debited to the plant asset account (for example, **Delivery Equipment**) at the time of purchase.

Estimated Useful Life of a Plant Asset

The *estimated useful life* of a plant asset is the number of years the asset is expected to be used before it wears out, becomes outdated, or is no longer needed by the business. The number of years a plant asset can be used varies from one asset to another. A delivery truck might have a useful life of six years. A building, on the other hand, might have a useful life of thirty years.

In estimating useful life, the accountant considers past experiences with the same type of asset. The Internal Revenue Service (IRS) also publishes guidelines on the estimated useful lives for many types of assets.

Estimated Disposal Value of a Plant Asset

At some point a plant asset will be replaced, sold, or discarded. Usually this occurs while the asset still has some monetary value. For example, if a business buys a new delivery truck, the old delivery truck can often be traded in to reduce the price of the new truck.

Did You Know?

Games

Creating software games can cost millions of dollars per game. As the largest game developer, Electronic Arts is well rewarded for its investments, earning over $1.5 billion a year selling electronic games.

Great Ideas *From the Classroom of...*

Calculating Depreciation Challenge students by explaining the other three methods of depreciation and the formulas for calculating each. Have students create an electronic spreadsheet to compare the calculations on a given asset. Provide the following information: the cost of the asset, estimated useful life, estimated salvage value, and estimated number of units the asset will produce. When the spreadsheet is complete, compare the different methods and discuss the reasons for choosing one method over another.

Stephen Stengel
William Floyd High School
Mastic Beach, New York

2 TEACH

GUIDED PRACTICE

Reading Accounting

- Have students skim the text to identify terms that are unfamiliar to them. Tell students to make a list of the terms and either look them up in the *Glossary* at the back of the book or in a dictionary. L1
- Have students list accounting terms and other English words that cause them difficulties. Ask a language teacher to help explain the terms to them. ELL

Visual Learning

Current and Plant Assets, p. 626

Use the illustration on this page to explain the characteristics of each type of asset.

Concept Development: Allocating the Cost of Plant Assets

Discussion: Explain the term "allocating." Give a simple example of how the cost of a $3,000 computer can be spread over a five-year period. Have students suggest ways to determine the amount to allocate each year. Ask them to justify their reasoning. L1

Concept Development: Estimating Depreciation of a Plant Asset

Discussion: Emphasize that depreciation is estimated because it is impossible to know at the time of purchase the actual useful life of the asset and its disposal value. Mention that certain guidelines are used to estimate depreciation: (1) past experience, (2) information published by the IRS, and (3) manufacturers' estimates. L1

2 TEACH (Cont'd.)

Teaching Tips

Point out that depreciation is an accounting term used to describe the allocation of cost. Depreciation does not change the actual market value of the asset. Some assets, especially buildings, appreciate in value while they are being depreciated.

Emphasize the phrase "allocating the cost," and remind students that the cost of earning revenue must be matched to that revenue each fiscal period. Discuss the phrase "expensing an asset," and point out that it means converting the cost of an asset into an expense. With depreciation, this is done over a period of years.

Straight-line depreciation is quite common because of its ease of calculation. You may want to briefly describe other methods of depreciation and point out that businesses use the method that is most beneficial for their individual situations.

Review vertical analysis and how to calculate percentages based on net sales.

The Office Depot 2001 Annual Report
Refer students to pages A-39–A-48 in the back of the book.

The estimated value of a plant asset at its replacement time is called **disposal value**. The disposal value assigned to a plant asset is an estimate that is based on previous experience. The IRS also publishes guidelines on disposal values.

Depreciation Method

There are several depreciation methods. In this course you will learn a simple, widely used depreciation method called the straight-line method. **Straight-line depreciation** equally distributes the depreciation expense over an asset's estimated useful life. Other methods of computing depreciation include units-of-production and accelerated methods.

- Units-of-production method estimates useful life measured in units of *use* rather than units of *time*.
- Accelerated depreciation methods are based on the theory that an asset loses more value in the early years of its useful life than in the later years. Two types of accelerated depreciation are the *sum-of-the-years'-digits* method and the *declining-balance* method.

ACCOUNTING TIPS

Disposal Value

Disposal value is also referred to as trade-in, salvage, scrap, or residual value.

ANALYZING FINANCIAL REPORTS

The Income Statement: Vertical Analysis

You learned about classified financial statements in earlier chapters. One reason for classifying financial statements is to make it easier to analyze the information they report. One type of analysis used is **vertical analysis.** With vertical analysis, each dollar amount on the statement is stated as a percentage of a base amount. In the case of the income statement, the base amount is net sales. Net sales is 100 percent, and all other amounts for that same year are stated as a percentage of net sales.

Look at Office Depot's Consolidated Statements of Earnings (their income statement). To complete a vertical analysis, each amount is calculated as a percentage of net sales. Here's a sample calculation showing cost of goods sold and gross profit as proportions of net sales.

Sales	$167,155	100.0%
Cost of goods sold	115,212	68.9
Gross profit	$ 51,943	31.1

Calculations:

$115,212 ÷ $167,155 = 68.9%

$51,943 ÷ $167,155 = 31.1%

Analyze the Report:

Use Office Depot's Consolidated Statements of Earnings on page A-46 to answer these questions:

1. Complete a vertical analysis of net earnings (income) to sales for the past three years as reported on the statement of earnings.
2. Explain how net income has changed in relation to net sales over the three years.

ANALYZING FINANCIAL REPORTS

Analyze the Report (Answers)

1. Net income as a percentage of sales is:
   2001 1.8% ($201,043 ÷ $11,154,081)
   2000 0.4% ($49,332 ÷ $11,569,696)
   1999 2.5% ($257,638 ÷ $10,272,060)
2. Looking at the trend, net earnings (income) as a percentage of sales increased sharply from 2000 to 2001, after a severe drop from 1999 to 2000.

SECTION 1 Check Your Understanding

Now that you have studied this section, complete the following questions and problems.

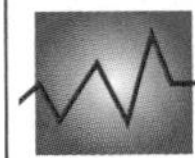

Thinking Critically

1. What is the difference between plant assets and current assets?
2. List three examples of plant assets that are depreciated. Which plant asset should not be depreciated?

Communicating Accounting

As the accounting manager for Small Tykes Playworld, you are trying to convince the owners, Barbara and Bryson Billingsley, to purchase computers for the children to use. You must explain to them that the $20,000 investment can be depreciated and that they will be able to deduct the depreciation on the tax return of the business. Select a classmate with whom you can brainstorm the four factors affecting the estimate of depreciation. Together, prepare your recommendations and practice your presentation for your next meeting with the Billingsleys.

Problem 23–1 Classifying Asset Accounts

Listed below are the assets of New England Sports Equipment Inc.

Accounts Receivable	Office Equipment
Building	Office Furniture
Cash in Bank	Petty Cash Fund
Change Fund	Prepaid Insurance
Delivery Equipment	Store Equipment
Land	Supplies
Merchandise Inventory	

Instructions In your working papers, indicate whether each asset listed is a current asset or a plant asset by placing a check mark in the correct column. The first account is completed as an example.

Asset	Current Asset	Plant Asset
Accounts Receivable	✓	

RETEACHING SECTION 1

Explaining the Straight-Line Method of Depreciation Several methods can be used to calculate the depreciation amounts for plant assets. Businesses choose a method based on the asset. The straight-line depreciation distributes the depreciation expense equally over the estimated useful life of the asset. This method assumes that depreciation of the asset depends only on the passage of time. To calculate the depreciation, you need to know the cost of the asset, its estimated useful life, and the estimated disposal value.

3 ASSESS

Thinking Critically (Answers)

1. Plant assets are used for more than one accounting period; current assets are consumed or converted to cash in one accounting period.
2. All plant assets except land are depreciated. Examples: buildings, automobiles, equipment.

Communicating Accounting (Answers)

Answers will vary. Students should address cost of the asset ($20,000), estimated useful life (3–5 years), disposal value (perhaps $500), and depreciation method used.

Problem 23–1 (Answers)

Building, plant
Cash in Bank, current
Change Fund, current
Delivery Equipment, plant
Land, plant
Merchandise Inventory, current
Office Equipment, plant
Office Furniture, plant
Petty Cash Fund, current
Prepaid Insurance, current
Store Equipment, plant
Supplies, current

Chapter Reviews and Working Papers Refer students to the Chapter 23 workbook pages to answer *Check Your Understanding* activities.

4 CLOSE

Section Wrap-Up

Writing: Have students write a paragraph explaining how to expense an asset and why it is done. L1

1 FOCUS

Introducing the Section
In this section students will learn how to calculate straight-line depreciation. They'll also learn how to determine the amount to be depreciated and to calculate book value.

Section Concepts
- How to calculate the annual depreciation of a plant asset.
- How to calculate depreciation for a partial year.
- How to determine the book value of a plant asset.

Visual Learning

Section 2 Focus

Use **Transparency 23–2** to introduce section concepts.

BELL RINGER

Analyzing: Have students make a list of the plant assets in your classroom (such as tables, chairs, desks, computers, calculators). Then ask students to think about the useful life of each item. Will computers last as long as desks? Have students decide how long to depreciate each item. L1

Concept Development: Calculating Depreciation
Discussion: Explain and illustrate how estimated annual depreciation is calculated using the example in the textbook. You may want to review the recording of a transaction for the purchase of the delivery equipment. L1

Demonstration Problem
Step-by-Step Practice
Use demonstration problem 23–1 to give students practice in calculating estimated depreciation.

SECTION 2

Calculating Depreciation

What You'll Learn
- How to calculate the annual depreciation of a plant asset.
- How to calculate depreciation for a partial year.
- How to determine the book value of a plant asset.

Why It's Important
Businesses must maintain accurate records of each plant asset and its related depreciation.

KEY TERMS
accumulated depreciation
book value

When an asset is used by a business over a period of several years, depreciation is calculated. Depreciation allocates the cost of the asset over the asset's useful life. This results in the cost of the asset being matched against revenue that the asset generates. In this section you will learn how to calculate depreciation.

Calculating Depreciation

On Your Mark Athletic Wear purchased a delivery truck on January 5 for $16,500 cash. The truck has an estimated disposal value of $1,500 and an estimated useful life of five years. The purchase of the truck is recorded in On Your Mark's general journal as follows:

GENERAL JOURNAL — PAGE 2

	DATE		DESCRIPTION	POST. REF.	DEBIT	CREDIT	
1	20--						1
2	Jan.	5	Delivery Equipment		16 500 00		2
3			Cash in Bank			16 500 00	3
4			Check 2205				4

To calculate depreciation, you need to know the cost of the truck, the estimated useful life, and the estimated disposal value.

First calculate the amount to be depreciated:

Original Cost	−	Estimated Disposal Value	=	Amount to be Depreciated
$16,500	−	$1,500	=	$15,000

The estimated disposal value represents the part of the asset's cost that the business expects to recover. Therefore, the estimated disposal value should not be treated as an expense.

Next calculate the annual depreciation expense using the straight-line method:

Amount to be Depreciated	÷	Estimated Useful Life	=	Annual Depreciation Expense
$15,000	÷	5	=	$3,000

The annual depreciation expense for the delivery truck is $3,000.

ACCOUNTING Flashbacks

MONEY SYSTEMS
In the late 600s BC, the Mediterranean city-state of Lydia was the first to set prices and develop a money system using coins—a departure from the existing barter system.

RESOURCE MANAGER

Reproducible Masters
- Lesson Plans
- Chapter Reviews and Working Papers (CRWP) TAE
- Demonstration Problems

Transparencies
- Section Focus Transparency
- Teaching Transparencies
- Source Document Transparencies
- Solution Transparencies

Multimedia
- ExamView CD-ROM
- Electronic Learning Center CD-ROM
- Interactive Lesson Planner CD-ROM
- Electronic Field Trips in Accounting

Calculating Depreciation Expense for Part of a Year

The $3,000 depreciation expense is for a full year. Suppose that On Your Mark purchased the delivery truck on April 5 instead of January 5. During the first year, the delivery truck will be used for only nine months. Therefore, the depreciation expense is calculated for nine months.

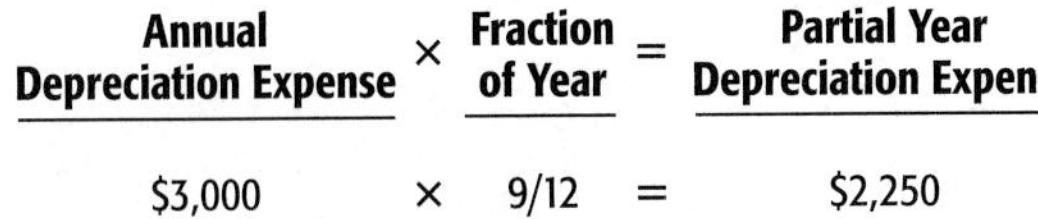

Annual Depreciation Expense	×	Fraction of Year	=	Partial Year Depreciation Expense
$3,000	×	9/12	=	$2,250

Plant Asset Records

Businesses maintain records for each plant asset and the depreciation taken for that asset. As you can see in **Figure 23–1**, this record provides detailed information about the delivery truck, including:

1. the date of purchase
2. the original cost
3. the estimated useful life
4. annual depreciation
5. accumulated depreciation
6. book value at the end of each year

Use the lower part of the plant asset record to prepare the depreciation schedule. The amount of depreciation expense accumulates from one year to the next. **Accumulated depreciation** is the total amount of depreciation for a plant asset that has been recorded up to a specific point in time. The accumulated depreciation at the end of the third year is $9,000.

The far right column of the depreciation schedule shows the **book value** of the plant asset, the original cost less accumulated depreciation.

At the end of the third year, the book value of the delivery truck is $7,500 ($16,500 − $9,000). Notice that the book value of the delivery truck at the end of five years is $1,500. This is the truck's estimated disposal value. Under the straight-line method, the truck is not depreciated below its estimated disposal value.

ACCOUNTING TIPS

Book Value

Book value = Original cost − Accumulated depreciation

Key Points

Cost Allocation

After a plant asset is purchased, its cost is allocated over its estimated useful life.

PLANT ASSET RECORD

ITEM Delivery Truck — GENERAL LEDGER ACCOUNT Delivery Equipment
SERIAL NUMBER 2911-50041 — MANUFACTURER VanPower
PURCHASED FROM Winding Creek Auto — EST. DISPOSAL VALUE $1,500.00
ESTIMATED LIFE 5 years 3 — LOCATION Company Garage
DEPRECIATION METHOD Straight-line — DEPRECIATION PER YEAR $3,000.00 4

DATE	EXPLANATION	ASSET			ACCUMULATED DEPRECIATION 5			BOOK VALUE
		DEBIT	CREDIT	BALANCE	DEBIT	CREDIT	BALANCE	
1 1/5/2004	Purchased	16,500 2		16,500				6 16,500
12/31/2004						3,000	3,000	13,500
12/31/2005						3,000	6,000	10,500
12/31/2006						3,000	9,000	7,500
12/31/2007						3,000	12,000	4,500
12/31/2008						3,000	15,000	1,500

Figure 23–1
Plant Asset Record

COOPERATIVE LEARNING ACTIVITY

Pairs Check Ask students to use the straight-line method to calculate the annual depreciation on the following plant assets. When students have completed the calculations, they should compare their answers with those of a partner. If any answers differ, the pairs should work together to find the correct answer.

1. Copy machine: original cost, $22,100; disposal value, $4,500; useful life, 4 years.
2. Delivery van: original cost, $18,500; disposal value, $7,000; useful life, 5 years.
3. Fork lift: original cost, $25,900; disposal value, $10,900; useful life, 8 years.

(Copy machine, $4,400; delivery van, $2,300, fork lift, $1,875)

2 TEACH

GUIDED PRACTICE

Reading Accounting

- Have students read the depreciation equations and study the relationship of each item to the calculation of depreciation expense. L1

Concept Development: Calculating Depreciation Expense for Part of a Year

Discussion: Describe a plant asset that requires a partial year's calculation (a delivery truck purchased in April rather than January). Explain the formula for a partial year. L1

Demonstration Problem Step-by-Step Practice

Use demonstration problem 23–2 to give students practice in calculating depreciation for a partial year.

Concept Development: Plant Asset Records

Discussion: Explain the information on the plant asset record and why the record is kept. Point out that a new entry is made on the record for each year of the asset's life. Explain how to calculate accumulated depreciation. L1

Visual Learning

Figure 23–1 Plant Asset Record

Use **Transparency 23–3** to discuss the information on this form.

Thinking Algebraically

Conceptualize: Have students write an equation expressing the calculation for depreciation. (Example: annual depreciation = (a − b) ÷ x) L2

3 ASSESS

Thinking Critically (Answers)

1. Amount to be depreciated is divided by the number of years of the asset's estimated useful life.
2. Date of purchase, original cost, estimated useful life, annual depreciation, accumulated depreciation, and book value at end of each year.

Computing in the Business World (Answer)

Annual depreciation expense = $10,125

Problem 23–2 (Answers)

Cash register $420, $60, $40
Computer $5,000, $1,000, $166.66
Conference table $1,800, $72, $36
Del. truck $30,000, $6,000, $1,500
Desk $2,880, $144, $132

Problem 23–3 (Answers)

Book Value:
10/1/2001, $12,500
12/31/2001, $11,960
12/31/2002, $9,800
12/31/2003, $7,640
12/31/2004, $5,480
12/31/2005, $3,320
09/31/2006, $1,700

Chapter Reviews and Working Papers Refer students to the Chapter 23 workbook pages to answer *Check Your Understanding* activities.

4 CLOSE

Section Wrap-Up

Writing: Have students write a paragraph explaining how to calculate depreciation using the straight-line method. L1

SECTION 2 Check Your Understanding

Now that you have studied this section, complete the following questions and problems.

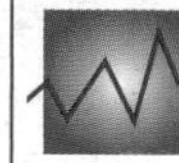

Thinking Critically

1. When using the straight-line method, how is the annual depreciation expense calculated?
2. What type of information does the plant asset record contain?

Computing in the Business World

Office furniture for Teen Counseling Center is estimated at a total value of $45,000 with a 10 percent disposal value. The estimated useful life is four years. Calculate the annual depreciation expense for the office furniture.

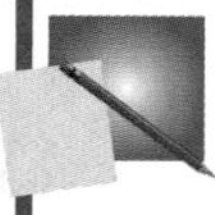

Problem 23–2 Calculating Depreciation Expense

Instructions

For each of the following plant assets:
(1) calculate the amount to be depreciated,
(2) calculate the annual depreciation expense,
(3) calculate the depreciation expense for the first year.

Use the form provided in your working papers.

	Plant Asset	Months Owned First Year	Original Cost	Estimated Disposal Value	Estimated Useful Life
1.	Cash register	8	$ 450	$ 30	7 years
2.	Computer	2	6,500	1,500	5 years
3.	Conference table	6	1,900	100	25 years
4.	Delivery truck	3	36,400	6,400	5 years
5.	Desk	11	3,180	300	20 years

Problem 23–3 Completing a Plant Asset Record

Use the following information to complete the blank asset record found in your working papers. The company uses the straight-line method for depreciating all plant assets. Item Purchased: Xerox Copier - Serial No. X42599757, $12,500, from K&C Office Equipment.

Purchased: 10/1/2001
Estimated Life: 5 years
Location: Executive Offices
Estimated Disposal Value: $1,700

RETEACHING SECTION 2

Calculating Depreciation To review the steps for calculating depreciation expense for part of a fiscal year, provide the following scenario: A business purchased and installed a new $3,400 computer on August 10. The computer has an estimated useful life of three years and no disposal value. Guide students through the following steps: (1) Review the formula to calculate depreciation for a full year. (2) Stress that the depreciation must be calculated for the number of months the plant asset is owned during the fiscal year. (3) Develop a formula for the partial year. (4) Ask students to calculate the depreciation. (5) Have students prepare a depreciation schedule.

Accounting for Depreciation Expense at the End of a Year

After depreciation on plant assets is calculated, adjustments are made to record depreciation for the period. These adjustments bring the general ledger in agreement with the plant asset records.

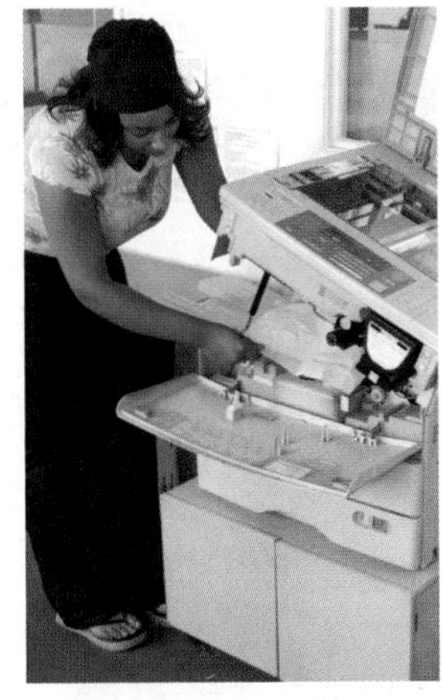

Adjusting for Depreciation Expense

When a plant asset is purchased, the accountant sets up a depreciation schedule for the asset, like the one shown in **Figure 23–1.** The amount of depreciation expense for each plant asset is recorded in the accounting records at the end of the year. The information to record the adjustments for depreciation comes from the plant asset records.

Many businesses prepare a summary of depreciation for each type of plant asset. For example, a business may have ten delivery trucks. Each truck has its own plant asset record. At the end of the year, the depreciation expense for all ten trucks is totaled. This total is entered on a summary form under the name of the asset account, in this case, **Delivery Equipment. Figure 23–2** shows On Your Mark's depreciation summary form for its plant assets.

As you can see, On Your Mark's total depreciation expense for the year is $33,000. This amount includes the depreciation expense for all of the plant assets. The accumulated depreciation for all of On Your Mark's plant assets is $100,250.

What You'll Learn

- How to record adjusting entries in the general journal for depreciation.
- How to record depreciation adjustments on a work sheet.
- How to report **Depreciation Expense** and **Accumulated Depreciation** on financial statements.

Why It's Important

Adjustments are made to record depreciation. This allows businesses to present up-to-date financial information about plant assets.

2004 SUMMARY OF DEPRECIATION EXPENSE
December 31, 2004

Asset	Cost	Depreciation Expense	Depreciation to Date
Building	50,000	2,500	8,125
Delivery Equipment	16,500	3,000	9,000
Office Equipment	50,000	2,500	8,125
Store Equipment	250,000	25,000	75,000
Totals	366,500	33,000	100,250

Figure 23–2 Depreciation Summary Form

RESOURCE MANAGER

Reproducible Masters
- Lesson Plans
- Chapter Reviews and Working Papers (CRWP) TAE
- Demonstration Problems

Transparencies
- Section Focus Transparency
- Teaching Transparencies
- Source Document Transparencies
- Solution Transparencies

Multimedia
- ExamView CD-ROM
- Electronic Learning Center CD-ROM
- Interactive Lesson Planner CD-ROM
- Electronic Field Trips in Accounting

1 FOCUS

Introducing the Section

Now that students have learned how to calculate depreciation, they're ready to learn how to record depreciation expense in the accounting records.

Section Concepts
- How to record adjusting entries in the general journal for depreciation.
- How to record depreciation adjustments on a work sheet.
- How to report Depreciation Expense and Accumulated Depreciation on financial statements.

Visual Learning

Section 3 Focus

Use **Transparency 23–4** to introduce section concepts.

BELL RINGER

Compare and Contrast: Ask students to think back to the adjusting entries for accounts such as supplies or merchandise. How are the plant asset and accumulated depreciation accounts similar at the end of the fiscal period? (All need balances brought up to date.) Ask students what they would do to adjust the depreciation accounts. L1

Visual Learning

Figure 23–2 Depreciation Summary Form

Use **Transparency 23–5** to call students' attention to the summary of estimated depreciation expense. Point out that "Depreciation to Date" is the same as accumulated depreciation.

CHAPTER 23
SECTION 3, PAGES 633–641

2 TEACH
GUIDED PRACTICE

Reading Accounting

- Have students look at each illustration and read the related text describing the content of the illustration. Ask students to note how the text explains the information in the illustration. L1

Concept Development: Adjusting for Depreciation Expense

Discussion: Point out to students that plant asset records are used to determine depreciation for a fiscal year. Like other expenses of the business, depreciation is reported on the financial statements.

Note that the total cost of the plant assets, as recorded in the general ledger, must agree with the total value of plant assets on the depreciation summary form. This agreement is one proof that the accountant is recording all the depreciation for the fiscal year.

Mention that a credit to a plant asset account, such as Delivery Equipment, signals that the asset was sold, traded in, or discarded. L1

Teaching Tip

As a reinforcement activity, have students prepare a depreciation schedule for the computer in Problem 23–2 on page 632. The schedule should cover 6 years.

Math Review for Accounting Photocopy appropriate *Activity Sheets* for students who need additional practice in basic math skills.

Combining Math Functions

When combining mathematical functions, such as calculating and adding sales tax to a sale amount, \$184.00 + (\$184.00 × 0.05):

- start with the multiplication first (184 × 0.05),
- then add (184).

The adjustment for depreciation affects two accounts: **Depreciation Expense** and **Accumulated Depreciation.**

Depreciation Expense

Depreciation Expense is an expense account. During the year the account has a zero balance because the adjustment for depreciation is recorded at the end of the period. **Depreciation Expense** is reported on the income statement. At the end of the year, **Depreciation Expense** is closed to **Income Summary.**

There is a depreciation expense account for each type of plant asset. Some examples are:

- **Depreciation Expense—Delivery Equipment** (trucks, vans, automobiles)
- **Depreciation Expense—Office Furniture** (desks, chairs, filing cabinets)

Accumulated Depreciation

The balance of **Accumulated Depreciation** represents the total amount of depreciation expensed since the asset was purchased. There is an accumulated depreciation account for each type of plant asset. Typical account names are:

- **Accumulated Depreciation—Delivery Equipment**
- **Accumulated Depreciation—Building**

Accumulated Depreciation is classified as a contra asset account. The balance of a contra account reduces the balance of its related account. In the case of an accumulated depreciation account, the related account is a plant asset account. For example, if the asset account is **Delivery Equipment,** the contra asset account is **Accumulated Depreciation—Delivery Equipment**.

Accumulated Depreciation	
Debit – Decrease Side	Credit + Increase Side Normal Balance Side

Key Points

Normal Balances

The normal balance of an asset account, such as **Store Equipment**, is a debit. The normal balance of a contra asset account, such as **Accumulated Depreciation—Store Equipment,** is a credit.

The rules of debit and credit for an accumulated depreciation account are opposite those for an asset account. The balance of an accumulated depreciation account is reported on the balance sheet as a decrease to its related plant asset account.

Account Name

Asset	Expense	Contra Asset
Del. Equip.	Depr. Exp.—Del. Equip.	Accum. Depr.—Del. Equip.
Office Equip.	Depr. Exp.—Office Equip.	Accum. Depr.—Office Equip.
Store Equip.	Depr. Exp.—Store Equip.	Accum. Depr.—Store Equip.

Math Skill Builder Activity

Combining Math Functions Have students practice combining math functions while using the calculator with this exercise. At the back-to-school sale, students wanted to purchase three pairs of jeans that were priced at \$25 a pair. The sales tax in the state is 6% (or substitute your state's sales tax percentage). How much will students pay in taxes? What is the total amount of the purchase? (Tax, \$4.50; total purchase, \$79.50)

Preparing the Adjustment for Depreciation Expense

Let's learn how to record depreciation of plant assets. Look at On Your Mark's depreciation schedule in **Figure 23–1** on page 631. The annual depreciation expense for the delivery truck is $3,000.

Adjustment

On December 31 the accounting clerk for On Your Mark records the depreciation for the delivery truck.

ANALYSIS

Identify 1. The accounts affected are **Depreciation Expense—Delivery Equipment** and **Accumulated Depreciation—Delivery Equipment.**

Classify 2. **Depreciation Expense—Delivery Equipment** is an expense account. **Accumulated Depreciation—Delivery Equipment** is a contra asset account.

+/− 3. Both **Depreciation Expense—Delivery Equipment** and **Accumulated Depreciation—Delivery Equipment** are increased by $3,000.

DEBIT-CREDIT RULE

4. Increases to expense accounts are recorded as debits. Debit **Depreciation Expense—Delivery Equipment** for $3,000.
5. Increases to contra asset accounts are recorded as credits. Credit **Accumulated Depreciation—Delivery Equipment** for $3,000.

T ACCOUNTS

6.

Depreciation Expense—Delivery Equipment	
Debit +	Credit −
3,000	

Accumulated Depreciation—Delivery Equipment	
Debit −	Credit +
	3,000

Similar adjustments are made to record depreciation for other plant assets, such as buildings and office equipment.

Analyzing the Accumulated Depreciation Account

Suppose this is the end of the third year of the estimated useful life of On Your Mark's delivery truck. For each year the same adjustment was made to record the depreciation of the delivery truck:

- a debit to **Depreciation Expense—Delivery Equipment**
- a credit to **Accumulated Depreciation—Delivery Equipment.**

2 TEACH (Cont'd.)

Visual Learning

Adjustment

Use **Transparency** 23–6 to guide students through the analysis of the entry to record depreciation.

Teaching Tips

Some businesses may estimate depreciation and make a monthly entry. An adjustment is made at the end of the year to reflect actual depreciation.

Remind students that accumulated depreciation of all plant assets should agree with balances in the general ledger. Such agreement proves that depreciation expense has been recorded for each plant asset.

Research: Have students interview local business owners and managers to learn the types of assets their businesses depreciate. Ask students to share their findings in class. L1

Chapter Review and Working Papers

Refer students to the *Study Plan* located at the beginning of Chapter 23 in the workbook.

REINFORCING STUDY SKILLS

Test-Taking Strategy Students who do well on tests not only know the material they have studied but also know how to take tests. Point out that different types of test questions—multiple choice, true-false, and essay questions—require different strategies and ways of thinking. Some students may need specific practice with test questions.

2 TEACH (Cont'd.)

Visual Learning

Figure 23–3 Work Sheet with Depreciation Adjustments

Using **Transparency 23–7**, trace the parts of the adjustment for depreciation expense for the fiscal year. Point out the amounts extended to the Balance Sheet and Income Statement columns. Remind students that Accumulated Depreciation is a contra asset account, so its balance is extended to the Balance Sheet section. Depreciation Expense is a temporary account, so its balance is extended to the Income Statement section.

Teaching Tips

Point out that after the adjusting entry for depreciation is analyzed, the adjustments for depreciation are written in the Adjustments section of the work sheet. Remind students that the purpose of an adjusting entry is to bring account balances up to date prior to reporting them on the financial statements.

Call attention to the T account for Accumulated Depreciation—Delivery Equipment. Point out that the $9,000 balance represents the total amount of the cost expensed to date.

Strategies for Teaching International Accounting

To enrich study of international accounting, refer to the additional critical thinking activities in the booklet.

On Your Mark
Work
For the Year Ended

	ACCT. NO.	ACCOUNT NAME	TRIAL BALANCE DEBIT	TRIAL BALANCE CREDIT	ADJUSTMENTS DEBIT	ADJUSTMENTS CREDIT
8	140	Delivery Equipment	16 500 00			
9	142	Accum. Depr.—Delivery Equip.		6 000 00		(e) 3 000 00
10	145	Office Equipment	50 000 00			
11	147	Accum. Depr.—Office Equipment		5 625 00		(f) 2 500 00
23	615	Depr. Expense—Delivery Equip.	—		(e) 3 000 00	
24	620	Depr. Expense—Office Equip.	—		(f) 2 500 00	
25						

Figure 23–3 Work Sheet with Depreciation Adjustments

After the books are closed each year, the **Depreciation Expense—Delivery Equipment** account has a zero balance. (Remember that expense accounts are closed at the end of each year.) In contrast, the **Accumulated Depreciation—Delivery Equipment** account shows the total amount of depreciation expensed since the asset was purchased. At the end of the third year, the total is $9,000.

Accumulated Depreciation—
Delivery Equipment

Debit	Credit	
–	+	
	3,000	(first year depreciation)
	3,000	(second year depreciation)
	3,000	(third year depreciation)
	Bal. 9,000	

International ACCOUNTING

Dating Documents

When dating documents for international use, writing out the month can eliminate confusion or misinterpretation. For example, in the U.S., the month is followed by the day and year: November 1, 2005, or 11/1/05. In other countries, the day is often followed by the month and then the year: 1 November 2005 or 1/11/05.

Recording Depreciation Adjustments on a Work Sheet

After the adjustment for depreciation is prepared, it is entered in the Adjustments section of the work sheet.

Refer to **Figure 23–3.** Locate the accumulated depreciation accounts in the Trial Balance Credit column ($6,000 and $5,625). Notice that the depreciation expense accounts do not have balances in the Trial Balance section. Adjustments (e) and (f) are entered in the Adjustments section to show the depreciation adjustments for the year. Note that the depreciation expense accounts are debited and the accumulated depreciation accounts are credited. Also note that no adjustments are made to the asset accounts.

Each amount is extended to the other work sheet columns.

	Column Extended to	
Account	**Adjusted Trial Balance**	**Financial Statement**
Del. Equip.	Debit (unchanged)	Balance Sheet
Accum. Depr.—Del. Equip.	Credit (increased)	Balance Sheet
Office Equip.	Debit (unchanged)	Balance Sheet
Accum. Depr.—Office Equip.	Credit (increased)	Balance Sheet
Depr. Exp.—Del. Equip.	Debit (increased)	Income Statement
Depr. Exp.—Office Equip.	Debit (increased)	Income Statement

Teaching International ACCOUNTING

Dating Documents Gather examples of documents using a variety of date formats. Ask students to bring in additional examples of documents. Display all the documents for students to review. Ask the students to convert the date(s) on each document to the U.S. format. Compare answers and follow up with a group discussion. Ask students to comment on which format they prefer, and have them explain why they prefer that format.

Athletic Wear
Sheet
December 31, 20--

	ADJUSTED TRIAL BALANCE		INCOME STATEMENT		BALANCE SHEET	
	DEBIT	CREDIT	DEBIT	CREDIT	DEBIT	CREDIT
8	16,500.00				16,500.00	
9		9,000.00				9,000.00
10	50,000.00				50,000.00	
11		8,125.00				8,125.00
23	3,000.00		3,000.00			
24	2,500.00		2,500.00			
25						

Figure 23–3 Work Sheet with Depreciation Adjustments (cont.)

Reporting Depreciation Expense and Accumulated Depreciation on Financial Statements

Figure 23–4 shows placement of the depreciation expense accounts on the partial income statement of On Your Mark.

On Your Mark Athletic Wear
Income Statement
For the Year Ended December 31, 20--

Operating Expenses				
Depreciation Expense—Delivery Equip.			3,000 00	
Depreciation Expense—Office Equip.			2,500 00	
Total Operating Expenses				94,351 00
Operating Income				51,342 00

Figure 23–4 Income Statement

CONNECT TO . . . ENGLISH

In Accounting, *capital* refers to money used to start up or grow a new business. The term comes from the Latin word for head–*caput.* In ancient times, nomadic herdsmen measured their wealth by the number of animals they had, a number reached by counting heads.

Figure 23–5 shows placement of the plant asset and related accumulated depreciation accounts. Both types of accounts appear in the Assets section of the balance sheet. Notice that the accumulated depreciation account is listed immediately below the related plant asset account.

For **Delivery Equipment:**

- The original cost is entered in the first amount column ($16,500).
- The accumulated depreciation is entered in the first amount column ($9,000).
- The difference between cost and accumulated depreciation is entered in the second amount column ($7,500).

INTERDISCIPLINARY CONNECTIONS ACTIVITY

English Have students explore the origins of common words used in the financial industry. For example, you could have students locate a definition or word origin for such terms as: *barter, dollar, cents, tax*. Once students have located this information, ask them to write sentences highlighting the terms and using them correctly. Encourage students to add to the word list with terms or expressions they hear most often.

2 TEACH (Cont'd.)

Concept Development: Reporting Depreciation Expense and Accumulated Depreciation on Financial Statements

Discussion: Emphasize to students that Depreciation Expense represents the portion of an asset that has become an expense during a fiscal period. That expense account is thus reported on the income statement. Accumulated Depreciation is a contra asset account, which means its balance represents a reduction in assets. The balances of all accumulated depreciation accounts are reported on the balance sheet to show the changes in assets during the fiscal period. L1

Visual Learning

Figure 23–4 Income Statement

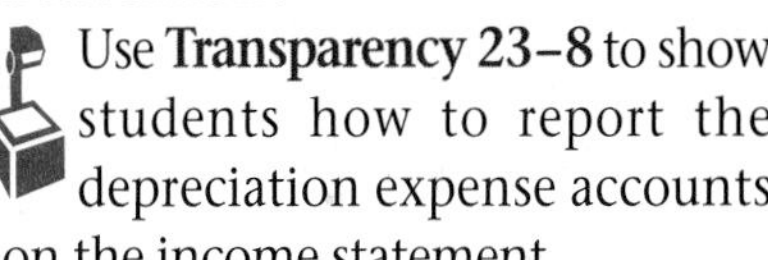

Use **Transparency 23–8** to show students how to report the depreciation expense accounts on the income statement.

Demonstration Problem Step-by-Step Practice

Use demonstration problem 23–3 to give students practice calculating and entering depreciation adjustments on the work sheet.

Critical Thinking: Point out the adjustments for depreciation expense in Figure 23–3. Ask students why the depreciation expense accounts had no balance prior to the adjustments. (The accounts were closed in the previous period and this period's depreciation is yet to be recorded when the trial balance is prepared.) L1

2 TEACH (Cont'd.)

Visual Learning

Figure 23–5 Balance Sheet
Use **Transparency 23–9** to show students how to report accumulated depreciation balances on the balance sheet.

Teaching Tip
Point out how the balance of the accumulated depreciation account reduces the balance of its related asset account on the balance sheet. Subtracting the accumulated depreciation from the asset account balance results in the book value of asset.

Concept Development: Journalizing Adjusting Entries for Depreciation Expense
Discussion: Review why data in the Adjustments columns of the work sheet must be journalized. Remind students that the work sheet is a working document, not a record of accounting entries. To update the account balances that are affected by adjustments, journal entries must be recorded and posted. L1

Demonstration Problem Step-by-Step Practice
Use demonstration problem 23–4 to give students practice in reporting the depreciation accounts on the income statement and balance sheet.

Figure 23–5
Balance Sheet

On Your Mark Athletic Wear Balance Sheet December 31, 20--			
Assets			
Delivery Equipment		16 500 00	
Less: Accum. Depr.—Delivery Equip.		9 000 00	7 500 00
Office Equipment		50 000 00	
Less: Accum. Depr.—Office Equip.		8 125 00	41 875 00

The $7,500 is the book value of the delivery equipment. The book value of each plant asset reported on the balance sheet should be the same as that shown on the plant asset record.

Journalizing Adjusting Entries for Depreciation Expense

After the work sheet is completed and the financial statements are prepared, adjustments for depreciation expense are recorded in the general journal. The information for the journal entries is taken directly from the Adjustments section of the work sheet.

Adjustment

Record the December 31 adjusting journal entries for depreciation.

ANALYSIS

Identify 1. The accounts affected are **Depreciation Expense—Delivery Equipment, Depreciation Expense—Office Equipment, Accumulated Depreciation—Delivery Equipment**, and **Accumulated Depreciation—Office Equipment.**

Classify 2. **Depreciation Expense—Delivery Equipment** and **Depreciation Expense—Office Equipment** are expense accounts. **Accumulated Depreciation—Delivery Equipment** and **Accumulated Depreciation—Office Equipment** are contra asset accounts.

+/− 3. **Depreciation Expense—Delivery Equipment** is increased by $3,000. **Depreciation Expense—Office Equipment** is increased by $2,500. **Accumulated Depreciation—Delivery Equipment** is increased by $3,000. **Accumulated Depreciation—Office Equipment** is increased by $2,500.

DEBIT-CREDIT RULE

4. Increases in expense accounts are recorded as debits. Debit **Depreciation Expense—Delivery Equipment** for $3,000 and **Depreciation Expense—Office Equipment** for $2,500.
5. Increases in contra asset accounts are recorded as credits. Credit **Accumulated Depreciation—Delivery Equipment** for $3,000 and **Accumulated Depreciation—Office Equipment** for $2,500.

MEETING SPECIAL NEEDS

Students with Orthopaedic Impairments Students with orthopaedic impairments should be made to feel that they are a part of all class activities. Include these students in field work (interviews, surveys, etc.) and field trips. If students cannot participate, involve them in preliminary planning—choosing the site for a field trip or planning an itinerary—or provide an alternate, related activity.

T ACCOUNTS

6.

Depreciation Expense— Delivery Equipment		Accumulated Depreciation— Delivery Equipment	
Debit + 3,000	Credit −	Debit −	Credit + 3,000

Depreciation Expense— Office Equipment		Accumulated Depreciation— Office Equipment	
Debit + 2,500	Credit −	Debit −	Credit + 2,500

JOURNAL ENTRY

7.

GENERAL JOURNAL — PAGE 21

	DATE		DESCRIPTION	POST. REF.	DEBIT	CREDIT	
1	20--						1
2	Dec.	31	Depr. Exp.—Del. Equip.		3 000 00		2
3			Accum. Depr.—Del. Equip.			3 000 00	3
4		31	Depr. Exp.—Office Equip.		2 500 00		4
5			Accum. Depr.—Office Equip.			2 500 00	5
6							6

Journalizing Closing Entries for Depreciation Expense

After adjusting entries are journalized and posted, the next step in the accounting cycle is to close the ledger. In the second closing entry, you'll remember, accounts with debit balances in the Income Statement Debit column of the work sheet are closed to **Income Summary.** This closing entry includes the depreciation expense accounts.

When this closing entry is posted to the general ledger, the balances of the depreciation expense accounts are reduced to zero.

Closing

Second Closing Entry—Depreciation accounts only.

ANALYSIS

Identify 1. The accounts affected are **Depreciation Expense—Delivery Equipment, Depreciation Expense—Office Equipment,** and **Income Summary.**

Classify 2. **Depreciation Expense—Delivery Equipment** and **Depreciation Expense—Office Equipment** are expense accounts. **Income Summary** is a temporary capital account.

+/− 3. **Depreciation Expense—Delivery Equipment** is decreased by $3,000 and **Depreciation Expense—Office Equipment** is decreased by $2,500; the total decrease is $5,500. The $5,500 is transferred to the **Income Summary** account.

2 TEACH (Cont'd.)

Visual Learning

Adjustment

Use **Transparency 23–10** to guide students through the analysis of the journal entry to record depreciation expense.

Concept Development: Journalizing Closing Entries for Depreciation Expense

Discussion: Review the closing process with students, and point out that Depreciation Expense is closed at the end of the fiscal period with the other expense accounts. Remind students that since expense accounts have debit balances, they are closed with credits. L1

Demonstration Problem Step-by-Step Practice

Use demonstration problem 23–5 to give students practice in journalizing adjusting entries for depreciation.

CRITICAL THINKING ACTIVITY

Analyzing Information Ask students to identify which of the following assets are classified as plant and equipment assets: building, cash, computer, copy machine, fax machine, merchandise inventory, office furniture, land, supplies. After classifying the assets, have them decide which are depreciated and which are not. (Plant assets include the building, computer, copy machine, fax machine, and land. Only the land is not depreciated.)

2 TEACH (Cont'd.)

Visual Learning

Closing

Use **Transparency 23–11** to guide students through the analysis and recording of the entry to close the depreciation expense accounts.

Teaching Tip

Remind students that when the closing entries are posted to the general ledger, the Depreciation Expense accounts will have zero balances and will be ready to record depreciation expense for the next fiscal period.

GO TO Strategies for Teaching Ethics in Accounting

Photocopy the Chapter 23 *Student Activity Sheet* for students. Answers are also provided in the booklet.

DEBIT-CREDIT RULE

4. To transfer the expenses to the **Income Summary** account, debit **Income Summary** for $5,500.
5. Decreases in expense accounts are recorded as credits. Credit **Depreciation Expense—Delivery Equipment** for $3,000 and **Depreciation Expense—Office Equipment** for $2,500.

T ACCOUNTS

6.

Income Summary

Debit	Credit
5,500	

Depreciation Expense—Delivery Equipment

Debit +	Credit –
3,000	Clos. 3,000

Depreciation Expense—Office Equipment

Debit +	Credit –
2,500	Clos. 2,500

JOURNAL ENTRY

7.

GENERAL JOURNAL PAGE 22

	DATE		DESCRIPTION	POST. REF.	DEBIT	CREDIT	
1	20--						1
2	Dec.	31	Income Summary		5 500 00		2
3			Depr. Exp.—Del. Equip.			3 000 00	3
4			Depr. Exp.—Office Equip.			2 500 00	4
5							5

A MATTER OF ETHICS

Who Will They Believe?

Imagine that you are the newest employee—an accounting clerk—for a small book publishing company. After nearly a year, you believe you have discovered evidence of embezzlement. You're not sure who is responsible, but you suspect the department manager or the senior accountant. You wonder if you should tell someone. Who can you tell? Who would believe you?

Ethical Decision Making:

- What are the ethical issues?
- What are the alternatives?
- Who are the affected parties?
- How do the alternatives affect the parties?
- What would you do?

Teaching A MATTER OF ETHICS

Who Will They Believe? Bring in an organization chart showing several levels of management responsibility. Have students look at the chart and think about positions within an organization. If a department manager is suspected of embezzlement, who is that person's boss? Discuss with students the role of the human resources department, which may be one place to turn for advice. You may also want to assign extra credit and have students research "whistle-blowers" in newspaper and magazine articles. Or students might research the federal law protecting whistle-blowers from retaliation by an employer.

SECTION 3 Check Your Understanding

Now that you have studied this section, complete the following questions and problems.

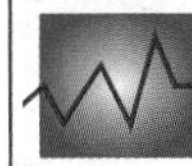

Thinking Critically

1. Why are depreciation adjusting entries recorded at the end of the period?
2. What does the balance of an accumulated depreciation account represent?

Communicating Accounting

You and your best friend, Paulina, are discussing whether or not to prepare plant asset records and a depreciation summary form for the equipment you purchased to start your screen printing business, Supreme T-Shirt Outfitters. Paulina says it's too much work. What would you say to convince her of the need to prepare and maintain the depreciation records?

Problem 23–4 Analyzing a Source Document

Instructions In your working papers:

(1) Record the purchase in the general journal page 4.

(2) Record the partial depreciation expense for the first year in the general journal, page 7.
 (a) Disposal value—$200
 (b) Estimated useful life—5 years
 (c) The company's fiscal year ends on December 31.

(3) Record the annual depreciation, one year later, in the general journal, page 13.

All Purpose Office Equipment
996 Lake Drive, Sacramento, CA 94203

INVOICE NO. 14492

DATE: June 4, 20--
ORDER NO.: 22688
SHIPPED BY: UPS
TERMS: Cash

TO Universal Auto Supply
1422 Central Blvd.
Sacramento, CA 94203

QTY.	ITEM	UNIT PRICE	TOTAL
1	Xerox Copy Machine Serial Number 24X612987	$ 3,200.00	$ 3,200.00
	Sales Tax		256.00
	Total		$ 3,456.00

Problem 23–5 Preparing a Depreciation Schedule and Journalizing the Depreciation Adjusting Entry

Quade Corporation bought a copy machine on January 7 of the current year for $2,360. It has an estimated useful life of five years and an estimated disposal value of $100.

Instructions In your working papers:

(1) Prepare a depreciation schedule for the copy machine using the straight-line method of depreciation. (Use the form provided in your working papers.)

(2) Journalize the adjustment for depreciation on the copy machine at the end of the first year.

(3) Journalize the closing entry for the expense account affected by the adjusting entry.

(4) What is the book value of the asset after five years? Is this the same as the disposal value?

RETEACHING SECTION 3

Using a Contra Account When recording depreciation expense of a plant asset, some students may want to credit the asset account for the amount of the depreciation. Explain that the only time a plant asset account is credited is when the asset is sold, traded in, or discarded. When depreciation is allocated, the amount of depreciation is recorded in the Accumulated Depreciation account, which is a contra asset account. The contra account balance decreases the plant asset balance.

3 ASSESS

Thinking Critically (Answers)

1. To show depreciation expense for each plant asset for the period.
2. Asset cost allocated as depreciation expense to date.

Communicating Accounting (Answer)

Depreciation expense is worth tracking because it reduces income taxes. Keeping good records saves time in calculating depreciation and preparing financial statements and tax documents.

Problem 23-4 (Answers)

1. June 4: Dr. Office Equip. $3,456; Cr. Cash in Bank $3,456; Inv. 14492
2. Dec. 31: Dr. Depr. Exp.—Off. Equip. $379.87; Cr. Accum. Depr.—Off. Equip. $379.87
3. Dec. 31: Dr. Depr. Exp.—Off. Equip. $651.21; Cr. Accum. Depr.—Off. Equip. $651.20

Problem 23–5 (Answers)

1. Book Value: Jan. 7, $2,360; Yr. 1, $1,908; Yr. 2, $1,456; Yr. 3, $1,004; Yr. 4, $552; Yr. 5, $100
2. Dr. Depr. Exp.—Off. Equip. $452; Cr. Accum. Depr.—Off. Equip. $452
3. Dr. Inc. Summary $452; Cr. Depr. Exp.—Off. Equip. $452
4. $100; yes

Chapter Reviews and Working Papers Refer students to the Chapter 23 workbook pages to answer *Check Your Understanding* activities.

4 CLOSE

Section Wrap-Up

Writing: Have students write a paragraph explaining how adjusting entries affect the information reported on financial statements. L1

SCANS in the Workforce

Foundation Skills Connection

Problem Solving

Hold a classroom discussion about workplace behavior and ask students to solve a common problem—the absentee worker. They may have personal experience with how their own workload changed when a co-worker was absent. Did it make them angry that they were asked to do more work? How would they solve the problem of absenteeism on the job? L1

Workplace Competencies Connection

Understanding Systems

Ask students to design a list of items they would need to know when being hired by a new company. In order to understand expectations and function within the guidelines of the new employer, what questions would they ask? How can they go about educating themselves about work requirements? Have students talk with a local employer about systems currently used for indoctrinating new employees. L2

Organizing and Maintaining Information

Tell students they are working for their employer as an office manager. Their job today is to create a travel itinerary for a new employee and to provide step-by-step instructions for retaining receipts and tracking expenses. Students may use their creativity in designing the itineraries and writing instructions. Have students submit all completed work to you for approval. L3

ACCOUNTING CAREERS IN FOCUS

CHRISTINE SPAGNOLA
Controller
SFX Broadcasting of PA, Inc.

Q: How does one get the experience to be a controller?

A: Work for a small company where you perform many functions. I worked for a small company where I didn't make a lot of money, but I did receivables, payables, closings, bad debt, annual reports, auditing, and payroll.

Q: What's difficult about being controller for a broadcasting company?

A: There are frequent buy-outs. Each time the company is sold, I have to do a new chart of accounts, a new budget, and a new projection. So there is a lot of redundant work. It is also hard to motivate a staff under these conditions. They may be determined to prove themselves to the new owners at first, but eventually they get tired of the changes and leave.

Q: How does a person keep his or her job through the changes?

A: Make yourself valuable to the organization. Show them you're an asset. Find the issues that need to be brought to their attention. Don't wait for them to ask you. Call them and tell them what you think.

Q: What skills are most important to a controller?

A: Problem solving. You have to be able to see things other people can't see. If you are given a new problem, you have to be able to complete the task. You have to make things happen.

Tips from . . .

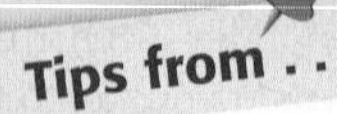

Higher positions do not mean shorter hours. Executives surveyed averaged 54 hours a week, with one-third working longer hours now than five years ago. Employees wanting to advance as a company grows will often work additional hours.

CAREER FACTS

Nature of the Work: Oversee staff, make reports, budget, and keep financial reporting on track during transitions.
Training or Education Needed: A bachelor's degree in accounting.
Aptitudes, Abilities, and Skills: Accounting, time-management skills, problem-solving skills, communication skills, and interpersonal skills.
Salary Range: $60,000 and up depending on location and company revenues.
Career Path: Start by working for small company to learn a variety of skills, then move up through other companies to become a controller.

Thinking Critically: In what ways could you demonstrate to a company that you are a valuable employee?

ACCOUNTING CAREERS IN FOCUS

Thinking Critically (Answers)

To show that you are valuable, demonstrate an understanding of the business. Show an understanding of computer systems and demonstrate an interest in your work. Also, be eager to find solutions to problems in the workplace.

ROBERT HALF CORNER

Telecommuting The 40-hour work week is increasing to a 50- or 60-hour week. To save time, many people work at home and telecommute. Using telephone lines, modems, computers, and satellites, some employees can work from home offices. The time normally spent commuting can instead be spent on work.

CHAPTER 23 SUMMARY

SUMMARY CHAPTER 23

KEY CONCEPTS

1. Plant assets are long-lived assets used in the production or sale of other assets or services over several accounting periods.
2. A plant asset is depreciated so that its cost is spread over its useful life.
3. To calculate the annual depreciation expense of an asset, you must know its cost, estimated useful life, estimated disposal value, and depreciation method.
4. To calculate annual depreciation:

   Original Cost − **Estimated Disposal Value** = **Amount to be Depreciated**

   Amount to be Depreciated ÷ **Estimated Useful Life** = **Annual Depreciation Expense**

5. When depreciation is recorded, two accounts are affected:
   Accumulated Depreciation and **Depreciation Expense.**
6. To calculate depreciation for part of a year: **Annual Depreciation Expense** × **Fraction of Year** = **Partial Year Depreciation Expense**
7. To calculate book value: **Original Cost** − **Accumulated Depreciation** = **Book Value**
8. To record depreciation:

Depreciation Expense—Description of Asset	
Debit + xx	Credit −

Accumulated Depreciation—Description of Asset	
Debit −	Credit + xx

9. On the balance sheet, the accumulated depreciation accounts are listed immediately below their related plant asset accounts.
10. To close depreciation expense accounts:

Income Summary	
Debit xx	Credit

Depreciation Expense	
Debit +	Credit − xx

Chapter 23 Quiz

Student Class Instructor
Date Assigned Date Completed

CHAPTER 23 QUIZ

Plant Assets and Depreciation

QUESTIONS (Completion)

Directions: Fill in the blank with the term that best completes each sentence.

1. Land and buildings are examples of ______.
2. The estimated value of a plant asset at the end of its useful life is its ______.
3. Allocating the cost of an asset equally over a period of years is ______ depreciation.
4. The original cost of a plant asset less its accumulated depreciation is its ______.
5. The total amount of depreciation at the end of each period is ______.
6. The account used to show the cost of using an asset for the fiscal period is ______.
7. Accumulated Depreciation is a ______ asset account.
8. The adjustment for depreciation is calculated and entered on the ______.
9. The book value of a plant asset is reported on the ______.
10. The cost of depreciation for a fiscal period is reported on the ______.

 Chapter Quizzes • 25

QUESTIONS (Completion)

1. Land and buildings are examples of ______.
2. The estimated value of a plant asset at the end of its useful life is its ______.
3. Allocating the cost of an asset equally over a period of years is ______ depreciation.
4. The original cost of a plant asset less its accumulated depreciation is its ______.
5. The total amount of depreciation at the end of each period is ______.
6. The account used to show the cost of using an asset for the fiscal period is ______.
7. Accumulated Depreciation is a ______ asset account.
8. The adjustment for depreciation is calculated and entered on the ______.
9. The book value of a plant asset is reported on the ______.
10. The cost of depreciation for a fiscal period is reported on the ______.

ANSWERS

1. plant assets
2. disposal value
3. straight-line
4. book value
5. accumulated depreciation
6. Depreciation Expense
7. contra
8. work sheet
9. balance sheet
10. income statement

REVIEW AND ACTIVITIES CHAPTER 23

USING KEY TERMS

See the *Glossary* for the definitions of these terms. Have teams volunteer to share their definitions and examples in class. Discuss any differences between teams in use of the terms.

Understanding Accounting Concepts and Procedures

(Answers)

1. Plant assets are long-lived assets used over several accounting periods. Current assets are either used up or converted to cash during one accounting period.
2. Because it will wear out from normal use, become outdated, or no longer needed by the business.
3. Charging a portion of the plant asset's cost over the number of years of the asset's estimated productive life as depreciation expense.
4. Because land never wears out or becomes obsolete.
5. (a) Cost, (b) estimated useful life, (c) estimated disposal value, and (d) depreciation method used.
6. (Original Cost − Estimated Disposal Value) ÷ Estimated Useful Life = Estimated Annual Depreciation Expense
7. To provide detailed information about an individual plant asset, including date of purchase, original cost, annual depreciation, accumulated depreciation, book value, estimated useful life, estimated disposal value, and depreciation method used.
8. At the end of the fiscal period through an adjusting entry.
9. Depreciation Expense and Accumulated Depreciation.
10. A contra plant asset account.
11. Income Summary.

CHAPTER 23 REVIEW AND ACTIVITIES

USING KEY TERMS

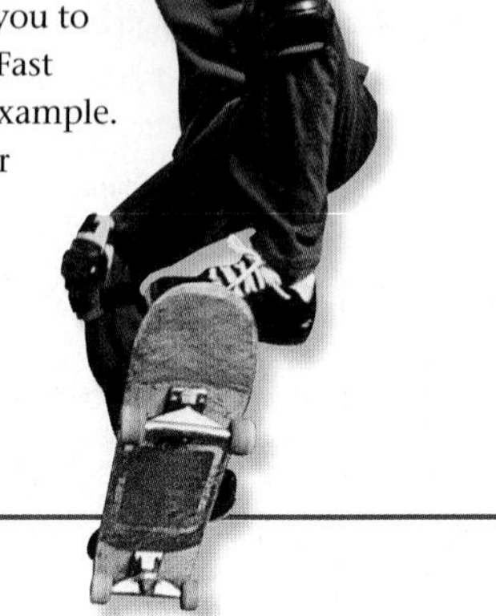

You have just been hired as the plant accountant for Fast Runner, a large manufacturer of inline skates and skateboards. To do your job well, you must be able to understand and apply accounting procedures for plant assets and depreciation. Your immediate boss is the CEO for Fast Runner, Rob Myers. Rob wants you to define the following terms and give him some examples related to Fast Runner. Pair up with a colleague to discuss each term and find an example. Then write your ideas on a note pad for quick reference during your meeting with Rob. Good luck!

accumulated depreciation	disposal value
book value	plant assets
current assets	straight-line depreciation
depreciation	

Understanding Accounting Concepts and Procedures

Instructions

On a separate sheet of paper, answer the following questions:

1. What distinguishes a plant asset from a current asset?
2. Why is the useful life of a plant asset limited?
3. What is meant by "allocating the cost" of a plant asset?
4. Why is the cost of land not depreciated?
5. What four factors affect the depreciation calculation?
6. How is the annual depreciation expense for a plant asset calculated under the straight-line method?
7. What is the purpose of a plant asset record?
8. When is the depreciation on a plant asset recorded?
9. Which two accounts are affected by an adjusting entry for depreciation?
10. What is the classification of the **Accumulated Depreciation** account?
11. To which account are the depreciation expense accounts closed at the end of the period?

ASSESSMENT RESOURCES

Choose assessment strategies from the following pages to evaluate your students' progress.

Student Edition
Check Your Understanding, pp. 629, 632, 641
Chapter 23 Problems, pp. 647–649
Analyzing Financial Reports, p. 628

Assessment and Evaluation Masters
Chapter 23 Study Plan, *Glencoe Workbook (CRWP)*
Chapter 23 Self-Test, *Glencoe Workbook (CRWP)*
Chapter 23 Test, *Chapter Tests* Booklet
Chapter 23 Activity, *School-to-Work Handbook*
Chapter 23 **Exam***View*

Teacher Wraparound Edition
Critical Thinking Activity, p. 639
Reteaching Sections 1–3, pp. 629, 632, 641
Chapter 23 Quiz, p. 643

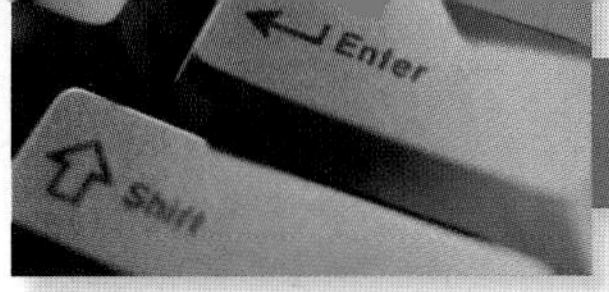

Case Study...

Merchandising Business: Photography Studio

Karina Ludmiko has been photographing weddings and parties as a hobby for several years and has decided to open a business called The Photo Studio. The studio consists of a consultation room, a developing lab, and a portrait studio. Karina has come to you seeking help in setting up the accounting records for the business.

Thinking Critically:

1. Which accounts might be in the chart of accounts for The Photo Studio?
2. Assume that the photography equipment used by The Photo Studio cost $25,000, has a useful life of ten years, and has no salvage value. Set up a depreciation schedule.
3. Explain to Karina how depreciation of the photography equipment appears on the balance sheet and income statement.

interNET CONNECTION

Depreciating Assets

As you learned in this chapter, business furniture and equipment are depreciated over their useful life. For tax purposes the IRS determines the period of time over which to depreciate qualifying property. Do you know what kinds of items can be depreciated? Let's check with the IRS to find out.

Do This:

1. Locate the IRS Web site.
2. Using the site's search feature, locate the IRS publication that provides information about depreciating business equipment and furniture.
3. List five items that can be depreciated according to the IRS.
4. Over what time period should each item be depreciated?

Conducting an Audit with Alex

Brookside Sports Equipment Inc. purchased a new cash register for $3,900 on August 3 from Best Office Equipment. The cash register has an estimated useful life of ten years and an estimated disposal value of $300. Review the journal entry below and answer the following questions.

1. What is wrong with the adjustment for depreciation made on December 31?
2. Because of the error, is the book value of the cash register too high or too low?

GENERAL JOURNAL PAGE 61

	DATE		DESCRIPTION	POST. REF.	DEBIT	CREDIT	
1	20--						1
2	Dec.	31	Depr. Exp.—Store Equip.		360 00		2
3			Accum. Depr.—Store Equip.			360 00	3
4							4

Workplace Skills

Working with Diverse Cultures

An increasing number of businesses are opening international offices. Your ability to work with a variety of ethnic, social, educational, and gender groups indicates your acceptance of cultural diversity.

On the Job:

As the owner of Cool Runnings, a manufacturer of skis, ice skates, and snowboards, you are committed to hiring employees from diverse cultures. You decide to offer workshops on cultural diversity, which will teach your employees techniques for cultural acceptance.

Thinking Critically:

Develop a list of ten items to discuss in your workshops. These should be issues that deal with cultural awareness and gender issues in the workplace.

interNET CONNECTION www.glencoe.com

Do This (Answers)

1. Locate the IRS site online. Try using these search terms: IRS, Internal Revenue Service, or Department of the Treasury. Web address: www.irs.gov
2. Try using these search terms: depreciation or depreciating assets. Publication 946, *How to Depreciate Assets.*
3. Computers, trucks, furniture, agricultural equipment.
4. Computers, 5 years; trucks, 5 years; furniture, 7 years; agricultural equipment, 7 years.

Case Study...

Thinking Critically (Answers)

1. Answers may vary. Possible accounts include Cash in Bank, Photography Revenue, Photography Equipment, Supplies, and Utilities Expense.
2. *Book Value*: first year, $22,500; second year, $20,000; third year, $17,500; fourth year, $15,000; fifth year, $12,500; sixth year, $10,000; seventh year, $7,500; eighth year, $5,000; ninth year, $2,500; tenth year, $0
3. Depreciation expense for the period is shown on the Income Statement, in the expenses section. Accumulated depreciation is shown on the Balance Sheet as a contra account to Photography Equipment.

Workplace Skills

Thinking Critically (Answers)

Answers will vary. Students should list items relating to cultural awareness.

Conducting an Audit with Alex

(Answers)

1. It should have been for $150, because it was only for five months of depreciation.
2. Too low.

Internet Resources and Activities Handbook

Refer students to the booklet for additional Internet activities.

PEACHTREE CORNER

Entering Depreciation Adjustments

Select the **General Journal Entry** option from the ***Tasks*** menu to enter adjustments for depreciation. To save time, students can record multiple adjustments in one, multi-part entry.

Tasks Analysis Options Reports
Quotes/Sales Orders
Sales/Invoicing...
Receipts...
Finance Charge...
Select for Deposit...
Purchase Orders...
Purchases/Receive Inventory...
Select for Payment...
Payments...
Write Checks...
Time/Expense
Select for Payroll Entry...
Payroll Entry...
General Journal Entry...
Inventory Adjustments...
Assemblies...
Account Reconciliation...
Void Checks...
Action Items...
System

As a reminder, students can also use the General Ledger navigation aid to access the **General Journal Entry** option and the General Ledger reports.

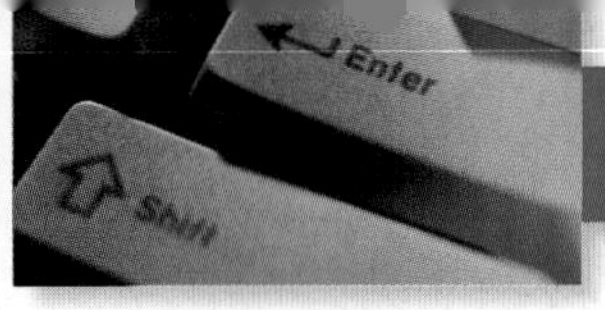

Recording Depreciation

Making the Transition from a Manual to a Computerized System

Task	Perform Accounting Procedures Using Manual Methods	Perform Accounting Procedures Using Automated Methods
Recording depreciation	1. Estimated annual depreciation is calculated when a fixed asset is purchased. 2. Each accounting period, an adjusting entry is journalized and posted for each plant asset account in the general ledger. 3. The Depreciation Expense account is closed at the end of the fiscal year.	1. Estimated annual depreciation is calculated when a fixed asset is purchased. 2. A depreciation journal entry is recorded for the month's amount. The journal entry can be automatically posted each month as a recurring entry. 3. Amounts are posted to the Depreciation Expense and Accumulated Depreciation accounts. Their balances are automatically updated.

Recording Depreciation

Peachtree Question	Description
How do I set up accounts required for depreciation entries in Peachtree?	1. Select **Chart of Accounts** from the ***Maintain*** menu. 2. Enter the account number for the new asset to be depreciated. 3. Enter the account name. For example, Delivery Equipment. 4. Select Fixed Asset as the account type. 5. Set up account numbers and names for the Accumulated Depreciation account and the Depreciation Expense account for this asset in the same manner. Select the appropriate account type for each new account.
How do I record depreciation for fixed assets in Peachtree?	1. Select **General Journal Entry** from the ***Tasks*** menu. 2. Enter the transaction to record the depreciation expense for the current period. 3. Select the Recur icon. 4. Select the number of times and how often you want this transaction to recur. (Each month? Each quarter? Each year?) 5. Click OK to save.
What does the software do "behind the scenes"?	1. When you select the account type for accounts such as Fixed Assets, Accumulated Depreciation, or Depreciation Expense, the software then positions these accounts in the appropriate places on the financial statements. 2. Using the Recur option for journal entries tells the system to post the entry at specified intervals to the accounts you have indicated.

For detailed instructions: See the **Peachtree User Guide** in your Glencoe Working Papers.

Peachtree® Answers to Frequently Asked Questions

Q: Can you edit a general journal entry from an earlier period after you close the fiscal year?
A: No, you cannot edit a General Journal entry after you close the fiscal year. You must make a correcting entry using the General Journal option, or you can restore data from a backup disk made before closing and then make the correction.

For additional information, refer to your *Glencoe Peachtree Accounting User Guide.*

APPLICATION OPTIONS

Problem 23–6 Opening a Plant Asset Record

On July 10 Sunset Surfwear purchased a scanner from Taunton Equipment for $1,500. Taunton Equipment charged Sunset Surfwear $200 to install the scanner. The scanner has an estimated useful life of four years and an estimated disposal value of $260.

Instructions Prepare a plant asset record, including the depreciation schedule for the new scanner. Use the form provided in your working papers.

Serial number: TMC46312
General ledger account: **Office Equipment**
Location: Main Street store
Depreciation method: Straight-line
Manufacturer: Brothers Company

Analyze: How did you determine the book value at the end of each period?

Complete chapter problems one of three ways:

1 **Manual** Glencoe Working Papers

or

2 **Peachtree Complete Accounting** Software

or

3 **QuickBooks** Templates (Problems 23–8, 23–10)

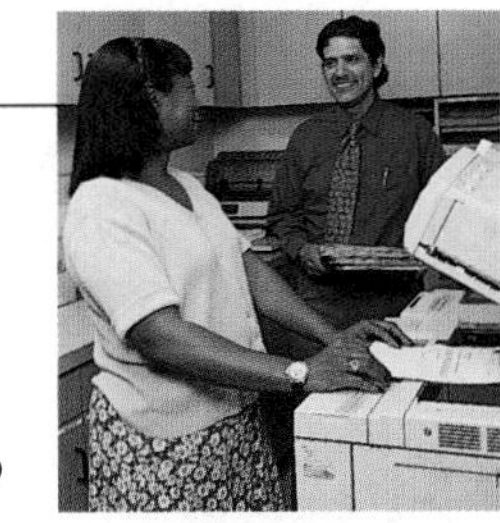

Problem 23–7 Recording Adjusting Entries for Depreciation

The following adjustments for depreciation were entered on the work sheet for InBeat CD Shop for the year ended December 31.

	Adjustments	
	Debit	Credit
Store Equipment		
Accumulated Depreciation—Store Equipment		(e) 3,800
Office Equipment		
Accumulated Depreciation—Office Equipment		(f) 1,400
Depreciation Expense—Store Equipment	(e) 3,800	
Depreciation Expense—Office Equipment	(f) 1,400	

Instructions Record the adjusting entries on general journal page 11.

Analyze: How does the adjustment affect the book value of the store equipment?

Peachtree®

SMART GUIDE

Step-by-Step Instructions: Problem 23–7

1. Select the problem set for InBeat CD Shop (Prob. 23–7).
2. Rename the company and set the system date.
3. Record the depreciation adjusting entries.
4. Print a General Journal report and proof your work.
5. Answer the Analyze question.
6. End the session.

TIP: Use the **General Journal Entry** option to record adjusting entries.

Problem 23–6 (Answers)
Opening a Plant Asset Record

Book Value:
July 2008, $1,700
Dec. 2008 $1,520
Dec. 2009, $1,160
Dec. 2010, $800
Dec. 2011, $440
Dec. 2012, $260

Analyze: Book value is equal to cost minus accumulated depreciation.

Problem 23–7 (Answers)
Recording Adjusting Entries for Depreciation

Dec. 31: Dr. Depr. Exp.—Store Equip. $3,800; Cr. Accum. Depr.—Store Equip. $3,800
Dec. 31: Dr. Depr. Exp.—Office Equip. $1,400; Cr. Accum. Depr.—Office Equip. $1,400

Analyze: The adjustment lowers book value.

EXTENDING THE CONTENT

Determining the Book Value of a Car One item that students may already associate with depreciation is a car. Ask students if they know the book value of their family car (or their own car). Have students contact a car dealer and/or bank in your area to research the book value of a specific car over a five-year period. Students may be surprised to find out how much a car depreciates the first year. Point out that the IRS allows businesses to depreciate cars and trucks used in the operation of the business. A business can deduct the depreciation as a business expense.

PROBLEM CHAPTER 23

Problem 23-8 (Answers) Reporting Depreciation Expense on the Work Sheet and Financial Statements

1. (a) Dr. Depr. Exp.—Office Equip. $2,500; Cr. Accum. Depr.—Office Equip. $2,500
   (b) Dr. Depr. Exp.—Store Equip. $1,200; Cr. Accum. Depr.—Store Equip. $1,200
2. Adjusted TB Totals $162,350
3. Net Income $11,355; Retained Earnings $35,355; Total Assets $90,150

Analyze: $59,750

Problem 23-9 (Answers) Calculating and Recording Depreciation Expense

1. Book Value: First Year $403,500 Second Year $387,900
2. Dec. 31: Dr. Depr. Exp.—Manu. Equip. $6,500; Cr. Accum. Depr.—Manu. Equip. $6,500
3. Dec. 31: Dr. Depr. Exp.—Manu. Equip. $6,500; Cr. Accum. Depr.—Manu. Equip. $6,500

Analyze: $6,500 1st year, $22,100 2nd year

Problem 23-10 (Answers) Calculating and Recording Adjustments

Adjustments:

(a) Dr. Inc. Summary $1,300; Cr. Merch. Inv. $1,300
(b) Dr. Supplies Exp. $3,400; Cr. Supplies $3,400
(c) Dr. Insurance Exp. $5,000; Cr. Prepaid Insurance $5,000
(d) Dr. Depr. Exp.—Delivery Truck $3,000; Cr. Accum. Depr.—Delivery Truck $3,000
(e) Dr. Depr. Exp.—Store Equip. $1,200; Cr. Accum. Depr.—Store Equip. $1,200
(f) Dr. Depr. Exp.—Building $6,000; Cr. Accum. Depr.—Building $6,000
(g) Dr. Fed. Inc. Tax Exp. $1,850; Cr. Fed. Inc. Tax Pay. $1,850

(Continued)

Peachtree®

SMART GUIDE

Step-by-Step Instructions: Problem 23-8

1. Select the problem set for Shutterbug Cameras (Prob. 23-8).
2. Rename the company and set the system date.
3. Record the adjustments for depreciation using the **General Journal Entry** option.
4. Print a General Journal report and proof your work.
5. Print an Income Statement, a Statement of Retained Earnings, and a Balance Sheet.
6. Answer the Analyze question.
7. End the session.

TIP: Select the predefined financial statements (Income Statement and Balance Sheet).

Problem 23-8 Reporting Depreciation Expense on the Work Sheet and Financial Statements

The trial balance of Shutterbug Cameras appears on the work sheet included in your working papers. All adjustments, except those for depreciation, are already recorded on the work sheet.

Instructions

(1) Record the following adjustments for depreciation expense on the work sheet.
   (a) Depreciation for office equipment is $2,500.
   (b) Depreciation for store equipment is $1,200.
(2) Complete the work sheet.
(3) Prepare an income statement, statement of retained earnings, and balance sheet for Shutterbug Cameras for the year ended December 31.

Analyze: What are the total current assets?

Peachtree®

SMART GUIDE

Step-by-Step Instructions: Problem 23-9

1. Select the problem set for Cycle Tech Bicycles (Prob. 23-9).
2. Rename the company and set the system date.
3. Calculate the depreciation for the first two years.
4. Record the depreciation adjustment for the first year using the **General Journal Entry** option.
5. Print a General Journal report and proof your work.
6. Answer the Analyze question.
7. End the session.

Problem 23-9 Calculating and Recording Depreciation Expense

Cycle Tech Bicycles purchased manufacturing equipment on August 1 for $410,000. The equipment has an estimated useful life of 25 years and an estimated disposal value of $20,000. The partial depreciation schedule found in your working papers is set up for the equipment.

Instructions

(1) Calculate annual depreciation, accumulated depreciation, and book value for each of the first two years. The fiscal year ends December 31. Use the form provided in your working papers.
(2) Calculate the depreciation adjustment to be entered on the work sheet at the end of the first year. Use T accounts to show the accounts debited and credited.
(3) Journalize the adjustment for depreciation at the end of the first year, general journal page 21.
(4) Post the adjusting entry to the general ledger accounts.

Analyze: What is the balance of the accumulated depreciation account at the end of the first and second years?

HOME AND COMMUNITY CONNECTIONS ACTIVITY

Dealing with Depreciation Ask students to talk with a parent or a professional who may know about depreciation. If a parent has a home office, she or he may have chosen to depreciate office equipment, office space, or an automobile used for business. In the workplace, students may be able to locate someone who handles the depreciation of facilities and equipment for their employer. How often are the items depreciated? Why do they find it necessary to depreciate? Ask volunteers to share their findings with the class.

Problem 23–10 Calculating and Recording Adjustments

The December 31 trial balance of Rivers Edge Canoe & Kayak is included in your working papers.

Instructions

(1) Calculate and record end-of-period adjustments on the work sheet.
- (a) Ending **Merchandise Inventory** is $15,000.
- (b) Supplies on hand total $1,450.
- (c) The amount of the expired insurance premium is $5,000.
- (d) Use the following information to calculate the estimated annual depreciation expense.

Plant Asset	Cost	Estimated Disposal Value	Estimated Useful Life
Store Equipment	$ 13,000	$ 1,000	10 years
Delivery Truck	32,000	2,000	10 years
Building	160,000	10,000	25 years

- (e) The total federal income tax expense for the year is $4,250.

(2) Complete the work sheet.
(3) Journalize and post the adjusting entries on page 16 of the general journal.
(4) Journalize and post the closing entries on page 16 of the general journal.

Analyze: What is the total depreciation expense for the year?

Peachtree®

SMART GUIDE

Step-by-Step Instructions: Problem 23–10

1. Select the problem set for River's Edge Canoe & Kayak (Prob. 23–10).
2. Rename the company and set the system date.
3. Calculate and record the end-of-period adjustments.
4. Print a General Journal report and proof your work.
5. Print an Income Statement and a Balance Sheet.
6. Close the fiscal year.
7. Print a Post-Closing Trial Balance.
8. Answer the Analyze question.
9. End the session.

Problem 23–11 Examining Depreciation Adjustments

On May 2, Buzz Newsstand purchased a new machine from Yong Manufacturing Co. The machine cost $2,700, with an estimated disposal value of $100 and an estimated useful life of eight years.

On December 31 the adjustment for depreciation for the first year was entered: **Accumulated Depreciation—Store Equipment** was credited for $325, and **Depreciation Expense—Store Equipment** was debited for $325.

Instructions

Answer the following questions regarding this adjustment:

(1) What is wrong with the adjustment for depreciation made on December 31? What is the correct entry?
(2) One year from now, another adjustment for this machine will be entered on the work sheet. Assume the error from the previous year is not corrected. What amount should be entered in the Adjustments section for annual depreciation expense?

Analyze: If the original error is not corrected, will the net income for the period be too high or too low?

ADDRESSING MULTIPLE LEARNING STYLES

Visual/Spatial Learner Ask students to identify a business that they are famliar with or where they would like to work. Have them gather photos and ads from magazines that illustrate examples of plant assets for that business; for example, office furniture, computers, fax machines, copiers, delivery vehicles, construction equipment, and so on. Ask students to arrange these images in a collage and share the collage with the class. In their presentation, students should explain how or why the business uses the assets illustrated and estimate the useful life of each of the assets.

Problem 23–10 (Answers) Calculating and Recording Adjustments (continued)

Closing entries:

Dec. 31: Dr. Sales $180,000; Cr. Inc. Summary $180,000

Dec. 31: Dr. Inc. Summary $140,450; Cr. Purchases $96,000, Trans. In $5,000, Adv. Exp. $3,500, Depr. Exp.—Del. Truck $3,000, Depr. Exp.—Store Equip. $1,200, Depr. Exp.—Building $6,000, Fed. Corp. Inc. Tax Exp. $4,250, Gas Exp. $1,400, Ins. Exp. $5,000, Misc. Exp. $5,400, Supplies Exp. $3,400, Utilities Exp. $6,300

Dec. 31: Dr. Inc. Summary $38,250; Cr. Retained Earnings $38,250

Ending debit balances:

Merchandise Inventory $15,000
Supplies $1,450
Prepaid Insurance $1,000

Ending credit balances:

Accum. Depr.—Delivery Truck $19,000
Accum. Depr.—Store Equip. $7,200
Accum. Depr.—Building $66,000
Federal Corporate Income Tax Payable $1,850
Retained Earnings $58,770

Analyze: $10,200

Problem 23–11 (Answers) Examining Depreciation Adjustments

1. Amount is overstated. The equipment was owned for eight months, and the depreciation recorded is for an entire year. Correct amount is $216.67.
2. $216.67.

Analyze: It will be too low.

CHAPTER 24 Resource Manager

Section Resources

	Objectives & Standards	Activities & Features	Reproducible Masters
Chapter Opener *Uncollectible Accounts Receivable*	• Explain the direct write-off method and the allowance method of accounting for uncollectible accounts. • Determine uncollectible accounts receivable. • Record uncollectible accounts receivable using the direct write-off method. • Calculate bad debits expense. • Journalize the adjusting entry for estimated uncollectible accounts. • Record uncollectible accounts receivable using the allowance method. • Journalize the entry to record the collection of an account that was previously written off. • Describe two methods that can be used to estimate uncollectible accounts expense. **National Standards for Business Education**: IA13, IA16, IIA3, IIA4, IIA9, IIA10	Exploring the Real World of Business, p. 650 Workplace Connections, p. 651	School-to-Work Handbook
Section 1 *The Direct Write-Off Method*	• Why businesses extend credit. • The direct write-off method of accounting for uncollectible accounts. • Record direct write-off of uncollectible accounts receivable. • How to record the collection of an account that was previously written-off under the direct write-off method.	Did You Know?, p. 653 Accounting Tips, p. 653 A Matter of Ethics, p. 656	Demonstration Problems Strategies for Teaching Ethics in Accounting
Section 2 *The Allowance Method*	• The concept of matching uncollectible accounts with revenue. • The allowance method of accounting for uncollectible accounts. • Record adjustments for uncollectible accounts on a work sheet. • Record estimated uncollectible amounts on financial statements. • How to journalize the adjusting entry for uncollectible accounts. • How to write off an uncollectible account receivable using the allowance method. • How to record collection of an account written off by the allowance method.	Connect To, p. 659 Math Hints, p. 661 Analyzing Financial Reports, p. 665	Demonstration Problems Math Review for Accounting
Section 3 *Estimating Uncollectible Accounts Receivable*	• Use the percentage of net sales method to determine the estimated uncollectible accounts expense. • Use the aging of accounts receivable method to determine estimated uncollectible accounts expense.	International Accounting, p. 668 Accounting Flashbacks, p. 668	Strategies for Teaching International Accounting Demonstration Problems Internet Resources and Activities Handbook

KEY

Posters · Transparency · Software · Videocassette · Blackline Masters · CD-ROM · Portfolio

MULTIMEDIA RESOURCE

Peachtree	QuickBooks	Spreadsheets	Videos	CD-ROMs
Problem 24–4 *Using the Direct Write-Off Method* Problem 24–5 *Calculating and Recording Estimated Uncollectible Accounts Expense* Problem 24–6 *The Allowance Method* Problem 24–7 *Estimating Uncollectible Accounts Expense* Problem 24–8 *Reporting Uncollectible Amounts* 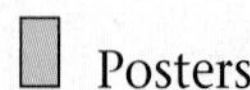 Problem 24–9 *Using the Allowance Method for Write-Offs*	Problem 24–4 *Using the Direct Write-Off Method* Problem 24–6 *The Allowance Method*	None in this chapter.	***Video Segment: Business Ethics*** After viewing this video, students will be able to exercise judgment in evaluating ethical situations.	***Electronic Learning Center (ELC), Chapter 24*** This program is ideal for visual learners since it incorporates video images, animation, and graphics to enliven the content of each lesson. ***Interactive Lesson Planner (ILP), Chapter 24*** This CD-ROM combines the versatility of an electronic lesson planner with the convenience of teacher classroom resources.

SCANS Correlation Chart

FOUNDATION SKILLS

Basic Skills:	Reading	Writing	Math	Listening	Speaking	
Thinking Skills:	Creative Thinking	Decision Making	Problem Solving	Seeing Things in the Mind's Eye	Knowing How to Learn	Reasoning
Personal Qualities:	Responsibility	Self-Esteem	Sociability	Self-Management	Integrity/Honesty	

WORKPLACE COMPETENCIES

Resources:	Allocating Time	Allocating Money	Allocating Material and Facility Resources	Allocating Human Resources		
Information:	Acquiring and Evaluating Information	Organizing and Maintaining Information	Interpreting and Communicating Information	Using Computers to Process Information		
Interpersonal Skills:	Participating as a Member of a Team	Teaching Others	Serving Clients/ Customers	Exercising Leadership	Negotiating to Arrive at a Decision	Working with Cultural Diversity
Systems:	Understanding Systems	Monitoring and Correcting Performance	Improving and Designing Systems			
Technology:	Selecting Technology	Applying Technology to Task	Maintaining and Troubleshooting Technology			

*Highlighted blocks indicate areas covered in the chapter. Additional SCANS skills are also covered throughout the *Teacher Wraparound Edition.*

Assessment

Student Edition
- Check Your Understanding, pp. 657, 666, 670
- Chapter 24 Problems, pp. 675–677

Assessment and Evaluation Masters
- Chapter 24 Study Plan, *Glencoe Workbook*
- Chapter 24 Self-Test, *Glencoe Workbook*
- Chapter 24 Test, *Chapter Tests* Booklet
- Chapter 24 Activity, *School-to-Work Handbook*
- Chapter 24 **Exam***View*

Teacher Wraparound Edition
- Critical Thinking Activity, p. 664
- Reteaching Section 1, p. 657
- Reteaching Section 2, p. 666
- Reteaching Section 3, p. 670
- Chapter 24 Quiz, p. 671

Transparencies

	Teaching Transparencies	Solution Transparencies
Section 1:	24–1, 24–2, 24–3, 24–4, 24–5	Problem 24–1
Section 2:	24–6, 24–7, 24–8, 24–9, 24–10, 24–11, 24–12, 24–13, 24–14	Problem 24–2
Section 3:	24–15, 24–16, 24–17	Problem 24–3
End of Chapter:		Problems 24–4, 24–5, 24–6, 24–7, 24–8, 24–9

TEACHER CLASSROOM RESOURCES

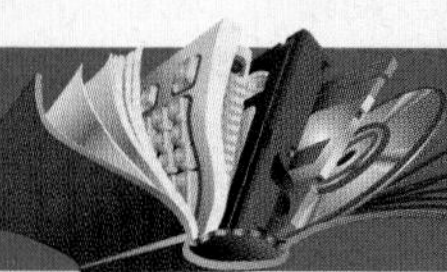

This is a representation of key blackline masters available in the Teacher Classroom Resources.

Teaching Aids

Transparency Examples

Section Focus Transparencies

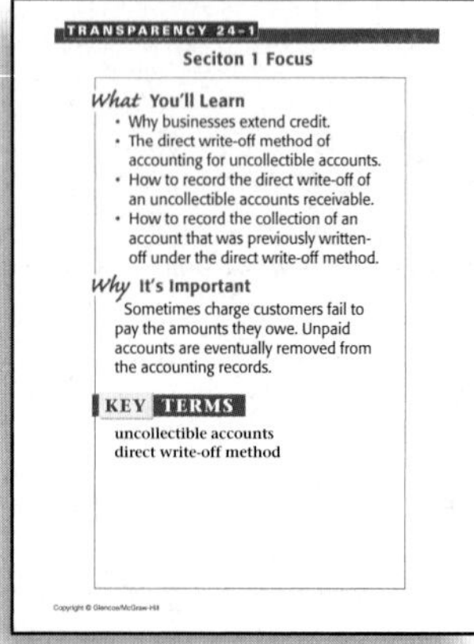

TRANSPARENCY 24-1

Seciton 1 Focus

What You'll Learn

- Why businesses extend credit.
- The direct write-off method of accounting for uncollectible accounts.
- How to record the direct write-off of an uncollectible accounts receivable.
- How to record the collection of an account that was previously written-off under the direct write-off method.

Why It's Important

Sometimes charge customers fail to pay the amounts they owe. Unpaid accounts are eventually removed from the accounting records.

KEY TERMS

uncollectible accounts
direct write-off method

Teaching Transparencies

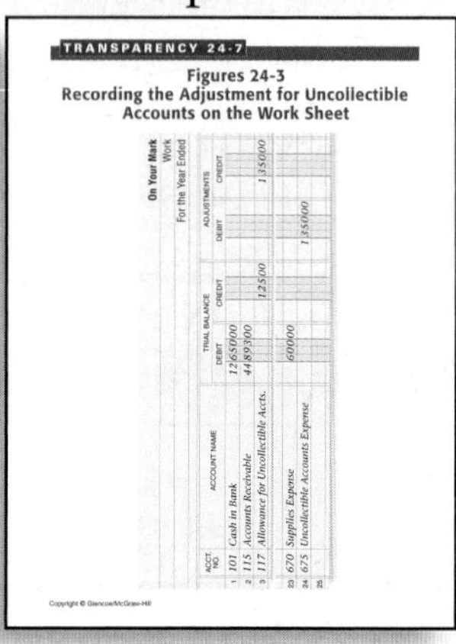

TRANSPARENCY 24-7

Figures 24-3
Recording the Adjustment for Uncollectible Accounts on the Work Sheet

Teaching Transparencies

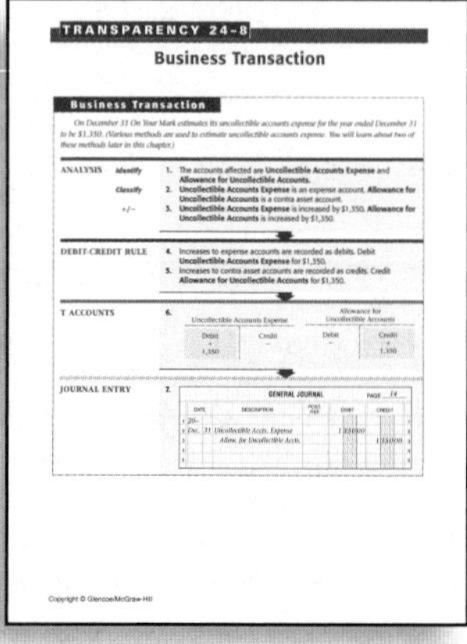

TRANSPARENCY 24-8

Business Transaction

Solution Transparencies

Working Papers for End-of-Chapter Problems

Problem 24-4 Using the Direct Write-Off Method

Demonstration Problems

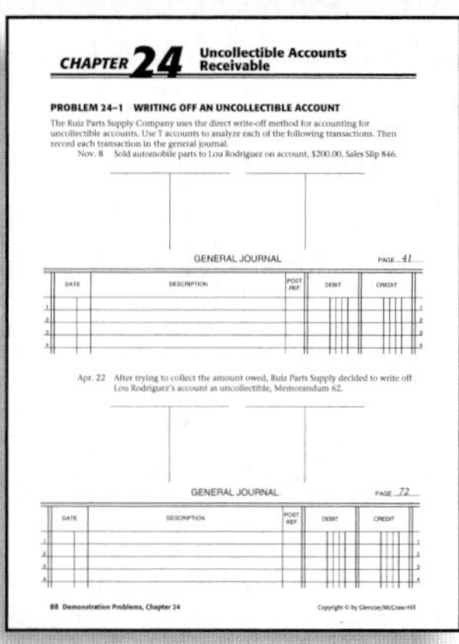

CHAPTER 24 Uncollectible Accounts Receivable

PROBLEM 24-1 WRITING OFF AN UNCOLLECTIBLE ACCOUNT

Lesson Plans

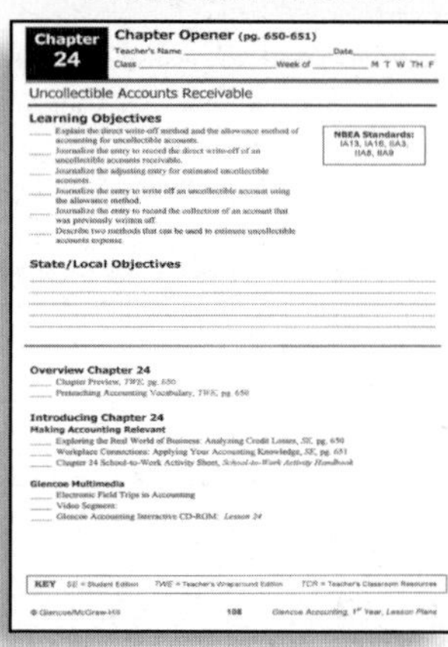

Chapter 24 Chapter Opener (pg. 650-651)

Uncollectible Accounts Receivable

Learning Objectives

State/Local Objectives

Block Scheduling

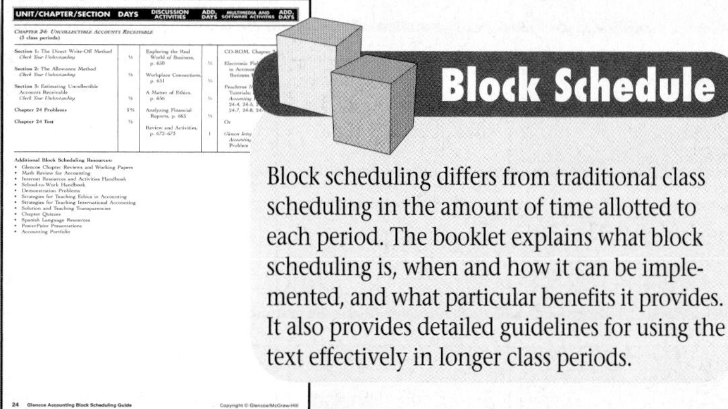

Block Schedule

Block scheduling differs from traditional class scheduling in the amount of time allotted to each period. The booklet explains what block scheduling is, when and how it can be implemented, and what particular benefits it provides. It also provides detailed guidelines for using the text effectively in longer class periods.

Enrichment and Application

Strategies for Teaching Ethics in Accounting

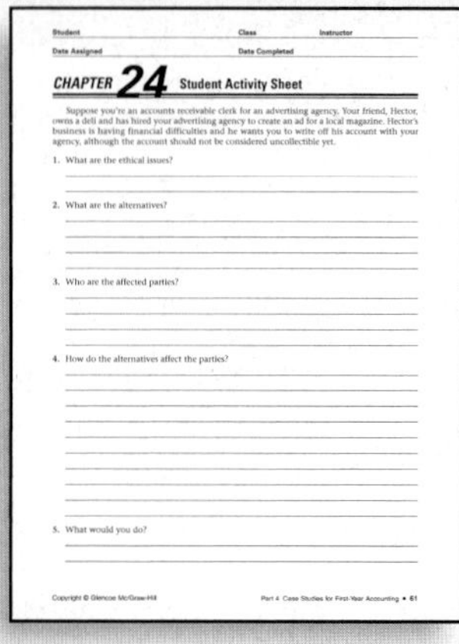

CHAPTER 24 Student Activity Sheet

1. What are the ethical issues?
2. What are the alternatives?
3. Who are the affected parties?
4. How do the alternatives affect the parties?
5. What would you do?

Strategies for Teaching International Accounting

Chapter 24 Language and Written Communications: *How Many Languages Do You Speak?*

Business Languages

Communication-Verbal and Nonverbal

School-to-Work Handbook

CHAPTER 24 SCHOOL-TO-WORK ACTIVITY

Uncollectible Accounts Receivable

Meeting Different Ability Levels

Chapter Reviews and Working Papers (CRWP)

Working Papers

Review

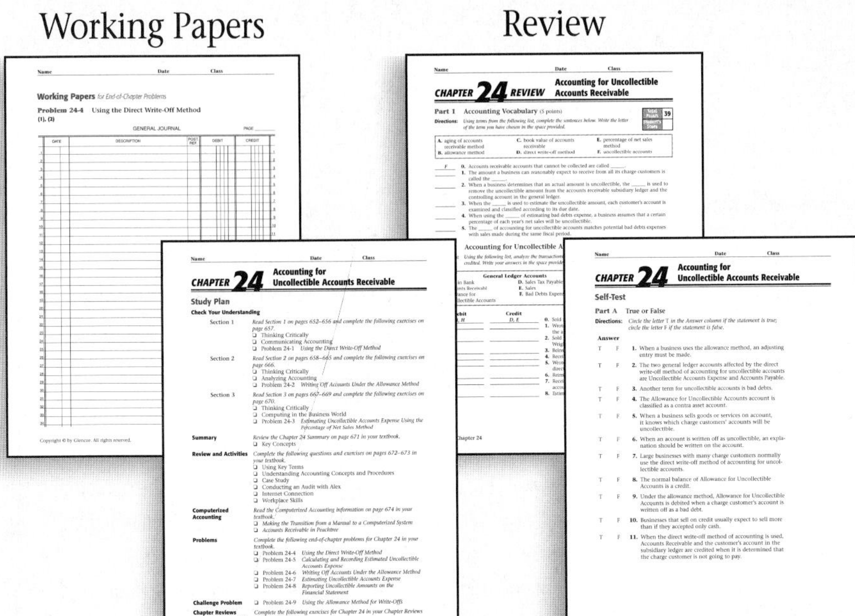

Student Study Plan

Self-Test

Real-World Multimedia CD-ROM

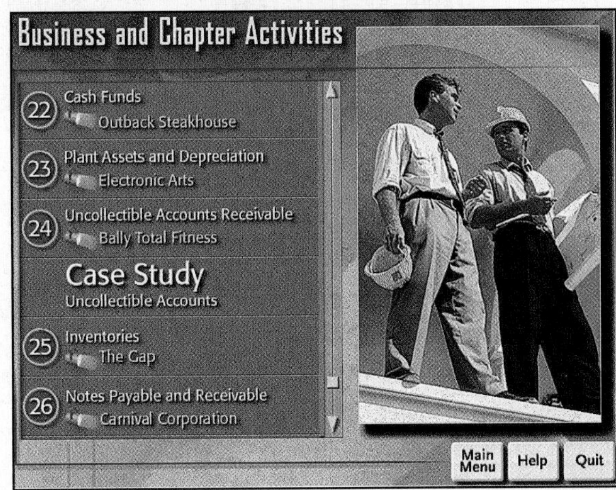

Teaching Resources at a Glance

Application Resources

- Glencoe Chapter Review and Working Papers, SE and TAE
- School-to-Work Handbook, SE and TM
- Accounting Portfolio, SE and TM

Reproducible Masters

- Demonstration Problems
- Lesson Plans
- Block Scheduling
- Spanish Language Resources

Glencoe Accounting Professional Development Series

- Strategies for Teaching Ethics in Accounting
- Accounting Competitive Event Review
- Math Review for Accounting
- Strategies for Teaching International Accounting
- Internet Resources and Activities Handbook

Transparency Package

- Section Focus Transparencies
- Teaching Transparencies
- Source Document Transparencies
- Solution Transparencies

Performance Assessment

- **Exam***View* CD-ROM
- Chapter Tests
- Chapter Quizzes
- Unit Tests
- Audit Tests
- Printed Testbank

Multimedia Resources

- Electronic Learning Center:
  - Multimedia CD-ROMs
  - Peachtree software, tutorials, templates, and solutions
  - Spreadsheet templates
- Using QuickBooks with Glencoe Accounting
- Interactive Lesson Planner
- Electronic Field Trips in Accounting
- PowerPoint Presentation
- Web site: glencoeaccounting.glencoe.com

Key to Ability Levels

Each section gives skill-building activities. Each activity has been labeled for use with students of various learning styles and abilities.

L1 Level 1 activities are basic activities and should be within the range of all students.

L2 Level 2 activities are average activities and should be within the range of average and above average students.

L3 Level 3 activities are challenging activities designed for the ability range of above average students.

ELL ELL activities should be within the ability range of English Language Learners.

Assessment and Evaluation

Chapter Tests

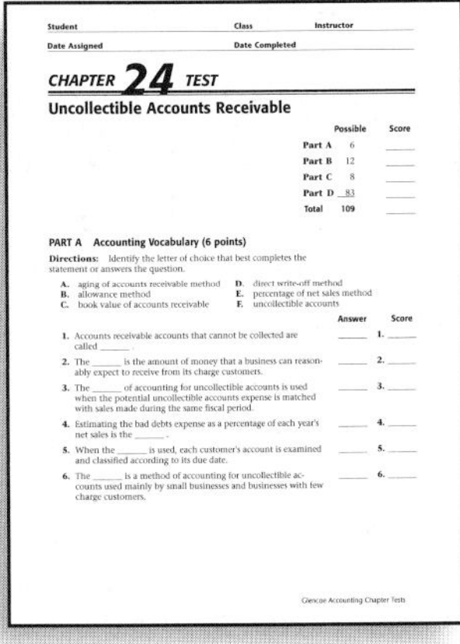

Chapter Quiz

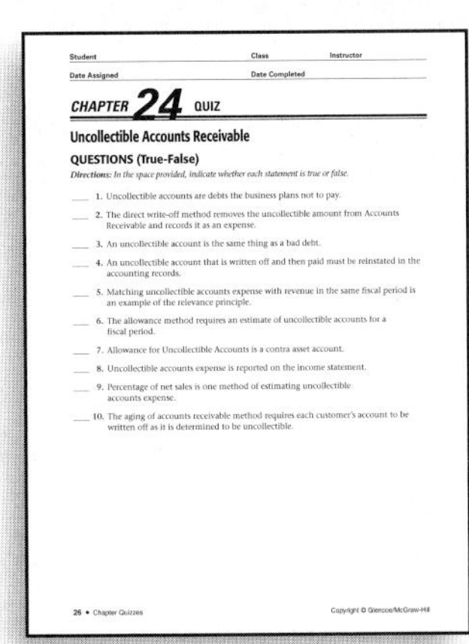

Correlations to National Standards for Business Education

(See pages T50–T51 for a detailed correlation chart.)

Standards: IA13, IA16, IIA3, IIA4, IIA9, IIA10

Chapter Preview

Although businesses check to make sure that customers buying on account are good credit risks, sometimes those customers do not pay. In this chapter students will learn how businesses allow for uncollectible accounts receivable and how they adjust the accounting records to reflect unpaid customer balances.

Section Overviews

- Section 1—*The Direct Write-Off Method*
- Section 2—*The Allowance Method*
- Section 3—*Estimated Uncollectible Accounts Receivable*

Chapter Vocabulary

uncollectible accounts
direct write-off method
allowance method
book value of accounts receivable
percentage of net sales method
aging of accounts receivable method

Preteaching Accounting Vocabulary

Oral Exercise: Explain each of the terms to students. Relate terms to concepts students already know. For example, they already know what net sales is, so they might logically conclude that the percentage of net sales method is a proportion of net sales that will become uncollectible. Ask for volunteers to use each term in a sentence relating to uncollectible accounts receivable. L1

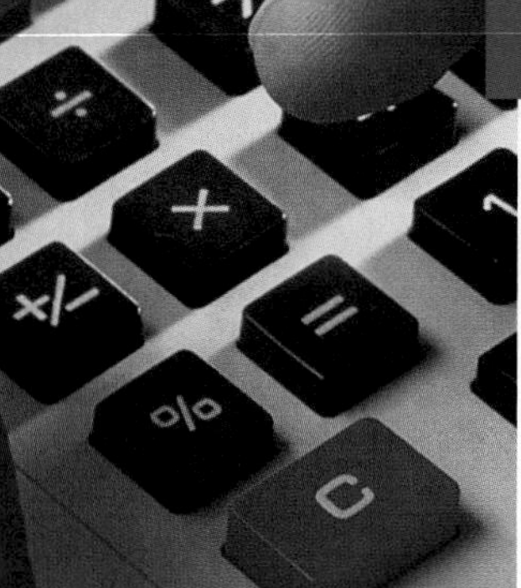

Uncollectible Accounts Receivable

Learning Objectives

When you have completed this chapter, you will be able to:

- Explain the direct write-off method and the allowance method of accounting for uncollectible accounts.
- Determine uncollectible accounts receivable.
- Record uncollectible accounts receivable using the direct write-off method.
- Calculate bad debts expense.
- Journalize the adjusting entry for estimated uncollectible accounts.
- Record uncollectible accounts receivable using the allowance method.
- Journalize the entry to record the collection of an account that was previously written off.
- Describe two methods that can be used to estimate uncollectible accounts expense.

Exploring the Real World of Business

ANALYZING CREDIT LOSSES

Personal fitness is a major contributing element to good health and longevity. One company that has made its mark in the personal fitness industry is **Bally Total Fitness,** a national chain of health clubs. **Bally** fitness clubs offer members the use of exercise equipment and free weights, aerobics classes, swimming pools, and racquetball courts. The clubs also sell sports clothing and equipment and nutritional products. The company operates 350 clubs in 29 states and Canada. **Bally** charges its members annual or monthly fees to use the club facilities.

When a company such as **Bally** cannot collect payment for items charged by a club member, they must write off the debt in their accounting records. Too many write-offs will affect earnings and may cause the company to raise membership fees for all members to cover the losses.

What do you think?

If you worked for **Bally Total Fitness,** what would you do to help minimize losses from people who do not pay their debts?

Bally Total Fitness

Exploring the Real World of Business

Bally Total Fitness
Bally claims approximately four million members for its fitness clubs. Members not only have access to local clubs; they can also check out Bally products and news online (www.ballyfitness.com) and locate clubs in other areas they might visit while traveling.

What do you think? (Answers)
Answers will vary. Students might mention making credit checks on all charge customers, keeping a list of customers who gave bad checks to avoid accepting checks from those same people, and setting a policy of accepting only cash or bankcards.

Workplace Connections

Applying Your Accounting Knowledge

When people cannot pay their debts, businesses have to decide what to do about their losses. Retailers and banks are examples of businesses that are likely to have customers who fail to pay what they owe. When amounts owed to a business cannot be collected, the business records them in the accounting records. In this chapter, you'll learn how to estimate and record uncollectible amounts.

Investigate:

1. In your workplace, does the business have customers who fail to pay what they owe?
2. How does the business handle amounts it cannot collect?

651

Glencoe Accounting Online

Visit the *Glencoe Accounting* Web site at **glencoeaccounting.glencoe.com** for additional activities and information.

GLENCOE MULTIMEDIA

Electronic Field Trips in Accounting *Video Segment: Business Ethics*
After viewing this video, students will be able to exercise judgment in evaluating ethical situations.

Glencoe Accounting: Electronic Learning Center *Chapter 24*
The CD-ROM program is ideal for visual learners since it incorporates video images, animation, and graphics to enliven the content of each lesson.

INTRODUCING
CHAPTER 24

Making Accounting Relevant

Workplace Connections: Applying Your Accounting Knowledge

Discussion: Many people use credit cards to buy the things they need and want. Sometimes people use too much credit, and they can't pay their debts. When this happens, the debtor may get a bad credit rating, making it harder or more costly to use credit in the future. The business does not get its payments and may have trouble paying its own debts as a result.

Investigate (Answers)

1. Answers may vary. Most businesses that extend credit to customers do eventually have some uncollectible debts.
2. Answers may vary. If the debts are small, the business may just write them off. For larger debts, the business may send collection letters. If that fails, the business may sell the debt to another company, which will then try to collect.

School-to-Work Activity

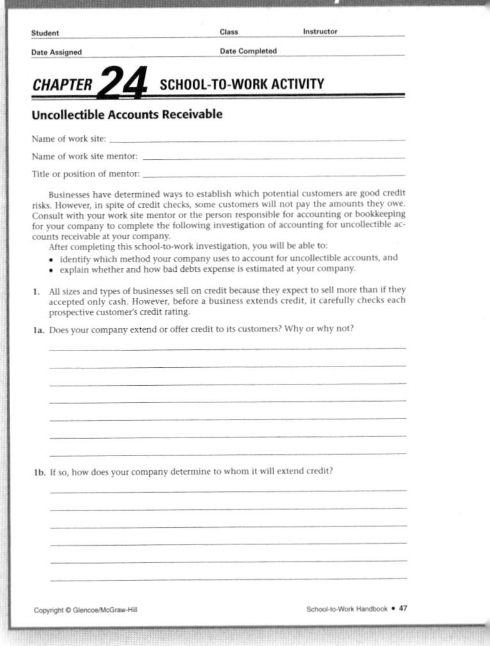

Student ________ Class ________ Instructor ________

Date Assigned ________ Date Completed ________

CHAPTER 24 SCHOOL-TO-WORK ACTIVITY

Uncollectible Accounts Receivable

Name of work site: ________

Name of work site mentor: ________

Title or position of mentor: ________

Businesses have determined ways to establish which potential customers are good credit risks. However, in spite of credit checks, some customers will not pay the amounts they owe. Consult with your work site mentor or the person responsible for accounting or bookkeeping for your company to complete the following investigation of accounting for uncollectible accounts receivable at your company.

After completing this school-to-work investigation, you will be able to:

- identify which method your company uses to account for uncollectible accounts, and
- explain whether and how bad debts expense is estimated at your company.

1. All sizes and types of businesses sell on credit because they expect to sell more than if they accepted only cash. However, before a business extends credit, it carefully checks each prospective customer's credit rating.

1a. Does your company extend or offer credit to its customers? Why or why not?

1b. If so, how does your company determine to whom it will extend credit?

 School-to-Work Handbook • 47

1 FOCUS

Introducing the Section

In this section students will learn why businesses extend credit and how they deal with customer accounts that remain uncollected. Students will learn how to record uncollectible accounts in the accounting system using the direct write-off method.

Section Concepts

- Why businesses extend credit.
- The direct write-off method of accounting for uncollectible accounts.
- How to record the direct write-off of an uncollectible accounts receivable.
- How to record the collection of an account that was previously written off under the direct write-off method.

Visual Learning

Section 1 Focus

Use **Transparency 24–1** to introduce section concepts.

BELL RINGER

Compare and Contrast: Have students discuss how loaning money to a friend or family member is a way of extending credit. Ask what they did to collect the debt. If the debt was not repaid, what did they do? Have students discuss nonpayment of debts from the viewpoint of the business whose customers fail to pay their debts. L1

SECTION 1

The Direct Write-Off Method

What You'll Learn

- Why businesses extend credit.
- The direct write-off method of accounting for uncollectible accounts.
- How to record the direct write-off of an uncollectible accounts receivable.
- How to record the collection of an account that was previously written-off under the direct write-off method.

Why It's Important

Sometimes charge customers fail to pay the amounts they owe. Unpaid accounts are eventually removed from the accounting records.

KEY TERMS

uncollectible accounts
direct write-off method

In previous chapters, you learned that many businesses sell goods or services on account. Some charge customers cannot or will not pay the amounts they owe. Businesses such as JCPenney or Mervyn's routinely deal with customers who do not pay their accounts. These uncollectible accounts are eventually removed from the accounting records.

Extending Credit

Selling goods and services on credit is a standard practice for businesses of all sizes and types. Businesses sell on credit because they expect to sell more than if they accepted only cash. The additional sales on account result in higher profits.

Before a business extends credit, it should check each prospective customer's credit rating. This credit check helps the business determine the customer's ability to pay the amounts charged on account. Retail stores often ask customers to complete a credit application. They also rely on reports from credit card companies and local retail credit bureaus. Wholesalers and manufacturers use reports from wholesale credit bureaus and national credit-rating organizations such as Dun & Bradstreet to check their customers' creditworthiness.

An **uncollectible account**, or *bad debt,* is created when a customer fails to pay the amount due on account. An account that is uncollectible becomes an expense to the business. The account receivable is removed from the accounting records, and an expense is recorded.

There are two ways to handle uncollectible accounts: the direct write-off method and the allowance method. In this section, we will look at the direct write-off method.

The Direct Write-Off Method

The direct write-off method is used primarily by small businesses and those with few charge customers. Under the **direct write-off method**, when the business determines that the amount owed is not going to be

RESOURCE MANAGER

Reproducible Masters
- Lesson Plans
- Chapter Reviews and Working Papers (CRWP) TAE
- Demonstration Problems

Transparencies
- Section Focus Transparency
- Teaching Transparencies
- Source Document Transparencies
- Solution Transparencies

Multimedia
- Exam*View* CD-ROM
- Electronic Learning Center CD-ROM
- Interactive Lesson Planner CD-ROM

paid, the uncollectible account is removed from the accounting records. **Uncollectible Accounts Expense** is debited and **Accounts Receivable** (both controlling and subsidiary) is credited.

Let's look at an example of how this method is used to record uncollectible accounts receivable.

> **Did You Know?**
>
> **Consumer Debt**
>
> U.S. consumer credit-card and installment debt totals over $1 trillion dollars. When divided by the population, consumer debt averages over $3,900 for each person in the United States.

Writing Off an Uncollectible Account

On June 4 On Your Mark Athletic Wear sold football equipment on account to Robert Galvin for $250 plus $15 sales tax. The original transaction was recorded as a debit to **Accounts Receivable** (controlling) for $265 and credits to **Sales** for $250 and **Sales Tax Payable** for $15. Also, the subsidiary account **Accounts Receivable—Robert Galvin** was debited for $265.

For over a year, On Your Mark tried to collect this account. The length of time is one consideration used to determine uncollectible accounts receivable. It is now apparent that Robert Galvin is not going to pay the $265.

What this means to On Your Mark is that the business must decrease its **Accounts Receivable** account and increase its expense related to uncollectible accounts. In effect, the business must decrease total assets and increase total expenses when a customer fails to pay a debt.

> **ACCOUNTING TIPS**
>
> **Direct Write-Off Method**
>
> The direct write-off method is the only method a business can use for income tax purposes.

Business Transaction

On August 25 On Your Mark wrote off as uncollectible Robert Galvin's account for $265, Memorandum 170.

ANALYSIS	***Identify***	1. The accounts affected are **Uncollectible Accounts Expense, Accounts Receivable** (controlling), and **Accounts Receivable—Robert Galvin** (subsidiary).
	Classify	2. **Uncollectible Accounts Expense** is an expense account. **Accounts Receivable** (controlling) and **Accounts Receivable—Robert Galvin** (subsidiary) are asset accounts.
	+/−	3. **Uncollectible Accounts Expense** is increased by $265. **Accounts Receivable** (controlling) and **Accounts Receivable—Robert Galvin** (subsidiary) are decreased by $265.
DEBIT-CREDIT RULE		4. Increases to expense accounts are recorded as debits. Debit **Uncollectible Accounts Expense** for $265. 5. Decreases to asset accounts are recorded as credits. Credit **Accounts Receivable** (controlling) and **Accounts Receivable—Robert Galvin** (subsidiary) for $265.

2 TEACH

GUIDED PRACTICE

> **Reading Accounting**
>
> - Have students skim the text of this section and identify the main points. Ask them to write a brief description of each point. L1
> - Have students interview local businesspeople who speak their first language to find information on a business's guidelines for extending credit and how they handle uncollectible accounts. ELL

Concept Development: Extending Credit

Discussion: Review the different types of credit checks a business may make before selling to a customer on credit. If time permits, use a resource person to discuss safeguards a business can take to reduce its number of uncollectible accounts. Students should understand that granting credit is risky, but most businesses believe that the increase in revenue will offset the uncollectible accounts. L1

Concept Development: The Direct Write-Off Method

Discussion: Give students an example of a sale of merchandise on account. After recording the transaction in general journal form, inform students that for a year efforts have been made to collect this account. Management has decided that the customer is not going to pay. Analyze the write-off of the uncollectible account using T accounts. Mention that the direct write-off method is used because the expense is being charged directly for the uncollectible amount at the time it is determined to be uncollectible. L1

Great Ideas *From the Classroom of...*

Bridging the Gap Between the Classroom and Work

Employees often refer to a set of procedures that provide step-by-step instructions for completing a task. Have students develop a procedure guide or outline (a "Go By") for each chapter. The activity will require students to correlate writing, reading, problem solving, and analysis skills with accounting activities. Students can use their guides for problem solving, evaluation, and testing procedures, with emphasis placed on where to go to find the correct procedure or answer.

Robert E. Turner
University of Louisiana at Monroe
Monroe, Louisiana

2 TEACH (Cont'd.)

Visual Learning

Business Transaction

Using **Transparency 24–2**, help students analyze how the uncollectible account affects the accounting records of a business.

Figure 24–1 Ledger Accounts After an Uncollectible Write-Off

Use **Transparency 24–3** to point out the impact of an uncollectible account on the Accounts Receivable controlling account and the customer's account in the accounts receivable subsidiary ledger.

Teaching Tips

Use T accounts to review the recording of the original sale to Robert Galvin.

Ask a resource person from a credit bureau or a credit manager to speak to your class about credit and how it is used by business.

Demonstration Problem Step-by-Step Practice

Use demonstration problem 24–1 to give students practice in analyzing and recording the transaction to write off an uncollectible account using the direct write-off method.

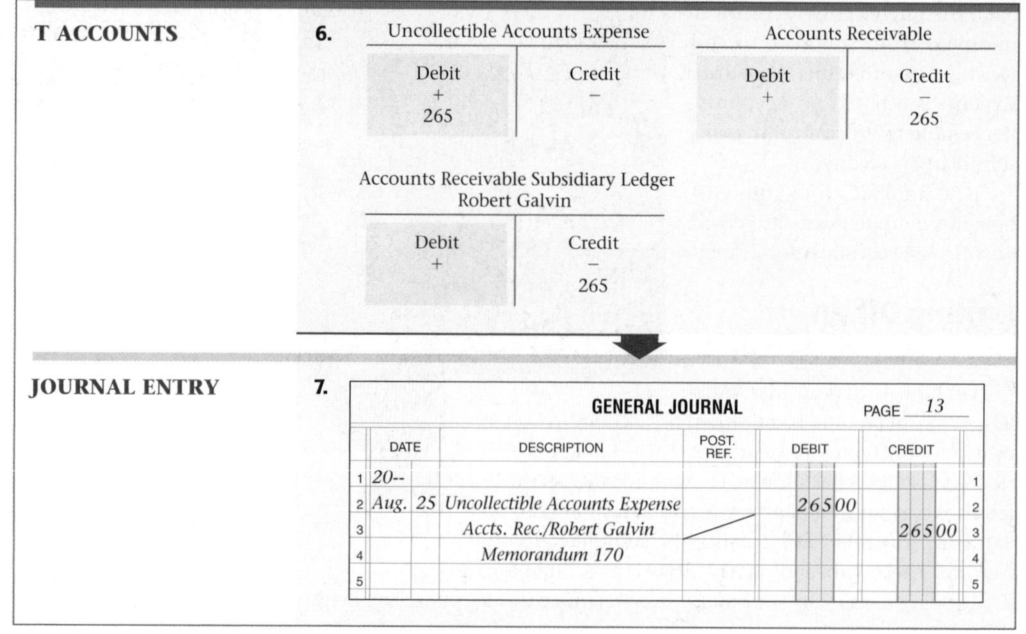

T ACCOUNTS

6.

Uncollectible Accounts Expense	
Debit +	Credit –
265	

Accounts Receivable	
Debit +	Credit –
	265

Accounts Receivable Subsidiary Ledger
Robert Galvin

Debit +	Credit –
	265

JOURNAL ENTRY

7.

GENERAL JOURNAL PAGE 13

	DATE		DESCRIPTION	POST. REF.	DEBIT	CREDIT	
1	20--						1
2	Aug.	25	Uncollectible Accounts Expense		265 00		2
3			Accts. Rec./Robert Galvin			265 00	3
4			Memorandum 170				4
5							5

Figure 24–1 shows how this transaction is posted to the general ledger and the accounts receivable subsidiary ledger.

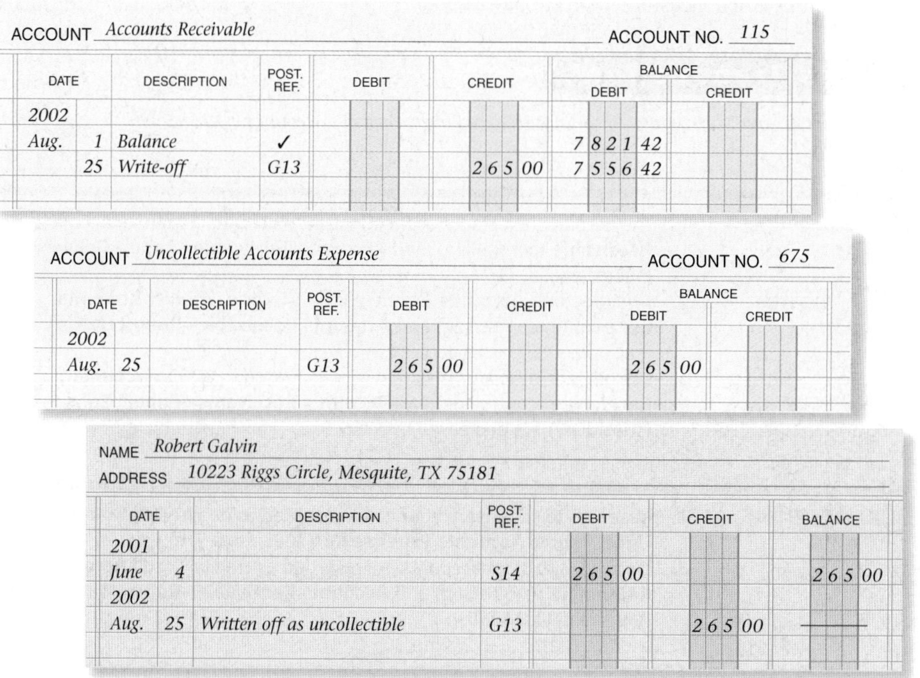

ACCOUNT *Accounts Receivable* ACCOUNT NO. *115*

DATE		DESCRIPTION	POST. REF.	DEBIT	CREDIT	BALANCE DEBIT	BALANCE CREDIT
2002							
Aug.	1	Balance	✓			7 8 2 1 42	
	25	Write-off	G13		2 6 5 00	7 5 5 6 42	

ACCOUNT *Uncollectible Accounts Expense* ACCOUNT NO. *675*

DATE		DESCRIPTION	POST. REF.	DEBIT	CREDIT	BALANCE DEBIT	BALANCE CREDIT
2002							
Aug.	25		G13	2 6 5 00		2 6 5 00	

NAME *Robert Galvin*
ADDRESS *10223 Riggs Circle, Mesquite, TX 75181*

DATE		DESCRIPTION	POST. REF.	DEBIT	CREDIT	BALANCE
2001						
June	4		S14	2 6 5 00		2 6 5 00
2002						
Aug.	25	Written off as uncollectible	G13		2 6 5 00	—

Figure 24–1 Ledger Accounts after an Uncollectible Write-off

COOPERATIVE LEARNING ACTIVITY

Brainstorming Share this scenario with students: The Amish Furniture Company has tried for 13 months to collect on the Lamplighter Family Restaurant's account. The furniture company managers have determined that this charge customer is not going to pay its debt. Ask students how the business should record this decision and what effect it will have on the business. (Students should conclude that the Accounts Receivable account should be removed from the books and that the removal represents an expense to the business. If you choose, do not give students the answer but instead let them read the chapter and find the answer on their own.)

Notice the explanation entered in Robert Galvin's account. When an account is written off as uncollectible, it is important to note on the subsidiary ledger that the account was written off, not paid off.

Collecting a Written-Off Account

Occasionally, a charge customer whose account was written off as uncollectible will later pay the amount owed. When this happens:

- First, the customer's account is reinstated, or reentered in the accounting records.
- Second, the cash receipt is recorded.

Key Points

Uncollectible Accounts
To write off an account under the direct write-off method: Debit: **Uncollectible Accounts Expense** Credit: **Accounts Receivable** (controlling and subsidiary).

Business Transaction

On September 5 On Your Mark received $265 from Robert Galvin, whose account was written off as uncollectible on August 25, Memorandum 176 and Receipt 1109. First reinstate the account receivable.

ANALYSIS

Identify 1. The accounts affected are **Accounts Receivable** (controlling), **Accounts Receivable–Robert Galvin** (subsidiary), and **Uncollectible Accounts Expense.**

Classify 2. **Accounts Receivable** (controlling) and **Accounts Receivable–Robert Galvin** (subsidiary) are asset accounts. **Uncollectible Accounts Expense** is an expense account.

+/− 3. **Accounts Receivable** (controlling) and **Accounts Receivable–Robert Galvin** (subsidiary) are increased by $265. **Uncollectible Accounts Expense** is decreased by $265.

DEBIT-CREDIT RULE

4. Increases to asset accounts are recorded as debits. Debit **Accounts Receivable** (controlling) and **Accounts Receivable–Robert Galvin** (subsidiary) for $265.
5. Decreases to expense accounts are recorded as credits. Credit **Uncollectible Accounts Expense** for $265.

T ACCOUNTS

6.

Accounts Receivable	
Debit + 265	Credit −

Uncollectible Accounts Expense	
Debit +	Credit − 265

Accounts Receivable Subsidiary Ledger
Robert Galvin

Debit + 265	Credit −

HOME AND COMMUNITY CONNECTIONS ACTIVITY

Credit Bureau Have students talk with family members about obtaining a credit report from a credit bureau. Many families have had credit checks run when they purchased a home, took out a car loan, or applied for a new credit card. Without divulging the family finances, students can find out what is involved in requesting a credit check, what information they can receive, and how companies use this information to choose people to whom they will extend credit.

2 TEACH (Cont'd.)

Visual Learning

Business Transaction
Use **Transparency 24–4** to guide students through the analysis and recording of the entry to reinstate an account that has been written off as uncollectible.

Demonstration Problem
Step-by-Step Practice
Use demonstration problem 24–2 to give students practice in analyzing and recording amounts collected from a customer whose account has been written off.

Teaching Tip
Point out that the entry to reinstate a previously written-off account is the reverse of the entry to write off the account.

2 TEACH (Cont'd.)

Visual Learning

Figure 24–2 Robert Galvin Account

Using **Transparency 24–5,** have students describe each journal entry posted to the account. Have students discuss the journal in which each entry was recorded and why that journal was used.

Teaching Tip

Point out to students that the direct write-off method is typically used by businesses that have few uncollectible accounts. A business that sells on credit frequently may need to plan for some losses from uncollectible accounts and record the anticipated amount in the accounting records. Students will learn about other methods of accounting for uncollectible accounts in the next section.

Strategies for Teaching Ethics in Accounting

Photocopy the Chapter 24 *Student Activity Sheet* for students. Answers are also provided in the booklet.

JOURNAL ENTRY

7.

GENERAL JOURNAL — PAGE 14

	DATE		DESCRIPTION	POST. REF.	DEBIT	CREDIT	
1	20--						1
2	Sept.	5	Accts. Rec./Robert Galvin	/	265 00		2
3			Uncollectible Accts. Expense			265 00	3
4			Memorandum 176				4
5							5

After this transaction is posted, the cash receipt is recorded as a debit to **Cash in Bank** for $265 and a credit to **Accounts Receivable** (controlling) for $265. Also, the subsidiary account **Accounts Receivable—Robert Galvin** is credited for $265. Receipt 1109 is the source document for this entry.

Figure 24–2 shows Robert Galvin's subsidiary ledger account, which contains data about: the sale, the write-off, the reinstatement, and the cash receipt.

NAME *Robert Galvin*
ADDRESS *10223 Riggs Circle, Mesquite, TX 75181*

DATE		DESCRIPTION	POST. REF.	DEBIT	CREDIT	BALANCE
2001						
June	4		S14	265 00		265 00
2002						
Aug.	25	Written off as uncollectible	G13		265 00	—
Sept.	5	Reinstated	G14	265 00		265 00
	5		G14		265 00	—

Figure 24–2 Robert Galvin Account

A MATTER OF ETHICS

Uncollectible Accounts

Suppose you're an accounts receivable clerk for an advertising agency. Your friend, Hector, owns a deli and has hired your advertising agency to create an ad for a local magazine. Hector's business is having financial difficulties and he wants you to write off his account with your agency, although the account should not be considered uncollectible yet.

Ethical Decision Making:

- What are the ethical issues?
- What are the alternatives?
- Who are the affected parties?
- How do the alternatives affect the parties?
- What would you do?

Teaching A MATTER OF ETHICS

Uncollectible Accounts Ask students whether a friend or family member has ever asked for a favor that turned out to be more involved than the student expected. Once one favor was granted, did the friend or family member begin to expect other favors? Have students discuss when doing a good deed for a friend could turn into unethical behavior. How would they decide where to draw the line on doing favors that involved questionable actions?

SECTION 1 Check Your Understanding

Now that you have studied this section, complete the following questions and problems.

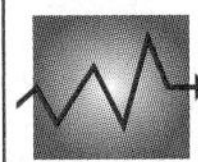

Thinking Critically

1. Before a business extends credit, it needs to approve potential credit customers. What are some items a business needs to evaluate? Why is it important for a business to verify these before extending credit?
2. Explain the use of the direct write-off method of accounting for uncollectible accounts.

Communicating Accounting

As an accounting clerk for The Music Connection, you are responsible for accounts receivable and uncollectible accounts. Six months ago a new dance club in town purchased a high-priced, state-of-the-art music system from your company. This account is still unpaid. Write a letter to the management of the dance club and request payment. In your letter indicate that if payment is not received within 30 days, the account will be turned over to a bill collection agency.

Problem 24–1 Using the Direct Write-Off Method

The Parker Supply Company uses the direct write-off method of accounting for uncollectible accounts.

Instructions In your working papers:

(1) Record the following transactions on page 21 of the general journal.

(2) Post the transactions to the appropriate accounts.

Parker Supply Company MEMORANDUM 78

TO: Accounting Clerk
FROM: Jon Herbert, Collection Manager
DATE: November 30, 20--
SUBJECT: Account write-off

It has been determined by the collection department that Account No. 4698214, Sonya Dickson, in the amount of $630, is uncollectible. This memo is your authorization to write this amount off as uncollectible. Thank you.

Date	Transactions
Apr. 10	Sold merchandise on account to Sonya Dickson, $600 plus $30 sales tax, Sales Slip 928.
Nov. 30	Wrote off Sonya Dickson's account as uncollectible, $630, Memorandum 78.
Dec. 30	Received $630 from Sonya Dickson in full payment of her account. This account was written off on November 30, Memorandum 89 and Receipt 277.

RETEACHING SECTION 1

Writing Off Uncollectible Accounts Give students extra practice using the direct method of writing off and reinstating uncollectible accounts by writing several examples on the chalkboard. As students analyze each example, enter amounts in T accounts at the chalkboard. Be sure students include both the Accounts Receivable controlling account and the subsidiary account. Have students explain why each entry is being made. Also use T accounts to review the accounts involved when a customer's account is reinstated.

3 ASSESS

Thinking Critically (Answers)

1. The prospective customer's credit rating and credit history. Businesses need to know whether their credit customers are likely to pay their debts.
2. Accounts Receivable is credited when it is determined that the charge customer is not going to pay. The loss of the uncollectible amount is charged to Uncollectible Accounts Expense.

Communicating Accounting (Answers)

Answers will vary. Students should write a formal letter and use any recipient's name. Letters should explain the company's policy on bill collection, the time that has already expired, and the urgency of receiving payment.

Problem 24–1 (Answers)

See the TAE of *Chapter Reviews and Working Papers* for journal entries.

Ending debit balances:
Cash in Bank $10,058; Accounts Receivable $7,290; Uncollectible Accts. Exp. $928; Accts. Rec./Sonya Dickson $0

Ending credit balances:
Sales Tax Pay. $278; Sales $24,760

Chapter Reviews and Working Papers Refer students to the Chapter 24 workbook pages to answer *Check Your Understanding* activities.

4 CLOSE

Section Wrap-Up

Writing: Have students write a paragraph explaining why businesses extend credit and how they record losses from customers who do not pay. L1

1 FOCUS

Introducing the Section

In this section students will learn how to apply the allowance method of accounting for anticipated uncollectible accounts. They'll record journal entries for writing off and collecting accounts using the allowance method.

Section Concepts

- The concept of matching uncollectible accounts with revenue.
- The allowance method of accounting for uncollectible accounts.
- How to record the adjustment for uncollectible accounts on the work sheet.
- How to record estimated uncollectible amounts on the financial statements.
- How to journalize the adjusting entry for uncollectible accounts.
- How to write off an uncollectible account receivable using the allowance method.
- How to record the collection of an account written off by the allowance method.

Visual Learning

Section 2 Focus

Use **Transparency 24–6** to introduce section concepts.

BELL RINGER

Analyzing: Tell students that they use a monthly budget. They need all their income to pay each month's expenses. Ask what they would do if they loaned $20 to a friend who promised to repay it in two weeks. The friend was then laid off and couldn't repay the loan. (Students might mention decreasing expenses. Relate this exercise to matching revenue and expenses.) L1

SECTION 2

The Allowance Method

What You'll Learn

- The concept of matching uncollectible accounts with revenue.
- The allowance method of accounting for uncollectible accounts.
- How to record the adjustment for uncollectible accounts on the work sheet.
- How to record estimated uncollectible amounts on the financial statements.
- How to journalize the adjusting entry for uncollectible accounts.
- How to write off an uncollectible account receivable using the allowance method.
- How to record the collection of an account written off by the allowance method.

Why It's Important

The allowance method of accounting for uncollectible accounts conforms to the matching principle.

KEY TERMS

allowance method
book value of accounts receivable

In Section 1 you learned that the direct write-off method is used by:

- small businesses
- businesses with few credit customers
- all businesses for tax purposes

Businesses that have many credit customers use the allowance method of accounting for uncollectible accounts. This method allows businesses to match revenue with the expenses incurred to earn that revenue. In this section you will learn about the allowance method and continue to journalize transactions involving uncollectible accounts.

Matching Uncollectible Accounts Expense with Revenue

When the direct write-off method of accounting for uncollectible accounts is used, an unpaid account is written off when the business determines that it will not be paid. Under the direct write-off method, it often happens that the sale is recorded in one period, and the uncollectible accounts expense is recorded in the following period. This violates the matching principle.

One of the fundamental principles of accounting is that *revenue should be matched with the expenses incurred in generating that revenue.* This means that expenses incurred to earn revenue should be deducted in the same period that the revenue is recorded. The uncollectible accounts expense should be reported in the year in which the sale takes place. However, the uncollectible account expense is usually not determined with certainty until some future period. That is, a credit sale in the year 2005 may not be determined to be uncollectible until some time in 2006. In order to conform to the matching principle, the credit sales are recorded in the year 2005 and an *estimate* of the uncollectible accounts expense is also recorded in 2005.

The estimate of uncollectible accounts expense is recorded as an end-of-period adjustment. The adjusting entry meets two objectives:

(1) **Accounts Receivable** is reduced to the amount the business can reasonably expect to receive.

RESOURCE MANAGER

Reproducible Masters
- Lesson Plans
- Chapter Reviews and Working Papers (CRWP) TAE
- Demonstration Problems

Transparencies
- Section Focus Transparency
- Teaching Transparencies
- Source Document Transparencies
- Solution Transparencies

Multimedia
- Exam*View* CD-ROM
- Electronic Learning Center CD-ROM
- Interactive Lesson Planner CD-ROM

(2) The estimated uncollectible accounts expense is charged to the current period.

Let's look at this method of accounting for uncollectible accounts.

The Allowance Method

The **allowance method** of accounting for uncollectible accounts matches the estimated uncollectible accounts expense with sales made during the same period. At the end of the period, the accountant must calculate bad debts expense that will result from the sales made during the period. The estimated uncollectible accounts expense is recorded as an adjustment on the work sheet. The two accounts affected by this adjustment are **Uncollectible Accounts Expense** and **Allowance for Uncollectible Accounts.**

When the adjustment is made, the business does not know exactly which charge customers will not pay the amounts they owe. Therefore, the estimated uncollectible amount cannot be credited to **Accounts Receivable** (neither controlling nor subsidiary). Since **Accounts Receivable** cannot be used to record the estimated uncollectible amount, another account is opened. This account is **Allowance for Uncollectible Accounts.**

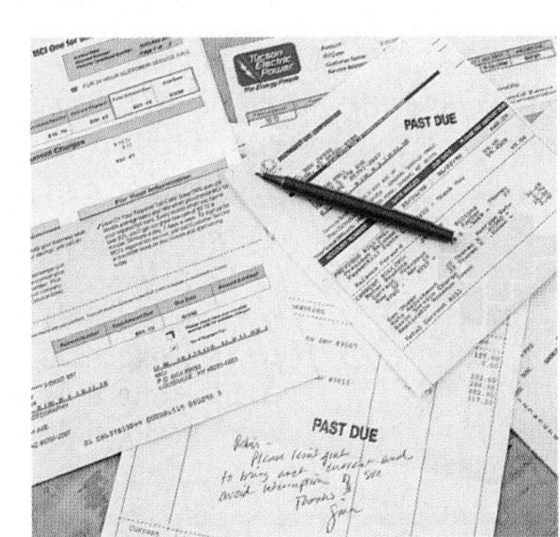

Allowance for Uncollectible Accounts is used to summarize the *estimated* uncollectible accounts receivable of the business. It is classified as a contra asset account.

Allowance for Uncollectible Accounts	
Debit – Decrease Side	Credit + Increase Side Normal Balance

Allowance for Uncollectible Accounts appears on the balance sheet as a deduction from **Accounts Receivable.** By using **Allowance for Uncollectible Accounts:**

- The balance of **Accounts Receivable** still equals the total of the customer accounts in the subsidiary ledger.
- The balance of **Allowance for Uncollectible Accounts** represents the amount the business *estimates* to be uncollectible.
- The difference between **Accounts Receivable** and **Allowance for Uncollectible Accounts** represents the book value of accounts receivable.

The **book value of accounts receivable** is the amount the business can reasonably expect to collect from the accounts receivable. **Figure 24–3** illustrates how this adjustment is recorded and extended on the work sheet.

Notice that **Allowance for Uncollectible Accounts** has a $125 balance in the Trial Balance Credit column. This balance is carried over from

CONNECT TO . . . HISTORY

The first recorded Olympic Games took place in Olympia, Greece in 776 BC. The competitive sporting event was a religious festival meant to honor the gods and the dead. To the ancient Greeks, Olympic winners were considered heroes, and in some city-states they didn't have to pay taxes.

INTERDISCIPLINARY CONNECTIONS ACTIVITY

History The Summer Olympics in 2004 will be held in Athens, Greece. Your students may find it interesting to look up some of the improvements necessary to prepare this ancient city for the games and the many spectators. To keep up with the latest and greatest happenings surrounding Olympic games preparation, visit the Athens 2004 Web site (www.athens.olympics.org/en). Or key in Athens 2004 and search for other Web sites.

2 TEACH

GUIDED PRACTICE

Reading Accounting

- Have students skim the section and make a list of the terms and accounting vocabulary they do not know. Tell them to use the *Glossary* and a dictionary to learn the terms. L1

Concept Development: Matching Uncollectible Accounts Expense with Revenue

Discussion: Ask students this question: When the direct write-off method is used for uncollectible accounts, does the write-off usually occur during the fiscal year in which the sale on account was made? During the discussion, give examples of charge sales from one fiscal period that are written off in a later fiscal period. Stress that if this occurs often, revenue received during the period is not being matched with expenses. Brainstorm how revenue from charge sales can be matched with all expenses, including losses from uncollectible accounts, for the same period. L1

Concept Development: The Allowance Method

Discussion: Summarize the important facts concerning the use of the allowance method for uncollectible accounts. Then analyze the adjusting entry using T accounts. Explain why an allowance account is used rather than recording amounts from losses in the Accounts Receivable account. L1

2 TEACH (Cont'd.)

Visual Learning

Figure 24–3 Recording the Adjustment for Uncollectible Accounts on the Work Sheet

Using **Transparency 24–7**, guide students through the recording of the adjusting entry for uncollectible accounts expense. Have students explain why each account affected is extended to the Balance Sheet and Income Statement sections.

Business Transaction

Using **Transparency 24–8**, have students analyze the adjusting entry for recording uncollectible accounts expense.

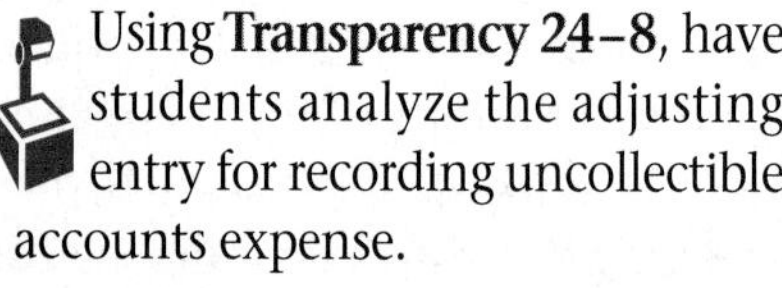

Demonstration Problem Step-by-Step Practice

Use demonstration problem 24–3 to give students practice in applying the allowance method of adjusting for uncollectible accounts.

Teaching Tips

Choosing the proper method of estimated uncollectible accounts expense is important because the business must use the method chosen consistently.

Emphasize that Allowance for Uncollectible Accounts is used to record an amount the business estimates it will not collect from charge customers. It is a contra asset account, and its balance decreases the asset Accounts Receivable.

Point out that the book value of accounts receivable represents the estimated amount of accounts receivable a business will collect from its charge customers.

Figure 24–3 Recording the Adjustment for Uncollectible Accounts on the Work Sheet

On Your Mark
Work
For the Year Ended

	ACCT. NO.	ACCOUNT NAME	TRIAL BALANCE DEBIT	TRIAL BALANCE CREDIT	ADJUSTMENTS DEBIT	ADJUSTMENTS CREDIT
1	101	Cash in Bank	12 650 00			
2	115	Accounts Receivable	44 893 00			
3	117	Allowance for Uncollectible Accts.		125 00		(b)1 350 00
23	670	Supplies Expense	600 00			
24	675	Uncollectible Accounts Expense			(b)1 350 00	
25						

Business Transaction

On December 31 On Your Mark estimates its uncollectible accounts expense for the year ended December 31 to be $1,350. (Various methods are used to estimate uncollectible accounts expense. You will learn about two of these methods later in this chapter.)

ANALYSIS

Identify 1. The accounts affected are **Uncollectible Accounts Expense** and **Allowance for Uncollectible Accounts.**

Classify 2. **Uncollectible Accounts Expense** is an expense account. **Allowance for Uncollectible Accounts** is a contra asset account.

+/− 3. **Uncollectible Accounts Expense** is increased by $1,350. **Allowance for Uncollectible Accounts** is increased by $1,350.

DEBIT-CREDIT RULE

4. Increases to expense accounts are recorded as debits. Debit **Uncollectible Accounts Expense** for $1,350.
5. Increases to contra asset accounts are recorded as credits. Credit **Allowance for Uncollectible Accounts** for $1,350.

T ACCOUNTS

6.

Uncollectible Accounts Expense	
Debit + 1,350	Credit −

Allowance for Uncollectible Accounts	
Debit −	Credit + 1,350

JOURNAL ENTRY

7.

GENERAL JOURNAL — PAGE 15

	DATE		DESCRIPTION	POST. REF.	DEBIT	CREDIT	
1	20--		Adjusting Entries				1
2	Dec.	31	Uncollectible Accts. Expense		1 350 00		2
3			Allow. for Uncollectible Accts.			1 350 00	3
4							4
5							5

MAKING CONNECTIONS TO DAILY LIFE

Offering a Loan Ask students what factors they would consider before deciding whether to loan money to a friend. Relate their responses to the safeguards that businesses employ when extending credit; i.e., requiring references, verifying financial ability to repay, and completing credit checks.

Athletic Wear							
Sheet							
December 31, 20--							
ADJUSTED TRIAL BALANCE		INCOME STATEMENT		BALANCE SHEET			
DEBIT	CREDIT	DEBIT	CREDIT	DEBIT	CREDIT		
12 650 00				12 650 00		1	
44 893 00				44 893 00		2	
	1 475 00				1 475 00	3	
600 00		600 00				23	
1 350 00		1 350 00				24	
						25	

Figure 24–3 Recording the Adjustment for Uncollectible Accounts on the Work Sheet (continued)

previous years. If the previous years' uncollectible accounts exactly equaled the estimate, **Allowance for Uncollectible Accounts** would have a zero balance. This seldom happens.

Also notice that the new balance is extended first to the Adjusted Trial Balance Credit column and then to the Balance Sheet Credit column.

Math Hints

Calculating Percentages

An easier way to calculate percentages or ratios is:

- to round dollar amounts to the nearest whole,
- then use the rounded amounts in your calculations.

Reporting Estimated Uncollectible Amounts on the Financial Statements

The **Uncollectible Accounts Expense** account appears on On Your Mark's income statement as an expense. The placement of the **Uncollectible Accounts Expense** account is shown in the partial income statement in **Figure 24–4**.

Figure 24–4 Reporting Uncollectible Accounts on the Income Statement

On Your Mark Athletic Wear Income Statement For the Year Ended December 31, 20--				
Operating Expenses				
Supplies Expense			600 00	
Uncollectible Accounts Expense			1 350 00	
Total Operating Expenses				38 345 00
Operating Income				24 698 00

On the balance sheet, **Allowance for Uncollectible Accounts** is listed immediately below **Accounts Receivable** in the Assets section. The partial balance sheet of On Your Mark is shown in **Figure 24–5**.

Figure 24–5 Reporting Allowance for Uncollectible Accounts on the Balance Sheet

On Your Mark Athletic Wear Balance Sheet December 31, 20--			
Assets			
Cash in Bank			12 650 00
Accounts Receivable		44 893 00	
Less: Allowance for Uncollectible Accounts		1 475 00	43 418 00

Math Skill Builder Activity

Calculating Percentages Have students practice calculating percentages by giving them this word problem: Mark Grayson was doing some early back-to-school shopping and wanted to hit the store sales. He found a pair of athletic shoes regularly priced at $72.50, with a 25% discount; a duffel bag priced at $33.93, with a 20% discount; and a parka priced at $56.45, with a 50% discount. What is the price for each item after the discount? (Shoes = $54.38; duffel bag = $27.14; parka = $28.23)

2 TEACH (Cont'd.)

Visual Learning

Figure 24–4 Reporting Uncollectible Accounts on the Income Statement

Using **Transparency 24–9**, point out that the estimated amount of uncollectible accounts is an expense to the business and is reported with other expenses on the income statement.

Figure 24–5 Reporting Allowance for Uncollectible Accounts on the Balance Sheet

Using **Transparency 24–10**, explain the reporting of uncollectible accounts on the balance sheet. Ask students what the amount of $43,418 represents. (Book value of Accounts Receivable)

Teaching Tips

Emphasize that the allowance for uncollectible accounts aids in determining the appropriate balance to report for Accounts Receivable. Without allowing for uncollectible accounts, the business would overstate its assets, thus misleading readers of its financial reports.

Point out that managers would compare actual uncollectible amounts with the estimate to determine that estimated amounts are correct. Managers would also track uncollectible amounts to determine whether the business should revise its credit rules.

Math Review for Accounting
Photocopy appropriate *Activity Sheets* for students who need additional practice in basic math skills.

2 TEACH (Cont'd.)

Demonstration Problem Step-by-Step Practice
Use demonstration problem 24–4 to give students practice in preparing partial financial statements to report uncollectible accounts.

Visual Learning

Figure 24–6 Journalizing and Posting the Adjusting Entry for Uncollectible Accounts

Using **Transparency 24–11**, review the journal entry for the uncollectible accounts adjustment.

Teaching Tips

Remind students that an adjusting entry for uncollectible accounts is journalized only at the end of the fiscal period.

After students read the paragraphs under "Writing Off Uncollectible Accounts Receivable," pose this question: When the allowance method is used and it is clear that a charge customer is not going to pay the amount owed, how is the uncollectible amount removed from the accounting records? Have students brainstorm the journal entry that must be made. Then analyze the entry using T accounts and stressing why the allowance account is used rather than the expense account.

Key Points

Allowance for Uncollectible Accounts
The balance of Allowance for Uncollectible Accounts reduces the balance of Accounts Receivable.

Notice that the balances of **Accounts Receivable** and **Allowance for Uncollectible Accounts** are entered in the first amount column. The difference between the two balances—the book value of accounts receivable—is entered in the second amount column.

Journalizing the Adjusting Entry for Uncollectible Accounts

After the work sheet is completed and the financial statements are prepared, the adjusting entries are journalized. The information for the adjusting entries is found in the Adjustments section of the work sheet as shown in **Figure 24–3.**

Figure 24–6 shows how the adjusting entry for the estimated uncollectible accounts expense is recorded in the general journal and posted to the appropriate general ledger accounts.

GENERAL JOURNAL — PAGE 14

	DATE		DESCRIPTION	POST. REF.	DEBIT	CREDIT	
1	20--		Adjusting Entries				1
2	Dec.	31	Uncollectible Accounts Expense	675	1 350 00		2
3			Allowance for Uncollectible Accts.	117		1 350 00	3
4							4

ACCOUNT Allowance for Uncollectible Accounts — ACCOUNT NO. 117

DATE		DESCRIPTION	POST. REF.	DEBIT	CREDIT	BALANCE DEBIT	BALANCE CREDIT
20--							
Dec.	1	Balance	✓				125 00
	31	Adjusting Entry	G14		1 350 00		1 475 00

ACCOUNT Uncollectible Accounts Expense — ACCOUNT NO. 675

DATE		DESCRIPTION	POST. REF.	DEBIT	CREDIT	BALANCE DEBIT	BALANCE CREDIT
20--							
Dec.	31	Adjusting Entry	G14	1 350 00		1 350 00	

Figure 24–6 Journalizing and Posting the Adjusting Entry for Uncollectible Accounts

At the end of the period, the balance of the **Uncollectible Accounts Expense** account is closed, along with the balances of the other expense accounts, to **Income Summary. Uncollectible Accounts Expense** has a zero balance at the beginning of the next period. The balance of **Allowance for Uncollectible Accounts** is not affected by the closing entries. Its balance at the beginning of the next period is $1,475.

Writing Off Uncollectible Accounts Receivable

When it becomes clear that a charge customer is not going to pay the amount owed, the uncollectible account is removed from the accounting records.

MEETING SPECIAL NEEDS

Students with Hearing Impairments Students with hearing impairments take in most information visually. As a result, they will tire more quickly than other students. Periodically check to ensure that the student understands the material being presented. Do so by asking questions; do not rely simply on the student's assurances.

Allowance for Uncollectible Accounts acts as a reservoir—at the end of the period, it is "filled up" by the adjusting entry. The account balance is saved until it is needed some time in the future. When a charge customer's account finally proves uncollectible, the business dips into that reservoir to write off the account. In other words, **Allowance for Uncollectible Accounts** is reduced when a specific account is written off. Let's look at an example.

Business Transaction

On April 18, after many attempts to collect the amount owed, On Your Mark decides to write off the account of Megan Sullivan for $150, Memorandum 236.

ANALYSIS

Identify 1. The accounts affected are **Allowance for Uncollectible Accounts, Accounts Receivable** (controlling), and **Accounts Receivable–Megan Sullivan** (subsidiary).

Classify 2. **Allowance for Uncollectible Accounts** is a contra asset account. **Accounts Receivable** (controlling) and **Accounts Receivable–Megan Sullivan** (subsidiary) are asset accounts.

+/– 3. **Allowance for Uncollectible Accounts** is decreased by $150. **Accounts Receivable** (controlling) and **Accounts Receivable–Megan Sullivan** (subsidiary) are decreased by $150.

DEBIT-CREDIT RULE

4. Decreases to contra asset accounts are recorded as debits. Debit **Allowance for Uncollectible Accounts** for $150.
5. Decreases to asset accounts are recorded as credits. Credit **Accounts Receivable** (controlling) and **Accounts Receivable–Megan Sullivan** (subsidiary) for $150.

T ACCOUNTS

6.

Allowance for Uncollectible Accounts

Debit –	Credit +
150	

Accounts Receivable

Debit +	Credit –
	150

Accounts Receivable Subsidiary Ledger
Megan Sullivan

Debit +	Credit –
	150

JOURNAL ENTRY

7.

GENERAL JOURNAL PAGE 16

	DATE		DESCRIPTION	POST. REF.	DEBIT	CREDIT	
1	20--						1
2	Apr.	18	Allow. for Uncollectible Accts.		150 00		2
3			Accts. Rec./Megan Sullivan	✓		150 00	3
4			Memorandum 236				4
5							5

CHAPTER 24
SECTION 2, PAGES 658–666

2 TEACH (Cont'd.)

Visual Learning

Business Transaction

Using **Transparency 24–12**, guide students through the analysis and recording of the entry to write off an uncollectible account.

Demonstration Problem
Step-by-Step Practice

Use demonstration problem 24–5 to give students practice in making entries to write off uncollectible accounts using the allowance method.

Chapter Reviews and Working Papers

Refer students to *Study Plans* located at the beginning of Chapter 24 in the workbook.

REINFORCING STUDY SKILLS

Active Listening Techniques Learning through listening may be difficult for many students because people speak at an average of about 200 words a minute, while they think at a rate about four times faster. Unless a person is consciously focusing on the speaker's words, the mind tends to wander onto other subjects during the extra time, such as daydreaming or thinking about everyday events and plans. Remind students that an important technique for active listening is to ask questions during the speaker's presentation or lecture to clarify information or to review a point.

2 TEACH (Cont'd.)

Visual Learning

Business Transaction

Using **Transparency 24–13,** have students analyze the transaction to record the receipt of payment from a customer whose account has been written off.

Teaching Tip

Remind students that no expense account is affected by a write-off using the allowance method.

Making Decisions: Point out that once a customer has paid the amount owed, the reinstated account has a zero balance and is in good standing. Ask students to discuss whether a business should once again grant credit to a customer who had previously failed to pay an account balance on time. Have students decide whether they would or would not grant credit. Ask for the reasons for their decisions. L1

With the allowance method, an expense account is not affected by the write-off of a specific account. The expense is recorded as an adjusting entry.

Collecting an Account Written Off by the Allowance Method

A charge customer whose account was written off as uncollectible might later pay the amount owed. When this happens:

- First, reinstate the customer's account.
- Second, record the cash receipt.

Business Transaction

On November 19 On Your Mark received a check for $150 from Megan Sullivan, whose account was written off April 18, Memorandum 294 and Receipt 2243.

ANALYSIS

Identify 1. The accounts affected are **Accounts Receivable** (controlling), **Accounts Receivable—Megan Sullivan** (subsidiary), and **Allowance for Uncollectible Accounts.**

Classify 2. **Accounts Receivable** (controlling) and **Accounts Receivable—Megan Sullivan** (subsidiary) are asset accounts. **Allowance for Uncollectible Accounts** is a contra asset account.

+/− 3. **Accounts Receivable** (controlling) and **Accounts Receivable—Megan Sullivan** (subsidiary) are increased by $150. **Allowance for Uncollectible Accounts** is increased by $150.

DEBIT-CREDIT RULE

4. Increases to asset accounts are recorded as debits. Debit **Accounts Receivable** (controlling) and **Accounts Receivable—Megan Sullivan** (subsidiary) for $150.
5. Increases to contra asset accounts are recorded as credits. Credit **Allowance for Uncollectible Accounts** for $150.

T ACCOUNTS

6.

Accounts Receivable

Debit +	Credit −
150	

Allowance for Uncollectible Accounts

Debit −	Credit +
	150

Accounts Receivable Subsidiary Ledger
Megan Sullivan

Debit +	Credit −
150	

CRITICAL THINKING ACTIVITY

Predicting Consequences Point out to students that the normal balance side of Allowance for Uncollectible Accounts is a credit. Could the account ever have a debit balance? Have students explain. (Yes. If the actual amount of accounts written off totaled more than the amount that was estimated, the account would have a debit balance instead of its normal credit balance.)

JOURNAL ENTRY

7.

	GENERAL JOURNAL			PAGE 18		
	DATE	DESCRIPTION	POST. REF.	DEBIT	CREDIT	
1	20--					1
2	Nov. 19	Accts. Rec./Megan Sullivan	/	150 00		2
3		Allow. for Uncollectible Accts.			150 00	3
4		Memorandum 294				4
5						5

After this transaction is posted, the cash receipt transaction is journalized and posted. **Figure 24–7** shows Megan Sullivan's account after the cash receipt transaction is posted. The account shows that:

(1) The account was declared uncollectible and was written off.
(2) The account was reinstated.
(3) The account was collected in full.

NAME *Megan Sullivan*
ADDRESS *883 Bisbee Drive, Dallas, TX 75211*

DATE		DESCRIPTION	POST. REF.	DEBIT	CREDIT	BALANCE
20--						
Jan.	1	Balance	✓			150 00
Apr.	18	Written off as uncollectible	G16		150 00	—
Nov.	19	Reinstated	G18	150 00		150 00
	19		G18		150 00	—

Figure 24–7 Megan Sullivan Account

ANALYZING FINANCIAL REPORTS

The Balance Sheet

In the last chapter, you learned about vertical analysis of the income statement. Another type of analysis is **horizontal analysis.** Horizontal analysis is the comparison of the same items on a financial statement for two or more accounting periods. For example, you might compare changes in depreciation or uncollectible amounts from one year to the next.

Look at the Office Depot balance sheet on page A-45. You'll see financial data for two years. The earlier year is the base year. Amounts in the current year are compared to the base year. To complete a horizontal analysis, the amounts for the base year (2000) are subtracted from the current year (2001). The result is the amount of the increase or decrease over the base year. These amounts are then calculated as percentages of the base year amounts.

▶ **Analyze the Report:**

Use the Office Depot balance sheet to complete the following:

1. By what amount and percentage did total assets and total stockholders' equity change from 2000 to 2001?
2. How does horizontal analysis provide useful information to a reader of an annual report?

ANALYZING FINANCIAL REPORTS

Analyze the Report (Answers)

1. Changes in major categories:

Total Assets:	+$135,309	($4,331,643 − $4,196,334)
	+3.22%	($135,309 ÷ $4,196,334)
Total Stockholders' Equity:	+$247,187	($1,848,438 − $1,601,251)
	+15.44%	($247,187 ÷ $1,601,251)

2. It shows how certain balances have changed since the previous accounting period. Such analysis allows users to examine the financial data for relationships and trends.

2 TEACH (Cont'd.)

Visual Learning

Figure 24–7 Megan Sullivan Account

Using **Transparency 24–14**, have students describe each of the entries in the subsidiary ledger account.

Teaching Tip

Review horizontal analysis and how percentages are used to compare amounts from one year to the next. Remind students that the earlier year is the base year and that all percentages are calculated using base year amounts.

The Office Depot 2001 Annual Report
Refer students to pages A-39–A-48 in the back of the book.

CHAPTER 24
SECTION 2, PAGES 658–666

3 ASSESS

Thinking Critically (Answers)

1. Reduce Accounts Receivable to the amount the business expects to receive, and charge estimated uncollectible amounts to the current fiscal period.
2. An estimate is made of the amount(s) owed by charge customers that will go unpaid. Using an estimate allows a company to match expenses and revenue for the period.

Analyzing Accounting (Answers)

Students should prepare a line graph with graph paper or computer software. Use graphs as a basis for discussing the abuse of credit in the business world.

Problem 24–2 (Answers)

See the TAE of *Chapter Reviews and Working Papers* for journal entries.
Ending debit balances:
Cash in Bank $10,470; Accts. Rec. $19,350; Uncoll. Accts. Exp. $1,850; Accts. Rec./Jack Bowers $0
Ending credit balances:
Allow. for Uncoll. Accounts $3,050

Chapter Reviews and Working Papers Refer students to the Chapter 24 workbook pages to answer *Check Your Understanding* activities.

4 CLOSE

Section Wrap-Up

Demonstration: Make up a scenario for an uncollectible account. Have different students analyze the transaction using T accounts and make a journal entry to write off and then reinstate the uncollectible account using the allowance method. L1

SECTION 2 Check Your Understanding

Now that you have studied this section, complete the following questions and problems.

Thinking Critically

1. What two objectives are met by the uncollectible accounts adjustment at the end of the period?
2. Explain the use of the allowance method of accounting for uncollectible accounts.

Analyzing Accounting

A review of the books for Mary Sawyer's business, The Secret Garden, revealed a disturbing trend. Her uncollectible accounts continue to increase. You suspect that Mary is far too nice about extending "in store" credit. You strongly recommend that she change her credit policies and collect on the outstanding accounts for this year. However, Mary just doesn't seem to understand the big picture, and she requested an illustration. Using a line graph, map out the uncollectibles for the past five years using the figures given below.

Year 1 $1,500
Year 2 $1,875
Year 3 $2,300
Year 4 $2,422
Year 5 $2,800

Problem 24–2 Writing Off Accounts Under the Allowance Method

Taylor Furniture Company Inc. uses the allowance method of accounting for uncollectible accounts.

Instructions In your working papers:
(1) Record the following transactions in the general journal on page 24.
(2) Post the transactions to the appropriate accounts.
(3) Prepare the Assets section of the balance sheet for Taylor Furniture Company Inc. using the partial general ledger in your working papers. The balance of other asset accounts are **Merchandise Inventory**, $42,000; **Supplies**, $1,500; and **Prepaid Insurance**, $1,200.

Date	Transactions
May 4	Using the allowance method, wrote off the account of Jack Bowers for $1,050 as uncollectible, Memorandum 241.
Nov. 18	Received $1,050 from Jack Bowers in full payment of his account, which was written off May 4, Memorandum 321 and Receipt 1078.
Dec. 31	The adjusting entry for the estimated uncollectible accounts expense for the year ended December 31 was $1,850.

RETEACHING SECTION 2

Explaining the Allowance Method In explaining the allowance method, try to get students to think of the allowance account as a worst-case scenario. The allowance is the business's best guess as to the amount it might lose as a result of credit customers not making their payments. As the possibility of a nonpayment turns into reality, the amount of the lost revenue must be taken out of the allowance account and turned into a definite expense (Uncollectible Accounts Expense).

Estimating Uncollectible Accounts Receivable

Under the allowance method of accounting for uncollectible accounts, businesses estimate the uncollectible accounts expense at the end of the period. In this section you will learn about two methods used to estimate uncollectible accounts expense.

Estimating Uncollectible Accounts Expense

The percentage of net sales and the aging of accounts receivable are two ways a business may calculate an estimate of uncollectible accounts expenses. These estimates are based on judgment and past experience.

Percentage of Net Sales Method

When using the **percentage of net sales method** for estimating uncollectible accounts expense, the business assumes that a certain percentage of each year's net sales will be uncollectible. To find the adjustment for uncollectible accounts expense:

(1) Determine the percentage.
(2) Calculate net sales.
(3) Multiply net sales by the percentage.
(4) Enter the amount calculated above on the work sheet.

Let's see how this method works. First, the percentage is determined. As you can see, in recent years On Your Mark's actual uncollectible accounts have been approximately 2 percent of net sales. On this basis, On Your Mark's accountant believes that the 2 percent figure should be used to estimate uncollectible accounts expense.

Year	Net Sales	Uncollectible Accounts	Percentage
2005	$ 59,000	$1,062	(1.8%)
2006	65,000	1,430	(2.2%)
2007	67,000	1,273	(1.9%)
Totals	$191,000	$3,765	(2.0%)

Second, the amount of net sales is calculated. Remember that net sales equals sales minus sales discounts and sales returns and allowances.

What You'll Learn

- How to use the percentage of net sales method to determine the estimated uncollectible accounts expense.
- How to use the aging of accounts receivable method to determine estimated uncollectible accounts expense.

Why It's Important

In order to use the allowance method, uncollectible accounts expense is estimated at the end of the period.

KEY TERMS

percentage of net sales method
aging of accounts receivable method

RESOURCE MANAGER

Reproducible Masters
- Lesson Plans
- Chapter Reviews and Working Papers (CRWP) TAE
- Demonstration Problems

Transparencies
- Section Focus Transparency
- Teaching Transparencies
- Source Document Transparencies
- Solution Transparencies

Multimedia
- ExamView CD-ROM
- Electronic Learning Center CD-ROM
- Interactive Lesson Planner CD-ROM

1 FOCUS

Introducing the Section

In this section students will learn how businesses estimate the amount of their uncollectible accounts expense.

Section Concepts

- How to use the percentage of net sales method to determine the estimated uncollectible accounts expense.
- How to use the aging of accounts receivable method to determine estimated uncollectible accounts expense.

Visual Learning

Section 3 Focus

Use **Transparency 24–15** to introduce section concepts.

BELL RINGER

Estimating: Tell students they are planning a car wash to raise money for new band uniforms. Have them create a plan outlining costs, prices, and expected profits. Then ask how they chose costs and prices. Discuss estimating and how it is based on experience and analyzing similar data or situations—just as businesses analyze data to estimate uncollectible accounts. L1

Concept Development: Estimating Uncollectible Accounts Expense

Discussion: Point out that to match revenues earned with expenses, uncollectible accounts expense must be estimated at the end of a fiscal period. Under the allowance method, the amount of uncollectible accounts is an estimate. Have students name factors that could cause an estimate to be off. L1

2 TEACH

GUIDED PRACTICE

Reading Accounting

- Have students read the chart in Figure 24–8. Have them discuss the ease of understanding information presented in a table versus the same information given in a narrative format. L1

Teaching Tips

Demonstrate the percentage of net sales method of estimating uncollectible accounts. Have students practice estimating uncollectible accounts by making up several balances for these accounts: Sales, Sales Discounts, Sales Returns and Allowances, and different percentages of estimated net sales uncollectible.

The percentage of net sales method is used here because it is fairly easy for students to understand. Point out that other methods are also used to estimate uncollectible accounts. Each business chooses a method that is reasonable for its particular circumstances.

Visual Learning

Figure 24–8 Computer-Generated Analysis of Accounts Receivable

Using **Transparency 24–16**, explain the categories (ages) of accounts receivable. Point out that in most situations, the older the account receivable, the less likely the business is to collect the amount owed.

Strategies for Teaching International Accounting

To enrich study of international accounting, refer students to the additional critical thinking activities in the booklet.

International ACCOUNTING

Decimal Points

If you work in international business, you may encounter some numbers written like this: 439,45 or 15,2. Don't worry, a number hasn't gotten lost. In Zimbabwe, for example, commas are used in the same way decimal points are used in the U.S. In Germany, decimal points indicate thousands, while commas indicate tenths: 17.203,6 in Germany is the same as 17,203.6 in the U.S.

ACCOUNTING Flashbacks

COLLECTING TAXES

The ancient Greek city-state of Mycenae kept records of every person's wealth to help in collecting taxes. Taxes were taken in the form of wheat, livestock, and honey.

As shown, net sales for On Your Mark is $67,500.

Sales		$74,500
Less: Sales Discounts	$3,000	
Sales Returns and Allowances	4,000	− 7,000
Net Sales		$67,500

Third, the uncollectible accounts expense for the current year is determined by multiplying net sales by the percentage. On Your Mark's uncollectible accounts expense for the period is estimated to be $1,350 ($67,500 × .02).

Under this method, the amount calculated is recorded as the adjustment on the work sheet and later entered into the accounting records by journalizing the adjusting entry. At the beginning of the next period, **Allowance for Uncollectible Accounts** will have a credit balance of $1,475 ($1,350 adjustment plus $125 existing balance in the account).

The Aging of Accounts Receivable Method

When using the **aging of accounts receivable method**, the uncollectible accounts expense is based on the date each customer account is due. This method assumes that the longer an account is overdue, the less likely it is to be collected. To find the adjustment for uncollectible accounts expense:

(1) "Age," or classify and group, each account according to due date.
(2) Determine a percentage for each group.
(3) Multiply the amount per group by the percentage per group and add the results.
(4) Enter on the work sheet the total estimated uncollectible amount (calculated above) adjusted by any balance in **Allowance for Uncollectible Accounts.**

Let's look at an example. First, each customer account is "aged," or classified and grouped according to its due date.

The computer printout in **Figure 24–8** is an analysis of On Your Mark's "aged" accounts receivable. As you can see, each customer account is placed in a group according to due date.

On Your Mark Athletic Wear
ANALYSIS OF ACCOUNTS RECEIVABLE
December 31, 20--

Account ID	Customer's Name	Total Amount Owed	Not Yet Due	Days Past Due 1–30	31–60	61–90	Over 90
DIM	Joe Dimaio	$ 300.00	$ 300.00				
GAL	Robert Galvin	50.00		$ 50.00			
KLE	Casey Klein	800.00					$ 800.00
MON	Anita Montero	200.00	200.00				
RAH	Shashi Rahim	175.00			$ 175.00		
RAM	Gabriel Ramos	1,000.00	1,000.00				
SUL	Megan Sullivan	40.00				$ 40.00	
TAM	Tammy's Fitness	225.00	225.00				
WON	Kim Wong	306.50		306.50			
YOU	Lara Young	750.00	750.00				
	TOTALS	$ 3,846.50	$ 2,475.00	$ 356.50	$ 175.00	$ 40.00	$ 800.00

Figure 24–8 Computer-Generated Analysis of Accounts Receivable

Teaching International ACCOUNTING

Converting Foreign Amounts Provide students practice in converting foreign numbers by asking them to convert the following amounts into U.S. dollars. As part of the activity, have students research where to find current exchange rates. (Many major newspapers and business newspapers print exchange rates.)

300,000 lira (Turkey)	65 pounds (United Kingdom)
500 euros (European Union)	2,400 rand (South Africa)
85 reals (Brazil)	190 rupees (India)
780 yen (Japan)	400 new shekels (Israel)

Next, the accountant for On Your Mark estimates what percentage of each group will be uncollectible. The percentages range from 2 to 80 percent.

Third, the total amount for each group is multiplied by the percentage for that group. The resulting amounts are the estimated uncollectible amounts for each group. The total of all the estimated uncollectible amounts represents the end-of-period balance of **Allowance for Uncollectible Accounts.** The computer printout in **Figure 24–9** illustrates how the estimated uncollectible amount is determined from the accounts receivable analysis in **Figure 24–8.** As you can see, On Your Mark estimates that a total of $729.26 of its accounts will be uncollectible.

On Your Mark Athletic Wear
AGING OF ACCOUNTS RECEIVABLE
Estimated Uncollectible Amount
December 31, 20--

Age Group	Amount	Estimated Percentage Uncollectible	Estimated Uncollectible Amount
Not yet due	$ 2,475.00	2%	$ 49.50
1–30 days past due	356.50	4%	14.26
31–60 days past due	175.00	10%	17.50
61–90 days past due	40.00	20%	8.00
Over 90 days past due	800.00	80%	640.00
Total	$ 3,846.50		$ 729.26

Figure 24–9 Accounts Receivable Aging Schedule

Finally, an adjustment is entered on the work sheet. This adjustment will bring the balance of **Allowance for Uncollectible Accounts** to the estimate of $729.26.

Suppose the balance of **Allowance for Uncollectible Accounts** reported in the Trial Balance Credit column is $49.80. To determine the adjustment, subtract the balance of **Allowance for Uncollectible Accounts** from the total estimated uncollectible amount. The adjustment amount is $679.46 ($729.26 − $49.80).

After the adjusting entry is journalized and posted, the balance of **Allowance for Uncollectible Accounts** is $729.26 (the balance as determined by the aging schedule).

Uncollectible Accounts Expense

Debit +	Credit −
Adj. 679.46	

Allowance for Uncollectible Accounts

Debit −	Credit +
	Bal. 49.80
	Adj. 679.46
	Bal. 729.26

Key Points

The Adjustment Amount

The amount of the adjustment entered on the work sheet is as follows:

Net Sales Method: Net sales multiplied by the percentage.

Aging of Accounts Receivable Method: The estimated uncollectible amount adjusted by the existing **Allowance for Uncollectible Accounts** balance.

ADDRESSING MULTIPLE LEARNING STYLES

Visual/Spatial Learner Ask students to create a chart to illustrate the analysis of the aged accounts receivable shown in Figure 24–8 on page 668. The chart should include the total amount owed and the four categories for the number of days past due. The account numbers and customer names are not pertinent to the chart. If computers are available, have the students enter the data in a spreadsheet and then create the chart. Students should choose a chart type appropriate for illustrating the data.

2 TEACH (Cont'd.)

Visual Learning

Figure 24–9 Accounts Receivable Aging Schedule

Using **Transparency 24–17,** point out the totals from Figure 24–8 listed in each age group. Explain that business managers choose percentages for each age group based on the company's past experience.

Teaching Tip

Explain that the aging schedule shows amounts yet to be collected. The amount of uncollected accounts generally decreases as the time period of the age groups increases. Note also that as the number of days an account remains uncollected increases, the estimated percentage also increases.

Demonstration Problem
Step-by-Step Practice

Use demonstration problem 24–6 to give students practice estimating uncollectible accounts using the percentage of net sales and the aging of accounts receivable methods.

Thinking Algebraically

Extrapolating: Tell students that the Video Vault has tracked its uncollectible accounts and found these percentages: Qtr. 1, 3.4%; Qtr. 2, 4.3%; Qtr. 3, 3.7%; Qtr. 4, 3.0%. Ask students what percentage the company should use to estimate uncollectible accounts for next year. (Avg. = 3.6%) L1

CHAPTER 24
SECTION 3, PAGES 667–670

3 ASSESS

Thinking Critically (Answers)

1. Customers' accounts are categorized by due dates. A percentage of each category is estimated to be uncollectible. The total of all categories represents the end-of-period balance of Allowance for Uncollectible Accounts.
2. The balance of Allowance for Uncollectible Accounts is subtracted from the total estimated uncollectible amount. That total represents the adjustment amount.

Computing in the Business World (Answers)

Year 1: 3.5%; Year 2: 4%; Year 3: 3%; Year 4: 2%

Problem 24–3 (Answers)

Uncollectible Accounts Expense:
Andrews Co. $2,800.02
The Book Nook $2,047.81
Cable Inc. $2,550.00
Davis Inc. $1,282.40
Ever-Sharp Co. $1,164.38

Dec. 31: Dr. Uncollectible Accounts Expense $1,282.40; Cr. Allowance for Uncollectible Accounts $1,282.40

Chapter Reviews and Working Papers Refer students to the Chapter 24 workbook pages to answer *Check Your Understanding* activities.

4 CLOSE

Section Wrap-Up

Writing: Have students write a paragraph describing two ways of estimating uncollectible accounts and giving examples of how each is used. L1

SECTION 3 Check Your Understanding

Now that you have studied this section, complete the following questions and problem.

Thinking Critically

1. Explain the aging of accounts receivable method of estimating uncollectible accounts expense.
2. How do you determine the adjustment of uncollectible accounts expense when using the net sales method and the aging of accounts receivable method?

Computing in the Business World

Hernando's Card Shop is planning to expand. Before they expand, the owner wants to review the uncollectible accounts. Hernando asks you to calculate the percentage of uncollectible accounts per year.

	Net Sales	Uncollectible Accounts
Year 1	$23,000	$ 800
Year 2	28,750	1,200
Year 3	46,000	1,345
Year 4	52,000	1,150

Problem 24–3 Estimating Uncollectible Accounts Expense Using the Percentage of Net Sales Method

Listed below are the end-of-period account balances for several stationery and office supply companies. Each company uses the percentage of net sales method to estimate its uncollectible accounts expense. The percentage used by each company is also listed.

Instructions Using the form provided in your working papers:

(1) Calculate the amount of the adjustment for uncollectible accounts expense using the percentage of net sales method.
(2) Record the adjusting entry for the estimated uncollectible accounts expense for Davis Inc.

	Sales	Sales Discounts	Sales Returns and Allowances	Percentage of Net Sales Uncollectible
Andrews Co.	$142,360	$1,423	$ 936	2
The Book Nook	209,100	3,180	1,139	1
Cable Inc.	173,270	1,730	1,540	1½
Davis Inc.	65,460	650	690	2
Ever-Sharp Co.	95,085	900	1,035	1¼

RETEACHING SECTION 3

Aging Accounts Receivable Aging accounts receivable is classifying each customer's balance according to the date the account is due. Ask students where they get the information for aging the accounts receivable (the accounts receivable ledger). Have students refer to Figure 24–9 on page 669 and ask them why the amounts in the Estimated Percentage Uncollectible column get increasingly larger with the number of days past due. (The longer an account is overdue, the less likely it will be collected.) Explain that the business determines these percentages based on past experience with uncollectible accounts.

CHAPTER 24 SUMMARY

KEY CONCEPTS

1. Customer accounts that are uncollectible are an expense to the business. When it is apparent that a customer account is uncollectible, it is written off using either the direct write-off method or the allowance method.
2. Recording the direct write-off of an accounts receivable:
   Debit: **Uncollectible Accounts Expense** Credit: **Accounts Receivable** (controlling/subsidiary)
3. When a charge customer whose account was previously written off pays the amount owed, the account is first reinstated before the cash receipt is recorded.
4. Recording reinstatement of an account written off using the direct write-off method:
   Debit: **Accounts Receivable** (controlling/subsidiary) Credit: **Uncollectible Accounts Expense**
5. The allowance method of accounting for uncollectible accounts enables the business to match sales and uncollectible accounts expense in the same period.
6. **Allowance for Uncollectible Accounts** is a contra asset account and is shown on the balance sheet as a deduction from **Accounts Receivable.**
7. The book value of accounts receivable is the **Accounts Receivable** balance minus the **Allowance for Uncollectible Accounts** balance. It is the amount the business can reasonably expect to receive from all accounts receivable.
8. Recording the adjusting entry using the allowance method:
   Debit: **Uncollectible Accounts Expense** Credit: **Allowance for Uncollectible Accounts**
9. Recording the write-off of a specific uncollectible account under the allowance method:
   Debit: **Allowance for Uncollectible Accounts** Credit: **Accounts Receivable** (controlling/subsidiary)
10. Recording the reinstatement of an account written off using the allowance method:
   Debit: **Accounts Receivable** (controlling/subsidiary) Credit: **Allowance for Uncollectible Accounts**
11. Two common methods used to estimate uncollectible accounts expense are the percentage of net sales method and the aging of accounts receivable method.
12. Calculating uncollectible accounts expense using the percentage of net sales method:

   Net Sales × Percentage of Net Sales Estimated Uncollectible = Uncollectible Accounts Expense

13. Calculating uncollectible accounts expense using the aging of accounts receivable method:

Age Group	Amount	×	Estimated Percentage Uncollectible	=	Estimated Uncollectible Amount
Not yet due	XXXXX		XX		XXXX
1–30 days past due	XXXXX		XX		XXXX
31–60 days past due	XXXXX		XX		XXXX
61–90 days past due	XXXXX		XX		XXXX
91–180 days past due	XXXXX		XX		XXXX
Over 180 days past due	XXXXX		XX		XXXX
Total					**XXXX**
Allowance for Uncollectible Accounts, end of period					

SUMMARY CHAPTER 24

Chapter 24 Quiz

Student ____ Class ____ Instructor ____
Date Assigned ____ Date Completed ____

CHAPTER 24 QUIZ

Uncollectible Accounts Receivable

QUESTIONS (True-False)

Directions: In the space provided, indicate whether each statement is true or false.

____ 1. Uncollectible accounts are debts the business plans not to pay.
____ 2. The direct write-off method removes the uncollectible amount from Accounts Receivable and records it as an expense.
____ 3. An uncollectible account is the same thing as a bad debt.
____ 4. An uncollectible account that is written off and then paid must be reinstated in the accounting records.
____ 5. Matching uncollectible accounts expense with revenue in the same fiscal period is an example of the relevance principle.
____ 6. The allowance method requires an estimate of uncollectible accounts for a fiscal period.
____ 7. Allowance for Uncollectible Accounts is a contra asset account.
____ 8. Uncollectible accounts expense is reported on the income statement.
____ 9. Percentage of net sales is one method of estimating uncollectible accounts expense.
____ 10. The aging of accounts receivable method requires each customer's account to be written off as it is determined to be uncollectible.

QUESTIONS (True-False)

1. Uncollectible accounts are debts the business plans not to pay.
2. The direct write-off method removes the uncollectible amount from Accounts Receivable and records it as an expense.
3. An uncollectible account is the same thing as a bad debt.
4. An uncollectible account that is written off and then paid must be reinstated in the accounting records.
5. Matching uncollectible accounts expense with revenue is an example of the relevance principle.
6. The allowance method requires an estimate of uncollectible accounts for a fiscal period.
7. Allowance for Uncollectible Accounts is a contra asset account.
8. Uncollectible accounts expense is reported on the income statement.
9. Percentage of net sales is one method of estimating uncollectible accounts expense.
10. The aging of accounts receivable method requires each customer's account to be written off as it is determined to be uncollectible.

ANSWERS

1. False
2. True
3. True
4. True
5. False
6. True
7. True
8. True
9. True
10. False

REVIEW AND ACTIVITIES CHAPTER 24

USING KEY TERMS

See the *Glossary* for the definitions of these terms. Have students share their "help sheets" in class. Discuss how teaching a topic to someone else aids the learning process.

Understanding Accounting Concepts and Procedures

(Answers)

1. Direct write-off method, allowance method. The allowance method is likely to be used by a large business, the direct write-off method by a business that sells mainly for cash.
2. To make it obvious the account was written off, not paid off.
3. The first journal entry reinstates the customer's account; the second records the cash receipt.
4. The matching principle—because revenue is not matched with expenses incurred to earn that revenue.
5. Uncollectible Accounts Expense is debited; Allowance for Uncollectible Accounts is credited.
6. It is a contra account to Accounts Receivable.
7. By subtracting the balance of Allowance for Uncollectible Accounts from the Accounts Receivable account.
8. Using direct write-off, Accounts Receivable and the customer's account are credited; Uncollectible Accounts Expense is debited. With the allowance method, Accounts Receivable and the customer's account are also credited, but the account debited is Allowance for Uncollectible Accounts.
9. Percentage of net sales and aging of accounts receivable.
10. $12,600.
11. The aging of accounts receivable method.

CHAPTER 24 REVIEW AND ACTIVITIES

USING KEY TERMS

You applied for your CPA license and are in the process of studying for the big exam. You need a quick review on uncollectible accounts. You decide to write a description of each key term and show its relationship to **Accounts Receivable.** Your college professor recommends that you teach this unit to his Accounting students as another way to fully comprehend the material. Use the terms below to create your "help sheet."

- aging of accounts receivable method
- allowance method
- book value of accounts receivable
- direct write-off method
- percentage of net sales method
- uncollectible accounts

Understanding Accounting Concepts and Procedures

Instructions

Answer the following questions on a separate sheet of paper:

1. Name two methods of accounting for uncollectible accounts. Which method is likely to be used by a large business with many charge customers? Which method is likely to be used by a business that sells mainly on a cash basis?
2. Why is an entry made in the Description column of the subsidiary ledger when a customer's account is written off?
3. Describe the two journal entries needed to record the collection of an account that was previously written off.
4. Explain which accounting principle is violated when the direct write-off method of accounting for uncollectible accounts is used.
5. Under the allowance method, which two general ledger accounts are affected by the adjusting entry to record the estimated uncollectible account expense for the period?
6. What is the classification of the account **Allowance for Uncollectible Accounts?**
7. How is the book value of accounts receivable determined?
8. Explain the difference between the write-off of a customer's account using the direct write-off method and the allowance method.
9. Name two methods that can be used to estimate the uncollectible accounts expense.
10. If a company had net sales of $630,000 and estimates that its uncollectible accounts will be 2 percent of net sales, what is the amount of the adjustment?
11. Which method of estimating uncollectible accounts analyzes each customer account?

ASSESSMENT RESOURCES

Choose assessment strategies from the following pages to evaluate your students' progress.

Student Edition

Check Your Understanding, pp. 657, 666, 670
Chapter 24 Problems, pp. 675–677
Analyzing Financial Reports, p. 665

Assessment and Evaluation Masters

Chapter 24 Study Plan, *Glencoe Workbook (CRWP)*
Chapter 24 Self-Test, *Glencoe Workbook (CRWP)*
Chapter 24 Test, *Chapter Tests* Booklet
Chapter 24 Activity, *School-to-Work Handbook*
Chapter 24 Exam*View*

Teacher Wraparound Edition

Critical Thinking Activity, p. 664
Reteaching Sections 1–3, pp. 657, 666, 670
Chapter 24 Quiz, p. 671

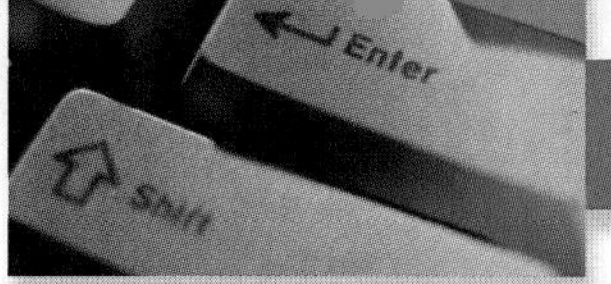

CHAPTER 24 REVIEW AND ACTIVITIES

Case Study...

Merchandising Business: Formal Wear

The Black Tie sells and rents tuxedos and formal dresses. They require a down payment to reserve an outfit. The balance is recorded as an account receivable and is due ten days after the outfit is returned.

The Black Tie accepts cash, credit cards, and personal checks. Recently the store has encountered problems collecting accounts receivable. Two customers failed to return their outfits altogether.

Thinking Critically:

1. Suggest a store policy that would help avoid losses from uncollectible accounts and outfits that are not returned.
2. What customer issues might arise if you restrict payment to cash or credit cards only? How can you overcome these issues?

interNET CONNECTION

Outsourcing Accounts Receivable

Outsourcing of accounts receivable is growing at a rapid rate. Since sales on account directly affect cash flow, timely collection of accounts receivable is a measure of a business's success. Businesses seek ways to reduce the expense associated with processing, monitoring, and collecting accounts receivable.

Do This:

1. Conduct research on the Web to find out what it means to outsource accounts receivable. Use search terms like "outsourcing" or "accounts receivable."
2. List three advantages of outsourcing accounts receivable.
3. What is the difference between outsourcing and using a collection agency?

Conducting an Audit with Alex

Peggy Matero, owner of Matero Department Store, uses the allowance method to account for uncollectible accounts. The March 30, 20-- trial balance shows a debit balance of $300 in the **Uncollectible Accounts Expense** account. You discovered that Jan Anderson's account for $300 was written off on March 1 using the direct write-off method instead of the allowance method.

Instructions

What entry was recorded in the general journal on March 1? Which entry should have been recorded in the general journal on March 1?

Workplace Skills

Interpreting and Communicating Information

Presenting information in the most effective method is a powerful workplace skill.

On the Job:

The Clothes Horse, a well-known retailer of men's apparel, is closing its doors. The store wants to collect all accounts receivable before closing.

Thinking Critically:

1. Design a letter to send to all customers with outstanding balances.
2. Design a second collection letter to send to customers with outstanding balances after four weeks have passed.

interNET CONNECTION www.glencoe.com

Do This (Answers)

1. Outsourcing is the use of outside resources to perform activities handled by internal staff. When outsourcing accounts receivable, management contracts with a service provider to handle all aspects of the company's accounts receivable (www.outsourcing.com).
2. Some advantages are the reduction and control of costs, gain of expertise not available internally, quick payments, free capital for other uses, and increased inflow of cash.
3. A collection agency deals only with accounts that are delinquent. An outsourcing company handles all accounts receivable (www.creditworthy.com).

Case Study...

Thinking Critically (Answers)

1. Answers will vary. The store might require a large deposit for rental. Also, they could require payment in advance.
2. Answers will vary. Some customers prefer to pay by check or debit card. Allowing customers to pay by check is better service because it gives them more options, but there is a risk of having checks returned for insufficient funds. The store might accept checks if they are guaranteed by a credit card.

Workplace Skills

Thinking Critically (Answers)

1. Answers will vary. Students should submit a one-page letter with the following points included: how and why the Clothes Horse is closing, why uncollectible accounts are a problem, how customers can close out personal accounts.
2. Answers will vary. Students should try to come up with a more persuasive appeal for payment.

Conducting an Audit with Alex

(Answers)

Mar. 1: Dr. Uncollectible Account Expense $300; Cr. Accts. Rec./Jan Anderson $300
Mar. 1: Dr. Allowance for Uncollectible Accounts $300; Cr. Accts. Rec./Jan Anderson $300

Internet Resources and Activities Handbook

Refer students to the booklet for additional Internet activities.

PEACHTREE CORNER

Uncollectible Accounts

Use the **Receipts** option to write off an uncollectible account. Set the cash GL Account either to **Uncollectible Accounts Expense** (Direct Method) or to **Allowance for Uncollectible Accounts** (Allowance Method). After recording a cash receipt for a reinstated account, be sure to change the cash account back to **Cash in Bank**.

Tasks Analysis Options Reports
Quotes/Sales Orders
Sales/Invoicing...
Receipts...
Finance Charge...
Select for Deposit...

Choose the **Sales/Invoicing** option to reinstate an account that was previously written off. Change the GL Account on the Apply to Sales tab either to **Uncollectible Accounts Expense** (Direct Method) or to **Allowance for Uncollectible Accounts** (Allowance Method). Be sure to set the sales tax to $0.00.

Tasks Analysis Options Reports
Quotes/Sales Orders
Sales/Invoicing...
Receipts...
Finance Charge...
Select for Deposit...

You can also access the Accounts Receivable reports and the **Receipts** and **Sales/Invoicing** options by using the Sales navigation aid.

Writing Off Uncollectible Accounts Receivable

Making the Transition from a Manual to a Computerized System

Task	Perform Accounting Procedures Using Manual Methods	Perform Accounting Procedures Using Automated Methods
Preparing an Aged Accounts Receivable Report	1. Examine each customer account and organize based on due date. 2. Using accounting stationery, list each customer's account in the appropriate past date columns.	1. A preformatted report feature allows the accountant to generate an aging schedule. The software pulls data from information stored in the accounts receivable ledgers.
Writing off an uncollectible account	1. Determine the method to be used to write-off uncollectible accounts. 2. Record a general journal entry to record the write-off. 3. Post the entry to the general ledger and subsidiary ledger. 4. Calculate new balances for the accounts.	1. Determine the method to be used to write-off uncollectible accounts. 2. Outstanding invoices due are stored in the computerized system and tied to the customer's ID. 3. Using the Customer ID, the invoice due is assigned to the account, Allowance for Uncollectible Accounts.

Accounts Receivable

Peachtree Question	Description
How do I set up defaults for the aging of Accounts Receivable ledgers in Peachtree?	1. From the ***Maintain*** menu, select **Default** Information. 2. Select Customers to set or to change default information. (In Peachtree, Accounts Receivable ledgers are referred to as customer accounts.) 3. Click on the Account Aging Tab. 4. Set default for how accounts are to be aged.
How do I write off an uncollectible account in Peachtree?	1. Select **Receipts** from the ***Tasks*** menu. 2. Enter the Customer ID. 3. In the Cash Account field, select Allowance for Uncollectible Accounts. 4. Click the Apply to Invoices tab. 5. Select the Pay box next to the invoices you wish to write off. 6. Click Save.
What does the software do "behind the scenes"?	The customer's account, the list of unpaid invoices, the Accounts Receivable account, and the Allowance for Uncollectible Accounts are updated.

For detailed instructions: See the **Peachtree User Guide** in your Glencoe Working Papers.

Peachtree® Answers to Frequently Asked Questions

Q: Why do some Peachtree reports fail to show all of the transactions?

A: By default, most Peachtree reports show only those transactions entered in the current period. If you enter transactions over multiple periods, you must change the report date option. For example, change the date range to include the entire year.

For additional information, refer to your *Glencoe Peachtree Accounting User Guide*.

APPLICATION OPTIONS

Problem 24–4 Using the Direct Write-Off Method

Sunset Surfwear uses the direct write-off method of accounting for uncollectible accounts.

Instructions

(1) In your working papers, record the following transactions on page 14 in the general journal.
(2) Post the transactions to the appropriate accounts.

Date	Transactions
June 1	Wrote off the $288.75 account of Alex Hamilton as uncollectible, Memorandum 223.
4	Wrote off the $243.60 account of Helen Jun as uncollectible, Memorandum 249.
14	Wrote off the $57.75 account of Nate Moulder as uncollectible, Memorandum 255.
22	Received $288.75 from Alex Hamilton in full payment of his account, Memorandum 298 and Receipt 944.
29	Wrote off the $100.80 account of Martha Adams as uncollectible, Memorandum 329.

Analyze: When an account is written off, what is the impact on **Accounts Receivable** and **Uncollectible Accounts Expense?**

Problem 24–5 Calculating and Recording Estimated Uncollectible Accounts Expense

InBeat CD Shop uses the percentage of net sales method of accounting for uncollectible accounts. At the end of the period, the following account balances appeared on InBeat's trial balance:

Accts. Rec.	$110,000	Allow. for Uncoll. Accts.	$ 4,000
Sales	900,000	Sales Ret. and Allow.	50,000
Sales Disc.	10,000	Uncoll. Accts. Expense	—

Instructions

(1) In your working papers, determine the amount of the adjustment for uncollectible accounts for the period ended June 30. Management estimates that uncollectible accounts will be 1 percent of net sales.
(2) Journalize the adjusting entry on page 8 in the general journal.
(3) Post the adjusting entry to the general ledger accounts.

Analyze: Determine the book value of accounts receivable.

Complete chapter problems one of three ways:

1 **Manual** Glencoe Working Papers

or

2 **Peachtree Complete Accounting** Software

or

3 **QuickBooks** Templates (Problems 24–4, 24–6)

Peachtree®

SMART GUIDE

Step-by-Step Instructions: Problem 24–4

1. Select the problem set for Sunset Surfwear (Prob. 24–4).
2. Rename the company and set the system date.
3. Record the transactions to write off bad debts using the **Receipts** option.
4. Record the transaction (June 22) to reinstate Alex Hamilton's account **(Sales/Invoicing)** and enter the receipt **(Receipts)**.
5. Print the following reports: Cash Receipts Journal, Sales Journal, Customer Ledgers, and General Ledger.
6. Answer the Analyze question.
7. End the session.

TIP: Remember to set the Cash *G/L Account* field to **Uncollectible Accounts Expense** when you write off a bad debt.

EXTENDING THE CONTENT

Exploring Credit Card Debt Annual credit card debt is about $200 billion in the United States. Businesses have seen an increase in credit card delinquencies that exceed 90 days past due or that are no longer collectible. Have students research the topic "credit card debt" to determine current statistics. Ask them to respond to the following questions: What is the most recent estimate of credit card debt? What percentage of today's credit card debt is determined uncollectible? How do businesses attempt to recover these uncollectible debts? What effect does credit card debt have on national consumer debt and personal bankruptcies?

PROBLEMS CHAPTER 24

Problem 24–4 (Answers) Using the Direct Write-Off Method

Journal entries:

June 1: Dr. Uncollectible Accounts Exp. $288.75; Cr. Accts. Rec./Alex Hamilton $288.75; Memo 223

June 4: Dr. Uncollectible Accounts Exp. $243.60; Cr. Accts. Rec./Helen Jun $243.60; Memo 249

June 14: Dr. Uncollectible Accounts Exp. $57.75; Cr. Accts. Rec./Nate Moulder $57.75; Memo 255

June 22: Dr. Accts. Rec./Alex Hamilton $288.75; Cr. Uncollectible Accounts Exp. $288.75; Memo 298

June 22: Dr. Cash in Bank $288.75; Cr. Accts. Rec./Alex Hamilton $288.75; Receipt 944

June 29: Dr. Uncollectible Accounts Exp. $100.80; Cr. Accts. Rec./Martha Adams $100.80; Memo 329

Ending debit balances:

Cash in Bank $10,938.91
Accounts Receivable $7,325.60
Uncollectible Accounts Exp. $402.15

Analyze: Accounts Receivable is decreased, Uncollectible Accounts Expense is increased.

Problem 24–5 (Answers) Calculating and Recording Estimated Uncollectible Accounts Expense

Adjustment for Uncollectible Accounts $8,400

June 30: Dr. Uncollectible Accounts Exp. $8,400; Cr. Allowance for Uncollectible Accounts $8,400

Ending balances:

Allowance for Uncoll. Accts. $12,400
Uncollectible Accounts Exp. $8,400

Analyze: $97,600

PROBLEMS CHAPTER 24

SOURCE DOCUMENT PROBLEM

Problem 24–6 (Answers) Writing Off Accounts Under the Allowance Method

See TAE of *Chapter Reviews and Working Papers* for journal entries.

Ending debit balances:
Cash in Bank $9,437.79
Accounts Receivable $20,723.75
Income Summary $3,000.00

Ending credit balances:
Allowance for Uncollectible Accounts $3,917.00

Total Assets $62,444.54

Analyze: $16,806.75

Problem 24–7 (Answers) Estimating Uncollectible Accounts Expense

Total amount owed $7,211
Not yet due $3,997; 1–30 days $1,255; 31–60 days $743; 61–90 days $601; 91–180 days $319; Over 180 days $296

Estimated uncollectible amount $780.19

June 30: Dr. Uncollectible Accounts Exp. $638.19; Cr. Allowance for Uncollectible Accounts $638.19

Ending balances:
Accounts Receivable $7,211.00
Allowance for Uncollectible Accounts $780.19
Uncollectible Accounts Exp. $638.19

Analyze: $6,430.81

Peachtree®

SMART GUIDE

Step-by-Step Instructions: Problem 24–5

1. Select the problem set for InBeat CD Shop.
2. Rename the company and set the system date.
3. Record the uncollectible accounts adjustment using the **General Journal Entry** option.
4. Print the General Journal and General Ledger reports.
5. Answer the Analyze question.
6. End the session.

Peachtree®

SMART GUIDE

Step-by-Step Instructions: Problem 24–6

1. Select the problem set for Shutterbug Cameras.
2. Record the uncollectible accounts transactions.
3. Record the adjustment for estimated uncollectible accounts.
4. Record the closing entry for **Uncollectible Accounts Expense** using the **General Journal Entry** option.
5. Print reports: Cash Receipts Journal, Sales Journal, Customer Ledgers, General Journal, General Ledger, and Balance Sheet.
6. Answer the Analyze question.
7. End the session.

SOURCE DOCUMENT PROBLEM

Problem 24–6

Use the source documents in your working papers to record the transactions for this problem.

SOURCE DOCUMENT PROBLEM

Problem 24–6 Writing Off Accounts Under the Allowance Method

Shutterbug Cameras uses the allowance method of accounting for uncollectible accounts.

Instructions

(1) In your working papers, record the following transactions on page 9 in the general journal.
(2) Post the transactions to the appropriate accounts.
(3) Prepare the Assets section of the balance sheet for Shutterbug Cameras using the partial general ledger in the working papers. The balances of other asset accounts are **Merchandise Inventory**, $33,000; **Supplies**, $2,000; and **Prepaid Insurance**, $1,200.

Date	Transactions
June 2	Wrote off the $593.25 account of Kalla Booth as uncollectible, Memorandum 329.
9	Wrote off the $840 account of Click Studios as uncollectible, Memorandum 343.
10	Received $131.25 from Jimmy Thompson in full payment of his account, which was written off on November 10, Memorandum 349 and Receipt 210.
12	Wrote off the $945 account of FastForward Productions as uncollectible, Memorandum 474.
30	Recorded the adjusting entry for estimated uncollectible accounts for the period. The uncollectible accounts expense estimate is based on 2 percent of the net sales of $150,000.
30	Recorded the closing entry for **Uncollectible Accounts Expense.**

Analyze: What is the book value of the accounts receivable after the closing entries are posted?

Problem 24–7 Estimating Uncollectible Accounts Expense

Cycle Tech Bicycles uses the allowance method of accounting for uncollectible accounts. The company estimates the uncollectible amount by aging its accounts receivable accounts.

Instructions

(1) Complete the analysis of accounts receivable that is included in your working papers.
(2) Calculate the estimated uncollectible amount. Use the form provided in your working papers.

ACCOUNTING ISSUES

International Auditing Differences The auditing of financial statements in other countries varies by content, level of detail, and application of auditing standards. For example, German standards are brief and address audit policies and procedures at a general level. The United Kingdom's standards are more extensive but are not as detailed as U.S. standards. Other countries have different audit rules. The Securities and Exchange Commission is working with the International Federation of Accountants and the International Organization of Securities Commissions to standardize international audit practices.

(3) Journalize the June 30 adjusting entry for uncollectible accounts expense on page 11 of the general journal. Before the adjusting entry, **Allowance for Uncollectible Accounts** had a credit balance of $142.

(4) Post the adjusting entry to the general ledger accounts.

Analyze: Calculate the book value of accounts receivable.

Problem 24–8 Reporting Uncollectible Amounts on the Financial Statements

The work sheet for River's Edge Canoe & Kayak is included in your working papers. The trial balance is complete, and all of the adjustments are entered except the one required for uncollectible accounts.

Instructions

(1) Record the adjustment for uncollectible accounts expense in the Adjustments section of the work sheet. Uncollectible accounts are estimated to be 1.5 percent of net sales. Label the adjustment (a).

(2) Complete the work sheet.

(3) Prepare an income statement, a statement of retained earnings, and a balance sheet.

(4) Record the adjusting entries on page 18 of the general journal.

(5) Post the adjusting entries. Record and post the closing entries.

Analyze: What is the balance of **Allowance for Uncollectible Accounts** before and after the adjusting entry?

Problem 24–9 Using the Allowance Method for Write-Offs

Buzz Newsstand uses the allowance method for uncollectible accounts.

Instructions

In your working papers, journalize the following transactions on page 13 in the general journal. Post the transactions to the account of Lee Adkins.

Date	Transactions
Jan. 14	Wrote off the $194.50 account of Lee Adkins as uncollectible, Memorandum 498.
June 25	Received a check for $30 from Lee Adkins on account, Memorandum 767 and Receipt 98.
Dec. 10	Received notice that Lee Adkins declared bankruptcy. Received 40 percent of the balance not paid, Receipt 288 and Memorandum 941.

Analyze: If the direct write-off method was used instead of the allowance method, which account would you debit when writing off an account?

Peachtree®

SMART GUIDE

Step-by-Step Instructions: Problem 24–7

1. Select the problem set for Cycle Tech Bicycles.
2. Rename the company and set the system date.
3. Complete the analysis of the accounts receivable provided in your working papers.
4. Based on your analysis, record the uncollectible accounts adjustment using the **General Journal Entry** option.
5. Print a General Journal and General Ledger report to proof your work.
6. Answer the Analyze question.
7. End the session.

Step-by-Step Instructions: Problem 24–8

1. Select the problem set for River's Edge Canoe.
2. Rename the company and set the system date.
3. Record the uncollectible accounts adjustment.
4. Print a Balance Sheet and an Income Statement.
5. Click the Save Pre-closing Balances button.
6. Close the fiscal year.
7. Print a Post-Closing Trial Balance.
8. Answer the Analyze question.
9. End the session.

Step-by-Step Instructions: Problem 24–9

1. Select the problem set for Buzz Newsstand.
2. Rename the company and set the system date.
3. Record the uncollectible accounts transactions.
4. Print the following reports: Cash Receipts Journal, Sales Journal, and Customer Ledgers.
5. Answer the Analyze question.
6. End the session.

SOLUTION NOTES

Problem 24–8 (Answers) Reporting Uncollectible Amounts on the Financial Statements

Adjustment amount $2,239.35
Adjusted TB totals $217,728.80
Net Income $36,745.85
Ending Retained Earnings $46,510.00
Total Assets $92,889.10

See the TAE of *Chapter Reviews and Working Papers* for journal entries.

Ending debit balances:
Merchandise Inventory $35,761.50
Supplies $975.00
Prepaid Insurance $1,100.00

Ending credit balances:
Allow. for Uncoll. Accts. $2,639.35
Accum. Depr.—Store Equip. $4,110.00
Fed. Corp. Inc. Tax Pay. $1,806.00
Retained Earnings $46,510.00

Analyze: $400, $2,639.35

Problem 24–9 (Answers) Using the Allowance Method for Write-Offs

Jan. 14: Dr. Allow. for Uncollectible Accounts $194.50; Cr. Accts. Rec./Lee Adkins $194.50; Memo 498

June 25: Dr. Accts. Rec./Lee Adkins $194.50; Cr. Allow. for Uncollectible Accounts $194.50; Memo 767

June 25: Dr. Cash in Bank $30.00; Cr. Accts. Rec./Lee Adkins $30.00; Receipt 98

Dec. 10: Dr. Cash in Bank $65.80; Cr. Accts. Rec./Lee Adkins $65.80; Receipt 288

Dec. 10: Dr. Allow. for Uncollectible Accounts $98.70; Cr. Accts. Rec./Lee Adkins $98.70; Memo 941

Analyze: Uncollectible Accounts Expense

CHAPTER 25 Resource Manager

Section Resources

	Objectives & Standards	Activities & Features	Reproducible Masters
Chapter Opener *Inventories*	• Explain the importance of maintaining accurate inventory records. • Explain the difference between a periodic and a perpetual inventory system. • Take a physical inventory count and record inventories. • Determine the cost of merchandise inventory using the specific identification; first-in, first-out; last-in, first-out; and weighted average cost methods. • Assign a value to merchandise inventory using the lower-of-cost-or-market rule. • Explain the accounting principles of consistency and conservatism. • Define the accounting terms introduced in this chapter. **National Standards for Business Education**: IA16, IIA6	Exploring the Real World of Business, p. 678 Workplace Connections, p. 679	School-to-Work Handbook
Section 1 *Determining the Quantity of Inventories*	• The purpose of the **Merchandise Inventory** account. • The difference between a periodic and a perpetual inventory system.	Did You Know?, p. 680 A Matter of Ethics, p. 682	Demonstration Problems Strategies for Teaching Ethics in Accounting
Section 2 *Determining the Cost of Inventories*	• How to determine the cost of the merchandise on hand. • How to use the four inventory costing methods.	Connect To, p. 685 International Accounting, p. 686 Accounting Flashbacks, p. 687 Analyzing Financial Reports, p. 687 Accounting Careers in Focus, p. 689	Demonstration Problems Strategies for Teaching International Accounting
Section 3 *Analyzing the Inventory Costing Methods*	• How to choose an inventory costing method. • The effect of the inventory costing method on gross profit. • How to use the lower-of-cost-or-market method. • How to apply to inventory the accounting principles of consistency and conservatism.	Accounting Tips, p. 690 Spreadsheet Hints, p. 691	Demonstration Problems Math Review for Accounting Internet Resources and Activities Handbook

KEY

Posters — Transparency — Software — Videocassette
Blackline Masters — CD-ROM — Portfolio

MULTIMEDIA RESOURCE

Peachtree

- Problem 25–4 *Calculating the Cost of Ending Inventory*
- Problem 25–7 *Reporting Ending Inventory on the Income Statement*
- Problem 25–8 *Calculating Cost of Merchandise Sold and Gross Profit on Sales*

QuickBooks

- Problem 25–4 *Calculating the Cost of Ending Inventory*
- Problem 25–8 *Calculating Cost of Merchandise Sold and Gross Profit on Sales*

Spreadsheets

- Problem 25–6 *Calculating Gross Profit on Sales*

Videos

Video Segment: Inventory
After viewing this video, students will be able to describe the products for which a business must take an annual inventory. Have students explain why a business must determine a value for its inventory and give an example of one inventory valuation method.

CD-ROMs

Electronic Learning Center (ELC), Chapter 25
This program is ideal for visual learners since it incorporates video images, animation, and graphics to enliven the content of each lesson.

Interactive Lesson Planner (ILP), Chapter 25
This CD-ROM combines the versatility of an electronic lesson planner with the convenience of teacher classroom resources.

SCANS Correlation Chart

FOUNDATION SKILLS

Basic Skills:	Reading	Writing	Math	Listening	Speaking	
Thinking Skills:	Creative Thinking	Decision Making	Problem Solving	Seeing Things in the Mind's Eye	Knowing How to Learn	Reasoning
Personal Qualities:	Responsibility	Self-Esteem	Sociability	Self-Management	Integrity/Honesty	

WORKPLACE COMPETENCIES

Resources:	Allocating Time	Allocating Money	Allocating Material and Facility Resources	Allocating Human Resources		
Information:	Acquiring and Evaluating Information	Organizing and Maintaining Information	Interpreting and Communicating Information	Using Computers to Process Information		
Interpersonal Skills:	Participating as a Member of a Team	Teaching Others	Serving Clients/ Customers	Exercising Leadership	Negotiating to Arrive at a Decision	Working with Cultural Diversity
Systems:	Understanding Systems	Monitoring and Correcting Performance	Improving and Designing Systems			
Technology:	Selecting Technology	Applying Technology to Task	Maintaining and Troubleshooting Technology			

*Highlighted blocks indicate areas covered in the chapter. Additional SCANS skills are also covered throughout the *Teacher Wraparound Edition.*

Assessment

Student Edition
- Check Your Understanding, pp. 683, 688, 692
- Chapter 25 Problems, pp. 697–699

Assessment and Evaluation Masters
- Chapter 25 Study Plan, *Glencoe Workbook*
- Chapter 25 Self-Test, *Glencoe Workbook*
- Chapter 25 Test, *Chapter Tests* Booklet
- Chapter 25 Activity, *School-to-Work Handbook*
- Chapter 25 **Exam***View*

Teacher Wraparound Edition
- Critical Thinking Activity, p. 697
- Reteaching Section 1, p. 683
- Reteaching Section 2, p. 688
- Reteaching Section 3, p. 692
- Chapter 25 Quiz, p. 693

Transparencies

	Teaching Transparencies	Solution Transparencies
Section 1:	25–1, 25–2, 25–3, 25–4	Problem 25–1
Section 2:	25–5	Problem 25–2
Section 3:	25–6	Problem 25–3
End of Chapter:		Problems 25–4, 25–5, 25–6, 25–7, 25–8

TEACHER CLASSROOM RESOURCES

This is a representation of key blackline masters available in the Teacher Classroom Resources.

Teaching Aids

Transparency Examples

Section Focus Transparencies

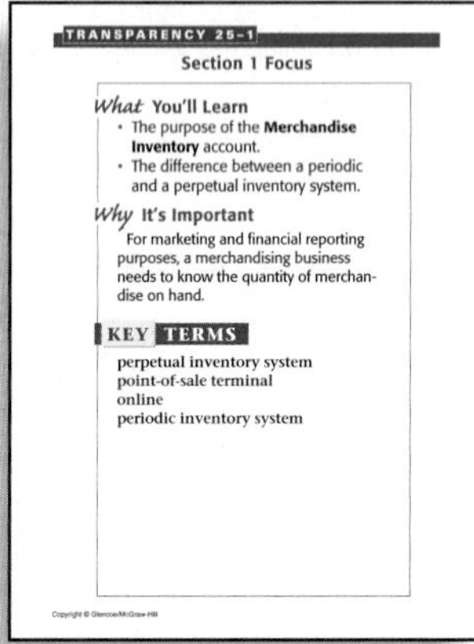

TRANSPARENCY 25-1

Section 1 Focus

What You'll Learn
- The purpose of the **Merchandise Inventory** account.
- The difference between a periodic and a perpetual inventory system.

Why It's Important

For marketing and financial reporting purposes, a merchandising business needs to know the quantity of merchandise on hand.

KEY TERMS

perpetual inventory system
point-of-sale terminal
online
periodic inventory system

Teaching Transparencies

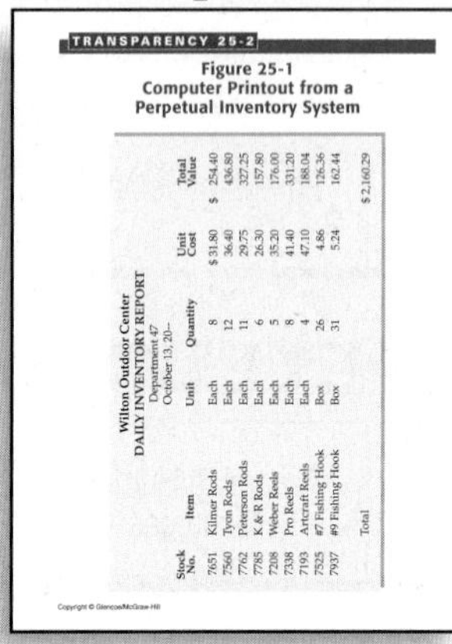

TRANSPARENCY 25-2

Figure 25-1
Computer Printout from a Perpetual Inventory System

Wilton Outdoor Center
DAILY INVENTORY REPORT
Department 47
October 13, 20--

Stock No.	Item	Unit	Quantity	Unit Cost	Total Value
7651	Kilmer Rods	Each	8	$ 31.80	$ 254.40
7560	Tyen Rods	Each	12	36.40	436.80
7762	Peterson Rods	Each	11	29.75	327.25
7785	K & R Rods	Each	6	26.30	157.80
7208	Weber Reels	Each	5	35.20	176.00
7338	Pro Reels	Each	8	41.40	331.20
7193	Aircraft Reels	Each	4	47.10	188.04
7325	#7 Fishing Hook	Box	26	4.86	126.36
7937	#9 Fishing Hook	Box	31	5.24	162.44
	Total				$ 2,160.29

Teaching Transparencies

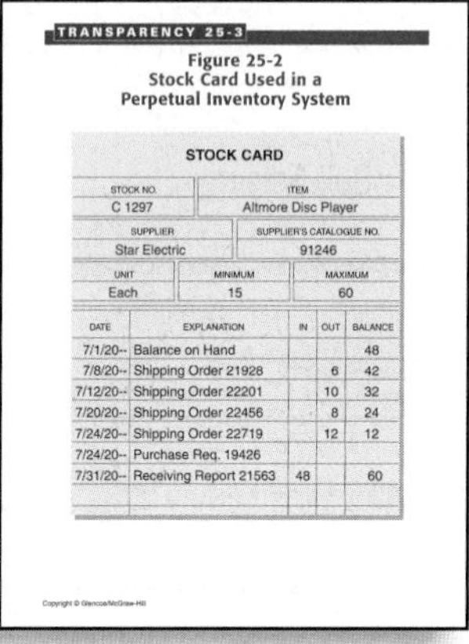

TRANSPARENCY 25-3

Figure 25-2
Stock Card Used in a Perpetual Inventory System

STOCK CARD

STOCK NO.	ITEM
C 1297	Altmore Disc Player

SUPPLIER	SUPPLIER'S CATALOGUE NO.
Star Electric	91246

UNIT	MINIMUM	MAXIMUM
Each	15	60

DATE	EXPLANATION	IN	OUT	BALANCE
7/1/20--	Balance on Hand			48
7/8/20--	Shipping Order 21928		6	42
7/12/20--	Shipping Order 22201		10	32
7/20/20--	Shipping Order 22456		8	24
7/24/20--	Shipping Order 22719		12	12
7/24/20--	Purchase Req. 19426			
7/31/20--	Receiving Report 21563	48		60

Solution Transparencies

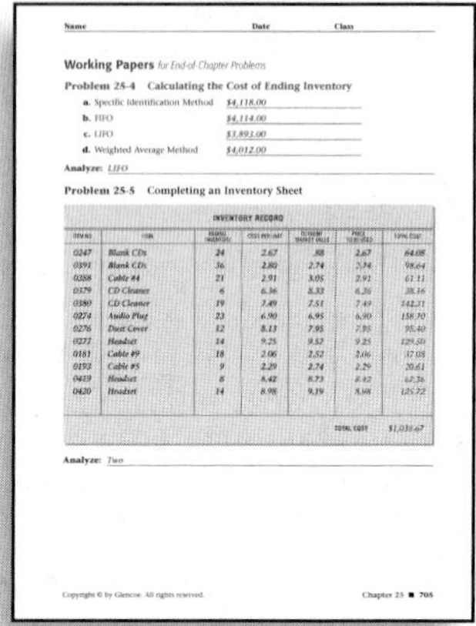

Working Papers for End-of-Chapter Problems

Problem 25-4 Calculating the Cost of Ending Inventory

Problem 25-5 Completing an Inventory Sheet

Demonstration Problems

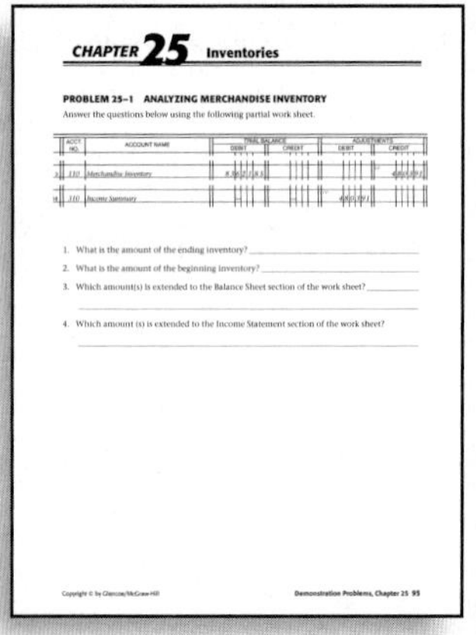

CHAPTER 25 Inventories

PROBLEM 25-1 ANALYZING MERCHANDISE INVENTORY

Lesson Plans

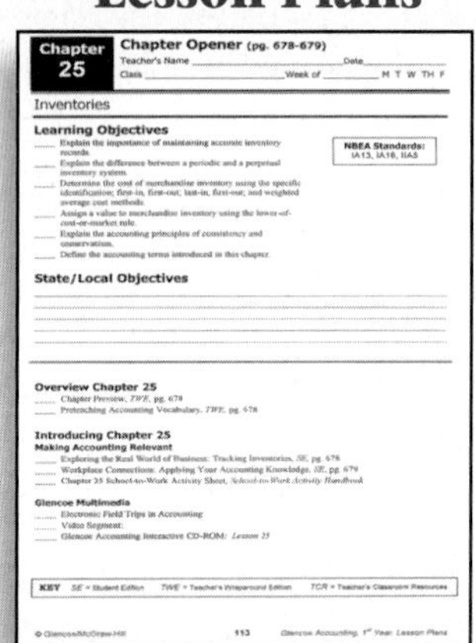

Chapter 25 — Chapter Opener (pg. 678–679)

Inventories

Learning Objectives

State/Local Objectives

Overview Chapter 25

Introducing Chapter 25

Glencoe Multimedia

Block Scheduling

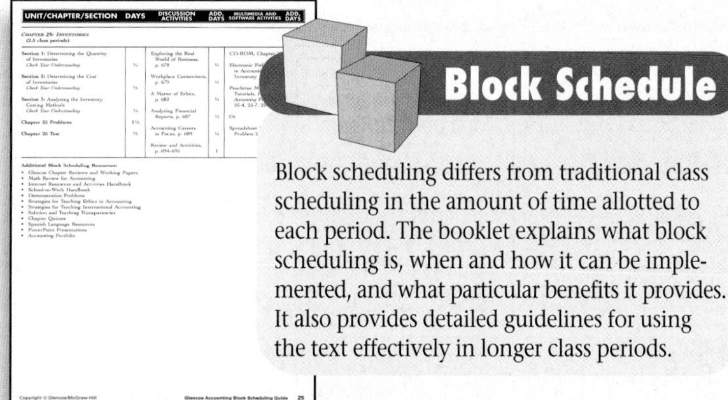

Block Schedule

Block scheduling differs from traditional class scheduling in the amount of time allotted to each period. The booklet explains what block scheduling is, when and how it can be implemented, and what particular benefits it provides. It also provides detailed guidelines for using the text effectively in longer class periods.

Enrichment and Application

Strategies for Teaching Ethics in Accounting

CHAPTER 25 Student Activity Sheet

Strategies for Teaching International Accounting

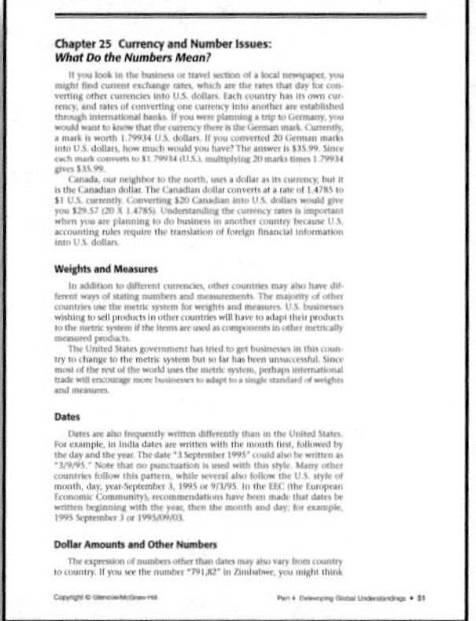

Chapter 25 Currency and Number Issues: What Do the Numbers Mean?

School-to-Work Handbook

CHAPTER 25 SCHOOL-TO-WORK ACTIVITY

Inventories

Meeting Different Ability Levels

Chapter Reviews and Working Papers (CRWP)

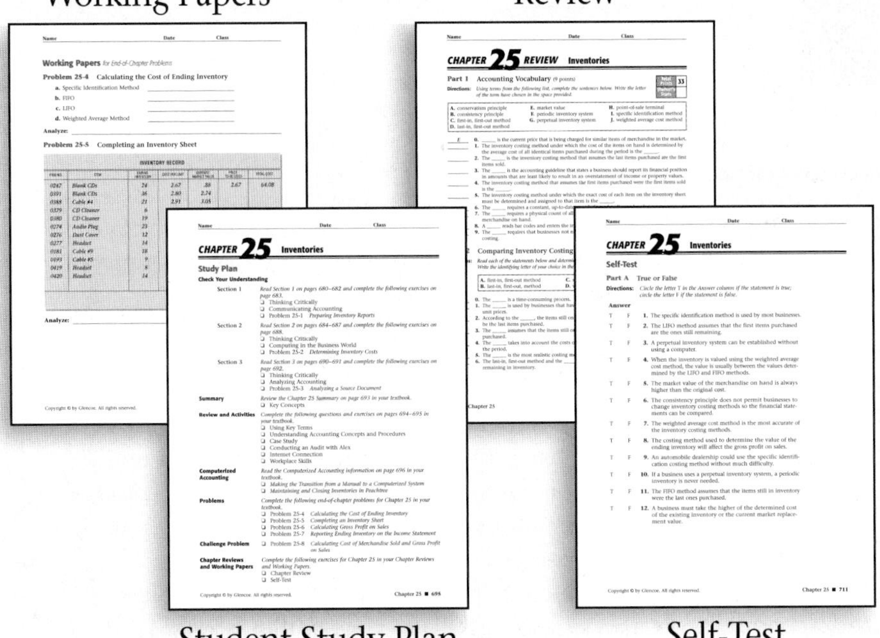

Real-World Multimedia CD-ROM

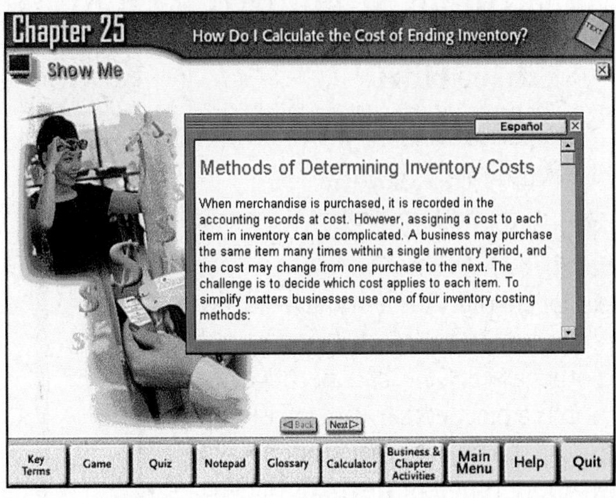

Key to Ability Levels

Each section gives skill-building activities. Each activity has been labeled for use with students of various learning styles and abilities.

L1 Level 1 activities are basic activities and should be within the range of all students.

L2 Level 2 activities are average activities and should be within the range of average and above average students.

L3 Level 3 activities are challenging activities designed for the ability range of above average students.

ELL ELL activities should be within the ability range of English Language Learners.

Assessment and Evaluation

Chapter Tests

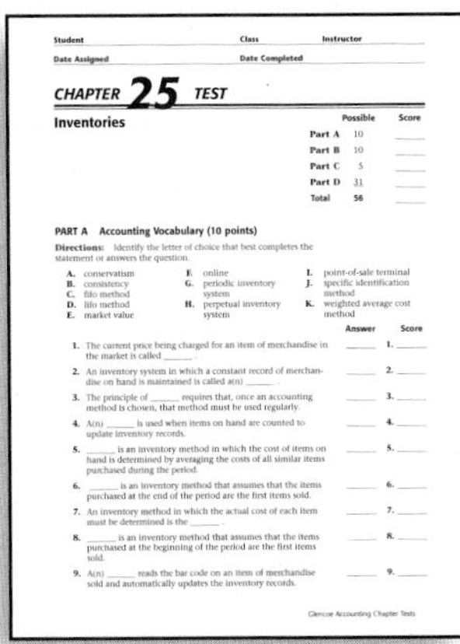

Chapter Quiz

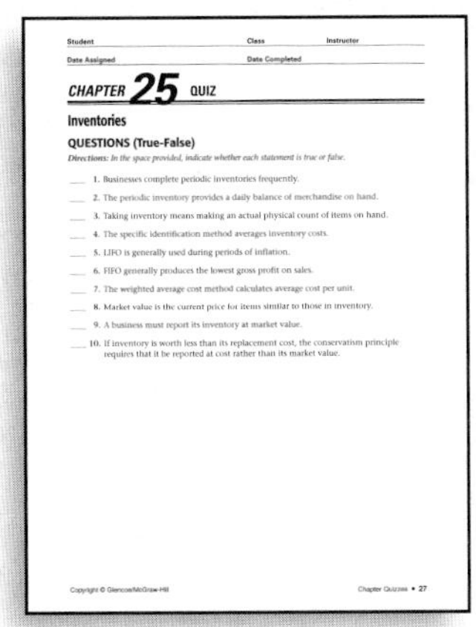

Teaching Resources at a Glance

Application Resources

- Glencoe Chapter Review and Working Papers, SE and TAE
- School-to-Work Handbook, SE and TM
- Accounting Portfolio, SE and TM

Reproducible Masters

- Demonstration Problems
- Lesson Plans
- Block Scheduling
- Spanish Language Resources

Glencoe Accounting Professional Development Series

- Strategies for Teaching Ethics in Accounting
- Accounting Competitive Event Review
- Math Review for Accounting
- Strategies for Teaching International Accounting
- Internet Resources and Activities Handbook

Transparency Package

- Section Focus Transparencies
- Teaching Transparencies
- Source Document Transparencies
- Solution Transparencies

Performance Assessment

- **Exam***View* CD-ROM
- Chapter Tests
- Chapter Quizzes
- Unit Tests
- Audit Tests
- Printed Testbank

Multimedia Resources

- Electronic Learning Center:
  - Multimedia CD-ROMs
  - Peachtree software, tutorials, templates, and solutions
  - Spreadsheet templates
- Using QuickBooks with Glencoe Accounting
- Interactive Lesson Planner
- Electronic Field Trips in Accounting
- PowerPoint Presentation
- Web site: glencoeaccounting.glencoe.com

OVERVIEW
CHAPTER 25

Correlations to National Standards for Business Education

(See pages T50–T51 for a detailed correlation chart.)

Standards: IA16, IIA6

Chapter Preview

In earlier chapters students have learned about internal controls that protect cash and other assets. One asset needing protection is a business's inventory of merchandise. In this chapter students will learn about different methods of determining the quantity of merchandise on hand and four methods for assigning a value to that merchandise.

Section Overviews

- Section 1—*Determining the Quantity of Inventories*
- Section 2—*Determining the Cost of Inventories*
- Section 3—*Analyzing the Inventory Costing Methods*

Chapter Vocabulary

perpetual inventory system
point-of-sale terminal
online
periodic inventory system
specific identification method
first-in, first-out method
last-in, first-out method
weighted average cost method
consistency principle
market value
conservatism principle

Preteaching Accounting Vocabulary

Oral Exercise: Write all the new terms on the chalkboard. Have students read the list and suggest ideas for each term's meaning. Explain terms, and then ask students to use each term in context in a sentence. L1

CHAPTER 25

Inventories

Learning Objectives

When you have completed this chapter, you will be able to:

- Explain the importance of maintaining accurate inventory records.
- Explain the difference between a periodic and a perpetual inventory system.
- Take a physical inventory count and record inventories.
- Determine the cost of merchandise inventory using the specific identification; first-in, first-out; last-in, first-out; and weighted average cost methods.
- Assign a value to merchandise inventory using the lower-of-cost-or-market rule.
- Explain the accounting principles of consistency and conservatism.
- Define the accounting terms introduced in this chapter.

Exploring the Real World of Business

TRACKING INVENTORIES

Have you ever wondered where the **Gap** got its name? The original store, selling jeans and records, was named for a cultural phenomenon known as "the generation gap." Since its beginning in 1969, the **Gap** has expanded to a full line of clothing, kids clothes, and accessories.

With inventories of clothes for its Banana Republic stores, Old Navy locations, GapKids stores, and the **Gap** outlets, you can imagine how important the tracking of merchandise inventory must be. Each store tracks its own inventory and prepares regular reports on items sold and items left in stock. Studying inventory reports helps the store managers decide which items sell best in their particular markets.

What do you think?

If you worked for the **Gap,** what information would you want on an inventory report to help you decide which clothing lines to stock?

Gap

Exploring the Real World of Business

Gap

Like many other retailers, Gap has joined the e-commerce trend by setting up an online store for consumers to shop via the Internet (www.gap.com). Online shoppers can browse through new styles and sign up for e-mail alerts about special promotions and new products.

What do you think? (Answers)

Answers may vary. The inventory report might include items sold; the sizes, colors, and styles; quantities sold; unit costs; and frequency of restocking orders. Using this report, managers could decide which items, colors, sizes, and styles are most popular with customers.

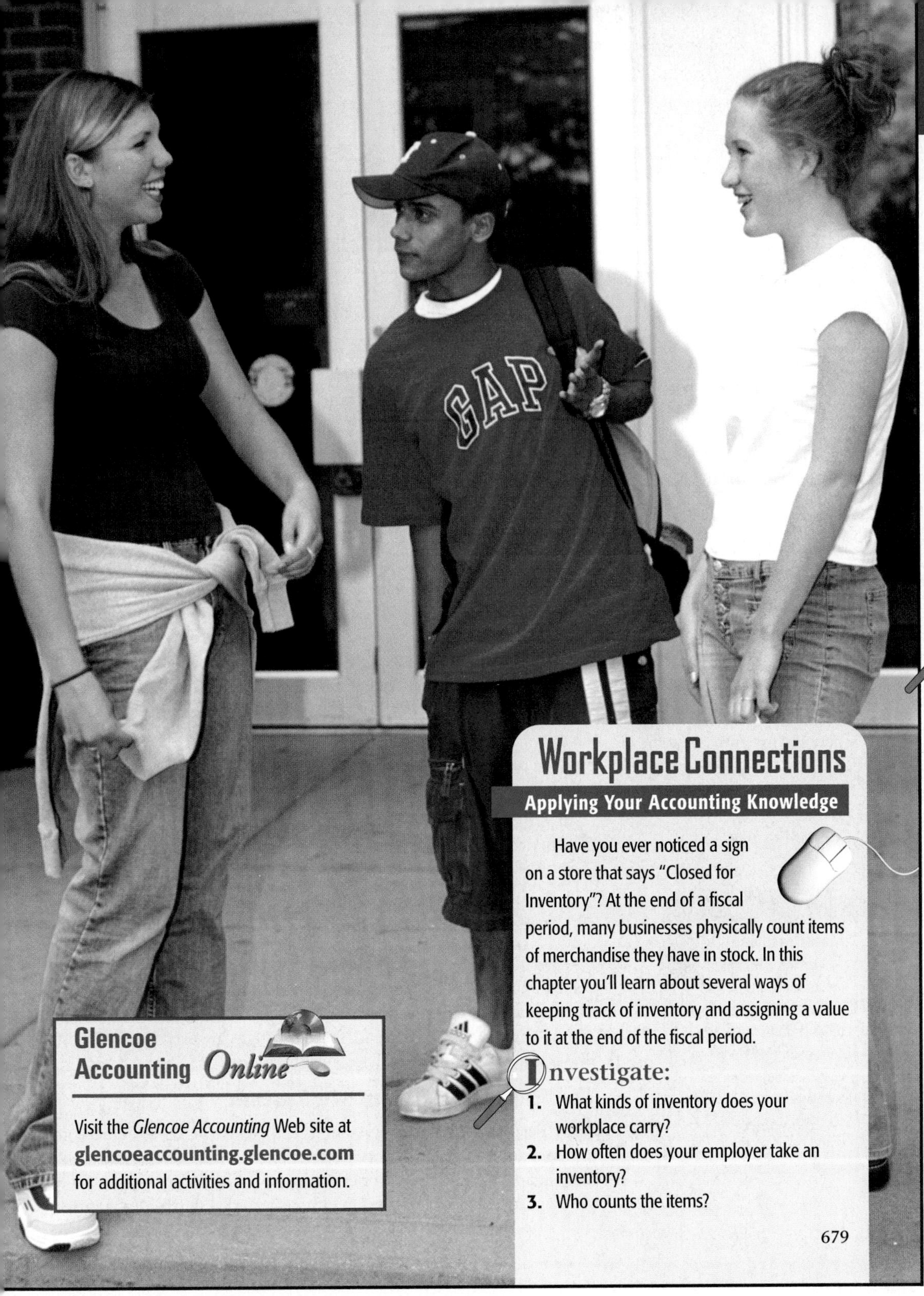

Workplace Connections

Applying Your Accounting Knowledge

Have you ever noticed a sign on a store that says "Closed for Inventory"? At the end of a fiscal period, many businesses physically count items of merchandise they have in stock. In this chapter you'll learn about several ways of keeping track of inventory and assigning a value to it at the end of the fiscal period.

Investigate:

1. What kinds of inventory does your workplace carry?
2. How often does your employer take an inventory?
3. Who counts the items?

Glencoe Accounting Online

Visit the *Glencoe Accounting* Web site at **glencoeaccounting.glencoe.com** for additional activities and information.

679

INTRODUCING CHAPTER 25

Making Accounting Relevant

Workplace Connections: Applying Your Accounting Knowledge

Discussion: Businesses have different types of inventories. Service businesses have inventories of supplies and other assets used to operate the business. Manufacturers have inventories of parts used to make finished products. Retailers have inventories of merchandise for sale. Have students think of local companies and discuss the types of inventories the companies might have.

Investigate (Answers)

1. Answers will vary. For example, restaurants might have inventories of supplies such as food, paper goods, and eating utensils. The local copy shop would have inventories of paper and copier supplies.
2. Answers will vary. For tax purposes, inventory must be taken at least once a year.
3. Answers will vary. Most businesses have their regular employees count items in inventory.

School-to-Work Activity

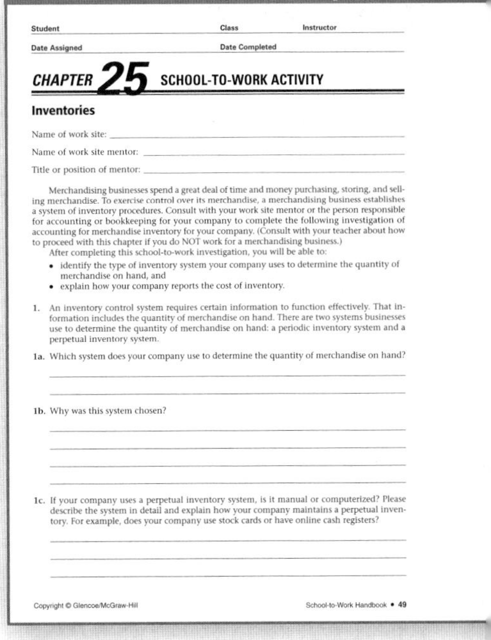

Student ____ Class ____ Instructor ____

Date Assigned ____ Date Completed ____

CHAPTER 25 SCHOOL-TO-WORK ACTIVITY

Inventories

Name of work site: ____

Name of work site mentor: ____

Title or position of mentor: ____

Merchandising businesses spend a great deal of time and money purchasing, storing, and selling merchandise. To exercise control over its merchandise, a merchandising business establishes a system of inventory procedures. Consult with your work site mentor or the person responsible for accounting or bookkeeping for your company to complete the following investigation of accounting for merchandise inventory for your company. (Consult with your teacher about how to proceed with this chapter if you do NOT work for a merchandising business.)

After completing this school-to-work investigation, you will be able to:

- identify the type of inventory system your company uses to determine the quantity of merchandise on hand, and
- explain how your company reports the cost of inventory.

1. An inventory control system requires certain information to function effectively. That information includes the quantity of merchandise on hand. There are two systems businesses use to determine the quantity of merchandise on hand: a periodic inventory system and a perpetual inventory system.

1a. Which system does your company use to determine the quantity of merchandise on hand?

1b. Why was this system chosen?

1c. If your company uses a perpetual inventory system, is it manual or computerized? Please describe the system in detail and explain how your company maintains a perpetual inventory. For example, does your company use stock cards or have online cash registers?

 School-to-Work Handbook • 49

GLENCOE MULTIMEDIA

Electronic Field Trips in Accounting *Video Segment: Inventory*

After viewing this video, students will be able to explain why a business must determine a value for its inventory and give an example of one inventory valuation method.

Glencoe Accounting: Electronic Learning Center *Chapter 25*

The CD-ROM program is ideal for visual learners since it incorporates video images, animation, and graphics to enliven the content of each lesson.

1 FOCUS

Introducing the Section

In this section students will learn about ways of keeping track of the inventory and of verifying the amount of inventory on hand at a given time.

Section Concepts

- The purpose of the Merchandise Inventory account.
- The difference between a periodic and a perpetual inventory system.

Visual Learning

Section 1 Focus

Use **Transparency 25–1** to introduce section concepts.

BELL RINGER

Recording Inventories: Have students record inventories of items in your classroom. Make up a blank inventory sheet and have students count desks, chairs, computers, and so on. When finished, have students compare items counted and totals. Identify differences. Ask students how they decided which items in the room to count. L1

Concept Development: Merchandise Inventory

Discussion: Emphasize the importance of accurate inventory records, both for internal control and reporting purposes. Inaccurate inventory data will cause inaccurate reporting of the net income or loss, resulting in financial statements that do not present a true picture of financial position. L1

Demonstration Problem Step-by-Step Practice

Use demonstration problem 25–1 to review the adjustment for merchandise inventory.

SECTION 1

Determining the Quantity of Inventories

***What* You'll Learn**

- The purpose of the **Merchandise Inventory** account.
- The difference between a periodic and a perpetual inventory system.

***Why* It's Important**

For marketing and financial reporting purposes, a merchandising business needs to know the quantity of merchandise on hand.

KEY TERMS

perpetual inventory system
point-of-sale terminal
online
periodic inventory system

In a merchandising business, it is essential to maintain control over the merchandise that is purchased, stored, and sold. To keep control of its merchandise, a business establishes a system of inventory procedures. Can you imagine the problems that a store like Wal-Mart or a manufacturer like Toyota would encounter if they didn't have an inventory system?

Merchandise Inventory

Earlier you learned that goods purchased by a business for resale to customers are called merchandise. The **Merchandise Inventory** account shows the cost of goods purchased for resale. **Merchandise Inventory** is the only account reported on both the balance sheet (as a current asset) and on the income statement (to calculate the cost of merchandise sold).

Merchandise Inventory typically is one of the largest asset accounts. By tracking merchandise, a business knows:

- how much merchandise is sold,
- which items are selling well, and
- which items, when sold, should not be replaced.

To function efficiently, an inventory control system tracks the quantity and cost of merchandise purchased, on hand, and sold.

Did You Know?

Manufacturing

Gap Inc. does not manufacture any of the hundreds of retail products that earn its revenue of around $13 billion a year. The company uses suppliers in several different countries to produce its brand-name products.

Determining the Quantity of Inventories

Two methods are used to track merchandise: the perpetual inventory system and the periodic inventory system. Perpetual inventory systems are used by most large businesses as well as smaller ones with automated accounting systems. Periodic inventory systems are used by small businesses that maintain manual accounting records.

The Perpetual Inventory System

A **perpetual inventory system** keeps a constant, up-to-date record of merchandise on hand. This system reports what merchandise is on hand at any point in time. Under the perpetual inventory system, every time a purchase or sale occurs, an entry is recorded in the **Merchandise**

RESOURCE MANAGER

Reproducible Masters
- Lesson Plans
- Chapter Reviews and Working Papers (CRWP) TAE
- Demonstration Problems

Transparencies
- Section Focus Transparency
- Teaching Transparencies
- Source Document Transparencies
- Solution Transparencies

Multimedia
- Exam*View* CD-ROM
- Electronic Learning Center CD-ROM
- Interactive Lesson Planner CD-ROM
- Electronic Field Trips in Accounting

Inventory account. Also, after every sale the cost of merchandise sold is recorded in the accounting records.

When a business uses a perpetual inventory system, management can obtain the quantity on hand and cost of any item at any point in time. The business can reorder items when the quantity on hand is low. This avoids loss of sales due to inadequate inventory. **Figure 25–1** shows an example of a computer printout for a perpetual inventory system.

Wilton Outdoor Center
DAILY INVENTORY REPORT
Department 47
October 13, 20--

Stock No.	Item	Unit	Quantity	Unit Cost	Total Value
7651	Kilmer Rods	Each	8	$ 31.80	$ 254.40
7560	Tyon Rods	Each	12	36.40	436.80
7762	Peterson Rods	Each	11	29.75	327.25
7785	K & R Rods	Each	6	26.30	157.80
7208	Weber Reels	Each	5	35.20	176.00
7338	Pro Reels	Each	8	41.40	331.20
7193	Artcraft Reels	Each	4	47.10	188.40
7525	#7 Fishing Hook	Box	26	4.86	126.36
7937	#9 Fishing Hook	Box	31	5.24	162.44
	Total				$ 2,160.65

Figure 25–1 Computer Printout from a Perpetual Inventory System

Computers help to maintain a perpetual inventory system. Many businesses use electronic cash registers, known as **point-of-sale terminals**. These terminals are **online** to a central computer system. Online means that the terminal or cash register is linked to the computer. These machines read bar codes that identify the item being sold. The computer records the sale and automatically updates the inventory information. Also, the cost and quantity of merchandise that is purchased is entered into the computer, and the inventory records are updated.

Businesses that have not yet automated their operations may also use a perpetual inventory system. Instead of point-of-sale terminals and computers, they use stock record sheets or cards. **Figure 25–2** shows a stock card used in a perpetual inventory system. For every purchase and sale, the amount of increase or decrease is recorded on the stock card. For example, when merchandise is purchased, the quantity received is recorded in the In column of the stock card. When items are sold, the quantity is recorded in the Out column.

Figure 25–2 Stock Card Used in a Perpetual Inventory System

STOCK CARD

STOCK NO.	ITEM
C 1297	Altmore Disc Player

SUPPLIER	SUPPLIER'S CATALOGUE NO.
Star Electric	91246

UNIT	MINIMUM	MAXIMUM
Each	15	60

DATE	EXPLANATION	IN	OUT	BALANCE
7/1/20--	Balance on Hand			48
7/8/20--	Shipping Order 21928		6	42
7/12/20--	Shipping Order 22201		10	32
7/20/20--	Shipping Order 22456		8	24
7/24/20--	Shipping Order 22719		12	12
7/24/20--	Purchase Req. 19426			
7/31/20--	Receiving Report 21563	48		60

The Periodic Inventory System

Another commonly used system of determining the quantity of merchandise on hand is a periodic inventory system. Under the **periodic inventory system**, inventory records are updated only after a physical count of merchandise on hand is made. Under this system, inventory records are not adjusted for every purchase and sale.

Great Ideas *From the Classroom of...*

Illustrating Inventory Methods To help explain the "whys" of inventories, set up displays to illustrate the various methods. Use a display with plastic flowers to teach the specific identification method. Use milk jugs to explain the first-in, first-out method. Use a basket of potatoes to demonstrate the last-in, last-out method. Label each method with the cost and the weighted average cost.

Scott A. Arcand
Columbus High School
Columbus, Nebraska

2 TEACH

GUIDED PRACTICE

Reading Accounting

- Have students read the forms in this section and identify the type of information provided on each form. Ask how this information fits into accounting records. L1
- Have students interview local businesspeople who speak their first language and learn about the business's inventory practices. ELL

Concept Development: Determining the Quantity of Inventories

Discussion: Point out that a perpetual inventory system provides quick access to inventory data and should produce better inventory management decisions. Discuss how large department stores use perpetual inventory systems with the aid of computers. Ask students to notice what happens the next time they purchase an item at a store that uses electronic cash registers. They should notice the cashier entering or scanning a number that identifies the item for perpetual inventory. L1

Visual Learning

Figure 25–1 Computer Printout from a Perpetual Inventory System

Using **Transparency 25–2**, point out the information included in a perpetual inventory system.

Figure 25–2 Stock Card Used in a Perpetual Inventory System

Use **Transparency 25–3** to explain how each new item ordered is recorded in the perpetual inventory system.

CHAPTER 25

SECTION 1, PAGES 680–683

2 TEACH (Cont'd.)

Teaching Tips

Point out that even with a perpetual inventory system, a physical count should be taken at least once a year to determine errors or theft and to establish the taxable value of inventory. A physical count is part of internal inventory controls.

The periodic inventory system is probably familiar to most students who have noticed local retailers taking inventory. Discuss the amount of time needed to complete this type of inventory, which is why most businesses do this type of inventory infrequently.

Businesses using a periodic inventory system need a physical count of all merchandise at least once a year.

Visual Learning

Figure 25–3 Inventory Sheet

Use **Transparency 25–4** to explain the types of information recorded on an inventory sheet. Ask students who have participated in an inventory to relate their experiences and describe the types of information they recorded when taking an inventory.

Strategies for Teaching Ethics in Accounting

Photocopy the Chapter 25 *Student Activity Sheet* for students. Answers are also provided in the booklet.

The Physical Inventory Count

Businesses take a physical count of their merchandise at least once a year. This is called *taking inventory.* Businesses using the periodic inventory system take a physical count to update their accounting records.

For businesses with many items in inventory, the process of identifying and counting all items of merchandise is very time-consuming. For this reason, inventory is usually counted when it is at its lowest level. Seasonal businesses take physical counts and record inventories at the end of the peak selling period after most of the merchandise has been sold. A ski shop, for instance, would probably take inventory in May or June.

The total number of a particular item on hand is recorded on an inventory card or an inventory sheet. **Figure 25–3** shows a typical inventory sheet. The inventory sheet lists the stock number of the item, a description of the item, the quantity on hand, the unit cost, and the total cost of the inventory item on hand.

INVENTORY SHEET

DATE Jan. 5, 20-- CLERK Arlene Stone PAGE 8

STOCK NO.	ITEM	UNIT	QUANTITY	UNIT COST		TOTAL VALUE	
1901	Needles	Pkg	24	1	14	27	36
2132	Thread	Spool	12		65	7	80
2136	Thread	Spool	18		55	9	90
3245	Zipper	Each	18	1	50	27	00
1917	Pins	Box	24		79	18	96
4971	Buttons	Pkg	12		89	10	68
4993	Tape Measure	Each	15	1	49	22	35
			TOTAL FOR THIS SHEET			789	14

Figure 25–3 Inventory Sheet

A MATTER OF ETHICS

Keeping Promotional Items

Imagine that you just got a job in the cosmetics department of a large department store like Macy's. You have access to free samples—such as shampoo, moisturizer, lipstick, and nail polish—offered by manufacturers to get customers to try their products. This is great! You'll never have to buy these products again. You figure by using them, you're helping to promote them.

Ethical Decision Making:

- What are the ethical issues?
- What are the alternatives?
- Who are the affected parties?
- How do the alternatives affect the parties?
- What would you do?

Teaching A MATTER OF ETHICS

Keeping Promotional Items Ask students how many of them have purchased a bottle of cologne or some type of makeup at a department store because the store was offering a free gift or sample with a purchase. Have students discuss whether they would have bought the item without the gift or at a different store if it had been offering a gift. Would they have decided not to buy the item if the store personnel had said they were out of free gifts? Ask students to discuss the impact of free samples and gifts on store sales and how the taking of samples by workers could affect sales.

Check Your Understanding

Now that you have studied this section, complete the following questions and problems.

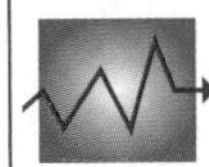

Thinking Critically

1. Why do seasonal businesses take inventory at the end of the peak selling period?
2. What is the difference between a periodic and a perpetual inventory system?

Communicating Accounting

Natural Wonder offers products organically grown or made from organic materials. Its products include clothing, jewelry, gardening materials, and hair and body care products. The store is interested in a system that will keep an accurate count of inventory. Discuss the different inventory systems and explain how frequently each system is updated.

Problem 25–1 Preparing Inventory Reports

In your working papers, complete the manual inventory sheet for Carole's Gift Shop. Use today's date and your name as the clerk.

Stock No.	Item	Unit	Quantity	Unit Cost
1790	Greeting Cards	Doz.	32	6.00
2217	Plush Toys	Each	20	2.50
1900	Balloons	Doz.	12	.50
1201	Wrapping Paper	Each	30	1.12
1205	Ribbon	Spool	25	.75
3495	Novelty Buttons	Doz.	12	2.50
2722	Music Boxes	Doz.	6	60.00
4200	Party Supplies	Doz.	10	6.50
1907	Gift Boxes	Doz.	5	2.75
1742	Vases	Doz.	2	12.50

RETEACHING SECTION 1

Comparing Inventory Systems Have students take an inventory of the contents of their lockers, recording each item of information on an inventory sheet. Once the inventory has been completed, discuss the use of the perpetual inventory system versus the periodic inventory system. If students kept a perpetual inventory of their lockers, each time they opened their lockers and changed the contents they would need to record that change on their inventory sheets. In a periodic inventory system, they could take a new inventory at the end of the school year.

3 ASSESS

Thinking Critically (Answers)

1. Their inventory should be at its lowest level and easier to count.
2. With a periodic system, an actual count of merchandise on hand is made at specific (periodic) intervals. A perpetual inventory system keeps a daily record of merchandise on hand.

Communicating Accounting (Answers)

Answers will vary. Students might mention that a perpetual inventory system provides up-to-date records of merchandise on hand; the balance of Merchandise Inventory can be determined at any time; the cost of merchandise sold can be determined easily. A periodic inventory system requires a time-consuming physical count of all merchandise on hand; before the count, no up-to-date inventory records are available.

Problem 25–1 (Answer)

Total value of inventory $794.10

Chapter Reviews and Working Papers Refer students to the Chapter 25 workbook pages to answer *Check Your Understanding* activities.

4 CLOSE

Section Wrap-Up

Writing: Have students write a paragraph explaining why a business maintains inventory records and two means of tracking inventory. L1

1 FOCUS

Introducing the Section

In this section students will learn four methods used to place a value on the inventory once it has been counted. Students will learn the specific identification method, FIFO, LIFO, and the weighted average cost method.

Section Concepts

- How to determine the cost of the merchandise on hand.
- How to use the four inventory costing methods.

Visual Learning

Section 2 Focus

Use **Transparency 25–5** to introduce section concepts.

BELL RINGER

Consulting: If you have access to a Monopoly™ game, bring in the real estate pieces (or use other items to represent buildings). Divide students into teams and then distribute several pieces to each team. Tell students that they operate a real estate investment company, and they need to determine the total value of their real estate holdings. Have students assign a value to each building and calculate a total for their real estate inventory. After reviewing the types of inventory valuation methods, ask students which method they used to value their inventory. L1

Demonstration Problem Step-by-Step Practice

Use demonstration problem 25–2, Part A, to have students calculate inventory cost using specific identification.

SECTION 2

Determining the Cost of Inventories

What You'll Learn

- How to determine the cost of the merchandise on hand.
- How to use the four inventory costing methods.

Why It's Important

Much time and effort is spent determining the cost of merchandise inventory because it appears on both the balance sheet and the income statement.

KEY TERMS

specific identification method
first-in, first-out method
last-in, first-out method
weighted average cost method

Once the quantity of merchandise on hand is determined, the cost of that merchandise is calculated. There are four inventory costing methods used to assign costs to merchandise.

Methods of Determining Inventory Costs

When merchandise is purchased, it is recorded in the accounting records at cost. However, assigning a cost to each item in inventory can be complicated. A business may purchase the same item many times within a single inventory period, and the cost may change from one purchase to the next. The challenge is to decide which cost applies to each item. To simplify matters businesses use one of four inventory costing methods:

- specific identification
- first-in, first-out
- last-in, first-out
- weighted average cost

The Specific Identification Costing Method

Under the **specific identification method**, the exact cost of each item is determined and assigned to that item. The actual cost of each item is obtained from the invoice.

The specific identification method is most often used by businesses that sell a small number of items with high unit prices. Appliance stores, automobile dealerships, and furniture stores often use this method. Let's look at an example.

The Disk Jockey Electronics Store uses the periodic inventory system. It started the year with a beginning inventory of 15 laser disc players. During the period the store purchased an additional 50 players. When a physical inventory count was taken on May 31, there were 12 players still on hand. The cost of the players was calculated as follows:

Date	Description	Units	Cost		Total
June 1	Beginning inventory	15	$250	=	$ 3,750
Aug. 4	Purchase	20	250	=	5,000
Dec. 8	Purchase	10	253	=	2,530
Feb. 27	Purchase	10	258	=	2,580
May 1	Purchase	10	260	=	2,600
	Total	65			$16,460

Using the specific identification method, the accountant checks the invoices to find the actual cost of each of the 12 players still on hand at the end of May. The accountant found the following:

RESOURCE MANAGER

Reproducible Masters
- Lesson Plans
- Chapter Reviews and Working Papers (CRWP) TAE
- Demonstration Problems

Transparencies
- Section Focus Transparency
- Teaching Transparencies
- Source Document Transparencies
- Solution Transparencies

Multimedia
- Exam*View* CD-ROM
- Electronic Learning Center CD-ROM
- Interactive Lesson Planner CD-ROM
- Electronic Field Trips in Accounting

4 purchased @ $253 each	=	$ 1,012
5 purchased @ $258 each	=	1,290
3 purchased @ $260 each	=	780
12 players (ending inventory)		$3,082

The cost of ending inventory is $3,082. Once the cost of ending inventory is calculated, the cost of merchandise sold can be computed:

Purchases available for sale
– Cost of ending inventory
Cost of merchandise sold

In this example the cost of the laser disc players sold using the specific identification method is $13,378:

	Units	Cost
Cost of players available for sale	65	$16,460
Less ending inventory	12	3,082
Cost of merchandise sold	53	$13,378

The First-In, First-Out Costing Method

The **first-in, first-out method (FIFO)** of assigning cost assumes that the first items purchased (first in) are the first items sold (first out). The **FIFO** method assumes that the items purchased most recently are the ones on hand at the end of the period. The physical flow of most merchandise is first-in, first-out. For example, think about milk that is stocked by a supermarket. Since milk is perishable, the supermarket stocks the shelves with the milk it purchased first. As that milk is sold, later purchases of milk are added at the back of the shelves.

Let's apply the **FIFO** costing method to our laser disc player example.

Date	Description	Units	Cost		Total
June 1	Beginning inventory	15	$250	=	$ 3,750
Aug. 4	Purchase	20	250	=	5,000
Dec. 8	Purchase	10	253	=	2,530
Feb. 27	Purchase	10	258	=	2,580
May 1	Purchase	10	260	=	2,600
	Total	65			$16,460

Under the FIFO method, the items purchased first are assumed to be the items sold first. In other words, the 53 players sold are assumed to be as follows:

	Units
Beginning inventory	15
Aug. 4	20
Dec. 8	10
Feb. 27	8
Total sold	53

The items remaining in inventory are:

		Units
Feb. 27	(10 – 8 sold)	2
May 1		10
Total		12

CONNECT TO . . .
CIVICS

The 16th Amendment gives Congress the power to "lay and collect taxes on incomes, from whatever sources derived, without apportionment among several States, and without regard to any census or enumeration." It was passed in 1913 in response to an 1895 Supreme Court verdict that declared a federal income tax unconstitutional.

2 TEACH

GUIDED PRACTICE

Reading Accounting

- Have students make a note card for each of the four costing methods. Tell them to read the section on each method and make notes on key points. L1

Concept Development: Methods of Determining Inventory Costs

Discussion: Before introducing the methods of assigning costs to ending inventory, discuss the problems a business may have in determining costs. Very few businesses can assign exact costs to all items on hand, so estimated costing methods are used. When presenting the specific identification costing method, emphasize that this is the most accurate method since exact costs are used. L1

Demonstration Problem Step-by-Step Practice

Use demonstration problem 25–2, Part B, to give students practice in calculating inventory cost using the FIFO method.

Teaching Tips

Have students name different types of businesses that could use the specific identification method with success (e.g., art galleries, auto dealers).

Mention that FIFO and LIFO are acronyms. Have students think of other acronyms such as CPA or FASB.

INTERDISCIPLINARY CONNECTIONS ACTIVITY

Civics One of the reasons businesses take inventory and assign a value is to determine taxes owed on major assets. Individuals also pay taxes on one of their assets, which is the property they own. In 1978 California voters began a property tax revolt. Voters overwhelmingly approved a referendum, popularly known as Proposition 13, to roll back property taxes by 57 percent. Fears that deep cuts in public services would result proved unfounded. Other areas of the country followed California's lead, and the voters in many communities continue to vote down increases in their property taxes. Voters' support for state and federal representatives also frequently hinges on representatives' stands on tax issues.

2 TEACH (Cont'd.)

Teaching Tips

When presenting FIFO and LIFO, put an example on the chalkboard and have students determine the costs under each method. After calculating the costs, ask students to compare the results. Which method gives the lowest cost?

Point out that businesses pay taxes on their inventories, so they want to use an inventory valuation that results in the lowest value for ending inventory.

Critical Thinking: Explain to students that in periods of rising costs, the LIFO method will usually yield a lower ending inventory amount than the FIFO method. Ask students to explain why. (When costs are rising, the last items in the inventory cost more than the first ones. Using LIFO, the higher-cost items are assumed to be sold, leaving the lower-cost items in inventory and thus resulting in a lower inventory valuation.) L2

Demonstration Problem Step-by-Step Practice

Use demonstration problem 25–2, Part C, to give students practice in calculating inventory costs using the LIFO method.

Strategies for Teaching International Accounting

To enrich study of international accounting, refer students to the additional critical thinking activities in the booklet.

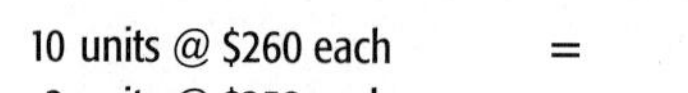

The cost of the ending inventory using the FIFO method is:

10 units @ $260 each	=	$2,600
2 units @ $258 each	=	516
12 units		$ 3,116

The cost of merchandise sold using the FIFO method is $13,344:

	Units	
Cost of players available for sale	65	$16,460
Less ending inventory	12	3,116
Cost of merchandise sold	53	$13,344

The Last-In, First-Out Costing Method

The **last-in, first-out method (LIFO)** of assigning inventory cost assumes that the last items purchased (last in) are the first items sold (first out). The LIFO method assumes that the items purchased first are still on hand at the end of the period. The earliest costs, therefore, are the ones used to assign a cost to the inventory. The physical flow of a stone and gravel company is last-in, first-out. When new gravel is purchased and delivered, it is deposited on top of the existing gravel. As gravel is taken from the top of the pile, the first gravel used is the last gravel delivered.

Let's return to the laser disc player example and apply the LIFO costing method.

Date	Description	Units	Cost		Total
June 1	Beginning inventory	15	$250	=	$ 3,750
Aug. 4	Purchase	20	250	=	5,000
Dec. 8	Purchase	10	253	=	2,530
Feb. 27	Purchase	10	258	=	2,580
May 1	Purchase	10	260	=	2,600
	Total	65			$16,460

International ACCOUNTING

Holiday Observances

When working with international clients, familiarize yourself with their local observances of holidays. Over 70 percent of the holidays celebrated each year change annually. Some countries have such diverse ethnic populations that they observe religious holidays for over 10 major religions!

Using the LIFO method, the 12 players remaining in stock are from the beginning inventory of 15 units. The cost of the ending inventory is $3,000 (12 units @ $250 each).

The cost of merchandise sold using the LIFO method is $13,460:

	Units	
Cost of players available for sale	65	$16,460
Less ending inventory	12	3,000
Cost of merchandise sold	53	$13,460

The Weighted Average Cost Method

A fourth method of assigning inventory costs is the weighted average cost method. The **weighted average cost method** assigns the average cost to each unit in inventory. The average cost is calculated by:

- adding the number of units on hand at the beginning of the period and the number of units purchased
- adding the cost of the units on hand at the beginning of the period and the cost of the units purchased
- dividing the total cost by the total number of units

Teaching International ACCOUNTING

Holiday Observances Approximately 70 percent of the world's population follows one of these religions: Christianity, Islam, Hinduism, or Buddhism. Divide the class into five groups, and assign the first four groups one religion to research. Have groups identify their religion's major tenets and also find out how the religion affects the business practices and types of products consumers may purchase. Students should also address challenges firms face to accommodate differences in religious holidays, dietary restrictions or customs, and Sabbath days. Ask the fifth group to research the countries in which these four religions are dominant. Have groups share their findings with the class.

The average cost per unit is used to determine the cost of the ending inventory. Again, we will use the Disk Jockey example to apply the weighted average cost method.

Date	Description	Units	Cost		Total
June 1	Beginning inventory	15	$250	=	$ 3,750
Aug. 4	Purchase	20	250	=	5,000
Dec. 8	Purchase	10	253	=	2,530
Feb. 27	Purchase	10	258	=	2,580
May 1	Purchase	10	260	=	2,600
	Total	65			$16,460

The average cost per player is $253.23 ($16,460 ÷ 65 units).

The cost of the ending merchandise inventory using the weighted average cost method is $3,038.76 (12 units × $253.23).

The cost of merchandise sold using the weighted average cost method is $13,421.24:

	Units	
Cost of players available for sale	65	$16,460.00
Less ending inventory	12	3,038.76
Cost of merchandise sold	53	$13,421.24

The following table illustrates the different inventory costing methods for Disk Jockey. Once an inventory costing method is selected, it is applied consistently.

Method	Cost of Players Sold	Ending Inventory
Specific identification	$13,378.00	$3,082.00
FIFO	13,344.00	3,116.00
LIFO	13,460.00	3,000.00
Weighted average	13,421.24	3,038.76

ACCOUNTING *Flashbacks*

EARLY INVENTIONS

In 1948, John Bardeen, William Shockley, and Walter H. Brattain announced the development of the three-electrode solid-state transistor. This invention permitted the miniaturization of computers and other electronic devices.

ANALYZING FINANCIAL REPORTS

Inventories

In this chapter, you learned how to count and assign a value to inventory on hand at the end of a fiscal period. Knowing how much inventory is on hand helps managers make decisions about how much product to make. For example, too much inventory means the business has not sold what it has produced, and its money is tied up in the inventory. Managers would want to find out why the product is not selling as well as they expected when they set production numbers.

▶ Analyze the Report:

Use the Office Depot balance sheet and "To Our Shareholders" message on pages A-40–A-45 to answer these questions.

1. How did merchandise inventories for Office Depot change from 2000 to 2001?
2. What might be some reasons for this change?

CHAPTER 25
SECTION 2, PAGES 684–688

2 TEACH (Cont'd.)

Teaching Tips

Briefly discuss average costs. For students who need a math review, assign problems in the *Math Review for Accounting* booklet.

Point out that the weighted average cost method is often used by businesses dealing in such products as oil and grain.

Explain that the average cost method usually yields an amount between the LIFO and FIFO amounts.

Demonstration Problem
Step-by-Step Practice

Use demonstration problem 25–2, Part D, to give students practice in calculating inventory costs using the weighted average cost method.

Thinking Algebraically

Developing Formulas: Have students develop formulas they could use for calculating inventory cost subtotals and totals in a spreadsheet. Using LIFO as an example, they might label each column A, B, C, D, E and write formulas to multiply across a row and add a column. (Example: = B1 * C1 * D1 to multiply amounts in row 1 and =SUM(E1: E5) to calculate a total) L2

The Office Depot 2001 Annual Report

Refer students to pages A-39–A-48 in the back of the book.

ANALYZING FINANCIAL REPORTS

Analyze the Report (Answers)

1. Inventories decreased by $161,303,000 ($1,420,825,000 – $1,259,522,000) from 2000 to 2001. This is a decrease of 11.35 percent ($161,303,000 ÷ $1,420,825,000 = 0.1135).
2. Answers may vary. It is most likely that Office Depot's inventory is lower because of implementation of improved inventory and warehouse operations. The company also undertook more disciplined capital spending that may have impacted inventory purchases.

CHAPTER 25
SECTION 2, PAGES 684–688

3 ASSESS

Thinking Critically (Answers)

1. It is the most realistic costing method because it assigns the actual cost to each item in inventory. Most businesses that have a low unit volume of merchandise with high unit prices use this type of inventory method.
2. LIFO assumes that the last items purchased are the first items sold. This means that the ending inventory is made up of the oldest items. FIFO assumes that the first items purchased are the first items sold; therefore, the ending inventory is made up of the newest items.

Computing in the Business World (Answer)

Cost of merchandise sold $30,125

Problem 25-2 (Answers)

(a) Specific identification $472.55
(b) FIFO $477.25
(c) LIFO $465.25
(d) Weighted average cost $470.52

Chapter Reviews and Working Papers Refer students to the Chapter 25 workbook pages to answer *Check Your Understanding* activities.

4 CLOSE

Section Wrap-Up

Presentation: Divide students into four teams. Assign a different inventory costing method to each team. Have teams prepare a one- to two-minute presentation explaining their method, how it is used to value inventories, and which businesses typically use the method. L2

SECTION 2 Check Your Understanding

Now that you have studied this section, complete the following questions and problems.

Thinking Critically

1. What type of business would use the specific identification costing method?
2. Contrast the LIFO and FIFO inventory costing methods.

Computing in the Business World

Foxfire Golf Club Pro Shop uses the specific identification method for inventory control. At the beginning of the year, Foxfire had 30 golf club sets on hand. The golf club sets were purchased for $800 each. An additional 12 golf club sets were purchased during the year at $875 each. When inventory was taken at the end of the season, 5 golf sets were still on hand. The remaining 5 sets were valued at $875 each. Using the FIFO method of inventory valuation, what was the total cost of merchandise sold?

Problem 25–2 Determining Inventory Costs

The following items were purchased by Kudos Leather Goods during the month of April:

April 2	34 wallets @ $12.95 each
April 8	24 wallets @ $13.10 each
April 18	15 wallets @ $13.25 each
April 26	20 wallets @ $13.27 each

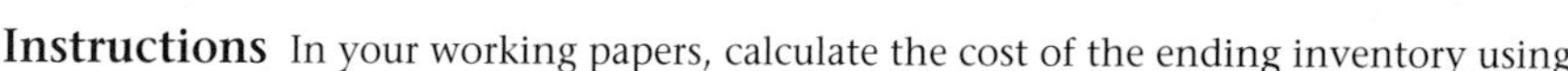

On April 1 the business had in inventory 19 wallets valued at $12.90 each. On April 30 the business had 36 wallets in inventory; of these wallets, 8 were purchased on April 2, 15 were purchased on April 8, 3 were purchased on April 18, and 10 were purchased on April 26.

Instructions In your working papers, calculate the cost of the ending inventory using:

(a) the specific identification method
(b) the FIFO method
(c) the LIFO method
(d) the weighted average method

RETEACHING SECTION 2

Explaining Inventory Costing Methods Remind students that there is a key word in each of the inventory costing methods that will help them remember which prices to use. In the specific identification method, the key word is "specific," and the actual cost of each item is determined. In the FIFO method, "F" for "first" tells students that the first items purchased are assumed to have been sold. Using the LIFO method, "L" for "last" tells students that the last items purchased are assumed to have been sold. The key word in the weighted average cost method is "average," and the average cost for each unit is calculated.

ACCOUNTING CAREERS IN FOCUS

ERIC MONGO
Accounts Payable Accounting Assistant
KICU-TV, Channel 36

Q: How did you get interested in accounting?
A: I developed the interest while working in a family business. I worked as a temp for about three months, then realized that my boss was really smart. I knew I could learn much from her and get more experience than I could get in a class.

Q: What do you do on a typical day?
A: It depends on the week. My functions have recently been expanded to include payroll. If it is a payroll week, from Monday through Wednesday I process payroll in the morning. In the afternoons, I do journal entries. On regular weeks, I pick up the mail and classify the invoices we've received by how each of them is to be paid. I also talk to vendors about payment and to company employees about their checks.

Q: Is a degree necessary for a position as an accounting assistant?
A: Companies often require a bachelor's degree of some kind. They also require some experience, especially if you don't have an accounting or finance degree. You need basic accounting skills. Companies are reluctant to hire someone who has to be taught everything from the beginning.

Q: What is the future like for an accounting assistant?
A: There are quite a lot of openings to go into from here, such as international business or auditing. Accounting is good experience if you want to run your own business.

Tips from . . . Robert Half International Inc.

Many executives believe a good team player is one who can meet deadlines. Everyone must help keep a project on track. If you don't, everyone else has to work harder to compensate.

CAREER FACTS

Nature of the Work: Organize and process invoices and checks; journal entries; data entry.
Training or Education Needed: A bachelor's degree, and some accounting experience.
Aptitudes, Abilities, and Skills: Accounting, time-management skills, problem-solving skills, accuracy, and communication skills.
Salary Range: $25,000 to $35,000 depending on company size and industry.
Career Path: Start as an entry-level bookkeeper, then take on more difficult tasks and eventually move up as you develop more skills.

Thinking Critically: How might you get the basic accounting experience you need for an entry-level accounting position?

SCANS in the Workforce

Foundation Skills Connection

Self-Management
Lead your students in an exercise of self-evaluation. Ask them to evaluate themselves on these questions: (1) Can they set realistic personal goals? (2) Can they motivate themselves to achieve their goals? (3) Can they take constructive criticism? (4) Would they consider themselves self-starters? Students who answer "yes" to all four questions may consider themselves excellent self-managers. Urge students with fewer positive responses to work toward improving their weak areas. L1

Workplace Competencies Connection

Allocating Time
Help students learn the skills of efficient time management. Ask students to bring in or create daily and weekly schedules. Have them map out time commitments for one week and monitor how their actual time use matches their planned time frame. At the end of one week, have students share their insights and discuss ways they can adjust their schedules. L2

Applying Technology to Tasks
Ask students to imagine they are being hired as the accounting manager for a small advertising agency. The agency has been reluctant to move its financial recordkeeping to computers. What types of accounting activities can be more easily handled with the use of technology? Have students create a list or table identifying possible accounting jobs, and assign those jobs a technological application. L3

ACCOUNTING CAREERS IN FOCUS

Thinking Critically (Answers)
Start with a position such as data entry or filing, during high school or college; be willing to learn and take on responsibilities; accumulate skills and knowledge; go through a temporary agency to get an entry-level position.

ROBERT HALF CORNER

The Accountant's Changing Role
CFOs predict that issues and responsibilities outside of traditional accounting functions will occupy 37 percent of a senior accountant's time five years from now.

1 FOCUS

Introducing the Section
Now that students have learned how to apply different inventory costing methods, in this section they'll learn why a business chooses a particular method.

Section Concepts
- How to choose an inventory costing method.
- The effect of the inventory costing method on gross profit.
- How to use the lower-of-cost-or-market method.
- How to apply to inventory the accounting principles of consistency and conservatism.

Visual Learning

Section 3 Focus

Use **Transparency 25–6** to introduce section concepts.

BELL RINGER

Analyzing: Ask students how the local price for gasoline has changed over the past few weeks. Chances are it has gone up a few pennies, then down again. Have students analyze why gasoline prices change. Point out that the price today is the market price. L1

Concept Development: Choosing an Inventory Costing Method

Discussion: Discuss the effects of the different methods on the cost of merchandise sold. Point out that there is no right or wrong method, but rather one that is best for a particular business given current economic conditions. You may also want to discuss long-term and short-term economic projections and current price trends. This section may be confusing to students, but it is important for them to understand why inventory costing decisions are made. L1

SECTION 3

Analyzing the Inventory Costing Methods

What You'll Learn
- How to choose an inventory costing method.
- The effect of the inventory costing method on gross profit.
- How to use the lower-of-cost-or-market method.
- How to apply to inventory the accounting principles of consistency and conservatism.

Why It's Important

It is essential that business owners and managers understand how the choice of an inventory costing method affects the financial statements.

KEY TERMS

consistency principle
market value
conservatism principle

A business may use any one of the four inventory costing methods. Careful consideration is given to this choice because it affects the gross profit reported by the business.

Choosing an Inventory Costing Method

When a business applies the same accounting methods from one period to the next, the business is applying the **consistency principle**. Once a business chooses an inventory costing method, the business must use it consistently. This helps owners and creditors compare financial reports from one period to another.

Businesses are permitted to change costing methods but must declare the reasons for changing and how the change will affect the financial statements. In addition, the business must get permission for the change from the Internal Revenue Service.

When making a decision about which inventory costing method to use, the owner or manager compares the four methods and selects the one that is likely to be the most beneficial to the company. The owner or manager will consider the present economic conditions and the future economic outlook. He or she will also consider whether prices and demand for the product will remain stable, will increase, or will decrease.

ACCOUNTING TIPS

Cost of Inventory

Businesses must know the cost of inventory in order to purchase insurance on the inventory, pay income and personal property taxes, and prepare financial statements.

Comparing the Four Methods of Determining Inventory Cost

The cost of ending inventory affects the cost of merchandise sold, which in turn affects the income or loss reported on the income statement. Remember:

Sales
– Cost of merchandise sold
Gross profit on sales
– Operating expenses
Net income (loss)

The following table compares Disk Jockey's gross profit on sales using the four inventory costing methods. All of the laser disc players were sold for $320 each. Total sales are $16,960 (53 units × $320).

RESOURCE MANAGER

Reproducible Masters
- Lesson Plans
- Chapter Reviews and Working Papers (CRWP) TAE
- Demonstration Problems

Transparencies
- Section Focus Transparency
- Teaching Transparencies
- Source Document Transparencies
- Solution Transparencies

Multimedia
- ExamView CD-ROM
- Electronic Learning Center CD-ROM
- Interactive Lesson Planner CD-ROM
- Electronic Field Trips in Accounting

	Specific Identification	First-In, First-Out	Last-In, First-Out	Weighted Average
Sales	$16,960.00	$16,960.00	$16,960.00	$16,960.00
Less: Cost of merchandise sold	13,378.00	13,344.00	13,460.00	13,421.24
Gross profit on sales	$ 3,582.00	$ 3,616.00	$ 3,500.00	$ 3,538.76

Over the year the cost of the laser disc players increased from $250 to $260. As shown in the table, in a period of rising prices, the LIFO method results in the lowest gross profit on sales. The FIFO method results in the highest gross profit on sales.

Businesses pay income taxes on income earned. As shown above, the inventory costing method used by a business can increase or decrease its taxes.

Key Points

The Effect of Inventory Costing on Net Income
A company's gross profit on sales and net income are affected by the inventory costing method used.

Reporting Inventory Cost Using the Lower-of-Cost-or-Market Rule

The cost of the inventory is reported on the income statement and the balance sheet. The cost of the ending inventory that appears on the financial statements is the lower of cost (calculated using one of the four inventory methods) or market value.

Market value is the current price that is charged for similar items of merchandise in the market. Market value is the cost at which the inventory items could be replaced at the date of the financial statements.

Let's look at an example. Assume that Disk Jockey determines that the current market value of the laser disc players is $248 each. At market the players are worth $2,976 ($248 × 12 units). Assume also that Disk Jockey uses the FIFO inventory costing method. Under this method the cost of the ending inventory was $3,116.

Following the lower-of-cost-or-market rule, Disk Jockey will report inventory at $2,976.

Lower of cost (FIFO)	$3,116
or	
Market	2,976

Cost is the most common basis for reporting inventory. Occasionally inventory may be worth less than its cost. For example, some merchandise items may deteriorate or become obsolete. If the market value of such items is less than the cost, the difference is a loss to the business. In such a case, it is more conservative to report inventory at market value.

The **conservatism principle** is another principle of accounting. To be conservative is to take the safe route. In reporting the financial position of a business, the conservatism principle states that it is best to present amounts that are least likely to result in an overstatement of income or assets. The lower-of-cost-or-market rule is conservative for two reasons:

(1) Decreases in inventory value (losses) are recognized when they occur, but increases in inventory value are not recorded.
(2) Inventory as reported on the balance sheet is never greater, but may be less, than the actual cost of the inventory.

Spreadsheet Hints

Understanding Spreadsheet Formulas
Spreadsheet formulas identify the cells affected, rather than the amounts themselves. For example:
- to subtract the cost of merchandise sold from net sales, you might enter +E5-E16, where net sales are in E5 and cost of merchandise sold is in E16.

Math Skill Builder Activity

Understanding Spreadsheet Formulas To help students understand how to use and interpret spreadsheet formulas, have students set up a spreadsheet using the information on sales and cost of merchandise sold at the top of page 691. Ask students to write the formulas to calculate gross profit on sales for each of the four inventory costing methods. Each spreadsheet program uses different ways to denote formulas. Students may need to refer to spreadsheet user guides. (Example: In cell B3, enter the formula =B1–B2)

2 TEACH

GUIDED PRACTICE

Reading Accounting
- Have students turn each heading in this section into a question and mentally answer each question. L1

Concept Development: Comparing the Four Methods of Determining Inventory Cost

Discussion: Emphasize that specific identification is the only method that reports actual inventory cost. Discuss the effects of using the four methods in periods of increasing costs and decreasing costs. Point out that the *higher* the cost of the ending inventory the *lower* the cost of merchandise sold. The *lower* the cost of merchandise sold, the higher the gross profit. L1

Concept Development: Reporting Inventory Cost Using the Lower-of-Cost-or-Market Rule

Discussion: When discussing the lower-of-cost-or-market rule, review the conservatism principle and why it is applied to the reporting of inventory cost. L1

GO TO Demonstration Problem Step-by-Step Practice
Use demonstration problem 25–3 to give students practice in calculating and comparing inventory costs. Use demonstration problem 25–4 to have students report inventory cost.

GO TO Math Review for Accounting
Photocopy appropriate *Activity Sheets* for students who need additional practice in basic math skills.

3 ASSESS

Thinking Critically (Answers)

1. So the IRS can ensure that the business pays the proper amount of taxes to state and federal governments as determined by the costing method used.
2. It is thought to be a conservative approach since losses, or decreases, in inventory value are recognized when they occur and increases in market value are never recorded; and inventory values reported on the balance sheet are never greater, but may be less, than the actual cost of the inventory.

Analyzing Accounting (Answer)

Of the four methods, the LIFO method affords the highest gross profit.

Problem 25–3 (Answers)

1. Ending inventory $575.90
2. Gross profit $214.30

Chapter Reviews and Working Papers Refer students to the Chapter 25 workbook pages to answer *Check Your Understanding* activities.

4 CLOSE

Section Wrap-Up

Demonstration: Give students this example: sales, $68,400; cost of merchandise sold under specific identification, $56,800; FIFO, $56,600; LIFO, $56,720; weighted average, $56,670. Have students calculate gross profit under each method and explain how each method affects income taxes paid by the business. (Specific ID, $11,600; FIFO, $11,800; LIFO, $11,680; weighted avg., $11,730) L1

SECTION 3 Check Your Understanding

Now that you have studied this section, complete the following questions and problems.

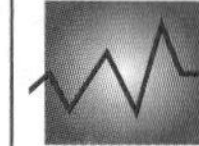

Thinking Critically

1. If a business wants to change its inventory costing method, why must it get permission from the Internal Revenue Service?
2. Explain why the lower-of-cost-or-market rule for inventory valuation is a conservative approach.

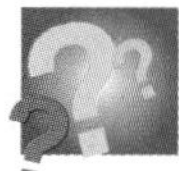

Analyzing Accounting

The management of Baby Steps Children's Store wants to report the largest gross profit on sales. Using the graph, compare the gross profit on sales for the four inventory costing methods. Which method results in the largest gross profit on sales?

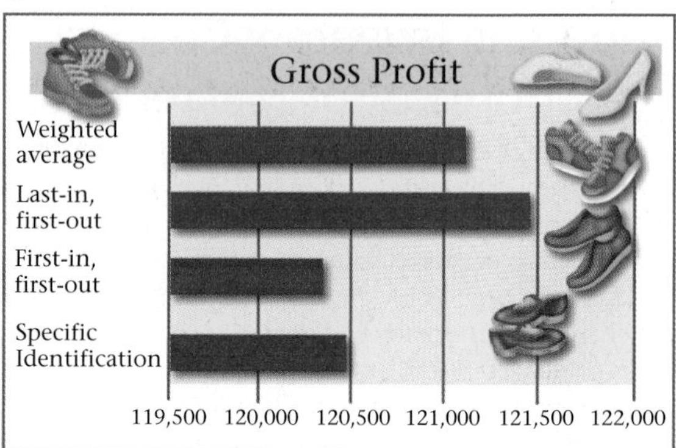

Problem 25–3 Analyzing a Source Document

Read the following memorandum and complete the assigned task.

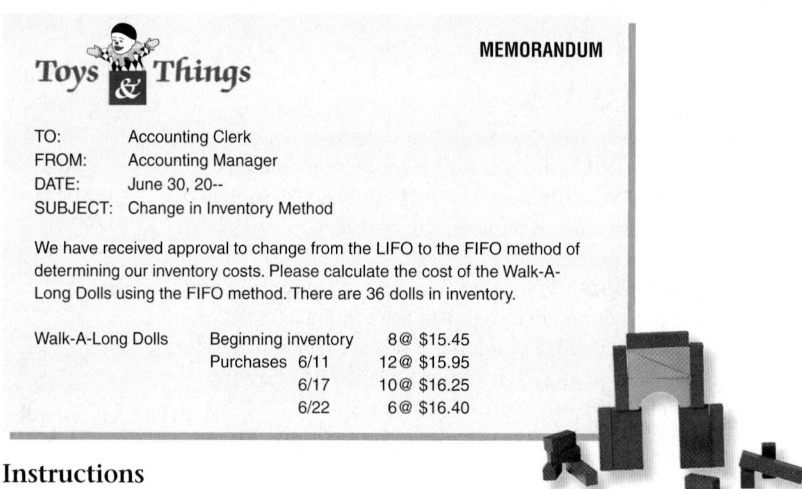

Toys & Things

MEMORANDUM

TO: Accounting Clerk
FROM: Accounting Manager
DATE: June 30, 20--
SUBJECT: Change in Inventory Method

We have received approval to change from the LIFO to the FIFO method of determining our inventory costs. Please calculate the cost of the Walk-A-Long Dolls using the FIFO method. There are 36 dolls in inventory.

Walk-A-Long Dolls	Beginning inventory		8 @ $15.45
	Purchases	6/11	12 @ $15.95
		6/17	10 @ $16.25
		6/22	6 @ $16.40

Instructions

1. What is the new value of the ending inventory?
2. Assume that all 36 dolls were sold for $21.95. What is the gross profit for this item?

RETEACHING SECTION 3

Comparing the Inventory Costing Methods If inventory prices remain consistent, all four inventory costing methods provide similar results. However, in a market where prices are constantly rising and falling, each costing method yields different results. Therefore, it is important that business owners and managers know how to choose an inventory costing method. They will want to consider current economic conditions and the future economic outlook when they decide which costing method to use.

CHAPTER 25 SUMMARY

KEY CONCEPTS

1. It is important for a business to keep accurate inventory records so that the financial statements are correct.
2. Most businesses take a physical inventory count at least once a year.
3. Inventory Systems

Perpetual	Periodic
Provides current inventory records at any point in time.	A physical count of all merchandise on hand is required to update inventory records.

4. Perpetual inventory systems are used by most large businesses. Periodic inventory systems are often used by small businesses that maintain manual accounting records.
5. Inventory Costing Methods

Specific identification method	The exact cost of each item is tracked.
First-in, first-out method (FIFO)	Assumes that the first items purchased are the first items sold.
Last-in, first-out method (LIFO)	Assumes that the last items purchased are the first items sold.
Weighted average cost method	Uses an average cost for each inventory item.

6. A company's gross profit on sales and net income are affected by the inventory costing method used.
7. A business must be consistent with the inventory costing method it uses. A change in inventory valuation method must be approved by the Internal Revenue Service.
8. The cost of ending inventory affects the cost of merchandise sold, which in turn affects the income or loss reported on the income statement.
9. The lower-of-cost-or-market rule is a conservative approach to costing inventory. On the financial statements, ending inventory is reported at the lower of cost (using one of the costing methods) or market value.

ANSWERS

1. False
2. False
3. True
4. False
5. True
6. False
7. True
8. True
9. False
10. True

SUMMARY CHAPTER 25

Chapter 25 Quiz

Student Class Instructor
Date Assigned Date Completed

CHAPTER 25 QUIZ

Inventories

QUESTIONS (True-False)

Directions: In the space provided, indicate whether each statement is true or false.

___ 1. Businesses complete periodic inventories frequently.
___ 2. The periodic inventory provides a daily balance of merchandise on hand.
___ 3. Taking inventory means making an actual physical count of items on hand.
___ 4. The specific identification method averages inventory costs.
___ 5. LIFO is generally used during periods of inflation.
___ 6. FIFO generally produces the lowest gross profit on sales.
___ 7. The weighted average cost method calculates average cost per unit.
___ 8. Market value is the current price for items similar to those in inventory.
___ 9. A business must report its inventory at market value.
___ 10. If inventory is worth less than its replacement cost, the conservatism principle requires that it be reported at cost rather than its market value.

 Chapter Quizzes • 27

QUESTIONS (True-False)

1. Businesses complete periodic inventories frequently.
2. The periodic inventory provides a daily balance of merchandise on hand.
3. Taking inventory means making an actual physical count of items on hand.
4. The specific identification method averages inventory costs.
5. LIFO is generally used during periods of inflation.
6. FIFO generally produces the lowest gross profit on sales.
7. The weighted average cost method calculates average cost per unit.
8. Market value is the current price for items similar to those in inventory.
9. A business must report its inventory at market value.
10. If inventory is worth less than its replacement cost, the conservatism principle requires that it be reported at cost rather than its market value.

USING KEY TERMS

See the *Glossary* for the definitions of these terms. Have students share their advertisements in class. Discuss any differences in use of the terms.

Understanding Accounting Concepts and Procedures

(Answers)

1. Merchandise is the largest asset for most businesses and needs protection from theft and loss.
2. In a periodic system, a physical count of merchandise is made to determine cost. In a perpetual system, a daily record of merchandise is kept.
3. To provide accurate information for financial statements and determine accuracy of a perpetual system.
4. Keeping a constant record of merchandise on hand would be too difficult for large-volume businesses without a computerized system.
5. A business can quickly determine the balance of Merchandise Inventory since all purchases and sales of merchandise are recorded immediately.
6. FIFO assumes that items purchased first are sold first. Items in inventory are the last items purchased and their cost is the most recent cost.
7. The costing method affects cost of merchandise sold, which then changes gross profit and net income. The higher the cost of merchandise sold, the lower the gross profit and net income, and conversely.
8. A business should value its inventory at the cost calculated by one of the costing methods or at market value, whichever is lower; the rule results in a conservative statement of inventory value, with losses recognized before goods are sold and increases in market value never recorded.

CHAPTER 25 REVIEW AND ACTIVITIES

USING KEY TERMS

Grandma's Toy Attic is in the process of changing from a manual to an automated system of inventory control. You, as the owner, plan to hire an inventory supervisor who understands accounting principles, inventory control, and business economics as well as computer applications. You decide to run an advertisement in your local newspaper to find the most qualified individual. Use the terms listed below and write an advertisement to attract applicants for the inventory supervisor position. You are encouraged to give your newspaper some layout ideas for the advertisement. Also, use these terms to create a job description.

- conservatism principle
- consistency principle
- first-in, first-out method
- last-in, first-out method
- market value
- online
- periodic inventory system
- perpetual inventory system
- point-of-sale terminal
- specific identification method
- weighted average cost method

Understanding Accounting Concepts and Procedures

Instructions

On a separate sheet of paper, answer the following questions:

1. Why should a company have a control system for its merchandise inventory?
2. What is the difference between a periodic and a perpetual inventory system?
3. Why is a physical inventory count taken at least once a year?
4. Why is it difficult for some businesses to use a perpetual inventory system?
5. What advantage is there in using a perpetual inventory system?
6. What is meant by the phrase "with the FIFO method, the inventory is based on the most recent costs"?
7. How does the inventory costing method affect gross profit on sales and net income?
8. What is the lower-of-cost-or-market rule, and why is it used?

ASSESSMENT RESOURCES

Choose assessment strategies from the following pages to evaluate your students' progress.

Student Edition
Check Your Understanding, pp. 683, 688, 692
Chapter 25 Problems, pp. 697–699
Analyzing Financial Reports, p. 687

Assessment and Evaluation Masters
Chapter 25 Study Plan, *Glencoe Workbook (CRWP)*
Chapter 25 Self-Test, *Glencoe Workbook (CRWP)*
Chapter 25 Test, *Chapter Tests* Booklet
Chapter 25 Activity, *School-to-Work Handbook*
Chapter 25 **Exam***View*

Teacher Wraparound Edition
Critical Thinking Activity, p. 697
Reteaching Sections 1–3, pp. 683, 688, 692
Chapter 25 Quiz, p. 693

Case Study...

Merchandising Business: Home Building and Supply

Remodeling a kitchen? Adding a deck to your home? Home Helper is a building supply store that sells everything from lightbulbs to lumber, cabinet fixtures to appliances. Because it stocks many sizes and varieties of building products, the store has a huge inventory.

You work for a local CPA firm that has been hired to evaluate the store's inventory procedures. The store manager wants to make sure the store is using the most appropriate inventory costing method.

Thinking Critically:

Think about the types of products stocked by a home building supply store. Of the four inventory costing methods you have studied in this chapter, recommend the best method for Home Helper. Assume that costs are expected to remain stable over the next few years. Explain the reasons for your recommendation.

interNET CONNECTION

Inventory Management

Inventory management can be a nightmare without the proper organization and technology. A variety of perpetual inventory management systems exist that help the business owner keep track of inventory quantities as well as sales and product orders. Bar codes and advanced database systems are just two tools available to businesses.

Do This:

Locate Web sites that deal with inventory management products. Try key words like "point-of-sale," "bar codes," and "inventory."

1. List three companies that offer inventory management products.
2. Name one inventory management product.
3. What are the benefits of using inventory technology?

Conducting an Audit with Alex

Instructions Verify the accuracy of the inventory sheet below. Correct any errors on a separate sheet of paper.

INVENTORY SHEET

DATE 11/30/20-- CLERK Janet Milhouse PAGE 17

STOCK NO.	ITEM	UNIT	QUANTITY	UNIT COST	TOTAL VALUE
2184	Socks	Pair	27	2 19	59 13
2724	Hat	Each	31	7 95	246 54
4163	Gloves	Pair	14	12 40	137 60
2261	Gloves	Pair	9	14 80	133 20
3290	Mittens	Pair	17	14 70	299 90
			TOTAL FOR THIS SHEET		875 47

Workplace Skills

Selecting Equipment and Tools

Many business tasks that are done manually can be performed in a fraction of the time if automated. Selecting equipment and software to achieve desired outcomes, demonstrates your evaluation skills.

On the Job:

Your manager, Richard Smythe, has decided to switch from a manual inventory system to an automated perpetual system.

Thinking Critically:

Write a proposal to Mr. Smythe that emphasizes the benefits of using a perpetual inventory system. Specifically address time savings and revenue possibilities.

Case Study...

Thinking Critically (Answers)

Answers will vary. Evaluate students' responses for a logical progression of ideas.

Workplace Skills

Thinking Critically (Answers)
Answers will vary. Some advantages are that it allows immediate determination of quantities on hand with their respective costs, and it can signal when an item needs to be reordered.

Conducting an Audit with Alex

(Answers)
Values:
2184 Hat $246.45
4163 Gloves $173.60
3290 Mittens $249.90

Total $862.28

GO TO Internet Resources and Activities Handbook
Refer students to the booklet for additional Internet activities.

interNET CONNECTION www.glencoe.com

Do This (Answers)

1. Answers may vary. Here are some examples:
   EDP System Services, Inc. (www.abarcode.com)
   Great Lakes Software (www.greatlakessoftware.com)
   Advanced Point of Sale (www.aposme.com)
2. Answers may vary. EDP System Services, Inc. has a system called CheckMate.
3. Answers may vary. Possibly the greatest benefit of an automated system is that it can tie together all of the inventory related functions of the business.

PEACHTREE CORNER

Inventory Records

Use the **Inventory Items** option in the ***Maintain*** menu to add, update, or delete inventory items. To set up an inventory record, enter the item ID, description, price, general ledger accounts, costing method, and cost.

Maintain Tasks Analysis Op
Customers/Prospects...
Vendors...
Employees/Sales Reps...
Chart of Accounts...
Inventory Items...
Item Prices...
Job Costs

Choose the **Inventory** option in the ***Reports*** menu to access the inventory reports, including the Inventory Valuation Report, Cost of Goods Sold Journal, and Item Costing Report.

Reports Services Window
Accounts Receivable...
Accounts Payable...
Payroll...
General Ledger...
Financial Statements...
Inventory...
Jobs...

You can also access Inventory reports and the **Purchases/Receive Inventory** and **Inventory Items** options by using the Inventory navigation aid.

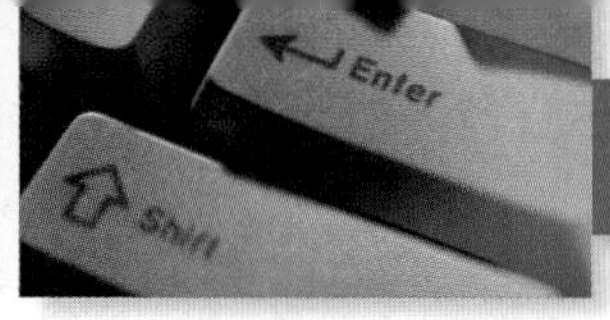

Inventory Costing

Making the Transition from a Manual to a Computerized System

Task	Perform Accounting Procedures Using Manual Methods	Perform Accounting Procedures Using Automated Methods
Determining the cost of inventories in a perpetual inventory system	1. Enter purchases of merchandise onto stock cards. 2. Enter sales of items onto stock cards. 3. At period end, calculate number and value of remaining inventory items.	1. When the accounting system is set up, the costing method must be determined. Many computerized systems link the cash register to the accounting system. 2. Purchases of merchandise update not only the general ledger but also update the inventory records. 3. As sales are made, the system updates the inventory records. 4. Inventory quantities and values are available when needed.

Maintaining and Costing Inventories

Peachtree Question	Description
How are inventory records set up in Peachtree?	1. Select **Default Inventory** from the ***Maintain*** menu. 2. Select Inventory Items. 3. Click the G/L Accts/Costing tab and enter the G/L account numbers for sales and purchases. 4. Click the Taxes/Shipping tab and enter a (✓) if sales taxes are to be collected on items sold. Click OK. 5. From the ***Maintain*** menu, select **Inventory Items.** 6. Enter Item ID codes, descriptions, price, and costing method (FIFO, LIFO, or Average) for all inventory items. 7. The costing method cannot be changed once transactions have been posted against the item.
How do I track inventory?	1. When recording sales or purchases of inventory items, use the established item codes. With each transaction, the system will update the inventory records.
How do I generate inventory reports?	1. From the ***Reports*** menu, choose **Inventory.** 2. Select Inventory Valuation Report from the reports list. Quantities on hand and values for each item are displayed based on the costing method default.
What does the software do "behind the scenes"?	1. Peachtree tracks the inventory items and automatically updates the quantities after each transaction. 2. The Cost of Merchandise Sold G/L account will contain all transactions.

For detailed instructions: See the **Peachtree User Guide** in your Glencoe Working Papers.

Peachtree® Answers to Frequently Asked Questions

Q: Can you change the inventory valuation method for an inventory item?
A: No. If you have entered no transactions for the item, delete the record and re-enter.
Q: How do you correct a **Purchases/Receive Inventory** transaction if you enter the wrong quantity or item number?
A: Choose the **Purchases/Receive Inventory** option, click *Open*, and select the invoice you want to correct. Make changes and save the updated invoice.
For additional information, refer to your *Glencoe Peachtree Accounting User Guide.*

CHAPTER 25 PROBLEMS

APPLICATION OPTIONS

Problem 25–4 Calculating the Cost of Ending Inventory

Sunset Surfwear sells wet suits. On January 2 there were 21 wet suits, at a total cost of $4,809 in inventory.

Date	Description	Wet Suits	Cost	Total
Jan. 2	Beginning inventory	21	$229	$ 4,809
Jan. 3	Purchase	10	235	2,350
Mar. 17	Purchase	6	238	1,428
July 27	Purchase	12	240	2,880
Sept. 27	Purchase	10	241	2,410
Nov. 29	Purchase	6	244	1,464
	Total	65		$ 15,341

At the end of the year, there were 17 wet suits in ending inventory. Of these, 1 was purchased on July 27, 10 were purchased on September 27, and 6 were purchased on November 29.

Instructions Assign a cost to the ending inventory using the following:

(a) the specific identification method
(b) the FIFO method
(c) the LIFO method
(d) the weighted average cost method

Analyze: Which inventory method resulted in the lowest cost of the ending inventory?

Problem 25–5 Completing an Inventory Sheet

InBeat CD Shop assigns a cost to its inventory using the lower-of-cost-or-market rule. In your working papers, there is a partial inventory record. As an example, the first line of the inventory record has been completed.

INVENTORY RECORD

Item No.	Item	Ending Inventory	Cost per Unit	Current Market Value	Price to be Used	Total Cost
0247	Blank CDs	24	2.67	2.88	2.67	64.08

Continued

Complete chapter problems one of four ways:

1 **Manual** Glencoe Working Papers

or

2 **Peachtree Complete Accounting** Software

or

3 **QuickBooks** Templates (Problems 25–4, 25–8)

or

4 **Spreadsheet** Templates (Problem 25–6)

Peachtree®

SMART GUIDE

Step-by-Step Instructions: Problem 25–4

1. Select the problem set for Sunset Surfwear (Prob. 25–4).
2. Rename the company and set the system date.
3. Print the following reports: Inventory Valuation Report, Cost of Goods Sold Journal, and Item Costing Report.
4. End the session.

TIP: Set the date range for the Cost of Goods Sold Journal to include data for the entire year.

PROBLEMS CHAPTER 25

Problem 25–4 (Answers) Calculating the Cost of Ending Inventory

Specific Identification $4,114
FIFO $4,114
LIFO $3,893
Weighted Average $4,012

Analyze: LIFO

Problem 25–5 (Answers) Completing an Inventory Sheet

Total cost of items:

0247 $64.08
0391 $98.64
0388 $61.11
0379 $38.16
0380 $142.31
0274 $158.70
0276 $95.40
0277 $129.50
0181 $37.08
0193 $20.61
0419 $67.36
0420 $125.72

Total Cost $1,038.67

Analyze: LIFO and Specific Identification

CRITICAL THINKING ACTIVITY

Interpreting Information Have students explain reasons why a physical count at the end of an accounting period may not match the Merchandise Inventory account balance even when a perpetual inventory system is maintained. Would a computerized inventory system guarantee totally accurate records? (Stock cards may not be completed accurately or consistently, or merchandise may be taken from stock without approval. Use of a computerized system would not guarantee perfect records. Some errors could still occur, such as the wrong product code or the wrong number being entered. Even with a computerized system, employees may steal merchandise from the company's inventory.)

Problem 25-6 (Answers) Calculating Gross Profit on Sales

Specific Identification $17,729.61
FIFO $17,835.01
LIFO $17,664.54
Weighted Average $17,700.97

Analyze: FIFO

Problem 25-7 (Answers) Reporting Ending Inventory on the Income Statement

Cost of merchandise sold:
FIFO $11,520
LIFO $11,782
Weighted Average $11,636

Gross profit on sales:
FIFO $7,380
LIFO $7,118
Weighted Average $7,264

Analyze: FIFO

SPREADSHEET SMART GUIDE

Step-by-Step Instructions: Problem 25-6

1. Select the spreadsheet template for Problem 25-6.
2. Enter your name and the date in the spaces provided on the template.
3. Complete the spreadsheet using the instructions in your working papers.
4. Print the spreadsheet and proof your work.
5. Save your work and exit the spreadsheet program.

Instructions Complete the inventory record. Do the following:

(1) Select the lower-of-cost-or-market value. Enter that amount in the Price to be Used column.
(2) Calculate the total cost of each item by multiplying the units in ending inventory by the Price to be Used column.
(3) Add the amounts in the Total Cost column to determine the total cost of the ending inventory.

Analyze: How many of the items used market value rather than actual cost?

Problem 25-6 Calculating Gross Profit on Sales

Using the four inventory costing methods, Shutterbug Cameras summarized the cost of its ending inventory as follows:

Specific Identification	First-In, First-Out	Last-In, First-Out	Weighted Average Cost
$21,476.00	$21,581.40	$21,410.93	$21,447.36

Shutterbug Cameras also reported the following amounts:

Net sales	$53,874.92
Purchases available for sale	57,621.31

Instructions Using the above information, determine the cost of merchandise sold and the gross profit on sales for each of the inventory costing methods.

Analyze: Which method resulted in the largest gross profit on sales?

Peachtree® SMART GUIDE

Step-by-Step Instructions: Problem 25-7

1. Select the problem set for Cycle Tech Bicycles (Prob. 25-7).
2. Rename the company and set the system date.
3. Print the following reports: Inventory Valuation Report, Cost of Goods Sold Journal, and Item Costing Report.
4. Print an Income Statement and a Balance Sheet.
5. End the session.

TIP: Remember to set the date range for the Cost of Goods Sold Journal to include data for the entire year.

Problem 25-7 Reporting Ending Inventory on the Income Statement

Cycle Tech Bicycles operates on a fiscal year beginning January 1. At the beginning of the year, the shop had in stock six Model #8274, ten-speed bicycles, valued at $2,364 (6 bicycles @ $394 each). During the year the business made the following purchases:

Date	Bicycles	Cost		Total
Jan. 20	4	$399	=	$ 1,596
Mar. 5	5	415	=	2,075
Apr. 23	7	419	=	2,933
Aug. 14	4	423	=	1,692
Oct. 3	6	430	=	2,580
Nov. 17	3	435	=	1,305
Total Purchases	29			$12,181

There were seven bicycles in inventory at the end of the period. During the year the bicycles sold for $675 each.

ADDRESSING MULTIPLE LEARNING STYLES

Verbal/Linguistic Learner Several key terms in this chapter—*perpetual inventory system; periodic inventory system; first-in, first-out method; last-in, first-out method; conservatism principle;* and *consistency principle*—can be confusing. Ask students to define the terms in their own words. Then have students exchange definitions with a partner to critique.

Instructions

(1) Calculate the cost of the ending inventory using the FIFO, LIFO, and weighted average cost methods.
(2) Using the costs calculated in (1), determine the cost of merchandise sold for each inventory costing method.
(3) Prepare a partial income statement for each inventory costing method showing sales and the calculation of gross profit on sales. Assume that the sales and purchases are net amounts.

Analyze: Which method resulted in the lowest cost of merchandise sold?

Problem 25–8 Calculating Cost of Merchandise Sold and Gross Profit on Sales

Buzz Newsstand started the month of May with the following inventory of disposable cameras:

Stock No.	Brand	Units on Hand	Unit Cost	Selling Price
3845	Lenox	4	$9.60	$ 17.95
4931	Lancaster	6	8.40	17.29
9265	Paterson	3	8.10	16.88
4850	McMahon	5	7.60	15.95

Buzz Newsstand uses the FIFO method to calculate the cost of its merchandise inventory. The May 31 physical inventory count indicated:

Lenox	4 cameras	Paterson	7 cameras
Lancaster	5 cameras	McMahon	5 cameras

Instructions

(1) How many units of each of the four cameras were sold during May?
(2) Using the chart provided in your working papers, calculate the gross profit on sales for each type of camera.

Date	Transactions
May 2	Purchased 10 Lancaster cameras at $8.45 each.
4	Purchased 5 McMahon cameras at $7.80 each.
9	Purchased 6 Lenox cameras at $9.95 each plus a $4 transportation charge.
14	Purchased 5 Paterson cameras at $8.25 each.
17	Purchased 8 Lancaster cameras at $8.60 each.
19	Purchased 4 Lenox cameras at $10.10 each plus a $5 transportation charge.
27	Purchased 8 Paterson cameras at $8.30 each.
29	Purchased 4 Lancaster cameras at $8.85 each.

Analyze: Which camera sold the most number of units in May?

Peachtree®

SMART GUIDE

Step-by-Step Instructions: Problem 25–8

1. Select the problem set for Buzz Newsstand (Prob. 25–8).
2. Rename the company and set the system date.
3. Record all of the purchases transactions using the **Purchases/Receive Inventory** option.
4. Record the transportation charges using the **Payments** option.
5. Record the camera sales using the **Receipts** option.
6. Print a Purchases Journal, Cash Disbursements Journal and a Cash Receipts Journal to proof your work.
7. Print the following reports: Inventory Valuation Report, Cost of Goods Sold Journal, and Item Costing Report.
8. Answer the Analyze question.
9. End the session.

TIP: Determine the quantity sold for each camera and enter the sales as a multi-part cash receipt. Record the total sales for each camera on the last day of the month.

SOURCE DOCUMENT PROBLEM

Problem 25–8

Use the source documents in your working papers to record the transactions for this problem.

CHALLENGE PROBLEM

Problem 25–8 (Answers) Calculating Cost of Merchandise Sold and Gross Profit on Sales

Units sold:
#3845, 10
#9265, 9
#4931, 23
#4850, 5

Gross profit on sales:
#3845, $72.40
#4931, $202.57
#9265, $78.07
#4850, $41.75

Analyze: The model that sold the most units was #4931.

MEETING SPECIAL NEEDS

Students with Learning Disabilities Students with learning disabilities may not be able to communicate well in written form. Consider giving these students oral examinations or allowing them to present oral reports. Students who are able to use a computer could provide written materials. Finally, you might have an aide take dictation from the student.

CHAPTER 26 Resource Manager

Section Resources

	Objectives & Standards	Activities & Features	Reproducible Masters
Chapter Opener *Notes Payable and Receivable*	• Explain how promissory notes are used by businesses. • Calculate due dates and maturity values of notes payable and notes receivable. • Explain the difference between interest-bearing and noninterest-bearing notes. • Calculate interest due on notes payable and notes receivable. • Record notes payable and notes receivable. • Journalize transactions involving notes payable and notes receivable. • Define the accounting terms introduced in this chapter. **National Standards for Business Education**: IIB1, IIB3, IIB4	Exploring the Real World of Business, p. 700 Workplace Connections, p. 701	School-to-Work Handbook
Section 1 *Promissory Notes*	• How promissory notes are used. • How to determine the due date, interest expense, and maturity value of a promissory note.	International Accounting, p. 704 Did You Know?, p. 705 A Matter of Ethics, p. 706	Demonstration Problems Strategies for Teaching International Accounting Strategies for Teaching Ethics in Accounting
Section 2 *Notes Payable*	• The differences between interest-bearing and noninterest-bearing notes. • How to record notes payable transactions. • How to calculate and record bank discounts.	Connect To, p. 709 Accounting Tips, p. 710 Accounting Flashbacks, p. 712 Calculator Hints, p. 714 Analyzing Financial Reports, p. 714	Demonstration Problems Math Review for Accounting
Section 3 *Notes Receivable*	• How to record the issuance of a note receivable. • How to record payments on a note receivable.		Demonstration Problems Internet Resources and Activities Handbook

KEY

Posters | Transparency | Software | Videocassette
Blackline Masters | CD-ROM | Portfolio

MULTIMEDIA RESOURCE

Peachtree	QuickBooks	Spreadsheets	Videos	CD-ROMs
Problem 26–6 *Recording Transactions for Interest-Bearing Notes Payable* Problem 26–7 *Recording Transactions for Noninterest-Bearing Notes Payable* Problem 26–8 *Recording Notes Payable and Notes Receivable* Problem 26–9 *Recording Notes Payable and Notes Receivable* Problem 26–10 *Renewing a Note Receivable*	Problem 26–6 *Recording Transactions for Interest-Bearing Notes Payable* Problem 26–10 *Renewing a Note Receivable*	None in this chapter.	***Video Segment: Accounting All Around You*** After viewing this video, students will be able to describe the role that accounting plays in providing decision-making information in a private enterprise economy.	***Electronic Learning Center (ELC), Chapter 26*** This program is ideal for visual learners since it incorporates video images, animation, and graphics to enliven the content of each lesson. ***Interactive Lesson Planner (ILP), Chapter 26*** This CD-ROM combines the versatility of an electronic lesson planner with the convenience of teacher classroom resources.

SCANS Correlation Chart

FOUNDATION SKILLS

Basic Skills:	Reading	Writing	Math	Listening	Speaking	
Thinking Skills:	Creative Thinking	Decision Making	Problem Solving	Seeing Things in the Mind's Eye	Knowing How to Learn	Reasoning
Personal Qualities:	Responsibility	Self-Esteem	Sociability	Self-Management	Integrity/Honesty	

WORKPLACE COMPETENCIES

Resources:	Allocating Time	Allocating Money	Allocating Material and Facility Resources	Allocating Human Resources		
Information:	Acquiring and Evaluating Information	Organizing and Maintaining Information	Interpreting and Communicating Information	Using Computers to Process Information		
Interpersonal Skills:	Participating as a Member of a Team	Teaching Others	Serving Clients/ Customers	Exercising Leadership	Negotiating to Arrive at a Decision	Working with Cultural Diversity
Systems:	Understanding Systems	Monitoring and Correcting Performance	Improving and Designing Systems			
Technology:	Selecting Technology	Applying Technology to Task	Maintaining and Troubleshooting Technology			

*Highlighted blocks indicate areas covered in the chapter. Additional SCANS skills are also covered throughout the *Teacher Wraparound Edition.*

Assessment

Student Edition
- Check Your Understanding, pp. 707, 715, 718
- Chapter 26 Problems, pp. 723–725

Assessment and Evaluation Masters
- Chapter 26 Study Plan, *Glencoe Workbook*
- Chapter 26 Self-Test, *Glencoe Workbook*
- Chapter 26 Test, *Chapter Tests* Booklet
- Chapter 26 Activity, *School-to-Work Handbook*
- Chapter 26 **Exam***View*

Teacher Wraparound Edition
- Critical Thinking Activity, p. 705
- Reteaching Section 1, p. 707
- Reteaching Section 2, p. 715
- Reteaching Section 3, p. 718
- Chapter 26 Quiz, p. 719

Transparencies

	Teaching Transparencies	Solution Transparencies
Section 1:	26–1, 26–2, 26–3, 26–4	Problems 26–1, 26–2
Section 2:	26–5, 26–6, 26–7, 26–8, 26–9, 26–10, 26–11	Problems 26–3, 26–4
Section 3:	26–12, 26–13, 26–14	Problem 26–5
End of Chapter:		Problems 26–6, 26–7, 26–8, 26–9, 26–10

TEACHER CLASSROOM RESOURCES

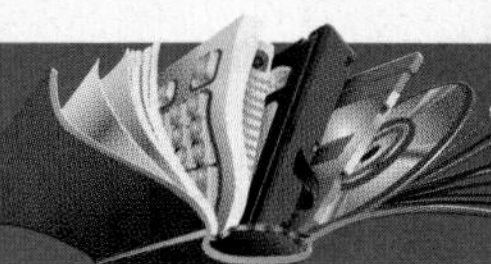

This is a representation of key blackline masters available in the Teacher Classroom Resources.

Teaching Aids

Transparency Examples

Section Focus Transparencies

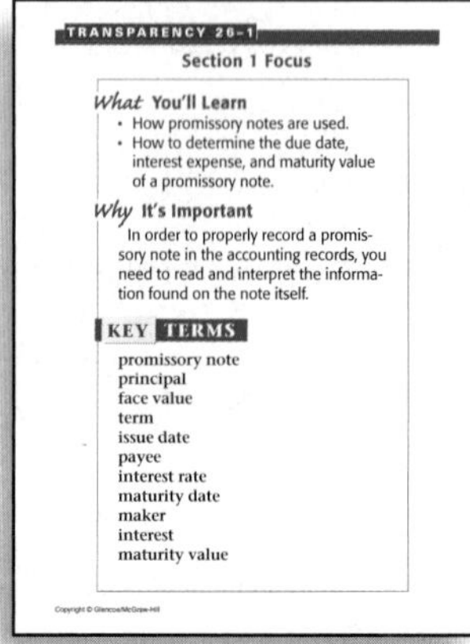

TRANSPARENCY 26-1

Section 1 Focus

What You'll Learn
- How promissory notes are used.
- How to determine the due date, interest expense, and maturity value of a promissory note.

Why It's Important

In order to properly record a promissory note in the accounting records, you need to read and interpret the information found on the note itself.

KEY TERMS

promissory note
principal
face value
term
issue date
payee
interest rate
maturity date
maker
interest
maturity value

Teaching Transparencies

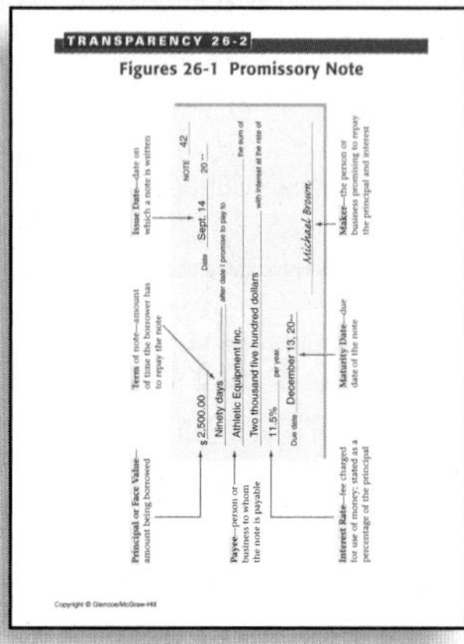

TRANSPARENCY 26-2

Figures 26-1 Promissory Note

Source Document Transparencies

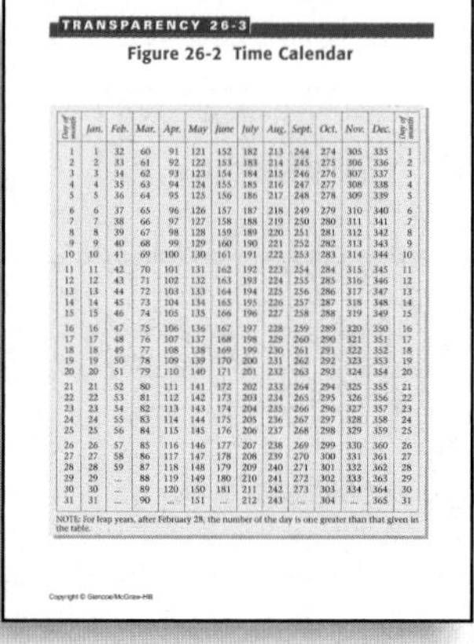

TRANSPARENCY 26-3

Figure 26-2 Time Calendar

Solution Transparencies

Problem 26-6 Recording Transactions for Interest-Bearing Notes Payable

Demonstration Problems

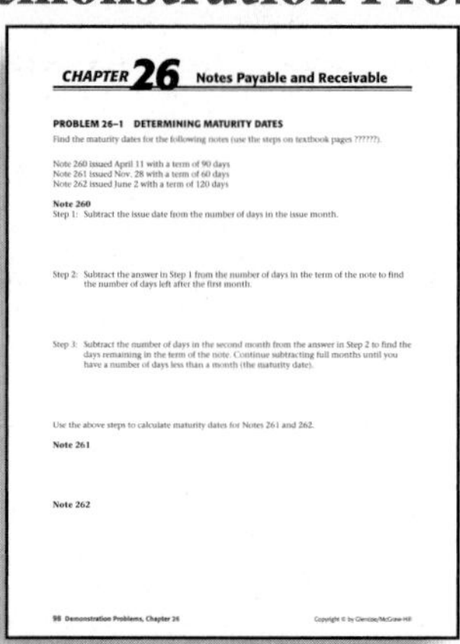

CHAPTER 26 Notes Payable and Receivable

PROBLEM 26-1 DETERMINING MATURITY DATES

Lesson Plans

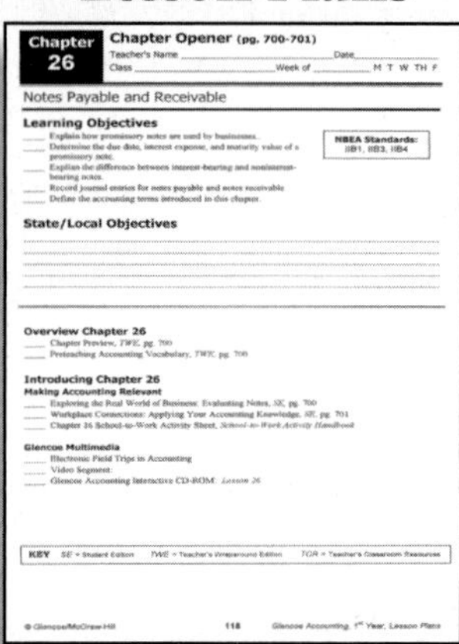

Chapter 26 Chapter Opener (pg. 700–701)

Notes Payable and Receivable

Learning Objectives

State/Local Objectives

Block Scheduling

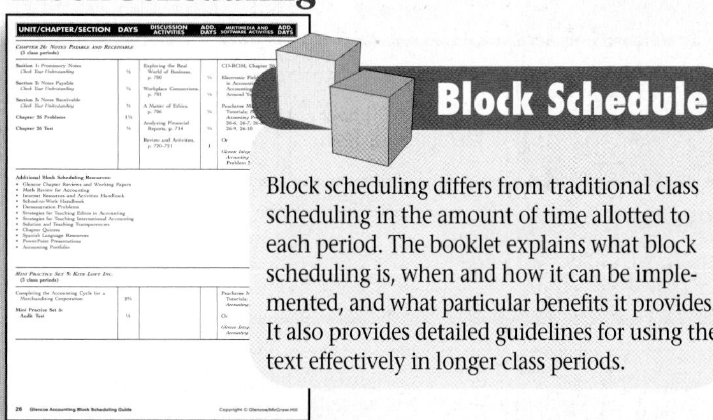

Block Schedule

Block scheduling differs from traditional class scheduling in the amount of time allotted to each period. The booklet explains what block scheduling is, when and how it can be implemented, and what particular benefits it provides. It also provides detailed guidelines for using the text effectively in longer class periods.

Enrichment and Application

Strategies for Teaching Ethics in Accounting

CHAPTER 26 Student Activity Sheet

Strategies for Teaching International Accounting

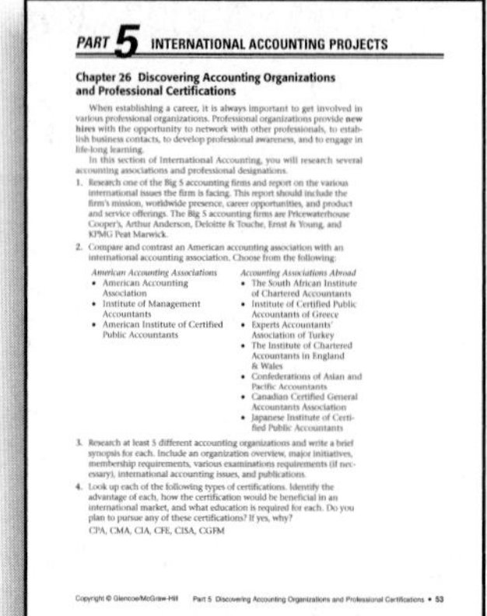

PART 5 INTERNATIONAL ACCOUNTING PROJECTS

Chapter 26 Discovering Accounting Organizations and Professional Certifications

School-to-Work Handbook

CHAPTER 26 SCHOOL-TO-WORK ACTIVITY

Notes Payable and Receivable

Meeting Different Ability Levels

Chapter Reviews and Working Papers (CRWP)

Working Papers

Review

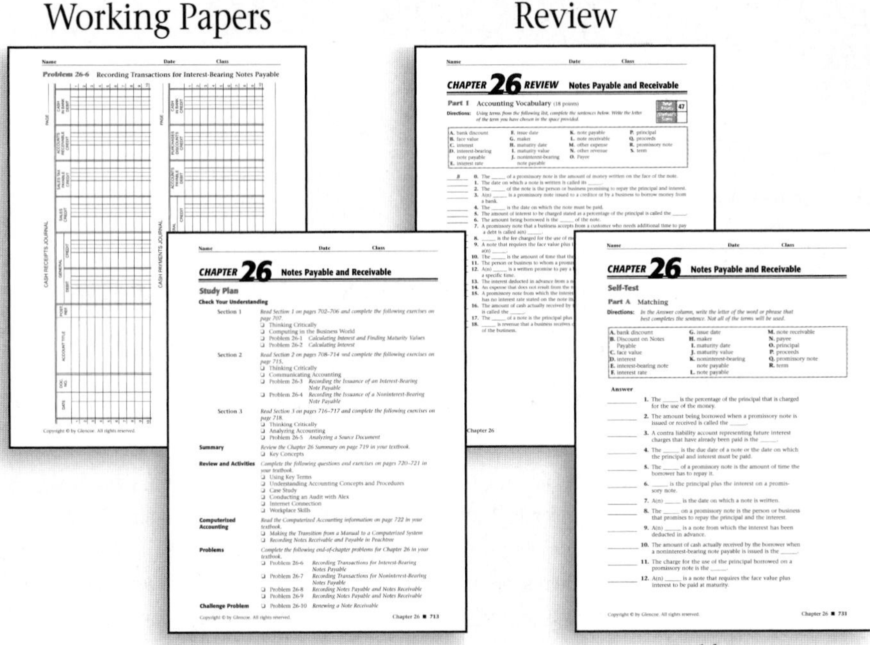

Student Study Plan

Self-Test

Real-World Multimedia CD-ROM

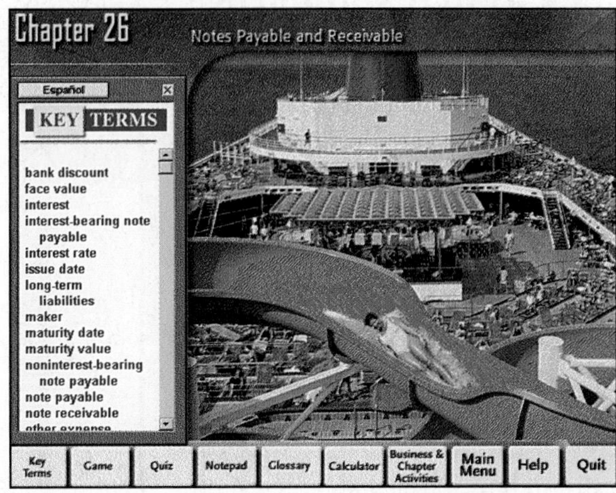

Key to Ability Levels

Each section gives skill-building activities. Each activity has been labeled for use with students of various learning styles and abilities.

L1 Level 1 activities are basic activities and should be within the range of all students.

L2 Level 2 activities are average activities and should be within the range of average and above average students.

L3 Level 3 activities are challenging activities designed for the ability range of above average students.

ELL ELL activities should be within the ability range of English Language Learners.

Assessment and Evaluation

Chapter Tests

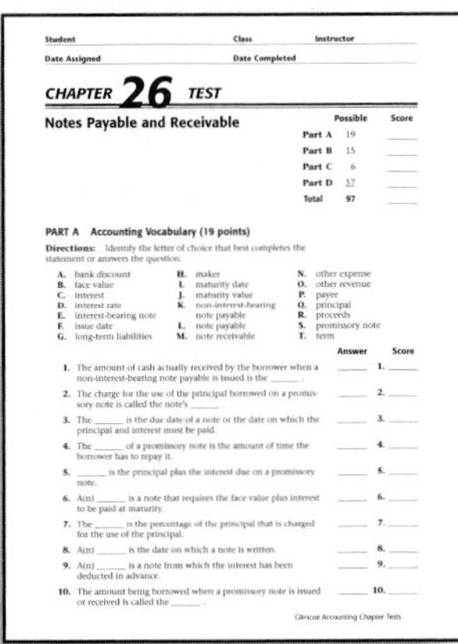

Chapter Quiz

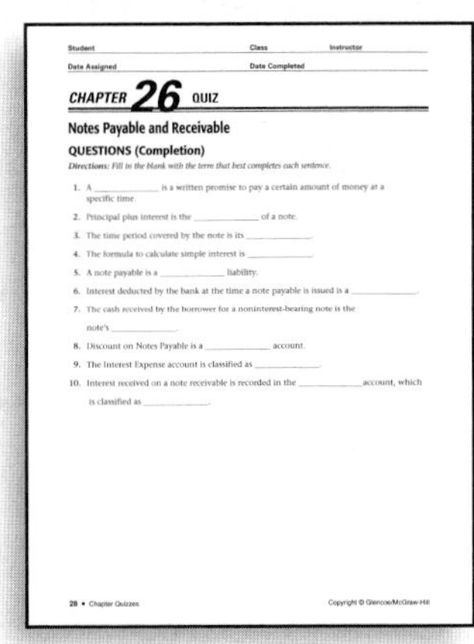

Teaching Resources at a Glance

Application Resources

- Glencoe Chapter Review and Working Papers, SE and TAE
- School-to-Work Handbook, SE and TM
- Accounting Portfolio, SE and TM

Reproducible Masters

- Demonstration Problems
- Lesson Plans
- Block Scheduling
- Spanish Language Resources

Glencoe Accounting Professional Development Series

- Strategies for Teaching Ethics in Accounting
- Accounting Competitive Event Review
- Math Review for Accounting
- Strategies for Teaching International Accounting
- Internet Resources and Activities Handbook

Transparency Package

- Section Focus Transparencies
- Teaching Transparencies
- Source Document Transparencies
- Solution Transparencies

Performance Assessment

- **Exam***View* CD-ROM
- Chapter Tests
- Chapter Quizzes
- Unit Tests
- Audit Tests
- Printed Testbank

Multimedia Resources

- Electronic Learning Center:
  - Multimedia CD-ROMs
  - Peachtree software, tutorials, templates, and solutions
  - Spreadsheet templates
- Using QuickBooks with Glencoe Accounting
- Interactive Lesson Planner
- Electronic Field Trips in Accounting
- PowerPoint Presentation
- Web site: glencoeaccounting.glencoe.com

OVERVIEW CHAPTER 26

Correlations to National Standards for Business Education

(See pages T50–T51 for a detailed correlation chart.)

Standards: IIB1, IIB3, IIB4

Chapter Preview

This chapter concludes the unit on accounting for special procedures. In this chapter students will learn how to record notes payable and receivable. They'll also learn the characteristics of notes and how to calculate interest on various types of notes.

Section Overviews

- Section 1—*Promissory Notes*
- Section 2—*Notes Payable*
- Section 3—*Notes Receivable*

Chapter Vocabulary

promissory note
principal
face value
term
issue date
payee
interest rate
maturity date
maker
interest
maturity value
note payable
long-term liabilities
interest-bearing note payable
noninterest-bearing note payable
bank discount
proceeds
other expense
note receivable
other revenue

Preteaching Accounting Vocabulary

Oral Exercise: Discuss the definitions of the new terms in class. Ask students to give their own examples of terms and explain how each is used in accounting. L1

CHAPTER 26

Notes Payable and Receivable

Learning Objectives

When you have completed this chapter, you will be able to:

- Explain how promissory notes are used by businesses.
- Calculate and record notes payable and notes receivable.
- Explain the difference between interest-bearing and noninterest-bearing notes.
- Journalize transactions involving notes payable.
- Journalize transactions involving notes receivable.
- Define the accounting terms introduced in this chapter.

Exploring the Real World of Business

EVALUATING NOTES

Can you imagine your next vacation aboard a cruise ship? Then check out the cruises offered by **Carnival Cruise Lines. Carnival** is known for its "Fun Ships," which offer on-board entertainment that appeals to all ages. Cruise lines offer fitness facilities, gaming, movies, guest entertainers and shows, musical revues, and of course plenty of food, fresh air, and sunshine. One of **Carnival's** ships, the Conquest, is the largest "Fun Ship" ever constructed, measuring 110,000 tons. This ship has ten decks of passenger rooms and public spaces!

When **Carnival** buys a new cruise ship, the amount of the purchase order is staggering. The **Carnival** Conquest costs $500 million. Like other companies that make very large purchases, the company may choose to borrow money for the purchase by issuing a note payable.

What do you think?

In addition to a note payable, can you think of at least two other ways a company might pay for a large purchase?

Carnival Corporation

Exploring the Real World of Business

Carnival Corporation

Through a subsidiary company, Cunard, Carnival owns one of the world's most famous ships, the *Queen Elizabeth 2*. Other Carnival companies are Windstar Cruises, Costa Cruises, Seabourn Cruise Line, Holland America Line, and Holland America Tours.

What do you think? (Answers)

Answers may vary. Public corporations might issue stock to raise capital for large purchases. Corporations might also sell bonds, which pay interest and have a specific maturity date. Smaller companies might sell part ownership in the company to a venture capitalist.

INTRODUCING CHAPTER 26

Workplace Connections

Applying Your Accounting Knowledge

Have you or your parents ever bought a new or used car? Chances are you made a down payment and then signed a note payable for the rest of the purchase price. When businesses buy costly items, such as manufacturing equipment or even an office building, they also sign a note payable. In this chapter, you'll learn how to calculate the interest on a business note and record the total amount payable.

Investigate:

Have you noticed any items that were purchased by your employer that may have required signing a note payable? This might include purchases like equipment, buildings, vehicles, or land.

Glencoe Accounting Online

Visit the *Glencoe Accounting* Web site at **glencoeaccounting.glencoe.com** for additional activities and information.

701

Making Accounting Relevant

Workplace Connections: Applying Your Accounting Knowledge

Discussion: Bring to class several annual reports for well-known corporations. Have students go through the reports looking at balance sheets to find examples of the companies' long-term liabilities. Point out that these liabilities represent notes payable issued by the companies.

Investigate (Answers)

Answers will vary. Most businesses use notes payable. Businesses that own land and buildings probably financed at least part of the purchase price by signing a note payable. Businesses that rent may have used a note payable to buy equipment, such as display cabinets or delivery trucks.

School-to-Work Activity

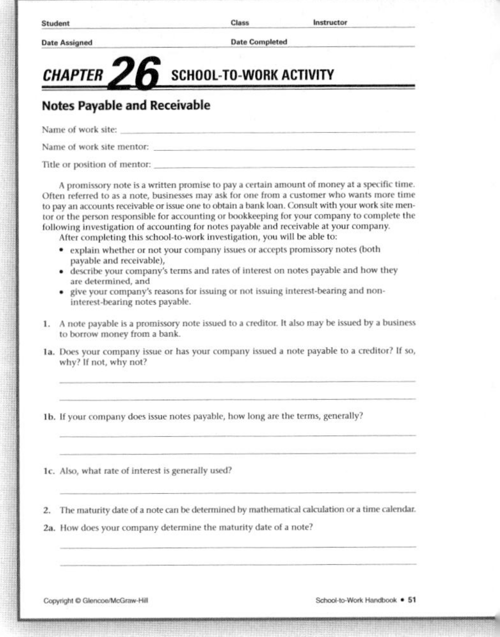

Student ____________ Class ____________ Instructor ____________

Date Assigned ____________ Date Completed ____________

CHAPTER 26 SCHOOL-TO-WORK ACTIVITY

Notes Payable and Receivable

Name of work site: ____________

Name of work site mentor: ____________

Title or position of mentor: ____________

A promissory note is a written promise to pay a certain amount of money at a specific time. Often referred to as a note, businesses may ask for one from a customer who wants more time to pay an accounts receivable or issue one to obtain a bank loan. Consult with your work site mentor or the person responsible for accounting or bookkeeping for your company to complete the following investigation of accounting for notes payable and receivable at your company.

After completing this school-to-work investigation, you will be able to:

- explain whether or not your company issues or accepts promissory notes (both payable and receivable),
- describe your company's terms and rates of interest on notes payable and how they are determined, and
- give your company's reasons for issuing or not issuing interest-bearing and non-interest-bearing notes payable.

1. A note payable is a promissory note issued to a creditor. It also may be issued by a business to borrow money from a bank.

1a. Does your company issue or has your company issued a note payable to a creditor? If so, why? If not, why not?

1b. If your company does issue notes payable, how long are the terms, generally?

1c. Also, what rate of interest is generally used?

2. The maturity date of a note can be determined by mathematical calculation or a time calendar.

2a. How does your company determine the maturity date of a note?

 School-to-Work Handbook • 51

GLENCOE MULTIMEDIA

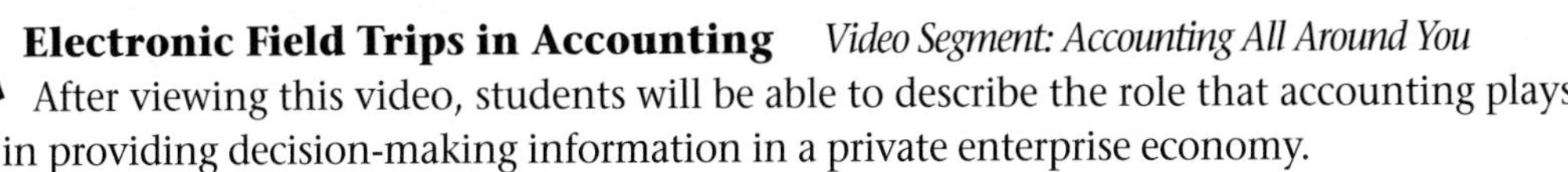

Electronic Field Trips in Accounting *Video Segment: Accounting All Around You*

After viewing this video, students will be able to describe the role that accounting plays in providing decision-making information in a private enterprise economy.

Glencoe Accounting: Electronic Learning Center *Chapter 26*

The CD-ROM program is ideal for visual learners since it incorporates video images, animation, and graphics to enliven the content of each lesson.

1 FOCUS

Introducing the Section
In this section students will learn the features of a promissory note, how to calculate due dates, and how to calculate simple interest on a note.

Section Concepts
- How promissory notes are used.
- How to determine the due date, interest expense, and maturity value of a promissory note.

Visual Learning

Section 1 Focus
 Use **Transparency 26–1** to introduce section concepts.

BELL RINGER

Calculating: Tell students that they have just signed a note to buy a used car for $3,500 at 8% interest for three years. Have students determine how much interest they will pay. How much will their monthly payments be? ($3,500 at 8% for 3 years = $280 × 3 years = $840 + $3,500 = $4,340 ÷ 36 = $120.56. Actual monthly payments would be less if payments were calculated using an amortization table.) L1

Concept Development: A Promise to Pay
Discussion: Explain that a promissory note is simply a promise to repay a specific amount of money. The note contains all the information about the amount of money owed, who owes it and to whom, and the terms of repayment. Spend time explaining each part of the promissory note illustrated in Figure 26–1. L1

SECTION 1

Promissory Notes

What You'll Learn
- How promissory notes are used.
- How to determine the due date, interest expense, and maturity value of a promissory note.

Why It's Important
In order to properly record a promissory note in the accounting records, you need to read and interpret the information found on the note itself.

KEY TERMS
- promissory note
- note payable
- note receivable
- principal
- face value
- term
- issue date
- payee
- interest rate
- maturity date
- maker
- interest
- maturity value

If you or a member of your family have ever purchased a car, then you may have signed a note to pay for the vehicle over a certain period of time. You may have signed a note with a company like Ford Motor Credit or with a bank. For large purchases, and sometimes even small ones, customers will promise to pay the debt over a period of time instead of paying for the item at the time of the purchase. In this chapter you'll learn how to calculate and record notes payable and notes receivable.

A Promise to Pay

A **promissory note** is a written promise to pay a certain amount of money at a specific time. "Promissory note" is often shortened to "note." Promissory notes are formal documents that are evidence of credit granted or received.

A **note payable** is a promissory note issued to a creditor. A **note receivable** is a promissory note that a business accepts from a customer.

To be upheld in a court of law, a promissory note must contain certain information, which is shown in **Figure 26–1.**

Determining the Maturity Date of a Note

When a note is signed, the maker agrees to repay the note within a certain period of time, usually expressed in days or months. This period of time is the **term** of the note. Both the term and the **issue date** (date on which the note is signed) are needed to determine the **maturity date** (due date) of a note.

Let's use the promissory note in **Figure 26–1** as our example. In signing this note, Michael Brown, manager of On Your Mark Athletic Wear, agreed to pay Athletic Equipment Inc. the principal plus interest 90 days from September 14. To determine the maturity date:

RESOURCE MANAGER

Reproducible Masters
- Lesson Plans
- Chapter Reviews and Working Papers (CRWP) TAE
- Demonstration Problems

Transparencies
- Section Focus Transparency
- Teaching Transparencies
- Source Document Transparencies
- Solution Transparencies

Multimedia
- Exam*View* CD-ROM
- Electronic Learning Center CD-ROM
- Interactive Lesson Planner CD-ROM

1. Determine the number of days remaining in the month in which the note is issued. No interest is charged for the issue date, so subtract the date of the note from the number of days in the month.	30 days −14 days 16 days	in September issue date is September 14
2. Determine the number of days remaining after the first month. To do this, subtract the days calculated in Step 1 from the term of the note.	90 days −16 days 74 days	term of note in September remaining
3. Subtract the number of days in the next month (October) from the number of days remaining after Step 2.	74 days −31 days 43 days	 in October remaining
4. Subtract the number of days in the next month (November) from the days remaining after Step 3.	43 days −30 days 13 days	 in November remaining
5. Since there are only 13 days remaining, the due date is 13 days into the next month (December).	The due date for this note is December 13.	

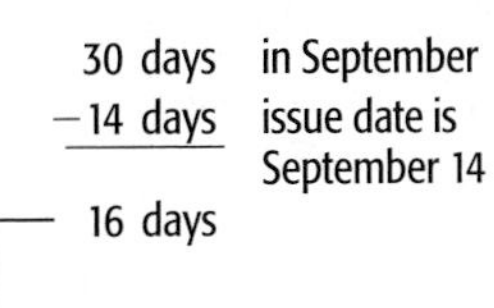

Number of Days in Months

January, March, May, July, August, October, and December have 31 days.

April, June, September, and November have 30 days.

February has 28 days (29 days in a leap year).

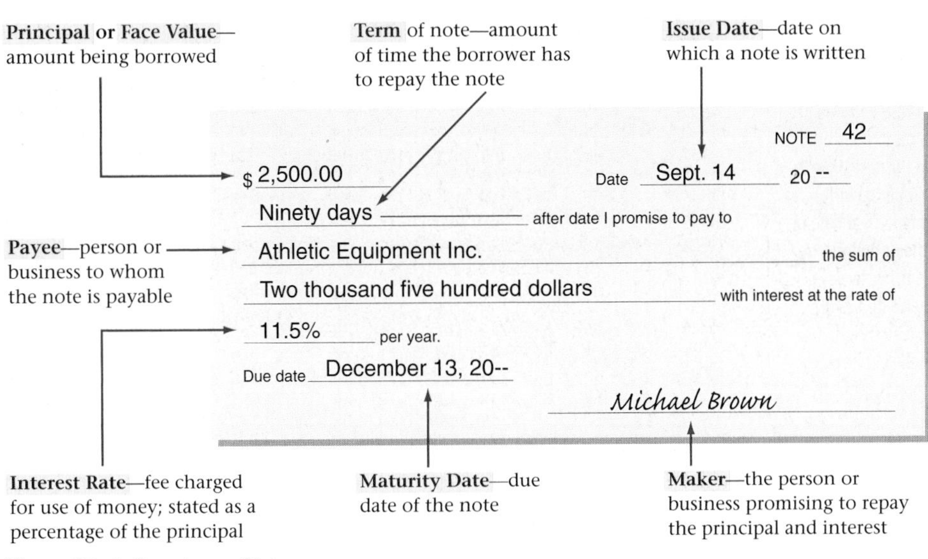

Figure 26–1 Promissory Note

Great Ideas *From the Classroom of...*

Comparing Interest-Bearing and Noninterest-Bearing Notes Compare and discuss the following scenario: You borrow $5,000 at 7 percent interest for 90 days. Bank A accepts interest-bearing notes, whereas Bank B accepts only noninterest-bearing notes. Compute the repayment of each loan, compare the two banks, and discuss. (Bank A: $5,000 principal + $86.30 interest = $5,086.30 maturity value; Bank B: $5,000 principal + $0 interest = $5,000 maturity value − $86.30 bank discount = $4,913.70 proceeds)

Donald J. Guerrieri
Norwin Senior High School
Greensburg, Pennsylvania

2 TEACH

GUIDED PRACTICE

Reading Accounting

- Have students read the steps for calculating the due date of a note (page 703), paying close attention to the logic in the calculations. Then give students another example and have them calculate the due date. Have students bring a calendar to class to use in this activity. L1
- Have students visit a local bank to obtain loan information printed in their first language. ELL

Concept Development: Determining the Maturity Date of a Note

Discussion: Emphasize that the maturity date is important because that is the date on which the total principal and interest must be paid, minus any interim payments made. Demonstrate the calculations for determining the maturity date using the steps on this page (703) and the time calendar on page 704. L1

Visual Learning

Figure 26–1 Promissory Note

Using **Transparency 26–2**, have students identify each part of a promissory note. Point out that the signed noted is a legal document requiring the signer to perform according to its terms.

2 TEACH (Cont'd.)

Demonstration Problem Step-by-Step Practice

Use demonstration problem 26–1 to give students practice in calculating maturity dates for promissory notes.

Teaching Tips

Invite a local banker or businessperson who works with promissory notes to discuss them with the class. Prepare students for the resource person by helping them gain a working knowledge of notes. Be sure that students understand the purposes for either issuing or receiving a note. Ask the resource person to give specific examples of how notes are used.

Give students several examples of note terms and have students use both the mathematical method and the time calendar to calculate maturity dates.

Visual Learning

Figure 26–2 Time Calendar

Use **Transparency 26–3** to show students how to find a maturity date using a time calendar.

Strategies for Teaching International Accounting

To enrich study of international accounting, refer to the additional critical thinking activities in the booklet.

Some businesses and banks use time calendars to calculate the maturity date of a note. **Figure 26–2** shows an example of a time calendar. The time calendar has two sets of days: (1) the day of the month (left and right columns), and (2) the day of the year, by month (middle column).

To calculate a maturity date using the time calendar, follow these steps:

1. Locate the issue date of the note (for example, 14) in the Day of month column. Move across the month columns to the issue month (September). In our example September 14 is the 257th day of the year.
2. Add the number of days in the term of the note (90) to the day of the year. The sum of the two numbers is 347 (257 + 90).
3. Find the number 347 in the month columns. The 347th day of the year is in December. The maturity month is December. Move across to the Day of month column. The 347th day of the year corresponds to the 13th day of the month. The due date of the note is December 13.

Gender Roles

In the U.S., women's roles are more varied than in many other cultures. In countries where women play little part in business, American businesswomen may find it particularly challenging to negotiate or express their opinions. In certain cultures, females are not permitted to drive a vehicle, wear bright colors, make eye contact, or shake hands with a male.

Day of month	*Jan.*	*Feb.*	*Mar.*	*Apr.*	*May*	*June*	*July*	*Aug.*	*Sept.*	*Oct.*	*Nov.*	*Dec.*	*Day of month*
1	1	32	60	91	121	152	182	213	244	274	305	335	1
2	2	33	61	92	122	153	183	214	245	275	306	336	2
3	3	34	62	93	123	154	184	215	246	276	307	337	3
4	4	35	63	94	124	155	185	216	247	277	308	338	4
5	5	36	64	95	125	156	186	217	248	278	309	339	5
6	6	37	65	96	126	157	187	218	249	279	310	340	6
7	7	38	66	97	127	158	188	219	250	280	311	341	7
8	8	39	67	98	128	159	189	220	251	281	312	342	8
9	9	40	68	99	129	160	190	221	252	282	313	343	9
10	10	41	69	100	130	161	191	222	253	283	314	344	10
11	11	42	70	101	131	162	192	223	254	284	315	345	11
12	12	43	71	102	132	163	193	224	255	285	316	346	12
13	13	44	72	103	133	164	194	225	256	286	317	347	13
14	14	45	73	104	134	165	195	226	257	287	318	348	14
15	15	46	74	105	135	166	196	227	258	288	319	349	15
16	16	47	75	106	136	167	197	228	259	289	320	350	16
17	17	48	76	107	137	168	198	229	260	290	321	351	17
18	18	49	77	108	138	169	199	230	261	291	322	352	18
19	19	50	78	109	139	170	200	231	262	292	323	353	19
20	20	51	79	110	140	171	201	232	263	293	324	354	20
21	21	52	80	111	141	172	202	233	264	294	325	355	21
22	22	53	81	112	142	173	203	234	265	295	326	356	22
23	23	54	82	113	143	174	204	235	266	296	327	357	23
24	24	55	83	114	144	175	205	236	267	297	328	358	24
25	25	56	84	115	145	176	206	237	268	298	329	359	25
26	26	57	85	116	146	177	207	238	269	299	330	360	26
27	27	58	86	117	147	178	208	239	270	300	331	361	27
28	28	59	87	118	148	179	209	240	271	301	332	362	28
29	29	...	88	119	149	180	210	241	272	302	333	363	29
30	30	...	89	120	150	181	211	242	273	303	334	364	30
31	31	...	90	...	151	...	212	243	...	304	...	365	31

NOTE: For leap years, after February 28, the number of the day is one greater than that given in the table.

Figure 26–2 Time Calendar

Teaching International ACCOUNTING

Gender Roles Invite an international cultural guest speaker to talk with your class about the role of women in business in her or his native country. Ask students to prepare questions in advance and set aside time for questions and answers. Follow up by having students write a summary of what they learned and how they would feel about traveling to a foreign country to conduct business.

Calculating Interest on a Note

Interest is the fee charged for the use of money. The **interest rate** is the interest stated as a percentage of the principal. The interest on a promissory note is based on three factors:

- principal
- interest rate
- term of the note

The formula used to calculate interest is:

Interest = Principal × Interest Rate × Time

Interest rates are usually stated on an annual basis; that is, they are usually based on a borrowing period of one year. To find the interest on a promissory note for one year, multiply the principal by the interest rate. For example, the interest on an 11.5%, $2,500 promissory note for one year is $287.50 ($2,500 × .115 = $287.50).

If the term of a promissory note is less than one year, the time in the calculation is expressed as a fraction of one year. The fraction may be stated in days or months. For example, on September 14 On Your Mark signed a note for $2,500 at 11.5% interest for 90 days. Since the term of the note is expressed in days, 365 days is used as the denominator of the time fraction. The interest is calculated as follows:

Principal	×	Interest Rate	×	Time	=	Interest
$2,500	×	.115	×	90/365	=	$70.89

The interest on the note shown in **Figure 26–1** is $70.89.

On the maturity date, On Your Mark will repay the maturity value of the note. **Maturity value** is the principal plus the interest. In our example the maturity value is $2,570.89 ($2,500.00 + $70.89).

If the term of this note had been three months instead of 90 days, the denominator of the time fraction would be 12. The interest would be calculated as follows:

Principal	×	Interest Rate	×	Time	=	Interest
$2,500	×	.115	×	3/12	=	$71.88

The maturity value would be $2,571.88 ($2,500.00 + $71.88)

Did You Know?

Travel

The cruise ship business became more popular after a television program called *The Love Boat.* Popularity of vacation cruises has meant operating profits of $2 billion for the three biggest cruise lines: Carnival, Royal Caribbean, and Princess.

Key Points

Interest Rates

Interest rates are stated for a period of one year. To calculate interest on a note signed for a period of less than one year, express the term of the note as a fraction of one year.

Calculating Interest Using an Interest Table

To calculate interest, businesses and banks often use an interest table similar to the one shown in **Figure 26–3**.

2 TEACH (Cont'd.)

Concept Development: Calculating Interest Due on a Note

Discussion: Review with the class the arithmetic skills needed to calculate interest. Stress that interest rates are usually stated on an annual basis. Show students how to determine interest for one year. Then demonstrate calculations for less than a year. For example, if annual interest is $287.50 and the note is for 90 days, have students calculate the interest on the note ($287.50 × 90 = $25,875 ÷ 365 = $70.89). L1

Teaching Tips

The full year—365 days—is used in the examples here since banks or businesses using computers to calculate interest generally use the full year. Some businesses use 360 days as the basis for one year.

Remind students that "term" means "time" and that "face value" is usually the same as principal.

Thinking Algebraically

Solving for Unknowns: Tell students that they are planning to purchase a large-screen television for $880. The store will allow them to pay for the television over 12 months and will charge interest of $83.60. Ask students how they would find the interest rate. L2

Demonstration Problem Step-by-Step Practice

Use demonstration problem 26–2 to give students practice in calculating interest and maturity value.

CRITICAL THINKING ACTIVITY

Making Comparisons Ask students to describe the similarities and differences between a note payable and an account payable. (They are both liabilities. An account payable is open credit for items purchased on account. A note payable is based on a written promise to pay on a certain date in the future. A note payable can be issued to a creditor or to borrow money from a bank. Interest is usually charged on a note payable.)

2 TEACH (Cont'd.)

Concept Development: Calculating Interest Using an Interest Table

Discussion: Demonstrate how to use the interest table, giving students several examples and having them practice finding interest amounts. If possible, borrow several interest tables from a local bank and have students use them to calculate the interest on notes. L1

Visual Learning

Figure 26–3 Interest Table

Use **Transparency 26–4** to show students how to calculate interest using an interest table.

Teaching Tip

Point out that the interest table is based on 100, which means that interest is calculated per $100 of principal. Before using the interest factor, you need to find the multiples of 100 for the principal of the note.

Strategies for Teaching Ethics in Accounting

Photocopy the Chapter 26 *Student Activity Sheet* for students. Answers are also provided in the booklet.

SIMPLE INTEREST ON $100 (365 DAY BASIS)

DAY	11.50 % INTEREST	DAY	11.75 % INTEREST	DAY	12.00 % INTEREST	DAY	12.25 % INTEREST	DAY	12.50 % INTEREST	DAY	12.75 % INTEREST
30	0.945205	30	0.965753	30	0.986301	30	1.006849	30	1.027397	30	1.047945
60	1.890411	60	1.931507	60	1.972603	60	2.013699	60	2.054795	60	2.095890
90	2.835616	90	2.897260	90	2.958904	90	3.020548	90	3.082192	90	3.143836
120	3.780822	120	3.863014	120	3.945205	120	4.027397	120	4.109589	120	4.191781
150	4.726027	150	4.828767	150	4.931507	150	5.034247	150	5.136986	150	5.239726
180	5.671233	180	5.794521	180	5.917808	180	6.041096	180	6.164384	180	6.287671
210	6.616438	210	6.760274	210	6.904110	210	7.047945	210	7.191781	210	7.335616
240	7.561644	240	7.726027	240	7.890411	240	8.054795	240	8.219178	240	8.383562
270	8.506849	270	8.691781	270	8.876712	270	9.061644	270	9.246575	270	9.431507
300	9.452055	300	9.657534	300	9.863014	300	10.068493	300	10.273973	300	10.479452
330	10.397260	330	10.623288	330	10.849315	330	11.075342	330	11.301370	330	11.527397
360	11.342466	360	11.589041	360	11.835616	360	12.082192	360	12.328767	360	12.575342
365	11.500000	365	11.750000	365	12.000000	365	12.250000	365	12.500000	365	12.750000
366	11.531507	366	11.782192	366	12.032877	366	12.283562	366	12.534247	366	12.784932

Figure 26–3 Interest Table

Let's use On Your Mark's note as an example. To calculate interest using an interest table:

- Find the term of the note in the Day column, 90.
- Follow the row across until you reach the column for the interest rate, 11.5%. Where the Day row and the Interest column meet is a factor, 2.835616. The factor is based on a principal amount of $100.
- Divide the principal of the note by 100. The result is 25 ($2,500 ÷ 100).
- Multiply the result by the factor to find the interest. The interest is $70.89 (25 × 2.835616).

In this example the interest calculated using the equation and the interest table are the same. Sometimes there are small differences caused by rounding.

A MATTER OF ETHICS

Is the Boss Always Right?

Imagine that you work for a large property management company. Your boss, Joan, is the senior accountant; and her boss, Frank, is vice president. For the past several months, Joan has been coming to work late, taking long lunches, and leaving early. When Frank calls, she has asked you to tell him that she is "away from her desk." You think Frank is getting suspicious, and you're starting to feel guilty for lying.

Ethical Decision Making:

- What are the ethical issues?
- What are the alternatives?
- Who are the affected parties?
- How do the alternatives affect the parties?
- What would you do?

Teaching A MATTER OF ETHICS

Is the Boss Always Right? Ask students whether they've ever been in a situation where a friend has asked them to say or do something that made them uncomfortable, such as telling the friend's parents a lie or covering for the friend at work. How do students decide what actions to take? Relate their responses to a business situation, and ask how they would deal with the situation if they were business owners who suspected employees of taking time away from the job.

Check Your Understanding

Now that you have studied this section, complete the following questions and problems.

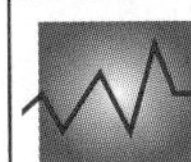

Thinking Critically

1. If the interest rate for a promissory note is stated on an annual basis, and if the promissory note has a term that is less than one year, how is the interest for the note calculated?
2. Explain how to use an interest table to calculate interest on a loan.

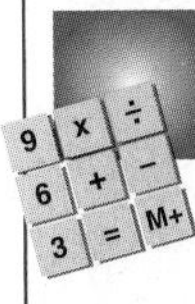

Computing in the Business World

Marty Herick is the owner of CyberAction, a new computer-game store. Marty has just signed a promissory note with Excelsior Bank. He plans to use the loan to purchase and update his interactive computer-game inventory. Using the formula, what is the interest on the $20,000 90-day note with a 10.5% interest rate? What is the maturity value?

Problem 26–1 Calculating Interest and Finding Maturity Values

Instructions Using the formula, compute the interest and maturity values for each of the following notes. Record your answers in your working papers. Use the interest table to check your computations.

	Principal	Interest Rate	Term
1.	$ 4,000	11.5%	60 days
2.	10,000	11.75%	90 days
3.	6,500	12.75%	60 days
4.	900	12.25%	120 days
5.	2,400	12%	180 days

Problem 26–2 Calculating Interest

Instructions Calculate the interest for each of the following notes. Record your answers in your working papers.

	Principal	Interest Rate	Term
1.	$600	15%	90 days
2.	3,500	12%	60 days
3.	9,600	9%	4 months
4.	2,500	10%	180 days
5.	1,500	11.5%	6 months

RETEACHING SECTION 1

Comparing Promissory Notes and Installment Loans Contrast the promissory note with an installment loan for a car. Students are probably familiar with the idea of making monthly car payments through an installment loan. A promissory note is a single-payment loan. It is repaid with one payment after a specified period of time. Such notes are generally offered for short periods of time, usually less than a year. An installment loan for a car, however, is repaid in several equal payments over a specified period of time.

3 ASSESS

Thinking Critically (Answers)

1. Time is calculated and expressed as a fraction of a year; annual interest is multiplied by the fraction to determine interest for the period.
2. Find the term in the Day column. Find the interest rate column. Where the two intersect is the factor used to calculate the interest.

Computing in the Business World (Answers)

Interest $2,100
Maturity value $22,100

Problem 26–1 (Answers)

1. Int. $75.62, mat. value $4,075.62
2. Int. $289.73, mat. value $10,289.73
3. Int. $136.23, mat. value $6,636.23
4. Int. $36.25, mat. value $936.25
5. Int. $142.03, mat. value $2,542.03

Problem 26–2 (Answers)

1. $22.19
2. $69.04
3. $288.00
4. $123.29
5. $86.25

Chapter Reviews and Working Papers Refer students to the Chapter 26 workbook pages to answer *Check Your Understanding* activities.

4 CLOSE

Section Wrap-Up

Demonstrate: Give students the example of a 60-day note for $300 at 8.5% annual interest. Have them calculate the interest and the maturity value of the note. Have them calculate the maturity date from today's date. (Int. $4.19, mat. value $304.19) L1

SECTION 2

Notes Payable

1 FOCUS

Introducing the Section

In this section students will learn how to calculate interest and maturity value for an interest-bearing note payable and to record both in the accounting system. They will also learn how to calculate the bank discount and proceeds for a noninterest-bearing note.

Section Concepts

- The differences between interest-bearing and noninterest-bearing notes.
- How to record notes payable transactions.
- How to calculate and record bank discounts.

Visual Learning

Section 2 Focus

Use **Transparency 26–5** to introduce section concepts.

BELL RINGER

Analyzing: Ask students whether they have ever purchased an item on layaway. If so, they (or their parents) signed a promise to repay the amount over a period of months. Obtain copies of layaway agreements from local stores and have students read the agreements to identify the terms and the interest charged. L1

What You'll Learn

- The differences between interest-bearing and noninterest-bearing notes.
- How to record notes payable transactions.
- How to calculate and record bank discounts.

Why It's Important

Many businesses issue and make payment on notes payable.

KEY TERMS

long-term liabilities
interest-bearing note payable
noninterest-bearing note payable
bank discount
proceeds
other expense

In this section you will journalize transactions involving notes payable. Recall that a note payable is a promissory note issued to a creditor. For example, a note payable may be issued by a business to borrow money from a bank. Notes issued by a business are recorded in the **Notes Payable** account. **Notes Payable** is a liability account; its normal balance is a credit. When the due date of a note extends beyond one year, the note is classified as a long-term liability. **Long-term liabilities** are debts that mature after one year.

There are two types of notes that are frequently issued by businesses: interest-bearing notes and noninterest-bearing notes.

Interest-Bearing Notes Payable

A note that requires the face value plus interest to be paid on the maturity date is called an **interest-bearing note payable**. On an interest-bearing note, the face value and principal are the same amount. The note issued by On Your Mark (in Section 1) is an interest-bearing note. Its maturity value is $2,570.89 ($2,500.00 face value + $70.89 interest).

Let's record an interest-bearing note payable.

Recording the Issuance of an Interest-Bearing Note Payable

Business Transaction

On April 3 On Your Mark borrowed $7,000 from State Street Bank and issued a 90-day, 12% note payable to the bank, Note 6.

ANALYSIS		
	Identify	1. The accounts affected are **Cash in Bank** and **Notes Payable.**
	Classify	2. **Cash in Bank** is an asset account. **Notes Payable** is a liability account.
	+/−	3. **Cash in Bank** is increased by $7,000. **Notes Payable** is increased by $7,000.

RESOURCE MANAGER

Reproducible Masters
- Lesson Plans
- Chapter Reviews and Working Papers (CRWP) TAE
- Demonstration Problems

Transparencies
- Section Focus Transparency
- Teaching Transparencies
- Source Document Transparencies
- Solution Transparencies

Multimedia
- Exam*View* CD-ROM
- Electronic Learning Center CD-ROM
- Interactive Lesson Planner CD-ROM

DEBIT-CREDIT RULE	**4.** Increases to asset accounts are recorded as debits. Debit **Cash in Bank** for $7,000. **5.** Increases to liability accounts are recorded as credits. Credit **Notes Payable** for $7,000.

T ACCOUNTS

6.

Cash in Bank	
Debit +	Credit −
7,000	

Notes Payable	
Debit −	Credit +
	7,000

JOURNAL ENTRY

7.

GENERAL JOURNAL PAGE 12

	DATE		DESCRIPTION	POST. REF.	DEBIT	CREDIT	
1	20--						1
2	Apr.	3	Cash in Bank		7 000 00		2
3			Notes Payable			7 000 00	3
4			Note 6				4
5							5

Recording the Payment of an Interest-Bearing Note Payable

The maturity date of the note payable is July 2. You can verify this by using the time calendar in **Figure 26–2**. The interest is $207.12:

Principal	×	Interest Rate	×	Time	=	Interest
$7,000	×	.12	×	90/365	=	$207.12

The maturity value of the note is $7,207.12 ($7,000.00 principal + $207.12 interest).

CONNECT TO . . . HISTORY

To control inflation and high prices, Napoleon created the Bank of France and required that every citizen pay taxes after he became Emperor of France in 1799. The taxes were deposited in the bank and used by the government to make loans to businesses.

Business Transaction

On July 2 On Your Mark issued Check 3892 for $7,207.12 payable to State Street Bank in payment of the note payable issued April 3.

ANALYSIS		
	Identify	**1.** The accounts affected are **Notes Payable**, **Interest Expense**, and **Cash in Bank.**
	Classify	**2.** **Notes Payable** is a liability account. **Interest Expense** is an expense account. **Cash in Bank** is an asset account.
	+/−	**3.** **Notes Payable** is decreased by $7,000. **Interest Expense** is increased by $207.12. **Cash in Bank** is decreased by $7,207.12.

INTERDISCIPLINARY CONNECTIONS ACTIVITY

History The first income tax was adopted in England in 1799 and abolished from 1816 to 1842. In the United States, income tax was used as a temporary tax during the American Civil War. In 1894 the income tax was again enacted. Later it was declared to be unconstitutional, so an amendment to the U.S. Constitution was adopted in 1913 to once again allow government to levy a tax on income.

2 TEACH

GUIDED PRACTICE

Reading Accounting

- Have students obtain sample copies of notes from local banks. Tell them to read the notes and decide what information should be recorded in an accounting system. L1

Concept Development: Interest-Bearing Notes Payable

Discussion: Role-play borrowing $7,000 from a bank by signing an interest-bearing note. After the role-play, analyze the transaction using T accounts. Then illustrate how the transaction is recorded in the general journal. Review how to calculate interest. Stress that when an interest-bearing note is due, the principal and the interest must be paid. Review how the maturity value is determined. L1

Visual Learning

Business Transaction

Using **Transparency 26–6**, analyze the transaction for issuing a note payable. Point out that when a note payable is issued, a liability is created. The liability is recorded in the Notes Payable account.

Demonstration Problem Step-by-Step Practice

Use demonstration problem 26–3 to give students practice in analyzing and recording the issuance of an interest-bearing note payable.

2 TEACH (Cont'd.)

Visual Learning

Business Transaction

Using **Transparency 26–7**, have students analyze the transaction paying off the note payable. Point out that interest paid on money borrowed to operate the business is a business expense; thus, the amount of interest is recorded in the Interest Expense account.

Teaching Tip

Point out that the interest expense on the note payable is not actually recorded in the accounting records until the interest is paid—even though the note payable may have been signed and the liability created some time before.

Demonstration Problem Step-by-Step Practice

Use demonstration problem 26–4 to give students practice in analyzing and recording the payment of an interest-bearing note payable.

Concept Development: Noninterest-Bearing Notes Payable

Discussion: Role-play the signing of a $1,500 noninterest-bearing note payable at the bank. Explain the difference between an interest-bearing note and a noninterest-bearing note at the time it is signed (interest charges are deducted at the time a noninterest-bearing note is signed rather than being paid at maturity). Illustrate how the proceeds of a noninterest-bearing note are determined. L1

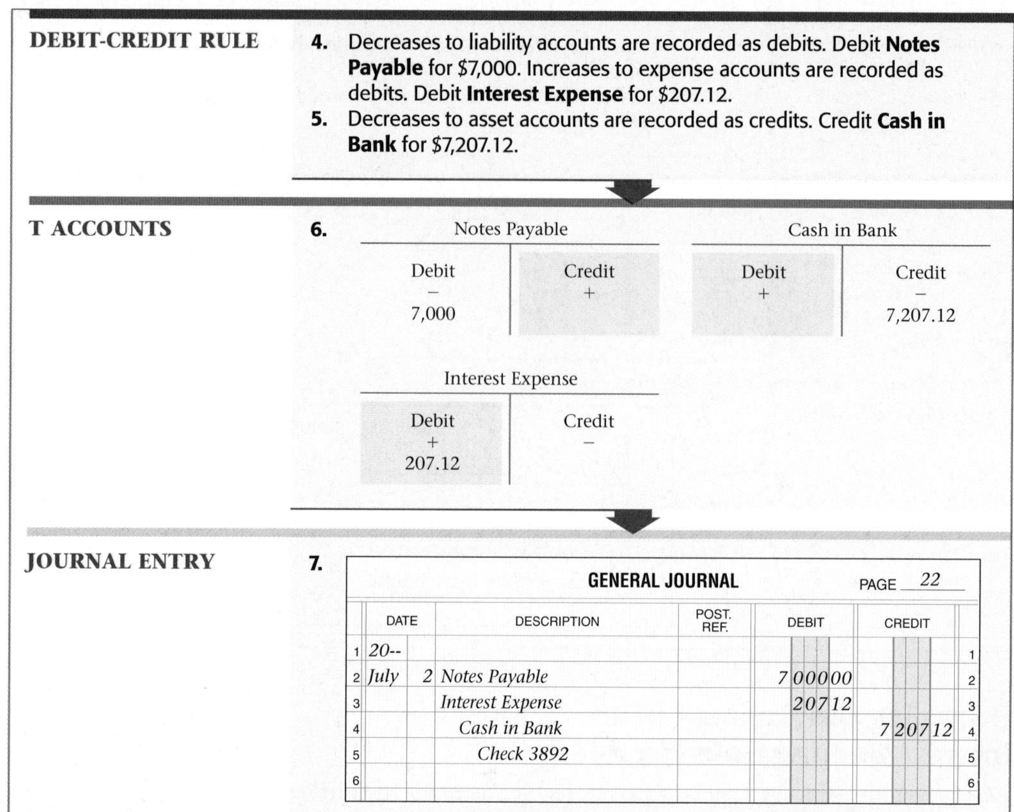

DEBIT-CREDIT RULE

4. Decreases to liability accounts are recorded as debits. Debit **Notes Payable** for $7,000. Increases to expense accounts are recorded as debits. Debit **Interest Expense** for $207.12.
5. Decreases to asset accounts are recorded as credits. Credit **Cash in Bank** for $7,207.12.

T ACCOUNTS

6.

Notes Payable	
Debit −	Credit +
7,000	

Cash in Bank	
Debit +	Credit −
	7,207.12

Interest Expense	
Debit +	Credit −
207.12	

JOURNAL ENTRY

7.

GENERAL JOURNAL — PAGE 22

	DATE		DESCRIPTION	POST. REF.	DEBIT	CREDIT	
1	20--						1
2	July	2	Notes Payable		7 000 00		2
3			Interest Expense		207 12		3
4			Cash in Bank			7 207 12	4
5			Check 3892				5
6							6

ACCOUNTING TIPS

Liabilities and the Law

Liabilities are debts. They are claims recognized by law. If a company fails to pay its liabilities, the law gives creditors the right to force the sale of the company's assets so that the company can pay its debts. Creditors have rights over owners. Creditors must be paid in full before the owners receive anything, even if payment of the debts uses up all the assets of a business.

Noninterest-Bearing Notes Payable

Sometimes a bank requires a borrower to pay the interest on a note in advance. On the issue date, the bank deducts the interest from the face value of the note. This reduces the amount of money received by the borrower. When interest is deducted in advance from the face value of the note, the note is called a **noninterest-bearing note payable**. The note is "noninterest-bearing" because there is no interest rate stated on the note. The interest deducted in advance is called the **bank discount**. The interest rate used to calculate the bank discount is called the discount rate. The cash received by the borrower is called the **proceeds**. The proceeds equal the face value of the note minus the bank discount.

For a noninterest-bearing note payable, the maturity value is the same as the face value. This is because the interest is deducted from the face value on the issue date. **Figure 26–4** shows an example of a noninterest-bearing note payable.

Calculating Noninterest-Bearing Notes Payable

Let's calculate the proceeds of the noninterest-bearing note payable shown in **Figure 26–4**. The note was discounted at a rate of 12% by First Federal Bank, Note 13.

HOME AND COMMUNITY CONNECTIONS ACTIVITY

Researching Notes Have students visit their local banks to gather literature or information on promissory notes or noninterest-bearing and interest-bearing loans. What type of notes (loans) are available at the bank? What is the minimum age requirement? When do the loans need to be repaid? Once students have gathered the necessary information, ask them to write a paragraph about each type of promissory note available at their banks.

NOTE 13

$ 1,500.00 Date June 12 20 --

Ninety days after date I promise to pay to

First Federal Bank the sum of

One thousand five hundred dollars.

Due date September 10, 20--

Michael Brown

Figure 26–4 Noninterest-Bearing Note Payable

The first step is to calculate the bank discount, which is the interest on the note. (Note that the formula is similar to the one used to compute interest on an interest-bearing note.)

Face Value	×	Discount Rate	×	Time	=	Bank Discount
$1,500	×	.12	×	90/365	=	$44.38

The bank discount is subtracted from the face value of the note to determine the proceeds. The proceeds are $1,455.62 ($1,500.00 – $44.38).

Recording the Issuance of a Noninterest-Bearing Note Payable

The bank discount is recorded in a contra liability account called **Discount on Notes Payable**. The normal balance of the **Discount on Notes Payable** account is a debit. The bank discount is the future interest expense on the note. However, the bank discount is not recorded in an expense account because the interest expense is not yet incurred.

Key Points

Comparison of Interest-Bearing and Noninterest-Bearing Notes

Interest-Bearing
Proceeds = Face Value
Maturity Value > Face Value

Noninterest-Bearing
Proceeds < Face Value
Maturity Value = Face Value

Business Transaction

On June 12 On Your Mark signed a $1,500, 90-day noninterest-bearing note payable that First Federal Bank discounted at a rate of 12%, Note 13.

ANALYSIS		
	Identify	1. The accounts affected are **Cash in Bank**, **Discount on Notes Payable**, and **Notes Payable.**
	Classify	2. **Cash in Bank** is an asset account. **Discount on Notes Payable** is a contra liability account. **Notes Payable** is a liability account.
	+/−	3. **Cash in Bank** is increased by $1,455.62. **Discount on Notes Payable** is increased by $44.38. **Notes Payable** is increased by $1,500.00.

REINFORCING STUDY SKILLS

Surveying Techniques From time to time, remind students of the steps in the reading technique SQ3R. After surveying the section heads and subheads, students should turn them into questions that can then guide their reading; for example, "What is a promissory note?" or "How do you determine the maturity date of a note?"

2 TEACH (Cont'd.)

Visual Learning

Figure 26–4 Noninterest-Bearing Note Payable

Using **Transparency 26–8**, have students study the note. Discuss why no interest rate is stated on the note.

Teaching Tips

Point out that for a noninterest-bearing note, face value equals maturity value.

Write this formula on the chalkboard: Face Value – Bank Discount = Proceeds. Give students several examples and have them calculate the proceeds.

If a note is not due until after a fiscal period ends, an adjusting entry may be necessary.

Demonstration Problem Step-by-Step Practice

Use demonstration problem 26–5 to give students practice in calculating the discount and proceeds for a note.

Critical Thinking: Point out that the cost of borrowing is higher with a noninterest-bearing note that has the same rate as an interest-bearing note. Have students explain why. (With notes having the same interest rate and term, the noninterest-bearing note will cost more because interest is deducted at the beginning of the note. The business has the use of less money for the term of the note, thus increasing the effective borrowing rate.) L2

Chapter Reviews and Working Papers

Refer students to *Study Plans* located at the beginning of Chapter 26 in the workbook.

2 TEACH (Cont'd.)

Visual Learning

Business Transaction

Using **Transparency 26–9**, guide students through the analysis and recording of the issuance of a noninterest-bearing note.

Figure 26–5 Reporting Noninterest-Bearing Notes Payable on the Balance Sheet

Use **Transparency 26–10** to discuss how to report a note payable in the liabilities section of the balance sheet. Have students compare the note payable amount and the discount with the June 12 general journal entry. Remind students that the balance of the note will be included in total liabilities.

Demonstration Problem Step-by-Step Practice

Use demonstration problem 26–6 to give students practice in recording the issuance of a noninterest-bearing note payable.

Teaching Tips

Use of the Discount on Notes Payable account may be confusing to students. Point out that the Interest Expense account is not debited until the note payable is actually paid. Discount on Notes Payable is used to reflect the difference between the amount of the note and the amount of money (the proceeds) the business actually receives by issuing the note.

Discuss why Discount on Notes Payable is a contra account for Notes Payable.

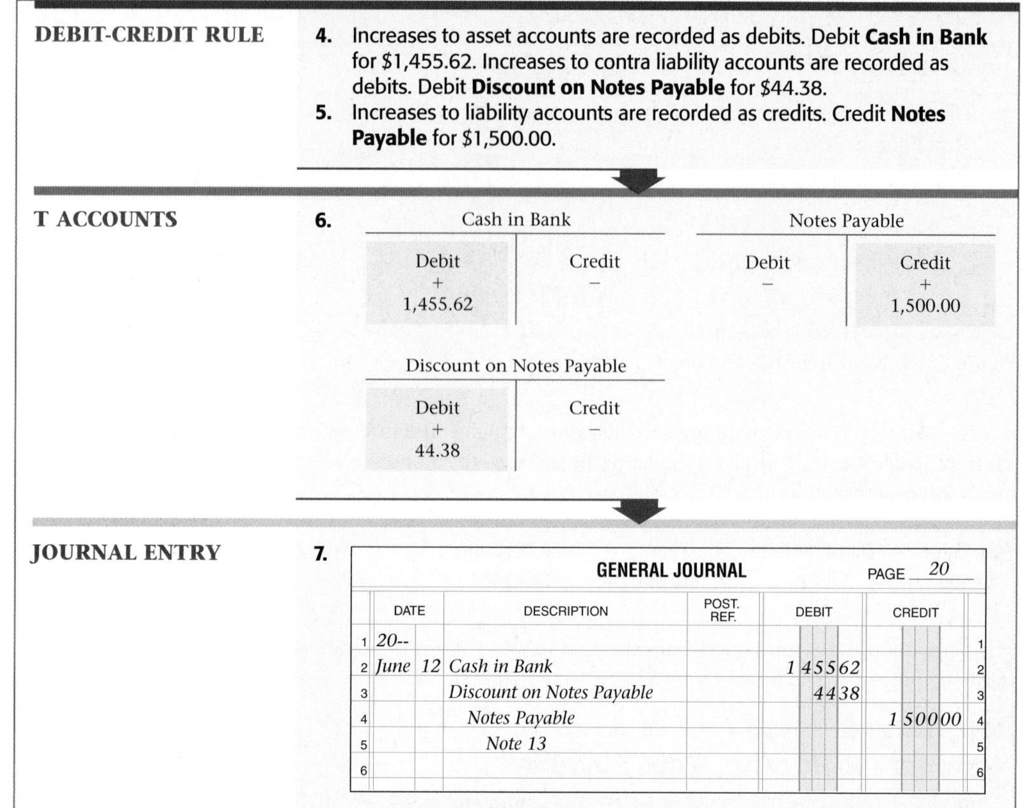

DEBIT-CREDIT RULE

4. Increases to asset accounts are recorded as debits. Debit **Cash in Bank** for $1,455.62. Increases to contra liability accounts are recorded as debits. Debit **Discount on Notes Payable** for $44.38.
5. Increases to liability accounts are recorded as credits. Credit **Notes Payable** for $1,500.00.

T ACCOUNTS

6.

Cash in Bank	
Debit +	Credit −
1,455.62	

Notes Payable	
Debit −	Credit +
	1,500.00

Discount on Notes Payable	
Debit +	Credit −
44.38	

JOURNAL ENTRY

7.

GENERAL JOURNAL — PAGE 20

	DATE		DESCRIPTION	POST. REF.	DEBIT	CREDIT	
1	20--						1
2	June	12	Cash in Bank		1 455 62		2
3			Discount on Notes Payable		44 38		3
4			Notes Payable			1 500 00	4
5			Note 13				5
6							6

The **Discount on Notes Payable** account is reported on the balance sheet as a deduction from **Notes Payable**. The difference between the **Notes Payable** account and the **Discount on Notes Payable** account is the book value of notes payable. **Figure 26–5** shows the Liabilities section of the balance sheet for On Your Mark on June 30. The book value of notes payable is $1,455.62, ($1,500 − $44.38).

ACCOUNTING *Flashbacks*

ACCOUNTING DEGREES

In the early 1970s, only about 10 percent of undergraduate degrees in accounting were awarded to women. By 2001, women earned more than half of all undergraduate accounting degrees.

On Your Mark Athletic Wear
Balance Sheet
June 30, 20--

Liabilities			
Notes Payable		1 500 00	
Less: Discount on Notes Payable		44 38	1 455 62

Figure 26–5 Reporting Noninterest-Bearing Notes Payable on the Balance Sheet

MEETING SPECIAL NEEDS

English Language Learners Students who are English language learners may avoid asking questions in class. Periodically, have all the students in the class write down one to three questions on the content of the chapter. The questions should concern something that they do not understand, such as the meaning of a particular word or how to record a particular transaction. Collect the questions, read them aloud, and discuss ways of finding the answers.

Recording the Payment of a Noninterest-Bearing Note Payable

When the noninterest-bearing note payable is due, On Your Mark will pay First Federal Bank the face value of the note.

Business Transaction

On September 10 On Your Mark issued Check 4241 for $1,500 to First Federal Bank in payment of the June 12 noninterest-bearing note payable.

ANALYSIS *Identify* *Classify* +/−

1. The accounts affected are **Notes Payable** and **Cash in Bank.**
2. **Notes Payable** is a liability account. **Cash in Bank** is an asset account.
3. **Notes Payable** is decreased by $1,500. **Cash in Bank** is decreased by $1,500.

DEBIT-CREDIT RULE

4. Decreases to liability accounts are recorded as debits. Debit **Notes Payable** for $1,500.
5. Decreases to asset accounts are recorded as credits. Credit **Cash in Bank** for $1,500.

T ACCOUNTS

6.

Notes Payable	
Debit −	Credit +
1,500	

Cash in Bank	
Debit +	Credit −
	1,500

JOURNAL ENTRY

7.

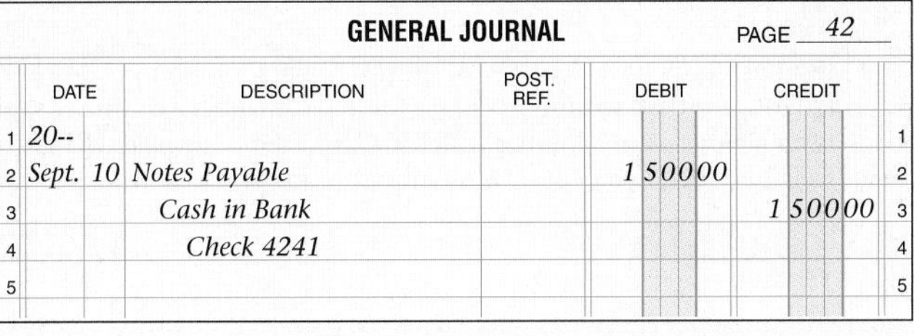

GENERAL JOURNAL — PAGE 42

	DATE		DESCRIPTION	POST. REF.	DEBIT	CREDIT	
1	20--						1
2	Sept.	10	Notes Payable		1 500 00		2
3			Cash in Bank			1 500 00	3
4			Check 4241				4
5							5

When a noninterest-bearing note payable matures, the amount of the bank discount is recognized as an expense. The bank discount is transferred from the **Discount on Notes Payable** account to the **Interest Expense** account. As you can see from the T accounts, **Interest Expense** is debited for $44.38 and **Discount on Notes Payable** is credited for $44.38. When this transaction is recorded, the balance of the **Discount on Notes Payable** account is reduced to zero.

2 TEACH (Cont'd.)

Visual Learning

Business Transaction

Using **Transparency 26–11,** analyze the transaction paying off a note payable. Guide students through the entry to record the transaction in the general journal.

Interview: Have students interview a loan representative at a local bank to find out the types of business loans the bank provides. Tell students to ask what the bank requires for collateral and what form of note a business signs when it borrows money. If possible, have students obtain a blank copy of a note to share in class, along with their findings. L1

GO TO **Math Review for Accounting** Photocopy appropriate *Activity Sheets* for students who need additional practice in basic math skills.

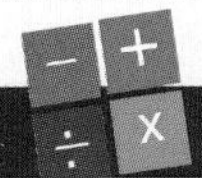

Math Skill Builder Activity

(Refer to the *Calculator Hints* activity on page 714.)

Calculating Time Help students practice calculating time by having them complete this application. Cory Sampson needed to calculate the overtime hours worked for the weekend staff at the amusement park. Following are the employees, the time clocked in, and their time clocked out. Have students calculate the hours worked for each person.

Marissa Earnhardt: In 6:30 A.M., Out 11:10 A.M.

Victor Negron: In 12 NOON, Out 6:15 P.M.

(Marissa = 4¾ hours; Victor = 5¾ hours)

CHAPTER 26
SECTION 2, PAGES 708–715

2 TEACH (Cont'd.)

Visual Learning

General Journal, p. 714
Use the illustration of the general journal on this page to explain how to record the entry for payment of the non-interest-bearing note.

Teaching Tip

Remind students that a compound entry involving two or more debits or credits is used to save journalizing and posting time.

Demonstration Problem Step-by-Step Practice
Use demonstration problem 26–7 to give students practice in analyzing and recording the payment of a noninterest-bearing note.

Research: Have students research the loan programs offered by the Small Business Administration (www.sba.gov). Ask students to summarize their findings in a one- to two-page report. L2

The Office Depot 2001 Annual Report
Refer students to pages A-39–A-48 in the back of the book.

Calculating Time

You can use a calculator to find total time worked by rounding a time to the nearest quarter hour and entering the decimal amount. For example:

- to find the hours between 8:13 and 12:04,
- enter 12 − 8.25.

The result is 3¾ hours.

Interest Expense	
Debit +	Credit −
9/10 44.38	

Discount on Notes Payable	
Debit +	Credit −
6/12 44.38	9/10 44.38

You could record two separate journal entries:

(1) the payment of the noninterest-bearing note payable (in the cash payments journal)
(2) the interest expense (in the general journal)

It is simpler, however, to prepare one compound entry:

GENERAL JOURNAL PAGE 43

	DATE		DESCRIPTION	POST. REF.	DEBIT	CREDIT	
1	20--						1
2	Sept.	10	*Notes Payable*		1 500 00		2
3			*Interest Expense*		44 38		3
4			*Cash in Bank*			1 500 00	4
5			*Discount on Notes Payable*			44 38	5
6			*Check 4241*				6
7							7

The **Interest Expense** account is classified as an other expense account. An **other expense** is a nonoperating expense. This means that the expense does not result from the normal operations of the business. Other expenses appear in a separate section on the income statement, as deductions from operating income.

ANALYZING FINANCIAL REPORTS

Evaluating Debt

Most businesses have debt—both short-term and long-term. Short-term debt refers to liabilities which are expected to be paid off within one year. Examples include accounts payable, short-term notes, and taxes. Long-term debt refers to liabilities which are expected to be paid off in more than one year. Businesses often incur long-term debt when borrowing money to expand business operations.

▶ Analyze the Report:

Use the balance sheet for Office Depot on page A-45 to answer these questions:

1. How much has accounts payable increased or decreased from 2000 to 2001?
2. What is the percentage change of the increase or decrease? (Round to the nearest one-tenth of a percent.)
3. How much has long-term debt—net of current maturities—increased or decreased from 2000 to 2001?
4. What is the percentage change of the increase or decrease? (Round to the nearest one-tenth of a percent.)
5. What do you think is meant by the phrase "net of current maturities"?

ANALYZING FINANCIAL REPORTS

Analyze the Report (Answers)

1. $76,026,000 decrease ($1,136,994,000 − $1,060,968,000)
2. 6.7% ($76,026,000 / $1,136,994,000)
3. $58,730,000 decrease ($374,061,000 − $315,331,000)
4. 15.7% ($58,730,000 / $374,061,000)
5. "Net of current maturities" refers to the portion of long-term debt that will not mature within the next 12 months.

SECTION 2 Check Your Understanding

Now that you have studied this section, complete the following questions and problems.

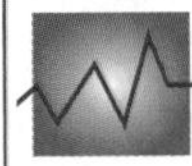

Thinking Critically

1. How is the interest charge calculated for an interest-bearing note and a noninterest-bearing note?
2. What two journal entries (or one compound entry) are prepared when a noninterest-bearing note payable matures and is paid?

Communicating Accounting

You design brochures to highlight New South Bank's many financial products. Today you were asked to prepare a brochure explaining the value of noninterest-bearing notes. You may design your brochure by hand or on a computer.

Problem 26–3 Recording the Issuance of an Interest-Bearing Note Payable

On June 12 Frank's Lobster Pound issued a $9,000, 120-day, 12% note payable to American Bank of Commerce.

1. Which account is debited? What is the debit amount?
2. Which account is credited? What is the credit amount?
3. What is the classification of each account?
4. What is the maturity value of the note?

Problem 26–4 Recording the Issuance of a Noninterest-Bearing Note Payable

On October 14 Canton Car Care Center issued a $10,000, 60-day, 12% noninterest-bearing note payable to Canton National Bank.

1. Which accounts are debited and which are credited? What are the debit and credit amounts?
2. Compute the bank discount. What are the proceeds?

RETEACHING SECTION 2

Calculating and Recording Notes Payable Before introducing how to record a note payable, have students role-play borrowing $10,000 from a bank by signing a 60-day, 11 percent, interest-bearing note. After the role-play, ask the students to calculate the interest, analyze the transaction, determine which ledger accounts are affected, and indicate in which journal the transaction should be recorded. (Interest, $183.33; Cash in Bank debit, $10,000; Notes Payable credit, $10,000; cash receipts journal)

3 ASSESS

Thinking Critically (Answers)

1. Interest charge for both is based on a percentage of the note's face value.
2. Payment of the note is recorded in the cash payments journal; interest expense, in the general journal.

Communicating Accounting (Answers)

Students may use any style for brochures. Points could include how interest is calculated, an example, and how to determine maturity value.

Problem 26–3 (Answers)

1. Cash in Bank $9,000
2. Notes Payable $9,000
3. Cash in Bank, asset; Notes Payable, liability
4. $9,355.07

Problem 26–4 (Answers)

1. Cash in Bank, Dr. $9,802.74; Discount on Notes Payable, Dr. $197.26; Notes Payable, Cr. $10,000
2. Disc. $197.26, Proceeds $9,802.74

Chapter Reviews and Working Papers Refer students to the Chapter 26 workbook pages to answer *Check Your Understanding* activities.

4 CLOSE

Section Wrap-Up

Demonstration: Have students calculate the interest and maturity value on a $12,000, 8.5% interest-bearing note payable. Then have them change the note to a noninterest-bearing note and calculate the discount and proceeds. ($1,020, $13,020; $1,020, $10,980) L1

1 FOCUS

Introducing the Section

In this section students will continue their study of notes by learning how to record entries for notes receivable.

Section Concepts

- How to record the issuance of a note receivable.
- How to record payments on a note receivable.

Visual Learning

Section 3 Focus

Use **Transparency 26–12** to introduce section concepts.

BELL RINGER

Compare and Contrast: Draw an IOU promising to pay students three pieces of candy or a soda, and photocopy enough to give one to each student. Include dates and terms on the IOUs. Have students discuss what is represented by the IOU. Ask them to compare this note with one a business might receive from a customer to pay for merchandise purchased. L1

Concept Development: Accounting for Notes Receivable

Discussion: Point out the difference between a note receivable and a note payable. Review the reasons for a business to accept a note receivable. Discuss the Notes Receivable account, and point out that it has the same rules of debit and credit as Accounts Receivable. L1

Demonstration Problem Step-by-Step Practice

Use demonstration problem 26–8 to give students practice in recording the receipt of a note receivable.

SECTION 3

Notes Receivable

What **You'll Learn**

- How to record the issuance of a note receivable.
- How to record payments on a note receivable.

Why **It's Important**

Many businesses accept notes receivable and receive payments on those notes.

KEY TERMS

other revenue

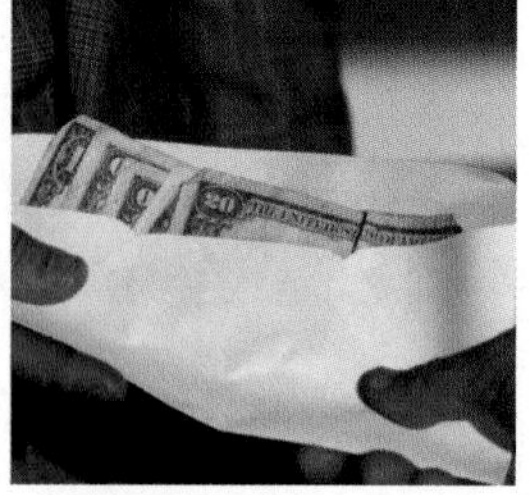

In this section you will journalize transactions involving notes receivable. Have you ever loaned someone money and asked that they repay the loan by a specific date? If so, you understand the basic concept of a note receivable. Sometimes a loan like this may include payment of a specified amount of interest; other times no interest is expected.

Accounting for Notes Receivable

Sometimes a customer needs additional time to pay his or her account receivable. The customer may be asked to sign a promissory note. The customer replaces the account receivable with the note. Promissory notes that a business accepts from customers are called notes receivable.

Notes Receivable is an asset account, and its normal balance is a debit. A note receivable is due on a specific date and carries an interest charge for the term of the note.

The interest earned on a note receivable is recorded in the **Interest Income** account. **Interest Income** is an other revenue account. **Other revenue** accounts track nonoperating revenue that a business receives from activities outside the normal operations of the business. Other revenue appears in a separate section on the income statement, as an increase to operating income.

Recording the Receipt of a Note Receivable

Business Transaction

On March 1 On Your Mark sold $1,750 of merchandise on account to Joe Dimaio. That transaction was recorded in On Your Mark's sales journal. Joe cannot pay his account by the due date. On April 8 On Your Mark received a 60-day, 12.5% note dated April 6 for $1,750 from Joe Dimaio to settle the account receivable, Note 4.

ANALYSIS		
	Identify	1. The accounts affected are **Notes Receivable**, **Accounts Receivable** (controlling), and **Accounts Receivable—Joe Dimaio** (subsidiary).
	Classify	2. **Notes Receivable**, **Accounts Receivable** (controlling), and **Accounts Receivable—Joe Dimaio** (subsidiary) are asset accounts.
	+/−	3. **Notes Receivable** is increased by $1,750. **Accounts Receivable** (controlling) and **Accounts Receivable—Joe Dimaio** (subsidiary) are decreased by $1,750.

RESOURCE MANAGER

Reproducible Masters
- Lesson Plans
- Chapter Reviews and Working Papers (CRWP) TAE
- Demonstration Problems

Transparencies
- Section Focus Transparency
- Teaching Transparencies
- Source Document Transparencies
- Solution Transparencies

Multimedia
- **Exam***View* CD-ROM
- Electronic Learning Center CD-ROM
- Interactive Lesson Planner CD-ROM

DEBIT-CREDIT RULE	**4.** Increases to asset accounts are recorded as debits. Debit **Notes Receivable** for $1,750. **5.** Decreases to asset accounts are recorded as credits. Credit **Accounts Receivable** (controlling) for $1,750. Also credit **Accounts Receivable–Joe Dimaio** (subsidiary) for $1,750.

T ACCOUNTS

6.

Notes Receivable

Debit +	Credit –
1,750	

Accounts Receivable

Debit +	Credit –
	1,750

Accounts Receivable Subsidiary Ledger
Accounts Receivable—Joe Dimaio

Debit +	Credit –
	1,750

JOURNAL ENTRY

7.

GENERAL JOURNAL PAGE 13

	DATE		DESCRIPTION	POST. REF.	DEBIT	CREDIT	
1	20--						1
2	Apr.	8	Notes Receivable		1 750 00		2
3			Accts. Rec./Joe Dimaio			1 750 00	3
4			Note 4				4

Recording the Receipt of Cash for a Note

The note from Joe Dimaio is due on June 5. The maturity value of the note is $1,785.96 ($1,750.00 principal + $35.96 interest).

Principal	×	**Interest Rate**	×	**Time**	=	**Interest**
$1,750	×	**.125**	×	**60/365**	=	**$35.96**

Business Transaction

On June 7 On Your Mark received a check dated June 5 for $1,785.96 from Joe Dimaio in payment of the $1,750 note of April 6 plus interest of $35.96, Receipt 996.

JOURNAL ENTRY

GENERAL JOURNAL PAGE 18

	DATE		DESCRIPTION	POST. REF.	DEBIT	CREDIT	
1	20--						1
2	June	7	Cash in Bank		1 785 96		2
3			Notes Receivable			1 750 00	3
4			Interest Income			35 96	4
5			Receipt 996				5

MAKING CONNECTIONS TO DAILY LIFE

Loan Repayment Plans Ask students if they have ever borrowed money from a parent or a friend. How long did it take to pay the money back? Did they pay the money back in one payment, or did they make several payments until the loan was paid in full? Point out that if the student had borrowed the money from a bank or other lending institution, the bank would have charged a fee (interest) for the use of the money and would have set a specific date for the total to be repaid.

2 TEACH

GUIDED PRACTICE

Reading Accounting

- Have students copy the two business transactions on pages 716–717 onto notebook paper. Then have them read the transactions and underline the key words that tell them what to record in the accounting records. L1

Visual Learning

Business Transaction

Use **Transparency 26–13** to guide students through the analysis and recording of the receipt of a note receivable.

Business Transaction

Using **Transparency 26–14**, have students analyze the transaction for receipt of payment on a note receivable. Draw T accounts on the chalkboard and have students tell you how each account is affected. Then review the journal entry to record the transaction.

Teaching Tips

Explain to students why businesses ask their customers to sign promissory notes instead of just extending the due date of an account receivable.

Review the calculation of interest before analyzing the receipt of cash in payment of the note receivable.

Demonstration Problem Step-by-Step Practice

Use demonstration problem 26–9 to give students practice in recording the receipt of payment for a note receivable.

3 ASSESS

Thinking Critically (Answers)

1. Like a note payable, a note receivable has a stated value, is due on a specific future date, and carries an interest charge for the term of the note.
2. Interest income is recorded as a credit to Interest Income. Interest income increases the income accounts.

Analyzing Accounting (Answers)

Answers may vary. Students must compare interest rates before making a final recommendation. Have students team together to review the graph and formulate reasons for their recommendations.

Problem 26–5 (Answers)

June 12: Dr. Cash in Bank $2,426.03, Discount on Notes Payable $73.97; Cr. Notes Payable $2,500; Note 55

Chapter Reviews and Working Papers Refer students to the Chapter 26 workbook pages to answer *Check Your Understanding* activities.

4 CLOSE

Section Wrap-Up

Record Notes Receivable: Using the IOUs from the Bell Ringer activity, assign a monetary value to the items described in the IOUs. Have students prepare journal entries to record notes receivable. L1

SECTION 3 Check Your Understanding

Now that you have studied this section, complete the following questions and problems.

Thinking Critically

1. Explain the similarities between a note payable and a note receivable.
2. How is interest income recorded in the accounting records?

Analyzing Accounting

Your accounting manager has just finished a graph illustrating the possible interest-bearing notes available from the region's banks. Review the graph and give your boss your recommendation of which bank will provide the best loan value.

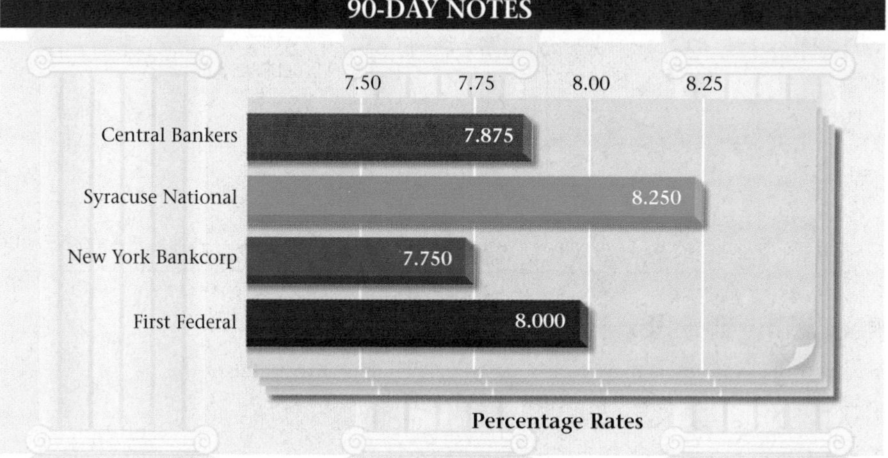

Problem 26–5 Analyzing a Source Document

Instructions Examine the note illustrated here. In your working papers, make the appropriate journal entry on page 14 of the general journal for Eli's Catering Company. The note was discounted at a rate of 12% by First Federal Bank.

NOTE 55

$ 2,500.00 Date June 12 20 --

Ninety days after date I promise to pay to

First Federal Bank the sum of

Two thousand five hundred and no/100 dollars.

Due date September 10, 20--

Owner, Eli's Catering Co.

RETEACHING SECTION 3

Calculating and Recording Notes Receivable Give students this example: A customer of Business Express, Drew Simpkins, signed a 30-day, 11.75 percent note for $3,450 to pay an account receivable. Ask students to analyze the issuance of the note and its payment, indicating accounts affected and journals used to record each transaction. (At signing, Notes Receivable is debited for $3,450, and Accounts Receivable/Drew Simpkins are credited for $3,450. The entry is recorded in the general journal. At payment, Cash in Bank is debited for $3,483.78, Notes Receivable is credited for $3,450, Interest Income is credited for $33.78. The entry is made in the cash receipts journal.)

CHAPTER 26 SUMMARY

KEY CONCEPTS

1. A promissory note is a written promise to pay an amount of money by a specific future date.
2. Promissory notes issued by businesses to creditors or banks to obtain a loan are called notes payable. **Notes Payable** is a liability account.
3. Interest is the fee charged to the issuer of a promissory note for the use of money. Interest is calculated as a percentage of the face value of the note, based on a borrowing period of one year. Borrowing periods of less than one year are expressed as fractions of a year.
4. Calculating interest on a note:
   Interest = Principal × Interest Rate × Time
5. For interest-bearing notes, interest is paid on the maturity date of the note. The maturity value of an interest-bearing note equals the principal (face value) plus the interest.
6. A noninterest-bearing note payable is a note from which the interest is deducted in advance. The interest deducted in advance is called the bank discount. The cash received by the borrower is called the proceeds. For a noninterest-bearing note payable, the maturity value is the same as the face value.
7. Calculating a bank discount:
   Face Value × Discount Rate × Time = Bank Discount
8. When a noninterest-bearing note payable is paid, the bank discount is transferred from **Discount on Notes Payable** to **Interest Expense.**
9. The **Discount on Notes Payable** account is reported on the balance sheet as a deduction from **Notes Payable**. The difference between the two account amounts is the book value of notes payable.
10. Promissory notes accepted by businesses from charge customers are called notes receivable. **Notes Receivable** is an asset account.

Chapter 26 Quiz

Student ______ Class ______ Instructor ______
Date Assigned ______ Date Completed ______

CHAPTER 26 QUIZ

Notes Payable and Receivable

QUESTIONS (Completion)

Directions: Fill in the blank with the term that best completes each sentence.

1. A ______ is a written promise to pay a certain amount of money at a specific time.
2. Principal plus interest is the ______ of a note.
3. The time period covered by the note is its ______.
4. The formula to calculate simple interest is ______.
5. A note payable is a ______ liability.
6. Interest deducted by the bank at the time a note payable is issued is a ______.
7. The cash received by the borrower for a noninterest-bearing note is the note's ______.
8. Discount on Notes Payable is a ______ account.
9. The Interest Expense account is classified as ______.
10. Interest received on a note receivable is recorded in the ______ account, which is classified as ______.

28 • Chapter Quizzes

QUESTIONS (Completion)

1. A ______ is a written promise to pay a certain amount of money at a specific time.
2. Principal plus interest is the ______ of a note.
3. The time period covered by the note is its ______.
4. The formula to calculate simple interest is ______.
5. A note payable is a ______ liability.
6. Interest deducted by the bank at the time a note payable is issued is a ______.
7. The cash received by the borrower for a noninterest-bearing note is the note's ______.
8. Discount on Notes Payable is a ______ account.
9. The Interest Expense account is classified as ______.
10. Interest received on a note receivable is recorded in the ______ account, which is classified as ______.

ANSWERS

1. promissory note
2. maturity value
3. term
4. I = P × R × T
5. long-term
6. bank discount
7. proceeds
8. contra liability
9. other expense
10. Interest Income, other revenue

USING KEY TERMS

See the *Glossary* for the definitions of these terms. Ask for volunteers to write their groupings of terms on the chalkboard. Ask the class whether they agree with the placement of terms within groups. Discuss any differences.

Understanding Accounting Concepts and Procedures

(Answers)

1. Maker issues the note; payee receives the note.
2. A business might receive a promissory note in exchange for an account receivable a customer cannot pay by the due date. A business might issue a promissory note to borrow money from a bank.
3. Interest = Principal × Rate × Time
4. Multiply the principal times the interest rate times the time, which is stated as a fraction of a year.
5. Interest-bearing notes and noninterest-bearing notes payable. When the interest is paid is the difference between the two. Interest on an interest-bearing note is paid at maturity. Interest on a noninterest-bearing note is paid at issue.
6. Principal of the note plus interest charged equals maturity value.
7. Interest is the charge for the use of borrowed money that is paid on the maturity date of the loan. Bank discount is the charge for the use of borrowed money that is paid the day the money is borrowed.
8. The amount of the bank discount (interest) is determined and subtracted from the principal.
9. It is a contra liability account and has a normal debit balance.
10. Because the revenue or expense results from activities that are outside the normal operations of the business.

USING KEY TERMS

Imagine you are employed by the Carnival Corporation as a staff accountant. You have been asked to discuss the notes payable and receivable of the company with the accounting clerks. Prepare note cards containing the terms below. Arrange these terms in meaningful groups. Explain why you have grouped terms together. Are they related? Are they part of the same thing? Is one the result of another? Are they opposites?

bank discount	noninterest-bearing note payable
face value	note payable
interest	note receivable
interest-bearing note payable	other expense
interest rate	other revenue
issue date	payee
long-term liabilities	principal
maker	proceeds
maturity date	promissory note
maturity value	term

Understanding Accounting Concepts and Procedures

Instructions

On a separate sheet of paper, answer the following questions:

1. Name the two parties to a promissory note. Which party issues the note? Which party receives the note?
2. Describe a situation in which a business might (a) receive a promissory note and (b) issue a promissory note.
3. What is the formula to calculate interest?
4. How is the interest on a note calculated if the term is less than one year?
5. Name two types of notes a business may issue. What is the major difference between the two?
6. How is the maturity value of an interest-bearing note determined?
7. What is the difference between interest and a bank discount?
8. When a noninterest-bearing note payable is issued, how are the proceeds calculated?
9. How is the **Discount on Notes Payable** account classified? What is its normal balance?
10. Why are interest income and interest expense reported separately on the income statement?

ASSESSMENT RESOURCES

Choose assessment strategies from the following pages to evaluate your students' progress.

Student Edition
Check Your Understanding, pp. 707, 715, 718
Chapter 26 Problems, pp. 723–725
Analyzing Financial Reports, p. 714

Assessment and Evaluation Masters
Chapter 26 Study Plan, *Glencoe Workbook (CRWP)*
Chapter 26 Self-Test, *Glencoe Workbook (CRWP)*
Chapter 26 Test, *Chapter Tests* Booklet
Chapter 26 Activity, *School-to-Work Handbook*
Chapter 26 **Exam***View*

Teacher Wraparound Edition
Critical Thinking Activity, p. 705
Reteaching Sections 1–3, pp. 707, 715, 718
Chapter 26 Quiz, p. 719

Case Study...

Merchandising Business: Restaurant/Retail Shop

Moreno's Italian Oven is a local restaurant with a deli that offers takeout pastas and sauces. It is open seven days a week for lunch and dinner. The restaurant seats 60 patrons in a day and averages 90 percent capacity.

The space adjacent to the restaurant is available, and Moreno's is considering expanding. The cost of remodeling the space and buying additional kitchen and restaurant equipment is estimated at $200,000. The rent on the additional space is $1,200 a month.

Thinking Critically:

1. If Moreno's could double the number of customers it serves in a week, how many customers would the restaurant serve?
2. If each customer spends an average of $12 for a meal, how much additional revenue would the restaurant earn in a day if it expands and maintains 90 percent capacity?

interNET CONNECTION

Notes Payable: Car Loans

Thinking about buying a car? Most of us need a loan to finance the purchase. Wondering how much your monthly payment will be? Let's find out!

Do This:

Assume you are purchasing a used Ford Mustang from a friend and your bank is offering an interest rate of 10.5%. You've agreed to pay $12,500 for the car. You would like to pay the loan over three years. Locate a mortgage or loan calculator on the Internet.

You will be asked for the following information:

Loan term or months to repay the loan: 36 months
Loan amount: $12,500
Interest rate: 10.5%
What is your monthly payment?

Conducting an Audit with Alex

On May 1 Artist's Loft borrowed $8,000 from American National Bank. The art supply company issued an interest-bearing 90-day, 12% note payable to the bank, Note 5. The following journal entry was made to record the transaction.

GENERAL JOURNAL PAGE 18

	DATE		DESCRIPTION	POST. REF.	DEBIT	CREDIT	
1	20--						1
2	May	1	Cash in Bank		7 230 40		2
3			Notes Payable			7 230 40	3
4			Note 5				4
5							5

Instructions Determine whether the entry above is correct. If not, why?

Workplace Skills

Allocating Time, Money, Materials, Space, and Staff

Being resourceful on the job includes allocating time, money, materials, space, and staff efficiently. Budgeting, acquiring materials, assessing employee talents, and allocating time to activities are a few examples of acting competently.

On the Job:

You have been offered a full-time job with Good Times Amusement Park. Before you accept the job, you must purchase a car to get you to and from work.

Thinking Critically:

Make a list of the potential costs involved in owning a car. Make a list of potential costs involved in other modes of transportation. How would owning a car impact the use of your time? How might it affect your budget?

Case Study...

Thinking Critically (Answers)

1. 756
2. $648

Workplace Skills

Thinking Critically (Answers)

Answers will vary. Some possibilities include bicycling, walking, and various forms of public transportation.

Conducting an Audit with Alex

(Answers)

The note is an interest-bearing note. When first issued, the note should have been recorded as a debit to Cash in Bank and a credit to Notes Payable for the full $8,000. The entry to record the interest would be made at the time the interest is paid.

Internet Resources and Activities Handbook

Refer students to the booklet for additional Internet activities.

interNET CONNECTION www.glencoe.com

Do This (Answers)

1. There is a loan calculator at www.carseverything.com.
2. The monthly payment is $406.28.

PEACHTREE CORNER

Notes Receivable

On the **Tasks** menu, select **Receipts** (not the **General Journal Entry** option) to record a transaction when a customer offers a note in exchange for an extension of time on an outstanding receivable balance. For information on recording the entry, see Answers to Frequently Asked Questions on this page.

Tasks Analysis Options Reports
Quotes/Sales Orders
Sales/Invoicing...
Receipts...
Finance Charge...
Select for Deposit...
Purchase Orders...

Notes Payable

Use the **Payments** option to record a transaction when a company issues a note to a vendor in place of an amount owed on account. Change Cash (GL Account) to **Notes Payable.** Mark the invoice as "paid" and post the transaction. Peachtree debits **Accounts Payable** and the vendor's subsidiary account and credits **Notes Payable.** Reset the Cash account before recording other cash payments.

Tasks Analysis Options Reports
Quotes/Sales Orders
Sales/Invoicing...
Receipts...
Finance Charge...
Select for Deposit...
Purchase Orders...
Purchases/Receive Inventory...
Select for Payment...
Payments...
Write Checks...

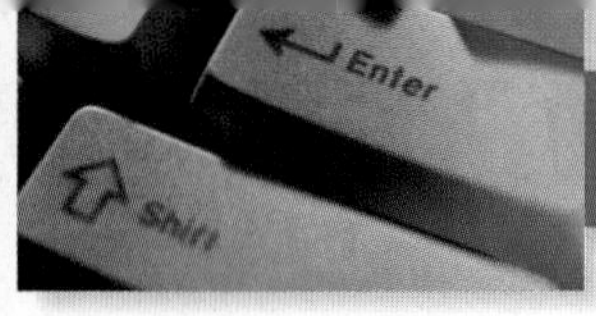

Notes Receivable and Payable

Making the Transition from a Manual to a Computerized System

Task	Perform Accounting Procedures Using Manual Methods	Perform Accounting Procedures Using Automated Methods
Recording notes receivable and payable transactions	1. Using the general journal, record the receipt or issuance of the note. 2. Post the entry to the appropriate accounts in the general ledger and subsidiary ledgers. 3. Journalize and post the entry to record the receipt or payment of cash and interest. 4. Calculate new balances for all accounts affected.	1. Using the general journal, record the receipt or issuance of the note. The entry is automatically posted to the appropriate accounts. 2. Use the Receipts menu item or the Payments menu item to record receipts or payment of notes.

Recording Notes Receivable and Payable

Peachtree Question	Description
How do I record the issuance of a note payable?	1. From the ***Tasks*** menu, select **Receipts.** 2. Accept the Cash in Bank account number as the G/L account. 3. Enter a Reference number, usually the note number. 4. Click on the Apply to Revenues tab. 5. Enter the Notes Payable account number and the note amount.
How do I record the receipt of a note receivable?	1. From the ***Tasks*** menu, select **Receipts.** 2. Accept the Cash in Bank account number as the G/L account. 3. Enter a Reference number, usually the note number. 4. Enter the Notes Receivable account number and the amount of the note. 5. Enter the Interest Income account number and the amount of interest received.
How do I record the receipt of a note as an extension of an existing account receivable?	1. From the ***Tasks*** menu, select **Receipts.** 2. Enter the customer ID. 3. Enter a Reference number, usually the note number. 4. Enter the Notes Receivable account number. 5. Click the Apply to Invoices tab. 6. Select the pay boxes next to the invoices that the note will pay.
What does the software do "behind the scenes"?	Journal entries are posted to the appropriate G/L accounts and subsidiary accounts for all payments and receipts.

For detailed instructions: See the **Peachtree User Guide** in your Glencoe Working Papers.

Peachtree® Answers to Frequently Asked Questions

Q: How do you record the exchange of a promissory note for an account receivable?

A: Use the **Receipts** option and change Cash (GL Account) to Notes Receivable. Then mark the invoice as "paid" and post the transaction. Peachtree debits Notes Receivable (instead of Cash in Bank) and credits Accounts Receivable and the customer's subsidiary ledger account. Be sure to reset the Cash account before you record any other cash receipts.

For additional information, refer to your *Glencoe Peachtree Accounting User Guide.*

APPLICATION OPTIONS

Problem 26–6 Recording Transactions for Interest-Bearing Notes Payable

Instructions In your working papers, record the following transactions in a cash receipts journal (page 22) and a cash payments journal (page 26).

Date	Transactions
Jan. 14	Sunset Surfwear borrowed $1,500 from First One Bank by issuing a 90-day, 12% interest-bearing note payable, Note 78.
Apr. 14	Issued Check 168 for $1,544.38 to First One Bank in payment of the $1,500 note issued on January 14, plus interest of $44.38.
May 31	Borrowed $12,400 from Merchant's Bank and Trust by issuing a 90-day, 12.5% interest-bearing note, Note 79.
Aug. 29	Paid Merchant's Bank and Trust the maturity value of the note issued on May 31, $12,782.19, Check 284.

Analyze: On January 14 the balance in the **Notes Payable** account was zero. What is the balance of the **Notes Payable** account on August 30?

Problem 26–7 Recording Transactions for Noninterest-Bearing Notes Payable

Instructions In your working papers, record the following transactions in a cash receipts journal (page 14) and a cash payments journal (page 16).

Date	Transactions
June 10	InBeat CD Shop borrowed $6,000 from BankOne by issuing a 60-day, noninterest-bearing note payable (proceeds, $5,901.37) that the bank discounted at 10%, Note 67.
Aug. 9	Issued Check 205 for $6,000 in payment of the note issued June 10 and recorded the interest expense.
30	Borrowed $16,000 from Citizens Bank by issuing a 120-day, noninterest-bearing note payable less the 10.5% bank discount of $552.33, Note 68.
Dec. 28	Issued Check 398 in payment of the note issued on August 30 and recorded the interest expense.

Analyze: What is the interest expense associated with these notes?

Complete chapter problems one of three ways:

1 **Manual** Glencoe Working Papers

or

2 **Peachtree Complete Accounting** Software

or

3 **QuickBooks** Templates (Problems 26–6, 26–10)

Peachtree®

SMART GUIDE

Step-by-Step Instructions: Problem 26–6

1. Select the problem set for Sunset Surfwear (Prob. 26–6).
2. Rename the company and set the system date.
3. Record the transactions using the **Receipts** and **Payments** options. Enter each transaction in the proper accounting period (month).
4. Print a Cash Receipts Journal and a Cash Disbursements Journal to proof your work.
5. Answer the Analyze question.
6. End the session.

TIP: Set the date range on the journal reports to print the transactions for all of the periods.

Problem 26–6 (Answers) Recording Transactions for Interest-Bearing Notes Payable

Cash receipts journal entries:

Jan. 14: General Cr. $1,500 (Notes Payable); Cash in Bank Dr. $1,500

May 31: General Cr. $12,400 (Notes Payable); Cash in Bank Dr. $12,400

Cash payments journal entries:

Apr. 14: General Dr. $1,500 (Notes Payable), $44.38 (Interest Expense); Cash in Bank Cr. $1,544.38

Aug. 29: General Dr. $12,400 (Notes Payable), $382.19 (Interest Expense); Cash in Bank Cr. $12,782.19

Analyze: Zero

Problem 26–7 (Answers) Recording Transactions for Noninterest-Bearing Notes Payable

Cash receipts journal entries:

June 10: Cash in Bank Dr. $5,901.37; General Cr. $6,000 (Notes Payable); General Dr. $98.63 (Disc. on Notes Payable)

Aug. 30: Cash in Bank Dr. $15,447.67; General Cr. $16,000 (Notes Payable); General Dr. $552.33 (Disc. on Notes Payable)

Cash payments journal entries:

Aug. 9: General Dr. $6,000 (Notes Payable), $98.63 (Interest Expense); General Cr. $98.63 (Disc. on Notes Payable); Cash in Bank Cr. $6,000

Dec. 28: General Dr. $16,000 (Notes Payable), $552.33 (Interest Expense); General Cr. $552.33; Cash in Bank Cr. $16,000

Analyze: $650.96

EXTENDING THE CONTENT

Researching Interest Rates Assign students in pairs and ask them to contact a local bank or other lending institution to determine the current interest rate for car loans. Ask students to compare this rate with the current prime rate. Have students share their findings in class. List all the sources for car loans on the chalkboard so students can compare the various rates.

Problem 26–8 (Answers) Recording Notes Payable and Notes Receivable

Cash receipts journal entries:

Mar. 19: Cash in Bank Dr. $9,000; General Cr. $9,000 (Notes Payable)

Sept. 29: Cash in Bank Dr. $1,981.21; General Cr. $1,900 (Notes Receivable), $81.21 (Interest Income)

Oct. 6: Cash in Bank Dr. $2,648.96; General Cr. $2,700 (Notes Payable); General Dr. $51.04 (Disc. on Notes Payable)

Cash payments journal entries:

June 17: General Dr. $9,000 (Notes Payable), $266.30 (Interest Expense); Cash in Bank Cr. $9,266.30

Dec. 5: General Dr. $2,700 (Notes Payable), $51.04 (Interest Expense); General Cr. $51.04 (Disc. on Notes Payable); Cash in Bank Cr. $2,700

General journal entry:

June 4: Dr. Notes Receivable $1,900; Cr. Accts. Rec./Greg Kellogg $1,900; Note 6

Analyze: $317.34

Peachtree®

SMART GUIDE

Step-by-Step Instructions: Problem 26–7

1. Select the problem set for InBeat CD Shop (Prob. 26–7).
2. Rename the company and set the system date.
3. Record the transactions using the **Receipts** and **Payments** options. Enter each transaction in the proper accounting period (month).
4. Print a Cash Receipts Journal and a Cash Disbursements Journal to proof your work.
5. Answer the Analyze question.
6. End the session.

Peachtree®

SMART GUIDE

Step-by-Step Instructions: Problem 26–8

1. Select the problem set for Cycle Tech Bicycles (Prob. 26–8).
2. Rename the company and set the system date.
3. Record the transactions using the **Receipts** and **Payments** options.
4. Print a Cash Receipts Journal and a Cash Disbursements Journal to proof your work.
5. Answer the Analyze question.
6. End the session.

TIP: Use the **Receipts** option to record a transaction where a customer replaces an accounts receivable obligation with a promissory note.

Problem 26–8 Recording Notes Payable and Notes Receivable

Instructions In your working papers, record the following transactions in a cash receipts journal (page 47), cash payments journal (page 56), and general journal (page 19) for Cycle Tech Bicycles.

Date	Transactions
Mar. 19	Borrowed $9,000 from Desert Palms Savings and Loan by issuing a 90-day, 12% interest-bearing note payable, Note 87.
June 4	Received a 120-day, 13% note receivable for $1,900 from Greg Kellogg as a time extension on his account receivable, Note 6.
17	Paid Desert Palms Savings and Loan the maturity value of the note issued on March 19, Check 2784.
Sept. 29	Received a check from Greg Kellogg for the maturity value of the note dated June 1, Receipt 628.
Oct. 6	Borrowed $2,700 from Jonesboro Bank and Trust by issuing a 60-day, noninterest-bearing note payable discounted at 11.5%, Note 88.
Dec. 5	Prepared a check for the note issued on October 6 and recorded the interest expense, Check 3954.

Analyze: How much did Cycle Tech pay in interest for the notes payable?

Problem 26–9 Recording Notes Payable and Notes Receivable

The following is a partial list of accounts used by River's Edge Canoe & Kayak.

101	Cash in Bank	205	Notes Payable
115	Accounts Receivable	207	Discount on Notes Payable
120	Notes Receivable	415	Interest Income
201	Accounts Payable	640	Interest Expense

Instructions In your working papers, record the following transactions in a cash receipts journal (page 67), cash payments journal (page 73), and general journal (page 27).

ADDRESSING MULTIPLE LEARNING STYLES

Verbal/Linguistic Learner Promissory notes can be very lengthy and the language can be difficult to understand. However, when signing a promissory note, it is very important to know what the agreement actually states. Provide copies of a promissory note from a bank or other lending institution for students to review. Have students read the note and analyze the terms of the agreement. Discuss with the class questions they have about the terms. Allow the students to respond to their classmates' questions by providing their own interpretations of the words.

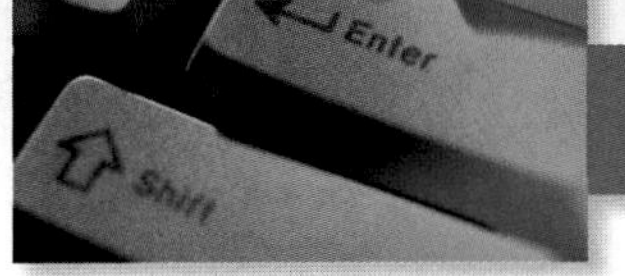

Date	Transactions
May 7	Borrowed $4,000 from Union Bank by issuing a 60-day, 9.5% noninterest-bearing note, Note 284.
15	Issued a $3,000, 90-day, 9% interest-bearing note to Trailhead Canoes in place of the amount owed on account, Note 285.
21	Received a 120-day, 10% note for $1,200 from Cathy Wilcox for an extension of time on her account, Note 94.
July 6	Issued Check 4711 in payment of the noninterest-bearing note given to Union Bank on May 7.
Aug. 13	Issued Check 5044 for the maturity value of the note issued to Trailhead Canoes on May 15.
Sept. 17	Received a check from Cathy Wilcox for the maturity value of the note dated May 21, Receipt 5921.

Analyze: How much interest did Cathy Wilcox pay River's Edge Canoe & Kayak?

Peachtree®

SMART GUIDE

Step-by-Step Instructions: Problem 26–9

1. Select the problem set for River's Edge Canoe & Kayak (Prob. 26–9).
2. Rename the company and set the system date.
3. Record the transactions using the **Receipts** and **Payments** options.
4. Print a Cash Receipts Journal and a Cash Disbursements Journal to proof your work.
5. Answer the Analyze question.
6. End the session.

TIP: Use the **Payments** option to record a transaction where a company issues a promissory note to a vendor to replace an outstanding accounts payable balance.

Problem 26–10 Renewing a Note Receivable

SOURCE DOCUMENT PROBLEM

Occasionally, on the maturity date, a note may be renewed instead of being paid. When this occurs, (1) the interest on the first note is paid, (2) the first note is canceled, and (3) a new note for the same principal amount is issued, usually at a higher interest rate. Buzz Newsstand had the following transactions.

Instructions In your working papers, record the following transactions on general journal page 24.

Date	Transactions
Mar. 14	Sold merchandise on account to Saba Nadal for $1,800, plus sales tax of $108.00, terms 30 days, Sales Slip 388.
Apr. 13	Accepted a 60-day, 9% note for $1,908.00 from Saba Nadal in place of the account receivable, Note 416.
June 12	Received the interest due from Saba Nadal for the note dated April 13 and agreed to renew the note at 10% for 90 days, Receipt 1387 and Note 417.
Sept. 10	Received a check from Saba Nadal for the maturity value of the note issued June 12, Receipt 1555.

Analyze: On September 10, before the payment was recorded, what was the balance of the Notes Receivable account for Saba Nadal?

Peachtree®

SMART GUIDE

Step-by-Step Instructions: Problem 26–10

1. Select the problem set for Buzz Newsstand (Prob. 26–10).
2. Rename the company and set the system date.
3. Record the transactions in the correct period.
4. Print a Sales Journal, Cash Receipts Journal, and a General Journal.
5. Answer the Analyze question.
6. End the session.

SOURCE DOCUMENT PROBLEM

Problem 26–10

Use the source documents in your working papers to record the transactions for this problem.

Problem 26–9 (Answer) Recording Notes Payable and Notes Receivable

Cash receipts journal entries:

May 7: Cash in Bank Dr. $3,937.53; General Cr. $4,000 (Notes Pay.); General Dr. $62.47 (Disc. on Notes Pay.)

Sept. 17: Cash in Bank Dr. $1,239.45; General Cr. $1,200 (Notes Rec.), $39.45 (Interest Income)

Cash payments journal entries:

July 6: General Dr. $4,000 (Notes Pay.), $62.47 (Interest Exp.); General Cr. $62.47 (Disc. on Notes Pay.); Cash in Bank Cr. $4,000

Aug. 13: General Dr. $3,000 (Notes Pay.), $66.58 (Int. Exp.); Cash in Bank Cr. $3,066.58

General journal entries:

May 15: Dr. Accts. Pay./Trailhead Canoes $3,000; Cr. Notes Pay. $3,000; Note 285

May 21: Dr. Notes Rec. $1,200; Cr. Accts. Rec./Cathy Wilcox $1,200; Note 94

Analyze: $39.45

SOURCE DOCUMENT PROBLEM

Problem 26–10 (Answers) Renewing a Note Receivable

Mar. 14: Dr. Accts. Rec./Saba Nadal $1,908; Cr. Sales $1,800, Sales Tax Pay. $108; Sales Slip 388

Apr. 13: Dr. Notes Rec. $1,908; Cr. Accts. Rec./Saba Nadal $1,908; Note 416

June 12: Dr. Cash in Bank $28.23; Cr. Interest Income $28.23; Receipt 1387

June 12: Dr. Notes Rec. (Note 417) $1,908; Cr. Notes Rec. (Note 416) $1,908; Note 417

Sept. 10: Dr. Cash in Bank $1,955.05; Notes Rec. $1,908, Interest Income $47.05; Receipt 555

Analyze: $1,908

COOPERATIVE LEARNING ACTIVITY

Create-a-Problem Assign students to teams of four or five. Ask each team to create a problem to be solved. Students can create problems similar to those provided at the end of the chapter. The team must solve the problem and write the solution on a separate sheet of paper. When the solutions are completed, the teams trade their problem with other teams, keeping the solutions hidden. When teams have solved the problem they received, they compare their solutions to the original solutions. If the solutions do not match, the teams work together to find the errors. If the solutions match, the teams may trade again with another team and continue the same process.

INTRODUCING *MINI PRACTICE SET 5*

Mini Practice Set Overview
This mini practice set is a comprehensive activity that requires students to complete an entire accounting cycle for a merchandising business organized as a closely held corporation. In this activity students will analyze and record business transactions for Kite Loft Inc., a store that sells kites and paper airplanes. Students must decide which journal to use to record each of the transactions. Students will also post, prove cash, and complete the end-of-period work for the business.

Most students should be able to complete this practice set manually within three to four class periods.

Source documents and accounting stationery are included in the student workbook, *Chapter Reviews and Working Papers*.

Mini Practice Set Concepts
- How to analyze, journalize, and post transactions using special journals and the general journal.
- How to prove cash.
- How to prepare a schedule of accounts receivable and a schedule of accounts payable.
- How to prepare a trial balance and a work sheet.
- How to prepare financial statements.
- How to journalize and post adjusting and closing entries.
- How to prepare a post-closing trial balance.
- How to complete the accounting cycle within an assigned time frame.

Visual Learning

Mini Practice Set Focus, p. 726
Discuss with students the accounting concepts and procedures they will apply in this mini practice set.

Completing the Accounting Cycle for a Merchandising Corporation

KITE LOFT INC.

What You'll Learn
- How to analyze, journalize, and post transactions using special journals and the general journal.
- How to prove cash.
- How to prepare a schedule of accounts receivable and a schedule of accounts payable.
- How to prepare a trial balance and a work sheet.
- How to prepare financial statements.
- How to journalize and post adjusting and closing entries.
- How to prepare a post-closing trial balance.
- How to complete the accounting cycle within an assigned time frame.

Why It's Important
In Unit 4, you studied the complete accounting cycle for a merchandising corporation that uses special journals. Now you will apply what you have learned as you work through the accounting cycle for Kite Loft Inc.

Kite Loft Inc.

Company Background: The Ramspart family owns and operates a wholesale-retail merchandising business organized as a corporation. The business, called Kite Loft Inc., sells a variety of kites and paper airplanes to regional and local toy store businesses.

Your teacher will assign a due date for this project. Working with Kite Loft Inc. will give you an opportunity to complete the accounting cycle within an assigned time frame.

Keeping the Accounting Records for Kite Loft Inc.: Kite Loft Inc. uses special journals and a general journal to record its business activity.

Max Martin, Kite Loft's previous accounting clerk, has already journalized and posted the transactions for December 1 through December 15. The transactions recorded thus far are included in the accounting stationery in your working papers. The transactions for December 16 through December 31 are shown on the following pages.

Your Job Responsibilities: The forms for completing this activity are included in the working papers. As the accountant for Kite Loft:

(1) Record the remaining December transactions in the sales, cash receipts, purchases, cash payments, and general journals.
(2) Post the individual amounts from the five journals to the accounts receivable and accounts payable subsidiary ledgers daily.
(3) Post the individual amounts from the General columns of the cash receipts, purchases, cash payments, and general journal daily.
(4) Foot, prove, total, and rule the special journals at the end of the month.
(5) Post the column totals of the special journals to the general ledger. Use this order for posting: sales, cash receipts, purchases, and cash payments.
(6) Prove cash. The balance shown on check stub 619 is $22,752.83.
(7) Prepare a schedule of accounts receivable and a schedule of accounts payable.
(8) Prepare a trial balance on a ten-column work sheet for the year ended December 31.

TEACHING NOTES

(9) Complete the work sheet. Use the following December 31 adjustment information.

Merchandise Inventory	$24,850.43
Supplies inventory	120.00
Unexpired insurance	660.00
Total federal income taxes	4,500.00

(10) Prepare the income statement from the work sheet information.
(11) Prepare a statement of retained earnings.
(12) Prepare a balance sheet.
(13) Journalize and post the adjusting entries.
(14) Journalize and post the closing entries.
(15) Prepare a post-closing trial balance.

APPLICATION OPTIONS

CHART OF ACCOUNTS
Kite Loft Inc.

ASSETS

101 Cash in Bank
105 Accounts Receivable
110 Merchandise Inventory
115 Supplies
120 Prepaid Insurance
125 Office Equipment
130 Store Equipment

LIABILITIES

201 Accounts Payable
205 Federal Corp. Income Tax Payable
210 Sales Tax Payable

STOCKHOLDERS' EQUITY

301 Capital Stock
305 Retained Earnings
310 Income Summary

REVENUE

401 Sales
405 Sales Discounts
410 Sales Returns and Allowances

COST OF MERCHANDISE

501 Purchases
505 Transportation In
510 Purchases Discounts
515 Purchases Returns and Allowances

EXPENSES

605 Advertising Expense
610 Bankcard Fees Expense
615 Insurance Expense
620 Miscellaneous Expense
625 Rent Expense
630 Salaries Expense
635 Supplies Expense
640 Utilities Expense
650 Federal Corp. Income Tax Expense

Accounts Receivable Subsidiary Ledger

BES Best Toys
LAR Lars' Specialties
SER Serendipity Shop
SMA Small Town Toys
TOY The Toy Store

Accounts Payable Subsidiary Ledger

BRA Brad's Kites Ltd.
CRE Creative Kites Inc.
EAS Easy Glide Co.
RED Reddi-Bright Manufacturing
STA Stars Kites Outlet
TAY Taylor Office Suppliers

Complete activities one of three ways:

1 **Manual** Glencoe Working Papers

or

2 **Peachtree Complete Accounting** Software

or

3 **QuickBooks** Templates

MINI PRACTICE SET 5
PAGES 726–729

Visual Learning

Chart of Accounts, p. 727

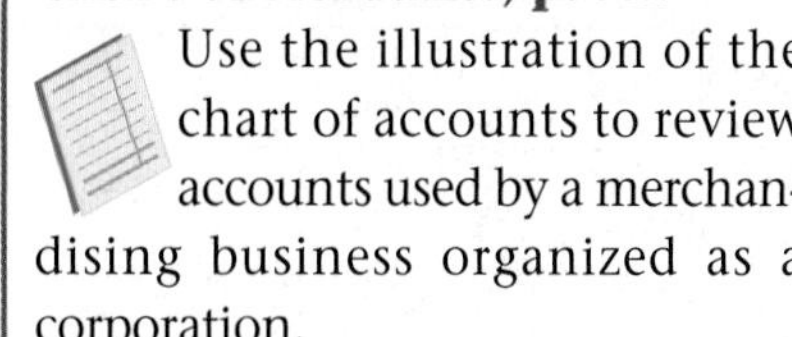

Use the illustration of the chart of accounts to review accounts used by a merchandising business organized as a corporation.

Teaching Tips

Have students give you the normal balance of each of the revenue and cost of merchandise accounts. Ask students to explain contra accounts and how they are used.

MAKING CONNECTIONS TO DAILY LIFE

Defining Market Value Ask students who have a personal computer at home whether the value of their computer is the same today as when they purchased it. They have probably already realized that the market value of their computer has depreciated because of the ongoing improvements in technology. Ask those students with home computers to contact a computer store to determine the approximate value of their components.

MINI PRACTICE SET 5
PAGES 726–729

SOURCE DOCUMENT PROBLEM

ANSWERS

Sales Journal totals:
Sales $13,424.00
Sales Tax Payable $805.44
Accounts Receivable $14,229.44

Cash Receipts Journal totals:
General $230.00
Sales $11,194.47
Sales Tax Payable $671.67
Accounts Receivable $14,007.90
Sales Discounts $225.90
Cash in Bank $25,878.14

Purchases Journal totals:
Accounts Payable $14,110.00
Purchases $13,905.00
General $205.00

Cash Payments Journal totals:
General Debit $7,033.80
Accounts Payable $14,765.00
Purchases Discounts $193.20
Cash in Bank $21,605.60

Net income $26,900.99

Cash proof $22,752.83

Schedule of Accounts Receivable $8,497.44
Schedule of Accounts Payable $6,645.00

Post-Closing Trial Balance totals $74,205.70

Peachtree®

SMART GUIDE

Step-by-Step Instructions:

1. Select the problem set for Kite Loft Inc. (MP–5).
2. Rename the company and set the system date.
3. Enter all of the sales on account using the **Sales/Invoicing** option.
4. Record and apply any sales returns.
5. Process all of the cash receipts using the **Receipts** option.
6. Enter the purchases on account using the **Purchases/Receive Inventory** option.
7. Record and apply any purchases returns.
8. Process all of the cash payments with the **Payments** option.
9. Record the adjusting entries.
10. Print the following reports: General Journal, Purchases Journal, Cash Disbursements Journal, Sales Journal, and Cash Receipts Journal.
11. Proof your work.
12. Print the following reports: General Ledger, Vendor Ledgers, and Customer Ledgers.
13. Print a General Ledger Trial Balance.
14. Print an Income Statement.
15. Print a Statement of Retained Earnings.
16. Print a Balance Sheet.
17. Close the fiscal year.
18. Print a Post-Closing Trial Balance.
19. Answer the Analyze questions.
20. End the session.

Business Transactions: Kite Loft Inc. had the following transactions for the month of December.

Date	Transactions
Dec. 16	Received Invoice 410 from Reddi-Bright Manufacturing for merchandise purchased on account, $1,475.00.
16	Paid the quarterly federal income tax installment of $1,050.00, Check 610.
16	Issued Check 611 for $2,548.00 to Brad's Kites Ltd. In payment of Invoice 112 for $2,600.00 less discount of $52.00.
17	Paid the monthly salaries by issuing Check 612 for $4,750.00.
17	Purchased $80.00 of supplies from Taylor Office Suppliers on account, Invoice 830.
17	Received a check for $1,965.60 from Best Toys in payment of Sales Slip 479 for $2,003.40 less a cash discount of $37.80, Receipt 358.
19	Sold merchandise on account to Best Toys, $2,600.00 plus $156.00 sales tax, Sales slip 484.
19	Prepared Receipt 359 for a $1,716.00 check received from Lars' Specialties in payment of Sales Slip 480 for $1,749.00 less a $33.00 cash discount.
20	Purchased merchandise on account from Brad's Kites Ltd., Invoice 215, $1,560.00.
20	Wrote Check 613 to Creative Kites Inc. to apply on account, $375.00.
21	Prepared Credit Memorandum 44 for $106.00 for the return of $100.00 in merchandise by Best Toys, plus sales tax of $6.00.
23	Sold merchandise to Lars' Specialties on account, $1,580.00 plus sales tax of $94.80, Sales Slip 485.
23	Received a check from Serendipity Shop to apply on account, Receipt 360 for $300.00.
23	Paid Easy Glide Co. For Invoice 326 for $1,890.00 less a $37.80 discount, Check 614 for $1,852.20.
26	Received from The Toy Store a check for $1,102.40 in payment of Sales Slip 483 for $1,123.60 less a cash discount of $21.20, Receipt 361.
26	Returned defective merchandise purchased on account from Brad's Kites Ltd., $150.00, Debit Memorandum 28.
26	Received Invoice 335 from Easy Glide Co. for merchandise purchased on account totaling $1,630.00.
28	Wrote Check 615 for $120.00 to the *Daily Examiner* for a monthly advertisement.
28	Small Town Toys sent a check for $450.00 to apply on account, Receipt 362.
29	Paid Stars Kites Outlet $1,625.00 on account, Check 616.

Continued

ACCOUNTING ISSUES

THE GASB The principal purpose of the Governmental Accounting Standards Board (GASB) is to establish and improve standards of state and local governmental accounting and financial reporting. Their mission is to ensure that financial reporting provides useful information for users of financial reports and guides and educates the public reading those financial reports. The due process the GASB must follow before issuing its standards is stringent, and it encourages broad public participation in the standard-setting process.

Date	Transactions (cont.)
29	Sold to The Toy Store $1,990.00 of merchandise on account, plus $119.40 sales tax, Sales Slip 486.
30	Issued Check 617 to Reddi-Bright Manufacturing for $700.00 to apply on account.
30	Sold merchandise totaling $560.00 plus $33.60 sales tax to the Serendipity Shop on account, Sales Slip 487.
31	Recorded the bank service charge of $10.00 and the bankcard fee of $150.00, from December bank statement.
31	Paid transportation charges of $51.60 for merchandise shipped from Easy Glide Co., Check 618.
31	Recorded cash sales of $3,995.10 plus $239.71 in sales tax, Tape 41.
31	Recorded bankcard sales of $1,736.27 plus sales tax of $104.18, Tape 41.

Peachtree®

SMART GUIDE

TIP: To save time entering transactions, group them by type and then enter the transactions in batches.

TIP: Always verify the *G/L Account* field when you enter a purchases on account transaction.

TIP: You should back up your Peachtree files before you perform the year-end closing.

Analyze:

1. Which customer owes Kite Loft Inc. the most money at the end of December? How much do they owe?
2. On the cash receipts journal, what is the total amount of the **Cash in Bank** debit that will be posted to the general ledger?
3. On the work sheet, what is the Adjusted Trial Balance debit and credit column total?

SOLUTION NOTES

MINI PRACTICE SET 5

PAGES 726–729

Analyze:

1. Best Toys; $2,650.00
2. $25,878.14
3. $181,304.37

This is a representation of key resources available in the *Glencoe Accounting* program.

interNET CONNECTION

Use the following Web resources to introduce, reinforce, or stimulate discussion on unit topics.

- Case Studies
- Study Plans
- Career Corner
- Real-Life Applications
- Self-Assessment Quizzes
- Games for the Classroom
- Ethics and the Profession

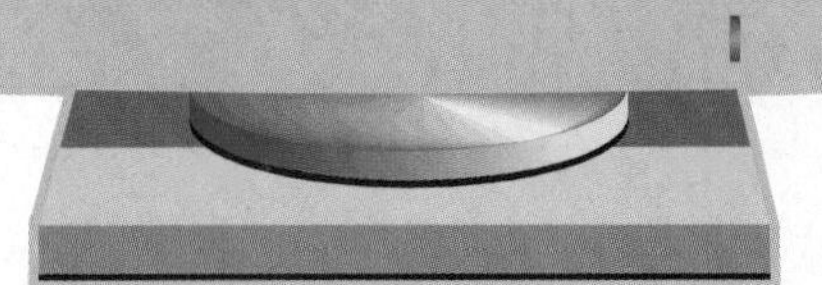

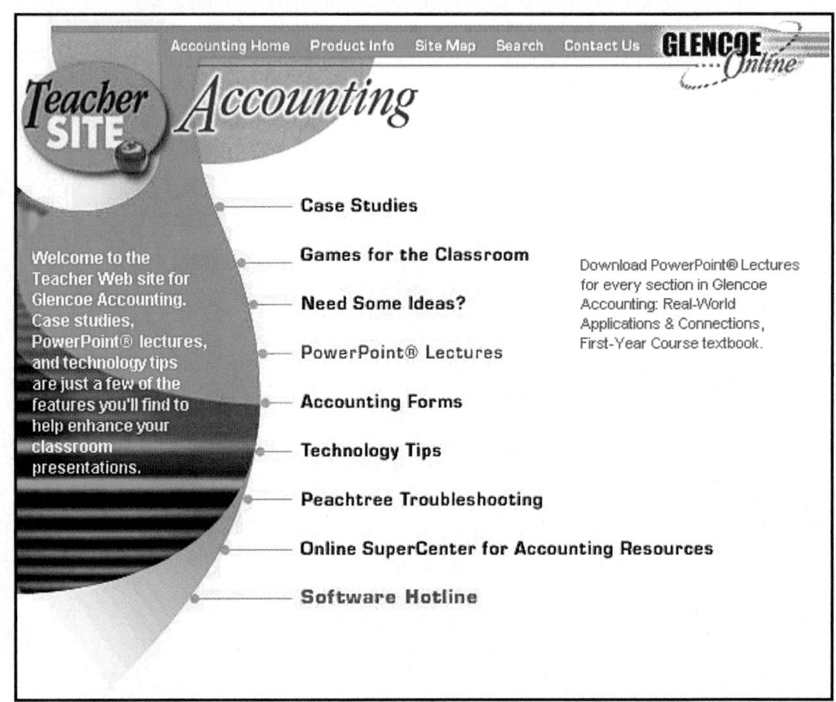

GLENCOE ACCOUNTING BULLETIN BOARD POSTER

Virtual Business® CD-ROM

Virtual Business **is a fully visual marketing and business simulation that lets students start and run their own business. For more information on the simulation, visit the teacher page on the** ***Glencoe Accounting*** **Web site.**

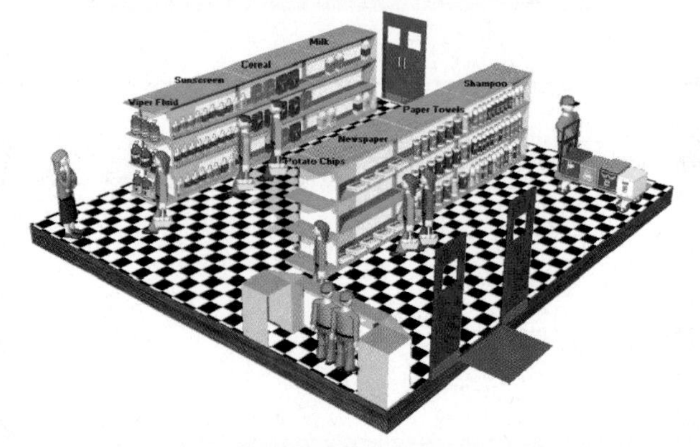

Accounting in Action

Unit Video Portfolio

Integrating *Electronic Field Trips* into Your Accounting Instruction

The *Electronic Field Trip* videos provide an excellent introduction to key accounting concepts taught in the textbook. You may want to use this video segment in **Unit 6.** The title of the video segment is:

- *Partnerships and Corporations*

Mini Practice Set

Fine Finishes

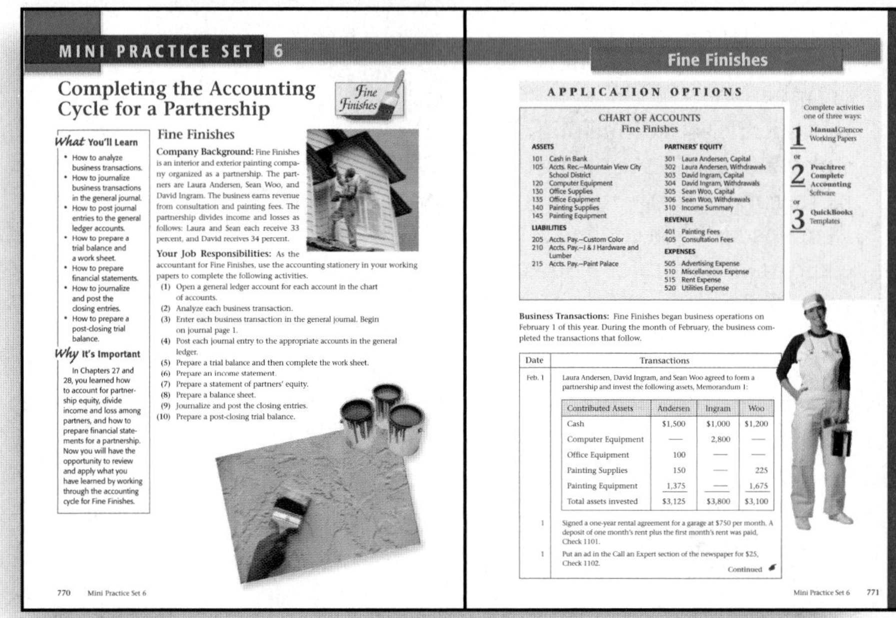

MINI PRACTICE SET 6

Completing the Accounting Cycle for a Partnership

What You'll Learn

- How to analyze business transactions.
- How to journalize business transactions in the general journal.
- How to post journal entries to the general ledger accounts.
- How to prepare a trial balance and a work sheet.
- How to prepare financial statements.
- How to journalize and post the closing entries.
- How to prepare a post-closing trial balance.

Why It's Important

In Chapters 27 and 28, you learned how to account for partnership equity, divide income and loss among partners, and how to prepare financial statements for a partnership. Now you will have the opportunity to review and apply what you have learned by working through the accounting cycle for Fine Finishes.

Fine Finishes

Company Background: Fine Finishes is an interior and exterior painting company organized as a partnership. The partners are Laura Andersen, Sean Woo, and David Ingram. The business earns revenue from consultation and painting fees. The partnership divides income and losses as follows: Laura and Sean each receive 33 percent, and David receives 34 percent.

Your Job Responsibilities: As the accountant for Fine Finishes, use the accounting stationery in your working papers to complete the following activities.

(1) Open a general ledger account for each account in the chart of accounts.
(2) Analyze each business transaction.
(3) Enter each business transaction in the general journal. Begin on journal page 1.
(4) Post each journal entry to the appropriate accounts in the general ledger.
(5) Prepare a trial balance and then complete the work sheet.
(6) Prepare an income statement.
(7) Prepare a statement of partners' equity.
(8) Prepare a balance sheet.
(9) Journalize and post the closing entries.
(10) Prepare a post-closing trial balance.

770 Mini Practice Set 6

Fine Finishes

APPLICATION OPTIONS

CHART OF ACCOUNTS
Fine Finishes

ASSETS
101 Cash in Bank
105 Accts. Rec.—Mountain View City School District
120 Computer Equipment
130 Office Supplies
135 Office Equipment
140 Painting Supplies
145 Painting Equipment

LIABILITIES
205 Accts. Pay.—Custom Color
210 Accts. Pay.—J & J Hardware and Lumber
215 Accts. Pay.—Paint Palace

PARTNERS' EQUITY
301 Laura Andersen, Capital
302 Laura Andersen, Withdrawals
303 David Ingram, Capital
304 David Ingram, Withdrawals
305 Sean Woo, Capital
306 Sean Woo, Withdrawals
310 Income Summary

REVENUE
401 Painting Fees
405 Consultation Fees

EXPENSES
505 Advertising Expense
510 Miscellaneous Expense
515 Rent Expense
520 Utilities Expense

Complete activities one of three ways:
1 **Manual** Glencoe Working Papers
or
2 **Peachtree Complete Accounting** Software
or
3 **QuickBooks** Templates

Business Transactions: Fine Finishes began business operations on February 1 of this year. During the month of February, the business completed the transactions that follow.

Date	Transactions
Feb. 1	Laura Andersen, David Ingram, and Sean Woo agreed to form a partnership and invest the following assets, Memorandum 1:

Contributed Assets	Andersen	Ingram	Woo
Cash	$1,500	$1,000	$1,200
Computer Equipment	—	2,800	—
Office Equipment	100	—	—
Painting Supplies	150	—	225
Painting Equipment	1,375	—	1,675
Total assets invested	$3,125	$3,800	$3,100

Date	Transactions
1	Signed a one-year rental agreement for a garage at $750 per month. A deposit of one month's rent plus the first month's rent was paid, Check 1101.
1	Put an ad in the Call an Expert section of the newspaper for $25, Check 1102.

Continued

Mini Practice Set 6 771

*Can be found after Chapter 28

Assessment and Evaluation

Unit 6 Test

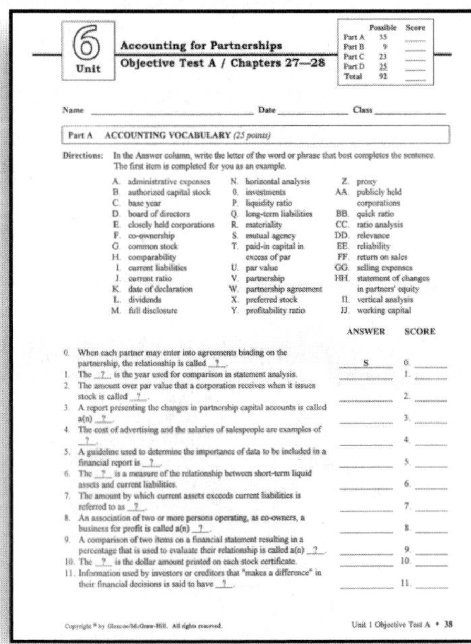

6 Unit

Accounting for Partnerships
Objective Test A / Chapters 27—28

	Possible	Score
Part A	35	___
Part B	9	___
Part C	23	___
Part D	25	___
Total	92	___

Name ______ Date ______ Class ______

Part A ACCOUNTING VOCABULARY *(25 points)*

Directions: In the Answer column, write the letter of the word or phrase that best completes the sentence. The first item is completed for you as an example.

A. administrative expenses
B. authorized capital stock
C. base year
D. board of directors
E. closely held corporations
F. co-ownership
G. common stock
H. comparability
I. current liabilities
J. current ratio
K. date of declaration
L. dividends
M. full disclosure
N. horizontal analysis
0. investments
P. liquidity ratio
Q. long-term liabilities
R. materiality
S. mutual agency
T. paid-in capital in excess of par
U. par value
V. partnership
W. partnership agreement
X. preferred stock
Y. profitability ratio
Z. proxy
AA. publicly held corporations
BB. quick ratio
CC. ratio analysis
DD. relevance
EE. reliability
FF. return on sales
GG. selling expenses
HH. statement of changes in partners' equity
II. vertical analysis
JJ. working capital

ANSWER SCORE

0. When each partner may enter into agreements binding on the partnership, the relationship is called _?_. S 0. ___
1. The _?_ is the year used for comparison in statement analysis. 1. ___
2. The amount over par value that a corporation receives when it issues stock is called _?_. 2. ___
3. A report presenting the changes in partnership capital accounts is called a(n) _?_. 3. ___
4. The cost of advertising and the salaries of salespeople are examples of _?_. 4. ___
5. A guideline used to determine the importance of data to be included in a financial report is _?_. 5. ___
6. The _?_ is a measure of the relationship between short-term liquid assets and current liabilities. 6. ___
7. The amount by which current assets exceeds current liabilities is referred to as _?_. 7. ___
8. An association of two or more persons operating, as co-owners, a business for profit is called a(n) _?_. 8. ___
9. A comparison of two items on a financial statement resulting in a percentage that is used to evaluate their relationship is called a(n) _?_. 9. ___
10. The _?_ is the dollar amount printed on each stock certificate. 10. ___
11. Information used by investors or creditors that "makes a difference" in their financial decisions is said to have _?_. 11. ___

Copyright © by Glencoe/McGraw-Hill. All rights reserved. Unit 1 Objective Test A • 38

Accounting Portfolio

Unit 6 Model Résumé

Student ______ Class ______ Instructor ______

Date Assigned ______ Date Completed ______

Unit 6 *Accounting Portfolio*

Model Resume

Most employers you contact will expect to see a resume. Resumes present a picture of you: your personal information (address, telephone number), work experience, education, activities, and personal or work references. Look at the sample resume below, then use the form on the next page to write your own resume.

Marcia Steiner
982 Johnson Road
Charlotte, NC 28206
(704) 844-9615

Career Objective: To work in a challenging position in the accounting or financial group for a major corporation.

Experience: *9/96 to present*
ACCOUNTING CLERK, The Marietta Corporation
1684 Lake Drive
Charlotte, NC 28217
(704) 882-4736
Part-time job keeping accounting records for the retail division; primary responsibilities are to maintain accounts payable accounts.
6/96 to 9/96
STOCKPERSON, BookSeller Factory Outlet
337 Mallard Crossing Mall
Charlotte, NC 28262
(704) 645-0611
Responsible for stocking and retrieving retail merchandise. Summer position.

Education: Jefferson Davis High School. Honor roll last three years, president of Business Professionals of America chapter, member of business program in computerized accounting.

Activities: Business Professionals of America, Youth for the Environment Club, National Honor Society, Volunteer for Walk for Hunger.

References: Mrs. Yolanda Morrison, 118 Hollow Tree Court, Charlotte, NC 28226
Marianne Watson, Walk for Hunger, 15 Rockwell Road, Charlotte, NC 28269

Copyright © Glencoe/McGraw-Hill Accounting Portfolio 40

Enrichment and Extension

Accounting Competitive Event Review

Student ______ Class ______ Instructor ______

Date Assigned ______ Date Completed ______

Accounting for Partnerships

In a partnership, two or more people agree to operate a business as co-owners. Partnerships are most often found in professional fields such as law and in small service businesses. Most business transactions are recorded in the same way by a proprietorship, a partnership, or a corporation. Differences arise in accounting for the partners' equity.

Accounting for a partnership also involves accounting for the income or loss of the business. There are many ways partners may divide income or loss. Usually, it is based on the services and capital contributed to the business.

For further information: See Chapters 27 and 28, First Year; Chapters 14 and 15, Advanced.

For additional practice: Additional Reinforcement Problems 27A and 28A.

On a separate sheet of paper, answer the following questions.

True/False

1. Each partner has unlimited liability for the debts of the partnership.
2. A partnership has a limited life. It ends with the death or withdrawal of a partner.
3. Any partner can make valid contracts for a partnership.
4. The general ledger of a partnership will include a single capital account, whose balance represents the combined equity of all partners.
5. If the assets of a sole proprietorship are to be transferred to a partnership at amounts different from those shown in the financial records of the proprietorship, any resulting gain or loss is shared equally by all of the partners.
6. On the balance sheet of a partnership, each partner's investment is shown in a separate capital account in the Partners' Equity section.
7. The agreement between the partners should include all provisions to which the partners have agreed.
8. The balance sheet of a partnership is very different from the balance sheet of a sole proprietorship.
9. The partners' equity accounts consist of separate capital accounts but only one withdrawals account.
10. When a partner invests noncash assets in the partnership, they are valued at their current market values.
11. A partnership can have only two owners.
12. Partners can divide partnership earnings in any manner they choose.
13. The persons who have agreed to form a partnership must file an application to operate with the state.

Multiple Choice

14. Federal income tax is levied (A) on a partnership based on its total net income, (B) on the partners for their individual shares of the reported partnership income, (C) on the partnership income and on the partners' share of the partnership income, (D) on the partners only when they make withdrawals from the partnership for personal use.
15. The entry to record the investment of cash in a partnership by one partner would consist of (A) a debit to the partner's capital account and a credit to Cash in Bank, (B) a debit to Cash

Copyright © Glencoe/McGraw-Hill Accounting Competitive Event Review • 51

Unit Objectives

1. Correctly use accounting terminology related to the partnership form of business organization.
2. Describe the accounting principles and practices applying to partnerships.
3. Demonstrate the recording of equity transactions for partners.
4. Report partnership information on financial statements.
5. Record entries needed to liquidate a partnership.

Unit 6 Contents

EXTENDING THE QUOTE

As a child, **Helen Keller** existed in a world without sight or sound. A remarkable teacher named Anne Sullivan helped Helen learn to communicate using sign language. With Anne's help, Helen attended school, eventually graduating with honors from Radcliffe College. Helen went on to become a world-famous author and lecturer, communicating with a world she could not see or hear.

UNIT 6

Accounting for Partnerships

In this unit. . .

You will learn how to keep accounting records for a business organized as a partnership. Although accounting for a partnership has many similarities to accounting for a sole proprietorship and a corporation, there are a few different procedures that must be applied as you record transactions for the partnership. You'll learn the procedures involved in accounting for partners' equity and in dividing net income or loss among the partners. You will explore the transactions of **Surfside Bike and Skate Rentals**, a service company owned by Molly Gill and Don Putman. Also in this unit, you will learn about ethics in the accounting profession.

Alone we can do so little;
together we can do so much.
—Helen Keller
American Lecturer with
Hearing and Visual Impairments

730

Great Ideas *From the Classroom of...*

Accounting Spell Down Ask students to analyze transactions and journal entries from a chapter problem in a "spell down" format. Choose a transaction from a chapter problem and then ask the students the following questions: What journal? Debit? Credit? Subsidiary ledger?, and so forth. Present a certificate to the winner.

Jerry Hawes
East Jordan High School
East Jordan, Michigan

OVERVIEW
UNIT 6

POWER READING STRATEGIES

To get the most out of your reading:

Predict what the section will be about.

Connect what you read with your own life.

Question as you read to make sure you understand the content.

Respond to what you've read.

In Your Journal . . .

A business partnership has many unique features and characteristics. It's an association of two or more persons to operate a business as co-owners. Imagine yourself in a couple of years. You and a friend are planning to open a business together.

1. What kind of business will it be?
2. What are the major characteristics of the partnership?
3. What are its advantages? Disadvantages?
4. When you are finished, discuss your responses with a partner in class.

In Your Journal. . .

Teacher Guidelines Have students add to their accounting portfolios by completing and including the *In Your Journal* writing activities. Ask for volunteers to share their answers to the questions. Have students discuss whether they would prefer to be sole proprietors, partners in a business, or employees of a small, medium-sized, or large business. Have students think about the advantages and disadvantages of each option and how their individual goals and personal interests might be used to decide which option is best for them. P

Previewing the Chapters

The three chapters in this unit focus on the accounting procedures that are specific to the partnership form of business organization and the role of ethics in accounting. In Chapter 27 students will learn characteristics of partnerships and how to record partnership data. Chapter 28 continues with financial statements and the liquidation of partnership assets. Chapter 29 introduces the study and application of ethics in accounting.

Tying to Previous Knowledge

Unit 6 expands on the concept of the private enterprise system introduced in Unit 1. Students learn characteristics of the partnership form of business organization, how to record financial information for a partnership from inception to liquidation, and the role of ethics in accounting.

BULLETIN BOARD

Glencoe Poster Teaching Tip

Studies of successful entrepreneurs show that they have certain traits that contribute to their success. Ask students what they think these traits might be. Then have them answer the questions on the poster to see if they think they are potential entrepreneurs.

CHAPTER 27 Resource Manager

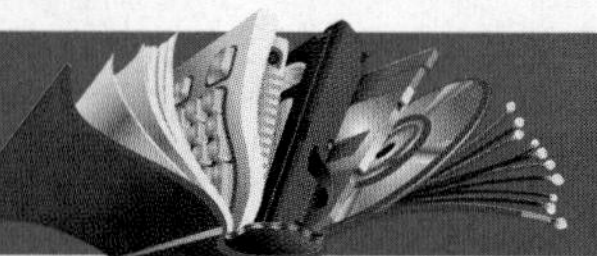

Section Resources

	Objectives & Standards	Activities & Features	Reproducible Masters
Chapter Opener *Introduction to Partnerships*	• Identify the characteristics of a partnership. • Identify the various accounting functions involved with a partnership. • Account for investments in a partnership. • Account for partners' withdrawals. • Allocate profits and losses to the partners by different methods. • Define the accounting terms introduced in this chapter. **National Standards for Business Education**: IA15, IA16, IIC1, IVA1, IVA2	Exploring the Real World of Business, p. 732 Workplace Connections, p. 733	School-to-Work Handbook
Section 1 *Partnership Equity*	• The characteristics of a partnership. • How to account for partners' investments. • How to account for partners' withdrawals.	Did You Know?, p. 734 Connect To, p. 735 Accounting Tips, p. 736 A Matter of Ethics, p. 737	Demonstration Problems Strategies for Teaching Ethics in Accounting
Section 2 *Division of Income and Loss*	• How to divide profits and losses equally. • How to divide profits and losses based on a fractional share. • How to divide profits and losses based on partners' investments.	International Accounting, p. 739 Accounting Flashbacks, p. 740 Calculator Hints, p. 741 Analyzing Financial Reports, p. 743	Demonstration Problems Strategies for Teaching International Accounting Math Review for Accounting Internet Resources and Activities Handbook

KEY

Posters · Blackline Masters · Transparency · CD-ROM · Software · Portfolio · Videocassette

MULTIMEDIA RESOURCE

Peachtree

- Problem 27–6 *Recording Investments of Partners*
- Problem 27–7 *Sharing Losses Based on Capital Balances*
- Problem 27–8 *Partners Withdrawals*
- Problem 27–9 *Preparing Closing Entries for a Partnership*

QuickBooks

- Problem 27–7 *Sharing Losses Based on Capital Balances*
- Problem 27–8 *Partners Withdrawals*

Spreadsheets

- Problem 27–5 *Calculating the Percentage of Each Partner's Capital Investment*

Videos

Video Segment: Partnerships and Corporations
After viewing this video, students will be able to describe the organizational differences between partnerships and corporations. Have students list the major advantages and disadvantages of partnerships.

CD-ROMs

Electronic Learning Center (ELC), Chapter 27
This program is ideal for visual learners since it incorporates video images, animation, and graphics to enliven the content of each lesson.

Interactive Lesson Planner (ILP), Chapter 27
This CD-ROM combines the versatility of an electronic lesson planner with the convenience of teacher classroom resources.

SCANS Correlation Chart

FOUNDATION SKILLS

Basic Skills:	Reading	Writing	Math	Listening	Speaking	
Thinking Skills:	Creative Thinking	Decision Making	Problem Solving	Seeing Things in the Mind's Eye	Knowing How to Learn	Reasoning
Personal Qualities:	Responsibility	Self-Esteem	Sociability	Self-Management	Integrity/Honesty	

WORKPLACE COMPETENCIES

Resources:	Allocating Time	Allocating Money	Allocating Material and Facility Resources	Allocating Human Resources		
Information:	Acquiring and Evaluating Information	Organizing and Maintaining Information	Interpreting and Communicating Information	Using Computers to Process Information		
Interpersonal Skills:	Participating as a Member of a Team	Teaching Others	Serving Clients/ Customers	Exercising Leadership	Negotiating to Arrive at a Decision	Working with Cultural Diversity
Systems:	Understanding Systems	Monitoring and Correcting Performance	Improving and Designing Systems			
Technology:	Selecting Technology	Applying Technology to Task	Maintaining and Troubleshooting Technology			

*Highlighted blocks indicate areas covered in the chapter. Additional SCANS skills are also covered throughout the *Teacher Wraparound Edition.*

Assessment

Student Edition
- Check Your Understanding, pp. 738, 744
- Chapter 27 Problems, pp. 749–751

Assessment and Evaluation Masters
- Chapter 27 Study Plan, *Glencoe Workbook*
- Chapter 27 Self-Test, *Glencoe Workbook*
- Chapter 27 Test, *Chapter Tests* Booklet
- Chapter 27 Activity, *School-to-Work Handbook*
- Chapter 27 **Exam***View*

Teacher Wraparound Edition
- Critical Thinking Activity, p. 742
- Reteaching Section 1, p. 738
- Reteaching Section 2, p. 744
- Chapter 27 Quiz, p. 745

Transparencies

	Teaching Transparencies	Solution Transparencies
Section 1:	27–1, 27–2, 27–3	Problem 27–1
Section 2:	27–4	Problems 27–2, 27–3
End of Chapter:		Problems 27–4, 27–5, 27–6, 27–7, 27–8, 27–9, 27–10

TEACHER CLASSROOM RESOURCES

This is a representation of key blackline masters available in the Teacher Classroom Resources.

Teaching Aids

Transparency Examples

Section Focus Transparencies

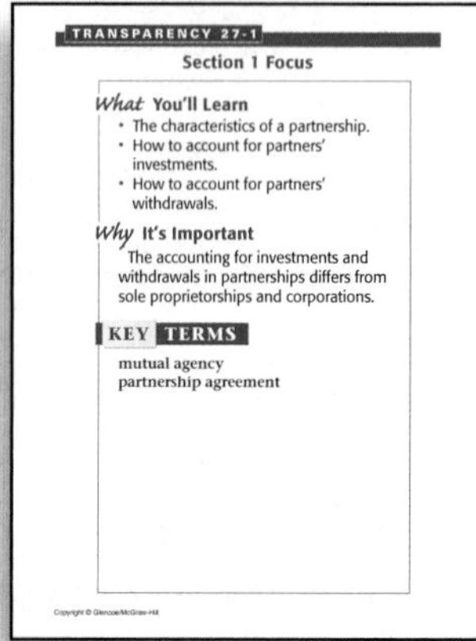

TRANSPARENCY 27-1

Section 1 Focus

What You'll Learn
- The characteristics of a partnership.
- How to account for partners' investments.
- How to account for partners' withdrawals.

Why It's Important

The accounting for investments and withdrawals in partnerships differs from sole proprietorships and corporations.

KEY TERMS

mutual agency
partnership agreement

Teaching Transparencies

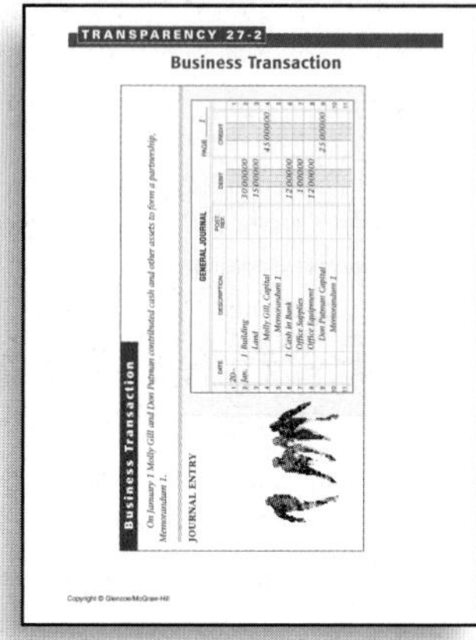

TRANSPARENCY 27-2

Business Transaction

Teaching Transparencies

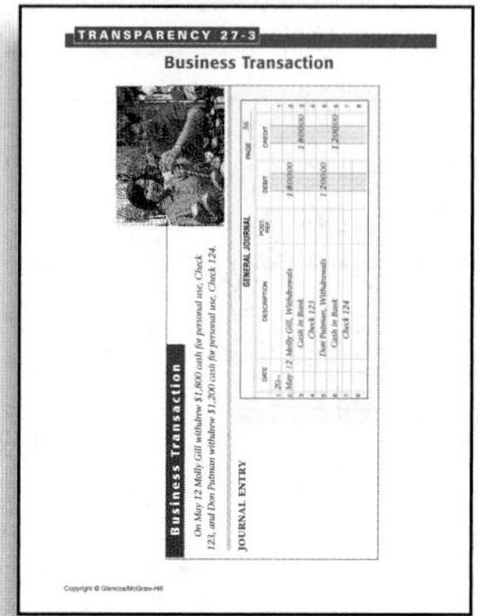

TRANSPARENCY 27-3

Business Transaction

Solution Transparencies

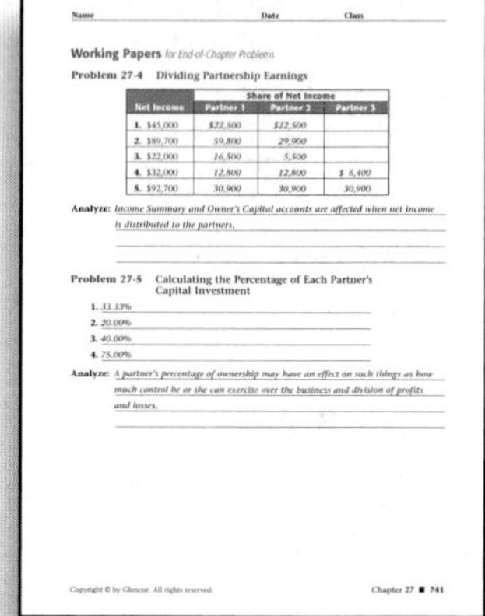

Working Papers for End-of-Chapter Problems

Problem 27-4 Dividing Partnership Earnings

Problem 27-5 Calculating the Percentage of Each Partner's Capital Investment

Demonstration Problems

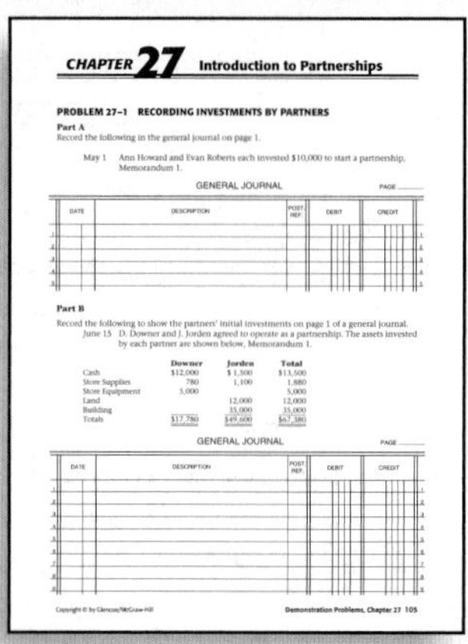

CHAPTER 27 Introduction to Partnerships

PROBLEM 27-1 RECORDING INVESTMENTS BY PARTNERS

GENERAL JOURNAL

Lesson Plans

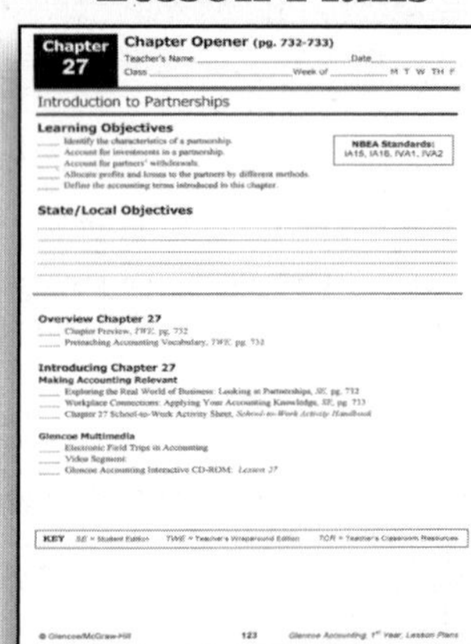

Chapter 27 Chapter Opener (pg. 732-733)

Introduction to Partnerships

Learning Objectives

State/Local Objectives

Overview Chapter 27

Introducing Chapter 27

Glencoe Multimedia

Block Scheduling

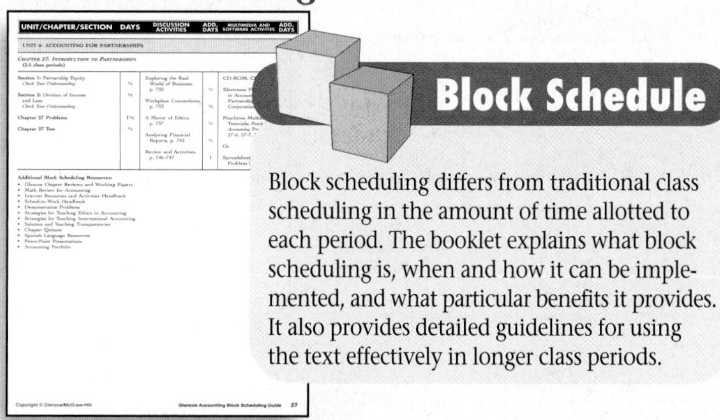

Block Schedule

Block scheduling differs from traditional class scheduling in the amount of time allotted to each period. The booklet explains what block scheduling is, when and how it can be implemented, and what particular benefits it provides. It also provides detailed guidelines for using the text effectively in longer class periods.

Enrichment and Application

Strategies for Teaching Ethics in Accounting

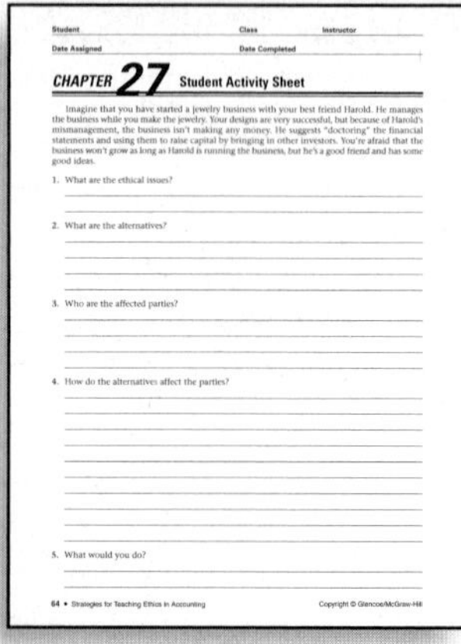

CHAPTER 27 Student Activity Sheet

1. What are the ethical issues?
2. What are the alternatives?
3. Who are the affected parties?
4. How do the alternatives affect the parties?
5. What would you do?

Strategies for Teaching International Accounting

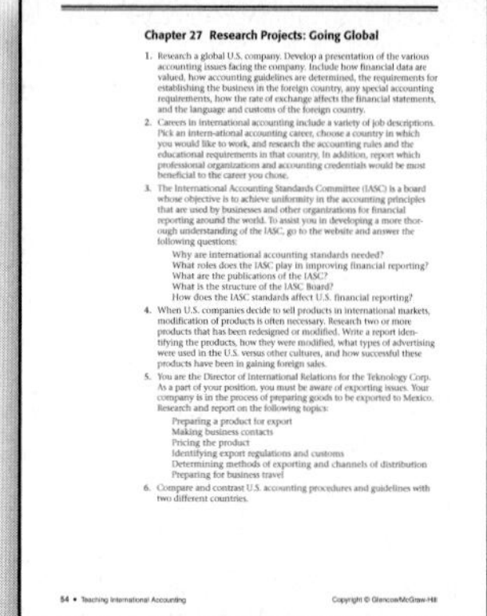

Chapter 27 Research Projects: Going Global

School-to-Work Handbook

CHAPTER 27 SCHOOL-TO-WORK ACTIVITY

Introduction to Partnerships

Meeting Different Ability Levels

Chapter Reviews and Working Papers (CRWP)

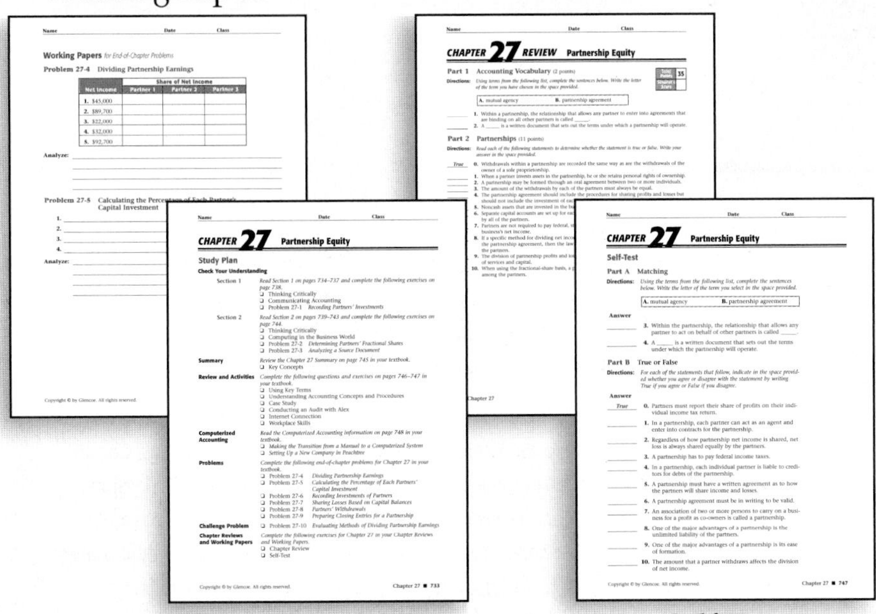

Real-World Multimedia CD-ROM

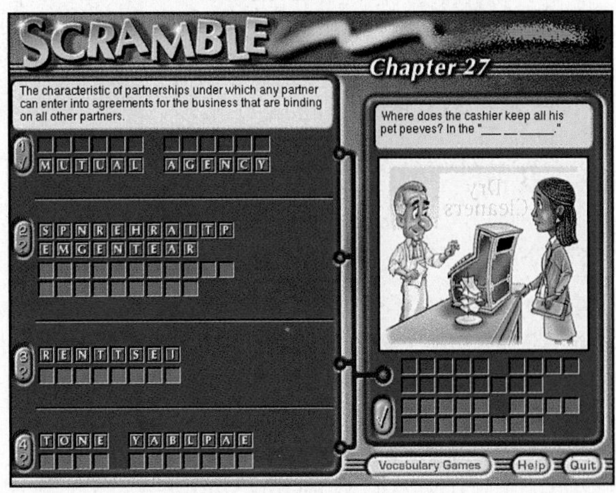

Key to Ability Levels

Each section gives skill-building activities. Each activity has been labeled for use with students of various learning styles and abilities.

L1 Level 1 activities are basic activities and should be within the range of all students.

L2 Level 2 activities are average activities and should be within the range of average and above average students.

L3 Level 3 activities are challenging activities designed for the ability range of above average students.

ELL ELL activities should be within the ability range of English Language Learners.

Teaching Resources at a Glance

Application Resources

- Glencoe Chapter Review and Working Papers, SE and TAE
- School-to-Work Handbook, SE and TM
- Accounting Portfolio, SE and TM

Reproducible Masters

- Demonstration Problems
- Lesson Plans
- Block Scheduling
- Spanish Language Resources

Glencoe Accounting Professional Development Series

- Strategies for Teaching Ethics in Accounting
- Accounting Competitive Event Review
- Math Review for Accounting
- Strategies for Teaching International Accounting
- Internet Resources and Activities Handbook

Transparency Package

- Section Focus Transparencies
- Teaching Transparencies
- Source Document Transparencies
- Solution Transparencies

Performance Assessment

- **Exam***View* CD-ROM
- Chapter Tests
- Chapter Quizzes
- Unit Tests
- Audit Tests
- Printed Testbank

Multimedia Resources

- Electronic Learning Center:
  - Multimedia CD-ROMs
  - Peachtree software, tutorials, templates, and solutions
  - Spreadsheet templates
- Using QuickBooks with Glencoe Accounting
- Interactive Lesson Planner
- Electronic Field Trips in Accounting
- PowerPoint Presentation
- Web site: glencoeaccounting.glencoe.com

Assessment and Evaluation

Chapter Tests

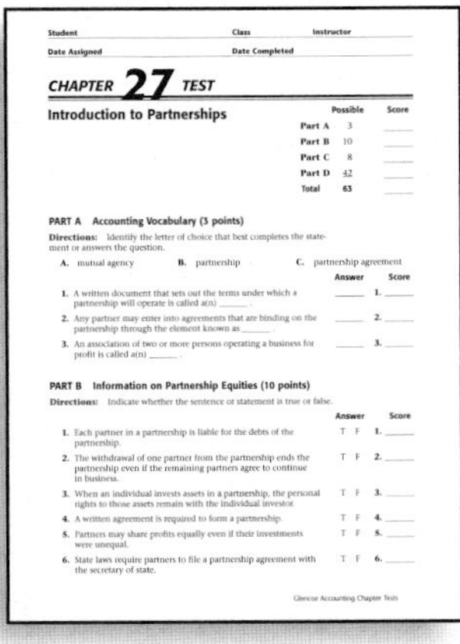

Chapter Quiz

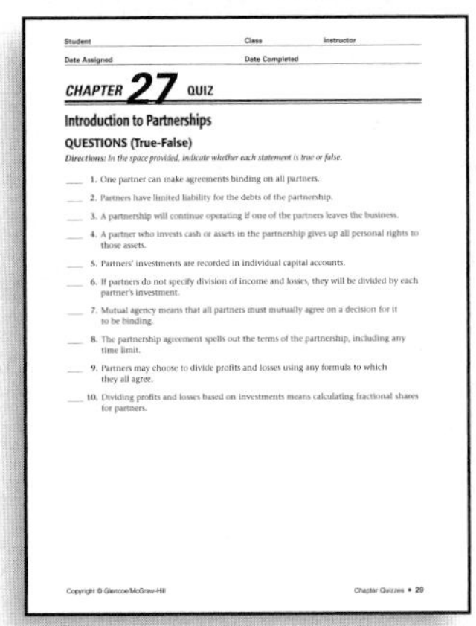

OVERVIEW CHAPTER 27

Correlations to National Standards for Business Education

(See pages T50–T51 for a detailed correlation chart.)

Standards: IA15, IA16, IIC1, IVA1, IVA2

Chapter Preview

In this chapter students learn what a partnership is, its advantages and disadvantages, and the entries needed to record partners' equity. Students also learn how to record the division of net income and losses between partners.

Section Overviews

- Section 1—*Partnership Equity*
- Section 2—*Division of Income and Loss*

Chapter Vocabulary

mutual agency
partnership agreement

Preteaching Accounting Vocabulary

Oral Exercise: Ask for volunteers to explain the meaning of each term. Then discuss the terms in relation to accounting for partnerships. L1

CHAPTER 27

Introduction to Partnerships

Learning Objectives

When you have completed this chapter, you will be able to:

- Identify the characteristics of a partnership.
- Identify the various accounting functions involved with a partnership.
- Account for investments in a partnership.
- Account for partners' withdrawals.
- Allocate profits and losses to the partners by different methods.
- Define the accounting terms introduced in this chapter.

Exploring the Real World of Business

LOOKING AT PARTNERSHIPS

Does the name Edward Teach ring a bell? Better known as Blackbeard the Pirate, he was notorious for raiding the East Coast of America in the early 1700s. The wreck of Blackbeard's flagship, *Queen Anne's Revenge,* was recently discovered off the coast of North Carolina. The ship had been lying in the North Carolina waters since it sank in 1718. Among the items found in the shipwreck are a bronze bell dating from 1709, the brass barrel of a blunderbuss, a cannonball, and several cannons.

The search and recovery of Blackbeard's ship is a partnership venture between the state of North Carolina and a private research firm, **Intersal,** that specializes in excavating historic shipwrecks. **Intersal** became interested in *Queen Anne's Revenge* after an eyewitness account of the ship's sinking was found in historical archives in London. This partnership between **Intersal** and North Carolina will last for the length of time it takes **Intersal** to excavate the wreck and recover the ship's artifacts.

What do you think?

What other types of partnerships can you name?

Intersal

Exploring the Real World of Business

Intersal

As they explore the wreck of the *Queen Anne's Revenge,* Intersal's divers keep a log of the artifacts they find. Working with representatives of the North Carolina Department of Cultural Resources, the divers have recovered artifacts that will be displayed in the North Carolina Maritime Museum.

What do you think? (Answers)

Professionals such as CPAs, doctors, lawyers, and architects often organize as partnerships. Businesses may also form temporary partnerships to work on projects, such as a software company working with a movie company to produce an interactive video.

Workplace Connections

Applying Your Accounting Knowledge

Going into business with someone else can be smart when two or more people have complementary business skills and resources that can help a business succeed. Business partners should agree about each person's responsibility in the business and how profits and losses will be shared. In this chapter, you'll learn how a defined partnership agreement helps avoid conflict and benefits the smooth operation of the business.

Investigate:

1. As an employee, you agree to follow the employer's rules. What are some rules in your workplace?
2. How do they help you and your co-workers avoid conflict?
3. If conflicts occur, how are they resolved?

Glencoe Accounting Online

Visit the *Glencoe Accounting* Web site at **glencoeaccounting.glencoe.com** for additional activities and information.

INTRODUCING CHAPTER 27

Making Accounting Relevant

Workplace Connections: Applying Your Accounting Knowledge

Discussion: Business partners often bring different skills and experience to the partnership. For example, one partner might have marketing and sales experience while another has financial and management experience. The combination of skills can help the business be successful.

Investigate (Answers)

1. Answers may vary. Many employers have a policy manual setting out rules employees are expected to follow. Rules might include working hours, holidays, or procedures for handling specific job tasks.
2. Answers may vary. Rules help prevent conflict because employees know what is expected of them.
3. Answers will vary. Some managers prefer to have employees work out conflict themselves; others prefer to help resolve issues causing the conflict.

School-to-Work Activity

Student ____ Class ____ Instructor ____

Date Assigned ____ Date Completed ____

CHAPTER 27 SCHOOL-TO-WORK ACTIVITY

Introduction to Partnerships

Name of work site: ____

Name of work site mentor: ____

Title or position of mentor: ____

As you know, a partnership is an association of two or more persons to operate, as co-owners, a business for profit. Any type of business may be organized as a partnership, although some types are more common than others. Consult with your work site mentor or one of the owners to complete the following investigation of your company's organization as a partnership. (Consult with your teacher about how to proceed with this chapter if you do NOT work for a partnership.)

After completing this school-to-work investigation, you will be able to:

- discuss the advantages and disadvantages of your company being organized as a partnership, and
- describe the general characteristics of your company's partnership agreement.

1. A partnership has certain characteristics. They include ease of formation, unlimited liability, limited life, mutual agency, and co-ownership of partnership property.

1a. Why was the company organized as a partnership?

1b. What do the owners see as the advantages and disadvantages of their business being a partnership?

Advantages: ____

Disadvantages: ____

GLENCOE MULTIMEDIA

Electronic Field Trips in Accounting *Video Segment: Partnerships and Corporations*

After viewing this video, students will be able to describe the organizational differences between partnerships and corporations and list the major advantages and disadvantages of both.

Glencoe Accounting: Electronic Learning Center *Chapter 27*

The CD-ROM program is ideal for visual learners since it incorporates video images, animation, and graphics to enliven the content of each lesson.

1 FOCUS

Introducing the Section
In this section students will learn the characteristics of a partnership, the advantages and disadvantages of this form of business organization, how to record the equity invested by partners, and how to account for withdrawals each partner may make.

Section Concepts
- The characteristics of a partnership.
- How to account for partners' investments.
- How to account for partners' withdrawals.

Visual Learning

Section 1 Focus
 Use **Transparency 27–1** to introduce section concepts.

BELL RINGER

Compare and Contrast: Ask students to create a table with two columns. In column 1 they are to write a list of the characteristics of a sole proprietorship. In column 2 they are to write a list of the characteristics of partnerships. Have students share their tables and discuss how a partnership differs from a sole proprietorship. You may also want to do this as a group exercise and write the table on the chalkboard. L1

SECTION 1

Partnership Equity

***What* You'll Learn**
- The characteristics of a partnership.
- How to account for partners' investments.
- How to account for partners' withdrawals.

***Why* It's Important**
The accounting for investments and withdrawals in partnerships differs from sole proprietorships and corporations.

KEY TERMS
mutual agency
partnership agreement

As you learned in Chapter 2, a partnership is an association of two or more persons to operate, as co-owners, a business for profit. Any type of business may be organized as a partnership. For example, Intersal is a company that salvages historic shipwrecks. Intersal entered into a partnership with the state of North Carolina to salvage the *Queen Anne's Revenge*, Blackbeard's ship. Partnerships, however, are more common in businesses that provide professional services. For example, accounting and legal firms are often organized as partnerships. Each partner can have his or her own clients, yet share with the other partners the expenses of operating an office.

Characteristics of a Partnership

The partnership form of business organization has certain unique features. Let's look at some of them.

Ease of Formation

Like a sole proprietorship, there are no special legal requirements that must be met to form a partnership. A partnership is automatically formed when two or more persons agree to operate as partners. A partnership is a voluntary arrangement. No one can be forced into a partnership or required to continue as a partner.

Unlimited Liability

Each partner is *personally* liable for the debts of the partnership. This means that if the partnership's creditors cannot be paid out of the assets of the partnership, a partner's personal assets may be used to pay the partnership's debts.

Limited Life

A partnership may end for a number of reasons, including death, withdrawal, bankruptcy, or incapacity of any partner. A partnership may also end when the project for which the partnership was formed is completed, or when the time period set by the partners has expired. For example, two architects may agree to combine their talents to design and oversee the construction of a building. When the building is completed, the partnership is dissolved.

Did You Know?

Shipwrecks
Perhaps the most famous shipwreck ever found was that of the *Titanic.* The salvage company RMS Titanic, Inc., has spent over $25 million collecting over 6,000 Titanic artifacts from the site of the shipwreck.

RESOURCE MANAGER

Reproducible Masters
- Lesson Plans
- Chapter Reviews and Working Papers (CRWP) TAE
- Demonstration Problems

Transparencies
- Section Focus Transparency
- Teaching Transparencies
- Source Document Transparencies
- Solution Transparencies

Multimedia
- Exam*View* CD-ROM
- Electronic Learning Center CD-ROM
- Interactive Lesson Planner CD-ROM
- Electronic Field Trips in Accounting

Mutual Agency

Each partner is an agent of the partnership. In other words, any partner can, in the name of the firm, enter into agreements that are binding on all other partners. This relationship is known as **mutual agency**.

Co-ownership of Partnership Property

When a partner invests assets in the partnership, he or she gives up all personal rights of ownership. All of the partnership assets are co-owned by the partners.

Advantages and Disadvantages of a Partnership

One of the most important advantages of a partnership is that it provides the opportunity to bring together the abilities, experiences, and resources of two or more individuals. A partnership is easy to form; the only requirement is the agreement of the partners. Members of a partnership are usually able to make decisions without holding a formal meeting of the partners. Although a partnership must have a legal purpose, there are few other restrictions. Finally, federal and state income taxes are not levied against the partnership. Each partner pays personal income taxes on his or her share of the net income of the business.

There are, of course, disadvantages to the partnership form. As discussed earlier, a partnership has a limited life, each partner is personally liable for the debts of the partnership, and all partners may be held responsible for the decisions of one partner. In addition, a partner cannot transfer his or her interest in the partnership without the consent of the other partners. The ability to work together without major disagreements, however, may be the greatest test of the partnership form of organization.

The Partnership Agreement

A partnership may be formed when two or more individuals orally agree to operate a business as co-owners. However, it is advisable to have a written partnership agreement. A **partnership agreement** is a document that sets out the terms under which the partnership will operate. There is no standard form for a partnership agreement. It should, however, include the following types of information:

1. the name and address of each partner
2. the name, location, and nature of the partnership
3. the date of the agreement and the length of time the partnership is to exist
4. the investment of each partner
5. the duties, rights, and responsibilities of each partner
6. the amount of withdrawals allowed each partner
7. the procedure for sharing profits and losses
8. the procedure for distributing assets when the partnership is dissolved

Each partner should sign the agreement.

CONNECT TO . . . CIVICS

On April 2, 1792, an act of Congress created the United States Mint and established the national coinage system. Supervision of the mint was delegated to the secretary of state, but the mint became an independent agency in 1799 and a bureau of the Treasury Department in 1873.

2 TEACH

GUIDED PRACTICE

Reading Accounting

- Obtain a copy of a sample partnership agreement and have students read and summarize the key points. L1
- If possible, identify local ethnic businesses that are organized as partnerships. Have students interview the business owners in their first language to learn about the partnership. ELL

Concept Development: Characteristics of a Partnership

Discussion: Discuss each characteristic of a partnership and explain why each is an advantage or disadvantage to this form of business organization. L1

Concept Development: The Partnership Agreement

Discussion: Most people who form partnerships should have a written agreement spelling out what each partner is to do and how the earnings or losses are to be divided. Such agreements help to avoid future conflict. L1

INTERDISCIPLINARY CONNECTIONS ACTIVITY

Civics The first U.S. coins were minted at the Philadelphia Mint in 1793. The coins were silver half-*dismes* and *dismes*. Dismes was how the modern word *dime* was then spelled. Coins are still in use today, and their production is based on demand. Federal Reserve banks determine demand and then request additional coins through the Bureau of the Mint. After minting, the coins are shipped directly to the Federal Reserve banks.

CHAPTER 27
SECTION 1, PAGES 734–738

2 TEACH (Cont'd.)

Teaching Tip
Of the three types of business organization discussed in this textbook, the partnership is the least common—probably because it is more difficult for two or more people to agree on how a business is to be run. In addition, mutual agency often makes the partnership less acceptable to those who do not want to be bound by others' decisions.

Concept Development: Accounting for Partners' Equity

Discussion: Compare the recording of an investment in a partnership to the recording of the same investment in a sole proprietorship and a corporation. Point out that sales, expenses, purchases, cash receipts and payments, cost of merchandise sold, assets, and liabilities do not differ from one form of business organization to another. The major differences have to do only with the recording of business ownership, or equity. L1

Visual Learning

Business Transaction
Display **Transparency 27–2** to review the general journal entry to record the equity invested by each partner in the business. You may want to use T accounts on the chalkboard to show how each capital account is affected.

Demonstration Problem Step-by-Step Practice
Use demonstration problem 27–1 to give students practice in analyzing and recording investments by partners.

Key Points

Partnership Accounts
In a partnership, there are separate capital and withdrawals accounts for each partner.

ACCOUNTING TIPS

Withdrawals
A partnership rewards partners in the form of partnership profits. Partners are not paid as employees of the business. Instead, active partners withdraw money on a weekly or monthly basis in anticipation of their share of annual profits.

Accounting for Partners' Equity

After completing this chapter and Chapter 28, you will be able to identify the various accounting functions involved with a partnership.

Accounting for owners' equity for a partnership is basically the same as for a sole proprietorship. While a sole proprietorship has only one capital account, a partnership has two or more capital accounts. A separate capital account is set up for each partner to record that partner's investment in the business. Each partner also has a separate withdrawals account.

Recording the Investments of the Partners

When a partnership is formed, the value of cash and other assets invested by each partner is listed in the partnership agreement. Separate entries are then made to record each partner's investment in the business. Let's look at an example.

On January 1 Molly Gill and Don Putman agree to form a partnership to operate a business. The name of the partnership is Surfside Bike & Skate Rentals. Each partner agrees to invest the following assets in the new business.

	Gill	Putman
Cash		$12,000
Office supplies		1,000
Office equipment (market value)		12,000
Building (market value)	$30,000	
Land	15,000	
Total assets invested	$45,000	$25,000

When assets other than cash are invested in a partnership, the asset accounts are debited for the market value of the assets.

Business Transaction

On January 1 Molly Gill and Don Putman contributed cash and other assets to form a partnership, Memorandum 1.

JOURNAL ENTRY

GENERAL JOURNAL — PAGE 1

	DATE		DESCRIPTION	POST. REF.	DEBIT	CREDIT	
1	20--						1
2	Jan.	1	Building		30 000 00		2
3			Land		15 000 00		3
4			Molly Gill, Capital			45 000 00	4
5			Memorandum 1				5
6		1	Cash in Bank		12 000 00		6
7			Office Supplies		1 000 00		7
8			Office Equipment		12 000 00		8
9			Don Putman, Capital			25 000 00	9
10			Memorandum 1				10
11							11

Great Ideas *From the Classroom of...*

Analyzing a Partnership Amanda and Lorenzo were partners who started from nothing, built their business together, and worked hard to make the business grow. The death of Lorenzo ended the business, and Lorenzo's will leaves everything to his wife. Now an accountant tells Amanda there was never a partnership. Everything was in Lorenzo's name and Amanda's was not even on the bank statements. What did Amanda do wrong? (She made the mistake of not creating a written agreement, and she waited too long to find an accountant and a lawyer to advise her.)

F. Barry Haber
Fayetteville State University
Fayetteville, North Carolina

Recording Additional Investments

Any additional investments by the partners are recorded in a similar manner. For example, in April each partner agreed to invest $5,000 cash in the business. **Cash in Bank** is debited for $10,000 and the two partners' capital accounts are credited for $5,000 each.

Recording Withdrawals by the Partners

During the year partners may withdraw cash or other assets for personal use, according to the terms of the partnership agreement. The amount of the withdrawal is debited to the partner's withdrawals account and credited to the appropriate asset account. The amounts withdrawn by the partners do not have to be equal.

Key Points

Partnership Investments When a partner invests noncash assets in the business, they are recorded in the partnership accounts at the market value of the assets.

Business Transaction

On May 12 Molly Gill withdrew $1,800 cash for personal use, Check 123, and Don Putman withdrew $1,200 cash for personal use, Check 124.

JOURNAL ENTRY

GENERAL JOURNAL — PAGE 36

	DATE		DESCRIPTION	POST. REF.	DEBIT	CREDIT	
1	20--						1
2	May	12	Molly Gill, Withdrawals		1 800 00		2
3			Cash in Bank			1 800 00	3
4			Check 123				4
5			Don Putman, Withdrawals		1 200 00		5
6			Cash in Bank			1 200 00	6
7			Check 124				7
8							8

A MATTER OF ETHICS

Partner Loyalty

Imagine that you have started a jewelry business with your best friend Harold. He manages the business while you make the jewelry. Your designs are very successful, but because of Harold's mismanagement, the business isn't making any money. He suggests "doctoring" the financial statements and using them to raise capital by bringing in other investors. You're afraid that the business won't grow as long as Harold is running the business, but he's a good friend and has some good ideas.

Ethical Decision Making:

- What are the ethical issues?
- What are the alternatives?
- Who are the affected parties?
- How do the alternatives affect the parties?
- What would you do?

2 TEACH (Cont'd.)

Teaching Tips

Remind students that once assets are invested in the business, they are owned by the partnership, not the individual partners.

When partners invest items other than cash, asset values are usually agreed to by the partners. Old book values need not be used, except for tax purposes.

Visual Learning

Business Transaction

Use **Transparency 27–3** to discuss the withdrawal of cash from the business by each of the partners. Use T accounts on the chalkboard to show the effect of the withdrawals on each partner's withdrawals account. Also review the effect of withdrawals on the partners' capital accounts.

Demonstration Problem Step-by-Step Practice

Use demonstration problem 27–2 to give students practice in analyzing and recording withdrawals by partners.

Strategies for Teaching Ethics in Accounting

Photocopy the Chapter 27 *Student Activity Sheet* for students. Answers are also provided in the booklet.

Teaching A MATTER OF ETHICS

Partner Loyalty Have students discuss the meaning of loyalty. Ask them questions such as these: Are they obligated to be loyal to a friend even when the friend wants to do something dishonest? Should they be loyal even if their loyalty results in significant personal or business costs? Ask students to suggest ways the business might be saved other than creating false (and illegal) accounting records. For example, Harold might take a management course or turn to professional mentors, such as members of SCORE, for help.

3 ASSESS

Thinking Critically (Answers)

1. A separate capital account is set up for each partner to record that partner's investment in the business.
2. Noncash assets are recorded at market value; asset accounts are debited and the contributing partner's capital account is credited.

Communicating Accounting (Answers)

Answers will vary. Students' agreements should include the points listed on page 735.

Problem 27-1 (Answers)

June 1: Dr. Cash in Bank $1,200, Accts. Rec. $2,000, Merch. Inv. $8,000, Equip. $5,000, Van $12,000, Off. Furn. $1,000; Cr. Matthew Deck, Capital $29,200; Memo 1

June 1: Dr. Cash in Bank $2,300, Accts. Rec. $7,000, Merch. Inv. $5,000, Equip. $12,000, Off. Furn. $500; Cr. Jennifer Rusk, Capital $26,800; Memo 1

Chapter Reviews and Working Papers Refer students to the Chapter 27 workbook pages to answer *Check Your Understanding* activities.

4 CLOSE

Section Wrap-Up

Writing: Have students write a paragraph describing the characteristics of a partnership and giving reasons why they would or would not start a business with a partner. L1

SECTION 1 Check Your Understanding

Now that you have studied this section, complete the following questions and problem.

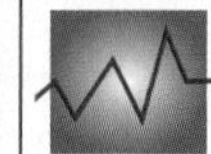

Thinking Critically

1. How is the owners' equity account set up for a partnership?
2. When a partner invests noncash assets in a business, describe how the investment is recorded in the accounting records.

Communicating Accounting

Choose a classmate and discuss a partnership for a business the two of you would like to own and operate. Use your creativity and spell out the details. Prepare a partnership agreement. Include details about what each partner will contribute to the business. Be sure the partners sign the agreement to make it a legal and binding document.

Problem 27–1 Recording Partners' Investments

On June 1 Matthew Deck and Jennifer Rusk agree to combine their sole proprietorships into a new business, Dreamscapes Catering, organized as a partnership. The partnership will take over all the assets of the two proprietorships. The assets invested by Deck and Rusk are listed below.

Instructions Prepare the journal entries required to record the investment by each partner. Use page 1 of the general journal in your working papers. The source document is Memorandum 1.

Investments	Deck	Rusk
Cash	$ 1,200	$ 2,300
Accounts receivable	2,000	7,000
Merchandise	8,000	5,000
Equipment	5,000	12,000
Van	12,000	– –
Office Furniture	1,000	500

RETEACHING SECTION 1

Recording Additional Investments of Capital Ask a student to name the accounts debited and credited when Chris Chan invests $15,000 in a sole proprietorship. (Cash in Bank is debited for $15,000 and Chris Chan, Capital is credited for $15,000.) Then ask another student to name the accounts debited and credited if Chris Chan invests $9,000 and Kim Swartz invests $6,000 in a partnership. (Cash in Bank is debited for $15,000; Chris Chan, Capital is credited for $9,000; and Kim Swartz, Capital is credited for $6,000.)

Division of Income and Loss

At the end of each accounting period, the net income or net loss from partnership operations is divided among the partners. Partners may divide the income or loss among themselves in any way they choose. The specific method should be defined in the partnership agreement. If it is not, the law provides that net income or net loss be divided equally among the partners.

What You'll Learn

- How to divide profits and losses equally.
- How to divide profits and losses based on a fractional share.
- How to divide profits and losses based on partners' investments.

Why It's Important

Partnership profits and losses are divided among the partners according to the partnership agreement.

Dividing Profits and Losses

There are many ways for partners to divide profits and losses. The division is generally based on the services and capital contributed by the partners to the partnership. For example, if the partners share equally in the work of the business, but one partner has invested more capital, it seems only fair that the one who has invested more should profit more.

When the profits of the accounting period are divided, each partner's capital account is increased. If the business incurs a net loss for the accounting period, the capital account of each partner is decreased.

Let's look at three methods that can be used to distribute partnership profits or losses. We'll use two examples for each method: a net income of $24,000 and a net loss of $12,000.

Dividing Profits and Losses Equally

The easiest way to divide a partnership's net income or net loss is equally. This method is often used when all partners invest equal amounts of capital and share equally in the work of the business.

The partnership agreement for Surfside Bike & Skate Rentals states that the profits or losses are to be divided between the two partners equally. During the first year of operation, the partnership earned a net income of $24,000. Each partner's share is $12,000 ($24,000 ÷ 2).

Remember that the balance of the **Income Summary** account is the net income or net loss for the period. In the third closing entry, **Income Summary** is closed to capital. On December 31 the balance of **Income Summary**, a $24,000 credit, is divided equally between the two partners.

GENERAL JOURNAL PAGE 66

	DATE		DESCRIPTION	POST. REF.	DEBIT	CREDIT	
1	20--		Closing Entries				1
2	Dec.	31	Income Summary		24 000 00		2
3			Molly Gill, Capital			12 000 00	3
4			Don Putman, Capital			12 000 00	4
5							5

International ACCOUNTING

Business Attire

Learning what is appropriate to wear or not wear when conducting business in another country is important. No matter where you go, it is generally safest to dress in conservative business attire.

RESOURCE MANAGER

Reproducible Masters
- Lesson Plans
- Chapter Reviews and Working Papers (CRWP) TAE
- Demonstration Problems

Transparencies
- Section Focus Transparency
- Teaching Transparencies
- Source Document Transparencies
- Solution Transparencies

Multimedia
- ExamView CD-ROM
- Electronic Learning Center CD-ROM
- Interactive Lesson Planner CD-ROM
- Electronic Field Trips in Accounting

1 FOCUS

Introducing the Section

In this section students will learn how to divide the net income earned by the business (or the net losses) between the partners. They will divide earnings using equal shares and fractional shares and show the effect of each on the partners' capital accounts.

Section Concepts

- How to divide profits and losses equally.
- How to divide profits and losses based on a fractional share.
- How to divide profits and losses based on partners' investments.

Visual Learning

Section 2 Focus

Use **Transparency 27–4** to introduce section concepts.

BELL RINGER

Calculating: Divide the class into groups and give each group a supply of fake money (perhaps $1,400). Tell the groups the money represents net income. Have groups choose a basis for dividing the money among three partners. Tell students that each partner invested $10,000 and that two of the partners work in the business while the third does not. After they divide the net income, have students calculate the return on each partner's investment. L2

Concept Development: Dividing Profits and Losses

Discussion: Point out that partners can choose to divide profits and losses any way they want. The method of division should be spelled out in the partnership agreement. L1

2 TEACH

GUIDED PRACTICE

Reading Accounting

- Have students list the three ways of dividing net income/losses described in the section. As they read, have them make notes about each means of dividing income and losses. L1

Visual Learning

General Journal and T Accounts, p. 739

Use the illustration of the general journal and the T accounts on this page to analyze the entry to record an equal division of net income between partners.

Demonstration Problem Step-by-Step Practice

Use demonstration problem 27–3 to give students practice in dividing profits and recording them in a general journal.

Strategies for Teaching International Accounting

To enrich study of international accounting, refer students to the additional critical thinking activities in the booklet.

ACCOUNTING Flashbacks

INVESTIGATING FRAUD

To fight white-collar crime, the Private Securities Litigation Reform Act was passed in 1996, requiring auditors to be more aggressive in looking for fraud in the companies they audit.

After the journal entry is posted, the balance of Molly Gill's capital account is $62,000 and the balance of Don Putman's capital account is $42,000.

Molly Gill, Capital		Don Putman, Capital	
Debit –	Credit + Bal. 50,000 Clos. 12,000 Bal. 62,000	Debit –	Credit + Bal. 30,000 Clos. 12,000 Bal. 42,000

If the partnership incurs a net loss of $12,000 for the period, each partner's share of the net loss is $6,000 ($12,000 ÷ 2).

On December 31 the balance of **Income Summary**, a $12,000 debit, is divided equally between the two partners.

GENERAL JOURNAL PAGE 66

	DATE		DESCRIPTION	POST. REF.	DEBIT	CREDIT	
1	20--		*Closing Entries*				1
2	Dec.	31	*Molly Gill, Capital*		6 000 00		2
3			*Don Putman, Capital*		6 000 00		3
4			*Income Summary*			12 000 00	4
5							5

After the journal entry is posted, the balance of Molly Gill's capital account is $44,000 and the balance of Don Putman's capital account is $24,000.

Molly Gill, Capital		Don Putman, Capital	
Debit – Clos. 6,000	Credit + Bal. 50,000 Bal. 44,000	Debit – Clos. 6,000	Credit + Bal. 30,000 Bal. 24,000

Key Points

Distribution of Net Income or Net Loss

If the partnership agreement does not explain how net income or net loss is to be distributed, the net income or net loss is shared equally among the partners.

Dividing Profits and Losses on a Fractional Share Basis

Another way to divide net income or loss is to assign each partner a stated fraction of the total. The size of the fraction usually depends on (1) the amount of each partner's investment and (2) the value of each partner's services to the business.

Suppose that the Surfside Bike & Skate Rentals partnership agreement states that the profits or losses are to be divided between the two partners on the following basis: Gill, two-thirds and Putman, one-third.

Teaching International ACCOUNTING

(Refer to the *International Accounting* feature on page 739.)

Business Attire Proper attire plays an important role in conducting business successfully, both in the United States and in other countries. Tell students they are traveling to Japan to meet with Akira Nishimura, a long-time client. During their visit, they will make a presentation at a business luncheon, go golfing, and attend a formal banquet. Divide students into five groups and ask each group to find magazine pictures that illustrate appropriate attire for the following: the plane ride, the business luncheon, the golf outing, and the formal banquet. Students should gather pictures to illustrate appropriate dress for both males and females.

When partners share net income or loss on a fractional share basis, the basis is often stated as a ratio. For example, Gill's two-thirds and Putman's one-third could be expressed as a 2:1 ratio (2 to 1). To turn a ratio into a fraction, add the figures and use the total as the denominator of the fraction.

2:1 = (2 + 1 = 3) = ⅔ and ⅓

The division of the $24,000 net income based on a 2:1 ratio is calculated as follows:

Gill's share:	$24,000 × ⅔ =	$16,000
Putman's share:	$24,000 × ⅓ =	$8,000

The December 31 closing entry is shown below:

GENERAL JOURNAL PAGE 66

	DATE		DESCRIPTION	POST. REF.	DEBIT	CREDIT	
1	20--		Closing Entries				1
2	Dec.	31	Income Summary		24 000 00		2
3			Molly Gill, Capital			16 000 00	3
4			Don Putman, Capital			8 000 00	4
5							5

After the journal entry is posted, the balance of Molly Gill's capital account is $66,000 and the balance of Don Putman's capital account is $38,000.

Molly Gill, Capital

Debit −	Credit +
	Bal. 50,000
	Clos. 16,000
	Bal. 66,000

Don Putman, Capital

Debit −	Credit +
	Bal. 30,000
	Clos. 8,000
	Bal. 38,000

If the partnership incurs a net loss of $12,000 for the period, the December 31 distribution based on a 2:1 ratio is calculated as follows:

Gill's share:	($12,000) × ⅔ =	($8,000)
Putman's share:	($12,000) × ⅓ =	($4,000)

On December 31 the closing entry is as follows:

GENERAL JOURNAL PAGE 66

	DATE		DESCRIPTION	POST. REF.	DEBIT	CREDIT	
1	20--		Closing Entries				1
2	Dec.	31	Molly Gill, Capital		8 000 00		2
3			Don Putman, Capital		4 000 00		3
4			Income Summary			12 000 00	4
5							5

Calculator Hints

Floating Decimal Point

Most calculators have a floating decimal point, which means that the calculator places the decimal in the correct position.

For example:

- if you multiply 0.055 × 1,860
- then the answer will show the decimal in the correct place at 102.3.

Math Skill Builder Activity

Floating Decimal Point Have students use pocket calculators or desk calculators to solve these problems.

- Shoes that cost $45.00 have been discounted 25%.
- The projected revenue for the store shows a 10% increase over the $15,000 they made last year.
- You owe $850 on your credit card plus a 12% interest charge.

(Discount, $11.25; total cost, $33.75; projected increase, $1,500; total revenue, $16,500; interest on the balance, $102, total owed, $952.)

2 TEACH (Cont'd.)

Teaching Tips

Remind students that when one partner receives more profits, that partner also takes more losses.

Present other net income amounts and have students calculate the division. You can also use more than two partners in these examples.

Remind students that closing entries are made as the last step in the accounting cycle to transfer net income or loss to the capital accounts.

Visual Learning

General Journals and T Accounts, pp. 740–741

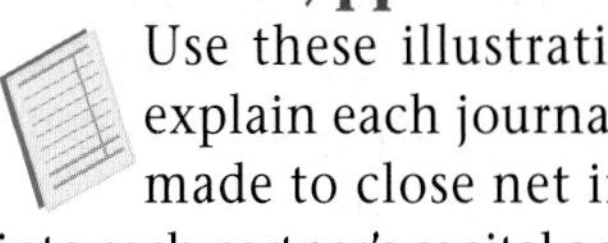

Use these illustrations to explain each journal entry made to close net income into each partner's capital account.

Demonstration Problem Step-by-Step Practice

Use demonstration problem 27–4 to give students practice in dividing a partnership loss using a fractional-share basis.

Math Review for Accounting

Photocopy appropriate *Student Activity Sheets* for students who need additional practice in basic math skills.

CHAPTER 27
SECTION 2, PAGES 739–744

2 TEACH (Cont'd.)

Teaching Tips

Partners' original investments are often used as a basis for dividing income and losses. When capital balances are used, decisions must be made about whether to count additional investments or withdrawals during the period. A weighted average might be used to avoid problems with amounts withdrawn and reinvested before the end of the year.

Visual Learning

General Journal, p. 742

Use the illustration of the general journal at the bottom of this page to explain the division of net income based on each partner's investments. Point out that this type of division is a way of calculating each partner's fractional share.

Thinking Algebraically

Designing Linear Equations: Have students write a linear equation to calculate each partner's share based on the capital invested by Gill and Putman. (Example: Gill's share = a ÷ c = x × i, or $50,000 ÷ $80,000 = 0.625 × $24,000 = $15,000) L2

After the journal entry is posted, the balance of Molly Gill's capital account is $42,000 and the balance of Don Putman's capital account is $26,000.

Molly Gill, Capital	
Debit −	Credit +
Clos. 8,000	Bal. 50,000
	Bal. 42,000

Don Putman, Capital	
Debit −	Credit +
Clos. 4,000	Bal. 30,000
	Bal. 26,000

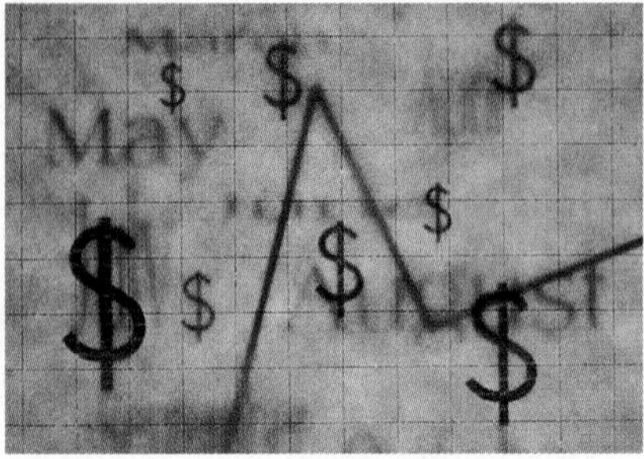

Dividing Profits and Losses Based on Capital Investments

Profits and losses can also be divided on the basis of the capital contributed by the individual partners. To do this, compute the percentage of each partner's capital investment.

$$\frac{\text{Individual Partner's Investment}}{\text{Total Partnership Investment}} = \text{Partner's Percentage}$$

Then multiply the net income or net loss by each partner's percentage.

Molly Gill and Don Putman made the following capital investments:

Molly Gill	$50,000
Don Putman	$30,000
Total investment	$80,000

Gill's Percentage $\frac{50,000}{80,000} = 62.5\%$

Putman's Percentage $\frac{30,000}{80,000} = 37.5\%$

Each partner's share of the $24,000 net income is calculated as follows:

Gill's share	$24,000 × .625 = $15,000
Putman's share	$24,000 × .375 = $9,000

The December 31 closing entry is as follows:

GENERAL JOURNAL — PAGE 66

	DATE		DESCRIPTION	POST. REF.	DEBIT	CREDIT	
1	20--		Closing Entries				1
2	Dec.	31	Income Summary		24 000 00		2
3			Molly Gill, Capital			15 000 00	3
4			Don Putman, Capital			9 000 00	4
5							5

After the journal entry is posted, the balance of Molly Gill's capital account is $65,000 and the balance of Don Putman's capital account is $39,000.

CRITICAL THINKING ACTIVITY

Interpreting Information Tell students they are advising Maria and Julio, who have the cash to start a restaurant business but little experience in managing a restaurant. Maria and Julio have decided to invite Shana, an experienced restaurant manager, to join the partnership. Shana has no cash to invest, but wants an equal share in the business. Should Maria and Julio offer Shana an equal share? Why or why not? (Effective management will be a key factor in the success of the restaurant. With an equal share, Shana will have as much incentive as Maria and Julio to make the business successful. Also, Shana may have more responsibility in managing the business and may work more hours.)

Molly Gill, Capital	
Debit	Credit
−	+
	Bal. 50,000
	Clos. 15,000
	Bal. 65,000

Don Putman, Capital	
Debit	Credit
−	+
	Bal. 30,000
	Clos. 9,000
	Bal. 39,000

If the partnership incurs a net loss of $12,000 for the period, the December 31 distribution is calculated as follows:

Gill's share	($12,000) × .625	=	($7,500)
Putman's share	($12,000) × .375	=	($4,500)

On December 31 the closing entry is as follows:

GENERAL JOURNAL PAGE *66*

	DATE		DESCRIPTION	POST. REF.	DEBIT	CREDIT	
1	*20--*		*Closing Entries*				1
2	*Dec.*	*31*	*Molly Gill, Capital*		*7 500 00*		2
3			*Don Putman, Capital*		*4 500 00*		3
4			*Income Summary*			*12 000 00*	4
5							5

After the journal entry is posted, the balance of Molly Gill's capital account is $42,500 and the balance of Don Putman's capital account is $25,500.

Molly Gill, Capital	
Debit	Credit
−	+
Clos. 7,500	Bal. 50,000
	Bal. 42,500

Don Putman, Capital	
Debit	Credit
−	+
Clos. 4,500	Bal. 30,000
	Bal. 25,500

ANALYZING FINANCIAL REPORTS

Analyzing Partners' Equity

Financially speaking, the major difference between partnerships and other forms of business ownership is in the equity of the business. In partnerships, two or more people invest equity in the business. When the business earns revenue from its operations, the partners split the revenue in some agreed-upon proportion. The revenue represents a return on their investment of partnership equity.

You learned how to calculate return on equity in Chapters 10 and 21. To review, return on equity is the profit of the business stated as a percentage of equity.

$$\text{Return on Equity} = \frac{\text{Net Income}}{\text{Equity}}$$

In the case of a partnership, each partner may have invested a different amount of equity, so the return might be different for each.

▶ Analyze the Report:

Use the balances in the T accounts for partners Putman and Gill on page 741 to answer these questions.

1. Using a total net income of $24,000, calculate the return on total partnership equity.
2. Using an equal split of net income, calculate the return on each partner's equity.
3. Which partner earned the better return? Explain your answer. Why is this percentage different than the return on total equity?

2 TEACH (Cont'd.)

Visual Learning

General Journal and T Accounts, p. 743

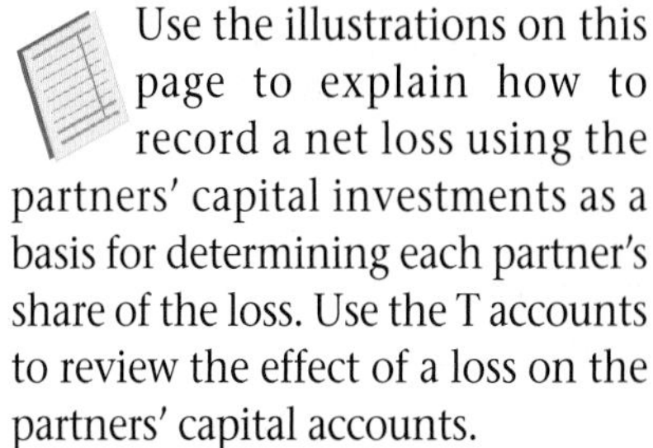

Use the illustrations on this page to explain how to record a net loss using the partners' capital investments as a basis for determining each partner's share of the loss. Use the T accounts to review the effect of a loss on the partners' capital accounts.

Teaching Tip

Give students other examples of partners' capital investments and have them calculate each partner's share.

Application: Tell students that three partners invested $12,000 each to start a new business at the beginning of January. On July 1 Partner A invested an additional $12,000. Partner B invested $6,000 on October 1. Partner C made no additional investments. None of the partners withdrew cash or assets from the business. Calculate the total equity and each partner's share of equity at the end of the year. Express the partners' shares as a ratio. (Total $54,000; Partner A, $24,000; Partner B, $18,000; Partner C, $12,000; ratio of 2:1.5:1) L1

ANALYZING FINANCIAL REPORTS

Analyze the Report (Answers)

1. 30%
2. Gill's return on equity is 24%, and Putman's return on equity is 40%.
3. Putman earned the better return. This is because he made the same amount of money with a smaller investment. The percentage is different for the individual partners than for total equity because they are splitting the income equally, yet they do not have the same amount of funds invested.

CHAPTER 27
SECTION 2, PAGES 739–744

3 ASSESS

Thinking Critically (Answers)

1. Net income or loss is shared equally among partners.
2. Net income (or loss) is multiplied by each partner's fractional share. The resulting amounts are then distributed to partners' capital accounts.

Computing in the Business World (Answers)

1. Mary Jo, 62.5%; partner, 37.5%
2. $12,000
3. Mary Jo Perry

Problem 27–2 (Answers)

1. 3/4, 1/4
2. 5/9, 3/9, 1/9
3. 3/8, 2/8, 2/8, 1/8
4. 2/4, 1/4, 1/4
5. 2/3, 1/3

Problem 27–3 (Answers)

Nov. 13: Dr. Cash in Bank $20,000; Cr. Walters, Capital $8,000, Yount, Capital $12,000

Chapter Reviews and Working Papers Refer students to the Chapter 27 workbook pages to answer *Check Your Understanding* activities.

4 CLOSE

Section Wrap-Up

Demonstration: Tell students that a partnership earned net income of $28,500. The two partners share income and losses on a 2-to-1 basis. Have students divide the income and explain the entry made to transfer the amount to each partner's capital account. L1

SECTION 2 Check Your Understanding

Now that you have studied this section, complete the following questions and problems.

Thinking Critically

1. If the partnership agreement doesn't specify a method, which method is used to divide income and losses among the partners?
2. Describe how to divide net income or net loss to each partner based on a fractional share basis.

Computing in the Business World

You and your best friend, Mary Jo Perry, operate an ice cream kiosk at the local outdoor shopping mall. You agree to divide profits and losses based on the capital investments made by each partner. Calculate the share of profit and loss due to each partner.

Your investment	$15,000
Mary Jo Perry's investment	25,000
Net income	32,000

1. What is the percentage of investment by each partner?
2. What is your share of the profit?
3. If there is a loss, which partner will have the largest share of the loss?

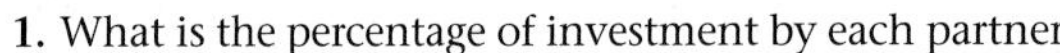

Problem 27–2 Determining Partners' Fractional Shares

Below are the ratios used by several partnerships to divide net income or net loss.

Instructions Determine the fractions that are used to calculate each partner's share of net income or net loss. Use the form provided in your working papers.

1. 3:1
2. 5:3:1
3. 3:2:2:1
4. 2:1:1
5. 2:1

Problem 27–3 Analyzing a Source Document

The deposit slips for Mr. Walter's and Ms. Yount's investments in the partnership of Walter and Yount Tax Service are presented here.

Instructions Prepare a journal entry to record the investments by the partners. Use the journal provided in your working papers.

Nations National Bank of U.S.A.
Auburn, Alabama 36831

Date November 13 20 --

Checks and other items are received for deposit subject to the terms and conditions of this bank's collection agreement.

Walter & Yount Tax Service
200 Market Square
Rockford, Alabama 35136

⑆011006534561⑆ 4509871⑈

BE SURE EACH ITEM IS ENDORSED

	DOLLARS	CENTS
CASH		
CHECKS (List Singly)		
1 234/67	8,000	00
2 Walter		
3		
4		
5		
6		
7		
8		
TOTAL	8,000	00

Nations National Bank of U.S.A.
Auburn, Alabama 36831

Date November 13 20 --

Checks and other items are received for deposit subject to the terms and conditions of this bank's collection agreement.

Walter & Yount Tax Service
200 Market Square
Rockford, Alabama 35136

⑆011006534561⑆ 4509871⑈

BE SURE EACH ITEM IS ENDORSED

	DOLLARS	CENTS
CASH		
CHECKS (List Singly)		
1 234/89	12,000	00
2 Yount		
3		
4		
5		
6		
7		
8		
TOTAL	12,000	00

RETEACHING SECTION 2

Calculating Percentages Students who are having difficulty apportioning partnership income or losses may need to review calculations involving percentages. Explain that to find a percentage of a number, you change the percentage to a decimal, then multiply it by the number. Students often make the mistake of putting the decimal point in the wrong place in the answer. Work through some examples with students so that they understand how to change the percent to a decimal and where to place the decimal in the answer.

CHAPTER 27 SUMMARY

KEY CONCEPTS

1. A partnership is an association of two or more persons to operate, as co-owners, a business for profit.
2. The actions of one partner acting on behalf of the partnership are binding on all partners. This is known as mutual agency.
3. In a partnership a capital account and a withdrawals account are set up for each partner.
4. Recording the investment of partners in a partnership:

Cash in Bank (or other asset)	
Debit + xx	Credit –

Individual Partner's Capital	
Debit –	Credit + xx

5. Recording cash withdrawals by partners:

Individual Partner's Withdrawals	
Debit + xx	Credit –

Cash in Bank	
Debit +	Credit – xx

6. The net income or net loss of a partnership is divided among the partners according to the terms set forth in the partnership agreement and is usually based on the contribution of services and capital by the partners.
7. Dividing profits among partners:

Individual Partner's Capital	
Debit –	Credit + xx

Income Summary	
Debit xx	Credit

8. Dividing losses among partners:

Individual Partner's Capital	
Debit – xx	Credit +

Income Summary	
Debit	Credit xx

SUMMARY CHAPTER 27

Chapter 27 Quiz

Student ____ Class ____ Instructor ____
Date Assigned ____ Date Completed ____

CHAPTER 27 QUIZ

Introduction to Partnerships

QUESTIONS (True-False)

Directions: In the space provided, indicate whether each statement is true or false.

____ 1. One partner can make agreements binding on all partners.
____ 2. Partners have limited liability for the debts of the partnership.
____ 3. A partnership will continue operating if one of the partners leaves the business.
____ 4. A partner who invests cash or assets in the partnership gives up all personal rights to those assets.
____ 5. Partners' investments are recorded in individual capital accounts.
____ 6. If partners do not specify division of income and losses, they will be divided by each partner's investment.
____ 7. Mutual agency means that all partners must mutually agree on a decision for it to be binding.
____ 8. The partnership agreement spells out the terms of the partnership, including any time limit.
____ 9. Partners may choose to divide profits and losses using any formula to which they all agree.
____ 10. Dividing profits and losses based on investments means calculating fractional shares for partners.

 Chapter Quizzes • 29

QUESTIONS (True-False)

1. One partner can make agreements binding on all partners.
2. Partners have limited liability for the debts of the partnership.
3. A partnership will continue operating if one of the partners leaves the business.
4. A partner who invests cash or assets in the partnership gives up all personal rights to those assets.
5. Partners' investments are recorded in individual capital accounts.
6. If partners do not specify division of income and losses, they will be divided by each partner's investment.
7. Mutual agency means that all partners must mutually agree on a decision for it to be binding.
8. The partnership agreement spells out the terms of the partnership, including any time limit.
9. Partners may choose to divide profits and losses using any formula to which they all agree.
10. Dividing profits and losses based on investments means calculating fractional shares for partners.

ANSWERS

1. True
2. False
3. False
4. True
5. True
6. False
7. False
8. True
9. True
10. True

REVIEW AND ACTIVITIES
CHAPTER 27

USING KEY TERMS

See the *Glossary* for the definitions of these terms. Ask for volunteers to share their letters in class. Discuss any differences in the use of terms.

Understanding Accounting Concepts and Procedures

(Answers)

1. Ease of formation, unlimited liability, limited life, mutual agency, co-ownership of property.
2. Advantages: ease of formation, few legal restrictions, no income taxes on partnership earnings; disadvantages: limited life, unlimited liability, and mutual agency.
3. Because it sets out terms under which the partnership will operate.
4. Name/address of partners; name, location, nature of partnership; date of agreement/time limits; investment of each partner; duties, rights, responsibilities of partners; withdrawals allowed partners; procedures for sharing profits and losses; procedure for distributing assets upon dissolution.
5. Current market value to accurately reflect partner's contribution.
6. Capital invested or skills, services, and time provided by each partner.
7. Equally, on a fractional basis, or according to the partners' investments.
8. Equally
9. One partner will receive 3/7 of any profit or loss; the other partner will receive the remaining 4/7.
10. The first two closing entries are the same. In the third closing entry, the balance of Income Summary is closed into the partners' capital accounts according to a specified division. In the fourth entry, each withdrawals account is closed separately into the partner's capital account.

CHAPTER 27 REVIEW AND ACTIVITIES

USING KEY TERMS

You and your friend Marianne Shelton have discussed forming a partnership to provide desktop publishing and layout services to local businesses. You have chosen a business name: The Perfect Paper. You are ready to launch your business idea, but need Marianne to agree so that you can obtain a business loan. Using the terms listed below, write a letter to Marianne and formally invite her to join you in this venture.

- mutual agency
- partnership agreement

Understanding Accounting Concepts and Procedures

Instructions

On a separate sheet of paper, answer the following questions:

1. List five characteristics of a partnership.
2. List three advantages and three disadvantages of the partnership form of business organization.
3. Why is a written partnership agreement important?
4. What information is usually included in a partnership agreement?
5. When assets other than cash are invested in a partnership, at what amount are the assets recorded?
6. What factors do partners usually consider when deciding on how the profits and losses of the partnership will be divided?
7. Name three methods partners might use to divide profits and losses.
8. How are profits divided when there is no written agreement?
9. What does it mean to share profits at a ratio of 3:4?
10. How do the closing entries of a partnership differ from those of a sole proprietorship?

ASSESSMENT RESOURCES

Choose assessment strategies from the following pages to evaluate your students' progress.

Student Edition
Check Your Understanding, pp. 738, 744
Chapter 27 Problems, pp. 749–751
Analyzing Financial Reports, p. 743

Assessment and Evaluation Masters
Chapter 27 Study Plan, *Glencoe Workbook (CRWP)*
Chapter 27 Self-Test, *Glencoe Workbook (CRWP)*
Chapter 27 Test, *Chapter Tests* Booklet
Chapter 27 Activity, *School-to-Work Handbook*
Chapter 27 **Exam***View*

Teacher Wraparound Edition
Critical Thinking Activity, p. 742
Reteaching Sections 1–2, pp. 738, 744
Chapter 27 Quiz, p. 745

CHAPTER 27 REVIEW AND ACTIVITIES

Case Study...

Partnership: Dentists

Arturo Garcia and Marcela Melendez are partners in Family Dental Center. They share equally the revenue and the costs of office rent, utilities, insurance, and salaries for the four people who work for them.

You just graduated from dental school. Arturo and Marcela offer you a partnership in their practice. Since you lack their years of experience, they offer you a 20 percent interest in return for a $40,000 investment.

Thinking Critically:

1. Assume that the revenue for the dental practice averages $10,000 a week. If you become a partner, you could generate additional revenue of $3,500 a week. Compute your 20 percent share of the revenue.
2. Assume that total expenses for the dental practice are $6,000 a week. Compute your share of the expenses.
3. Do you think that the 20% interest return in the partnership is a good deal? Would you negotiate a different arrangement? Explain.

Conducting an Audit with Alex

The partnership agreement states that partners Mary, Yoto, and Sally are to share profits in the ratio of 3:2:1. Allan, the chief accountant, divided the net income of $86,000 as follows:

Mary's share	=	$43,000
Yoto's share	=	$28,000
Sally's share	=	$15,000

Instructions Are profits calculated properly? If not, recalculate the partners' shares on a separate sheet of paper.

*inter*NET CONNECTION

Limited Liability Partnership

A Limited Liability Partnership is a hybrid entity—a cross between a partnership and a corporation.

Do This:

1. Search the Web to learn about this form of business ownership. The Limited Liability Partnership (LLP) is referred to as a pass-through entity. What does this mean?
2. Contrast the liability of owners of a Limited Liability Partnership with that of a regular partnership.

Workplace Skills

Negotiating

Can you work toward an agreement between those who disagree? If you can listen to opposing opinions, present facts and arguments, and help bring others to a compromise, then you are able to facilitate negotiations.

On the Job:

Several years ago two of your friends decided to create a business partnership so they could open a sports restaurant—The Gold Medal. You discover that the restaurant now is in jeopardy of closing because the partners are arguing about expansion plans. Because you can negotiate and mediate differences, you were asked to help your friends resolve their conflict.

Thinking Critically:

1. Meet with the partners (two of your classmates) and role-play the conflict. Have the partners talk about the problems connected with the restaurant expansion. Act as the mediator and write down all the issues mentioned.
2. Write down possible solutions for each of the identified problems.
3. Present your recommendations to the partners. Help them decide whether or not it is appropriate to expand the restaurant.

*inter*NET CONNECTION www.glencoe.com

Do This (Answers)

1. A pass-through entity means that the taxable income or loss is reported directly on the tax returns for the owners.
2. Doing business as a partnership exposes the partners to personal liability for all obligations of the partnership. The LLP protects the partners of the business from liabilities associated with the professional misconduct of another partner.

Case Study...

Thinking Critically (Answers)

1. $2,700/week
2. $1,200/week
3. Answers may vary. A variety of factors are involved but $1,500 a week translates to $78,000 a year from a $40,000 investment. The only real answer to this question depends on what other options you have for investing your time and money.

Workplace Skills

Thinking Critically (Answers)

1. Students should team with a group of three, with one student acting as the negotiator. Ask each team to develop a list of possible problems connected with this case.
2. The student who is acting as the negotiator should write out a set of recommended solutions for each problem listed.
3. Listen to the team discussions. As you circulate through the classroom, note where students are having meaningful discussions and then ask them to share their observations and solutions with the entire class.

Conducting an Audit with Alex

(Answers)

Correct shares:
Mary $43,000
Sally $28,666.67
Yoto $14,333.33

Internet Resources and Activities Handbook

Refer students to the booklet for additional Internet activities.

PEACHTREE CORNER

Partnership Transactions

Select **General Journal Entry** from the ***Tasks*** menu to record the partnership transactions presented in this chapter. The textbook illustrates the various transactions using general journal entries.

Tasks Analysis Options Reports
- Quotes/Sales Orders
- Sales/Invoicing...
- Receipts...
- Finance Charge...
- Select for Deposit...
- Purchase Orders...
- Purchases/Receive Inventory...
- Select for Payment...
- Payments...
- Write Checks...
- Time/Expense
- Select for Payroll Entry...
- Payroll Entry...
- General Journal Entry...
- Inventory Adjustments...
- Assemblies...
- Account Reconciliation...
- Void Checks...
- Action Items...
- System

As a reminder, your students can also use the General Ledger navigation aid to access the **General Journal Entry** option and the General Ledger reports.

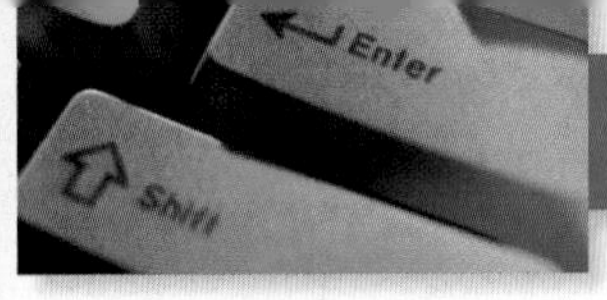

Starting a New Company

Making the Transition from a Manual to a Computerized System

Task	Perform Accounting Procedures Using Manual Methods	Perform Accounting Procedures Using Automated Methods
Starting a new company	1. Determine the form of business ownership. 2. Create a chart of accounts. 3. Open a general ledger account for each account. 4. Record the journal entry for the initial investment by the owner(s). 5. Post the opening entry to the appropriate ledger accounts.	1. Use the New Company Setup routine offered with most computerized accounting systems. 2. You will follow a checklist that will prompt you to enter general information about the business, as well as specific information about the accounting records.

Setting Up a New Company

Peachtree Question	Description
What information will I enter in the New Company Setup routine?	1. Setting up a new company in Peachtree is completed in two parts. 2. Part 1 requires: • company name and address • tax id • business form (type) • chart of accounts • posting method • accounting period • fiscal year 3. Part 2 requires: • customer defaults • statement and invoice options • vendor defaults • inventory defaults • payroll defaults
What does the software do "behind the scenes"?	1. The company information that you define in Part 1 will appear on all reports, statements, invoices, checks, etc. 2. The business form will determine the type of chart of accounts and relationships of G/L accounts. 3. The defaults that you define for customer and vendor accounts will apply to all transactions that you enter. 4. The accounting period, fiscal year, and posting options that you define set the parameters for the accounting records.

For detailed instructions: See the **Peachtree User Guide** in your Glencoe Working Papers.

Peachtree® Answers to Frequently Asked Questions

Q: Can you use the **Close Fiscal Year** option to automatically close a partnership?

A: Peachtree does not automatically record each partner's share of profit or loss. To record the split, set up one partner's capital account as "retained earnings." Set remaining capital account(s) to "equity—doesn't close." Peachtree then posts the profit/loss to "retained earnings" and automatically generates the closing entries. You then adjust the partners' capital accounts based on the partnership agreement.

For additional information, refer to your *Glencoe Peachtree Accounting User Guide.*

PROBLEMS
CHAPTER 27

APPLICATION OPTIONS

Problem 27–4 Dividing Partnership Earnings

Listed below are the net income and the method of dividing net income or net loss for several partnerships.

Instructions Use the form provided in your working papers to determine each partner's share of the net income.

Net Income	Method of Dividing Partnership Earnings
1. $45,000	Equally: 2 partners
2. $89,700	Fractional share: 2/3, 1/3
3. $22,000	Fractional share: 3:1
4. $32,000	Fractional share: 2/5, 2/5, 1/5
5. $92,700	Equally: 3 partners

Analyze: What accounts are affected when net income is distributed to the partners?

Problem 27–5 Calculating the Percentage of Each Partner's Capital Investment

Listed below are the individual partner's investments for several partnerships.

Instructions Using the form provided in your working papers, calculate each partner's percentage ownership in the partnership.

	Individual Partner's Investment	Total Partnership Investment
1.	$60,000	$180,000
2.	25,000	125,000
3.	11,250	28,125
4.	30,000	40,000

Analyze: Why is it important to know each partner's percentage of the total partnership investment?

Problem 27–6 Recording Investments of Partners

On May 1, Jason Pua and Roy Nelson formed the partnership called JR Landscaping. Jason contributed $8,100 cash and all of his landscaping equipment. The equipment was purchased by Jason for $2,500 last year. The market value of this equipment is now $1,800. Roy contributed $1,000 cash and his truck that has a market value of $5,600 presently.

Continued

Complete chapter problems one of four ways:

1. **Manual** Glencoe Working Papers

or

2. **Peachtree Complete Accounting** Software

or

3. **QuickBooks** Templates (Problems 27–7, 27–8)

or

4. **Spreadsheet** Templates (Problem 27–5)

SPREADSHEET SMART GUIDE

Step-by-Step Instructions: Problem 27–5

1. Select the spreadsheet template for Problem 27–5.
2. Enter your name and the date in the spaces provided on the template.
3. Complete the spreadsheet using the instructions in your working papers.
4. Print the spreadsheet and proof your work.
5. Save your work and exit the spreadsheet program.

Problem 27–4 (Answers) Dividing Partnership Earnings

1. $22,500 for each partner
2. $59,800 for partner 1, $29,900 for partner 2
3. $16,500 for partner 1, $5,500 for partner 2
4. $12,800 for partner 1, $12,800 for partner 2, $6,400 for partner 3
5. $30,900 for partner 1, $30,900 for partner 2, $30,900 for partner 3

Analyze: The partners' individual capital accounts and Income Summary.

Problem 27–5 (Answers) Calculating the Percentage of Each Partner's Capital Investment

1. 33.33%
2. 20.00%
3. 40.00%
4. 75.00%

Analyze: A partner's percentage of ownership may have an effect on such things as how much control he or she can exercise over the business and division of profits and losses.

EXTENDING THE CONTENT

Inviting an Attorney to Speak to the Class Invite an attorney to visit your class and talk with your students about the legal issues involved in setting up a partnership. Ask the attorney to describe how she or he assists individuals in forming a partnership. Included in the discussion should be the examples of mutual agency and advantages and disadvantages of a partnership. Have the attorney also discuss the pitfalls partners face when they do not have a partnership agreement. Set aside time for students to ask questions.

PROBLEMS CHAPTER 27

Problem 27-6 (Answers) Recording Investments of Partners

May 1: Dr. Cash in Bank $8,100, Landscaping Equip. $1,800; Cr. Jason Pua, Capital $9,900; Memo 1

May 1: Dr. Cash in Bank $1,000, Truck $5,600; Cr. Roy Nelson, Capital $6,600; Memo 1

Analyze: Jason Pua, Capital has a balance of $9,900. Roy Nelson, Capital has a balance of $6,600.

Problem 27-7 (Answers) Sharing Losses Based on Capital Balances

Share percentages:

M. DeJesus .4375

N. Faircloth .5625

Dec. 31: Dr. M. DeJesus, Capital $12,468.75, N. Faircloth, Capital $16,031.25; Cr. Income Summary $28,500

Analyze: $21,031.25

Problem 27-8 (Answers) Partners' Withdrawals

Dec. 31: Dr. Pane, Withdrawals $2,500, Graff, Withdrawals $2,500, Nu, Withdrawals $2,500; Cr. Cash in Bank $7,500

Analyze: Pane, Capital; Graff, Capital; Nu, Capital

Peachtree®

SMART GUIDE

Step-by-Step Instructions: Problem 27-6

1. Select the problem set for JR Landscaping (Prob. 27-6).
2. Rename the company, change the accounting period to May 1–May 31, 2008, and set the system date.
3. Enter the transactions to record the investment by each partner using the **General Journal Entry** option.
4. Print a General Journal report and proof your work.
5. Answer the Analyze question.
6. End the session.

Instructions Prepare the journal entries required to record the investment by each partner. Use page 1 of the general journal in your working papers. The source document is Memorandum 1.

Analyze: What are the balances in the partners' capital accounts after the formation of the partnership?

Problem 27-7 Sharing Losses Based on Capital Balances

Mariela DeJesus and Natasha Faircloth started the partnership In Shape Fitness with capital balances of $35,000 for Mariela and $45,000 for Natasha. They agreed to share profits and losses on the basis of their capital balances. The net loss for their first year of operation was $28,500.

Instructions Prepare the journal entry required to divide the loss between the partners. Use the journal in your working papers to record your entry.

Analyze: If Mariela took a $1,500 withdrawal, what was her capital account balance on December 31 after the closing entries were posted?

Peachtree®

SMART GUIDE

Step-by-Step Instructions: Problem 27-7

1. Select the problem set for In Shape Fitness (Prob. 27-7).
2. Rename the company and set the system date.
3. Record the entry to divide the loss between the two partners using the **General Journal Entry** option.
4. Print a General Journal report and proof your work.
5. Answer the Analyze question.
6. End the session.

Problem 27-8 Partners' Withdrawals

Graff, Nu, and Pane are partners in Travel Essentials. They agreed that partnership withdrawals would be 10 percent each based upon the profits recorded for the year. In the first year of operation, the partnership reported $25,000 in profits.

Instructions Prepare the entry to record the withdrawals of Graff, Nu, and Pane based on the partnership agreement. Use the journal paper provided in your working papers.

Analyze: If the partnership had a loss, what account(s) would be debited for the partners' withdrawals?

MEETING SPECIAL NEEDS

Gifted Provide an opportunity for gifted students to make a contribution to the class. Suggest that students express themselves in a variety of ways including drawing, creative writing, or acting. Allow these students to work independently on a bulletin-board display or a report. They could survey local businesses, collect copies of annual reports, or interview local businesspeople.

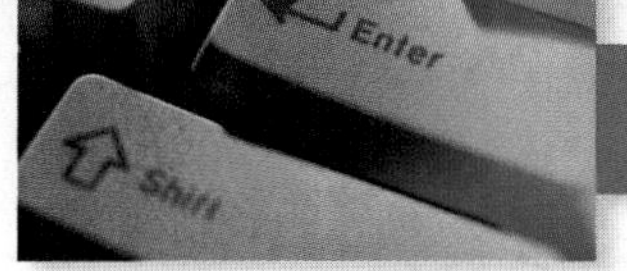

Problem 27–9 Preparing Closing Entries for a Partnership

Barbara Scott and Martin Towers are partners in the firm of Ten Column Accounting Services. Their partnership agreement states that Scott and Towers share net income or net loss in a 3:2 ratio.

At the end of the period, December 31, the business had a net loss of $9,700. During the period Scott withdrew $6,600 and Towers withdrew $5,400.

Instructions In your working papers, do the following:

(1) Journalize the closing entries to divide the net loss between the partners and to close the withdrawals accounts. Use general journal page 14.

(2) Post the closing entries to the general ledger accounts.

Analyze: What were the ending balances for the Scott and Towers capital accounts?

CHALLENGE PROBLEM

Problem 27–10 Evaluating Methods of Dividing Partnership Earnings

Jo Garrity, Maureen O'Riley, and David White decided to form a partnership called OnTime Copy Shop. The partners will invest the following assets in the business:

	Garrity	O'Riley	White
Cash	0	$22,000	$40,000
Supplies	0	5,000	2,000
Equipment	0	7,500	4,000
Building	$50,000	0	0
Land	15,000	0	0

They are considering the following plans for the division of net income or net loss:

1. Equally
2. Garrity, 20%; O'Riley, 40%; White, 40%
3. In the same ratio as the beginning balances of their capital accounts

Instructions Assume that the business had a net income of $17,500. Calculate the division of net income under each of the three plans.

Analyze: Which method would O'Riley prefer and why?

Peachtree® SMART GUIDE

Step-by-Step Instructions: Problem 27–8

1. Select the problem set for Travel Essentials (Prob. 27–8).
2. Rename the company and set the system date.
3. Enter the transactions to record the partners' withdrawals using the **General Journal Entry** option.
4. Print a General Journal report and proof your work.
5. Answer the Analyze question.
6. End the session.

Peachtree® SMART GUIDE

Step-by-Step Instructions: Problem 27–9

1. Select the problem set for Ten Column Accounting Services (Prob. 27–9).
2. Rename the company and set the system date.
3. Record the entry to divide net loss between partners using General Journal Entry option.
4. Print a General Journal report and proof your work.
5. Answer the Analyze question.
6. End the session.

ADDRESSING MULTIPLE LEARNING STYLES

Verbal/Linguistic Learner Tell students that they have decided to start a new computer retail business in your local area. Although they have sufficient funds to invest in the business to get it started, they will need a partner to help them make the business successful. Ask students to prepare a list of the personal qualities they would want in a business partner. Beside each quality, ask them to write a reason for choosing that quality. Have students share their lists with classmates. Then ask them to describe how their own personal qualities would mesh with the qualities they described for a partner.

Problem 27–9 (Answer) Preparing Closing Entries for a Partnership

Journal entries:

Dec. 31: Dr. Barbara Scott, Capital $5,820, Martin Towers, Capital $3,880; Cr. Income Summary $9,700

Dec. 31: Dr. Barbara Scott, Capital $6,600; Cr. Barbara Scott, Withdrawals $6,600

Dec. 31: Dr. Martin Towers, Capital $5,400; Cr. Martin Towers, Withdrawals $5,400

Ending credit balances:

Barbara Scott, Capital $54,892
Martin Towers, Capital $40,321

Analyze: Barbara Scott, Capital $54,892; Martin Towers, Capital $40,321

Problem 27–10 (Answers) Evaluating Methods of Dividing Partnership Earnings

Equally:

Garrity $5,833.33
O'Riley $5,833.33
White $5,833.34

Garrity, 20%; O'Riley, 40%; White 40%

Garrity $3,500
O'Riley $7,000
White $7,000

Capital account balance ratios:

Garrity $7,817.87
O'Riley $4,149.48
White $5,532.65

Analyze: O'Riley would prefer the second method because it would give him a larger share of the income.

CHAPTER 28 Resource Manager

Section Resources

	Objectives & Standards	Activities & Features	Reproducible Masters
Chapter Opener *Financial Statements and Liquidation of a Partnership*	• Prepare an income statement for a partnership. • Prepare a statement of partners' equity. • Prepare the Partners' Equity section of a balance sheet. • Account for partnership liquidation losses. • Account for partnership liquidation gains. • Prepare the final entry to liquidate a partnership. • Define the accounting terms introduced in this chapter. **National Standards for Business Education**: IA14, IIC1, IVA1, IVA2	Exploring the Real World of Business, p. 752 Workplace Connections, p. 753	School-to-Work Handbook
Section 1 *Financial Statements for a Partnership*	• How to show the division of net income among partners on the income statement. • How to prepare a statement of changes in partners' equity. • How to prepare the Partners' Equity section of a balance sheet.	Did You Know?, p. 754 A Matter of Ethics, p. 755	Demonstration Problems Strategies for Teaching Ethics in Accounting
Section 2 *Liquidation of a Partnership*	• How to record losses in a partnership liquidation. • How to record gains in a partnership liquidation. • How to record the cash distribution required to liquidate a partnership.	Accounting Tips, p. 757 International Accounting, p. 758 Connect To, p. 759 Accounting Flashbacks, p. 760 Math Hints, p. 761 Analyzing Financial Reports, p. 761	Strategies for Teaching International Accounting Demonstration Problems Math Review for Accounting Internet Resources and Activities Handbook

KEY

Posters · Transparency · Software · Videocassette
Blackline Masters · CD-ROM · Portfolio

MULTIMEDIA RESOURCE

Peachtree	QuickBooks	Spreadsheets	Videos	CD-ROMs
Problem 28–5 *Liquidating the Partnership with losses on the Sale of Noncash Assets* Problem 28–6 *Recording a Gain or Loss on the Sale of Noncash Assets by a Partnership* Problem 28–8 *Liquidating the Partnership*	Problem 28–6 *Recording a Gain or Loss on the Sale of Noncash Assets by a Partnership* Problem 28–8 *Liquidating the Partnership*	Problem 28–4 *Preparing an Income Statement and Balance Sheet for a Partnership* Problem 28–9 *Completing End-of-Period Activities for a Partnership*	***Video Segment: Partnerships and Corporations*** After viewing this video, students will be able to describe the organizational differences between partnerships and corporations. Have students list the major advantages and disadvantages of a corporation.	***Electronic Learning Center (ELC), Chapter 28*** This program is ideal for visual learners since it incorporates video images, animation, and graphics to enliven the content of each lesson. ***Interactive Lesson Planner (ILP), Chapter 28*** This CD-ROM combines the versatility of an electronic lesson planner with the convenience of teacher classroom resources.

SCANS Correlation Chart

FOUNDATION SKILLS

Basic Skills:	Reading	Writing	Math	Listening	Speaking	
Thinking Skills:	Creative Thinking	Decision Making	Problem Solving	Seeing Things in the Mind's Eye	Knowing How to Learn	Reasoning
Personal Qualities:	Responsibility	Self-Esteem	Sociability	Self-Management	Integrity/Honesty	

WORKPLACE COMPETENCIES

Resources:	Allocating Time	Allocating Money	Allocating Material and Facility Resources	Allocating Human Resources		
Information:	Acquiring and Evaluating Information	Organizing and Maintaining Information	Interpreting and Communicating Information	Using Computers to Process Information		
Interpersonal Skills:	Participating as a Member of a Team	Teaching Others	Serving Clients/ Customers	Exercising Leadership	Negotiating to Arrive at a Decision	Working with Cultural Diversity
Systems:	Understanding Systems	Monitoring and Correcting Performance	Improving and Designing Systems			
Technology:	Selecting Technology	Applying Technology to Task	Maintaining and Troubleshooting Technology			

*Highlighted blocks indicate areas covered in the chapter. Additional SCANS skills are also covered throughout the *Teacher Wraparound Edition.*

Assessment

Student Edition
- Check Your Understanding, pp. 756, 762
- Chapter 28 Problems, pp. 767–769

Assessment and Evaluation Masters
- Chapter 28 Study Plan, *Glencoe Workbook*
- Chapter 28 Self-Test, *Glencoe Workbook*
- Chapter 28 Test, *Chapter Tests* Booklet
- Chapter 28 Activity, *School-to-Work Handbook*
- Chapter 28 **Exam***View*

Teacher Wraparound Edition
- Critical Thinking Activity, p. 767
- Reteaching Section 1, p. 756
- Reteaching Section 2, p. 762
- Chapter 28 Quiz, p. 763

Transparencies

	Teaching Transparencies	Solution Transparencies
Section 1:	28–1, 28–2, 28–3, 28–4	Problems 28–1, 28–2
Section 2:	28–5, 28–6	Problem 28–3
End of Chapter:		Problems 28–4, 28–5, 28–6, 28–7, 28–8, 28–9

TEACHER CLASSROOM RESOURCES

This is a representation of key blackline masters available in the Teacher Classroom Resources.

Teaching Aids

Transparency Examples

Section Focus Transparencies

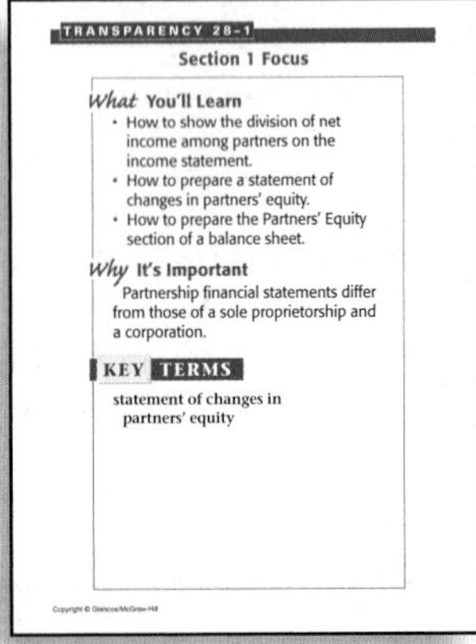

TRANSPARENCY 28-1

Section 1 Focus

What You'll Learn
- How to show the division of net income among partners on the income statement.
- How to prepare a statement of changes in partners' equity.
- How to prepare the Partners' Equity section of a balance sheet.

Why It's Important

Partnership financial statements differ from those of a sole proprietorship and a corporation.

KEY TERMS

statement of changes in partners' equity

Teaching Transparencies

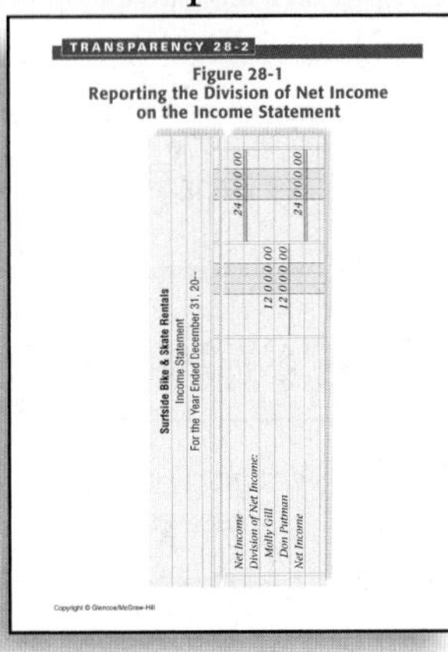

TRANSPARENCY 28-2

Figure 28-1
Reporting the Division of Net Income on the Income Statement

Source Document Transparencies

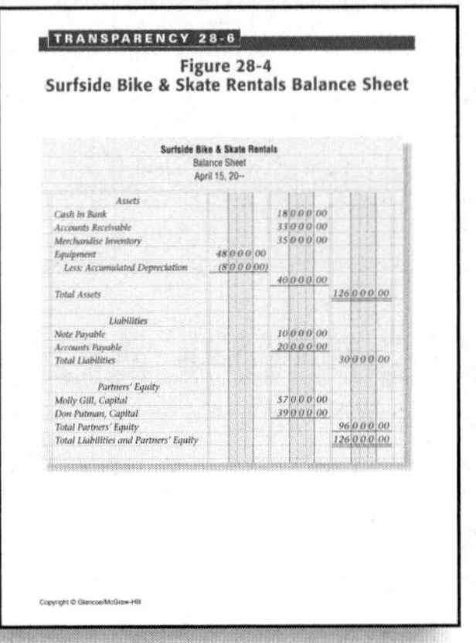

TRANSPARENCY 28-6

Figure 28-4
Surfside Bike & Skate Rentals Balance Sheet

Solution Transparencies

Working Papers for End-of-Chapter Problems

Problem 28-4 Preparing an Income Statement and Balance Sheet for a Partnership

Demonstration Problems

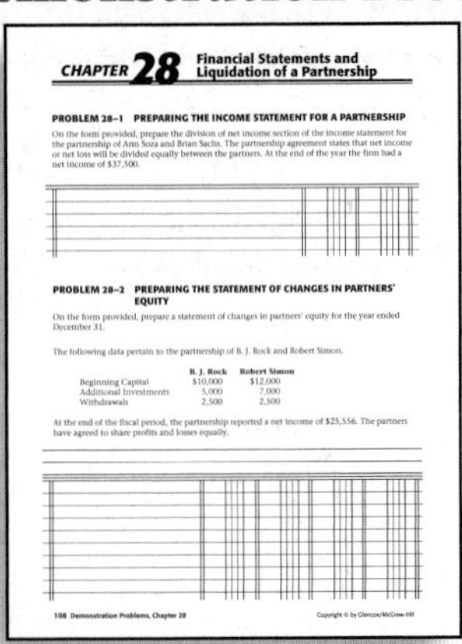

CHAPTER 28 Financial Statements and Liquidation of a Partnership

PROBLEM 28-1 PREPARING THE INCOME STATEMENT FOR A PARTNERSHIP

PROBLEM 28-2 PREPARING THE STATEMENT OF CHANGES IN PARTNERS' EQUITY

Lesson Plans

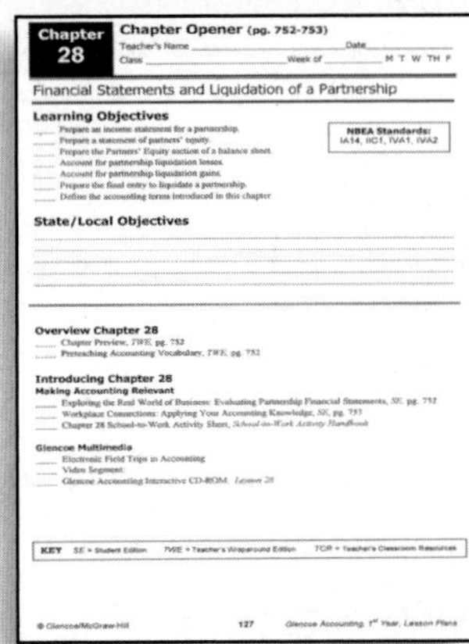

Chapter 28 Chapter Opener (pg. 752-753)

Financial Statements and Liquidation of a Partnership

Learning Objectives

State/Local Objectives

Block Scheduling

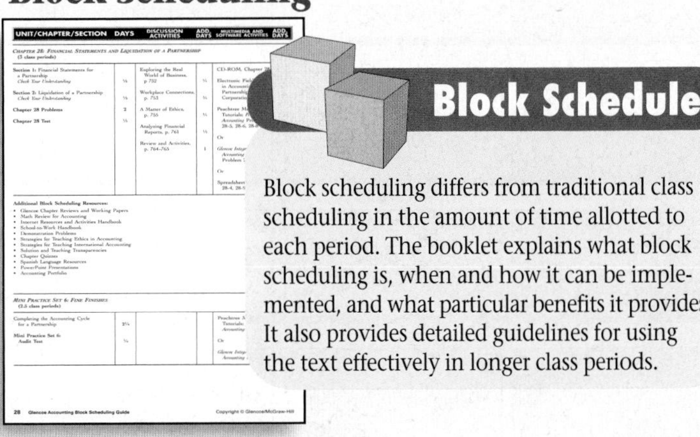

Block Schedule

Block scheduling differs from traditional class scheduling in the amount of time allotted to each period. The booklet explains what block scheduling is, when and how it can be implemented, and what particular benefits it provides. It also provides detailed guidelines for using the text effectively in longer class periods.

Enrichment and Application

Strategies for Teaching Ethics in Accounting

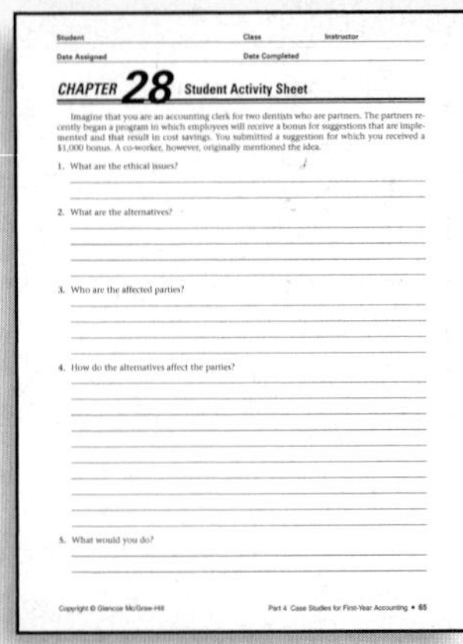

CHAPTER 28 Student Activity Sheet

1. What are the ethical issues?
2. What are the alternatives?
3. Who are the affected parties?
4. How do the alternatives affect the parties?
5. What would you do?

Strategies for Teaching International Accounting

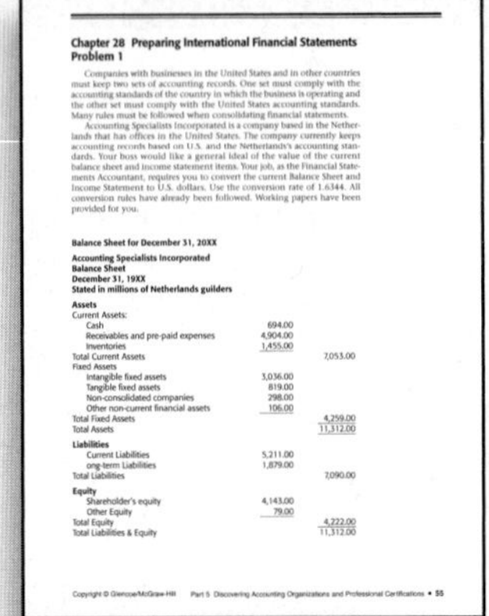

Chapter 28 Preparing International Financial Statements
Problem 1

School-to-Work Handbook

CHAPTER 28 SCHOOL-TO-WORK ACTIVITY

Financial Statements and Liquidation of a Partnership

Meeting Different Ability Levels

Chapter Reviews and Working Papers (CRWP)

Working Papers

Review

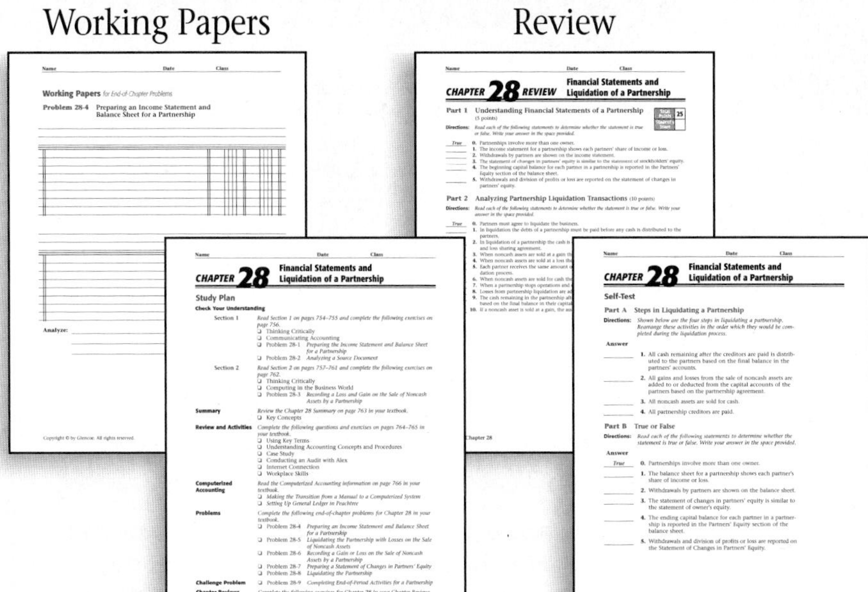

Student Study Plan

Self-Test

Real-World Multimedia CD-ROM

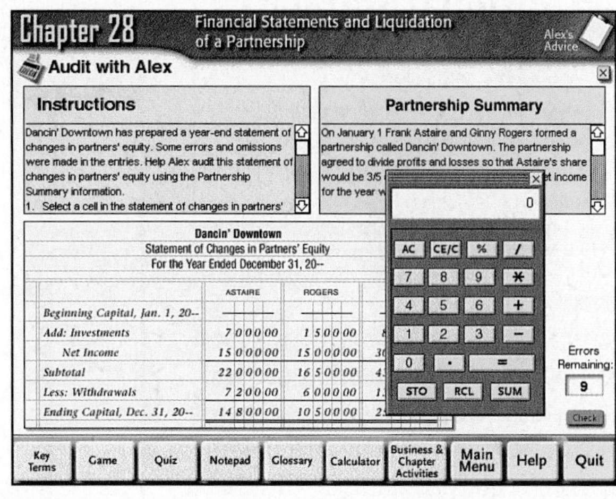

Key to Ability Levels

Each section gives skill-building activities. Each activity has been labeled for use with students of various learning styles and abilities.

L1 Level 1 activities are basic activities and should be within the range of all students.

L2 Level 2 activities are average activities and should be within the range of average and above average students.

L3 Level 3 activities are challenging activities designed for the ability range of above average students.

ELL ELL activities should be within the ability range of English Language Learners.

Teaching Resources at a Glance

Application Resources

- Glencoe Chapter Review and Working Papers, SE and TAE
- School-to-Work Handbook, SE and TM
- Accounting Portfolio, SE and TM

Reproducible Masters

- Demonstration Problems
- Lesson Plans
- Block Scheduling
- Spanish Language Resources

Glencoe Accounting Professional Development Series

- Strategies for Teaching Ethics in Accounting
- Accounting Competitive Event Review
- Math Review for Accounting
- Strategies for Teaching International Accounting
- Internet Resources and Activities Handbook

Transparency Package

- Section Focus Transparencies
- Teaching Transparencies
- Source Document Transparencies
- Solution Transparencies

Performance Assessment

- **Exam***View* CD-ROM
- Chapter Tests
- Chapter Quizzes
- Unit Tests
- Audit Tests
- Printed Testbank

Multimedia Resources

- Electronic Learning Center:
  - Multimedia CD-ROMs
  - Peachtree software, tutorials, templates, and solutions
  - Spreadsheet templates
- Using QuickBooks with Glencoe Accounting
- Interactive Lesson Planner
- Electronic Field Trips in Accounting
- PowerPoint Presentation
- Web site: glencoeaccounting.glencoe.com

Assessment and Evaluation

Chapter Tests

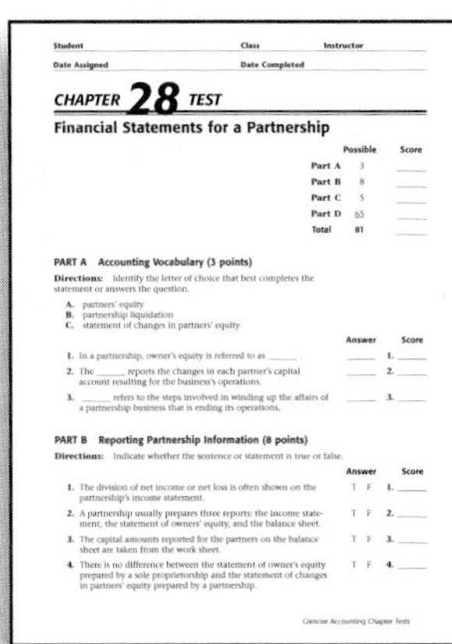

Chapter Quiz

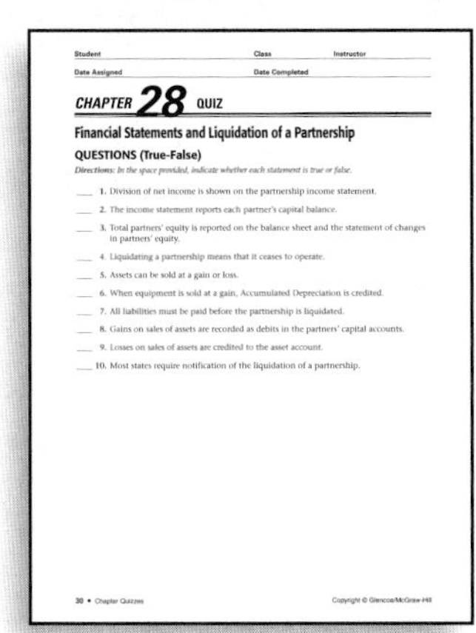

OVERVIEW CHAPTER 28

Correlations to National Standards for Business Education

(See pages T50–T51 for a detailed correlation chart.)

Standards: IA14, IIC1, IVA1, IVA2

Chapter Preview

Recording business transactions for a sole proprietorship, partnership, or corporation is essentially the same except for those transactions directly affecting the ownership equity accounts. In this chapter students will learn how to record transactions related to the capital accounts of a partnership.

Section Overviews

- Section 1—*Financial Statements for a Partnership*
- Section 2—*Liquidation of a Partnership*

Chapter Vocabulary

statement of changes in partners' equity
partnership liquidation

Preteaching Accounting Vocabulary

Oral Exercise: Have students explain the meaning of each of the terms. Then ask for several volunteers to use each term in the context of an accounting system. Discuss any differences in the way students use terms. L1

CHAPTER 28

Financial Statements and Liquidation of a Partnership

Learning Objectives

When you have completed this chapter, you will be able to:

- Prepare an income statement for a partnership.
- Prepare a statement of partners' equity.
- Prepare the Partners' Equity section of a balance sheet.
- Account for partnership liquidation losses.
- Account for partnership liquidation gains.
- Prepare the final entry to liquidate a partnership.
- Define the accounting terms introduced in this chapter.

Exploring the Real World of Business

EVALUATING PARTNERSHIP FINANCIAL STATEMENTS

Look around you and think about the number of products that are made from trees—paper, furniture, homes, and boats. One company that provides raw materials for such products is **Plum Creek Timber Company.** The company owns 7.8 million acres of timberland in the United States (increasing from just two million acres in the last decade) and follows strict environmental principles, including reforestation and soil conservation.

Plum Creek originally started as a partnership in 1989. Its success in timberland ownership and manufacturing is enhanced by its leadership in environmental stewardship. Through the use of habitat conservation plans, the Sustainable Forestry Initiative® Program, and various conservation agreements with local, state, and federal agencies, **Plum Creek** protects wildlife, native fish, and their ecosystems wherever they conduct business.

In 1999 **Plum Creek** became a real estate investment trust, which combines investors' capital for the purpose of purchasing and owning real estate.

Plum Creek

What do you think?

Can you think of at least two other types of partnerships?

Exploring the Real World of Business

Plum Creek Timber Company

Plum Creek is currently the second largest timberland owner in the United States. The company operates as a real estate investment trust. Investors can buy or sell shares in the REIT on the New York Stock Exchange.

What do you think? (Answers)

Answers may vary. Other types of limited partnerships may include law firms, accounting firms, medical practice firms, dental practices, real estate investment firms, and architectural companies.

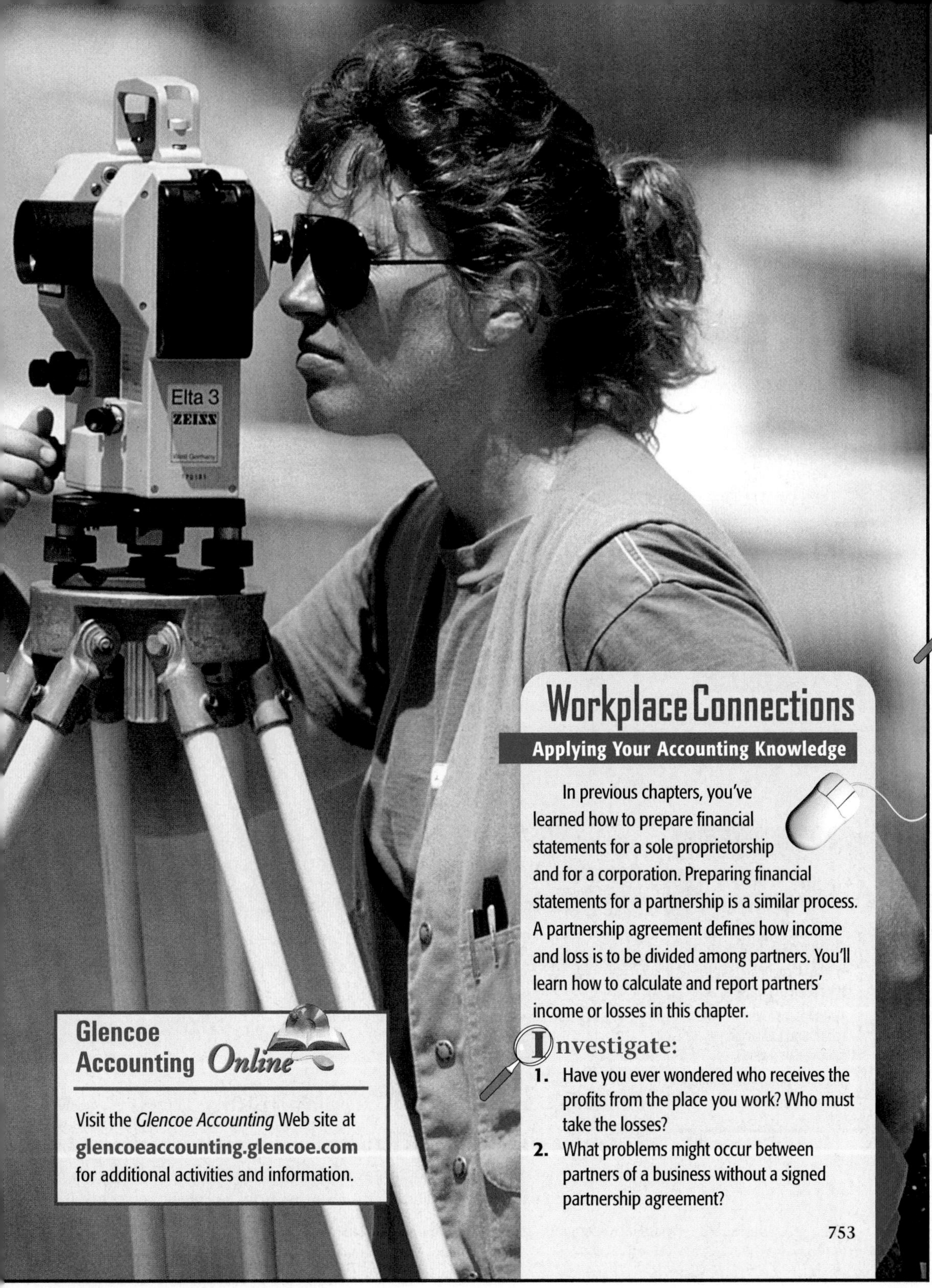

Workplace Connections

Applying Your Accounting Knowledge

In previous chapters, you've learned how to prepare financial statements for a sole proprietorship and for a corporation. Preparing financial statements for a partnership is a similar process. A partnership agreement defines how income and loss is to be divided among partners. You'll learn how to calculate and report partners' income or losses in this chapter.

Investigate:

1. Have you ever wondered who receives the profits from the place you work? Who must take the losses?
2. What problems might occur between partners of a business without a signed partnership agreement?

Glencoe Accounting Online

Visit the *Glencoe Accounting* Web site at **glencoeaccounting.glencoe.com** for additional activities and information.

753

INTRODUCING CHAPTER 28

Making Accounting Relevant

Workplace Connections: Applying Your Accounting Knowledge

Discussion: Plum Creek was originally organized as a limited partnership. A limited partnership offers some of the advantages of the corporate form of business organization in that the partners' liability is limited to their investments. Have students think about local companies and identify those that may be organized as partnerships.

Investigate (Answers)

1. Answers may vary. In a partnership, the ones in the partnership receive the profits and take the losses.
2. Answers may vary. Without an agreement, one partner that invests less than the others share equally in the profits.

School-to-Work Activity

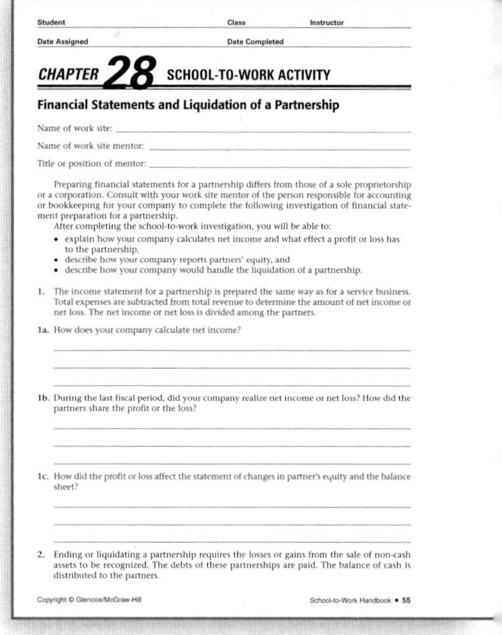

Student ______ Class ______ Instructor ______

Date Assigned ______ Date Completed ______

CHAPTER 28 SCHOOL-TO-WORK ACTIVITY

Financial Statements and Liquidation of a Partnership

Name of work site: ______

Name of work site mentor: ______

Title or position of mentor: ______

Preparing financial statements for a partnership differs from those of a sole proprietorship or a corporation. Consult with your work site mentor of the person responsible for accounting or bookkeeping for your company to complete the following investigation of financial statement preparation for a partnership.

After completing the school-to-work investigation, you will be able to:

- explain how your company calculates net income and what effect a profit or loss has to the partnership,
- describe how your company reports partners' equity, and
- describe how your company would handle the liquidation of a partnership.

1. The income statement for a partnership is prepared the same way as for a service business. Total expenses are subtracted from total revenue to determine the amount of net income or net loss. The net income or net loss is divided among the partners.

1a. How does your company calculate net income?

______

1b. During the last fiscal period, did your company realize net income or net loss? How did the partners share the profit or the loss?

______

1c. How did the profit or loss affect the statement of changes in partner's equity and the balance sheet?

______

2. Ending or liquidating a partnership requires the losses or gains from the sale of non-cash assets to be recognized. The debts of these partnerships are paid. The balance of cash is distributed to the partners.

School-to-Work Handbook • 55

GLENCOE MULTIMEDIA

Electronic Field Trips in Accounting *Video Segment: Partnerships and Corporations*
After viewing this video, students will be able to describe the organizational differences between partnerships and corporations.

Glencoe Accounting: Electronic Learning Center *Chapter 28*
The CD-ROM program is ideal for visual learners since it incorporates video images, animation, and graphics to enliven the content of each lesson.

CHAPTER 28
SECTION 1, PAGES 754–756

1 FOCUS

Introducing the Section

In this section students will prepare financial statements reporting the partners' division of net income (or loss) and changes in partners' equity.

Section Concepts

- How to show the division of net income among partners on the income statement.
- How to prepare a statement of changes in partners' equity.
- How to prepare the Partners' Equity section of a balance sheet.

Visual Learning

Section 1 Focus

Use **Transparency 28–1** to introduce section concepts.

BELL RINGER

Research: Have students choose a partner and plan a school activity. Tell partners to assign responsibility for each part of the plan. Have partners share their plans in class. If they were being paid for their work, how would they decide to split the money? L1

Concept Development: The Income Statement

Discussion: Partners must agree on how income and losses are to be divided. Investments by each partner are often the basis used. L1

Visual Learning

Figure 28–1 Reporting the Division of Net Income on the Income Statement

Use **Transparency 28–2** to show students the entry to report net income for each partner.

SECTION 1

Financial Statements for a Partnership

***What* You'll Learn**

- How to show the division of net income among partners on the income statement.
- How to prepare a statement of changes in partners' equity.
- How to prepare the Partners' Equity section of a balance sheet.

***Why* It's Important**

Partnership financial statements differ from those of a sole proprietorship and a corporation.

KEY TERMS

statement of changes in partners' equity

At the end of the year, Deloitte & Touche LLP, one of the "Big Four" accounting firms, prepares financial statements including an income statement, a statement of changes in partners' equity, and a balance sheet.

The Income Statement

The income statement for a partnership is prepared in the same way as for any service business. Expenses are subtracted from revenue to determine the net income or loss. Although it is not required, the division of net income or net loss among the partners may be shown on the income statement.

The partnership agreement of Surfside Bike & Skate Rentals states that net income or net loss will be divided equally between the partners. At the end of the year, the firm had a net income of $24,000. Each partner's share is $12,000. **Figure 28–1** illustrates how to report the division of net income on the income statement.

Surfside Bike & Skate Rentals
Income Statement
For the Year Ended December 31, 20--

Net Income		24 000 00
Division of Net Income:		
Molly Gill	12 000 00	
Don Putman	12 000 00	
Net Income		24 000 00

Figure 28–1 Reporting the Division of Net Income on the Income Statement

Did You Know?

Natural Products

The Amazon rain forests are the source of many natural substances used to treat health problems such as hypertension, diabetes, migraine headaches, and indigestion. Companies selling such natural products earn billions of dollars in revenue.

The Statement of Changes in Partners' Equity

The **statement of changes in partners' equity** reports the change in each partner's capital account resulting from business operations. It is

RESOURCE MANAGER

Reproducible Masters
- Lesson Plans
- Chapter Reviews and Working Papers (CRWP) TAE
- Demonstration Problems

Transparencies
- Section Focus Transparency
- Teaching Transparencies
- Source Document Transparencies
- Solution Transparencies

Multimedia
- Exam*View* CD-ROM
- Electronic Learning Center CD-ROM
- Interactive Lesson Planner CD-ROM

similar to the statement of changes in owner's equity for a sole proprietorship, except that there is a separate column for each partner. **Figure 28–2** shows the statement of changes in partners' equity for Surfside Bike & Skate Rentals. Notice that the net income is divided between the partners.

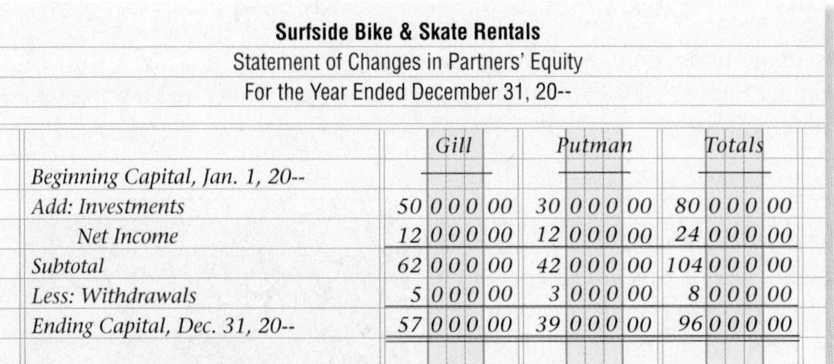

Surfside Bike & Skate Rentals
Statement of Changes in Partners' Equity
For the Year Ended December 31, 20--

	Gill	Putman	Totals
Beginning Capital, Jan. 1, 20--			
Add: Investments	50 000 00	30 000 00	80 000 00
Net Income	12 000 00	12 000 00	24 000 00
Subtotal	62 000 00	42 000 00	104 000 00
Less: Withdrawals	5 000 00	3 000 00	8 000 00
Ending Capital, Dec. 31, 20--	57 000 00	39 000 00	96 000 00

Figure 28–2 Statement of Changes in Partners' Equity

The Balance Sheet

For a partnership the Owners' Equity section of the balance sheet is referred to as the Partners' Equity section. Each partner's capital account is listed separately in the Partners' Equity section. (See **Figure 28–3**.) The capital account amounts reported on the balance sheet are from the statement of changes in partners' equity.

Surfside Bike & Skate Rentals
Balance Sheet
December 31, 20--

Partners' Equity			
Molly Gill, Capital		57 000 00	
Don Putman, Capital		39 000 00	
Total Partners' Equity			96 000 00
Total Liabilities and Partners' Equity			126 000 00

Figure 28–3 The Partners' Equity Section of the Balance Sheet

A MATTER OF ETHICS

Using Another Person's Idea

Imagine that you are an accounting clerk for two dentists who are partners. The partners recently began a program in which employees will receive a bonus for suggestions that are implemented and that result in cost savings. You submitted a suggestion for which you received a $1,000 bonus. A co-worker, however, originally mentioned the idea.

Ethical Decision Making:

- What are the ethical issues?
- What are the alternatives?
- Who are the affected parties?
- How do the alternatives affect the parties?
- What would you do?

Teaching A MATTER OF ETHICS

Using Another Person's Idea Have students discuss whether they have ever taken credit for someone else's work or if they've been in the situation where someone else copied their work or ideas. How did they deal with the situation? Ask students to take sides and debate the issue. For example, some students may say the person who submits an idea should get the credit. Others may think the originator of the idea should get the credit. Some may say the two could share the credit.

2 TEACH

GUIDED PRACTICE

Reading Accounting

- Have students read each financial statement and write a sentence or two describing what they read. L1

Visual Learning

Figure 28–2 Statement of Changes in Partners' Equity
Use **Transparency 28–3** to discuss how this statement differs from a statement of changes in owner's equity.

Figure 28–3 The Partners' Equity Section of the Balance Sheet
Use **Transparency 28–4** to explain the split of partners' capital.

Concept Development: The Statement of Changes in Partners' Equity and the Balance Sheet

Discussion: Explain that this statement is similar to the statement of changes in owner's equity for a sole proprietor.

Remind students that the partners' balance sheet is similar to that for a sole proprietorship. L1

Demonstration Problem Step-by-Step Practice

Use demonstration problems 28–1, 28–2, and 28–3 to have students prepare the financial statements.

Strategies for Teaching Ethics in Accounting

Photocopy the Chapter 28 *Student Activity Sheet* for students. Answers are also provided in the booklet.

CHAPTER 28
SECTION 1, PAGES 754–756

3 ASSESS

Thinking Critically (Answers)

1. Income statement, statement of changes in partners' equity, balance sheet.
2. Statement of partners' equity contains separate column for each partner.

Communicating Accounting (Answers)

Answers will vary. The downside to making additional investments is that you have to provide the cash. On the other hand, extra cash may allow for expansion and higher profits.

Problem 28–1 (Answers)

Division of net income:
Goldman $14,000, Jones $21,000
Partners' Equity:
Goldman $37,000, Jones $68,000

Problem 28–2 (Answers)

Bass $7,200
Buie $7,200
Anderson $3,600
Norman $3,600
Dunham $2,400
Ruppe $2,400

Chapter Reviews and Working Papers Refer students to the Chapter 28 workbook pages to answer *Check Your Understanding* activities.

4 CLOSE

Section Wrap-Up

Writing: Have students write a paragraph describing financial statements for a partnership and what each statement reports. L1

SECTION 1 Check Your Understanding

Now that you have studied this section, complete the following questions and problems.

Thinking Critically

1. What financial statements are prepared for a partnership?
2. What is the difference between a statement of changes in owner's equity and a statement of changes in partners' equity?

Communicating Accounting

Maurice Lance and Terry Klaus are partners in a business called M&T Computer Solutions. Maurice wants to contribute more money to the partnership. Terry, on the other hand, is satisfied with his initial investment. Choose a classmate and role play the partners. Discuss the pros and cons of additional investments.

Problem 28–1 Preparing the Income Statement and Balance Sheet for a Partnership

Information related to the operations of the Goldman and Jones partnership follows.

Instructions In your working papers, prepare the division of income section of the income statement and the Partners' Equity section of the balance sheet.

1. Goldman and Jones share profits in the ratio of 2:3.
2. Net income for the year ended December 31, 20-- was $35,000.
3. The January 1 capital balance for Goldman was $23,000.
4. The January 1 capital balance for Jones was $47,000.

Problem 28–2 Analyzing a Source Document

Instructions In your working papers or on a separate sheet of paper, determine each partner's share of the gain.

N *Buie Norman & Company*
CERTIFIED PUBLIC ACCOUNTANTS

Minutes of the Partners' Meeting
January 12, 20--

The partnership sold equipment for a gain of $26,400. The partners agreed to share the gain as follows:

Larry Bass, CPA	6/22
John Buie, CPA	6/22
Teri Anderson, CPA	3/22
Robert Norman, CPA	3/22
Paula Dunham, CPA	2/22
John Ruppe, CPA	2/22

RETEACHING SECTION 1

Comparing Similarities in Statement of Changes in Equity The statement of changes in partners' equity is similar to the statement of changes in owner's equity for a sole proprietorship. Have students compare Figure 28–2 on page 755 with Figure 9–6 on page 211. Point out that the only difference in these two figures is that the statement of partners' equity shows a separate column for each partner.

Liquidation of a Partnership

A partnership does not have an unlimited life. Partnerships end because of death or incapacity of a partner, upon completion of a project, or at the end of a specified time period. In this section you will learn about the procedures followed to dissolve a partnership.

What You'll Learn

- How to record losses in a partnership liquidation.
- How to record gains in a partnership liquidation.
- How to record the cash distribution required to liquidate a partnership.

Why It's Important

When a partnership is liquidated, the gains or losses from the sale of noncash assets are recognized, the debts of the partnership are paid, and the balance of cash is distributed to the partners.

KEY TERMS

partnership liquidation

Ending the Partnership

Settling the affairs of the partnership business when it ends is referred to as **partnership liquidation**. In the liquidation process, all partnership assets are converted to cash and all partnership debts are paid. Any remaining cash is then paid to the individual partners. The process involves the following four steps:

1. All noncash assets are sold for cash.
2. All gains or losses from the sale of noncash assets are added to or deducted from the capital accounts of the partners based on the partnership agreement.
3. All partnership creditors are paid.
4. Any cash remaining after the creditors are paid is distributed to the partners based on the final balance in the partners' accounts.

ACCOUNTING TIPS

The Seasoned Accountant

What do seasoned accountants know that new recruits do not? Experienced accountants know more about the nature of particular business fields, what can go wrong and why, and what is and is not important. This experience is sometimes called "good judgment."

Liquidation of Surfside Bike & Skate Rentals

Let's explore the liquidation of the Surfside Bike & Skate Rentals partnership. **Figure 28–4** shows the balance sheet on the date the partners decided to end Surfside Bike & Skate Rentals.

RESOURCE MANAGER

Reproducible Masters
- Lesson Plans
- Chapter Reviews and Working Papers (CRWP) TAE
- Demonstration Problems

Transparencies
- Section Focus Transparency
- Teaching Transparencies
- Source Document Transparencies
- Solution Transparencies

Multimedia
- Exam*View* CD-ROM
- Electronic Learning Center CD-ROM
- Interactive Lesson Planner CD-ROM

1 FOCUS

Introducing the Section
In this section students will learn what happens when a partnership is liquidated. They will learn how to record partnership losses and gains and any distributions made to the partners from liquidation of the partnership assets.

Section Concepts
- How to record losses in a partnership liquidation.
- How to record gains in a partnership liquidation.
- How to record the cash distribution required to liquidate a partnership.

Visual Learning

Section 2 Focus
Use **Transparency 28–5** to introduce section concepts.

BELL RINGER

Analyzing: Divide students into teams. Tell students that a local partnership is going out of business. Have teams make a list of possible reasons why the partners may be closing the business. (Some reasons include death or retirement of a partner, business losses, desire to relocate to another area, or poor outlook for future business success.) L1

Concept Development: Ending the Partnership

Discussion: A partnership ends when one or more of the partners dies or wants out of the business. With successful businesses, the remaining partner may be allowed to buy the full interests of other partners and turn the business into a sole proprietorship. With unsuccessful businesses, the partners sell the assets and distribute the cash. L1

2 TEACH

GUIDED PRACTICE

Reading Accounting

- Have students find a sample partnership agreement at the library. Ask them to read the agreement and summarize at least three main topics. L1
- Have students find a partnership agreement written in their first language. Ask them to summarize at least three main points. ELL

Concept Development: Liquidation of Surfside Bike & Skate Rentals

Discussion: Point out that one of the characteristics of the partnership form of organization is its limited life. If one or more of the partners wants to end the partnership, the business will cease to exist. L1

Visual Learning

Figure 28–4 Surfside Bike & Skate Rentals Balance Sheet

Review balance sheet information using **Transparency 28–6.**

Concept Development: The Liquidation Process

Discussion: Point out that when a partnership is liquidated, all the assets of the business must be sold. The resulting gains or losses are then recorded in the business's accounting system. L1

Strategies for Teaching International Accounting

To enrich study of international accounting, refer to the additional critical thinking activities in the booklet.

Figure 28–4 Surfside Bike & Skate Rentals Balance Sheet

Surfside Bike & Skate Rentals
Balance Sheet
April 15, 20--

Assets			
Cash in Bank		18 000 00	
Accounts Receivable		33 000 00	
Merchandise Inventory		35 000 00	
Equipment	48 000 00		
Less: Accumulated Depreciation	(8 000 00)		
		40 000 00	
Total Assets			126 000 00
Liabilities			
Note Payable		10 000 00	
Accounts Payable		20 000 00	
Total Liabilities			30 000 00
Partners' Equity			
Molly Gill, Capital		57 000 00	
Don Putman, Capital		39 000 00	
Total Partners' Equity			96 000 00
Total Liabilities and Partners' Equity			126 000 00

International ACCOUNTING

Social Etiquette

Being sensitive to the cultural differences in any business or social setting can prevent potential misunderstandings. For example, in most Latin American countries, people tend to stand very close to one another. When an American (who naturally stands about an arm's length away) backs away from a Latin associate during a conversation, it can be considered offensive.

The Liquidation Process

Gill and Putman share profits and losses equally and agree to end the partnership based on the April 15 balance sheet. The liquidation process requires that all partnership assets be converted to cash, debts be paid, and the remaining cash be distributed to the partners. There were five transactions over a period of weeks that involved ending the partnership.

Sale of Partnership Accounts Receivable at a Loss

On April 20 the $33,000 in accounts receivable are sold to a finance broker for $29,000. The sale of the receivables results in a $4,000 ($29,000 – $33,000) loss to the partnership. The loss is divided equally between Gill and Putman. The entry to record the sale of the receivables and distribute the loss is as follows:

GENERAL JOURNAL PAGE 109

	DATE		DESCRIPTION	POST. REF.	DEBIT	CREDIT	
1	20--						1
2	Apr.	20	Cash in Bank		29 000 00		2
3			Molly Gill, Capital		2 000 00		3
4			Don Putman, Capital		2 000 00		4
5			Accounts Receivable			33 000 00	5
6			Receipt 341				6
7							7

Teaching International ACCOUNTING

Role-Playing Social Etiquette A great deal of communication is nonverbal, such as hand gestures, facial expressions, posture and stance, and interpersonal distance. Ask two students to role-play a business conversation, with one person from the United States and the other from Latin America. Ask the "Latin American" to move very close (to within about 10 inches) to the other person. After the conversation, ask the U.S. person if he or she was uncomfortable with the distance between them. Discuss with the class that typically people in the United States maintain a larger distance between speakers than do people in many other countries, who may be insulted if a person moves back from them.

The individual balances in the accounts receivable subsidiary ledger are credited for a total of $33,000.

Sale of Partnership Merchandise at a Loss

On April 29 the merchandise inventory, which cost $35,000, is sold for $32,000 to a discount warehouse. The sale results in a $3,000 ($32,000 – $35,000) loss to the partnership. The loss is divided equally between the partners. The entry to record the sale of the inventory and distribute the loss is as follows:

GENERAL JOURNAL — PAGE 110

	DATE		DESCRIPTION	POST. REF.	DEBIT	CREDIT	
1	20--						1
2	Apr.	29	Cash in Bank		32 000 00		2
3			Molly Gill, Capital		1 500 00		3
4			Don Putman, Capital		1 500 00		4
5			Merchandise Inventory			35 000 00	5
6			Receipt 363				6
7							7

Sale of Partnership Equipment at a Gain

The partnership owns equipment that cost $48,000 and has accumulated depreciation of $8,000. The book value of the equipment is $40,000 ($48,000 – $8,000).

On May 5 the equipment is sold to a dealer for $42,000 resulting in a gain of $2,000 ($42,000 – $40,000). The gain is divided equally between the partners. The entry to record the sale of the equipment and distribute the gain is as follows:

GENERAL JOURNAL — PAGE 111

	DATE		DESCRIPTION	POST. REF.	DEBIT	CREDIT	
1	20--						1
2	May	5	Accum. Depr.—Equipment		8 000 00		2
3			Cash in Bank		42 000 00		3
4			Molly Gill, Capital			1 000 00	4
5			Don Putman, Capital			1 000 00	5
6			Equipment			48 000 00	6
7			Receipt 371				7
8							8

CONNECT TO . . . MATHEMATICS

The abacus is an ancient Chinese calculating device with two columns of beads strung on reeds that is still used by many Asians to perform arithmetic. In a 1946 contest between a Japanese abacist and an early computer, the traditional device won easily after two days of competition.

CHAPTER 28
SECTION 2, PAGES 757–762

2 TEACH (Cont'd.)

Demonstration Problem Step-by-Step Practice

Use demonstration problem 28–4 to give students practice in analyzing and recording the sale of partnership accounts receivable at a loss.

Visual Learning

General Journal, p. 759 Use the illustration of the general journal at the top of this page to explain the entry to record the sale of partnership merchandise at a loss. Point out that the partners' capital accounts are debited to show the decrease caused by selling the merchandise at a loss.

General Journal, p. 759 Use the illustration of the general journal at the bottom of this page to explain the entry to record a gain on the sale of equipment. Point out the debit to the Accumulated Depreciation account. Remind students that this account has a normal credit balance because it is a contra asset account. The debit reduces the balance in Accumulated Depreciation to zero.

INTERDISCIPLINARY CONNECTIONS ACTIVITY

Mathematics How do people who use an abacus learn to read the numbers and perform mathematics functions? In the illustration shown at the right, the abacist would read the numbers closest to the middle bar. Beads above the bar count five; those below, one. Reading from left to right, the number would be 139 (1, 3, 4 + 5 = 9).

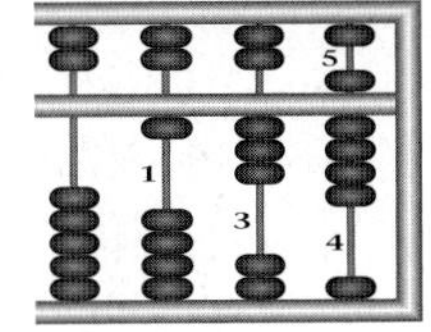

2 TEACH (Cont'd.)

Visual Learning

General Journal, p. 760

Use the illustration of the general journal on this page to discuss how to record payments made to clear the partnership's short- and long-term debts.

T Accounts, p. 760

Use the T accounts to summarize the liquidation transactions to date (sale of the accounts receivable at a loss for $29,000—$2,000 loss for each partner; sale of merchandise at a loss for $32,000—$1,500 loss for each partner; sale of partnership equipment at a gain for $42,000—$1,000 gain for each partner; and the payment of the partnerships debts totaling $30,000).

Thinking Algebraically

Creating Equations: Have students write an extended equation expressing the four liquidation entries described in this section. Ask students also to express the same relationships if they do not know whether assets will be sold at a gain or a loss. (Example: cash − loss on receivables − merchandise loss + equipment gain − liabilities; cash ± receivables ± merchandise ± equipment − liabilities) L2

Math Review for Accounting
Photocopy appropriate *Activity Sheets* for students who need additional practice in basic skills.

The Payment of Partnership Liabilities

On May 11 the partnership mails Check 234 to pay the bank note and Checks 235 through 238 to pay the accounts payable balances. The entry to record the transactions is as follows:

GENERAL JOURNAL — PAGE 112

	DATE		DESCRIPTION	POST. REF.	DEBIT	CREDIT	
1	20--						1
2	May	11	Notes Payable		10 000 00		2
3			Accounts Payable		20 000 00		3
4			Cash in Bank			30 000 00	4
5			Checks 234–238				5
6							6

The individual balances in the accounts payable subsidiary ledger are debited for a total of $20,000. This entry brings the **Accounts Payable** account to zero.

Only three accounts remain in the ledger after all the noncash assets are sold and the debts of the partnership are paid: **Cash in Bank; Molly Gill, Capital;** and **Don Putman, Capital.**

Cash in Bank

Debit	Credit
Bal. 18,000	30,000
29,000	
32,000	
42,000	
Bal. 91,000	

Molly Gill, Capital

Debit	Credit
2,000	Bal. 57,000
1,500	1,000
	Bal. 54,500

Don Putman, Capital

Debit	Credit
2,000	Bal. 39,000
1,500	1,000
	Bal. 36,500

ACCOUNTING *Flashbacks*

THE INTERNET
The Internet was created in the 1960s for military communication. Today, it is also used commercially for tasks such as promoting businesses, posting financial information, and conducting research.

Now cash can be distributed to the partners based on the final balances in their capital accounts: Gill, $54,500 and Putman, $36,500.

Final Distribution of Cash

On May 15 the partnership is ended by distributing the balance of **Cash in Bank** to Gill and Putman. The final transaction to end the partnership is recorded as follows:

Math Skill Builder Activity

Using Ratios Have students practice using ratios by calculating the amount each partner will receive in the following examples:

1. Two partners share earnings of $12,000 on a 3:2 basis.
2. Three partners share a loss of $16,000 on a 2:1:1 basis.
3. Two partners share liquidation cash of $35,000 on a 4:3 basis.

(1. $7,500/$4,800 2. $8,000/$4,000/$4,000 3. $20,000/$15,000)

DATE		DESCRIPTION	POST. REF.	DEBIT	CREDIT	
1	20--					1
2	May 15	Molly Gill, Capital		54 500 00		2
3		Don Putman, Capital		36 500 00		3
4		Cash in Bank			91 000 00	4
5		Checks 239 and 240				5
6		To dissolve the partnership				6
7						7

GENERAL JOURNAL — PAGE 113

Calculating Purchases Return

When calculating the amount of a purchases return:

- be sure to subtract the amount of the return *before* calculating any discounts to be taken.

Legal Requirements for Dissolving a Partnership

Terms of dissolution may have been stated in the partnership agreement. Any terms laid out in that agreement must be followed when the partnership ends. If the partnership did not have a stated agreement, the laws of the state apply. Most states require that the partnership file a document stating that the entity has been dissolved. If the business has employees, the partnership must also notify the appropriate state and federal tax agencies.

ANALYZING FINANCIAL REPORTS

Evaluating Partnership Operating Results

You learned in earlier chapters how to calculate ratios to help you evaluate the financial health of corporations that publish their operating results in annual reports. Owners and managers of businesses that do not make their financial information public are also interested in these measures of financial health.

$$\text{Return on Sales} = \frac{\text{Net Income}}{\text{Sales}}$$

$$\text{Current Ratio} = \frac{\text{Current Assets}}{\text{Current Liabilities}}$$

$$\text{Quick Ratio} = \frac{\text{Cash \& Receivables}}{\text{Current Liabilities}}$$

Return on sales is a measure of how much profit the business is earning for each dollar of total revenue. Other key measures are the current and quick ratios, which show a company's ability to repay it's debts.

Analyze the Report:

Use the balance sheet on page 758 to answer these questions:

1. Assume that Surfside Bike and Skate Rentals earned sales revenue of $192,000 and net income of $24,000 for the fiscal period just ended. Calculate the return on sales.
2. Analyze the company's liquidity based on the current ratio and the quick ratio.
3. Write one to two paragraphs describing the financial health of Surfside Bike and Skate Rentals based on your analysis of their financial information.

ANALYZING FINANCIAL REPORTS

Analyze the Report (Answers)

1. 12.5%
2. Current ratio 2.87; quick ratio 1.7
3. Answers may vary. The ratios show good financial condition.

Extension Activity: Have students make decisions using appropriate accounting concepts. Would they make a loan to this business? Would they enter this partnership? If yes, what percentage of ownership would they purchase?

2 TEACH (Cont'd.)

Visual Learning

General Journal, p. 761

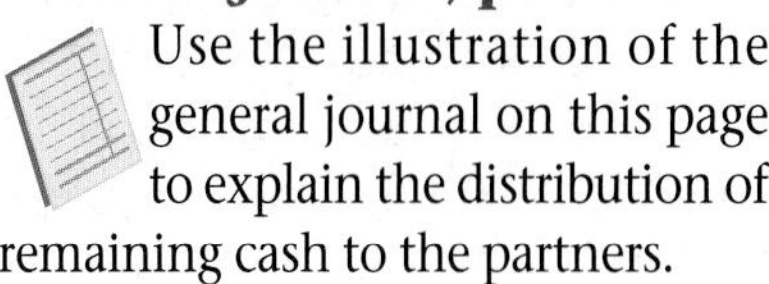

Use the illustration of the general journal on this page to explain the distribution of remaining cash to the partners.

Demonstration Problem Step-by-Step Practice

Use demonstration problem 28–5 to give students practice in analyzing and recording entries needed to liquidate a partnership.

Teaching Tip

Point out that had the partnership lacked enough cash to pay its debts after selling the receivables and equipment, the partners would have been required to invest the additional money needed to pay off all partnership debts. Unlike corporate investments, where liability is limited to the amount of the investment, partnerships have no limits on liability. The partners' personal assets can be taken to pay off the partnership's debts.

Research: Have students research any laws relating to forming and liquidating partnerships in your state. Ask students to make a short (1- to 2-minute) presentation to share their findings with the class. L2

Discussion: Have students identify the various accounting functions involved with a partnership. (Investment by partners, division of profits and losses, partner withdrawals, preparing financial statements, liquidation) L1

3 ASSESS

Thinking Critically (Answers)

1. (a) Noncash assets are sold. (b) Gains or losses from sale of noncash assets are added to or deducted from partners' capital accounts based on their profit-and-loss-sharing agreement. (c) All creditors are paid. (d) Cash remaining after creditors are paid is distributed to the partners based on the final balance in the partners' accounts.
2. The cash remaining after all the partnership debts are paid is distributed to the individual partners, according to their capital account balances.

Computing in the Business World (Answer)

$63,250

Problem 28–3 (Answers)

Sept. 4: Dr. Cash in Bank $38,000, Gunther, Capital $3,500, Pertee, Capital $3,500; Cr. Merchandise Inventory $45,000

Sept. 15: Dr. Cash in Bank $29,000; Cr. Gunther, Capital $1,000, Pertee, Capital $1,000, Office Equipment $27,000

Chapter Reviews and Working Papers Refer students to the Chapter 28 workbook pages to answer *Check Your Understanding* activities.

4 CLOSE

Section Wrap-Up

Drawing Conclusions: Have students explain how to liquidate a partnership with assets greater than liabilities. Then have them describe how to liquidate a partnership with liabilities greater than assets. L1

SECTION 2 Check Your Understanding

Now that you have studied this section, complete the following questions and problems.

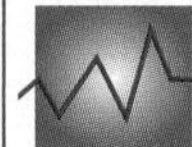

Thinking Critically

1. What steps are involved in liquidating a partnership?
2. Explain how to distribute the cash that remains after a partnership sells all of its noncash assets and pays all of its debts.

Computing in the Business World

Max & Tex novelty store, a partnership, is ending. You are to help liquidate the partnership. Listed below are the remaining assets and liabilities of the business. Max & Tex share profits and losses equally.

Assets		Liabilities	
Cash in Bank	$20,000	Accounts Payable	$15,500
Accounts Receivable	$12,000	**Partners' Equity**	
Merchandise Inventory	$42,000	Marilyn Max, Capital	$59,250
Equipment	$60,000	Tom Tex, Capital	$59,250

Liquidation Transactions:

1. Customers will pay their accounts in full before the liquidation date.
2. Merchandise inventory was sold for $40,000 resulting in a $2,000 loss to the partnership.
3. Equipment was sold to a local retailer for $70,000 resulting in a gain of $10,000.
4. Accounts payable will be paid in full.

Instructions How much cash will each partner receive at final liquidation?

Problem 28–3 Recording a Loss and Gain on the Sale of Noncash Assets by a Partnership

Partners Gunther and Pertee share profits equally. In the process of ending the business, they sell all the partnership's noncash assets. The transactions for the sales follow.

Instructions Record the transactions in general journal form in your working papers. Use general journal page 275.

Date	Transactions
Sept. 4	The merchandise inventory, which cost $45,000, was sold for $38,000.
15	The office equipment, with a book value of $27,000, was sold for $29,000.

RETEACHING SECTION 2

Liquidating a Partnership Explain that a liquidation occurs when both the partnership and the business end. Assets are sold, debts are paid, and the remaining cash is distributed to the partners. The sale of assets, recognition of gains and losses on asset sales, payments of debts, and the division of remaining cash are all recorded in the business accounting system to show the effect of each part of the liquidation process. The accounting records thus provide a full picture of the business from beginning to end.

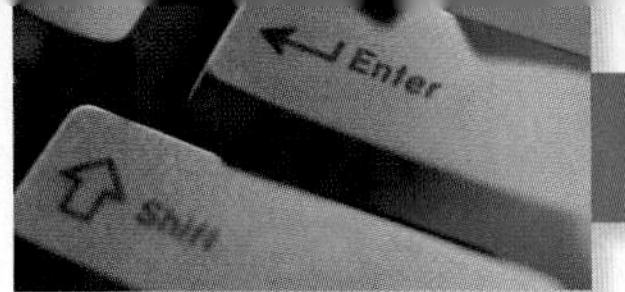

CHAPTER 28 SUMMARY

KEY CONCEPTS

1. The income statement of a partnership may have a special section showing the division of profits or losses among partners.
2. The balance sheet of a partnership contains a capital section titled Partners' Equity.
3. Partnerships prepare a statement of changes in partners' equity. This statement reflects beginning balances, investments, and withdrawals of each partner.
4. The process of ending a partnership is called partnership liquidation.
5. When partners agree to end the partnership:
   - All noncash assets are sold for cash.
   - All gains or losses from the sale of noncash assets are added to or deducted from the capital accounts of the partners based on the partnership agreement.
   - All partnership creditors are paid.
   - Any cash remaining after creditors are paid is distributed to the partners based on the final balance in the partners' accounts.
6. Each partner's share of gains and losses from the sale of noncash assets is added to or deducted from the partner's capital account.
7. In liquidation, creditors are paid before any partnership assets are distributed to the partners.
8. Terms of dissolution may be stated in a partnership agreement. In lieu of an agreement, laws of the state apply.
9. Upon dissolution, the partnership should notify any applicable taxing authority.

Great Ideas *From the Classroom of...*

Accounting for Partnerships To present partnership equity, use the analogy of three people contributing to the creation of a pie. One person invests money for ingredients, a second supplies the recipe, and a third makes the pie. The investments of time and money are measurable; the investment of knowledge is not measurable. When the pie is complete, it can be divided equally or split up proportionally based on each person's investment. The equity of a partnership is created by two or more people who decide how to split profit or loss.

William B. Hoyt
Wilton High School
Wilton, Connecticut

SUMMARY CHAPTER 28

Chapter 28 Quiz

Student ____ Class ____ Instructor ____
Date Assigned ____ Date Completed ____

CHAPTER 28 QUIZ

Financial Statements and Liquidation of a Partnership

QUESTIONS (True-False)
Directions: In the space provided, indicate whether each statement is true or false.
___ 1. Division of net income is shown on the partnership income statement.
___ 2. The income statement reports each partner's capital balance.
___ 3. Total partners' equity is reported on the balance sheet and the statement of changes in partners' equity.
___ 4. Liquidating a partnership means that it ceases to operate.
___ 5. Assets can be sold at a gain or loss.
___ 6. When equipment is sold at a gain, Accumulated Depreciation is credited.
___ 7. All liabilities must be paid before the partnership is liquidated.
___ 8. Gains on sales of assets are recorded as debits in the partners' capital accounts.
___ 9. Losses on sales of assets are credited to the asset account.
___ 10. Most states require notification of the liquidation of a partnership.

30 • Chapter Quizzes

QUESTIONS (True-False)

1. Division of net income is shown on the partnership income statement.
2. The income statement reports each partner's capital balance.
3. Total partners' equity is reported on the balance sheet and the statement of changes in partners' equity.
4. Liquidating a partnership means that it ceases to operate.
5. Assets can be sold at a gain or loss.
6. When equipment is sold at a gain, Accumulated Depreciation is credited.
7. All liabilities must be paid before the partnership is liquidated.
8. Gains on sales of assets are recorded as debits in the partners' capital accounts.
9. Losses on sales of assets are credited to the asset account.
10. Most states require notification of the liquidation of a partnership.

ANSWERS

1. True	5. True	8. False
2. False	6. False	9. False
3. True	7. True	10. True
4. True		

OVERVIEW CHAPTER 28

USING KEY TERMS

See the *Glossary* for the definitions of these terms. Ask for volunteers to share their descriptions in class. Discuss any differences in use of terms.

Understanding Accounting Concepts and Procedures

(Answers)

1. Income statement, statement of changes in partners' equity, and balance sheet.
2. The equity section of the balance sheet is called partners' equity rather than owner's equity or stockholders' equity; it reports each partner's capital account.
3. Settling the affairs of the partnership when it ends.
4. A partnership can be liquidated for many reasons including death of a partner, completion of a project, or at the end of a specified time period.
5. (a) All noncash assets are sold for cash. (b) All gains or losses from the sale of noncash assets are added to or deducted from the capital accounts of the partners based on the partnership agreement. (c) All creditors are paid. (d) Any remaining cash is distributed to the partners based on the final balances in their capital accounts.
6. Accounts Receivable, Cash in Bank, partners' capital accounts.
7. In the manner specified in the partnership agreement.
8. The partners' capital accounts are debited when noncash assets are sold at a loss; they are credited when noncash assets are sold at a gain.
9. Cash remaining after all creditors have been paid is distributed to the partners according to the ending balances in their capital accounts.

CHAPTER 28 REVIEW AND ACTIVITIES

USING KEY TERMS

Imagine that you have been asked to explain the following terms and how they might relate to a timber company organized as a partnership. Review the information about Plum Creek Timber Company on page 752 and prepare a short description of the terms below.

partnership liquidation
statement of changes in partners' equity

Understanding Accounting Concepts and Procedures

Instructions

On a separate sheet of paper, answer the following questions:

1. What three financial statements are prepared for a partnership at the end of a period?
2. How does the balance sheet for a partnership differ from that for a sole proprietorship and corporation?
3. What is the meaning of partnership liquidation?
4. List several reasons why partners liquidate a partnership.
5. What are the four steps required to liquidate a partnership?
6. When selling partnership accounts receivable at a loss, what accounts are affected?
7. How are the gains and losses from the sale of noncash assets distributed when a partnership ends?
8. What happens to the partners' capital accounts when noncash assets are sold at a loss? At a gain?
9. When dissolving a partnership, what is the final transaction?

ASSESSMENT RESOURCES

Choose assessment strategies from the following pages to evaluate your students' progress.

Student Edition
Check Your Understanding, pp. 756, 762
Chapter 28 Problems, pp. 767–769
Analyzing Financial Reports, p. 761

Assessment and Evaluation Masters
Chapter 28 Study Plan, *Glencoe Workbook (CRWP)*
Chapter 28 Self-Test, *Glencoe Workbook (CRWP)*
Chapter 28 Test, *Chapter Tests* Booklet
Chapter 28 Activity, *School-to-Work Handbook*
Chapter 28 **Exam***View*

Teacher Wraparound Edition
Critical Thinking Activity, p. 767
Reteaching Sections 1–2, pp. 756, 762
Chapter 28 Quiz, p. 763

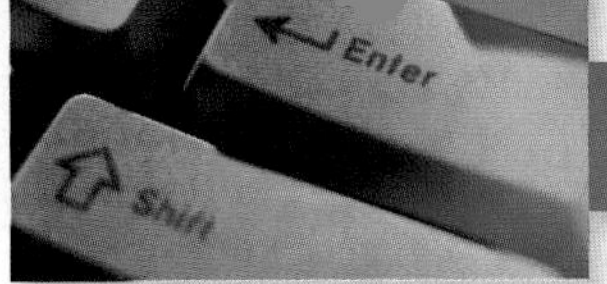

Case Study...

Partnership: Building and Design

Barnes Construction is a homebuilder that wants to expand into commercial real estate. The company has a client who owns 10 acres of land on which she wants to build an apartment complex. Barnes is looking for a partner to help design and build the apartments.

Slater Architectural Design is a firm of architects and builders that has been looking for new projects. Barnes and Slater agree to form a partnership to design and build the apartments. The contract to build the apartments is for $10,400,000. Based on estimated costs, the project should provide net profits of 18 percent.

Thinking Critically:

1. If Barnes and Slater agree to share revenue and expenses equally, how much profit will each partner earn?
2. To limit each partner's liability to this project only, what information should be in the partnership agreement?

interNET CONNECTION

Financial Statements for Partnerships

While the partnerships you studied in this chapter resulted from two or more individuals combining resources and skills to market products or services, partnerships are also possible between corporations.

Competitors AT&T and Sprint have found it profitable to form partnerships and joint ventures with telecommunication companies in other countries to enhance their competitive advantage in the global marketplace.

Do This:

1. Visit the Web sites for AT&T and Sprint.
2. List a partnership or joint venture that each company has formed with another telecommunications company.

Conducting an Audit with Alex

Ann Martha, the accountant for the R&P partnership, made an entry in the partnership books after some of the noncash assets were sold at a loss of $13,000. The remainder of the assets were sold at a gain of $4,000.

The capital balances before the distribution of gains and losses were Roberts, $40,000 and Patrick, $30,000. Roberts and Patrick shared profits and losses based on: Roberts, ⅔; Patrick, ⅓. Martha made the following entry to distribute the balance of cash after all the debts were paid.

Roberts, Capital	$ 34,000
Patrick, Capital	$ 27,000
Total	$ 61,000

Instructions Review Martha's calculations. If incorrect, re-compute the distribution of cash.

Workplace Skills

Self-Esteem

If you are an optimistic thinker and exhibit knowledge of your own skills and abilities, you display the elements of strong self-esteem.

On the Job:

Ten years ago you and your high school teammate opened a small sports and nutrition center. A large national sports center complex has opened in a nearby shopping mall, and your business has dropped significantly. You and your partner have decided to close the center and liquidate the assets.

Thinking Critically:

1. Make a list of all the pros and cons of liquidating a business.
2. Make a list of the tasks necessary to complete the liquidation. Prioritize the items on the list.

INTRODUCING CHAPTER 28

Case Study...

Thinking Critically (Answers)

1. $936,000
2. Answers may vary. The partnership agreement should include such items as the sharing of profits and losses, what each company will do/provide in order to complete the project, and the terms/conditions for final liquidation when the project is complete.

Workplace Skills

Thinking Critically (Answers)

1. Answers may vary. Liquidation means that the partners will not have a chance to make the business bounce back to profitability, but it also ends their exposure to the potential for further losses.
2. Answers may vary. Students should base their responses on the steps for liquidation listed in the chapter.

Conducting an Audit with Alex

(Answer)

The final balances are correct.

Internet Resources and Activities Handbook

Refer students to the booklet for additional Internet activities.

interNET CONNECTION www.glencoe.com

Do This (Answers)

1. AT&T: www.att.com and Sprint: www.sprint.com
2. AT&T has a joint venture with BT (British Telecom); Sprint has a joint venture with France Telecom.

PEACHTREE CORNER

Partnership Liquidation

Use the **General Journal Entry** task option to record the transactions to liquidate a partnership. The textbook ilustrates the various transactions using general journal entries.

Tasks Analysis Options Reports
- Quotes/Sales Orders
- Sales/Invoicing...
- Receipts...
- Finance Charge...
- Select for Deposit...
- Purchase Orders...
- Purchases/Receive Inventory...
- Select for Payment...
- Payments...
- Write Checks...
- Time/Expense
- Select for Payroll Entry...
- Payroll Entry...
- General Journal Entry...
- Inventory Adjustments...
- Assemblies...
- Account Reconciliation...
- Void Checks...
- Action Items...
- System

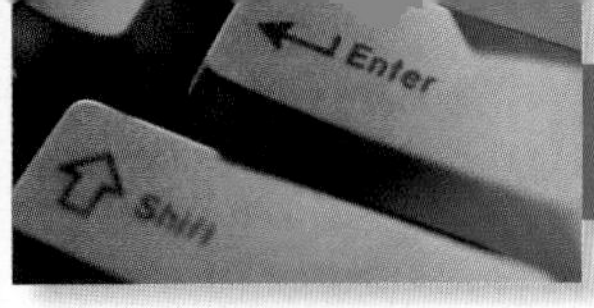

Setting Up the General Ledger

Making the Transition from a Manual to a Computerized System

Task	Perform Accounting Procedures Using Manual Methods	Perform Accounting Procedures Using Automated Methods
Setting up general ledger accounts with balances	1. Using accounting stationery, open a general ledger account for accounts based on the expected transactions of the business. 2. Record the balance of each account. Ideally, end-of-period balances should be used, therefore ensuring the accounting records were in balance when transferred.	1. Create a chart of accounts, selecting from predefined charts offered, or by entering select accounts based on the expected transactions for the business. 2. Enter the beginning balance for each account.

Setting up the General Ledger

Peachtree Question	Description
How do I convert a manual accounting general ledger system into Peachtree?	1. Create a general ledger account in Peachtree for each account in the manual system. From the ***Maintain*** menu, select **Chart of Accounts**. 2. Enter the account number, name, and account type for all accounts. 3. Click the arrow for Beginning Balances. 4. Select the period from which the balance was taken. 5. Enter the beginning balance for each account. 6. Click Save when all balances have been entered and the Trial Balance Difference at the bottom of the screen is 0.00.
What does the software do "behind the scenes"?	1. Peachtree will not post the beginning balances to the general ledger accounts until the trial balance is in balance. 2. Once the trial balance is in balance, Peachtree posts the amounts to the general ledger. 3. Transactions for the current period can then be entered.

For detailed instructions: See the **Peachtree User Guide** in your Glencoe Working Papers.

Peachtree® Answers to Frequently Asked Questions

Q: Can you print a Statement of Changes in Partners' Equity report using the Peachtree software?

A: No, Peachtree does not include an option to print a Statement of Changes in Partners' Equity report. You must manually prepare this report using the partners' beginning capital balances and each partners' share of profit or loss.

For additional information, refer to your *Glencoe Peachtree Accounting User Guide.*

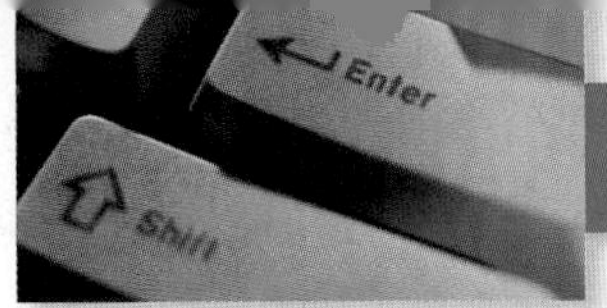

APPLICATION OPTIONS

Problem 28–4 Preparing an Income Statement and Balance Sheet for a Partnership

Joy Webster and Diana Ruiz have been in business since the beginning of the year. Now at the end of the year, they would like to know how the partnership has done in its first year of operation. Joy and Diana stated in the partnership agreement that they will share profits equally. The net income for the year was $5,780. The January 1 capital balances for both partners were $0. Joy invested $6,000 cash in the partnership throughout the year, and withdrew $1,800. Diana invested $5,500 cash in the partnership, and withdrew $1,200.

Instructions In your working papers, prepare the Division of Income section of the income statement and the Partners' Equity section of the balance sheet for the partnership.

Analyze: What are the ending balances in the partners' capital accounts?

Complete chapter problems one of four ways:

1. **Manual** Glencoe Working Papers

or

2. **Peachtree Complete Accounting** Software

or

3. **QuickBooks** Templates (Problems 28–6, 28–8)

or

4. **Spreadsheet** Templates (Problems 28–4, 28–9)

Problem 28–5 Liquidating the Partnership with Losses on the Sale of Noncash Assets

Guice and Ward decide to end their partnership on September 21. They share profits and losses equally. The account balances of the partnership as of that date are listed below.

Cash	$6,500
Inventory	8,800
Equipment (book value)	2,700
Accounts Payable	4,000
Guice, Capital	6,800
Ward, Capital	7,200

The inventory was sold for $5,000. The equipment was sold for $2,000. All of the accounts payable will be paid in full with the cash.

Instructions In your working papers, prepare the journal entries to record the liquidation of this partnership. Use general journal page 85.

Analyze: Before the final distribution to the partners, did the partners' capital account balances increase or decrease as a result of the liquidation of the partnership? Why?

SPREADSHEET SMART GUIDE

Step-by-Step Instructions: Problem 28–4

1. Select the spreadsheet template for Problem 28–4.
2. Enter your name and the date in the spaces provided on the template.
3. Complete the spreadsheet using the instructions in your working papers.
4. Print the spreadsheet and proof your work.
5. Save your work and exit the spreadsheet program.

PROBLEMS CHAPTER 28

Problem 28–4 (Answers) Preparing an Income Statement and Balance Sheet for a Partnership

Net income, each partner $2,890

Partners' equity: Webster, Capital $7,090; Ruiz, Capital $7,190

Analyze: Webster, Capital $7,090; Ruiz, Capital $7,190

Problem 28–5 (Answers) Liquidating the Partnership with Losses on the Sale of Noncash Assets

Sept. 21: Dr. Cash in Bank $5,000, Guice, Capital $1,900, Ward, Capital $1,900; Cr. Inventory $8,800

Sept. 21: Dr. Cash in Bank $2,000, Guice, Capital $350, Ward, Capital $350; Cr. Equip. $2,700

Sept. 21: Dr. Accts. Pay. $4,000; Cr. Cash in Bank $4,000

Sept. 21: Dr. Guice, Capital $4,550, Ward, Capital $4,950; Cr. Cash in Bank $9,500

Analyze: The capital balances decreased because the inventory and the equipment were both sold at a loss.

CRITICAL THINKING ACTIVITY

Identifying Assumptions Kayla and Ray went into an equal partnership two years ago when they opened their marina. Now, they would both like more time to enjoy sailing, so they have decided to invite Pete into the partnership. Pete does not have the capital to invest, but he is willing to manage the business, which would allow Kayla and Ray to become "silent partners" in the business. What type of negotiations should transpire before bringing Pete into the business? (Kayla and Ray should decide on the amount of time each partner will work, percentage of profit/loss for each, and decision-making authority. The three of them need to discuss all issues of operating the partnership.)

PROBLEMS CHAPTER 28

Problem 28–6 (Answers) Recording a Gain or Loss on the Sale of Noncash Assets by a Partnership

May 29: Dr. Cash in Bank $12,775, Hudson, Capital $1,293.75, Franklin, Capital $431.25; Cr. Equip. $14,500
June 2: Dr. Cash in Bank $6,900, Hudson, Capital $675, Franklin, Capital $225; Cr. Accts. Rec. $7,800
June 4: Dr. Cash in Bank $1,900, Hudson, Capital $675, Franklin, Capital $225; Cr. Merchandise Inventory $2,800

Analyze: All gains or losses must be recognized and all partnership debts paid prior to distributing cash to liquidate a partnership.

Problem 28–7 (Answers) Preparing a Statement of Changes in Partners' Equity

Ending capital balances:
Farmer $61,088
Romans $59,588
Total $120,676

Analyze: $61,088

Problem 28–8 (Answer) Liquidating the Partnership

Oct. 15: Dr. Cash in Bank $95,000, Royka, Capital $5,000, Martinez, Capital $5,000; Cr. Inventory $105,000
Oct. 15: Dr. Note Pay. $10,000; Cr. Cash in Bank $10,000
Oct. 15: Dr. Royka, Capital $40,000, Martinez, Capital $55,000; Cr. Cash in Bank $95,000

Analyze: Royka will receive $32,500; Martinez, $47,500.

Peachtree®

SMART GUIDE

Step-by-Step Instructions: Problem 28–5

1. Select the problem set Problem 28–5.
2. Rename the company and set the system date.
3. Record the transactions to liquidate the partnership using the **General Journal Entry** option.
4. Print a General Journal report and proof your work.
5. Answer the Analyze question.
6. End the session.

Peachtree®

SMART GUIDE

Step-by-Step Instructions: Problem 28–6

1. Select the problem set Problem 28–6.
2. Rename the company and set the system date.
3. Record the transactions to liquidate the partnership using the **General Journal Entry** option.
4. Print a General Journal report and proof your work.
5. Answer the Analyze question.
6. End the session.

Problem 28–6 Recording a Gain or Loss on the Sale of Noncash Assets by a Partnership

Hudson and Franklin are in the process of liquidating their partnership. They share profits and losses in a 3:1 ratio. They have sold all of the partnership's noncash assets. The transactions for the sales follow.

Date	Transactions
May 29	The equipment, with a book value of $14,500, was sold for $12,775.
June 2	The $7,800 in accounts receivable was sold to a finance broker for $6,900.
4	The merchandise inventory, which cost $2,800 was sold for $1,900.

Instructions In your working papers, record the journal entries for the sale of noncash assets. Use general journal page 120.

Analyze: Why must these losses be distributed to the partners' capital accounts before any cash is paid out to the partners?

Problem 28–7 Preparing a Statement of Changes in Partners' Equity

On January 1 Carol Farmer and Jim Romans formed a partnership called Research Consultants. Each partner invested $50,000 in cash on that date. The partnership agreement stated that the net income or loss would be shared equally.

During the year Farmer invested an additional $2,000 and withdrew $7,500 for personal use. Romans invested an additional $1,500 and withdrew $8,500. Net income for the first year was $33,176.

Instructions In your working papers, prepare a statement of changes in partners' equity for the year ended December 31.

Analyze: What was the balance in Farmer's capital account after earnings were distributed?

ADDRESSING MULTIPLE LEARNING STYLES

Naturalistic Learner Some students learn most effectively by observing their natural environment and collecting information through their observations. Have students work in groups to observe a local organization, such as a museum, a park, or a zoo. During their observations, ask students to make notes about the activities taking place. For example, students might observe animals being fed and cared for in a zoo. How would the cost of these activities be categorized and recorded in an accounting system? Have each group create charts and make a presentation of its findings to the class. Ask groups to describe how their observations relate to an accounting system the organization might use.

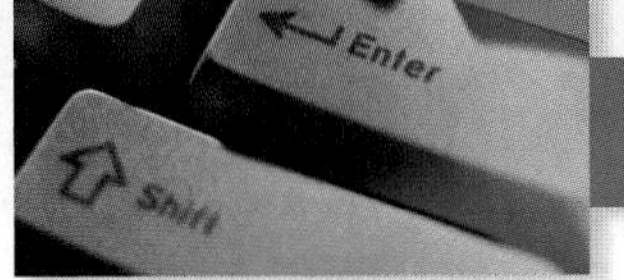

Problem 28–8 Liquidating the Partnership

On October 15 Martinez and Royka decide to end their partnership. Their assets consist of $10,000 in cash and inventory that cost $105,000 and was sold for $95,000. Their only liability is a note payable for $10,000 that will be paid in full. Their capital balances are Martinez, $60,000 and Royka, $45,000. They share profits and losses equally.

Instructions In your working papers, prepare the journal entries to record the liquidation of the partnership.

Analyze: If the inventory was sold for $80,000, how much cash would each partner receive at the final dissolution of the partnership?

Peachtree®

SMART GUIDE

Step-by-Step Instructions: Problem 28–8

1. Select the problem set Problem 28–8.
2. Rename the company and set the system date.
3. Record the transactions to liquidate the partnership using the **General Journal Entry** option.
4. Print a General Journal report and proof your work.
5. Answer the Analyze question.
6. End the session.

Problem 28–9 Completing End-of-Period Activities for a Partnership

Richard Smooth and Carrie Overhill are partners in the firm of R&C Roofing. They agreed to divide net income or loss on the following basis: Smooth, ¾; Overhill, ¼.

The completed work sheet for R&C Roofing for the year ended December 31 appears in your working papers.

Instructions In your working papers:

(1) Prepare an income statement for the partnership.
(2) Prepare a statement of changes in partners' equity.
(3) Prepare a balance sheet.
(4) Journalize the adjusting and closing entries, beginning on page 27 of the general journal.

Analyze: If Smooth or Overhill had not taken the withdrawals, what would the total equity balance have been at year end?

SPREADSHEET SMART GUIDE

Step-by-Step Instructions: Problem 28–9

1. Select the spreadsheet template for Problem 28–9.
2. Enter your name and the date in the spaces provided on the template.
3. Complete the spreadsheet using the instructions in your working papers.
4. Print the spreadsheet and proof your work.
5. Save your work and exit the spreadsheet program.

EXTENDING THE CONTENT

Exploring Partnerships in Your Community Invite one or more successful business partners in the community to speak to your class about working with a partner. Ask the speakers to share with students some history about the partnership. For example, ask them to share information about when the partnership was formed, how they became involved in the partnership, what goals they set, what plans they made for accomplishing their goals, and how they and their partner(s) work together to implement their plans. Also ask them to share any experiences they might have in ending a partnership or changing the members within a partnership.

CHALLENGE PROBLEM

Problem 28–9 (Answers) Completing End-of-Period Activities for a Partnership

Ending capital balances:
Smooth $53,305, Overhill $16,027

Net income $26,356
Total Assets $77,277

Adjusting entries:

Dec. 31: Dr. Office Supplies Exp. $335; Cr. Office Supplies $335
Dec. 31: Dr. Roofing Supplies Exp. $11,470; Cr. Roofing Supplies $11,470
Dec. 31: Dr. Insurance Exp. $1,200; Cr. Prepaid Insurance $1,200
Dec. 31: Dr. Depr. Exp.—Office Equip. $185; Cr. Accum. Depr.—Office Equip. $185
Dec. 31: Dr. Depr. Exp.—Truck $3,900; Cr. Accum. Depr.—Truck $3,900
Dec. 31: Dr. Depr. Exp.—Building $1,200; Cr. Accum. Depr.—Building $1,200

Closing entries:

Dec. 31: Dr. Consulting Fees $15,900, Roofing Fees $62,750; Cr. Income Summary $78,650
Dec. 31: Dr. Income Summary $52,294; Cr. Advertising Exp. $2,400, Depr. Exp.—Office Equip. $185, Depr. Exp.—Truck $3,900, Depr. Exp.—Building $1,200, Insurance Exp. $1,200, Office Supplies Exp. $335, Roofing Supplies Exp. $11,470, Salaries Exp. $28,109, Truck Exp. $1,400, Utilities Exp. $2,095
Dec. 31: Dr. Income Summary $26,356; Cr. Smooth, Capital $19,767, Overhill, Capital $6,589
Dec. 31: Dr. Smooth, Capital $8,700; Cr. Smooth, Withdrawals $8,700
Dec. 31: Dr. Overhill, Capital $8,100; Cr. Overhill, Withdrawals $8,100

Analyze: $86,132

INTRODUCING
MINI PRACTICE SET 6

Mini Practice Set Overview
This activity gives students the opportunity to record transactions and complete an accounting cycle for a business organized as a partnership. In the activity students will apply their knowledge of accounting procedures by analyzing normal business transactions for a partnership called Fine Finishes. The business has three partners, and students will determine each partner's share of earnings or losses based on the partner's stated percentage of ownership.

Most students should be able to complete this activity manually within two to three class periods.

Source documents and accounting stationery for completing the activity are included in the workbook, *Chapter Reviews and Working Papers*.

Mini Practice Set Concepts
- How to analyze business transactions.
- How to journalize business transactions in the general journal.
- How to post journal entries to the general ledger accounts.
- How to prepare a trial balance and a work sheet.
- How to prepare financial statements.
- How to journalize and post the closing entries.
- How to prepare a post-closing trial balance.

Visual Learning

Mini Practice Set Focus, p. 770
Discuss with students the accounting procedures they will use to complete this mini practice set.

MINI PRACTICE SET 6

Completing the Accounting Cycle for a Partnership

Fine Finishes

***What* You'll Learn**
- How to analyze business transactions.
- How to journalize business transactions in the general journal.
- How to post journal entries to the general ledger accounts.
- How to prepare a trial balance and a work sheet.
- How to prepare financial statements.
- How to journalize and post the closing entries.
- How to prepare a post-closing trial balance.

***Why* It's Important**

In Chapters 27 and 28, you learned how to account for partnership equity, divide income and loss among partners, and how to prepare financial statements for a partnership. Now you will have the opportunity to review and apply what you have learned by working through the accounting cycle for Fine Finishes.

Fine Finishes

Company Background: Fine Finishes is an interior and exterior painting company organized as a partnership. The partners are Laura Andersen, Sean Woo, and David Ingram. The business earns revenue from consultation and painting fees. The partnership divides income and losses as follows: Laura and Sean each receive 33 percent, and David receives 34 percent.

Your Job Responsibilities: As the accountant for Fine Finishes, use the accounting stationery in your working papers to complete the following activities.

(1) Open a general ledger account for each account in the chart of accounts.
(2) Analyze each business transaction.
(3) Enter each business transaction in the general journal. Begin on journal page 1.
(4) Post each journal entry to the appropriate accounts in the general ledger.
(5) Prepare a trial balance and then complete the work sheet.
(6) Prepare an income statement.
(7) Prepare a statement of partners' equity.
(8) Prepare a balance sheet.
(9) Journalize and post the closing entries.
(10) Prepare a post-closing trial balance.

ADDRESSING MULTIPLE LEARNING STYLES

Intrapersonal and Interpersonal Learners Divide students into pairs and ask each pair to reflect on themselves as business partners who have agreed to operate a business as co-owners. What personal qualities do each of them have that would be valuable in the business relationship? Do they like to share responsibility, help solve problems, and help make decisions? Have each pair decide what kind of business they could open and manage together. Finally, have each pair list some of the duties and responsibilities involved in operating their business and decide on who would handle each responsibility.

Fine Finishes

APPLICATION OPTIONS

CHART OF ACCOUNTS
Fine Finishes

ASSETS		PARTNERS' EQUITY	
101	Cash in Bank	301	Laura Andersen, Capital
105	Accts. Rec.—Mountain View City School District	302	Laura Andersen, Withdrawals
120	Computer Equipment	303	David Ingram, Capital
130	Office Supplies	304	David Ingram, Withdrawals
135	Office Equipment	305	Sean Woo, Capital
140	Painting Supplies	306	Sean Woo, Withdrawals
145	Painting Equipment	310	Income Summary
LIABILITIES		**REVENUE**	
205	Accts. Pay.—Custom Color	401	Painting Fees
210	Accts. Pay.—J & J Hardware and Lumber	405	Consultation Fees
215	Accts. Pay.—Paint Palace	**EXPENSES**	
		505	Advertising Expense
		510	Miscellaneous Expense
		515	Rent Expense
		520	Utilities Expense

Complete activities one of three ways:

1. **Manual** Glencoe Working Papers

or

2. **Peachtree Complete Accounting** Software

or

3. **QuickBooks** Templates

Business Transactions: Fine Finishes began business operations on February 1 of this year. During the month of February, the business completed the transactions that follow.

Date	Transactions
Feb. 1	Laura Andersen, David Ingram, and Sean Woo agreed to form a partnership and invest the following assets, Memorandum 1:

Contributed Assets	Andersen	Ingram	Woo
Cash	$1,500	$1,000	$1,200
Computer Equipment	—	2,800	—
Office Equipment	100	—	—
Painting Supplies	150	—	225
Painting Equipment	1,375	—	1,675
Total assets invested	$3,125	$3,800	$3,100

Date	Transactions
1	Signed a one-year rental agreement for a garage at $750 per month. A deposit of one month's rent plus the first month's rent was paid, Check 1101.
1	Put an ad in the Call an Expert section of the newspaper for $25, Check 1102.

Continued

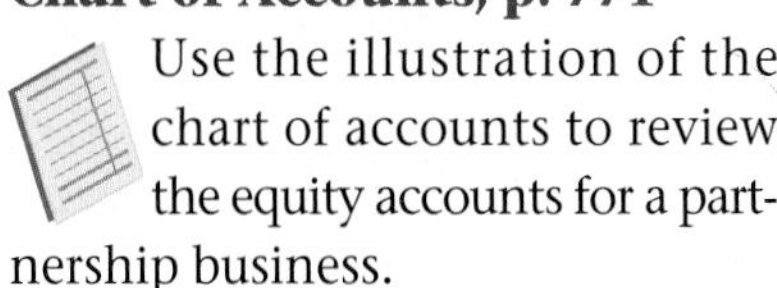

Visual Learning

Chart of Accounts, p. 771
Use the illustration of the chart of accounts to review the equity accounts for a partnership business.

Teaching Tip

Remind students that partners should have a written partnership agreement spelling out each person's responsibilities, ownership interest, and share of net income or loss. The agreement also should spell out how a partner who wishes to sell her or his share may do so.

HOME AND COMMUNITY CONNECTIONS ACTIVITY

Learning About Partnerships Ask students to work in teams of at least two students to a team. Have students visit at least one business that is operated as a partnership. Tell students to observe and note how the business operates, who makes the business decisions for the business, and what their future plans are for continuing their partnership. Then have each team of students present its findings and draw conclusions about the future success of the business.

SOURCE DOCUMENT PROBLEM

ANSWERS

Trial Balance totals $15,805

Net Income $3,233

Ending Capital balances:
Andersen $2,891.89
Ingram $3,599.22
Woo $2,866.89
Total $9,358.00

Total Assets $9,843
Total Liabilities $485

Post-Closing Trial Balance totals $9,843

Peachtree®

SMART GUIDE

Step-by-Step Instructions:

1. Select the problem set for Fine Finishes (MP–6).
2. Rename the company and set the system date.
3. Record all of the business transactions using the **General Journal Entry** option.
4. Print a General Journal report and proof your work.
5. Print a General Ledger report.
6. Print a General Ledger Trial Balance.
7. Print an Income statement and a Balance Sheet.
8. Click the save Pre-Closing Balances button in the Glencoe Smart Guide Window.
9. Record the closing entries using the **General Journal Entry** option.
10. Print a general journal report and proof your work.
11. Print a Post-Closing Trial Balance.
12. Answer the Analyze questions.
13. End the session.

TIP: Peachtree can only close a fiscal year. To close a monthly fiscal period, enter the closing entries using the **General Journal Entry** option.

Date	Transactions (cont.)
1	Paid deposit of $100 to utility company to start electric service, Check 1104.
1	Paid telephone company $175 to begin phone service and run dedicated line for computer, Check 1105.
2	Awarded a contract to paint a kitchen and family room for the McGuires. Collected $250 deposit, Receipt 1.
2	Bought paint and border stencils from Custom Color for $200 on account, Invoice 742.
2	Issued check 1103 for $55 for a business license to operate in the city of Mountain View, Colorado (Miscellaneous Expense).
4	Purchased $115 in office supplies, Check 1106.
5	Finished painting the kitchen and family room for the McGuires. Collected final payment of $450, Receipt 2.
6	Joined Mountain View Chamber of Commerce by purchasing membership of $45 (Miscellaneous Expense), Check 1107.
8	Bought painting equipment on account for $375 from Paint Palace, Invoice 1162.
10	Received $60 for color and painting consultation, Receipt 3.
12	Finished painting the cafeteria at the elementary school. Issued Invoice 101 to Mountain View City School District for $835.
14	Sent Check 1108 for $200 to Custom Color on account.
15	Andersen, Ingram, and Woo each made a withdrawal of $650 for personal use, Checks 1109, 1110, and 1111 respectively.
15	Awarded a contract to paint exterior of the Wicker and Hartel law office building. Received deposit of $1,000, Receipt 4.
16	Spent $135 for new paint brushes (Painting Supplies), Check 1112.
16	Bought paint from Custom Color for $395 on account, Invoice 750.
17	Received and paid Invoice 303 from Mountain View Realtors for ad in real estate brochure for $77, Check 1113.
18	Received $125 for painting consultation, Receipt 5.
19	Wrote Check 1114 for $85 to repair computer printer (Miscellaneous Expense).
21	Paid Paint Palace $375 on account, Check 1115.
22	Finished painting the Wicker and Hartel law office building. Collected final payment of $2,000, Receipt 6.
24	Bought $90 of lumber (Painting Supplies) on account from J & J Hardware and Lumber, Invoice 207.

Continued

MAKING CONNECTIONS TO DAILY LIFE

Business Failures Have students check the local newspapers or talk with area business owners about partnerships that have not succeeded in their community. Why did the businesses fail? Did the partnerships liquidate, dissolve, or merge with a larger entity? What advice do other business leaders have that would help a new partnershp to become successful?

Date	Transactions (cont.)
25	Received $575 for painting and making minor repairs to a garage, Receipt 7.
28	Andersen, Ingram, and Woo each made a withdrawal of $650 for personal use, Checks 1116, 1117, and 1118 respectively.

Analyze:

1. What is the balance in the **Laura Andersen, Capital** account after the closing entries have been posted?
2. What is the balance in the **David Ingram, Capital** account after the closing entries have been posted?
3. What is the balance in the **Sean Woo, Capital** account after the closing entries have been posted?
4. What is the net income for the partnership for the month ended February 28, 20--?

SOLUTION NOTES

MINI PRACTICE SET 6
PAGES 770–773

Analyze:

1. $2,891.89
2. $3,599.22
3. $2,866.89
4. $3,233.00

CHAPTER 29 Resource Manager

Section Resources

	Objectives & Standards	Activities & Features	Reproducible Masters
Chapter Opener *Ethics in Accounting*	• Explain the meaning of Business Ethics. • Describe the components of an effective business ethics program. • Identify the role of the accountant in business ethics. • Discuss how ethical behavior benefits individuals, business, and society. • Explain the concepts of integrity, objectivity, independence, competence, and confidentiality as related to the accounting profession. • Identify the professional organizations that establish codes of ethics for accountants. • Define the accounting terms introduced in this chapter. **National Standards for Business Education**: IIIA5	Exploring the Real World of Business, p. 774 Workplace Connections, p. 775	School-to-Work Handbook
Section 1 *The Nature of Ethics*	• The meaning of personal and business ethics. • The components of an effective business ethics program. • How the behavior of the accountant contributes to the public trust. • How ethical behavior effects individuals, business, and society.	International Accounting, p. 777 Did You Know?, p. 779 A Matter of Ethics, p. 779	Strategies for Teaching International Accounting Demonstration Problems
Section 2 *Ethics in the Accounting Profession*	• Why professional organizations create codes of ethics. • What key principles of conduct govern the accountant. • Who creates codes of ethics for the accounting profession.	Accounting Flashbacks, p. 782 Math Hints, p.782 Connect To…, p.783	Strategies for Teaching Ethics in Accounting Internet Resources and Activities Handbook

KEY

Posters
Blackline Masters
Transparency
CD-ROM
Software
Portfolio
Videocassette

MULTIMEDIA RESOURCE

Peachtree	QuickBooks	Spreadsheets	Videos	CD-ROMs
None in this Chapter.	None in this Chapter.	None in this Chapter.	***Video Segment: Business Ethics*** Have students describe the ethical decision-making process.	***Electronic Learning Center (ELC), Case Study*** The case study titled "Cash Control and Theft" is ideal for teaching ethics since it offers several scenarios for students to calculate losses and discuss employee theft and ethics. ***Interactive Lesson Planner (ILP), Chapter 29*** This CD-ROM combines the versatility of an electronic lesson planner with the convenience of teacher classroom resources.

SCANS Correlation Chart

FOUNDATION SKILLS

Basic Skills:	Reading	Writing	Math	Listening	Speaking	
Thinking Skills:	Creative Thinking	Decision Making	Problem Solving	Seeing Things in the Mind's Eye	Knowing How to Learn	Reasoning
Personal Qualities:	Responsibility	Self-Esteem	Sociability	Self-Management	Integrity/Honesty	

WORKPLACE COMPETENCIES

Resources:	Allocating Time	Allocating Money	Allocating Material and Facility Resources	Allocating Human Resources		
Information:	Acquiring and Evaluating Information	Organizing and Maintaining Information	Interpreting and Communicating Information	Using Computers to Process Information		
Interpersonal Skills:	Participating as a Member of a Team	Teaching Others	Serving Clients/ Customers	Exercising Leadership	Negotiating to Arrive at a Decision	Working with Cultural Diversity
Systems:	Understanding Systems	Monitoring and Correcting Performance	Improving and Designing Systems			
Technology:	Selecting Technology	Applying Technology to Task	Maintaining and Troubleshooting Technology			

*Highlighted blocks indicate areas covered in the chapter. Additional SCANS skills are also covered throughout the *Teacher Wraparound Edition.*

Assessment

Student Edition
- Check Your Understanding, pp. 780, 784
- Chapter 29 Problems, pp.788–789

Teacher Wraparound Edition
- Critical Thinking Activity, p. 783
- Chapter 29 Quiz, p. 785

Assessment and Evaluation Masters
- Chapter 29 Study Plan, *Glencoe Workbook*
- Chapter 29 Self-Test, *Glencoe Workbook*
- Chapter 29 Test, *Chapter Tests* Booklet
- Chapter 29 Activity, *School-to-Work Handbook*
- Chapter 29 **Exam***View*

Transparencies

	Teaching Transparencies	Solution Transparencies
Section 1:		Problems 29–1, 29–2
Section 2:		Problem 29–3
End of Chapter:		Problems 29–4, 29–5, 29–6, 29–7, 29–8, 29–9, 29–10, 29–11, 29–12

TEACHER CLASSROOM RESOURCES

This is a representation of key blackline masters available in the Teacher Classroom Resources.

Teaching Aids

Transparency Examples

Section Focus Transparencies

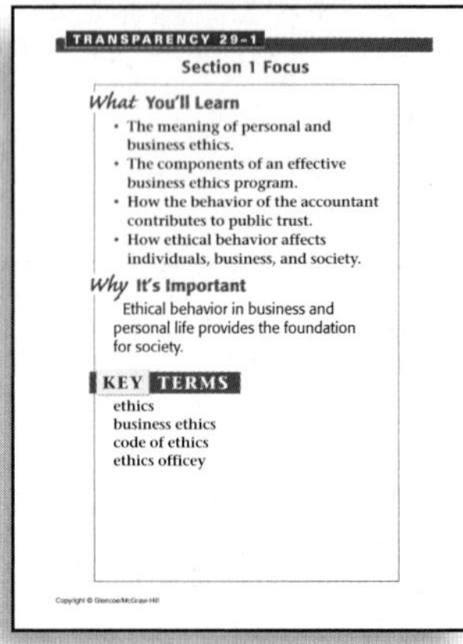

TRANSPARENCY 29–1

Section 1 Focus

What You'll Learn

- The meaning of personal and business ethics.
- The components of an effective business ethics program.
- How the behavior of the accountant contributes to public trust.
- How ethical behavior affects individuals, business, and society.

Why It's Important

Ethical behavior in business and personal life provides the foundation for society.

KEY TERMS

ethics
business ethics
code of ethics
ethics officey

Section Focus Transparencies

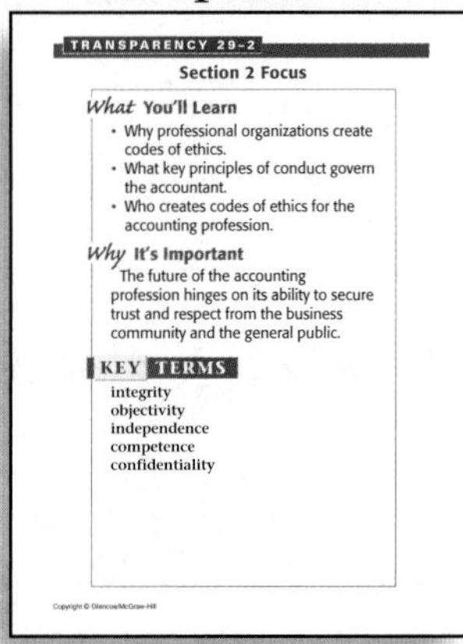

TRANSPARENCY 29–2

Section 2 Focus

What You'll Learn

- Why professional organizations create codes of ethics.
- What key principles of conduct govern the accountant.
- Who creates codes of ethics for the accounting profession.

Why It's Important

The future of the accounting profession hinges on its ability to secure trust and respect from the business community and the general public.

KEY TERMS

integrity
objectivity
independence
competence
confidentiality

Solution Transparencies

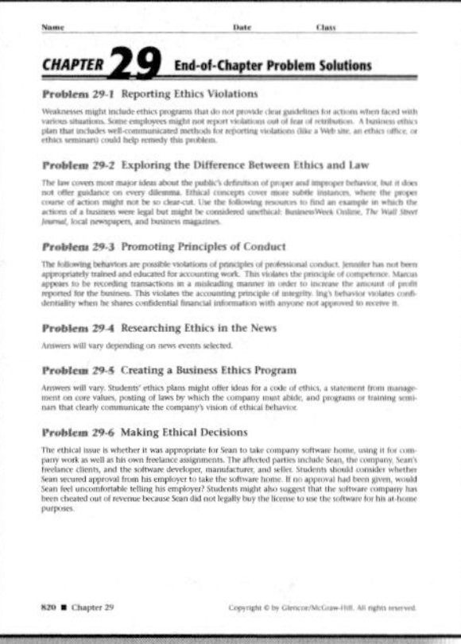

CHAPTER 29 End-of-Chapter Problem Solutions

Problem 29-1 Reporting Ethics Violations

Problem 29-2 Exploring the Difference Between Ethics and Law

Problem 29-3 Promoting Principles of Conduct

Problem 29-4 Researching Ethics in the News

Problem 29-5 Creating a Business Ethics Program

Problem 29-6 Making Ethical Decisions

Solution Transparencies

CHAPTER 29 REVIEW Ethics in Accounting

Part 1 Accounting Vocabulary

Demonstration Problems

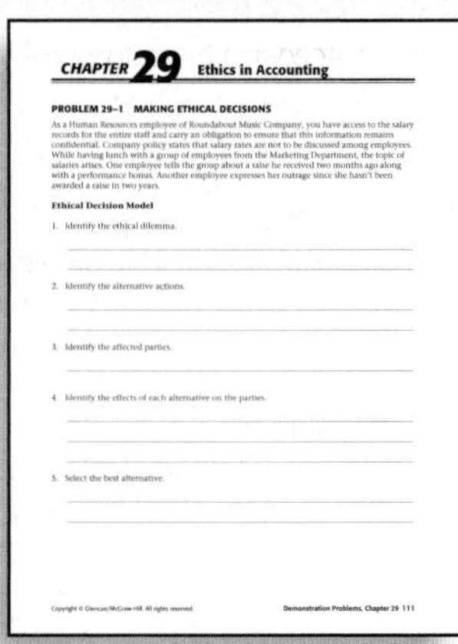

CHAPTER 29 Ethics in Accounting

PROBLEM 29–1 MAKING ETHICAL DECISIONS

Ethical Decision Model

1. Identify the ethical dilemma.
2. Identify the alternative actions.
3. Identify the affected parties.
4. Identify the effects of each alternative on the parties.
5. Select the best alternative.

Lesson Plans

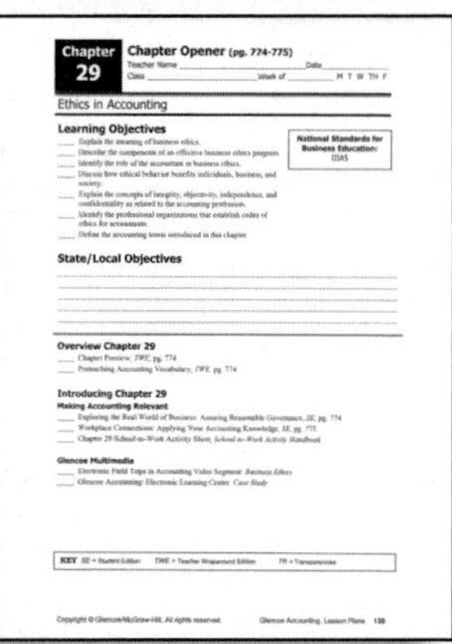

Chapter 29 Chapter Opener (pg. 774–775)

Ethics in Accounting

Learning Objectives

State/Local Objectives

Overview Chapter 29

Introducing Chapter 29

Glencoe Multimedia

Block Scheduling

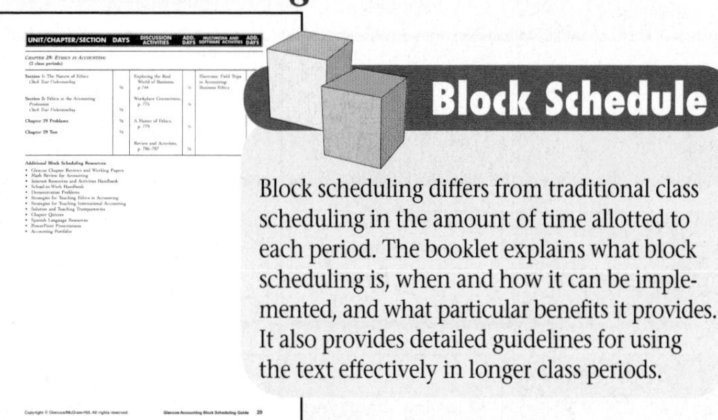

Block Schedule

Block scheduling differs from traditional class scheduling in the amount of time allotted to each period. The booklet explains what block scheduling is, when and how it can be implemented, and what particular benefits it provides. It also provides detailed guidelines for using the text effectively in longer class periods.

Enrichment and Application

Strategies for Teaching Ethics in Accounting

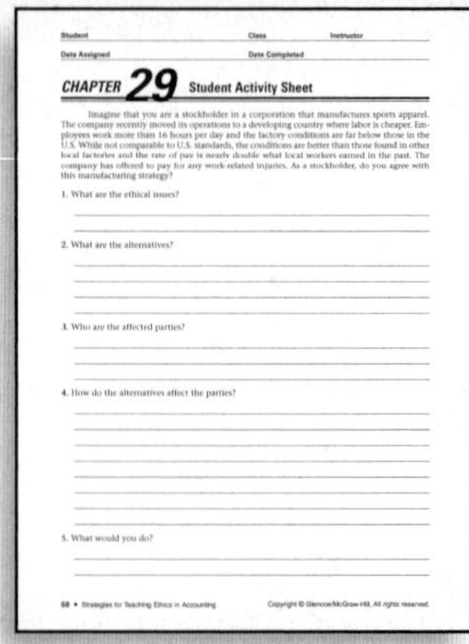

CHAPTER 29 Student Activity Sheet

1. What are the ethical issues?
2. What are the alternatives?
3. Who are the affected parties?
4. How do the alternatives affect the parties?
5. What would you do?

Strategies for Teaching International Accounting

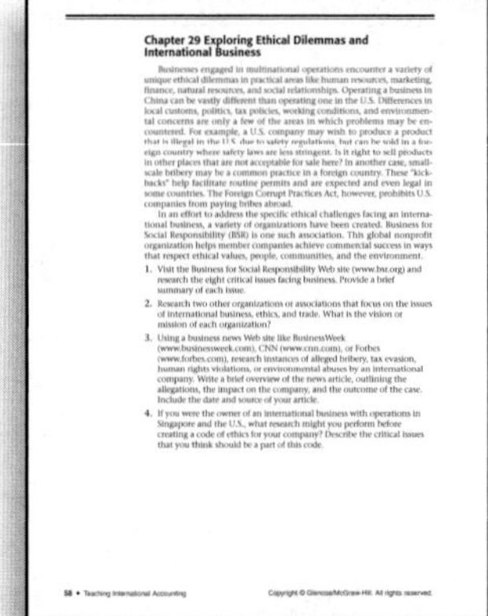

Chapter 29 Exploring Ethical Dilemmas and International Business

School-to-Work Handbook

CHAPTER 29 SCHOOL-TO-WORK ACTIVITY

Ethics in Accounting

Meeting Different Ability Levels

Chapter Reviews and Working Papers (CRWP)

Working Papers

Review

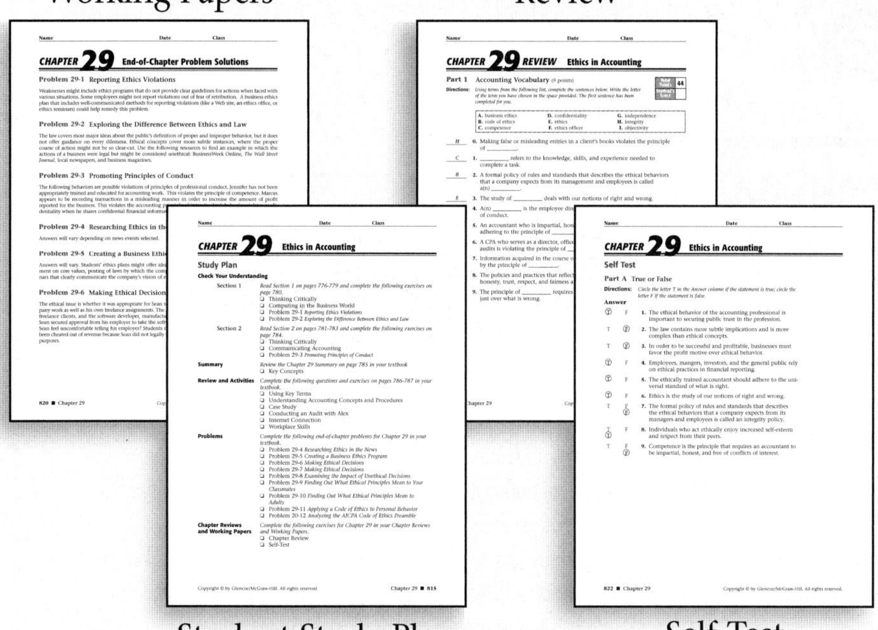

Student Study Plan

Self-Test

Real-World Multimedia CD-ROM

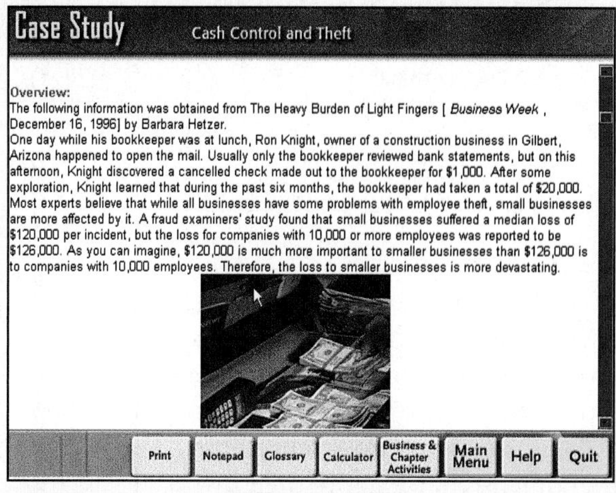

Key to Ability Levels

Each section gives skill-building activities. Each activity has been labeled for use with students of various learning styles and abilities.

L1 Level 1 activities are basic activities and should be within the range of all students.

L2 Level 2 activities are average activities and should be within the range of average and above average students.

L3 Level 3 activities are challenging activities designed for the ability range of above average students.

ELL ELL activities should be within the ability range of English Language Learners.

Assessment and Evaluation

Chapter Tests

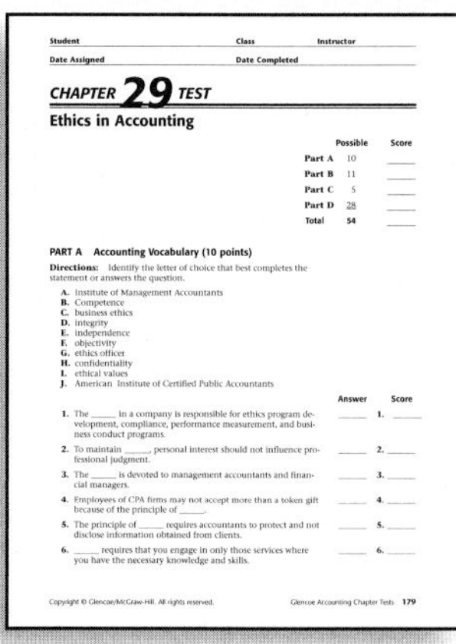

Chapter Quiz

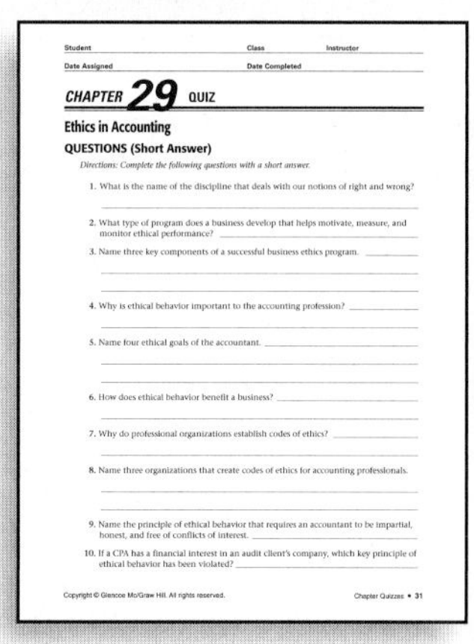

Teaching Resources at a Glance

Application Resources

- Glencoe Chapter Review and Working Papers, SE and TAE
- School-to-Work Handbook, SE and TM
- Accounting Portfolio, SE and TM

Reproducible Masters

- Demonstration Problems
- Lesson Plans
- Block Scheduling
- Spanish Language Resources

Glencoe Accounting Professional Development Series

- Strategies for Teaching Ethics in Accounting
- Accounting Competitive Event Review
- Math Review for Accounting
- Strategies for Teaching International Accounting
- Internet Resources and Activities Handbook

Transparency Package

- Section Focus Transparencies
- Teaching Transparencies
- Source Document Transparencies
- Solution Transparencies

Performance Assessment

- **Exam***View* CD-ROM
- Chapter Tests
- Chapter Quizzes
- Unit Tests
- Audit Tests
- Printed Testbank

Multimedia Resources

- Electronic Learning Center:
  - Multimedia CD-ROMs
  - Peachtree software, tutorials, templates, and solutions
  - Spreadsheet templates
- Using QuickBooks with Glencoe Accounting
- Interactive Lesson Planner
- Electronic Field Trips in Accounting
- PowerPoint Presentation
- Web site: glencoeaccounting.glencoe.com

OVERVIEW CHAPTER 29

Correlations to National Standards for Business Education

(See pages T50–T51 for a detailed correlation chart.)

Standards: IIIA5

Chapter Preview

In this chapter students learn about ethics as related to their personal lives, to the business world, and to the accounting professional. They learn how businesses create an effective ethics program and they explore their own ethical decision-making process. Students will gain an understanding of which organizations create codes of ethics for accountants and how the behaviors of accountants influence public trust.

Section Overviews

- Section 1—*The Nature of Ethics*
- Section 2—*Ethics in the Accounting Profession*

Chapter Vocabulary

ethics
business ethics
code of ethics
ethics officer
integrity
objectivity
independence
competence
confidentiality

Preteaching Accounting Vocabulary

Writing Exercise: Using 3 x 5 note cards, ask students to write each new term on a separate card. As they study the chapter, ask them to write the definition to each term on the appropriate card. L1

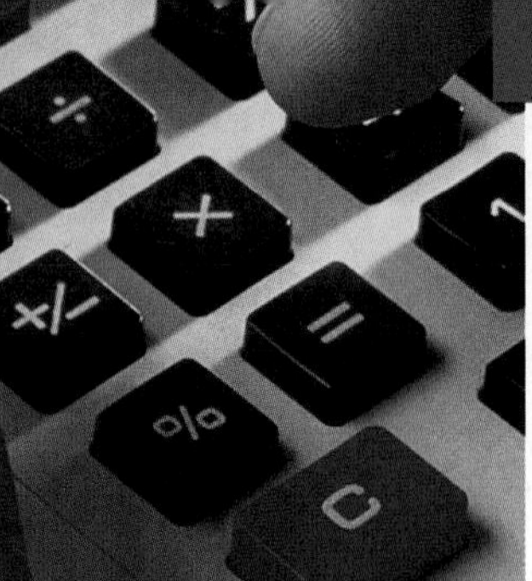

CHAPTER 29

Ethics in Accounting

Learning Objectives

When you have completed this chapter, you will be able to:

- Explain the meaning of business ethics.
- Describe the components of an effective business ethics program.
- Identify the role of the accountant in business ethics.
- Discuss how ethical behavior benefits individuals, business, and society.
- Explain the concepts of integrity, objectivity, independence, competence, and confidentiality as related to the accounting profession.
- Identify the professional organizations that establish codes of ethics for accountants.
- Define the accounting terms introduced in this chapter.

Exploring the Real World of Business

ASSURING RESPONSIBLE GOVERNANCE

In your school, you probably have a student government organization that influences student body policies and makes decisions on student issues. The term "governance" refers to the exercise of authority, administration, and decision making for a population or an organization.

The success or failure of business depends on ethical corporate governance and accounting practices. The Institute of Internal Auditors, an international professional organization, believes that now, more than ever, the internal auditor must play a strong and visible role in governance and internal control processes.

Internal auditors work within a business to review the company's financial, manufacturing, marketing, and human resources data. They make sure that the company operates according to its agreements with suppliers, government, and customers. In addition, the internal auditor establishes plans to safeguard assets and to use resources of the business economically.

What do you think?

Internal auditors evaluate procedures used to safeguard the resources of a business. What are some of these resources?

Institute of Internal Auditors

Exploring the Real World of Business

Institute of Internal Auditors

In April 2002, the Institute of Internal Auditors presented a position paper titled "Recommendations for Improving Corporate Governance" to the U.S. Congress. The Institute addressed issues like independence of auditors and mandatory internal audit functions for publicly traded companies.

What do you think? (Answers)

Answers will vary. The resources of a business may include cash, plant assets, and inventory. A business also possesses more intangible assets such as information, reputation, and popularity with customers. The internal auditor should prepare and monitor a strategy to protect these assets.

Workplace Connections

Applying Your Accounting Knowledge

Do you, or anyone you know, work for a fast food restaurant? Whether selling burgers, tacos, or salads, these restaurants must ensure that the food they sell is safe for consumption. They must also provide a safe and sanitary place for their customers to eat.

Investigate:

1. What risks do you think a fast food restaurant faces in regard to customer health?
2. What kinds of internal controls would you suggest to guard against these risks?

775

Glencoe Accounting *Online*

Visit the *Glencoe Accounting* Web site at **glencoeaccounting.glencoe.com** for additional activities and information.

INTRODUCING CHAPTER 29

Making Accounting Relevant

Workplace Connections: Applying Your Accounting Knowledge

Discussion: Take a poll of students who work, or have worked, in fast-food restaurants. Make a list of these restaurants on the board. Ask students to describe the interior and exterior setting of these businesses. Based on these settings, what potential safety or health hazards exist? L1

Investigate (Answers)

1. Answers will vary. Students may suggest that safe food preparation must be of primary concern to avoid health hazards to customers. The risk of food poisoning or food contamination must be addressed to avoid lawsuits and bad publicity.
2. Answers will vary. Students may suggest internal controls that ensure proper refrigeration of foods, frequent monitoring of expiration dates on food, strict adherence to health standards, and frequent health and safety checks within restaurants.

School-to-Work Activity

Student ____ Class ____ Instructor ____

Date Assigned ____ Date Completed ____

CHAPTER 29 SCHOOL-TO-WORK ACTIVITY

Ethics in Accounting

Name of work site: ____

Name of work site mentor: ____

Title or position of mentor: ____

In order to remain profitable and successful, businesses need to earn the respect and trust of their employees, managers, customers, and vendors by creating and maintaining ethical environments. Consult with your work site mentor to complete the following investigation on ethics in the workplace.

After completing the STW investigation, you will be able to:

- Explain the role of ethics in accounting.

1. Explain the meaning of business ethics for your company.

1a. Interview the human resources manager, president, or manager of your company and inquire about the business vision as related to ethics. Are business ethics important to the managers of the company? Why?

1b. Obtain a copy of the stated mission statement or goals of the business. Does this mission statement contain elements related to ethics?

2. Describe the components of the business ethics program at your company.

 School-to-Work Handbook • 57

GLENCOE MULTIMEDIA

Electronic Field Trips in Accounting *Business Ethics*

After viewing this video, students will gain exposure to the kinds of ethical dilemmas that occur in the workplace. Have students describe the ethical decision-making process.

Glencoe Accounting: Electronic Learning Center *Case Study*

The case study titled "Cash Control and Theft" is ideal for teaching ethics since it offers several scenarios for students to calculate losses and discuss employee theft and ethics.

CHAPTER 29
SECTION 1, PAGES 776–780

1 FOCUS

Introducing the Section

In this section students learn how businesses establish effective ethics programs and create a code of ethics. They also learn how the ethical behavior of the accountant plays a role in securing public trust and in the success of a business.

Section Concepts

- The meaning of personal and business ethics.
- The components of an effective business ethics program.
- How the behavior of the accountant contributes to public trust.
- How ethical behavior affects individuals, business, and society.

BELL RINGER

Active Learning: Before students arrive for class, leave three personal objects like your keys, daytimer, or photos on desks in your class. Observe what students do when they discover the misplaced items. Ask students to describe how they decided what to do with these items. Discuss how individuals in society decide how they will behave and treat each other. L1

Concept Development: What Are Ethics?

Discussion: Ask students to name behaviors that they think are ethically wrong. Then ask for ethically good acts. Lead a class discussion about where we, as individuals in society, learn these ideas of right and wrong. L1

SECTION 1

The Nature of Ethics

What You'll Learn

- The meaning of personal and business ethics.
- The components of an effective business ethics program.
- How the behavior of the accountant contributes to public trust.
- How ethical behavior affects individuals, business, and society.

Why It's Important

Ethical behavior in business and personal life provides the foundation for society.

KEY TERMS

ethics
business ethics
code of ethics
ethics officer

Have you ever been faced with a difficult decision about a particular course of action or behavior? Did you consider how you would feel about the action or how others would view your choice? Did you consider how your behavior would affect others? If so, you've probably encountered an ethical dilemma.

What Are Ethics?

Ethics is the study of our notions of right and wrong. In its broadest sense, ethics deals with human conduct in relation to what is morally good and bad. The term "ethics" often refers to a set of basic principles. Life is complex and individuals are faced with a variety of situations. A person's ethics, or basic principles, can provide guidelines for action when faced with ethical dilemmas.

The basic values found in a system of personal ethics exist in systems of business ethics as well. Business ethics are not very different from ethics in general.

What Are Business Ethics?

Business ethics are the policies and practices that reflect a company's core values such as honesty, trust, respect, and fairness. The ethics of a business can be seen by the way employees and customers are treated and how the company attends to shareholder value, community service, supplier relationships, and regulatory law. Review the following components to understand how a business ethics program can be established.

The Law As a Guide

When discussing ethical performance, the relationship between law and ethics should be considered. While law and ethics both define proper and improper behavior, law attempts to formally define the general public's ideas about what makes something right or wrong. The law

RESOURCE MANAGER

Reproducible Masters
- Lesson Plans
- Chapter Reviews and Working Papers (CRWP) TAE

Transparencies
- Solution Transparencies

Multimedia
- ExamView CD-ROM
- Electronic Learning Center CD-ROM
- Interactive Lesson Planner CD-ROM
- Electronic Field Trips in Accounting

describes a minimum acceptable level of correct behavior. Ethical concepts have more subtle implications and are more complex than written rules of law. For example, although a business may be well within the law to advertise certain products to teenagers, it may not be the "right" or "ethical" thing to do. A business may use law as a guide, but must consider ethical principles and standards as well.

Statements of Company Values

If you have heard the phrase, "actions speak louder than words," then you are familiar with one of the best methods of maintaining a strong business ethics program. People learn their standards and values by observing what others do, not necessarily by what they say.

In addition to setting good examples of ethical behavior, a well-defined framework of ethical concerns and core values must be stated. A **code of ethics** is a formal policy of rules and standards that describes the ethical behaviors that a company expects from its management and employees. The following topics are often addressed within a code of ethics:

- Conflicts of interest
- Product quality and testing
- Customer relations
- Employee relations
- Suppliers and consultants
- Expense reports
- Security
- Political contributions
- Environmental actions
- International business
- Workplace safety
- Technology
- Whistle-blowing

Training and Outreach

After a code of ethics is created, it is important to communicate that policy properly. Distribution of the written code, along with formal training, helps employees understand the importance of these policies and gives them realistic and concrete examples of what to do when faced with an ethical dilemma.

International ACCOUNTING

Business Ethics

Knowing about the culture in which a company operates is critical to understanding the subtle points of what is considered unethical. For example, in the U.S. it would not be proper to bring an expensive gift to an initial meeting with a prospective client–it could be viewed as a bribe. In Japan, however, it is considered impolite not to bring a gift.

Key Points

Modeling Behavior

Employees learn ethical standards of an organization by watching the behaviors of their employers and managers.

2 TEACH

GUIDED PRACTICE

Reading Accounting

- Have students outline the chapter by writing the major heads and subheads, leaving space between the entries. As they read, have them write notes about the content or identify the key terms defined in that section. **L1**
- For students who have difficulty connecting text information to real world situations, ask especially helpful students to describe practical examples of the academic concepts in the text. **ELL**

Concept Development: What Are Business Ethics?

Discussion: Ask volunteers to describe recent situations in the news or in their personal experience in which a business acted unethically. Have the class describe the proper or "ethical" behavior in these situations. **L1**

Strategies for Teaching International Accounting

To enrich the study of international accounting, refer to the additional critical thinking activities in the booklet.

ACCOUNTING ISSUES

Sharing the Responsibility for Ethics Accountants are only one part of a broad group responsible for the integrity of financial systems. Company executives, stock markets, and securities commissions are all part of the complex infrastructure of the business world. Because each group deals with different responsibilities, the goals can often be at odds. Though some critics of the accounting profession feel that more standards and regulations are needed, others believe that systems and rules are only as strong as the people who observe and apply them. It boils down to ethics—not only professional ethics—but the personal ethics of individuals.

2 TEACH (Cont'd.)

Demonstration Problem Step-by-Step Practice

Use demonstration problem 29-1 to show students how to use the ethical decision model.

Concept Development: What Is the Accountant's Role?

Discussion: Write the following ethical goals on the board or transparency:

- Avoid harm to stockholders.
- Optimize the interests of the public.
- Adhere to universal standards of what is right.
- Respect the human rights of all.

Ask students to suggest reasons why actions that support these goals would lend credibility to the profession of accounting. L1

Teaching Tip

In order to demonstrate the importance of the role of the accountant, lead a class discussion of the 2002 case of Enron. Ask volunteers to describe the basic elements of the case or outline the case for your students. Include the actions of the Arthur Andersen auditors. Ask students whether they think the auditors acted to optimize the interests of the public and adhered to universal standards of what is right. What influences may have interfered with these objectives?

Concept Development: Who Benefits from Ethical Behavior?

Discussion: Ask a volunteer from your class to describe a situation in which he or she acted ethically. How did the person benefit? How did others benefit? L1

Ethics Committees

Ethics committees and ethics officers play an important role in developing and enforcing ethical processes. An **ethics officer** is the employee directly responsible for creating business conduct programs, evaluating performance, and enforcing standards of conduct. As ethical dilemmas surface, these officials help settle disputed issues and resolve problems. Once a hearing has been held and all issues have been resolved, an enforcement phase may follow.

Enforcement

Effective enforcement is necessary to achieve an ethical work environment. A company's code of ethics might contain penalties for violations that include performance appraisal notes, probation, suspension, demotion, or termination.

What Is the Accountant's Role?

Key Points

Public Trust
The practices of the accountant directly reflect the credibility of a business and the integrity of the accounting profession.

Accountants play a major role in the operation, management, and development of business. In such roles, they can face many ethical dilemmas. For example, if an accountant's manager gives instructions to record the physical inventory at its original costs when it is obvious that the inventory's value has decreased, what should the accountant do? If an auditor finds questionable accounting practices within a client's financial reporting, yet knows the client is a major source of revenue for his or her firm, what action should be taken?

As you can see, the actions and behaviors of accountants play a critical role in the maintenance of public trust in the business community. The accountant's opinions, practices, and behaviors directly impact how the company is viewed, and how the profession, in turn, is assessed.

In general, the ethically trained accountant should focus on the following goals:

- Avoid harm to stockholders.
- Optimize the interests of the public.
- Adhere to universal standards of what is right.
- Respect the human rights of all.

Key Points

Positive Returns
Good ethics are good for business. These positive returns include employee loyalty, improved sales and company reputation, strengthened financial performance, and a decrease in consumer complaints.

Specific responsibilities of the accounting profession are expressed in the various codes of ethics created by major organizations. These codes of ethics are addressed in Section 2 of this chapter.

Who Benefits from Ethical Behavior?

While it may seem obvious that ethical behavior naturally benefits individuals, business, and society, the following discussion addresses specific benefits to each group.

Individuals

Acting ethically produces benefits that can affect the course of your life and the lives of others. These benefits include increased self-esteem,

Great Ideas *From the Classroom of...*

Multicultural Awareness Students love money! I ask students who have traveled to Latin America, Europe, Asia, or who come from different countries to bring coins or currency from those countries to show the class. We use the Internet to look up current monetary values from other countries. Students pick a country or draw names from a hat, convert the currency into American dollars, and report their findings to the class.

Martha Ramirez
McCallum High School
Austin, TX

contentment, and self-respect. Ethical behavior also paves the way for achieving life goals. Your honesty, trustworthiness, and integrity will allow you to find a satisfying career with the type of organization that shares your core values.

As you act ethically, you will also enjoy the benefit of acceptance in a society where appropriate behavior is rewarded and honored. As you focus more on the common good, rather than selfish interests, you will earn trust and respect from friends, co-workers, employers, and society in general. Finally, ethical behavior will dramatically improve the quality of your decisions.

Business

A 1999 DePaul University study indicated that companies that made commitments to an ethics code provided more than twice the value to shareholders than those that did not. A study by Walker Information, a shareholder research firm, supports this finding, reporting that "good corporate behavior" leads to positive business outcomes.

Society

Society can be viewed as the sum of all social relationships between humans. Therefore, it is easy to understand why our individual actions contribute to the overall nature of our society. We cannot expect our society to become more ethical unless individuals and businesses commit to ethical behaviors.

As businesses act in ethical ways, new wealth for society is created. In the realm of ethical financial reporting, the public can be confident in the data provided and make informed investment decisions. In turn, greater capital funding is available for growth and productivity, yielding strong and healthy economies.

Did You Know?

Internal Control

The Institute of Internal Auditors was established in 1941 with 24 members. Today, the Institute has more than 75,000 members from over 100 countries. John B. Thurston, a utility company employee, was among the first to promote greater understanding of the internal auditing function.

Key Points

The Sum of the Parts

The behavior of individuals and business contributes to the overall ethical performance of society.

A MATTER OF ETHICS

Working Conditions

Imagine that you are a stockholder in a corporation that manufactures sports apparel. The company recently moved its operations to a developing country where labor is cheaper. Employees work more than 16 hours per day and the factory conditions are far below those in the U.S. While not comparable to U.S. standards, the conditions are better than those found in other local factories and the rate of pay is nearly double what local workers earned in the past. The company has offered to pay for any work-related injuries. As a stockholder, do you agree with this manufacturing strategy?

Ethical Decision Making:

- What are the ethical issues?
- What are the alternatives?
- Who are the affected parties?
- How do the alternatives affect the parties?
- What would you do?

2 TEACH (Cont'd.)

Teaching Tip

Lead a class discussion on how ethical behavior can benefit society by describing films in which the characters fought for ethical solutions to business or societal problems. How did the ethical behaviors of the films' character contribute to benefits enjoyed by society or the individual?

Concept Development: Business

Discussion: Describe the following scenario to the class: A business chooses to voluntarily recall a product that it discovers has a safety flaw. Ask students to list ways in which this action will benefit the company. Have them consider both short-term and long-term benefits. L1

Teaching A MATTER OF ETHICS

Working Conditions U.S. goods are often manufactured in foreign countries. Investors and consumers recognize a growing need for the close monitoring of factory manufacturing practices to ensure that goods are produced under equitable conditions. Have students first discuss the issue of moving manufacturing operations to a developing country from the management's perspective. Have them list ways in which this decision will benefit the company. Then ask students to discuss the issue from a U.S. manufacturing employee's perspective. How might this person be affected? How do students think manufacturing workers in the developing country will view this opportunity?

3 ASSESS

Thinking Critically (Answers)

1. Answers will vary. A business can be ethical and financially successful.
2. Effective examples of behavior from upper management; communication; adherence to law; training; enforcement. Elements lacking will vary.
3. Adhering to universal standards of what is right and respecting human rights. Challenges may include the balance between the profit motive and ethical goals.

Computing in the Business World (Answers)

1. (a) Net loss = ($3,000)
   (b) Net income = $5,000
   (c) Net income = $29,000
2. Answers will vary.

Problem 29–1 (Answers)

Answers will vary but might include fear of retribution. Remedies include a well-communicated plan for reporting violations.

Problem 29–2 (Answers)

Answers will vary. Law covers major ideas about proper and improper behavior. It does not offer guidance on every dilemma. Ethical concepts cover more subtle instances.

Chapter Reviews and Working Papers Refer students to the Chapter 29 workbook pages to answer *Check Your Understanding* activities.

4 CLOSE

Section Wrap-Up

Creating Posters: Ask students to create colorful posters that might encourage others to act ethically in both their personal and business lives. L1

SECTION 1 Check Your Understanding

Now that you have studied this section, complete the following questions and problems.

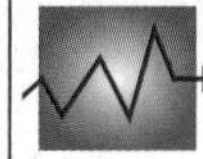

Thinking Critically

1. Supporters of ethical business practices say that good ethics are good for business. Do you agree? What conflicts might arise between the motives for maximum profits and good corporate citizenship?
2. Discuss the components needed to create a strong business ethics program. Which element do you think is most lacking in U.S. business today? Explain your answer.
3. Describe how an ethically trained accountant can contribute to ethical conduct in a business. What challenges might exist in this relationship?

Computing in the Business World

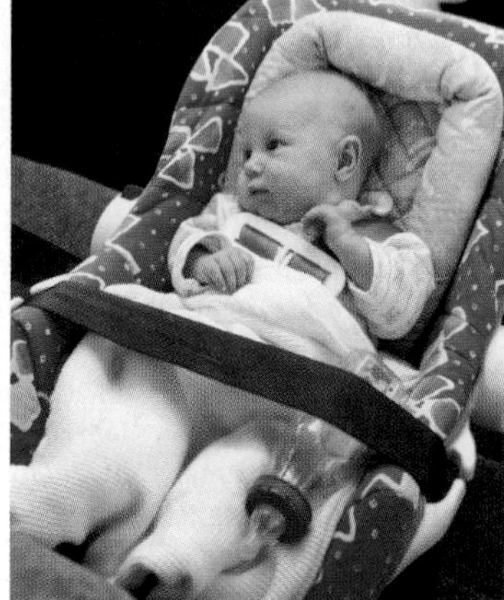

Assume that you are the chief financial officer for a major manufacturer of infant car seats. The lead product designer informs management that installation of a new latch system would improve product safety by 25 percent. The new latch system will add $4 to production costs per car seat. Current production costs are $52.50 per seat and the product sells for $69.50. Management wants to compare the effect on net income if they raise the product price by (a) $1, (b) $2, or (c)$5.

1. If the company sells 8,000 car seats in a year, what is the effect on net income for each proposed price increase scenario? Assume fixed operating costs are $115,000 annually.
2. As an officer of the company, what factors (other than pricing) do you think should be considered when making product design changes?

Problem 29–1 Reporting Ethics Violations

Instructions Results from Walker Information's 2001 study on business integrity state that 65 percent of employees who know about an ethical violation choose not to report it. What weaknesses in a company's ethical environment might be responsible for such a finding? Discuss the components of a strong business ethics plan that could be applied to resolve this situation.

Problem 29–2 Exploring the Difference Between Ethics and Law

Instructions Adhering to legal regulations is the first step in behaving ethically. Explain why ethical behavior extends beyond the law. Describe one situation in which a company might act within the boundaries of the law, yet still engage in an unethical act.

MEETING SPECIAL NEEDS

Students with Behavior Disorders Students with behavior disorders may have trouble understanding the idea of "ethical" or "acceptable" behaviors when faced with an especially tricky ethical dilemma. As you work through an ethical decision-making model with the class, involve this student in an active way by asking them to write the questions and answers on the board as the class offers alternative courses of action and suggested behaviors.

Ethics in the Accounting Profession

Professional organizations are often separated from other organizations by a code of conduct or a code of ethics. To build public trust, most accountants voluntarily join a professional organization and accept the standards of conduct expected by the organization.

However, ethical behavior requires commitment beyond a few rules of conduct. No ethics code or written rules can apply to all situations that might arise on the job. Day-to-day job experiences often test an individual's personal judgment and personal ethics.

Written codes of ethics are generally designed to encourage ideal behavior. However, the codes must be both realistic and enforceable. Professional organizations are charged with enforcing the rules of conduct outlined in their codes.

What You'll Learn

- Why professional organizations create codes of ethics.
- What key principles of conduct govern the accountant.
- Who creates codes of ethics for the accounting profession.

Why It's Important

The future of the accounting profession hinges on its ability to secure trust and respect from the business community and the general public.

KEY TERMS

integrity
objectivity
independence
competence
confidentiality

What Are the Key Principles?

Certain principles provide the framework for rules of conduct that an accountant is expected to follow. These principles include integrity, objectivity, independence, competence, and confidentiality.

Integrity

The principle of **integrity** requires that accountants choose what is right and just over what is wrong. Guidance for behaving with integrity suggests the accountant ask the following questions: Is this what a person of integrity would do? Have I made a right and just decision? Have I maintained the spirit of ethical conduct?

How do you explain the concept of integrity as related to the accounting profession? Making false or misleading entries in a client's books violates the accounting principle of integrity. Failing to correct false and misleading financial statements also violates integrity. Integrity helps accountants establish the trust necessary for others to rely on their professional judgment.

Objectivity

Every year publicly traded corporations must submit financial statements to the Securities and Exchange Commission. The financial statements are audited by certified public accountants (CPAs).

CHAPTER 29
SECTION 2, PAGES 781–784

1 FOCUS

Introducing the Section

In this section students learn why professional organizations create codes of ethics. They learn that the key principles of integrity, objectivity, independence, competence, and confidentiality are expected of the accounting professional.

Section Concepts

- Why professional organizations create codes of ethics.
- What key principles of conduct govern the accountant.
- Who creates codes of ethics for the accounting profession.

BELL RINGER

Identify: Describe the following to your class: A student hires an attorney to discuss a private family matter that may require litigation. Later, the student learns that the attorney gave him the wrong information and also shared the story with a personal friend. Ask students: How would you describe the conduct of the attorney? Did the attorney act as the student would expect of a professional? Use this scenario to introduce the ideas of competence, confidentiality, and codes of conduct. L1

Strategies for Teaching Ethics in Accounting

Photocopy the Chapter 29 *Student Activity Sheet* for students. Answers are also provided in the booklet.

RESOURCE MANAGER

Reproducible Masters

- Lesson Plans
- Chapter Reviews and Working Papers (CRWP) TAE
- Demonstration Problems

Transparencies

- Solution Transparencies

Multimedia

- Exam*View* CD-ROM
- Electronic Learning Center CD-ROM
- Interactive Lesson Planner CD-ROM
- Electronic Field Trips in Accounting

2 TEACH

GUIDED PRACTICE

Reading Accounting

Have students take notes about concepts in this section. Then pair students and have them "teach" each other the concepts using their notes. L2

Concept Development: What Are the Key Principles?

Discussion: Write the following terms on the chalkboard or a transparency:

- Integrity
- Objectivity
- Independence
- Competence
- Confidentiality

Define each term as it relates to the accounting field. Challenge students to describe fictional situations in which an accountant violates these principles. L1

ACCOUNTING Flashbacks

CONFLICTS OF INTEREST
Prior to 2002, public accounting firms were allowed to perform audit services as well as a wide range of consulting services for the same client. Lack of auditor independence is believed to be one of the factors that led to Enron Corporation's fall. The Sarbanes-Oxley Act of 2002 prohibits independent auditors from performing certain consulting services for an audit client.

Math Hints

Beyond the Numbers
When weighing alternative actions for an ethical dilemma, remember that not all factors can be measured in numbers or dollars. The effect on morale and potential harm to others must be considered in nonnumeric ways.

CPAs who perform audits are known as "independent auditors." They do not work for the companies they audit. For example, suppose that Paul Corporation needs to give audited financial statements to the SEC. Paul Corporation hires Findlay & Partners, a public accounting firm. Five CPAs who work for Findlay & Partners go to the offices of Paul Corporation and perform the audit. Paul Corporation is the *client* and Findlay & Partners is the *independent auditor.* The work of the independent auditor is critical. Many different users of financial information depend on audited financial statements when making decisions.

The principle of **objectivity** requires that accountants be impartial, honest, and free of conflicts of interest. When forming professional judgments, accountants should not be influenced by personal interests or relationships with others.

Independence

CPAs who audit public companies must maintain a position of independence. **Independence** in this sense means that the CPA does not have a financial interest in the company being audited. An investment in the company or a loan from the company would interfere with the independence required of an auditor. Serving as a director, officer, or employee of the company would also demonstrate a lack of independence.

An accountant must act in such a way that maintains the general public's confidence in the services provided by a professional. Even if the accountant's financial interest is minor and unimportant, the relationship could be suspect, and the accountant would be considered to lack independence. Even non-CPA employees in a public accounting firm may not accept more than token gifts from clients.

Competence

Accountants must engage only in services in which they are competent. **Competence** refers to the knowledge, skills, and experience needed to complete a task. Accountants are expected to maintain an appropriate level of competence through continuing education and to continually improve the quality of professional services. Services should be rendered promptly, carefully, thoroughly, and in accordance with appropriate technical and ethical standards. A commitment to learning and professional improvement must continue throughout the accountant's professional life.

Confidentiality

Accountants learn about everything from individual salaries to business strategies. How do you explain the concept of confidentiality as related to the accounting profession? **Confidentiality** is the requirement that information

HOME AND COMMUNITY CONNECTIONS ACTIVITY

Identifying Desirable Ethical Traits Ask students to interview managers of mid-sized businesses in the community to find out what qualities and qualifications are desired when hiring an accounting professional. Have students create a list of questions, then schedule an appointment with the manager of a business. Ask students to pay special attention to any discussion regarding honesty, integrity, or other key principles of conduct. After the interview, have students share their findings with the class.

acquired in the course of work be protected and not be disclosed without the appropriate legal or professional responsibility to do so. Information should not be used for personal gain.

Who Writes the Codes of Ethics?

Several accounting organizations provide guidelines to assist in ethical decision making.

American Institute of Certified Public Accountants

The AICPA is the national organization of certified public accountants. Members of the AICPA voluntarily accept standards of professional behavior that are much more strict than those required by the law. The following preamble in the AICPA's Code of Professional Conduct emphasizes the importance of ethical standards for CPAs.

AICPA Code of Professional Conduct Preamble

> Membership in the American Institute of Certified Public Accountants is voluntary. By accepting membership, a certified public accountant assumes an obligation of self-discipline above and beyond the requirements of laws and regulations.
>
> These Principles of the Code of Professional Conduct of the American Institute of Certified Public Accountants express the profession's recognition of its responsibilities to the public, to clients, and to colleagues. They guide members in the performance of their professional responsibilities and express the basic tenets of ethical and professional conduct. The Principles call for an unswerving commitment to honorable behavior, even at the sacrifice of personal advantage.[1]

Institute of Management Accountants

The IMA is the leading professional organization devoted exclusively to management accountants and financial managers. Unlike accountants in public practice who audit other companies, management accountants usually have a job in a single company.

The IMA helps accountants develop both personally and professionally through education, certification, and association with other professionals. Members of the IMA have a responsibility to maintain professional competence, uphold professional standards of confidentiality, avoid conflicts of interest, and communicate information fairly and objectively.

Institute of Internal Auditors

The IIA was introduced at the beginning of the chapter. Like other professional organizations, the IIA expects its members to demonstrate competence and to follow the principles of integrity, objectivity, and confidentiality. The IIA's code of ethics is necessary and appropriate because of the public trust placed in internal auditors.

[1] Preamble, *Online posting*, AICPA Code of Professional Conduct Section 51, 3 October 2002, <http://www.aicpa.org/about/code/archive/preamble.htm>

CONNECT TO . . . HEALTH

Tobacco products have been consumed in the U.S. since the early 1600s. Tobacco companies spend approximately $5 billion annually in advertising and promoting tobacco sales. Scientists and doctors accept that tobacco consumption is an important contributing factor in cancer and heart disease. What ethical issues come to mind as you consider the facts above?

Key Points

Guidelines

A code of ethics can't cover the details of every situation that might occur. The code provides principles that can be applied to a variety of unexpected situations.

2 TEACH (Cont'd.)

Concept Development: Who Writes the Codes of Ethics?

Discussion: Divide the class into three groups and assign each group to one of the following: AICPA, IMA, or IIA. Have each group read the text discussion of their assigned organization and present a brief overview to the rest of the class. L1

Teaching Tip

As you discuss each professional organization, remind students that an accountant might belong to all these groups depending on his or her specialty. This professional would therefore be held accountable to each organization's code of ethics or code of conduct.

Thinking Algebraically

Conceptualize: Ask students to think about the following situation and its effect on net income algebraically. A company must spend an additional $20,000 annually to make safety improvements to their products. These expenditures increase customer satisfaction and increase sales by $22,000 annually. (Additional Safety Expenses − Additional Revenue = Net Effect On Income; $20,000 − $22,000 = $2,000 increase)

CRITICAL THINKING ACTIVITY

Encouraging Ethical Behavior To encourage ethical behavior in the business world, some believe that government should play an increased role using financial incentives, legislation, and penalties. Others feel that government's role should be minimized. Ask students to discuss how they think corporations should be encouraged to become more ethical. What role should government play? (Students might consider how their own ethical behaviors are encouraged. Do they act ethically because of laws or fear of penalties? Are they motivated by their own sense of right and wrong?)

CHAPTER 29
SECTION 2, PAGES 781–784

3 ASSESS

Thinking Critically (Answers)

1. Exercising professional judgment free from economic, financial, and relationship incentives.
2. Answers will vary, but may include owning stock in an audit client company.
3. Strengthens ethical climate, lending credibility.

Communicating Accounting (Answers)

Answers will vary. Membership grants professionals some additional degree of legitimacy and respect in the eyes of the public.

Problem 29–3 (Answers)

Jennifer has not been appropriately trained and educated for accounting work. This violates the principle of competence. Marcus appears to be recording transactions in a misleading manner in order to increase the amount of profit reported for the business. This violates the accounting principle of integrity. Ing's behavior violates confidentiality when he shares confidential information with anyone not approved to receive it.

Chapter Reviews and Working Papers Refer students to the Chapter 29 workbook pages to answer *Check Your Understanding* activities.

4 CLOSE

Section Wrap-Up

Writing: Have students write a paragraph describing how the three professional organizations discussed in this section differ in their focus. L1

SECTION 2 Check Your Understanding

Now that you have studied this section, complete the following questions and problems.

Thinking Critically

1. Explain the concept of independence as it relates to the profession of accounting.
2. Describe a situation in which the principle of independence might be threatened for an accountant.
3. Describe the role of the internal auditor and how the Institute of Internal Auditors' code of ethics helps establish public trust.

Communicating Accounting

Your friend Samantha recently graduated with a degree in accounting. As a member of the American Institute of Certified Public Accountants, you encourage her to become a CPA and join the organization. Draft an e-mail message to your friend that includes reasons why you think she should join the AICPA and how she will benefit from the membership.

Problem 29–3 Promoting Principles of Conduct

Instructions Read the following scenario. Identify and discuss behaviors that you feel might violate the key principles of conduct for accountants.

In your new position as accounting manager with Triple B Markets, you supervise three staff accountants: Jennifer, Marcus, and Ing. You become aware of the following situations:

- Jennifer, a new employee, has never worked as an accountant, but scored high marks in her college math classes.
- Marcus often records payments of utilities as assets instead of expenses because he wants to show a higher net income for the business.
- You overheard Ing talking with a friend on the phone about the payroll details of the company.

COOPERATIVE LEARNING ACTIVITY

Group Discussion Divide the class into two groups. Ask one group to play the role of internal auditors. Ask the other to act as senior management for a clothing manufacturing company. Have the group of internal auditors list items of possible concern regarding employee safety, consumer safety and satisfaction, and the environment. What suggestions do the internal auditors have that might ensure corporate responsibility in these areas? What responses or concerns does the management team have? Do their concerns consider impact on profits?

CHAPTER 29 SUMMARY

KEY CONCEPTS

1. Ethics is the study of our notions of right and wrong. The term "ethics" also refers to a set of basic principles.
2. Business ethics are the policies and practices that reflect a company's core values such as honesty, trust, respect, and fairness.
3. Components of a business ethics program include adherence to written law, a written and well-communicated code of ethics, training, and enforcement.
4. The behaviors and practices of the accountant are critical to public trust in the business as well as the integrity of the accounting profession.
5. An ethically trained accountant should focus on the following goals: avoiding harm to stockholders, optimizing the interests of the public, adhering to the universal standards of what is right, and respecting the human rights of all.
6. Ethical behavior benefits the individual, business, and society at large.
7. Integrity is the principle that requires accountants to choose what is right and just over what is wrong.
8. Objectivity is the principle that requires accountants to be impartial, honest, and free of conflicts of interest.
9. Independence is the principle that requires CPAs to have no financial interest in the company being audited.
10. Competence is the principle that requires accountants to have the knowledge, skills, and experience needed to complete a task.
11. Confidentiality is the principle that requires accountants to protect and not disclose information acquired in the course of work unless they have a legal or professional responsibility to do so.
12. Professional organizations are often separated from other organizations by a code of professional conduct.
13. Professional accountants are distinguished by their willingness to accept a high degree of responsibility to the public.
14. The American Institute of Certified Public Accountants is the national professional organization of certified public accountants.
15. The Institute of Management Accountants serves management accountants and financial managers.
16. The Institute of Internal Auditors is a worldwide professional group that specializes in internal auditing.

SUMMARY CHAPTER 29

Chapter 29 Quiz

Student ____ Class ____ Instructor ____
Date Assigned ____ Date Completed ____

CHAPTER 29 QUIZ

Ethics in Accounting

QUESTIONS (Short Answer)

Directions: Complete the following questions with a short answer.

1. What is the name of the discipline that deals with our notions of right and wrong?
2. What type of program does a business develop that helps motivate, measure, and monitor ethical performance?
3. Name three key components of a successful business ethics program.
4. Why is ethical behavior important to the accounting profession?
5. Name four ethical goals of the accountant.
6. How does ethical behavior benefit a business?
7. Why do professional organizations establish codes of ethics?
8. Name three organizations that create codes of ethics for accounting professionals.
9. Name the principle of ethical behavior that requires an accountant to be impartial, honest, and free of conflicts of interest.
10. If a CPA has a financial interest in an audit client's company, which key principle of ethical behavior has been violated?

 Chapter Quizzes • 31

QUESTIONS (Short Answer)

1. What is the name of the discipline that deals with our notions of right and wrong?
2. What type of program does a business develop that helps motivate, measure, and monitor ethical performance?
3. Name three key components of a successful business ethics program.
4. Why is ethical behavior important to the accounting profession?
5. Name four ethical goals of the accountant.
6. How does ethical behavior benefit a business?
7. Why do professional organizations establish codes of ethics?
8. Name three organizations that create codes of ethics for accounting professionals.
9. Name the principle of ethical behavior that requires an accountant to be impartial, honest, and free of conflicts of interest.
10. If a CPA has a financial interest in an audit client's company, which key principle of ethical behavior has been violated?

ANSWERS

1. ethics
2. business ethics program
3. adherence to written law, a written and well-communicated code of ethics, and training and enforcement
4. secures public trust
5. avoid harm to stockholders, optimize the interests of the public, adhere to universal standards of what is right, and respect the human rights of all
6. good corporate behavior leads to positive business outcomes
7. demonstrate a willingness to accept a high degree of responsibility to the public
8. AICPA, IIA, IMA
9. objectivity
10. independence

USING KEY TERMS

See *Glossary* for the definitions of these terms. Ask students to share definitions in class or in groups.

Understanding Accounting Concepts and Procedures

(Answers)

1. People learn acceptable behaviors by observing what others do, not necessarily by what they say.
2. Distribute the code to personnel; provide training and examples of what to do when faced with ethical dilemmas.
3. Termination, suspension, probation, demotion, or performance appraisal notes.
4. Impacts how the company is viewed, and how the profession, in turn, is assessed.
5. Avoid harm to stockholders; optimize the interests of the public; adhere to universal standards of what is right; respect the human rights of all.
6. Enhances self-esteem, contentment and self-respect. Earns trust and respect from friends, co-workers, employers, and society.
7. Improved shareholder value and positive business outcomes: employee loyalty, improved sales, and company reputation.
8. Establishes standards of behavior.
9. Accountants choose what is right and just over what is wrong.
10. Free of conflicts of interest; no financial interest in the audited company; have required knowledge and skills.
11. Requires accountants protect and not disclose information acquired in the course of work unless they have a legal or professional responsibility to do so.

USING KEY TERMS

As the new training director for a public accounting firm, you have been instructed to design and present a program to employees on the importance of ethical behavior. A list of terms, which you are to use in your program, is shown below. Write a complete definition for each term. For each term, write one or two sentences describing its importance to the success of the firm.

business ethics	ethics officer
code of ethics	independence
competence	integrity
confidentiality	objectivity
ethics	

Understanding Accounting Concepts and Procedures

Instructions

On a separate sheet of paper, answer the following questions:

1. Explain what the phrase "actions speak louder than words" means.
2. How can a company communicate a code of ethics to its employees?
3. What kinds of penalties are sometimes imposed on employees who violate a company's code of ethics?
4 What role does the accountant play in maintaining public trust in the business community?
5. List four goals of an ethically trained accountant.
6. How does acting ethically benefit an individual?
7. How does a business benefit from acting ethically?
8. What is the purpose of an ethics code for a professional organization?
9. Explain the concept of integrity as related to the accounting profession.
10. Explain the concepts of objectivity, independence, and competence as related to the accounting profession.
11. Explain the concept of confidentiality as related to the accounting profession.

ASSESSMENT RESOURCES

Choose assessment strategies from the following pages to evaluate your students' progress.

Student Edition
Check Your Understanding, pp. 780, 784
Chapter 29 Problems, pp. 788–789

Assessment and Evaluation Masters
Chapter 29 Study Plan, *Glencoe Workbook (CRWP)*
Chapter 29 Self-Test, *Glencoe Workbook (CRWP)*
Chapter 29 Test, *Chapter Tests* Booklet
Chapter 29 Activity, *School-to-Work Handbook*
Chapter 29 **Exam***View*

Teacher Wraparound Edition
Critical Thinking Activity, p. 783
Chapter 29 Quiz, p. 785

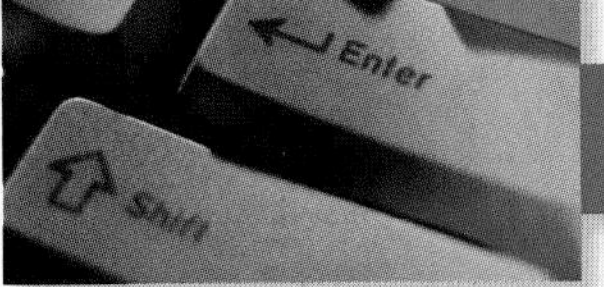

Case Study...

CPA Firm: Audits

Chris Snyder is an audit supervisor for an accounting firm. She and her staff will be auditing the financial records of Gemma Industries in the near future. The CEO of Gemma has invited Chris and staff to arrive one day earlier than the audit date to play a round of golf at an exclusive country club of which the CEO is a member. They have also been invited for dinner at an expensive restaurant that same evening.

Thinking Critically:

1. Should Chris and her staff accept the invitation?
2. If not, how should Chris turn down the invitation without offending the CEO and possibly losing a client?
3. What ethical issue could arise if Chris accepts the invitation?

Conducting an Audit with Alex

One of Alex's clients is a company that owns a hospital. As you review the hospital's various sources of income, you discover the hospital received a large donation from a pharmaceutical company. The hospital's code of ethics states that contributions from suppliers, in this case a pharmaceutical company, are not permitted.

Instructions:

1. Write a memo to Alex that gives your recommendation for action in this situation.
2. In your memo, discuss the reasons you think the hospital's code of ethics does not allow contributions from pharmaceutical companies.

interNET CONNECTION

Code of Professional Conduct

Certain principles provide the framework for rules of conduct that an accountant is expected to follow.

Do This:

1. Look at the American Institute of Certified Public Accountants Web site.
2. What guidance is provided to help AICPA members follow the code of conduct?
3. List three suggestions given by the AICPA.
4. Explain how the guidelines might help you in your personal behavior.

Workplace Skills

Acquiring and Analyzing Information

In order to ensure adequate internal controls for a business, you must be able to acquire and analyze relevant information.

On the Job:

You supervise three accounts payable clerks in your job at Blake's Auto Supply Company. Two clerks routinely process invoices on Friday and mail checks on Monday. The other clerk prepares checks on Monday and mails them on Tuesday. She uses Friday to verify subsidiary ledgers and double-check the calculations on invoices due. All checks must be processed through the data entry department, which has experienced a high turnover lately. Data entry clerks are often absent on Fridays and the entire accounting department must share one printer. You would like all three clerks to follow the same procedures and wonder why there are differences in how they handle their jobs.

Thinking Critically:

1. Prepare a list of questions to ask your employees that will help you assess the situation.
2. What resource factors might influence the way your clerks perform their duties?

interNET CONNECTION www.glencoe.com

Do This (Answers)

1. www.aicpa.org
2. The purpose of the Code of Professional Conduct of AICPA is to guide members in the performance of their professional responsibilities and toward a commitment to honorable behavior, even at the sacrifice of personal advantage.
3. Members' understanding and voluntary actions, reinforcement by peers and public opinion, and disciplinary proceedings when needed against members who fail to comply.
4. Answers will vary.

Case Study...

Thinking Critically (Answers)

1. The team should decline the invitation.
2. Chris should thank the CEO for the invitation and reject politely, citing company policy that does not permit employees to accept social invitations from clients.
3. The team may compromise the ethical principle of objectivity. Accountants must be impartial, honest, and free of conflicts of interest.

Workplace Skills

Thinking Critically (Answers)

1. Questions will vary, but may include issues of time management and accuracy.
2. Answers will vary. Students may suggest that the availability of data entry persons may be a factor, or that there may be resource considerations in the mailroom or printer availability.

Conducting an Audit with Alex

(Answers)

1. Memos will vary.
2. Students should demonstrate an understanding that contributions from suppliers may give the impression that the hospital will show partiality towards that supplier by way of large purchases.

Internet Resources and Activities Handbook

Photocopy additional Internet activities for your students to complete.

Problem 29-4 (Answer) Researching Ethics in the News
Answers will vary depending on news events selected.

Problem 29-5 (Answer) Creating a Business Ethics Program
Answers will vary, but plans may include a code of ethics, a statement from management on core values, company functions or meetings in which the ethical guidelines are communicated, posting of laws by which the company must abide, and training seminars.

Problem 29-6 (Answer) Making Ethical Decisions
The ethical issue is whether it was appropriate for Sean to take company software home, using it for company work as well as his own freelance assignments. The affected parties include Sean, the company, Sean's freelance clients, and the software developer, manufacturer and seller. Students should consider whether Sean secured approval from his employer to take the software home. If no approval had been given, would Sean feel uncomfortable telling his employer? Students might also suggest that the software company was cheated out of revenue because Sean did not legally buy the license to use the software for his at-home purposes.

Problem 29-7 (Answer) Making Ethical Decisions
The ethical issue is whether Randy and Kyung have taken company property in violation of their agreement. Students may suggest that Randy's work in cultivation of relationships with his clients is not the "property" of his previous employer. Students must decide what the company intended when using the word "property" in the agreement.

Problem 29-4 Researching Ethics in the News

Instructions Using the library, newspaper, or the Internet, find three recent examples of businesses accused of engaging in unethical practices. For each example, describe the practices of the company, any legal charges involved, and why you think the business chose this course of action.

Problem 29-5 Creating a Business Ethics Program

Instructions Imagine that you are the ethics officer for a national chain of coffeehouses. Prepare a one- or two-page outline for a business ethics plan that covers the main issues you think are relevant to the operations of this company. Include outline headings for a code of ethics, enforcement measures, and how you will communicate the ethics plan to the employees and managers of the company.

Problem 29-6 Making Ethical Decisions

Instructions Sean McGee works as a graphics designer for a large design firm. In his job, he utilizes dozens of expensive software programs that the company purchased for its employees. Because Sean often takes work home to finish for his deadlines, he copied all the software programs and installed them on his personal computer. In addition to the work he does for his employer, he also takes freelance jobs for extra cash. What are the ethical issues? Who are the affected parties? Do you think Sean has made an ethical decision? Why or why not? What actions would you have taken?

Problem 29-7 Making Ethical Decisions

Instructions Randy Simpson and Kyung Won worked as recruiters for a national job placement company. The company provided them with a database filled with potential companies that might use a placement service, as well as qualified applicants who are seeking jobs. After working together for several years, Randy and Kyung decided to open a recruiting agency themselves. They had previously signed agreements not to take any property of the company with them if they left.

When Randy and Kyung were setting up their new offices, Kyung noticed Randy downloading files from floppy disks to his computer. When questioned, Randy said he had copied his list of clients in addition to names of potential new clients and qualified applicants. Kyung was worried that this act

ADDRESSING MULTIPLE LEARNING STYLES

Naturalistic Learner Ask your students to visit an outdoor environment like a public park, beach, lake, or desert. These settings are used by many people, yet must be treated with respect. Ask students to spend time in their selected environment and make a list of the types of ethical dilemmas that might occur in these settings. For example, students may notice that visitors to a public park do not observe notices prohibiting littering or prohibiting entry to fragile landscapes. Ask them to consider what types of behaviors are commonly expected of users of public outdoor spaces.

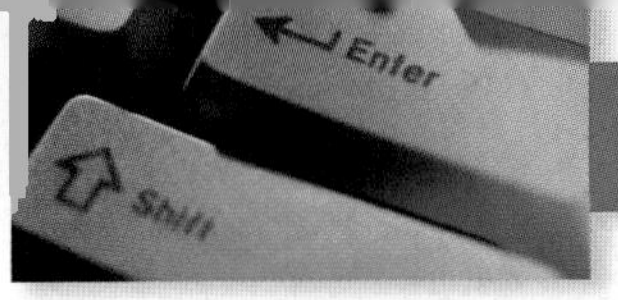

was a violation of the agreement they had signed. Randy maintained that he had built solid relationships with his clients, and that he was entitled to take their contact information. As for the names of applicants, he argued, "These people need jobs. If I can help make that happen, I should." What are the ethical issues? What would you do if you were Kyung?

Problem 29–8 Examining the Impact of Unethical Decisions

Instructions Assume that the accountant for a drug manufacturing company made the decision to record the company's ending drug inventory at an amount higher than its actual worth. How does this decision affect gross profit and net income for that accounting period? In what ways might this decision affect shareholder value? How might this affect confidence in the company's financial statements in the future?

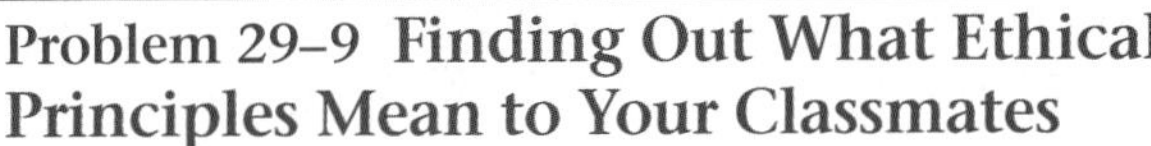

Problem 29–9 Finding Out What Ethical Principles Mean to Your Classmates

Instructions Make a list of the five ethical principles found in the chapter. Take the list with you and ask your friends how they think the principles might influence their everyday life. Report your results in class.

Problem 29–10 Finding Out What Ethical Principles Mean to Adults

Instructions Ask adults how they think the five principles of ethics found in this chapter influence professional behavior. Share your results in class.

Problem 29–11 Applying a Code of Ethics to Personal Behavior

Instructions Write a code of ethics that you feel would help guide the behavior of students in school organizations. Interview students outside your class for help with ideas.

Problem 29–12 Analyzing the AICPA Code of Ethics Preamble

Instructions Look up the AICPA Preamble in the text. List two key points covered in each of the two paragraphs. Are the points important to your everyday behavior? Why or why not?

MAKING CONNECTIONS TO DAILY LIFE

Code of Ethics Most companies create a code of ethics or code of conduct that is distributed to its employees. This code outlines acceptable behaviors and company values so that employees clearly understand what is expected of them. Ask students who hold part-time jobs to request a copy of their company's code of ethics to bring to class. Students may also choose to bring in a code of ethics from their parent's or a friend's workplace. Ask students to outline the primary topics found in the code.

Problem 29–8 (Answer) Examining the Impact of Unethical Decisions

This decision would overstate gross profit and net income for the accounting period. It would lead investors to believe that the company is performing better than it actually is. Inflated stock prices and a general overstatement of company value in the marketplace might result. If this error were revealed, the public would be less likely to trust the reliability of the financial statements.

Problem 29–9 (Answer) Finding Out What Ethical Principles Mean to Your Classmates

Answers will vary depending on outcome of interviews.

Problem 29–10 (Answer) Finding Out What Ethical Principles Mean to Adults

Answers will vary depending on outcome of interviews.

Problem 29–11 (Answer) Applying a Code of Ethics to Personal Behavior

Answers will vary.

Problem 29–12 (Answer) Analyzing the AICPA Code of Ethics Preamble

Paragraph one: membership is voluntary, assumes self-discipline above and beyond the rquirements of laws and regulations.

Paragraph two: responsibility to the public, clients, and colleagues; unswerving commitment to honorable behavior.

INTRODUCING APPENDIX A

Appendix A Overview

As students study the accounting cycle for a service business in Chapters 3 through 11, you may wish to introduce the preparation of adjusting entries. Use this appendix after your students study Chapter 8 to illustrate how to calculate, record, and post adjusting entries for supplies and prepaid insurance. If you prefer to cover the topic of adjusting entries later in the course, you may use Chapter 18 where adjustments for a merchandising business are covered.

Appendix A Concepts

- How to identify general ledger accounts that require adjustments.
- How to calculate end-of-period adjustments for a service business.
- How to record end-of-period adjustments for a service business.
- How to update accounts through adjusting entries for a service business.
- How to enter adjustments on a ten-column work sheet.
- How to complete the Adjusted Trial Balance section of a work sheet.

Visual Learning

Appendix A Focus

Use **Transparency APPA-1** to introduce the concepts and terms students will learn in this appendix.

Appendix Vocabulary

adjustment
premium

Preteaching Accounting Vocabulary

Writing Exercise: Ask students to write a sentence using both vocabulary terms. Explain the meaning of the terms as related to accounting and adjusting entries. L1

Adjustments for a Service Business Using a Ten-Column Work Sheet

What You'll Learn

- How to identify general ledger accounts that require adjustments.
- How to calculate end-of-period adjustments for a service business.
- How to record end-of-period adjustments for a service business.
- How to update accounts through adjusting entries for a service business.
- How to enter adjustments on a ten-column work sheet.
- How to complete the Adjusted Trial Balance section of a work sheet.

Why It's Important

Certain general ledger accounts require adjustments before the net income or net loss for the period can be determined and the work sheet completed.

KEY TERMS

adjustment
premium

The ten-column work sheet is prepared in the same manner as the six-column work sheet in Chapter 8. The additional columns are for the Adjustments and Adjusted Trial Balance sections. The ten-column work sheet has five amount sections instead of three.

The Trial Balance Section

The information for the Account Name and Trial Balance sections comes from the general ledger accounts. The end-of-period balance for each account is entered in the appropriate amount column of the Trial Balance section. In Chapter 8 you entered the final account balances in the correct column and completed the Trial Balance section by totaling and ruling the columns.

The Need for Adjustments

Up to this point the general ledger account balances have been changed by journal entries made to record transactions that are supported by source documents. However, not all changes in account balances are the result of daily business transactions. There are no source documents for the changes in account balances caused by the internal operations of a business or the passage of time. Such changes are recorded through adjustments made to the account balances at the end of the accounting period. An **adjustment** is an amount that is added to or subtracted from an account balance to bring that balance up-to-date.

In this appendix you will learn how to calculate end-of-period adjustments for a service business, Maximum Delivery Service. Every adjustment affects at least one permanent account and one temporary account. Two examples of general ledger accounts that need adjusting at the end of the accounting period are **Supplies** and **Prepaid Insurance**.

Adjusting the Supplies Account

All businesses purchase some sort of supplies for the operation of the business. Paper, pens and pencils, ink cartridges, and staples are common business supplies. When supplies are purchased, the asset account **Supplies** is debited (increased). Supplies may be purchased by paying cash or on account.

TEACHING NOTES

Purchasing Supplies

When supplies are purchased for cash, the asset account **Supplies** is increased, so it is debited for the amount of the purchase. **Cash in Bank** is also an asset account, and it is decreased (credited). On February 14 Maximum Delivery Service purchased supplies for $300, Check 229.

GENERAL JOURNAL — PAGE 11

	DATE		DESCRIPTION	POST. REF.	DEBIT	CREDIT	
1	20--						1
2	Feb.	14	Supplies		300 00		2
3			Cash in Bank			300 00	3
4			Check 229				4
5							5

When supplies are purchased on account, the **Supplies** account is again debited. Since additional money is owed to a creditor, the liability account, **Accounts Payable**, is credited. On August 21 Maximum Delivery Service purchased $400 worth of supplies on account from Shade Supply Company, Invoice 28714.

GENERAL JOURNAL — PAGE 14

	DATE		DESCRIPTION	POST. REF.	DEBIT	CREDIT	
1	20--						1
2	Aug.	21	Supplies		400 00		2
3			Accts. Pay.—Shade Supply Co.			400 00	3
4			Invoice 28714				4
5							5

Calculating the Adjustment for Supplies

Each time supplies are purchased, the **Supplies** account is debited for the amount of the purchase. For example, Maximum Delivery Service had $100 in supplies on hand at the beginning of the period. During the period the company made two purchases of supplies for $300 and $400. The final balance in the **Supplies** account in the general ledger on December 31 is $800 ($100 + $300 + $400). However, some of these supplies have been used or consumed during the period. Supplies are used every day. It is inefficient to keep daily records of all supplies used on a daily basis.

At the end of the period, Maximum Delivery Service does not have all $800 in supplies. Most of the supplies have been used. By examining the remaining supplies, Maximum determines that only $200 worth of the supplies are still on hand. This means $600 of supplies have been used or

APPENDIX A
PAGES A-1–A-12

Concept Development: The Trial Balance Section

Discussion: Remind students that the amounts to be entered in the Trial Balance section of the work sheet are taken from the general ledger accounts and placed in the appropriate Debit or Credit column. L1

Concept Development: The Need for Adjustments

Discussion: Lead a class discussion on the topic of the internal operations of a business. Point out that items like office supplies are purchased and initially recorded as assets. Over time, these supplies are used, but no entries have been made to account for this use. Explain that an adjustment is needed at the end of the period to bring the balance of the Supplies account up to date. L1

Concept Development: Adjusting the Supplies Account

Discussion: Explain that an adjustment to the Supplies account is an amount that is subtracted from the existing balance to record the supplies consumed during the period. L1

Visual Learning

General Journals, p. A-2

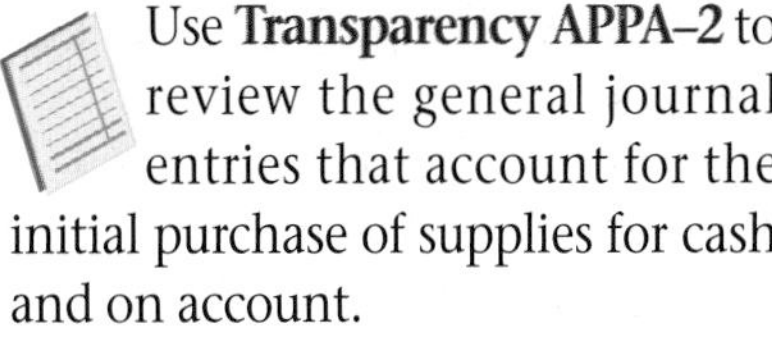

Use **Transparency APPA–2** to review the general journal entries that account for the initial purchase of supplies for cash and on account.

MEETING SPECIAL NEEDS

Students with Learning Disabilities Students with learning disabilities may have difficulty following the multiple steps involved in completing the ten-column work sheet and recording appropriate adjustments. Create a checklist of ordered tasks involved in completing the ten-column work sheet. Include the following tasks: complete the trial balance section, determine accounts to be adjusted, compute adjustments, complete the Adjustments section, complete the Adjusted Trial Balance section, extend amounts to the Balance Sheet and Income Statement sections, and compute net income on the work sheet. Students should check off each item on their list as they complete each task.

APPENDIX A
PAGES A-1–A-12

Concept Development: Calculating the Adjustment for Supplies

Discussion: Explain that the balance of the Supplies account should only reflect the value of supplies still on hand at the end of the period. First, students should determine the true amount of supplies on hand at the end of the period. Next, this amount should be subtracted from the existing balance of the account to determine the amount of the adjustment required. L1

Concept Development: Entering the Supplies Adjustment on the Work Sheet

Discussion: Once the Supplies account adjustment amount has been calculated, explain that this adjustment must be entered accurately on the work sheet. Point out that the amount will be entered in the Adjustments Debit column on the Supplies Expense account line and entered in the Adjustments Credit column on the Supplies account line. L1

Visual Learning

Adjustment Analysis
Use **Transparency APPA–3** to demonstrate the analysis and entry required to adjust the Supplies account.

consumed during the period ($800 – $200 = $600). The account balance for **Supplies** must be adjusted to report a final balance of $200. The account balance must be reduced by $600.

As supplies are used, they become expenses of the business. At the end of the period, adjustments are made to transfer the costs of the assets consumed from the asset accounts (permanent accounts) to the appropriate expense accounts (temporary accounts).

Entering the Supplies Adjustment on the Work Sheet

The Adjustments section of the work sheet is used to enter the necessary adjustments for the period. Since $600 worth of supplies were used during the period, the **Supplies** account is decreased, or credited, for this amount. The account **Supplies Expense** is increased, or debited, for $600.

Adjustment

ANALYSIS	*Identify*	1. The accounts affected are **Supplies** and **Supplies Expense**.
	Classify	2. **Supplies** is an asset account (permanent). **Supplies Expense** is an expense account (temporary).
	+/–	3. **Supplies** is decreased by $600. **Supplies Expense** is increased by $600.
DEBIT-CREDIT RULE		4. Increases to expense accounts are recorded as debits. Debit **Supplies Expense** for $600. 5. Decreases to asset accounts are recorded as credits. Credit **Supplies** for $600.
T ACCOUNTS		6.

Supplies Expense		Supplies	
Debit +	Credit –	Debit +	Credit –
600			600

The adjustment for **Supplies** in the Adjustments section of the work sheet is shown in **Figure A–1**. To enter the adjustment on the work sheet, follow these steps:

1. In the Adjustments Debit column, enter the debit amount of the adjustment ($600) on the Supplies Expense line.
2. In the Adjustments Credit column, enter the credit amount of the adjustment ($600) on the Supplies line.

On the work sheet, the debit and credit parts of each adjustment are given a unique label. The label consists of a small letter in parentheses and is placed just above and to the left of the adjustment amounts. The supplies adjustment is labeled (a).

REINFORCING STUDY SKILLS

Proofing Completed Work Remind students that when completing the ten-column work sheet it is easy to make errors. Offer these hints for proofing completed work:

- Consider the types of errors that might occur. Double check for these particular problems.
- Double check column headings, amounts, and placement on the work sheet.
- Always add columns twice to verify that calculations are accurate.
- The Adjustments column should always contain a debit entry for every credit entry. Verify that each debit has a corresponding credit.

Maximum Delivery Service
Work Sheet
For the Year Ended December 31, 20--

ACCT. NO.	ACCOUNT NAME	TRIAL BALANCE DEBIT	TRIAL BALANCE CREDIT	ADJUSTMENTS DEBIT	ADJUSTMENTS CREDIT	ADJUSTED TRIAL BALANCE DEBIT	ADJUSTED TRIAL BALANCE CREDIT
101	*Cash in Bank*	7 264 00				7 264 00	
105	*Accts. Rec.—Wein Corp.*	336 00				336 00	
110	*Accts. Rec.—Mike Cassidy*	917 00				917 00	
115	*Supplies*	800 00			(a) 600 00	200 00	
120	*Prepaid Insurance*	750 00			(b) 250 00	500 00	
125	*Office Equipment*	11 364 00				11 364 00	
130	*Delivery Equipment*	14 600 00				14 600 00	
201	*Accts. Pay.—Gillespie Co.*		1 774 00				1 774 00
205	*Accts. Pay.—Shade Supply Co.*		200 00				200 00
210	*Accts. Pay.—Trip Travel*		2 632 00				2 632 00
301	*Kevin Chan, Capital*		16 734 00				16 734 00
302	*Kevin Chan, Withdrawals*	2 500 00				2 500 00	
303	*Income Summary*						
401	*Delivery Revenue*		28 724 00				28 724 00
501	*Advertising Expense*	3 083 00				3 083 00	
505	*Insurance Expense*			(b) 250 00		250 00	
510	*Maintenance Expense*	710 00				710 00	
515	*Rent Expense*	6 500 00				6 500 00	
520	*Supplies Expense*			(a) 600 00		600 00	
525	*Utilities Expense*	1 240 00				1 240 00	
	Totals	50 064 00	50 064 00	850 00	850 00	50 064 00	50 064 00

Figure A–1 Ten-Column Work Sheet (Partial) Showing the Adjusted Trial Balance

Adjusting the Prepaid Insurance Account

Businesses buy insurance to protect against losses from hazards such as theft, fire, and flood. Insurance policies cover varying time periods, such as six months or one year. The cost of insurance protection is called the **premium**. A premium is paid in advance at the beginning of the covered period. Insurance paid in advance is an asset because, until the insurance protection expires, it represents a benefit to the business. The insurance premium is recorded in the asset account, **Prepaid Insurance**.

On November 1 Maximum Delivery Service paid a six-month insurance premium of $750, Check 314.

GENERAL JOURNAL PAGE *19*

DATE		DESCRIPTION	POST. REF.	DEBIT	CREDIT
20--					
Nov.	*1*	*Prepaid Insurance*		*750 00*	
		Cash in Bank			*750 00*
		Check 314			

APPENDIX A
PAGES A-1–A-12

Visual Learning

Figure A-1 Ten-Column Work Sheet (Partial) Showing the Adjusted Trial Balance

Use **Transparency APPA–4** to demonstrate how the supplies adjustment is reflected on the ten-column work sheet. Remind students to be sure that one side of the entry is recorded in the Debit column and the other in the Credit column of the Adjustments section.

Concept Development: Adjusting the Prepaid Insurance Account

Discussion: Remind students that businesses often pay for insurance at the beginning of a covered period and record the payment as an asset.

Explain that at the end of an accounting period, the asset account should be reduced by the amount of the premium that has been used by debiting the Insurance Expense account and crediting the Prepaid Insurance account. **L1**

Visual Learning

General Journal, p. A-4

Use **Transparency APPA–5** to remind students of the journal entry made when recording the payment of an insurance premium paid in advance of the insurance coverage period.

TEACHING NOTES

APPENDIX A
PAGES A-1–A-12

Visual Learning

Adjustment Analysis

Use **Transparency APPA–6** to demonstrate the analysis and debits and credits for the adjustment to the Prepaid Insurance account.

Concept Development: Completing the Work Sheet

Discussion: Write the following task list associated with completing the work sheet on the board:

1. Complete the Trial Balance section
2. Enter the adjustments; verify that debits equal credits
3. Complete the Adjusted Trial Balance section
4. Extend amounts to the Balance Sheet and Income Statement sections
5. Total Balance Sheet and Income Statement columns and compute net income or net loss L1

Concept Development: Completing the Adjusted Trial Balance Section

Discussion: Point out that new account balances must be computed for each account with an adjustment. These new balances are entered in the appropriate line and column of the Adjusted Trial Balance section. Account balances that were not affected by adjustments are simply extended to the Adjusted Trial Balance section. L1

At the end of December, the balance in the **Prepaid Insurance** account is still $750. However, two months of the six months of coverage have expired.

Nov. 1–Dec. 31		Jan. 1–Apr. 30		
Expired		Not Expired		
$250	+	$500	=	$750

The monthly cost of the insurance is $125 ($750 ÷ 6 = $125). Since the coverage for November and December has expired, $250 ($125 x 2) of the $750 in the premium has been used. The asset account **Prepaid Insurance** must be decreased (credited) for $250. The amount of insurance expired is charged to the expense account **Insurance Expense**. In this adjustment **Insurance Expense** is debited for $250.

Adjustment

ANALYSIS

Identify 1. The accounts affected are **Prepaid Insurance** and **Insurance Expense**.

Classify 2. **Prepaid Insurance** is an asset account (permanent). **Insurance Expense** is an expense account (temporary).

+/– 3. **Prepaid Insurance** is decreased by $250. **Insurance Expense** is increased by $250.

DEBIT-CREDIT RULE

4. Increases to expense accounts are recorded as debits. Debit **Insurance Expense** for $250.
5. Decreases to asset accounts are recorded as credits. Credit **Prepaid Insurance** for $250.

T ACCOUNTS

6.

Insurance Expense	
Debit + 250	Credit –

Prepaid Insurance	
Debit +	Credit – 250

To enter the adjustment on the work sheet, follow these steps:

1. In the Adjustments Debit column, enter the debit amount of the adjustment ($250) on the Insurance Expense line. Since this is the second adjustment, label it (b).
2. In the Adjustments Credit column, enter the credit amount of the adjustment ($250) on the Prepaid Insurance line. Label it (b) also.

Completing the Work Sheet

After the adjustments are entered on the work sheet, the Adjusted Trial Balance section can be completed. This section of the work sheet shows the updated balances of all the general ledger accounts.

ACCOUNTING ISSUES

Audit of Adjusting Entries As independent auditors perform audits for clients, they are responsible for assessment of the risk of material misstatement of financial condition due to fraud. One of the guidelines provided by the AICPA concerns adjusting entries made by the company. Auditors should perform a detailed review of the company's quarter-end and year-end adjusting entries and investigate any entries that appear unusual.

Completing the Adjusted Trial Balance Section

To complete this section, the balance of each account in the Trial Balance section is combined with the adjustment, if any, in the Adjustments section. The new balance is then entered in the appropriate Adjusted Trial Balance column.

Refer to **Figure A–2** on pages A–7 and A–8 and look at how new balances are computed. If there is no adjustment, the account balance shown on the Trial Balance section is simply extended to the same column (Debit or Credit) in the Adjusted Trial Balance section. After all account balances are extended to the Adjusted Trial Balance section, both columns are totaled. If total debits equal total credits, this section is proved. A double rule is drawn under the totals and across both columns.

Extending Amounts to the Balance Sheet and Income Statement Sections

Beginning with line 1, each account balance in the Adjusted Trial Balance section is extended to the appropriate column of either the Balance Sheet section or the Income Statement section. Remember, the Balance Sheet section includes the asset, liability, and owner's equity accounts. The Income Statement section includes the revenue and expense accounts.

Showing Net Income on the Work Sheet

The Income Statement and Balance Sheet sections of the work sheet are totaled. The net income (or net loss) is entered on the work sheet as shown in **Figure A–2**.

Journalizing and Posting the Adjusting Entries

The journal entries that update the general ledger accounts at the end of a period are called adjusting entries. The source of information for journalizing the adjusting entries is the Adjustments section of the work sheet. The accounts debited and credited in the Adjustments section are entered in the general journal.

Before recording the first adjusting entry, the words "Adjusting Entries" are written in the Description column of the general journal. This heading eliminates the need to write an explanation after each adjusting entry.

The first adjustment, labeled (a) on the work sheet, is recorded in the general journal as a debit to **Supplies Expense** for $600 and a credit to **Supplies** for $600. The second adjustment is a debit to **Insurance Expense** for $250 and a credit to **Prepaid Insurance** for $250.

After the adjusting entries are recorded in the general journal, they are posted to the general ledger accounts. Once the adjusting entries are posted, the general ledger accounts are up-to-date. Refer to **Figure A–3** on page A–9 to see how to record end-of-period adjustments and update accounts through adjusting entries.

TEACHING NOTES

Concept Development: Extending Amounts to the Balance Sheet and Income Statement Sections

Discussion: Inform students that all permanent account balances should be extended to the Balance Sheet section, and all temporary account balances should be extended to the Income Statement section. The Income Summary account is extended to the Income Statement section because it is a temporary account used only at the end of a fiscal period. Emphasize that the totals for the two financial statement sections do not match because the net income or loss has yet to be calculated and added to the subtotals. L1

Concept Development: Showing Net Income on the Work Sheet

Discussion: Explain to students that the net income or loss for the period is computed by finding the difference between the Debit and the Credit columns of the Income Statement section. Finding the difference between the Debit and Credit columns of the Balance Sheet should yield the same amount. After the net income or loss is recorded, the Balance Sheet and Income Statement columns should be equal. L1

Concept Development: Journalizing and Posting the Adjusting Entries

Discussion: Remind students that the entries on the work sheet are simply a way to organize information. The actual adjusting entries must still be recorded in the general journal and posted to the general ledger to bring all accounts up to date. L1

Concept Development: The Steps in the Accounting Cycle

Discussion: Explain to students that when adjustments are made at the end of a fiscal period, an additional step is added to the basic accounting cycle. After financial statements are prepared, adjusting entries must be journalized and posted, therefore creating one additional step in the cycle. **L1**

The Steps in the Accounting Cycle

There are additional general ledger accounts that need to be adjusted at the end of the period. You will learn the reasons and procedures for adjusting other accounts throughout this textbook.

Figure A–2 Work Sheet Showing Ending Adjusted Balances and Net Income

Maximum
Work
For Year Ended

	ACCT. NO.	ACCOUNT NAME	TRIAL BALANCE DEBIT	TRIAL BALANCE CREDIT	ADJUSTMENTS DEBIT	ADJUSTMENTS CREDIT
1	101	*Cash in Bank*	7,264.00			
2	105	*Accts. Rec.—Wein Corp.*	336.00			
3	110	*Accts. Rec.—Mike Cassidy*	917.00			
4	115	*Supplies*	800.00			(a) 600.00
5	120	*Prepaid Insurance*	750.00			(b) 250.00
6	125	*Office Equipment*	11,364.00			
7	130	*Delivery Equipment*	14,600.00			
8	201	*Accts. Pay.—Gillespie Co.*		1,774.00		
9	205	*Accts. Pay.—Shade Supply Co.*		200.00		
10	210	*Accts. Pay.—Trip Travel*		2,632.00		
11	301	*Kevin Chan, Capital*		16,734.00		
12	302	*Kevin Chan, Withdrawals*	2,500.00			
13	303	*Income Summary*				
14	401	*Delivery Revenue*		28,724.00		
15	501	*Advertising Expense*	3,083.00			
16	505	*Insurance Expense*			(b) 250.00	
17	510	*Maintenance Expense*	710.00			
18	515	*Rent Expense*	6,500.00			
19	520	*Supplies Expense*			(a) 600.00	
20	525	*Utilities Expense*	1,240.00			
21			50,064.00	50,064.00	850.00	850.00
22		*Net Income*				
23						
24						
25						
26						
27						
28						
29						
30						
31						
32						
33						
34						
35						
36						
37						
38						
39						
40						
41						

TEACHING NOTES

When adjustments are made at the end of the period, this procedure becomes an additional step in the accounting cycle. After Step 7—*Prepare financial statements*, Step 8 is *Journalize and post the adjusting entries*. The final two steps in the cycle remain the same. We now have a ten-step cycle instead of a nine-step cycle.

Delivery Service
Sheet
December 31, 20--

ADJUSTED TRIAL BALANCE		INCOME STATEMENT		BALANCE SHEET	
DEBIT	CREDIT	DEBIT	CREDIT	DEBIT	CREDIT
7 264 00				7 264 00	
336 00				336 00	
917 00				917 00	
200 00				200 00	
500 00				500 00	
11 364 00				11 364 00	
14 600 00				14 600 00	
	1 774 00				1 774 00
	200 00				200 00
	2 632 00				2 632 00
	16 734 00				16 734 00
2 500 00				2 500 00	
	28 724 00		28 724 00		
3 083 00		3 083 00			
250 00		250 00			
710 00		710 00			
6 500 00		6 500 00			
600 00		600 00			
1 240 00		1 240 00			
50 064 00	50 064 00	12 383 00	28 724 00	37 681 00	21 340 00
		16 341 00			16 341 00
		28 724 00	28 724 00	37 681 00	37 681 00

Figure A–2 Work Sheet Showing Ending Adjusted Balances and Net Income (continued)

Visual Learning

Figure A-2 Work Sheet Showing Ending Adjusted Balances and Net Income

Use **Transparencies APPA–7a** and **APPA–7b** to illustrate how ending balances are represented on the work sheet and how net income is computed. Remind students that without the entry for net income or loss, the Balance Sheet and Income Statement section columns will not equal.

TEACHING NOTES

APPENDIX A
PAGES A-1–A-12

Visual Learning

Figure A-3 Adjusting Entries Posted to the General Ledger

Use **Transparency APPA–8** to show how adjusting entries are recorded in the general journal and then posted to individual ledger accounts. Ask students to describe the net effect to these accounts.

GENERAL JOURNAL — PAGE 22

	DATE		DESCRIPTION	POST. REF.	DEBIT	CREDIT	
1	20--		Adjusting Entries				1
2	Dec.	31	Supplies Expense	520	600 00		2
3			Supplies	115		600 00	3
4		31	Insurance Expense	505	250 00		4
5			Prepaid Insurance	120		250 00	5
6							6

ACCOUNT Supplies — ACCOUNT NO. 115

DATE		DESCRIPTION	POST. REF.	DEBIT	CREDIT	BALANCE DEBIT	BALANCE CREDIT
20--							
Jan.	1	Balance				100 00	
Feb.	14		G11	300 00		400 00	
Aug.	21		G14	400 00		800 00	
Dec.	31	Adjusting Entry	G22		600 00	200 00	

ACCOUNT Prepaid Insurance — ACCOUNT NO. 120

DATE		DESCRIPTION	POST. REF.	DEBIT	CREDIT	BALANCE DEBIT	BALANCE CREDIT
20--							
Nov.	1		G19	750 00		750 00	
Dec.	31	Adjusting Entry	G22		250 00	500 00	

ACCOUNT Insurance Expense — ACCOUNT NO. 505

DATE		DESCRIPTION	POST. REF.	DEBIT	CREDIT	BALANCE DEBIT	BALANCE CREDIT
20--							
Dec.	31	Adjusting Entry	G22	250 00		250 00	

ACCOUNT Supplies Expense — ACCOUNT NO. 520

DATE		DESCRIPTION	POST. REF.	DEBIT	CREDIT	BALANCE DEBIT	BALANCE CREDIT
20--							
Dec.	31	Adjusting Entry	G22	600 00		600 00	

Figure A–3 Adjusting Entries Posted to the General Ledger

RETEACHING APPENDIX A

Journalize and Post Adjusting Entries On a piece of notebook paper, have students write the end-of-period adjustment based on the following scenario: supplies beginning balance: $2,000; supplies purchased: $1,500; supplies ending balance: $500. (Debit Supplies Expense, $3,000; Credit Supplies, $3,000.) Then have students open general ledger accounts and post two entries: one entry for the purchases and one entry for the adjustment. (Students should show the following beginning balances: Supplies, $2,000; Supplies Expense, $0.)

Problem A–1 Analyzing Adjustments

Information related to accounts requiring adjustments on the work sheet for the year ended December 31 for Magner's Advertising Center follows.

Instructions In your working papers, indicate the amount of each adjustment, which account is debited, and which account is credited.

(1) The Trial Balance section shows a balance of $4,239.80 for **Supplies**. The amount of supplies actually on hand at the end of the period is $912.15.

(2) Magner's paid an annual insurance premium of $4,920.00 on October 1.

Problem A–2 Analyzing Adjustments

Ace Advertising Agency has the following information regarding supplies. The beginning balance in the general ledger account **Supplies** on August 1 was $214.00. On August 13, the agency purchased $302.00 worth of supplies. On August 26, they purchased additional supplies for $176.00. At the end of August, Ace counted the supplies and determined that supplies worth $273.00 were still on hand.

Instructions Answer the following questions regarding the **Supplies** account.

(1) What amount should be entered in the Trial Balance section of the work sheet for **Supplies**? Which column should be used?

(2) What amount should be entered in the Adjustments section of the work sheet for **Supplies**? Which column should be used?

(3) Should any other amount be entered in the Adjustments section? If yes, answer these questions:
- **a.** Which account?
- **b.** Which column?
- **c.** What amount?

(4) What amounts should be entered in the Adjusted Trial Balance section? For each amount, list the name of the account and specify which column should be used (Debit or Credit).

SOLUTION NOTES

Problem A–1 (Answers) Analyzing Adjustments

1. Amount of Adjustment: $3,327.65 (Debit Supplies Expense, Credit Supplies)
2. Amount of Adjustment: $1,230.00 (Debit Insurance Expense, Credit Prepaid Insurance)

Problem A–2 (Answers) Analyzing Adjustments

1. $692.00; Debit
2. $419.00; Credit
3. a) Supplies Expense
   b) Debit
   c) $419.00
4. Supplies $273.00; Debit Supplies Expense $419.00; Debit

Problem A–3 (Answers) Entering Adjustments and Preparing an Adjusted Trial Balance

Trial Balance totals: $50,022.00
Adjustments section totals: $2,188.00
Adjusted Trial Balance totals:
$50,022.00

Problem A–3 Entering Adjustments and Preparing an Adjusted Trial Balance

The general ledger for Schellhorn's Water Slide shows the following account balances on December 31, the end of the fiscal period.

Instructions In your working papers:

(1) Prepare the Trial Balance section of the work sheet. The account names are entered on the work sheet.

(2) Enter the adjustments for **Office Supplies** and **Prepaid Insurance** in the Adjustments section. The data for the adjustments is as follows:

(a) The cost of supplies on hand on December 31 is $492.

(b) The insurance premium expired is $860.

(3) Extend the amounts and complete the Adjusted Trial Balance section.

101	Cash in Bank	$10,230
105	Accts. Rec.—Chiara Adin	519
110	Accts. Rec.—Miguel Hendrickson	207
115	Office Supplies	1,820
120	Prepaid Insurance	1,290
125	Office Equipment	3,117
130	Water Slide Equipment	14,204
201	Accts. Pay.—Northern Slide Co.	6,281
205	Accts. Pay.—Advertising World	1,559
210	Accts. Pay.—Merit Cleaning	332
301	Phil Schellhorn, Capital	12,641
302	Phil Schellhorn, Withdrawals	1,400
303	Income Summary	---
401	Slide Revenue	29,209
501	Advertising Expense	1,350
505	Insurance Expense	---
510	Maintenance Expense	719
515	Rent Expense	12,800
520	Office Supplies Expense	---
525	Utilities Expense	2,366

SOLUTION NOTES

Problem A–4 Preparing a Ten-Column Work Sheet

The general ledger for Ryan's Canoe Rentals shows the following account balances on December 31, the end of the fiscal period.

Instructions In your working papers:

(1) Prepare the Trial Balance section of the work sheet. The account names are entered on the work sheet.

(2) Enter the adjustments for **Office Supplies** and **Prepaid Insurance** in the Adjustments section. The data for the adjustments is as follows:

(a) Ryan's determines that 20 percent of the supplies purchased are still on hand on December 31.

(b) The insurance premium expired is $1,337.

(3) Extend the amounts and complete the Adjusted Trial Balance section.

(4) Extend the appropriate amounts to the Balance Sheet and Income Statement sections and determine the net income or net loss for the period.

101	Cash in Bank	$13,826
105	Accts. Rec.—Nancy Burrows	803
110	Accts. Rec.—Patrick Chang	519
115	Supplies	2,880
120	Prepaid Insurance	2,292
125	Office Equipment	3,117
130	Rental Equipment	14,204
135	Canoes	20,182
201	Accts. Pay.—South Canoe Co.	6,991
205	Accts. Pay.—H & T Advertising	2,046
210	Accts. Pay.—Cassidy's Equipment	855
301	Ryan Gillespie, Capital	38,619
305	Ryan Gillespie, Withdrawals	3,700
310	Income Summary	---
401	Rental Revenue	31,624
402	Lesson Revenue	3,475
501	Advertising Expense	2,730
505	Insurance Expense	---
510	Maintenance Expense	1,664
515	Rent Expense	14,900
520	Supplies Expense	---
525	Utilities Expense	2,793

PROBLEMS
APPENDIX A

Problem A-4 (Answers) Preparing a Ten-Column Work Sheet

Trial Balance totals: $83,610.00

Adjustments section totals: $3,641.00

Adjusted Trial Balance totals: $83,610.00

Net Income: $9,371.00

SOLUTION NOTES

INTRODUCING APPENDIX B

Appendix B Overview

In this appendix students will learn to use the numeric keypad by touch. They will learn the proper hand and finger positions and practice entering columns of numbers. Many jobs, from accounting and store clerks to data entry operators, require the use of a numeric keypad for fast and efficient calculations.

Appendix B Concepts

- How to use the numeric keypad by touch.

Visual Learning

Appendix B Focus

Use **Transparency APPB–1** to emphasize the importance of learning to use the ten-key numeric keypad. Ask students to describe how they have used such a keypad in the past.

Appendix Vocabulary

home keys

Preteaching Accounting Vocabulary

Oral Discussion: Ask students to venture the meaning of the term "home keys" as it relates to their keyboard. Draw comparisons to the terms "home base," "place of origin," or "home plate." L1

Concept Development: Key Locations

Discussion: Ask students to look at the numeric keypad on their keyboards. Ask them how many rows they see. How many keys are within a row? Explain that the placement of certain keys such as the Enter key can vary depending on the equipment. L1

APPENDIX B

Using the Numeric Keypad

***What* You'll Learn**

- How to use the numeric keypad by touch.

***Why* It's Important**

Most accounting jobs require the use of a numeric keypad, either for data entry or calculation.

KEY TERMS

home keys

Ten-key numeric keypads are found on electronic calculators and computer keyboards. When you are keying quantities of numerical data, your ability to use the numeric keypad by touch will make your task easier and faster.

Key Locations

The ten-key numeric keypad is usually arranged into four rows of three keys. The locations of the 1 to 9 keys are the same on all equipment. The locations of the 0 (zero), decimal, and Enter keys—as well as other function keys—vary depending on the equipment. Some typical arrangements are illustrated as follows:

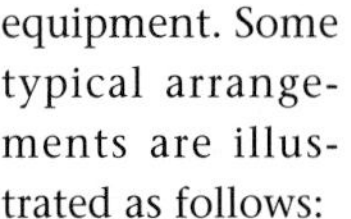

Home Position

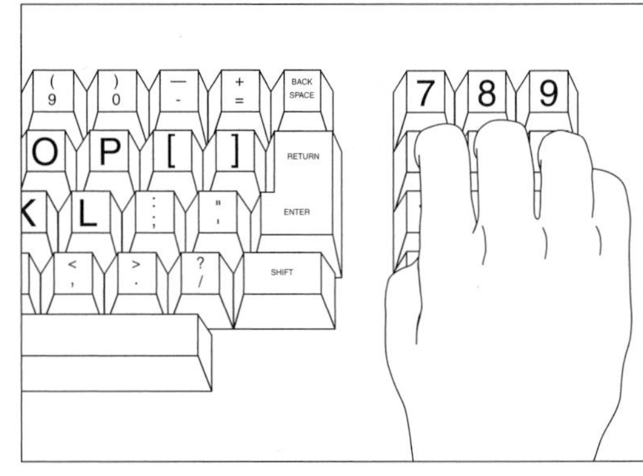

On the ten-key numeric keypad, the 4-5-6 keys are called the **home keys.** These keys are the "starting point" from which you will operate the other number keys. The index finger of your right hand should rest on the 4 key, your middle finger on the 5 key, and your ring finger on the 6 key. Most keypads have a special "help" on the home keys so you can easily locate them: there may be a raised dot on the 5 key or the surfaces of the 4-5-6 keys may be concave (indented).

From the home keys, you reach up or down to tap other keys. The index finger is also used for the 7 and 1 keys. The middle finger is used for the 8 and 2 keys. The ring finger is used for the 9 and 3 keys.

The fingers used for the 0 (zero), decimal, and Enter keys depend on the arrangement of the keypad. On some keypads, the thumb is used to tap the 0 (zero) key and the ring finger for the decimal key. The Enter

MAKING CONNECTIONS TO DAILY LIFE

Using the Ten-Key Numeric Keypad Ask students to describe instances in which they think they might use a ten-key numeric keypad in their daily lives. Have them consider the following tasks: reconciling checkbooks, using computerized calculators to calculate employment earnings, using desktop calculators to complete math problems, or entering amounts on a computerized cash register on the job.

key on a computer may be operated by the little finger or the thumb, depending on its location.

On an electronic calculator, numbers are entered by using function keys: plus (+), minus (–), multiply (×), divide (÷), and so on. A computer keypad has different function keys for multiply (*) and divide (/). On an electronic calculator, the asterisk (*) is used for the total.

The fingers used to operate these keys depend on the keys' location on the keyboard. Locate these keys on your keypad and determine the correct fingers to use to operate them.

Entering Numbers by Touch

Throughout the remaining pages of this appendix, you will demonstrate use of the numeric keypad by touch. That is, you will enter numbers on the keypad without looking at your fingers.

Your practice consists of adding columns of numbers. If you are using an electronic calculator, tap the plus (+) key after you have entered a number in a column. After entering all the numbers in a column, tap the total (*) key. If you are using a computer spreadsheet program, tap the Enter key after you have entered a number in a column. This will force a line break; each time you strike the Enter key, the cursor will move to the next line. After entering all the numbers in a column, use the software function or formula to add the numbers.

Using the 4-5-6 Keys

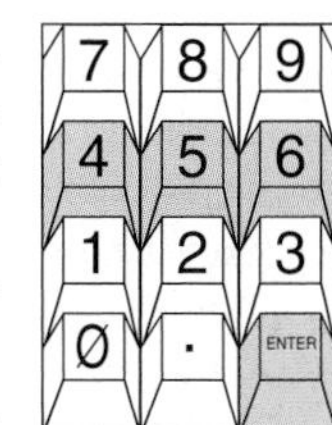

1. Demonstrate use of the numeric keypad by touch. Locate the 4-5-6 keys (the home keys) on your keypad. Also locate the Enter key if you're using a computer or the plus key if you're using a calculator.
2. Place your index finger on the 4 key, your middle finger on the 5 key, and your ring finger on the 6 key.
3. To enter a number, tap the number keys, one at a time, in the same order as you read the digits from left to right. Always keep your fingers on the home keys.
4. When you have entered the last digit, tap the Enter key (computer) or the plus key (calculator).
5. Using the following problems, practice entering columns of numbers. Practice at a comfortable pace until you feel confident about each key's location.
6. After entering all of the numbers in a column, add the numbers using the software (computer) or tap the total key once (calculator).

1.	2.	3.	4.	5.	6.
444	555	666	456	554	664
555	666	454	654	445	445
666	444	545	465	564	566
456	654	446	556	664	645
564	546	646	656	565	465
646	465	546	465	655	654

TEACHING NOTES

APPENDIX B
PAGES A-13–A-16

Concept Development: Home Position

Discussion: Explain to students that the home position is the "starting point" from which all keys are operated. Ask students to gently place the index finger of their right hand on the 4 key, the middle finger on the 5 key, and the ring finger on the 6 key. Centering the hand over these keys will ensure all other keys can be easily reached. L1

Visual Learning

Keypads

Use **Transparency APPB–2** to illustrate typical ten-key numeric configurations.

Concept Development: Entering Numbers by Touch

Discussion: Emphasize that the skill of operating the ten-key by touch means that students should not look at their fingers while entering numbers. Inform students that they will be entering columns of numbers and tapping the plus (+) key after each number if using a calculator. If using a computer, they should tap the Enter key after each number. L1

Concept Development: Using the 4-5-6 Keys

Discussion: Explain that students should first familiarize themselves with the home keys, or the 4-5-6 keys. Ask students to look at the list of practice columns. After a student's hand is placed in the home position, the student can begin tapping one number key at a time, reading the digits from left to right. L1

Column totals are provided in margins and also appear in the *Chapter Reviews and Working Papers* student edition.

1. 3,331
2. 3,330
3. 3,303
4. 3,252
5. 3,447
6. 3,439

APPENDIX B
PAGES A-13–A-16

Concept Development: Using the 1, 7, and 0 Keys

Discussion: Ask students to close their eyes and visualize the left column of numbers on the numeric keypad. Inform them that they will use the index finger and thumb for this side of the keypad. The index finger will reach up to strike the 7 key or reach down to tap the 1 key. The 0 (zero) key will be tapped with the thumb. L1

1. 2,947
2. 1,517
3. 2,834
4. 750
5. 1,540
6. 940

Concept Development: Using the 3 and 9 Keys

Discussion: Have students draw a quick sketch of the numeric keypad on a sheet of paper. Ask them to shade in the 9 and 3 keys. Explain that they will use the ring finger to reach down to the 3 key and up to the 9 key. As they practice the columns of numbers, remind them to keep their fingers in the home key position. L1

1. 3,591
2. 3,237
3. 3,693
4. 3,333
5. 3,654
6. 3,930

Using the 1, 7 and 0 Keys

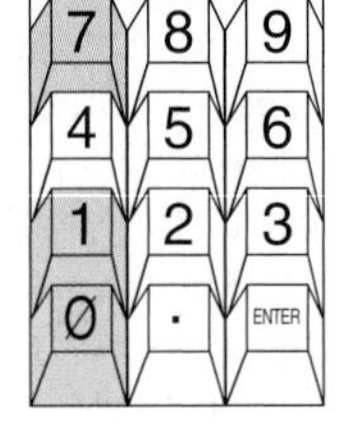

1. Demonstrate use of the numeric keypad by touch. Locate the 1, 7 and 0 (zero) keys on your keypad.
2. Place your fingers on the home keys.
3. Practice the reach from the home keys to each new key. Reach down to the 1 key and up to the 7 key with your index finger. Be sure to return your finger to the home keys after tapping the 1 and 7 keys. Strike the 0 (zero) key with your thumb.
4. Using the following problems, practice adding columns of numbers containing the new keys. Practice at a comfortable pace until you feel confident about each key's location. Be sure to keep your fingers in home-key position.

1.	2.	3.	4.	5.	6.
444	014	140	107	011	141
471	107	701	074	170	117
174	740	701	104	710	417
741	101	704	007	004	047
710	114	471	411	471	104
407	441	117	047	174	114

Using the 3 and 9 Keys

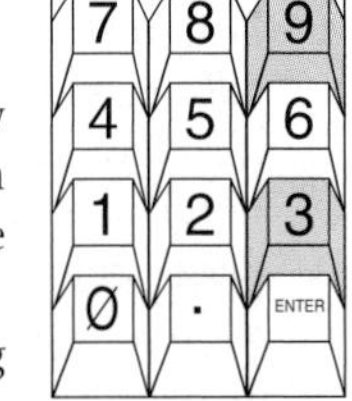

1. Locate the 3 and 9 keys on your keypad.
2. Place your fingers on the home keys.
3. Practice the reach from the home keys to each new key. Reach down to the 3 key and up to the 9 key with your ring finger. Be sure to return your finger to the home keys after tapping the 3 and 9 keys.
4. Using the following problems, practice adding columns of numbers containing the new keys. Practice at a comfortable pace until you feel confident about each key's location. Be sure to keep your fingers in home-key position.

1.	2.	3.	4.	5.	6.
666	669	339	966	939	699
999	663	363	393	363	936
333	936	336	966	393	939
963	396	936	633	639	336
639	936	636	393	369	696
399	363	996	993	369	939

Using the 2 and 8 Keys

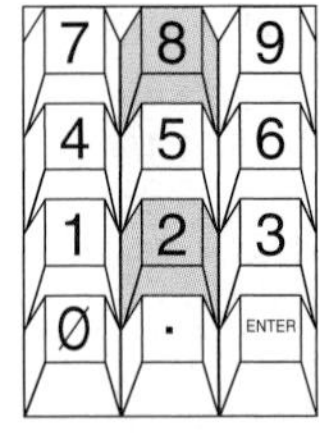

1. Locate the 2 and 8 keys on your keypad.
2. Place your fingers on the home keys.
3. Practice the reach from the home keys to each new key. Reach down to the 2 key and up to the 8 key with your middle finger. Be sure to return your finger to the home keys after tapping the 2 and 8 keys.

REINFORCING STUDY SKILLS

Concentration and Visualization Correct hand and finger placement is not the only factor in successful keyboarding. Consider the following:

- **Visualize.** Use visualization and instinct as you hone your keypad skills.
- **Concentrate.** Block out external distractions and focus on the task at hand.
- **Be a beginner.** Do not be pressured with speed goals; instead focus on key locations and hand position.
- **Minimize head movement.** Try to work as much as possible without looking at your hand. If necessary, pause to remember where the needed key is located.

4. Using the following problems, practice adding columns of numbers containing the new keys. Practice at a comfortable pace until you feel confident about each key's location. Be sure to keep your fingers in home-key position.

1.	2.	3.	4.	5.	6.
555	228	885	285	582	828
888	852	285	258	558	825
222	522	825	525	582	852
582	252	588	858	825	258
822	528	258	582	525	885
522	855	852	825	582	282

Using the Decimal Key

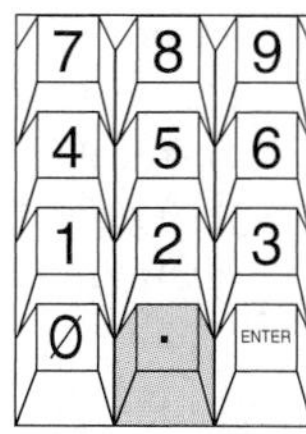

1. Locate the decimal key on your keypad.
2. Place your fingers on the home keys.
3. Depending on the arrangement of keys on your numeric keypad, you may use your thumb, your middle finger, or your ring finger to tap the decimal key. Practice the reach from the home keys to the decimal key. Be sure to return your finger to the home keys after tapping the decimal key.
4. Using the following problems, practice adding columns of numbers containing the decimal key. Practice at a comfortable pace until you feel confident about the key's location. Be sure to keep your fingers in home-key position.

1.	2.	3.	4.	5.	6.
.777	.978	.998	8.78	7.88	8.79
.888	.987	.879	8.89	7.87	7.98
.999	.878	.787	8.87	8.97	9.89
.789	.987	.878	7.88	9.77	9.87
.897	.789	.797	9.87	7.97	7.89
.978	.797	.899	7.98	8.79	9.78

7.	8.	9.	10.	11.	12.
468.	48.2	.8	284.0	41.87	154.88
.489	2,537.	5,827.	100.	4,057.4	888.
214.2	852.	.024	8.45	89.45	.0082
7.12	3.978	18.73	56.0	2.25	200.08
6,394.4	257.0	85.00	23.00	20.0	632.48
.58	.2684	1.045	.89	36.248	64.1

13.	14.	15.	16.	17.	18.
267.50	425.21	1.25	467.54	65.27	9.78
4.19	414.50	0.18	95.14	102.38	5.94
87.64	1,684.84	585.56	6,926.95	8,216.58	652.25
654.84	49.95	7.50	35.00	1,852.84	3,782.70
1,750.67	720.65	11.60	7.13	4.60	39.25
141.82	77.61	23.55	154.95	79.15	36.87

APPENDIX B

PAGES A-13–A-16

Concept Development: Using the 2 and 8 Keys

Discussion: Explain to students that the center of the keypad is operated by the middle finger, reaching up to the 8 key and down to the 2 key. As students practice entering the columns of numbers, have them work at a slow pace until they are comfortable with each key's position. L1

1. 3,591
2. 3,237
3. 3,693
4. 3,333
5. 3,654
6. 3,930

Concept Development: Using the Decimal Key

Discussion: Ask students to find the decimal key on their keypads. Explain that the placement of the key will determine which finger should be used to tap the decimal key. The thumb, middle finger, or ring finger may be used. L1

1. 5.328
2. 5.416
3. 5.238
4. 52.27
5. 51.25
6. 54.20

7. 7,084.789
8. 3,698.4464
9. 5,932.599
10. 472.34
11. 4,247.218
12. 1,939.5482

13. 2,906.66
14. 3,372.76
15. 629.64
16. 7,686.71
17. 10,320.82
18. 4,526.79

Supplemental exercises appear in the *Chapter Reviews and Working Papers.*

TEACHING NOTES

INTRODUCING APPENDIX C

Appendix C Overview

Although many small businesses have switched their record keeping to computers, some businesses may still use a combination journal. This appendix provides an option for you to have your students learn how to use a combination journal. In this appendix students will learn how to record transactions; total, prove, and rule the journal; and post from the journal.

Appendix C Concepts

- How to record business transactions in a multicolumn journal.
- How to post from the combination journal.
- How to total, prove, and rule the combination journal.

Visual Learning

Appendix C Focus

Use **Transparency APPC–1** to discuss the activities students will complete in the combination journal.

Appendix Vocabulary

combination journal

Preteaching Accounting Vocabulary

Demonstration: Define the combination journal for students. Using a combination journal, show students how its columns "combine" all the columns of the special journals into one journal. L1

Concept Development: The Combination Journal

Discussion: Review the columns in the combination journal and ask students to tell you the special journals in which each of these column headings appear. The combination journal is just what its name implies: a combination of special and general journals into one journal. L1

APPENDIX C

Recording Transactions in the Combination Journal

***What* You'll Learn**

The purpose of the combination journal.

- How to record business transactions in a multicolumn journal.
- How to post from the combination journal.
- How to total, prove, and rule the combination journal.

***Why* It's Important**

The combination journal is used primarily by small businesses and professional businesses (doctors, dentists, lawyers, etc.) which usually have one accounting clerk who records repetitious transactions. The accounting concepts, procedures, and applications associated with a combination journal can easily be adapted to a computerized accounting system.

KEY TERMS

combination journal

In earlier chapters you learned that businesses that have a large volume of financial transactions use special journals to record those transactions. Special journals, you'll remember, are designed for recording a "special" kind of business transaction.

Although special journals are ideally used in large businesses, they are not very practical for small service and retail businesses with few employees. Such businesses usually have only one accounting clerk. It is impractical for one clerk to record transactions in five different journals. At the same time, using only a general journal is very time consuming. For many small businesses, one journal is used—a combination journal.

The Combination Journal

As its name implies, a **combination journal** is a multicolumn journal that combines the features of the general journal and the special journals into one book of original entry. Like the special journals, the combination journal has special amount columns that are used to record transactions that occur frequently. In addition, the combination journal has General Debit and Credit columns in which to record transactions for which there are no special amount columns. Therefore, all the transactions of a business can be recorded in a single, multicolumn journal.

A business designs its combination journal to fit its own special needs. The number of columns, the selection of the special columns, and the arrangement of the columns will depend upon the type of business and the transactions that take place. Most businesses, however, use combination journals with between 10 and 13 columns.

The arrangement of the columns varies from one business to another. The columns should be arranged to make recording and posting easy and accurate. For example, look at On Your Mark Athletic Wear's combination journal in **Figure 1.** The Date, Account Name, Document Number, and posting Reference columns are located at the far left. These columns are followed by the General Debit and Credit columns.

COMBINATION

	DATE	ACCOUNT NAME	DOC. NO.	POST. REF.	GENERAL		ACCOUNTS RECEIVABLE	
					DEBIT	CREDIT	DEBIT	CREDIT
1								
2								
3								

Figure 1 The Combination Journal

TEACHING NOTES

The General columns are followed by the special amount columns for **Accounts Receivable, Sales, Sales Tax Payable, Accounts Payable, Purchases,** and **Cash in Bank**.

Notice that the line numbers appear to the left and right sides of each page of the journal. These line numbers help the accounting clerk avoid writing amounts on the wrong lines.

Using the Combination Journal

A properly designed combination journal can be used efficiently for recording every possible business transaction.

- Receipts of cash are recorded in the Cash in Bank Debit column.
- Cash payments are entered in the Cash in Bank Credit column.
- The purchase of merchandise, for cash or on account, is recorded in the Purchases Debit column.
- Transactions affecting creditor accounts are written in the Accounts Payable Debit and Credit columns.
- The sale of merchandise is recorded in the Sales Credit and Sales Tax Payable Credit columns.
- Transactions affecting charge customer accounts are entered in the Accounts Receivable Debit and Credit columns.
- General ledger accounts for which there are no special columns are recorded in the General Debit and Credit columns. Adjusting and closing entries, for example, would be recorded in the General Debit and Credit columns.

On Your Mark Athletic Wear's business transactions for the month of June are recorded in the combination journal shown in Figure 2.

Key Points

Recording Transactions

When recording transactions, use the line numbers as a guide to avoid writing amounts on the wrong line.

Proving and Posting the Journal

Like special journals, an important feature of the combination journal is that it saves time in both recording and posting transactions. The amounts entered in the General columns are posted on a daily basis to the appropriate general ledger accounts. Amounts entered in the Accounts Receivable and Accounts Payable columns are also posted on a daily basis to the appropriate charge customer or creditor accounts in the accounts receivable and accounts payable subsidiary ledgers. At the end of the month, the combination journal is footed, proved, totaled, and ruled. Totals of the special amount columns of the combination journal are then posted to the general ledger accounts named in the column headings. **Figure 2** shows how the combination journal will look at the end of the month after all postings have been made.

Key Points

Recording Transactions

The General columns are used to record any amount for which no special columns are provided.

JOURNAL PAGE ______

SALES CREDIT	SALES TAX PAYABLE CREDIT	ACCOUNTS PAYABLE DEBIT	ACCOUNTS PAYABLE CREDIT	PURCHASES DEBIT	CASH IN BANK DEBIT	CASH IN BANK CREDIT	
							1
							2
							3

APPENDIX C
PAGES A-17–A-24

Visual Learning

Figure 1 The Combination Journal

Use **Transparency APPC–2** to review the column headings in the combination journal. As you review each heading, ask students which general journal or special journal column this column replaces.

Concept Development: Using the Combination Journal

Discussion: Point out that recording entries in a combination journal is no different than recording entries in the special journals. Each business sets up column headings to meet its special needs. Business transactions are analyzed to determine the accounts affected and then recorded in the appropriate journal column. L1

Concept Development: Proving and Posting the Journal

Discussion: Point out that proving the combination journal follows the same process as proving any of the special journals. The columns are pencil footed, totals are proved, and the journal is ruled. Column totals are posted at the end of the month, while amounts in the Accounts Receivable and Accounts Payable columns are posted daily. L1

MEETING SPECIAL NEEDS

English Language Learners Before new topics are discussed in class, provide students who are English language learners a course outline that indicates when chapters are likely to be covered. Giving these students a chance to preview the chapter and study the new vocabulary before the topic is covered will enhance their understanding of the topic. It will also help students be ready to absorb information from class discussions.

Visual Learning

Figure 2 Recording Transactions in a Combination Journal

Use **Transparency APPC–3a** to review the recording of transactions in a multicolumn journal. Point out amounts that are posted daily and the column totals that are posted at the end of a month.

COMBINATION

	DATE		ACCOUNT NAME	DOC. NO.	POST. REF.	GENERAL DEBIT	GENERAL CREDIT	ACCOUNTS RECEIVABLE DEBIT	ACCOUNTS RECEIVABLE CREDIT
1	20--								
2	June	6	Cash Sales	T61	—				
3		8	Sales Discounts	R62	405	8 00			
4			Casey Klein		✓				424 00
5		10	Tammy's Fitness Club	S75	✓			530 00	
6		13	Office Equipment	I011	145	650 00			
7			Geary Office Supply		✓				
8		14	Sales Returns and Allowances	CM5	410	90 00			
9			Sales Tax Payable		220	5 40			
10			Lara Young		✓				95 40
11		15	Gabriel Ramos	M12	✓			80 00	
12			Shashi Rahim		✓				80 00
13		16	Computer Solutions	I003	✓				
14		18	Supplies	I214	130	100 00			
15			Geary Office Supplies		✓				
16		21	FastLane Athletics	CK350	✓				
17			Purchases Discounts		510		6 00		
18		23	Utilities Expense	CK351	680	175 00			
19		24	Purchases	CK352	—				
20		26	Salaries Expense	CK353	665	3200 00			
21			Social Security Tax Payable		212		198 40		
22			Medicare Tax Payable		213		46 40		
23			Employees' Federal Income Tax Payable		205		480 00		
24			Employees' State Income Tax Payable		206		70 40		
25		26	Payroll Tax Expense	P.Reg.	657	456 00			
26			Social Security Tax Payable		212		198 40		
27			Medicare Tax Payable		213		46 40		
28			Federal Unemployment Tax Payable		214		25 60		
29			State Unemployment Tax Payable		215		185 60		
30		27	Supplies	CK354	130	500 00			
31		28	Champion Store Supply	DM10	✓				
32			Purchases Returns and Allowances		515		90 00		
33		29	Supplies	M13	130	125 00			
34		30	Purchases		501		125 00		
35			Totals			5 309 40 5309 40	1 472 20 1472 20	6 1 0 00 610 00	5 9 9 40 599 40
36						(✓)	(✓)	(115)	(115)
37									

Daily
Post each amount in the General, Accounts Payable, and Accounts Receivable columns to the general ledger. The account number recorded in the Post Ref. column indicates that posting has been completed.

Figure 2 Recording Transactions in a Combination Journal

REINFORCING STUDY SKILLS

Reading Graphs Point out to students that reading charts, graphs, and technical illustrations is an important part of learning a subject such as accounting. The same reading techniques that are used with narrative can also be applied to reading graphs and other illustrations. For example, read the title and/or caption. In a table, read the headings on rows and columns. In diagrams, read the descriptive labels.

JOURNAL PAGE 7

SALES CREDIT	SALES TAX PAYABLE CREDIT	ACCOUNTS PAYABLE DEBIT	ACCOUNTS PAYABLE CREDIT	PURCHASES DEBIT	CASH IN BANK DEBIT	CASH IN BANK CREDIT	
							1
1250 00	75 00				1325 00		2
					416 00		3
							4
500 00	30 00						5
							6
			650 00				7
							8
							9
							10
							11
							12
			4200 00	4200 00			13
							14
			100 00				15
		200 00					16
						194 00	17
						175 00	18
				300 00		300 00	19
							20
							21
							22
							23
						2404 80	24
							25
							26
							27
							28
							29
						500 00	30
		90 00					31
							32
							33
							34
1750 00 1750 00	105 00 105 00	290 00 290 00	4950 00 4950 00	4500 00 4500 00	1741 00 1741 00	3573 80 3573 80	35
(401)	(220)	(201)	(201)	(501)	(101)	(101)	36
							37

End of Month
Post the column totals for Sales, Sales Tax Payable, Purchases, and Cash in Bank to the general ledger. Account numbers in parentheses indicate that posting has been completed.

Figure 2 Recording Transactions in a Combination Journal (Cont.)

Visual Learning

Figure 2 Recording Transactions in a Combination Journal (Continued)

Use **Transparency APPC–3b** to review the remaining columns in the combination journal. Point out column totals that are posted at the end of a month.

TEACHING NOTES

Problem C–1 (Answers) Analyzing Transactions for Combination Journal Entries

Dec. 2: Dr. General; Cr. Cash in Bank
Dec. 5: Dr. Accts. Rec.; Cr. Sales, Sales Tax Payable
Dec. 10: Dr. General; Cr. Accounts Receivable
Dec. 13: Dr. Accounts Payable; Cr. General
Dec. 15: Dr. Cash in Bank; Cr. Accounts Receivable
Dec. 18: Dr. Accounts Payable; Cr. General, Cash in Bank
Dec. 22: Dr. General; Cr. General
Dec. 25: Dr. General; Cr. General, Cash in Bank
Dec. 25: Dr. General; Cr. General
Dec. 30: Dr. Cash in Bank; Cr. Sales, Sales Tax Payable
Dec. 31: Dr. General; Cr. General

Problem C–1 Analyzing Transactions for Combination Journal Entries

John Dunn owns The Country Store, a small retail store. He uses a combination journal with the following columns.

- General Debit
- General Credit
- Accounts Receivable Debit
- Accounts Receivable Credit
- Sales Credit
- Sales Tax Payable Credit
- Accounts Payable Debit
- Accounts Payable Credit
- Purchases Debit
- Cash in Bank Debit
- Cash in Bank Credit

Instructions Use the form provided in your working papers. For each of the following selected transactions, indicate in which column(s) of the combination journal the debit and credit parts of the entry would be recorded. The first transaction has been completed as an example.

Date	Trans.	General		Accounts Receivable		Sales Cr.	Sales Tax Payable Cr.	Accounts Payable		Purchases Dr.	Cash in Bank	
		Dr.	Cr.	Dr.	Cr.			Dr.	Cr.		Dr.	Cr.
Dec. 1	Debit	✓										
	Credit								✓			

Date	Transactions
Dec. 1	Purchased a computer on account from King's Computer Outlet.
2	John Dunn withdrew cash for personal use.
5	Sold merchandise on account to Bernard Peterson, plus sales tax.
10	Issued Credit memo 14 to Tom Tray, a charge customer, for the return of merchandise sold on account plus sales tax.
13	Issued Debit Memo 20 to Cory distributors for the return of merchandise purchased from them on account.
15	Received a check from Bernard Peterson in full payment of his account.
18	Issued a check to Cory Distributors in payment of our account less the purchases return and less a purchases discount.
22	John Dunn invested a calculator in the business.
25	Issued a check for the monthly payroll less deductions for FICA.
25	Recorded the employer's payroll tax liabilities for FICA taxes, federal unemployment tax, and state unemployment tax.
30	Recorded cash sales plus sales tax.
31	Recorded the adjusting entry for the office supplies consumed during the period.

ACCOUNTING ISSUES

Accessing and Sharing Information Regardless of whether they are dealing with clients, vendors, or colleagues, accountants must be able to access a wide range of information from many locations and share it with others near and far. Innovations in technology provide many tools for the accountant to use. Among these tools are cellular phones, fax machines, pagers, PDAs (personal digital assistants) and handheld computers, laptop computers, video conferencing, E-mail and voice mail, and the Internet.

Problem C–2 Recording Transactions/Totaling, Proving, and Ruling the Combination Journal

Craig Glasser is a physician who operates a family medical practice, Glasser Family Medical Center. He uses the combination journal found in your working papers.

Instructions

(1) Record the following transactions on page 17 of the combination journal.
(2) Total, prove, and rule the combination journal.

Date	Transactions
Oct. 1	Received $2,100 in medical fees from patients, Receipt 90.
2	Issued Check 414 for the cash purchase of $120 of office supplies.
4	Purchased medical supplies on account from Wharton laboratories, Invoice 14006 for $1,950, terms n/60.
6	Craig Glasser invested medical equipment valued at $750 in the medical practice, Memorandum 30.
8	Billed a patient, Daniel O'Connell, $150 for his annual physical, Statement 40.
9	Completed lab services for Carl Fisher and billed him $160, Statement 41.
11	Purchased a new examination table (medical equipment) on account from Medical Suppliers, Invoice L163 for $1,452.50, terms n/45.
13	Billed Patricia Vallano $300 for medical services, Statement 42.
15	Issued Check 415 for $2,004.81 for the monthly salaries expense of $2,500.00 less deductions: social security tax, $155.00; Medicare tax, $36.25; employees' federal income taxes, $209.00; employees' state income taxes, $94.94.
15	Recorded the employer's payroll tax liabilities: social security tax, $155; Medicare tax, $36.25; federal unemployment taxes, $20; state unemployment taxes, $145; payroll register.
18	Issued Debit memo 16 to Wharton Laboratories for $200 for the return of medical supplies purchased on account.
20	Paid the telephone bill, Check 416 for $110.
22	A check for $110 was received from John Marshall to apply on his account, Receipt 91.
	Continued

Problem C–2 (Answers) Recording Transactions/ Totaling, Proving, and Ruling the Combination Journal

Combination Journal column totals:

General Debit $7,438.75
General Credit $1,801.44
Accounts Receivable Debit $705
Accounts Receivable Credit $185
Medical Fees Credit $2,550
Laboratory Fees Credit $255
Accounts Payable Debit $200
Accounts Payable Credit $3,402.50
Medical Supplies Debit $1,950
Cash in Bank Debit $2,285
Cash in Bank Credit $4,384.81

SOLUTION NOTES

Problem C-3 (Answers) Recording Transactions, Totaling, Proving, and Ruling the Combination Journal

Combination Journal column totals:
General Debit $3,580.68
General Credit $871.69
Accounts Receivable Debit $408.50
Accounts Receivable Credit $506.25
Sales Credit $3,300
Sales Tax Payable Credit $148.50
Accounts Payable Debit $660
Accounts Payable Credit $900
Purchases Debit $700
Cash in Bank Debit $3,489.82
Cash in Bank Credit $3,112.56

Date	Transactions
25	Craig Glasser withdrew $1,250 cash from the business, Check 417.
28	Received $75 from Daniel O'Connell to apply on his account, Receipt 92.
31	Sent Statement 43 for $95 to Donna Gordon for lab services completed on account.
31	Issued Check 418 for the November rent of $900.

Problem C–3 Recording Transactions, Totaling, Proving, and Ruling the Combination Journal

Sunset Surfwear is a small merchandise business specializing in a variety of surfwear items. Sunset Surfwear uses a combination journal with these amount columns.

General Debit	Accounts Payable Debit
General Credit	Accounts Payable Credit
Accounts Receivable Debit	Purchases Debit
Accounts Receivable Credit	Cash in Bank Debit
Sales Credit	Cash in Bank Credit
Sales Tax Payable Credit	

Instructions In your working papers:

(1) Record the following transactions on page 12 of the combination journal.

(2) Total, prove, and rule the combination journal.

Date	Transactions
Dec. 1	Issued Check 151 for $700 to Pine Valley Realty for the monthly rent.
2	Received a check for $204.82 from Martha Adams in payment of her account of $209 less a discount of $4.18, Receipt 303.
3	Purchased $400 of merchandise on account from Kelley Apparel, Invoice 479 dated December 2, terms 2/10, n/30.
4	Issued Check 152 for $75 to The Knight Crier for advertisements.
5	Issued Check 153 for $230.30 to Neilson Store Equipment in payment of their invoice for $235.
6	Sent Credit memo 35 to Alex Hamilton for damaged merchandise returned, $50 plus $2.25 sales tax.
8	Sold merchandise on account to Nate Moulder, $100 plus sales tax of $4.50, Sales Slip 205.

Continued

SOLUTION NOTES

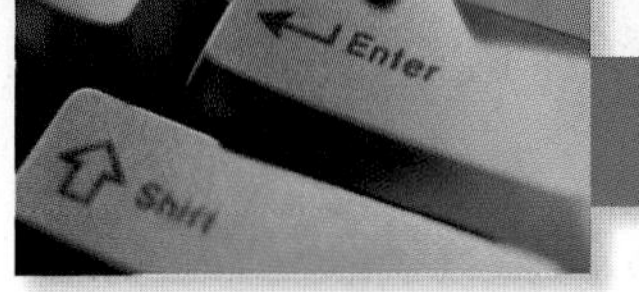

Date	Transactions (Cont.)
10	Discovered that $95 received on account from Helen Jan on November 16 had been journalized and posted to Harriett Junell's account, Memorandum 16.
11	Recorded the monthly salaries of $2,100 less deductions: social security tax, $130.20; Medicare tax, $30.45; employees' federal income taxes, $326; and employees' state income taxes, $48.09; Check 154 for $1,565.26.
11	Recorded the employer's payroll tax liabilities: social security tax, $130.20; Medicare tax, $30.45; federal unemployment tax, $16.80; state unemployment tax, $121.80; payroll register.
12	Sent Check 155 for $392 to Kelley Apparel in payment of Invoice 479 less a discount of $8.
15	Received $150 from Martha Adams to apply on her account, Receipt 304.
18	Issued Debit Memorandum 20 to Waverunner Designs for $25 for the return of merchandise purchased on account.
24	Sold $200 in merchandise on account to Westwood High School Athletics plus sales tax of $9, Sales Slip 206.
26	Purchased $300 of merchandise on account from Capital Accessories, Invoice 601.
28	Purchased store equipment on account from Neilson Store Equipment, $200, Invoice 609.
29	Paid a $150 electric bill for the month by issuing Check 156 to Dukane Power Company.
31	Recorded cash sales of $3,000, plus $135 sales taxes, Tape 52.

Problem C–4 Recording Adjusting and Closing Entries in a Combination Journal

A partial work sheet for December 31 for In Beat CD Shop is shown in your working papers.

Instructions

(1) Record the adjusting entries in the combination journal. Then total, prove, and rule the General columns of the journal.

(2) Record the closing entries in the combination journal. Then total, prove, and rule the General columns of the journal.

Problem C-4 (Answers) Recording Adjusting and Closing Entries in a Combination Journal

General column totals:
Adjusting entries $5,370
Closing entries $94,750

SOLUTION NOTES

INTRODUCING APPENDIX D

Appendix D Overview

Use of the accrual basis in accounting helps businesses match revenue for a period with the expenses incurred to earn that revenue. Under the accrual basis, revenue is recognized when a sale is made regardless of whether the resulting cash has actually been received. Likewise, interest is matched to the fiscal period when it is earned or incurred, not when it is actually received or paid.

Appendix D Concepts

- The difference between a cash and accrual basis of accounting.
- In what instances accruals are needed.
- In what instances deferrals are needed.
- How to record adjusting entries.
- How to record accrual entries.
- How to calculate interest receivable.
- How to calculate interest due and payable.

Visual Learning

Appendix D Focus

Use **Transparency APPD–1** to introduce the concepts students will learn in this appendix.

Appendix Vocabulary

cash basis of accounting
accrual basis of accounting
accruals
deferrals
accrued revenue
accrued expense
unearned revenue
prepaid expense

Preteaching Accounting Vocabulary

Demonstration: Write the terms "accruals" and "deferrals" on the chalkboard. Explain the meaning of each term. Write "increases" beside accruals; write "delays" beside deferrals. Explain how each relates to the term. Then have students look at the remaining terms and discuss their meaning. L1

APPENDIX D

The Accrual Basis of Accounting

What You'll Learn

- The difference between a cash and accrual basis of accounting.
- In what instances accruals are needed.
- In what instances deferrals are needed.
- How to record adjusting entries.
- How to record accrual entries.
- How to calculate interest receivable.
- How to calculate interest due and payable.

Why It's Important

Most businesses use the accrual basis of accounting, recognizing revenue when earned and expenses when incurred.

KEY TERMS

cash basis of accounting
accrual basis of accounting
accruals
deferrals
accrued revenue
accrued expense
unearned revenue
prepaid expense

Some small businesses keep their financial records on a cash basis. The **cash basis of accounting** recognizes and records revenues when cash is received and expenses only when cash is paid out. Often, however, cash is received and payments are made in an accounting period other than the period in which the original transaction took place. For example, a landscaping service performs work for a client in December, but the customer may not be required to pay until January of the next year. However, if the revenue is not recorded for the service performed in December, the financial statements may not present fairly the business earnings for the year just ended. To overcome this, the accounting profession requires that most businesses use what is called the **accrual basis of accounting**. In accrual accounting, revenues are recognized and recorded when earned, and expenses are recognized and recorded when they are actually incurred. The system for accrual accounting focuses on when earned and incurred rather than on when collected and paid.

Accruals and Deferrals

The accrual basis of accounting requires that accountants recognize revenue when the business makes a sale or performs a service, regardless of when the company receives the cash. Expenses are recognized as incurred, whether or not the business has paid out the cash. To accrue revenue means to record an amount in anticipation of future receipts and to accrue an expense means to record an amount in anticipation of a future payment. Accrual accounting involves two types of revenues and expenses: accruals and deferrals.

Accruals

Accruals relate to *transactions which have not yet been recorded* in the accounts. The word "accrue" means to accumulate or amass. Accruals for unrecorded revenues and expenses are required when:

1. *A revenue has been earned but not yet received.* For example, interest earned on a note receivable in one accounting period but not collected until the next accounting period.
2. *An expense has been incurred but not yet paid.* For example, you may earn wages from April 27 to April 30, but your employer may not pay your check to you until May 5.

Accruals are revenues or expenses that are gradually earned or incurred over time. In order to report a company's financial position fairly, accruals should be recognized in the accounting period in which they belong.

TEACHING NOTES

Deferrals

Deferrals are for *transactions that have been recorded* in the accounts. The word "defer" means to wait or delay. Deferrals are for receipts that are not earned and for payments that are not expenses.

1. *Cash may have been received but not yet earned.* For example, rent received in advance when some of the rental time is in one accounting period and the balance is in the next accounting period.
2. *Cash may have been paid but the expenses not incurred.* For example, when premiums on insurance are paid covering part of one accounting period and the balance covers the next accounting period.

Adjusting entries are required to: **(1)** recognize unrecorded accrued revenues and expenses or **(2)** allocate recorded deferred revenues and expenses to the appropriate accounting period.

Key Points

Accrual Basis of Accounting

With the accrual basis of accounting, revenue is recorded when it is earned, and expenses are recorded when they are incurred.

Accrued Revenue

Accrued revenue is revenue that has been earned but not received or recorded. Examples of unrecorded accrued revenues include unpaid fees for services completed and rent earned but not yet received. The accrued revenue example that follows is for unpaid interest earned on a note receivable.

Business Transaction

On December 5, Rapid Growth Co. accepted a $5,000, 90-day, 9% note receivable from a charge customer, Janie Pippa. Pippa issued the note as an extension on her charge account. Rapid Growth Co. recorded the transaction as a debit of $5,000 to ***Notes Receivable*** *and a credit of $5,000 to* ***Accounts Receivable*** *and Janie Pippa's account in the subsidiary ledger. On December 31, 26 days of interest had been earned (accrued) on the note receivable: $5,000 × .09 × 26/365 = $32.05. An adjusting entry is required on December 31 to record the amount of interest income earned from December 5 to the year ending December 31.*

ANALYSIS

Identify 1. For the adjusting entry, the accounts **Interest Receivable** and **Interest Income** are affected.

Classify 2. **Interest Income** is a revenue account. **Interest Receivable** is an asset account.

+/− 3. **Interest Income** is increased and **Interest Receivable** is increased.

DEBIT-CREDIT RULE

4. Increases to assets are recorded as debits. Debit **Interest Receivable** for $32.05.
5. Increases to revenues are recorded as credits. Credit **Interest Income** for $32.05.

T ACCOUNTS

6.

Interest Receivable		Interest Income	
Debit + Adj. 32.05	Credit −	Debit −	Credit + Adj. 32.05

APPENDIX D
PAGES A-25–A-32

Concept Development: Accruals and Deferrals

Discussion: Very few companies are able to use a cash basis of accounting because it may not allow for the matching of revenue and expenses. Review the definitions of accruals and deferrals. Point out that accruals are items that accumulate or increase. In accounting, accruals are amounts that have accumulated but have not yet been recorded in the accounting records.

Deferrals are items that are delayed or "deferred." Deferrals are used in accounting when an amount applies to two or more accounting periods. L1

Concept Development: Accrued Revenue

Discussion: Businesses often earn revenue before the actual cash is received. A primary example is interest on a note receivable. The business earns interest each day, but it is not recorded until the payment of the interest is received. L1

Visual Learning

Business Transaction

Use **Transparency APPD–2** to analyze the adjusting entry to record interest earned but not recorded during the period.

REINFORCING STUDY SKILLS

Research Skills Many students are unfamiliar with the best ways of using the research services available in school and public libraries. Point out that information now comes not only from books and journals but also from computerized databases, microfilm, computer software, and videos. Assign students to groups and give each group a selected topic to research. Ask students to report on how they used technology to do their research.

APPENDIX D
PAGES A-25–A-32

Teaching Tips

Remind students that a transaction to record interest is an example of accrued revenue. Also point out that interest on a promissory note is paid in one payment at the maturity date; no interest is received during the term of the note.

Visual Learning

General Journal, p. A-27

Use the illustration in the textbook to discuss the transaction involving receipt of payment for a note receivable and interest on the note.

Concept Development: Accrued Expenses

Discussion: Accrued expenses are amounts the business owes that have not yet been entered in the accounting records. Point out that students who have part-time jobs earn money each day they work, but they are not paid until the end of a week or perhaps two weeks. Their earnings are accrued expenses for the employer.

Have students ask their parents when they pay property taxes on their homes. Many people pay property taxes through their monthly mortgage payments. The mortgage company collects the tax money and pays it to the local government when it comes due. People who pay rent also pay property tax, but in a hidden way. Rental payments cover the building owner's costs, which include property taxes on all the rental units. L1

JOURNAL ENTRY

7.

GENERAL JOURNAL — PAGE 18

	DATE		DESCRIPTION	POST. REF.	DEBIT	CREDIT	
1	20--		Adjusting Entries				1
2	Dec.	31	Interest Receivable		32 05		2
3			Interest Income			32 05	3
4							4

On March 5, Rapid received a check from Janie Pippa for $5,110.96, the maturity value of the note ($5,000.00 principle + $110.96 interest). Of the total interest, $32.05 had been earned and recorded in the previous accounting period. The remaining $78.91 should be recorded as income earned in the *current* fiscal year.

In the entry for the receipt of Janie's payment, **Cash in Bank** is debited for $5,110.96, the total amount of cash received. **Notes Receivable** is credited for $5,000.00. **Interest Receivable** is credited for $32.05 since the amount owed has now been received. **Interest Income** is credited for $78.91, the amount of the interest earned that applies to the current accounting period. The entry for this transaction is shown below.

Key Points

Adjusting Entries

Adjusting entries must be recorded when (1) there are unrecorded revenues and expenses at the end of the accounting period, and (2) there are recorded revenues and expenses that must be allocated over two or more accounting periods.

GENERAL JOURNAL — PAGE 24

	DATE		DESCRIPTION	POST. REF.	DEBIT	CREDIT	
1	20--						1
2	Mar.	5	Cash in Bank		5 110 96		2
3			Notes Receivable			5 000 00	3
4			Interest Receivable			32 05	4
5			Interest Income			78 91	5
6			Receipt 416				6
7							7

Accrued Expenses

Most expenses are recorded when they are paid, or a liability is incurred. There are, however, some business expenses that have not been paid—but accrue daily—and are not recorded until an adjusting entry is made at the end of the fiscal period. Some examples of these **accrued expenses** are salaries or wages earned by working employees but not yet paid to them, property taxes owed but not yet paid, and interest accrued on unpaid notes payable. The example that follows shows how to calculate interest due and payable.

Business Transaction

On November 1, Rapid Growth Co. signed a $2,000, 90-day, 12% note payable for the purchase of equipment from Taylor Equipment. Rapid Growth Co. recorded the transaction as a debit of $2,000 to **Equipment** *and a credit of $2,000 to* **Notes Payable**. *On December 31, 60 days of interest was owed (accrued) on the note payable: $2,000 × .12 × 60/365 = $39.45. An adjusting entry is required on December 31 to record the amount of interest expense incurred from November 1 to the year ending December 31.*

TEACHING NOTES

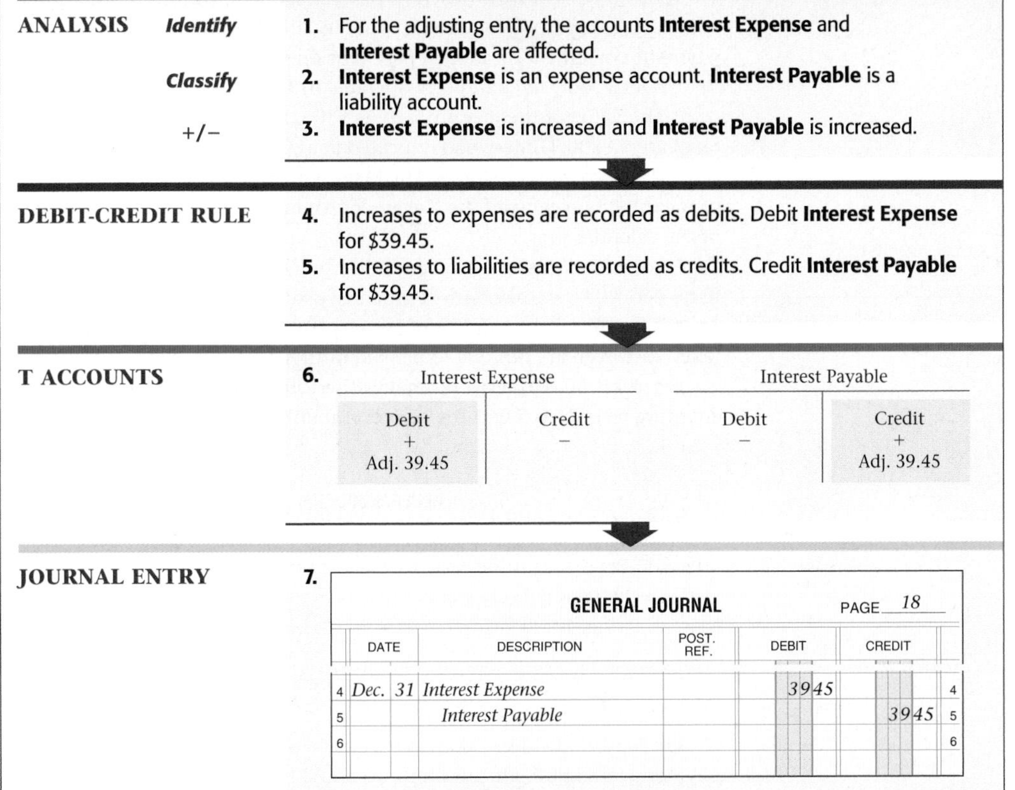

ANALYSIS

Identify 1. For the adjusting entry, the accounts **Interest Expense** and **Interest Payable** are affected.

Classify 2. **Interest Expense** is an expense account. **Interest Payable** is a liability account.

+/− 3. **Interest Expense** is increased and **Interest Payable** is increased.

DEBIT-CREDIT RULE

4. Increases to expenses are recorded as debits. Debit **Interest Expense** for $39.45.
5. Increases to liabilities are recorded as credits. Credit **Interest Payable** for $39.45.

T ACCOUNTS

6.

Interest Expense	
Debit +	Credit −
Adj. 39.45	

Interest Payable	
Debit −	Credit +
	Adj. 39.45

JOURNAL ENTRY

7.

GENERAL JOURNAL PAGE 18

	DATE		DESCRIPTION	POST. REF.	DEBIT	CREDIT	
4	Dec.	31	Interest Expense		39 45		4
5			Interest Payable			39 45	5
6							6

On March 5, Rapid sent a check to Taylor Equipment for $2,059.18, the maturity value of the note ($2,000.00 principle + $59.18 interest). Of the total interest expense, $39.45 had already been owed as of December 31. That amount was recorded as an adjusting entry in the previous accounting period. The remaining $19.73 should be recorded as expense for the *current* fiscal year.

In the entry for the payment of the note, **Notes Payable** is debited for $2,000.00. **Interest Expense** is debited for $19.73, the amount of interest expense incurred that applies to the current accounting period. **Interest Payable** is debited for $39.45 since the amount that was accrued has now been paid. **Cash in Bank** is credited for $2,059.18, the total amount of cash paid. The entry for this transaction is shown below.

GENERAL JOURNAL PAGE 24

	DATE		DESCRIPTION	POST. REF.	DEBIT	CREDIT	
7	Mar.	5	Notes Payable		2 000 00		7
8			Interest Expense		19 73		8
9			Interest Payable		39 45		9
10			Cash in Bank			2 059 18	10
11			Check # 1597				11

APPENDIX D
PAGES A-25–A-32

Visual Learning

Business Transaction

Use **Transparency APPD–3** to help students analyze and journalize the adjusting entry to record an accrued expense.

Teaching Tip

Point out that business expenses build up during the year and may be recorded only at the end of the period through an adjusting entry. Examples are interest owed on notes or taxes owed to local, state, and federal governments.

MEETING SPECIAL NEEDS

English Language Learners If you have special needs students, enlist the help of a language specialist when preparing exams and reviewing reading assignments. The specialist may identify potential problems with the language used in the exam. The specialist can offer suggestions on wording, sentence structure, and level of vocabulary that may increase the ELL students' comprehension without compromising the integrity of the exam. You can use this same procedure for textbooks and other assigned readings.

APPENDIX D

PAGES A-25–A-32

Concept Development: Deferrals

Discussion: Ask students whether they have ever bought tickets to a music concert or to a sporting event weeks or even months before the event. The payments they made for the tickets were unearned revenue for the company selling the tickets because the concert or sporting event had yet to take place. To match the expenses of producing the concert or event, the company will defer recognizing the revenue. The unearned revenue is treated as a liability (because the company is obligated to act since it has received payment) until it is earned. L1

Visual Learning

General Journal, p. A-29

Use the general journal illustration to explain the payment of an accrued expense. Contrast this entry with the preceding adjusting entry. The adjusting entry records the debt that is owed; the second entry records the actual payment.

To acquire cash with which to provide services, communities impose a tax on real property. Property taxes are usually paid twice a year, with each payment covering a six-month period or one-half the annual tax.

Underwood Merchandisers operates in the building on the land they own. The value of the real property is $300,000. The total annual property taxes are $7,800. Underwood is located in a state where property taxes must be paid in May and November. The May payment covers the first six months of the calendar year, and the November payment covers the last six months of the calendar year.

Underwood's fiscal period ends on April 30. As a result, at the end of its fiscal period, Underwood owes property taxes of $2,600 ($7,800 × 4/12 or $3,900 × 4/6) for the months of January, February, March and April. These taxes, however, are not due to be paid until May.

On April 30, Underwood makes the following adjustment to the accounting records to reflect the correct amount of property tax for the period.

GENERAL JOURNAL PAGE *26*

	DATE		DESCRIPTION	POST. REF.	DEBIT	CREDIT	
1	*20--*		*Adjusting Entries*				1
2	*Apr.*	*30*	*Property Tax Expense*		*2 600 00*		2
3			*Property Tax Payable*			*2 600 00*	3
4							4

On May 15, Underwood wrote a check for the semiannual property tax payment of $3,900. Of this amount, $2,600 is an expense charged to the prior fiscal period and $1,300 is an expense charged to the current accounting period. The entry in May to record this payment is shown in the general journal below.

GENERAL JOURNAL PAGE *33*

	DATE		DESCRIPTION	POST. REF.	DEBIT	CREDIT	
1	*20--*						1
2	*May*	*15*	*Property Tax Expense*		*1 300 00*		2
3			*Property Tax Payable*		*2 600 00*		3
4			*Cash in Bank*			*3 900 00*	4
5			*Check 401*				5

Deferrals

Sometimes a business receives cash or a receivable for revenue that has not yet been earned. Cash is also paid out for expenses before those expenses are actually incurred. So that a business can more fairly show its financial condition, unearned revenue and prepaid expenses must be deferred (postponed) and allocated to the proper fiscal periods.

REINFORCING STUDY SKILLS

Exam Preparation Tips When preparing for exams, students need some guidelines in knowing what material to study. Offer these tips as general guidelines for test preparation:

- Review all terminology—know the definition and be able to apply it by using it in a sentence.
- Check the main headings and subheadings in each chapter—be able to give a description of each heading.
- Review the chapter-ending summaries, questions, and problems.
- Ask a friend to "quiz" them about items in the sections to be tested.

Unearned Revenue

Unearned revenue is revenue received before it is actually earned. Examples include cash received in advance for rental properties, for season tickets to various events, for insurance premiums, and for work to be performed in the future. Because the business has an obligation to deliver the merchandise or perform the service for which it has already received payment, unearned revenue represents a current liability for the business.

Boyce Real Estate rents space in its building to a tax accountant. On November 1, the accountant paid Boyce $1,200 in advance for rent covering the months of November through April. The entry to record this transaction is shown below.

GENERAL JOURNAL PAGE 55

	DATE		DESCRIPTION	POST. REF.	DEBIT	CREDIT	
1	20--						1
2	Nov.	1	Cash in Bank		1 200 00		2
3			Unearned Rental Income			1 200 00	3
4			Receipt 181				4

As the business delivers the merchandise or performs the service, it earns a part of the advance payment. The earned portion must be transferred from the liability account to a revenue account through an adjusting entry made at the end of the period.

When Boyce's fiscal period ends on December 31, the company will have earned rental income of $400 for two of the six months paid in advance ($1,200 × 1/3). The adjusting entry to record the rental income is shown below.

GENERAL JOURNAL PAGE 65

	DATE		DESCRIPTION	POST. REF.	DEBIT	CREDIT	
1	20--		Adjusting Entries				1
2	Dec.	31	Unearned Rental Income		400 00		2
3			Rental Income			400 00	3
4							4

Prepaid Expenses

A **prepaid expense** is an expense paid in advance. Examples include the purchase of office supplies, premiums paid on insurance policies, rent paid in advance on the use of property or equipment, and bank discounts on non-interest-bearing notes payable. Examples of adjustments for prepaid expenses appear in Chapter 18 of this textbook.

Key Points

Unearned Revenue

Revenue received in advance is usually recorded in a liability account. That account must be adjusted at the end of the fiscal period to recognize the amount of revenue earned during the period.

Visual Learning

General Journal, p. A-30

Use the second general journal entry to discuss the entry to transfer unearned revenue to the revenue account. Ask students to explain why this adjusting entry is needed.

Concept Development: Prepaid Expenses

Discussion: Sometimes businesses pay for items before they are actually used. For example, if a business rents office space, the rent is usually due on the first of the month for the entire month's rent. Students who have cars will be familiar with the concept of prepaid expenses since they must make payments for insurance in advance of the period covered by the insurance. L1

TEACHING NOTES

Problem D–1 (Answers) Identifying Accruals and Deferrals

1. Unearned Revenue
2. Prepaid Expense
3. Unearned Revenue
4. Accrued Expense
5. Unearned Revenue
6. Accrued Revenue
7. Accrued Expense
8. Accrued Expense
9. Accrued Revenue
10. Prepaid Expense
11. Unearned Revenue

Problem D–2 (Answers) Recording Adjusting Entries

June 30: Dr. Office Supplies Expense $7,400; Cr. Office Supplies $7,400
June 30: Dr. Salaries Expense $900; Cr. Salaries Payable $900
June 30: Dr. Interest Receivable $59.18; Cr. Interest Income $59.18
June 30: Dr. Unearned Rental Income $250; Cr. Rental Income $250

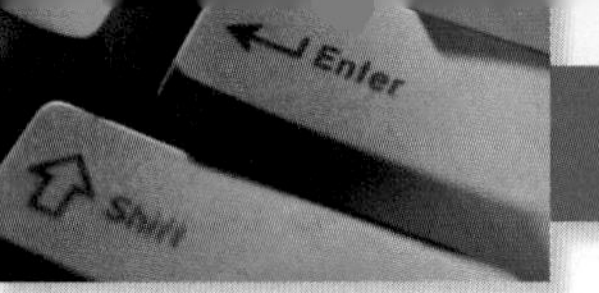

Problem D–1 Identifying Accruals and Deferrals

Instructions Use the form in your working papers that is similar to the one below. For each item listed below, indicate by placing a check mark in the correct column whether the item is a prepaid expense, unearned revenue, an accrued expense, or accrued revenue. The first item has been completed as an example.

1. Rent received in advance for a two-year rental of a computer.
2. A two-year premium paid on a fire insurance policy.
3. Tuition collected in advance by a university.
4. Interest on an interest-bearing note payable due next year.
5. Cash received for a three-year subscription to a magazine.
6. Fees due for the completed designs for three of five buildings.
7. Property taxes incurred for the last three months of the fiscal period.
8. Salaries owed but not yet paid.
9. Interest on an interest-bearing note receivable that matures in the next accounting period.
10. Office supplies purchased.
11. Cash received for season tickets for home football games.

Item	Prepaid Expense	Unearned Revenue	Accrued Expense	Accrued Revenue
1.		✓		

Problem D–2 Recording Adjusting Entries

The Gore Paper Company uses the accrual basis of accounting. Its fiscal period ends on June 30. The following account balances appear in the company's general ledger as of year-end.

Cash in Bank	$34,616	Office Supplies Expense	$0
Interest Receivable	0	Salaries Expense	75,000
Office Supplies	8,335	Rental Income	0
Salaries Payable	0	Interest Income	0
Unearned Rental Income	1,000		

SOLUTION NOTES

Instructions Record the adjusting entries on general journal page 14 in your working papers.

(1) The office supplies on hand as of June 30 are valued at $935.
(2) Gore's 5-day weekly payroll totals $1,500. Salaries have been earned but not yet paid or recorded, for June 28–30.
(3) On June 30, 30 days of interest had accrued on an $8,000, 90-day, 9% note receivable from a charge customer.
(4) Of the $1,000 recorded in the Unearned Rental Revenue account, $250 had been earned as of June 30.

Problem D–3 Recording Transactions for Notes Payable

The Villareal Corporation uses the accrual basis of accounting. Its fiscal period ends on December 31. On November 15, the Villareal Corporation borrowed $9,500 from the Second National Bank by issuing a 120-day, 9.5% interest-bearing note payable.

Instructions Record the following transactions on general journal page 41.

(1) The issuance of the note payable (Note 7).
(2) The adjusting entry to record the amount of accrued interest payable at year-end.
(3) The payment of the note on the maturity date (Check 411).

Problem D–4 Recording Accrued Expenses

The Cassenada's Dance Company uses the accrual basis of accounting. Located in Seattle, Washington, the company's fiscal year-end is July 31. Property taxes are paid in June and December. Total annual property taxes on the studio and parking lot are $12,000.

Instructions

(1) Record the payment made on June 30 for the first six months' property tax in the general journal, page 22.
(2) Record the adjusting entry necessary at the fiscal year-end, July 31.

Problem D–3 (Answers) Recording Transactions for Notes Payable

Nov. 15: Dr. Cash in Bank $9,500; Cr. Notes Payable $9,500; Note 7
Dec. 31: Dr. Interest Expense $113.74; Cr. Interest Payable $113.74
Mar. 15: Dr. Notes Payable $9,500, Interest Payable $113.74, Interest Expense $182.97; Cr. Cash in Bank $9,796.71; Check 411

Problem D–4 (Answers) Recording Accrued Expenses

June 30: Dr. Property Tax Expense $6,000; Cr. Cash in Bank $6,000
July 31: Dr. Property Tax Expense $1,000; Cr. Property Tax Payable $1,000

SOLUTION NOTES

INTRODUCING APPENDIX E

Appendix E Overview

In this appendix students will learn about tax forms and procedures for filing a personal tax return. They will learn how to calculate taxable earnings and to complete a Form 1040EZ.

Appendix E Concepts

- How income tax evolved in this country.
- The need for a federal income tax.
- The principle of voluntary compliance.
- The purpose of certain tax forms.
- How to prepare Form 1040EZ.

Visual Learning

Appendix E Focus

Use **Transparency APPE–1** to discuss the accounting concepts students will learn in this appendix.

Appendix Vocabulary

adjusted gross income
e-file system
Form 1099
Form 1040EZ
Form W-2
Form W-4
taxable income
teleFile
voluntary compliance

Preteaching Accounting Vocabulary

Oral Discussion: Write each term on the chalkboard, then ask students for the meaning. Discuss how each term relates to the federal income tax system. L1

Federal Personal Income Tax

What You'll Learn

- How income tax evolved in this country.
- The need for a federal income tax.
- The principle of voluntary compliance.
- The purpose of certain tax forms.
- How to prepare Form 1040EZ.

Why It's Important

Every person should understand our income tax system and exercise voluntary compliance to assure needed revenue for federal departments and programs. Tax forms should be accurately prepared and filed on time.

KEY TERMS

voluntary compliance
Form W-4
Form 1099
Form 1040EZ
adjusted gross income
taxable income
e-file system
TeleFile

In order to become an informed and contributing member of society, every individual should have a basic knowledge of our federal income tax system. For the system to work fairly and efficiently, everyone must pay their fair share in an accurate and timely manner.

Creating the Federal Income Tax System

When this country was founded in 1776, a federal personal income tax system did not exist. At that time, it was the responsibility of the individual state to tax its residents and raise revenue for needed expenditures. The first personal income tax was created in 1862 in an effort to finance the cost of the Civil War. A commission levied taxes on a small percentage of people in order to generate needed revenue. However, this tax was abolished in 1872, soon after the war ended. A federal personal income tax was again proposed in 1895 but was declared unconstitutional.

It was not until 1913 that Congress ratified the 16th Amendment to the Constitution that enabled the federal government to levy a tax on individuals based on personal income. The income tax system was established under the principle of **voluntary compliance**. This means that all individual taxpayers are responsible for filing their tax return. All taxpayers must report their taxable income, accurately calculate the income tax owed, and file the necessary forms on time.

The Internal Revenue Service (IRS) also has responsibilities under our present tax system. The IRS must administer the tax laws fairly and process tax returns in an efficient manner

Tax Forms and Procedures

For the federal tax system to run efficiently, certain tax forms must be prepared and filed by all income earning individuals. For personal income tax, the earning period is from January 1 through December 31. Every individual has from January 1 until April 15 of the next year to file a tax return and pay the government all taxes owed for the previous year.

For most taxpayers, the most common and largest form of income is the gross earnings paid to them by employers. Other common forms of taxable income include interest earned on savings accounts and investments, stock dividends, rental income, and profits from business operations run as sole proprietorships or partnerships.

Federal Withholding Tax

A certain amount is withheld from each paycheck by the employer. This system of "pay as you earn" was enacted during the early 1940s.

TEACHING NOTES

Since the exact amount earned for the year will not be determined until the end of December, the amount of taxes withheld from each employee's paycheck is an *estimate* of the amount the employee will owe at the end of the year. As you learned in Chapter 12, each employee fills out a **Form W-4** when they begin work. This indicates to the employer how much to withhold for federal income tax from each paycheck. For more information on completing Form W-4, refer back to Chapter 12, pages 293–294.

Reporting Earned Income

Individual taxpayers receive two common federal forms to report income for the year. The first is Form W-2. This form is prepared by employers and reports to employees and the federal government the total gross wages for the year and the amount withheld from employees' wages to pay the federal income tax. This form is given to the employees in the month of January so the information is available for employees to complete their individual tax returns. To review the Form W-2, refer to Chapter 13, page 334.

Reporting Interest Income

The other common form used to report income is **Form 1099**. This form reports interest earned in savings accounts and is prepared by banks or other institutions. Interest from all 1099 forms is added together and the total interest earned for the year is reported on your federal tax return.

Key Points

Completing Your Tax Form

You must receive all of your W-2 and 1099 forms before you complete your tax return.

Preparing and Filing a Federal Income Tax Return

The most common tax return prepared by students is Form 1040EZ.

Preparing Form 1040EZ

To file **Form 1040EZ**, the following requirements must be met:

1. Taxable income from wages and tips must be less than $50,000.
2. Interest income must be less than $400.

A completed Form 1040EZ is presented in Figure 2 on page A-36. To complete this form, use the following steps:

1. Enter your name, address, and social security number.
2. Check the box on the next line if you want $3 to go to the Presidential Election Campaign Fund.
3. Add the amount(s) in box 1 of your Form(s) W-2 and put that amount on line 1 of the form. This should be the total gross earnings from **all** of your jobs this year.
4. Add the total interest received, as reported on Form(s) 1099, and enter the total amount of interest on line 2.
5. Add lines 1 and 2 and put the total on line 4. This is your adjusted gross income. Your **adjusted gross income** is your total income for the year.
6. Since you are a student, you are probably claimed as a dependent by your parents or guardians. On line 5, check YES.
7. Go to the worksheet for dependents on the back of the form and complete A. through G. Enter the amount from G on line 5 on the front of the form.

ACCOUNTING ISSUES

Filing Taxes In 2001, the Internal Revenue Service reported that 31 percent of personal income tax returns were transmitted electronically. In 2000, the number of electronically filed returns was 27.8 percent. The IRS projects that 35.5 percent of taxpayers will use electronic filing methods when filing 2002 tax returns.

APPENDIX E

PAGES A-33–A-38

Concept Development: Creating the Federal Income Tax System

Discussion: Take a poll and ask students whether they are in favor of the federal income tax program. For students who answer "no," ask how they would pay for services such as highways, airports, education, and so on. Point out that without tax dollars, governments could not provide many of the services that citizens take for granted. For example, without tax dollars the federal government could not build highways; nor could most local governments since they receive much of their highway budgets from the federal government. Most people could not afford to build their own roads! L1

Concept Development: Tax Forms and Procedures

Discussion: Ask students who have part-time jobs to describe the forms they receive for filing a tax return. Point out that employers are required by law to report each employee's earnings and taxes withheld to the IRS. The employer also is required by January 31 to send a summary of earnings and taxes (Form W-2) to employees for use in filing their personal tax returns. L1

Concept Development: Preparing and Filing a Federal Income Tax Return

Discussion: Bring to class one or more copies of an Internal Revenue Service booklet with instructions and tax tables for filing a personal tax return. Have students look through the booklets, then read the instructions for preparing the 1040EZ form. If you cannot obtain booklets, photocopy a blank 1040EZ form (available in the public library) for students. Ask students who have filed tax returns to share their experiences with the class. L1

APPENDIX E
PAGES A-33–A-38

Concept Development: Using the IRS *e-file* System

Discussion: If your school has an Internet connection, have students access the IRS Web site and locate information about electronic filing. Ask students to make notes about requirements and procedures for filing electronically and then hold a class discussion for students to share the information. L1

Visual Learning

Figure 1 Completed Tax Computation Worksheet

Use **Transparency APPE–2** to explain the information required for the Tax Computation Worksheet.

8. Subtract line 5 from line 4 and enter the amount on line 6. This is your **taxable income**.
9. Add the amounts in box 2 of your Form(s) W-2 and enter the amount on line 8. This is the amount *already* deducted from your wages to pay your federal tax liability.
10. Enter the amount from line 8 on line 10.
11. Take the amount entered on line 6, and look up the amount of your actual tax liability on the tax table.
12. Complete the Tax Computation Worksheet for Certain Dependents and enter the amount on line 11 of Form 1040EZ.
13. If line 10 is greater than line 11, then you have paid in more than you owe and are entitled to a **refund.** Enter the amount of the overpayment on line 12a.
14. If line 11 is greater than line 10, then you still owe the federal government more money. Enter the amount you still owe on line 13.

If additional money is owed, you must include a check for the entire amount when you file the tax return. Sign the return and enter the date and your occupation on the designated lines.

Before your file your tax return, Form 1040EZ, make sure you do the following:

1. Check all calculations.
2. Attach Copy B (one copy) of each of your W-2's, which are supplied to you by your employer(s).
3. File the return by April 15.

Using the IRS *e-file* System

You can file electronically by using the ***e-file* system**. Forms and information are available on the Internet or by fax. By first completing the tax forms, you can use your personal computer to file the return.

Using the IRS *TeleFile* system, you can file your tax return using a Touch-Tone phone. You first complete the ***TeleFile*** *Tax Record,* which is similar to Form 1040EZ, call a toll free number, and follow the instructions on the computerized message. Most taxpayers who use Form 1040EZ can file by phone.

Figure 1 Completed Tax Computation Worksheet

Tax Computation Worksheet for Certain Dependents—Line 11

1. Figure the tax on the amount on Form 1040EZ, line 6. Use the Tax Table. **1.** *84.00*
2. Is the amount on line 1 more than the amount shown below for your filing status?
   • Single — $900
   • Married filing jointly — $1,800
   ☐ **Yes.** If **single,** enter $300; if **married**, enter $600
   ☒ **No.** Divide the amount on line 1 by 3.0. . . . . **2.** *28.00*
3. Subtract line 2 from line 1. Enter the result here and on Form 1040EZ, line 11. . . . . **3.** *56.00*

TEACHING NOTES

Form **1040EZ** — Department of the Treasury–Internal Revenue Service
Income Tax Return for Single and Joint Filers With No Dependents (P) **20--**
OMB No. 1545-0675

Label (See Page 12.) Use the IRS label. Otherwise please print or type

LABEL HERE		
Your first name and initial: *Joan J.*	Last name: *Bustelos*	Your social security number: *031 XX XXXX*
If a joint return, spouse's first name and initial	Last name	Spouse's social security number
Home address (number and street). If you have a P.O. box, see page 7.: *84 Elm Street*	Apt. no.	▲ Important! ▲ you **must** enter your SSN(s) above.
City, town or post office, state, and ZIP code. If you have a foreign address, see page 7.: *Norwalk, VA 23514*		

Presidential Election Campaign (See page 12.)
Note: *Checking "Yes" will not change your tax or reduce your refund.*
Do you, or spouse if a joint return, want $3 to go to this fund? ▶ You: ☑ Yes ☐ No Spouse: ☐ Yes ☐ No

Income — Attach Form(s) W-2 here. Enclose, but do not attach, any payment.

1	Total wages, salaries, and tips. This should be shown in box 1 of your W-2 form(s). Attach your W-2 form(s).	1	4,954 00
2	Taxable interest. If the total is over $400, you cannot use Form 1040EZ	2	167 00
3	Unemployment compensation, qualified state tuition program earnings and Alaska Permanent Fund dividends (see page 14).	3	
4	Add lines 1, 2, and 3. This is your **adjusted gross income.**	4	5,121 00
5	Can your parents (or someone else) claim you on their return? **Yes.** Enter amount from worksheet on back. ☑ **No.** ☐ If **single,** enter 7,450.00. If **married,** enter 13,400.00 See back for explanation	5	4,550 00
6	Subtract line 5 from line 4. If line 5 is larger than line 4, enter 0. This is your **taxable income.** ▶	6	571 00

Note. You **must** check Yes or No

Credits, payments, and tax

7	Rate reduction credit. See worksheet on page 14.	7	
8	Enter your Federal income tax withheld from box 2 of your W-2 form(s).	8	218 00
9a	**Earned income credit (EIC).** See page 15.	9a	
b	Nontaxable earned income. 9b		
10	Add lines 7, 8, and 9a. These are your **total credits and payments.** ▶	10	218 00
11	**Tax.** If you checked "Yes" on line 5, see page 20. Otherwise, use the amount on **line 6 above** to find your tax in the tax table on pages 24–28 of the booklet. Then, enter the tax from the table on this line.	11	56 00

Refund — Have it directly deposited! See Page 20 and fill in 12b, 12c, and 12d

12a	If line 10 is larger than line 10, subtract line 10 from line 11. This is your **refund.** ▶	12a	162 00
▶ b	Routing number ▶ c Type: ☐ Checking ☐ Savings		
▶ d	Account number		

Amount you owe

13	If line 11 is larger than line 10, subtract line 10 from line 11. This is **the amount you owe.** See page 21 for details on how to pay. ▶	13	

Third party desgnee — Do you want to allow another person to discuss this return with the IRS (see page 22)? ☐ **Yes.** Complete the following. ☐ **No**
Designee's name ▶ Phone no. ▶( ) Personal identification number(PIN) ▶

Sign here — Joint return? See page 11. Keep a copy for your records
Under penalties of perjury, I declare that I have examined this return, and to the best of my knowledge and belief, it is true, correct, and accurately lists all amounts and sources of income I received during the tax year. Declaration of preparer (other than the taxpayer) is based on all information of which the preparer has any knowledge.

Your signature	Date	Your occupation	Daytime phone number
Joan J. Bustelos	*3/19/20--*	*clerk*	*(123) 555-2000*
Spouse's signature if a joint return, **both** must sign.	Date	Spouse's occupation	

Paid Preparer's use only

Preparer's signature ▶	Date	Check if self-employed ☐	Preparer's SSN or PTIN
Firm's name (or yours if self-employed), address, and ZIP code ▶		EIN	
		Phone no. ( )	

For Disclosure, Privacy Act, and Paperwork Reduction Act Notice, see page 23 Cat. No. 12616G Form **1040EZ 20--**

Figure 2 Completed Form 1040EZ

APPENDIX E
PAGES A-33–A-38

Visual Learning

Figure 1 Completed Form 1040EZ

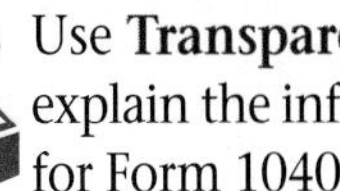

Use **Transparency APPE–3a** to explain the information required for Form 1040EZ.

Teaching Tips

Obtain blank copies of Form 1040EZ and have students complete their own returns. For students who do not work, provide an example of annual wages earned and taxes withheld for use in completing a return.

Ask students who earn some of their wages as tips how they keep track of their total tips throughout the year for reporting on their tax returns.

TEACHING NOTES

Visual Learning

Figure 2 Completed Form 1040EZ (Continued)

Use **Transparency APPE–3b** to explain the second page of Form 1040EZ.

Teaching Tip

Read the sections of Form 1040EZ with students to make sure they understand what information is required and how to enter it on the form.

Form 1040EZ (20– –) Page **2**

Use this form if

- Your filing status is single or married filing jointly.
- You (and your spouse if married) were under 65 January 1, 20– –, and not blind at the end of 20– –.
- You do not claim any dependents.
- Your taxable income (line 6) is less than $50,000.
- You do not claim a student loan interest deduction (see page 8) or an education credit.
- You had **only** wages, salaries, tips, taxable scholarship or fellowship grants, enemployment compensation, qualified state tuition program earnings, or Alaska Permanent Fund dividends, and your taxable interest was not over $400. **But** if you earned tips, including allocated tips, that are nor included in box 5 and box 7 of your W-2, you may not be able to use Form 1040EZ. See page 13. If you are planning to use Form 1040EZ for a child who received Alaska Permanent Fund dividends, see page 14.
- You did not receive any advance earned income credit payments.

If you are not sure about your filing status, see page 11. If you have questions about dependents, use TeleTax topic 354 (see page 6). If you **cannot use this form,** use TeleTax topic 352 (see page 6).

Filling in your return

For tips on how to avoid common mistakes, see page 30

If you received a scholarship or fellowship grant or tax–exempt interest income, such as on municipal bonds, see the booklet before filling in the form. Also, see the booklet if you received a Form 1099–INT showing Federal income tax withheld or if Federal income tax was withheld from your unemployment compensation or Alaska Permanent Fund dividends.
Remember, you must report all wages, salaries, and tips even if you do not get a W–2 form from your employer. You must also report all your taxable interest, including interest from banks, savings and loans, credit unions, etc., even if you do not get a Form 1099–INT.

Worksheet for dependents who checked "Yes" on line 5

(keep a copy for your records)

Use this worksheet to figure the amount to enter on line 5 if someone can claim you (or your spouse if married) as a dependent, even if that person chooses not to do so. To find out if someone can claim you as a dependent, use TeleTax topic 354 (see page 6).

A. Amount, if any, from line 1 on front . . . . 4,954.00 + 250.00 Enter total ▶ **A.** 5,204.00
B. Minimum standard deduction. . . . . **B.** 750.00
C. Enter the **larger** of line A or line B here. . . . . **C.** 5,204.00
D. Maximum standard deduction. If **single,** enter 4,550.00; if **married,** enter 7,600.00. . . . . **D.** 4,550.00
E. Enter the **smaller** of line C or line D here. This is your standard deduction. . . . . **E.** 4,550.00
F. Exemption amount.
- If single, enter 0
- If married and—
  —both you and your spouse can be claimed as dependents, enter 0.
  —only one of you can be claimed as a dependent, enter 2,900.00

F. 0
G. Add lines E and F. Enter the total here and on line 5 on the front. . . . . **G.** 4,550.00

If you checked "No" on line 5 because no one can claim you (or your spouse if married) as a dependent, enter on line 5 the amount shown below that applies to you.
- Single, enter 7,450.00. This is the total of your standard deduction (4,550.00) and your exemption (2,900.00).
- Married, enter 13,400.00. This is the total of your standard deduction (7,600.00), your exemption (2,900.00), and your spouse's exemption (2,900.00).

Mailing return

Mail your return by **April 15, 20– –.** Use the envelope that came with your booklet. If you do not have that envelope, see the back cover for the address to use.

Form **1040EZ** (20– –)

Figure 2 Completed Form 1040EZ (cont.)

ACCOUNTING ISSUES

Accounting for Managed Health Care The trend toward managed health care has had a significant impact on financial reporting and tax planning for health-care providers. When these providers turn to CPAs for help, the CPA must be familiar with managed care terminology and the terms of contracts their clients have signed. The AICPA provides *Audits of Providers of Health Care Services,* a guide containing a glossary of health-care and accounting terms useful in determining proper financial statement presentation and sample financial statements for various types of health-care providers.

Problem E–1 Preparing Form 1040EZ

Michael Feld is a junior at Lewiston High School. He lives with his parents at 274 West Polomia Drive in Hanksville, Ohio, 03856. Mike's social security number is 036-23-8825. If Mike must pay any tax, he wants the $3 to go to the Presidential Election Campaign Fund.

Mike worked full-time last summer at Harriet's Sub Shop as a counter clerk. He received a Form W-2 which stated that he had total gross wages of $4,806.00 and $192.00 was deducted for federal income tax.

Mike also had a savings account. The Kingsman National Bank sent him Form 1099 which stated he had earned interest of $113.00 on his account.

Mike lives at home with his parents and is claimed as a dependent on their tax return.

Instructions Using the information above, prepare Form 1040EZ for Mike Feld. A blank Form 1040EZ is provided in your working papers. Use the tax chart in your working papers to calculate the federal income tax.

Problem E–2 Preparing Form 1040EZ

Alicia DeSantis is a senior at Georgetown High School. She lives at 825 Patterson Street in Montville, Texas, 09436. Her social security number is 043-73-8217. She worked part-time during the school year at the Hilltop Deli and full-time during the summer as a lifeguard and swimming instructor at the Montville town pool.

If Alicia must pay some income tax on her earnings this year, she wants the $3 to go to the Presidential Election Campaign Fund. Alicia lives with her mother and is claimed as a dependent on her mother's tax return.

Her Form W-2 from the deli reported that she earned $1,736.00 during the year and $112.00 was deducted for federal income tax. The town of Montville sent her a W-2 that reported she earned $3,927.00 during the summer and $184.00 was deducted for federal income tax.

Alicia opened a savings account at the local bank that sent her a Form 1099 that stated she earned $118.50 in interest last year. She also had another savings account set up for college that paid her $201.70 in interest.

Instructions Prepare Form 1040EZ for Alicia. A blank Form 1040EZ is provided in your working papers. Use the tax charts in your working papers to calculate the tax owed.

Problem E–1 (Answers)
Preparing Form 1040EZ
Taxable earnings $369.00
Tax $36.00
Refund $156.00

Problem E–2 (Answers)
Preparing Form 1040EZ
Taxable earnings $1,433.20
Tax $144.00
Refund $152.00

SOLUTION NOTES

INTRODUCING
APPENDIX F

Appendix F Overview

Excerpts from Office Depot's annual report and the related "Analyzing Financial Reports" activities in the student textbook will give your students an understanding of how financial data is used in the "real world." The "Analyzing Financial Reports" features based on Office Depot begin in Chapter 14 and end with Chapter 26.

It is important for students to understand that annual reports are just one result of collecting and disseminating financial data. Business managers also use financial data to help them make decisions about the day-to-day operations of the business. The goal of the "Analyzing Financial Reports" activities is to help students gain a basic knowledge of how to evaluate and analyze financial data.

General Company Information

Office Depot, Inc.
2200 Old Germantown Road
Delray Beach, FL 33445
Telephone: 561-438-4800
Fax: 561-438-4001

Corporate Web site
www.officedepot.com

Stock Information
Office Depot's stock is traded on the New York Stock Exchange under the stock symbol ODP.

Auditors
Office Depot's financial statements are audited by Deloitte & Touche LLP.

Office DEPOT®
What you need. What you need to know.℠

Excerpts from the Office Depot 2001 Annual Report

Intended for Use in Chapters 14–26

In this appendix, we present excerpts from the 2001 Annual Report of Office Depot, a publicly held corporation. These reports were selected to illustrate many of the concepts discussed in this textbook. Since only portions of the Annual Report are presented here, please refer to the Office Depot Web site at www.officedepot.com for the entire 2001 Annual Report. Not all of the terminology and policies appearing in this report are consistent with our text discussions. This illustrates some of the diversity that exists in financial reporting.

Company Profile

Office Depot, Inc. is the world's largest supplier of office products and services. The Company sells office supplies, business machines, computers, computer software and office furniture, as well as copy, print, reproduction, mailing and shipping services to small office/home office (SoHo), medium and large businesses in the United States and 17 other countries around the globe. Office Depot operates under brand names Office Depot®, Viking Office Products®, Viking Direct®, 4Sure.com®, Computers4Sure.com®, Solutions4Sure.com®, The Office Place®, and Sands & McDougall™. The Company markets its products through multiple distribution channels, including office supply retail stores, direct mail, global Internet sites, business-to-business e-commerce, and various sales forces. Office Depot has approximately 45,000 employees, and its common stock is traded on the New York Stock Exchange under symbol ODP.

Financial Highlights

(in millions, except per share data)

	2001	2000	1999
Sales[1]	**$11,154.1**	$11,569.7	$10,272.1
Operating Profit[1]	**354.4**	110.2	413.4
Net Earnings	**201.0**	49.3	257.6
Diluted Earnings per Share	**0.66**	0.16	0.69
Return on Common Stockholders' Equity	**11.7%**	2.8%	13.1%
Excluding Impact of Charges and Credits			
Net Earnings	**$ 242.0**	$ 222.2	$ 326.9
Diluted Earnings per Share	**0.79**	0.70	0.86
Working Capital	**$ 704.7**	$ 790.8	$ 687.0
Total Assets	**4,331.6**	4,196.3	4,276.2
Common Stockholders' Equity	**1,848.4**	1,601.3	1,907.7

[1] Certain amounts in prior year financial statements have been reclassified to conform to current year presentation.

ACTIVITIES

Creating Financial Visuals Have students work in teams to create a chart or graph that depicts sales, operating profit, and net earnings for 2001, 2000, and 1999. Explain that charts or graphs are often used in financial presentations and annual reports in order to clearly represent relevant and pertinent data.

To Our Shareholders:

When I accepted leadership of Office Depot 20 months ago, our Company faced significant challenges. Growth in the U.S. office supply superstore industry was beginning to mature and we had not responded effectively to the changing competitive environment. We had lost sight of some of our core competencies and competitive advantages, and we had allowed parts of our business to become too complex and inefficient. We had been slow to address issues in underperforming businesses and assets. Worst of all, our Company and our management team had lost the loyalty of our shareholders and the confidence of our employees, who viewed our direction as unclear and our future as uncertain. • These challenges became even more daunting in 2001, as we faced a weak U.S. economy; softness in the computer hardware, software and furniture sectors; unfavorable foreign currency translation; and declining consumer confidence. As our delicate economy teetered on the brink of recession, the tragic events of September 11th gave the final push that sent it over the edge, creating a difficult, stormy and uncertain economic environment.

We are encouraged by Office Depot's progress in 2001, and we firmly believe it demonstrates the strength of our Company's true earnings potential.

Turning the Tide

Our efforts to strengthen Office Depot started in early fall of 2000, when our new leadership team conducted a critical assessment of Office Depot that redefined our destination and plotted a strategic course to get there. Throughout 2001, we continued this process, driving operating improvements that we expect to yield tangible results in the years ahead. • Our initiatives were careful and thorough. We sharpened our focus on our core competencies. We improved efficiencies and instituted disciplined capital spending. We introduced dramatic improvements in the management of our supply chain, our inventory, and our warehouse operations. We closed stores, cut costs in underperforming regions in North America and redeployed capital to our highly profitable and fast-growing international markets. We elevated the delivery of "fanatical" customer service to our first priority, and we established quality indices and ambitious new performance benchmarks. We fostered a management culture that gives our leaders and managers greater responsibility and makes them accountable for results. And we established new corporate values that form the basis for the way we do business and serve as a foundation for our future. • We also devoted significant energy and resources to making Office Depot a more compelling place to work and shop. We improved opportunities across the Company for our employees, and we tied recognition and reward directly to performance. We renewed our commitment to diversity, which appropriately reflects our diverse customers, suppliers and communities in which we live and work. We undertook new measures in our North American Retail stores to make shopping at Office Depot a more informative and customer-friendly experience by remerchandising, upgrading and resigning all 859 of our retail superstores. • These collective management and operating initiatives enabled Office Depot to perform well in light of the difficult economic environment. Total sales declined four percent to $11.2 billion, compared with $11.6 billion in 2000. Comparable worldwide sales in the 849 stores and 39 delivery centers that have been open for more than one year declined two percent, compared with an increase of seven percent in 2000. At the same time, however, our highly profitable International business delivered to record sales and profits, despite negative foreign currency translation. International now accounts for 27 percent of our Company's total segment operating income. Driven by a dramatic improvement in gross margins across our business segments, earnings per share (excluding charges and credits discussed in management's discussion and analysis), rose to $0.79, an increase of 13 percent, compared with $0.70 in 2000. Free cash flow rose to $540 million, a substantial improvement from $49 million in 2000. Stronger cash flow and an emphasis on better cash management enabled us to repay short-term debt, fund working capital needs and build our financial flexibility. • We also achieved marked progress in other vitally important areas of the Company. Employee turnover, a key measure of employee satisfaction, declined 29 percent from a year ago. Our quality and customer satisfaction measurements rose and our retail and warehouse Customer Service Indices hit all-time highs. Our in-stock positions, order-fill rates, line-fill rates and on-time deliveries also improved. In addition, inventory turns rose, accounts receivables declined and

APPENDIX F
PAGES A-39–A-48

Concept Development: Purpose of an Annual Report

Discussion: Prior to assigning the "Analyzing Financial Reports" activity in Chapter 14, you may want to review this appendix. Discuss the basic components found in an annual report and then give an overview of the excerpts found on pages A-39–A-48. Discuss how an annual report provides information to stockholders, employees, financial analysts, and the general public about the direction of the company, its mission, and its financial condition and operating results. L1

Teaching Tip

Collect other annual reports, or have students write to companies of their choice to request annual reports. (Many annual reports can be downloaded from the Internet.) Use the reports to build a classroom library. Have students review the reports to compare not only financial data but also letters to shareholders and mission statements.

Concept Development: Letter to Shareholders

Analyze: Ask students to read the letter to shareholders in its entirety. Then have students answer these questions in their own words:

1. Did sales increase or decrease in 2001 as compared to 2000? (decreased 4%)
2. What is the trend in employee turnover? (declined 29%) L1

ACTIVITIES

Evaluating the Letter to Shareholders Based on the ideas expressed in the letter to shareholders, ask students to give an overall impression of the company's condition. Were students encouraged by what they read? Did the letter give a strong indication of the company's direction? What questions, if any, came to mind while reading the letter?

APPENDIX F
PAGES A-39–A-48

Concept Development: Cash Flow

Analyze: Pose the following questions to students: What amount of free cash flow was available to Office Depot in 2001? ($540 million) Is this an increase or decrease over the previous year? (increase) Ask students to analyze why this additional cash is a positive indicator, and have them describe ways in which these funds might be used to improve the financial stability of the company. L1

Concept Development: The Value of Human Resources

Discussion: Lead a class discussion about the importance of employee satisfaction, loyalty, and expertise. Emphasize the potential impacts to customer satisfaction, sales, and employee retention and training. Point out how these factors ultimately affect shareholder value. L1

North American warehouse operating costs, as a percentage of sales, decreased to the lowest level in five years. • We are highly encouraged by Office Depot's progress in 2001, and we firmly believe it demonstrates the strength of our Company's true earnings potential once the U.S. and world economies regain stability and return to growth. But Office Depot's story in 2001 is about far more than financial results and operating improvements. It is about a company that has a crystal-clear vision of where it is going and how it is going to get there. It is about a new management team with the experience, skills and financial acumen to help the Company to achieve its goals. It is about our customers who reward us through their loyalty and our shareholders who once again have confidence that we can drive shareholder value. Moreover, it is about our approximately 45,000 worldwide employees, who have regained their trust in Office Depot and reaffirmed their conviction that we can become one of the world's great companies.

Forging Ahead

As we enter 2002, we are sharply focused on leveraging the momentum we have created to expand Office Depot's business. We are seeking new ways to drive sales, manage costs and increase shareholder value. We are undertaking new branding and advertising initiatives that will define the differences between Office Depot and our competitors. We are pursuing fanatical customer service, while leveraging our immense knowledge of our customer base to target our customers more effectively. In addition, we are integrating all of our business channels to make an even more seamless shopping experience for our customers. We expect these actions and others to accelerate growth across all three of our business segments. • At the same time, we are certain that we will continue to face short-term economic challenges that will call for us to make tough decisions and complicated choices. The economy, rapid shifts in technology and fundamental changes in the way Corporate America does business are likely to present new trials at every turn. But we are equally certain that there has never been a better time to invest in our future, as both our Company's foundation and the opportunities to grow our global industry leadership position are stronger than ever before. • As I consider the journey on which Office Depot embarked in 2001, my greatest single surprise is not the fact that our employees responded to the marked change in leadership and direction; rather it is *how* they responded to this change—quickly, willingly, and with enormous teamwork and cooperation. I am extremely grateful to the skilled and talented people at Office Depot for their commitment, loyalty, support, trust and confidence. I look to our Company's future with great enthusiasm, not merely because I know that we can achieve our goals, but also because I know that we will achieve those goals by working harmoniously and synergistically, *together*.

We believe that there has never been a better time to invest in our future, as the opportunities to grow our leadership position are stronger than ever.

Bruce Nelson
Chairman and Chief Executive Officer
March 2002

ACTIVITIES

Analyzing Operating Costs In his letter to shareholders, Bruce Nelson discusses the decline of accounts receivable and decrease of operating costs as a percentage of sales. Ask students to explain why each of these trends reflects a positive condition for Office Depot.

Office Depot, Inc.

Financial Highlights

(In thousands, except per share amounts and statistical data)

	2001	2000[4]	1999	1998	1997
Statements of Earnings Data:					
Sales[1]	**$11,154,081**	$11,569,696	$10,272,060	$8,997,738	$8,108,714
Cost of goods sold and occupancy costs	**7,983,973**	8,479,437	7,450,575	6,484,699	5,963,521
Gross profit	**3,170,108**	3,090,259	2,821,485	2,513,039	2,145,193
Store and warehouse operating and selling expenses[1]	**2,343,394**	2,409,478	2,023,055	1,683,973	1,482,179
General and administrative expenses[1]	**451,722**	453,784	328,108	288,028	241,430
Facility closure costs	**8,436**	110,038	40,425	—	—
Other operating expenses	**12,125**	6,733	16,524	136,279	22,703
Operating profit	**354,431**	110,226	413,373	404,759	398,881
Interest income	**13,058**	11,502	30,176	25,309	7,570
Interest expense	**(44,302)**	(33,901)	(26,148)	(22,356)	(21,680)
Miscellaneous income (expense), net	**(9,057)**	4,632	(3,514)	(18,985)	(13,180)
Earnings before income taxes	**314,130**	92,459	413,887	388,727	371,591
Income taxes	**113,087**	43,127	156,249	155,531	136,730
Net earnings	**$ 201,043**	$ 49,332	$ 257,638	$ 233,196	$ 234,861
Earnings per share[2]:					
Basic	**$ 0.67**	$ 0.16	$ 0.71	$ 0.64	$ 0.65
Diluted	**0.66**	0.16	0.69	0.61	0.62
Statistical Data:					
Facilities open at end of period:					
United States and Canada:					
Office supply stores	**859**	888	825	702	602
Customer service centers	**24**	25	30	30	33
Call centers	**13**	7	7	8	8
International[3]:					
Office supply stores	**143**	132	118	87	39
Customer service centers	**23**	19	19	18	17
Call centers	**15**	14	14	13	12
Balance Sheet Data:					
Working capital	**$ 704,676**	$ 790,752	$ 687,007	$1,293,370	$1,093,463
Total assets	**4,331,643**	4,196,334	4,276,183	4,025,283	3,498,891
Long-term debt, excluding current maturities	**317,552**	598,499	321,099	470,711	447,020
Common stockholders' equity	**1,848,438**	1,601,251	1,907,720	2,028,879	1,717,638

[1] *Certain amounts in prior year financial statements have been reclassified to conform to current year presentation.*

[2] *Earnings per share amounts previously reported for 1997 and 1998 have been restated to reflect the three-for-two stock split declared on February 24, 1999.*

[3] *Includes facilities in our International Division that we wholly own or lease, as well as those that we operate through licensing and joint venture agreements.*

[4] *Includes 53 weeks in accordance with our 52–53 week reporting convention.*

APPENDIX F

PAGES A-39–A-48

Concept Development: Gross Profit

Discuss: Ask a student to write the 2001 and 2000 sales, cost of goods sold and occupancy costs, and gross profit amounts on the chalkboard.

Point out to students that while sales and cost of goods sold decreased in 2001, gross profit increased over the prior year. Lead a class discussion about why this might occur. L1

Concept Development: Business Operations

Discuss: Have students review the data presented in the section labeled "Statistical Data." Ask them to recall statements made in the letter to the shareholders that relate to the data presented here. L1

ACTIVITIES

Analyzing Financial Data Ask students to review the dollar amounts presented in the Financial Highlights for 2001 and 2000. Have them pay special attention to the items that contributed to net earnings, comparing 2000 figures to 2001 figures. Which specific line item seems to have had the largest impact on the dip in net earnings in 2000? (Facility closure costs)

Concept Development: Sales by Product Group

Interpret: Have students describe the trends for sales within product groups over the past three years. Ask students for ideas on how a company like Office Depot might improve sales of office furniture. L1

Management's Discussion and Analysis of Financial Condition and Results of Operations

Results of Operations

Fiscal 2001 was a year of improved operational performance across the Company and increased overall earnings compared to 2000, even in the face of difficult economic conditions and a decline in our consolidated sales. Diluted earnings per share improved to $0.66 from $0.16 in 2000, and down from $0.69 in 1999. Fiscal year 2000 was adversely affected by charges associated with a comprehensive business review that resulted in the closing of 70 retail stores, the write-down of certain assets and the elimination of some employee positions. Additional store closure and impairment costs, the write-down of certain Internet investments, settlement of certain employee claims and gain on the sale of our London warehouse were recognized in 2001. Without these charges and credits, EPS was $0.79 in 2001 and $0.70 in 2000. See Charges and Credits section below for additional discussions on these items.

[Note to the student: The Charges and Credits section has been omitted from this selection of excerpts. For the complete 2001 Annual Report, please use the Office Depot Web site (www.officedepot.com).]

Overall

(Dollars in Millions)	**2001**		2000		1999	
Sales	**$11,154.1**	**100.0%**	$11,569.7	100.0%	$10,272.1	100.0%
Cost of goods sold and occupancy costs	**7,984.0**	**71.6%**	8,479.4	73.3%	7,450.6	72.5%
Gross profit	**3,170.1**	**28.4%**	3,090.3	26.7%	2,821.5	27.5%
Store and warehouse operating and selling expenses	**2,343.4**	**21.0%**	2,409.5	20.8%	2,023.1	19.7%
Store and warehouse operating profit	**$ 826.7**	**7.4%**	$ 680.8	5.9%	$ 798.4	7.8%

Our overall sales decreased 4% in 2001 and increased 13% in 2000, while comparable sales decreased 2% in 2001 and grew 7% in 2000. Fiscal year 2000 included 53 weeks in accordance with our 52–53 week accounting convention. Adjusting 2000 to a 52-week basis, sales decreased 2% in 2001. The overall sales decrease in 2001 reflects a 10% decrease in our North American Retail Division, a 4% increase in our Business Services Group and a 6% increase in our International Division. Sales across the United States were adversely affected in 2001 by the slowing domestic economy. Additionally, the decline in sales of our North American Retail Division reflects our decision to close 73 stores during 2001, following our comprehensive business review performed in the latter part of 2000. The largest percentage sales increases in 2000 were realized in our BSG segment, driven most significantly by the growth in our contract and Internet businesses. E-commerce sales have improved in all periods, increasing almost 60% in 2001 to $1.6 billion. Also contributing significantly to our sales growth in 2000 was the continued expansion of our store base.

ACTIVITIES

Analysis of Financial Reports Ask students to review the table labeled "Overall" that follows the "Results of Operations" section. The table presents percentages alongside each dollar value. Ask students to determine and explain whether these percentages represent horizontal or vertical analyses. (vertical) Although the percentages are presented in a horizontal format, they are actually the result of vertical analysis (restating each dollar amount as a percentage of a base amount).

Our worldwide sales by product group were as follows:

	2001	2000	1999
General office supplies	**44.2%**	41.7%	41.0%
Technology products	**46.3%**	47.5%	47.5%
Office furniture	**9.5%**	10.8%	11.5%
	100.0%	100.0%	100.0%

In both 2001 and 2000, our sales mix shifted toward our core office supply items. Sales of technology products decreased significantly in 2001, reflecting to a large extent, a general slowing of technology-related product sales in the overall economy. Moreover, many more general and specialty retailers outside the office products retail segment (including discount retailers, drug store chains and warehouse club retailers) have broadened their assortments of technology products. Technology products generally have lower profit margins compared to many of the core office supplies. Also, within the technology products category, the mix shifted from technology hardware and software towards machine supplies. Sales of office furniture declined, reflecting lower volume and unit prices in 2001 and lower average selling prices during 2000, as many business customers deferred large purchases because of concerns about the economy.

Our overall gross profit percentages fluctuate as a result of numerous factors, including competitive pricing pressures; changes in product, catalog and customer mix; emergence of new technology; suppliers' pricing changes; as well as our ability to improve our net product costs through growth in total merchandise purchases. Additionally, our occupancy costs may vary as we add stores and CSCs in new markets with different rental and other occupancy costs, and as we relocate and/or close existing stores in current markets.

In mid-2000, we reduced prices for paper and machine supplies across all of our domestic sales channels in response to competitive pressures from discount clubs and other non-traditional sellers of those supply items. These price reductions, along with increased product costs, primarily for paper and machine supplies, had the most significant effect on our decreased gross profit percentage in 2000 compared to 1999. These two product groups accounted for approximately 34% of our total sales mix in 2000.

Store and warehouse operating and selling expenses consist of personnel costs; maintenance and other facility costs; advertising expenses; delivery and transportation costs; credit card and bank charges and certain other operating and selling costs. These costs, expressed as a percentage of sales, increased in both 2001 and 2000. The increase in 2001 reflects the impact of declining sales on the ratio, while the increase in 2000 is primarily the result of higher personnel and warehouse costs. In 2001, we scaled back our personnel-related costs in response to weaker sales. Other expenses, such as credit card fees and delivery fees, have also declined along with sales. In 2000, however, we experienced higher delivery- and personnel-related costs in our warehouse operations as third-party carriers increased their rates, and our facility integration efforts took longer to complete than originally planned. We also had a significant increase during 2000 in personnel expenses in our domestic stores, largely related to wage pressures stemming from a tight labor market. Also included in this category are certain charges and credits that affect the comparisons of on-going operations and are more fully discussed below.

[Note to the student: Charges and credits mentioned above have been omitted from this selection of excerpts. For the complete 2001 Annual Report, please use the Office Depot Web site (www.officedepot.com).]

APPENDIX F

PAGES A-39–A-48

Concept Development: Product Mix

Discuss: Point out to students that Office Depot's sales in technology products decreased significantly in 2001. Have students review the reasons given by the company for this decline and ask for additional factors that might have had an impact. L1

Concept Development: Store and Warehouse Operating and Selling Expenses

Identify: List the following items on the board: personnel costs, maintenance and other facility costs, advertising expenses, delivery and transportation costs, credit card and bank charges, and warehouse costs.

Explain that these items comprise the overall category of "Store and Warehouse Operating and Selling Expenses" for Office Depot. L1

ACTIVITIES

Creating a Business Strategy Ask students to imagine that they are on the management team of a large office supply retail company. Ask them how they might create a pricing structure for their products and how they would decide what products to offer. Have them consider what they might charge their customers to deliver orders and what pay rate they might establish for store clerks, warehouse workers, and cashiers. Explain that these decisions must be based on market competition, cost of products, overhead costs, and consumer demand.

Concept Development: Consolidated Balance Sheets

Discussion: Remind students that large corporations often have balance sheets for individual divisions, and that they are often compiled into a single, consolidated balance sheet for the company as a whole. Office Depot's divisions, or "segments," are the North American Retail Division, the Business Services Group (BSG), and the International Division. L1

Office Depot, Inc.

Consolidated Balance Sheets

(In thousands, except share and per share amounts)

	December 29, 2001	December 30, 2000
Assets		
Current assets:		
Cash and cash equivalents	**$ 563,410**	$ 151,482
Receivables, net of allowances of $32,682 in 2001 and $34,461 in 2000	**781,476**	896,333
Merchandise inventories, net	**1,259,522**	1,420,825
Deferred income taxes	**148,490**	157,779
Prepaid expenses	**53,292**	72,670
Total current assets	**2,806,190**	2,699,089
Property and equipment, net	**1,110,011**	1,119,306
Goodwill, net	**249,560**	219,971
Other assets	**165,882**	157,968
Total assets	**$4,331,643**	$4,196,334
Liabilities and Stockholders' Equity		
Current liabilities:		
Accounts payable	**$1,060,968**	$1,136,994
Accrued expenses and other liabilities	**612,999**	580,966
Income taxes payable	**109,026**	37,118
Current maturities of long-term debt	**318,521**	153,259
Total current liabilities	**2,101,514**	1,908,337
Deferred income taxes and other credits	**64,139**	88,247
Long-term debt, net of current maturities	**315,331**	374,061
Zero coupon, convertible subordinated notes	**2,221**	224,438
Commitments and contingencies		
Stockholders' equity:		
Common stock—authorized 800,000,000 shares of $.01 par value; issued 385,538,340 in 2001 and 378,688,359 in 2000	**3,855**	3,787
Additional paid-in capital	**1,007,088**	939,214
Unamortized value of long-term incentive stock grant	**(2,578)**	(2,793)
Accumulated other comprehensive loss	**(71,273)**	(53,490)
Retained earnings	**1,717,734**	1,516,691
Treasury stock, at cost—82,443,170 shares in 2001 and 82,190,548 shares in 2000	**(806,388)**	(802,158)
Total stockholders' equity	**1,848,438**	1,601,251
Total liabilities and stockholders' equity	**$4,331,643**	$4,196,334

The accompanying notes are an integral part of these statements.
[Note to the student: For complete accompanying notes, refer to the 2001 Annual Report on the Office Depot Web site.]

Assets:
Things the company owns.
- **Cash.**
- **Receivables.** Money owed to the company.
- **Merchandise Inventories.** Products waiting to be sold.
- **Property and Equipment.** Buildings, machinery, trucks, etc.
- **Deferred income taxes, Prepaid expenses, Goodwill, Other assets.** These are other assets the company has that have value.

Liabilities:
What the company owes.
- **Current liabilities.** Bills, payroll due, taxes and other obligations that have to be paid within a year.
- **Long-term debt, net of current maturities.** This is the amount owed with due dates that are more than one year in the future.
- **Deferred income taxes and other credits; Zero coupon, convertible subordinated notes.** These are other obligations that are due more than one year in the future.

TEACHING NOTES

Office Depot, Inc.

Consolidated Statements of Earnings

(In thousands, except per share amounts)

	2001	2000	1999
Sales	**$11,154,081**	$11,569,696	$10,272,060
Cost of goods sold and occupancy costs	**7,983,973**	8,479,437	7,450,575
Gross profit	**3,170,108**	3,090,259	2,821,485
Store and warehouse operating and selling expenses	**2,343,394**	2,409,478	2,023,055
General and administrative expenses	**451,722**	453,784	328,108
Facility closure costs	**8,436**	110,038	40,425
Other operating expenses	**12,125**	6,733	16,524
Operating profit	**354,431**	110,226	413,373
Other income (expense):			
Interest income	**13,058**	11,502	30,176
Interest expense	**(44,302)**	(33,901)	(26,148)
Miscellaneous income (expense), net	**(9,057)**	4,632	(3,514)
Earnings before income taxes	**314,130**	92,459	413,887
Income taxes	**113,087**	43,127	156,249
Net earnings	**$ 201,043**	$ 49,332	$ 257,638
Earnings per share:			
Basic	**$ .67**	$ .16	$ .71
Diluted	**.66**	.16	.69

The accompanying notes are an integral part of these statements.
[Note to the student: For complete accompanying notes, refer to the 2001 Annual Report on the Office Depot Web site.]

Statement of Earnings

- **Sales.** Total sales of the company minus the value of product discounted or returned.
- **Cost of goods sold and occupancy costs.** Cost of goods sold is the actual cost to the business of the merchandise sold to customers. Occupancy costs include rent, common area maintenance, taxes, and utilities. Cost of goods sold and occupancy costs are reported on the same line based on the industry's general practices.
- **Gross profit.** Net sales minus cost of goods sold and occupancy costs.
- **Store and warehouse operating and selling expenses.**
- **General and administrative expenses.**
- **Facility closure costs.**
- **Other operating expenses.**
- **Operating profit.** Income earned from normal business activities.
- **Other income and expense.**
- **Earnings before income taxes.** Income taxes are federal and state taxes paid or due based on the company's taxable income.
- **Net earnings.** The "bottom line," or final earnings after taxes have been deducted.

Concept Development: Cost of Goods Sold

Discussion: Remind students that the cost of merchandise sold, or cost of goods sold, is computed using the following equation:

Beginning merchandise
+ Purchases
+ Transportation In
− Purchases Discounts
− Purchases Returns & Allowances
− Ending Inventory
= Cost of Goods Sold

Point out that Office Depot presents a total cost of goods sold instead of the individual amounts that comprise this amount. L1

ACTIVITIES

Analyzing the Consolidated Statements of Earnings Students learned how to perform horizontal analysis of financial statements in Chapter 19. Ask students to prepare a horizontal analysis of the Office Depot Consolidated Statements of Earnings for 2001 and 2000. Use the following check figures to verify their work. (Sales decreased by 3.59%, Gross Profit increased by 2.58%, Operating Profit increased by 221.55%, Net Earnings increased by 307.53%)

Concept Development: Statement of Stockholders' Equity

Discussion: Remind students that the statement of stockholders' equity reports the changes in all of the stockholders' equity accounts during the period and provides information about the transactions that affected these accounts. Point out that Office Depot's Consolidated Statements of Stockholders' Equity contains data for 1999, 2000, and 2001. Identify the types of transactions that had an impact on stockholders' equity in 2001: exercise of stock option plans, issuance of stock under employee stock option plans, 401K matching contributions, direct stock purchase plans, net earnings, adjustments for foreign currency translations, and acquisition of treasury stock. L1

Office Depot, Inc.

Consolidated Statements of Stockholders' Equity

(In thousands, except share amounts)

	Common stock shares	Common stock amount	Additional paid-in capital	Unamortized value of long-term incentive stock grant	Accumulated other comprehensive income (loss)	Comprehensive income (loss)	Retained earnings	Treasury stock
Balance at December 26, 1998	373,817,704	$3,738	$ 838,122	$(2,874)	$(18,078)		$1,209,721	$ (1,750)
Comprehensive income:								
Net earnings						$ 257,638	257,638	
Foreign currency translation adjustment					(28,319)	(28,319)		
Unrealized gain on investment securities, net of tax					62,127	62,127		
Comprehensive income						$ 291,446		
Acquisition of treasury stock								(501,361)
Retirement of treasury stock	(3,245,170)	(32)	(1,718)					1,750
Grant of long-term incentive stock	130,000	1	2,127	(2,127)				
Exercise of stock options (including income tax benefits)	4,457,024	45	72,865					
Issuance of stock under employee stock purchase plans	712,431	7	9,240					
Matching contributions under 401(k) and deferred compensation plans	320,906	3	5,423					
Conversion of LYONs® to common stock	23,710		329					
Payment for fractional shares in connection with 3-for-2 stock split	(4,166)		(93)					
Amortization of long-term incentive stock grant				936				
Balance at December 25, 1999	376,212,439	3,762	926,295	(4,065)	15,730		1,467,359	(501,361)
Comprehensive income:								
Net earnings						$ 49,332	49,332	
Foreign currency translation adjustment					(7,093)	(7,093)		
Realized gain on investment securities, net of tax					(62,127)	(62,127)		
Comprehensive income (loss)						$(19,888)		
Acquisition of treasury stock								(300,797)
Grant of long-term incentive stock	25,000		199	(199)				
Cancellation of long-term incentive stock	(50,000)		(819)	600				
Exercise of stock options (including income tax benefits)	424,809	4	(1,984)					
Issuance of stock under employee stock purchase plans	1,372,566	14	9,713					
Matching contributions under 401(k) and deferred compensation plans	703,545	7	5,810					
Amortization of long-term incentive stock grant				871				

ACTIVITIES

Stockholders' Equity Accounts Remind students that all ending balances for stockholders' equity accounts are represented on both the balance sheet and the statement of stockholders' equity. Ask students to trace each amount presented on the balance sheet to the statement of stockholders' equity.

Office Depot, Inc.

Consolidated Statements of Stockholders' Equity *(continued)*

(In thousands, except share amounts)

	Common stock shares	Common stock amount	Additional paid-in capital	Unamortized value of long-term incentive stock grant	Accumulated other comprehensive income (loss)	Comprehensive income (loss)	Retained earnings	Treasury stock
Balance at December 30, 2000	378,688,359	$3,787	$ 939,214	$(2,793)	$(53,490)		$1,516,691	$(802,158)
Comprehensive income:								
Net earnings						$201,043	201,043	
Foreign currency translation adjustment					(17,783)	(17,783)		
Comprehensive income (loss)						$183,260		
Acquisition of treasury stock								(4,254)
Grant of long-term incentive stock	80,000	1	764					
Exercise of stock options (including income tax benefits)	5,604,810	55	56,430					
Issuance of stock under employee stock purchase plans	751,400	8	6,712					
Matching contributions under 401(k) and deferred compensation plans	413,771	4	3,957					
Direct Stock Purchase Plans			11					24
Amortization of long-term incentive stock grant				215				
Balance at December 29, 2001	**385,538,340**	**$3,855**	**$1,007,088**	**$(2,578)**	**$(71,273)**		**$1,717,734**	**$(806,388)**

The accompanying notes are an integral part of these statements.

[Note to the student: For complete accompanying notes, refer to the 2001 Annual Report on the Office Depot Web site.]

Stockholders' Equity
This is called the "book value" of the owners' stake in the company. It includes proceeds the company received from the initial and subsequent sales of stock to the public, plus accumulated profits, called *retained earnings.*
This book value is not the same as the market value of stock on the public stock market, called "market value." The stock market determines in its own ways whether the company is worth more than the book value of what it owns minus what it owes. For example, a company's stock price changes regularly without regard to the value of the assets and liabilities it uses to run the company.

APPENDIX F
PAGES A-39–A-48

Concept Development: Treasury Stock

Discussion: Ask students to note the activity for treasury stock for the years 1999, 2000, and 2001 on the Consolidated Statements of Stockholders' Equity. Explain that treasury stock is a corporation's own stock that has been issued and reacquired. Emphasize that stockholders benefit when the corporation repurchases common stock because there are fewer shares of outstanding stock to share any increases in the company's value. No dividends, voting rights, or liquidation preferences apply to treasury stock. A corporation may buy back its own stock in order to create demand for the stock and thus increase its market value. L1

ACTIVITIES

Return on Sales Ask students to compute the return on sales for Office Depot for 2001, 2000, and 1999, using the Consolidated Statements of Earnings on page A–46. Remind them that this ratio examines the portion of each sales dollar that represents profit. (2001, 1.80%; 2000, 0.43%; 1999, 2.51%)

Problem 3A (Answers)
Determining the Effects of Business Transactions on the Accounting Equation

Ending debit balances:
Cash in Bank $40,500
Accts. Rec. $300
Office Furniture $1,000
Computer Equip. $5,000
Office Equip. $3,000

Ending credit balances:
Accts. Pay. $300
Pamela Wong, Capital $49,500

Analyze:
(A) $8,000
(B) $49,800
(C) $49,800
(D) Yes

APPENDIX G

Additional Reinforcement Problems

APPLICATION OPTIONS

Complete appendix problems one of two ways:

1 **Manual** Glencoe Working Papers

or

2 **Spreadsheet** Templates (Problems 3A, 23A, and 26A)

SPREADSHEET SMART GUIDE

Step-by-Step Instructions: Problem 3A

1. Select the spreadsheet template for Problem 3A.
2. Enter your name and the date in the spaces provided on the template.
3. Complete the spreadsheet using the instructions in your working papers.
4. Print the spreadsheet and proof your work.
5. Save your work and exit the spreadsheet program.

Chapter 3, Problem 3A Determining the Effects of Business Transactions on the Accounting Equation

Pamela Wong started her own business called Thunder Graphics Desktop Publishing.

Instructions Use the form provided in your working papers. For each of the following transactions:

(1) Identify the accounts affected.
(2) Write the amount of the increase (+) or decrease (−) in the space provided on the form.
(3) Determine the new balance for each account.

Trans. No.	Transactions
1	Pamela Wong, the owner, opened a checking account for the business by depositing $48,000 of her personal funds.
2	Paid the monthly rent of $1,500.
3	Bought office furniture on account for $1,000.
4	Pamela Wong invested $3,000 of office equipment in the business.
5	Paid cash for a new computer for the business, $5,000.
6	Paid for an advertisement in the local newspaper, $200.
7	Completed graphic desktop publishing services for a client and sent a bill for $800.
8	Paid $700 on account for the office furniture bought earlier.
9	Received $500 on account from a client.
10	Pamela Wong withdrew $1,000 for personal use.
11	Received $400 cash for desktop publishing services completed for a client.

Analyze: After analyzing all of the transactions, answer the following questions.

(a) What was the total amount of equipment assets?
(b) What is the total amount of assets?
(c) What are the total liabilities and owner's equity?
(d) Is the accounting equation in balance?

HOME AND COMMUNITY CONNECTIONS ACTIVITY

Investigating Community Benefits Have students get to know the community in which they live. Divide students into groups of three or four. Have students visit the local chamber of commerce or help them locate a visitor's guide to their city. What are some of the recreational benefits the city offers? What event(s) might bring the most revenue to their city? How many public services are available? (parks, bike trails, community fairs, sporting events, and museums) Have students create a list of activities or community services, the cost of each, the availability, and the location of each. Post completed lists so students can compare their findings.

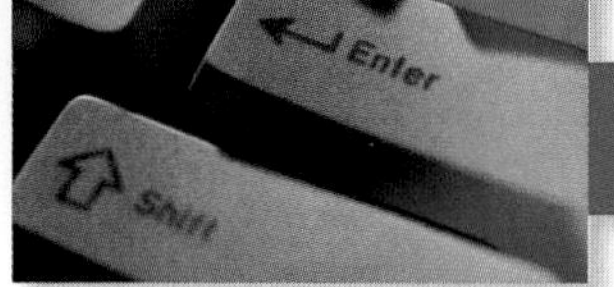

Chapter 4, Problem 4A Analyzing Transactions Affecting Assets, Liabilities, and Owner's Equity

Thunder Graphics Desktop Publishing had the following transactions. A partial list of the accounts used to record and report business transactions appear below.

101 Cash in Bank	201 Accounts Payable—Computer Warehouse, Inc.
110 Accounts Receivable—Roger McFall	205 Accounts Payable—Pro Computer Company
125 Office Equipment	301 Pamela Wong, Capital
130 Office Furniture	
135 Computer Equipment	

Instructions On the forms provided in your working papers:

(1) Prepare a T account for each account listed above.
(2) Analyze and record each of the following business transactions in the appropriate T accounts. Identify each transaction by number.
(3) After recording all transactions, compute and record the account balance and identify the normal side of each T account.
(4) Add the balances of those accounts with normal debit balances.
(5) Add the balances of those accounts with normal credit balances.

Trans. No.	Transactions
1	Pamela Wong invested $30,000 into the business.
2	Invested office equipment, valued at $650, into the business.
3	Bought a computer on account from Computer Warehouse, Inc. for $9,360.
4	Bought new office equipment for $1,550, Check 100.
5	Bought new office furniture on account from Computer Warehouse, Inc. for $1,250.
6	Sold the older office equipment on account to Roger McFall for $650.
7	Paid $3,000 on account to Computer Warehouse Inc., Check 101.
8	Received $400 on account from Roger McFall.
9	Paid $3,500 on account to Computer Warehouse Inc., Check 102.
10	Bought computer hardware from Pro Computer Company for $775.

Analyze: Is the accounting equation in balance?

Chapter 5, Problem 5A Analyzing Transactions Affecting Revenue, Expenses, and Withdrawals

Pamela Wong owns and operates Thunder Graphics Desktop Publishing. A partial list of the chart of accounts appears in your working papers.

Instructions On the forms provided in your working papers:

(1) Prepare a T account for each account listed above.
(2) Analyze and record each of the following business transactions in the appropriate T accounts. Identify each transaction by number.
(3) After recording all transactions, compute a balance for each account.
(4) Test for the equality of debits and credits.

Continued

ACCOUNTING ISSUES

CPAs who work for or with not-for-profit organizations (NPOs) must make certain they apply the correct generally accepted accounting principles. Some NPOs are under Financial Accounting Standards Board jurisdiction; others are considered governments and are subject to Governmental Accounting Standards Board jurisdiction. To determine if NPOs are government, CPAs must refer to the *Applicability of GASB Standards*, an advisory paper that helps resolve questions about which hierarchy a particular entity should follow.

Problem 4A (Answers) Analyzing Transactions Affecting Assets, Liabilities, and Owner's Equity

Ending debit balances:
Cash in Bank $22,350
Accts. Rec.—Roger McFall $250
Office Equip. $1,550
Office Furniture $1,250
Computer Equip. $10,135

Ending credit balances:
Accts. Pay.—Pro Computer Company $775
Accts. Pay.—Computer Warehouse Inc. $4,110
Pamela Wong, Capital $30,650

Sum of debit balances $35,535
Sum of credit balances $35,535

Analyze: Yes

Problem 5A (Answers) Analyzing Transactions Affecting Revenue, Expenses, and Withdrawals

Ending debit balances:
Cash in Bank $24,620
Accts. Rec.—Adams, Bell, and Cox $425
Computer Equip. $1,400
Office Equip. $650
Maintenance Exp. $145
Rent Exp. $750
Utilities Exp. $260
Pamela Wong, Withdrawals $150

Ending credit balances:
Accts. Pay.—Computer Warehouse Inc. $700
Design Income $2,050
Pamela Wong, Capital $25,650

Total debits/credits $28,400

Analyze: $2,050

PROBLEMS
APPENDIX G

Problem 6A (Answers) Recording General Journal Transactions

Jan. 1: Dr. Cash in Bank $900; Cr. Design Income $900; Receipt 545

Jan. 3: Dr. Office Furniture $2,400; Cr. Cash in Bank $400, Accts. Pay.—Computer Warehouse Inc. $2,000; Check 801/Invoice CW402

Jan. 7: Dr. Advertising Exp. $300; Cr. Accts. Pay.—Solutions Software $300; Invoice SS60

Jan. 10: Dr. Cash in Bank $500, Accts. Rec.—Adams, Bell, and Cox Inc. $3,000; Cr. Print Production Income $3,500; Receipt 546/Invoice TG90

Jan. 15: Dr. Pamela Wong, Withdrawals $1,500; Cr. Cash in Bank $1,500; Check 802

Jan. 17: Dr. Maintenance Exp. $175; Cr. Cash in Bank $175; Check 803

Jan. 20: Dr. Computer Equip. $4,000; Cr. Accts. Pay.—Pro Computer Company $4,000; Invoice 783

Jan. 27: Dr. Accts. Pay.—Computer Warehouse Inc. $1,000; Cr. Cash in Bank $1,000; Check 804

Jan. 29: Dr. Accts. Pay.—Solutions Software $300; Cr. Cash in Bank $300; Check 805

Jan. 31: Dr. Office Equip. $200; Cr. Pamela Wong, Capital $200; Memorandum 40

Analyze: $1,400

Trans. No.	Transactions
1	Pamela Wong invested $25,000 in the business.
2	Bought a new computer on account from Computer Warehouse, Inc. for $1,400.
3	Ms. Wong invested office equipment, valued at $650, in the business.
4	Paid the rent for the month, $750, Check 207.
5	Wrote Check 208 for $145 for minor repairs to the equipment.
6	Completed graphics design work on account for Adams, Bell, and Cox, Inc., $850.
7	Paid the $175 utility bill, Check 209.
8	Deposited the daily design receipts in the bank, $1,200.
9	Sent Check 210 for $700 to Computer Warehouse, Inc. as payment on account.
10	Received $425 from Adams, Bell, and Cox, Inc.
11	Ms. Wong withdrew $150 for personal needs.
12	Paid the $85 telephone bill, Check 211.

Analyze: How much design income did the business record in the above transactions?

Chapter 6, Problem 6A Recording General Journal Transactions

Instructions On the form provided in your working papers, record the following transactions for the month of January on page 7 of the general journal for Thunder Graphics Desktop Publishing.

Date	Transactions
Jan. 1	Received $900 for completion of design work for Designers Boutique, Receipt 545.
3	Purchased a desk, chairs, and table valued at $2,400 from Computer Warehouse, Inc. Made a down payment of $400 and agreed to pay the balance within 60 days, Check 801/Invoice CW402.
7	Ran a $300 special feature ad in Solutions Software's monthly magazine on account, Invoice SS60.
10	Completed a $3,500 print production job for Adams, Bell, and Cox, Inc. Received a down payment of $500 and agreed to receive the balance within 30 days, Receipt 546/ Invoice TG90.
15	Pamela Wong withdrew $1,500 from the business for personal use, Check 802.
17	Paid a carpenter $175 to install a new office door, Check 803.
20	Purchased a $4,000 computer system from Pro Computer Company on account, Invoice 783.
27	Paid Computer Warehouse, Inc. $1,000 to apply on our account, Check 804.
29	Wrote Check 805 for $300 to Solutions Software in payment of an ad purchased on July 7.
31	Pamela Wong invested a $200 file cabinet in the business, Memo 40.

Analyze: How much cash did the business receive during January?

CRITICAL THINKING ACTIVITY

Locating Back-Ordered Items The accounting clerk for Richland Supplies, an auto supplies store, paid an invoice in March. In April the clerk realized that some of the items listed on the invoice were back ordered and had never been received. Where would the accounting clerk find a record of the back-ordered items, and how could this error have been avoided? (The back-ordered items would have been noted on the packing slip. The error could have been avoided if the accounting clerk had verified the invoice against the packing slip before approving payment of the invoice.)

Chapter 7, Problem 7A Journalizing and Posting Transactions

The balances in the general ledger accounts of Thunder Graphics are shown below.

101	Cash in Bank	$ 10,000
110	Accounts Receivable—Roger McFall	---
125	Office Equipment	2,500
135	Computer Equipment	3,000
201	Accts. Pay.—Computer Warehouse Inc.	---
301	Pamela Wong, Capital	8,000
302	Pamela Wong, Withdrawals	4,000
401	Design Revenue	9,000
405	Print Production Revenue	4,000
505	Maintenance Expense	1,200
510	Miscellaneous Expense	300

Instructions On the forms provided in your working papers:

(1) Open the accounts in the general ledger with their beginning balances as of March 1 of the current year.
(2) Record March transactions on page 15 of the general journal.
(3) Post each journal entry to the appropriate accounts in the ledger.
(4) Prove the ledger by preparing a trial balance.

Date	Transactions
Mar. 1	Pamela Wong invested additional assets in the business: cash, $3,000, and office equipment, $500, Memorandum 75.
5	Paid $600 to Premier Painters for painting the office, Check 912.
7	Discovered that $1,500 in design revenue was incorrectly journalized and posted to the **Print Production Revenue** account last month, Memorandum 76.
9	Purchased $3,600 computer system from Computer Warehouse, Inc. on account, Invoice CW204.
12	Deposited $4,000 into the checking account. $3,000 was earned from design revenue and $1,000 from print production revenue, Receipts 300–310.
15	Completed print production for Roger McFall. Sent him a bill for $600, Invoice TG601.
20	Discovered that $50 in miscellaneous expense was incorrectly journalized and posted to the **Maintenance Expense** account, Memorandum 77.
25	Pamela Wong withdrew $2,000 from the business, Check 913.
28	Received $300 from Roger McFall to apply to his account, Receipt 311.
31	Issued Check 914 for $1,800 to Computer Warehouse, Inc. to apply on our account.

Analyze: What is the balance in the cash account on March 31?

PROBLEMS APPENDIX G

Problem 7A (Answers) Journalizing and Posting Transactions

Ending debit balances:
Cash in Bank $12,900
Accts. Rec.—Roger McFall $300
Office Equip. $3,000
Computer Equip. $6,600
Pamela Wong, Withdrawals $6,000
Maintenance Exp. $1,750
Miscellaneous Exp. $350

Ending credit balances:
Accts. Pay.—Computer Warehouse Inc. $1,800
Pamela Wong, Capital $11,500
Design Revenue $13,500
Print Production Revenue $4,100

Trial balance totals $30,900

Analyze: $12,900

SOLUTION NOTES

Problem 8A (Answers)
Preparing a Six-Column Work Sheet
Trial Balance column totals $43,561

Analyze: Net income $6,219

Problem 9A (Answers)
Interpreting Financial Information
Net Income $1,457

Analyze: Expenses $11,491

Chapter 8, Problem 8A Preparing a Six-Column Work Sheet

The final balances in the general ledger of Thunder Graphics Desktop Publishing at the end of May are listed below.

101	Cash in Bank	$16,095
105	Accts. Rec.—Adams, Bell, and Cox Inc.	1,729
110	Accts. Rec.—Roger McFall	281
113	Accts. Rec.—Designers Boutique	---
115	Accts. Rec.—Pat Cooper	714
120	Office Supplies	228
125	Office Equipment	5,027
130	Office Furniture	2,940
135	Computer Equipment	8,200
201	Accts. Pay.—Computer Warehouse Inc.	4,027
205	Accts. Pay.—Pro Computer Company	2,441
207	Accts. Pay.—Solutions Software	---
301	Pamela Wong, Capital	24,927
305	Pamela Wong, Withdrawals	2,400
310	Income Summary	---
401	Design Revenue	8,116
405	Print Production Revenue	4,050
501	Advertising Expense	735
505	Maintenance Expense	1,335
510	Miscellaneous Expense	285
520	Rent Expense	3,100
530	Utilities Expense	492

Instructions Use the form in your working papers to prepare a work sheet for the month ended May 30.

Analyze: How much net income or net loss did Thunder Graphics have for the month of May?

Chapter 9, Problem 9A Interpreting Financial Information

You are applying for a job with Thunder Graphics Desktop Publishing. The job includes preparing financial statements. In order to determine your ability to do the job, the owner, Pamela Wong, has given you the following information. At the beginning of the last fiscal period, the **Pamela Wong, Capital** account had a balance of $46,295. At the end of the period, the account showed a balance of $49,152. During the period, Ms. Wong made an additional investment of $2,000 and had withdrawals of $600. The revenue for the period was $12,948.

Analyze: Use the form provided in your working papers to determine the total expenses for the period.

MAKING CONNECTIONS TO DAILY LIFE

Purchasing on Account Ask students if they have ever purchased items on account. When buying on account, the customer receives a receipt for the items purchased. Once the invoice (or credit card statement) is received, the customer should compare the amounts on their receipts to the amounts shown on the invoice to verify that the charges are accurate. Ask students if they or their parents have ever experienced any inaccurate charges on their invoices. Then discuss with the class the pros and cons of purchasing on account.

APPENDIX G PROBLEMS

Chapter 10, Problem 10A Preparing Closing Entries

The work sheet of Thunder Graphics Desktop Publishing for the year ended December 31 is presented in your working papers.

Instructions Using the information in the work sheet, prepare the four journal entries to close the temporary capital accounts. Use general journal page 21 provided in your working papers.

Analyze: What is the balance in the **Pamela Wong, Capital** account after the closing entries?

Chapter 11, Problem 11A Recording Deposits in the Checkbook

On October 20, Pamela Wong, owner of Thunder Graphics Desktop Publishing, deposited the following in the checking account of the business.

Cash: $800

Checks: Boyden Company; drawn on National Bank of Commerce; Monroe; ABA No 45-1204; $50.29.
Gail's Supplies; drawn on Regent Bank; Rayville; ABA No 49-3401; $255.48.
Clinton Co.; drawn on Sun Federal Savings and Loan; Bastrop; ABA No 52-6429; $788.40.

On October 21, Pamela Wong received the electricity bill from Central Utilities for $314.69 for September 17 to October 18 service.

The October bank statement for Thunder Graphics listed a bank service charge of $21.80, dated October 23.

Instructions On the forms provided in your working papers:

(1) Complete a deposit slip using the October 20 information.
(2) Record the deposit on check stub 1068 using $2,468.14 as the balance brought forward.
(3) Complete check stub 1068 and prepare Check 1068 to Central Utilities. Use October 22 as the date and sign your name as drawer.
(4) Record this service charge in the checkbook on check stub 1069.
(5) Journalize the entry for the bank service charge in the general journal. Use October 25 as the date.
(6) Answer the following questions.
  (a) What was the amount carried forward from check stub 1067?
  (b) What was the checkbook balance before writing Check 1068?
  (c) What was the total amount deposited on October 20?
  (d) Identify the payee of Check 1068.
  (e) What was the balance brought forward on check stub 1069?

Analyze: What is the checkbook balance after all of the above transactions have been recorded?

PROBLEMS APPENDIX G

Problem 10A (Answers) Preparing Closing Entries

Dec. 31: Dr. Design Income $24,000, Print Production Income $15,000; Cr. Income Summary $39,000

Dec. 31: Dr. Income Summary $25,300; Cr. Rent Exp. $12,000, Maintenance Exp. $3,200, Advertising Exp. $2,000, Utilities Exp. $4,800, Office Supplies Exp. $1,800, Miscellaneous Exp. $1,500

Dec. 31: Dr. Income Summary $13,700; Cr. Pamela Wong, Capital $13,700

Dec. 31: Dr. Pamela Wong, Capital $8,000; Cr. Pamela Wong, Withdrawals $8,000

Analyze: $20,000

Problem 11A (Answers) Recording Deposits in the Checkbook

1. Total deposit $1,894.17
2. Subtotal $4,362.31
3. Checkbook balance $4,047.62
4. Subtotal $4,025.82
5. Oct. 25: Dr. Miscellaneous Exp. $21.80; Cr. Cash in Bank $21.80; October Bank Service Charge
6. (a) $2,468.14; (b) $4,362.31; (c) $1,894.17; (d) Central Utilities; (e) $4,047.62

Analyze: $4,025.82

SOLUTION NOTES

Problem 12A (Answers)
Preparing a Payroll Register

Earnings:
Regular $1,121.76
Overtime $36.71
Total $1,158.47

Deductions:
Social Security Tax $71.83
Medicare Tax $16.79
Federal Income Tax $91.00
State Income Tax $17.38
Hospital Insurance $25.20
Other $9.75
Total $231.95

Net Pay $926.52

Analyze: $1,158.47

Problem 13A (Answers)
Recording Payroll Transactions

Dec. 17: Dr. Salaries Exp. $968.60; Cr. Social Security Tax Pay. $60.05, Medicare Tax Pay. $14.05, Employees' Federal Income Tax Pay. $145.00, Employees' State Income Tax Pay. $14.52, Hospital Insurance Pay. $25.20, Union Dues Pay. $9.75, Cash in Bank $700.03; Check 831/ Payroll Register 12/17

Dec. 17: Dr. Payroll Tax Exp. $134.14; Cr. Social Security Tax Pay. $60.05, Medicare Tax Pay. $14.04, Federal Unemployment Tax Pay. $7.75, State Unemployment Tax Pay. $52.30; Payroll Register 12/17

Dec. 17: Dr. Employees' Federal Income Tax Pay. $334.00, Social Security Tax Pay. $311.58, Medicare Tax Pay. $73.02; Cr. Cash in Bank $718.60; Check 832

Dec. 17: Dr. Employees' State Income Tax Pay. $192.92; Cr. Cash in Bank $192.92; Check 833

Analyze: $718.60

Chapter 12, Chapter 12A Preparing a Payroll Register

Thunder Graphics Desktop Publishing has four employees. They are paid on a weekly basis with overtime paid for all hours worked over 40. The overtime rate is 1½ times the regular hourly rate of pay. The names of the employees and other information needed to prepare the payroll are as follows.

Employee No.	Employee	Status	Exemptions	Rate/Hour	Union
173	Don Hoffman	M	1	$6.95	No
168	Manual Gongas	S	0	7.10	Yes
167	Riley Sullivan	M	2	7.40	Yes
175	Marcy Jackson	S	1	6.95	Yes

During the week ended Oct. 15, Gongas worked 41 hours, Sullivan worked 39¼ hours, Jackson worked 42½ hours, and Hoffman worked 39¾ hours.

Instructions On the form provided in your working papers:

(1) Prepare a payroll register. The date of payment is October 15. List employees in alphabetical order by last name.
  (a) Compute FICA taxes at 6.2% for social security and 1.45% for Medicare.
  (b) Use the tax table in Chapter 12 to determine federal income taxes. The state income tax is 1.5% of gross earnings.
  (c) All employees have a deduction for hospital insurance that is $4.75 for single employees and $7.85 for married employees.
  (d) Union members pay weekly dues of $3.25.

(2) After the payroll information is entered in the payroll register, total the columns and check the accuracy of the totals.

Analyze: What are the total earnings for the week for all of Thunder Graphics' employees?

Chapter 13, Problem 13A Recording Payroll Transactions

Thunder Graphics Desktop Publishing pays its employees each week. The payroll register for the week ended December 17 is shown in your working papers.

Instructions On the forms provided in your working papers:

(1) Record the payment of the payroll on page 34 of the general journal. Check 831 was written on December 17 to pay the payroll.
(2) Compute the employer's payroll taxes (FICA tax rates, 6.2% social security, 1.45% Medicare; state unemployment tax rate, 5.4%; federal unemployment tax rate, 0.8%).
(3) Record the journal entry for the employer's payroll taxes.
(4) Record the payment of all FICA and employees' federal income taxes, Check 832. The previous account balances were: **Employees' Federal Income Tax Payable**, $189, **Social Security Tax Payable**, $191.48, and **Medicare Tax Payable**, $44.92.
(5) Record the income tax payment to the state, Check 833. The balance in the **Employees' State Income Tax Payable** account before the December 17 payroll was $178.40.

Analyze: What was the amount of Check 832?

ACCOUNTING ISSUES

Improved Accounting and Auditing Standards On July 30, 2002, the Sarbanes-Oxley Act of 2002 was signed into law. The Act applies in general to publicly held companies and their audit firms, and provides a variety of new rules related to audit oversight, committees, reporting, and client services created to help protect auditor independence. It also created the Public Company Accounting Oversight Board that issues and adopts standards set by other groups and recognized organizations for audit firm quality controls. The Board is empowered to regularly inspect registered accounting firms' operations and investigate potential violations of securities laws, standards, competency, and conduct.

Chapter 14, Problem 14A Recording and Posting Sales and Cash Receipt Transactions

On January 1, T-Shirt Trends, a merchandising business, had the following balances in its general ledger and accounts receivable subsidiary ledger.

General Ledger	
101 Cash In Bank	$ 7,500
115 Accounts Receivable	10,920
215 Sales Tax Payable	1,500
401 Sales	18,620
405 Sales Discounts	1,400
410 Sales Returns and Allowances	300

Accounts Receivable Subsidiary Ledger	
MOR Morales, Gabriela	$ 420
ROU Roundabout Fashions	3,150
SAM Samstead Fashions	5,250
SAN Sandpiper Sports Club	2,100

Instructions On the forms provided in your working papers:

(1) Open the general ledger accounts and record the January 1 balances.
(2) Open the customer accounts in the accounts receivable subsidiary ledger and record the January 1 balances.
(3) Record the January transactions. Use page 12 in the general journal.
(4) Post the transactions to the general ledger and accounts receivable subsidiary ledger accounts.

Date	Transactions
Jan. 1	Received a check for $3,087 from Roundabout Fashions payment of their $3,150 account less a 2% cash discount of $63, Receipt 82.
4	Gabriela Morales notified us that $40 in T-shirts were defective. Issued Credit Memorandum 20 for $42, which includes a 5% sales tax of $2.
9	Sold $1,000 in merchandise plus a sales tax of $50 to Roundabout Fashions on account, Sales Slip 90.
15	Sandpiper Sports Club sent us a check in payment of their $2,100 account less a 2% cash discount, Receipt 83.
17	Granted Samstead Fashions $252 credit for the return of $240 in merchandise plus a $12 sales tax, Credit Memorandum 21.
20	Received a check from Roundabout Fashions in payment of their $1050 account balance less a cash discount of $21, Receipt 84.
25	Samstead Fashions sent us a check for $2,000 to apply on their account, Receipt 85.
31	Cash sales for the month were $5,000 plus $250 in sales tax, Tape 44.
31	Bankcard transactions for the month were $6,000 plus $300 in sales tax, Tape 44.

Analyze: What is the balance in the **Accounts Receivable** account at the end of January?

PROBLEMS
APPENDIX G

Problem 14A (Answers) Recording and Posting Sales and Cash Receipt Transactions

Ending debit balances:
Cash in Bank $27,224
Accts. Rec. $3,376
Sales Discounts $1,526
Sales Ret. and Allow. $580
Accts. Rec.—Gabriella Morales $378
Accts. Rec.—Samstead Fashions $2,998

Ending credit balances:
Sales Tax Pay. $2,086
Sales $30,620

Analyze: $3,376

SOLUTION NOTES

Problem 15A (Answers) Recording Purchases and Cash Payment Transactions

Mar. 2: Dr. Accts. Pay./Dancing Wind Clothing Manufacturers $7,000; Cr. Cash in Bank $6,790, Purchases Disc. $210; Check 5500
Mar. 4: Dr. Purchases $2,800; Cr. Accts. Pay./Wilmington Shirt Factory $2,800; Invoice WSF123
Mar. 6: Dr. Transportation In $180; Cr. Cash in Bank $180; Check 5501
Mar. 8: Dr. Accts. Pay./Wilmington Shirt Factory $300; Cr. Purchases Ret. and Allow. $300; Debit Memo 44
Mar. 10: Dr. Prepaid Insurance $3,400; Cr. Cash in Bank $3,400; Check 5502
Mar. 12: Dr. Supplies $175; Cr. Accts. Pay./Carter Office Supply $175; Invoice 97
Mar. 14: Dr. Accts. Pay./Wilmington Shirt Factory $2,500; Cr. Purchases Disc. $75, Cash in Bank $2,425; Check 5503
Mar. 19: Dr. Accts. Pay./Carter Office Supply $50; Cr. Supplies $50; Debit Memo 45
Mar. 25: Dr. Salaries Exp. $4,000; Cr. Employees' Federal Income Tax Pay. $600, Employees' State Income Tax Pay. $240, Social Security Tax Pay. $248, Medicare Tax Pay. $58, Cash in Bank $2,854; Check 5504
Mar. 30: Dr. Accts. Pay./Carter Office Supply $125; Cr. Cash in Bank $125; Check 5505

Analyze: $2,854

Chapter 15, Problem 15A Recording Purchases and Cash Payment Transactions

Business transactions for the month of March for T-Shirt Trends are presented below. A partial general ledger appears in your working papers.

Instructions On the form provided in your working papers, record March transactions on page 11 of the general journal.

Date	Transactions
Mar. 2	Issued Check 5500 for $6,790 to Dancing Wind Clothing Manufacturers in payment of their $7,000 invoice less a 3% cash discount.
4	Purchased $2,800 in merchandise on account from Wilmington Shirt Factory, Invoice WSF123, terms 2/10, n/30.
6	Wrote Check 5501 for $180 to Mario's Trucking for delivery of merchandise shipped from Wilmington Shirt Factory, FOB shipping point.
8	Received a credit allowance of $300 from Wilmington Shirt Factory for damaged merchandise, issued Debit Memo 44.
10	Received a premium notice from Keystone Insurance Company for $3,400, issued Check 5502.
12	Bought $175 in supplies from Carter Office Supply on account, Invoice 97, terms n/30.
14	Paid Wilmington Shirt Factory the $2,500 balance owed less a 2% cash discount, Check 5503.
19	Returned $50 in supplies to Carter Office Supply, issued Debit Memorandum 45.
25	Paid employees gross earnings of $4,000. Rates for taxes withheld are: Employees' Federal Income Tax, 15%; State Income Tax, 6%; Social Security Tax, 6.2%; and Medicare Tax, 1.45%. Issued Check 5504 for the net amount.
30	Wrote Check 5505 to Carter Office Supply for the amount due on our account.

Analyze: How much was the net paid to employees on March 25?

Chapter 16, Problem 16A Recording and Posting Sales, Cash Receipts, and General Journal Transactions

T-Shirt Trends, a retail merchandising store, uses special journals for recording its business transactions. On May 1, the store had the following balances in its general ledger and accounts receivable subsidiary ledger accounts.

Continued

SOLUTION NOTES

General Ledger	
101 Cash in Bank	$ 4,700
115 Accounts Receivable	7,250
135 Supplies	300
215 Sales Tax Payable	600
401 Sales	40,000
405 Sales Discounts	1,500
410 Sales Returns and Allowances	500

Accounts Receivable Subsidiary Ledger	
HAL Hal's Fitness Studios	$ 1,500
HIO Dave Hioki	200
MOR Gabriela Morales	100
ROU Roundabout Fashions	2,000
SAM Samstead Fashions	2,500
SAN Sandpiper Sports Club	900
WIL Virginia Williams	50

Instructions On the forms provided in your working papers:

(1) Open the accounts and enter beginning balances in T-Shirt Trends' general ledger.
(2) Open the customers' accounts in the accounts receivable subsidiary ledger and record the beginning balances.
(3) Record the following transactions in the sales journal (page 9), the cash receipts journal (page 10), and the general journal (page 2).
(4) Post to the customer accounts daily from the journals.
(5) Post the entries in the General Credit column of the cash receipts journal daily.
(6) Post general journal entries daily.
(7) Foot, prove, total, and rule the sales and cash receipts journals.
(8) Post the column totals from the special journals.
(9) Prepare a schedule of accounts receivable.

Date	Transactions
May 1	Received a check for $50 from Virginia Williams in payment of her account, Receipt 202.
3	Sandpiper Sports Club sent a check for $882 in payment of their $900 account less 2% cash discount, Receipt 203.
5	Sold Virginia Williams $300 in merchandise plus 5% sales tax of $15, Sales Slip 404.
7	Received a check for $1,470 from Hal's Fitness Studios in payment of their $1,500 account balance less 2% cash discount, Receipt 204.
9	Virginia Williams returned $100 in merchandise plus sales tax of $5, issued Credit Memo 50.
11	Sold $700 in merchandise on account to Sandpiper Sports Club plus sales tax of $35, terms, 2/10, n/30, Sales Slip 405.
13	Dave Hioki sent a check for $100 to apply on his account, Receipt 205.
14	Received $25 from the sale of supplies to Hanson's Market, Receipt 206.
15	Cash sales amounted to $2,000 plus sales tax of $100, Tape 27.
15	Bankcard sales were $1,500 plus sales tax of $75, Tape 27.
18	Issued Credit Memo 51 to Roundabout Fashions for $210 which included $200 in defective merchandise and a sales tax of $10.
	Continued

PROBLEMS APPENDIX G

Problem 16A (Answers) Recording and Posting Sales, Cash Receipts, and General Journal Transactions

Sales Journal column totals:
Sales Cr. $4,200
Sales Tax Pay. Cr. $210
Accts. Rec. Dr. $4,410

Cash Receipts Journal column totals:
General Cr. $25
General Dr. $3,500
Sales Tax Pay. Cr. $175
Accts. Rec. Cr. $4,800
Sales Disc. Dr. $48
Cash in Bank Dr. $8,452

General Journal entries:
May 9: Dr. Sales Ret. & Allow. $100, Sales Tax Pay. $5; Cr. Accts. Rec./ Virginia Williams $105; Credit Memo 50
May 18: Dr. Sales Ret. & Allow. $200, Sales Tax Pay. $10; Cr. Accts. Rec./ Roundabout Fashions $210; Credit Memo 51

Ending debit balances:
Cash in Bank $13,152
Accts. Rec. $6,545
Supplies $275
Sales Disc. $970
Sales Ret. and Allow. $800
Accts. Rec./Hal's Fitness Studios $3,150
Accts. Rec./Dave Hioki $100
Accts. Rec./Gabriella Morales $210
Accts. Rec./Roundabout Fashions $890
Accts. Rec./Samstead Fashions $1,250
Accts. Rec./Sandpiper Sports Club $735
Accts. Rec./Virginia Williams $210

Ending credit balances:
Sales Tax Pay. $795
Sales $44,200

Analyze: $6,545; Yes

CRITICAL THINKING ACTIVITY

Advantages/Disadvantages of Bank Credit Cards When a business accepts a bank credit card for payment of a credit sale, the business usually pays between 2 and 6 percent of the sale amount to the bank that issued the credit card. What are the advantages to the business of allowing customers to use bank credit cards for their purchases? (When a business accepts a bank credit card, the business can treat the sale as a cash sale since its money comes from the bank. The bank, rather than the business, has the responsibility of collecting the money from the customer. A disadvantage is that the business must pay a fee to the bank for taking on the responsibility of collecting from the customer.)

Problem 17A (Answers) Recording Special Journal and General Journal Transactions

Sales Journal column totals:
Sales credit $5,000
Sales Tax Pay. credit $250
Accts. Rec. debit $5,250

Cash Receipts Journal column totals:
General credit $75
Sales credit $11,700
Sales Tax Pay. credit $585
Accts. Rec. credit $4,825
Sales Disc. debit $86
Cash in Bank debit $17,099

Purchases Journal column totals:
Accts. Pay. credit $12,150
Purchases debit $10,000
General debit $2,150

Cash Payment Journal column totals:
General debit $5,400
General credit $513
Accts. Pay. debit $6,425
Purchases Disc. credit $122
Cash in Bank credit $11,190

Date	Transactions
22	Sold $3,000 in merchandise on account to Hal's Fitness Studios plus 5% sales tax of $150, Sales Slip 406.
23	Samstead Fashions sent us a check for $1,250 to apply to their account, Receipt 207.
24	Received a check for $100 from Gabriela Morales in payment of her account, Receipt 208.
27	Sold Gabriela Morales $200 in merchandise plus 5% sales tax of $10, Sales Slip 407.
28	Roundabout Fashions sent us a check for $900 to apply on their account, Receipt 209.

Analyze: What is the ending balance in the **Accounts Receivable** account? Does this agree with the total of subsidiary ledgers?

Chapter 17, Problem 17A Recording Special Journal and General Journal Transactions

T-Shirt Trends, a retail merchandising business, uses special journals to record its business transactions.

Instructions On the forms provided in your working papers:

(1) Record the July transactions in the sales journal (page 15), cash receipts journal (page 16), purchases journal (page 15), cash payments journal (page 16), and general journal (page 3).
(2) Foot, prove, total, and rule the special journals.
(3) Prove cash. The beginning cash in bank balance is $7,500. The check stub balance at the end of the month is $13,394.

Date	Transactions
July 2	Sold $500 in merchandise on account to Dave Hioki plus 5% sales tax, Sales Slip 333.
2	Purchased $1,400 in merchandise on account from Cherokee Productions, Inc., Invoice 7001, terms 2/10, n/30.
3	Issued Check 535 for $1,960 in payment of Dancing Wind Clothing Manufacturers $2,000 invoice less a 2% discount.
4	Received $1,764 from Hal's Fitness Studios in payment of our $1,800 invoice less a 2% discount, Receipt 200.
5	Issued Credit Memo 27 to Gabriela Morales for the return of $100 in merchandise plus $5 sales tax.
6	Purchased $2,000 in store equipment on account from Carter Office Supply, Invoice CO123, terms n/30.
6	Received $2,450 from Sandpiper Sports Club in payment of our $2,500 invoice less a 2% discount, Receipt 201.
7	Sold $1,000 in merchandise on account plus 5% sales tax to Virginia Williams, Sales Slip 334.

Continued

SOLUTION NOTES

Date	Transactions
7	Issued Debit Memo 14 for $300 to Wilmington Shirt Factory for credit taken on damaged merchandise.
8	Wrote Check 536 to Chapel Hills Realtors in payment of monthly rent of $900.
8	Sold old office equipment for $75 cash to Ann Martin, an employee, Receipt 202.
9	Purchased $3,000 in merchandise on account from CompuRite Solutions, Invoice CR79, terms 2/10, n/30.
10	Sold $3,500 in merchandise plus 5% sales tax on account to Roundabout Fashions, Sales Slip 335.
12	Bought $150 in supplies from Palace Party Supplies, on account, Invoice 876.
13	Issued Check 537 for $1,600 to Academy Insurance Company for annual business insurance premium.
14	Wrote Check 538 to CompuRite Solutions for $2,940 in payment of Invoice CR79 for $3,000 less 2% discount.
15	Cash sales amounted to $3,000 plus 5% sales tax, Tape 29.
15	Bankcard sales were $5,000 plus 5% sales tax, Tape 29.
18	Purchased $1,100 in merchandise on account from Sullivan Screen Printers, Invoice 423, terms 2/10, n/30.
20	Purchased $750 in merchandise for cash from Cherokee Productions, Inc., Check 539.
22	Paid the monthly utility bill, $150, Check 540.
23	Purchased $4,500 in merchandise on account from Dancing Wind Clothing Manufacturers, Invoice 777, terms, 2/10, n/30.
24	Received $510 from Dave Hioki to apply on his account, Receipt 203.
24	Wrote Check 541 to Sullivan Screen Printers for $1,078 in payment of Invoice 423 for $1,100 less a 2% discount.
26	Issued Debit Memo 15 for $200 to Dancing Wind Clothing Manufacturers for the return of merchandise.
31	Cash sales amounted to $2,200 plus $110 sales tax, Tape 30.
31	Bank card sales amounted to $1,500 plus $75.00 sales tax, Tape 30.
31	Wrote Check 542 to pay the payroll of $2,000 (Gross Earnings) for the pay period ended July 31. The following amounts were withheld: employees' federal income taxes, $300; FICA taxes, $124 for social security and $29 for Medicare; employees' state income taxes, $60.
31	Recorded the employer's payroll taxes (FICA tax rate, 6.2% for social security, and 1.45% for Medicare; federal unemployment tax rate, 0.8%; and state unemployment rate, 5.4%).

Analyze: In the purchases journal, what is the total of the Purchases Debit column?

Problem 17A (Answers) Recording Special Journal and General Journal Transactions (cont'd)

General Journal entries:

July 5: Dr. Sales Ret. and Allow. $100, Sales Tax Pay. $5; Cr. Accts. Rec./ Gabriela Morales $105; Credit Memo 27

July 7: Dr. Accts. Pay./Wilmington Shirt Factory $300; Cr. Purchases Ret. and Allow. $300; Debit Memo 14

July 26: Dr. Accts. Pay./Dancing Wind Clothing Manufacturers $200; Cr. Purchases Ret. and Allow. $200; Debit Memo 15

July 31: Payroll Tax Exp. $277; Cr. Social Security Tax Pay. $124, Medicare Tax Pay. $29, Federal Unemployment Tax Pay. $16, State Unemployment Tax Pay. $108; July 31 Payroll

Ending Cash $13,394

Analyze: $10,000

ACCOUNTING ISSUES

Recording Environmental Remediation Liabilities When a company is responsible for environmental clean-up, the exact amounts for the clean-up may not be known for many years. Since the amounts are not fixed and are not determinable at a specific time, companies need guidance regarding when and how these environmental remediation liabilities should be reflected on their balance sheets. In 1996 the Accounting Standards Executive Committee of the AICPA issued a statement of position to provide CPAs guidance in helping their clients determine how the liabilities should be measured and when the liabilities should be recognized in financial statments and related disclosures.

PROBLEMS APPENDIX G

Problem 18A (Answers) Calculating Adjustments and Preparing the Ten-Column Work Sheet
Adjusted Trial Balance column totals $229,288

Net Income $12,836

Analyze: $7,768

Problem 19A (Answers) Preparing Financial Statements
Net Income $28,145

Total Assets $108,987

Ending Retained Earnings $38,956

Analyze: $38,956

Problem 20A (Answers) Journalizing Closing Entries
Dec. 31: Dr. Sales $94,412, Purchases Disc. $750, Purchases Ret. and Allow. $455; Cr. Income Summary $95,617
Dec. 31: Dr. Income Summary $72,573; Cr. Sales Disc. $867, Sales Ret. and Allow. $1,735, Purchases $35,000, Transportation In $1,700, Advertising Exp. $900, Bankcard Fees Exp. $647, Federal Corp. Income Tax Exp. $5,343, Insurance Exp. $1,200, Miscellaneous Exp. $369, Rent Exp. $18,000, Supplies Exp. $2,612, Utilities Exp. $4,200
Dec. 31: Dr. Income Summary $23,044; Cr. Retained Earnings $23,044

Analyze: $23,044

Chapter 18, Problem 18A Calculating Adjustments and Preparing the Ten-Column Work Sheet

A partially completed work sheet for T-Shirt Trends is shown in your working papers. Adjustments need to be made to the following items at year-end.

Data for Adjustments	
Merchandise Inventory, December 31	$47,394
Supplies on hand, December 31	678
Insurance premium expired during the period	1,260
Additional federal corporate income tax owed	168

Instructions On the form provided in your working papers, complete the December 31 work sheet for T-Shirt Trends. Make the necessary adjustments on the work sheet.

Analyze: What is the total of the Adjustments columns on the work sheet?

Chapter 19, Problem 19A Preparing Financial Statements

The completed work sheet for T-Shirt Trends for the year ended December 31 appears in your working papers.

Instructions On the forms provided in your working papers, prepare the following financial statements:
(1) The income statement for the fiscal year ended December 31.
(2) A statement of retained earnings.
(3) A balance sheet.

Analyze: What is the balance in the **Retained Earnings** account at December 31?

Chapter 20, Problem 20A Journalizing Closing Entries

The account balances for T-Shirt Trends appear in your working papers as of December 31.

Instructions On the form provided in your working papers, journalize all the closing entries on page 17 in the general journal.

Analyze: What was the balance in the **Income Summary** account before it was closed to **Retained Earnings**?

Chapter 21, Problem 21A Recording Stockholders' Equity Transactions

T-Shirt Trends was organized as a publicly held corporation on September 1 and authorized to issue 10,000 shares of $100 par, $8 preferred stock, and 25,000 shares of $50 par common stock.

Continued

ACCOUNTING ISSUES

The SEC The Securities and Exchange Commission (SEC) is an independent, nonpartisan regulatory agency that is responsible for administering the federal securities laws. The purpose of these laws is to protect investors in securities markets. The laws also ensure that investors have access to disclosure of all material information concerning publicly traded securities. In addition, the SEC regulates firms engaged in the purchase or sale of securities, people who provide investment advice, and investment companies.

Instructions On the form provided in your working papers, record the following transactions on page 1 of the general journal.

Date	Transactions
2007	
Sept. 1	Issued 4,000 shares of $8 preferred stock at $100 per share, Receipt 101.
12	Issued 12,000 shares of common stock at $50 per share, Receipt 102.
Nov. 15	Received $52.50 per share for 2,500 shares of common stock issued, Receipt 215.
Dec. 16	Received $5,000 for 50 shares of $8 preferred stock issued, Receipt 298.
2008	
Mar. 24	Issued 1,000 shares of common stock at $55 per share, Receipt 389.
Aug.15	Declared a dividend of $32,400 on 4,050 shares of $8 preferred stock outstanding, payable on September 15 to stockholders of record on September 1, Memorandum 316.
15	Declared cash dividend of 25¢ per share on 15,500 shares of common stock outstanding, payable on September 30 to stockholders of record on September 1, Memorandum 317.
Sept.15	Paid preferred stock dividend declared August 15, Check 1763.
30	Paid common stock dividend declared August 15, Check 1802.
Dec. 31	Prepared the closing entries in the general journal to close **Income Summary** for the net income of $102,600 and to close the two **Dividends** accounts.

Analyze: How much was the total dividend declared on preferred stock on August 15? How much was declared on the common stock on August 15?

Chapter 22, Problem 22A Maintaining a Petty Cash Register

Maureen Miller operates T-Shirt Trends, a T-shirt specialty business. She established a petty cash fund on February 1 by writing Check 336 for $100. She also records all petty cash disbursements in a petty cash register. Petty cash disbursements are usually made for expenses such as office supplies, delivery expense, miscellaneous expenses, and advertising expense.

Instructions On the forms provided in your working papers:

(1) Record the establishment of the petty cash fund on the first line of the petty cash register, page 1.
(2) Record each of the following petty cash disbursements in the petty cash register.
(3) Foot, prove, total, and rule the petty cash register at the end of the month.
(4) Reconcile the petty cash fund. An actual cash count of the fund shows a balance of $5.68.
(5) Check 362 was issued to replenish the petty cash fund. Record the replenishment information in the petty cash register.

Continued 

PROBLEMS APPENDIX G

Problem 21A (Answers) Recording Stockholders' Equity Transactions

2007:

Sept. 1: Dr. Cash in Bank $400,000; Cr. $8 Preferred Stock $400,000; Receipt 101

Sept. 12: Dr. Cash in Bank $600,000; Cr. Common Stock $600,000; Receipt 102

Nov. 15: Dr. Cash in Bank $131,250; Cr. Common Stock $125,000, Paid-in Capital in Excess of Par—Common $6,250; Receipt 215

Dec. 16: Dr. Cash in Bank $5,000; Cr. $8 Preferred Stock $5,000; Receipt 298

2008:

Mar. 24: Dr. Cash in Bank $55,000; Cr. Common Stock $50,000, Paid-in Capital in Excess of Par—Common $5,000; Receipt 389

Aug. 15: Dr. Dividends—Preferred $32,400; Cr. Dividends Pay.—Preferred $32,400; Memorandum 316

Aug. 15: Dr. Dividends—Common $3,875; Cr. Dividends Pay.—Common $3,875; Memorandum 317

Sept. 15: Dr. Dividends Pay.—Preferred $32,400; Cr. Cash in Bank $32,400; Check 1763

Sept. 30: Dr. Dividends Pay.—Common $3,875; Cr. Cash in Bank $3,875; Check 1802

Dec. 31: Dr. Income Summary $102,600; Cr. Retained Earnings $102,600

Dec. 31: Dr. Retained Earnings $36,275; Cr. Dividends—Preferred $32,400, Dividends—Common $3,875

Analyze: $32,400; $3,875

COOPERATIVE LEARNING ACTIVITY

Make and Defend Assign students to groups of three and ask them to look at the stock listings in the financial pages of a daily newspaper such as *The Wall Street Journal* or have them find stock listings at a Web site. Ask each group to select three companies and then compare the stock price and dividends paid for each company. Each group should decide which stock they would buy. In making their decisions, groups should consider the dividends paid and the price-earnings ratio (current market value per share divided by earnings per share). Ask each group to present and defend its decision before the class.

Problem 22A (Answers)
Maintaining a Petty Cash Register
Petty Cash Register totals:
Payments $90.07
Office Supplies $25.55
Delivery Exp. $19.80
Misc. Exp. $17.52
General $27.20

Analyze: Short by $4.25; expense.

Problem 23A (Answers)
Calculating and Recording Depreciation Expense
1. Annual depreciation $26,000
2. Dec. 31: Dr. Depreciation Expense—Delivery Truck $6,500, Cr. Accumulated Depreciation—Delivery Truck $6,500
   Dec. 31: Dr. Depreciation Expense—Delivery Truck $26,000, Cr. Accumulated Depreciation—Delivery Truck $26,000
3 (a) Cost minus estimated disposal value divided by useful life times partial year—$78,900 − $900 = $78,000 ÷ 3 = $26,000 × 1/4 = $6,500
  (b) $72,400
  (c) $46,400
  (d) Annual depreciation times partial year

Analyze: $78,000; Accumulated Depreciation—Delivery Truck

Date	Transactions
Feb. 1	Paid $1.20 for postage due on a letter, Voucher 101.
3	Purchased a $9 ad in the *Towne Sentinel* paper, Voucher 102.
5	Bought a ream of typing paper for $4.75, issued Voucher 103.
6	Paid $6 for a mailgram, Voucher 104.
8	Issued Voucher 105 for $9.90 to Express Couriers in payment for the delivery of packages.
10	Paid the newscarrier $4.10 for daily newspapers and issued Voucher 106.
13	Bought pens, pencils, and memo pads for $6.60, Voucher 107.
15	Purchased a $9.50 advertisement in a local trade journal, Voucher 108.
19	Issued Voucher 109 for $8.70 for office supplies.
22	Express Couriers delivered financial data from a client, $9.90, Voucher 110.
26	Issued Voucher 111 for $2.12 for additional postage due on mail.
27	Bought an ad in the *Towne Sentinel* for $8.70 and issued Voucher 112.
28	Purchased a typewriter ribbon for $5.50, issuing Voucher 113.
28	Voided Voucher 114 due to an error.
28	Issued Voucher 115 for $4.10 to the newscarrier.

Analyze: At the end of February, was cash short or over? By what amount? Should this be recorded as a revenue or an expense?

SPREADSHEET SMART GUIDE

Step-by-Step Instructions: Problem 23A

1. Select the spreadsheet template for Problem 23A.
2. Enter your name and the date in the spaces provided on the template.
3. Complete the spreadsheet using the instructions in your working papers.
4. Print the spreadsheet and proof your work.
5. Save your work and exit the spreadsheet program.

Chapter 23, Problem 23A Calculating and Recording Depreciation Expense

The T-Shirt Trends Company purchased a delivery truck on October 12, 2004, at a cost of $78,900. The delivery truck has an estimated useful life of three years and an estimated disposal value of $900.

Instructions On the forms provided in your working papers:

(1) Prepare a depreciation schedule for the delivery truck using the straight-line method.
(2) Record the following transactions on general journal page 41. Post the transactions to the ledger accounts provided.
(3) Answer the following questions.
  (a) How did you determine the depreciation from October 12 to December 31?
  (b) What was the book value of the truck on December 31, 2004?
  (c) What was the book value of the truck on December 31, 2005?
  (d) How did you determine the annual depreciation on December 31, 2005?

Date	Transactions
2004	
Dec. 31	Recorded the adjusting entry for the year's depreciation expense on the delivery truck.
2005	
Dec. 31	Recorded the adjusting entry for the year's depreciation expense on the delivery truck.

HOME AND COMMUNITY CONNECTIONS ACTIVITY

Keeping a Home Inventory Many insurance companies recommend that homeowners keep a personal inventory of all their valuable assets. Ask students to check with their family to see if such an inventory exists. If it does, have them ask where the inventory is kept for protection. How often is it updated? Have pictures been taken of valuable jewelry or keepsakes? What does the homeowner's insurance policy allow for replacement of items that become lost, stolen, or destroyed by a fire or flood? Ask students to write a paragraph on their findings.

Analyze: How much depreciation expense will be recorded over the useful life of the asset? Which account will show the depreciation recorded over the asset's useful life?

Chapter 24, Problem 24A Calculating and Recording Uncollectible Accounts Expense

T-Shirt Trends uses the allowance method of accounting for uncollectible accounts. At the end of the fiscal period, the following accounts appeared on T-Shirt's trial balance.

Accounts Receivable	$ 18,647.25
Allowance for Uncollectible Accounts	1,060.50
Sales	452,612.00
Sales Discounts	5,431.35
Sales Returns and Allowances	13,578.36
Uncollectible Accounts Expense	0.00

Instructions On the forms provided in your working papers:

(1) Determine the amount of the adjustment for uncollectible accounts for the fiscal period ended December 31. Management estimates that uncollectible accounts will be 1.25% of net sales.
(2) Journalize the adjusting entry in the general journal, page 10.
(3) Post the adjusting entry to the general ledger accounts.
(4) Determine the book value of accounts receivable.

Analyze: When an account is written off in the next fiscal period, what account will be debited?

Chapter 25, Problem 25A Accounting for Inventories

The Shoooot-It Camera Shop uses a one-year fiscal period beginning January 1. At the beginning of the fiscal period, the shop had a beginning inventory of film valued at $867.90 (526 rolls at $1.65 per roll). During the year, the shop made the following purchases:

January 13	400 rolls of film @ $1.67	=	$ 668
March 2	600 rolls of film @ $1.73	=	1,038
April 14	300 rolls of film @ $1.76	=	528
July 8	700 rolls of film @ $1.79	=	1,253
September 3	200 rolls of film @ $1.81	=	362
November 19	300 rolls of film @ $1.83	=	549
Totals	2,500 rolls		$4,398

There were 621 rolls of film in inventory at the end of the fiscal year.

Instructions On the form provided in your working papers, calculate the cost of the ending inventory using the specific identification, FIFO, LIFO, and weighted average cost methods. For the specific identification method, 165 of the rolls were purchased on September 3 and 456 were purchased on November 19.

Analyze: Which inventory valuation method gives the highest value to Shoooot-It's ending inventory?

Problem 24A (Answers) Calculating and Recording Uncollectible Accounts Expense

1. Uncollectible Accts. Exp. $5,420.03
2. Dr. Uncollectible Accounts Expense $5,420.03; Cr. Allow. for Uncollectible Accounts $5,420.03
3. Balance Allowance for Uncollectible Accounts $6,480.53; balance Uncollectible Accounts Expense $5,420.03
4. Book value of Accts. Rec. $12,166.72

Analyze: Allowance for Uncollectible Accounts

Problem 25A (Answers) Accounting for Inventories

Cost of Ending Inventory:
Specific identification $1,114.89
FIFO $1,127.59
LIFO $1,026.55
Weighted average $1,080.54

Analyze: Specific identification

MAKING CONNECTIONS TO DAILY LIFE

Point-of-Sale Information Ask students to bring in cash register receipts identifying products that they have purchased. Explain that many cash registers are point-of-sale terminals through which inventory cost records are updated at the time of the sale. Have students look at their receipts to determine whether they contain inventory numbers that help the store track inventory sold. Ask students to name local businesses that use point-of-sale terminals.

PROBLEMS APPENDIX G

Problem 26A (Answers) Calculating Current and Future Interest

1. Maturity date Jan. 9, current year $5.70, following year $2.44
2. Maturity date Jan. 20, current year $9.21, following year $4.60
3. Maturity date Jan. 8, current year $384.16, following year $37.48
4. Maturity date Feb. 3, current year $42.74, following year $55.89
5. Maturity date Mar. 10, current year $136.23, following year $184.32
6. Maturity date Mar. 7, current year $65.59, following year $37.97
7. Maturity date Jan. 26, current year $79.56, following year $47.02
8. Maturity date Apr. 1, current year $19.95, following year $19.95
9. Maturity date Mar. 1, current year $10, following year $20
10. Maturity date May 1, current year $90, following year $72

Analyze: The notes maturing on Feb. 3, Mar. 1, and Mar. 10 will have more interest in the following year.

Problem 26B (Answers) Recording Noninterest Bearing Notes Payable

Jan. 15: Dr. Cash in Bank $11,644.93, Disc. on Notes Pay. $355.07; Cr. Notes Pay. $12,000; Note 45

Apr. 15: Dr. Notes Pay. $12,000, Interest Exp. $355.07; Cr. Cash in Bank $12,000, Disc. on Notes Pay. $355.07; Check 2561

Oct. 31: Dr. Cash in Bank $17,230.68, Disc. on Notes Pay. $769.32; Cr. Notes Pay. $18,000; Note 46

Dec. 31: Dr. Interest Exp. $391.07; Cr. Disc. on Notes Pay. $391.07

Analyze: $746.14

SPREADSHEET SMART GUIDE

Step-by-Step Instructions: Problem 26A

1. Select the spreadsheet template for Problem 26A.
2. Enter your name and the date in the spaces provided on the template.
3. Complete the spreadsheet using the instructions in your working papers.
4. Print the spreadsheet and proof your work.
5. Save your work and exit the spreadsheet program.

Spreadsheet PROBLEM Chapter 26, Problem 26A Calculating Current and Future Interest

Frequently, notes that are issued or received in one fiscal period do not mature until the next fiscal period. As a result, the interest expense paid or the interest income received applies to two different fiscal periods. Listed below is the information for 10 different notes.

Instructions On the form provided in your working papers, determine the following for each note.

(1) Determine the maturity date. Assume February has 28 days.

(2) Determine what portion of the interest applies to the current year and what portion of the interest applies to the following year. December 31 is the end of the fiscal period.

	Amount	Issue Date	Interest Rate	Term
1.	$ 1,100	December 10	9%	30 days
2.	700	November 21	12%	60 days
3.	17,100	October 10	10%	90 days
4.	4,000	December 5	15%	60 days
5.	15,000	November 10	6.5%	120 days
6.	3,000	September 8	7%	180 days
7.	6,600	November 17	10%	70 days
8.	840	October 1	9.5%	6 months
9.	1,200	December 1	10%	3 months
10.	2,700	August 1	8%	9 months

Analyze: Which of the notes will have more interest expense next year than this year?

Chapter 26, Problem 26B Recording Noninterest Bearing Notes Payable

Your company, National Paper Supplies, frequently borrows money for short periods from First Bank by issuing promissory notes.

Instructions In your working papers, record the following transactions on page 6 of the general journal.

Date	Transactions
Jan. 15	Borrowed $12,000 from First Bank by issuing a 90-day, noninterest-bearing note payable that the bank discounted at 12%, Note 45.
Apr. 15	Issued Check 2561 for $12,000 in payment of the note issued Jan.15 and recorded the interest expense.
Oct. 31	Borrowed $18,000 from First Bank by issuing a 120-day, noninterest-bearing note payable that the bank discounted at 13%, Note 46.
Dec. 31	Made an adjusting entry to record the accrued interest expense for Note 46 at year-end.

Analyze: What was the total interest expense incurred in the current year for Notes 45 and 46?

COOPERATIVE LEARNING ACTIVITY

Categorize Categorizing accounts helps in preparing the financial statements. Assign students in pairs and give them a long list of account titles and balances. Ask each pair to analyze, classify, and organize the accounts, then prepare a balance sheet and income statement. After pairs prepare financial statements, have each pair work with another pair in the class to compare their answers. If the solutions do not agree, the pairs are to work together to find and correct the errors.

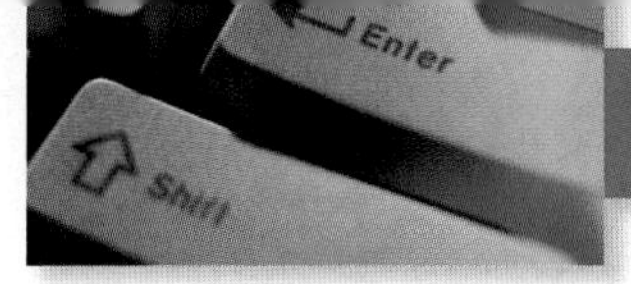

Chapter 27, Problem 27A Recording Partners' Investments

On June 15, Walter Cohen and Janice Connor agreed to combine their individual sole proprietorships into one firm organized as a partnership called Cohen & Connor Legal Services. The partners were to invest all the assets of their two former businesses. Those assets are listed below.

	Cohen	Connor
Cash	$247,000	$517,500
Accounts Receivable	78,000	
Merchandise Inventory	123,000	
Equipment	154,500	

Instructions Prepare the general journal entries (page 1) required to record the partners' investments. The source document is Memorandum 1.

Analyze: What is the total of all the assets contributed to the new partnership?

Chapter 28, Problem 28A Liquidation of a Partnership

The partnership of Joyce, Jane, and Jill is dissolving. The partnership account balances as of November 30, 2004 are:

Cash	$ 8,000	Accounts Payable	$ 8,000
Accounts Receivable	16,000	Joyce, Capital	10,800
Inventory	8,000	Jane, Capital	13,200
Equipment	3,000	Jill, Capital	3,000

Profits and losses are shared 4:5:1 to Joyce, Jane, and Jill respectively.

Date	Transactions
Dec. 1	The accounts receivable are sold for $15,000.
Dec. 8	The inventory is sold for $7,000.
Dec. 15	The equipment is sold for $5,000.
Dec. 23	The accounts payable are paid in full.
Dec. 24	The balance of cash is distributed to the partners.

Instructions Prepare the entries required to liquidate the partnership. Start with general journal page 213.

Analyze: What was the gain or loss on any of the assets that were sold?

Problem 27A (Answers) Recording Partners' Investments

June 15: Dr. Cash in Bank $247,000, Accts. Rec. $78,000, Merchandise Inventory $123,000, Equip. $154,500; Cr. Walter Cohen, Capital $602,500; Memorandum 1

June 15: Dr. Cash in Bank $517,500; Cr. Janice Connor, Capital $517,500; Memorandum 1

Analyze: $1,120,000

Problem 28A (Answers) Financial Statements for a Partnership

Dec. 1: Dr. Cash in Bank $15,000, Joyce, Capital $400, Jane, Capital $500, Jill, Capital $100; Cr. Accts. Rec. $16,000

Dec. 8: Dr. Cash in Bank $7,000, Joyce, Capital $400, Jane, Capital $500, Jill, Capital $100; Cr. Inventory $8,000

Dec. 15: Dr. Cash in Bank $5,000; Cr. Joyce, Capital $800, Jane, Capital $1,000, Jill, Capital $200, Equip. $3,000

Dec. 23: Dr. Accts. Pay. $8,000; Cr. Cash in Bank $8,000

Dec. 24: Dr. Joyce, Capital $10,800, Jane, Capital $13,500, Jill, Capital $2,700; Cr. Cash in Bank $27,000

Analyze: There was a $2,000 gain on the sale of equipment.

COOPERATIVE LEARNING ACTIVITY

Pairs Check Sam and Charles began a partnership. Using a fractional-share basis, calculate how the net income of $30,565 should be distributed under each of the independent situations described here. (a) Sam and Charles invested equal amounts. (b) Sam invested 3/4 of the assets and Charles invested 1/4 of the assets. (c) Sam invested $30,000 and Charles invested $90,000. (Allow students to compare answers with a partner. (a) Sam $15,282.50; Charles $15,282.50; (b) Sam, $22,923.75; Charles, $7,641.25; (c) Sam, $7,641.25; Charles, $22,923.75.)

APPENDIX H

Answers to *Check Your Understanding* Problems

Chapter 1

Problem 1-1
Perform an honest analysis of likes and dislikes. Use the chart on page 8 to help identify skills and traits you possess.

Problem 1-2
Use the personal career profile form (Figure 1-1) as a reference for the types of information. List personal information (values, interests, skills, etc.) and then select three possible careers.

Problem 1-3
The possibility for individuals with accounting degrees vary but include careers as: tax accountants, auditors, management accountants, controllers, or chief financial officers.

Problem 1-4
For the accountants mentioned in the section:

Drew Taylor – Interested in working with numbers and music.
Maya Cruz – Involved in environmental causes, studied accounting.
Shelley Hale – Interested in fashion, good with math and logic.

Problem 1-5

PricewaterhouseCoopers	www.pwcglobal.com
Deloitte & Touche	www.deloitte.com/us
Ernst & Young	www.ey.com
KPMG	www.kpmg.com

Problem 1-6
Use local Yellow Pages to find information.

Chapter 2

Problem 2-1
Perform an honest analysis of personal traits. Try to relate the answers to personal activities and experiences that correspond with entrepreneurship.

Problem 2-2
The situations such as these have opposing viewpoints. The drop in sales could be a sign that some improvements are in order. On the other hand, some owners will be reluctant to invest more money in a business where sales are down. More information will be needed in order to make a final decision.

Problem 2-3
Greenwood Sky Divers is the name of the business entity. It has been in business for six years, and is a "going concern." The accounting period for Greenwood Sky Divers is one year.

Chapter 3

Problem 3-1

1. $10,000
2. $26,000
3. $3,000
4. $26,000
5. $6,000
6. $13,000
7. $16,000
8. $8,000
9. $21,000
10. $20,000
11. $35,000
12. $4,500

Problem 3-2

1. Cash in Bank increased $30,000. Jan Swift, Capital increased $30,000.
2. Office Equipment increased $700. Jan Swift, Capital increased $700.
3. Cash in Bank decreased $4,000. Computer Equipment increased $4,000.
4. Office Equipment increased $5,000. Accounts Payable increased $5,000.
5. Accounts Receivable increased by $700. Office Equipment decreased $700.
6. Cash in Bank decreased $2,000. Accounts Payable decreased $2,000.

Problem 3-3

1. Cash in Bank decreased by $50. Jan Swift, Capital decreased by $50.

2. Cash in Bank increased by $1,000. Jan Swift, Capital increased by $1,000.
3. Cash in Bank decreased by $600. Jan Swift, Capital decreased by $600.
4. Cash in Bank decreased by $800. Jan Swift, Capital decreased by $800.
5. Cash in Bank increased by $200. Accounts Receivable decreased by $200.

Chapter 4

Problem 4-1

Office Equipment – asset, debit, credit, debit
Accounts Payable – liability, credit, debit, credit
Accounts Receivable – asset, debit, credit, debit
R. Lewis, Capital – owner's equity, credit, debit, credit

Problem 4-2

1a. The asset Office Equipment is increased. Increases in assets are recorded as debits.
b. The liability Accounts Payable is increased. Increases in liabilities are recorded as credits.
2a. The asset Office Furniture is increased. Increases in assets are recorded as debits.
b. The owner's capital account Alice Roberts, Capital is increased. Increases in the owner's capital account are recorded as credits.
3a. The liability Accounts Payable is decreased. Decreases in liabilities are recorded as debits.
b. The asset Cash in Bank is decreased. Decreases in assets are recorded as credits.

Chapter 5

Problem 5-1

Cash in Bank—asset, debit, credit, debit
Accounts Receivable—asset, debit, credit, debit
Airplanes—asset, debit, credit, debit
Accounts Payable—liability, credit, debit, credit
Caroline Palmer, Capital—owner's equity, credit, debit,credit
Caroline Palmer, Withdrawals—owner's equity, debit,credit, debit
Flying Fees—revenue, credit, debit, credit
Advertising Expense—expense, debit, credit, debit
Food Expense—expense, debit, credit, debit
Fuel and Oil Expense—expense, debit, credit, debit
Repairs Expense—expense, debit, credit, debit

Problem 5-2

1. Dr. Utilities Expense; Cr. Cash in Bank
2. Dr. Accounts Receivable; Cr. Service Fees
3. Dr. John Albers, Withdrawals; Cr. Cash in Bank
4. Dr. Advertising Expense; Cr. Cash in Bank

Chapter 6

Problem 6-1

1. JayMax Office Suppliers
2. Dario's Accounting Firm
3. April 9, 20--
4. $479
5. Fax Machine
6. $299
7. Payable in 30 days

Problem 6-2

Step 1 D
Step 2 F
Step 3 E
Step 4 B
Step 5 A
Step 6 C

Problem 6-3

1. Passenger Van, asset, increase, debit; Cash in Bank, asset, decrease, credit
2. Utilities Expense, expense, increase, debit; Cash in Bank, asset, decrease, credit
3. Cash in Bank, asset, increase, debit; Day Care Fees, revenue, increase, credit

Chapter 7

Problem 7-1

Cash in Bank $10,000 Dr.
Accounts Receivable – Mark Cohen $2,000 Dr.
Accounts Payable – Jenco Industries $1,000 Cr.
Tom Torrie, Capital $35,000 Cr.
Admissions Revenue $0

Problem 7-2

Account Balances:
Cash in Bank $10,000 (Dr.)
David Serlo, Capital $10,000 (Cr.)

Problem 7-3

May 20: Dr. Office Equip. $1,500;
Cr. Computer Equip. $1,500; Memorandum 47

Problem 7-4

July 7: Dr. Advertising Expense $300;
Cr. Rent Expense $300; Memoradum 13

Chapter 8

Problem 8-1

Store Equipment, asset, debit
Rent Expense, expense, debit
Service Fees Revenue, revenue, credit
Accounts Payable–Rubino Supply, liability, credit
Scott Lee, Capital, owner's equity, credit

APPENDIX H ANSWERS

Advertising Expense, expense, debit
Accounts Receivable–John Langer, asset, debit
Scott Lee, Withdrawals, owner's equity, debit
Maintenance Expense, expense, debit
Office Supplies, asset, debit

Problem 8-2

1. Hailey Office Supply
2. Garmot Electrical Co.
3. June 15
4. $6.23
5. Two
6. The invoice number is 220

Problem 8-3

Store Equipment, Balance Sheet, debit
Rent Expense, Income Statement, debit
Service Fees Revenue, Income Statement, credit
Accounts Payable–Rubino Supply, Balance Sheet, credit
Scott Lee, Capital, Balance Sheet, credit
Advertising Expense, Income Statement, debit
Accounts Receivable–John Langer, Balance Sheet, debit
Scott Lee, Withdrawals, Balance Sheet, debit
Maintenance Expense, Income Statement, debit
Office Supplies, Balance Sheet, debit

Chapter 9

Problem 9-1

1. Stratford Learning Ctr.
2. $832
3. Sandra Miller
4. Payment on account
5. August 21
6. Rose Hughes
7. Roxbury

Problem 9-2

1. $62,500
2. $29,915
3. $29,470
4. $10,630
5. $7,060
6. $25,010

Problem 9-3

Return on Sales = 20.53%

Chapter 10

Problem 10-1

1. Dr. Ticket Revenue $6,000; Cr. Income Summary $6,000
2. Dr. Income Summary $3,100; Cr. Gas and Oil Expense $700, Miscellaneous Expense $600, Utilities Expense $1,800

Problem 10-2

1.,2. Dr. Utilities Expense $129; Cr. Cash in Bank $129
3.,4. Dr. Income Summary $129; Cr. Utilities Exp. $129

Problem 10-3

Accts. Rec.–Linda Brown, Balance Sheet, No, Yes
Advertising Expense, Income Statement, Yes, No
Cash in Bank, Balance Sheet, No, Yes
Exercise Class Revenue, Income Statement, Yes, No
Exercise Equipment, Balance Sheet, No, Yes
Income Summary, N/A, Yes, No
Laundry Equipment, Balance Sheet, No, Yes
Maintenance Expense, Income Statement, Yes, No
Membership fees, Income Statement, Yes, No
Miscellaneous Expense, Income Statement, Yes, No
Office Furniture, Balance Sheet, No, Yes
Rent Expense, Income Statement, Yes, No
Repair Tools, Balance Sheet, No, Yes
Ted Chapman, Capital, Balance Sheet, Yes, Yes
Ted Chapman, Withdrawals, Balance Sheet, Yes, No
Utilities Expense, Income Statement, Yes, No

Chapter 11

Problem 11-1

1.,2. Total Deposit $967.08
3. Balance $2,394.24
4. Balance $2,394.24
5. Balance $2,119.24

Problem 11-2

1. $100
2. $25
3. Miscellaneous Expense

Chapter 12

Problem 12-1

Longas, Jane: 43, $7.25, $290, $32.63, $322.63
Lang, Richard: 38, $7.80, $296.40, $0, $296.40
Quinn, Betty: 44 1/4, $8.30, $332.00, $52.91, $384.91
Sullivan, John: 39 1/2, $8.30, $327.85, $0, $327.85
Talbert, Kelly: 40, $7.50, $300.00, $0, $300.00
Trimbell, Gene: 42 1/2, $9.75, $390.00, $36.56, $426.56
Varney, Heidi: 34 1/4, $8.75, $299.69, $0, $299.69
Wallace, Kevin: 46, $9.25, $370.00, $83.25, $453.25

Problem 12-2

Cleary, Kevin: S, 0, $155.60, $9.65, $2.26, $16, $3.11, $31.02, $124.58
Halley, James: S, 1, $184.10, $11.41, $2.67, $12, $3.68, $29.76, $154.34
Hong, Kim: S, 0, $204.65, $12.69, $2.97, $23, $4.09, $42.75, $161.90
Jackson, Marvin: M, 1, $216.40, $13.42, $3.14, $6, $4.33, $26.89, $189.51
Sell, Richard: M, 2, $196.81, $12.20, $2.85, $0, $3.94, $18.99, $177.82
Totals: $957.56, $59.37, $13.89, $57, $19.15, $149.41, $808.15

APPENDIX H ANSWERS

Problem 12-3
Medicare $4.57
Social Security $19.53
Federal Income Tax $32
Problem 12-4
Check number 79, net pay $263.94

Chapter 13

Problem 13-1

1. $2,193.40
2. $31.80
3. $503.25
4. $33.75
5. $1,690.15

Problem 13-2
Social Security Tax Payable $299.87
Medicare Tax Payable $70.13
Federal Unemployment Tax Payable $38.69
State Unemployment Tax Payable $261.18
Problem 13-3
Employee's federal income tax, payroll entry
Employer's social security tax, payroll tax entry
U.S. savings bonds, payroll entry
Employers' Medicare tax, payroll tax entry
Federal unemployment tax, payroll tax entry
Employees' state income tax, payroll entry
Union dues, payroll entry
Employees' social security tax, payroll entry
State unemployment tax, payroll tax entry
Employee's Medicare tax, payroll entry
Problem 13-4
April 30: Dr. Social Security Tax Payable $318.55, Medicare Tax Payable $113.28, Employee's Federal Income Tax Payable $286; Cr. Cash in Bank $717.83
April 30: Dr. State Income Tax Payable $205.60; Cr. Cash in Bank $205.60
Problem 13-5
Dr. Payroll Tax Exp. $1,328.07, Cr. Soc. Sec. Tax Pay. $82.34, Cr. Medicare Tax Payable $19.26, Cr. Fed. Inc. Tax Pay. $184.00, Cr. State Inc. Tax. Pay. $26.56, Cr. Hosp. Ins. Prem. Pay. $20.00, Cr. Cash in Bank $995.91

Chapter 14

Problem 14-1
Ending account balances:
Cash in Bank $554
Accounts Receivable $3,000
Sales $3,554
Problem 14-2
Sept. 1: Dr. Accts. Rec.—James Palmer $318; Cr. Sales $300, Sales Tax Pay. $18; Sales Invoice 101
Sept. 4: Dr. Accts. Rec.—Anna Rodriguez $636; Cr. Sales $600, Sales Tax Pay. $36; Sales Invoice 102
Sept. 7: Dr. Sales Ret. + Allow. $300, Sales Tax Pay. $18; Cr. Accts. Rec.—James Palmer $318; Credit Memo. 15
Sept. 19: Dr. Sales Ret. + Allow. $40, Sales Tax Pay. $2.40; Cr. Accts. Rec.—Anna Rodriguez $42.40; Credit Memo. 16
Problem 14-3
May 15: Dr. Cash in Bank $1908; Cr. Sales $1800, Sales Tax Payable $108; Tape 40
Problem 14-4
Mar. 1: Dr. Cash in Bank $140.40; Cr. Sales $130, Sales Tax Payable $10.40; Sales Slip 49
Mar. 5: Dr. Accts. Rec./Kelly Wilson $324; Cr. Sales $300, Sales Tax Payable $24; Sales Slip 55
Mar. 17: Dr. Cash in Bank $810; Cr. Sales $750, Sales Tax Payable $60; Tape 65

Chapter 15

Problem 15-1

1. Case Construction Company
2. Westmoreland Paint and Supply Company
3. 7894
4. November 15, 20--
5. December 1, 20--
6. 25 gallons
7. 5
8. White, gray, brown, beige and peach.
9. $20.00
10. $500.00

Problem 15-2
Sept. 2: Dr. Purchases $900; Cr. Accts. Pay./Sunrise Novelty Supply $900; Invoice SN110
Sept 7: Dr. Accts. Pay./Sunrise Novelty Supply $50; Cr. Purchases Returns and Allowances $50; Debit Memorandum 18
Problem 15-3
Nov. 12: Dr. Accts. Pay./Kaleidoscope Comics $16.00; Cr. Purchases Ret. and Allow. $16.00; Debit Memo 559
Problem 15-4
May 1: Dr. Purchases $10,500; Cr. Cash in Bank $10,500; Check 1150
May 5: Dr. Transportation In $325; Cr. Cash in Bank $325; Check 1151
May 7: Dr. Prepaid Insurance $2,500; Cr. Cash in Bank $2,500; Check 1152

Chapter 16

Problem 16-1
Post $12,000 to Sales credit column.
Post $720.00 to Sales Tay Pay. credit column.
Post $12,720 to Accts. Rec. debit column.

APPENDIX H ANSWERS

Problem 16-2

1. Sales credit $820, Sales Tax Payable credit $41, Accounts Receivable debit $861
2. Ending Balance $1,161

Problem 16-3

Totals:

General credit $105
Sales credit $6,200
Sales Tax Payable credit $372
Accounts Receivable credit $5,580
Sales Discounts debit $110
Cash in Bank debit $12,147
Total debits/credits $12,257

Chapter 17

Problem 17-1

Column totals:

Accounts Payable $4,550
Purchases $3,600
General $950

Problem 17-2

Ending Cash in Bank balance $5,610.59

Problem 17-3

Nov. 2: Dr. Accts. Pay./Colonial Products Inc. $900; Cr. Purchases Discounts $27, Cash in Bank $873; Check 104

Chapter 18

Problem 18-1

1. Greater
2. $1,533
3. Merchandise Inventory
4. Income Summary

Problem 18-2

1. Amount $2,454.70
   Account debited, Supplies Expense
   Account credited, Supplies
2. Amount $740
   Account debited, Insurance Expense
   Account credited, Prepaid Insurance
3. Amount $105
   Account debited, Federal Corporate Income Tax Expense
   Account credited, Federal Corporate Income Tax Payable

Problem 18-3

1. $9,995
2. Balance Sheet
3. $3,710
4. $155

Problem 18-4

1. Rotary Supply Corporation
2. 6
3. $177.09
4. Accounts Payable—K & L Electrical
5. Purchases Returns and Allowances

Chapter 19

Problem 19-1

1. Kevin Cleary, Capital
2. Capital Stock
3. Capital Stock and Retained Earnings

Problem 19-2

Subtotal $70.25, sales tax $2.81
Total $73.06

Problem 19-3

1. $96,506
2. $16,703
3. $27,783
4. $17,148

Problem 19-4

1. Office Equipment, Merchandise Inventory.
2. Federal Unemployment Tax Payable.
3. It increased by $16,379.43, or 12.73%.
4. 95.47%
5. The increase in Accounts Receivable indicates that either the company is selling more product or is less efficient at collecting payments. The decrease in Accounts Payable indicates that the company is paying bills earlier. In order to see the whole picture one would need to be able to analyze the data in relation to the other financial statements.
6. The company prepaid for a new insurance contract.

Chapter 20

Problem 20-1

Accounts Receivable, no
Bankcard Fees Expense, yes, credited, debited
Capital Stock, no
Cash in Bank, no
Equipment, no
Fed. Corp. Income Tax Expense, yes, credited, debited
Fed Corp. Income Tax Payable, no
Income Summary, yes, depends (loss = credit), depends (loss = credit)
Insurance Expense, yes, credited, debited
Merchandise Inventory, no
Miscellaneous Expense, yes, credited, debited
Prepaid Insurance, no
Purchases, yes, credited, debited

APPENDIX H ANSWERS

Purchases Discounts, yes, debited, credited
Purchases Returns and Allowances, yes, debited, credited
Retained Earnings, yes, depends (loss = credit), depends (loss = credit)
Sales, yes, debited, credited
Sales Discounts, yes, credited, debited
Sales Returns and Allowances, yes, credited, debited
Sales Tax Payable, no
Supplies, no
Supplies Expense, yes, credited, debited
Transportation In, yes, credited, debited
Utilities Expense, yes, credited, debited

Problem 20-2

July 12: Dr. Rent Exp. $750; Cr. Cash in Bank $750

Problem 20-3

Collecting and verifying source documents
Analyzing business transactions
Journalizing business transactions
Posting journal entries to ledgers
Preparing a trial balance
Completing the work sheet
Preparing financial statements
Journalizing and posting adjusting entries
Journalizing and posting closing entries
Preparing a post-closing trial balance

Chapter 21

Problem 21-1

1. 30,000 shares of common stock were issued at par, $10 per share in cash.
2. 2,000 shares of preferred stock were issued at par, $100 per share in cash.
3. 50,000 shares of common stock, par $10, were issued at $14 per share.

Problem 21-2

1. $87,500
2. $262,500

Problem 21-3

Apr. 1: Dr. Dividends—Common $5,679; Cr. Dividends Payable—Common $5,679; Memorandum 37
Apr. 30: Dr. Dividends Payable—Common $5,679; Cr. Cash in Bank $5,679; Check 221

Problem 21-4

The transactions that are reported on the statement of stockholders' equity are 2,3,6, and 8.

Chapter 22

Problem 22-1

1. Net cash $1,016.84
   Cash short $5
2. Mar 31: Dr. Cash in Bank $1,016.84, Cash Short and Over $5; Cr. Sales $964, Sales Tax Payable $57.84

Problem 22-2

1. Net cash $1,595.77
   Cash over $10
2. Apr. 14: Dr. Cash in Bank $1,595.77; Cr. Sales $1,496, Sales Tax Pay. $89.77, Cash Short and Over $10

Problem 22-3

Check $39.51

Chapter 23

Problem 23-1

Accounts Receivable, current
Building, plant
Cash in Bank, current
Change Fund, current
Delivery Equipment, plant
Land, plant
Merchandise Inventory, current
Office Equipment, plant
Office Furniture, plant
Petty Cash Fund, current
Prepaid Insurance, current
Store Equipment, plant
Supplies, current

Problem 23-2

Cash register $420, $60, $40
Computer $5,000, $1,000, $166.66
Conference table $1,800, $72, $36
Delivery truck $30,000, $6,000, $1,500
Desk $2,880, $144, $132

Problem 23-3

Book Value:
10/01/2001, $12,500
12/31/2001, $11,960
12/31/2002, $9,800
12/31/2003, $7,640
12/31/2004, $5,480
12/31/2005, $3,320
09/31/2006, $1,700

Problem 23-4

1. June 4: Dr. Office Equipment $3,456; Cr. Cash in Bank $3,456; Invoice 14492
2. Dec. 31: Dr. Depreciation Expense $379.87; Cr. Accumulated Depreciation $379.87
3. Dec. 31: Dr. Depreciation Expense $651.20; Cr. Accumulated Depreciation $651.20

Problem 23-5

1. Book Value:
   Jan. 7, $2,360
   First year, $1,908

APPENDIX H ANSWERS

Second year, $1,456
Third year, $1,004
Fourth year, $552
Fifth year, $100

2. Dec. 31: Dr. Depr. Exp.—Office Equip. $452; Cr. Accum. Depr.—Office Equip. $452
3. Dec. 31: Dr. Income Summary $452; Cr. Depr. Exp.—Office Equip. $452
4. $100, Yes

Chapter 24

Problem 24-1

Journal Entries

Apr. 10: Dr. Accts. Rec./Sonya Dickson $630; Cr. Sales $600, Sales Tax Pay. $30; Sales Slip 928

Nov. 30: Dr. Uncollectible Accounts Expense $630; Cr. Accts. Rec./Sonya Dickson $630; Memorandum 78

Dec. 30: Dr. Accts. Rec./Sonya Dickson $630; Cr. Uncollectible Accounts Expense $630; Memorandum 89

Dec. 30: Dr. Cash in Bank $630; Cr. Accts. Rec./Sonya Dickson $630; Receipt 277

Ledger Balances

Ending debit balances:

Cash in Bank $10,058
Accounts Receivable $7,290
Uncollectible Accounts Expense $928
Accts. Rec./Sonya Dickson $0

Ending credit balances:

Sales Tax Pay. $278
Sales $24,760

Problem 24-2

Journal Entries

May 4: Dr. Allowance for Doubtful Accounts $1,050; Cr. Accts. Rec./Jack Bowers $1,050; Memorandum 241

Nov. 18: Dr. Accts. Rec./Jack Bowers $1,050; Cr. Allowance for Doubtful Accounts $1,050; Memorandum 321

Nov. 18: Dr. Cash in Bank $1,050; Cr. Accts. Rec./Jack Bowers $1,050; Receipt 1078

Dec. 31: Dr. Uncollectible Account Expense $1,850; Cr. Allowance for Uncollectible Accounts $1,850

Ledger Balances

Ending debit balances:

Cash in Bank $10,470
Accounts Receivable $19,350
Uncollectible Account Expense $1,850
Accts. Rec./Jack Bowers $0

Ending credit balances:

Allowance for Doubtful Accounts $3,050

Problem 24-3

(1) Uncollectible Accounts Expense:
Andrews Co. $2,800.02
The Book Nook $2,047.81
Cable Inc. $2,550.00
Davis Inc. $1,282.40
Ever-Sharp Co. $1,164.38

(2) Dec. 31: Dr. Uncollectible Account Expense $1,282.40; Cr. Allowance for Uncollectible Accounts $1,282.40

Chapter 25

Problem 25-1

Preparing Inventory Reports

Total value of inventory $794.10

Problem 25-2

Determining Inventory Costs

a. $472.55
b. $477.25
c. $465.25
d. $470.52

Problem 25-3

1. Ending inventory $575.90
2. Gross profit $214.30

Chapter 26

Problem 26-1

1. Interest $75.62, Maturity value $4,075.62
2. Interest $289.73, Maturity value $10,289.73
3. Interest $136.23, Maturity value $6,636.23
4. Interest $36.25, Maturity value $936.25
5. Interest $142.03, Maturity value $2,542.03

Problem 26-2

1. Interest $22.19
2. Interest $69.04
3. Interest $288.00
4. Interest $123.29
5. Interest $86.25

Problem 26-3

1. Cash in Bank $9,000
2. Notes Payable $9,000
3. Cash in Bank , asset; Notes Payable, liability
4. $9,355.07

Problem 26-4

1. Cash in Bank is debited for $9,802.74; Discount on Notes Payable is debited for $197.26; Notes Payable is credited for $10,000.
2. Discount $197.26, Proceeds $9,802.74

APPENDIX H ANSWERS

Problem 26-5

June 12: Dr. Cash in Bank $2,426.03, Discount on Notes Payable $73.97; Cr. Notes Payable $2,500; Note 55

Chapter 27

Problem 27-1

June 1: Dr. Cash in Bank $1,200, Accts. Rec. $2,000, Merchandise Inventory $8,000, Equipment $5,000, Van $12,000, Office Furniture $1,000; Cr. Matthew Deck, Capital $29,200; Memorandum 1

June 1: Dr. Cash in Bank $2,300, Accts. Rec. $7,000, Merchandise Inventory $5,000, Equipment $12,000, Office Furniture $500; Cr. Jennifer Rusk, Capital $26,800; Memorandum 1

Problem 27-2

1. 3/4, 1/4
2. 5/9, 3/9, 1/9
3. 3/8, 2/8, 2/8, 1/8
4. 2/4, 1/4, 1/4
5. 2/3, 1/3

Problem 27-3

Nov. 13: Dr. Cash in Bank $20,000; Cr. Walter, Capital $8,000, Yount, Capital $12,000

Chapter 28

Problem 28-1

Division of Net Income:
Goldman $14,000
Jones $21,000
Partners' Equity:
Goldman $37,000
Jones $68,000

Problem 28-2

Shares of gain:
Bass $7,200
Buie $7,200
Anderson $3,600
Norman $3,600
Dunham $2,400
Ruppe $2,400

Problem 28-3

Sept. 4: Dr. Cash in Bank $38,000, Gunther, Capital $3,500, Pertee, Capital $3,500; Cr. Merchandise Inventory $45,000

Sept. 15: Dr. Cash in Bank $29,000; Cr. Gunther, Capital $1,000, Pertee, Capital $1,000, Office Equipment $27,000

Chapter 29

Problem 29-1

Weaknesses might include ethics programs that do not provide clear guidelines for action when faced with various situations. Some employees might not report violations out of fear of retribution. A business ethics plan that includes well-communicated methods for reporting violations (like a Web site, an ethics office, or ethics seminars) could help remedy this problem.

Problem 29-2

The law covers most major ideas about the public's definition of proper and improper behavior, but it does not offer guidance on every dilemma. Ethical concepts cover more subtle instances, where the proper course of action might not be so clear-cut. Use the following resources to find an example in which the actions of a business were legal but might be considered unethical: *Business Week* Online, *The Wall Street Journal*, local newspapers, and business magazines.

Problem 29-3

The following behaviors are possible violations of principles of professional conduct. Marcus appears to be recording transactions in a misleading manner in order to increase the amount of profit reported for the business. This violates the accounting principle of integrity. Jennifer has not been appropriately trained and educated for accounting work. This violates the principle of competence. Ing's behavior violates confidentiality when he shares confidential financial information with anyone not approved to receive it.

Glossary

A

401(k) plan An employee contributes a portion of gross earnings to an account in the 401(k) plan and does not pay income tax on the contributed earnings.

account Subdivision under the three sections of the accounting equation used to summarize increases and decreases in assets, liabilities, and owner's equity.

accountant A person who handles a broad range of jobs related to the making of choices and decisions about the design of a business's accounting system and the preparation and explanation of financial reports.

accounting clerk Entry-level job that can vary with the size of the company from specialization in one part of the system to a wide range of recordkeeping tasks.

accounting cycle The accounting period of a business is separated into activities that help the business keep its accounting records in an orderly fashion.

accounting equation The basis for keeping all accounting records in balance. Assets = liabilities + owner's equity

accounting period A period of time covered by an accounting report.

accounting system A systematic process of recording and reporting the financial information resulting from business transactions.

accounts payable The amount of money owed, or payable, to the creditors of a business.

accounts payable subsidiary ledger A separate ledger that contains accounts for all creditors; it is summarized in the **Accounts Payable** controlling account in the general ledger.

accounts receivable The total amount of money owed to a business.

accounts receivable subsidiary ledger A separate ledger that contains accounts for all charge customers; it is summarized in the **Accounts Receivable** controlling account in the general ledger.

accumulated depreciation The total amount of depreciation for a plant asset that has been recorded up to a specific point in time.

accumulated earnings The employee's year-to-date gross earnings, or the employee's gross earnings from the beginning of the year through the end of each pay period.

adjustment An amount that is added to or subtracted from an account balance to bring that balance up-to-date.

administrative expenses Costs related to the management of a business (for example, office expenses).

aging of accounts receivable method A method of estimating bad debts expense in which each customer's account is examined and classified by age; the age classifications are multiplied by certain percentages; and the total estimated uncollectible amounts are added to determine the end-of-period balance of **Allowance for Uncollectible Accounts**.

allowance Reduces the amount of income tax to be withheld.

allowance method A method of accounting for uncollectible accounts in which an estimate is made of the amount of sales on account for which payment will not be received.

assets Property or items of value owned by a business.

authorized capital stock The maximum number of shares of stock a corporation may issue.

B

balance sheet A report of the balances in all asset, liability, and owner's equity accounts at the end of the period.

bank discount The interest charge deducted in advance on a non-interest-bearing note payable.

bank service charge A fee the bank charges for maintaining bank records and processing bank statement items for the depositor.

bank statement An itemized record of all the transactions in a depositor's account over a given period, usually a month.

bankcard A card issued by a bank that can be used to withdraw cash and to make payments for goods and services at many businesses in place of writing checks.

bankcard fee A fee charged for handling bank card sales slips; it is usually based on the total dollar volume of the bank card sales processed.

base year A year or period that is used for comparison in financial statements analysis.

beginning inventory The merchandise a business has on hand at the beginning of a fiscal period.

board of directors A group of people, elected by the common stockholders, who are responsible for the affairs of a corporation.

book value The value of an asset at a specific point in time. For a plant asset, it equals the initial cost of the plant asset minus the accumulated depreciation.

book value of accounts receivable The amount the business can reasonably expect to receive from all its charge customers.

business entity Exists independently of its owner's personal holdings. The accounting records and reports are maintained separately and contain financial information related only to the business.

business ethics The policies and practices that reflect a company's core values such as honesty, trust, respect, and fairness.

business transaction A business event, such as the buying, selling, or exchange of goods, that causes a change in the assets, liabilities, or owner's equity of a business.

C

calendar year Period for which a business begins on January 1 and ends on December 31.

canceled checks Checks paid by the bank and deducted from the depositor's account.

capital Money supplied by investors, banks, or owners of a business. Refers to the dollar value of assets contributed to the business.

Capital Stock The account that represents the total amount of investment in the corporation by its stockholders (owners).

cash discount The amount a customer can deduct from the amount owed for purchased merchandise if payment is made within a certain time.

cash payments journal A special journal used to record all transactions in which cash is paid out or decreased.

cash receipt The cash received by a business.

cash receipts journal A special journal used to record all transactions in which cash is received.

cash sale A transaction in which the business receives full payment for the merchandise sold at the time of the sale.

certified public accountant A public accountant who has passed the licensing exam on accounting theory, practice, auditing, and business law. (CPA)

change fund An amount of money, consisting of varying denominations of bills and coins, that is used to make change in cash transactions.

charge customer A customer to whom a sale on account is made.

chart of accounts A list of all the accounts and their assigned account numbers, used in journalizing transactions.

charter A legal written permission that gives a corporation certain rights and privileges and spells out the rules under which the corporation is to operate.

check A written order from a depositor telling the bank to pay a stated amount of cash to the person or business named on the check.

check stub A source document that lists the same information that appears on a check and shows the balance in the checking account before and after each check is written.

checking account Allows a person or business to deposit cash in a bank and to write checks against the account balance.

closely held corporation A corporation, often owned by a few people or by a family, that does not offer its stock for sale to the general public.

closing entries Journal entries made to close, or reduce to zero, the balances in the temporary capital accounts and to transfer the net income or net loss for the period to the capital account.

code of ethics A formal policy of rules and standards that describe the ethical behaviors that a company expects from its management and employees.

commission An amount paid to an employee based on a percentage of the employee's sales.

common stock The stock issued by a corporation when it is authorized to issue only one class of stock.

comparability The accounting principle that allows the financial information from one period to be compared to that of another period; also, the comparison of financial information of two or more businesses.

competence The principle that requires accountants to have the knowledge, skills, and experience needed to complete a task.

Glossary

compound entry A journal entry with two or more debits or two or more credits.

computerized accounting system A system in which financial information is recorded by entering it into a computer.

confidentiality The principle that requires accountants to protect and not disclose information acquired in the course of work unless they have a legal or professional responsibility to do so.

conservatism principle Accounting guideline requiring that accountants choose the safer, or more conservative, method when there is a choice of procedures.

consistency principle The consistent use of an inventory costing method helps owners and creditors compare financial reports from one period to another.

contra account An account whose balance is a decrease to another account.

controlling account An account that acts as a control on the accuracy of the accounts in a related subsidiary ledger; its balance must equal the total of all the account balances in the subsidiary ledger.

corporation Business organization that is recognized by law to have a life of its own.

correcting entry An entry made to correct an error in a journal entry discovered after posting.

cost of merchandise The actual cost to the business of the merchandise sold to customers.

credit An agreement to pay for a purchase at a later time; an entry to the right side of a T account.

credit cards Cards containing a customer's name and account number presented when buying merchandise on account.

credit memorandum A form that lists the details of a sales return or sales allowance.

credit terms Terms that set out the time allowed for payment for a sale on account.

creditor A person or business that has a claim to the assets of a business; a person or business to which money is owed.

current assets Assets that are either used up or converted to cash during the normal operating cycle of the business, usually one year.

current liabilities Debts of the business that must be paid within the next accounting period.

current ratio The relationship between current assets and current liabilities; calculated by dividing the dollar amount of current assets by the dollar amount of current liabilities.

D

debit An amount entered on the *left* side of the T account.

debit memorandum The form a business uses to notify its supplier (creditor) of a return or allowance.

deduction An amount that is subtracted from an employee's gross earnings.

deposit slip A bank form listing the cash and checks to be deposited.

depositor A person or business that has cash on deposit in a bank.

depreciation Allocating the cost of a plant asset over an asset's useful life.

direct deposit The depositing of an employee's net pay directly into her or his personal bank account; usually made through electronic funds transfer.

direct write-off method A procedure in which an uncollectible account is removed from the accounts receivable subsidiary ledger and the controlling account in the general ledger when a business determines that the amount owed is not going to be paid.

discount period The period of time within which an invoice must be paid if a discount is to be taken.

disposal value The estimated value of a plant asset at its replacement time; often called trade-in value or salvage value.

dividend A return on the investments by the stockholders of a corporation; charged against the corporation's retained earnings.

double-entry accounting A financial recordkeeping system in which each transaction affects at least two accounts; for each debit there must be an equal credit.

drawee The bank on which a check is written.

drawer The person who signs a check.

due dates The date by which an invoice must be paid.

E

electronic badge readers Employee is issued an identification badge with a magnetic strip that contains employee information. When the employee inserts the identification badge into the badge reader, the magnetic strip is scanned and information is transferred directly to the computer.

Electronic Federal Tax Payment System (EFTPS) Larger businesses deposit income tax payments by electronic funds transfer.

Electronic Funds Transfer System (EFTS) Allows banks to transfer funds among accounts quickly and accurately without the exchange of checks.

employee's earnings record An individual payroll record prepared for each employee; includes data on earnings, deductions, net pay, and accumulated earnings.

ending inventory The merchandise a business has on hand at the end of a fiscal period.

endorsement An authorized signature written or stamped on the back of a check representing receipt and deposit or payment of check.

entrepreneur A person who transforms ideas for products or services into real-world businesses.

equity The total financial claims to the assets, or property, of a business.

ethics The study of our notions of right and wrong; a set of basic principles.

ethics officer The employee directly responsible for creating business conduct programs, evaluating performance, and enforcing standards of conduct.

expense The cost of the goods or services that are used to operate a business; expenses decrease owner's equity.

external controls The measures and procedures provided outside the business to protect cash and other assets.

F

face value The amount written on the face of a promissory note; usually the same as the principal.

Federal Tax Deposit Coupon A form sent with payment for FICA and federal income taxes or federal unemployment taxes to indicate the total amount of taxes being paid.

Federal Unemployment Tax Act (FUTA) Requires employers to pay unemployment taxes.

financial accounting Reporting information to external users (individuals not directly involved in the day-to-day operations of the business).

financial claims Legal rights to an item.

financial reports Summarized information about the financial status of a business.

financial statements Prepared to summarize the changes resulting from business transactions that occur during an accounting period.

first-in, first-out method An inventory costing method that assumes that the first items purchased (first in) were the first items sold (first out).

fiscal year An accounting period of twelve months.

FOB destination Shipping terms specifying that the supplier pays the shipping cost to the buyer's destination.

FOB shipping point Shipping terms specifying that the buyer pays the shipping charge from the supplier's shipping point.

footing A column total written in small pencil figures.

Form 940 The employer's unemployment tax return; it includes both federal and state unemployment taxes paid during the year.

Form 941 The employer's quarterly federal tax return; it reports the accumulated amounts of FICA and federal income tax withheld from employees' earnings for the quarter, as well as FICA tax owed by the employer.

Form W-2 A form that provides the employee with a summary of earnings and amounts withheld for federal, state, and local taxes; also called a wage and tax statement.

Form W-3 The Transmittal of Wage and Tax Statements, filed with the federal government to summarize the information contained on the employees' Forms W-2.

for-profit business Business that operates to earn money for its owners.

free enterprise system A system in which people are free to produce the goods and services they choose.

full disclosure Accounting guideline requiring that a financial report include enough information so that it is complete.

Glossary

G

general journal An all-purpose journal in which all the transactions of a business may be recorded.

general ledger The group of accounts used by a business.

generally accepted accounting principles (GAAP) A set of rules used by accountants to prepare financial reports.

going concern The assumption that a business entity will continue to operate for an indefinite time.

gross earnings The total amount of money an employee earns in a pay period.

gross profit on sales The amount of profit made during the fiscal period before expenses are deducted; it is found by subtracting the cost of merchandise sold from net sales.

H

home keys The 4-5-6 keys on a numeric keypad.

horizontal analysis The comparison of the same items on financial statements for two or more accounting periods and the analysis of changes from one period to the next.

I

income statement A report of the net income or net loss for a fiscal period; sometimes called a "profit and loss" statement.

Income Summary account The account in the general ledger used to summarize the revenue and expenses for the fiscal period.

independence The principle that requires CPAs to have no financial interest in the company being audited.

integrity The principle that requires accountants to choose what is right and just over what is wrong.

interest The fee charged for the use of money.

interest rate The fee charged for the use of the principal when a loan is made.

interest-bearing note payable A note that requires the face value plus interest to be paid at maturity.

internal controls Steps a business takes to protect cash (for example, limiting the number of persons handling cash).

inventory The items of merchandise a business has in stock.

investments Those assets owned by a business but not used in the operation of the business.

invoice A bill; a form that lists the quantity, description, unit price, and total cost of the items sold and shipped to a buyer.

issue date The date on which a promissory note is written.

J

journal A chronological record of all of the transactions of a business.

journalizing The process of recording business transactions in a journal.

L

last-in, first-out method An inventory costing method that assumes that the last items purchased are the first items sold.

ledger A book or file containing a separate page for each business account; serves as a permanent record of financial transactions.

ledger account form The accounting stationery used to record financial information about specific accounts.

liabilities Amounts owed to creditors; the claims of creditors to the assets of the business.

lifestyle The way you use your time, energy, and resources.

liquidity ratio The measure of a business's ability to pay its current debts as they become due and to provide for unexpected needs of cash.

long-term liabilities Debts that are not required to be paid within the next accounting period.

loss The result of a company's spending more than it receives in revenue.

M

maker The person or business promising to repay the principal and interest when a loan is made.

management accounting Reporting information to management, often referred to as accounting for *internal* users of accounting information.

manual accounting system A system in which accounting information is recorded and processed by hand.

manufacturing business A business that transforms raw materials into finished products through the use of labor and machinery.

market value The current price that is being charged for similar items of merchandise in the market.

matching principle Principle stating that expenses are compared to revenues for the same period.

materiality An accounting guideline stating that relatively important data should be included in financial reports.

maturity date The due date of a promissory note; the date on which the principal and interest must be paid.

maturity value The principal plus interest on a note that must be paid on the maturity date.

memorandum A brief written message that describes a transaction that takes place within a business.

merchandise Goods bought for resale to customers.

merchandising business A business that buys goods (for example, books or clothing) and then sells those goods for a profit.

mutual agency The characteristic of partnerships under which any partner can enter into agreements for the business that are binding on all other partners.

N

net income The amount of revenue that remains after expenses for the period are subtracted.

net loss The amount by which total expenses exceed total revenue.

net pay The amount left after total deductions are subtracted from gross earnings.

net purchases The total cost of all merchandise purchased during a fiscal period, less any purchases discounts, returns, or allowances.

net sales The amount of sales for the period less any sales discounts, returns, or allowances.

networking Making contacts with people to share information and advice.

noninterest-bearing note payable A note from which the interest is deducted at the time the note is made; a promissory note that has no stated rate of interest on its face.

normal balance The increase side of an account: assets, debit side; liabilities and capital, credit side. The word *normal* used here means usual.

note payable A promissory note issued to a creditor.

note receivable A promissory note that a business accepts from a customer or other person who owes the business money.

not-for-profit organization An organization that does not operate for the purpose of making a profit.

NSF check A check returned to the depositor by the bank because there are not sufficient funds in the drawer's checking account to cover the check.

O

objectivity The principle that requires accountants to be impartial, honest, and free of conflicts of interest.

on account When a business or individual buys an item on credit.

online The direct link-up of a terminal or cash register to a centralized computer system.

operating expenses The cash spent or assets consumed to earn revenue for a business; operating expenses do not include federal income tax expense.

operating income The taxable income of a corporation.

other expense A non-operating expense; an expense that does not result from the normal operations of the business.

other revenue Non-operating revenue that a business receives from activities outside its normal operations.

outstanding checks Checks that have been written but have not yet been presented to the bank for payment.

Glossary

outstanding deposits Deposits that have been made and recorded in the checkbook but do not appear on the bank statement.

overtime rate Employers are required to pay overtime when employees covered by these laws work more than 40 hours per week.

owner's equity Owner's claims to the assets of the business.

P

packing slip A form that lists the items included in the shipment.

Paid-in Capital in Excess of Par The account that represents the amount of cash received by a corporation over the stock's par value.

par value The dollar amount assigned to each share of stock when the corporation's charter is approved; used to determine the amount credited to the capital stock account.

partnership Business owned by two or more persons, called partners, who agree to operate the business as co-owners.

partnership agreement A written document that sets out the terms under which the partnership will operate.

partnership liquidation Ending a partnership involves winding up the affairs of the partnership business.

pay period The amount of time over which an employee is paid.

payee The person or business to whom a check is written or a note is payable.

payroll A list of the employees and the payments due to each employee for a specific pay period.

payroll clerk Responsible for preparing the payroll.

payroll register A form that summarizes information about employees' earnings for each pay period.

Payroll Tax Expense Account where the employer's payroll taxes are recorded.

percentage of net sales method A method of estimating uncollectible debts expense in which a business assumes that a certain percentage of each year's net sales will be uncollectible.

periodic inventory system An inventory system in which the number of items on hand is determined by a physical count.

permanent accounts Accounts that are continuous from one accounting period to the next; balances are carried forward to the next period (for example, assets, liabilities, and owner's capital accounts).

perpetual inventory system An inventory system in which a constant, up-to-date record of the amount of merchandise on hand is maintained.

personal interest tests Tests that uncover personal preferences you can use to research potential careers and determine which ones match your particular interests.

personality A set of unique qualities that makes us different from all other people.

petty cash disbursement A payment made from the petty cash fund.

petty cash fund Cash kept on hand for making small, incidental cash payments.

petty cash register A record of all disbursements made from the petty cash fund.

petty cash requisition A form requesting money to replenish the petty cash fund.

petty cash voucher A form that provides proof of payment from the petty cash fund.

petty cashier The person responsible for maintaining the petty cash fund and for making petty cash disbursements.

physical inventory An actual count of all the merchandise on hand and available for sale.

plant assets Long-lived assets that are used in the production or sale of other assets or services over several accounting periods.

point-of-sale terminal Electronic cash register.

post-closing trial balance Prepared to verify that total debits equal total credits after the closing entries are posted.

posting The process of transferring information from the general journal to individual general ledger accounts, the fourth step in the accounting cycle.

preferred stock Stock whose owners have certain privileges over common stockholders.

premium The amount paid for insurance.

principal The amount of money being borrowed on a promissory note.

proceeds The amount of cash actually received by a borrower on a non-interest-bearing note payable.

processing stamp A stamp placed on a creditor's invoice that outlines the steps to be followed in processing the invoice for payment.

profit The amount of revenue earned above the expenses incurred to operate the business.

profitability ratio Ratios used to evaluate the earnings performance of a business during the accounting period (for example, return on common stockholders' equity).

promissory note A written promise to pay a certain amount of money at a specific future time.

property Items of value that are owned or controlled by a business; economic resources of a business.

property rights Creditors' and owners' financial claims to the assets of a business.

proving cash The process of determining whether the amounts of cash recorded in the accounting records of a business and in its checkbook agree.

proving the ledger Adding all debit balances and all credit balances of ledger accounts and then comparing the two totals to see whether they are equal.

proxy A document that transfers a stockholder's voting rights to someone else.

public accounting Accounting services that range from tax preparation to merger and acquisition consultation; a variety of accounting services offered to businesses.

publicly held corporation A corporation whose stock is widely held, has a large market, and is usually traded on a stock exchange.

purchase order A written offer to a supplier to buy certain items.

purchase requisition A written request that a certain item or items be ordered.

Purchases account The account used to record the cost of merchandise purchased during a fiscal period.

purchases allowances A price reduction given when a business keeps unsatisfactory merchandise it has bought.

purchases discount Term used by the buyer to refer to a cash discount offered for early payment.

purchases journal A special journal used to record all transactions in which items are bought on account.

purchases returns The return to the supplier for full credit of merchandise bought on account.

Q

quick ratio A measure of the relationship between short-term assets and current liabilities.

R

ratio analysis Involves the comparison of two amounts on a financial statement and the evaluation of the relationship between these amounts.

receipt A form that serves as a record of cash received.

reconciling the bank statement The process of determining any differences between a bank statement balance and a checkbook balance.

relevance A characteristic of accounting requiring that information "make a difference" in reaching a business decision.

reliability A characteristic requiring that accounting information be reasonably free of bias and error.

report form A format for preparing the balance sheet in which the classifications of accounts are listed one under another.

restrictive endorsement A check endorsement that restricts or limits how a check may be handled (for example, "For Deposit Only").

retailer A business that sells to the final user, the consumer.

retained earnings Earnings held by a corporation and not paid to stockholders as a return on their investment.

return on sales The portion of each sales dollar that represents profit. To calculate this ratio, divide net income by sales.

revenue Income earned from the sale of goods and services.

revenue recognition Accounting principle that states that revenue is recognized and recorded on the date it is earned even if cash has not been received.

ruling A single line drawn under a column of figures to signify that the entries above the rule are to be added or subtracted; a double rule under an amount signifies a total.

Glossary

S

Salaries Expense The expense account used to record employees' earnings.

salary A fixed amount of money paid to an employee for each pay period.

sale on account The sale of merchandise that will be paid for at a later date.

Sales A revenue account to record the amount of the merchandise sold.

sales allowance A price reduction granted for damaged goods kept by the customer.

sales discount A cash discount.

sales journal A special journal used to record only the sale of merchandise on account.

sales return Any merchandise returned for credit or a cash refund.

sales slip A form that lists the details of a sale.

sales tax A tax levied by a city or state on the retail sale of merchandise.

schedule of accounts payable A list of all creditors in the accounts payable ledger, the balance in each account, and the total amount owed to all creditors.

schedule of accounts receivable A list of each charge customer, the balance in the customer's account, and the total amount due from all customers.

selling expenses Expenses incurred in selling or marketing the merchandise or services sold by a business.

service business Provides a needed service for a fee.

signature card A card containing the signature(s) of the person(s) authorized to write checks on a checking account.

skills Activities that you perform well.

slide error Accidental misplacement of a decimal point in an amount.

sole proprietorship A business owned by one person.

source document A paper prepared as evidence that a transaction occurred.

special journals Multicolumn journals that have columns reserved for the recording of specific types of transactions.

specific identification method An inventory costing method in which the exact cost of each item in inventory is determined and assigned; used most often by businesses that have a low unit volume of merchandise with high unit prices.

State Unemployment Tax Act (SUTA) Requires employers to pay unemployment taxes.

statement of changes in owner's equity A financial statement prepared to summarize the effects of business transactions on the capital account.

statement of changes in partners' equity A financial statement that reports the changes in each partner's capital account as a result of business operations.

statement of retained earnings A statement that reports the changes that have taken place in the **Retained Earnings** account during the fiscal period; prepared as a supporting document for the balance sheet.

statement of stockholders' equity A statement that reports the changes that have taken place in all of the stockholders' equity accounts during the period.

stockholders' equity The value of the stockholders' claims to the assets of the corporation.

stop payment order A demand by the drawer that the bank not honor a certain check.

straight-line depreciation A method of equally distributing the cost of a plant asset over the asset's estimated useful life.

subsidiary ledger A ledger that is summarized in a controlling account in the general ledger.

T

T account An account shaped like a "T" that is used for analyzing transactions.

temporary capital accounts Accounts used to record information during the fiscal period that will be transferred to a permanent capital account at the end of the period.

term The length of time the borrower has to repay a promissory note.

tickler file A file that contains a folder for each day of the month; invoices are placed in the folders according to their due dates.

time card A record of the time an employee arrives at work, the time the employee leaves, and the total number of hours worked each day.

transposition error Occurs when two digits within an amount are accidentally reversed, or transposed.

trial balance A proof of the equality of total debits and credits, the fifth step in the accounting cycle.

U

uncollectible accounts An account receivable that cannot be collected, sometimes called a bad debt.

unemployment taxes Taxes collected to provide funds for workers who are temporarily out of work; usually paid only by the employer.

V

values Concepts or ideas held important or worthwhile.

vertical analysis A method of analysis that requires the restating of each dollar amount reported on a financial statement as a percentage of a base amount reported on the same statement.

voiding a check Canceling a check by writing the word "Void" across the front in ink.

W

wage An amount of money paid to an employee at a specified rate per hour worked.

weighted average cost method An inventory costing method in which all purchases of an item are added to the beginning inventory of that item; the total cost is then divided by the total units to obtain the average cost per unit.

wholesaler A business that sells to retailers.

withdrawal The removal of cash or another asset from the business by the owner for personal use.

work sheet A working paper used to collect information from ledger accounts for use in completing end-of-fiscal-period work.

working capital The amount by which current assets exceed current liabilities.

Index A

A

Index

B

C

Index A

Index

Index A

J

K

L

M

N

Index

Index A

Index

Q

R

S

Index A

T

Index B

Real-World Applications and Connections

Index B

Index B

Index B

Photo Credits

Cover photography by: Masterfile/Imtek Imagineering(b); Jordon Miller(t)

Selected spot photography provided by: Corbis Digital Stock; EyeWire Image Library; & Photo Disc, Inc.

AFP/Corbis xv, 573; Thomas J. Abercrombie/National Geographic Society 734(b); Adam Smith/FPG International LLC 142(b); Lori Adamski Peek/Tony Stone Images 360; American Airlines 96(c); Amwell/Tony Stone Images 556(b); Eric Antoniou/ Corbis 32; Bill Aron/Photo Edit 101, 327(b), 393(b), 629, 776(t), 631; Robert Aschenbrenner/Tony Stone Images 621(b); Joe Atlas/Artville 482(bl); Bruce Ayres/ Tony Stone Images 67(b), 79; Bill Bachman/Leo de Wys 166(b); Bill Bachmann/Photo Edit 614(t), 701; Davis Barber/Photo Edit 89(b); Barros & Barros/The Image Bank 9(b), 632(t); Harry Bartlett/Stone xix; 775; Paul Barton/The Stock Market 715(t); Ben & Jerry's Homemade, Inc. 122(b), 796, 799; Brain Bielmann/Index Stock 619(b); Ken Biggs Tony Stone Images 215(b); Nathan Bilow/Tony Stone Images 438; Warren Bolster/Tony Stone Images 381(c); D. Boone/ Corbis-Westlight 75; Mathew Borkoski/Index Stock 782; Daniel Bosler/Tony Stone Images 164, 358(b), 601(t), 744; Deborah Boyd/World Wildlife Fund 5; Robert Brenner/Photo Edit 323, 367(b); Gary Brettracher/Image State xiii(b), 483; Michelle D. Bridwell/PhotoEdit 679; P. Broze/Leo de Wys 605(b); Peter Cade/Tony Stone Images 769; Melanie Carr/ Image State 781; Melanie Carr/Index Stock 616(c); Tom Carroll/International Stock 299(b); Aaron Chang/The Stock Market 172(b); Ron Chapple/FPG International LLC 340(c); Steve Chenn/Corbis-Westlight 694(b), 768(c); Ken Chernnus/FPG International LLC 663; Cleo/Photo Edit 595(b); Dennis Cody/FPG International LLC 366; Stewart Cohen/Tony Stone Images 216(b), 521, 681; Connie Coleman/Tony Stone Images 30; Comstock, Inc. xii(m), 350(t), 401(t), 472, 530(t), 584(t); Corbis 777(t); Gary Conner/Corbis 597; Gary A. Conner/ Photo Edit 157(b), 235; Tom Craig/FPG International LLC 322(t); David K. Crow/Photo Edit 98; Jim Cummins/FPG International LLC 16(b); Robert E. Daemmrich/Tony Stone Images 92(b), 170, 276(b); Michael Kevin Dal/The Stock Market 415(b); Michael Daly/The Stock Market207(t), 428; Dennis Degnan/ Westlight 582; Uli Degwert/International Stock 73; Danita DeJane viii(b), 120(bl), 628(b), 687(b); David de Lossy/The Image Bank 136(b); Thomas Del Brase/ Tony Stone Images(m), 284(t),338(t); Dewys & Japack/ Leo de Wys 495(b); Dewys/D & J Heaton/Leo de Wys 517; George Diebold/The Stock Market 338(b); Digital Vision 50(b), 287; Joseph Drivas/The Image Bank 532; Robert Essel/Corbis 776(b); Eyewire/Stone 95 638; Jon Feingersh/The Stock Market 403, 495(t); Myrleen Ferguson/Photo Edit 8(t), 555; Bob Firth/ International Stock 192; Kim Fowler/Leo de Wys 46(c); David Fraizer Photolibrary 316(b), 689(b), 754(b), 759; David R. Frazier/Tony Stone Images, 136(t); Tony Freeman/Photo Edit 57(b), 60, 83, 104(b), 224(b), 757(c); Robert Frerck/Tony Stone Images 14(b); Tim Fuller Photography xv(b), 6(b), 12 (all except br) 52 , 56, 59, 106(b), 117(c), 128, 129, 133, 139, 153, 194, 201(b), 210(b), 212, 225(br), 260, 264, 270, 309(b), 322(b), 357, 378(c), 387, 410(b), 421, 492, 564(b), 570(b), 579(b), 614(b), 659, 685, 738(t), 746(c); Robert Ginn/Photo Edit 199(b); GK & Vikki Hart/Petco Inc. 474(b); Spencer Grant/Photo Edit 258(b), 292, 449; Ernst Grasser/Stone 126(b); Vincent Graziani/ International Stock 265(b); Jeff Greenberg/Photo Edit 22(t), 103; Brain Haimer/Photo Edit 627(b), 755; David Hanilton/The Image Bank 90(c); Chris Harvey/Stone ix(b), 231; John Henley/The Stock Market 672(b); Ed Honowitz/Tony Stone Images 18, 49; Ted Horowitz/The Stock Market 15, 596(b); Richard Hutchings/Photo Edit 391; Miwako Ikeda/International Stock 306(b); Index Stock 9(t), 50(b), 65(b), 148(b), 196(b), 271, 291, 372, 451, 463, 518, 622(b), 750(b); David Joel/Tony Stone Images 707; Johnny Stockshooter/International Stock 484(b); Mark A. Johnson/The Stock Market 688(t); Chris Jones/The Stock Market/538(b); R.W. Jones/ Corbis-Westlight 408, 543(b), 750(c); Mark Joseph/ Tony Stone Images 490; Kalunzy & Thatcher/FPG International LLC 487(t); Bonnie Kamin/Photo Edit 326; Ronnie Kaufman/Corbis 121; Chuck Keeler/Tony Stone Images 99; Michael A. Keller/The Stock Market 369; John P. Kelley/The Image Bank 350(b); Michael Krasowitz/FPG International LLC 20, 33, 186, 269; Bob Krist/Leo de Wys 13; Gary D. Landsman/The Stock Market/Corbis xii(b), 419, 691; Brian Leng/ Corbis-Westlight xix(tl), 4(t), 6(t), 14(t), 24(t), 26(t), 32(t), 44(t), 46(t), 50(t), 57(t), 70(t), 72(t), 78(t), 96(t), 120(t), 122(t), 126(t), 150(t), 152(t), 157(t), 166(t), 180(t), 182(t), 202(t), 204(t), 210(t), 256(t), 258(t), 265(t), 286(t), 288(t), 293(t), 299(t), 314, 316(t), 322(t), 327(t), 352(t), 354(t), 358(t), 367(t), 386(t), 388(t), 393(t), 402(t), 418(t), 420(t), 429(t), 448(t), 450(t), 458(t), 482(t),484(t), 491(t), 493, 514(t), 516(t), 522, 531(t), 548(t), 550(t), 556(t), 572(t), 574(t), 579(t), 585(t), 600(t), 605(t), 624(t), 626(t), 630, 633(t), 650(t), 652(t), 658(t), 667(t), 678(t), 680(t), 684, 690(t), 700(t), 702(t), 708(t), 730(t), 732(t), 734(t), 739, 752(t), 754(t), 757(t), 774, 782, 790, 806, 824; Larry Levine/Washington Metropolitan Area Transit Authority viii(b), 181; RobLewine/Corbis 549; Romilly Lockyer/The Image Bank 214; Dick Luria/FPG International LLC 458(b), 612; Renee Lynn/Tony Stone Images 343(b); David Madison/Tony Stone Images 273; Nadine Markova/ The Stock Market 187(b); Chuck Mason/International Stock xi(b), 246, 287, 513(b); Don Mason/The Stock Market xi(t), 257, 356; Masterfile xvi(c), 642(t), 689(t); Dennis MacDonald/Photo Edit 138, 653(t);

Tom McCarthy/Photo Edit 462; Tom McCarthy/The Stock Market 293(b), 337; Kathy McLaughlin/The Image Works 731; Cathlyn Melloan/Tony Stone Images 388(c); Lawrence Migdale/Tony Stone Images/35; Michael Moore/Microsoft Corporation xvi(t); Kaz Mori/The Image Bank 8(b); Gray Mortimore/Allsport 12(br); Mugshots/The Stock Market 520, 751(b); Jeffry W. Myer/Index Stock 457; Andy Newman/Carnival Corporation 720(c); Michael Newman/Photo Edit 11, 23(b), 106(t), 255(b); 232(b), 359, 452, 494, 648(c), 657; Dennis O'Clair/Tony Stone Images 36, 43, 84(b), 257; 390; Pat Olear/Photo Edit 207(b), 583; Kunio Owaki/The Stock Market x(b), 203, 666(t); Gabe Palmer/The Stock Market 466; Vladimar Pcholkin/FPG International LLC 433; Jose Pelaez/The Stock Market/Corbis 38(b), 370, 402(b), 486, 667(b), 705, 718(t), 756, 762; Stephen Peters/Tony Stone Images 536; PhotoDisc/Stone 124(t), 519; 764(c), 766; Tom Prettyman/PhotoEdit 753; P. Proehl/The Image Bank 167; Radlund & Associates/Artville 482(br); A. Ramey/Photo Edit 40(c); Patrick Ramsey/International Stock 248(b); Dick Reed/The Stock Market 48; Ken Reid/FPG International LLC 217; Rhino Records 315; Jon Riley/Tony Stone Images 321(t), 576, 713; Marc Romanelli/The Image Bank 227; Laurie Rubin/The Image Bank 708(b); Jeff Rutman/Index Stock xviii(t), 733; SW Productions/Index Stock 285; Eric Sanford/International Stock 567(c); Chuck Savage/The Stock Market 767(b); Vincent Serbin/Leo de Wys 105; Nancy Simmerman/Tony Stone Images 117(b); Frank Siteman/Photo Edit 683(t); Frank Siteman/Tony Stone Images 86(b), 228(b); Ariel Skelley/The Stock Market 296, 641, 711(t); Skjold/Photo Edit 648(b); Don Smetzer/Tony Stone Images 96(b), 253(b), 568(c); Joe Sohm/The Stock Market 62(b); Tom Stewart/The Stock Market 392; David Stoecklein/Corbis viii(t), 151; 351, 509(b), 724(b); David Strick/Outline vii(c), 45; Superstock 7, 25, 71, 109, 112(b), 154, 156, 158, 165(b), 173(br), 205(t), 208, 209, 279(b), 280(b), 304, 311, 353, 431, 455, 471, 504, 531(b), 578, 581, 585(b), 602, 604(t), 609, 634, 658(b), 682, 690(b), 737, 777(b); Sygma/Corbis vi(m), 45; Ed Taylor/FPG International LLC 50(c); Peter Taylor/Allsport 274(b); Telegraph Colour Library/FPG International LLC 735; Chris Thomaidis/Tony Stone Images 742; Jay Thomas/International Stock 147(b); K. Tiedge/Corbis-Westlight iv, v, vii(tl), viii, ix(t), x(t), xi(t), xii(t), xiii(t), xiv(t), xv(t), xvi(t), xvii(t), xix(t), 500; Mike Tima/Tony Stone Images 384(b); Tony Stone Images 642(b); T. Tracy/FPG International LLC 577(b); William Taufic/Corbis 267, Uniphoto, Inc., 110(b), 702(b); Randy Ury/The Stock Market xvi(b); Susan Van Etten/PhotoEdit 368; Jeremy Walker/Tony Stone Images 477(b); Karl & Jill Wallin/FPG International LLC 676(b); Carl Weatherly/Tony Stone Images 542(b); Rosemary Weller/Tony Stone Images vii(tr), 42(t), 274(t); Charlie Westerman/International Stock 40(b); Dana C. White/Dana White Productions 27, 54, 72(b), 80, 131, 152(b), 258(c), 263, 288(c), 290, 321(b), 329(b), 354(b), 363, 364, 395, 420(b), 424, 429(b), 440, 450(b), 484(c), 487(b), 506, 516(b), 523, 526, 550(b), 574(b), 593(b), 600(b), 608, 626(b), 628(t), 647(b), 652(b), 655, 670, 680(b), 687(t); Lee White Photography 515, 599; William Whitehurst/The Stock Market 575; Darrell Wong/Tony Stone Images 413(b); Caroline Wood/International Stock 736; Ted Wood/Tony Stone Images 68; David Young-Wolff/Photo Edit 3, 16(t), 26(b), 42(b), 130, 149(b), 182(b), 200(b), 204(b), 222, 351, 387, 544(b), 625, 626, 633, 644(b), 651; David Young-Wolff/Tony Stone Images 233; Jeff Zaruba/The Stock Market 530(b)

Glencoe's Business Transaction Analysis Model

Business Transaction

On October 1 Maria Sanchez took $25,000 from personal savings and deposited that amount to open a business checking account in the name of Roadrunner Delivery Service, Memorandum 1.

Roadrunner Delivery Service — MEMORANDUM 1
155 Gateway Blvd.
Sacramento, CA 94230

TO: Accounting Clerk
FROM: Maria Sanchez
DATE: October 1, 20--
SUBJECT: Contributed personal funds to the business

I have contributed $25,000 from my personal savings for a deposit to the business, Roadrunner Delivery Service.

ANALYSIS

Identify 1. The accounts **Cash in Bank** and **Maria Sanchez, Capital** are affected.

Classify 2. **Cash in Bank** is an asset account. **Maria Sanchez, Capital** is an owner's capital account.

+/− 3. **Cash in Bank** is increased by $25,000. **Maria Sanchez, Capital** is increased by $25,000.

DEBIT-CREDIT RULE

4. Increases in asset accounts are recorded as debits. Debit **Cash in Bank** for $25,000.
5. Increases in the owner's capital account are recorded as credits. Credit **Maria Sanchez, Capital** for $25,000.

T ACCOUNTS

6.

Cash in Bank	
Debit + 25,000	Credit −

Maria Sanchez, Capital	
Debit −	Credit + 25,000

JOURNAL ENTRY

7. GENERAL JOURNAL — PAGE *1*

	DATE		DESCRIPTION	POST. REF.	DEBIT	CREDIT	
1	*20--*						1
2	*Oct.*	*1*	*Cash in Bank*		*25 000 00*		2
3			*Maria Sanchez, Capital*			*25 000 00*	3
4			*Memorandum 1*				4
5							5